Contents

INTRODUCTION 4

Where to go 5
When to go 10
Author picks 11
Things not to miss 12
Itineraries 20

BASICS 22

Getting there 23
Getting around 25
Accommodation 29
Food and drink 31
The media 34
Festivals 35
Sports and outdoor pursuits 37
Shopping 38
Work and study 38
Travel essentials 39

THE GUIDE 44

1 Rome and Lazio 45
2 Piemonte and Valle d'Aosta 131
3 Liguria 171
4 Lombardy and the Lakes 215
5 Trentino-Alto Adige 305
6 Venice and the Veneto 347
7 Friuli-Venezia Giulia 437
8 Emilia-Romagna 465
9 Tuscany 513
10 Umbria 625
11 Le Marche 677
12 Abruzzo and Molise 713
13 Campania 739
14 Puglia 803
15 Basilicata and Calabria 843
16 Sicily 873
17 Sardinia 943

CONTEXTS 980

History 981
Italian art 998
Italian architecture 1007
An A–Z of Italian film 1014
Books 1019
Italian 1024
Glossary of artistic and architectural terms 1030

SMALL PRINT & INDEX 1031

Introduction to **Italy**

Ask an Italian where they would most like to live, and the odds are that they will say "right here" – and, indeed, Italy really does have it all: one of the most diverse and beautiful landscapes in Europe; the world's greatest hoard of art treasures (many on display in spectacular cities and buildings); a relatively benign climate; and, most important of all for many, a delicious and authentic national cuisine. The country is not perfect – its historic cities have often been marred by development, beyond the showpiece sights the infrastructure is visibly straining, and corruption is rife – but as a visitor many of the old clichés still ring true; once you've visited, you may never want to travel anywhere else.

Italy might be the world's most celebrated tourist destination, but it only became a unified state in 1861, and as a result Italians often feel more loyalty to their region than to the nation as a whole – something manifest in its different cuisines, dialects, landscapes and often varying standards of living. However, if there is a single national Italian characteristic, it's to embrace life to the full – in the hundreds of local festivals taking place across the country on any given day to celebrate a saint or the local harvest; in the importance placed on good food; in the obsession with clothes and image; and in the daily ritual of the collective evening stroll or *passeggiata* – a sociable affair celebrated by young and old alike in every town and village across the country.

There is also the enormous **cultural legacy**: Tuscany alone has more classified historical monuments than any country in the world; there are considerable remnants of the Roman Empire all over Italy, most notably in Rome itself; and every region retains its own relics of an artistic tradition generally acknowledged to be among the world's richest. Yet if all you want to do is chill out, there's no reason to be put off. There are any number of places to just lie on a beach, from the resorts filled with regimented rows of sunbeds and parasols favoured by the Italians themselves, to secluded and less developed

PIAZZA DEI SIGNORI, VERONA

spots. And if you're looking for an active holiday, there's no better place: mountains run the country's length – from the Alps and Dolomites in the north right along the Apennines, which form the spine of the peninsula; skiing and other winter sports are practised avidly; and wildlife of all sorts thrives in the national parks.

Where to go

Rome, Italy's capital and the one city in the country that owes allegiance neither to the north or south, is a tremendous city quite unlike any other, and in terms of historical sights outstrips everywhere else in the country by some way. It's the focal point of **Lazio**, in part a poor and sometimes desolate region whose often rugged landscapes, particularly south of Rome, contrast with the more manicured beauty of the other central areas. **Piemonte** and **Lombardy**, in the northwest, make up Italy's richest and most cosmopolitan region, and the two main centres, Turin and Milan, are its wealthiest cities. In their southern reaches, these regions are flat and scenically dull, especially Lombardy, but in the north the presence of the Alps shapes the character of each: skiing and hiking are prime activities, and the lakes and mountains of Lombardy are time-honoured tourist territory. **Liguria**, the small coastal province to the south, has long been known as the "Italian Riviera" and is accordingly crowded with sunseekers for much of the summer. Nonetheless, it's a beautiful stretch of coast, and its capital,

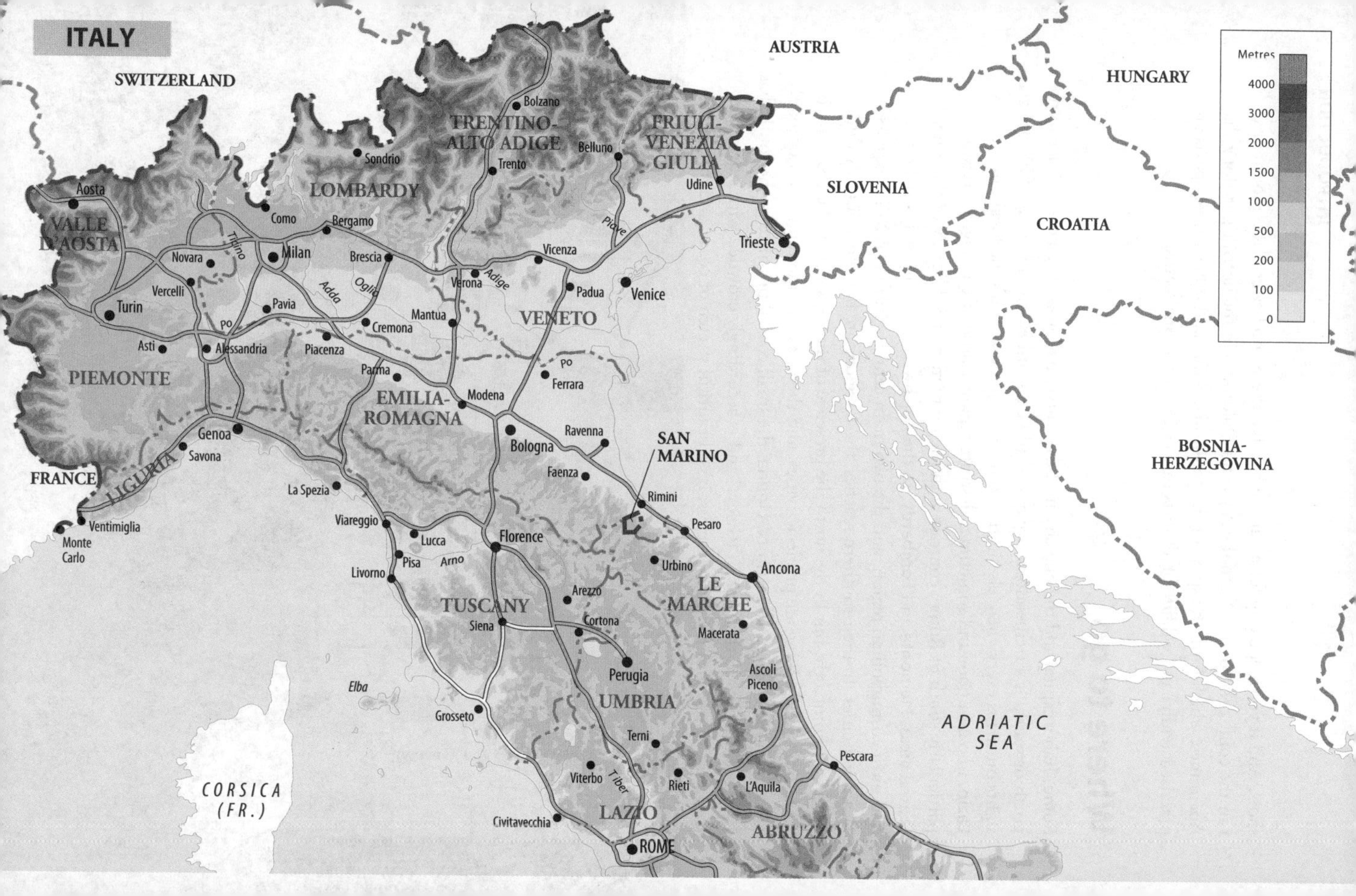
ITALY
SWITZERLAND
AUSTRIA
HUNGARY
SLOVENIA
CROATIA
BOSNIA-
HERZEGOVINA
FRANCE
Metres
4000
3000
2000
1500
1000
500
200
100
0
TRENTINO-
ALTO ADIGE
FRIULI-
VENEZIA
GIULIA
LOMBARDY
VALLE
D'AOSTA
PIEMONTE
LIGURIA
VENETO
EMILIA-
ROMAGNA
SAN
MARINO
TUSCANY
LE
MARCHE
UMBRIA
LAZIO
ABRUZZO
ADRIATIC
SEA
CORSICA
(FR.)
Elba
Aosta
Como
Sondrio
Bolzano
Trento
Belluno
Udine
Trieste
Bergamo
Milan
Novara
Vercelli
Turin
Pavia
Brescia
Verona
Vicenza
Padua
Venice
Mantua
Cremona
Piacenza
Asti
Alessandria
Parma
Modena
Ferrara
Bologna
Ravenna
Genoa
Savona
Faenza
Rimini
Pesaro
La Spezia
Ventimiglia
Monte
Carlo
Viareggio
Lucca
Pisa
Livorno
Florence
Urbino
Ancona
Arezzo
Siena
Cortona
Macerata
Perugia
Ascoli
Piceno
Grosseto
Terni
Viterbo
Rieti
L'Aquila
Pescara
Civitavecchia
ROME
Ticino
Adda
Oglio
Adige
Piave
Po
Arno
Tiber

MOLISE
Campobasso
Foggia
Formia
Benevento
Volturno
CAMPANIA
Naples
Salerno
PUGLIA
Bari
Brindisi
Potenza
Matera
Taranto
Lecce
BASILICATA
Capri
Ischia
Pontine Islands
Porto Torres
Sassari
Olbia
SARDINIA
Iglesias
Cagliari
TYRRHENIAN SEA
CALABRIA
Cosenza
Catanzaro
Ustica
Aeolian Islands
Messina
Reggio di Calabria
Palermo
Trapani
Egadi Islands
Mazara del Vallo
Enna
Catania
SICILY
Agrigento
Siracusa
Ragusa
IONIAN SEA
Pantelleria
TUNISIA
ALGERIA
N
0
100
kilometres

FACT FILE

- Napoleon claimed Italy was "too long", and who can disagree? The **distance** from the tip of the country's "toe" to its northern border is about 1380km.
- Italy became a **nation state** in 1861, under King Vittorio Emanuele II, and has been a **democratic republic** since 1946, when the monarchy was abolished by popular referendum.
- The **parliament** consists of two houses, the Senate (315 seats) and the Chamber of Deputies (630 seats); both sit for five-year terms of office. The country has an elected **president**, but real power lies with the **prime minister**, who is generally the leader of the party with the biggest majority in the Chamber of Deputies.
- Italy's population is just under 60 million, of whom almost three million live in the capital, Rome. The country is divided geographically and administratively into twenty regions, of which five are autonomous.
- Italy has the lowest **birth rate** in Europe, and twenty percent of the population is over 65.
- The average Italian eats 23 kilos of **pasta** annually, and the nation drinks a staggering fourteen billion cups of **coffee** every year.
- There's still a significant **gender divide** in Italy, with the country ranked at number 81 in the world, in a recent gender gap survey. And in the country of the *pizzaiolo*, a shocking seventy percent of men claim never to have used an oven.

Genoa, is a vibrant, bustling port town with a long seafaring tradition.

Much of the most dramatic mountain scenery lies within the smaller northern regions. In the far northwest, the tiny bilingual **Valle d'Aosta** is home to some of the country's most frequented ski resorts, and is bordered by the tallest of the Alps – the Matterhorn and Mont Blanc. In the northeast, **Trentino-Alto Adige**, another bilingual region and one in which the national boundary is especially blurred, marks the beginning of the Dolomites mountain range, where Italy's largest national park, the Stelvio, lies amid some of the country's most memorable landscapes.

The Dolomites stretch into the northeastern regions of the **Veneto** and **Friuli-Venezia Giulia**. However, here the main focus of interest is, of course, Venice: a unique city, and every bit as beautiful as its reputation would suggest (although this means you won't be alone in appreciating it). If the crowds are too much, you could visit an arc of historic towns outside the city – Verona, Padua and Vicenza, all centres of interest in their own right, although rather overshadowed by their illustrious neighbour. To the south, the region of **Emilia-Romagna** was at the heart of Italy's postwar industrial boom and enjoys a standard of living on a par with Piemonte and Lombardy, although it's also a traditional stronghold of the Italian Left. Its coast is popular among Italians, and Rimini is about Italy's brashest (and trendiest) seaside resort, renowned for its nightlife. You may do better to ignore the beaches altogether, however, and concentrate on the historic centres of Ravenna, Ferrara, Parma and the regional capital of Bologna, one of Italy's liveliest, most historic but least appreciated cities – and traditionally Italy's gastronomic and academic capital.

Central Italy represents perhaps the most commonly perceived image of the country, and **Tuscany**, with its classic rolling countryside and the art-packed towns of Florence, Pisa and Siena, to name only the three best-known, is one of its most visited regions. Neighbouring **Umbria** is similar in all but its tourist numbers, though it gets busier

every year, as visitors flock into towns such as Perugia, Spoleto and Assisi. Further east still, **Le Marche** has gone the same way, with old stone cottages being turned into foreign-owned holiday homes; the highlights of the region are the ancient towns of Urbino and Ascoli Piceno. South of Le Marche, the hills begin to pucker into mountains in the twin regions of **Abruzzo** and **Molise**, one of Italy's remotest areas, centring on one of the country's highest peaks – the Gran Sasso d'Italia.

The south proper begins with the region of **Campania**, whose capital, Naples, is a unique, unforgettable city, the spiritual heart of the Italian south. It's close to some of Italy's finest ancient sites in Pompeii and Herculaneum, not to mention the country's most spectacular stretch of coast around Amalfi and the islands in its bay, most famously Capri. **Basilicata** and **Calabria**, which make up the instep and toe of Italy's boot, are harder territory but still rewarding, the emphasis less on art, more on the landscape and quiet, relatively unspoilt coastlines. **Puglia**, the "heel" of Italy, has underrated pleasures, too, notably the landscape of its Gargano peninsula, the souk-like qualities of its capital, Bari, and the Baroque glories of Lecce in the far south. As for **Sicily**, the island is really a place apart, with a wide mixture of attractions ranging from some of the finest preserved Hellenistic treasures in Europe to a couple of Italy's most appealing beach resorts in Taormina and Cefalù, not to mention some gorgeous upland

THE SCOOP ON ITALIAN ICE CREAM

The taste of real Italian ice cream, eaten in Italy, is unbeatable. **Gelato** is the country's favourite dessert, and there's no better way to end the day, as the locals do, than strolling through the streets with a cone in hand enjoying the cool of the evening. Italian ice cream really is better than any other, and like most Italian food this is down to the use of local whole milk and eggs, and a focus on natural production methods and the provenance of ingredients (pistachios from Bronte in Sicily, lemons from Amalfi, hazelnuts from the Langhe in Piemonte).

Everywhere but the tiniest village has at least one *gelateria*. If you want to sample the very best, avoid places where the *gelato* is displayed in fluffy, whipped mounds – the volume is achieved by artificial thickeners – and steer clear of brightly coloured ice cream, a sure sign of chemical additives. There's usually a veritable cornucopia of **flavours** (*gusti*) to choose from. You'll find the classics – like lemon (*limone*) and hazelnut (*nocciola*) – everywhere, and you'll often see newfangled flavours too, with the current trend for savoury *gelato* reaching even small-town *gelaterie*. Anyone for a scoop of Gorgonzola?

ITALIAN FOOTBALL

Calcio – football, or soccer – is Italy's national sport, and enjoys a big following across the country. It's usually possible to get tickets to see one of the top sides – as long as they're not playing each other – and it's one of the best introductions to modern Italian culture you'll find.

Since World War II, Italian football has been dominated by **Inter** and **AC Milan** (of Milan) and **Juventus** (Turin), who have between them won the *scudetto* or **Serie A** (Italy's premier division) 70 times. It's a testament to the English origins of the game that AC Milan, as well as another big club, Genoa, continue to use anglicized names, and to sport the cross of St George in their insignia. Unfortunately, the other thing that has been copied from the English is hooliganism, which remains a problem in Italian football, along with a latent degree of racism, and, perhaps most notoriously, corruption – the country has been hit by scandal after scandal, most recently the match-fixing "Last Bet" controversy, which has seen over a hundred people investigated since 2011, among them high-profile footballers. As well as Juventus, AC Milan and Inter, the two Rome clubs, **AS Roma** and to a lesser extent **SS Lazio**, regularly do well, although Lazio's star has faded in recent years and their fans are perceived as among the worst examples of Italy's right-wing lunatic fringe. In Tuscany, **Fiorentina** reckon themselves a big club, while in the south **Napoli** are beginning to relive their Eighties "glory days", when they were led by Diego Maradona, although they still struggle to fill their giant eighty-thousand capacity stadium. We've given details of the big city clubs in the Guide, but wherever you are, grab one of Italy's three sports papers – *Gazzetta dello Sport*, *Corriere dello Sport* and *Tuttosport* – to see what's on.

scenery. Come this far south and you're closer to Africa than Milan, and it shows in the climate, the architecture and the cooking, with couscous featuring on many menus in the west of the island. **Sardinia**, too, feels far removed from the Italian mainland, especially in its relatively undiscovered interior, although you may be content just to laze on its fine beaches, which are among Italy's best.

When to go

If you're planning to visit popular areas, especially beach resorts, avoid July and especially August, when the weather can be too hot and the crowds at their most congested. In August, when most Italians are on holiday, you can expect the crush to be especially bad in the resorts, and the scene in the major historic cities – Rome, Florence, Venice – to be slightly artificial, as the only people around are fellow tourists. The nicest time to visit, in terms of the weather and lack of crowds, is from April to June, and in September or October. If you're planning to swim, however, bear in mind that only the south of the country is likely to be warm enough outside the May to September period. For more information and a temperature chart, check Basics (see page 40).

Author picks

Our writers have travelled the length and breadth of Italy over the years, visiting both its world-famous sights and its remote, untouristed corners; their Italian highlights are below.

Hit the beach With 7600km of coastline, Italy is a great place to hang out on the beach. We love surfy Levanto in Liguria (see page 205), rugged Torre Guaceto in Puglia (see page 832) and the beautifully wild Riserva Naturale dello Zingaro in Sicily (see page 939).

Unspoilt towns Nowhere in Europe are there so many towns and villages where time seems to have stood still. Our favourites? The palaces and porticoes of Ferrara, Emilia-Romagna (see page 494), the perfectly preserved village of Pienza, Tuscany (see page 611), atmospheric Urbino, Le Marche, one of the cultural capitals of the Renaissance (see page 678), and the Baroque whimsy of Lecce, Puglia (see page 833).

Ancient places Standout ancient sites include Ostia Antica, Lazio (see page 108), Paestum, Campania (see page 801), Agrigento, Sicily (see page 932), Su Nuraxi, Sardinia (see page 958) and the amazing Neolithic Sassi of Matera, Basilicata (see page 849).

Hot, hot, hot? Italy lies at the centre of the most volcanic regions in Europe, something you can experience first-hand by climbing Vesuvius (see page 768), Etna (see page 910) or Stromboli (see page 903), or, more easily, by visiting the Solfatara just outside Naples (see page 765).

Road trips There are any number of great routes, not least the spectacular Amalfi Coast road in Campania (see page 791), the Chiantigiana road in Tuscany (see page 557), the Alghero to Bosa coast road in Sardinia (see page 960) and the Great Dolomites Road, Trentino-Alto Adige (see page 306).

Underground Italy Italy is full of subterranean wonders, like the amazing Toirano caves, Liguria (see page 194), the catacombs of Rome (see page 82), and Palermo (see page 877), and Napoli Sotterranea, a labyrinth of ancient runnels beneath Naples, Campania (see page 748).

> Our author recommendations don't end here. We've flagged up our favourite places – a perfectly sited hotel, an atmospheric café, a special restaurant – throughout the Guide, highlighted with the ★ symbol.

LEVANTO, LIGURIA

PIAZZA TRENTO E TRIESTE, FERRARA

20 things not to miss

It's not possible to see everything that Italy has to offer in one trip – and we don't suggest you try. What follows is a selective taste, in no particular order, of the country's highlights: outstanding buildings and ancient sites, spectacular natural wonders, great food and idyllic beaches. Each highlight has a page reference to take you straight into the Guide, where you can find out more. Coloured numbers refer to chapters in the Guide section.

1 AMALFI COAST

See page 791

Everyone should see the stunning Amalfi Coast at least once in their life.

2 THE UFFIZI, FLORENCE

See page 528

One of Italy's most celebrated collections of art, and Florence's most essential attraction.

3 NEAPOLITAN PIZZA

See page 762

You can eat pizza all over Italy, but nowhere is it quite as good as in its hometown of Naples.

4 VATICAN MUSEUMS, ROME

See page 88

The largest and richest collection of art and culture in the world. You'd be mad to miss it.

5 SICILY'S GREEK RUINS

See pages 916, 908 and 932

The ancient theatres at Siracusa and Taormina are magnificent summer stages for Greek drama, while the temple complex at nearby Agrigento is one of the finest such sites outside Greece itself.

5

6
7
8

6 HIKING IN THE DOLOMITES

See page 310

The spiky landscape of the Dolomites is perfect hiking country, covered in dramatic long-distance trails.

7 MATERA

See page 849

A truly unique city, sliced by a ravine containing thousands of *Sassi* – cave dwellings gouged out of the rock that were inhabited until the 1950s

8 BASILICA DI SAN FRANCESCO, ASSISI

See page 646

The burial place of St Francis and one of Italy's greatest church buildings, with frescoes by Giotto and Simone Martini.

9 CENTRO STORICO, ROME

See page 54

There's so much to see in Rome that aimlessly wandering the city's fantastic old centre can yield a surprise at every turn, whether it's an ancient statue, a marvellous Baroque fountain or a bustling piazza.

10 THE LAST SUPPER, MILAN

See page 233

Leonardo da Vinci's mural for the refectory wall of Santa Maria delle Grazie is one of the world's most resonant images.

11 LECCE

See page 833

This exuberant city of Baroque architecture and opulent churches is one of the must-sees of the Italian South.

12 PIAZZA SAN MARCO, VENICE

See page 353

Crowded or not, this is one of Europe's grandest urban spaces and home to Italy's most exotic cathedral.

13 LAKE COMO

See page 265

If you can escape the hordes, Como in the Italian Lakes region is utterly beguiling, with stunning scenery and plenty of activities.

14 GIOTTO'S FRESCOES, PADUA

See page 405

The artist's frescoes in Padua's Cappella degli Scrovegni constitute one of the great works of European art.

15 AGRITURISMI

See page 31

Farmstays and rural retreats are one of Italy's lesser-known specialities and can be among the country's most spectacular and bucolic places to stay.

12

13
14
15

16 SARDINIA'S BEACHES

See page 976

There are plenty of places to sun-worship in Italy, but Sardinia's coastline ranks among the most beautiful.

17 DUOMO, FLORENCE

See page 522

Florence's cathedral dome is instantly recognizable – and is one of the world's most significant engineering feats.

18 URBINO

See page 678

This so-called "ideal city" and art capital, created by Federico da Montefeltro, the ultimate Renaissance man, is one of the most memorable of all Italian provincial cities.

19 PARCO NAZIONALE D'ABRUZZO

See page 725

Italy's third-largest national park, and probably its wildest, with marvellous walking and wildlife.

20 POMPEII AND HERCULANEUM

See page 769 and 767

Probably the two best-preserved Roman sites in the country, destroyed and at the same time preserved by the eruption of Vesuvius in AD 79.

18
19
LE SACERDOS IVL
20

Tailor-made trips

Italy is a large and complex destination and you can't hope to savour it all on one visit; indeed, experiencing and appreciating the country properly, in all its aspects, is arguably a lifetime's work. The trips below give a flavour of what the country has to offer and what we can plan and book for you at www.roughguides.com/trips.

FOODIES' ITALY

Think of Italy and you think of food, and with so many regional variations you can try something different everywhere you go.

❶ **Alba, Piemonte** If you're here at the right time of year you may be able to sample the town's extraordinary white truffles; and at any time you can taste the excellent local wine. See page 153

❷ **Genoa, Liguria** The food of Liguria, and in particular Genoa, is among the country's most distinctive: the home of pesto, focaccia, *farinata* and great fish and seafood. See page 172

❸ **Bologna, Emilia-Romagna** Regarded as the culinary capital of Italy and by far the best place to take a course in mastering Italian cuisine. See page 466

❹ **Norcia, Umbria** Famous nationwide for all kinds of pork products, from *guanciale* to *pancetta*, and – in season – superb black truffles too. See page 664

❺ **Rome** The "cucina povera" of Rome isn't the country's best-known regional cuisine, but it's one of the tastiest, with gutsy pasta dishes and a focus on offal and the poorer cuts of meat – perfect for the more adventurous foodie. See page 46

❻ **Naples, Campania** There's nothing like tasting pizza in the city where it was invented. See page 740

❼ **Sicily** With Arabic, Spanish and Greek culinary influences, Sicily's cuisine is unique, and there are plenty of tempting specialities to sample, from *caponata* to *cannoli*. See page 874

ITALY OUTDOORS: MOUNTAINS AND WATER

Italy has a wonderful mix of high mountains, lakes and sea, making it the ideal country for an outdoor holiday.

❶ **Gran Paradiso, Valle d'Aosta** Some of the most beautiful and best-organized high-altitude trekking in the country. See page 165

❷ **Alta Via, Liguria** This long-distance high-level hiking trail takes you the length of Liguria, and offers a very different view of the region than the resorts on the coast. See page 198

❸ **Riva del Garda, Lombardy** There's no better place in the country for quality windsurfing and sailing. See page 296

❹ **Vie ferrate, Trentino-Alto Adige** High-altitude climbing the Italian way, using the fixed ladders and pegs of the northern Dolomites. See page 317

❺ **Gran Sasso, Abruzzo** The Gran Sasso national park holds the highest peaks of the Apennines, including the 2900m Corno Grande. See page 718

❻ **Porto Pollo, Sardinia** Sardinia's northern Costa Smeralda is the home of all manner of waterborne activities, not least fantastic opportunities for kitesurfing. See page 972

ITALY INDOORS: ART AND CULTURE

No country in the world boasts the same volume of cultural artefacts, and you can stumble across great art displayed in fine historic buildings just about anywhere – or follow our tailored cultural itinerary below.

❶ **Venice** Italy's greatest maritime state, ossified in stone and oils. See page 348

❷ **Padua, Veneto** The amazingly preserved Giotto frescoes of Padua's Scrovegni chapel, dating back to the fourteenth century, are one of the absolute highlights of Western European art. See page 403

❸ **Mantua, Lombardy** Two palaces, plastered with the work of two very different artists – Mantegna's beautiful refined frescoes in the Palazzo Ducale and Giulio Romano's later Mannerist experiment in the Palazzo Te. See page 249

❹ **Arezzo, Tuscany** Home to a hugely famous fresco cycle by Piero della Francesca, and to other works by the fifteenth-century painter. See page 617

❺ **Florence** Birthplace of the Italian Renaissance, with Ghiberti's famous bronze door, Brunelleschi's dome, and, er, the Uffizi too. See page 516

❻ **Assisi, Umbria** Assisi's basilica is covered top to toe with fourteenth-century frescoes – one of the greatest artworks you can see in a church. See page 646

❼ **Rome** Where to start? One of the great things about Rome is the chance to see some of the world's greatest paintings in the places they were meant for – best of all are the many works by Caravaggio that remain in the city. See page 46

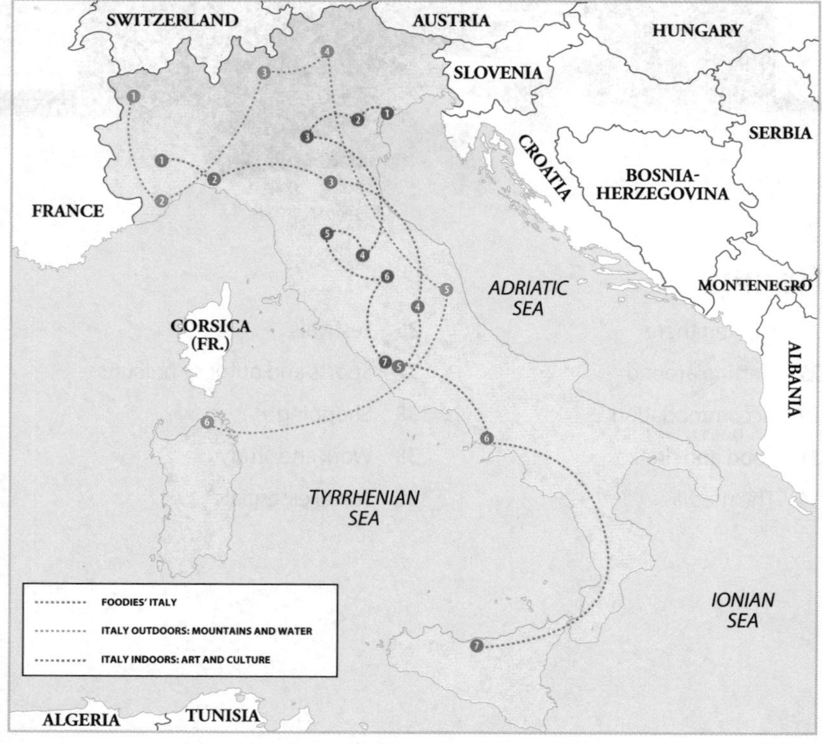

SHOPFRONT IN VERONA

Basics

23 Getting there

25 Getting around

29 Accommodation

31 Food and drink

34 The media

35 Festivals

37 Sports and outdoor pursuits

38 Shopping

38 Work and study

39 Travel essentials

Getting there

There are regular direct flights to Italy from the UK and the US, while airlines from Australia, New Zealand and South Africa fly via Asian or European cities. Price-comparison sites such as Ⓦ skyscanner.net and Ⓦ edreams.com are invaluable for bargain-hunting, though it is usually cheaper to make bookings direct through an operator's website. Rail connections with the rest of Europe are also good and link well into the comprehensive national network.

Flights from the UK and Ireland

Of the scheduled **airlines** flying to Italy, British Airways (Ⓦ ba.com) and Alitalia (Ⓦ alitalia.com) regularly serve most of the country including Trieste, Turin, Genoa, Verona, Venice, Milan, Rome, Bologna, Florence, Palermo, Pisa, Naples, Bari, Brindisi, Reggio Calabria, Cagliari and Catania. The majority of the routes are from London but British Airways also flies from Edinburgh, Aberdeen, Newcastle, Leeds/Bradford and Manchester. Aer Lingus (Ⓦ aerlingus.com) has direct flights from Dublin to Milan, Bologna, Catania, Naples and Pisa. Of the **low-cost carriers**, easyJet (Ⓦ easyjet.com), TUI (Ⓦ tui.co.uk), Jet2 (Ⓦ jet2.com), flybe (Ⓦ flybe.com), Norwegian Air (Ⓦ norwegian.com) and Ryanair (Ⓦ ryanair.com) fly from London and numerous smaller airports to bases throughout Italy and its islands.

Prices depend on how far in advance you book, the popularity of the destination, and the **season**: unless you book well in advance, flying between June and September will cost more than in the depths of winter (excluding Christmas and New Year). Note also that it is generally more expensive to fly at weekends. Book far enough in advance with one of the low-cost airlines and you can pick up a ticket for under £60 return, excluding hold luggage, even in summer; book anything less than three weeks in advance and this could triple in price. Scheduled airline fares, booked within a month of travel, will cost £150–250 during winter, spring and autumn, and £250–350 in summer; booking in advance in summer will save you £100 or so.

Flights from the US and Canada

Between them, Delta (Ⓦ delta.com), Alitalia (Ⓦ alitalia.com) and American Airlines (Ⓦ aa.com) offer daily flights from New York, Boston, Atlanta, Los Angeles, Miami and Chicago to Rome and Milan; one short layover greatly extends the network. In addition, many European carriers fly to Italy (via their capitals) from all major US and Canadian cities – for example British Airways (Ⓦ ba.com) via London, Lufthansa (Ⓦ lufthansa.com) via Frankfurt and KLM (Ⓦ klm.com) via Amsterdam.

The **direct scheduled fares** don't vary as much as you might think, and you'll more often than not be basing your choice around things like flight timings, routes and gateway cities, ticket restrictions, and even the airline's reputation for comfort and service. The cheapest **round-trip fares** to Rome or Milan, travelling midweek in low season, start at around US$650 for indirect flights from New York, or US$1300 for nonstop flights, rising to US$750 (US$1500 nonstop) in spring and fall, and US$950 (US$1600 nonstop) during the summer. Add another US$100–200 for flights from LA, Miami and Chicago.

Air Canada (Ⓦ aircanada.com) and Alitalia have nonstop flights **from Toronto and Montreal** to Rome for around Can$600 nonstop in low season, or Can$800 nonstop in summer.

Flights from Australia, New Zealand and South Africa

There are no nonstop flights to Italy **from Australia** or **New Zealand**. From either country you are likely to get most flexibility by travelling with Malaysia Airlines (Ⓦ malaysiaairlines.com), Emirates (Ⓦ emirates.com), British Airways (Ⓦ ba.com.fly) or Qantas (Ⓦ qantas.com.au). Round-trip fares to Rome from the main Australian cities go for Aus$1100–1500 in low season, and around Aus$1800 in high season; from New Zealand, round-trip fares cost from around NZ$1800 in low season up to NZ$3000 in high season.

A BETTER KIND OF TRAVEL

At Rough Guides we are passionately committed to travel. We believe it helps us understand the world we live in and the people we share it with – and of course tourism is vital to many developing economies. But the scale of modern tourism has also damaged some places irreparably, and climate change is accelerated by most forms of transport, especially flying. We encourage our authors to consider the carbon footprint of the journeys they make in the course of researching our guides.

Various carriers serve **South Africa**, usually with a stop in their European or Middle Eastern hub. Return fares start at around ZAR5000 return from Johannesburg, or around ZAR7000–8000 from Cape Town or Durban.

Trains

Travelling by **train** to Italy from the UK can be an enjoyable and environmentally friendly way of getting to the country, and you can stop off in other parts of Europe on the way. Most trains pass through Paris and head down through France towards Milan. A standard-class return **fare** from London to Paris using Eurostar (2hr 15min) starts at £72; travelling by high-speed TGV from Paris to Milan (7hr 20min) costs from €39.

The Franco-Italian Thello **sleeper** runs every evening from Paris to Venice via Milan, Brescia, Verona, Vicenza and Padua; it departs from Paris Gare de Lyon at 7.10pm, and arrives in Venice 14hr later. Those heading straight to Rome (14hr from Paris) need to change trains in Milan. Accommodation is in four- and six-berth couchettes, and one-, two- and three-berth cabins – the more you pay, the fewer people you share with; women can opt to share with other women if they are travelling alone. All services have a restaurant car and a steward who looks after each carriage. Prices vary hugely depending on the time of year and demand. If you buy tickets online in advance, you can pay as little as £50, including a couchette, or £225 with a two-bed sleeper.

If you really want to push the boat out, the Venice Simplon-**Orient-Express** (Ⓦ belmond.com) runs from London to Venice, offering around 30hr of pampered luxury starting from £2129, including all meals.

Advance booking on trains is essential (and can often save you a lot of money); there are also discounts for children and rail-pass holders. When booking trains, bear in mind that if you travel via Paris on Eurostar you will have to change stations, so you should give yourself a good hour (more like 1hr 30min if you have to queue for metro tickets) to travel on the metro from the Gare du Nord to the Gare de Lyon. Allow more time for the return journey across Paris, as there is a minimum thirty-minute check-in for Eurostar departures. Note that there are no left-luggage lockers at the Gare de Bercy.

The **Man in Seat 61** website (Ⓦ seat61.com) offers exhaustive information on travelling by train, with details of routes, times and fares.

Rail passes

Interrail (Ⓦ interrail.eu) and **Eurail** (Ⓦ eurail.com) Passes offer unlimited rail travel throughout Italy and other European countries; you can buy them before leaving home, but they're also available at many European mainline stations at the international ticket desks. Italy-only passes are also available (see page 26). If you use a EuroCity (domestic) or Le Frecce high-speed trains, a supplement of €10 applies (€15 for first class).

Interrail

Interrail Passes are only available to European citizens and official residents (if you aren't a European citizen but can prove that you live in Europe, you can use an Interrail Pass), and are not valid in the country of residence. They come in first- and second-class. The Interrail Global Pass is available for travel in a combination of countries for five days within a ten-day period, ten days within a 22-day period, 15 consecutive days, 22 consecutive days or one month unlimited. Under-11s travel free of charge (up to a maximum of two children). Young people aged 12–27 and senior travellers (60-plus) are entitled to a discounted rate. There are also various promotions throughout the year – check the website for details.

Pass holders can use all of the trains run by the national railways in Europe. For high-speed and night trains you need to reserve in advance, and a fee may apply.

Eurail

A **Eurail Pass** is for non-European residents and comes in a variety of forms: a Flexi pass (ten or fifteen days unlimited travel in 26 countries over two months); the Eurail Selectpass (up to four countries over 5, 6, 8, 10 or 15 days); two- or three-country passes (four or more days of free travel within a two-month period); or Italy only (three or more days of free travel within a two-month period). The pass must be purchased before arrival in Europe and allows first- and second-class train travel. As with the Interrail Pass, pass holders can use all trains run by the national railways in Europe. You need reservations for high-speed and night trains; a fee may also apply. There are various promotions throughout the year when you can purchase passes at a discounted rate – check the website for details.

There are numerous small-group and saver versions, and certain passes can be purchased at main European train stations at the international ticket desks, although it works out cheaper to buy them online (see page 25).

Buses

It's difficult to see why anyone would want to travel to Italy by **bus**. Eurolines does, however, have bargain

offers, and tickets cost from £62 one-way from London to Milan, taking a gruelling 30 hours – check the website for the latest timetables.

Busabout is a popular option with backpackers, offering various Italian tours as well as Europe-wide hop-on-hop-off services (from £169 for three stops).

Package and special interest holidays

As well as the travel agents offering **flight-and-accommodation package** deals, an increasing number of operators organize **specialist holidays** to Italy – covering walking, art and archeology, food and wine, and short breaks to coincide with opera festivals or even football matches. If you want to rent a car in Italy, it's worth checking **fly-drive** deals with tour operators (and flight agents) before you leave.

RAIL CONTACTS

Eurostar ⓣ 0343 218 6186, ⓦ eurostar.com.

International Rail ⓣ 0871 231 0790, ⓦ internationalrail.com. Friendly company offering a wide variety of rail options including Eurostar, international sleepers and ferry crossings.

The Man in Seat Sixty-One ⓦ seat61.com. Up-to-date, user-friendly advice on how to use rail systems around the world.

Trainline ⓣ 00 33 1318 62421 ⓦ trainline.eu. Train and coach website and app selling tickets on behalf of over 180 carriers across more than 35 countries in Europe.

BUS CONTACTS

Busabout UK ⓣ 0845 026 7576, ⓦ busabout.com.

Eurolines UK ⓣ 0871 781 8177, ⓦ eurolines.eu.

AGENTS AND OPERATORS

TRAVEL AGENTS

North South Travel UK ⓣ 01245 608 291, ⓦ northsouthtravel.co.uk. Friendly, competitive travel agency, offering discounted fares worldwide. Profits are used to support projects in the developing world, especially the promotion of sustainable tourism.

STA Travel UK ⓣ 0333 321 0099, US ⓣ 1800 781 4040, Australia ⓣ 134 782, New Zealand ⓣ 0800 474 400, South Africa ⓣ 0861 781 781; ⓦ statravel.com. Worldwide specialists in independent travel; also student IDs, travel insurance, car rental, rail passes and more. Good discounts for students and under-26s.

Trailfinders UK ⓣ 020 7084 6500, Ireland ⓣ 01 677 7888; ⓦ trailfinders.com. One of the best-informed and most efficient agents for independent travellers.

Travel CUTS Canada ⓣ 1800 667 2887; ⓦ travelcuts.com. Canadian youth and student travel firm.

USIT Ireland ⓣ 01 602 1906, Northern Ireland ⓣ 028 9032 7111; ⓦ usit.ie. Ireland's main student and youth travel specialists.

PACKAGE TOURS

Central Holidays US ⓣ 1800 935 5000, ⓦ centralholidays.com. Offers tours combining Tuscany, Cinque Terre and the Lakes, among other popular holiday spots.

CIT US & Canada ⓣ 1800 387 0711, ⓦ cittours.ca; Australia ⓣ 1300 380 992, ⓦ cit.com.au. Huge range of well-organized themed holidays and tours, plus advice for independent travellers on hotels.

Citalia UK ⓣ 01293 839 105, ⓦ citalia.com. Long-established Italy specialists.

Long Travel UK ⓣ 01694 722 193, ⓦ long-travel.co.uk. Well-established company creating tailor-made holidays in various Italian regions including Puglia, Tuscany, Sicily and the Aeolian Islands.

SPECIALIST AND CULTURAL TOURS

Abercrombie & Kent UK ⓣ 01242 386 500, US ⓣ 1 800 554 7016; ⓦ abercrombiekent.com. This high-end operator offers art-focused tours led by experts from Christie's.

ACE Cultural Tours UK ⓣ 01223 841 055, ⓦ aceculturaltours.co.uk. Specialist, academic-led tours focusing on such subjects as art, architecture and gardens.

Alternative Travel Group UK ⓣ 01865 315 678, ⓦ atg-oxford.co.uk. Walking and cycling holidays.

Backroads US ⓣ 1800 462 2848, ⓦ backroads.com. Cycling and hiking holidays, as well as culinary tours.

Context Travel US ⓣ 1800 691 6036, ⓦ contexttravel.com. Themed walking tours for the "intellectually curious" in Rome, Florence, Venice, Milan, Naples and Tuscany, either in small groups of up to six or privately.

Elite RetrEat UK ⓣ 020 7460 1098, ⓦ eliteretreatitalia.com. High-end tailor-made holidays specializing in bespoke wine and culinary experiences.

Martin Randall Travel UK ⓣ 020 8742 3355, ⓦ martinrandall.com. Small-group cultural holidays with experts on art, architecture, music, history, gastronomy and wine.

MT Sobek US ⓣ 1888 831 7526, ⓦ mtsobek.com. Adventures for keen hikers and rafters, plus cultural explorations, family trips and wellness journeys.

Walkabout Gourmet Adventures Australia ⓣ 02 9871 5526, ⓦ walkaboutgourmet.com. Gourmet walking holidays from Piedmont to Sicily.

Getting around

Italy is a big country and unless you opt for a one-base holiday you will probably find yourself travelling a fair bit. Both rail and bus services are good value and relatively efficient, while regular ferries service the islands and local buses link more out-of-the-way areas. Internal flights can be worthwhile for some of the longer journeys – and may even work out cheaper than travelling by train.

Naturally, you'll have most flexibility with your own transport.

We've detailed train, bus and ferry frequencies in the "Arrival and departure" sections within the Guide; note that these usually refer to regular working-day schedules (Mon–Sat); services can be much reduced or even nonexistent on Sundays and in August.

By rail

The Italian train system is one of the least expensive in Europe, reasonably comprehensive and, in the north of the country at least, pretty efficient. Italian trains are run by **Ferrovie dello Stato Italiane** (Ⓦfsitaliane.it), under the brand name **Trenitalia** (Ⓣ89 20 21, Ⓦtrenitalia.com), operating a comprehensive network across the country with numerous types of train. Sleeper trains connect the major Italian cities with cities such as Paris, Vienna, Hamburg and Barcelona. Le Frecce, comprising Frecciarossa, Frecciargento and Frecciabianca, is the country's swish high-speed train network, with trains reaching up to 360km/hr, offering daily connections between the main cities. Book tickets in advance for the best fares. Seat reservations are required for all these services – even if you have a rail pass you'll need to pay a €10 or €15 supplement.

Intercity and **Eurocity** trains are fast and comfortable, connecting main towns, with a number of Eurocity trains crossing the border to connect with European cities. Regionale trains can be very slow, stopping at virtually all stations with a population higher than zero. No reservation is necessary, and there's no need to buy in advance for these.

NTV (Nuovo Trasporto Viaggiatori) is a private company whose high-speed **Italo** trains (Ⓦitalotreno.it) connect a number of destinations in Italy, from Bolzano in Alto Adige to Salerno in Campania. There are also a number of smaller **privately run** lines, using separate stations but charging similar fares to the FS trains. Where they're worth using, these are detailed in the Guide.

> **STAMP IT**
>
> All stations have yellow validating machines in which passengers must stamp their ticket before embarking on their journey. However, if your ticket is booked for a specific train, validation is not necessary. If in doubt, ask. Look out for the machines as you come onto the platform: if you fail to **validate your ticket** you'll be given a hefty on-the-spot fine.

Timetables and fares

Timings and route information are posted at train stations. Check the Trenitalia website (Ⓦtrenitalia.com) for the latest schedules.

Fares are inexpensive, calculated by the kilometre and easy to work out for each journey. The timetables give the prices per kilometre, but as a rough guide, a second-class one-way fare from Milan to Verona (1hr 50min) currently costs about €22 by Intercity, €13 on Regionale. Return tickets are valid within two months of the outward journey, but as two one-way tickets cost the same it's hardly worth bothering. **Children** aged 4–12 qualify for a fifty percent discount on all journeys, and children under four (not occupying a seat) travel free.

There are huge savings to be had by booking in advance online, especially for Le Frecce high-speed trains. As a rough guide, a Frecciarossa high-speed train from Rome to Milan costs from €45 for the three-hour journey.

Rail passes

A **rail pass** is unlikely to be worthwhile for an Italy-only trip. Prices are low and as you need to have a reservation for the faster trains, the convenience of a pass is outweighed by the extra queues and booking fees.

Europe-wide **InterRail** and **Eurail** passes (see page 24) are accepted on the Trenitalia network, though you will still have to book for certain trains and pay a supplement for travel on the Freccia trains; children's, youth (under-26) and group tickets are available.

By bus

Trains don't go everywhere and sooner or later you'll probably have to use **regional buses** (*autobus*). Nearly all places are connected by some kind of bus service, but in out-of-the-way towns and villages schedules can be sketchy and are drastically reduced – sometimes nonexistent – at weekends, especially on Sundays. Bear in mind also that in rural areas schedules are often designed with the working and/or school day in mind – meaning an early start if you want to catch that day's one bus out of town, and occasionally a complete absence of services during school holidays.

There's no national **bus company**, though a few regional ones do operate beyond their own immediate area. **Bus terminals** (*autostazione*) are often conveniently located next to the train station; wherever possible we've detailed their whereabouts in the text. In smaller towns and villages, most buses pull in at the central piazza; timetables are widely available. Buy **tickets** immediately before you travel from the

TIMETABLE READING

On **timetables** – and parking signs – *lavorativo* or *feriale* is the word for the Monday-to-Saturday service, represented by two crossed hammers; *festivo* means that a train runs only on Sundays and holidays, symbolized by a Christian cross.

Some other common terms on timetables are:

escluso sabato	not including Saturdays
si effettua fino al …	running until …
si effettua dal …	starting from …
giornalmente	daily
prenotazione obbligatoria	reservation obligatory
estivo	summer
invernale	winter

bus station ticket office, or on the bus itself; on longer hauls you can try to buy them in advance online direct from the bus company, but seat reservations are not normally possible. If you want to get off, ask *Posso scendere?*; "the next stop" is *la prossima fermata*.

City buses are always cheap, usually costing around €1.20. **Tickets** are commonly available from newsagents and tobacconists. Once on board, you must validate your ticket in the machine at the front or back of the bus. The whole system is based on trust, though in most cities checks for fare-dodging are regularly made, and hefty spot-fines are levied against offenders.

By car

Travelling **by car** in Italy is relatively painless, though cities and their ring roads can be hard work. The roads are good, the motorway network very comprehensive, and the notorious Italian drivers rather less erratic than their reputation suggests – in the north of the country at least. The best plan is to avoid driving in cities as much as possible; the congestion, proliferation of complex one-way systems and confusing signage can make it a nightmare.

Bear in mind that **traffic** can be heavy on main roads (particularly over public holiday weekends and throughout August) and appalling in city centres. Rush hour during the week usually runs from 7.30am to 9am and from 5pm to 9pm, when roads in and around the major cities can be gridlocked.

Although Italians are by no means the world's worst drivers they don't win any **safety** prizes either. The secret is to make it very clear what you're going to do – and then do it. A particular danger for unaccustomed drivers is the large number of scooters that can appear suddenly from the blind spot or dash across junctions and red lights with alarming recklessness.

Most **petrol stations** have someone who will fill the tank for you, with some giving the choice of self-service (*fai da te*). Petrol stations, in particular the small stations in the more remote locations, often have the same working hours as shops, which means they'll be closed for a couple of hours at midday, will shut up shop at around 7pm and are likely to be closed on Sundays (this does not apply to petrol stations on motorways, which are always open). Outside these times many have a self-service facility for which you pay into a machine between the pumps by bank note or, more rarely, credit card; these are often not well advertised so you might need to go onto the forecourt to check.

Rules of the road

Rules of the road are straightforward: drive on the right; at junctions, where there's any ambiguity, give precedence to vehicles coming from the right; observe the speed limits – 50km/hr in built-up areas, 110km/hr on dual carriageways (90km/hr when it's raining) and 130km/hr on autostradas (110km/hr in the rain); for camper vans, these limits are 50km/hr, 80km/hr and 100km/hr respectively – and don't drink and drive. Drivers need to have their dipped headlights on while using any road outside a built-up area.

The centres of many Italian towns and villages have a **Zona Traffico Limitato** (ZTL; restricted traffic area), where vehicle access is for residents only. These zones are marked by a red-rimmed circular road sign giving the hours and days of the limitation and are vigorously enforced, often by police on the ground as well as by cameras. Note that car-rental companies invariably pass the fine on. That said, if you are staying at a hotel within a ZTL area you can normally drive in to drop off your bags or even park if the hotel has parking, but you must make sure you give your number plate to your hotel so they can register it with the local authorities, thereby avoiding a fine. Double check with your hotel first.

If you're bringing your own car, as well as current insurance, you need a valid driving licence and an international driving permit if you're a non-EU licence holder. It's compulsory to carry your car documents and passport while you're driving, and you can be fined

WALK/DON'T WALK

It's worth bearing in mind that cars do not automatically stop at **pedestrian crossings** in Italy. Even on crossings with traffic lights you can be subjected to some close calls. Note that when there's a green light for pedestrians to go, it may be green for one of the lines of traffic too.

on the spot if you cannot present them when stopped by the police. It's also obligatory to carry a warning triangle and a fluorescent jacket in case of breakdown. For more information, consult Ⓦtheaa.com.

Note that it is a legal requirement to have snow tyres or chains on board between mid-November and mid-April when travelling on motorways; you will incur a hefty fine if you're not suitably equipped.

Motorway driving

The majority of **motorways** (*autostrade*) are toll roads. Take a ticket as you join the motorway and pay on exit; the amount due is flashed up on a screen in front of you. Paying by cash is the most straightforward option – booths are marked "cash/*contanti*" and colour-coded white. Avoid the Telepass lane (colour-coded yellow), for which you have to have a linked bank account. Be alert as you get into lane as traffic zigzags in and out at high speed to get pole position at the shortest-looking queue. Since other roads can be frustratingly slow, tolls are well worth it over long distances, but be prepared for queues at exits at peak times, and rates can mount up on a long journey.

Parking

Parking can be a problem. Don't be surprised to see cars parked just about anywhere, notably on pavements and seemingly working tram lines and at bus stops – it would be unwise to follow suit. Parking attendants are especially active in tourist areas and if you get fed up with driving around and settle for a space in a *zona di rimozione* (tow-away zone), don't expect your car to be there when you get back.

Most towns and villages have pay-and-display areas just outside the centre, but they can get very full in high season. An increasing number of towns operate a colour-coded parking scheme: **blue-zone** parking spaces (delineated by a blue line) usually have a maximum stay of one or two hours; they cost around €0.70–1.50/hour (pay at meters, to attendants wearing authorizing badges or buy scratchcards from local tobacconists) but are sometimes free at lunchtimes, after 8pm and on Sundays. Meters can usually be fed the night before to allow a lie-in in the morning. Much coveted **white-zone** spaces (white lines) are free; **yellow-zone** areas (yellow lines) are for disabled drivers or delivery zones. In smaller towns, to use the designated areas, it's handy to have a mini clock-like dial which you set and display in the windscreen, to indicate when you parked and that you're still within the allowed limit. Rental cars generally come equipped with these, and some tourist offices have them too.

Car parks, usually small, enclosed garages, are universally expensive, costing up to €20 a day in big cities; it's not unknown for hotels to state that they have parking and then direct you to the nearest paying garage. Parking at night is easier than during the day, but make sure you're not parked in a street that turns into a market in the morning or on the one day of the week when it's cleaned in the small hours, otherwise you're likely to be towed.

Never leave anything visible in the car when you're not using it, including the radio. Certain cities have appalling reputations for theft – in Naples, some rental agencies won't insure a car left anywhere except in a locked garage. A patrolled car park is probably the safest overnight option, especially if you have foreign plates.

Breakdown

In the event of a **breakdown**, call Ⓣ116 or the ACI (the national motoring association) on Ⓣ803 116, who will send someone out – this is expensive if you need a tow, unless you already have cover with a motoring organization in your home country. Alternatively, consult the Yellow Pages (*Pagine Gialle*) under "*Autoriparazioni*" for specialized repair shops.

Car rental

Car rental in Italy can be pricey, especially in high season and in smaller towns – around €200–300/week for a small hatchback, with unlimited mileage, if booked in advance. In bigger cities there are savings to be made – in Rome, for example, booking in advance and shopping around, you can rent a small car for a week for under £100. Local firms can be less expensive and often have an office at the airport – as do all the major chains – but generally the best deals are to be had by arranging things in advance; you can compare rates and book at Ⓦcarrentals.co.uk. You need to be over 21 to rent a car in Italy and will need a credit card to act as a deposit when picking up your vehicle. If booking with a small local company, be sure to check whether CDW is included in the price before booking. **Sat nav systems** are available to rent with cars from many outlets; reserve in advance.

Camper van rental

Camper van or mobile home holidays are becoming increasingly popular in Italy – it's convenient, facil-

ities in campsites are usually dependable (see page 31), and more and more resorts have created free camper-van parking areas (*sosta camper*). Blurent (Ⓦ blurent.com), Comocaravan (Ⓦ comocaravan.it) and Magicamper (Ⓦ magicamper.com) are among the companies offering new (or newish) quality vehicles for rent. Prices are usually around €900 for a four-berth vehicle for a week in high season, with unlimited mileage.

By plane

Like most European countries, internal airfares in Italy have been revolutionized in the last decade or so. **Budget airlines** open and close every season and there are often special deals being advertised; it pays to shop around and, as always, book as far in advance as you can.

DOMESTIC AIRLINES

Air Dolomiti Ⓦ airdolomiti.eu.
Alitalia Ⓦ alitalia.com.
Blue Panorama Ⓦ blue-panorama.com.
Meridiana Ⓦ airitaly.com.

By ferry and hydrofoil

Italy has a well-developed network of **ferries** and **hydrofoils** operated by a number of different private companies. Large car-ferries connect the major islands of Sardinia and Sicily with the mainland ports of Genoa, Livorno, La Spezia, Civitavecchia, Fiumicino and Naples, while the smaller island groupings – the Bay of Naples islands, the Pontine islands, the Aeolian islands – are usually linked to a number of nearby mainland towns. The larger lakes in the north of the country are also well served with regular boats and ferries in season, although these are drastically reduced in winter.

Fares are quite expensive, with hydrofoils costing around twice as much as ferries, and on some of the more popular services – to Sardinia, for example – you should book well in advance in summer, especially if you're taking a vehicle across. Remember, too, that sailings are cut outside the summer months, and some services stop altogether. You'll find a broad guide to journey times and frequencies in the "Arrival and departure" sections within the Guide; for full schedules and prices, check Ⓦ directferries.co.uk or the Italian website Ⓦ traghetti.com.

By bike and motorbike

Cycling is a very popular sport and mode of transport in much of Italy. Italians in small towns and villages are welcoming to cyclists, and hotels and hostels will take your bike in overnight for safekeeping. On the islands, in the mountains, around the Italian Lakes, in major resorts and larger cities, it's usually possible to **rent** a bike, but in rural areas rental facilities are few and far between.

Serious cyclists might consider staying at one of a chain of hotels (Italy Bike Hotels; Ⓣ 39 0541 307 531, Ⓦ italybikehotels.it) that cater specifically for cycling enthusiasts. Each hotel has a secure room for your bike, a maintenance workshop, overnight laundry facilities, suggested itineraries and group-tour possibilities, a doctor on hand and even dietary consultation. Bikes can be taken on local and slower Regionale trains if you buy a *supplemento bici* (bike supplement) for €3.50, or for free in a bike bag; on faster Eurostar or equivalent trains cycles must be placed in bike bags.

An alternative is to tour by **motorbike**, though there are relatively few rental places. **Mopeds** and **scooters** are comparatively easy to find: virtually everyone in Italy can ride one and although they're not really built for long-distance travel, for shooting around towns and islands they're ideal. Helmets are compulsory.

Accommodation

There is an infinite variety of accommodation in Italy: mountain monasteries, boutique hotels, youth hostels, self-catering villas, family-run B&Bs and rural farmhouses. While rarely particularly cheap, standards are fairly reliable.

In popular resorts and the major cities **booking ahead** is advisable, particularly during July or August, while for Venice, Rome and Florence it's pretty much essential to book ahead from Easter until late September and over Christmas and New Year. The phrases in our Language section (see page 1024) should help you get over the language barrier.

Hotels

Italy has some of the most memorable hotels in Europe, ranging from grand hotels oozing *belle époque* glamour to boutique hotels on the cutting edge of contemporary design. As is commonplace throughout Europe, Italian hotels are given an official rating of between one and five stars based on facilities and services, such as the number of rooms with en-suite bathroom or telephone, whether there is a restaurant on site, and whether there is 24-hour service. This means that the star rating is no guide to a hotel's subtler, more subjective charms, such as the style of decor or the friendliness or helpfulness of staff.

In very busy places at peak times of the year it's not unusual to have to stay for a minimum of three nights, and many proprietors will add the price of **breakfast** to your bill whether you want it or not. Make sure to check whether breakfast is included and, if it's not, you can always grab a brioche and a cappuccino from a bar. Be warned, too, that in major resorts you will often be obliged to take **half or full board** in high season. Note that people travelling alone may sometimes have to pay for a double room even when they only need a single, though it can also work the other way round – if all their **single rooms** are taken, a hotelier may well put you in a double room but only charge the single rate.

Bed and breakfasts

Bed and breakfast schemes are becoming a very popular alternative form of accommodation. The best ones offer a real flavour of Italian home life, though they're not necessarily cheaper than an inexpensive hotel, and they rarely accept credit cards. Some places going under the name are actually little different from private rooms, with the owners not living on the premises, but you'll invariably find them clean and well maintained. The most recent trend is for boutique B&Bs, often in stylishly revamped old *palazzi*. Check out Ⓦbbitalia.it, Ⓦbbplanet.it and Ⓦbed-and-breakfast.it.

Hostels

There is a good network of private and HI **hostels** throughout the country – from family-friendly institutions on the edge of large cities to sociable town-centre backpacker-focused options. **Rates** are roughly €20 for a dorm bed, while for a double you could be paying anything upwards of €60. You can easily base a tour of the country around them, although for two people travelling together they don't always represent a massive saving on the cheapest double hotel room. If you're travelling on your own, on the other hand, hostels are usually more sociable and can work out a lot cheaper; many have facilities such as inexpensive restaurants and self-catering kitchens that enable you to cut costs further.

HI hostels are members of the official International Youth Hostel Federation, and you'll need to be a member of the organization in order to use them – you can join through your home country's youth hostelling organization (see below) or often at the hostel on arrival. You need to reserve well ahead in the summer, most conveniently by using Ⓦhostelbookers.com or Ⓦhostelworld.com.

In some cities, it's also possible to stay in **student accommodation** vacated by Italian students in July and August. Accommodation is generally in individual rooms and can work out a lot cheaper than a hotel room. Again you'll need to book in advance: for details, see Ⓦitaly.accommodationforstudents.com.

Monasteries and convents

You will also come across accommodation operated by **religious organizations** – convents (normally for women only), welcome houses and the like, again with a mixture of dormitory and individual rooms, which can sometimes be a way of cutting costs as well as meeting like-minded people. Most operate a curfew of some sort, and you should bear in mind that they don't always work out any cheaper than a bottom-line one-star hotel. Information can be found in the local tourist offices.

An online agency, Monastery Stays (Ⓦmonasterystays.com), offers a centralized booking service for over five hundred convents and monasteries around Italy. There are no restrictions on age, sex or faith, all rooms have private bathrooms and few places have early curfews.

Self-catering

Self-catering is becoming an increasingly feasible option for visitors to Italy's cities. High prices mean that renting rooms or an **apartment** can be an attractive, cost-effective choice. Usually in well-located positions in city centres, and available for a couple of

ACCOMMODATION PRICES

An increasing number of hotels are beginning to base room prices on **demand**, rather than simply on season, particularly those that have booking facilities online. In addition **rates** vary greatly between the south and north of Italy, as well as between tourist hot spots and more rural areas. Although we have given a price reflective of the **cheapest standard high-season double** booked a couple of months in advance, be aware that there are increasingly huge fluctuations in price. As a rule, substantial discounts are to be had by booking **online** well in advance, or by looking for last-minute hotel bargains online on sites such as Ⓦlastminute.com, Ⓦbooking.com or Ⓦlaterooms.com.

AGRITURISMO

The **agriturismo** scheme, which allows the owners of country estates, vineyards and farms to rent out converted barns and farm buildings to tourists, has boomed in recent years. Usually these comprise a self-contained flat or building, though a few places just rent rooms on a bed-and-breakfast basis. While some rooms are still annexed to working farms or vineyards, many are smart, self-contained rural holiday properties; attractions may include home-grown food, swimming pools and a range of outdoor activities. Many *agriturismi* have a minimum-stay requirement of one week in busy periods.

Rates start at around €120/night for self-contained places with two bedrooms. Tourist offices keep lists of local properties; alternatively, you can search one of the agriturismo websites – try Ⓦ agriturismo.it, Ⓦ agriturismo.com, Ⓦ agriitalia.it and Ⓦ agriturist.it.

nights to a month or so, they come equipped with bedding and kitchen utensils, and there's nothing like shopping for supplies in a local market to make you feel part of Italian daily life.

If you don't intend to travel around a lot it might be worth renting a **villa** or farmhouse for a week or two. Most tend to be located in the affluent northern areas of Italy, especially Tuscany and Umbria, although attractive options are also available on Sicily and Sardinia and other rural locations too. They don't come cheap, but are of a high standard and often enjoy marvellous locations.

VILLA AND APARTMENT COMPANIES

Bridgewater UK Ⓣ 0161 787 8587, Ⓦ bridgewatertravel.co.uk. Family owned and managed company sourcing exclusive villas in Italy.

CV Villas UK Ⓣ 0203 355 0756, Ⓦ cvvillas.com. Great website listing luxury holiday villas including designer villas, dog-friendly villas, villas for two, and more.

Friendly Rentals UK Ⓣ 0800 520 0373, Ⓦ friendlyrentals.com. Well-run company offering properties in Milan, Florence, Venice and Rome to suit most budgets.

HomeAway UK Ⓦ homeaway.co.uk. This site puts you in touch directly with the owners of over a thousand Italian properties.

Ilios Travel UK Ⓣ 01444 225 633, Ⓦ iliostravel.com. High-quality selection of country mansions and villas, in various parts of the country.

Italian Breaks UK Ⓣ 020 8666 0407, Ⓦ italianbreaks.com. Accommodation for a range of budgets.

Livingitalia Italy Ⓣ 39 06 3211 0998, Ⓦ livingitalia.com. Apartments in Florence and Rome.

Owners Direct UK Ⓦ ownersdirect.co.uk. User-friendly website advertising thousands of villas and apartments across Italy, booked direct through the owner.

Mountain refuges

If you're planning on hiking and climbing, check out the **rifugi** network, consisting of almost eight hundred mountain huts owned by the Club Alpino Italiano (**CAI**; Ⓣ 02 205 7231, Ⓦ cai.it). Nonmembers can use them for around €24 a night, though make sure you book well in advance, especially in the height of summer. There are also private *rifugi* that charge around double this. Most are fairly spartan, with bunks in unheated dorms, but their settings can be magnificent and usually leave you well placed to continue your hike the next day. Note that the word *rifugio* can be used for anything from a smart chalet-hotel to a snack bar at the top of a cable-car line.

Camping

Camping is popular in Italy and there are plenty of sites, mostly on the coast, in the mountains and around the lakes, and generally open April to September (though winter "camping" – in caravans and camper vans – is common in ski areas). The majority are well equipped and often have bungalows, mainly with four to six beds. On the coast in high season you can expect to pay a daily rate of around €12/person plus €10–15/tent or caravan and €8/vehicle; unless otherwise stated, prices in the Guide are for two people. Local tourist offices have details of nearby sites, or see Ⓦ camping.it.

Food and drink

The importance Italians attach to food and drink makes any holiday in the country a treat. The southern Italian diet especially, with its emphasis on olive oil, fresh and plentiful fruit, vegetables and fish, is one of the healthiest in Europe, and there are few national cuisines that can boast so much variety in both ingredients and cooking methods. Italy's wines, too, are among the finest and most diverse in the world.

Italian food remains determinedly regional. Northern Italian cuisine includes the butter-, cream- and truffle-rich cooking of the French-influenced northwest, the Tyrolean ham, sausage and dumplings of the

NO SMOKING

Smoking is banned in all enclosed public spaces in Italy. Any restaurant or bar that wants to allow smoking has to follow very stringent rules in isolating a separate room – including doors and special air conditioning. Needless to say this is beyond the pockets of most places and so the majority remain no-smoking throughout, except for restaurants with outdoor terraces and gardens.

northeast, and the light basil, fish and pine nut dishes of Liguria. Food in central Italy is characterized by the hearty wood-roasted steaks of rural Tuscany and the black truffles, hams and salamis of Umbria, while in traditional trattorias of Rome, offal reigns supreme. Continuing south, the classic vegetables of the Mediterranean take over, with plump juicy tomatoes featuring heavily. In Sicily, history is enshrined in rich, fragrant dishes such as aubergine *caponata*, fish couscous, and almond-milk- and jasmine-scented *granitas*, the abiding legacy of Arab rule.

Restaurants

Traditionally, a trattoria is a cheaper and more basic purveyor of home-style cooking (*cucina casalinga*), while a *ristorante* is more upmarket. *Osterie* are common too, basically an old-fashioned restaurant or pub-like place specializing in home cooking, though some upmarket places with pretensions to established antiquity borrow the name. A pizzeria is always best with a *forno a legna* (wood-burning oven) rather than an electric one. In mid-range establishments, pasta dishes go for €7–14, while the main fish or meat courses will normally cost between €12 and €18.

The menu

Traditionally, lunch (*pranzo*) and dinner (*cena*) start with an **antipasto** (literally "before the meal"), a course consisting of various cold cuts of meat, fish or vegetable dishes, generally costing €8–12. Some places offer self-service antipasto buffets. The next course, the **primo**, involves soup, risotto or pasta, and is followed by the **secondo** – the meat or fish course, usually served alone, except for perhaps a wedge of lemon or tomato. Fish will often be served whole or by weight – 250g is usually plenty for one person, or ask to have a look at the fish before it's cooked. Note that by law, any ingredients that have been frozen need to be marked (usually with an asterisk and "*surgelato*") on the menu. Vegetables or salads – **contorni** – are ordered and served separately: potatoes can come as fries (*patate fritte*), but you can also find boiled (*lesse*) or roast (*arrosto* or *al forno*) potatoes, while salads are either green (*verde*) or mixed (*mista*) and vegetables (*verdure*) usually come very well boiled. Afterwards, you'll have a choice of **desserts** (*dolci*) – sometimes just ice cream or *macedonia* (fresh fruit salad), but often home-made items, like apple or pear cake (*torta di mele/pere*), *tiramisù* or trifle (*zuppa inglese*). **Cheeses** (*formaggi*) are always worth a shot if you have any room left; ask to try a selection of local varieties.

You will need quite an appetite to tackle all these courses and it's perfectly acceptable to order less. If you're not sure of the size of the portions, start with a pasta or rice dish and ask to order the *secondo* when you've finished the first course. And don't feel shy about just having an antipasto and a *primo*; they're probably the best way of trying local specialities anyway.

At the end of the meal ask for the **bill** (*il conto*); bear in mind that almost everywhere you'll pay a **cover charge** (*coperto* – effectively a service charge) of €1.50–3 a head, with prices varying depending on the quality of the establishment. In many trattorias the bill amounts to little more than an illegible scrap of paper; if you want to check it, ask for a **receipt** (*ricevuta*). If service isn't included it's common just to leave a couple of coins as a **tip**, unless you're particularly pleased with the service, in which case, leave up to ten percent. In more expensive places, service (*servizio*) will often be added on top of the cover charge, generally about ten percent; if it isn't, leave what you feel is appropriate for the service you received – up to ten percent.

Breakfast

Most Italians start their day in a bar, their **breakfast** (*prima colazione*) consisting of a coffee and a *brioche* or *cornetto* – a croissant often filled with jam, custard or chocolate, which you usually help yourself to from the counter and eat standing at the bar. It will cost between €1.30 and €1.60, more if you sit down. Breakfast in a hotel is all too often a limp affair of bread, pastries and processed meats, often not worth the price.

Pizza and snacks

Italy remains the best place to eat **pizza** – it usually comes thin and flat, not deep-pan, and the choice of toppings is fairly limited, with none of the dubious pineapple and sweetcorn variations. For a quality pizza opt for somewhere with a wood-fired oven (*forno a legna*) rather than a squeaky-clean electric one, so that the pizzas arrive blasted and bubbling on the surface

and with a distinctive charcoal taste. This adherence to tradition means that it's unusual to find a good pizzeria open at lunchtime; it takes hours for a wood-fired oven to heat up to the necessary temperature.

On the whole **pizzerias** don't sell much else besides pizza, soft drinks and beer. A basic cheese and tomato *margherita* can cost from €4 to €8, depending on how fancy the pizzeria is. More elaborate pizzas will cost from around €6–10, and it's quite acceptable to cut it into slices and eat it with your fingers. Consult our food glossary (see page 1027) for the different varieties.

For a lunchtime snack, you can grab a slice of *pizza al taglio*, a large slice of pizza; take it away or eat at one of the small casual tables that are usually available. **Sandwiches (panini)** are pretty substantial, a bread stick or roll packed with any number of fillings. A sandwich bar (*paninoteca*) in larger towns and cities, and in smaller places a grocer's shop (*alimentari*), will normally make you up whatever you want. Bars, particularly in the north, may also offer *tramezzini*, ready-made sliced white bread with mixed fillings.

Other sources of quick snacks are **markets**, where fresh, flavoursome produce is sold, often including cheese, cold meats, warm spit-roast chicken and *arancini*, deep-fried balls of rice with meat (*rosso*) or butter and cheese (*bianco*) filling that are traditionally from Sicily. **Bread shops** (*panetterie*) often serve slices of pizza or focaccia (bread with oil and salt topped with rosemary, olives or tomato). **Supermarkets**, also, are an obvious stop for a picnic lunch: larger branches are on the outskirts of cities, while smaller supermarkets can be found in town centres.

Vegetarians and vegans

The quality of fruit and vegetables in Italy is excellent, with local, seasonal produce available throughout the country. There are numerous pasta sauces without meat, some superb vegetable antipasti and, if you eat fish and seafood, you should have no problem at all. Salads, too, are fresh and good. Outside the cities and resorts, you might be wise to check if a dish has meat in it (*C'è carne dentro?*) or ask for it "*senza carne e pesce*" to make sure it doesn't contain poultry or prosciutto.

Vegans will have a much harder time, though pizzas without cheese (*marinara* – nothing to do with fish – is a common option) are a good stand-by, and vegetable soup (*minestrone*) is usually just that.

Drinks

Although *un mezzo* (half-litre carafe of house wine) is a standard accompaniment to a meal, there's not a great emphasis on dedicated **drinking** in Italy. Public drunkenness is rare, young people don't devote their nights to getting wasted, and women especially are frowned on if they're seen to be overindulging. Nonetheless there's a wide choice of alcoholic drinks available, often at low prices. Soft drinks, crushed-ice drinks and, of course, mineral water are widely available.

Where to drink

Traditional **bars** are less social centres than functional places and are all very similar to each other – brightly lit places, with a counter, a coffee machine and a handful of tables. This is the place to come for a cappuccino in the morning, and a quick coffee or a drink in the afternoon – people don't generally idle away evenings in bars. Indeed in some more rural areas it's difficult to find a bar open much after 8pm.

It's cheapest to drink standing at the counter, in which case you pay first at the cash desk (*la cassa*), present your receipt (*scontrino*) to the barperson and give your order. If there's waiter service, just sit where you like, though bear in mind that this will cost up to twice as much as standing at the bar, especially if you sit outside (*fuori*) – the difference is shown on the price list as *tavola* (table). Late-night bars and pubs rarely operate on the *scontrino* system; you may be asked to pay up front, in the British manner, or be presented with a bill. If not, head for the counter when you leave – the barperson will have kept a surprisingly accurate tally.

Real enthusiasts of the grape should head for an **enoteca**, a dedicated wine bar, generally with a decent variety of wines available by the glass. Cities offer a much greater variety of places to sit and drink in the evening, with Italy's larger metropolises such as Rome, Milan and Turin offering plenty of places with live music or DJs.

Coffee and tea

Always excellent, **coffee** can be taken small and black (espresso, or just *caffè*), which costs around €1 a cup, or white and frothy (cappuccino, for about €1.30), but there are scores of variations. If you want your espresso watered down, ask for a *caffè lungo* or, for something more like a filter coffee, an *Americano*; espresso with a drop of milk is a *caffè macchiato*; very milky is *caffè latte* or (in the south) *latte macchiato* (ordering just a "*latte*" will get you a glass of milk). Coffee with a shot of alcohol – and you can ask for just about anything – is *caffè corretto*. Many places also serve decaffeinated coffee; in summer you might want to have your coffee cold (*caffè freddo*).

If you're not up for a coffee, there's always **tea**. In summer you can drink this cold, too (*tè freddo*) – excellent for taking the heat off. Hot tea (*tè caldo*) isn't'

very popular at all; it comes with lemon (*con limone*) unless you ask for milk (*con latte*). A small selection of herbal teas (*infusion* or *tisane*) are generally available: camomile (*camomilla*) and peppermint (*menta*) are the most common.

Soft drinks and water

There are various **soft drinks** (*analcolici*) to choose from. Slightly fizzy, bitter drinks like San Bittèr or Crodino are common, especially at *aperitivo* time. A **spremuta** is a fresh fruit juice, squeezed at the bar, usually orange, but sometimes lemon or grapefruit. There are also crushed-ice **granitas**, big in Sicily and offered in several flavours, available with or without whipped cream (*panna*) on top. Otherwise you'll find the usual range of fizzy drinks and concentrated juices: the home-grown Italian version of Coke, Chinotto, is less sweet and good with a slice of lemon. **Tap water** (*acqua del rubinetto*) is quite palatable in some places, undrinkable in others: it's perfectly safe to drink (see page 40), though few Italians would dream of imbibing it. **Mineral water** (*acqua minerale*) is ubiquitous, and available both still (*naturale, liscia* or *senza gas*) and sparkling (*frizzante* or *con gas*).

Beer and spirits

Beer (*birra*) usually comes in one-third or two-third litre bottles, or on tap (*alla spina*), measure for measure more expensive than the bottled variety. A small beer is a *piccola* (20cl or 25cl), a larger one (usually 40cl) a *media*. The cheapest and most common brands are the Italian Moretti, Peroni and Dreher, all of which are very good; if this is what you want, either state the brand name or ask for *birra nazionale* or *birra chiara* – otherwise you could end up with a more expensive imported beer. You may also come across darker beers (*birra nera, birra rossa* or *doppio malto*), which have a sweeter, maltier taste and in appearance resemble stout or bitter.

All the usual **spirits** are on sale and known mostly by their generic names. There are also Italian brands of the main varieties: one of the country's best brandies is Vecchia Romagna. A generous shot costs about €1.50, imported stuff much more.

You'll also find **fortified wines** like Martini, Cinzano and Campari; ask for a Campari-soda and you'll get a ready-mixed version from a little bottle; a slice of lemon is a *spicchio di limone*, ice is *ghiaccio*. You might also try Cynar – an artichoke-based sherry often drunk as an aperitif with water.

There's also a daunting selection of **liqueurs**. Amaro is a bitter after-dinner drink or *digestivo*; Amaretto much sweeter with a strong taste of almond; Sambuca a sticky-sweet aniseed concoction, traditionally served with a coffee bean in it and set on fire (though, increasingly, this is something put on to impress tourists). A shot of clear grappa is a common accompaniment to a coffee and can range from a warming palate-cleanser to throat-burning firewater, while another sweet alternative, originally from Sorrento, is *limoncello*, a lemon-based liqueur best drunk in a frozen vase-shaped glass. *Strega* is another drink you'll see behind every bar, yellow, herb-and-saffron-based stuff in tall, elongated bottles: about as sweet as it looks but not unpleasant.

Wine

From sparkling prosecco to deep-red chianti, Italy is renowned for its wines. However, it's rare to find the snobbery often associated with "serious" wine drinking. Light **reds** such as those made from the *dolcetto* grape are hauled out of the fridge in hot weather, while some full-bodied **whites** are drunk at near room temperature. In restaurants you'll invariably be offered red (*rosso*) or white (*bianco*) – though rosé (*rosato*) is slowly becoming more available. The local stuff (*vino sfuso*) can be great or awful – there's no way of telling without trying – but it is inexpensive at an average of around €5 a litre, and you can always order just a glass or a quarter-litre (*un quarto*) to see what it's like. Bottled wine is pricier but still very good value; expect to pay €9–20 a bottle in a mid-priced restaurant, and less than half that from a shop or supermarket. In bars you can buy a decent glass of wine for about €3.

The media

Italy's decentralized press serves to emphasize the strength of regionalism in the country. Local TV is popular, too, in the light of little competition from the national channels. If you know where to look, journalistic standards can be high but you might find yourself turning to foreign TV channels or papers if you want an international outlook on events.

Newspapers

The **Italian press** is largely regionally based, with just a few newspapers available across the country. The centre-left *La Repubblica* (Ⓦ repubblica.it) and authoritative right-slanted *Corriere della Sera* (Ⓦ corriere.it) are the two most widely read, published nationwide with local supplements, but originating in Rome and Milan respectively. Provincial newspapers include *La Stampa* (Ⓦ lastampa.it), the daily of Turin, and *Il Messaggero* (Ⓦ ilmessaggero.it) of Rome – both rather stuffy, establishment sheets. *Il Mattino* (Ⓦ ilmattino.

it) is the more readable publication of Naples and the Campania region, while other southern editions include the *Giornale di Sicilia* (Ⓦgds.it) and the *Gazzetta del Sud* (Ⓦgazzettadelsud.it). The traditionally radical *Il Manifesto* (Ⓦilmanifesto.info) has always been regarded as one of the most serious and influential sources of Italian journalism. Perhaps the most avidly read newspapers of all, however, are the specialist sports papers, most notably the *Corriere dello Sport* (Ⓦcorrieredellosport.it) and the pink *Gazzetta dello Sport* (Ⓦgazzetta.it) – both essential reading if you want an insight into the Italian football scene.

English-language newspapers can be found for around three times their home cover-price in all the larger cities and most resorts, usually a day late, though in Milan, Rome and Turin you can sometimes find papers on the day of publication. In remoter parts of the country it's not unusual for foreign papers to be delayed by several days.

TV and radio

Italian TV is renowned for its cheesy quiz shows, variety programmes and chat-shows squeezed in between countless advertisements. Of the three national channels, RAI 1, 2 and 3 have a number of worthwhile programmes and documentaries, although the intelligent, satirical shows are often indecipherable to foreigners who have anything less than an encyclopaedic knowledge of Italian politics from the last fifty years. **Satellite television** is widely distributed across the region, and hotels with three stars and above usually offer a mix of BBC World News, CNN, and French-, German- and Spanish-language news channels, as well as MTV and Eurosport.

As for **radio**, the most serious RAI channel is RAI 3, while the most listened-to pop radio stations are RTL (102.5 FM) and Radio Deejay (frequency depends on where you are listening – find them on Ⓦradiodeejay.it).

Festivals

Whether religious, traditional or cultural, there are literally thousands of festivals in Italy and sometimes the best are those that you come across unexpectedly in smaller towns.

Perhaps the most widespread local event in Italy is the **religious procession**, which can be a very dramatic affair. **Good Friday** is celebrated – particularly in the south – by parading models of Christ through the streets accompanied by white-robed, hooded figures singing penitential hymns. Many processions have strong pagan roots, marking important dates on the calendar and only relatively recently sanctified by the Church.

Despite the dwindling number of practising Catholics in Italy, there has been a revival of **pilgrimages** over the last couple of decades. These are as much social occasions as spiritual journeys with, for example, as many as a million pilgrims travelling through the night, mostly on foot, to the **Shrine of the Madonna di Polsi** in the inhospitable Aspromonte mountains in Calabria. Sardinia's biggest festival, the **Festa di Sant'Efisio**, sees a four-day march from Cagliari to Pula and back, to commemorate the saint's martyrdom.

Recently there's been a revival of the **carnival** (*carnevale*), the last fling before Lent, although the anarchic fun of the past has generally been replaced by elegant, self-conscious affairs, with ingenious costumes and handmade masks. The main places are Venice, Viareggio in Tuscany and Acireale in Sicily.

Many festivals invoke local pride in **tradition**. Medieval contests like the **Palio** horse race in Siena perpetuate allegiances to certain competing clans, while other towns put on crossbow, jousting and flag-twirling contests, accompanied by marching bands in full costume. These festivals are highly significant to those involved, with fierce rivalry between participants.

There are literally hundreds of **food festivals**, sometimes advertised as **sagre**, and usually celebrating the regional speciality with dancing, brass bands and noisy fireworks. Every region has them – look in the local papers or ask at the tourist office.

The country's **arts festivals**, particularly in central Italy, are often based in ancient amphitheatres or within medieval walls and occasionally mark the work of a native composer. Major concerts and opera are usually well advertised and extremely popular, so book well in advance.

A festival calendar

Some of the highlights are listed here – more appear in the Guide. Note that dates change from year to year, so contact the local tourist office for specifics.

JANUARY

Milan Epifania (Jan 6). Costumed parade of the Three Kings from the Duomo to Sant'Eustorgio, the resting place of the bones of the Magi.

Rome Epifania (Jan 6). Toy and sweet fair in Piazza Navona, to celebrate the Befana, the good witch who brings toys and sweets to children who've been good, and coal to those who haven't.

FEBRUARY

Sicily Festa di Sant'Agata (Feb 3–5). Riotous religious procession in Catania.

Carnevale (weekend before Lent). Carnival festivities in Venice (carnevale.venezia.it), Viareggio (viareggio.ilcarnevale.com), Foiano della Chiana, near Arezzo (carnevaledifoiano.it), Cento, near Ferrara (carnevalecento.com), plus many towns throughout Italy.
Ivrea Battle of the Oranges (Carnival Sun–Shrove Tues). A messy few days when processions through the streets are an excuse to pelt each other with orange pulp; storicocarnevaleivrea.it.
Agrigento Almond Blossom Festival (ten days in mid-Feb). Colourful celebration of spring with folk music from around the world.

MARCH

Rome Rome Marathon (usually Sun in late March, or early April). A 42km run though Rome's centre, starting at the Roman Forum and ending at the Colosseum; maratonadiroma.it.

APRIL

Nocera Terinese (Calabria) Rito dei Vattienti (Easter Sat). Macabre parade of flagellants whipping themselves with shards of glass.
Florence Lo Scoppio del Carro (Easter Sun). A symbolic firework display outside the Duomo after Mass.
Milan Salone Internazionale del Mobile (a week in mid-April). The city becomes a showcase for the world's best furniture and industrial design.

MAY

Cocullo, Abruzzo Festival of snakes (May 1). One of the most ancient festivals celebrating the patron saint, San Domenico Abate, in which his statue is draped with live snakes and paraded through town.
Gubbio, Umbria Corsa dei Ceri (May 15). Three 6m-high wooden figures, representing three patron saints, are raced through the old town by *ceraioli* in medieval costume.
Siracusa, Sicily Greek Drama festival (mid-May to end June). Classical plays performed by international companies in the spectacular ruins of the ancient Greek theatre.
Countrywide Cantine Aperte (last Sat & Sun). Wine estates all over Italy open their cellars to the public.

JUNE

Noto, Spello, Genzano Infiorata (weekend in May or June). Spectacular flower art festival in which dried petals are used to create large-scale artworks in the streets.
Florence Calcio Storico Fiorentino (early June with final on June 24th). Four teams wearing historical costume compete in a combination of football, rugby and wrestling originating in sixteenth-century Florence.
Verona Arena opera season (late June to late Aug); arena.it.
Ravello Ravello Festival (late June to late Aug). Amalfi Coast opera and chamber music festival; ravellofestival.com.
Amalfi, Genoa, Pisa, Venice Regatta of the Maritime Republics (first Sat & Sun in June). Costumed procession and a race in replica Renaissance boats. Venue alternates yearly; 2016 is Amalfi's turn.
Pisa Game of the Bridge (last Sat). A costumed parade and mock battle between rival teams on the town's main bridge.

JULY

Siena Palio (July 2). Medieval bareback horse race in the Campo.
Palermo Festino di Santa Rosalia (second week). A five-day street party to celebrate the city's patron saint.
Perugia Umbria Jazz Festival (second week). Italy's foremost jazz event, attracting top names from all over the world; umbriajazz.com.
Lucca Summer Festival (throughout July). International rock and pop artists perform all month; summer-festival.com.
Venice Festa del Redentore (third Sun). Venice's main religious festival, marked with a fireworks display.

AUGUST

Countrywide Ferragosto (Aug 15). National holiday with local festivals, water fights and fireworks all over Italy.
Siena Second Palio horse race (Aug 16).
Pesaro Rossini Opera Festival (two weeks in mid-Aug); rossinioperafestival.it.
Ferrara Ferrara Buskers Festival (mid-end Aug). Gathering of some of the world's best street performers; ferrarabuskers.com.

SEPTEMBER

Venice La Regata di Venezia (first Sun). The annual trial of strength for the city's gondoliers and other expert rowers; it starts with a procession of historic craft along the Canal Grande. regatastoricavenezia.it
Venice (early Sept). The world's oldest International Film Festival; labiennale.org.
Naples Festa di San Gennaro (Sept 19). Festival for the city's patron saint with crowds gathering in the cathedral to witness the liquefaction of San Gennaro's blood.

OCTOBER

Marino, Rome Sagra dell'Uva (first weekend). One of the country's most famous wine festivals, with fountains literally flowing with wine. sagradelluvamarino.it
Perugia EuroChocolate (ten days in mid-Oct). Italy's chocolate city celebrates. eurochocolate.com
Alba Truffle Festival (early Oct to late Nov). An opportunity to sample the prestigious white truffle along with the region's superb wines, some of the world's finest. fieradeltartufo.org

NOVEMBER

Countrywide Olive oil festivals all over Italy.

DECEMBER

Milan Oh bej! Oh bej! (Dec 7). The city's patron saint, Sant'Ambrogio, is celebrated with a huge street market around the Castello Sforzesco and a day off work and school for all.
Milan (Dec 7). Milan opera season starts with an all-star opening night at La Scala.
Orvieto Umbria Jazz Winter (end Dec to early Jan); umbriajazz.com.

Sports and outdoor pursuits

Spectator sports are popular in Italy, especially the hallowed *calcio* (football), and there is undying national passion for frenetic motor and cycle races. For visitors to Italy, the most accessible activities are centred on the mountains – where you can climb, ski, paraglide, raft, canoe or simply explore on foot or cycle – and the lake and coastal regions, with plenty of opportunities for swimming, sailing and windsurfing; Campania, Calabria and Sicily are particularly popular for scuba diving and snorkelling.

Football

Football – or **calcio** – is the national sport, followed fanatically by millions of Italians, and if you're at all interested in the game it would be a shame to leave the country without attending a *partita* or football match. The **season** starts around the middle of August, and finishes in June. **Il campionato** (the championship) is split into four principal divisions, with the twenty teams in the Serie A being the most prestigious. Matches are normally played on Sunday afternoons, although Saturday, Sunday evening and Monday games are becoming more common. See Ⓦ legaseriea.it for results, a calendar of events and English links to the official team websites. English-language Italian football sites are also worth a look – Ⓦ football-italia.net or Ⓦ footballitaliano.co.uk.

Tickets

Inevitably, **tickets** for Serie A matches are not cheap, starting at €15–25 for "*Curva*" seats where the *tifosi* or hard-core fans go, rising to €30–50 for the more widely available *distinti* tickets in the corners of the stadium, €60–100 for "*Tribuna*" seats along the side of the pitch, and €150 or more for the more comfortable "*Poltroncina*", cushioned seats in the centre of the *Tribuna*. Once at the football match, get into the atmosphere of the occasion by knocking back *borghetti*, a coffee liqueur.

You can get tickets from sites like Ⓦ www.listicket.it or Ⓦ seatwave.com, which will either sell you a ticket or give you details of the nearest outlet. You must carry photo ID when you purchase a ticket and when you go to a game.

Other spectator sports

Italy's chosen sport after football is **basketball**, introduced from the United States after World War II. Most cities have a team, and Italy is now ranked among the foremost in the world. The teams currently vying for the top spot are Montepaschi Siena, Olimpia Milano, Virtus Bologna, Banco di Sardegna Sassari and Dinamo Sassari. For more details on fixtures and the leagues, see Ⓦ eurobasket.com/italy/basketball.as.

In a country that has produced Ferrari, Maserati, Alfa Romeo and Fiat, it should come as no surprise that **motor racing** gives Italians such a buzz. There are grand prix tracks at Monza near Milan (home of the Italian Grand Prix) and at Imola, where the San Marino Grand Prix is held.

The other sport popular with participants and crowds of spectators alike is **cycling**. At weekends especially, you'll often see a club group out, dressed in bright team kit, whirring along on their slender machines. The annual Giro d'Italia (Ⓦ giroditalia.it) in May/early June is a prestigious event that attracts scores of international participants, closing down roads and creating great excitement.

Outdoor activities

With the Alps right on the doorstep, it's easy to spend a weekend **skiing** or **snowboarding** from Milan, Turin or Venice. Some of the most popular ski resorts are Sestriere and Bardonecchia in Piemonte, Cervinia and Courmayeur in Valle d'Aosta, the Val Gardena and Val di Fassa in the stunning Dolomite mountains of Trentino-Alto Adige and the Veneto – home to one of Italy's best-known and most exclusive resorts, Cortina d'Ampezzo. Further south you can ski at the small resorts of Abetone and Amiata in Tuscany, Monte Vettore in Le Marche, Gran Sasso and Maiella in Abruzzo, Aspromonte in Calabria and on Mount Etna in Sicily. Contact the regional tourist offices for information about accommodation, ski schools and prices of lift passes.

All these mountain resorts make equally good bases for summer **hiking** and **climbing**, and most areas have detailed maps with itineraries and marked paths. For less strenuous treks, the rolling hills of Tuscany and Umbria are perfect walking and **mountain-bike** country and numerous tour operators offer independent or escorted tours. Many tourist offices also publish booklets suggesting itineraries.

The extensive Italian coast offers all the usual seaside resort activities including plenty of opportunities for **sailing** and **windsurfing**. **Scuba diving** is popular in Sicily and off most of the smaller islands – you can either join a diving school or rent equipment if you're an experienced diver. You can get a guide and map suggesting **sailing itineraries** round the coast of southern Italy from the Italian State Tourist Office (see page 43).

Watersports aren't just restricted to the coast and can be found in places such as lakes Como and Garda

in the north, and Trasimeno and Bolsena further south towards Rome. River **canoeing**, **canyoning** and **rafting** are popular in the mountain areas of the north of the country.

Horseriding is becoming increasingly popular in rural areas, and most tourist offices have lists of local stables (*maneggi*). Some agriturismi (see page 31) also have riding facilities and sometimes offer daily or weekly treks and night rides. Note that Italians rarely wear or provide riding hats.

Shopping

There is no shortage of temptation for shoppers and souvenir-hunters in Italy, with the country's age-old expertise in textiles, ceramics, leather and glassware available in all price ranges.

There are factory outlets across the country, particularly for clothes and other textiles but also for pottery and glass; local tourist offices will be able to point you in the right direction. Rural areas usually have good basketware, local terracotta or ceramic items as well a veritable banquet of locally produced wine, olive oils, cheeses, hams and salamis. It's always worth rooting out the local speciality, even in urban centres: Turin is known for its chocolate, Milan is famous for designer clothes and furniture, Venice for glassware and lace, Florence for leather goods, Sicily and Perugia for ceramics.

Every large village and town has at least one weekly **market** and though these are usually geared towards household goods, they can be useful for picking up cheap clothing, basketware, ceramics and picnic ingredients.

Prices are mainly in line with most of Western Europe and are always a little higher in the north of the country and urban areas. **Credit/debit cards** are increasingly acceptable, with swipe-and-pin machines the norm – though some small shops may still accept only cash. **Haggling** is uncommon in most of Italy but in markets you might like to try your luck; ask for *uno sconto* (a discount) and see where it gets you. Bargaining is not practised when buying food, however, or in shops.

If you're resident outside the EU you are entitled to a rebate for the **VAT** (or *IVA*) paid on items over €155. You need to ask for a special receipt at the time of purchase and allow your goods to be checked at the airport and the receipt stamped when you leave the country.

Work and study

All EU citizens are eligible to work and study in Italy. Work permits are pretty impossible for non-EU citizens to obtain: you must have the firm promise of a job that no Italian could do before you can even apply to the Italian embassy in your home country.

Red tape

EU citizens staying for more than ninety days must visit the local *ufficio anagrafe* (registry office) to obtain a stamped **Dichiarazione di Presenza** (declaration of presence), within eight days of arrival. Non-EU citizens need to apply for a **Permesso di Soggiorno** (permit to stay) specifying the reason for their stay (for work, study and so on). You can pick up a "kit" at the post office (see page 41), which contains the necessary forms and instructions (in Italian only). Once completed, you submit the forms at the post office and keep the receipt as proof: *permessi* can take up to three months to obtain.

The other bureaucratic requirement is the **codice fiscale** (tax number), which is essential for most things in Italy including buying a transport pass, opening a bank account or renting a flat. It can be obtained free from the local *Ufficio delle Entrate* (tax office) or through an Italian consular office or embassy in your home country. To find a local office, check agenziaentrate.gov.it.

Work options

One obvious work option is to **teach English**, for which the demand has expanded enormously in recent years. You can do this through a language school or via freelance private lessons. For less reputable schools, you can get away without any qualifications, but you'll need to show a TEFL (Teaching of English as a Foreign Language) certificate for the more professional – and better-paid – establishments. For the main language schools, it's best to apply in writing before you leave (check tefl.com or look for the ads in British newspapers *The Guardian* and *The Times Education Supplement*), preferably before the summer. If you're looking on the spot, check the local English-language press and do the rounds on foot, but don't bother trying in August when everything is closed. The best teaching jobs are with a university as a *lettore*, a job requiring fewer hours than the language schools and generally paying more. Universities require English-language teachers in most faculties, and you can write to the individual faculties. Strictly speaking you could get by without any knowledge of Italian, though it obviously helps, especially when setting up private classes.

There's also the possibility of **holiday rep work** in the summer, especially around the seaside resorts, while in winter you may consider working in the

ski resorts. These are good places for finding **bar or restaurant work** too. You'll have to ask around for both types of job, and some knowledge of Italian is essential. **Au pairing** is another option: again sift through the ads in locally produced English-language publications in the big cities, or try one of the dedicated websites such as Ⓦ aupair.com.

Study programmes

One way of spending time in Italy is to combine a visit with **learning the language**, either as part of an overseas study scheme or by applying directly to a language school when you arrive.

AFS Intercultural Programs US Ⓣ 1800 AFS INFO, Ⓦ afs.org. Runs student exchange programmes to destinations around the world.
American Institute for Foreign Study US Ⓣ 866 906 2437, Ⓦ aifs.com. Language study and cultural immersion for the summer or school year.
ASA Cultural Tours Australia Ⓣ 03 9822 6899, Ⓦ asatours.com.au. Study tours focusing on art, architecture and culture.
British Council UK Ⓣ 0161 957 7755, Ⓦ britishcouncil.org. Has an informative website with current teaching vacancies, as well as downloadable teaching resources.
Erasmus Ⓦ erasmusprogramme.com. Europe-wide university-level initiative enabling students to study abroad for one year.
International House UK Ⓣ 020 7611 2400, Ⓦ ihworld.com. Reputable English-teaching organization which offers language courses, teacher training and teaching positions in Italy.
Italian Cultural Institute UK Ⓣ 020 7235 1461, Ⓦ iiclondra.esteri.it. The official Italian government agency for the promotion of cultural exchanges between Britain and Italy. A number of scholarships are available to British students wishing to study at Italian universities.
Road Scholar US Ⓣ 800 454 5768, Ⓦ roadscholar.org. Runs activity programmes in Italy for the over-60s.

Travel essentials

Climate

Italy's **climate** is one of the most hospitable in the world, with a general pattern of warm, dry summers and mild winters. There are, however, marked regional variations, ranging from the more temperate northern part of the country to the firmly Mediterranean south. Summers are hot and dry along the coastal areas, especially as you move south, cool in the major mountain areas – the Alps and Apennines. Winters are mild in the south of the country, Rome and below, but in the north they can be at least as cold as anywhere in the northern hemisphere, with snow in winter.

Costs

In general, the south is much less expensive than the north. As a broad guide, expect to pay most in Venice, Milan, Florence and Bologna, less in Rome, while in Naples and Sicily prices drop quite a lot.

You should be able to survive on a **budget** of about €50–60/day if you stay in a hostel, have lunchtime snacks and a cheap evening meal. If you stay in a budget hotel and eat out twice a day, you'll spend closer to €140–160/day.

Some **basics** are reasonably inexpensive, such as transport and, most notably, food, although drinking can be pricey unless you stick to wine. **Room rates** are in line with much of the rest of Europe, at least in the major cities and resorts. Bear in mind, too, that the **time of year** can make a big difference. In July and August, when the Italians take their holidays, hotel prices can escalate, especially in coastal areas; in low season, however, you can often negotiate much lower rates.

There are a few **reductions** and discounts for ISIC members and under-18s (and often for under-26s), but only in the major cities and for entry into state museums and sites.

Crime and personal safety

Despite what you hear about the Mafia, most of the **crime** you'll come across as a visitor to Italy is of the small-time variety, prevalent in the major cities and the south of the country, where pickpockets and gangs of *scippatori* or "snatchers" operate. Crowded streets or markets and packed tourist sights are the places to be wary of; *scippatori* work on foot or on scooters, disappearing before you've had time to react. As well as handbags, they whip wallets, tear off visible jewellery and, if they're really adroit, unstrap watches. You can minimize the risk of this happening by being discreet: don't flash anything of value, keep a firm hand on your camera, and carry shoulder-bags slung across your body. Never leave anything valuable in your car, and try to park in car parks on well-lit, well-used streets. On the whole it's a good idea to avoid badly lit areas completely at night and deserted inner-city areas by day. For help in an emergency, call Ⓣ 112.

Carabinieri, with their military-style uniforms and white shoulder-belts, deal with general crime, public order and drug control, while the **Vigili Urbani** are mainly concerned with directing traffic and issuing parking fines; the **Polizia Stradale** patrol the motorways. The **Polizia Statale**, the other general crime-fighting force, enjoy a fierce rivalry with the **Carabinieri**. As at the tourist office for the address of the *Carabinieri* barracks, *questura* or police station (in smaller places it may be just a local *commissariato*).

AVERAGE DAILY TEMPERATURES AND RAINFALL

	Jan	Feb	Mar	Apr	May	Jun	Jul	Aug	Sep	Oct	Nov	Dec
FLORENCE												
Max/min (ºC)	11/3	13/3	16/6	18/8	24/12	27/17	32/18	32/19	27/15	21/12	15/7	11/4
Rainfall (mm)	51	55	74	78	76	72	44	48	82	102	80	76
MILAN												
Max/min (ºC)	7/-3	9/-2	14/2	17/5	23/10	27/14	28/17	28/17	23/12	18/7	12/2	3/-2
Rainfall (mm)	63	62	78	78	85	65	67	86	74	98	96	96
NAPLES												
Max/min (ºC)	12/4	13/5	16/7	19/9	25/14	27/17	29/18	29/18	27/17	24/13	18/19	13/7
Rainfall (mm)	92	83	75	68	45	48	18	22	68	130	110	138
PALERMO												
Max/min (ºC)	14/7	14/7	17/8	20/12	25/15	28/19	29/21	30/22	27/18	25/15	20/12	17/10
Rainfall (mm)	70	45	50	50	20	10	5	20	42	75	70	60
ROME												
Max/min (ºC)	13/4	14/4	16/6	18/8	24/13	27/16	28/18	29/18	26/17	23/13	18/8	13/5
Rainfall (mm)	103	98	68	65	48	34	23	33	68	94	128	110

Electricity

The supply is 220V, though anything requiring 240V will work. Plugs either have two or three round pins: a multi-plug adapter is very useful.

Entry requirements

British, Irish and other EU citizens can enter Italy and stay as long as they like on production of a valid **passport**. Citizens of the United States, Canada, Australia and New Zealand need only a passport, too (valid for at least three months beyond the planned date of departure from Italy), but are limited to stays of 90 days. South Africans require a Schengen visa, which entitles them to travel through many of the countries in the Eurozone. All other nationals should consult the Italian embassy in their own country about visa requirements.

Health

As a member of the European Union, Italy has **free reciprocal health agreements** with other member states. EU citizens are entitled to treatment within Italy's public healthcare system at reduced cost, or sometimes for free if on a temporary stay, on production of a **European Health Insurance Card** (EHIC). The EHIC is free of charge and valid for at least three years, and entitles you to the same treatment as an Italian. In the UK, you can apply for the card on ⓣ 0300 330 1350 or ⓦ nhs.uk. In Ireland, apply at your local health office or online (ⓦ hse.ie). The card should take seven–ten days to come through, but it's worth allowing a week or so longer. Non-EU citizens should take out health insurance, though the Australian Medicare system also has a reciprocal healthcare arrangement with Italy.

Vaccinations are not required, and Italy presents no more health worries than anywhere else in Europe; the worst that's likely to happen is suffering from the extreme heat in summer. The **water** is perfectly safe to drink and you'll find public fountains in squares and city streets everywhere, though look out for *acqua non potabile* signs, indicating that the water is unsafe to drink. It's worth taking **insect repellent** with you in summer.

Italian **pharmacists** (*farmacisti*) are well qualified to give you advice on minor ailments and to dispense prescriptions; a handful of pharmacies are open all night in the bigger towns and cities. A rota system operates, and you should find the address of the one currently open on any *farmacia* door or listed in the local paper. If you need to see a **doctor** (*medico*), take your EHIC with you to get free treatment and prescriptions for medicines at the local rate – about ten percent of the price of the medicine.

In an **emergency**, go straight to the *Pronto Soccorso* (casualty) of the nearest hospital (*ospedale*), or phone the emergency line ⓣ 112 and ask for an *ambulanza*. Major train stations and airports also often have first-aid stations with doctors on hand.

Incidentally, try to avoid going to the **dentist** (*dentista*) while you're in Italy. These aren't covered by your EHIC or the health service, and for the smallest problem you'll pay through the teeth.

Insurance

Even though EU healthcare privileges apply in Italy, you'd do well to take out an **insurance policy** before travelling to cover against theft, loss, illness or injury. A typical policy usually provides cover for the loss of baggage, tickets and – up to a certain limit – cash or cheques, as well as cancellation or curtailment of your journey. Most policies exclude so-called **dangerous sports**, such as scuba diving, windsurfing and trekking, unless an extra premium is paid. Many policies can be tailor-made to exclude coverage you don't need – for example, sickness and accident benefits can often be excluded or included at will.

If you do take **medical cover**, ascertain whether benefits will be paid as treatment proceeds or only after your return home, and whether there is a **24-hour medical emergency number**. When securing **baggage cover**, make sure the per-article limit will cover your most valuable possession. If you need to **make a claim**, you should keep receipts for medicines and medical treatment, and if you have anything stolen, you must obtain an official statement from the police (see page 39).

Internet

Wi-fi access is standard in hostels and hotels. Cities often have several wi-fi zones, usually run by the local council. Access is generally via a card with a username and pin number. Details of how to access wi-fi zones are usually posted on signs or stickers around town. Alternatively, try a mobile wi-fi service like Ⓦwitourist.com.

Laundries

You should be able to find a **laundry** (*lavanderia*) in most towns. Coin-operated laundries are rare outside large cities, and even there, numbers are sparse; more common are service-wash laundries, but these are more expensive.

LGBTQ & Italy

Homosexuality is legal in Italy, and the age of consent is 16. Attitudes are most tolerant in the northern cities: Bologna is generally regarded as the LGBTQ capital, and Milan, Turin and Rome all have well-developed scenes; there are also a few *spiagge gay* (gay beaches) dotted along the coast: among the more popular LGBTQ resorts is Rimini. Away from the big cities and resorts, though, activity is more covert. In the south especially, overt displays of affection between (all) men – linking arms during the *passeggiata*, kissing in greeting and so on – are common, though the line determining what's acceptable is finely drawn. The **national LGBTQ organization**, ARCI-Gay (Ⓣ051 095 7241, Ⓦarcigay.it) is based in Bologna but has branches in most big towns. The website Ⓦpatroc.com has a wealth of information on LGBTQ events in the major cities.

Mail

Post office opening hours are usually Monday to Friday 8.30am to 7.30pm and Saturday 8.30am-12.30pm. **Stamps** (*francobolli*) are sold in *tabacchi*, too, as well as in some gift shops in the tourist resorts; they will often also weigh your letter. The Italian postal system is one of the slowest in Europe so if your letter is urgent make sure you send it "*posta prioritaria*", which has varying rates according to weight and destination. Letters can be sent *poste restante* to any Italian post office by addressing them "*Fermoposta*", along with the name and surname or passport number of the recipient and the details of the receiving post office including the postcode. When picking something up take your passport, and make sure they check under middle names and initials – and every other letter when all else fails – as filing is often diabolical.

Maps

The **town plans** throughout the Guide should be fine for most purposes, and practically all tourist offices give out maps of their local area for free.

The clearest and best-value large-scale commercial **road map** of Italy is the Touring Club Italiano 1:400,000, which covers the country in three separate maps (north, south and central Italy). TCI also produces excellent 1:200,000 maps of the individual regions, which are indispensable if you are touring a specific area.

For **hiking** you'll need a map of at least a scale of 1:50,000. Tabacco and Freytag & Berndt cover northern Italy's major mountain areas to this scale, but for more detailed 1:25,000 maps, the Istituto Geografico Centrale, Kompass and Edizioni Multigraphic cover central and northwest Italy and the Alps. The Club Alpino Italiano (Ⓦcai.it) is also a good source of hiking maps; we've supplied details of branches in Italy throughout the Guide.

Money

Italy's currency is the **euro** (€; note that Italians pronounce it "eh-uro"), which is split into 100 cents (*centesimi*). You can check the current **exchange rate** at Ⓦxe.com.

The easiest way to get euros is to use your **debit card** in an ATM machine (*bancomat*); there's usually a charge but it's no more expensive than getting money any other way. The daily limit for withdrawal is €250. It's more expensive to use a **credit card** to withdraw cash; check charges before you travel. Credit and debit cards are widely accepted in hotels and most restaurants, though some of the smaller restaurants, B&Bs and shops are cash-only, so check first. Visa and MasterCard are the most commonly accepted cards, with American Express also accepted in some places.

PUBLIC HOLIDAYS

January 1 *Primo dell'anno*, New Year's Day.
January 6 *Epifania*, Epiphany.
Pasquetta Easter Monday.
April 25 *Giorno della Liberazione*, Liberation Day.
May 1 *Festa dei Lavoratori/Primo Maggio*, Labour Day.
June 2 *Festa della Repubblica*, Republic Day.
August 15 *Ferragosto*, Assumption of the Blessed Virgin Mary.
November 1 *Ognissanti*, All Souls' Day.
December 8 *Immacolata*, Immaculate Conception of the Blessed Virgin Mary.
December 25 *Natale*, Christmas.
December 26 *Santo Stefano*, St Stephen's Day.

Travellers' cheques (available through American Express and Visa) are increasingly rare and generally more hassle than they're worth, but if you do use them, note that buying online in advance usually works out cheapest. It's advisable to buy euro travellers' cheques rather than dollars or pounds sterling since you won't have to pay commission when you cash them. Many travellers find that **Cash Passports** – a prepaid currency card that is loaded up before travelling and can be used in some shops and most ATMs in Italy – are a secure, convenient alternative. Mastercard (Ⓦcashpassport.com), post offices and various banks offer the service.

Banking hours are normally Monday to Friday from 8.30am until 1.30pm, and then for an hour in the afternoon (usually between 2.30 & 4pm). Outside banking hours, the larger hotels will change money, while larger towns have exchange bureaux.

Opening hours and public holidays

Traditionally most **shops and businesses** open Monday to Saturday from around 8am until 1pm, and from about 4pm until 7pm, with additional closures on Monday mornings, though these days an increasing number of shops remain open all day. Traditionally, everything except bars and restaurants closes on Sunday, though most towns have a *pasticceria* open in the mornings, while in large cities and tourist areas, Sunday shopping is becoming more common.

Most **churches** open in the early morning, around 7 or 8am for Mass, and close around noon, opening up again at 4pm and closing at 7 or 8pm. In more remote places, some will only open for early morning and evening services, while others are closed at all times except Sundays and on religious holidays; if you're determined to take a look, you may have to ask around for the key. Another problem is that lots of churches, monasteries, convents and oratories are **closed for restoration** (*chiuso per restauro*), though you might still be able to persuade someone to show you around.

Most museums, galleries and archeological sites throughout the country **close on Mondays.**

Public holidays

Whereas it can be fun to stumble across a local festival, it's best to know when the national holidays are as almost everything shuts down. In **August**, particularly during the weeks either side of Ferragosto (Aug 15), when most of the country flees to the coast and mountains, many towns are left half-deserted, with shops, bars and restaurants closed and a reduced

public transport service. Local religious holidays don't necessarily close down shops and businesses, but they do mean that accommodation space may be tight. During official **national holidays**, however, everything closes down except bars, restaurants and some national museums and monuments.

Phones

Mobile (cell) phones in Italy work on the GSM European standard, usually compatible with phones from the UK, the rest of Europe, Australia and New Zealand, but not the US and Canada, which use a different system. If you're from the EU, roaming in Italy incurs no extra fees – you can call, text and use mobile data as if you were at home. If you're from outside the EU, make sure you have a booster package or have made the necessary arrangements with your provider. Alternatively, pick up an Italian pay-as-you-go SIM from any mobile phone provider; take a form of ID (passport is best) as they'll need to register the SIM in your name.

INTERNATIONAL CALLS

To make **international calls from Italy**, dial 00, then the destination's country code, before the rest of the number. Note that the initial zero is omitted from the area code when dialling the UK, Ireland, Australia and New Zealand from abroad.

Australia 00 + 61
New Zealand 00 + 64
UK 00 + 44
US and Canada 00 + 1
Ireland 00 + 353
South Africa 00 + 27

The **country code** for dialling Italy from abroad is T +39.

Time

Italy is always one hour ahead of Britain, seven hours ahead of US Eastern Standard Time and ten hours ahead of Pacific Time.

Tourist information

Before you leave home, it may be worth contacting the Italian State Tourist Office (ENIT; W enit.it) for a selection of maps and brochures, though you can usually pick up much the same information from tourist offices in Italy. Most towns, major train stations and airports in Italy have a **tourist office**, "APT" (Azienda Promozione Turistica) or "IAT" (Ufficio Informazioni Accoglienza Turistica), which vary in usefulness (and helpfulness) but usually provide at least a town plan and local listings guide. In smaller villages there is sometimes a "Pro Loco" office that has much the same kind of information, but with more limited opening times.

Travelling with children

Children are adored in Italy and will be made a fuss of in the street, and welcomed and catered for in bars and restaurants. Hotels often won't charge to put a cot in your room, but if they do it's usually around €20–30. Kids pay less on trains and can generally expect discounts for museum entry: prices vary, but 11–18-year-olds are usually admitted at a reduced rate on production of some form of ID (although sometimes this applies only to EU citizens). Under-11s – or sometimes only under-4s – have free entry.

Supplies for **babies** and small children are pricey: nappies and milk formula can cost up to three times as much as in other parts of Europe. Discreet breast-feeding is widely accepted – even smiled on – but nappy changing facilities are few. Branches of the children's clothes and accessories chain, Prénatal, have changing facilities and a feeding area, but otherwise you may have to be creative. High chairs are unusual too, although establishments in tourist areas tend to be better equipped.

Check out W italyfamilyhotels.it, an organization of hotels across Italy with facilities from cots and bottle warmers in rooms to baby-sitters, play areas and special menus.

Travellers with disabilities

Italy isn't generally geared towards disabled travellers, though people are usually helpful and progress is gradually being made in accessible accommodation, transport and public buildings.

Public transport access can be challenging in Italy, although low-level buses are gradually being introduced in towns and some trains have disabled facilities.

CONTACTS AND RESOURCES

Accessible Italy San Marino T 378 941111, W accessibleitaly.com. San Marino-based operation offering an English-speaking accessible accommodation advice, organized tours and tailor-made trips in Italy.

Irish Wheelchair Association IRE T 01 818 6400, W iwa.ie. Useful information for wheelchair users about travelling abroad.

Society for Accessible Travel & Hospitality (SATH) US T 212 447 7284, W sath.org. Information on accessibility and advice on travelling with any kind of disability.

CLEMENS XI
PONT·MAX·
FONTIS ET FORI
ORNAMENTO
ANNO SAL·
MDCCXI
PONTIF·XI
M·AGRIPPA

Rome and Lazio

46 Rome

112 Northern Lazio

119 Southern Lazio

THE PANTHEON, ROME

1

Rome and Lazio

Rome is the most fascinating city in Italy, which makes it arguably the most fascinating city in the world: you could spend a month here and still only scratch the surface. It's an ancient place packed with the relics of over two thousand years of inhabitation, yet it's so much more than an open-air museum: its culture, its food, its people make up a modern, vibrant city that would be worthy of a visit irrespective of its past. As a historic centre, it is special enough; as a contemporary European capital, it is utterly unique.

The former heart of the mighty Roman Empire, and still the home of the papacy, the city is made up of layers of history. There are Rome's ancient features, most visibly the Colosseum, the Forum and Palatine Hill; but beyond these there's an almost uninterrupted sequence of monuments – from early Christian basilicas and Romanesque churches to Renaissance palaces and the fountains and churches of the Baroque period, which perhaps more than any other era has determined the look of the city today. The modern epoch has left its mark too, from the ponderous Neoclassical architecture of the post-Unification period to prestige projects like Zaha Hadid's MAXXI exhibition space. These various eras crowd in on one another to an almost overwhelming degree: medieval churches sit atop ancient basilicas above Roman palaces; houses and apartment blocks incorporate fragments of eroded Roman columns, carvings and inscriptions; and roads and piazzas follow the lines of ancient amphitheatres and stadiums.

Beyond Rome, the region of **Lazio** inevitably pales in comparison, but there is plenty to draw you there, not least the landscape, which varies from the green hills and lakes of the northern reaches to the drier, more mountainous south. It's a relatively poor region, its lack of identity the butt of a number of Italian jokes, but it's the closest you'll get to the feel of the Italian South without catching the train to Naples. Much of the area can be easily seen on a day-trip from the capital, primarily the ancient sites of **Ostia Antica** and the various attractions of **Tivoli**. Further afield, in northern Lazio, the Etruscan sites of **Tarquinia** and **Cerveteri** provide the most obvious tourist focus, as does the pleasant provincial town of **Viterbo** and the gentle beauty of lakes **Bracciano**, **Vico** and **Bolsena**. The south arguably holds Lazio's most appealing enclaves, not least unpretentious resorts like **Terracina** and **Sperlonga**, and the island of **Ponza** – one of the most alluring spots on the entire western coast.

Rome

You won't enjoy **ROME** if you spend your time trying to tick off sights. However, there are some places that it would be a pity to leave the city without seeing. The **Vatican** is perhaps the most obvious one, most notably **St Peter's** and the amazing stock of loot in the Vatican Museums; and the star attractions of the ancient city – the **Forum** and **Palatine**, the **Colosseum** – are worth a day or two in their own right. There are also the churches, fountains and works of art from the period that can be said to most define Rome, the Baroque, and in particular the works of Borromini and Bernini, whose efforts compete for space and attention throughout the city. Bernini was responsible for the Fountain of the Four Rivers in the city's most famous square, **Piazza Navona**, among other things; but arguably his best sculptural work is in the **Galleria Borghese**, or in various churches, like his statue of St Theresa in Santa Maria della Vittoria. Borromini, his great rival at the time, built the churches of San Carlo alle Quattro

SCULPTURE OF PAULINE BONAPARTE IN GALLERIA BORGHESE

Highlights

❶ **Pantheon** The most complete ancient Roman structure in the city. See page 54

❷ **Capitoline Museums** The august complex containing some of Rome's finest ancient sculpture and paintings. See page 63

❸ **Galleria Borghese** One of the city's finest art galleries – and home to the cream of the work of the city's favourite sculptor, Bernini. See page 85

❹ **Vatican Museums** Quite simply the largest and richest collection of art in the world. See page 88

❺ **Ostia Antica** The old port of Rome is one of the best-preserved and most intriguing ancient sites in the country. See page 108

❻ **Tivoli** The site of Hadrian's villa, as well as the splendid landscaped gardens of Villa d'Este. See page 109

❼ **Subiaco** St Benedict's two monasteries are among Italy's most spiritual and peaceful locations. See page 123

HIGHLIGHTS ARE MARKED ON THE MAPS ON PAGES 48 & 50

Fontane and Sant'Ivo, both buildings intricately squeezed into small sites – Borromini's trademark. Other great palaces are themselves treasure-troves of great art, such as the **Doria Pamphilj** and **Palazzo Barberini**; and there are some unmissable museums, including the galleries of the **Capitoline** and the main collections of the **Museo Nazionale Romano** in the Palazzo Altemps and Palazzo Massimo, all of which hold staggering collections of the cream of the city's ancient art and sculpture. And finally there's the city itself: stroll through the *centro storico* in the early morning, through Trastevere at sunset, or gaze down at the roofs and domes from the Janiculum Hill on a clear day, and you'll quickly realize that there's no place in Italy like it.

The **city centre** is divided neatly into distinct blocks. The warren of streets that makes up the **centro storico** occupies the hook of land on the left bank of the River Tiber, bordered to the east by Via del Corso and to the north and south by water. From here Rome's central core spreads south and east: down towards Campo de' Fiori; across Via del Corso to the major shopping streets and alleys around the **Spanish Steps**; to the

OFFALLY GOOD: TRADITIONAL ROMAN CUISINE

Roman cooking is traditionally dominated by the earthy cuisine of the working classes, with a little influence from the city's centuries-old Jewish population thrown in. Although you'll find all sorts of **pasta** served in Roman restaurants, spaghetti is common, as is the local speciality of *bucatini* or thick-cut hollow spaghetti (sometimes called *tonnarelli*), served *cacio e pepe* (with pecorino and ground black pepper), *alla carbonara* (with beaten eggs, cubes of pan-fried *guanciale* – cured pork cheek, similar to bacon – and pecorino or Parmesan), *alla gricia* (with pecorino and *guanciale*), and *all'amatriciana* (with *guanciale*, tomato and bacon).

Fish features most frequently in Rome as salt cod – *baccalà* – best eaten Jewish-style, deep-fried. **Offal** is also key, and although it has been ousted from many of the more refined city-centre restaurants, you'll still find it on the menus of more traditional places, especially those in Testaccio. Most favoured is *pajata*, the intestines of an unweaned calf. Look out, too, for *coda alla vaccinara*, oxtail stewed in a rich sauce of tomato and celery; *abbacchio*, milk-fed lamb roasted to melting tenderness with rosemary, sage and garlic; *abbacchio allo scottadito*, grilled lamb chops eaten with the fingers; and *saltimbocca alla romana*, thin slices of veal cooked with a slice of prosciutto and sage on top. **Artichokes** (*carciofi*) are the quintessential Roman vegetable, served *alla romana* (stuffed with garlic and mint and stewed) and in all their unadulterated glory as *alla giudea* – flattened and deep-fried in olive oil. Another not-to-be-missed side dish is *fiori di zucca* – batter-fried courgette blossom, stuffed with mozzarella and a sliver of marinated anchovy. Roman **pizza** has a thin crust and is best when baked in a wood-fired oven (*forno a legna*), but you can also find lots of great pizza by the slice (*pizza al taglio*). Lazio's **wine** is enjoying a bit of a resurgence and is often better than most people think. Nonetheless you'll still mostly see wines from the Castelli Romani (most famously Frascati) to the south, and from around Montefiascone (Est! Est!! Est!!!) in the north – both excellent, straightforward whites, great for sunny lunchtimes or as an evening *aperitivo* – but you'll also find wines from other regions and newer producers.

major sites of the **ancient city** to the south; and to the expanse of the **Villa Borghese** park to the north. The left bank of the river is a little more distanced from the main hum of the city centre, home to the Vatican and St Peter's, and, to the south of these, **Trastevere** – even in ancient times a distinct entity from the city proper, although nowadays as much of a focus for tourists as anywhere, especially at night.

Brief history

Rome's early **history** is interwoven with legend. Rea Silvia, a vestal virgin and daughter of a local king, Numitor, had twin sons – the product, she alleged, of a rape by Mars. The two boys were abandoned and found by a wolf, who nursed them until their adoption by a shepherd. He named them **Romulus and Remus**, and they became leaders of the community and later laid out the boundaries of the city on the Palatine Hill. Before long it became apparent that there was only room for one ruler, and they quarrelled, Romulus killing Remus and becoming in 753 BC the city's first **monarch**, to be followed by six further kings.

The Roman Republic and Empire

Rome as a kingdom lasted until about 507 BC, when the people rose up against the tyrannical King Tarquinius and established a **Republic**. The city prospered, growing greatly in size and subduing the various tribes of the surrounding areas. By the time it had fought and won the third Punic War against its principal rival, **Carthage**, in 146 BC, it had become the dominant power in the Mediterranean.

The history of the Republic was, however, also one of **internal strife**, marked by factional fighting among the patrician ruling classes, and the ordinary people, or plebeians. This all came to a head in 44 BC, when **Julius Caesar**, having proclaimed himself dictator, was murdered by conspirators concerned at the growing concentration of power into one man's hands. A brief period of turmoil ensued, giving way, in 27

1

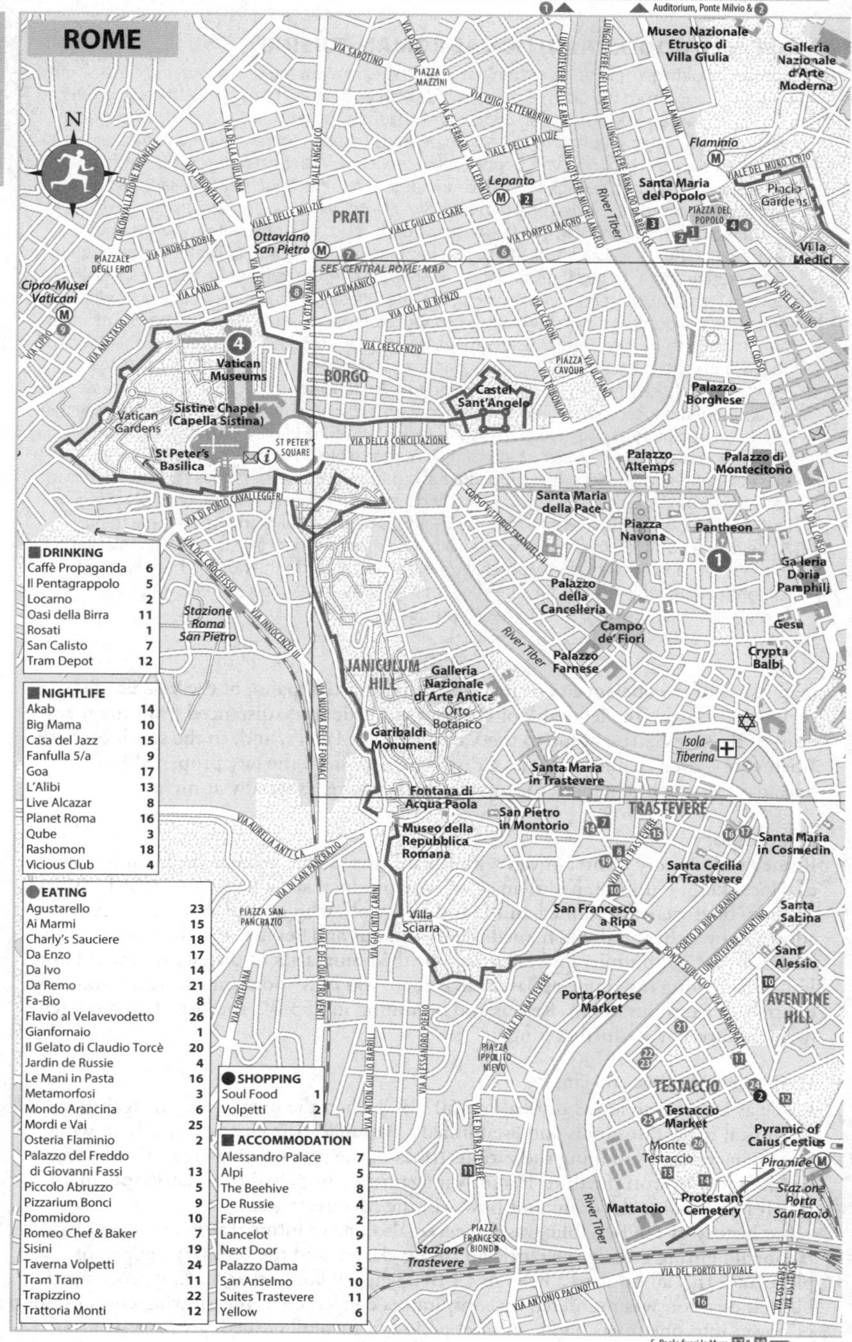
ROME
Auditorium, Ponte Milvio & 2
Museo Nazionale Etrusco di Villa Giulia
Galleria Nazionale d'Arte Moderna
Flaminio
Lepanto
Santa Maria del Popolo
Piazza del Popolo
Pincio Gardens
Villa Medici
PRATI
Ottaviano San Pietro
SEE 'CENTRAL ROME' MAP
Cipro-Musei Vaticani
Vatican Museums
Sistine Chapel (Capella Sistina)
Vatican Gardens
St Peter's Basilica
St Peter's Square
BORGO
Castel Sant'Angelo
Piazza Cavour
Palazzo Borghese
Palazzo Altemps
Palazzo di Montecitorio
Santa Maria della Pace
Piazza Navona
Pantheon
Galleria Doria Pamphilj
Palazzo della Cancelleria
Campo de' Fiori
Gesù
Crypta Balbi
Palazzo Farnese
River Tiber
Stazione Roma San Pietro
JANICULUM HILL
Galleria Nazionale di Arte Antica
Orto Botanico
Garibaldi Monument
Isola Tiberina
Santa Maria in Trastevere
Fontana di Acqua Paola
San Pietro in Montorio
Museo della Repubblica Romana
TRASTEVERE
Santa Maria in Cosmedin
Santa Cecilia in Trastevere
San Francesco a Ripa
Villa Sciarra
Santa Sabina
Sant' Alessio
AVENTINE HILL
Porta Portese Market
TESTACCIO
Testaccio Market
Monte Testaccio
Pyramid of Caius Cestius
Piramide
Protestant Cemetery
Mattatoio
Stazione Porta San Paolo
Stazione Trastevere
S. Paolo fuori le Mura, 17 & 18
DRINKING
Caffè Propaganda 6
Il Pentagrappolo 5
Locarno 2
Oasi della Birra 11
Rosati 1
San Calisto 7
Tram Depot 12
NIGHTLIFE
Akab 14
Big Mama 10
Casa del Jazz 15
Fanfulla 5/a 9
Goa 17
L'Alibi 13
Live Alcazar 8
Planet Roma 16
Qube 3
Rashomon 18
Vicious Club 4
EATING
Agustarello 23
Ai Marmi 15
Charly's Sauciere 18
Da Enzo 17
Da Ivo 14
Da Remo 21
Fa-Bìo 8
Flavio al Velavevodetto 26
Gianfornaio 1
Il Gelato di Claudio Torcè 20
Jardin de Russie 4
Le Mani in Pasta 16
Metamorfosi 3
Mondo Arancina 6
Mordi e Vai 25
Osteria Flaminio 2
Palazzo del Freddo di Giovanni Fassi 13
Piccolo Abruzzo 5
Pizzarium Bonci 9
Pommidoro 10
Romeo Chef & Baker 7
Sisini 19
Taverna Volpetti 24
Tram Tram 11
Trapizzino 22
Trattoria Monti 12
SHOPPING
Soul Food 1
Volpetti 2
ACCOMMODATION
Alessandro Palace 7
Alpi 5
The Beehive 8
De Russie 4
Farnese 2
Lancelot 9
Next Door 1
Palazzo Dama 3
San Anselmo 10
Suites Trastevere 11
Yellow 6

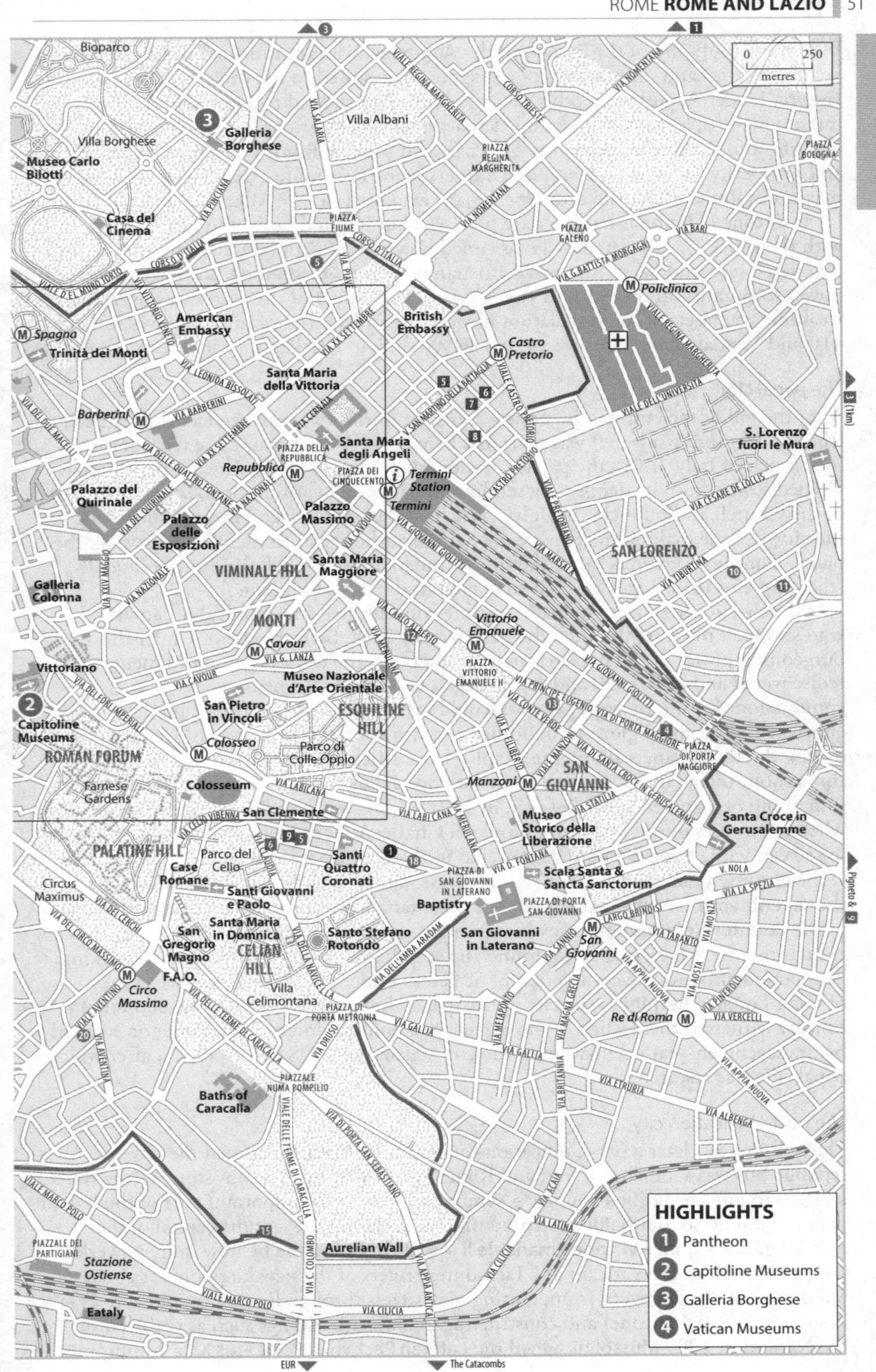
Bioparco
Villa Borghese
Galleria Borghese
Museo Carlo Bilotti
Casa del Cinema
Villa Albani
American Embassy
Spagna
Trinità dei Monti
British Embassy
Castro Pretorio
Policlinico
Santa Maria della Vittoria
Barberini
Santa Maria degli Angeli
Repubblica
Termini Station
Termini
S. Lorenzo fuori le Mura
Palazzo del Quirinale
Palazzo delle Esposizioni
Palazzo Massimo
SAN LORENZO
Galleria Colonna
VIMINALE HILL
Santa Maria Maggiore
MONTI
Vittorio Emanuele
Cavour
Vittoriano
Museo Nazionale d'Arte Orientale
Capitoline Museums
San Pietro in Vincoli
ESQUILINE HILL
Colosseo
Parco di Colle Oppio
ROMAN FORUM
Farnese Gardens
Colosseum
San Clemente
Manzoni
SAN GIOVANNI
Museo Storico della Liberazione
Santa Croce in Gerusalemme
PALATINE HILL
Parco del Celio
Case Romane
Santi Quattro Coronati
Scala Santa & Sancta Sanctorum
Circus Maximus
Santi Giovanni e Paolo
Baptistry
San Gregorio Magno
Santa Maria in Domnica
CELIAN HILL
Santo Stefano Rotondo
San Giovanni in Laterano
San Giovanni
F.A.O.
Circo Massimo
Villa Celimontana
Re di Roma
Baths of Caracalla
Aurelian Wall
Stazione Ostiense
Eataly
EUR
The Catacombs
Pigneto
0 250 metres
HIGHLIGHTS
1 Pantheon
2 Capitoline Museums
3 Galleria Borghese
4 Vatican Museums

BC, to the founding of the **Empire** under **Augustus**, who transformed Rome, building arches, theatres and monuments of a magnificence suited to the capital of an expanding empire. Under Augustus, and his successors, the city swelled to a population of a million, its people housed in cramped apartment blocks or *insulae*; crime in the city was rife, and the traffic apparently on a par with today's. But it was a time of peace and prosperity too, with the empire's borders being ever more extended, reaching their maximum limits under the Emperor Trajan, who died in 117 AD.

The **decline of Rome** is hard to date precisely, but it could be said to have started with the Emperor Diocletian, who assumed power in 284 and divided the empire into two parts, East and West. The first Christian emperor, **Constantine**, shifted the seat of power to Byzantium in 330, and Rome's period as capital of the world was over; the wealthier members of the population moved east and a series of invasions by Goths in 410 and Vandals about forty years later served only to quicken the city's ruin.

The papal city

After the fall of the empire, the **pope** – based in Rome owing to the fact that St Peter (the Apostle and first pope) was martyred here in 64 AD – became the temporal ruler over much of Italy. It was the papacy, under **Pope Gregory I** ("the Great") in 590, that rescued Rome from its demise. By sending missions all over Europe to spread the word of the Church and publicize its holy relics, he drew pilgrims, and their money, back to the city, in time making the papacy the natural authority in Rome. The pope took the name "Pontifex Maximus" after the title of the high priest of classical times (literally "the keeper of the bridges", which were vital to the city's well-being).

As time went on, power gradually became concentrated in a handful of **families**, who swapped the top jobs, including the papacy itself, between them. Under the burgeoning power of the pope, churches were built, the city's pagan monuments rediscovered and preserved, and artists began to arrive in Rome to work on commissions for the latest pope, who would invariably try to outdo his predecessor's efforts with ever more glorious buildings and works of art. This process reached a head during the Renaissance: Bramante, Raphael and Michelangelo all worked in the city throughout their careers, and the reigns of **Pope Julius II** and his successor, **Leo X**, were something of a golden age. However, in 1527 all this was brought abruptly to an end, when the armies of the Habsburg monarch Charles V swept into the city, occupying it for a year, while **Pope Clement VII** cowered in the Castel Sant'Angelo.

The ensuing years were ones of yet more restoration, and perhaps because of this it's the **seventeenth century** that has left the most tangible impression on Rome, the vigour of the **Counter-Reformation** throwing up huge sensational monuments like the Gesù church that were designed to confound the scepticism of the new Protestant thinking. This period also saw the completion of St Peter's under **Paul V**, and the ascendancy of Gian Lorenzo **Bernini** as the city's principal architect and sculptor. The **eighteenth century** witnessed the decline of the papacy as a political force, a phenomenon marked by the seventeen-year occupation of the city starting in 1798 by Napoleon, after which papal rule was restored.

The post-Unification city

Thirty-four years later a pro-Unification caucus under **Mazzini** declared the city a republic but was soon chased out, and Rome had to wait until troops stormed the walls in 1870 to join the unified country – symbolically the most important part of the Italian peninsula to do so. **Garibaldi** wasted no time in declaring the city the capital of the new kingdom – under **Vittorio Emanuele II** – and confining the by now quite powerless pontiff, **Pius IX**, to the Vatican. The Piemontese rulers of the new kingdom set about building a city fit to govern from, cutting new streets through Rome's central core (Via Nazionale, Via del Tritone) and constructing grandiose buildings such as the Altar of the Nation. In 1929 **Mussolini** signed the **Lateran Pact** with **Pope Pius XI**, a compromise

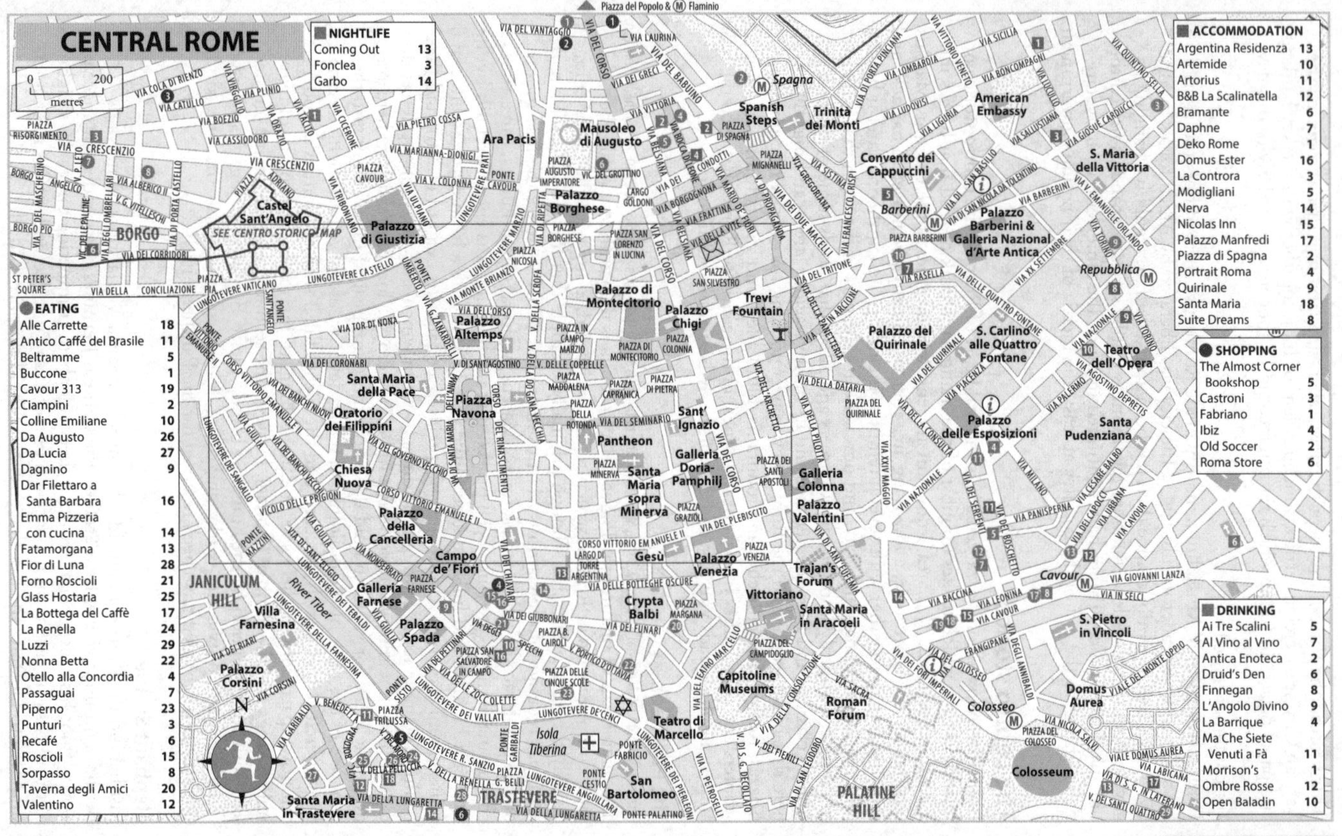
CENTRAL ROME
0 200 metres
NIGHTLIFE
Coming Out 13
Fonclea 3
Garbo 14
EATING
Alle Carrette 18
Antico Caffè del Brasile 11
Beltramme 5
Buccone 1
Cavour 313 19
Ciampini 2
Colline Emiliane 10
Da Augusto 26
Da Lucia 27
Dagnino 9
Dar Filettaro a Santa Barbara 16
Emma Pizzeria con cucina 14
Fatamorgana 13
Fior di Luna 28
Forno Roscioli 21
Glass Hostaria 25
La Bottega del Caffè 17
La Renella 24
Luzzi 29
Nonna Betta 22
Otello alla Concordia 4
Passaguai 7
Piperno 23
Punturi 3
Recafé 6
Roscioli 15
Sorpasso 8
Taverna degli Amici 20
Valentino 12
ACCOMMODATION
Argentina Residenza 13
Artemide 10
Artorius 11
B&B La Scalinatella 12
Bramante 6
Daphne 7
Deko Rome 1
Domus Ester 16
La Controra 3
Modigliani 5
Nerva 14
Nicolas Inn 15
Palazzo Manfredi 17
Piazza di Spagna 2
Portrait Roma 4
Quirinale 9
Santa Maria 18
Suite Dreams 8
SHOPPING
The Almost Corner Bookshop 5
Castroni 3
Fabriano 1
Ibiz 4
Old Soccer 2
Roma Store 6
DRINKING
Ai Tre Scalini 5
Al Vino al Vino 7
Antica Enoteca 2
Druid's Den 6
Finnegan 8
L'Angolo Divino 9
La Barrique 4
Ma Che Siete Venuti a Fà 11
Morrison's 1
Ombre Rosse 12
Open Baladin 10
SEE 'CENTRO STORICO' MAP
Piazza del Popolo & Flaminio

which forced the Vatican to accept the new Italian state and in return recognized the Vatican City as sovereign territory, independent of Italy, together with the key basilicas and papal palaces in Rome which remain technically independent of Italy to this day.

The contemporary city

During **World War II**, Mussolini famously made Rome his centre of operations until his resignation as leader in July 1943. The city was liberated by Allied forces in June 1944. The Italian republic since then has been a mixed affair, regularly changing its government (if not its leaders) every few months until a series of **scandals** forced the old guard from office. Things have continued in much the same vein, with the city symbolizing, to the rest of the country at least, the inertia of their nation's government.

The centro storico

Immediately north of Piazza Venezia is the real heart of Rome – the **centro storico** or historic centre, which makes up most of the triangular chunk of land that bulges into a bend in the Tiber. This area, known in ancient Roman times as the Campus Martius, was outside the city centre, a low-lying area that was mostly given over to barracks and sporting arenas, together with several temples, including the Pantheon. Later it became the heart of the Renaissance city, and nowadays it's the part of the town that is densest in interest, an unruly knot of narrow streets and alleys that holds some of the best of Rome's classical and Baroque heritage and its most vivacious street- and nightlife. It's here that most people find the Rome they've been looking for – a city of crumbling piazzas, Renaissance churches and fountains, blind alleys and streets humming with scooters and foot traffic. It's part of the appeal of the centre of Rome that even the most aimless ambling leads you past some breathlessly beautiful and historic spots.

The Pantheon

Piazza della Rotonda • Mon–Sat 8.30am–7.30pm, Sun 9am–6pm, public hols 9am–1pm • Free • T 06 6830 0230, W pantheonroma.com

The main focus of picturesque Piazza della Rotonda is the **Pantheon**, easily the most complete ancient Roman structure in the city and, along with the Colosseum, visually the most impressive. Though originally a temple that formed part of Marcus Agrippa's redesign of the Campus Martius in around 27 BC – hence the inscription on the porch facade, which translates as "Marcus Agrippa, son of Lucius, three-time consul, made this" – it's since been proved that the building was entirely rebuilt by the Emperor Hadrian and finished around the year 125 AD. It's a formidable architectural achievement even now: the diameter is precisely equal to its height (43.3m), and the oculus (the hole in the centre of the dome) – from which shafts of sunlight descend to illuminate the musty interior – is a full 8.7m across. Most impressively, there are no visible arches or vaults to hold the whole thing up; instead they're sunk into the concrete of the walls of the building. In its heydey it would have been richly decorated, the coffered ceiling heavily stuccoed and the niches filled with the statues of gods, but now, apart from its sheer size, the main things of interest are the tombs of two Italian kings and the **tomb of Raphael**, between the second and third chapel on the left, with an inscription by the humanist bishop Pietro Bembo: "Living, great Nature feared he might outvie Her works, and dying, fears herself may die." The same kind of sentiments might well have been reserved for the Pantheon itself.

Elephant Statue

Just behind the Pantheon, outside the church of Santa Maria sopra Minerva, is Bernini's diminutive **Elephant Statue**. The statue is Bernini's most endearing piece of work, if not his most characteristic: a cheery elephant trumpeting under the weight of the obelisk he carries on his back – a reference to Pope Alexander VII's reign and supposed to illustrate the fact that strength should support wisdom.

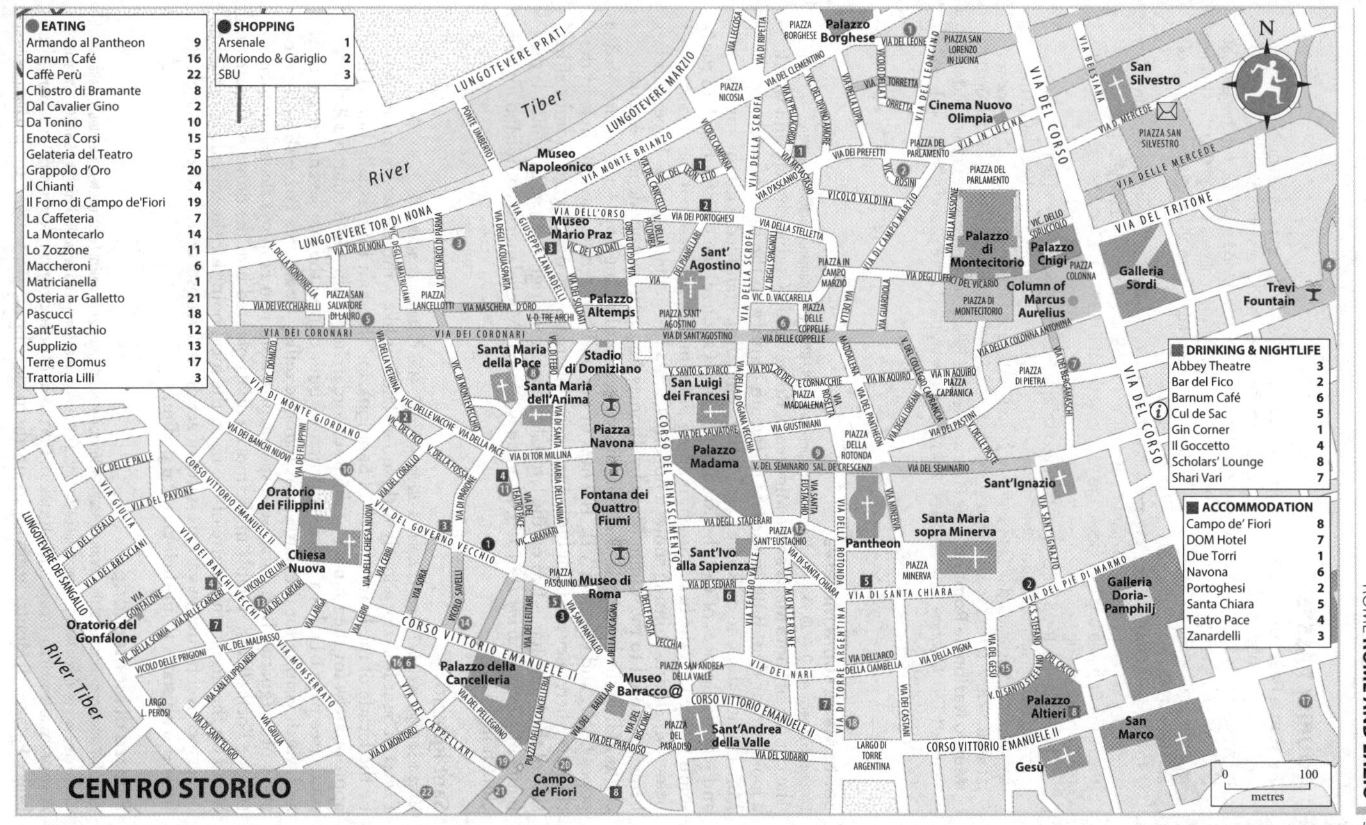
CENTRO STORICO
EATING
Armando al Pantheon 9
Barnum Café 16
Caffè Perù 22
Chiostro di Bramante 8
Dal Cavalier Gino 2
Da Tonino 10
Enoteca Corsi 15
Gelateria del Teatro 5
Grappolo d'Oro 20
Il Chianti 4
Il Forno di Campo de'Fiori 19
La Caffeteria 7
La Montecarlo 14
Lo Zozzone 11
Maccheroni 6
Matricianella 1
Osteria ar Galletto 21
Pascucci 18
Sant'Eustachio 12
Supplizio 13
Terre e Domus 17
Trattoria Lilli 3
SHOPPING
Arsenale 1
Moriondo & Gariglio 2
SBU 3
DRINKING & NIGHTLIFE
Abbey Theatre 3
Bar del Fico 2
Barnum Café 6
Cul de Sac 5
Gin Corner 1
Il Goccetto 4
Scholars' Lounge 8
Shari Vari 7
ACCOMMODATION
Campo de' Fiori 8
DOM Hotel 7
Due Torri 1
Navona 6
Portoghesi 2
Santa Chiara 5
Teatro Pace 4
Zanardelli 3
0 100 metres
N
Trevi Fountain
San Silvestro
Galleria Sordi
Palazzo Chigi
Column of Marcus Aurelius
Palazzo di Montecitorio
Cinema Nuovo Olimpia
Palazzo Borghese
Sant'Ignazio
Galleria Doria-Pamphilj
San Marco
Palazzo Altieri
Gesù
Santa Maria sopra Minerva
Pantheon
Sant'Agostino
San Luigi dei Francesi
Palazzo Madama
Sant'Ivo alla Sapienza
Sant'Andrea della Valle
Palazzo Altemps
Stadio di Domiziano
Piazza Navona
Fontana dei Quattro Fiumi
Museo di Roma
Museo Barracco
Museo Mario Praz
Museo Napoleonico
Santa Maria dell'Anima
Santa Maria della Pace
Palazzo della Cancelleria
Campo de' Fiori
Oratorio dei Filippini
Chiesa Nuova
Oratorio del Gonfalone
Tiber
River
River Tiber
VIA DEL CORSO
CORSO VITTORIO EMANUELE II
CORSO DEL RINASCIMENTO
VIA DEI CORONARI
LUNGOTEVERE MARZIO
LUNGOTEVERE PRATI
LUNGOTEVERE TOR DI NONA
LUNGOTEVERE DEI SANGALLO
VIA GIULIA
VIA DEL TRITONE

1

TOURIST PASSES

The **Roma Pass** (T 06 0608, W romapass.it) costs €38.50 (valid for three days) or €28 (valid for two days) entitles you to travel for free on buses, trams and the metro, gives you free admission to two major sights or museums of your choice (just one sight for the cheaper pass) and reduced entry to many more. Perhaps most importantly, it allows you to skip the queue at major sights – quite a lifesaver at the Colosseum. It's available from all museums in the circuit and tourist information kiosks.

The Vatican's **Omnia Card** (W omniakit.org) gives free, fast-track access to the Vatican Museums, St Peter's, Carcer Tullianum, as well as a free Roma Pass; you also get a free trip on the Roma Cristiana bus tour (see page 95). However, at €113 (valid 72hr), you're paying a lot to jump the queues.

A new offering, the S.U.P.E.R ticket ("Seven Unique Places to Experience in Rome"), allows entry to several archeological sites, including the Colosseum and areas of the Palatine that are off-limits to standard ticket-holders. It costs €20, is valid for two days and can be booked at T 06 3996 7700 or W coopculture.it. You can also visit the four museums that make up the **Museo Nazionale Romano** – the Palazzo Altemps, Palazzo Massimo, Crypta Balbi and the Terme di Diocleziano – on one ticket, valid for seven days. It costs €12 and is available from each location.

Santa Maria sopra Minerva

Piazza della Minerva 42 • Daily 10.30am–12.30pm & 3.30–7pm • T 06 6992 0384, W santamariasopraminerva.it/en

The church of **Santa Maria sopra Minerva** is Rome's only Gothic church, and worth a look just for that. Built in the late thirteenth century on the ruins of a temple to Minerva, it's also one of Rome's art-treasure churches, crammed with the tombs and self-indulgences of wealthy Roman families. Of these, the Carafa chapel, in the south transept, is the best known, holding Filippino Lippi's fresco of the *Assumption*, below which one painting shows a hopeful Carafa (the religious zealot, Pope Paul IV) being presented to the Virgin Mary by Thomas Aquinas; another depicts Aquinas confounding the heretics in the sight of two beautiful young boys – the future Medici popes Leo X and Clement VII. The lives of Leo and Clement come full circle in the church, where they are both buried and remembered by two very grand tombs either side of the high altar – Leo on the left, Clement on the right – close by which is the figure of *Christ Bearing the Cross*, a serene work that Michelangelo completed for the church in 1521.

Sant'Ignazio

Piazza di Sant'Ignazio • Daily 7.30am–12.20pm & 3–7.20pm • T 06 679 4406, W santignazio.gesuiti.it

Piazza di Sant'Ignazio, a lovely little square laid out like a theatre set, is dominated by the facade of the Jesuit church of **Sant'Ignazio**. The saint isn't actually buried here; appropriately, for the founder of the Jesuit order, he's in the Gesù church a little way south (see page 61). It's a spacious structure, built during the late seventeeth century, and worth visiting for the marvellous Baroque ceiling by Andrea Pozzo showing the entry of St Ignatius into paradise, a spectacular work that employs sledgehammer trompe l'oeil effects, notably in the mock cupola painted into the dome of the crossing. Stand on the disc in the centre of the nave, the focal point for the ingenious rendering of perspective: figures in various states of action and repose, conversation and silence, fix you with stares from their classical pediment.

Palazzo di Montecitorio

Piazza di Montecitorio • First Sun of the month 10.30am–3.30pm; closed July, Aug & first half of Sept; hourly guided tours (Italian only); 30min • Free; pick up tickets first at the Infopoint on Via Uffici del Vicario, on the corner of Via della Missione • T 06 67 601, W camera.it

A short walk north from Sant'Ignazio, **Piazza di Montecitorio** takes its name from the bulky **Palazzo di Montecitorio** on its northern side, home since 1871 to the Italian

parliament. You can only visit by guided tour, but for those who speak Italian and have even the slightest interest in Italy's notoriously shaky parliamentary system, a visit can be very worthwhile. Next door to Palazzo di Montecitorio is **Piazza Colonna**, home to Palazzo Chigi – the prime minister's official residence – and the Column of Marcus Aurelius (see page 70).

Sant'Agostino

Piazza di Sant'Agostino 80 • Daily 7.30am–noon & 4–7.30pm • ⓣ 06 6880 1962

A few minutes west of the Palazzo di Montecitorio, the Renaissance facade of the church of **Sant'Agostino** takes up one side of a drab piazza of the same name. It's not much to look at from the outside, but a handful of art treasures might draw you in. Just inside the door, the serene statue of the *Madonna del Parto*, by Sansovino, is traditionally invoked during pregnancy and is accordingly surrounded by offerings in pink and baby blue. Further into the church, take a look at Raphael's vibrant fresco of Isaiah, on the third pillar on the left, beneath which is another work by Sansovino, a craggy *St Ann, Virgin and Child*. But the biggest crowds gather around the first chapel on the left, where the *Madonna and Pilgrims* by Caravaggio – a characteristic work of what was at the time almost revolutionary realism – shows two peasants with dirty clothes praying at the feet of a sensuous Mary and Child.

Palazzo Altemps

Piazza Sant'Apollinare 46 • Tues–Sun 9am–7.45pm • €10, or €12 combined ticket with Palazzo Massimo (see page 78), Terme di Diocleziano (see page 77) and Crypta Balbi, valid for three days; free first Sun of the month • ⓣ 06 3996 7700, ⓦ coopculture.it

A five-minute walk west of Sant'Agostino, Piazza Sant'Apollinare is home to the beautifully restored **Palazzo Altemps**, part of the Museo Nazionale Romano (see page 56), and housing the cream of its collections of Roman statuary. On the **ground floor** at the far end of the courtyard's loggia is a statue of the Emperor Antoninus Pius, and, around the corner, a couple of heads of Zeus and Pluto and a bust of Julia, the daughter of the Emperor Augustus. There are two almost identical statues of Apollo the Lyrist, a magnificent statue of Athena taming a serpent, pieced together from fragments found near the church of Santa Maria sopra Minerva, and, just off the far corner of the courtyard, a Dionysus with a satyr and panther, found on the Quirinale Hill. Restoration works on the *palazzo* brought to light the remains of a Roman **domus** from the fourth to fifth century AD, which you can peer down at from a room off the south side of the courtyard.

On the **first floor** you get a slightly better sense of the original building – some of the frescoes remain and the north loggia retains its original, late sixteenth-century decoration, simulating a vine-laden pergola. Among the objects on display there's a fine statue of Hermes, a wonderful statue of a warrior at rest and a charmingly sensitive portrayal of Orestes and Electra from the first century AD by a sculptor called Menelaus – his name is carved at the base of one of the figures. In a later room stands a colossal head of Hera, now thought to be a head of **Antonia** (Mark Antony's daughter and mother of Caligula and Claudius), and – what some consider the highlight of the entire collection – the famous **Ludovisi throne**, embellished with a delicate relief portraying the birth of Aphrodite. Further on, the Great Room of Galata – whose huge fireplace is embellished with caryatids and lurking ibex, the symbol of the Altemps family – has the so-called *Suicide of Galatian*, apparently commissioned by Julius Caesar to adorn his Quirinal estate. Also here, an incredible sarcophagus depicts a battle between the Romans and barbarians in graphic, almost viscerally sculptural detail.

Via dei Coronari

West of Palazzo Altemps, narrow **Via dei Coronari**, and some of the streets around, are the fulcrum of Rome's **antiques** trade. Although the prices are as high as you might

1

expect in such a location, there's a huge number of shops (Via dei Coronari consists of virtually nothing else) selling a tremendous variety of stuff, and a browse along here makes for an absorbing bit of sightseeing.

Piazza Navona

The pedestrianized **Piazza Navona**, lined with cafés and restaurants and often thronged with tourists, street artists and pigeons, is Rome's most famous square, and as picturesque as any in Italy. It takes its oval shape from the first-century-AD Stadio di Domiziano (see below), the principal venue of the athletic events and later chariot races that took place in the Campus Martius. Until the mid-fifteenth century the ruins of the arena were still here, overgrown and disused, but the square was given a face-lift in the mid-seventeenth century by Pope Innocent X, who built most of the grandiose palaces that surround it.

Sant'Agnese in Agone

Piazza Navona • Tues–Sat 9.30am–1pm & 3–7pm, Sun 9am–1pm & 3–8pm • ⓣ 06 6819 2134, ⓦ santagneseinagone.org

Pope Innocent X commissioned Borromini to design the facade of the church of **Sant'Agnese in Agone** on the piazza's western side. The story goes that the 13-year-old St Agnes was stripped naked before the crowds in the stadium as punishment for refusing to marry, whereupon she miraculously grew hair to cover herself. The church, typically squeezed into the tightest of spaces by Borromini, is supposedly built on the spot where it all happened.

Fontana dei Quattro Fiumi

Opposite Sant'Agnese in Agone, the **Fontana dei Quattro Fiumi** (Fountain of the Four Rivers), one of three fountains that punctuate the square, is a masterpiece by Bernini, Borromini's archrival. It's said that all the figures are shielding their eyes in horror from Borromini's church facade (Bernini was disdainful of the less successful Borromini, and their rivalry is well documented), but the fountain had actually been completed before the facade was begun. The grand complexity of rock, which represents the four great rivers of the world, is topped with an Egyptian obelisk, brought here by Pope Innocent X from the Circus of Maxentius.

Stadio di Domiziano

Via di Tor Sanguigna 3 • Mon–Fri & Sun 10am–7pm, Sat 10am–8pm • €8 • ⓣ 06 4568 6100, ⓦ stadiodomiziano.com

Just north of Piazza Navona lie the remains of the **Stadio di Domiziano** (Stadium of Domitian), built in around 86 AD as a Roman venue for the Greek athletic games, of which the emperor Domitian was a fan. The underground site holds the well-preserved remains of a small section of the stadium, the towering archways giving a sense of its former size (it once held around thirty thousand spectators) – though you can also get a reasonable view from the balcony at street level.

San Luigi dei Francesi

Piazza San Luigi dei Francesi 5 • Mon–Fri 9.30am–12.45pm & 2.30–6.30pm, Sat 9.30am–12.15pm & 2.30–6.30pm, Sun 11.30am–12.45pm & 2.30–6.30pm • ⓣ 06 688 271, ⓦ saintlouis-rome.net

On the eastern side of Piazza Navona, the French national church of **San Luigi dei Francesi** is worth a look, mainly for its works by Caravaggio. In the last chapel on the left are three paintings: *The Calling of St Matthew*, in which Christ points to Matthew, who is illuminated by a shaft of sunlight; *The Inspiration of St Matthew*, where Matthew is visited by an angel as he writes the Gospel; and *The Martyrdom of St Matthew*. Caravaggio's first public commission, these paintings were actually rejected at first, partly on grounds of indecorum, and it took considerable reworking by the artist before they were finally accepted.

Sant'Ivo alla Sapienza

Corso del Rinascimento 40 • Sun 9am–noon; closed July & Aug • ⓣ 06 686 4987, ⓦ sivoallasapienza.eu

Between the Pantheon and Piazza Navona, accessible from Corso del Rinascimento, the rather blank facade of the **Palazzo della Sapienza** cradles the church of **Sant'Ivo** – from the outside at least, one of Rome's most impressive churches, with a playful facade designed by Borromini. Though originally built for the Barberini pope, Urban VIII, the building actually spans the reign of three pontiffs. Each of the two small towers is topped with the weird pyramidal groupings that are the symbol of the Chigi family (representing the hills of Monti dei Paschi di Siena), and the central cupola spirals helter-skelter to its zenith, crowned with flames that are supposed to represent the sting of the Barberini bee, their family symbol. The inside, too, is very cleverly designed, light and spacious given the small space the church is squeezed into, rising to the tall parabolic cupola.

Museo di Roma

Piazza San Pantaleo 10 • Tues–Sun 10am–7pm; last entry 1hr before closing • €9.50, free first Sun of the month • ⓣ 06 0608, ⓦ museodiroma.it

Overlooking the south side of Piazza Navona, the eighteenth-century Palazzo Braschi is the home of the **Museo di Roma**, which has a permanent collection relating to the history of the city from the Middle Ages to the present day. The building itself is probably the main attraction – particularly the magnificent Sala Nobile where you enter, and the main staircase – but some of the paintings are of interest, showing views of the city during different eras, and frescoes from demolished palaces provide decent enough highlights.

Piazza Pasquino and Via del Governo Vecchio

The triangular space of **Piazza Pasquino** is named after the small battered torso that still stands in the corner. Pasquino is perhaps the best known of Rome's "talking statues" of the Middle Ages and Renaissance times, on which anonymous comments on the affairs of the day would be attached – comments that had a serious as well as a humorous intent, and gave us our word "pasquinade". **Via del Governo Vecchio** leads west from here, and is home – along with the narrow streets around – to some of the *centro storico*'s liveliest restaurants and bars.

Campo de' Fiori and the Ghetto

Just south of the *centro storico* proper, this is Rome's old centre part two, a similar neighbourhood of cramped, wanderable streets opening out into small squares flanked by churches. However, it's less monumental and more of a working quarter, as evidenced by its main focus, **Campo de' Fiori**, whose fruit and veg stalls are a marked contrast to the pavement artists of Piazza Navona. Close by are the dark alleys of the old **Jewish Ghetto**, and the busy traffic junction of Largo di Torre Argentina.

Campo de' Fiori

Campo de' Fiori is in many ways Rome's most appealing square, home to a lively fruit and vegetable market (Mon–Sat 7am–2pm), and flanked by restaurants and cafés. No one really knows how the square came by its name, which means "field of flowers", but one theory holds that it was derived from the Roman Campus Martius, which used to cover most of this part of town. Another claims it is named after Flora, the mistress of Pompey, whose theatre used to stand on what is now the square's northeast corner – a huge complex by all accounts, and the supposed location of Julius Caesar's assassination. Later, Campo de' Fiori was an important point on papal processions between the Vatican and the major basilicas of Rome, and a site of public

1

executions. The most notorious killing was of Giordano Bruno, a late sixteenth-century freethinker who was denounced to the Inquisition; his trial lasted for years and he is commemorated by a statue in the middle of the square.

Palazzo Farnese

Piazza Farnese • Tours in English Wed 5pm, in French or Italian Mon, Wed & Fri 3pm, 4pm & 5pm; 45min • €9; book several weeks in advance and bring your passport; no admission to under-10s • ⓦ inventerrome.com

Just south of Campo de' Fiori, **Piazza Farnese** is a quite different square, with great fountains spurting out of lilies – the Farnese emblem – into marble tubs brought from the Baths of Caracalla, all overlooked by the sober bulk of the **Palazzo Farnese** itself. Begun in 1514 by Antonio da Sangallo the Younger, the *palazzo* was finished off after the architect's death by Michelangelo, who added the top tier of windows and cornice. The building now houses the **French Embassy** but is open to those organized enough to book in advance – worth doing to see the amazing Baroque ceiling frescoes of Annibale Carracci in one of the rear reception rooms.

Galleria Spada

Piazza di Capo di Ferro 3 • Daily (except Tues) 8.30am–7.30pm • €5; free first Sun of the month • ⓣ 06 683 2409, ⓦ galleriaspada.beniculturali.it

If you can't get in to the Palazzo Farnese, make do instead with the Palazzo Spada and the **Galleria Spada** inside; walk right through the courtyard to the back of the building. Its four rooms, decorated in the manner of a Roman noble family's home, have two portraits of Cardinal Bernardino Spada by Reni and Guercino, and the building itself is a treat, its facade frilled with stucco adornments. Left off the small courtyard, there's a crafty **trompe l'oeil** by Borromini – a tunnel whose actual length is multiplied about four times through the architect's tricks with perspective.

Via Giulia

Via Giulia runs parallel to the Tiber from the Ponte Sisto, and was laid out by Julius II to connect the bridge with the Vatican. The street was conceived as the centre of papal Rome, and Julius commissioned Bramante to line it with imposing palaces. Bramante didn't get very far with the plan, as Julius was soon succeeded by Leo X, but the street quickly became a popular residence for wealthier Roman families, and is still packed full with stylish *palazzi* and antiques shops.

Museo di Scultura Antica Giovanni Barracco

Corso Vittorio Emanuele II 166/A • Tues–Sun: June–Sept 1–7pm; Oct–May 10am–4pm • Free • ⓣ 06 0608, ⓦ museobarracco.it

Just north of Campo de' Fiori, the **Museo di Scultura Antica Giovanni Barracco** holds a small but high-quality collection of ancient sculpture that was donated to the city at the turn of the century by one Baron Barracco. There are some fine ancient Egyptian pieces and ceramics and statuary from classical Greece and Rome. Highlights include a head of the young Rameses II, next to a bust of an Egyptian priest, a Roman figure of an athlete from an ancient Greek original and a highly realistic depiction of a bitch washing herself, from the fourth century BC.

Largo di Torre Argentina and around

Largo di Torre Argentina is a large square, frantic with traffic circling around the ruins of four Republican-era temples, and home to a thriving cat sanctuary (daily noon–6pm; ⓣ 06 4542 5240, ⓦ romancats.com). On the far side of the square, the **Teatro Argentina** (ⓦ teatrodiroma.net) was built in 1731, according to legend over the spot in Pompey's theatre where Julius Caesar was assassinated. In 1816 it was the venue for the first performance of Rossini's *Barber of Seville*, which was not a success: Rossini was apparently booed into taking refuge in a nearby pastry shop.

The Gesù

Via degli Astalli 16 • Daily 7am–12.30pm & 4–7.45pm • ⓣ 06 697 001, ⓦ chiesadelgesu.org

A short walk east of Largo di Torre Argentina, the church of the **Gesù** is a huge structure, high and wide, with a single-aisled nave and short transepts edging out under a huge dome. The headquarters of the Jesuits, it was ideal for the large and fervent congregations the order wanted to attract – indeed, it has since served as the model for Jesuit churches everywhere. The facade is by Giacomo della Porta, the staggeringly rich interior the work of Vignola. Look out for the glitzy tomb of the order's founder, St Ignatius, topped by a huge globe of lapis lazuli representing the earth; and the paintings by the Genoese painter Baciccia in the dome and the nave – the *Triumph in the Name of Jesus* oozes out of its frame in a tangle of writhing bodies, flowing drapery and stucco angels clinging on like limpets.

Rooms of St Ignatius

Via degli Astalli 16 • Mon–Sat 4–6pm, Sun 10am–noon • Free

Next door to the Gesù, the **Rooms of St Ignatius** occupy part of the first floor of the Jesuit headquarters, and are the rooms where St Ignatius lived from 1544 until his death in 1556. There are bits and pieces of memorabilia relating to the saint, but the true draw is the decorative corridor outside, designed by Andrea Pozzo in 1680 – a superb exercise in perspective on a minimized scale, giving an illusion of a grand hall in a relatively small space.

Via Portico d'Ottavia and around

Cross over to the far side of Via Arenula and you're in what was once the city's **Jewish Ghetto**, a crumbling area of narrow, switchback streets and alleys, easy to lose your way in. There was a Jewish population in Rome as far back as the second century BC, and although much depleted now, it still numbers sixteen thousand (around half Italy's total), and the quarter is thriving. There are a few kosher restaurants, bakers and butchers on and around the main artery of the Jewish area, **Via Portico d'Ottavia**. This leads down to the **Portico d'Ottavia**, a second-century-BC gate, rebuilt by Augustus and dedicated to his sister in 23 BC. There's a walkway (daily 9am–7pm, until 6pm in winter) through the ancient fish market to the adjacent amphitheatre of the **Teatro di Marcello**. Begun by Julius Caesar, finished by Augustus, this was pillaged in the fourth century and not properly restored until the Middle Ages, after which it became a formidable fortified palace for a succession of different rulers, including the Orsini family. On the other side of Via Portico d'Ottavia, narrow Via della Reginella leads to **Piazza Mattei**, whose **Fontana delle Tartarughe**, or "turtle fountain", is a delightful, late sixteenth-century creation, perhaps restored by Bernini.

The Synagogue and Museo Ebraico

Lungotevere Cenci X • **Synagogue tours** Hourly; same days and hours as museum; 20min • Free • **Museum** April–Sept Mon–Thurs & Sun 10am–5.15pm, Fri 10am–3.15pm; Sept–March Mon–Thurs & Sun 10am–5pm, Fri 9am–2pm; closed Jewish hols • €11 • ⓣ 06 6840 0661, ⓦ museoebraico.roma.it

The Ghetto's principal Jewish sight is the huge **Synagogue** by the river, built in 1904 and very much dominating all around with its bulk – not to mention the *carabinieri* who stand guard 24 hours a day. The only way to see the building is on one of the regular guided tours it runs in English, afterwards taking in the Synagogue's **Museo Ebraico**. The interior of the building is impressive, rising to a high, rainbow-hued dome; tours are excellent, giving good background on the building and Rome's Jewish community in general, and the museum underneath holds one of the most important collections of Judaica in Europe.

Isola Tiberina

Almost opposite the Syngagogue, the **Ponte Fabricio** crosses the river to **Isola Tiberina.** Built in 62 BC, it's the only classical bridge to remain intact without help from the

restorers (the Ponte Cestio, on the other side of the island, was partially rebuilt in the nineteenth century). As for the island, it's a calm respite from the city centre proper, with its originally tenth-century church of **San Bartolomeo** worth a peep inside for its ancient columns and an equally ancient wellhead on the altar steps, carved with figures relating to the founding of the church. The figures include St Bartholomew himself, who also features in the painting above the altar, hands tied above his head, on the point of being skinned alive – his famous and gruesome mode of martyrdom. Beyond the island, you can see the **Ponte Rotto** (Broken Bridge) – all that remains of the first stone bridge to span the Tiber, originally built between 179 and 142 BC.

Piazza Venezia and around

Piazza Venezia is not so much a square as a road junction, and a busy one at that. Flanked on all sides by imposing buildings, it's a dignified focal point for the city in spite of the traffic, and a spot you'll find yourself returning to time and again given its proximity to both the medieval and Renaissance centre of Rome and the bulk of the ruins of the ancient city.

The Vittoriano

Piazza Venezia 3 • **Exterior** Mon–Thurs 9.30am–7.30pm • Free • **Lifts** Daily 9.30am–7.30pm • €7 • T 06 678 0664

Piazza Venezia is dominated by the marble monstrosity that is the Vittorio Emanuele Monument or **Vittoriano**, erected at the beginning of the twentieth century as the "Altar of the Nation" to commemorate Italian Unification. It has been variously likened in the past to a typewriter (because of its shape) and, by American GIs, to a wedding cake. It's great fun clambering up and down the sweeping terraces and flights of steps, cutting through eventually to the Capitoline Museums behind. There are things to see inside (a large Unification museum and the Complesso del Vittoriano, a space for high-profile temporary exhibitions), but the main interest is on the outside: the Tomb of the Unknown Soldier at the top of the first flight of steps; the equestrian statue of Vittorio Emanuele II, one of the world's largest, on the next level; the terraces above this; and finally the **lifts** which whisk you to the terrace at the top – not cheap. The views are all-encompassing, and of course this is the one place in Rome from which you can't see the Vittoriano.

Museo Nazionale di Palazzo Venezia

Via del Plebiscito 118 • Tues–Sun 8.30am–7.30pm; last entry 1hr before closing • €10; free first Sun of the month • T 06 6999 4388, W museopalazzovenezia.beniculturali.it

Forming the western side of the piazza, **Palazzo Venezia** was the first large Renaissance palace in the city, built for the Venetian Pope Paul II in the mid-fifteenth century and for a long time the embassy of the Venetian Republic. More famously, **Mussolini** moved in here while in power, occupying the vast Sala del Mappamondo and making his declamatory speeches to the huge crowds below from the small balcony facing onto the piazza. Nowadays it's a venue for great exhibitions and home to the **Museo Nazionale di Palazzo Venezia**, a museum of Renaissance arts and crafts, with a number of fifteenth-century devotional paintings, bronzes and sculpture.

San Marco

Piazza di San Marco 52 • Tues–Fri 10am–1pm & 4–6pm, Sat & Sun 10am–1pm & 4–8pm • T 06 679 5205, W sanmarcoevangelista.it

Adjacent to the Palazzo Venezia on its southern side, the church of **San Marco** is the Venetian church in Rome – and one of its most ancient basilicas. Standing on the spot where the apostle is supposed to have lived while in the city, it was rebuilt in 833 and added to by various Renaissance and eighteenth-century popes. Look out for the apse mosaic dating from the ninth century, which shows Pope Gregory offering his church to Christ.

Palazzo Valentini

Via IV November 119/A • Tours daily (except Tues) 9.30am–6.30pm; 1hr 30min • €12; booking essential • ⓣ 06 32 810, ⓦ palazzovalentini.it

Just off Piazza Venezia, the late sixteenth-century **Palazzo Valentini** is the home of Rome's regional government but is also the location of an ancient Roman baths and residential complex. You have to take a tour to see them, but they succeed pretty well in bringing the excavations to life, with glass floors and catwalks taking you through the site and technology that re-creates the rooms as they might have looked in ancient times. The tour ends with a video explaining the story of the nearby Column of Trajan (see page 69).

The Capitoline Hill

The real pity about the Vittoriano is that it obscures views of the **Capitoline Hill** behind – once the spiritual and political centre of the Roman Empire. Apart from anything else, this hill has contributed key words to the English language, including, of course, "capitol", and "money", which comes from the temple to Juno Moneta that once stood up here and housed the Roman mint. The Capitoline also played a significant role in medieval and Renaissance times: the flamboyant fourteenth-century dictator Cola di Rienzo stood here in triumph in 1347 and was murdered here by an angry mob seven years later – a humble statue marks the spot.

Santa Maria in Aracoeli

Piazza del Campidoglio 4; access via Aracoeli staircase, or avoid the steps by going via Piazza del Campidoglio or the back of the Vittoriano • Daily: May–Sept 9am–6.30pm; Oct–April 9.30am–5.30pm • ⓣ 06 6976 3839

The church of **Santa Maria in Aracoeli** crowns the highest point on the Capitoline Hill, built on the site of a temple where, according to legend, the Tiburtine Sybil foretold the birth of Christ. Reached by a steep flight of steps erected by Cola di Rienzo in 1348, or more easily by cutting through from the Vittoriano or Campidoglio, it's one of Rome's most ancient basilicas, with, in the first chapel on the right, some fine frescoes by Pinturicchio recording the life of San Bernardino. The church is also known for its role as keeper of the "Bambino", a small statue of the infant Christ, said to have healing powers, carved from the wood of a Gethsemane olive tree. The statue was stolen in 1994 and a copy now stands in its place, in a small chapel to the left of the high altar.

The Capitoline Museums

Piazza del Campidoglio • Daily 9.30am–7.30pm • €11.50, €12.50 combined ticket with Centrale Montemartini (see page 82) • ⓣ 06 0608, ⓦ museicapitolini.org

Next to the steps up to Santa Maria is the **cordonata**, an elegant, gently rising ramp, topped with two Roman statues of Castor and Pollux, leading to one of Rome's most elegant squares, **Piazza del Campidoglio**. The square was designed by Michelangelo in the last years of his life for Pope Paul III (though it wasn't in fact completed until the late seventeenth century); Michelangelo balanced the piazza, redesigning the facade of what is now the **Palazzo dei Conservatori** and projecting an identical building across the way, known as the **Palazzo Nuovo**. Both are angled slightly to focus on **Palazzo Senatorio**, Rome's town hall. In the centre of the square Michelangelo placed an equestrian statue of Emperor Marcus Aurelius, which had previously stood for years outside San Giovanni in Laterano. After careful restoration, the original is now behind a glass wall in the Palazzo dei Conservatori, and a copy has taken its place at the centre of the piazza.

The Palazzo dei Conservatori and Palazzo Nuovo together make up the **Capitoline Museums**, containing some of the city's most important ancient sculpture and art.

Palazzo dei Conservatori

The **Palazzo dei Conservatori** holds the larger, more varied collection. Among its many treasures are the so-called *Spinario*, a Roman statue of a boy picking a thorn out of his

foot; the Etruscan bronze she-wolf nursing the mythic founders of the city; and the Hannibal Room, covered in wonderfully vivid fifteenth-century paintings recording Rome's wars with Carthage, and so named for a rendering of Hannibal seated impressively on an elephant.

The wonderfully airy **new wing** holds the original statue of Marcus Aurelius, formerly in the square outside, alongside a giant bronze statue of Constantine, or at least his head, hand and orb. Nearby stands the rippling bronze of Hercules, behind which are part of the foundations and a retaining wall from the original temple of Jupiter here, discovered when the work for the new wing was undertaken. When museum fatigue sets in you can climb up to the floor above to the second-floor **café**, whose terrace commands one of the best views in Rome.

The second-floor **pinacoteca** holds Renaissance painting from the fourteenth century to the late seventeenth century. Highlights include a couple of portraits by Van Dyck, a penetrating *Portrait of a Crossbowman* by Lorenzo Lotto, a pair of paintings from 1590 by Tintoretto and a very fine early work by Lodovico Carracci, *Head of a Boy*. In one of the two large main galleries, there's a vast picture by Guercino, depicting the *Burial of Santa Petronilla* (an early Roman martyr who was the supposed daughter of St Peter), and two paintings by Caravaggio, one a replica of the young John the Baptist which hangs in the Galleria Doria Pamphilj, the other an early work known as *The Fortune-Teller.*

Palazzo Nuovo

The **Palazzo Nuovo** across the square – also accessible by way of an underground walkway that holds the **Galleria Lapidaria**, a collection of Roman marble inscriptions – is the more manageable of the two museums, with some of the best of the city's Roman sculpture crammed into half a dozen or so rooms. Among them is the remarkable statue *Dying Gaul*, as well as a *Satyr Resting* that was the inspiration for Nathaniel Hawthorne's book *The Marble Faun*, and the red marble *Laughing Silenus*. There are also busts and statues of Roman emperors and other famous names: a young Augustus, a cruel Caracalla and, the centrepiece, a life-size portrait of Helena, the mother of Constantine, reclining gracefully. Don't miss the coy, delicate *Capitoline Venus*, housed in a room on its own.

San Pietro in Carcere and the Carcer Tullianum

Clivo Argentario 1 • Daily: entry every 30min 8.30am–4.30pm • €10; joint ticket with Colosseum, Forum and Palatine €20; booking essential • 06 6992 4652, tullianum.org

On the left side of the Palazzo Senatorio (as you face it from the Campidoglio) steps lead down to the little church of **San Pietro in Carcere**, built above the ancient **Carcer Tullianum** (also known as the **Mamertine Prison**), where spies, vanquished soldiers and other enemies of the Roman state were incarcerated, and where both St Peter and St Paul are thought to have been held. It's now part of a multimedia-assisted tour, taking in the depths of the jail, including the column to which St Peter was chained, along with the spring the saint is said to have used to baptize his guards and other prisoners.

Piazza Bocca della Verità

On the south side of the Capitoline Hill, down towards the Tiber, Via del Teatro di Marcello meets the riverside main drag at the **Piazza Bocca della Verità**, home to two of the city's better-preserved Roman temples, the **Temple of Portunus** and the **Temple of Hercules Victor** – the oldest surviving marble structure in Rome and long known as the Tempio Rotondo because of its circular shape. Both date from the end of the second century BC and are worth a look as fine examples of Republican-era places of worship.

Santa Maria in Cosmedin

Piazza Bocca della Verità 18 • Daily 10am–5pm • 06 678 7759

The church of **Santa Maria in Cosmedin**, on the far side of the square, is a typically Roman medieval basilica with a huge marble altar and a colourful and ingenious Cosmati-work marble mosaic floor – one of the city's finest. Outside in the portico, and giving the square its name, is the **Bocca della Verità** (Mouth of Truth), an ancient Roman drain cover in the shape of an enormous face that in medieval times would apparently swallow the hand of anyone who hadn't told the truth. It was particularly popular with husbands anxious to test the faithfulness of their wives; now it is one of the city's biggest tour-bus attractions.

Ancient Rome

There are remnants of the ancient Roman era all over the city, but the most concentrated and central grouping – which for simplicity's sake we've called **Ancient Rome** – is the area that stretches southeast from the Capitoline Hill. Mussolini ploughed the Via dei Fori Imperiali road through here in the 1930s, with the intention of turning it into one giant archeological park, and this to some extent is what it is. You could spend a good day or so picking your way through the rubble of what was once the heart of the ancient world.

The Colosseum

Daily: mid-Feb to mid-March 8.30am–5pm; mid- to end March 8.30am–5.30pm; April–Aug 8.30am–7.15pm; Sept 8.30am–7pm; Oct 8.30am–6.30pm; Nov to mid-Feb 8.30am–4.30pm; last entry 1hr before closing • €12 combined ticket with Forum (see page 66) and Palatine Hill (see page 68), valid for two days; first Sun of the month free • T 06 3996 7700, W coopculture.it

The **Colosseum** is perhaps Rome's most awe-inspiring ancient monument, an enormous structure that despite the depredations of nearly two thousand years of earthquakes, fires, riots, wars and, not least, plundering for its seemingly inexhaustible supply of ready-cut travertine blocks, still stands relatively intact – a recognizable symbol not just of the city of Rome, but of the entire ancient world. Sitting in the middle of a traffic roundabout, it was eaten away by pollution and cracked by the vibrations of cars and the metro – until a huge, 25-million-euro renovation, funded by Italian shoe giant Tod's and completed in 2018, uncovered a much sprucer structure.

The basic structure has served as a model for stadiums around the world. You'll not be alone in appreciating it and during summer the combination of people and scaffolding can make a visit more like touring a contemporary building site than an ancient monument. But visit late in the evening or early morning before the tour buses have arrived, and the arena can seem more like the marvel it really is.

ANCIENT ROME: TICKETS AND TOURS

A single **ticket** (€12) covers the **Colosseum**, **Forum and Palatine Hill** and is valid for two days; you're allowed to visit each attraction once during this time, and the Forum and Palatine Hill count as one site, so have to be visited at the same time. **Queues** can be a problem, particularly at the Colosseum, and while they do move quickly, during summer they're rarely less than 100m long and are often besieged by touts. Your best bet is to buy your ticket **online in advance** (booking fee of €2 in addition to the ticket price; W coopculture.it), or buy it at either entrance to the Forum early in the morning when things are usually quieter. Alternatively, holders of the RomaPass, Omnia Card and S.U.P.E.R ticket (see page 56) are allowed to use a different queue.

If you **book a tour** you will generally be allowed to skip the line. There are guided tours of the Colosseum daily (10.15am–5.15pm; roughly every 30min–1hr; 45min; €5), as well as daily tours of the underground area, the upper tiers and the arena floor – areas usually closed to the public (€9; advance booking essential). **Night tours** of the Colosseum are also available (usually mid-May to Oct Mon–Wed & Sun; €20), which include a visit to the underground areas. All tours can be booked through W coopculture.it.

Originally known as the Flavian Amphitheatre (the name Colosseum is a much later invention), it was begun around 72 AD by the Emperor Vespasian. Inside, there was room for a total of around sixty thousand people seated and ten thousand or so standing. Seating was allocated according to social status, with the emperor and his attendants naturally occupying the best seats in the house, and the social class of the spectators diminishing as you got nearer the top. There was a labyrinth below that was covered with a wooden floor and punctuated at various places with trapdoors that could be opened as required, and lifts to raise and lower the animals that took part in the games. The floor was covered with canvas to make it waterproof and the canvas was covered with several centimetres of sand to absorb blood; in fact, our word "arena" is derived from the Latin word for sand.

The Arch of Constantine

Next to the Colosseum is the huge **Arch of Constantine**, placed here in the early decades of the fourth century AD after Constantine had consolidated his power as sole emperor. The arch demonstrates the deterioration of the arts during the late stages of the Roman Empire – most of the sculptural decoration here had to be removed from other monuments. The round medallions are taken from a temple dedicated to the Emperor Hadrian's lover, Antinous, and show Antinous and Hadrian engaged in a hunt; the other pieces, taken from the Forum of Trajan, show Dacian prisoners captured in Trajan's war.

The Roman Forum

Entrances Largo della Salara Vecchia, halfway down Via dei Fori Imperiali; at the Arch of Titus near the Colosseum; by the Temple of Venus; and on Via di San Gregorio (via the Palatine) **Exits** Largo della Salaria Vecchia; Via di San Gregorio (via the Palatine); behind the Arch of Septimius Severus, near the Capitoline Hill; and by the Basilica of Maxentius, by the church of Santa Francesca Romana • Daily: mid-Feb to mid-March 8.30am–5pm; mid- to end March 8.30am–5.30pm; April–Aug 8.30am–7.15pm; Sept 8.30am–7pm; Oct 8.30am–6.30pm; Nov to mid-Feb 8.30am–4.30pm; last entry 1hr before closing • €12 combined ticket with Colosseum (see page 65) and Palatine Hill (see page 68), valid for two days; free first Sun of the month • Ⓦ coopculture.it

The five or so acres that make up the **Roman Forum** were once the heart of the Mediterranean world, and, although the glories of ancient Rome are hard to glimpse here now, there's a symbolic allure to the place, and at certain times of day a desolate drama, that make it one of the most compelling sets of ruins anywhere in the world.

Via Sacra to the Curia

You need some imagination and a little history to really appreciate the place but the public spaces are easy enough to discern, especially the spinal **Via Sacra**, the best-known street of ancient Rome, along which victorious emperors and generals would ride in procession to give thanks at the Capitoline's Temple of Juno. Towards the Capitoline Hill end of the Via Sacra, the large cube-shaped building is the **Curia**, meeting place of the Senate, which was built on the orders of Julius Caesar as part of his programme for expanding the Forum, although what you see now is a third-century-AD reconstruction. Inside (under restoration at the time of writing), three wide stairs rise left and right, on which about three hundred senators could be accommodated with their folding chairs.

Arch of Septimius Severus and around

Near the Curia, the **Arch of Septimius Severus** was constructed in the early third century AD by his sons Caracalla and Galba to mark their father's victories in what is now Iran. Next to the arch, the low brown wall is the **Rostra**, from which important speeches were made (it was from here that Mark Anthony most likely spoke about Caesar after his death), to the left of which are the long stairs of the **Basilica Julia**, built by Julius Caesar in the 50s BC after he returned from the Gallic wars. A bit further along, on the right,

rails mark the site of the **Lacus Curtius**, the spot where, according to legend, a chasm opened during the earliest days of the city and the soothsayers determined that it would only be closed once Rome had sacrificed its most valuable possession into it. Marcus Curtius, a Roman soldier who declared that Rome's most valuable possession was a loyal citizen, hurled himself and his horse into the void and it duly closed.

Temple of Castor and Pollux and House of the Vestal Virgins

Next to the Basilica Julia, the enormous pile of rubble topped by three graceful Corinthian columns is the **Temple of Castor and Pollux**, dedicated in 484 BC to the divine twins or Dioscuri, who appeared miraculously to ensure victory for the Romans in a key battle. Beyond here, the **House of the Vestal Virgins** is a second-century-AD reconstruction of a building originally built by Nero: four storeys of rooms set around a central courtyard, fringed by the statues or inscribed pedestals of the women themselves, with the round Temple of Vesta at the near end.

The Basilica of Maxentius and the Arch of Titus

Almost opposite the House of the Vestal Virgins, a shady walkway to the left leads to the **Basilica of Maxentius**, in terms of size and ingenuity probably the Forum's most impressive remains. Begun by Maxentius, it was continued by his co-emperor and rival, Constantine, after he had defeated him at the Battle of the Milvian Bridge in 312 AD. From here the Via Sacra climbs more steeply to the **Arch of Titus**, built by Titus's brother, Domitian, after the emperor's death in 81 AD, to commemorate his victories in Judea in 70 AD and his triumphal return from that campaign.

The Palatine Hill

Access is from the Roman Forum or from Via di San Gregorio, near the Colosseum • Daily: mid-Feb to mid-March 8.30am–5pm; mid- to end March 8.30am–5.30pm; April–Aug 8.30am–7.15pm; Sept 8.30am–7pm; Oct 8.30am–6.30pm; Nov to mid-Feb 8.30am–4.30pm; last entry 1hr before closing; House of Livia and House of Augustus accessible via the S.U.P.E.R ticket (see page 56) • €12 combined ticket with Colosseum (see page 65) and Forum (see page 66), valid for two days; free first Sun of the month • Ⓦ coopculture.it

Rising above the Roman Forum, the **Palatine Hill** is supposedly where the city of Rome was founded, and is home to some of its most ancient remains. In a way it's a greener, more pleasant site to tour than the Forum. In the days of the Republic, the Palatine was the most desirable address in Rome (the word "palace" is derived from Palatine), and big names continued to colonize it during the imperial era, trying to outdo each other with ever larger and more magnificent dwellings.

Along the main path up from the Forum, the **Domus Flavia** was once one of the most splendid residences, and, to the left, the top level of the gargantuan **Domus Augustana** spreads to the far brink of the hill. You can look down from here on its vast central courtyard with fountain and wander to the brink of the deep trench of the **Stadium**. On the far side of the Stadium, the ruins of the Domus and **Baths of Septimius Severus** cling to the side of the hill, while the large grey building nearby houses the **Museo Palatino**, which contains an assortment of statuary, pottery and architectural fragments that have been excavated on the Palatine during the last 150 years. Beyond the Domus Flavia is the **Cryptoporticus**, a long passage built by Nero to link the vestibule of his Domus Aurea (see page 75) with the Palatine palaces, and decorated with well-preserved Roman stuccowork at the far end, towards the **House of Livia**. The latter has been recently restored and can be visited on daily tours, its courtyard and inner rooms decorated with mosaic floors and frescoes depicting mythological scenes. The structure was originally believed to have been the residence of Livia, the wife of Augustus, but it's now identified as simply part of the neighbouring **House of Augustus**, which is also accessible on guided tours. Visits take in the vividly frescoed rooms, some of which are very well-preserved, with designs on rich Pompeian-red backgrounds.

Climb up the steps near the House of Livia and you're in the bottom corner of the **Farnese Gardens**, among the first botanical gardens in Europe, laid out by Cardinal

Alessandro Farnese in the mid-sixteenth century and now a tidily planted retreat from the exposed heat of the ruins. The gardens surround the foundations of the **Domus Tiberiana**, a once lavish palace begun by Nero, embellished by Tiberius and extended by Hadrian a century or so later.

The Circus Maximus

On its southern side, the Palatine Hill drops down to the **Circus Maximus**, a long, thin, green expanse bordered by heavily trafficked roads that was the ancient city's main venue for chariot races; at one time this arena had a capacity of up to 400,000 spectators.

The Imperial Forums and Trajan's Markets

Imperial Forums Via dei Fori Imperiali • No access • Ⓦ capitolium.org • Metro Colosseo or bus to Via dei Fori Imperiali • **Trajan's Markets** Via IV Novembre 94 • Daily 9.30am–7.30pm; last entry 1hr before closing • €11.50, free first Sun of the month • Ⓣ 06 0608, Ⓦ mercatiditraiano.it

The **Imperial Forums** were built as ancient Rome grew in power and the Forum proper became too small. The ruins of forums built by Caesar, Augustus and Trajan, among others, line either side of the Via dei Fori Imperiali, and are still being excavated. With the exception of Trajan's markets, access to the area isn't possible, though from mid-April to mid-November, sound and light shows offer grandstand views of the illuminated forums of Augustus and Caesar (Ⓦ viaggioneifori.it). The **Forum of Trajan** was constructed at what was probably the very pinnacle of Roman power and prestige and incorporates the crescent of shops and arcades known as **Trajan's Markets**. Accessible from Via IV Novembre, the Great Hall here is an impressive two-storey space, and incorporates a number of finds from the Imperial Forums, including a colossal head of Constantine, a torso of a warrior, part of the temple of the Forum of Augustus and a bit of the frieze from Casear's temple of Venus Genetrix – three columns of which still stand in the Forum of Caesar across the road, and are viewable from the terrace upstairs. Afterwards descend to the Via Biberatica, whose shops and taverns wind around the bottom of the arcade before climbing to the belvedere for a better view over the Forum proper, the most notable remains of which are the column stumps of the massive **Basilica Ulpia** and the enormous **Column of Trajan** next to it – erected to celebrate the emperor's victories in Dacia (modern Romania) in 112 AD, and covered from top to bottom with reliefs commemorating the highlights of the campaign.

The Tridente

The northern part of Rome's centre is sometimes known as the **Tridente** on account of the trident shape of the roads leading down from the apex of Piazza del Popolo – **Via di Ripetta**, **Via del Corso** and **Via del Babuino**. The area east of Via del Corso, focusing on **Piazza di Spagna**, was historically the artistic quarter of the city, and eighteenth- and nineteenth-century Grand Tourists would come here in search of the colourful and exotic; institutions like *Caffè Greco* and *Babington's Tea Rooms* were the meeting places of the local expat community for close on a couple of centuries. Today these institutions have given ground to more latter-day traps for the tourist dollar, and the area around Via dei Condotti is these days strictly international designer territory. But the air of a Rome being discovered – even colonized – by foreigners persists, even if most of those hanging out on the Spanish Steps are flying-visit teenagers.

Via del Corso

The central prong of the Tridente and the boundary of the historic centre to the east, **Via del Corso** is Rome's main thoroughfare, leading all the way from Piazza Venezia at its southern end up to Piazza del Popolo to the north. On its eastern side, it gives onto the swish shopping streets that lead up to Piazza di Spagna; on the western side the web

of streets tangles its way right down to the Tiber. It is Rome's principal shopping street, home to a mixture of upmarket boutiques and chain stores that make it a busy stretch during the day, full of hurrying pedestrians and crammed buses, but relatively dead after dark.

Galleria Doria Pamphilj

Via del Corso 305 • **Gallery** Daily 9am–7pm; last entry 1hr before closing • €12, including audioguide in English • T 06 679 7323, W doriapamphilj.it • **Private apartments** Tours Tues–Sun; book in advance via E info.rm@trustfdp.it or T 331 164 1490

North of Piazza Venezia, the first building on the left of Via del Corso is the Palazzo Doria Pamphilj, one of the city's finest Rococo palaces. Inside is the **Galleria Doria Pamphilj**, perhaps the best of Rome's private art collections. The Doria Pamphilj family still lives in part of the building, and you're guided through the gallery by way of a free audio-tour narrated by the urbane Jonathan Pamphilj.

The **picture gallery** extends around the main courtyard, the paintings displayed in old-fashioned style, crammed in frame-to-frame, floor-to-ceiling. It has perhaps Rome's best concentration of Dutch and Flemish paintings, with a rare Italian work by Brueghel the Elder showing a naval battle being fought outside Naples, a highly realistic portrait of two old men by Quentin Metsys and a Hans Memling *Deposition* in the furthest rooms off the main gallery, as well as a further Metsys painting – the fabulously ugly *Moneylenders and their Clients* – in the main gallery, close to Annibale Carracci's bucolic *Flight into Egypt*. Also in the rooms off the courtyard are three paintings by Caravaggio – *Repentant Magdalene* and *John the Baptist*, and his wonderful *Rest on the Flight into Egypt* – hanging near *Salome with the Head of St John*, by Titian. The gallery's most prized treasures, however, are in a small room on their own – a Bernini bust of the Pamphilj pope Innocent X and Velázquez's famous, penetrating painting of the same man. All in all it's a marvellous collection of work, displayed in a wonderfully appropriate setting.

Guided tours take in the sumptuous **private apartments**, some of which were lived in until recently, hence the family photos dotted around the place.

Piazza Colonna

Piazza Colonna is flanked on its north side by the late sixteenth-century **Palazzo Chigi**, the official residence of the prime minister. The **Column of Marcus Aurelius**, which gives the piazza its name, was erected between 180 and 190 AD to commemorate military victories in northern Europe.

Piazza di Spagna

Via del Babuino leads down from Piazza del Popolo to **Piazza di Spagna**, a long straggle of a square almost entirely enclosed by buildings and centring on the distinctive boat-shaped **Barcaccia** fountain, the last work of Bernini's father. It apparently remembers the great flood of Christmas Day 1598, when a barge from the Tiber was washed up on the slopes of Pincio Hill here.

Keats-Shelley House

Piazza di Spagna 26 • Mon–Sat 10am–1pm & 2–6pm • €5 • T 06 678 4235, W keats-shelley-house.org

Facing directly onto Piazza di Spagna, opposite the fountain, is the house where the poet John Keats died in 1821. It now serves as the **Keats-Shelley House**, an archive of English-language literary and historical works and a museum of manuscripts and literary memorabilia relating to the Keats circle of the early nineteenth century – namely the poet himself, Shelley and Mary Shelley, and Byron (who at one time lived across the square). Among many bits of manuscript, letters and the like, there's a silver scallop-shell reliquary containing locks of Milton's and Elizabeth Barrett Browning's hair, while Keats's death mask, stored in the room where he died, captures a resigned grimace. Keats didn't really enjoy his time in Rome, referring to it as his "posthumous

life": he was tormented by his love for Fanny Brawne and spent months in pain before he died, confined to the rooming house with his artist friend Joseph Severn to whom he remarked that he could already feel "the flowers growing over him".

The Spanish Steps

The **Spanish Steps** (Scalinata di Spagna) sweep down in a cascade of balustrades and balconies to Piazza di Spagna. In the nineteenth century they were the hangout of young hopefuls waiting to be chosen as artists' models, and nowadays the scene is not much changed, with the steps providing the venue for international posing and flirting late into the summer nights. The only Spanish thing about them, incidentally, is the fact that they lead down to the Spanish Embassy, which also gave the piazza its name.

Trinità dei Monti

Piazza della Trinità dei Monti • Tues–Sat 10am–7pm, Sun 10am–5pm • ⓣ 06 679 4179

At the top of the Spanish Steps is the **Trinità dei Monti**, a largely sixteenth-century church designed by Carlo Maderno and paid for by the French king. Its rose-coloured Baroque facade overlooks the rest of Rome from its hilltop site, and it's worth clambering up just for the views. Do look inside for a couple of works by Daniele da Volterra, notably a soft, flowing fresco of the *Assumption* in the third chapel on the right, which includes a portrait of his teacher Michelangelo, and a *Deposition* across the nave.

Piazza del Popolo

The oval-shaped expanse of **Piazza del Popolo** is a dignified meeting of roads, now pedestrianized, laid out in 1538 by Pope Paul III (Alessandro Farnese) to make an impressive entrance to the city. The monumental **Porta del Popolo** went up in 1655, and was the work of Bernini, whose patron Alexander VII's Chigi family symbol – the heap of hills surmounted by a star – can clearly be seen above the main gateway. The square's main attraction is the unbroken view it gives all the way down Via del Corso to the central columns of the Vittoriano. If you get to choose your first view of the centre of Rome, make it this one.

Santa Maria del Popolo

Piazza del Popolo 12 • Mon–Thurs 7.30am–noon & 4–7pm, Fri & Sat 7.30am–7.30pm, Sun 7.30am–noon & 4.30–7pm • €1 to illuminate paintings • ⓣ 06 361 0836, ⓦ www.santamariadelpopolo.it

On the far side of the piazza, hard against the city walls, **Santa Maria del Popolo** holds some of the best Renaissance art of any Roman church. It was originally erected here in 1099 over the supposed burial place of Nero, in order to sanctify what was believed to be an evil place. Inside, the Chigi chapel, second on the left, was designed by Raphael for Agostino Chigi in 1516. Michelangelo's protégé, Sebastiano del Piombo, was responsible for the altarpiece, and two of the sculptures in the corner niches, of Daniel and Habakkuk, are by Bernini. But it's two pictures by Caravaggio in the left-hand chapel of the north transept that attract the most attention. These are typically dramatic works – one, the *Conversion of St Paul*, showing Paul and horse bathed in a beatific radiance; the other, the *Crucifixion of St Peter*, depicting Peter as an aged but strong figure, dominated by the muscular figures hoisting him up.

Ara Pacis

Lungotevere in Augusta, at Via Tomacelli • Daily 9.30am–7.30pm; last entry 1hr before closing • €10.50 • ⓣ 06 0608, ⓦ arapacis.it

Via Ripetta runs southwest from Piazza del Popolo into **Piazza del Augusta Imperatore**, an odd square of largely Mussolini-era buildings, dominated by the massive **Mausoleum of Augustus**, burial place of the emperor and his family and now under long-term restoration.

On the far side of the square, the **Ara Pacis** or "Altar of Augustan Peace" is now enclosed in a controversial purpose-built structure designed by the New York-based architect Richard Meier, its angular lines and sheer white surfaces dominating the Tiber

1

side of the square. The altar is a more substantially recognizable Roman remain than the mausoleum, a marble block enclosed by sculpted walls built in 13 BC, probably to celebrate Augustus's victory over Spain and Gaul and the peace it heralded. It's a superb example of Roman sculpture, with a frieze on one side showing the imperial family at the height of its power: Augustus, his great general Marcus Agrippa and Augustus's wife Livia, followed by a victory procession containing her son – and Augustus's eventual successor – Tiberius and niece Antonia, the latter caught simply and realistically turning to her husband, Drusus. On the opposite side the veiled figure is believed to be Julia, Augustus's daughter.

The Trevi Fountain and around

Across Via del Tritone from the area around Piazza di Spagna and the heart of the Tridente area, the web of streets around the famous **Trevi Fountain** is well worth exploring, and provides a relatively quiet route down to Piazza Venezia, avoiding what is perhaps Via del Corso's least interesting and most traffic-congested stretch.

The Trevi Fountain

The **Trevi Fountain**, or Fontana di Trevi, is one of Rome's more surprising sights, and easy to stumble on by accident – a huge, very Baroque gush of water over statues and rocks built onto the backside of a Renaissance palace and fed by the same source that surfaces at the Barcaccia fountain in Piazza di Spagna. There was a previous Trevi fountain, designed by Alberti, around the corner in Via dei Crociferi, a smaller, more modest affair by all accounts, but Urban VIII decided to upgrade it in line with his other grandiose schemes of the time and employed Bernini, among others, to design an alternative. Work didn't begin, however, until 1732, when Niccolò Salvi won a competition held by Clement XII to design the fountain, and even then it took thirty years to finish the project. Salvi died in the process, his lungs destroyed by the time spent in the dank waterworks of his construction. The fountain is now a popular hangout and, of course, the place you come to chuck in a coin if you want to guarantee your return to Rome. You might also remember Anita Ekberg frolicking in the fountain in *La Dolce Vita*, though any attempt at re-creating the scene would be met with an immediate reaction by the police here.

In 2015 the fountain underwent a €2.2 million **restoration** – the most comprehensive in its history – funded by the Italian fashion house Fendi.

Galleria Colonna

Via della Pilotta 17 • Sat 9am–1.15pm; guided tours in English at noon; terrace café March–Oct Sat same hours; gardens not open to the public • €12, including guided tour • ⓣ 06 678 4350, ⓦ galleriacolonna.it

A short stroll south from the Trevi Fountain brings you to the **Galleria Colonna**, part of the Palazzo Colonna complex and home to one of the city's best collections of fine art still in private hands. The building itself is worth visiting for the massive chandelier-decked Great Hall, but the paintings, too, are worthy of attention, not least the two lascivious depictions of *Venus* and *Cupid* (one by Bronzino, the other Ghirlandaio) that eye each other across the room – once considered so risqué that clothes were painted on them and have only recently been removed. Through the Great Hall is the gallery's collection of landscapes by Dughet (Poussin's brother-in-law), and beyond that a small group of other high-quality works: Carracci's early and unusually spontaneous *Bean Eater*, Tintoretto's *Portrait of an Old Man* and a *Portrait of a Gentleman* caught in supremely confident pose by Veronese.

The Time Elevator

Via dei SS. Apostoli 20 • Daily 10.30am–7.30pm; shows every hour, lasting 45min • Adults €12, 5–12s €9; not suitable for children under 5 • ⓣ 06 6992 1823, ⓦ time-elevator.it

Not far from the Galleria Colonna, the **Time Elevator** is a multimedia film show of the history of Rome from its founding to the present day, with visitors strapped into a chair that moves around a bit like a flight simulator – a half-hour or so the kids might enjoy.

The Quirinale and around

Of the hills that rise up on the eastern side of the centre of Rome, the **Quirinale** is perhaps the most appealing, home to some of the city's finest palaces, but also to some of Rome's greatest art collections, not least in the **Palazzo Barberini**.

Piazza Barberini

Piazza Barberini, a frenetic traffic junction at the top end of the busy shopping street of Via del Tritone, was named after Bernini's **Fontana del Tritone**, which gushes a high jet of water in the centre of the square. Traditionally, this was the Barberini family's quarter of the city; they were the greatest patrons of Gian Lorenzo Bernini, and the sculptor's works in their honour are thick on the ground around here. He finished the Tritone fountain in 1644, going on shortly after to design the **Fontana delle Api** (Fountain of the Bees) at the bottom end of Via Veneto. Unlike the Tritone fountain you could walk right past this; it's a smaller, quirkier work, with a broad scallop shell studded with the bees that were the symbol of the Barberini.

Palazzo Barberini: Galleria Nazionale d'Arte Antica

Via delle Quattro Fontane 13 • Gallery Tues–Sun 8.30am–7pm; last entry 1hr before closing • €12 combined ticket with Palazzo Corsini (see page 84), valid three days; free first Sun of the month • T 06 482 4184, W barberinicorsini.org • Tours of the eighteenth-century apartments Tues–Fri 8.30am–4pm • Free; advance booking advisable through E gan-aar.settecento@beniculturali.it

On the southern side of Piazza Barberini, **Palazzo Barberini** houses the **Galleria Nazionale d'Arte Antica**, a rich patchwork of art, mainly Italian and focused on the early Renaissance to late Baroque period. Perhaps the most impressive feature of the gallery is the building itself, worked on at different times by the most favoured architects of the day – Bernini, Borromini, Maderno – and the epitome of Baroque grandeur. In an impressive show of balanced commissioning, there are two main staircases, one by Bernini and a second by his rival Borromini, and the two couldn't be more different – the former an ordered rectangle of ascending grandeur, the latter a more playful and more organic spiral staircase. But the palace's first-floor **Salone di Cortona** is its artistic high spot, with a ceiling frescoed by Pietro da Cortona that is one of the best examples of exuberant Baroque trompe l'oeil you'll ever see, a manic rendering of *The Triumph of Divine Providence* that almost crawls down the walls to meet you. Note the bees – the Barberini family symbol – flying towards the figure of Providence.

Ground floor

The collection is divided into three sections, the first of which, on the **ground floor**, has the oldest works, from the **medieval** to the early **Renaissance**. Among the numerous Madonnas, highlights include the *Madonna Advocata* in Room 1, the gallery's oldest work, a panel painting dating to c.1075, and Fra' Filippo Lippi's warmly maternal *Tarquinia Madonna* in Room 3, painted in 1437 and introducing background details, notably architecture, into Italian religious painting for the first time.

First floor

The second section, on the **first floor**, is the core of the collection, with works taking you through the **Renaissance** and **Baroque** eras, and including Raphael's beguiling *Fornarina*, a painting of a Trasteveran baker's daughter thought to have been the artist's mistress (Raphael's name appears clearly on the woman's bracelet), although some experts claim the painting to be the work of a pupil. Later rooms have works by Tintoretto and Titian, and an impressive array of **portraiture**: Bronzino's rendering

of the marvellously erect *Stefano Colonna*, a portrait of *Henry VIII* by Hans Holbein and another of *Erasmus of Rotterdam* by Quentin Metsys. Next door are two unusually small paintings by El Greco, *The Baptism of Christ* and *Adoration of the Shepherds*, and then, further on, a couple of rooms of work by Caravaggio – notably *Judith and Holofernes* – and his followers, for example the seventeenth-century Neapolitan Ribera, and the Dutch Terbrugghen and Jan van Bronckhorst.

Top floor

The galleries on the **top floor** finish off the collection by taking you from the **late Baroque era**, starting with works by more Neapolitan Baroque painters and their acolytes, most significantly Luca Giordano and the Calabrian Matia Preti, whose dark, dramatic canvases again owe a huge debt to Caravaggio. Next door, Bernini's portrait of *Urban VIII* has been rightfully reinstated in the pope's own palace, while the final rooms cover the late seventeenth and eighteenth centuries, with a number of cityscapes of Rome by Gaspar van Wittel and classic Venetian scenes by Guardi and Canaletto.

Via Veneto

Via Veneto bends north from Piazza Barberini up to the southern edge of the Borghese gardens, its pricey bars and restaurants lining a street that was once the haunt of Rome's beautiful people, made famous by Fellini's *La Dolce Vita*. Those days are long gone, however, and Via Veneto isn't really any different from other busy streets in central Rome – a pretty, tree-lined road, but with a fair share of expensive tack trying to cash in on departed glory.

Santa Maria della Concezione and the Convento dei Cappuccini

Via Veneto 27 • **Church** Daily 7am–noon & 3–7pm • T 06 487 1185 • **Convento dei Cappuccini** Daily 9am–7pm • €8.50, including museum • T 06 8880 3695, W cappucciniviaveneto.it

A little way up Via Veneto on the right, the Capuchin church of **Santa Maria della Concezione** was a sponsored creation of the Barberini, though it's not a particularly significant building in itself and most people come to see its **Capuchin cemetery**, Convento dei Cappuccini, one of Rome's more macabre and bizarre sights. Here, the bones of four thousand monks are set into the walls of a series of chapels, a monument to "Our Sister of Bodily Death" in the words of St Francis, which was erected in 1793. The bones appear in abstract or Christian patterns or as fully clothed skeletons, their faces peering out of their cowls in various twisted expressions of agony. An attached **museum** fills you in on the background.

San Carlino alle Quattro Fontane

Via del Quirinale 23 • Mon–Sat 10am–1pm • T 06 488 3261

Heading southeast of Palazzo Barberini, along Via delle Quattro Fontane, brings you to the seventeenth-century church of **San Carlo alle Quattro Fontane**. This was Borromini's first real design commission, and in it he displays all the ingenuity he later became famous for, cramming the church elegantly into a tiny and awkwardly shaped site. Outside the church are the four **fountains** that give the street and church their name, each cut into a niche in a corner of the crossroads that marks this, the highest point on the Quirinal Hill.

Sant'Andrea al Quirinale

Via del Quirinale 29 • Tues–Sun 9am–noon & 3–6pm • Rooms of St Stanislaus €2 • T 06 487 4565, W santandrea@gesuiti.it

The domed church of **Sant'Andrea al Quirinale**, on Via del Quirinale, is a great piece of design ingenuity: Bernini planned it as a kind of flat oval shape to fit into its wide but shallow site, and it's unusual and ingenious inside. Upstairs, the rooms where the Polish saint St Stanislaus Kostka lived (and died) in 1568 focus on a disturbingly lifelike painted statue of Stanislaus lying on his deathbed.

Palazzo del Quirinale

Piazza del Quirinale • Visit by obligatory guided tour Tues, Wed, Fri, Sat & Sun 9.30am–4pm; book at least 5 days in advance • 1hr 20min tour €1.50, 2hr 30min tour €10 • ☎ 06 3996 7557, Ⓦ palazzo.quirinale.it

Opposite Sant'Andrea is the featureless wall of the **Palazzo del Quirinale**, a sixteenth-century structure that was the official summer residence of the popes until Unification, when it became the royal palace. It's now the home of Italy's president, and it's worth braving the security for a glimpse of the style in which popes, despots, kings and now presidents like to live, with a fine set of state rooms and works of art. Two **tours** visit the palace's interior. The first (1hr 20min) starts with a fragment of Melozzo da Forlì's fifteenth-century fresco of Christ, painted for the apse of Santi Apostoli, and takes in the sumptuous rooms of the piano nobile, including the Hall of Mirrors and Hall of Tapestries; the second (2hr 20min) goes on to see the palace's porcelain collection, a museum of carriages and the gardens. You can appreciate the *palazzo*'s exceptional siting from the **Piazza del Quirinale**, from which views stretch right across the centre of Rome.

Scuderie del Quirinale

Via XXIV Maggio 16 • Exhibitions around €15 • ☎ 06 3996 7500, Ⓦ scuderiequirinale.it

The eighteenth-century papal stables, or **Scuderie del Quirinale**, face the Palazzo del Quirinale from across the square. Imaginatively restored as display space for major exhibitions, they feature an impressive equestrian spiral staircase winding up to the exhibition rooms. The modern glass staircase on the side of the building offers the best view over Rome from the Quirinale by far.

Santa Maria della Vittoria

Via XX Settembre 17 • Daily 8.30am–noon & 3.30–6pm • ☎ 06 4274 0571

The church of **Santa Maria della Vittoria** was built by the Baroque-era architect Carlo Maderno and its interior is one of the most elaborate examples of Baroque decoration in Rome: its ceiling and walls are pitted with carving, and statues are crammed into remote corners as in an overstuffed attic. The church's best-known feature, Bernini's carving *The Ecstasy of St Theresa*, the centrepiece of the sepulchral chapel of Cardinal Cornaro, is a deliberately melodramatic work featuring a theatrically posed St Theresa, who lays back in groaning submission beneath a mass of dishevelled garments in front of the murmuring cardinals.

Monti, Termini and the Esquiline

Immediately north of the Colosseum, the **Esquiline Hill** is the highest and largest of the city's seven hills. Formerly one of the most fashionable residential quarters of ancient Rome, it's nowadays a mixed area that together with the adjacent Viminale Hill make up the district known as **Monti**, an appealing and up-and-coming quarter of cobbled streets and neighbourhood bars and restaurants. It's also an area that most travellers to Rome encounter at some point – not just because of key sights like the basilica of **Santa Maria Maggiore**, but also because of its proximity to **Termini** station, whose environs shelter many of Rome's budget hotels.

Domus Aurea

Viale della Domus Aurea 1 • Sat & Sun 8.30am–6.15pm; entry by guided tour only, limited to groups of 25 people; check the website for changing opening hours • €16 • Book in advance on ☎ 06 3996 7700 or Ⓦ coopculture.it

Currently undergoing a decade-long, €39-million restoration, the city's most intriguing and magnificent ancient building, the **Domus Aurea**, or "Golden House", partially reopened to the public in late 2014. Once covering a vast area between the Palatine and Esquiline, it was built by the Emperor Nero to glorify himself in typical excessive fashion. Rome was accustomed to Nero's excesses, but it had never seen anything like the Golden House before; the facade was supposed to have been coated in solid gold,

there was hot and cold running water in the baths, and the grounds held vineyards, game and a lake where mock nautical battles were staged. Nero didn't get to enjoy it for long: he died a couple of years after it was finished, and later emperors were determined to erase it from Rome's cityscape. Vespasian built the Colosseum over the lake and Trajan built his baths on top of the rest of the complex. It was pretty much forgotten until its **wall paintings** were discovered by Renaissance artists, including Raphael and Pinturicchio, who descended ladders into what they first believed was some kind of mystical cave.

Engaging **tours** take you through a series of chilly rooms (dress warmly, even in summer), beautifully decorated with garlands of flowers, fruit, vines and foliage. Virtual reality glasses are provided, with which you can view the site as it would have been. The tours also deal with the problems faced by the restorers: the roots of the trees in the Colle Oppio park above have embedded themselves in the roof, and the long-term plan is to remove the existing park and create a landscaped garden on a thinner layer of soil, to ease the pressure on the palace below.

Monti

Between Via Cavour and Via Nazionale, and up as far as the church of Santa Maria Maggiore, is the small area that has come to be known as **Monti**. Once the ancient city's slum district, it's now an atmospheric, vibrant quarter focusing on lively **Piazza Madonna dei Monti**; **Via dei Serpenti** and **Via del Boschetto** lead north from the square, both crammed with appealing bars and restaurants.

San Pietro in Vincoli

Piazza di San Pietro in Vincoli 4/A • Daily 8am–12.30pm & 3–7pm; closes 6pm Oct–March • ⓣ 06 9784 4952

San Pietro in Vincoli is one of Rome's most delightfully plain churches. It was built to house an important relic, the **chains** (*vincoli*) that bound St Peter when imprisoned in Jerusalem and those that held him in the Mamertine Prison, which supposedly miraculously fused together when they were brought into contact with each other. The chains can still be seen beneath the high altar, but most people come to see the **tomb of Pope Julius II** at the far end of the southern aisle, which occupied Michelangelo on and off for much of his career. The artist eventually gave it up to paint the Sistine Chapel – the only statues that he managed to complete are the *Moses*, *Leah* and *Rachel*, which remain here, and two *Dying Slaves* (now in the Louvre). The figures are among the artist's most captivating works, especially *Moses*: because of a medieval mistranslation of scripture, he is depicted with satyrs' horns instead of the "radiance of the Lord" that Exodus tells us shone around his head. Nonetheless this powerful statue is so lifelike that Michelangelo is alleged to have struck its knee with his hammer and shouted "Speak, damn you!"

Santa Maria Maggiore

Piazza di Santa Maria Maggiore • **Basilica** Daily 7am–6.45pm • Free • ⓣ 06 6988 6800, ⓦ www.vatican.va/various/basiliche/sm_maggiore/index_en.html • **Museum** Daily 9.30am–6.30pm • €3 • **Loggia and apostolic palace** Daily 9.30am–6.30pm • €5, including tour • **Domus Romana** Tours Sat & Sun; book in advance • €5, including tour

Via Cavour opens out at Piazza Esquilino to reveal **Santa Maria Maggiore**, one of the city's greatest basilicas, and with one of Rome's best-preserved Byzantine interiors – a fact belied by its dull eighteenth-century exterior. The present structure dates from about 420 AD, and was completed during the reign of Sixtus III; it survives remarkably intact, the broad nave fringed on both sides with strikingly well kept mosaics. The chapel in the right transept holds the elaborate tomb of Sixtus V, decorated with frescoes and stucco reliefs portraying events from his reign. Outside this is the tomb of the Bernini family, including Gian Lorenzo himself, while opposite, the Pauline Chapel is home to the tombs of the Borghese pope Paul V and his immediate predecessor Clement VIII. The high altar contains the relics of St Matthew, among other Christian

martyrs, but it's the mosaics of the arch that really dazzle, a vivid representation of scenes from the life of Christ.

Tours take in the **loggia** above the main entrance, whose thirteenth-century mosaics of the "legend of the snow" are worth seeing, and the **apostolic palace**, which holds the portraits of popes associated with the basilica and a splendid spiral staircase by Bernini. Underneath the basilica there's a **museum** which sports what even by Roman standards is a wide variety of relics.

Santa Prassede

Via di Santa Prassede 9/A • Mon–Sat 7am–noon & 3–6.30pm, Sun 7.30am–12.30pm & 4–6.30pm • €1 to light the mosaics • Ⓣ 06 488 2456

Across the road from Santa Maria Maggiore, the ninth-century church of **Santa Prassede** occupies an ancient site, where it's claimed St Prassede harboured Christians on the run from the Roman persecutions. She apparently collected the blood and remains of the martyrs and placed them in a well where she herself was later buried; a red marble disc in the floor of the nave marks the spot. In the southern aisle, the Chapel of St Zeno was built by Pope Paschal I as a mausoleum for his mother, Theodora, and is decorated with marvellous ninth-century mosaics which make it glitter like a jewel-encrusted bowl. The chapel also contains a fragment of a column supposed to be the one to which Christ was tied when he was scourged.

Palazzo delle Esposizioni

Via Nazionale 194 • Tues–Fri & Sun noon–8pm, Sat noon–11pm • Usually €10–12.50 • Ⓣ 06 3996 7500, Ⓦ palazzoesposizioni.it

About halfway along workaday Via Nazionale, the imposing **Palazzo delle Esposizioni** was designed in 1883 by Pio Piacentini (father of the more famous Marcello, favourite architect of Mussolini) and now hosts regular large-scale exhibitions and cultural events. It also houses a cinema, an excellent art and design bookshop and a café in its basement, plus the fancy *Open Colonna* restaurant up above.

Piazza della Repubblica

At the top of Via Nazionale, **Piazza della Repubblica** is typical of Rome's nineteenth-century regeneration, a stern and dignified semicircle of buildings that was until recently rather dilapidated but is now – with the help of the very stylish *Palazzo Naiadi* hotel and a branch of gourmet food emporium Eataly – resurgent, centring on a fountain surrounded by languishing nymphs and sea monsters.

Santa Maria degli Angeli

Piazza della Repubblica • Mon–Sat 7.30am–6.30pm, Sun 7.30am–7.30pm • Ⓣ 06 488 0812

Piazza della Repubblica actually follows the outlines of the Baths of Diocletian, the remains of which lie across the piazza and are partially contained in the church of **Santa Maria degli Angeli**. It's a huge, open building, with an interior standardized by Vanvitelli into a rich eighteenth-century confection. The pink granite pillars, at 3m in diameter the largest in Rome, are original, and the main transept formed the main hall of the baths. The meridian that strikes diagonally across the floor here was until 1846 the regulator of time for Romans (today a cannon shot is fired daily at noon from the Janiculum Hill).

Terme di Diocleziano

Via Enrico di Nicola 79 • Tues–Sun 9am–7.30pm; last entry 1hr before closing • €10, or €12 combined ticket with Palazzo Altemps (see page 57), Crypta Balbi and Palazzo Massimo, valid for three days; free first Sun of the month • Ⓣ 06 3996 7700, Ⓦ archeoroma.beniculturali.it

Behind Santa Maria degli Angeli, the huge halls and courtyards of the **Museo delle Terme di Diocleziano**, or **Diocletian's baths**, have been renovated; they and an attached Carthusian monastery now hold what is probably the least interesting part of the **Museo Nazionale Romano** (see page 56). The museum's most evocative part is

1 the large cloister of the church whose sides are crammed with statuary, funerary monuments and sarcophagi and fragments from all over Rome. The galleries that wrap around the cloister hold a reasonable if rather academically presented collection of pre-Roman and Roman finds.

Palazzo Massimo

Largo di Villa Peretti • Tues–Sun 9am–7.45pm • €10, or €12 combined ticket with Palazzo Altemps (see page 57), Crypta Balbi and Terme di Diocleziano (see above), valid for three days; free first Sun of the month • ☎ 06 3996 7700, Ⓦ archeoroma.beniculturali.it

Across from Santa Maria degli Angeli, the **Palazzo Massimo** is a superb collection of Greek and Roman **antiquities**, second only to the Vatican's. Start in the **basement**, where there are displays of exquisite gold jewellery from the second century AD, and the mummified remains of an 8-year-old girl, along with a fantastic coin collection. The **ground floor** is devoted to statuary of the early empire, including a gallery with an unparalleled selection of unidentified busts found all over Rome – amazing pieces of portraiture, and as vivid a representation of patrician Roman life as you'll find. At the far end of the courtyard are more busts, this time identifiable as members of the imperial family: a bronze of Germanicus, a marvellous small bust of Caligula, several representations of Livia, Tiberius, Antonia and Drusus and a life-size statue of Augustus, piously dressed as the high priest of Rome with his toga covering his head.

The first and second floors

The **first floor** has sculpted portraits of the various imperial dynasties in roughly chronological order, starting with the Flavian emperors – the craggy determination of Vespasian, the pinched nobility of Nerva – and leading on to Trajan, who appears with his wife Plotina as Hercules, opposite a bust of his cousin Hadrian. The collection continues with the Antonine emperors – Antoninus Pius in a heroic nude pose and in several busts, flanked by likenesses of his daughter Faustina Minor. Faustina was the wife of Antoninus's successor, Marcus Aurelius, whose bust is in the corridor outside. Further on are the Severans, with the fierce-looking Caracalla looking across past his father Septimius Severus to his brother Geta, whom he later murdered.

The **second floor** takes in some of the finest Roman frescoes and mosaics ever found, among them a stunning set of frescoes from the **Villa di Livia**, depicting an orchard dense with fruit and flowers and patrolled by partridges and doves; wall paintings rescued from what was perhaps the riverside villa of Augustus's daughter Julia and Marcus Agrippa; and mosaics showing four chariot drivers and their horses, so finely crafted that from a distance they look as if they've been painted.

Termini station

The low white facade of **Termini station** (so named for its proximity to the Baths or "Terme" of Diocletian), and the vast, bus-crammed hubbub that is Piazza dei Cinquecento in front, is many people's first experience of Rome. The station is an ambitious piece of modern architectural design that was completed in 1950 and still entirely dominates the streets around with its low-slung, futuristic lines.

San Lorenzo fuori le Mura

Piazzale del Verano 3 • Daily 7.30am–12.30pm & 4–8pm (winter 3.30–7pm) • ☎ 06 446 6184

A short walk east of Termini, the studenty neighbourhood of San Lorenzo takes its name from the basilica of **San Lorenzo fuori le Mura** – one of the great pilgrimage churches of Rome, fronted by a columned portico and with a lovely twelfth-century cloister to its side. The original church here was built over the site of St Lawrence's martyrdom by Constantine. It is actually a combination of three churches built at different periods – one a sixth-century reconstruction of Constantine's church, which now forms the chancel, another a fifth-century church from the time of Sixtus III, both joined by a basilica from the thirteenth century.

The Celian Hill and San Giovanni

Some of the animals that were to die in the Colosseum were kept in a zoo up on the **Celian Hill**, just behind the arena, the furthest south of Rome's seven hills and probably still its most peaceful, with the park of **Villa Celimontana** at its heart. Just east, **San Giovanni** is named after the basilica complex at its centre, which was, before the creation of the separate Vatican city state, the headquarters of the Catholic Church.

Santi Giovanni e Paolo and Case Romane

Church Piazza dei Santi Giovanni e Paolo 13 • Daily 8.30am–noon & 3.30–6pm • T 06 700 5745 • **Case Romane** Clivo di Scauro • Mon & Thurs–Sun 10am–1pm & 3–6pm; entry every 30min • €8 • T 06 7045 4544, W caseromane.it

At the summit of the Celian Hill, the church of **Santi Giovanni e Paolo**, marked by its colourful campanile, is dedicated to two government officials who were beheaded here in 316 AD after refusing military service; a railed-off tablet in mid-nave marks the shrine where the saints were martyred and buried. Around the corner are the remains of what is believed to their house, the **Case Romane**. The ten rooms are patchily frescoed with pagan and Christian subjects, including the Stanza dei Genii, with winged youths and cupids, and the courtyard or nymphaeum, which has a marvellous fresco of a goddess being attended on.

San Gregorio Magno

Piazza di San Gregorio 1 • Daily 9am–1pm & 3.30–7.30pm; ring the bell marked "portineria" to gain admission • T 06 700 8227

The road descends from the Case Romane to the church of **San Gregorio Magno**, founded by St Gregory, who was a monk here before becoming pope in 590 AD. Gregory was an important pope, stabilizing the city after the fall of the empire and effectively establishing the powerful papal role that would endure for the best part of the following 1500 years. Today's rather ordinary interior doesn't really do justice to the historical importance of the church, but the lovely Cosmati floor remains intact, and the chapel at the end of the south aisle has a beautifully carved bath showing scenes from St Gregory's life along with his marble throne, a beaten-up specimen that actually predates the saint by five hundred years.

San Clemente

Via Labicana 95 • Mon–Sat 9am–12.30pm & 3–6pm, Sun noon–6pm; last entrance to lower church 30min before closing • Church free; lower church €10 • T 06 774 0021, W basilicasanclemente.com

Down below the Celian Hill, five minutes' walk from the Colosseum, the church of **San Clemente** is one of the most visited sights of Rome, a cream-coloured twelfth-century basilica that's a conglomeration of three places of worship, encapsulating perhaps better than any other the continuity of history in the city. The ground-floor church is a superb example of a medieval basilica: its facade and courtyard face east in the archaic fashion, there are some fine, warm mosaics in the apse and – perhaps the highlight of the main church – a chapel with frescoes by Masolino, showing scenes from the life of St Catherine. Downstairs there's the nave of an earlier church, dating to 392 AD, and on a third level a dank Mithraic temple of the late second century where you can see a statue of Mithras slaying the bull and the seats on which the worshippers sat during their ceremonies.

San Giovanni in Laterano

Piazza di San Giovanni in Laterano 4 • **Basilica** Daily 7am–6.30pm • Free • **Cloisters** Daily 9am–6pm • €2 • **Baptistry** Daily 9am–12.30pm & 4–7pm • Free • T 06 6988 6433

At the far end of Via San Giovanni in Laterano, a ten-minute walk from the Colosseum, the basilica of **San Giovanni in Laterano** is officially Rome's cathedral, the seat of the pope as bishop of Rome, and was for centuries the main papal residence. There has been a church on this site since the fourth century, the first of which was established by Constantine, and the present building, reworked by Borromini in the

mid-seventeenth century, evokes Rome's staggering wealth of history with a host of features from different periods. The **doors** to the church were taken from the Curia of the Roman Forum, while much of the **interior** dates from 1600, when Clement VIII had the church remodelled for that Holy Year. The first pillar on the left of the right-hand aisle shows a fragment of Giotto's fresco of Boniface VIII, proclaiming the first Holy Year in 1300. Further on, a more recent monument commemorates Sylvester I – "the magician pope", bishop of Rome during much of Constantine's reign – and incorporates part of his original tomb, said to sweat and rattle its bones when a pope is about to die. Outside, the **cloisters** are one of the most pleasing parts of the complex, decorated with early thirteenth-century Cosmati work and with fragments of the original basilica arranged around in no particular order. Rooms off to the side form a small **museum**, displaying various papal artefacts.

Next to the basilica, the **baptistry** is the oldest surviving example in the Christian world, a mosaic-lined, octagonal structure built during the fifth century that has been the model for many such buildings since.

Scala Santa and Sancta Sanctorum

Piazza di San Giovanni in Laterano 14 • **Scala Santa** Mon–Sat 6.30am–7pm, Sun 7am–7pm; Oct–March closes 30min earlier • Free • **Sancta Sanctorum** Mon–Sat 9.30am–12.40pm & 3–5.10pm; entrance is by guided tour only, booked at the entrance to the Scala Santa • €3.50 • 329 751 1111, scala-santa.com

Across Piazza di Porta San Giovanni from the San Giovanni basilica is a building housing the **Scala Santa**, said to be the staircase from Pontius Pilate's house down which Christ walked after his trial. The 28 steps are protected by boards, and the only way you're allowed to climb them is on your knees, which pilgrims do regularly – although there is also a staircase to the side for the less penitent. At the top, the **Sancta Sanctorum** or chapel of San Lorenzo holds an ancient (sixth- or seventh-century) painting of Christ said to be the work of an angel, hence its name – *acheiropoeton*, or "not done by human hands".

Museo Storico della Liberazione

Via Tasso 145 • Tues–Sun 9.30am–12.30pm, Tues, Thurs & Fri also 3.30–7.30pm • Free • 06 700 3866, museoliberazione.it

Five minutes' walk from the San Giovanni basilica, the **Museo Storico della Liberazione** is a very different sort of attraction, occupying two floors of the building in which Nazi prisoners were held and interrogated during the wartime Occupation. It's a moving place and deliberately low key, with the original cells left as they were, including two isolation cells marked with the desperate notes and messages from the people held here. Other rooms display artefacts pertaining to the years of occupation, including one dedicated to the 335 victims of the Fosse Ardeatine massacre, a mass execution carried out by the Germans in 1944.

The Aventine Hill and south

The leafy **Aventine Hill** is the southernmost of the city's seven hills and the heart of plebeian Rome in ancient times. These days the working-class quarters of the city are further south, in earthy **Testaccio** and up-and-coming **Ostiense**, and the Aventine is in fact one of the city's more upmarket residential areas, dotted with villas and gardens, and one of the few places in the city where you can escape the traffic. Further south lie the magnificent basilica of **San Paolo fuori le Mura** and the **Via Appia Antica** with its atmospheric catacombs.

Santa Sabina

Piazza Pietro d'Illiria 1 • Daily 8.15am–12.30pm & 3.30–6pm • 06 579 401

A short way up Via Santa Sabina, the church of **Santa Sabina** is a strong contender for Rome's most beautiful basilica: high and wide, its nave and portico were restored

back to their fifth-century appearance in the 1930s. Look especially at the main doors, which boast eighteen panels carved with Christian scenes, forming a complete illustrated Bible that includes one of the oldest representations of the Crucifixion in existence. The **views** from the orange-tree-filled gardens outside are splendid – right across the Tiber to the centre of Rome and St Peter's.

The Baths of Caracalla

Viale delle Terme di Caracalla 52 • Daily 9am–1hr before sunset; last entry 1hr before closing; tours Sun 3pm (Italian only) • €8; free first Sun of the month; tours free • T 06 3996 7700, W coopculture.it

Southeast of the Aventine, the **Baths of Caracalla** give a far better sense of the scale and monumentality of Roman architecture than most of the extant ruins in the city. The baths are no more than a shell now, but the walls still rise to very nearly their original height. There are many fragments of mosaics – none spectacular, but quite a few bright and well preserved – and it's easy to discern a floor plan. Virtual reality goggles, available from the ticket office (€7), do a good job of bringing the ruins to life. As for Caracalla, he was one of Rome's worst rulers, and it's no wonder there's nothing else in the city built by him. The baths are used as the venue for the **Teatro dell'Opera**'s summer season – one of Mussolini's better ideas – and attending an opera performance here allows you to see the baths at their most atmospheric.

Testaccio

On the far side of the Aventine Hill, across Via Marmorata, the solid working-class neighbourhood of **Testaccio** is a tight-knit community with a market and a number of bars and small trattorias that was for many years synonymous with the slaughterhouse that sprawls down to the Tiber just beyond. In recent years the area has become trendy, property prices have soared, and some unlikely juxtapositions have emerged, with vegetarian restaurants opening their doors in an area still known for the offal dishes served in its traditional trattorias, and gay and alternative clubs standing cheek-by-jowl with the car-repair shops gouged into Monte Testaccio. Testaccio's historic **market** (Mon–Sat 7am–3.30pm) occupies an airy space between Via Galvani and Via Alessandro Volta, and is a great place to pick up a picnic lunch.

The slaughterhouse, or **Mattatoio**, once the area's main employer, is now used for concerts and innovative exhibitions of contemporary art (Tues–Sun 2–8pm; tickets around €6; W mattatoioroma.it). Opposite, **Monte Testaccio** gives the area its name, a 35m-high mound created out of the shards of Roman amphorae that were dumped here. It's an odd sight, the ceramic curls visible through the tufts of grass that crown its higher reaches, with bars and restaurants hollowed out of the slopes below.

The Protestant Cemetery

Via Caio Cestio 6 • Mon–Sat 9am–5pm, Sun 9am–1pm • Donation of at least €3 expected • T 06 574 1900, W cemeteryrome.it

Via Zabaglia leads from Monte Testaccio to Via Caio Cestio, a left turn up which takes you to the entrance of the **Protestant Cemetery**, one of the shrines to the English in Rome and a fitting conclusion to a visit to the Keats-Shelley House (see page 70), since it is here that both poets are buried, along with a handful of other well-known names. In fact, the cemetery's title is a misnomer – the cemetery is reserved for non-Roman Catholics so you'll also find famous Italian atheists, Christians of the Orthodox persuasion and the odd Jew or Muslim buried here.

Most visitors come here to see the **grave of Keats**, who lies next to the painter Joseph Severn in the furthest corner of the less crowded, older part of the cemetery, his stone inscribed as he wished with the words "Here lies one whose name was writ in water." Severn died much later than Keats but asked to be laid here nonetheless, together with his brushes and palette. Shelley's ashes were brought here at Mary Shelley's request and interred in the newer part of the cemetery.

1

The pyramid of Caius Cestius

Piazzale Ostiense • **Pyramid** 1st Sat & Sun of the month at 10.30am, after a visit to the Museo della Via Ostiense opposite; free; or guided tours in Italian on 2nd, 3rd & 4th Sat & Sun at 11am; €5.50; book in advance for either option • T 06 574 3193 • **Cat shelter** Daily 2–4pm • W igattidellapiramide.it

The most distinctive landmark in this part of town is the mossy pyramidal tomb of one **Caius Cestius**, who died in 12 BC. Cestius had spent some time in Egypt, and part of his will decreed that all his slaves should be freed – the white pyramid you see today was thrown up by them in only 330 days of what must have been joyful building. You can visit the **cats** that live here, and the volunteers who care for them, in the afternoon.

Centrale Montemartini

Via Ostiense 106 • Tues–Sun 9am–7pm • €7.50, or €12.50 combined ticket with Capitoline Museums (see page 63), valid 7 days • T 06 0608 • W centralemontemartini.org

It's a ten-minute walk south down Via Ostiense from the pyramid of Caius Cestius to the **Centrale Montemartini**, a former electricity generating plant. Originally requisitioned to display the cream of the Capitoline Museums' sculpture while the main buildings were being renovated, it was so popular that it became the Capitoline's permanent outpost. The huge rooms of the power station are ideally suited to showing ancient sculpture, although the massive turbines and furnaces have a fascination of their own. Among many compelling objects are the head, feet and an arm from a colossal statue, once 8m high, found in Largo Argentina; a large Roman copy of *Athena*; a fragmented mosaic of hunting scenes; and an amazingly naturalistic statue of a girl seated on a stool with her legs crossed, from the third century BC.

San Paolo fuori le Mura

Via Ostiense 186 • **Basilica** Daily 7am–7pm • Free • **Cloister, chapel & archeological area** Daily 9am–6pm • €4 • T 06 4543 4185, W abbaziasanpaolo.net • Metro B to San Paolo

Some 2km south of the Porta San Paolo, the basilica of **San Paolo fuori le Mura** is one of the four patriarchal basilicas of Rome, occupying the supposed site of St Paul's tomb, where he was laid to rest after being beheaded nearby. A devastating fire in 1823 means that the church you see now is largely a nineteenth-century reconstruction but it's a very successful rehash, and it's impossible not to be awed by the space of the building inside. Some parts of the building did survive the fire. In the south transept, the paschal candlestick is a remarkable piece of Romanesque carving, supported by half-human beasts and rising through entwined tendrils and strangely human limbs and bodies to scenes from Christ's life. The bronze aisle doors date from 1070 and were also rescued from the old basilica, as was the thirteenth-century tabernacle by Arnolfo di Cambio. The arch across the apse is original, too, embellished with mosaics donated by the Byzantine queen Galla Placidia in the sixth century.

The **cloister** holds probably Rome's finest piece of Cosmatesque work, its spiralling, mosaic-encrusted columns enclosing a peaceful rose garden. Just off here, the **Relics Chapel** houses a set of artefacts, including the remains of Pope Gregory VII, and, beyond, the **pinacoteca**, a gallery of ecclesiastical art. Also off the cloister, an **exhibition gallery** holds vessels from the treasury and fragments of statuary recently excavated in the early medieval monastic complex south of the basilica. The **excavations** themselves, accessed via the glass staircase by the shop, were opened to the public in 2018.

Via Appia Antica and the catacombs

The best way to get to Via Appia Antica is by bus – #118 stops at Via del Teatro di Marcello (to the right of the staircase up to the Campidoglio), the Colosseum, the Circus Maximus and Terme di Caracalla, or you can take #218 (Mon–Wed, Sat & Sun) from Piazza Porta San Giovanni or #660 from Colli Albani metro station (line A)

Starting at the Porta San Sebastiano, the **Via Appia Antica** (or Appian Way) is the most famous of Rome's consular roads that used to strike out in every direction from the ancient city. It was built by one Appio Claudio in 312 BC, and is the only Roman

landmark mentioned in the Bible. During classical times it was the most important of all the Roman trade routes, carrying supplies through Campania to the port of Brindisi It remains an important part of early Christian Rome, its verges lined with numerous pagan and Christian sites, including most famously the underground burial cemeteries or catacombs of the first Christians. The **information office** for the area is at Via Appia Antica 58 (T 06 513 5316, W parcoappiaantica.it); you can pick up a good map and rent bikes here.

Catacombs of San Callisto

Via Appia Antica 110–126 • Daily (except Wed) 9am–noon & 2–5pm; closed end Jan to end Feb; tours 45min • €8 • T 06 513 0151, W catacombe.roma.it

Around 1km from the Porta San Sebastiano, the **Catacombe di San Callisto** are the largest of Rome's catacombs, founded in the second century AD; many of the early popes (of whom St Callisto was one) are buried here. The site also features some well-preserved seventh- and eighth-century frescoes, and the crypt of Santa Cecilia, who was buried here after her martyrdom before being shifted to the church dedicated to her in Trastevere.

Catacombe di San Sebastiano

Via Appia Antica 136 • Mon–Sat 10am–4.30pm; closed Dec • €8 • T 06 785 0350, W catacombe.org

The **Catacombe di San Sebastiano**, 500m further on from San Callisto, are situated under a basilica that was originally built by Constantine on the spot where the bodies of the apostles Peter and Paul are said to have been laid for a time. Tours take in paintings of doves and fish, a contemporaneous, carved oil lamp and inscriptions dating the tombs themselves. The most striking features, however, are not Christian at all, but three pagan tombs (one painted, two stuccoed) discovered when archeologists were burrowing beneath the floor of the basilica upstairs.

Trastevere and the Janiculum Hill

Across the river from the centre of town, on the right bank of the Tiber, the district of **Trastevere** was the artisan area of the city in classical times, neatly placed for the trade that came upriver from Ostia to be unloaded nearby. Outside the city walls, Trastevere (the name means "across the Tiber") was for centuries heavily populated by immigrants, and this separation lent the neighbourhood a strong identity that lasted well into the twentieth century. Nowadays it's a long way from the working-class quarter it used to be, often thronged with tourists lured by the charm of its narrow streets and closeted squares. However, it is among the most pleasant places to stroll in Rome, particularly peaceful in the morning, lively come the evening, as dozens of trattorias set tables out along the cobbled streets, and still buzzing late at night when its **bars and clubs** provide a focus for one of Rome's most dynamic night-time scenes.

Santa Maria in Trastevere

Piazza Santa Maria in Trastevere • Daily 7.30am–9pm; Aug 8am–noon & 4–9pm • T 06 581 4802

The heart of Trastevere is **Piazza Santa Maria in Trastevere**, a large square that takes its name from the **church** in its northwest corner, whose facade mosaics were beautifully restored in 2018. The church is thought to have been the first Christian place of worship in Rome, built on a site where a fountain of oil is said to have sprung on the day of Christ's birth. Inside, the mosaics are among the city's most impressive: Byzantine-inspired works in the apse depict a solemn yet sensitive parade of saints thronged around Christ and Mary, while underneath a series of panels shows scenes from the life of the Virgin by the painter Pietro Cavallini. Beneath the high altar on the right, an inscription – "FONS OLEI" – marks the spot where the oil is supposed to have sprung up.

1

Galleria Nazionale di Arte Antica – Palazzo Corsini

Via della Lungara 10 • Daily except Tues 8.30am–7pm • €12 combined ticket with Palazzo Barberini (see page 73), valid for three days; free first Sun of the month • T 06 6880 2323, W barberinicorsini.org

Cutting north from Piazza Santa Maria in Trastevere, you come to **Palazzo Corsini**, an unexpected cultural attraction on this side of the river. It's a relatively small collection, and only takes up a few rooms of the giant palace, which was a fitting final home for Queen Christina of Sweden, who renounced Protestantism and with it the Swedish throne in 1655, bringing her library and fortune to Rome to the delight of the Chigi pope, Alexander VII. Among the highlights are works by Rubens, Van Dyck, Guido Reni and Caravaggio, and the curious **Corsini Throne**, thought to be a Roman copy of an Etruscan throne of the second or first century. Cut out of marble, its back is carved with warriors in armour and helmets, below which is a boar hunt with wild boars the size of horses pursued by hunters.

Villa Farnesina

Via della Lungara 230 • Mon–Sat 9am–2pm & second Sun of the month 9am–5pm; guided tours in English Sat at 10am • €6, guided tours €4, second Sun of the month (with obligatory guided tour) €15 • T 06 6802 7268, W villafarnesina.it

Across the road from the Palazzo Corsini is the **Villa Farnesina**, built during the early sixteenth century for the banker Agostino Chigi, and one of the earliest Renaissance villas, with opulent rooms decorated with frescoes by some of the masters of the period. Most people come to view the Raphael-designed painting **Cupid and Psyche** in the now glassed-in loggia, completed in 1517 by the artist's assistants. The painter and art historian Vasari claims Raphael didn't complete the work because his infatuation with his mistress – "La Fornarina", whose father's bakery was situated nearby – was making it difficult to concentrate. Nonetheless it's mightily impressive: a flowing, animated work bursting with muscular men and bare-bosomed women. Raphael did, however, apparently manage to finish the **Galatea** in the room next door, whose bucolic country scenes are interspersed with Galatea on her scallop-shell chariot and a giant head in one of the lunettes which was once said to have been painted by Michelangelo, but is now attributed to the architect of the building, Peruzzi. The ceiling illustrates Chigi's horoscope constellations, frescoed by the architect of the building, Peruzzi, who also decorated the upstairs Salone delle Prospettive, where trompe l'oeil balconies give views onto contemporary Rome – one of the earliest examples of the technique.

Santa Cecilia in Trastevere

Piazza di Santa Cecilia, off Piazza dei Mercanti • **Basilica & crypt** Daily 10am–1pm & 4–7pm • Basilica free, crypt €2.50 • **Singing gallery** Mon–Sat 10am–12.30pm • €2.50 • T 06 589 9289

One of Trastevere's most intriguing attractions is the church of **Santa Cecilia in Trastevere**, whose antiseptic eighteenth-century appearance belies its historical associations. A church was originally built here over the site of the second-century home of St Cecilia, whose husband Valerian was executed for refusing to worship Roman gods and who herself was subsequently persecuted for Christian beliefs. The story has it that Cecilia was locked in the caldarium of her own baths for several days but refused to die, singing her way through the ordeal (Cecilia is patron saint of

PORTA PORTESE FLEA MARKET

Trastevere at its most disreputable but also most characteristic can be witnessed on Sunday, when the **Porta Portese flea market** stretches down from the Porta Portese gate down Via Portuense to Trastevere train station in a congested medley of antiques, old motor spares, cheap clothing, household goods, bric-a-brac, antiques and assorted junk. It starts around 7am, and you should come early if you want to buy, or even move – most of the bargains, not to mention the stolen goods, have gone by 10am, by which time the crush of people can be intense. It's pretty much all over by lunchtime.

music). Her head was finally half hacked off with an axe, though it took several blows before she finally succumbed. Below the high altar, Stefano Maderno's limp statue of the saint shows her incorruptible body as it was found when exhumed in 1599, with three deep cuts in her neck. Downstairs, excavations of the baths and the rest of the Roman house are on view in the crypt, but more alluring by far is the **singing gallery** above the nave, where Pietro Cavallini's late thirteenth-century fresco of the *Last Judgement* – all that remains of the decoration that once covered the entire church – is a powerful, amazingly naturalistic piece of work for its time.

The Janiculum Hill

Bus #115 crosses the hill from Viale di Trastevere (near Porta Portese) to the Gianicolo terminal on the Vatican side

It's about a fifteen-minute walk up Via Garibaldi from the centre of Trastevere to the summit of the **Janiculum Hill** – not one of the original seven hills of Rome, but the one with the best and most accessible views of the centre. Follow Vicolo del Cedro from Via della Scala and take the steps up from the end, cross the main road, and continue on the steps that lead up the hill to the Passeggiata del Gianicolo and then to **Piazzale Garibaldi**. Spread out before you are some of the best **views** in Rome, taking in pretty much the whole of the city, while just below is the spot from which a cannon is fired at noon each day for Romans to check their watches.

Villa Borghese and north

Some of the area immediately north of Rome's city centre is taken up by its most central park, **Villa Borghese**, which serves as valuable outdoor space for both Romans and tourists as well as hosting some of the city's best **museums**. The neighbourhoods beyond, Flaminio and the other residential districts of north central Rome, were until recently not of much interest in themselves, but the **Auditorium** complex and the cutting-edge **MAXXI** have inspired fresh interest in the area.

Pincio Gardens

On the edge of the Villa Borghese, overlooking Piazza del Popolo, the **Pincio Gardens** were laid out by Valadier in the early nineteenth century. Fringed with dilapidated busts of classical and Italian heroes, they give fine views over the roofs, domes and TV antennae of central Rome, right across to St Peter's and the Janiculum Hill.

Galleria Borghese

Piazzale del Museo Borghese 5 • Tues–Sun 9am–7pm; July–Oct also open Fri & Sat 7–10pm; admission on timed tickets every 2hr (last entry 5pm); pick up tickets 30min before admission time • €15, (including booking fee) or €2 first Sun of the month • Prebook at least a day in advance; at least two weeks best in summer at T 06 32810 or W galleriaborghese.it; limited number of last-minute tickets available; ask at the ticket office 30min after the start of any 2hr entry slot

On the far eastern edge of the Villa Borghese park, the wonderful **Galleria Borghese** was built in the early seventeenth century by Cardinal Scipione Borghese, and turned over to the state in 1902. Today it's one of Rome's great treasure houses of art and should not be missed; be sure to book in advance.

The ground floor

The **ground floor** contains mainly **sculpture**: a mixture of ancient Roman items and seventeenth-century works, roughly linked together with late eighteenth-century ceiling paintings showing scenes from the Trojan War. Highlights include, in the first room off the entrance hall, Canova's famously erotic statue *Paolina Borghese* – sister of Napoleon and married (reluctantly) to the reigning Prince Borghese – posed as Venus. Next door, there's a marvellous statue of *David* by **Bernini**, the face of which is a self-portrait of the sculptor, and, further on, a dramatic, poised statue of *Apollo and Daphne* that captures the split second when Daphne is transformed into a laurel tree, with her

fingers becoming leaves and her legs tree trunks. Next door, the Emperors' Hall has another Bernini sculpture, *The Rape of Persephone*, dating from 1622, a coolly virtuoso work that shows in melodramatic form the story of the abduction to the underworld of the beautiful nymph Persephone. The last room contains a variety of paintings by Cardinal Scipione's protégé **Caravaggio**, notably the *Madonna of the Grooms* from 1605, a painting that at the time was considered to have depicted Christ far too realistically to hang in a central Rome church. Look also at *St Jerome*, captured writing at a table lit only by a source of light that streams in from the upper left of the picture, and his *David Holding the Head of Goliath*, sent by Caravaggio to Cardinal Scipione from exile in Malta, where he had fled to escape capital punishment for various crimes, and perhaps the last painting he ever did.

The first floor

The **upstairs gallery** is one of the richest small collections of **paintings** in the world. In the first room are several important paintings by Raphael, including his *Deposition*, painted in 1507 for a noble of Perugia in memory of her son. Look out also for *Lady with a Unicorn* and *Portrait of a Man* by Perugino, and a copy of the artist's tired-out *Julius II*, painted in the last year of the pope's life, 1513. In further rooms there are more early sixteenth-century paintings; prominent works include Cranach's *Venus and Cupid with a Honeycomb*, Lorenzo Lotto's touching *Portrait of a Man*, and in the opposite direction a series of self-portraits by Bernini at various stages of his long life. Next to these are a lifelike bust of *Cardinal Scipione* executed by Bernini in 1632, and a smaller bust of *Pope Paul V*, also by Bernini. Beyond here, in a further room, is a painting of *Diana* by Domechino, depicting the goddess and her attendants doing a bit of target practice, and Titian's *Sacred and Profane Love*, painted in 1514 when he was about 25 years old, to celebrate the marriage of the Venetian noble Niccolò Aurelio.

Galleria Nazionale d'Arte Moderna

Viale delle Belli Arti 131 • Tues–Sun 8.30am–7.30pm; last entry 45min before closing • €8 • ⓣ 06 3229 8221, ⓦ gnam.beniculturali it

In addition to the Galleria Borghese, the Villa Borghese has two other major museums and of them, the **Galleria Nazionale d'Arte Moderna** is probably the less compulsory – a lumbering, Neoclassical building housing a collection of nineteenth- and twentieth-century Italian paintings and a few foreign artists. There are paintings by Courbet, Cézanne and Van Gogh, and a twentieth-century collection upstairs including work by Modigliani, De Chirico, Boccioni and the Futurists, and postwar canvases by the likes of Mark Rothko, Jackson Pollock and Cy Twombly, who lived in Rome for much of his life.

Museo Nazionale Etrusco di Villa Giulia

Piazzale di Villa Giulia 9 • Tues–Sun 9am–8pm; last entry 1hr before closing • €8; free first Sun of the month • ⓣ 06 322 6571, ⓦ villagiulia.beniculturali.it

A harmonious collection of courtyards, loggias, gardens and temples put together in a playful Mannerist style for Pope Julius III in the mid-sixteenth century, the Villa Giulia now houses the **Museo Nazionale Etrusco di Villa Giulia**, the world's primary collection of Etruscan treasures (along with the Etruscan collection in the Vatican). Part of the collection is housed in nearby **Villa Poniatowski**, but its open limited hours (Wed & Thurs 3–6pm). Not much is known about the Etruscans, but they were a creative and civilized people, evidenced here by a wealth of sensual sculpture, jewellery and art. The most famous exhibit, in the octagonal room in the east wing, is the remarkable **Sarcophagus of the Married Couple** (dating from the sixth century BC) from Cerveteri – a touchingly lifelike portrayal of a husband and wife lying on a couch. Look also at the delicate and beautiful *cistae*, drum-like objects, engraved and adorned with figures, which were supposed to hold all the things needed for the care of the body after death. Other highlights include marvellously intricate pieces of gold jewellery, delicately

worked into tiny horses, birds, camels and other animals; a drinking horn in the shape of a dog's head that is so lifelike you almost expect it to bark; a *holmos*, or small table, to which the maker attached 24 little pendants around the edge; and a bronze disc breastplate from the seventh century BC decorated with a weird, almost modern abstract pattern of galloping creatures.

MAXXI

Via Guido Reni 4/A • Tues, Wed & Fri–Sun 11am–7pm, Thurs 11am–10pm; last entry 1hr before closing • €12 • ⓣ 06 320 1954, ⓦ fondazionemaxxi.it • Metro Flaminio, then tram #2

A ten-minute tram journey north of Piazza del Popolo, **MAXXI** is a museum of twenty-first-century art and architecture. Opened to much fanfare in 2010 in a landmark building by the Anglo-Iraqi architect Zaha Hadid, it's primarily a venue for temporary exhibitions of contemporary art and architecture (though it does have small collections of its own), but the building, a simultaneously jagged and curvy affair, is worth a visit in its own right, with its long, unravelling galleries and a towering lobby encompassing the inevitable café and bookstore.

The Vatican

On the west bank of the Tiber, just across from the city centre, the **Vatican City** was established as a sovereign state in 1929, a tiny territory surrounded by high walls on its far western side and on the near side opening its doors to the rest of the city and its pilgrims in the form of **St Peter's** and its colonnaded piazza. The city-state's one thousand inhabitants have their own radio station, daily newspaper, postal service and indeed security service in the colourfully dressed Swiss Guards. It's believed that St Peter was buried in a pagan cemetery on the Vatican hill, giving rise to the building of a basilica to venerate his name and the siting of the headquarters of the Catholic Church here. Stretching north from St Peter's, the Renaissance papal palaces are now home to the **Vatican Museums** – quite simply, the largest, most compelling and perhaps most exhausting museum complex in the world.

Piazza San Pietro

Perhaps the most famous of Rome's many piazzas, Bernini's **Piazza San Pietro** doesn't disappoint, although its size isn't really apparent until you're right on top of it, its colonnade arms symbolically welcoming the world into the lap of the Catholic Church. The obelisk in the centre was brought to Rome by Caligula in 36 AD and was moved here in 1586, when Sixtus V ordered that it be erected in front of the basilica, a task that took four months and was apparently done in silence, on pain of death. The matching fountains on either side are the work of Carlo Maderno (on the right) and Bernini (on the left). In between the obelisk and each fountain, a circular stone set into the pavement marks the focal points of an ellipse, from which the four rows of columns on the perimeter of the piazza line up perfectly, making the colonnade appear to be supported by a single line of columns.

St Peter's

Basilica Daily: April–Sept 7am–7pm; Oct–March 7am–6.30pm • Free • **Treasury** Daily: April–Sept 8am–7pm; Oct–March 8am–6.15pm • €6 • **Grottoes** Daily: April–Sept 8am–6pm; Oct–March 7am–5.30pm • **Dome** Daily: April–Sept 8am–6pm; Oct–March 8am–5pm • €10 via lift, €8 climbing the 551 stairs • ⓣ 06 6988 1662

The Basilica di San Pietro, better known to many as **St Peter's**, is the principal shrine of the Catholic Church, built on the site of St Peter's tomb, and worked on by the greatest Italian architects of the sixteenth and seventeenth centuries. You have to go through security before entering, and the **queues** can be long unless you get here before 9am or after 5pm. Bear in mind that you need to observe the **dress code** to enter, which means no bare knees or shoulders – a rule that is very strictly enforced.

The interior

Entering the basilica, the first thing you see is Michelangelo's graceful **Pietà** on the right, completed when he was just 24. Following an attack by a vandal in 1972, it sits behind glass, strangely remote from the life of the rest of the building. Further into the church, the **dome** is breathtakingly imposing, rising high above the supposed site of St Peter's tomb. With a diameter of 41.5m it is Rome's largest dome, supported by four enormous piers, decorated with reliefs depicting the basilica's "major relics": St Veronica's handkerchief, which was used to wipe the face of Christ; the lance of St Longinus, which pierced Christ's side; and a piece of the True Cross. On the right side of the nave, the bronze **statue of St Peter** is another of the most venerated monuments in the basilica, its right foot polished smooth by the attentions of pilgrims. Bronze was also the material used in Bernini's wild, spiralling **baldacchino**, a massive 26m high, cast out of 927 tonnes of metal removed from the Pantheon roof in 1633. Bernini's feverish sculpting decorates the apse, too, his bronze *Cattedra* enclosing the chair of St Peter, though more interesting is his **monument to Alexander VII** in the south transept, with its winged skeleton struggling underneath the heavy marble drapes upon which the Chigi pope is kneeling in prayer.

The treasury and grottoes

An entrance off the south aisle, under a giant monument to Pius VIII, leads to the **treasury**, which has among many riches the late fifteenth-century bronze tomb of Pope Sixtus IV by Pollaiuolo. Steps lead down by Bernini's statue of St Andrew to the **grottoes**, which extend right under the footprint of the main church. The majority of the popes are buried here, including John Paul II.

The roof and dome

You can make the ascent to the **roof** and **dome** by taking the entrance to the right of the basilica complex. The views from the gallery around the interior of the dome give you a sense of the huge size of the church, and from there you can make the (challenging) ascent to the lantern at the top of the dome, from which the **views** over the city are as glorious as you'd expect.

The Vatican Museums

Viale Vaticano 13 • Mon–Sat 9am–6pm, last entrance at 4pm; last Sun of each month 9am–2pm, last entrance at 12.30pm; closed public and religious hols; end April–Oct also open Fri 7–11pm, last entrance 9.30pm, online booking obligatory • €17; tickets prebooked online €4 extra; last Sun of the month free • Ⓦ museivaticani.va • Tours in groups no larger than six are available through Context Travel; 4hr; €110/person; Ⓦ contexttravel.com

However much you may have enjoyed Rome's other museums, nothing else in the city quite measures up to the **Vatican Museums**, a fifteen-minute walk from St Peter's out of the north side of Piazza San Pietro. So much booty from the city's history has ended up here, from both classical and later times, and so many of the Renaissance's finest artists were in the employ of the pope, that not surprisingly the result is a set of museums stuffed with enough exhibits to put most other European collections to shame.

The Pinacoteca

If the **Pinacoteca** is on your list, it's best to visit it first – turn right at the top of the stairs. Housed in a separate building, it ranks highly among Rome's picture galleries, with works from the early to High Renaissance right up to the nineteenth century. Among early works is the stunning Simoneschi triptych by Giotto; the *Martyrdom of Sts Peter and Paul*, painted in the early 1300s for the old St Peter's; works by Masolino, Fra' Angelico and Fra' Filippo Lippi; and Melozzo da Forlì's musical angels – fragments of a fresco commissioned for the church of Santi Apostoli. Raphael has a room to himself, where you'll find his *Transfiguration*, which he had nearly completed when he died in 1520, the *Coronation of the Virgin*, painted when he was only 19 years old,

THE VATICAN MUSEUMS: PLANNING A VISIT

As its name suggests, the Vatican Museums complex actually holds a series of museums on very diverse subjects – displays of classical statuary, Renaissance painting, Etruscan relics, Egyptian artefacts, not to mention the furnishings and decoration of the building itself. There's no point in trying to see everything, at least not on one visit, and the only features you really shouldn't miss are the **Raphael Rooms** and the **Sistine Chapel**. Above all, decide how long you want to spend here, and what you want to see, before you start; you could spend anything from an hour to a whole day here, and it's easy to collapse from museum fatigue before you've even got to your target. Also, bear in mind that the collections are in a constant state of restoration, and are often closed and shifted around with little or no notice – so check Ⓦ museivaticani.va for up-to-date details.

In high season at least there is likely to be a **queue** to get into the museums; even if you get here before opening you may still have to stand in line for a while. Arriving late morning or after lunch can often mean a shorter wait, and it's also a good idea to **avoid Mondays**, when many of the city's other museums are closed. But the best thing to do is to **book online**, thereby jumping the queues altogether.

and, on the left, the *Madonna of Foglino*, showing Sts John the Baptist, Francis of Assisi and Jerome. Take a look also at the most gruesome painting in the collection, Poussin's *Martyrdom of St Erasmus*, which shows the saint being "drawn" prior to "quartering".

Museo Gregoriano Egizio

The **Museo Gregoriano Egizio** isn't one of the Vatican's main highlights, but it has a distinguished collection of ancient Egyptian artefacts, including some vividly painted mummy cases (and two mummies), along with *canopi*, the alabaster vessels into which the entrails of the deceased were placed. There's also a partial reconstruction of the Temple of Serapis from Hadrian's villa near Tivoli, along with another statue of his lover, Antinous, who drowned close to the original temple in Egypt and so inspired Hadrian to build his replica.

Museo Pio-Clementino

The **Museo Pio-Clementino** is home to some of the Vatican's best classical statuary, including two statues that influenced Renaissance artists more than any others: the serene *Apollo Belvedere*, a Roman copy of a fourth-century-BC original, and the first-century-BC *Laocoön*, which shows a Trojan priest being crushed by serpents for warning of the danger of the Trojan horse – perhaps the most famous classical statue ever. There are also busts and statues of the Roman emperors, fantastic Roman floor mosaics and the so-called *Venus of Cnidos*, the first known representation of the goddess.

Museo Gregoriano Etrusco

A grand staircase, the Simonetti Stairs, leads up to the **Museo Gregoriano Etrusco**, which holds sculpture, funerary art and applied art from the sites of southern Etruria – a good complement to Rome's specialist Etruscan collection in the Villa Giulia. Especially worth seeing are the finds from the Regolini-Galassi tomb, from the seventh century BC, discovered near Cerveteri, which contained the remains of three Etruscan nobles, two men and a woman; the breastplate of the woman and her huge *fibia* (clasp) are of gold. There's also armour, a bronze bedstead, a funeral chariot and a wagon, as well as a great number of enormous storage jars, in which food, oil and wine were stored for use in the afterlife.

Galleria dei Candelabri and Galleria degli Arazzi

Outside the Etruscan museum, the staircase leads back down to the main Sistine route, taking you first through the **Galleria dei Candelabri**, the niches of which are adorned

with huge candelabra taken from imperial Roman villas, and the **Galleria degli Arazzi** (Gallery of Tapestries), with Belgian tapestries to designs by the school of Raphael.

Galleria delle Carte Geografiche

Next comes the **Galleria delle Carte Geografiche** (Gallery of Maps), which is as long as the previous two galleries put together. It was decorated in the late sixteenth century at the behest of Pope Gregory XIII to show all of Italy, the major islands in the Mediterranean and the papal possessions in France, as well as large-scale maps of the maritime republics of Venice and Genoa.

The Raphael Rooms

The **Raphael Rooms** formed the private apartments of Pope Julius II, and when he moved in here he commissioned Raphael to redecorate them in a style more in tune with the times. Raphael died in 1520 before the scheme was complete, but the two rooms that were painted by him, as well as others completed by pupils, stand as one of the highlights of the Renaissance. The **Stanza di Eliodoro**, the first of the Raphael Rooms proper, was painted by three of Raphael's students five years after his death, and is best known for its painting the *Mass of Bolsena*, which relates a miracle that occurred in the town in northern Lazio in the 1260s, and, on the window wall opposite, the *Deliverance of St Peter*, showing the saint being assisted in a jailbreak by the Angel of the Lord. The other main room, the **Stanza della Segnatura** or Pope's Study, was painted in the years 1508–11, when Raphael first came to Rome, and comes close to the peak of the painter's art. The *School of Athens*, on the near wall as you come in, steals the show, a representation of the triumph of scientific truth in which all the great minds from antiquity are represented. It pairs with the *Disputation of the Sacrament* opposite, which is a reassertion of religious dogma – an allegorical mass of popes, cardinals, bishops, doctors and even the poet Dante.

The Appartamento Borgia

Outside the Raphael Rooms, the **Appartamento Borgia** was inhabited by Julius II's hated predecessor, Alexander VI, and is nowadays host to a large collection of modern religious art, although its ceiling frescoes, the work of Pinturicchio in the years 1492–95, are really the main reason to visit.

The Sistine Chapel

Steps lead up from the Appartamento Borgia to the **Sistine Chapel**, a huge barn-like structure that serves as the pope's official private chapel and the scene of the conclaves of cardinals for the election of each new pontiff. The ceiling frescoes here, and painting of the *Last Judgement* on the altar wall, are probably the most viewed paintings in the world: it's estimated that on an average day about fifteen thousand people trudge through here to take a look. Bear in mind that photography is strictly prohibited and it's also officially forbidden to speak – a rule that is rampantly ignored.

The walls of the chapel were decorated by several prominent painters of the Renaissance – Pinturicchio, Perugino, Botticelli and Ghirlandaio. Anywhere else they would be pored over very closely indeed. As it is, they are entirely overshadowed by Michelangelo's **ceiling frescoes**, commissioned by Pope Julius II in 1508. They depict scenes from the Old Testament, from the *Creation of Light* at the altar end to the *Drunkenness of Noah* over the door. Look at the pagan sibyls and biblical prophets which Michelangelo also incorporated in his scheme, including the figure of the prophet Jeremiah – a brooding self-portrait of an exhausted-looking Michelangelo.

On the altar wall of the chapel, the **Last Judgement** was painted by the artist more than twenty years later. It took four years, again single-handed, and is probably the most inspired and homogeneous large-scale painting you're ever likely to see, the technical virtuosity of Michelangelo taking a back seat to the sheer exuberance of the

work. The centre is occupied by Christ, turning angrily as he gestures the condemned to the underworld. Below, a group of angels blast their trumpets to summon the dead from their sleep: on the left, they awaken from their tombs and are either levitated to heaven or pulled by angels who take them before Christ. At the bottom right, Charon, keeper of the underworld, swings his oar at the damned souls as they fall off the boat into the waiting gates of hell.

The Braccio Nuovo and Museo Chiaramonti

The Braccio Nuovo and Museo Chiaramonti both hold classical sculpture, although be warned that they are the Vatican at its most overwhelming – close on a thousand statues crammed into two long galleries. The **Braccio Nuovo** was built in the early 1800s to display classical statuary that was particularly prized, and it contains, among other things, probably the most famous extant image of Augustus, and a bizarre-looking statue depicting the Nile, whose yearly flooding was essential to the fertility of the Egyptian soil. The 300m-long **Museo Chiaramonti** is especially unnerving, lined as it is with the chill marble busts of hundreds of nameless, blank-eyed ancient Romans, along with the odd deity. It pays to have a leisurely wander, for there are some real characters here: sour, thin-lipped matrons; kids, caught in a sulk or mid-chortle; and ancient old men with sagging flesh.

Castel Sant'Angelo

Lungotevere Castello 50 • Daily 9am–7.30pm; last entry 1hr before closing • €14; free first Sun of the month • ⓣ 06 681 9111, ⓦ castelsantangelo.com

The great circular hulk of the **Castel Sant'Angelo** marks the edge of the Vatican, designed and built by Hadrian as his own mausoleum. Renamed in the sixth century, when Pope Gregory the Great witnessed a vision of St Michael here that ended a terrible plague, the building was converted by the papal authorities for use as a fortress; a raised walkway (the **Passetto di Borgo**) was built to link it with the Vatican as a refuge in times of siege or invasion.

Inside, a spiral ramp leads up into the centre of the mausoleum, over a drawbridge, to the main level at the top, where a small palace was built to house the papal residents in appropriate splendour. Pope Paul III had some especially fine renovations made, including the beautiful Sala Paolina, whose gilded ceiling displays the Farnese family arms. Elsewhere, the rooms hold swords, armour, guns and the like, while others are lavishly decorated with grotesques and paintings (don't miss the bathroom of Clement VII on the second floor, with its prototype hot and cold water taps and mildly erotic frescoes). Below are dungeons and storerooms that can be glimpsed from the spiralling ramp, testament to the castle's grisly past as the city's most notorious Renaissance prison. The quiet **café** upstairs offers one of the best views of Rome.

ARRIVAL AND DEPARTURE — ROME

BY PLANE

Rome has two airports: Leonardo da Vinci, better known as Fiumicino, which handles the majority of scheduled flights, including easyJet's; and Ciampino, where you'll arrive if you're travelling with Ryanair. Information on both airports is available at ⓣ 06 65 951 and ⓦ adr.it.

Fiumicino The airport is linked to the centre of Rome by a direct train, the Leonardo Express, which takes 32min to get to Termini and costs €14; services begin at 6.23am, leaving every 15–30min until 11.23pm. Slower trains leave every 15–30min to Trastevere (27min), Ostiense (32min) and Tiburtina (48min) stations; the latter two are stops on Rome's metro. Tickets cost €8. Alternatively, there are various buses, all taking about 45min to get to the centre: COTRAL has around eight services a day to Termini's Piazza dei Cinquecento (5.45am–1.45am; €7 one-way; ⓦ cotralspa.it); SIT Bus Shuttle runs to Via Marsala 5, by Termini, and to Via Crescenzio in the Vatican area (7.15am–12.40pm; every 30–45min; €6 one way; ⓦ sitbusshuttle.com); Terravision runs to Via Marsala 29, by Termini (5.35am–11pm; every 30min; €5.80 one way; ⓦ terravision.eu); and T.A.M. buses run to Via Giolitti on the south side of Termini, and to Stazione Ostiense (5.40am–11.30pm; roughly every 30min; €6 one way; ⓦ tambus.it). As for taxis, you'll pay a fixed price of €48 for the 40–50min journey to the centre.

Ciampino From Ciampino, three companies run roughly every 30min–1hr to Termini: Terravision (8.15am–12.15am; Ⓦ terravision.eu), SIT Bus Shuttle (7.45am–12.15am; Ⓦ sitbusshuttle.it) and Schiaffini (4am–11.45pm; Ⓦ romeairportbus.com); tickets cost around €6 one way and the journey takes 30–45 min. If you don't want to go to Termini, and are staying near a metro stop on the A line (near the Spanish Steps or Via Veneto areas, for example), you could alternatively take an ATRAL bus from the airport to Anagnina metro station at the end of metro line A (6.10am–10.40pm; every 40min; 10min; €1.20 one way, plus €1.20/suitcase; Ⓦ atral-lazio.com), and take a metro from there to your destination (€1.50). The fixed price for taxis into the city centre is €30 (30–40min).

BY TRAIN

Termini Travelling by train from most places in Italy, or indeed Europe, you arrive at Termini station, centrally placed for all parts of the city and meeting point of the two metro lines and many city bus routes. There are left-luggage facilities here, on the lower level by platform 24 (daily 6am–11pm; €6/piece for the first 5hr, then €1/hr for 6–12hr, then €0.50/hr). Selected routes around Lazio are handled by the Regionali platforms of Termini station (a 5min walk beyond the end of the regular platforms).

Other stations As for other train stations in Rome, Tiburtina is a stop for some north–south intercity trains, and certain parts of Lazio and elsewhere, as are Ostiense, Trastevere, San Pietro and Tuscolana. The Roma-Nord line station on Piazzale Flaminio runs to Viterbo, and the Roma Lido/Porta San Paolo station next to Piramide metro station serves stations down to Ostia Lido (including Ostia Antica).

Destinations Rome (Termini) to: Ancona (every 1–2hr; 3hr 40min–4hr 10min); Anzio/Nettuno (hourly; 1hr); Bologna (every 10–20min; 2hr); Cerveteri* (every 30min–1hr; 45min); Civitavecchia* (at least every 30min; 1hr 10min); Florence (every 10–30min; 1hr 30min); Formia (at least every 30min; 1hr 5min–1hr 25min); Latina (every 15–30min; 35–45min); Milan (every 10–30min; 3hr–3hr 40min); Naples (at leastevery 30min; 1hr 10min–2hr 20min); Pescara (6 daily; 3hr 50min–5hr); Tarquinia* (hourly; 1hr 30min). Rome (Ostiense) to: Bracciano* (every 30min; 1hr); Viterbo* (hourly; 1hr 50min). Rome (Roma-Nord line from Piazzale Flaminio) to: Saxa Rubra (14 daily; 15min); Viterbo (4 daily; 2hr 40min). Rome (Roma Lido/Porta San Paolo) to: Ostia Antica (every 10–15min; 25min).

* Trains also run from Rome Trastevere and Roma San Pietro.

BY BUS

The main station for buses from outside the Rome area is Tiburtina; from here, take metro line B to Termini for buses, trains and metro line A. COTRAL (Ⓣ 06 7205 7205, Ⓦ cotralspa.it) runs a number of useful bus routes: to Tivoli, Subiaco and Palestrina (from Ponte Mammolo metro station; line B); to Cerveteri and Civitavecchia (from Cornelia metro station; line A); to San Felice Cireco, Terracina, Sabaudia and Nettuno (near Anzio; from Laurentina metro station; line B); to the Castelli Romani and Nettuno (from Anagnina metro station; line A); and to Bracciano, Viterbo and around (from Saxa Rubra station; on the Roma-Nord train line).

Destinations Ariccia (every 15min; 40min); Bracciano (every 20–40min; 1hr); Castel Gandolfo (9 daily; 35min); Cerveteri (every 20–50min; 1hr); Civitavecchia (every 30min–1hr; 1hr 40min); Frascati (every 15–30min; 30min); Grottaferrata (12 daily; 40min); Nettuno (every 30–45min; 1hr 40min); Palestrina (hourly; 1hr); Sabaudia (3–5 daily; 1hr 40min); San Felice Circeo (3–5 daily; 2hr); Subiaco (every 30–45min; 2hr); Terracina (2–4 daily; 2hr 15min); Tivoli (every 10min; 45min); Viterbo (every 30min; 1hr 30min).

BY CAR

Coming into the city by car can be confusing and isn't advisable unless you're used to driving in Italy and know where you are going to park. If you are coming from the north on the A1 autostrada take the exit "Roma Nord"; from the south, take the "Roma Est" exit. Both lead you to the Grande Raccordo Anulare (GRA), which circles the city and is connected with all of the major arteries into the city centre – Via Cassia from the north, Via Salaria from the northeast, Via Tiburtina or Via Nomentana from the east, Via Appia Nuova and the Pontina from the south, Via Prenestina and Via Casilina or Via Cristoforo Colombo from the southeast, and Via Aurelia from the northwest.

GETTING AROUND

The best way to get around the centre of Rome is to walk. However, the ATAC-run **public transport** system, incorporating buses, metros and trams, is cheap, reliable and as quick as the clogged streets allow. There's an **information office** in Piazza dei Cinquecento outside Termini station (daily 8am–8pm); Ⓦ atac.roma.it has information in English and a route planner; and the Muoversi a Roma website (Ⓦ muovi.roma.it) has a **journey planner** that uses real-time data to find the quickest route.

By bus Buses run till around midnight, when a network of nightbuses comes into service, accessing most parts of the city and operating until about 5.30am.

By metro The metro operates from 5.30am to 11.30pm (till 1.30am on Fri and Sat). Its two main lines, A (red) and B (blue), crossing at Termini, only have a few stops in the city centre. The most useful on metro line A are Ottaviano (for the Vatican), Flaminio (near Piazza del Popolo), Spagna (by the Spanish Steps), Barberini (at Piazza Barberini), Repubblica (at

METRO AND TRAINS

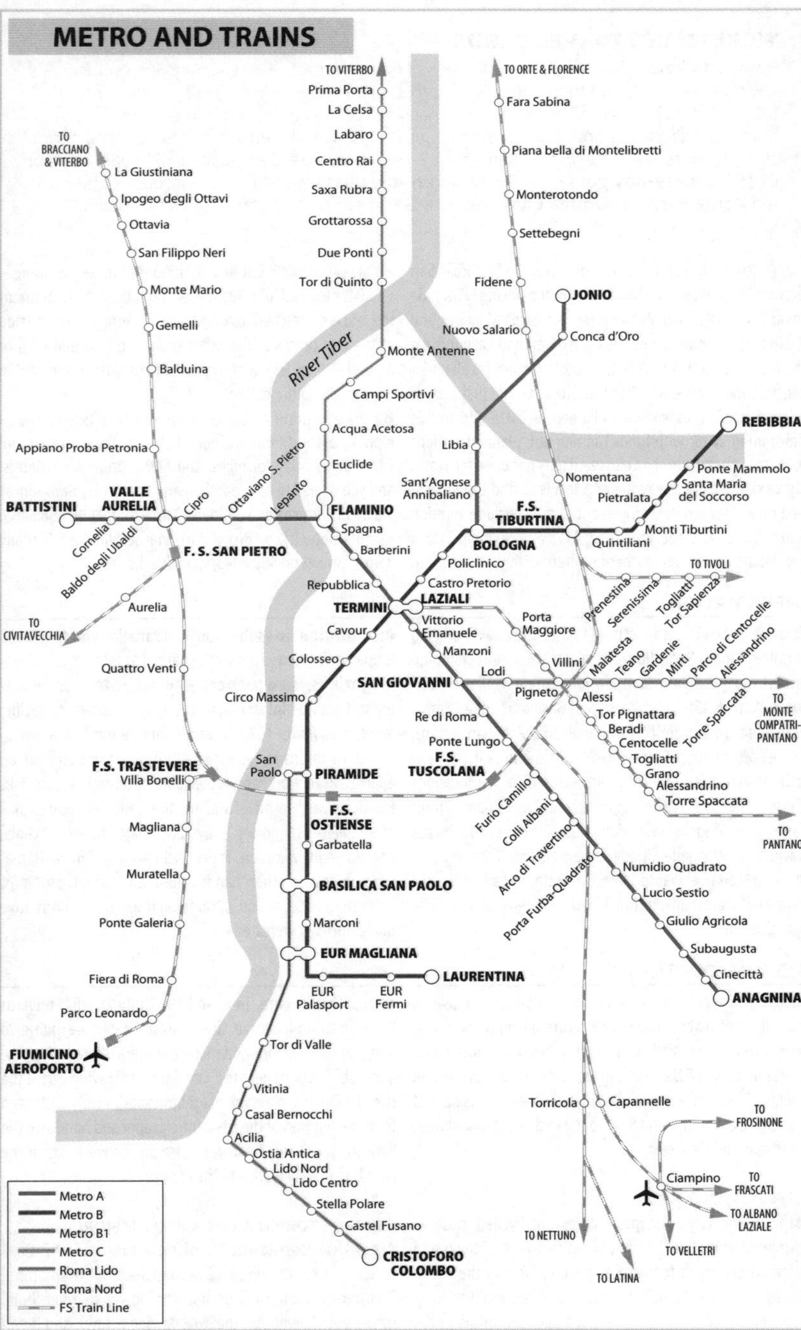

TICKETS AND TRAVEL CARDS

Flat-fare **tickets** (known as BIT) on all forms of transport cost €1.50 each and are good for any number of bus and tram rides and one metro ride within 100 minutes of validating them – bus tickets should be stamped in machines on board the bus. You can buy tickets from *tabacchi*, newsstands and ticket machines located in all metro stations and at major bus stops. If you're using transport extensively it's worth getting a **day-pass** for €7, a 48hr pass for €12.50, a **three-day pass** for €18, or a **seven-day pass** for €24. Public transport is free with the **Roma Pass** and **Omnia Card** (see page 56). There are hefty fines for fare-dodging.

Piazza Repubblica) and San Giovanni (near the Basilica di San Giovanni in Laterano); on line B, useful stops include Piramide (near Testaccio); Circo Massimo (by the Circus Maximus and Palatine Hill); Colosseo (by the Colosseum) and Cavour (near the Monti district). A new line, C, most of which is still under construction, crosses line A at San Giovanni. The first section opened in 2014, extending to Pigneto in 2015 and to San Giovanni in 2018; with funds running out, planned stations at Piazza Venezia and the Colosseum may not open for years

By taxi The easiest way to get a taxi is to find the nearest taxi rank (*fermata dei taxi*) – central ones include Termini, Piazza Venezia, Largo Argentina, Piazza di Spagna, Piazza del Popolo and Piazza Barberini. Alternatively, you can call a taxi (T 06 0609), but bear in mind that these cost more – €3.50 for the call, plus the meter starts ticking the moment the taxi is dispatched to collect you. A journey from one side of the city centre to the other should cost around €15, or around €20 on Sun or at night. All taxis carry a rate card in English giving the current tariff.

By bike Renting a bike or scooter is an efficient way of nipping around Rome's clogged streets. Rates are around €4/hr or €13/day for bikes, and €40–80/day for scooters, and you'll need to have a full driving licence. Try Barberini at Via della Purificazione 84 (daily 9am–7pm; T 06 488 5485, W rentscooter.it), or Bici e Baci, Via del Viminale 5 (daily 8am–7pm; T 06 482 8443, W bicibaci.com).

INFORMATION

Tourist office There are official tourist offices at Fiumicino Terminal 3 (daily 8am–9pm); in the Arrivals hall at Ciampino airport (daily 8.30am–6pm); inside Termini by Platform 24 (daily 8am–6.45pm); at Via di San Basilio 51 (daily 8am–6pm) and on Via dei Fori Imperiali (daily 9.30am–7pm). Rome's official tourist website is W turismoroma.it.

Information kiosks These are located in key locations around the city centre (generally open 9.30am–7pm): Castel Sant'Angelo (Via della Conciliazione 4); Piazza Navona (Piazza delle Cinque Lune); Portico d'Ottavia (Via di Santa Maria del Pianto 1); Trevi Fountain (Via Minghetti); Vatican (Piazza San Pietro); Via Nazionale (Palazzo delle Esposizioni).

Information lines The tourist information line T 06 0608 is open daily 9am–7pm (calls charged at local rates)

Magazines, newspapers and websites For what's-on and listings information, the English expat magazine, *Wanted in Rome* (€2; W wantedinrome.com) is a useful source of information, especially if you're looking for an apartment or work, and is available at central newsstands. For those with a bit of Italian, the daily arts pages of *Il Messaggero* list movies, plays and major musical events, and *La Repubblica* on Thurs includes the "Trova Roma" supplement, another handy guide to current offerings. W inromenow.com and W romeing.it are both informative Rome-focused websites.

ACCOMMODATION

There's plenty of accommodation in Rome, and overall the choice of **hotels** in the city centre has improved a lot over recent years, with lots of new boutique hotels and contemporary **B&Bs** opening up. But it's always worth booking in advance, especially when the city is at its busiest – from Easter to July, and Sept to the end of Oct, and during Christmas and New Year.

HOTELS AND B&BS

Many of the city's cheapest places are located close to Termini station, but this isn't the nicest part of town and there are plenty of moderately priced places in the *centro storico* or around Campo de' Fiori. However, you'll need to book well in advance to be sure of a cheaper option in the centre. The Tridente, Trevi and the Quirinale Hill, towards Via Veneto and around the Spanish Steps, are home to more upscale accommodation, although there are a few affordable options here too. Consider also staying across the river in Prati, a pleasant neighbourhood, nicely distanced from the hubbub of the city centre proper and handy for the Vatican, or in lively Trastevere, also on the west side of the river but an easy walk into the centre.

CENTRO STORICO AND CAMPO DE' FIORI

Argentina Residenza Via di Torre Argentina 47 T 06 6880 9533, W argentinaresidenza.com; map p.53. This former noble carriage-house is now a six-room hotel by the people who run the *Navona* (see below), and it's an

elegant affair, with antique ceilings combining well with the well-chosen modern furnishings and amenities. **€210**

Campo de' Fiori Via del Biscione 6 ⓣ 06 6880 6865, ⓦ hotelcampodefiori.com; map p.55. A friendly place in a nice location with rooms in a plush, boutique style. The sixth-floor roof terrace has great views, and the hotel also owns a number of small apartments nearby. **€393**

DOM Hotel Via Giulia 131 ⓣ 06 683 2144, ⓦ domhotelroma.com; map p.55. A newcomer to Rome's luxury boutique hotel scene, *DOM Hotel* goes all out for opulence in its 24 rooms and suites, all moody greys and browns, dramatic lighting and splashy statement art. On the ground floor, boudoir-esque restaurant and cocktail bar *Achilli al DOM* is thronged with hip young things after dark. **€418**

USEFUL TRANSPORT ROUTES

BUSES

#23 Piazzale Clodio–Piazza Risorgimento–Ponte Vittorio Emanuele–Ponte Garibaldi–Via Marmorata–Piazzale Ostiense–Centrale Montemartini–Basilica di S. Paolo.

#30 Express (Mon–Sat only) Piazzale Clodio–Piazza Mazzini–Piazza Cavour–Corso Rinascimento–Largo Argentina–Piazza Venezia–Lungotovere Aventino–Via Marmorata–Piramide–Via C. Colombo–EUR.

#40 Express Termini–Via Nazionale–Piazza Venezia–Largo Argentina–Piazza Pia/Castel Sant'Angelo.

#60 Express Piazza Venezia– Via Nazionale– Porta Pia–Via Nomentana.

#62 Stazione Tiburtina–Via Nomentana/Villa Torlonia–Porta Pia–Piazza Barberini–Via del Corso–Piazza Venezia–Corso V. Emanuele–Lungotevere Santo Spirito–Piazza Pia.

#64 Termini–Piazza della Repubblica–Via Nazionale–Piazza Venezia–Largo Argentina–Corso V. Emanuele–Stazione S. Pietro.

#75 Via Poerio (Monteverde)–Via Induno–Porta Portese–Testaccio–Circus Maximus–Colosseum–Via Cavour–Termini.

#118 Via Appia Antica–Terme di Caracalla–Circus Maximus–Piazza Venezia–Colosseum–Terme di Caracalla–Via Appia Antica.

#492 Stazione Tiburtina–Termini–Piazza Barberini–Via del Corso–Piazza Venezia–Largo Argentina–Corso del Rinascimento–Piazza Cavour–Piazza Risorgimento–Cipro (Vatican Museums).

#590 Same route as metro line A but with access for disabled; runs every 1hr 30min Mon, Tues, Wed, Sat & Sun.

#660 Largo Colli Albani–Via Appia Nuova–Via Appia Antica.

#714 Termini–Santa Maria Maggiore–Via Merulana–San Giovanni in Laterano–Terme di Caracalla–EUR.

#910 Termini–Piazza della Repubblica–Galleria Borghese–Auditorium–Piazza Mancini.

TRAMS

#2 Piazzale Flaminio–Viale delle Belle Arti–Palazzetto dello Sport–Piazza Mancini.

#3 Viale delle Belle Arti–Piazza Buenos Aires–Viale Regina Margherita–San Lorenzo–Piazza di Santa Croce in Gerusalemme–Colosseum–Circus Maximus–Piazzale Ostiense.

#8 Stazione Trastevere–Piazza Mastai–Viale Trastevere–Via Arenula/Largo Argentina–Piazza Venezia.

#14 Termini–Piazza Vittorio Emanuele–Porta Maggiore–Via Prenestina (Pigneto).

#19 Porta Maggiore–San Lorenzo–Piazzale Verano–Viale Regina Margherita–Viale Belle Arti–Villa Giulia–Ottaviano–Piazza Risorgimento.

NIGHTBUSES

#N1 Same route as metro line A.

#N2 Same route as metro line B.

#N7 Piazzale Clodio–Via Ripetta–Corso del Rinascimento–Largo Argentina–Piazza Venezia–Via Nazionale–Termini.

#N8 Viale Trastevere–Piazza Venezia–Via Nazionale–Termini.

#N10 Piazzale Ostiense–Lungotevere De' Cenci–Via Crescenzio–Viale Belle Arte–Viale Regina Margherita–Via Labicana–Colosseum–Circus Maximus–Piazzale Ostiense.

TOURIST BUSES

Big Bus ⓣ 06 488 2625, ⓦ bigbustours.com. There are several hop-on-hop-off buses in Rome, operating on similar double-decker buses on much the same route around the main sights, with audioguide included in the ticket price. The Big Bus service departs from Termini station and stops at most of the major sights every 10–20min from 8.30am to 7pm, and tickets cost €32, or €28.80 online (24hr) it's €39 or €35.10 online for the 48hr version, which also includes the Catacombs and the Baths of Caracalla.

Roma Cristiana ⓣ 06698961, ⓦ romeandvaticanpass.com. The Vatican's tourist bus service, with commentary, links Rome's major basilicas and other Christian sites, starting in front of Termini on Piazza dei Cinquecento, and also at St Peter's. Services run daily every 10–15min between 9am (9.30am St Peter's) and 6.30pm (6.45pm St Peter's), and tickets are included in the OMNIA Card (see page 56).

1

Domus Ester Via di San Salvatore in Campo 38 ⓣ06 6813 9414, ⓦnew.estercampodefiori.com; map p.55. Tucked away on a tranquil alley in the heart of the Ghetto, *Domus Ester* offers good value given its location, a 5min walk from Campo de' Fiori. The rooms are small but spotless and crisply painted, with wood-beamed ceilings and gleaming bathrooms. There are several flights of stairs and no lift. **€146**

Due Torri Vicolo del Leonetto 23 ⓣ06 6880 6956, ⓦhotelduetorriroma.com; map p.55. This little hotel was once a residence for cardinals, and later served as a brothel. Completely remodelled, it retains a homely feel and some of its rooms have lovely rooftop views. A good location just north of Piazza Navona. **€229**

Navona Via dei Sediari 8 ⓣ06 6830 1252, ⓦhotelnavona.com; map p.55. Friendly hotel in a building that dates back to the first century AD, built on the ancient Roman baths of Agrippa. Some of the rooms have wonderful coffered ceilings, though the general aesthetic leans towards modern simplicity, with wood floors, designer Perspex chairs and modish padded headboards. **€225**

Portoghesi Via dei Portoghesi 1 ⓣ06 686 4231, ⓦhotelportoghesiroma.it; map p.55. Decent, classically furnished rooms, a stone's throw from most *centro storico* attractions. Breakfast on the roof terrace, with a view of St Peter's dome, is a high point. **€200**

Santa Chiara Via di S. Chiara 21 ⓣ06 687 2979, ⓦalbergosantachiara.com; map p.55. A friendly hotel in a great location, on a quiet street behind the Pantheon. Tastefully furnished rooms, too, some of which overlook the church of Santa Maria sopra Minerva. **€285**

★ **Teatro Pace** Via del Teatro Pace 33 ⓣ06 687 9075, ⓦhotelteatropace.com; map p.55. This beautifully restored *palazzo*, a few paces from Piazza Navona, has an impressive Baroque spiral staircase (no lift) and four floors of elegant rooms with original wood beams, floor-sweeping drapes and luxurious bathrooms. **€169**

Zanardelli Via G. Zanardelli 7 ⓣ06 6821 1392, ⓦhotelnavona.com; map p.55. Run by the same people as the *Navona*, this is the slightly more lavish alternative, just north of Piazza Navona, in a building which used to be a papal residence and has many original features. The rooms are quite elegant, with antique iron beds, silk-lined walls and modern amenities, but still decently priced. **€189**

THE TRIDENTE, TREVI AND THE QUIRINALE

Daphne Via degli Avignonesi 20 ⓣ06 8953 8471, ⓦdaphne-rome.com; map p.53. A welcoming *pensione* run by an American woman and her Roman husband. Bright, nicely renovated modern rooms in two good locations either side of Piazza Barberini, and as much advice as you need on how to spend your time in Rome. Some cheaper rooms have shared bathrooms. **€180**

★ **De Russie** Via del Babuino 9 ⓣ06 328 881, ⓦroccofortehotels.com; map p.50. Coolly elegant and understated, this is the abode of choice for visiting movie stars and hip travellers spending someone else's money. **€870**

★ **Deko Rome** Via Toscana 1 ⓣ06 4202 0032, ⓦdekorome.com; map p.53. This six-room hotel, run by friendly and efficient Marco and Serena, gets everything right, from the complimentary minibar to the smooth service. The rooms are modern and spotless, and it's in a great location too. It's understandably popular, so book ahead. **€202**

Modigliani Via della Purificazione 42 ⓣ06 4281 5226, ⓦhotelmodigliani.com; map p.53. On a quiet street just off Piazza Barberini, this family-run hotel is tastefully decorated and has a delightful garden courtyard. Splash out on one of the superior rooms, whose balconies have a view of St Peter's. **€144**

Palazzo Dama Lungotevere Arnaldo da Brescia 2 ⓣ06 8956 5272, ⓦpalazzodama.com; map p.50. This five-star villa hotel has whimsical decor and an air of glamour. An eclectic art collection lines the grand staircase – the centrepiece a chandelier from the Plaza in New York. The outdoor pool and bar is a chic summertime hangout **€177**

Piazza di Spagna Via Mario de' Fiori 61 ⓣ06 679 3061, ⓦwww.hotelpiazzadispagna.it; map p.53. This small hotel, just a few minutes' walk from the Spanish Steps, is a good alternative to the sumptuous palaces that characterize this area. Friendly, and family-owned and -run, it has comfortable rooms, all with a/c and TV, and some with jacuzzis. There's a little roof garden, too. **€210**

★ **Portrait Roma** Via di Bocca di Leone 23 ⓣ06 6938 0742, ⓦlungarnocollection.com; map p.53. This converted townhouse with fourteen suites, owned by the Salvatore Ferragamo fashion house and dotted with the late designer's shoe lasts and other fashiony details, is a bastion of luxury and comfort. Prices are eye-watering, but the suites are superbly appointed, and there's a lovely rooftop bar. Service is unstuffy and ultra-friendly. **€864**

MONTI, TERMINI AND THE ESQUILINE

Alpi Via Castelfidardo 84 ⓣ06 444 1235, ⓦhotelalpi.com; map p.50. One of the more peaceful yet convenient options close to Termini, with pleasant, if somewhat small, en-suite rooms and a flower-filled terrace. **€232**

Artemide Via Nazionale 22 ⓣ06 489 911, ⓦhotelartemide.it; map p.53. The handsome *Artemide* combines an imposing, old-world feel with a warm welcome and service that's second to none. The comfortable rooms come with a free minibar, breakfast is five-star, and the rooftop bar-restaurant is a lovely spot on a sunny day. There's a swish spa too. Rates are significantly lower in low season. **€502**

Artorius Via del Boschetto 13 ⓣ06 482 1196, ⓦhotelartoriusrome.com; map p.53. On a cobbled Monti street and with just ten rooms, decorated in classic style, this family-run hotel is an appealing budget option. The attractive courtyard makes a pleasant spot for breakfast in fine weather and for drinks after dark. **€117**

★ **B&B La Scalinatella** Via Urbana 48 ⓣ06 488 0547 or ⓣ339 525 6537, ⓦlascalinatellaroma.com; map p.53. This fabulous three-room B&B, run by friendly sisters Annamaria and Elisabetta, is in a seventeenth-century *palazzo* in bustling Monti. The rooms are beautifully furnished with whitewashed wood beams, antique furniture and spacious modern bathrooms. The B&B is three floors up with no lift. **€150**

★ **The Beehive** Via Marghera 8 ⓣ06 4470 4553, ⓦthe-beehive.com; map p.50. This cheery and friendly ecological – and economical – hotel is run by an American couple and has fairly basic but very well-decorated doubles (a few with private bathrooms) and more spartan dorms. There's a cosy lounge, an on-site café serving breakfast (extra) and a peaceful garden that feels like a real haven so close to Termini. **€80**

Nerva Via Tor de' Conti 3 ⓣ06 679 3764, ⓦhotelnerva.com; map p.53. Right by the Roman Forum, and once a dowdy three-star, *Nerva* has undergone a dramatic transformation into a modern boutique hotel, with rooms decorated in cool monochrome. **€299**

Nicolas Inn Via Cavour 295 ⓣ06 9761 8483, ⓦnicolasinn.com; map p.53. A brief stroll from the Colosseum, this B&B is run by a friendly American-Italian couple who are keen to make guests feel at home and offer a concierge service – impressive at this price. The rooms are a good size, spotless and elegant. Breakfast is included but is served in a nearby bar. **€180**

Quirinale Via Nazionale 7 ⓣ06 4707, ⓦhotelquirinale.it; map p.53. Giuseppe Verdi greeted the Teatro dell'Opera crowds here after the 1893 Rome premiere of *Falstaff*, and it's still a pleasantly old-fashioned place. The rooms – large and antique-filled, with spacious marble bathrooms – are excellent value. **€205**

Suite Dreams Via Modena 5 ⓣ06 4891 3907, ⓦsuitedreams.it; map p.53. Simple yet stylish rooms with good-sized bathrooms, and nice details like a DVD library for guests' use. **€134**

THE CELIAN HILL, SAN GIOVANNI AND THE AVENTINE

★ **Lancelot** Via Capo d'Africa 47 ⓣ06 7045 0615, ⓦlancelothotel.com; map p.50. Just 2min from the Colosseum, this friendly family-run hotel has rooms with oriental carpets on wood or terrazzo floors, and an attractive bar. Half board also available. **€192**

Palazzo Manfredi Via Labicana 125 ⓣ06 7759 1380, ⓦpalazzomanfredi.com; map p.53. This hotel couldn't help but be a haven, given the traffic and tourist mayhem outside, but its lobby, rooms and fabulous top-floor restaurant are an oasis of peace and tranquillity. Its fourteen rooms and suites (as well as a number of luxury apartments nearby) are thoughtfully and very stylishly furnished and equipped. The views of the Colosseum from some of them (and from the rooftop bar and restaurant) are arguably Rome's best. **€700**

San Anselmo Piazza Sant'Anselmo 2 ⓣ06 570 057, ⓦaventinohotels.com; map p.50. One of the most peaceful places to stay in Rome's most upscale residential neighbourhood, the *San Anselmo* has beautifully furnished rooms, each with a different theme. Breakfast is good, there's a nice lounge and garden, and parking is free. **€150**

FIVE GREAT HOTEL BARS

Achilli al DOM, DOM Hotel see page 95
De Russie see page 96
Gin Corner, Hotel Adriano see page 103
Locarno see page 104
Palazzo Dama see page 96

TRASTEVERE, THE VATICAN AND PRATI

Bramante Vicolo delle Palline 24 ⓣ06 6880 6426, ⓦhotelbramante.com; map p.53. Located on an attractive corner of a busy shopping area near the Vatican, this place provides four-star amenities at three-star prices, with nicely furnished en-suite rooms, some with views of St Peter's dome. **€160**

★ **Farnese** Via Alessandro Farnese 30 ⓣ06 321 1953, ⓦfarnese.hotelinroma.com; map p.50. Another grand aristocratic residence that has been turned into a comfortable, mid-range hotel. The rooms, some featuring private balconies, have handmade walnut furniture and marble bathrooms, while the rooftop breakfast room offers a great view of the Vatican. **€178**

★ **Santa Maria** Vicolo del Piede 2 ⓣ06 589 4626, ⓦhotelsantamariatrastevere.it; map p.53. Just steps from Piazza Santa Maria in the heart of Trastevere, the rooms of this small three-star surround an orange-tree-filled garden, giving the feel of a place far removed from the city. The hotel has free bikes for guests to use, and serves a free snack buffet in the afternoon. **€203**

Suites Trastevere Viale Trastevere 248 ⓣ347 074 4086; map p.50. A tram ride from Trastevere's bustle, at the Porta Portese end of Viale Trastevere, this boutique B&B offers something a bit different. The rooms are themed around Roman sights – one has a trompe l'oeil of the Pantheon's oculus on the ceiling, another is emblazoned with Villa Borghese views. Breakfast – including owner Marco's grandmother's coffee cake – is served at a communal table in the kitchen. **€120**

HOSTELS

Alessandro Palace Via Vicenza 42, Termini T 06 446 1958, W alessandropalace.com; map p.50. This has been voted one of the top hostels in Europe, and it sparkles with creative style. Pluses include no lockout or curfew, a roof terrace for cocktail parties and a funky new restaurant that serves up pizza, burgers and the like to hungry backpackers. Wi-fi and satellite TV are free, but breakfast costs extra. You can stay in dorm beds or en-suite private rooms. Dorms €18, doubles €100

La Controra Via Umbria 7, around Via Veneto T 06 9893 7366, W lacontrora.com; map p.53. In an excellent location near Piazza Barberini, this new hostel has very helpful staff and a relaxed, arty feel, with quirky geometric wallpaper in the dorms and en-suite doubles. The spacious lounge has a big-screen TV and wi-fi, and there's a large communal kitchen. Dorms €36, doubles €98

★ **Next Door** Via Nomentana 316, Nomentano T 349 522 7371, W nextdoorguesthouse.com; map p.50. If you're after a party hostel, look elsewhere: this impeccably decorated guesthouse is more about beautiful design than pizza parties. The seven-bed dorm and private rooms are decked out in a mix of moody greys and zingy brights. Breakfast isn't provided but there's a kitchen and large terrace for guests' use. About 20min by bus from the centre. Dorms €27, doubles €70

★ **Yellow** Via Palestro 44, Termini T 06 4938 2682, W the-yellow.com; map p.50. The *Yellow* is hands-down central Rome's best hostel if you're looking to make new friends. There are various types of dorm on offer, plus en-suite private rooms. There's a lively scene in the downstairs bar, with cheap drinks and regular pub crawls organized. Dorms €28, doubles €116

CAMPING

Camping Tiber Via Tiberina Km1400 T 06 3361 0733, W campingtiber.com. Right beside the Tiber, this place is quiet, spacious and friendly, with a supermarket, bar/pizzeria, swimming pool and really hot showers; it has some hundred bungalows (with bath), as well as three camping areas. It's about an hour from central Rome by public transport. Dorms €6, tent pitches €27, double bungalow with bath €25

EATING

Rome is a great place to eat: its denizens know a good deal about freshness and authenticity, and can be very demanding when it comes to the quality of the dishes they are served. Most city-centre restaurants offer standard Italian menus, with the emphasis on **traditional Roman** dishes, although a few more adventurous places have been popping up of late; plus there are numerous establishments dedicated to a variety of **regional cuisines**. The city is also blessed with an abundance of good **pizzerias**, churning out thin, crispy-baked Roman pizza from wood-fired ovens. In recent years a number of successful exponents of the thicker, airier, Neapolitan style have also found favour.

COFFEE, SNACKS AND LUNCH

Rome has plenty of places in which to refuel during a long day's sightseeing, and it's easy to find places that aren't just targeted at tourists. Most bars sell panini and sandwiches (*tramezzini*), and there are plenty of stand-up *rosticcerie* for roast chicken and the like. The following are some of our favourite places for a good-quality, unpretentious lunch or snack.

CENTRO STORICO

Chiostro del Bramante Via Arco della Pace 5 T 06 6880 9036, W chiostrodelbramante.it; map p.55. This *caffetteria*-bistro is an atmospheric hideaway located on the first-floor loggia of a historic fifteenth-century palace. A great venue for breakfast, lunch (salads, risottos), cakes and *aperitivi* at reasonable prices. Mon–Fri 10am–8pm, Sat & Sun 10am–9pm; lunch served 11.30am–3pm; closed Aug.

Enoteca Corsi Via del Gesù 87–88 T 06 679 0821; map p.55. An old-fashioned Roman trattoria and wine shop where you eat what they happen to have cooked that morning. The menu changes each day, and as it's cheap it gets very busy at lunchtimes – you may have to wait for a table. Mon, Tues & Sat noon–3.30pm, Wed–Fri noon–3.30pm & 7–10.30pm; closed 4 weeks July–Aug.

La Caffeteria Piazza di Pietra 65 T 06 679 8147; map p.55. Great Neapolitan café that imports its pastries daily from Naples. The coffee is among Rome's best, though it's not particularly cheap. Daily 7.30am–10pm.

Lo Zozzone Via del Teatro Pace 32 T 06 6880 8575; map p.55. This Rome legend, just around the corner from Piazza Navona and with outside seating, serves *pizza bianca* stuffed with whatever you like, as well as pizza and Roman dishes. Daily 10am–11pm, later in summer.

Pascucci Via di Torre Argentina 20 T 06 686 4816; map p.55. This tiny stand-up *centro storico* bar serves your choice of fresh fruit whipped up with ice and milk – the ultimate Roman refreshment on a hot day. Mon–Sat 6am–midnight.

Sant'Eustachio Piazza Sant'Eustachio 82 T 06 6880 2048; map p.55. The home of what many consider to be Rome's best coffee, roasted on the premises and perennially popular. Take it at the bar for the fully authentic (and cheaper) experience. Nice coffee-based sweets and cakes too. Mon–Thurs & Sun 7.30am–1am, Fri 7.30am–1.30am, Sat 7.30am–2am.

Supplizio Via dei Banchi Vecchi 43 T 06 8987 1920; map p.55. Not really a restaurant, but more than a café, this place is a mecca for street-food fans. It's named for its *supplì* (deep-fried rice balls with various additions; from €3), but other fried goodies and sandwiches are also available. Mon–Sat 11.30am–4pm & 4.30–10pm.

ICE CREAM

★ Fatamorgana Piazza degli Zingari 5, Monti ⓣ06 4890 6955, ⓦgelateriafatamorgana.com; map p.53. One of the top *gelaterie* in Rome, serving up scoops of creative and seasonal flavours. Gluten-free options are also available. There are other branches by Piazza San Cosimato in Trastevere (ⓣ06 580 3615), on Via dei Chiavari near Campo de' Fiori (ⓣ06 8881 8437) and on Via Leone IV in Prati. Tues–Sun 1.30–11pm/12am, until 9.30pm in winter, plus occasionally Mon in summer.

Fior di Luna Via della Lungaretta 96, Trastevere ⓣ06 6456 1314; map p.53. Seasonality, invention and fair trade are the buzz words at this Trastevere establishment. If you're feeling adventurous try the donkey milk *gelati*. Easter–Oct daily 11.30am–11pm, Oct–Easter Tues–Sun 10.30am–9pm.

Gelateria del Teatro Via dei Coronari 65, Centro Storico ⓣ06 4547 4880; map p.55. The *laboratorio* is on view at this *gelateria*, where traditional flavours are executed with great panache. Unusually for central Rome there is seating both inside and out at no extra charge. Daily: Sept–May 11am–10.30pm; June–Aug 11am–midnight.

Il Gelato di Claudio Torcè Viale Aventino 59, Aventine ⓦilgelatodiclaudiotorce.com; map p.50. One of three outlets serving the outstanding ice cream of Claudio Torcè, founder of the city's natural *gelato* movement. Flavours range from classic chocolate to habanero pepper. Mon & Tues 11am–9pm, Wed–Sun 11am–midnight.

Palazzo del Freddo di Giovanni Fassi Via Principe Eugenio 65/67A ⓣ06 446 4740, ⓦpalazzodelfreddo.it; map p.50. This huge old-school ice-cream parlour is a piece of Roman cultural history and has been doing business since 1880. It's no longer the best in town but is still a solid choice. Mon–Thurs noon–midnight, Fri & Sat noon–12.30am, Sun 10am–midnight; winter closes 10pm Mon–Thurs & Sun.

CAMPO DE' FIORI AND THE GHETTO

Barnum Café Via del Pellegrino 87 ⓣ06 6476 0483, ⓦbarnumcafe.com; map p.55. This friendly circus-themed café with free wi-fi is handy for breakfast, coffee and cake or a light lunch. After dark, it's a relaxing bar (see page 103) with great cocktails, and there's a popular nightly *aperitivo* buffet. Mon 9am–midnight, Tues–Sat 9am–2am.

Caffè Perù Via di Monserrato 46 ⓣ06 687 9548; map p.55. A real slice of old Rome, this timewarp bar just off Campo de' Fiori does a fine cappuccino and is notable for its friendly service – a rarity in central Rome. There's seating inside as well as a few hotly contested tables on the cobbles outside. Mon–Sat 6.30am–2am, Sun 9am–9pm.

Forno Roscioli Via dei Chiavari 34 ⓣ06 686 4045, ⓦsalumeriaroscioli.com; map p.55. Old bakery that's associated with the swanky restaurant and deli around the corner and does great bread, lots of types of pizza and other savoury and sweet delights. Mon–Sat 7am–7.30pm, Sun 8am–6pm.

Il Forno di Campo de' Fiori Campo de' Fiori 22 ⓣ06 6880 6662; map p.55. This bakery on the corner of Campo de' Fiori does all sorts of goodies, including fantastic *pizza al taglio*. No seating. Mon–Sat 7.30am–2.30pm & 4.45–8pm; closed Sat afternoon in Aug.

THE TRIDENTE

Buccone Via di Ripetta 19 ⓣ06 361 2154; map p.53. This wine shop is a good, atmospheric spot for lunch in the Tridente/Piazza del Popolo area, with tables laid out amid its bottle-lined shelves and a menu that changes daily, with salads and cold-cut platters, as well as a few hot daily specials. A meal with a glass of wine costs around €20. Mon–Thurs 12.30–3pm, Fri & Sat 12.30–3pm & 7.30–10.30pm.

Punturi Via Flavia 48 ⓣ06 487 0391; map p.53. A historic gastronomia, with superb pizza by the slice and a handful of hot dishes (lasagne, arancini)– at lunch time. Mon–Fri 8am–8pm, Sat 8am–8pm.

THE ESQULINE, MONTI AND TERMINI

Antico Caffé del Brasile Via dei Serpenti 23 ⓣ06 488 2319; map p.53. Reliable old Monti standby that has been selling great coffee, sandwiches, snacks and cakes for over a century. Mon–Sat 6am–8pm, Sun 7am–3pm.

Dagnino Galleria Esedra Via E. Orlando 75 ⓣ06 481 8660; map p.53. Good for both a coffee and snack or a light lunch, this long-established Sicilian bakery is a peaceful retreat in the Termini area, with tables outside on a small 1960s shopping arcade. Daily 7am–11pm.

La Bottega del Caffè Piazza Madonna dei Monti 5 ⓣ06 474 1578; map p.53. Bang in the heart of Monti, this is a good place for breakfast or a lunchtime snack, with tables outside on this peaceful square. Mon–Sat 8am–2am, Sun 9am–2am.

TESTACCIO

★ Mordi e Vai Mercato Testaccio (Box 15), Via B. Franklin ⓣ06 339 1343 344; map p.50. Head to Sergio Esposito's stand in Testaccio Market for one of the finest sandwiches you'll ever taste. Crusty rolls are filled on the spot with classics of *cucina romana* such as beef stew, tripe or veal kidneys. Take a number and wait your turn: you won't regret it. Mon–Sat 8am–2.30pm.

Taverna Volpetti Via A. Volta 8; map p.50. This casual restaurant is attached to the famous deli of the same name, around the corner at Via Marmorata 47. It serves all the Roman classics, from charcuterie boards to carbonara. Mon & Sun noon–11pm, Tues–Sat noon–11pm.

★ **Trapizzino** Via Giovanni Branca 88 ⓣ 06 4341 9624, ⓦ trapizzino.it; map p.50. A great spot for a taste of Roman street food. The patented *trapizzino* (a hybrid of *tramezzino* and *pizza*) is a pocket of pizza bread filled with a stew of your choice: Roman tripe, tongue, or meatballs if you're feeling less adventurous. There are also vegetarian options and a good selection of bottled beers, as well as stools on which to perch. Tues–Sat noon–1am.

TRASTEVERE

La Renella Via del Moro 15 ⓣ 06 581 7265; map p.53. Lovely bakery right in the heart of Trastevere, with great focaccia and *pizza al taglio*. Takeaway or eat on the premises at its long counter. Summer Mon–Thurs & Sun 7am–midnight, Fri & Sat 7am–3am; winter daily 7am–10pm.

Sisini Via San Francesco a Ripa 137 ⓣ 06 589 7110; map p.50. Hole-in-the-wall pizzeria that does great slices, as well as roast chicken and potatoes, *supplì* and all the usual *rosticceria* fare. Mon–Sat 10.30am–9.30pm.

VILLA BORGHESE AND NORTH

Gianfornaio Piazzale Ponte Milvio 35/37; map p.50. Just across the ancient Ponte Milvio, this is the place for a snack lunch if you're visiting the Auditorium or MAXXI, with great *pizza al taglio* and lots of other goodies. Mon–Sat 7.30am–9pm, Sun 9am–3pm.

THE VATICAN AND PRATI

Fa-Bìo Via Germanico 43 ⓣ 06 6452 5810 ⓦ fa-bio.com; map p.50. There's often a queue out of the door at this tiny café, which makes delicious made-to-order sandwiches, juices and salads from organic (bio) ingredients. There are a few stools to sit on. Mon–Fri 10.30am–5.30pm, Sat 10.30am–4pm.

Mondo Arancina Via Marcanonio Colonna 38 ⓣ 06 9761 214; map p.50. Great *pizza al taglio*, but the real treats here are the *arancini* – deep-fried rice balls – which come in lots of varieties, all delicious and just €2.50 each. Daily 8am–midnight.

Pizzarium Bonci Via della Meloria 43; map p.50. Undoubtedly Rome's best pizza-by-the-slice joint, with creatively topped pizzas you won't find anywhere else. Top-notch ingredients and a new seating area make this a great spot near(ish) the Vatican Museums. Mon–Sat 11am–10pm, Sun noon–4pm & 6–10pm.

RESTAURANTS AND PIZZERIAS

There are lots of good restaurants in the *centro storico*, and it's surprisingly easy to find places that are not tourist traps – prices in all but the really swanky restaurants remain pretty uniform throughout the city. The area around Via Cavour and Termini is packed with inexpensive places, but you're better off heading to the nearby student area of San Lorenzo, where you can often eat far better for the same money, or to Monti. South of the centre, Testaccio is well endowed with good, inexpensive trattorias; Trastevere, across the river, has more and more samey tourist joints but a little research will pay off.

CENTRO STORICO

★ **Armando al Pantheon** Salita de' Crescenzi 30 ⓣ 06 6880 3034; map p.55. Surprisingly unpretentious surroundings and honestly priced, great-quality food in this long-standing staple close to the Pantheon (open since 1961). Reservations required. Mon–Fri 12.30–3pm & 7–11pm, Sat 12.30–3pm.

Dal Cavalier Gino Vicolo Rosini 4 ⓣ 06 687 3434; map p.55. Down a small alley by the parliament building, Gino presides over his bustling restaurant with unhurried authority, serving a determinedly trad Roman menu at keen prices – mains €10–15. It's been very much discovered by tourists, but at heart it remains a locals' joint. No credit cards. Mon–Sat 1–3pm & 8–10.30pm.

★ **Da Tonino** Via del Governo Vecchio 18–19 ⓣ 333 587 0779; map p.55. Basic but delicious Roman food is the order of the day at this unmarked *centro storico* favourite. A full meal with wine will set you back less than €25. The few tables fill up quickly, so come early or be prepared to queue. Mon–Sat noon–3.30pm & 7–11pm.

La Montecarlo Vicolo Savelli 12 ⓣ 06 686 1877, ⓦ lamontecarlo.it; map p.55. This hectic pizzeria serves crisp, blistered pizza, along with heaped dishes of pasta. Tables outside in summer, but be prepared to queue. Cheap and cheerful. Tues–Sun noon–1am.

Maccheroni Piazza delle Coppelle 44 ⓣ 06 6830 7895; map p.55. Solid, inexpensive fare in a perfect location on a pretty little square a stone's throw from the Pantheon. Daily 12.30–3pm & 7–11.30pm.

★ **Trattoria Lilli** Via di Tor di Nona 23 ⓣ 06 686 1916; map p.55. One of the city centre's best and most untouristed old-style trattorias, with a great selection of classic, well-prepared Roman staples. Tues–Sat 12.30–3pm & 7.30–11pm, Sun 12.30–3pm.

CAMPO DE' FIORI AND THE GHETTO

Dar Filettaro a Santa Barbara Largo dei Librari 88; map p.53. A fish-and-chip shop without the chips. Paper-covered Formica tables (outdoors in summer), cheap wine, beer and fried cod, a timeless Roman speciality. Mon–Sat 5.30–11.10pm.

★ **Emma Pizzeria con cucina** Via Monte della Farina 28 ⓣ 06 6476 0475, ⓦ emmapizzeria.com; map p.53. The Roscioli clan have a hand in this great new pizzeria near Campo de' Fiori. As one might imagine, the pizza

(from €8) is excellent, but there are also pasta dishes and *secondi*, delicious *fritti* (try the *supplì* or *fiori di zucca*) and an unusually good wine and beer list. Some outdoor seating. Daily 12.30–3pm & 7–11.30pm.

Grappolo d'Oro Piazza della Cancelleria 80 ⓣ06 686 4118; map p.55. This place remains relatively untouched by the hordes in nearby Campo de' Fiori, and serves imaginative Roman cuisine in a traditional trattoria atmosphere at moderate prices – pasta dishes for €10 and mains, including Roman-style lamb, around €17. Mon, Tues & Thurs–Sat 12.30–3pm & 6.30–11pm, Wed 6.30–11pm, Sun 12.45–3.30pm & 6.30–11pm.

★ **Nonna Betta** Via del Portico d'Ottavia 16 ⓣ06 6880 6263, ⓦnonnabetta.it; map p.53. The best kosher restaurant in the Ghetto serves all the classics of Jewish Roman cuisine, from deep-fried artichokes to anchovies with curly endive. Mon & Wed–Sun noon–5pm & 6–10.30pm.

Osteria ar Galletto Piazza Farnese 102 ⓣ06 686 1714, ⓦristoranteargallettoroma.com; map p.55. This long-running Campo favourite no longer quite has the provincial trattoria feel that made it so special but it still serves good, wholesome Roman food at pretty decent prices, and has some tables on the splendid Piazza Farnese. Daily 12.30–3pm & 7.30–11pm.

Piperno Monte de' Cenci 9 ⓣ06 6880 6629; map p.53. This stalwart of the Jewish Ghetto is not the cheapest but is perhaps the best place for a real Roman blow-out, either in its elegant dining room or on the square outside. A great place to try classics like *baccalà*, Roman *fritti* and some of the classic pasta dishes. Tues–Sat 12.45–2.20pm & 7.45–10.20pm, Sun 12.45–2.20pm.

★ **Roscioli** Via dei Giubbonari 21/22 ⓣ06 687 5287; map p.53. Is it a deli, a wine bar, or a fully fledged restaurant? Actually it's all three, and you can either just have a glass of wine and some cheese or go for the full menu, which has great pasta dishes and *secondi* at lunch and dinner. Incredibly high-quality ingredients mean it isn't cheap, but the *carbonara* is legendary. Mon–Sat 12.30–4pm & 7pm–midnight.

Taverna degli Amici Piazza Margana 37 ⓣ06 6992 0637, ⓦlatavernadegliamici.net; map p.53. Long-established restaurant on the fringes of the Ghetto, with lots of outside tables. The menu is unadventurous, with lots of Roman classics as well as pizzas, and prices are moderate. Daily 11am–11pm.

THE TRIDENTE AND QUIRINALE

Beltramme Via della Croce 39; map p.53. This very old-fashioned *fiaschetteria* (originally it sold only wine, by the *fiasco* or flask) is always packed and fairly pricey, but if you want authentic Roman food, atmosphere and service, this is the place. No credit cards. Daily 11.30am–11.30pm.

Ciampini Viale Trinità dei Monti; map p.53. Across the road from the French Academy, *Ciampini* has a great setting in an enclosed garden overlooking the roofs and domes below. There are pasta dishes and salads for around €12, as well as fish, steaks and chicken from the grill. It's a good place for kids, who can watch the turtles playing in the fountain between courses. Daily 12.30–3.30pm–7–11pm.

Colline Emiliane Via degli Avignonesi 22 ⓣ06 481 7538; map p.53. Just down from Piazza Barberini, on a quiet backstreet not far from the Trevi Fountain, this cosy family-run restaurant serves excellent Emilian food at moderate prices (mains around €18). Tues–Sat 12.45–2.45pm & 7.30–10.45pm, Sun 12.45–2.45pm.

Il Chianti Via del Lavatore 81–82/A ⓣ06 678 7550; map p.55. This Tuscan restaurant and wine bar is quite a find, with good spreads of cold meats and cheeses, and full meals of pasta, pizza and beef dishes. Daily noon–1am.

Jardin de Russie Hotel de Russie, Via del Babuino 9 ⓣ06 3288 8870, ⓦroccofortehotels.com; map p.50. It's the magical terrace garden that makes this restaurant. Service is faultless and quality high – with equally high prices. Weekday brunch (€45 per head) is a treat. Daily 12.30–3pm & 7.30–11pm.

Matricianella Via del Leone 4 ⓣ06 683 2100; map p.55. Handily placed just off Via del Corso, this old favourite serves classic Roman food, either in the bustling main dining room or on the outdoor terrace. A great city-centre choice. Mon–Sat 12.30–3pm & 7.30–11pm.

Otello alla Concordia Via della Croce 81 ⓣ06 678 1454; map p.53. In a little courtyard just off Via della Croce, this place used to be one of Fellini's favourites – he lived just a few blocks away on Via Margutta – and remains an elegant yet affordable choice in the heart of Rome. Mon–Sat 12.30–3pm & 7.30–11pm, Sun 12.30–3pm.

Piccolo Abruzzo Via Sicilia 237 ⓣ06 4282 0176; map p.50. A five-minute stroll up the unprepossessing Via Sicilia from Via Veneto, this is a great alternative to the glitzy, mob-run places on the Dolce Vita street. No menu, just a seemingly endless parade of Abruzzese and other goodies plonked on your table at regular intervals – all for around €35 a head. Be sure to come hungry. Mon–Sat 12.30–3pm & 6.30pm–11pm.

Recafé Piazza Augusto Imperatore 9 ⓣ06 6813 4730; map p.53. The entrance on Via del Corso is a Neapolitan café, while on the square you can enjoy proper Neapolitan pizzas, good pasta and salad dishes and excellent grilled *secondi* at

FIVE GREAT ROMAN RESTAURANTS

Armando al Pantheon see page 100
Dal Cavalier Gino see page 100
Flavio al Velavevodetto see page 102
Nonna Betta see page 101
Trattoria Lilli see page 100

moderate prices. Neapolitan sweets and *fritti* too. Mon–Thurs & Sun noon–midnight, Fri & Sat noon–12.30am.

THE ESQUILINE, MONTI AND SAN LORENZO

Alle Carrette Via Madonna dei Monti 95 ⊕06 679 2770; map p.53. This long-standing Monti pizza joint serves great thin and crispy Roman pizzas and deep-fried *baccalà*, and also does great desserts. It's cheap, too. Daily noon–3pm & 7pm–midnight; in winter open for dinner daily, lunch Fri–Sun.

Cavour 313 Via Cavour 313; map p.53. This lovely old wine bar makes a handy retreat after seeing the ancient sites. Lots of wines and delicious (though not cheap) snacks and salads. Mon–Thurs 12.30–2.45pm & 6–11.30am, Fri & Sat 12.30–2.45pm & 6pm–midnight, Sun 12.30–2.45pm & 7–11pm; July & Aug closed Sun.

★ **Pommidoro** Piazza dei Sanniti 44 ⊕06 445 2692; map p.50. Family-run Roman trattoria in San Lorenzo that's been around forever. The speciality is great Roman homecooking, very seasonal, with an emphasis on grilled lamb and game, cooked on a big open grill. All the pasta classics too, with a great *carbonara* among other things. Mon–Sat 12.30–3pm & 7–11pm.

Terre e Domus Largo di Foro di Traiano 84 ⊕06 6994 0273; map p.55. Situated just off Piazza Venezia – a relative restaurant desert – this place couldn't be more central. It serves up classic Roman and Lazio dishes in a bright contemporary interior. Stop by for the evening *aperitivo* buffet (from 6pm) to enjoy the view of Trajan's Column without the crowds. Daily 7.30am–12.30am.

Tram Tram Via dei Reti 44–46 ⊕06 490 416; map p.50. In a grungy location but cosy inside, this cool and animated San Lorenzo restaurant serves good Roman classics, Pugliese seafood dishes and unusual salads. Tues–Sun 12.30–3.30pm & 7.30–11.30pm.

★ **Trattoria Monti** Via di San Vito 13/A ⊕06 446 6573; map p.50. Small, family-run restaurant that specializes in the cuisine of the Marche region – which means great pasta, interesting cabbage-wrapped starters and mainly meaty *secondi*. It's pricey (at least €45/person) but popular – book at least two days in advance. Tues–Sat 1–2.45pm & 8–10.45pm, Sun 1–2.45pm.

Valentino Via del Boschetto 37 ⊕06 488 0643; map p.53. With only a faded Peroni sign above the door, this trattoria is easy to miss. Inside, it's always buzzing, with closely packed tables. You'll find lots of grilled meat options, plus a scamorza (grilled cheese) menu. Mon–Sat 12.30–2pm & 8–11pm.

THE CELIAN HILL AND SAN GIOVANNI

Charly's Sauciere Via San Giovanni in Laterano 270 ⊕06 7049 5666; map p.50. If the background *chansons* don't make you think you're in France – albeit a mythical one from the 1930s – the menu certainly will, with lots of French classics. Moderate to high prices – soups and starters around €12, mains €22. It's just a 5min walk from the Colosseum. Mon–Sat 7.30–11.30pm.

Luzzi Via San Giovanni in Laterano 88 ⊕06 709 6332; map p.53. Midway between San Giovanni in Laterano and the Colosseum, this bustling restaurant is a good choice amid the tourist joints of the neighbourhood. The food is hearty and no-frills, there's outside seating and it's extremely cheap – *secondi* go for €7–13. There are pizzas, too. Daily except Wed noon–midnight.

TESTACCIO

Agustarello Via G. Branca 98 ⊕06 574 6585; map p.50. Moderately priced Testaccio place serving genuine Roman cuisine – all the offal classics, as well as great steaks and pork chops – in a simple, old-fashioned atmosphere. *Primi* go for around €12, mains €12–18. Mon–Sat 12.30–3pm & 7.30–11.30pm.

Da Remo Piazza Santa Maria in Liberatrice 44 ⊕06 574 6270; map p.50. No-nonsense Testaccio pizzeria serving some of the crispiest thin-crust Roman pizzas you'll find. Mon–Sat 7pm–1am; closed 3 weeks in Aug.

★ **Flavio al Velavevodetto** Via di Monte Testaccio 97 ⊕06 574 4194, ⊛ristorantevelavevodetto.it; map p.50. Very reasonable restaurant carved out from Monte Testaccio. All the standard Roman classics are on offer, as well as some fish dishes, and its outdoor patios are a delightful venue for summer meals. Daily 12.30–3pm & 7.45–11pm.

TRASTEVERE

Ai Marmi Viale Trastevere 53–59 ⊕06 580 0919; map p.50. Nicknamed "the mortuary" because of its stark interior and marble tables, this place serves unique "supplì al telefono" (deep-fried rice balls, so named because of the string of mozzarella it forms when you take a bite), fresh baccalà and good Roman pizza. Daily (except Wed) 6.30pm–2.20am.

Da Augusto Piazza de Renzi 15 ⊕06 580 3798; map p.53. A Trastevere old-timer serving Roman basics outside on the cobbles in the summer months. You can get a good meal for about €15 here, including a glass of robust house wine. Expect offerings such as pasta and soup starters, and daily meat and fish specials – not haute cuisine, but decent, hearty Roman cooking. No bookings taken, and no credit cards. Daily 12.30–3pm & 8–11pm.

Da Enzo Via dei Vascellari 29 ⊕06 581 2260, ⊛daenzoal29.com; map p.50. A tiny restaurant close to the river in Trastevere that does tasty basic Roman food at decent prices – a million miles away from some of the glitzy new places that have opened up over in the district's busier quarter. Mon–Sat 12.30–3pm & 7.30–11pm.

Da Ivo Via di San Francesco a Ripa 158 ⊕06 581 7082; map p.50. The archetypal Trastevere pizzeria, almost in danger of becoming a caricature, but still good. Arrive early

to avoid a chaotic queue. Mon & Wed–Sat 7.30pm–1am, Sun noon–4pm & 7.30pm–1am.

Da Lucia Vicolo del Mattonato 2 ☎06 580 3601; map p.53. Outdoor Trastevere dining in summer is at its traditional best at this wonderful old Roman trattoria. *Spaghetti cacio e pepe* is the speciality. Get here early for a table outside. Tues–Sun 12.30–3pm & 7.30–11pm.

Glass Hostaria Vicolo dè Cinque 58 ☎06 5833 5903; map p.53. Trastevere's smartest dining option is this Michelin-starred restaurant, with renowned chef Cristina Bowerman in the kitchen. On the menu you might find tagliatelle with wild asparagus, black garlic and lemon, or crab with truffle sauce. The nine-course tasting menu is €150. Tues–Sun 7.30–11.30pm.

★ **Le Mani in Pasta** Via dei Genovesi 37 ☎06 581 6017; map p.50. This small and cosy restaurant cooks up fantastic pasta and fish dishes; a full meal with wine will set you back €40–50 per head. It's often very crowded, so it's worth reserving. Tues–Sun 12.20–3pm & 7.30–11.30pm.

VILLA BORGHESE AND NORTH

★ **Metamorfosi** Via Giovanni Antonelli 30 ☎06 807 6839, ⓦmetamorfosiroma.it; map p.50. Roy Caceres' Michelin-starred *Metamorfosi* in super-smart Parioli is an absolute delight, with spectacular food served with grace, but not pomposity, in the elegantly restrained dining room. The tasting menus are excellent value for such quality (€100 for six dishes, €130 for ten). Mon–Fri 12.30–2.30pm & 8–10.30pm, Sat 8–10.30pm.

Osteria Flaminio Via Flaminia 279 ☎06 323 6900, ⓦosteriaflaminio.com; map p.50. This airy and informal bistro-style restaurant is convenient for MAXXI and the Auditorium. Expect to pay around €35 per head for a full meal with wine. Daily 12.30–2.30pm & 7.30pm–11.30pm.

THE VATICAN AND PRATI

Passaguai Via Pomponio Leto 1 ☎06 8745 1358, ⓦpassaguai.it; map p.53. Run by the same people as *Sorpasso* (see below), this basement wine bar serves great platters of cheese, cold cuts, salads and various other snacks to go with its excellent choice of wine. Always busy, with a great vibe. Mon–Fri 10am–2am, Sat & Sun 6pm–2am.

Romeo Chef & Baker Villa Silla 26 ☎06 3211 0120, ⓦromeo.roma.it; map p.50. Not only a restaurant, but also a wine bar, baker's and grocer's, so you have no excuse not to pop in, either for a quick glass of wine and a plate of cheese, or for a full meal enjoyed in the relentlessly futuristic interior. It's not especially cheap – *primi* are €14–17, *secondi* €16–20 – but the food is pretty good. Tues–Sat 4am–2am, Sun noon–2am.

Sorpasso Via Properzio 31/33 ☎06 8902 4554, ⓦsorpasso.info; map p.53. Wine bar and restaurant with a great choice of wines by the glass, and a menu that runs from cheese and cold cuts to risotto and pasta dishes that change daily, along with steaks and other mains. Enjoy the full menu in the back room, or just snack at the table outside or by the marble-topped bar. Mon–Fri 7.30am–1am, Sat 9am–1am.

DRINKING

There's no shortage of **bars** in Rome. There's also been a recent upsurge in **wine bars** (*enoteche* or *vinerie*); the old ones have gained new cachet, and newer ones are springing up too, often with accompanying gourmet menus or just plates of salami and cheese. Bear in mind that there is sometimes considerable crossover between Rome's bars, restaurants and clubs. For the most part, the places we have listed are drinking spots, but you can eat, sometimes quite substantially, at many of them, and several could be classed just as easily as clubs, with loud music and occasionally even an entrance charge. Campo de' Fiori, Monti, Trastevere and Testaccio are the densest and most happening parts of town.

CENTRO STORICO

Abbey Theatre Via del Governo Vecchio 51 ☎06 686 1341, ⓦabbey-rome.com; map p.55. The most central and perhaps most convivial Irish pub in the city, with a good mix of Italians and expats, regular sport on TV and live music, as well as basic pub food. Daily noon–2am.

Bar del Fico Piazza del Fico 26 ☎06 889 2321; map p.53. One of the nicest places for an outside drink in the *centro storico*, on its own peaceful square but right at the heart of Rome's urban buzz. You can also eat here in the evenings. Daily 8am–2am.

★ **Cul de Sac** Piazza Pasquino 73 ☎06 6880 1094, ⓦenotecaculdesacroma.it; map p.55. Busy, long-running wine bar with an excellent wine list, a great city-centre location with outside seating, and decent wine-bar food – cold meats, cheeses, salads and soups. One of the best *centro storico* locations for a snack. Daily 8am–2am.

Gin Corner Hotel Adriano, Via di Pallacorda 2 ☎06 9453 4255, ⓦhoteladriano.com; map p.55. Dedicated to all things gin, the *Gin Corner* in the *Hotel Adriano* is tended by expert bar staff. Tell them what you like and they'll come up with something to hit the spot. Daily 6pm–midnight.

CAMPO DE' FIORI AND THE GHETTO

Barnum Café Via del Pellegrino 87 ☎306 6476 0483, ⓦbarnumcafe.com; map p.55. Café by day (see page 99), great cocktail bar by night, this trendy spot lies just off Campo de' Fiori, but its cocktails are a million miles from the watery mojitos normally found in the piazza. Mon 9am–midnight, Tues–Sat 9am–2am.

1

FIVE GREAT WINE BARS

Cul de Sac see page 103
Il Goccetto see page 104
La Barrique see page 104
L'Angolo Divino see page 104
Passaguai see page 103

Il Goccetto Via dei Banchi Vecchi 14 ⓣ 06 686 4268; map p.55. A short walk from Campo de' Fiori, this is one of the city centre's nicest wine bars, with lots of options by the glass and good plates of cheese and salami to go with them. Mon 6.30pm–midnight, Tues–Sat noon–2.30pm & 6.30pm–midnight.

L'Angolo Divino Via dei Balestrari 12 ⓣ 06 686 4413; map p.53. A peaceful haven after the furore of Campo de' Fiori, this wine bar has a large selection of wine, and simple wine-bar food – bread, cheese, cold cuts, soups and the like. Tues–Sat 10.30am–3pm & 5pm–1.30am, Mon & Sun 5pm–1.30am; closed one week in Aug.

★ **Open Baladin** Via degli Specchi ⓣ 06 683 8989; map p.53. Central Rome's ultimate birreria, operated by the Baladin brewing company, and with a stark, modern interior and literally hundreds of mainly artisanal Italian beers to choose from. Daily noon–2am.

Scholars' Lounge Via del Plebiscito 101/B ⓣ 06 6920 2208, ⓦ scholarsloungerome.com; map p.55. One of the better city-centre Irish pubs, with regular live music and giant screens showing Premier League football and other sports. Mon–Fri 11am–3am, Sat & Sun 10am–3am.

THE TRIDENTE AND QUIRINALE

Antica Enoteca Via della Croce 76/B ⓣ 06 679 0896, ⓦ anticaenoteca.com; map p.53. This friendly wine bar is one of Rome's oldest, and has a lively, casual feel despite the high-rent district. It serves lots of wines by the glass, as well as a selection of hot and cold dishes. Mon & Wed–Sun noon–1pm.

★ **Locarno** Via della Penna 22 ⓣ 06 361 0841, ⓦ hotellocarno.com; map p.50. The slightly decadent atmosphere graced with hip cocktail-sippers and a clubby backroom make the *Locarno* Rome's most egalitarian hotel bar. It's frequented by literati, artists, princes, paupers, poseurs, fashionistas and just ordinary folk, and warm weather adds a roof terrace to the mix. Daily 7pm–1am.

Rosati Piazza del Popolo 5 ⓣ 06 322 5859; map p.50. This bar hosted left-wingers, bohemians and writers in years gone by, and although that's no longer really the case its cocktails and food still draw the crowds. A nice place from which to watch the action on Piazza del Popolo. Daily 7.30am–11.30pm.

THE ESQULINE, MONTI AND TERMINI

Ai Tre Scalini Via Panisperna 251 ⓣ 06 4890 7495; map p.53. Great, easy-to-miss little Monti bar, cosy and comfortable, with a good wine list, beer on tap and food that runs from cheese and salami plates to a good *melanzane parmigiana*. Daily 12.30pm–1am.

Al Vino al Vino Via dei Serpenti 19 ⓣ 06 485 803; map p.53. Seriously good wine bar situated on the Monti district's most happening street. Snacks too – generally Sicilian specialities. Daily 10am–2pm & 6pm–midnight.

Druid's Den Via San Martino ai Monti 28 ⓣ 06 4890 4781, ⓦ druidspubrome.com; map p.53. Appealing Irish pub near Santa Maria Maggiore with a genuine Celtic feel (and owners). It has a mixed expat/Italian clientele, and is not just for the homesick. Daily noon–2am.

Finnegan Via Leonina 66 ⓣ 06 474 7026, ⓦ finnegan pub.com; map p.53. Another of the area's crop of Irish pubs, with live football on TV, pool, and a friendly expat crowd. There's seating outside, too, on this bustling Monti street. Daily 1pm–1am.

La Barrique Via del Boschetto 41/B ⓣ 06 4782 5953; map p.53. This lovely Monti wine bar is a great spot for an *aperitivo*, and platters of meats and cheeses keep pre-dinner hunger pangs at bay. Mon–Sat 1–3pm & 7pm–12.30am.

THE CELIAN HILL AND SAN GIOVANNI

Caffè Propaganda Via Claudia 15 ⓣ 06 9453 4255, ⓦ caffepropaganda.it; map p.50. This studiedly informal Celio restaurant has a bar area in the front room with an impressive display of bottles presided over by Rome cocktail star Patrick Pistolesi, the barman-in-chief. Mon–Fri noon–3.30pm & 6.30pm–2am, Sat & Sun noon–2am.

Il Pentagrappolo Via Celimontana 21/B ⓣ 06 709 6301, ⓦ ilpentagrappolo.com; map p.50. Celio wine bar with lots of good wines by the glass, cheese plates and the usual cold cuts; food is served right up until 1am, and there's live piano music several nights a week. Tues–Sun noon–3pm & 6pm–1am.

THE AVENTINE AND TESTACCIO

Oasi della Birra Piazza Testaccio 41; map p.50. Subterranean Testaccio bar with a beer selection that would rival anywhere in the world and plenty of wine to choose from as well, plus generous plates of cheese and salami. Mon–Sat 5pm–1.30am, Sat 5pm–2am, Sun 6pm–1am.

Tram Depot Via Marmorata 13 ⓣ 06 4178 0081; map p.50. Fashioned from an old tram and with (only) outside tables, this kiosk is open all day for drinks and snacks, but really comes into its own from *aperitivo* time onwards. Mon–Thurs 7.30am–midnight, Fri–Sun 7.30am–2am.

TRASTEVERE

★ **Ma Che Siete Venuti a Fà** Via Benedetta 25 ⓣ 06 9727 5218; map p.53. You'll find an amazing choice of artisanal beers from all over the world in this cosy Trastevere

1

bar – most of them you won't find anywhere else in the city, or even Italy. Daily 11am–2am.

Ombre Rosse Piazza Sant'Egidio 12/13 ⊕06 588 4155; map p.53. A people-watching spot that has become a Trastevere institution, especially for a morning cappuccino, but it's also good for light meals and evening drinks. Daily 10am–2am.

San Calisto Piazza San Calisto 4; map p.50. This bar attracts a huge, slighly scruffy crowd on late summer nights; the booze is cheap, and you can sit at outside tables for no extra cost. During the day it's simply a great spot to sip a cappuccino in the sunshine. Mon–Sat 6am–2am.

THE VATICAN AND PRATI

Morrison's Via Ennio Quirino Visconti 88 ⊕06 322 2265, ⊕morrisons.it; map p.5353⊠ An Irish themed pub – although not all is as it seems, for as well as the usual beers and (good) pub food they also make spectacularly good cocktails, and have a top-notch whisky and gin selection. Daily 4pm–2am.

NIGHTLIFE

Roman nightlife is a lot cooler and more varied than it used to be. There are a few smart **clubs**, principally in the centre of town, but also quite a few smaller and more **alternative clubs** and **live music venues**, mainly confined to the neighbourhoods of Testaccio and Ostiense, and in up-and-coming Pigneto and Prenestino to the east of Termini – though bear in mind that some clubs close during Aug or move to summer premises in Ostia or Fregene.

CLUBS

Akab Via di Monte Testaccio 69 ⊕06 5725 0585, ⊕akabcave.com; map p.50. *Akab* is built into an old carpenter's shop on two floors, one on ground level, the other a cave-like room below. Head down for Thursday's popular "Milkshake" (r'n'b, hip-hop) night. Thurs–Sat 11pm–5am.

Goa Via Libetta 13 ⊕06 574 8277, ⊕goaclub.com; map p.50. This long-running Ostiense club is where all the biggest DJs that come to Rome spin. There's a superb sound system playing techno, house and drum'n'bass, and a loungey bar area. Thurs–Sat 11.30pm–5am.

Rashomon Via degli Argonauti 16 ⊕391 730 7386, ⊕rashomonclub.com; map p.50. A two-room live music space with good music and DJ sets at weekends. Fri & Sat 11pm–4am.

Shari Vari Via di Torre Argentina 78 ⊕06 6880 6936, ⊕sharivari.it; map p.55. Full of glammed-up Romans, Shari Vari is one of the city's newest clubs. Set over different levels and with lots of cosy nooks, it's great for people-watching. Saturday's club tunes draw the crowds, but Tuesday's electronica and Sunday's jazz nights are fun too. Tues–Sun midnight–4am.

Vicious Club Via Achille Grandi 7/a ⊕06 7061 4349, ⊕viciousclub.com; map p.50. Its interior lined with mirrors and black walls, Vicious Club's underground feel marks it out from many Roman clubs. It's a cocktail bar Monday to Wednesday, and the rest of the week it hosts djs. Friday's Rock'n Yolk night (indie, nu-wave, electronica, rap) is popular, and there's a monthly gay night. Mon–Sat 10pm–4am.

LIVE MUSIC VENUES

★ **Big Mama** Vicolo S. Francesco a Ripa 18 ⊕06 581 2551, ⊕bigmama.it; map p.50. Trastevere-based jazz/blues club of long standing, hosting nightly acts. Monthly membership costs €8, and then entry is free except for star attractions (when it's important to book ahead). Tues–Sat (and occasionally on Mon) 9pm–1.30am, concerts begin at 10.30pm; closed June to mid-Sept.

Casa del Jazz Viale di Porta Ardeatina 55 ⊕06 704 731, ⊕casajazz.it; Metro B Piramide, or bus #714 from Termini; map p.50. This converted villa in leafy

LGBTQ BARS AND CLUBS

Coming Out Via di San Giovanni in Laterano 8 ⊕06 700 9871, ⊕comingout.it; map p.53. If any area has developed as Rome's LGBTQ zone, it is the stretch between the Colosseum and San Clemente. This little pub is the epicentre of the scene, frequented mostly by a younger clientele. Daily 7am–5.30am.

Garbo Vicolo di Santa Margherita 1/A ⊕06 5832 0782, ⊕garbobar.it; map p.53. Friendly bar, just behind Piazza Santa Maria in Trastevere, with a relaxed atmosphere and a nice setting. Daily 9pm–6am.

L'Alibi Via Monte Testaccio 44 ⊕320 354 1185, ⊕lalibi.it; map p.50. This predominantly, but by no means exclusively, male venue is one of Rome's oldest gay clubs, situated in the heart of the city's alternative night scene in Testaccio. It's no longer quite cutting-edge, but is a good all-round hangout, with a multiroom cellar disco, an upstairs open-air bar and a big terrace to enjoy in the warm months. Oct to mid-June Wed–Sat 11.30pm–5am.

Qube Via di Portonaccio 212 ⊕06 438 5445; map p.50. This club plays host to the extremely successful Muccassassina ("Killer Cow"; ⊕muccassassina.com) gay and drag night every Fri. 11pm–4am, though check website for dates as opening can be irregular.

1

surroundings is the ultimate jazz-lovers' complex, with a book and CD store and restaurant, recording studios and a 150-seat auditorium that hosts jazz names most nights of the week. Admission €12–25. Show times generally 9pm.

Fanfulla 5/a Via Fanfulla da Lodi 5a ☎ 06 8902 1632; Metro C Pigneto; map p.50. Just off Via Prenestina, this intimate space hosts live music and assorted cultural happenings, and also has a bar. Daily 10pm–3am.

Fonclea Via Crescenzio 82/A ☎ 06 689 6302, ⓦ fonclea.it; map p.53. Busy and happening basement bar in the Vatican area that hosts regular live music – usually jazz, soul and funk. Happy hour 6–8.30pm. Daily 6pm–2am; concerts start at 9.30pm.

Live Alcazar Via Cardinale Merry del Val 14 ☎ 340 560 1705, ⓦ alcazarlive.it; map p.50. An ex-cinema has been given new life with the opening of this new venue that mixes music, theatre, cinema, art and comedy. Mon–Thurs are (original language) film nights, while Thurs–Sun there's live music, cocktails and a happy-hour buffet. A restaurant overlooks the stage. Daily 7pm–2am.

Planet Roma Via del Commercio 36 ☎ 06 574 7826, ⓦ planetroma.com; map p.50. Housed in an ex-factory off Via Ostiense, this venue has space for up to seven simultaneous events – live music, DJs, exhibitions or theatre. Check website for listings and hours.

ENTERTAINMENT

Even locals would admit that Rome is a bit of a backwater for the performing arts. Relatively few international-class performers put in an appearance here, and there have been significant cutbacks to the city's cultural funds in recent years. Nevertheless, what the arts scene may lack in quality is made up for by the charm of the city's settings. The summer **opera** performances at the Baths of Caracalla are resounding occasions, while Rome's **summer festival** – ⓦ estateromana.comune.roma.it – ensures a good range of classical music, opera, theatre and cinema throughout the warmer months, often in picturesque locations.

CLASSICAL MUSIC AND OPERA

Auditorium Parco della Musica Viale P. de Coubertin 30 ☎ 06 6006 0900, box office ☎ 892 101, ⓦ auditorium.com. This landmark musical complex is Rome's most prestigious venue. It is home to the city's premier orchestra, the Accademia Nazionale di Santa Cecilia, who are resident part of the year in its largest hall, while two smaller venues host smaller chamber, choral, recital and experimental works. Box office daily 11am–8pm.

Oratorio del Gonfalone Via del Gonfalone 32/A ☎ 06 687 5952, ⓦ www.oratoriogonfalone.eu. This lovely theatre stages performances of chamber music, with an emphasis on the Baroque, every Thurs at 8.30pm and Sun at 11am, with the season running from mid-Oct to mid-May. Tickets cost €20–25; telephone reservations are strongly recommended.

Teatro dell'Opera di Roma Piazza Beniamino Gigli 1 ☎ 06 4816 0255, ⓦ operaroma.it. Nobody compares it to La Scala, but cheap tickets are a lot easier to come by at Rome's opera and ballet venue – they start at around €20 for opera, less for ballet – and important artists do sometimes perform here. If you buy the very cheapest tickets, bring some high-powered binoculars, as you'll need them in order to see anything at all. Don't miss the summer opera season, set in the Baths of Caracalla. Box office Mon–Sat 10am–6pm, Sun 9am–1.30pm.

FILM

Casa del Cinema Largo Marcello Mastroianni 1 ☎ 06 0608, ⓦ casadelcinema.it. Right by the Porta Pinciana entrance to the Villa Borghese, this cinema hosts film premieres, festivals, reruns and retrospectives, often in the original language. In summer it moves outside, among Villa Borghese's umbrella pines.

L'Isola di Roma Isola Tiberina ⓦ isoladiroma.it. This summer festival sees films screened daily on the Tiber island – few in their original language, but there are occasional special events that bring in directors or actors for films in

CALCIO

Rome's two big **football** teams are **AS Roma** (ⓦ asroma.it) and **SS Lazio** (ⓦ sslazio.it). Roma and Lazio currently play on alternate weekends between Sept and May at the Stadio Olimpico (ⓦ stadiodi.it/olimpico-roma), northwest of the city centre, though Roma are due to move to a new stadium in the coming years. You can buy **tickets** through booking agencies such as ⓦ listicket.it and ⓦ ticketone.it, but it's cheapest to get them from one of the dedicated outlets for Roma (Piazza Colonna 360 on Via del Corso) or Lazio (Via Calderini 66 near the Stadio Olimpico). You need to carry photo ID when you buy a ticket and when you go to the game. To get to the **Stadio Olimpico** on public transport, you can take tram #2 from Piazzale Flaminio to Piazza Mancini or bus #910 from Termini and then walk across the river; alternatively, take bus #32 from Piazza Risorgimento or #628 from Via del Plebiscito by Piazza Venezia.

the original language. The setting is magical and there are good food stalls, too.

Multisala Barberini Piazza Barberini 24/26 ⓣ06 8639 1361, ⓦmultisala.barberini.18tickets.it. This central cinema offers first-run English-language films, some in the original language.

Nuovo Olimpia Via in Lucina 16 ⓣ06 861 1068, ⓦnuovoolimpia.ccroma.18tickets.it. Very central, just off Via del Corso, with two screens, and featuring films in their original language most days.

SHOPPING

At first glance, you may wonder where to start when it comes to **shopping** in a busy city like Rome. In fact the city promises a more appealing shopping experience than you might think, and there are plenty of colourful shopping streets. There are some vibrant **markets** too: Porta Portese (see page 84) is chaotic but fun, while the market at Testaccio (Mon–Sat 7am–3.30pm) is great for foodie souvenirs. **Fashion** straight from the catwalk is well represented on the streets close to the Spanish Steps, where you'll find all the major A-list designers; more mainstream and chain fashion stores cluster on Via del Corso, Via Cola di Rienzo (near the Vatican) and Via Nazionale; while the streets of the Monti district are home to an increasing number of stylish independent boutiques, as is Via del Governo Vecchio in the *centro storico*. Or just follow your nose – in Rome you're almost bound to stumble across something interesting.

BOOKS, MUSIC AND STATIONERY

★ **The Almost Corner Bookshop** Via del Moro 45 ⓣ06 583 6942; map p.53. Of all Rome's English bookshops, this stalwart Trastevere store is the best bet for having the very latest titles and lots of Rome-related reading. Mon–Thurs 10am–7.30pm, Fri–Sun 10am–8pm.

Fabriano Via del Babuino 172; map p.53. This long-running chain sells bright and contemporary stationery, wallets and briefcases. Daily 10am–8pm.

Soul Food Via di S. Giovanni in Laterano 192–194; map p.50. This vinyl junkie's paradise has lots of stuff from the 1960s and 1970s, and genuinely enthusiastic staff too. Tues–Sat 10.30am–1.30pm & 3.30–7.30pm.

CLOTHES AND ACCESSORIES

★ **Arsenale** Via del Pellegrino 172 ⓣ06 686 1380; map p.55. Just off Campo de' Fiori, this funky womenswear boutique has great dresses by the owner Patrizia Pieroni and lots of other stuff by small independent designers. Mon 3.30–7.30pm, Tues–Sat 10am–7.30pm.

Ibiz Via dei Chiavari 39; map p.53. Great leather bags, purses and rucksacks in exciting contemporary designs made on the premises. Mon–Sat 10am–7.30pm.

SBU Via di San Pantaleo 68–69; map p.55. The bafflingly named Strategic Business Unit offers hip menswear – mainly Italian, with the odd Japanese import – including their popular own-brand jeans. There's a small womenswear section too, plus cool, affordable jewellery. Mon–Sat 10am–7pm.

FOOD AND WINE

Castroni Via Cola di Rienzo 196; map p.53. Huge, labyrinthine food store that's a great place to stock up a large selection of Italian treats including chocolates, pastas, sauces and olive oils – plus a café. There's another city-centre branch are at Via Frattina 79, near the Spanish Steps. Mon–Sat 8.30am–8pm.

Moriondo & Gariglio Via del Pie' di Marmo 21–22; map p.55. The city centre's most sumptuous and refined handmade-chocolate shop – great for exquisitely wrapped gifts. Mon–Fri 9am–7.30pm.

★ **Volpetti** Via Marmorata 47; map p.50. It's worth seeking out this Testaccio deli, which is truly one of Rome's very best. If you're lucky, one of the staff will let you sample their incredible *mozzarella di bufala*. They also have a great *tavola calda* round the corner. Mon–Fri 8.30am–2pm & 4.30–8.15pm, Sat 8.30am–8.30pm.

GIFTS

Old Soccer Via di Ripetta 30; map p.53. Old-fashioned Italian football shirts from around €70 – ironically enough, made in England. Daily 10am–7.30pm.

Roma Store Via della Lungaretta 63; map p.53. Not a football merchandise store but a shop selling classic perfumes, scented soaps, lotions and candles. Only the very finest from Italy, France and England. Daily 10am–8pm.

DIRECTORY

Dentist Absolute Dentistry at Via G. Pisanelli 3 (ⓣ06 3600 3837, ⓦabsolutedentistry.it) is English-speaking and has a 24hr emergency service on ⓣ339 250 7016.

Embassies Australia, Via Bosio 5 ⓣ06 852 721; Britain, Via XX Settembre 80a ⓣ06 4220 0001; Canada, Via Zara 30 ⓣ06 85444 3937; Ireland, Villa Spada, Via Giacomo Medici ⓣ06 585 2381; New Zealand, Via Clitunno 44 ⓣ06 853 7501; US, Via Veneto 121 ⓣ06 46741.

Emergencies Police or any emergency service ⓣ113; *Carabinieri* ⓣ112; Fire ⓣ115; Ambulance ⓣ118. Both the police and the *carabinieri* have offices in Termini. Otherwise the *questura* (main police office) is at Via San Vitale 15, off Via Nazionale; report any thefts to the police here.

Hospitals If you are seriously ill or involved in an accident, go straight to the *Pronto Soccorso* (casualty) of the nearest hospital, or phone ⓣ113 and ask for *ospedale* or *ambulanza*.

The most central hospitals with emergency facilities are Fatebenefratelli on the Isola Tiberina (T 06 68371), San Giovanni at Via A. Aradam 8 (T 06 77051) and Santo Spirito, near the Vatican at Lungotevere in Sassia 1 (T 06 68351).
Internet Many of Rome's cafés and bars, and most of its hotels, offer free wi-fi. If you need an internet café, try *AntiCafé* at Via Veio 4/B, San Giovanni (Mon–Fri 9am–9pm, Sat & Sun 10am–9pm; T 06 7049 4442); or *Yex* at Piazza Sant'Andrea della Valle 1, near Campo de' Fiori (daily 9am–10pm; T 06 9727 3136).
Lost property For lost property call T 06 6769 3214 (Mon, Tues, Wed & Fri 8.30am–1pm, Thurs 8.30am–5pm); the office is at Circonvallazione Ostiense 191 (Garbatella Metro).
Pharmacies Piram, Via Nazionale 228 (T 06 488 0754), is open 24hr.
Post office The main post office is on Piazza S. Silvestro (Mon–Fri 8.20am–7.05pm, Sat 8.20am–12.35pm).

Out from the city: Ostia Antica and Tivoli

You may find there's quite enough in Rome to keep you occupied during your stay, but it can be a hot, oppressive city and if you're around long enough you shouldn't feel any guilt about seeing something of the countryside. **Tivoli**, less than an hour by bus east of Rome, is a small town famous for the travertine quarries nearby, the landscaped gardens and parks of its Renaissance villas, and a fine ancient Roman villa just outside. **Ostia**, in the opposite direction near the sea, and similarly easy to reach on public transport, was home to the port of Rome in classical times, and the well-preserved site is well worth seeing.

Ostia Antica

Viale dei Romagnoli 717 • Tues–Sun: Nov to mid-Feb 8.30am–4.30pm; mid-Feb to mid-March 8.30am–5pm; late March 8.30am–5.30pm; end March to Aug 8.30am–7.15pm; Sept 8.30am–7pm; Oct 8.30am–6.30pm; last entry 1hr before closing; Museo Ostiense 8.30am–1hr before the site closing time • €10, or €12 if there's an exhibition on; free first Sun of the month • T 06 5635 0215, W www.ostiaantica.beniculturali.it

There are two Ostias: one a rather over-visited seaside resort, **Lido di Ostia**; the other, one of the finest ancient Roman sites – the excavations of **OSTIA ANTICA** – which are on a par with anything you'll see in Rome itself (or indeed elsewhere in Italy) and easily merit the half-day journey out from the city.

The site of Ostia Antica marked the coastline in classical times, and the town that grew up here was the port of ancient Rome, a thriving place whose commercial activities were vital to the city further upstream. The **excavations** are relatively free of tourists, and it's much easier to reconstruct a Roman town from these than from any amount of pottering around the Roman Forum. The site is also very spread out, so be prepared for a fair amount of walking.

The site

The main street, the **Decumanus Maximus**, leads west from the entrance, past the **Baths of Neptune** on the right (where there's an interesting mosaic) to the town's commercial centre, otherwise known as the **Piazzale delle Corporazioni**, for the remains of shops and trading offices that still fringe the central square. These represented commercial enterprises from all over the ancient world, and each was once fronted by a mosaic of boats, fish and suchlike to denote their trade as well as their origin. Flanking the southern side of the square, the **theatre** has been much restored but is nonetheless impressive, enlarged by Septimius Severus in the second century AD to hold up to four thousand people; it hosts theatre performances in the summer. Further along, the Decumanus Maximus runs past the substantial remains of one of Ostia's largest **horrea** (warehouses), buildings that once stood all over the city. Turn right up **Via dei Molini**, then left, to reach the **House of Diana**, probably the best-preserved private house in Ostia, with a dark, mysterious set of rooms around a central courtyard, with a *mithraeum* (a shrine devoted to the cult of Mithras) at the back. Just along the street is the delightful **Thermopolium** – an ancient Roman café, complete with seats outside, a high counter, display shelves and even wall paintings of parts of the menu. Just beyond

the Thermopolium are the high brick walls of the **Capitolium**, Ostia's most important temple, dating from the second century AD, overlooking the shattered columns of the **Forum** and the **Temple of Rome and Augustus**. Further on down the main street, more *horrea*, superbly preserved and complete with pediment and names inscribed on the marble, merit a detour off to the right; although you can't enter, you can peer into the courtyard. Beyond, the **House of Cupid and Psyche** has a courtyard you can walk into, its rooms clearly discernible on one side, a colourful marbled floor at the top and a columned nymphaeum, with marble niches, on the right.

Next door to the site's café-restaurant, the **Museo Ostiense** holds a variety of articles from the site, including a statue of Mithras killing a bull and some fine sarcophagi and statuary from the imperial period.

ARRIVAL AND DEPARTURE — OSTIA ANTICA

By train Take the metro to Piramide station (line B), then go up the escalator, turn left and go down the steps to Roma-Lido station, where you can take a train to Ostia Antica; you can do the whole journey with a single €1.50 metro ticket. The site is a 5min walk from the station.

By car There's a car park at the site.

Tivoli

Perched high on a hill just 40km from Rome, **TIVOLI** has always been something of a retreat from the city. In classical days it was a retirement town for wealthy Romans; later, during Renaissance times, it became the playground of the city's most well-to-do families, who built their country villas out here. Nowadays the moneyed classes have mostly gone, but Tivoli does very nicely on the fruits of its still-thriving travertine business, exporting the precious stone worldwide (the quarries line the main road into town from Rome). To do justice to its gardens and villas – especially if Villa Adriana is on your list, as indeed it should be – you'll need time, so it's worth setting out early.

Villa d'Este

Piazza Trento 5 • Mon 2pm–1hr before sunset, Tues–Sun 8.30am–1hr before sunset; June–Sept closes 10.45pm (last entrance 9.45pm) • €10; free first Sun of the month • ⓣ 199 766 166, ⓦ www.villadestetivoli.info • The Villa d'Este is a 2min walk from Tivoli's Piazza Garibaldi

Tivoli's major sight is the **Villa d'Este**, across the main square of Largo Garibaldi. The country villa of Cardinal Ippolito d'Este, it has been restored to its original state, with beautiful Mannerist frescoes in its seven ground-floor rooms showing scenes from the history of the d'Este family in Tivoli. Most people, however, come here to see the **garden**, which peels away down the hill in a succession of terraces dotted with **fountains**. Among the highlights are the Fontana dell'Ovato on the right, topped with statues on a curved terrace around artificial mountains, behind which is a rather dank arcade. Beyond are the dark, gushing Grottoes of the Sibyls and behind them the Fontana dell'Organo, a giant and very elaborate water-organ which plays every couple of hours; right in front, the similarly large Fontana del Nettuno ejects a massive torrent down into a set of central fish ponds. Finish up on the far side of the garden, where the Rometta or "Little Rome" has reproductions of the city's major buildings and a boat holding an obelisk.

Villa Gregoriana

Piazza Tempio di Vesta • March Tues–Sun 10am–5pm; April–June & Sept daily 10am–6.30pm; July & Aug 10am–8pm; Oct 10am–4/6.30pm; Nov to mid-Dec 10am–4pm; last entry 1hr before closing • €6 • ⓣ 0774 332 650, ⓦ visitfai.it/parcovillagregoriana • Turn right off Piazza Garibaldi to Piazza Santa Croce and follow Via del Trevio through the pedestrianized old town to Piazza del Plebiscito, where Via Palatina continues down to the bridge over the gorge; cross over, and the back entrance is just around the corner on the left – a 10min walk in all

Tivoli's second main attraction, the **Villa Gregoriana**, isn't actually a villa at all, but an impressively wild set of landscaped **gardens**, created when Pope Gregory XVI diverted the flow of the river here in 1831 to ease the periodic flooding of the town. At least as interesting and beautiful as the d'Este estate, it remains less well known and less visited,

1

and has none of the latter's conceits – its vegetation is lush and overgrown, descending into a gorge over 60m deep.

There are two main **waterfalls** – the larger Grande Cascata on the far side, and a small Bernini-designed one at the neck of the gorge. The best thing to do is walk the main path in reverse, starting at the back entrance, over the river, and winding down to the bottom of the canyon. The ruins of a Republican-era villa cling to the far side of the gorge, and you can peek into them and then catch your breath down by the so-called Grotto of the Mermaid, before scaling the other side to the Grotto of Neptune, reached by a tunnelled-out passage through the rock, where you can sit right by the roaring falls. The path leads up from here to an exit and the substantial remains of an ancient **Temple of Vesta**, which marks the main entrance to the villa. You can take a breather at the small **café** here, and the view is probably Tivoli's best – down into the chasm and across to the high green hills that ring the town.

Villa Adriana

Largo Marguerite Yourcenar 1 • Daily 8.30am–1hr before sunset; ticket office closes 1hr before • €10; free first Sun of the month • ⓣ 0774 382 733, ⓦ coopculture.it • The CAT #4 bus from Tivoli's Piazza Garibaldi stops right outside the villa (roughly every 45min, 6 daily on Sun); buses also run direct from Rome (see page 95)

Just outside town, at the bottom of the hill, **Villa Adriana** casts the invention of the Tivoli popes and cardinals very much into the shade. This was probably the largest and most sumptuous villa in the Roman Empire, the retirement home of the Emperor Hadrian for a short while between 135 AD and his death three years later, and it occupies an enormous site. There's no point in doing it at a gallop and, taken with the rest of Tivoli, it makes for a long day's sightseeing.

The site is one of the most soothing spots around Rome, its stones almost the epitome of romantic, civilized ruins. The imperial palace buildings proper are in fact one of the least well preserved parts of the complex, but much else is clearly recognizable. Hadrian was a great traveller and a keen architect, and parts of the villa were inspired by buildings he had seen throughout the empire. The massive **Pecile**, for instance, through which you enter, is a reproduction of a building in Athens; and the **Canopus**, on the opposite side of the site, is a liberal copy of the sanctuary of Serapis near Alexandria, its long, elegant channel of water fringed by sporadic columns and statues leading up to a **Temple of Serapis** at the far end. Nearby, a **museum** displays the latest finds from the ongoing excavations, though most of the extensive original discoveries have found their way back to Rome. Walking back towards the entrance, make your way across the upper storey of the so-called Pretorio, a former warehouse, and down to the remains of two bath complexes. Beyond is a fishpond with a **cryptoporticus** (underground passageway) winding around underneath, and behind that the relics of the emperor's imperial apartments. The **Teatro Marittimo**, adjacent, with its island in the middle of a circular pond, is the place to which it's believed Hadrian would retire at siesta time to be sure of being alone.

ARRIVAL AND DEPARTURE — TIVOLI

By bus COTRAL buses for Tivoli leave every 10min from outside Ponte Mammolo metro station in Rome (line B), dropping off on Tivoli's main square, Piazza Garibaldi (50min). There are 7 buses a day (Mon–Sat) from Ponte Mammolo to Villa Adriana (ⓦ cotralspa.it), dropping off 300m from the site; the more frequent Rome–Tivoli buses stop 1km from the site – ask the driver to drop you off.

By train Trains run hourly from Tiburtina station (on metro line B) to Tivoli (40–50min).

EATING AND DRINKING

Pizzeria Reginella Via Sante Viola 4/6 ⓣ 0774 333 729. A couple of minutes' walk from the Villa d'Este, this friendly, casual pizzeria with outdoor tables also serves home-made pasta dishes and healthy salads; you can eat very well here

1

for little more than €10. Daily 10.30am–11.30pm, closes 9.30pm in winter.

Sibilla Via Sibilla 50 ⊕ 0774 335 281, ⊛ ristorantesibilla.com. Overlooking the Villa Gregoriana, right by the back entrance, this is one of the best restaurants in Tivoli. Roman cuisine, and great pasta in particular (ravioli *alla gricia* €9), and a fantastic setting if you can bag an outside table. Service is pretty good, too. Tues–Sun 12.30–3pm & 7.30–10.30pm.

Northern Lazio

Northern Lazio, or "Alto Lazio", is quite a different entity from the region south of the capital. Green and wooded in the centre, with few large towns, its steadily more undulating hills hint at the landscapes of Tuscany and Umbria further north. With determination (and, ideally, a car), you can see much of it on day-trips from Rome. Foremost among the area's attractions is the legacy of the **Etruscans**, a sophisticated pre-Roman people swathed in mystery. To the west, some of their most important sites are readily accessible by road or rail – principally the necropolises at **Cerveteri** and **Tarquinia**. Alternatively there's the town and lake at **Bracciano**, and beaches from Tarquinia to **Civitavecchia** – playgrounds for hot and bothered Romans on summer weekends. **Viterbo**, the medieval "city of popes", can serve as a base if you're thinking of a two- or three-day visit, particularly if you're touring without a car. It's close to some fine examples of the region's Mannerist villas and gardens at **Caprarola** and **Bagnaia** – and the amazing monster park at **Bomarzo.**

Etruria and the coast

D.H. Lawrence had pretty much the last word on the plain, low hills stretching **north from Rome** towards the Tuscan border, describing the landscape as "lifeless looking … as if it had given up its last gasp and was now forever inert." His *Etruscan Places*, published in 1932, is one of the best introductions to this pre-Roman civilization and its cities, which, one or two beaches excepted (see page 114), are the main reasons for venturing out here.

Cerveteri

CERVETERI provides the most accessible Etruscan taster from Rome. The settlement here dates back to the tenth century BC. Once known as Caere, it ranked among the top three cities in the twelve-strong Etruscan federation, its wealth derived largely from the mineral-rich **Tolfa hills** to the northeast – a gentle range that gives the plain a much-needed touch of scenic colour. In its heyday, the town spread over 150 hectares (something like thirty times its present size), controlling territory 50km up the coast. By the third century BC, Caere was under Roman control, leading to the decline of Etruscan

LAZIO PUBLIC TRANSPORT

The **Lazio transport system** is divided into seven zones, which spread out concentrically from Rome, and it's possible to buy **season tickets** to travel within them. The **BIRG** (Biglietto Integrato Regionale Giornaliero) is valid all day (until midnight) for unlimited travel on the state railway, COTRAL buses and the Rome metro, but not buses to the airport; prices range from €3.30 to €14 depending on the number of zones. A €9.30 ticket, covering four zones, for example, will get you from Rome to Viterbo. You can also buy three-day passes (**BTR**; Biglietto Turistico Regionale) for €8.90–39.20, and weekly passes (**CIRS**; Carta Integrata Regionale Settimanale) for €13.50–61.50. Vendors – train and bus ticket offices, newspaper stands and tobacconists – can advise you on the required zone, or see ⊛ atac.roma.it. Note that **COTRAL** buses often follow the school-day schedule during the week and run much less frequently on weekends, especially **Sundays**.

CIVITAVECCHIA

The only reason to break a journey in **CIVITAVECCHIA**, 30km north of Cerveteri, is to catch a **ferry to Sardinia**: there are two daily crossings to Olbia (5hr 30min–8hr 15min) and one daily to Cagliari (10hr 30min), as well as a couple of sailings weekly to Arbatax (10hr) and Porto Torres (6hr 30min). Ferries also run to **Sicily** (3 weekly; 14hr). The **docks** are in the city centre at the end of Viale Garibaldi beside the Forte Michelangelo, a ten-minute walk from the **train station**. Beware of taxis (both legal and otherwise) lurking at the port and station: they charge outrageous prices to shuttle you and your luggage around town. If you're planning on staying the night, it's best to arrange a pick-up with your hotel. There is no left-luggage office at the port; you can leave luggage at the train station or at Largo della Pace.

There are **tourist info points** in the port area (W civitavecchia.portmobility.it), in Largo della Pace (daily 6.30am–7.30pm), Varco Vespucci (daily 7am–11pm) and at the Terminal Autostrade del Mare (Mon & Wed 10am–5pm, Tues & Thurs 9.30am–5pm, Fri 10am–2pm). **COTRAL buses** depart from Porta Tarquinia, 100m from Largo della Pace, for Cerveteri, Tarquinia and Viterbo. Free regular **shuttles** whisk passengers from the fortress to the departure piers.

culture in the region. The present town is a thirteenth-century creation, dismissed by D.H. Lawrence – and you really can't blame him – as "forlorn beyond words".

Necropoli di Banditaccia

Piazzale Mario Moretti • Tues–Sun 8.30am–sunset • €6, or €8 combined ticket with the Museo Nazionale Cerite (see below); free first Sun of the month • T 06 994 0651, W tarquinia-cerveteri.it • The necropolis site is just over 1km away from the bus stop at Piazza Aldo Moro and is well signposted from the town; you can take bus D from the piazza but it's a fairly simple walk

The **Necropoli di Banditaccia**, or Etruscan Necropolis, is the largest extant Etruscan burial site. From the seventh to second centuries BC, some fifty thousand Etruscans were buried in this literal city of the dead, weird and fantastically well preserved with complete streets and homes. The Etruscan elite did not practise cremation, preferring to have their remains laid on beds or in sarcophagi carved directly out of the rock. The tombs were kitted out like homes, complete with beds, furniture and wall decorations. Of the nineteen show-tombs, try to see the **Tomba Bella** (Tomb of the Bas-Reliefs), **Tomba dei Letti Funebri** (Tomb of the Funeral Beds) and the **Tomb of the Capitals**. There's a bar-restaurant on site.

Museo Nazionale Cerite

Piazza Santa Maria 1 • Tues–Sun 8.30am–7.30pm • €6, or €8 combined ticket with the Necropoli di Banditaccia (see above) • T 06 994 0651, W tarquinia-cerveteri.it

The **Museo Nazionale Cerite** lies at the top of the old quarter in the sixteenth-century Castello Ruspoli. It has two large rooms containing a fraction of the huge wealth that was buried with the Etruscan dead – vases, terracottas and a run of miscellaneous day-to-day objects; most of the best stuff, though, has been whisked away to Villa Giulia in Rome (see page 86).

ARRIVAL AND DEPARTURE — CERVETERI

By bus The best way to get to Cerveteri is from Rome's Cornelia station (on metro line A) by COTRAL bus (every 20–50min; 1hr); buses drop off in Piazza Aldo Moro. The same Rome–Cerveteri bus also links to the train station 7km away.

By train Trains from Termini, Ostiense, Trastevere and San Pietro stations run to Ladispoli-Cerveteri station (every 30min–1hr; 45min). From here there's a Seatour bus that runs to the site four times daily (Tues–Sat).

Tarquinia

The necropolis at **TARQUINIA** is second only to Cerveteri among northern Lazio's Etruscan sites. Founded in the tenth century BC, the city's population peaked at around one hundred thousand but the Roman juggernaut triggered its decline six

hundred years later and only a warren of graves remains. The town itself is pleasant, its partial walls and crop of medieval towers making it a good place to pass an afternoon after seeing the ruins. Its museum is also the region's finest outside Rome.

Necropoli di Tarquinia

Via Monterozzi Marina • Tues–Sun 8.30am–sunset • €6, or €8 including museum (see below); free first Sun of the month • Buses (every 30min–1hr, less frequent on Sun) run from the central Barriera San Giusto, or it's a 20min walk: follow Via Umberto I from Piazza Cavour, pass through the Porta Romana, cross Piazza Europa, follow Via IV Novembre/Via delle Croci up the hill, and the site is on the left; a free shuttle runs between the necropolis and the museum (9.15am–12.10pm & 4–7.20pm; every 20–30min) • T 0766 840 000, W tarquinia-cerveteri.it

Once the artistic, cultural and probably political capital of Etruria, the wooden city has now all but vanished and all that is left is the **Necropoli di Tarquinia**. Since the eighteenth century, six thousand tombs have been uncovered, but grave-robbing is common (thieves are known as *tombaroli*). Fresh air and humidity have also damaged the wall paintings and attempts at conservation mean tombs are open on a rotating basis.

In the **tombs**, some of the frescoes depict the inhabitants' expectations of the afterlife: scenes of banqueting, hunting and even a *ménage à trois*. The famed Tomba dei Caronti makes a darker prediction, with demons greeting the deceased. The earliest paintings emphasize mythical and ritualistic scenes, but the sixth- to fourth-century works – in the dell'Orco, degli Auguri and della Caccia e Pesca tombs – show greater social realism. This style is a mixture of Greek, indigenous Etruscan and eastern influences: the ease and fluidity points to a civilization at its peak. Later efforts grow increasingly morbid with purely necromantic drawings – enough to discourage picnic lunches on the pleasant, grassy site.

Museo Nazionale Tarquiniense

Piazza Cavour 2 • Tues–Sun 8.30am–7.30pm • €6, or €8 including necropolis (see above); free first Sun of the month • T 0766 850 080, W tarquinia-cerveteri.it

In town, the **Museo Nazionale Tarquiniense** has a choice collection of Etruscan finds, sensitively housed in an attractive Gothic-Renaissance *palazzo*. The ground floor exhibits superb sculpted sarcophagi, many decorated with warm and human portraits of the deceased. Upstairs are displays of exquisite Etruscan gold jewellery, painted ceramics, bronzes, candlesticks, heads and figures. The impressive top floor houses the collection's finest piece – the renowned **winged horses** (fourth century BC), probably from a temple frieze. The Sala delle Armi boasts panoramic views of the countryside and sea.

ARRIVAL AND DEPARTURE — TARQUINIA

By train Trains run roughly hourly to Tarquinia from Rome's Termini and Ostiense stations, on the same train line as Cerveteri (Tarquinia is about 40min further on); journey time is around 1hr 30min from Termini, about 1hr from Ostiense. The train station is 2km below the town centre, connected with the central Barriera San Giusto by regular bus BC.

EATING AND DRNKING

La Capanna del Buttero Via della Tuscia 21 T 347 545 8184. An alternative to the café in the necropolis is this cosy restaurant about a 10min walk away, which serves up rustic local fare, with a big open grill and an emphasis on meaty

TARQUINIA LIDO

Reachable by bus from the train station, or the Barriera San Giusto, **Tarquinia Lido** is a fairly developed stretch of coast, with lots of bars, restaurants and hotels lining its sandy beaches, some of which are free, and it might just hit the spot after a dose of the Etruscans – as might the adjacent nature reserve and bird sanctuary, adapted from the nearby salt marshes.

mains (two courses with wine around €30). Nov–May daily (except Tues) 12.30–2.30pm & 7.30–10.30pm.

Bracciano and around

Around 30km northwest of Rome, **BRACCIANO** is a small town that was catapulted into the news when Tom Cruise and Katie Holmes got married at the castle here in 2006. The town is nothing spectacular, with the castle the only sight as such, but it enjoys a great position on the western shore of the **lake** it gives its name to, which is a wonderful place to swim, enjoy watersports or just eat excellent lake fish in one of the shoreline restaurants.

Castello Odescalchi

Via del Lago 2 • April to mid-Oct Tues–Sat 10am–noon & 3–6pm, Sun 9am–12.30pm & 3–6.30pm; mid-Oct to March Tues–Fri 10am–noon & 2–4pm, Sat & Sun 10am–12.30pm & 2.30–5pm • €8.50 • T 06 9980 4348, W odescalchi.it

Tom and Katie tied the knot at the imposing **Castello Odescalchi**, which dominates the town, a late fifteenth-century structure privately owned by the Odescalchi family. The outer walls, now mostly disappeared, contained the rectangular piazza of the medieval town; the view from the ramparts is worth the admission price alone.

Lago di Bracciano

The **Lago di Bracciano** fills an enormous volcanic crater, a smooth, roughly circular expanse of water that's popular – but not too popular – with Romans keen to escape the city's summer heat; its shores are fairly peaceful even on summer Sundays. The best place to **swim** is from the beach at Lungolago Argenti, a ten-minute walk along Via del Lago from Bracciano Town. You can rent a boat and picnic on the beach – or eat in one of the nearby restaurants.

ARRIVAL AND DEPARTURE — BRACCIANO

By train Bracciano's train station is reasonably central, just a 10min walk from the castle and centre of town. Trains run to Bracciano from Roma Ostiense every 30min (direction Viterbo), or hourly on Sundays, and take just over 1hr (less from Trastevere and San Pietro, where they also stop).

By bus There are COTRAL buses to Bracciano from Saxa Rubra station on the Roma Nord line (trains from Flaminio station) every 20–40min, which take around 1hr.

EATING AND DRINKING

Gens Trebonia Via Garibaldi 53, Trevignano T 06 998 5096. This bar-restaurant is a stylish spot for fresh fish on a terrace overlooking the lake; expect to pay around €25/head. Wed–Sun noon–midnight.

Ristorantino del Castello Piazza Mazzini 14, Bracciano T 333 778 2055, W ristorantinodelcastello.it. Perhaps the town's best restaurant, reasonably priced and right next to the castle, with a cosy, wood-beamed dining room and a roaring fire in winter. Mon & Wed–Sun noon–11.30pm.

Viterbo

The capital of its province, and indeed of northern Lazio as a whole, **VITERBO** is easily the region's most historic centre, a medieval town which, during the thirteenth century, was once something of a rival to Rome. It was, for a time, the residence of popes, a succession of whom relocated here after friction in the capital, and today there are some vestiges of its vanquished prestige – a handful of grand palaces and medieval churches, enclosed by an intact set of walls. The town is a well-kept place and refreshingly untouched by much tourist traffic; buses and trains run frequently to Rome and you can comfortably see Viterbo in a day, but it makes the best base for seeing the rest of northern Lazio.

1

Piazza del Plebiscito

If there is a centre to Viterbo it's **Piazza del Plebiscito**, girdled almost entirely by fifteenth- and sixteenth-century buildings. The lions and palm trees that reflect each other across the square are the city's symbols, repeated, with grandiose echoes of Venice, all over town. You can peek into the fine Renaissance courtyard of the main, arcaded building of the **Palazzo dei Priori**. The council chamber is decorated with a series of murals depicting Viterbo's history right back to Etruscan times in a weird mixture of pagan and Christian motifs – a melange continued across the square in the church of **Sant'Angelo**.

Via San Lorenzo and the Quartiere San Pellegrino

Roads fork in many directions from Piazza del Plebiscito. Most interesting is **Via San Lorenzo**, which sweeps past the pretty Piazza di Gesù to the macabrely named **Piazza della Morte** – the "Square of Death", so-called after the paupers and abandoned corpses that were buried here by the monks. A left from here leads to Viterbo's oldest district, the **Quartiere San Pellegrino**, a tight mess of hilly streets, home to a number of art and antique shops.

Palazzo dei Papi

Via del Ginnasio 8 • Daily: summer 10am–1pm & 3–7pm (Aug closes 8pm); winter 10am–1pm & 3–6pm; last entry 45min before closing • €9 combined ticket with the Museo Colle del Duomo (see below)

Piazza San Lorenzo is flanked by the town's most historic buildings, chief among which is the **Palazzo dei Papi**, a thirteenth-century structure with impressive views from its loggia looking over the green gorge that cuts into central Viterbo. Most of the palace is closed to the public but you can visit the Aula del Conclave, venue of the election of half a dozen or so popes.

The Duomo and Museo Colle del Duomo

Opposite the Palazzo dei Papi, the **Duomo** is a plain Romanesque church that has an elegant striped floor and an understated beauty unusual among Italian churches. Some of its treasure is held in the **Museo Colle del Duomo** next door (summer daily 10am–1pm & 3–7pm, Aug closes 8pm; winter Tues–Sun 10am–1pm & 3–6pm; €9 combined ticket with the Palazzo dei Papi).

Corso Italia and Santa Rosa

Via Roma leads off Piazza del Plebiscito to become Viterbo's main commercial street, **Corso Italia**, scene of a busy *passeggiata* early evening. At its far end, steps lead up from the right side of Piazza Verdi to the church of **Santa Rosa**, where the desiccated corpse of the town's patron saint can be seen in the second chapel on the right– a slightly grotesque, doll-like figure dressed up in a nun's habit. On September 3 each year an icon of the saint is paraded through town to the accompaniment of much revelry and fireworks (W macchinasantarosa.viterbo.it).

Museo Nazionale Etrusco

Piazza della Rocca 21/B • Tues–Sun 8.30am–7.30pm • €6 • T 0761 325 929

From Piazza Verdi, Via Matteotti leads up to Piazza della Rocca, a large square dominated by the fierce-looking **Rocca Albornoz**, home of the small **Museo Nazionale Etrusco**, whose archeological collection includes displays of locally unearthed Roman and Etruscan artefacts.

ARRIVAL AND INFORMATION — VITERBO

By train Unusually for a small town, Viterbo has three train stations; the most useful, the Porta Romana station south of the centre, is on the Roma–Viterbo line from Ostiense, Trastevere and San Pietro (every 2hr; 1hr 50min from Ostiense). Trains on the Roma-Nord line run from Piazzale Flaminio, by metro A Flaminio (5 daily; 2hr 35min).

By bus The main bus depot is a 10min walk from the centre on the Tangenziale Ovest. Take a local train from Flaminio station to Saxa Rubra, from where there are COTRAL buses every 30min to Viterbo. There are also buses from Viterbo's bus station to Tarquinia (8–9 daily, fewer on Sun; 1hr).

Tourist information The tourist office is in Piazza Martiri d'Ungheria, also known as Piazza del Sacrario (Tues–Sun: April–mid-Aug & mid-Sept to Oct 10am–1pm & 3–7.30pm; mid-Aug to mid-Sept 10am–7.30pm; Nov–March 10am–1pm & 3–7pm; ⓣ 0761 226 427).

ACCOMMODATION

Al Melograno Strada S. Caterina ⓣ 347 828 3753, ⓦ almelograno.net. Just outside Viterbo, this is a lovely B&B with simple but nicely furnished rooms just a short walk from the Terme dei Papi, Viterbo's hot springs. **€80**

B&B dei Papi Via del Ginnasio ⓣ 0761 346 451, ⓦ bbdeipapi.it. Modern design in a fairy-tale setting. This lovely old vine-clad mansion is right in the town centre and has beautiful rooms furnished with flair and filled with antiques. There's also a suite with a canopy bed. **€150**

Tuscia Via Cairoli 41 ⓣ 0761 344 400, ⓦ tusciahotel.com. Large and central hotel with clean though rather dated rooms, and a bright roof terrace that's a pleasant spot for breakfast. **€82**

EATING AND DRINKING

★ **Antica Taverna** Via S. Agostino 12 ⓣ 0761 305 502. This cosy, grotto-like trattoria with stone walls and wooden tables serves up excellent pasta dishes and melt-in-the-mouth Fiorentina steaks. A full meal with wine will set you back less than €25. Mon–Sat 12.30–3pm & 7.30–10.30pm.

Buongusto Piadineria Corso Italia 107 ⓣ 393 661 9127. Recently opened in the heart of Viterbo's historic centre, hole-in-the-wall *Buongusto Piadineria* is the perfect spot for lunch on the run. *Piadine* (flatbreads) are the order of the day here, with numerous different fillings, all fresh and delicious. Tues–Fri & Sun noon–3pm & 7–10.30pm, Sat noon–3pm & 7–11pm.

Il Grottino Via della Cava 7 ⓣ 0761 290088. The "Little Cave" offers a bountiful *antipasto della casa* (one portion feeds two), tasty pasta dishes and hearty, rib-sticking mains such as rabbit in wine. Expect to pay around €30/head for a full meal. Tues–Sat 12.45–2.30pm & 7.45–10pm, Sun 12.45–2.30pm.

Around Viterbo

Viterbo makes an appealing and practical base for seeing the rest of northern Lazio, especially the places that aren't really feasible on a day-trip from the capital. To the south, **Lago di Vico** and **Caprarola**, home to the magnificent Palazzo Farnese, make worthwhile excursions, while east of Viterbo the Mannerist **Villa Lante** at **Bagnaia** is easily reached on public transport, as are – from the same era – the bizarre gardens of **Bomarzo** and the shores of **Lago di Bolsena** further north.

Lago di Vico

The smallest of northern Lazio's lakes is the only one deemed worthy of nature-reserve status. **LAGO DI VICO** is a former volcanic crater ringed by mountains, the highest of which, Monte Fogliano, rises to 963m on the western shore. The **Via Cimina** traverses the summit ridges and is a popular scenic drive, dotted with restaurants, but there's a quieter road (closed to cars) near the shoreline, and lovely spots to swim from, with small beaches.

Caprarola

A few kilometres southeast of Viterbo, the small town of **CAPRAROLA** is home to the **Palazzo Farnese**, which, like the villas at Bagnaia and Bomarzo, ranks among the high points of sixteenth-century Italian Mannerism.

The Palazzo Farnese

Piazza Farnese 1 • Tues–Sun 8.30am–7.30pm • €5; free first Sun of the month • ⓣ 0761 646 052

The **Palazzo Farnese** stands huge and imposing at the top of the town's steep main street, Via Nicolai. Begun by Antonio da Sangallo the Younger for Pierluigi Farnese in the early 1520s, it was originally more a castle than a palace, situated at the centre of the Farnese family lands. Later, Cardinal Alessandro Farnese took up residence here, hiring Vignola in 1559 to modify the building while retaining its peculiar

1

pentagonal floor plan. Vignola was among the most accomplished architects of the late Renaissance, and his creation here exemplifies the Mannerist style at its best.

A magnificently decorated spiral staircase ascends to the **main rooms** on the first floor. The first and last rooms are perhaps the best: the former has a super-embellished grotto-like fountain and pictures of local communities including Caprarola itself (the central scene is an imaginary one); the latter, the Sala del Mappamondo, boasts huge painted maps of the known world and a wonderful ceiling fresco of the constellations. Outside are the villa's celebrated **gardens**. The garden retreat in the woods, the so-called Casino del Piacere (House of Pleasure), is the main attraction, with a water staircase, fountains, terraces and a loggia.

ARRIVAL AND DEPARTURE — CAPRAROLA

By bus Without your own car, it's best to use Viterbo as a base and take a bus (Mon–Sat 5 daily; 25min) from here to Caprarola. Alternatively, take a local train from Rome's Flaminio station to Saxa Rubra, from where there are three daily COTRAL buses to Caprarola (1hr 10min).

ACCOMMODATION AND EATING

Bella Gioia Via Antonio Tempesta 3 ⓣ 0761 646 963. This simple and inexpensive trattoria is very conveniently located off to the left of Piazza Romei in front of the palace. Generous portions, and good service too. Daily noon–3pm & 7–10pm; closed Tues evening in winter.

La Rocca Piazza Romeo Romei 7 ⓣ 0761 646 411, ⓦ bblarocca.it. Not far from the *palazzo*, this cosy B&B with two en-suite double rooms, and one twin, is your best bet in a town with few hotels if you decide to stay over **€60**

Villa Lante, Bagnaia

Via Jacopo Barozzi 71, Bagnaia • Tues–Sun 8.30am–1hr before sunset • €5; free first Sun of the month • ⓣ 0761 288 008 • Easily reached from Viterbo on hourly bus #6 (#6F on Sun) from Piazza Verdi or Viale Trieste; alternatively, there are the infrequent trains of the Roma-Nord line (2hr 30min) from Piazzale Flaminio, by metro A Flaminio

About 5km east of Viterbo, **BAGNAIA** isn't much of a town, but like Caprarola further south it's completely dominated by a sixteenth-century palace, the **Villa Lante**, whose small but superb estate is considered Vignola's masterpiece and a supreme creation of Mannerist garden art. Sacheverell Sitwell pronounced it "the most lovely place of the physical beauty of nature in all Italy or in all the world". A short walk uphill from the main square, the **villa** is actually two buildings, built twenty years apart for different cardinals, but symmetrically aligned as part of the same architectural plan. Only a couple of rooms are open to the public, but the **gardens** are the main draw, some of the period's best preserved, and a summing-up of Mannerist aspirations, ranged over five gently sloping terraces. The route takes in various watery adventures – waterfalls, lakes and the like – and among numerous fountains and low hedges surface plenty of humorous or symbolic touches. Look for the ubiquitous shrimp motif, symbol of the villa's first patron Cardinal Gambara, allegories of the four elements, and a cascade designed as an elongated crayfish.

Parco dei Mostri, Bomarzo

Località Giardino Bomarzo • Daily: April–Oct 8.30am–7pm; Nov–March 8.30am–sunset • €10 • ⓣ 0761 924 029, ⓦ sacrobosco.it • Six buses a day run from Viterbo and from Orte (40min from Rome by train) to Bomarzo's Piazza Matteotti (20min), from where it's a signposted 10min walk downhill

Some 12km northeast of Bagnaia, the village of **BOMARZO** is home to another Mannerist creation, the **Parco dei Mostri**, and a greater contrast to the Villa Lante's restrained elegance would be hard to find. The "Monster Park" – also known as the Sacro Bosco (Sacred Wood) – was built in 1552 by the hunchbacked Duke of Orsini, who set out to parody Mannerist self-glorification by deliberate vulgarity. The result is like a sixteenth-century theme park of fantasy and horror, and the park is one of northern Lazio's primary tourist attractions. Throughout, there are dank, mossy sculptures of tortoises, elephants, a whale, a mad laughing mask, dragons, nymphs,

butterflies and plenty more. Highlights include a perfect octagonal temple, dedicated to Orsini's wife, and a crooked, slanting house that makes your head spin. Numerous cryptic inscriptions dot the park and add to the mystery. The site has a **café**, bar, and ample picnic tables and spaces among the trees.

Lago di Bolsena

North along the Via Cassia from Viterbo, **Lago di Bolsena** is a popular destination, though rarely overcrowded; its western shore is more picturesque, and better for camping rough. On the northern shore of the lake, **BOLSENA** is the main focus, a relaxed and likeable place that's worth a brief stop. The town itself is set back from the water, around the main square, Piazza Matteotti, off which run medieval nooks and alleyways to the deconsecrated thirteenth-century church of **San Francesco**, which occasionally hosts concerts and exhibitions. The adjacent sixteenth-century portal is the entrance to the medieval *borgo*, with the well-preserved thirteenth-century **Rocca Monaldeschi** perched over its western end. Inside the castle is the local **museum** (May to mid-July & Sept Mon–Fri 10am–1pm & 3.30–7.30pm, Sat & Sun 10am–7.30pm; mid-July to mid-Sept daily 10am–8pm; mid-Sept to end Sept Mon–Fri 10am–1pm & 3–7pm; Sat & Sun 10am–7pm; Oct–April Mon 3–6pm, Tues–Fri 10am–1pm & 3–6pm, Sat & Sun 10am–6pm; €5), with modest displays on underwater archeology and Villanovan and Etruscan finds, plus stunning views from the ramparts.

East of Piazza Matteotti, the twelfth-century basilica of **Santa Cristina** conceals a good Romanesque interior behind a wide Renaissance facade added in 1494. Cristina, daughter of the town's third-century Roman prefect, was tortured by her father for her Christian beliefs, eventually being thrown into the lake with a stone round her neck; miraculously, the rock floated, though Cristina was martyred soon after. Adjoining the chapel is the Grotta di Santa Cristina, once part of early Christian **catacombs** (daily: summer 10am–noon & 4–6pm; winter 10am–noon & 3.30–5pm; €4).

There's a nice stretch of free **beach** by the *Naiadi Park* hotel, about 750m south of the main town.

ARRIVAL AND DEPARTURE — LAGO DI BOLSENA

By bus There are hourly COTRAL buses from Viterbo to Bolsena (45min).

ACCOMMODATION AND EATING

Hotel Holiday Viale Armando Diaz 38 ⓣ 0761 796 900, ⓦ lnx.hotelholidaybolsena.it. Rooms with views over the lake, and a pool set in beautifully tended gardens make this the top choice in the area. There's an on-site restaurant too. Closed Nov–March. €100

La Pineta Viale Diaz 48 ⓣ 0761 799 801, ⓦ lapinetabolsena.it. Lovely restaurant with a terrace and garden that serves exquisite fixed-price tasting menus featuring fish from the lake for €25–30. Mon–Wed & Sun 12.30–3pm, Fri & Sat 12.30–3pm & 7.30–10.30pm.

★ **Osteria del Borgo Dentro** Corso Cavour 5 ⓣ 0761 797 167. Best of the town centre's few restaurants, specializing in lake fish and with tasty pizzas too. Eat under brick arches on the restaurant's lovely covered terrace. Tues–Sun noon–2.20pm & 7.30–10pm.

Southern Lazio

The saying goes that the Italian South begins with the first petrol station below Rome, and certainly there's a radically different feel here. Green wooded hills give way to flat marshy land and harsh unyielding mountains that possess a poor, almost desperate, look in places – most travellers skate straight through en route to Naples. But the **coast** merits a more unhurried route south – its resorts, especially **Terracina** and **Sperlonga**, are fine places to take it easy after the rigours of the capital. And **Ponza**, a couple of hours offshore, is – out of high season, at least – one of Italy's undiscovered treasures. **Inland**, too, there are rewarding points to head for: the day-trip towns of the **Castelli**

Romani; the peaceful retreat of **Subiaco**, set amid glorious scenery; and Cassino and its nearby abbey of **Montecassino**, where some of the fiercest fighting of World War II took place.

The Castelli Romani

Just free of the sprawling southern suburbs of Rome, the sixteen towns that make up the **Castelli Romani** date back to pre-Roman times. These hills – the **Colli Albani** – have long charmed rich and powerful urbanites, who also treasure the spectacular views of Lago Albano and the area's extraordinary white **wines**, which benefit from the rich volcanic soil and cooling breezes from the nearby Tyrrhenian Sea. The region is now pretty heavily built up, with most of the historic centres ringed by unprepossessing suburbs, and summer weekends see traffic jams of Romans trooping out to local trattorias. But off-peak, it's worth the journey, either as an excursion from Rome or a stop on the way south.

Frascati

At just 20km from Rome, **FRASCATI** is the nearest of the Castelli towns and also the most striking, with a nice old centre and some great places to eat and drink. Its main square, **Piazza Marconi**, is dominated by the majestic **Villa Aldobrandini**, designed by Giacomo della Porta at the turn of the sixteenth century. The Baroque *palazzo* is off-limits, but the **gardens** are open on weekday mornings (ask at the tourist office on Piazza Marconi; free). Sadly the elaborate water theatre, where statues once played flutes, is not in top form, but the view from the front terrace is superb, with Rome visible on a clear day. You can also visit the impressively remodelled **Scuderie Aldobrandini**, or stables, of the Villa, at Piazza Marconi 6 (Tues–Fri 10am–6pm, Sat & Sun 10am–7pm; €5; ⓣ06 941 7196), where a collection of Roman finds have been assembled from the nearby site of Tusculum, and an extra floor added for local art exhibitions.

Just beyond here is the pedestrianized old centre, which revolves around the two squares of **Piazza San Pietro** and **Piazza del Mercato**. Frascati is also about the most famous of the Colli Albani **wine** towns: ask at the tourist office for details of winery tours and tastings, and local *fraschette* – rustic, rough-and-ready bars serving up local wine, often produced in the owner's vineyard.

Abbazia San Nilo, Grottaferrata

Corso del Popolo 128 • Church Mon–Sat 9am–noon & 3.30–7pm; monastery Sat & Sun: May–Sept tours at 5pm; Oct–April tours at 4pm • Free • ⓣ069 459 309

Some 3km south of Frascati, **GROTTAFERRATA** is also known for its wine and for its eleventh-century **Abbazia San Nilo**, at the bottom of the main Corso del Popolo – a Greek Orthodox monastery surrounded by high defensive walls and a now-empty moat. The monastery itself is only open briefly at weekends, but most days you can visit the little church of Santa Maria, which has a very ancient and atmospheric Byzantine-style interior decorated with thirteenth-century mosaics above the high altar, and, in the chapel of St Nilo off to the right, some big, busy frescoes by Domenichino. Look in also on the so-called **Crypta Ferrata**, a first-century-AD edifice where Mary supposedly appeared to saints Bartholomew and Nilo and they resolved to build a church here.

Castel Gandolfo

To the southwest of Grottaferrata, the road joins up with the ancient Roman Via Appia, which travels straight as an arrow down the west side of Lago Albano. The first significant stop is **CASTEL GANDOLFO**. Set 400m above Lago Albano, the town is a pleasantly airy place, which enjoys great views over the lake. It's best known as

the **Pope's summer retreat**, though it depends on the individual – Pope Francis has never used the palace here, reportedly finding it too luxurious for his frugal tastes, so much so that in 2016 he opened it as a museum (tours hourly: Mon–Fri 9am–1pm, Sat 9am–4pm, Sun 10am–1.45pm; €11; museivaticani.va). Twenty rooms display papal vestments and furniture, including the pope's simple bedroom with its single bed. Afterwards, you can take the minibus that tours the lavish Barberini Garden (1hr; €20). The main Piazza della Libertà is a pleasant oblong of cafés and papal souvenir shops at the end of which is the imposing bulk of the Papal Palace itself. Below the town, there's a lido along the lakeshore with lots of restaurants and pizzerias and a small stretch of grey **beach**. The road leads down from the main highway, just north of Castel Gandolfo's old centre.

Ariccia

ARICCIA enjoys a dramatic location on the ancient Via Appia, poised between two gorges and with spectacular views on all sides. The main road crosses the town's central piazza, a well-proportioned square that owes its appearance to Baroque master Bernini. His Pantheon-inspired church of **Santa Maria dell'Assunzione** sits across the Piazza della Repubblica from the massive **Palazzo Chigi**, whose *piano nobile* is home to the Chigi collections of paintings, sculpture and objects of applied art (guided tours Tues–Fri 11am, 4pm & 5.30pm, Sat & Sun hourly 10.30am–12.30pm & 4–7pm, opens and closes one hour earlier Oct–March afternoons; €8; 06 933 0053, palazzochigiariccia.it) and the small Baroque Museum (€6); at weekends you can also visit the private apartment of Cardinal Flavio Chigi (€6). Locally, Bernini's fame here is eclipsed by the town's most famous food, **porchetta** – roast pork, which is served in *fraschette*, rustic taverns, clustered on Via Borgo San Rocco.

Museo delle Navi, Nemi

Via Tempio di Diana 13 • Daily 9am–7pm • €3 • 06 939 8040

The town of **NEMI**, built high above the tiny crater lake, isn't much to write home about, but it's famous for its **strawberries** (the annual Sagra delle Fragole takes place on the first Sunday in June) and its local **Museo delle Navi** below the town on the lake's northern shore. This vast hangar-like building was purpose-built by Mussolini to hold two ancient Roman pleasure boats, floating villas built by Caligula that were unearthed here in 1930. In the last days of the German occupation in 1944 they were set on fire, so apart from a few plans and wooden shutters that survived, what you see today are modern reconstructions of the imperial ships. The building itself is worth the trip, and also holds finds from the ships (though the best are in the Palazzo Massimo in Rome) and stretches of a Roman road that passes right through the site.

ARRIVAL AND INFORMATION — THE CASTELLI ROMANI

By bus COTRAL buses serve most of the major towns in the area from Rome's Anagnina metro station (line A), with services every 15–30min to Frascati (25min), every 15min–1hr to Albano, from where it's a 20min walk to Ariccia (35min) and every 15–30min to Castel Gandolfo (30min).

By train Trains depart hourly from Termini station for Frascati (30min; for Grottaferrata take bus 1 or 5 from Frascati), as well as other towns in the region, Marino (35min) and Albano (55min), from where buses connect to Genzano, where you can catch a bus to Nemi (Mon–Sat).

Tourist office Frascati's tourist office is the best for the region and very conveniently located at Piazza Marconi 5 (daily 10am–7pm; 06 9418 4406).

ACCOMMODATION AND EATING

FRASCATI

Cantina da Santino Via Pietro Campana 27 06 9429 8110, cantinadasantino.it. This cave-like place is one of the few genuine *fraschette* left in town. Take a seat at one of the communal wooden tables and the friendly owner will pour you a tumbler of wine produced in his own vineyard. No food is served but you can bring your own from the nearby market. Daily 10.30am–1.30pm & 4.30–9pm.

1

★ **Colonna** Piazza del Gesù 12 T 06 9401 8088, W hotelcolonna.it. The twenty rooms of this small hotel are furnished in comfortable, traditional style and are a decent size with large bathrooms; there's a friendly welcome and you couldn't be more central. Free parking too. €95

Pinocchio Piazza del Mercato 21 T 06 941 6694, W hotelpinocchio.it. This small hotel has seven large, simply furnished rooms. Downstairs there's a cosy restaurant with a biggish outside terrace and a much more extensive menu than most of the other more basic Frascati offerings, with lots of bruschettas, good, ultra-thin Roman pizzas from €7, a large array of pasta dishes under €10, and meat and fish mains for around €16. Mon–Fri 7am–10.45pm, Sat & Sun noon–3pm & 7–10.45pm. €75

CASTEL GANDOLFO

Trattoria Lo Spuntino Via Oratorio 1 T 06 936 0226, W ristorantelospuntino.com. Just off Piazza della Libertà, this pint-sized trattoria has a few cosy tables indoors and two tables on the street outside, which enjoy a side-on view of the lake. The cooking is hearty, tasty and well priced, and there are fixed-price menus (from €21 for two courses). Mon, Tues & Thurs–Sun 12.30–3pm & 7.30–10pm.

ARICCIA

L'AriccIarola Via Borgo S. Rocco 7 T 06 933 3100. One of a number of restaurants on this street, just outside Ariccia's old centre, with tables outside and a traditional and affordable menu featuring classic *primi* and *secondi* at reasonable prices. You could try the grilled steak or local pork, washed down with a litre of cheap local wine. Or just order cheese and cold cuts from the amazing spread at the counter. Mon–Fri 6pm–midnight, Sat & Sun noon–3pm & 6pm–midnight.

Palestrina

PALESTRINA was built on the site of the ancient Praeneste, originally an Etruscan settlement and later a favoured resort for patrician Romans. "Cool Praeneste", as Horace called it, was the site of an enormous Temple of Fortune whose foundations more or less determine the modern centre, which steps up the hillside in a series of terraces.

Palazzo Barberini and the Museo Nazionale Archeologico Prenestino

Piazza della Cortina • Daily 9am–8pm; last entry 1hr before closing; guided tours (in Italian) Sun at 11.30am • €5, includes access to sanctuary of Fortuna Primigenia; free first Sun of the month • T 06 953 8100

The stepped streets of Palestrina encourage casual strolling, but you need to save your energy for the real attraction, the **Palazzo Barberini**, right on top of the hill, which houses the **Museo Nazionale Archeologico Prenestino**, originally built in the eleventh century and greatly modified in 1640. The palace and the terraces below were carved out of a Republican temple which previously stood on this site, and the views are magnificent from the top, surveying the countryside around as far as the eye can see. Among the collection's highlights are a number of ancient Roman pieces found locally: a torso of *Fortune* in slate-grey marble; Etruscan funerary *cistae*; and, the museum's prize possession, a marvellous first-century-BC *Mosaic of the Nile* housed at the very top of the building, which traces the flooding river from source to delta, chronicling everyday Egyptian life in amazing detail.

ARRIVAL AND DEPARTURE — PALESTRINA

By bus The COTRAL bus from Rome runs from Ponte Mammolo on metro B (roughly hourly Mon–Sat; 1hr), terminating at Via degli Arcioni, from where the trudge up to the town is a steep one.

ACCOMMODATION AND EATING

Altavista Holiday Home Via degli Scacciati 30 T 333 620 5004, W altavistaroma.it. Right by the archeological museum, this immaculate apartment is run by the extremely helpful Jennifer, who is full of advice on what to see in the area. The two bedrooms have wood-beamed ceilings and are cosily funished with antiques, and there are panoramic views of town from the kitchen balcony. €240

Zi' Rico Via E. Toti 2–4 T 06 8308 2532, W zirico.it. Signed off the main Corso, *Zi' Rico* isn't the sort of restaurant you'd expect to find on a Palestrina backstreet. The decor is elegant and the food seriously good. The creative *primi* include potato and salt cod ravioli in a chickpea and rosemary cream, while braised veal cheek with Barolo wine sauce is a standout *secondo*; expect to pay upwards of €30 a head. Tues–Sat 12.30–3pm & 8–11pm, Sun 12.30–2.30pm.

Subiaco

Around 35km northeast of Palestrina, **SUBIACO** is beautifully set around a hill topped by the Rocca Abbazia castle, and close to Monte Liviato – one of Lazio's premier ski resorts. Purpose-built for workmen on Nero's grand villa (very meagre traces of which survive), Subiaco became the contemplative base of St Benedict in the fifth century. The hermit dwelled in a mountain cave here for three years before leaving to found the monastery at Montecassino (see page 124), but his legacy continues today in the shape of two **monastic complexes** just outside town. There's nothing much to the town centre – the nicest bit is arguably the riverside, where there's a crumbling medieval bridge over the fast-flowing Aniene, footpaths, and even the chance to go canoeing; international competitions take place here in the first half of May.

Monastero di Santa Scolastica

Guided tours only daily 9am–12.15pm & 3.30–6.15pm • Free, though you should tip the guide • ⓦ benedettini-subiaco.org • It's a 3km walk along the Jenne road from the main bus stop – follow the signs left before the bridge

The **Monastero di Santa Scolastica** is the closer (and larger) of the town's monastic complexes, the home of St Benedict's first foundation and home to around twenty monks; it was also where the first book to be printed in Italy came off the press in 1465. You can also stay overnight here (see page 124). Dedicated to Benedict's twin sister, the monastery's most notable features are its three delightful **cloisters**. The first is from the Renaissance period; the second, one of the oldest Gothic works in Italy, dates from the thirteenth century and is lushly planted and fragrant; and the third is a Cosmati work with lovely arcades of pillars taken from a nearby ancient Roman villa (said to have belonged to Nero). Off the second cloister you can see the facade of the monastery's plain church, a Neoclassical edifice inside the shell of the original Gothic church. The church contains the embalmed body of a local saint, Chelidonia, who inhabited a cave in the vicinity in the eleventh century. A little **shop** sells products made from the monks' recipes, including honey grappa and an intriguing-sounding "absinthe elixir".

Monastero di San Benedetto

Daily 9am–12.30pm & 3–6pm • Free • ⓦ sacrospecosubiaco.it

Some 2km up the road from the Monastero di Santa Scolastica, the landscape grows more dramatic as it approaches the craggy **Monastero di San Benedetto**, nicknamed the "swallow's nest". Founded in the Middle Ages, it is today home to just four resident monks. This is the more interesting monastery of the two in Subiaco, and certainly the more dramatically sited, set in the middle of tree-clad hills that radiate utter tranquillity. Its **church**, too, is a wonderful collage of religious paintings: its upper level has frescoes of the fourteenth-century Sienese school and fifteenth-century Perugian school, while the lower levels incorporate Benedict's cave, all raw authentic rock except for a serene statue by Raggi, a disciple of Bernini. From here a spiral staircase leads up to the **chapel of San Gregorio**, containing a 1224 picture of St Francis – pre-stigmata – that's reckoned to be the first portrait of the saint painted from life. In the other direction, the so-called **Scala Santa**, flanked by various images of death, descend to the chapel where Benedict preached to shepherds, its floor strewn with offerings, and a terrace and garden that used to be the burial place of the monastery's monks, overlooking the lush valley.

ARRIVAL AND DEPARTURE — SUBIACO

By bus Subiaco and its monasteries are a reasonable day-trip from Rome's Ponte Mammolo station (every 30–45min; 2hr;). Three daily buses also service Frosinone, a transport hub; useful if you're heading south to Campania.

1

ACCOMMODATION AND EATING

Foresteria di Monastero di Santa Scolastica 0774 85 569, benedettini-subiaco.it. If Subiaco's location makes you want to linger, and it should, why not book a room at the monastery, whose rooms, situated in separate chalet blocks in front of the main complex, are open to pilgrims and tourists alike. They're not exactly monkish cells but are pretty simply furnished, with twin beds and small en-suite bathrooms with showers. The monastery also serves food in the main building (half board €51/person). €74

La Panarda Piazza Emilio Blenio 4 0774 822 731. Near the river and the old bridge, this restaurant serves hearty home cooking. The owner also has a butcher's shop, and the meat is top-notch – try the succulent *tagliata*. A full meal will set you back around €30 a head. Thurs–Tues noon–3.30pm & 7–10.30pm.

Abbazia di Montecassino, Cassino

Abbey Daily 8.45am–7pm • Free • **Museum** Mid-March to Oct daily 8.45am–7pm, Nov to mid-March Sun 9am–5pm • €5 • abbaziamontecassino.org • Train from Rome or Frosinone, then bus from train station to abbey (3 daily at 9.55am, 12.30pm & 3.15pm; 20min)

The town of **CASSINO** in the southeast corner of Lazio was fairly comprehensively destroyed during World War II, and has very little appeal (except for Fiat enthusiasts, who coo over the factory here), but it is the site of an important monastery, the **Abbazia di Montecassino** – itself the scene of fierce fighting during one of the seminal battles of the war. After St Benedict left Subiaco in 529, three ravens supposedly guided him to this spot, where he founded one of the most important and influential Christian complexes in the world. Its monks spread the word as far away as Britain and Scandinavia, while developing the tradition of culture and learning that was at the core of the Benedictine order. Ironically, the abbey's strategically vital position, perched high on a mountaintop between Rome and Naples, was its downfall. A succession of invaders coveted and fought over this vantage point, and the buildings were repeatedly destroyed.

During World War II, the abbey came to be the lynchpin of the German presence in this part of Italy. After a battle that lasted almost six months, the Allies – a mixture of Poles, New Zealanders and Indian troops – eventually bombed it to ruins in May 1944, sacrificing several thousand lives in the process. The austere medieval architecture has been faithfully re-created, but it's really more impressive for its position. Much is not open to the public, and its sterile white central courtyard is engaging only for the views of the surrounding hills and the Polish war cemetery below. The hideously ornate Baroque church has a small **museum** containing old manuscripts and the like.

The Pontine Marshes

South of the Castelli Romani lie the **Pontine Marshes**, until eighty-odd years ago a boggy plain prone to malaria and populated by only a few inhabitants and water buffalo. Julius Caesar hoped to drain the area, but was assassinated before he could carry out the plan. Instead Mussolini reclaimed the region in 1928 – building a series of spanking-new towns and exposing fertile, fresh farmland.

Sermoneta

The crumbling medieval hill-town of **SERMONETA** is a bit of a gem, with a magical, otherworldly air and views right over the plains and beyond to the sea. Its walls were erected to safeguard against the Saracens and later the struggles between the papacy and other kingdoms, which raged throughout the Middle Ages. The well-preserved **Castello Caetani** (guided tours hourly: April & May Tues & Thurs–Sun 10am–noon & 3–6pm; June–Sept daily 10am–noon & 3–6pm; €8; fondazionecaetani.org/castello), erected in the 1200s by the feudal Caetani family, is well worth seeing – a near-perfect example of the medieval system of moats, portcullises, drawbridges and tunnels designed

to render the place practically impregnable. Inside, there is a huge display of arms, armour, catapults and ancient cannons, plus the vast siege cisterns and silos.

Giardino di Ninfa

Most weekends of the following months, but check website for exact days: March–June 9am–noon & 2.30–6pm; July–Sept 9am–noon & 3–6.30pm; Oct & Nov 9am–noon & 2–4pm; 1hr guided tours only, every 10min • €15 • booking obligatory via Ⓦ giardinodininfa.eu

Tucked away in the hills, the ruins of the ancient town of **Ninfa** form part of a remarkable set of **gardens** huddled at the base of a cliff. The temples of Ninfa inspired the poetry of Pliny the Elder, and the settlement grew into a thriving fortified village in the twelfth century, before bandits, mercenaries and malaria destroyed it, leading to it being dubbed the "Pompeii of the Middle Ages". In the early twentieth century the long-ruined town was given some spectacular landscaping and transformed into a garden, where wild and domestic flowers, shrubs and trees flourish among charming rivulets, waterfalls and ponds: the design is spontaneous, whimsical and entirely enchanting.

ARRIVAL AND DEPARTURE — THE PONTINE MARSHES

By train Trains run from Rome to Latina Scalo, at the centre of the Pontine Marshes, every 15–45min (35min). There are buses from Latina to Sermoneta (Mon–Sat 2–6 daily; 50min); to reach Ninfa, there are free shuttles on garden opening days, or take a taxi from the station (Ⓣ 0773 632 292).

ACCOMMODATION AND EATING

Ostello San Nicola Via G. Matteotti 1, Sermoneta Ⓣ 0773 30 381, Ⓦ sannicola-hostel.com. A thirteenth-century convent complete with Gothic church and fading frescoes, and a mixture of dorm beds and private rooms, plus a communal kitchen. Breakfast €3. Dorms €22, doubles €44

Simposio al Corso Corso Garibaldi 33, Sermoneta Ⓣ 339 284 6905, Ⓦ simposio.it. This restaurant specializes in hearty pasta dishes and grilled meats; try their *pasta al trombolotto*, in a sauce that combines porcini mushrooms with lemon oil and fourteen herbs. From May to Sept, you can eat in their pergola-covered garden restaurant, *Il Giardino del Simposio*, the other side of the triangular main square at Via della Conduttura 2. Daily 10am–11pm.

The southern Lazio coast

The **Lazio coast to the south** of Rome is a more attractive proposition than the northern stretches. Its towns have a bit more charm, the water is cleaner, and in the further reaches, beyond the flats of the Pontine Marshes and Monte Circeo, the shoreline begins to pucker into cliffs and coves that hint gently at the glories of Campania – all good either for day-trips and overnight outings from the city, or for a pleasingly wayward route to Naples.

Anzio

About 50km south of Rome, and fairly free of the pull of the capital, **ANZIO** is worth visiting both for its **beaches** and its history – much of the town was damaged during a difficult Allied landing here on January 22, 1944, to which two military **cemeteries** (one British, another, at nearby **Nettuno**, American), as well as a small museum, bear testimony. It was also a favoured spot of the Emperor Nero, who was born here in 37AD, and later built the harbour and decorated the town with statues. The ruins of his villa spread along the cliffs above and even down onto the beach, which stretches north from the town centre. Regular ferries run from Anzio to Ponza (see page 128).

ARRIVAL AND DEPARTURE — ANZIO

By train Trains run to Anzio from Rome every hour and take about 1hr. The station is 10min from the centre of town and the waterfront.

1

EATING AND DRINKING

Fraschetta del Mare Piazzale Orazio 5 ⓣ06 984 6240. Anzio hosts a thriving fishing fleet and has some great seafood restaurants, including this place, where they will bring you an endless supply of fishy specialities depending on the day's catch, for a fixed price of €16 a head. Tues–Sun noon–3pm & 7.30–11pm.

Pierino Piazza C. Battisti 3 ⓣ06 984 5683. Opposite the Municipio, a block back from Piazza Garibaldi and the waterfront, this is one of central Anzio's better restaurants, with great fish and pasta. A full meal will set you back around €70. Tues–Sun 1–3.30pm & 7pm–midnight.

San Felice Circeo

About 50km south of Anzio, **SAN FELICE CIRCEO** is a picturesque small town of weathered stone houses that is split between the busy lower town and pretty upper town. In summer, the lower town's marina can be unpleasantly crowded, bursting with fancy motor launches and yachts, its sandy beaches crowded with bodies and roads clogged with flashy cars. To escape the overpopulated sand, rent a boat at Circeo Mare, Via Ammiraglio Bergamini 124 (ⓣ0773 542 638, ⓦcirceomare.it), to visit the famous **Grotta della Maga Circe**. The town's main road winds up past the upper town, eventually arriving at the summit of Monte Circeo, where there's an ancient **temple** with marvellous views.

ARRIVAL AND INFORMATION — SAN FELICE CIRCEO

By bus Buses arrive in the lower town from Via Domenichelli and depart for Rome Laurentina (5 daily; 1hr 40min), Latina (6–8 daily; 50min) and Terracina (2 daily; 50min). A local minibus service connects the lower town to the historical centre above.

Tourist office Just off the town's main Piazza Vittorio Veneto, on Piazza Lanzuisi (Mon–Wed & Fri–Sun 9am–5pm; ⓣ0773 541 7770); also serves as an office for the Circeo national park (see box, below).

ACCOMMODATION AND EATING

Claro de Lua Strada del Sole 9 ⓣ0773 354 8425. Smart and stylish, with lovely rooms looking across the sea to the Pontine islands, a small spa and candlelit barbecues in a panoramic gazebo. €172

Locanda degli Artisti Via Ammiraglio Bergamini 48 ⓣ340 612 1388. A creative restaurant in the port with a grassy terrace overlooking the port, and excellent fish and pasta dishes (around €15) on the menu. Mon & Tues 4.30–11.30pm, Thurs–Sun 12.30–3.30pm & 7.30–11.30pm.

Terracina

A further 15km down the coast from San Felice, **TERRACINA** is an immediately likeable little town, divided between a tumbledown old quarter high on the hill and a lively newer area by the sea. During classical times, it was an important staging post on the Appian Way, which meets the ocean here; nowadays it's primarily a seaside resort with good beaches and frequent connections with the other points of interest, including daily ferries and hydrofoils to Ponza (see page 128). Apart from the scrubby oval of sand fringing the centre, Terracina's **beaches** stretch west pretty much indefinitely from the main harbour and are large enough to be uncrowded.

THE PARCO NAZIONALE DEL CIRCEO

The pine groves, beach-front and lake of Sabaudia, together with Monte Circeo and the offshore Zannone island, form the **Parco Nazionale del Circeo** (ⓦwww.parcocirceo.it). Created in 1934, this park preserves something of the marshes' wildlife and natural beauty, and is a fine spot for appreciating **flora and fauna** as well as **archeological ruins**: there are over a hundred sites in varying states of preservation. The park's office in San Felice Circeo (see above) can supply information and suggest **hikes**.

Piazza Municipio and around

The centre of the old quarter is **Piazza Municipio**, which occupies the site of the Roman forum – complete with the original steps and slabs – and now focuses on the colonnade of the town's **Cattedrale** (daily 8am–noon & 4.30–7pm), with its elegant campanile. An endearing church with a fine mosaic floor and a beautiful tile-studded pulpit and twisted mosaic candlestick, it was built within the shell of a Roman temple dedicated to the gods Augustus and Roma. The town's more impressive Roman ruins lie just through the stone archway, where the **Capitolium**, dating back to around 50 BC, sits in its own small piazza. Back on Piazza Municipio, the **Museo Civico Pio Capponi** (July & Aug Mon 9am–2pm, Tues–Sat 9am–2pm & 3–9pm, Sun 10am–1pm & 5–9pm; Sept–June Mon 9am–2pm, Tues–Sat 9am–8pm, Sun 9am–1pm & 3–6pm; €3) has finds from the Roman town.

Temple of Jupiter Anxur

Piazzale Loffredo • July–Sept 9am–midnight; Oct–June 9am–sunset • €7 • ☎ 348 818 5541 • Directly after the stone archway and before the Capitolium remains, turn right onto Via Anxur and follow this road for 200m, from where a road winds to the top (40min); you can also take bus #0 (9 daily) from Piazza Mazzini, the Capitolium or the museum; if coming by car, you'll find a car park at the top

Terracina's main attraction is the **Temple of Jupiter Anxur**, which crowns the hill above town. The temple may date back to the first century BC and was connected to Terracina by some lengthy walls; these days it's an impressive if rather ruinous complex, with tremendous views up the coast, and a **café**.

ARRIVAL AND DEPARTURE — TERRACINA

By bus There are hourly buses to Terracina from San Felice (20min), and 2–4 daily buses from Rome Laurentina on metro line B (2hr 20min); you can change at Terracina for Sperlonga (30min).

By train From Rome Termini you need to change at Priverno-Fossanova (1hr 20–1hr 40min).

ACCOMMODATION AND EATING

Centosedici Lungomare Circe 116 ☎ 0773 764 110, @ centosedici.it. Bright, white minimalist rooms with lots of seaside motifs in a revamped villa on the seafront. They have a popular restaurant too, with a menu that constantly changes depending on the day's catch. Restaurant Tues–Sun noon–2.30pm & 6.30–10.30pm. **€100**

★ **Enoteca St Patrick** Corso Anita Garibaldi 56 ☎ 0773 703 170, @ st-patrick.it. No it's not an Irish bar, but a great little *enoteca* in Terracina's upper town that serves delicious plates of cheese and cold cuts, as well as pasta and other hot dishes, washed down with excellent local wines, in a relaxed and buzzy atmosphere. Daily (except Tues) 7pm–12.45am.

La Tana degli Artisti Via Villa Franca 34 ☎ 333 759 0258. This central option is fairly simple, with just ten tables, but dishes are beautifully presented, and the fish and service are both excellent. For a full meal expect to pay €50 a head. Mon–Fri 8–11pm, Sat 7.30–11.30pm, Sun 1–2.30pm & 8–11pm.

Sperlonga and around

The coast south of Terracina is probably Lazio's prettiest stretch, the cliff punctured by tiny beaches signposted enticingly from the road. **SPERLONGA**, built high on a rocky promontory, is a fashionable spot for Roman and Neapolitan families, its whitewashed houses, arched alleys and stepped narrow streets almost Moorish in feel. Both the old upper town and modern lower district are almost given over entirely to tourists during summer, but it's still a pleasant spot, with cars not allowed into the old centre. There are **beaches** either side of Sperlonga's headland, and although a lot of space is private, it's never too difficult to find a decent spot.

Villa of Tiberius

Daily 8.30am–7.30pm • €5 • Head south along the beach from town and turn off at the unmarked stone path before the Tiberio Club beach club; alternatively, from the historic centre, follow the pathway from the end of Via del Corso

A couple of kilometres south of Sperlonga, the remains of the **Villa of Tiberius** are the only real sight of note but are well worth a visit. The villa is right by the beach, and you

1

can stroll around the excavations, as well as walking into the cave where fish still dart about Tiberius's fishpond. There's also a small and extremely engaging museum, the **Museo Archeologico Nazionale Sperlonga**, which contains finds from the villa and its attached grotto, the setting for imperial banquets.

ARRIVAL AND INFORMATION — SPERLONGA

By train The nearest train station is Fondi, 8km away, from where there are buses into town (☎ 0771 519 067); buy tickets on the bus. Otherwise, a taxi (☎ 338 377 2737 or ☎ 339 754 5297) will cost around €25.

By bus COTRAL buses run from Formia (hourly; 30min), Gaeta (hourly; 20min) and Terracina (2 daily; 30min), with stops along Via Cristoforo Colombo in the lower town.

Tourist offices On Via del Porto, the road that winds round the headland to the left of the main beach (summer daily 8am–8pm; ☎ 0771 557 341), and another on Via del Municipio 9 (same hours; ☎ 0771 557 524).

ACCOMMODATION AND EATING

Corallo Corso S. Leone 3 ☎ 0771 548 060, ⓦ www.corallohotel.net. A great choice if you want to be up in the old town, just off Piazza della Repubblica, with beautifully and individually furnished rooms, some with large and panoramic balconies. €200

L'Angolo Via Tiberio ☎ 0771 548 808, ⓦ langolosperlonga.it. On the sandy southern beach, this large, reasonably priced restaurant does down-to-earth pasta with seafood, such as spaghetti with clams, and Neapolitan-style pizzas. Daily 11am–12.30am.

Laocoonte Da Rocco Via C. Colombo 4 ☎ 0771 548 122. The best restaurant in the lower town, right by the beach and serving excellent fish dishes on a patio overlooking the sea (fish fry €16). Tues–Sun 12.30pm–11pm.

The Pontine islands

Scattered across the sea between Rome and Naples, the **Pontine islands** are relatively unknown to foreign travellers. Volcanic in origin, only two are inhabited – the small island of Ventotene and its larger neighbour **Ponza**. The latter bustles with Italian tourists, especially Romans, between mid-June and the end of August, but at any other time, it's yours for the asking.

Ponza

The group's main island, **PONZA**, is only 8km long and 2km across at its widest point. **Ponza Town** is a sight to behold: a jumble of pastel-coloured, flat-roofed houses heaped above a pink semicircle of promenade that curls around the harbour. It makes a marvellous place to rest up for a few days. Although the island lacks specific sights, Ponza is great for aimless wanderings; in the early evening, locals parade along the yellow-painted **Municipio** arcade of shops and cafés. For lazing and swimming, there's a small, clean **cove** in the town.

Chiaia di Luna beach

A ten-minute walk across the island from Ponza Town, the **Chiaia di Luna beach** is a slender rim of sand edging a sheer sickle cliff – though be warned that the waves here are much choppier than on the sheltered side facing the mainland, and the beach is intermittently closed for safety reasons.

EXPLORING PONZA BY BOAT

For real seclusion, rent a **boat** for the day from the **Spiaggia di Sant'Antonio** in Ponza Town (€50–180) and take your time circumnavigating the island and exploring its remote coves. The **Cooperativa Barcaioli Ponzesi** (☎ 0771 809 929, ⓦ barcaioliponza.it) offers boat trips around the island and excursions to uninhabited Palmarola and Zannone from €15/person.

Le Forna and the Piscina Naturale

The only other real settlement on Ponza is **LE FORNA**, a wide, green bay dotted with huddles of houses. The beach here is small and grubby, so follow the path down from the road, around the bay to the rocks: the water of the so-called **Piscine Naturali** is lovely and clear, perfect for sheltered swimming when the fishing boats have finished for the day. The settlement straggles on from Le Forna towards the sharp northern end of the island, where the road ends abruptly and a steep stony path (to the right) leads down to more rocks where you can swim.

ARRIVAL AND INFORMATION — PONZA

By ferry Formia has year-round services to Ponza, with two ferry crossings daily (2hr 30min) and two daily hydrofoils (1hr 20min). There are also connections from Terracina in summer, with 1–2 ferries daily (2hr 40min), as well as summer ferries from both Anzio (1–2 daily; 1hr 20min) and, usually, Naples (to Ponza 2hr 55min, to Ventotene 1hr 50min). Buses connect the port with other points on the island every 10min (hourly in winter).

Tourist office On Via Molo Musco in Ponza Town (daily 9am–1pm & 4–8pm; T 0771 80031, W prolocodiponza.it).

ACCOMMODATION AND EATING

L'Aragosta Via Carlo Pisacane 13 T 0771 80102. The most appealing of a few restaurants in Ponza's main harbour is this place, specialising in seafood (try the *carbonara di mare* – with prawns instead of the classic bacon) and perfectly located to watch the sunset over Ponza's hills. Mon & Wed–Sun 7.30pm–1am.

Ortensia Via Piscine Naturali T 0771 808 922, W hotelortensia.it. The best and most convenient option in Le Forna is this serene and chic hotel, with lovely en-suite rooms with private balconies, and its own restaurant with a nice terrace overlooking the sea (half board €30/person). **€165**

★ **Piccolo Hotel Luisa** Via Chiaia di Luna T 0771 80128, W www.piccolohoteluisa.it. A 5min walk from the port, this family-run small hotel has spick-and-span rooms, plus some apartments up the road. Breakfast is a feast, with pancakes and home-made pastries among other treats, served on the terrace. **€80**

Piemonte and Valle d'Aosta

132 Turin (Torino)

151 Saluzzo

153 Alba and Langhe Roero

155 Asti

157 Northern Piemonte

160 Valle d'Aosta's Bassa Valle

161 Aosta and around

165 Gran Paradiso National Park

167 The northwest: around Mont Blanc

BAROLO VINEYARDS

Piemonte and Valle d'Aosta

2

In the extreme northwest of Italy, fringed by the French and Swiss Alps and grooved with deep valleys, Piemonte and Valle d'Aosta are among the least "Italian" regions in the country. Piemontesi spoke French until the end of the nineteenth century and Piemontese dialects reflect Provençal influence; Valle d'Aosta is bilingual and in some valleys the locals, whose ancestors emigrated from Switzerland, still speak a dialect based on German. Piemonte (literally "at the foot of the mountains") is one of Italy's wealthiest regions, known for its fine wines and food, and for being home to huge Italian corporations such as Fiat and Olivetti. Italy's longest river, the mighty Po, begins here, and the towns of its vast plain have grown rich on both manufacturing and rice, cultivated in sweeping paddy fields.

Turin, on the main rail and road route from France to Milan, is the obvious first stop and retains a freshly restored Baroque core, with a cornucopia of galleries and museums. South of Turin, **Alba** is a good base for visiting the region's wine cantinas. **Asti**, to the southeast, comes to life during its famous medieval Palio, or horse race. For the rest of the region, winter sports and walking are the favourite activities, with **Sestriere** being the main skiing centre, while the ascent of **Monviso** in the far west appeals to the climbing fraternity.

Bordered by Europe's highest mountains, **Mont Blanc**, Monte Rosa and the Matterhorn, veined with valleys and studded with castles, the **Valle d'Aosta** region is picturesque. The Aosta Valley cuts across it, following the River Dora to the foot of Mont Blanc. It's in the more scenic tributary valleys that you'll want to linger, and **Aosta**, the regional capital, makes an excellent staging post on the way to the smaller mountain resorts.

Straddling the two provinces is the protected zone of Italy's oldest and largest national park, the **Gran Paradiso**. The mountain *rifugi* and hotels here become packed in summer but development is purposely restrained to preserve pristine conditions.

Although the western shore of **Lago Maggiore** is actually in Piemonte, we've covered all the lakes in the "Lombardy and the Lakes" chapter (see page 216).

GETTING AROUND — **PIEMONTE AND VALLE D'AOSTA**

PIEMONTE

Travelling in Piemonte is fairly easy – the network of trains and buses here is comprehensive, and your own transport is only necessary for the out-of-the-way villages. You can get to most places from Turin, while Alba makes a good base for Le Langhe, and Saluzzo for the western valleys.

VALLE D'AOSTA

Using public transport to explore the Valle d'Aosta is tricky: buses run from Piemonte along the main valley past most of the castles, but services connecting the tributary valleys are infrequent. Trains are less regular and run only as far as Pré-St-Didier, so, for serious exploration, your own vehicle is useful

Turin (Torino)

TURIN's renovated, gracious Baroque avenues and squares, opulent palaces and splendid collections of Egyptian antiquities and Northern European paintings, as well as appealing pedestrian-only areas, make it a pleasant surprise to those who might have been expecting satanic factories and little else. Ever since the major spruce-up for the 2006 Winter Olympics, Turin's emphasis has been on promoting its historic urban charms, such as its

ALPINE IBEX

Highlights

❶ **White truffles** This very costly speciality is shaved onto pasta, and enjoyed with excellent local Barolo or Barbaresco wines. See page 135

❷ **The Museo Egizio, Turin** A dazzling collection of Egyptian antiquities in a city rich in museums. See page 138

❸ **Sacra di San Michele** The views of the surrounding valley from this fortified abbey are well worth the steep walk up here. See page 150

❹ **Langhe-Roero and Monferrato** Sample some of the country's finest wines from the rolling vineyards of Langhe-Roero and Monferrato. See page 153

❺ **Gran Paradiso National Park** Italy's first national park preserves Alpine valleys and peaks that are home to ibex, chamois and golden eagles. See page 165

❻ **Mont Blanc** Enjoy excellent views of this awe-inspiring mountain from the top of the Skyway cable car just outside Courmayeur. See page 168

HIGHLIGHTS ARE MARKED ON THE MAP ON PAGE 134

genteel *belle époque* cafés and traditional chocolate treats – not to mention an array of walking tours that explore the city's extraordinary, vivid heritage (see page 145).

The grid street plan of Turin's Baroque centre makes it easy to find your way around. **Via Roma** is the central spine of the city, lined with designer shops and ritzy cafés. It's punctuated by the city's most elegant piazzas: at one end Piazza Carlo Felice, boasting a small park; in the middle Piazza San Carlo, close to which are some of the more prestigious museums; and at the other end Piazza del Castello, with its royal palaces.

TRUFFLES, CAT'S TONGUES AND LADY'S KISSES – THE CUISINE OF PIEMONTE AND VALLE D'AOSTA

Piemonte and Valle d'Aosta are a paradise for gastronomes and connoisseurs of vintage wines. Rich Piemontese cuisine betrays close links with France through dishes like *fonduta* (fondue) and its preference for using **butter** and **cream** in cooking. Piemonte is perhaps most famous for its **white truffles**, the most exquisite of which come from around the town of Alba and are ferociously expensive. They are most often used in the form of shavings to subtly perfume a dish of pasta or a risotto. Watch out too for porcini mushrooms, chestnuts, and *bagna cauda* – a sauce of oil, anchovies, garlic and butter, also served as a fondue (the city of Asti celebrates this much-loved dish with a three-day event; see Ⓦ bagnacaudaday.it). *Agnolotti* (pasta filled with meat) is the best-known dish, followed by meat *buji* (boiled) or ***brasato*** (braised in wine). **Cheeses** to look out for are *tomini*, *robiole* and *tume*.

The **sweets**, too, are marvellous: *spumone piemontese*, a mousse of mascarpone cheese with rum; *panna cotta*, smooth cooked cream; and light pastries like *lingue di gatto* (cat's tongues) and *baci di dama* (lady's kisses). The best known is the *bonet*, a confection of chocolate and *amaretti*. Turin is also credited as the home of *zabaglione*, an egg yolk, sugar and Marsala mixture used to fill pastries.

The hills of Langhe-Roero and Monferrato produce traditional **wines** such as Barolo, Barbaresco and Barbera. These fine reds need ageing, and Barolo in particular can be very expensive. Everyday wines are made from the *dolcetto* grape, notably Dolcetto d'Alba. Probably the most famous is the sweet sparkling wine, Asti (wine makers dropped the "spumante" from the name in 1994 in a bid for a new image) – there has been a trend in recent years to make dry *spumante* too. Martini & Rossi and Cinzano vermouths are also produced in and around Turin, a fusion of the region's wines with at least thirteen of the wild herbs that grow on its mountains. The traditional version, now a brand name, is Punt e Mes ("point and a half") – one part bitter to half a part sweet.

On either side are pedestrianized shopping streets, more relaxed than Via Roma. North is **Piazza della Repubblica**, a huge square with the largest open-air market in Europe. To the east the porticoes of Via Po lead to Piazza Vittorio Veneto, slanting down to the **River Po**, from where it's a short walk to the **Monte dei Cappuccini**, with its stunning views of the city and the Alps. A stroll southward from Piazza Vittorio brings you to the extensive Parco del Valentino. Beyond here is the **Museo Nazionale dell'Automobile di Torino** and the **Lingotto Centre**, home to the Pinacoteca Giovanni e Marella Agnelli, displaying the Fiat magnates' superb private art collection, while the hills across the river are crowned by the **Basilica di Superga**. Further south, beyond the city limits, lies the royal **Stupinigi Hunting Lodge**. Outside the city limits to the northwest stands the jewel in Turin's crown, the magnificent **Venaria Reale** palace and gardens. A couple of notable sights in the area around Turin can be easily visited on a day-trip, including the **Sacra di San Michele** and the imposing **Forte di Finestrelle**, in the bucolic Chisone Valley.

Brief history

Although originally a Roman settlement, it was the Savoy dynasty that left the largest impression on Turin: from 1563 the city was the seat of the **Savoy dukes**, who persecuted Piemonte's Protestants and Jews, censored the press and placed education of the nobles in the fanatical hands of the Jesuits. The Savoys gained a royal title in 1713. After more than a century of military and diplomatic wrangling with foreign powers, Duke Carlo Alberto di Savoia teamed up with the liberal politician of the Risorgimento, Cavour, who used the royal family to lend credibility to the Italian Unification movement. In 1860, Sicily and southern Italy were handed over to Vittorio Emanuele, successor to Carlo Alberto, thereby elevating him to sovereign of all Italy. Turin became the new country's **capital**, but only two years later, political turmoil moved the court to Florence, and then finally in 1870, to Rome. Turin fell into the

hands of the petty Piemontese nobility and quickly became a provincial backwater. Nevertheless, it retained its regal centre: its cafés lavishly encumbered with chandeliers, carved wood, frescoes and gilt – only slightly less ostentatious than the rooms of the **Savoy palaces**, fourteen in all, and now all listed as UNESCO World Heritage sites.

World War I brought plenty of work to the city, but also food shortages, and, in 1917, street riots erupted, establishing Turin as a focus of labour activism. Gramsci led

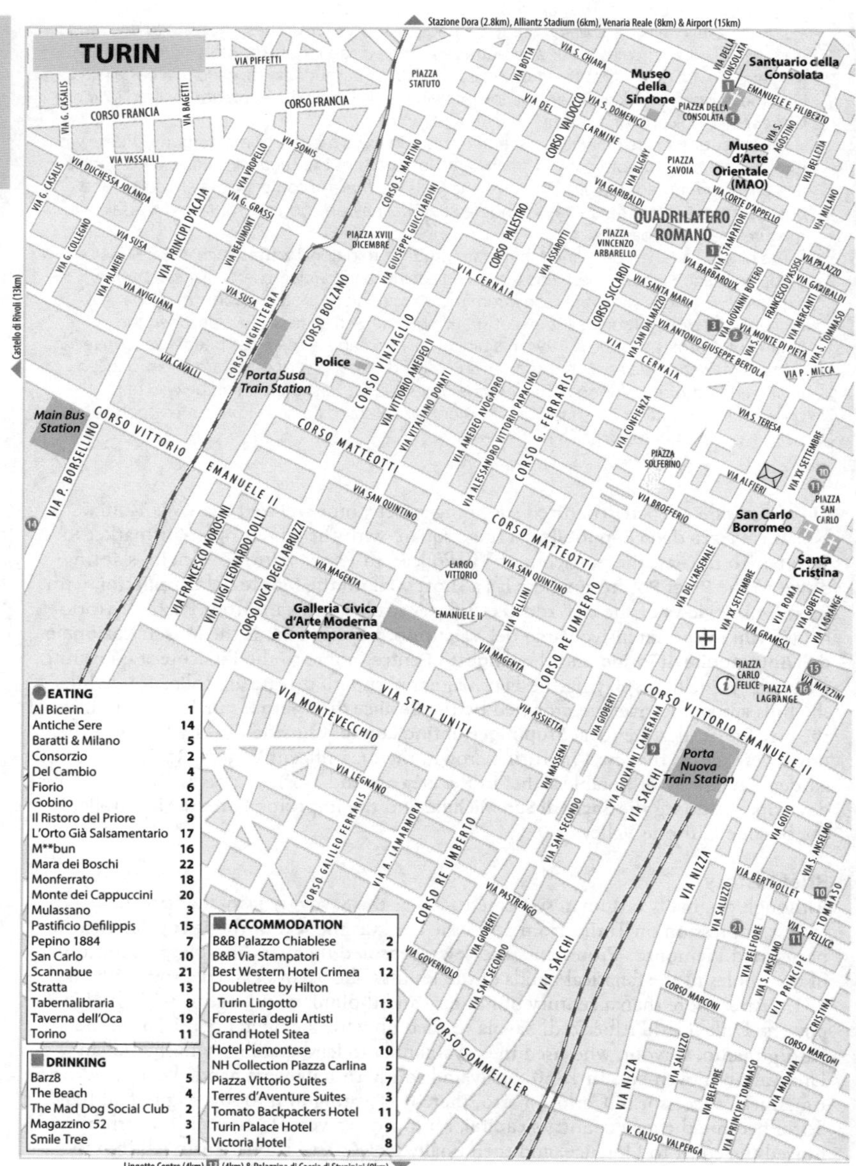

occupations of the **Fiat factory**, going on to found the Communist Party. By the 1950s, Turin's population had soared to 700,000, mainly migrant workers from the poor south housed in shanty towns and shunned by the Torinesi. By the 1960s Fiat's workforce had grown to 130,000, with a further half million dependent on the company. Today there are fewer people involved in the industry, and Fiat's famous Lingotto factory is now a shopping centre and conference space; the gap left behind has been filled by some of the

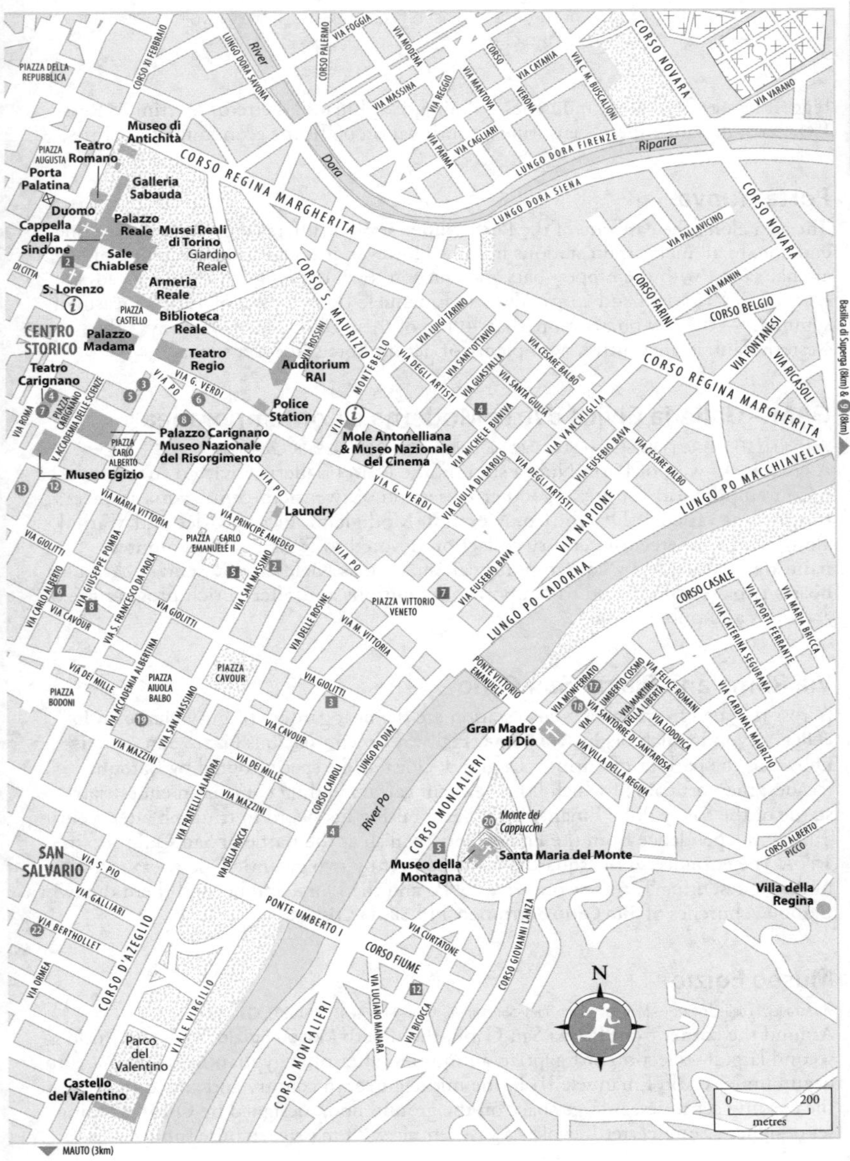

THE TORINO+PIEMONTE CARD

The **Torino+Piemonte Card** (€25 for 24hr, €35 for 48hr, €42 for 72hr or €51 for five days; Ⓦ turismotorino.org/card) is valid for one adult and one child under 12 and allows free entry to a number of establishments including museums, castles, fortresses and Piemonte's royal residences. It also gives reductions at a number of sights including the panoramic lift in the Mole Antonelliana, boats on the River Po, the tram to Superga and the City Sightseeing bus (see page 146), plus discounts on guided tours, adventure parks and activities in the region. The card is available to buy online, from tourist offices, at the Castello di Rivoli, La Venaria Reale and the Palazzina di Caccia di Stupinigi.

biggest names from other industries – Pininfarina, Einaudi, Ferrero, Martini & Rossi, Lavazza and many others – ensuring a continuation of Turin's economic prosperity.

Porta Nuova

The area along the east side of the **Porta Nuova** station suffers from the usual seediness endemic to all major train stations in Italy. However, it is enjoying something of a renaissance, with the hippest bars and clubs in town opening among the arcades (*portici*) of Via Nizza and Corso Vittorio Emanuele II, so typical of Turin's measured symmetry – the city boasts more than 40km of these colonnaded walkways. The western flank is uneventful, with plenty of decent hotels in quiet streets.

GAM – Galleria Civica d'Arte Moderna e Contemporanea

Via Magenta 31 • Tues–Sun 10am–6pm • €10, free first Tues of the month • Ⓣ 011 442 9518, Ⓦ gamtorino.it

A few blocks west of Porta Nuova station, the **GAM** (Galleria Civica d'Arte Moderna e Contemporanea) features a good cross-section of twentieth-century masterpieces by artists as varied as De Chirico, Morandi, Modigliani, Picasso, Klee and Warhol, along with a nineteenth-century collection devoted to Italian and Piemontese painting, and works by contemporary artists such as Kiefer and Baselitz. GAM also boasts two areas dedicated to temporary exhibitions and offers a rich programme of activities and publications.

Via Roma and Piazza San Carlo

Across the road from Porta Nuova station are the neat gardens of busy **Piazza Carlo Felice**, beyond which begins **Via Roma**. Halfway down, spacious **Piazza San Carlo** is known as the parlour of Turin; it's a grand, cloister-like space fronted by Baroque facades, the porticoes of which house elegant cafés. Holding court is an equestrian statue of the Savoy duke Emanuele Filiberto raising his sword in triumph after securing Turin's independence from the French and Spanish at the Battle of San Quintino in 1574. The entrance to the square is watched over by two gigantic Fascist-era reclining nudes representing Turin's two rivers, the Po and the Dora, and beyond them the twin Baroque churches of **San Carlo Borromeo** and **Santa Cristina**.

Museo Egizio

Via Accademia delle Scienze 6 • Mon 9am–2pm, Tues–Sun 9am–6.30pm • €13 • Ⓣ 011 440 6903, Ⓦ museoegizio.it

Around the corner from Piazza San Carlo, the superb **Museo Egizio** holds the world's second largest collection of Egyptian antiquities (after the Egyptian Museum in Cairo), begun under Carlo Emanuele III in the mid-eighteenth century and added to over the ensuing centuries. A large space on the ground floor, designed by Oscar-winning set designer Dante Ferretti, evokes a vast temple with massive granite sphinxes, gods

and pharaohs looming out of the subdued lighting. Upstairs, you'll find decorated mummy cases and an intriguing assortment of everyday objects and even food – eggs, pomegranates and grain, recognizable despite their shrivelled, darkened state. The collection's highlights are a **statue of Ramses II** and the **Tomb of Kha and Merit**. The tomb, discovered in 1906 at Deir el-Medina, is that of a 1400 BC architect, Kha, and his wife Merit. Kha's burial chamber contains after-life supplies, including a board game to while away the posthumous hours, as well as his own personal illustrated copy of the Egyptian Book of the Dead. And to ensure that Merit kept up appearances, she was provided with a cosmetic case, wig, comb and tweezers.

Museo Nazionale del Risorgimento Italiano

Via Accademia delle Scienze 5; entrance at Piazza Carlo Alberto 8 • Tues–Sun 10am–6pm • €10 • ⓣ 011 562 1147, ⓦ museorisorgimentotorino.it

Via Roma heads north through the heart of Turin, passing near some of the significant monuments of the Savoys and Italian Unification. With its rounded façade, Palazzo Carignano is one of the city's first expressions of the Baroque, and was the seat of both the Subalpine Parliament and of the first Italian Parliament. The first floor contains the **Museo Nazionale del Risorgimento Italiano**, home to a library, historic archives and two iconic parliamentary chambers. Displays include documents, flags, weapons, war memorabilia and paintings that trace the life and events that led to the unification of Italy. The Chamber of Deputies of the Subalpine Parliament was used between 1848 and 1860, while the adjacent Chamber of Deputies of the Kingdom of Italy was built between 1863 and 1871, and is embellished with gorgeous frescoes by Francesco Gonin.

Musei Reali di Torino

Piazzetta Reale 1 • Tues–Sun 8.30am–7.30pm; Biblioteca Reale Mon–Fri 8am–7pm, Sat 8am–2pm • €12 • ⓣ 011 521 1106, ⓦ museireali.it

Located in the heart of the city, the **Musei Reali di Torino** complex includes the Palazzo Reale (Royal Palace), the Armeria Reale, the Biblioteca Reale, the Cappella della Sindone, the Galleria Sabauda, the Museo di Antichità, the Giardini Reali and the Sale Chiablese,

At the heart of the complex lies the sixteenth-century **Palazzo Reale**, the residence of the kings of Sardinia until 1859 and then of Vittorio Emanuele II, King of Italy, until 1865. A wonderful staircase by Domenico Ferri decorated with eighteenth-century statues leads up to the first floor, while the palace's sumptuous rooms are gilded virtually top to bottom, with furniture dating from the seventeenth to nineteenth centuries.

On the right-hand side of the Palazzo Reale, the **Armeria Reale** boasts beautiful frescoed ceilings, and a collection of more than 1200 pieces of armour and weapons spanning seven centuries and several continents started by King Carlo Alberto in 1837.

LITERARY TURIN

Turin has been home to many major literary figures. Rousseau and Ruskin, Nietzsche, Flaubert and Twain all enjoyed sojourns here. Casanova wrote: "In Turin, the fair sex is most delightful, but the police regulations are troublesome to a degree." Melville wondered at the architecture, commenting that even the poor breakfasted in elegant coffee shops. But perhaps Turin's most famous literary resident is **Primo Levi**. Born at 75 Corso Re Umberto in 1919, Levi graduated in Chemistry from Turin University in 1941 before joining the partisans. Captured by the Nazis in 1944, he spent the rest of the war In Auschwitz. Returning to Turin, he wrote his two masterpieces, *If This Is a Man* and *The Truce*. You can visit the Centro Internazionale di Studi Primo Levi at Via del Carmine 13 (ⓦ www.primolevi.it).

Carlo Alberto was also behind the **Biblioteca Reale**, which he founded in 1837. Its collections include manuscripts, miniatures, engravings and more than two thousand drawings by artists including Michelangelo, Raphael, Tiepolo and Rembrandt. The library also contains Carlo Alberto's acquisition of drawings by Leonardo da Vinci.

Wedged between the Palazzo Reale and the Duomo is the seventeenth century **Cappella della Sindone,** designed by architect Guarino Guarini to house the burial shroud of Jesus Christ. Today the shroud is housed in the Duomo (see page 140).

Behind the Palazzo Reale, the **Galleria Sabauda** was built around the Savoys' private collection, and displays more than seven hundred artworks by Italian and European artists dating from the thirteenth to twentieth centuries, with works by Rubens, van Dyck, Mantegna, Veronese and Botticelli – to name a few.

The excellent **Museo di Antichità** was also built around the Savoys' private collection and displays objects from the Paleolithic to the Renaissance eras, with a section of the museum dedicated to Turin's archeological history.

Behind the palace and museums, the seventeen-acre **Giardini Reali** (Royal Gardens) are embellished with flowerbeds, statues and marble fountains depicting Triton and sea nymphs.

Finally, the **Sale Chiablese**, located in Palazzo Chiablese, host a range of temporary exhibitions by international artists that span a variety of eras, from the Roman ages to the end of the twentieth century.

Palazzo Madama

Piazza del Castello • **Museo Civico d'Arte Antica** Mon & Wed–Sun 10am–6pm • €10, free first Wed of the month • Ⓣ 011 443 3501, Ⓦ palazzomadamatorino.it

First fortress, later medieval castle and subsequently private residence of two powerful duchesses of the House of Savoy, **Palazzo Madama** is the work of renowned eighteenth-century architect Filippo Juvarra, its grand staircase a masterpiece of European Baroque. The building houses the **Museo Civico d'Arte Antica**, with displays spanning various eras. In the basement, you'll find stone sculptures, mosaics and jewellery from the Middle Ages, while the ground floor showcases medieval and Renaissance art. The first floor and the Baroque rooms are embellished with lavish decorations and house seventeenth- and eighteenth-century paintings, and on the second floor you'll find decorative art including pottery, glasswork and fabrics. You can climb the panoramic tower to soak in the city views.

The Duomo

Piazza S. Giovanni • Daily 7am–12.30pm & 3–7pm • Free

Behind the Palazzo Reale – and reached through a small passage – is the fifteenth-century **Duomo**. The only example of Renaissance architecture in Turin, it was severely damaged in a fire in 1997. It is most famous as the home of the **Turin Shroud** (see box, opposite), though the reconstruction of the fantastic Holy Shroud Chapel, designed by Guarini in 1668, has yet to be completed. Most of the time you can't see the Shroud; it is locked away and officially only on display once every 25 years (the last time was during the Milan Expo in 2015). However, it is sometimes brought out for special occasions (it's worth checking at the tourist office). There's a photographic reproduction, on which the face of a bearded man, crowned with thorns, is clearly visible, together with marks supposed to have been left by a double-thonged whip, spear wounds, and bruises that could have been caused by carrying a cross.

Relics of Turin's days as a small Roman colony are visible from outside the Duomo: the scant remains of a **theatre** and the impressive **Porta Palatina** – two sixteen-sided towers flanking an arched passageway.

SHROUDED IN MYSTERY

During the devastating Duomo fire of 1997, a quick-thinking fireman rescued from a blazing chapel what has been called "the most remarkable forgery in history", the **Turin Shroud** – a linen sheet bearing the image of a man's body – claimed to be the shroud in which Christ was wrapped after his crucifixion. One of the most famous medieval relics, it made world headlines in 1988 after carbon-dating tests carried out by three universities each concluded it was a fake, made between 1260 and 1390. Since 1988, the Shroud has continued to be a tissue of contention between true believers and true scientists. Most recently, in 2005, an American chemist posited that somehow all three carbon tests were mistakenly conducted on a medieval patch and that the oldest parts of the fabric were in the target age range. But even if the cloth itself were proven of biblical vintage, that's just the starting point. Unless the Vatican gives full access (supremely unlikely) to a whole army of impartial experts to test the fragile fabric – including DNA tests of the supposed bloodstains – the Shroud's authenticity will always remain a simple matter of faith.

2

Santuario della Consolata

Piazza della Consolata • Daily 6.30am–7pm • Free • Ⓦ laconsolata.org

West of Piazza della Repubblica stands the royal **Santuario della Consolata**, built to house an ancient statue of the Madonna, Maria Consolatrice, the protector of the city. Designed by Guarini, its Neoclassical facade is pink and white, while the interior has an impressive decorative altar by Juvarra. Don't miss the vast array of votive objects devout Torinesi have offered to the statue, including silver hearts, medals, crochet work and even shoulder pads donated by officers as a thanks for protection in war, along with an impressive body of over 3000 ex-voto paintings depicting everything from war scenes to hospital wards.

Museo d'Arte Orientale (MAO)

Via S. Domenico 11 • Tues–Fri 10am–6pm, Sat & Sun 11am–7pm • €10 • Ⓣ 011 443 6927, Ⓦ maotorino.it

Housed in the historic Palazzo Manzonis, the **Museo d'Arte Orientale (MAO)**, displays an extraordinary range of Asian works distributed over five galleries, with a focus on South Asia and Southeast Asia, China, Japan, the Himalayas and Asian Islamic Countries. Among the objects on display are sculptures from India, Gandhara and the Khmer period, seventeenth-century Japanese folding screens, Tibetan Buddhist ritual instruments, Chinese Neolithic pottery, and an important collection of glazed tiles and pottery from the Islamic countries of Asia.

Museo Nazionale del Cinema

Via Montebello 20 • Mon & Wed–Fri & Sun 9am–8pm, Sat 9am–11pm • €11, or €15 including the lift to the top, €8 for lift only • Ⓣ 011 813 8560, Ⓦ museocinema.it

Halfway down Via Po, a left turn onto Via Montebello brings you to the huge **Mole Antonelliana**, whose bishop's-hat dome, topped by a pagoda-like spire balancing on a mini-Greek temple, is a distinctive landmark. Designed as a synagogue in the nineteenth century by the eccentric architect Antonelli, the building was ceded to the local council by Turin's Jewish community while still under construction because of escalating costs. Today, it houses the excellent **Museo Nazionale del Cinema**, which celebrates Turin's involvement with cinema since the early twentieth century, when it was one of the first Italian cities to import and experiment with the new medium. The museum covers the early days of the magic lantern and experimental moving pictures, the development of the cinema as a global phenomenon, and twenty-first-century special effects.

Santa Maria di Monte dei Cappuccini

Piazzale Monte dei Capuccini • Daily 8.30–noon & 3–7.30pm • Free

Perched on **Monte dei Cappuccini** on the opposite side of the river from Piazza Vittorio Veneto (just a fifteen-minute walk away), is the late Renaissance-style church of **Santa Maria del Monte**. It's worth heading up to the terrace outside the church for spectacular views of the city and beyond – on a clear day you can see the snowcapped Alps that wrap around the city, including the pyramid-shaped Monviso, the source of the River Po. Next door to the church, the **Museo della Montagna**, at Piazzale Monte dei Capuccini 7 (Tues–Sun 10am–6pm; €10; ⓦ museomontagna.org), provides an insight into Alpine culture and mountaineering, as well as hosting photography exhibitions.

2

Parco del Valentino

The grounds of the riverside **Parco del Valentino** make a pleasant place to wind down after the hum of the city centre. There are two **castles** here: the **Rocca** and the ornate **Castello Valentino**, another Savoy residence that today is the seat of the university's architecture faculty.

Borgo e Rocca Medievale

Viale Virgilio 107 • **Grounds** Daily 9am-10pm • **Rocca** Tues–Sun 9.30am–7pm • €5 • ⓣ 011 443 1701, ⓦ borgomedievaletorino.it

The **Borgo e Rocca Medievale** dates from an industrial exhibition held in 1884. The Borgo is a reconstructed medieval village whose houses are a true synthesis of Piemonte and Valle d'Aosta medieval dwellings, built with the same materials as the originals and using the same construction techniques. The centrepiece of the village, the **Rocca** is a fifteenth-century castle, which, although bogus, conjures up a picture of life in a medieval castle far better than many of the originals.

MAUTO (Museo Nazionale dell'Automobile di Torino)

Corso Unità d'Italia 40 • Mon 10am–2pm, Tues-Sun 10am-7pm (last admission 1hr before closing time) • €12 • ⓦ museoauto.it

Three kilometres south along the river from Parco del Valentino, the excellent **Museo Nazionale dell'Automobile di Torino** – or **MAUTO** – traces the development of the automobile from early vehicles, handcrafted for a privileged minority, to the cult objects they have become today. The collection of 200 original vehicles is beautifully presented, with interactive displays including an F1 driving simulator, a photo corner with dress-up area and the chance to rent a supercar (you can even charge your electric car here). Vehicles that are not part of the permanent collection are stored and repaired in the basement Open Garage, which can be visited by prior reservation.

The Lingotto Centre

Via Nizza 250 • Pinacoteca Giovanni e Marella Agnelli Tues–Sun 10am–7pm • €8 • ⓦ pinacoteca-agnelli.it • Tram #1 or bus #35 from Piazza Carlo Felice or take the metro to Lingotto

Formerly the original Fiat factory, the **Lingotto Centre** has been redesigned by Renzo Piano to house an exhibition space, auditorium and shopping centre, as well as the **Pinacoteca Giovanni e Marella Agnelli**, a priceless collection of artworks donated by the head of the Fiat dynasty and his wife. The paintings are housed in a glass and metal gallery called the *scrigno* (jewellery case), which overlooks the test track on top of the former Fiat car works. The collection consists of works of art dating from between the XVIII and XX centuries, with pieces by Canaletto, Tiepolo, Manet, Renoir, Matisse, Picasso and Modigliani, along with two statues by Canova.

2

Basilica di Superga

Strada Basilica di Superga 75 • **Royal tombs and apartment** Only visitable on guided tours (in Italian, with explanatory hand-outs in English) March–Oct Thurs–Tues 10am–1.30pm & 2.30–7pm; Nov–Feb Sat & Sun only 10am–1.30pm & 2.30–6pm • Tombs €5, Apartment €5 • **Dome** Opening times are weather dependent • €3, Basilica free • T 011 899 7456, W basilicadisuperga.com • Tram #15 & bus #61 run from Piazza Castello to Stazione Sassi, while bus #68 runs from Stazione Porta Nova to Stazione Sassi, from where the Sassi-Superga train runs hourly on the hour (Mon & Wed–Fri €4 single, €6 return; Sat, Sun & holidays €6 single, €9 return)

The **Basilica di Superga**, a Filippo Juvarra creation, stands high on a hill above the city. In 1706 Duke Vittorio Amedeo climbed the hill in order to study the positions of the French and Spanish armies who had been besieging the city, and vowed that he would erect a temple to the Madonna on this site if she were to aid him in the coming battle. Turin was spared, and the duke immediately set Juvarra to work, producing over the next 25 years the circular basilica you see today. The elegant dome, pierced by windows and supported on pairs of white columns, is flanked by delicately scalloped onion-domed towers and rises above a Greek temple entrance. In the crypt are the 66 Royal Tombs of the House of Savoy; they're impressive, elaborately decorated with magnificent marble statues and motifs. As well as the tombs, you can visit the Royal Apartment, commissioned in the eighteenth-century by Duke Vittorio Amedeo II as a pied-a-terre for the Savoy Family when visiting Superga. Many Torinesi come here to visit the commemorative plaque of the 1949 Torino football team, all of whom were killed when their plane crashed into the side of the hill. The most atmospheric approach to the Baroque basilica is on the **Sassi-Superga train**, which runs – complete with its original 1884 carriages – along a 3km-long track and climbs over 400m.

Palazzina di Caccia di Stupinigi

Piazza Principe Amedeo 7 • Tues–Fri 10am–5.30pm, Sat & Sun 10am–6.30pm • €12 • T 011 620 0634, W ordinemauriziano.it • Tram #4 from Porta Nuova (direction Drosso), then change at Castello di Mirafiori to bus #41 (direction Orbassano); get off at stop "Stupinigi".

The Savoy dynasty's luxurious hunting lodge, the **Palazzina di Caccia di Stupinigi** was built in the 1730s to a design by Juvarra and is perhaps his finest work. The exterior of the palace has been restored, while the interior is as luxurious as ever, and incorporates the **Museo d'Arte e Ammobiliamento**, a collection of art and furniture from other Savoy palaces. The oval Salone Centrale is a dizzying triumph of optical illusion that merges fake features with real in a superb trompe l'oeil. Other rooms are decorated with hunting motifs – and even the chapel is dedicated to Sant'Uberto, patron saint of hunting.

Castello di Rivoli – Museo d'Arte Contemporanea

Piazza Mafalda di Savoia, Rivoli • Tues–Fri 10am–5pm, Sat & Sun 10am–7pm • €8.50 • W castellodirivoli.org, Take the metro to Borgata Paradiso (20min) then catch bus #36 (20min) to Piazza Martiri; from here it's a pleasant stroll to the castle or catch shuttle bus #36 up to the entrance

West of Turin, the **Museo d'Arte Contemporanea** is housed in the Baroque **Castello di Rivoli**, one-time residence of the Savoy family. It's the most important collection of postwar art in Italy, with works by Jeff Koons, Carl Andre and Claes Oldenburg, as well as Arte Povera artists such as Mario Merz and Alighiero Boetti.

Venaria Reale

Piazza della Repubblica 4 • **Palace** • End June to end Aug Tues–Thurs 10am–5pm, Fri & Sat 10am–7pm, Sun 10am–7.30pm; end Aug to mid-Oct Tues-Fri 10am–6pm, Sat & Sun 10am–7.30pm; mid-Oct to end June Tues–Fri 9am–5pm, Sat & Sun 9am–6.30pm • **Gardens** • March Tues–Fri 9am–5pm, Sat & Sun 9am–6.30pm; April to end June Tues–Sun 9am–6.30pm; end June to end Aug Tues–Thurs 10am–6pm, Fri & Sat 10am–7pm, Sun 10am–7.30pm; end Aug to mid-Oct Tues–Fri 10am–6pm, Sat & Sun 10am–7.30pm; mid-Oct to end Oct Tues–Fri 9am–5pm, Sat & Sun 9am–6.30pm; Nov–Jan Tues–Sun 9am–4pm • €25 for palace, gardens and temporary exhibitions

• 011 499 2333, lavenaria.it • Shuttle bus Venaria Express from Piazza Vittorio Veneto and Piazza Castello (Tues–Fri €3.40 return, Sat & Sun €7 or €4 with Torino+Piemonte Card) or City Sightseeing bus (see page 146)

Begun in 1659 for Carlo Emanuele II, the magnificent **Venaria Reale** was originally used as a hunting lodge, dedicated to the goddess Diana. The palace was completed in the 1700s, and includes the Great Gallery, the Stables, the Orangery and the Clock Tower. The palace contains masterpieces from the Savoy collections housed in the sumptuous Baroque rooms. The outside is no less impressive, with a hazel grove, rose garden and kitchen garden, not to mention the Great Pond with its own gondolas.

ARRIVAL AND DEPARTURE — TURIN

By plane Turin's airport, Caselle (011 567 6361 or 011 567 6362, aeroportoditorino.it), is 17km north of the city and is used by domestic and international traffic. The quickest and most convenient way to reach the centre is by Sadem bus (every 15–30min, every 30min on Sun; sadem.it), with services travelling to Porta Susa and Porta Nuova train stations (50min; €6.50, or €7.50 on the bus). Trains take much longer as they travel to Dora-GTT Station (19min; €3 – also valid for 2hr on buses and trams or for one metro ride), from where you'll have to change train or catch a bus to reach the city centre. The flat-rate taxi service to or from the airport costs about €30 (30min).

By train Turin's main train station is Porta Susa on Corso Bolzano, west of the centre. Some trains also stop at Porta Nuova on Corso Vittorio Emanuele II at the southern end of Via Roma, which is more convenient for the city centre. See trenitalia.com for timetables.

Destinations Alba (hourly; 1hr 10min–1hr 30min); Aosta (hourly; 2hr 30min); Asti (hourly; 30min–1hr); Ivrea (hourly; 1hr 10min); Milan (Milano Centrale; every 30min; 50min–1hr 30min); Novara (every 30min; 50min–1hr 50min).

By bus The main bus station at Corso Vittorio Emanuele II, 131/H (autostazionetorino.it) is the arrival and departure point for most intercity and all international buses; however, local buses to Saluzzo arrive at, and leave from, Torino Esposizioni near Corso Massimo d'Azeglio. Bus #9 runs along Corso Vittorio Emanuele II from the main bus station to Porta Nuova. See gtt.to.it for timetables.

Destinations Aosta (8 daily; 2–3hr); Cervinia (1 Sun; 2hr 15min); Courmayeur (7 daily; 4hr); Ivrea (12 daily; 1hr 15min); Saluzzo (10 daily; 1hr 20min).

By car All the international companies have rental offices at the airport and in the city: Avis, 37 Via Giusti 1 corner Corso Bolzano (011 440 9231; airport 011 470 1528); Europcar, Via Nizza 94 (011 650 3603; airport 011 567 8048); and Hertz, Porta Susa Railway Station, Corso Bolzano 14i (348 123 6396; airport 011 567 8166). Parking spaces are marked with blue lines on the road and cost €1.30–2.50/hr. More expensive parking lots lie under some main piazzas. Beware of Turin's one-way systems as you enter and leave the city, and note that on weekday mornings (Mon–Fri 7.30–10.30am) you can't drive into the ZTL zone in the city centre.

INFORMATION

Tourist office Piazza del Castello at Via Garibaldi (Mon–Sat 9.30am–12.30pm & 2.30–5pm, Sun 10am–1pm; turismotorino.org) provides a good range of information and sells the Torino+Piemonte Card (see page 138). It also organizes Made in Torino tours on Fridays and Mondays to the region's major industrial plants, from chocolate and coffee producers to car factories (see turismotorino.org/en/made-torino-tour-excellent). There's also an info point at Piazza Carlo Felice (daily 9am–1pm & 2–6pm), while the tourist information hotline is 011 535 181.

GETTING AROUND

On foot The best way to see Turin is by walking. Almost all of the major sights can be reached from Porta Nuova station, and the mainly pedestrian centre means that walking is stress-free.

WALKING TOURS IN TURIN

Pedestrian-friendly Turin is a fine place to take a **walking tour**, with several different themes on offer. Perhaps the most intriguing is based on the city's reputation as one of the three great European centres of the occult (along with London and Prague). To visit some of the noted sites, relating to both black and white magic, check out somewhere.it (011 668 0580) for its Magic Turin evening walking and bus tour (Thurs & Sat; 9pm at Piazza Statuto 15; 2hr 30min; €25). It also runs a number of other tours, including Subterranean Turin (Fri; 8.30pm from Corso Bolzano 44; 3hr; €29.50). Reserve through the website or check the tourist office site for further tour options (turismotorino.org/en/your-trip/tourist-products).

2

By metro Turin's metro service (gtt.to.it) is limited but fast, efficient, safe and clean. Single tickets cost €1.70 and are valid for 100min, but 24hr (€4), 48hr (€7.50) and 72hr (€10) options are also available.

By tram and bus If you're pushed for time you should take advantage of the city's fast and efficient overground network (gtt.to.it). Tickets, valid for 100min, must be bought before you board – they cost €1.70 each from *tabacchi* and newsstands. Useful routes include tram #4, which heads north through the city from Porta Nuova along Via XX Settembre close to Piazza della Repubblica; metro line 1 between Porta Nuova and the Lingotto Centre; and bus #61 or #68 from Porta Nuova across the river to the Sassi-Superga tramway.

City Sightseeing Torino This red double-decker plies a hop-on-hop-off circular route (Lines A & B €22 valid 24hr, Lines A, B & C €25 valid 48hr, Line C €12, valid 24hr; www.city-sightseeing.it/en/turin) that takes in the major sights. There are three lines: Line A, Line B and Line C that travels to the Allianz Stadium and Juventus Museum and on to La Venaria Reale and the Castello di Rivoli. You can hop on at Piazza del Castello and at all the other stops along the route; buy tickets on the bus.

By car Driving your own car in the city is best avoided: much of the centre is pedestrianized and the complicated one-way system means you risk getting lost or getting a ticket. There is also restricted access in the city centre (for details, see comune.torino.it/trasporti/ztl).

By taxi Taxi ranks are found on most of the main squares in the centre of Turin, as well as at the bus and train stations and the airport, or call 011 5730 or 011 5737. Most hotels can organize a taxi service for you.

By bike With its wide avenues, relatively car-free centre, grid system and some 40km of bicycle paths, many along the picturesque rivers, Turin is ideal for cyclists. A bike-sharing system, with over a hundred drop-off points, makes this a great way to see the city; a 4hr pass costs €8, 48hr pass valid for 8hr of use €13 (tobike.it).

ACCOMMODATION

Turin has attractive hotels in every quarter. Demand is usually high, especially during the skiing season and trade fairs (when prices also rise), so it's a good idea to phone in advance. Be aware that some places offer special weekend packages – and that a few hotels close in Aug, which is low season for Turin. The tourist office website lists all of the city's hotels (turismotorino.org/accommodation), and you can book via the website too.

HOTELS

B&B Palazzo Chiablese Vicolo San Lorenzo 1 333 886 2670 bbpalazzochiablese.com; map p.136. A lovely B&B in the heart of town offering three tastefully furnished rooms embellished with antique furniture and lively works of art. €130

B&B Via Stampatori Via Stampatori 4 339 2581 330 viastampatori.it; map p.136. Located in a 16th-century palazzo, this pleasant B&B offers airy rooms with parquet floors, chocolate-brown furnishings and crisp bed linen. Breakfast is served on a terrace overlooking a pretty courtyard. €110

Best Western Hotel Crimea Via Mentana 3 011 660 4700, hotelcrimea.it; map p.136. Conveniently located for exploring the Monte dei Cappuccini (it's a short uphill walk away), the rooms at this hotel are rather small, although bathrooms are modern and staff welcoming. Breakfast is basic. €189

Doubletree by Hilton Turin Lingotto Via Nizza 230 011 664 2781, hiltonhotels.it; map p.136. Located in the Lingotto Centre, this business hotel has modern interiors – a glass-fronted elevator takes you up to the rooms, and there's a leafy bar with high ceilings. Guests have access to the Centre's well-equipped gym. €190

Foresteria degli Artisti Via degli Artisti 15 011 837 785, foresteriadegliartisti.it; map p.136. Run by a charming family, this cosy attic apartment with kitchenette has parquet floors with rugs and plenty of books that give the place a warm, lived-in feel. The friendly owner, who lives next door, bakes cakes which she serves for breakfast. The family has a number of other apartments in the heart of town on Piazza Vittorio. €90

★ **Grand Hotel Sitea** Via Carlo Alberto 35 011 517 071, grandhotelsitea.it; map p.136. This charming hotel on a pedestrianized street in the heart of town offers attractive and spacious rooms with period furnishings. The breakfast buffet is generous, and there's a great restaurant and bistrot too. The staff will help you navigate the city. €150

Hotel Piemontese Via Berthollet 21 011 669 8101, hotelpiemontese.it; map p.136. In the fashionable district of San Salvario, the rooms here are welcoming – some have bare brick walls, while the top floor attic suites are cosy and feature wooden beams and bathtubs; the walls are embellished with black-and-white photos of the local area. €140

★ **NH Collection Piazza Carlina** Piazza Carlo Emanuele II 15 011 860 1611, nh-hotels.com; map p.136. A modish hotel offering stylish rooms with parquet flooring and grey furnishings, some with cedar bedheads; the retro bathrooms have black-and-white tiles, and there's a fourth-floor herb and spice garden that provides the restaurant with greens. €179

Piazza Vittorio Suites Piazza Vittorio Veneto 13 011 034 1610, torinosuites.com; map p.136. Right in the centre of town on Piazza Vittorio, these self-catering apartments have one or two bedrooms sleeping up to four people; all are equipped with a kitchenette. €120

Terres d'Aventure Suites Via Santa Maria 1 ⓣ389 434 2699, ⓦsuitestorino.it; map p.136. Parquet floors, smooth clean lines and minimalist design are predominant at this B&B which offers five rooms with modern bathrooms and glass-fronted showers. €100

Turin Palace Hotel Via Sacchi 8 ⓣ011 082 5321, ⓦturinpalacehotel.com; map p.136. This historic hotel opened in 1850, but had a complete revamp in 2015. The comfortable rooms feature modern amenities, and all are painted in light pink and blue tones and embellished with Expressionist works of art. There's a spa with hot tub, sauna and steam room, and a stylish rooftop terrace that is a great spot for an aperitivo. €198

Victoria Hotel Via Nino Costa 4 ⓣ011 561 1909, ⓦhotelvictoria-torino.com; map p.136. Centrally located, this friendly hotel has a quiet pleasant courtyard that is a perfect spot to enjoy a coffee or aperitif in summer. The rooms are comfortable, and there's a lovely spa with swimming pool and jacuzzi. €240

HOSTELS

★ **Tomato Backpackers Hotel** Via Silvio Pellico 11 ⓣ011 020 9400, ⓦtomato.to.it; map p.136. Characterful hostel in the happening San Salvario district, with a cosy lounge area and a small open-air courtyard. The rooms have recycled tomato tin lampshades, while wooden fruit and veg crates serve as bedside tables. Free tea and coffee all day in the little bar area. Dorms €25.50, doubles €76

2

EATING AND DRINKING

It's worth taking your time over a drink, snack, pastry or ice cream in one of the fin-de-siècle cafés that are a Turin institution: prices are steep, but the elegant *belle époque* interiors – often with touches of Art Nouveau (known as "Liberty" style in Italy) – more than compensate. The city also has plenty of good restaurants in which to sample local cuisine.

CAFÉS, PASTICCERIE AND GELATERIE

★ **Al Bicerin** Piazza della Consolata 5 ⓣ011 436 9325, ⓦbicerin.it; map p.136. This tiny, beautiful café has been here since 1763 and age has not withered it – it's *the* place to try a *bicerin* (€6.50). Thurs–Tues 8.30am–7.30pm.

Baratti & Milano Piazza del Castello 29 ⓣ011 440 7138, ⓦbarattiemilano.it; map p.136. Established in 1873, this café has a well-preserved nineteenth-century interior of mirrors, chandeliers and carved wood, where genteel Torinese ladies sip tea. Great hot chocolate and ice cream. Tues–Sun 8am–8pm.

Fiorio Via Po 8 ⓣ011 817 3225, ⓦfioriocaffegelateria.com; map p.136. Turin's most historic café, once patronized by Nietzsche, presumably for its legendary *gelato* and signature cappuccino (€1.30 at the bar; €3.50 at the tables). Mon–Thurs & Sun 8am–1am, Fri & Sat 8am–2am.

Gobino Via Lagrange 1 ⓣ011 566 0707, ⓦguidogobino.it; map p.136. Gobino is definitely in the running for producing the most delicious chocolates in the world. A sampling, at the very least, is not to be missed. Other boutiques at Via Cagliari 15/B and Corso Vittorio Emanuele II 172. Mon 3–8pm, Tues–Sun 10am–8pm.

★ **Mara dei Boschi** Via Berthollet 30/H ⓣ011 076 9557, ⓦmaradeiboschi.it; map p.136. The best *gelateria* in the city, serving exquisite ice cream made with fresh fruits. There are more than twenty flavours on offer, most scribbled on a blackboard – don't miss the chocolate fondant with orange. Two flavours €2.50. Mon 3–11pm, Tues–Sun 11.30am–11pm.

Mulassano Piazza del Castello 15 ⓣ011 547 990, ⓦcaffemulassano.com; map p.136. Dating from 1900, this inviting café has marble fittings and a striking ceiling. It's the favoured spot of actors and singers from the nearby Teatro Regio. Mon–Sat 7.30am–midnight, Sun 8am–midnight.

Pepino 1884 Piazza Carignano 8 ⓣ011 542 009; map p.136. This historical café on the piazza once supplied the Royal Household. It's also Europe's oldest *gelateria* – it was here that *pinguino* ice cream was invented, which comes in six flavours (€2.50). Daily 9.30am–9.30pm.

San Carlo Piazza S. Carlo 156 ⓣ011 532 586, ⓦsancarlocaffe.it; map p.136. Heroes of the Risorgimento once met in this café/restaurant/ice-cream parlour, now regally

TURIN'S CHOCOLATE

Make sure you leave some room to sample one of Turin's signature products – **chocolate**, brought to the city by the Savoy family in 1559. Best known is the hazelnut milk chocolate Gianduiotto, which dates back to the nineteenth century. Some even claim that it was the Torinesi who introduced chocolate to France when chocolate making for export began in 1678.

You can sample the finest chocolate products in all Turin's historic establishments, confectionery shops and chocolate factories: Gianduiotti, pralines, various cakes, hot chocolate, and the distinctive *bicerin*, which is a bit like a cappuccino but fortified with brandy, cream and chocolate. The supreme Torinese spot to buy chocolate is *Gobino* (see above).

restored with gilt pilasters and an immense chandelier. An incredibly smooth cappuccino will cost you €1.50 at the bar. Mon–Fri 7am–midnight, Sat & Sun 8am–midnight.

Stratta Piazza S. Carlo 191 011 547 920, stratta1836.it; map p.136. One of the oldest and most beautiful shops in the city, *Stratta* has been making sweet delights since 1836, beautifully displayed in the window. Tues–Sat 9am–7pm, Sun 9.30am–7pm.

2

Torino Piazza S. Carlo 204 011 545 118, caffe-torino.it; see map.136. A plush place for a leisurely coffee (€1.20 at the bar, €3.50 at the tables). Illustrious regulars have included writer Cesare Pavese and Luigi Einaudi (a Torinese economist who became the second president of the Italian Republic). Daily 8am–midnight.

RESTAURANTS

CENTRO STORICO

Del Cambio Piazza Carignano 2 011 546 690, delcambio.it; map p.136. Historic, lavish shrine to Piemontese food, much frequented by expense-account types. A great opportunity to feast on traditional dishes such as Cavour's favourite of *finanziera* (veal, sweetbreads and porcini, cooked with butter and wine). Prices are extravagant – around €30 for a starter – and booking is advisable. Tues–Sat 12.30–2.30pm & 7.30–10.30pm, Sun 12.30–2.30pm.

L'Orto Già Salsamentario Via Monferrato 14A 011 1994 1750 lortogiasalsamentario.it; map p.136. An excellent vegan and raw food restaurant serving all manner of delicious homemade specialities in attractive interiors, including quinoa with cream of courgette, oven baked veggies and cannellini beans (€9) and *polpette* ("meat" balls) made with lentils, carrots, millet and leeks (€10). *Primi* €9, *secondi* €11. Tues–Sun 7.30–10.30pm.

Mbun** Corso Siccardi 8/A 011 561 097, mbun.it; map p.136. A great alternative to *McDonald's*, *M**Bun* (*bun* means "good" in Torinese dialect) is a fast-food member of the Slow Food revolution, focusing on locally sourced meat, biodegradable utensils and organic produce. Although the speciality here is the burgers (from €6.50), you'll find plenty of local specialities too, as well as gluten-free and vegetarian options. Also at Via Rattazzi 4. Daily noon–11pm, Fri & Sat until midnight.

Monferrato Via Monferrato 6 011 819 0661, ristorantemonferrato.com; map p.136. Established in 1820, this is one of the city's oldest restaurants although interiors have a modern feel. It's a popular spot among locals who come to enjoy tasty authentic cuisine in a convivial environment. *Primi* €10, *secondi* €18. Mon–Sat 12.30–2.30pm & 7.45–10.30pm.

Pastificio Defilippis Via Lagrange 39 011 542 137, pastificiodefilippis.it; map p.136. This *pastificio* (pasta maker) serves tasty, freshly made pasta dishes (€12), plus other meals such as grilled salmon with orange and ginger compote (€16), with seating at high tables overlooking the pedestrianized street. There's a deli counter too, selling freshly made pasta in a variety of intriguing shapes. Mon–Fri 12.30–3pm & 7.30–10.30pm, Sat & Sun 12.30–3.30pm & 7.30–10.30pm; deli counter Tues–Fri 10am–2pm & 4.30–7.30pm, Sat 10–7.30pm, Sun 10am–2pm.

Tabernalibraria Via Bogino 5 011 812 8028, tabernalibraria.to.it; map p.136. A pleasant restaurant with over 250 bottles on its wine list, and a few tables lining the pavement in summer. The food is great, with hearty portions of traditional Italian cuisine. *Primi* €12, *secondi* €14. Mon–Sat noon–2.30pm & 7.15–11.45pm, Sun noon–2.30pm.

Taverna dell'Oca Via dei Mille 24 011 837 547, tavernadelloca.com; map p.136. A bustling restaurant tucked away on a pleasant square that specializes in goose dishes (*Taverna dell'Oca* translates as "Goose Tavern"); there's a goose tasting menu (€37), a seafood tasting menu (€35) and a Piedmontese tasting menu (€32) as well as very reasonably priced dishes at lunchtime. *Primi* €12, *secondi* €18. Tues–Fri 12.15–2.15pm & 7.45–11pm, Sat 7.45–11pm, Sun 12.15–2.45pm & 7.45–11pm.

QUADRILATERO ROMANO

Consorzio Via Monte di Pietà 23 011 276 7661, ristoranteconsorzio.com; map p.136. Pleasantly trendy Slow Food spot, serving traditional dishes with a twist. In autumn try the handmade *tajarin* (a thin version of tagliatelle) with grated truffles supplied by the owner's

TURIN'S FESTIVALS

For most of September, the **MITO** festival (011 247 87, mitosettembremusica.it) mixes jazz, world music, classical music and performance art at various venues in Turin and Milan, while **Traffic**, Turin's free rock festival, takes place in Parco Dora in July (kappafuturfestival.it). There are also three annual international **film festivals** – the Torino Film Festival (torinofilmfest.org), the Torino Lovers Film Festival – Torino LGBTQI Visions (loversff.com) and the Festival CinemAmbiente (cinemambiente.it) – plus the Salone del Libro **book** fair (salonelibro.it) and a biennial **food** event (salonedelgusto.com).

father who is a truffle hunter in Piemonte. *Primi* €12, *secondi* €16. Mon–Fri 12.30–2.30pm & 7.30pm–1am, Sat 7.30pm–1am.

SAN SALVARIO

★ **Scannabue** Largo Saluzzo 25/H ⓣ011 669 6693, ⓦscannabue.it; map p.136. This excellent restaurant is reminiscent of a Parisian bistro with dark brown and olive green interiors and seating on leather benches. The menu features Piemontese dishes, with a number of meat options including rabbit, beef and pork. Dishes from €12. Daily 12.30–2.30pm & 7.30pm–10.30am.

OUT OF THE CENTRE

★ **Antiche Sere** Via Cenischia 9 ⓣ011 385 4347; map p.136. This lovely family-run *osteria* in a quiet residential neighbourhood west of the centre has interiors with dark wooden furniture and framed black-and-white photos. The hearty seasonal dishes are scribbled on recycled paper, and there's a lovely vine-shaded terrace for the summer months. *Primi* €8, *secondi* €12. Mon–Sat 7.30pm–1am.

Il Ristoro del Priore Strada della Basilica di Superga 75 ⓣ011 899 7456, ⓦristorodelpriore.com; map p.136. Located in the same complex as the Basilica di Superga, this is a great spot to try some traditional dishes in a welcoming setting. There's a Piemontese menu (€25) featuring local specialities, and a three-course *menù turistico* for €14. Thurs–Tues 12–2.30pm.

★ **Monte dei Cappuccini** Salita al CAI Torino 12 ⓣ011 660 0302; map p.136. Located on the Monte dei Cappuccini, this restaurant has exceptional views of Turin. Seating is on a pleasant leafy terrace, and the menu features seasonal Piemontese dishes, such as prime *fassone* meat and home-made pasta dishes with fresh truffles. *Primi* €12, *secondi* €15. Tues–Sat 12.30–2.15pm & 7.30–10pm, Sun 12.30–2.15pm.

DRINKING AND NIGHTLIFE

Turin's nightlife is a reasonably varied mix of clubs and bars. A good place for a quiet drink is the tranquil medieval area, the **Quadrilatero Romano**, around Piazza Emanuele Filiberto and Via Santa Chiara. The up-and-coming **San Salvario** neighbourhood, near the train station, has plenty of **bars** and clubs serving up live music and killer cocktails, while the bars on Piazza Vittorio are busy especially in the summer months, with tables pouring out onto the city's spectacular square. Many of the city's *vinerie* – wine bars – offer generous aperitivi.

Barz8 Corso Moncalieri 5 39 ⓣ339 533 1352; map p.136. This small bar south of the river shakes up some great cocktails using fresh ingredients, and over one hundred types of vodka and more than forty types of gin and vermouth. The youngish crowd spills out onto the pavement in summer. Tues–Sun 6pm–3am.

The Beach Via Murazzi del Po 22 ⓣ392 288 3024, ⓦthebeachmurazzi.it; map p.136. This happening club right by the river gets particularly crowded on Thurs and Fri evenings when top-class DJs spin techno and electronica. Thurs–Sun 8.30pm–3am.

★ **The Mad Dog Social Club** Via Maria Vittoria 35A ⓣ011 812 0874 ⓦthemaddog.it; map p.136. Set out to resemble an American 1920's speakeasy, this welcoming cocktail bar with bare brick walls shakes up great Prohibition-inspired cocktails. Live jazz and blues add to the atmosphere. Mon–Sat 9pm–2am.

Magazzino 52 Via Giolitti 52/A ⓣ011 427 1938 ⓦmagazzino52.it; map p.136. This welcoming wine bar and restaurant is a great spot to enjoy some of Piedmont's excellent reds, including Barolo and Barbaresco. There are plenty of delicious nibbles and plates to choose from. Mon–Sat 10.30–2.30pm & 6pm–midnight; closed Sat lunch.

★ **Smile Tree** Piazza della Consolata 9/C ⓣ331 1848 136, ⓦsmiletree.it; map p.136. Award-winning mixologists shake up inventive cocktails (€9) with a twist at this popular bar on Piazza della Consolata. The interior features bottles hanging from the ceiling, and there's seating on the square in the summer. A vegan *aperitivo* is served daily 7–10pm (€12). Tues, Wed & Sun 7pm–2am, Thurs–Sat 7pm–3am.

ENTERTAINMENT

Turin's cultural life is suitably comprehensive for a place of this size. For what's-on listings and opening hours, check the pages of the Turin daily, *La Stampa*, particularly its Friday supplements *"Torino Sette"*. Alternatively, look out for free listings magazines and promo leaflets in bars and restaurants around town. Torino Cultura in Piazza del Castello at Via Garibaldi (ⓦtorinocultura.it) has a free ticket-reservation service.

RAI National Symphony Orchestra Arturo Toscanini Auditorium, Piazza Rossaro ⓣ011 810 4653, ⓦosn.rai.it. One of the most prestigious orchestras in Italy, offering a rich programme of classical music concerts and events throughout the year. Ticket office (at Via Rossini 15) Tues & Wed 10am–2pm, Thurs & Fri 3–7pm and 1hr before performances.

Teatro Regio Piazza del Castello 215 ⓣ011 881 5241, ⓦteatroregio.torino.it. The city's opera house is one of the best in the country and is recognizable from its pod-like 1970s architecture. Ticket office Tues–Fri 10.30am–6pm, Sat 10.30am–4pm and 1hr before performances.

Teatro Stabile Via Rossini 8 ⓣ011 516 9555, ⓦteatrostabiletorino.it. One of Italy's principal national

theatres, the Stabile is acclaimed for its productions of major works by nineteenth- and twentieth-century European playwrights; performances are usually at the sumptuous Carignano Theatre, as well as at the Gobetti and Fonderie Limone theatres. Ticket office Tues–Sat 1–7pm and 1hr before performances.

DIRECTORY

Books and newspapers Libreria Luxemburg, Via Cesare Battisti 7, has an excellent range of British and American paperbacks and magazines. English-language newspapers can be bought from most newsagents in the city centre, in particular the one at the Porta Nuova station.

Exchange Outside normal banking hours you can exchange money at Porta Nuova station at Forexchange by platforms 5 and 6 (Mon–Sat 7.30am–7.45pm, Sun 10am–6pm).

Football Turin's two teams, Juventus and Torino, play on Sat and Sun afternoons at respectively the Allianz Stadium, Strada Comunale di Altessano 131, and the Stadio Olimpico, Via Filadelfia 88. You can get to the Juventus Stadium by bus #72 from Via Bertola or from the metro Bernini stop and then bus #9 only on match days; the Stadio Olimpico on line #4 from Porta Nuova station or #10 from Porta Susa. Although Juventus has been voted the most popular team in Italy, most locals support the underdogs, Torino.

Hospital Ospedale Molinette, Corso Bramante 88–90 (011 633 1633); for 24hr emergency medical attention call 118.

Laundries Lav@sciuga, Via S. Massimo 4, with other branches at Via Vanchiglia 10, Via S. Anselmo 9, Via Madama Cristina 85 and Piazza della Repubblica 5 (lavasciuga.torino.it).

Markets Piazza della Repubblica, known as Porta Palazzo, hosts Europe's largest outdoor market (Mon–Fri 8.30am–1.30pm, Sun 8.30am–6.30pm) selling mainly fruit and vegetables, but also clothes and, in the indoor market hall, cheeses, bread, meat, fish and *salumi*. Behind Porta Palazzo is the Saturday Balôn (6am–5pm), or flea market, and the monthly Gran Balôn market (second Sun of month 8am–7pm). There's often heavily discounted designer fashion (from end-of-line clearances) at the Crocetta market around Via Cassini and Via Marco Polo (Mon–Fri mornings & all day Sat) and Piazza Benefica market (Mon–Fri 7am–2pm, Sat 7am–2.30pm) – not exactly street-market prices, but still much cheaper than in the shops.

Pharmacy Comunale 42, Via XX Settembre 5, is open all night (7.30pm–9am).

Police The police station is at Via Verdi 11 (011 818 2011). For emergencies call 112.

Post office The central post office is at Via Vittorio Alfieri 10 (Mon–Fri 8.30am–7pm, Sat 8.30am–12.30pm).

Sacra di San Michele

Via alla Sacra 14 • Mid-March to mid-Oct Tues–Sat 9.30am–12.30pm & 2.30–6pm, Sun 9.30am–noon & 2.30–6pm; mid-Oct to mid-March Tues–Sat 9.30am–12.30pm & 2.30–5pm, Sun 9.30am–noon & 2.30–5pm • €8 • 011 939 130, sacradisanmichele.com • Take the train to Susa or Bardonecchia from Turin's Porta Nuova station and get off at Avigliana station (every 30min; 28min); from here it's a 14km taxi drive (€25) to the Sacra; on Wed, Sat, Sun & public hols between Apr 1st and Nov 1st there is a shuttle bus service connecting Avigliana station to the Sacra (€4 return; 40min); alternatively, travel to S. Ambrogio station (hourly; 43min) from where it's a 90min uphill walk to the Sacra.

A forbidding fortified abbey anchored atop a rocky hill, the **Sacra di San Michele** is best approached via the small town of Sant'Ambrogio. From here, the steep ninety-minute hike is well worth the effort, both for the views and for the opportunity to soak up the atmosphere. Climbing up to the abbey and hewn into the rock, a long flight of stairs – the Scalone dei Morti (Stairs of the Dead) – sets a morbid tone, for it was here that the skeletons of the monks used to be laid out for local peasants to come and pay their respects and to remind them of human frailty. The Romanesque entrance arch to the Gothic-Romanesque abbey church is carved with signs of the zodiac. If you don't fancy the climb, and have your own car, you can drive up to the abbey from the nearby town of Avigliana.

Forte di Fenestrelle

Visitable only on a guided tour July & Aug daily 10am–noon & 2.30–6pm; Sept–June Thurs–Mon 10am–noon & 2.30–6pm • €5 • Book tours 24hr in advance on 0121 83 600, fortedifenestrelle.it • The Sadem bus to Sestriere from the corner of Corso Vittorio Emanuele II and Via Sacchi in Turin stops at Forte di Fenestrelle (6 daily; 1hr 50min); check www.sadem.it for timetables

Near the picturesque slate-roofed hamlet of Usseaux, whose weather-worn old walls are decorated with colourful murals, the impressive **Forte di Fenestrelle** sits at an altitude of nearly 2000m. Comprising three different forts connected by staircases, it's the largest defensive structure ever constructed in Europe. Known as "The Great Wall of

PIEMONTE'S SKI RESORTS

Piemonte's main **ski areas** – Oulx, Claviere, Cesana, Sestriere, Sansicario, Sauze d'Oulx and Pragelato – collectively constitute some 400km of interconnected runs, known as **ViaLattea** (The Milky Way; vialattea.it). They are well used by British tour operators and all had their facilities upgraded in 2006, when they hosted the Alpine events of the Winter Olympics. You can gain access to the ski area from Pragelato on the Pattemouche-Anfiteatro cableway: a daily lift-pass covering all the resorts costs €36.

Sestriere was the dream resort of Fiat baron Gianni Agnelli, who conceived it as an aristocratic mountain retreat. Today, the reality is a bland resort dominated by two cylindrical towers, though the mountain is impeccable – the choice for World Cup and Olympic ski races. Nearby modern **Bardonecchia** is a weekenders' haunt, with small chalet-style hotels and more than 100km of runs – it's not directly connected to the ViaLattea, and is run by the Bardonecchia ski company (bardonecchiaski.com).

Piemonte", it was started by the Savoys in 1728 and took some 122 years to complete. The gigantic fortification has now been restored and much of the wall's length can be visited: the longest guided tour (€15) takes you up all of the four thousand steps and back – a strenuous seven-hour trek.

EATING **FORTE DI FENESTRELLE**

Cafè des Forçats Piazza d'Armi 0121 83 600. Located within the Forte di Fenestrelle, this café and restaurant is a great spot to refuel once you've tackled the fort's thousands of steps; the home cooking features hearty portions of traditional dishes. July & Aug daily 9am–6pm; Sept–June Thurs–Mon 9am–6pm.

Saluzzo

A flourishing medieval town, and later the seat of one of Piemonte's few Renaissance courts, **SALUZZO**, 57km south of Turin, retains much of its period appeal. Flaking ochre-washed terraces and Renaissance houses line cobbled streets that climb up to a castle, from where you can enjoy views of the town. A pleasant place to stay, the town makes a good base for walks in the Po, Varaita and Maira valleys, which cut through the foothills of the Monviso mountain towards France (see page 153).

Torre Civica

Salita al Castello 26 • April–Sept Fri 10am–12.30pm, Sat & Sun 10am–12.30pm & 3–6.30pm; Oct–March Fri 10.30am–12.30pm, Sat & Sun 10.30am–12.30pm & 2–5pm • €3, combined ticket with Museo Civico €6

Just below the castle, the **Torre Civica** was built in 1462 under the Marquisate of Ludovico I, and forms part of the old town hall building. From the top of the tower, at a height of 48m, you get great views over the town and surrounding areas – though you'll have to climb the 130 steps first.

San Giovanni

Via San Giovanni • Daily 8am–noon & 2.30–6.30pm • Free

South of the castle, the Gothic church of **San Giovanni** boasts a number of impressive thirteenth- and fourteenth-century frescoes. It's also home to the tomb of the leading light of Renaissance Saluzzo, Marchese Ludovico II, anachronistically depicted as a medieval knight beneath a fancily carved canopy.

Casa Cavassa

Via San Giovanni 5 • Tues, Thurs, Fri & Sat 10am–1pm & 2–6pm, Sun 10am–1pm & 2–7pm; Nov to early Jan Sun only 10am–1pm & 2–6pm• €5, combined ticket with Torre Civica €6 • ⓦ casacavassa.it

Near the San Giovanni church, the Renaissance **Casa Cavassa** is a fifteenth-century palace with an arcaded courtyard that now houses the town's **Museo Civico**. Inside are period furniture and paintings, including the gorgeously gilded *Madonna della Misericordia*, with the Madonna sheltering Ludovico, his wife and the population of Saluzzo in the folds of her cloak.

Castiglia

Piazza Castello • Mon & Thurs–Sat 10am–1pm & 2–6pm, Sun 10am–1pm & 2–7pm; Nov to early Jan Sun only 10am–1pm & 2–6pm • €7

Perched above town, the thirteenth-century Castello dei Marchesi, or **Castiglia**, houses a museum that provides an insight into the history of the Marquisate of Saluzzo (captions in Italian only). Downstairs, you can visit the former prisons, where displays trace the history of the prison system. Ask the museum staff to take you to the guardhouse from where there are lovely views of the town and beyond.

Castello della Manta

March to mid-Dec Tues–Sun 10am–6pm • €8, including audioguide • ⓣ 0175 87 822 ⓦ fondoambiente.it/luoghi/castello-della-manta • A 5min ride on bus #91 or #96 from outside the train station

Just south of Saluzzo, the **Castello della Manta** was a medieval fortress that was transformed into a refined residence in the fifteenth century. Though from the outside it's as plain and austere as Saluzzo's castle, it houses evocative late-Gothic frescoes in the Baronial Hall. One of these illustrates the myth of the Fountain of Youth, elderly people processing towards the magical waters while others impatiently rip off their clothes to plunge in.

ARRIVAL AND INFORMATION — SALUZZO

By bus Saluzzo has excellent bus links, with regular services from Turin (line #91), and into the Po, Varaita and Maira valleys. For timetables, see ⓦ atibus.it.

Destinations Paesana (Po Valley; Mon–Sat 11 daily, 3 on Sun; 2hr); Turin (hourly; 1hr 25min); Val Varaita (3 daily; 1hr 15min).

Tourist office Piazza Risorgimento 1 (April–Sept Tues–Sun 10am–12.30pm & 3–6.30pm; Oct–March Tues–Sun 10am–noon & 3–6pm; ⓣ 0175 46 710, ⓦ saluzzoturistica.it).

ACCOMMODATION

Agriturismo Camisassi Via Torino 75 ⓣ 0175 249 673, ⓦ agriturismocamisassi.it. This sixteenth-century farmhouse is part agriturismo, part hotel. The former has ten en-suite rooms, two with kitchenette, some of which feature open-brick walls and tiled floors; breakfast is not included. The hotel offers comfortable a/c rooms (€90) with breakfast included. **€64**

★ **San Giovanni Resort** Via S. Giovanni 9/A ⓣ 0175 45 420, ⓦ sangiovanni-relais.com. Part of the fifteenth-century monastery complex, this is the loveliest hotel in town, with rooms overlooking the cloisters. There's a café in the cloisters too, and a wonderful restaurant in the basement featuring arched ceilings. **€135**

EATING AND DRINKING

Interno 2 Due Via Martiri Liberazione 2 ⓣ 0175 248 907, ⓦ internodue.it. One of Saluzzo's best restaurants, offering traditional regional cuisine in a welcoming setting; the menu changes weekly. On Fri and Sat evenings there are live music gigs and DJ sets in the bar area. Tues–Fri & Sun noon–3pm & 6.30–midnight, Sat 7pm–4am.

Le Quattro Stagioni Via Volta 21 ⓣ 0175 47 470, ⓦ ristorantele4stagioni.it. The menu here includes salads (€10), pizzas (€6.50) and a selection of Piemontese dishes such as gnocchi Val Varaita (€10), but the real draw is the shaded courtyard surrounded by ancient walls. Daily noon–2.15pm & 7–11.30pm; closed Sat lunch.

Locanda Corona di Ferro Via Martiri della Liberazione 48 ⓣ 0175 218 975, ⓦ coronadiferro.it. Tucked away on a little lane and giving onto a courtyard, this pleasant

restaurant serves creatively presented regional dishes such as ravioloni (large ravioli) stuffed with ricotta and spinach (€14). In summer customers can dine outside in the courtyard. Thurs–Tues noon–2.30pm & 7.30–10pm.

2

Castello di Racconigi

Via Morosini 3, Racconigi • Tues–Sun 9am–7pm • €5 • ⓦ polomusealepiemonte.beniculturali.it

About 25km northeast of Saluzzo is the **Castello di Racconigi**, one of Piedmont's former Royal Residences of the House of Savoy. Built in the twelfth century as a small fortress, it later became the summer hunting residence of the Carignano branch of the Savoy Family· Interiors are embellished with stuccos, frescoes and elaborate furnishings, while the gardens have a nineteenth-century structure, with waterways, caves, statues and ponds.

Santuario di Vicoforte

Mon–Sat 7am–12pm & 2.30–7pm, Sun 7am–12.30pm & 2.30–7.30pm • ⓣ 0174 565 555 ⓦ santuariodivicoforte.it

A one-hour drive southeast of Saluzzo, the **Santuario di Vicoforte** is a baroque masterpiece boasting the largest elliptical dome in the world. Created over the course of two centuries by architects Ascanio Vitozzi and Francesco Gallo, the sanctuary is embellished with spectacular trompe l'oeil frescoes. You can explore the building's ancient walkways and climb to the top of the dome with Magnificat, a tour run by local company Kalatà (by advance booking only; see ⓦ magnificat-italia.com for details).

Alba and Langhe Roero

The town of **Alba** and the surrounding **Langhe and Roero** hills (protected by UNESCO World Heritage status) signify two things: **white truffles** and **red wine**. The exquisite truffles are more delicate and aromatic than the black variety found further south, whereas most of the area's very different wines all come from the same grape, the Nebbiolo. The final taste is dependent on the soil: tuff-rich soil produces the grapes for the light red Nebbiolo; calcium and mineral-rich soil for the more robust Barolo, the "King of wines and the wine of Kings". The entire picturesque area around Alba is dotted with attractive hill-towns, castles, wineries and cantinas, such as **Barolo** and **Pollenzo**. Ask at the tourist office for one of the excellent free maps and suggestions for wine tours.

Alba

Whether or not you want to taste the extraordinary wines, **ALBA** is worth the visit for its alluring mix of red-brick medieval towers, Baroque and Renaissance palaces and

HIKING AROUND THE PO VALLEY

West of Saluzzo, the source of the River Po rises from the uncontaminated environment of the Po River Natural Park. Towards the end of the valley, the Alpine-style resort of **Crissolo** is the jumping-off point for the 5km hike (or take a minibus in summer) to the **Pian del Re**, a plain around the source of the Po, for a view of one of the passes legend claims Hannibal and his elephants used.

Crissolo is also a good base for climbing **Monviso** (3841m), one of Piemonte's highest mountains; it's a long (about 6hr) rocky scramble from the *Quintino Sella rifugio*, two to three hours beyond the Pian del Re. The walk to the *rifugio* is lovely, passing a series of **mountain lakes**; or you can do a circuit of the lakes, turning off the main trail just before Lago Chiaretto, from where a path leads past Lago Superiore and back to Pian del Re.

cobbled streets. And if you come in early October, you might catch the town's hilarious annual donkey race – a skit on nearby Asti's prestigious Palio.

The town's only sight as such is its late-Gothic **Duomo**, standing confectionery-pink on the central Piazza Risorgimento. But Alba is primarily a place to stroll and eat. Leading up to the centre from Piazza Michele Ferrero, the main drag of **Via Vittorio Emanuele II** is a fine, bustling street, with Alba's local produce on display – wines, truffles, cheeses, weird and wonderful mushroom varieties, and the wickedly sticky *torta di nocciole*, a deliciously nutty cake. Via Cavour is a pleasant medieval street, behind which the **donkey race** and displays of medieval pageantry attract the crowds during the October festival. In October and November Alba hosts the world-famous **White Truffle Fair** (ⓦfieradeltartufo.org), when you could blow your whole budget on a knobbly truffle or a meal in one of the many swanky restaurants. At the end of April/ beginning of May, the **Vinum wine festival** gives you the chance to taste five hundred local wines.

2

ARRIVAL, INFORMATION AND TOURS — ALBA

By train There are direct trains from Turin's Porta Susa (hourly; 1hr18min) and Torino Lingotto stations (hourly; 1hr11min).

By bus Buses leave from the bus station at Piazzale Dogliotti. Services from Alba don't reach all the surrounding hill-villages, so if you want to explore these your own transport is best. A number of bus companies travel to the city, each with their own stops dotted around the outskirts of town; if coming from Turin, you're best off travelling by train as you'll alight right in the city centre.

Destinations Barolo (3 daily Mon–Sat; 30min); Turin (Mon–Sat hourly; 1hr 55min).

Tourist office Piazza Risorgimento 2 (End Nov to end March Mon–Fri 9am–-6pm, Sat & Sun 9.30am–6pm; Apr to end Sept Mon–Fri 9am–6.30pm, Sat & Sun 10am–6.30pm; Oct to end Nov Mon–Fri 9am–6.30pm, Sat & Sun 9am–7pm; ⓣ0173 35 833, ⓦlangheroero.it).

Archeology tours A team of young archeologists run monthly Alba Sotterranea (Underground Alba) tours that visit Roman ruins around the town (ⓦambientecultura.it); book in advance via the tourist office.

ACCOMMODATION

Casa Dellatorre Via Pertinace 20 ⓣ0173 441 204, ⓦcasadellatorre.net. This pleasant B&B and café on a narrow cobbled street in the centre of Alba has three comfortable rooms furnished with French-style antiques giving onto a little courtyard. Service is friendly and informal; breakfast is served at the café. **€140**

Casa Scaparone Località Scaparone 45 ⓣ0173 33 946, ⓦcasascaparone.it. A wonderful agriturismo in beautiful surroundings just outside Alba. Breakfast includes home-made jams and bread, and the restaurant uses home-grown organic ingredients. The rooms are spacious with many of the original beams and floorboards restored: the feel is rustic chic. **€110**

Palazzo Finati Via Vernazza 8 ⓣ0173 366 324, ⓦpalazzofinati.it. Nine rooms in a nineteenth-century building with lovely frescoes that have been carefully restored. Walls are decorated with works of art by local artists (available for purchase), while the rooms feature antique furniture. Staff are friendly and helpful. **€180**

Villa La Favorita Località Altavilla 12 ⓣ338 471 5005, ⓦvillalafavorita.biz. Set on a hillside amid raspberry, cherry and hazelnut trees, this friendly hotel has rooms decorated in an eclectic style – the furniture and paintings date from the early nineteenth century to the 1950s. The garden is the perfect spot for a sundowner, and there's an open-air hot-tub, too. The hotel also produces its own wines. **€140**

EATING AND DRINKING

Lalibera Via Elvio Pertinace 24 ⓣ0173 293 155, ⓦlalibera.com. A welcoming restaurant with stylish modern interiors serving traditional seasonal dishes; pastas and bread are home-made. *Primi* €12, *secondi* €14. Mon 8–11pm, Tues–Sat 12–2pm & 8–11pm.

La Piola Piazza Risorgimento 4 ⓣ0173 442 800, ⓦlapiola-alba.it. Located opposite the tourist office in the picturesque heart of the historical centre, this is a popular spot to try some local Piemontese dishes such as *agnolotti del plin* (€15). Mon–Sat 12.15–2.30pm & 7.15–10pm.

Osteria dei Sognatori Via Macrino 8 ⓣ333 787 9230. With welcoming interiors featuring wooden furniture, this simple *osteria* serves hearty portions of local dishes; the menu, scribbled on recycled paper, changes daily with *primi* at €8 and *secondi* at €10. Daily noon–2pm & 7.30–10pm; closed Wed lunch.

Barolo

A few kilometres south of Alba, in the heart of the **Langhe**, the most famous spot is **BAROLO**, which gives its name to one of the premier Italian wines. It's a small village with peach- and ochre-washed houses set among extensive vineyards. A steady stream of wealthy gastronomes and wine connoisseurs come here for the **Enoteca Regionale del Barolo** (March Wed & Fri–Mon 10am–5.30pm, April to mid-Sept Thurs–Tues 10am–6.30pm, mid-Sept to end of Nov daily 10am–6.30pm, early to mid-Dec Thurs–Mon 10am–5.30pm; ⓣ0173 56 277, ⓦenotecadelbarolo.it) and the **WiMu Wine Museum** (daily: mid-March to mid-Nov 10.30am–7pm; mid-Nov to early Dec plus Christmas 10.30am–6pm; €8; ⓣ0173 386 697, ⓦwimubarolo.it), housed in a turreted castle on Piazza Falletti, while for a more quirky take on the wine industry, there's the original **Museo dei Cavatappi**, or Corkscrew Museum, at Piazza Castello 4 (Fri–Wed 10am–1pm & 2–6.30pm; €4; ⓣ0173 560 539, ⓦmuseodeicavatappi.it).

ACCOMMODATION AND EATING — BAROLO

★ Locanda in Cannubi Via Crosia 13 ⓣ0173 56 294 ⓦlocandaincannubi.it. Surrounded by rolling vineyards, the views from this glass-fronted restaurant are exceptional. The food is great too, with tasty seasonal dishes served in a refined setting. The four-course taster menu is €50; otherwise, *primi* €13, *secondi* €18. There are also a couple of comfortable rooms (€100) and an apartment sleeping four (€250). Thurs–Tues 12.30–2pm & 7.45–9.30pm; closed Sun eve.

Pollenzo

Though not as famous as Barolo, the pretty village of **POLLENZO**, situated just south of the Alba–Bra road, merits a visit. The buildings at Piazza Vittorio Emanuele 13 are of particular note: once home to the Agenzia di Pollenzo, King Carlo Alberto's headquarters for viticultural trials, they now belong to the Slow Food association and house the University of Gastronomic Sciences and the **Banca del Vino** (Tues–Sat 10am–7pm & Sun 10am–1pm; €3, or €8–20 for guided tours and tasting; ⓦbancadelvino.it), as well as a hotel and restaurant. Stored in the Savoy wine cellars, the Wine Bank keeps wines from all over Italy – a vault of the best vintages. Professional sommeliers guide you through the wine-tasting sessions, and it's an essential stopping-point for all wine lovers.

ACCOMMODATION AND EATING

Albergo dell'Agenzia Via Fossano 21 ⓣ0172 458 600, ⓦalbergoagenzia.it. Housed in the same beautiful building as the Banca del Vino, this four-star hotel has an inviting swimming pool along with a sauna, steam room and hot-tub. The rooms are comfortable with stone floors and rugs that lend the place a rustic touch; the restaurant serves creative traditional dishes in an elegant setting. **€240**

Carpe Noctem et Diem Via Amedeo di Savoia 5 ⓣ339 1019 233, ⓦcarpenoctemetdiem.it. Set in the old royal stables, this fabulous family-run restaurant offers Piemontese dishes with a contemporary touch including creative takes on vitello tonnato (cold sliced veal covered in a tuna and mayonnaise sauce; €13), raviolini del plin ai tre arrosti (ravioli stuffed with three types of meat; €13) and slow-cooked brasato al Barolo (braised beef with Barolo wine €18). Don't miss the tiramisú sabaudo made with sheep ricotta (€7). *Primi* €13, *secondi* €18. Tues 12.30–2pm, Wed–Sun 12.30–2pm & 7.30–9.30.

La Corte Albertina Via Amedeo di Savoia 8 ⓣ0172 458 410, ⓦalbergocortealbertina.it. In lush surroundings, this hotel offers a peaceful haven and its rooms have been furnished in keeping with the philosophy of calm. A/c and wi-fi in all rooms. As you would expect from a hotel wed to the Slow Food principles, its restaurant is exemplary, as is the wine list. **€120**

2

Asti

Some 30km northeast of Alba, **ASTI** was one of the most important towns in medieval times. Today its province is capital of Italy's sparkling-wine industry and the most famous producer of **Asti Spumante**. Each September, this small town becomes the focus of attention as it gears up for its **Palio**, the oldest in Italy. On the day of the race, the first Sunday in September, there's a thousand-strong **procession** of citizens dressed as their medieval ancestors, before the frenetic bare-backed horse race around Piazza Alfieri – followed by the awarding of the *palio* (banner) to the winner and all-night partying.

The rest of the year, Piazza Alfieri and the former Palio site, Piazza Campo del Palio, together host the region's largest open-air market (Wed & Sat). On the second weekend of September Piazza Campo del Palio houses the **Festival delle Sagre** during which stalls sell traditional dishes and wines in a reconstructed traditional village, and hundreds of people dress in costume to evoke agricultural life. If you want to sample Asti Spumante or other wines from the region and the rest of Italy, come for the **Douja d'Or, the National Show of Selected Wines** held from the second Friday to the third Sunday in September.

Collegiata di San Secondo

Piazza San Secondo • Daily 7.30am–7pm • Free

Dedicated to the Patron Saint of Asti, the present **Collegiata di San Secondo** church was built between the thirteenth and fifteenth centuries. Of the previous building only the Romanesque bell tower remains, along with the central part of the crypt that holds the saint's remains. Among the most notable works found within the church are a polyptych and a panel painting by Gandolfino d'Asti, along with traces of frescoes that date from the 1300s and 1400s.

Corso Alfieri

The main street, **Corso Alfieri**, slices through town from Piazza Alfieri, with the medieval complex of **San Pietro in Consavia** at no. 2 (Tues–Sun Nov–March 10am–1pm & 3–6pm; April–Oct 10am–1pm & 4–7pm; free). The **Duomo** on Piazza Cattedrale (daily 8.30am–noon & 3–5.30pm; free) is one of the most beautiful examples of Gothic architecture in Piemonte. Children will enjoy visiting the **Museo Paleontologico** at Corso Alfieri 381 (Mon–Thurs 10am–4pm, Sat & Sun: summer 10am–1pm & 4–7pm, winter 10am–1pm & 3–6pm; ⓦ museodeifossili.org; €3), while Palazzo Alfieri, which houses the **Museo Alfieriano** (Tues–Sun 10am–7pm; entry with smarTicket) in Palazzo Alfieri, Corso Alfieri 375, was once the childhood home of Italian dramatist and poet Vittorio Alfieri. The **Museo Civico Sant'Anastasio (Tues–Sun April–Oct 10am–1pm & 4–7pm, Nov–March 10am–1pm & 3–6pm;** entry with smarTicket) houses the remains of a Benedictine monastery and a beautiful Romanesque crypt. A fine example of eighteenth-century architecture, Palazzo Mazzetti, at Corso Alfieri 357, houses the **Civic Museum** (Tues–Sun 10am–7pm; last entry at 6pm €10; ⓦ palazzomazzetti.it), with its excellent collection of paintings and frescoes from the seventeenth to the twentieth centuries. You can climb to the top of the **Torre Troyana,** (April–Oct Tues–Sun 10am–7pm; entry with smarTicket) the most representative of the city's medieval towers.

ARRIVAL & INFORMATION — ASTI

By train Regular direct trains connect Turin to Asti in as little as 35min (every 30min).

Tourist office Piazza Alfieri 34 (Mon–Sat 9am–1pm & 2–6pm, Sun 9am–1pm & 1.30–5.30pm; ⓣ 0141 530 357, ⓦ astiturismo.it). At Palazzo Mazzetti (ⓦ palazzomazzetti.it) you can purchase a SmarTicket (€5) that grants access to a number of museums dotted around town.

ACCOMMODATION

★ **La Villa** Via Torino 7, Mombaruzzo ⊕0141 793 890, ⊕lavillahotel.net. A wonderful hotel 30km southeast of Asti nestled among rolling vineyards. The fifteen light and airy rooms feature local antiques and handcrafted furniture; a couple have freestanding bathtubs, and others have walk-in showers. The restaurant serves excellent Italian cuisine using local ingredients (four-course menu €49), and there are wine-tasting sessions featuring the region's excellent wines. There's a lovely swimming pool, too. **€220**

Relais Cattedrale Via Cattedrale 7 ⊕0141 092 099, ⊕relaiscattedrale.it. In the centre of town, this place is decorated in a hotchpotch of styles – there are frescoes from the seventeenth centuries, lamps from the 1970s, furniture from North Africa, Turkey and Lebanon, and ancient stone sinks. But this eclectic approach works, and the spacious, individually furnished rooms feature handmade beds. **€130**

2

EATING AND DRINKING

Campanarò Corso Alfieri 36 ⊕0141 33 252, ⊕campanaro.net. A friendly family-run place offering a range of Piemontese specialities (most gluten-free) – try the unusual *agnolotti gobbi monferrini* (€10), pasta stuffed with rabbit, pork and veal served with a glass of Barbera wine that is then poured over the *agnolotti*. There's an extensive wine list listing only local wines from Monferrato, Langhe and Roero. Thurs–Tues noon–3pm & 7.30–10.30pm; closed Sat lunch.

Osteria del Diavolo Piazza San Martino 6 ⊕0141 30 221, ⊕osteriadeldiavolo.it. Excellent friendly *osteria* with tables spilling out onto the pretty square in the summer months; the cuisine is both Ligurian and Piemontese, and includes tasty dishes such as *Battuta di razza piemontese e baccalà* (raw meat and salted codfish; €10). Mon–Sat 7.30–10.30pm.

Tastè Vin Via C. Vassallo 2 ⊕0141 320 017. This cosy wine bar, grocer's and restaurant, with a few tables lining the street, offers wines by the glass (from €3), and a weekly changing menu scribbled on the blackboard. It's a great spot to buy some local food to take home – or simply to enjoy a preprandial drink and a bite to eat in the cosy interior. *Primi* €9, *secondi* €12. Wed–Fri noon–2.30pm & 6.30pm–midnight, Sat & Sun 6.30pm–midnight.

Northern Piemonte

The main attraction of northern Piemonte is the mountains, especially the dramatic Alpine **Valsesia**, which winds up to the foot of Monte Rosa on the Swiss border. On the way is the industrial town of Ivrea and one of the region's most visited sanctuaries, the **Santuario di Oropa** near **Biella**. From here you're well poised for either Piemonte's mountains or those of Valle d'Aosta, a few kilometres west. Worth a slight detour is the magical train ride that starts at **Domodossola**, conveniently en route if you're heading for Switzerland.

Ivrea

IVREA, 53km north of Turin, is the home of Italian electronics manufacturer Olivetti, whose headquarters is located on the banks of the river. Dotted around the city are the modernist estates built between the 1930s and 1980s to house the company's employees – their original design reflects the town's rich architectural heritage, and today they form part of MAAM, the city's Open Air Museum of Modern Architecture (you can download a map of the buildings at ⊕ivreacittaindustriale.it or pick one up from the tourist office). There's also a little museum, the Laboratorio-Museo Tecnologic@mente (⊕museotecnologicamente.it) housing a wonderful collection of old Olivetti typewriters, although it's only open a couple of days a month – check the website or with the tourist office for the latest opening times. Today, the town is mostly known for its spectacular **carnival** (⊕storicocarnevaleivrea.it) that falls in February or March – featuring piping, drumming, masked balls, historic processions and fireworks – that culminates in a bizarre three-day "Battle of the Oranges" when the whole town turns out to pelt each other with oranges – you have to wear a red hat if you don't want to be a target.

Museo Civico Pier Alessandro Garda

Piazza Ottinetti • Mon–Wed & Fri 9am–1pm, Thurs 9am–1pm & 2.30–6.30pm, Sat 3–7pm, first Sun of month 3–7pm • €5 • 0125 634 155, museogardaivrea.it

Located in the former monastery of Santa Chiara, the **Museo Civico Pier Alessandro Garda** displays exhibits from the Neolithic age up to the modern day. It also houses a beautiful collection of oriental art including watercolours on pith paper, incense burners in the shape of animals and plants, and a wonderful nineteenth-century picnic set made of wood, pearl, silk, gold and silver. The Croff Collection displays a valuable collection of paintings, drawings and documents.

2

Castello di Masino

Caravino • March & Nov Wed–Sun 10am–5pm; April, May & Oct Tues–Sun 10am–6pm; June–Sept Tues–Fri 10am–6pm, Sat & Sun 10am–7pm • €10 including 45min guided tour • 0125 778 100, visitfai.it/castellodimasino

About 13km southeast of Ivrea, the **Castello di Masino** is an eleventh-century royal palace surrounded by pretty gardens and commanding lovely views over the plain of Canavese. The castle was the residence of the earls of Valperga for ten centuries; its well-preserved interior houses seventeenth-century portraits and frescoes, damasks, pottery and antiques in thirty sumptuous rooms.

The five lakes of Ivrea

The area around Ivrea is peppered with five small **lakes**, two of which – **Sirio** and **Pistono** – have small beaches where you can sunbathe and swim. Sirio has a café and private beach area with loungers, while the pleasant *La Monella* trattoria at Pistono is a great spot to grab a sundowner in summer.

ARRIVAL AND INFORMATION — IVREA

By bus The bus station is at Via Dora Baltea Movicentro, with 2 daily (except Sat) services to Biella (1hr 15min).

By train The train station is at Corso Costantino Nigra 73.
Destinations Aosta (hourly; 58min); Biella (hourly; 1hr 45min); Torino (hourly; 1hr 10min).

Tourist information Piazza Ottinetti (Mon 9am–1pm, Tues, Wed & Fri 9am–1pm & 3–5pm, Thurs 9am–1pm & 2.30-6.30pm, Sat 9am–1pm & 3-7pm, first Sun of the month 3–7pm; 0125 618 131, turismotorino.org).

ACCOMMODATION

Agriturismo La Perulina Via San Pietro Martire 35 0125 45 222, laperulina.it. A laidback agriturismo that produces its own honey and has goats, geese, pigs, chickens and even an ostrich. The three rooms are simply furnished, and the welcoming owner Gianpietro rustles up hearty set meals for €26. **€65**

Spazio Bianco Via Patrioti 17 0125 196 1620, spaziobiancoivrea.it. This welcoming place has six themed rooms that recall Ivrea's culture and traditions – the Carnival room is decorated in orangey-red to honour the battle of the oranges that takes place every year, while the Erbaluce room features pastel tones and celebrates the area's white wine grape. **€110**

EATING AND DRINKING

La Mugnaia Via Arduino 53 0125 40 530, mugnaia.com. One of the town's best restaurants, this is a great spot to try some local specialities including oven-cooked Piemontese *fassone* (€19), a rare breed of Italian beef prized for its excellent meat. *Primi* €14, *secondi* €17. Tues–Fri 7.30–10pm, Sat & Sun 12.30–2.30pm & 7.30–10pm.

La Piazzetta Via Amedeo di Castellamonte 23 0125 642 867. Delicious home-cooking at this friendly restaurant managed and run by an all-female team. The menu changes weekly, and includes local specialities such as nettle flan with fresh tomatoes. *Primi* €11, *secondi* €14. Mon–Fri noon–3pm & 7.30–midnight, Sat 7.30pm–midnight.

Osteria San Maurizio Via Guarnotta 1 0125 189 3509, osteria-san-maurizio.it. A warm and welcoming *osteria* with vaulted brick ceilings, wooden furniture and black-and-white photos of Ivrea decorating the walls. Ingredients are mainly sourced from the local area, and the menu changes every two weeks or so. *Primi* €12, *secondi* €15. Tues–Fri 12.30–2.30pm & 7.30–10pm, Sat 7.30–10pm, Sun 12.30–3pm.

Biella and the Santuario di Oropa

To the northeast of Turin lies the provincial capital of **BIELLA**, known for its wool industry: the town's periphery is studded with nineteenth-century industrial chimneys, while the hilltop upper town is where the wool barons built their mansions and villas. Its small medieval quarter, reached by funicular, is worth a wander, too. The **Santuario di Oropa** lies about 11km northwest, while 6km southeast of the city, the **Ricetto di Candelo** is one of Europe's best-preserved medieval fortifications – a number of Italian movies have been filmed here.

2

Santuario di Oropa

Via Santuario di Oropa 480 • **Complex** Daily 6am–midnight; **Ancient Basilica** daily 7.am–7pm; **Upper Basilica** • Mon–Sat 9am–4pm & Sun 9am–5pm • Free • **Gallery of the Nativity Scenes** • Mon–Sat 9am–4pm & Sun 9am–5pm • Free • **Museum** July & Aug Tues–Sun 10am–12.30pm & 2.30–5pm; May, June & Sept Sat & Sun only; Oct–Apr Sun only • €3 • ☎ 015 2555 1200, ⓦ santuariodioropa.it • Bus #360 from Biella's train station (7 daily; 40min)

The most important Marian sanctuary in the Alps, the **Santuario di Oropa** was founded in the fourth century by St Eusebio, the first Bishop of Vercelli, to house a black statue of the Madonna and Child. It's the most venerated of Piemonte's shrines, with the Ancient Basilica being its spiritual centre. It's not a secluded mountain hideaway, however – the sanctuary has developed into a self-sufficient village, with shops, restaurants and accommodation for pilgrims, plus a **museum** containing archeological finds, jewels and liturgical fittings, a Monumental Cemetery, a Botanical Garden (May–Sept), an Adventure Park and Sacro Monte, home to 12 chapels dedicated to the life of Mary. From the sanctuary, a cable car takes visitors to Lago Mucrone (7min; 1900m), a good starting point for hikes.

ARRIVAL AND INFORMATION — BIELLA

By train Biella has two train stations (the main one is San Paolo), with trains running regularly from Turin (usually changing at Santhia) and taking about 1hr 30min and Milan (change at Novara; 1hr 45min).

By bus There are two buses daily between Biella and Ivrea (bus #380 from the train station; 1hr 10min), 10 daily buses to Vercelli (#55 from the train station; 1hr) and seven daily buses to the Santuario (bus #2 from the train station; 40min). See ⓦ atapspa.it for timetables.

Tourist office Piazza Vittorio Veneto 3 (Mon–Fri 9am–5pm, Sat 9am–12.30pm & 2.30–5.30pm; ☎ 015 351 128, ⓦ atl.biella.it).

ACCOMMODATION

Al Ricetto B&B Via San Sebastiano 35, Candelo ☎ 015 253 8838, ⓦ alricetto.it. This small B&B in Candelo, 6km southeast of Biella, has two lovely rooms with parquet flooring, wooden furniture and crimson rugs; there are two connecting bedrooms on the first floor, while the top floor houses a large, cosy attic room. **€60**

B&B Del Piazzo Corso del Piazzo 14 ☎ 340 158 1357, ⓦ bbdelpiazzo.blogspot.it. Run by a friendly mother and son, this welcoming B&B in the heart of the old town has three spacious rooms furnished with antiques. There's a terrace with lovely views of the surrounding area, where breakfast is served in the summer. Shared bathroom **€64**, private bathroom **€80**.

EATING

La Civetta Piazza Cucco 10/B ☎ 015 26 342, ⓦ lacivettadibiella.it. A charming little place with colourful chairs and copper pots dangling from the ceiling. The food is very reasonable, with *primi* €8, *secondi* €11. On warm evenings, you can sit under the cobbled colonnade, or there's seating on the first floor which also houses a little bookstore. Thurs–Mon 5pm–1am.

Osteria Due Cuori Piazza Cisterna 11 ☎ 015 30 145. A pleasant restaurant serving excellent fare on one of Biella's prettiest squares. The menu changes seasonally, with *primi* at €12, *secondi* at €16. Try the delicious *torcetti*, sugar-coated biscuits that have been made here since 1859. Tues–Fri 7.30–10.30pm; Sat & Sun 12.30–2.30pm & 7.30–10.30pm.

Valsesia

Heading on into the northern heights, the main road follows the River Sesia to the foot of multi-peaked Monte Rosa, whose massive bulk dominates five Italian valleys

and spreads north into Switzerland. Flanked by dark pine-wooded slopes topped with a toothed ridge of rock, **VALSESIA** is the easternmost valley, and it's also the greenest and most dramatic. Plenty of **treks** can be done here in summer, and the valley is also popular for **canoeing** and **rafting**: several centres organize classes and excursions – the tourist office can advise on these and trekking routes. In winter, the area is popular with **skiers**.

2

Sacro Monte di Varallo

Varallo • Basilica Daily 8.30am–12.20pm & 2.15–6.30pm (winter until 5.30pm); Grounds 24hr• Free • ⓦ sacromontedivarallo.org • Take the bus from Alagna to Varallo (every 2–3hr; 1hr), then it's a 30min uphill walk to Sacro Monte, or catch the cable car from Varallo town (€5 return)

Some 40km before Alagna, the main road along the valley passes through the town of Varallo, where the UNESCO World Heritage Site of **Sacro Monte di Varallo** is well worth a visit. Built at the end of the fifteenth century, it houses a basilica and 45 beautiful chapels with more than eight hundred life-size painted figures in wood and terracotta.

Alagna

At the head of the valley, right below Monte Rosa, **ALAGNA** is the most convenient place in the valley to stay. It has a cluster of traditional dwellings built by the age-old Swiss religious sect known as the Walsers, who have maintained their unique language and culture here for at least seven centuries. To find out more about the community, visit the little **Walser Museum**, in a quaint wooden house on Frazione Pedemonte dating from 1628, which showcases how the Walsers once lived (July & Aug Mon–Fri 3–6pm, Sat & Sun 10am–noon & 3–6pm; Sept–June Sat & Sun 2–5pm; €3).

ARRIVAL AND INFORMATION — ALAGNA

By bus Buses from Turin (ⓦ canovaspa.it) run to Varallo (1–2 daily; 2hr 15min), from where ATAP buses travel to Alagna (1hr; no services on Sun). In Aug there are direct buses from Milan to Alagna (1 daily; 3hr 20min; ⓦ baranzelli.it). Timetables are subject to frequent change. Call the tourist office in Varallo (ⓣ 0163 564 404) for the latest schedule.

Tourist office Piazza Grober 1 (July–Sept & Dec–April Daily 9.30am–12.30pm & 3–6pm; Oct, Nov, May & June Mon, Wed & Thurs 9.30am–12.30pm, Fri, Sat & Sun 9.30–12.30pm & 3–6pm; ⓣ 0163 922 988, ⓦ atlvalsesiavercelli.it).

ACCOMMODATION AND EATING

★ **Dir Und Don** Piazza Regina Margherita 1 ⓣ 0163 922 642. Housed in the former stable of a seventeenth-century Walser house, this attractive restaurant has rustic wooden interiors and a *menù walser* for €25; in summer, there are a handful of tables on the little square. Wed–Mon noon–2pm & 7–10.30pm.

★ **Zimmer Casa Prati** Frazione Casa Prati 6 ⓣ 0163 922 802, ⓦ zimmercasaprati.com. A lovely place featuring rustic cosy interiors decorated with ancient objects of the Walser tradition, including books, photographs and warm fabrics. Breakfast consists of sweet and savoury homemade delights as well as meats and cheeses from the area. There's a wellness area with steam room, sauna and relaxation zone too – perfect to soothe those aching muscles after a day on the slopes. €110

Domodossola and the border

At the foot of the Simplon Pass, and on the main train line between Milan and Bern, in Switzerland (15 trains daily from Novara), is the little town of **DOMODOSSOLA**. With its arcaded medieval centre and market square, it warrants a visit in its own right, but is more famous as the starting point of a scenic **train ride**, La Vigezzina–Centovalli, which connects Domodossola with **Locarno**, in Switzerland, taking in the vineyards and chestnut forests of the Val Vigezzo and Centovalli along the way. Although the ride is pricier than the regular train, it's well worth it; Interrail Passes are valid. The journey takes an hour and a half, but you can get off at any of the pretty

flower-strewn stations en route; when you want the next train to stop, raise the red-and-white signal on the platform.

Valle d'Aosta's Bassa Valle

Heading north from Piemonte into **Valle d'Aosta**, the A5 and SS26 road snake their way through the **BASSA VALLE** (Lower Valley), peppered with ancient forts and castles. The Valle d'Aosta is dominated by the highest mountains in Europe, namely Mont Blanc, Gran Paradiso, Monte Rosa and the Matterhorn, and in winter the region sees plenty of **skiers** from Turin and Milan thanks to its excellent resorts. In summer it's a popular destination too, with plenty of outdoor sports including **mountain climbing** and **trekking**.

Forte di Bard

Bard • Tues–Fri 10am–6pm, Sat & Sun 10am–7pm; open daily 10am–7pm last week of July & throughout August; closed mid-Nov to early Dec • Fort free; Museo delle Alpi €8; Prisons €4; Museo Ferdinando €9; joint ticket for all three museums €15; Le Alpi dei Ragazzi €6 • T 0125 833 811, W fortedibard.it • The nearest station is Hone-Bard, with hourly trains from Ivrea (20min) and Aosta (40min): the fortress is 500m from the station

The **Forte di Bard** is the region's most important example of military architecture. The original structure dates from 1034, although the present building was built in the early nineteenth century. It stretches over three levels that are connected by glass-fronted lifts commanding lovely views over the rooftops of the little town of Bard that spills into the valley below. The fort houses the **Museo delle Alpi**, with displays on Alpine life; the former **prisons** with 24 cells; the **Museo Ferdinando** which explores the development of defence strategy in fortifications and the concept of boundaries from political, economic and cultural views; and **Le Alpi dei Ragazzi**, an interactive museum for children that allows visitors to experience a virtual ascent of Mont Blanc.

Castello di Issogne

Piazza Castello, Issogne • April–Sept daily 9am–7pm; Oct–March Tues–Sun 10am–1pm & 2–5pm • €5, guided tours only • T 0125 929 373 • The nearest train station is Verrès, with regular trains from Ivrea (30min) and Aosta (30min): the castle is a 15min walk from the station

Although the site where the castle stands had been occupied since Roman times, the **Castello di Issogne** was built in the early fifteenth century by Ibleto of Challant. Its courtyard houses a pretty wrought-iron fountain in the shape of a pomegranate tree and a frescoed portico depicting scenes of daily life, with a beautiful stone spiral staircase leading to the first floor. Look out for the graffiti, mostly in French and Latin, that has been left over the centuries on the frescoed walls both in the courtyard and in the rooms.

Castello di Fénis

Frazione Chez Sapin 1, Fénis • April–Sept daily 9am–7pm; Oct–March Tues-Sun 10am–1pm & 2-5pm • €7, guided tours only • T 0165 764 263 • There's a direct bus from Aosta to Fénis (every 2hr; 30min): check W savda.it for timetable

Backed by wooded hills and encircled by two rows of turreted walls, the **Castello di Fénis** is the result of various building campaigns between the twelfth and fifteenth centuries. The original manor house belonged to the Challants, Viscounts of Aosta, who added a semicircular stairway in the courtyard in the early fifteenth century. The courtyard is adorned with wonderful frescoes, including a courtly St George rescuing a princess from the clutches of a dragon,

overlooked by a tribe of wise men and prophets brandishing moral maxims on curling scrolls.

ACCOMMODATION AND EATING — BASSA VALLE

Agriturismo Maison Rosset Passaggio Rosset 1, Nus ⊤0165 767 176, ⓦmaisonrosset.it. A pleasant agriturismo in the centre of Nus offering rooms and apartments, some with a kitchenette. A procession of dishes flows in the dining area with excellent home-made cuisine that uses ingredients from the agriturismo's farm and vegetable garden; the restaurant is also open to non-guests. **€80**

Al Maniero Frazione Pied de Ville 58, Issogne ⊤0125 929 219, ⓦristorantealmaniero.it/almaniero.asp. A short walk from the Castello di Issogne, this restaurant serves great dishes prepared with local ingredients. The Valdostana menu costs €24, while *primi* start at €9 and *secondi* at €12. There are also six simple but comfortable rooms (€90). Tues–Sun 12.30–2.30pm & 7.30–9.30pm.

Aosta and around

AOSTA, the attractive mountain-valley capital of Valle d'Aosta province, is an ideal base for exploring the northwest of the region. Surrounded by the Alps, the town's key attraction is its position, with access to the lovely valleys of the Parco Nazionale del Gran Paradiso (see page 165), the ski resorts of **Mont Blanc** and a sprinkling of castles, such as the impressive **Castello di Sarre**.

Aosta

Founded by the Romans in 25 BC, **AOSTA** was primarily an imperial military camp, vestiges of which can be seen in the town's impressive Roman ruins. In the east, the dignified **Arco di Augusto** celebrates the Roman victory over the Salassi, a tribe from

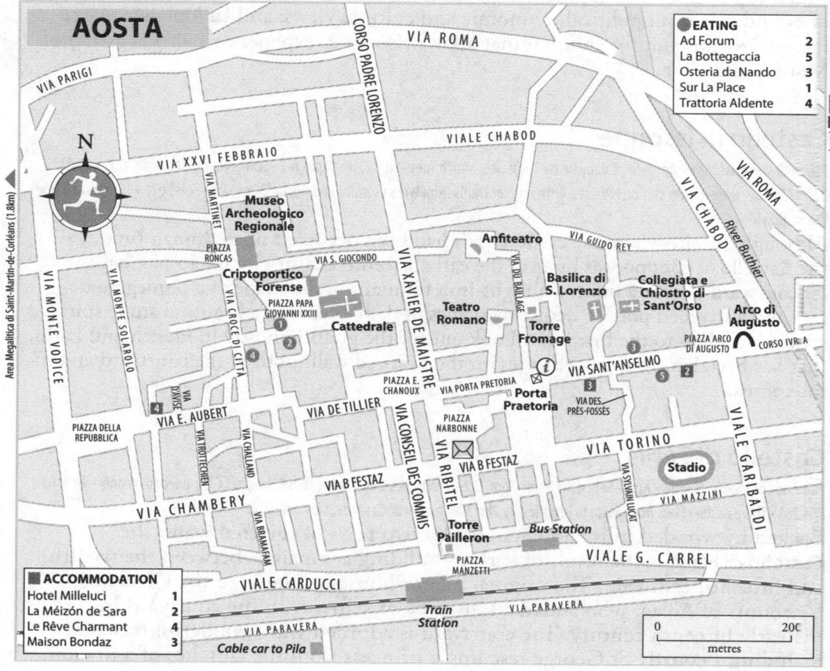

the Italian side of the Little St Bernard Pass. It was erected in 25 BC to honour the Emperor Augustus, after whom the town was named. Beyond is a well-preserved **Roman bridge**, its single arch spanning the dried-up River Buthier, while to the west is one of the town's most impressive sights, the **Porta Praetoria**, whose two parallel triple-arched gateways served as the main entrance into the Roman town.

Teatro Romano

Via Porta Pretoria, on the corner Via du Baillage • Daily: April–Sept 9am–7pm; Oct–March 10am–1pm & 2–5pm • €7 (includes entry to the Criptoportico Forense, Museo Archeologico Regionale and the Chiesa Paleocristiana di San Lorenzo)

An elegant section of the four-storey facade of the **Teatro Romano** remains, 22m high and pierced with arched windows. Likely to have seated between three thousand and four thousand spectators, it was one of the few Roman theatres to have originally been roofed.

Collegiata e Chiostro di Sant'Orso

Piazzetta Sant'Orso • Daily 9am–5.30pm; Frescoes: check with the tourist office for latest viewing times • Free

The **Collegiata e Chiostro di Sant'Orso** houses a number of eleventh-century **frescoes** hidden up in its roof: you can examine them at close quarters from specially constructed walkways, though they are only visible at limited times of the year. The fifteenth-century choir stalls are carved with a menagerie of holy men and animals, ranging from bats and monkeys to a tonsured monk. There are even better carvings on the capitals of the Romanesque **cloisters** – mostly scenes from the story of Christ.

Cattedrale

Piazza Giovanni XXIII • **Cathedral** Mon–Sat 6.30am–noon & 3–7pm, Sun 7am–noon & 3–7pm • Free • **Frescoes** Check with the tourist office for latest viewing times • €5 • **Museum** Daily 3–5pm • €4, Museum & Frescoes €6 • Ⓦ cattedraleaosta.it

Aosta's **cattedrale** has a Gothic interior with carved choir stalls, sporting fantastic creatures, a lion and a snail nestled among the saints. Like Sant'Orso, it has some impressive tenth-century frescoes hidden in the roof, saved for posterity by the lowering of the ceiling in the fourteenth century; you can visit these on a guided tour. There's also a small **museum** displaying a collection of precious artefacts including a carved wooden Gothic altarpiece and engraved silver relic busts set with crystals and gemstones.

Criptoportico Forense

Piazza Giovanni XXIII • Daily: April–Sept 9am–7pm; Oct–March 10am–1pm & 2–5pm • €7 (includes entry to the Teatro Romano, Museo Archeologico Regionale and the Chiesa Paleocristiana di San Lorenzo)

The well-preserved **Criptoportico Forense** is a vaulted passage built beneath the Roman forum – such constructions were common in Roman times and probably served as protected walkways. It is thought they may have had a political and liturgical function, connecting the sacred temple with the public square.

Museo Archeologico Regionale

Piazza Roncas 12 • Daily April–Sept 9am–7pm; Oct–March 10am–1pm & 2-5pm • €7 (includes entry to the Teatro Romano, Criptoportico Forense and the Chiesa Paleocristiana di San Lorenzo)

The **Museo Archeologico Regionale** has interesting exhibits on the settlements in and around Aosta since Neolithic times. Displays include artefacts from the Celtic Salassi tribe who ended up being sold as slaves by the Romans.

Area Megalitica di Saint-Martin-de-Corléans – Museo e Parco Archeologico

Corso Saint-Martin-de-Corléans 258 • April–Sept 9am–7pm; Oct–March Tues–Sun 10am–1pm & 2–5pm • €7

Occupying an area of just under 2.5 acres on the western fringes of the city, the **Area Megalitica di Saint-Martin-de-Corléans** narrates the cultural development of man from the late Stone Age to the present day. It's home to a number of megalithic monuments

– menhirs, standing stones, burial grounds, dolmen tombs – that suggest it was for centuries an important worship and burial site.

ARRIVAL AND INFORMATION — AOSTA

By train The train station is on Piazza Manzetti, south of the centre.

Destinations Ivrea (hourly; 1hr); Pré-St-Didier (9 daily; 40–50min); Sarre (9 daily; 10min); Turin (hourly; 2hr).

2

By bus You can get to most places within the region by bus from the bus station on Via G. Carrel, but some of the more remote valleys are served only by buses running at school times out of season (contact the tourist office for timetables and check savda.it for routes).

Destinations Cogne (6 daily; 50min); Courmayeur (hourly; 1hr); Pont Valsavarenche (via Villeneuve; 2–3 daily; 1hr 30min); Pré-St-Didier (hourly; 50min); Rhêmes Notre Dame (via Villeneuve; 3 daily; 1hr10min).

Tourist office Piazza Porta Praetoria 3 (daily 9am–7pm; 0165 236 627, lovevda.it).

ACCOMMODATION

Hotel Milleluci Località Porossan-Roppoz 15 0165 44 274, hotelmilleluci.com; map p.162. This four-star hotel 2km east of the city centre has comfortable rooms with wooden furnishings and dark olive-green tapestries. There's an outdoor pool, an open-air Jacuzzi and a spa with sauna, steam room and hot tub. Breakfast consists of local cheeses, cold cuts and home-made cakes. **€200**

La Méizón de Sara Via Sant'Anselmo 134 393 182 6737, lameizondesara.com; map p.162. A stone's throw from the Arco di Augusto, this friendly place in a late nineteenth-century building has rustic rooms named after local sights and mountains. **€100**

★ **Le Rêve Charmant** Via Vaudan Marchè 6 0165 238 855, lerevecharmant.com; map p.162. A welcoming hotel with cosy wooden interiors. The six bedrooms have rustic wardrobes and parquet floors with crimson rugs; some have bathrooms with built-in steam rooms. **€114**

Maison Bondaz Rue Saint-Anselme 36 345 637 3351, maisonbondaz.com; map p.162. In a building with traditional character, two rooms at this friendly little place have small balconies; all feature modern bathrooms with glass showers. A hearty breakfast is served in the ground-floor dining area. **€125**

EATING AND DRINKING

Ad Forum Via M. de Sales 11 0165 548 510, adforum-enoteca.com; map p.162. The real draw of this café, restaurant and wine bar by the cathedral is its spacious garden – a pleasant spot to enjoy a drink in summer. There are occasional live music performances too. Café & bar daily 10am–midnight; restaurant 12–2.20pm & 7–10.45pm; Oct–May closed Mon.

La Bottegaccia Via Sant'Anselmo 90 338 816 9229; map p.162. A popular wine bar and deli whose counter overflows with cheeses, cold cuts and local products to take home as gifts; otherwise enjoy a glass of wine (€4.50) and a cheese and meat platter (€7) at one of the small wooden tables. Tues–Sun 10am–11pm.

Osteria da Nando Via S. Anselmo 99 0165 44 455, osterianando.com; map p.162. A pleasant restaurant with a vaulted interior and a handful of tables on the street in summer serving tasty local specialities including *fonduta* (cheese fondue; €15) and *crèpes alla valdostana* (with local fontina cheese and ham; €12). Wed–Mon noon–3pm & 7.30–10pm; closed Wed lunch.

Sur La Place Piazza della Cattedrale 0165 548 661, surlaplace.it; map p.162. A small informal bistro with outdoor seating in a glass-fronted veranda looking across the square to the church. Dishes use local ingredients where possible. *Primi* €10, *secondi* €16. Daily noon–3pm & 4pm–midnight.

Trattoria Aldente Via Croce di Città 34 0165 194 596 aldentetrattoria.eu; map p.162. A characterful trattoria with a weekly changing menu featuring a range of home-cooked dishes from Valle d'Aosta. Dining is in two areas – the front room has rustic furniture and chequered tablecloths, while the second dining area has vaulted stone walls from the seventeenth century. *Primi* €11, *secondi* €16. Daily noon–2.30pm & 7–10.30pm.

Castello di Sarre

Località Lalex, Sarre • April–Sept daily 9am–7pm; Oct–March Tues–Sun 10am–1pm & 2–5pm• €5 • Buses from Aosta (every 45min; 15min) run on urban line 2 and 7 (svap.it) or the regional Aosta-Courmayeur service (savda.it); from the bus stop, walk up the main road and take the unmarked turning just before the tollbooth

West of Aosta are a number of **castles**, the best of which is the thirteenth-century **Castello di Sarre**, the former hunting lodge of Vittorio Emanuele II. The king stamped the halls of the castle with his astounding taste in interior decor, pushing

the hunting-lodge motif to its limits, with horns of wild ibex lining the main gallery and thousands of white chamois skulls studding the stuccoed festoons. The walls are also lined with portraits and sculptures of members of the House of Savoy, as well as paintings dedicated to royal hunting expeditions in the nearby valleys.

Pont d'Aël

Pondel • April–Sept daily 9am–7pm; Oct Sat & Sun 10am–1pm & 2–5pm • €3 • Catch a bus (ⓦ svap.it) from Aosta to Cogne and hop off at Pondel

In the little hamlet of Pondel, en route to Cogne, the **Pont d'Aël** aqueduct was built of masonry and stone in the third century BC. The ingenious structure functioned as a bridge and aqueduct and is remarkably well preserved – today, you can still walk across the bridge on what was once the aqueduct, then head back through the covered passageway that cuts through the middle of the bridge.

Colle del Gran San Bernardo

North of Aosta, the **Colle del Gran San Bernardo** (2473m) leads the way into Switzerland. Named after the famous monastery that for centuries provided shelter to travellers on the main pilgrim route from Northern Europe to Rome, it was the home of the eponymous big brown-and-white dogs which rescued Alpine travellers in distress. The history of the mountain pass is documented in the **museum** (June–Sept daily 10am–6pm; CHF10) housed in the monastery-hospice, although you'll need your passport to visit as it's situated over the border in Switzerland. The pass is open only in summer, but the border is open year-round by way of a tunnel.

Gran Paradiso National Park

For some of the area's most beautiful mountains and valleys, head to the **Gran Paradiso National Park** (ⓦ pngp.it) – Italy's first national park, spread around the valleys at the foot of 4061m-high Monte Gran Paradiso. The park's three valleys – **Cogne, Valsavarenche** and **Val di Rhêmes** – are popular, but tourist development has been cautious and well organized. The hotels are good and the campsites not too vast. There are a few mountain *rifugi* and *bivacchi* (unoccupied shelters) between which run well-marked footpaths. Though it's primarily a summer resort for walkers, the cross-country skiing is also good, and every winter a 45km **Gran Paradiso trek** is organized at Cogne (contact the tourist office in Cogne for details). The starting point for the ascent of Gran Paradiso itself is **Pont** in

WILDLIFE IN GRAN PARADISO NATIONAL PARK

Gran Paradiso National Park owes its foundation to King Vittorio Emanuele II, who donated his extensive hunting park to the state in 1922, ensuring that the population of **ibex** that he and his hunters had reduced to near extinction would, after all, survive. There are now around 3500 ibex here and about six thousand **chamois**, living most of the year above the tree line but descending to the valleys in winter and spring. The most dramatic sightings are during the mating season in November and December, when you may see pairs of males fighting it out for a female. You might also spy **golden eagles** nesting, and there are a number of rare **Alpine flowers**, most of which can be seen in the botanical garden in the Val di Cogne.

the Valsavarenche, while Cogne gives access to the Alta Via 2, a long, high-level mountain trail.

GETTING AROUND **GRAN PARADISO NATIONAL PARK**

By bus Regular buses run throughout the year from Aosta to Cogne, Rhêmes and Valsavarenche (see ⓦsvap.it and ⓦsavda.it for the latest timetables).

By car If you're using your own transport, access to the Rhêmes and Valsaverenche valleys is via the village of Introd, about 2km from Villeneuve.

2

Val di Cogne

Val di Cogne is the most popular and most dramatic section of the park. Its lower reaches are narrow, the road running above the fast-flowing Grand Eyvia River overlooked by sheer mountains. The valley broadens out around the main village, **COGNE**, surrounded by gentle green meadows and glacier-covered mountains. Here, you can visit the **Maison de Gerard Dayné**, Frazione Sonvuella 30 (June & Sept Tues–Sun 2–6.30pm; July & Aug daily 10am–1pm & 2–6.30pm; Oct Fri, Sat & Sun 2–6.30pm; Nov–June by advance booking only; ask at the tourist office or call ⓣ0165 749 665; €5), to see inside a typical nineteenth-century Valdaostan house evocative of the traditional rustic lifestyle.

The small village of **VALNONTEY**, 2.5km southwest of Cogne, is the starting point for a steep, three-hour walk up to the *Rifugio V. Sella* (ⓣ0165 74 310, ⓦrifugiosella.com; Easter–Sept), a demanding hike that's incredibly popular in summer. The path passes the **Paradisia Alpine Botanical Garden** (daily June & early Sept 10am–5.30pm; July & Aug 10am–6.30pm; €3), with rare Alpine flora, then zigzags up through a forest and onto exposed mountainside before reaching the *rifugio*. At the mountain tarn of Lago Loson, a fifteen-minute walk from the *rifugio*, you may well spot ibex or more timid chamois. Hardened hikers who can cope with a stretch of climbing (difficulty "E") can press on over the **Colle de Lauson** to the Val di Rhêmes.

INFORMATION **VAL DI COGNE**

Tourist office In the centre of Cogne at Via Bourgeois 34 (daily 9am–1pm & 3–6pm; ⓣ0165 74 040, ⓦcogneturismo.it), the tourist office has maps with descriptions in English of walks, one of which is an easy, scenic stroll that follows the river.

ACCOMMODATION

★ **Bellevue** Rue Grand Paradis 22, Cogne ⓣ0165 74 825, ⓦhotelbellevue.it. A luxurious property with cosy rustic interiors and wooden furniture, some dating from the sixteenth century. Its award-winning spa has grottos and treatment rooms in traditional-style chalets. Afternoon tea is served by a crackling fire in winter. €250

★ **Les Trompeurs** Via Grappein 81, Cogne ⓣ0165 74 805, ⓦlestrompeurs.it. A wonderful B&B with homely interiors – the six rooms are comfortable and snug, with wooden furniture and parquet flooring, and there's a small living area with sofas by a fireplace. There's a garden area with deckchairs, a trampoline and a small children's play area. €110

Hotel Miramonti Viale Cavagnet 31, Cogne ⓣ0165 74 030, ⓦmiramonticogne.com. A four-star hotel with crimson interiors, a cosy lounge and bar area, and most rooms commanding views of the Gran Paradiso National Park. Classic rooms are comfortable, while the more spacious Romantic rooms (€240) are decorated with Imperial-style furniture, French silk tapestries and Carrara marble bathrooms. There's a lovely spa area with two whirlpools, a sauna and steam room. €190

CAMPING

Gran Paradiso Frazione Valnontey 58 ⓣ0165 749 204, ⓦcampeggiogranparadisocogne.it. This pleasant campsite in Valtontey has a café, shop, laundry, volleyball pitch and barbecues; gas can be provided. Open mid-May to mid-Sept. Pitches €7, per person €6

EATING

Lou Bequet Frazione Crétax, Cogne 93 ⓣ0165 74 651, ⓦloubequet.it. In a peaceful location by the river just west of town, this pleasant restaurant serves local dishes with a twist; the menu includes risotto cooked in white wine with leeks, apples and *mocetta*, a local ham (€10.50). Thurs–Mon 12.15–2pm & 7.15–9pm, Tues 12.15–2pm.

Lou Ressignon Rue Mines de Cogne 22, Cogne ⓣ0165 74 034, ⓦlouressignon.it. This place has been going since 1966, serving hearty soups and stews, with the likes of beef *tartar* (€14) served with *bagna cauda* (a dip made with garlic and anchovies), and a popular *seupetta à la Cogneintze* (risotto with croutons and fontina cheese; €13). Thurs–Mon 12.15–2pm & 7.15–9pm.

Valsavarenche

Valsavarenche, the next valley west of Val di Cogne, has stunning mountain scenery and great trekking. The most popular route is the ascent of Gran Paradiso, from **Pont**. Though considered the easiest of the higher Alps, it is a climb rather than a hike, with no path marked beyond the *Rifugio Vittorio Emanuele II* (ⓣ0165 95 920, ⓦrifugiovittorioemanuele.com; mid-March to mid-Sept), two and a half hours from Pont.

INFORMATION — VALSAVARENCHE

Park information The National Park visitors' centre is at Dégioz 65,(first half of July, second half of Aug & early Sept Thurs–Tues 2.30–6.30pm; mid July–mid Aug Daily 10am–1pm & 2.30–6.30pm; ⓣ0165 753011, ⓦgrand-paradis.it).

ACCOMMODATION AND EATING

Agriturismo Lo Mayen Frazione Bien 1, Località Bien, 2km outside Degioz ⓣ0165 905 735. An agreeable agriturismo with pleasant rustic rooms in a quiet location by the river. €70

Hostellerie du Paradis L'Eau Rousse, Maisonasse, 3km south of Degioz ⓣ0165 905 972, ⓦhostellerieduparadis.it. A cosy family-run place offering a living area with coffee-table books and an open fire, plus comfortable en-suite rooms; breakfast is served in a small dining area with low arched ceilings. Rates are half board. €150

Pont Breuil Località Pont ⓣ0165 95 458, ⓦcampingpontbreuil.com. This campsite has a well-stocked site shop (there's no other for kilometres around), and ibex come down to graze on the grassy meadow around the tents. The views are spectacular and you are in the very midst of nature. There are also a couple of chalets (minimum stay one week; €700). Closed mid-Sept to mid-May. Pitches €4, per person €6

★ **Refuge du Tétras-Lyre** Pont ⓣ335 600 1921, ⓦrifugiotetraslyre.it. A cosy rustic *rifugio* a short walk from where the road ends at Pont; the rooms are comfortable, with stone walls and wooden ceilings, while the communal areas are decorated with Alpine curios. The welcoming restaurant serves hearty portions of local fare. Dorms €23, doubles €80

Val di Rhêmes

Headed by glaciers, **Val di Rhêmes** is the least touristy of the valleys, and the hamlet of **BRUIL**, at the end of the valley, is the best place to base yourself. It's here that most of the **walks** start from, including a fairly easy path along the river to a waterfall, the Cascata di Goletta. From here you can continue to the mountain lake of Goletta and the *Rifugio Gian Federico Benevolo* (ⓣ0165 936 143, ⓦrifugiobenevolo.com; March–Sept, closed first half of June), taking in some splendid views on the way.

ACCOMMODATION — VAL DI RHÊMES

Hotel Granta Parey Località Chanavey 23 ⓣ0165 936 104, ⓦrhemesgrantaparey.com. A stone's throw away from the area's only chair lift, 1km west of Bruil, this three-star hotel has a lovely, well-equipped spa with gym, an agreeable restaurant and simple, comfortable rooms. €70

The northwest: around Mont Blanc

Dominated by the snowy peaks of **Mont Blanc** (Monte Bianco to the Italians), the northern reaches of Valle d'Aosta are spectacular and very popular. The most sensational views are from the cable cars that glide and swoop across the mountain from **Courmayeur**, while the resort of **La Thuile**, which hosted the Women's Skiing World Cup in 2016, offers superb winter sports.

2

La Thuile

LA THUILE's excellent **ski** area links with the French resort of La Rosière, offering a combined total of 150km of runs. It's also a great spot for **mountain biking**, with more than fifteen different tracks (it hosted the International Mountain Bike World Series in 2014). In summer, you can tackle the two-hour **walk** from La Thuile up to the **Testa d'Arpy**, a natural balcony with a bird's-eye view towards Mont Blanc, or take the path from town to **Lago d'Arpy** (45min), a lovely spot to enjoy a picnic. Three kilometres south of the town, path 3 leads from the pretty **Rutor waterfalls** up to Rutor Glacier (3hr 30min).

ARRIVAL AND INFORMATION — LA THUILE

By bus In winter, shuttle buses connect Turin airport, Milan Malpensa, Milan Linate, Bergamo, Verona and Geneva airports to La Thuile (daily except Tues; see airporttransferservices.com for details).

By train The closest train station to La Thuile is Pré-St-Didier; buses connect the station to La Thuile (11 daily; 20min).

Destinations Aosta (every 1–2hrs; 50min).

Tourist office Via M. Collomb 36 (daily 9am–12.30pm & 2.30–6.30pm; 0165 884 179, lovevda.it). There's also a helpful information kiosk on Piazza Cavalieri di Vittorio Venoto (Mon–Sat 9am–12.30pm & 2–6pm; 0165 883 049, lathuile.it).

ACCOMMODATION AND EATING

Chalet Eden Frazione Villaret 74 0165 885 050, chaleteden.it. Right by the slopes, this four-star hotel has comfortable rooms with wooden interiors; some bathrooms have stone basins. The hotel's *Coq au Vin* restaurant (open to non-residents) serves excellent cuisine using organic produce. €200

La Crèche Via Paolo Debernard 5/A. A welcoming restaurant with stone walls and wooden beams where the chef often greets the customers – the menu includes traditional Italian dishes, plus Mediterranean and local specialities. *Primi* €11, *secondi* €15. Daily noon–2.30pm & 7–10pm.

★ **Lo Tatà** Frazione Petite Golette 103 0165 884 132. A welcoming, cosy restaurant with rustic Alpine interiors and serving excellent local dishes; the bubbling wood-fire oven pizzas are exquisite, too. Daily noon–2.30pm & 7–10.30pm.

Courmayeur

Located at the foot of Mont Blanc, **COURMAYEUR** is the smartest and most popular of Valle d'Aosta's ski resorts. It's the region's oldest Alpine resort – indeed, Italy's first alpine guides association was established here in 1850. The scenery is magnificent, the skiing good, and the area is equally popular in summer, with excellent climbing, mountain biking, rafting, angling and 100km of walking trails: the tourist office can advise on routes. The **thermal baths** in Pré-Saint-Didier, 6km south of Courmayeur (Mon–Thurs 9.30am–9pm, Fri 8.30am–11pm, Sat 8am–11pm, Sun 8am–9pm; €50; qcterme.com/en/pre-saint-didier) are a lovely spot to soothe aching muscles after a day's skiing or hiking.

Skyway Monte Bianco

Strada Statale 26, Entreves • Daily 7.30am–5pm; every 20min • €52 • 0165 89 925, montebianco.com

The rotating glass-fronted **Skyway Monte Bianco cable car** provides 360-degree views and three stations with bars and restaurants. The top station, **Punta Helbronner** (3466m) has a circular scenic terrace with stunning views of the western Alps' highest peaks, including Mont Blanc, Monte Rosa and the Matterhorn. From here, you can take the Panoramique cable car (compagniedumontblanc.fr) to Aiguille du Midi, from where another cable car takes you down to Chamonix in France.

ARRIVAL AND INFORMATION — COURMAYEUR

By bus Buses arrive at Piazzale Monte Bianco just by the pedestrianized centre of town. There are buses from Aosta (hourly; 1hr), Milan (4 daily, with 1 direct and 3 via Aosta; 3hr 45min) and Turin (3 daily via Aosta; 3hr 20min).

Tourist office Piazzale Monte Bianco 15 (mid-July to end Aug & Christmas period daily 9am–1pm & 2–7pm, Jan to mid-Apr, end Aug to mid-Sept & Dec 1st to 24th 9–1pm & 2.30–6.30pm; mid-Apr to mid-July & Oct 9–1pm & 2.30-6pm; 0165 842 060; courmayeurmontblanc.it or courmayeur.com).

ACCOMMODATION

★ **Auberge de la Maison** Entreves, 2.5km north of Courmayeur 0165 869 811, aubergemaison.it. A wonderful Alpine inn in the picture-perfect hamlet of Entreves at the foot of Mont Blanc – the decor is rustic but elegant, and the comfortable living areas have armchairs, antique furniture and nineteenth-century paintings. The spa has a sauna, steam room and a small heated swimming pool. **€190**

Hotel La Grange Entreves, 2.5km north of Courmayeur 0165 869 733, lagrange-it.com. A family-run and pet-friendly place in a fourteenth-century building with stone-and-wood floors; the rooms are simply furnished but cosy, especially those on the attic floor. There's a small gym and sauna, too. **€160**

EATING AND DRINKING

Chalet Plan Gorret Strada Plan Gorret 45 0165 841 988 chaletplangorret.it. About 1 mile from the centre of Courmayeur, this rustic Alpine lodge is a great place for a filling meal of local specialities. In winter, you'll find warming soups (minestrone with fontina cheese €12), cheese fondue (€12) and polenta with porcini mushrooms (€16). Summer & peak winter season daily 12.30–2.30pm & 7–10pm; otherwise, closed Tues and open only for dinner during the week, with lunch and dinner Fri–Sun.

Du Tunnel Via Circonvallazione 80 0165 841 705, pizzeriadutunnel.it. The town's best pizzeria is often packed, so make sure you book ahead; its laidback wood-panelled interiors are warm and cosy, and there's a mezzanine level with a handful of tables too. Pizzas from €7. Daily noon–3pm & 7pm–midnight.

Liguria

172 Genoa

190 The Riviera di Ponente

199 The Riviera di Levante

PORTOVENERE

Liguria

Sheltering on the seaward side of the mountains that divide Piemonte from the coast, Liguria is the classic introduction to Italy. There's an unexpected change as you cross the French border: the Italian Riviera, as Liguria's commercially developed strip of coast is known, has more variety of landscape and architecture and is generally less frenetic than its French counterpart. And its mountains, draped with terraced vineyards and olive groves and speckled with pretty old villages, offer respite from the standard format of beach, beach and more beach.

The chief city of the region is **Genoa**, an ancient, sprawling port with a fascinating labyrinthine old quarter complemented by its thriving modern dockside district and a vibrant social and ethnic mix. Genoa straddles the apex of Liguria's arching coast and marks the midway point of the Italian Riviera, dividing it in two distinct halves. The **Riviera di Ponente** to the west is more the developed stretch, a long ribbon of hotels and resorts packed in summer months – particularly August – with Italian families. **San Remo**, the *grande dame* of Riviera resorts, is flanked by hillsides covered with glasshouses, and is a major centre for the worldwide export of flowers; **Albenga** and **Noli** are attractive medieval centres that have also retained a good deal of character; while **Finale Ligure** is a pleasantly laidback seaside town with plenty of outdoor activities.

On Genoa's eastern side is the more rugged **Riviera di Levante**, a mix of mountains and fishing villages, originally accessible only by boat. Drawn by its remoteness, the Romantics "discovered" the Riviera in the early nineteenth century, preparing the way for other artists and poets and subsequently the first package tourists. It's still wild and extremely beautiful in places, although any sense of remoteness has long gone. Resorts like **Portofino** are among the most expensive in the country, although nearby **Santa Margherita Ligure** and **Rapallo** make great bases for exploring the surrounding coastline by train or car, as does the pretty fishing village of **Camogli**. Walks on **Monte di Portofino** and through the dramatic coastal scenery of the **Cinque Terre** take you through scrubland and vineyards for memorable views over broad gulfs and jutting headlands. At the far end of the Riviera is the busting mercantile port and naval base of **La Spezia**, its shimmering **Golfo dei Poeti** bookended by the picturesque coastal towns of **Portovenere** and **Lerici**.

In a **car**, the shore road is overall a disappointment as the coast is extremely built up, but you can get a much better sense of the region's beauty by taking the east–west autostrada which cuts through the mountains a few kilometres inland by means of a mixture of tunnels and viaducts. Fleeting bursts of daylight between tunnels give glimpses of the string of resorts along the coast, silvery olive groves and a brilliant sea. It's ten times quicker, too. However, the real plus of Liguria is that so many of the coastal resorts are easily accessible by **train**, with regular services stopping just about everywhere, and, because the track is forced to squeeze along the narrow coastal strip, the views are wonderful and the stations invariably located in the centre of town.

Genoa

GENOA (**Genova** in Italian) is "the most winding, incoherent of cities, the most entangled topographical ravel in the world". So said Henry James, and the city – Italy's sixth largest, and one of the busiest in Europe – is still marvellously eclectic, vibrant

CATTEDRALE DI SAN LORENZO

Highlights

❶ **Genoa** With its rabbit warren of medieval streets, revamped port area and clutch of first-rate museums and churches, Genoa could easily justify a week of your time. See page 172

❷ **Cinque Terre** Five picturesque villages shoehorned into one of the most rugged parts of Liguria's coastline and linked by highly scenic, coastal walking paths. See page 206

❸ **Finale Ligure** This classic Ligurian family resort is one of the most laidback beach towns in Italy, and a hub for outdoor adventure sports. See page 192

❹ **Camogli** A gorgeous fishing village pressed against the coast, Camogli makes a lovely base for walks and boat trips around the Portofino headland and beyond. See page 199

❺ **Portovenere** A postcard-perfect marina at the mouth of the Gulf of Poets, crammed with a colourful row of tower-houses. See page 211

❻ **Levanto** Family-friendly, unpretentious beach town that makes a great and authentically Italian base from which to explore the Cinque Terre. See page 205

HIGHLIGHTS ARE MARKED ON THE MAP ON PAGE 174

and full of rough-edged style; indeed "La Superba", as it was known at the height of its powers, boasts more zest and intrigue than all the surrounding coastal resorts put together. Stretching behind the recently revitalized old port, the **old town** is a dense and fascinating warren of medieval alleyways, increasingly brightened with new shops, restaurants, and bars, as well as a series of large *palazzi*. These, built in the sixteenth and seventeenth centuries by Genoa's wealthy mercantile families are now transformed into museums and art galleries. The tidying-up hasn't completely sanitized the old town, however; much of the city's core – between the two stations and the waterfront – retains a dark and slightly menacing air, but the overriding impression is of a buzzing hive of activity. Food shops nestle in the portals of former palaces, carpenters' workshops are sandwiched between designer furniture outlets, and everything is surrounded by a crush of people and the squashed vowels of the impenetrable Genoese dialect that has, over the centuries, absorbed elements of Neapolitan, Calabrese and Portuguese. Aside from the cosmopolitan street life, you should seek out the **Cattedrale di San Lorenzo**, the **Palazzo Ducale** and the Renaissance palaces of **Via Garibaldi**, which contain the cream of Genoa's art collections, as well as furniture and decor from the grandest days of the city's past.

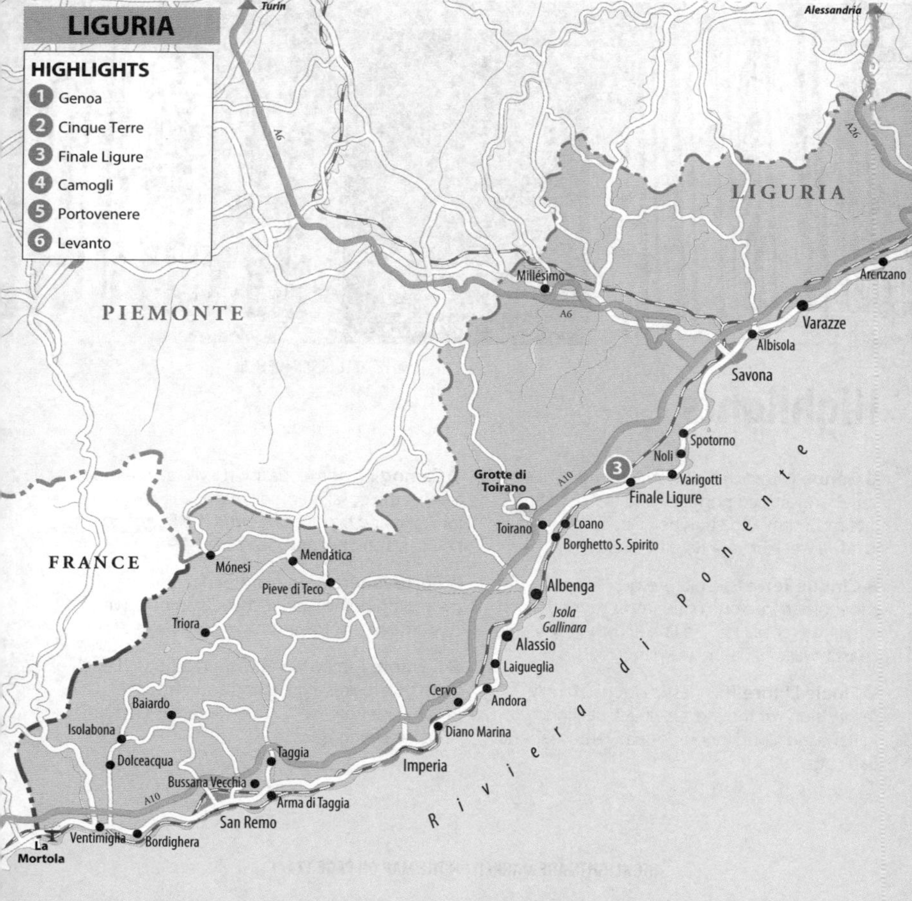

Brief history

Genoa made its money at sea, through trade, colonial exploitation and piracy. It was one of the four major Italian maritime republics (the others being Venice, Pisa and Amalfi), and a local superpower with its own well-developed system of government that lasted several hundred years. By the thirteenth century, after playing a major part in the **Crusades**, the Genoese were roaming the Mediterranean, bringing back ideas as well as goods: the city's architects were using Arab pointed arches a century before the rest of Italy. The San Giorgio banking syndicate effectively controlled the city for much of the fifteenth century, and cold-shouldered **Columbus** (who had grown up in Genoa) when he sought funding for his voyages. With Spanish backing, he opened up new Atlantic trade routes that ironically would later reduce Genoa to a backwater. Following foreign invasion, in 1768 the Banco di San Giorgio was forced to sell the Genoese colony of Corsica to the French, and a century later, the city became a hotbed of radicalism: **Mazzini**, one of the main protagonists of the Risorgimento, was born here, and in 1860 **Garibaldi** set sail for Sicily with his "Thousand" from the city's harbour. Around the same time, Italy's industrial revolution began in Genoa, with steelworks and shipyards spreading along the coast. These suffered heavy

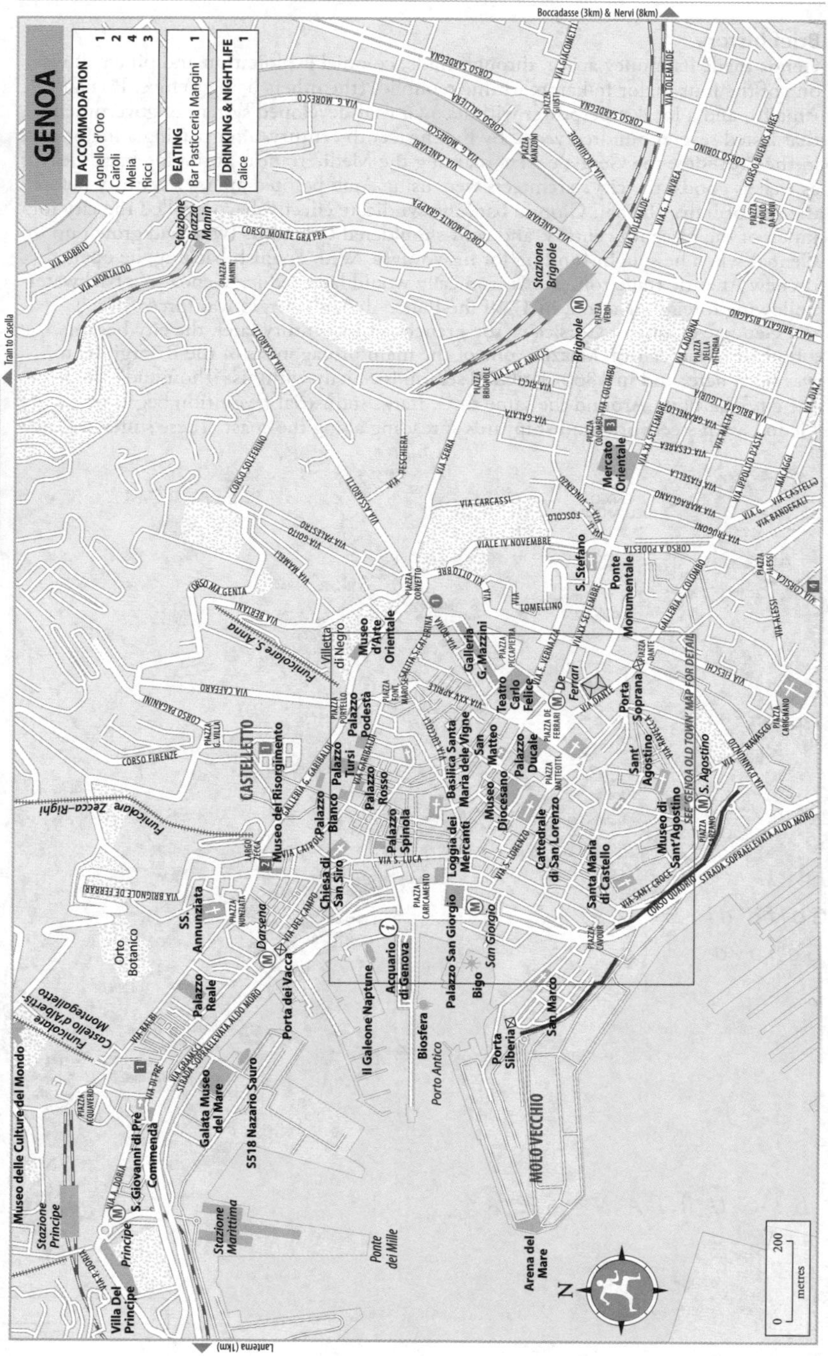

GENOA
ACCOMMODATION
Agnello d'Oro 1
Cairoli 2
Melia 4
Ricci 3
EATING
Bar Pasticceria Mangini 1
DRINKING & NIGHTLIFE
Calice 1
Boccadasse (3km) & Nervi (8km)
Train to Casella
Lantema (1km)
Stazione Principe
Museo delle Culture del Mondo
Villa Del Principe
Principe
S. Giovanni di Prè
Commendà
Funicolare Castello d'Albertis-Montegalletto
Galata Museo del Mare
SS18 Nazario Sauro
Stazione Marittima
Ponte dei Mille
Palazzo Reale
Orto Botanico
SS. Annunziata
Darsena
Porta dei Vacca
Il Galeone Naptune
Acquario di Genova
Biosfera
Porto Antico
Palazzo San Giorgio
Bigo
San Giorgio
Porta Siberia
San Marco
MOLO VECCHIO
Arena del Mare
Funicolare Zecca–Righi
CASTELLETTO
Museo del Risorgimento
Chiesa di San Siro
Palazzo Bianco
Palazzo Tursi
Palazzo Rosso
Palazzo Spinola
Palazzo Podestà
Loggia dei Mercanti
Basilica Santa Maria dele Vigne
Museo Diocesano
San Matteo
Palazzo Ducale
Cattedrale di San Lorenzo
Santa Maria di Castello
Museo di Sant'Agostino
Sant' Agostino
S. Agostino
Porta Soprana
Teatro Carlo Felice
De Ferrari
Galleria G. Mazzini
Museo d'Arte Orientale
Villetta di Negro
Funicolare S. Anna
SEE 'GENOA OLD TOWN' MAP FOR DETAIL
S. Stefano
Ponte Monumentale
Mercato Orientale
Brignole
Stazione Brignole
Stazione Piazza Manin
Piazza Manin
Corso Monte Grappa
Via Montaldo
Via Bobbio
Corso Solferino
Via Assarotti
Via Serra
Via Peschiera
Via Carcassi
Viale IV Novembre
Via XX Settembre
Corso A Podestà
Via Fieschi
Via Ravasco
Corso Quadrio
Strada Sopraelevata Aldo Moro
Via Balbi
Via Cairoli
Via Garibaldi
Via S. Luca
Via Dante
Via Galata
Via Colombo
Corso Torino
Corso Buenos Aires
Via Tolemaide
Corso Sardegna
Corso Galliera
Viale Brigata Bisagno
Via Diaz
Piazza Corvetto
Piazza Dante
Piazza de Ferrari
Piazza Caricamento
Piazza Cavour
Piazza Carignano
Piazza Verdi
Piazza Manzoni
Piazza Colombo
Piazza Brignole
Corso Firenze
Corso Paganini
Via Caffaro
Corso Magenta
Via Bertani
N
0 200 metres

PESTO AND SEAFOOD – THE STAPLES OF LIGURIAN CUISINE

Liguria may lie in the north of Italy, but its benign Mediterranean climate, and to some extent its cooking, belong further south. Traditionally, the recipes from this region make something out of nothing, and the best-known Ligurian speciality is **pesto**, the simplest of dishes. Invented by the Genoese to help their long-term sailors fight off scurvy, it's made with chopped basil, garlic, pine nuts and grated sharp cheese (pecorino or Parmesan) ground together in olive oil. It's used as a sauce for pasta (often flat *trenette* noodles, or knobbly little potato-flour shapes known as **trofie**), or served with a few boiled potatoes and green beans, or stirred into soup to make *minestrone alla genovese*. Look out also for pasta, usually *Pansotti*, served with a creamy hazelnut sauce – *salsa di noci*; and other typical dishes like **cima alla genovese** (cold, stuffed veal); *tomaxelle* (veal meatballs); **torta pasqualina** (a spinach and cheese pie with eggs); **sardenaira** (a Ligurian pizza made with tomatoes, onions and garlic); and, of course, the ubiquitous golden focaccia bread, often flavoured with olives, sage or rosemary, or covered with toppings. There are lots of things with chickpeas too, which grow abundantly along the coast and crop up most regularly in *farinata*, a kind of chickpea pancake displayed in broad, round baking trays.

Otherwise, **fish** dominates – not surprising in a region where more than two thirds of the population lives on the coast. Local **anchovies** are a common antipasto, while pasta with a variety of fish and seafood sauces appears everywhere (mussels, scampi, octopus and clams are all excellent); you'll find delicious *polpo* (octopus), usually served cold with potatoes, good swordfish, and dishes like *ciuppin* or fish soup, *burrida di seppie* (cuttlefish stew), fish *in carpione* (marinated in vinegar and herbs), or just a good *fritto del Golfo* (mixed fish fry-up). Salt cod (*baccalà*) and wind-dried cod (*stoccofisso*) are also local favourites. Many restaurants in Rapallo and along the Tigullio coast serve *bagnun*, a dish based on anchovies, tomato, garlic, onion and white wine, and in Cinque Terre and Levanto you'll often see **gattafin** – a delicious deep-fried vegetable pasty. Liguria's soil and aspect aren't well suited to vine-growing, although plenty of local **wine** – mainly white – is quite drinkable. The steep, terraced slopes of the Cinque Terre are home to some decent eponymous white wine and a sweet, expensive dessert wine called Sciacchetrà, made from partially dried grapes. From the Riviera di Ponente, look out for the crisp whites of Pigato (from Albenga) and Vermentino (from Imperia), as well as the acclaimed Rossese di Dolceacqua, Liguria's best red.

3

bombing in World War II, and the subsequent economic decline hobbled Genoa for decades. Things started to look up in the 1990s: state funding to celebrate the 500th anniversary of Columbus's 1492 voyage paid to renovate many of the city's late-Renaissance palaces and the old port area, with Genoa's most famous son of modern times, **Renzo Piano** (co-designer of Paris's Pompidou Centre), taking a leading role. The results of a twelve-year programme that saw Genoa becoming a **European Capital of Culture** in 2004 are evident all over the city.

Piazza de Ferrari and around

If Genoa has a centre it's probably **Piazza de Ferrari**, a mainly pedestrian, open space that separates the old part of Genoa from the nineteenth-century city. Focused on a large fountain, it's overlooked by a statue of Garibaldi in front of the grand facade of the **Teatro Carlo Felice**, a rather war-torn, messed-about-with building that doesn't have much to recommend it architecturally, but as the city's principal opera house hosts some fine performances.

Palazzo Ducale

Piazza Matteotti 9 • Daily 9am–7pm • Free • **Torre Grimaldi** Late July–Aug Tues–Sun 10.30am–8pm; guided tours Sept to late July Sat 3pm • €5 • ☎ 010 817 1600, Ⓦ palazzoducale.genova.it

One side of Piazza de Ferrari is taken up by a flank of the sixteenth-century **Palazzo Ducale** (its main facade faces nearby Piazza Matteotti, which you can reach by way

THE CARD MUSEI

If you're planning to visit a number of museums, it might be worth buying the city's **museum card**, or *Card Musei*, which costs €12 for 24hr (€15 including public transport), or €20 for 48hr (€25 including public transport). It's valid for most of Genoa's museums and gives discounts at others. You can buy the card at tourist offices, civic museums or the bookshops at the Muse di Strada Nuova (see page 182).

of the palace's main arcade). The Palazzo Ducale was home to the doge of Genoa between 1384 and 1515, and its huge vaulted atrium makes a splendid venue for regular exhibitions. In summer, parts of the rest of the building are also open to the public for exhibitions, and you can visit the vast hall of the Maggior Consiglio upstairs, where massive chandeliers hang above the space once occupied by the four hundred Genoese nobles who ruled the maritime republic. You can also view the Doge's Chapel, perhaps the most frescoed room of all time, and from there climb up to the **Torre Grimaldi** for the views and some of the grimmest dungeons you'll ever see: home for a while to Garibaldi and another Italian patriot, Jacopo Ruffini, who cut his own throat here in 1833.

The Gesù

Piazza Matteotti • Mon–Sat 7am–1pm & 3.30–7.30pm, Sun 8am–1pm & 4–10pm • Free

Piazza de Ferrari feeds through to the more regular open space of Piazza Matteotti. On its corner is the **Gesù**, designed by Pellegrino Tibaldi at the end of the sixteenth century, and which contains a mass of marble and gilt stucco and some fine Baroque paintings, including Guido Reni's *Assumption* in the right aisle and two works by Rubens: *The Miracles of St Ignatius* on the left and *The Circumcision* on the high altar.

The Old Town

Old Genoa's main artery, **Via San Lorenzo**, leads from Piazza Matteotti down to the port, a pedestrianized stretch that makes for a busy evening *passeggiata*, and a handy reference point when negotiating the **old town**, which it effectively splits in two, an atmospheric confusion of tiny alleyways (*caruggi*) that spreads either side and upwards from the waterfront as far as **Via Garibaldi** to the north. The *caruggi* are lined with high buildings, usually six or seven storeys, set very close together. Grocers, textile workshops and bakeries jostle for position with boutiques, design outlets and goldsmiths amid a flurry of shouts, smells and scrawny cats. The cramped layout of the area reflects its medieval politics. Around the thirteenth and fourteenth centuries, the city's principal families – Doria, Spinola, Grimaldi and Fieschi – marked out certain streets and squares as their territory, even extending their domains to include churches: to pray in someone else's chapel was to risk being stabbed in the back. New buildings on each family's patch had to be slotted in wherever they could, resulting in a maze of crooked alleyways that was the battleground of dynastic feuds lasting well into the eighteenth century.

Cattedrale di San Lorenzo

Piazza San Lorenzo • Daily 9am–noon & 3–6pm • Free

On the eastern side of Via San Lorenzo, the **Cattedrale di San Lorenzo** anchors the square of the same name, its facade an elaborate confection of twisting, fluted columns and black-and-white striped stone that was added by Gothic craftsmen from France in the early thirteenth century. The stripes here, like other examples throughout the city, were a sign of prestige: families could use them only if they had a permit, awarded for "some illustrious deed to the advantage of their native city". While the rest of Genoa's

churches were portioned out between the ruling dynasties, the cathedral remained open to all.

The **interior** has some well-preserved Byzantine frescoes of the *Last Judgement* above the main entrance, and is home, off the left aisle, to the large Renaissance chapel of St John the Baptist, whose ashes – legend has it – once rested in the thirteenth-century sarcophagus. After a particularly bad storm in medieval times, priests carried his casket through the city down to the port to placate the sea, and a procession still takes place each June 24 in honour of the saint.

Museo del Tesoro

Piazza San Lorenzo • Mon–Sat 9am–noon & 3–6pm & Sun 3–6pm • €6; €12 including Museo Diocesano • ⓣ 010 209 1863

Just past the chapel of St John the Baptist and housed in an atmospheric crypt, the **Museo del Tesoro** holds a polished quartz plate on which, legend says, Salome received John the Baptist's severed head; a green bowl brought to Genoa in the eleventh century and believed once to have been the Holy Grail; and a reliquary believed to contain a lock of the Virgin Mary's hair.

Museo Diocesano

Via Tommaso Reggio 20 • Mon & Wed–Sun noon–6pm • €8; €12 including Museo del Tesoro • ⓣ 010 247 5127, ⓦ museodiocesanogenova.it

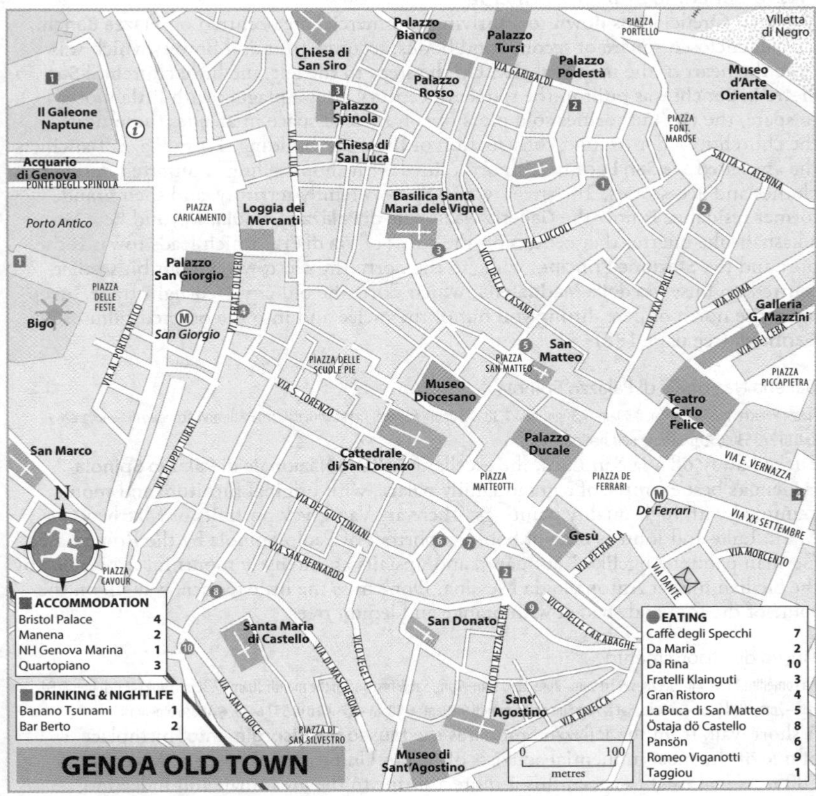

Behind the cathedral, the **Museo Diocesano** occupies a partially frescoed cloister and the medieval buildings that surround it, and displays religious art and sculpture, including paintings by Luca Cambiaso. Look out for the dozen or so dyed blue cloths from the early sixteenth century depicting various scenes from the Passion of Christ.

Piazza Soziglia and around

The busiest and more obviously appealing part of old Genoa lies to the north of Via San Lorenzo. Just off the cathedral's square, tiny **Piazza Invrea** gives on to the shopping square of the **Campetto** and adjacent **Via degli Orefici**, "Street of the Goldsmiths". Much of the jewellery here is still made by hand at upper-storey workshops around the Campetto, which links to the genteel sliver of **Piazza Soziglia**, crowded with stalls and café tables. From here **Via Luccoli** heads north, with glitzy boutiques and design outlets galore, while a few streets to the east is one of the city's prettiest little squares, **Piazza San Matteo**. This lay in the territory of the Doria family, who went one step further than merely striping the twelfth-century church of **San Matteo** (Mon–Sat 7.30am–6.30pm & Sun 9.30am–6.30pm; free) and ordered elaborate testimonials to the family's worthiness to be carved on the facade of the church and their adjoining palaces; inside, the tomb of the patriarch and sea captain Andrew Doria lies in the crypt.

Piazza Banchi to Stazione Principe

Via degli Orefici leads down to a thriving commercial area centred on **Piazza Banchi**, a small enclosed square of secondhand books, records, fruit and flowers which was once the heart of the medieval city. Up the steps to the left, the little church of **San Pietro in Banchi** was built in the sixteenth century after a plague; with little money to spare, the city authorities sold plots of commercial space in arcades underneath the church in order to fund construction of the main building. From Piazza Banchi the animated **Via San Luca** heads north, lined with shops selling counterfeit designer clothes and accessories. The street was in Spinola family territory, and their grand, former residence is now the **Galleria Nazionale di Palazzo Spinola**. Beyond here lies a kasbah-like quarter that centres on the street of **Via di Pre**, which leads towards the port and the **Stazione Principe**, while to the north the old town is a fair bit seedier, centred on busy **Via della Maddalena**, which skirts the old city's red-light trade. Steep lanes rise north of here, lifting you out of the melee and into the ordered calm of **Via Garibaldi** (see page 182).

Galleria Nazionale di Palazzo Spinola

Piazza Pellicceria 1 • Tues–Sat 8.30am–7.30pm, Sun 1.30–7.30pm • €6, joint ticket with Palazzo Reale and Acquario di Genova €26 • 010 270 5300, palazzospinola.beniculturali.it

Tucked away off Via San Luca, the excellent **Galleria Nazionale di Palazzo Spinola** is Genoa's best example of a grand family palace, with original furniture and rooms crammed with high-quality paintings. There are Van Dyck portraits of Matthew, Mark, Luke and John as men of books, a portrait of Paolo Spinola by the Rome-based German painter Angelika Kaufmann, and upstairs an intensely mournful *Ecce Homo* by the Sicilian master Antonello da Messina. Don't miss the little terrace, way up on the spine of the roof and shaded with orange and lemon trees.

Museo del Risorgimento

Via Lomellini 11 • April–Oct Tues & Fri 9am–2pm, Wed 9am–7pm, Sat & first Sun of the month 10am–7.30pm; Nov–March Tues & Fri 9am–2pm, Wed 9am–6.30pm, Sat & first Sun of the month 9.30am–6.30pm • €5 • 010 557 6430, museidigenova.it

A short walk from the Palazzo Spinola is the **Museo del Risorgimento**, birthplace of one of the most influential activists of Italian Unification, Giuseppe Mazzini, in 1805. As you might expect, this is quite a shrine to the great man and indeed to

the Risorgimento in general, with documents and relics from Mazzini's life, lots of paintings and other artworks relating to the Unification struggle, and personal effects from other local heroes, including Mazzini's fellow Genoese, Goffredo Mameli and Nino Bixio.

Palazzo Reale

Via Balbi 10 • Tues–Fri 9am–7pm, Sat & Sun 1.30pm–7pm • €6, joint ticket with Palazzo Spinola and Acquario di Genova €26 • ⓣ 010 2705230, ⓦ palazzorealegenova.beniculturali.it

The vast **Palazzo Reale** was built by the Balbi family in the early seventeenth century and later occupied by the Durazzo dynasty and the Savoyard royals. A large atrium overlooks an elegant courtyard garden, while a grand staircase leads to the ballroom, with gilt stucco ceiling, and several rooms to the left, one of which is a stunning hall of mirrors; Joseph II, Emperor of Austria, is said to have remarked in 1784 that the palace appeared more of a royal residence than his own simple pad back in Vienna. On the other side of the palace are the royal quarters: a chapel gallery behind the ballroom, covered in trompe l'oeil frescoes from the seventeenth and eighteenth centuries; the adjacent throne room, dotted with dozens of "C.A." monograms in honour of Carlo Alberto, King of Savoy, and two large and dramatic paintings by the Neapolitan master Luca Giordano; and a lavish audience room with a grand portrait of a tight-lipped Caterina Durazzo-Balbi painted by Van Dyck in 1624 during his six-year stay in Genoa. Alongside, the king's bedchamber has Van Dyck's first canvas of the *Crucifixion*, dating from 1627 (though this is occasionally displayed elsewhere), and on the seaward side of the palace, the queen's quarters feature a hyper-naturalistic *St Lawrence* by Bernardo Strozzi and a ghostly pale *Crucifixion* by Luca Giordano.

3

Museo delle Culture del Mondo

Corso Dogali 18 • April–Sept Tues, Wed & Fri 10am–6pm, Thurs 1–10pm, Sat & Sun 10am–7pm; Oct–March Tues–Fri 10am–5pm, Sat & Sun 10am–6pm • €6 • ⓣ 010 272 3820, ⓦ museidigenova.it

Via Balbi leads eventually to Piazza Acquaverde and the Stazione Principe, but in the heights above the station (and reachable by *ascensore* from the piazza), is one of the city's more overlooked sights, the **Museo delle Culture del Mondo**, housed in the grand neo-Gothic home of the nineteenth-century adventurer Captain D'Albertis, who spent much of his later life filling its rooms with masks, musical instruments, pottery, paintings, stuffed animals and more picked up during voyages to the Americas, Africa and Oceania.

Via San Bernardo to Piazza Sarzano

The section of the old town south of Via San Lorenzo is less visited than the districts to the north, and more residential – it's inhabited mostly by students and young professionals – with a lively bar culture in the surrounding alleys. From the cathedral and Piazza Matteotti, narrow **Salita Pollaiuoli** plunges you into the gloom between high buildings down to a crossroads with **Via San Bernardo**, one of Genoa's most vibrant old-town streets, with grocers and bakers trading behind the portals of palaces decorated in the fifteenth and sixteenth centuries. On the south side of the crossroads tiny **Piazza San Donato** is overlooked by a crumbling, bare Romanesque church with a Roman architrave over its door and an octagonal Byzantine-style campanile. Beyond, Stradone Sant'Agostino is home to a quirky array of bars and workshops, with Via Ravecca at the end, leading eastward to the twin-towered stone gateway of the **Porta Soprana**, featuring impressive Gothic arches – beyond which lies the nineteenth-century city.

Museo di Sant'Agostino

Piazza Sarzano • April to early Oct Tues–Fri 9am–7pm, Sat & Sun 10am–7.30pm; early Oct to March Tues–Fri 9am–6.30pm, Sat & Sun 9.30am–6.30pm • €5 • ⓣ 010 251 1263, ⓦ museidigenova.it

To the north of Piazza Sarzano is the (rebuilt) thirteenth-century church of **Sant'Agostino**, whose unique triangular cloister houses the **Museo di Sant'Agostino**, which displays fragments of sculpture through Genoa's long history. Among the highlights is a fragment of the tomb of Margherita of Brabant, sculpted in 1312 by Giovanni Pisano; the tomb of the first doge of Genoa, Simone Boccanegra, from 1363; and a collection of fifteenth-century paintings by northern Italian artists.

Santa Maria di Castello

Salita Santa Maria di Castello 15 • 10am–1pm & 3–6pm • Donation • ⓣ 347 995 6740, ⓦ santamariadicastello.it

Concealed among the narrow, winding *caruggi* of the old town, about five minutes' walk west of Stradone Sant'Agostino (and about the same distance east of the port), this twelfth-century Romanesque **basilica** was once the highest esteemed in Genoa. Incorporating the remains of Roman-era fortifications and a Byzantine-era castle, the rambling complex features three cloisters and a museum that houses a trove of medieval and Renaissance artwork, including many items brought from other Dominican convents and monasteries.

The Musei di Strada Nuova

Via Garibaldi • April–early Oct Tues–Fri 9am–7pm, Sat & Sun 10am–7.30pm; early Oct–March Tues–Fri 9am–6.30pm, Sat & Sun 9.30am–6.30pm • €9 combined ticket includes all three palaces; tickets sold at the office on the ground floor of the Palazzo Tursi • Audio guide €5 • ⓣ 010 557 2193, ⓦ museidigenova.it

When newly made fortunes encouraged Genoa's merchant bankers to move out of the cramped old town in the mid-sixteenth century, artisans' houses were pulled down to make way for the Strada Nuova, later named **Via Garibaldi**. To walk along the surprisingly narrow street is to stroll through a Renaissance architect's drawing pad – sculpted facades, stuccowork and medallions decorate the exteriors of the three-storey *palazzi*, while some of the large courtyards are almost like private squares. Three of the street's finest *palazzi* – **Bianco**, **Rosso** and **Tursi** – have been re-branded the **Musei di Strada Nuova** and together they hold the city's finest collection of old masters.

Palazzo Bianco

Via Garibaldi 11

The **Palazzo Bianco** was built between 1530 and 1540 for the important Genoese family, the Grimaldis. Its gallery houses the world's largest collection of Genoese and Ligurian painting – including work by Cambiaso, Piola, Castiglione and Castello – alongside works by Flemish and Dutch masters such as Gerard David and Hans Memling.

Palazzo Tursi

Via Garibaldi 9

The Palazzo Bianco provides access to the next-door **Palazzo Tursi**, the largest of Genoa's palaces, with an imposing main courtyard. It's the site of the town hall, so much of it is closed to the public, but you can wander around and admire more paintings, ceramics and furniture. Don't miss, too, the **Sala Paganiniana**, on the first floor – a couple of rooms dedicated to the great Italian violinist Niccolò Paganini, who was born in Genoa in 1782. The prime exhibits are his two violins – the *cannone*, the great man's Guarneri violin made in 1743, along with a copy of it made in Paris in 1834, which he is said to have preferred.

Palazzo Rosso

Via Garibaldi 18

Across the road from the Palazzo Tursi, the **Palazzo Rosso** has a splendid first-floor picture gallery, with paintings by mainly fifteenth- and sixteenth-century Italian

PORTO ANTICO TICKETS

If you are visiting several of the Porto Antico attractions, it's probably worth buying a **combined ticket**. These are available in various combinations, such as the Aquarium and Galata Museo del Mare (€42, children €30), or the **Acquario Village** ticket (€52, children €37), covering pretty much everything at the port, including the Aquarium, Biosfera, Bigo and Galata Museo del Mare. All the combined tickets can be bought at the attractions themselves or online at Ⓦ acquariodigenova.it.

artists – Andrea del Sarto, Mattia Preti, Guercino and a whole room of works by local Bernardo Strozzi – along with a choice few northern European works by the likes of Roger van der Weyden, Dürer and Gerard David. The rooms on the floor above have been restored to their original Baroque grandeur, bedecked with chandeliers, mirrors, frescoed ceilings and an excess of gilding, and there's a series of splendid portraits by Van Dyck of the Brignole-Sale family, who built the palace in 1671. On the floor above this is a mock-up of the refined twentieth-century apartment of the former director of Genoa's museums, an odd mixture of classic and modern furniture and old masters, and above this a rooftop terrace that offers fantastic views of the city centre.

The Porto Antico

It's a short stroll from Piazza Banchi into the open spaces of Genoa's old port or **Porto Antico** – more integrated now with the city than it has perhaps ever been, and indeed totally revitalized over the past two decades, its old warehouses converted into exhibition spaces, concert halls, museums and waterfront cafés, bars and restaurants. The sea once came up to the vaulted arcades of Via Sottoripa, which runs alongside the large pedestrianized space of **Piazza Caricamento**, above which the *sopraelevata*, or elevated highway, shoots along the waterfront.

Palazzo di San Giorgio

Piazza Caricamento • Volunteer-guided tours first Sat of the month 10am–noon; must book by Thurs of previous week • Free • Ⓣ 333 778 1977, Ⓔ genova@delegazionefai.fondoambiente.it

The **Palazzo di San Giorgio**, a fortified palace built in 1260 from the stones of a captured Venetian fortress, is now home to the harbour authorities. After the great sea battle of Curzola in 1298, the Genoese used the building to keep their Venetian prisoners under lock and key; among them was one Marco Polo, who met a Pisan writer named Rustichello inside and spun tales of adventure to him of worlds beyond the seas. After their release, Rustichello published the stories in a single volume that became *The Travels of Marco Polo*. The bright and intricately-painted outer façade stands in stark contrast to the thoroughly modernized harbour, a solitary nod to the past, while the medieval rooms inside have been beautifully restored.

The Bigo

Elevator March, April, Sept & Oct Mon 2–6pm, Tues–Sun 9am–7pm; June–Aug Mon 4–11pm, Tues–Sun 10am–11pm; Jan, Feb, Nov & Dec Sat & Sun 10am–5pm • €4, children €3 • Ⓣ 010 23 451, Ⓦ acquariodigenova.it/bigo-panoramic

Beyond the Palazzo di San Giorgio, the visual centrepiece of the resurgent waterfront is the **Bigo** – a curious multiarmed contraption designed by Renzo Piano, intended to recall the harbourside cranes of old. It consists of a tent-roofed exhibition/concert space where waterside performances are given in summer and an ice rink is set up in winter, next to which stands a circular **elevator** that ascends 40m in the air to let visitors see Genoa "as it is seen by the seagulls".

The Acquario di Genova

Ponte Spinola • March–June, Sept & Oct Mon–Fri 9am–8pm, Sat & Sun 8.30am–9pm; July daily 8.30am–10.30pm; Aug daily 8.30am–midnight; Nov–Feb Mon–Fri 9.30am–8pm, Sat & Sun 9.30am–9pm; last entry 2hr before closing • €26, ages 4–12 €18 • T 010 23 451, W acquariodigenova.it

North of the Bigo, the **Acquario di Genova** is the city's pride and joy, parked like a giant ocean liner on the waterfront, with seventy tanks housing sea creatures from all the earth's major habitats. It houses the world's biggest reconstruction of a Caribbean coral reef, complete with moray eels, turtles and angelfish, and lots of larger beasts too – sharks, dolphins, seals, an enclosure of penguins and the usual rays in their petting pools. It's a great aquarium by any standards, one of Europe's largest by capacity, and boasts a fashionably ecology-conscious slant with excellent background information in Italian and English.

Biosfera

Ponte Spinola • Daily: March & Oct 10am–6pm; April–Sept 10am–7pm; Nov–Feb 10am–5pm • €5 • T 010 234 5659, W acquariodigenova.it/biosfera

3

Alongside the aquarium, the futuristic-looking **Biosfera** is a steel-and-glass Renzo Piano-designed sphere – a hothouse, basically – enclosing a small tropical ecosystem, complete with trees, flowers, insects and the odd tropical bird. It's crammed with vegetation inside, warm and atmospheric, and well worth a quick tour – though you can see it all in ten minutes.

Il Galeone Neptune

Porto Antico • Daily 10am–6pm • €6

Moored at the next pier along from the Biosfera, **Il Galeone Neptune** is a kitsch, full-size replica of a seventeenth-century galleon. Built to feature in the 1986 Roman Polanski film *Pirates*, it has a huge, colourful Neptune figurehead, and several decks to explore. It's fun to stumble around the low-beamed interior, convincingly dark and cannon-crammed, and then to emerge onto the open deck, which is similarly kitted out with cannons, ropes and rigging – and a poop deck to declaim from.

Galata Museo del Mare

Calata de Mari 1 • March–Oct daily 10am–7.30pm; Nov–Feb Tues–Fri 10am–6pm, Sat & Sun 10am–7.30pm • €13, children €8, €19/€14 including submarine • T 010 234 5655, W galatamuseodelmare.it

About five minutes' walk from the Aquarium, a giant glass building houses the wonderful **Galata Museo del Mare**, detailing on four floors the history of Genoa and its relationship with the sea. The ground floor covers the era of Christopher Colombus – with letters by and portraits of the great mariner – and the era of the Genoese galleys, with lots of background on the oarsmen who powered them as well as a full-size replica. There are also displays on the silver trade and one of the greatest galley commanders of them all, Andrea Doria. One floor up are models of later sailing ships, from the last days of the Genoese republic to the brigantines of the nineteenth century (including another full-size example), while perhaps the most involving part of the museum is the top-floor exhibition on the **steamship era**, in particular Italian immigration to the US. Outside, it's worth paying extra to don a hard hat and climb aboard the moored submarine, the **S518 Nazario Sauro**, whose interior is described in detail with an English audioguide. It's pretty much what you would expect – claustrophobic and tricky to negotiate; you will be glad of the hard hat.

The Stazione Marittima and Ponte dei Mille

Beyond the redeveloped part of the port lies the *fin-de-siècle* **Stazione Marittima**, the ferry terminal for services to Corsica, Sardinia, Sicily and Tunisia (see page 187). Just

in front, the **Ponte dei Mille** (Jetty of the Thousand) is so called for **Giuseppe Garibaldi**, ex-mercenary and spaghetti salesman, who persuaded his thousand Red Shirts to set off for Sicily in two clapped-out paddle steamers, armed with just a few rifles and no ammunition. Their mission, to support a Sicilian uprising and unite the island with the mainland states, greatly annoyed some northern politicians, who didn't want anything to do with the undeveloped south.

Villa del Principe

Piazza del Principe 4 • Daily 10am–6pm • €9 • ⓣ 010 255 509, ⓦ doriapamphilj.it/genova

Between the port and the station, and with oddly peaceful, contained gardens (despite the views over the cranes and containers of the port and the buzzing activity of the *sopraelevata*), the **Villa del Principe** was built in the early 1530s by the sea commander and doge of Genoa, Andrea Doria. Doria made his reputation and fortune attacking Turkish fleets and Barbary pirates and liberating the Genoese republic from the French and Spanish. Though often overlooked, it's a grand old palace with plenty to recommend it, not least the central **Loggia of the Heroes**, whose walls depict the twelve naval warriors of the illustrious Doria family, bearded heroes in Roman dress who fought and won key naval battles between the thirteenth and fifteenth centuries. Next door, the **Hall of the Giants** is decorated with a ceiling fresco showing Jupiter striking the rebellious giants with thunderbolts, an enormous decorative marble chimneypiece, two amazing Belgian tapestries depicting the deeds of Alexander the Great and a picture of an aged, red-eyed Doria that's quite at odds with Bronzino's portrait next door which shows him as a muscle-bound sea god. The magnificent Golden Gallery beyond has seen better days, but continues the Roman theme with its Roman generals in each lunette, culminating with Doria himself at the far end, his foot on the head of a beaten Turk. In the opposite wing, Sebastiano del Piombo's striking portrait of Doria is perhaps the best-known representation of the great sea captain, painted in 1526 when he became commander of the papal fleet.

3

The Lanterna

Via Milano 134 • Sat & Sun 2.30–6.30pm • €6, €2 for park only • ⓣ 349 280 9485, ⓦ lanternadigenova.it • It's a 15min walk south of the Dinegro metro stop

The promenade walk around the port from the Stazione Marittima takes about twenty-five minutes to reach the old emblem of Genoa, the sixteenth-century **Lanterna** – a forty-metre-tall lighthouse that stands on a rocky outcrop. The interior has been restored as a museum, and it's worth climbing the 172 steps to reach the panoramic terrace for wonderful views over the harbour.

Modern Genoa

In the nineteenth century, Genoa began to expand beyond its old-town constraints. The newer districts begin with the large, central **Piazza de Ferrari**, from where **Via XX Settembre** runs a straight course east through the commercial centre of the city towards Stazione Brignole. This grand boulevard features big department stores, clothes shops and pavement cafés beneath its arcades, prized delicatessens in the side streets around Stazione Brignole and Piazza Colombo, and a bustling covered **Mercato Orientale** partway along, in the cloisters of an old Augustinian monastery. At the eastern end of Via XX Settembre, the park outside the Stazione Brignole extends south into **Piazza della Vittoria**, a huge and dazzling white square built during the Fascist period that now serves as the long-distance bus station. Walking north from Piazza de Ferrari takes you up to the elegant **Piazza Corvetto** – built by the Austrians in the nineteenth century and now a major confluence of traffic and people.

Museo d'Arte Orientale Edoardo Chiossone

Piazzale Mazzini 4, Villetta di Negro • April to early Oct Tues 9am–7pm, Wed–Sat & Sun 10–7.30pm; early Oct–Mar Tues–Fri 9am–6.30pm, Sat & Sun 9.30am–6.30pm • €5 • ☎ 010 542 285, 🌐 museidigenova.it

On the far side of busy Piazza Corvetto, a thoughtful-looking statue of Giuseppe Mazzini marks the entrance to the **Villetta di Negro**, a lushly landscaped park whose artificial waterfalls and grottoes scale the hill. At the top, the **Museo d'Arte Orientale Edoardo Chiossone** holds a collection of oriental art that includes eighteenth-century sculpture and paintings and samurai armour. Chiossone was a printer and engraver for the Italian mint, who, on the strength of his banknote-engraving skills, was invited by the Meiji dynasty to establish the Japanese Imperial Mint. He lived in Japan from 1875 until his death in Tokyo in 1898, building up a fascinating and extensive collection.

The funiculars

3

If you're not satisfied with the view from the Villetta di Negro, you can take the Art Nouveau-style public lift from **Piazza del Portello** up to the **Castelletto**, which offers a great panorama over the port and the roofs of the old town. There's also a **funicular** from the same place up to the residential **Sant'Anna** district, although the views from here aren't as good, and another from Largo Zecca, further west, to the suburb of **Righi**, where locals come for extended sessions of family dining in the various panoramic restaurants.

Boccadasse and Nervi

From Brignole, there are regular buses to Boccadasse (#31; 15min) and trains to Genova Nervi station (20min)

Within surprisingly close reach of Genova's city centre are some pleasantly peaceful coastal retreats worth the short bus or train ride. Heading east of Brignole, the first you'll reach is **Boccadasse**, a picturesque huddle of pastel-painted houses overlooking a pebble beach, while just beyond it is the similarly low-key fishing village of Vernazzola. At the city's easternmost tip, a further five kilometres down the coast, is the **Passeggiata Anita Garibaldi a Nervi**, a popular seaside promenade that hugs the rocky shoreline in both directions from Nervi station. Named after Garibaldi's wife and comrade-in-arms, it connects Nervi's scenic harbour on the western end to the tiny beach of Capolungo, taking in rock pools and the occasional restaurant and bar along the way.

ARRIVAL AND DEPARTURE — GENOA

By plane The Aeroporto Cristoforo Colombo (☎ 010 60 151, 🌐 airport.genova.it) is 6km west of the city centre and is connected to it by the Volabus service, which runs roughly every 40min throughout the day to Stazione Principe, Piazza de Ferrari and Stazione Brignole (30min); tickets cost €6 (or €5 online) and include one hour of public transport in the city. Taxis pull up outside the Arrivals building and charge a fixed price of €7/person to Stazione Principe, €8 to Brignole (minimum three people); otherwise a taxi will cost you about €25 to the city centre.

BOAT TRIPS FROM GENOA

Plenty of boat trips leave from Genoa's harbour, most heading to the Riviera di Levante. Consorzio Liguria Via Mare (☎ 010 256 712, 🌐 liguriaviamare.it) runs 1hr boat trips around Genoa's port, departing from the quayside by the Aquarium (late April–Sept Mon–Fri 2.15pm & 5.20pm, Sat & Sun 2pm, 3.20pm & 5pm; €6), and summer excursions east along the Riviera, including San Fruttuoso and Portofino (€26) and the Cinque Terre (Monterosso; €40). It also runs summer whale-watching trips, departing roughly twice per week at 1.30pm (returning 6.30pm; check the website for dates; €35). Golfo Paradiso (☎ 0185 772 091, 🌐 golfoparadiso.it) also runs regular services east along the coast to Recco, Camogli and the Cinque Terre.

GENOA CITY TOURS

Various operators offer tours of Genoa, all starting from opposite the aquarium in Piazza Caricamento. Pippo runs a **mini-train** around the city centre (40min; hourly departures daily 10am–5pm; April–Oct until 7pm Sat & Sun; €8, children €4; ⓦ alphacoop.it/trenino); **Citysightseeing Genoa** organizes hour-long **open-top bus** tours with commentary (late Mar to early Nov daily 9.30am–5pm every 30min; €15, children €8; ⓦ city-sightseeing.it); the tourist office offers guided walking tours (Sat & Sun 10am; €14) as well as audioguides (€11.50) for self-guided walks through the old town.

By train Genoa has two main train stations: Stazione Principe, on Piazza Acquaverde, just north of the port and west of the centre, and Stazione Brignole on Piazza Verdi, east of the old town. Most trains stop at both stations, which are also well connected by metro line and bus (#36, among others). Train information is available from ⓣ 06 3000. Genoa is on the fast line between Milan and Rome, with regular, slower trains also plying the coastal routes in both directions.

Destinations Camogli (every 30min; 50min); Finale Ligure (every 30min–1hr; 45min–1hr); La Spezia (every 30min–1hr; 1hr–1hr 30min); Levanto (every 30min–1hr; 1hr 10min–2hr); Milan (25 daily; 1hr 30min); Pisa (16 daily; 1hr 40min–2hr); Rapallo (every 30min; 30–50min); Rome (10 daily; 4–5hr); San Remo (17 daily; 1hr 40min–2hr); Sestri Levante (every 30min–1hr; 1hr).

By bus Buses heading to the city outskirts, the Riviera and inland arrive on Piazza della Vittoria, a few minutes' walk south of Brignole, though for most places you're better off taking the train.

By ferry Genoa is one of Italy's biggest passenger ports, not just for cruise ships but also serving a range of ferry routes. See ⓦ moby.it, ⓦ gnv.it and ⓦ tirrenia.it for up-to-date schedules.

Destinations Arbatax, Sardinia (2 weekly; 15hr); Barcelona (3 weekly; 19hr 30min); Bastia (1–2 daily; 6hr 15min); Olbia (2–3 daily; 11hr); Palermo (daily; 21hr); Porto Torres (1–2 daily; 10–12hr); Tunis (6 weekly; 22–24hr).

INFORMATION

Tourist offices The central tourist office is at Via Garibaldi 12/R (daily 9am–6.20pm; ⓣ 010 557 2903, ⓦ visitgenoa.it). There's also an information centre by the Old Harbour on Piazza Caricamento (daily 9am–5.50pm), in the airport's arrival hall (daily 10am–8pm) and at the cruise terminal (hours coincide with cruise ship arrivals).

GETTING AROUND

By public transport The best way to get around the city is to walk, though the metro line is handy for getting across town. The line links Stazione Principe with Stazione Brignole, with the most useful stops at San Giorgio (for the Porto Antico) and Piazza de Ferrari. Tickets cost €1.50 and are valid for 1hr 30min, including use of the lifts and funiculars that scale the city's many hills; a one-way ticket for the funicular alone costs €0.90. You can also buy a Genovapass, a 24hr transport ticket for €4.50 (four people €9 for 24hr), or a museum card that includes public transport (see page 178): see ⓦ amt.genova.it for more information.

By car There are a dozen or so central car parks, all of which cost around €2.50/hr, €15–25/day; the largest is beneath Piazza della Vittoria (24hr), and there are several others in and around the Porto Antico. The old quarter is barred to traffic. On the street, blue painted lines mean you'll have to pay for parking (Mon–Sat 8am–8pm).

Car rental Europcar, Via Cararegis 42 (ⓣ 010 595 5428; airport ⓣ 010 650 4881); Hertz, Via E. Ruspoli 78 (ⓣ 010 592 101; airport ⓣ 010 651 2422); Maggiore, Corso Sardegna 275 (ⓣ 010 839 2153; airport ⓣ 010 651 2467).

By taxi Taxi fares start at €4.20 plus €1.28/km within the city (minimum fare €7.20), although prices from the airport are fixed for groups (see page 186). Prominent taxi stands are at Stazione Brignole, Stazione Principe, Piazza de Ferrari, Piazza Dante, Piazza Caricamento and Piazza Nunziata. You can also call ⓣ 010 5966 or book online at ⓦ 5966.it.

ACCOMMODATION

Genoa has a good range of accommodation options, though many are either characterless chain hotels or characterful but dowdy budget choices. The area just west of Stazione Brignole (Piazza Colombo and Via XX Settembre) remains preferable to anything around Stazione Principe, and there's a handful of quality hotels in the old quarter.

Agnello d'Oro Vico Monachette 6 ⓣ 010 246 2084, ⓦ hotelagnellodoro.it; map p.176. Just off Via Balbi and a 10min walk from the heart of Genoa's old town, this three-star hotel is handy for Stazione Principe (500m), with spacious, modernized rooms – some with balconies – and a pleasant little rooftop terrace. **€90**

Bristol Palace Via XX Settembre 35 ⓣ 010 592 541, ⓦ hotelbristolpalace.it; map p.179. Well located where

MAKING SENSE OF GENOA ADDRESSES

Genoa is one of a handful of Italian cities with a double system of street numbering: commercial establishments, such as bars and restaurants, have **red** numbers (rosso), while all other buildings have **black** numbers (nero) – and the two systems don't run in tandem. This means, for example, that Via Banchi 35/R might be next door to Via Banchi 89/N, but several hundred metres from Via Banchi 33/N.

the old town meets the new town, this has long been among the city's posher options, although its slightly tired air means it's often possible to pick up a bargain. The rooms are spacious and well equipped, bathrooms have baths and the lovely elliptical staircase that stretches up to its nineteenth-century roof is worth looking in for alone. **€144**

Cairoli Via Cairoli 14/4 ⓣ 010 246 1454, ⓦ hotelcairoligenova.com; map p.176. A superior three-star, with a choice of doubles, triples and family rooms, all brightly furnished, modern, en-suite and soundproof. The location, on the edge of the old town but handy for Principe station, is excellent, and there's also a roof terrace and two apartments for rent. **€80**

Manena Vico alla Chiesa della Maddalena 9/1 ⓣ 010 860 8890, ⓦ manenahostel.it; map p.179. Situated on the edge of the old town, down a lane just off Via Garibaldi, with clean five-, eight- and twelve-bed dorms. The friendly, energetic staff arrange free city tours and weekend pub crawls, and the somewhat cramped shared spaces make it a good place to meet fellow travellers. Dorms **€25**

Melia Via Corsica 5 ⓣ 010 531 5111, ⓦ melia-hotels.com; map p.176. Housed in a grand, black Fascist-era building in the leafy Carignano neighbourhood, the sleek lines of this large (99 rooms), contemporary hotel are spot-on. Choose from standard or much larger deluxe doubles, both of which have Nespresso machines and slick bathrooms with TV screens that project onto the mirrors. There's a comfy bar, a restaurant, a gym and a pool. Good if you want somewhere slightly apart from Genoa's hubbub, yet only a 5min walk from Piazza de Ferrari. **€150**

NH Genova Marina Molo Ponte Calvi 5 ⓣ 010 253 91, ⓦ nh-collection.com; map p.179. Jutting into the water from the Porto Antico just opposite the aquarium, this stylish hotel makes a convenient base for the harbor and Old Town, with comfortable wood-panelled rooms, some of them with balconies overlooking the marina and views stretching all the way to La Lanterna. On-site parking garage €20/day. **€120**

Quartopiano Piazza di Pellicceria 2/4 ⓣ 348 742 5779, ⓦ quarto-piano.it; map p.179. In a great location, a few steps from the Palazzo Spinola, this small B&B is an oasis of peace and elegance, with ultra-stylish, minimalist rooms, a cool, contemporary sitting room and a rooftop terrace with a hot tub. Though there's no elevator at this fourth-floor hotel and it can be a bit tricky to find, it's certainly among the best choices in the old town. **€105**

Ricci Piazza Colombo 4 ⓣ 010 592 746, ⓦ hotelricci.com; map p.176. This reliable two-star is conveniently set a few steps west of Stazione Brignole and a five-minute walk east of Piazza de Ferrari. Rooms are spotless, well-equipped and – aside from the somewhat cramped economy rooms – spacious, some of them overlooking a lively and sharply symmetrical piazza. **€150**

EATING

Genoa is one of the very the best Italian cities for dining out, with plenty of cheap trattorias and fancy restaurants. You can readily find *farinata* and focaccia at street outlets, particularly in the old town, where there is also a good choice of places to enjoy *pasta al pesto*, *pansotti alle noce* and any number of classic Ligurian fish and seafood dishes.

CAFÉS AND PASTICCERIE

Bar Pasticceria Mangini Piazza Corvetto 3 ⓣ 010 564 013; map p.176. One of Genoa's most venerable *pasticcerie*, in business since the early 1800s and still top-notch today, with a fantastic array of pastries and seats outside overlooking the bustle of Piazza Corvetto. Daily 7.30am–8.30pm.

Caffè degli Specchi Salita Pollaiuoli 43/R ⓣ 010 256 685; map p.179. A prime spot since 1908 for Genoese artists, writers and intellectuals to take coffee while admiring themselves in the mirrors (*specchi*) that cover the magnificent tiled bar downstairs. The upstairs restaurant has a small menu of hot dishes (lasagne al pesto Genovese, €10) – great for lunch, and very popular. Mon–Sat 7.30am–9.30pm, Sun 8.30am–9pm.

Fratelli Klainguti Piazza Soziglia 98–100/R ⓣ 010 860 2628; map p.179. An Austrian-style café dating from 1828, with cakes, coffee and ice cream under chandeliers and tables on the busy square outside. A good spot for lunch – it serves sandwiches, pasta dishes and salads – and breakfast: they still produce the hazelnut croissant known as a Falstaff (€1.70), much esteemed by Giuseppe Verdi, who spent forty winters in Genoa ("Thanks for the Falstaff, much better than mine," he wrote to the bakers). Daily 7.30am–7.30pm.

Romeo Viganotti Vico Dei Castagna 14/R ⓣ 010 251 4061, ⓦ romeoviganotti.com; map p.179. Hidden

down a small alley near the Cattedrale di San Lorenzo, this tiny chocolate and pastry shop, first opened in 1866, has become a Genoese institution, its shelves stacked with delicious handmade works of art. Its adjacent *gelateria* is also excellent. Mon–Sat 7.30am–7.30pm, Sun 8.30am–6.30pm; closed Aug.

RESTAURANTS

★ **Da Maria** Vico Testadoro 14/R ⓣ 010 581 080; map p.179. No frills at this rough-and-ready trattoria on a side street off Via XXV Aprile, yet it's won wide renown for its unpretentious atmosphere and daily-changing menu of authentic Genoese dishes at unbeatable prices: just €12 for a two-course meal and drink. Tables fill up fast, so get there early. When it's especially busy, diners are often seated side by side, making it a great spot to chat with locals. Mon–Sat noon–3pm, Thurs & Fri 7–10pm.

Da Rina Mura delle Grazie 3/R ⓣ010 246 6475, ⓦristorantedarina.it; map p.179. Family-run and expertly so, *Da Rina* has been going for sixty years and is what passes for posh in Genoa, serving simple, high-quality Genoese cooking down near the waterfront. There's nothing like tucking into their fish soup of the day (€22) in the wonderfully serene dining room while glimpsing the rushing traffic outside. Prices are high to moderate, the clientele ever-so-slightly middle-aged, but the food can't be faulted – it's mostly fish, with a few meat dishes too. Tues–Sun 12–3pm & 7.30–11pm; closed Aug.

★ **Gran Ristoro** Via Sottoripa 29/R ⓣ010 247 3127; map p.179. The humble appearance of this hole-in-the-wall sandwich shop belies its city-wide fame. Tucked away along the old arcades of Via Sottoripa, it's filled with locals around lunchtime and its vast array of meats and fillings allows for endless combinations of custom sandwiches (from €4). If you're feeling overwhelmed, let them guide you towards building the sandwich of your dreams. Mon–Sat 11.45am–3.30pm.

La Buca di San Matteo Via David Chiossone 5/R ⓣ010 236 2389, ⓦlabucadisanmatteo.it; map p.179. Cosy place down an alley off Piazza San Matteo, and spread out over several rooms with vaulted ceilings – one has a glass floor under which lies the restaurant's namesake, an old well discovered during renovation. The menu is classic Ligurian and reasonably priced (*pansoti* with walnut sauce €12; stuffed, seabass ravioli with shrimp ragù €14) with a great selection of wines. Book ahead. Daily noon–3pm & 7–11pm.

Östaja dö Castello Salita S. Maria di Castello 32/R ⓣ010 860 2064; map p.179. A great old-town, family-run trattoria serving good, inexpensive fish and seafood specialities, such as octopus with potatoes and grilled prawns and a few land-based classics (Ligurian-style braised rabbit, €8). Pasta dishes from €6, mains €8–12. Tues–Fri noon–2pm & 7.30–10pm, Sat noon–2pm & 7.30–10.30pm.

Pansön Piazza delle Erbe 5/R ⓣ010 246 8903, ⓦristorantepanson.com; map p.179. Venerable Genoese institution, in the same family since 1790, with an attractive location on this tucked-away yet lively piazza. The food is excellent, highly traditional, and reasonably priced: antipasti and *primi* start at €9 and *secondi* at €13. Mon–Sat 12.30–2.30pm & 7.30–10.30pm, Sun 12.30–2.30pm.

★ **Taggiou** Via Superiore del Ferro 8/R ⓣ375 631 3019; map p.179. Housed in a former butcher shop, this is more of a wine bar and delicatessen than a restaurant, but very popular, drawing crowds at lunch and dinner for its great selection of Italian wine, plates of cold cuts and cheese, sandwiches, and blackboard of hot dishes – typically various pastas, *polpettone* or *involtini*. Good-value lunch specials (pasta plus a glass of water or wine and a coffee for €8). Mon noon–3pm & 6–10pm, Tues–Thurs noon–3pm & 6–11pm, Fri noon–3pm & 6pm–midnight, Sat 6pm–midnight, Sun 6pm–11pm.

DRINKING AND NIGHTLIFE

Banano Tsunami Ponte Embriaco ⓣ010 247 2970; map p.179. Floating at the end of a jetty off the Porto Antico, *Banano Tsunami* is one of Genoa's biggest and best-known clubs. Enjoy an *aperitivi* (from €6) as the sun goes down over the water, or show up later when it's rolled into a full-fledged nightclub, with two dancefloors and three bars. April–Oct lounge bar daily 6pm–10pm; club Wed–Sat 11.30pm–3am.

Bar Berto Piazza delle Erbe 6/R ⓣ010 275 8157; map p.179. Narrow little stand-up café-bar founded in 1904 by Signor Berto, and decorated with colourful bits of broken tile from the nearby ceramics centre of Albisola. With lots of seating out on the square, it's a trendy spot for locals to people-watch with a coffee, beer or a reasonably priced light meal. Sun–Thurs 10am–1am, Fri & Sat 10am–2am.

Calice Spianata di Castelletto 9/R ⓣ010 246 6820; map p.179. Take the funicular up to the Castelletto to reach this tiny wine bar, with a few seats in the cool, vaulted interior and panoramic views outside. It's great value, too – just €3 for a glass of wine or €5 for a plate of cold cuts and cheeses. Mon–Thurs 11am–2pm & 5–9pm, Fri & Sat 11am–2pm & 4–11pm.

3

DIRECTORY

Bookshops Feltrinelli, Via Ceccardi 16 (Mon–9am–8pm, Sun 10am–8pm), has English-language paperbacks and other books.

Consulates UK Piazza Verdi 6/A (ⓣ010 574 0071); US, Via Dante 2 (ⓣ010 584 492).

Football Genoa has two major teams – Genoa, the

oldest team in Italy, founded in 1893 as the Genoa Cricket and Athletic Club, originally for British expats only, and their fierce rivals, Sampdoria. Both teams play at the 36,000-capacity Luigi Ferraris stadium, northeast of Stazione Brignole. Bus #13 from Piazza Caricamento, bus #37 from Piazza de Ferrari, or bus #34 from Stazione Principe pass near th e stadium, or you can walk it in 15–20min from Brignole. Tickets start at around €20 for seats in the end stands, and can be bought from the ticket windows on the ground floor of the stadium, or in advance at the Sampdoria Point at Via Cesarea 107/R (Mon 3.30–7.30pm, Tues–Sat 9.30am–7.30pm), ⓣ010 860 2722, ⓦsampdoriapoint.com; or the Genoa Store at Via al Porto Antico 4 (Tues–Sun 10am–7pmⓣ010 595 9709, ⓦgenoacfc.it), or online at ⓦlisticket.com.

Hospitals Ospedale Galliera, Via Volta Alessandro 8 (ⓣ010 56 321), is the city's most central hospital, situated about 500m southwest of Piazza Vittoria. In an emergency call ⓣ118.

Pharmacies Farmacia Pescetto, close to Stazione Principe at Via Balbi 185/R (ⓣ010 261 609), is open 24hr.

Police Carabinieri ⓣ112; Polizia ⓣ113; coastguard police ⓣ010 27 771. Genoa's police HQ is south of Brignole at Via Armando Diaz 2 (ⓣ010 53 661).

Post office The main post office at Via Dante 4B/R (Mon–Fri 8.20am–7.05pm, Sat 8.20am–12.35pm) has two desks with English-speaking staff. Sub-post offices at both train stations are open the same hours.

3

The Riviera di Ponente

Tracing a slow arc southwest of Genoa, the **Riviera di Ponente** (Coast of the Sunset), is Liguria's most built-up stretch, home to practical, unpretentious resorts, functional towns and the occasional attractive medieval quarter. The beaches are sandy and the prices relatively low, making it a popular holiday spot for Italian families. Almost every settlement along the coast from Genoa to San Remo is a resort of some kind, and extremely busy during July and especially August, when prices are at their highest. But there are some gems among the run-of-the-mill holiday towns, not least the likeable resort of **Finale Ligure**, nearby **Noli**, with its alley-laden old centre, the medieval centre of **Albenga** and the grand old resort of **San Remo**, which can also make a good base for exploring sections of the **Alta Via dei Monti Liguri** (see page 198).

Savona

Some 50km along the coast from Genoa, **SAVONA** is the Ligurian coast at its most functional, a port city that was substantially rebuilt after a hammering in World War II. However, its ugly outskirts hide a picturesque if small medieval centre, and although you're unlikely to stay long, it is worth a look, especially when it's taken over on summer Saturdays by a huge antiques and bric-a-brac market. The town's main claim to fame is as the "Città dei Papi" (City of Popes), after local boy Francesco Della Rovere, who became Pope Sixtus IV in 1471, and his nephew Giuliano, who became Pope Julius II in 1503. Both men left a huge legacy, not least in the Vatican's Sistine Chapel, which Sixtus IV built and Julius II famously commissioned Michelangelo to decorate.

The Duomo

Piazza del Duomo • **Duomo** Daily 9am–7pm • Free • **Sistine Chapel** Sat & Sun 10am–12.30pm & 4–6pm; closed afternoons in July & Aug • €2

Savona's atmospheric old quarter lies to the right of the main, arcaded Via Paleocapa, and focuses on the **Duomo**, a huge building that was constructed in the early seventeenth century to replace an earlier church destroyed by the Genoese. It was a Franciscan convent, and is the city's main memorial to the powerful Delle Rovere family – in the church itself and also in its own **Sistine Chapel**, off the cloister, which was built as a funerary monument by Pope Sixtus IV for his parents. Their simple Renaissance memorials survive, along with some fragments of fresco, though the rest has since been dolled up in a flashy Rococo style that's quite at odds with the cathedral. Inside, there's a column from the original church frescoed with a Madonna and Child in a side chapel, while the major remnant is the well-preserved inlaid wood choir, an early sixteenth-century gift of Sixtus IV's nephew Julius II, which

CASELLA BY TRAIN

There's no better way to explore inland Liguria than by taking a narrow-gauge **train** which leaves roughly every ninety minutes from Genoa's Piazza Manin (about 1km north of Stazione Brignole; reachable by bus #34 or #36 from Stazione Principe). They start off climbing through the Val Bisagno and coil northwards up to **Casella**, in a wooded dell at the foot of Monte Maggio, just over an hour from Genoa. Return fares to Casella are €9 (T 010 837 321, W ferroviagenovacasella.it). Casella is the trailhead for a number of hiking routes in the picturesque **Valle Scrivia** and has a handful of hotels and restaurants.

shows the Apostles and other saints with Christ at the centre flanked on either side by Sixtus IV and Julius II.

Fortezza di Priamàr

Corso Giuseppe Mazzini 1 • Daily: early June to mid-Sept daily 9am–midnight; mid-Sept to early June 9am–6.30pm • Free • **Museo Archeologico** Mid-June to mid-Sept Thurs 4.30–7.30pm, Sat & Sun 10am–2pm & 5–7pm; mid-Sept to mid-June Thurs 3–6pm, Sat & Sun 10am–2pm & 4–6pm • €4 • T 019 822 708, W museoarcheosavona.it

3

Across the road from the old town, right by the sea, the huge **Fortezza di Priamàr** was built in 1528 by the Genoese as a sign of their superiority over the defeated Savonese. From the eighteenth to the early twentieth century it became a major military prison that hosted Giuseppe Mazzini during the Risorgimento. It's a sprawling complex, with grassy turrets, keeps and courtyards, the ruins of a cathedral at the top and a monastery in front. However, the main thing to see is the **Museo Archeologico e della Città**, spread out over the first and second floors with Greek and Etruscan bits and bobs along with some Islamic and Byzantine ceramics. Just below and to the right of the fortress there's a small beach.

ARRIVAL AND INFORMATION — SAVONA

By train Savona's train station is a 10min walk from the old quarter, across the River Letimbro: go left out of the station and follow the road across the river, turning right just past the large car park to get to the end of Via Paleocapa.

Tourist office On the harbour at Via dei Maestri d'Ascia 7/R (open Sat, Sun and days when cruise ships moor 9am–1pm; T 370 329 0922).

ACCOMMODATION AND EATING

NH Savona Via A. Chiodo 9 T 019 803 211, W nh-hotels.com. Sleek, modern rooms with standard mod cons at this reliable business hotel chain, in the revamped harbour district of Darsena, amid plenty of good restaurants and cafés and a short walk from the old town. On-site parking garage €15/day. **€130**

Vino e Farinata Via Pia 15/R T 019 528 4360, W vinoefarinata.it. Set along the busiest pedestrian street in the heart of the old town, this *farinata* place is a Savona institution, with a takeaway counter in front and dining room out back serving *frittura del Golfo*, squid and fish soup (€8), and, of course, great *farinata* (€3/5.50 half/full serving). Service can be a bit hit-and-miss, though you'll pay less than €20 for a couple of courses. Tues–Sat noon–2pm & 6.30–9.30pm, Sun until 9pm.

Noli

Pressed against a beach moored with old fishing boats, tiny **NOLI** is one of the most peaceful and remote settlements along the Riviera di Ponente. Beyond the pleasant, palm-fringed promenade, the tangled alleys of the old town are home to a handful of **medieval towers** built to reflect the wealth of Noli's nobles during its thirteenth- and fourteenth-century heyday as a thriving independent republic. Of these, the most impressive are the **Torre dei Quattro Canti** in the centre of town and the **Torre Comunale**, by the beach. There's little to keep you in Noli for long, but it's worth a visit for the quaint atmosphere and the short stroll up to its crumbling hilltop castle.

Chiesa di San Paragorio

Via Collegio 2 • July–Sept Thurs 5–7pm, Sat & Sun 10am–noon & 5–7pm; April, Sept & Oct Thurs 4–6pm, Sat & Sun 10am–noon & 4–6pm; Nov–Mar Thurs 3–4pm, Sat & Sun 10.30am–noon & 3–4.30pm • €2

Just outside the old city walls stands Noli's most fascinating memorial to the past, an eleventh-century Romanesque cathedral built on the remains of a centuries-older church. Named a national monument by King Umberto I, it has since been largely renovated, and there's a local association of volunteers guides to show you around inside, pointing out its frescoes, tombs and re-used columns. They'll also lead you to the thousand-year-old crypt, set within a pair of ruined chapels built half a millennium earlier still.

ARRIVAL AND INFORMATION — NOLI

By bus Buses run to Noli every 30min from Finale Ligure (15min) and Savona (30min).

Tourist office Beneath the town hall tower at Piazza Milite Ignoto (June–Sept Fri–Sun 9.30am–1pm & 3.30–7pm; April–May & Oct Sat 9.30am–1pm & 2–5.30pm, Sun 9.30am–1pm); T 347 022 4031, W nolitourism.com.

3

ACCOMMODATION AND EATING

Da Pino Corso Italia 23 T 0197 485 648, W ristorantedapinonoli.it. Modern little place on the edge of the old town serving excellent cooked and raw fish dishes, including an Italian interpretation of sashimi. The daily changing menus are good value (from €25). Be sure to book ahead for dinner. Tues–Sun 12.30–2pm & 8–10pm.

Miramare Corso Italia 2 T 0197 48 926, W hotelmiramarenoli.it. Well situated and as close to the beach as it gets in Noli, with spacious, clean rooms, the best of which have private terraces and great sea views, set in a sixteenth-century building attached to a medieval home. Perhaps unsurprisingly, the decor is a bit dated. Excellent buffet breakfast. €130

Finale Ligure

FINALE LIGURE, half an hour from Savona, is a full-on Italian resort, in summer crowded with Italian families who pack the outdoor restaurants, seafront fairground and open-air cinema, or take an extended *passeggiata* along the promenade and through the old alleys. It's a thoroughly enjoyable place for all that, with a long sandy beach that stretches the entire length of the town and a busy, buzzy vibe that lasts long into the evening.

At its centre is **Finalmarina**, with a palm-lined promenade and a small quarter of narrow shopping streets set back from the seafront, focused on the arcaded Piazza Vittorio Emanuele II. At the eastern end of town, **Finalpia** is a small district on the other side of the River Sciusa, with the twelfth-century church of Santa Maria di Pia (rebuilt in florid, early eighteenth-century style) and the adjacent sixteenth-century cloistered abbey at its centre. **Finalborgo**, 2km inland, is perhaps the most attractive part of Finale, a medieval walled quarter overlooked by bare rock faces that are a favourite with free climbers who gather at *Bar Centrale* in Finalborgo's Piazza Garibaldi at weekends. It's also become a thriving hub for mountain bikers (see box, below). Finalborgo has quite a chichi air, and is a nice place to eat, shop, wander the old streets, or take a look at the array of prehistoric remains and other local artefacts at the **Museo Archeologico del Finale** in the cloisters of the convent of Santa Caterina (Tues–Sun: July & Aug 10am–noon & 4–7pm; Sept–June 9am–noon & 2.30–5pm; €5; W museoarcheofinale.it).

ARRIVAL AND INFORMATION — FINALE LIGURE

By train Finale Ligure's train station is at the western end of Finalmarina, the main part of town, just a 5min walk from the main street and the seafront.

By bus Bus #31 connects the train station in Finalmarina to Finalborgo and Finalpia (roughly every 40min).

Tourist office On the seafront boulevard at Via S. Pietro 14 (Tues–Sat 9.30am–12.30pm & 2.30–6pm, T 019 681 019).

THE RIVIERA DEI FIORI BY BIKE

There is no shortage of **cycle routes** linking Liguria's mountainous interior with the coast, particularly along the Riviera dei Fiori, the stretch of shoreline centred around San Remo, ,along which the annual Milan–San Remo "Classicissima" has run since 1907. Finale Ligure makes a great hub for cycling and mountain biking along the Riviera, with well-kept trails and plenty of bike outfits and tour operators, among them ProRide (ⓦ proridefinale.it), which offers year-round uplifts into the hills for €10 per bike.

Among the most popular **mountain bike trails** is the 125km Via del Sale, which begins in Limone Piemonte and winds through the Maritime Alps in the far west of Liguria, tracing a stretch of the Alta Via dei Monti Liguri (see page 198) before reaching the coast at Ventimiglia. Meanwhile, the less adventurous can enjoy long stretches of level cycle paths that hug the coast while occasionally making use of old, paved-over railway lines – such as the 24km greenway from Ospedaletti to San Lorenzo al Mare that passes through San Remo (see page 196).

ACCOMMODATION

Medusa Vico Bricchieri 7 ⓣ 019 692 545, ⓦ medusahotel.it. Right on the beach and just a 5min walk from the station, this friendly hotel is housed in a beautifully renovated seventeenth-century palazzo. It has spotless rooms – the best ones with sea views (€160) – and a buffet breakfast served on a beautiful terrace. **€120**

Hotel Rosita Via Manie 67 ⓣ 019 602 437, ⓦ hotelrosita.it. This friendly, family-run hotel is set about 2km from the edge of town in the hills above Finalpia, with large, a/c rooms and a communal terrace overlooking the sea. Treat yourself to a four course, home-cooked dinner at the superb on-site restaurant. Free parking. **€115**

Residenza San Valentino Piazza Oberdan 8 ⓣ 327 071 2710, ⓦ residencesanvalentino.it. On the outskirts of Finalpia about 15min walk from the train station, these bright, comfortable and modern a/c apartments come equipped with kitchens and balconies with glimpses of the sea. There's a friendly café and bar downstairs, and big discounts out of season. **€130**

CAMPSITES

Camping del Mulino Via Castello, Finalpia ⓣ 019 601 669, ⓦ campingmulino.it. A 10min walk inland from the centre of Finalpia, up winding Via Castello, this site has peaceful, shady pitches, great views up the valley and well-priced bungalows (sleeping two–four) too. Pitches **€27**, bungalows **€75**

Il Villaggio di Giuele & Eurocamping Calvisio Via Calvisio 37, Finalpia ⓣ 019 601 240, ⓦ eurocampingcalvisio.it. Well-run riverside site, about 1500m inland from the seafront at Finalpia, with pitches for tents and caravans and a holiday "village" with a selection of apartments. Facilities include two pools, a decent restaurant and shops. There's also a shuttle bus service into town. Great for kids. April–Nov. Pitches around **€38**

EATING AND DRINKING

Ai Torchi Via dell'Annunziata 12, Finalborgo ⓣ 019 690 531, ⓦ ristoranteaitorchi.com. This refined restaurant occupies an ancient olive-oil factory in Finalborgo and serves expensive pasta and fish dishes (risotto with artichokes and prawns €18) with care and some style. Wed–Mon 12.30–2.30pm & 8–10pm; closed Jan–early Feb.

Alla Vecchia Maniera Via Roma 25, Finalmarina ⓣ 019 692 562. A central and unpretentious place to eat local fish and seafood (tuna *carpaccio* €15), but it's popular – book in advance if you can, especially if you want to sit outside. Thurs–Sun noon–2.30pm & 7–9pm.

★ **Chiesa** Vico Gandolino 12, Finalmarina ⓣ 018 692 516. A small, canteen-like place with a daily-changing menu of good, cheap dishes: *primi* start at €5 and mains at €6. Popular with locals, it serves up tasty pasta and roasts, fish dishes, rabbit and *baccalà*. Check out also its *salumeria*, around the corner on the main street at Via Pertica 13, which is the best central option for picking up delicious picnic supplies. Mon–Sat noon–2pm.

Albenga

The small market town of **ALBENGA** is one of the most attractive places along this part of the Ligurian coast, an ex-port whose estuary silted up long ago but left a wanderable old quarter, still within medieval walls and following the grid pattern of its ancient Roman predecessor, Albingaunum.

In the centre of town, **Piazza San Michele** is home to the elegant **cathedral** (daily 8am–7pm; free), the main part of which was built in the eleventh century and enlarged in the early fourteenth. Just beyond, in the Torre Comunale, the **Museo Civico Ingauno** (Tues–Sun: mid-Sept–mid-June 10am–12.30pm & 2.30–6.30pm, mid-June–mid-Sept 9.30am–noon & 3.30–7.30pm; €3.50; ⓣ018 251 215) is home to an array of Roman masonry and fragments, including a patch of first-century mosaic floor. Around the corner from the museum, the ingenious fifth-century **baptistry** combines a ten-sided exterior with an octagonal interior. Inside are fragmentary mosaics showing the Apostles represented by twelve doves. Behind the baptistry to the north, the archbishop's palace houses the diverting **Museo Diocesano**, Via Episcopio 5 (April–Sept Tues–Sat 9.30am–12.30pm & 3.30–6.30pm, Sun 10am–12.30pm & 3.30–6pm; Oct–Mar Tues 9.30am–12.30pm & 3–5pm, Wed–Sat 9.30am–12.30pm & 3–6pm; €5; ⓣ347 808 5811), where there are paintings by Lanfranco and Guido Reni. The archbishop's partially frescoed bedchamber, next door to his private chapel, is also decorated with fifteenth-century frescoes. A few metres from here, at the junction of Via Medaglie d'Oro and Via Ricci, the arched, thirteenth-century **Loggia dei Quattro Canti** marks the centre of the Roman town, while some 500m further north, beyond the city's largest gate, **Porta Molino**, and along Viale Pontelungo, is the elegant, arcaded **Pontelungo bridge**. Built in the twelfth century to cross the river, which shifted course soon afterwards, it now makes an odd sight, half-submerged alongside the modern road.

In the opposite direction, five minutes' walk beyond the train station, lies Albenga's seafront and **beaches** – mostly sandy and with a couple of reasonable free sections.

ARRIVAL AND INFORMATION — ALBENGA

By train Albenga's train station is 800m east of the old town; turn left outside the station and cross the road to follow Viale Martiri della Libertà to the town centre and its old quarter.

Tourist office Just east of the old town at Viale Martiri della Libertà 1 (Mon–Sat 9am–12.30pm & 4–7.30pm, Sun 9am–12.30pm; ⓣ0182 568 5223).

ACCOMMODATION AND EATING

Da Puppo Via Torlaro 20 ⓣ0182 51 853, ⓦdapuppo.it. Just off Via Medaglie d'Oro, this is a basic canteen-like trattoria with daily specials and a great menu of cheap grilled staples, from smoked swordfish *carpaccio* (€8.50) to Argentinian steaks. Also a good spot for pizza (from €4) and *farinata* (€3.50). July–Sept Tues–Sun 6.30–10pm; Oct–June Tues–Sat 12.15–2pm & 6.30–10pm.

Marisa Via Pisa 28 ⓣ0182 50 241, ⓦmarisahotel.com. Between the train station and the seafront amid a good number of cafés and restaurants, this small family-run hotel is a 10–15min walk from the old town. It has clean and spacious a/c rooms, some with sea views and balconies, and all nicely furnished with LCD-screen TVs. **€140**

The Caves of Toirano

Via alle Grotte Toirano • Daily: July & Aug 9.30am–12.30pm & 2–5.30pm; Sept–June 9.30am–12.30pm & 2–5pm; tours leave every 30min and last 1hr 10min • €13 • ⓣ0182 98 062, ⓦtoiranogrotte.it • Take a train from Albenga or Finale Ligure to the resort of Loano, where bus #81 departs for the caves once a day at 2.45pm (20min; returns from the caves 5.15pm) and for the centre of Toirano (a 20min walk from the caves) several times throughout the day; check ⓦtpllinea.it for the latest timetable

Just outside the village of Toirano, a few kilometres inland, are the spectacular **Caves of Toirano**. They lie up a track a kilometre or so beyond the main part of the village, and are quite well developed as an attraction, with plenty of parking and a café and shop. Well worth seeing, the caves are made up of two accessible complexes connected by a man-made tunnel. The first, the so-called **Grotta della Bàsura**, or "Witch's Cave", was inhabited some twelve thousand years ago, and you can see well-marked foot- and handprints to prove it, as well as the well-preserved

RIOMAGGIORE, CINQUE TERRE

bones of bears who lived here around twenty thousand years earlier. Beyond, the **Grotta di Santa Lucia Inferiore** has some remarkable stalagmite and stalactite formations, including stone flowers and rare, rounded stalactites; outside and above, the grotto and church of **Santa Lucia Superiore** holds a natural spring that was dedicated in the Middle Ages to St Lucy, patron saint of eyesight, after several miraculous cures were effected here. You too can have a drink – bottles are left out for the purpose.

Imperia

3 Some 30km west of Albenga is the provincial capital of **IMPERIA**, a sprawling settlement formed in 1923 when Mussolini linked twin townships on either side of the River Impero. Imposing **Porto Maurizio**, on the western bank, is the more likeable of the two, ascending the hillside in a series of zigzags from a marina and small beach, with its stepped old quarter dominated by a massive, late eighteenth-century cathedral and a series of Baroque churches and elegant villas. Quieter **Oneglia**, 2km east, is a more workaday place, devoted to fishing and the olive industry, most manifest in local producer Fratelli Carli's **Museo dell'Olivo** behind the old train station at Via Garessio 11 (Mon–Sat 9am–12.30pm & 3–6.30pm; €5; T 0183 295 762, W museodellolivo.com): its modern displays are devoted to the history of the olive hereabouts and in particular the green nectar it produces.

ACCOMMODATION AND EATING — IMPERIA

Corallo Imperia Corso Garibaldi 29 T 0183 666 264, W coralloimperia.it. Light, airy rooms all with sea views, a spacious sundeck and an abundant breakfast buffet served in the roof garden, weather permitting. **€120**

Croce di Malta Via Scarincio 148 T 0183 667 020, W hotelcrocedimalta.com. Overlooking the old harbour in an excellent location, the rooms at this long-established hotel are spotless if a bit characterless – the best ones have nice sea views (€98). **€90**

Osteria dai Pippi Via dei Pellegrini 9 T 0183 652 122. Friendly restaurant close to the waterfront in Porto Maurizio, serving a small menu of mainly regional dishes but also a few surprises, including slow-cooked rabbit (€14), great gnocchi and excellent desserts. Book ahead. Mon & Wed–Sat 7–10pm, Sun 12–3pm & 7–10pm

San Remo

Set on a broad, sweeping bay between twin headlands, **SAN REMO** had its heyday as a classy resort in the sixty years or so up to the outbreak of World War II, when the Empress Maria Alexandrovna headed a substantial Russian community in the town (Tchaikovsky completed *Eugene Onegin* and wrote his Fourth Symphony in San Remo in 1878). Some of the grand hotels overlooking the sea, especially those near the train station, are now grimy and crumbling, but others in the ritzier, western parts of town are still in pristine condition, opening their doors to Europe's remaining aristocrats season after season. San Remo is blessed with the Italian Riviera's most famous **casino**, and remains a showy and attractive town, with a good beach and a labyrinthine old town standing guard over the palm-laden walkways below.

Corso Matteotti

San Remo's main artery is the largely pedestrianized **Corso Matteotti**, lined with cocktail bars, *gelaterie*, cinemas and clothes stores, which runs through the commercial centre of town. At no. 143, the Renaissance Palazzo Borea d'Olmo houses the **Museo Civico** (Tues–Sat 9am–7pm; €5), with the usual array of local archaeological finds, paintings and items relating to the Risorgimento (Garibaldi spent quite a bit of time in San Remo).

The Casino

Corso degli Inglesi 18 • Sun–Thurs 2.30pm–2.30am, Fri & Sat 3pm–3.30am; slots Sun–Thurs 10am–2.30am, Fri & Sat 10am–3.30am; guided tours July & Aug Sat 9.30am • Free; guided tours €3 • ⊕ 0184 59 51, ⓦ casinosanremo.it

At the far end of Corso Matteotti is the town's landmark **Casino**, an ornate white palace with grand staircases and distinctive turrets which epitomizes the town's old-fashioned *fin-de-siècle* charm. It's a theatre too, and hosts San Remo's long-running festival of popular song every March. Anyone can visit, as long as you have your passport (you don't even need to dress up); or you can see the gaming rooms, roof garden and theatre on regular **guided tours** throughout the summer; the entrance is from the side entrance to the theatre on the left.

The Cathedral and La Pigna

The area just above San Remo's main street and Casino is probably its most atmospheric, where busy Via Palazzo gives way to a warren of narrow streets and eventually the mainly Romanesque **Cattedrale di San Siro** (Mon–Sat am–11.45 & 3–5.45pm, Sun 8am–12.15pm & 4–7pm; free), decorated with unusual twelfth-century bas reliefs above each of its side doors and with a very ancient feel within; note the fifteenth-century processional black crucifix in the right aisle.

Above here is **La Pigna** or "The Pine Cone", perhaps San Remo's most fascinating quarter, accessible up steep lanes north of Piazza Eroi Sanremesi and Piazza Cassini. Known for its kasbah-like arched passageways and alleys, it remains remarkably ungentrified – and a stark contrast to the crisp and bustling modern streets down below.

The seafront

Beyond the Casino, the palm-lined boulevard of **Corso Imperatrice** stretches along the **seafront** west of the centre, just back from which the impressive onion-domed **Russian Orthodox church**, built in the 1920s, is a manifestation of San Remo's former Russian community (Tues–Sun 9.30am–12.30pm & 3–6.30pm; €1 donation), though it's more impressive outside than in. Opposite there are some small stretches of **beach**, while in the other direction, Corso Mombello takes you down to the **Porto Vecchio**, full of high-end boats and lined with restaurants and cafés, just east of which is another, larger stretch of beach.

3

ARRIVAL AND INFORMATION — SAN REMO

By train San Remo's modern underground train station is east of the town centre on Corso Cavallotti. It's a 5min walk east from here along Corso Garibaldi to the end of Corso Matteotti.

By bus The main bus station is on Piazza Colombo, right in the centre of town at the eastern end of Corso Matteotti.

ACCOMMODATION

Alexander Corso Garibaldi 123 ⊕ 0184 504 591, ⓦ hotelalexandersanremo.com. This welcoming hotel is only 5min from the train station in a beautiful *belle époque* building surrounded by pleasant gardens, where a buffet breakfast is served in good weather. Rooms are well kept, with a/c and flatscreen TVs. There's parking at the rear (€10) and free bike loan for guests. **€124**

Paradiso Via Roccasterone 12 ⊕ 0184 571 211, ⓦ paradisohotel.it. If you want a quiet location above the town's bustle but only a short walk from the sea, this is the place, a family-run hotel with sunny, modern rooms, a secluded garden, a pool and underground parking (€12). Rates are cut in half during the off-season, but it's good value any time of the year. **€100**

Royal Hotel Corso Imperatrice 80 ⊕ 0184 5391, ⓦ royalhotelsanremo.com. A grand white presence above San Remo's western seafront, this is how they did things in times gone by, and it's the place to stay if you're dressing for dinner and gambling at the Casino below. Great facilities – three restaurants, a tennis court and a vast, heated, salt-water swimming pool set in a tropical garden – and large, beautifully appointed rooms. **€400**

Villaggio dei Fiori Via Tiro a Volo 3 ⊕ 0184 660 635, ⓦ villaggiodeifiori.it. Facility-laden campsite about 2km west of town with space for tents and caravans, plus pricey chalets and bungalows for rent. Open all year but best to book in advance in high season. Pitches around **€34**, chalets **€140**

3

THE ALTA VIA DEI MONTI LIGURI

The **Alta Via dei Monti Liguri** is a long-distance high-level trail covering the length of Liguria, from Ventimiglia in the west across the ridgetops to Ceparana on the Tuscan border above La Spezia in the east – a total distance of some 442km. The mountains, which form the connection between the Alps and the Apennines, aren't high – rarely more than 1500m – meaning that the scenic route, which makes full use of the many passes between peaks, is relatively easy-going. The whole thing would take weeks to complete, but has been divided up into 43 stages of between two and four hours each, making it easy to dip in and out. Trail support and maintenance is good, with *rifugi* dotted along the path and distinctive waymarks (red-white-red "AV" signs).

Unfortunately, **access** to most parts of the Alta Via from the main coastal towns can be tricky, and requires juggling with route itineraries and bus timetables. For **information** on the Alta Via, the Associazione Alta Via dei Monti Liguri (T 010 2485 2200, W altaviadeimontiliguri.it; information phone line open Mon–Fri 9am 1pm & 2–4pm; T 800 445 445) produces a full-colour wall-map of the route, along with detailed English descriptions and timings of all 43 stages. Club Alpino Italiano (W cai.it) offices in the major towns have information on *rifugi*, though it's worth the €5 subscription fee to access a more exhaustive list of accommodation and dining options along the way from Alta Via Info H24 (W altaviainfoh24.com), which also provides the latest updates on closures.

EATING AND DRINKING

Il Dehor del Marinaio Corso Nazario Sauro 23 T 0184 506 721, W facebook.com/pg/ildehordelmarinaiosanremo. Deservedly the most popular of the strip of tightly-crammed, casual restaurants overlooking San Remo's old marina. Serves classic if slightly pricey seafood favourites like fried calamari (€18) and spaghetti with clams (€15). Tues–Sun 11.30am–3pm & 7–11.45pm.

Cantine Sanremesi Via Palazzo 7 T 0184 572 063. Cosy, vaulted wine bar, in business since the 1930s, with a few tables outside that make a good lunch stop. It serves great focaccia, lots of pasta dishes and Ligurian specialities like potato and octopus salad and *sardenaira*. Most dishes are €10 or less. Tues–Sun 12.30–3pm & 5.30–10.30pm.

Nuovo Piccolo Mondo Via Piave 7 T 0184 509 012. Charming trattoria with tables outside in an alley off Corso Matteotti, serving delicious Ligurian specialities like swordfish *carpaccio* (€13.50) and *polpo e patate* (€17) The owner speaks good English. No credit cards. Mon 12.30–2pm, Tues–Sat 12.30–2pm & 7.30–9.30pm.

Bussana Vecchia

7km east of San Remo • From San Remo, take the bus towards Bussana or Arma di Taggia and ask the driver to drop you at the trail up to Bussana Vecchia (a 15min hike)

Capping a hilltop, the picturesque village of **Bussana Vecchia** is worth a wander for its winding medieval alleys, many of which remain overgrown with weeds. Abandoned by its eight hundred or so residents following a devastating earthquake in 1887, the village was resettled in the 1960s by a small community of artists who built their homes and studios out of the rubble. These days there's also a good handful of cafés and restaurants, most of them around the entrance to the village.

Giardini Botanici Hanbury

Corso Montecarlo 43, Mortola Inferiore • Daily: March to mid-June & mid-Sept to mid-Oct 9.30am–6pm, mid-June to mid-Sept 9.30am–7pm, mid-Oct to Feb 9.30am–5pm; Nov–Feb closed Mon • €9 • T 0184 229 507, W giardinihanbury.com • Bus #1a from Via Cavour or the train station in Ventimiglia (approx hourly, no service 3–5pm; 15min)

Some 11km west of San Remo, just near the French border, the village of Mortola Inferiore is famed for the spectacular hillside **Giardini Botanici Hanbury**. The gardens were laid out in 1867 by Sir Thomas Hanbury, a London spice merchant who set up home here, and are highly atmospheric, with hidden corners and pergola-covered walks tumbling down to the sea.

The Riviera di Levante

The coast **east of Genoa**, dubbed the **Riviera di Levante** (Coast of the Sunrise), is more varied and beautiful than its counterpart to the west, though not always the ideal destination for a get-away-from-it-all holiday. Its picturesque series of charming towns and villages that once eked out a living from fishing and coral diving have been transformed by decades of tourism. Still, it's a glorious and rugged stretch of coast, its cliffs and bays covered with pine and olive trees and plenty of appealing resorts. The footpaths crisscrossing the headland that stretches to the upmarket resort of **Portofino** are a great way to get off the beaten track, and the harbour towns on each side – **Camogli** towards Genoa and **Santa Margherita** in the Golfo di Tigullio – are well worth a visit. Other highlights include big, feisty resorts like **Rapallo**, and smaller, quieter places like **Sestri Levante.** Further east, the main road (though not the railway) heads inland, bypassing the laidback beach town of **Levanto** and the spectacular **Cinque Terre** coast (now a national park and great, organized walking country). The road joins the train line again at the naval port of **La Spezia**, a short hop from the alluring towns of **Portovenere** and **Lerici** (the latter almost in Tuscany) on either side of the Golfo dei Poeti.

Camogli

CAMOGLI was the "saltiest, roughest, most piratical little place", according to Dickens when he visited the town. Though it still has the "smell of fish, and seaweed, and old rope" that the author relished, its rough edges are long gone and it's now one of the most attractive resorts along this stretch of the coast. The town's name, a contraction of *Casa Mogli* (House of Wives), comes from the days when voyages lasted for years and the women ran the port while the men were away. In its day Camogli supported a huge fleet of seven hundred vessels, which once saw off Napoleon. The town declined in the age of steam, but has since been reborn as a classy getaway.

Camogli's serried towers of nineteenth-century apartment blocks line up above the waterfront and a small promontory topped with the medieval **Castello della Dragonara**. On one side of the castle there's a busy **harbour**, crammed with fishing boats, and on the other a section of pebble **beach** backed by a long promenade of bars and restaurants. Camogli is also known for its annual **Sagra del Pesce** (second weekend in May), when thousands of fresh fish are cooked in a giant frying pan in Piazza Colombo by the Marina; €6 a head gets you a souvenir plate to fill up with fish.

ARRIVAL AND INFORMATION — CAMOGLI

By train The train station is just inland and uphill from the centre of Camogli, a 5min walk.

Tourist office Not far from the train station at Via XX Settembre 33 (June–Sept Mon 10am–noon & 4.15–7.15pm, Tues–Sat 9.15am–12.15pm & 4.15–7.15pm, Sun 9.15am–12.15pm; Oct–May Mon 10am–noon & 3.30–6.30pm, Tues–Sat 9.15am–12.15pm & 3.30–6.30pm, Sun 9.15am–12.15pm; **T** 0185 771 066, **W** camogliturismo.it).

ACCOMMODATION

Augusta Via Piero Schiaffino 100 **T** 0185 770 592, **W** htlaugusta.com. Just above the harbour and a 5min walk from the train station, this is a good-value family-run hotel with clean and attractive a/c rooms, all en suite. **€120**

Casmona Salita Pineto 13 **T** 0185 770 015, **W** casmona.com. Up towards the train station from the town centre, this seafront hotel is housed in a recently renovated nineteenth-century villa with light, airy rooms with balconies, satellite TV and excellent sea views. Parking available nearby (€15 per day). **€190**

Cenobio dei Dogi Via Cuneo 34 **T** 0185 7241, **W** cenobio.it. Set just below the train station at the southern end of the beach, this is Camogli's most traditional upmarket alternative, a lavish hotel that was once the summer palace of Genoa's doges. As well as great views over the bay, it has its own park, beach, pool, tennis courts and restaurants. Rooms with sea views start at €380. **€270**

Villa Rosmarino Via Figari 38 **T** 0185 771 580, **W** villa

3

COASTAL FERRIES

FERRIES FROM GENOA, CAMOGLI AND PORTOFINO

In summer, dozens of **boats** serve points along the Tigullio coast and beyond. There are shuttles between Genoa's Porto Antico and Camogli, San Fruttuoso and Portofino, several times a day (see page 186). **Golfo Paradiso**, Via Scalo 3, Camogli (0185 772 091, golfoparadiso.it) runs year-round ferries connecting Camogli with tranquil **Punta Chiappa** and **San Fruttuoso**, both ideal for a spot of swimming and basking in the sun (€11 return to Punta Chiappa, €14 return to San Fruttuoso). From July to early September, there are also ferries from Camogli to the **Cinque Terre** (€31 return) and **Portovenere** (€32 return).

OTHER SERVICES

Another line – **Servizio Marittimo Tigullio**, Piazza Mazzini 33, Santa Margherita Ligure (0185 284 670, traghettiportofino.it) – shuttles hourly in summer between **Rapallo**, **Santa Margherita**, **Portofino** and **San Fruttuoso**, taking around fifteen minutes between each town and thirty minutes between Portofino and San Fruttuoso (Rapallo to San Fruttuoso costs €18 return). They also run services down the coast to the **Cinque Terre** (€36 return from Rapallo), as well as lovely **night excursions** to Portofino (July Sat only, Aug Fri & Sat; €15 return).

rosmarino.com. Just out of town, though only a 15min walk from the train station, this boutique hotel is perhaps Camogli's best option, and certainly its most relaxing. Set in a nineteenth-century *palazzo*, its six cool white rooms are hung with contemporary art and face onto lush, manicured grounds and a pool. **€270**

EATING

La Camogliese Via Garibaldi 76 0185 776 027. Better value than its seafront neighbours, with a great view and a reliable menu, including tasty *vongole* and mussels with pasta, focaccia *di Recco*, *pansotti alle noce* and *trofie al pesto*. Fish of the day costs from €18–22. On summer evenings, book ahead. April–Oct 12.30–3pm & 7.30–11pm; Dec–Mar 12.30–2.30pm & 7.30–10.30pm; closed Nov.

Nonna Nina Viale Molfino 126, San Rocco 0185 773 835, nonnanina.it. Perhaps Camogli's best choice, about a 10min walk from the seafront up on the Portofino headland, in a gorgeous old house with a garden overlooking the sea. Menus change with the seasons but you can expect wonderful Ligurian specialities such as *trofiette al pesto*. Count on about €40 for a full meal with wine. Thurs–Tues 12.30–2.30pm & 7.30–10pm. Closed Nov & last two weeks of Jan.

San Fruttuoso

The enchanting thousand-year-old abbey of **SAN FRUTTUOSO** is one of the principal draws along this stretch of the Riviera, occupying a picturesque little bay at the southern foot of Monte di Portofino. The only way to get here is on foot or by boat. On summer weekends, the tiny pebble beach and church may be uncomfortably crowded, but out of season (or at twilight, courtesy of an overnight stay or the occasional night cruise), San Fruttuoso is a peaceful, excellent place for doing very little.

Abbazia di San Fruttuoso

Daily: June to mid-Sept 10am–5.45pm; April, May & late Sept 10am–4.45pm; Jan–March & Oct–Dec 10am–3.45pm • €7 • 0185 772 703

The **Abbazia di San Fruttuoso** was originally built to house the relics of the third-century martyr St Fructuosus, which were brought here from Spain after the Moorish invasion in 711. It was rebuilt in 984 with an unusual Byzantine-style cupola and distinctive waterside arches, and later became a Benedictine abbey that exerted a sizeable degree of control over the surrounding countryside. The Doria family took over in the sixteenth century, adding the defensive **Torre dei Doria** nearby, and the small, elegant church, with its compact little cloister and half-dozen Doria tombs.

Cristo degli Abissi

Off the headland, a 1954 bronze statue known as the **Cristo degli Abissi** (Christ of the Abyss) rests eight fathoms (15m) down on the sea bed, to honour the memory of divers who have lost their lives at sea and to protect those still working beneath the waves. Taxi-boats queue up to take you there.

ARRIVAL — SAN FRUTTUOSO

By boat Dozens of boats shuttle backwards and forwards from practically every harbour along the coast in peak season: Golfo Paradiso (see page 200) charges €14 return from Camogli.

ACCOMMODATION — SAN FRUTTUOSO

From May to October there are a few options for staying in San Fruttuoso.

Da Giovanni Via S. Fruttuoso 10 ⓣ 0185 770 047, ⓦ dagiovanniristorante.com. As central as it gets in San Fruttuoso, this is also the largest and best of the tiny enclave's restaurants, serving tasty seafood and pesto dishes (pasta with *pesto genovese*, €15). It also has a handful of nicely renovated a/c rooms, each with private bathroom and a view of the bay. Advance booking is essential. **€180**

Locanda del Parco Viale Rainusso 1 ⓣ 335 194 3665, ⓦ locandadelparcodiportofino.it. A 2min walk around the ridge to the south of San Fruttuoso's main beach, this friendly B&B has five rustic but spotless rooms just up from a smaller, quieter beach. Pack food supplies in advance to avail yourself of the communal kitchen. **€180**

3

Portofino

Situated at the end of a narrow and treacherously winding road just 5km south of Santa Margherita, **PORTOFINO** is an appealing place, tucked into a protected inlet surrounded by lush cypress- and olive-clad slopes. It's an A-list resort that has attracted high-flying bankers, celebs and their hangers-on for years, as evidenced by the flotillas of giant yachts usually anchored just outside. The tiny place manages to be both attractive and off-putting at the same time, with a quota of fancy shops, bars and restaurants that would suit somewhere twice its size, and unashamedly expensive accommodation – luxury is really the point of Portofino.

Northwest from the village, steeply stepped paths head through vineyards and orchards to Olmi and on to **San Fruttuoso** (see page 200), while the best sandy **beach** is the sparkling cove at **Paraggi**, 2km back towards Santa Margherita on the coast road (buses will stop on request) – not exactly remote, but less formal than Portofino and with a small stretch of pebbly sand and a couple of bars set back from the water.

To get a sense of Portofino's idyllic setting follow the footpath which heads south from the harbour up onto the headland. Five minutes from the village is the church of **San Giorgio**, said to contain relics of St George, and a further ten minutes up is the spectacularly located **Castello Brown** (April–May & Sept–Oct daily 10am–6pm; Jun–Aug daily 10am–7pm; Nov–March Sat & Sun 10am–5pm; €5; ⓦ castellobrown.com), from whose terrace there are breathtaking views of a pint-sized Portofino. The castle, which dates from Roman times and now frequently hosts art and photography exhibitions, is named after its former owner, British Consul Montague Yeats Brown, who bought it in 1867 and set about transforming it. In 1870 he planted two pines on the main terrace for his wedding – one for him and one for his wife, Agnes Bellingham – and they remain a prominent feature today. The scenic path continues for a kilometre or so, down to the **Faro** (lighthouse) on the very tip of the promontory. The only way back is up the same path.

ARRIVAL AND INFORMATION — PORTOFINO

By bus and ferry Regular buses connect Portofino with nearby Santa Margherita (every 15–20min); they're supposed to take 15min but can take longer and indeed, in summer it can be quicker and easier to jump on one of the ferries linking Portofino with Santa Margherita (one-way/return €7/12) and Rapallo (one-way/return €9/15).

Tourist office Via Roma 35 (April Wed–Sun 10am–2pm; May–Oct Tues–Sun10am–6pm; Nov–Mar Sat & Sun 10am–2pm; ⓣ 0185 269 024).

ACCOMMODATION

Belmond Splendido Salita Baratta 16 ⓣ 0185 267 801, ⓦ belmond.com. High above the village, this is the place to stay if money is no object, with fabulously lush grounds and stupendous views. Although it is a little way out, the pool, tennis courts, views and two restaurants may mean you won't want to leave anyway. For those who prefer to be in the thick of things there is another, smaller location, linked by free shuttle – the *Splendido Mare* – down in the port, with slightly humbler rates (rooms without sea views start at €850). Both branches closed Nov to late March. **€1800**

Eden Vico Dritto 18 ⓣ 0185 269 091, ⓦ hoteleden portofino.com. Set within its own delightful gardens in the centre of town, this is perhaps Portofino's best-value option, its simply furnished rooms equipped with tiny bathrooms and balconies looking onto the pretty garden. Rates drop drastically midweek out of season. **€210**

EATING AND DRINKING

Chuflay Via Roma 2 ⓣ 0185 269 020. Right on the harbour, the *Splendido Mare's* waterfront restaurant has a relatively small, fairly international menu at lunchtime and more exciting Ligurian dishes in the evening. The food is great, especially the fish and seafood, and the location can't be bettered, though you can expect to pay upwards of €100 for a full meal. April–Oct daily 12.30–3.30pm & 7.30–11pm.

3

Il Pitosforo Molo Umberto I 9 ⓣ 0185 269 020, ⓦ pitosforo-portofino.it. Perhaps the most established of Portofino's waterfront choices, offering a postcard-perfect view of the colourful strip of tower-houses across the harbour. The Ligurian dishes here are top-notch, especially the seafood, but again – be prepared to face a hefty tab, around €100 for a full meal. Book ahead during summer months. Wed–Sun 12.30–2.30pm & 7–10.30pm.

Trattoria Concordia Via del Fondaco 5 ⓣ 0185 269 207. A friendly, family-run restaurant about a minute's walk up the road from the bus station, *Concordia* is a local favourite for its daily-caught seafood, and – by Portofino standards – reasonable prices: a full meal with wine will cost about €60. Wed–Sun noon–2.30pm & 7–10.30pm; closed Feb.

Santa Margherita Ligure

SANTA MARGHERITA LIGURE is a small, thoroughly attractive, palm-laden resort, tucked into an inlet and replete with grand hotels, garden villas and views of the glittering bay. In the daytime, trendy young Italians cruise the streets or whizz around the harbour on jet skis, while the rest of the family sunbathes or crams the *gelaterie*. Santa Margherita is far cheaper to stay in than Portofino and a bit less crowded than Rapallo, and makes a good base both for taking boats and trains up and down the coast and for exploring the countryside on foot.

The town is in two parts: one set around a harbour and gardens and a small town beach, and a second, more commercial harbour around the headland. In between there's a small **castle**, and behind this the shady gardens of the sixteenth-century **Villa Durazzo** (June to mid-Sept 9am–7pm; mid-Sept to May 9am–5pm; free; ⓦ villadurazzo.it), the lavishly decorated rooms of which can be glimpsed on guided tours (June to mid-Sept 9.30am–1pm & 2–6pm; mid-Sept to May 9.30am–1pm & 2–5pm; €5.50). There's a decent if small town **beach**, but the best beaches are out of town, accessible by bus: south towards Portofino is Paraggi (see page 201), while to the north the road drops down to a patch of beach in the bay of **San Michele di Pagana**. In addition to its beach bars and crystal-clear water, a *Crucifixion* by Van Dyck in the church of San Michele may prove an added incentive for a visit.

ARRIVAL AND INFORMATION — SANTA MARGHERITA LIGURE

By train Santa Margherita's train station overlooks the harbour, a 5min walk from the town centre and seafront.

By bus Buses for Portofino, San Michele and Rapallo stop right outside the tourist office.

Tourist office On the waterfront Piazza Vittorio Veneto (June–Sept daily 9am–1pm & 3–7pm; Mar–May & Oct daily 10am–noon & 2–4pm; Nov–Feb Fri–Sun 10am–noon & 2–4pm; ⓣ 0185 287 485).

ACCOMMODATION

Flory Via Luigi Bozzo 3 ⓣ 0185 286 435, ⓦ hotelflory.it. A friendly mid-priced hotel nicely located on a quiet side street, with good-sized rooms, most with a/c and some en suite. There's also a panoramic roof terrace and free bike loan for guests. Parking nearby for €20/day. Ten percent discount with this book. **€135**

Lido Palace Via Doria 3 ⓣ0185 285 821, ⓦlidopalacehotel.com. This impressive seafront hotel is right by Santa Margherita's small beach and has spacious, modern rooms, with a choice of hill or sea view. There's a restaurant, bar and fitness centre, although its major asset is the fact that it's the most central of the town's upmarket hotels. Parking offered nearby for €30/day. **€220**

EATING AND DRINKING

★ **Angolo 48** Via Palestro 48 ⓣ0185 286 650. Stylish and very popular place on a busy corner in the heart of the old town, with an excellent variety of reasonably priced Ligurian meat and pasta dishes (lasagne al pesto €12) and friendly service, a well-stocked bar and a gluten free menu. Book ahead. Daily 6–10pm.

Trattoria Baicin Via Algeria 5 ⓣ0185 286 763. A good-value family-run seafood restaurant right in the centre of town, just back from the waterfront park with outdoor seating in a tiny alley. It serves Ligurian specialities such as swordfish with tomato sauce and olives, a great *fritto misto* and home-made pasta with pesto. Four-course tourist menu for €25. Tues–Sun noon–3pm & 7–10.30pm.

Rapallo

3

RAPALLO is larger and has a more urban feel than anywhere else along the coast. It's a highly developed resort with an expanse of glass-fronted restaurants and plush hotels crowding around a south-facing bay. In the early part of the twentieth century it was a backwater, and writers in particular came for the bay's extraordinary beauty, of which you now get an inkling only early in the morning or at dusk. Max Beerbohm lived in Rapallo for the second half of his life, and attracted a literary circle to the town; Ezra Pound wrote the first thirty of his *Cantos* here between 1925 and 1930; D.H. Lawrence stayed for a while, and Hemingway also dropped by (but came away muttering that the sea was flat and boring). There's a pleasant **old town** tucked away behind the seafront hotels, but otherwise the town's landmarks are the large **marina** and the small, sixteenth-century **castle** (daily: June–Sept 4–7pm; Oct–May 3–6pm; free), now converted into an exhibition space. Despite the beauty of the bay, there's not much to Rapallo's **beaches**: there's a free patch of shingle right by the castle, and some pay-beaches on the other side of the bay close to the Riviera. For panoramic views over Rapallo's pretty stretch of

WALKS AROUND PORTOFINO

The Portofino headland – protected as the Parco Naturale Regionale di Portofino (ⓦparcoportofino.it) and encircled by cliffs and small coves – is one of the most rewarding areas for **walking** on the Riviera coast. At 612m, **Monte di Portofino** is high enough to be interesting but not so high as to demand any specialist hiking prowess. The trails cross slopes of wild thyme, pine and holm oak, enveloped in summer in the constant whirring of cicadas. From the summit, the view over successive headlands is breathtaking. Not many people walk these marked paths, maybe because their early stages are fairly steep – but they aren't particularly strenuous, levelling off later and with plenty of places to stop. One of the best trails skirts the whole headland, beginning in **Camogli**, on the western side of the promontory. The path rises gently for 1km south to **San Rocco** (30–40min from Camogli), then follows the coast south to a viewpoint above Punta Chiappa, before swinging east to the scenic **Passo del Bacio** (200m), rising to a hair-raising ridgetop and then descending gently through the olive trees and palms to **San Fruttuoso** (3hr from Camogli). It continues east over a little headland and onto the wild and beautiful clifftops above **Punta Carega**, before passing through the hamlets of Prato, Olmi and Cappelletta and down steps to Portofino (4hr 30min from Camogli).

There are plenty of shorter routes too. From San Rocco, an easier path forks inland up to **Gaixella** and **Pietre Strette** (452m), before leading down again through the foliage to San Fruttuoso (2hr 30min from Camogli). Meanwhile, from **Ruta**, a tiny village 250m up on the north side of Monte di Portofino (served by buses from Camogli, Santa Margherita and Rapallo), a little-trod trailheads up to the summit of the mountain (1hr), or diverts partway along to take you across country to Olmi and on to Portofino (3hr from Ruta).

coast, head to the **cable car** (daily: 9am–12.30am & 2–6pm; Oct–April closes 4.45pm; every 30min; about 10min; one-way €6; return €10) station, about five-hundred metres north of the castle to be whisked to the tiny mountain hamlet of Montallegro, home to a fifteenth-century sanctuary and a couple of restaurants.

ARRIVAL AND INFORMATION — RAPALLO

By train Rapallo's train station is a 5min walk from the sea on Piazza Molfino.

By bus Services run every 15min between Rapallo and Santa Margharita (10–15min), stopping at the Santa Margherita end of the seafront and at the train station.

Tourist office Lungomare V. Veneto 38 (Feb, Mar, Dec & Nov: daily except Wed; 10am–noon & 3–5pm; April & Oct daily except Wed; 9.30am–12.30pm & 2.30–5.30pm; May & Sept daily 9am–1pm & 3–5pm; June–August daily 9am–1pm & 5–7pm; ⓣ 0185 230 346).

ACCOMMODATION

Albergo La Vela Via Milite Ignoto 19 ⓣ 0185 50 551, ⓦ eliteristorante.it. Reliable cheapie on the third floor of an old building just steps from the old town and the castle, with simple, decent rooms, most with balconies and shared bathrooms. Basic breakfast served in the downstairs restaurant. **€60**

Excelsior Palace Via S. Michele di Pagana 8 ⓣ 0185 230 666, ⓦ excelsiorpalace.it. Rapallo's flagship five-star hotel, at the western edge of town high above the shore, has hosted an impressive list of dignitaries over the last century or so, from King Farouk to George Clooney. Rooms are splendidly lavish, while there's a state-of-the-art spa and two refined, romantic restaurants. In summer, you can take a dip in the pair of infinity pools at the hotel's beach club. **€455**

Riviera Piazza IV Novembre 2 ⓣ 0185 50 248, ⓦ hotelrivierarapallo.com. Hemingway wrote his short story *Cat in the Rain* while staying in this *belle époque* family-owned hotel overlooking the sea in 1923. Service is good and rooms have been beautifully renovated – it's worth the extra euros for one with a balcony overlooking the sea. **€170**

EATING AND DRINKING

Da Mario Piazza Garibaldi 23 ⓣ 0185 51 736, ⓦ trattoriadamario.com. Moderate prices, and great seafood served on outside tables under Rapallo's medieval arcades. Pasta dishes €8–12, mains €14–20. Very popular, so you may need to book ahead or wait for a table. Thurs–Tues 12.30–2pm & 7.30–10pm.

Il Castello Via Castello 6 ⓣ 00185 52 426, ⓦ facebook.com/pg/barenotecailcastello. There's one of the best views in town from the terrace of this friendly bar and enoteca, extending over the water directly opposite the castle. An excellent spot for an afternoon focaccia or an evening *aperitivo*. Mon, Tues & Fri–Sun 11.30am–midnight, Wed & Thurs 11.30am–3pm.

Sestri Levante

Some 20km east of Rapallo, **SESTRI LEVANTE** is another large resort, though with a quite different feel to its brasher neighbours, its centre set on a narrow isthmus between two bays – the Bay of Fables, with a broad sandy beach decked with umbrellas, and the quieter Bay of Silence, a picturesque curve of sand overlooked by bobbing fishing boats. A former fishing village, the town has a relaxed feel, and is one of the nicer places to stay along this stretch of coast, with a number of decent hotels in its old quarter within easy walking distance of the town's beaches.

ARRIVAL AND INFORMATION — SESTRI LEVANTE

By train The train station is on Piazza Caduti di Via Fani, a 10min walk from the beach at the end of Viale Roma in the modern part of town.

Tourist office In a kiosk between the old centre and the train station at Corso Colombo 50 (daily 9am–1pm & 2–5pm; ⓣ 0185 478 530).

ACCOMMODATION

Due Mari Vico del Coro 18 ⓣ 0185 42 695, ⓦ duemarihotel.it. This recently renovated four-star overlooks both bays towards the south end of Sestri, with gardens, indoor and outdoor pools, parking and fairly large, palatial rooms. **€220**

Portobello Piazza Giacomo Matteotti 54 ⓣ 331 131 3137. Ideally situated between both bays at the end of the main pedestrian drag, this friendly, family-run B&B has comfortable, well-kept rooms, most decked with old paintings and some with ceiling frescoes. Generous breakfast buffet. **€129**

EATING AND DRINKING

L'Osteria Mattana Via XXV Aprile 34 ⓣ0185 457 633, ⓦosteriamattana.com. Canteen-like restaurant with long communal tables serving Ligurian specialities chalked up on blackboards – great *farinata* (€6), seafood spaghetti (€12), *burrida di seppie* (cuttlefish stew; €13) and the like – all good, simple stuff, and sometimes accompanied by live jazz. Cash only. Sun–Thurs 7.30–10.30pm, Fri & Sat 12.30–2.30pm & 7.30–10.30pm; closed Mon Oct–April.

Millelire Via XXV Aprile 149/153 ⓣ0185 41 191. Lively bar and café that's popular among locals and tourists alike. A good spot for focaccia and snacks at lunchtime, cocktails and occasional live music later on. Mon–Sat 7.30am–2am.

Levanto

Anchoring the westernmost point of the Cinque Terre, the quiet and unpretentious little resort of **LEVANTO** feels quite cut off by Ligurian standards, though that is precisely its charm, particularly after time spent among the crowds of the Cinque Terre. There's a sandy **beach** that attracts a surfy crowd, inexpensive hotels and good transport links that make it perhaps the best base for exploring the area. As well as a number of **trails** and **cycle paths** heading south to Monterosso, there's also a wonderful new cycle path that heads north along an abandoned old railway track – it runs for 6km from Levanto to Bonassola and Framura, giving beautiful coastal views in between long stretches through dark tunnels. Levanto itself has few sights – only the **Loggia Comunale** on the central Piazza del Popolo, the black-and-white-striped church of **Sant'Andrea** across the road in the old part of town, and the odd surviving stretch of medieval wall – but it's a pleasant, and for the most part, thoroughly Italian seaside resort.

3

ARRIVAL, INFORMATION AND GETTING AROUND — LEVANTO

By train The train station is a 10min walk inland from the seafront.

Tourist office In the town centre on Piazza Cavour (Mon–Sat 9am–1pm & 3–7pm, Sun 9am–1pm; ⓣ0187 808 125, ⓦvisitlevanto.it).

By ferry From mid-April to late Oct, ferries leave Levanto daily at 10am and 2pm for Portovenere, stopping in each of the towns of the Cinque Terre (except Corniglia) and returning from Portovenere at 5pm (open return ticket €35).

Bike rental Cicli Raso at Via Garibaldi 63 (daily 9.30am–12.30pm & 3.30–7pm; ⓣ0187 802 511) rents out bikes at €10/day or €6/half-day.

ACCOMMODATION

Acqua Dolce Via Semenza 5 ⓣ0187 808 465, ⓦcampingacquadolce.com. Right by the medieval walls of the old town, this is the most central of several decent campsites in the area around Levanto, with terraced plots and a good restaurant on-site. Pitches €32

Europa Via Dante Alighieri 41 ⓣ0187 808 126, ⓦwww.europalevanto.com. This charmingly old-fashioned hotel is among the most comfortable places to stay in the centre of Levanto. Recently refurbished, its rooms are clean and pleasant with all the standard mod cons and some with balconies (€145). There's also a wonderful buffet breakfast. €120

La Rosa dei Venti Via della Compera 2 ⓣ0187 808 165, ⓦlarosadeiventilevanto.com. Homey, welcoming B&B in a central position beside the town's old harbour and just two minutes from the beach. Clean, comfortable rooms, some with a/c, and an abundant breakfast. €120

Ospitalia del Mare Via S. Nicolò ⓣ0187 802 562, ⓦospitalialevanto.com. A clean, modern hostel set in a rambling old hospital, a 5min walk from the beach and 10min from the station. Accommodation includes beds in four-, six- and nine-bed dormitories as well as private doubles and singles, and there's a nice terrace and a basic breakfast. Dorms €24.50, doubles €68

EATING AND DRINKING

Antica Trattoria Centro Corso Italia 25 ⓣ0187 808 157. One of Levanto's longest-established restaurants, with plenty of space: inside, streetside or on a cosy garden terrace out back. Excellent seafood pasta dishes (*tagliolini di fritti di mare* €13) and the best service in town. Wed–Mon 12.30–2.30pm & 7–11pm.

Bruna Piazza Staglieno 42 ⓣ0187 807 796. With a few tables outside and a fairly bare interior, there's nothing immediately alluring about this place, but the pizzas are top-notch and reasonably priced (€4.50–8.50). Popular among locals, so you may have to wait for a table. Tues–Sun 6–11pm.

Pochi Intimi Via Garibaldi 1 ⓣ0187 807 118. In a quiet part of the old town with both indoor and outdoor seating on Levanto's prettiest piazzetta, this restaurant is popular for its well-rounded menu of pasta, seafood and meats (€10–30), as well as its excellent, if a bit pricey, tasting menus (€60). Book ahead. Mon–Sat 7–11pm.

The Cinque Terre

The breathtaking folded coastline of the **Cinque Terre** (Five Lands) stretches between the beach resort of Levanto and the port of La Spezia. It's named for five tiny villages – **Monterosso**, **Vernazza**, **Corniglia**, **Manarola** and **Riomaggiore** – wedged into a series of coves between sheer cliffs, and it is their rugged beauty as well as their comparative remoteness that makes them the unrivaled highlight of the Riviera. While the scenery is certainly lovely, it's also the convenience that makes the Cinque Terre so popular: the trails aren't particularly arduous – it's pretty flat most of the way, the villages are not too far apart and all have plenty of amenities and places to stay – and if you get fed up with walking you can always jump on a train (or a boat) to the next village. No surprise, then, that the area is teeming with travellers during summer, and the villages have lost some of their character to the tide of kitschy souvenir shops and overpriced restaurants. Outside of August, however, you should certainly try to take in at least part of the area – it's well worth it, especially if you use quieter and more authentic Levanto (see page 205) or even La Spezia (see page 209) as a base.

3

Monterosso

Tucked into a bay on the east side of the jutting headland of Punta Mesco, **MONTEROSSO** is the chief village of the Cinque Terre. It's the largest of the five – population 1700 – and the most developed, conjoined with the modern beach resort of **Fegina** whose shingle beach strings along the shore by Monterosso's station; there's a free section right by the station. Jutting into the sea to the east is a rocky headland, on top of which sits the seventeenth-century **Convento dei Cappuccini**, while at its tip the sixteenth-century **Torre Aurora** is the most impressive remnant of the town's once formidable defences against Saracen raids. Beyond the headland, the old village is a pleasant tangle of streets around the striped thirteenth-century church of **San Giovanni Battista**. Coastal ferries stop in the little harbour, and there's another, smaller stretch of shingle beach, again with a small free section.

Vernazza

A few headlands east of Monterosso, **VERNAZZA**, which many consider to be the loveliest of the five villages, sits behind the only natural harbour on this rocky coast. The narrow lanes with their tall, colourful houses are typical of the area, and the cramped village is overlooked by stout medieval bastions and a watchtower, built by the Genoese after they'd destroyed the previous castle in 1182 to punish the locals for piracy. The village's main street, Via Roma, leads down from the station to Piazza Marconi and the small harbour, where the Gothic church of **Santa Margherita di Antiochia**, with its elegant octagonal campanile, overlooks the small town beach.

Corniglia

CORNIGLIA is the smallest and remotest of the Cinque Terre villages, clinging to a high cliff 90m above the sea, its only access to the water (and the train station) via a long flight of steps. Floral-decorated squares fill the village, and the little Gothic church of **San Pietro** boasts an exquisite, marble rose window. Oddly for a hilltop village, Corniglia stands out for its **beach**: on the southern side of the village's rocky promontory is the **Spiaggone di Corniglia**, a narrow stretch of pebbles that has relatively easy access from the footpath towards Manarola.

Manarola

MANAROLA vies with Vernazza for the claim of being the Cinque Terre's most photogenic town, its pastel-shaded houses either squeezed into a cleft in the cliffs or crowded impossibly up the sides of the prominent headland of dark rock. The station is on the other side of the headland, connected to the main part of the village by a tunnel, from where you can either turn left up the hill, past a small **museum** devoted to the local white dessert wine, Sciacchetrà, and eventually to the fourteenth-century

HIKING IN THE CINQUE TERRE

Most people come to the Cinque Terre to **walk**, with its most popular route being the coastal **Blue Path** (*Sentiero Azzurro*) – **path no. 2** – from Riomaggiore to Monterosso. Severe flooding and landslides have led to much of it being closed over recent years, including the popular Via dell'Amore (see below). At the time of writing, however, almost the whole route has been reopened – the only exceptions are the sections between Manarola and Corniglia (expected to reopen in the summer of 2019) and between Riomaggiore and Manarola (spring 2021), though a small portion of the latter route – leading out of Manarola – is already accessible. Check ⓦwww.parconazionale5terre.it for the latest updates on trail closures. It's certainly well worth doing as much of the Blue Path as you can, especially out of season – start early to avoid the worst of the crowds. To do so, you'll need a **Cinque Terre Card** (€7.50/€14.50 for one/two days; €12/€23 for one/two days including unlimited use of trains and local buses), which you can buy at any train station within the Cinque Terre as well as in La Spezia and Levanto, or at any of the Blue Path's starting points.

All the park's other marked routes, including the inland **High Path** (*Sentiero Alto*), are free and mostly much steeper. The most challenging is path no. 1, which runs 25km from Portovenere to Levanto – a great walk to do over a couple of days with an overnight stop. Another rewarding walk is **path no. 10**, which leads from Monterosso station up through pine woods and onto a flight of steps that emerge at the Sant'Antonio church on the high point of the Punta Mesco headland (1hr), giving a spectacular panorama along the length of the Cinque Terre coastline.

3

church of San Lorenzo, or left around the main square down the main street to Manarola's pretty **harbour**. You can swim from the rocks or the slipway down into the harbour – the water is lovely – but there's no beach. Bear in mind also that the park's most popular walk is from Manarola to Riomaggiore on the paved **Via dell'Amore**, though only a small portion of it was open at the time of writing (see above).

Riomaggiore

Lively **RIOMAGGIORE** is the easternmost village of the Cinque Terre, and its relatively easy road link to the outside world makes it also the most crowded of the five. Nonetheless, its vivid multicoloured houses piling up the steep slopes above the romantic little harbour give the place a charm untempered by the café crowds, especially the higher you climb. Like Manarola, the train station is connected to the main part of the village by a tunnel (and to its upper town by a lift), which brings you out at the bottom of the main street. From here you can either head down the hill beneath the rail track to the harbour – where you can rent snorkels and kayaks or continue along to the small stony beach just around the headland to the left – or up the main street, which is home to the bulk of Riomaggiore's rooms and restaurants.

GETTING AROUND — THE CINQUE TERRE

By train Slow trains run between Levanto and La Spezia (roughly every 20min; 30min), most of them stopping at every village.

By boat Boats from every company on the Riviera shuttle along this bit of coast all summer. Be sure to confirm which of the four waterside villages you'll be stopping at (Corniglia has no harbour), and specify if you want a one-way ticket, rather than the more usual return.

On foot The most satisfactory way to get around is on foot: a network of trails (see box, above) links the villages along the coast or up on the ridgetops, which offer spectacular views. However, the coastal path in particular can get uncomfortably crowded throughout the summer months.

By car Trying to tour the area by car or motorbike truly isn't worth the effort. All five villages have road access, but streets are narrow and exceptionally steep, and parking is limited – you'd do better to leave your vehicle in Levanto or La Spezia.

INFORMATION

Tourist offices Much of the area is protected as the Parco Nazionale delle Cinque Terre (ⓦparconazionale5terre.it) and there are information offices – called Cinque Terre Points – at the train stations of each of the five villages as

well as La Spezia and Levanto (daily 8am–8pm; La Spezia ⓣ 0187 743 500; Riomaggiore ⓣ 0187 920 633; Manarola ⓣ 0187 760 511; Corniglia ⓣ 0187 812 523; Vernazza ⓣ 0187 812 533; Monterosso ⓣ 0187 817 059; Levanto ⓣ 0187 801 312). They sell Cinque Terre Cards and can provide maps, itinerary advice and guide services.

Accommodation booking The national park website runs a hotel booking service, and you can also book apartments and hotels through Arbaspaa (ⓣ 0187 920 783, ⓦ arbaspaa.com), based in Manarola.

ACCOMMODATION

3

MONTEROSSO

Amici Via Buranco 36 ⓣ 0187 817 544, ⓦ hotelamici.it. In the old part of Monterosso, this hotel is among the town's more affordable options, with a rooftop garden lined with deckchairs and views of the sea, as well as a good restaurant. **€180**

Porto Roca Via Corone 1 ⓣ 0187 817 502, ⓦ portoroca.it. Perched on the cliffs east of town, this is Monterosso's top hotel, overlooking the beach to the west and steep, terraced hills to the east. Bedrooms are imaginatively and beautifully decorated, some with terraces, sun loungers and gorgeous views (from €340), though these can also be enjoyed from the gorgeous infinity pool, the sun deck or the restaurant's broad terrace. Closed early Nov to early April. **€280**

VERNAZZA

Barbara Piazza Marconi 30 ⓣ 0187 812 398, ⓦ albergobarbara.it. This third- and fourth-floor hotel has an unbeatable position right on the harbour in Vernazza, and nine simple yet comfortable rooms, some en suite (from €100) and others with shared bathrooms – a couple have superior views over the harbour (€150). **€75**

CORNIGLIA

Ostello di Corniglia Via alla Stazione 3 ⓣ 0187 812 559, ⓦ ostellocorniglia.com. A choice of two dormitories with eight beds in each and four private doubles. Light sleepers be warned: it's very close to the church's belltower. Reception daily 7am–1pm & 3pm–midnight. There's a 1.30am curfew. Dorms **€27**, doubles **€65**

MANAROLA

Ca' d'Andrean Via Discovolo 101 ⓣ 0187 920 040, ⓦ cadandrean.com. Just below the church, this freshly renovated hotel takes pride in its service and airy rooms, some of which have nice balconies (€165); breakfast (€7) is taken in the lovely garden in summer. **€145**

Marina Piccola Via Birolli 120 ⓣ 0187 920 770, ⓦ hotelmarinapiccola.com. Down near the harbour, this has twelve cool and modern rooms, most of them with lovely sea views. Its restaurant offers a raft of reasonably priced fish dishes, including good *fritto misto*, and has a terrace right on the harbour. Minimum of two nights' stay April–Oct. **€150**

Ostello Cinque Terre Via Riccobaldi 21 ⓣ 0187 920 039, ⓦ hostel5terre.it. A reliable hostel with six-bed dorms – clean, friendly and well situated near the church of San Lorenzo at the upper end of Manarola. Very popular, so book in advance in summer. Check-in hours from 4–8pm. Dorms **€33**, doubles **€70**

RIOMAGGIORE

Il Boma Via C. Colombo 99 ⓣ 0187 920 395, ⓦ ilboma.it. Three simple rooms in a great position in the heart of Riomaggiore, 200m up the main street from the station – a good and affordable Cinque Terre base. The rooms are beautifully kept and breakfast is served in your room. **€110**

La Scogliera Salita Castello 174 ⓣ 340 344 1785, ⓦ la-scogliera.it. In an enviable spot pressed against the sea about five minutes' walk from the train station, this family-run hotel consists of just one room and two well-equipped apartments (with kitchens) stacked one on top of the other. Both the room's shutters and the apartments' terraces face right onto the water and the cliffs from which bathers launch themselves in summer months. Double **€120**, apartments **€170**

EATING AND DRINKING

MONTEROSSO

Il Moretto Piazza Colombo 1/3 ⓣ 0187 817 483. Right on the central square, with plenty of seating and a fairly typical Ligurian menu, as well as a few more adventurous dishes – there's grilled swordfish (€15), Ligurian steaks (€13–22) and a good vegetarian selection. Consistently good cooking and service. Wed–Mon noon–3pm & 6–10pm.

VERNAZZA

Belforte Via Gerolamo Guidoni 42 ⓣ 0187 812 222, ⓦ ristorantebelforte.it. With views over the sea at the far western edge of town, this longtime favourite is known for its inventive seafood and homemade pasta dishes, among them a delicious prawn curry (€16) and squid ink tagliolini served with shrimps and seaweed (€16). Wed–Mon noon–3pm & 7–9.30pm.

CORNIGLIA

A Cantina de Mananan Via Fieschi 117 ⓣ 0187 821 166, ⓔ manaman@libero.it. Cosy, cluttered *osteria* with excellent pesto and chalkboard menu crammed with both seafood and land-based fare (Ligurian-style rabbit €20) – all made with

locally sourced products. It's one of Corniglia's most popular choices, and a good spot to sample the Cinque Terre's Sciacchetrà wine, so book ahead. Wed–Mon 12.30–2.30pm & 7.30–pm.

MANAROLA

La Scogliera Via Birolli 103 ⓣ0187 920 747. Right on the main street down to the harbour, this serves a fine signature spaghetti with clams (€12) on its outside terrace, along with great lobster pasta and tuna *carpaccio*. Pizzas too (from €6.50). Sat–Thurs 11am–11pm.

RIOMAGGIORE

Dau Cila Via San Giacomo 65 ⓣ0187 760 032, ⓦristorantedaucila.com. In a cosy, vaulted space just steps from the water, this recently renovated restaurant and bar offers a good range of seafood dishes – try the sea bass ravioli (€16) or the spaghetti with anchovies (€15) – plus a well-stocked wine cellar. Daily 12.30–3pm & 7–10.30pm.

The Golfo dei Poeti

After the beauty of the Golfo Paradiso and Golfo del Tigullio, and the drama of the Cinque Terre, Liguria still has a final flourish. Hard up against the Tuscan border is the majestic Golfo di La Spezia, an impressively sweeping panorama of islands and rough headlands renamed the **Golfo dei Poeti** in 1919 by Italian playwright Sem Benelli for the succession of romantic souls who fell in love with the place. Petrarch was the first; Shelley lived and died on these shores; Byron was another regular; and D.H. Lawrence passed the pre-World War I years here. The town at the head of the gulf is workaday **La Spezia**, a major naval and shipbuilding centre with a fine art gallery. Small resorts line the fringes of the bay, linked by buses that hug the twisting roads or boats that shuttle across the glittering blue water. The most picturesque of these are **Portovenere**, sitting astride a spit of land to the southwest, **Lerici**, on the southeastern shore, and tiny **Tellaro**, just a short bus ride further south.

3

La Spezia

Most travellers only stay in **LA SPEZIA** long enough to change trains. Its sprawling mercantile port and the largest naval base in the country aren't particular draws for tourists. However, the city has at least one genuinely compelling sight in its **Museo Amedeo Lia**, probably the finest collection of medieval and Renaissance art in Liguria.

The town centre and seafront

Sandwiched between the hills and the sea, La Spezia proved an early attraction to conquerors, but it took Napoleon to capitalize on what is one of Europe's finest natural harbours and construct a naval complex at La Spezia early in the nineteenth century. Later the town was a prime target in World War II and much of the centre was rebuilt following Allied bombing. It is now a largely pedestrianized grid of streets behind the palm-fringed harbourfront promenade of **Viale Mazzini** and busy **Via Chiodo**, focused around the main pedestrian spine of Via del Prione and the central market square of **Piazza Cavour**, with a great selection of fish and other stalls. Wander through the city's blend of old town alleyways and nostalgic *belle époque* boulevards, which contrast with examples of Fascist architecture, such as La Spezia's main post office, and the superyachts docked at the flashy new marina of **Porto Mirabello**, across the footbridge at the bottom of the harbour.

Museo Amedeo Lia

Via del Prione 234 • Tues–Sun 10am–6pm • €10 • ⓣ0187 731 100 • ⓦmuseolia.spezianet.it

Right in the heart of town, in a restored seventeenth-century Franciscan convent, the **Museo Amedeo Lia** has a large and surprisingly interesting collection of bronzes, illuminated manuscripts and paintings, including lots of fourteenth- and fifteenth-century Italian works. Among the highlights are Pontormo's sharp-eyed *Self-Portrait*, a supremely self-assured *Portrait of a Gentleman* by Titian, and Bellini's *Portrait of an Attorney*, as well as bronzes by Giambologna and Ammanati. Upstairs, be sure to search

FERRIES FROM LA SPEZIA

Dozens of boats make excursions throughout the summer – and on certain days in winter too – between La Spezia and just about every port along this coast, leaving from the waterfront Passeggiata Morin at the far end of Via del Prione. The most popular route is to **Portovenere and the Cinque Terre**, which operates daily in season, taking 45min to Portovenere and just under 2hr to Monterosso. Return prices range from €12 to Portovenere to €35 for the whole Cinque Terre; a one-way ticket to the Cinque Terre is €18. The main operator **Consorzio Maríttimo Turistico**, "5 Terre–Golfo dei Poeti", Via Don Minzoni 13, La Spezia (T 0187 732 937, W navigazionegolfodeipoeti.it), which also runs to Palmaria for €12 return and circles each of the islands of the Golfo dei Poeti (see page 212) for €22 return.

out one of the museum's most celebrated items – the *Madonna Dolente*, a half-statue in polychrome terracotta of a sorrowful Madonna by Benedetto da Maiano.

3

Museo Tecnico Navale

Viale Giovanni Amendola 1 • Daily 8.30am–7.30pm • €1.55 • T 0187 784 763

At the western end of the seafront is the vast naval **Arsenale**. There's no public admittance to the complex, but just to the left of the entrance the engaging **Museo Tecnico Navale** contains wonderful figureheads, model ships, submersibles, maps and other nautical artefacts.

ARRIVAL AND DEPARTURE — LA SPEZIA

By train The train station is a 10min walk from the town centre and a 5min walk from the pedestrianized Via del Prione.

By bus Buses stop at various points around town – on Via Chiodo at the end of Via del Prione, on Piazza Chiodo in front of the naval arsenal, at the train station and also on Piazza Cavour. Bus #L runs to Lerici every 10min and takes around 30min; bus #P runs roughly every 30min to Portovenere from Via Chiodo and takes 25min.

INFORMATION

Tourist offices There's a helpful tourist office by the Amedeo Lia museum at Via del Prione 222 (daily 10am–6pm; T 0187 026 152, W myspezia.it), while there's another office (daily 9am–1pm) on the right-hand side of the train station's forecourt.

ACCOMMODATION

Crismar Vicolo dello Stagno 7 T 0187 778 539, W hotelcrismar.it. Nine small but spotless, en suite a/c rooms, conveniently set in the pedestrianized centre of town – a 10min walk from both the train station and the waterfront and only 50m south of the Museo Amedeo Lia. There's also a communal kitchen and breakfast is served in the cosy little courtyard. Free use of bikes for guests. **€130**

Mary Via Fiume 177 T 0187 743 254, W hotelmary.it. The nicest of the hotels grouped around the train station, with simply but decently furnished rooms with a/c and flatscreen TV. Very friendly, with a pleasant downstairs lounge and breakfast room. There are a few smaller doubles with French beds (€90). **€100**

EATING AND DRINKING

La Pia Via Magenta 12 T 0187 739 999, W lapia.it. La Spezia institution and family favourite off Via del Prione, with great focaccia, pizza and delicious farinata (around €3) to eat in or take away. There's also a newer branch by the water at Porto Mirabello. Mon–Sat 10am–10pm.

★ **Osteria della Corte** Via Napoli 86 T 0187 715 210, W osteriadellacorte.com. About a 5min walk southeast of the station, this is the town's top restaurant, offering excellent, locally sourced and reasonably priced Ligurian cuisine (*primi* from €12–16 and meat and fish *secondi* from €15–30), plus the odd themed menu for around €35. Great service, too. Book ahead. Mon 6–11pm, Tues–Sun 11.30am–3.30pm & 6–11.30pm.

Toa degli Aranci Via Daniele Manin 23 T 0187 826 416. Great, friendly place where you can eat as much as you want, with a fantastic array of forty-odd kinds of bruschette (around €5), generous plates of cheese and/or *salumi*, along with a rotating menu of *primi* and *secondi* – though there are always steaks. Dine inside or on the lovely terrace hung with fairy lights. Book ahead at weekends. Mon–Sat 7.30pm–midnight.

Portovenere

The ancient, narrow-laned town of **PORTOVENERE** sits astride a spit of land on the very tip of the southwestern arm of the Golfo dei Poeti, blessed with breathtaking views, a memorably tranquil atmosphere and a string of three islets just offshore, each smaller and rockier than the last (see page 212).

The town's characteristic rose- and yellow-painted tower-houses form a defensive wall along the photogenic harbourfront, Calata Doria, a busy waterside strip lined with cafés and restaurants and known as the **Palazzata**. Up above, the town's main street, **Via Capellini**, runs parallel, and both continue to the end of the promontory to join at the thirteenth-century church of **San Pietro**, which was built over the ruins of a Roman temple to Venus, goddess of love (hence the town's name), and occupies a fantastic location overlooking the sea. You can enjoy the view from the attached loggia, and afterwards head through the gate in the nearby wall to the rocky cove of the **Grotto Arpaia**, a favoured spot of Lord Byron, who swam across the bay from here to visit Shelley at San Terenzo. To this day, the gulf has the nickname of the "Baia di Byron".

Back in the main part of town, steps lead up from Via Capellini to the bare twelfth-century church of **San Lorenzo**, and above here to the remains of the sixteenth-century **Castello Doria** (daily 10.30am–6.30pm; €5), where you can amble around the ramparts enjoying yet more great views. The tiny but clean **beach**, right in the centre, is good for paddling, though not much else. Otherwise most people swim from the rocks off the Calata Doria, the rocky cove of Grotto Arpaia, or a couple of crowded shingle beaches one or two kilometres back towards La Spezia.

3

ARRIVAL AND INFORMATION — PORTOVENERE

By bus Bus #P runs from La Spezia's Via Chiodo to within a few hundred metres of Portovenere's harbourfront (roughly every 30min; 25min).

By ferry There several ferries daily between Portovenere and Lerici (35min; €13 return), while Consorzio Marittimo Turistico (T 0187 732 987, W navigazionegolfodeipoeti.it) runs 7–9 daily ferries to the Cinque Terre (one way to Riomaggiore & Manarola €13; Vernazza & Monterosso €18; Levanto €20).

Tourist office Right in the centre of town, just back from the beach at Piazza Bastreri 7 (daily 10am–noon & 3–6pm; closed Wed Oct–May; T 0187 790 691, W prolocoportovenere.it).

ACCOMMODATION

Genio Piazza Bastreri 8 T 0187 790 611, W hotelgenioportovenere.com. Pressed against the city walls next to the tourist office, this is Portovenere's least expensive and most convenient hotel, with nice if undistinguished rooms, some with balconies facing the sea (€120), and parking nearby (€10 per day). **€100**

Grand Hotel Portovenere Via Garibaldi 5 T 0187 777 751, W portoveneregrand.com. Towering over the north end of the marina, Portovenere's top hotel occupies a beautifully restored Franciscan convent. Rooms are bright, stylish and flush with mod-cons, and some have arched balconies overlooking the colourful town (€675). Perhaps the town's best harbor view can be enjoyed from the big terrace of the hotel's airy restaurant and bar, where guests are served a sumptuous breakfast. Free parking in the hotel's private garage (though only with direct booking). **€290**

Locanda La Lucciola Via dell'Olivo 101 T 0187 790 145, W locandalalucciola.com. On the waterfront about 5min out of town towards La Spezia (and just opposite from a bus stop), with lovely, bright, contemporary rooms with sea views and balconies. Breakfast is served in the downstairs restaurant and pizzeria, and there's parking nearby for €12/day. **€150**

Ostello Portovenere Via del Comune 1 T 0187 792 606, W hostel5terre.it. Sharing a building with a school, Portovenere's only hostel is a short walk from the bus stop, up the stairs beyond the *Grand Hotel*. It has spacious and well-kept mixed and female only four- to eight-bed dorms and a few private rooms, some with good views of the town. A simple breakfast is included. Limited reception hours (check-in time 4–8pm), so arrange early or late arrivals in advance. Dorms **€26**, doubles **€85**

EATING AND DRINKING

Antica Osteria del Carugio Via Capellini 66 T 0187 790 617, W anticaosteriadelcarugio.com. Right in the heart of the medieval town, this century-old osteria offers a cosy, vaulted setting and a good selection of affordable

ISLANDS OF THE GOLFO DEI POETI

Of the three islands that lie south of the peninsula, all but the nearest are in a military zone and so can only be viewed from the water. **Isola Palmaria** is the largest, just across the water, and regular boats shuttle back and forth from Portovenere for €5 return. Its main attraction is the Grotta Azzurra, which you can reach by boat, and a couple of beaches. Next is the **Isola del Tino**, a rocky islet marked with a lighthouse and the remains of a Romanesque abbey. Finally, the even tinier **Isola del Tinetto** was also once home to a monastic community. For a quick glimpse of each island, including a stop at the Grotta Azzurra, join a "3 Islands Tour" from Portovenere (€13) or La Spezia (€22) – best to sit on the right side of the boat.

specialities, among them stuffed mussels (€12) – cultivated on poles in Portovenere's harbour. Fri–Wed noon–2.30pm & 6.30–11pm.

3

La Piazzetta Via Capellini 56 0187 791 682. Relaxed little spot for focaccia and panini (from €4), with a good selection of wines, friendly service and tables outside on a tiny square. Daily 10am–10pm.

Portivene Via Capellini 94/98 0187 792 722. Despite a somewhat overbearing nautical theme, this tiny, welcoming Ligurian kitchen with cute tables on Portovenere's narrow main drag has some excellent seafood and pasta dishes at affordable prices (*gnocchi di mare* €12). Great-value daily menu including wine and coffee (starting from €20). Tues–Sat noon–3pm & 7–10pm, Sun noon–3pm.

Lerici

Towards the eastern end of the Golfo dei Poeti, **LERICI** is the largest and best known of the string of small resorts stretching around the coast from La Spezia. Its garden villas, seafront bars, trattorias and gift shops are grouped around the circular main square of **Piazza Garibaldi**, while outdoor restaurants along the busy quaysides provide an attractive setting as the sun goes down. Steps lead up from the harbour (you can also take an elevator) to the **Castello di San Giorgio** at the top of the town (mid-March to mid-Oct Tues–Sun 10.30am–1pm & 2.30–6pm, stays open until midnight in July & Aug; mid-Oct to mid-March Tues–Fri 10.30am–12.30pm, Sat & Sun 10.30am–12.30pm & 2.30–5.30pm; €6, family ticket €12), which has fabulous views across to Portovenere and back to La Spezia. Inside there's a small Gothic chapel and a museum documenting prehistoric dinosaur life in the area. Finally, there are **beaches** five minutes' walk north of town towards San Terenzo.

ARRIVAL AND DEPARTURE — LERICI

By bus Bus #L runs roughly every 10min to link Lerici's seafront with La Spezia's Via Chiodo (30min) and the train station (35min). Leaving Lerici, wait at the stop on the corner of the central Piazza Garibaldi.

By ferry There are several ferries daily between Portovenere and Lerici (35min; €13 return).

ACCOMMODATION AND EATING

Jeri Via Mazzini 20 0187 967 605, ristorantejeri.it. Right by the steps to the castle and just above the fish market, this place serves up the freshest fish and seafood on its scenic terrace, with views over the Golfo dei Poeti: there are great-value fixed-priced lunch menus from €25 and tasting menus for €37.50. Tues–Fri noon–2.15pm & 7–10.30pm, Sat 7–10.30pm.

Shelley & delle Palme Via Biaggini 5 0187 968 204, hotelshelley.it. Smallish and quite plain rooms, most with nice balconies and wonderful views over to Palmaria and Portovenere, with just the lazy clinking of the rigging in the boats below to lull you to sleep. Superior rooms (€190) are much larger and better furnished, with bigger balconies and baths. €150

Tellaro

Buses link Tellaro with Lerici's Piazza Garibaldi until around midnight (roughly every 45min; 15min)

Among the most picturesque seaside towns in all of Italy, the secluded village of **Tellaro** lies 5km south of Lerici along a winding road through the hills. Its pastel-coloured houses are crammed together over the tiny harbour, while furthest out to sea stands the

artfully weathered San Giorgio **church**. It's worth the bus ride from Lerici to wander the town's narrow *carrugi* down to the water, and there's a handful of good restaurants and guesthouses along the main road into town in case you're tempted to linger.

Lombardy and the Lakes

216 Milan

244 Southern Lombardy

255 Northern Lombardy: lakes and mountains

VIEW FROM CAMPANONE, BERGAMO

Lombardy and the Lakes

Lombardy, Italy's richest region, often seems to have more in common with its northern European neighbours than with the rest of Italy. Given its history, this is hardly surprising: it was ruled for almost two centuries by the French and Austrians and takes its name from the northern Lombards, who ousted the Romans. As a border region, Lombardy has always been vulnerable to invasion, just as it has always profited by being a commercial crossroads. Emperors from Charlemagne to Napoleon came to Lombardy to be crowned king – and big business continues to take Lombardy's capital, Milan, more seriously than Rome.

The region's people, ranging from Milanese workaholics to cosseted provincial urbanites, hardly fit the popular image of Italians – and, in truth, they have little time for most of their compatriots. This has led to the rise of the **Lega Nord** over the last fifteen years, a political party nominally demanding independence from Rome, although working in the government there in coalition, and successfully exploiting the popular sentiment that northern taxes sustain the inefficient, workshy south.

Sadly all this economic success has taken its toll on the landscape: industry chokes the peripheries of towns, sprawls across the Po plain and even spreads its polluting tentacles into the Alpine valleys. Traffic, too, is bad, with many roads – autostradas and lakeside lanes alike – gridlocked at peak times. Nonetheless, Lombardy's towns and cities retain medieval cores boasting world-class art and architecture, and the stunning scenery of the **Italian Lakes** – **Orta, Maggiore**, **Como, Iseo** and **Garda** – never fails to seduce.

Milan's lowland neighbours – **Cremona** and **Mantua** – flourished during the Middle Ages and Renaissance and retain much character. To the north, Lombardy is quite different, the lakes and valleys sheltering fewer historic towns, the cities of **Bergamo** and **Brescia** excepted. Reaching into the high Alps, lakes Maggiore, Como, Garda and their lesser-celebrated siblings have long been popular tourist territory with both Italians and foreigners.

Although the western shore of Lake Maggiore and the northern and eastern shores of Lake Garda fall outside Lombardy (in Piemonte, Trentino and Veneto respectively), the **Lakes region** and its resorts are all covered in this chapter.

Milan

The dynamo behind the country's "economic miracle" in the 1950s, **MILAN** is an Italian city like no other. It's foggy in winter, muggy and mosquito-ridden in summer, and is closer in outlook, as well as distance, to London than to Palermo. It's a historic city, with a spectacular cathedral and enough ancient churches and galleries to keep you busy for a week, but there are also bars and cafés to relax in, and the contemporary aspects of the place represent the cutting edge of Italy's fashion and design industry. Milan wears its history on its well-tailored sleeve: medieval buildings nestle next to nineteenth-century splendour, rickety trams trundle past overgrown bombsites left from World War II and Fascist-era bombastic facades. But the Milanese keep the best for themselves: peep through a doorway into one of Milan's fabulous courtyards and you will be smitten.

The obvious focal point of central Milan is Piazza del Duomo, which, as well as being home to the city's iconic **Duomo**, leads on to the elegant **Galleria Vittorio Emanuele** and Piazza della Scala, home to the world-famous **opera house**. Heading northwest from

THE HISTORIC MILLE MIGLIA CAR RACE

Highlights

❶ **Roof of Milan's Duomo** Wander around the roof of the world's largest Gothic cathedral with the best views of the city and the mountains beyond. See page 224

❷ **The Last Supper** Leonardo da Vinci's mural for the refectory wall of Santa Maria delle Grazie is one of the world's most resonant images. See page 233

❸ **Shopping in Milan** Steel yourself for the ultimate shopping trip in the fashion and design capital of the world. See page 242

❹ **Certosa di Pavia** This Carthusian monastery is a fantastic construction rising out of the rice fields near Pavia. See page 244

❺ **Cycling around Mantua** Rent a bike and explore elegant Mantua and the surrounding waterways. See page 254

❻ **Lake Como** Hemmed in by mountains, beautiful Lake Como is an unmissable stop for unrepentant romantics. See page 265

❼ **Bergamo Alta** Bergamo's medieval upper town is an enchanting spot to spend an evening. See page 276

❽ **Mille Miglia** This historic race sees hundreds of classic and vintage cars set off from the centre of Brescia. See page 287

HIGHLIGHTS ARE MARKED ON THE MAP ON PAGE 218

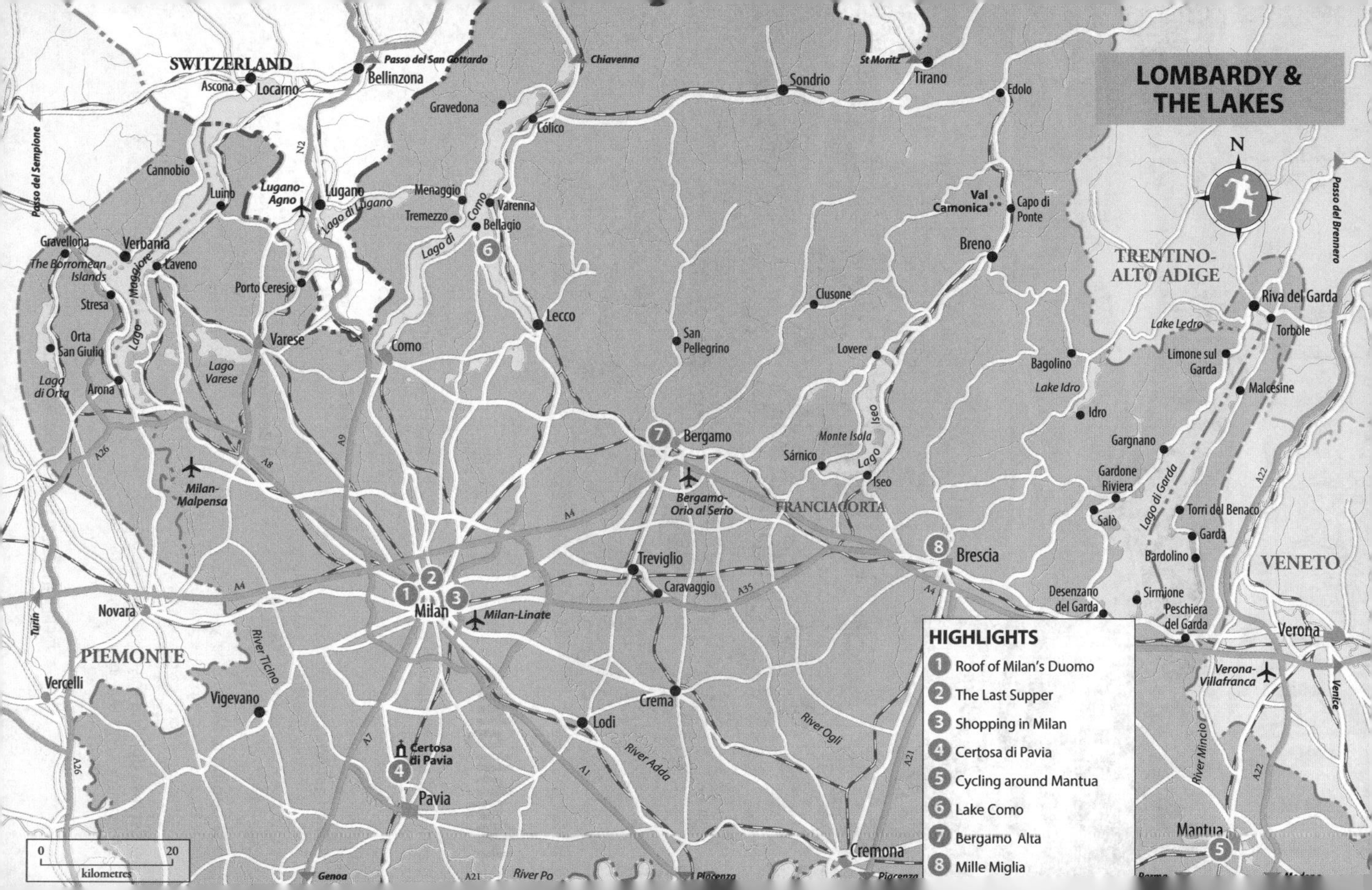
LOMBARDY & THE LAKES
N
HIGHLIGHTS
1 Roof of Milan's Duomo
2 The Last Supper
3 Shopping in Milan
4 Certosa di Pavia
5 Cycling around Mantua
6 Lake Como
7 Bergamo Alta
8 Mille Miglia
SWITZERLAND
PIEMONTE
TRENTINO-ALTO ADIGE
VENETO
FRANCIACORTA
Passo del Sempione
Passo del San Gottardo
Chiavenna
St Moritz
Passo del Brennero
Turin
Genoa
Piacenza
Venice
Locarno
Ascona
Bellinzona
Gravedona
Cólico
Sondrio
Tirano
Edolo
Cannobio
Luino
Lugano-Agno
Lugano
Lago di Lugano
Menaggio
Varenna
Tremezzo
Bellagio
Lago di Como
Val Camonica
Capo di Ponte
Breno
Gravellona
Verbania
The Borromean Islands
Laveno
Lago Maggiore
Porto Ceresio
Stresa
Orta San Giulio
Lago di Orta
Arona
Varese
Lago Varese
Como
Lecco
San Pellegrino
Clusone
Lovere
Bagolino
Lake Idro
Idro
Lake Ledro
Riva del Garda
Torbole
Limone sul Garda
Malcesine
Gargnano
Gardone Riviera
Salò
Lago di Garda
Torri del Benaco
Garda
Bardolino
Sirmione
Peschiera del Garda
Desenzano del Garda
Verona
Verona-Villafranca
Mantua
River Mincio
Monte Isola
Lago Iseo
Sárnico
Iseo
Bergamo
Bergamo-Orio al Serio
Brescia
Milan-Malpensa
Novara
Milan
Milan-Linate
Treviglio
Caravaggio
Vercelli
Vigevano
River Ticino
Crema
Lodi
River Adda
River Ogli
Certosa di Pavia
Pavia
Cremona
River Po
A4
A8
A9
A26
A35
A7
A1
A21
A22
N2
0
20
kilometres

THE LAKES AND THEIR FEATURES

Although they share many things – dreamy vistas, quality local cooking and sheer romance, to name but a few – the Italian Lakes each have a very different character and it's worth thinking about the type of holiday you're looking for before you book.

Activity holidays The mountainous regions behind all the Lakes provide great hiking and mountain-biking opportunities but the combined winds to its north and the presence of Monte Baldo make Lake Garda, and in particular its northern shore, the destination for on- and off-water thrill seekers.

Incurable romantics Watch the sun set behind Isola San Guilio on Lake Orta or from the Lake Como waterfront at Varenna or, alternatively, hole up in Gargnano on Lake Garda for a winter like D.H. Lawrence and his mistress did in 1912.

Visiting lakeside villas Lake Como offers the best selection of romantic waterfront residences with dreamy gardens to visit, although *belle époque* villas and sumptuous *palazzi* are dotted around the shore lines of all the lakes.

Wine tasting With Franciacorta and the various DOC regions to the south and southeast of Lake Garda – including Bardolino, Valpolicella and Lugana – you're never far from somewhere to try a local vintage or two.

Botanic gardens The microclimate of this corner of Lake Maggiore make the Isole Borromee and gardens in Verbania some of the most glorious gardens on the lakes, although competition is steep.

Travelling by public transport A quick train ride from Milan, Varenna is at the heart of the most spectacular part of Lake Como, from where an excellent boat service will ferry you around to explore further.

Holidaying with kids With older children you can't beat the activities available on and around Lake Garda – from windsurfing or castle climbing to the theme and water parks in the southeast of the lake. Younger children might enjoy better the shorter distances around the centre of Lake Como, the family-friendly resort of Cannobio on Lake Maggiore or the dragon stories linked with Lake Orta.

Piazza del Duomo along the shopping street of Via Dante takes you to the imperious **Castello Sforzesco** and the extensive **Parco Sempione** beyond. North, the well-heeled neighbourhoods of **Brera** and **Moscova** are the haunt of Milan's most style-conscious citizens. Here you'll find the fine-art collection of the **Pinacoteca di Brera** and, nearby, the so-called **Quadrilatero d'Oro** (Golden Quadrangle), a concentration of top designer fashion boutiques. Slightly further north is Milan's most pleasant park, the **Giardini Pubblici**. Southwest of the Duomo, the shopping streets of Via Torino take you to the **Ticinese** district, a focal point at *aperitivo* time, and home to a couple of the city's most beautiful ancient churches. Continuing south to the **Navigli** leads to the bar and restaurant area around the city's remaining canals. West of the cathedral, the **Museo Archeologico** gives a taste of Roman Milan, while the basilica of Milan's Christian father, **Sant'Ambrogio**, is a couple of blocks away. A little further west stands the church of **Santa Maria delle Grazie** and the adjacent refectory building, holding Leonardo da Vinci's *The Last Supper*.

Brief history

Milan first stepped into the historical limelight in 313 AD when Emperor Constantine issued the **Edict of Milan**, granting Christians throughout the Roman Empire the freedom to worship for the first time. The city, under its charismatic bishop, **Ambrogio** (Ambrose), swiftly became a major centre of Christianity; many of today's churches stand on the sites, or even retain parts, of fourth-century predecessors.

Medieval Milan rose to prominence under the **Visconti** dynasty, who founded the florid late-Gothic **Duomo**, and built the nucleus of the **Castello** – which, under their successors, the **Sforza**, was extended to house what became one of the most luxurious courts of the Renaissance. The last Sforza, Lodovico, commissioned **Leonardo da Vinci** in 1495 to paint *The Last Supper*.

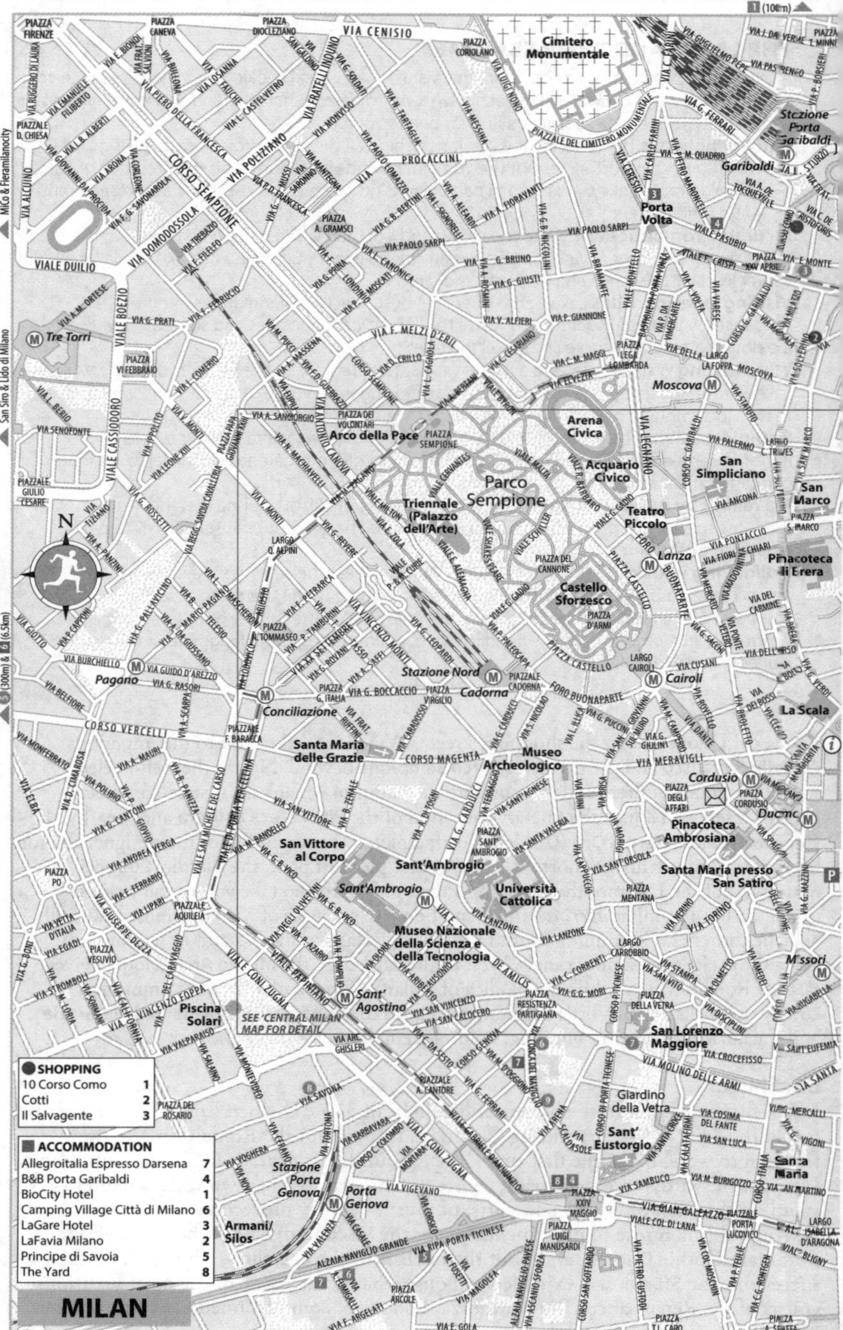
MILAN
SHOPPING
10 Corso Como 1
Cotti 2
Il Salvagente 3
ACCOMMODATION
Allegroitalia Espresso Darsena 7
B&B Porta Garibaldi 4
BioCity Hotel 1
Camping Village Città di Milano 6
LaGare Hotel 3
LaFavia Milano 2
Principe di Savoia 5
The Yard 8
SEE 'CENTRAL MILAN' MAP FOR DETAIL
MiCo & Fieramilanocity
San Siro & Lido di Milano
Cimitero Monumentale
Stazione Porta Garibaldi
Garibaldi
Porta Volta
Moscova
Tre Torri
Arco della Pace
Arena Civica
Acquario Civico
Parco Sempione
Triennale (Palazzo dell'Arte)
Teatro Piccolo
San Simpliciano
San Marco
Lanza
Castello Sforzesco
Pinacoteca di Brera
Stazione Nord
Cadorna
Cairoli
Pagano
Conciliazione
La Scala
Santa Maria delle Grazie
Museo Archeologico
Cordusio
Duomo
Pinacoteca Ambrosiana
San Vittore al Corpo
Sant'Ambrogio
Università Cattolica
Santa Maria presso San Satiro
Museo Nazionale della Scienza e della Tecnologia
Missori
Piscina Solari
Sant' Agostino
San Lorenzo Maggiore
Giardino della Vetra
Sant' Eustorgio
Stazione Porta Genova
Porta Genova
Armani/ Silos
Santa Maria
CORSO SEMPIONE
CORSO VERCELLI
CORSO MAGENTA
VIALE DUILIO
VIA CENISIO
FORO BUONAPARTE
VIA MERAVIGLI
ALZAIA NAVIGLIO GRANDE
VIALE CONI ZUGNA

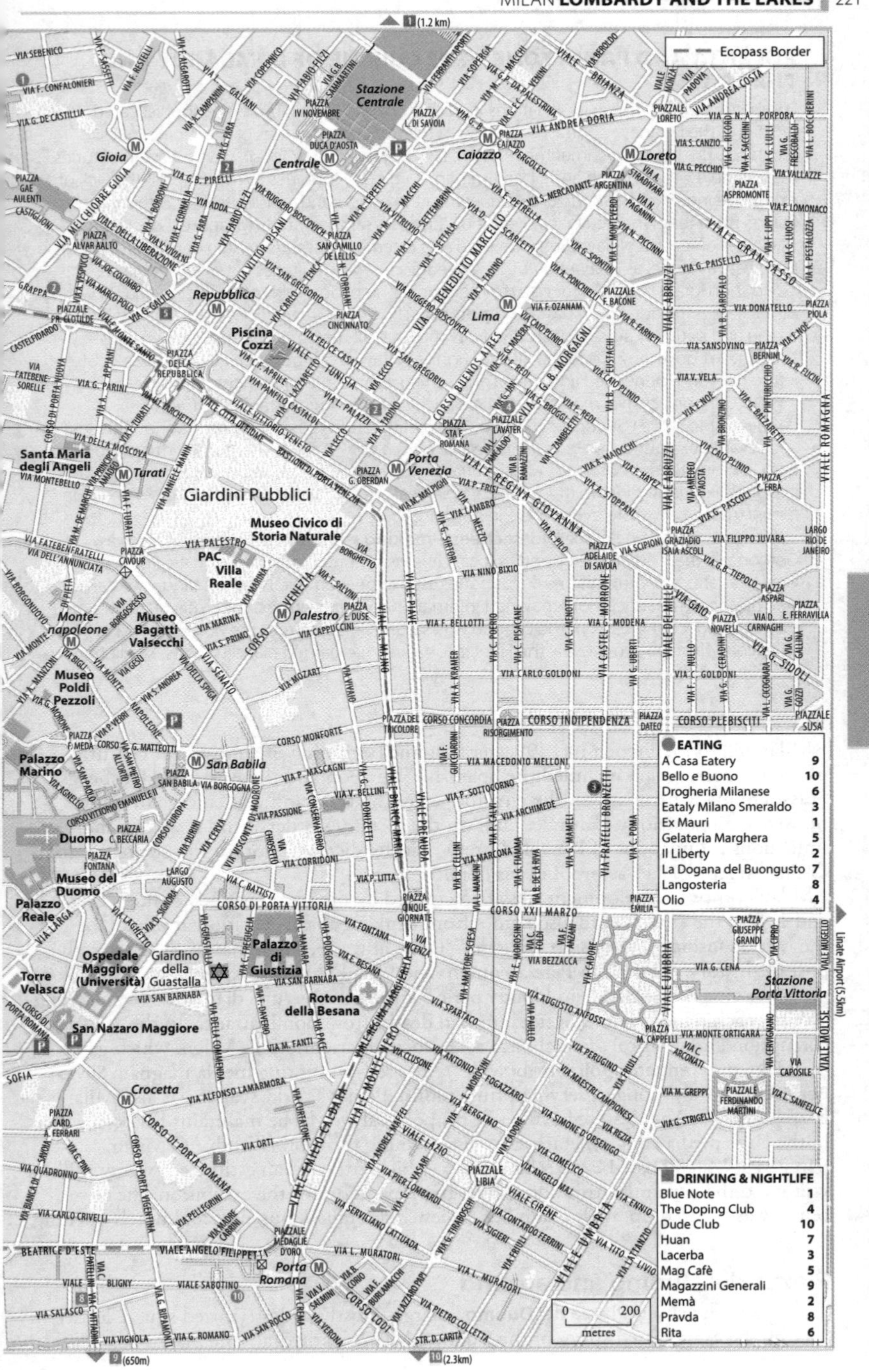
1 (1.2 km)
Ecopass Border
Stazione Centrale
Centrale
Gioia
Caiazzo
Loreto
Repubblica
Lima
Piscina Cozzi
Porta Venezia
Turati
Santa Maria degli Angeli
Giardini Pubblici
Museo Civico di Storia Naturale
PAC
Villa Reale
Palestro
Montenapoleone
Museo Bagatti Valsecchi
Museo Poldi Pezzoli
Palazzo Marino
San Babila
Duomo
Museo del Duomo
Palazzo Reale
Ospedale Maggiore (Università)
Giardino della Guastalla
Palazzo di Giustizia
Rotonda della Besana
Torre Velasca
San Nazaro Maggiore
Crocetta
Porta Romana
Stazione Porta Vittoria
Linate Airport (5.5km)
VIALE BRIANZA
VIA ANDREA DORIA
VIALE GRAN SASSO
VIALE ABRUZZI
CORSO BUENOS AIRES
VIA BENEDETTO MARCELLO
VIA G. B. MORGAGNI
VIALE REGINA GIOVANNA
CORSO VENEZIA
VIALE PIAVE
VIALE L. MAINO
CORSO INDIPENDENZA
CORSO PLEBISCITI
CORSO CONCORDIA
CORSO MONFORTE
CORSO DI PORTA VITTORIA
CORSO XXII MARZO
VIALE CASTEL MORRONE
VIA FRATELLI BRONZETTI
VIALE DEI MILLE
VIALE UMBRIA
VIALE MOLISE
VIALE ROMAGNA
VIALE MONTE NERO
VIALE EMILIO CALDARA
CORSO DI PORTA ROMANA
CORSO LODI
VIALE ANGELO FILIPPETTI
9 (650m)
10 (2.3km)
0 200 metres
EATING
A Casa Eatery 9
Bello e Buono 10
Drogheria Milanese 6
Eataly Milano Smeraldo 3
Ex Mauri 1
Gelateria Marghera 5
Il Liberty 2
La Dogana del Buongusto 7
Langosteria 8
Olio 4
DRINKING & NIGHTLIFE
Blue Note 1
The Doping Club 4
Dude Club 10
Huan 7
Lacerba 3
Mag Cafè 5
Magazzini Generali 9
Memà 2
Pravda 8
Rita 6

POLENTA AND PANETTONE – THE CUISINE OF LOMBARDY AND THE LAKES

Lombardy is distinctive in its variations in culinary habits. For example, the sophisticated recipes of the Milanese contrast sharply with the more rustic dishes of the Alpine foothills and lakes. The latter are sometimes known as *piatti poveri* (poor food): devised over centuries, these employ imagination and often time-consuming techniques to make up for the lack of expensive ingredients. *Risotto alla Milanese*, on the other hand, golden yellow with saffron, is Milan's most renowned culinary invention – and, it is said, only truly Milanese if cooked with the juices of roast veal flavoured with sage and rosemary. *Ossobucco* (shin of veal) is another Milanese favourite, as is *panettone*, the soft, eggy cake with sultanas eaten at Christmas.

The short-grain rice used for **risotto** is grown in the paddy fields of the Ticino and Po valleys; other staples include green pasta and **polenta**. The latter – made from maize meal which is boiled and patiently stirred for around forty minutes, all the time watched with an eagle eye so it doesn't go lumpy – is found all over northern Italy. It can be eaten straightaway, or else left to cool and then sliced and grilled and served as an accompaniment to meat.

From Cremona comes *mostarda di frutta* (pickled fruit with mustard), the traditional condiment to serve with *bollito misto* (boiled meats). Stuffed pastas come in various guises – for example, around the Po Valley *tortelli alla zucca* (ravioli filled with pumpkin) or around Bergamo and Brescia *casoncei* (ravioli stuffed with sausage meat). Veal is eaten hot or cold in dishes like *vitello tonnato* (thin slices of cold veal covered with tuna mayonnaise) and wild *funghi* (mushrooms) are everywhere in autumn.

Lombardy is also one of the largest **cheese-making** regions in the country. As well as Gorgonzola there are numerous other local cheeses: among the best known are Parmesan-like Grana Padano, smooth, creamy mascarpone (used in sweet dishes) and the tangy, soft taleggio.

4

Although Lombardy is not renowned internationally for its **wines**, supermarket shelves bulge with decent reds from the Oltrepò Pavese, and "Inferno" from the northern areas of Valtellina, while around Brescia, the Franciacorta area has earned plaudits for its excellent sparkling whites.

Milan fell to the French in 1499, marking the beginning of almost four centuries of foreign rule, which included the Spanish, Napoleon and the Austrian Habsburgs. **Mussolini** made his mark on the city, too: arrive by train and you emerge into the massive white Stazione Centrale, built on the dictator's orders. And it was on the innocuous roundabout of Piazzale Loreto that the dictator's corpse was strung up for display in April 1945 as proof of his demise.

Milan's postwar development was characterized by the boom periods of the 1950s and 1980s: the city's wealth also comes from banking and its position at the top of the world's **fashion** and **design** industries. Politically, too, Milan has been key to Italy's postwar history. A bomb in Piazza Fontana in 1969 that killed sixteen people signalled the beginning of the dark and bloody period known as the **Anni di piombo**, when secret-service machinations led to over a hundred deaths from bomb attacks. In the 1980s, corruption and political scandal once again focused attention on Milan, which gained the nickname **Tangentopoli** ("Bribesville"). The self-promoting media magnate **Silvio Berlusconi** – Italy's longest serving prime minister since World War II – is also Milan born and bred. And despite having lost his political weight he maintains his power base in the city's media conglomerates as well as owning the football club AC Milan.

In 2015, Milan hosted **Expo Milano 2015**, which attracted an estimated twenty million visitors to the city and surrounding area. In preparation for the exhibition, the city centre was spruced up, with a number of new restaurants, museums and hotels opening.

Piazza del Duomo and around

The hub of the city is **Piazza del Duomo**, a large, mostly pedestrianized square lorded over by the exaggerated spires of the **Duomo**, Milan's cathedral. The piazza was

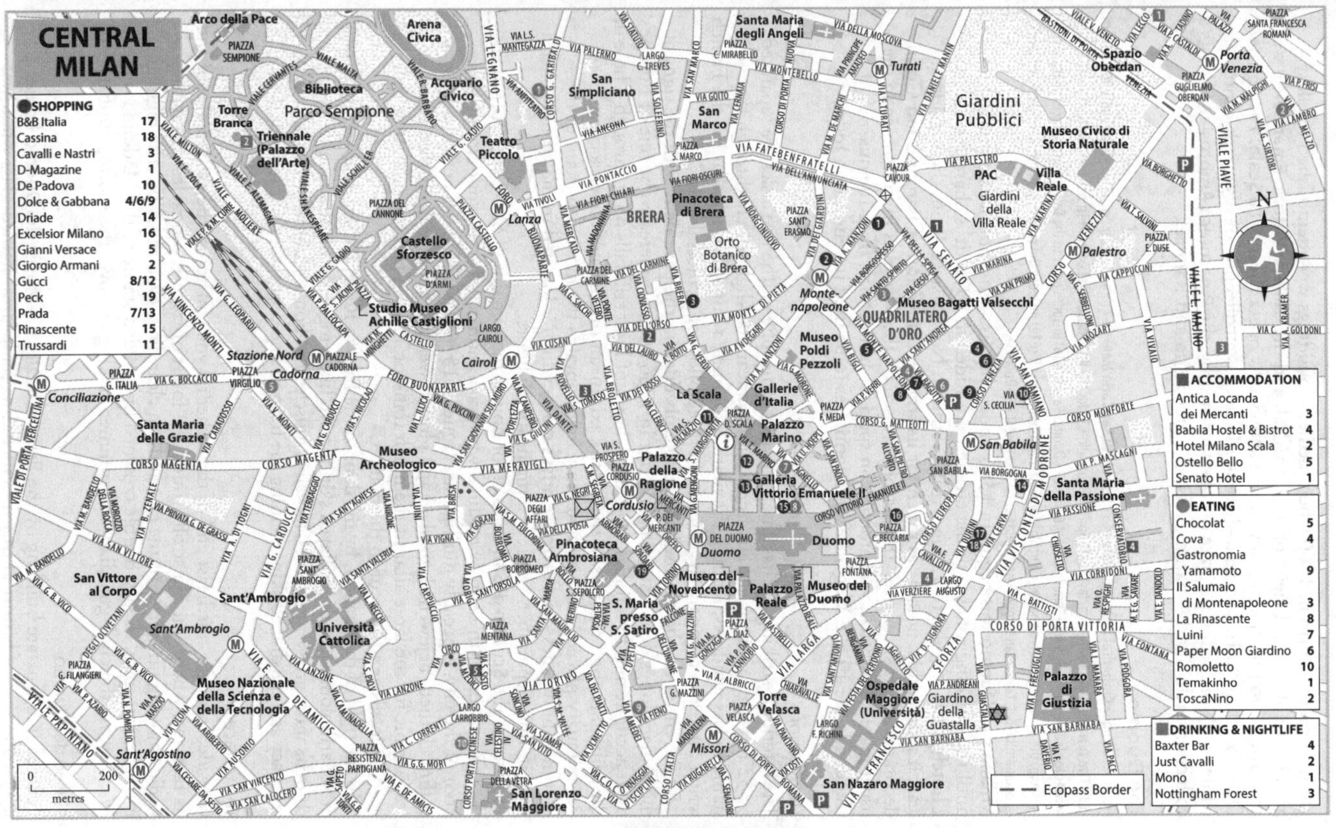
CENTRAL MILAN
SHOPPING
B&B Italia 17
Cassina 18
Cavalli e Nastri 3
D-Magazine 1
De Padova 10
Dolce & Gabbana 4/6/9
Driade 14
Excelsior Milano 16
Gianni Versace 5
Giorgio Armani 2
Gucci 8/12
Peck 19
Prada 7/13
Rinascente 15
Trussardi 11
ACCOMMODATION
Antica Locanda dei Mercanti 3
Babila Hostel & Bistrot 4
Hotel Milano Scala 2
Ostello Bello 5
Senato Hotel 1
EATING
Chocolat 5
Cova 4
Gastronomia Yamamoto 9
Il Salumaio di Montenapoleone 3
La Rinascente 8
Luini 7
Paper Moon Giardino 6
Romoletto 10
Temakinho 1
ToscaNino 2
DRINKING & NIGHTLIFE
Baxter Bar 4
Just Cavalli 2
Mono 1
Nottingham Forest 3
Ecopass Border
0 200 metres
N
Arco della Pace
Arena Civica
Biblioteca
Parco Sempione
Torre Branca
Triennale (Palazzo dell'Arte)
Acquario Civico
Teatro Piccolo
Castello Sforzesco
Studio Museo Achille Castiglioni
San Simpliciano
San Marco
Santa Maria degli Angeli
BRERA
Pinacoteca di Brera
Orto Botanico di Brera
Giardini Pubblici
Museo Civico di Storia Naturale
Spazio Oberdan
Porta Venezia
Turati
PAC
Villa Reale
Giardini della Villa Reale
Palestro
Montenapoleone
Museo Bagatti Valsecchi
QUADRILATERO D'ORO
Museo Poldi Pezzoli
Gallerie d'Italia
La Scala
Palazzo Marino
Galleria Vittorio Emanuele II
San Babila
Santa Maria della Passione
Stazione Nord
Cadorna
Cairoli
Lanza
Conciliazione
Santa Maria delle Grazie
Museo Archeologico
Palazzo della Ragione
Cordusio
Pinacoteca Ambrosiana
Duomo
Museo del Novecento
Palazzo Reale
Museo del Duomo
S. Maria presso S. Satiro
Università Cattolica
Sant'Ambrogio
San Vittore al Corpo
Museo Nazionale della Scienza e della Tecnologia
Sant'Agostino
Torre Velasca
Missori
Ospedale Maggiore (Università)
Giardino della Guastalla
Palazzo di Giustizia
San Nazaro Maggiore
San Lorenzo Maggiore
4

given its present form in 1860 when medieval buildings were demolished to allow grander, unobstructed views of the cathedral, and the **Galleria Vittorio Emanuele II** was constructed to link the piazza with the showy new opera theatre, **La Scala**. Facing the Duomo, Mussolini's **Palazzo dell'Arengario** houses a collection of twentieth-century art, while south of medieval **Piazza dei Mercanti** nearby, the **Pinacoteca Ambrosiana** boasts a collection including Leonardo da Vinci, Caravaggio and Raphael.

The Duomo

Piazza del Duomo • **Cathedral** Daily 8am–7pm • €3 • **Scurolo di San Carlo** Mon–Fri 11am–5.30pm, Sat 11am–5pm, Sun 1.30–3.30pm • €3 • **The terraces** Daily 9am–7pm, last ticket 6pm • €9 to walk, €13 for the lift • **Museo del Duomo** Thurs–Tues 10am–6pm • €3 • **Archeological Area** • Daily 9am–7pm, last ticket 6pm • €7 • Duomo Pass A (€16) includes entry to the Duomo, the terraces by lift, the museum, the archeological area and the Church of San Gottardo; Duomo Pass B (€12) includes the same sights, but the terraces on foot • Ⓦ duomomilano.it; tickets can be purchased online at Ⓦ ticketone.it • Ⓜ Duomo

Milan's vast **Duomo** was begun in 1386 under the Viscontis, but not completed until the finishing touches to the facade were added in 1938. It is characterized by a hotchpotch of styles that range from Gothic to Neoclassical. From the **outside** at least it's incredible, notable as much for its strange confection of Baroque and Gothic decoration as its sheer size. The marble, chosen by the Viscontis in preference to the usual material of brick, was brought on specially built canals from the quarries of Candoglia, near Lake Maggiore, and continues to be used in renovation today.

The interior

4

The **interior** is striking for its dimension and atmosphere. The five aisles are separated by 52 towering piers, while an almost subterranean half-light filters through the stained-glass windows, lending the marble columns a bone-like hue that led the French writer Suarez to compare the interior to "the hollow of a colossal beast".

By the entrance, the narrow brass strip embedded in the pavement with the signs of the zodiac alongside is a **sundial**, laid out in 1786 and considered to be one of Europe's most accurate and functional sundials. A beam of light still falls on it through a hole in the ceiling, though changes in the Earth's axis mean that it's no longer accurate.

A reliquary placed in the apsidal semicircle contains the most important of the Duomo's holy relics – **a nail from Christ's cross**, which is lowered to the ground once a year, in mid-September, where it remains for 40 hours.

Close by, the **Scurolo di San Carlo** crypt houses the remains of San Carlo Borromeo, the zealous sixteenth-century cardinal who was canonized for his work among the poor of the city, especially during the Plague of 1576–1577. He lies here in a glass coffin, clothed, bejewelled, masked and gloved, wearing a mitre. Borromeo was also responsible for the large altar in the north transept, erected to close off a door that was used by locals as a shortcut to the market.

To the right of the chancel, by the door to the Palazzo Reale, the sixteenth-century statue of **St Bartholomew**, with his flayed skin thrown like a toga over his shoulder, is one of the church's more gruesome statues, its veins, muscles and bones sculpted with anatomical accuracy and the draped skin retaining the form of knee, foot, toes and toenails.

The terraces

Outside, from the northeast end of the cathedral you can access the **cathedral roof and its terraces**, where you can stroll around the forest of tracery, pinnacles and statues while enjoying fine views of the city and, on clear days, even the Alps. The highlight is the central spire, its lacy marble crowned by a gilded statue of the Madonna – the *Madonnina*, the city's guardian – in summer looking out over the rooftop sunbathers.

Museo del Duomo

Located in a separate building by the Palazzo Reale, the **Museo del Duomo** houses a large collection of historical treasures including sculptures, stained-glass windows,

paintings, tapestries and embroideries from the fifteenth to the twentieth centuries. The Tesoro del Duomo showcases a collection of antique objects, including ivory diptychs dating from the fifth to the ninth century.

Archeological Area

Dating back between the fourth and fourteenth centuries, the **Archeological Area** houses the remains of a vast episcopal complex of the city, which extended both over the space the Duomo occupies today and over the square that lies opposite. Here you'll see the remains of the fourth-century **Battistero San Giovanni alle Fonti,** where the city's patron saint, Ambrogio, baptized St Augustine in 387 AD.

Museo del Novecento

Palazzo dell'Arengario, Piazza Duomo 8 • Mon 2.30–7.30pm, Tues, Wed, Fri & Sun 9.30am–7.30pm, Thurs & Sat 9.30am–10.30pm • €10 • Ⓦ museodelnovecento.org • Ⓜ Duomo

The **Museo del Novecento** houses an excellent collection of twentieth-century art. The permanent collection begins with paintings from the avant-garde movements, with works by Picasso, Braque, Kandinsky, Modigliani and Klee, moving on to Futurism, with Italian masters such as Boccioni, Carrà and Severini, before passing on to masterpieces by de Chirico, Morandi and Martini, the Novecento movement and Abstract art. The top floor is dedicated to Lucio Fontana, and there are works by Alberto Burri and Italian Informalism masters too. Linked by a glass bridge, the gallery spaces spill into the adjacent Palazzo Reale, with the final section devoted to the Sixties, Seventies and the Italian Arte Povera movement. There are regular temporary exhibitions that shed light on Italian art.

Biblioteca Pinacoteca Ambrosiana

Piazza Pio XI 2 • Tues–Sun 10am–6pm • €15 • Ⓦ www.ambrosiana.eu • Ⓜ Duomo

Five minutes' walk southwest of the Piazza, just off Via Torino, lies the **Biblioteca Pinacoteca Ambrosiana**, founded by Cardinal Federico Borromeo in the early seventeenth century. In the face of Protestant reforms, the Cardinal was concerned to defend Catholic traditions not only through doctrine and liturgy, but also by educating the faithful about their Catholic origins. To this end he set about collecting paintings and ancient manuscripts, assembling one of the largest libraries in Europe. You can visit the original reading room and other rooms, but the main attraction is the world's largest collection of Leonardo da Vinci's drawings and writings, known as the **Codice Atlantico Leonardo.**

The extensive **art collection** is stamped with Borromeo's taste for Jan Brueghel, sixteenth-century Venetians and some of the more kitsch followers of Leonardo. Among many mediocre works, there is a rare painting by Leonardo da Vinci, *Portrait of a Musician*, a cartoon by Raphael for the School of Athens, and a Caravaggio considered to be Italy's first still life. The prize for the quirkiest exhibit is shared between a pair of white gloves that Napoleon reputedly wore at Waterloo, and a lock of Lucrezia Borgia's hair – displayed for safe-keeping in a glass phial ever since Byron (having decided that her hair was the most beautiful he had ever seen) extracted a strand as a keepsake from the library downstairs, where it used to be kept unprotected.

Piazza dei Mercanti

Northwest out of Piazza del Duomo, at the start of pedestrianized Via Dante which leads to the Castello Sforzesco, lies **Piazza dei Mercanti**, the commercial centre of medieval Milan. The square is dominated by the thirteenth-century **Palazzo della Ragione**, where council meetings and tribunals were held on the upper floor, with markets under the porticoes below. The stone relief on the facade above the arcade shows the rather forlorn-looking Oldrado da Tresseno, the mayor who commissioned the building in 1228, astride his horse. Opposite, the striped black-and-white marble

Loggia degli Orsi, built in 1316, was where council proclamations were made and sentences announced. The coats of arms of the various districts of Milan are just about visible beneath the grime left by Milanese smog.

Galleria Vittorio Emanuele II

Leading off to the north of Piazza del Duomo is the gaudily opulent **Galleria Vittorio Emanuele II**, a cruciform glass-domed gallery designed in 1865 by Giuseppe Mengoni, who was killed when he fell from the roof a few days before the inaugural ceremony. The circular mosaic beneath the glass cupola is composed of the symbols that made up the cities of the newly unified Italy: Romulus and Remus for Rome, a fleur-de-lys for Florence, a white shield with a red cross for Milan and a bull for Turin – it's considered good luck to spin round three times on the bull's testicles, hence the indentation in the floor.

The *galleria* was designed as a covered walkway between the Piazza del Duomo and Piazza della Scala to the north; nicknamed the "*salotto*" – or drawing room – of Milan, it used to be the focal point for the parading Milanese on their *passeggiata*. These days, visitors rather than locals are more likely to swallow the extortionate prices at the gallery's cafés, which include the historic *Zucca*, now *Camparino*, with its glorious 1920s tiled interior, and the newer *Ristorante Cracco* by owner and chef Carlo Cracco. Shops, too, are aimed at visitors to the city, with top designer stores occupying most of the gallery. Somehow, however, the *galleria* still manages to retain most of its original dignity, helped along by quietly elegant boutiques including the handsome 80-year-old Prada shop in the centre.

La Scala

Largo Ghiringhelli 1 • Museum daily 9am–5.30pm • €9 • Ⓦ teatroallascala.org • Ⓜ Duomo

The world-famous Teatro alla Scala opera house, popularly known as **La Scala**, was commissioned by Empress Maria Theresa of Austria from the architect Piermarini and many of the leading names in Italian opera had their major works premiered here, including Bellini, Donizetti and Rossini. But it is **Giuseppe Verdi** who is most closely associated with the opera house and whose fame was consolidated here in 1842 with the first performance of *Nabucco*, with its perfectly timed patriotic sentiments. The post-World War II period saw another breathtaking roll call of top composers and musical performers – among them Schoenberg, Lucio Berio, Rudolf Nureyev and Maria Callas – while Toscanini, perhaps the most influential conductor of all time, devoted more than fifty years to the theatre. Today, La Scala is embarking on a new direction – when Riccardo Chailly replaced Daniel Baremboim as musical director in 2015 he pledged to put the Italian repertoire centre-stage once again. Details of **tickets** for a performance can be found on page 242.

Tucked into one corner of the theatre, a **museum** features costumes, sets, composers' death masks, plaster casts of conductors' hands and a rugged statue of Puccini in a capacious overcoat. A visit to the auditorium is included in the admission price, providing there is no rehearsal taking place; times when the auditorium is empty are listed fortnightly at Ⓦ museoscala.org/bestview-online. Temporary exhibitions also take place at the museum and are included in the admission price. Guided tours of the theatre, as well as the chance to visit the Ansaldo Workshops where sets are crafted and costumes made, are possible upon reservation.

Gallerie d'Italia

Via Manzoni 10 • Tues–Sun 9.30am–7.30pm, Thurs until 10.30pm • €10 • Ⓦ gallerieditalia.com • Ⓜ Montenapoleone

Housed in a splendid eighteenth-century Neoclassical *palazzo* with its original decoration unchanged, the wonderful **Gallerie d'Italia** is worth visiting for the building alone. Formerly a bank – note the cashier desks within – the gallery now houses an exceptional collection of Italian art that once belonged to the likes of the Emperor

of Austria and various kings of Italy. The two hundred works on display span just over a century of Italian art from 1798 to 1911, from Antonio Canova's bas-reliefs to masterpieces by Futurist Umberto Boccioni. The emphasis is on nineteenth-century Lombard paintings that aimed to confirm Milan's importance as the country's centre for artistic production at the time.

Piazza Castello and around

At the far end of the pedestrianized Via Dante, the Castello Sforzesco rises imperiously from Foro Buonaparte, a road laid out by Napoleon in self-tribute. He had a vision of a grand new centre for his Italian capital, designed along Roman lines, but he only got as far as constructing an arena, a triumphal arch and these two semicircular roads before he lost Milan to the Austrians. The arena and triumphal arch still stand half-forgotten behind the castle on the edges of the **Parco Sempione**, the city centre's largest patch of green and once the castle's garden and hunting grounds.

Castello Sforzesco

Piazza Castello • Daily 7am–8pm, closes at 6pm in winter • Free • ⓦ milanocastello.it • Ⓜ Cairoli or Cadorna

With its crenellated towers and fortified walls, the red-brick **Castello Sforzesco** is one of Milan's most striking landmarks. The result of numerous rebuildings, it was begun by the Viscontis, destroyed by mobs rebelling against their regime in 1447, and rebuilt by their successors, the Sforzas. Under Lodovico Sforza the court became one of the most powerful, luxurious and cultured of the Renaissance, renowned for its ostentatious wealth and court artists like Leonardo and Bramante. Lodovico's days of glory came to an end when Milan was invaded by the French in 1499, and from then until the end of the nineteenth century the castle was used as a barracks by successive occupying armies. Just over a century ago it was converted into a series of museums. Ongoing restoration means that parts of the complex may be closed when you visit.

The *castello*'s buildings are grouped around three courtyards: through the **Filarete Tower** (rebuilt in 1905, having been destroyed in the sixteenth century by an explosion of gunpowder) you enter the larger of the three, the dusty-looking parade ground. It's not until you're through the gateway opposite that you begin to sense a Renaissance castle: this is the **Corte Ducale**, which formed the centre of the residential quarters and is now the home of the castle's museums. The **Rocchetta**, to your left, was the most secure part of the fortress and is now used for temporary exhibitions. The gateway ahead leads to the Parco Sempione.

The museums

Tues–Sun 9am–5.30pm • Combined ticket €5; free entry on first and third Tues of the month

The ticket office, on your right as you enter the Corte Ducale, gives access to the **Museo d'Arte Antica**, a succession of rooms containing an extensive collection of ancient artefacts saved from the city's churches and archeological excavations. More interesting, however, are the castle rooms themselves, especially the **Sala delle Asse**, designed by Leonardo da Vinci; his black-and-white preparatory sketches were discovered in the 1950s. In the courtyard you will find the museum's star exhibit: Michelangelo's **Rondanini Pietà**, which the artist worked on during the last days of his life. It's an unfinished but oddly powerful work; much of the marble is unpolished and a third arm, indicating a change of position for Christ's body, hangs limply from a block of stone to his right.

Upstairs, the **Museo delle Arti Decorative** exhibits furniture and decorative arts through the ages, including fascinating early works by the great twentieth-century Milanese designer, Gio Ponti. The Torre Falconiere (Falconry Tower) next door holds the castle's **art collection** containing numerous paintings by Lombard artists such as Foppa and Bramantino, as well as minor Venetian works, including some Canalettos. The best are all

grouped together in Room XIII and include Antonello da Messina's *St Benedict*, originally part of a five-piece polyptych, of which two panels are in the Uffizi in Florence.

Across the courtyard, in the castle cellars, are the smaller **Egyptian collection**, with displays of mummies, sarcophagi and papyrus fragments from The Book of the Dead, and the deftly lit **prehistoric collection** – an assortment of finds from the Iron Age burial grounds of the Golasecca civilization.

The Parco Sempione

Park Dawn to dusk • Free • **Acquario Civico** Tues–Sun 9am–5.30pm • €5; free entry first and third Tues of the month • verdeacqua.eu • **Torre Branca** Mid-May to mid-Sept Tues, Thurs & Fri 3–7pm & 8.30pm–midnight, Wed 10.30am–12.30pm, 3–7pm & 8.30pm–midnight, Sat & Sun 10.30am–2pm, 2.30–7.30pm & 8.30pm–midnight; mid-Sept to mid-May Wed 10.30am–12.30pm & 4–6.30pm, Sat 10.30am–1pm, 3–6.30pm & 8.30pm–midnight, Sun 10.30am–2pm & 2.30–7pm • €5; free Wed for over-65s • 02 331 4120 • Cairoli or Cadorna

The **Parco Sempione**, the city centre's largest area of greenery, was laid out in the castle's old hunting grounds and orchards. It can make a refreshing break from the city's traffic-choked roads, with a playground for younger kids, grass to sprawl or kick a football on and a café or two. On the eastern edge of the park is the **Arena Civica**, a Colosseum-inspired area where mock chariot races and naval battles were held to entertain Napoleon's generals. Nearby, in a pretty Liberty building, the **Acquario Civico** focuses on marine life in Italian fresh- and saltwater environments: its small collection of tanks will keep children entertained for a spell. Opposite, on the western edge, the **Torre Branca**, designed by Gio Ponte on the occasion of the fifth Triennale in 1933, offers a birds-eye view of the city.

4

Triennale

Viale Emilio Alemagna 6 • Tues–Sun 10.30am–8.30pm • Single exhibitions €5–9, all exhibitions €12 • 02 724 341, triennale.org • Cadorna

The Palazzo dell'Arte or **Triennale**, located in the Palazzo dell'Arte on the western reaches of the park, was designed by Giovanni Muzio in 1931. The building played a pivotal role in the development of Milan's importance in the world of design, providing a permanent home for the triennial design exhibition held here since the 1930s. The *palazzo* holds the excellent **Triennale Design Museum** and other good-quality temporary exhibitions of design, architecture, fashion, new media and contemporary art. The building is also home to the Teatro dell'Arte, which regularly hosts musical and theatrical performances. There's a bookshop, a great café-bar, an outdoor café and a rooftop restaurant.

Studio Museo Achille Castiglioni

Piazza Castello 27 • Tues–Sat 1hr guided tours (by reservation) at 10am, 11am & noon; Thurs also at 6.30pm, 7.30pm & 8.30pm • €10 • 02 805 3606, fondazioneachillecastiglioni.it • Cadorna or Cairoli

Design enthusiasts should not miss the **Studio Museo Achille Castiglioni**, just outside the park gates. Born in 1918, Castiglioni was one of Italy's foremost designers of furniture, lighting and other objects. His studio is jam packed with drawings, models and sketches, as well as prototypes of some of his most famous works. Guided tours are carried out by Castiglioni's son Carlo and daughter Giovanna.

Brera and Moscova

Due north of La Scala, **Via Brera** sets the tone for Milan's arty quarter: small galleries nestle in the lanes surrounding the Accademia di Belle Arti and Pinacoteca di Brera. As you'll notice from the café prices and designer styles of those who can afford to sit outside them, these cobbled streets are the terrain of the urban rich.

Across Via Fatebenefratelli, the stylish bars and traditional trattorias continue north through the neighbourhood of **Moscova**, home to the offices of the *Corriere della Sera*

newspaper. A good area for shopping and browsing, Corso Garibaldi, Via Solferino and Via San Marco lead up to the bastion in Piazza XXV Aprile, which marks the beginning of **Corso Como**, a trendy street full of bars, clubs and boutiques, which in turn leads up to the train and bus station of Porta Garibaldi. Here you reach Milan's financial district, at the heart of which is Piazza Gae Aulenti, flanked by towering skyscrapers and office blocks. Don't miss the city's famous Bosco Verticale, a pair of eco-friendly residential towers blanketed in trees and plants. The up-and-coming neighbouring area of Isola is home to an array of restaurants and bars.

Pinacoteca di Brera

Via Brera 28 • Tues–Sun 8.30am–7.15pm • €10, audioguide €5 • Ⓦ pinacotecabrera.org • Ⓜ Lanza or Montenapoleone

Milan's most prestigious art gallery, the **Pinacoteca di Brera** was opened to the public in 1809 by Napoleon, who filled the building with works looted from the churches and aristocratic collections of French-occupied Italy. It's big: your visit will probably be more enjoyable if you're selective, dipping into the collection guided by your own personal tastes.

Room VI

Exiting the three rooms of early medieval works brings you face to face with the stunningly powerful *The Dead Christ*, a painting by Andrea Mantegna, the court artist in fifteenth-century Mantova responsible for the Camera degli Sposi (see page 252). One of Mantegna's sons had died around the time he was working on this painting and the desolation in the women's faces and the powerful sense of bereavement emanating from the work seem autobiographical. In the same room, the *Pietà* by Mantegna's brother-in-law, Giovanni Gentile, is another beautifully balanced work of grief and pain that has been deemed "one of the most moving paintings in the history of art".

Room VIII

Next door in Room VIII, the impressive *St Mark Preaching in St Euphemia Square* introduces an exotic note, the square bustling with turbaned men, veiled women, camels and even a giraffe. Gentile Bellini, who had lived and worked in Constantinople for several years, died before the painting was complete, so it was finished off by his brother Giovanni for the Scuola Grande di San Marco in Venice.

Room IX

Another theatrical work hanging nearby is Paolo Veronese's depiction of *Supper in the House of Simon*; it got him into trouble with the Inquisition, who considered the introduction of frolicking animals and unruly kids unsuitable subject matter for a religious painting. Tintoretto's *Pietà* was more starkly in tune with requirements of the time, a scene of intense concentration and grief over Christ's body, painted in the 1560s. Nearby in the same room is another Tintoretto, *The Finding of the Body of Saint Mark in Alexandria*: the dramatic use of perspective coupled with mystical use of light and shadow create a truly operatic ensemble.

Room XXIV

The pride of the Brera collection, room XXIV contains three paintings ranked among the highest expression of Renaissance culture in art: Piero della Francesca's haunting *Madonna and Child with Saints* and *Federigo da Montefeltro*, which is the most arresting, with its stylized composition and geometric harmony, and, on the wall opposite, *Christ at the Column*, the only known painting by the architect Bramante. Take a look, too, at Raphael's altarpiece, the *Marriage of the Virgin*, whose lucid, languid Renaissance mood stands in sharp contrast to the grim realism of Caravaggio's deeply human *Supper at Emmaus* (Room XXIX), set in a dark tavern.

The rest of the gallery

Less well known but equally naturalistic are the paintings of Lombardy's brilliant eighteenth-century realist, Ceruti – known as Il Pitochetto (The Little Beggar) for his unfashionable sympathy with the poor, who stare out with reproachful dignity from his canvases (Room XXXVI).

On display at Brera Modern in the recently restored Citterio Palace, there is also a small collection of modern works from the Jesi donation, which is particularly strong on the Futurists and also includes paintings by Morandi, Modigliani, De Chirico and Carrà, as well as abstract sculpture by Marino Marini and Medardo Rosso.

Quadrilatero d'Oro

The Roman thoroughfare **Via Manzoni** leads north from La Scala to Porta Nuova, one of the medieval entrances to the city forming one side of the **Quadrilatero d'Oro**. Comprising a few hundred square metres bordered by Via Montenapoleone, Via Sant'Andrea, Via della Spiga and Via Manzoni, the quarter is home to shops of all the big international and Italian fashion names, along with design studios and contemporary art galleries. This is Milan in its element and the area is well worth a wander if only to see the city's better-heeled residents in their natural habitat.

Museo Bagatti Valsecchi

Via Gesù 5 • Tues–Sun 1–5.45pm • €9 • ⓣ 02 7600 6132, ⓦ museobagattivalsecchi.org, Ⓜ Montenapoleone or San Babilia

4

In a house linking Via Santo Spirito with Via Gesù 5, just off Via Montenapoleone, is the **Museo Bagatti Valsecchi**, an absorbing private museum affording an intriguing insight into the tastes of the Bagatti Valsecchi brothers, Giuseppe and Fausto. Taking the nineteenth-century fashion for collecting to an extreme, in 1883 they built a Renaissance-style home, inspired by the Palazzo Ducale in Mantova, in which to house their Renaissance collections, as well as a home for their families. All the rooms are richly decorated with carved fireplaces, painted ceilings and heavy wall-hangings and paintings. The fireplace in the drawing room perfectly illustrates the brothers' eclectic approach to decoration: the main surround is sixteenth-century Venetian, the frescoes in the middle are from Cremona, and the whole ensemble is topped off with the Bagatti Valsecchi coat of arms. Modern conveniences were incorporated into the house but not allowed to ruin the harmony, so the shower in the bathroom is disguised in a niche, and the piano, which was not realized as an instrument until the eighteenth century, is incorporated within a cabinet. Look out also for touching domestic items, such as the nursery furniture for Giuseppe's children.

Museo Poldi Pezzoli

Via Manzoni 12 • Wed–Mon 10am–6pm • €10 • ⓣ 02 794 889, ⓦ museopoldipezzoli.it, Ⓜ Montenapoleone

Halfway between La Scala and Porta Nuova, the eclectic **Museo Poldi Pezzoli** comprises pieces assembled by the nineteenth-century collector Gian Giacomo Poldi Pezzoli. Much of this is made up of rather dull rooms of clocks, watches, cutlery and jewellery, but the Salone Dorato upstairs contains a number of intriguing paintings, including a portrait of a portly *San Nicola da Tolentino* by Piero della Francesca, part of an altarpiece on which he worked intermittently for fifteen years. St Nicholas looks across at two works by Botticelli; one a gentle *Madonna del Libro*, among the many variations of the Madonna and Child theme which he produced at the end of the fifteenth century, and the other a mesmerizing *Deposition*, painted towards the end of his life in response to the monk Savonarola's crusade against his earlier, more humanistic canvases. Also in the room is the museum's best-known portrait, *Portrait of a Young Woman* by Antonio Pollaiuolo, whose anatomical studies are evidenced in the subtle suggestion of bone structure beneath skin.

Around the Giardini Pubblici

At the top of Piazza Cavour, on the northern side of Porta Nuova, are the **Giardini Pubblici** (dawn – dusk; Ⓜ Palestro, Ⓜ Turati or Ⓜ Porta Venezia), stretching over to Porta Venezia. Milan's most attractive green space, it was designed by Piermarini shortly after he completed La Scala. Re-landscaped in the nineteenth century to give a more rustic look, the park, with its shady avenues, children's play areas and small lake, is ideal for a break from the busy streets. Across the road, the **Giardini della Villa Reale** is an urban oasis reserved for those with children under 13. With a small area of swings, lawns, shady trees and a little pond with ducks, turtles and giant carp, it makes a perfect bolthole. Located within the Galleria Reale is the **Galleria d'Arte Moderna Milano (GAM)** (Tues–Sun 9–5.30pm; €5), which displays a collection of works from the nineteenth century.

Corso Venezia, which leads back down from here to San Babila and the centre, is lined with nineteenth-century palaces. Hereabouts are the city homes of many of Milan's most moneyed residents, including the rooftop apartments of Domenico Dolce and Stefano Gabbana.

Villa Necchi Campiglio

Via Mozart 14 • Wed–Sun 10am–6pm • €12, free for National Trust members; entrance by 1hr guided tours only • Ⓣ 02 763 40121, Ⓦ fondoambiente.it • Ⓜ Palestra or Porta Venezia

Beautiful **Villa Necchi Campiglio** showcases the tastes and way of life of the privileged Milan bourgeoisie in the heady days of the twentieth century. Built in the 1930s by the Milanese architect Piero Portaluppi for an industrialist who had made his fortune from sewing machines, the villa, complete with a lovely garden, swimming pool and tennis court, will perhaps be familiar from the film *I Am Love* where it starred alongside Tilda Swinton. It is an Art Deco beauty, beautifully preserved with a sweeping walnut stairway, marble bathrooms, brass radiator covers and the original kitchen and pantry.

4

The Ticinese district

Leading southwest away from the Duomo, past the chain stores of Via Torino, the city takes on a different, slightly more alternative air. The main thoroughfare of the **Ticinese district**, the Corso di Porta Ticinese, has become a focus for street fashion and is lined with small boutiques and bars. The area really comes into its own at *aperitivo* time, especially during summer when people spill on to the pedestrian streets from the numerous bars and cafés. The neighbourhood also boasts two of Milan's most important churches – and most rewarding sights – **San Lorenzo Maggiore** and **Sant'Eustorgio**.

San Lorenzo Maggiore

Corso di Porta Ticinese 35 • **Church** Mon–Fri 8am–6.30pm, Sat & Sun 9am–7pm • **Cappella di Sant'Aquilino** Mon–Fri 8am–6.30pm, Sat & Sun 9am–7pm • €4 • Ⓣ 02 8940 4129 • Ⓦ sanlorenzomaggiore.com • Tram #3

Towards the northern end of Corso Ticinese stands **San Lorenzo Maggiore**, a graceful building with a quiet dignity, somewhat at odds with the skateboarding and partying that goes on in the piazza outside. Founded in the fourth century, it was built with masonry salvaged from various Roman buildings. The sixteen Corinthian columns outside – the **Colonne di San Lorenzo** – were placed here in the fourth century as a portico to the church. To the right of the altar, the **Cappella di San Aquilino** was probably built as an imperial mausoleum. The lunettes in the Roman octagonal room hold beautiful fourth-century mosaics, which would originally have covered all the walls, while beneath the relics of Sant'Aquilino steps lead down to what is left of the original foundations, a jigsaw of fragments of Roman architecture.

Sant'Eustorgio

Piazza Sant'Eustorgio 1 • Portinari chapel Tues–Sun 10am–6pm • €6 • Ⓦ santeustorgio.it • Trams #3, #9 & #10

Heading south down Corso Ticinese, you come to **Sant'Eustorgio**, a fourth-century church built to house the bones of the Magi, said to have been brought here by Sant'Ambrogio. It was expanded in the eleventh century, and in the twelfth century was virtually destroyed by Barbarossa, who seized the Magi's bones and deposited them in Cologne's cathedral. Some of the bones were returned in 1903 and are kept in a reliquary placed above the altar of the Magi. The Roman sarcophagus tucked away in the right transept is the one in which, according to tradition, the relics of the Magi arrived.

Cappella Portinari

A must-see while here is the **Cappella Portinari** or chapel, accessed round to the left of the main entrance. The beautiful chapel consciously recalls Brunelleschi's San Lorenzo in Florence, with two domed rooms, the smaller one housing the altar. It has been credited with being Milan's first true Renaissance building because of its simple geometric design; the mixture of Lombard terracotta sculpture and Florentine monochromatic simplicity makes an enchanting stylistic fusion. It was commissioned by an unknown architect in the 1460s to house the remains of St Peter the Martyr, who was struck on the head with a billhook, resulting in him becoming the patron saint for headache sufferers.

The Navigli

4

The southern end of Corso di Porta Ticinese is guarded by the nineteenth-century **Arco di Porta Ticinese**, marking the beginning of Milan's canal – or **Navigli** – neighbourhood, once a bustling industrial area and these days a focus for the city's nightlife, although it is scruffy and often disappointing in the harsh light of day. The best time to visit is in the evening when the quarter's many restaurants and bars come alive, although the

MILAN'S CANALS

Improbable though it may seem, less than fifty years ago Milan was still a viable port – and less than a hundred years ago several of its main arteries – including Via Senato and Via San Marco – were busy waterways.

In the twelfth century, the first **canals** linked irrigation channels and the various defensive moats of the city. Later, in 1386, the **Naviglio Grande** was opened, linking the city to the River Ticino and thus Lake Maggiore. It was Gian Galeazzo Visconti, however, who was really responsible for the development of the system, in the fourteenth century to transport the building materials for the Duomo, especially marble from Lake Maggiore.

Travellers were also seen on the canals: the ruling families of the north used them to visit one another; Prospero and Miranda escaped along the Navigli in *The Tempest*; and they were still plied by the Grand Tourists in the eighteenth century – Goethe, for example, describes the hazards of journeying by canal.

A number of rivers and canals were added to the system over the centuries. The Spanish developed the **Darsena** to the south in 1603 and under Napoleon's regime the **Naviglio Pavese** was made navigable all the way to Pavia and down to the River Po, and so to the Adriatic. During the Industrial Revolution, raw materials like coal, iron and silk were brought into the city, and handmade products transported out with an efficiency that ensured Milan's commercial and economic dominance of the region. The process of covering over the canals began in the 1930s, to make way for the city's trams and trolley buses. In the 1950s, desperately needed materials were floated in for reconstructing the badly bombed city but by the mid-1970s, only a handful of canals were left uncovered; the last working boat plied the waters in 1979.

The best way to explore Milan's waterways is on a relaxing **boat trip**. These run between April and mid-September when the canals are not being dredged or cleaned; for more information ask at the tourist office, call Ⓣ 02 667 9131 or check Ⓦ navigazionenavigli.it.

monthly Sunday **antiques street-market** (last Sun of month; closed July and Aug) also brings a vivacious focus to the waterways.

Naviglio Grande and Naviglio Pavese

South from the Darsena (the main goods dock), the **Naviglio Grande** and the **Naviglio Pavese**, respectively the first and last of the city's canals to be completed, lead into the plains of Lombardy. This was once Milan at its grittiest. Some of the warehouses and traditional tenement blocks, or *case di ringhiera*, have been refurbished and become prime real estate but you'll still find plenty of unreconstructed corners. Craftsmen and artists have moved in and although the overpriced craft and antique shops won't hold your attention for long, a wander round the streets, popping into open courtyards, will give you a feel of the neighbourhood. Take a look at the prettified Vicolo dei Lavandai (Washerwomen's Alley), near the beginning of the Naviglio Grande, where washerwomen scrubbed smalls in the murky canal waters.

Porta Genova

Five minutes' walk west from the Naviglio Grande is **Porta Genova**, the train station for Milan's southern outskirts. It is also the name given to one of Milan's up-and-coming areas. Across the tracks from the train station, bars and restaurants have moved in and disused warehouses and factories are being reclaimed by photographers, fashion houses and designers. Giorgio Armani has an exhibition space and workshops here, as does Prada.

Santa Maria delle Grazie and around

Due west from the Duomo, on Corso Magenta, stands the attraction that brings most visitors to Milan – the beautiful terracotta-and-brick church of **Santa Maria delle Grazie**, famous for its mural of **The Last Supper** by Leonardo da Vinci. More ancient exhibits are on display at the city's **Museo Archeologico,** while the nearby **Sant'Ambrogio** is one of the city's loveliest churches.

Santa Maria delle Grazie

Piazza Santa Maria delle Grazia, Via Magenta • Ⓜ Cadorna or Conciliazione

The beautiful terracotta-and-brick church of **Santa Maria delle Grazie** was first built in Gothic style by the fifteenth-century architect Guiniforte Solari. It was part of the Dominican monastery that headed the Inquisition for over one hundred years in the late fifteenth and sixteenth centuries. Soon after its completion, Lodovico Sforza commissioned Bramante to rework and model the Gothic structure into a grand dynastic mausoleum. Bramante promptly tore down the existing chancel and replaced it with a massive dome supported by an airy Renaissance cube. Lodovico also intended to replace the nave and facade, but was unable to do so before Milan fell to the French, leaving an odd combination of styles – Gothic vaults, decorated in powdery blues, reds and ochre, illuminated by the light that floods through the windows of Bramante's dome. A side door leads into Bramante's cool and tranquil cloisters, from where there's a good view of the sixteen-sided drum the architect placed around his dome.

The Last Supper

Leonardo's *The Last Supper* – signposted **Cenacolo Vinciano** – is one of the world's great paintings and most resonant images. Henry James likened the painting to an "illustrious invalid" that people visited with "leave-taking sighs and almost death-bed or tip-toe precautions"; certainly it's hard, when you visit the fragile painting, not to feel that it's the last time you'll see it. A twenty-year restoration has re-established the original colours using contemporary descriptions and copies, but that the work survived at all is something of a miracle. Leonardo's decision to use oil paint rather

than the more usual faster-drying – and longer-lasting – fresco technique with watercolours led to the painting disintegrating within five years of its completion. A couple of centuries later Napoleonic troops billeted here used the wall for target practice. And, in 1943, an Allied bomb destroyed the building, amazingly leaving only *The Last Supper*'s wall standing.

A Last Supper was a conventional theme for refectory walls, but Leonardo's decision to capture the moment when Christ announces that one of his disciples will betray him imbues the work with an unprecedented sense of drama.

Goethe commented on how very Italian the painting was in that so much is conveyed through the expressions of the characters' hands; the group of Matthew, Thaddaeus and Simon on the far right of the mural could be discussing a football match or the latest government scandal in any bar in Italy today. The only disciple not gesticulating or protesting in some way is the recoiling Judas who has one hand clenched while a bread roll has just dropped dramatically out of the other. Christ is calmly reaching out to share his bread with him while his other hand falls open in a gesture of sacrifice.

If you feel you need any confirmation of the emotional tenor or accomplishment of the painting, take a look at the contemporary *Crucifixion* by Montorfano on the wall at other end of the refectory: not a bad fresco in itself, but destined always to pale in comparison with Leonardo's masterpiece.

Museo Archeologico

Corso Magenta 15 • Tues–Sun 9am–5.30pm • €5, free entry first and third Tues of the month • T 02 8844 5208, W comune.milano.it/museoarcheologico • M Cadorna

Bits and pieces of Roman buildings can be found across the city centre, but the **Museo Archeologico** presents more domestic examples of Milan's Roman heritage. Housed in the ex-Monastero Maggiore (don't miss the beautiful Church of San Maurizio next door, also accessible from the museum), the museum has some compelling displays of glass phials, kitchen utensils and jewellery from Roman Milan. The inner cloister is home to the remains of a Roman dwelling dating from the first to third century AD, as well as some beautiful frescoes from the thirteenth to fourteenth centuries. From here a walkway leads to a building on Via Nirone, which houses findings from the Early Middle Ages and the Etruscan and Greek eras.

Sant'Ambrogio

Piazza Sant'Ambrogio 15 • Mon–Sat 7.30am–12.30pm & 2.30–7pm, Sun 7.30am–1pm & 3–8pm • Free • W basilicasantambrogio.it • M Sant'Ambrogio

The church of **Sant'Ambrogio** was founded in the fourth century by Milan's patron saint, St Ambrose. The saint's remains still lie in the church's crypt, but there's nothing left of the original church in which his most famous convert, St Augustine, first heard

THE LAST SUPPER: BOOKING INFORMATION AND TOURS

Visits to *The Last Supper* must be booked far in advance, at least one month (about three in summer and at weekends). If it's fully booked when you ring, try asking about cancellations on the day: people don't always turn up for the early morning slots so it might be worth enquiring at the desk. At your allotted hour, once you've passed through a series of air-filtering systems along the rebuilt sides of what was the monastery's largest courtyard, your fifteen-minute slot face-to-face with the masterpiece begins.

Viewing times Tues–Sun 8.15am–7pm (last entry 6.45pm).

Reservations Mon–Sat 8.30am–6.30pm on T 02 9280 0360; for online bookings use W musei.lombardia.beniculturali.it.

Admission €13, plus €2 booking fee; free first Sun of the month (bookings necessary).

Tours Alternatively, try one of the city tours (see page 237), which can include entrance to view the painting.

EVIL PERSONIFIED

Leonardo spent two years on his *Last Supper* mural, wandering the streets of Milan searching for and sketching models. When the monks complained that the face of **Judas** was still unfinished, Leonardo replied that he had been searching for over a year among the city's criminals for a sufficiently evil visage, and that if he didn't find one he would use the face of the prior. Whether or not Judas is modelled on the prior is unrecorded, but Leonardo's Judas does seem, as Vasari wrote, "the very embodiment of treachery and inhumanity".

him preach. The present twelfth-century church, the blueprint for many of Lombardy's Romanesque basilicas is, however, one of the city's loveliest, reached through a colonnaded quadrangle with column capitals carved with rearing horses, contorted dragons and an assortment of bizarre predators. Inside, it is embellished with works by Italian Renaissance painters Ambrogio Bergognone, Bernardino Luini and Bernardino Lanino. To the left of the nave, a freestanding Byzantine pillar is topped with a "magic" bronze serpent, flicked into a loop and symbolizing Aaron's rod – an ancient tradition held that on the Day of Judgement it would crawl back to the Valley of Josaphat. Look, too, at the pulpit, a superb piece of Romanesque carving decorated with reliefs of wild animals and the occasional human, most of whom are intent upon devouring one another. Below the pulpit is the Sarcophagus of Stilicho, which dates back to the fourth century. There are other relics further down the nave, notably the ciborium, reliefed with the figures of saints Gervasius and Protasius – martyred Roman soldiers in their twenties whose clothed bodies flank that of St Ambrose in the crypt. A nineteenth-century autopsy revealed that they had been killed by having their throats cut. Similar investigations into St Ambrose's remains restored the reputation of the anonymous fifth-century artist responsible for the mosaic portrait of the saint in the Cappella di San Vittorio in Ciel d'Oro (to the right of the sacristy). Until then it was assumed that Ambrose owed his crooked face to a slip of the artist's hand, but the examination of his skull revealed an abnormally deep-set tooth, suggesting that his face would indeed have been notably asymmetric. The Golden Altar is a masterpiece from the ninth century, inlaid with precious stones from the Byzantine court and families close to the Emperor.

ARRIVAL AND DEPARTURE — MILAN

BY PLANE

Milan has two airports. Malpensa is the city's main airport, 50km northwest of the city near Lake Maggiore, with domestic and long haul flights arriving here. Domestic and short-haul European flights serve the much smaller Linate; located only 7km east of Milan, it's particularly convenient to reach the city centre (enquiries for both on 02 232 323; daily 6am–11pm). Bergamo-Orio al Serio (see page 281), sometimes also touted as Milan, is a comfortable 45min away.

Malpensa (milanomalpensa-airport.com). Direct buses, operated by Autostradale (autostradale.com), Terravision (terravision.eu) and Air Pullman (malpensashuttle.com), run from Malpensa airport to Stazione Centrale, Milan's main train station (every 15–20min; 1hr; €8–10). There's a fast train, the Malpensa Express (www.malpensaexpress.it) from the airport to Milano Cadorna-Stazione Nord (every 30min; 37min; €13) and Milano Centrale (every 30min; 58min; €13), also stopping at Milano Porta Garibaldi. A taxi (taximilano.it) from Malpensa to the centre (around 40min) costs €95.

Linate (milanolinate-airport.com). Regular airport buses connect Linate with Piazza Luigi di Savoia, on the east side of Stazione Centrale (every 20min; 25min; €5; autostradale.it; 02 720 01304; buy ticket on board). Ordinary ATM urban transport buses (#73; €1.50; atm.it) also run every 10min between Linate and Via Gonzaga (Duomo), and take around 30min; tickets must be bought before you get on the bus from the airport newsagent, or, if you have change, from the ticket machine at the bus stop. A taxi to the centre from the rank outside will cost around €30.

BY TRAIN

Most international and domestic trains pull in at the monumental Stazione Centrale, northeast of the city centre on Piazza Duca d'Aosta, at the hub of the metro network on lines M2 and M3. Other services, especially those from stations in the Milan region – Bergamo, Pavia, Como and the other western lakes – terminate at smaller stations around the city, Porta Garibaldi, Lambrate, Porta Genova and Milano Nord, all on M2 (the metro stop for Milano Nord is "Cadorna"), although these

often also stop at Stazione Centrale. There are separate train enquiries lines for Ferrovie dello Stato (T 892 021, W trenitalia.com) and for TreNord (T 02 7249 4949, W trenord.it).

MILANO STAZIONE CENTRALE

Destinations Bergamo (hourly; 45min); Brescia (every 45min; 1hr 20min); Certosa di Pavia (9 daily; 20min); Como (hourly; 40min); Cremona (3 daily; 1hr 25min); Desenzano (every 30min; 1hr); Lecco (every 2hr; 50min); Pavia (every 30min; 25min); Peschiera (hourly; 1hr 17min); Stresa (9 daily; 1hr 10min); Varenna (every 2hr; 1hr 10min); Verbania-Pallanza (9 daily; 1hr 20min); Verona (hourly; 1hr 35min).

MILANO LAMBRATE

Destinations Bergamo (hourly; 45min); Brescia (hourly; 1hr 20min); Certosa di Pavia (9 daily; 20min); Cremona (3 daily; 1hr 25min); Desenzano (2 daily; 1hr); Pavia (every 25min; 25min); Peschiera (2 daily; 1hr 10min); Verona (hourly; 1hr 35min).

MILANO NORD CADORNA

Destinations Como (every 30min; 1hr 5min); Varese (every 30min; 1hr).

MILANO PORTA GARIBALDI

Destinations Bergamo (every 40min; 55min); Chiasso (hourly; 1hr 15min); Como (7 daily; 30min); Cremona (3 daily; 1hr 30min); Lecco (hourly; 1hr); Luino (4 daily; 1hr 40min); Stresa (9 daily; 1hr 30min); Verbania-Pallanza (9 daily; 1hr 35min).

BY BUS

Bus station International and long-distance buses, and many regional buses, arrive at and depart from Lampugnano bus station on Via Giulio Latta (M Lampugnano).

Private buses Regular buses (W safduemila.com) run from Malpensa airport to several regional towns around the lakes.

BY CAR

If you're driving, try to avoid arriving during the morning and evening rush hours (approximately 7.30–10am & 4.30–7pm) when Milan's ring road, the infamous Tangenziale, is often gridlocked.

GETTING AROUND

Milan's street plan resembles a spider's web, with roads radiating out from the central Piazza del Duomo. The bulk of the city is encircled by two concentric ring roads following the medieval and Spanish walls of the city, while the suburbs and industrial estates spill out towards a third ring, the Tangenziale, which links the main motorways. The city centre is just about compact enough to explore on foot, though the public transport system is easy to master if you're flagging or going a long way.

BY PUBLIC TRANSPORT

Metro The metro (W atm.it) has four lines: the red M1, green M2, yellow M3 and lilac M5, as well as the blue suburban railway line *passante ferroviario*. The main intersections are Stazione Centrale, Duomo, Cadorna (Milano Nord) and Loreto (see below). The front of each metro train shows the station at the end of the line. Services run from around 6am to midnight.

Buses and trams Most bus and tram stops display the route and direction of travel. Services run from around 4am to 2am, after which nightbuses take over, following the metro routes throughout the night.

Enquiries For all public transport enquiries (W atm.it) the information offices at the Duomo or Stazione Centrale

MILAN TOURS

Canal boat cruises Naviglio Lombardi (02 9227 3118, navigazionenavigli.it) runs four cruise itineraries along the Navigli (mainly April–Oct; €14/person).

City Sightseeing Buses City Sightseeing Milano (milano.city-sightseeing.it) and Milano Open Tour (www.milanopentour.com) both offer hop-on-hop-off bus tours that run along different routes around central Milan, with fares starting from €10.

City Tours Zani Viaggi (www.zaniviaggi.it) and Autostradale Viaggi (lookmitours.com) both offer a range of city tours, with some including entrance to *The Last Supper*. Advance booking highly recommended.

San Siro tour Tours around the home of AC Milan and InterMilan (see page 245).

metro stations are helpful, and have English-speaking staff.

Tickets These are valid for 75min, cost €1.50 and can be used for one metro trip and as many bus and tram rides as you want. They are on sale at tobacconists, bars and at the metro station newsagents; most outlets close at 8pm, so it's best to buy a few tickets in advance if you intend to use public transport after this time, or get a carnet of ten for €13.80. Some stations have automatic ticket machines, although only the newer ones give change. You can also buy a 24hr (€4.50) or 48hr pass (€8.25). Remember to validate your ticket in the orange machines when you enter the metro and board buses and trams, as inspections are common.

BY TAXI

Taxis Don't bother trying to flag a taxi down, as they don't cruise the streets. Your best bet is to phone one of the following numbers (operators speak English): 02 6767, 02 4040 or 02 8585. Say where you are and the operator will check how long before a cab can get to you (usually under 5min) and then give you a code to quote to the driver. Alternatively, there are a number of taxi ranks around town – including in Piazza del Duomo, Largo Cairoli, Piazza San Babila and Stazione Centrale. All cabs are metered and prices are reasonable, although in the daytime Milan's traffic-filled streets can quickly start to push fares up.

BY CAR

Congestion charge Driving your own car in the city is best avoided: the streets are congested and street parking nigh on impossible in the evenings and on Saturdays. If you do bring a car, you'll need to buy a pass to enter the central Area C (Mon–Fri 7.30am–7.30pm, Thurs until 6pm; €5) – an initiative to cut pollution and congestion in the city centre. The pass must be bought on the day of entry or up to midnight of the day afterwards. Payments can be made at authorized newsagents and tobacconists, or, in English, over the phone (02 4868 4001) or online (comune.milano.it/areac).

Parking Head for one of the numerous central car parks, costing around €3/hr, less if you stay longer than four hours. Central options include Autosilo Diaz, Piazza Diaz 6, just south of Piazza del Duomo; Garage Traversi, on Via Bagutta, close to Piazza San Babila; Parking Majno, on Viale Majno near Porta Venezia. Blue lines along the street denote "pay and display" parking: prices vary from zone to zone but are displayed on the sign. Parking within yellow lines is for residents only.

Car rental All the international companies have car rental offices at the airports and in the city centre including Avis (02 8901 0645), Europcar (02 6698 7826), Hertz (02 6698 5151) and Maggiore (02 669 0934).

BY BIKE

Cycling Milan is easily explored by bike: the terrain is flat, there is little of the aggression that you see on the streets of London or New York, and it is easy to head off down a quiet side road and get away from it all. Do be careful with the tram lines though. Three companies offer bike-sharing services: **Bike Mi** (02 4860 7607, bikemi.com), OFO (ofo.com) and Mobike (mobike.com), with rates starting from €0.30 for 30min.

4

INFORMATION

Tourist office InfoMilano (Mon–Fri 9am–7pm & Sat 9am–6pm, Sun 10am-6pm; visitamilano.it and yesmilano.it); check website for address.

ACCOMMODATION

Accommodation in Milan is expensive, with prices soaring during Fashion Week and the Milan Furniture Fair – if you can, avoid visiting the city during major events as not only will you come across extortionate prices, but you'll be hard pushed to find availability at most hotels.

HOTELS

The hotels below have been divided into three areas –the Station area, covering places within a 20min walk of the Stazione Centrale; the districts around Piazza del Duomo, all within a half-hour stroll of the cathedral, and the area around the Navigli, Milan's canals.

STAZIONE CENTRALE AND AROUND

★ **BioCity Hotel** Via Edolo 18 02 6670 3595, biocityhotel.it; Sondrio or Central F.S. map p.220. An excellent budget choice with immaculate, tastefully furnished rooms 750m north of Stazione Centrale. The hotel prides itself on being ecofriendly – complimentary beauty products are organic and biodegradable, bathrooms feature recycled toilet paper, and breakfast includes home-made cakes, organic jams and eggs. **€99**

LaGare Hotel Via G.B. Pirelli 20 02 872 5241, lagarehotelmilano.it; map p.220. A business hotel offering stylish, comfortable rooms, a large rooftop terrace with views over Milan's skyline and a trendy spa with fitness area, sauna, steam room and salt room. **€220**

Principe di Savoia Piazza della Repubblica 17 02 62 301, dorchestercollection.com; map p.220. Opened in 1927, this historic hotel next to Stazione Centrale offers sumptuous interiors with period furnishings and marble bathrooms. The hotel bar has long attracted the Milanese jet set for an *aperitivo*, while *Acanto* restaurant serves creative Italian cuisine. **€310**

AROUND PIAZZA DEL DUOMO

Antica Locanda dei Mercanti Via San Tomaso 6 02 805 4080, locanda.it; Cairoli; map p.223. Tucked away near the castle, this quietly elegant *locanda* offers individually decorated rooms; two even have their own leafy roof terraces. Rooms have parquet or *graniglia* (marble grit) flooring and are flooded with natural light. **€225**

Hotel Milano Scala Via dell'Orso 7 02 870 961, hotelmilanoscala.it; Cairoli or Montenapoleone; map p.223. A stone's throw away from La Scala, this four-star hotel offers rooms decorated with large images of opera, dance and backstage scenes from the historical archives of La Scala. The suites are each named after a different opera, and there's a rooftop terrace where drinks are served. **€252**

★ **Senato Hotel** Via Senato 22 02 781 236 senatohotelmilano.it; map p.223. A stylish boutique hotel a short walk from the Fashion District with attractive black, white and golden interiors. Set around a sleek interior courtyard, the airy rooms have oak wood flooring, brass lamps and black armchairs, while light dishes can be ordered throughout the day at the pleasant *Senato Caffé*. **€245**

AROUND THE NAVIGLI

Allegroitalia Espresso Darsena Via Conca del Naviglio 20 02 899 19809, espressodarsena.it; map p.220. In an enviable location along Milan's trendy Conca del Naviglio, this budget hotel is brightened up with vibrant splashes of orange. Standard rooms are very poky, so opt for a higher category room if you can. They have smart TVs, black-and-white chequered showers and open-fronted wardrobes. Breakfast is generous, and guests are entitled to ten percent off at various restaurants in the area. **€135**

★ **The Yard** Piazza XXIV Maggio 8 02 8941 5901, theyardmilano.com; map p.220. This fashionable boutique hotel bursts with character, with interiors packed with curios and sporting memorabilia that the owner has collected over the years. Themed rooms are mainly sports-related although you'll also find British style interiors in some, with plenty of tweed, hunting prints and wooden furniture. The cool bar serves up great cocktails, while the restaurant attracts a hip crowd. **€279**

B&BS AND APARTMENTS

B&B Porta Garibaldi Viale Pasubio 8 02 2906 1419 or 335 804 4030, portagaribaldi.it; Garibaldi FS; map p.220. This colourful B&B close to Porta Garibaldi station features a comfortable mini apartment with kitchenette. The friendly owner lives next door and is always happy to help with suggestions. Complimentary bicycles, too. **€130**

★ **LaFavia Milano** Via Carlo Farini 4 347 784 2212, lafaviamilano.com; Garibaldi FS; map p.220. A charming B&B in a nineteenth-century building with warm and welcoming rooms decorated in different styles, featuring retro armchairs and lamps, hand-woven carpets and designer wallpaper. Breakfast is served on the leafy roof terrace garden. The owners also manage a number of attractive apartments in the area. **€110**

HOSTELS AND CAMPING

Babila Hostel & Bistrot Via Conservatorio 2A 02 3658 8490, babilahostel.it; map p.223. Tucked away in a residential neighbourhood east of the city centre, this hostel has a boutique hotel feel, with grey arched ceilings and marble fireplaces. Dorms are brightened up with colourful lockers and reading lamps, there's a chill out room with yoga mats and beanbags, and a living area with Playstation and table football. Dorms **€24**, doubles **€90**

Camping Village Città di Milano Via G. Airaghi 61 02 4820 7017, campingmilano.it; M1 to De Angeli, then bus #72; map p.220. West of the city a metro trip and a bus ride away, this campsite offers accommodation in two and three-bed bungalows, cabins with double rooms, quirky tents shaped like VW vans, as well as in suspended tents that seemingly float in the trees. You'll also find stylish eco suites with floor-to-ceiling glass windows. Open all year. Tents **€7.50** plus **€10**/person, doubles **€70**, bungalows **€105**

★ **Ostello Bello** Via Medici 4 02 3658 2720, www.ostellobello.com; Missori; map p.223. This trendy hostel brims with character, with a lively communal area and bar featuring mismatched coloured furniture, black and white murals and plenty of fun curios. Dorms have reading lamps and lockers, and there's a cosy kitchen stacked with free food for guests. Dinner is included, too. Dorms **€39**, doubles **€109**

EATING

Whether you're looking for a neighbourhood trattoria, want to watch models pick at their salads or crave a bit of well-priced ethnic food, Milan has it all – usually within easy reach of wherever you're staying. If you don't fancy a sit-down meal, make the most of the Milanese custom of **aperitivo** to curb your hunger.

LUNCH AND SNACKS

★ **Bello e Buono** Viale Sabotino 14 ⓣ02 9455 3407, ⓦbelloebuonogastronomia.it; ⓜPorta Romana; map p.220. This tiny laidback place, attracting students from nearby Bocconi University, offers exceptional home cooking at incredible prices. Expect traditional Mediterranean recipes that have been passed down from generation to generation – the *melanzane parmigiana* is to die for. The pasta and bread are home-made, too. Lunch will set you back about €10. Daily noon–midnight.

Eataly Milano Smeraldo Piazza XXV Aprile 10 ⓣ02 4949 7301, ⓦeataly.net; map p.220. This large food emporium is a real foodie's delight, selling all manner of Italian produce from cold cuts to cheeses and freshly-made pastas. Grab a slice of pizza or focaccia at the bakery counter or take a seat at one of the food outlets that serve a variety of dishes, including pastas, fish and meat mains. Daily 8.30am–midnight.

La Rinascente Top floor, Via San Raffaele 2 ⓣ02 866 371, ⓦrinascente.it; ⓜDuomo; map p.223. Enjoy one of the best views in town with a plate of nibbles or a full-blown meal, although the service is not always of the same quality as the food. The space is divided between the city's best bread-makers, mozzarella specialists, sushi chefs, experts in Milanese cooking and chocolatiers to provide a gourmet pick-and-mix to please all tastes. Choose a table on the terrace outside and you can almost reach over and feed the gargoyles on the Duomo roof. Daily 10am–midnight.

Luini Via S. Radegonda 16 ⓦluini.it; ⓜDuomo; map p.223. A city institution that's been serving *panzerotti* (deep-fried mini-*calzone*) round the corner from the Duomo for over 150 years; be prepared to queue. There are a couple of benches in nearby Piazza San Fedele if you want to eat sitting down. Mon 10am–3pm, Tues–Sat 10am–8pm.

★ **Romoletto** Corso di Porta Ticinese 14 ⓣ02 8347 2458, ⓦromolettostreetfood.com; map p.223. This is a great little spot to refuel on delicious Roman street food as you explore town. The pizza slices (from €3.50) are divine, thinner and crunchier than Neapolitan pizza, and there are a dozen types to choose from. You'll also find *supplì* (€2), fried rice balls traditionally made with meat and tomatoes and stuffed with melted mozzarella. Mon–Wed 11am–10pm, Thurs–Sat 11am–11pm, Sun noon–8pm.

CAFÉS AND GELATERIE

★ **Chocolat** Via Boccaccio 9 ⓣ02 4810 0597, ⓦchocolatmilano.it; ⓜCadorna; map p.223. A sleek, stylish café and *gelateria* offering 26 delicious flavours, including seven chocolate options such as orange chocolate, rum chocolate and ginger chocolate. Their ice cream is blended with unusual ingredients such as chilli, aniseed and vinegar. The café also offers delicious cakes that can be enjoyed at the tables on the ground floor or on the mezzanine. Mon–Fri 7.30am–1am, Sat 8am–1am, Sun 10am–1am.

Cova Via Montenapoleone 8 ⓣ02 7600 5599, ⓦpasticceriacova.com; ⓜMontenapoleone; map p.223. Fin-de-siècle surroundings set the scene for this elegant tearoom dating from the Napoleonic era. Discreet service and starched linen accompany the mouthwatering chocolate delicacies, although naturally they don't come cheap. Mon–Sat 7.45am–8.30pm, Sun 9.30am–7.30pm.

Gelateria Marghera Via Marghera 33 ⓣ02 468 641; ⓜWagner or ⓜDe Angeli; map p.220. A popular *gelateria* displaying large tubs of tasty ice cream; flavours include seasonal fruits as well as the classics. Be prepared to queue. Sun–Thurs 11am–11pm, Fri & Sat 11am–12.30am.

RESTAURANTS

★ **A Casa Eatery** Via Conca del Naviglio 37 ⓣ02 3674 3350 ⓦacasaeatery.it; map p.220. Tucked away off Via Conca del Naviglio, this charming restaurant brims with character. Interiors are set out to resemble a mid-twentieth century home, with vintage 1950s and 1960s furnishings

4

UN APERITIVO

An Italian custom that has been honed to a fine art in Milan is the **aperitivo**, or predinner drink. Between 6 and 9pm the city unwinds over a drink and a bite to eat. As well as another opportunity to preen and pose, *aperitivo* time – or happy hour as it is also called – is a boon for budget travellers: counters often groan under the weight of hot and cold food, all of which is included in the price of your drink (somewhere between €5 and €10, depending on the establishment). Take a plate and help yourself, although if you're really planning to fill up, it'll go down better if you go back several times rather than piling your plate high. If you're on a budget and choose your venue wisely, you won't need to spend another penny on food all night. Most *aperitivo* bars evolve as the evening goes on: the lights dim, the volume of the music increases and you can settle in for the night.

in the dining areas and books lining shelves in the cosy library room. Expect hearty homemade cooking (primi €13, secondi €16); there's a great value lunch menu on weekdays, with dishes priced €8–10. Daily 12.30–3pm & 7.30–11pm.

★ **Drogheria Milanese** Via Conca del Naviglio 7 ⓣ 02 5811 4843, ⓦ droghieriamilanese.it; ⓜ Sant'Ambrogio or ⓜ Sant'Agostino; map p.220. This fashionable bistro-style restaurant has a welcoming interior with low-hanging light bulbs and a long communal table. The menu features Mediterranean and international dishes, including pasta, burgers and fish; most dishes can be ordered in half-portions – great for sampling different options. Daily noon–3pm & 7pm–midnight.

Ex Mauri Via Federico Confalonieri 5 ⓣ 02 6085 6028, ⓦ exmauri.com; ⓜ Isola; map p.220. An atmospheric restaurant with bare-brick walls, mismatched chairs and exposed pipework serving traditional Italian recipes with a twist. The menu features regional dishes prepared with local ingredients, along with Milanese favourites such as risotto alla milanese (€14) and tasty home-made desserts (€7). Mon–Fri noon–2pm & 8–11pm.

4

★ **Gastronomia Yamamoto** Via Amedei 5 ⓣ 02 3674 1426; map p.223. This friendly family-run deli and restaurant serves authentic Japanese fare in two attractive dining areas that take inspiration from traditional 1960s and 1970s Japanese interiors. Tuck into meat and vegetable curry (€13), stewed *hijiki* (cooked seaweed; €6) or *unadon* (steamed rice topped with grilled eel; €15) or grab a bento (€12) for lunch on the go. Mon–Sat 12.30–3pm & 7.30–11pm.

★ **Il Liberty** Viale Monte Grappa 6 ⓣ 02 2901 1439, ⓦ il-liberty.it; map p.220. A smart restaurant with a business-oriented clientele serving exquisite creative takes on traditional Italian dishes such as wrapped aubergine *parmigiana* (€23) and Milanese veal cutlet with tomato salad, basil and green lemon zest (€29) There's a great-value two-course business lunch for €20; at other times, *primi* cost around €18, *secondi* €26. Mon–Fri 12.30–2.30pm & 7.30–11pm, Sat 7.30–11pm.

Il Salumaio di Montenapoleone Via Santo Spirito 10/Via Gesù 5 ⓣ 02 760 01123, ⓦ ilsalumaio dimontenapoleone.it; ⓜ San Babila or Montenapoleone; map p.223. Set in the lovely courtyard of the Palazzo Bagatti Valsecchi, this chic, relaxed corner of Milan attracts a well-heeled clientele. Pop in just for coffee, an *aperitivo* or for a full lunch or dinner. The menu is a simple list of Milanese/Italian staples sourced from the delicatessen of the same name. *Primi* €22, *secondi* €28. Daily noon–10.30pm.

★ **La Dogana del Buongusto** Via Molino delle Armi 48 ⓣ 02 8324 2444, ⓦ ladoganadelbuongusto.it; ⓜ Sant'Ambrogio or ⓜ Crocetta; map p.220. Warm and welcoming family-run restaurant serving exceptional cuisine in a rustic interior with cavernous exposed brick walls, wooden ceilings and old-world knick-knacks. The hearty cold cut platters (€13) include wild boar and deer ham, and the menu includes some excellent Milanese dishes. The 30cm meat *brochette* served with baked potato and herb flavoured butter (€22) is a must. Mon–Fri 12.30–2.30pm & 7.30pm–12.30am, Sat 7.30pm–1.30am.

★ **Langosteria** Via Savona 10 ⓣ 02 5811 1649, ⓦ langosteria.com; ⓜ Porta Genova or ⓜ Sant'Agostino; map p.220. This atmospheric restaurant with an understated interior serves some of Milan's best fish and seafood dishes. The oyster bar is the perfect spot for a pre- or postprandial drink, while seating is in a series of individually furnished rooms featuring maritime ornaments, including an upturned boat. The Catalan-style King Crab is superb, as is the scampi tartar with foie gras, with main courses around €30. Its sister-restaurant, *Langosteria Bistrot* (Via Bobbio 2), offers similar cuisine in a more informal setting. Mon–Sat 7pm–midnight, oyster bar open until 1am.

Olio Piazzale Lavater 1 ⓣ 02 2052 0503 ⓜ Porta Venezia; map p.220. Giving onto a leafy little square, this pleasant restaurant serves delicious pugliese specialities, with the likes of broad beans and chicory (€11) and orecchiette pasta with black pork ragu (€15) featuring on the menu. Interiors are welcoming, with pleasant touches here and there (table tops made of ceramic tiles; quirky lamps made with corscrews). Upon arrival you'll be given a small bottle of pugliese olive oil to enjoy during the meal – it's yours to take home when you leave. Wed–Sun 12.30–2.30pm & 7.30–11.30pm, Tues open for dinner only.

Paper Moon Giardino Via Bagutta 12 ⓣ 02 7600 9895, ⓦ papermoongiardino.com; map p.223. Set in a gorgeous Neoclassical building in the city's Fashion District, elegant *Paper Moon Giardino* features original terrazzo floors, vaulted frescoed ceilings and stylish designer chairs. Mirrors create a sense of space, while quirky portraits of celebrities add a pinch of fun. The focus is on delicious fish dishes such as wild seabass tartar (€22) and homemade pasta served with fresh basil pesto and raw shrimps (€1[illegible]). In summer, tables spill out into a lovely peaceful courtyard. Daily 12.30–3.30pm & 7.30–11.30pm.

Temakinho Corso Giuseppe Garibaldi 59 ⓣ 02 72[illegible]1 6158, ⓦ temakinho.com; map p.223. This hugely popular restaurant with several branches throughout Italy serves Japanese/Brazilian fusion cuisine. The menu includes sushi rolls (€10) and *temaki* (cone shaped pieces of *nori* with rice and fish; €7), plus various different flavours of caipirinha. Daily noon–3.30pm & 7pm–midnight.

ToscaNino Via Melzo angolo Via Lambro ⓣ 02 74[illegible]8 1354, ⓦ toscanino.com; ⓜ Porta Venezia; map p.220. The counter of this Tuscan deli-restaurant groans with Tuscan produce, from cold cuts to cheeses, while the menu features Tuscan specialities such as *pappa al pomodoro*

(a thick Tuscan bread soup; €10) and juicy *bistecca alla fiorentina* (T-bone steak; €6/100gr). Perfect for an informal lunch, a relaxed dinner or an *aperitivo*. Mon–Sat 11.30am–3.30pm & 6.30pm–midnight, Sun 12.30–3.30pm.

DRINKING

★ **Baxter Bar** Largo Augusto 1 ⓣ371 139 6734; map p.223. This stylish bar with toweringly high ceilings screams retro-chic, with marble, leather and brass marrying with designer lamps and pastel coloured walls. Laidback 1930s swing tracks set the mood, while the drinks list features classics (from €12) alongside creative cocktails prepared with seasonal ingredients. Tues–Sat 5–11pm.

The Doping Club The Yard Hotel, Piazza XXIV Maggio 8 ⓣ02 8941 5901, ⓦthedopingclub.com; map p.220. Located in the lounge of *The Yard* hotel (see page 238), this fashionable bar serves creative cocktails (€12) prepared by award-winning mixologists in a cool and wacky setting. Expect plenty of comfy velvet couches and interiors jam-packed with all manner of curios, from sporting memorabilia to hatboxes. If you manage to get your hands on the password, you may be able to sneak into the speakeasy at the back. Daily 5pm–2am.

Huan Via Ripa di Porta Ticinese 69 ⓣ02 8976 0637, ⓦhuanmilano.com; map p.220. This stylish dim sum bar serves creative cocktails with an oriental touch (think shiitake mushroom-inflused vodka, Nori seaweed-infused Campari and bamboo liqueur). The *aperitivo* includes oriental nibbles, including wasabi peas, rice crackers and dumplings served in a bamboo steamer. Tues & Wed 6pm–1am, Thurs & Fri 6pm–2am, Sat 12.30–2.30pm & 6pm–2am, Sun 12.30–2.30pm & 6pm–1am.

★ **Lacerba** Via Orti 4 ⓣ02 545 5475, ⓦlacerba.it; map p.220. A popular *aperitivo* (6–9.30pm; €8–10) spot attracting a young alternative crowd for its laidback atmosphere; seating is on colourful stools and worn sofas, while shelves are decorated with knick-knacks from toy trains to umbrellas. Mon–Thurs 6pm–1am, Fri & Sat 6pm–2am.

Mag Cafè Ripa di Porta Ticinese 43 ⓣ02 3956 2875; map p.220. This cosy little place has plenty of character and atmosphere, with quirky paintings, antique cabinets and mismatched armchairs dotted about. A café during the day, in the evenings it morphs into a popular bar serving great cocktails. Daily 7.30am–2am.

★ **Nottingham Forest** Viale Piave 1 ⓣ02 798 311, ⓦnottingham-forest.com; ⓜPorta Venezia; map p.223. Arguably one of Milan's best cocktail bars, shaking up all manner of creatively presented drinks (€12), each served in different funky glasses and containers (there's even a cocktail served in a first aid kit) in an intimate environment. Tues–Sat 6.30pm–2am, Sun 6pm–1am.

Pravda Via Carlo Vittadini 6; ⓜPorta Romana; map p.220. Offering over 150 types of vodka from across the world, this is a definite favourite among Milanese students who flock here for potent cocktails made with fresh fruit and juices (€7), and typically enjoyed on the little pavement outside. Daily 6.30pm–1am.

★ **Rita** Via Angelo Fumagalli 1 ⓣ02 837 2865; ⓜPta Genova; map p.220. This discreet little bar just off Porta Ticinese shakes up creative cocktails using the freshest ingredients around. *Aperitivo* includes delicious finger food as well as tapas-sized portions of Mediterranean dishes that change daily. Daily 6.30pm–2am.

4

NIGHTLIFE

Milan's **nightlife** traditionally centres on two main areas: the designer-label streets around Corso Como and Via Brera and the canal-side Navigli and the adjacent Ticinese quarter, south of the city, where a more mixed clientele enjoys the lively bars, restaurants and nightclubs, some of which host regular live bands. But there are numerous other pockets around Porta Venezia, Corso Sempione and Porta Romana, as well as Isola, north of Porta Garibaldi, where trendy bars and restaurants have started to spring up. Milan's relatively small size and car-and-scooter culture mean that people are happy to drive to places out of the centre, so some of the more popular bars and clubs we recommend below may require a bus, a bike or a short taxi ride.

LIVE-MUSIC VENUES AND CLUBS

The city's clubs are at their hippest midweek, particularly on Thurs – at weekends out-of-towners flood in and any self-respecting Milanese trendy either stays at home or hits a bar. There are a number of lively central clubs for a good dance around Corso Como, otherwise you might need to grab a cab to some of the more out-of-the-way places. In summer some clubs move out to waterside venues at the Idroscalo, by Linate airport. Many have obscure door policies, often dependent on the whim of the bouncer; assuming you get in, you can expect to pay €15–30 entry, which usually includes your first drink. As for live music, Milan scores high on jazz and there are regular gigs by local bands.

★ **Blue Note** Via Borsieri 37 ⓣ02 6901 6888, ⓦbluenotemilano.com; ⓜGaribaldi FS or Isola; map p.220. Top-name jazz club located in the alternative neighbourhood of Isola, just north of Stazione Garibaldi. Quality bookings and a relaxed atmosphere make this place an excellent venue. There's a small restaurant too, as well as the bar. Tues–Sun 7.30pm–midnight.

Dude Club Via Boncompagni 44 ⓦdude-club.net; map p.220. Electronica and techno music are the flavours at this club, which hosts regular international DJ sets – check

the website for details of who's playing. Entry €10–15. Fri & Sat 11pm–5am.

Just Cavalli Torre Branca, Via Luigi Camoens ⓣ02 311 817, ⓦjustcavallimilano.com; ⓜCadorna; map p.223. A chic, glamorous club that is *the* place to go if you want to be surrounded by beautiful people. Offering comfortable cushioned seating, the candle-lit outdoor garden is a great spot for an *aperitivo*. Entry €15. Daily 7.30pm-5am.

Magazzini Generali Via Pietrasanta 14 ⓣ02 539 3948, ⓦmagazzinigenerali.it; tram #24; map p.220. Ex-warehouse that's become a Milan institution with a mixture of popular club nights and live music. Wed, Fri & Sat 11pm–5am.

OPERA

LA SCALA

At La Scala in Piazza della Scala (info ⓣ02 7200 3744, ⓦteatroallascala.org), one of the world's most prestigious opera houses, the opera, ballet and concert season runs from Dec 7 through to July and from Sept to Nov. Tickets range from €5 to 300 (the average price is about €90), with sales for performances starting two months before the Premier, and seats selling out very quickly.

Advance tickets Tickets can be bought online at ⓦteatroallascala.ticketone.it (subject to a twenty percent booking fee) or in person at the Box Office at the theatre in Largo Ghiringhelli (subject to a ten percent booking fee; box office daily 10.30am–6pm).

Same-day sales Some tickets for each performance are set aside for sale on the day; 140 cheap limited-view gallery tickets are available for each performance with a maximum purchase of one ticket/person. A list of names is compiled at the box office at 1pm, with tickets to be collected and paid for at 5pm. Last minute remaining tickets are sold 1 hour before each performance with a twenty five percent reduction in price. Check the website or ask at the box office for the latest information.

SHOPPING

4

Milan is synonymous with shopping. If your pockets are not deep enough to tackle the big-name designer boutiques you could always rummage through last season's leftovers at the many factory outlets around town, or check out the city's wide range of medium- and budget-range clothes shops. Milan also excels in furniture and design, with showrooms from the world's top companies, plus a handful of shops offering a selection of brands and labels under one roof.

DEPARTMENT STORES

10 Corso Como Corso Como 10 ⓦ10corsocomo.com; ⓜMoscova or ⓜGaribaldi FS; map p.220. A Milan institution selling a small range of perfectly selected design and fashion items, as well as books and music, with a café and art gallery, too. Daily 10.30am–7.30pm, Wed & Thurs 10.30am–9pm.

Excelsior Milano Galleria del Corso 4 ⓦexcelsiormilano.com; ⓜDuomo; map p.223. Seven-storey department store in an old cinema building reworked by Jean Nouvel offers a multi-brand pick-and-mix representing the very latest in high-end fashion and design, and rounded off by a tempting foodie floor including a café, bistro and bar. Daily 10am–8.30pm.

Rinascente Piazza Duomo 14 ⓦrinascente.it; ⓜDuomo; map p.223. Milan's best one-stop shop: each department is divided up into boutiques so browsing among the designer goods, from bed linen to bridal wear, toasters to top-quality togs, is a joy. The top-floor food hall is a great refuelling stop (see page 239). Mon–Sat 9.30am–10pm, Sun 10am–10pm.

FASHION

Milan's top-name fashion stores are mainly concentrated in three areas. The Quadrilatero d'Oro – Via Montenapoleone

LGBTQ & MILAN

Milan is one of Italy's most LGBTQ-friendly cities and while many of its nightspots welcome a mixed crowd, they often hold specific LGBTQ nights, too. Naturally, see-and-be-seen venues are Milan's forte, though there is also a choice of more relaxed, as well as more hardcore establishments. The city's main LGBTQ neighbourhood is Porta Venezia, with plenty of LGBTQ-friendly venues clustered along and around Via Lecco.

Memà Largo Bellintani 2 ⓣ02 9286 9193 ⓜPorta Venezia; map p.220. Giving onto a lovely little square, this Sicilian bar serves a great *aperitivo* buffet with all manner of Sicilian specialities including *pane cunzato* (bread topped with cheese, tomatoes and anchovies). It's a great spot to mingle. Sun–Fri 5pm–3am, Sat 7am–3am.

Mono Via Lecco 6; ⓜPorta Venezia; map p.223. This LGBTQ-friendly, vintage cocktail bar has 1960s decor and a happy hour 6.30–9.30pm. The musical flavour is indie, rock and electro with DJ sets Thurs, Fri & Sat. Tues & Sun 6.30pm–1am, Wed & Thurs 6.30pm–1.30am, Fri & Sat 6.30pm–2am.

Via della Spiga and around – is the place for Versace, Prada et al. Corso di Porta Ticinese houses funkier, more youth-oriented shops – independents as well as global names like Diesel, Carhartt and Stussy. Head to Corso Vittorio Emanuele or Via Torino for mid-range chains, including MaxMara, Benetton and Stefanel, plus H&M and Zara.

DESIGNER CLOTHES

Cavalli e Nastri Via Brera 2 ⓣ02 7200 0449, ⓦcavallienastri.com; ⓜmontenapoleone; map p.223. The ultimate in vintage chic offers exquisite pieces to complement any wardrobe or home from their Brera showroom. Sun noon–7.30pm, Mon–Sat 10.30am–7.30pm.

Dolce & Gabbana Menswear, Corso Venezia 15 ⓣ02 7602 8485; womenswear and shoes, Via della Spiga 2 ⓣ02 795 747; D&G trendy line including D&G junior, Corso Venezia 7 ⓣ02 7600 4091; ⓦdolcegabbana.com; ⓜSan Babila; map p.223. Go through to the courtyard on the ground floor of the eighteenth-century palace for the menswear collection to find a space dedicated to enhancing your shopping experience. There's an old-fashioned barber's, a small grooming centre and the *Bar Martini*, popular with beautiful people of all nationalities. All Mon–Sat 10am–7pm.

Gianni Versace Via Montenapoleone 11 ⓣ02 7600 8528, ⓦversace.com; ⓜMontenapoleone or ⓜSan Babila; map p.223. Unusually for Versace, this store, spread over five storeys, is nothing if not understated. The clean lines provide a perfect backdrop for the luxurious ostentation of the clothes, shoes and accessories in glinting gold and swirling colours. Mon–Sat 10.30am–7.30pm, Sun 11am–7pm.

Giorgio Armani Via Manzoni 31 ⓣ02 7231 8600, ⓦarmani.com; ⓜMontenapoleone; map p.223. This temple to all things Giorgio is more a mini-shopping centre than a shop. There are boutiques for all his ranges – women's- and menswear, furnishings and houseware – accompanied by *Armani Café*, a relaxed pavement café, and *Nobu*, a pricey, high-tech Japanese restaurant that's been one of the places in town to be seen for years. With a hotel, chic bar, book corner selling design and coffee-table books, a florists' and a chocolate counter offering monogrammed sugary confections, you really won't need to spend your money anywhere else in town. Mon–Sat 10am–8pm, Sun 11am–7.30pm.

Gucci Via Montenapoleone 5–7 & Galleria Vittorio Emanuele II ⓣ02 771 1271, ⓦgucci.com; ⓜMontenapoleone or ⓜSan Babila; map p.223. Every desirable fashion item imaginable is available in the warren of sleek showrooms in Montenapoleone, while the newer store in the Galleria Vittorio Emanuele II has the *Gucci café*, where you can get a freshly squeezed fruit juice or a coffee accompanied by an exquisite chocolate – sporting the famous GG symbol, of course – all in an atmosphere of elegant minimalism. Daily 10am–7pm.

Prada Galleria Vittorio Emanuele II 62 ⓣ02 8721 1450; womenswear, Via Montenapoleone 8 ⓣ02 7602 0273; ⓦprada.com; ⓜDuomo; map p.223. The original Prada store, complete with walnut display cabinets and swirling staircase, dating from 1913, stands on a side corner in the centre of the Galleria Vittorio Emanuele II. Mon–Sat 10am–7.30pm, Sun 10am–7pm.

Trussardi Piazza della Scala 5 ⓣ02 8068 8242, ⓦtrussardi.com; ⓜDuomo; map p.223. A spacious boutique spread across three floors. The uber-chic *Trussardi Alla Scala* café occupies the ground floor, serving some of the best cocktails in town. On the floor above the soft leather bags and crisp home lines is the formal Michelin-starred restaurant, and one floor higher still is a gallery space that's worth checking out for contemporary art and fashion exhibitions. Daily 10am–8pm.

FACTORY STORES

D-Magazine Via Manzoni 44 ⓣ02 3651 4365, ⓦdmag.eu; ⓜmontenapoleone; map p.223. Rails of different designer labels for both men and women, squished next to the golden rectangle; discounts on major fashion brands such as Dior, Gucci and Grifoni from last season, including purses, handbags, shoes, necklaces, earrings and other fashion accessories. Daily 10am–7.30pm.

Il Salvagente Via Bronzetti 16, 15min east of San Babila by bus ⓣ02 7611 0328 ⓦsalvagente.com; bus #60 or #62; map 220. The *grande dame* of Milan's outlet stores where, with a little rummaging, you can bag a designer label for around a third of its original price. Mon 3–7.30pm, Tues–Sat 10am–7.30pm, Sun 11–2pm & 3–7pm.

DESIGN AND FURNITURE

B&B Italia Via Durini 14 ⓣ02 764 441, ⓦbebitalia.com; ⓜSan Babila; map p.223. International name that specializes in stylish contemporary furniture by big names in Italian modern design. Mon 3–7pm, Tues–Sat 10am–7pm.

Cassina Via Durini 16 ⓣ02 7602 0745, ⓦcassina.com; ⓜSan Babila; map p.223. The showroom of this legendary Milanese company, which worked with all the greats in Italian design in the 1950s, is always worth a visit for both new designs and its range of twentieth-century design classics including Eames, De Stijl and Rennie Mackintosh chairs. Mon–Sat 10am–7pm.

De Padova Via Santa Cecilia 7 ⓣ02 777 201, ⓦdepadova.com; ⓜSan Babila; map p.223. Two floors of elegant own-brand furniture and houseware artfully displayed in a stylish showroom including collections by Vico Magistretti and Patricia Urquiola. Mon 10am–6pm, Tues–Sat 10am–7pm.

Driade Via Borgogna 8 ⓣ 02 799 957, ⓦ driade.com; ⓜ Montenapoleone; map p.223. A wonderful multi-brand store with its own designs, as well as work by designers like Ron Arad and Philippe Starck. The collection includes furniture, tableware, kitchen and bathroom accessories. Mon–Sat 10am–7pm.

FOOD AND DRINK

Cotti Via Solferino 42 ⓣ 02 2900 1096, ⓦ enotecacotti.it; ⓜ Moscova; map p.220. A treasure-trove of wines and liqueurs from across the country is accompanied by an array of gourmet treats – both sweet and savoury. Tues–Sat 9am–1pm & 3–8pm.

Peck Via Spadari 9 ⓣ 02 802 3161, ⓦ www.peck.it; ⓜ Duomo; map p.223. Three storeys of top-priced Italian delicacies, from olive oil and home-made chocolate to mouthwatering prosciutto, cheeses, and an impressive wine cellar. There's also a café on the first floor and a swish cocktail bar and restaurant round the corner at Via Cantù 3. Mon 3–8pm, Tues–Sat 9am–8pm, Sun 10am–5pm.

DIRECTORY

Consulates Australia, Via Borgogna 2 ⓣ 02 7767 4200, ⓦ italy.embassy.gov.au; Canada, Piazza Cavour 3 ⓣ 02 6269 4238, ⓦ canadainternational.gc.ca; Ireland, Piazza San Pietro in Gessate 2 ⓣ 02 5518 7569, ⓦ dfa.ie; New Zealand, Via Terraggio, 17 ⓣ 02 7217 0001, ⓦ mfat.govt.nzSouth Africa, Vicolo San Giovanni sul Muro 4 ⓣ 02 885 8581, ⓦ dirco.gov.za; UK, Via San Paolo 7 ⓣ 02 723 001, ⓦ gov.uk; US, Via Principe Amadeo 2/10 ⓣ 02 290 351, ⓦ it.usembassy.gov.

Exchange Banks usually offer the best rates, but out of normal banking hours you can change money at the Forexchange at Stazione Centrale (daily 7.30am–10.30pm). The airports all have exchange facilities.

Hospital There is a 24hr casualty service at the Ospedale Maggiore Policlinico, Via Francesco Sforza 35 (ⓣ 02 55 031, ⓦ policlinico.mi.it), a short walk from Piazza del Duomo. Emergency ⓣ 112.

Left luggage Stazione Centrale (daily 6am–11pm; €6/5hr, then small increments per hour).

Pharmacy The pharmacy in the Stazione Centrale has English-speaking assistants; on Piazza del Duomo try Carlo Erba. Rotas for all night pharmacies are published in *Corriere della Sera*, and are usually posted on *farmacia* doors.

Police ⓣ 112. Headquarters at Via Fatebenefratelli 11 (ⓣ 02 62 261), near the Pinacoteca di Brera.

Post office Via Cordusio 4 (Mon–Fri 8.30am–7pm, Sat 8.30am–12.30pm). Stamps for letters and postcards can be bought from the many *tabacchini* around the city.

Southern Lombardy

Strung across the broad plain of the River Po in southern Lombardy, a belt of well-preserved ancient towns offers a handful of spectacular masterpieces of art and architecture against the backdrop of comfortable provincial life.

Just outside the ancient town of **Pavia**, the fabulous **Certosa monastery complex** makes an attractive introduction to this part of Lombardy. To the east, **Cremona**, birthplace of the violin, has a neat, well-preserved centre that's worth popping in to visit. **Mantua**, on the eastern edge of the region, is Lombardy's most visually appealing city: the powerful Gonzaga family ruled for three hundred years from an extravagant ducal palace and later the Palazzo Te, on the outskirts of the city, which contains some of the finest (and most steamily erotic) fresco-painting of the entire Renaissance.

Certosa di Pavia

April: Tues–Sun 9–11.30am & 2.30–5.30pm; May–Sept 9–11.30am & 2.30–6pm; Oct–March Tues–Sat 9–11.30am & 2.30–4.30pm, Sun 9am–11.30am & 2.30–5pm • Free • ⓦ certosadipavia.it

Among the rice fields around 40km south of Milan, one of the most extravagant monasteries in Europe, the **Certosa di Pavia** (Charterhouse of Pavia), was commissioned by the Duke of Milan, Galeazzo II Visconti in 1396 as the family mausoleum. Visconti intended the church here to resemble Milan's late-Gothic cathedral and the same architects and craftsmen worked on the construction. It took a century to build; by the time it was finished tastes had changed (and the Viscontis had been replaced by the Sforzas). As a work of art the monastery is one of the most important testimonies to the transformation from late-Gothic to Renaissance and Mannerist styles, but it also affords a wonderful insight into the lives and beliefs of the Carthusian monks.

CALCIO CRAZY

Milan has two rival football teams – **Inter Milan** and **AC Milan** – which share the G. Meazza or San Siro stadium, playing on alternate Sundays. In 1899 AC (Associazione Calcio or Football Association) Milan was founded by players from the Milan Cricket and Football Club. Eight years later, a splinter group broke away to form Inter in reaction to a ruling banning foreigners playing in the championships. Inter – or the Internationals – were traditionally supported by the middle classes, while AC Milan, with its socialist red stripe, claimed the loyalty of the city's working class. This distinction was blown apart in the mid-1980s when the ardent capitalist Silvio Berlusconi bought the ailing AC and revived its fortunes, leaving many an AC fan with a moral quandary. Their twice-yearly derbies are a highlight of the city's calendar and well worth experiencing live.

Tours There are hourly guided tours around Stadio San Siro stadium (Museum at Entrance 8; daily 9.30am–6pm; €7; tours €17 including museum entry; ⓣ 02 404 2432, ⓦ sansirotour.com; Ⓜ San Siro Stadio), which includes a visit to the club's museum. Match tickets can be bought here. You can also buy tickets for AC Milan matches on the team's website at ⓦ tickets.acmilan.com, while for Inter they're at ⓦ inter.it.

You can see the church unaccompanied, but to visit the rest of the monastery you need to join a **guided tour** of just under an hour (free but contributions welcomed), led by one of the monks released from the strict vow of silence. Tours run regularly – basically when enough people have gathered. They're in Italian, but well worth doing – even if you don't understand a word – as they allow you to visit the best parts of the monastery complex.

4

The church

The monastery lies at the end of a tree-lined avenue, part of a former Visconti hunting range that stretched all the way from Pavia's *castello*. Encircled by a high wall, the complex is entered through a central gateway bearing a motif that recurs throughout the monastery – "GRA-CAR" or "Gratiarum Carthusiae", a reference to the fact that the Carthusian monastery is dedicated to Santa Maria delle Grazie, who appears in numerous works of art in the church. Beyond the gateway is a gracious courtyard, with the seventeenth-century Ducal Palace on the right-hand side and outbuildings along the left. Rising up before you is the fantastical **facade** of the **church**, festooned with inlaid marble, twisted columns, statues and friezes. Despite more than a century's work by leading architects, the facade remains unfinished: the tympanum was never added, giving the church its stocky, truncated look.

The interior

Inside, the Gothic design of the church was a deliberate reference to Milan's Duomo, but it has a lighter, more joyous feel, with its painted ceiling, and light streaming in through the one hundred windows high up in the walls. The elaborate seventeenth-century gates to the transept and highly decorated altar, at the far end, are opened when a tour is about to start.

The sculptural highlights of the church lie in the two wings of the transept. In the centre of the north transept lies the stone **funerary monument** of the greatest of the dukes of Milan, Ludovico il Moro, and his wife Beatrice d'Este, neither of whom is actually buried here. The exquisite detail of the statue is an important document of sixteenth-century fashions with its tasselled latticework dress and glam-rock platform shoes. The south transept contains the magnificent **mausoleum** of the founder of the monastery, Gian Galeazzo Visconti, by Cristoforo Romano, including a carving of Gian Galeazzo presenting a model of the Certosa to the Virgin. Both he and his wife, Isabella di Valois, are buried here.

The monastery

Opposite the mausoleum is the door to the delightful **small cloister**, with fine terracotta decoration and a geometric garden around a fountain where monks shared the communal part of their lives, meeting here to pace the courtyard during their weekly ration of talking time. In the adjacent **refectory**, the monks would eat together in silence on Sundays and holy days; the Bible was read throughout the meal from the pulpit (with a hidden entrance in the panelling). The dining room is divided by a blind wall, which allowed the monastery to feed lay workers and guest pilgrims without compromising the rules of their closed order. Further on, the **great cloister** is stunning for its size and tranquillity. It is surrounded on three sides by the **monks' houses**, each consisting of two rooms, a chapel, a garden and a loggia, with a bedroom above. The hatches to the side of the entrances were designed to enable food to be passed through without any communication. The final call is the Certosa **shop**, stocked with honey, chocolate, souvenirs and the famous Chartreuse liqueur.

ARRIVAL AND DEPARTURE — CERTOSA DI PAVIA

By train The most efficient way of travelling here is on the S13 train line operated by Trenord, which connects a number of stations, including Milano Porta Garibaldi, Milano Repubblica and Milano Porta Venezia to the Certosa di Pavia (every 30min; 37min). Turn left out of the station and walk around the Certosa walls until you reach the monastery entrance – a 15min walk.

4

Cremona

A cosy provincial town in the middle of the Po plain, **CREMONA** is renowned for its **violins**. Ever since Andrea Amati established the first violin workshop here in 1566, followed by his son, grandson (Nicolò) and pupils Guarneri and – most famously – **Antonio Stradivari** (1644–1737), Cremona has been a focus for the instrument. Today the city is home to an internationally famous school of violin making, as well as the excellent **Museo del Violino**.

Cremona has some fine Renaissance and medieval buildings, and its cobbled streets make for some pleasant wandering, but it's a modest sort of place: target it as a half-day trip from Bergamo or Milan, en route towards the rich pickings of Mantua.

Piazza del Comune

At the centre of Cremona is the splendid **Piazza del Comune**, dominated by monumental architecture. In the northeast corner looms the Romanesque **Torrazzo** (daily 10am–1pm & 2.30–6pm; €5, joint ticket with Baptistry €6), at 112m one of Italy's tallest brick medieval towers, built in the mid-thirteenth century and bearing a fine Renaissance clock dating from 1583. The belltower houses the **Museo Verticale del Torrazzo**, which is dedicated to the measurement of time, while its 502 steps can be climbed for excellent views.

Adjacent to the Torrazzo stands the **Duomo** (Mon–Sat 10.30am–noon & 3.30–5.30pm, Sun 12–12.30pm & 3–5pm; free), connected to it by way of a Renaissance loggia. The Duomo's huge facade, made up of classical, Romanesque and fancy Gothic elements, focuses on a rose window from 1274. The interior is dimly lit, marked by the dark stone of its piers, and covered in complex sixteenth-century frescoes, including a trompe l'oeil by Pordenone on the west wall showing the *Crucifixion* and *Deposition*. Also of note are the fifteenth-century pulpits, decorated with finely tortured reliefs.

The south side of Piazza del Comune features the octagonal **Baptistry** (daily 10am–1pm & 2.30–6pm; €3, joint ticket with Torrazzo €6) dating from the late twelfth century. Its vast bare-brick interior is rather severe, though lightened by the twin columns in each bay and a series of upper balconies.

RIZZOLI
RIZZOLI
RIZZOLI

Directly opposite the Duomo, the **Palazzo del Comune** (Mon–Sat 9am–6pm, Sun 10am–6pm; free), built in the thirteenth century, is a typical example of Lombard architecture. It houses the municipal administration and its halls display exhibitions of local painters and photographers.

Museo del Violino

Piazza Marconi 5 • Tues–Sun 10am–6pm • €7 • Ⓦ museodelviolino.org

Located in what was the School of Violin Making in the 1930s, the wonderful **Museo del Violino** houses a collection of priceless instruments, as well as an auditorium where recitals are regularly held. The museum traces the origins and history of violins and other stringed instruments, with some fine examples by Nicolò Amati, Antonio Stradivari and Giuseppe Guarneri del Gesù, plus a collection of tools used by Stradivari. For more violin-based activity, you can also visit the open studios of some of Cremona's violin-makers' **workshops**: the tourist office (see page 248) has details.

Museo Civico Ala Ponzone

Via Ugolani Dati 4 • Tues–Sun10am–5pm • Ⓦ musei.comune.cremona.it

A pleasant ten-minute stroll north of Piazza del Comune, the pilastered Palazzo Affaitati is home to the **Museo Civico Ala Ponzone**. Here, you can see some fine displays of Cremonese art, plus an important collection of guitars and mandolins donated to the museum in 2013 by Carlo Alberto Carutti.

4

Church of San Sigismondo

Largo Bianca Maria Visconti • Daily 8am–noon & 3–5.30pm, although hours vary; call ahead to check • Ⓣ 0372 801 700 • Catch bus #D or #E from Piazza Roma

On the outskirts of Cremona, the **church of San Sigismondo**, built in the fifteenth century, boasts some of Italy's best Mannerist decor. Its highlights include Camillo Boccaccino's soaring apse fresco and Giulio Campi's *Annunciation*, in which Gabriel floats in mid-air.

ARRIVAL, INFORMATION AND GETTING AROUND — CREMONA

By train Cremona's train station is on Via Dante, a 10min walk north of the main Piazza del Comune, and linked to Piazza Roma in the centre by bus #D or #E.

Destinations Mantua (8 daily; 1hr); Milan (every 2hr; 1hr 10min).

By bike Cremona has a bike sharing system (Ⓦ comune.cremona.it/node/426145); a 24hr subscription costs €8.

Guided tours Target Turismo (Ⓦ targetturismo.com) organizes a range of excellent cultural tours around the city.

Tourist office The tourist office, at Piazza del Comune 5, opposite the Torrazzo (Jan, Feb, July & Aug daily 10am–4.30pm; March–June & Sept–Dec daily 10am–6pm; Ⓣ 0372 407 081, Ⓦ turismocremona.it) has details of classical concerts around town, as well as information about the cultural programmes organized by A. Ponchielli Theatre, Corso Vittorio Emanuele II 52, including theatre, ballet, opera and concerts. It can also arrange visits to the theatre on request.

ACCOMMODATION

Astoria Via Bordigallo Domenico 19 Ⓣ 0372 461 616 Ⓦ hotelastoriacremona.com. A central three-star hotel just a few steps away from the cathedral offering modern en-suite rooms with LED TVs; staff are friendly and welcoming. **€90**

B&B Il Violino Via Francisco Arisi 3 Ⓣ 0372 462 030, Ⓦ ilviolinocremona.it. This pleasant B&B has three well-appointed apartments sleeping up to four, each with a kitchenette – the owner stocks the fridge with breakfast ingredients before guests' arrival. **€100**

Locanda Torriani Via Janello Torriani 7 Ⓣ 0372 30 017, Ⓦ locandatorriani.it. A friendly *locanda* and restaurant offering spacious well-equipped apartments in a lovely seventeenth-century building. There's an excellent restaurant too, whose courtyard has incredible views of the Torrazzo. **€120**

EATING AND DRINKING

Numerous cosy *osterie* serve Cremona's specialities: *gran bollito cremonese* – a mixture of boiled meats, served with *mostarda di Cremona*, fruit suspended in a sweet mustard syrup. The excellent *gastronomie* around Corso Garibaldi

make good places to put together a picnic.

★ **Cascina** Lago Scuro, Stago Lombardo 0372 57 487. A wonderful seventeenth-century farmhouse serving superb local cuisine in a dining room with high ceilings. During the week, the restaurant is only open for groups of ten or more, although there are occasional openings – call to check. Set menu €33. Book ahead. Sat 7–10.30pm, Sun noon–2pm.

Hosteria 700 Piazza Gallina 1 0372 36 175, hosteria700.com A lovely *osteria* with original eighteenth-century frescoes decorating the walls. It specializes in delicious home-made pastas and risotto dishes (there are over twenty types), including the signature speck ham, scamorza cheese and rocket. Mon 12.30–2.30pm. Wed–Sun 12.30–2.30pm & 7.30–10.30pm.

Osteria La Sosta Via Sicardo 9 0372 456 656, osterialasosta.it. A pleasant spot to try some local specialities including *gnocchi vecchia Cremona* (oven-baked gnocchi with salami); in winter there are plenty of hearty dishes such as *cotechino* (pork sausage) served with sweet and sour cabbage and mustard. *Primi* €12, *secondi* €15. Tues–Sat noon–2pm & 7.30–10pm, Sun noon–2pm.

Mantua (Mantova)

Aldous Huxley called it the most romantic city in the world. With a skyline of domes and towers rising above its three encircling lakes, **MANTUA** (Mantova) is undeniably evocative. This was where Romeo heard of Juliet's supposed death, and where Verdi set *Rigoletto*. Its history is one of equally operatic plots, most of them acted out by the **Gonzaga**, one of Renaissance Italy's richest and most powerful families, who ruled the town for three centuries. Its cobbled squares retain a medieval aspect, and there are two splendid palaces: the **Palazzo Ducale**, containing Mantegna's stunning fresco of the Gonzaga family and court, and **Palazzo Te**, whose frescoes by the flashy Mannerist Giulio Romano encompass steamy erotica and illusionistic fantasy. Mantua's lakes, and the flat surrounding plain, offer numerous boat cruises and cycling routes.

4

The centre of Mantua is made up of four attractive squares, each connected to the next. Lively Piazza Mantegna is overlooked by the massive **Basilica di Sant'Andrea**. Beside it is the lovely Piazza delle Erbe, with fine arcades facing the medieval **Rotonda** church. To the north, through medieval passageways and across Piazza Broletto, the long, cobbled slope of Piazza Sordello is dominated by the **Palazzo Ducale**, the fortress and residence of the Gonzaga, packed with Renaissance art. Mantua's other great palace stands in its own gardens 1.5km south of the historic centre – **Palazzo Te**, adorned with sensational frescoes.

Basilica di Sant'Andrea

Piazza Mantegna • Daily 8am–noon & 3–7pm • santandreainmantova.it

Dominating **Piazza Mantegna** – a wedge-shaped open space at the end of the arcaded shopping thoroughfares of Corso Umberto and Via Roma – is the facade of Leon Battista Alberti's church of **Sant'Andrea**, an unfinished basilica that says a lot about the ego of Lodovico II Gonzaga, who commissioned it in 1470. He felt that the existing medieval church was neither impressive enough to represent the splendour of his state nor large enough to hold the droves of people who packed in every Ascension Day to see the holy relic of Christ's blood which had been found on the site. Lodovico brought in the court architect, Luca Fancelli, to oversee Alberti's plans. There was a bitchy rivalry between the two, and when, on one of his many visits, Alberti fell and hurt a testicle, Fancelli gleefully told him: "God lets men punish themselves in the place where they sin." Work started in earnest after Alberti's death in 1472, and took more than two decades to complete.

The Classical **facade** is focused on an immense triumphal arch supported on giant pilasters. **Inside**, the vast, column-free space is roofed with one large barrel-vault, echoing the facade. The octagonal balustrade at the crossing stands above the crypt where the holy relic is kept in two vases, copies of originals designed by Cellini and stolen by the Austrians in 1846; to see them, ask the sacristan. The painter Mantegna is buried in the first chapel on the left, his tomb topped with a bust of the artist that is

said to be a self-portrait. The wall-paintings in the chapel were designed by Mantegna and executed by students, Correggio being one.

Piazza delle Erbe

Beside Sant'Andrea, Piazza Mantegna gives way to atmospheric **Piazza delle Erbe**, with a small daily market and cafés sheltering in the arcades below the thirteenth-century **Palazzo della Ragione.** Sunk below the present street level is the eleventh-century **Rotonda di San Lorenzo** (Mon–Fri 10am–1pm & 3–6pm, Sat & Sun 10am–6pm), which was partially demolished in the sixteenth century and used as a courtyard by the surrounding houses. Rebuilt in 1908 and beautifully restored in recent years, it still contains traces of twelfth- and thirteenth-century frescoes.

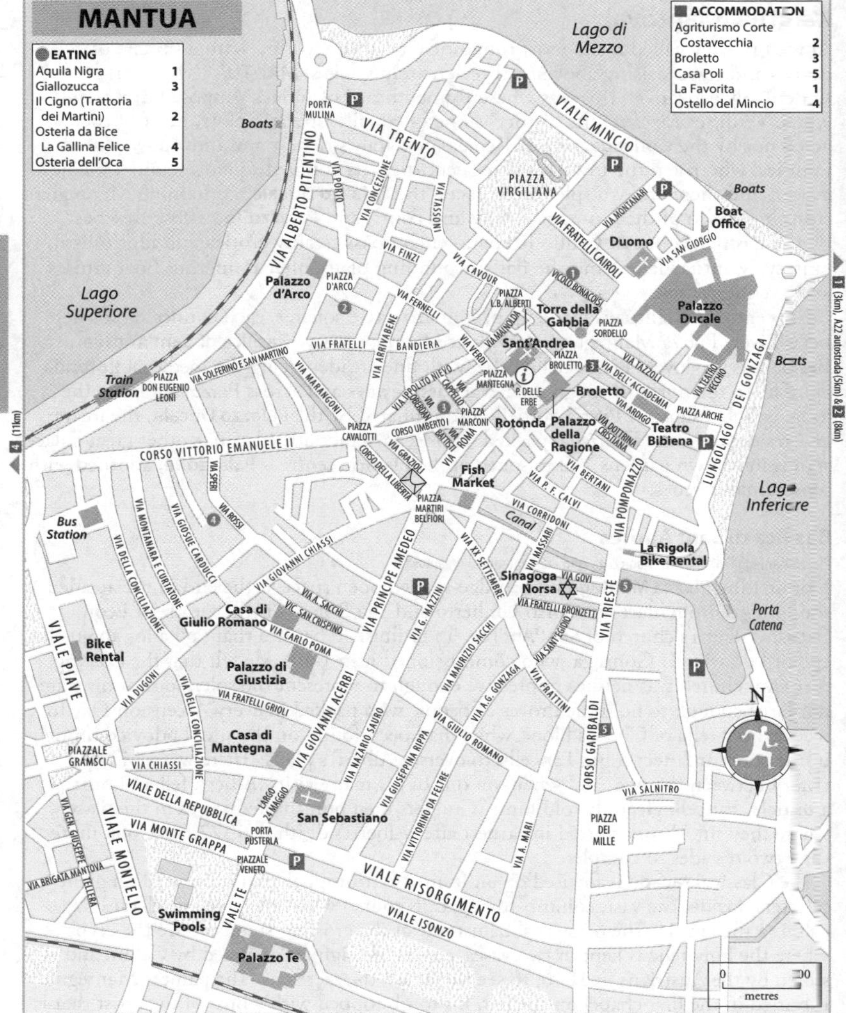

THE GONZAGA

At the time of the coup of 1328, when **Luigi Gonzaga** seized Mantua from the Bonacolsi, the **Gonzaga** family were wealthy local landowners living outside Mantua on vast estates with an army of retainers. Luigi nominated himself Captain of the People, a role which quickly became hereditary, eventually growing to that of marquis.

Mantua's renaissance began in 1459, when a visiting pope complained that it was muddy, marshy and riddled with fever. This spurred his host, **Lodovico II Gonzaga**, to give the city a face-lift, ranging from paving the squares and repainting the shops to engaging **Andrea Mantegna** as court artist and calling in the prestigious architectural theorist **Leon Battista Alberti** to design the monumental church of Sant'Andrea, one of the most influential buildings of the early Renaissance. Later, Lodovico's grandson, **Francesco II** (1466–1519), swelled the family coffers by hiring himself out as a mercenary – money his wife, **Isabella d'Este**, spent amassing a prestigious collection of paintings, sculpture and objets d'art.

Under Isabella's son, **Federico II**, Gonzaga fortunes reached their height; his marriage in 1531 to the heiress of the duchy of Monferrato procured a ducal title for the family, while he continued the policy of self-glorification by commissioning an out-of-town villa – the **Palazzo Te** – for himself and his mistress. Federico's descendants were for the most part less colourful characters, one notable exception being **Vincenzo I**, whose debauchery and corruption provided the inspiration for Verdi's licentious duke in *Rigoletto*. After Vincenzo's death in 1612, the then-bankrupt court was forced to sell many of the family treasures to Charles I of England (many are still in London's Victoria and Albert Museum), just three years before the arrival of the Habsburgs.

Piazza Broletto

At the northern end of Piazza delle Erbe, a passage leads under the red-brick **Broletto**, or medieval town hall, into the smaller **Piazza Broletto**, where you can view two reminders of how "criminals" were treated under the Gonzagas. The bridge to the right has metal rings embedded in its vault, to which victims were chained by the wrists, before being hauled up by a pulley and suspended in mid-air; and on your far left – actually on the corner of Piazza Sordello – the tall, medieval **Torre della Gabbia** has a cage attached in which prisoners were displayed.

Teatro Bibiena

Via Accademia 47 • Tues–Fri 10am–1pm & 3–6pm, Sat & Sun 10am–6pm • €2

A diversion up Via Accademia leads to the Baroque **Teatro Bibiena**, a splendid, intimate theatre, its curved walls lined with boxes. Mozart gave the inaugural concert here on January 16, 1770, a few days before his fourteenth birthday. His father was fulsome in his praise for the building, calling it "the most beautiful thing in its genre that I have ever seen".

The Duomo

Piazza Sordello • Daily 7am–noon & 3–7pm • Free

Northeast of Piazza Broletto, **Piazza Sordello** is a large, sombre, rectangular square, headed by the Baroque facade of the **Duomo**. Flanked by touristy pavement cafés and grim crenellated palaces built by the Bonacolsi (the Gonzagas' predecessors) the Duomo conceals a rich interior, designed by Giulio Romano after the church had been gutted by fire in 1545.

Palazzo Ducale

Piazza Sordello • Tues–Sun 8.15am–7.15pm, last entry 6.20pm • €12, audioguides €5 • For conservation reasons, access to the Camera degli Sposi is limited to 1500 people a day; from mid-March to mid-June and Sept to mid-Oct, it is advisable to book a timed slot for admission to this room in advance on T 041 241 1897 (press 1 for English-speaking operators; Mon–Fri 9am–6pm, Sat 9am–2pm) or via the website W www.ducalemantova.org – booking costs €1 extra • W mantovaducale.beniculturali.it

The Palazzo del Capitano and Magna Domus form the core of the **Palazzo Ducale**, an enormous complex that was once the largest palace in Europe. Covering 34,000 square

metres, in its heyday it had a population of more than a thousand; when it was sacked by the Habsburgs in 1630 eighty carriages were needed to carry away the two thousand works of art contained in its five hundred rooms.

Rooms 1–14

Visits to the Palazzo Ducale start in the Corte Vecchia, the oldest wing of the palace. In the **Sala del Morone** (room 1) hangs a painting from 1494 by Domenico Morone showing the expulsion of the Bonacolsi from Piazza Sordello, with the Duomo sporting its old, Gothic facade (replaced in the eighteenth century). In the **Sala del Pisanello** (room 3) are the fragments of a half-finished fresco by Pisanello, discovered in 1969 behind two layers of plaster.

The splendid Neoclassical **Sala degli Specchi** (Hall of Mirrors; room 6) was originally an open loggia, bricked up in 1773; the barrel-vaulted ceiling holds a fresco depicting teams of horses being driven from Night to Day. In the **Sala degli Arcieri** (Hall of Archers; room 7), a huge canvas by Rubens shows the Gonzaga family of 1604 seated comfortably in the presence of the Holy Trinity; look out for Vincenzo with his handlebar moustache. The picture was originally part of a huge triptych, but Napoleonic troops carried off two-thirds of it in 1797 (one part is now in Antwerp, the other in Nancy) and chopped the remaining third into saleable chunks of portraiture; some gaps remain. Around the room is a curious frieze of horses, glimpsed behind curtains. Beyond the **Sala del Labirinto** (room 9), named for the maze on its painted and gilded wooden ceiling, the **Sala di Amore e Psiche** (room 11) is an intimate space with a wooden floor and an eighteenth-century *tondo* of Cupid and Psyche in the ceiling.

Rooms 15–17: Camera degli Sposi

From here follow signs along corridors, down stairs and over a moat into the fourteenth-century **Castello di San Giorgio**, which contains the palace's principal treasure: Mantegna's frescoes of the Gonzaga family in the **Camera degli Sposi** (also called the Camera Picta) in room 17. Painted between 1465 and 1474, they're naturalistic pieces of work, giving a vivid impression of the Marquis Lodovico, his wife Barbara and their family, and of the relationships between them. In the main fresco Lodovico discusses a letter with a courtier while his wife looks on; their youngest daughter leans on her mother's lap, about to bite into an apple, while an older son and daughter look towards the door, where an ambassador from another court is being welcomed. The other fresco, divided into three sections, shows Lodovico welcoming his son Francesco back from Rome. In the background are the Holy Roman Emperor Frederick III and the king of Denmark. Don't forget to look up: the ceiling features another nice piece of trompe l'oeil, in which two women, peering down from a balustrade, have balanced a tub of plants on a pole and appear to be on the verge of letting it tumble into the room.

Rooms 18–37: Corte Nuova and Corte Vecchia

Next comes the sixteenth-century **Corte Nuova** wing, designed by Giulio Romano for Federico II Gonzaga. After several formal audience rooms you come to the **Sala di Troia** (room 22), decorated with Romano's brilliantly colourful scenes from the *Iliad* and *Aeneid*. The adjacent **Galleria dei Marmi** (room 23), with delicate floral and wildlife motifs, looks out over the Cortile della Cavallerizza (Courtyard of the Riding School). Along the courtyard's long side runs the immense **Galleria della Mostra** (room 24), once hung with paintings by Titian, Caravaggio, Brueghel and others, all now dispersed; in their place are 64 Roman marble busts. Push on through the smaller rooms and up more stairs to the stunning **Sala dello Zodiaco** (room 33), whose late sixteenth-century ceiling is spangled with stars and constellations. The adjoining Rococo **Sala dei Fiumi** (room 34) features an elaborate painted allegory of Mantua's six rivers, flanked by two over-the-top stucco-and-mosaic fountains.

Save some wonder for rooms 35–37, beside the Sala dello Zodiaco. These comprise the **Stanze degli Arazzi**, three rooms (and a small chapel) altered in the eighteenth century to house nine sixteenth-century Flemish tapestries of exceptional virtuosity, depicting stories from the Acts of the Apostles, made from Raphael's cartoons for the Sistine Chapel (now in London's Victoria and Albert Museum).

South of the centre

South of the central squares, Giulio Romano's **Fish Market** – to the left off Piazza Martiri Belfiori – a short covered bridge over the river, is still used as a market building. Following Via Principe Amedeo south brings you to the **Casa di Giulio Romano**, off to the right at Via Poma 18, overshadowed by the monster-studded Palazzo di Giustizia. The house was meant to impress the sophisticated, who would have found the licence taken with the Classical architecture witty. A five-minute walk away on busy Via Acerbi stands the austere brick **Casa del Mantegna**, now a contemporary art space (hours and admission vary).

San Sebastiano

Largo Ventiquattro Maggio • Mid-March to mid-Nov Tues–Sun 10.30am–12.30pm & 3–5pm • €1.50

The church of **San Sebastiano**, the work of Alberti, is famous as the first Renaissance church to be built on a central Greek-cross plan, described as "curiously pagan" by Nikolaus Pevsner. Lodovico II's son was less polite: "I could not understand whether it was meant to turn out as a church, a mosque or a synagogue." The bare interior – now deconsecrated – is dedicated to Mantua's war dead.

4

Palazzo Te

Viale Te 13 • end of March–end of Oct Mon 1–7.30pm & Tues–Sun 9am–7.30pm (last entry 6.30pm); end of Oct–end of March Mon 1–6.30pm, Tues–Sun 9am–6.30pm, last entry 5.30pm • €12 • Ⓦ palazzote.it

A twenty-minute walk from the centre of Mantua, at the end of the long spine of Via Principe Amedeo and Via Acerbi, the **Palazzo Te** is the later of the city's two Gonzaga palaces, and equally compelling. Set in its own grounds, the *palazzo* was designed by Giulio Romano in the 1520s for playboy Federico Gonzaga and his mistress, Isabella Boschetti. It's the artist's greatest work and a renowned Renaissance pleasure dome – originally an island connected to the mainland by bridge, an ideal location for an amorous retreat away from Federico's wife and the restrictions of life in the Palazzo Ducale. Although the upstairs rooms display paintings and antiquities, the main reason for visiting is to see Giulio's amazing decorative scheme on the ground floor.

Camera del Sole and Sala dei Cavalli

A tour of the palace is like a voyage around Giulio's imagination, a sumptuous world where very little is what it seems. In the **Camera del Sole**, the sun and the moon are represented by a pair of horse-drawn chariots viewed from below, giving a fine array of human and equine bottoms on the ceiling. The **Sala dei Cavalli** holds portraits of prime specimens from the Gonzaga stud-farm (which was also on the island), standing before an illusionistic background in which simulated marble, fake pilasters and mock reliefs surround views of painted landscapes through nonexistent windows.

Sala di Amore e Psiche

The function of the **Sala di Amore e Psiche**, further on, is undocumented, but the graphically erotic frescoes, and the proximity to Federico's private quarters, are powerful clues. The ceiling paintings tell the story of Cupid and Psyche with more dizzying *sotto in su* ("from the bottom up") works by Giulio, while the walls are covered with orgiastic wedding-feast scenes, at which drunken gods in various states of undress are attended by a menagerie of real and mythical beasts. On one wall, Mars and Venus are climbing out of the bath together, their cave watered by a river-god lounging above

EXPLORING MANTUA: BIKES AND BOATS

Several companies offer **cruises** on Mantua's lakes – bulges in the course of the River Mincio – and on the river itself down to its confluence with the Po, ranging from 1hr jaunts (around €10) up to full-day voyages as far as Ferrara and Venice (around €90/€140). All run daily but must be **booked in advance**: usually a day ahead, but sometimes an hour or so will do. The leading company is Motonavi Andes Negrini, whose ticket office is at Via San Giorgio 2 (T 0376 322 875, W www.motonaviandes.it), three minutes' walk from its jetty on Lago Inferiore, or try Navi Andes (T 0376 324 506, W naviandes.com), based at its jetty on Lago di Mezzo. Alternatives include the Barcaioli del Mincio (T 0376 349 292, W fiumemincio.it), local boatmen operating small craft upstream from Grazie di Curtatone, about 8km west of Mantua.

Many of the boats accept bikes, so you can make a great day-trip – a morning on the boat, a picnic lunch at, say, Rivalta, then a gentle cycle ride back in the afternoon. The tourist office has a good map (also on its website) detailing cycle routes, plus information on bus, boat and train combinations.

who is gushing with deliberately ambiguous liquid flowing from his beard, a vessel he's holding and his genitals. Other scenes show Olympia about to be raped by a half-serpentine Jupiter, and Pasiphae disguising herself as a cow in order to seduce a bull – all watched over by the giant Polyphemus, perched above the fireplace, clutching the pan-pipes with which he sang of his love for Galatea before murdering her lover.

4

Sala dei Giganti

Polyphemus and his fellow giants are revenged in the extraordinary **Sala dei Giganti** beyond – "the most fantastic and frightening creation of the whole Renaissance", according to the critic Frederick Hartt – showing the destruction of the giants by the gods. As if in some kind of advanced disaster movie, the destruction appears to be all around: cracking pillars, toppling brickwork and screaming giants, mangled and crushed by great chunks of architecture, appearing to crash down into the room. Stamp your feet and you'll discover another parallel to modern cinema – the sound effects that Giulio created by turning the room into an echo chamber.

ARRIVAL AND INFORMATION — MANTUA

By train The train station is a 10min walk west of the centre. Destinations Bologna (2 daily; 1hr 35min); Milan (9 daily; 1hr 50min); Modena (hourly; 45min); Verona (hourly; 50min).

By bus Buses pull in alongside the train station, although services from Verona drop off first in the more convenient Piazza Sordello. Destinations Brescia (every 2hr; 1hr 40min); Milan (1 daily; 2hr 15min); Peschiera (hourly; 1hr 10min).

Tourist office Piazza Mantegna 6, on the corner of Portici Broletto (Mon 9am–1.30pm & 2.30–4pm, Tues–Sun 9am–1.30pm & 2.30–6pm; Oct–April closes at 5pm; T 0376 432 432, W turismo.mantova.it).

GETTING AROUND

By bike Although Mantua is small enough to cover on foot – the walk south to Palazzo Te is just 20min –it's also a great place to explore by bike (see above). The best rental places are Mantua Bike (T 348 415 5679, W mantuabike.it) and Mantova Bike Experience (T 338 120 8689, W mantovabikexperience.com) which run a drop-off bike service and organize guided bike tours of the local area

By bus Bus #CC runs along a circular route linking the train station, the central squares and Palazzo Te.

ACCOMMODATION

Agriturismo Corte Costavecchia Via Cavallare 11, Strada Ghisiolo, San Giorgio di Mantova T 0376 248 812, W costavecchia.it; map p.250. Dating from the fifteenth century, this lovely agriturismo 10km northeast of Mantova was once a convent; it offers warm and welcoming rustic rooms in a pleasant rural setting, and has a very good restaurant serving local specialities. €99

Broletto Via Accademia 1 T 0376 326 784, W hotelbroletto.com; map p.250. A comfortable hotel in the heart of the old town with attractive rooms, if a bit small;

all are en suite, most with showers. **€110**

Casa Poli Corso Garibaldi 32 ☎0376 288 170, hotelcasapoli.it; map p.250. This friendly design hotel offers comfortable, stylish rooms with parquet flooring and walls decorated with black-and-white photos. Breakfast is served in the courtyard in warmer months, and the jovial staff can advise on activities in and around the city. **€160**

La Favorita Via S. Cognetti de Martiis 1 ☎0376 254 711, hotellafavorita.it; map p.250. In an unusual location by a shopping centre on the northeastern outskirts of town, this hotel is a pleasant surprise, offering comfortable modern rooms and efficient service. Bus #12 connects it to the city centre. **€160**

Ostello del Mincio Via Porto 23, Rivalta ☎340 930 0509, ostellodelmincio.it; map p.250. Pleasant hostel 10km west of town, in a sleepy village on the River Mincio, with boat trips plus canoes and bicycles to rent. It stands 5km from Castellucchio train station (on the Cremona–Mantua line), and the hourly bus #13 (Mantua–Asola; apam.it) stops outside. There are double and family rooms as well as dorms. Dorms **€20**, doubles **€50**

EATING

Mantua has plenty of excellent, reasonably priced restaurants, many serving local specialities like *spezzatino di Mantova* (donkey stew), *agnoli in brodo* (pasta stuffed with cheese and sausage in broth) or the delicious *tortelli di zucca* (sweet pumpkin-filled pasta).

Aquila Nigra Vicolo Bonacolsi 4 ☎0376 327 180, aquilanigra.it; map p.250. A formal restaurant housed in an elegant *palazzo* just off Piazza Sordello, serving delicious seasonal dishes complemented by an impressive wine list. The fish and, especially, seafood are highly regarded. Menus are €70/€80. There's also a contemporary bistro next door with a shorter menu and lower prices. Tues–Sat noon–2pm & 8–10pm, Sun noon–2pm.

★ **Giallozucca** Corte dei Sogliari 4 ☎335 686 9686, giallozucca.it; map p.250. The walls of this restaurant are decorated with old Beatles' record sleeves; wine bottles line shelves, while books pour over a piano at the front of the dining room. The cuisine changes regularly, and is exceptionally creative and very reasonably priced, too. *Primi* €10, *secondi* €15. Thurs 7.30–10pm, Fri–Tues 12.30–2.30pm & 7.30–10pm.

Il Cigno (Trattoria dei Martini) Piazza d'Arco 1 ☎0376 327 101 ristoranteilcignomantova.it; map p.250. Wonderful restaurant occupying a sixteenth-century mansion in a quiet corner away from the centre, with seating in a pleasant open-air courtyard. Choose from the seasonal menu, which includes tasty *tortelli di zucca* with *amaretti*. Service is discreet yet welcoming. Expect to pay around €80/person. Wed–Sun 12.15–2pm & 7.30–9.30pm.

Osteria da Bice La Gallina Felice Via Carbonati 4/6 ☎0376 288 368; map p.250. A short walk from the train station, this lovely little *osteria* serves a great-value weekday lunch for about €10 in a welcoming setting; there's also seating in an outdoor courtyard. Tues–Sat 12.15–2.30pm & 8–10pm, Sun 12.15–2.30pm.

★ **Osteria dell'Oca** Via Trieste 10 ☎0376 327 171, osteriadelloca.it; map p.250. A laidback *osteria* with a cosy and atmospheric interior that serves tasty home-made Mantuan dishes; the traditional *risotto alla mantovana* with sausage and the *tortelli di zucca* (both €12) are particularly good, and are served in a copper pan. Wed–Mon noon–2.30pm & 7.30–10pm; closed Sun eve.

4

Northern Lombardy: lakes and mountains

"One can't describe the beauty of the **Italian lakes**, nor would one try if one could." Henry James's sentiment hasn't stopped generations of writers producing reams of purple prose in the attempt. Yet, in truth, the Lakes just about deserve it: their beauty is extravagant, and it's not surprising that the most romantic and melodramatic of Italy's opera composers – Verdi, Rossini and Bellini – rented villas here in which to work. British and German Romantic poets also enthused about the Lakes, and in doing so planted them firmly in northern-European imaginations. The result is an influx every summer of tourists from cooler climes, come to savour the Italian dream and to take gulps at what Keats called "the beaker of the warm south".

Garda is the largest lake, and one of the best centres in Europe for windsurfing and sailing. It is also visually stunning, especially in its mountainous northern stretches – yet **Como** matches (or, some say, betters) it, with forested slopes rising directly from the water's edge. On both lakes, the luxuriance of the waterfront vegetation is equalled by the opulence of the local villas and *palazzi*; both also offer good hiking in the mountainous hinterland.

GETTING AROUND THE LAKES

Lakes Garda, Como and Maggiore are all well served by ferries and hydrofoils, which dock at jetties that are usually conveniently positioned on the main lakeside piazzas: travelling by water makes a lot more sense than struggling through lakeside traffic. All three also have useful **car ferry** routes across the centre of the lakes.

For **timetables and fares** covering all three lakes, check Ⓦ navigazionelaghi.it or consult the posters displayed at every lakeside jetty (and local tourist offices). Prices aren't expensive – the two-hour voyage from Como to Bellagio is €10.40, for example, while it costs €8.60 to take a small car across Lake Como from Bellagio to Cadenabbia – and there are good-value day-passes available, with some discounts for children and EU citizens over 65.

Trains serve a handful of points on the lakes, and **buses** run up and down the shores. Tourist offices can advise about routes and timings. Public transport between the lakes is not very good – you're probably better off renting your own car if you're planning on exploring more than one lake.

Further west, **Maggiore** is less popular yet just as beautiful, with several sedate fin-de-siècle resorts. There are, however, some good walks, and superb formal gardens adorning Isola Bella and other grand villas. Nearby, the picture-postcard Orta San Giulio, the main village on **Lake Orta** – with its steepled offshore islet – is well worth a visit; while it's a popular spot for Milanese and Torinesi, it's still largely off the tourist radar for international travellers, and is a wonderfully romantic place to hole up.

Southwest of Garda, **Brescia** is a treat as a day-trip, while its neighbour **Bergamo** is a lovely place to stay, with an old walled hilltop quarter that ranks as one of the most alluring in Italy.

Note that in winter (Nov–Easter) most hotels around the lake close down and attractions may be shut.

Lake Maggiore

For generations of overland travellers, weary of journeying over the Alps, **LAKE MAGGIORE** (Lago Maggiore) has been a first taste of Italy: the sight of limpid blue waters, green hills and exotic vegetation is evidence of arrival in the warm south. With palms and oleanders lining the lakeside promenades and a peaceful, serene air, Maggiore – at 66km, Italy's longest lake – may not be somewhere for thrill-seekers, but it is seductively relaxing.

The majority of tourists head for the western shore, from where the sumptuous gardens and villas of the **Borromean islands** are within easy reach. The genteel old resort of **Stresa** is still a convenient base, linked by high-speed train to Milan (1hr) and by bus and boat to all points around the lake. Further north across the bay, pretty **Verbania** is also well connected by train, bus and ferry, while further north still, enchanting **Cannobio** – the last stop before Switzerland – is popular with families and a good place from which to explore Maggiore's hilly hinterland. The highlight of Maggiore's eastern shore is **Santa Caterina del Sasso**, a tiny monastery hewn out of the rock face, although there's also good **hiking** into the hills behind the more northern villages.

Stresa

The Maggiore of the tourist brochures begins at **STRESA**, whose popularity as a resort started in 1906, when the Simplon Tunnel opened, the final link in a chain of railways connecting Lake Geneva to Milan, and thus northern Europe to the Mediterranean. International trains, including the *Orient Express*, were routed through Stresa, which quickly became a holiday retreat for Europe's high society.

Today, Stresa is a bustling little place, but its greatest days have passed. Stroll the floral promenade, take in the lake views – which are worth coming for – head out to the islands, then retire to a waterside bench with an ice cream.

Parco Pallavicino

Via Sempione Sud 8 • March–Sept 9am–7pm (last entry 5.30pm); Oct & Nov 9am–6pm (last entry 4.30pm) • €11 • ⓣ 0323 933 478, ⓦ parcopallavicino.it

A 2km drive south of Stresa is **Parco Pallavicino**, a beautiful 44-acre park that harbours over 50 species of mammals and exotic birds. Once you enter the park from the lakefront road, a gorgeous shaded pathway zigzags up the hillside, bypassing the ground's nineteenth-century Neoclassical mansion and leading up to the farmhouse and gardens. It's a great spot for families, with a playground and petting farm with goats, deer, Shetland ponies and donkeys, along with enclosures home to zebras, owls, parrots and coati.

Mottarone

Separating Stresa from Lake Orta (see page 263) is the **Mottarone** mountain (1491m). Its wooded western slopes are a favourite destination for rambles and family outings, while the impressive views from the top stretch to Monte Rosa on the Swiss border. The mountain is accessed by a **cable car** (*funivia*), rising from the Carciano ferry stop, 750m north of Stresa (see ⓦ stresa-mottarone.it for details).

ARRIVAL AND INFORMATION — STRESA

By train Stresa is an hour from Milano Centrale on the fast trains heading for Switzerland; slower trains also run from Milano Centrale and Milano Porta Garibaldi. Taxis wait outside the station. Alternatively walk right to the crossroads, then left on Via Duchessa di Genova for 200m down to the lakefront.

Destinations Milano Centrale (approx. hourly; 55min).

By bus Buses from Milan Malpensa airport (Terminals 1 and 2) run along the western shore of Lake Maggiore between April and Oct (€12; booking essential 48hr in advance; ⓣ 0323 552 172, ⓦ safduemila.com). Buses connect Orta San Giulio to Stresa, dropping passengers off in the square by the *imbarcadero*.

Destinations Malpensa (April–Oct 6 daily; 1hr); Orta San Giulio (mid-June to early Sept 3 daily; 1hr).

By boat Stresa is at the centre of a network of boats serving the Borromean islands as well as ferries heading up and down the lake. Private boat-taxis also leave from Stresa for trips to the islands. The *imbarcadero* is on Piazza Marconi, across the main road from the village centre.

Destinations Arona (approx hourly; 1hr); Intra (every 30min; 55min); Isola Bella (every 30min; 10min); Isola Madre (every 30min; 30min); Pallanza (every 30min; 35min); Santa Caterina (hourly; 15min); Villa Taranto (every 30min; 45min).

Tourist office Piazza Marconi 16, beside the *imbarcadero* (daily 10am–12.30pm & 3–6.30pm; Nov–Feb closed Sat afternoon & Sun; ⓣ 0323 31 308, ⓦ stresaturismo.it & ⓦ distrettolaghi.it).

ACCOMMODATION AND EATING

Il Clandestino Via Rosmini 5 ⓣ 0323 30 399, ⓦ ristoranteilclandestino.com. The emphasis here is on fish – high-quality wild fish mostly from the Mediterranean that is expertly prepared by chef and owner Franco, who creates a new menu every two months or so. The pasta is all handmade, and there are a couple of meat-based dishes, too. *Primi* €20, *secondi* €25. Mon, Wed & Thurs 7–11pm, Fri, Sat & Sun 12.15–2pm & 7–11pm.

Grand Hotel de Iles Borromées Corso Umberto I 67 ⓣ 0323 938 938, ⓦ borromees.com. This lakeside palace dating from 1863 has hosted international royalty, celebrities and high society. Hemingway was a regular and the hotel features in *A Farewell to Arms*. Even if you're not staying, pop in to take a look at the pretty gardens – non-guests are welcome to take a stroll. **€308**

La Luna nel Porto Corso Italia 60 ⓣ 0323 934 466, ⓦ lalunanelporto.it. Ideal for self-caterers, this place features twelve spacious suites measuring between 35 and 70m2, each with its own balcony or terrace. The rooms are painted in different colours, and the superior suites with sofa beds can sleep up to four. The suites have their own kitchenettes, which can be used by guests staying for a minimum of five days. **€155**

Osteria Mercato Piazza Capucci 9 ⓣ 0323 346 245 ⓦ osteriamercatostresa.com. This great little *osteria* serves some of the best food in town. Expect nicely presented Italian dishes prepared using local seasonal ingredients, with the likes of suckling pig, duck leg and ravioli stuffed with veal, saffron and marrow sauce all featuring on the menu. *Primi* €11, *secondi* €15. Wed–Mon 11.30am–3pm & 7–11pm.

★ **La Palma** Lungolago Umberto I ⓣ 0323 32 401, ⓦ hlapalma.it. The real draw at this welcoming four-star hotel on the lakefront is the rooftop terrace with loungers and a large open-air jacuzzi; the glass-fronted gym, sauna and steam room all have wonderful views of the lake

4

islands. The comfortable rooms are decorated in natural tones, with thick curtains and low lighting. €165

La Rampolina Via Someraro 13, Campino di Stresa 0323 923 415 larampolina.com. In a spectacular location overlooking the lake and the Isole Borromee, this bustling tavern and restaurant above Stresa serves hearty dishes prepared with fresh seasonal ingredients (lake fish, cheeses and cold cuts from the Valli Ossolane, mushrooms and chestnuts in the autumn). Sit back at one of the tables on the terrace and soak in the gorgeous panoramic views. *Primi* €11, *secondi* €16. Tues–Sun 11.30–3.30pm & 6pm–1am.

★ **Relais Casali della Cisterna** Strada Vecchia alle Sale 8, Belgirate 0322 7570, casalidellacisterna.it. Six kilometres south of Stresa, tucked away on the hillside in the small town of Belgirate, this welcoming place has twelve well-appointed rooms named after plants and sailing boats; there's a lovely garden to relax in and a play area for children, as well as bikes for guests' use. €130

★ **Sky Bar** La Palma Hotel, Lungolago Umberto I 0323 32 401, hlapalma.it. On the seventh floor of the *Hotel Palma*, this lounge bar and restaurant serves light lunches including salads, burgers and pasta dishes (€15–18) between 12.30 and 2.30pm, but the terrace really comes alive at sunset for *aperitivo* time; this is the spot to enjoy a cocktail or two while soaking up the exceptional views of the lake islands from the lounge chairs and inviting sofas. Daily noon–midnight.

Lo Stornello Via Cavour 35 0323 30444 ristorantelostornello-stresa.it. An intimate restaurant with tables neatly packed together in a dining area with light grey walls with wine bottles encased in small niches. The food is particularly good, with Mediterranean specialities such as sea bass ravioli (€11) and cod with cream of peas and turmeric (€11). There's a great value lunch menu for €19. Daily 12-10pm.

Taverna del Pappagallo Via Principessa Margherita 46 0323 30 411, tavernapappagallo.com. One of the best spots in town to grab a bubbling pizza (€5.50), straight from the open wood fire; they also serve traditional Piemontese dishes including home-made pastas, risottos and lake fish. Thurs–Tues noon–2pm & 6.30–10pm.

Il Vicoletto Vicolo del Poncivo 3 0323 932 102, ristorantevicoletto.com. This welcoming restaurant serves tasty Italian cuisine in a pleasant setting; the menu, scribbled on a blackboard at the entrance, is very reasonable indeed, with *primi* at €11 and *secondi* at €15. There are a few tables on a small terrace in the summer. Fri–Wed noon–2pm & 6.30–10pm.

4

The Borromean islands

Lake Maggiore's leading attractions are three lush islands rising from the bay between Stresa and Pallanza. All three are often dubbed the **Borromean islands** (Isole Borromee), though strictly speaking only two are property of the Borromeo family (originally bankers, raised to nobility in the 1450s and still prominent locally), namely Isola Bella and Isola Madre.

Isola Bella

Mid-March to mid-Oct daily 9am–6.15pm (last admission 5.30pm) • €17; same-day joint ticket with Isola Madre €24; audioguide €3; book at least one day in advance for a 1hr guided tour of the palace in English (€55) • 0323 933 478, isoleborromee.it

Romantics – if they can bear the crowds and the sheer hyperbole – will be knocked for six: the short voyage from Stresa to **Isola Bella** is Italian Lakes fantasy brought to life. In 1630, Carlo III Borromeo began a redesign of this modest rock: soil was brought across from the mainland, a villa, fountains and statues were built, white peacocks imported, and terraces of orange and lemon trees, camellias, magnolias, box trees, laurels and cypresses carved out. Carlo's son Vitaliano died in 1690 with most of the work completed. As well as roaming

LAGO MAGGIORE EXPRESS

A highlight of any Lake Maggiore holiday, the **Lago Maggiore Express** (lagomaggioreexpress.com; one day €34, two days €44) combines rail and ferry travel to explore the lake and mountains while dipping into Switzerland too (so, don't forget your passport).

One of the best routes involves heading up to the mountain town of Domodossola by train from Stresa, then catching the spectacular narrow-gauge Vigezzina Cento Valli railway to Locarno in Switzerland. Here you have time to explore and have lunch before boarding the ferry for a relaxed three-hour cruise back to Stresa. The trip can be enjoyed both clockwise and anticlockwise, and there are various starting points, including Arona, Stresa, Baveno, Domodossola and Locarno.

the sumptuous Baroque gardens, complete with obelisks and classical statuary, dip into the island's opulent *palazzo*, which boasts a banqueting hall, ballroom, throne room and a three-storey domed *salone*, as well as mirror- and shell-encrusted grottoes down at water level.

Isola Madre

Mid-March to mid-Oct daily 9am–6.15pm (last admission 5.30pm) • €13.50; same-day joint ticket with Isola Bella €24; audioguide €3; book at least one day in advance for a 1hr guided tour of the palace in English (€55) • ⓣ 0323 933 478, ⓦ isoleborromee.it

Larger but less visited than its neighbour, **Isola Madre** has a beautiful extensive garden – home to azaleas, rhododendrons, palm and citrus trees, a colony of parrots and Europe's largest Kashmir cypress – alongside a small, tasteful *palazzo* housing a collection of eighteenth-century puppets.

Isola Superiore

Closest to shore, Hemingway's favourite island, **Isola Superiore**, is commonly known as **Isola dei Pescatori**, as it was once populated by fishermen. Despite the trinket shops, the island retains a certain charm that is best enjoyed after the crowds have left in the evening. There are no sights bar a cluster of attractive old houses, but it has some decent restaurants and is a good spot for a picnic.

ARRIVAL AND DEPARTURE — THE BORROMEAN ISLANDS

By ferry Public ferries (ⓦ navigazionelaghi.it) shuttle frequently between the islands (every 30min) linking them to Stresa (10min), Carciano, Baveno and Pallanza. Private boat-taxis leave more frequently (every 20min), connecting Stresa to the three islands.

ACCOMMODATION AND EATING

Il Fornello Bottega con Cucina Via Lungo Lago Vittorio Emanuele 18, Isola Bella ⓣ 338 794 5408. Tucked away on a pebbled flight of steps in a former smokehouse, this restaurant-deli is a great little spot to grab some food or a drink as you explore the island. Take your pick of cold cuts, cheeses, pastas and sauces at the counter and then sit back on the terrace and enjoy the lake views. Cold cut platters €14, pastas €10. Daily 9.45am–6.15pm.

Verbano Via Ugo Ara 2 ⓣ 0323 30 408, ⓦ hotelverbano.it. To avoid the crowds, book a night at this tranquil little spot dating from 1895. Its rooms feature contemporary furnishings, with black and white photos of the lake decorating the walls. The real draw is the excellent restaurant with shaded terraces at the water's edge, serving delicious local specialities including a range of lake-fish dishes. *Primi* €17, *secondi* €26. Booking essential. Restaurant open daily noon–2.30pm & 7–9.30pm. **€185**

Verbania

Across the bay from Stresa lies **VERBANIA** (a conglomerate town including neighbouring villages Suna, Intra and Pallanza), whose title recalls *Lacus Verbanus*, the Roman name for verbena-fringed Lake Maggiore. Car ferries shuttle between Intra and Laveno on the eastern shore. Pallanza is a relaxed, pretty little corner with a ferry jetty and views across to the Borromean islands, while behind its manicured flower beds busier Intra's cobbled centre has local shops and boutiques for all pockets.

Villa Taranto

Via Vittorio Veneto 111 • Daily March 8.30–6.30pm (last entry 5.30pm); April–Sept 8.30am–7.30pm (last entry 6.30pm); first half of Oct 9am–5.30pm (last entry 4.30pm); mid Oct–early Nov 9am–5pm (last entry 4pm) • €11 • ⓣ 0323 556 667, ⓦ villataranto.it

Verbania's balmy climate prompted Captain Neil McEacharn, scion of a Scottish industrial family, to buy the lakeside **Villa Taranto** in 1931. The sixteen hectares of botanical gardens that he created remain exceptional, housing twenty thousand plants, including giant Amazonian lilies, lotus blossoms, Japanese maples and more, laid out with geometric precision. You need at least a couple of hours to do the place justice; there is also a pleasant **café**.

ARRIVAL AND INFORMATION — VERBANIA

By boat From Intra, just north of Pallanza, a car ferry shuttles frequently over to Laveno (every 20min; 20min), from where trains run direct to Milan, and roads connect to Varese and the A8 autostrada. Verbania has several landing stages – Intra, Villa Taranto and Pallanza – served by boats heading to the Borromean islands, Stresa and beyond. You can also combine boat and train services from here, on the Lago Maggiore Express (see page 258).

By train Verbania-Pallanza train station is on the Stresa–Domodossola main line with trains from Milan (Centrale and Porta Garibaldi). Buses travelling to Omegna or taxis cover the 8km into the town centre.

Tourist offices The main tourist office is at Via Ruga 44 (Mon–Sat 9.30am–12.30pm & 3–5pm; ⊕0323 503 249 ⓦverbania-turismo.it).

ACCOMMODATION

Aquadolce Via Cietti 1, Pallanza ⊕0323 505 418, ⓦhotelaquadolce.it. A pleasant option whose thirteen well-furnished rooms have sturdy wooden furniture and prints of flowers adorning the walls. Rooms with lake views are €10–15 more than those facing the rear of the building. **€80**

★ **Grand Hotel Majestic** Via Vittorio Veneto 32, Pallanza ⊕0323 509 711, ⓦgrandhotelmajestic.it. This charming hotel is set in a peaceful location on the lakefront, its main entrance giving onto a quiet one-way system and cycling route. The lovely garden stretches out to the lakefront, with a small sandy beach and deckchairs; there's an inviting pool, sauna and well-equipped gym too. It feels a little creaky around the edges but that's what lends it charm. **€186**

Pesce d'Oro Via Troubetzkoy 136, Suna ⊕0323 504 445, ⓦhotelpescedoro.it. A popular family-run hotel in Suna, a 10min walk west of Pallanza, that has been going strong for over three decades; rooms are simple and comfortable and prices affordable. There's also an annexe with self-catering apartments. **€70**

EATING & DRINKING

★ **La Casera** Piazza Daniele Ranzoni 19 ⊕0323 581123. This superb deli is a real delight –shelves groan with all manner of local produce from cheeses and olive oils to pates and wines. It's a great little spot to grab savoury delights for a picnic or a sandwich on the go – or sit back at one of the small tables and enjoy an *aperitivo* as you nibble on cheese and cold cut platters. Mon–Sat 8am–10pm, Wed 8am–7pm.

Estremadura Via Troubetzkoy 142 ⊕0323 504 282. This friendly bar owned by award-winning mixologist Cinzia Ferro is known for offering more than 250 cocktails (€6), along with beers and spirits, as well as light snacks and a few bites. Fortnightly art exhibitions brighten up the walls of the warm interior; there's also seating outside. Daily 6pm–2am.

Il Portale Via Sassello 3 ⊕0323 505 486, ⓦristoranteilportale.it. This Michelin-starred restaurant is one of the very best around, serving delicious nouvelle-style cuisine with *primi* around €20 and *secondi* around €40. Tues, Wed & Thurs 7–10pm, Fri, Sat & Sun noon–2pm & 7–10pm.

Cannobio

CANNOBIO, 25km north of Pallanza (and 5km from the Swiss border), is one of Lake Maggiore's most appealing places to stay and a good base for exploring the lake. The village leads back from the water, its lakefront piazza of pastel-washed houses giving onto a tightly tangled web of stepped alleyways and stone houses. On Sunday mornings the local **market** takes over the waterfront selling everything from fresh produce to leather goods. The town's only sight is the **Santuario della Pietà**, a Bramante-inspired church beside the landing stage with a curious openwork cupola, built to house a painting of the Pietà which supposedly bled in 1522. On the northern edge of the village is a blue-flag **beach**, backed by pleasant lawns with trees and picnic tables.

Inland along the Val Cannobina

Extending behind Cannobio, the wooded **Val Cannobina** offers beautiful views and little-visited stone-built hamlets. An easy **riverside cycle path** heads off into the valley to the **Orrido di Sant'Anna**, an impressive rocky gorge surrounded by wooded slopes that is a popular picnic spot. Beside the Roman bridge and the chapel is a small river beach and restaurant (see below). The Orrido is also accessible on the summer miniature train and by car off the Val Cannobina road.

ARRIVAL AND INFORMATION — CANNOBIO

By bus Buses run approximately hourly from Verbania (35min): see timetables at vcotrasporti.it.

By boat Cannobio has regular ferry links up and down the lake as well a good service across to Luino.

Tourist office Largo alla Chiesa 3 (Mon–Sat 9am–noon & 4–7pm, Sun 9am–noon; 0323 71212, procannobio.it); there's an infopoint at Piazza Martiri della Libertà (March–Oct Daily 10am–2pm & 3–7pm; 0323 060088; cannobio4you.it).

GETTING AROUND

By bus Every 30min in summer, an evening shuttle bus (June–Aug 6.30pm–1am; €1) runs a 15min circular tour around town and up to the Orrido.

By bike Living Lake (329 569 2378, livinglake.it) rent 125cc Vespas (€65/day) at the Infopoint kiosk at Via Darbedo 5.

ACCOMMODATION

Antica Stallera Via P. Zacchero 7 0323 71 595, anticastallera.com. This three-star hotel in the heart of town has a garden restaurant overlooked by simple, modern en-suite rooms decorated in warm hues. **€129**

Hotel Cannobio Piazza Vittorio Emanuele III 6 0323 739 639, hotelcannobio.com. Right on the waterfront, this historic hotel has well-appointed rooms offering lovely lake views. The staff are attentive and friendly, and the restaurant has a terrace looking out to the water. **€195**

★ Hotel Pironi Via Marconi 35 0323 70 624, pironihotel.it. This hotel is a real charmer, edged into a narrow fifteenth-century ex-monastery on a cobbled lane in the village centre. Rooms are light, bright and attractive, and there's a cosy living area with sofas and armchairs where you can while away a few hours on a rainy day. **€160**

★ Park Hotel Villa Belvedere Via Casali Cuserina 2 0323 70 159, villabelvederehotel.it. About 1km west of the village centre, this lovely hotel has spacious rooms, painted in warm colours. The walls are adorned with abstract art, and there are a couple of apartments plus a house with a kitchenette. The well-manicured gardens have deck chairs and hammocks, and there's an inviting swimming pool. **€160**

4

EATING AND DRINKING

L'Imbuto Piazza XXVII-XXVIII Maggio 12 0323 70026 ristorantelimbuto.it. This laidback restaurant on the lakefront serves tasty pastas (€12), fish dishes (€14) and bubbling pizzas (€7) in white and airy Meditearrean-style interiors. Daily noon–3pm & 6–11pm.

La Streccia Via Merzagora 5 0323 70 575, ristorantelastreccia.it. Up a narrow alley behind the lakefront, this is a reliable choice in town for very good Piemontese food – including home-made breads and pasta – in a rustic, low-ceilinged dining room. *Primi* €10, *secondi* €17; two-course menu €18 or €24. Fri–Wed noon–3pm & 6–10pm.

★ Grotto Sant'Anna Via Sant'Anna 30, Traffiume 0323 70 682. With stone tables perched outside above the gushing water of the Sant'Anna Gorge, this traditional restaurant serves surprisingly creative Italian cuisine. On the menu you'll find the likes of porcini mushroom soufflé and cream of potatoes and rosemary (€13.50) and baked quail breast (€21) while the wine list focuses on Piedmont's excellent wines. Tues–Sat noon–1.30pm & 7–9.30pm, Sun noon–1.30pm & 7–9pm.

Scurone Piazza Vittorio Emanuele III, Traversa Scurone 7 348 888 1916, scurone.it. Tucked away in a quaint little alleyway, this small wine bar and café with a vaulted ceiling was once a sailing boat workshop. Today, it's a great spot for an *aperitivo* or snack – there are cold platters of meats and cheeses (€15), plus light dishes including burrata cheese with anchovies (€12) and marinated vegetables (€7). Mon, Tues, Thurs & Fri 11am–3pm & 5–11pm, Sat 10 & Sun 10am–11pm, Wed 5pm–11pm.

Luino

On Maggiore's eastern shore, the commercial town and rail hub of **LUINO** is besieged every Wednesday by people pouring in for its large weekly **market** – dodge the fake-label handbag and novelty stalls to seek out the tasty food section, piled high with salami and cheeses from all over Italy and Switzerland. Roads are jam-packed from 7am onwards and extra boats and buses serve Luino all day long. Outside market day, the town's attractions include a strollable *centro storico* and frescoes probably of the school of Bernardino Luini, a follower of Leonardo, at the **Church of San Pietro in Campagna.**

ARRIVAL AND INFORMATION — LUINO

By bus Buses connect Luino with towns up and down the eastern shoreline: for more details see muoversi.regione.lombardia.it or ctpi.it.

By boat Boats from Luino head across to Cannobio as well as to other Italian towns and over the border to Locarno and Ascona in Switzerland. On Wed there are extra sailings to

service the market.

Tourist office Via della Vittoria (Mon–Sat 10am–1pm & 3–6pm; 0332 530 019, vareselandoftourism.it).

ACCOMMODATION

Camin Hotel Colmegna Via Palazzi 1, 3km north of Luino 0332 510 855, caminhotel.com. One of the best accommodation options on the eastern side of the lake, this eighteenth-century building is tucked into the rock just where the shore road enters a tunnel, so the lakeside gardens are wonderfully tranquil and the swimming areas are difficult to beat. It's a friendly, family-orientated place, with light, bright and comfortable rooms and a moderately priced restaurant. The property also manages a number of good-value apartments (from €90) dotted around the area, too. **€160**

Laveno

Roughly 25km south of Luino, **LAVENO** is a significant transport hub with car-ferries shuttling over to the western shore at Verbania-Intra, plus various rail links with Milan. Its pleasant little centre, focused around Piazza Fontana, is worth a wander while you wait for your ferry. Just south of the centre on the lakefront in the neighbourhood of Cerro, a fine sixteenth-century porticoed former monastery houses the **Museo Internazionale Design Ceramico** at Via Lungolago Perabò 5 (Fri & Sun 2–7pm, Sat 10am–1pm & 2–7pm; €5; midec.org), with its strong collection of mainly twentieth-century ceramics.

ARRIVAL AND INFORMATION — LAVENO

4

By train Laveno-Mombello Nord station is a terminus for trains from Milano Nord/Cadorna. The town's other station, Laveno-Mombello, 1km south of the centre, is served by trains from Luino to Milano Porta Garibaldi (change at Gallarate).

By boat Car ferries from Verbania-Intra (see page 259) dock directly in front of the Laveno-Mombello Nord train station.

Tourist office Piazzale Ferrovie Nord (Tues–Sun 10am–4pm; 0332 667 223, vareselandoftourism.com).

Santa Caterina del Sasso

Via Santa Caterina 13, off the main SP69 between Cellina and Reno • March daily 9am–noon & 2–5pm; April–Oct daily 9am–noon & 2–6pm; Nov–Feb Sat & Sun 9am–noon & 2–5pm • Free • santacaterinadelsasso.com

One of the most popular sights on the lake, the hermitage of **Santa Caterina del Sasso** is a beautiful little cliffside **monastery** – visible only from the water – that is well worth a visit, though it can get crowded. It is most atmospherically reached by one of the many ferries from around the lake. The site dates back to 1170, when a local sailor was caught in a storm, invoked the help of St Catherine of Alexandria and survived: he withdrew to a cave, where local people began construction of a votive chapel. By 1620 fourteen monks lived here; today, it is still home to a small community of Benedictine monks.

The complex is tiny: you could walk from one end to the other in three minutes. Steep steps and a sparkling new lift take you down from the upper entrance or up from the jetty to the lovely entrance gallery (1624), with arches looking out over the lake, which leads to the South Convent. Inside is the Gothic Chapterhouse, decorated with a pristine fresco from 1439 of St Eligius healing a horse. Ahead, beneath the four Gothic arches of the Small Convent (1315) is the church, with its stubby Romanesque belltower and graceful Renaissance porch; a fresco of *God the Father*, dated 1610, adorns the Baroque vault above the high altar.

Rocca di Angera

Via Rocca Castello 2 • March–Oct 9am–5.30pm • €10 • isoleborromee.it

Standing on a spur looking out across to the western shore, the **Rocca di Angera** was once a stronghold and strategic point for controlling lake traffic. Today, it houses a couple of great museums and also hosts contemporary art exhibitions. On the ground floor, the wonderful **Museo della Bambola e del Giocattolo (Museum of Dolls and Toys)**

is the largest of its kind in Europe, showcasing over 1000 antique dolls and toys made with wood, wax, porcelain, cloth and papier-mâché. Don't miss the first-floor **Sale Storiche (Historical Halls)**, in particular the beautiful Sala di Giustizia, embellished with a 13th century cycle of frescoes depicting battle scenes. On display are portraits of the Borromeo family and a rare collection of Italian majolica.

Lake Orta

The locals call **LAKE ORTA** (Lago d'Orta) "Cinderella", capturing perfectly the reticent beauty of this small lake, with its deep blue waters and intriguing island. Lying west of Lake Maggiore, wholly within Piemonte, it is unmissable for **Orta San Giulio**, the most captivating medieval village on this – or, perhaps, any – Italian lake, with narrow, cobbled lanes snaking between the wrought-iron balconies of tall, pastel-washed *palazzi*. The village is unforgettably romantic, but consequently popular with day-trippers: on summer Sundays the approach roads are jammed with traffic (though the charm returns after dark). If you can, visit midweek or out of season.

Orta San Giulio

Occupying the tip of a peninsula on the lake's eastern shore, **ORTA SAN GIULIO** is a seductive little bolthole with charm and character in spades. The pace of life is slow, with everything revolving around the main waterside square, **Piazza Motta**, which is lined on three sides by faded butterscotch facades and open on the fourth to the lake and island. *Gelaterie*, terrace cafés and restaurants share space under the arcades with traditional shops and boutiques. Opposite the lake, Salita della Motta steps steeply upward towards the fifteenth-century Baroque church of **Santa Maria Assunta** and the **Sacro Monte** (see page 263) along a lovely wide lane where the Renaissance Palazzo Gemelli vies for your attention with Orata's oldest house, **Casa dei Nani**, named for its tiny windows. Back on Piazza Motta, head northward on the main street, Via Olina – cobbled, and barely 3m wide – through the village and out for a stroll or a sunbathe on the lakeside promenade. Lauded by UK Poet Laureate Carol Ann Duffy plus regulars from all over the world, the annual **Poetry on the Lake** festival (ⓦpoetryonthelake.org) takes place here, with a plethora of events including readings, workshops and competitions on land and water.

4

Isola San Giulio

Basilica: April–Sept Mon noon–6.45pm, Tues–Sun 9.30am–6.45pm; Oct–March Mon 2–5pm, Tues–Sun 9.30am–noon & 2–5pm • Free

Motorboats do the five-minute run more or less on demand out from Orta San Giulio to the **Isola San Giulio**, dominated by a white convent and the Romanesque tower of its basilica. According to legend, the island was the realm of dragons until 390 AD, when Julius, a Christian from Greece, crossed the lake using his staff as a rudder and his cloak as a sail, banished the monsters, founded a sanctuary and thus earned himself sainthood. The resulting **Basilica di San Giulio** has an impressively lofty interior. Much of its decoration, including the vaulting, dates from a Baroque eighteenth-century refit, but frescoes from as early as the fourteenth century survive. The fine **pulpit** was carved from local stone in the early twelfth century with symbols of the Four Evangelists and images of good winning over evil: note the crocodile/dragon locked in battle with the phoenix.

From the church, it takes twenty minutes to walk round the island on its one cobbled lane, past a shop, a restaurant and some enticingly scenic picnic spots.

Sacro Monte di San Francesco

Via Sacro Monte • Grounds open 24hr; Chapels open daily: end of March–end of Oct 9am–6.30pm; end of Oct–end of March 9am–4.30pm • ⓦsacromonte-orta.com

Above Orta, the **Sacro Monte di San Francesco** consists of 21 chapels containing life-size, painted terracotta statues acting out scenes from the Bible and the life of San

Francesco. It winds around the wooded hillsides, making up a devotional route still followed by pilgrims, though as many visitors come simply to admire the breathtaking views of the lake and inhale the pine-scented air.

ARRIVAL AND INFORMATION — ORTA SAN GIULIO

By train Orta-Miasino train station – on the little-used Novara–Domodossola branch line (change at Novara from/to Milano Centrale) – is around 2km east of the historic centre: turn right to take the foot path out of the station and walk downhill for about 20min to reach Orta San Giulio.

By bus Three buses a day link Stresa (1hr; mid-June to early Sept) with Piazzale Prarondo just outside the pedestrianized part of the village.

By car The village and the island of San Giulio are traffic-free: follow signs to the big car parks on the hillside above town. From here take the *trenino* (see below) or pick any of the footpaths heading downhill.

Tourist office The tourist office is in the car park on Via Panoramica (daily 10.30am–1pm & 2–6pm; 0322 90 5163, distrettolaghi.it and comune.ortasangiulio.no.it).

GETTING AROUND

By boat Motor launches depart frequently from Piazza Motta year round (9am–6pm; €4.50 return) to Isola San Giulio. From April to early Oct a cheaper public ferry crosses the lake to Pella (Mon–Fri hourly, Sat & Sun every 20min; 15min) and to Omegna (2 daily, 3 daily on Thurs for market day; 50min).

By trenino The village tourist train, the *trenino*, runs between the minigolf centre (from where it's a short walk down to the pedestrianized centre) and the car park by Villa Crespi, then on to the Sacro Monte at peak times (March, April & Oct daily 9am–5.30pm; May–Sept daily 9am–6pm; Nov–Feb Sat & Sun by prior reservation; €3 one way, €5 return)

ACCOMMODATION

4

★ **B&B Al Dom** Via Giovanetti 57 335 249 613, aldom57.com. Located in a pretty building on the lakefront, this lovely B&B has four welcoming rooms set on two floors; the entrance flooring is a handmade reproduction of eighteenth-century tiles, while the wrought-iron and wooden banister is original. There's a small leafy garden with camellias, maple and camphor trees, and a terrace with deckchairs right by the lake. **€165**

Hotel Aracoeli Piazza Motta 34 0322 905 173, ortainfo.com. This small hotel right on the main square features seven contemporary rooms with modern industrial-style fittings; you'll find painted concrete floors, hanging light bulbs and walk-in showers, and pretty vistas over the town's rooftops. Check-in is in the building right by Ristorante Olina down the street. **€130**

★ **La Darbia** Via per Miasino 389 311 3813 ladarbia.com. These self-catering apartments enjoy a lovely location on the hillside above Orta San Giulio, offering panoramic views of the lake and the island. There's an attractive swimming pool nestled amid vineyards, and there are a couple of small play areas for children. A great option for families. **€210**

Il Giardinetto Via Pronvinciale 1, Pettenasco 0323 89118, giardinettohotel.com. A five-minute drive from Orta San Giulio, this three-star hotel right on the water offers simple rooms with lake views. There's a swimming pool, private beach and a lovely terrace restaurant serving excellent local cuisine. **€107**

San Rocco Via Gippini 11 0322 911 977, hotelsanrocco.it. In an unbeatable location on the edge of the village right on the water, this four-star hotel set in a former convent offers recently refurbished rooms, and an inviting lakeside terrace and swimming pool where you could easily while away your entire holiday. **€190**

EATING AND DRINKING

★ **Blu Lago Café** Piazza Motta angolo Via Roma 2 0322 969 893. Under the same management as *Casa Fantini*, this excellent café and gourmet snack bar serves delicious homemade Italian cuisine in an attractive setting. The cocktails (from €7.50), prepared by award-winning mixologists, are superb too. It's a great place for lunch or a sundowner away from the tourist crowds of Orta San Giulio. Daily 11am–1am.

Il Giardinetto Via Provinciale 1 0323 89 118, giardinettohotel.com. Located 3.5km north of Orta San Giulio, this hotel restaurant serves creative local cuisine on a pleasant terrace overlooking the lake; the wine cellar has over four hundred wines. It's a great spot to get away from the crowds of Orta San Giulio and soak up the pretty lake views while enjoying good food at reasonable prices. *Primi* €14, *secondi* €18. Daily 12.30–2.30pm & 7.30–10pm.

★ **L'Ustaria Cà dal Rat** Via Novara 66 0322 905 120 lustaria.it. This pleasant restaurant tucked away to the south of Orta San Giulio has a quiet lakefront location. The friendly chef prepares delicious Italian dishes that follow the seasons, with the likes of raw ombrina fish and red prawns served with soybean sprouts (€14), and spinach flavoured gnocchi with tomato and gorgonzola (€12). Thurs–Tues noon–3pm & 5.30–11pm; open Wednesdays in July & Aug.

★ **Osteria San Martino** Vicolo Chiuso 8, Frazione Crabbia, Pettenasco ⓣ 0323 197 5177. This welcoming trattoria with exposed wooden beams and bare stone walls serves authentic Italian cooking. Expect hearty seasonal dishes prepared with local ingredients, with plenty of game, polenta, delicious soups and pasta dishes made with fresh greens from the veggie garden. *Primi* €10, *secondi* €15. Wed–Fri 7–11pm, Sat noon–2pm & 7pm–midnight, Sun noon–2pm & 7pm–midnight.

★ **Pan & Vino** Piazza Motta 37 ⓣ 393 858 3293. This excellent deli and café is the best spot in town to grab some cheeses, cold cuts and bread for a picnic by the lake. Light dishes (€8) are served in the vaulted interior or at tables that spill onto the square, and the all-day *aperitivo* includes a platter of local cheese, salami and ham: there's English breakfast, too. Thurs–Tues 10am–10pm.

★ **Villa Crespi** Via Fava 18 ⓣ 0322 911 902, ⓦ villacrespi.it. MasterChef Italy judge Antonino Cannavacciuolo has won this world-class restaurant two Michelin stars. Located in a turreted Moorish villa dating from 1879, this ornate restaurant has decor as singular as its creative cooking. The €150 Carpe Diem tasting menu mixes the best of the chef's native Naples with his adoptive Piemonte cuisine. Tues 7.30–9.30pm, Wed–Sun 12.30–2pm & 7.30–9.30pm.

Lake Como

Of all the Italian Lakes, it's the forked **LAKE COMO** (Lago di Como) that comes most heavily praised: Wordsworth thought it "a treasure which the earth keeps to itself". Today, despite huge visitor numbers, the lake is still surrounded by abundant vegetation: zigzagging slowly between shores by boat can seem impossibly romantic. As well as lakeside villas to visit, there is also some great walking to be done in the mountainous hinterland hereabouts. The principal towns – **Como** and **Lecco** – are at the southernmost tips of their own branches of the lake – Ramo di Como and Ramo di Lecco – while narrow winding roads follow the shoreline above and through erstwhile fishermen's villages past *belle époque* houses and Neoclassical villas up to the Centro Lago or centre of the lake. Here three small towns stand out as the highlight of the lakes: **Varenna** and **Bellagio** for unrepentant romantics, and **Menaggio** if you want a pleasant, affordable base for walking, swimming or cycling. To the north, the Alto Lago is much more sedate, with the towns of Gravedona ed Uniti and Domaso making for good bases for sports enthusiasts, with hiking, mountain biking, windsufing and sailing aplenty.

4

GETTING AROUND — LAKE COMO

By boat Boats stop at many villages on the lake, supplemented by car ferries shuttling from Cadenabbia and Menaggio across to Bellagio and Varenna.

By bus and train The #C10 bus (ⓦ asfautolinee.it) runs northwards from Como, stopping everywhere on the shoreline to Colico, from where the train takes you back to Lecco and the #C40 bus to Como. The #C30 links Como and Bellagio.

By car The lakeside roads are busy and narrow, and there are pay and display car parks on the edge of all the villages.

Como

Standing astride main routes to and from Switzerland, **COMO** is a comfortable, ancient town, much of its wealth coming from the factories dotted around the outskirts which produce luxury silk items for the fashion houses of Milan, Paris and New York. The town reaches around a small bay at the southernmost tip of the western fork of the lake, but Como gets on with life relatively regardless of the lake and the visitors passing through.

At the centre of the bay, lakeside **Piazza Cavour** is bounded by hotels and the main ferry jetty. To the northwest the lakeside promenade curls through a pleasant park to Villa Olmo, while to the northeast the road curves round to the funicular station up to Brunate and on to Villa Geno. Via Plinio leads back from Piazza Cavour to the tourist office and the eminently wanderable once-walled quarter: the crisscross of pedestrianized cobbled lanes reflect their Roman origins and offer the town's main sight – the Duomo – plus plenty of window shopping and shady pavement cafés.

The Duomo

Piazza del Duomo • Daily 7.30am–7.30pm • Free • ⓦ cattedrale.diocesidicomo.it

Work began on Como's splendid **Duomo** in 1396, when Gothic held sway, but wasn't completed until 1744, with the addition of a Baroque cupola. The church is reckoned to be Italy's best example of Gothic-Renaissance fusion: the fairy-tale pinnacles, rose windows and symbolic images are Gothic, while the rounded portals and statues of classical figures such as Pliny the Elder and Younger flanking the main door exemplify the Renaissance spirit. Inside, the Gothic aisles are hung with rich Renaissance tapestries, some woven with perspective scenes.

Palazzo Terragni (Ex Casa del Fascio)

Piazza del Popolo

In striking contrast to the town's medieval buildings, across the train tracks behind the Duomo stands the definitive example of Rationalist architecture by Como-born Giuseppe Terragni. Built as the headquarters for the local Fascist party in the 1930s, this light, deftly functional building is now dubbed **Palazzo Terragni** and houses the Guardia di Finanza. From a distance the angular building is almost transparent: you can see right through its loggia to the wooden hills behind.

The lakeside park

Northwest of Piazza Cavour, a **lakeside park** curves along the water; it's currently being refurbished (and has been for several years) but it's worth persevering past the hoardings and going in. Inside the **Tempio Voltiano** (Tues–Sun 10am–6pm; €4),

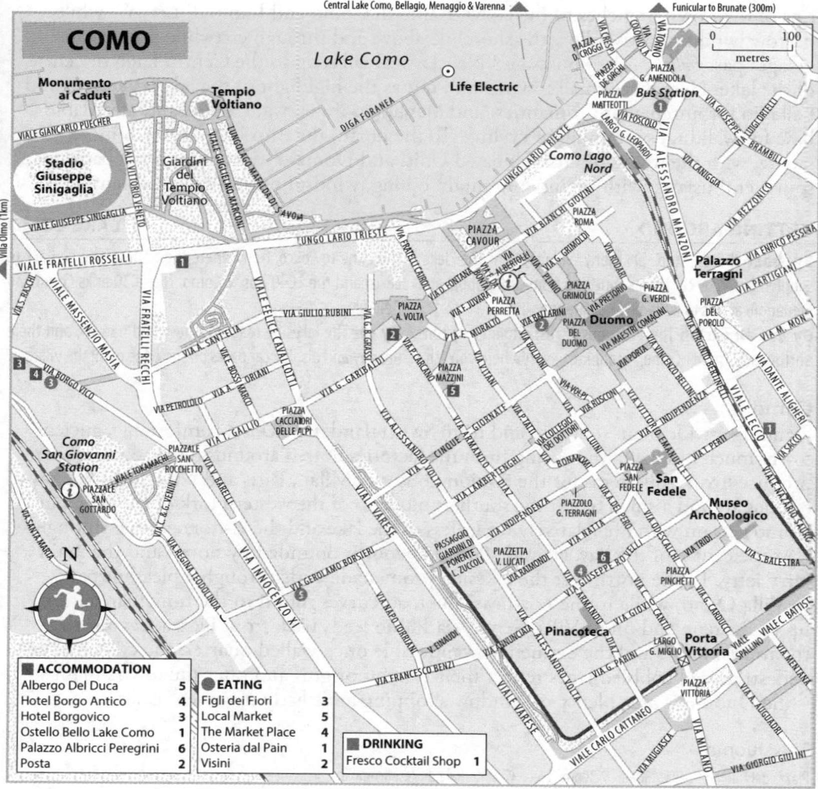

dedicated to Alessandro Volta, a Como man and pioneer in electricity who gave his name to the volt, there's a small museum displaying some of his instruments. Next door, the stark **Monumento ai Caduti**, a memorial to the dead of World War I, was built by Terragni to the design of the Futurist architect Antonio Sant'Elia, who was killed in 1916 aged 28. Ten minutes' walk beyond, past the Seaplane hangar, the **Villa Olmo** is a Neoclassical pile which is compellingly illuminated at night. It hosts conferences and temporary exhibitions, but its **gardens** (daily: summer 7am–11pm; winter 7am–7pm; free) are the biggest draw.

Brunate

Funicular Piazza Alcide de Gaspari • Daily every 15–30min; Sept–May 6am–10.30pm; June–Aug 6am–midnight • €5.50 return • Ⓦ funicolarecomo.it

From the base station of the **funicular** northwest from Piazza Cavour, it takes seven minutes to creep up the hillside past the gardens of wonderful nineteenth-century villas to **Brunate**, a small hilltop resort that has a few bars and restaurants and great views of the lake. It is also a good starting point for hikes – from a couple of hours to a two-day trip along mule paths to Bellagio; the tourist office has details of routes.

ARRIVAL AND DEPARTURE — COMO

By plane There are a handful of direct trains to Como San Giovanni railway station from Milan-Malpensa Airport (every 2hr; 1hr30min). Trains to Como Nord Lago involve a change at Saronno (hourly; 1hr20min).

By train The main train station is Como San Giovanni (Como S.G.), on the fast line from Milano Centrale to Chiasso and also served by several trains from Milano Garibaldi. The station lies about a 10min walk west of the centre. Como Nord Lago station – the terminus of a line from Milano Nord/Cadorna – stands on the lakefront Piazza Matteotti, alongside the old quarter and the bus station.

By bus The bus station is right on the water on Piazza Matteotti. Services link Como with the lake's western shore (#C10); Bellagio (#C30); Lecco (#C40/#D41); and Bergamo (#C46/#D46). See timetables at Ⓦ asfautolinee.it.

Destinations Bellagio (hourly; 1hr 10min); Bergamo (Mon–Sat 7 daily; 2hr); Lecco (daily; 1hr 10min); Menaggio (hourly; 1hr 10min).

By ferry Boats dock at the jetties on Piazza Cavour, where you also buy tickets. There are regular services to all points along the lake as well as fast *aliscafi* services. In summer, private companies run evening cruises and day-trips around Centro Lago, the centre of the lake. In winter boats operate around the first basin only.

Destinations Bellagio (7 to 15 daily; 45min–2hr 10min); Cernobbio (every 20min; 15min); Colico (3 to 8 daily; 1hr 50min–4hr); Menaggio (7 to 15 daily; 50min–2hr 25min); Varenna (7 to 9 daily; 1hr–2hr 40min).

INFORMATION

Tourist office The very helpful tourist office is at Via Albertolli 7 (Ⓣ 031 269 712 Ⓦ visitcomo.eu). There is also an information point at Como San Giovanni railway station.

ACCOMMODATION

Albergo Del Duca Piazza Mazzini 12 Ⓣ 031 264 859, Ⓦ albergodelduca.it; map p.266. The simple rooms here overlook either a picturesque old-town square or a small internal area. The attached family-run restaurant serves traditional Italian dishes as well as pizzas. **€130**

Hotel Borgo Antico Via Borgo Vico 47 Ⓣ 031 338 0150, Ⓦ borgoanticohotelcomo.it; map p.266. On the eastern fringes of town, this inviting three-star hotel is a good mid-range option, with welcoming spic-and-span rooms painted in mellow green and yellow hues, featuring modern bathrooms with rain showers. Five ground-floor rooms also have little private terraces. **€138**

Hotel Borgovico Via Borgo Vico 91 Ⓣ 031 570 107, Ⓦ hotelborgovico.it; map p.266. A friendly, intimate hotel with only thirteen rooms, most featuring wrought-iron headboards and wooden beams. There's a small courtyard where breakfast is served in the warmer months. **€130**

Ostello Bello Lake Como Viale Fratelli Rossi 9 Ⓣ 031 570 889, Ⓦ ostellobello.com; map p.266. Great hostel a short walk from the Como landing stage, with bright industrial-style interiors (bare walls, hanging light bulbs, exposed pipes), a hugely popular bar and a spic-and-span kitchen stocked with plenty of free food for guests. Dinner is included, too. Dorms **€33**, doubles **€129**

★ **Palazzo Albricci Peregrini** Via Giuseppe Rovelli 28 Ⓣ 331 2305 764 Ⓦ palazzoalbricciperegrini.it; map p.266. This lovely family-run boutique hotel is a real delight: giving onto an internal courtyard, the attractive rooms have reclaimed fittings including vintage armchairs

and industrial lamps. Breakfast is a real feast, with plenty to suit all tastes, from eggs Benedict to cow and goat's milk yoghurt. It's one of the very few hotels on the lake that is open year-round. **€230**

★**Posta** Via Garibaldi 2 031 276 9011, postadesignhotel.com; map p.266. This small design hotel has fourteen rooms set on four floors right in the heart of town. The walls are embellished with framed silk scarves, and the modern rooms are spacious and comfortable with stylish marble bathrooms. There's a pleasant café and bar on the ground floor. **€160**

EATING

Figli dei Fiori Via Borgovico 39/A 031 571 077 figlideifiori.com; map p.266. This flower shop doubles as a lovely bistro, with seating in a rustic leafy dining area. The cuisine is creatively presented, yet simple at heart, prepared using local ingredients and following traditional recipes. There's a great value business lunch Tues–Fri for €13/€15. *Primi* €9, *secondi* €14. Tues–Sun noon–1am.

★**Local Market** Via Borsieri 21/A 031 413 0093 localmarketcomo.com. This stylish deli is a great spot to grab an informal bite throughout the day (€6–10) or to enjoy a laidback *aperitivo* (€12). Dishes are all homemade using fresh local ingredients, while wines have been carefully selected from small and medium-size producers. Mon–Sat 10am–10pm.

4

★**The Market Place** Via Rovelli 51 031 270 712 themarketplace.it; map p.266. This attractive restaurant serves beautifully presented dishes using local seasonal ingredients, prepared by a young and enthusiastic team. The set menu will set you back €70. Mon 7pm–11pm, Tues–Sat noon–2.30pm & 7–11pm.

Osteria dal Pain Piazza Giovanni Amendola 4 031 306270; map p.266. Tucked away to the east of town, this traditional osteria serves authentic home cooking in a simple setting. Portions are hearty and generous, with a focus on regional specialities such as polenta uncial (€10) and *risotto col persico* (risotto with lake fish; €17). Tues–Sun noon–3pm & 7–11pm.

Visini Via Francesco Ballarini 9 031 242 760 visini.it; map p.266. This deli is a great spot to put together a tasty lunch of cold cuts, cheeses and freshly made cooked dishes such as lasagne and seabass. It doubles as a lunch spot and wine bar too, offering local specialities and wines from the area. *Primi* €12, *secondi* €16. Mon–Sat 8.30am–7.30pm.

DRINKING

★**Fresco Cocktail Shop** Viale Lecco 23 393 731 5649 frescococktailshop.it; map p.266. At this itsy-bitsy cocktail bar expert mixologists serve up superb drinks (€12–15) prepared using aromatic herbs, spices, flowers, citrus fruits and even essential oils that add a touch of sweetness. Jazz and swing tunes nicely complement the 1940s-themed interiors. Wed–Mon 6pm–1am.

Ramo di Como

The scenic **Ramo di Como** – the Como branch of the lake – is the stuff of tourist brochures: wooded mountain slopes protect the villages crammed onto the narrow shoreline from extremes of temperature, and lush gardens abound. Many of the opulent villas that line this stretch are still privately owned by industrialists and celebrities – George Clooney is a much-fêted resident of Laglio.

Western shore: Cernobbio to Isola Comacina

A stone's throw outside Como town, the village of **CERNOBBIO** comprises a compact quarter of old houses, loomed over by Monte Bisbino (1325m). The broad lakeside piazza is bordered by glitzy boutiques and the upmarket hotels that characterize the village, including the famous, palatial **Villa d'Este** hotel (villadeste.it) beloved of celebrities and the super-rich.

The old road leaving Cernobbio, the **SP71 Vecchia Regina**, is what this part of Lake Como is all about. The narrow road weaves by lush gardens and celebrity-owned villas, through the little hamlets of Urio, Carate and Laglio and along the waterside to Brienno and Argegno.

From Sala Comacina or nearby **Ossuccio** – drop in at the eleventh-century **church** and **Antiquarium**, while you're there (Via Somalvico; Tues, Wed & Fri–Sun 10am–5pm; €2) – catch a row boat (€7) over to **Isola Comacina** (daily: mid-March to June, Sept & Oct 10am–5pm; July & Aug 10am–6pm; isola-comacina.it), Lake Como's only island – wild, unkempt and dotted with the ruins of nine abandoned churches.

Occupied by the Romans, it later attracted an eclectic mix of dethroned monarchs, artists, future saints and Emperor Federico Barbarossa. Wander the island at will, or book for dinner at its famous **restaurant** (see below).

The eastern shore

The rugged cliffs of the **eastern shore**, north of Como, are stepped into terraces where small village communities cling on to the rock. The boats that zigzag their way up the lake are as good a way as any of sampling the landscapes. Tiny Torno's tranquil lakeside plaza belies its medieval importance as a rival of Como and the string of visiting celebrities – from Byron and Shelley to Stendhal and Rossini – at Villa Pliniana. In spring, water pours down through gorges in tiny Nesso, fed by the mountains behind. The road continues on to Bellagio (see page 272).

ACCOMMODATION AND EATING — RAMO DI COMO

★ **Domus Plinii** Via Alle Rive 28/30, Faggeto Lario ☎ 031 225 5832, 🌐 domusplinii.com. This friendly boutique hotel offers thirteen apartments that ooze plenty of character. The decor is vintage 1950s, 1960s and 1970s, with original designer pieces complementing quirky geometric wallpaper patterns. There's a swimming pool and an excellent affiliated watersports centre. **€250**

Locanda dell'Isola Comacina Isola Comacina ☎ 0344 55 083, 🌐 comacina.it. The same six-course set menu (€77; no credit cards) has been served by father and son at this island's famous restaurant since 1948. The highlight is the elaborate "exorcism by fire" at the end of every meal to ward off a curse laid on the island in 1169 by the Bishop of Como. Decent food and an infectious atmosphere make this less gimmicky and more enjoyable than it sounds. Wed–Mon noon–2pm & 7–9pm; in summer open daily.

Nest on the Lake Frazione Sostra 17/19 ☎ 031 914 372, 🌐 nestonthelake.com. Right on the water's edge, this small family-run hotel offers simple spotless rooms, all with balconies looking out towards the lake. It's quiet and peaceful, with steps leading down to an attractive pebbly beach. The family own a great restaurant a short walk away. **€120**

★ **Villa Aurora** Frazione Sossana 2, Lezzeno ☎ 031 914 645, 🌐 hotelauroralezzeno.com. This lovely hotel has pleasant rooms with wooden flooring and plenty of light, plus a restaurant and lakeside terrace with dreamy views across to Villa Balbianello; there are more stylish rooms (€130) in an annexe across the road. **€100**

4

Centro Lago: western shore

Halfway up the lake, where the Como, Lecco and Colico branches meet, is the **Centro Lago**, the most scenically attractive part of the lake, hosting its three most sought-after destinations. If you have just one day to spend on Lake Como spend it here.

The western side north of the sheltered shore around **Tremezzo** boasts two of the lake's most famous villas – **Villa del Balbianello** and **Villa Carlotta**, while just north lies the busy village resort of **Menaggio** with some great hiking in the surrounding hills. Opposite on the eastern shore, trapped between towering cliffs, stands the alluring waterfront village of Varenna (see page 274). Midway between the two, occupying a headland jutting into the lake, nestles **Bellagio** (see page 272), a picture-perfect village of steps and cobbled alleys.

Villa del Balbianello

Via Guida Monzino 1 • Mid-March to mid-Nov Tues & Thurs–Sun 10am–6pm • Villa €20, gardens only €10 • 🌐 fondoambiente.it

Access to **Villa del Balbianello** is chiefly by boat from Lenno but you can also walk through the grounds (roughly 800m from Lenno). The house is a classic eighteenth-century set piece, but it's the romantic **gardens** that inspire, with gravel paths between lush foliage, and stone urns framing spectacular views. Parts of *Star Wars: Episode II* and the 2006 version of the James Bond classic *Casino Royale* were filmed here.

Mezzegra

Euphemistic signposts in the pretty village of **Mezzegra** direct you to the gateway of a house where on April 28, 1945, Mussolini and his mistress Clara Petacci were shot dead by partisans, having been arrested the night before as they tried to escape to Switzerland. Their bodies were taken to Milan and hung upside down outside a petrol station as proof that the Fascist leader was dead.

THE GREENWAY

The **Greenway** is an enchanting 10km trail of paths and waterside lanes that links Colonno with Cadenabbia, passing through unspoilt countryside past ancient churches, Roman relics and lakeside villas. The route can be broken down into forty-minute sections and combined with the ferry service, or the whole walk takes three and a half hours. Maps are available in English from the tourist office (see below).

Villa Carlotta

Via Regina 2, loc. Tremezzo, Tremezzina • Daily: end of March–Sept 9am–7.30pm; Oct 9am–6.30pm; late-Oct–early Nov 10am–5pm • €10 • villacarlotta.it

Tremezzo became a popular resort in the nineteenth century and is best known for **Villa Carlotta**, located on the lakefront road but best glimpsed from the water (there's a public boat stop just by the entrance). Pink, white and exceptionally photogenic, this grand house – built in 1690 – was given by a Prussian princess to her daughter Carlotta as a wedding present. It now houses a collection of pompous eighteenth-century statuary, including masterpieces such as Canova's Palamede, and boasts beautifully ordered eight-acre **gardens**, rich with camellias, rhododendrons and azaleas.

ACCOMMODATION AND EATING — CENTRO LAGO: WESTERN SHORE

4

Alberghetto La Marianna Via Regina 57, Cadenabbia 0344 43 095, la-marianna.com. Wonderful old hotel-restaurant just north of Cadenabbia on the lakefront road run by a welcoming husband-and-wife team. The eight balconied rooms look over the road to the water and there's a good, informal restaurant serving traditional Lakes cuisine (two-course menu €36, four courses €55). **€115**

La Darsena Via Regina 3, Tremezzo 0344 43 166, ladarsena.it. Located in what was once a boat repair workshop, this friendly family-run place has comfortable rooms painted in mellow colours; there's also an excellent terrace restaurant with wonderful views of the lake. **€129**

La Fagurida Via Rogaro 17 0344 40676, lafagurida.it. Up above the lake a short drive from Tremezzo, this traditional family-run restaurant is welcoming and cosy, jam packed with pots and pans dangling from the ceiling and family curios – old irons, ceramic plates – lining the shelves. It's a great spot for an authentic meal in a laidback setting. *Primi* €10, *secondi* €14. Tues–Sun 12.30–2pm & 7–10pm.

Menaggio

MENAGGIO, 34km north of Como, a lively and bustling village resort, is a good base for hiking and cycling in the mountains as well as sunbathing and swimming. **Hiking possibilities** range from a two-and-a-half-hour walk to the pretty village of Codogna, to a trek through the Sentiero delle Quattro Valli, which leads for 50km through four valleys to Valsolda on Lake Lugano. There's a beach and vast pool at the **Lido**, as well as boat rental and other activities.

ARRIVAL AND INFORMATION — MENAGGIO

By boat Boats and ferries dock about a 5min walk from the main lakefront square, Piazza Garibaldi. The car ferry across to Bellagio leaves every 30min from Cadenabbia, 3.5km south of Menaggio.

By bus Bus #C10 links Menaggio with Como and the other villages and towns on the western shore of the lake.

Tourist office Piazza Garibaldi 3 (daily 9.30am–12.30pm & 2–6pm; Oct–March closed Mon; 0344 32 924, menaggio.com). A very well organized office, with English-language information on everything, including Menaggio's numerous hiking possibilities.

ACCOMMODATION

Garni Corona Largo Cavour 3 0344 32 006, hotelgarnicorona.com. This family-run three-star bang on the main square has been welcoming guests since 1964. The refurbished interiors offer pleasant rooms, some with lake views and balcony. **€150**

Grand Hotel Menaggio Via IV Novembre 77 0344 30 640, www.grandhotelmenaggio.com. The best of Menaggio's grand hotels because of its lakeside swimming pool, though you are paying for location. The anonymous carpeted rooms are comfortable, but nothing special. **€220**

Ostello La Primula Via IV Novembre 106 0344 32 356, lakecomohostel.com. Just south of Menaggio,

this friendly hostel has lovely views of the lake and access to a private stretch of beach. Rooms are simple and clean, and there are kayaks (€10/hr), bikes (€15/half day) and e-bikes (€19-25/half-day) for rent, along with table tennis and football facilities. They also offer cooking classes, Italian language courses and guided bike and sailing tours, while a three-course meal at the restaurant will set you back €13.50. Dorms €22, doubles €64

EATING AND DRINKING

Il Ristorante di Paolo Largo Cavour 5 ⓣ0344 32 133. This pleasant restaurant has plenty of outside tables by the lakefront and a series of dining rooms inside. The atmosphere is relaxed but elegant, and dishes are prepared using fresh local ingredients. *Primi* €15, *secondi* €20. Wed–Mon 12am–2.30pm & 7pm–10pm.

Trattoria La Vecchia Magnolia Via Per Plesio 6 ⓣ0344 30567. Great food, affordable prices and an extensive menu are what make this simple trattoria one of the most popular places in Menaggio. On the menu you'll find the likes of risotto with taleggio cheese and rosemary (€10) and grilled black Angus with rocket and balsamic vinegar (€16); there are pizzas (€6), too. Tues–Sun noon–2pm & 6.45–9.30pm.

Alto Lario

The **Alto Lario**, or Northern Lake Como, is little explored compared to the southern part of the lake, which swarms with tourists for much of the year. While the lakeside towns here are by no means as gorgeous as Bellagio or Varenna, they still have picturesque historical centres along with one of the lake's best museums at **Dongo**. The towns of **Gravedona ed Uniti** and **Domaso** make good bases for sports enthusiasts; this is the windiest part of the lake, with excellent **windsurfing**, sailing and kitesurfing, and there are great **hikes** and mountain bike trails, too. The Via dei Monti Lariani is a beautiful 125km trail that follows an ancient route across the mountains to Alpine pastures: it starts at Cernobbio and winds up the western lakeshore to Sorico – allow at least six days to hike the entire stretch.

Museo della Fine della Guerra

Piazza Paracchini 6 , Dongo • Tues–Sun 10am–1pm & 3–6pm • €5 • ⓣ0344 82 572, ⓦmuseofineguerradongo.it

About 12km north of Menaggio, the town of **DONGO** is where Fascist leader Benito Mussolini was captured by Resistance partisans; he was shot the next day near Tremezzo (see opposite). Housed in the Palazzo Manzi, Dongo's former town hall on the main square, the excellent **Museo della Fine della Guerra** is dedicated to the end of the war, with multilingual interactive exhibits on the Resistance movement on Lake Como. The museum's displays include original archive footage, video clips and a handful of objects used by partisans, including a MAS-36 rifle, plus eyewitness accounts of the capture and execution of Mussolini.

Gravedona ed Uniti and Domaso

Just over 4km north of Dongo, **GRAVEDONA ED UNITI** is a pretty town with cobbled streets set around a curving bay. There's little to do in the town itself except stroll along the waterfront or get lost in the narrow streets, although the surrounding area makes excellent hiking terrain. Just over 1km east, the little town of **DOMASO** is home to a couple of small family-run **vineyards** that are worth a visit (ⓦcantineangelinetta.com and ⓦsorsasso.com).

INFORMATION — ALTO LARIO

Tourist office Infopoint Gravedona ed Uniti, Piazza Trieste ⓣ0344 85005 ⓦnorthlakecomo.net (end March–end Oct 9.30am–1pm & 3–6.30pm); Infopoint Dongo, Piazza Paracchini ⓣ0344 82572 ⓦnorthlakecomo.net (Tues–Sun 10am–12.30pm & 3–5.30pm).

ACCOMMODATION AND EATING

Cà dè Mätt Via al Castello 6, Gravedona ⓣ0344 85 640. Tucked away in a fifteenth-century building on a narrow little lane in Gravedona's historical centre, this friendly restaurant has seating on a small terrace overlooking the rooftops, as well as in a cosy vaulted dining area; ingredients are sourced locally, and the seasonal menu features

excellent lake-fish dishes. *Primi* €13, *secondi* €20. Daily noon–2.30pm & 7–10.30pm; Sept–June closed Wed.

Residence Il Giardino di Lory Via Lubiana, Domaso ⓣ334 921 1979, ⓦilgiardinodilory.com. Perched on a hillside above Domaso, these self-catering apartments have stunning views of the lake and the surrounding area; the rooms are modern and comfortable, and there's a swimming pool, children's play area and BBQ facilities, too. **€115**

Ristorante dei Pescatori Via Case Sparse 219, Domaso ⓣ0344 96 088, ⓦristorantedeipescatori.com. A laidback waterside restaurant with lake views; as the name suggests (it translates as "Fishermen's restaurant") the emphasis is on lake-fish dishes. Prices are extremely reasonable, with three-course menus priced between €22 and €30. There are also four simple rooms for rent (€80). Thurs–Sun noon–2.30pm & 7–9.30pm, Tues noon–2.30pm; June–Sept open daily.

Villa Vinicia Via Regina 135, Domaso ⓣ339 621 8247, ⓦvillavinicia.it. Located in a beautiful historical building dating back to 1680, this friendly place has rooms, apartments and suites with original bare stone walls (there are original frescoed ceilings in some), all with kitchenette and a/c units. There's a children's playground, a small garden with mountain views, a BBQ for guests, a swimming pool and a whirlpool tub. **€160**

Centro Lago: Bellagio

Cradled by cypress-spiked hills on the tip of the Triangolo Lariano – the triangle of mountainous land between the Como and Lecco branches of the lake – **BELLAGIO** has been called the most beautiful town in Italy. With a promenade planted with oleanders and limes, fin-de-siècle hotels painted shades of butterscotch, peach and cream, and a hilly old quarter of steep cobbled streets and alleyways – to say nothing of its spectacular mid-lake location – it's easy to see why Bellagio has become so popular. These days, the alleys are lined with upmarket boutiques and souvenir shops; town life plays second fiddle to tourism, but this is still a charming, attractive resort.

4

The waterfront

Bellagio's first hotel, the *Genazzini*, opened in 1825; its second, the *Florence*, opened in 1852. The two flank Bellagio's scenic **waterfront** to this day, and passenger boats dock midway between them (the *Genazzini* is now the *Metropole*). The **views** from here westwards to the mountains above Cadenabbia are simply lovely; spending an afternoon watching the shadows lengthen, as the ferries parade to and fro, is pure Bellagio.

The village centre

The old quarter at the heart of the village is tiny, with three streets parallel to the waterfront connected by seven steep, perpendicular, stepped alleyways. At the top is a piazza with the eleventh-century Romanesque church of **San Giacomo**, alongside a tower which is all that's left of Bellagio's medieval defences.

Punta Spartivento

A stroll along the road 350m north of the village brings you to the **Punta Spartivento**, the "Point Which Divides the Winds", at the very tip of Bellagio's promontory. There's a tiny harbour here, a handkerchief-sized park where you could enjoy a picnic and a pleasant restaurant from which to drink in the unique panorama.

Pescallo

Ten minutes' walk east of Bellagio on an attractive footpath through vineyards, the enchanting little harbour of **Pescallo**, a fishing port since Roman times, offers a tremendous view of the Grigne mountains looming over the Lecco branch of the lake. There's nothing here but a small hotel and restaurant (see opposite) and a handful of fishing boats.

Villa Serbelloni

April–Oct Tues–Sun 11am–3.30pm • €9; buy tickets 15min in advance from the Promo Bellagio office on Piazza della Chiesa

Bellagio is blessed with luxuriant flora, some of which you can admire on a guided **tour** of the gorgeous park of the **Villa Serbelloni**. The villa, now owned by the

Rockefeller Foundation and maintained as a study centre, is splendidly sited on a hill above the town.

Villa Melzi

April–Oct daily 9.30am–6.30pm • €6.50 • ⓦ giardinidivillamelzi.it

South of town, the lake promenade continues for about 500m to the gardens of the **Villa Melzi**, a luxuriant affair crammed with azaleas, rhododendrons, ornamental lemon trees, cypresses, palms, camellias and even sequoia. The gardens extend to the fishing hamlet of **Loppia**, a picturesque retreat.

ARRIVAL AND INFORMATION — BELLAGIO

By boat Boats arrive frequently from Tremezzo, Cadenabbia, Menaggio and Varenna. Passenger ships and hydrofoils dock at the main Piazza Mazzini; car ferries dock 150m south by the car parks. Tickets are available from the jetties.

By bus or car By road, Bellagio is 30km from Como (served by bus #C30) on a narrow, scenic road coiling along the rocky cliffs. Bellagio is mainly car free; pay and display car parks line the approach road.

Tourist office The tourist office on Piazza Mazzini (Mon–Sat 9am–12.30pm & 1–5.30pm, Sun 10am–noon & 2.30–5.30pm; ⓣ 031 950 204, ⓦ bellagiolakecomo.com) has information on activities including hiking, mountain biking and watersports.

ACCOMMODATION

Bellagio Salita Grandi 6 ⓣ 031 952 202, ⓦ hotelbellagio.it. Tucked away on a narrow street in the centre of town, this pleasant two-star hotel has clean and comfortable rooms; being one of the highest buildings in town, it has wonderful views from its top-floor rooms, particularly from room 404 with its large windows. **€155**

★ **Belvedere** Via Valassina 31 ⓣ 031 950 410, ⓦ belvederebellagio.com. Sitting on a hilltop above town, this lovely hotel in its own attractive grounds has a swimming pool and wonderful views over the Lecco arm of the lake. Rooms are spacious, with parquet flooring and rain showers in the bathroom. There's a small library room with TV, plus some apartments with kitchenettes. **€375**

Borgo Le Terrazze Via Panoramica 3 ⓣ 031 950 049, ⓦ borgoleterrazze.com. This pleasant hotel offering both rooms and apartments is set in an enviable location on the hillside overlooking Bellagio – the views from here are simply stunning. The spacious rooms feature pastel-coloured walls and en-suite bathrooms; all have terraces or balconies. There's an attractive swimming pool, too. **€165**

Florence Piazza Mazzini ⓣ 031 950 342, ⓦ hotelflorencebellagio.it. Run by the same family for over a century, this attractive hotel overlooking the main square has tastefully furnished rooms with four-poster beds, wooden floors and marble bathrooms. **€155**

★ **Hotel du Lac** Piazza Mazzini 32 ⓣ 031 950 320, ⓦ bellagiohoteldulac.com. Commanding a great location directly opposite Bellagio's docking station, this three-star offers spic-and-span rooms with cream-coloured furnishings, with some brightened up with bolder splashes of colour. There's an attractive rooftop terrace with sun loungers. **€195**

La Pergola Piazza del Porto 4, Pescallo ⓣ 031 950 263, ⓦ lapergolabellagio.it. Welcoming en-suite rooms with balconies overlooking the lake and a vine-covered restaurant below in this enchanting fishing hamlet. The only downside is that the staff are not as welcoming as one would expect from such a cosy little place. It's a good 15min walk over the hill from Bellagio, so you'll probably need your own transport (or taxi). **€150**

4

EATING AND DRINKING

Alle Darsene di Loppia Via Melzi D'Eril, frazione Loppia ⓣ 031 952 069, ⓦ ristorantedarsenediloppia.com. The real draw of this pleasant restaurant in the hamlet of Loppia, a little south of Bellagio, is the lovely shaded terrace – a perfect spot to enjoy a meal as boats bob in the harbour. Call ahead to bag one of the outside tables. *Primi* €20, *secondi* €25. Tues–Sun noon–2.30pm & 7–9.30pm.

La Punta Punta Spartivento 19 ⓣ 031 951 888, ⓦ ristorantelapunta.it. With lovely views over the Punta Spartivento, where the Ramo di Como meets the Ramo di Lecco, this is a great family-run spot to enjoy some seafood in an atmospheric open-air setting. One of the owners, a fisherman, supplies the restaurant daily with fresh fish. *Primi* €13, *secondi* €16. Daily 9am–10pm.

Lido di Bellagio Lungo Lario Marconi ⓣ 031 951 195, ⓦ lidodibellagio.com. Bellagio's nightlife centres around the Lido south of town; this place gets packed on weekend nights when youngsters from all around the lake head here for the good cocktails and pumping music. Cover charge €15–30. The bar provides a boat service from Cadenabbia (return €5). During the day you can come and use the beach (loungers €10/day) or grab a bite to eat for lunch. Mon–Thurs 10am–6.30pm, Fri & Sat 10am–4am, Sun 10am–7.30pm.

Ristoro Forma & Gusto Salita Mella 13 ⓣ031 951 030. An informal restaurant with tables out on the cobbled lanes, serving wood-fired pizzas (€7) and other mains (*primi* from €11). Its sister-restaurant, *Terrazza Barchetta*, which sits above, offers tasty Italian dishes in a more formal setting. Daily noon–10.30pm; Nov–end March closed Tues, open lunch only weekdays and lunch & dinner weekends.

Silvio Via Carcano 10/12, Loppia ⓣ031 950 322, ⓦbellagiosilvio.com. A great restaurant for authentic lake cuisine served under a vine-shaded terrace overlooking the lake. *Primi* €11, *secondi* €23. Daily 12.15–2.30pm & 7.15–10.30pm.

Trattoria San Giacomo Salita Serbelloni 45 ⓣ031 950 329. Located at the top of the picturesque Salita Serbelloni, this bustling trattoria serves hearty meat dishes including *ossobuco di vitello*, deer and wild boar with polenta. Grab a cushion and sit on the steps as you wait for a table, drink in hand. *Primi* €10, *secondi* €12. Wed–Mon noon–2.30pm & 7–9.30pm.

Centro Lago: Varenna

Gazing back at Bellagio's Punta Spartivento from the eastern shore of the lake, **VARENNA** is perhaps the loveliest spot on Lake Como. With no through traffic, shaded by pines and planes and almost completely free of souvenir shops, the village oozes character. This is the quiet side of the lake, less visited and with fewer places to stay, and the highlight of the eastern shore, if not the region.

The village

As well as the fourteenth-century **San Giorgio** on the main piazza, Varenna also hosts one of the oldest churches on the lake, the eleventh-century **San Giovanni Battista** opposite, with well-preserved, fragmentary frescoes depicting St George, St Christopher and St John the Baptist. Varenna's other main sights are botanical: the nineteenth-century **Villa Cipressi** (April–Oct daily 9.30am–6pm; June, July & Aug open until 7pm; €5; ⓦhotelvillacipressi.it), on the southern fringe of the village, has terraced gardens tumbling down to the lake that make a perfect spot to relax. The adjacent **Villa Monastero** gardens (March daily 10am–5pm; April & Oct daily 10am–6pm; May–Aug daily 9.30am–7pm; Sept daily 9.30am–6pm; gardens €5, gardens & house museum €8; ⓦvillamonastero.eu) are even more lavish. Built on the site of a twelfth-century convent, the splendid villa has fourteen furnished rooms that visitors can wander around. A twenty-minute walk south of Piazza San Giorgio leads to **Fiumelatte**, a waterfall visible between March and Oct (free) that is known to be one of Italy's shortest waterways at only 250m from source to lake.

4

Castello di Vezio

March–Oct daily 10am–sunset • €4 • ⓦcastellodivezio.it

A steep forty-minute walk along the Scabium footpath opposite Villa Monastero leads to spectacular views from the landscaped ruins of the **Castello di Vezio**, allegedly founded by the Lombard Queen Theodolinda in the seventh century. There are regular falconry displays (check the website for the latest schedules) and a good outside restaurant-café serving local specialities.

Abbazia di Piona

Daily 9am–noon & 2.30–6pm • Free • ⓣ0341 940 331, ⓦabbaziadipiona.it

About 16km north of Varenna on the eastern shore, a minor road branches down to the tranquil twelfth-century Romanesque **Abbazia di Piona**, perched on a headland. A shop by the gates sells bottles of the monks' fiery herb liqueur.

ARRIVAL AND INFORMATION — VARENNA

Thanks to its rocky shoreline, Varenna is split into two halves. Boats dock to the north, above which stands the train station. Some 300m south via the main road – or the *passarella*, a scenic walkway which clings to the rocks – is the main village.

By train Regular trains from Milano Centrale and Lecco pull in at Varenna-Esino station, a steep 5min walk uphill from the boat landing stage. The station is unstaffed; if you haven't got a return ticket you can buy one at Cafè al Barilott at Via IV Novembre 6, the official Trenord reseller of Varenna,

or from the I Viaggi del Tivano travel agency at the station (☎0341 814 009, ⓦtivanotours.com) for a fee.

Destinations Bergamo (hourly, changing at Lecco; 1hr 15min); Lecco (every 20min; 20-40min); Milano Centrale (16 daily; 1hr3min).

By boat Ferries shuttle between Varenna, Bellagio, Menaggio and other points. Car ferries cross to Bellagio and Menaggio.

Tourist office Via 4 Novembre 7 (Jan–March Tues–Sat 9.30am–1pm & 2–5.30pm, Sun 9.30am–1pm; April Tues–Sat 10am–1pm & 2.30–6pm, Sun 9.30am–3pm; May Tues–Sun 10am–1pm & 2.30–6pm; June–Sept Mon–Thurs 10am–1pm & 2–7pm, Fri–Sun 10am–6pm; Oct daily 9am–1pm & 2–6pm; Dec 9.30am–1pm & 2–5.30pm, Sun 9.30am–1pm; closed Nov; ☎0341 830 367, ⓦvarennaturismo.com).

ACCOMMODATION

★ **Albergo Milano** Via XX Settembre 35 ☎0341 830 298, ⓦvarenna.net. This friendly hotel tucked away on a narrow lane behind the waterfront is run by a charming couple. Some of the modern rooms have great lake views, and there are also a couple of apartments (€150) with kitchenette nearby. There's a lovely terrace with a great restaurant, too. **€190**

Casa Stacy Piazza San Giorgio 3 ☎342 008 6536, ⓦcasastacy.com. Friendly American-run B&B with three locations dotted around town, featuring four comfortable rooms and three apartment suites. At Piazza San Giorgio, two rooms have kitchenettes, and there's a communal kitchen with living area, as well as a lovely rooftop terrace with stunning views over the town and the lake. Check-in is at Contrada dei Cavalli 3. **€135**

Hotel Du Lac Via del Prestino 11 ☎0341 830 238, ⓦalbergodulac.com. Built in 1823, this relaxed four-star hotel right on the water has spacious and comfortable rooms, and most have lovely views. Sit on the vine-shaded terrace and drink in the vista. **€190**

EATING AND DRINKING

Al Prato Piazza Al Prato ☎348 712 4389. A local fisherman supplies fresh fish to this friendly restaurant and wine bar – try the *merenda* (afternoon snack), consisting of either cheese (€15) or meat platters (€12). Wed–Mon noon–3pm & 6.30–10.30pm.

Il Cavatappi Via XX Settembre ☎0341 815 349, ⓦcavatappivarenna.it. Tiny restaurant with just a handful of tables, tucked away in the thicket of lanes off the main square. *Primi* €12, *secondi* €18. Mon & Tues 6.30–9pm, Thurs–Sun noon–2pm & 6.30–9pm 6.30–9pm.

La Passerella ☎0341 830 369. The best place in town to grab an ice cream – even if you're lactose intolerant. All the ice creams here are made with water (the chocolate flavoured ice cream consists of melted chocolate – divine); there are over twenty flavours, including white chocolate with coconut and Nutella. Daily 11am–11pm.

La Vista Via XX Settembre 35 ☎0341 830 298. Part of *Albergo Milano*, this restaurant has a beautiful lake-view terrace that's ideal for an intimate dinner of light, tasty Mediterranean cuisine. There's a three-course menu for €40, while four courses will set you back €48. Wed–Mon 7–10pm; during the warmer months of the year open also for lunch on weekends 12.30–2.30pm.

Osteria Quatro Pass Via XX Settembre 20 ☎0341 815 091, ⓦquattropass.com. Set back from the lake in a vaulted cellar, this welcoming *osteria* serves authentic, seasonal cuisine at modest prices: *primi* €12, *secondi* €20. Daily noon–2.30pm & 6.30–10pm.

4

Ramo di Lecco

The Lecco branch of the lake to the southeast is often dubbed "Lago di Lecco", even though it is an integral part of the whole: it's austere and fjord-like, at its most atmospheric in the morning mists. At its foot is the workaday town of **LECCO**, 30km east of Como, with the brooding Grigne mountain range above, which is a magnet for keen mountain climbers. Lecco is largely a commercial centre with only a couple of tourist attractions; literary types might appreciate **Villa Manzoni**, Via Guanella 7 (Tues–Fri 9.30am–6pm, Sat & Sun 10am–6pm; €6), the childhood home of Alessandro Manzoni, author of the great nineteenth-century Italian novel *I Promessi Sposi* ("The Betrothed"); otherwise, pop into the lakefront **Basilica** and then climb the bell tower, Italy's second highest, from where there are lovely views of the city, the lake and the mountains; the bell tower is open only on certain days (check the website for the latest dates and timings at ⓦcampaniledilecco.it).

ARRIVAL AND INFORMATION — LECCO

By train Lecco is directly linked with Milan and is the hub for changing trains if you're connecting between Lake Como and Bergamo.

Destinations Bergamo (hourly; 45min); Como (6 daily; 1hr

5min); Milano Centrale (10 daily; 45min); Varenna (every 30min; 20–40min).

By bus #C40/#D41 bus links Lecco with Como, #D10 serves Bellagio and #D35 shuttles between Lecco and Valsassina (asfautolinee.it).

Destinations Bellagio (every 2hr; 50min); Como (every 2hr; 1hr 10min).

By boat Boats from Bellagio to Lecco run daily in summer and at weekends in spring and autumn; there is no service in winter.

Tourist office The tourist office at Piazza XX Settembre 23 (daily 9am–1pm & 2–6pm; 0341 295 720, lakecomo.com) has information on mountain hikes in Valsassina, sports activities, events and accommodation.

ACCOMMODATION

Casa sull'Albero Viale Penati 5/7 0341 188 0440, casa-sullalbero.eu. This minimalist design hotel is all glass and timber, with large floor-to-ceiling windows throughout making the most of the surrounding scenery. It's particularly eco-friendly, with natural materials, solar panels and Tesla car charging points. Breakfast offers a very good selection of local produce, including cold cuts, cheeses and locally made jams. **€140**

Bergamo

Just 50km northeast of Milan, yet much closer to the mountains in look and feel, **BERGAMO** comprises two distinct parts – **Bergamo Bassa**, the city centre on the plain, and medieval **Bergamo Alta**, 100m above. Bergamo Bassa is a harmonious mixture of medieval cobbled quarters blending into late nineteenth- and early twentieth-century town planning, while Bergamo Alta is one of northern Italy's loveliest urban centres, with strollable lanes and a lively, easy-going pace of life.

4

Bergamo owes much of its magic to the Venetians, who ruled the town for over 350 years, adorning facades and open spaces with the Venetian lion, symbol of the Republic, and leaving a ring of gated walls. Now worn, mellow and overgrown with creepers, these kept armies out until the French invaded in 1796.

Bergamo Alta: the upper town

With its steep, narrow streets, flanked by high facades and encircled by sixteenth-century walls, **Bergamo Alta** – the upper town – remains in appearance largely as it was in the Middle Ages. The main public spaces – **Piazza Vecchia** and adjacent **Piazza del Duomo** – combine medieval austerity with the grace of later, Renaissance design. The funicular railway from the lower town arrives at the tiny station on Piazza Mercato delle Scarpe from where the main street, beginning as Via Gombito and continuing as Via Colleoni after Piazza Vecchia, follows the line of the Roman *decumanus maximus*, topped and tailed by evidence of Bergamo's military past – the **Rocca** to the east, the **Cittadella** to the west. Just beyond the Cittadella, through Porta Sant Alessandro, another funicular ride whisks you up to the highest point of town, San Vigilio.

Torre del Gombito

Via Gombito 13 • Early April–early Oct Tues–Sun entrance at 10am, 10.45am, 11.30am, 2.30pm, 3.15pm & 4pm; timed slots must be booked in advance at the tourist office • 035 242 226

The twelfth-century **Torre del Gombito** looms 52m above Bergamo Alta's main street. It's worth climbing up to the top of the tower for incredible views over the old town and the valley below – book a time slot at the tourist office on the ground floor before heading up.

Piazza Vecchia

Bergamo's magnificent **Piazza Vecchia** is enclosed by a harmonious miscellany of buildings, ranging from wrought-iron-balconied houses containing cafés and restaurants to the opulent Palladian-style civic library. Le Corbusier proclaimed this "the most beautiful square in Europe", and it's certainly a striking space. The piazza was the scene of joyous celebrations in 1797, when the French formed the Republic of Bergamo: the square was carpeted with tapestries and transformed into an open-air ballroom in

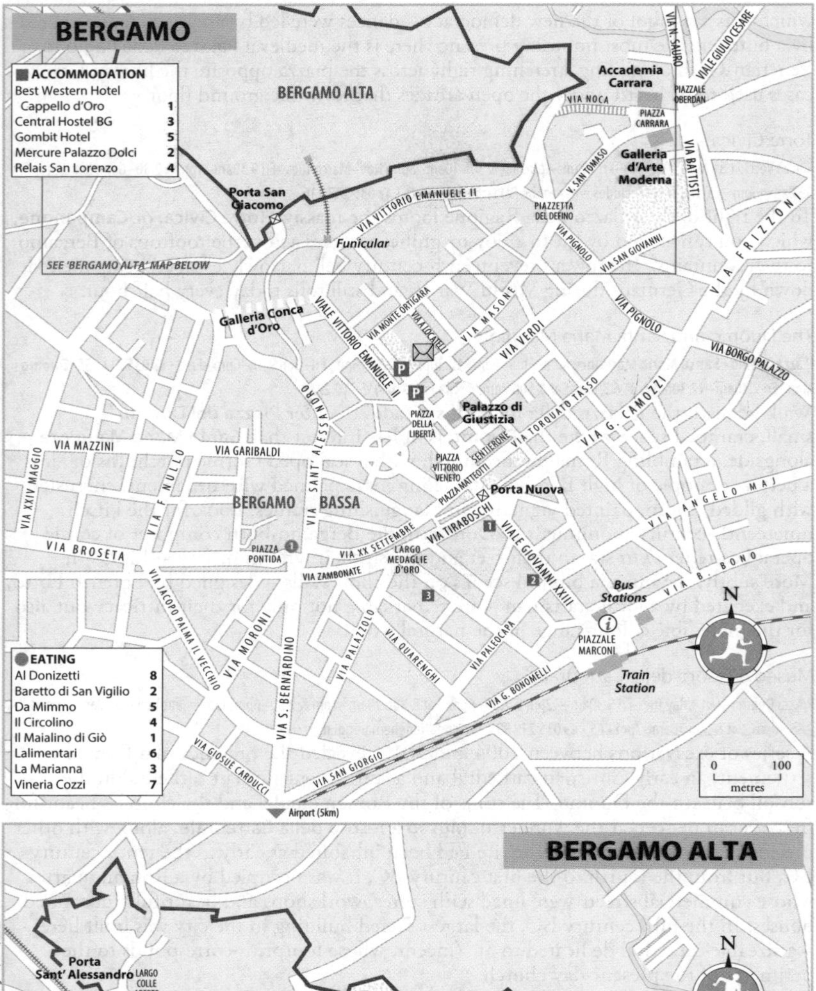

BERGAMO

ACCOMMODATION

Best Western Hotel Cappello d'Oro	1
Central Hostel BG	3
Gombit Hotel	5
Mercure Palazzo Dolci	2
Relais San Lorenzo	4

EATING

Al Donizetti	8
Baretto di San Vigilio	2
Da Mimmo	5
Il Circolino	4
Il Maialino di Giò	1
Lalimentari	6
La Marianna	3
Vineria Cozzi	7

BERGAMO ALTA
Accademia Carrara
Galleria d'Arte Moderna
Porta San Giacomo
Funicular
SEE 'BERGAMO ALTA' MAP BELOW
Galleria Conca d'Oro
Palazzo di Giustizia
Porta Nuova
BERGAMO BASSA
Bus Stations
Train Station
PIAZZALE MARCONI
PIAZZA DELLA LIBERTÀ
PIAZZA VITTORIO VENETO
PIAZZA MATTEOTTI
PIAZZA PONTIDA
LARGO MEDAGLIE D'ORO
PIAZZALE OBERDAN
PIAZZA CARRARA
PIAZZETTA DEL DEFINO
VIA N. SAURO
VIALE GIULIO CESARE
VIA NOCA
VIA BATTISTI
V. SAN TOMASO
VIA VITTORIO EMANUELE II
VIA PIGNOLO
VIA SAN GIOVANNI
VIA FRIZZONI
VIA BORGO PALAZZO
VIA MONTE ORTIGARA
VIA A. LOCATELLI
VIA MASONE
VIA VERDI
VIALE VITTORIO EMANUELE II
VIA SANT' ALESSANDRO
VIA TORQUATO TASSO
VIA G. CAMOZZI
SENTIERONE
VIA MAZZINI
VIA GARIBALDI
VIA F. NULLO
VIA XXIV MAGGIO
VIA BROSETA
VIA XX SETTEMBRE
VIA TIRABOSCHI
VIA ANGELO MAJ
VIA B. BONO
VIALE GIOVANNI XXIII
VIA ZAMBONATE
VIA JACOPO PALMA IL VECCHIO
VIA MORONI
VIA S. BERNARDINO
VIA PALAZZOLO
VIA QUARENGHI
VIA PALEOCAPA
VIA G. BONOMELLI
VIA GIOSUÈ CARDUCCI
VIA SAN GIORGIO
N
0 100 metres
Airport (5km)

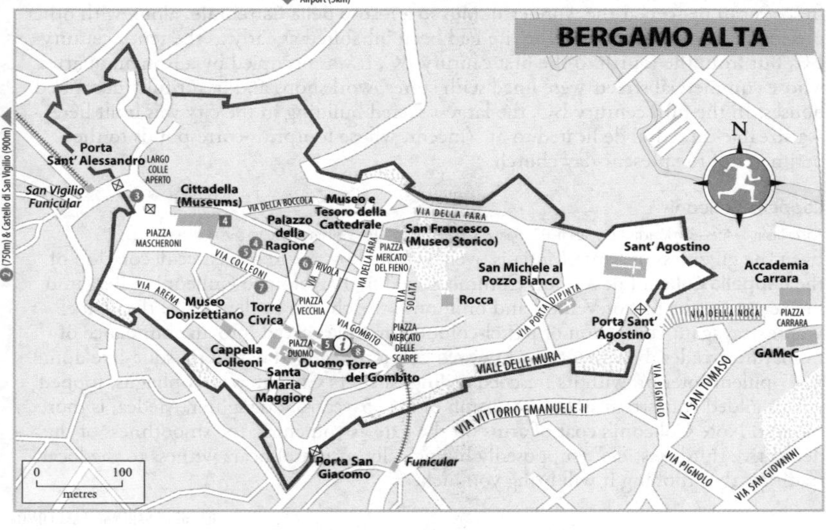

4

which – as a symbol of the new democracy – dances were led by an aristocrat partnered by a butcher. The most imposing presence here is the medieval **Palazzo della Ragione**, a Venetian-Gothic building stretching right across the piazza opposite the library. Court cases used to be heard under the open arcades that form the ground floor.

Torre Civica

Piazza Vecchia 8 • April–Oct Tues–Fri 10am–6pm, Sat & Sun 10am–8pm; Nov–March Tues–Fri 9.30am–1pm & 2.30–6pm, Sat & Sun 9.30am–6pm • €5; the ticket includes entry to the Palazzo del Podestà • T 035 247 116

To the right of the Palazzo della Ragione looms the massive **Torre Civica**, or **Campanone**, which you can ascend by lift to enjoy magnificent views across the rooftops of Bergamo to the mountains. The tower's seventeenth-century bell narrowly escaped being melted down by the Germans during World War II, and still tolls today every half-hour.

The Duomo and Santa Maria Maggiore

Piazza Duomo • **Santa Maria Maggiore** Mon–Thurs 9am–12.30pm & 2.30–6pm, Fri–Sun 9am–6pm • Free • T 035 211 355• **Duomo** Mon–Fri 7.30am–12.30pm & 3–6.30pm, Sat & Sun 7am–7pm • Free • T 035 210 223

Walk beneath the Palazzo della Ragione's arcades to enter **Piazza del Duomo** – a small, cramped space where the **Duomo** is of less interest than **Santa Maria Maggiore** alongside, a rambling Romanesque church with a scalloped Gothic porch. Inside, it is a perfect example of high Baroque, its ceiling marzipanned with ornament, encrusted with gilded stucco, painted vignettes and languishing statues. Look for the kitsch nineteenth-century monument to Donizetti, the Bergamo-born composer of comic opera: bas-relief *putti* stamp their feet and smash their lyres in misery at his death. More subtly, the intarsia biblical scenes on the choir stalls – designed by Lorenzo Lotto, and executed by a local craftsman – are remarkable not only for their intricacy but also for the incredible colour-range of the natural wood.

4

Museo e Tesoro della Cattedrale

Piazza Duomo • Oct–May Tues-Fri 9.30am–12pm & 2.30–6pm, Sat & Sun 10am–1pm & 2.30–6pm; June–Sept Tues-Fri 10am–1pm & 2–6.30pm, Sat & Sun 10am–7pm • €5 • T 035 2?9 893, W fondazionebernareggi.it

A series of excavations between 2004 and 2012 revealed the presence of a Roman settlement, an early Christian cathedral and a subsequent Roman cathedral in the subsoil beneath the Duomo. The ruins of the Roman citadel and the church's beautiful frescoes can be seen at the wonderful **Museo e Tesoro della Cattedrale**, along with other precious objects found here. The site had been inhabited as early as the tenth century BC, but from the fourth to the first century BC, it was occupied by a Roman quarter whose commercial streets were lined with stores, workshops and beautifully decorated houses. In the fifth century BC, the largest sacred building in the city was built here – a sizeable cathedral dedicated to St Vincent, whose footprint corresponds to the perimeter of the present-day church.

Cappella Colleoni

Piazza Duomo • Tues–Sun March–Oct 9.30am–12.30pm & 2–6.30pm; Nov–Feb 9.30am–12.30pm & 2–4.30pm • Free

Even the glitziness of Santa Maria is overshadowed by the Renaissance decoration of the **Cappella Colleoni** next door. Commissioned by Bartolomeo Colleoni, a Bergamo mercenary in the pay of Venice, and built onto the church in the 1470s, the chapel is an extravagant confection of pastel-coloured marble carved into an abundance of miniature arcades, balustrades and twisted columns, capped with a mosque-like dome. The opulent interior, with its frescoed ceiling, shelters Colleoni's sarcophagus, topped with a gilded equestrian statue; the tomb of his 15-year-old daughter, Medea, is more modest. Note Colleoni's coat of arms on the gate as you enter; the smoothness of the decorative third "testicle" (supposedly biologically accurate) bears witness to the local tradition that rubbing it will bring you luck.

VILLAGE OF VARENNA, LAKE COMO

Museo Donizettiano

Via Arena 9 • Tues–Fri 10am–1pm, Sat & Sun 10am–1pm & 3–6pm • €5 • ⓣ 035 247 116, ⓦ bergamoestoria.it

Partway up Via Arena, a frescoed doorway opens into the grounds of the Santa Grata monastery, also home to the **Museo Donizettiano**. One of the masters of the "bel canto" opera style (along with Bellini and Rossini), Gaetano Donizetti (1797–1848), who was born and died in Bergamo, is celebrated for his melodramatic lyricism, which reached a peak in *Lucia di Lammermoor*. The museum contains portraits of the maestro, original letters and scores, his imperial-style bed and his patron's fortepiano.

Ex Convento di San Francesco (Museo Storico)

Piazza Mercato del Fieno 6/A • **Museum** June–Sept Tues–Fri 10am–1pm & 2.30–6pm, Sat & Sun 10am–7pm; Oct–May Tues–Sun 9.30am–1pm & 2.30–6pm • €1• ⓦ museodellestorie.bergamo.it

Built between the end of the thirteenth century and the early fifteenth century, the **Ex Convento di San Francesco** has a beautiful thirteenth-century cloister. The convent was supressed in 1797, and later used as a hospital, prison, penal institution and in the 1930s as a primary school. Today the building houses temporary exhibitions spanning the history of the city from the eighteenth century to 1945.

The Rocca (Museo Storico)

Piazzalle Brigata Legnano • June–Sept Tues–Fri 10am–1pm & 2.30–6pm, Sat & Sun 10am–7pm; Oct–May Tues–Sun 9.30am–1pm & 2.30–6pm • €5 • ⓦ bergamoestoria.it

4

The beautiful **Rocca** gardens make a great spot for a picnic, with stunning views over the Città Alta, plus cannons and armoured vehicles that children can clamber over. The gardens were probably the site of the Roman Capitol, rebuilt and reinforced in the 1330s. Inside the Rocca, the nineteenth-century section of the **Museo Storico** focuses on the Italian Wars of Unification, the Risorgimento, in which Bergamo had a very proud role and earned itself the name the "Città dei Mille" after the thousand volunteers from the city who went to join Garibaldi's army.

The Cittadella

The narrow, pedestrianized **Via Colleoni** is lined with boutiques, delicatessens and pastry shops selling sweet polenta cakes topped with chocolate birds. At the top of the street Piazza Mascheroni lies at the entrance to the **Cittadella**, a military stronghold built by Barnabo Visconti, now housing a small theatre and two didactic (Italian labelling only) museums of archeology and natural history.

The Colle Aperto and San Vigilio

The **Colle Aperto** is an open hillside beyond the city walls. Just through the Porta Sant'Alessandro, leading off Colle Aperto, a funicular trundles up the short track to the hamlet of **San Vigilio** – it's also a pleasant but very steep walk up a cobbled lane overlooking villas and gardens. At the top perches San Viglio, with a couple of lovely restaurants, castle ruins and more wonderful vistas across the ornate gardens of Bergamo's most prestigious summer retreats.

Returning to Colle Aperto, you can follow the old **walls** around the circumference of the upper town – the whole circuit takes a couple of hours, with the most picturesque stretch lying between the Colle Aperto and Porta San Giacomo (from where a long flight of steps leads down into Bergamo Bassa alongside the vegetable patches and orchards growing in the shade of the walls).

Bergamo Bassa: the lower town

Bergamo Bassa spreads north from the train station in a comfortable blend of Neoclassical ostentation, Fascist severity and tree-lined elegance. At the heart of the busy streets, midway along the main Viale Papa Giovanni XXIII, the mock-Doric temples of the **Porta Nuova** mark the **Sentierone**, a favourite spot for Bergamo's citizens to meet and

stroll. Frowning down on the square is the **Palazzo di Giustizia**, built in the bombastic rectangular style of the Mussolini era. Via XX Settembre to the west is the main focus for Bergamo's shoppers, with a selection of quality mainstream stores. From the Sentierone, Via Tasso leads east into the oldest part of the Città Bassa, formed in the Middle Ages as overspill from the upper town; shady **Via Pignolo** has a largely unchanged appearance, with many architectural features – balconies, mullioned windows – surviving.

Galleria d'Arte Moderna e Contemporanea (GAMeC)

Via San Tomaso 53 • Mon & Wed–Sun 10am–7pm, Thurs until 10pm • Free; charge for temporary exhibitions varies • ⓣ 035 270 272, ⓦ gamec.it

As well as hosting temporary exhibitions, often of world-class stature, the **Galleria d'Arte Moderna e Contemporanea (GAMeC)** has a small, but impressive, permanent collection. Among paintings by Kandinsky and Graham Sutherland are bronzes by the twentieth-century Bergamo-born sculptor Giacomo Manzù plus a collection of abstract works by Atanasio Soldati, Luigi Veronesi and Alberto Magnelli.

Accademia Carrara

Piazza Giacomo Carrara 82 • Early June–late Sept Wed–Mon 10am-7pm; early Oct–late May Wed–Mon 9.30–5.30pm • €12 • ⓣ 035 234 396, ⓦ lacarrara.it

Established in 1796 by Count Giacomo Carrara as a school of painting and gallery, the **Accademia Carrara** is today one of Italy's greatest art museums. With more than 1800 artworks, the gallery holds masterpieces such as Botticelli's *The Story of Virginia the Roman* (1500–1510), Pisanello's *Ritratto di Lionello d'Este* (c. 1441), Andrea Mantegna's *Madonna col Bambino* (1475) and The Resurrection of Christ (1492-93), recently attributed to the great Renaissance master, Titian's *Madonna col Bambino in un Paesaggio* (c. 1507), Raffaello's *San Sebastiano* (c.1502–03) and Canaletto's *Il Canal Grande da palazzo Balbi* (1728).

4

ARRIVAL AND DEPARTURE — BERGAMO

BY PLANE

Bergamo's Orio al Serio airport (ⓣ 035 326 323, ⓦ orioaeroporto.it) – also called "Milan-Bergamo" – is 4km southeast of Bergamo city centre.

From the airport to central Bergamo City bus #1 (daily every 20min 5.20am–midnight; 15min; ⓦ atb.bergamo.it) runs to the bus station: most also continue to the funicular base station and into the Città Alta. A taxi into Bergamo (ⓣ 035 451 9090) costs around €35.

From the airport to Milan The following bus companies connect the airport daily to Milano Centrale station (1hr; €5): Orioshuttle (every 30min 4.25am–midnight; ⓣ 035 330 706, ⓦ orioshuttle.it), Autostradale (every 30min 7.45am–12.15am; ⓣ 035 322 915, ⓦ autostradale.it) and Terravison (every 30min 4.05am–1am; ⓣ 331 299 9450, ⓦ terravision.eu). A taxi to Milan costs over €120.

BY TRAIN

Bergamo's train station is at the southernmost end of the Città Bassa's central avenue, Viale Papa Giovanni XXIII: it's a long walk from the Città Alta but well linked by bus (#1) with the airport, the upper town and the funicular station. Left-luggage facilities are a 2min walk away just outside the bus station (see below). There are fast trains from Milan (Centrale and Lambrate) and Brescia, and slower ones from Como, Cremona and Lecco.

Destinations Brescia (hourly; 50min); Como San Giovanni (with a change in Monza; hourly; 1hr 25min); Cremona (via Treviglio or Milan; every 30min; 2hr) Lecco (hourly; 40min); Milano Centrale or Porta Garibaldi (hourly; 50min).

BY BUS

Bergamo bus station is behind the lower town tourist office, opposite the train station and has a secure, automated left-luggage facility just outside (€4/24hr).

Destinations Clusone (11 daily; 1hr); Lovere (hourly; 1hr 10min); Sarnico (hourly; 55min).

INFORMATION AND GUIDED WALKS

Tourist information Tourist offices can be found in the Orio al Serio airport arrivals hall (daily 8am–9pm; ⓣ 035 320 402, ⓦ turismo.bergamo.it), in Piazzale Marconi opposite the train station in Città Bassa (daily 9am–12.30pm & 2–5.30pm; ⓣ 035 210 204, ⓦ comune.bergamo.it/turismo) and at Via Gombito 13 at the base of

the Torre Gombito in Città Alta (daily 9am–5.30pm; ☎ 035 242 226).

Tours The Gruppo Guide Turistiche Città di Bergamo runs guided walking tours of the old town (Wed, Sat & Sun at 3pm; 2hr; €10; ☎ 035 344 205, bergamoguide.it), which leave from just outside the tourist office at Via Gombito 13.

GETTING AROUND

By funicular A funicular (daily 7am–12.13am) runs every few minutes on the steep route between Viale Vittorio Emanuele II in the Città Bassa (the extension of Viale Papa Giovanni) and Piazza Mercato delle Scarpe in the Città Alta. A separate funicular also runs from just behind Colle Aperto in the upper town up to San Vigilio. Purchase an ordinary ticket (75min; €1.30), a *biglietto turistico giornaliero* (24hr; €3.50, or €5 including the airport), or a *biglietto turistico 3 giorni* (valid for three days; €7), all of which are usable on city buses and funiculars.

By tourist train The tourist train Gulliberg links the upper funicular station (Città Alta) to the Colle Aperto (Sun & public holidays every 30min 2–7pm; €3 return).

By bike, scooter and micro-car Electric bikes, scooters and micro-cars can be rented from Eco-rent, Viale Papa Giovanni XXIII 57, c/o Urban Center (☎ 035 529 3888, eco-rent.it) by the bus station in the lower town.

ACCOMMODATION

Bergamo is not somewhere to arrive without a reservation, even out of season: **accommodation** is pricey and, in the centre, fairly limited. There are a handful of atmospheric hotels in the Città Alta, with mostly business hotels in the Città Bassa. As always B&Bs provide a good, low-key alternative – there are several located in attractive buildings in Bergamo Alta; consult bedandbergamo.it.

4

UPPER TOWN

★ **Gombit Hotel** Via Mario Lupo 6 ☎ 035 247 009, gombithotel.it; map p.277. A fashionable design hotel housed in a thirteenth-century building with a stone tower: the stylish interiors feature exposed walls and pastel-coloured furnishings. **€225**

Relais San Lorenzo Piazza Mascheroni 9/A ☎ 035 237 383, relaisanlorenzo.com; map p.277. This luxury hotel features sleek, stylish rooms in shades of brown and cream looking onto a peaceful cloister. Its atmospheric restaurant is a must visit for non-guests too, carved into the basement with seating amid ancient Roman and medieval walls. Facilities include a spa and a lovely terrace overlooking the lower city. **€265**

LOWER TOWN

Best Western Hotel Cappello d'Oro Viale Papa Giovanni XXIII 12 ☎ 035 422 2711, hotelcappellodoro.it; map p.277. Just a few hundred metres from the train station, this pet-friendly four-star hotel has welcoming rooms with tasteful decor. Facilities include a sauna and gym. At breakfast there's a choice of organic and gluten-free cereal and croissants. **€140**

Central Hostel BG Via Ghislanzoni 30 ☎ 035 211 359, centralhostelbg.com; map p.277. Right in the centre of the lower town and handy for the train station, this hostel has simple dorms as well as private rooms. There's an in-house pub that's open until 1am, a TV room, free international calls, parking, laundry facilities, and free bikes to borrow. Dorms **€25**, doubles **€56**

Mercure Palazzo Dolci Viale Papa Giovanni XXIII 100 ☎ 035 227 411, mercure.com; map p.277. This four-star chain hotel is in a good location in the lower town, a short walk from the station. With stylish, if slightly anonymous, swish contemporary interiors and good soundproofing, it's excellent value. **€160**

EATING

One of the pleasures of Bergamo is its food and drink, whether you're assembling picnics from the many *salumerie* and bakeries in the upper town – most lining the main streets of Via Gombito and Via Colleoni – or grazing around the city's *osterie*. The town's signature dish is **polenta**, often served with veal or local game; polenta *taragna* is a creamy cheese and butter combination. *Casoncelli* – ravioli stuffed with sausage meat and served with sage and melted butter – is another favourite. **Booking ahead** is recommended, and essential at weekends.

Al Donizetti Via Gombito 17/A ☎ 035 242 661, donizetti.it; map p.277. Located in the old cheese market, this pleasant bar with seating on a breezy shaded portico serves tasty cheese and cold cut platters (€11.50) that go down a treat with a glass of one of the many wines on offer. Choose from goat's cheeses, *prosciutti crudi*, bresaola, *salumi d'oca* (goose) and more. Mon–Fri & Sun 11am–midnight, Sat 11am–12.30am.

Baretto di San Vigilio Via Castello 1 ☎ 035 253 191, baretto.it; map p.277. A stylish, classic restaurant, whose shaded terrace is an unbeatable spot for a long, lazy summer lunch or for a balmy evening with wonderful views and lovely food. The *menù degustazione* will set you back €45/head. *Primi* €16, *secondi* €20. There's a good-value lunch deal on weekdays for €25. Mon–Fri 11am–2.30pm, Sat 10am–1am, Sun 9am–1am.

★ **Da Mimmo** Via Bartolomeo Colleoni 17 ☎ 035 218 5 35, ristorantemimmo.com; map p.277. In a

former post office building, this is an excellent family-run restaurant, where the recipes have been passed down for generations. It serves hearty dishes and exquisite pizzas on a large shaded terrace in summer, or in the welcoming interior on cold winter days. Try the excellent Regina Margherita pizza with buffalo mozzarella (€9). Daily noon–2.30pm & 7–11pm; closed Tues lunch.

Il Circolino Vicolo Sant'Agata 19 ⓣ035 218 568, ⓦilcircolinocittaalta.it; map p.277. This laidback, informal place with a huge leafy garden serves up large portions of great-value dishes made with ingredients from the area. Lunch menu Mon–Fri €10–14; otherwise *primi* from €8, *secondi* from €8.50. Daily 11am–1am.

Il Maialino di Giò Piazza Pontida 37 ⓣ035 215 840, ⓦilmaialinodigio.it; map p.277. A lively little deli and bar with hams hanging from the ceiling that is particularly popular at *aperitivo* time for its tasty cold cut platters (€8). It's a great spot to grab a sandwich (€4), too. Mon–Sat 10am–11pm, Sun 10am–4pm.

Lalimentari Piazza Vecchia 8/12 ⓣ035 233 043, ⓦlalimentari.it; map p.277. A friendly little restaurant, breakfast and wine bar serving traditional regional cuisine made from high-quality seasonal ingredients – including a number of polenta-based dishes (€15), the area's much-loved casoncelli (€12) and hearty rabbit mains (€18). Cheeses and cold cuts are all local, as are the majority of wines they stock (the extensive wine list features over eight hundred labels). Daily 8.30am–1am.

La Marianna Largo Colle Aperto 4 ⓣ035 237 027, ⓦlamarianna.it; map p.277. Bergamo's historic ice cream parlour, beneath balconies dripping with geraniums, serves the best ice cream in town. They even claim to have invented the flavour *stracciatella*. Tues–Sat 7.30am–11pm, Sun 8am–11pm.

Vineria Cozzi Via Colleoni 22/A ⓣ035 238 836, ⓦvineriacozzi.it; map p.277. A historic wine bar and restaurant on the main thoroughfare in the upper town with a great selection of local wines and grappas. There's a network of pretty dining rooms behind the bar where excellent, traditional dishes are served. Customers can order a lovely two-course picnic meal (€30), served in a pretty picnic basket with tablecloths and cutlery. Daily 10.30am–3pm & 6.30pm–midnight.

4

Lake Iseo

The least known of the Italian Lakes, pretty **Lake Iseo** is popular with hikers and outdoor sports enthusiasts. The S-shaped lake is home to Europe's largest lake island, **Monte Isola**, which is a great place to explore by bike. The lake's main town and transport hub is **Iseo**, off the A4 Turin to Venice motorway and linked via a fast road north to the prehistoric UNESCO rock carvings of the Val Camonica by a series of tunnels.

ARRIVAL AND INFORMATION — LAKE ISEO

By train Iseo train station is served by slow trains on the Brescia–Edolo line, and lies at the far eastern end of Via XX Settembre, 450m inland from the *imbarcadero*, which is located just off the main square at the western end of the town centre.

Destinations Borgonato–Adro (4 daily; 6min); Bornato Calino (4 daily; 10min); Brescia (approx hourly; 30min); Edolo (8 daily; 1hr 30min); Pisogne (hourly; 30min); Rovato Città (4 daily; 20min).

By bus Buses from Brescia stop at Iseo, as do local buses from along the lake. From Bergamo, head to Sarnico, or take a train to Brescia, then switch to an Iseo-bound bus or train.

Destinations Lovere (2 daily; 45min); Pisogne (2 daily; 30min).

By boat Iseo is a ferry hub for the lake with regular services to towns around the lake between March and Sept; ferries to Monte Isola run year round. Iseo is also a departure point for the lake cruise services. The *imbarcadero* is located just off the main square at the western end of the town centre.

Tourist office Lungolago Marconi 2 (April–Sept Mon–Sat 10am–12.30pm 3–6pm, Sun 9.30am–12.30pm; Oct–March Mon–Fri 10am–12.30pm & 3–6pm, Sat 10am–12.30pm; ⓣ030 374 8733, ⓦiseolake.info).

ACCOMMODATION AND EATING

Relais I Due Roccoli Via S. Bonomelli, Località Invino ⓣ030 982 2977, ⓦidueroccoli.com. Tucked away on a hillside offering gorgeous views of the lake and the island, this laidback four-star is set in a restored farmhouse and former hunting lodge. Rooms are simply furnished, the atmosphere is unpretentious, and the attractive restaurant is very good, serving creatively presented Italian dishes. There's a small swimming pool and tennis court. €176

★ **Trattoria Cacciatore** Via Molini 28, Sulzano ⓣ030 985 184, ⓦtrattoriacacciatore.it. In a panoramic location on a hillside above Sulzano, this bustling family-run trattoria is a great spot for some authentic home cooking in an informal setting. The cuisine is excellent, with the likes of tagliolini pasta with goose meat ragu (€9), suckling pig (€13) and dried sardines with polenta (€12) featuring on the menu. Wed–Sun noon–2pm & 7.30–10pm, Mon noon–2pm.

Monte Isola (Mont'Isola or Montisola)

The pretty lake island of **MONTE ISOLA** is a peaceful spot, whose perimeter promenade is dotted with restaurants, while smaller paths crisscross the interior commanding lovely views. The best way to explore the island is by bike (available for rent at Peschiera Maraglio; €3.50/hour) or on foot. On the island's western shore, the **Museo della Rete** (by advance booking only, call ⊤345 914 3707, ⓦwww.laretesrl.it) provides an insight into its history, when the islanders produced hundreds of fishing nets – today they make mainly sporting nets and hammocks.

ARRIVAL AND INFORMATION — MONTE ISOLA

By boat There are four landing stages around the island: Peschiera (nearest to Sulzano on the mainland) and Sensole on the south side, Carzano (opposite Sale Marasino) and Siviano on the north. Ferries shuttle over from Iseo and other points frequently.

Tourist office Località Peschiera Maraglio 150 (Jan & Feb Thurs–Sun 10am–2pm; March Thurs–Sat 10am–2pm, Sun 10am–4pm; April Thurs & Fri 10am–2pm, Sat & Sun 10am–4pm; May Mon 10am–2pm, Thurs & Fri 10am–2pm, Sat & Sun 10am–4pm; June–Sept Mon–Fri 10am–4pm, Sat & Sun 10am–5pm; Oct–Dec Fri 10am–2pm, Sat & Sun 10am–4pm; ⊤030 982 5088, ⓦvisitmonteisola.it).

ACCOMMODATION AND EATING

Castello Oldofredi Via Peschiera Maraglio 58 ⊤030 982 5294, ⓦoldofrediresidence.it. Located on a hill in the picturesque village of Peschiera Maraglio, this four-star hotel in a restored medieval mansion has welcoming double rooms as well as apartments with modern amenities. Facilities include a swimming pool and a restaurant with a lovely terrace. Doubles **€120**, apartments **€150**

★ **Villarzilla** Via Olzano 18, Olzano ⊤329 117 8552, ⓦbbvillarzilla.it. Run by a friendly family, this lovely B&B with books scattered everywhere features natural materials such as wood and stone. The three warm rooms are filled with objects from the family's time in India, and are decorated with mismatched rustic furniture (all made by the owner). Book ahead. **€75**

4

Franciacorta

Between Iseo and Brescia, the hilly wine-producing area of FRANCIACORTA got its name from the religious communities that lived here from the eleventh century onwards: they were exempt from tax and known as the Corti Franche, or free courts. This small region is best known for its **Franciacorta DOCG** (Denominazione di Origine Controllata e Garantita), Italy's most refined sparkling wine: first made in the 1960s, it is produced according to Champagne methods. The area has more than a hundred vineyards, many of which are open for **tours** and **tasting sessions (by advanced booking)**, as well as some excellent Michelin-starred restaurants, plus more laidback trattorias where you can sample both the local wine and traditional regional dishes. A

FRANCIACORTA WINERIES

The secret of **Franciacorta's sparkling wine** lies in a second fermentation in the bottle which can last from eighteen to sixty months. Usually a blend of Chardonnay and Pinot Noir or Blanc grapes, the sparkling wine comes in various types: Not Dosed/Pas Dosé (extremely dry), Extra Brut, Brut Satèn (a light silky-smooth mixture), Sec, Demisec and Rosé. Some of its best-known **producers** are Bellavista (ⓦterramoretti.it), Belucchi (ⓦberlucchi.it), Ca'del Bosco (ⓦwww.cadelbosco.com) and Majolini (ⓦmajolini.it) but all the vineyards have their own story and often lovely headquarters in ancient farmhouses or villas. Most guided tours end with a tasting and very competitive prices are offered in the *cantina* shops, where they can usually arrange shipping back home. The Consortium Franciacorta (Via. Verdi 53, Erbusco; ⊤030 776 0477, ⓦfranciacorta.net) can give advice on which vineyards to visit, or you could be guided by local suggestions; make sure you book an appointment with the wineries you're planning on visiting. On Saturdays and Sundays between July and September buses tour the Franciacorta wine route, while in mid-September on even years, the **Festival Franciacorta** sees wineries open for tasting sessions and local restaurants offering themed seasonal menus.

good way to visit some of them is to follow the **Strada del Vino Franciacorta** (pick up a map from tourist offices or hotels, or check Ⓦstradadelfranciacorta.it), which winds through the region for 80km, via vineyards, hotels and restaurants, with well-planned routes for cars, cyclists and walkers ranging from a couple of hours to a day or two.

ARRIVAL AND DEPARTURE — FRANCIACORTA

By train Trains on the Brescia–Edolo line link Iseo with several small stations in the Franciacorta region. Bikes are permitted on board.

Destinations Borgonato–Adro (hourly; 5min); Bornato Calino (hourly; 10min); Cazzago San Martino (4 daily; 15–30min); Rovato (5 daily; 15–30min).

ACCOMMODATION AND EATING

★**Al Rocol** Via Provinciale 79, Ome Ⓣ030 685 2542, Ⓦalrocol.com. This family-run agriturismo has agreeable rooms in a peaceful setting; the friendly owners organize wine-tasting sessions and the restaurant (open to non-guests Fri & Sat 7–9pm, Sun noon–2pm & 7–9pm) comes highly recommended for its outstanding home cooking. The seasonal menu includes traditional Italian staples. *Primi* €8.50, *secondi* €13 **€80**

★**Due Colombe** Borgo Antico San Vitale, Via Foresti 13, Borgonato di Cortefranca Ⓣ030 982 8227, Ⓦduecolombe.com. In an ancient farmhouse now housing a grappa distillery, this Michelin-starred restaurant dishes up exceptional gourmet cuisine with its roots in Franciacorta traditions. Tasting menu €75–95/head, mains €25. Tues–Fri 7.30–10pm, Sat 12.30–2pm & 7.30–10.30pm, Sun 12.30–2pm.

Brescia

Surrounded by vine-covered hills, the ancient settlement of **BRESCIA** is a wealthy city boasting Roman remains, Renaissance squares and a medieval centre with the outstanding museum complex of **Santa Giulia**. The city is also known for its legendary **Mille Miglia** car race in May, when hundreds of beautiful classic vehicles set off from the city centre to Rome and back.

Piazza della Loggia

Brescia's centre comprises a compact cluster of piazzas linked by cobbled streets. The main square, **Piazza della Loggia**, is also the prettiest, dating from 1433, when the city invited Venice to protect it from Milan's power-hungry Viscontis. The Venetian influence is clearest in the fancy **Loggia**, in which both Palladio and Titian had a hand, and the **Torre dell'Orologio**, modelled on the campanile in Venice's Piazza San Marco. Below it, a monument commemorates the Fascist bombing, in 1974, of a trade-union rally here, in which eight people were killed and over a hundred injured: you can still see the blast damage on the pillar. Alongside is the **Porta Bruciata**, a defensive medieval tower-gate. Streets connect south into the austere, Fascist-built **Piazza della Vittoria**, under the stern gaze of the monumental post-office building.

Piazza Paolo VI and the duomos

Duomo Nuovo and Duomo Vecchio daily 8am–noon & 2–4pm • Free

Passages from Piazza della Loggia and Piazza della Vittoria lead east across galleried Via X Giornate through to **Piazza Paolo VI**, one of the few squares in Italy to have two cathedrals – the **Duomo Nuovo**, its Neoclassical facade concealing an 80m-tall cupola, and the adjacent twelfth-century **Duomo Vecchio**, or **Rotonda**, a circular church of local stone, sunk below the current level of the piazza. Inside, glass set into the transept pavement reveals the remains of Roman baths (a wall and geometrical mosaics) and the apse of an eighth-century basilica, which burned down in 1097. The crypt is supported on a random array of reused Roman columns.

Parco Archeologico di Brescia Romana

Via Musei 55 • Tues–Fri 9am–5pm, Sat & Sun 10am–6pm • €8 • Ⓦbresciamusei.com

In the **Parco Archeologico di Brescia Romana** it's possible to admire the incredibly well-preserved Roman ruins of ancient Brixia (today Brescia). Built in the first century BC and featuring lavish decoration, the **Santuario Repubblicano** houses wonderfully preserved wall paintings that are the only surviving monumental example of Republican Roman painting in northern Italy. At the centre of a terraced sanctuary and dominating the site is the **Capitolium** , where it's possible to admire original flooring in coloured marble slabs, fragments of magnificent cult statues and limestone altars. An installation brings the ruins to life with narrative voices and images. By the Capitolium is the **Teatro Romano**, which dates to the Augustan period and is connected to the temple via the Chamber of Pillars. You can also see the cavea, the theatre's tiered seating space on the slop of Cidneo Hill where spectactors once sat to watch performances.

Museo di Santa Giulia

Via dei Musei 81/B • Tues–Fri 9am–5pm, Sat 10am–9pm & Sun 10am–6pm • €10 • Ⓦ bresciamusei.com

Brescia's fabulous civic **Museo di Santa Giulia** is housed in an ex-Benedictine convent built over what was a Roman quarter of frescoed villas. The layers of history on show make this a fascinating place to spend a couple of hours. Inside are three churches: twelfth-century **San Salvatore**, which includes the remains of a crypt built in 762; **Santa Maria in Solario**, covered in frescoes painted mainly by the Renaissance artist Floriano

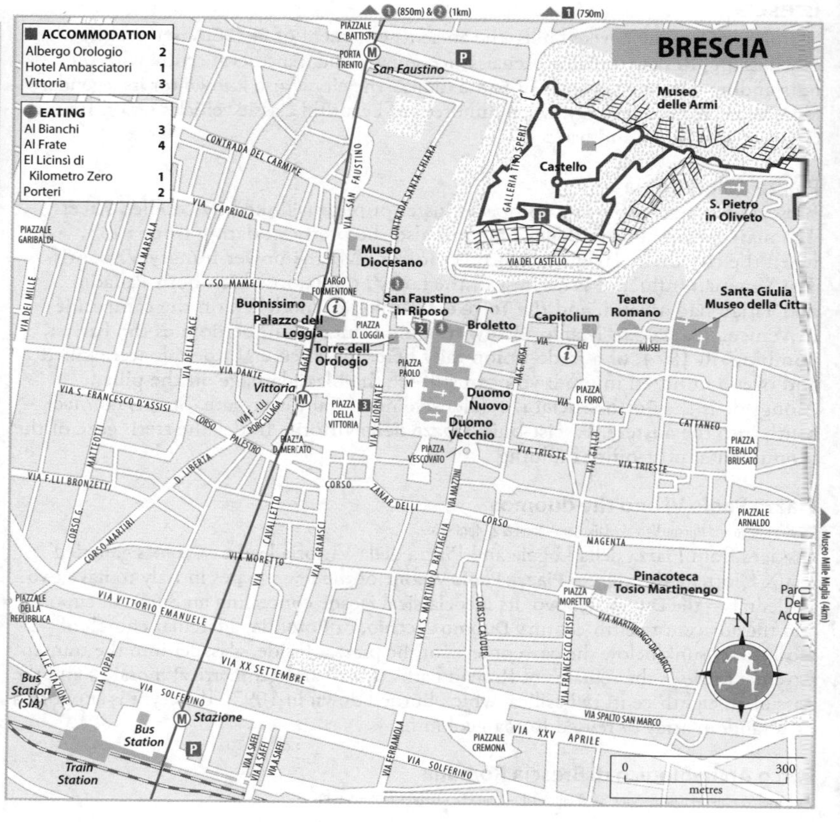

Ferramola; and the late sixteenth-century church of **Santa Giulia**, with further frescoes by Ferramola. The museum holds a collection of artefacts chronicling the city's history, including a life-size Roman *Winged Victory* in bronze; beautiful Roman mosaic floors and frescoed walls preserved in situ; and the eighth-century wooden cross of Desiderius, first-century King of the Lombards, studded with more than two hundred gemstones.

Pinacoteca Tosio Martinengo

Piazza Moretto 4 • Tues–Fri 9am–5pm, Sat 10am–9pm & Sun 10am–6pm • €8 • W bresciamusei.com

Housed in a historic sixteenth century building, the **Pinacoteca Tosio Martinengo** has been the home of the city's art collection since 1908. Showcasing paintings and applied art objects, the exhibition starts with works of the fourteenth century, followed by Raphael's Christ Blessing (1505) and Angel (1500–1501), before moving on to sixteenth century Brescian painting with works by Vincenzo Foppa, Romanino and Girolamo Savoldo, as well as Giacomo Ceruti's poignantly humane Beggars. The collection ends with a sculpture by Canova and two monumental paintings by Francesco Hayez.

The Castello

Via del Castello 9 • Museums Tues–Fri 9am–5pm, Sat & Sun 10am–6pm • €5 • W bresciamusei.com

Perched on a hill overlooking the town, Brescia's **Castello** is Europe's second largest fortification. It was begun in the fifteenth century by Luchino Visconti and added to by the Venetians, French and Austrians. Today, it houses the **Museo delle Armi Luigi Marzoli,** which has one of the most extensive collections of arms and weaponry in Europe.

4

Museo Mille Miglia

Viale della Bornata 123 • Daily 10am–6pm • €8 • T 030 336 5631, W museomillemiglia.it

Housed in an eleventh-century monastery complex, the **Museo Mille Miglia** showcases dozens of classic vehicles with photos, vintage posters, old-style petrol pumps and memorabilia from past Mille Miglia car races. The museum consists of nine sections covering the period from 1927 to the present day. The pathway displays cars belonging to private collectors that are still used during the annual Mille Miglia race (W millemiglia.it).

ARRIVAL AND DEPARTURE — BRESCIA

By car Brescia is well connected to Milan (approx 40min drive away) via the Torino–Venezia motorway.

By train The town is served by mainline trains from Milano Centrale, Verona, Desenzano/Sirmione and Venice, as well as slower trains from Lecco, Bergamo, Cremona and Parma. The easiest way to reach the historical centre from the train station is by hopping on the metro for one stop to Vittoria station; alternatively it's a ten-minute walk.

Destinations Bergamo (hourly; 50min); Cremona (hourly; 55min); Desenzano/Sirmione (hourly; 20min); Iseo (approx hourly; 40min); Lecco (hourly; 1hr 55min); Milano Centrale (every 30min; 1hr); Verona (every 30min; 35min).

By bus Flanking the train station are two bus stations – the main Stazione Autolinee, with buses from Verona, Mantua, Iseo, Bergamo-Orio al Serio airport and Brescia-Montichiari airport, and the SIA bus station, with buses from Desenzano, Salò, Riva, Idro and Val Trompia.

Destinations Cremona (hourly; 1hr 15min); Desenzano (at least hourly; 1hr); Gargnano (every 30min; 1hr 25min); Iseo (8 daily; 40min–1hr); Mantua (hourly; 1hr 25min); Riva del Garda (3 daily; 2hr 5min); Salò (at least every 30min; 55min); Verona (hourly; 2hr 20min).

INFORMATION

Tourist office Piazza Paolo VI (daily 9am–7pm; T 030 306 1266, W bresciatourism.it); and at Piazzale Stazione train station (daily 9am–7pm; T 030 837 8559). At both offices you can buy the Brescia Card (€15/24hr; €20/48hr), which includes access to various museums in the city, along with public transport, and bike and car sharing.

GETTING AROUND

By metro Brescia's metro has one efficient line running daily until midnight (until 1am on Saturdays). As the city centre is easily explorable on foot, you're likely to only use it to get from the train station to the centre (Vittoria or San

Faustino are the most central stops; 1 stop €1.40 or €3 for 24hr including buses in Zone 1).

On foot Central Brescia is compact and mainly pedestrianized, making it safe and pleasant to wander on foot.

ACCOMMODATION

Albergo Orologio Via Beccaria 17 ⓣ030 375 5411, ⓦalbergoorologio.it; map p.286. Right in the heart of town, a stone's throw from the Piazza della Loggia, this attractive little hotel with wooden furniture is one of the city's most atmospheric places to stay, matching the warm welcome and genial service. Breakfast is €5 per person. **€99**

Hotel Ambasciatori Via Crocefissa di Rosa 92 ⓣ030 399 114, ⓦambasciatori.net; map p.286. This friendly family-run four-star hotel offers spacious rooms with parquet flooring and Persian rugs, and a seventh-floor fitness centre with views over the castle. Bus #10 stops just outside the hotel and runs to the city centre, while Marconi metro station is 200m away. **€99**

Vittoria Via X Giornate 20 ⓣ030 768 7200, ⓦhotelvittoria.com; map p.286. Brescia's most upmarket hotel has a spacious rooftop terrace with gorgeous views of the Duomo; the interior retains its original 1930s parquet floors, and the rooms are comfortable. **€130**

EATING

Central Brescia has plenty of reasonably priced places to eat, specializing in local dishes such as *casoncei* (large meat-filled ravioli) and *brasato d'asino* (donkey stew). Many menus feature pasta stuffed with (or polenta smothered in) *bagòss*, a local cheese – rich, spicy and flavourful.

Al Bianchi Via Gasparo da Salò 32 ⓣ030 292 328, ⓦosteriaalbianchi.it; map p.286. Historic restaurant in a quiet central location. A popular spot, serving a variety of tasty, well-priced local dishes, specializing in Brescian meaty mains. Thurs–Mon 9am–2.30pm & 4.30–11pm.

Al Frate Via dei Musei 25 ⓣ030 377 0550, ⓦalfrate.com; map p.286. A popular restaurant decorated with vintage posters and serving great traditional dishes in an informal setting; there are also a few tables out on the street. Mon 7.30–11pm, Tues–Sun 12.30–2.30pm.

El Licinsì di Kilometro Zero Via Montegrappa 15&17 ⓣ030 8370 717 ⓦkilometri-zero.it; map p.286. This food hall sells all manner of locally produced delights, from cold cuts and cheeses to liqueurs and wines. It's a great spot to stock up on foodie goodies for friends back at home, or to stop by for an informal bite. Tues–Sun noon–2.30pm & 6.30–11.30pm.

★ **Porteri** Via Trento 52 ⓣ030 380 947, ⓦtrattoriaporteri.it; map p.286. This cosy rustic trattoria with wooden interiors and open brick walls decorated with curios and copper pots and pans serves excellent local dishes. Try the *malfatti al bagòss* (€13), a local speciality similar to gnocchi made with spinach stuffed with cheese. The attached deli provides the restaurant with excellent cold cuts and a great selection of local cheeses. Tues–Sat noon–2pm & 8–10pm, Sun noon–2pm.

4

Lake Garda

LAKE GARDA (Lago di Garda) is the largest lake in Italy (52km long by 17km wide): it's so big that it alters the local climate, which is milder and – thanks to a complex pattern of lake breezes – sunnier than might be expected. It's also the most popular of the lakes, attracting around seven percent of all tourists to Italy and acting as a bridge between the Alps and the rest of the country. The narrow north of the lake is tightly enclosed by mountains that drop sheer into the water with villages wedged into gaps in the cliffs. Further south, the lake spreads out comfortably, flanked by gentle hills and lined by placid holiday resorts.

In the south, **Desenzano** is a cheery spot with the advantage of good transport links, plus proximity to the very popular and scenically impressive **Sirmione**. On the western shore are the old Venetian town of **Salò** and **Gargnano**, the lake's best destination, a small village that remains largely unspoilt. The mountainous scenery is spectacular on the approach to the genteel resort of **Riva del Garda** at the head of the lake. It's a handsome town with a long history and is a focal point for sports and water activities.

On Lake Garda's **eastern shore**, aim for **Torbole** if you're an outdoors enthusiast. To the south, the very popular resort of **Malcesine** has direct access up to Monte Baldo, which tops 2100m, as does **Brenzone**, comprising a string of attractive little harbours and a good base for walks and mountain-bike rides into Monte Baldo behind. **Torri del Benaco**, a little to the south, is an attractive corner that has avoided the worst of the crowds.

GETTING AROUND

By bus Regular buses ply the main roads along all three shores. For buses on the northern shore in the Trentino region see Ⓦ ttesercizio.it; for buses in the Veneto region on the eastern shore, take a look at Ⓦ atv.verona.it; and for buses on the western shore in the Lombardy region go to Ⓦ muoversi.regione.lombardia.it.

By boat The water offers the most relaxing form of transport, with at least hourly boat services between the main resorts plus several sightseeing and evening cruise services in summer. Two car ferries cross the lake (Maderno–Torri del Benaco, and Limone–Malcesine). Services are significantly reduced in winter; Ⓦ navigazionelaghi.it has all the details.

By car On summer weekends don't be surprised to find heavy traffic on the scenic lakeshore road, which has one lane in each direction (often squeezing round villages and through tunnels). There is pay and display parking outside all the villages but there can be queues in summer.

INFORMATION

For information on resorts and activities all round the lake – which fall into three different regions and therefore tourism authorities, consult Ⓦ visitgarda.com. Each region also has its own useful website on the lake – Ⓦ gardalombardia.com, Ⓦ gardatrentino.it and Ⓦ lagodigardaveneto.com – and each tourist office on the northern and western shore has a **hotel-booking service** with a display board showing which hotels have vacancies (also available out of hours).

Sirmione

At the bottom of the lake, the long narrow promontory of **SIRMIONE** is lined with hotels leading up to the very pretty village accessed through ancient castle walls. It's in a striking location, although the narrow cobbled lanes creak under the weight of ice cream parlours and the strain of a million overnight visitors a year. Your best bet is to press on through the crowded lanes of the village, past the ferry dock on Piazza Carducci and out to the grassy park and cypress-clad hills at the head of the peninsula. Sirmione is one of northern Italy's top spa destinations and many come to take the waters or enjoy a day in the health and beauty centre (Ⓦ termedisirmione.com).

Rocca Scaligera

Tues–Sat 8.30am–7.30pm, Sun 8.30am–1.30pm • €4

Sirmione's picture-postcard looks owe much to the fairy-tale castle at its entrance. Built when the Della Scala/Scaligeri family of Verona expanded and fortified their territory in the thirteenth century, the **Rocca Scaligera**, with boxy towers, is almost entirely

THEME PARKS: GARDALAND AND CANEVAWORLD

The **theme parks** around the southeast corner of the lake are a good day out for all ages. **GARDALAND** is the biggest theme park in the area (Daily April–Sept, with other openings during the year – check the website for the latest schedules; €40.50, children under 10 €32.50, children less than 1m tall free; discounts for part-day and multi-day tickets; Ⓣ 045 644 9777, Ⓦ gardaland.it), and includes the small but well-planned **SeaLife aquarium** nearby. It's pricey but well thought out with lots of shade, water games and rides for all ages from around 3 upwards. Parking costs an extra €5, or take the free shuttle bus which runs from Peschiera train station, 2km away.

Gardaland Resort Via Palù 11, Castelnuovo Ⓣ 045 640 4000, Ⓦ gardaland.it. Gardaland is home to three themed hotels: *Gardaland Hotel*, echoing the world of dreams and fairytales; *Gardaland Adventure Hotel*, with themed rooms recalling the park's adventure activities; and *Gardaland Magic Hotel*, with rooms dedicated to the world of magic. Free shuttle buses connect all three hotels with the theme park. Check the website for special offers. Family packages from €287

A little north, **CANEVAWORLD RESORT** (Ⓣ 045 696 9900, Ⓦ canevaworld.it) comprises two adjacent parks: **Movieland** (mid-April to mid-Sept daily 10am–6pm, later opening in July & Aug; Oct Sat & Sun 10am–6pm; €29, €23 for kids under 1.40m high), with fake movie sets and shows revealing the secrets of special effects; and Caneva **Aquapark** (mid-May to mid-Sept daily 10am–6pm; July & Aug until 7pm; €29, €23 for kids under 1.40m high), with slides, flumes, pools and a pirate island. Children under 1m go free at both parks, and free buses shuttle every 30min (mornings only) to Canevaworld from Peschiera station.

4

surrounded by water. It dates from the thirteenth century. You're free to roam around the walls – the enclosed harbour is especially photogenic – and climb the towers: 77 steps lead up to the keep, followed by another 92 to the top of the highest tower, from where views over the rooftops of Sirmione are gorgeous.

Grotte di Catullo

Tues–Sat 8.30am–7.30pm, Sun 9.30am–6.30pm; Nov–Feb grounds close at 5pm • €6

At the far end of the promontory, a pleasant fifteen-minute stroll from the castle, stand the remains of a first century BC/AD Roman villa, the **Grotte di Catullo**, purportedly belonging to Roman poet Catullus, though the evidence is scant. The ruins, scattered among ancient olive trees, are lovely, and offer superb views across the lake. On the site, an archeological museum houses fragments of frescoes and artefacts that were unearthed in the area.

Lido delle Bionde

Partway along the route to the Roman ruins, a path heads down to water level to a shingle beach, the **Lido delle Bionde**, where you can eat, drink, swim in the lake or sunbathe on the pontoon or nearby rocks. Alternatively, turn right when you reach the water and follow the walkway along to the public beach by the village, where there is also room to paddle.

4

ARRIVAL AND INFORMATION — SIRMIONE

By bus The bus station is at the end of Viale Marconi by the tourist office and the entrance to the walled village.

Destinations Brescia (hourly; 1hr 10min); Desenzano (at least hourly; 20min); Verona (hourly; 1hr).

By boat The *imbarcadero* is on Piazza Carducci. Regular boats link Sirmione with the resorts at the southern end of the lake while a reduced number of boats also head to the towns to the north of the lake.

By car Sirmione is closed to traffic; if you are staying at a hotel in the centre with parking you will be granted special access to the historical core. There is plenty of pay and display parking at the end of the approach road, Viale Marconi.

Tourist office Via Marconi 2 (daily 9am–12.30pm & 3–6pm; Nov–April closed Sat afternoon & Sun; ⓣ 030 374 8721, ⓦ provincia.brescia.it and ⓦ gardalombardia.com).

ACCOMMODATION

Hotel Catullo Piazza Flaminia 7 ⓣ 030 990 5811, ⓦ hotelcatullo.it. A pet-friendly three-star hotel with a laidback atmosphere offering simply furnished, spacious rooms; there's a rooftop terrace with lovely views over the lake. €150

Hotel Marconi Via Vittorio Emanuele II 51 ⓣ 030 916 007, ⓦ hotelmarconi.net. A welcoming hotel right on the lakefront, offering comfortable rooms and a lovely outdoor area with sunbeds facing the lake. Classic rooms decorated in light tones are in the main building, while a side building houses refurbished contemporary rooms. All rooms have balconies. €120

EATING

La Rucola Via Strentelle 3 ⓣ 030 916 326, ⓦ ristorantelarucola.it. A sophisticated little spot near the castle, this is the top gourmet restaurant in town with one Michelin star. Prices are high: expect to pay more than €80/head. Fri–Wed 12.30–2pm & 7.30–10.30pm.

Desenzano del Garda

At Garda's southwest extremity, **DESENZANO** is a good access point to the lake. Its attractive waterfront squares – Piazza Malvezzi and Piazza Matteotti – are lined with bars and restaurants, while nearby the **Roman villa** on Via Crocifisso (Tues–Sun 8.30am–7pm; Nov–Feb closes 4.30pm; €4) displays some good mosaics. Looming over the town, the **castle** offers spectacular views.

ARRIVAL AND INFORMATION — DESENZANO

By train The town has a good train service on the fast Milan–Brescia–Verona line.

Destinations Brescia (hourly; 20min); Milano Centrale (hourly; 1hr 10min); Venice (approx hourly; 1hr 40min);

Verona (approx every 30min; 30min).

By bus Regular buses serve the western shore of the lake as well as linking the town with Brescia and Sirmione to the east. Destinations Brescia (every 30min; 35min); Riva (hourly; 1hr 50min); Salò (9 daily; 40min); Sirmione (at least hourly; 20min).

By boat Regular ferries zip between Sirmione and the towns on the lower eastern shore while fast services leave several times a day for Riva at the top of the lake, calling at most larger villages on both shores along the way.

Tourist office Via Porto Vecchio 34, just off the main square on the old harbour (June–Sept Mon–Sat 10am–12.30pm & 2–6pm, Sun 10am–1pm & 2–6pm; Oct–May Mon–Fri 10am–12.30pm & 2–5pm, Sat 9.30am–12.30pm; ⓣ 030 374 8726, ⓦ comune.desenzano.brescia.it); there's also an infopoint at the train station (Jan–March Mon–Fri 9am–6pm, Sat 9am–7pm; April–Nov Mon–Thurs 9am–7pm, Fri & Sat 9am–8pm; ⓦ provincia.brescia.it/turismo).

ACCOMMODATION

Relais Il Giardino Segreto Via Curiel 2 ⓣ 030 917 2294, ⓦ relaisilgiardinosegreto.it. A friendly family-run hotel with just four rooms, each individually themed – the Red Lantern room features Far Eastern decor, with wooden chests and scarlet hues, while the Desert room is decorated in light sandy yellow colours. €95

Isola del Garda

Guided tours only April–Oct • €31–38 depending on starting point • ⓣ 328 612 6943, ⓦ isoladelgarda.com

Off the Valtenesi shore in front of San Felice del Benaco, the elongated **ISOLA DEL GARDA** is the lake's largest island, formerly the site of an ancient monastery once visited by St Francis. The old buildings were replaced around 1900 by a fanciful **villa** in Venetian neo-Gothic style. Lush Italianate terraced **gardens** lead down to the lake, alongside Mediterranean shrubs, cypresses, cedars, bay trees and more.

The Cavazza family own and live on the island and it is visitable only on a **guided tour** between Easter and the end of October. Trips run from several points around the lake, most frequently from Salò, Garda, Bardolino, Gardone Riviera and elsewhere. The fare covers return boat transport and a two-hour guided tour, including a tasting of local products.

4

Salò

SALÒ, splendidly sited on its own bay, is one of Garda's more handsome towns. Capital of the Magnifica Patria – a grouping of lake communes – for more than four hundred years until the fall of the Venetian Republic in 1797, it retains something of its old-fashioned hauteur, exemplified by the grand seventeenth-century town hall, directly on the lakefront by the ferry dock, and the unfinished Renaissance facade of the **Duomo** (daily 8.30am–12.30 & 3.30–7pm; free), which holds paintings by Romanino. On the outskirts of town, the Museo di Salò, known as **MuSa** (Via Brunati 9; daily 10am–8pm; ⓦ museodisalo.it; €14), houses a collection of art from the fifteenth century to the present day, alongside a series of scientific displays, including two original seismographs from the 1950s.

From 1943 to 1945, Salò was the nominal capital of Italy, as the Nazis installed Mussolini here at the head of a puppet regime in a failed attempt to hold off the Allied advance. It's now something of a yachties' town, with a less touristy profile than its neighbours, offering everything you'd want – long, quiet waterfront promenade, great views, alluring old quarter – but without the crowds.

ARRIVAL AND INFORMATION — SALÒ

By bus Buses stop on Largo Dante Alighieri.

Destinations Brescia (every 30min; 1hr); Desenzano (9 daily; 50min); Gargnano (every 30min; 25min); Riva (3 daily; 1hr 15min).

By boat Regular ferries and cruises leave for destinations around the lake from the *imbarcadero* at the end of Piazza della Vittoria.

Tourist office Piazza Sant'Antonio 4 (mid April–Oct daily 10am–12.30pm & 2.30–6.30pm; Nov–mid April Mon–Fri 10am–12.30pm & 2–5pm, Sat 10am–12.30pm; ⓣ 030 374 8745, ⓦ gardalombardia.com).

ACCOMMODATION

Panorama Cinque Via del Panorama 5 ⓣ 348 321 1020, ⓦ panoramacinque.com. A friendly B&B overlooking the lake with modern stylish interiors and a well-manicured garden that is a lovely spot to enjoy breakfast – home-made

cakes, jams, cheeses and cold cuts are all available. **€100**

★Villa Arcadio Hotel & Resort Via Palazzina 2 ⓣ0365 42 281, ⓦhotelvillaarcadio.it. Set on a hillside amid olive and citrus groves and commanding wonderful views of the lake, this four-star property is located in a nineteenth-century monastery. The interiors feature original frescoes while rooms have contemporary furnishings and en-suite marble bathrooms. The restaurant serves exceptional Mediterranean cuisine with a twist, and there's a swimming pool, too. **€330**

EATING AND DRINKING

★Locanda del Benaco Lungolago Zanardelli 44 ⓣ0365 20 308, ⓦlocandadelbenaco.com. This stylish boutique hotel with minimalist rooms (doubles €180) has an excellent restaurant right on the lakefront serving delicious Mediterranean cuisine – the shrimp tartare (€16) is to die for. Wed–Mon noon–2.30pm & 7.30–10pm.

Osteria di Mezzo Via di Mezzo 10 ⓣ0365 290 966, ⓦosteriadimezzo.it. A great *osteria* tucked away off Salò's main strip, serving both lake fish and meat dishes including duck foie gras (€20) and fritto misto fish fillets from the lake (€18). *Primi* €15, *secondi* €18. Wed–Mon noon–2.30pm & 7–9.30pm.

Pasticceria Vassalli Via San Carlo 86 ⓣ0365 20 752, ⓦpasticceriavassalli.com. Those with a sweet tooth will love this *pasticceria* serving all manner of home-made confectionery – spring and summer see plenty of citrus-themed delights, including lemon biscuits and lemon sweets filled with liquor. Daily 8am–8pm.

Gardone Riviera

Just 2km east of Salò, **GARDONE RIVIERA** was once the most fashionable of Lake Garda's resorts and still retains its symbols of sophistication, with lush gardens, opulent Art Nouveau villas in spacious park-like grounds and a smattering of ritzy hotels. **Gardone Sotto**, the old village on the lakeside, comprises a cobbled street and a couple of piazzas sandwiched between the busy Corso Zanardelli road and the lake. **Gardone Sopra** spreads across the hillside above, with a tiny centre at the chapel and piazza just by the entrance to Il Vittoriale.

4

Giardino Botanico André Heller

Via Roma 2, Gardone Sopra • March–Oct daily 9am–7pm • €12 • ⓦhellergarden.com

Gardone's success as a health retreat and winter resort was in great part due to its famously consistent climate which has also encouraged the exotic **Giardino Botanico André Heller**, laid out just above Gardone Sotto in 1912 by Arturo Hruska, dentist to the Russian tsar, and now owned by Heller, an artist. Bamboo, waterlilies, camphor trees, banana plants and more, set amid artificial cliffs and streams, are interspersed with sculptures and modern artworks.

Il Vittoriale

Via Vittoriale 12 • Daily: end March–mid Oct 9am–8pm; mid Oct–end March 9am–5pm • €16 • Tickets can be restricted at peak times (Sun, national holidays, some days in July & Aug), when you should arrive 1hr or more before the opening time to be sure of entry • ⓣ0365 296 511, ⓦvittoriale.it

On the hillside above Gardone, **Il Vittoriale** was the home of Italy's most notorious twentieth-century writer, Gabriele d'Annunzio (see page 293). A deeply idiosyncratic complex, it gives an insight into the poet's eccentric character, and is a hugely popular destination with Italians.

D'Annunzio's personality makes itself felt from the start in the Prioria's two reception rooms – one a chilly and formal room for guests he didn't like, the other warm and inviting for those he did. Mussolini was apparently shown to the former, where the mirror has an inscription reputedly aimed at him: "Remember that you are made of glass and I of steel." Dining with d'Annunzio was never a reassuring experience: in the glitzy dining room, as a warning to greedy guests, pride of place was given to a gilded tortoise that had died of overeating. The rest of the house is no less bizarre: the bathroom has a bathtub hemmed in by hundreds of objects, ranging from Persian ceramic tiles and Buddhas to toy animals; and the Sala del Mappamondo contains an Austrian machine gun and an oversized edition of *The Divine Comedy*, as well as the huge globe for which it is named. Suspended from the ceiling of the auditorium

GABRIELE D'ANNUNZIO

Born in 1863, Gaetano Rapagnetta – who took the name **Gabriele d'Annunzio** (Gabriel of the Annunciation) – is often acclaimed as one of Italy's greatest poets, though he became better known as a soldier and socialite, leading his own private army and indulging in much-publicized affairs with numerous women, including the actress Eleonora Duse (when berated by his friends for treating her cruelly, he simply replied, "I gave her everything, even suffering.") He was a fervent supporter of Mussolini, providing the Fascist Party with their (meaningless) war cry *"eia! eia! alalá!"* – though Mussolini eventually found his excessive exhibitionism an embarrassment and in 1921 presented d'Annunzio with the Vittoriale villa, ostensibly to reward his patriotism, in reality to shut him up. d'Annunzio died in the house in 1938, suffering a brain haemorrhage while sitting at his desk in the Zambracca room, which remains untouched.

adjoining the house is the biplane that d'Annunzio used in a daring flight over Vienna in World War I.

Outside amid the cypress trees is the prow of the battleship *Puglia*, used in d'Annunzio's so-called "Fiume adventure". Fiume (now Rijeka), on the North Adriatic, had been promised to Italy before they entered World War I, but was handed to Yugoslavia instead. Incensed, d'Annunzio gathered an army, occupied Fiume and returned home a hero. Amid the gardens above stands d'Annunzio's mausoleum, a Fascistic array of angular travertine stonework.

ARRIVAL AND INFORMATION — GARDONE RIVIERA

By bus Regular services connect Gardone with villages and towns along the western shore of the lake. Buses stop at several points along the main road; ask at the tourist office. Destinations Brescia (every 30min; 1hr 5min); Limone (3 daily; 1hr); Riva del Garda (3 daily; 1hr 15min).

By boat The *imbarcadero* is just by Piazza Wimmer in Gardone Sotto. Services leave for around the lake with a reduced service in autumn..

Tourist office Corso Repubblica 1 in Gardone Sotto (June–mid Sept daily 10am–12.30pm & 3–6.30pm; mid Sept–May Mon–Sat 10am–12.30pm & 2.15–6pm; ⓣ 030 374 8736, ⓦ gardalombardia.com)

ACCOMMODATION

★ **B&B Due di Moro** Via Ceriolo 23/25 ⓣ 0365 20 101, ⓦ duedimoro.com. A rustic yet stylish B&B made entirely with natural materials. The cosy rooms have wooden beams and modern bathrooms, while large windows ensure plenty of light; each room has its own private terrace from where you can soak in the stunning lake views. The veggie restaurant serves healthy organic dishes, with plenty on offer for vegans, too. **€105**

Hotel Villa Florida Corso Zanardelli 113 ⓣ 0365 21 836, ⓦ hotelvillaflorida.com. Thoughtfully run by a charming family, who are a fascinating wealth of information on the history of the area. The attractive rooms are good-sized suites with kitchen corners and balconies offering lovely lake views. Large pool and pretty grounds, as well as bike storage and a bike maintenance room. **€199**

Locanda Agli Angeli Via Dosso 7 ⓣ 0365 20 991, ⓦ agliangeli.biz. Right by Il Vittoriale, this small, family-run place offers rooms decorated with wooden Indonesian furnishings, a veranda, a small swimming pool and a peaceful location. Parking is complimentary for guests. **€145**

EATING

Il Fiore di Zucca Via Trieste 16 ⓣ 0365 20458 ⓦ ilfioredizucca.it. Tucked away in the back streets of Gardone, this is an excellent spot for a tasty lunch of Roman specialities, including stuffed zucchini flowers and *cacio e pepe* pasta. There's a shaded courtyard for warm, sunny days. *Primi* €9, *secondi* €12. Wed–Mon 11.30am–2.30pm & 7–10pm.

Osteria Antico Brolo Via Carere 10 ⓣ 0365 21 421 ⓦ ristoranteanticobrolo.it. In the heart of Gardone, this pleasant, welcoming eighteenth-century *osteria* is one of the town's best restaurants; there are a few tables in the courtyard in summer. The cuisine is creative with *primi* at €13, and *secondi* at €16. Tues–Sun 12.30–2pm & 7–10pm.

Toscolano Maderno

Barely 3km east of Gardone, the road passes through the twin *comune* of **TOSCOLANO MADERNO**, which straddles the delta of the Toscolano River. A car ferry crosses from

4

here to Torri del Benaco on the western shore of the lake, and there's a decent beach. The valley behind has a tradition of paper making dating from the fourth century – following the riverside road up into the beautiful, wooded valley brings you past many disused **paper mills** to the **Fondazione Valle delle Cartierie**, with a well-presented **museum** offering an insight into the processes and importance of the industry (April–Sept daily 10am–6pm; Oct Sat & Sun 10am–6pm; €7). This is also a lovely area for shady walks or picnics.

ARRIVAL AND INFORMATION — TOSCOLANO MADERNO

By bus Local and longer-distance buses stop at various points along the main road.

Destinations Brescia (9 daily; 1hr 10min); Gargnano (9 daily; 10min); Riva del Garda (5 daily; 1hr).

By boat The *imbarcadero* is just off the main road on Lungolago Zanardelli. Services run to villages round the lake and regular car ferries cross throughout the year to Torri del Benaco (see page 299).

Tourist office Viale Ugo Foscolo 5 (daily 9.30am–noon & 3–8pm; ☎ 0365 641 330).

Gargnano

Some 15km north of Salò, **GARGNANO** is the prettiest village on Lake Garda. Traffic runs above and slightly inland here, leaving the old village itself noise-free. In addition, the narrow, difficult road north of town means tour buses don't bother trying to reach Gargnano. Still more a working village than a resort, it's the perfect spot to unwind for a day or two – D.H. Lawrence stayed here while writing *Twilight in Italy*, a work which is beautifully evocative of Lake Garda's attractions. If you tire of relaxing in a waterfront café by one of the tiny ports, you can wander around the abandoned olive factory, the lakefront villas with their boathouses, or the harbourside, former **Palazzo Comunale**, which has two cannonballs wedged in its wall dating from the naval bombings of 1866 during the war of independence from the Austrians.

San Francesco

Church June–Sept daily 8am–6pm; Oct–May daily 8am-4.30pm • **Cloister** April–Sept daily 9.30am–6pm • Free

Aside from the Palazzo Comunale, the main sight in Gargnano is the simple Romanesque church of **San Francesco**, built in 1289. The attached monastery became a citrus-fruit warehouse at the end of the nineteenth century. Its cloister has columns carved with citrus fruits, a reference to the Franciscans' introduction of the crop to Europe.

San Giacomo di Calino

Via San Giacomo

A stroll along the road which leads north out of Gargnano from the harbour takes you for 3km past the beach and through olive and lemon groves, past the *Villa Feltrinelli* (see below), to the tiny eleventh-century chapel of **San Giacomo di Calino**. On the side facing the lake, under the portico where the fishermen keep their equipment, is a thirteenth-century fresco of St Christopher, patron saint of travellers.

LEMON HOUSES

Lake Garda's western shore is dubbed the **Riviera del Limone** for the citrus orchards that once flourished here. The crop, introduced by the Franciscans in the fourteenth century, was cultivated in the *limonaie*, or "lemon houses" that are still in evidence, although many of the stone-pillared constructions were abandoned last century when Sicilian lemons became cheaper to produce. Several structures around the lake are open to visitors; head for Gargnano (see page 294), Limone (see page 295) or Torri del Benaco (see page 299).

GARGNANO

ARRIVAL AND DEPARTURE

By bus Buses stop at Piazza Boldini on the main road, by the multistorey car park opposite the tourist office.

Destinations Brescia (hourly; 1hr 27min); Desenzano (5 daily; 1hr); Riva (5 daily; 50 min); Salò (hourly; 30min).

By boat The regular ferry services round the lake pull in at the *imbarcadero* by the little harbour lined with orange trees on Piazza Feltrinelli.

INFORMATION AND ACTIVITIES

Tourist office Pro Loco, Piazzale Boldini 2, on the main road by the multistorey car park (April–Sept daily 9.30am–12.30pm & 2.30–6.30pm; ⓣ0365 791 243, ⓦgardalombardia.com).

Bikes and surfing OKSurf, Via Remembranza 30 (ⓣ328 471 7777, ⓦoksurf.it), rents stand-up paddle boards (€10), mountain and electric bikes (€25/day), and also runs windsurfing and kitesurfing courses for adults and children (2hr group lessons including equipment €55).

Sailing Every Sept hundreds of boats take to the waters off Gargnano for the round-Garda yacht race, the Centomiglia (ⓦcentomiglia.it). It's been celebrated for over sixty years and attracts top international sailors and locals alike. The village celebrates with open-air concerts and markets.

ACCOMMODATION

Du Lac Via Colletta 21, Villa di Gargnano ⓣ0365 71 107, ⓦhotel-dulac.it. Run by the same family as the *Gardenia* – standards are high, the welcome is warm and the rooms are comfortable and unfussy. Six of them look over the lake, with a balcony or terrace. Antique furniture, en-suite bathrooms and a/c come as standard. **€110**

Gardenia Via Colletta 53, Villa di Gargnano ⓣ0365 71 195, ⓦhotel-gardenia.it. A lovely family-run hotel in a nineteenth-century lakeside villa. The public areas feature beautifully maintained 1950s decor and fittings while the guest rooms have been completely renovated with big comfy beds, well-appointed bathrooms and airy lake views. **€130**

Riviera Via Roma 1 ⓣ0365 72 292, ⓦgarniriviera.it. Comfortable, good-value en-suite rooms in an enviable lakeside position in the village centre. Breakfast is served on the lovely waterside terrace, and there's parking 200m from the hotel for €3/day. **€85**

★ **Villa Sostaga** Via Sostaga 19, Navazzo ⓣ0365 791 218, ⓦvillasostaga.com. On the hillside above Gargnano, this handsome villa is a wonderful bolthole with lovely rooms, spacious grounds and a pool. The views are breathtaking, the welcome genuine and the restaurant excellent (see below). **€250**

4

EATING AND DRINKING

La Tortuga Via XXIV Maggio 5 ⓣ0365 71 251, ⓦristorantelatortuga.it. Intimate Michelin-starred restaurant decorated in red tones serving top-rate creative cuisine. A meal will set you back about €90 a head. Wed–Mon 7.30–9.30pm.

Villa Sostaga Via Sostaga 19, Navazzo ⓣ0365 791 218, ⓦvillasostaga.com. The restaurant at this hillside hotel restaurant commands wonderful views over the lake, and serves well-judged seasonal, local cuisine including home-made pastas. There's a Fish of the Lake taster menu for €55. Daily 1–2.30pm & 7.30–10pm.

The SP38 road to Tremosine

North of Gargnano the lake road skirts the water, passing through treacherously narrow road tunnels. Just after the windsurfing destination Campione del Garda there's a turning to the village of Pieve on the high plateau of the Tremosine (signposted Tremosine and Via Benaco). Not for the faint-hearted or large vehicles, the breathtakingly narrow **SP38** road, described by Winston Churchill as "the eighth wonder of the world", switchbacks its way up the mountain through the scenic Brasa Gorge to the Alpine plains above.

Limone sul Garda

The last lakeside town in Lombardy, 20km from Gargnano on a tongue of land surrounded by rugged mountains, is **LIMONE SUL GARDA** (ⓦvisitlimonesulgarda.com). Although famous for its lemon cultivation – a commercial concern until the 1920s – the name derives from its location at what was the frontier (*limen* in Latin) of the Kingdom of Italy and the Austro-Hungarian Empire. Limone is undeniably pretty, a stone-built village jammed onto a slender slope between the mountains and the lake, but with some one million overnight visitors a year and plenty of souvenir shops, it

does feel rather touristy. The town's main attraction is the **Limonaia del Castèl** (April–Oct daily 10am–6pm; €2), a lemon house and museum that sheds light on the history of lemons in the area.

ACCOMMODATION — LIMONE SUL GARDA

Hotel Monte Baldo Via Porto 29 ⓣ0365 954 021, ⓦmontebaldolimone.it. A welcoming little three-star hotel hugging the rock front. It has twelve comfortable rooms with en-suite bathrooms, the staff are friendly, and there's a good restaurant, too. **€118**

Riva del Garda

Dramatically located beneath sheer cliffs at the northwest tip of the lake, **RIVA DEL GARDA** is unmistakeably a holiday town, but it has a long history and the pedestrianized old quarter is still full of character. Riva is a tranquil town that serves as a good base for outdoor activities, with windsurfing, canyoning, climbing and surfing aplenty in the area.

Piazza III Novembre

Riva's showpiece main square, **Piazza III Novembre** (named to celebrate the arrival of Italian forces in 1918), is an attractive, cobbled space, its medieval Lombard and Venetian facades lined up on three sides below the rugged face of Monte Rocchetta, the fourth side open to the lake.

4

Dominating Piazza III Novembre is the thirteenth-century **Torre Apponale**, 34m high and climbable inside for sensational lake views (mid-March to May Tues–Sun 10am–6pm; June–Sept daily 10am–6pm; Oct Tues–Sun 10am–6pm; €2). In the middle of the square are **Palazzo Pretorio**, dating from 1375, and the Venetian **Casa del Comune**, completed in 1482, while to one side, behind the *imbarcadero* looms a 1920s-era hydroelectric **power station** (ⓦwww.hydrotourdolomiti.it). Designed to exploit the 500m drop in water level from Lake Ledro to this point, its multimedia installations shed light on how water is turned into energy, and can be visited by private tour (guided tours daily 9am–5pm; call 0461 032 486 or email ⓔbooking@hydrotourdolomiti.it to book; €15).

The Rocca & Museo Alto Garda (MAG)

Piazza Cesare Battisti 3/A • Museo Alto Garda (MAG): mid-March to May & Oct Tues–Sun 10am–6pm; June–Sept daily 10am–6pm • €5 • ⓦmuseoaltogarda.it

The stout **Rocca** was originally built in 1124 but has been much altered since, not least by the Austrians, who lopped some height off the main tower in 1852 and turned the fortress into a barracks. It now houses the **Museo Alto Garda (MAG)**, with temporary exhibits on the ground floor, an art gallery upstairs and displays of archeology and local history upstairs again.

Parco Grotta Cascata Varone

Tenno • Daily: March & Oct 9am–5pm; April & Sept 9am–6pm; May–Aug 9am–7pm; Nov–Feb 10am–5pm • €6 • ⓦcascata-varone.com • Bus #1 from the centre of Riva (15min)

Three kilometres north of Riva, the **Parco Grotta Cascata Varone** is a gorge and waterfall system where you can penetrate the canyon on a series of catwalks, as the waters of the River Magnone thunder down from almost 100m above. There's a small bar and picnic area on site.

ARRIVAL AND INFORMATION — RIVA DEL GARDA

By bus Riva's bus station is about 1km north of the lakefront, on Viale Trento, but all intercity buses drop off at the *imbarcadero* (if approaching from Limone) or Viale Carducci (if approaching from Torbole).

Destinations Brescia (3 daily; 2hr 5min); Desenzano (9 daily; 1hr 50min); Malcesine (approx hourly; 25min); Salò (9 daily; 1hr 15min); Torbole (approx every 30min; 5min); Torri del Benaco (approx hourly; 1hr); Verona (hourly; 2hr 20min).

By boat The *imbarcadero* stands beside Piazza III Novembre. Riva is one of the hubs for lake ferries, with fast services heading to the larger villages and resorts around the lake.

Tourist information Largo Medaglie d'Oro (mid March–end April daily 9am–6pm; end April–Sept daily 9am–7pm; Oct–mid March Mon–Fri 9am–6pm, Sat & Sun 9.30am–12.30pm & 2–6pm; ⓣ 0464 554 444, ⓦ gardatrentino.it).

ACCOMMODATION

Lido Palace Viale Goisuè Carducci 10 ⓣ 0464 021 899, ⓦ lido-palace.it. Set in private grounds on the lakefront, this five-star hotel has stylish modern interiors, a spa and an excellent restaurant with floor-to-ceiling windows looking out towards Riva's rocky mountains. **€450**

Luise Viale Rovereto 9 ⓣ 0464 550 858, ⓦ hotelluise.com. The entrance of this contemporary hotel is decorated with 350 vintage travel tags. The comfortable rooms feature a bike, typewriter or map theme, and there's a swimming pool and garden at the back with a children's play area. The food is worth a mention, too – the bread and ice cream are both home-made, and there's a great hearty buffet breakfast. **€159**

★ **Vivere Suites** Via Epifanio Gobbi 30, Arco ⓣ 335 634 5428, ⓦ agrivivere.com. Set amid vineyards 5km north of Riva, this sleek and stylish pad offers spacious contemporary suites, some with kitchenette and most with living areas, plus an inviting swimming pool. With only six rooms, it feels more like a home – guests are given their own access key for the main gate, and most of the time you'll have the place to yourself. **€290**

EATING AND DRINKING

Il Gallo Piazza S. Rocco 12 ⓣ 0464 556 200, ⓦ osteriailgallo.com. A great little place beneath the porticoes, just off the main square. There's a short menu of simple local mountain staples and the owner will reel off many more dishes. The good wine list of Trento wines and the relaxed atmosphere make this a fine spot to settle down for the evening. *Primi* €8, *secondi* €12. Daily noon–2pm & 6–10pm.

★ **Sud** Via A. Gazzoletti 15 ⓣ 0464 088 079. Run by a friendly young bunch, with sloppy pizzas (€6) as authentic as they get. The *pizzaiolo* is Neapolitan and ingredients are imported from southern Italy (hence the name). The menu also includes pasta and fish dishes – or just grab a takeaway *cuoppo* (mixed fried fish in a paper cone; €16) to munch on as you explore town. Wed–Mon noon–2.45pm & 6.30–10.30pm; open daily in summer.

Spiaggia degli Olivi Via Giardini di Porta Orientale 5 ⓣ 0464 755 353, ⓦ spiaggiadegliolivi.it. This is probably Riva's liveliest nightlife spot – it's a great place to enjoy an *aperitivo* as you soak in the lake and harbour views from the terrace. The restaurant serves traditional Italian dishes prepared with fresh seasonal ingredients from around the lake. Tues–Sun 11am–3pm & 6–10.30pm.

4

Torbole sul Garda

TORBOLE SUL GARDA, 4km east of Riva and simply known as Torbole, played an important role in the fifteenth-century war between Milan and Venice, when a fleet of warships was dragged overland here and launched into the lake. Nowadays the water still dominates, since Torbole's main diversions are sailing and windsurfing; enthusiasts come here from all over Europe, attracted by ideal wind conditions.

INFORMATION — TORBOLE SUL GARDA

Tourist office Lungolago Conca d'Oro 25 (mid March–end April daily 9.30am–12.30pm & 2–5.30pm; end April–Sept daily 9am–1pm & 3–7pm; Oct–mid March Mon–Sat 9.30am–12.30pm & 2–5.30pm; ⓣ 0464 505 177, ⓦ gardatrentino.it).

ACCOMMODATION

Hotel Centrale Piazza Goethe 13 ⓣ 0464 505 234, ⓦ hotelcentraletorbole.it. Tucked away just behind the lakefront and facing a pretty little square, this family-run hotel has comfortable modern rooms with parquet flooring and contemporary furnishings. There's an attached pizzeria. **€110**

Hotel Lago di Garda Via Lungolago Conca d'Oro 11 ⓣ 0464 505 111, ⓦ hotellagodigarda.it. Facing the water, this hotel offers modern rooms in neutral tones; there's a fitness area and a restaurant offering lovely views of the lake. **€180**

Malcesine

Occupying a headland backed by the slopes of Monte Baldo, the small lakefront village of **MALCESINE**, 14km south of Torbole, boasts a pretty, historic core overlooked by the battlements of a medieval castle: it is a picture-perfect backdrop for an Italian Lakes

LAKE GARDA SPORTS AND ACTIVITIES

All around Lake Garda, there are places were you can rent out mountain bikes, e-bikes, windsurfing equipment and much more at reasonable prices, though the northern shore around **Riva**, **Arco** and **Torbole** is the real hub for sporting activity – see Ⓦgardatrentino.it for details. The Lake Garda website (Ⓦvisitgarda.com) also has details of schools and sports companies around the lake, while another useful website is Ⓦ360gardalife.com. All prices below are approximate; check details directly or with local tourist offices.

WATERSPORTS

Top of the list is **watersports**, with a clutch of local outfits offering **windsurfing**: first-timers can get individual tuition (€60/hr) or there are group lessons at various grades (€80/3hr). If you're already proficient, you can rent a board for €70 a day. **Sailing** is also popular, with beginners' courses in a dinghy or catamaran (€80/2hr) and boat rental (€100/half-day, depending on the size of boat). For a list of windsurfing schools on the northern shore of the lake see Ⓦgardatrentino.it/en/Lake-Garda-Windsurfing-Schools, while for sailing see Ⓦgardatrentino.it/en/Lake-Garda-Sailing-School.

CLIMBING, TREKKING AND CANYONING

With over a dozen good locations within easy reach of the lake, **canyoning** is a good bet (April–Oct only; half-day €75, full day €150; Ⓦcanyonadv.com). Several companies offer more traditional **Alpine activities** – free-climbing, *via ferrata*, trekking and so on; check Ⓦmmove.net for details or Ⓦgardatrentino.it/en/Canyoning-Centers-Lake-Garda. For hiking see Ⓦgardatrentino.it/en/Hiking-Guides-Lake-Garda, while for climbing see Ⓦgardatrentino.it/en/Climbing-Courses-Lake-Garda.

PARAGLIDING

Paragliding – notably off Monte Baldo above Malcesine – is a spectacular way to get an eagle's-eye view of the lake. Check out Ⓦtandemparagliding.eu and Ⓦparaglidingmalcesine.it

4

holiday – but hardly undiscovered. In season the lanes are packed with holiday-makers and it's a very popular choice for weddings.

Castello Scaligero

Via Castello 39 • Daily: April–Oct 9.30am–6.30pm; Nov–March 9.30am–5.30pm • €6

Malcesine's main sight is the thirteenth-century **Castello Scaligero**, built, like Sirmione's (see page 289), by the Della Scala family of Verona. Goethe was imprisoned here briefly in 1786, having been arrested on suspicion of being a spy: he'd been caught making sketches of the castle's towers, which still loom over the old village.

Monte Baldo

Cable car: March–Oct daily every 30min 8am–6.45pm • €22 return • Ⓦfuniviedelbaldo.it

For a change of perspective and a breath of mountain air, head up **Monte Baldo**. There are well-marked trails up the mountain, or you can take the **cable car** (*funivia*), which rises more than 1600m in ten minutes. The trip alone is well worthwhile, with slowly revolving cable cars giving splendid views of the lake and mountains. At the top, footpaths let you explore the summit ridge.

There are several trips a day for cyclists to transport their bikes to the top; you can **rent a mountain bike** at Bike Xtreme, next to the cable car (€25/day; daily 8am–7pm; Ⓣ045 740 0105; Ⓦxtrememalcesine.com) and make a panoramic descent down easy trails to the shore. Be prepared for queues of walkers in summer, and skiers in winter.

ARRIVAL AND INFORMATION — MALCESINE

By bus The bus station is on the main lakeside road, with the old village spreading out below.

Destinations Riva (approx hourly; 30min); Torri del Benaco (approx hourly; 35min); Verona (approx hourly; 1hr 45min).
By boat From the central square Piazza Statuto, stepped lanes head down to the old port and the *imbarcadero*. Car ferries cross to Limone and regular ferries leave for destinations all around the lake.
Tourist information The tourist office is beside the bus station on the main road, at Via Gardesana 238 (daily 9am–4.45pm; T 045 740 0444, W visitmalcesine.com).

ACCOMMODATION

Aurora Piazza Vittorio Emanuele 10 T 045 740 0114, W aurora-malcesine.com. This family-run hotel in the heart of town is one the few hotels that stays open year round; the simple rooms are neat and tidy, and all have a/c. €98

Locanda Monte Baldo Località San Michele T 045 740 0612, W locandamontebaldo.com. This family-run place has an enviable location halfway up the Monte Baldo cable-car route; the views are wonderful, and there's an inviting swimming pool and a great restaurant, too. At the time of writing, the rooms were under renovation – check the website for the new prices.

EATING

La Pace Via Casella 1 T 045 740 0057, W ristorantelapacemalcesine.com. A pretty restaurant at the foot of the castle by the old port, good for a cosy meal on cooler days and with lots of tables outside in summer. *Primi* €10–18, *secondi* €12–24. Daily 11am–10.30pm.

Locanda Monte Baldo Località San Michele T 045 740 0612, W locandamontebaldo.com. A stone's throw from the cable car's intermediate station, this is a great spot to stop for lunch and soak in the views from the restaurant's panoramic terrace. The cuisine is home-made, with plenty of local dishes on offer. The tasting menu will set you back €40, while *primi* are €14 and *secondi* are €18. Daily noon–5.30pm & 6.30–9.30pm.

4

Brenzone

South of Malcesine, the elongated community of **BRENZONE** encompasses five lakeside villages dotted along 5km of shoreline, as well as a clutch of hamlets clinging to the mountainsides above, nestled among olive trees (the small hamlet of Prada sits 1000m above the water). The tourist office in the waterfront hamlet of **Porto** has maps and information about **walking and mountain biking** in the hills – including Path 33, which climbs (in about 2hr 15min) from just above Porto on a steep, scenic forest trail to **Prada Alta**, a village at 1000m. Other paths lead to the ruins of a Roman villa, a pair of eleventh-century churches and the wonderfully atmospheric abandoned medieval hamlet of Campo.

A short way south of Porto lies the centre of Brenzone, **Magugnano**, in reality no more than a little cluster of alleyways by the water. It's a perfect spot for a quiet meal: gaze across the lake and watch as the ferries glide into the lake barely 10m away. A kilometre or more south, you come to the pretty hamlet of **Castelletto**, home to a highly recommended restaurant.

ACCOMMODATION AND EATING — BRENZONE

Alla Fassa Via Nascimbeni 11, Castelletto T 045 743 0319, W ristoranteallafassa.com. Highly recommended restaurant with a delightful lakeside terrace serving very tasty lake-fish dishes. There's a good wine list too. Around €40 a head. Wed–Mon noon–2pm & 7–9.30pm.

Hotel Brenzone Via XX Settembre 26, Magugnano T 045 742 0388, W hotelbrenzone.eu. Built in 1911, this hotel has an appealingly old-fashioned atmosphere in its public rooms; the bedrooms have been modernized and there's a genuine welcome from the Brighenti family who run it. Closed mid-Oct to mid-April. €160

Torri del Benaco

TORRI DEL BENACO, 13km south of Brenzone, is one of the prettiest villages on this side of the lake. Part of its tenth-century walls still stand, notably the West Tower of the lakefront castle, which was overhauled in 1383 by the Della Scala of Verona. During the following centuries, Torri was a financial centre, controlling trade and imposing customs duties.

ANCIENT ROCK CARVINGS

In 1964, **rock carvings** dating from the Bronze Age, around 1500 BC, were discovered in the hills between Torri and San Vigilio. Since then 250 rocks with over three thousand figures have been discovered, with more being unearthed all the time. The carvings often represent warriors, sometimes on horseback, as well as fishermen, boats and religious worship. A **7km walk** from Torri del Benaco (or slightly longer from Garda) takes you through oak woods on the slopes of the hills behind the lake to see some of the carvings in situ: ask at the tourist office for details.

Torri's old centre – which consists of one long cobbled street, **Corso Dante**, crisscrossed with tunnelling alleyways and lined with mellow stone *palazzi* – is quiet and appealing. The swallowtail battlements of the **Castello Scaligero** stand guard over the quaint harbour at one end of the village, while there's a green park and shingle beach at the northern end.

Santuario Madonna della Corona

Spiazza • Daily 7am–6pm • Free • madonnadellacorona.it • Shuttle bus €1.80 one way, €3 return

Tucked away inland, about a 40min drive from Torri del Benaco, is the impressive **Santuario Madonna della Corona**, a church hewn into the rock face 774m above sea level. Legend says that the Shrine of our Lady of the Corona made its way here thanks to angelic intervention in 1522 from the island of Rhodes. A more spacious building was constructed in 1625, although much of the church you see today dates back to 1974. Interiors house an array of sculptures and bronze casts, as well as over one hundred ex-votos displayed on the walls. It's the impressive setting that is the real draw though: nestled among wooden slopes, the sanctuary appears to be suspended mid-air.

From the town of Spiazzi, a long series of steps lead down to the entrance; alternatively, a shuttle bus takes visitors to the monastery along a paved road.

4

Castello Scaligero

Viale Fratelli Lavanda 2 • Daily: April to mid-June & mid-Sept to Oct 9.30am–12.30pm & 2.30–6pm; mid-June to mid-Sept 9.30am–1pm & 4.30–7.30pm • €5 • 045 629 6111 • museodelcastelloditorridelbenaco.it

The buildings of the **Castello Scaligero** house an engaging display of local fishing and olive-oil making traditions as well as information on the area's prehistoric rock carvings (see box, below). The castle also boasts one of the oldest working *limonaie*, or glasshouses, on the lake, dating from 1760, built to protect the lemon trees inside during cold weather (see page 294).

ARRIVAL AND INFORMATION — TORRI DEL BENACO

By bus Buses pull in at the bus stop on the main road, Via Gardesana, near the tourist office.

Destinations Malcesine (approx hourly; 35min); Riva (approx hourly; 1hr); Verona (approx hourly; 1hr 15min).

By boat Regular ferries serve towns across the lake, with car ferries crossing to Toscolano Maderno throughout the year (see page 256).

By car If you're driving, park in the pay and display area by the castle walls: the old centre is off-limits to cars.

Tourist office Via Gardesana 5 (daily 10am–7pm; 045 629 6482, torri-del-benaco.net).

ACCOMMODATION

Gardesana Piazza Calderini 5 045 722 5411, gardesana.eu. In an unbeatable location, the harbourside classic *Gardesana* has hosted the likes of Churchill, Maria Callas, Laurence Olivier and Vivien Leigh. The three-star rooms are comfortable and you can choose between a view of the harbour and castle or the lake (with or without a balcony). **€150**

Garnì Onda Via per Albisano 28 045 722 5895, garnionda.com. Budget hotel 100m up from the centre. Each simple but spotlessly clean room has its own balcony or terrace and the friendly owners provide lots of local knowledge on hikes, bike rides and restaurants. Closed Nov–Feb. **€100**

EATING AND DRINKING

La Casa degli Spiriti Via Monte Baldo 28, Costermano sul Garda ⊕045 620 0766, ⊚casadeglispiriti.it. Set high on a hill and commanding wonderful views of the lake, this restaurant serves formal fine dining in a glass-fronted room (tasting menu €130), with a more casual bistro (daily 10am–10pm) serving brunch and burgers. It's a great spot for an *aperitivo* (€15), too. Daily noon–2.30pm & 7–10.30pm; closed Tues & Wed in winter.

Punta San Vigilio

Four kilometres south of Torri, **PUNTA SAN VIGILIO** is a private promontory set back from the main road, home to a historic **hotel** in a sixteenth-century villa surrounded by olive and citrus groves, an excellent restaurant, and a **taverna** (see below) that is one of the most romantic spots on the lake to enjoy a sundowner. It is also home to two lovely parks: **Parco Baia delle Sirene** (last two weeks of May daily 10am–7pm; €8, after 3pm €5; June–Sept Mon–Sat 9.30am–8pm, Sun 9am–8pm; €12, after 2.30pm €9, after 4.30pm €5; ⊚parcobaiadellesirene.it), with an attractive, well-equipped beach, and **Parco San Vigilio** (same opening times as Parco Baia delle Sirene; €18, after 3pm €15, 2hr visit before 3pm excluding Sundays €8; ⊚parcosanvigilio.com), a calm and relaxed spot with a lovely swimming pool, sunbeds, private gazebos, and a café.

ACCOMMODATION AND EATING — PUNTA SAN VIGILIO

Locanda San Vigilio Punta San Vigilio ⊕045 725 6688, ⊚locanda-sanvigilio.it. An impossibly romantic hotel, a favourite with Churchill and various other heads of state, with just seven doubles and a handful of suites in a beautiful lakeside location amid olive groves and cyprus trees. The restaurant is excellent, serving traditional Italian dishes in an intimate dining area. €200

Taverna San Vigilio Punta San Vigilio ⊕045 725 5190, ⊚locanda-sanvigilio.it. On a tiny horseshoe harbour beside the hotel, this taverna with tables spilling out onto the jetty is a wonderfully romantic spot for a coffee or an *aperitivo*. On Fri & Sat evenings in summer there is a buffet (€45) laid out in the olive groves above the café. Daily: Sept–May 10am–10pm; June–Aug 10am–12.30am.

4

Bardolino

About 4km south of Punta San Vigilio is the spruce resort of **BARDOLINO**, home of light, red Bardolino wine. The town is at its most animated in mid-September during the bibulous **Festa dell'Uva**; otherwise, strolling the lush palm- and pine-shaded promenade is the main activity. On Thursdays the promenade is taken over by the weekly market.

If you have your own transport, grab a map from the tourist office and head off along the **Strada del Bardolino** (⊚stradadelbardolino.com) to enjoy the inland countryside, taking in wineries and olive-oil producers on the way.

ARRIVAL AND INFORMATION — BARDOLINO

By boat Bardolino is well linked to the towns and villages up and down the lake, with both regular and fast ferry services (see page 256).

By bus The #62/#64 bus runs from Verona to Riva del Garda throughout the year stopping at Bardolino en route.

Destinations Malcesine (hourly; 50min); Peschiera (hourly; 25min); Riva (6 daily; 1hr 15min); Torri del Benaco (hourly; 15min); Verona (6 daily; 1hr 5min).

Tourist office Piazzale Aldo Moro (Mon–Sat 9am–7pm, Sun 9am–2pm; ⊕045 721 0078).

ACCOMMODATION AND EATING

★ **Prati Palai** Strada Palai 11 ⊕342 529 1971, ⊚pratipalai.it. Nestled amid olive groves on a hillside overlooking the lake, this welcoming B&B set in an old farmhouse offers spacious well-appointed rooms; there's a swimming pool with loungers commanding lovely views of the lake. €210

Rambaldi Apartments Piazza Guerrieri 1A ⊕ 045 621 1261 ⊚rambaldiapartments.com. Right in the heart of town, these pleasant apartments come in a variety of decor and sizes: contemporary apartments overlooking an attractive green courtyard; rustic attic apartments with wooden ceiling beams and stone floors; colourful and stylish pads with high ceilings and open-plan kitchens. There's a swimming pool and a great pizzeria within the same complex. €130

Peschiera del Garda

Surrounded by Venetian walls, **PESCHIERA DEL GARDA** makes a good base for hikes, canoe trips and bike rides around the lake, as well as being the starting point of a 45km **cycle route** running along the River Mincio to Mantua. With good bus and train connections to major Italian cities, exploring the lake and its surrounding area from here is relatively easy. On May 11 each year, the town floods with pilgrims who travel here to visit the **Shrine of Madonna del Frassino**, where the Virgin Mary is said to have appeared in 1511.

ARRIVAL AND INFORMATION — PESCHIERA DEL GARDA

By train The train station is on Viale della Stazione, a 10min-minute walk from the town centre.

Destinations Brescia (hourly; 30min); Milan (hourly; 1hr 7min); Trieste (3 daily; 2hr 50min); Turin (5 daily; 3hr); Venice (hourly; 1hr 15min); Verona (2 hourly; 17min).

By bus Buses drop passengers off at the train station and at the port.

Destinations Mantua (hourly; 1hr); Verona airport (June–Oct hourly; 30min).

By boat The *imbarcadero* is just by the harbour in the town centre, with regular ferries to all major destinations around the lake.

Tourist office Piazzale Bettelloni 15 (mid March–May daily 9am–2pm & 3–6pm; June–mid Sept daily 9am–7pm; mid Sept–mid Oct daily 9am–2pm & 3–6pm; mid Oct–mid March Mon & Fri 9am–2pm, Sat & Sun 9am–1pm & 2–5pm; T 045 755 0810, W tourismpeschiera.com).

ACCOMMODATION

★ **Meet Hostel** Via Benaco 14 T 045 824 0950, W meethostel.com. A stylish hostel with spotless and spacious en-suite rooms, and a large communal area dotted with colourful chairs and musical instruments including a guitar and piano. There's a wonderful rooftop terrace with bar where films are screened in summer, plus table football, table tennis and a pool table; meals cost a bargain €5. Dorms €23, doubles €75

Valeggio sul Mincio

From Peschiera del Garda, a popular cycling route meanders along the Mincio River to arrive in **Valeggio sul Mincio**, a pretty town renowned for its delicious tortellini, small pasta pockets stuffed with all manner of specialities. On the third Tuesday in June, the Festa del Nodo d'Amore sees more than three thousand diners tucking into tortellini at a 1km-long table on the Ponte Visconteo. With over forty family-run restaurants dotted around town, it makes for a great day-trip from Peschiera – hop on a bike and trace the 48km cycle route, refuelling in Valeggio for lunch. Make sure you head to **Borghetto del Mincio**, the town's most attractive neighbourhood; with its picture-perfect houses and water gently cascading alongside the buildings, you'll feel as if you've stepped into a film set.

Parco Giardino Sigurtà

Via Cavour 1 • Daily April–Sept 9am–7pm (last entry 6pm); March, Oct & Nov 9am–6pm (last entry 5pm) • €14 • T 045 637 1033, W sigurta.it

One of Valeggio's main attractions is the **Parco Giardino Sigurtà**, a lovely park occupying 600,000 square metres of wooded slopes and verdant lawns. In spring, it's carpeted with a rainbow of flowers, including irises, roses, dahlias, and more than one million tulips. Little ones will enjoy the educational farm, home to donkeys, chickens, ducks, goats and turkeys, while older children will enjoy getting lost in the maze, whose hedges are made with 1500 yew trees. You can explore the park on foot, by train or rent an electric golf cart at the entrance and zip around the paved pathways, stopping off at points of interest along the way.

EATING

Alla Borsa Via Goito 2 T 045 795 0093 W ristoranteborsa.it. At this bustling restaurant, experienced nonne lovingly prepare Valeggio's speciality at incredible speed in the kitchen, using over 250 eggs per day to create about 20,000

tortellini. This is one of the town's most famous restaurants, offering a traditional yet sophisticated setting, and al fresco dining in the warmer months of the year. A full meal will set you back about €35-40. Thurs–Mon noon–2pm & 7–9.30pm; mid Nov–mid March closed Sun eve.

Bue D'Oro Via Alessandro Sala 3 ⓣ045 795 2451 ⓦbuedorovaleggio.it. Run since 1927 by the Zara family, this contemporary restaurant serves delicious tortellini as well as plenty of other dishes (seared tuna; braised pork cheek; beef tartar) in a bright and breezy setting. Tues 7–10pm, Wed–Sun 11am–1pm & 7–10pm.

4

Trentino-Alto Adige

311 Trento
315 Rovereto
316 The Dolomiti di Brenta
320 East of Trento
323 The Catinaccio and Gruppo di Sella
327 Bolzano (Bozen)
333 Alpe di Siusi (Seiser Alm)
334 Northeast of Bolzano
338 Cortina d'Ampezzo
340 Merano and around
342 Parco Nazionale dello Stelvio

LAGO DI BRAIES

5

Trentino-Alto Adige

Draped across the high Alps, where Italy, Austria and Switzerland collide and their cultures blur, Italy's northernmost region is a major draw for holiday-makers who mostly come for winter skiing, summer hiking and tranquil year-round vistas. However, in past times this region was far from today's peaceful vacation paradise; a string of castles along the Adige (Etsch) Valley bear witness to the cut and thrust of medieval politics, and World War I saw prolonged and ferocious fighting, with Italian and Austrian troops battling it out in the harsh conditions of the Alpine ridges. Armies of brightly attired skiers and sturdily booted hikers have long since replaced the troops, invading the sunny slopes on ski and board or marching along one of the hundreds of dramatic trails that crisscross the landscape.

As its double-barrelled name suggests, the region is made up of two areas: **Trentino**, the southern part, is 98 percent Italian-speaking and the cuisine and architecture belong predominantly to the south rather than the Alps. By contrast, the mountainous terrain around Bolzano – known both as the Südtirol (South Tyrol) and **Alto Adige** – was only annexed to Italy at the end of World War I (see page 327). Here, onion-domed churches dot vineyards and forests, street signs are in German and Italian and the landscape is redolent of illustrations from the Brothers Grimm. German is the dominant tongue, though immigrants from Italy's south rarely speak anything other than Italian. Both Trentino and Alto Adige enjoy autonomy from central government, along with one of the highest standards of living in Italy.

The region is dominated by the barren, jagged rock walls of the **Dolomites**. Some of the most eye-catching peaks in Europe, these vast massifs have been eroded over the last 200 million years into a weird and wonderful array of needles, towers and pinnacles. In 2009 the range was added to the UNESCO World Natural Heritage List for their unique geology – they began life around 250 million years ago as a giant coral reef beneath the ancient Tethys Ocean – and for their diverse ecosystem, abundant in rare flora and fauna. Numerous cable cars rise from the region's small resorts enabling you to hike at 2000–3000m, with a web of well-marked **trails** lasting from a gentle day-hike to a two-week trek. Views of this spectacular landscape can also be savoured from the comfort of luxurious **spa hotels**, with first-rate regional cuisine and a unique selection of treatments from bathing in thermal water to "dry baths" involving lying swaddled in sheep's wool or mountain hay.

Down in the valleys, Trentino-Alto Adige has a flourishing **cultural scene**, with cutting-edge galleries and museums, such as Trento's **MUSE** science museum and Bolzano's **Museion** gallery. The regional capital **Trento** has an atmospheric old centre and an enviable quality of life, while **Bolzano**, Alto Adige's chief town, makes an engaging base for exploring the region, with its star attraction the famous "Ice Man" (see page 329). Verdant hillsides planted with **vineyards** can be visited as part of the Strada del Vino wine-tasting route, and the valley floor is carpeted with apple trees which produce the principal ingredient for Südtirol's delicious *strudel*.

Both Trento and Bolzano are transport hubs, reachable by train via Verona and Innsbruck, and by bus from Bergamo and other airports. The scenic Great Dolomites Road links Bolzano with Cortina d'Ampezzo. **Merano**, in the northwest, is another hub, serving the Val Venosta (Vinschgau) and its side valleys which take you deep into the mountains of the **Parco Nazionale dello Stelvio**, straddling the border with Lombardy.

PIAZZA DUOMO, TRENTO

Highlights

❶ **Mountain refuges** Bunk down in some of Central Europe's most isolated and vista-rich locations. See page 311

❷ **Dolomiti Superski** With more than 1200km of pistes and over 450 lifts connecting twelve different ski areas, there's a vast choice of slopes for all levels. See page 311

❸ **Trento** Surrounded by mountains, this beautiful city combines Austro-Hungarian and Renaissance architecture with a laidback vibe. See page 311

❹ **Alpine lakes** Enjoy the beauty of the region's majestic Alpine lakes, such as Lago Carezza, Lago di Braies and Lago di Toblino. See pages 314, 323 and 338

❺ **The Dolomiti di Brenta** Paths through this rugged cluster of peaks are far less trodden but no less spectacular, with waterfalls, vast glaciers and pristine lakes. See page 316

❻ **The Pale di San Martino** One of the most spectacular hiking areas in the Dolomites, with a great choice of high-altitude trails. See page 322

❼ **Ice Man** The star exhibit at Bolzano's Museo Archeologico is the incredibly well preserved "Ice Man", discovered in the Ötzaler Alps in 1991. See page 329

HIGHLIGHTS ARE MARKED ON THE MAP ON PAGE 308

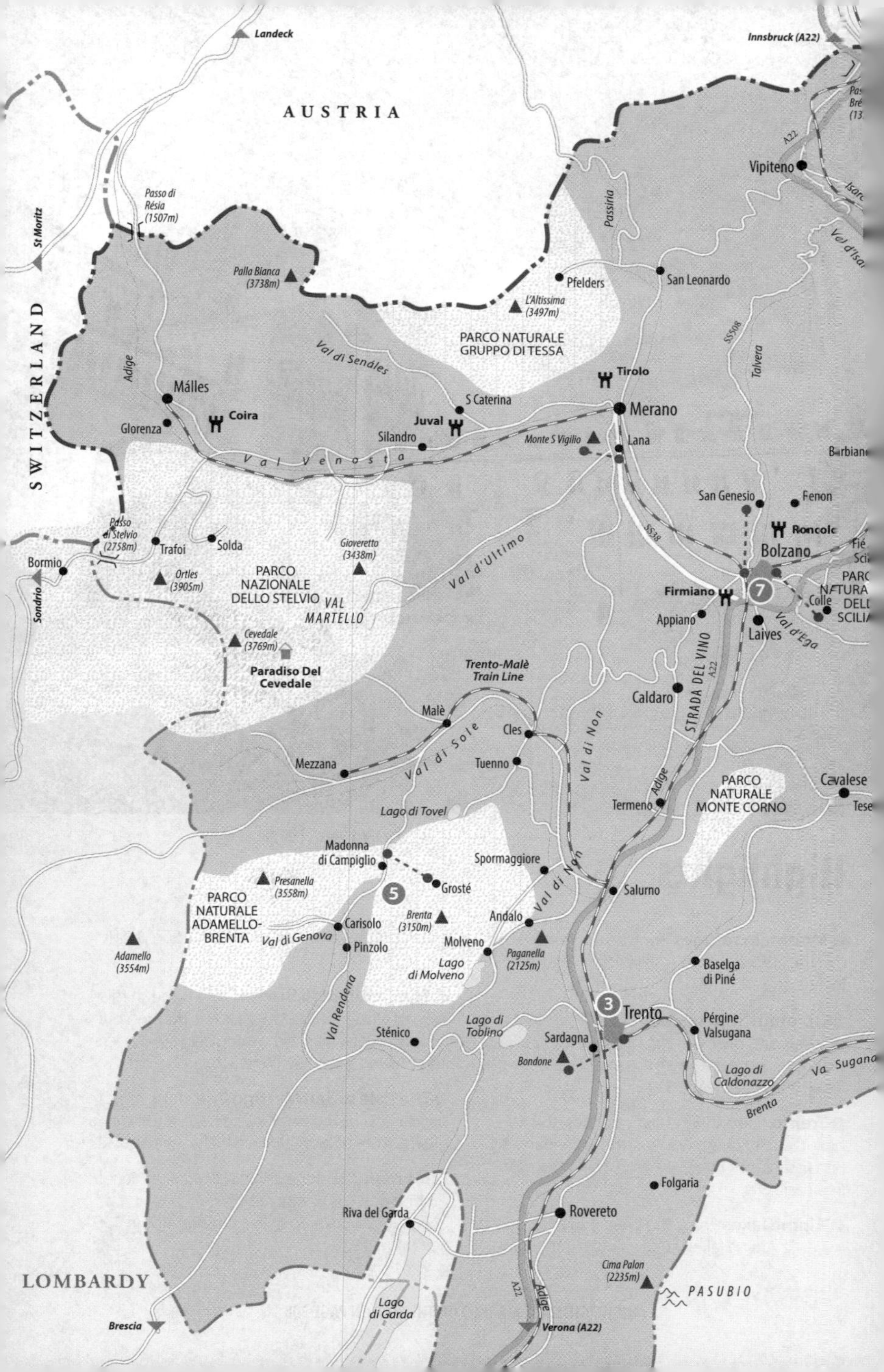

Landeck
Innsbruck (A22)
AUSTRIA
SWITZERLAND
St Moritz
Passo di Résia (1507m)
Palla Bianca (3738m)
L'Altissima (3497m)
Pfelders
San Leonardo
Passiria
Vipiteno
A22
SS508
Talvera
PARCO NATURALE GRUPPO DI TESSA
Val di Senáles
Adige
Málles
Coira
Juval
S Caterina
Tirolo
Merano
Glorenza
Silandro
Monte S Vigilio
Lana
Val Venosta
San Genesio
Fenon
Roncolc
SS38
Bolzano
Passo di Stelvio (2758m)
Trafoi
Solda
Gioveretto (3438m)
Val d'Ultimo
Bormio
Sondrio
Ortles (3905m)
PARCO NAZIONALE DELLO STELVIO
VAL MARTELLO
Firmiano
Colle
Appiano
Laives
Val d'Ega
Cevedale (3769m)
Paradiso Del Cevedale
STRADA DEL VINO
Trento-Malè Train Line
Caldaro
Malè
Cles
Val di Sole
Val di Non
Mezzana
Tuenno
Cavalese
PARCO NATURALE MONTE CORNO
Termeno
Lago di Tovel
Madonna di Campiglio
Spormaggiore
Grosté
Presanella (3558m)
Salurno
PARCO NATURALE ADAMELLO-BRENTA
Brenta (3150m)
Andalo
Carisolo
Val di Genova
Pinzolo
Molveno
Paganella (2125m)
Adamello (3554m)
Lago di Molveno
Baselga di Piné
Val Rendena
Trento
Pérgine Valsugana
Sténico
Lago di Toblino
Sardagna
Bondone
Lago di Caldonazzo
Brenta
Folgaria
Rovereto
Riva del Garda
Cima Palon (2235m)
PASUBIO
LOMBARDY
Lago di Garda
Brescia
Verona (A22)

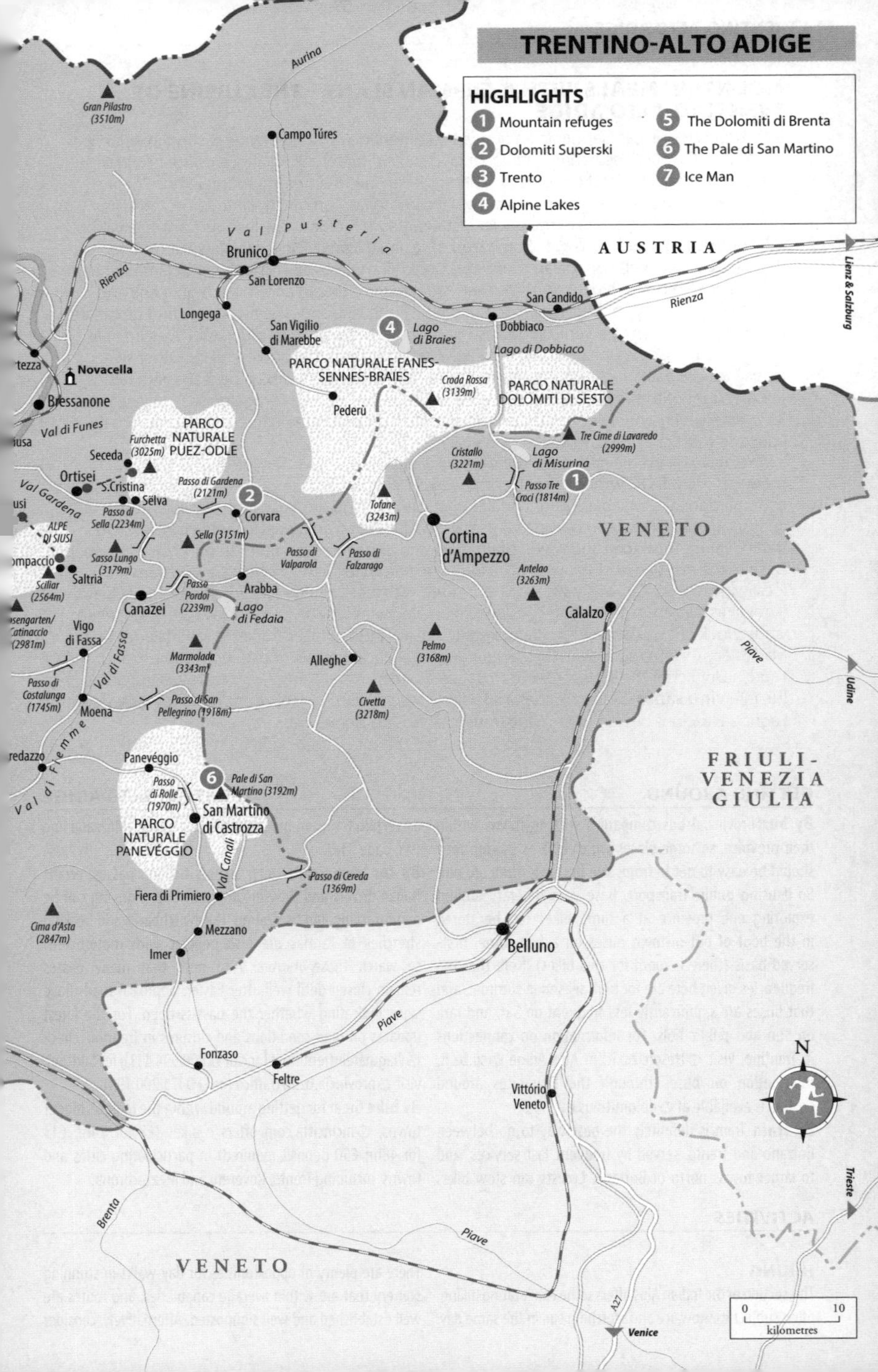
TRENTINO-ALTO ADIGE
HIGHLIGHTS
1 Mountain refuges
2 Dolomiti Superski
3 Trento
4 Alpine Lakes
5 The Dolomiti di Brenta
6 The Pale di San Martino
7 Ice Man
AUSTRIA
VENETO
FRIULI-VENEZIA GIULIA
VENETO
Aurina
Gran Pilastro (3510m)
Campo Túres
Val Pusteria
Brunico
San Lorenzo
Rienza
Longega
San Vigilio di Marebbe
Lago di Braies
San Candido
Dobbiaco
Lago di Dobbiaco
Lienz & Salzburg
PARCO NATURALE FANES-SENNES-BRAIES
Croda Rossa (3139m)
PARCO NATURALE DOLOMITI DI SESTO
Pederù
Novacella
Bressanone
Val di Funes
PARCO NATURALE PUEZ-ODLE
Furchetta (3025m)
Seceda
Ortisei
S.Cristina
Sëlva
Val Gardena
Passo di Gardena (2121m)
Corvara
Passo di Sella (2234m)
ALPE DI SIUSI
Sella (3151m)
Sasso Lungo (3179m)
Saltria
Sciliar (2564m)
Passo Pordoi (2239m)
Arabba
Lago di Fedaia
Canazei
Vigo di Fassa
Val di Fassa
Tre Cime di Lavaredo (2999m)
Lago di Misurina
Cristallo (3221m)
Passo Tre Croci (1814m)
Tofane (3243m)
Cortina d'Ampezzo
Passo di Valparola
Passo di Falzarago
Antelao (3263m)
Calalzo
Piave
Udine
Marmolada (3343m)
Pelmo (3168m)
Alleghe
Civetta (3218m)
Passo di Costalunga (1745m)
Moena
Passo di San Pellegrino (1918m)
Val di Fiemme
Panevéggio
Pale di San Martino (3192m)
Passo di Rolle (1970m)
San Martino di Castrozza
PARCO NATURALE PANEVÉGGIO
Val Canali
Passo di Cereda (1369m)
Fiera di Primiero
Cima d'Asta (2847m)
Mezzano
Imer
Belluno
Piave
Fonzaso
Feltre
Vittório Veneto
Brenta
Piave
Trieste
A27
Venice
N
0
10
kilometres

MOUNTAIN MEALS WITH A GERMAN SLANT – THE CUISINE OF TRENTINO-ALTO ADIGE

Alto Adige cuisine has Germanic traditions, while Trentino cooking blends mountain influences with Italian flavours. The hearty traditional food is great for refuelling after a day of hiking or skiing and the quality of produce is exceptional, even in the simplest mountain hut. For finer dining, adventurous chefs are reworking old recipes to fashion much lighter dishes, and it is well worth trying out some of the pricier restaurants we list for a new take on local specialities.

A **traditional meal** starts with some kind of salami (*lucaniche* in local dialect), often paper-thin slices of salt beef, or Tyrolean *canederli* – bread dumplings spiked with speck (smoked ham) often served in broth (*brodo*). You'll also see *strangolapreti* (bread and spinach gnocchi) and *schlutzkrapfen* (spinach-filled pasta) on the menu. Fresh lake and river fish, game and rabbit are popular as *secondi*, as are venison goulash or boiled cured pork with sauerkraut. Desserts are often based on apples, pears or plums, readily available from the local orchards. Other sweet treats include *apfel strudel*, *sachertorte* and *kaiserschmarren*, a scrambled pancake with raisins.

A highlight of the year for food- and wine-lovers is the autumn Törggelen season (see page 333), when everyone heads for the hills to sample the new vintage and snack on mountain ham and roast chestnuts, followed by a walk.

Vines have been cultivated here since before Roman times, and Trentino-Alto Adige produces more **DOC wines** than any other region in Italy. Most famous are the Pinot Grigios and Chardonnays, which are bright and aromatic from being grown at high altitudes and in cool conditions. These also provide wine makers with the raw material for some outstanding traditional-method sparkling wines, often marketed under the spumante Trentino Classico label. Despite the excellence of the whites, including the aromatic slightly sweet Gewürztraminer, local wine makers actually make more reds often with local varieties like Teroldego and Schiava (known as Vernatsch in German-speaking areas). Red wines made from Schiava are good when young: look out for the pale red Kalterersee (Caldaro) and the fuller, fruitier St Magdalene (Santa Maddalena); those made from the Lagrein grape variety are more robust, such as the strong, dark Lagrein Dunkel, or the Kretzer rosé from Bolzano's vineyards at Gries. Also worth seeking out is the rare **vino santo** (not to be confused with *vin santo* from Tuscany) from Trentino's Valle dei Laghi – a luscious dessert wine made from local Nosiola grapes.

GETTING AROUND — TRENTINO-ALTO ADIGE

By bus Provincial bus companies stick to towns within their province, so some places which look as though they should be easy to get to from, say, Bolzano, often are not. So if using public transport, base your itinerary around exploring one province at a time. Bikes can be stored in the boot of out-of-town buses on a first-come, first-served basis (there is room for two bikes). Note that the frequencies given here are for high season in summer, and that buses are significantly less frequent on Sat, and rare on Sun and public hols. For information on connections in Trentino, visit Ⓦ ttesercizio.it; in Alto Adige Ⓦ sii.bz.it. Information on buses through the Dolomites around Cortina is available at Ⓦ dolomitibus.it.

By train Train is definitely the best way to go between Bolzano and Trento, served by frequent fast services, and to larger towns north of Bolzano. Cyclists can stow bikes on certain trains on the private Trento–Malè–Mezzana line (see page 314).

By car With scenic, steep ascents to high passes, erratic Italian drivers and slow-moving tour buses, driving can be nerve-racking and frustrating. The switchbacks and bucking stretches of tarmac are also popular with motorbikers, so watch those mirrors. Also note that many passes remain closed until well after Easter: approach roads have signs indicating whether the pass is open. For the latest updates on road conditions and closures in Trentino, check Ⓦ viaggiareintrentino.it (or call ⓣ 800 994 411); for Südtirol, visit Ⓦ provincia.bz.it/traffico (or ⓣ 0471 200 198).

By bike Great for getting around within the region's bigger towns, Ⓦ bicincitta.com offers e-bikes (€8 for 24hr, €13 for 48hr; €50 deposit required) in participating cities and towns, including Trento, Rovereto and Mezzocorona.

ACTIVITIES

HIKING

This section of the Italian Alps offers some exhilarating hiking, often subject to snow, ice and scorching sun in the same day. There are plenty of opportunities for day-walks in stunning scenery that are within average capabilities, and routes are well established and well signposted. Alternatively, consider

tackling one of the longer trails known as *alte vie* (literally "high ways"), almost all of which run north–south, including the most popular pair: the Alta Via 1 (150km; from Lago di Braies to Belluno), perhaps the easiest route; and the tougher Alta Via 2 (185km; from Bressanone to Feltre). Along the way there are plenty of mountain huts for meals and overnight accommodation. Some of the initial ascents are strenuous, but once you are up on the ridges the paths level out and afford stupendous views across the valleys and glaciers. Parts of the trails are exposed, or have snowfields across them, but there are usually detours you can take to avoid these. In Trentino two well-planned circuits provide spectacular views, the Dolomiti Panorama Trek (W visittrentino.info) and the Dolomiti Brenta Trek (W dolomitibrentatrek.it).

Guides Gillian Price's *Trekking in the Dolomites* covers Alte Vie 1 and 2 and outlines Vie 3–6; her *Shorter Walks in the Dolomites* outlines fifty day-walks of varying levels of difficulty.

Maps To plan your own routes through the Dolomites, the Kompass 1:50,000 maps are on sale in every bookshop and tourist office throughout the region: check which sheets you'll need at W kompass.de. Paths are numbered and easy to follow – just look out for the red-and-white blaze on rocks and trees by the side of the path along the way.

Websites W dolomiti.it and W visitdolomites.com are good sources of general information on the area, while W visittrentino.it and W south-tirol.com have details on mountain refuges, transport, hiking, skiing and agriturismo accommodation. W meteotrentino.it provides the latest on snow conditions in Trentino from Dec onwards, or check the national winter weather website W meteomont.net.

CLIMBING

Salewa Cube The Dolomites are prime climbing territory, but if you fancy some practice beforehand, the mammoth Salewa Cube (Waltraud-Gebert-Deeg-Strasse 4; T 0471 188 6867, W salewa-cube.com) in Bolzano, is Italy's largest climbing hall with 2000 square metres of climbing walls, including outdoor climbing and bouldering areas. An all-day ticket costs €13 and buses #10A or #10B from Piazza Walther will get you near.

RIFUGI

A network of solidly constructed mountain huts – *rifugi* (refuges) – provides dormitory accommodation (and often double or quad rooms), meals and a bar: most also have hot showers. Blankets are provided, but you must bring your own sheet sleeping bag – or you can usually buy one at the hut for around €10. *Rifugi* are generally open from June until late Sept, and many also operate in the skiing season, subject to weather conditions. If you're relying on *rifugi* for accommodation, you should definitely call ahead – nobody is ever turned away, but overflow accommodation is either on a mattress in the bar or, *in extremis*, the hen house. If you are a member of the Club Alpino Italiano (W cai.it) or the Alpenverein Südtirol (W alpenverein.it), the overnight rate at CAI-run *rifugi* is around €12; if not, expect to pay around €25, or €40–50 for a bunk, breakfast and dinner – good value for hearty home-cooking and local wine in some pretty remote locations. Emergency calls can be made from most *rifugi*; to call Soccorso Alpino (Alpine Rescue), dial T 118. A directory of refuges is available at W trentinorifugi.com and W trekking.suedtirol.info.

SKIING

When to come Trentino-Alto Adige is home to many of Italy's top ski resorts that are popular with families and with a laidback atmosphere. Jan and Feb are the best months to come; March can also be good, although by mid-April the winter season is over. Italian tourist offices have details of Settimane Bianche (White Weeks), when bargain package deals include full or half-board accommodation and a ski-pass – although be wary of deals late in the season when the snow deteriorates fast on south-facing slopes. There's also summer skiing from June to Nov on the glacier slopes of Stelvio Pass (W passostelvio.com) although this is dependent on the state of the glacier and there being a good dump of snow the winter before.

Dolomiti Superski In the eastern Dolomites twelve different ski areas are linked to create the world's largest ski area with 1200km of runs and 450 cable cars and lifts. You can access all these areas and lifts with the Dolomiti Superski pass (€258–322 for seven days; W dolomitisuperski.com), which covers Cortina d'Ampezzo, Plan de Corones, Alta Badia, Val Gardena/Alpe di Siusi, Val di Fassa/Carezza, Arabba/Marmolada, San Martino di Castrozza/Passo Rolle, Valle Isarco, Alpe Lusia-S. Pellegrino, Tre Cime, Val di Fiemme/Obereggen and Civetta.

Other resorts The ski area of Campiglio Dolomiti di Brenta-Val di Sole Val Rendena (W valdisole.net) offers 150km of runs and 62 lifts, while at Passo Tonale you can ski at 3000m. The Paganella plateau just off the Brenner motorway is popular for downhill skiing, cross-country skiing and ski mountaineering. Check out details of chair lifts, altitude and length of runs at W visittrentino.info and W suedtirol.info.

Trento

Overshadowed by Monte Bedone, just 13km away, **TRENTO** is beautifully situated, encircled by mountains and exuding an easy-going pace of life. Visitors inevitably gravitate to the central, café-lined Piazza del Duomo, all fading frescoes and

cobblestones, with fashionable shops, boutiques and restaurants occupying the narrow streets that lead off it. Mammoth, moss-covered city walls lurk beyond.

Trento was known as Tridentum to the Romans, a name celebrated by the eighteenth-century Neptune fountain in the central **Piazza Duomo**. From the tenth to the eighteenth centuries, the city was a powerful bishopric ruled by a dynasty of princes; it was the venue of the Council of Trent between 1545 and 1563, when the Catholic Church, threatened by the Reformation in northern Europe, met to plan its counterattack. Later, throughout the nineteenth century, ownership of the city, which remained in Austrian hands, was hotly contested, and it only became properly part of Italy in 1919, following World War I.

The Duomo

Piazza Duomo • **Duomo** Daily 6.30am–noon & 2.30–8pm • Free • **Crypt** Mon–Sat 10am–noon & 2.30–5.30pm • €1.50 • Ⓣ 0461 231 293, Ⓦ cattedralesanvigilio.it

Started in the thirteenth century, but not completed until the sixteenth, Trento's **Duomo** hosted the three most significant meetings of the Council of Trent. Inside, an enormous, carved marble *baldachino*, held over the altar by four chunky Baroque barley-twist columns, is a replica of the one in St Peter's, Rome. However, by far the

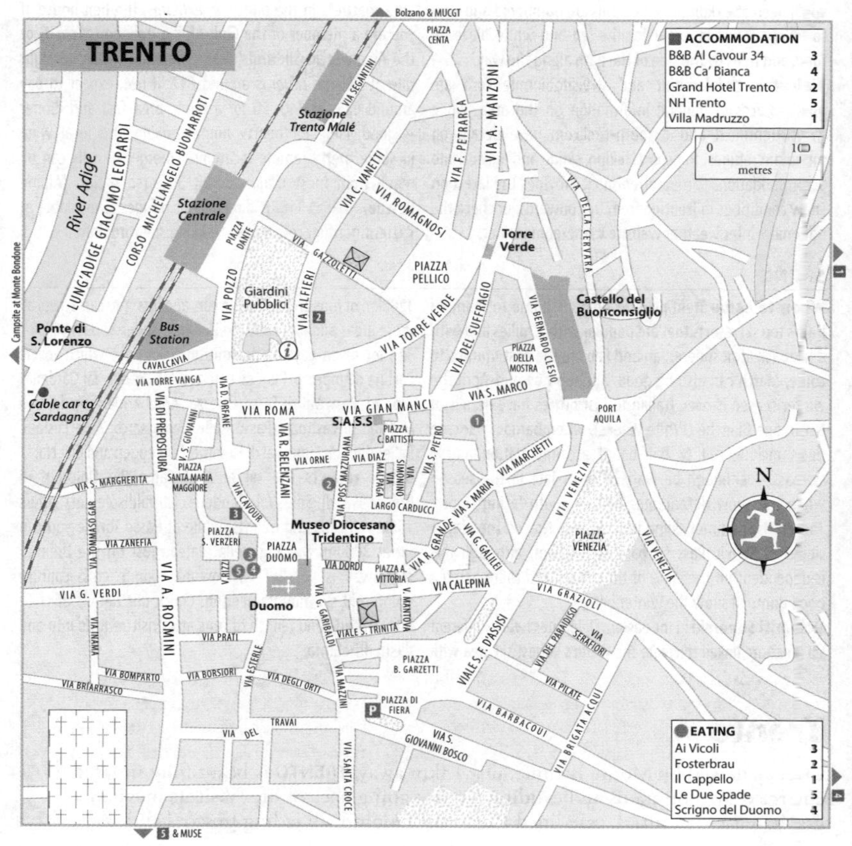

FESTIVALS AND EVENTS

Wine-related festivities abound across the region, with almost every village celebrating its vintages, harvest or related traditions – ask local tourist offices for details. The biggest wine bash, the **Festa in Vino** takes place in the sixteen towns along the South Tyrolean Wine Road from late April to mid-June, with tours, music, tastings and myriad other events. The month of events comes to a climax with the **Night of the Cellars** when wine producers open their doors on the final night: see Ⓦ suedtiroler-weinstrasse.it for further details.

There are plenty of summer concerts, but possibly the best event is the **Suoni delle Dolomiti** series of jazz, folk and world music concerts by artists from all over the world: the concept is an original one – you hike (sometimes with the artists) to the chosen location, which may be a wood, perhaps, or a rocky gully, then listen to the concert. Performances are in the early afternoon and sometimes at dawn: Ⓦ isuonidelledolomiti.it has details of concerts, local accommodation and walking times to venues. In the best Central European tradition, vast **Christmas markets** take over the historic centres of Trento and Bolzano, as well as most towns in the region: for details, see Ⓦ visittrentino.it or Ⓦ christkindlmarkt.it.

most interesting part of the building lies beneath the cathedral, where a **medieval crypt** and foundations of an early Christian basilica built over the tomb of St Vigilio, the third bishop of Trento, were discovered in 1977.

Museo Diocesano Tridentino

Piazza Duomo 18 • June–Sept Wed–Mon 10am–1pm & 2–6pm; Oct–May Mon & Wed–Sat 9.30am–12.30pm & 2–5.30pm, Sun 10am–1pm & 2–6pm • €7 • Ⓣ 0461 234 419, Ⓦ museodiocesanotridentino.it

Next to the Duomo, the **Museo Diocesano Tridentino**, housed in the Palazzo Pretorio, includes large annotated paintings of the sessions of the Council of Trent and some carved altarpieces from the church of San Zeno in the Val di Non. The building is appealing in itself, too, with its fishtail battlements, heavy studded doors and a view from the upper storey of the frescoed palaces around the square.

Castello del Buonconsiglio

Via Bernardo Clesio 5 • Tues–Sun: early May to Oct 10am–6pm; Nov to early May 9.30am–5pm • €8 • Ⓣ 0461 233 770, Ⓦ buonconsiglio.it

The most powerful of the Trento princes was Bernardo Clesio, who in the late fifteenth and early sixteenth centuries built up much of the city's art collection, a good proportion of which is held in the **Castello del Buonconsiglio**, another venue of the Council of Trent. It's really two castles: the thirteenth-century **Castelvecchio** and the extension built in 1530 called the **Magno Palazzo**, in which several rooms frescoed with classical subjects by the Dossi family and Romanino lead off an inner courtyard. Upstairs in the **Museo Provinciale d'Arte**, the highlight is the *Ciclo dei Mesi* (Cycle of the Months), where frescoes dating from 1391 to 1407 show scenes of farming and courtly life.

S.A.S.S.

Piazza Cesare Battisti • Tues–Sun: June–Sept 9.30am–1pm & 2–6pm; Oct–May 9am–1pm & 2–5.30pm • €2.50

During renovation work on Trento's theatre in the 1990s, archeologists discovered around 1700 square metres of a Roman road – complete with sewage system – along with buildings and remains of the city walls dating from between 1000 BC and 400 AD. This is now the **S.A.S.S.** (Spazio Archeologico Sotterraneo del Sas), an underground archeological area where you can see all the mosaics, buildings, courtyards and artisans' dwellings from the visitor centre, built on a level with the existing road.

5

MUSE

Corso del Lavoro e della Scienza 3 • Sept–June Tues–Fri 10am–6pm, Sat & Sun 10am–7pm; July Tues–Sun 10am–7pm; Aug daily 10am–7pm; Wed year-round 10am–9pm • €10 • ⓣ 0461 270 311, ⓦ muse.it

Spread over six floors, Trento's Museo delle Scienze, or **MUSE**, is located in a futuristic structure designed by architect Renzo Piano. The museum houses exhibitions on Alpine ecosystems, with the top floors examining the highest peaks and glaciers and the basement taking visitors below sea level. It is one of the region's top draws, with permanent exhibitions as well as temporary displays, and plenty of interactive exhibits.

Museo degli Usi e Costumi della Gente Trentina (MUCGT)

Via Mach 2, San Michele all'Adige • Tues–Sat 9am–12.30pm & 2.30–6pm • €6 • ⓣ 0461 650 314, ⓦ museosanmichele.it • Take the Trento–Malè–Mezzana line from Trento to Grumo San Michele, from where it's a 10min walk

Some 15km northeast of Trento, the **Museo degli Usi e Costumi della Gente Trentina** – or **MUCGT** – at San Michele All'Adige, gives a real flavour of what life in Trentino was like until the twentieth century. One of the largest museums of its kind in Europe, it has exhibits that range from re-creations of village houses (complete with muddy boots drying by the stove) to displays on hunting, grazing and wine making.

Lago di Toblino

Take bus #201 from Trento to Padergnone (every 30min–2hr; 30min)

Seventeen kilometres west of Trento, the sixteenth-century Castel Toblino sits on a verdant peninsula stretching out into the beautiful **Lago di Toblino**. The region's best-known lake fortress, it boasts a stunning location surrounded by mountains. There's an upmarket restaurant in the castle itself (ⓣ0461 864 036, ⓦcasteltoblino.com) and a lovely cycle route around one side of the lake tracing the lakeside road.

ARRIVAL AND INFORMATION — TRENTO

By train Trento's main train station is on Piazza Dante. A separate station belonging to the privately-run Trento–Malè–Mezzana railway for the Val di Non is on Via Dogana 2, just beyond the train station (follow platform 1 for 100m heading north).

Destinations Bologna (13 daily; 2hr–3hr); Bolzano (every 15–30min; 30–50min); Bressanone (13 daily; 1hr 10min; or change in Bolzano); Grumo San Michele (at least hourly; 30min); Malè (9 daily; 1hr 40min); Rovereto (at least 2 hourly; 15min); Venice (1 direct daily at 4.04pm; 2hr; at least hourly with change in Verona; 2hr 30min–3hr); Verona (2 hourly; 1hr–1hr 20min).

By bus Trento makes a good base for exploring the Dolomites, because of its bus services. The bus station is on Via Pozzo, just 200m south of the train station.

Destinations Canazei (4 daily; 2hr 45min); Madonna di Campiglio (4 daily, more in winter; 2hr 8min); Molveno (4 daily, train and bus; change at Mezzolombardo; 1hr 30min); Predazzo (7 daily; 1hr 51min); San Martino di Castrozza (4 daily, bus and train connection; 3hr); Vigo di Fassa (4 daily; 2hr 20min).

Tourist office The tourist office at Piazza Dante 24 (daily 9am–7pm; ⓣ0461 216 000, ⓦdiscovertrento.it) sells the useful Trento Rovereto Card (€20 for 48hr) and the Trentino Guest Card (€40 for seven days), each offering free city transport and admission to major museums and castles. You can also get the latter for free by booking two nights at one of the hotels listed on ⓦvisittrentino.info.

GETTING AROUND

By bike Trento's cycle-path network is excellent and it's linked via the Valle dell Adige cycle path to Bolzano in the north and Verona to the south, with many charming towns and villages en route. You get free bike rental with a Trento Rovereto Card or a Trentino Guest Card (see above).

By cable car A cable car runs from just east of San Lorenzo bridge, near Trento's bus station (every 15–30min until 10.30pm; one-way/return €3/€5), to the lower slopes of the towering Monte Bondone, from where you get a wonderful view.

Taxis Radiotaxi, Via Degasperi 27 (ⓣ0461 930 002)

ACCOMMODATION

★ **B&B Al Cavour 34** Via Cavour 34 ⓣ349 415 5814, ⓦalcavour34.it; map p.312. About five minutes' walk from the train station, this friendly B&B run by an enthusiastic young couple, has four bright, colourful rooms (two of which can sleep up to four). Breakfast is served at a communal table, and includes home-made cakes, ham,

eggs and cheeses. Covered parking for bikes available. **€130**

B&B Ca' Bianca Via Gabbiolo 22 ⓣ348 820 8977, ⓦcabiancatrento.it; map p.312. This family-friendly B&B lies four kilometres east of the Trento's historic centre, with just two rooms (one sleeping up to four) and a gorgeous garden in the back with kiwi fruit, strawberries, figs, apples and pears. Breakfast includes home-made jams, honey, yogurt, cold cuts and cheeses. **€70**

Grand Hotel Trento Piazza Dante 20 ⓣ0461 271000, ⓦgrandhoteltrento.com; map p.312. Conveniently set just across the park from the train station, this charming four-star has a grand old lobby and large, comfortable rooms with big bathtubs – although decor is strikingly dated. There's a roof terrace affording views over the centre, a pricey restaurant and café and a plentiful breakfast. Paid parking (€11 per day) and bike storage available underground. **€140**

NH Trento Via Adalberto Libera ⓣ0461 366 111, ⓦnh-hotels.com; map p.312. A stone's throw from MUSE, this modern, glass-fronted four-star hotel has light and airy rooms and spacious suites (€350). Facilities include parking (€7 per night), bike and ski storage and a small gym. **€230**

Villa Madruzzo Via Ponte Alto 26 ⓣ0461 986 220, ⓦvillamadruzzo.com; map p.312. Set in the hills above Trento, this peaceful four-star hotel has classic rooms with nineteenth-century furniture in the main historic villa, which is connected by an underground passageway to an annexe with stylish modern rooms. There's an indoor swimming pool and a lovely garden area. **€130**

EATING

You'll eat well in Trento and the surrounding area, and foodies might consider a winter visit as, from late Nov until Christmas, hundreds of food and craft stalls fill the streets to celebrate the feast of St Lucy. For some local wine tasting, head to the *cantine* in the suburbs and villages around Trento, all marked on the map from the tourist office.

Ai Vicoli Piazza S. Verzeri 1 ⓣ0461 260 673 ⓦaivicoli.it; map p.312. With a lovely setting on a tiny piazza close to the Duomo, this distinctive restaurant serves up dishes that skilfully combine tradition and innovation (*primi* around €15; *secondi* €22) as well as a wide range of local wines. Mon–Sat 11.30am–3pm & 6.30pm–midnight.

★ **Fosterbrau** Via Oss Mazzurana 38, Trento ⓣ0461 235 590, ⓦforst-trento.it; map p.312. Cosy, wood-panelled restaurant and brewery in the centre of the old town. The menu recommends pairings of Forst beer to match the generously portioned Tirolian comfort foods like canederli, schnitzel, würstel and gulash. Mains around €15 and good-value three-course menus for €30 including drinks. Daily noon–2.30pm & 7–11pm.

Il Cappello Piazzetta B. Lunelli ⓣ0461 235 850, ⓦosteriailcappello.it; map p.312. A friendly *osteria* in the heart of town serving regional dishes like homemade *pappardelle* with duck ragù (€13.50). There's a dining area with an open-plan kitchen on the ground floor, while below is a candlelit vaulted basement; in summer there's seating outside. Tues–Sat noon–2pm & 7.30–10pm, Sun noon–2pm.

Le Due Spade Via Don Arcangelo Rizzi 11 ⓣ0461 234 343, ⓦleduespade.com; map p.312. The atmospheric wood-panelled interior of this first-rate *osteria* is almost as much a reason to come as the excellent food. The €30 lunch menu is a real bargain for this quality; otherwise the menu is divided into "sea" (taster menu €75) and "mountains" (taster menu €65). *Primi* €16, *secondi* €20. Mon 7.30–10pm, Tues–Sat noon–2pm & 7–10pm.

★ **Scrigno del Duomo** Piazza Duomo 29 ⓣ0461 220 030, ⓦscrignodelduomo.com; map p.312. One of the city's most elegant dining options is this restaurant in a series of nicely renovated underground cellars that incorporate Roman-era walls and medieval frescoes. Tasting menus cost around €65, while there's a more casual and affordable menu (*primi* and meat platters from around €13) in the ground floor bistro and wine-bar, which spreads tables onto the main square – a great spot for an *aperitivo*. The wine list features over four hundred labels. Daily 11am–2.30pm & 5–11.30pm.

DIRECTORY

Doctor Guardia Medica, Via Paolo Orsi 1 (ⓣ0461 904 298; ⓦapss.tn.it), offers out-of-hours medical service Mon–Fri 8pm–8am and from Sat 8am to Mon 8am.

Hospitals In an emergency, call ⓣ118. Casualty ⓣ0461 903 111 at the Ospedale Santa Chiara, Largo Medaglie d'Oro 9.

Markets There are food markets in Piazza Vittoria (Mon–Sat mornings) and Piazza Dante (Sat mornings) and a weekly market in the historic centre (Thurs mornings).

Pharmacies Dall'Armi, Piazza del Duomo 10; Alla Madonna, Via Manci 42; S. Chiara, Via S. Croce 57.

Police Via Maccani 148 (ⓣ0461 889 111).

Post office Piazza A. Vittoria 20 (Mon–Fri 8.20am–7.05pm, Sat 8.20am–12.35pm; ⓣ0461 275 349).

Rovereto

Some 20km to the south of Trento and a mere 13km from Lago di Garda, **ROVERETO** is a small picturesque town, with stylish *palazzi* containing university faculties which give

the town a youthful, lively atmosphere. Its main attraction is the outstanding **MART** gallery, though it's also home to the world's largest ringing **bell**, at Colle di Miravalle, which tolls a hundred times daily (at 9.30pm & at noon on Sun) to honour the war dead. The bell is in a little park (daily: Jan–Feb & Nov–Dec 9am–4.30pm; Mar & Oct 6pm; April–Sept 9am–7pm; €4; 0464 434 412, fondazioneoperacampana.it), where there are lovely views which you can admire while listening to the bell toll.

MART

Corso Bettini 43 • Tues–Thurs, Sat & Sun 10am–6pm, Fri 10am–9pm • €11; €14 combined with Casa d'Arte Futurista Depero • mart.trento.it

Designed by Mario Botta, **MART (Museo di Arte Moderna e Contemporanea)** hosts world-class exhibitions and is one of Trentino's unmissable experiences. The spectacular building, with spacious galleries wrapped around a central circular atrium flooded with light, is impressive enough even before you view the art inside. Skilfully curated, themed exhibitions use works loaned from institutions and individuals around the world as well as drawing on the gallery's collection of 30,000 paintings, design pieces and sculptures by names including the great Italian Futurist Fortunato Depero, Felice Casorati, Giorgio de Chirico and Giorgio Morandi. A smaller nearby branch, the **Casa d'Arte Futurista Depero** (Via Portico 38; Tues–Sun 10am–6pm; €7) displays Depero's large cloth collages, tapestries, furniture and other design pieces.

Museo Storico Italiano della Guerra

Via Castelbarco 7 • Tues–Sun 10am–6pm • €7.50 • 0464 438 100, museodellaguerra.it

Perched above town in Rovereto's castle, the **Museo Storico Italiano della Guerra** is one of Italy's major museums dedicated to the Great War. It houses an extensive collection of 5700 weapons and arms, 1300 uniforms mainly from the nineteenth and twentieth centuries, military vehicles, bombs, projectiles and flags, as well as 190 pieces of artillery, some of which were used during World War II.

ARRIVAL AND INFORMATION — ROVERETO

By train Rovereto's train station is located at the western end of Corso Rosmini, with MART just north of the eastern end. Buses #1, #3 and #6 linke the two. Alternatively, pick up an e-bike via bicincitta.com (see page 310).

Destinations Bolzano (2 hourly; 1hr); Trento (2 hourly; 15min); Venice (at least hourly; 2–3hr, change in Verona); Verona (2 hourly; 1hr).

Tourist office Piazza Rosmini 21 (Mon, Sat & Sun 10am–1pm; Tues–Fri 9am–1pm & 2–6pm; 0464 430 363, visitrovereto.it).

ACCOMMODATION AND EATING

Casa del Pittore Via Acquedotto 8 0464 486 856, casadelpittore.it. This was formerly the house of a painter (as its name suggests), whose works of art are displayed in the entrance area. The rooms are furnished with antiques purchased at flea markets over the years, and there's a pleasant garden and terrace. **€85**

Osteria del Pettirosso Corso Bettini 24 0464 422 463, osteriadelpettirosso.it. Cosy restaurant set in a pair of beautifully renovated, stone-vaulted cellars, with a menu that includes tasty specialities such as *canederli* (dumplings made of bread soaked with milk; €9), gourmet sandwiches (€5–6) and plates of locally-sourced cured meats and cheeses (€12). There's live jazz roughly every fortnight on Fri (Sept–May). Mon–Sat noon–2.30pm & 7.30–10pm, Sun noon–2.30pm.

The Dolomiti di Brenta

With their saw-toothed peaks and glaciers, the **Dolomiti di Brenta**, northwest of Trento, have a rougher character than the better-known Dolomitic peaks to the east – and their trails are far less well-trodden. While they are steep, few peaks rise above 3000m and the paths are easy to follow, though the walking is strenuous. Climbers come here

VIE FERRATE

Vie ferrate (literally "iron ways") are an Italian phenomenon, consisting of fixed metal ladders, pegs and cables that climbers clip onto with karabiners, making otherwise difficult routes accessible. Many *vie ferrate* began life in the late nineteenth century as mountaineering took off as a sport in Europe; Alpini troops put others in place during World War I to help the soldiers fighting in the mountains. In the decades since then, volunteers from local Club Alpino Italiano groups have created many more.

Kompass maps show *vie ferrate* as a line of little black dots or crosses, so you can easily avoid them – they are definitely not for beginners or vertigo-sufferers. To use them, you need to be confident at belaying and have the proper **equipment** (including helmet, ropes, two self-locking karabiners and a chest- or seat-harness). Incidentally, it's not advisable to climb a *via ferrata* in a thunderstorm either, as it might just become one long lightning conductor.

Once you've done a few straightforward paths up in the mountains you may be inspired to tackle some *ferrate*, and there are plenty of specialist **guides** who can show you the ropes – though you'll need to book at least a week ahead in high season. Guides charge by the hour, so save money by getting a small group together. Many of the *rifugi* are run by mountain guides, or you can enrol in a mountain skills course: both Trentino and Alto Adige provincial tourist offices keep lists of guides and mountaineering schools. Alternatively, contact the Collegio Guide Alpine del Trentino, Vicolo Galasso 19, Trento (T 0461 981 207, W guidealpinetrentino.it), an organization for Alpine guides in Trentino; for Alto Adige, contact Verband der Südtiroler Berg- und Skiführer, Piazza Fiera 1, Bolzano (T 0471 976 357, W bergfuehrer-suedtirol.it).

for the towers of **Cima Tosa** and **Cima Brenta**, accessible by *vie ferrate* – iron "ladders" knocked into the rock (see page 317). If you are looking for easier strolls, **Val Genova** has a gentler beauty, with a woodland path taking you past a number of waterfalls cascading down the mountainside.

The range is circled by a good but slow and winding road, the southern half of which passes through the quiet lake resort of **Molveno**. The Trento-to-Madonna di Campiglio road takes you past the frescoed churches and wooded valleys of the Val Rendena before arriving at **Campiglio** itself, the best base for skiing in the area, and a transport hub for walkers and climbers. The northern half of the Brenta mountains is bounded by the Val di Non and the Val di Sole, both served by the privately-run Trento–Malè–Mezzana railway.

Pinzolo and the Val Genova

Buses from Trento to Madonna di Campiglio skirt Monte Bondone and wind their way past a series of patchy hills and villages to Lago di Toblino. From here, the road continues west, turning into the Val Rendena at Tione di Trento, where a more remote landscape of pasture and forest begins. Two settlements worth jumping off the bus for are the ski village of **PINZOLO** and **CARISOLO**, which lie just a couple of kilometres apart on the main road, for their well-preserved sixteenth-century frescoes of the *danse macabre*.

Chiesa di San Vigilio

Pinzolo • June–Sept Tues–Sat 9.30–11am & 3.30–5pm, Sun 3–4.30pm; otherwise on request • Free T 0465 447 501.

Simone Baschenis was one of a family of itinerant artists who decorated several small churches in Trentino in the 1500s. Among them was Pinzolo's Romanesque **Chiesa di San Vigilio**. On the south facade, a band of skeletons playing trumpets and bagpipes accompanies a procession representing the social order of the day – from emperors, cardinals and finely dressed ladies to soldiers, beggars and even a cherubic toddler who has a mini skeleton friend to remind him of his own mortality. Inside is a fine *Annunciation* from the thirteenth century, attributed to the Tuscan school,

and other works by Simone Baschenis, among them the *Life of San Vigilio*, the young Bishop of Trento.

Chiesa di Santo Stefano

2km west of Carisolo • June & Sept Tues–Sun 4–6pm; July & Aug Tues–Sat 10am–11.30am & 4–6pm, Sun 10am–11.30am • Free audioguides available in the church

Decorated by the same artists as the Chiesa di San Vigilio, the modest **Chiesa di Santo Stefano** perches on a huge chunk of granite just off the road into the beautiful **Val Genova**. Near the start of the valley you'll see a sign pointing down a track to the church which has more frescoes of the *danse macabre* by the Baschenis on an outside wall, and others inside the spare, Gothic interior depicting the legend of Charlemagne's passage through the Val di Campiglio on the way to his coronation in Rome.

Ponte Verde and the Cascata di Nardis

The Val Genova road out of Carisolo follows a cascading river up through woods to an information point at **Ponte Verde**, 4km west of Carisolo. Footpaths lead from here past several waterfalls, spectacular in the spring melt and after rain, or in winter when they are frozen solid and a glacial turquoise inside. Most impressive is the **Cascata di Nardis**, a five-minute walk from Ponte Verde, where several channels spill down the granite rock walls of the mountainside.

Ponte Maria, Malga Bedole and the Adamello glaciers

A 4.5km walk or bike ride from Cascata di Nardis will bring you to **Ponte Maria** (cars are only allowed beyond this point before 9.45am or after 6.30pm), from where a shuttle bus runs (July & Aug daily, every 30min) another 8.5km to **Malga Bedole** (1584m), a settlement used by shepherds in summer. A two- to three-hour hike from there along trail 212 is *Rifugio Città di Trento* (T 0465 501 193, W sat.tn.it; mid-June to mid-Sept & April; access in snowy weather is from Passo Tonale by cable car) at 2480m, within reach of the **Adamello glaciers**.

Madonna di Campiglio

The major village in the Val Rendena is **MADONNA DI CAMPIGLIO**, an upmarket ski resort 70km from Trento known as "Campiglio" for short. This is where the Austro-Hungarian aristocracy holidayed in the nineteenth century, although not much from that era remains – what you see now is very much a twentieth-century resort, with hotel balconies groaning under the weight of geraniums. Winter sports and a quiet summer hiking season are Campiglio's forte, and the climbing and walking in the Dolomiti di Brenta are superb.

Reaching the trailheads

The best way to approach the trailheads is by cable car from **Carlo Magno**, 3km north of the village centre, to Groste (daily: mid-June to mid-Sept 8.30am–12.30pm & 2–5pm; €12.80 one way, €18.80 return). If you're not into hard trekking, an alternative is to take the **Cinque Laghi** cable car (July to early Sept daily 8.30am–12.50pm & 2–5.20pm; €9 one way, €12.30 return) from the centre of the village west into the Presanella group. A scenic two-and-a-half-hour route will take you via **Lago Ritorto** back down to the valley.

Molveno and Andalo

On the other side of the Brenta mountain range from Campiglio is the lakeside village of **MOLVENO**, with the slightly smaller town of **ANDALO** 4km away by road or beautiful wooded trail. Both are known for the quality of their wild **mushrooms**, and many

WALKING IN THE BRENTA MASSIF

From the **GROSTE** Pass (2437m) planning your own routes is easy enough if you have a decent hiking map. *Rifugio Graffer* (T 0465 441 358, W graffer.com; open year round) is a fifteen minute walk from the cable-car terminus, at 2261m. Head out along trail 316 nearby, which crosses the boulder-strewn slopes towards the *Sella* and *Tuckett rifugi* at 2272m (both T 0465 441 226, W sat.tn.it; June 20–Sept 20). The latter is named after the most prodigious of nineteenth-century climbers, Francis Fox Tuckett, who climbed in this range, opening up a difficult new route called the Bochetta di Tuckett. As ice axes hadn't been invented, he negotiated snowfields with a ladder and alpenstock (long staff), and carried joints of meat and wine for mountaintop breakfasts.

Trail 328 (becoming 318) starts just past the *Sella* and *Tuckett* refuges, bringing you (in about 4hr from Groste) to *Rifugio Brentei* (T 0465 441 244, W rifugiobrentei.it; mid-June to mid-Sept), set at 2179m, midway between the Cima Brenta and Cima Tosa mountain peaks. If you stay overnight here, next day, if you can cope with snowfields, you can extend your walk by trekking up to the Bocca di Brenta and crossing over the ridge to meet trail 319 down to Molveno, or simply return to Campiglio via trails 318 and 316 (3hr 30min).

Italians come here to pick them, after buying a mushrooming licence (€5/day, €20/week) from the local *comune* or the tourist office at Andalo (see below). Each year forty thousand or so Italians suffer mushroom poisoning, so only pick them if you know what you are doing.

Parco Faunistico di Spormaggiore

April & May Sat & Sun 9.30am–6pm; June–Sept daily 9.30am–6.30pm; Oct Sat & Sun 10am–5.30pm • €8 • T 0461 653 622, W parcofaunistico.tn.it • Bus #611 (every 1–2hr) from Molveno (30min) or Mezzocorona (20min)

About 14km northeast of Molveno, the **Parco Faunistico di Spormaggiore** was founded in 1994 to educate visitors on the region's native fauna, and to conserve some of the endangered predators that used to live in the area. In the enclosed outdoor areas, you can see brown bears, wolves, lynxes, foxes, wildcat, deer and owls. The nearby **Museo Casa del Parco Orso** (May, June & Sept Sat & Sun 10am–1pm & 2–6.30pm; July & Aug Mon–Fri 2–6.30pm, Sat & Sun 10am–1pm & 2–6.30pm; €3) in the village of Spormaggiore is dedicated to the region's bears and the Parco Naturale Adamello Brenta.

Lago di Tovel

At the northeastern end of Parco Naturale Adamello Brenta is one of the region's prettiest lakes, its calm turquoise surface reflecting the craggy peaks of the Brenta Dolomites. It's also known as Lago Rosso for its former tendency to turn a deep red in the summer, a phenomenon caused by an abundance of algae, and although it hasn't happened in the last half century there's a museum dedicated to the spectacle on the lake's shores (April to mid-June & mid-Sept to Oct Sat & Sun 10am–1pm & 2–6pm; mid-June to mid-Sept daily 10am–1pm & 2–6pm; T 0463 451 033;free). Tovel is easily reached by car (parking €6) via Cles in the Val di Non, and in summer months bus #616 runs twice daily from Tuenno (30min) and Cles (40min).

ARRIVAL AND INFORMATION — DOLOMITI DI BRENTA

By bus Express bus services run from Madonna di Campiglio, Pinzolo and Carisolo to Bedole once daily in the morning, returning late afternoon. A dozen buses a day run from Trento to Madonna di Campiglio's main square (2hr) and there are handily timed services that coincide with arrivals and departures of the train (approx hourly) to Malè, 23km north.

Tourist offices Via Pradalago 4, Madonna di Campiglio (daily 9am–1pm & 3–7pm; T 0465 447 501, W campigliodolomiti.it); and Piazza Dolomiti 1, Andalo (Mon–Sat 8.30am–12.30pm & 3.30–6.30pm, Sun 9.30am–noon & 4–6.30pm; T 0461 585 836).

5

ACCOMMODATION

PINZOLO

★ **Casa al Campo** Via Al Pont 4 ⊤0465 500 290, ⓦcasalcampo.com. A lovely agriturismo with pigs, chickens, ducks and geese. Its eight cosy rooms have wooden floors and there's a pretty garden with deck chairs in summer. You can sample its own hams and fresh garden produce at the excellent restaurant. **€95**

MADONNA DI CAMPIGLIO

Hotel Diana Via Cima Tosa 52 ⊤0465 441 011, ⓦhoteldiana.net. An attractive and welcoming four-star hotel in the heart of Madonna di Campiglio, set right at the foot of the ski runs (some rooms have excellent views over the resort's black run where championships are often held); rooms have oak, spruce and Swiss pine fittings, and there's a small cellar for wine tasting sessions. **€160**

Maso Mistrin Viale Dolomiti di Brenta 93 ⊤0465 507 293, ⓦmasomistrin.com. About 6km south of Madonna di Campiglio, on the road to Carisolo, this pleasant hotel has rooms named after flowers; interiors feature rustic wooden fittings, and there are three apartments with kitchenettes. There's also a pleasant garden with table tennis in the summer and a tennis court nearby. **€98**

East of Trento

If soaring peaks get your pulse racing, a trip **east of Trento** to a group of stunningly bare peaks called the **Pale di San Martino** is unmissable. Now 2000m above sea level, the range was formed as a coral reef sixty million years ago – white shells crunch underfoot as you walk, and the pale rock reflects light, even at dawn. The Pale are part of the **Parco Naturale Paneveggio**, an area of gently rolling woods and summer pastures with many walks, trails and campsites. The nearest resort is **San Martino di Castrozza**, the terminus for buses travelling from Trento along the **Valsugana** and the **Val di Fiemme**.

Imer and Mezzano

The road from Trento to San Martino passes through the archetypal tourist villages of **IMER** and, a couple of kilometres east, **MEZZANO**, dotted with beautiful woodcarving sculptures made by the town's inhabitants. The wide Val di Primiero, in which they're located, has hay meadows spreading either side, and makes a good place to walk or cycle, with cycle tracks linking the villages and easy paths running into the foothills.

Fiera di Primiero

Around 3km beyond Mezzano, **FIERA DI PRIMIERO** is a large resort and market town. It's a major crossroads in the area, from where buses run up to the beginning of the Val Canali and to Passo Cereda (1369m). The mountains around Fiera were worked for silver, iron and copper from the thirteenth century, and miners' guilds paid for the town's late-Gothic **parish church** near the fortified Palazzo delle Miniere (where the precious metals were guarded before being sent to the mint). Inside the church is a beautiful painting of *The Hunt of the Mystic Unicorn* and a fine fifteenth-century carved altar showing scenes from the Virgin Mary's life. Recent excavations have brought to light the remains of a **paleo-Christian basilica** dating from the fifth to sixth centuries. It's well worth a stroll round the village – paintings made in the sixteenth century on the outside of some of the older houses have survived the elements.

San Martino di Castrozza

The road into **SAN MARTINO DI CASTROZZA** twists and turns, and you feel like you're in the middle of nowhere until the resort's new hotels appear. As far back as the Middle

Ages, travellers and pilgrims stopped here for the night, staying at the monastery, of which only traces remain. Today, it's one of the smarter Dolomite resorts, and visitors come here for skiing and hiking – roughly hourly buses south to Fiera di Primiero and Imer, and cable-car routes into the mountains make San Martino one of the best walking bases in the area.

Parco Naturale Paneveggio

T 0439 64 854, **W** parcopan.org

Beyond San Martino, traffic files up to **Passo di Rolle**, a beautiful stretch of high moorland dotted with avalanche breaks and a few sheep. There are only two buses a day, so a car really helps here. The Passo di Rolle falls within the **Parco Naturale Paneveggio**, which protects a vast area of ancient woodland as well as the high peaks of the Pale di San Martino, prime hiking country. Crisscrossed by nature trails and ancient paved paths called *reversi*, the park gives you a sense of rural life on the summer pastures and in the forest, and makes an atmospheric venue for open-air concerts in the Suoni delle Dolomiti series (see page 313).

Predazzo

Out of the confines of the Parco Naturale Paneveggio, **PREDAZZO** is the first town you come to in the **Val di Fiemme**, which lies between two immense mountain massifs: the Latemar and the Catena di Lagorai. Predazzo has become something of a pilgrimage site for geologists, owing to the extensive collection of local rocks and fossils in the **Museo Geologico delle Dolomiti** next to the church at Piazza Santi Filippo e Giacomo 1 (July–Sept Tues–Fri 10am–6pm, Sat & Sun 10am–7pm; €10; **T** 0462 500 366). Surprisingly accessible to non-experts, the displays include samples of the Dolomitic calcite rock first identified by the elaborately named French mineralogist Dieudonné Sylvain Guy Tancrède de Gratet de Dolomieu.

Tesero

Between Predazzo and Cavalese, the only reason to stop at the village of **TESERO** is to view the small but intriguing **Chiesa di Sant'Eliseo**, next to the parish church. This is decorated with a fresco called the *Cristo della Domenica* ("Christ of the Sabbath") – around the Christ figure are depictions of activities you mustn't do on a Sunday and tools you mustn't use. Crossbow shooting, music playing and wood chopping are on the list and the fresco also shows a couple in bed; apparently you aren't supposed to do that on the Sabbath either. If you just want to stop to view the fresco, there's free parking outside the church.

Cavalese

Built around its colourful church tower and still sporting a cobbled main street, **CAVALESE**, the chief town of the Val di Fiemme, makes for an engaging afternoon halt. In the centre of Cavalese, the **Palazzo della Magnifica Comunità**, at Piazza Cesare Battisti 2 (July to mid-Sept Wed–Mon 10am–noon & 3– 6.30pm; €5; **T** 0462 340 812, **W** palazzomagnifica.eu), is a fabulously frescoed medieval palace that has been painstakingly restored. It was the Bishop of Trento's grand summer palace, and now houses a small **museum and gallery** containing some original valley statutes, carefully kept in wood-panelled rooms, with fine wooden ceilings and painted friezes. The building's lack of fortifications indicates that Trento's bishop felt safe from the armed rebellions that had plagued him in the city, and its exterior is covered in frescoes depicting St Vigilio (Trento's patron saint).

5

HIKING IN THE PALE DI SAN MARTINO

The most dramatic part of the Paneveggio national park is the **Pale di San Martino** – a large plateau surrounded by razor-sharp peaks that range from 2600m to 3200m in altitude. You should be prepared for snow, wind and rain, even in the summer, as well as scorching sunlight and the most stupendous views. There are two main entry points – the **Val Canali** (accessed from Fiera di Primiero) and the **cable car** from San Martino di Castrozza.

The **Val Canali** was described by Amelia Edwards in the nineteenth century as the most "lonely, desolate and tremendous scene to be found this side of the Andes". Things have changed slightly since then with the arrival of the Alta Via 2 walking route which runs through here, but the valley retains a feeling of isolation. Buses from Fiera di Primiero run to the trailheads of the valley. *Rifugio Treviso* (T 0439 62 311; mid-June to Sept) is a possible overnight stop, or there's the more comfortable *Cant del Gal* (see page 322), further down the valley.

A stiff ascent from the *Cant del Gal* brings you onto the **Altopiano delle Pale** at Passo di Pradidali, where white partridges and stoats inhabit the barren plateau and the silence is broken every so often by a trickle of falling stones. About three hours along you'll reach *Rifugio Pradidali* at 2278m (T 0439 64 180, W rifugiopradidali.com; mid-June to Sept).

The fastest and easiest route into the Pale di San Martino is via **cable car** from San Martino. The Colverde funicular (June 14th–Sept 20th daily 8am–4.45pm; T 0439 68 204, W impiantices.it) from the village runs to the foot of the Pale, from where the Rosetta chair lift takes you up to the *Rifugio Rosetta* (T 0439 68 308, W rifugiorosetta.it; June16 th–Sept 23rd daily, late Sept & Oct Sat & Sun), perched 2581m up the western edge of the Altopiano. From the Rosetta chair-lift terminus, you can hike onwards to *Rifugio Pradidali* (2hr and 30min south) and either take the ambitious walk over the **Passo di Ball** to San Martino or descend into the Val Canali to reach the *Cant del Gal*.

INFORMATION — EAST OF TRENTO

FIERA DI PRIMIERO

Tourist office Via Dante 6 (mid-June to mid-Sept & mid-Dec to Easter Mon–Sat 9am–12.30pm & 3.30–6.30pm, Sun 9.30am–12.30pm; rest of year Mon–Sat 8.30am–12.30pm & 3.20–6pm; T 0439 62 407).

SAN MARTINO DI CASTROZZA

Tourist office Via Passo Rolle 165 (mid-June to mid-Sept & mid-Dec to Easter daily 9am–12.30pm & 3.30–6.30pm; rest of year Mon–Sat 9am–12.30 & 2.30–5.30pm; T 0439 768 867, W sanmartino.com).

PARCO NATURALE PANEVEGGIO

Visitor centres The park has three visitor centres: San Martino, Via Laghetto 27 (late June to early Oct daily 9am–12.30pm & 3–6.30pm; T 0439 768 859); Casa del Parco at Villa Welsperg, Val Castelpietra 2 in the Val Canali (Jan–May & Oct–Dec 9.30am–12.30pm & 2–5pm, June 9am–12.30pm & 3–6pm, July & Aug 9am–6pm, Sept 9am–12.30pm & 12.30am–5.30pm; T 0439 765 973); and Terra Foresta, the main Paneveggio centre, which is along the SS50 road from Predazzo up to the Passo Rolle (mid-June to mid-Sept daily 9am–12.30pm & 2–5.30pm; T 0462 576 283).

CAVALESE

Tourist office Via Fratelli Bronzetti 60 (Mon–Sat 9am–noon & 3.30–7pm; mid-July & Aug also Sun 9am–noon; T 0462 241 111, W visitfiemme.it).

ACCOMMODATION AND EATING

MEZZANO

Camping Calavise Localita Pezze di Imèr 36 T 0439 67 468, W campingcalavise.it. Well signposted from Imer, this enjoyable and well-fitted campsite boasts a pizzeria, bar and swimming pool and live music in summer. Pitches €9.50, per adult €7.50

SAN MARTINO DI CASTROZZA

★ **Chalet Prà delle Nasse** Via Cavallazza 24 T 0439 768 893, W ristorante-da-anita.com. A lovely family-run place with cosy wooden interiors and fires lit on the chilly evenings; the spacious rooms all have balconies with views of the surrounding countryside. The hearty breakfast includes delicious home-made pies and cakes, along with savoury dishes including speck and eggs, while the restaurant serves excellent home-made meals. €150

PARCO NATURALE PANEVEGGIO

Cant del Gal Localita Val Canali 1, Tonadico T 0439 62 997, W cantdelgal.it. Opened in 1951, this hotel

is the perfect spot to relax after a long trek, with nine simply furnished rooms, and free electric bikes for guests. Its restaurant (open to non-residents) follows traditional recipes using local products; the *canederli verdi* with spinach and herbs, and ricotta and nut gnocchi (both €8) are good, while meat lovers can opt for the lamb (€12) or deer (€14) ribs. Rates are half-board. Daily noon–2pm & 7–9pm; closed Nov & early June. **€110**

TESERO

Castelir Via Nazionale 57 0462 810 001, castelir.it. About 2.5km east of Tesero, this lovely ecofriendly hotel nestles among verdant meadows: its pinewood rooms are spacious and inviting. There's also a cosy wellness centre, with a sauna, a hot tub and an outdoor heated pool that is great in winter when the ground is covered in snow. **€180**

CAVALESE

Costa Salici Via Costa dei Salici 10 0462 340 140, costasalici.com. A longtime favourite, with pinewood interiors, serving great local and Italian dishes including *pappardelle* or lasagne with deer bolognaise (€12). There's an attractive garden that gets lively around *aperitivo* time. Tues–Sun noon–2pm & 7–10pm.

Laurino Via Antoniazzi 14 0462 340 151, hotelgarnilaurino.com. Conveniently set just off the main road through town, this cosy seventeenth-century building has rooms decorated in Tyrolean style with Alpine antiques and local artwork. There's an open-air hot tub, sauna and steam room as well as a generous breakfast. **€160**

The Catinaccio and Gruppo di Sella

The **Catinaccio** (or **Rosengarten**) range is one of the best-known sights in the Dolomites, its unmistakeable bare-rock pinnacles appearing on brochures, guides and myriad souvenirs. This immense wall of stone along the edge of the 3000m-high massif takes on a famously rosy glow at sunset, and the mountain plays a lead role in the area's best-known myths and legends. Trails across this mountain are popular with mainly Italian and German walkers and, although the zigzag paths to the peaks can be crowded in August, once you're above the cable-car line, there's plenty of wilderness to lose yourself in.

Access is simple enough from **Vigo di Fassa**, the main place to stay in the Val di Fassa, which splits off from the Val di Fiemme north of Predazzo at Moena. If you travel these roads and trails, you pass through one of the heartlands of **Ladino** culture (see page 324).

At the head of the Val di Fassa, **Canazei** makes a good springboard for the high plateaux of the **Gruppo di Sella**, and the gentler trail of the **Viel del Pan**, which leads down to the tiny resort of **Arabba**. On the northern side of the Sella group, **Corvara** is a much larger resort with a sizeable Ladin population.

Catinaccio

The **Catinaccio** range was described by nineteenth-century writer Theodor Christomannos as a "gigantic fortification … the gate into the kingdom of immortal ghosts, of high-flying giants". The area's German name, **Rosengarten** (rose garden), derives from the legend of Laurin, king of the dwarves, who used to grow roses here. The king, angered when he was prevented from being with his beloved princess Similde, put a spell on the roses so that no one would see them again by day or night, but forgot to include dawn and dusk, which is when the low sun gives the rock its fiery glow.

The **trails** across the range cater for all levels of hiking ability; however, the going gets tough on the ridges, from where you can see as far as the Stubaier Alps, on the border with Austria. The most popular approach to Catinaccio is from the hamlet of Vigo di Fassa, served by buses on the Trento–Canazei route. Once you're above the tree line, *rifugi* abound, serving hordes of summer walkers – if you're looking for wilderness trekking, you may want to go elsewhere.

Lago Carezza

Twelve kilometres west of Vigo di Fasso on the Bolzano road, stunning **Lago Carezza** nestles amid thick forest, surrounded by jagged peaks. At an altitude of 1834m, its

LADIN COUNTRY

The **Ladins** (*Ladini* in Italian, *Ladinisch* in German) are a community of around thirty thousand people living in the Gardena, Badia, Fassa, Livinallongo and Ampezzo valleys around the Sella massif. They're united by their ancient language – Ladin – which was once spoken over a wide area, from Austria down to the River Po (in what's now Emilia-Romagna). The Dolomitic Ladin language, preserved by the relative remoteness of the territory, is linked to Swiss Romansch (there are about thirty-five thousand speakers in the east of Switzerland) and Friulan (more than 400,000 speakers in the Friuli region of Italy).

The history of the Ladins is recorded in their epics, which recount tales of battles, treachery and reversals of fortune. Around 400 AD, the Ladins were constantly threatened with invasion by Germanic tribes from the north and others from the Po Valley. Christianity later emerged as a major threat, but the Ladins absorbed and transformed the new religion, investing the new saints with the powers of more ancient female divinities.

The **Museo Ladin de Fascia**, Strada de Sèn Jan 5 (mid-June to mid-Sept daily 9am–12.30pm & 3–7pm; mid-Sept to Oct & Dec to mid-June Tues–Sat 3–7pm; €5; ⓣ 0462 760 182, ⓦ istladin.net), between Vigo di Fassa and Pozza di Fassa, is devoted to traditional Ladin working life and provides a fascinating introduction to Ladin culture, with intriguing exhibits on the language and history. It also has exhibits scattered throughout the territory, including a restored nineteenth-century cooperage (Botega da Pinter) at Via Dolomiti 3 in **Moena**; a restored watermill (Molin de Pezol) at Via Jumela 6 in **Pera di Fassa**; and a working, antique sawmill (La Sia) at Via Pian Trevisan in **Penia**, just outside Canazei. Tourist offices throughout the area have details of festivals, exhibitions and events.

crystal-clear waters are fed by underwater springs. There's a viewing platform, a path with benches from where you can soak in the wonderful views, and a handful of simple restaurants by the parking lot.

Canazei and around

CANAZEI, a buzzing summer and winter resort at the head of the Val di Fassa is a stepping stone to the stupendous high road passes between here and Cortina d'Ampezzo. It's also a good base for walking in the Gruppo di Sella or strolling along a much easier trail – the **Viel del Pan** opposite glacier-topped Marmolada.

The road to the Passo Pordoi

With your own vehicle, it's well worth driving the **switchback road** of 27 bends that climbs for 12km out of Canazei towards the **Passo Pordoi**. Although it's often busy with busloads of tourists heading for the scenic Great Dolomites Road and determined cyclists making the 1000m ascent, the view when you get there is unforgettable.

Halfway along the road, the cable car at Pradel leads to **Passo di Sella** (2240m), one of the most impressive of the Dolomite passes. Paths climb from here onto the jagged peaks of the **Sasso Lungo** (Langkofel) and follow the ridges down onto the Alpe di Siusi. Just past Pradel the road forks. Straight ahead is the **Gruppo di Sella** – an arid lunar plateau surrounded by pink, dolomitic peaks. A right-hand turning takes you up to the **Passo Pordoi** (2242m), an astonishing vantage point between the Gruppo di Sella and Marmolada, from where mountains radiate in every direction. In the foreground, the Sasso Lungo look like a jagged, gloved hand, flanked by two prominent peaks; the Gruppo di Sella is squat and chunky; and Sciliar (Schlern), just visible in the distance, comprises a flat rocky tabletop, culminating in two peaks. A small road winds downwards to Passo Falzarego, and ultimately Cortina d'Ampezzo.

From the Passo Pordoi you can join Alta Via 2, or walk a short section of it known as the Viel del Pan (see box, below). Most tourist buses and plenty of bikers stop at the collection of cafés and stalls at the pass.

MOUNTAIN HUT IN PASSO PORDOI

Rifugio-Hütte
Forcella Pordoi
2848 m

5

A WALK ALONG THE VIEL DEL PAN

If you're not a great walker, this easy twenty-minute stroll from the Passo Pordoi provides a good way to enjoy terrific Dolomite vistas. Pick up the **Alta Via 2 trail** just past the *Albergo Savoia*, from where a narrow path traverses the mountainside opposite the glaciers of Marmolada. From the seventeenth century this path was on the grain-smuggling route called the **Viel del Pan** ("trail of bread" in Venetian dialect), and it remained busy enough in the nineteenth century for the Guardia di Finanza to set up armed patrols along it. The contrast between the glacier on Marmolada and the peaks of the Sella group is superb. The easiest option is to return the same way to the Passo Pordoi, or you can continue on the same path to Lago Fedaia, from where irregular buses in summer run back to Canazei.

Marmolada

Cable car: daily late June to mid-Sept 9am–4pm; early Dec to early April 8.40am–4.30pm • €30 return for all three lifts; €24 for the first two • ⓣ 0437 522 984, ⓦ funiviemarmolada.com

To be whisked to the top of the Dolomites' highest peak, head to the cable car station in Malga Ciapela (1450m) – about 20km southeast of Canazei – for the three-leg trip to **Punta Rocca** (3265m). When the weather is clear the views from the panoramic terrace here are hard to match. Between the second and third lifts (at almost 3000m), there's a restaurant and a fascinating war museum, **Marmolada Grande Guerra** (museomarmoladagrandeguerra.com; entry included in price of return cable car trip), recently re-modelled to commemorate a century since World War One, when entire Austrian battalions overwintered inside the glacier, blasting 12km of tunnels tens of metres deep under the ice and rock.

Corvara and around

The central town of the Ladin ethnic group, **CORVARA** is primarily a ski resort, and it also makes a good base for the excellent trails of the nearby Fanes Park (see page 338), a bus ride away, where most of the Ladin legends are based. Some 4.5km north of Corvara is **La Villa**, a small village with a fairy-tale sixteenth-century castle.

ARRIVAL AND INFORMATION — CATINACCIO AND GRUPPO DI SELLA

By bus Between mid-June and mid-Sept there are buses daily from Canazei to Passo Pordoi (8 daily; 30min) and Corvara (9 daily; 1hr 20min; transfer in Plan di Gralba), from where there are regular buses to Brunico (hourly; 1hr), which is on the rail line into Austria.

Tourist office Strada Col Alt 36, Corvara (Mon–Sat 8am–noon & 3–7pm, Sun 9am–noon & 4–6pm; ⓣ 0471 836 176, ⓦ altabadia.org).

ACCOMMODATION AND EATING

VIGO DI FASSA

★ **Agritur Agua Biencia** Località Ramon ⓣ 345 286 5410, ⓦ agrituraguabiencia.it. This lovely agriturismo has nine well-appointed rooms, some with rustic Ladin-style interiors. There's a pleasant garden and an open-air hot tub with stunning views of the mountains, and a small indoor pool and sauna as well as cows, ducks, llamas and alpacas. The agriturismo produces its own yogurt and milk. **€140**

L Chimpl da Tamion Hotel Gran Mugon, Strada de Tamion 3 ⓣ 0462 769 108, ⓦ hotelgranmugon.com. Set in a quiet hamlet some 4km south of Vigo di Fassa, this excellent Michelin-starred restaurant is in a friendly hotel with simple rooms (€160 half board) in a peaceful setting. The three-course set menu is very reasonably priced at €38, though it is only open for dinner. Mon–Sat 8–9.45pm.

CANAZEI

Enoteca Valentini Streda do Ruf de Antermont 6 ⓣ 0462 601 134, ⓦ enotecavalentini.com. Run by a family of sommeliers, this deli and wine bar is a great spot to stock up on excellent local produce and bottles of wine – it's jam-packed with local foodstuffs including home-made jams, polenta, speck and dried mushrooms. In winter you can get cosy with a glass of wine (€3.50) and a cheese and meat platter (€16.50) at the bar (Nov–Mar daily 3.30–8.30pm). Daily 9am–12.30pm & 3.30–7.30pm.

La Cacciatora Via Strèda de Contrin 26, Alba di Canazei ⓣ 0462 601 411, ⓦ lacacciatora.it. This large chalet-style

hotel has a cosy wood-panelled lounge with a welcoming fire in winter. The panorama suites are worth the extra €40, with modern interiors and spacious bathrooms. There's a complimentary afternoon buffet of nibbles and home-made cakes daily, and facilities include a heated indoor pool, sauna, steam room, wine cellar and gym. Rates are half board. **€244**

CORVARA

Rosa Alpina Strada Micurá de Rü 20, San Cassiano in Badia 0471 849 500, rosalpina.it. The luxurious "Alpine Rose" is a cool, luscious and extremely hip spa-hotel. Take a dip in the pool, indulge in a few spa treatments and dine in the highly rated *St Hubertus* restaurant, one of many on-site, but be warned – you could easily part with €1000 a day. **€500**

Villa Resi Via Col Alt 22 0471 836 097, villaresi.it. Excellent-value B&B in the centre of town with spotless, simply-furnished and identically priced (per person) rooms and apartments with kitchenettes. There's a lush little garden and free parking on the premises. **€80**

Bolzano (Bozen)

The gently historic capital of Alto Adige, **BOLZANO** (largely known by its German name, **Bozen**) straddles the junction of the jade-hued Alpine waters of the Talvera (Talfer) and Isarco (Eisack) rivers. Winter and summer see the town's 100,000 population swell with tourists, as it makes a good jumping-off point for exploring the surrounding mountainscape. Bolzano's centre maintains a relaxed pace of life, its highlight for most visitors being "Ötzi" the **prehistoric Ice Man**.

Brief history

Located in a predominantly sunny, sheltered bowl, for centuries Bolzano was a valley market town and way station whose fortunes in the Middle Ages swayed as the counts of Tyrol and the bishops of Trento competed for power. The town passed to the Habsburgs in the fourteenth century, then at the beginning of the nineteenth century Bavaria took control, opposed by Tyrolese patriot and military leader Andreas Hofer. His battle in 1809 to keep the Tyrol under Austrian rule was only temporarily successful, as in the same year the Austrian emperor ceded the Tyrol to the Napoleonic kingdom of Italy. More changes followed, as Bolzano was handed back to Austria until World War I, whereupon it passed, like the rest of the province, to Italy.

Piazza Walther and the Duomo

Piazza Duomo • Duomo Mon–Sat 10am–noon & 2–5pm • Free • **Treasury** Tues–Sat 10am–12.30pm • €3 • 0471 978 676

THE ITALIANIZATION OF THE TYROL

The **South Tyrol** (Südtirol) was Italy's reward for cooperating with the Allies during World War I. But when Mussolini's Fascists came to power in 1923 the region was renamed Alto Adige after the upper reaches of the Adige River, and despite the fact that German speakers outnumbered Italian speakers by around ten to one, a process of sometimes brutal Italianization was imposed on the area. Cartographers remade maps, substituting Italian place names (often made up) for German; people were forced to adopt Italian names; the teaching of German in schools was banned and stonemasons even chipped away German inscriptions from tombstones. World War II then intervened, and by 1946, Austria and Italy came to an agreement ratified under the Paris Peace Treaty that Austria would give up its claim to the region on condition that Italy took steps to redress some of the cultural damage perpetrated under Fascism.

Successive governments have channelled funds into the area allowing the region more independence than ever before and much greater say in local law. Over the last few years, Italy's central and regional governments have become more tolerant of ethnic diversity and, increasingly, German is the language of preference in Südtirol.

Bolzano's heart is **Piazza Walther**, whose pavement cafés, around its statue of the *Minnesänger* (troubadour) Walther von der Vogelweide, are the town's favoured meeting places. The southern flank is dominated by the **Duomo**, a church converted into a cathedral as recently as 1964. Built in the fourteenth and fifteenth centuries, and restored following bomb damage during World War II, it sports a strikingly multi-coloured ceramic roof and elaborately carved spire. The interior's beautiful vaulted ceiling and magnificent, lizard-adorned pulpit are worth a look, as is the treasury directly beneath the tower, with a collection of old relics such as bibles, breviaries, priestly garb and gold and silver statuary.

Chiesa dei Domenicani

Piazza Domenicani • Mon–Sat 9.30am–5pm, Sun noon–6pm • Free • ☎ 0471 973 133

A couple of streets west of Piazza Walther, the **Chiesa dei Domenicani** has frescoes of fifteenth-century courtly life painted on the walls of its decaying cloisters, framed by a growth of stone tracery. Inside, the **Cappella di San Giovanni**, built at the beginning of the fourteenth century, resembles a Byzantine church, retaining frescoes by painters of the Giotto school, including a *Triumph of Death*, underneath a star-spangled vault.

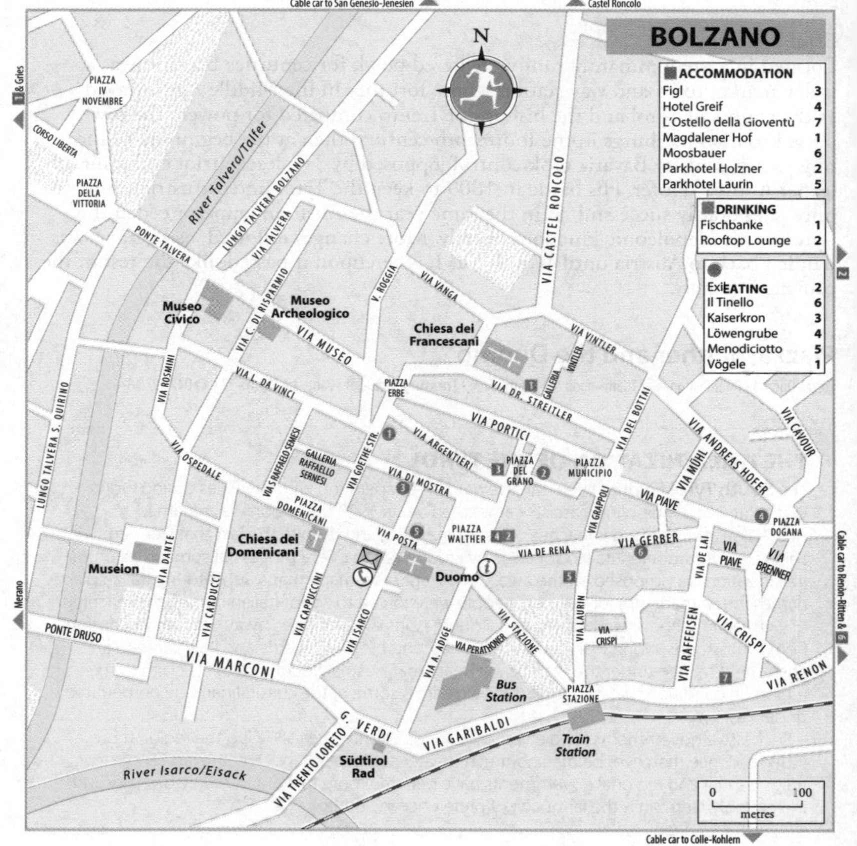

THE ÖTZI CULT

Since Europe's most famous ice man was discovered on a lonely Alpine mountainside in 1991, an entire culture has sprouted around this anonymous Ladin forebear. **Conspiracy theories** have come thick and fast with some "revealing" Ötzi to be a Peruvian mummy transported to the Alps for publicity purposes. Others have claimed to be his direct descendants, while the "Ötzi diaries", which appeared in the wake of the infamous "Hitler diaries", were quickly dismissed as tomfoolery. The "Ötzi curse" stems from the fact that he was found on a palindromic date (19.9.1991), and indeed some people linked with the discovery have since died unexpectedly, while one woman has even offered to bear a child using Ötzi's 5000-year-old sperm – she was politely rejected.

Museo Archeologico

Via Museo (Museumstrasse) 43 • Tues–Sun 10am–6pm; also open Mon 10am–6pm in July, Aug & Dec • €9 • ⓣ 0471 320 100, ⓦ iceman.it

Bolzano's top attraction is the **Museo Archeologico**, a superb and informative exhibition built around the **Ice Man**, a frozen, mummified body discovered in the ice of the Ötzaler Alps in 1991, just 92m from the border with Austria. At first a policeman estimated the body – nicknamed "Ötzi" – to be around 100 years old; he was out by around 5200 years, as later experts dated the corpse to around 3300 BC. Visitors queue up to peer into the €200,000-per-year, temperature-controlled cell where the surprisingly diminutive Ötzi lies dry-frozen, his complexion that of cured ham and glistening with tiny ice crystals. The rest of the exhibits include possessions found on or around the body – his still serviceable bearskin cap, his longbow and arrows, firelighting gear, a shamanic first-aid kit – as well as an incredibly realistic, life-size silicon model showing what experts think Ötzi would have looked like and numerous displays and films explaining how he came to be preserved on the mountainside.

Museion

Via Dante 6 • Tues–Sun 10am–6pm, Thurs closes at 10pm • €7; free after 6pm on Thurs • ⓦ museion.it

Bolzano's museum of contemporary art, **Museion**, is housed in a strikingly modern building, a futuristic glass cube. The museum has a collection of more than four thousand pieces, and exhibitions change every few months or so – check the website to see what's on.

Piazza della Vittoria

Across the River Talvera (Talfer) a riverside walk upstream brings you to the Ponte Talvera where Bolzano's German and Gothic quarter ends and **Piazza della Vittoria** signals the beginning of the 1930s Functionalist quarter, much of it laid out by Mussolini's favourite architect, Marcello Piacentini. The Fascist-period triumphal arch (1928) on the square, known as the Monument to Victory, has long sparked controversy, not least due to its inscription: "Here is the border of the Motherland. Set the banners down. From this point on we educated others with language, law and culture." It was bombed by German-speaking separatists in the late 1970s and closed for years until 2012. Today, there's an award-winning permanent exhibition entitled "BZ '18–'45" (Oct–Mar Tues–Sat 10.30am–12.30pm & 2.30–4.30pm; April–Sept Tues, Wed & Fri–Sun 11am–1pm & 2–5pm, Thurs 3–9pm; free; ⓦ monumenttovictory.com) in the crypt below the restored monument, which tactfully treats both the Fascist decades and the Nazi occupation.

ARRIVAL AND INFORMATION — BOLZANO

By train Bolzano's train station is a few minutes' walk southeast of Piazza Walther through a scruffy park on Via Stazione. Timetables at ⓦ sii.bz.it

Destinations Bressanone (every 30min; 30min); Merano (every 30min; 40min); Trento (every 15–30min; 30–50min); Vipiteno (every 30min; 1hr).

5

THE MUSEUMOBIL CARD

The **Museumobil card** (mobilcard.info) gives free unlimited use of public transport (buses, regional trains and certain *funivie*) in the region, and free access to more than ninety museums (almost all museums in the Alto Adige): a three-day card costs €30, and a seven-day card €34. It's available from every tourist office across the Alto Adige.

By bus Bolzano's bus station, centrally placed at Via Perathoner 4, serves most (but not all) the small villages and resorts in the province.

Destinations Cavalese (hourly; 1hr 25min; first train to Ora (Auer) then bus); Corvara (6 daily; 2hr 30min; via Plan/Wolkenstein or Ortisei); Merano (hourly; 50min): Siusi (every 30min; 40min).

Tourist office Via Alto Adige 60 (Mon–Fri 9am–7pm, Sat 9.30am–6pm, May–Oct also Sun 10am–3pm; 0471 307 000, bolzano-bozen.it).

GETTING AROUND

By bike Fixed-gear bikes are available right in the centre at Viale Stazione/Bahnhofsallee and mountain and e-bikes at Südtirol Rad (0473 201 500, suedtirol-rad.com) in Piazza Verdi Platz.

By car Hertz has branches at the airport (0471 254 266) while Maggiore is 1km north at Via Galvani 1f (0471 971 531). You can park at Parcheggio Piazza Walther; Central Parking, Piazza Stazione; or Parcheggio Bolzano Centro, Via Mayr-Nusser: all charge about €2.50/hr.

By taxi Radio Taxi is your best bet (0471 981 111).

ACCOMMODATION

Figl Piazza del Grano 9 0471 978 412, figl.net; map p.328. This shuttered guesthouse in the Corn Market has been serving guests for a century so must be doing something right. Rooms are simple, cheerful, business-standard affairs with stock-issue bathrooms. Breakfast (an extra €4–16) can be taken in the wood-panelled restaurant or out on the piazza. Parking is €15 a night. **€142**

★ **Hotel Greif** Piazza Walther 0471 318 000, greif.it; map p.328. This stylish hotel just off the main square has 33 spacious rooms, each individually designed with its own character and atmosphere. Interiors feature blond wood and polished timber floors, contemporary art, plus bathrooms made of eleven types of marble. Guests can use the garden and pool at *Grief's* sister hotel, the *Parkhotel Laurin*, while the trendy rooftop bar is one of the coolest in town. **€209**

L'Ostello della Gioventù Via Renon 23 0471 300 865, ostello.bz; map p.328. This cheerful hostel is one of a chain in the South Tyrol offering good-quality, low-cost accommodation to young people and families with children. Private rooms are a bit of a squeeze, although they are great value; there are no double or twin rooms (singles only; €33), but extra beds can be added. Facilities include a small kitchen, board games, table tennis and the use of laundry facilities. Dorms **€24.50**

Magdalener Hof Via Rencio 48/A 0471 978 267, magdalenerhof.it; map p.328. Two kilometres east of town, this hotel has bright, recently renovated rooms in the original wing and more stylish and spacious ones with trendy armchairs and in the more modern complex (€195). There's a pleasant garden with outdoor swimming pool and a lounge bar and restaurant (both open to non-guests) with seating on a pleasant terrace. **€174**

★ **Parkhotel Holzner** Via del Paese 18, Soprabolzano 0471 345 231, parkhotel-holzner.com; map p.328. This gorgeous hotel is at the top of the Renon cable car in a spectacular location overlooking the mountains and valley below. Set in an Alpine Art Nouveau building, the attractive rooms in the main building are each unique, some featuring renovated old wooden furniture or pretty floral patterned wallpaper. Facilities include a panoramic tower, an inviting pool and a lovely garden, ideal for children to run around, or for adults to enjoy a drink or two at sunset and soak in the great views. **€408.50**

Parkhotel Laurin Via Laurin 4 0471 311 000, laurin.it; map p.328. Built in 1910, this smart hotel is set in a verdant garden oasis with a small summer swimming pool, children's play area, bar and gourmet restaurant. The Art Deco-styled rooms are restful and understated; some have terraces and others balconies. The food in the secluded open-air restaurant is first rate and the same menu is available in the lounge bar, with its *King Laurin* fresco (1911) by Jugendstil artist Bruno Goldschmitt. Guests can use their bikes (with child seats available) for free and get discounted parking across the street (€13). **€191**

CAMPING

Moosbauer Via Merano 101, 5km from the city centre on the main Bolzano–Merano road 0471 918 492, moosbauer.com; map p.328. This campsite is one of the best in the area, with clean facilities and a family-friendly atmosphere. There's a restaurant and inviting swimming pool with sun loungers, too. Pitches **€19.40**, per adult **€11.10**

EATING

Piazza delle Erbe is the place to go for a quick eat, packed as it is with stalls selling *wurstel*, *apfel strudel*, local cheeses, hams, breads and fabulous fruit and salads, with no shortage of exuberant bars and cafés offering beer and inexpensive fare. As for **nightlife** there are pubs aplenty, with Fri- and Sat-night crowds spilling out onto the street; for a local aperitif, ask for a Veneziana (Aperol, champagne or prosecco, ice and a slice of lemon).

CAFÉS AND GELATERIE

Exil Piazza del Grano 2/A ⓣ0471 971 814; map p.328. A popular spot that attracts quite a crowd for its laidback, welcoming atmosphere; the interior is airy, and in summer seating spills out onto the street. It's a good spot for a light lunch, with salads (around €8) and bruschetta (€6) on the menu. Mon–Thurs 8am–9pm, Fri 8.30am–11pm, Sat 9.30am–11pm.

Menodiciotto Piazza Parrocchia 7 ⓣ0471 324 787; map p.328. Just across from the Duomo, this *gelateria* serves 24 flavours of ice cream (all gluten-free); the seasonal fruit flavours only use water (no milk). Daily 10.30am–10.30pm.

RESTAURANTS

Il Tinello Via Crispi 9B/Via Conciapelli 38 ⓣ0471 324 711, ⓦtinello.bz.it; map p.328. Tucked away on a narrow street, this place rustles up home-made Italian-Mediterranean fare – the speciality is the home-made tagliatelle, which comes with a variety of sauces including shrimps, lemon juice and olive oil (€9.80) or spicy sausage, olives and tomatoes (€9.50). Mon–Sat noon–2.15pm & 7–10pm.

★ **Kaiserkron** Piazza della Mostra 2 ⓣ0471 980 214, ⓦkaiserkron.bz; map p.328. Fine dining in a beautiful Baroque building or outside on the quiet, elegant piazza. The very fairly-priced menu features Italian and international dishes with local influences – try dishes such *schlutzkrapfen* (half-moon-shaped ravioli) with ricotta, spinach and melted butter (€13) or line-caught sea bass fillet with Romanesco broccoli and pesto (€27). Mon–Sat noon–2pm & 7–9.30pm.

★ **Löwengrube** Piazza Dogana 3 ⓣ0471 970 032, ⓦloewengrube.it; map p.328. This trendy restaurant and lounge bar is housed in the city's oldest *stube*, with frescoes dating back to the sixteenth century. Wine and cheese tastings take place in the cellar (book ahead), while in summer dining is on a smart terrace. The cuisine is Italian with a twist, with the likes of foie gras ice cream and baked *paccheri* stuffed with a prawn and buffalo curd (€13). Six-course tasting menu for €60. Mon–Sat 11am–3pm & 6pm–midnight.

Vögele Via Goethe 3 ⓣ0471 973 938, ⓦvoegele.it; map p.328. This historic nineteenth-century restaurant was once a meeting point for philosophers and poets, including Goethe. Dining is in a series of partitioned areas on the first floor, or in a cosy wooden dining room on the ground floor. The menu features both Italian and heartier Alpine meat dishes with mains around €15. There are also lighter dishes served at lunch until 4pm and at dinner until 11pm. Mon–Sat 11am–2pm & 7–10pm.

DRINKING

★ **Fischbanke** Via Dr Streiter 24 ⓣ340 5707 468; map p.328. Laidback bar and café where you can enjoy a glass of wine (€4) at marble counters that once made up the city's fish market – hence the name. The enthusiastic owner creates a relaxed ambience, and you can snack on an array of bruschette (€7–16) stacked high with local produce. March–Nov Mon–Sat 11am–9pm.

★ **Rooftop Lounge** Via della Rena 28 ⓣ0471 318 000, ⓦgreif.it; map p.328. The leafy rooftop lounge of the *Hotel Greif* is a stylish spot to enjoy a summer evening sundowner as you soak in the views of town. Creative cocktails are prepared by experienced barman Christian Gruber, with exciting takes on classics, such as Asian mojito made with refreshing ginger and Japanese shiso leaves. The terrace closes at 11pm, although the action then continues on the ground floor in the hotel's fashionable *Grifoncino* bar (year round Mon–Sat 5pm–1am). May–Sept Mon–Sat 5pm–midnight.

Around Bolzano

Bolzano makes a great base for a few easy half-day trips to visit various **castles** and fortresses that almost ring the city. For wine buffs, it's good to know that Bolzano is located at the head of the **Strada del Vino** or Wine Road (Südtiroler Weinstrasse), which runs south to the border with Trentino.

Castel Roncolo

Tues–Sun: mid-March to Oct 10am–6pm; Nov to mid March 10–5pm • €8 • ⓦrunkelstein.info • Free shuttle bus from Piazza Walther (every 15–30min)

Just 5km from Bolzano, the thirteenth-century **Castel Roncolo** (Schloss Runkelstein) contains probably the best secular frescoes in Europe, showing people hunting and

5

dancing, and other scenes from courtly life. In the Sala del Torneo, look out for a fresco showing a fishing party: in the background a noble is offering a fish to a lady – the medieval equivalent of an indecent proposal. Pier Paolo Pasolini filmed some of his *Decameron* (1971) here.

Castello d'Appiano

Hocheppanerweg • April–Oct Thurs–Tues 10am–6pm • Chapel by hourly guided tour (20min) €4; 11am–4pm); grounds free • T 0471 662 206, W hocheppan.it

Around 8km southwest of Bolzano, high above the village of **APPIANO** (Eppan), a clutch of thirty or so fortresses and castles can be seen from the ruined battlements of **Castello Appiano** (Schloss Hocheppan). In the castle chapel, secular frescoes show women flirting at the altar and one of the earliest representations of the South Tyrolean *knödel*, or dumpling. From the car park it's a thirty-minute uphill walk, rewarded by stunning views, and there's a pleasant café and restaurant with outdoor seating within the castle walls.

Castel Firmiano/Sigmundskron

Sigmundskronerstrasse 53 • Late March to mid-Nov Fri–Wed 10am–6pm • €12 • T 0471 631 264, W messner-mountain-museum.it • Bus #9 from Bolzano bus station

One of the most imposing fortresses in the area is **Firmiano/Sigmundskron**, perched on an outcrop of porphyry rock which made it a strategic base for the Bishop of Trento in the tenth century before falling into ruin in the sixteenth. The site was brought back from the dead in 2003 by mountaineer Reinhold Messner, who transformed it into the flagship of his group of mountain museums. A trail leads up and through the castle towers that contain a vast collection of paintings, sculptures – and objects such as a huge prayer wheel – celebrating the Himalayas, the Alps and the world's other lofty locations.

Strada del Vino

Fans of the grape are well catered for around Bolzano, with a **Strada del Vino** or Wine Road (W weinstrasse.com) enabling visitors to combine sightseeing with tastings. The 40km route proper begins at **Nalles** (Nals) just north of Bolzano, but you can also join it at **Appiano** (Eppan) and wend your way through sunny vineyards to **Salurno** (Salurn) halfway between Bolzano and Trento. This is one of the oldest wine-growing areas of all German-speaking regions – some claim the tradition goes back to the Iron Age – and it's also one of the smallest in Italy. Certainly, the wine industry was well established in Roman times, with the colonists from down south finding that locally made barrels with metal hoops were much better for transporting wine back to Rome than their clay amphorae. The vines in the region are often strung on wide pergolas, the traditional method of viticulture here, which allows the Ora breeze blowing from Lake Garda to circulate around the grapes, giving a beneficial cooling effect. Others are on hillsides too steep for machinery, so all work still has to be done by hand.

BOLZANO'S CABLE CARS

A trip up in any of Bolzano's three **cable cars** gives a small taste of the high peaks that surround the city: for fares and times on all three cable cars, see W sii.bz.it. The first ascends from **Via Renòn** (Rittnerstrasse), a ten-minute walk from the train station, to Soprabolzano (Oberbozen; €6 one-way/€10 return), where you can ride the scenic, narrow gauge Renon Railway to Collalbo (€3.50/€6). Alternatively the **San Genesio/Jenesien** cable car (€3/€5) offers stupendous views of the Catinaccio/Rosengarten massif – the station is at Via Sarentino, 1.5km north of the town centre along the river (bus #12 or #14). On the high Alpine pastures at the top, you'll see blond-maned Haflinger horses grazing. The third cable car (€4/€8) goes to **Colle/Kohlern** from the station across the river south of the train station at Ponte Campiglio. In operation since 1908, it is the oldest cable car in the world.

TÖRGGELEN SEASON

A good time to sample Alto Adige's wine is in the autumn during the **Törggelen season**. This roughly coincides with the arrival of the *Neuien* – the first bottles of new, young wine – from about the end of September to the beginning of December. It traditionally marks the passage of the year, celebrating a golden time of clear autumnal weather before winter sets in. Farmers and innkeepers lay on a spread of speck (smoked ham), a bread called *schüttelbrot* and roast chestnuts, accompanied by wines from the surrounding hills.

The route's main halt is **CALDARO** (Kaltern), home to many sixteenth-century buildings in Uberetsch style, combining northern Gothic and southern Renaissance architectural details. Wines from the vineyards around this small village have won numerous awards; one of the best places to taste them is *Punkt* (ⓦwein.kaltern.com), a wine bar/information point on the main square. Alternatively, two **cellars** near the village centre also offer wine tasting – Kellerei Kaltern (ⓦkellereikaltern.com) and Erste & Neue Kellerei (ⓦerste-neue.it). Within walking distance, too, on the Wine Road on the way to Lake Caldaro, the producer Manincor (ⓦmanincor.com) is well worth a visit for its combination of modern architecture and traditional estate buildings, as well as its fine vintages.

Another centre to head for is the village of **TERMENO** (Tramin), from which the varietal Gewürztraminer gets its name.

Alpe di Siusi (Seiser Alm)

The grasslands of the **Alpe di Siusi** (**Seiser Alm**), to the east of Bolzano, are Europe's largest Alpine plateau, extending over sixty square kilometres above the rest of the valley bordered by **Sciliar** (Schlern), a flat-topped, sheer mountain which splits off at one end into two peaks. The lush summer pastures 2000m above sea level are superb for mountain biking and hiking, especially now that the area, protected by the **Parco Naturale dello Sciliar**, is closed to road traffic (except for guests of hotels on the Alpe) between 9am and 5pm.

If you are travelling by bus to **Siusi** (Seis) from Bolzano you can stash mountain bikes in the luggage compartment of the bus. The service passes through **FIÈ AM SCILIAR** (Völs am Schlern), famous for inventing the curative "hay bath".

Compaccio and Saltria

From Siusi you can ascend to **COMPACCIO** (Compatsch) on the plateau by a connecting bus service or by cable car (mid-May to mid-Sept 8am–7pm; mid-Sept to early Nov 8am–6pm). Compaccio is the starting point for many excellent day-hikes, such as the two-and-a-half-hour trek to *Tierser Alpl* or a climb of similar length to *Rifugio Bolzano al Monte Pez*. You can get the views the easier way by taking the chair lift to *Restaurant Bullaccia/Puflatsch*, enjoying a coffee and *buchweizentorte* (buckwheat and redcurrant cake) when you get there.

A shuttle bus from Compaccio runs to **SALTRIA** (Saltner), about 5km to the east (every 30min; 15min), where a smattering of hotels are more or less the only buildings. Here, horses graze on the tough grass, picking their way between the bogs and streams, and the main evidence of human activity is dairy farming and some logging in the woods.

Val Gardena (Grödnertal)

Trails and chair lifts connect the Alpe di Suisi with the **Val Gardena** (**Grödnertal**), a valley with plenty of squeaky-clean guesthouses linked by a continuous stream of

5

tourist buses making their way along the Great Dolomites Road to Cortina d'Ampezzo. The main village in the valley, **Ortisei** (Sankt Ulrich), has for centuries been a big producer of religious sculpture and, more recently, hand-carved wooden toys, with several families each keeping their own particular design going. Almost three thousand woodcarvers in the valley still make furniture and religious statues, but Ortisei, like the neighbouring villages of **Santa Cristina** (Sankt Christina) and **Selva** (Wolkenstein), is now mainly a ski resort, within easy reach of the **Sella Ronda**, a route of ski runs and lifts encircling the Sella mountain range that takes a whole day to complete. From Ortisei you can also ascend via cable car to **Seceda**, the start of one of the most picturesque day-hikes in the entire region. It takes around an hour and a half to complete the loop from the mountain summit station, a relatively easy path that at one point edges the spiky, razor sharp ridges of the Fermeda peaks.

ARRIVAL AND INFORMATION — ALPE DI SIUSI (SEISER ALM)

By bus There are connections from Bolzano to Siusi (every 30min; 40min) and Ortisei (hourly; 1hr 15min), and from Siusi to Ortisei (hourly; 30min).

Tourist office This office at Compatsch 50 in Compaccio (Mon–Fri 8.15am–12.30pm, Sat 8.15am–noon; ☎ 0471 709 600, ⓦ seiseralm.it) handles information for the entire area.

ACCOMMODATION AND EATING

SIUSI

Adler Mountain Lodge Via Piz 11, Castelrotto ☎ 0471 723 077, ⓦ adler-lodge.com. Light floods in through floor-to-ceiling windows at this stylish Alpine lodge with modern interiors – it has tastefully decorated suites in natural larch plus chalets with log fires and private saunas. There's a heated outdoor pool and a panoramic hay sauna, and they rent out ski equipment in winter and bikes in summer. Rates are full board per person and the minimum stay is three nights. €326

★ **Gostner Schwaige** Via San Vigilio 7, Siusi ☎ 347 836 8154, ⓦ aussergost.com. Not-to-be-missed, this welcoming family-run chalet-restaurant serves exceptional dishes that are beautifully presented, often with colourful edible flowers – you can even have a flower salad. The mouthwatering breakfast baskets (€15) features cheese, butter and jams made on the premises, or try the tasty *kaiserschmarrn*, shredded pancake with raisins. There are also four comfortable suites on offer (€160). Daily 9am–10pm.

Hotel Arvina Via Patener 4, Siusi ☎ 0471 706 436, ⓦ hotelarvina.com. This ecofriendly hotel features welcoming and attractive rooms in natural materials including local wood; the rooms have added touches such as glass partitions filled with hay to give the place a rustic touch. The restaurant is one of the best in the area, serving traditional and international dishes (half board €204). €164

SALTRIA

Tirler Saltria 59 ☎ 0471 727 927, ⓦ hotel-tirler.com. All the rooms have balconies or terraces, and feature heated clay walls, plus pine and larch furnishings, whose essential oils are said to have a relaxing effect. There's a hay sauna, as well as an attractive heated indoor and outdoor pool, and a good, vegan-friendly restaurant to boot. Rates are half board. €280

Northeast of Bolzano

The route **northeast of Bolzano** along the **Isarco** (Eisacktal) Valley is one of the main routes between Italy and northern Europe, crossing the border into Austria at the famous Brenner Pass (1375m), the lowest in the Alps. Protestant reformer Martin Luther was one of many travellers to have walked over the Brenner Pass on his epic journey to Rome in 1510. A motorway and high-speed train line to Innsbruck now make light work of the distance, and the ancient towns of **Bressanone** (Brixen) and **Vipiteno** (Sterzing) are engaging places on the way to stretch the legs. Nearby is the wild protected area called the **Parco Naturale Fanes-Sennes-Braies** accessible via the **Val Pusteria** (Pustertal), a side valley off the Isarco. If you are planning to walk any of the long-distance walking trails known as **alte vie** (literally "high ways") you will almost certainly visit the Val Pusteria, as most of the trails launch from there. Train is the best way to reach it, with a line branching off the main Bolzano–Innsbruck tracks

at **Fortezza** (Franzenfeste) and serving the drowsy settlements of the Val Pusteria, the market town of **Brunico** (Bruneck) and **Dobbiaco** (Toblach), from where there are buses to Cortina d'Ampezzo.

Bressanone (Brixen)

Wonderfully medieval **BRESSANONE** (**Brixen**), the principal settlement in the Val d'Isarco, is well worth a halt or even a couple of days for its atmospheric old town and some fine places to stay. This entirely German-speaking town was an independent state for a thousand years, its bishops in a constant state of rivalry with the neighbouring counts of Tyrol based in Merano. The bishops' palace, next to the Duomo, still serves as the town's epicentre.

Duomo

Piazza del Duomo (Domplatz) • Daily 7am–8pm • Free

Destroyed by fire in the eleventh century and rebuilt in its current Baroque style in the eighteenth, the **Duomo** is Bressanone's most imposing building. Inside, it's decorated in faux marble, glass chandeliers and lots of gilding, but the really interesting part lies to the side, in the fantastically ornate **cloisters**, which were frescoed in the fourteenth century.

Hofburg Palace

Piazza Palazzo Vescovile (Hofburgplatz) 2 • Mid-March to Oct Tues–Sun 10am–5pm; late Nov to early Jan daily 10am–5pm only Nativity collection open • €8; late Nov to early Jan €5 • T 0472 830 505, W hofburg.it

Built as a residence for the bishops of Bressanone, the beautiful **Hofburg Palace** is one of Alto Adige's most important historical buildings, with its splendid inner courtyard lined by Renaissance loggias on three floors. It houses the **Museo Diocesano**, displaying a collection of medieval, Baroque, Classical and Romantic works of art, along with vestments belonging to Bressanone's bishop-princes. There's also an impressive collection of Nativity scenes, including a rather fun exhibition of terracotta statuettes.

Pharmaziemuseum

Via Ponte Aquila (Adlerbrückengasse) 4 • July & Aug Mon–Fri 2–6pm, Sat 11am–4pm; Sept–June Tues & Wed 2–6pm, Sat 11am–4pm • €3.50 • T 0472 209 112, W pharmaziemuseum.it

An unexpected gem above the town's oldest family-run pharmacy, the **Pharmaziemuseum** boasts a weird and wonderful selection of antique vials and pillboxes, pharmaceutical apparatus, and sumptuously illustrated medical manuals from the late sixteenth century.

Abbazia Novacella (Neustift)

Grounds Mon–Sat 10am-4pm • Free • **Library, Museum, Art Gallery & Basilica** By guided tour only Mon–Sat 10am, 11am, 2pm, 3pm & 4pm; mid-July to mid-Sept also noon & 1pm; Jan–March closed Mon • Guided tours €9 • T 0472 836 189, W abbazianovacella.it

Just 3km from the town centre, and a pleasant thirty-minute stroll along the river from the centre of town, the **Abbazia Novacella** is the most important abbey in the Südtirol. It's known for its beautiful Baroque library, art collection and museum, as well for the well-regarded wine produced here and sold direct to the public. The medieval cloisters are also well worth viewing.

ARRIVAL AND INFORMATION — BRESSANONE (BRIXEN)

By train The train station is 500m southwest of the historical centre along Via Stazione.

Destinations Bolzano (roughly every 30min; 35min), Brennero (every 20–30min; 50min; change here for Innsbruck).

By bus The bus station is on Via Dante near the town centre.

Destinations Bolzano (7 daily; 55min); Brunico (every 30min; 1hr); Ortisei (7 daily; 1hr); Siusi (hourly; 1hr).

Tourist office Viale Ratisbona 9 (Mon–Fri 8.30am–12.30pm & 2–6pm, Sat 9am–1pm & 1.30pm–5pm; T 0472 275 252, W brixen.org).

5

BRIXEN CARD

The **Brixen Card** is available free to anyone staying at registered accommodation in and around Bressanone, and gives free access to public transport, the Acquarena pool, all Südtirol's museums and much more: see brixencard.info for details.

ACCOMMODATION

Elephant Via Rio Bianco 4 0472 832 750, hotelelephant.com. This historic, family-run hotel is one of the oldest in the Dolomites, with forty-four comfortable rooms, a lovely garden, pool and a pair of fine restaurants, of which the *Elephant* is renowned for its mouthwatering steak tartare (€25). The elephant theme, including two beautiful murals, refers to an incident in the sixteenth century, when an elephant is said to have stopped in Bressanone on its way from India to Vienna – a gift to the Archduke Maximilian of Austria. **€248**

Goldener Adler Via Ponte Aquila 9 0472 200 621, goldener-adler.com. Built in 1500, this hotel in the heart of Bressanone's old town is decorated with historic furnishings, including a wonderful old stove that is still used today to heat part of the building. The standard rooms are simple – go for a spacious superior room with brushed parquet flooring. There's a little sauna and steam room, too. **€180**

Löwenhof Via Lago di Varna 60 0472 836 216, loewenhof.it. Hotel and campsite complex, with a large outdoor swimming pool, in meadowland 2km north of Bressanone in Varna (Vahrn); several buses travel here on weekdays, fewer at weekends. Campsite closed Nov–March. Doubles **€106**, pitches **€12.50** plus **€8.50** per person

★ **Pupp** Via Mercato Vecchio 36 0472 268 355, small-luxury.it. A stylish hotel with modern decor – the Chocolate room is decorated in dark brown hues, while the light and airy Cream room has blond wood floors. Some of the rooms have a private terrace with hot-tub. The rich buffet breakfast includes fresh bread and pastries made at the hotel's *pasticceria* across the road. **€301**

Tallero Via Mercato Vecchio 35 0472 830 577, tallero.it. In a pretty pastel-coloured building, this modern hotel has simple rooms with wooden furniture, and some with small balconies. There's an attached café on the ground floor with tables lining the street. **€135**

EATING AND DRINKING

Der Traubenwirt Portici Minori/Kleine Lauben 9 0472 836 552, traubenwirt.it. Generous portions of beef *gulasch* (€18.20), wienerschnitzel (€18.90) and grilled polenta with chanterelles (€19.50) are served up at this friendly restaurant with outdoor seating; there's also a weekly changing menu featuring seasonal produce, and pizzas (€6), too. Snacks and drinks are available outside meal times. Daily 11.30am–2.30pm & 6pm–11pm.

Finsterwirt Vicolo del Duomo/Domgasse 3 0472 835 343, finsterwirt.com. This elegant, old-fashioned restaurant, with nineteenth-century oil paintings on the walls and a grandfather clock, serves excellent local specialities such as veal head, tongue and cheek (€18) and *canederli di polenta* (€18) served with cheese produced in *malghe* (mountain dairies). Seating is inside or on a pretty vine-shaded terrace. Tues–Sat 11.30am–2.15pm & 6.30–9.15pm, Sun 11.30am–2.15pm.

Valentina Via Millan 14 0472 833 625, pizzeriavalentina.com. Laid-back, family-friendly pizzeria about a kilometre south of the centre, with delicious charcoal-cooked pizzas (around €5) as well pasta, schnitzel and desserts. Tues–Sun 11:30am–2pm & 5.30–11pm.

Val Pusteria (Pusertal)

The entrance to the **Val Pusteria** (**Pusertal**), a wide, sleepy valley of cornfields and hay meadows skirting the northern edge of the Dolomites, lies 4km north of Bressanone. This is a rural area where dippers dart in and out of streams in the side valleys and the sawing of timber cuts through the air. Higher up, you're likely to see marmots – timid creatures similar to guinea pigs – or more likely hear them, as they give out a piercing whistle as a warning before speeding off to their burrows; on the scree-covered slopes, chamois betray their presence with a tumbling of stones.

Many of the region's long-distance *alte vie* **footpaths** start in the Val Pusteria: Alta Via 1 starts from Lago di Braies (Pragser Wildsee), Alta Via 3 from Villabassa (Niederdorf), Alta Via 4 from San Candido (Innichen) and Alta Via 5 from Sesto (Sexten). The valley is served by bus from Brunico (see below), and by train from Fortezza (Franzensfeste).

Brunico (Bruneck)

An influx of people from the surrounding villages arrives daily in the otherwise quiet market town of **BRUNICO (Bruneck)**, which is also the transport hub of the region. Brunico was the home of the best-known Tyrolean painter and woodcarver **Michael Pacher** (c.1435–98), who straddled German Gothic and the more spare Italian styles. His *Vine Madonna* can be found in its original setting in the parish church of the village of San Lorenzo, 4km to the southwest, though there's something unsavoury about this Madonna and her pudgy child gripping a bunch of black grapes.

Brunico Castle, on Schlossweg 2, houses a branch of the **Messner Mountain Museum** (Wed–Mon: mid-May to Oct 10am–6pm; Boxing Day–April noon–6pm; €10) focusing on the sherpas of Nepal.

Capriz Feinkäserei

Via Val Pusteria 1/B • Daily 9am–7pm • Museum €3 • ⓣ 0472 869 268, ⓦ capriz.it

Just off the main road to Braies, some 17km west of Brunico, the **Capriz Feinkäserei** goats' cheese factory and museum is set in a stylish modern building. There's an excellent museum showing the process of cheese making with fun interactive exhibits, and you can look into the factory through floor-to-ceiling windows to watch the cheese being made. There's a well-stocked shop selling a selection of cheeses, and an attached café serving goats' cheese sandwiches and more.

Schloss Taufers

Self-guided visit of the castle complex • Only available May to early Nov daily 10am–6pm (last entry 5pm) • €5 • **Guided tour** Castle and rooms (50min) • Daily: Nov–Jan at 10am, 11am, 3pm & 4pm; Feb–June & Sept–Oct at 10am, 11am, 2pm, 3.15pm & 4.30pm; July & Aug roughly every 30min from 10am–5pm • €8 • ⓣ 0474 678 053, ⓦ burgeninstitut.com

North of Brunico extends the remote Val di Tures where the principal attraction is medieval **Schloss Taufers**, in the valley's main settlement, **CAMPO TURES** (Sand in Taufers). Its dungeons boast a gruesome array of torture instruments, and there are frescoes by Pacher, but the most appealing aspect of the castle is its setting: stark grey walls, bristling with towers, stand in contrast to the glistening backdrop of the Zillertal glaciers.

ARRIVAL AND INFORMATION — BRUNICO (BRUNECK)

By train The train station is a short walk southeast of the town centre, with trains to Dobbiaco (every 30min; 35min).

By bus Buses leave from near the train station, and run to destinations along the Val Pusteria.

Destinations Bressanone (every 30min; 1hr); Campo Tures (every 30min; 35min); Corvara (roughly hourly; 1hr).

Tourist office Rathausplatz 7 (July & Aug Mon–Fri 9am–7pm, Sat 9.30am–12.30pm & 3–6pm; Sept–June Mon–Fri 9am–12.30pm & 3–6pm, Sat 9.30am–12.30pm; ⓣ 0474 555 722, ⓦ bruneck.com).

ACCOMMODATION AND EATING

Agnello Bianco Via Stuck 5 ⓣ 0474 411 350, ⓦ weisseslamm.it. Rustic Alpine-style furnishings at this family-run restaurant serving reasonably-priced, traditional Tyrolean specialities like buckwheat *canederli* with speck (€8.50). An emphasis on seasonal produce, including asparagus in spring and hearty meats in autumn. Mon–Sat

THE MESSNER MOUNTAIN MUSEUM

Bressanone-born climber and explorer **Reinhold Messner** is renowned for having made the first ascent of Everest without oxygen in 1978 and for being the first human to climb all fourteen of the world's peaks over 8000m. Having retired from climbing, Messner set up an inspiring and engaging **museum** (ⓦ messner-mountain-museum.it) in his home region, dedicated to the world's mountain ranges and the cultures of the people who inhabit them. The museum is spread over six branches – Firmian at Schloss Sigmundskron, Ortles near Solda, the Dolomites branch south of Cortina d'Ampezzo, Juval in the Val Venosta, Ripa at Brunico Castle and Corones – occupying some pretty spectacular and remote places.

5

noon–2pm & 7–11pm.

Am Schloss Via Centrale 14 ⓣ345 437 0402, ⓦamschloss.it. In the centre of Brunico, within a few metres of the river and overlooking the town's main pedestrian street, this small B&B has a few spacious, spotless rooms and a decent breakfast. Parking available at an extra charge (€15). **€180**

Parco Naturale Fanes-Sannes-Braies

For dramatic mountain vistas and not-too-crowded paths – plus an insight into some of the Ladin legends (see page 324) – head for the **Parco Naturale Fanes-Sannes-Braies**, southeast of Brunico. If you have a limited amount of time to spend in this beautiful protected area, you should aim for the upper slopes of **Alpe di Fanes**, where you pick up some of the best ridgeway paths. Footpaths cross the grassy plateaus, passing the rocks of **Castel de Fanes**, home of Dolasilla, the mythical princess of the Ladini, and an area called the Marmot Parliament. The lakes are fed by underground streams, which you can sometimes hear, burbling deep beneath your feet.

Another way to see the park is to walk the (often busy) section of Alta Via 1 that runs through it, a hike that takes three to four days, with overnight stops at refuges. The trail starts at **Lago di Braies** (Pragser Wildsee), a spectacular deep-green lake surrounded by pines, 8km off the main road through the Val Pusteria – according to legend, the lake is a gateway to an underground kingdom. Parking beside the lake costs €6 per day, while several buses daily (hourly; July–Sept every 30min; 30min) connect the lake with Dobbiaco.

Also accessible from Brunico by cable car is the **Plan de Corones**, surrounded by jagged peaks. Here, legend has it, Dolasilla was crowned a warrior princess at the top of the mountain with the *raiëta* – a crystal that harnessed powerful forces. Making the most of the views from the plateau (2275m) is the final piece of Reinhold Messner's constellation of mountain museums, the **MMM Corones** (daily June to early Oct & late Nov to mid April 10am–4pm; ⓣ0474 501 350, ⓦmessner-mountain-museum.it; €10). The museum's displays wander from K2 to the Matterhorn, laying out the history of modern mountaineering. It also offers a glimpse into Messner's own childhood, including his climb of Heiligkreuzkofel (2907m), which rises within view to the south – 'the most difficult climb in my whole life.'

Vipiteno (Sterzing)

Straddling the busy road north over the Brenner Pass to Innsbruck, **VIPITENO** (**Sterzing**) is typically Tyrolean, with geranium-filled balconies and wood-panelled old inns. The porticoed main street, however, **Via Città Nuova** (Neustadtstrasse), is more reminiscent of locations further south, lined with elegant, battlemented *palazzi* erected in Renaissance times by a locally based Florentine bank. At one end, the **Zwölferturm clock tower** divides the old town from the new: the roof was rebuilt in 1867 after fire destroyed the fifteenth-century original. The town is especially pretty on summer nights when it's lit by lanterns and there's often a local festival, with live music and foodie specialities.

ARRIVAL AND INFORMATION — VIPITENO

By train The train station is in Via Stazione, a short walk east of the town centre.

Destinations Bolzano (every 30min; 1hr); Brennero (at least hourly; 20min; change here for Innsbruck).

Tourist office Piazza Città/Stadtplatz 3 (Mon–Sat 8.30am–noon & 2.30–6pm; ⓣ0472 765 325, ⓦvipiteno.com).

Cortina d'Ampezzo

Dubbed the "Pearl of the Dolomites", **CORTINA D'AMPEZZO** is well and truly part of the mountains of Trentino-Alto Adige, even though it officially belongs to the Veneto

TRE CIME DI LAVAREDO

About a 15min drive (or 30min bus ride) east of Cortina, this trio of massive spires (Drei Zinnen), the tallest of which – Cima Grande – rises just shy of 3000m, is high among the most iconic vistas in the Dolomites. The **trail circling the peaks** is one of the most accessible, too, its trailhead easily reached via a toll road (€30 per car) from the pretty lake town of **Misurina**, from where there are also frequent buses in summer months (€10 return). The refuges along the route get extremely crowded in high season, so be sure to call ahead to book – the first of them, Rifugio Auronzo (T 0435 39002, W rifugioauronzo.it), is right at the trailhead.

region next door. An upmarket ski resort – think an Italian St Moritz – Cortina boasts a gorgeous setting, surrounded by a great circle of mountains, and it's had a starring role in many films, including *The Pink Panther*, *For Your Eyes Only* and *Cliffhanger*.

After hosting the **Winter Olympics** in 1956, Cortina swiftly became *the* resort to be seen in and in the 1960s you were just as likely to spot movie stars such as Brigitte Bardot and Sophia Loren sauntering down the Corso Italia as people in ski boots. Nowadays, the VIPs it attracts tend to be titans of Italian industry – the Agnellis, Benettons, Barillas and the president of Ferrari all frequent the resort – and the population swells from six thousand to around forty thousand during the ski season (roughly Christmas to Easter).

ARRIVAL AND INFORMATION — CORTINA D'AMPEZZO

By train The nearest train station is Calalzo di Cadore, 35km southeast; buses to Cortina are timed to coincide with trains.

By bus Express bus services run by Cortina Express (W cortinaexpress.it) run to Cortina from Venezia airport and Mestre train station, as well as Bologna train station during the ski season. The bus station is on Via Marconi, above town.

Destinations Calalzo (16 daily; 1hr); Dobbiaco (roughly every 2hr; 45min).

Tourist office Corso Italia 81 (June–Sept & Dec–March Mon–Sun 8.30am–8pm; Oct, Nov, April & May Mon–Sat 9am–1pm & 2–7pm, Sun 10am–1pm; T 0436 869 086, W infodolomiti.it).

ACCOMMODATION

★ **Ambra** Via XXIX Maggio 28 T 0436 867 344, W hotelambracortina.it. A four-star boutique hotel in a central location a short walk from Corso Italia, the town's main artery; the rooms are furnished with antiques and wooden fittings which give the place a cosy rustic touch. **€300**

Baita Fraina Località Fraina 1,5km south of Cortina T 0436 3634, W baitafraina.it. A lovely B&B tucked away on a mountainside a short drive or a half-hour walk from Cortina; the cosy interiors are wood-panelled, with black-and-white family photos and a couple of beautiful majolica heaters. The restaurant comes particularly recommended, with dishes such as spaghetti with stewed onion (€11) and deer fillet (€24). **€180**

Camping Rocchetta Via Campo di Sopra 1 T 0436 5063, W campingrocchetta.it. Set about a 20min walk south from the centre, this well-run and well-fitted site is the best of Cortina's camping options, with friendly staff, a good offering of facilities and pleasant pitches beside the Boite River. No bookings accepted – first come, first served. Pitches **€11**, per adult **€10**

Rosapetra Zuel di Sopra 1 T 0436 869 062, W rosapetracortina.it. A five-star boutique spa resort; most of the rooms have private terraces, while the suites have a mezzanine floor with a second bedroom, or a bathroom with rustic wooden hot-tub. There's a small bar and a restaurant, along with a gym and spa with heated pool, steam room and sauna (open to non-guests for €40/day). **€420**

EATING AND DRINKING

★ **Agriturismo El Brite de Larieto** Strada per Passo Tre Croci, 6km east of Cortina T 368 700 8083, W elbritedelarieto.it. A friendly agriturismo and farmhouse, where pigs, cows, goats, hens and even a couple of Shetland ponies roam about. The restaurant serves excellent dishes using top-quality produce sourced directly from the farm, such as mixed *canederli* (€14) and sausage with polenta (€15). You can buy cheeses and cold cuts from the agriturismo's shop down the road or grab a picnic basket brimming with local produce for €15 (inclusive of blanket; July & Aug only). Book ahead. July–Aug daily noon–3pm & 8–10pm; Sept–June Fri–Wed noon–3pm & 8–10pm.

Ariston Via Marconi 10 T 0436 866 705, W ristoranteaaristoncortina.it. Cortina's best pizzas (€6.50) come

5

bubbling out of the wood-fired oven at this bustling family-run pizzeria. There are also plenty of pasta and meat dishes (from €12), and a good selection of pastries and desserts as well as a handful of tables outside in summer. Fri–Wed noon–2.30pm & 7–10.30pm. Closed early June–early July & Nov.

★ **Baita Pie Tofana** Località Rumerlo, 5km west of Cortina ⓣ 0436 4258, ⓦ baitapietofana.it. In a pretty spot beside the chair lift to Tofana, this rustic mountain restaurant makes a great stop after hitting the slopes, though in and of itself it's well worth the trip from Cortina. There is a good range of meat and vegetarian options, a lengthy wine list, excellent desserts and arguably the region's best home-made *casunziei all'ampezzana* €12.50) – half-moon-shaped ravioli stuffed with beetroot and ricotta and topped with melted butter and poppy seeds. Daily noon–11pm.

Enoteca Baita Fraina Largo delle Poste 17 ⓣ 0436 862 218, ⓦ baitafraina.it. Run by a family of sommeliers, this wine bar in the heart of Cortina is a great spot to enjoy a glass of wine (from €3) as you nibble on a cheese or cold cut platter (€13). Wed–Mon 10.30am–2.30pm & 5.30–10.30pm.

Pontejèl Largo Poste 11 ⓣ 0436 863 828, ⓦ hotelpontejelcortina.it. Ladin and international dishes are served at this family-run restaurant, with home-made fig, smoked ricotta and speck *cappelloni* (folded pasta squares; €12) and calf liver with onion (€22) both featuring on the menu. It's part of the *Pontejèl* hotel, which has seven simple rooms (€140). Thurs–Tues noon–2.30pm & 7–10pm.

Merano and around

An hour north by train from Bolzano, **MERANO** (Meran) lies in an attractive, broad stretch of the Adige (Etsch) Valley. Neatly tended apple orchards and vineyards cover almost every square centimetre of the lower slopes and valley floor, but when you look upwards the scale changes due to the two great mountain ranges – the Ortles (Ortler) and the Giogaia di Tessa (Texelgruppe) encircling the town. Closer geographically and in looks to the Swiss and Austrian Alps than the Dolomites, the grandeur of the landscape turns up a notch here – and a simple event like a summer storm becomes a drama, with the whole valley reverberating to the rumble of thunder.

A well-heeled **spa town**, relaxed, stylish and packed with affluent shoppers, Merano has a mild climate that attracted Central Europeans at the beginning of last century after Empress Elizabeth of Austria – known as Sissi – chose the town for her winter cure. The *époque* bequeathed a resort of fin-de-siècle hotels, gardens and elegant promenades.

Duomo

Piazza del Duomo • Daily 9am–7pm • Free

At the eastern end of the fabulously arcaded Laubengasse/Via Portici is the town's **Duomo**, dedicated to St Nicholas. Pure Gothic in and out, it was one of the first cathedrals to be built in the style in Tyrol. The most notable features are its intricate stained-glass windows, attractive ceramic floor and the 83m-high clock tower, South Tyrol's tallest.

Terme Merano

Plaza Terme 9 • Daily 9am–10pm • €19 for a day-ticket for the inside and outdoor pools, €25 for pools plus sauna • ⓣ 0473 252 000, ⓦ termemerano.it

Sitting impressively on the river's south bank is Merano's sparkling spa complex **Terme Merano**, with fifteen indoor pools (open year round) and a raft of wellness, spa and fitness facilities, all contained inside a huge steel-and-glass cube designed by architect Matteo Thun. Treatments often use local South Tyrolean produce such as apples, grapes, wool, hay and chestnuts. There are also ten outdoor pools (open from mid-May to mid-Sept), including a full-length heated pool in a large park –

it's a great spot to while away a summer's afternoon and soak in the views of the surrounding mountains.

Trauttmansdorff Castle and Touriseum

Via Valentino 51/A • April to mid-Oct daily 9am–7pm, last 2 weeks of Oct daily 9am–6pm first 2 weeks of Nov daily 9am–5pm; June, July & Aug Fri until 11pm • €13 • ⓣ 0473 255 600, ⓦ trauttmansdorff.it or ⓦ www.touriseum.it • Take bus #4 or #1B to the Botanischer Garten stop

Set amid the town's botanical gardens, **Trauttmansdorff Castle** is the former residence of Empress Elisabeth and houses the fascinating **Touriseum** (Museum of Tourism). It explores the relationship between political events, social change and the rise of tourism in the South Tyrol over the past couple of centuries using entertaining and often hands-on displays.

ARRIVAL AND INFORMATION — MERANO

By train Merano's train station is on Piazza Stazione, a 15min walk from the centre of town along Corso Libertà.

Destinations Bolzano (roughly every 30min; 40min); Mals (at least hourly; 1hr 10min); Silandro (at least hourly; 50min).

By bus Buses arrive and depart from the train station.

Destinations Bolzano (9 daily; 45min); Lana (approx every 15min; 17min).

Tourist office Corso Libertà 45 (Mon–Fri 9am–6pm, Sat 9am–4pm, Sun 10am–12.30pm; ⓣ 0473 272 000, ⓦ meran.eu).

ACCOMMODATION

Camping Hermitage Via Val di Nova 29 ⓣ 0473 232 191, ⓦ einsiedler.com. Situated the hills about 4km east of town and linked by frequent buses to the centre (10min; every 20min), this family-friendly site has pitches equipped with power and cable TV and plenty of amenities, including a nice pool, sauna and solarium. There's also an on-site pizzeria and a garden café, and you can reserve a private bathroom for €11 per day. Pitches **€14**, per adult **€12.40**

★ **Castel Fragsburg** Via Fragsburg 3 ⓣ 0473 244 071, ⓦ fragsburg.com. On a mountainside above the city, this upmarket, seventeenth-century hunting lodge has a quiet refined atmosphere; the charming rustic rooms feature Alpine-style fittings, and the spa offers a range of holistic treatments, plus yoga and meditation retreats. The Michelin-starred restaurant serves top-notch food and has a panoramic terrace with tremendous views. **€350**

Hotel Terme Merano Piazza Terme 1 ⓣ 0473 259 000, ⓦ hoteltermemerano.com. With an underground passage to the Terme Merano (free entry for guests), this hotel is the perfect spot to while away days in the thermal baths. The hotel also has its own rooftop spa with swimming pool and sauna and great views over the town. Rates are half-board only. **€440**

Miramonti Via S. Caterina/St Kathreinstrasse 14, Hafling ⓣ 0473 279 335, ⓦ hotel-miramonti.com. Southeast of Merano by 12km, this stylish boutique hotel is perched on a mountainside with views to die for. The bright rooms are decorated in earthy tones, and there's a spa with swimming pool. The wonderful restaurant has a glass-fronted panoramic platform. **€346**

★ **Ottmanngutt** Via Verdi/Verdistrasse 18 ⓣ 0473 449 656, ⓦ ottmanngut.it. Set in a 700-year-old building, this elegant family-run B&B surrounded by vineyards and cypress trees just a 5min walk from the town centre has nine well-appointed rooms furnished with antiques. Cultural events are held here monthly, and the B&B also produces its own wine, which guests may sample. **€308**

EATING AND DRINKING

Bistro Pienzenau Via Pienzenau 6 ⓣ 0473 235 979, ⓦ bistro.pienzenau.com. A 15min walk from the Trauttmansdorff Castle, this pleasant restaurant is set in a fourteenth-century fortress surrounded by greenery. The innovative Mediterranean cuisine includes a number of fish dishes such as salmon tartare with orange marinated fennel (€14) and homemade potato dumplings with swordfish and aubergines (€14). April–Oct Tues–Sat 12.30–2.30pm & 6.30–9.30pm, Sun 12.30–2.30pm.

★ **Miil** Via Palade/Gampenstrasse 1 ⓣ 0473 563 733, ⓦ miil.info. About 8km south of Merano, this restaurant is well worth the journey. It's located by a watermill, with a cosy, wooden-beamed interior and a leafy patio for summer dining. The top-notch creative dishes use seasonal ingredients, and there's an attached wine shop and pretty garden where ducks and pheasants roam freely. Five-course menu €70 (an extra €35 with wine). Mon–Fri noon–3.30pm & 7pm–midnight.

Onkel Taa's Bahnhofstrasse 17, Töll ⓣ 0473 967 342; take bus #5613. This unmissable place, around 6km northwest of Merano, is located in the Bad Egart Habsburg museum, though the colourful restaurant, bedecked in knick-knacks, resembles a museum itself. Onkel Taa cooks up some scrumptious Alpine fare (mains around €15), most

of which is made with local ingredients. Tues–Sat noon–3pm & 6.30–11pm, Sun noon–3pm.

Sissi Via Galilei/Galileistrasse 44 ⓣ 0473 231 062, ⓦ sissi.andreafenoglio.com. The best place to dine in town is the pricey yet understated *Sissi* where renowned Italian chef Andrea Fenoglio puts a sophisticated twist on traditional Alpine and Mediterranean dishes. *Primi* €20, *secondi* €32. Tues 7–10pm, Wed–Sun 12.15–2.30pm & 7–10pm.

Around Merano

Merano is a good base for exploring some seriously remote mountainscapes as well as discovering one of the most significant castles in the region, **Tirolo**, and **San Leonardo**, birthplace of local nineteenth-century hero, Andreas Hofer.

Castel Tirolo

Schlossweg 24, Tirol • Mid-March to early Dec Tues–Sun 10am–5pm, Aug until 6pm; audioguides €4 • €7 • ⓣ 0473 220 221, ⓦ schlosstirol.it

On the northern outskirts of Merano, the beautiful twelfth-century **Castel Tirolo** houses an interesting museum on daily life in the Middle Ages. Such was the influence of its owners, the Counts of Tirol, that the whole Tyrol region takes its name from the castle. Below it is **Brunnenburg**, a neo-Gothic pile of fishtail battlements and conical towers, where American poet Ezra Pound spent the last years of his life.

Museum Passeier

Via Passiria 72, San Leonardo • Mid-March to June & Oct to early Nov Tues–Sun 10am–6pm; Aug & Sept daily 10am–6pm • €8 • ⓣ 0473 659 086, ⓦ museum.passeier.it • Bus #240 from Merano (every 30min; 35min)

San Leonardo (Sankt Leonhard), some 20km to the north of Merano, is the birthplace of **Andreas Hofer**. Originally an innkeeper, wine merchant and cattle dealer, Hofer fought for the Tyrol's return to Austria after it had been ceded to Bavaria in 1805, becoming a hero of the people after successful uprisings against occupying Bavarian and Napoleonic troops. However, larger political forces overtook him and Hofer was arrested in 1810 and executed under Napoleon's orders in Mantua. His birthplace now houses the small **Museum Passeier**, dedicated to Hofer.

Val d'Ultimo (Ultental)

A traditional place of hiding in an area renowned for mountain warfare, the **Val d'Ultimo** (Ultental) to the southwest of Merano remained relatively isolated and closed to outsiders until the early twentieth century. The road into the valley begins its ascent just south of Merano at **LANA** and ends at the remote village of **SANTA GERTRUDE** (Sankt Gertraud), the terminus for buses along the valley and a great base for walks around the valley. The road from here carries on until the Lago di Fontana Bianca (Weissbrunnsee), which is only a 1hr 30min hike over rock-strewn moorland to *Rifugio Canziani* aka *Höchster Hütte* (ⓣ 0473 798 120, ⓦ rifugiocanziani.it; early June to late Oct), surrounded by the glaciers and peaks of **Gioveretto** (Zufrittspitze). Hourly buses from Merano and Lana make the trip along the valley to Santa Gertrude, while you can catch a second bus for the Lago di Fontana Bianca (15min; also hourly).

Parco Nazionale dello Stelvio

The **Parco Nazionale dello Stelvio** (or the Stilfser National Park) is one of Italy's major national parks: it extends north to the Swiss Engadine and southwest into Lombardy and covers the whole **Ortles** (Ortler) mountain range. The park is topped by one of Europe's largest glaciers (the Ghiacciaio dei Forni) and crossed by the **Passo dello Stelvio** (2758m; see page 343), which misses being the highest pass in the Alps by just 12m.

CROSSING THE PASSO DELLO STELVIO

The white-knuckle drive across the Ortles mountains over the **Passo dello Stelvio** (Stelvio Pass) to Bormio follows a convoluted route consisting of 48 numbered switchbacks and turns. Motorbikers love the thrill and the views while cyclists see the climb as the ultimate challenge – it's often an important stage of the Girò d'Italia. It's one of the last Alpine passes to open to traffic each year, sometimes staying closed until July if there's been a late fall of snow. You can access the pass **by bus** from Malles, one early morning, the other mid-afternoon.

Ski tourism has made its mark, and the park is as crisscrossed by lifts as anywhere in the Alps, but it's still a remarkable place. People come here for the high trails and glacier skiing in summer, or for the chance of seeing **wildlife** such as the red and roe deer, elk, chamois, golden eagle and ibex. A railway line running from Merano to Malles and connecting buses from stations along the way into the side valleys makes all places of interest below easily accessible.

The Val Venosta (Vinschgau)

Extending west from Merano, the **Val Venosta (Vinschgau)** is the main approach to the Stelvio park, and while it's often busy with traffic a rural feel remains away from the road. Every weekend during July and August, one or other of the villages holds a summer **street festival**, with live music, beer gardens and fresh produce. One of the best is the **Marmor e Marillen** (Marble and Apricots) in early August in the tiny village of **Lasa (Laas)**, when you can sample *marillenknödel* – sweet potato dumplings filled with whole apricots and rolled in sugar and breadcrumbs.

Castello Juval

Late March to June & Sept to early Nov Thurs–Tues 10am–4pm • €10 • Ⓣ 0471 631 264, Ⓦ messner-mountain-museum.it

At the Vinschgau village of Kastelbell, 20km from Merano, the dramatic, thirteenth-century **Castello Juval** houses another branch of the Messner Mountain Museum and is also the summer residence of the famous mountaineer Reinhold Messner. Inside, there's a superb collection of Tibetica, an assembly of paintings depicting the world's holy peaks, from Kailash to Uluru, an Expedition Cellar packed with old climbing gear that's been to some pretty lonely places, and a reasonable *osteria*.

Glorenza

The ancient walled village of **GLORENZA** (Glurns), 2.5km before the railway ends at Malles, has a population of less than nine hundred, but still enjoys special privileges conferred in 1294 when it was a salt-trading centre. An architectural gem, the settlement boasts numerous porticoes and merchants' houses dating back to the sixteenth century, as well as well-preserved defences.

Churburg

Visits are by 1hr guided tour every 15min; mid-March to Oct Tues–Sun 10am–noon & 2–4.30pm • €10 • Ⓦ churburg.com

End of the line for the railway comes at Malles (Mals) where the castle at **Coira**, more frequently known by its German name of **Churburg**, was owned by the lords of Matsch at the beginning of the thirteenth century. Back then, it was just one castle in a whole chain stretching from Bavaria to just north of Milan and was battled over by various knights – their suits of armour, some weighing nearly 25kg, can be seen in the **armoury**.

5

The side valleys

Three main **side valleys** thread their way from the Val Venosta into the foothills of the Ortles range: the Val Martello (Martelltal), the Val di Trafoi (Trafoiertal) and the Val di Solda (Suldental).

Val Martello

Buses run regularly from Coldrano (Goldrain) into the stunning **VAL MARTELLO** (Martelltal), passing silver birch woods, the ruins of Castel Montani and an aviary for falcons at Morter along the way. At the head of the valley, **Paradiso del Cevedale** (2088m) is one of the busiest bases for climbers and cross-country skiers, lying close to Monte Cevedale (Zufallspitze; 3769m); other trails lead across high passes to Val d'Ultimo and Val di Solda.

Val di Trafoi

TRAFOI is a beautifully situated hamlet perched at 1543m by the side of the road towards the beginning of the main climb up to the Stelvio Pass. The uninterrupted views of the mighty **Ortles** are stupendous, and the slopes remarkably unsullied by tourism. A cable car makes the ascent from Trafoi to *Rifugio Forcola* (T 0473 613047) at 2250m, from where a fine path (4hr) continues up and round to the pass which until 1918 marked the frontier between Italy, Switzerland and Austria. On your way, you pass the **Pizzo Garibaldi** (Dreisprachenspitze), a spur of rock celebrated – at least in the German and Romansh names – as the symbolic meeting place for the three main languages of the area.

Val di Solda

The isolated Val di Solda is a tributary valley off the Val di Trafoi. At its head lies the hamlet of **SOLDA** (Sulden), a major climbing and skiing centre since the nineteenth century. Here, a small **museum**, in the same building as the school by the *Post Hotel* (daily 10am–11pm; €3), celebrates Solda's existence as a mountain resort, displaying photos and finds from local glaciers. Nearby, the **MMM Ortles** ice museum (Wed–Mon: late May to mid-Oct & mid-Dec to April 2–6pm; July & Aug 1–7pm; T 0473 613 577, W messner-mountain-museum.it; €8) is another branch of Reinhold Messner's network of mountain museums. As well as exhibits on the nearby glaciers of the Ortles, the highlight is a jagged skylight giving the impression you're at the bottom of a crevasse, looking up.

Although Solda attracts fairly serious climbers and skiers, there are also easy paths (2hr) up to *Rifugio-Albergo Città di Milano* at 2581m (*Schaubachhütte*; T 0473 613 024; late June to early Oct & Dec–May), plus the more difficult trail (3hr) to *Rifugio Payer* at 3029m (*Payerhütte*; T 0473 613 010; mid-June to Sept), a fantastic viewpoint and base for the ascent of **Ortles** (Ortler). At 3905m high, it was the tallest mountain of the old Austrian Empire before the border changed, and was once marked on local maps as "The End of the World".

ARRIVAL AND DEPARTURE — PARCO NAZIONALE DELLO STELVIO

If you don't have your own vehicle, train is the easiest way to travel along the Val Venosta, from where you can access the park. Bus services run from the railway line into the side valleys of Martello, Trafoi and Solda. Check W sii.bz.it for bus and train timetables.

By train The privately operated Vinschgaubahn/Ferrovia della Val Venosta runs every 30min between Merano and Malles (Mals; 1hr 15min) and gives access to several villages along the valley, connecting with local bus services. Trains also carry bicycles for an additional €7.

By bus There are services from Malles to Glorenza (hourly; 5min); from Spondigna to Trafoi (10 daily; 40–45min) and Solda (hourly; 50min); and from Goldrain to Martello (hourly; 15min).

INFORMATION

Tourist offices There are offices at Solda, Via Principale 72 (Mon–Sat 9am–noon & 3–6pm; ⓣ0473 613 015, ⓦortlergebiet.it); Silandro, Kapuzinerstrasse 10 (Mon–Fri 8.30am–12.30pm & 2–6pm, Sat 8.30am–12.30pm; ⓣ0473 730 155, ⓦvinschgau.net); and Malles, Via S. Benedetto 1 (July & Aug daily 8.30am–noon & 3–6pm; Sept–June Mon–Fri 8.30am–noon & 3–6pm, Sat 8.30am–noon; ⓣ0473 831 190, ⓦvinschgau.it).

Website For general information on the area, visit ⓦstelviopark.bz.it.

ACCOMMODATION

PRATO ALLO STELVIO

Residence Sägemühle Via delle Spine/Dornweg 12 ⓣ0473 616 078, ⓦsaegemuehle.it. A stylish campsite and residence that has pitches as well as welcoming rooms and apartments (€115) with rustic wooden interiors and modern amenities. There's an indoor swimming pool, too. Doubles **€100**, pitches **€12** plus **€15.15** per person

GLORENZA

Hotel Gasthof Grüner Baum Piazza della Città/Stadtplatz 7 ⓣ0473 831 206, ⓦgasthofgruenerbaum.it. This lovely sixteenth-century hotel on Glorenza's main square has been sensitively restored in minimalist style, with brass lamps and white oiled wood. The rooftop lounge has views over to the Ortler region. **€132**

TRAFOI

Hotel Bella Vista Dorf 17 ⓣ0473 611 716, ⓦbella-vista.it. This welcoming, family-friendly hotel has spacious panoramic rooms, and food is served in a pleasant dining room that opens onto an inviting garden with stunning views of the mountains. **€162**

SOLDA

Hotel Nives Haupstrasse 71 ⓣ0473 613 422, ⓦsulden-nives.com. Right in the heart of town, this hotel with attached pizzeria and café has great-value modern rooms; the doubles are spacious with wooden interiors and spotless en-suite bathrooms, while the Basecamp rooms have bunk beds that sleep up to four (€119.60). **€93**

Venice and the Veneto

348 Venice (Venezia)

401 The Veneto

VIEW FROM ACCADEMIA BRIDGE, VENICE

6

Venice and the Veneto

The first-time visitor to Venice arrives full of expectations, most of which turn out to be well founded. All the photographs you've seen of the Palazzo Ducale, of the Basilica di San Marco, of the palaces along the Canal Grande – they've simply been recording the extraordinary truth. All the bad things you've heard about the city turn out to be right as well. Economically and socially ossified, it is losing hundreds of residents by the year and plays virtually no part in the life of modern Italy. It's deluged with tourists and occasionally things get so bad that pedestrian one-way systems are imposed in the tourist hot-spots. And it's expensive – the price of a good meal almost anywhere else in Italy will get you a lousy one in Venice, and its hoteliers make the most of a situation where demand will always far outstrip supply.

As soon as you begin to explore Venice, though, every day will bring its surprises, for this is an urban landscape so rich that you can't walk for a minute without coming across something that's worth a stop. And although it's true that the city can be unbearably crowded, things aren't so bad beyond the magnetic field of San Marco, and in the off-season it's possible to have parts of the centre virtually to yourself. As for keeping your costs down, Venice does have some good-value eating places, and you can, in the quieter months, find a bed without spending a fortune.

Tourism is far from being the only strand to the economy of the **Veneto**, the surrounding region of which Venice is the capital. The rich, flat land around the Po supports some of Italy's most productive farms and vineyards, and industrial development around the main towns rivals even the better-known areas around Milan, making the region one of the richest in Europe. At Marghera, just over the lagoon from Venice, the Veneto has the largest industrial complex in the country, albeit one that is now in decline. **Padua** and **Verona** are the main tourist attractions after Venice, thanks mainly to the former's masterpieces by Giotto, and the latter's gorgeous medieval *centro storico*. None of the other towns of the Veneto can match the cultural wealth of these two, but there are nonetheless plenty of places that justify a detour – the Palladian city of **Vicenza**, for instance, the fortified settlements of **Castelfranco** and **Cittadella**, and the idyllic upland town of **Asolo**.

For outdoor types, the interesting terrain lies in the northern part of the Veneto, where the wooded slopes of the foothills soon give way to the savage precipices of the eastern Dolomites. Because most of the high peaks of the Dolomites lie within Trentino-Alto Adige, and the eastern Dolomites are most easily explored as part of a tour of the range as a whole, the area of the Veneto north of **Belluno** is covered in Chapter Five. Similarly, the eastern shore of Lake Garda is covered as part of the Lakes region in Chapter Four.

Venice (Venezia)

The monuments that draw the largest crowds in Venice are the **Basilica di San Marco** – the mausoleum of the city's patron saint – and the **Palazzo Ducale** – the home of the doge and all the governing councils. Certainly these are the most dramatic structures in the city: the first a mosaic-clad emblem of Venice's Byzantine origins, the second perhaps the finest of all secular Gothic buildings. But every parish rewards exploration, and a roll call of the churches worth visiting would feature over fifty names, and a list of the important paintings and sculptures they contain would be twice as long.

WOMAN IN COSTUME AT VENICE'S CARNEVALE

Highlights

❶ **Basilica di San Marco, Venice** San Marco is an amazing sight with its 4000 square metres of golden mosaics. See page 353

❷ **The Accademia, Venice** Masterpieces by Titian, Bellini, Veronese and Tintoretto feature strongly in the world's best collection of Venetian painting. See page 364

❸ **Punta della Dogana, Venice** If you have even the slightest interest in contemporary art, make time for the Dogana – the best collection of its kind in Europe. See page 366

❹ **Carnevale** Venice's carnival is the most famous, but if you want a less touristic event, head for Verona, where the whole town turns out for a procession of more than eighty floats. See page 400

❺ **Giotto frescoes, Padua** Giotto's frescoes in the Cappella degli Scrovegni constitute one of the pivotal works in the history of European art. See page 405

❻ **Vicenza** The well-heeled city of Vicenza is renowned above all for the buildings of Palladio, perhaps the most influential architect ever. See page 412

❼ **Verona** Cradled in a tight curve of the Adige River, Verona is a fabulously handsome city. See page 418

HIGHLIGHTS ARE MARKED ON THE MAPS ON PAGES 350 AND 358

6

Two of the distinctively Venetian institutions known as the **scuole** retain some of the outstanding examples of Italian Renaissance art – the **Scuola di San Rocco**, with its sequence of pictures by Tintoretto, and the **Scuola di San Giorgio degli Schiavoni**, decorated with a gorgeous sequence by Carpaccio.

Although many of the city's treasures remain in the buildings for which they were created, a sizeable number have been removed to Venice's **museums**. The one that should not be missed is the **Accademia**, an assembly of Venetian painting that consists of virtually nothing but masterpieces; other prominent collections include the museum of eighteenth-century art in the **Ca' Rezzonico**, the **Museo Correr** (the civic museum of Venice) and the city's superb showcase for contemporary art, the **Punta della Dogana.**

Venice's cultural heritage is a source of endless fascination, but you should also allow time just to wander – the anonymous parts of the city reveal as much of the city's essence as the highlighted attractions. And equally indispensable for a full understanding of Venice's way of life and development are expeditions to the outer **islands** of the lagoon.

Brief history

Small groups of fishermen and hunters were living on the mudbanks of the Venetian lagoon at the start of the Christian era, but the first mass migration was provoked

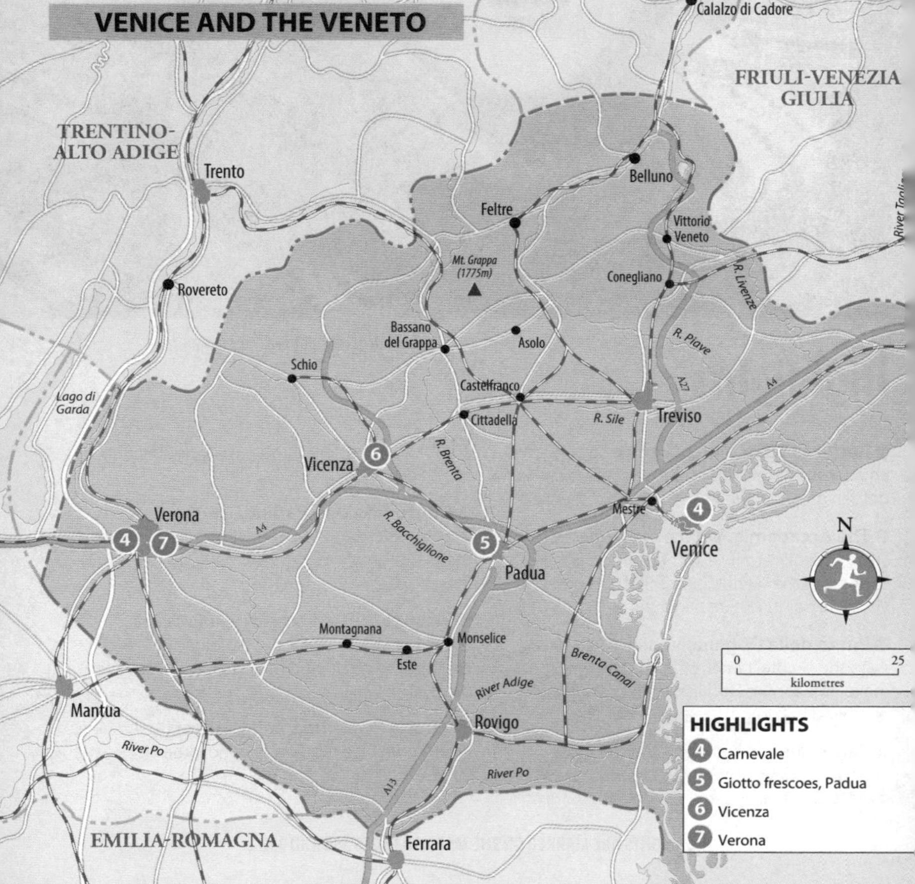

FRUITS OF THE SEA: THE CUISINE OF THE VENETO

Venice specializes in fish and **seafood**, together with exotic ingredients like pomegranates, pine nuts and raisins, harking back to its days as a port and merchant city. The surrounding Veneto vies with Lombardy for the risotto-making crown. The end product tends to be more liquid than those to the west, usually with a seafood base although peas (*bisi* in the local dialect) are also common, as are other seasonal vegetables including spinach, asparagus and pumpkin. The red salad-leaf radicchio also has its home in the Veneto, as does the renowned Italian dessert, **tiramisu**. Polenta is eaten, too, while **pork** in all forms features strongly, together with heavy **soups** of beans, rice and root vegetables.

Pastries and **sweets** are also an area of Venetian expertise. Look out for the thin oval biscuits called *baicoli*, the ring-shaped cinnamon-flavoured *bussolai* (a speciality of the Venetian island of Burano) and *mandorlato*, a cross between nougat and toffee, made with almonds.

The Veneto has been very successful at developing **wines** with French and German grape varieties, notably Merlot, Cabernet, Pinot Bianco, Pinot Grigio, Müller-Thurgau, Riesling, Chardonnay and Gewürztraminer. The quintessentially Italian Bardolino, Valpolicella and Soave are all from the Verona area, while the increasingly popular **prosecco** is produced in vineyards around Conegliano. **Grappa**, the local firewater, is associated particularly with the upland town of Bassano di Grappa, where every *alimentari* stocks a dozen varieties. Made from grape husks, juniper berries or plums, grappa is very much an acquired taste.

by the arrival in the Veneto of **Attila the Hun**'s hordes in 453, and the rate of settlement accelerated when the **Lombards** swept into northern Italy in 568. The loose confederation of island communes that developed owed political allegiance to **Byzantium.** But with the steep increase in the population of the islands the ties with the empire grew weaker, and in 726 the settlers chose their own leader of the provincial government – the first **doge**.

The control of Byzantium soon became no more than nominal, and the inhabitants of the lagoon signalled their independence through one great symbolic act – the theft of the body of **St Mark** from Alexandria in 828. St Mark displaced Byzantium's St Theodore as the city's patron, and a basilica was built alongside the doge's castle to accommodate the relics. These two buildings – the **Basilica di San Marco** and the **Palazzo Ducale** – were to remain the emblems of the Venetian state and the repository of power within the city for almost one thousand years.

Before the close of the tenth century the Venetian **trading networks** were well established through concessions granted by Byzantium in the markets of the East. By the early twelfth century Venetian merchants had won exemption from all tolls within the eastern empire and were profiting from the chaos that followed the **First Crusade**, launched in 1095. Prosperity found expression in the fabric of the city: the basilica and many of its mosaics are from this period. The **Fourth Crusade**, diverted to Constantinople by the Venetians, set the seal on their maritime empire. They brought back shiploads of treasure (including the horses of San Marco) from the **Sack of Constantinople** in 1204, but more significant was the division of the territorial spoils, which left "one quarter and half a quarter" of the Roman Empire under Venice's sway and gave it a chain of ports that stretched to the Black Sea.

After the **Sack of Rome** in 1527 the whole Italian peninsula, with the exception of Venice, came under the domination of Emperor Charles V. Hemmed in at home, Venice saw its overseas territory further whittled away by the Turks as the century progressed: by 1529 the **Ottoman Empire** extended right along the southern Mediterranean to Morocco, and even the great naval success at **Lepanto** in 1571 was followed by the surrender of Cyprus.

The decline continued throughout the 1600s and by the eighteenth century Venice had become a political nonentity: the playground of Europe, a city of casinos and perpetual festivals. **Napoleon** finally brought the show to an end: on May 12, 1797, the Maggior Consiglio met for the last time, voting to accede to Napoleon's demand that

6

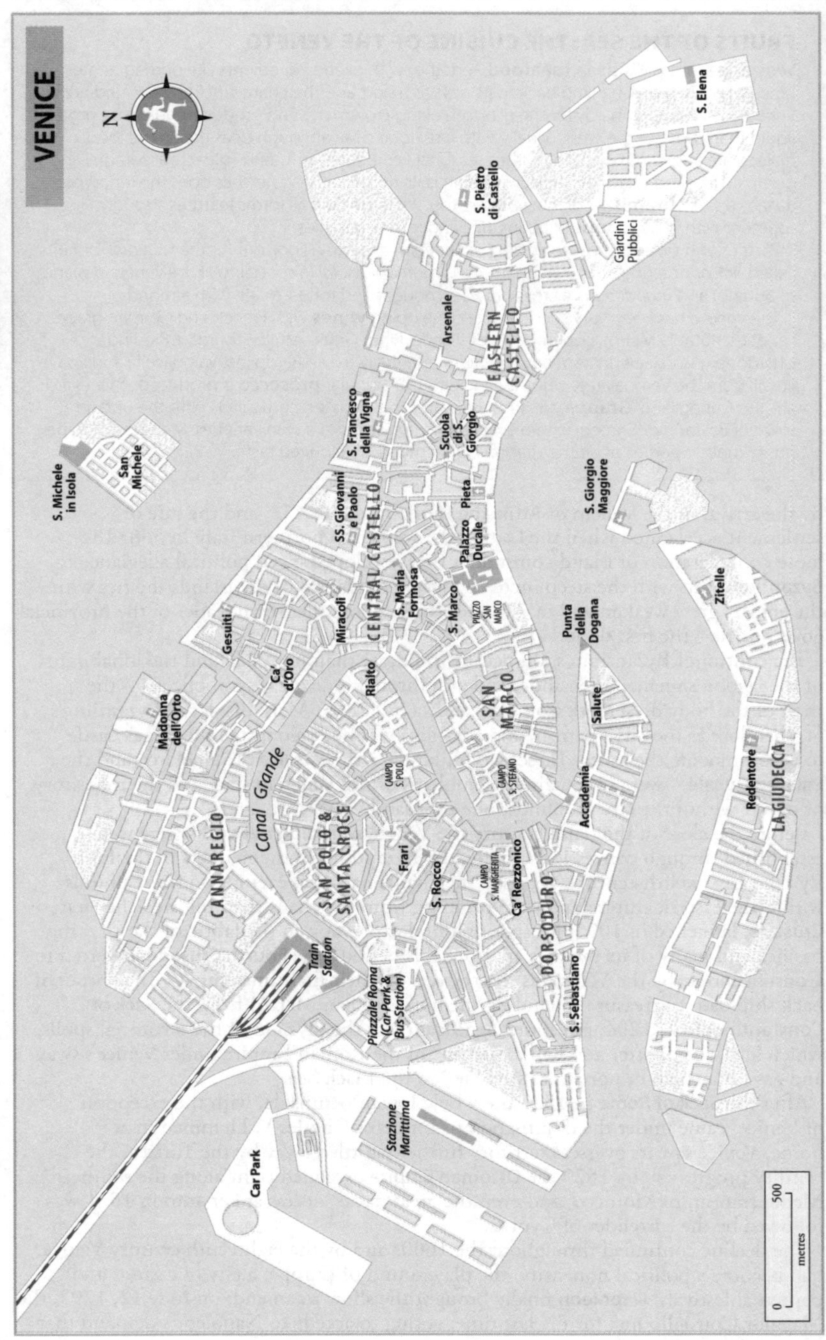
VENICE
N
S. Michele in Isola
San Michele
S. Elena
S. Pietro di Castello
Giardini Pubblici
Arsenale
EASTERN CASTELLO
S. Francesco della Vigna
Scuola di S. Giorgio
S. Giorgio Maggiore
SS. Giovanni e Paolo
CENTRAL CASTELLO
Pieta
Palazzo Ducale
Miracoli
S. Maria Formosa
Zitelle
Gesuiti
S. Marco
PIAZZO SAN MARCO
Punta della Dogana
Ca' d'Oro
Rialto
SAN MARCO
Salute
Madonna dell'Orto
Canal Grande
CAMPO S. POLO
CAMPO S. STEFANO
Accademia
Redentore
LA GIUDECCA
SAN POLO & SANTA CROCE
CANNAREGIO
Frari
S. Rocco
CAMPO S. MARGHERITA
Ca' Rezzonico
DORSODURO
S. Sebastiano
Train Station
Piazzale Roma (Car Park & Bus Station)
Stazione Marittima
Car Park
0
500
metres

THE SESTIERI OF VENICE

The 121 islands of central Venice are divided into six districts known as **sestieri**, and the houses within each *sestiere* are numbered in a sequence that makes sense solely to the functionaries of the post office – this explains how buildings facing each other across an alleyway can have numbers that are separated by hundreds.

Venice's main thoroughfare, the **Canal Grande**, divides the city in half – three *sestieri* to the west and three to the east. On the east side of the Canal Grande is the *sestiere* of **San Marco**, the area where the majority of the essential sights are clustered, and accordingly the most expensive and most crowded zone. East of San Marco is **Castello**, and to the north is **Cannaregio** – both of which become more residential, and quieter, the further you get from the centre. On the other side of the Canal Grande, the largest of the *sestieri* is **Dorsoduro**, stretching from the fashionable quarter at the southern tip of the canal to the docks in the west. **Santa Croce**, named after a now-demolished church, roughly follows the curve of the Canal Grande from Piazzale Roma to a point just short of the Rialto, where it joins the smartest and commercially most active of the districts on this bank – **San Polo**.

it dismantle the machinery of government. After Waterloo, Venice fell to the Austrians and remained a Habsburg province until united with the Kingdom of Italy in 1866.

The need for a more substantial economic base led, in the wake of World War I, to the construction of the industrial centre across the lagoon at **Marghera**, adjacent to Mestre, which in 1933 was connected to Venice by a road link. After World War II Mestre-Marghera's growth accelerated greatly, and the mainland conurbation has continued to expand, to the detriment of the *centro storico*. The factories of Mestre-Marghera are essential to the economy of the province, but have caused problems too: apart from polluting the lagoon, they have siphoned many people out of Venice and into the cheaper housing of Mestre, making Mestre-Marghera today more than three times larger than the historic centre of Venice and the outlying islands, where the population has dropped since World War II from around 170,000 to not much over 50,000. No city has suffered more from the tourist industry than Venice, but the place would barely survive without them.

San Marco

The section of Venice enclosed by the lower loop of the Canal Grande – a rectangle smaller than 1000m by 500m – is, in essence, the Venice of the travel brochures. The plush hotels are concentrated here, in the *sestiere* of **San Marco**, as are the swankier shops and the best-known cultural attractions of the city.

"The finest drawing-room in Europe" was how Napoleon described its focal point, the **Piazza San Marco** – the only piazza in Venice, all other squares being *campi* or *campielli*. Less genteel phrases might seem appropriate on a suffocating summer afternoon, but the Piazza has been congested for centuries. Its parades, festivities and markets have always drawn visitors, the biggest attraction being the trade fair known as the **Fiera della Sensa**, which kept the Piazza buzzing for the fortnight following the Ascension Day ceremony of the Marriage of Venice to the Sea; nowadays the Piazza is the focal point of the Carnevale shenanigans. The coffee shops of the Piazza were a vital component of eighteenth-century high society, and the square's three historic cafés – **Florian, Quadri** and **Lavena** – are still the most expensive in town.

Basilica di San Marco

Piazza San Marco • **Basilica di San Marco** Open to tourists Mon–Sat 9.30am–4.45pm, Sun 2–5pm • Free; sanctuary €2.50, treasury €3 • **Loggia dei Cavalli** Daily 9.45am–4.45pm • €5 • ⓦ basilicasanmarco.it

The **Basilica di San Marco** is the most exotic of Europe's cathedrals, and no visitor can remain dispassionate when confronted by it. Herbert Spencer loathed it – "a fine

6

TOURIST PASSES

MUSEUM PASSES

There are two museum cards for the city's civic museums (Ⓦvisitmuve.it). The **Musei di Piazza San Marco card** costs €20 (€13 for ages 6–14, students under 26, EU citizens over 65 and Rolling Venice Card holders), is valid for three months, and covers the Palazzo Ducale, Museo Correr, Museo Archeologico and the Libreria Sansoviniana.

The **Museum Pass**, costing €24/€18, covers these four, plus all the other civic museums: Ca' Pésaro (the modern art and oriental museums), Ca' Rezzonico, Casa Goldoni, Museo di Storia Naturale, Museo del Merletto (Burano), Museo del Vetro (Murano) and the Palazzo Mocenigo costume museum. It's valid for six months.

Both passes allow one visit to each attraction and are available from any of the participating museums. The sights covered by the Musei di Piazza San Marco card can be visited only with a museum card; at the other places you have the option of paying an entry charge just for that attraction. Accompanied disabled people have free access to all civic museums.

CHURCH PASS

Eighteen churches are part of the ever-expanding **Chorus Pass** scheme (Ⓦchorusvenezia.org), whereby a €12 ticket (€8 for students up to 29; family ticket €24) allows one visit to each of the churches over a one-year period; the individual entrance fee at each of the participating churches is €3. The churches involved are: the Frari; the Gesuati; the Redentore; San Giacomo dell'Orio; San Giobbe; San Giovanni Elemosinario; San Pietro di Castello; San Polo; San Sebastiano; San Stae; Sant'Alvise; Santa Maria dei Miracoli; Santa Maria del Giglio; Santa Maria Formosa; Santo Stefano; San Vidal; San Giacomo di Rialto; San Giuseppe di Castello. The Chorus Pass is available at each of these churches and the tourist offices.

VENEZIA UNICA

For tourists who intend to do some intensive sightseeing, the city has a complicated scheme called **Venezia Unica** (Ⓦveneziaunica.it), in which you choose a menu of services online (museum passes, water-buses, wi-fi networks, public toilets etc), and are then quoted a price that also includes discounts to some other museums and exhibitions. Note that there are two versions of the Venezia Unica pass: this one, which is for tourists; and the "frequent users" pass, which is a travel permit for long-stayers. Given that the three-day version of the Venezia Unica pass costs more than €80 if you want public transport included, and that its period of validity begins when you collect it (whereas ACTV travel cards (see page 387) are valid from the moment you first use them), for most visitors it's best just to buy a Travel Card and/or Museum Pass when you arrive.

ROLLING VENICE CARD

Visitors aged between 6 and 29 are eligible for a **Rolling Venice** card, which gives discounts at certain shops, restaurants, museums and exhibitions (details are given in a leaflet that comes with the card) and entitles holders to a 72-hour ACTV travel card (not valid for the airport bus) for just €22. The Rolling Venice card costs €6 and is available from the tourist offices on production of a passport.

sample of barbaric architecture", but to John Ruskin it was a "treasure-heap … a confusion of delight". It's certainly confusing, increasingly so as you come nearer and the details emerge; some knowledge of the history of the building helps bring a little order out of chaos.

Brief history

According to the **legend of St Mark's annunciation**, the Evangelist was moored in the lagoon, on his way to Rome, when an angel appeared and told him that his body would rest there. (The angel's salute – *Pax tibi, Marce evangelista meus* – is the text cut into the book that the Lion of St Mark is always shown holding.) This tale seems to have been invented in the thirteenth century, partly as backdated justification for the

theft of the body of St Mark from its tomb in Alexandria in **828**. As soon as the holy remains had arrived in Venice, work began on a shrine to house them.

Modelled on Constantinople's Church of the Twelve Apostles, the shrine of St Mark was consecrated in 832, but in 976 both the church and the Palazzo Ducale were burnt down. The present basilica was finished in 1094 and embellished over the succeeding centuries. Every trophy that the doge stuck onto his church (this church was not the cathedral of Venice but the doge's own chapel) was proof of Venice's secular might and so of the spiritual power of St Mark.

The exterior

Of the exterior features that can be seen easily from the ground, the **Romanesque carvings** of the **central door** demand the closest attention – especially the middle arch's figures of the months and seasons and outer arch's series of the trades of Venice. The carvings were begun around 1225 and finished in the early fourteenth century. Take a look also at the mosaic above the doorway on the far left – *The Arrival of the Body of St Mark* – which was made around 1260 (the only early mosaic left on the main facade) and includes the oldest known image of the basilica.

The narthex

From the Piazza you pass into the vestibule known as the **narthex**, which is decorated with thirteenth-century **mosaics** of Old Testament scenes on the domes and arches; *The Madonna with Apostles and Evangelists*, in the niches flanking the main door, date from the 1060s and are the oldest mosaics in San Marco.

Loggia dei Cavalli

A steep staircase goes from the church's main door up to the **Museo di San Marco** and the **Loggia dei Cavalli**. Apart from giving you an all-round view, the loggia is also the best place from which to inspect the Gothic carvings along the apex of the facade. The **horses** outside are replicas, the genuine articles having been removed inside. Stolen from the Hippodrome of Constantinople in 1204 during the Fourth Crusade, the horses are probably Roman works of the second century – the only such ancient group, or *quadriga*, to have survived.

The interior's mosaics

With its undulating floor of twelfth-century patterned marble, its plates of eastern stone on the lower walls and its four thousand square metres of **mosaics** covering every other centimetre of wall and vaulting, the interior of San Marco is the most opulent of any cathedral. One visit is not enough – there's too much to take in at one go, and the shifting light reveals and hides parts of the decoration as the day progresses; try calling in for half an hour at the beginning and end of a couple of days.

The majority of the mosaics were in position by the middle of the thirteenth century; some date from the fourteenth and fifteenth centuries, and others were created as recently as the eighteenth century to replace damaged early sections. Some of the best are the following: on the west wall, above the door, *Christ, the Virgin and St Mark*; in the west dome, *Pentecost*; on the arch between the west and central domes, the *Crucifixion* and *Resurrection*; in the central dome, *Ascension*; and in the east dome, *Religion of Christ Foretold by the Prophets*.

The sanctuary

From the south transept you can enter the **sanctuary** where, behind the altar, you'll find the most precious of San Marco's treasures – the **Pala d'Oro** (Golden Altar Panel). Commissioned in 976 in Constantinople, the Pala was enlarged, enriched and rearranged by Byzantine goldsmiths in 1105, then by Venetians in 1209 (to incorporate some less cumbersome loot from the Fourth Crusade) and again (finally)

VENICE IN FLOOD

Called the *acqua alta*, the **winter flooding** of Venice is caused by a combination of seasonal tides, fluctuations in atmospheric pressure in the Adriatic and persistent southeasterly winds, and has always been a feature of Venetian life. In recent years, however, it has been getting worse: between 2000 and 2013 there were eight highest-category floods, which is more than in the preceding fifty years. If the siren sounds, you can expect a serious flood in three to four hours' time. A system of plank walkways is immediately set up in the low-lying parts of the city. The usual high-tide season is October to March, with the worst flooding between November and February. Most floods, though, are minor, and cause no disruption at all.

A grand plan is being implemented to protect the city, involving building a **tidal barrier** across the three entrances to the lagoon. The barrier has aroused considerable opposition, both to its cost and to its potential environmental impact. However, mounting concern about global warming gave the matter some urgency and work finally began on the barrier in 2003. Delays, corruption and engineering problems have dogged the project, which is now scheduled for completion in 2021, though few Venetians think it'll be functioning by then, if ever.

in 1345. The completed screen holds 83 enamel plaques, 74 enamelled roundels, 38 chiselled figures, 300 sapphires, 300 emeralds, 400 garnets, 15 rubies, 1300 pearls and a couple of hundred other stones.

The treasury

Tucked into the corner of the south transept is the door of the **treasury**, installed in a thick-walled chamber which is perhaps a vestige of the first Palazzo Ducale. This dazzling warehouse of chalices, icons, reliquaries, candelabra and other ecclesiastical appurtenances is an unsurpassed collection of Byzantine work in silver, gold and semiprecious stones. Particularly splendid are a twelfth-century Byzantine incense burner in the shape of a domed church and a gilded silver Gospel cover from Aquileia, also made in the twelfth century.

The rest of the basilica

Back in the main body of the church, there's still more to see on the lower levels of the building. Don't overlook the **rood screen**'s marble figures of The Virgin, St Mark and the Apostles, carved in 1394 by the dominant sculptors in Venice at that time, Jacobello and Pietro Paolo Dalle Masegne. The **pulpits** on each side of the screen were assembled in the early fourteenth century from miscellaneous panels (some from Constantinople); the new doge was presented to the people from the right-hand one. The tenth-century **Icon of the Madonna of Nicopeia** (in the chapel on the east side of the north transept) is the most revered religious image in Venice; it used to be one of the most revered in Constantinople.

Palazzo Ducale

Piazzetta San Marco • Daily: April–Oct 8.30am–7pm; Nov–March 8.30am–5.30pm • Entrance with Museum Pass or Musei di Piazza San Marco card • W palazzoducale.visitmuve.it

Architecturally, the **Palazzo Ducale** is a unique mixture: the style of its exterior, with its geometrically patterned stonework and continuous tracery walls, can only be called Islamicized Gothic, whereas the courtyards and much of the interior are based on classical forms – a blending of influences that led Ruskin to declare it "the central building of the world". Unquestionably, it is the finest secular building of its era in Europe, and the central building of Venice. The Palazzo Ducale was far more than the residence of the doge – it was the home of all of Venice's governing councils, its law courts, a sizeable number of its civil servants and even its prisons. All power in the Venetian Republic and its domains was controlled within this one building.

At the head of the network was the **doge**, the one politician to sit on all the major councils of state and the only one elected for life; he could be immensely influential in policy and appointments, and restrictions were accordingly imposed on his actions to reduce the possibility of his abusing that power – his letters were read by censors and he wasn't permitted to receive foreign delegations alone. The privileges of the job far outweighed the inconveniences though, and men campaigned for years to increase their chances of election.

The Porta della Carta and courtyard

Like the Basilica, the Palazzo Ducale has been rebuilt many times since its foundation in the first years of the ninth century. The principal entrance to the *palazzo* – the **Porta della Carta** – is one of the most ornate Gothic works in the city. It was commissioned in 1438 by Doge Francesco Fóscari from Bartolomeo and Giovanni Bon, but the figures of Fóscari and his lion are replicas – the originals were pulverized in 1797 as a favour to Napoleon. Fóscari's head survived the hammering, however, and is on display inside.

Tourists enter through a doorway on the lagoon side. Once through the ticket hall you emerge in the **courtyard**, opposite the other end of the passageway into the *palazzo* – the **Arco Fóscari**. The itinerary begins on the left side of the courtyard, where the finest of the capitals from the *palazzo*'s exterior arcade are displayed in the **Museo dell'Opera**.

The Anticollegio

Upstairs, the route takes you through the doge's private apartments, then on to the **Anticollegio**, the room in which embassies had to wait before being admitted to the presence of the doge and his cabinet. This is one of the richest rooms in the Palazzo Ducale for paintings: four pictures by Tintoretto hang on the door walls, and facing the windows is Veronese's *Rape of Europa*.

The Sala del Collegio and Sala del Maggior Consiglio

The cycle of paintings on the ceiling of the adjoining **Sala del Collegio** is also by Veronese, and he features strongly again in the most stupendous room in the building – the **Sala del Maggior Consiglio**. Veronese's ceiling panel of *The Apotheosis of Venice* is suspended over the dais from which the doge oversaw the sessions of the city's general assembly; the backdrop is **Tintoretto**'s immense *Paradiso*, painted towards the end of his life with the aid of his son, Domenico. At the opposite end there's a curiosity: the frieze of portraits of the first 76 doges (the series continues in the Sala dello Scrutinio – through the door at the far end) is interrupted by a painted black veil, marking the place where **Doge Marin Falier** would have been honoured had he not been beheaded for conspiring against the state in 1355.

The Bridge of Sighs and the prisons

A couple of rooms later you descend to the underbelly of the Venetian state, crossing the **Ponte dei Sospiri**, or **Bridge of Sighs**, to the **prisons**. Before the construction of

THE ITINERARI SEGRETI

If you want to see the rooms in which the day-to-day administration of Venice took place, take the **Itinerari Segreti del Palazzo Ducale**, a fascinating 75-minute **guided tour** through the warren of offices and passageways that interlocks with the public rooms of the building. There are six tours daily, in English at 9.55am, 10.45am and 11.35am; the price is €20 (or €14 with Museum Pass) and includes admission to the rest of the Palazzo Ducale. Tickets can be booked up to 48hr in advance through Ⓦ visitmuve.it; for visits on the next or same day go in person to the Palazzo Ducale ticket desk.

6

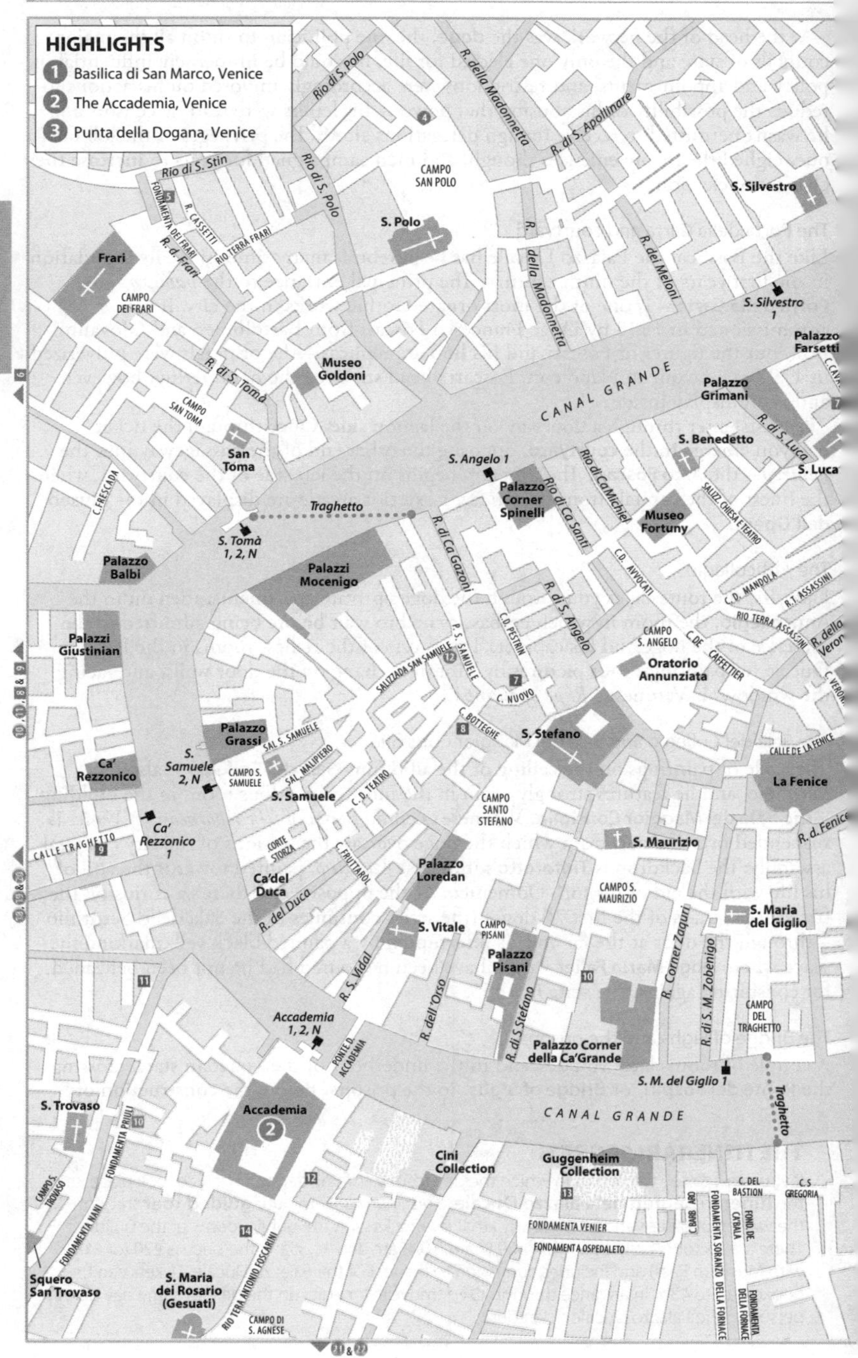
HIGHLIGHTS
1 Basilica di San Marco, Venice
2 The Accademia, Venice
3 Punta della Dogana, Venice
Frari
CAMPO DEI FRARI
S. Polo
CAMPO SAN POLO
S. Silvestro
S. Silvestro 1
Palazzo Farsetti
Museo Goldoni
CANAL GRANDE
Palazzo Grimani
S. Benedetto
S. Luca
San Toma
CAMPO SAN TOMA
S. Angelo 1
Palazzo Corner Spinelli
Museo Fortuny
Traghetto
S. Tomà 1, 2, N
Palazzo Balbi
Palazzi Mocenigo
CAMPO S. ANGELO
Oratorio Annunziata
Palazzi Giustinian
Palazzo Grassi
S. Stefano
La Fenice
Ca' Rezzonico
S. Samuele 2, N
CAMPO S. SAMUELE
S. Samuele
CAMPO SANTO STEFANO
Ca' Rezzonico 1
S. Maurizio
Palazzo Loredan
Ca'del Duca
CAMPO S. MAURIZIO
S. Maria del Giglio
S. Vitale
CAMPO PISANI
Palazzo Pisani
CAMPO DEL TRAGHETTO
Accademia 1, 2, N
Palazzo Corner della Ca'Grande
S. M. del Giglio 1
S. Trovaso
Accademia
Cini Collection
Guggenheim Collection
Squero San Trovaso
S. Maria dei Rosario (Gesuati)
CAMPO DI S. AGNESE
Rio di S. Polo
R. della Madonnetta
R. di S. Apollinare
Rio di S. Stin
R. dei Meloni
R. di S. Tomà
R. d. Frari
RIO TERRA FRARI
R. di Ca Gazoni
R. di S. Angelo
Rio di Ca Santi
Rio di CaMichiel
C.D. AVVOCATI
C.D. MANDOLA
RIO TERRA ASSASSINI
SALIZZADA SAN SAMUELE
C. NUOVO
C. BOTTEGHE
CALLE DE LA FENICE
R. d. Fenice
R. del Duca
R. S. Vidal
R. dell'Orso
R. di S Stefano
R. Corner Zaguri
R. di S. M. Zobenigo
PONTE D. ACCADEMIA
FONDAMENTA PRIULI
FONDAMENTA NANI
RIO TERA ANTONIO FOSCARINI
FONDAMENTA VENIER
FONDAMENTA OSPEDALETO
FONDAMENTA SORANZO DELLA FORNACE
CALLE TRAGHETTO
C. FRESCADA
CAMPO S. TROVASO
C. DEL BASTION
C.S GREGORIA
21 & 22

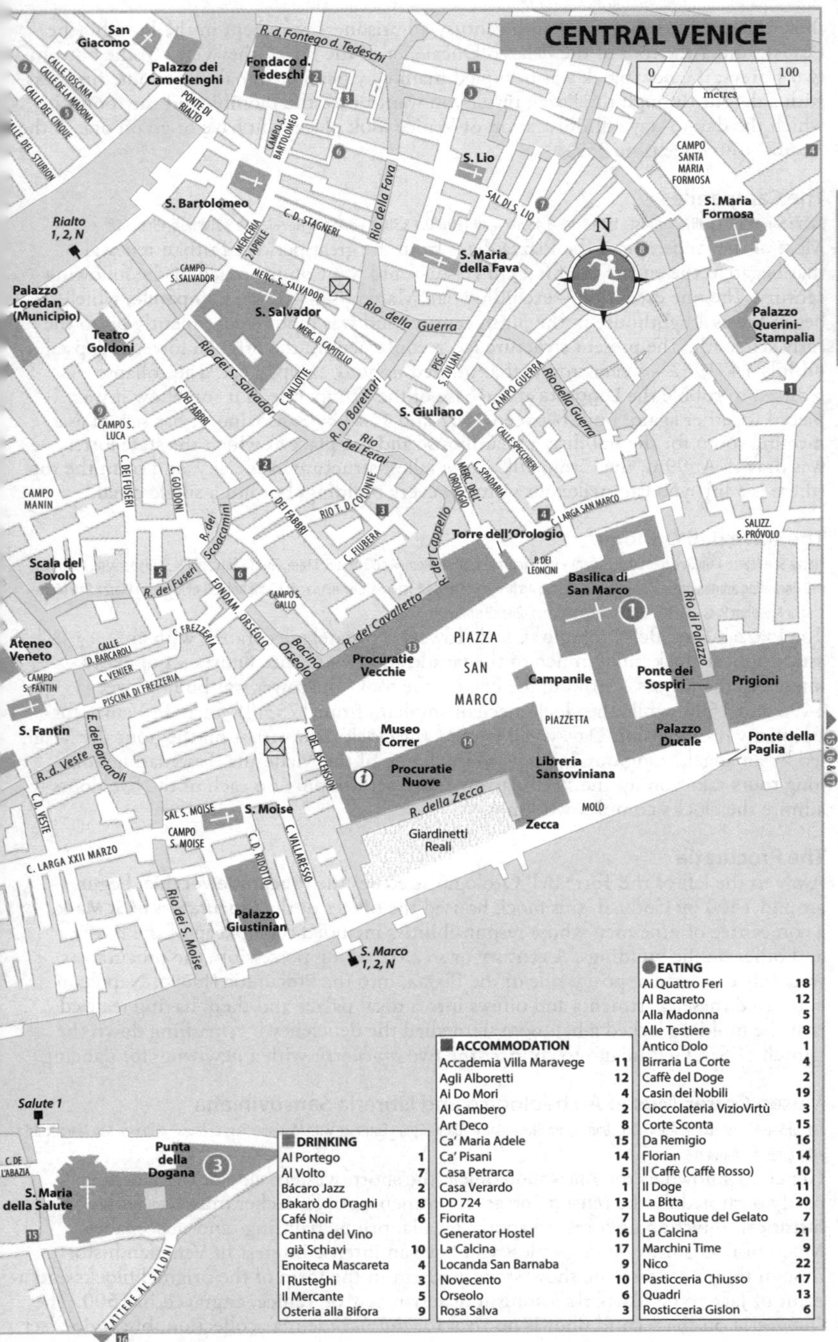

DRINKING

Al Portego	1
Al Volto	7
Bácaro Jazz	2
Bakarò do Draghi	8
Café Noir	6
Cantina del Vino già Schiavi	10
Enoiteca Mascareta	4
I Rusteghi	3
Il Mercante	5
Osteria alla Bifora	9

ACCOMMODATION

Accademia Villa Maravege	11
Agli Alboretti	12
Ai Do Mori	4
Al Gambero	2
Art Deco	8
Ca' Maria Adele	15
Ca' Pisani	14
Casa Petrarca	5
Casa Verardo	1
DD 724	13
Fiorita	7
Generator Hostel	16
La Calcina	17
Locanda San Barnaba	9
Novecento	10
Orseolo	6
Rosa Salva	3

EATING

Ai Quattro Feri	18
Al Bacareto	12
Alla Madonna	5
Alle Testiere	8
Antico Dolo	1
Birraria La Corte	4
Caffè del Doge	2
Casin dei Nobili	19
Cioccolateria VizioVirtù	3
Corte Sconta	15
Da Remigio	16
Florian	14
Il Caffè (Caffè Rosso)	10
Il Doge	11
La Bitta	20
La Boutique del Gelato	7
La Calcina	21
Marchini Time	9
Nico	22
Pasticceria Chiusso	17
Quadri	13
Rosticceria Gislon	6

these cells in the early seventeenth century all prisoners were kept in the Piombi (the Leads), under the roof of the Palazzo Ducale, or in the Pozzi (the Wells) in the bottom two storeys; the new block was occupied mainly by petty criminals. The route finishes with a detour through the Pozzi, but if you want to see the Piombi, and the rooms in which the day-to-day administration of Venice took place, you have to go on one of the "secret" tours (see page 357).

The Campanile

Piazza San Marco • Daily: April 1st–15th 9am–4.45pm; April 16th–Oct 8.30am–8.45pm; Nov–March 9.30am–4.45pm • €8

Most of the landscape of the Piazza dates from the great period of urban renewal that began at the end of the fifteenth century and went on for much of the following century. The one exception – excluding San Marco itself – is the **Campanile**, which began life as a lighthouse in the ninth century and was modified frequently up to the early sixteenth. The present structure is a reconstruction: the original tower collapsed on July 14, 1902 – a catastrophe that injured nobody except a cat. The collapse reduced to rubble the **Loggetta** at the base of the Campanile, but somehow it was pieced together again; built between 1537 and 1549 by Sansovino, it has served as a meeting room for the nobility, a guardhouse and the place at which the state lottery was drawn. At 99m, the Campanile is the tallest structure in the city, and from the top (there is a lift) you can make out virtually every building, but not a single canal.

The Torre dell'Orologio

Piazza San Marco • Guided tours daily 10am–5pm; tours in English Mon–Wed 10am & 11am, Thurs–Sun 2pm & 3pm; booking essential • €12 (including admission to Museo Correr, Museo Archeologico and Libreria Sansoviniana) or €7 for holders of Musei di Piazza San Marco card or Museum Pass • T 848 082 000, W torreorologio.visitmuve.it

The Piazza's **Torre dell'Orologio** (Clock Tower) is ornately decorated, with an astronomical clock filling much of the facade and two bronze figures – popularly known as the Moors – striking the bell on the roof. The tower was built between 1496 and 1506, while the clock mechanism dates from 1753. If you're in Venice for Epiphany or Ascension Day, you'll witness the clock's star turn – on the hour the Magi, led by an angel, troop out and bow to the figure of the Madonna. Fascinating hour-long **tours** take you up the steep narrow staircase, stopping on each of the five floors to admire the clock's complex workings.

The Procuratie

Away to the left of the Torre dell'Orologio stretches the **Procuratie Vecchie**; begun around 1500 by Codussi, this block housed the offices of the **Procurators of St Mark,** a committee of nine men whose responsibilities included the upkeep of the Basilica and other public buildings. A century or so after taking possession, the procurators were moved to the opposite side of the Piazza, into the **Procuratie Nuove**. Napoleon converted these apartments and offices into a royal palace and then, having realized that the building lacked a ballroom, remedied the deficiency by smashing down the church of San Geminiano to connect the two *procuratie* with a new wing for dancing.

Museo Correr, Museo Archeologico and Libreria Sansoviniana

Piazza San Marco • Daily: April–Oct 10am–7pm; Nov–March 10am–5pm • Entrance with Museum Pass or Musei di Piazza San Marco card • W correr.visitmuve.it

Generally known as the **Ala Napoleonica**, the short, western side of the Piazza is partly occupied by the **Museo Correr**, an immense triple-decker museum with a vast **historical collection** of coins, weapons, regalia, prints, paintings and miscellanea. Much of this is heavy going unless you have an intense interest in Venetian history, though there's at least one show-stopping item in the form of the original blocks and a print of Jacopo de' Barbari's astonishing aerial view of Venice, engraved in 1500. The **Quadreria** on the second floor is no rival for the Accademia's collection, but it does set

out clearly the evolution of painting in Venice from the thirteenth century to around 1500, and it contains some gems – the most famous being the **Carpaccio** picture usually known as *The Courtesans*, although its subjects are really a couple of bored-looking bourgeois ladies.

The archeological museum

Accessed from within the Correr, the **Museo Archeologico** is a somewhat scrappy museum, with cases of Roman coins and gems, fragments of sarcophagi and inscriptions, headless statues and bodiless heads interspersed with the odd Bronze Age, Egyptian or Assyrian relic.

The library

From the archeological museum you pass into the hall of the **Libreria Sansoviniana**, described by Palladio as "perhaps the richest and most ornate building to be created since the times of ancient Greece and Rome". Paintings by Veronese, Tintoretto, Andrea Schiavone and others cover the walls and ceiling, gazing down on selected volumes from the library's immense collection; Titian's *Allegory of Wisdom* occupies the central panel of the ceiling of the anteroom, beyond which lies the intended approach to the library, a magnificent staircase encrusted with stuccowork by Vittoria.

The Piazzetta

The **Piazzetta** – the open space between San Marco and the waterfront pavement known as the Molo – was the area where the politicians used to gather before meetings. Facing the Palazzo Ducale is Sansovino's masterpiece, the **Libreria Sansoviniana** (see above), which is attached to his first major building in Venice, the **Zecca** (Mint), built between 1537 and 1545 on the site of the thirteenth-century mint. By the beginning of the fifteenth century the city's prosperity was such that the Venetian coinage was in use in every European exchange, and the doge could with some justification call Venice "the mistress of all the gold in Christendom".

The Piazzetta's two **columns** were brought here from the Levant at the end of the twelfth century, in company with a third, which fell off the barge and still lies somewhere just off the Molo. The figures perched on top are St Theodore (the original is in the Palazzo Ducale), patron saint of Venice when it was dependent on Byzantium, and a Chimera, customized to look like the Lion of St Mark. Public executions were carried out between the columns, the techniques employed ranging from straightforward hanging to burial alive, head downwards. Superstitious Venetians avoid passing between them.

North of the Piazza

The **Mercerie**, a chain of streets that starts under the Torre dell'Orologio and finishes at the Campo San Bartolomeo, is the most direct route between San Marco and the Rialto Bridge, and has always been the main land thoroughfare of the city and a prime site for its shopkeepers. For those immune to the charms of window-shopping there's little reason to linger until you reach the church of **San Salvador**.

San Salvador

Campo San Salvador • June–Aug Mon–Sat 9am–noon & 4–7pm, Sun 4–7pm; Sept–May Mon–Sat 9am–noon & 3–7pm, Sun 3–7 pm • Free

At its northern end, the Mercerie veers right at the church of **San Salvador** or Salvatore, which was consecrated in 1177. The facade, applied in 1663, is less interesting than the sixteenth-century interior, cleverly planned in the form of three Greek crosses placed end to end. It has a couple of late Titian paintings – an altarpiece of the *Transfiguration* (1560) and an *Annunciation* (1566), whose awkward angel is often blamed on the great man's assistants. The wall of the south transept is occupied by the tomb of Caterina Cornaro (see page 431).

Campo San Bartolomeo

Campo San Bartolomeo, terminus of the Mercerie, is at its best in the evening, when it's often as packed as any bar in town. To show off their new wardrobes the Venetians take themselves off to the Piazza, but Campo San Bartolomeo is one of the favoured spots to just meet friends and talk. The **church of San Bartolomeo** (Tues, Thurs & Sat 10am–noon) has a landmark campanile, but its interior isn't thrilling: its organ panels, beautifully painted by Sebastiano del Piombo, are now housed in the Accademia.

Campo San Luca and Campo Manin

To the west of San Salvador lies **Campo San Luca**, another focus of after-work gatherings but not as much of a pressure cooker as San Bartolomeo. Beyond Campo San Luca is **Campo Manin**, on the south side of which is a sign for the nearby spiral staircase known as the **Scala del Bovolo** (*bovolo* means "snail shell" in Venetian dialect), a piece of flamboyant engineering dating from around 1500.

Museo Fortuny

Campiello San Beneto • Daily (except Tues) 10am–6pm • Entry charge varies according to what's on – usually €10 • fortuny.visitmuve.it

The **Museo Fortuny** lies west of Campo Manin, tucked away in a spot you'd never accidentally pass. Mariano Fortuny (1871–1949) was a painter, architect, engraver, photographer and sculptor, who was also famous for making silk dresses that were said to be fine enough to be threaded through a wedding ring. Design and photography exhibitions are held pretty much constantly in the Museo Fortuny, and how much of the building you get to see depends on how extensive the show is – often only a couple of rooms are used. And in high season you'll have to queue, as the *palazzo* is so fragile that only 75 people are allowed in at a time.

West of the Piazza

Leaving the Piazza **by the west side**, through the colonnade of the Ala Napoleonica, you enter another major shopping district, but one that presents a contrast to the frenetic Mercerie: here the big Italian fashion houses rule the roost. Most visitors hurry through this part of the city **en route to the Accademia**, but it does have a handful of sights worth stopping for.

San Moisè

Campo San Moisè • Mon–Sat 9.30am–12.30pm • Free

In naming the church of **San Moisè** ("Saint Moses") the Venetians were following the Byzantine custom of canonizing Old Testament figures while simultaneously honouring Moisè Venier, who paid for a rebuilding in the tenth century – the church was founded back in the eighth. Its facade, featuring a species of camel unknown to zoology, was designed in 1668 by Alessandro Tremignon and sculpted largely by **Heinrich Meyring**, a follower of Bernini. And if you think this is in questionable taste, wait till you see the miniature mountain that Tremignon and Meyring created as the main altarpiece, representing *Mount Sinai with Moses Receiving the Tablets*.

Campo San Fantin and La Fenice

Halfway along the Calle Larga XXII Marzo, on the right, is the Calle del Sartor da Veste, which takes you over a canal and into the **Campo San Fantin**, where the Renaissance church of **San Fantin** has a graceful domed apse by Sansovino. Across the *campo* is Venice's largest and oldest theatre, **La Fenice**, which opened in December 1792 as a replacement for the San Benedetto opera house after it burned down; La Fenice ("The Phoenix") itself was rebuilt in 1836 after the place had been wrecked by fire, and rebuilt yet again after another blaze – deliberately started – on the night of January 29, 1996. Tours of the magnificently restored interior with an audioguide cost €9.

Santa Maria del Giglio

Campo Santa Maria del Giglio • Mon–Sat 10am–5pm • €3, or Chorus Pass

On the main road to the Accademia, a very odd church awaits – **Santa Maria del Giglio**, otherwise known as Santa Maria Zobenigo. You can stare at its exterior all day and still not find a single Christian image: the statues are of the five Barbaro brothers who financed the rebuilding of the church in 1678; Virtue, Honour, Fame and Wisdom hover respectfully around them; and the maps in relief depict the towns that the brothers graced during their military and diplomatic careers. The interior, full to bursting with devotional sculptures and pictures (notably *The Evangelists* by **Tintoretto**), overcompensates for the impiety of the exterior.

Santo Stefano

Campo Santo Stefano • Mon–Sat 10am–5pm • Free; sacristy €3, or Chorus Pass

The tilting campanile that looms into view over the vapid church of San Maurizio (now a museum of musical instruments) belongs to **Santo Stefano**, which stands at the end of the spacious **Campo Santo Stefano**. The church of Santo Stefano dates from the thirteenth century, but was rebuilt in the fourteenth and altered again in the first half of the fifteenth; the Gothic doorway and the ship's-keel roof both belong to this last phase. The best paintings are in the sacristy: *The Agony in the Garden*, *The Last Supper* and *The Washing of the Disciples' Feet*, all late works by Tintoretto.

Palazzo Grassi

Campo San Samuele 3231 • €18 combined ticket with Punta della Dogana (see page 366) • Ⓦ palazzograssi.it

A short distance to the northwest of Campo Santo lies the gigantic **Palazzo Grassi**, which in 2005 was acquired by a consortium headed by **François Pinault**, France's pre-eminent collector of modern art. A couple of years later, Pinault acquired the Dogana di Mare, which has become the main showcase for his vast collection, while the Grassi stages immense art shows that also draw heavily on works owned by him.

Dorsoduro

Some of the finest architecture in Venice, both domestic and public, is to be found in the *sestiere* of **Dorsoduro**, a situation partly attributable to the stability of its sandbanks – Dorsoduro means "hard back". Yet for all its attractions, not many visitors wander off the strip that runs between the main sights of the area – Ca' Rezzonico, the Accademia, the Salute and the Punta della Dogana.

The Accademia

Campo della Carità • Mon 8.15am–2pm, Tues–Sun 8.15am–7.15pm • €12 • Ⓦ gallerieaccademia.it

The **Galleria dell'Accademia** is one of the finest specialist collections of European art, following the history of Venetian painting from the fourteenth to the eighteenth centuries. With San Marco and the Palazzo Ducale, it completes the triad of obligatory tourist sights in Venice, but admissions are restricted to batches of three hundred people at a time, so queues can be huge in high season.

Occupying the former church and convent of the Scuola della Carità, the Accademia has recently been expanded to create new ground-floor galleries for some three hundred paintings that were previously in storage; the upper floor focuses on art up to the seventeenth century, with the lower galleries being devoted mainly to later artists, though there is some chronological overlap. One-off exhibitions of modern and contemporary art are also held in the new rooms.

The early Renaissance

The gallery is laid out in a roughly chronological succession of rooms going anticlockwise. The first room at the top of the stairs is the fifteenth-century assembly

room of the Scuola della Carità, and contains work by the earliest known Venetian painters, of whom **Paolo Veneziano** (from the first half of the fourteenth century) and his follower **Lorenzo Veneziano** are the most absorbing.

Room 2 moves on to works from the late fifteenth and early sixteenth centuries, with large altarpieces that are contemplative even when the scenes are far from calm. **Carpaccio**'s strange and gruesome *Crucifixion and Glorification of the Ten Thousand Martyrs of Mount Ararat* (painted around 1512) and his *Presentation of Jesus in the Temple* accompany works by **Giovanni Bellini** and **Cima da Conegliano**, both of whom feature strongly in the next room, along with fine paintings by **Sebastiano del Piombo**

The High Renaissance

Rooms 6 to 8 introduce the heavyweights of **High Renaissance** Venetian painting, most notably **Tintoretto**, **Titian, Paolo Veronese** and **Lorenzo Lotto**. Room 10 is dominated by epic productions, with an entire wall filled by **Paolo Veronese**'s *Christ in the House of Levi*. Originally called *The Last Supper*, this picture provoked a stern reaction from the Court of the Holy Office: "Does it appear to you fitting that at our Lord's last supper you should paint buffoons, drunkards, Germans, dwarfs and similar indecencies?" Veronese responded simply by changing the title, which made the work acceptable. The pieces by **Tintoretto** in here include three legends of St Mark: *St Mark Rescues a Slave* (1548), which was the painting that made his reputation; *The Theft of the Body of St Mark*; and *St Mark Saves a Saracen* (both 1560s). Tintoretto's love of physical and psychological drama, the energy of his brushstrokes and the sometimes uncomfortable originality of his colours and poses are all displayed in this group. Opposite is **Titian's last painting**, a *Pietà* intended for his own tomb in the Frari.

In addition to more work by Tintoretto, room 11 houses a number of works by **Giambattista Tiepolo**, the most prominent painter of **eighteenth-century** Venice, including two shaped fragments rescued from the Scalzi (1743–45) and *The Translation of the Holy House of Loreto* (1743), a sketch for the same ceiling. In the rooms that follow, some minor seventeenth- and eighteenth-century paintings are still on show; they will eventually be moved downstairs.

The Vivarinis, the Bellinis and Carpaccio

The top part of the Carità church now forms the huge **room 23**, which houses works mainly from the fifteenth and early sixteenth centuries, the era of two of Venice's most significant artistic dynasties, the **Vivarini** and **Bellini** families. The extraordinary *Blessed Lorenzo Giustinian* by **Gentile Bellini** is one of the oldest surviving Venetian canvases, and was possibly used as a standard in processions, which would account for its state. In the same room you'll also find an exquisite *St George* by **Mantegna**, **Piero della Francesca**'s *St Jerome*, a batch of paintings by **Hieronymus Bosch and Giorgione**'s enigmatic *Tempest*.

There's more from Gentile Bellini over in **room 20**, which is entirely filled by the cycle of *The Miracles of the Relic of the Cross*, a cycle of pictures painted around 1500 for the Scuola di San Giovanni Evangelista. All of the paintings are replete with fascinating local details, but particularly rich are Gentile Bellini's *Recovery of the Relic from the Canale di San Lorenzo* and *Procession of the Relic in the Piazza*, and **Carpaccio**'s *Cure of a Lunatic*. The next room contains a complete cycle of pictures by Carpaccio illustrating the *Story of St Ursula*, painted for the Scuola di Sant'Orsola at San Zanipolo (1490–94). The sequence depicts the legend of Ursula, a Breton princess who undertook a pilgrimage with a company of 11,000 virgins, which ended with their massacre by the Huns.

Finally, in room 24 (the former hostel of the Scuola), there's **Titian**'s *Presentation of the Virgin* (dating from 1539). It was painted for the place where it hangs, as was the triptych by **Antonio Vivarini** and **Giovanni d'Alemagna** (1446).

The ground-floor galleries

Nothing in the new ground-floor galleries matches the impact of the upper rooms, but there are some fine pieces here, by artists such as **Canaletto** and **Guardi**, along with **Pietro Longhi**'s quasi-documentary interiors, a series of pastel portraits by **Rosalba Carriera**, and a quantity of sculptures and reliefs by the great neoclassical sculptor **Antonio Canova**.

The Guggenheim Collection

Calle San Cristoforo 701 • Daily (except Tues) 10am–6pm • €15 • ⓦ guggenheim-venice.it

Within five minutes' walk of the Accademia, east beyond the Campo San Vio, is the unfinished **Palazzo Venier dei Leoni**, home of Peggy Guggenheim for thirty years until her death in 1979 and now the base for the **Guggenheim Collection**. Her private collection is a quirky choice of mainly excellent pieces from her favourite modernist movements and artists. Prime pieces include Brancusi's *Bird in Space* and *Maestra*, De Chirico's *Red Tower* and *Nostalgia of the Poet*, Max Ernst's *Robing of the Bride*, sculpture by Laurens and Lipchitz, and paintings by Malevich.

Santa Maria della Salute

Campo della Salute • Daily 9am–noon & 3–5.30pm • Sacristy €4

The massive **Santa Maria della Salute**, better known simply as the **Salute**, was built to fulfil a Senate decree of October 22, 1630, that a new church would be dedicated to Mary if the city were delivered from the plague that was ravaging it – an outbreak that killed about a third of the population. Work began in 1631 on **Baldassare Longhena**'s design and the church was consecrated in 1687. On November 21, for the Festa della Salute (*salute* meaning "health"), a pontoon bridge is built across the Canal Grande to the steps of the church, where people pray for, or give thanks for, good health.

In 1656, a hoard of **Titian** paintings from the suppressed church of Santo Spirito was moved here and is now housed in the **sacristy**. The most prominent of these is the altarpiece *St Mark Enthroned with Saints Cosmas, Damian, Sebastian and Rocco* (the plague saints). *The Marriage at Cana*, with its dramatic lighting and perspective, is by **Tintoretto** (1561), and features likenesses of a number of the artist's friends.

The Punta della Dogana

Fondamenta della Dogana alla Salute • Daily (except Tues) 10am–7pm • €18 combined ticket with Palazzo Grassi • ⓦ palazzograssi.it

On the point where the Canal Grande and the Giudecca canal merge stands the huge, late seventeenth-century **Dogana di Mare** (Customs House), which in 2009 reopened as the **Punta della Dogana** exhibition space. Financed by François Pinault, the co-owner of Palazzo Grassi, the Dogana – like the Grassi – has been beautifully renovated to designs by Tadao Ando, and is unquestionably one of the world's great showcases for contemporary art. The entry charge is savage, but well over one hundred works from Pinault's collection are usually on display here at any one time, and he has invested in most of the really big names of the current art scene, so you can expect to see pieces by the likes of Cindy Sherman, Luc Tuymans, Thomas Schütte, Jeff Koons and Marlene Dumas, to name but a few.

The Zattere and San Sebastiano

Known collectively as the **Zattere**, the sequence of waterfront pavements between the Punta della Dogana and the Stazione Marittima is now a popular place for a stroll or an alfresco meal, but was formerly the place where most of the bulky goods coming into Venice were unloaded onto floating rafts called *zattere*.

The Gesuati

Fondamenta delle Zattere ai Gesuati • Mon–Sat 10am–5pm • €3, or Chorus Pass • ⓦ chorusvenezia.org

The principal monument on the Zattere is the church of Santa Maria del Rosario, invariably known as the **Gesuati**; rebuilt in 1726–43, about half a century after the church was taken over from the order of the Gesuati by the Dominicans, it was designed by **Giorgio Massari** and is notable mainly for its paintings by **Giambattista Tiepolo**, who created the first altarpiece on the right, *The Virgin with SS. Catherine of Siena, Rose and Agnes* (c.1740), and the three magnificent ceiling panels of *Scenes from the Life of St Dominic* (1737–39).

San Trovaso

Campo San Trovaso • Mon–Sat 2.30–5.30pm • Free

A diversion to the right after the Gesuati takes you past the **squero di San Trovaso**, one of only two gondola workshops left in Venice, and on to the church of **San Trovaso**. Its paintings include a fine pair by **Tintoretto** (*The Temptation of St Anthony* and *The Last Supper*) and two large scenes that were begun by Tintoretto and completed by his son and other assistants: *The Adoration of the Magi* and *The Expulsion from the Temple*.

San Sebastiano

Campo San Sebastiano • Mon–Sat 10am–5pm • €3, or Chorus Pass • Ⓦ chorusvenezia.org

At the end of the Zattere the barred gates of the Stazione Marittima deflect you away from the waterfront and towards the church of **San Sebastiano**. Built between 1505 and 1545, this was the parish church of **Paolo Veronese**, who provided most of its paintings and is buried here. He was first brought in to paint the ceiling of the sacristy with a *Coronation of the Virgin* and the *Four Evangelists*, followed by the *Scenes from the Life of St Esther* on the ceiling of the church. He then painted the dome of the chancel (since destroyed), and with the help of his brother, Benedetto, moved on to the walls of the church and the nuns' choir. The paintings around the high altar and the organ came last, being painted in the 1560s.

Campo Santa Margherita and around

Campo Santa Margherita is the social heart of Dorsoduro, and is one of the most appealing squares in the whole city. Piazza San Marco is overrun with tourists, but Campo Santa Margherita – the largest square on this side of the Canal Grande – belongs to the Venetians and retains a spirit of authenticity. Ringed by houses that date back as far as the fourteenth century, it's spacious and at the same time modest, taking its tone not from any grandiose architecture but from its cluster of market stalls and its plethora of bars and cafés, which draw a lot of their custom from the university.

Scuola Grande dei Carmini

Campo Santa Margherita 2617 • Daily 11am–5pm • €5 • Ⓦ scuolagrandecarmini.it

In Campo Santa Margherita's southwest extremity stands the **Scuola Grande dei Carmini**, once the Venetian base of the Carmelite order. Originating in Palestine towards the close of the twelfth century, the Carmelites blossomed during the Counter-Reformation, when they became the shock-troops through whom the cult of the Virgin was disseminated as a response to the inroads of Protestantism. As happened elsewhere in Europe, the Venetian Carmelites became immensely wealthy, and in the 1660s they called in an architect – probably Longhena – to redesign the property they had acquired. The core of this complex, which in 1767 was raised to the status of a *scuola grande* (see below), is now effectively a showcase for the art of **Giambattista Tiepolo**, who in the 1740s painted the wonderful ceiling of the upstairs hall.

Santa Maria del Carmelo

Campo dei Carmini • Mon–Sat 2.30–5.30pm • Free

Adjacent to the Scuola Grande dei Carmini is **Santa Maria del Carmelo** – usually known simply as the **Carmini**, and identifiable from a long way off thanks to the statue of the

THE SCUOLE OF VENICE

The Venetian institutions known as the **scuole** seem to have originated in the early thirteenth century, with the formation of the flagellant orders, whose public scourgings were intended to purge the sins of the world. The **Scuole Grande**, drawing much of their membership from the wealthiest professional and mercantile groups, received subscriptions that allowed them to fund lavish **architectural and artistic projects**, of which the Scuola Grande di San Rocco (see page 372) is the most spectacular example. The **Scuole Minore**, united by membership of certain guilds (for example goldsmiths at the Scuola dei Battioro e Tiraori), or by common nationality (as with San Giorgio degli Schiavoni, the Slavs' *scuola*), generally operated from far more modest bases. Yet all *scuole* had the same basic functions – to provide assistance for their members (dowries, medical aid and so on), to offer a place of communal worship and to distribute alms and services in emergencies.

Like many Venetian institutions, the *scuole* came to an end with **Napoleon**, who disbanded them in 1806. The Scuola di San Giorgio degli Schiavoni (see page 381) and Scuola Grande di San Rocco, however, were revived in the middle of the nineteenth century and continue to function as charitable bodies in the magnificently decorated buildings that they commissioned centuries ago. A third *scuola*, San Giovanni Evangelista, was reinstituted in the twentieth century.

Virgin atop the campanile. A dull series of Baroque paintings illustrating the history of the Carmelite order covers a lot of space inside, but the second altar on the right has a fine *Nativity* by Cima da Conegliano (before 1510), while Lorenzo Lotto's *SS. Nicholas of Bari, John the Baptist and Lucy* (1529) – featuring what Bernard Berenson ranked as one of the most beautiful landscapes in all Italian art – hangs on the opposite side of the nave.

San Pantalon

Campo San Pantalon • Mon–Sat 10am–noon & 1–3pm • Free

A short distance to the north of Campo Santa Margherita rises the raw brick hulk of **San Pantalon**, which possesses a *Coronation of the Virgin* by Antonio Vivarini and Giovanni d'Alemagna (in the chapel to the left of the chancel) and Veronese's last painting, *San Pantaleone Healing a Boy* (second chapel on right). The church also boasts the most melodramatic ceiling in the city: *The Martyrdom and Apotheosis of San Pantaleone*, which kept Gian Antonio Fumiani busy from 1680 to 1704.

Ca' Rezzonico

Fondamenta Rezzonico 3136 • Daily (except Tues): April–Oct 10am–6pm; Nov–March 10am–5pm • €10, or Museum Pass • Ⓦ carezzonico.visitmuve.it

The eighteenth century, the period of Venice's political senility, was also the period of its last grand flourish in the visual and decorative arts. The main showcase for the art of that era, the **Museo del Settecento Veneziano** spreads through most of the enormous **Ca' Rezzonico**, which the city authorities bought in 1934 specifically as a home for the museum. Recently restored, it's a spectacular building, furnished and decorated mostly with genuine eighteenth-century items and fabrics: where originals weren't available, the eighteenth-century ambience has been preserved by using modern reproductions. The applied arts of the eighteenth century are not to everyone's taste, but the paintings by the Tiepolo family and Pietro Longhi's affectionate Venetian scenes should justify the entrance fee.

San Polo and Santa Croce

Two *sestieri* are covered in this section: **San Polo**, which extends from the Rialto market to the Frari area; and **Santa Croce**, a far less sight-heavy district which lies to the north

of San Polo and reaches right across to Piazzale Roma. There are two main routes through these districts: one runs between the Rialto and the Scalzi Bridge; the other takes you in the opposite direction from the Rialto, down towards the Accademia. Virtually all the essential sights lie around these two routes.

The Rialto Bridge

The famous **Ponte di Rialto** (Rialto Bridge), the perpetually thronged link between San Marco and San Polo, superseded a succession of wooden structures – one of Carpaccio's *Miracles of the True Cross*, in the Accademia, shows what one of the old drawbridges looked like. The decision to construct a stone bridge was taken in 1524, and the job was awarded to the aptly named **Antonio da Ponte**, whose top-heavy design was described by Edward Gibbon as "a fine bridge, spoilt by two rows of houses upon it". Until 1854, when the first Accademia Bridge was built, this was the only point at which the Canal Grande could be crossed on foot.

The Rialto district

West of the Rialto Bridge, the relatively stable building land drew some of the earliest lagoon settlers to the high bank (*rivo alto*) that was to develop into the **Rialto district**. While the political centre of the new city grew up around San Marco, the Rialto became the commercial zone. It was through the markets of the Rialto that Venice earned its reputation as the bazaar of Europe. Virtually anything could be bought or sold here: Italian fabrics, precious stones, silver plate and gold jewellery, and spices and dyes from the Orient. After a fire destroyed everything in the area except the church in 1514, work began on the **Fabbriche Vecchie** (the arcaded buildings along the Ruga degli Orefici and around the Campo San Giacomo); Sansovino's **Fabbriche Nuove** (running along the Canal Grande from Campo Cesare Battisti) followed about thirty years later.

The Rialto market

Today's **Rialto market** may be a lot tamer than that of Venice at its peak, but it's still one of the liveliest spots in the city, and one of the few places where it's possible to stand in a crowd and hear nothing but Italian spoken. There's a shoal of memento-sellers by the church and along the Ruga degli Orefici; the market proper lies between them and the Canal Grande – mainly fruit stalls around the **Campo San Giacomo** and vegetable stalls and butchers' shops as you go through to the Campo Battisti, after which you come to the fish market, which is now threatened with closure because of the city's declining population.

San Giacomo di Rialto

Campo San Giacomo • Mon–Sat 10am–5pm • €3, or Chorus Pass • chorusvenezia.org

Venetian legend asserts that the city was founded on Friday, March 25, 421 AD at exactly noon; from the same legend derives the claim that the church of **San Giacomo di Rialto** was founded in that year, and is thus the oldest church in Venice. Whether it is or not, what is not disputed is that the church was rebuilt in 1071 and that parts of the present structure date from then. Like so many of Venice's underused churches, San Giacometto (as it's known to Venetians) has been pressed into service as a concert venue, with Vivaldi featuring heavily, as ever; the church functions largely as a ticket office and also houses some music instruments from the Artemio Versari collection, more of which is on display at San Maurizio (see page 364).

San Cassiano

Campo San Cassiano • Daily 9am–noon & 5–7pm • Free

The church of **San Cassiano** is a building you're bound to pass as you wander west from the Rialto. Don't be put off by its barn-like appearance: it contains three paintings

by **Tintoretto**: *The Resurrection*, *The Descent into Limbo* and *The Crucifixion,* the last of which is one of the most arresting pictures in Venice – a startling composition dominated not by the Cross but by the ladder on which the executioners stand.

Ca' Pésaro

Calle Pésaro 2076 • Tues–Sun: April–Oct 10am–6pm; Nov–March 10am–5pm • €14 for both museums, or Museum Pass • ⓦ capesaro.visitmuve.it

6

The immense **Ca' Pésaro** was bequeathed to the city at the end of the nineteenth century by the Duchessa Felicità Bevilacqua La Masa, an energetic patron of the arts who stipulated in her will that the *palazzo* should provide studio and exhibition space for impoverished young artists. Although exhibitions were later held at Ca' Pésaro, and the Bevilacqua La Masa foundation still promotes progressive art, the Duchess's plans were never fully realized, and in place of the intended living arts centre the *palazzo* became home to the city's **modern art gallery** and, later, the **Museo Orientale**.

Galleria Internazionale d'Arte Moderna

The name of the **Galleria Internazionale d'Arte Moderna** is slightly misleading. A few of the non-Italian heavyweights of modern art are here: Klimt, Rodin, Kandinsky, Matisse, Klee, Nolde, Picasso, Ernst and Miró are all present, in small quantities. But in essence this is a selective overview of Italian art in the late nineteenth and twentieth centuries, consisting largely of pieces bought from the Biennale, or acquired from exhibitions held here from 1908 to 1924, when Ca' Pésaro had a reputation for being one of the most daring venues in the country.

Museo Orientale

In the top-storey rooms of Ca' Pésaro you'll find the **Museo Orientale**, which is built around a hoard of artefacts amassed by the Conte di Bardi (a Bourbon prince) during a long Far Eastern voyage in the nineteenth century. It's a tightly packed array of porcelain, ceremonial armour, netsuke, musical instruments, clothing, paintings and enough swords, daggers and lances to equip a private army. Many of the pieces are exquisite – look out for an incredibly intricate ivory-and-coral chess set, and a room full of marvellous lacquerwork.

Museo di Storia Naturale

Salizzada del Fontego dei Turchi 1730 • Tues–Fri 9am–5pm, Sat & Sun 10am–6pm • €8, or Museum Pass • ⓦ msn.visitmuve.it

The superb **Museo di Storia Naturale**, or Museum of Natural History, occupies one of the Canal Grande's most striking buildings, the **Fondaco dei Turchi** (see page 372). The opening sequence of rooms takes you through the fossil collection, which has been laid out in such a way as to trace the process of evolution – the fossilized animal tracks set into the floor are a typically imaginative touch. Beyond, there are rooms devoted to locomotion (with separate sections for land, water and air), an extraordinary miscellany of items gathered by Giovanni Miani during his 1859–60 expedition to trace the source of the Nile, a hideous array of African hunting trophies harvested by Giuseppe de Reali and – in the long room overlooking the Canal Grande – a splendid sequence of cabinets illustrating the development of the study of natural history in Venice.

San Polo

Mon–Sat 10am–5pm • €3, or Chorus Pass • ⓦ chorusvenezia.org

The largest square in Venice after the Piazza, the **Campo San Polo** used to be the city's favourite bullfighting arena as well as the site of weekly markets and occasional fairs. At the southern end of the square, the church of **San Polo** should be visited for *The Last Supper* by **Tintoretto** and **Giandomenico Tiepolo**'s *The Stations of the Cross*, a series painted when the artist was only 20.

The Frari

Campo dei Frari • Mon–Sat 9am–6pm, Sun 1–6pm • €3, or Chorus Pass

The Franciscans were granted a large plot of land near San Polo in about 1250, not long after the death of St Francis. Replacement of their first church by the present Santa Maria Gloriosa dei Frari – more generally known simply as the **Frari** – began in the mid-fourteenth century and took more than a hundred years. This mountain of brick is not an immediately attractive building but its collection of paintings, sculptures and monuments makes it a guaranteed highlight of anyone's visit to Venice.

Wherever you stand in the Frari, you'll be facing something that rewards your attention. Apart from the Salute and the Accademia, the Frari is the only building in Venice with more than a single significant work by **Titian**. One of these – *The Assumption*, painted in 1518 – you will see almost immediately as you look towards the altar, a swirling, dazzling piece of compositional bravura for which there was no precedent in Venetian art. The other Titian masterpiece here, the *Madonna di Ca' Pésaro*, was equally innovative in its displacement of the figure of the Virgin from the centre of the picture.

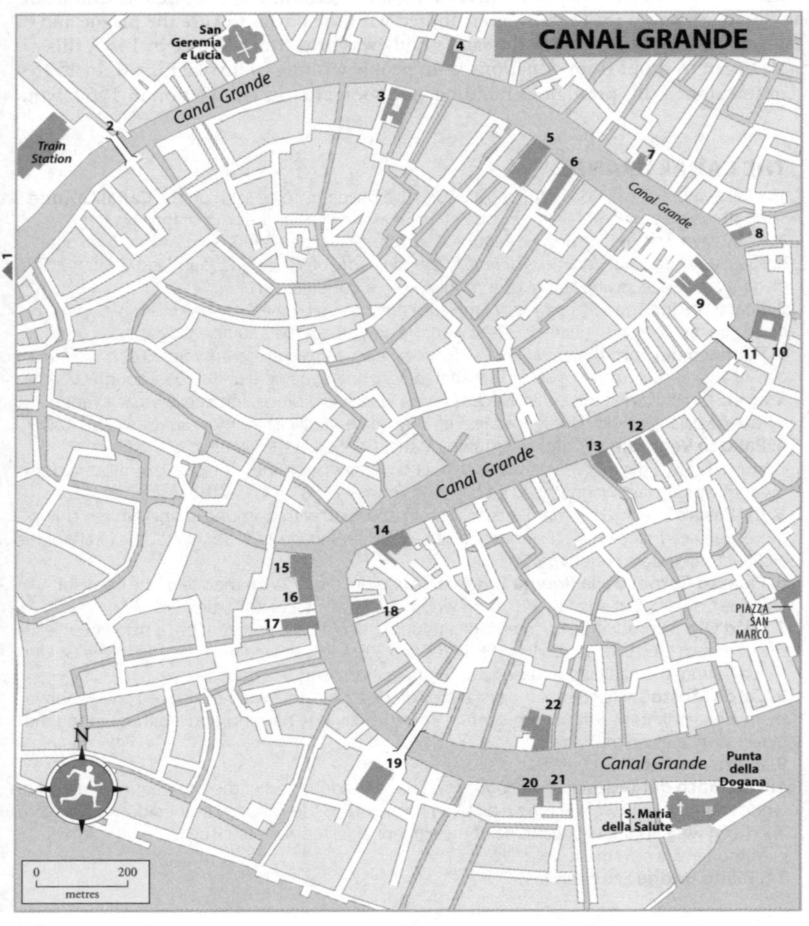

Two funerary monuments embodying the emergence in Venice of Renaissance sculptural technique flank the Titian *Assumption*: on the left is the tomb of Doge Niccolò Tron, by **Antonio Rizzo** and assistants, dating from 1476; on the right, the more chaotic tomb of Doge Francesco Fóscari, carved by **Antonio and Paolo Bregno** shortly after Fóscari's death in 1457. Head through the door in the right transept for the sacristy, where on the altar stands a picture that alone would justify a visit to the Frari – the *Madonna and Child with Saints Nicholas of Bari, Peter, Mark and Benedict*, painted in 1488 by **Giovanni Bellini**.

Two massive tombs take up much of the nave. One is the bombastic monument to Titian, built in the mid-nineteenth century on the supposed site of his grave. Opposite is a tomb of similarly pompous dimensions but of redeeming peculiarity: the mausoleum of Canova, erected in 1827 by his pupils, following a design he had made for the tomb of Titian.

Scuola Grande di San Rocco

Campo San Rocco • Daily 9.30am–5.30pm • €10 • ⓦ scuolagrandesanrocco.it

At the rear of the Frari is a place you should on no account miss: the **Scuola Grande di San Rocco**. St Rocco (St Roch) was attributed with the power to cure the plague and other serious illnesses, so when the saint's body was brought to Venice in 1485, this *scuola* began to profit from donations from people wishing to invoke his aid. In 1515 it commissioned this prestigious building, and soon after its completion in 1560, work

THE CANAL GRANDE

The following is a selection of the most impressive buildings to be seen on the **Canal Grande**. To see both banks at once, make sure you get a seat at the front or the back of the *vaporetto*.

1. Calatrava Bridge The newest feature of Venice's cityscape is officially known as the Ponte della Costituzione, but Venetians generally use the name of its designer, Santiago Calatrava. The elegant arc of steel, stone and glass is modelled on a gondola's hull.

2. Scalzi Bridge The successor of an iron structure put up by the Austrians in 1858–60, which had to be replaced in the early 1930s to give the new steamboats sufficient clearance.

3. Fondaco dei Turchi A private house from the early thirteenth century until 1621, the Fondaco dei Turchi was then turned over to Turkish traders, who stayed here until 1838. Though over-restored, the building's towers and arcade give a reasonably precise picture of what a Veneto-Byzantine palace would have looked like. It's now the natural history museum (see page 370).

4. Palazzo Vendramin-Calergi Begun by Mauro Codussi at the very end of the fifteenth century, this was the first Venetian palace built on Renaissance lines. The *palazzo*'s most famous resident was Richard Wagner, who died here in February 1883. It's now the casino.

5. Ca' Pésaro The thickly ornamented Ca' Pésaro, bristling with diamond-shaped spikes and grotesque heads, took half a century to build – work finished in 1703, long after the death of the architect, Baldassare Longhena. See page 370.

6. Palazzo Corner della Regina This *palazzo* was built in 1724 on the site of the home of Caterina Cornaro, Queen of Cyprus, from whom the palace takes its name.

7. Ca' d'Oro Incorporating fragments of a thirteenth-century palace that once stood on the site, the gorgeous Ca' d'Oro was built in the 1420s and 30s, and acquired its nickname – "The Golden House" – from the gilding that used to accentuate its carving. See page 376.

8. Ca' da Mosto The arches of the first storey of the Ca' da Mosto and the carved panels above them are remnants of a thirteenth-century Veneto-Byzantine building, and are thus among the oldest structures on the canal.

9. Rialto market See page 369.

10. Fondaco dei Tedeschi The *fondaco* was once headquarters of the city's German merchants, who as early as 1228 were leasing a building here. In 1505 the Fondaco burned down; Giorgione and Titian were commissioned to paint the exterior of its replacement. The remnants of their contribution are now in the Ca' d'Oro.

11. Rialto Bridge See page 369.

began on the decorative scheme that was to put the Scuola's rivals in the shade – a cycle of more than fifty major paintings by **Tintoretto**.

The Tintoretto paintings

To appreciate the evolution of Tintoretto's art you have to begin in the smaller room on the upper storey, the **Sala dell'Albergo**. In 1564 the Scuola held a competition for the contract to paint its first picture. Tintoretto won the contest by rigging up a finished painting in the very place for which the winning picture was destined – the centre of the ceiling. The protests of his rivals, who had simply submitted sketches, were to no avail. Virtually an entire wall of the Sala is occupied by the stupendous *Crucifixion*. As Ruskin's loquacious guide to the cycle concludes: "I must leave this picture to work its will on the spectator; for it is beyond all analysis, and above all praise."

In the main upper hall, the Old Testament subjects depicted in the three large panels of the **ceiling**, with their references to the alleviation of physical suffering, are coded declarations of the Scuola's charitable activities: *Moses Striking Water from the Rock*, *The Miracle of the Brazen Serpent* and *The Miraculous Fall of Manna*. The paintings around the walls, all based on the New Testament, are an amazing feat of sustained inventiveness, in which every convention of perspective, lighting, colour and even anatomy is defied. A caricature of the irascible Tintoretto (with a jarful of paint brushes) is incorporated into the trompe l'oeil carvings by the seventeenth-century sculptor Francesco Pianta.

12. Palazzo Loredan and Palazzo Farsetti These neighbouring *palazzi* are heavily restored Veneto-Byzantine palaces of the thirteenth century; now the town hall.
13. Palazzo Grimani Work began on the immense Palazzo Grimani in 1559, to designs by Sanmicheli, but was not completed until 1575, sixteen years after his death. See page 380.
14. The Mocenigo palaces Four houses that once belonged to the Mocenigo family stand side by side on the Canal Grande's sharpest turn: the **Palazzo Mocenigo-Nero**, a late sixteenth-century building, once home to Byron; the double **Palazzo Mocenigo**, built in the eighteenth century; and the **Palazzo Mocenigo Vecchio**, a Gothic palace remodelled in the seventeenth century.
15. Ca' Fóscari The largest private house in Venice at the time of its construction (c.1435), Ca' Fóscari was the home of Doge Francesco Fóscari, whose extraordinarily long term of office (34 years) came to an end with his forced resignation.
16. The Palazzi Giustinian These twinned palaces were built in the mid-fifteenth century for two brothers who wanted attached but self-contained houses.
17. Ca' Rezzonico Longhena's gargantuan Ca' Rezzonico was begun in 1667 as a commission from the Bon family, but they were obliged to sell the still unfinished palace to the Rezzonico, a family of stupendously wealthy Genoese bankers. Among its subsequent owners was Pen Browning, whose father Robert died here in 1889. See page 368.
18. Palazzo Grassi This vast *palazzo* was built in 1748–72 by Massari, and was the last great house to be raised on the Canal Grande. See page 364.
19. Accademia Bridge As the larger *vaporetti* couldn't get under the iron Ponte dell'Accademia built by the Austrians in 1854, it was replaced in 1932 by a wooden structure, later reinforced with steel.
20. Palazzo Venier dei Leoni In 1759 the Venier family, one of Venice's richest dynasties, began rebuilding their home, but this *palazzo*, which would have been the largest palace on the canal, never progressed further than the first storey. The stump of the building is occupied by the Guggenheim Collection (see page 366).
21. Palazzo Dario This exquisite little *palazzo* was built in the late 1480s, and the multicoloured marbles of the facade are characteristic of the work of the Lombardo family.
22. Palazzo Corner della Ca' Grande The palace that used to stand here was destroyed when a fire lit to dry out a stock of sugar ran out of control. Sansovino's design – built from 1545 – is notable for its rugged lower-storey stonework, which makes it the prototype for the Ca' Pésaro and Ca' Rezzonico.

Displayed on easels, either in the *sala* or main hall – they are often moved – are a handful of paintings that are easy to miss, given the competition. *Christ Carrying the Cross* is now generally thought to be an early **Titian**, though some still maintain Giorgione's authorship; Titian's *Annunciation* is similarly influenced by the earlier master. Two early **Tiepolo** paintings, also on easels, relieve the eyes with a wash of airy colour.

The paintings on the ground floor were created between 1583 and 1587, when Tintoretto was in his late 60s. The turbulent *Annunciation* is one of the most original images of the event ever painted, and there are few Renaissance landscapes to match those of *The Flight into Egypt* and the small paintings of *St Mary Magdalen* and *St Mary of Egypt*.

San Rocco

Campo San Rocco • Daily 9.30am–5.30pm • Free

Yet more paintings by Tintoretto adorn the church of **San Rocco**. On the south wall of the nave you'll find *St Roch Taken to Prison*, and below it *The Pool of Bethesda* – though only the latter is definitely by Tintoretto. In the chancel are four large works, all of them difficult to see properly: the best are *St Roch Curing the Plague Victims* (lower right) and *St Roch in Prison* (lower left).

Cannaregio

In the northernmost section of Venice, **Cannaregio**, you can go from the bustle of the train station and the tawdry Lista di Spagna to areas which, although no longer rural (Cannaregio comes from *canna*, meaning "reed") are still among the quietest and prettiest parts of the whole city. The district also has the dubious distinction of containing the world's original **ghetto**.

The Scalzi

Fondamenta dei Scalzi • Daily 8am–noon & 4–7pm • Free

Right next to the station stands the **Scalzi**, or Santa Maria di Nazareth. Built by Baldassare Longhena in the 1670s for the barefoot (*scalzi*) order of Carmelites, the church has frescoes by Giambattista Tiepolo in the first chapel on the left and the second on the right, but his major work on the ceiling was destroyed in 1915 by an Austrian bomb. A couple of fragments, now in the Accademia, were all that was salvaged. The second chapel on the left is the resting place of **Lodovico Manin** (d.1802), Venice's last doge. The bare inscription set into the floor – "Manini Cineres" (the ashes of Manin) – is a fair reflection of the low esteem in which he was held.

San Geremia e Lucia

Campo San Geremia e Lucia • Mon–Sat 8am–noon & 4–6pm, Sun 9.30am–12.15pm • Free

The church of **San Geremia e Lucia**, east of the Scalzi, is chiefly notable for being the present home of **St Lucy**, martyred in Syracuse in 304. In one version of her legend, Lucy's response to an unwanted suitor who praised her beautiful eyes was to pluck out the offending organs and hand them to him, saying "Now let me live for God"; in another version, she was blinded by her executioner. She is the patron saint of the blind and those afflicted with ocular ailments, and is usually depicted holding her eyes on a dish. The glass case on the high altar contains her desiccated body. Architecturally, the church's main point of interest is the twelfth-century campanile, one of the oldest in the city.

Palazzo Labia

The ballroom of the **Palazzo Labia**, next door to San Geremia, contains frescoes by Giambattista Tiepolo and his assistants (1745–50) illustrating the story of *Antony and Cleopatra*. The present owners, RAI (the state radio and TV service), occasionally allow

public access – the tourist office will have the current details, or contact ⓔ direzione.veneto@rai.it.

The Ghettoc

The Venetian **Ghetto** was, in a sense, the first in the world: the word comes from the Venetian dialect *getar* (to found), or *geto* (foundry), which is what this area was until 1390. In 1516 all the city's Jews were ordered to move to the island of the Ghetto Nuovo. Distinctive badges or caps had to be worn by all Jews, and there were various economic and social restraints on the community, although oppression was lighter in Venice than in most other parts of Europe. When Jews were expelled en masse from Spain in 1492 and Portugal in 1497, many came here.

The Jewish population grew to about five thousand and, even though they were allowed to spread into the **Ghetto Vecchio** (called the "old ghetto" because that's where the foundries used to be) and the **Ghetto Nuovissimo**, there was gross overcrowding. As the Ghetto buildings were not allowed to be more than a third higher than the surrounding houses, the result was a stack of low-ceilinged storeys – seven floors are not unusual. Napoleon removed the gates of the Ghetto in 1797 but Venice's Jews didn't achieve equal rights with other Venetians until Unification with Italy in 1866. In a corner of the *campo* a series of reliefs by **Arbit Blatas** commemorates the two hundred Venetian Jews deported to the death camps during World War II – their names and ages are inscribed on a separate memorial entitled *The Last Train*. Today Venice's Jewish population of around six hundred is spread all over the city, but the Ghetto remains the centre of the community.

Museo Ebraico and the scole

Daily except Sat & Jewish hols: June–Sept 10am–7pm; Oct–May 10am–5.30pm; regular tours (in English) of the synagogues run throughout the day • Museum €8, museum and tour €12

Each wave of Jewish immigrants established its own **synagogue** and four of the most significant – the ornate Scola Levantina (founded in 1538), the Scola Spagnola, the beautiful Scola al Canton and the Scola Italiana – can be viewed in a fascinating **tour** of the area organized by the **Museo Ebraico** in Campo Ghetto Nuovo; the collection in the museum itself consists mainly of silverware, embroidery and other liturgical objects.

Sant'Alvise

Campo Sant'Alvise • Mon–Sat 10am–5pm • €3, or Chorus Pass • ⓦ chorusvenezia.org

A few minutes' walk north of the Ghetto stands the church of **Sant'Alvise**, which was commissioned by Antonia Venier, daughter of Doge Antonio Venier, after the saint appeared to her in a vision in 1388. The church has one outstanding picture, *The Road to Calvary* by Tiepolo, painted in 1743. His *Crown of Thorns* and *Flagellation*, slightly earlier works, are on the right-hand wall of the nave.

Madonna dell'Orto

Campiello Madonna dell'Orto • Mon–Sat 10.30am–4.30pm • €3

A circuitous stroll eastward from Sant'Alvise brings you to the Gothic church of **Madonna dell'Orto**. Dedicated to St Christopher in about 1350, the church was renamed after a large stone Madonna by Giovanni de' Santi, found discarded in a local vegetable garden (*orto*), began to work miracles. Brought inside the church in 1377, the figure can still be seen (now heavily restored) in the Cappella di San Mauro through a door at the front end of the right aisle. This was Tintoretto's parish church – he's buried in the chapel to the right of the high altar – and there are a number of his paintings here, notably the colossal *Making of the Golden Calf* and *The Last Judgement*, which flank the main altar.

Ca' d'Oro

Calle Ca' d'Oro • Mon 8.15am–2pm, Tues–Sat 8.15am–7.15pm • €6, or more when special exhibitions are on; free on first Sun of the month • ⓦ cadoro.org

The **Strada Nova** – the main thoroughfare of Cannaregio – was carved through the houses in 1871–72 and is now a bustling shopping street. Nearly halfway along is the inconspicuous *calle* named after, and leading to, the **Ca' d'Oro**, a spectacular Gothic palace that now houses the **Galleria Giorgio Franchetti**. Its main attraction is the *St Sebastian* painted by **Mantegna** shortly before his death in 1506, although the collection of sculpture has more outstanding items, notably **Tullio Lombardo**'s beautifully carved *Young Couple*, and superb portrait busts by Bernini and Alessandro Vittoria.

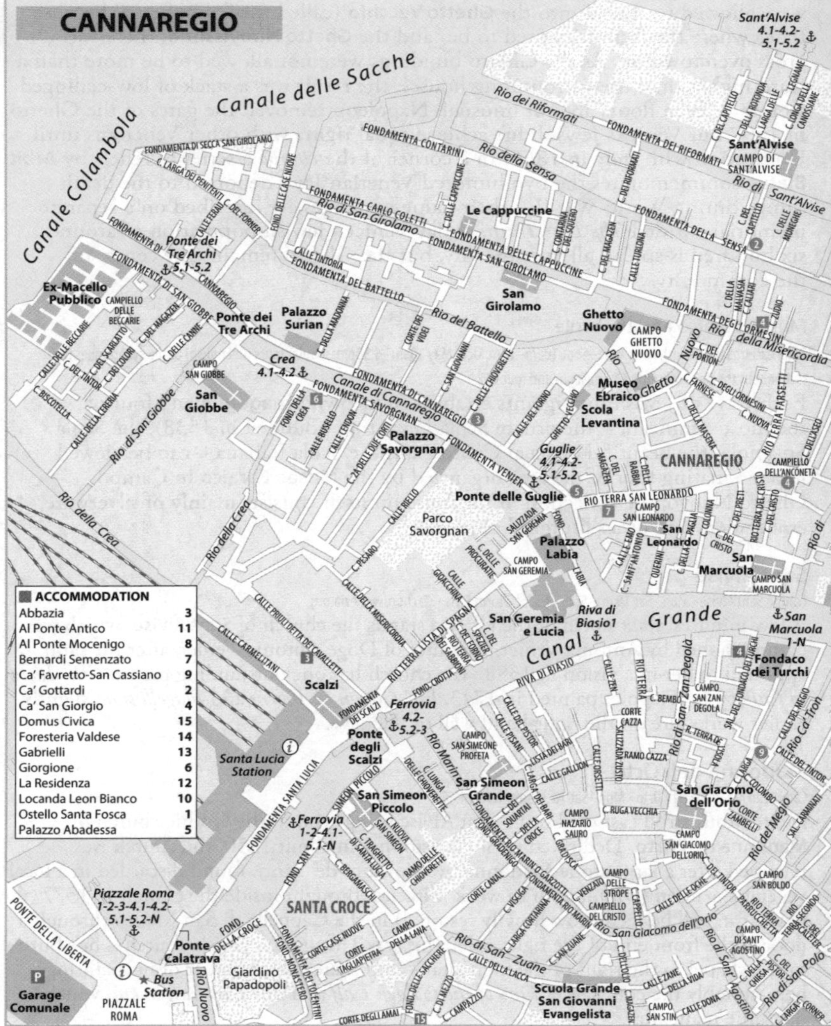

San Giovanni Crisostomo

Campo San Giovanni Crisostomo • Mon–Sat 10am–noon & 3.30–6.30pm, Sun 3.30–6.30pm • Free

Tucked into the southernmost corner of Cannaregio stands **San Giovanni Crisostomo** (John the Golden-Mouthed), named after the famously eloquent Archbishop of Constantinople. An intimate church with a compact Greek-cross plan, it was possibly the last project of Mauro Codussi, and was built between 1497 and 1504. It possesses two outstanding altarpieces: in the chapel to the right hangs one of the last works by **Giovanni Bellini**, *SS Jerome, Christopher and Louis of Toulouse*, painted in 1513 when the artist was in his 80s; and on the high altar, **Sebastiano del Piombo**'s *St John Chrysostom with SS John the Baptist, Liberale, Mary Magdalen,*

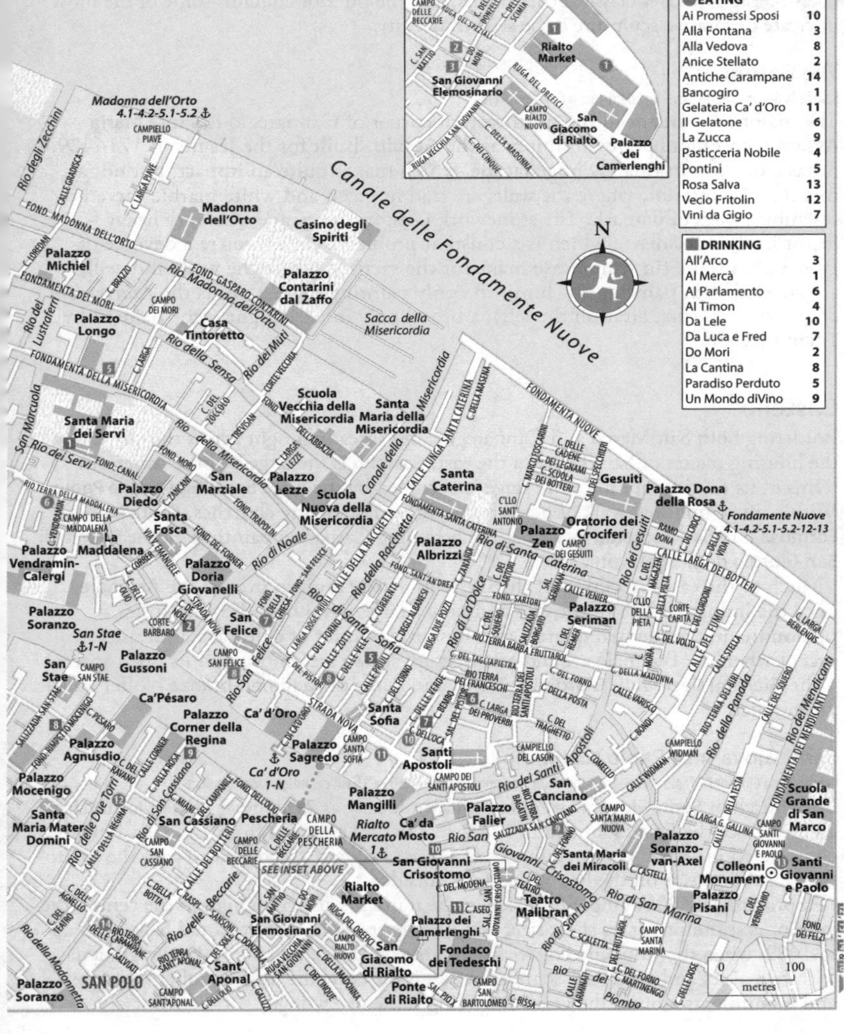

Agnes and Catherine, painted in 1509–11. On the left side is a marble panel of the *Coronation of the Virgin* by Tullio Lombardo, a contrast with his more playful stuff in the nearby Miracoli.

The Miracoli

Campiello dei Miracoli • Mon–Sat 10am–5pm • €3, or Chorus Pass • chorusvenezia.org

The exquisite marble-clad church of Santa Maria dei Miracoli, known simply as the **Miracoli**, sits on the lip of a canal on the very edge of Cannaregio. Thought to have been designed by Pietro Lombardo, it was built in the 1480s to house a painting of the Madonna (still the altarpiece) that was believed to have performed a number of miracles, such as reviving a man who'd spent half an hour lying at the bottom of the Giudecca canal. Typically for Renaissance architecture in Venice, richness of effect takes precedence over classical correctness, and the interior contains some of the most intricate decorative sculpture to be seen in the city.

The Gesuiti

Salizzada dei Spechieri • Mon–Fri 10am–noon & 4–6pm • Free

The major monument in the northeastern corner of Cannaregio is **Santa Maria Assunta**, commonly known simply as the **Gesuiti**. Built for the Jesuits in 1714–29, it has a disproportionately huge facade, which makes quite an impact, but not as much as the **interior**, where the walls are clad in green and white marble carved to resemble swags of damask. The stonework is astonishing, and also very heavy – a factor in the subsidence which is a constant problem. Unless you're a devotee of Palma il Giovane (in which case make for the sacristy, where the walls and ceiling are covered with paintings by him), the only painting to seek out is the *Martyrdom of St Lawrence* (first altar on the left), a broodingly intense night scene painted by **Titian** in 1558.

Castello

Bordering both San Marco and Cannaregio, and spreading right across the city to the housing estates of Sant'Elena in the east, **Castello** is the largest of the *sestieri*. In terms of its tourist appeal, centre stage is occupied by the huge **Santi Giovanni e Paolo.** Within a few minutes' walk of here are two other fascinating churches, **Santa Maria Formosa** and **San Zaccaria**, as well as the beguiling Carpaccio paintings in the **Scuola di San Giorgio degli Schiavoni**.

Much of the eastern section of the Castello *sestiere* is given over to the **Arsenale**, once the industrial hub of the city and now a large naval base. Beyond it lies a predominantly residential quarter that has little to offer of cultural significance, except when the Biennale art and architecture shows are on, though its open spaces – the **Giardini Garibaldi**, **Giardini Pubblici** and **Parco della Rimembranza** – offer a little green relief.

Santi Giovanni e Paolo (Zanipolo)

Campo Santi Giovanni e Paolo • Mon–Sat 9am–6pm, Sun noon–6pm • €3.50 • basilicasantigiovanniepaolo.it

The church of **Santi Giovanni e Paolo** – known locally as **Zanipolo** – is the Dominicans' equivalent of the Frari, founded in 1246, rebuilt and enlarged from 1333, and finally consecrated in 1430. The sarcophagus of Doge Giacomo Tiepolo, who gave the site to the Dominicans, is on the left of the door outside.

Approximately 90m long, 38m wide at the transepts and 33m high in the centre, the **interior** is stunning for its sheer size, and is more spacious than it would have been up to 1682, when the wooden choir was demolished. The simplicity of the design, a nave with two aisles and gracefully soaring arches, is offset by the huge number of tombs and monuments around the walls, including those of 25 doges.

The south aisle and south transept

In the **south aisle** you'll find Giovanni Bellini's superb polyptych *St Vincent Ferrer with Saints Christopher and Sebastian*, with an *Annunciation* and pietà above. At the far end of this aisle, before you turn into the transept, you'll see a small shrine with the **foot of St Catherine of Siena**: most of her body is in Rome, her head is in her house in Siena and other relics are scattered about Italy.

The **south transept** has a painting by Alvise Vivarini, *Christ Carrying the Cross* (1474), and Lorenzo Lotto's *St Antonine* (1542), painted in return for nothing more than his expenses and permission to be buried in the church. Sadly, Lotto was eventually driven from his home town by the jealousies and plots of other artists (including Titian), and died in a monastery at Loreto.

The chancel and the rest of the church

On the right of the **chancel** is the tomb of Doge Michele Morosini, selected by Ruskin as "the richest monument of the Gothic period in Venice". The Renaissance tomb of Doge Andrea Vendramin, opposite, was singled out as its antithesis – only the half of the effigy's head that would be visible from below was completed by the artist, a short cut denounced by Ruskin as indicative of "an extreme of intellectual and moral degradation". Tullio Lombardo is thought to have been the sculptor.

In 1867 a fire wrecked the **Cappella del Rosario**, at the end of the north transept, destroying paintings by Tintoretto, Palma il Giovane and others; of their replacements, the best are **Veronese**'s ceiling panels and *Adoration*. Funerary sculpture is the main attraction of the north aisle. To the left of the sacristy door is the monument to Doge Pasquale Malipiero by Pietro Lombardo, one of the earliest in Renaissance style in Venice.

Scuola Grande di San Marco

Campo Santi Giovanni e Paolo • Tues–Sat, plus first Sun of month, 9.30am–5.30pm; pharmacy Mon 2–5pm • €5 • Ⓦ scuolagrandesanmarco.it

After its suppression in the early nineteenth century, the **Scuola Grande di San Marco** provided a sumptuous facade and foyer for Venice's hospital for the best part of two hundred years. The **facade** was started by Pietro Lombardo and Giovanni Buora in 1487, half a century after the *scuola* moved here from its original home over in the Santa Croce *sestiere*, and was finished in 1495 by Mauro Codussi.

In 2013, after the restructuring of the hospital, the main rooms of the *scuola* were opened to the public. A Codussi staircase leads up to the huge **Sala Capitolare**, whose spectacular golden ceiling hangs over an impressive collection of old medical instruments and books. A cycle of Tintoretto paintings of scenes from the life and afterlife of St Mark used to adorn the walls of the Sala Capitolare; these were removed after the fall of the Republic, but the originals of *The Transport of the Body of St Mark* and *St Mark Blesses the Lagoon Islands*, both by Tintoretto and his son Domenico, are still in place. The adjacent **Sala dell'Albergo** was similarly stripped of its paintings by

THE COLLEONI MONUMENT

When the *condottiere* **Bartolomeo Colleoni** died, he left a handsome legacy to the republic on condition that a monument should be erected to him in the square in front of San Marco, an impossible proposition to Venice's rulers with their cult of anonymous service to the state. They got around this dilemma by interpreting the will in a way that allowed them to raise the monument in front of the Scuola Grande di San Marco, rather than the Basilica, and still claim the money. In 1481 the commission for the monument was won by **Andrea Verrocchio**, who was working on the piece when he died at the end of June 1488. **Alessandro Leopardi** was called in to finish the work and produce the plinth for it, which he gladly did – even adding his signature on the horse's girth and appending *del Cavallo* to his name.

Gentile and Giovanni Bellini, Giovanni Mansueti, Paris Bordone and Palma il Vecchio; amazingly accurate digital reproductions have replaced them.

Next door, the rooms of the disbanded Scuola di Santa Maria della Pace are now home to a collection of specimens of anatomical pathology and a reconstruction of an old **pharmacy**.

San Francesco della Vigna

Campo San Francesco • Mon–Sat 8am–12.30pm & 3–6.30pm, Sun 3–6.30pm • Free

The church of **San Francesco della Vigna**, to the east of Zanipolo, takes its name from the vineyard that was here when the Franciscans were given the site in 1253. The present church building was begun in 1534, designed and supervised by Sansovino, but the design was modified during construction and Palladio was later brought in to provide the facade. Some fine works of art are to be seen inside, including Giambattista Tiepolo's frescoes in the **Cappella Sagredo**, a *Sacra Conversazione* by Veronese, sculptures of Prophets and Evangelists by the Lombardo family and their assistants (in the chapel to the left of the chancel) and a large *Madonna and Child Enthroned* by **Antonio da Negroponte**. And don't overlook the tranquil fifteenth-century cloisters.

Santa Maria Formosa

Campo Santa Maria Formosa • Mon–Sat 10am–5pm • €3, or Chorus Pass • Ⓦ chorusvenezia.org

South of San Zanipolo lies the atmospheric **Campo Santa Maria Formosa**. The eponymous **church** was founded by St Magnus, Bishop of Oderzo, in the seventh century, having been inspired by a dream in which he saw a buxom (*formosa*) figure of the Madonna. The present building is another Codussi design, dating from 1492. Palma il Vecchio's altarpiece *St Barbara*, the church's outstanding picture, was admired by George Eliot as "an almost unique presentation of a hero-woman".

Pinacoteca Querini-Stampalia

Campo Santa Maria Formosa 5252 • Tues–Sun 10am–6pm • €14 • Ⓦ querinistampalia.it

The Palazzo Querini-Stampalia, just round the corner from Santa Maria Formosa, houses the **Pinacoteca Querini-Stampalia**. Although there is a batch of Renaissance pieces – such as Palma il Vecchio's marriage portraits of Francesco Querini and Paola Priuli Querini (for whom the palace was built), and **Giovanni Bellini**'s *Presentation in the Temple* – the general tone of the collection is set by the culture of eighteenth-century Venice, a period to which much of the palace's decor belongs. The winningly inept pieces by **Gabriel Bella** form a comprehensive record of Venetian social life in that century, and the more accomplished genre paintings of **Pietro and Alessandro Longhi** feature prominently as well. Exhibitions are often held in the museum's ground-floor rooms, which were brilliantly refashioned in the 1960s by Carlo Scarpa, who also designed the entrance bridge and the garden – an ensemble that constitutes one of Venice's extremely rare examples of first-class modern architecture.

Palazzo Grimani

Ramo Grimani 4858 • Tues–Sun 8.15am–7.15pm • €6.50 (more during special exhibitions); free first Sun of the month • Ⓦ palazzogrimani.org

One of the most impressive palaces in the city stands on the island immediately to the south of Santa Maria Formosa. Turn first left off Ruga Giuffa and you'll be confronted by the land entrance of the gargantuan sixteenth-century **Palazzo Grimani**, once owned by the branch of the Grimani family whose collection of antiquities became the basis of the Museo Archeologico. The neo-Roman interior, featuring some of the most spectacular rooms in the city (the tribune, with its huge skylight, is especially dramatic), has been beautifully restored and furnished with a miscellany of objets d'art.

San Zaccaria

Campo San Zaccaria • Mon–Sat 10am–noon & 4–6pm, Sun 4–6pm • Free, Cappella di Sant'Atanasio and Cappella di San Tarasio €2

The towering church of **San Zaccaria**, a pleasing mixture of Gothic and Renaissance, was started by Antonio Gambello and finished after his death in 1481 by Mauro Codussi, who was responsible for the facade from the first storey upwards. Inside is one of the city's most stunning altarpieces, a *Madonna and Four Saints* by Giovanni Bellini. A small fee gets you into the rebuilt remnants of the old church, the **Cappella di Sant'Atanasio and Cappella di San Tarasio**, where you'll find an early Tintoretto, *The Birth of John the Baptist*, and three wonderful altarpieces by Antonio Vivarini and Giovanni d'Alemagna.

The Pietà

Riva degli Schiavoni • Tues–Fri 10.15am–noon & 3–5pm, Sat & Sun 10.15am–1pm & 2–5pm • €3

The principal promenade of Castello, the **Riva degli Schiavoni**, has one outstanding monument: the **Pietà**, or Santa Maria della Visitazione. **Vivaldi** wrote many of his finest pieces for the orphanage attached to the church, where he worked as violin-master (1704–18) and later as choirmaster (1735–38). Giorgio Massari won a competition to redesign the church in 1736, and it's possible that Vivaldi advised him on its acoustics; building didn't actually begin until 1745, and the facade was finished only in 1906. The white and gold interior is crowned by a superb ceiling painting of *The Glory of Paradise* by **Giambattista Tiepolo**, who also painted the ceiling panel above the high altar. Today the Pietà is in effect a **concert hall** and ticket office: the in-house orchestra plays Vivaldi two or three times a week, with the *Four Seasons* always on the bill.

San Giorgio dei Greci and the Museo Dipinti Sacri Bizantini

Campiello dei Greci • **Church** Mon & Wed–Sat 9am–12.30pm & 2.30–4.30pm, Sun 9am–1pm • Free • **Museum** Daily 9am–5pm • €4

Stroll north along the flank of the Pietà and you'll come to **San Giorgio dei Greci**, focal point of the city's Greek community. The Greek presence was strong in Venice from the eleventh century, and grew stronger after Constantinople's capture by the Turks in 1453; by the close of the fifteenth century they had founded their own church, college and school here. The paintings on the church's iconostasis include several by a sixteenth-century Cretan artist called **Michael Damaskinós** and a few Byzantine pieces dating back as far as the twelfth century.

The *scuola* adjoining the church is home to the **Museo Dipinti Sacri Bizantini**, a collection of predominantly fifteenth- to eighteenth-century icons, many of them by the *Madoneri*, the school of Greek and Cretan artists working in Venice in that period.

Scuola di San Giorgio degli Schiavoni

Calle dei Furlani 3259A • Mon 2.45–6pm, Tues–Sat 9.15am–1pm & 2.45–6pm, Sun 9.15am–1pm • €5

The ground-floor hall of the **Scuola di San Giorgio degli Schiavoni** is one of the most beautiful rooms in Europe. Venice's resident Slavs (*Schiavoni*), most of whom were traders, set up a *scuola* to look after their interests in 1451; the present building dates from the early sixteenth century, and the whole interior looks more or less as it would have then. Entering it, you step straight from the street into the lower hall, the walls of which are decorated with a superb cycle of pictures created by Vittore Carpaccio between 1502 and 1509. Outstanding among them is *The Vision of St Augustine*, depicting the moment that Augustine, while writing to St Jerome, had a vision of Jerome's death.

The Arsenale

The dockyards and factories of the **Arsenale** were the foundations on which Venice's mercantile and military supremacy rested. A corruption of the Arabic *darsin'a* (house of industry), its very name is indicative of the strength of the city's trading links with the eastern Mediterranean. Construction of the Arsenale began in the early years of

the twelfth century, and by the third decade of the fifteenth century it had become the base for some 300 shipping companies, operating around 3000 vessels in excess of 200 tonnes.

Expansion of the Arsenale continued into the sixteenth century – Sanmicheli's covered dock for the state barge (the *Bucintoro*) was built in the 1540s, for example, and da Ponte's gigantic rope factory (the Tana) in 1579. By then, though, the maritime strength of Venice was past its peak; militarily, too, despite the conspicuous success at Lepanto in 1571, Venice was on the wane. When Napoleon took over the city in 1797 he burned down the wharves, sank the last *Bucintoro* and confiscated the remnant of the Venetian navy.

There's no public access to the Arsenale complex except during the Biennale, but you can get a look at part of it from the bridge connecting the Campo Arsenale and the Fondamenta dell'Arsenale. The main **gateway**, built by Antonio Gambello in 1460, was the first structure in Venice to employ the classical vocabulary of Renaissance architecture. The four **lions** to the side of the gateway must be the most photographed in the city: the two on the right were probably taken from Delos (at an unknown date); the larger pair were brought back from Piraeus in 1687 by Francesco Morosini after the reconquest of the Morea.

Museo Storico Navale

Campo San Biagio 2148 • Daily 10am–6pm (Padiglioni delle Navi opens at 10.30am) • €10 • When we went to press, the museum was only partially open and its future is uncertain; it's probable that you'll find major sections closed, and ticket prices accordingly reduced. See www.marina.difesa.it for more information

Occupying a vast old granary at the mouth of the Arsenale canal, the rambling **Museo Storico Navale** is chiefly of interest for its models of Venetian craft, from gondolas to the state barge known as the *Bucintoro* (these models were the equivalents of blueprints), and it gives a comprehensive picture of the working life of the Arsenale and the smaller boatyards of Venice. A couple of hundred metres along the *fondamenta*, at the foot of the wooden Arsenale bridge, a second section of the museum, the **Padiglioni delle Navi**, has a large collection of craft with Venetian connections.

San Pietro di Castello

Campo San Pietro • Mon–Sat 10am–5pm • €3, or Chorus Pass • chorusvenezia.org

San Pietro di Castello, the city's cathedral throughout the life of the Venetian Republic (San Marco was regarded as the doge's church), lies on the island of **San Pietro**, a slightly down-at-heel area where the chief activity is the repairing of boats. A church was raised here as early as the seventh century, but the present building was built nearly a millennium later, with a facade designed in the mid-sixteenth century by **Palladio**. Inside, the body of Lorenzo Giustiniani, the first Patriarch of Venice, who died in 1456, lies in the glass case within the elaborate high altar; otherwise there's little of interest.

The main approach to San Pietro is **Via Garibaldi**, the busiest commercial area in the eastern district and the widest street in the city, formed in 1808 when the greater part of the canal connecting the Bacino di San Marco to the broad inlet of the Canale di San Pietro was filled in. Head along the right-hand side of the street to reach Ponte di Quintavalle, which will take you across to the island.

The northern islands

The islands lying to the north of Venice – **San Michele**, **Murano**, **Burano** and **Torcello** – are the places to visit when the throng of tourists in the main part of the city becomes too oppressive; Murano has been a glass-producing centre for hundreds of years, while Burano was once renowned for its lace work. The main *vaporetto* stop for the northern islands is **Fondamente Nove** (or Nuove).

San Michele

A church was founded on **San Michele**, the innermost of the northern islands, in the tenth century, and a monastery was established in the thirteenth. Its best-known resident was Fra Mauro (d.1459), whose map of the world – the most accurate of its time – is now a precious possession of the Libreria Sansoviniana. The monastery was suppressed in the early nineteenth century, but in 1829, after a spell as an Austrian prison for political offenders, it was handed back to the Franciscans, who look after the church and the cemetery to this day.

San Michele in Isola

Daily: April–Sept 7.30am–6pm; Oct–March 7.30am–4pm • Free

The high brick wall around the cemetery gives way by the landing stage to the elegant white facade of **San Michele in Isola**, designed by Mauro Codussi in 1469. With this building, Codussi not only helped introduce Renaissance architecture to Venice, but also promoted the use of Istrian stone. Easy to carve yet resistant to water, it had been used as damp-proofing at ground level, but never before for a complete facade; it was to be used on the facades of most major buildings in Venice from the Renaissance onwards. Attached on the left, and entered from within the church, is the dainty **Cappella Emiliana**, built around 1530 by **Guglielmo dei Grigi**.

The cemetery

Daily: April–Sept 7.30am–6pm; Oct–March 7.30am–4pm

The main part of the island, through the cloisters, is the city **cemetery**, which was established by Napoleonic decree. The majority of Venetians lie here for just ten years or so, when their bones are dug up and removed to an ossuary: only those who can afford it stay longer. The cemetery is laid out in sections, the most dilapidated of which is for the Protestants (no. XV), **Ezra Pound**'s final resting place; Nobel laureate Joseph Brodsky is buried here too. In section XIV are the Greek and Russian Orthodox graves, including the restrained memorial stones of **Igor and Vera Stravinsky** and the more elaborate tomb of **Serge Diaghilev**.

Even with the grave-rotation system, the island is reaching full capacity, so in 1998 a competition was held for the **redevelopment** of San Michele. The winning entry, from English architect David Chipperfield, places a sequence of formal courtyards alongside a new funerary chapel and crematorium. The new section is an austerely beautiful place, resembling a cross between a necropolis and a philosopher's retreat.

Murano

The **glass-blowing industry** is what made **Murano** famous all over Europe, and today its furnaces constitute Venice's sole surviving manufacturing zone. The main *fondamente* of Murano are given over almost entirely to shops selling glasswork, and it's difficult to walk more than a few metres on this island without being invited to step inside a showroom – and once inside, you're likely to be pressured into forking out for some piece of kitsch which may not even have been made here. However, some of the showrooms have furnaces attached, and you shouldn't pass up the chance to see these astoundingly skilful craftsmen in action, even if they're only churning out little glass ponies and other knick-knacks.

The glass furnaces were moved to here from Venice as a safety measure in 1291, and so jealously did the Muranese guard their industrial secrets that for a long while they had the European monopoly on glass mirror-making. The glass-blowers of Murano were accorded various privileges not allowed to other artisans, such as being able to wear swords. From 1376 the offspring of a marriage between a Venetian nobleman and the daughter of a glass-worker were allowed to be entered into the *Libro d'Oro*, unlike the children of other cross-class matches.

6

San Pietro Martire

Fondamenta dei Vetrai • Mon–Fri 8am–7pm, Sat 11am–7pm, Sun noon–5pm • Free

When the Venetian Republic fell to Napoleon in 1797, there were seventeen churches on Murano; today only two are open. The Dominican church of **San Pietro Martire**, which was begun in 1363 and largely rebuilt after a fire in 1474, contains a handful of fine paintings, most notably **Giovanni Bellini**'s large *Madonna and Child with St Mark, St Augustine and Doge Barbarigo*; a later altarpiece by Bellini – an *Assumption* – has been in restoration for years, but may return soon. On the opposite side of the church, two pieces by Veronese stand out – *St Agatha in Prison* and *St Jerome in the Desert.*

Museo del Vetro

Fondamenta Giustinian 8 • Daily: April–Oct 10am–6pm; Nov–March 10am–5pm • €10, or €12 with Museo del Merletto (Burano), or Museum Pass • Ⓦ museovetro.visitmuve.it

The seventeenth-century Palazzo Giustinian is now home to the **Museo del Vetro** (Glass Museum), which reopened in 2015 after extensive renovation. The museum features glasswork dating back to the first century and examples of Murano glass from the fifteenth century onwards, and now has a large ground-floor space for one-off shows. Perhaps the most celebrated single item is the dark-blue Barovier marriage cup, dating from around 1460; it's on show in room 2 on the first floor, along with some splendid Renaissance enamelled and painted glass. But every room contains some amazing creations: a chalice with a spiral stem as slender as a strand of spaghetti; sixteenth-century platters that look like discs of scored ice; an eighteenth-century formal garden in miniature; and some stupendously ugly nineteenth-century pieces, such as the life-sized cockerel with individual glass feathers. A separate room is devoted to Murano beads and the techniques of Murano glass-making – look out for the extraordinary *murrine*, the patterned glass made by fusing and stretching of differently coloured rods.

Santi Maria e Donato

Calle San Donato • Mon–Sat 9am–noon & 3.30–7pm, Sun 3.30–7pm • Free

Murano's finest building is the Veneto-Byzantine church of **Santi Maria e Donato**, which was founded in the seventh century and rebuilt in the twelfth. Its beautiful **mosaic floor**, dated 1141 in the nave, mingles abstract patterns with images of beasts and birds – an eagle carries off a deer; two roosters carry off a fox slung from a pole. The church was originally dedicated to Mary, but in 1125 was rededicated when the relics of St Donatus were brought here from the Greek island, Kefalonia. Four splendid bones from an unfortunate dragon that was slain by the holy spit of Donatus are now hanging behind the altar. Above these, in the apse, is a fine twelfth-century mosaic of the Madonna.

Burano

After the peeling plaster and eroded stonework of the other lagoon settlements, the small, brightly painted houses of **Burano** come as something of a surprise. Local tradition says that the colours once enabled each fisherman to identify his house from out at sea, but nowadays the colours are used simply for decorative effect.

This is still largely a fishing community, the lagoon's main yield being shellfish of various kinds, such as *vongole* (tiny clams) and small crabs. The lives of the women of Burano used to be dominated by the **lace** industry, but the production of handmade lace is no longer a large-scale enterprise, and most of the stuff sold in the shops lining the narrow street leading from the *vaporetto* stop is produced by machine, outside Italy.

Museo del Merletto

Piazza Galuppi • Tues–Sun: April–Oct 10am–6pm; Nov–March 10am–5pm • €5, or €12 with Museo del Vetro (Murano), or Museum Pass • Ⓦ museomerletto.visitmuve.it

The Scuola del Merletto, home of the **Museo del Merletto**, is simply a school rather than a confraternity-cum-guild – unlike all other craftspeople in Venice, the lacemakers

had no guild to represent them, perhaps because the workforce was exclusively female. It was opened in 1872, when the indigenous crafting of lace had declined so far that it was left to one woman, Francesca Memo, to transmit the necessary skills to a younger generation of women. Although the *scuola* has not operated as a full-time school since the late 1960s and is now almost moribund, a few courses are still held here.

Reopened in 2011 after a major restoration, the *scuola*'s **museum** showcases around 150 examples of exquisite Murano lacework, along with paintings and a profusion of other documentation. The most engrossing, and poignant, display is the live demonstration by master lacemakers – these women are almost certainly the last practitioners of this highly specialized and exacting art.

Torcello

Torcello was settled as early as the fifth century, became the seat of the Bishop of Altinum from 638, and the home of about twenty thousand people by the fourteenth century, before being eclipsed by Venice – by the end of the fifteenth century Torcello was largely deserted and today fewer than a dozen people remain in residence.

Santa Maria dell'Assunta

Piazza di Torcello • Daily: March–Oct 10.30am–6pm; Nov–Feb 10am–5pm • €5

The main reason people come to Torcello today is to visit Venice's first cathedral, **Santa Maria dell'Assunta**, a Veneto-Byzantine building that evolved from the original seventh-century church. A stunning twelfth-century **mosaic** of the Madonna and Child, on a pure gold background, covers the semi-dome of the apse, resting on an eleventh-century mosaic frieze of the Apostles. In the centre of the frieze, below the window, is St Heliodorus, the first Bishop of Altinum, whose remains were brought here by the first settlers. It's interesting to compare this image with the gold-plated face mask given to his remains in a Roman sarcophagus in front of the original seventh-century altar. Ruskin described the view from the **campanile** as "one of the most notable scenes in this wide world", a verdict you can test for yourself (for a fee) if the campanile isn't undergoing one of its frequent bouts of restoration.

Santa Fosca

Piazza di Torcello • Daily 10am–4.30pm • Free

Santa Fosca was built in the eleventh and twelfth centuries for the body of the martyred St Fosca, brought to Torcello from Libya some time before 1011 and now resting under the altar. Though much restored, the church retains the Greek-cross form and a fine exterior apse; the bare interior, with beautiful marble columns and elegant brick arches, exudes a tranquillity that no number of visitors can quite destroy.

Museo di Torcello

Piazza di Torcello • Tues–Sun: March–Oct 10.30am–5.30pm; Nov–Feb 10am–5pm • €3

The well-laid-out **Museo di Torcello** includes thirteenth-century beaten-gold figures, jewellery, mosaic fragments (including pieces from the cathedral's *Last Judgement*, in which the hands of several artists can be distinguished) and a mishmash of pieces relating to the history of the area.

The southern islands

The islands in the section of the lagoon to the south of the city, enclosed by the **Lido** and **Pellestrina**, are scattered over a larger expanse of water than the northern lagoon, but the nearer islands – notably **San Giorgio Maggiore**, **La Giudecca** and **San Lazzaro** – are the more interesting ones. The farther-flung settlements of the southern lagoon have played a significant role in the history of Venice, but nowadays they have little going for them other than the pleasure of the trip.

San Giorgio Maggiore

May–Sept Mon–Sat 9.30am–6.30pm, Sun 8.30–10.30am & 2.30–6.30pm; Oct–April Mon–Sat 9.30am–dusk, Sun 8.30–10.30am & 2.30pm–dusk • Free, campanile €6

6

Palladio's church of **San Giorgio Maggiore**, facing the Palazzo Ducale across the Bacino di San Marco, is one of the most prominent and familiar of all Venetian landmarks. It is a startling building, with an impact that's enhanced by its isolation on an island of its own. The Venetians were the first to cover church interiors with white stucco, and the technique is used to dazzling effect in San Giorgio Maggiore – "Of all the colours, none is more proper for churches than white; since the purity of colour, as of the life, is particularly gratifying to God", wrote Palladio. Of its paintings, two stand out: Tintoretto's *The Fall of Manna* and *The Last Supper*, which hang in the chancel and were painted as a pair in 1592–94, the last years of the artist's life. On the left of the choir a corridor leads to the lift that takes you up the **campanile**, perhaps the best vantage point in the city.

The monastery

Guided tours hourly (in English or French at least 3 daily), daily: April–Sept 10am–5pm; Oct–March 10am–4pm • €13 • Ⓦ cini.it

Since the early ninth century there's been a church on this island, and at the end of the tenth century the lagoon's most important Benedictine monastery was established here. Now the home of the **Fondazione Giorgio Cini**, a cultural institute that hosts conferences and courses here, the monastery is one of the architectural wonders of the city. Two adjoining cloisters form the heart of the complex: the **Cloister of the Bay Trees**, planned by Giovanni Buora and built by his son Andrea in the two decades up to 1540; and the **Cloister of the Cypresses**, designed in 1579 by Palladio. Inside, there's a 128m-long **dormitory** by Giovanni Buora (c.1494), a **double staircase** (1641–43) and **library** (1641–53) by Longhena and, approached by an ascent through two anterooms, a magnificent **refectory** by Palladio (1560–62). A dazzlingly accurate reproduction of Veronese's great *Marriage at Cana* fills the end wall of the refectory; the original, stolen by Napoleon's army, is now in the Louvre.

La Giudecca

In the earliest records of Venice, the island of **La Giudecca** was known as Spina Longa, a name clearly derived from its shape; the modern name might refer to the Jews (*Giudei*) who were based here from the late thirteenth century until their removal to the Ghetto, or to the disruptive noble families who, from the ninth century, were shoved onto this chain of islets to keep them out of mischief (*giudicati* meaning "judged"). Before the banks of the Brenta became prestigious, the Giudecca was where the wealthiest aristocrats of early Renaissance Venice built their villas, and in places you can still see traces of their gardens. Wealth is still present, in the form of the luxury *Cipriani* and *Hilton* hotels at either end of the island; the latter occupies the immense Mulino Stucky, once a flour mill. In between are the workshops, boatyards and housing estates that make Giudecca one of the few places in Venice where tourism doesn't prevail.

The Redentore

Campo del Santissimo Redentore • Mon–Sat 10am–5pm • €3, or Chorus Pass • Ⓦ chorusvenezia.org

The Franciscan church of the **Redentore**, designed by Palladio in 1577, is the Giudecca's main monument. In 1575–76 Venice suffered an outbreak of bubonic plague that killed nearly fifty thousand people – virtually a third of the city's population. The Redentore was built in thanks for Venice's deliverance, and every year the doge and his senators attended a Mass in the church on the Feast of the Redentore. The procession walked to the church over a pontoon bridge from the Zattere, a ceremony perpetuated by the people of Venice on the third Sunday in July.

As in San Giorgio, the complex white surfaces of the Redentore modulate the natural light to draw the eye – and the mind – inward and upward. In the side chapels you'll

find a couple of pictures by Francesco Bassano and an *Ascension* by Tintoretto and his assistants, but the best paintings – including a *John the Baptist* by **Jacopo Bassano**, a *Baptism of Christ* by **Paolo Veronese** and *Madonna with Child and Angels* by **Alvise Vivarini** – are in the sacristy, which is rarely opened.

San Lazzaro degli Armeni

No foreign community has a longer pedigree in Venice than the Armenians: they were established by the end of the thirteenth century, and for around five hundred years have had a church within a few metres of the Piazza (in Calle degli Armeni). They are far less numerous now, and the most conspicuous sign of their presence is the island by the Lido, **San Lazzaro degli Armeni**, identifiable from the city by the onion-shaped top of its campanile.

The monastery

Guided tours daily, at 3.25pm • €6 • The #20 boat leaves San Zaccaria 15min before the tour starts and returns within 10min of the end

The Roman Catholic Armenian **monastery** was founded in 1717 by Manug di Pietro (known as Mechitar, "The Consoler"), and derived its name from the island's past function as a leper colony – Lazarus being the patron saint of lepers. The Armenian monks have always had a reputation as scholars and linguists, and the monastery's collection of precious books and manuscripts, some going back to the fifth century, is a highlight of the tour, along with a Tiepolo ceiling panel and the room in which Byron stayed while lending a hand with the preparation of an Armenian-English dictionary.

The Lido

For about eight centuries, the **Lido** was the focus of the annual hullaballoo of Venice's "Marriage to the Sea", when the doge went out to the Porto di Lido to drop a gold ring into the brine and then disembarked for Mass at San Nicolò al Lido. It was then an unspoilt strip of land, and remained so into the nineteenth century. By the twentieth century, however, it had become the smartest bathing resort in Italy, and although it's no longer as chic as it was when Thomas Mann set *Death in Venice* here, there's not much room on its beaches in summer. Unless you're staying at one of the seafront hotels, you won't be made welcome on the prime stretch of Lido sand. The ungroomed public beaches are at the northern and southern ends of the island.

ARRIVAL AND DEPARTURE — VENICE

BY PLANE

MARCO POLO AIRPORT

Venice's Marco Polo airport is a little over 7km north of the *centro storico*, on the edge of the lagoon.

Buses into the city The most inexpensive way of getting into the city is to take one of the bus services to the terminal at Piazzale Roma: the ATVO (Azienda Trasporti Veneto Orientale; @atvo.it) coach, which departs every 30min and takes around 20min (€8), or the ACTV (Azienda del Consorzio Trasporti Veneziano; @actv.it) bus #5, which is equally frequent but usually takes a little longer (it's a local bus service, so it picks up and puts down passengers between the airport and Piazzale Roma), and also costs €8.

TRAVEL CARDS

ACTV produces **Tourist Travel Cards** valid for **24 hours** (€20), **48 hours** (€30), **72 hours** (€40) and **seven days** (€60), which can be used on all ACTV services within Venice. Holders of a Rolling Venice Card (see page 354) can get a 72-hour ACTV card for €22. A supplement of €6/journey is payable if you want to use an ACTV pass for the airport buses. Travel cards are available from the tourist offices, at Piazzale Roma, the train station and the airport, and at the Ca' d'Oro, Rialto, Accademia, San Marco, San Zaccaria, Arsenale, Zattere, Fondamente Nove and Tronchetto *vaporetto* stops.

6

For €14 you can buy an ACTV bus+boat ticket, which gets you to Piazzale Roma then gives you one *vaporetto* journey of up to 90min.

Water-buses into the city If you'd prefer to approach the city by water, you could take one of the Alilaguna water-buses, which operate on three routes from the airport: the fare is €15 to any stop in central Venice, and €8 to Murano. All services are hourly, and the journey time to San Marco is usually a little over an hour.

Tickets and travel cards Ticket offices for Alilaguna, ATVO and ACTV buses are in the arrivals hall; in addition to single tickets, you can also get ACTV travel cards (see page 387) here – a wise investment for most visitors. ACTV passes are not valid on the Alilaguna service, nor on the ATVO bus.

Taxis into the city Water-taxi drivers tout for business in and around the arrivals hall. This is the most luxurious means of getting into the city, but it's expensive: you'll pay in the region of €110 to San Marco, for up to six people. Ordinary car-taxis cost about €50 to Piazzale Roma.

TREVISO AIRPORT

Treviso, 30km to the north of Venice, is a very small airport used chiefly by charter companies and budget airlines, some of which provide a bus link from the airport into Venice. An ATVO bus service to Venice's Piazzale Roma meets the incoming Ryanair flights; the fare is €12 one way and the journey takes 1hr 10min. Much quicker are the Barzi buses (10–15 daily) from Treviso airport to Tronchetto (Venice's main car park) – also costing €12, they take just 40min.

BY TRAIN OR BUS

Arriving by train or long-distance bus, you simply get off at the end of the line. The Piazzale Roma bus station and Santa Lucia train station are just a 5min walk from each other, linked by the Ponte della Costituzione, at the top of the Canal Grande, and both are well served by *vaporetto* services to the core of the city. Buses run from Piazzale Roma to various parts of the Veneto, but trains are generally quicker, more frequent, and no more expensive. Main Veneto train services from Venice are as follows:

Destinations Bassano (hourly; 1hr 15min–1hr 40min); Conegliano (every 30min; 50min–1hr 10min); Padua (every 15min; 25–50min); Treviso (every 30min; 30–40min); Verona (every 30min; 1hr 10min–2hr 25min); Vicenza (every 30min; 30min–1hr 15min).

BY CAR

Visitors arriving by car must leave their vehicle either on the mainland or in one of the city's car parks.

City car parks Prices at the Piazzale Roma car park or the ever-expanding Tronchetto, Europe's largest car park, vary according to the time of year, the length of stay and the size of car, but it's never cheap, and in summer the tailbacks can be horrendous. It's better to use the less expensive car parks on the mainland.

Mainland car parks There's an open-air San Giuliano car park at Mestre (open summer, Easter and during Carnevale), linked by ACTV buses with central Venice or, alternatively, the terminal at Fusina, just south of Mestre, open year-round and connected by water-buses with Piazza San Marco (ACTV passes not valid).

GETTING AROUND

Venice has two interlocking street systems – the canals and the pavements. The #1, #2 and the night service all shuttle along the Canal Grande, but most **water-buses** skirt the city centre, connecting points on the periphery and the outer islands. Taking a water-bus is usually the quickest way of getting between far-flung points, but in many cases the speediest way of getting from A to B is **on foot** – you don't have to run, for instance, to cover the distance from the Piazza to the Rialto Bridge a lot quicker than the #1.

WATER-BUSES

There are two basic types of boat: *vaporetti*, which are the lumbering workhorses used on the Canal Grande and other heavily used routes, and *motoscafi*, smaller vessels employed on routes where the volume of traffic isn't as great.

Fares The standard fare is an exorbitant €7.50 for a single journey (but there's a €5 ticket for one-stop trips such as a crossing from San Zaccaria to San Giorgio Maggiore, or Záttere to Giudecca); the ticket is valid for 75min, and for any number of changes of water-bus, as long as you're travelling from point A to point B – it cannot, in other words, be used as a return ticket. Should you have more than one piece of large luggage, you're supposed to pay €7.50 for each additional item. Children under 4 travel free.

Tickets Tickets are available from most landing stages, from *tabacchi*, from shops displaying the ACTV sign, from the tourist offices and from the ACTV office at Piazzale Roma (daily: summer 6am–11.30pm; winter 6am–8pm). Tickets can also be bought on board at the standard price, as long as you ask the attendant as soon as you get on board; if you are caught without a valid ticket, you could be liable for a spot-fine of between 40 and 150 times the ticket price. Note that all tickets and travel cards have to be swiped before each journey at the meter-like machines which are at every stop.

TRAGHETTI

There are just four bridges spanning the Canal Grande – the Ponte Calatrava (at Piazzale Roma), Ponte dei Scalzi (at the train station), Ponte di Rialto and Ponte dell'Accademia – so the *traghetti* (gondola ferries) that cross it can be useful time-savers. Costing €2 (€0.70 if you're a resident), they are also the only cheap way of getting a ride on a gondola, albeit a stripped-down version, with none of the trimmings

WATER-BUS ROUTES

What follows is a run-through of the **routes** that visitors are most likely to find useful. Be warned that so many services call at San Marco, San Zaccaria, Rialto, Piazzale Roma and the train station that the stops at these points are spread out over a long stretch of waterfront, so you might have to walk past several stops before finding the one you need. Note also that the San Marco stop has two sections – San Marco Vallaresso and San Marco Giardinetti – which are just metres from each other, and that the San Zaccaria stop is as close to the Piazza as are the San Marco stops.

DAYTIME ROUTES

#1: The #1 is the slowest of the water-buses, and the one you're likely to use most often. It starts at Piazzale Roma, calls at every stop on the Canal Grande except San Samuele, works its way along the San Marco waterfront to Sant'Elena, then goes over to the Lido. The #1 runs every 20min between 5am and 6.20am, every 10min between 6.20am and 10pm, and every 20min between 10pm and 11.40pm. There's also a #1B service, which runs shuttles between Piazzale Roma and Rialto from 9.30am to 4.30pm, every 12min.

#2: The timetable of the #2 is immensely complicated but basically, from around 9am to 5pm, its clockwise route takes it from San Zaccaria to San Giorgio Maggiore, Giudecca (Zitelle, Redentore and Palanca), Zattere, San Basilio, Sacca Fisola, Tronchetto, Piazzale Roma and the train station, then down the Canal Grande (calling only at Rialto, San Tomà, San Samuele and Accademia) to San Marco Giardinetti; the anticlockwise version calls at the same stops. It runs in both directions every 12min. From around 5am to 9am, however, the route is truncated, with the #2 running back and forth between San Zaccaria and Rialto, via Giudecca, every 20min (ie it doesn't cover the lower section of the Canal Grande). In summer the #2 is extended out to the Lido, via Giardini.

#4.1/4.2: The circular service runs right round the core of Venice, with a short detour at the northern end to San Michele and Murano. The #4.1 travels anticlockwise, the #4.2 clockwise, and both run every 20min from about 6.10am to 7.30pm; after that, the #4.1/4.2 together act as a shuttle service between Murano and Fondamente Nove, running every 20min until around 11.20pm.

#5.1/5.2: Similar to the #4.1/4.2, this route also circles Venice, but heads out to the Lido (rather than Murano) at the easternmost end of the loop. The #5.1 runs anticlockwise, the #5.2 clockwise, and both run fast through the Giudecca canal, stopping only at Zattere, San Basilio and Santa Marta between San Zaccaria and Piazzale Roma. Both run every 20min from around 6am to midnight. In the early morning (4.30–6.20am) the #5.1 doesn't do a complete lap of the city – instead it departs every 20min from Fondamenta Nove and proceeds via the train station and Zattere to the Lido, where it terminates; from about 11pm to 12.20am the #5.2 goes no farther than the train station.

#12: For most of the day, from 4.20am until 11.20pm, the #12 runs every 30min from Fondamente Nove (approximately hourly after 8.40pm), calling first at Murano-Faro before heading on to Mazzorbo, Burano (from where there is a connecting shuttle to Torcello) and Treporti; it runs with the same frequency in the opposite direction.

NIGHT SERVICE

#N: The main night service (11.30pm–4.30am) is a selective fusion of the #1 and #2 routes, running every 30min from the Lido to San Zaccaria via the Canal Grande, train station, Piazzale Roma, Tronchetto, Zattere and Giudecca – and vice versa. Other night services connect Venice with Murano and Burano, running to and from Fondamente Nove (every hour for Burano; every 30min for Murano) between 11.30pm and 4.15am.

and no padded seats: most locals stand rather than sit. There used to be almost thirty gondola *traghetti* across the Canal Grande, but today there are just seven, and most of these are virtually defunct; only two are in frequent operation – Santa Sofia–Rialto and San Tomà–Sant'Angelo. Their hours are irregular, but 8am–7pm is fairly standard in summer.

WATER-TAXIS

Venice's water-taxis are sleek and speedy vehicles that can penetrate most of the city's canals, and can carry up to ten people. Unfortunately they are possibly the most expensive form of taxi in Western Europe, with even a short trip from the train station to Rialto costing around €50. All sorts of surcharges are levied as well: €10 for each extra person if there are more than five people in the party; €5 for each piece of luggage in excess of five items; €20 for a ride between 10pm and 7am.

Hiring a taxi There are five ways of getting a taxi: go to one of the main stands (at Piazzale Roma, the train station, Rialto and San Marco Vallaresso); find one in the process of disgorging its passengers; call one by phone (T 041 522 2303); email at E info@motoscafivenezia.it; or book through

6

the website, ⓦ motoscafivenezia.it. If you phone for one, you'll pay a surcharge, of course. And if your hotel concierge calls a taxi for you, the surcharge could be even worse.

GONDOLAS

The gondola is no longer a form of transport but rather an adjunct of the tourist industry. But however much the gondola's image has become tarnished, it is an astonishingly graceful craft, perfectly designed for negotiating the tortuous and shallow waterways: a gondola displaces so little water, and the gondoliers are so dexterous, that there's hardly a canal in the city they can't negotiate.

Fares To hire one costs €80/40min for up to six passengers, rising to €100 between 7pm and 8am; you pay an extra €40 for every additional 20min, or €50 from 7pm to 8am. Further hefty surcharges will be levied should you require the services of an on-board accordionist or tenor. Even though the tariff is set by the local authorities, it's been known for gondoliers to extort even higher rates than these – if you do decide to go for a ride, establish the charge before setting off.

Gondola stands To minimize the chances of being ripped off, only take a boat from one of the following official gondola stands: west of Piazza San Marco at Calle Vallaresso, Campo San Moisè or Campo Santa Maria del Giglio; immediately north of the Piazza at Bacino Orseolo; on the Molo, in front of the Palazzo Ducale; outside the *Danieli* hotel on Riva degli Schiavoni; at the train station; at Piazzale Roma; at Campo Santa Sofia, near the Ca' d'Oro; at San Tomà; or by the Rialto Bridge on Riva Carbon.

INFORMATION

Tourist office Venice's main tourist office is at Calle dell'Ascensione 71/F, in the corner of the Piazza's arcades (daily 9am–7pm; ⓣ 041 523 0399; ⓦ veneziaunica.it); this is also the main outlet for information on the rest of the Veneto. Another office is located at the station (daily 8am–9pm). Other offices are in the airport arrivals area (daily 9am–7pm) and at the multistorey car park at Piazzale Roma (daily 7am–8pm).

Listings magazines The English-Italian magazine *Un Ospite di Venezia* (ⓦ unospitedivenezia.it) gives information on exhibitions and events, plus extras such as *vaporetto* timetables; it's free from the reception desks of many four- and five-star hotels. The fullest source of information, though, is *VENews* (€3; ⓦ venezianews.it), published ten times each year and sold at newsstands all over the city.

ACCOMMODATION

Limitless demand for holiday accommodation has made Venice the most expensive city in Western Europe, and the **high season** here is longer than anywhere else in the country – it officially runs from March 15 to Nov 15 and then from Dec 21 to Jan 6, but many places don't recognize the existence of a low season any more. Several hotels, on the other hand, lower their prices in Aug, the month in which many Italians – including Venetian restaurateurs and bar owners – decamp to the beaches and the mountains. It's wisest to book your place at least three months in advance; if you're planning a peak-season visit, six months would be more sensible.

HOTELS AND LOCANDE

Venice has well in excess of three hundred hotels, ranging from spartan one-star joints to five-star *lusso* establishments charging over €1500/night for the best double room in high season. Bear in mind that you pay through the nose for your proximity to Piazza San Marco, so if you want maximum comfort for your money, decide how much you can afford and then look for a place outside the San Marco *sestiere* – after all, it's not far to walk, wherever you're staying. If you are looking for a small family-run establishment, a *locanda* – guesthouse – might fit the bill: Venice's best *locande* offer a standard of accommodation equivalent to three- or even four-star hotels (24hr room service is just about the only facility they don't provide), but often at a lower cost.

SAN MARCO

★Ai Do Mori Calle Larga S. Marzo 658 ⓣ 041 528 9293, ⓦ hotelaidomori.com; map p.358. Very friendly, and situated a few paces off the Piazza, this is a top recommendation for budget travellers. The top-floor room has a private terrace looking over the roofs of the Basilica and the Torre dell'Orologio, and is one of the most attractive (and, of course, expensive) one-star rooms in the city. All rooms have their own bathroom. **€160**

Al Gambero Calle dei Fabbri 4687 ⓣ 041 522 4384, ⓦ locandaalgambero.com; map p.358. Three-star hotel in an excellent position a short distance off the north side of the Piazza; many of the 26 rooms overlook a canal that's on the standard gondola route from the Bacino Orseolo. There's a busy restaurant on the ground floor. **€250**

Art Deco Calle delle Botteghe 2966 ⓣ 041 277 0558, ⓦ locandaartdeco.com; map p.358. This cosy *locanda* has a seventeenth-century *palazzo* setting, but the interior is strewn with 1930s and '40s objects, and the pristinely white bedrooms have modern wrought-iron furniture. **€210**

★Casa Petrarca Calle delle Schiavini 4386 ⓣ 041 520 0430, ⓦ casapetrarca.com; map p.358. A very hospitable one-star, one of the cheapest hotels within a stone's throw of the Piazza – but make sure you contact them first, as it only has seven rooms. **€180**

Fiorita Campiello Nuovo 3457 ⓣ 041 523 4754, ⓦ locandafiorita.com; map p.358. Welcoming *locanda*

with just ten rooms, so it's crucial to book well in advance. Rooms are all en suite and decorated in eighteenth-century style, and many are spacious. **€180**

★ **Novecento** Calle del Dose 2683 ⓣ 041 241 3765, ⓦ locandanovecento.it; map p.358. Beautiful, intimate and very welcoming *locanda* with nine individually decorated doubles and luxurious bathrooms. Styling is ethnic/eclectic (furnishings from Morocco, China, Japan and Egypt), and there's a small courtyard for breakfast. **€280**

Orseolo Corte Zorzi 1083 ⓣ 041 520 4827, ⓦ locandaorseolo.com; map p.358. Three four-room B&Bs are joined to form this superb family-run *locanda* overlooking the Orseolo canal, 50m north of Piazza San Marco. Most rooms are spacious and light, the breakfasts are substantial and the staff extremely hospitable. Entrance is through a gate in Campo S. Gallo. **€260**

Rosa Salva Calle Fiubera 951 ⓣ 041 241 3323, ⓦ rosasalvahotel.it; map p.358. If you're looking for a stylish but not madly expensive hotel right in the heart of the city, you can't do better than the new *Rosa Salva* hotel. Run by the family who own the city's best-known *pasticceria*-caffès (there's a branch next door), it has 22 rooms (mostly spacious, by the standards of central Venice) that are furnished and decorated in contemporary style, in which bare wood, leather and soft metallic tones predominate. This zone of San Marco is very busy in high season, but soundproofed windows keep noise to a minimum. **€260**

DORSODURO

Accademia Villa Maravege Fondamenta Bollani 1058 ⓣ 041 521 0188, ⓦ pensioneaccademia.it; map p.358. Once the Russian embassy, this three-star seventeenth-century villa has a devoted following, not least on account of its garden, which occupies a promontory at the convergence of two canals, with a view of a small section of the Canal Grande. **€250**

Agli Alboretti Rio Terrà Foscarini 884 ⓣ 041 523 0058, ⓦ aglialboretti.com; map p.358. Friendly and popular family-run three-star, well situated right next to the Accademia. The rooms are quite plain, but all have a/c and TV, and its high-season prices compare very favourably with those of most others in this category. **€180**

★ **Ca' Maria Adele** Rio Terrà dei Catecumeni 111 ⓣ 041 520 3078, ⓦ camariaadele.it; map p.358. Five of the twelve rooms in this very upmarket *locanda* are so-called "theme rooms", with every item designed to enhance a particular atmosphere – the Sala Noir, for example, is a "voluptuous and hot" creation in cocoa and spice tones. The non-themed accommodation is less artfully conceived (and a lot cheaper), but spacious and very comfortable. **€500**

★ **Ca' Pisani** Rio Terà Foscarini 979/A ⓣ 041 240 1411, ⓦ capisanihotel.it; map p.358. This glamorous 29-room four-star, just a few metres from the Accademia, created quite a stir when it opened in 2000, partly because of its location, on the opposite side of the Canal Grande from its top-echelon peers, but chiefly because of its high-class retro look. Taking its cue from the Art Deco style of the 1930s and 1940s, the *Ca' Pisani* makes heavy use of dark wood and chrome, a welcome break from the Renaissance and Rococo flourishes that tend to prevail in Venice's upmarket establishments. **€300**

DD 724 Ramo da Mula 724 ⓣ 041 277 0262, ⓦ thecharminghouse.com; map p.358. In a city awash with nostalgia, the cool high-grade modernist style of this *locanda*, right by the Guggenheim, comes as a refreshing change. It has just seven rooms, each of them impeccably cool and luxurious – and not a Murano chandelier in sight. As you'll see on the website, the same team runs a couple of other similarly sleek properties: a *palazzo* by Santa Maria Formosa, containing four suites; and a single apartment close to *DD 724*. **€370**

★ **La Calcina** Zattere ai Gesuati 780 ⓣ 041 520 6466, ⓦ lacalcina.com; map p.358. Charismatic three-star hotel in the house where Ruskin wrote much of *The Stones of Venice*. From the more expensive rooms you can gaze across to the Redentore, a church that gave him apoplexy. All rooms have parquet floors (unusual in Venice) and antique wooden furniture. Its restaurant is good, too. **€300**

★ **Locanda San Barnaba** Calle del Traghetto 2785 ⓣ 041 241 1233, ⓦ locanda-sanbarnaba.com; map p.358. Exceptionally pleasant and nicely priced *locanda* right by the Ca' Rezzonico. The "superior double" rooms have eighteenth-century frescoes on the ceilings, and one has a really enormous bath. **€180**

SAN POLO AND SANTA CROCE

Al Ponte Mocenigo Fondamenta Rimpetto Mocenigo 2063, Santa Croce ⓣ 041 524 4797, ⓦ alpontemocenigo.com; map p.376. The relaxed and welcoming Ponte Mocenigo is one of the best two-stars in the city. Located in a quiet quarter of Santa Croce, but close to the San Stae *vaporetto* stop, the main building has just ten rooms, which are focused on a beautiful little courtyard where breakfast is served in good weather. Most of the rooms are a good size, with the best ones overlooking the San Stae canal. The rooms in the adjacent annexe are comfortable too, but it's better to be in the main building. **€150**

★ **Ca' Favretto-San Cassiano** Calle della Rosa, Santa Croce 2232 ⓣ 041 524 1768, ⓦ sancassiano.it; map p.376. Beautiful 35-room four-star with some rooms looking across the Canal Grande towards the Ca' d'Oro. Has very helpful staff, a nice courtyard garden and a grand entrance hall. It was once the home of the nineteenth-century painter Giacomo Favretto, and is fitted out in the style of the period. Discounts for stays of three days or more. **€280**

★ **Ca' San Giorgio** Salizada del Fontego dei Turchi 1725, Santa Croce ⓣ 041 275 9177, ⓦ casangiorgio.com; map p.376. Exposed timber beams and walls of raw

6

brick advertise the age of the Gothic *palazzo* that's occupied by this fine little *locanda*, while the bedrooms are tastefully and very comfortably furnished in quasi-antique style. The gorgeous top-floor suite has its own rooftop terrace. **€230**

CANNAREGIO

Abbazia Calle Priuli 68 041 717 333, abbaziahotel.com; map p.376. One of Cannaregio's most restful hotels, the light-filled *Abbazia* occupies a former Carmelite monastery (the monks attached to the Scalzi still live in a building adjoining the hotel) and provides three-star amenities without losing its air of quasi-monastic austerity. There's a delightful garden too, and the staff are exceptionally helpful. **€200**

★ Al Ponte Antico Calle dell'Aseo 5768 041 241 1944, alponteantico.com; map p.376. This plush four-star *residenza*, a few metres upstream of the Rialto Bridge, is one of the best small hotels in the city. Decorated throughout in eighteenth-century style, with lashings of gold and blue satin in the bedrooms, it has four grades of accommodation – the best rooms, the "Deluxe", have huge windows that open onto the Canal Grande. Exceptionally nice staff, too. **€330**

Bernardi Semenzato Calle dell'Oca 4366 041 522 7257, hotelbernardi.com; map p.376. Very well priced two-star hidden in a tiny alleyway close to Campo S. Apostoli, with bright, basic and good-sized rooms. **€110**

Ca' Gottardi Calle Noal 2283 041 275 9333, cagottardi.com; map p.376. A smart and very welcoming three-star boutique hotel, located just off Strada Nova, the main route through Cannaregio. The prevailing décor is a modern facsimile of eighteenth-century style, and many of the rooms overlook the Rio de Noal, which opens into the Canal Grande opposite Ca' Pesaro. **€250**

Giorgione Calle Larga dei Proverbi 4587 041 522 5810, hotelgiorgione.com; map p.376. This plush but very reasonably priced four-star, very close to Santi Apostoli, has a more personal touch than many of the city's upmarket hotels – it has been run by the same family for many generations. Amenities include a quiet garden and a pool table, and some of the 76 well-equipped rooms have a small private terrace. **€240**

Locanda Leon Bianco Corte Leon Bianco 5629 041 523 3572, leonbianco.it; map p.376. Friendly and charming three-star in a superb location not far from the Rialto Bridge, tucked away beside the decaying Ca' da Mosto. There are only eight rooms, but three of them overlook the Canal Grande (for which you pay a premium, of course) and most of the others are spacious and tastefully furnished– one room even has a huge fresco copied from a Tiepolo ceiling. **€210**

★ Palazzo Abadessa Calle Priuli 4011 041 241 3784, abadessa.com; map p.376. This gorgeous four-star *residenza d'epoca* is a meticulously restored *palazzo* behind the church of Santa Sofia; all fifteen of its bedrooms (some of them huge) are nicely furnished with genuine antiques, and there's a lovely secluded garden as well. **€300**

CASTELLO

Casa Verardo Calle della Chiesa 4765 041 528 6127, casaverardo.it; map p.358. A fine three-star hotel occupying a nicely refurbished sixteenth-century *palazzo* between San Marco and Campo Santa Maria Formosa. There are 23 well-equipped rooms with a breakfast terrace downstairs, a small garden, a sun lounge at the top and another terrace attached to the priciest of the rooms. **€230**

Gabrielli Riva degli Schiavoni 4110 041 523 1580, hotelgabrielli.it; map p.376. Occupying a beautifully converted Gothic palace, the 103-room *Gabrielli* offers four-star comforts and *Danieli*-style views across the Bacino di San Marco for a fraction of the price of the *Danieli*. It also has an attractive little courtyard and a lovely small garden. **€250**

★ La Residenza Campo Bandiera e Moro 3608 041 528 5315, venicelaresidenza.com; map p.376. This fourteenth-century *palazzo* is a mid-budget gem (in Venetian terms), occupying much of one side of a tranquil square just off the main waterfront. It's pricier than many two-stars, but the recently refurbished rooms are very spacious (rare at this price) and elegant, and the management extremely *simpatico*. Payment by cash is preferred for short stays. **€240**

HOSTELS

Venice has a large hostel over on Giudecca and a few other hostel-like establishments – most run by religious foundations – offering basic accommodation. Some of the latter are more expensive than one-star hotels and B&Bs; we've listed only the low-cost options.

Domus Civica Calle Campazzo, San Polo 3082 041 721 103, domuscivica.com; map p.376. This Catholic women's student hostel is open to tourists from mid-June to mid-Sept. Most rooms are double with running water; showers free; no breakfast; midnight curfew. Dorms **€30**

Foresteria Valdese Calle S. Maria Formosa, Castello 5170 041 528 6797, foresteriavenezia.it; map p.376. Run by Waldensians, this hostel is installed in a wonderful *palazzo* at the end of Calle Lunga S. Maria Formosa, with flaking frescoes in the rooms and a large communal salon. It has bedrooms ranging from singles to small dormitories that can accommodate up to ten; most of the smaller rooms have a private bathroom. Registration 9am–1pm & 6–8pm. Dorms **€40**, doubles **€115**

Ostello Santa Fosca S. Maria dei Servi, Cannaregio 2372 041 715 775, ostellosantafosca.it; map p.376. Student-run hostel in an atmospheric former Servite convent in a quiet part of Cannaregio, with rudimentary bedrooms sleeping two to seven people (some of the larger rooms are female-only), nearly all of them with

6

B&BS AND SELF-CATERING

As you may expect in a city in which demand is such that someone could get away with charging more than €100 for the privilege of sleeping on a mattress in the attic, much of Venice's accommodation is not terribly attractive, but many **B&Bs** are excellent, offering rooms that compare favourably with budget hotels – and some are in effect small-scale *locande*, with rooms of three-star standard or better. Full listings can be found at turismovenezia.it.

If you're staying in Venice for at least a week, it can be worth looking at a **self-catering apartment**. The best sources are veniceapartment.com, viewsonvenice.comand and homeaway.co.uk. AirBnB is of course another option, but be aware that this company – and others in the same business – has generated considerable ill-feeling in Venice, where it's seen as bearing a lot of responsibility for the dearth of affordable rented accommodation for local people; there is widespread support here for the sort of restrictions on AirBnB that have been imposed in Berlin.

shared bathrooms. 12.30pm curfew. Dorms **€25**

Generator Hostel Fondamenta delle Zitelle, Giudecca 86 041 523 8211, generatorhostels.com; map p.358. The city's former HI hostel, now thoroughly revamped as one of the Generator group of hostels, occupies a superb location looking over the water to San Marco. Rooms are bright, spacious, comfortable and even stylish, ranging from doubles to sixteen-bed mini-dorms (some of them female-only). Prices, however, are rather higher than you'll pay in a bog-standard hostel – double rooms here can cost as much as some three-stars. Breakfast and sheets are included in the price – but remember to add the expense of the boat from central Venice. No curfew. Dorms **€44**

CAMPING

There are some unlovely campsites near the airport – better to head out to the outer edge of the lagoon, to the Litorale del Cavallino, which stretches from Punta Sabbioni to Jesolo and has around sixty thousand pitches, many quite luxurious; from Punta Sabbioni the #14 *vaporetto* goes to San Zaccaria via the Lido. Alternatively, you could camp on the mainland at Fusina; a Linea Fusina water-bus links Fusina to the Zattere in central Venice (ACTV tickets not valid), taking 25min, with an hourly service from 8am until around 10pm (late May–Sept), or around 7.30pm for the rest of the year.

LITORALE DEL CAVALLINO

Marina di Venezia Via Montello 6 041 966 146, marinadivenezia.it. This big and well-equipped four-star site is a couple of kilometres from the Punta Sabbioni *vaporetto* stop, on the seaward side of the Litorale del Cavallino, adjoining the beach and the huge AquaMarina waterpark. Has a big range of accommodation, with seven-berth a/c chalets at the top. Open early May to mid-Oct. Tent pitch **€32** plus **€13** per person, chalets and bungalows from **€150**

Miramare Lungomare Dante Alighieri 29 041 966 150, camping-miramare.it. A three-star site, located at the mouth of the lagoon, very near the *vaporetto* stop, with bungalows and maxi caravans. Open April–Oct. Tent pitch **€20** plus **€9** per person, bungalows from **€80**

FUSINA

Camping Fusina Via Moranzani 93 041 547 0055, campingfusina.com. Situated at the mouth of the Brenta River, this is the closest campsite to central Venice. Marketing itself as a "tourist village", it has cabins as well as pitches for tents and campervans, plus a pizzeria, bar, beer garden, internet café and 24hr laundry. The boat stop for Venice is only 100m from the front gate, and there's a bus service too. Open all year. Tent pitch **€10** plus **€12** per person, cabins from **€50**

EATING

Venice has fewer good moderately priced **restaurants** than any other major Italian city, but there's a fair number of places serving genuine Venetian cuisine at sensible prices – which in the Venetian context means in the region of €35–40/person. A distinctive aspect of the Venetian social scene is the **bácaro**, which in its purest form is a bar that offers a range of snacks called **cicheti** (sometimes spelled *ciccheti*); the array will typically include *polpette* (small beef and garlic meatballs), *carciofini* (artichoke hearts), eggs, anchovies, *polipi* (baby octopus or squid) and tomatoes, peppers and courgettes cooked in oil. Some *bácari* also produce one or two more substantial dishes each day, such as risotto or seafood pasta. Excellent food is also served at many of Venice's **osterie** (or *ostarie*), the simplest of which are indistinguishable from *bácari*, while others have sizeable dining areas. We've classified our bars and restaurants according to which aspect of the business draws most of the customers, but if you're looking for a simple meal in a particular area of the city, be sure to check both bar and restaurant listings.

6

PICNICKING IN VENICE

The price of restaurants in Venice makes **picnicking** an attractive option, but you can't just spread your lunch wherever you like: by-laws forbid picnicking on the Piazza and other busy spots, and it's illegal to sit down on any bridge. To be on the safe side always use a bench, not the pavement.

The best places to buy food – especially fruit and veg – are the markets that are held in various squares every day except Sunday: the biggest and best is of course the **Rialto** (see page 369), but you'll also find stalls on **Campo Santa Maria Formosa (Castello)**, **Campo Santa Margherita (Dorsoduro)** and between **Ponte delle Guglie and Campiello dell'Anconeta** in **Cannaregio**. Fresh produce is also sold from barges moored by **Campo San Barnaba (Dorsoduro)** and at the top end of **Via Garibaldi (Castello)**. Virtually every parish has its **alimentari**, and Venice has many **supermarkets** too.

CAFÉS, PASTICCERIE AND GELATERIE

As in every Italian city, Venice's cafés are central to its social life, and you'll never be more than a couple of minutes from a decent one. In addition to their marvellous local confections, many *pasticcerie* also serve coffee, but will have at most a few bar stools. Calorie control is further jeopardized by Venice's terrific *gelaterie*.

SAN MARCO

Florian Piazza S. Marco 56–59 ⓣ 041 520 5641, ⓦ caffeflorian.com; map p.358. The most famous café in Venice began life in 1720, when Florian Francesconi's *Venezia Trionfante* (Venice Triumphant) opened for business here, and the place is still redolent of the eighteenth century, though the gorgeous interior – a frothy confection of mirrors, stucco and frescoes – is a nineteenth-century pastiche. Its prices match its pedigree: a simple cappuccino at an outside table will set you back around €12, and you'll have to take out a mortgage for a cocktail; if the "orchestra" is playing, you'll be taxed another €6 for the privilege of hearing them. (*Quadri* and *Lavena* levy a similar surcharge.) Daily 9am–midnight (but often closes earlier in winter); closed Tues in winter.

Marchini Time Campo S. Luca 4589 ⓣ 041 241 3087; map p.358. Sample the succulent *Marchini* pastries with a cup of top-grade coffee at this sleek café. Daily 7.30am–8.30pm.

Quadri Piazza S. Marco 120–124 ⓣ 041 522 2105; map p.358. *Quadri* can claim an even longer lineage than *Florian*, as coffee has been on sale here since the seventeenth century, and sit-down prices are in the same price league too, though you can save a lot by taking your cappuccino at the tiny bar. It's also the one Piazza café you're sure to find open late on a winter night. On the other hand, it's not as pretty as *Florian*, and its name doesn't have quite the same lustre, partly because Austrian officers patronized it during the occupation, while the natives stuck with *Florian*. Daily 9am–midnight.

DORSODURO

Il Caffè Campo S. Margherita 2963 ⓣ 041 528 7998; map p.358. Known locally as *Caffè Rosso* for its big red sign, this small, atmospheric, old-fashioned café-bar is a student favourite. Good sandwiches, and lots of seats outside in the *campo*. Mon–Sat 7am–1am.

★ **Il Doge** Campo S. Margherita 3058 ⓣ 041 523 4607; map p.358. Well-established, very friendly and extremely good hole-in-the-wall *gelateria*, which also does a superb *granita*. Mon–Sat 9am–midnight, Sun 9am–9pm, but often closes earlier in off-season; closed Nov & Dec.

Nico Zattere ai Gesuati 922 ⓣ 041 522 5293; map p.358. This café-*gelateria*, which has occupied its prime location overlooking the Giudecca canal for the best part of ninety years, is celebrated for an artery-clogging creation called a *gianduiotto da passeggio* – a paper cup with a block of praline ice cream drowned in whipped cream. Daily (except Thurs) 6.45am–10pm.

SAN POLO

Caffè del Doge Calle dei Cinque 609 ⓣ 041 522 7787, ⓦ caffedeldoge.com; map p.358. Fantastically good coffee (they supply many of the city's bars and restaurants), served in a chic minimalist setup very close to the Rialto Bridge. Daily 7am–7pm.

CANNAREGIO

Gelateria Ca' d'Oro Strada Nova 4273 ⓣ 041 522 8982; map p.376. A wide range of wonderfully smooth ice creams is served at Andrea Busolin's long-established shop. Daily 10am–midnight (10pm in winter).

Il Gelatone Rio Terà Maddalena 2063 ⓣ 041 720 631; map p.376. Despite the recent arrival of *Grom*, this place or the *Ca' d'Oro* would still win a local vote for the title Best Gelateria in Cannaregio. Daily: Oct–April 10am–9pm; May–Sept 10am–10.30pm.

Pasticceria Nobile Calle del Pistor 1318 ⓣ 041 720 731; map p.376. Established back in the 1930s, this is still the classiest café in Cannaregio, and is always thronged with locals at breakfast and after work; the pastries are excellent. Tues–Sun 7am–8.30pm; closed July & two weeks in Feb.

CASTELLO

★ **Cioccolateria VizioVirtù** Calle del Forner 5988 ⓣ 041 275 0149, ⓦ viziovirtu.com; map p.358. Venice's

best chocolates, and the most expensive *gelati* in town. Daily 10am–7pm; closed Aug.

La Boutique del Gelato Salizzada S. Lio 5727 ⊕ 041 522 3283; map p.358. Top-grade ice creams – as good as any in Venice – are created at this tiny outlet. Daily mid-Feb to Nov 10.30am–8.30pm (sometimes later in high season).

Pasticceria Chiusso Salizzada dei Greci 3306 ⊕ 041 523 1611; map p.358. An award-winning *pasticceria* (known locally as *Da Pierino*, after the owner), with terrific buttery home-made pastries and very nice coffee too. Always packed at the start of the day, as people drop in for a coffee and cornetto on their way to work. Mon, Tues & Thurs–Sun 7am–8pm.

Rosa Salva Campo SS. Giovanni e Paolo 6779 ⊕ 041 522 7949; map p.376. With its marble-topped bar and outside tables facing Zanipolo, this is the most characterful of the three *Rosa Salva* branches in the city. (The others are at Calle Fiubera 951 and Merceria S. Salvador 5020, both a short way north of the Piazza, and both closed on Sun.) The coffee and ice cream are superb. Daily 8am–8pm.

RESTAURANTS

Value for money tends to increase with distance from San Marco; plenty of restaurants within a short radius of the Piazza offer menus that seem to be reasonable, but you'll find the food unappetizing and the portions tiny. As a rule of thumb, avoid anywhere that advertises a "menù turistico". There are some notable concentrations of good-value restaurants: around Rialto market; around San Barnaba in Dorsoduro; and the western part of Cannaregio, around the Ghetto. In most cases, booking is advisable in high season, and you should also be aware that Venetians tend to eat early and that restaurateurs close early if trade is slack. If you're in town at a quiet time, don't turn up later than 8.30pm unless you're dining at one of the more expensive restaurants, which tend to keep longer hours.

SAN MARCO

Al Bacareto Calle Crosera S. Samuele 3447 ⊕ 041 528 9336, ⓦ osteriaalbacareto.it; map p.358. *Al Bacareto* has been in business for more than forty years and remains one of the most genuine places in the San Marco *sestiere*. In recent years it has been getting smarter and more expensive, but it's still fairly good value, with main courses in the €15–20 range – and if you're watching the pennies you can always eat at the bar, where the *cicheti* are outstanding. In summer there are seats outside. Mon–Sat 8am–3.30pm & 6.30–11pm.

Rosticceria Gislon Calle della Bissa 5424A; map p.358. The perpetually busy *Gislon* is a sort of glorified snack bar, serving pizzas, plates of meat and cheese, fried fish and other basic meals. There's a slightly less rudimentary restaurant upstairs, where prices are higher for no great increase in quality. Daily 9am–9.30pm.

DORSODURO

Ai Quattro Feri Calle Lunga S. Barnaba 2754/A ⊕ 041 520 6978; map p.358. A very popular *osteria* just off Campo San Barnaba, with a small menu that changes daily but often consists entirely of fish and seafood; most dishes are priced per 100g, so *secondi* will vary according to the size of the fish. Limited seating (some might find the place a bit too cramped), so booking is essential at all times. No credit cards. Mon–Sat noon–3pm & 7–10pm.

Casin dei Nobili Calle Lombardo 2765 ⊕ 041 241 1841; map p.358. Very popular with both locals and tourists, the *Casin* is a large and dependable trattoria-pizzeria with a nice open courtyard – pizzas are served only in the evenings, and are the best thing they do. The restaurant occupies part of a premises that was once notorious as an upper-class gambling-den-cum-bordello – hence the racy logo. Tues–Sun noon–3pm & 6–11pm.

★ **La Bitta** Calle Lunga S. Barnaba 2753/A ⊕ 041 523 0531; map p.358. Innovative fare at a welcoming little *osteria* that's remarkable for featuring hardly anything aquatic. Marcellino runs the kitchen while his wife Debora serves and cajoles the guests, offering expert guidance on the impressive wine and grappa list. Main courses are €20–30. Tiny dining room (and garden), so booking is essential. No credit cards. Mon–Sat 7–10pm.

La Calcina Zattere ai Gesuati 780 ⊕ 041 520 6466, ⓦ lacalcina.com; map p.358. Stretching onto the waterfront outside the *Calcina* hotel, to which it's attached, this is one of the most pleasant restaurants in Dorsoduro. The service is excellent, the food better than in the majority of restaurants in Venice (meat and fish dishes from around €20), and the view of Giudecca from the terrace is wonderful. Tues–Sun noon–3pm & 6.30–10.30pm.

SAN POLO AND SANTA CROCE

Alla Madonna Calle della Madonna 594 ⊕ 041 522 3824, ⓦ ristoranteallamadonna.com; map p.358. Roomy, loud and bustling seafood restaurant that's been going strong since the 1950s and is now run by the founder's son. Little finesse (the atmosphere is rather refectory-like), and service can be brisk, but many locals still rate its kitchen as one of the city's best. Prices have gone up noticeably of late, but it's still good value – reckon on around €45/person. Mon, Tues & Thurs–Sun noon–3pm & 7–10pm.

TOP 5 PLACES FOR OUTDOOR EATING

Al Gatto Nero see page 397
Alla Fontana see page 396
Alla Palanca see page 397
La Calcina see page 395
Venissa see page 397

6

★**Antiche Carampane** Rio Terrà delle Carampane 1911 ⓣ041 524 0165, ⓦantichecarampane.com; map p.376. If not the most tourist-friendly place in the city (a semi-jokey notice tells you there's "No lasagne, no pizza, no menu turistico"), the *Carampane* is a thoroughbred high-class Venetian trattoria, serving excellent seafood in a cosy interior – with outside seating in fine weather. The menu is brief and often wholly fish-based, and you'll pay in the region of €70 for three courses. Tues–Sat 12.30–2.30pm & 7.30–11pm.

Antico Dolo Ruga Vecchia S. Giovanni 778 ⓣ041 522 6546, ⓦanticodolo.it; map p.358. You can pop into this tiny and long-established *osteria* for a few *cicheti* and a glass of Merlot and come away just a few euros poorer; or you can take a table and eat an excellent meal for something in the region of €40. For lunch, the €20 plate of assorted *cicheti* is a tempting offer. Daily noon–10pm.

Bancogiro Sottoportego del Banco Giro 122 ⓣ041 523 2061; map p.376. This very smart *osteria*, in a splendid location in the midst of the Rialto market, was instrumental in making this zone fashionable, and though a number of similar operations have opened in the vicinity, none is better than *Bancogiro*. Come here to nurse a glass of fine wine beside the Canal Grande, or nip upstairs to the dining room for a well-prepared meal from the imaginative menu (around €20–25 for main courses). Tues–Sun 9am–midnight.

Birraria La Corte Campo San Polo 2168 ⓣ041 275 0570, ⓦbirrarialacorte.it; map p.358. If a pizza is all you want, this large bar-pizzeria-trattoria – occupying a former brewery on the north side of Campo San Polo – will do just fine. The rest of the menu is OK, but the pizzas are the thing – along with the beers, which feature strongly on the drinks list. The outside tables give you a grandstand view of Venice's second-largest square. Daily 10am–midnight (kitchen open noon–2.30pm & 6–10.30pm).

La Zucca Ponte del Megio 1762 ⓣ041 524 1570, ⓦlazucca.it; map p.376. Long a well-respected restaurant, *La Zucca* was once a vegetarian establishment (its name means "pumpkin") but now goes against the Venetian grain by featuring a lot of meat – chicken, lamb, beef – alongside the Eastern-inflected vegetable dishes. The quality remains high, prices are moderate (most mains are under €20) and the canalside setting is nice. Mon–Sat 12.30–2.30pm & 7–10.30pm.

Vecio Fritolin Calle della Regina 2262 ⓣ041 522 2881, ⓦveciofritolin.it; map p.376. The name translates as "the old frying-place", and one of its signature dishes is a succulent fry-up of estuary fish, but the *Vecio Fritolin* is esteemed nowadays for its distinctive take on Venetian fishy classics, making imaginative use of seasonal herbs and vegetables. Main courses are €25–30, and there's an excellent three-course set menu for €65. Mon & Thurs–Sun noon–2.30pm & 7–10.30pm, Wed 7–10.30pm only.

CANNAREGIO

Ai Promessi Sposi Calle dell'Oca 4367 ⓣ041 241 2747; map p.376. Run by former employees of *Alla Vedova* (see below), this moderately priced (mains around €15) and cosy little *osteria* specializes in *baccalà* and other traditional fish recipes. Excellent range of *cicheti* at the bar. Mon 6.30–10.15pm, Tues–Sun 11.30am–2.15pm & 6.30–10.15pm.

★**Alla Fontana** Fondamenta Cannaregio 1102 ⓣ041 715 077; map p.376. A great little trattoria, offering a small menu of classic Venetian maritime dishes, which changes daily according to what the boats have brought in; tables beside the canal are an added attraction in summer. Portions are generous and prices good – you'll pay about €40/person for two courses with house wine. Mon, Tues & Thurs–Sun 7.30–10.30pm; sometimes closes Sun in winter.

Alla Vedova Calle del Pistor 3912 ⓣ041 528 5324; map p.376. Located in an alley directly opposite the one leading to the Ca' d'Oro, this long-established little restaurant – formally called the *Ca' d'Oro*, but known to all as *Alla Vedova* – is fronted by a bar offering a mouthwatering selection of *cicheti* and a good range of wines. It's known as one of the best-value places in town (antipasti and main courses from around €10), so reservations are always a good idea. No credit cards. Mon–Wed, Fri & Sat 11.30am–2.30pm & 6.30–10.30pm, Sun 6.30–10.30pm.

★**Anice Stellato** Fondamenta della Sensa 3272 ⓣ041 720 744, ⓦosterianicestellato.com; map p.376. Located on one of the northernmost Cannaregio canals, this unfussy restaurant is a bit too remote for many tourists, but has become hugely popular in recent years, thanks to the superb quality of its kitchen. It is not inexpensive, however, with starters around €15 and main courses mostly in the €25–30 range. Booking always advisable. Mon 7.15–10pm, Tues–Sat 12.15–2pm & 7.15pm–10pm.

Pontini Fondamenta Pescheria 1268 ⓣ041 714 123; map p.376. From outside, this looks like any number of ordinary Venetian trattoria-bars, but it's a cut above the average: the staff are extraordinarily welcoming, and the menu consists of plain but high-quality Venetian *osteria* fare: *frittura mista*, squid-ink pasta, *baccalà* and so forth. Portions are generous too, and the prices very good, with mains under €15 and some delicious set meals for less than €30. It's popular with tourists and locals alike, so booking is advisable in high season. Mon–Sat 6.30am–10.30pm.

Vini da Gigio Fondamenta S. Felice 3628/A ⓣ041 528 5140, ⓦvinidagigio.com; map p.376. Though this family-run trattoria is firmly on the tourist map, it retains much of its authenticity and is still fairly good value by local standards, with most mains at around €25. It has two short but excellent menus – one for meat dishes, one for fish and seafood – and the wine list is remarkable. Reservations essential. Wed–Sun noon–2.30pm & 7–10pm.

CASTELLO

★Alle Testiere Calle Mondo Nuovo 5801 ⓣ 041 522 7220, ⓦ osterialletestiere.it; map p.358. Small, expensive but very special fish and seafood restaurant in the alley on the other side of the canal from the front of Santa Maria Formosa, with an ever-changing menu (starters around €25, mains €30 – and you're not allowed to order less than two courses) and a superb wine selection. In the evening there are sittings at 7pm and 9pm, to handle the demand – booking is essential. Tues–Sat noon–3pm & 7–11pm; closed Aug.

★Corte Sconta Calle del Pestrin 3886 ⓣ 041 522 7024; map p.358. Secreted in a lane to the east of San Giovanni in Bragora, with a lovely vine-covered courtyard, this restaurant is one of Venice's finest. You might find it difficult to resist ordering the day's specials, which could easily result in a bill not far short of €100 per person – and it would be just about the best meal you could get in Venice for that price. If expenditure is an issue, check the menu in the window carefully before going in (often the waiters will simply recite what's on offer rather than give you anything printed). Booking several days in advance is essential for most of the year. Tues–Sat 12.30–2pm & 7.15–10pm.

Da Remigio Salizzada dei Greci 3416 ⓣ 041 523 0089; map p.358. Old-style trattoria, serving straightforwardly excellent fish dishes and home-made gnocchi. The wine list is outstanding, too. Be sure to book – the locals (and ever-increasing numbers of tourists) pack this place every night. While many other restaurants have ramped up their prices in recent years, it remains good value for the quality – mains are around €15–20. Mon 12.30–2.30pm, Wed–Sun 12.30–3pm & 7.30–10pm.

MURANO

Busa alla Torre Campo S. Stefano 3 ⓣ 041 739 662. This is the best trattoria on Murano, and the outdoor seating makes it a pleasant place to while away an hour or two. Unfortunately, though, the kitchen is open for lunch only; for the rest of the day it functions as a café-bar. Tues–Sun 9am–5pm; kitchen open noon–3pm.

BURANO

Al Gatto Nero Fondamenta Giudecca 88 ⓣ 041 730 120, ⓦ gattonero.com. Founded way back in 1946, this is an outstanding trattoria, located just a minute's walk from the busy Via Galuppi, opposite the Pescheria. It's been run since the 1960s by the Bovo family, and what they don't know about the edible delicacies of the lagoon, and the wines of the region, isn't worth knowing. If you want one of the canalside tables, book a week ahead. You'll be spending in the region of €50–60 each, excluding wine. Tues–Sat 12.30–3pm & 7.30–9pm, Sun 12.30–3pm; closed one week in July & most of Nov.

TOP 5 PLACES FOR OUTDOOR DRINKING

Al Parlamento see page 398
Florian see page 394
Il Caffè see page 394
La Cantina see page 398
Nico see page 394

MAZZORBO

Venissa Fondamenta S. Caterina 3 ⓣ 041 52 72 281, ⓦ venissa.it. As soon as it opened, in 2010, *Venissa* become one of Venice's foodie havens. The personnel have changed since then, but the philosophy hasn't – this restaurant uses the resources of the lagoon and the restaurant's garden and vineyard to create a menu that mixes the traditional and the innovative to sometimes brilliant effect. Main courses are €40–50, and there are three fabulous set menus: five courses for €110, seven for €150, and nine for €175 (all excluding wine). The dining room is stylishly modern and intimate (booking is essential), and there are tables outside in good weather. In the adjoining wine bar there's a simpler and less expensive menu on offer, with mains courses at €20–25. Restaurant April–Oct Mon & Wed–Sun noon–3pm & 7–11pm; wine bar May–Oct Mon, Tues & Thurs–Sun 11am–11pm; Nov–April Mon, Tues & Thurs–Sun noon–3pm & 7–11pm.

GIUDECCA

Alla Palanca Fondamenta Ponte Piccolo 448 ⓣ 041 528 7719. If you want a low-cost sit-down lunch, you couldn't do better than to pop over to this bar-trattoria – the food is plain but fine, and the view of the city from the outside tables is magnificent. Meals are served from noon to 2.30pm; before and after that, it's one of Giudecca's busiest bars. Mon–Sat 7am–8.30pm.

Da Sandro Calle Michelangelo 53c ⓣ 041 520 0119. Having relocated from its original site amid the Giudecca boatyards, the *osteria* formerly known as *Mistrà* retains a canteen-like atmosphere and solid local following; the menu is of course strong on fish and seafood (mains around €20), but they do pizzas too, and the new location has a small garden. Mon & Wed–Sun noon–2.30pm & 6.30–11pm.

DRINKING

Most bars serve some kind of food, their counters usually bearing trays of the characteristically Venetian, fat little crustless sandwiches called *tramezzini*, which are stuffed with fillings such as egg and mushroom, egg and anchovy, or Parma ham and artichoke. Many bars will have a selection of *cicheti* as well, and even two or three more substantial

6

dishes. Venice is notoriously somnolent after dark, but are three areas in which you'll find a good concentration of lively bars: in and around Campo Santa Margherita; the Rialto market area; and in northern Cannaregio, along the canals to the north of the Ghetto.

SAN MARCO

Al Volto Calle Cavalli 4081 ⓣ041 522 8945, ⓦenotecaalvolto.com; map p.358. This dark little bar is an *enoteca* in the true sense of the word – 1300 wines from Italy and elsewhere, 100 of them served by the glass, some cheap, many not; good *cicheti*, too. Daily 10am–4pm & 6–10pm.

Bácaro Jazz Salizzada Fondaco dei Tedeschi 5546 ⓣ041 528 5249, ⓦbacarojazz.com; map p.358. A jazz-themed bar-restaurant that's proved a big hit with young Venetians and tourists, mainly on account of its late hours (a real rarity in Venice); there's food, but it's far from the best quality. Daily noon–3am.

★ **I Rusteghi** Corte del Tintor 5513 ⓣ041 523 2205, ⓦairusteghi.com; map p.358. A small *osteria*, secreted away in a tiny courtyard close to Campo San Bartolomeo, with great (if expensive) *cicheti*, a superb selection of wines (some of them very special indeed) and a congenial host – plus a few outside tables. Daily 11.30am–3pm & 6.30pm–midnight.

DORSODURO

Bakarò do Draghi Campo S. Margherita 3665 ⓣ041 528 9731, ⓦbakaro.it; map p.358. Taking its name from the two dragons on the wall opposite, this is a tiny, friendly café-bar with a good range of wines and snacks. The back room exhibits the work of local photographers and artists. Daily 10am–midnight.

Café Noir Crosera S. Pantalon 3805 ⓣ041 710 227; map p.358. A favourite student bar, often with live music on Tues. Mon–Fri 11am–2am, Sat & Sun 7pm–2am.

★ **Cantina del Vino già Schiavi** Fondamenta Nani 992 ⓣ041 523 0034, ⓦcantinaschiavi.com; map p.358. Known to Venetians as the *Cantinone* or *Al Bottegon*, this is a great bar and wine shop opposite San Trovaso. Excellent *cicheti* and generously filled panini too. Mon–Sat 8.30am–8.30pm.

Osteria alla Bifora Campo S. Margherita 2930 ⓣ041 523 6119; map p.358. A candlelit wood-beamed and brick interior, friendly service, good wine, excellent *cicheti*, and large plates of meat and cheese if you need more calories – the *Bifora* is one of several fine places for a pit stop on Campo Santa Margherita. Daily noon–2am.

SAN POLO AND SANTA CROCE

★ **All'Arco** Calle del'Ochialer 436 ⓣ041 520 5666; map p.376. A great stand-up Rialto bar, tucked under the end of the *sottoportego* (covered alley) opposite San Giovanni Elemosinario; does superb *sarde in soar* (sardines with sweet onions) and other snacks. Mon–Sat 8am–3pm.

Al Mercà Campo Cesare Battisti 213 ⓣ347 100 2583; map p.376. This minuscule stand-up Rialto bar is perfect for a quick little panino and glass of prosecco. Mon–Thurs 9am–2.30pm & 6–8pm, Fri & Sat closes 9.30pm.

★ **Da Lele** Campo dei Tolentini 183; map p.376. As you can tell by the opening hours, this tiny and utterly authentic micro-bar attracts a lot of custom from workers en route to or from Piazzale Roma. Sandwiches and rolls are made freshly to order, and wine by the glass costs less than €1. Mon–Fri 6am–8pm, Sat 6am–2pm.

Do Mori Calle Do Mori 429 ⓣ041 522 5401; map p.376. Hidden just off Ruga Vecchia San Giovanni, this single narrow room, with no seating, is packed every evening with homebound shopworkers, Rialto porters and locals just out for a stroll – plus, inevitably, a fair number of tourists. Delicious snacks, good range of wines, nice atmosphere. Mon–Sat 8am–8pm.

★ **Il Mercante** Fondamenta dei Frari 2564 ⓣ041 524 1877; map p.358. For many years this place – directly opposite the front door of the Frari – was a pretty belle époque-styled bar-café. Given a thorough revamp and a moody new colour scheme in 2016, it's now possibly the best cocktail bar in Venice. The upstairs gallery is a great spot to spend a late-night hour or two. Tues–Sat 7pm–2am.

CANNAREGIO

★ **Al Parlamento** Fondamenta Savorgnan 511 ⓣ041 244 0214; map p.376. This spacious and very friendly bar is the area's smartest, with pale wood furnishings and lengths of rope slung in rows across the ceiling to impart a touch of maritime cool. Good snacks and cocktails, tables beside the Cannaregio canal, and live music too. Daily 7.30am–1.30am.

Al Timon Fondamenta degli Ormesini 2754 ⓣ041 524 6066; map p.376. With its attractively spartan neo-traditional decor, this *osteria* is a big hit with Venice's students and 20-somethings – most nights, the crowd spills out onto the canalside. The meals are generally good (steaks are a speciality), but this is really a place for a snack and a drink or two with your mates. Daily 6pm–1am.

Da Luca e Fred Rio Terrà S. Leonardo 1518 ⓣ041 716 170; map p.376. Terrific gritty old *cichetteria*, serving excellent snacks and simple meals to a regular clientele, a few of whom are usually to be found sitting outside, watching the world go by. Very few tables inside, so if you want to eat here in winter, be prepared to wait for a space. Daily (except Tues) 9am–9pm.

La Cantina Strada Nova 3689 ⓣ041 522 8258; map p.376. Long-established *enoteca* with a good range of wines, and substantial and excellent (but not inexpensive) snacks. Daily 11am–11pm.

6

SHOPPING IN VENICE

With every passing year the population of Venice falls, while commercial rents increase. The result: small-scale family-run shops are an endangered species here. Venice has two major **shopping districts**: the **Mercerie**, connecting the Piazza to the area around the Rialto Bridge; and **Calle Larga XXII Marzo**, running west from the Piazza. These zones are almost monopolized by Italian mega-brands such as Gucci, Dolce e Gabbana and Prada, which you'll find in every other major tourist destination in Italy.

On the island of Murano you'll find a lot of showrooms selling **local glass**, but much of the cheaper stuff is mass-produced outside Italy – look for the "Vetro Artistico Murano" trademark, the sign of authenticity. With **Burano lace**, the situation is much the same: if it's not shockingly expensive, it's fake. In central Venice, one of the best outlets for real Burano lace is Kerer, Calle Canonica 4328A, Castello (T 041 523 5485, W kerer.it) – it's in the Palazzo Trevisan-Cappello, across the Ponte Cappello at the rear of the Basilica di San Marco. Likewise, most **Carnival masks** – the quintessential Venetian souvenirs – are manufactured abroad; for a terrific selection of handmade Venetian masks, go to Ca' Macana, Calle delle Botteghe 3172, Dorsoduro (T 041 277 6142, W camacana.com) – it's near San Barnaba church.

Paradiso Perduto Fondamenta della Misericordia 2540 T 041 720 581; map p.376. A real fixture on the Venice scene, *Paradiso Perduto* is packed to the rafters most nights with a predominantly young crowd. The restaurant section is like a boho refectory and the atmosphere at the tables is usually terrific, though there are many better kitchens in the neighbourhood. Go for the drinks, the *cicheti* and the buzz. Thurs–Mon 10am–midnight.

★ **Un Mondo diVino** Salizzada S. Canciano 5984/A T 041 521 1093; map p.376. Occupying a marble-fronted and wood-beamed old butcher's shop, this little *bácaro* has rapidly built up a great reputation, for its fantastic array of *cicheti*, its choice selection of wines and the warmth of its staff. Prices are quite steep, though. Daily 10am–11pm.

CASTELLO

Al Portego Calle Malvasia 6015 T 041 522 9038, W osteriaalportego.org; map p.358. In the middle of the day this bar is crammed with customers eating *cicheti* and in the evening there's often a queue for a place at one of the tiny tables, where some well-prepared basics (pasta, risotto, *fegato alla veneziana* etc) are served. No reservations are taken. Daily 10.30am–2.30pm & 5.30–10.30pm.

Enoiteca Mascareta Calle Lunga S. Maria Formosa 5183 T 041 523 0744, W ostemaurolorenzon.com; map p.358. First-rate and perpetually busy wine bar with delicious *cicheti* and a small menu of more substantial fare. The wine list is well chosen, and there's an unusually wide choice of gins too. . Daily 7pm–2am.

ENTERTAINMENT

Venice does not have a single club, and though there's a number of late-opening bars with DJs or live music, strict by-laws against late-night noise mean that the gig often entails nothing wilder than an aspiring singer-songwriter on acoustic guitar. The **Teatro Malibran** stages concerts by Italian rock outfits from time to time, but bands rarely come nearer than Padua, and the biggest names tend to favour Verona. Music in Venice, to all intents and purposes, means **classical music**.

OPERA AND CLASSICAL MUSIC

Classical concerts, with a very strong bias towards the eighteenth century (and Vivaldi in particular – barely a day goes by without a fancy-dress performance of the *Four Seasons*), are given at various venues, such as the Palazzo Prigione Vecchie, the Scuola Grande di San Giovanni Evangelista, the Scuola di San Teodoro, Palazzo Albrizzi, the Teatrino Grassi and the churches of Santo Stefano, the Frari, San Stae, San Samuele, San Vidal, San Giacomo di Rialto, the Ospedaletto and the Pietà. Tickets for concerts at these venues are usually €15–30, with reductions for students and children. The two big venues are as follows:

La Fenice Campo S. Fantin T 041 786 511, W teatrolafenice.it. The third-ranking Italian opera house after Milan's La Scala and Naples' San Carlo, La Fenice has opera and ballet performances throughout the year; classical concerts are held in the Fenice's Sale Apollinee. Seats for the opera cost €40–200 on most nights, but you'll pay rather more for the opening night of a production; prices are a little lower midweek than at the weekend. Tickets can be bought online, at the Fenice box office and at the Venezia Unica/Hellovenezia offices at Piazzale Roma and the train station.

Teatro Malibran Campiello del Teatro Malibran W teatrolafenice.it. The Malibran and La Fenice's Sale Apollinee share top billing as the city's prime venues for classical recitals; the Malibran also has occasional opera, jazz and rock shows. Tickets for the Malibran (around €25–70) can be bought at the Venezia Unica/Hellovenezia offices at Piazzale Roma and the train station; its own box office sells tickets only on the night of the concert, from around 1hr before the start.

6

FESTIVALS AND EVENTS

CARNEVALE

Venice's **Carnevale** (ⓦcarnivalofvenice.com) occupies the ten days leading up to Lent, finishing on Shrove Tuesday with a masked ball for the glitterati and dancing in the Piazza for the plebs. After falling out of fashion for many years, it was revived in 1979 and is now supported by the city authorities who organize various pageants and performances, beginning with the "Flight of the Angel" from the Campanile. Apart from these events, Carnevale is an endless parade: during the day people don costumes and go to the Piazza to be photographed, while business types do their shopping in the classic white mask, black cloak and tricorn hat. In the evening some congregate in the remoter squares, while those who have spent hundreds of euros on their costumes install themselves in the windows of *Florian* and pose. Masks are on sale throughout the year (few of them are actually made in Venice), but special mask and costume shops magically appear during Carnevale, and Campo San Maurizio sprouts a marquee with mask-making demonstrations and a variety of designs for sale.

LA SENSA AND THE VOGALONGA

From the twelfth century until the fall of the Republic, Ascension Day was marked by the ceremony of The Marriage of Venice to the Sea, a ritual which was followed by a huge trade fair called the Fiera della Sensa (*Sensa* being dialect for Ascension). Today the feast of **La Sensa** happens on the Sunday after Ascension Day, and features a feeble modern version of the ceremony, plus a gondola regatta. Far more spectacular is the **Vogalonga** or "long row", held a week later. Established in 1974, the Vogalonga is open to any crew in any class of rowing boat, and covers a 32km course from the Bacino di San Marco out to Burano and back, with the competitors setting off from in front of the Palazzo Ducale around 9am.

THE BIENNALE

The **Venice Biennale** (ⓦlabiennale.org), set up in 1895 as a showpiece for international contemporary art, is held from May to November of every odd-numbered year. The main site is by the Giardini Pubblici, with permanent pavilions for about forty countries plus space for a thematic international exhibition. This core part of the Biennale is supplemented by exhibitions in parts of the Arsenale that are otherwise closed to the public, such as the colossal Corderie or Tana (the former rope factory) and the Artiglierie (gun foundry). In addition, various sites throughout the city (such as the salt warehouses on the Zattere) are used as national pavilions and as venues for fringe exhibitions, installations and performances.

Some of the Biennale pavilions and various other buildings (usually the Corderie) are used in even-

FILM

In addition to the cinemas listed below, from late July to late Aug an open-air cinema is installed on Campo San Polo, usually with half a dozen non-dubbed English-language films on the programme. Films start each night at around 9pm, and it's worth an evening of anyone's holiday, if only for the atmosphere.

Giorgione Rio Terrà dei Franceschi 4612A, Cannaregio ⓣ041 522 6298. A small two-screen cinema: Sala B is used for less mainstream films than those shown in Sala A, and non-dubbed English-language films are shown on Tues from Oct to May.

Multisala Astra Via Corfu 12, Lido ⓣ041 526 5736. Another two-screener, running the same programmes as the Giorgione, but slightly out of synch.

Multisala Rossini Salizzada del Teatro 3997A, San Marco ⓣ041 241 7274. Occupying the vast old Teatro Rossini, the three-screen Multisala Rossini is Venice's chief outlet for mainstream films.

DIRECTORY

Banks Banks are concentrated around Campo San Luca and Campo Manin.

Consulates and embassies The nearest British consulate is in Milan. The nearest US consulate is also in Milan, but there's a consular agency at Marco Polo airport (ⓣ041 541 5944). Travellers from Ireland, Australia, New Zealand and Canada should contact their Rome embassies.

Hospital Ospedale Civile, Campo SS. Giovanni e Paolo (ⓣ041 529 4111).

Laundries Venice's self-service laundries are now virtually extinct; one survivor is to be found to the south of Campo Santa Maria Formosa, at Ruga Giuffa 4826 (daily 8.30am–8pm)

numbered years for an independent Biennale for **architecture**, a smaller-scale event which runs from June to mid-November; this overlaps with a brief **music** Biennale and a small **dance** Biennale.

THE FILM FESTIVAL

The **Venice Film Festival** (Ⓦlabiennale.org) – the world's oldest, founded in 1932 – takes place on the Lido every year in late August and/or early September. Tickets are available to the general public on the day before the performance, at the Palazzo del Cinemà and PalaBiennale ticket offices (both on the Lido) and at the Biennale HQ, a short distance west of the Piazza at Calle del Ridotto 1364A.

THE REGATA STORICA

Held on the first Sunday in September, the **Regata Storica** is the annual trial of strength and skill for the city's gondoliers and other expert rowers. It starts with a procession of historic craft along the Canal Grande course, their crews all decked out in period dress, followed by a series of races up the canal. The opening parade is a spectacular affair, and is followed by a race for young rowers in two-oared *pupparini*; the women come next (in boats called *mascarete*), followed by a race for canoe-like *caorline*; and then it's the men's race, in specialized two-man racing gondolas called *gondolini*.

LA FESTA DEL REDENTORE

For Venetians it's not Carnevale that's Venice's quintessential festival – it's the **Festa del Redentore**, which marks the end of the plague of 1576. Celebrated on the third Sunday in July and the preceding Saturday, the *festa* is centred on Palladio's church of the Redentore, which was built in thanksgiving for the city's deliverance from that terrible epidemic. On the Saturday the bishop of Venice marks the commencement of the festive weekend by leading a procession to the church, crossing the Giudecca canal on a bridge that's supported by dozens of boats that are strung across the waterway from the Zattere. By the evening the Bacino di San Marco is clogged with boats as people row out for a picnic on the lagoon, then at midnight there's the mother of all firework displays, after which it's traditional to row to the Lido for the sunrise.

LA FESTA DELLA SALUTE

Named after the church of the Salute, the **Festa della Salute** is a reminder of the plague of 1630–31, which killed one third of the city's population. The church was built after the outbreak, and every **November 21** people process to it over a pontoon bridge across the Canal Grande, to give thanks for good health, or to pray for it.

Lost property If you lose anything on the train or at the station, call Ⓣ041 785 531; at the airport call Ⓣ041 260 9222; on ACTV water- or land buses call Ⓣ041 272 2723; and anywhere in the city itself call Ⓣ041 274 8225.

Police To notify police of a theft or lost passport, report to the *questura* at Rampa S. Chiara 500, on the north side of Piazzale Roma (Ⓣ041 271 5511); in an emergency, ring Ⓣ113. There's a small police station on the Piazza, at no. 63.

Post offices Venice's central post office is at Calle delle Acque 5016, close to San Salvador (Mon, Tues, Thurs & Fri 8.20am–7pm, Sat 8.20am–12.30pm). The principal branch offices are located at Calle dell'Ascensione 1241 (off the west side of the Piazza; Mon, Tues & Thurs–Fri 8.20am–1.30pm, Sat 8.20am–12.30pm), Calle del Spezier 233 and Calle Priuli 3732 (both Cannaregio; same hours),Zattere 1507 (Dorsoduro; same hours), Campo San Polo 2012 (San Polo; same hours), Via Garibaldi 1641 (Castello; same hours), and Fondamenta Santa Eufemia 430 (Giudecca; same hours)

The Veneto

Virtually every acre of the **Veneto** bears the imprint of Venetian rule – Venice dominated this region for centuries and is still the capital of the province today. In **Belluno**, right under the crags of the Dolomites, the style of the buildings declares the town's former allegiance, while the Lion of St Mark looks over the market square of **Verona**, on the Veneto's western edge. On the flatlands of the Po basin (the southern

border of the region) and on farming estates all over the Veneto, the elegant **villas** of the Venetian nobility are still standing.

Yet the Veneto is as diverse culturally as it is geographically. The aspects of Verona that make the city so attractive were created long before the expansion of Venice's terra firma empire, and in **Padua** – a university seat since the thirteenth century – the civilization of the Renaissance displays a character quite distinct from that which evolved in Venice. Even in **Vicenza**, which reached its present form mainly during its long period of subservience, the very appearance of the streets is proof of a fundamental independence.

Nowadays the Veneto is one of Italy's wealthiest regions. Verona, Padua, Vicenza and **Treviso**, 30km north of Venice, are all major industrial and commercial centres, while intensive dairies, fruit farms and vineyards (around Conegliano, for example) have made the region a leading agricultural producer too. The Veneto's densest concentration of industry is at **Mestre** and **Marghera**, the grim conurbation through which road and rail lines from Venice pass before spreading out over the mainland. It's less a city than an economic life-support system for Venice, and the negative impression you get on your way through is entirely valid.

The Brenta

The southernmost of the three main rivers that empty into the Venetian lagoon, the **Brenta** caused no end of trouble for the earliest settlers in the area, with its frequent flooding and its deposits of silt. By the sixteenth century, though, the canalization of the river had brought it under control, and it became a favoured building site for the Venetian aristocracy. Some **villas** were built as a combination of summer residence and farmhouse – many, however, were intended solely for the former function. Around one hundred villas are left on the river between Padua and Venice, though only a handful are open to the public, of which two are outstanding: the **Villa Fóscari** and the **Villa Pisani** – both accessible by bus from Venice.

Villa Fóscari

Mira • April–Oct Tues, Wed & Fri–Sun 9am–noon • €10 • Ⓦ lamalcontenta.com • From Venice, you can take the ACTV Padua-bound bus via Dolo (hourly)

The **Villa Fóscari** at Malcontenta was designed in 1559 by Palladio (see page 415) and is the nearest of his villas to Venice. Most of Palladio's villas fall into two broad groups: those built on cohesive farming estates, with a central low block for living quarters and wings for storage and associated uses, such as the Villa Barbaro at Maser; and the single-block villas built for landowners whose fields were dispersed or unsuitable for the construction of a major building. The Villa Fóscari is the masterpiece of this second group, evoking the architecture of ancient Rome with its rusticated exterior, massive Ionic portico and two-storey main hall.

The frescoes in the living rooms include what is said to be a portrait of a woman of the Fóscari family who was exiled here as punishment for an amorous escapade, and whose subsequent misery was the source of the name Malcontenta. The reality is more prosaic – the area has long been known by that name, either because of some local discontent over development of the land or because of the political *malcontenti* who hid in the nearby salt marshes.

Villa Pisani

Strà • Tues–Sun: April–Sept 9am–8pm; Oct 9am–6pm; Nov–March 28th 9am–5pm • €10 house and garden, €4.50 garden only (free on first Sun of month) • Ⓦ villapisani.beniculturali.it • ACTV Padua-bound bus via Dolo (hourly) from Venice

The **Villa Pisani** (or Nazionale) at Stra, virtually on the outskirts of Padua, looks more like a product of the *ancien régime* than a house for the Venetian gentry. Commissioned when Alvise Pisani was elected Doge of Venice in 1735, it was the biggest such residence to be built in Venetian territory during that century. It has appealed to megalomaniacs ever since: Napoleon bought it from the Pisani in 1807 and handed it over to Eugène Beauharnais, his stepson and Viceroy of Italy; and in 1934 it was chosen for the first meeting of Mussolini and Hitler.

Most of what you see is unexciting and sparsely furnished, but stick with it for the ballroom – its ceiling is covered with a dazzling fresco, *The Apotheosis of the Pisani Family*, painted by **Tiepolo** at the age of 66. It shows the Pisani family, accompanied by Venice, being courted by the Arts, Sciences and Spirits of Peace, while Fame plays a fanfare in praise of the Pisani while the Madonna looks on with appropriate pride.

In the **grounds**, the long fish pond ends in front of a stable-block which from a distance might be mistaken for another grand house. Off to the right there's an impressive maze, which is closed in winter and whenever the weather is bad.

Padua (Padova)

Hemmed in by the sprawl that has accompanied its development as the most important economic centre of the Veneto, **PADUA** (Padova) is not immediately the most alluring city in northern Italy. It is, however, one of the most ancient, and plentiful evidence remains of its impressive lineage. A large student population creates a young, vibrant atmosphere, and yet in spite of having two big attractions – the **Giotto frescoes** and the **Basilica of St Antony** – Padua has the feel of a town that is just getting on with its own business.

Brief history

A Roman municipium from 45 BC, the city thrived until the barbarian onslaughts and the subsequent Lombard invasion at the start of the seventh century. Recovery was slow, but by the middle of the twelfth century, when it became a free commune, Padua was prosperous once again. Italy's second-oldest **university** was founded here in 1221, and a decade later the city became a place of pilgrimage following the death of **St Antony**.

In 1337 the **Da Carrara** family established control. Under their domination, Padua's cultural eminence was secured – Giotto, Dante and Petrarch were among those attracted here – but Carraresi territorial ambitions led to conflict with Venice, and in 1405 the city's independence ended with its conquest by the neighbouring republic. Though politically nullified, Padua remained an artistic and intellectual centre: Donatello and Mantegna both worked here, and in the seventeenth century Galileo researched at the university, where the medical faculty was one of the most ambitious in Europe. With the fall of the Venetian Republic the city passed to Napoleon and then to the Austrians, who ruled until Padua was annexed to Italy in 1866. Bombed several times by the Allies in World War II, the city has been extensively restored.

PADOVACARD

Costing €16 for 48 hours or €21 for 72 hours, the **PadovaCard** (ⓦ padovacard.it) allows one visit for one adult and one child under 14 to twelve sites in the city and environs, including the Capella degli Scrovegni, Musei Civici degli Eremitani and Palazzo della Ragione. There are further discounts on the other main attractions, as well as free parking in the Piazza Rabin car park by Prato della Valle, free travel on the APS buses, free bicycle rental and discounts at some bed and breakfasts. It's available from the tourist offices and at the Eremitani, or can be bought online at ⓦ cappelladegliscrovegni.it.

Corso Garibaldi

Corso del Popolo and its extension **Corso Garibaldi** lead south from the railway station, passing the 17m-tall structure of glass and steel designed by the architect **Daniel Libeskind** as a memorial to the victims of the September 11 attacks. Named *Memory and Light*, it contains part of a girder salvaged from the World Trade Center. A couple of minutes' walk further on are two

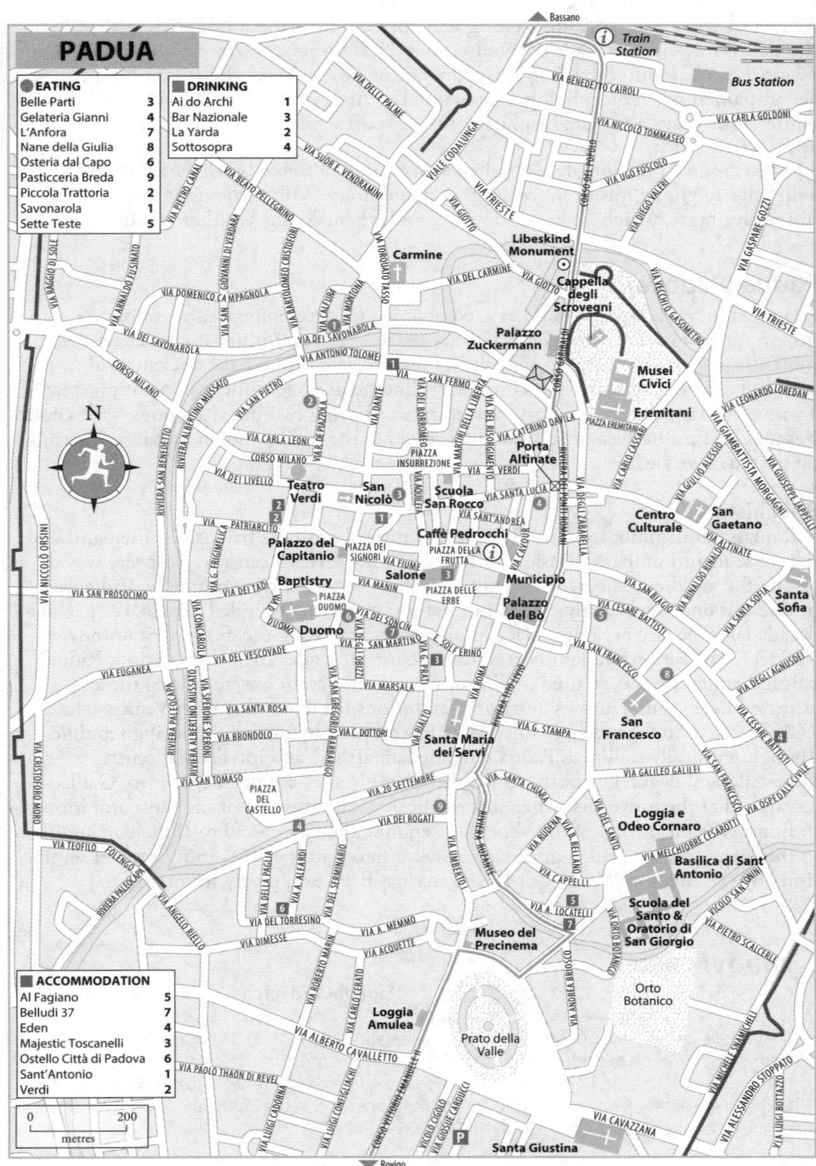

TICKETS FOR THE CAPPELLA DEGLI SCROVEGNI

The number of visitors permitted each day to the Cappella is strictly limited, so it's usually advisable to **book tickets in advance** – at least three or four days in summer, though in winter you may find there is no need to wait. Reservations can be made at the museum ticket desk, or by phoning Ⓣ 049 201 0020 (Mon–Fri 9am–7pm, Sat 9am–6pm), or online (at least 24hr in advance) at Ⓦ cappelladegliscrovegni.it. Tickets must be picked up from the ticket desk an hour before your **timed entry**; you have to be at the chapel waiting room five minutes before your allotted time. Once inside, the air humidity of the waiting room is adjusted down to that of the chapel while you watch a video about the frescoes, with just a meagre fifteen to twenty minutes allowed inside the chapel itself. **Tickets** cost €13 – which includes entry to the Musei Civici degli Eremitani and Palazzo Zuckermann– or €8 when the museum is closed (on Mon); the PadovaCard also gets you in free, but you still have to pay a €1 booking fee. From time to time the chapel is open in the evenings; on those days, you can book a double slot ("*doppio turno*"), which for €12 gives you forty minutes inside the chapel after 7pm.

6

of the city's biggest draws, the **Cappella degli Scrovegni** and **Musei Civici degli Eremitani**.

Cappella degli Scrovegni

Entry via the Musei Civici, Piazza Eremitani 8 • Daily 9am–7pm • Tickets must be prebooked (see page 405) • Ⓦ cappelladegliscrovegni.it

The **Cappella degli Scrovegni** was commissioned in 1303 by Enrico Scrovegni in atonement for his father's usury, which was so vicious that he was denied a Christian burial. **Giotto** covered the walls with illustrations of the life of Mary, the life of Jesus and the story of the Passion, and the finished fresco cycle is one of the high points in the development of European art – a marvellous demonstration of Giotto's innovative attention to the inner nature of his subjects. In terms of sheer physical presence and the relationships between the figures and their environment, Giotto's work takes the first important strides towards realism and humanism.

The Joachim series on the top row of the north wall (facing you as you walk in) is particularly powerful – note the exchange of looks between the two shepherds in the *Arrival of Joachim*. Beneath the main pictures are shown the Vices and Virtues in human (usually female) form, while on the wall above the door is a *Last Judgement* – in rather poor condition and thought to be only partly by Giotto. At the bottom is a portrait of Scrovegni presenting the chapel; his tomb is at the far end, behind the altar with its statues by **Giovanni Pisano**.

Musei Civici degli Eremitani

Piazza Eremitani 8 • Tues–Sun 9am–7pm • €10 combined ticket with the Palazzo Zuckermann, or €13 including the Cappella degli Scrovegni, or PadovaCard

Next to the chapel, the **Musei Civici degli Eremitani**, formerly the monastery of the Eremitani, is a well-presented museum complex that holds the Museo Archeologico and the Museo d'Arte Medioevale e Moderna. The **archeological collection**, on the ground floor, has an array of pre-Roman, Roman and paleo-Christian objects. Upstairs, the vast **Museo d'Arte** houses an assembly of fourteenth- to nineteenth-century art from the Veneto and further afield – a long walk through tracts of workaday stuff, though works by names such as Titian, Tintoretto and Tiepolo leaven the mix. Highlights are the Giotto *Crucifixion* that was once in the Scrovegni chapel, a fine *Portrait of a Young Senator* by Bellini and four mysterious landscapes by Titian and Giorgione.

Palazzo Zuckermann

Corso Garibaldi 33 • Tues–Sun 10am–7pm • €10 combined ticket with the Musei Civici degli Eremitani, or €13 including the Cappella degli Scrovegni, or PadovaCard

Across Corso Garibaldi, **Palazzo Zuckermann** houses two museums of specialist interest: the **Museo di Arti Applicate e Decorative** displays pottery, jewellery, textiles and furniture; while upstairs, the **Museo Bottacin** contains over 100,000 coins, medals and seals, making it one of the most important museums of its type in the world.

Eremitani church

Piazza Eremitani • Mon–Fri 7.30am–12.30pm & 3.30–7pm, Sat & Sun 9am–12.30pm & 4–7pm • Free

Next door to the Musei Civici stands the church of the **Eremitani**, which was built at the turn of the fourteenth century and wrecked by an Allied bombing raid in 1944. The worst aspect of the bombardment was the damage to **Mantegna**'s frescoes of the lives of St James and St Christopher; the fragments have been meticulously reassembled in the last chapel to the right of the high altar.

Palazzo del Bò

Via VIII Febbraio • Guided tours only: Mon–Fri 9.30am–5.30pm (in English 10.30am, 12.30pm, 4.30pm), Sat 9.30am–12.30pm (in English 10.30am & 12.30pm) • €7

A short distance south of the Eremitani stands the university's main block, the **Palazzo del Bò** – the name translates as "of the Ox", after an inn that used to stand here. Established in September 1221, the University of Padua is older than any other in Italy except that of Bologna, and the coats of arms that encrust the courtyard and Great Hall attest to the social and intellectual rank of its alumni. The first permanent anatomy theatre was built on this site in 1594, a facility that doubtless greatly helped William Harvey, who went on to develop the theory of blood circulation after taking his degree here in 1602. Galileo taught physics at the university from 1592 to 1610, declaiming from a lectern that is still on show. And in 1678 Elena Lucrezia Corner Piscopia became the first woman in the world to collect a university degree – her statue is in the courtyard.

Caffè Pedrocchi

Piazzetta Pedrocchi • Piano Nobile Tues–Sun 9.30am–12.30pm & 3.30–6pm • €4, or PadovaCard • caffepedrocchi.it

The Bò's neighbour, the Neoclassical **Caffè Pedrocchi** was once the city's main intellectual salon, and it was here that an abortive uprising against the Austrian occupation was launched on February 9, 1848. The building now has a multiplicity of functions: there's a glossy and expensive café-restaurant on the ground floor, and concert hall, conference centre and exhibition space upstairs.

A staircase on the Piazzetta Pedrocchi side of the building leads up to the **piano nobile**, where highly decorative rooms radiate off a central hall. You'll also find the **Museo del Risorgimento e dell'Età Contemporane** here: covering local history from 1797 until 1948, its rooms of uniforms and guns are of limited interest, but the films and photos from World War II are worth a look.

Palazzo della Ragione

Piazza delle Erbe • Tues–Sun: Feb–Oct 9am–7pm; Nov–Jan 9am–6pm • €6, or PadovaCard

The hub of the city is formed by the adjoining **Piazza della Frutta** and **Piazza delle Erbe**, still the sites of Padua's main markets, though nowadays it's mostly clothes rather than fruit that's on sale in the former. Butchers' stalls and bars occupy the arcades of the extraordinary building that separates the two piazzas – the **Palazzo della Ragione** or the **Salone**, as it's more commonly known.

The building was constructed in the 1210s, and the vast hall of the upper storey was originally divided into three parts, to accommodate the law courts for justice – hence the appellation *della Ragione*, meaning "of reason". Its decoration would once have been as astounding as its size, but the frescoes that Giotto and his assistants created here were destroyed by fire in 1420, though some by **Giusto de' Menabuoi** have survived. It was after this fire that the partition walls were removed, creating a

single enormous space, which was then painted by **Nicola Miretto** (1425–40), whose 333-panel astrological calendar covers all four walls. You're given a detailed exposition of them at the ticket desk.

The black stone in the far corner, called the *pietra del vituperio* (stone of insults), played a part in the judicial system: insolvent Paduans were obliged to sit on it three times, repeating the words "I renounce my wordly goods" prior to being expelled from the city. The gigantic wooden horse at the other end is modelled on Donatello's *Gattamelata* (see page 408), and was made for a joust in 1466.

The Duomo and Baptistry

Duomo Mon–Sat 7.30am–noon & 3.30–7.30pm, Sun 8am–1pm & 3.30–8.45pm • Free • **Baptistry** Daily 10am–6pm • €3, or PadovaCard

Blank outside and barren within, Padua's **Duomo** may be the only cathedral in Italy that contains nothing of interest. The adjacent Romanesque **baptistry**, however, is one of the delights of the city. Built by the Da Carrara in the thirteenth century, and still in use today, it's lined with fourteenth-century frescoes by Giusto de' Menabuoi, a cycle which makes a fascinating comparison with Giotto's more monumental work in the Cappella degli Scrovegni – the treeful of children watching Christ's entry into Jerusalem is a typically beguiling detail. The polyptych **altarpiece**, also by Menabuoi, was stolen in 1972 but quickly recovered, minus some of its wooden framework; it's flanked by startling frescoes of the Apocalypse. Don't overlook the **mausoleum of Fina Buzzaccharini** (on the wall opposite the altar), one of the Carrara family's most assiduous artistic patrons; she's shown on the front being presented to the Virgin by John the Baptist.

Basilica di Sant'Antonio

Piazza del Santo • **Basilica di Sant'Antonio** April–Oct daily 6.30am–7.45pm; Nov–March Mon–Sat 6.30am–6.45pm, Sun 6.30am–7.45pm • Free • **Museums** Tues–Sun 9am–1pm & 2–6pm • €3, or €7 with Scuola del Santo & Oratorio di San Giorgio

Within eighteen months of his death in 1231, St Anthony of Padua had been canonized and his tomb was attracting so many pilgrims that it became necessary to rebuild the small church in which he had been buried. The end product of the rebuilding – the immense **Basilica di Sant'Antonio**, or **Il Santo** – was completed in 1301.

The Cappella del Santo

The focal point of the building, the **Cappella del Santo**, is in the left aisle, where the saint's tomb is encompassed by a sequence of nine beautiful panels showing scenes from St Anthony's life. Carved between 1505 and 1577, by artists such as Antonio Lombardo, Tullio Lombardo and Jacopo Sansovino, these constitute the most important series of relief sculpture created in sixteenth-century Italy.

The rest of the church

Adjoining the chapel is the **Cappella della Madonna Mora** (named after its fourteenth-century French altar statue), which in turn lets onto the **Cappella del Beato Luca**, where St Anthony's body was first placed. Dedicated to Luca Belludi, St Anthony's closest companion, the latter chapel contains a fine fresco cycle by **Giusto de' Menabuoi**, including scenes from the lives of the Apostles Philip and James the Less, and *St Anthony revealing to Luca Belludi that Padua will be liberated from Ezzelino*, with an idealized version of the city, parts of it recognizable, as backdrop.

Back in the aisle, just before the Cappella del Santo, is Padua's finest work by **Pietro Lombardo**, the monument to Antonio Roselli (1467). More impressive still are the high altar's bronze sculptures and reliefs by **Donatello** (1444–45), the works that introduced Renaissance classicism to Padua. Unfortunately you can't get close enough to see them properly.

Built onto the furthest point of the ambulatory, the **Cappella delle Reliquie** or **del Tesoro** was designed in the 1690s by Filippo Parodi, a pupil of Bernini. Its most

GATTAMELATA

The main sight on Piazza del Santo, apart from the mighty basilica, is Donatello's monument to **Gattamelata** (which translates as "The Honeyed Cat"), as the *condottiere* Erasmo da Narni was known. He died in 1443 and this monument – the earliest large bronze sculpture of the Renaissance – was raised ten years later.

important relics are a thorn from Christ's crown, and St Anthony's tongue, vocal chords and jaw, which are kept in elaborate reliquaries in the central of the three niches behind the balustrade. Also on show are scraps of the saint's tunic, and the coffin in which his bones lay until the 1980s.

In the **Cappella di San Giacomo**, off the right aisle, there's a glorious *Crucifixion*, frescoed in the 1370s by Altichiero da Zevio, who also painted the scenes from the life of St James. Other things to seek out are the **monuments to Cardinal Pietro Bembo and Alessandro Contarini,** which face each other on the nave's second pair of columns and were both designed by Sanmicheli in the 1550s, and the **tomb of Gattamelata**, in the first chapel on the right.

Museo Antoniano and Museo della Devozione Populare

Parts of the cloisters, on the south side of the basilica, are occupied by the **Museo Antoniano** and the **Museo della Devozione Populare**. The former, on the first floor, is a collection of paintings (including a fresco of *SS. Anthony and Bernardine* by **Mantegna**), ornate incense-holders, ceremonial robes and other paraphernalia linked to the basilica; the latter, on the ground floor, is a history of votive gifts, with copious examples of the genre.

Scuola del Santo

Piazza del Santo • Tues–Sun 9am–1pm & 2–6pm • €3, or €7 combined ticket with the Oratorio di San Giorgio & Museo Antoniano

On the southern side of the basilica is the **Scuola del Santo**, a confraternity run on the same lines as the *scuole* of Venice, which was founded soon after Anthony's canonization, though this building dates only as far back as the early fifteenth century. The ground floor is still used for religious purposes, while upstairs is maintained pretty much as it would have looked in the sixteenth century, with its fine ceiling and paintings dating mainly from 1509–15. Four of the pictures are said to be by **Titian** – if any of these are genuine, they would be the earliest known extant works by him.

Oratorio di San Giorgio

Piazza del Santo • Tues–Sun 9am–1pm & 2–6pm • €3, or €7 combined ticket with the Scuola del Santo & Museo Antoniano

Joined to the Scuola del Santo, the **Oratorio di San Giorgio** was founded in 1377 as a mortuary chapel, and its frescoes by **Altichiero di Zevio** and **Jacopo Avanzi** were completed soon after. Recently restored, their work is an engaging and colourful narrative romp: the scenes from the life of St George on the left wall, for example, show not just the customary dragon-slaying, but also the saint being released by angels from a wheel of torture; and the opposite wall is adorned with a depiction of St Lucy remaining immoveable as her persecutors attempt to haul her off to a brothel with the help of a team of oxen.

Loggia e Odeo Cornaro

Via Cesarotti 37 • Feb–Oct Tues–Fri 10am–1pm, Sat & Sun 10am–1pm & 4–7pm • €3, or PadovaCard

Just northeast of the basilica is the **Loggia e Odeo Cornaro**, the remains of a set of buildings and gardens commissioned in 1524–30 by Alvise Cornaro, a local landowner, architectural theoretician and patron of the arts. The main attraction here is the **Odeo**, where Cornaro held concerts and literary gatherings; the vault of its octagonal chamber has Roman-style decorations with a series of grotesque figures, while the walls of the

shell-hooded niches are painted with watery landscapes. You can admire the ceiling of the adjoining loggia, but the theatre above is closed.

Orto Botanico

Via dell'Orto Botanico • April & May daily 9am–7pm; June–Sept Tues–Sun 9am–7pm; Oct Tues–Sun 9am–6pm; Nov–March Tues–Sun 9am–5pm • €10, or €5 with PadovaCard • ⓦ ortobotanicopd.it

A good place to relax after a visit to the basilica is the **Orto Botanico**, the oldest botanic gardens in Europe. Planted in 1545 by the university's medical faculty as a collection of medicinal herbs, the gardens have mainly kept their original layout. Goethe came here in 1786 to see a palm tree that had been planted in 1585; the selfsame tree still stands, the oldest in the garden. There is, however, a spectacular new section to the Orto Botanico: a 100-metre glasshouse that's divided into five sections, ranging from the tropical to the subarctic. The artificial climates are maintained by a self-sufficient system that utilises rainwater and solar energy to control the heating, ventilation, irrigation and electricity supply.

Prato della Valle

A little to the south of the basilica sprawls the **Prato della Valle**, claimed to be the largest piazza in Italy – though it's not so much a piazza as a small park encircled by major roads. The greenery in the centre follows the oval plan of the extinct Roman amphitheatre; the two rings of statues commemorate 78 worthy Paduans, both native and honorary.

Santa Giustina

Prato della Valle • Summer Mon–Fri 7.30am–noon & 3–8pm, Sat & Sun 6.30am–1pm & 3–8pm; winter Mon–Sat 8am–noon & 3–8pm, Sun 8am–1pm & 3–8pm • Free

In the southeast corner of the Prato looms the sixteenth-century **Basilica di Santa Giustina**, at 120m long, one of the world's largest churches. The exterior is a mighty box of raw brick and the interior is somewhat clinical, with little of interest except **Paolo Veronese**'s altarpiece of *The Martyrdom of St Justina*, some highly proficient carving on the choirstalls and a sarcophagus that reputedly once contained the relics of Luke the Evangelist (in the left transept).

In the right transept a stone arch opens onto the **Martyrs' Corridor**, named after the martyrs whose bones were found in the well that stands at the head of the corridor. At the end of the corridor is the **Sacellum di Santa Maria e San Prosdocimo**, burial place of St Prosdocimus. He was the first bishop of Padua back in the fourth century, when the church was founded, and is depicted here on a fifth-century panel.

Museo del Precinema

Prato della Valle 1 • Daily (except Tues) 10am–4pm • €5 • ⓦ minicizotti.it

At the northern end of the Prato, on the top floor of the Palazzo Angeli, you'll find the **Museo del Precinema – Collezione Minici Zotti**, a wonderful collection of shadow puppets, magic lanterns and other optical instruments (plus a few mechanical musical instruments) assembled by Laura Minici Zotti in the course of thirty years of research into the precursors of cinematography, and now run by the founder's son. Gorgeous contraptions with names such as the Praxinoscope, Zogroscope, Megalethoscope and the Panoptic Polyorama fill the rooms under the roof, from one of which you can survey the streets through a camera obscura.

ARRIVAL AND GETTING AROUND — PADUA

By train Trains arrive in the north of the city centre, just a few minutes' walk up Corso del Popolo from the old city walls.
Destinations Bassano (16 daily; 1hr 5min); Belluno (13 daily; 2hr–2hr 30min); Castelfranco (19 daily; 35min); Milan (24 daily; 2hr 30min); Venice (every 20min; 25–50min); Verona (every 30min; 45min–1hr 15min); Vicenza (every 20min; 15–30min).

By bus and tram The main APS bus station is next to the

train station at Piazzale della Stazione. Tickets for journeys around Padua cost €1.30, are valid for 75min and can be bought from any shop displaying the APS sign (tickets bought on-board cost €2). The tickets are also valid for the single-line tram system, which runs north–south through the city, via the station, the Musei Civici and Prato della Valle.

INFORMATION

Tourist offices There are tourist offices at the train station (Mon–Sat 9am–7pm, Sun 10am–4pm; ⓣ049 520 7415, ⓦturismopadova.it) and in the centre of the city at Galleria Pedrocchi 9, right next to *Caffè Pedrocchi* (same hours & phone).

ACCOMMODATION

Padua makes an obvious base for exploring the Veneto, as it's a main rail hub and it has plenty of reasonably priced accommodation. In high season, however, you should still **book ahead**, as the town draws thousands of pilgrims.

Al Fagiano Via Locatelli 45 ⓣ049 875 0073, ⓦalfagiano.com; map p.404. A friendly two-star, with forty rooms, each floor decorated in a different colour and with a bizarre selection of art. The rooms vary in size; ask for no.72, with its own large terrace. **€90**

Belludi 37 Via Luca Belludi 37 ⓣ049 665 633, ⓦbelludi37.it; map p.404. This slickly renovated *palazzo* near the Basilica di Sant'Antonio has fifteen tasteful rooms decorated in neutral tones. All rooms are spacious, with high ceilings, luxurious bathrooms and DVD players, but it's worth paying the extra for views of the basilica; the best is no. 107, with its own balcony. **€160**

Eden Via C. Battisti 255 ⓣ049 650 484, ⓦhotel edenpadova.it; map p.404. The *Eden* is a clean-cut modern one-star, and better than most other one-stars in the city in that the majority of the doubles are a good size and all have private bathrooms – but the singles are tiny. **€70**

Majestic Toscanelli Via dell'Arco 2 ⓣ049 663 244, ⓦtoscanelli.com; map p.404. The most appealing of the city's four-stars, with elegant, well-appointed rooms; it's located in the old Jewish quarter, just south of Piazza delle Erbe. **€150**

Ostello Città di Padova Via Aleardo Aleardi 30 ⓣ049 875 2219, ⓦostellopadova.it; map p.404. Padua's friendly HI hostel is in a quiet street in the south of the city; it's a 30min walk from the station, but the tram goes to nearby Prato della Valle. Beds are in six-bed dorms, with some four-bed rooms for families. Wi-fi and laundry facilities. Check-in 7–9.30am & 3.30–11pm; reception is closed between these times; 11.30pm curfew. Dorms **€20**

Sant'Antonio Via S. Fermo 118 ⓣ049 875 1393, ⓦhotelsantantonio.it; map p.404. A plain, unfussy and inexpensive three-star. Rooms at the back have views over the Ponte Molino; the nicest are nos. 311 and 312, on two levels, with a small sitting area upstairs. **€70**

Verdi Via Dondi dell'Orologio 7 ⓣ049 836 4163, ⓦalbergoverdipadova.it; map p.404. A friendly boutique three-star, very near to Piazza dei Signori. The fourteen rooms are all a good size and have modern furnishings. **€80**

EATING

As in any university city, there's plenty of choice when it comes to unpretentious **bars** and **restaurants**. Catering for the midday stampede of ravenous students, Padua's bars and cafés generally produce very good **snacks** too – there are dozens of places in and around Piazza delle Erbe, Piazza Duomo and Piazza dei Signori. Padua's **nightlife** tends to fluctuate in synch with term time; during the summer vacation things are rather somnolent. Of the local newspapers, the most comprehensive for **listings** is *Il Mattino*, but for more offbeat events check out the posters up around the city.

CAFÉS AND GELATERIE

Gelateria Gianni Via Calvi Pietro Fortunato 12; map p.404. This little *gelateria*, located just off Piazza Garibaldi, sells the best ice cream in Padua, without question. The menu of flavours is constantly changing, and often features mixtures you won't find anywhere else. Daily 10.30am–midnight.

Pasticceria Breda Via Umberto I 26, ⓦpasticceriabreda.it; map p.404. Founded in 1967, *Breda* is the creator of Padua's finest cakes, and the coffee is good too. Take a seat under the arcades and watch the passing traffic on one of Padua's smartest streets. Tues–Sun 7.30am–8pm.

RESTAURANTS

Belle Parti Via Belle Parti 11 ⓣ049 875 1822, ⓦristorantebelleparti.it; map p.404. The very elegant *Belle Parti*, just off Via Verdi, has long been ranked as one of Padua's finest restaurants. With mains upward of €30, it's not cheap, but the quality is unerringly high and the service perfect. A highlight of the antipasto menu is the *gran crudità di mare* – a local raw fish speciality (€34). Booking always advisable. Mon–Sat 12.30–2.30pm & 7.30–10.30pm.

★ **L'Anfora** Via dei Soncin 13 ⓣ049 656 629; map p.404. The best-known old-style *osteria* in central Padova, with *secondi* around €15, and delicious snacks at the bar. Mon–Sat 9am–11.30pm; kitchen open 12.30–3pm & 8–11pm.

Nane della Giulia Via Santa Sofia 1 ⓣ049 660 742; map p.404. There has been an *osteria* in this former

6

hospital since 1820. The present one is a trendy and unpretentious trattoria that serves reasonably priced Veneto specialities (*secondi* €10–15), using locally sourced and seasonal products. The summer garden is lovely too. Tues 7–11.30pm, Wed–Sun noon–2.30pm & 7–11.30pm.

★ **Osteria dal Capo** Via degli Obizzi 2 ⓣ049 663 105, ⓦosteriadalcapo.it; map p.404. This small, refined and very friendly trattoria, located just off Piazza del Duomo, has been serving food since the 1950s and is a secure Padua favourite, so booking is essential in the evenings. Main courses are €15 on average. Mon 7.30–11pm, Tues–Sat noon–2.30pm & 7.30–11pm.

Piccola Trattoria Via Rolando da Piazzola 21 ⓣ049 656 163, ⓦpiccolatrattoria.it; map p.404. Homely and very popular trattoria, with a distinctive menu that focuses on Sardinian specialities such as suckling pig, all superbly presented. Its *secondi* are around €16. Tues–Sat noon–2.30pm & 8–11pm.

Savonarola Via Savonarola 38 ⓣ049 875 9128, ⓦsavonarola-pizzeria-trattoria.it; map p.404. If all you want is a pizza, head for this pizzeria-trattoria just outside the city walls; service can be somewhat frenetic, but the atmosphere is always buzzy. Tues–Fri 12.30–2.30pm & 7.30pm–midnight, Sat & Sun 7pm–midnight.

Sette Teste Via Cesare Battisti 44 ⓣ347 040 5158, ⓦosteriasetteteste.it; map p.404. A very smart and hospitable modern *osteria*, with an excellent selection of wines at the bar and a nice Padovan-Venetian menu (€12–20 for *secondi*). *Baccalà* is always available, along with *fegato* and various beef dishes. Daily (except Tues) noon–11.45pm.

DRINKING

Ai do Archi Via Nazario Sauro 23; map p.404. Small wine bar off Piazza dei Signori, with a very lively vibe. Good music (often loud reggae) and a great atmosphere, with tasty bruschette and *crostini* to accompany your drinks. Daily 6.30pm–2am.

★ **Bar Nazionale** Piazza delle Erbe 41; map p.404. Situated by the steps leading up to the Palazzo della Ragione, this bar is the ideal place to people-gaze while you nurse an aperitif; the food is good too. Daily 8am–9pm.

La Yarda Via Dondi dall'Orologio 1; map p.404. Situated on the same cobbled square as the Liviano, this bar is packed with students every term-time evening, when the music is played loud, but it can be very peaceful at other times, especially if you sit at one of the tables in the shade of the piazza's trees. Mon–Sat 10am–midnight, Sun 6–11pm.

Sottosopra Via XX Settembre 77, ⓦsottosoprapadova.it; map p.404. The "Upside down" bar-bistro is an intriguing Anglo-Mediterranean mix, with a list of fifty teas to complement its menu of wines, snacks and light meals. Run by a very friendly couple, it attracts an unusually varied clientele, from retired couples to students. It's in a quiet part of town and has outdoor tables in summer. Tues–Fri noon–3pm & 7pm–1am, Sat noon–3pm & 6pm–1am, Sun 6pm–midnight (opens 5pm Sun in winter).

Vicenza

Being the focus of Italy's "Silicon Valley" and a major producer of steel, textiles, gold and jewellery, **VICENZA** is one of Italy's main wealth-generators, even if the economic malaise that has afflicted Italy in recent years has had a visible impact here. In 1404 Vicenza was absorbed by Venice, and the city's numerous Gothic palaces reflect its status as a Venetian satellite. But in the latter half of the sixteenth century the city was transformed by the work of an architect who owed nothing to Venice and was to influence every succeeding generation: Andrea di Pietro, alias **Palladio**. Within the girdle of industrial estates and factories, a lot of the *centro storico* looks much as it did when Palladio's buildings were constructed. This historic core is compact enough to be explored in a day, but the city and its environs really require a short stay to do them justice.

Corso Andrea Palladio

The main street of Vicenza, **Corso Andrea Palladio**, cuts right through the old centre from Piazza del Castello down to Piazza Matteotti, and is lined with *palazzi*, now occupied by shops, offices and banks. Palladio's last palace, the fragmentary **Palazzo Porto-Breganze**, stands on the southern side of Piazza Castello, at the top of the Corso; no. 163 on the Corso, the **Casa Cogollo**, is known locally as the Casa del Palladio, though he never lived here and few people think he designed it.

Pinacoteca di Palazzo Chiericati

Piazza Matteotti 37/39 • Tues–Sun: July & Aug 10am–6pm; Sept–June 9am–5pm • €7, or Vicenza Card

The Corso Palladio ends at one of the architect's most imperious buildings, the Palazzo Chiericati. It's now the home of the **Pinacoteca di Palazzo Chiericati**, where celebrated names such as Veronese, Memling, Tintoretto, Giambattista Tiepolo, Van Dyck, the Bassano family and Luca Giordano punctuate a picture collection that's given its backbone by Vicentine artists – notably Montagna, Buonconsiglio, Maffei and Carpioni. Though none of these local artists is likely to knock you flat, there are some intriguing pieces here: the tiny bronze plaquettes and rock-crystal carvings made by the once-famous Valerio Belli, for example, and Francesco del Cairo's orgasmic *Herodias with the Head of the Baptist*.

Teatro Olimpico

Piazza Matteotti 11 • Tues–Sun: July & Aug 10am–6pm; Sept–June 9am–5pm • €11, or Vicenza Card • Ⓦ teatrolimpicovicenza.it

Across the Piazza Matteotti from the Pinacoteca is the one building in Vicenza you shouldn't fail to go into – the **Teatro Olimpico**, the oldest indoor theatre in Europe. Approached in 1579 by the members of the Olympic Academy (a society dedicated to the study of the humanities) to produce a design for a permanent theatre, Palladio devised a covered amphitheatre based on his studies of Roman works. He died soon after work commenced, and the scheme was overseen by Scamozzi, who added the backstage perspective of a classical city, creating the illusion of long urban vistas by tilting the "streets" at an alarming angle. The theatre opened on March 3, 1585, and is still used for concerts and plays.

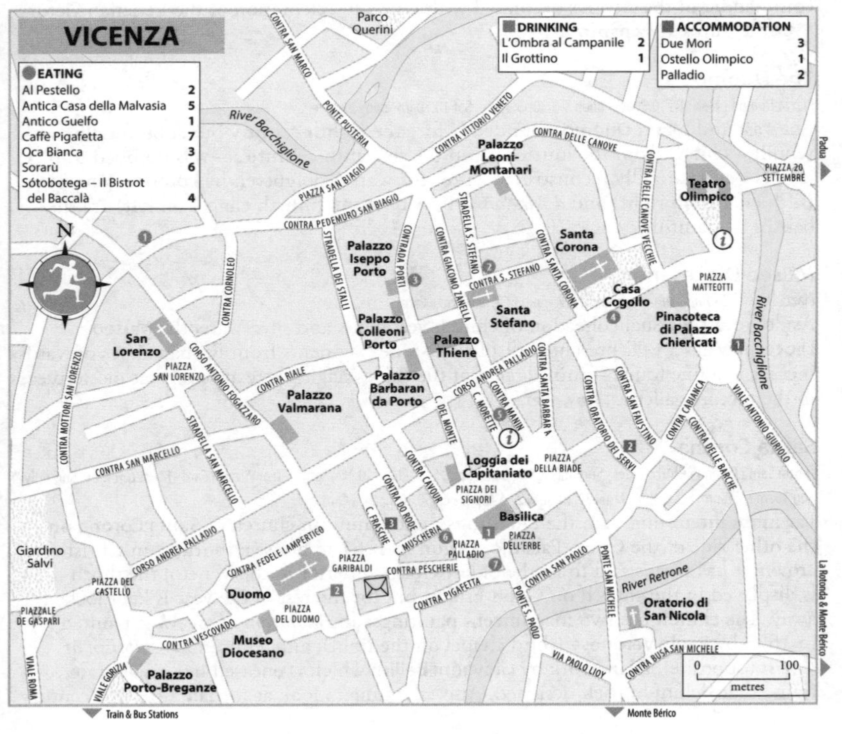

THE VICENZA CARD

The €15 **Vicenza Card** is valid for seven days and gives admission to the Palazzo Leoni Montanari, the Museo del Risorgimento, the Museo Diocesano, the Museo Naturalistico-Archeologico, the Palladio Museum, the Pinacoteca di Palazzo Chiericati, Santa Corona and Teatro Olimpico. The €18 family version of the card, for two adults and up to four children, is valid for three days. You can buy the Vicenza Card at all of the above museums except the Museo Naturalistico-Archeologico, Palazzo Chiericati and Santa Corona.

Piazza dei Signori

At the hub of the city, the **Piazza dei Signori**, stands the most portentous of Palladio's creations – the Palazzo della Ragione, widely known simply as the **Basilica**. Designed in the late 1540s, this was Palladio's first public project and the one that secured his reputation. The monumental regularity of the basilica disguises the fact that the Palladian building is effectively a stupendous piece of buttressing – the colonnades enclose the fifteenth-century hall of the city council, an unstable structure that had defied a number of previous attempts to prop it up. The vast Gothic hall (which had to be rebuilt after bomb damage in World War II) is now used for exhibitions, while on the ground floor, in the midst of the jewellers' shops, there's a new **Museo del Gioiello** (Tues–Fri 3–7pm, Sat & Sun 11am–7pm; €8; museodelgioiello.it). Billed as Italy's first jewellery museum, it has nine rooms arranged by slightly tenuous themes (Symbol, Magic, Function, Beauty, etc), and has the ambience of a shop in which nothing is for sale.

A late Palladian building, the unfinished **Loggia del Capitaniato**, faces the basilica across the Piazza dei Signori. Built as accommodation for the Venetian military commander of the city, it's decorated with reliefs in celebration of the Venetian victory over the Turks at Lepanto in 1571.

The Duomo

Piazza Duomo • Mon–Fri 10.30am–noon & 3.30–5.30pm, Sat 10.30am–noon 3 • Free

The vast and bland **Duomo**, founded before the eighth century but substantially rebuilt – chiefly from the fourteenth to the sixteenth centuries – was bombed to bits in 1944 and carefully reconstructed after the war. A polyptych by **Lorenzo Veneziano** (fifth chapel on right) and a *Madonna* by **Montagna** (fourth chapel on left) are the best of its paintings.

Museo Diocesano

Piazza Duomo 2 • Tues–Sun 10am–1pm & 2–6pm • €5, or Vicenza Card

Aside from the usual collection of church vestments and silverware, the **Museo Diocesano** has a well-presented display of stone fragments from Roman times onwards, including a fine fourth-century relief of the three Magi. There are no great masterpieces in the picture galleries, however.

Santa Corona

Contrà Santa Corona • **Church** Tues–Sun: July & Aug 9am–5pm, Sept–June 10am–6pm • €3, or Vicenza Card • **Museum** Tues–Sun: July & Aug 10am–1.45pm; Sept–June 9am–12.30pm & 2–4.45pm • €3.50, or Vicenza Card

Far more interesting than the Duomo is the Dominican church of **Santa Corona** on the other side of the Corso Palladio. Begun in 1261 to house a thorn from Christ's crown, it has what's said to be the oldest Gothic interior in the Veneto; the thorn itself is displayed in the church on Good Friday, but for the rest of the year is kept locked away. The church has two magnificent paintings: an *Adoration of the Magi* painted in 1573 by **Paolo Veronese** (third chapel on the right), and a luminous *Baptism of Christ* (opposite), a late work by **Giovanni Bellini** which is encased in an elaborate frame that Bellini himself designed. Also take time to look at the late fifteenth-century

inlaid **choirstalls**, the extraordinary seventeenth-century *pietra dura* **altarpiece** and the anonymous *Madonna* in the left aisle, which includes a view of Vicenza around 1500, added by Fogolino.

Santa Corona's cloisters now house the **Museo Naturalistico-Archeologico**, which includes various collections of skewered insects, stuffed birds and fossils; the highlight of the historical section is a fine fourth-century Roman mosaic.

Palazzo Leoni Montanari

Contrà Santa Corona 25 • Tues–Sun 10am–6pm • €5, or Vicenza Card • Ⓦ gallerieditalia.com

Now owned by the Sanpaolo banking group, the opulent Baroque **Palazzo Leoni Montanari** has been restored as a showcase for selections from the three art collections that the bank has accumulated over the years. In the profusely decorated rooms of the *piano nobile*, paintings by Canaletto, Francesco Guardi and Tiepolo feature in a survey of eighteenth-century Veneto art that also includes a room of quirky scenes of everyday Venetian life created by Pietro Longhi and his followers. Another room on this floor houses some sixth- to third-century BC ceramics from the necropolis of Ruvo di Puglia, while upstairs there's a thematic display of more than a hundred Russian icons (about a quarter of the bank's hoard), a remarkable and well-presented array that spans the period from the thirteenth century to the twentieth.

Palazzo Barbaran da Porto – Palladio Museum

Contrà Porti 11 • Tues–Sun 10am–6pm • €6, or Vicenza Card • Ⓦ palladiomuseum.org

Palladio's **Palazzo Barbaran da Porto**, which was designed around 1570 and subsequently embellished by others, is now occupied by the Centro Internazionale di Studi di Architettura "A. Palladio", which organizes Vicenza's prestigious annual architecture conference and has turned the *palazzo* into the **Palladio Museum**, a place "in which thinking about architecture is fostered". The focus is of course largely on Palladio, and it's brilliantly done, with large-scale cutaway models of most of his major buildings and a host of imaginative audiovisual displays. And the building is in itself impressive, especially the grand Salone di Cesare, where Palladio's patrons are represented in the guise of Roman emperors.

The outskirts – Monte Bèrico and the villas

Rising behind the rail line, **Monte Bèrico** has a number of attractions: an amazing view (on a clear day the horizon is a switchback of mountain peaks), a clutch of excellent paintings and one of Europe's most famous and imitated buildings. Buses for Monte

PALLADIO

Born in Padua in 1508, Andrea di Pietro della Gondola began his career as an apprentice stonemason in Vicenza. At 30 he became the protégé of a local nobleman, Count Giangiorgio Trissino, who gave the architect his classicized name, **Palladio**. Trissino directed Palladio's training and, perhaps most crucially, took him to Rome – the first of many trips he made sketching ancient Roman remains.

Between 1540 and his death in 1580 Palladio created around a dozen palaces and public buildings in Vicenza and an even larger number of villas on the Vicentine and Venetian farming estates in the surrounding countryside, as well as the churches of the Redentore and San Giorgio Maggiore in Venice. In 1570 he published **I Quattro Libri dell'Architettura**, or "The Four Books of Architecture". Earlier Renaissance architects had written important works of theory, but Palladio's was unique in its practical applicability, in that it combined a survey of Roman architecture and his own projects with a discussion of building methods – it was both a manual and a demonstration of the principles of harmony and proportion. The *Quattro Libri* became the reference book for generations of classical architects, making Palladio more influential than any other architect in Western history.

Bèrico leave the bus station approximately every ninety minutes from Monday to Saturday; on Sunday there is a more frequent service from Viale Roma. If you decide to walk, the most direct route from the basilica is to cross Ponte San Michele, carry on to Strada Pozzetto then along Contrà San Silvestro, which brings you to Viale Risorgimento; on the other side of this major road junction, Via Casanova leads to the **Portici**, an eighteenth-century arcade built to shelter the pilgrims on their way up to the church. The walk will take about half an hour from the centre.

Basilica di Monte Bèrico

Viale X Giugno • Summer Mon–Sat 6am–12.30pm & 2.30–7.30pm, Sun 6am–7pm; winter Mon–Sat 6am–12.30pm & 2.30–6pm, Sun 6am–7pm • Free

In 1426–28 Vicenza was struck by an outbreak of bubonic plague, in the course of which the Virgin appeared twice at the summit of Monte Bèrico to announce the city's deliverance. A chapel was raised on the spot that the Virgin had obligingly marked out for its construction, and it duly became a place of pilgrimage. It was enlarged later in the century, altered again in the sixteenth century and then, at the end of the seventeenth, replaced by the present **Basilica di Monte Bèrico**. Pilgrims regularly arrive here by the busload, and the glossy interior of the church, all gilding and fake marble, is immaculately maintained to receive them.

The basilica's best painting, Montagna's *Pietà* (1500), hangs in the chapel on the right side of the apse, while *The Supper of St Gregory the Great* (1572) by **Veronese** is in the old refectory of the adjoining monastery, which it shares with the fossil collection amassed by the resident Franciscans.

Museo del Risorgimento e della Resistenza

Viale X Giugno 87 • Tues–Sun: July & Aug 10am–2pm, Sept–June 9am–1pm & 2.15–5pm • Free

From the basilica, carry on towards the summit of the hill for some ten minutes and you come to the **Museo del Risorgimento e della Resistenza**. The museum houses an impressive display, paying particular attention to Vicenza's resistance to the Austrians in the mid-nineteenth century and to the efforts of the anti-fascist Alpine fighters a century later, but for many visitors the big attraction will be the extensive wooded **parkland** on the slopes below.

Villa Valmarana ai Nani

Stradella dei Nani 87 • March–Oct daily 10am–6pm • €10 • Ⓦ villavalmarana.com

Ten minutes' walk from the basilica is the **Villa Valmarana "ai Nani"** – go back down the hill, head along Via M. D'Azeglio for 100m, then turn right into the cobbled Via S. Bastiano, which ends at the villa. This is an undistinguished house made extraordinary by the decorations of Giambattista and Giandomenico Tiepolo. *Nani*, by the way, means "dwarfs", the significance of which becomes clear when you see the garden wall.

There are two parts to the house. The main block, the **Palazzina**, was frescoed by Giambattista, drawing his imagery from the epic poems of Virgil, Tasso and Ariosto – you're handed a brief guide to the paintings at the entrance. Giambattista also painted one wall of the **Foresteria**, the guest wing, but here the bulk of the work was done by his son. Giandomenico's scope was somewhat narrower than his father's (carnivals and bucolic pleasures were his favourite themes), and he doesn't quite have the senior Tiepolo's apparently effortless virtuosity, but a similar air of wistful melancholy pervades his scenes.

La Rotonda

Via della Rotonda 45 • Villa Wed & Sat, grounds Tues–Sun: both March 10–Nov 10 10am–noon & 3–6pm; rest of year 10am–noon & 2.30–5pm • €10 villa & grounds, €5 grounds only • Ⓦ villalarotonda.it

From Villa Valmarana the narrow Strada Valmarana descends to Palladio's Villa Capra, known as **La Rotonda**. La Rotonda is unique among Palladio's villas in that it was

designed not as the main building of a farm but as a pavilion in which entertainments could be held and the landscape enjoyed. Only a walk round the lavishly decorated rooms will fully reveal the subtleties of the Rotonda's design, which gives a strong impression of being as symmetrical as a square while in fact having a definite main axis. Unless you're an architecture student and really want to scrutinize the walls from point-blank range, the garden can be given a miss, as it's just a narrow belt of grass and gravel.

ARRIVAL AND INFORMATION — VICENZA

6

By train The station is a 10min walk southwest of the historic centre.

Destinations Castelfranco Veneto (16 daily; 30–40min); Cittadella (15 daily; 25min); Milan (25 daily; 1hr 50min–2hr 40min); Padua (every 20min; 15–30min); Thiene (20 daily; 25min); Treviso (hourly; 45min–1hr 15min); Venice (every 30min; 45min–1hr 20min); Verona (every 30min; 25min–1hr).

By bus The bus terminus is next to the train station.

Destinations Bassano (hourly; 1hr); Padua (every 30min; 30min–1hr).

Tourist offices The main tourist office is by the entrance to the Teatro Olimpico, at Piazza Matteotti 12 (daily 9am–5.30pm; T 0444 320 854, W visitvicenza.org)

ACCOMMODATION

Vicenza has no central one-star **hotels**, and most of the hotels in the upper categories are rather soulless places, aimed at businesspeople and attendees at the city's frequent conferences and trade fairs. The business traffic keeps demand high, so if you want to stay in Vicenza, always reserve a room in advance.

★ **Due Mori** Contrà Do Rode 26 T 0444 321 886, W hotelduemori.com; map p.413. Friendly old-fashioned two-star hotel by the Piazza dei Signori. Its rooms are mostly capacious, and are plainly but comfortably furnished; there's wi-fi throughout, but no TVs. €90

Ostello Olimpico Viale Antonio Giuriolo 9 T 0444 540 222, W ostellovicenza.com; map p.413. Vicenza's HI hostel occupies a three-storey Art Nouveau building very near the Teatro Olimpico. It's a spartan place, and it overlooks a busy road junction, but the staff are friendly and the location is central. Reception 7–10am & 3–11pm; check-in 3–11pm. Dorms from €22

Palladio Contrà Oratorio dei Servi 27 T 0444 325 347, W hotel-palladio.it; map p.413. Once a budget hotel, the *Palladio* has been totally transformed into sleek four-star, and is now the plushest hotel in the city centre. Its 23 rooms have minimalist modern furnishings, including comfortable Japanese mattresses and wall radiators that look like abstract paintings. Room 302 at the top has the largest balcony. €170

EATING

In contrast to Verona and Padua, good **restaurants** are not numerous in Vicenza's *centro storico* – which means it's sensible to book a table in high season. Popular **specialities** include *baccalà alla Vicentina* (made by marinating dried cod in milk and oil) and *sopressa*, a kind of salami from the Pasubio and Recoaro valleys, generally eaten with a slice of grilled polenta.

CAFÉS

Caffè Pigafetta Contrà Pescaria 12; map p.413. For many Vicentines, this is where the city's best coffee is served – it's certainly where you'll get the biggest choice of brews. The teas and pastries are excellent too. Mon–Sat 8am–8pm.

Sorarù Piazzetta Andrea Palladio; map p.413. Attractive old-world *pasticceria*-café in the shadow of the basilica. You can have a coffee and cake inside at the bar or at its outdoor tables, next to the statue of Palladio. Mon, Tues, Thurs & Fri 7.30am–1pm & 3.30–7.30pm, Sat & Sun 7.30am–7.30pm.

RESTAURANTS

★ **Al Pestello** Contrà S. Stefano 3 T 0444 323 721, W ristorantealpestello.it; map p.413. Homely, well-priced (*secondi* around €17) and long-established *ristorante* by San Stefano – one of the best places in town for sampling *baccalà alla Vicentina* and other local specialities. The dining room is quite small, but in summer there are a few tables in the street. Mon, Thurs & Fri 7.30–11pm, Sat & Sun 12.30–2.30pm & 7.30–11pm.

Antica Casa della Malvasia Contrà delle Morette 5 T 0444 543 704, W anticacasadellamalvasia.it; map p.413. This bustling restaurant, just off Piazza dei Signori, offers a good range of well-prepared local standards, at around €15 for *secondi*. The dining rooms are handsome and spacious (the colour scheme is a nice mix of pistachio and bare brick), and in good weather there are seats in the alleyway outside. Tues–Sat 11.30am–3pm & 7–11.30pm, Sun 7–11.30pm.

Antico Guelfo Contrà Pedemuro S. Biagio 90 T 0444 547 897, W anticoguelfo.it; map p.413. Run by young Padova-born chef Luca Menegon, the chic *Antico Guelfa* offers a small menu of imaginative dishes (typically three or four fish/meat, plus a vegetarian option), prepared with top-quality local ingredients. Main courses are around €20.

The bare-brick dining room is one of the nicest in the city, too. Mon & Wed–Sun noon–3pm & 7–11pm.

Oca Bianca Contrà Porti 20a ⊕0444 542 193, trattoriaocabianca.com; map p.413. A small, congenial and dependable no-frills trattoria a few minutes' walk from Piazza dei Signori. The menu always features *baccalà* but is otherwise often exclusively meaty; main courses are €10–15. Mon noon–2.30pm, Tues–Fri noon–2.30pm & 7.30–10.30pm, Sat 7.30–10.30pm.

★ **Sótobotega – Il Bistrot del Baccalà** Corso Palladio 196 ⊕0444 544 414, ⊕negozio.gastronomiailceppo.com; map p.413. The best place in town for lunch – the dining area consists of a single line of tables in the wine cellar of *Il Ceppo*, Vicenza finest delicatessen, and of the main emphasis is placed, unsurprisingly, on *baccalà* – there's even a *baccalà* tasting menu. But if salt cod isn't your thing, you can choose from the other high-quality light dishes on offer. The wines are excellent, too. Tues–Sun 11.30am–3.30pm.

6

DRINKING

L'Ombra al Campanile Contrà Fontana 2; map p.413. There are plenty of bars in the zone between the Duomo and the basilica, and this traditional and atmospheric *enoteca* – which occupies a locale that's been a bar for three hundred years and has been run by the same family for three generations – is the best of them. It has an excellent selection of wines, and nice sandwiches too. Daily 9am–2pm & 5–9pm.

Il Grottino Piazza delle Erbe 2; map p.413. The bars within the arcades of the basilica tend to attract more passing traffic, but the dimly lit *Grottino*, which occupies a cellar bar beneath the building, is more atmospheric than any of them, and has tables out in the open air too. The range of wines and snacks is very good, and there's also music sometimes. Mon–Fri 5pm–2am, Sat & Sun noon–2am.

Verona

With its Roman sites and streets of pink-hued medieval buildings, the irresistible city of **VERONA** has more in the way of historic attractions than any other place in the Veneto except Venice itself. Unlike Venice, though, it's not a city overwhelmed by the tourist industry, important though that is to the local economy. Verona is the largest city of the mainland Veneto, and its economic success is largely due to its position at the crossing of the major routes from Germany and Austria to central Italy and from the west to Venice and Trieste.

Set within the low amphitheatre that the wide River Adige has carved out of the hills, Verona conveys a sense of ease that you don't find in the region's other cities. As you walk past the great **Roman arena**, or along the embankments or over the bridges that span the broad curves of the Adige, you'll be struck by the spaciousness of the city. With cars and buses barred from many of the squares and narrow medieval lanes of the historic centre, this is a city that invites dawdling.

Brief history

Verona's initial development as a **Roman** settlement came about from its geographical position straddling the main lines of communication. A period of decline after the disintegration of the Roman Empire was followed by revival under the Ostrogoths, who in turn were succeeded by the Franks. By the twelfth century Verona had

THE BIGLIETTO UNICO AND VERONA CARD

A **biglietto unico**, costing €6, allows one visit to each of the four great churches of Verona: Duomo, San Fermo, San Zeno and Sant'Anastasia. It can be bought at any of these churches, which otherwise individually charge €2.50 for admission. The **Verona Card** (⊕veronacard.it) gives access to all of these churches, plus the Arena, Casa di Giulietta, Castelvecchio, Galleria d'Arte Moderna, Museo Lapidario, Teatro Romano, Arche Scaligeri, Tomba di Giulietta and Torre dei Lamberti (but you have to pay an extra €1 there for the lift), as well as unlimited travel on city buses. The 24-hour version of the card costs €18, the 48-hour version €22. It's available at *tabacchi* displaying the Verona Card sign (there's one at the station), at participating museums and at the tourist office; the period of validity begins when you first use it, not when you buy it.

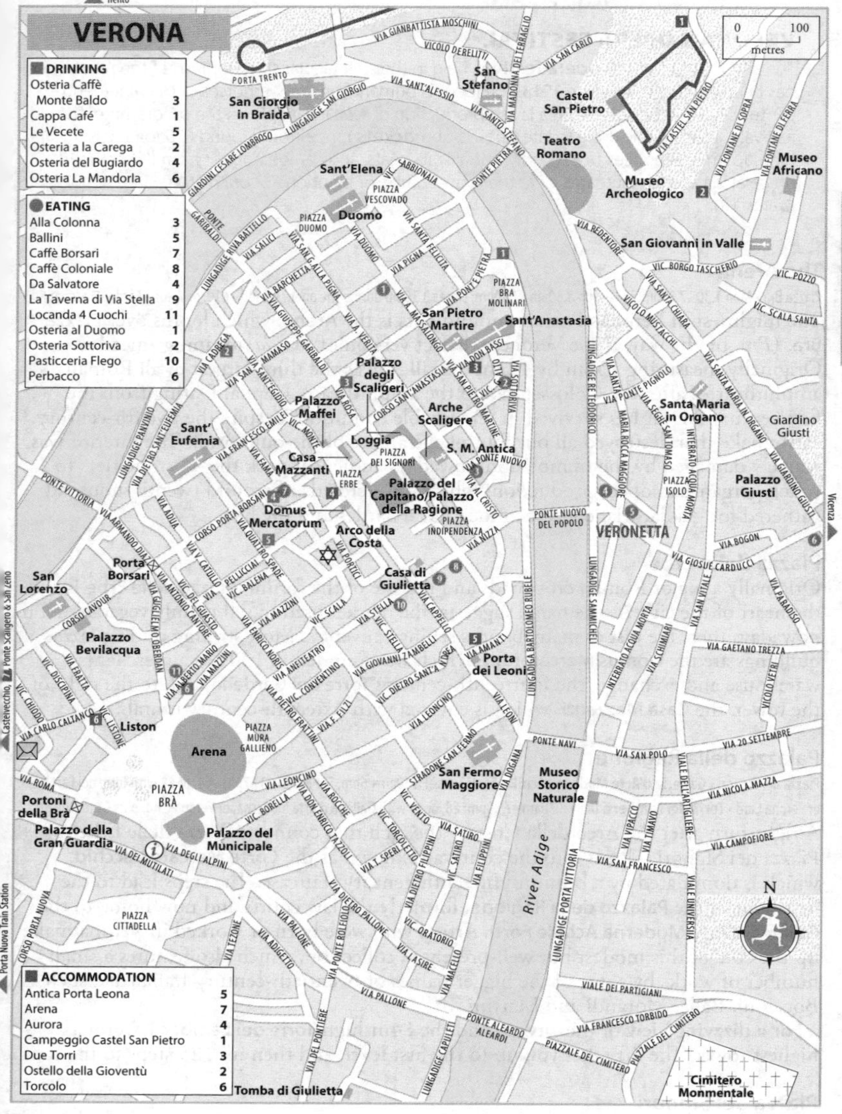

become a city-state, and in the following century it approached the zenith of its independent existence with the rise of the Scaligers. The ruthless Scaligers were at the same time energetic patrons of the arts, and many of Verona's finest buildings date from their rule.

With the fall of their dynasty a time of upheaval ensued, Gian Galeazzo Visconti of Milan emerging in control of the city. Absorption into the Venetian Empire came in 1405, and Verona was governed from Venice until the arrival of Napoleon. Verona's history thereafter shadowed that of Venice.

VERONA'S OPERA FESTIVAL

The city's world-famous **opera festival**, held in the spectacular surroundings of the Arena, has been a major draw since 1913. The focus is primarily on the warhorses of the nineteenth-century Italian repertoire, with a lavish production of *Aïda* invariably on the programme. The festival runs from mid-June to late August, and **tickets** range from around €25 for a perch high up on the terraces to €200 for central stalls seats, and can be bought from the ticket office at Via Dietro Anfiteatro, or at the tourist office, or by phone or online (T 045 800 5151, W arena.it).

The Arena

Piazza Brà • Mon 1.30–7.30pm, Tues–Sun 8.30am–7.30pm; closes 3.30pm during the opera season • €10, or Verona Card • W arena.it

The mightiest of Verona's Roman monuments is the **Arena**, which looms over **Piazza Brà**. (*Brà*, by the way, is the Veronese dialect version of *braida*, meaning "meadow".) Originally measuring 152m by 123m overall, it was the third-largest of all Roman amphitheatres after the Colosseum and the amphitheatre Capua. Dating from the first century AD, it has survived in remarkable condition, despite the twelfth-century earthquake that destroyed all but four of the arches of the outer wall. The interior was scarcely damaged by the tremor, and nowadays audiences pack the 44 stone tiers to watch gargantuan opera productions where once crowds of around twenty thousand gathered for gladiatorial contests, mock naval battles and the like.

Piazza delle Erbe

Originally a major Roman crossroads and the site of the forum, **Piazza delle Erbe** is still the heart of the city. As the name suggests, the market used to sell mainly vegetables, but nowadays there are just as many booths selling souvenirs. Most striking of the piazza's buildings are the **Domus Mercatorum**, which was founded in 1301 as a merchants' warehouse and exchange, the fourteenth-century **Torre del Gardello** and, to the right of the tower, the **Casa Mazzanti**, which is covered with sixteenth-century murals.

Palazzo della Ragione

Piazza dei Signori • **Galleria d'Arte Moderna Achille Forti** Tues–Fri 10am–6pm, Sat & Sun 11–7pm • €4, or €8 with Torre dei Lamberti, or Verona Card • **Torre dei Lamberti** Daily 8.30am–7.30pm; €6, or €8 with Galleria d'Arte Moderna, or Verona Card, plus €1 for the lift

A right turn after the Arco della Costa – the arch that connects Piazza delle Erbe to Piazza dei Signori – leads into the courtyard known as the **Corte Mercato Vecchio**, which is dominated by a beautiful fifteenth-century staircase. The steps lead to the first floor of the **Palazzo della Ragione**, formerly the law courts and now home to the **Galleria d'Arte Moderna Achille Forti**. Artists who were born or worked in Verona make up the core of this modest but well-presented collection, which also features a small number of works by some of the bigger names of twentieth-century Italian art, such as Boccioni, Balla, Morandi and Martini.

For a dizzying view of the city, ascend the 84m-high **Torre dei Lamberti**, Verona's highest tower. The lift takes you up to the first level, and then it's 125 steps to the top.

Piazza dei Signori

Piazza dei Signori used to be the chief public square of Verona. Facing you as you come into the square is the medieval **Palazzo degli Scaligeri**, residence of the Scaligers; extending from it at a right angle is the fifteenth-century **Loggia del Consiglio**, the former assembly hall of the city council and Verona's outstanding early Renaissance building. The rank of Roman notables along the roof includes Verona's most illustrious native poet, Catullus.

Arche Scaligeri

June–Sept daily 10am–1pm & 3–6pm • €1, or Verona Card

Passing under the arch linking the Palazzo degli Scaligeri to the Palazzo del Capitano, you come to the little Romanesque church of Santa Maria Antica, in front of which, within their own enclosure, are ranged the **Arche Scaligeri**, some of the most elaborate funerary monuments in Italy. Over the side entrance to the church, an equestrian statue of **Cangrande I** ("Big Dog"; died 1329) gawps down from his tomb's pyramidal roof; the statue is a copy, the original being displayed in the Castelvecchio. The canopied tombs of the rest of the clan are enclosed within a wrought-iron palisade decorated with ladder motifs, the emblem of the Scaligeri. **Mastino I** ("Mastiff"; died 1277), founder of the dynasty, is buried in the simple tomb against the wall of the church; Mastino II (died 1351) is to the left of the entrance, opposite the most florid of the tombs, that of **Cansignorio** ("Top Dog"; died 1375).

Sant'Anastasia

Piazza Sant'Anastasia • March–Oct Mon–Sat 9am–6pm, Sun 1–6pm; Nov–Feb Mon–Sat 10am–1pm & 1.30–5pm, Sun 1–5pm • €2.50, or biglietto unico, or Verona Card

Going on past the Arche Scaligeri, and turning left along Via San Pietro, you come to **Sant'Anastasia**, Verona's largest church. Started in 1290 and completed in 1481, it's mainly Gothic in style, with undertones of the Romanesque. The fourteenth-century carvings of New Testament scenes around the doors are the most arresting feature of its bare exterior; the interior's highlight is Pisanello's delicately coloured fresco *St George and the Princess* (high above the chapel to the right of the altar), a work in which the normally martial saint appears as something of a dandy.

San Pietro Martire

Piazza Sant'Anastasia • Sat & Sun 2–6pm • Free

On one side of the little piazza fronting Sant'Anastasia stands **San Pietro Martire**, deconsecrated since its ransacking by Napoleon. The highlight of the small interior is the vast and strange lunette fresco on the east wall. Painted in the early sixteenth century, it's an allegorical account of the Virgin's Assumption, though the bizarre collection of animals appears to have little connection with a bemused-looking Madonna.

The Duomo

Piazza Duomo • March–Oct Mon–Sat 10am–5.30pm, Sun 1.30–5.30pm; Nov–Feb Mon–Sat 10am–1pm & 1.30–5.30pm, Sun 1.30–5.30pm • €2.50, or biglietto unico or Verona Card

Verona's red-and-white-striped **Duomo** lies just round the river's bend, past the Roman Ponte Pietra. Consecrated in 1187, it's Romanesque in its lower parts, developing into Gothic as it goes up; the two doorways are twelfth century – look for the story of Jonah and the whale on the south porch, and the statues of Roland and Oliver, two of Charlemagne's paladins, on the west. In the first chapel on the left, an *Assumption* by Titian occupies an architectural frame by Sansovino, who also designed the choir. The door at the end of the left aisle gives access to the churches of **San Giovanni in Fonte** and, straight ahead, **Sant'Elena**, in front of which lie the remnants of the presbytery of a fourth-century basilica, whose form Sant'Elena roughly follows. Mosaics from the

"ROMEO'S HOUSE" AND "JULIET'S TOMB"

The Casa di Giulietta is the foremost of Verona's spurious **Romeo and Juliet** attractions, but the city has a couple of other shrines to the ill-fated couple: **"Romeo's house"**, a private dwelling at Via Arche Scaligere 4; and the **Tomba di Giulietta**, in the southeast of the city, in the cloister of the deconsecrated San Francesco al Corso (Mon 1.30–7.30pm, Tues–Sun 8.30am–7.30pm; €4.50, or €7 combined ticket with the Casa di Giuletta, or Verona Card; Oct–May free on first Sun of month), which also has a collection of frescoes that have been removed from various Veronese houses and churches, the oldest of them dating from 996.

second half of the fourth century can be seen in Sant'Elena itself, while the adjacent San Giovanni in Fonte contains a masterpiece of Romanesque sculpture: a large baptismal font covered with biblical scenes.

Casa di Giulietta

Via Cappello 23 • Mon 1.30–7.30pm, Tues–Sun 8.30am–7.30pm • €6, or €7 combined ticket with the Tomba di Giulietta,or Verona Card

South of Piazza delle Erbe on Via Cappello, you'll find the **Casa di Giulietta** – the busiest attraction in Verona, and the least substantial. Verona was the setting for Shakepeare's famous romance, but while the "Capulets" (Capuleti) and the "Montagues" (Montecchi) did exist, Romeo and Juliet themselves were entirely fictional creations, and the association of this house with Juliet is based on nothing more than its picturesque balcony. Notwithstanding the facts, a bronze Juliet has been shoved into a corner of the courtyard, and her right breast has been polished bright by the groping hands of school-age pilgrims hoping for luck in love. The house itself, constructed at the start of the fourteenth century, is in a fine state of preservation, but the rooms are largely empty and the displays reek of desperation: the bed from Zeffirelli's film of *Romeo and Juliet* is displayed as if it were an item of significance, for example, and there is even an area in which visitors can dispatch an email to "Juliet".

San Fermo Maggiore

Stradone San Fermo • March–Oct Mon–Sat 10am–6pm, Sun 1–6pm; Nov–Feb Mon–Sat 10am–1pm & 1.30–5pm, Sun 1–5pm • €2.50, or biglietto unico, or Verona Card

Via Cappello leads into Via Leoni with its Roman gate, the **Porta Leona**, and a segment of excavated Roman street, exposed 3m below today's street level. At the end of Via Leoni and across the road stands the red-brick church of **San Fermo Maggiore**, whose exterior betrays the fact that it consists of two churches combined. The Benedictines built the original one in the eighth century, then rebuilt it in the eleventh to honour the relics of St Fermo and St Roch (the former was supposedly martyred on this site); very soon after, flooding forced them to superimpose another church for day-to-day use, a structure greatly altered in the early fourteenth century by the Minorites. The Gothic upper church has numerous fourteenth-century frescoes and a fine wooden keel-vault. The now subterranean Romanesque lower church, entered from the right transept, has some well-preserved twelfth-century frescoes on its columns.

Porta Borsari

After the Arena and the Teatro Romano, Verona's most impressive Roman remnant is the **Porta Borsari**, on the junction of Via Diaz and Corso Porta Borsari. This was Verona's largest Roman gate; the inscription dates it at 265 AD, but it's almost certainly older than that.

Corso Cavour

Heading on from Porta Borsari down the busy thoroughfare of **Corso Cavour** you pass the small twelfth-century **San Lorenzo** before coming to the **Arco dei Gavi**; demolished by Napoleon's troops, it was rebuilt here in 1932. This is your best vantage point from which to admire the **Ponte Scaligero**, which was built by Cangrande II between 1355 and 1375. The retreating German army blew up the bridge in 1945, but the salvaged material was used for its reconstruction.

The Castelvecchio

Corso Castelvecchio 2 • Mon 1.30–7.30pm, Tues–Sun 8.30am–7.30pm • €6, or Verona Card

The fortress from which the Ponte Scaligero springs, the **Castelvecchio**, was commissioned by Cangrande II and became the stronghold for Verona's subsequent rulers. Opened as the city museum in 1925, it was damaged by bombing in World War II, but reopened in 1964 after restoration by **Carlo Scarpa**. Scarpa's conversion of

the Castelvecchio is one of his most impressive projects, leading the visitor through a labyrinth of chambers, courtyards and open-air walkways – a route fascinating to explore in itself, thanks largely to Scarpa's subtle use of materials and textures. Halfway through the itinerary, you'll come face to face with the equestrian figure of **Cangrande I**, removed from his tomb and strikingly displayed on an outdoor pedestal – a perfect demonstration of Scarpa's extraordinary ability to maximize the visual impact both of the objects in the museum and of the building itself.

The museum contains lots of fine medieval sculpture, an array of weapons and other artefacts, and a large collection of paintings, all perfectly displayed. Many of the pictures are unremarkable, but there are some outstanding pieces too – look out for the exquisite *Madonna of the Quails* by **Pisanello**, **Mantegna**'s *Holy Family*, the bizarre *Madonna of the Passion* by Crivelli, a *Madonna* by **Giovanni Bellini** and **Veronese**'s *Descent from the Cross*.

Basilica di San Zeno Maggiore

Piazza San Zeno • March–Oct Mon–Sat 8.30am–6pm, Sun 12.30–5pm; Nov–Feb Mon–Sat 10am–1pm & 1.30–5pm, Sun 12.30–5pm • €2.50, or biglietto unico, or Verona Card

A little over 1km northwest of the Castelvecchio is the **Basilica di San Zeno Maggiore**, one of the most significant Romanesque churches in northern Italy. A church was founded here, above the tomb of the city's patron saint, as early as the fifth century, but the present building and its campanile were put up in the first half of the twelfth century, with additions continuing up to the end of the fourteenth. Its large rose window dates from the early twelfth century, as does the magnificent portal, whose lintels bear relief sculptures representing the months and the miracles of St Zeno. The reliefs to the side of the portal, also from this period, show scenes from the Old and New Testaments and various allegorical scenes. Extraordinary bronze panels on the **doors** depict scenes from the Bible and more miracles of Zeno, in a style influenced by Byzantine and Ottoman art; most of those on the left date from around 1100, most of the right-hand panels from a century later. Wooden doors protect the panels from the elements, but they can be seen from inside the church.

Areas of the lofty and simple **interior** are covered with frescoes, dating from the twelfth to the sixteenth centuries. Diverting though these are, the most compelling painting is the high altar's luminous *Madonna and Saints* by **Mantegna**.

San Giorgio in Braida

Lungadige San Giorgio 6 • Thurs–Sat 10am–5.30pm, Sun 1–7pm • Free

On the north bank of the Adige River, across Ponte Garibaldi, stands **San Giorgio in Braida**, which in terms of its works of art is the richest of Verona's churches. A *Baptism* by Tintoretto hangs over the door, while the main altar, designed by Sanmicheli, incorporates a marvellous *Martyrdom of St George* by Paolo Veronese.

Teatro Romano and Museo Archeologico

Regaste Redentore 2 • Theatre and museum Mon 1.30–7.30pm, Tues–Sun 8.30am–7.30pm • €4.50, or Verona Card

Walking along the north bank of the river past the delightful Romanesque Santo Stefano and the Ponte Pietra, you come to the first-century-BC **Teatro Romano**; much restored, the theatre is used for concerts and plays. High above it, and reached by a lift, the **Museo Archeologico** occupies the buildings of an old convent. Its well-arranged collection features a number of Greek, Roman and Etruscan finds, including a magnificent Roman bronze head. Steps to the side of the theatre lead to the **Castel San Pietro**, built by the Austrians on the site of a Visconti castle that had been destroyed by Napoleon. An uningratiating building, its sole appeal is the view away from it.

Santa Maria in Organo

Piazzetta Santa Maria in Organo 1 • Thurs & Fri 10.30am–5.30pm, Sat 10am–4.30pm, Sun 11am–5.30pm • Free

In the heart of the **Veronetta** district, on the east bank of the Adige, stands the church of **Santa Maria in Organo**, which possesses what Vasari praised as the finest choirstall in Italy. Dating from the 1490s, this marquetry was the work of a Benedictine monk called Fra Giovanni, and is astonishing in its precision and use of perspective. There's more of his work in the sacristy.

Giardino Giusti

Via Giardino Giusti 2 • Daily: April–Sept 9am–8pm; Oct–March 9am–sunset • €7

Close to Santa Maria in Organo you'll find one of the finest formal gardens in the country, the sixteenth-century **Giardino Giusti**. After feuding between some of the heirs to the Giusti estate, the grounds and the splendid Palazzo Giusti (which is not open to the public) have been put up for sale, and rumour has it that it will become a luxury hotel. But for the time being the garden's fountains and shaded corners continue to provide the city's most pleasant refuge from the streets, as they have done for centuries – Goethe and Mozart both paid a visit, and were much impressed.

ARRIVAL AND GETTING AROUND — VERONA

By plane Verona's Valerio Catullo airport is at Villafranca, 12km away; ATV buses (6.30am–11.30pm; every 20min; €6) run to the bus terminal in front of the Porta Nuova train station.

By train From the main train station (Verona Porta Nuova) it's a 20min walk to Piazza Brà; there are regular buses from the station to the city centre.

Destinations Milan (every 30min; 1hr 20min–2hr); Padua (every 30min; 45min–1hr 20min); Venice (every 30min; 1hr 10min–2hr 20min); Vicenza (every 30min; 25–60min).

By car There are well-signed car parks just before Piazza Brà and at Piazza Isolo in Veronetta, or there is free parking across the river, beyond Santo Stefano.

By bus City buses leave from outside the train station. Tickets can be bought for €1.30 from inside the train station or from machines by the bus ranks, or for €2 on board; alternatively, you can get ten rides for €11.70 or a day pass for €4. Tickets are valid for 90min. The Verona Card (see page 418) also gives unlimited use of city buses.

INFORMATION

Tourist information The tourist office is by Piazza Brà, tucked into the old town walls at Via degli Alpini 9, just beyond the Palazzo del Municipale (summer Mon–Sat 9am–7pm, Sun 9am–6pm; winter Mon–Sat 10am–6pm, Sun 10am–4pm); ⓣ 045 806 8680, ⓦ tourism.verona.it & ⓦ veronatouristoffice.it). As well as providing information, it organizes walking tours, runs a hotel-booking service and can book tickets for the Arena.

ACCOMMODATION

Peak periods for Verona's hotel prices include the **opera season** (late June to early Sept) and the numerous trade fairs in the autumn. But given that Verona is one of Italy's major tourist cities, good-quality accommodation is strangely scarce here, so whatever time of year you're coming, **reserve** your room well in advance.

Antica Porta Leona Via Corticella Leoni 3 ⓣ 045 595 499, ⓦ anticaportaleona.com; map p.419. A very elegant four-star with 23 spacious rooms and a fitness centre in the basement, which has a small pool. All rooms have steam showers, while the five "opera suites" (their names and decor pay tribute to Verdi's masterpieces) are equipped with whirlpool baths. **€240**

Arena Stradone Porta Palio 2 ⓣ 045 803 2440, ⓦ albergoarena.it; map p.419. There are hardly any one-star hotels in central Verona – this one, next to Castelvecchio (not as close to the Arena as its name might suggest), has been refurnished quite recently, and is the best of the bunch. Rooms without private bathroom are €30 cheaper than en-suite rooms. **€125**

Aurora Piazza delle Erbe ⓣ 045 594 717, ⓦ hotelaurora.biz; map p.419. This three-star is one of the most attractive mid-range hotels in the city. Many rooms have a view of the Piazza delle Erbe, and the staff are welcoming and knowledgeable. Excellent buffet breakfast on a terrace overlooking the square. **€190**

Due Torri Piazza Sant'Anastasia 4 ⓣ 045 595 044, ⓦ hotelduetorri.duetorrihotels.com; map p.419. Located right next door to the church of Sant'Anastasia, the *Due Torri* began life as an inn on the Milan–Venice route, but for some time has been Verona's best-known five-star hotel. The 89 supremely comfortable rooms are decorated in nineteenth-century Imperial style, with lavish use of pink Veronese marble in the bathrooms. If you're pushing the boat out, this is the place to stay. **€270**

Ostello della Gioventù Salita Fontana del Ferro 15 ⓣ 045 590 360, ⓦ ostelloverona.it; bus #73, or #91 after 7.45pm and on Sun, from the station to Piazza

Isolo; map p.419. The official HI hostel is in the lovely setting of sixteenth-century Villa Francescatti. It has 241 beds, including some family rooms (bunk beds only); some rooms have frescoed ceilings, others a private terrace; many have splendid views over the rooftops. The midnight curfew is extended for guests with opera tickets. Price includes breakfast, and dinner is available for €8, if ordered in advance. Dorms **€18**, family rooms (per person) **€20**

★ **Torcolo** Vicolo Listone 3 ⓣ 045 800 7512, ⓦ hoteltorcolo.it; map p.419. An extremely welcoming two-star hotel within 100m of the Arena, just off Piazza Brà. It's run by two sisters who have been in the business for more than thirty years, and is a favourite with the opera crowds, so book ahead. Breakfast is an extra €10. **€150**

CAMPING

Campeggio Castel San Pietro Via Castel S. Pietro 2 ⓣ 045 592 037, ⓦ campingcastelsanpietro.com; bus #41 or #95 from the station to Via Marsala and then a steep walk up the hill; map p.419. This pleasant shady site out by the old city walls, the only place to camp near the centre of Verona, offers marvellous views over the city. Open April–Sept. From **€10** per pitch and **€10** per person

6

EATING

Your money goes a lot further in Verona than it does in Venice: numerous **trattorie** offer full meals for less than €30, and Verona's cuisine – which is much meatier and richer than Venice's, with horsemeat being a speciality – can also be sampled in many of the city's unpretentious **osterie**. All *osterie* serve both drinks (with snacks) and full meals; we've listed the ones in which the emphasis is on eating more than drinking under "Restaurants".

CAFÉS AND GELATERIE

★ **Ballini** Via S. Maria Rocca Maggiore 4A ⓦ gelateria ballini.it; map p.419. Andrea Ballini has built up a big following since opening his *gelateria* at the far end of the Ponte Nuovo in 2011. Flavours such as fig and almond are used in season, and his pear cooked in Valpolicella is delectable. The best ice cream in town. Mon–Fri 1–11pm, Sat & Sun noon–1.30pm & 3–11.30pm.

Caffè Borsari Via Porta Borsari 15/D; map p.419. Still known to many Veronese by its original name – *Caffè Tubino* – this homely little cave of a place serves what might be the finest coffee in Verona, and amazing hot chocolate too. Daily 7.30am–8pm.

Caffè Coloniale Piazzetta Viviani 14/C; map p.419. Good cakes, light meals and the best hot chocolate in the city, with an attractive outdoor terrace. Daily 7.30am–midnight.

Pasticceria Flego Via Stella 13/A ⓣ 045 803 2471; map p.419. In the opinion of many Veronese, *Flego* is the best *pasticceria* in town. For elegance it can't be beaten, and in addition to superb cakes and coffee, it has a long list of teas. There's a second branch at Porta Borsari 9. Both branches Tues–Sun 7.30am–7.30pm.

RESTAURANTS

Alla Colonna Largo Pescheria Vecchia 4 ⓣ 045 596 718; map p.419. In business for more than thirty years now, this is perhaps the best no-frills trattoria in the city centre, and it's packed most evenings, so booking is advisable. It's renowned for its *cotoletta* (veal cutlet), which comes in three sizes, the biggest of which is vast. Main courses begin at less than €10, and there's a €15 set lunch. Mon–Sat noon–2.30pm & 7–11.30pm.

Da Salvatore Piazza S. Tomaso 6 ⓣ 045 803 0366, ⓦ pizzeriadasalvatorevr.com; map p.419. Tucked under the arcades of a riverside road junction, this is the most stylish and the busiest pizzeria in Verona. Tues–Sat 12.30–2.30pm & 7–11pm, Sun 7–11pm.

La Taverna di Via Stella Via Stella 5c ⓣ 045 800 8008, ⓦ tavernadiviastella.com; map p.419. An excellent city-centre trattoria, with very professional service, generous portions of unpretentious local dishes, and modest prices, with main courses all under €20. Popular with locals and tourists alike, so reservations are sensible in summer. Mon 7.15–11pm, Tues & Thurs–Sun 12.15–2.15pm & 7.15–11pm.

★ **Locanda 4 Cuochi** Via Alberto Mario 12 ⓣ 045 803 0311, ⓦ locanda4cuochi.it; map p.419. Run by four young chefs, this stylish open-kitchen restaurant has a more inventive menu than many in Verona, though the emphasis is still very much on meat. The atmosphere is buzzy, cool and friendly, and prices are lower than you might expect – *secondi* are around €15. Tues 7.30–10.30pm, Wed–Sun 12.30–2.30pm & 7.30–10.30pm.

★ **Osteria al Duomo** Via Duomo 7/A ⓣ 045 800 7333; map p.419. There has been an *osteria* here for at least a century, and it still serves old Veronese favourites such as

VINITALY

As the Veneto produces more DOC wine than any other region in Italy, it's not surprising that Italy's main wine fair, **Vinitaly** (ⓦ vinitaly.com), is held in Verona. It takes place over four days in April and offers abundant sampling opportunities; day tickets cost about €50, less if you book online.

VERONA'S CARNIVAL

One of the most enjoyable days in the calendar is Verona's **Carnevale**. On the Friday before Shrove Tuesday, a huge procession winds through the centre from Piazza Brà. This is a local event with none of the masks and posing of Venice – just lots of people dressing up, loud music and confetti – though mind the kids who get carried away spraying white foam everywhere. The procession is led by a large character called the Papa del Gnocco – most of the city's restaurants serve gnocchi on that Friday.

6

pastissada (horse stew) and *bigoli* with *sugo d'asino* (donkey sauce). Prices are low (most *secondi* around €10), the decor is quirky (with a miscellany of musical instruments hanging on the walls), and the hosts are terrific. Mon–Sat 11.30am–2.30pm & 7pm–midnight.

Osteria Sottoriva Via Sottoriva 9 T 045 801 4323; map p.419. Medieval Via Sottoriva is one of most atmospheric streets in the city, and has several decent places to eat. None of its *osterie* is more convivial than this one, which serves Verona specialities at reasonable prices (mains all under €15), and in hefty portions. Tripe is something of a speciality, and horsemeat is always on the menu. In summer you can eat at the tables outside, under the arches. Daily except Wed 11am–3pm & 6–10.30pm.

Perbacco Via Carducci 48/A T 045 594 193, W trattoriaperbacco.com; map p.419. Located a short way out of the centre, near the Giusti gardens, this simple neighbourhood trattoria offers a small menu of traditional Veronese cooking at remarkably low prices – mains are all under €10. In good weather, tables in the vine-covered courtyard augment the small and intimate dining room. Mon, Tues & Thurs–Sat 12.30–2pm & 7.30–10pm.

DRINKING

Osteria Caffè Monte Baldo Via Rosa 12 T 045 803 0579, W osteriamontebaldo.com; map p.419. A very attractive and popular *osteria* near Piazza delle Erbe, with excellent antipasti and more substantial dishes (€12–20), and a wide range of wines available by the glass. The bottle-lined lower room opens out onto the street, which makes it particularly nice in summer, and there's another dining room upstairs. Unusually, the kitchen is in operation continuously from noon. Mon–Thurs 10am–11pm, Fri 10am–midnight, Sat 11am–midnight, Sun 11am–11pm.

Cappa Café Piazzetta Brà Molinari 1/A T 045 800 4516; map p.419. Just down from the Ponte Pietra, this smart bar has been popular since it opened way back in 1966; it can get very crowded at weekends, but you can always take your drink to one of the nearby benches, or lean on the parapet and gaze over the river. Mon–Sat 9am–2am, Sun 9am–midnight.

Le Vecete Via Pellicciai 32; map p.419. Big and atmospheric city-centre *osteria* with a delicious selection of the savoury tartlets known as *bocconcini*, and a menu of pasta dishes, risottos and other plain fare. The wine list is excellent, ranging from the swiggable to the very expensive. Daily noon–4pm & 6.30–11.30pm.

Osteria a la Carega Via Cadrega 8 T 045 806 9248, W osterialacarega.com; map p.419. Friendly, small and studenty *osteria* with a few outside tables in the side yard, and a fine selection of inexpensive wines, plus excellent *piadine* and simple meals. If you're wondering about the sign above the door – *carega* is Veronese dialect for "chair". Daily noon–2.30pm & 7–11pm.

Osteria del Bugiardo Corso Porta Borsari 17/A T 045 591 869, W buglioni.it/osteria; map p.419. This long-standing *osteria* is always thronged with locals grabbing a quick snack and a glass – the wine list is outstanding. There's a small meal menu too, but unless you enjoy eating elbow-to-elbow with strangers, it's maybe best to stick to the drinks and antipasti. Mon–Thurs & Sun 11am–midnight, Fri & Sat 11am–1am.

★ Osteria La Mandorla Via Alberto Mario 23 T 045 597 053; map p.419. This tiny, old-fashioned and hundred percent authentic bar is just a minute's stroll from the Arena; the atmosphere is great, and the wines and snacks are very good. Mon 5pm–2am, Tues–Sun 11am–2pm & 5pm–2am.

ENTERTAINMENT

Opera The city's opera festival is held in the Arena from mid-June to late Aug or early Sept (see page 420). For the rest of the year Verona's opera moves to the Teatro Filarmonico in Via Roma, off Piazza Brà (T 045 800 5151, W arena.it).

Classical music, theatre and dance A season of ballet and of Shakespeare and other dramatists in Italian is the principal summer fare at the Teatro Romano. Some events here are free; for the rest, if you don't mind inferior acoustics, park yourself on the steps going up the hill alongside the theatre. The city has two other major old venues: the Teatro Nuovo (W teatronuovoverona.it), at Piazza Viviani 10, which has plays and classical music; and the Teatro Ristori (W teatroristori.org), at Via Teatro Ristori 7, which presents music and dance.

Rock and jazz Big rock events crop up on the Arena's calendar, while June's Verona Jazz festival at the Teatro Romano attracts international names. The *Spettacoli* section of the local paper, *L'Arena*, is the best source of up-to-date information about what's on.

Treviso

One of the overlooked gems of the Veneto, **TREVISO** makes an ideal jumping-off point for the northern Veneto. Treviso was an important town long before its assimilation by Venice in 1389, and plenty of evidence of its early status survives in the form of Gothic churches, public buildings and, most dramatically of all, the paintings of **Tomaso da Modena** (1325–79), the major artist in northern Italy in the years immediately after Giotto's death. The general townscape within Treviso's sixteenth-century walls is appealing too – long porticoes and frescoed house facades give many of the streets an appearance quite distinct from that of other towns in the region, and wandering the maze of backstreets and canals is a pleasant way to while away an hour or two. Treviso was pounded during both world wars and on Good Friday 1944 was half destroyed in a single bombing raid, but enough survived or was rebuilt to restore the atmosphere of the old streets.

Piazza dei Signori

Piazza dei Signori is the town's focal point. On one side of the piazza stands the early thirteenth-century **Palazzo dei Trecento**, which was badly damaged in the 1944 bombing; the adjoining **Palazzo del Podestà** is a nineteenth-century concoction. Of more interest are the two conjoined churches at the back of the block on Piazza San Vito: **San Vito** and **Santa Lucia** (Mon–Fri 8am–noon, Sat & Sun 8am–noon & 3.30–6.30pm; free). The tiny chapel of Santa Lucia has extensive frescoes by Tomaso da Modena and his followers; San Vito has even older paintings in the alcove through which you enter from Santa Lucia.

The Duomo

Piazza del Duomo • Mon–Sat 7.30am–noon & 3.30–6.30pm, Sun 8am–1pm & 3.30–8pm • Free

Calmaggiore, the main street of the *centro storico*, stretches from Piazza dei Signori to the **Duomo**, which was founded in the twelfth century, much altered in succeeding centuries, and rebuilt after 1944. The interior is chiefly notable for its crypt – a thicket of twelfth-century columns with scraps of medieval mosaics – and the Cappella Malchiostro, which has frescoes by Pordenone and a much-restored *Annunciation* by Titian.

Musei Civici di Santa Caterina

Piazzetta Mario Botter • Tues–Sun 9am–12.30pm & 2.30–6pm • €6, or 10 with Museo Bailo • ⓦ museicivicitreviso.it

The finest frescoes in Treviso – Tomaso da Modena's *Life of St Ursula* – are displayed in the deconsecrated church of **Santa Caterina**, on Via Santa Caterina. Painted for a now-extinct church, the frescoes were detached from the walls in the late nineteenth century and now take pride of place in the impressive complex that now houses the city's main museum collections. The rest of the complex comprises an extensive archeological section and a collection of pictures that features work by Giandomenico Tiepolo, Francesco Guardi, Jacopo Bassano and Titian, and a wonderful portrait by Lorenzo Lotto.

Museo Luigi Bailo

Borgo Cavour 24 • Tues–Sun 10am–6pm • €6, or €10 with Santa Caterina museum • ⓦ museicivicitreviso.it

Treviso's newest museum, the **Museo Luigi Bailo**, is an extensive collection of art produced in the Treviso area in the twentieth century, beautifully displayed in a sixteenth-century monastery onto which has been fused a sleek and handsome modern gallery, built in 2015. The dominant presence is local-born **Arturo Martini** (1889–1947), more than 100 of whose works (paintings, sculptures and drawings) are on show.

San Nicolò and the seminario

Via San Nicolò • **Church** Mon–Fri 8am–noon & 3.30–6pm • Free • **Seminario** Mon–Fri: summer 8am–6pm; winter 8am–12.30pm & 3–5.30pm • Free

West of the centre, just over the River Sile from the train station, rises the severe Dominican church of **San Nicolò**, which has frescoes dating from the thirteenth to the sixteenth centuries. Some of the columns are decorated with paintings by Tomaso da Modena and his school, while the left wall of the chancel has a fine composite tomb created in 1500 by **Antonio Rizzo** (who did the sculpture) and **Lorenzo Lotto** (who painted the attendant pages).

For a comprehensive demonstration of Tomaso da Modena's talents you have to visit the adjoining **Seminario**, where the chapterhouse (*sala del capitolo*), to the left as you enter (you may need to ring the bell to get in), is decorated with forty portraits of members of the Dominican order, painted in 1352. Each shows a friar at study in his cell, but there is never a hint of the formulaic: one man is shown sharpening a quill, another checks a text through a magnifier, a third blows the surplus ink from his nib and a fourth scowls as if you've interrupted his work.

ARRIVAL AND INFORMATION — TREVISO

By plane The MOM #6 bus runs at least every 30min from the airport to Treviso train station, taking 15min; tickets (€1.30) can be bought in the arrival hall (tickets cost €3 if bought on board). For transport to Venice, see page 387.

By train Arriving at the train station on Piazza Duca d'Aosta, head straight across the bridge, bending slightly left at the first roundabout to reach the centre.

Destinations Castelfranco Veneto (15 daily; 25min); Cittadella (13 daily; 35min); Conegliano (every 30min; 15–25min); Venice (every 30min; 35min); Vicenza (13 daily; 45min–1hr 10min).

By bus Treviso's bus station is on Lungosile Antonio Mattei, up the road towards the centre from the train station.

Destinations Asolo (10 daily; 1hr); Bassano (hourly; 1hr 30min); Castelfranco Veneto (every 30min; 50min); Conegliano (every 30min; 45min); Padua (every 30min, hourly at weekends; 1hr 10min); Venice (every 30min; 35min).

Tourist office The tourist office is at Via Fiumicelli 30 (Mon 10am–1pm, Tues–Sat 10am–5pm, Sun 10am–4pm; ⓣ 042 254 7632, ⓦ visittreviso.it).

ACCOMMODATION

Il Focolare Piazza Ancilotto 4 ⓣ 0422 56 601, ⓦ albergoilfocolare.net. This pleasant and very central three-star, which for many years was known as the *Campeol*, has recently been thoroughly freshened up: the rooms are now light and simply furnished, though some are quite confined – an extra €20 or so will get you one of the larger ones. **€100**

★ **Locanda San Tomaso** Viale Burchiellati 5 ⓣ 0422 541 550 or ⓣ 346 951 3652, ⓦ locandasantomaso.it. The six rooms of this charming, family-run B&B have been decorated with painstaking attention to detail. All are spacious, and are nicely adorned with antiques, paintings and bric-a-brac. **€95**

★ **Maison Matilda** Via Jacopo Riccati 44 ⓣ 0422 582 212, ⓦ maisonmatilda.com. Treviso's first boutique hotel, located near the Duomo, adds a much-needed touch of style to the city's hotels: just five double rooms plus one suite, all furnished in an individual and unshowily sumptuous style, with roll-top baths, antique furnishings and floor-sweeping curtains. **€180**

EATING AND DRINKING

Treviso has some excellent **restaurants**, many of which feature radicchio, the bitter red lettuce, and *tiramisù*, which was invented here in the late 1960s. The **bars** and **cafés** around the Pescheria (fish market), which sits on its own island in the centre of the city, are always buzzing, while those clustered around the Palazzo dei Trecento are good for people-watching.

★ **Dai Naneti** Vicolo Broli 2. Standing at the mouth of the alley alongside the large Benetton store next to the Palazzo dei Trecento, this busy, rough-edged bar offers wines and superb panini and other snacks – but no coffee, and no seats. Mon–Sat 9am–2.30pm & 5.30–9pm.

★ **Due Torri** Via Palestro 8 ⓣ 0422 541 243. The *Antica Contrada delle Due Torri*, to give it its full name, offers a sophisticated take on local fish and meat specialities, and offers exceptional value – most main courses are in the region of €16. The brick-lined interior is inviting, and the well-informed staff are attentive. Daily except Tues 12.30–2.30pm & 7.30–11pm.

La Finestra Via Armando Diaz 24 ⓣ 0422 411292, ⓦ pizzerialafinestra.it. Possibly the best pizzas in Treviso, plus a small menu that usually features some excellent seafood and a vegetarian option. The look of the place is smartly minimalist, and in summer there are outside tables at the back of the restaurant. Mon & Wed–Sun noon–3pm & 7–11pm.

Muscoli Via Pescheria 23. The punters spill out onto the fish market island from the ever-popular *Muscoli*. Try the delicious fig and blue cheese sandwiches at the bar or go further inside for a more substantial meal – from just €10.

Mon–Tues & Thurs–Sat 8am–2pm & 5pm–midnight, Sun 8am–2pm.

Toni del Spin Via Inferiore 7 ⓣ0422 543 829, ⓦristorantetonidelspin.com. This convivial trattoria has been winning plaudits for many years. The risottos are excellent, and the *secondi* menu is packed with meaty Trevisan classics, such as *Bocconcini di vitello al radicchio* and *Coniglio alle olive*. Good value too, with most main courses under €15. Mon 7.30–10.30pm, Tues–Sun 12.30–2.30pm & 7.30–10.30pm.

6

Castelfranco

CASTELFRANCO VENETO once stood on the western edge of Treviso's territory, and the battlemented brick walls the Trevisans threw round the town in 1199 to protect it against the Paduans still encircle most of the old centre (or *castello*). Of all the **walled towns** of the Veneto, few bear comparison with Castelfranco, and the place would merit a visit on the strength of this alone, even without the magnificent painting by **Giorgione** that it also possesses.

The Duomo

Piazza San Liberale • Daily 8am–noon & 3–6pm • Free

Known simply as the **Castelfranco Madonna**, Giorgione's *Madonna and Child with Saints* hangs in the eighteenth-century **Duomo**, in a chapel to the right of the chancel. The left-hand saint is St Francis, but there are several possibilities for the right-hand figure, of which Nicasius and Liberale (patron saint of Castelfranco) are the leading contenders. Giorgione is the most elusive of all the great figures of the Renaissance, and so little is known for certain about his life that legends have proliferated to fill the gaps – for instance, the story that his premature death in 1510, aged 34 at most (his birthdate is unknown), was caused by bubonic plague caught from a lover. The paintings themselves have compounded the enigma and none is more mysterious than this one, in which a boldly geometrical composition is combined with an extraordinary fidelity to physical texture and the effects of light, while the demeanour of the figures suggests a sort of melancholy preoccupation.

ARRIVAL AND INFORMATION — CASTELFRANCO

By train Castelfranco is the major crossroads of the Veneto rail network. The station is on the south side of the *centro storico*, a 15min walk from the Duomo.

Destinations Belluno (12 daily; 1hr 20min–1hr 40min); Padua (19 daily; 35min); Treviso (15 daily; 25min); Venice (20 daily; 55min); Vicenza (16 daily; 40min).

Tourist office Via F.M. Preti 66 (Wed & Thurs 9.30am–12.30pm, Fri & Sat 9.30am–12.30pm & 3–6pm; ⓣ0423 491 416).

Cittadella

When Treviso turned Castelfranco into a garrison, the Paduans promptly retaliated by reinforcing the defences of **CITTADELLA**, 15km to the west, on the train line to Vicenza. The fortified walls of Cittadella were built in the first quarter of the thirteenth century, and are even more impressive than those of its neighbour. You enter the town through one of four rugged brick gateways; if you're coming from the train station it'll be the Porta Padova, the most daunting of the four, flanked by the **Torre di Malta**. The tower was built as a prison and torture chamber by the monstrous Ezzelino da Romano, known to those he terrorized in this region in the mid-thirteenth century as "The Son of Satan". His atrocities earned him a place in the seventh circle of Dante's *Inferno*, where he's condemned to boil eternally in a river of blood.

Bassano del Grappa

Situated on the River Brenta, **BASSANO** has expanded rapidly over the last few decades, though its historic centre – the area between the Brenta and the train station – remains

THE WAR MEMORIALS OF BASSANO

The two world wars took a particularly heavy toll on the Bassano area, and the town and its environs are strewn with memorials to the dead of those conflicts. The **Viale dei Martiri**, near the Duomo, is named after the Resistance fighters who were rounded up in the hills and hanged from trees along this street in September 1944. At one end of it is the **Piazzale Generale Giardino**, with its Fascist-style memorial to the general, who died in 1935; a World War I monument in similar vein stands below in the **Parco Ragazzi del'99**, named after the "Lads of '99", who as teenagers were slaughtered in the last phase of World War I.

The area's major **war memorial**, however, is 35km away on the summit of **Monte Grappa**. Built in 1935 on the spot where Italian troops repulsed the Austrian army's offensive in 1917, it's the burial place of some twelve thousand Italian and ten thousand Austro-Hungarian dead. From the summit (1775m) the strategic importance of the peak is obvious: on a clear day you can see as far as Venice.

largely unspoiled. For centuries a major producer of ceramics and wrought iron, Bassano is also renowned for its **grappa** distilleries and its culinary delicacies such as porcini mushrooms, white asparagus and honey. Although it has few outstanding monuments or fine architecture, Bassano's airy situation on the edge of the mountains and the quiet charm of the old streets make it well worth the trip.

Piazza Garibaldi

Piazza Garibaldi, one of the town's two main squares, is overlooked by the 42m-high **Torre Civica**, once a lookout tower for the twelfth-century inner walls, now a clock tower with spurious nineteenth-century battlements and windows.

Museo Civico

Piazza Garibaldi 34 • Mon & Wed–Sun 10am–7pm • €7

The cloister of the church of San Francesco now houses the **Museo Civico**, where the downstairs rooms are devoted to Roman and other archeological finds. Upstairs is a collection of sixteenth- to eighteenth-century work, including paintings by the da Ponte family, better known by the name **Bassano**. Elsewhere in the museum are some huge frescoes detached from a palace in Piazzetta Montevecchio, two luminous pictures by Bartolomeo Vivarini and a number of plaster works by **Canova**, two thousand of whose drawings are owned by the museum. There's also a room devoted to the great baritone **Tito Gobbi**, who was born in Bassano.

Ponte degli Alpini

Bassano's signature building is the **Ponte degli Alpini**, which takes its name from the Alpine soldiers who rebuilt the bridge in 1948. The present structure was designed by **Palladio** in 1568, and constructed in wood to make the bridge as flexible as possible – torrential meltwater would demolish an unyielding stone version. Badly damaged by the retreating German army in World War II, it was restored in accordance with Palladio's design.

Palazzo Sturm

Via Schiavonetti 40 • Mon & Wed–Sat 9am–1pm & 3–6pm• €5

From the Ponte degli Alpini follow Via Ferracina downstream for a couple of minutes and you'll come to the eighteenth-century **Palazzo Sturm**, which houses two museums. On the ground floor the Museo Remondini gives a well-illustrated account of the history of printing, with pride of place given to the Remondini printing works, which was founded in Bassano in the seventeenth century; upstairs is an extensive collection of the town's famed majolica ware.

ARRIVAL AND INFORMATION **BASSANO DEL GRAPPA**

By train The station lies on the eastern edge of the centre; walk up Via Chilesotti and pass through the city walls on the far side of the Viale delle Fosse to reach Piazza Garibaldi. Trains from Venice pull in fifteen times daily (1hr 15min–1hr 40min).

By bus Bus services from the train station connect with Asolo (6 daily) and Maser (4 daily); services are much less frequent on Sun.

Tourist office Piazza Garibaldi 34 (Mon & Wed–Sun 10am–7pm, Tues 3–7pm; ⓣ 0424 519 917, ⓦ bassano.eu).

ACCOMMODATION AND EATING

Al Caneseo Via Vendramini 20 ⓣ 042 422 8524. A rustic family-run restaurant with a small menu of Abruzzo and Veneto specialities. Most main courses are less than €10. Tues–Sun 12.30–3pm & 7.30pm–10.30pm.

Al Castello Via Bonamigo 19 ⓣ 0424 228 665, ⓦ hotelalcastello.it. Situated right by the castle at the top of the town, this is the only hotel in the old centre. It's a pleasant three-star with eleven rooms – best of all is no. 10, which has a small balcony overlooking the square. **€120**

★ **Alla Caneva** Via Matteotti 34 ⓣ 335 542 3560. A cosy *osteria* that does delicious snacks as well as more substantial dishes, including a range of grilled meats. Mon 9.30am–3pm, Wed–Sun 930 am–3pm & 5.30pm–midnight.

Ostello Don Cremona Via Chini 6 ⓣ 0424 219 137, ⓦ ostellobassanodelgrappa.it. The youth hostel is just south of the centre, with ninety beds, half of which are bunks. Check-in 2–9pm. Dorms from **€18**, doubles **€48**

6

Asolo

East of Bassano, the medieval hilltop town of **ASOLO** presides over a tightly grouped range of gentle peaks in the foothills of the Dolomites. Known as *la città dei cento orizzonti* ("the city of the hundred horizons"), the town has proved convivial to many writers and artists: at the end of the fifteenth century Cardinal Bembo, one of the most eminent literary figures of his day, coined the verb *asolare* to describe the experience of spending one's time in pleasurable aimlessness; Gabriele d'Annunzio wrote about the town; and Robert Browning's last published work – *Asolando* – was written here.

Museo Civico

Via Regina Cornaro 74 • Sat & Sun 9.30am–12.30pm & 3–6pm • €5

The hub of the town is **Piazza Garibaldi** (also known as Piazza Maggiore). Just off the piazza you'll find the **Museo Civico**, whose most diverting exhibits are the memorabilia of Asolo's celebrated residents, including the portraits, photos and personal effects of the actress **Eleonora Duse** (1858–1924). Almost as well known for her tempestuous love life as for her roles in works by Shakespeare, Hugo and Ibsen, she came to Asolo to seek refuge from gossip.

The Castello

Eleonora Duse gave her name to the theatre that is now up the road from the museum in the **Castello**, which from 1489 to 1509 was home to Asolo's most celebrated resident, **Caterina Cornaro.** Born into one of Venice's most powerful families, Caterina was married to Jacques II, King of Cyprus. Within a year Jacques was dead, and Caterina was pressurized into ceding Cyprus to the Republic. She was given the region of Asolo in compensation. Eventually Asolo, too, was taken away from her by the Emperor

GRAPPA IN BASSANO

There's nowhere better to sample Bassano's local firewater than **Nardini**, a **grappa distillery** founded in 1779 at the foot of the Ponte degli Alpini; these days the distilling process takes place elsewhere, but the original shop and bar are still functioning here (daily 8.30am–9.30pm; ⓦ nardini.it). You can also taste and buy the stuff in the **Museo della Grappa** at nearby Via Gamba 6 (daily 9am–7.30pm, free; ⓦ grappa.com), which is in effect a showcase for the Poli distillery.

Maximilian, and she sought asylum in Venice, where she died in 1510. The castle also contains a children's play area and a bar, and there are great views from its walls.

The Rocca

Sat & Sun 10am–6pm • €2

Asolo's ruined medieval fortress, the **Rocca**, is reached by taking Via Collegio up the hill from the back of Piazza Brugnoli (the car park next to Piazza Garibaldi) and going through the Porta Colmarian. Built on Roman foundations, the Rocca stands 350m above sea level, and the views are worth the effort of the climb.

6

Villa Barbaro, Maser

Via Cornuda 7, Maser • April–Oct Tues–Sat 10am–6pm, Sun 11am–6pm; Nov–March Sat & Sun 11am–5pm (but closed mid-Dec to early Feb) • €9 • villadimaser.it • Bus from Bassano or Treviso

The **Villa Barbaro**, or the **Villa di Maser**, 7km east of Asolo, is a masterpiece created by **Palladio** and adorned by **Paolo Veronese**, whose careers crossed here and nowhere else. Commissioned in the 1550s by Daniele and Marcantonio Barbaro, the villa was a working farm in which was embodied a classical vision – derived from writers such as Livy – of the harmony of architectural form and the well-ordered pastoral life. In the living quarters, the magnificent series of **frescoes** by Veronese make fantastic use of trompe l'oeil effects: servants peer round painted doors, a dog sniffs along the base of a fictional balustrade, a huntsman (possibly Veronese himself) steps into the house through an entrance that's a solid wall. There's a gorgeous formal garden at the rear of the house, and at the front stands Palladio's **Tempietto**, which was built in 1580, the year the architect died.

ARRIVAL AND INFORMATION — ASOLO

By bus and train There are six buses daily to Asolo from Bassano. From Venice, the quickest route is to take a train to Treviso, where you won't have to wait more than an hour for a bus to Asolo (some change at Montebelluna), though it can be longer on Sun – in addition to the direct services, all buses to Bassano go through Asolo and Maser. The bus drops you at the foot of the hill, from where a minibus takes you up into the town.

Tourist office Piazza Garibaldi 73 (Thurs–Sun 9.30am–12.30pm & 3–6pm; 0423 529 046, asolo.it).

ACCOMMODATION AND EATING

Asolo is an expensive little town, with two of the Veneto's flashiest **hotels**, the *Villa Cipriani* and *Al Sole*, but there are alternatives for those on more sensible budgets. Note that all accommodation is booked solid on the second Sun of every month, during the antiques fair.

★ **Agriturismo Sant'Andrea** Via Cornuda 72, Maser 0423 565 358, agrsantandrea.it. This friendly wine-making agriturismo, down the road from the Villa Barbaro, makes the perfect base for exploring the region. There are eleven plain but comfortable rooms, three with cooking facilities, and an ample buffet breakfast is provided. €75

Antica Osteria Al Bacaro Via Browning 165 042 355 150. Atmospheric and welcoming rustic *osteria* with a very local feel. The food is unpretentious and well prepared (the menu changes daily), and prices are reasonable, with *secondi* at €10–15. Daily except Wed noon–3pm & 6–10pm.

Duse Via Browning 190 0423 55 241, asolohotelduse.com. The only inexpensive hotel in the centre, this three-star has 14 rooms, most of them spacious. €120

★ **Locanda Baggio** Via Bassane 1, Casonetto 042 352 9648, locandabaggio.it. Located 1km northeast of the town in the hamlet of Casonetto, the Baggio family's restaurant offers superb and inventive cooking – the tasting menu (€65 per person, excluding wine) is a real treat. They also have an excellent wine list, from vineyards all over Italy, plus some foreign vintages, including wines from Slovenia and Lebanon. Tues–Sat noon–3pm & 7.30–10.30pm, Sun noon–3pm.

Conegliano

The hills surrounding **CONEGLIANO** are patched with vineyards, and the production of wine – prosecco in particular – is central to the economy of the town. Italy's first wine-growers' college was set up in Conegliano in 1876, and a couple of well-established

wine routes meet here: the **Strada dei Vini del Piave**, which runs for 68km southeast to Oderzo and concentrates on the region's red wines; and the more rewarding **Strada del Prosecco**, a 42km journey west to Valdobbiadene. The main square is given over to a medieval pageant in mid-June, the **Dama Castellana**, and the streets of Conegliano host a major **wine festival** on the last weekend in September.

The Duomo and around

Via XX Settembre • Daily 8am–noon & 3–7pm • Free

On the central street of the old town, Via XX Settembre, the most decorative feature is the unusual facade of the **Duomo**: a fourteenth-century portico, frescoed in the sixteenth century. The interior has been much rebuilt, but has a fine *Madonna and Child with Saints and Angels*, painted in 1493 by **Giambattista Cima**, the most famous native of Conegliano. Cima's birthplace, at the rear of the Duomo, has been restored and converted into the **Casa Museo di G.B. Cima** (Sat & Sun 4–7pm; free), which is replete with high-class reproductions of his work.

Alongside the Duomo is the **Sala dei Battuti** or Hall of the Flagellants, the frescoed meeting place of a local confraternity (July Sat & Sun 10am–noon & 4–6pm; Aug Sat & Sun 10am–noon; free). The pictures are mostly sixteenth-century, incorporating the weirdest *Ascension* you'll ever see, with the ascendant Christ half out of the frame and a pair of footprints left behind at the point of liftoff.

Museo Civico

Piazza San Leonardo • Tues–Sun 10am–12.30pm & 2.30–6pm• €2.50

The **Museo Civico** is housed in the tower of the *castello* on top of the hill. It has some damaged frescoes by Pordenone and a small bronze horse by Giambologna, but the main reason to visit is the climb to the tower's roof from where there's a fine panorama of the vine-clad landscape.

ARRIVAL AND INFORMATION — CONEGLIANO

By train Access to Conegliano itself is straightforward, as nearly all the regular Venice–Udine trains stop here. The station is on the southern edge of the old town, just 5min from the Duomo.

Destinations Belluno (8 daily; 55min); Venice (every 30min; 50–70min); Vittorio Veneto (every 40min–1hr; 25min).

Tourist office The tourist office at Via XX Settembre 132 (Tues & Wed 9am–1pm, Thurs–Sun 9am–1pm & 2–6pm; T 0438 21 230) is well stocked with information, including the latest list of recommended prosecco outlets and details of the wine routes.

ACCOMMODATION AND EATING

Canon d'Oro Via XX Settembre 131 T 0438 34 246, W hotelcanondoro.it. The first-choice hotel in town, this Best Western four-star is housed in one of the street's fine frescoed *palazzi*. It has a terraced garden to the rear, and whirlpool baths in the more expensive rooms. €110

★ **Trattoria Stella** Via Accademia 3 T 0438 22 178. An old-fashioned and immensely welcoming little trattoria in the heart of the old town, offering simple and honest home cooking, with decent house wine too. Mon–Sat noon–2.30pm & 7–10pm; closed Thurs eve.

Vittorio Veneto

Some 13km north of Conegliano, **VITTORIO VENETO** first appeared on the map in 1866 when the towns of **Ceneda** and **Serravalle** were knotted together and rechristened in honour of Italy's new king. A town hall was built midway between the two, with a new train station opposite, in a sort of no-man's-land.

Museo della Battaglia, Ceneda

Piazza Giovanni Paolo I • Tues–Fri 9.30am–12.30pm, Sat & Sun 10am–1pm & 3–6pm • €5 • W museobattaglia.it

Ceneda is primarily worth a visit for the **Museo della Battaglia**, which is housed in the sixteenth-century Loggia Cenedese, a good twenty-minute walk from the station. The

battle of Vittorio Veneto, which lasted from October 24 to November 3, 1918, was the triumphant final engagement of World War I for the Italian army (which is why most towns in Italy have a Via Vittorio Veneto) and this well-designed museum is dedicated to the climactic engagement. Upstairs, in the impressive Aula Civica Cenedese, crucial episodes in the history of Cèneda are depicted in nineteenth-century frescoes. The nondescript Duomo, on the same piazza, has nothing of interest inside.

Serravalle

Serravalle, wedged up against the mouth of a gorge, is an entirely different proposition from its partner. Most of the buildings on the stage-like Piazza Marcantonio Flaminio and the neighbouring streets date from the fifteenth and sixteenth centuries – the handsomest being the shield-encrusted Loggia Serravallese. This is now home to the **Museo del Cenedese** (Sat & Sun 10am–noon & 3–5/6pm; €3), a jumble of sculptural and archeological bits, detached frescoes and minor paintings. Your time will be more profitably spent in the church of **San Lorenzo dei Battuti** (same ticket and opening times), immediately inside the south gate, which is decorated with frescoes painted around 1450. Uncovered in 1953, it was then restored to rectify the damage done when Napoleon's soldiers used the chapel as a kitchen.

ARRIVAL AND INFORMATION — VITTORIO VENETO

By train The town's train station is just off Viale della Vittoria, the main Ceneda–Serravalle road.

Destinations Belluno (10 daily; 40min); Conegliano (10 daily; 20min).

By bus The bus station is across the main road from the train station, behind the post office. Bus #1 shuttles between the two towns every 30min.

Destinations Belluno (1 daily; 1hr); Conegliano (11 daily; 45min).

Tourist office Near the train station at Viale della Vittoria 110 (Mon 9.30am–12.30pm, Tues–Sun 9.30am–12.30pm & 3–6pm; T 0438 57 243).

Belluno

BELLUNO was once a strategically important ally of Venice, and today is the capital of a province that extends mainly over the eastern Dolomites (covered in Chapter 5). Belluno's main attraction is its position, in the lee of the mountains, but the old centre calls for an hour or two's exploration if you're passing through. The hub of the modern town is the wide **Piazza dei Martiri**.

Piazza del Duomo

Off the south side of **Piazza dei Martiri** a road leads to the **Piazza del Duomo**, the kernel of the old town. The sixteenth-century **Duomo**, which had to be completely reconstructed twice after earthquake damage, in 1873 and 1939, was originally the work of **Tullio Lombardo**, although the stately campanile was designed in 1743 by **Filippo Juvarra**, best known for his rebuilding of central Turin. The elegant interior has a good painting by Jacopo Bassano and another by Palma il Giovane.

Occupying one complete side of the Piazza del Duomo is the residence of the Venetian administrators of the town, the **Palazzo dei Rettori**, a frilly, late fifteenth-century building dolled up with Baroque trimmings. A relic of more independent times stands on the right – the twelfth-century **Torre Civica**, all that's left of the medieval castle.

Palazzo Fulcis

Via Roma 28 • Tues, Wed & Fri 9.30am–12.30pm & 3.30–6.30pm, Thurs 9.30am–12.30pm, Sat & Sun 10am–6pm • €8

The huge Palazzo Fulcis – Belluno's most important eighteenth-century building – has recently been refurbished to house the collections that used to be held by the Museo Civico. A substantial quantity of fine porcelain is on show here, but of wider appeal is the work of Belluno's three best-known artists, all of whom were born here between

1659 and 1676: the painters Sebastiano and Marco Ricci, and the virtuoso sculptor-woodcarver Andrea Brustolon (who features prominently in Venice's Ca' Rezzonico). All three are to be found in the top-floor galleries, where there's also an engaging series of artless *ex voto* paintings. Among the earlier art displayed on the floor below, the placid Paduan artist Bartolomeo Montagna stands out.

Piazza del Mercato and Via Mezzaterra

Leading out of Piazza del Duomo, Via Duomo ends at the **Piazza del Mercato**, a tiny square hemmed in by porticoed Renaissance buildings. The principal street of the old town, **Via Mezzaterra**, goes down to the medieval **Porta Rugo** (veer left along the cobbled Via Santa Croce about 100m from the end), from where the view up into the mountains is magnificent.

ARRIVAL AND INFORMATION — BELLUNO

Belluno's focus of attention lies to the north – the network of the Dolomiti Bus company radiates out from here, trains run regularly up the Piave Valley to Calalzo, and the tourist handouts are geared mostly to hikers and skiers.

By train No trains run straight from Venice to Belluno – you need to change at Conegliano or Castelfranco Veneto. You can also get to Belluno from Padua (directly or via Castelfranco; 13 daily; 2hr–2hr 30min).

Destinations Calalzo di Cadore (9 daily; 1hr 5min–1hr 20min), Conegliano (10 daily; 60min); Vittorio Veneto (10 daily; 40min).

Tourist office Piazza del Duomo 1 (Mon–Sat 9.30am–12.30pm & 2.30–6pm, Sun 10am–noon; ⓣ 0437 940 083, ⓦ infodolomiti.it).

ACCOMMODATION AND EATING

Cappello e Cadore Via Ricci 8 ⓣ 0437 940 246, ⓦ albergocappello.com. This long-established three-star hotel, tucked away off the main square, is the best place to stay in the centre of Belluno. Its 32 rooms are plain but comfortable and quiet, and some have whirlpool baths. **€90**

Terracotta Borgo Garibaldi 66 ⓣ 0437 291 692, ⓦ ristoranteterracotta.it. The friendly and elegant *Terracotta* is the best restaurant in central Belluno. Ingredients gathered from the mountains are the basis of the small but well-composed menu, which therefore changes with the seasons, but you can expect to find some excellent and inventive fish dishes at any time of year (most mains around €20). The set lunch menu, at €20 including a glass of wine and coffee, is a bargain. In summer, tables are set out in the lovely garden. Mon & Thurs–Sun noon–2pm & 7.30–9.30pm, Wed 7.30–9.30pm.

Friuli-Venezia Giulia

438 Trieste

448 Inland from Trieste: the Carso

450 The Triestine Riviera

452 Aquileia

454 Grado

455 Gorizia and around

457 Udine and around

461 Cividale del Friuli

CIVIDALE DEL FRIULI

Friuli-Venezia Giulia

Established only in 1963 and given special status as one of Italy's five semi-autonomous regions, Friuli-Venezia Giulia is odd, even in its name (Friuli is a corruption of the ancient name for modern-day Cividale, Foro Iulii "Forum of Julius", while Venezia Giulia, "Julian Venetia", also references the area's abiding association with Caesar). Bordering Austria to the north and Slovenia to the east, it has always been a major bone of contention among rival powers. Today, Slavic, Germanic and Italian populations all call it home and are fiercely proud of their local language, Friulano (a Romance language related to Swiss Romansch and Ladin). The area's landscapes are equally varied, with one-half Alps, about one-third limestone plateaux (carso) and the rest alluvial and gravel plains sloping down to the Adriatic.

The cities and towns here are as wildly dissimilar as one might expect. **Trieste**, the capital, is an urbanely elegant Habsburg creation, built by Austria to showcase the empire's only port. In spirit and appearance it is essentially Central European, a character it shares with **Gorizia**, to the north, though the latter has an even more Slavic flavour, and in fact straddles the border with Slovenia. Both cities benefit from castles looming on a central hilltop, affording memorable views, and provide access to walkabouts in the **Carso** – the windswept, limestone plateau that extends eastwards into Slovenia – while Trieste also boasts its very own **riviera**, complete with attractive beach resorts. A little further west, **Udine**'s architecture and art collections evoke Venice at its grandest, while UNESCO-listed **Cividale del Friuli** preserves a picturesque historic centre perched over the aquamarine Natisone River. The archeologically minded, however, head straight to **Aquileia** and the ruins of the Roman capital of Friuli, with its impressive basilica and huge paleo-Christian floor mosaic. From here it's south to the lagoon resort of **Grado**, which conceals a beautiful, early Christian centre surrounded by beach hotels.

Historically, what unites the region is its perennial role as a link between the Mediterranean and Central Europe. It has been repeatedly overrun from east and west and north, by the Romans, Huns, Goths, Lombards, Nazis and even the Cossacks. By turns, it has been lorded over by the Venetian Republic, Napoleonic France and the Austrian Empire. More recently, the area witnessed some of the most savage fighting of World War I, and World War II saw Fascism become especially virulent in Trieste, site of one of Italy's two death camps.

Today, right-wing and xenophobic tendencies are still strong. While most Friulani certainly want Italian nationality, the sociopolitical baggage of Rome and the south strike many as a drag. Currently, economic anxiety and general malaise about Italy's direction have resulted in something of a conservative resurgence.

Trieste

Framed by green hills and white limestone cliffs, **TRIESTE** looks out over the blue Adriatic, offering an idyllic panorama from its hilltop citadel, at least when the gale-force *bora* winds aren't blasting you off the seafront. But in any weather, there's a distinct atmosphere of grandeur with a cosmopolitan twist. The city's main squares are adorned with spectacular Neoclassical buildings, and the much-photographed canal, clustered with open-air cafés, is a reminder that, just like Venice and its lagoon, this

ANCIENT FLOOR MOSAIC IN THE BASILICA OF AQUILEIA

Highlights

❶ **Trieste** From the castle atop the San Giusto, take in a panoramic view of this elegant and atmospheric maritime city. See page 438

❷ **Grotta Gigante** One of the largest accessible caves in the world. See page 448

❸ **Aquileia** The glorious fourth-century mosaic pavements rank among the most important monuments of early Christendom. See page 452

❹ **Laguna di Grado** Hop on a boat and explore the lagoon, stopping off at one of the islands for a delicious fish or seafood lunch. See page 454

❺ **Udine's Piazza della Libertà** The central piazza of the provincial capital is a perfect example of classic Venetian architecture. See page 457

❻ **San Daniele del Friuli** Sample some of the world's finest prosciutto in its picturesque home town, just north of Udine. See page 461

❼ **Cividale del Friuli** This attractive small town was granted UNESCO World Heritage status for its extraordinary medieval monuments and art treasures, including the splendid eighth-century Tempietto Longobardo. See page 461

HIGHLIGHTS ARE MARKED ON THE MAP ON PAGE 440

city has enjoyed a glorious seafaring past, too. Like so many ports in Europe, there is a certain seediness here, particularly evident in some areas around the train station, although in recent years the city has been spruced up. The heart of modern Trieste is in the grid-like streets of the **Borgo Teresiano**, but no visit would be complete without a climb to the top of its hill, San Giusto, named for its patron saint and with the best views for kilometres around.

Brief history

Trieste dates from the third millennium BC, with Jason and the Argonauts alleged to have been among its earliest visitors. Roman ruins scattered around the city attest to its incorporation into the Roman Republic in 178 BC, when it was called Tergeste, from *terg* or market. However, with the exception of the castle and cathedral of San Giusto, and the tiny medieval quarter below it, the city's whole pre-nineteenth-century history is overwhelmed by the massive Neoclassical architecture of the **Borgo Teresiano** – named after the Empress Maria Theresa (1740–80), who poured money into the city. This was Trieste's golden age, as the Austrians spared no expense on embellishing what was to become the Habsburg Empire's only seaport. For a time, it even eclipsed Venice, but its heyday was short-lived and drew to an ignominious close after 1918, when the city was annexed to Italy. A grim period ensued under Mussolini as he rode roughshod over ethnic diversity.

HEARTY SOUPS, HAM AND WINE – THE CUISINE OF FRIULI-VENEZIA GIULIA

Food in Friuli-Venezia Giulia reflects its cultural eclecticism, with the legacy of the Austro-Hungarian era always present. The food tends to be hearty and uncomplicated, from thick soups to warming stews, such as the ubiquitous goulash. This is the home of **prosciutto**, the best of which comes from San Daniele, and you will be offered plates of *affettati* or home-cured meats as part of a meal or to accompany a glass of wine. Pasta and gnocchi come with a Friulian twist, sweet and salty flavours combined; try *cialzons*, a pasta filled with spinach, chocolate, raisins and nutmeg. *Jota* is the local soup, a bean and sauerkraut combination with the possible addition of pork or sausage, good on a cold day. Friuli's signature dish is **frico**, a type of potato cake; potato and Montasio cheese grated together, fried until golden brown and served up with polenta. Another speciality is *brovada*, made from wine-fermented turnips and served with sausage. Desserts tend towards cakes and pastries, usually filled with nuts, dried fruit and alcohol – look out for *presnitz*, *strukliji* and *gubana*. The Austrian influence makes itself felt in the form of *strudel*, filled with fruit or ricotta cheese.

Friuli-Venezia Giulia is Italy's third most important quality **wine** region, after Piedmont and Tuscany, and has long been acclaimed for its fragrant, elegant whites. The two premium regions are the Collio and the Colli Orientali del Friuli, hilly zones sharing a border with Slovenia. Tocai (now known as Friulano) or Sauvignon Vert is the most widely planted grape variety – pale in colour, it is usually drunk young and makes a perfect aperitif. Top reds include Cabernet Franc, Refosco or Terrano as it called around Trieste, and best of all, the obscure Schioppettino. Last but not least is the cult dessert wine Picolit, produced in very small quantities and commanding high prices. The Strada del Vino e dei Sapori del Friuli Venezia Giulia consists of six scenic food and wine touring routes – see the website for further details: Ⓦ tastefvg.it.

Lying on the political and ethnic faultline between the Latin and Slavic worlds, Trieste has long been a city of political turbulence. In the nineteenth century it was a hotbed of *irredentismo* – an Italian nationalist movement to "redeem" the Austrian lands of Trieste, Istria and Trentino. After 1918, tensions increased between the city's ethnic groups, with Slovenes suffering persecution at the hands of the rising Fascist regime. Trieste was annexed by the Germans in 1943 and then at the end of the war, the city and surrounding area became a "Free Territory" administered by the Allies before being divided between Italy and Yugoslavia in 1954. Trieste was awarded to Italy but lost its coastal hinterland, Istria, to Yugoslavia. It was a bitter settlement and the definitive **border settlement** was not reached until 1975. As Tito kept Istria, huge numbers of its fearful Italian population abandoned the peninsula: Fiume (Rijeka), for example, lost 58,000 of its 60,000 Italians. The Slovene population of the area around Trieste, previously in the majority, suddenly found itself treated as second-class citizens, with Italians dominant politically and culturally. In the last sixty years, the Slovene and Italian populations have mixed and intermarried and, along with other newer arrivals, have made Trieste one of the more multicultural cities in Italy.

Castello di San Giusto

Piazza della Cattedrale 3 • April–Oct Daily 10am–7pm; Nov–March Tues–Sun 10am–5pm • €3 • Ⓣ 040 309 362, Ⓦ castellodisangiustotrieste.it

At the very summit of the hill of San Giusto, the **Castello di San Giusto** is a fifteenth to seventeenth-century Habsburg fortress that overlooks the remnants of the Roman basilica and forum. A walk round its ramparts offers panoramic views of the city and busy port below, while beyond the city confines the high escarpment of the Carso looms over the Adriatic. Inside the castle, the **Museo Civico-Armeria** displays Venetian Renaissance furniture and an extensive weapons collection.

TRIESTE

● EATING	
Antica Hostaria Da Libero	12
Caffè degli Specchi	7
Caffè San Marco	2
Caffè Tommaseo	4
Chocolat	9
Da Pepi Buffet	5
Gelato Marco	8
Istriano	11
La Bomboniera	3
Menarosti	6
NerodiSeppia	10
Suban	1

■ ACCOMMODATION	
Albero Nascosto	6
B&B Atelier Lidia Polla	1
Casa Trauner	7
Continentale	3
Grand Hotel Duchi D'Aosta	4
Locanda alle Beccherie	5
Residenza Le 6A	2

■ DRINKING	
Gran Malabar	1
L'Etrusco	2
SaluMare	3

THE FVG CARD

Available at many hotels, travel agents and at all tourist offices, the **FVG Card** (€18/48hr, €21/72hr and €29/week) gives free admission to virtually all the city's public museums, several guided tours and free use of some public transport, including the *tranvia* (see page 450). It also gives discounts on some services, sports and recreation facilities, hotels and restaurants.

Cattedrale di San Giusto

Piazza della Cattedrale 2 • April–Oct Mon–Sat 7.30am–7pm, Sun 8am–8pm; Nov–March Mon–Sat 7.30am–12.30pm & 3.30–7pm, Sun 8am–1pm & 3.30–8pm • Free; campanile €1.50 • Ⓦ sangiustomartire.it

The **Cattedrale di San Giusto** is a fusion of two churches built on Roman ruins. Some ancient fragments remain: the base of the campanile has been chipped away to reveal the original pillars, the columns at the entrance are actually stelae from a Roman tomb and part of the Roman floor mosaic is incorporated in the present flooring. In around 1050 an earlier Christian chapel was replaced by two churches, the Basilica di Santa Maria Assunta and the Cappella di San Giusto. The site was further expanded in the early thirteenth century when the two adjacent buildings were bridged by a high-beamed vault, forming the current cathedral nave and leaving a double aisle on each side. Today, the cathedral is a typically Triestine synthesis of styles, with a serene, largely Romanesque interior, with the exception of the central apse, which was rebuilt in a more modern style in the twentieth century. The Cappella di Santa Maria Assunta (north aisle) has fine Byzantine-style mosaics of the *Coronation of the Virgin*, revealing the Byzantine roots of the style, while the Cappella di San Giusto (south aisle) has thirteenth-century frescoes of the life of the saint, framed between Byzantine pillars.

7

Civico Museo d'Antichità J.J. Winckelmann

Piazza Cattedrale 1 • April–Sept Tues–Sat 10am–1pm & 4–7pm, Sun 10am–7pm; Oct–March Tues–Sat 9am–1pm, Sun 10am–5pm • Free • Ⓣ 040 310 500, Ⓦ museoantichitawinckelmann.it

Named after German archaeologist and theorist of Ancient Art J.J. Winckelmann (1717-1768), who was murdered in Trieste by a man to whom he had shown off his gold and silver medals, the **Civico Museo d'Antichità J.J. Winckelmann** displays local archeological finds from prehistory to Roman times. It also houses a collection of Egyptian, Cypriot, Greek, Southern Italian and Etruscan objects. The museum's **Orto Lapidario** showcases ancient Roman inscriptions from Trieste, Aquileia and Istria, and houses a monument dedicated to Winckelmann, Greek and Roman sculptures, and the remains of a Roman Propylaeum.

The Città Vecchia

The tiny remnant of the **Città Vecchia** (Old Town) lies between the castle hill and the Stazione Marittima below. Newly restored, the area is delightful for a stroll despite the odd modern building inserted into its tilting medieval structures and cobbled lanes. The tiny, early Romanesque **San Silvestro**, on Via della Cattedrale (Thurs & Sat 10am–noon; free), is the city's oldest extant church; it's now used by adherents of the rare Helvetic-Waldensian sect. A short way below are the heavily restored remains of the **Teatro Romano**, built between the first and second centuries AD – in Roman times, the sea water reached the theatre walls. Today, it is some way inland and sometimes hosts performances during the city's spring–autumn festival season. There's little else of note in the old city, though mosaic enthusiasts may want to stop off at the remains of the **Basilica Paleocristiana** (Wed 10am–noon, or by appointment; free; Ⓣ 040 43 632) under the building at Via Madonna del Mare 11. The evocative **Arco di Riccardo**, on the nearby Piazza Barbacan, comprises reassembled remnants of the Roman walls dating from 33 BC, while excavation works nearby are revealing more traces of the city's ancient imperial past.

The Borgo Teresiano

To the north of the old centre, Trieste's "new" town, the **Borgo Teresiano**, is imposingly laid out in a Neoclassical style imported from nineteenth-century Vienna, with wide boulevards and a vast piazza on the waterfront. The focus of the main grid of streets is the picturesque **Piazza Sant'Antonio Nuovo**, with its small yacht basin overlooked by cafés and dominated by two churches: the Neoclassical hulk of Sant'Antonio Thaumaturgo and the smaller, more appealing Serbian Orthodox San Spiridione.

The real heart of town, however, is the grandiose **Piazza Unità d'Italia**, directly below the hill of San Giusto. Built mostly by Giuseppe Bruni in the late nineteenth century, the expanse of flagstones with one side open to the water is deliberately reminiscent of Venice's Piazza and Piazzetta – Trieste had commercially eclipsed the older city some years before. Projecting into the harbour nearby, the **Molo Audace**, named after the first boat of Italian soldiers to land here in 1918, is the venue for the evening *passeggiata*.

7

Museo Teatrale Carlo Schmidl

Via Rossini 4 • Tues–Sun April–Oct 10am–6pm; Nov–Mar 10am–5pm • €4 • T 040 675 4072, W museoschmidl.it

One of the city's gems, the little-visited **Museo Teatrale Carlo Schmidl** traces the history of music and theatre in Trieste from the eighteenth century to the present day. Displays include prints, photographs, manuscripts, marionettes, puppets, theatrical costumes and jewellery, along with a wonderful collection of musical instruments.

Museo Revoltella

Via Armando Diaz 27 • Wed–Mon April–Oct 9am–7pm; Nov–March 10am–7pm • €7 • T 040 675 4350, W museorevoltella.it

Trieste's principal museum is the **Museo Revoltella**, housed in a Viennese-style *palazzo* bequeathed to the city by the financier Baron Pasquale Revoltella in 1869. Its display of nineteenth-century stately-home furnishings and Triestine paintings is well worth a look, and the adjacent palace, redesigned by the architect Carlo Scarpa, houses an extensive collection of modern art, including works by Fontana, Guttoso, Carrà and De Chirico.

Museo Sartorio

Largo Papa Giovanni XXIII 1 • Tues, Wed & Thurs 10am–1pm, Fri & Sat 4–7pm, Sun 10am–7pm • Free • T 040 301 479, W museosartoriotrieste.it

The **Museo Sartorio** is set in an urban villa and has an interesting collection of ceramics, porcelain and pictures mainly from the nineteenth century; it gives you a good idea of how the well-to-do lived at that time. It is also home to an early fourteenth-century Santa Chiara triptych and an important collection of drawings by Tiepolo. The museum hosts temporary exhibitions and concerts in the summer. Incidentally, the villa was used by the Allies as their headquarters after World War II when the city was partitioned and occupied.

Risiera di San Sabba

Via Palatucci 5 • Daily 9am–7pm • T 040 826 202, W risierasansabba.it • Free • Bus #8 and #10

One of the darkest periods of modern European history is embodied by the **Risiera di San Sabba** on the outskirts of Trieste. This was one of only four major concentration camps in Italy and now houses a museum which serves as a reminder of Fascist crimes in the region. It is estimated that about 2000 prisoners were burned in the Risiera crematorium, although the exact number is uncertain. Many more passed through here before being transported to forced labour and concentration camps in other parts of Europe. The victims – Italians, Solvenians and Croats – were mostly members of the Resistance, suspected of collaborating with the partisans.

JOYCE IN TRIESTE

From 1905 to 1915, and again in 1919–20, **James Joyce** and his wife Nora lived in Trieste. While living here he wrote *The Dubliners* and *A Portrait of the Artist as a Young Man* and started work on *Ulysses*. He supported himself by teaching English at the Berlitz school where his most famous pupil was the Italian writer Italo Svevo. He lived a somewhat peripatetic life and you can visit his many homes and old haunts by picking up the walking-tour guide from the tourist office. After staying at Piazza Ponterosso 3 for a month, the Joyces moved to a third-floor flat at Via San Nicolò 30. There's a plaque in Via San Nicolò, and one at Via Bramante 4, quoting the postcard Joyce despatched in 1915 to his brother Stanislaus, whose Irredentist sympathies had landed him in an Austrian internment camp. The postcard announced that the first chapter of *Ulysses* was finished. Don't miss the wry bronze statue of the writer, strolling bemusedly across the little canal bridge of Via Roma.

ARRIVAL AND DEPARTURE — TRIESTE

By plane The airport is at Ronchi dei Legionari (T 0481 773 224, W triesteairport.it), 40km northwest of the city, connected to the city centre by regular trains (every 15–30min although there can be gaps of up to two hours – check W trenitalia.com for details; 29min; €4.05 Mon–Fri & €3.20 Sat & Sun); train services also connect the airport to Udine and Venice. Bus #51 travels to the bus station (every 30min, hourly from 7.35pm; 50min; €4.05 from the information point or the machine directly outside arrivals; freephone T 800 955 957, W aptgorizia.it). A taxi should cost about €65.

By train The train station is a 10min walk from the town centre.

Destinations Gorizia (every 30min–1hr; 45min); Udine (every 30min–1hr; 1hr 25min); Venice (every 30min; 2hr).

By bus Trieste's Piazza Libertà bus station is right by the train station.

Destinations Duino (hourly; 30min–1hr); Grado (14 daily; 1hr–1hr 30min); Monfalcone (for Aquileia and Grado; hourly; 45min).

By ferry This is an enjoyable way to travel to the coastal resorts such as Grado, though most services are infrequent and summertime only. Delfino Verde ferries (W delfinoverde.it) run to Grado, included on the FVG card (see page 443), while Trieste Lines (W triestelines.it) runs to Piran, Rovinj and Pola in Slovenia. Agemar, Piazza Duca degli Abruzzi 1/A (T 040 363 737, W agemar.it), is a travel agent selling ferry tickets to Greece, Albania and Croatia.

Destinations Barcola, Grignano and Sistiana (June–Sept 4 daily; 1hr 45min); Grado (mid-June to Aug 3 daily; 1hr 30min–2hr); Muggia (hourly; 30min); Piran (end June to Aug 1 daily; 30min); Pola (end June to Aug 1 daily on Fri, Sat & Sun; 2hr 45min); Rovinj (end June to Aug daily except Wed; 1hr 50min).

INFORMATION

Tourist office Via dell'Orologio 1, corner Piazza Unità d'Italia (May–Sept Mon–Sat 9am–7pm, Sun 9am–7pm; Oct–April Mon–Sat 9am–6pm, Sun 9am–1pm & 2–6pm; T 040 347 8312, W www.turismofvg.it). There's also an information point at the airport (Mon–Thurs 9am–7.30pm, Fri 9am–9.30pm, Sat 9am–1.30pm & 2–5.30pm, Sun 8.30am–7.30pm; T 0481 476 079).

GETTING AROUND

By bus City buses (freephone T 800 016 675, W triestetrasporti.it) cost €1.25 for any journey up to an hour. Timetables and tickets can be bought from newsagents, bars and *tabacchi*. Useful services include #30, which connects the train station with Via Roma and the waterfront; #24, which goes to/from Castello di San Giusto; and #6 (along with #36 in summer only) which links Trieste bus station with Miramare.

By car There are very few places to park in Trieste and the streets are congested. If you come with a car leave it in your hotel car park or use the waterfront public parking. Pick up a rental car at the airport, in town or from the port: Avis, Nuova Stazione Marittima (T 040 300 820, W avis.com); Europcar, Via Fabio Severo 5 (T 040 765 863, W europcar.it); Hertz, Nuova Stazione Marittima (T 040 322 0098, W hertz.com).

By taxi The best outfit is Radio Taxi (T 040 307 730).

ACCOMMODATION

★ **Albero Nascosto** Via Felice Venezian 18 T 040 300 188, W alberonascosto.it; map p.442. Stylish, small boutique hotel in the historical centre of Trieste. The building is beautifully renovated using good quality materials. Studio-apartments are bright, with kitchen unit, satellite TV, refrigerator, a/c and wi-fi. **€145**

★ **B&B Atelier Lidia Polla** Via del Coroneo 1 T 334 715 0231, W atelierlidiapolla.com; map p.442. Gregarious

TRIESTE'S COFFEE HERITAGE

Trieste's love affair with **coffee** dates from the mid-eighteenth century, when the port was given tax-free status by Habsburg Emperor Charles VI. The resultant boom in trade coincided with the coffee craze hitting Europe, in particular Vienna, and coffee beans destined for Austrian cafés became one of Trieste's biggest imports. Even today it's the leading coffee port in the Mediterranean – forty percent of Italy's coffee arrives here – and Trieste's denizens imbibe twice as much on average as their fellow countrymen. The city even has its own coffee terminology – if you order a cappuccino you'll get a *caffè macchiato*, so instead you should ask for a *caffè latte*.

One of the pleasures of walking around the city centre is the exotic scent of roasting beans emanating from choice establishments, known as *torrefazioni*. The city's most famous brand is Illy, founded in 1933 and producer of a world-renowned 100-percent Arabica blend. So supreme is the coffee culture in the city that Riccardo Illy, scion of the clan, has held the offices of mayor and regional president, among numerous other posts. Illy runs courses in coffee appreciation at the Università del Caffè (ⓦ unicaffe.it).

7

owner Laura has transformed the studio of her grandmother, the artist Lidia Polla, into a delightful B&B; the three rooms feature high ceilings and beautiful furniture, as well as Lidia's sculptures and paintings. The Madame Butterfly Room has Japanese motifs, and a gorgeous 1920s-style bathroom (all bathrooms are outside the rooms). There's a leafy terrace and breakfast is served in the cosy kitchen. €90

Casa Trauner Via delle Mura 26 ⓣ 040 372 7379, ⓦ gruppofama.com; map p.442. Tucked away on a little street in the historical centre, this renovated building is ideal for self-caterers; there are five spacious and modern apartments embellished with black-and-white photos of the city. The cosy attic room 5 on the top floor should be your first choice. €80

Continentale Via S. Nicolò 25 ⓣ 040 631 717, ⓦ continentalehotel.com; map p.442. A comfortable four-star hotel in the heart of town with 47 rooms over five floors; there are also sixteen modern apartments with kitchenette in an annexe close by. Breakfast is served at the attached restaurant with tables spilling onto the pedestrianized street. €120

Grand Hotel Duchi D'Aosta Piazza Unità d'Italia 2 ⓣ 040 760 0011, ⓦ duchi.eu; map p.442. Right on the main square, this historic hotel is one of the city's smartest, with cosy interiors featuring warm hues and crimson-coloured rugs. There's a basement spa with swimming pool, steam room and sauna. The hotel's *Harry's Grill* restaurant and bar is a pleasant, if pricey, spot to enjoy a coffee at one of the tables on the square. €129

★ **Locanda alle Beccherie** Via Beccherie 5 ⓣ 040 372 7379, ⓦ gruppofama.com; map p.442. The five apartments here are spacious, yet cosy, with modern open-plan kitchenettes. There is no reception; on arrival guests are met by the friendly owners and given a key to access the building. €90

Residenza Le 6A Via Santa Caterina 7 ⓣ 040 672 6715, ⓦ residenzale6a.it; map p.442. An agreeable place with charming rooms and a cosy living area where breakfast is served, plus a small communal terrace. Guests who stay for more than two nights have complimentary use of the house Vespa – perfect to explore the city's narrow little streets. The owners also manage a similar property on the third floor of the same building. €80

EATING

Trieste has a huge range of good-value **restaurants**: the best area to head for is pedestrian-only **Viale XX Settembre**, known as the Acquedotto ("aqueduct"), where citizens stroll in the evening. Via C. Battisti, east of Sant'Antonio, is good for **food shops**, while the lively Ghetto, Piazza Borsa and Via Torino are packed with happening bars for late-night **drinking** (see page 447).

CAFÉS, PASTICCERIE AND GELATERIE

Caffè degli Specchi Piazza Unità d'Italia 7 ⓣ 040 661 973, ⓦ caffespecchi.it; map p.442. Located in the centre of Trieste's main square, this historic café is a great place to indulge in an early evening *aperitivo*, afternoon tea or a spot of people-watching. Daily 8am–10pm.

★ **Caffè San Marco** Via C. Battisti 18/A ⓣ 040 064 1724, ⓦ caffesanmarcotrieste.eu; map p.442. This gorgeous, atmospheric café, restaurant and bookshop with Art Nouveau-style mahogany and mirrors opened in 1914; it quickly became a meeting point for political activists, and was closed a year later by the Austrians before reopening in 1919. Tues–Thurs 8.30am–11pm, Fri & Sat 8.30am–midnight, Sun 9am–9pm.

Caffè Tommaseo Piazza Tommaseo 4/C ⓣ 040 362 666, ⓦ caffetommaseo.it; map p.442. A rendezvous for Italian nationalists in the nineteenth century, this is the oldest surviving café and restaurant in Trieste and supposedly introduced *gelato* to the city. Daily 10am–11pm.

Chocolat Via Cavana 15/B ⓣ 040 300 524; map p.442. Paradise for chocolate lovers, this tiny place dishes up delicious hot chocolate – in summer it's served refreshingly

cold, and there are a handful of creamy ice-cream flavours to choose from, too. Tues–Sat 7.30am–8pm.

Gelato Marco Via Malcanton 16/A ⊕392 078 8230, ⊕gelatomarco.com; map p.442. This friendly *gelateria* offers more than forty flavours (all vegan and gluten free), including chocolate orange and *carsolina*, a creamy dessert from the area. There are *granite* (slush puppies) too, with exotic flavours such as mojito and pina colada. March–Nov Tues–Sun 10am–11.30pm.

★ **La Bomboniera** Via XXX Ottobre 3 ⊕040 632 752, ⊕pasticcerialabomboniera.com; map p.442. This historic *pasticceria* has been making home-baked Austro-Hungarian cakes and pastries (from €1.60) since it opened in 1848; even if you're not buying anything, it's worth popping in to look at the beautiful interior that has been lovingly preserved, with gorgeous nineteenth-century black-and-white floor tiles. Tues–Sat 9am–1pm & 5–8pm, Sun 9am–3pm.

RESTAURANTS

Antica Hostaria Da Libero Via Risorta 7/A ⊕040 301 113, ⊕hostariadalibero.com; map p.442. This old-fashioned establishment at the foot of the castle is virtually the last remaining genuine *osteria* in the city, with original wood-panelled walls lined with curios. The emphasis is on hearty meat dishes including goulash and gnocchi with wild boar. *Primi* €8, *secondi* €10. Mon 7.30–10.30pm, Tues–Sat 12.30–2pm & 7.30–10.30pm.

Da Pepi Buffet Via Cassa di Risparmio 3 ⊕040 366 858, ⊕buffetdapepi.it; map p.442. Traditional no-frills restaurant that's the perfect place for meat-based snacks and lunches. The speciality here is *bollito di maiale* – various cuts of pork, including sausages, cooked in broth and served up with mustard and horseradish, accompanied by *crauti*, fermented cabbage flavoured with cumin. Full meals about €20. Mon–Sat 8.30am–10pm.

Istriano Riva Grumula 6 ⊕040 306 664, ⊕osteria istriano.com; map p.442. Gregarious owner Giobi hops from table to table explaining the ingredients of his fish and seafood dishes; the menu changes regularly, and dishes of the day are jotted on a blackboard. Antipasti (€11) are the forte here, although mains are good too. Tues–Sat 12.30–2.30pm & 7.30–11pm, Sun 12.30–2.30pm.

★ **Menarosti** Via del Toro 12 ⊕040 661 077; map p.442. A truly atmospheric place not to be missed, this wonderful family-run fish restaurant feels like stepping back in time; the graceful interiors feature wooden wardrobes lined with china, and elderly family members sit at the tables removing cooked lobsters from their shells. *Primi* €12, *secondi* €18. Tues–Sat noon–2.30pm & 7–10pm, Sun noon–2.30pm.

★ **NerodiSeppia** Via Cadorna 23 ⊕040 301 377, ⊕trattorianerodiseppia.com; map p.442. One street back from the seafront, this bustling place is one of the city's best fish and seafood restaurants; the fish is as fresh as could be, and the menu changes regularly – it's always packed, so make sure you book ahead. *Primi* €12, *secondi* €16. Tues–Sat 12.30–2pm & 7.30–9.30pm.

Suban Via Comici 2/D ⊕040 54 368, ⊕suban.it; map p.442. Traditional dishes are perfectly prepared at this family-run restaurant. The food is Mittel-European with dishes such as cheese strudel with prosciutto (€13) and roasted veal shank (€16). The excellent wine list includes bottles from Slovenia. There's outdoor seating under the pergola in summer. A three-course meal costs about €50. Mon & Wed–Fri 7–10pm, Sat & Sun 12–2.30pm & 7–10pm.

DRINKING

★ **Gran Malabar** Piazza San Giovanni 6 ⊕040 636 226; map p.442. This small, nondescript corner bar is a Trieste institution not to be missed by wine connoisseurs; with more than six hundred varieties on offer and an authentic, laidback atmosphere, this is one of the best spots in the city to enjoy an *aperitivo* (from €3). There are meat and cheese platters, too. Mon–Sat 6.30am–9pm, Sun 7.30am–1pm.

L'Etrusco Via dei Capitelli 7/B ⊕348 005 8940 ⊕etruscotrieste.com; map p.442. A friendly wine bar and restaurant serving traditional Tuscan dishes such as *bistecca alla fiorentina* (flame-grilled T-bone steak; €4.80/100g) and *pappa al pomodoro* (Tuscan soup made with tomatoes, basil, garlic and bread; €5) and panino col lampredotto (tripe sandwich; €5). There's a Sunday brunch buffet (11am–4pm) for €20. Live music from jazz to bossanova on Thurs (8–11pm). Wed–Mon 11am–3pm & 6–11pm; June, July & Aug Wed–Mon 5pm–midnight.

★ **SaluMare** Via di Cavana 13/A ⊕040 322 9743, ⊕salumare.it; map p.442. This popular little seafood deli attracts quite a crowd in the early evening for a refreshing glass of wine and exquisite fish and seafood nibbles enjoyed at a long communal table on the pavement. Tues–Sat 11am–2pm & 6–9pm.

TRIESTE FESTIVALS AND EVENTS

The second Sunday of October sees the **Barcolana** (⊕barcolana.it), Italy's largest sailing regatta with over two thousand boats of all types skimming the bay; the race attracts thousands of spectators and there are ten days of festivities around the event. From spring to autumn, events abound, including at the **Teatro Verdi** (⊕040 672 2111, ⊕teatroverdi-trieste.com): for details, contact the tourist office or check *Il Piccolo*, Trieste's daily paper.

DIRECTORY

Hospital Ospedale Maggiore, Piazza dell'Ospitale 2 (T 040 399 1111); in an emergency dial T 112.

Police Via Tor Bandena 6 (T 040 379 0502). Otherwise call T 113.

Post office Piazza Vittorio Veneto 1 (Mon–Sat 8.20am–7.05pm, Sat 8.20am–12.35pm).

Inland from Trieste: the Carso

The **CARSO** is the Italian name for limestone uplands that rise from the Venetian plain south of Monfalcone and eventually merge into the Istrian plateau. Although within a thirty-minute bus ride of Trieste, it feels like an entirely different country, and is geologically, botanically and demographically distinct from anywhere else in Italy. Most of the Carso now lies within Slovenia (its Slovene name is Kras), and even the narrow strip inside Italy, which has a population of just twenty thousand, remains distinctively Slovene in culture, boasting places with names like Zagradec and Koludrovica.

7 The particular shape and look of the **karst landscape** is due to the weathering of the limestone bedrock by water and wind, and the surface of the plateau is studded with sinkholes left by streams which have formed vast caverns, underground lakes and rivers. This distinctive landscape and the unspoiled natural environment make for fine **walking**, and you can stop for refreshments at an *osmiza*, a rustic eating place where farmers sell their own produce, such as cured meats, cheese, olives, hard-boiled eggs, bread and wine (ask the tourist office for a list or check W osmize.com).

Like all limestone landscapes the **environment** is harsh: arid in summer and sometimes snowbound in winter. The thick-walled houses are built to withstand the blasts of the *bora*, the fierce northeasterly wind which can reach gusts of 145km/hr – when it's at its worst ropes are strung along the steeper streets in Trieste.

Grotta Gigante

Guided visits hourly on the hour April–Sept Tues–Sun 9am–5pm; Oct–March 10am–4pm; July & Aug also open Mon • €12 • T 040 327 312, W grottagigante.it

The **Grotta Gigante** is the Carso's main tourist attraction, and with good reason: it's one of the largest accessible caves in the world. At 98m high by 76m wide, the cave is large enough that the dome of St Peter's would fit comfortably inside. It's a steady 11°C inside, so bring warm clothes.

The cave is impressive in scale and, like most of the caves in the Carso, was created by the erosive action of a river, in this case the Timavo, which sank deeper and deeper underground before changing course (the cave is now dry). The fantastically shaped stalactites and stalagmites were formed by deposits of calcium carbonate and colourful metal oxides. Much more recently, ferns and moss have started to grow in what was previously a lifeless environment, thanks to photosynthesis triggered by electric lighting. In the centre of the cave there are two geodetic pendulums, scientific devices that measure the slow movements of the earth's crust, while at the bottom of the cave three seismometers play a vital role in the seismic monitoring of the Mediterranean area.

Rupingrande

Apart from the Grotta Gigante, the main sights to head for are in and around the village of **RUPINGRANDE** (aka Monrupino), 3km northeast of the cave. Here, the **Casa Carsica** at Località Rupingrande 31 (free; T 040 327 124, W kraskahisa.com/eng) is a typical rural home that puts on various cultural exhibitions, while the village itself hosts an important Slovene folk festival, the **Nozze carsiche** (Carsic Wedding) in August in

PIAZZA DELLA LIBERT À, UDINE

IOANNI MAVRO PRAES-

WALKS AROUND TRIESTE

Trieste tourist office (see page 445) publishes a useful map of the network of numbered footpaths in the Carso; it shouldn't be used for serious navigation but is a good guide. For serious hiking in the hills you need Tabacco's *Carso Triestino e Isontino Map #047*. Two walks near Trieste can be particularly recommended:

The Strada Vicentina Also known as the Napoleonica, the Strada Vicentina is some 3.7km long, contouring the hillside above the city, between the *Obelisco* campsite, 7km from Trieste, and the hamlet of Borgo Nazario (near Prosecco). It's a scenic, easy walk, partly shaded by trees and partly cut through by almost sheer limestone cliffs; on a clear day the views are superb. Access to the Strada Vicentina is easy: *Obelisco* is a stop on the *tranvia*, and the Borgo Nazario end is near Via San Nazario, where the #42 bus stops on its way back to Trieste station.

The Val Rosandra A miniature wilderness of limestone cliffs and sumac trees, the Val Rosandra is the local rock-climbing headquarters and is crisscrossed with walking paths. From the bus stop at Bagnoli Della Rosandra (bus #40 from Trieste), follow the road behind the square to Bagnoli Superiore where the marked hiking trails begin. Highlights include the remains of a Roman aqueduct, the little sanctuary church of Santa Maria in Siaris, and various pools and waterfalls. If you get as far as the tiny hamlet of Bottazzo – the last habitation before Slovenia – you'll see a sign indicating a friendship path linking communities on either side of the frontier.

odd-numbered years. A short walk east of the village is a fourteenth-century castle built to defend the area from Turkish incursions.

ARRIVAL AND DEPARTURE — THE CARSO

By bus Several bus services run to the Carso from Piazza Oberdan in central Trieste, including the #42 and #44.

By tram The most picturesque way up into the Carso is to take the *tranvia* (cable tramway; daily 7am–8pm; every 20min; €1.25, same ticket as for buses) from Trieste's Piazza Oberdan to the village of Opicina, at the edge of the plateau. From the tram stop, cross the square and catch bus #42 to Rupingrande and the Grotta Gigante. At the time of writing the *tranvia* was momentarily suspended; check triestetrasporti.it for the latest details.

EATING

Agriturismo Milic Località Sagrado 2, Sgonico 040 229 383, agriturismomilic.it. Tasty and reasonably priced country cooking since 1531, with everything produced on the farm, including the excellent wine. There are tables in the garden in summer, and specialities include home-cured meats, gnocchi and the mixed grill: four-course meals for €23. Book ahead. Fri–Sun 11.30am–9.30pm.

The Triestine Riviera

The thirty-odd kilometres of coastline either side of Trieste, from Muggia to the south and as far as Duino in the north, are optimistically known as the **TRIESTINE RIVIERA**. While beaches aren't as good as at nearby Grado, some fine walks, historic sites and castles make it worth a day-trip from Trieste.

ARRIVAL AND INFORMATION — THE TRIESTINE RIVIERA

By train There's a train from Trieste to Miramare, Bivio d'Aurisina and Sistiano (hourly; 10–20min).

By bus Frequent buses trace the coast road; #6 from Trieste's bus station (every 20min; also bus #36 in summer) runs to Miramare and Barcola, while bus #20 from Piazza Oberdan or the bus station (every 15min) runs to Muggia (45min). Bus #44 runs from Piazza Oberdan (every 30min) to Sistiana (45min) and Duino (50min).

By ferry In summer, ferries from Trieste's central dock call at all the coastal towns, including Muggia (10 daily; 30min), Barcola (4 daily mid-June to mid-Sept; 15min), Sistiana (4 daily mid-June to mid-Sept; 1hr 35min) and Grado (3 daily Tues–Sun mid-June to early Sept; 2 daily mid-May to mid-June & early–mid Sept; 1hr15min; free with FVG card).

Muggia

Directly south across the bay from Trieste, 11km away by road, **MUGGIA**, the last remnant of Venice's Istrian possessions, is a picturesque little town and a popular lunch spot for visitors from Trieste. It's best accessed by ferry (summer only), with the trip across the bay a good enough reason in itself to visit, but there are also appealing signs of the past, particularly in the brightly painted buildings on the main square. On the east side of the piazza, the fifteenth-century **Duomo** reveals its origins in its Venetian-Gothic arches and a bas-relief of Christ Pantocrator in the lunette above the main door; the handsome **Palazzo dei Rettori**, on the north side of the square, displays the telltale lion of St Mark, symbol of Venice's former hegemony here. The piazza is backed by a handful of narrow streets and tumbledown houses, many dating back to Venetian times.

On the seaward side of the piazza, the tiny *mandracchio* is now used as a basin for pleasure boats, while the working harbour just beyond is spoilt only by the unenviable view of Trieste's industrial backside.

EATING **MUGGIA**

Trattoria Splendor Via Dante Alighieri 47 ⓣ 040 275 262. This historic family-run restaurant opened here in 1897 and is hugely popular – make sure you arrive early to get a table. Seating is in a laidback, cosy dining area, and there are tables on the little square in summer. The menu changes daily, with plenty of delicious fish and seafood dishes to choose from. Wed–Mon 12–2.30pm & 7–9.30pm.

Barcola

BARCOLA, 2km northwest of Trieste, is the city's nearest beach resort. Developed during Trieste's great days at the end of the nineteenth century, it is now really a suburb that comes to life in summer, when all Trieste decamps here. Just short of the resort, perched on the slope of the limestone escarpment and offering stunning views along the coast, is the **Faro della Vittoria**, the world's third-tallest≈lighthouse.

Castello di Miramare

Castle Daily 9am–7pm • €8 • **Gardens** Daily: Jan & Feb 8am–4pm; March & Oct 8am–5pm; April, May & Sept 8am–6pm; June–Aug 8am–7pm; Nov & Dec 8am–3pm • Free • ⓣ 040 224 143, ⓦ castello-miramare.it

Standing at the tip of a rocky promontory 7km north of Trieste, the fairy-tale castle of **MIRAMARE** is the area's prime tourist attraction. Archduke Maximilian of Habsburg, the younger brother of Emperor Franz Joseph of Austria, built his dream castle and laid out its grounds between 1856 and 1870, but never lived to see it completed. He was duped into accepting Napoleon III's offer to become the Emperor of Mexico, and executed by a Mexican firing squad in 1867. His wife Carlotta went mad after his execution, and Archduke Franz Ferdinand stayed here on his way to his assassination in Sarajevo in 1914, giving rise to the legend that anyone who spends a night in Miramare will come to a bad end – when the British general Freybourg chose the castle as his headquarters at the end of the war, he slept in the garden.

The park and gardens, which are free, make an excellent spot for a picnic, but the real draw is the castle's kitsch **interior**, a remarkable example of regal decadence and over-the-top furnishings. The Monarchs' Salon, for instance, is embellished with portraits of a king of Norway, the Emperor of Brazil, a tsar of Russia – anyone, no matter how fraudulent or despotic, as long as they're nominal monarchs. The bedroom is full of images chronicling the construction of the castle. Other rooms are panelled and furnished like ship's quarters, reflecting Maximilian's devotion to the Austrian Navy.

Duino

The village of **DUINO**, 14km northwest along the coast from Trieste, is dominated by its two castles. Built around the eleven th century, the **Castello Vecchio** (by prior booking only ⓣ 040 208 120; €3) is now just a ruined eyrie above the sea, but has wonderful views of the nearby **Castello Nuovo**.

Castello Nuovo

Daily except Tues: mid- to end March & mid-Oct to Nov 9.30am–4pm; April–Sept 9.30am–5.30pm; first two weeks of Oct 9.30am–5pm • €8 • ⓣ 040 208 120, ⓦ castellodiduino.it • Bus #44 from Trieste

Seat of the princes of Thurn und Taxis, the **Castello Nuovo** was built in the early fifteenth century and its grounds opened to the public in 2003. Today, visitors can stroll through the lavishly decorated rooms, admire a massive doll's house given to the family by Napoleon III's widow and explore a history of the family's eighteenth-century pan-European postal service. Don't miss, too, the fantastic coastal views from the beautiful gardens and the top of the third-century Roman tower.

7

Sentiero Rilke

Near the Castello Nuovo, the **Sentiero Rilke** is a panoramic coastal footpath, named after Rainer Maria Rilke who began his famous *Duino Elegies* while staying at the castle. Apparently, while walking along the castle bastions in a gale he heard a voice asking, "Who, if I cried out, would hear me among the angelic orders?" and, so inspired, he started work on the Elegies. The path ends at Sistiana, where there's a large yacht harbour and a beach, of which the first 500m are open to the public.

Aquileia

Bordered by the Tagliamento in the west and the Isonzo in the east, the triangle of flatlands west of Trieste and south of Udine seems unpromising territory for a visitor – mile upon mile of maize fields, streams, market gardens and newish villages. Yet **AQUILEIA** was once the Roman capital of Friuli and is the most important archeological site in northern Italy. These unremarkable fields have yielded a wealth of Roman remains, while the glorious basilica here ranks among the most important monuments of early Christendom.

Brief history

Some 45km west of Trieste, Aquileia was established as a **Roman colony** in 181 BC, its location at the eastern edge of the Venetian plain – on the bank of a navigable river a few kilometres from the sea – being ideal for defensive and trading purposes. It became the nexus for all Rome's dealings with points east and north, and by 10 BC, when the Emperor Augustus received Herod the Great here, Aquileia was the fourth most important city in Italy, after Rome, Milan and Capua. In 314 AD the Patriarchate of Aquileia was founded, and under the first patriarch, Theodore, a great basilica was built. Sacked by Attila in 452 and again by the Lombards in 568, Aquileia lost the patriarchate to Grado, which was protected from invasion by its lagoons. Aquileia regained its primacy in the early eleventh century under Patriarch Poppo, who rebuilt the basilica and erected the campanile, a landmark for kilometres around. But regional power inevitably passed to Venice, and in 1751 Aquileia lost its patriarchate for the last time, to Udine. The sea has long since retreated, the River Natissa reduced to a reed-clogged stream, and Aquileia is now a quiet little town of 3500 people.

The basilica

Piazza Capitolo 1 • **Basilica** March & Oct daily 9am–6pm; April–Sept daily 9am–7pm; Nov–Feb Mon–Fri 10am–4pm, Sat & Sun 9am–5pm • **Basilica & Cripta degli Affreschi** €3; Basilica, Cripta degli Affreschi & Cripta degli Scavi €5 • **Belltower** March–Oct daily 9.30am–1.30pm & 2.30–6.30pm • €2 • ⓣ 0431 919 719, ⓦ basilicadiaquileia.it

A UNESCO World Heritage Site, Aquileia's vast **basilica**, just east of the main road reveals the town's rich history. The earliest part, Theodore's extraordinary **mosaic pavement** was discovered below the nave floor at the beginning of the twentieth century and is thought to be the oldest surviving remnant of any Christian church. The mosaic undulates the full length of the nave in a riotous sequence of colours, patterns and images – look for the blond angel bearing the laurel wreath and palm frond. Beyond the red line extending across the aisle, the Christian imagery begins with the story of Jonah, complete with waves, whale and fish. Other stunning mosaics from Theodore's original basilica, depicting a whole bestiary, have been discovered around the base of the campanile in the **Cripta degli Scavi** (access from inside the basilica).

In 1348 an earthquake destroyed much of Poppo's work, but the building is still superb, the Gothic elements of the reconstruction – all points above the capitals – harmonizing perfectly with the Romanesque below. The fine nave ceiling dates from the fifteenth century, while the steeple of the campanile dates from eleventh century. The ninth-century **Cripta degli Affreschi** under the chancel has superb twelfth-century frescoes telling the story of St Hermagora, the legendary first bishop of Aquileia, including a gory beheading and a moving descent from the Cross. Next door, a climb up the eleventh-century **belltower**, constructed with stones from the nearby Roman amphitheatre, gives views from the mountains to the coast.

Museo Archeologico Nazionale

Via Roma 1 • Tues–Sun 8.30am–7.30pm; last entry 7pm • €7 • ⓣ 0431 91 035, ⓦ museoarcheologicoaquileia.beniculturali.it

The **Museo Archeologico Nazionale** contains the finer Roman remnants found around Aquileia, ranging from precise surgical needles, delicate coloured glass and precious stones to great piles of jumbled masonry. The two courtyards resemble a junkyard of Roman stone, with hundreds of funerary monuments, including urns piled in neat pyramids. On the ground floor of the museum, two extraordinary bronze heads are displayed side by side: one is a fantastical relief in the Hellenistic style, the other a naturalistic bust with a cruel expression that may portray a dictator of the third century AD. Rows of marble sculptures and busts mostly derive from the Roman tombs that once lined the roads into Aquileia.

ARRIVAL AND INFORMATION — AQUILEIA

By bus An hourly bus from Udine stops here. From Trieste change at Monfalcone, and take the Grado bus that stops at Aquileia. Details on ⓦ aptgorizia.it and ⓦ saf.ud.it.

By train There are direct trains from Udine to Aquileia (9 daily; 25min). From Trieste, take the hourly train to Cervignano, and then bus #26 which coincides with train arrival time.

Tourist office In the Via Giulia Augusta bus terminal car park at the northern edge of town (April–Oct 9am–1pm & 1.30–5.30pm, Sun 9–1pm, Nov–March 9am–7pm; ⓣ 0431 919 491, ⓦ turismofvg.it).

ACCOMMODATION

B & B Casa di Giulia Via Giulia Augusta 21 ⓣ 043 191 8742, ⓦ casadigiulia.it. An attractive B&B offering three spacious rooms with wooden floors and nineteenth-century furnishings; two rooms have wooden ceiling beams that give the place a rustic touch. The cosy top-floor attic room is the nicest, with an airy modern bathroom. There's also a lovely garden that gives onto a beautifully preserved Roman road. **€70**

Hotel Patriarchi Via Giulia Augusta 12 ⓣ 0431 919 595, ⓦ hotelpatriarchi.it. On the main road not far from the bus terminal, this three-star hotel has simple comfortable rooms with wooden or carpeted floors, many with views of the basilica and belltower (add extra for these). The restaurant is good, too. **€80**

EATING AND DRINKING

La Capannina Via Gemina 10 ⓣ 0431 91 019, ⓦ ristorantelacapannina.net. A reliable café and restaurant in the centre of town offering outdoor seating. The focus is on fish dishes such as risotto with shrimps and porcini mushrooms, and grilled or fried calamari. *Primi* around €10, *secondi* €12. Thurs–Tues 9am–3pm & 5.30–11pm; open daily in summer.

Corallo Via Beligna 3 ⓣ 0431 91 065 ⓦ ristorante

coralloaquileia.it. On the main road, this laidback café and restaurant offers a great value two-course set lunch for €12, with a selection of fish and meat based *primi* and *secondi*. Seating is on a little shaded terrace in summer. Tues–Sun 11.30am–3pm & 6–10pm.

Grado

Some 11km south of Aquileia, isolated among lagoons, is the ancient island-town of **GRADO**, through which Aquileia once traded with Syria, Cyprus, Arabia and Asia Minor. Grado enjoyed its heyday under the Austrians who developed it as a health resort due to the presence of curative sand and waters – and there's still a **spa** here today (ⓦgradoit.it). Grado's **historic centre** has three early Christian buildings, grouped close together in the heart of a miniature network of old streets. It's also one of the best places in the northern Adriatic for relaxing on the **beach**; the water is safe, warm as a bath and shallow – indeed, the town's name comes from the gentle angle of its shore. The free beaches are at the eastern and western ends. Alternatively, you can take a **boat trip** round Grado's **lagoon** to explore some of its many islands.

7

Basilica di Santa Eufemia

Campo Patriarca Elia • Daily 8am–6pm; until 7pm in summer • Free

Grado's sixth-century **Basilica di Santa Eufemia** was heavily restored between the 1930s and 1950s, but preserves a bizarre parade of ill-matched nave pillars topped by an assortment of Corinthian capitals; it's thought that these were recycled from various Roman buildings in Aquileia. The pulpit is of similarly hybrid origins, perched on six slender Roman columns under a Venetian canopy that resembles an oriental tent. Venice's presence is also felt in the fourteenth-century silver *pala* on the high altar. The mosaic pavement is beautiful, the pattern being formed by an endless knot.

The baptistry and Santa Maria delle Grazie

Adjacent to the basilica, the octagonal **baptistry** (daily 8am–7pm; free) dates back to the fifth century. The church of **Santa Maria delle Grazie** (daily 8am–6pm, until 7pm in summer; free), on its far side, is from the same period and has another mongrel collection of columns and capitals. From the outside it's possible to see how the ground level has sunk over the centuries.

Laguna di Grado

Speedboats leave from Grado's Canale della Schiusa to Barbana Island (30min one way; return ticket €6; boat schedules are subject to frequent change – check ⓦmotoscafistigradesi.it for details); Motonave Nuova Cristina boats (ⓦmotorshipcristina.it also offer trips to various destinations around the lagoon, as well as further afield); private taxi boats cost about €100/day

Covering approximately ninety square kilometres, the **Laguna di Grado** is home to a myriad of canals and islands that can be visited by boat. The islands were once inhabited for months at a time by fishermen who travelled to Grado on Saturdays to stock up on supplies, and the lagoon is dotted with their *casoni*, traditional houses built with mud and reeds. After World War I most migrated to the city, and only three or four families live in the lagoon today, though a number of fishermen have kept their *casoni* and use them as second homes.

ARRIVAL AND INFORMATION — GRADO

By bus From Udine hourly buses depart for Grado (1hr 30min), stopping at Palmanova and Aquileia. From Trieste there are direct buses from mid-June to mid-Sept (every 2hr; 1hr 30min); the rest of the year, catch the train from Trieste to Cervignano (every 30min; 30min), then take a bus from there (hourly; 20min).

By ferry Between June and Aug there are three daily services (1hr 30min) from Trieste's Molo Audace to Grado's Molo Torpediniere.

Tourist office Viale Dante Alighieri 66 (May–Sept daily 9am–1pm & 2–7pm; Oct–April Mon–Sat 9am–1pm & 2–6pm, Sun 9am–1pm; ⓣ 0431 877 111, ⓦ turismofvg.it).

ACCOMMODATION

★ **Ai Ciodi** Località Anfora ⓣ 335 752 2209, ⓦ portobusoaiciodi.it. On the small fisherman's island of Anfora in the Laguna di Grado, the island's primary school has been converted into a hotel. Its solar-heated rooms are decorated with nautical-style murals, and all have modern amenities including flatscreen TVs and en-suite bathrooms. In the evenings you'll have the entire island to yourself. Rates are half board, so you can enjoy the outstanding cuisine at the attached restaurant (see below). **€170**

Alla Spiaggia Via Mazzini 2 ⓣ 0431 84 841, ⓦ albergo allaspiaggia.it. A pleasant place on the seafront with bright and airy rooms; the leafy open-air veranda with wicker chairs is a great spot to grab a book and unwind in summer. **€180**

Villa Erica Viale Dante Alighieri 69 ⓣ 0431 84 444, ⓦ hotel villaerica.com. Giving onto a pedestrianized street, this late nineteenth-century building has been tastefully restored; the graceful interiors exude olde worlde charm. Corridors are decorated with black-and-white prints, while some rooms have wooden furnishings and lagoon views. **€180**

Villa Marin Via dei Provveditori 20 ⓣ 0431 80 789, ⓦ villamarin.it. A one-star hotel with an excellent location right on the seafront; rooms are fairly small and a little dated but the wonderful sea views compensate. **€105**

Ville Bianchi Viale Dante Alighieri 50 ⓣ 0431 80 169, ⓦ villebianchi.it. Once exclusive holiday residences during the Austro-Hungarian Empire, these five restored villas with smart interiors nestle between the seafront and the historical centre. The communal areas are attractively furnished, while the pricey rooms have plainer decor. **€220**

7

EATING AND DRINKING

★ **Ai Ciodi** Località Anfora ⓣ 335 752 2209, ⓦ portobusoaiciodi.it. This exceptional fish and seafood trattoria on the island of Anfora has been run by the friendly Tognon family for over three decades – the fish is daily caught by Mauro and his two sons who lovingly prepare the simple but delicious dishes. Seating is on a breezy terrace looking onto the sea, and you can watch the chefs at work in the open-plan kitchen. A meal will set you back about €35. Easter to mid-Oct daily 11.30am–7pm.

Tavernetta all'Androna Calle Porta Piccola 6 ⓣ 0431 80 950, ⓦ androna.it. A smart restaurant that doesn't come cheap, although the fish and seafood dishes are among the best in town. There's a lovely outdoor terrace area in summer. *Primi* €18, *secondi* €22. Daily 7–10.30pm; Mon, Fri, Sat & Sun also open for lunch noon–2.30pm.

Zero Miglia Riva E. Dandolo 22 ⓣ 0431 80 287, ⓦ zeromiglia.it. Run by a cooperative of fishermen, this restaurant serves fish that couldn't get any fresher, with the boats docked on the bank just outside. The stylish interiors feature wooden floors and a marble worktop recalling counters at a fish market. *Primi* €12, *secondi* €14. Wed–Mon noon–2pm & 6–10pm; open daily in summer.

Gorizia and around

As with other towns in this region, the tranquillity of present-day **GORIZIA** – virtually midway along the Trieste–Udine rail line – belies its turbulent past. The castle that dominates the old centre was the power base of the dukes of Gorizia, who ruled the area for four centuries. After their eclipse, Venice briefly ruled the town at the start of the sixteenth century, before the Habsburgs took over. It was controlled from Vienna until August 8, 1916, when the Italian army occupied it. The border settlement after World War II literally split houses in Gorizia down the middle. Italy kept the town proper, but lost its eastern perimeter to what was then Yugoslavia, where the new regime resolved to build its own Gorizia: **Nova Gorica** – New Gorizia – is the result.

The town's appearance is distinctly Central European, stamped with the authority of Empress Maria Theresa. Numerous parks and gardens – thriving in the area's mild climate – further enhance the fin-de-siècle atmosphere. It's a major shopping town for Slovenes, which explains the large number of electrical, clothes and food shops, and the cafés and restaurants.

The Castello

Borgo Castello 36 • Mon 9.30am–11.30pm, Tues–Sun 10am–7pm • €3 • ⓣ 0481 535 146

The main sight in town is the **Castello**, built in the twelfth century with various defence structures added later; it was largely destroyed during World War I, then rebuilt. Inside, the **Museum of the Middle Ages** displays weaponry, paintings and models of the castle and town, plus an interesting collection of reproductions of ancient musical instruments made by local artisans. The terrace at the back of the castle provides great views of the city and beyond, and regularly hosts open-air concerts in summer.

Musei Provinciali di Borgo Castello

Borgo Castello 13 • Tues–Sun 9am–7pm • €6; combined entry with Palazzo Attems €7 • ☎ 0481 530 382

On the road leading up to the castle, the **Musei Provinciali di Borgo Castello** consists of three museums in the same building. The **Museo della Grande Guerra** documents life in Gorizia and the trenches during the Great War, with interactive exhibits, while the extensive **Collezione Archeologica** displays finds from the prehistoric period until the Renaissance. On the first floor of the building, the **Museo della Moda e delle Arti Applicate** includes a beautiful eighteenth-century silk-throwing machine and a section devoted to theatrical costumes.

Palazzo Attems Petzenstein

Piazza de Amicis 2 • Tues–Sun 10am–6pm • €6; combined entry with the Castello €7 • ☎ 0481 547 541

Built in the first half of the eighteenth century, the **Palazzo Attems** houses the city's **pinacoteca**, or art gallery. In the exhibition halls you can admire the monumental Pala Attems (1759) by Giambettino Cignaroli, portraits by Giuseppe Tomintz, and works by Austrian Josef Maria Auchentaller, one of the leading members – along with Gustav Klimt – of the Vienna Secession. On display are also paintings, engravings and sculptures by artists from Gorizia and Trieste from the first half of the twentieth century.

The Synagogue

Via Ascoli 19 • Tues & Thurs 5–7pm; first Sun of the month 10am–1pm • Free • ☎ 0481 532 115 • Ⓦ amicidisraelegorizia.it

Behind Palazzo Attems, in what was once the Jewish quarter, the Neoclassical **Synagogue** has an eighteenth-century wrought-iron gate adorned with floral motifs and swags, while the facade is crowned with the Tablets of the Law. The synagogue's ground floor houses a museum that traces the history of Judaism in Gorizia over the centuries.

Monastery Kostanjevica

Škrabčeva ulica 1, Nova Gorica • Mon–Sat 9am–noon & 3–5pm, Sun 3–5pm • €2 donation • Ⓦ samostan-kostanjevica.si • A 30min walk (2km) from Gorizia city centre

Over the border in Slovenia, the crypt of the Franciscan **Monastery Kostanjevica** (Castagnevizza in Italian) is the burial place of the last but one French king, Charles X. After being ousted by the bloodless revolution of July 1830 and sent into exile, the family eventually ended up in Gorizia in 1836, where the Habsburgs allowed them to stay, though Charles died of cholera just seventeen days after his arrival. The Bourbon Institute has asked for the return to France of the family's remains, but both the monks and the Slovenian government have refused, asserting that the royal relics now form part of Slovenia's history.

ARRIVAL AND INFORMATION — GORIZIA

By train Gorizia's train station is at Piazzale Martiri on the southwestern edge of the city, about 2km from the centre.
Destinations Trieste (every 30min; 50min); Udine (every 30min; 35min).

By bus The bus station is directly in front of the railway station. There are three daily services to Cividale (1hr).

Tourist office Corso Italia 9 (May–Sept Mon–Sat 9am–1pm & 2.30–6.30pm; Oct–April Mon–Sat 9am–1pm & 2–6pm, Sun 9am–1pm; ☎ 0481 535 764, Ⓦ turismofvg.it).

ACCOMMODATION

Bed & Breakfast Flumen Via Brigata Cuneo 20 ⓣ 0481 391 877, ⓦ bbflumen.it. Located 3km west of the city centre, this B&B has a beautiful location on the banks of the emerald River Isonzo; there are bikes for guests' use, the rooms are pleasant and the modern bathrooms have rainshowers. Two rooms have a mezzanine floor, and sleep up to three. €70

Palazzo Lantieri Piazza Sant'Antonio 6 ⓣ 0481 533 284, ⓦ palazzo-lantieri.com. This atmospheric fourteenth-century city residence is a glorious place to stay, complete with frescoes, surrounded by its own park and right in the centre of Gorizia. You'll be in good company, as both Goethe and Casanova stayed here. €140

Urban Homy Via Diacono 4 ⓣ 040 982 8095, ⓦ urbanhomy.com. Six stylish rooms and three apartments decorated with modern furnishings and heated with solar panels; some have terraces. They have apartments in Trieste and Ljubljana, too. €80

EATING AND DRINKING

Ai Tre Amici Via Oberdan 11 ⓣ 340 632 3992. A pleasant little place with friendly staff; the concise handwritten menu includes homemade pasta dishes as well as fish and meat mains prepared using local produce. *Primi* €10, *secondi* €15. Thurs–Tues 11.30am–2.30pm & 6.30–11.30pm.

★ **Alla Luna** Via Oberdan 13 ⓣ 0481 530 374. Atmospheric restaurant opened in the 1800s that brims with character; the cosy interior is packed with curios including pots, pans and kitchenware dangling from the ceiling, and seating is on cushioned benches. Waitresses are dressed in dirndls, and serve up excellent Mitteleuropean cuisine. Wed–Sun noon–3pm & 7–11pm.

Trattoria da Gianni Via Morelli 8/B ⓣ 0481 534 568. This simple place is renowned for its enormous portions of food. The menu includes a range of hand-rolled *strozzapreti* (a type of pasta) and gnocchi-based dishes, as well as hearty meat mains (€12.50). Wed–Fri 6pm–midnight; Sat & Sun 11am–3pm & 6pm–midnight.

Udine and around

UDINE, 71km northwest of Trieste, is the provincial capital and radically different to its larger sister city. Framed by mountains and hemmed in by sombre suburbs, the oval-shaped historic centre retains much of its Venetian charm. In many ways Udine harks back to the Venetian Republic, for which it was one of the most important cities, though, its canals, called *roggie*, are little more than rivulets compared to those in Venice. In addition to grand architecture, the churches and galleries here also boast scores of fine works by **Giambattista Tiepolo**, whose airy brilliance evokes the city's easy-going atmosphere. Two days is enough time to experience Udine's charms, though you may also want to factor in a visit to nearby **San Daniele del Friuli** to sample some of Italy's best prosciutto in its hometown.

Brief history

Along with Cividale (see page 461), Udine was one of the frontier towns of imperial Rome but it was not until the thirteenth century that it started to become a regional centre. Patriarch **Bertoldo di Andechs** (1218–51) can be seen as the father of Udine – he established two markets, moved the patriarchate from Cividale to the castle of Udine and set up a city council. In 1362 the dukes of Austria acquired the place by treaty, but not for long: Venice, now hungry for territory, captured Udine in 1420 after several assaults and sieges. The city was ruled by Venetian governors for almost four hundred years – until 1797, when the Venetian Republic surrendered to Napoleon. These days it's a centre of Friulian nationalism.

Piazza della Libertà

The place to start any exploration of Udine is at the foot of the hill, in the gorgeous **Piazza della Libertà**, a square whose architectural ensemble is matched by few cities in Italy. Here, the fifteenth-century **Palazzo del Comune** is a homage to the Palazzo Ducale in Venice, and the clock tower facing the *palazzo*, built in 1527, similarly has a Venetian model – the lion on the facade and the bronze Moors who strike the hours on top of the tower are references to the Torre dell'Orologio in Piazza San Marco. All Udine's points of interest are about a fifteen-minute stroll from the piazza.

The castello

Colle del Castello • Tues–Sun: April–Oct 10.30am–7pm; Nov–March 10.30am–5pm • €8; free with FVG Card • ⓣ 0432 127 2591, ⓦ civicimuseidiudine.it

Once the seat of the Friulian parliament, the sixteenth-century **castello** now houses a series of museums including the excellent **Galleria d'Arte Antica**, containing works by Carpaccio, Pordenone and Caravaggio. The **Galleria dei Disegni e delle Stampe** features a collection of nineteenth-century works, including drawings by Tiepolo, while the **Museo Friulano della Fotografia** displays a selection of original photographs and reprints. The

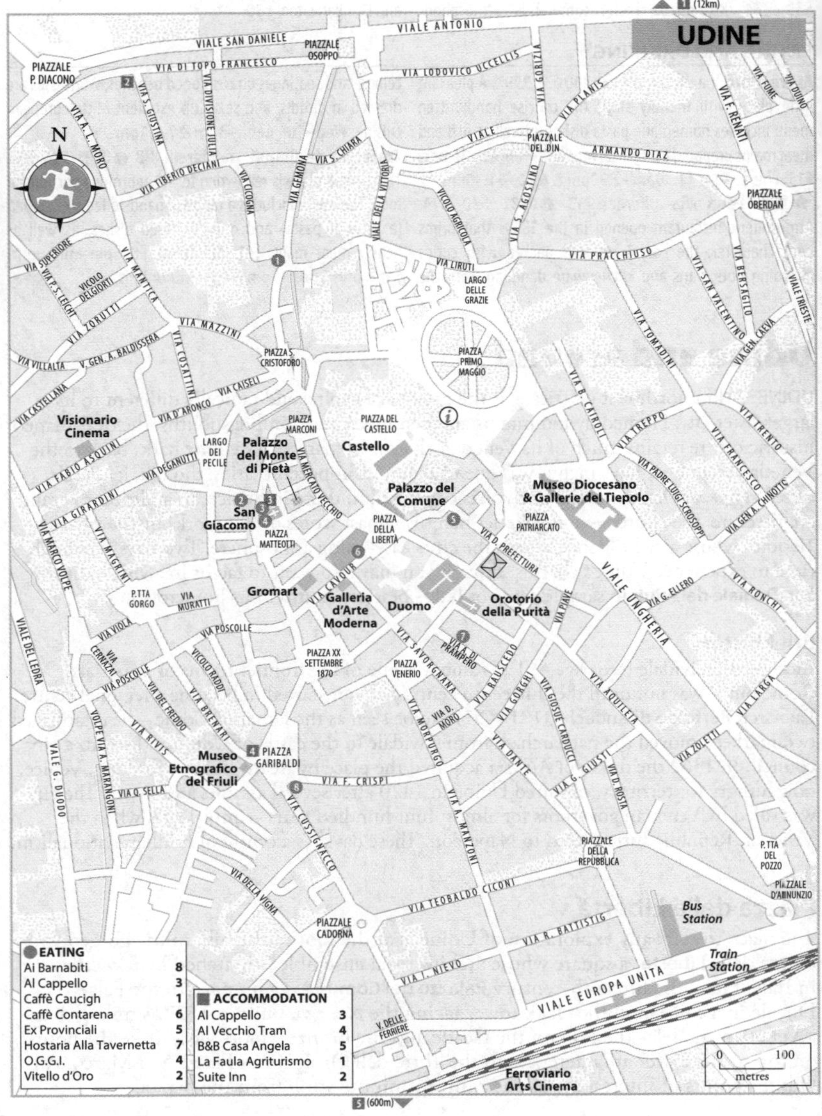

Museo Archeologico has a wonderful collection of artefacts, including vases from Magna Graecia, Roman tombs and cinerary urns. Finally, the **Museo del Risorgimento** traces local history from the fall of the State of Veneto up to its annexation by the Italian State.

Via Mercatovecchio

North from the Piazza della Libertà is **Via Mercatovecchio**, once the mercantile heart of the city and now one of the town's busiest shopping street. The little **Cappella del Monte di Pietà**, incorporated into the Palazzo del Monte di Pietà here, is a beauty: viewed through the glass booth from the street, the interior, with its cloudy Baroque frescoes by Giulio Quaglio (1694), has a pristine, subaqueous appearance.

Piazza Matteotti

Due west of Via Mercatovecchio lies the **Piazza Matteotti**, with galleries on three sides and the fine Baroque facade of San Giacomo on the fourth. The square's importance as the centre of public life in Udine is proved by the outside altar on the first-floor balcony of **San Giacomo**; Mass was celebrated here on Saturdays so that selling and buying could go on uninterrupted in the market below (the market has today moved to Piazza XX Settembre). As well as once being the town's main market, this was the setting for tournaments, plays and carnivals, and still sees summer festivals today. The fountain in the middle of the square was designed in 1543 by Giovanni da Udine, a pupil of Raphael, who also had a hand in building the castle.

7

Museo d'Arte Moderna e Contemporanea Casa Cavazzini

Via Cavour 14 • Tues–Sun: April–Oct 10.30am–7pm; Nov–March 10.30am–5pm • €5; free with FVG Card • ⓣ 0432 127 3772, ⓦ civicimuseiudine.it

Housed in the sixteenth-century Casa Cavazzini, the **Museo d'Arte Moderna e Contemporanea Casa Cavazzini** displays an excellent collection of modern paintings, drawings and sculpture, with works by De Chirico, Carrà, Willem de Kooning and Frank Stella. Look out, too, for the Casa Cavazzini's wonderful fourteenth-century frescoes that were uncovered during the restoration of the building.

The Duomo

Daily 7am–noon & 4–6.45pm • Free

South of Piazza della Libertà is the **Duomo**, a Romanesque construction that was given a Baroque refit in the eighteenth century. Altarpieces and frescoes by Giambattista Tiepolo are the main attraction – they decorate the first two chapels on the right and the Chapel of the Sacrament a little way beyond. There's a series of frescoes painted by Tiepolo in collaboration with his son, Giandomenico, in the tiny **Oratorio della Purità** opposite – ask the sacristan in the Duomo to show you.

Gallerie del Tiepolo

Piazza Patriarcato 1 • Wed–Mon 10am–1pm & 3–6pm • €7; free with FVG Card • ⓣ 0432 25 003, ⓦ musdioc-tiepolo.it

Udine's outstanding works of art are the Giambattista Tiepolo frescoes in the **Gallerie del Tiepolo** in the beautifully furnished **Palazzo Arcivescovile**. Painted in the late 1720s, these luminous and theatrical scenes add up to a sort of Rococo epic of the Old Testament. *Fall of the Rebel Angels* is the first work you see as you climb the staircase, while the finest room, the Gallery, is at the top, immediately on your right. Every surface is painted with either trompe l'oeil architectural details or scenes from the story of Abraham, Isaac and Jacob. To the left is a sequence of rooms decorated in rich colours: look out for Tiepolo's *Judgement of Solomon*

in the Red Room, and Bambini's wonderful *Triumph of Wisdom* in the serene Delfino library. Arranged around the Tiepolo galleries, the **Museo Diocesano** displays popular wooden sculptures from Friuli's churches spanning the Gothic, Renaissance and Baroque periods.

Museo Etnografico del Friuli

Borgo Grazzano 1 • Tues–Sun: April–Oct 10.30am–7pm; Nov–March 10.30am–5pm • €5; free with FVG Card • ⓣ 0432 127 2920, ⓦ civicimuseiudine.it

One of Udine's most engaging museums, the **Museo Etnografico del Friuli** provides an insight into the rich culture of the region, with a wonderful collection of objects on a wide range of themes including religion, medicine, music and national dress. Audiovisual displays bring the objects to life.

ARRIVAL AND INFORMATION — UDINE

7

By plane The nearest airport is Ronchi dei Legionari, 43km away, connected to Udine by regular bus #51 (1hr).

By train Udine's train station is in the south of the town, at Viale Europa Unità 40. From the station catch bus #1 to Piazza Libertà in the city centre (10min).

Destinations Cividale (hourly; 20min); Gorizia (every 30min; 35min); Trieste (hourly; 1hr–1hr 24min); Venice (hourly; 2hr).

By bus The bus station is across the road from the train station at Viale Europa Unità 31. Bus #1 travels to Piazza Libertà in the city centre (10min).

Destinations Aquileia (16 daily; 40min); Grado (12 daily; 1hr); San Daniele (Mon–Sat 8 daily, Sun 2 daily; 40min).

Tourist office Piazza I (Primo) Maggio 7 (Oct–April 9am–5.30pm; Sept–May 9am–6pm; June, July & Aug 9am–7pm; ⓣ 0432 295 972, ⓦ turismofvg.it).

ACCOMMODATION

★ **Al Cappello** Via Sarpi 5 ⓣ 0432 299 327, ⓦ osteria alcappello.it; map p.458. In an excellent location right in the heart of town, this *osteria* (see below) has a small *locanda* with six cosy rooms with private bathrooms – four-legged friends are welcome, too. **€100**

Al Vecchio Tram Via Brenari 28 ⓣ 0432 507 164, ⓦ hotelvecchiotram.com; map p.458. One of the best options in town, featuring minimalist decor and modern rooms in red and grey tones. There's also a pleasant outdoor breakfast area. **€120**

B&B Casa Angela Via Calatafimi 7 ⓣ 348 841 5093, ⓦ casaangela.it; map p.458. Excellent option in a renovated Art Nouveau building, a 10min walk from the city centre. Two attractive first-floor apartments (Camera Bianca is the nicest) with modern furnishings and kitchenettes. **€65**

★ **La Faula Agriturismo** Via Faola 5, Povoletto ⓣ 333 171 9514, ⓦ faula.com; map p.458. Set in idyllic countryside 14km north of Udine, this working farm has nine inviting rooms and three apartments with lovely antiques and wooden floorboards. It produces its own wine, and its chickens provide the restaurant with fresh eggs. Facilities include a swimming pool, a nine-course golf course and playground. Rates are half board; minimum three-night stay. **€129**

Suite Inn Via Di Toppo 25 ⓣ 0432 501 683, ⓦ hotel suiteinn-udine.com; map p.458. This pleasant hotel has spacious modern rooms with contemporary, en-suite bathrooms, and there are both electric bike and car charge points. The only downside is the location – it's on a main road a 10 to 15min walk from the centre of town. **€109**

EATING

Ai Barnabiti Piazza Garibaldi 3/A ⓣ 0432 25 150, ⓦ osteriaaibarnabiti.com; map p.458. This historic *osteria* with cosy rustic interiors is a great spot for a laidback *aperitivo* or a snack or two; the menu features salads and cold meats, while the wine list is scribbled on the blackboard. Mon–Thurs 10am–11pm, Fri & Sat 10am–1am.

Al Cappello Via Sarpi 5 ⓣ 0432 299 327, ⓦ osteria alcappello.it; map p.458. A trendy, convivial and welcoming place with tables and benches outside. Lively atmosphere, popular with locals, best for a snack and a glass of wine rather than a meal. Mid-Sept–May Tues–Sat 10.30am–3pm & 5.30–11.30pm, Sun 10.30am–3pm; June–mid-Sept closed Mon and Sun.

★ **Caffè Caucigh** Via Gemona 36 ⓣ 0432 502 719, ⓦ caffecaucigh.wixsite.com/caucigh; map p.458. The city's oldest café, with an attractive historic interior featuring marble tables, wooden chairs and old newspaper cuttings on the walls; there are Fri jazz sessions with Italian and international artists. Tues–Thurs 7am–11pm, Fri & Sat 7am–midnight, Sun 8am–10pm.

Caffè Contarena Via Cavour 1 ⓣ 0432 512 741; map p.458. An attractive café and wine bar looking out onto the beautiful Piazza della Libertà. It's a great spot for an afternoon coffee break, while the attached wine bar has an extensive list of wines available by the glass (€4). Mon–Thurs

FESTIVALS AND EVENTS IN UDINE

In summer there's a busy programme of cultural events in and around town: ask the tourist office for the fortnightly listings of events. Throughout the year the Visionario arts cinema at Via Asquini 33 (T 0432 204 933, W visionario.movie) holds cinematic events, jazz evenings and shows films in English on Mondays. The **Far East Film Festival**, one of the most comprehensive festivals of Asian film, is held here every year in April/May; details on W www.fareastfilm.com.

The **Friuli DOC** wine festival, held over four days in mid-September, has been an annual event since1995; food and wine lovers come from all over Europe to drink wine, take master classes, and sample the local food (W friuli-doc.it).

8am–9pm, Fri & Sat 8am–2am, Sun 9am–midnight.

Ex Provinciali Via della Prefettura 3 T 0432 512 073, W osteriaexprovinciali.it; map p.458. Once a bakery – you can still see the baker's oven – this friendly place with wooden tables and a marble counter is a great spot to grab an *aperitivo* or a dish or two; the menu includes home-made pastas and risotto dishes with a variety of seasonal toppings, all prepared with organic produce. *Primi* €10, *secondi* €13. Mon–Sat 11am–3.30pm & 6pm–midnight, Sun 6pm–midnight.

★ **Hostaria Alla Tavernetta** Via Artico di Prampero 2 T 0432 501 066, W allatavernetta.com; map p.458. One of Udine's best restaurants, serving regional dishes with a modern twist, including braised beef cheek in Refosco red wine served with polenta and corn (€18), and *cjarsons*, pasta made with potatoes, stuffed with wild herbs, and seasoned with butter, cinnamon and grated smoked ricotta (€12). Seating is available outside in summer, while in winter food is served in the cosy vaulted interior with a fireplace. Tues–Sat noon–3pm & 7pm–midnight; June–Aug closed Sat lunch & open Mon 7pm–midnight.

O.G.G.I. Via Sarpi 3/A T 0432 192 7573, W oggigelato.it; map p.458. An excellent *gelateria* with more than twenty flavours of ice cream as well as refreshing *granita*, including lemon, peach and apricot. In winter, it serves crêpes and waffles instead. Mon–Thurs & Sun 11am–11pm, Fri & Sat 11am–midnight.

Vitello d'Oro Via Erasmo Valvason T 0432 508 982, W vitellodoro.com; map p.458. The city's smartest restaurant has seating on a pleasant terrace in summer; the fish and seafood dishes here are good, particularly the popular fish and seafood tartare (€25). Mon 7–10pm, Tues & Thurs–Sun noon–3pm & 7–10pm; June–Aug closed Sun.

San Daniele del Friuli

Just over 20km northwest of Udine, the picturesque town of **SAN DANIELE DEL FRIULI** produces some of the world's finest **prosciutto** (W prosciuttosandaniele.it) thanks to the local microclimate that assists with the ham's ageing process. You can visit one of the town's many *prosciuttifici* for a tour round the processing plant and to sample some ham (W prosciuttosandaniele.it lists all the town's producers), or enjoy delicious cold cuts at one of the many *prosciutterie* in town; the *Osteria Ai Bintars*, at Via Trento Trieste 67 (W aibintars.com), is one of the best. The four-day culinary festival **Aria di Festa** (last weekend of June; W ariadifesta.it) celebrates the highly prized prosciutto as well as other regional sweet and savoury products. Prosciutto aside, the deconsecrated **Chiesa di Sant'Antonio Abate**, Via Garibaldi 12/A, is home to a stunning cycle of Renaissance frescoes, considered to be the most beautiful of the region.

Cividale del Friuli

Some 17km east of Udine, the UNESCO World Heritage Centre of **CIVIDALE DEL FRIULI** is a well-preserved medieval gem and one of the most beautiful towns in the area. Visitors are drawn to its dramatic setting, perched over the Natisone River, and to its art treasures. The town has ancient roots, having been founded in 50 BC by Julius Caesar at the picturesque point where the Natisone River valley opens into the plain. In the sixth century AD it became the capital of the first Lombard duchy, and in the eighth century the Patriarch of Aquileia moved here, inaugurating Cividale's most prosperous period. It has been the main commercial

centre of the Natisone Valley for two hundred years. Strolling around town is a pleasure, the pace of life leisurely and unhurried, with the historic centre lying between the train and coach stations, within the oval ring bisected by Via Carlo Alberto and Corso Mazzini.

Tempietto Longobardo

Via Monastero Maggiore 34 • April–Sept Mon–Fri 10am–1pm & 3–6pm, Sat & Sun 10am–6pm; Oct–March Mon–Fri 10am–1pm & 2–5pm, Sat & Sun 10am–5pm • €4, joint ticket with Museo Archeologico and Museo Cristiano e Tesoro del Duomo €9; free with FVG Card

The tiny **Tempietto Longobardo** chapel, poised above the Natisone, was built in the eighth century, though much of the elaborate stuccowork inside was reduced to rubble in an earthquake in 1222. Its delicate interior preserves faded frescoes and carved stalls from its use as a convent chapel in the late fourteenth century, but the highlight is an exquisite stucco arch on the west wall flanked by six female figures. These luminous, smiling statues are among the most splendid surviving works of art from the eighth century.

The Duomo

Piazza del Duomo • Daily 8am–7pm • Free

The highlight of Cividale's **Duomo** is a twelfth-century masterpiece of silversmithery: the *pala* (altarpiece) named after Pellegrino II, the patriarch who commissioned and donated it to the town. It depicts the Virgin seated between the archangels Michael and Gabriel, who are flanked by 25 saints and framed by more saints, prophets and the patron himself.

Museo Archeologico

Piazza del Duomo 13 • Mon 9am–2pm, Tues–Sun 8.30am–7.30pm • €4, joint ticket with Tempietto Longobardo and Museo Cristiano e Tesoro del Duomo €9; Free with FVG Card

The **Museo Archeologico** houses an excellent exhibition on the Lombards on the first floor, incorporating local finds including some beautiful gold brooches. On the ground floor is a hotchpotch of late Roman and early Christian pieces, the highlight being a second-century mosaic of a wild-eyed Neptune.

Museo Cristiano e Tesoro del Duomo

Via Candotti 1 • Oct–March Wed–Sun 10am–1pm & 3–5pm; April–Sept Wed–Sun 10am–1pm & 3–6pm • €4, joint ticket with Tempietto Longobardo and Museo Archeologico €9; Free with FVG Card • T 0432 730 403, W mucris.it

Two beautiful Lombard pieces are in the **Museo Cristiano e Tesoro del Duomo**, housed in the precincts of the fifteenth-century Duomo. The **Altar of Ratchis** was carved for Ratchis, Duke of Cividale and King of the Lombards at Pavia, who died as a Benedictine monk at Montecassino in 759 – an excellent digital reproduction gives an insight into the altar's original colours. The other highlight is the **Baptistry of Callisto**, named after Callisto de Treviso, the first Patriarch of Aquileia to move to Cividale. He lived here from 730 to 756 and initiated the building of the patriarchal palace, the cathedral and this octagonal baptistry, which used to stand beside the cathedral. It's constructed from older Lombard fragments, the columns and capitals dating from the fifth century.

The Ipogeo Celtico

South of the Piazza del Duomo, on Via Monastero Maggiore, is a cellar-like cavern called the **Ipogeo Celtico** (to visit, ask at the tourist office or the *All'Ipogeo* bar next

FESTIVALS IN CIVIDALE DEL FRIULI

Cividale hosts many festivals including **Mittelfest** (mittelfest.org), held each July, a celebration of Central European culture with concerts, theatre and dance. In August the **Palio di San Donato** (paliodicividale.it) transforms the town centre into a medieval stage, complete with fourteenth-century costumes, food, jousts and archery. The town's **chamber music festival** (perfezionamentomusicale.it) in August is a world-class event.

door; entry is free). This underground space was probably used as a tomb for Celtic leaders between the fifth and second centuries BC, but there is still some dispute as to whether it's man-made or was merely adapted by its users. Either way, the spectral faces carved on the walls make it a most unsettling place.

Ponte del Diavolo

Spanning the Natisone, the **Ponte del Diavolo** (Devil's Bridge) is a reconstruction of the original fifteenth-century structure destroyed during World War I. Of many legends concerning the bridge's demonic name, a favourite involves the devil agreeing to aid the speedy construction of the bridge in return for the soul of the first living thing to cross it – Cividale's wily inhabitants sent a hapless dog.

7

ARRIVAL AND INFORMATION — CIVIDALE DEL FRIULI

By train Cividale's train station is a 5min walk north of the city centre, and served hourly from Udine (20min); it's free with the FVG Card (see page 443).

By bus Three daily buses from Gorizia (1hr) pull in at Cividale's bus station, which is adjacent to the train station.

Tourist office Piazza Diacono 10 (daily: April–Sept 10am–1pm & 3–5pm; Oct–March 10am–noon & 2.30–4.30pm; 0432 710 460, cividale.net).

ACCOMMODATION

Al Pomo d'Oro Piazzetta S. Giovanni 20 0432 731 489, alpomodoro.com. This inn offers thirteen simple rooms, some with original columns dating back to the eleventh to thirteenth centuries, others with bare stone walls. Breakfast is enjoyed on a small terrace in summer, and features a selection of homemade cakes as well as other sweet and savoury dishes. **€90**

Locanda al Castello Via del Castello 12 0432 733 242, alcastello.net. A 20min walk from the town centre, this nineteenth-century building was formerly a Jesuit convent; spacious rooms in the main building are decorated with period furniture, while those in the annexe are slightly smaller. Facilities include an indoor pool, spa and good restaurant. **€120**

Orsone Via Darnazzacco 63 0432 732 053, orsone.com. Just over 4km south of Cividale, this stylish B&B has five rooms with views of rolling vineyards. The interiors are attractive, with spacious bathrooms, and there's an excellent attached restaurant and wine bar (see below). **€150**

EATING AND DRINKING

Antico Leon d'Oro Borgo di Ponte 24 0432 731 100, anticoleondoro.it. One of the town's best options, serving tasty regional dishes at reasonable prices, including *frico con patate* (a sort of omelette made with potatoes, onion and cheese; €6.50); alternatively try the *piatto del Friuli* (€13), which includes five or six seasonal specialities. Food is served in a pleasant courtyard in summer. Thurs–Tues 11am–3.30pm & 6.30pm–midnight.

★ **Orsone** Via Darnazzacco 63 0432 732 053, orsone.com. Owned by American restaurateur and TV personality Joe Bastianich, this cool little place with New York-style furnishings is somewhat unexpected in Cividale's countryside – juicy American burgers (€15) and Caesar salads (€12) are served here along with creative takes on dishes that blend Italian American culinary traditions. Cooking classes and wine-tasting sessions are held in the restaurant's vineyard across the road. Wed–Sun noon–2.30pm & 7–9.20pm.

Emilia-Romagna

466 Bologna and around
482 Modena and around
485 Reggio Emilia
487 Parma
491 Around Parma
492 East along the Via Emilia from Bologna
494 Ferrara
498 The Po Delta
499 Ravenna and around
506 Rimini
510 San Marino
511 San Leo

FORTRESS OF SAN LEO

Emilia-Romagna

Emilia-Romagna doesn't attract nearly the same volume of tourists as its neighbouring provinces of Lombardy, the Veneto and Tuscany, which is strange because it offers just as fine a distillation of the region's charms: glorious countryside, plenty of historic architecture and local cuisine renowned across the rest of Italy. It's also pretty easy to get around, with most of its main sites located along the Via Emilia, the dead-straight road laid down by the Romans in 187 BC that splits the province in two along its east–west axis, dividing the Apennine mountains in the south from the flat fields of the northern plain, the Pianura Padana.

Dotted along this road are some proud, historic towns, filled with restored medieval and Renaissance *palazzi*, the legacy of a handful of feuding families – the **Este** in Ferrara and Modena, the **Farnese** in Parma, and lesser dynasties in Ravenna and Rimini – who used to control the area before the papacy took charge. The largest urban centre, and the main tourist draw, is **Bologna**, the site of Europe's first university – and today best known as the gastronomic capital of Italy. It's one of the country's most beautiful cities with a mazy network of porticoed, medieval streets housing a collection of restaurants that easily live up to the town's reputation.

8

To the west are the wealthy, provincial towns of **Modena**, **Parma** and **Reggio Emilia**, easily reached by train, and each with their own charming historic centres and gastronomic delights, while to the east lies **Ravenna**, once the capital of the Western Roman Empire and today home to the finest set of Byzantine mosaics in the world. The Adriatic coast south is an overdeveloped ribbon of settlements, although **Rimini**, at its southern end, provides a spark of interest, with its wild seaside nightlife and surprisingly historic town centre.

Away from the central artery, Emilia-Romagna's **countryside** comes in two topographical varieties: flat or hilly. To the north lies one of the largest areas of flat land in Italy, a primarily agricultural region where much of the produce for the region's famed kitchens is grown. It also boasts a good deal of wildlife, particularly around the **Po Delta** on the Adriatic (a soggy expanse of marshland and lagoons that has become a prime destination for birdwatchers) and in **Ferrara**, just thirty minutes north of Bologna, one of the most important Renaissance centres in Italy. To the south are the **Apennines**, an area best explored using your own transport, sampling local cuisine and joining in the festivals; although it's still possible to get a taste of this beautiful region, far removed from the functional plain to the north, by bus. If you're a keen hiker, you might be tempted by the Grande Escursione Appenninica, a 25-day-long trek following the backbone of the range from refuge to refuge, which can be accessed from the foothills south of Reggio Emilia.

Bologna and around

Emilia's capital, **BOLOGNA**, is a thriving city whose light-engineering and high-tech industries have brought conspicuous wealth to the old brick palaces and porticoed streets. It's well known for its food – undeniably the richest in the country – and for its **politics**. "Red Bologna" became the Italian Left's stronghold and spiritual home, having evolved out of the resistance movement to German occupation during World War II. Consequently, Bologna's train station was singled out by Fascist groups in 1980 for a bomb attack in Italy's worst postwar terrorist atrocity – a glassed-in jagged gash in the station wall commemorates the tragedy in which 84 people died. In subsequent

FRESCO IN MODENA'S DUOMO

Highlights

❶ **Bologna's restaurants** A meal out in the gastronomic capital of Italy is a rite of passage for any true food-lover. See page 479

❷ **Duomo, Modena** One of the finest Romanesque buildings in Italy, with some magnificent decoration inside and out. See page 482

❸ **Gourmet Parma** Parma is inextricably linked to two great delicacies, Parma ham and Parmesan cheese, both of which can be sampled in the city or in the surrounding region. See page 490

❹ **Rocca Viscontea** Northern Emilia-Romagna's most majestic castle. See page 491

❺ **Brisighella festivals** This medieval village is known for its truffle, polenta and olive festivals in autumn. See page 494

❻ **Ravenna's mosaics** Unrivalled both in beauty and state of preservation, these mosaics are unmissable. See page 502

❼ **Rimini's nightlife** The hottest, loudest and wildest in the country. See page 510

❽ **San Leo** This spectacular ancient town on a rocky outcrop is a landmark for kilometres around. See page 511

HIGHLIGHTS ARE MARKED ON THE MAP ON PAGE 468

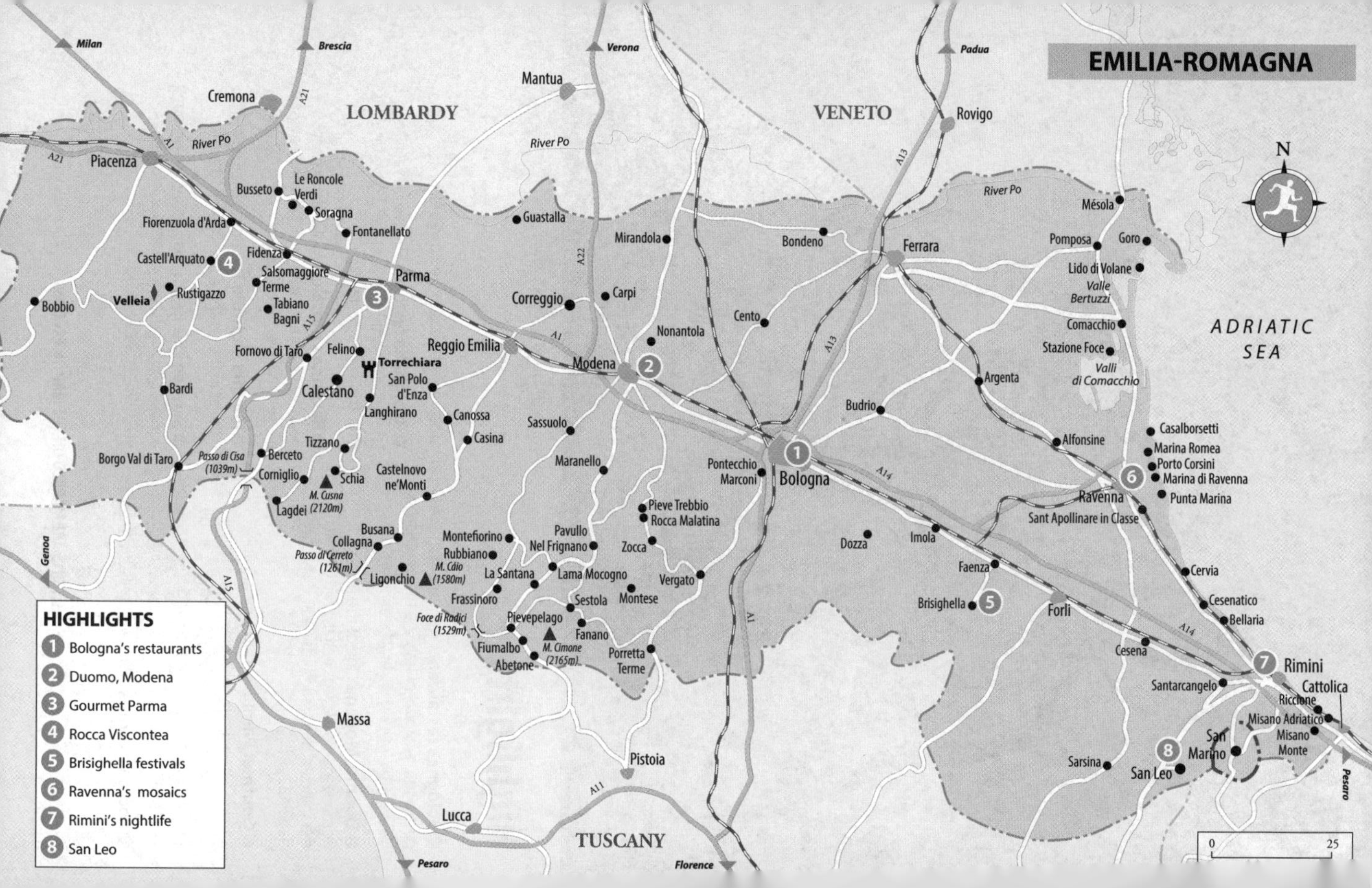
EMILIA-ROMAGNA
N
LOMBARDY
VENETO
TUSCANY
ADRIATIC SEA
Milan
Brescia
Verona
Padua
Genoa
Pesaro
Florence
Cremona
Mantua
Rovigo
Piacenza
River Po
A1
A21
A22
A13
A14
A15
A11
Busseto
Le Roncole Verdi
Soragna
Fontanellato
Fiorenzuola d'Arda
Castell'Arquato
Fidenza
Salsomaggiore Terme
Velleia
Rustigazzo
Bobbio
Tabiano Bagni
Parma
Guastalla
Mirandola
Bondeno
Ferrara
Mésola
Pomposa
Goro
Lido di Volane
Valle Bertuzzi
Correggio
Carpi
Cento
Nonantola
Comacchio
Stazione Foce
Valli di Comacchio
Reggio Emilia
Modena
Fornovo di Taro
Felino
Torrechiara
Calestano
San Polo d'Enza
Langhirano
Bardi
Canossa
Casina
Sassuolo
Argenta
Budrio
Alfonsine
Casalborsetti
Marina Romea
Porto Corsini
Marina di Ravenna
Punta Marina
Ravenna
Sant Apollinare in Classe
Tizzano
Berceto
Borgo Val di Taro
Passo di Cisa (1039m)
Corniglio
Schia
M. Cusna (2120m)
Lagdei
Castelnovo ne'Monti
Maranello
Pontecchio Marconi
Bologna
Pieve Trebbio
Rocca Malatina
Zocca
Dozza
Imola
Faenza
Brisighella
Forlì
Cervia
Cesenatico
Bellaria
Cesena
Rimini
Santarcangelo
Cattolica
Riccione
Misano Adriatico
Misano Monte
San Marino
San Leo
Sarsina
Busana
Collagna
Passo di Cerreto (1261m)
Ligonchio
M. Cáio (1580m)
Montefiorino
Rubbiano
La Santana
Pavullo Nel Frignano
Lama Mocogno
Vergato
Montese
Frassinoro
Sestola
Foce di Radici (1529m)
Pievepelago
Fiumalbo
Abetone
M. Cimone (2165m)
Fanano
Porretta Terme
Massa
Pistoia
Lucca
0
25
HIGHLIGHTS
1 Bologna's restaurants
2 Duomo, Modena
3 Gourmet Parma
4 Rocca Viscontea
5 Brisighella festivals
6 Ravenna's mosaics
7 Rimini's nightlife
8 San Leo

PARMA HAM, PARMESAN AND PASTA – THE CUISINE OF EMILIA-ROMAGNA

Emilia-Romagna has a just reputation for producing the richest, most lavish food in Italy, with its famous specialities of **Parmesan** cheese (*parmigiano-reggiano*), egg pasta, **Parma ham** (generically known as *prosciutto di Parma*) and balsamic vinegar. Despite its current foodie connotations, **balsamic vinegar** started off as a cottage industry, with many Emilian families distilling and then redistilling local wine to form a dark liquor that is then matured in wooden barrels for at least twelve years. Bologna is regarded as the gastronomic capital of Italy, and Emilia is the only true home of **pasta** in the North: often lovingly handmade, the dough is formed into *lasagne*, *tortellini* stuffed with ricotta cheese and spinach, pumpkin or pork, and other fresh pastas served with *ragù* (meat sauce), cream sauces or simply with butter and Parmesan – *alla parmigiana* usually denotes something cooked with Parmesan. Modena and Parma specialize in *bollito misto* – boiled **meats**, such as flank of beef, trotters, tongue and spicy sausage – while another Modenese dish is *zampone* – stuffed pig's trotter. The region is second only to Sicily for the amount of **fish** caught in its waters.

Regional **wines** are, like the landscapes and people, quite distinct. Emilia is synonymous with **Lambrusco**, but don't despair: buy only DOC Lambrusco and be amazed by the dark, often blackberry-coloured wine that foams into the glass and cuts through the fattiness of the typically meaty Emilian meal. There are four DOC zones for Lambrusco, three of them around Modena, while the fourth zone extends across the plains and foothills of the Apennines, in the province of Reggio Emilia. Other wines to try, both whites, are Trebbianino Val Trebbia and Monterosso Val D'Arda, while the lively Malvasia (also white) from the Colli di Parma goes well with the celebrated local ham.

In the flatter, drier Romagna province, the wines have less exuberance but more body and are dominated by Albana and Sangiovese. The sweeter versions of **Albana** bring out the peachy, toasted almond flavours of this white. The robust red of **Sangiovese**, from the hills around Imola and Rimini, comes in various "weights" – all pretty heavy. Much lighter is Cagnina di Romagna, which is best drunk young (within six months of harvest).

decades, the city's political leanings have been less predictable, although its "leftist" reputation continues to stick.

Bologna is certainly one of Italy's best-looking cities. Its centre is startlingly medieval in plan, a jumble of red brick, tiled roofs and balconies radiating out from the great central square of **Piazza Maggiore**. There are enough monuments and curiosities for several days' leisured exploration, including plenty of small, quirky museums, some tremendously grand Gothic and Renaissance architecture and, most conspicuously, the **Due Torri**, the city's own "leaning towers". Thanks to the **university**, there's always something happening – be it theatre, music or just the café and bar scene, which is among northern Italy's most convivial

Piazza del Nettuno and Piazza Maggiore

Bologna's city centre is compact, with most sights within easy reach of the main ring road. Lined with shops and bars, **Via dell'Indipendenza** runs from the train station to the centre, finishing up at the linked central squares of **Piazza Maggiore** and **Piazza del Nettuno.**

The Neptune Fountain

At the centre of Piazza del Nettuno, the **Neptune Fountain**, one of the most celebrated symbols of the city, was created by Giambologna in the late sixteenth century. Its extravagant – and, when first unveiled, highly controversial – composition sees a trident-wielding Neptune sat atop a pile of *putti* and mermaids – who are arranged rather indelicately astride dolphins with water shooting from their breasts. Beside the fountain is a wall lined with photographs of partisans who died in World War II, near a memorial to those killed in the 1980 train station bombing.

Palazzo Re Enzo and Palazzo Podestà

Piazza del Nettuno • Both *palazzi* open occasionally for special exhibitions

Across the square from the fountain, the **Palazzo Re Enzo** takes its name from its time as the prison-home of Enzo, king of Sicily, confined here by papal supporters for two decades after the Battle of Fossalta in 1249. Next door to the Palazzo Re Enzo, **Palazzo Podestà** fills the northern side of Piazza Maggiore, built in the fifteenth century at the behest of the Bentivoglio clan.

Palazzo d'Accursio

Piazza del Nettuno 6

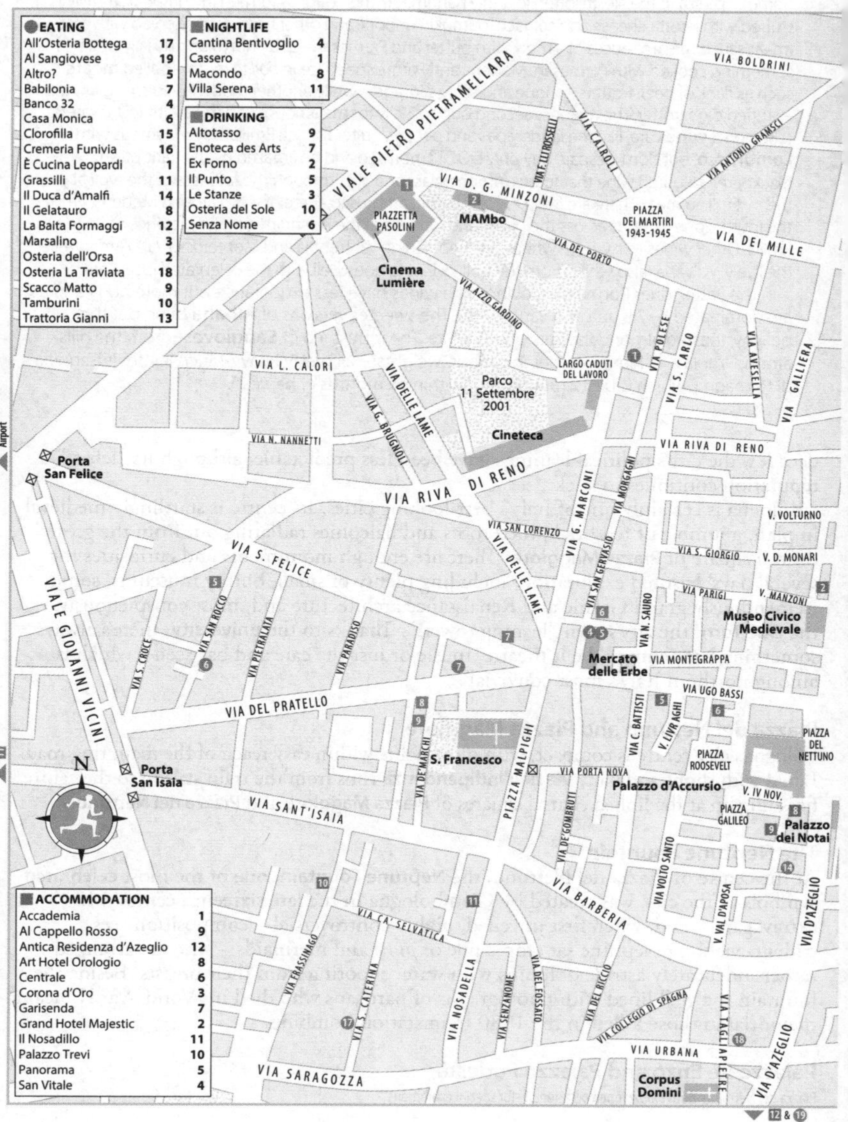

On the piazza's western edge, the **Palazzo d'Accursio** (or **Palazzo Comunale**) gives some indication of the political shifts in power, its facade adorned by a huge statue of Pope Gregory XIII as an affirmation of papal authority. The palazzo's upper storey houses the municipal art collection, the Collezioni Comunali d'Arte.

Collezioni Comunali d'Arte

Tues–Sun 10am–6.30pm • €5, free first Sun of the month

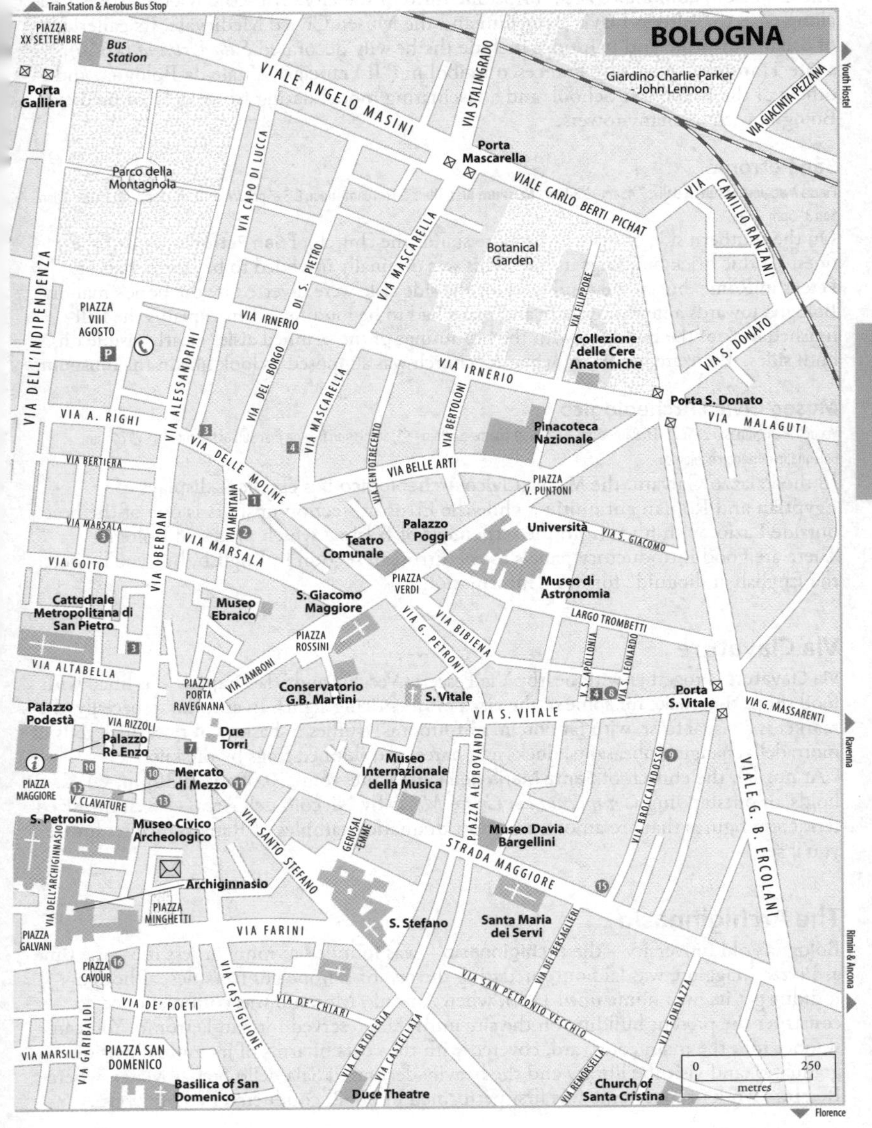

8

ROMAGNA VISIT CARD

If you're planning to stay in the area for a few days or more, consider investing in the **Romagna Visit Card**, which for €17 entitles you to free entry to 55 cultural sights across Ravenna, Forlì, Rimini and Ferrara, with discounted entry to many more. It's valid for a year, but you can visit each site once only. Buy the card at tourist offices or online at Ⓦ romagnavisitcard.it.

The **Collezioni Comunali d'Arte** forms one third of the city's Museo Civici d'Arte Antica, along with the Museo Davia Bargellini and the Museo Civico Medievale. Its galleries of ornate furniture and paintings include the heavily decorated *Sala Urbana* (1630), a late Tintoretto, works by Francesco Raibolini ("Il Francia"), Vitale da Bologna, and others of the Bolognese School, and a fascinating model dating from 1917 of medieval Bologna with its many towers.

San Petronio

Piazza Maggiore • **Church** Daily: 7.45am–6.30pm • **Museum** Tues, Thurs & Fri 10am–noon & 3–5pm, Wed 10am–1pm, Sat 10am–noon, Sun 3–5pm • Free

On the southern side of Piazza Maggiore stands the church of **San Petronio**, one of the finest Gothic brick buildings in Italy. This was originally intended to be larger than St Peter's in Rome, but money and land for the side aisle were diverted by the pope's man in Bologna towards a new university and plans had to be modified. This explains the half-finished look of the building, with the beginnings of the planned aisles clearly visible on both sides. There are models of what the church was supposed to look like in the **museum**.

8

Museo Civico Archeologico

Via dell'Archiginnasio 2 • Tues–Fri 9am–6pm, Sat & Sun 10am–6.30pm • €5, admission free on first Sun of the month • Ⓦ comune.bologna.it/museoarcheologico

In the Palazzo Galvani, the **Museo Civico Archeologico** has excellent displays of Egyptian and Roman antiquities, while the Etruscan section upstairs is one of the best outside Lazio, with finds from the settlement of Felsina, which predated Bologna. There are good introductory panels to the Etruscan section in English, but you'll need the English audioguide for more information.

Via Clavature

Via Clavature – together with nearby Via Pescerie Vecchie and Via Draperie – is lined with food shops that make for some of the city's most enticing sights. In autumn, especially, the market is a visual feast, with fat porcini mushrooms, truffles in baskets of rice, thick rolls of mortadella, hanging pheasants, ducks and hares, and skinned frogs by the kilo.

At no. 10, the church of **Santa Maria della Vita** (Tues–Sun 10.30am–6.30pm; €4) holds an outstanding *Compianto del Cristo Morto* by Niccolò dell'Arca – seven life-sized terracotta figures that are among the most dramatic examples of Renaissance sculpture you'll see.

The Archiginnasio

Bologna's old university – the **Archiginnasio** – was founded at more or less the same time as Piazza Maggiore was laid out, predating the rest of Europe's universities, although it didn't get its own home until 1565, when Antonio Morandi was commissioned to construct the present building on the site until then reserved for San Petronio. You can wander into the main courtyard, covered with the coats of arms of its more illustrious graduates, and visit the library and the heavily decorated Sala dello Stabat Mater, where Rossini's work of that name was first performed in 1842, conducted by Donizzetti.

Teatro Anatomico

Mon–Fri 10am–6pm, Sat 10am–7pm, Sun 10am–2pm, reduced hours in Aug • €3 • Ⓦ www.archiginnasio.it

The Archiginnasio's most interesting feature is the **Teatro Anatomico**, the original medical faculty dissection theatre dating from the seventeenth century, but re-created after suffering heavy damage in an Allied bombing raid in 1944. Tiers of seats surround an extraordinary professor's chair, covered with a canopy supported by figures known as *gli spellati* – "the skinned ones". Not many dissections went on, owing to prohibitions of the Church, but when they did (usually around carnival time), the general public used to turn up as much for the social occasion as for studying the body.

Piazza San Domenico

A few minutes south of the old university, down Via Garibaldi, is **Piazza San Domenico**, with its strange canopied tombs holding the bones of medieval law scholars. Bologna was instrumental in sorting out wrangles between the pope and the Holy Roman Emperor in the tenth and eleventh centuries, earning itself the title of *La Dotta* ("The Learned") and forming the basis for the university's prominent law faculties.

San Domenico

Piazza San Domenico 13 • **Church** Mon–Fri 9.30–noon & 3.30–6pm, Sat 9am–noon & 3.30–5pm, Sun 3.30–5pm • **Museum** Open on request Mon–Sat 9am–noon & 3.30–6pm, Sun 3–5pm • Free

The church of **San Domenico** was built in 1221 to house the relics of the founder of the Dominican Order. These were placed in the so-called *Arca di San Domenico* (on the right-hand side of the nave), the creation of Nicola Pisano, but also bearing three figures by **Michelangelo** (the display by the chapel tells you which are his). While you're in the church, look into the **Museo di San Domenico**, displaying a very fine polychrome terracotta bust of St Dominic by Niccolò dell'Arca along with paintings, reliquaries and vestments, and, beyond, the intricately inlaid mid-sixteenth-century choir stalls.

8

The university district

Bordered by Via Oberdan to the west and Strada Maggiore to the south, the eastern section of Bologna's *centro storico* preserves many of the older **university** departments, housed for the most part in large seventeenth- and eighteenth-century palaces. Bookshops, cafés and low-key restaurants make this atmospheric slice of studentville perfect for idling away an afternoon.

AFTER THE QUAKES

On May 20, 2012, pressure caused by the slow movement of the Apennines through the Po Valley caused a magnitude-6 **earthquake** to shake the Emilia-Romagna region. The first quake was followed in successive days by hundreds of aftershocks, leaving 27 people dead, forty-five thousand homeless and many historic structures damaged. The epicentre was in the province of Modena, and although the town itself was largely unaffected, the surroundings fared less well; many of the dead were workers in warehouses and factories which had not been constructed to withstand serious seismic movement. An important contributor to the local economy – the production of Grana Padano and Parmigiano-Reggiano cheeses – was affected when storage facilities collapsed, causing an estimated €100 million-worth of damage.

Further earthquakes in central Italy in recent years have put the spotlight on a widespread problem – the general disregard for planning permission. Whether the country's lax construction laws will be tightened up to protect against future disasters remains to be seen.

BOLOGNA'S PORTICOES

No other city has anything like the number of **porticoes** or covered walkways found in Bologna. In the city centre there are barely any stretches of pavement not topped by an ornate, arched covering. The first porticoes were built out of wood, some thirteenth-century examples of which still stand. They proved so popular that by the fourteenth century construction of stone or brick porticoes, high enough to accommodate people on horseback, were compulsory on all new streets. Today, some 38km still stand, including the longest portico in the world, leading from the city up to the Santuario di San Luca (see page 482).

The Due Torri

Daily: March–Oct 9am–7.30pm, last entrance 6.30pm; Nov–Feb 9.30am–5.45pm, last entrance 5pm • €5; pre-booking essential, either online or from the tourist office in Piazza Maggiore • duetorribologna.com

Via Rizzoli leads into the student district from Piazza del Nettuno, ending up at Piazza di Porta Ravegnana, where the **Torre degli Asinelli** and the perilously leaning **Torre Garisenda** next to it are together known as the **Due Torri**, two of the hundreds of towers that were scattered across the city in the Middle Ages. The former offers fantastic views, but it is not for the faint-hearted as its 498 steps go up round an open well.

Santo Stefano

Via S. Stefano 24 • Daily 9.15am–7.15pm; closes 6pm in winter • Free

Southeast of the Due Torri, Via Santo Stefano leads down to its medieval gateway, past a complex of four – but originally seven – churches, collectively known as **Santo Stefano**, set in a wide piazza. Three of the churches face onto the piazza, of which the striking polygonal church of **San Sepolcro**, reached through the church of **Crocifisso**, is about the most interesting. Inside, the bones of St Petronius provide a macabre focus typical of the relic-obsessed Middle Ages. A doorway leads from here through to **Santi Vitale e Agricola**, Bologna's oldest church, built from discarded Roman fragments in the fifth century.

Santa Maria dei Servi

Strada Maggiore • Mon 7.30am–12.30pm, Tues–Sun 7.30am–12.30pm & 4–7pm • Free

From Santo Stefano, you can follow Via Gerusalemme up to Strada Maggiore and the elegant fourteenth-century **Santa Maria dei Servi**, filled with frescoes by Vitale da Bologna – it's a rare chance to see the work of the so-called "father" of Bolognese painting *in situ*. The beautiful portico holds a festive market during the Christmas season.

Palazzo Poggi and La Specola

Via Zamboni 33 • Tues–Fri 10am–4pm, Sat & Sun 10am–6pm • €5 • 051 209 9398, sma.unibo.it

Around and along **Via Zamboni** are many of the old palaces housing various parts of the university. The main building, the **Palazzo Poggi**, is home to many of the university's small specialist museums on subjects as diverse as naval maps and charts, human anatomy, physics and natural history.

On the fourth floor, the fascinating 300-year-old **Specola** (currently only open to private tour groups; ask at the tourist office for the latest details), or observatory, attracts the most interest. Its small **Museo di Astronomia** is home to a number of eighteenth-century instruments and a frescoed map of the constellations.

Collezione delle Cere Anatomiche

Via Irnerio 48 • Mon–Fri 9am–1pm, Sat & Sun 10am–6pm • Free

The **Collezione delle Cere Anatomiche "Luigi Cattaneo"** might seem an odd place to visit, but it would be a shame to leave Bologna without seeing its beautiful, if rather morbid, **waxworks.** These were used until the nineteenth century for medical demonstrations, and the lurid anatomical cutaways, plus models of conjoined twins and deformed limbs, are as startling as any art or sculpture in the city – though not for the faint-hearted.

Pinacoteca Nazionale

Via delle Belle Arti 56 • Tues–Sun 8.30am–7.30pm • €6 • Ⓦ pinacotecabologna.beniculturali.it

The paintings in the **Pinacoteca Nazionale** concentrate mainly on the heavier religious works of Bolognese artists. There are early pieces, such as those by Vitale da Bologna, with later works by Il Francia and Tibaldi, as well as paintings from the city's most productive artistic period, the early seventeenth century.

San Giacomo Maggiore

Piazza Rossini • **San Giacomo Maggiore** Mon–Fri 7.30am–12.30pm & 3.30–6.30pm, Sat & Sun 8.30am–12.30pm & 3–6.30pm • **Oratorio di Santa Cecilia** Daily: June–Sept 10am–1pm & 3–7pm; Oct–May 10am–1pm & 2–6pm • Free

The church of **San Giacomo Maggiore** is a Romanesque structure begun in 1267 and enlarged over the centuries. The target here is the Bentivoglio Chapel, decorated with funds provided by one Annibale Bentivoglio to celebrate the family's victory in a local feud in 1488. Lorenzo Costa painted frescoes called *The Triumph of Life*, *The Triumph of Death* and *Madonna Enthroned* – in which she is surrounded by the Bentivoglio family. The altarpiece of the *Madonna and Child and Saints* is by Il Francia, while another chapel is home to a glorious polyptych by Paolo Veneziano (1346).

Next door, the walls of the **Oratorio di Santa Cecilia** are covered with exquisite frescoes commissioned by the Bentivoglio family in 1505 from the city's top artists of the day, Il Francia, Lorenzo Costa and Amico Aspertini. These depict ten scenes from the life of St Cecilia, patron saint of music, her husband St Valerian and his brother St Tiburtius. The oratory makes an atmospheric backdrop for free classical music concerts in summer (Ⓦ sangiacomofestival.it).

8

Museo Internazionale della Musica

Palazzo Sanguinetti, Strada Maggiore 34 • Tues–Sun 10am–6.30pm • €5, free first Sun of the month • Ⓦ www.museomusicabologna.it

The beautifully frescoed sixteenth-century **Palazzo Sanguinetti** is home to the **Museo Internazionale della Musica** displaying an impressive trove of musical instruments, original manuscripts and paintings, including a portrait of Vivaldi and one of J.C. Bach by Gainsborough.

Museo Ebraico

Via Valdonica 1/5 • Mon–Thurs & Sun 10am–6pm, Fri 10am–4pm • €4 • Ⓦ museoebraicobo.it

Situated in the old Jewish ghetto, the **Museo Ebraico** presents the history and migratory patterns of the once-thriving Jewish community in Emilia-Romagna, through rather dry display panels; it also has temporary exhibitions of works by Jewish artists.

North and west of Piazza Maggiore

There are fewer sights to the north and west of Bologna's central squares, although the refurbished covered market off **Via Ugo Bassi** (see page 480) is worth a visit. This street and busy **Via dell'Indipendenza** are lined with shops, while the market's bars and, further west, **Via del Pratello** are lively spots after dark.

Cattedrale Metropolitana di San Pietro

Via dell'Indipendenza 9 • Mon–Sat 7.30am–6.45pm, Sun 8am–6.45pm • Free

A couple of blocks north of Piazza del Nettuno, the city's cathedral, the **Cattedrale Metropolitana di San Pietro**, dates from the tenth century but has been rebuilt several times. It took its present shape in the seventeenth century, and is more enjoyable for its stately atmosphere than any particular features.

Museo Civico Medievale

Via Manzoni 4 • Tues–Sun 10am–6.30pm • €5, free first Sun of the month

The **Museo Civico Medievale** is housed in the Renaissance Palazzo Fava and decorated with frescoes by Carracci and members of the Bolognese School depicting the *History of Europa*, *Jason's Feats* and scenes from the *Aeneid*. The museum's collection includes bits of armour, ceramics, numerous tombs and busts of various popes and other dignitaries, and a *Madonna and Saints* by Jacopo della Quercia.

Basilica di San Francesco

Piazza San Francesco • Daily 6.45am–noon & 3.30–7pm • Free

West of Piazza del Nettuno, the **Basilica di San Francesco** is a Gothic brick pile supported by flying buttresses that was built in 1236, heavily restored in the 1920s and partly rebuilt after World War II. Inside there are a beautiful and very ornate altarpiece from 1392 and a pleasant cloister.

MAMbo – Museo d'Arte Moderna di Bologna

Via Don Minzoni 14 • Tues, Wed, Fri, Sat & Sun 10am–6.30pm, Thurs 10am–10pm • €6 • mambo-bologna.org • Bus #33 or #35 from the station

Known, inevitably perhaps, by the acronym **MAMbo**, the **Museo d'Arte Moderna di Bologna** is Bologna's answer to Bilbao's Guggenheim, with its large white galleries offering a thought-provoking overview of Italian art from the 1950s onwards. Opened in 2007, it forms the centrepiece of an ambitious cultural complex, the **Manifattura delle Arti** (Factory of Arts), which is also home to an arthouse cinema and film archive and performance spaces belonging to the university.

8

MAMbo currently also houses the **Museo Morandi** while its home in the Palazzo d'Accursio (see page 470) is being restored. The museum is dedicated to one of Italy's most important twentieth-century painters, Giorgio Morandi, who was best known for his captivating still lifes. Fans of Morandi can also visit the **Casa Morandi**, on the opposite side of the city at Via Fondazza 36 (open Fri–Sun by appointment, 051 649 6611), where the painter lived and worked for fifty years: recently restored, it includes his studio and nice touches such as a recipe written by his mother.

ARRIVAL AND DEPARTURE — BOLOGNA

BY PLANE

Marconi airport (051 647 9615, bologna-airport.it) is northwest of town, linked to the centre and the train station by the Aerobus (Linea BLQ; €6, buy tickets online or at the airport or train station ticket machines; aerobus.bo.it), which runs roughly every 15min and takes around 25min in light traffic. Taxis to the centre cost around €20.

BY TRAIN

The station is at Piazza delle Medaglie d'Oro. Buses #25 and #30 run to Piazza Maggiore or Via Rizzoli, or it's a 20min walk.

Destinations Ancona (every 30–45min; 1hr 45min–3hr 25min); Faenza (every 30min; 25–40min); Ferrara (every 30min–1hr; 25–50min); Florence (every 20min; 35min–1hr 40min); Forlì (every 30min; 35–50min); Milan (every 30min; 1–3hr); Modena (every 20min; 20–30min); Parma (every 20min; 55min–1hr 10min); Ravenna (every 30min–1hr; 1hr–1hr 20min); Reggio Emilia (every 20min; 35–50min); Rimini (every 20–40min; 50min–2hr 20min).

BY BUS

All long-distance buses terminate at the bus station (*autostazione*), 300m from the train station at Piazza XX Settembre 6. Bus #27 takes you to Via Rizzoli in the centre, otherwise it's a 20min walk.

BY CAR

Avoid bringing a car into central Bologna if possible: there are traffic restrictions all over town and the city centre is closed to private traffic between 7am and 8pm every day. If your hotel is in the historic centre you'll be allowed to bring your car in, but you'll need to inform your hotel first.

Car rental Try Avis, Via Nicolo dall'Arca 2/D (051 634 1632); Europcar, Via Cesare Boldrini 22B (051 353 665); Maggiore, Via Cairoli 4 (051 252 525); or the very competitive Sicily by Car, at the airport (051 647 2006). All the major companies also have desks at the airport.

Parking There are 24hr car parks on Piazza XX Settembre, adjacent to the bus station, and Piazza VIII Agosto.

FRESH FOOD SERVED FROM A SHOP IN BOLOGNA

AURICCHIO
STRAVECCHIO
AURICCHIO
STRAVECCHIO
€ 14,80 al kg
Giuncata
Burrata
con foglia
,90 al kg
tellini

INFORMATION

Tourist offices Bologna's main tourist office, Bologna Welcome, at Piazza Maggiore 1 (Mon–Sat 9am–7pm, Sun 10am–5pm; ⓣ 051 658 3111, ⓦ bolognawelcome.com), is packed with information, including details of gourmet tours and cookery courses. There's a second office at the airport (Mon–Sat 9am–7.30pm, Sun 9am–5pm; ⓣ 051 647 2201), plus detailed, up-to-date information on the website.

GETTING AROUND

On foot The best way to enjoy Bologna is on foot, strolling beneath some of the city's beautiful porticoes amid Italy's most courteous drivers. Two-hour guided sightseeing walking tours of the city in English leave from the main tourist office (Easter–Oct Mon, Fri & Sat 10.30am & 4.45pm, Tues–Thurs 4.45pm, Sun 3pm; Feb, March, Nov & Dec Mon, Fri, Sat & Sun 10.30am & 3pm, Tues–Thurs 10.30am; times can change, so call to check ⓣ 051 658 3111; €15).

By bike Demetra Social Bike at Via Capo di Lucca 37, near the bus station, rents bikes for €15/day.

By bus Buses (ⓦ tper.it) are fast and frequent. Tickets cost €1.30 each from *tabacchi*, newsstands and bus info kiosks, or €1.50 from ticket machines on board, and are valid on as many buses as you like within an hour and 15 minutes. If you plan to make frequent use of them it might be worth buying a day ticket for €5, or a Citypass (€12, valid for ten journeys).

By open-top bus The open-top, hop-on-hop-off City redbus (ⓣ 051 350 853, ⓦ cityredbus.com) makes a tour of the city starting from the train station (6–12 daily 10am–5.30pm; Jan & Feb Fri–Sun only; buses run later in high summer; €14, or €21 including the San Luca Express; see page 482).

By taxi Cotabo (ⓣ 051 372 727); CAT (ⓣ 051 4590).

ACCOMMODATION

8

Bologna's accommodation mostly caters for business travellers with only a few inexpensive hotels. During the **trade-fair peak** (March to early May & Sept–Dec) prices can more than double. Many hotels prefer to take block bookings during these times and making an individual reservation can be tricky. In July and Aug prices are much lower. The tourist office has a helpful and free booking service (Piazza Maggiore ⓣ 051 658 3111; airport ⓣ 051 647 2201), or you can do it yourself through ⓦ bolognawelcome.com. Note that Bologna hotels charge a **tourist tax** of €0.50–5/person/night, depending on the type of accommodation.

Accademia Via Belle Arti 6 ⓣ 051 232 318, ⓦ hotelaccademia.com; map p.470. In the heart of the university quarter, this large three-star hotel has modestly sized and furnished en-suite doubles, some with balconies. Periodic art shows decorate the public areas. All rooms have a/c. **€120**

Al Cappello Rosso Via de' Fusari 9 ⓣ 051 261 891, ⓦ alcappellorosso.it; map p.470. It may be one of the city's oldest hotels, with six centuries of service behind it, but the *Cappello Rosso* has moved with the times, now offering silk kimonos and a pillow menu in every room, a pet-care service and even allergy-proof rooms. Bedrooms are stylishly modern, large and comfortable – some decorated by artists, such as the Shock in Pink room, a homage to the fashion designer Elsa Schiaparelli. There's also a library-book-swapping service, and bikes and laptops for guests' use. **€195**

Antica Residenza d'Azeglio Via Massimo d'Azeglio 64 ⓣ 051 644 7389, ⓦ anticaresidenzadazeglio.it; map p.470. This B&B's five rooms are large, comfortable and elegantly decorated, with thoughtful touches such as wine and fresh fruit. Ultra-helpful hosts Agostino and Roberto provide a superb breakfast and are on hand to answer questions and make restaurant recommendations. Closed mid-Aug. **€150**

★ **Art Hotel Orologio** Via IV Novembre 10 ⓣ 051 745 7411, ⓦ art-hotel-orologio.com; map p.470. On a side street just south of Piazza Maggiore – look for the clock sign – this elegant four-star hotel has an air of understated luxury and well-equipped rooms. **€214**

Centrale Via della Zecca 2 ⓣ 051 006 3937, ⓦ albergocentralebologna.it; map p.470. Spacious, simple two-star in the heart of the city. Most of the 25 rooms come with bathrooms and a/c, and there are great views from the top floor. **€93**

★ **Corona d'Oro** Via Oberdan 12 ⓣ 051 745 7611, ⓦ hco.it; map p.470. Graced with a lovely wooden portico, the city's oldest, on its northern side, this hotel offers four-star opulence with parquet flooring throughout – the deluxe suite has a beautiful painted panel ceiling. The televisions are out of sight behind cupboard doors, a nice touch. **€280**

★ **Garisenda** Galleria del Leone 1/Via Rizzoli 9 ⓣ 051 224 369, ⓦ albergogarisenda.com; map p.470. The seven rooms here are basic – only three have private bathrooms (€92) – but the location is great and the welcome genuine. It's surprisingly quiet for its commercial location, above the Via Rizzoli shops right opposite the two towers. **€68**

Grand Hotel Majestic Via dell'Indipendenza 8 ⓣ 051 225 445, ⓦ grandhotelmajestic.duetorrihotels.com; map p.470. A luxurious five-star option in the heart of town. Rooms go all-out for glamour and elegance, with fabric-covered walls, heavy drapery, ornate beds and marble bathrooms. One of Bologna's Roman roads is preserved in the basement. **€360**

Il Nosadillo Via Nosadella 15c ⓣ 051 716 2926,

ⓦilnosadillo.com; map p.470. This small hostel in the old centre is more convenient than Bologna's official HI hostel, 6km out of town. As the staff aren't around all day, it feels more like a shared apartment than a hostel, with three mixed dorms sleeping five to eight. Bathrooms, kitchens and living room are shared. Dorms **€24**

★ **Palazzo Trevi** Via Frassinago 31 ⓣ051 580 230, ⓦpalazzotrevi.it; map p.470. An impeccably run six-room B&B a 5min walk from Piazza Maggiore. The rooms vary in size – some are very large – but all are comfortably furnished, with an attention to detail that goes beyond the usual B&B standard, such as complimentary wine and snacks. Breakfast is also excellent, taken on a pretty flower-filled terrace in summer. **€140**

Panorama Via Livraghi 1 ⓣ051 221 802, ⓦhotelpanoramabologna.it; map p.470. Offering excellent value, this fourth-floor one-star hotel has three- and four-bed rooms as well as large doubles and singles: it's a little old-fashioned but spotlessly clean. Only one room comes with private bath; the rest share clean and pleasant facilities down the corridor. Helpful owners. **€69**

★ **San Vitale** Via San Vitale 94 ⓣ051 225 966, ⓦalbergosanvitale.com; map p.470. A little hotel east of the two towers, which offers a rare treat – its own lush garden. The rooms are basic but spotless and all have private bathrooms with showers. The friendly owners provide a very warm welcome. No breakfast, but there ae plenty of options nearby. **€74**

EATING

Eating is important to the Bolognese, and its **restaurants** are said to be the best in Italy: indeed, the city is known as *La Grassa* ("The Fat One"), the result of a rich culinary tradition. Its. For a snack, head for the **Mercato di Mezzo**, the former market hall at Via Clavature 12 where you can buy salads, *calamari*, platters of ham and cheese plus wine and beer from different stalls and sit at convivial shared tables – or take away (daily 9am–midnight). The most convenient **supermarket** is the Co-op, at Via Garibaldi 1/D, next to Piazza Cavour (Mon–Sat 9am–8.30pm, Sun10am–7.30pm).

CAFÉS, GELATERIE AND PASTICCERIE

★ **Cremeria Funivia** Piazza Cavour 1 ⓣ051 656 9365; map p.470. It's impossible to find more perfectly executed, silky and richly flavoured *gelato* – try the classics, such as *bacio* and *zabaione*, or more innovative flavours like toasted pine nut, dubbed "Leonardo", and white chocolate with crunchy puffed rice – "San Luca". Worth queuing for. Tues–Sat noon–11.30pm, Sun 11am–11.30pm.

Il Duca d'Amalfi Piazza dei Celestini 3A ⓣ051 265 146; map p.470. Café-bar with a fine panelled wooden ceiling on a quiet square round the corner from Piazza Maggiore, where you can enjoy breakfast, lunch or an *aperitivo* with the locals. Tues–Sun 8am–9pm.

★ **Il Gelatauro** Via S. Vitale 98/B ⓣ051 230 049; map p.470. A 10min walk east of the centre, the charming Giovanni and his team serve up organic pastries, handmade chocolates, speciality wines, delicious hot chocolate and fantastic ice cream, in flavours that include pumpkin and cinnamon and the "Principe di Calabria", with bergamot, jasmine and sponge cake. Mon 8.30am–8pm, Tues–Thurs 8.30am–9.30pm, Fri & Sat 8.30am–10.30pm, Sun 8.30am–8.30pm; open later in high summer; closed Aug.

La Baita Formaggi Via Pescherie Vecchie 3 ⓣ051 223 940; map p.470. A renowned cheese shop, stuffed with tempting gourmet goodies. You can stop by at lunch for a generous platter of cold cuts and cheeses for around €12, washed down with a glass of the local wine. Daily 9am–11pm.

★ **Tamburini** Via Caprarie 1 ⓣ051 234 726; map p.470. A.F. Tamburini's fabulous delicatessen is a gourmet's delight, its ceiling thick with hanging hams and its counters bulging with giant cheeses. It's also got a popular café selling roasted meats and plates of filled pasta for around €5–7. Mon–Sat 8.30am–8pm, Sun 10am–6.30pm, wine bar Mon–Sat noon–12.30am, Sun noon–10.30pm.

RESTAURANTS

All'Osteria Bottega Via S. Caterina 51 ⓣ051 585 111; map p.470. One of the city's top choices for fine dining, featuring a masterfully prepared, meat-centric menu that might include roast rabbit in a white wine sauce with cannellini beans (€16) or braised pigeon with chicory (€20). The place is low-lit, cosy and tiny, so booking is a must. Tues–Sat 12.30–2.30pm & 8–11pm.

★ **Al Sangiovese** Vicolo del Falcone 2 ⓣ051 583 057, ⓦalsangiovese.com; map p.470. Tucked away on an unprepossessing backstreet by the Porta San Mamolo, this traditional trattoria serves excellent pasta dishes such as *strozzapreti* with porcini mushrooms, peas and ham (€8), as well as meaty mains (€12–16), washed down with a fine Sangiovese red from the family vineyard. Mon–Sat noon–2.30pm & 7–10.30pm.

Altro? Mercato delle Erbe, Via Ugo Bassi 25 ⓣ351 014 4191; map p.470. You could spend all day in *Altro?*, tucked into a side hall of the market. Have breakfast in the bar, lounge on the sofas for coffee, cross over the hall for a slice of organic pizza, a salad or a generously stuffed panino (€3–5), then doze on the sofas until it's *aperitivo* time back at the bar. But save room for supper – the restaurant uses fresh ingredients for delights such as the beef carpaccio with artichokes and Parmesan (€12). Booking essential. Mon–Fri 8am–11.30pm, Sat 8am–1am.

★ **Babilonia** Via Pratello 17 ⓣ051 221 154; map p.470. Iranian bar where revellers queue to fortify themselves with falafel and kebabs served in delicious crisp pitta bread or

FOODIE SOUVENIRS

Some of Bologna's most colourful sights are inside its many **food stores**, particularly those in the old market district between Piazza Maggiore and the Due Torri, epitomized by *Tamburini* at Via Caprarie 1 (see page 479). All manner of goodies are on offer, but look out in particular for *tagliatelle* and *tortellini* – said to have been invented by a Bolognese innkeeper trying to re-create the beauty of Venus's navel.

There's also a great **food market** in the city centre where you can pick up a tasty picnic or some gourmet souvenirs: the large and lively Mercato delle Erbe is at Via Ugo Bassi 2 (Mon–Thurs 7am–midnight, Fri & Sat 7am–2am, though many stalls close on Thurs & Sat afternoon); while Piazzetta Pasolini, near MAMbo, hosts a farmer's market (Sat 9am–2pm; mid-June to July and usually Aug Mon 5.30–9.30pm).

baguettes, from €4. You can also get a Nutella version. Mon–Thurs & Sun 6pm–1am, Fri & Sat 6pm–5am.

★ **Banco 32** Mercato delle Erbe, Via Ugo Bassi 25 T 051 269 522; map p.470. Spilling out of the old market hall on to a terrace, *Banco 32* is an exciting venture run by an Italian, French and English trio. Its tapas-style menu changes daily, with tasty standards such as *cartoccio di alici*, a little bag/cone of fried anchovies with fried vegetables (€10), plus unusual dishes like the aromatic tuna salad with spiced yoghurt (€8.50). No booking – you'll have to queue most evenings. Tues–Thurs 12.30–3.45pm & 7–10.30pm, Fri & Sat 12.30–3.45pm & 7–11pm.

Casa Monica Via S. Rocco 16 T 051 522 522; map p.470. The colourful, high-ceilinged interior of *Monica's* – a former car workshop – makes a refreshing change from the rather dark Bolognese restaurant norm. The menu varies daily, always something creative and light, such as carrot, ginger and almond soup or courgette flan with Gorgonzola cream; a full meal without wine will set you back around €40. Booking recommended. Daily 7pm–1am.

★ **Clorofilla** Strada Maggiore 64/C T 051 235 343; map p.470. This warmly inviting fish and vegetarian place is just the spot if the "fat of Bologna" has been weighing you down, offering enticing salads with predominantly organic products, including tofu and seitan dishes. A three-course meal with wine will set you back around €30. Mon–Sat noon–3pm & 7.30–11pm.

★ **È Cucina Leopardi** Via G. Leopardi 4 T 051 275; map p.470. Funky bistro with a lively buzz and wacky decor run by the celebrity chef Cesare Marretti – everyone seems to go into the kitchen to have a chat with the man himself. Small menu: three- to four-course lunch menus cost €10–20; dinner costs €19.50/30 for two/four courses. A bargain for cooking of this calibre. Daily noon–3.30pm & 8pm–midnight.

Grassilli Via del Luzzo 3 T 051 222 961; map p.470. Emilian dishes adapted with flair to suit modern tastes, accompanied by good service. The restaurant was founded by opera singer Francesco Grassilli, and the walls are crammed with pictures of opera singers who dined here. An experience to remember, though you'll need to book and it's above averagely priced (around €50 per person for a full meal, including wine). Thurs–Tues 12.30–2.30pm & 7.30–10.30pm; closed Sun eve.

Marsalino Via Marsala 13/D T 051 238 675; map p.470. Housed in a former dairy, this popular local *osteria* has outdoor seating on a terrace at the front. Booking essential. Mon–Sat noon–3pm & 6pm–1am, Sun 6pm–1am (kitchen closes at midnight).

★ **Osteria dell'Orsa** Via Mentana 1/F T 051 231 576; map p.470. Bustling, friendly and cheap, this is where both students and locals go for simple good food. Pastas (€6–8), salads (€8) and main dishes €10–12. Share one of the big tables and join in the pub-like conviviality. Daily 12.30pm–1am.

Osteria La Traviata Via Urbana 5/C T 051 331 298; map p.470. A simple, homely *osteria* with plenty of outdoor tables and great pasta dishes: this is a good place to try local speciality *tortellini in brodo* (€13). The *secondi* are mainly meaty grills for €15–22. Service can be patchy. Mon–Sat noon–2.30pm & 8–11pm.

★ **Scacco Matto** Via Broccaindosso 63/B T 051 263 404; map p.470. A welcoming and elegant dining space adorned with framed tarot and playing cards, this venue offers some of the city's most unusual flavours, featuring gourmet variants on traditional cuisine. Menu varies daily; superb wines. *Primi* from €14, *secondi* €16–20. Reservations a must. Tues–Fri 12.15–2.15pm & 7.45pm–11pm, Sat & Sun 7.45–11pm.

Trattoria Gianni Via Clavature 18 T 051 229 434; map p.470. Hidden down a narrow side-alley, this is one of the top options in Bologna: try the ultra-traditional *bolliti*, a variety of meats boiled in the Emilian way, or the fantastic home-made *tortellini*. Moderate prices: you can eat very well for €25–30 for two courses. Reservations recommended. Tues–Sat 12.30–2.15pm & 7.30–10.15, Sun 12.30–2.15pm.

DRINKING AND NIGHTLIFE

Bologna's **bar and club** culture thrives thanks to its huge student population, with a string of drinking places centred on and around Via Zamboni – Piazza Verdi pulls in the crowds on summer evenings with its open-air bars and live

music. West of the centre, there is a buzzing scene in the streets around the Mercato delle Erbe, while the nearby Via del Pratello is lined with bars and restaurants and draws more of a mixed (not exclusively studenty) crowd. The tourist office's website, ⓦ bolognawelcome.com, has details of life in the city after dark, or there's the useful *Bologna Spettacolo* (ⓦ bolognaspettacolo.it).

BARS

★ **Altotasso** Piazza San Francesco 6/D ⓣ 051 238 003; map p.470. Small *enoteca* near Via Pratello where the punters spill out on to the square. Great spread of *aperitivi*, with an emphasis on zero kilometre produce. Craft beers on tap and the wines are mostly local and organic. Mon–Thurs & Sun 4.30pm–3am, Fri & Sat 4.30pm–4am.

Enoteca des Arts Via San Felice 9 ⓣ 051 236 422; map p.470. This tiny, dark bar is a proper *enoteca* – all warm wood and dusty bottles – serving cheap local wine and preparing simple snacks (panini, cold meat platters) on request. Organizes regular tastings. Mon–Sat 4.30pm–2am.

Ex Forno Via Don Minzoni 14 ⓣ 051 649 3896; map p.470. Named after the old bakery that once stood here, this dimly lit cocktail bar inside MAMbo attracts a cultured and arty crowd. There are sometimes DJs at weekends, but it's more about the chat and the fancy *aperitivo* buffet (7–10pm), with tempura, platters of couscous and salads. Tues–Fri 7.30am–2am, Sat & Sun 10am–2am; closed three weeks in Aug.

★ **Il Punto** Via San Rocco 1G ⓣ 051 649 2895; map p.470. Laid back gay-friendly bar where the modern industrial feel is tempered by sofas and wooden fittings. They have one hundred bottled beers plus eight on tap, mainly Italian craft beers, and hold regular beer tastings and food pairings. The hamburgers and cheese and meat platters are delicious. Daily 5.30pm–1.30am.

★ **Le Stanze** Via del Borgo di San Pietro 1/A ⓣ 051 228 767; map p.470. Elegant place to unwind and sip wine and cocktails in the airy splendour of a former Bentivoglio chapel; there's a good *aperitivo* buffet 6.30–9pm (€1 extra for the first drink), but the bistro also serves pasta dishes and mains (from €9). The sixteenth-century frescoed ceilings, romantic candles and occasional art exhibitions produce an evocative atmosphere. Tues–Sun 11am–1am.

Osteria del Sole Vicolo Ranocchi 1/D ⓣ 347 968 0171; map p.470. There's been an *osteria* on this spot since 1465, and it retains a charmingly old-fashioned atmosphere. Turning the usual concept of BYO on its head, here you pick up a bite to eat in the nearby market and buy a glass of wine or two to wash it down with. Mon–Sat 10.30am–9.30pm.

Senza Nome Via Belvedere 11/B ⓣ 392 516 2896; map p.470. In the streets around the Mercato delle Erbe, the "Bar with No Name" is run by hard-of-hearing staff, which can be a relief if your Italian accent is weak – use sign language to order. Prices are low, the beers are mainly craft and the *aperitivi* are delicious (7–9pm). Mon–Thurs 10am–1.30am, Fri & Sat 10am–3am, Sun 2pm–midnight.

CLUBS AND LIVE MUSIC

★ **Cantina Bentivoglio** Via Mascarella 4/B ⓣ 051 265 416, ⓦ cantinabentivoglio.it; map p.470. This place has live jazz from around 10pm in the cellars of a sixteenth-century *palazzo*, and the food (snacks to full meals; mains €9–20) and wines are excellent. From mid-June to the end of July (Thurs–Sat), concerts take place outside as part of the Salotto del Jazz festival (see page 481). Daily 8pm–2am; closed Sun in summer.

8

★ **Cassero** Via Don Minzoni 18 ⓣ 051 649 4416, ⓦ cassero.it; map p.470. Housed on the "garden floor" in historic La Salara, one of the old city fortifications, this is the best of Bologna's LGBTQ clubs, with bar and entertainment. Events mainly Mon, Wed, Fri, Sat & Sun 9pm–5am.

Macondo Via Pratello 22; map p.470. There's music most evenings in the small back room at this popular venue, mainly jazz, blues and rock (8–10pm). There's a good spread of *aperitivi* to keep you going till the music starts (€2 extra with your drink). Tues–Sun 5pm–4am.

Villa Serena Via della Barca 1 ⓣ 340 782 1002; take bus #14 or #21 (direction: Stadio) and get off at the "Certosa" stop; map p.470. Spread over three floors, this buzzing live music and arts venue hosts exhibitions and installations throughout the year, but from mid-May to July it comes into its own with daily discos, live music or films. Tues–Thurs 8pm–3am, Fri & Sat 8pm–3.30am.

BOLOGNA FESTIVALS AND EVENTS

From mid-May to mid-October, Bologna hosts a summer arts festival called **bè bolognaestate** (ⓦ bolognaestate.it), with concerts, films and dance performances every evening. June/July sees the annual **Gay Pride** celebrations (ⓦ bolognapride.it), while from mid-June to July the **Salotto del Jazz** takes place in Via Mascarella, with live music under the stars on Thursday to Saturday nights. In spring and autumn, classical concerts are staged under the aegis of the **Bologna Festival** (ⓦ bolognafestival.it), for which the Teatro Manzoni at Via de' Monari (ⓦ auditoriumanzoni.it) is one of the main venues. Tickets cost from €12. The **Bologna Jazz Festival** in October and November sees concerts performed by international musicians in venues around town (ⓦ festivaljazzbologna.it).

ENTERTAINMENT

CINEMA

Cineteca Via Riva di Reno 72 ⓣ 051 219 4820, ⓦ cinetecadibologna.it. The arthouse cinema across the park from MAMbo specializes in restoring old films; its archive and Cinema Lumière are next to the Cassero centre (see above). The films are screened in the original language with Italian subtitles. Tickets €5–7. In July its films are screened for free in Piazza Maggiore.

DIRECTORY

Books There's a wide range of English books in the swish *Ambasciatori* bookshop at Via Orefici 19, as well as a wine bar and trattoria (Mon–Sat 9am–midnight, Sun 10am–midnight); or try Feltrinelli International at Piazza Ravegnana 1 (Mon–Sat 9am–8pm, Sun 10am–8pm).

Hospital In an emergency, dial ⓣ 118; or go to the Pronto Soccorso (24hr casualty) at the Ospedale Sant'Orsola-Malpighi, Via Massarenti 9 (ⓣ 051 214 1111); bus #14 from Via Rizzoli.

Left luggage At the station (daily 7am–9pm; first 5hr €6, 6th–12th hr €0.90/hr).

Pharmacy Lloyds Farmacia on Piazza Maggiore is open 24hr (ⓣ 051 239 690).

Police The *questura* is at Piazza Galileo 7 (ⓣ 051 640 1111).

Post office The main post office is on Piazza Minghetti (Mon–Fri 8.20am–7.05pm, Sat 8.20am–12.35pm).

Santuario di San Luca

Via di San Luca 36 • March–Oct Mon–Fri 7am–12.30pm & 2.30–7pm, Sat 7am–7pm, Sun 7am–7pm; Nov–Feb same days but closes 6pm • Free • Bus #20 from Via Rizzoli drops you at the start of the route at the Meloncello stop, southwest of the centre; from there you can walk or catch bus #58 – alternatively, the San Luca Express tourist train runs here from Piazza Maggiore (end Feb to Oct 5–10 daily; first departure 9.45am; 35min; €10, or €21 including the City redbus tour; (see page 478)

8

In the heat of the summer the hills that start almost as soon as you leave Bologna's gates take you high enough to catch some cooling breezes. The most obvious destination for a short trip is the eighteenth-century shrine of **Santuario di San Luca**, 4km southwest of the city centre but connected by way of the world's longest portico, which meanders across the hillside in a series of 666 arches – a shelter for pilgrims on the trek to the top.

Modena and around

Though only thirty minutes northwest by train, **MODENA** has a quite distinct identity from Bologna. It proclaims itself the "spiritual capital" of Emilia and has a number of claims to fame: great car names such as Ferrari, Lamborghini and Maserati are linked to the town (celebrated in Modena Terra di Motori every spring, when the piazzas are filled with classic models); the late Pavarotti was a native of Modena, his name commemorated in the Teatro Comunale Luciano Pavarotti; the area's balsamic vinegar has become a cult product in kitchens around the world, duly celebrated with an array of tastings and events in and around town in September and October; and the cathedral – a UNESCO World Heritage Site – is one of the finest Romanesque buildings in Italy. Modena's highlights include the rich collections of **paintings** and **manuscripts** built up by the Este family, who decamped here from Ferrara in 1598, after it was annexed by the Papal States, and who ruled the town until the nineteenth century. But really the city's appeal is in wandering its labyrinthine **old centre**, finishing off the day with some good food. The town's small, concentric medieval core is bisected by **Via Emilia**, which runs past the edge of **Piazza Grande**, the nominal centre of town, its stone buildings and arcades forming the focus of much of its life.

The Duomo

Piazza Grande • **Church** Mon 7am–12.30pm & 3.30–7pm, Tues–Sun 7am–7pm • Free • **Museums** Tues–Sun 9.30am–12.30pm & 3.30–6.30pm • €4, or €6 including the Torre Ghirlandina • **Torre Ghirlandina** April–Sept Tues–Fri 9.30am–1pm & 3–7pm, Sat & Sun 9.30am–7pm; Oct–March Tues–Fri 9.30am–1pm & 2.30–5.30pm, Sat & Sun 9.30am–5.30pm • €3, or €6 including the Musei del Duomo • ⓦ duomodimodena.it

Dominating Piazza Grande, the twelfth-century **Duomo** is one of the finest products of the Romanesque period in Italy and is on the UNESCO World Heritage list. Its most striking feature is the west facade whose portal is supported by two fierce-looking lions and fringed with marvellous reliefs – the work of one **Wiligelmo**, who also did the larger reliefs that run along the wall. Inside, under the choir is the plain stone coffin of St Geminianus, the patron saint of Modena – on his feast day, January 31, crowds come to visit his coffin, and a big market is held out in the main square.

Separated from the Duomo by the narrow Via Lanfranco are the **Musei del Duomo**, which includes the usual ecclesiastical artefacts, and the Museo Lapidario, which has Roman-age marbles from the Duomo. Next door looms the 86m-high **Torre Ghirlandina**, which you can climb for a bird's-eye view of the city.

Palazzo dei Musei

Viale Vittorio Veneto 5 • **Biblioteca Estense** Mon–Thurs 8.30am–7pm, Fri 8.30am–3.30pm, Sat 8.30am–1.30pm • Free • **Museo Civico Archeologico Etnologico** Tues–Fri 9am–noon, Sat & Sun 10am–1pm & 4–7pm • Free • **Galleria Estense** Tues–Sat 8.30am–7.30pm, Sun 2–7.30pm; first Sun of the month 8.30am–7.30pm • €6; first Sun of the month free

At the far, northwestern end of the centre, the **Palazzo dei Musei** houses the city museums and art galleries. Through an archway lined with Roman tombstones – nearby Piazza Matteotti was the site of a necropolis – a staircase leads to the **Biblioteca Estense**, on the first floor, where you can see letters sent by monarchs, popes and despots, with great wax seals, old maps and the prize treasure, Borso d'Este's Bible – the *Bibbia di Borso d'Este* – arguably the most decorated book in the world. The **Museo Civico Archeologico Etnologico**, on the second floor, has a large collection of artefacts of archeological and artistic significance, while on the top floor, the **Galleria Estense** is the highlight. Made up of the picture collection of the Este family, it contains paintings of the local schools, from the early Renaissance through to the works of the Carraccis, Guercino and Guido Reni.

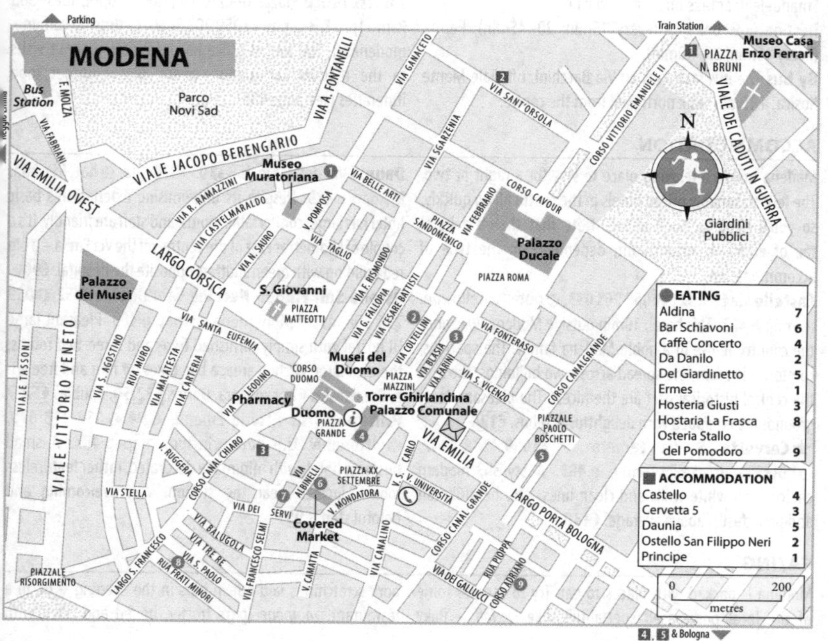

Museo Casa Enzo Ferrari

Via Paolo Ferrari 85 • Daily: April–Oct 9.30am–7pm; Nov–March 9.30am–6pm • €16, or €26 joint ticket with the Museo Ferrari in Maranello (see below) • museiferrari.com • There's a shuttle bus from the station (gate no. 4) every 1hr 30min, which also runs to the Ferrari Museum in Maranello; alternatively, it's a 5min walk

Fans of motor racing won't want to miss the two local sights inspired by the king of the sport, Enzo Ferrari: the Museo Ferrari (see below), and the **Museo Casa Enzo Ferrari**. The museum preserves Ferrari's original house, where he was born in 1898, while the futuristic gallery space alongside contains gleaming ranks of supercars and is covered by a bright yellow aluminium "bonnet" the colour of the prancing horse logo, designed by Jan Kaplický.

Museo Ferrari

Via Dino Ferrari 43, Maranello • Daily: April–Oct 9.30am–7pm; Nov–March 9.30am–6pm • €16, or €26 joint ticket with Museo Casa Enzo Ferrari (see above) • museiferrari.com • A shuttle bus runs from Modena train station and from the Museo Casa Enzo Ferrari (6 daily; 50min; €12 return); there's also a shuttle service from Bologna station – book tickets via the museum's website

Around 20km south of Modena in Maranello, the **Museo Ferrari** is an exhibition centre dedicated to the racing dynasty. On display are the cups and trophies won by the Ferrari team over the years and an assortment of Ferrari engines, along with vintage and contemporary examples of the cars themselves. There's also a shop stocking all manner of merchandise, from baseball caps to surfboards.

ARRIVAL AND INFORMATION — MODENA

8

By plane There's a shuttle from Bologna airport (see page 476) to Modena (9 daily; 50min; €15); buy tickets on the bus.

By train Modena's centre, marked by the main Piazza Grande, is a 10min walk southwest from the train station on Piazza Dante Alighieri, down the wide Corso Vittorio Emanuele II; or take buses #7 and #11.

Destinations Bologna (every 15min; 20–45min); Parma (every 15min; 25–40min).

By bus The bus station is on Via Bacchini, off Viale Monte Kosica, a 10min walk northeast from the centre.

By car There's free parking in Piazza Giovani di Tien An Men, beyond the stadium, though most hotels in the centre either have a garage or can give you free parking permits; driving in the centre's one-way system on weekdays can be a nightmare.

Tourist office Piazza Grande 14 (Mon 3–6pm, Tues–Sun 9am–1pm & 3–6pm; 059 203 2660, turismo.comune.modena.it). The tourist office has information about visits to the region's car manufacturers, plus gourmet food itineraries (see page 486).

ACCOMMODATION

Modena makes a relaxing place to stay for a night or two. The few reasonably priced hotels in the centre fill up quickly, so you'll need to book ahead. Note that there's a hotel tax of €0.50–4/person/night, depending on the type of accommodation.

Castello Via Pica 321 059 361 033, hotelcastello-mo.it; map p.483. This hotel, 10min outside Modena, was once the country house of a noble Modena family. The spacious, comfortable rooms are spread across two buildings; those in the central historical part are the nicest. The pleasant, leafy grounds are equipped with delightful gazebos. **€120**

★ **Cervetta 5** Via Cervetta 5 059 238 447, hotelcervetta5.com; map p.483. A stylish, modern choice – all white walls and clean lines. Very helpful staff and breakfast is above average. **€130**

Daunia Via del Pozzo 158 059 371 182, hoteldaunia.it; map p.483. Despite its unpromising exterior, this basic hotel has large, comfortable rooms, and staff are friendly. It's a couple of kilometres east of the centre, off the Via Emila – a big red building with green shutters opposite the hospital. **€90**

Ostello San Filippo Neri Via Sant'Orsola 48/52 059 234 598, ostellomodena.it; map p.483. Pleasant large HI hostel with simply furnished two- and three-bed rooms: there's a large kitchen area, a bar, bikes for rent and free wi-fi. Breakfast is €2 or so extra. Dorms **€22.50**, doubles **€52**

Principe Corso Vittorio Emanuele 94 059 218 670, vittoriahotels.it/hotelprincipe; map p.483. A small business hotel, with minimally decorated, rather featureless rooms, located near the station. Very welcoming and helpful staff. **€95**

EATING

Modena is packed with places to eat. Try to sample some of the local pork-based specialities, like *ciccioli* – flaky pork scratchings laid out in bars in the evening – or, in a restaurant, *zampone* (pig's trotter, boned and filled with

minced meat) or *cotechino* (the same, but stuffed inside a pig's bladder). The covered Mercato Albinelli (Mon–Sat 6.30am–2.30pm; Oct–May also Sat 4.30–7.30pm), just south of Piazza Grande, has a fantastic array of fresh vegetables, fruit and meat, as well as balsamic vinegars (a bottle of 25-year-old *tradizionale* goes for more than €70).

★ **Aldina** Via Albinelli 40 ⓣ 059 236 106; map p.483. Up on the first floor, this traditional, family-run restaurant is an example of what the Slow Food movement is all about. The simple, delicious, home-made dishes of the day are recited, not written, and the pastas are the crowning glory. About €16 for a full meal; no credit cards. Mon–Thurs 12.30–3pm, Fri & Sat 12.30–3pm & 8–10.30pm; closed Aug.

Bar Schiavoni Via Albinelli 13 ⓣ 059 243 073; map p.483. Good, popular choice for a great coffee, a glass of wine and delicious and inventive panini for around €5, as well as various fresh, gourmet creations. Mon–Fri 6am–8.30pm, Sat 6am–7.30pm.

Caffè Concerto Piazza Grande 26 ⓣ 059 222 232; map p.483. Large place that operates a buffet service during the day (noon–3pm; a plate of your choice, water and coffee for €16–19) and an à la carte restaurant at night (when prices are around double). Its main role, however, is as Modena's key meeting place and premier soiree spot. Regular DJ sets and live music. Mon–Fri 9.30am–2am, Sat & Sun 8am–2am.

Da Danilo Via Coltellini 51 ⓣ 059 225 498; map p.483. The archetypal Modena eating experience – regional specialities served in a cosy backstreet dining room. Be adventurous and try the mixed meat platter – including stuffed pig's trotters, cheek and tongue – for €16. Mon–Wed, Fri & Sat noon–3pm & 7–10.30pm, Thurs 7–10.30pm.

★ **Del Giardinetto** Piazzale Boschetti 1 ⓣ 059 234 448; map p.483. Popular local trattoria tucked away on a small square serving tasty risottos and pasta (from €7). In the evening – and Thurs lunch – it serves the Modenese speciality *gnoccho e tigelle*, a complete meal of breads, meats, cheese, jams, even Nutella (€15). Mon–Fri noon–3pm & 8pm–midnight, Sat 8pm–midnight.

Ermes Via Ganaceto 89–91 ⓣ 059 238 065; map p.483. A tiny eatery with a big local following, as authentic as it gets. The menu changes daily according to market finds. Three courses with wine €20; worth the queue. No credit cards. Mon–Sat noon–3pm; closed Aug.

★ **Hosteria Giusti** Vicolo Squallore 46 ⓣ 059 222 533; map p.483. This marvellous family-run place, set at the back of a 400-year-old *salumeria*, serves hearty home cooking at lunch only: try the traditional *tortellini in brodo* followed by pork slow-braised in white wine and herbs (*secondi* €10–18). There are only four tables, so book ahead, and pick up a jar of the home-made black cherry jam in the shop before you leave. Tues–Sat 12.30–3pm.

★ **Hostaria La Frasca** Via San Paolo 51 ⓣ 059 216 271; map p.483. Eating at this trattoria, another locals' favourite, is always an experience. There's no menu and the owner, who makes all her own pasta, speaks no English, but making yourself understood is half the fun. Booking is a good idea; meals cost around €30 a head. Terrace out front in summer. Daily 12.30–11pm.

Osteria Stallo del Pomodoro Largo Hannover 63 ⓣ 059 214 664; map p.483. Good for a relaxed dinner with friends – the high ceiling of this former stable can make it pretty noisy, so it's not the place for a romantic meal. Unusually, all of the dishes are available in gluten-free versions. The wine list is endless, and the waiters can advise on what best to pair with your ox cheek or roast lamb; a full meal costs around €35 without wine. Daily 12.30–2.30pm & 7.30–10.30pm.

8

Reggio Emilia

About 25km northwest of Modena, up the Via Emilia, is **REGGIO EMILIA**, a pleasant, well-heeled place with a handsome historic core. Though nicknamed "the red town" – in 1960 five protestors were killed by police during demonstrations designed to prevent Fascists joining the government – you wouldn't credit such a revolutionary past as you wander its quiet streets; these days, it's more associated with the high-end fashion house MaxMara.

Piazza San Prospero

The town is built around two central squares, Piazza Prampolini and **Piazza San Prospero**, which come alive on market days (Tues and Fri). Stalls specialize in rather tacky clothes – the shops surrounding the market are far more alluring, crammed with a mighty range of local produce such as salami and *parmigiano-reggiano*. Around the square, the buildings squeeze up so close to the church of **San Prospero** that they seem to have pushed it off-balance so that it now lurches to one side. Built in the sixteenth century, it's guarded by six lions in rose-coloured Verona marble.

Piazza Prampolini

Via Broletto leads through from Piazza San Prospero into **Piazza Prampolini**, skirting the side of the **Duomo**, which displays an awkward amalgamation of styles. Underneath the marble tacked on in the sixteenth century, it's possible to see the church's Romanesque facade, with incongruously Mannerist statues of Adam and Eve lounging over the medieval portal.

At right angles to the Duomo is the sugar-pink **Palazzo del Capitano del Popolo**. The Italian tricolour of red, white and green was proclaimed here as the official national flag of Italy when Napoleon's Cispadane Republic was formed in 1797. North of here on the edge of Piazza della Vittoria are the **Musei Civici** (July & Aug Tues–Sat 9am–noon & 9–11pm, Sun 9–11pm; Sept–June Tues–Fri 9am–1pm, Sat & Sun 10am–7pm; free), containing an eighteenth-century private collection of archeological finds, fossils and paintings. In the corner of the square, the **Galleria Parmeggiani** (July & Aug Tues–Sun 9–11pm; Sept–June Tues–Fri 9am–noon, Sat & Sun 10am–1pm & 4–7pm; free) houses an important collection of Spanish, Flemish and Italian art, including sculptures and bronzes, as well as costumes and textiles. Nearby stands the **Basilica della Ghiara** (advance booking necessary on T 0522 439 707; free), built in the seventeenth century and decorated with Bolognese School frescoes of scenes from the Old Testament and a *Crucifixion* by Guercino.

ARRIVAL AND INFORMATION — REGGIO EMILIA

By train Reggio is on the main rail line between Bologna and Milan. The train station is on Piazza Marconi, just east of the old centre.

By bus The bus station is behind the train station, on Piazzale Europa.

Tourist information The tourist office is at Via Farini 1A (Tues–Sat 9am–1pm & 2–6pm, Sun 9.30am–12.30pm; T 0522 451 152, W turismo.comune.re.it), while the helpful Club Alpino Italiano office, a 10min walk south of the centre at Viale dei Mille 32 (Wed 7–10pm, Thurs & Fri 6–7.30pm; closed most of Aug; T 0522 436 685, W caireggioemilia.it), has information on walking in the nearby hills, though nothing in English.

ACCOMMODATION

★ B&B Cantarelli Via Monzermone 3 T 329 714 9847, W cantarellibandb.com. A beautifully turned out, cosy retreat in the heart of town. Some rooms are in the rafters (be prepared to duck), and all are beautifully furnished. The extremely helpful owner will make restaurant reservations and provide information. There's no breakfast room but coffee and pastries are served in your room. **€75**

Posta Piazza del Monte 2 T 0522 432 944, W hotelposta.re.it. This four-star hotel in the historic Palazzo del Capitano del Popolo has great service, comfortable rooms and plenty of character. Free bikes are available for guests, and the owner can arrange visits to his family farm, to see the

HIT THE GOURMET TRAIL

Food is an integral part of the countryside between the Appenines and the Po, and the best way to get a feel of this is on a **gourmet tour**: Food Valley Travel (W foodvalleytravel.com) will take you to a dairy farm to see how milk is turned into Parmesan cheese, and some of the *aceterie* around Modena to see how the traditional balsamic vinegar is matured.

Local tourist offices can also advise you on **farms** and **vineyards** to visit – or you can head out on your own into the wooded foothills of the Apennines. Restaurant signs by the roadside invite you to try cuisine "*alla tua nonna*" – "like grandma used to make" – usually involving mortadella (cold pork sausage, spotted with lumps of fat and often flavoured with nutmeg, coriander and myrtle), salami or *crescente* (a kind of pitta bread eaten with a mixture of oil, garlic, rosemary and Parmesan). Higher in the mountains you can still find *ciacci* – chestnut-flour pancakes, filled with ricotta and sugar – and walnuts that go to make *nocino* liqueur.

In the foothills south of Reggio and Parma signs along the roadside advertise the local **parmigiano-reggiano** while the village of Casina, 27km from Reggio on the N63 to La Spezia, holds a popular **Fiera del Parmigiano** in early August, when the vats of cheese mixture are stirred with enormous wooden paddles. Buses run to Casina from Reggio hourly and take around an hour.

8

aking of the local *aceto di balsamico*. €90

tudent Hostel della Ghiara Via Guasco 6 ⓣ 0522 452 23, ⓦ www.ostelloreggioemilia.it. A basic, hundred-ed hostel, 1km from the station, with no curfew, and breakfast and internet included. The cloister and garden make a pleasant place to relax in summer. Half board is available for an extra €14. Dorms €19, doubles €45

ATING AND DRINKING

affè Arti E Mestieri Via Emilia S. Pietro 14 ⓣ 0522 432 02. A smart restaurant with a menu of updated classic shes from the region (€45 for three courses). In summer has a delightfully secluded garden terrace. Tues–Sat oon–2.30pm & 7.30–10.30pm, Sun noon–2.30pm.

Canossa Via Roma 37 ⓣ 0522 454 196. A few minutes' walk north of Piazza Prampolini, this ultra-traditional place is consistently popular with locals. Its specialities are antipasti and meaty grills, and a full meal costs around €30. Thurs–Tues 12.30–2pm & 7.30–10pm.

arma

ong reckoned to have one of the highest standards of living in Italy, **PARMA**, 28km long the Via Emilia northwest of Reggio, is a comfortable town, though its general air of ffluence has been shaken by the recent recession. You could easily fill a day or two seeing he sights and sampling the city's excellent **restaurants**. A visit to the **opera** can be an xperience – the audience are considered the toughest outside Milan's La Scala – and the ity's **works of art** are dominated by two great local artists, Correggio and Parmigianino.

anta Maria della Steccata

iazza Steccata 9 • **Church** Daily 7.30am–noon & 3–6.30pm • Free • **Museum** Mid-March to June & Sept–Nov Mon–Fri 9.30am–noon & 30–6pm, Sat & Sun 3.30–6pm; July & Aug Mon–Fri 9.30am–noon • €5 • ⓣ 0521 282 854

he Renaissance church of **Santa Maria della Steccata** was apparently built using ramante's original plan for St Peter's as a model. Inside there are frescoes by a number f sixteenth-century painters, notably **Parmigianino**, who spent the last ten years of is life on this work, eventually being sacked for breach of contract by the disgruntled hurch authorities. Also inside the church, the **Museo Costantiniano** includes the acristy, intricately carved in ebony in the seventeenth century, as well as precious ilverware, paintings and textiles.

he Duomo

iazza del Duomo • Daily 10am–7pm • Free

ive minutes' walk from Piazza Garibaldi, the slightly gloomy **Piazza del Duomo** forms art of the old *centro episcopale*, away from the shopping streets of the commercial entre. The Lombard-Romanesque **Duomo**, dating from the eleventh century, holds arlier work by Parmigianino in its south transept, executed when the artist was a pupil f **Correggio** – who painted the fresco of the *Assumption* in the central cupola. Finished n 1534, this is among the most famous of Correggio's works, the Virgin Mary floating up through a sea of limbs, faces and swirling clouds. One contemporary compared it to a "hash of frogs' legs", while Dickens thought it a sight that "no operative surgeon gone mad could imagine in his wildest delirium". A known miser, Correggio was paid with a sacksful of small change – the story goes that he carried the sack of coins home in the heat, caught a fever and died aged 40.

The Baptistry

Piazza del Duomo • Daily: March–Oct 10am–6.30pm; Nov–Feb 10am–4.30pm • Joint ticket with the Museo Diocesano €8

Just across the way from the Duomo is the beautiful twelfth-century octagonal **Baptistry**, its sugary pink-and-white Verona marble rising four storeys high. Its three

elaborately carved portals and frieze are the work of the architect Benedetto Antelami. Inside, sixteen arches frame thirteenth- and fourteenth-century frescoes under a beautifully painted dome.

The Bishop's Palace and Museo Diocesano

Piazza del Duomo • Daily: March–Oct 10am–6.30pm; Nov–Feb 10am–4.30pm • Joint ticket with the Baptistry €8

Piazza Duomo's other key sight is the **Bishop's Palace**, opposite the Duomo, built between the eleventh and thirteenth centuries. The palace's reception halls hold the **Museo Diocesano**, an unusually absorbing collection of ecclesiastical artefacts ranging from Roman to early medieval and Romanesque sections. The highlight is the collection of sculptures by Benedetto Antelami, depicting King David, King Solomon and the Queen of Sheba, among other figures.

San Giovanni Evangelista and the Spezieria di San Giovanni

Correggio features in the cupola of the church of **San Giovanni Evangelista** behind the Duomo, Piazzale San Giovanni 1 (church daily 8.30–11.45am & 3–6pm; monastery Mon–Wed, Fri & Sat 9–11.45am & 3–5pm; free) – with his fresco of the *Vision of St John at Patmos*. Next door, the **Spezieria di San Giovanni**, at Borgo Pipa 1 (Tues–Sun 8.30am–2pm; €2), is a thirteenth-century pharmacy with a medieval interior.

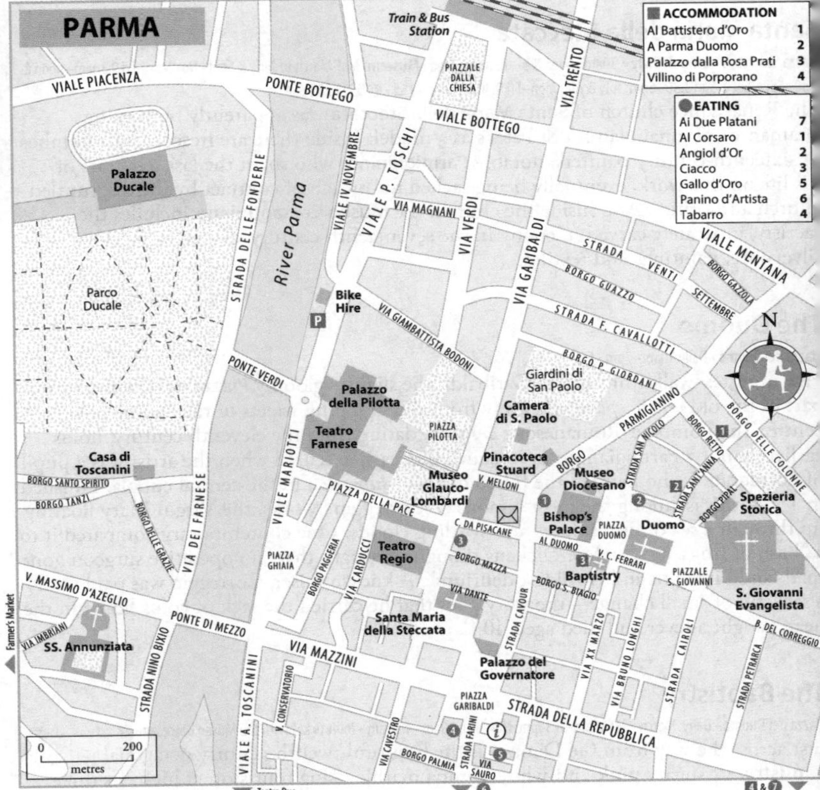

Pinacoteca Stuard

Borgo del Parmigianino 2 • Mon & Wed–Fri 10am–5pm, Sat & Sun 10.30am–6.30pm • Free

Housed in a former convent, the **Pinacoteca Stuard** holds 270 paintings from the fourteenth to the nineteenth centuries that used to form the private collection of the nobleman Giuseppe Stuard. Upon his death in 1834, the collection was bequeathed to the congregation of San Filippo Neri.

Camera di San Paolo

Via Melloni 3 • Mon–Sat 1.10–6.50pm • €6

A short walk northwest from Piazza del Duomo, the **Camera di San Paolo**, in the former Benedictine convent off Via Garibaldi, houses more frescoes by Correggio executed in 1519; above the fireplace, the abbess who commissioned the work is portrayed by Correggio as the goddess Diana.

Museo Glauco-Lombardi

Via Garibaldi 15 • Tues–Sat 9.30am–4pm, Sun 9.30am–7pm; closes at 2pm Sun in July & Aug • €5

The **Museo Glauco-Lombardi** has a display of memorabilia relating to Marie-Louise of Austria, who reigned here after the defeat of her husband Napoleon at Waterloo. She set herself up with another suitor (much to the chagrin of her exiled spouse) and expanded the Parma violet perfume industry.

Musei della Pilotta

Tues–Sat 8.30am–7pm, Sun 1–7pm • Joint ticket for Museo Archeologico Nazionale, Galleria Nazionale and Teatro Farnese €10; free first Sun of the month

It's hard to miss Parma's biggest monument, the brutal **Palazzo della Pilotta**, on Piazza della Pilotta, fronted by a vast expanse of lawn. Begun for Alessandro Farnese – the wily Pope Paul III – in the sixteenth century, the building was reduced to a shell by World War II bombing but was partly rebuilt and now houses a number of Parma's **museums**.

Museo Archeologico Nazionale

On the mezzanine, the **Museo Archeologico Nazionale** is worth a glance, with finds from the prehistoric lake villages around Parma, as well as the table top on which the Emperor Trajan notched up a record of his gifts to the poor.

Galleria Nazionale

Ⓦ gallerianazionaleparma.it

On the first floor, the city's main art gallery, the **Galleria Nazionale** is a sparse display of uninspiring paintings, but it's enlivened by a couple of frescoes by Correggio and two drawings by Parmigianino, as well as works by El Greco, Fra Angelico and Da Vinci, and the remarkable *Apostles at the Sepulchre* and *Funeral of the Virgin* by Carracci.

Teatro Farnese

Made completely of wood, the **Teatro Farnese** in the former arms room of the palace was almost entirely destroyed by bombing in 1944. Restored using the original plans, it has an extended semicircle of seats three tiers high inspired by Palladio's Teatro Olimpico at Vicenza, and is still used occasionally.

Across the river

Behind the Palazzo della Pilotta, the Ponte Verdi crosses the River Parma, bringing you to the **Parco Ducale** (daily: April–Oct 6am–midnight; Nov–March 7am–8pm; free), a set of eighteenth-century formal gardens arranged to offset the sixteenth-century

Palazzo Ducale, built for Ottaviano Farnese and now the offices of the carabinieri. Just south, the **Casa Natale Toscanini**, Via R. Tanzi 13 (Tues 9am–1pm, Wed–Sat 9am–1pm & 2–6pm, Sun 2–6pm; free), is the birthplace of the conductor who debuted in the Teatro Regio here (see page 491).

ARRIVAL AND DEPARTURE

PARMA

By train Parma's train station is a 15min walk from the central Piazza Garibaldi, or take bus #1, #8, #9 or #13.

By bus The bus station is next to the train station; take bus #1, #8, #9 or #13 to get to the centre.

Destinations Busseto/Le Roncole (6 daily; 1hr); Roncole Verdi (6 daily; 55min).

INFORMATION AND GETTING AROUND

Tourist office Piazza Garibaldi 1 (daily 9am–7pm; ⓣ 0521 218 889, ⓦ turismo.comune.parma.it).

Bike rental Bikes can be rented from several agencies, including La Cicletteria at Piazzale dalla Chiesa, near the train station (Mon–Fri 6am–10.30pm, Sat 9am–1pm & 3–7pm, Sun 10am–1pm & 2.30–7.30pm; €1.50/hr; ⓣ 0521 281 979).

ACCOMMODATION

★ **Al Battistero d'Oro** Strada Sant'Anna 22 ⓣ 338 490 4697, ⓦ albattisterodoro.it; map p.488. Two delightful rooms in a B&B filled with local eighteenth-century furniture belonging to the family of its friendly owner Patrizia. She can help with information and book restaurants and the like, and also rents out a well-equipped apartment round the corner. **€100**

8

A Parma Duomo Strada Sant'Anna 12 ⓣ 349 479 5701, ⓦ bbparma-centro.it; map p.488. This elegant B&B offers two spacious rooms, each with frescoed ceilings and modern furnishings. Host Giampaolo is endlessly helpful and hospitable. **€110**

★ **Palazzo dalla Rosa Prati** Piazza Duomo 7 ⓣ 0521 386 429, ⓦ palazzodallarosaprati.it; map p.488. Luxurious conversion of an old *palazzo* in the heart of town with fabulous rooms and suites – the deluxe suite looks out over the Baptistry, and if the lights are on in the evening you can see the frescoes. It's a friendly place – owned and run by the same family since the 1600s. Breakfast is served in the flashy café downstairs. **€135**

★ **Villino di Porporano** Strada Bodrio 26, Porporano, 4.5km from central Parma ⓣ 0521 162 6836, ⓦ villinodiporporano.com; map p.488. Some 7km south of the city, surrounded by gardens, this lovely, airy B&B – converted from an old barn – has a swimming pool and great views of the Apennines. Floating staircases lead to the five rustic-chic rooms, each beautifully decorated with antiques and luxurious touches such as fine linens and complimentary chocolates. **€150**

EATING

Given its reputation for ham and cheese, it is hardly surprising that Parma ham (*prosciutto di Parma*) and *parmigiano-reggiano* features strongly on menus, but you will also find other local specialities such as *guancia di manzo*, cheek of beef. You can eat more cheaply in the bars around Strada Farini, with snacks such as prosciutto stuffed into pastries and other local delights available for around €2 from the many bakeries. Picnic supplies can be bought at the Farmers' Market across the river on Via Imbriani (Sat 8am–noon).

★ **Ai Due Platani** Strada Budellungo 104/A, Località Coloreto, 7km from central Parma ⓣ 0521 645 626; map p.488. You can't go wrong with any dish at this fantastic trattoria, but the rosemary and duck *pappardelle* and beef braised in wine with crunchy polenta are standouts. Save room for the home-made vanilla ice cream, served in a huge tower that's wheeled round the tables at 10pm nightly. Booking essential. A full meal with wine will set you back €40–50. Mon noon–3pm, Wed–Sun noon–3pm & 7.30–10pm.

Al Corsaro Via Cavour 37 ⓣ 0521 235 402; map p.488. Good-value pizzeria filled with local regulars, where the bar is designed like a large boat. The service is very friendly and the pizzas (from €5) are delicious. Fri–Wed noon–2.45pm & 7pm–midnight.

Angiol d'Or Piazza Duomo ⓣ 0521 282 632; map p.488. Elegant restaurant that serves local specialities with a modern twist. Its fish dishes are tasty, and the spaghetti with prawns and courgettes is delicious (€12). The strong wine list is especially good on regional wines. Tues–Sun noon–3pm & 7–11pm.

★ **Ciacco** Strada Garibaldi 11 ⓣ 0521 234 063; map p.488. Jazzy artisan ice-cream parlour, named after a Dante character, where the range of seasonal ices includes some unusual flavours, such as the delicious pine nut, the curious liquorice sorbet or the "quasi cheesecake". Tues–Sun noon–11pm.

★ **Gallo d'Oro** Borgo della Salina 3 ⓣ 0521 208 846; map p.488. Atmospheric trattoria on a quiet side street off Strada Farini. Excellent filled pastas such as pumpkin ravioli (€8) are the main attraction, while the *secondi* include a tasty pig's cheek with apple sauce (€9). Daily noon–2.30pm & 7.30–11pm.

★Panino d'Artista Strada Farini 19–21 ⓣ0521 185 6150; map p.488. This narrow bar bustles with customers and serves a superb array of antipasti (a glass of wine plus a plateful of snacks €5). On the wine list look out for the Lamoretti wines from a family-run vineyard near Torrechiara. At their Verdi-themed restaurant next door, *La Cucina del Maestro*, the *risotto Verdi* is masterful (€12.50). Daily 8am–midnight.

★Tabarro Strada Farini 5/B ⓣ0521 200 223; map p.488. Cosy little wine bar with geometric-tiled floor, copper-topped bar and beer barrels as tables – a convivial spot for an *aperitivo*. The meat and cheese plates (from €7) are locally sourced. Tues–Thurs & Sun 5pm–midnight, Fri & Sat 5pm–1am.

ENTERTAINMENT

For nightlife in refined Parma, opera and theatre take precedence over clubs. In summer the city's entertainment options become more diverse – the piazzas host live jazz bands and during July and Aug locals flock to the garden behind Camera di San Paolo for a free season on Wed nights of old horror movies, dubbed into Italian (9.30pm; ⓦufficiocinema.it).

Teatro Due Next to the river at Viale Basetti 12/A ⓣ0521 230 242, ⓦteatrodue.org. The home of top theatre company L'Ensemble del Teatro Due, which performs between Oct and April.

Teatro Regio Via Garibaldi 16/A ⓣ0521 203 999, ⓦteatroregioparma.org. Theatre buffs should head to this imposing nineteenth-century opera house, closely associated with Verdi, who was born nearby in Busseto. The season runs from Jan to April, with a Verdi festival taking place in Oct.

Around Parma

The countryside **around Parma** is a strange mixture: some of the major roads follow bleak gorges, skirting the edge of blank rock walls for kilometres; others look as if they will lead precisely nowhere before emerging into meadows and orchards with rich farmland stretching into the distance.

Prime targets are any of the twenty **medieval castles** strung out across the foothills to the south, many built by the powerful Farnese dynasty. The website ⓦcastellidelducato.it has a useful map locating all the castles and can help you plan a tour. It's also worth buying a Castelli del Ducato card (€2), available from tourist offices or the castles themselves, that will give you a €1 reduction on admission fees and is valid for a year.

One of the finest castles is at **TORRECHIARA** (Mon–Sat 8.10am–1.50pm, Sun 10am–4pm; April–July open till 7.30pm on Sun; €4), about 18km south of Parma. It provides a superb vantage point over the surrounding area and also has frescoes by Bembo in its **Camera d'Oro**.

An hour's drive south is the hiking and skiing centre of **CORNIGLIO**. From here, buses squeeze themselves round the tight bends to the small villages of Monchio (16km), Trefiumi (20km) and Prato Spilla (23km from Corniglio), leaving you on the lower slopes of **Monte Malpasso** (1716m) – glistening with small lakes and tarns. Buses also run to **Lagdei** (14km), a starting point for further walks.

Castell'Arquato

Some 35km west of Parma is the beautiful **CASTELL'ARQUATO**, a nicely restored medieval town set on a hillside overlooking the Arda Valley. At the top of the town, Piazza del Municipio is lined with some stunning buildings. The thirteenth-century **Palazzo del Podestà** isn't open to the public, but you can visit the **Collegiata**, a magnificently preserved Romanesque monument with an eighth-century baptismal font in the right-hand **apse** (the entrance is round to the right; April–Sept 9am–12.30pm & 3–7pm; March–Oct 9.30am–noon & 2.30–5pm). The restored tower of the fourteenth-century **Rocca Viscontea** (March–June & 15 Aug–Oct Tues–Fri 10am–1pm & 3–6pm, Sat & Sun 10am–1pm & 3–6pm; July–14 Aug Mon–Fri open for tours only at 10.30am, 11.30am, 3.30pm, 4.30pm & 5.30pm, Sat & Sun 10am–1pm & 3–6pm; Nov–Feb Mon–Fri open for tours only at 10.30am, 2.30pm & 4pm; Sat & Sun 10am–1pm & 2–5pm; €5) offers amazing views of the surrounding countryside.

VERDI COUNTRY

About 30km northwest of Parma, the small village of **Le Roncole** marks the start of Verdi country. There are two **combined tickets for the Verdi sights**: the €10 ticket gets you into the Casa Barezzi, Verdi's birthplace and the Verdi Theatre, while the €11 ticket covers the Casa Barezzi and the Sant'Agata villa.

By the main road on Piazza Giovannino Guareschi – named after the author of the Don Camillo books who also lived here – you can visit the humble **house** where the composer was born (March & Oct 9.30am–12.10pm & 2.30–4.30pm; April–Sept Tues–Sun 9.30am–12.10pm & 2.30–5.10pm; Nov–Feb Sat & Sun 9.30am–12.10pm & 2.30–6.30pm; €5, or combined ticket). Some 5km up the road is **Busseto**, the childhood home of Verdi and the centre of the industry that has grown up around the composer. At one end of the arcaded main street the tourist office at Piazza Verdi 10 (Tues–Sun: April–Oct 9.30am–1pm & 3–6.30pm; Nov–March 9.30am–1pm & 2.30–5.30pm; T 0524 92 487, W bussetolive.com) can give you information about the sights and tickets for operas in the **Verdi Theatre** in the same building. Across the square, at Via Roma 119, the **Casa Barezzi** (March–Oct Tues–Sun 10am–12.30pm & 3–6.30pm; Nov Tues–Sun 10am–12.30pm & 2.30pm–5.30pm; Dec–Feb Sun 10am–12.30pm & 3–5.30pm; €5, or combined ticket; W museocasabarezzi.it) was the home of Antonio Barezzi, a wealthy merchant who spotted the young Verdi's talent and brought him in as a teacher for his daughter, Margherita, the future Mrs Verdi. It's now a museum to the maestro that contains the piano that Verdi played on and memorabilia such as the baton that Toscanini used to conduct his Verdi memorial concert in 1926. At the far end of Via Roma the town's newest Verdi museum is the **Verdi National Museum** (Jan & Feb Sat & Sun 10am–5.30pm; March–Dec Tues–Sat 10am–6.30pm, March closes 5.30pm; €9; W museogiuseppeverdi.it). Opened in 2009 in the Villa Pallavicino, the museum is little more than the glorified audioguide account of Verdi's life, hardly worth the entry fee. You'll need private transport to get to the last of the Verdi sights, the composer's **villa**, a couple of kilometres west of Busseto at **Sant'Agata di Villanova**, which contains a mock-up of the Milan hotel room where Verdi died: there's parking 300m along the road. It's open for 45min guided tours only (March–Oct Tues–Sun 9.30–11.45am & 2.30–6pm; Nov–Feb Sat & Sun 9.30–11.45am & 2–5pm, but closed much of Dec; €9, or combined ticket; W www.villaverdi.org).

8

ARRIVAL AND INFORMATION — CASTELL'ARQUATO

By bus/train From Parma take one of the frequent trains to Fiorenzuola on the main line to Piacenza (25min), from where six buses daily run to Castell'Arquato (22min), or take a taxi from Piazza Caduti.

Tourist office On the ground floor of the castellated medieval Palazzo del Podestà, at Piazza Municipio 1 (Tues–Sun 10am–1pm & 2–6pm; April & May also open Mon; T 0523 803 215, W castellarquatoturismo.it).

ACCOMMODATION AND EATING

Casa del Pane Piazza Europa 1 T 0523 806 084. For snacks and pastries you can't beat this thriving bakery/café which has outside tables with a view of the castle high above. Stop by in the evening for an *aperitivo* served with home-made snacks. Daily 7am–7.30pm.

Enoteca Comunale Piazza del Municipio T 0523 803 215. Housed on the ground floor of the Palazzo del Podestà, the bar offers light lunches and tasty cakes, and serves local wines such as Monterosso. You can sit outside and enjoy the view of the Rocca. Tues–Sun 10am–11pm.

La Rocca da Franco Piazza del Municipio T 0523 805 154, W larocca1964.it. This family-run restaurant has been serving typical Piacentine specialities in the town's main square since 1964. Try one of the tasting menus (€25–39) to sample local dishes such as *pisarei e fasò* (gnocchi with tomato and beans). Thurs–Tues 12.30–3pm & 7–10.30pm.

Leon d'Oro Piazza Europa 6 T 0523 803 222, W hotel-leondoro.com. A historic *palazzo* at the foot of the town, the friendly, family-run *Leon d'Oro* has comfortable, simply furnished doubles, some with balcony. €140

East along the Via Emilia from Bologna

East of Bologna, the Via Emilia passes through a clutch of small towns – some of them industrialized and mostly postwar, like Forlì, the unappealing administrative capital of the region, others, like **Faenza**, with medieval piazzas surrounded by towers and battlements.

Both started life as Roman way stations and were under the rule of the Papal States for much of their subsequent history. The **lowlands** to the north are farmed intensively, while on the southern side lie hilly vineyards and pastures, narrow gorges that lead up into the mountains and a couple of ski resorts around Monte Fumaiolo (1407m).

Faenza

As you travel east, cypress trees and umbrella pines, gentler hills and vineyards signal the fact that you're leaving Emilia and entering the Romagna – although strictly speaking there's no distinct boundary between the two regions. **FAENZA**, 50km from Bologna, gives its name to the faïence ware it has been producing for the last six hundred years. This style of decorated ceramic ware reached its zenith in the fifteenth and sixteenth centuries, and Faenza is still home to one of Italy's leading ceramics schools, teaching techniques of tin-glazing first introduced in the fourteenth century, as well as a major production centre, with small workshops down most of its side streets.

The town is worth a visit for the ivy-covered **Museo Internazionale delle Ceramiche** (April–Oct Tues–Sun 10am–7pm; Nov–March Tues–Fri 10am–1.30pm, Sat & Sun 10am–5.30pm; €8; ⓦmicfaenza.org) alone, one of the most important ceramic museums in the world. Housed at Viale Baccarini 19, this exhaustive collection includes early local work decorated in the characteristic blue and ochre, as well as pre-Columbian, Greco-Roman and Islamic pieces; although the highlight is perhaps the Sala Europa, featuring ceramic art by Picasso, Matisse and Chagall.

The rest of Faenza is an attractive town with buildings garnished with ceramic art and an appealing medieval centre formed by the long, crenellated **Palazzo del Podestà**, the **Piazza del Popolo** and the **Piazza della Libertà**, which is the scene of much activity on market days (Tues, Thurs and Sat). **Piazza Martiri della Libertà** – through an archway from Piazza del Popolo – is where you'll find more stalls selling cheese and other local foodstuffs. Each July the local *bambini* turn entrepreneur hosting their own colourful **children's market** on Thursday evenings in Piazza del Popolo (around 6.30–10.30pm), selling toys, books and bric-a-brac. Another good time to be in Faenza is for the **Palio del Niballo** (ⓦpaliodifaenza.it) on the fourth Sunday in June, when the five neighbourhoods of the town compete in a medieval jousting tournament.

8

ARRIVAL AND INFORMATION — FAENZA

By train Trains run from Faenza to Brisighella (every 1–2hr; 10–20min), Ravenna (every 2hr; 30–45min) and Rimini (every 30min; 40min–1hr 40min).

Tourist office Voltone Molinelli 2, on the west side of Piazza del Popolo (May–Sept Mon–Sat 9.30am–12.30pm & 3.30–6.30pm, Sun 9.30am–12.30pm; Oct–April Tues–Sat 9am–12.30pm & 3.30–5.30pm, closed Thurs afternoon; ⓣ0546 25 231, ⓦprolocofaenza.it).

ACCOMMODATION AND EATING

Osteria del Mercato Piazza Martiri della Libertà 13 ⓣ0546 680 797. This lively *osteria* on the northern side of the square (next to the terracotta relief) is located in several interlinking cellars and offers an excellent-value menu including authentic wood-fired pizzas (from €5.50) and a wide selection of pasta dishes and grilled meats. Mon–Fri noon–2.30pm & 7pm–midnight, Sat & Sun 7pm–midnight.

★ **Osteria La Baita** Via Naviglio 25/C ⓣ0546 21 584, ⓦlabaitaosteria.it. Developed from a small shop that sells local gastronomic specialities, *Osteria La Baita* is an inviting restaurant serving high-quality traditional dishes and an excellent selection of wines. The menu changes weekly and includes superb home-made pasta. *Primi* around €10, *secondi* €13–20. Tues–Sat 12.15am–2.15pm & 7.30–11pm.

★ **Treré** Via Naviglio 19 ⓣ0546 47 034, ⓦtrere.com. Charming agriturismo set amid vineyards 10km west of Faenza with large rooms and comfy apartments, an outdoor pool and lots of space for children to run around. The restaurant (Fri & Sat 7.30–10.30pm, Sun 12.30–2.30pm & 7.30–10.30pm) serves local specialities, using much of their own produce, including their award-winning wine. The buffet breakfast will keep you going all day. **€79**

Vittoria Corso Garibaldi 23 ⓣ0546 21 508, ⓦhotel-vittoria.com. The best hotel in town, the four-star *Vittoria* is a few blocks north of Piazza del Popolo and features nineteenth-century decor and a dining room with frescoed ceiling. A largely business clientele means it often has special offers at weekends. **€111**

Brisighella

South of Faenza, the medieval village of **BRISIGHELLA**, halfway up a hillside, is a food-lover's delight, famed both for its restaurants (visited by people from as far afield as Milan) and its **festivals of gastronomy** throughout the year, including the Sagra della Polenta (Oct), del Tartufo (truffle) and dell'Ulivo (both in Nov).

EATING — BRISIGHELLA

Cantina del Bonsignore Via Recuperati 4/A ⓣ 0546 81 889. This romantic restaurant with friendly staff offers an interesting, varied menu and a good wine list. The menu changes weekly and includes dishes such as *ravioli gratinati ai pinoli e profumo di tartufo* (baked ravioli with pine nuts and truffle; €8). Mon & Thurs–Sat 11.30am–2.30pm & 6.30–10.30pm, Tues & Wed 6.30–10.30pm, Sun 11.30am–10.30pm.

La Grotta Via Metelli 1 ⓣ 0546 81 488, ⓦ ristorantelagrotta.it. Set in an atmospheric underground cave, *La Grotta* serves creative Italian cuisine such as *strozzapreti con carciofi e piselli* (pasta with artichokes and peas; €10). There are also daily fixed-price menus based on both meat (€30) and fish (€35). Thurs–Tues noon–2.30pm & 7–11pm.

La Rocca Via delle Volte 10 ⓣ 0546 81 180, ⓦ albergolarocca.it. This hotel restaurant prides itself on using the freshest locally sourced ingredients for its menu of Romagnolo cuisine, offering home-made pasta dishes such as *tagliatelle all romagnola* (with sausage *ragù*, €7) and meat courses from €13. Tues–Sun noon–3pm & 7–10.30pm.

Ferrara

8

Thirty minutes' train ride north of Bologna, **FERRARA** was the residence of the Este dukes, an eccentric dynasty that ranked as a major political force throughout Renaissance times. The Este kept the main artists of the day in commissions and built a town which, despite a relatively small population, was – and still is – one of the most elegant urban creations of the period.

At the end of the sixteenth century, with no heir to inherit their lands, the Este were forced to hand over Ferrara to the papacy and leave for good. Life in the city effectively collapsed: eighteenth-century travellers found a ghost town of empty streets and clogged-up canals infested with mosquitoes. Since then Ferrara has picked itself up and dusted itself off, and is now a vibrant, provincial town that, with its grand squares, restored medieval palaces and portico-lined streets, looks a bit like a mini Bologna.

Ferrara's main sights are clustered together in an area that's easily explored on foot. The **castle** is the main focus, but several other palaces and museums offer reminders of the town's more glorious past. Ferrara's **market days** are Monday and Friday, with most activity taking place on Piazza Travaglio. On the first weekend of the month (except Aug) a large antiques market takes place between the Castello and the Duomo.

Castello Estense

Mon–Fri 9.30am–5.30pm, Sat & Sun 9.30am–6pm • €8 • ⓦ www.castelloestense.it

The bulky, moated **Castello Estense** dominates the centre of Ferrara, built in response to a late fourteenth-century uprising and generally held at the time to be a major feat of military engineering. Behind its impenetrable brick walls, the Este court thrived, supporting artists like Pisanello, Jacopo Bellini, Mantegna and the poets Ariosto and Tasso. You get a sense of the magnificence of the Este era in the *saletta* and Salone dei Giochi, or games rooms, decorated by Sebastiano Filippi with vigorous scenes of wrestling, discus throwing, ball tossing and chariot racing. You can also visit the castle dungeon and the poison room that served as a toxic pharmacy – both for the Este's political enemies.

Palazzo Municipale

Just south of the castle, the crenellated **Palazzo Municipale**, built in 1243 but much altered and restored since, holds statues of Niccolò III and son, Borso, on its facade –

though they're actually twentieth-century reproductions. Walk through the arch into the pretty, enclosed square of **Piazza del Municipio** for a view of the rest of the building.

The Duomo

Piazza della Cattedrale • Mon–Sat 7.30am–noon & 3.30–6.30pm, Sun 7.30am–12.30pm & 3.30–7pm • Free

Opposite the Palazzo Municipale, the **Duomo** is a mixture of Romanesque and Gothic styles and has a monumental facade, focused on a carved central portal that was begun in the mid-twelfth century and finished a century or so later. Much of the carving depicts the Last Judgement. Inside, the cathedral is much less intriguing than the exterior, with most of the best works having been moved to the nearby Museo della Cattedrale.

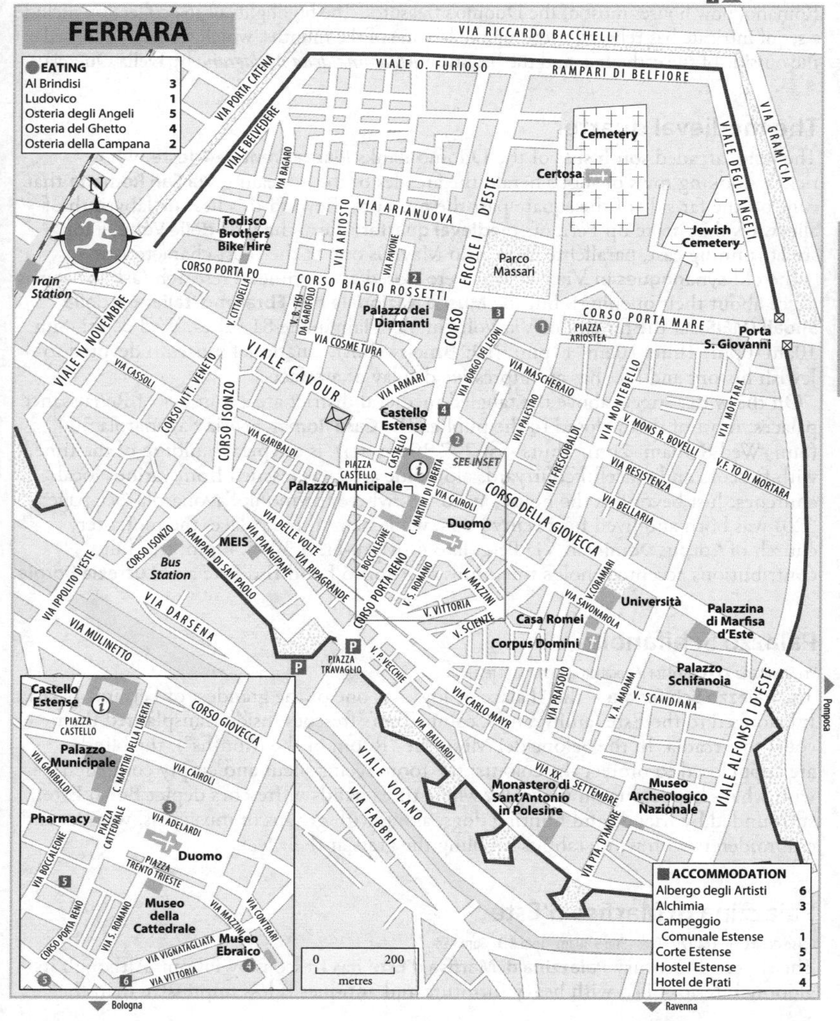

HIT THE STREETS – FERRARA BY BIKE

Ferrara is a *città della bicicletta*, where seemingly everyone makes the majority of their journeys by bike. Outside the centre, the roads are bordered by cycle lanes, while the centre is traffic-free although the streets are largely cobbled. You can **rent bicycles** at the station (to the left as you come out) from Pirani e Bagni (T 339 281 4002; closed Sat afternoon & Sun) or from Todisco Brothers at Corso Porta Po 102, a few minutes' walk from the station (T 346 139 4287, W noleggiobiciaferrara.it), for around €2/hr (€8/day). The tourist office has details of routes both within the city and out into the Po Delta Park: see W ferrarabike.com for details.

Museo della Cattedrale

Via San Romano • Tues–Sun 9.30am–1pm & 3–6pm • €6

Across the square from the cathedral, the **Museo della Cattedrale**, in the former church of San Romano, now houses most of the Duomo's treasures. The highlights of the collection include a set of intricate bas-reliefs illustrating the labours of the months, which formerly adorned the outside of the cathedral, and the beautiful *Madonna della Melagrana* by Della Quercia.

The medieval quarter

8

The long, arcaded south side of the Duomo flanks **Piazza Trento e Trieste**, whose rickety-looking rows of shops herald the arcades of the appealing **Via San Romano** that runs off the far side of the square past the museum. Beyond this lies the labyrinth of alleyways that make up Ferrara's **medieval quarter**; the arched **Via delle Volte**, a long street running east, parallel to Via Carlo Mayr, is one of the most characteristic.

The old **synagogues** in Via Mazzini were closed at the time of research (ask the tourist office about their opening), but the **Museo Nazionale dell'Ebraismo Italiano e della Shoah (MEIS),** at the far end of Via Volte in Via Piangipane 81 (Tues, Wed & Fri–Sun 10am–6pm, Thurs 10am–11pm; €10; W meisweb.it), a national museum devoted to Jewish history and life, has an impressive display of artefacts.

On the wider streets above the tangled medieval district are a number of Renaissance palaces, most of them closed to the public. The **Casa Romei**, at Via Savonarola 30 (Sun–Wed 8.30am–2pm, Thurs–Sat 2–7.30pm; €3), is a typical building of the time, with frescoes and graceful courtyards alongside artefacts rescued from various local churches. Just beyond is the house, at no. 19, where the monk Savonarola (see page 520) was born and lived for twenty years, while behind the palace, the monastery church of **Corpus Domini** at Via Pergolato 4 (Mon–Fri 3.30–5.30pm; free but contributions accepted) holds the tombs of Alfonso I and II d'Este and **Lucrezia Borgia**.

Palazzo Schifanoia

Via Scandiana 23 • Closed for restoration at the time of research

The **Palazzo Schifanoia** – the "Palace of Joy" – is one of the grandest of Ferrara's palaces. It belonged to the Este family, and Cosimo Tura's frescoes inside transplanted their court to Arcadia. In the Salone dei Mesi (the "Room of the Months"), the blinds are kept closed to protect the colours; the room seems silent and empty compared with what's happening on the walls, where three bands of frescoes depict Borso Este surrounded by friends and hunting dogs, along with groups of musicians, weavers and embroiderers with white rabbits nibbling the grass at their feet.

Palazzina di Marfisa d'Este

Corso della Giovecca 170 • Tues–Sun 9.30am–1pm & 3–6pm • €4

The sixteenth-century **Palazzina di Marfisa d'Este** has frescoes by Filippi. Although its gloomy interior filled with heavy furniture and antiques is less impressive than the

Schifanoia complex (see above), in summer the loggia and orange grove are a welcome refuge from the heat.

Museo Archeologico Nazionale

Via XX Settembre 124 • Tues–Sun 9.30am–5pm • €6

The **Museo Archeologico Nazionale** holds the city's well-organized archeological collections, most of which are finds from Spina, the Greco-Etruscan seaport and trading colony near Comacchio. Highlights include red-figure vases from the fifth century BC and many funerary objects from the ancient necropolis of Spina.

Monastero di Sant'Antonio in Polesine

Vicolo del Gambone • Mon–Fri 9.30–11.30am & 3.15–5pm, Sat 9.30–11.30am & 3.15–4.30pm • Donations expected • Bus #2 from the train station

In the southeast corner of the town is a gem of a place: the **Monastero di Sant'Antonio in Polesine**, with exquisite frescoes. Knock at the door of the convent and the nuns shepherd you into a chapel covered with works by the school of Giotto, including a rare *Flight from Egypt* in which Joseph carries Jesus on his shoulders.

North of the castle

There are some more impressive palaces **north of the castle**, on and around **Corso Ercole I d'Este** – named after Ercole I, who succeeded to the throne in 1441 after his father Niccolò III died, probably poisoned, and who promptly disposed of anyone likely to pose a threat. His reputation for coldness earned him nicknames such as "North Wind" and "Diamond" and his ambition led him to order the extension of the northern quarter of the city, the so-called "Herculean Addition", on such a grand scale that Ferrara doubled in size, with a boldly avant-garde planning system.

Palazzo dei Diamanti

Corso Ercole I d'Este 21 • Pinacoteca Nazionale Tues–Sun 10am–5.30pm • €6

The **Palazzo dei Diamanti**, a little way down the Corso on the left, named after the 8500 pink-and-white marble ashlars in the form of pyramids (or diamonds) that stud its facade, was at the heart of Ercole's town plan and is nowadays used for modern art exhibitions as well as being home to the **Pinacoteca Nazionale**, holding works from the Ferrara and Bologna schools, notably paintings by Dossi, Garofalo and Guercino, and a spirited *St Christopher* by "Il Bastianino" (Sebastiano Filippi).

ARRIVAL AND INFORMATION — FERRARA

By train Ferrara's train station is west of the city walls, a 30min walk along Viale Cavour to the centre of town, or take bus #1, #2, #9 or #3C (#2 is the most direct).

Destinations Bologna (every 30min; 30–50min); Ravenna (every 1–2hr; 1hr–1hr 30min); Rimini (4 daily; 1hr 30min–2hr 30min).

By bus The bus station lies just southwest of the main square, on Corso Isonzo, though buses from Bologna airport (8 daily; 1hr; €15; ⓦ ferrarabusandfly.com) pull in on Viale Cavour, by the Castello Estense, and the train station.

Destinations Comacchio (11 daily; 1hr 10min).

By car There is a large 24hr car park at the southern end of the city, outside the city walls on Via Darsena (€0.80/first hr, max €3.20).

Tourist office On the south side of the Castello courtyard, the tourist office (Mon–Sat 9am–6pm, Sun 9.30am–5.30pm; ⓣ 0532 209 370, ⓦ ferrarainfo.com) sells two-, three- or six-day tourist cards (€12/14/18), which give free access to the main sights of the city plus other discounts.

ACCOMMODATION

★ **Albergo degli Artisti** Via Vittoria 66 ⓣ 0532 761 038, ⓦ albergoartisti.it; map p.495. Friendly, unpretentious hotel in a modern block in the medieval quarter. Rooms are clean and quiet and are available with or without bathrooms;

FESTIVALS AND EVENTS IN FERRARA

One of the big annual events, held the last weekend in May, is the **Palio**, smaller than the famous Siena race, but still an exciting time to be here (ⓦpaliodiferrara.it). In August, the streets of the town ring to the annual **buskers' festival** (ⓦferrarabuskers.com), with musical offerings ranging from African drums to Dixieland bands, while the following month the skies are filled with giant blobs of colour as the **Ferrara Balloon Festival** (ⓦferrarafestival.it), one of the largest in Europe, gets under way.

one has a private kitchen, and there is also a small kitchen for general use. No breakfast, no credit cards. **€50**

Alchimia Via Borgo dei Leoni 122 ⓣ0532 186 4656, ⓦalchimiaferrara.it; map p.495. This renovated B&B offers sleek contemporary comfort in a fifteenth-century *palazzo*, a generous breakfast in the courtyard room and courteous staff. The hotel has a changing display of art, off-street parking and free bicycle rental. **€130**

Corte Estense Via Correggiari 4/A ⓣ0532 242 168, ⓦcorteestense.it; map p.495. Inviting and comfortable with a fantastic position in the heart of the town, this historic *palazzo* is a grand option with its oriental carpets, elegant courtyard and spacious rooms. **€80**

8

Hostel Estense Corso Biagio Rossetti 24 ⓣ0532 201 158, ⓦostelloestense.com; map p.495. Hostel situated northwest of the centre with huge, bright, spotlessly clean rooms with grand, wooden ceiling beams and a calm but friendly atmosphere; internet and wi-fi are available; always open. Breakfast included. Dorms **€20**, doubles **€45**

★ **Hotel de Prati** Via Padiglioni 5 ⓣ0532 241 905, ⓦhoteldeprati.com; map p.495. Very friendly and helpful family-run establishment dotted with interesting modern paintings by local artists; it has eight comfortable rooms with antique furniture, just a few minutes on foot from the town centre. **€85**

CAMPING

Campeggio Comunale Estense Via Gramicia 76 ⓣ0532 752 396, ⓦcampeggioestense.it; take bus #1 or #5 from the train station to Piazzale San Giovanni by the walls, from where it's a 10min walk north; map p.495. Campsite for tents and caravans on the northeast edge of town with helpful staff and a tranquil, relaxing atmosphere. Closed Feb. Two people in small pitch **€20.50**

EATING

Ferrara has a good range of restaurants and trattorias with prices to suit most pockets, plus a few bars in which to while away the evening with the locals. For self-caterers, Marchetti, on Via Cortevecchia 35, just south of the Palazzo Municipale (9am–1.30pm & 4.30–7.30pm; closed Thurs & Sun afternoon), is a great traditional delicatessen with a fine line in salamis, hams, seafood dishes and pastas.

Al Brindisi Via degli Adelardi 11 ⓣ0532 473 744, ⓦalbrindisi.net; map p.495. The unprepossessing exterior conceals Ferrara's oldest (at least fifteenth-century) *osteria*, once frequented by the likes of Cellini and Titian. The food is good and reasonably priced, with set menus ranging from €15 for the weekday lunch menu up to €50. Tues–Sun 11am–midnight; closed end Jan.

Ludovico Piazza Ariostea 7 ⓣ345 439 9981; map p.495. Welcoming café-bar set beneath arcades overlooking a pretty, grassy park (site of the city's Palio) and always filled with gossiping locals, particularly for the early evening *aperitivo*. Platters of cold cuts and cheeses (€4–12) and jumbo panini (€5) take their place alongside a large drinks menu. Tues–Thurs 10am–1am, Fri & Sat 10am–2am, Sun 10am–11pm.

Osteria degli Angeli Via delle Volte 4 ⓣ0532 764 376; map p.495. A bustling, welcoming place, with lots of different wines and a changing daily menu of good local dishes, with particular focus on pumpkin (*zucca*). *Primi* €11–15, *secondi* €14–19. Thurs–Tues noon–2.30pm & 7–10.30pm.

★ **Osteria del Ghetto** Via della Vittoria 26 ⓣ0532 764 936, ⓦosteriadelghetto.it; map p.495. On a Ghetto backstreet, running off the bustling Via Mazzini, this serves up all manner of fish specialities, such as *spaghetti marinara* (€13), as well as pork, beef or lamb for €13–18. Tues–Sun noon–2.30pm & 7.30–10.30pm.

★ **Osteria della Campana** Via Borgo dei Leoni 26 ⓣ0532 241 256; map p.495. Romantic, spacious spot down a narrow alleyway with an interesting menu of traditional specialities, local cheeses and home-made desserts. Highlights include the typical Ferrarese pasta dish with a new twist – *cappellacci con zucca* in a citrus sauce (€9). Tues–Sun 12.30–2.30pm & 7.30–10.30pm.

The Po Delta

East of Ferrara lies the **Po Delta**, an expanse of marshland and lagoons where the River Po splits into several channels, trickling to the sea, and small fingers of land poke out

into the Adriatic. Etruscan traders set up the port of Spina here between the fourth and third centuries BC, when the sea covered much of the land from Comacchio to Ravenna. Partly owing to drainage schemes, the briny waters have since retreated by 12km, and the area becomes a bit less marshy each year – an advantage for local farmers but a threat to the many varieties of sea and shore **birds** that inhabit the area. The two main lagoons of **Valli di Comacchio** and **Valle Bertuzzi** together form a major part of the Parco del Delta del Po (ⓦparcodeltapo.it), which with the surrounding wetlands now constitute one of Europe's most highly regarded birdwatching areas, providing a habitat for nesting and migrating birds, including heron, egret, curlew, avocet and tern.

Comacchio

The region's main centre, **COMACCHIO** is a small fishing town intersected by a network of canals, also accessible by boat tour, with a famous local attraction in its triple-bridge or **Trepponti**, built in 1634, which crosses three of the canals. Comacchio is an eel port and a good time to visit is in October when the Festival of the Eel sees wriggling masses of the creatures fished out of the canals on their way to the Sargasso Sea. Eel (*anguilla*) unsurprisingly takes centre stage in many local restaurants with other regional dishes like fish risotto and *fritto misto* particularly recommended.

ARRIVAL AND INFORMATION — COMACCHIO

By bus There is no train station in Comacchio so the only way to arrive is by bus from either Ferrara (10 daily; 1hr 10min) or Ravenna (6 daily; 1hr 10min).

Tourist office Via Agatopisto 3 (April–June & Sept–Oct Mon–Fri 9.30am–1pm & 3–6.30pm, Sat & Sun 9.30am–6.30pm; July & Aug daily 9.30am–6.30pm; Nov–March Tues–Sat 9.30am–1pm & 2.30–6pm, Sun 10am–5pm; ⓣ0533 314 154, ⓦturismocomacchio.it).

8

EATING

La Barcaccia Piazza XX Settembre 41 ⓣ0533 311 081. Situated opposite Comacchio's cathedral, *La Barcaccia* serves typical cuisine of the lagoon area with some particular dishes such as *ravioli di branzino e olive* (ravioli with sea bass and olives; €12) as well as fresh grilled and fried fish from €13. Tues–Sun 12.30–2.30pm & 7.15–10.30pm.

Vasco e Giulia Via Muratori 21 ⓣ0533 81 252. Unassuming trattoria run by a mother and two daughters and specializing in fish dishes. Aside from the local eel, which is served in different ways including the *risotto di anguilla* (€9.50), there's also a delicious *fritto misto di pesce* (mixed fried fish; €12). Tues–Sat 12.30–2.30pm & 7–10.30pm; closed Wed eve.

Ravenna and around

The main reason to visit **RAVENNA**, a few kilometres inland of the Adriatic coast, is simple – it holds a set of **mosaics** generally acknowledged to be the crowning achievement of Byzantine art. No fewer than eight of Ravenna's buildings have been designated UNESCO World Heritage sites. They date from a strange interlude in

BOAT TRIPS AROUND THE PO DELTA

The most evocative way of seeing the delta is by **boat**. Every spring free birdwatching trips are organized by the tourist office in Comacchio as part of the annual International Po Delta Birdwatching Fair (ⓦpodeltabirdfair.it). And between April and October voluntary groups run free boat tours on a typical marshland boat called a *batana* from its mooring at the fish market of Trepponti in Comacchio. Boat trips also set off from the harbour of Stazione Foce, south of Comacchio (March Sat & Sun 11am & 3pm; April to mid-June & mid-Sept to Oct daily11am & 3pm, mid-June to mid-Sept daily 11am & 6pm; ⓣ340 253 4267, ⓦvallidicomacchio.info; €12), accessible by car only; follow signs for "Museo delle Valli". More information is available at the tourist office in Comacchio (see page 499) or see ⓦpodeltatourism.it.

the city's history during the late Roman–early Byzantine period when this otherwise unremarkable provincial centre briefly became one of the most important cities in all of Europe (see below).

Tourism seems almost incidental and for a city that has such historic monuments, the centre feels surprisingly modern – a combination of Mussolini's building programme and Allied bombing that levelled much of the city during World War II. It's a pleasant enough place to spend a couple of days and, though it has some excellent bars and restaurants, it's the churches and mosaics that will monopolize your time. Nightlife is sparse, but a number of small **coastal resorts**, known as the lido towns, a dozen or so kilometres away provide some excitement in summer. And if you're looking for thrills and spills, the nearby **Mirabilandia** (ⓦmirabilandia.it), a Disneyesque theme park, brings in the crowds during summer.

Brief history

When Ravenna became capital of the **Western Roman Empire** sixteen hundred years ago, it was more by quirk of fate than design. The Emperor Honorius, alarmed by armies invading from the north, moved his court from Milan to this obscure town on the Romagna coast around 402; it was easy to defend, surrounded by marshland, and was situated close to the port of Classe – at the time the biggest Roman naval base on the Adriatic. After enjoying a period of great monumental adornment as chief city of the empire, Ravenna was conquered by the Goths in 476. However, the new conquerors were also Christians and continued to embellish the city lavishly,

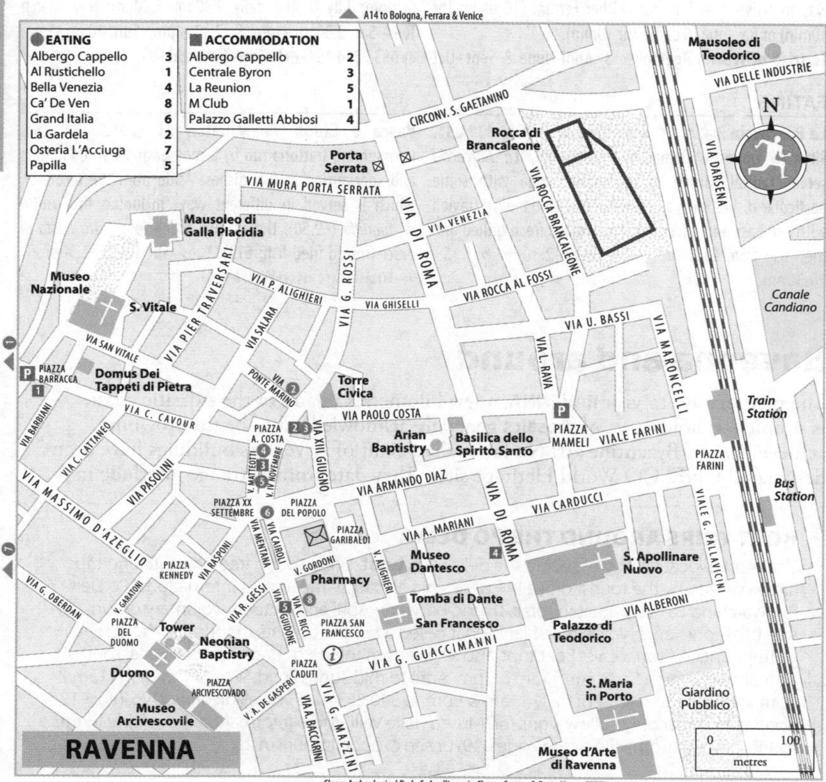

RAVENNA'S MUSEUM CARDS

Ravenna has three **museum cards**: a combined ticket covers the basilicas of San Vitale and Sant'Apollinare Nuovo, the Neonian Baptistry, the Mausoleo di Galla Placidia and the Museo Arcivescovile – all the church-controlled sites. The card is valid for seven days, costs €9.50 (March to mid-June there is an extra fee of €2 to enter the Mausoleo) and can be purchased from any participating site. Note that tickets for these sites cannot be purchased individually. For the state sites you can get a joint ticket for the Museo Nazionale, the Basilica di Sant'Apollinare in Classe and the Mausoleo di Teodorico (€10); this can be purchased at the sites. There is also a combined ticket for the Domus dei Tappeti di Pietra plus two smaller mosaic displays (€7).

particularly the Ostrogoth Theodoric, making it one of the most sought-after towns in the Mediterranean. In the mid-sixth century Byzantine forces annexed the city to the Eastern Empire and made it into an exarchate (province), under the rule of Constantinople. The Byzantine rulers were responsible for Ravenna's most glorious era, keen to outdo rival cities with magnificent palaces, churches and art. By the end of the eighth century, however, the glory years had passed. The city was captured by the Lombards, after which the Adriatic shoreline receded – an 11km-long canal now links Ravenna's port to the sea – and Ravenna sank slowly back into obscurity.

Piazza del Popolo and around

The centre of Ravenna is the **Piazza del Popolo**, an elegant open space, arcaded on two sides, laid out by the Venetians in the fifteenth century. Two columns dominate the western end of the square, bearing the figures of St Apollinaris, the patron saint of the city, and St Vitalis.

Tomba di Dante

Via Dante Alighieri • Mon–Fri 10am–6pm, Sat & Sun 10am–7pm • Free

A couple of blocks south of Piazza del Popolo, across Piazza Garibaldi, the **Tomba di Dante** is a small Neoclassical building which was put up in the eighteenth century to enclose the tomb of Dante. The poet had been chased out of Florence by the time he arrived in Ravenna, and he was sheltered here by the Da Polenta family – then in control of the city – while he finished his *Divine Comedy*.

San Francesco and the Museo Dantesco

Via Dante Alighieri 9 • **Church** Daily 7am–noon & 3–7pm • Free • **Museum** Tues–Sun 10am–6pm • €3

Dante died in 1321 and was laid to rest in the church of **San Francesco**, a much-restored building dating back to the fourth century. File down the stairs towards the tenth-century waterlogged crypt complete with swimming goldfish and remnants of a mosaic floor. The **Museo Dantesco** is off San Francesco's cloister and contains memorabilia of the poet and his final resting place.

The Duomo

Piazza del Duomo • Mon–Fri 8.30am–noon & 3–6pm, Sat & Sun 8.30am–noon & 3–7pm • Free

A couple of minutes' walk west of San Francesco, a group of buildings around **Piazza del Duomo** shelters the **Duomo** itself, with its cylindrical – and slightly tipsy – tower. Originally a fifth-century building, it was completely destroyed by an earthquake in 1733 and rebuilt in unexceptional style soon after.

Museo Arcivescovile

Piazza Arcivescovile • Daily: March–Oct 9am–7pm; Nov–Feb 10am–5pm • Museum card (see page 501)

The interesting **Museo Arcivescovile**, in the Bishop's Palace behind the Duomo, displays fragments of mosaics from around the city. However, the main attraction here is the palace's sixth-century Oratorio Sant'Andrea, which is adorned with mosaics of birds in a meadow above a Christ dressed in the armour, cloak and gilded leather skirt of a Roman centurion.

Neonian Baptistry

Piazza del Duomo • Daily: March–Oct 9am–7pm; Nov–Feb 10am–5pm • Museum card

The **Neonian Baptistry**, on the same side of the Duomo as the Museo Arcivescovile, by the belltower, is a conversion from a Roman bathhouse. The original floor level has sunk into the marshy ground, and the remains of the previous building are now 3m below. The choice of building was a logical one as baptisms involved total immersion in those days.

Basilica di Sant'Apollinare Nuovo and around

Via di Roma • Daily: March–Oct 9am–7pm; Nov–Feb 10am–5pm • Museum card

Via di Roma, lined with bland, official-looking palaces, cuts right through the modern centre of Ravenna and carries much of its traffic. Halfway up stands the **Basilica di Sant'Apollinare Nuovo**. Built by Theodoric in the sixth century, it contains some of Ravenna's most impressive mosaics, running the length of both sides of the nave. Each shows a line of martyrs – one side male, the other female – processing through avenues of date palms and bearing gifts for Christ and the Virgin enthroned. As a Goth, Theodoric belonged to the Arian branch of Christianity which didn't accept the absolute divinity of Christ. Theodoric dedicated the church to Jesus, but when the Byzantines took over they removed many of the mosaic figures that had been placed here under his reign and the church was rededicated to St Martin, who was known for his anti-heretic campaigns and is shown at the head of the line of male devotees. In the ninth century, it was rededicated yet again to St Apollinaris.

Five minutes' walk away up Via di Roma, next door to the Basilica dello Spirito Santo, is the **Arian Baptistry** (daily 8.30am–7.30pm, Nov–March closes at 4.30pm; €1), also built by Theodoric, with a fine mosaic ceiling showing the twelve Apostles and the baptism of Christ.

San Vitale

Via Fiandrini Benedetto • Daily: March–Oct 9am–7pm; Nov–Feb 10am–5pm • Museum card

Ravenna's main attractions lie in the area ten minutes' walk northwest of the city centre, around the **Basilica di San Vitale**, which holds the finest of the mosaics and is now gathered together into one big complex, including the mausoleum of Galla Placidia and the National Museum.

San Vitale, which was begun in 525 under Theodoric and finished in 548 under the Byzantine ruler Justinian, remains unique for an Italian building. Created to an Eastern-inspired arrangement of void and solid and dark and light, the design was the basis for the great church of Hagia Sofia in Istanbul, built fifteen years later.

The series of **mosaics** in the basilica starts with Old Testament scenes spread across the semicircular lunettes of the choir; the triumphal arch shows Christ, the Apostles and sons of St Vitalis. Further in, on the semi-dome of the apse, a beardless Christ stands between two angels, presenting a model of the church to St Vitalis and Bishop Ecclesius. Of the mosaics on the side walls of the apse, the two processional panels are the best surviving portraits of the Emperor Justinian and his wife Theodora – he's on the left and she's on the right – and a rich example of Byzantine mosaic technique. The minute glass *tesserae* are laid in sections, alternate rows set at slightly different angles to vary the reflection of light and give an impression of depth.

There were definite rules about who appeared where in mosaics – the higher up and further to the east, the more important or holy the subject. Colour is used emblematically, too, with gold backgrounds denoting either holiness or high status.

Mausoleo di Galla Placidia

Via Fiandrini Benedetto • Daily: March–Oct 9am–7pm; Nov–Feb 10am–5pm • Museum card; note that March to mid-June there is an extra €2 fee to enter the Mausoleo

Across the grass from the basilica is the tiny **Mausoleo di Galla Placidia** named after the half-sister of Honorius. The emperor's frequent absences left Galla in charge of the city and she was responsible for much of the grandeur of Ravenna's early days. Despite the name and the three sarcophagi inside, it's unlikely that the building ever held her bones. Galla Placidia was taken hostage when the Goths sacked Rome, and caused a scandal by marrying one of her kidnappers, Ataulf. She went into battle with him as his army forged south, and later they reigned jointly over the Gothic kingdom. When Ataulf was assassinated the Romans took her back for a ransom of corn, after which she was obliged to marry a Roman general, Constantius. Their son formally became the Emperor Valentinian III at the age of 6, and as his regent, Galla Placidia assumed control of the Western Empire.

Inside the *mausoleo*, filtered through thin alabaster windows, the light falls on mosaics that glow with a deep blue lustre, most in an earlier style than those of San Vitale, full of Roman and naturalistic motifs.

Museo Nazionale

Via Fiandrini Benedetto • Tues–Sun 8.30am–7.30pm • €6

Adjacent to San Vitale on the southern side, housed in the former cloisters of the church, the **Museo Nazionale** contains various items, such as fifteenth-century icons, early Byzantine glass and embroidery from Florence. Among the most eye-catching exhibits is a sixth-century statue of Hercules capturing a stag, possibly a copy of a Greek original.

Domus dei Tappeti di Pietra

Via Gianbattista Barbiani • March–Sept 10am–6.30pm; Oct to early Jan Mon–Fri 10am–5pm, Sat & Sun 10am–6pm • €4

Just a couple of hundred metres south of San Vitale, and accessed through the small church of Santa Eufemia, is one of the city's more recently discovered Byzantine treasures. Uncovered in the early 1990s, the **Domus dei Tappeti di Pietra**, which translates as the "House of Stone Carpets", is the remains of a palace from the late Roman–early Byzantine period. It comprises fourteen rooms, each adorned with intricately crafted floor and wall mosaics, the most striking of which shows figures representing the Four Seasons dancing hand in hand while another figure provides a musical accompaniment on a pan-flute.

Mausoleo di Teodorico

Via delle Industrie 14 • Daily 8.30am–7pm; Oct–March closes at 5.30pm • €4 or Museum Card

Still within Ravenna, but a bit of a hike north of the train station, lies one more early sixth-century monument that's worth visiting: the **Mausoleo di Teodorico**. This ten-sided curiosity is unique in Western architecture owing much to Syrian models of its day, and constructed of Istrian limestone. The 300-tonne cupola is a single, if cracked, chunk and no one knows how it was manoeuvred into place. Inside the decagonal second storey sits an ancient porphyry bathtub, pressed into use as the royal sarcophagus.

ARRIVAL AND DEPARTURE — RAVENNA

By train From the train station on Piazza Farini in the east of town, it's a 5min walk along Viale Farini and Via Armando Diaz to Ravenna's central square, Piazza del Popolo.

Destinations Bologna (hourly; 1hr–1hr 20min); Ferrara (hourly; 1hr 15min); Rimini (hourly; 50min–1hr).

By bus The bus station is across the tracks behind the train station, on Piazzale Aldo Moro.

Destinations Classe (every 30min; 15min); Marina di Ravenna (every 30min; 25min).

By car Parking is available – for around €1.20/hr – on various squares around the centre, including Piazza Barracca and Piazza Mameli.

INFORMATION AND GETTING AROUND

Tourist offices Piazza San Francesco 1 (Mon–Sat 8.30am–7pm, Sun 9.30am–5.30pm; ⊕0544 35 755, ⊕turismo.ravenna.it). The Classe tourist office is by the church at via Romea Sud 226 (Sat & Sun 10am–4pm; ⊕0544 473 661).

Bike rental With much of its centre pedestrianized, Ravenna is best explored by foot or on two wheels. Bikes can be rented from the Cooperativa San Vitale (Mon–Fri 7am–7pm; ⊕0544 37 031), the green building next to the train station, for €1.50/hr or €12/day; the office also gives out maps and holds left luggage.

ACCOMMODATION

8

Albergo Cappello Via IV Novembre 41 ⊕0544 219 813, ⊕albergocappello.it; map p.500. Old *palazzo* right in the heart of town that's been turned into an extremely stylish small hotel with just seven chic rooms each decorated in its own colour and style. It also has an excellent restaurant. **€129**

Centrale Byron Via IV Novembre 14 ⊕0544 212 225, ⊕hotelsravenna.it/Byron; map p.500. This great-value hotel offers comfortable, smart furnishings throughout and is located right in the heart of town. There's a friendly, family atmosphere and each of the well-appointed rooms has satellite TV and a/c in summer. **€77**

La Reunion Via Corrado Ricci 29 ⊕0544 212 949, ⊕lareunion.it; map p.500. Opposite the *Ca' De Ven* restaurant, *La Reunion* offers a range of bright mini-apartments for up to six people, each well equipped and with its own kitchen. Breakfast included. Bikes rented out. **€132**

M Club Piazza Francesco Baracca 26 ⊕333 955 6466, ⊕m-club.it; map p.500. A stylish B&B just a few minutes from San Vitale with six beautifully decorated rooms each with wood-beamed ceilings and carefully selected furnishings. Bike rental is included in the price. Closed end Nov to early Dec. **€102**

Palazzo Galletti Abbiosi Via di Roma 140 ⊕0544 31 313, ⊕palazzogallettiabbiosi.it; map p.500. Welcoming eighteenth-century palace, smartly refurbished with comfortable a/c singles and doubles, plus some very large rooms that sleep 4 or 5. Three of the rooms have fine painted ceilings and antique terracotta floors. Amenities include free bike hire, a gym, a garden and parking. **€123**

CAMPING

Adriano Camping Village Via dei Campeggi 7 ⊕0544 437 230, ⊕campingadriano.com; buses to Lidi di Comacchio or Lido Spina from outside Ravenna train station leaves 1.5km from the site; call the campsite to ask for a member of staff to pick you up. One of many campsites in the area, this one is in the coastal resort of Punta Marina Terme, 9km away, allowing easy access to the beach. There are a range of amenities and activities including a swimming pool, bike rental, entertainments and games, plus bungalows and mobile homes for rent. Open mid-April to mid-Sept. Pitches **€17**

EATING

Albergo Cappello Via IV Novembre 41 ⊕0544 240 128, ⊕albergocappello.it; map p.500. The hotel's elegant restaurant and wine bar are both excellent and offer a delicious and creative menu of home-made pasta and local meats and seafood. Try the ravioli al formaggio di fossa saltati con il burro, salvia e pinoli tostati (ravioli with butter, sage and toasted pine nuts; €13). Daily 12.30–2.30pm & 7–10.30pm.

Al Rustichello Via Maggiore 21 ⊕0544 36 043; map p.500. Consistently popular place a short walk from Piazza Baracca where the excitable owner tells you the menu (in English too) and serves food that an Italian grandmother would be proud of – the *cappelletti* with asparagus, *prosciutto* and cream is recommended (€10). Booking advised. Mon–Fri noon–2.15pm & 7.30–10.15pm.

Bella Venezia Via IV Novembre 16 ⊕0544 21 274, ⊕bellavenezia.it; map p.500. Come here for simple meals, expertly prepared – handmade pumpkin *cappelletti* (€8), *asparagi alla Bismarck* (asparagus topped with Parmesan and an egg), etc. Eat formally inside amid the starched tablecloths or informally outside watching the city pass by. Mon–Sat noon–3pm & 7–11pm.

★ **Ca' De Ven** Via C. Ricci 24 ⊕0544 30 163, ⊕cadeven.it; map p.500. Stunning wood-panelled *enoteca* with painted ceilings that has expanded into the airy glass-covered courtyard next door. It offers a simple menu of a few pizza and pasta dishes, as well as a selection of *piadine* for around €4.50. There's also a huge range of vintages to sample by the glass from €1.50 upwards. Tues–Sun 10am–

RAVENNA'S FESTIVALS

The **Ravenna Festival** in June and July attracts big names in the classical music world (Ⓦ ravennafestival.org) with performances taking place in various venues across town including churches, gardens and theatres, while the venerable **Jazz Festival** in May also draws international stars (Ⓦ ravennajazz.org). In October, local wines are in the spotlight at **Giovinbacco** (Ⓦ giovinbacco.it), and every two years the city also hosts **RavennaMosaico,** which celebrates contemporary mosaics and visual arts with exhibitions, workshops and concerts (Ⓦ ravennamosaico.it).

2.30pm & 6–10.30pm.

Grand Italia Piazza del Popolo 9/10 Ⓣ 393 903 3375, Ⓦ granditaliaravenna.business.site; map p.500. This extensive lounge, bar and restaurant offers everything from *gelato* sundaes to full meals, though it's best for a casual drink and a spot of people-watching on the piazza. Wine costs around €5 a glass, €8 with *aperitivi* (6–9pm). Daily 7am–midnight.

La Gardela Via Ponte Marino 3 Ⓣ 0544 217 147, Ⓦ ristorantelagardela.com; map p.500. Smart spot with a view of the Torre Civica (Ravenna's own leaning tower) and a varied menu of fish dishes and home-made pasta; classic *primi* are around €6–7, *secondi* €8–16, and there's a four-course Romagnolo tasting menu for €25. Fri–Wed noon–2.30pm & 7–10pm.

Osteria L'Acciuga Via Francesco Baracca 74 Ⓣ 0544 212 713; map p.500. With the decor based on the interior of a submarine, it's no surprise that this lively restaurant sells fish. The menu changes daily depending on the catch, ensuring quality and freshness; the five-course tasting menu (€42) is a good way to try a variety of dishes. Tues–Sat 12.30–2.30pm & 7.30pm–10.30pm; Sun 12.30–2.30pm.

Papilla Via IV Novembre 8 Ⓣ 0544 213 433; map p.500. Delicious ice creams in this smart *gelateria*, where the flavours include seasonal fruits and different combinations of nuts and chocolate. For a special treat they pour a little chocolate into the bottom of the cone. Daily 10am–midnight.

8

The Classe archeological park

Via Marabina 7 • July & Aug daily 5–10pm; Sept & Oct Sat & Sun 10am–6pm; call for the latest opening times • €5; 1hr guided tours €40 • Ⓣ 0544 478 100, Ⓦ parcoarcheologicodiclasse.it • Bus #4 or #176 from Ravenna's station (every 30min; 15min)

About 4km south of Ravenna, the ruins of the ancient Roman port of **Classe** were heavily looted for stone, but its remains are now on display. A new visitor centre gives an idea of how the site would have looked with the aid of multimedia displays; to view the site itself, take a tour with a member of the archeological team, as without a guide it's hard to make sense of the scattered remains. Tours cover the area's origins, its development into a military port and then a major commercial hub, contributing to Ravenna's evolution into the capital of the western Roman Empire. New structures, including the Basilica di San Severo, are still being excavated.

Sant'Apollinare di Classe

Via Romea Sud, 300m from the port of Classe • Mon–Sat 8.30am–7.30pm, Sun 1–7.30pm • €5 or Museum card; free first Sun of the month • Bus #4 or #44 from Ravenna's station (every 30min; 15min); for the return journey catch the bus from the main road

One building that survived the looting is the church of **Sant'Apollinare in Classe**, spared because it was the burial place of Ravenna's patron saint. Its fine mosaics include a marvellous allegorical depiction of the Transfiguration in the apse, with Christ represented by a large cross in a star-spangled universe.

Ravenna's seaside resorts

Buses leave from outside Ravenna's station: #60 or #70 to Marina di Ravenna, #70, #75, #80 or #85 for Punta Marina and #90 to Porto Corsini

There's easy access by bus through Ravenna's heavy industry belt to the nine lido towns nearby that total 35km of coast. **Marina di Ravenna** and **Punta Marina** are both crowded, lively places; for something quieter head north to the beaches at **Porto Corsini**, **Casalborsetti** and **Marina Romea**. Just before Porto Corsini, you pass the **Capanno**

Garibaldi, a reconstruction of the hut in which Garibaldi hid on his epic 800km march from Rome after the fall of the short-lived Roman republic in 1849. Garibaldi's life-long partner Anita, who often fought alongside him, died on the way and he was unable to stop for long enough to bury her.

Rimini

RIMINI, Italy's largest and most varied beach resort, has long been a traditional summer magnet for families and many Italians return year after year. But there is also an upmarket side to the town, with its boutique hotels, high-end restaurants and chichi clubs. And with that comes a less savoury aspect: Rimini is known throughout Italy for its fast living and chancy nightlife, and there's a thriving hetero- and transsexual prostitution scene alongside the town's more wholesome attractions.

The resort is best avoided in August, unless you have a penchant for teeming crowds. Out of season, it's pleasant enough, though bear in mind that many hotels, restaurants and shops are closed and the atmosphere along the seafront is almost eerily quiet.

Given that so much of Rimini was destroyed in the last war, it's surprising to find that the town has a much-ignored **old centre** that is worth at least a morning of your time. Located inland, past the station, it is an often unseen part of Rimini, made up of old stone buildings clustered around the beautiful twin squares of Piazza Tre Martiri and Piazza Cavour, and bordered by the port-canal and town ramparts. Unlike the touristy side of town, this quiet, refined community stays in business throughout the winter, albeit in a low-key, backwater sort of way. But it's the beach, the crowds and the wild nights that you really come for: Rimini is still the country's best place to party.

The beach

The main attraction of Rimini is the long, clean, sandy **beach** which is lined by largely indistinguishable three- to five-star hotels, all of which have parcelled up their own particular stretches of beach and equipped them with beach bars, volleyball courts, watersports outfitters and other such holiday essentials. Running behind the front is Viale Amerigo Vespucci, a brash drag crammed with souvenir shops, restaurants and video arcades.

Arco d'Augusto and Ponte di Tiberio

Founded in 286 BC as Ariminum, Rimini was once an important Roman colony. On the southern and northern edges of the old centre respectively sit two monuments from the first century AD, the **Arco d'Augusto** and **Ponte di Tiberio**. The patched-up Arco was built at the point where Via Emilia joined Via Flaminia, which came up from Rome. Rimini's other Roman remains consist of the **Anfiteatro**, of which there are sparse foundations off Via Roma.

Piazza Tre Martiri and Piazza Cavour

Just south of the well-preserved Ponte di Tiberio, **Piazza Cavour** and **Piazza Tre Martiri**, which largely follows the layout of the original Roman square, are the two main squares. Piazza Cavour boasts a statue of Pope Paul V and the Gothic **Palazzo del Podestà**; the square was rebuilt in the 1920s, and purists argue that it was ruined, although the fishtail battlements are still impressive enough. Opposite, beyond the sixteenth-century fountain incorporating Roman reliefs, the beautiful eighteenth-century **fish market** often shades antiques stalls worth a browse. A couple of blocks

north of Piazza Cavour, at Corso d'Augusto 162, stands the **Cinema Fulgor**, where, as a boy, the director **Federico Fellini** watched his first film. There have long been plans to open a museum here, dedicated to Rimini's most famous son; check at the tourist office for the latest information.

Museo della Città

Via L. Tonini 1 • May–Aug Tues & Wed 10am–1pm & 4.30–7.30pm, Thurs–Sun 10am–7.30pm; July & Aug also open Wed 9–11pm; Sept–April Tues–Sat 9.30am–1pm & 4–7pm, Sun 10am–7pm • €7, free on Wed and first Sun of the month

The **Museo della Città** has a collection of art dating from the fourteenth to the nineteenth centuries, the highlight of which is Giovanni Bellini's pietà. Also part of the museum, across the road on Piazza Ferrari, is the **Domus del Chirurgo**, where a glass-sided structure sits above the remains of a third-century Roman surgeon's house. The site has yielded numerous fascinating finds, including coins and bronze surgeon's instruments (such as forceps and pliers), which are now on display in the archeology gallery on the ground floor of the museum. What remains here are the foundations and a set of mosaic pavements, including one showing Orpheus surrounded by animals.

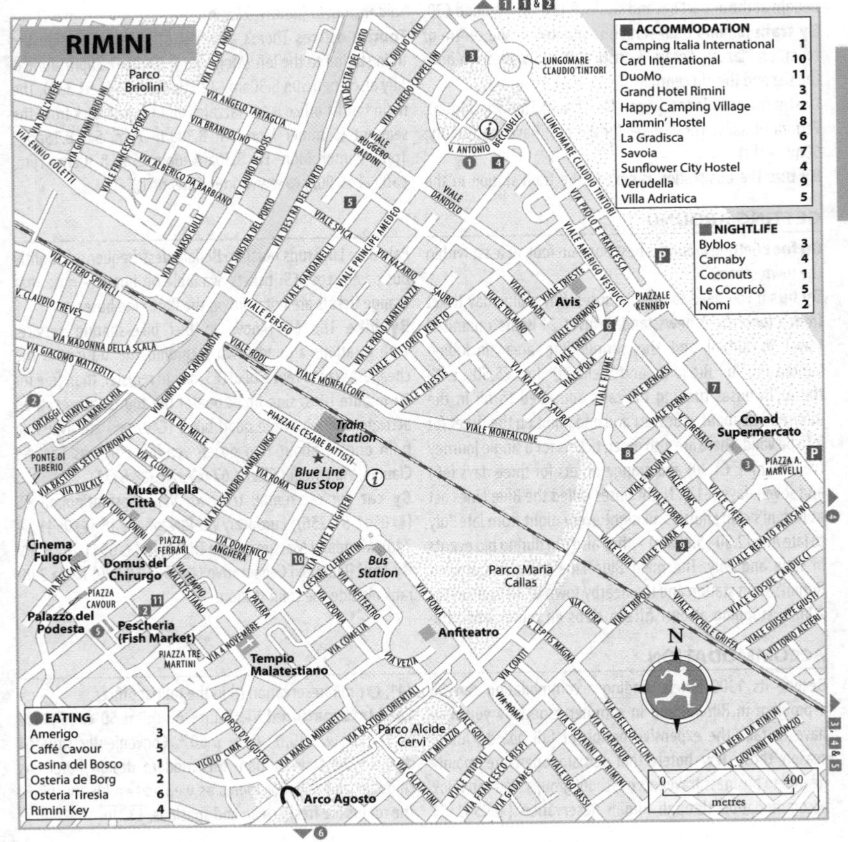

8

Tempio Malatestiano

Via IV Novembre • Mon–Fri 8.30am–12.30pm & 3.30–7pm, Sun 9am–1pm & 3.30–7pm, Sat 8.30am–12.30pm, 3.30–4.30pm & 6.30–7pm • Free

Rimini's best-known monument is the **Tempio Malatestiano**, which serves as the town's cathedral. Built by the Guelph family of Malatesta, it was originally a Franciscan Gothic church before being transformed in 1450 into a gorgeous monument to Sigismondo Malatesta, a notorious *condottiere* whose long list of alleged crimes included rape, incest and looting. Understandably, the pope of the time, Pius II, was less than impressed and publicly consigned an ambivalent Sigismondo to hell. Sigismondo was more concerned with his great love, Isotta degli Atti, and treated the *tempio* as a private memorial chapel to her. Their initials are linked in emblems all over the building, and the Malatesta family's favourite heraldic animal – a trumpeting elephant – appears almost as often. There are a number of fine artworks, now restored, to look out for, including a *Crucifix* attributed to Giotto, friezes and reliefs by Agostino di Duccio and a fresco by Piero della Francesca of Sigismondo himself.

ARRIVAL AND INFORMATION — RIMINI

By plane From Federico Fellini Airport (☎ 0541 715 711, ⓦ riminiairport.com), 8km south of Rimini, bus #9 goes to the train station every 20min; tickets cost €1.30, and can be bought at the airport bar and kiosks. A taxi costs around €20.

By train Rimini's train station is situated in the centre of town, on Piazzale Cesare Battisti, a 10min walk from both the sea and the old centre.

Destinations Bologna (every 10–15min; 1hr–1hr 30min); Ferrara (4 daily; 1hr 25min–2hr 25min); Ravenna (hourly; 50min–1hr).

By bus The bus station is next to the train station in the centre of town.

Destinations Rome (2 daily in summer, 2 weekly in winter; 6hr 30min–7hr 40min); San Marino (hourly; 45min); Santarcangelo (hourly; 25min).

Tourist offices There's a tourist office right outside the train station to the left (Mon–Sat 8.30am–7.30pm; June & July also open Sun 8.30am–12.30pm; ☎ 0541 51 331). The main tourist office is at Piazzale Fellini 3, just back from the seafront (summer Mon–Sat 8.30am–7pm, Sat 8.15am–1pm; winter Mon–Fri 8.30am–6pm, Sat 8.30am–1pm; ☎ 0541 56 902, ⓦ www.riminiturismo.it).

GETTING AROUND

On foot Getting around is best done on foot, at least within the town centre.

By bus If you need to use the buses, buy a blue day ticket from a *tabacchi* or newsstand; it gives 24 hours' unlimited travel in Rimini and the surrounding area (including Santarcangelo, Riccione and Bellaria) for €5.50, with the main buses running till 2am. You need to fill in the information about your start and end point on the ticket for it to be valid. There are also green tickets for a single journey (valid 75min; €1.30) and orange tickets for three days (€9) and seven days (€17). Night buses called the Blue Lines act as Rimini's club shuttles all night every night from late July to late Aug (2.30–5.40am) – they also run during big events in June and July. The main Blue Line trundles between Rimini's train station and the nearby town of Riccione every 20min, stopping at over fifteen clubs en route, while the Pale Blue Line runs north to Bellaria less frequently. Nightly bus passes cost €5; tickets available on board – note that orange tickets are not valid on the Blue Line buses.

By bike The Mi Muovo in Bici bike-sharing service, with locations around town including the station, is the cheapest way to rent a bike (€5/day to register, than free for 30-minute trips; sign up at one of the tourist offices, then activate online), while quad bikes (€40/day) are available from one of about two dozen vendors, such as Casadei Claudio, Viale Regina Elena 62 (☎ 328 388 6171).

By car For car rental, try Avis, Viale Costantinopoli 45 (☎ 0541 51 256); Europcar, Via Ravegnani 18 (☎ 0541 54 746); Mondaini Massimo, Viale Tripoli 16 (☎ 0541 782 646).

By taxi Radiotaxi Cooperative (☎ 0541 50 020) has a 24hr rank outside the train station.

ACCOMMODATION

Despite its 1300 hotels, finding accommodation can be a problem in Rimini, and in summer especially you may have to take the expensive option of full board. Out of season those few hotels that remain open are mainly geared to business travellers or school groups. You can book accommodation through Rimini Reservation (☎ 0541 51 441, ⓦ riminireservation.it) in the tourist offices.

Card International Via Dante Alighieri 50 ☎ 0541 26 412, ⓦ hotelcard.it; map p.507. Conveniently situated close to the train station, this modern design hotel has standard and superior rooms as well as two luxury suites. The rooms are fresh, clean and spacious. **€130**

★ **DuoMo** Via G. Bruno 28 ☎0541 24 215, Ⓦduomohotel.com; map p.507. In the heart of the old town, this designer hotel is swanky and self-consciously ultramodern. Through the automatic bright red doors, the reception desk is a giant, neon-adorned, flying stainless-steel doughnut, while the huge bedrooms are space-age and well equipped. Great breakfasts and very friendly staff. **€130**

Grand Hotel Rimini Parco Federico Fellini 1 ☎0541 56 000, Ⓦgrandhotelrimini.com; map p.507. A five-star vision of grand Fellini-esque luxury defines this historic property with a quietly refined ambience. It's right on the sea, surrounded by elegant lush grounds with its own beach, and the opulent rooms are graced by Venetian and French antiques. **€295**

Jammin' Hostel Viale Derna 22 ☎0541 390 800, Ⓦjamminrimini.com; map p.507. Popular, friendly hostel near the beach, which offers bikes, laundry and other services as well as events both in the hostel and in the town's bars. There's 24hr reception and free wi-fi. Breakfast included. Dorms **€16**, en-suite doubles **€64**

La Gradisca Viale Fiume 1 ☎0541 26 498, Ⓦhotellagradisca.it; map p.507. This is a luxurious four-star, where the whimsical decor inside and out is inspired by Fellini – in fact, the name itself comes from the maestro's unforgettable character in *Amarcord*. **€180**

Savoia Viale Lungomare Murri 13 ☎0541 396 600, Ⓦsavoiahotelrimini.com; map p.507. This plush seafront hotel was designed by Paolo Portoghesi and boasts every facility imaginable, including a spa, a swimming pool, a good seafood restaurant and a beach club. It's worth paying extra for the large, bright, sea-facing rooms, as the cheaper city-view rooms are rather small. **€185**

Sunflower City Hostel Viale Dardanelli 102 ☎0541 25 180, Ⓦsunflowerhostel.com; map p.507. Non-HI hostel open year-round with clean dorms, kitchen, bike rental and free wi-fi. It also operates a smaller beachside branch (Via Siracusa 25 ☎0541 373 432; March–Oct only). Dorms **€13**, doubles **€64**

★ **Verudella** Viale Tripoli 238 ☎389 612 2838, Ⓦhotelverudella.it; map p.507. This simple two-star with comfortable rooms is one of the town's best options, run by a friendly brother-and-sister team. In summer there's a three-night stay minimum, and half board generally required. **€80**

Villa Adriatica Viale Vespucci 3 ☎0541 54 599, Ⓦvilladriatica.it; map p.507. This stylish choice is a refurbished Art Nouveau villa, vintage 1880, with its own swimming pool. The pricier rooms come with wooden floors and larger beds. **€172**

CAMPING

Camping Italia International Via Toscanelli 112 ☎0541 732 882, Ⓦcampingitaliarimini.it; bus #4 from the station will drop you right outside at stop 14; map p.507. Around 3km north of the city centre, right on the seafront, this campsite boasts its own beach, plus all the facilities you'd expect. Camping for small tents as well as bungalows and mobile homes for rent. Two people plus pitch **€30**

Happy Camping Village Via Panzini 228, Bellaria 112 ☎0541 346 102, Ⓦhappycamping.it; bus #4 from the station will drop you right outside at stop 1; map p.507. Some 12km north of Rimini, this spacious campsite has a wealth of facilities, including a private beach, swimming pool, restaurant and supermarket. In addition to pitches for tents it also offers a hotel, bungalows and apartments to rent. Two people plus pitch **€38**

8

EATING

★ **Amerigo** Viale Amerigo Vespucci 137 ☎0541 391 338, Ⓦristoranteamerigo.it; map p.507. A welcoming, always bustling spot with a huge menu – all of it delicious – ranging from fresh *mozzarella di bufala* salads (€9.50) to seafood pastas (€9.50), as well as wood-fired pizzas (from €4) and *piadine* (€4.50). Mon–Fri 9am–6pm.

Caffè Cavour Piazza Cavour 13 ☎0541 785 123; map p.507. Good choice for a leisurely drink or a light meal, this elegant café serves sandwiches, *piadine* (€5–6) and salads (€8–10). Sit outside and admire the old Pescheria in the centre of the old town. Wed–Mon 7am–midnight.

Casina del Bosco Viale Beccadelli 15 ☎0541 56 295, Ⓦcasinadelbosco.it; map p.507. Among a row of similar establishments, this popular place offers a large selection of generously filled *piadine* – tuna and carrot (€5.50), roast beef, parmesan and rocket (€6.70) – with seating beneath shady trees. There are also home-made desserts and local craft beers. March–Oct daily 11.30am–2am.

★ **Osteria de Borg** Via Forzieri 12 ☎0541 56 074, Ⓦosteriadeborg.it; map p.507. Friendly, busy restaurant across the Ponte di Tiberio serving innovative regional cooking, such as *galletto al tegame* (wine-cooked chicken in a skillet; €12), fire-roasted steak (€16) and a dozen different vegetable dishes. Antipasti €8–15, *primi* €8.50–10, *secondi* €10–16. Their *menù degustazione* is excellent value at €35. Booking advised. Daily noon–4pm & 6pm–1am.

Osteria Tiresia Via XX Settembre 41 ☎0541 781 896, Ⓦosteriatiresia.it; map p.507. Popular haunt just outside the Arco d'Augusto. It's a great choice for meat-lovers, with delicious steaks (€20) and dishes such as rabbit with potatoes (€16) as well as a good-value choice of wines. Tues–Sat 7pm–midnight, Sun noon–3pm & 7pm–midnight.

Rimini Key Piazzale B. Croce 7 ☎0541 381 445; map p.507. Good-value set menus and pizzas, in a prime location for observing Rimini's evening *passeggiata* along the seafront. The house specialities include fish dishes such as *tortellini di pesce alle capesante* (*tortellini* with fish and scallops; €13). Pizzas from €4. Daily 11.30am–1am.

NIGHTLIFE

Rimini's nightlife is mainly concentrated on the seafront and in the fashionable enclave of Misano Monte, 15km south of Rimini and about 5km inland. Clubbing is a seasonal activity in Rimini, with full-on nightlife in summer, and few places open in winter. Even on a balmy July evening, things tend to start late with crowds cruising the bars from about 11pm onwards before heading off to the first club at around 1am. If you haven't got a car, or are drinking, use night buses (see page 508). For up-to-date **information** on the Rimini club scene, go to ⓦ riminiturismo.it, or ⓦ riviera.rimini.it for English-language listings.

Byblos Via Pozzo Castello 24, Misano Monte ⓣ 335 389 253, ⓦ byblosclub.com; map p.507. Set in a beautiful Mediterranean villa, with several different bars and dance areas as well as a restaurant and an outdoor courtyard with a swimming pool. Music includes house and 1970s/1980s funk. Fri–Sun 9pm–5am.

Carnaby Via Brindisi 20 ⓣ 0541 373 204, ⓦ carnaby.it; map p.507. Wildly popular club spread over three floors, the lowest of which is subterranean and appropriately named "The Cave". The music gets lighter and less intense the higher you go. Like its namesake, it swings. It's 5km south of the town centre, but there's a free shuttle service. Daily 10pm–5am.

Coconuts Via Lungomare Tintori 5 ⓣ 0541 24 422, ⓦ coconuts.it; map p.507. Right on the beach, this "Miami-style" club boasts palm trees, neon, salsa and podium dancers. As well as house music there are Latin nights with salsa and reggaeton. Attracts a slightly older crowd. Daily 6pm–4am.

Le Cocoricò Viale Chieti 44 ⓣ 327 441 6681, ⓦ cocorico.it; map p.507. Located in nearby Riccione, this is one of Italy's most celebrated clubs. There are five rooms, but the best DJs play under an enormous glass pyramid where thousands come to rave to the latest in Italian techno. Fri & Sat 11pm–6am.

Nomi Via G. Bruno 28 ⓣ 0541 24 215, ⓦ duomohotel.com; map p.507. The fashionable disco club in the *Duomo* hotel is a place to pose charmingly, rather than dance too intently and risk dishevelling your carefully crafted look. Instead, perch on one of the spring-like chairs surrounding the mirrored-steel central bar, then watch and be watched. Mon–Thurs & Sat 8–11pm, Fri & Sun 8pm–2am.

San Marino

Around 25km southwest of Rimini, the **REPUBLIC OF SAN MARINO** is an unashamed, though not entirely unpleasant, tourist destination that trades on its nearly two millennia of precariously maintained autonomy. Said to have been founded around 300 AD by a monk fleeing the persecutions of Diocletian, it claims to be the world's oldest constitutional republic and has been bumbling along ever since, outside the fierce battles and intrigues of mainstream Italian politics. Too small and inconsequential to be worth conquering, the republic has – save for a brief Borgia episode in the sixteenth century – been left largely to its own devices. Culturally, it is essentially Italian – there's no San Marinese language – but in legal, constitutional terms, it remains **independent**, electing its government, passing its own laws and maintaining an army of around a thousand. Important sources of revenue include its coins and postage stamps, which are much sought after by collectors, and it long benefited from its position as a tax haven, though this ended in 2014.

There's not a great deal to see. The ramparts and medieval-style buildings of the citadel above Borgomaggiore, restored in the last century, are mildly interesting; there's a **waxworks museum** in Via Lapicidi Marini 17 (daily: April–June & Sept 9am–6.30pm; July & Aug 9am–8pm; Oct–March 9am–12.30pm & 2–5.30pm; €7.50; ⓦ museodellecerersm.com); and there are same tacky souvenir shops and restaurants. You can also get your passport stamped, for €5, by the border guards or at the information office (see below). All the touristy tawdriness and weapon shops aside, however, it's a good place just to stroll around; the walk up through town to the **rocce**, the battlemented castles along the highest three ridges, is worth the effort for the all-round views. Below, in Borgomaggiore, Giovanni Michelucci's "fearless and controversial" church, built in the 1960s, has a roof that seems to cascade down in waves.

ARRIVAL AND INFORMATION — SAN MARINO

By bus The express bus leaves from Rimini's Piazza Marvelli via the station (hourly; 1hr; €5), and stops in Borgomaggiore, at the bottom of the funicular (*funivia*) that rises up to the medieval city walls (€4.50 return).

Tourist office Contrada Omagnano 20 (summer Mon–Fri 8.30am–6.30pm, Sat & Sun 9am–1.30pm & 2–6.45pm; winter Mon–Fri 8.30am–6pm, Sat & Sun 9am–1.30pm & 2–6pm; ⓣ 0549 882 914), by the top of the funicular.

San Leo

Fortress daily 9.30am–6pm • €9 • 4–7 shuttle buses daily from Piazza Dante in the village (5min)

Clamped to the summit of a dizzying precipice, the beautiful fortress of **SAN LEO** has only been part of Emilia-Romagna since 2006, when the town and five others voted in a referendum to leave Le Marche and join its northern neighbour. Generations have admired the fortress – Machiavelli praised it, Dante modelled the terrain of his Purgatory on it, and Pietro Bembo considered it Italy's "most beautiful implement of war".

Brief history

There's been a fortress at San Leo since the Romans founded a city on the rock. Later colonizers added to it until the fifteenth century, when Federico da Montefeltro set his military architect, Francesco di Giorgio Martini, the task of creating a new one. The walls were built on a slight inward slope and backed with earth, thus reducing the impact of cannonballs. Three large squares were incorporated for the manoeuvring of heavy cannons, and every point was defended with firing posts.

From the eighteenth century San Leo was used as a prison for enemies of the Vatican, of whom the most notorious was the womanizing Count of Cagliostro, a self-proclaimed alchemist, miracle doctor and necromancer. At first the charismatic heretic was incarcerated in a regular prison, but on the insistence of his guards, who were terrified of his diabolic powers, he was moved to the so-called **Pozzetto di Cagliostro** (Cagliostro's Well), now the fortress's most memorable sight. The only entrance was through a trapdoor in the ceiling, so that food could be lowered to him without the warden running the risk of engaging Cagliostro's evil eye. There was one window, triple-barred and placed so that the prisoner couldn't avoid seeing San Leo's twin churches. Cagliostro eventually died of an apoplectic attack, unrepentant after four years of being virtually buried alive.

The village

As well as the fortress, there's the pleasant old **village** to explore. St Leo arrived in the third century and converted the local population to Christianity, and the two village churches, though they failed to impress Cagliostro, are worth a visit. The **Pieve** was built in the ninth century, with material salvaged from a Roman temple to Jupiter, by Byzantine-influenced architects from Ravenna. Sunk into the ground behind the church is a sixth-century chapel founded by and later dedicated to St Leo, whose body lay here until 1014 when Henry II, Emperor of Germany, calling in at the town on his way home from defeating the Greeks and Saracens in Rome, decided to remove it to Germany. His plans were thwarted by the horses bearing the saint's body – after a short distance they refused to go any further, so St Leo's body was left in the small village of Voghenza near Ferrara. The heavy lid of the sarcophagus remains in San Leo's twelfth-century **Duomo**, dedicated to the saint.

ARRIVAL AND INFORMATION — SAN LEO

By bus Catch bus #160 from outside the train station in Rimini (see page 508) to Pietracuta (every 30min–1hr; 40min), then bus #102 on to San Leo (4 daily; 20min). From mid-June to mid-Sept there are direct services with bus #165.

Tourist office Piazza Dante 14 (daily 9am–6pm, open longer hours in summer; ⓣ 0541 916 306, ⓦ san-leo.it).

Tuscany

516 Florence (Firenze)

559 Pisa, Lucca and the coast

582 Siena

595 San Gimignano

600 Volterra

604 Southern Tuscany

617 Eastern Tuscany

FLORENCE DUOMO

9

Tuscany

The idea of Tuscany as an idyll of olive groves, vineyards, hill-towns and frescoed churches may be clichéd, but it is largely true. Late medieval Tuscany was the birthplace of Italian culture and in many ways remains the essence of what travellers imagine Italy to be, a place where art and landscape are fused in the kind of harmony familiar from Renaissance paintings. The national language evolved from the Tuscan dialect, a supremacy ensured by Tuscan writers such as Petrarch, Boccaccio and, most influential of all, Dante – who all wrote in the Tuscan vernacular. Indeed the era we know as the Renaissance, which played so large a role in forming the culture not just of Italy but of Europe as a whole, is associated more strongly with this part of the country than with anywhere else. Florence was the most active centre of the Renaissance, flourishing principally through the all-powerful patronage of the Medici dynasty. Every eminent artistic figure from Giotto onwards – Masaccio, Brunelleschi, Alberti, Donatello, Botticelli, Leonardo da Vinci, Michelangelo – is represented here, in an unrivalled gathering of churches, galleries and museums.

The problem is, of course, that the whole world knows about the attractions of **Florence**, with the result that the city can be off-puttingly busy in high season. **Siena** tends to provoke a less ambivalent response. One of the great medieval cities of Europe, it remains almost perfectly preserved, and holds superb works of art in its religious and secular buildings. In addition, its beautiful Campo – the central, scallop-shaped market square – is the scene of the **Palio**, when bareback horseriders career around the cobbles amid an extravagant display of pageantry. The cities of **Pisa** and **Lucca** have their own fair share of attractions and provide convenient entry points to the region, either by air (via Pisa's airport) or along the coastal rail route from Genoa. **Arezzo** and **Cortona** serve as fine introductions to Tuscany if you're approaching from the south (Rome) or east (Perugia).

Tucked away to the west and south of Siena, dozens of small **hill-towns** epitomize the region for many visitors. **San Gimignano**, the most famous, is worth visiting as much for its spectacular array of frescoes as for its bristle of medieval tower-houses, even if it has become far too popular for its own good. Both **Montepulciano** and **Pienza** are superbly located and dripping with atmosphere, but the best candidates for an authentic Tuscan hill-town escape are places such as **Volterra**, **Massa Marittima** or **Pitigliano**, where tourism has yet to undermine local character. You may find lesser-known sights even more memorable – remote monasteries such as **Monte Oliveto Maggiore** and **San Galgano**, or the sulphur spa of **Bagno Vignoni**. The one area where Tuscany fails to impress is its over developed **coast**, with beach-umbrella compounds filling every last scrap of sand. **Elba**, the largest of several Tuscan islands, offers great beaches and good hiking, but is busy in summer.

Finding **accommodation** can be a major problem in the summer, so you should definitely reserve in advance; Ⓦ turismo.intoscana.it is a useful resource, and includes details of **agriturismi**, family-run places dotted around the countryside offering anything from budget rooms in a farmhouse to luxury apartments in restored castles.

UFFIZI GALLERY, FLORENCE

Highlights

❶ **The Duomo, Florence** Climbing Brunelleschi's dome is a must. See page 522

❷ **The Uffizi, Florence** The world's greatest collection of Italian Renaissance paintings, now with a whole floor of new galleries. See page 528

❸ **Chianti** The country's most famous vineyards. See page 557

❹ **The Leaning Tower, Pisa** Still defying gravity and still continuing to amaze, the Leaning Tower is just one component of Pisa's spectacular medieval centre. See page 560

❺ **Lucca** A stunning array of Romanesque churches in this most urbane of Tuscan towns. See page 564

❻ **Siena Palio** Historic horse race, run over three frenetic laps of the town's spectacular cobbled main square. See page 583

❼ **Tuscan hill-towns** Tuscany's hill-towns epitomize the region for many visitors; San Gimignano is the most popular, but don't miss Montepulciano, Montalcino and Cortona. See pages 595, 607, 613 and 622

HIGHLIGHTS ARE MARKED ON THE MAP ON PAGE 516

9

Florence (Firenze)

Since the early nineteenth century **FLORENCE** has been widely celebrated as the most beautiful city in Italy. Stendhal staggered around its streets in a perpetual stupor of delight; the Brownings sighed over its charms; and E.M. Forster's *Room with a View* portrayed it as the great southern antidote to the sterility of Anglo-Saxon life. The pinnacle of Brunelleschi's stupendous cathedral dome dominates the cityscape, and the close-up view is even more breathtaking, with the multicoloured **Duomo** rising beside the marble-clad **Baptistry**. Wander from here down towards the River Arno and the attraction still holds: beyond the broad Piazza della Signoria – site of the towering **Palazzo Vecchio** – the river is spanned by the medieval, shop-lined **Ponte Vecchio**, with the gorgeous church of **San Miniato al Monte** glistening on the hill behind it.

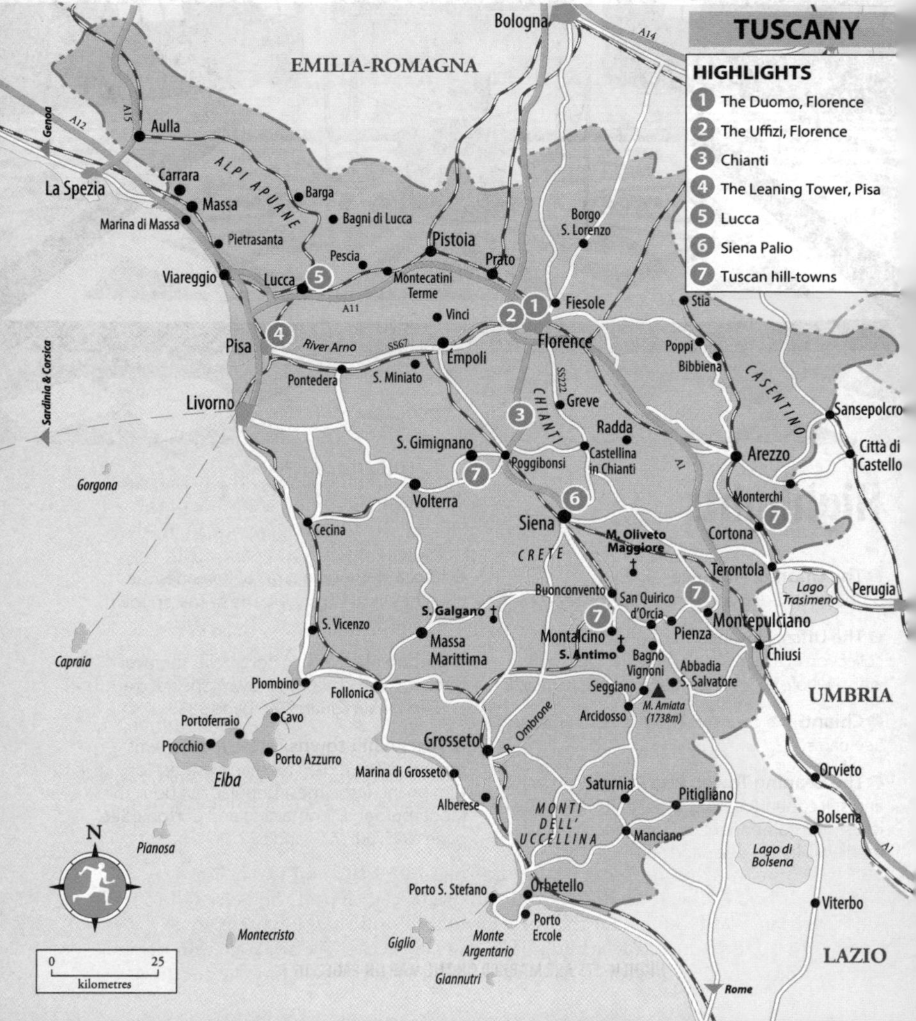

SOUPS, STEAKS AND BEANS – TUSCAN CUISINE

Tuscan cooking, with its emphasis on simple dishes using fresh, quality, local ingredients, has had a seminal influence on Italian cuisine. Classic Tuscan antipasti are peasant fare: bruschetta is stale bread, toasted and dressed with oil and garlic; *crostini* is toast and pâté. **Olive oil** is the essential flavouring, used as a dressing for salads and a medium for frying and to drizzle over bread or vegetables and into soups and stews just before serving. Tuscan bread is unsalted – a tradition thought to have its roots in a ploy to avoid the salt tax.

Soups are very popular – Tuscan menus almost always include either *ribollita*, a hearty stew of vegetables, beans and chunks of bread, or *zuppa di farro*, a thick soup with spelt (a barley-like grain). *Pappa col pomodoro* (bread and tomato soup) is another staple, while fish restaurants serve *cacciucco*, a spiced fish and seafood soup. White cannellini **beans** (*fagioli*) are another favourite, turning up in salads, with pasta (*tuoni e lampo*), with sausages in a stew (*fagioli all'uccelletto*) or just dressed with olive oil. Tuscany is not known for its **pasta**, but many towns in the south serve *pici*, thick, hand-rolled spaghetti with toasted breadcrumbs. **Meat** is kept plain, often grilled, and Florentines profess to liking nothing better than a good *bistecca alla fiorentina* (rare chargrilled steak), or the simple rustic dishes of *arista* (roast pork loin stuffed with rosemary and garlic) or *pollo alla diavola* (chicken flattened, marinated and then grilled with herbs). Hunters' fare such as *cinghiale* (wild boar) and *coniglio* (rabbit) often turns up in hill-town trattorias.

Spinach is often married with ricotta and gnocchi, used as a pasta filling, and in *crespoline* (pancakes) or between two chunks of *focaccia* and eaten as a snack. Sheep's milk pecorino is the most widespread Tuscan **cheese** (best in Pienza), but the most famous is the oval marzolino from the Chianti region, which is eaten either fresh or ripened. **Dessert** menus will often include *cantuccini*, hard, almond-flavoured biscuits to be dipped in a glass of Vinsanto (sweet dessert wine); Siena is the main source of sweet treats, including almond macaroons and *panforte*, a rich and very dense cake full of nuts and fruit.

Tuscany has some of Italy's finest **wines**. Three top names, which all bear the exclusive DOCG mark (and price tags to match), are Chianti Classico, Brunello di Montalcino and Vino Nobile di Montepulciano – not the sort of thing you'd knock back at a trattoria. There are dozens of other Chianti varieties, most of them excellent, but it can be difficult to find a bargain. Both Montalcino and Montepulciano produce *rosso* varieties that are more pocket-friendly, and other names to look for include Carmignano and Rosso delle Colline Lucchesi. Two notable whites are dry Vernaccia di San Gimignano and the fresh Galestro.

For art lovers, Florence has no equal in Europe. The development of the Renaissance can be plotted in the vast picture collection of the **Uffizi** and in the sculpture of the **Bargello** and the **Museo dell'Opera del Duomo**. Equally revelatory are the fabulously decorated chapels of **Santa Croce** and **Santa Maria Novella**, forerunners of such astonishing creations as Masaccio's superb frescoes in the **Cappella Brancacci**. The Renaissance emphasis on harmony and rational design is expressed with unrivalled eloquence in Brunelleschi's architecture, specifically in the churches of **San Lorenzo**, **Santo Spirito** and the **Cappella dei Pazzi**. While the full genius of Michelangelo, the dominant creative figure of sixteenth-century Italy, is on display in San Lorenzo's **Biblioteca Laurenziana** and the marble statuary of the **Cappelle Medicee** and the **Accademia**, every quarter of Florence can boast a church worth an extended call, and the enormous **Palazzo Pitti** south of the river constitutes a museum district on its own. If you're on a whistle-stop tour, note that it's not possible to simply stroll into the Cappella Brancacci, and that spontaneous visits to the Accademia and Uffizi are often difficult.

Brief history

The Roman colony of **Florentia** was established in 59 BC and expansion was rapid, based on trade along the Arno. In the sixth century AD the city fell to the barbarian hordes of Totila, then the Lombards and then Charlemagne's Franks. In 1078 Countess Mathilda of Tuscia supervised the construction of new fortifications, and in the year of her death – 1115 – granted Florence the status of

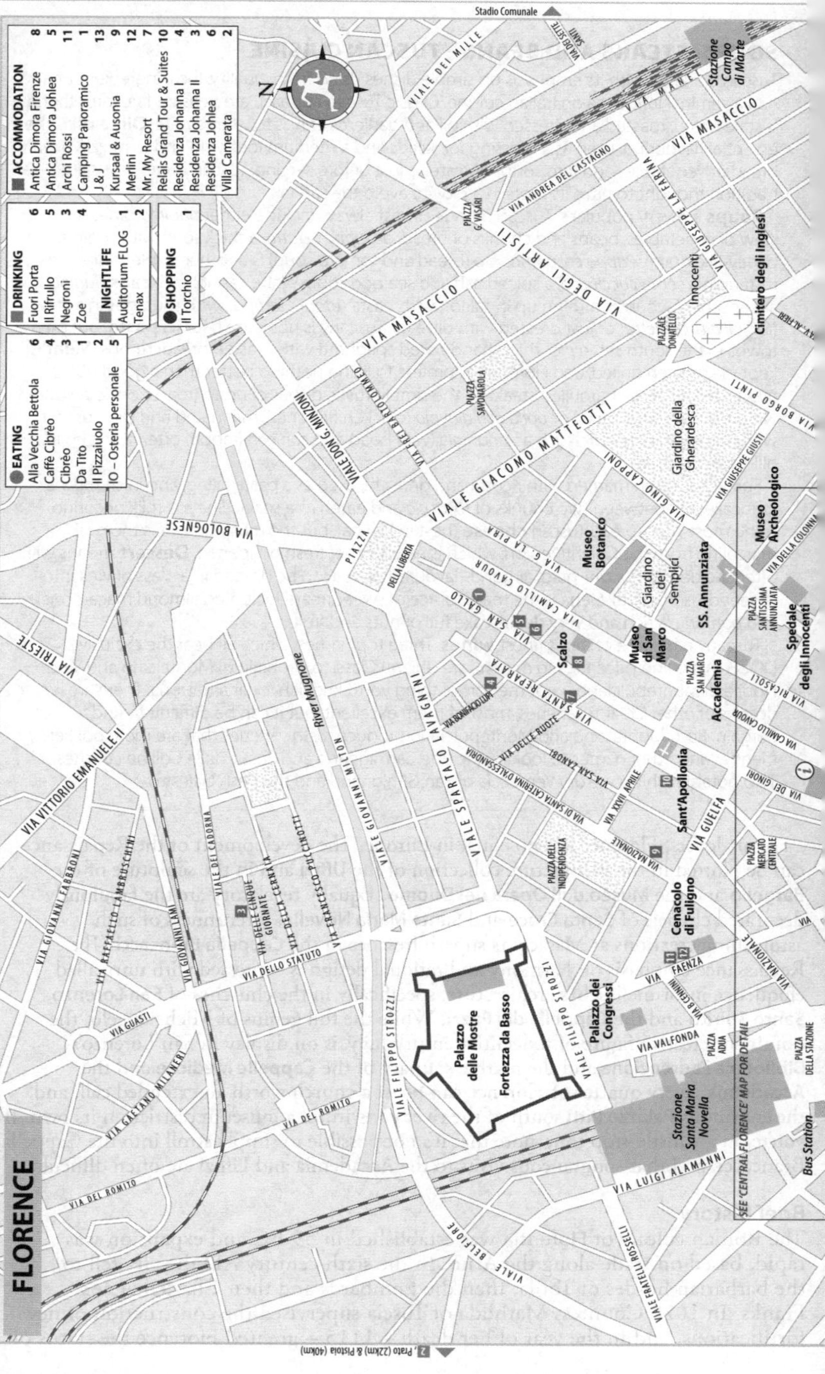

FLORENCE
EATING
Alla Vecchia Bettola 6
Caffè Cibrèo 4
Cibrèo 3
Da Tito 1
Il Pizzaiuolo 2
IO – Osteria personale 5
DRINKING
Fuori Porta 6
Il Rifrullo 5
Negroni 3
Zoe 4
NIGHTLIFE
Auditorium FLOG 1
Tenax 2
SHOPPING
Il Torchio 1
ACCOMMODATION
Antica Dimora Firenze 8
Antica Dimora Johlea 5
Archi Rossi 11
Camping Panoramico 1
J & J 13
Kursaal & Ausonia 9
Merlini 12
Mr. My Resort 7
Relais Grand Tour & Suites 10
Residenza Johanna I 4
Residenza Johanna II 3
Residenza Johlea 6
Villa Camerata 2
1 (3km)
1 & Fiesole (10km)
2 (5km)
2, Prato (22km) & Pistoia (40km)
Stadio Comunale
N
Stazione Campo di Marte
Stazione Santa Maria Novella
Bus Station
Palazzo delle Mostre
Fortezza da Basso
Palazzo dei Congressi
Cenacolo di Fuligno
Sant'Apollonia
Accademia
Museo di San Marco
SS. Annunziata
Spedale degli Innocenti
Museo Archeologico
Museo Botanico
Giardino dei Semplici
Giardino della Gherardesca
Cimitero degli Inglesi
Innocenti
Scalzo
River Mugnone
SEE 'CENTRAL FLORENCE' MAP FOR DETAIL
VIA VITTORIO EMANUELE II
VIA TRIESTE
VIA BOLOGNESE
VIALE DON G. MINZONI
VIA MASACCIO
VIALE DEI MILLE
VIA MANETTO
VIA ANDREA DEL CASTAGNO
VIA DEGLI ARTISTI
VIA GIUSEPPE LA FARINA
VIALE GIACOMO MATTEOTTI
VIA FRA BARTOLOMMEO
VIALE GINO CAPPONI
VIA BORGO PINTI
VIA G. LA PIRA
VIA CAMILLO CAVOUR
VIA SAN GALLO
VIA SANTA REPARATA
VIA DELLE RUOTE
VIA SAN ZANOBI
VIA XXVII APRILE
VIA GUELFA
VIA NAZIONALE
VIA FAENZA
VIA VALFONDA
VIA LUIGI ALAMANNI
VIALE FILIPPO STROZZI
VIALE SPARTACO LAVAGNINI
VIALE GIOVANNI MILTON
VIA FRANCESCO PUCCINOTTI
VIA DELLA CERNAIA
VIA DELLE CINQUE GIORNATE
VIALE DEI CADORNA
VIA DELLO STATUTO
VIA GIOVANNI LAMI
VIA RAFFAELLO LAMBRUSCHINI
VIA GIOVANNI FABBRONI
VIA GUASTI
VIA GAETANO MILANESI
VIA DEL ROMITO
VIALE BELFIORE
VIALE FRATELLI ROSSELLI
VIA RICASOLI
VIA DEI GINORI
VIA GIUSEPPE GIUSTI
VIA DELLA COLONNA
VIA BONIFACIO LUPI
VIA DI SANTA CATERINA D'ALESSANDRIA
PIAZZA DELLA LIBERTÀ
PIAZZA SAVONAROLA
PIAZZA G. VASARI
PIAZZALE DONATELLO
PIAZZA DELL'INDIPENDENZA
PIAZZA SAN MARCO
PIAZZA SANTISSIMA ANNUNZIATA
PIAZZA MERCATO CENTRALE
PIAZZA ADUA
PIAZZA DELLA STAZIONE

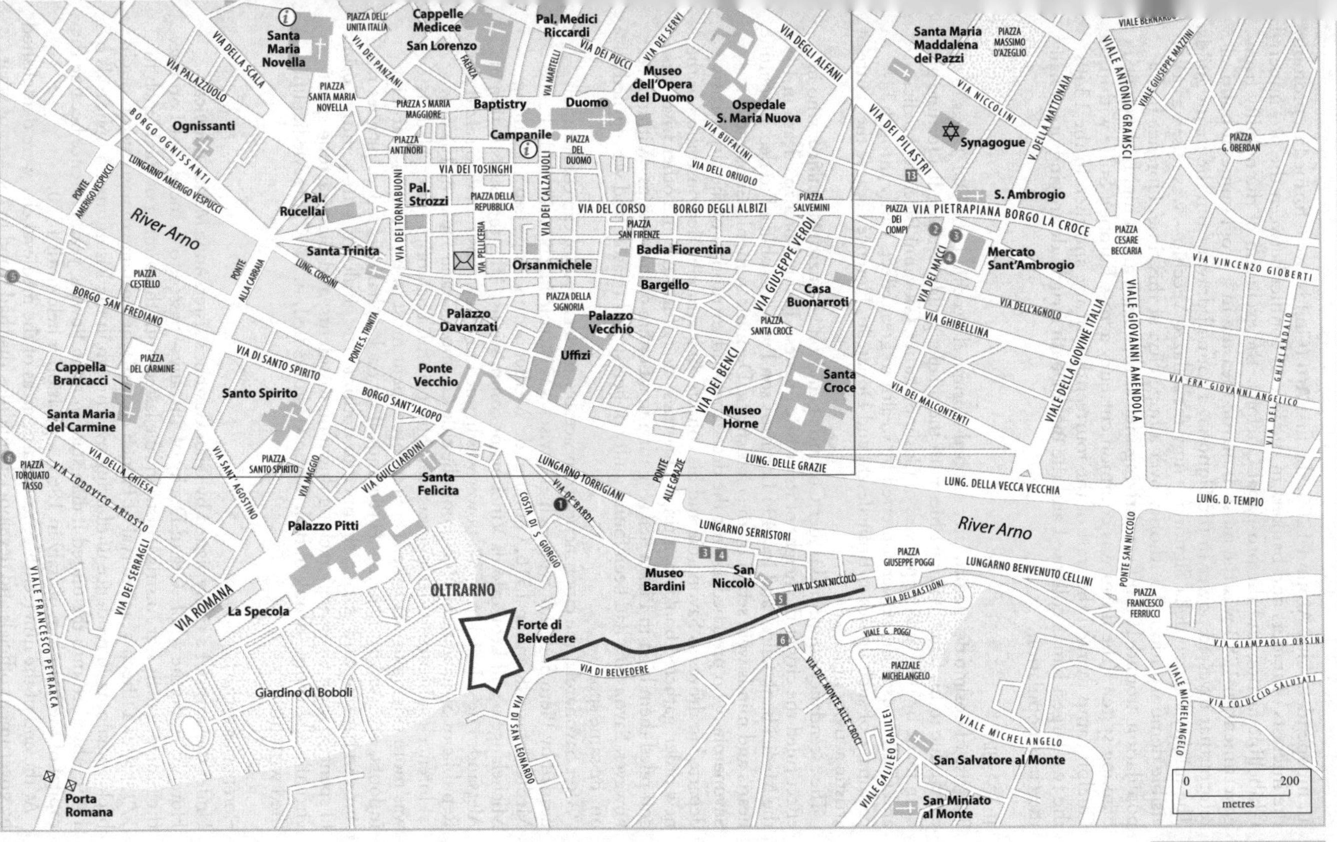
Santa Maria Novella
Ognissanti
Pal. Rucellai
Santa Trinita
Cappelle Medicee
San Lorenzo
Baptistry
Campanile
Pal. Strozzi
Palazzo Davanzati
Ponte Vecchio
Pal. Medici Riccardi
Duomo
Orsanmichele
Uffizi
Palazzo Vecchio
Museo dell'Opera del Duomo
Badia Fiorentina
Bargello
Ospedale S. Maria Nuova
Casa Buonarroti
Santa Croce
Museo Horne
Santa Maria Maddalena del Pazzi
Synagogue
S. Ambrogio
Mercato Sant'Ambrogio
River Arno
Museo Bardini
San Niccolò
Forte di Belvedere
OLTRARNO
Santa Felicita
Palazzo Pitti
Santo Spirito
Cappella Brancacci
Santa Maria del Carmine
La Specola
Giardino di Boboli
Porta Romana
San Salvatore al Monte
San Miniato al Monte
Piazza Santa Maria Novella
Piazza S Maria Maggiore
Piazza Antinori
Piazza dell' Unità Italia
Piazza del Duomo
Piazza della Repubblica
Piazza della Signoria
Piazza San Firenze
Piazza Salvemini
Piazza dei Ciompi
Piazza Santa Croce
Piazza Massimo D'Azeglio
Piazza Cesare Beccaria
Piazza G. Oberdan
Piazza Francesco Ferrucci
Piazza Giuseppe Poggi
Piazzale Michelangelo
Piazza Santo Spirito
Piazza del Carmine
Piazza Cestello
Piazza Torquato Tasso
Via della Scala
Via Palazzuolo
Borgo Ognissanti
Lungarno Amerigo Vespucci
Ponte Amerigo Vespucci
Via dei Panzani
Faenza
Via dei Tornabuoni
Via dei Tosinghi
Via Pellicceria
Via dei Calzaiuoli
Via Martelli
Via dei Pucci
Via dei Servi
Via del Corso
Borgo degli Albizi
Via dell' Oriuolo
Via Bufalini
Via degli Alfani
Via dei Pilastri
Via Niccolini
V. della Mattonaia
Viale Antonio Gramsci
Viale Giuseppe Mazzini
Viale Giovanni Amendola
Viale della Giovine Italia
Via Pietrapiana
Borgo La Croce
Via dei Macci
Via dell'Agnolo
Via Ghibellina
Via dei Malcontenti
Via Giuseppe Verdi
Via dei Benci
Lung. delle Grazie
Lung. della Vecca Vecchia
Ponte alle Grazie
Lung. Corsini
Ponte S. Trinita
Borgo Sant'Jacopo
Via Guicciardini
Via Maggio
Via di Santo Spirito
Ponte alla Carraia
Via Sant' Agostino
Via Romana
Via dei Serragli
Borgo San Frediano
Via della Chiesa
Via Lodovico Ariosto
Viale Francesco Petrarca
Lungarno Torrigiani
Via de' Bardi
Costa di S Giorgio
Via di San Leonardo
Via di Belvedere
Lungarno Serristori
Via di San Niccolò
Via del Monte alle Croci
Via dei Bastioni
Viale G. Poggi
Viale Galileo Galilei
Viale Michelangelo
Lungarno Benvenuto Cellini
Ponte San Niccolò
Lung. D. Tempio
Via Vincenzo Gioberti
Via Fra' Giovanni Angelico
Via del Ghirlandaio
Via Giampaolo Orsini
Via Coluccio Salutati
0
200
metres

an independent city. Around 1200, the first **Arti** (Guilds) were formed to promote the interests of traders and bankers in the face of conflict between the pro-imperial Ghibelline faction and the pro-papal Guelphs. The exclusion of the nobility from government in 1293 was the most dramatic measure in a programme of political reform that invested power in the **Signoria**, a council drawn from the major guilds. The mighty Palazzo della Signoria – now the Palazzo Vecchio – was raised as a visible demonstration of authority over a huge city: at this time, Florence had a population around 100,000, a thriving mercantile sector and a highly developed banking system (the florin was common currency across Europe). Strife within the Guelph camp marked the start of the fourteenth century, and then in the 1340s the two largest banks collapsed and the **Black Death** struck, destroying up to half the city's population.

The Medici

The rise of **Cosimo de' Medici**, later dubbed Cosimo il Vecchio ("the Old"), was to some extent due to his family's sympathies with the smaller guilds. The Medici fortune had been made by the banking prowess of Cosimo's father, Giovanni Bicci de' Medici, and Cosimo used the power conferred by wealth to great effect. Partly through his patronage of such figures as Brunelleschi and Donatello, Florence became the centre of artistic activity in Italy.

The ascendancy continued under Cosimo's grandson **Lorenzo il Magnifico**, who in effect ruled the city at the height of its artistic prowess. Before Lorenzo's death in 1492, the Medici bank failed, and in 1494 Lorenzo's son Piero was obliged to flee. Florentine hearts and minds were seized by the charismatic Dominican monk, **Girolamo Savonarola**, who preached against the decadence and corruption of the city. Artists departed in droves as Savonarola and his cohorts, in a symbolic demonstration of the new order, gathered books, paintings, tapestries, fancy furniture and other frivolities, and piled them high in Piazza della Signoria in a **Bonfire of the Vanities**. Within a year, however, Savonarola had been found guilty of heresy and treason, and was burned alive on the same spot.

After Savonarola, the city functioned peaceably under a republican constitution headed by Piero Soderini, whose chief adviser was **Niccolò Machiavelli**. In 1512 the Medici returned, and in 1516, Giovanni de' Medici became **Pope Leo X**, granting Michelangelo and Leonardo da Vinci major commissions. After the assassination of Alessandro de' Medici in 1537, power was handed to a new Cosimo, who seized the Republic of Siena and, in 1569, took the title **Cosimo I**, Grand Duke of Tuscany.

Florence's subsequent decline was slow and painful. Each of the later Medicis was more ridiculous than the last: **Francesco** spent most of his thirteen-year reign indoors, obsessed by alchemy; **Ferdinando II** sat back as harvests failed, plagues ran riot and banking and textiles slumped to nothing; the virulently anti-Semitic **Cosimo III** spent 53 years in power cracking down on dissidents; and **Gian Gastone** spent virtually all his time drunk in bed. When Gastone died, in 1737, the Medici line died with him.

Florence after the Medici

Under the terms of a treaty signed by Gian Gastone's sister, **Anna Maria Ludovica**, Florence – and the whole Grand Duchy of Tuscany – passed to Francesco of Lorraine, the future Francis I of Austria. Austrian rule lasted until the coming of the French in 1799; after a fifteen-year interval of French control, the Lorraine dynasty was brought back, remaining in residence until being overthrown in the Risorgimento upheavals of 1859. Absorbed into the united Italian state in the following year, Florence became the **capital** of the Kingdom of Italy in 1865, a position it held until 1870.

At the end of the nineteenth century, large areas of the medieval city were **demolished** by government officials and developers; buildings that had stood in the area of what

FLORENCE'S MUSEUMS: TICKETS AND INFORMATION

Tickets for the Uffizi, Palazzo Pitti and Boboli garden can be booked in advance online at wuffizi.it. This allows you to take your printout to the museums, and join the fast track queue.

All of Florence's state-run museums belong to an association called **Firenze Musei (Ⓦ firenzemusei.it)**, which sets aside a daily quota of tickets that can be **reserved in advance**. The Uffizi, the Accademia and the Bargello belong to this group, as do the Palazzo Pitti museums (including the Boboli garden), the Medici chapels, the archeological museum and the San Marco museum. Tickets for all are for a specified time slot, and in the most popular museums such as the Uffizi, tickets are often only available for slots from lunchtime onwards than for the morning, when tour groups tend to block book. There is a booking fee of €4 for Uffizi and Accademia, €3 for the rest. If you don't have internet access, tickets can also be booked via a Call Centre (Mon–Fri 8.30am–6.30pm, Sat 8.30am–12.30pm; Ⓣ 055 294 883). An English-speaking operator will allocate you a ticket for a specific hour, to be collected at the museum at a specific time, shortly before entry. Be aware, however, that the call centre gets very busy, and getting through can involve long holds. A better alternative is the under-publicized Firenze Musei booth at Orsanmichele, which is set into the wall of the church on the Via Calzaiuoli side (Mon–Sat 10am–5.30pm). Other options are the *My Accademia* bookshop, opposite the Accademia at Via Ricasoli 105r (Tues–Sun 8.15am–5pm); and the ticket offices of all the state museums (except the Accademia Gallery) during opening hours.

Prebooking is strongly recommended year round for the Uffizi and the Accademia, whose allocation of reservable tickets is often sold out weeks ahead.

The **Firenze Card**, costing a whopping €85, is valid for 72 hours (ie 3 days) from the first time you use it, and gives access to scores of museums and monuments in greater Florence (including all the big ones), plus unlimited use of public transport. It also enables you to bypass the queues at the major museums, which have separate gates for cardholders. You do, though, have to pack a hell of a lot into each day to make it worthwhile. The card can be bought at the Via Cavour and Piazza Stazione tourist offices, from the Uffizi, Bargello, Palazzo Pitti, Museo Bardini and Museo di Santa Maria Novella, and at Ⓦ firenzecard.it.

For Florence's **civic museums** – of which the main ones are the Museo Bardini, Museo Santa Maria Novella, Palazzo Vecchio and the Cappella Brancacci – the website is Ⓦ museicivicifiorentini.comune.fi.it.

Note that nearly all of Florence's major museums are routinely **closed on Monday**.

is now Piazza della Repubblica since the early Middle Ages were pulled down to make way for undistinguished office blocks, and old quarters around Santa Croce and Santa Maria Novella were razed. In 1944, the retreating German army blew up all the city's bridges except the Ponte Vecchio and destroyed acres of medieval architecture. A disastrous **flood** in November 1966 drowned several people and wrecked buildings and works of art, and restoration of the damage is still going on. Indeed, monuments and paintings are the basis of Florence's survival, a state of affairs that gives rise to considerable disquiet. The development of new industrial parks on the northern outskirts is the latest and most ambitious attempt to break Florence's ever-increasing dependence on its tourists.

Piazza del Duomo and around

Stepping out for the first time in Florence, it's almost impossible not to gravitate straight towards the square at the heart of Florence, **Piazza del Duomo**, beckoned by the iconic form of Brunelleschi's extraordinary dome, which dominates the cityscape in a way unmatched by any architectural creation in any other Italian city. Yet even though the magnitude of the **Duomo** is apparent from a distance, and even though you may have seen it in a thousand photos, the first full sight of the church and adjacent **Baptistry** still comes as a jolt, the colours of their patterned exteriors making a startling contrast with the dun-coloured buildings around them.

9

IL GRANDE MUSEO DEL DUOMO

The major sights of Piazza del Duomo are marketed as **Il Grande Museo del Duomo**. An €18 ticket, valid for 72 hours, gives a single admission to the Dome, the Campanile, Santa Reparata, the Museo dell'Opera del Duomo and the Baptistry, though be aware that booking a time slot in advance for the Dome is obligatory and that in high season you should do this several days ahead; the ticket can be bought online (ⓦ ilgrandemuseodelduomo.it) and at a ticket office at Piazza San Giovanni 7, opposite the north doors of the Baptistry. Online tickets need to be printed.

The Duomo (Santa Maria del Fiore)

Cathedral Mon–Wed & Fri 10am–5pm, Thurs 10am–4.30pm,& Sat 10am–4.45pm, Sun 1.30–4.45pm (may close for special events on religious festival days – check website) • Free • **Santa Reparata** Same hours as cathedral • €15 Il Grande Museo del Duomo ticket • **Dome** Mon–Fri 8.30am–7pm, Sat 8.30am–5.40pm • €15 Il Grande Museo del Duomo ticket • ⓦ operaduomo.firenze.it

It was sometime in the seventh century when the seat of the Bishop of Florence was transferred from San Lorenzo to the ancient church that stood on the site of the **Duomo**. In the thirteenth century, it was decided that a new cathedral was required, to better reflect the wealth of the city and to put the Pisans and Sienese in their place. In 1294 **Arnolfo di Cambio** designed a vast basilica focused on a domed tribune; by 1418 this project was complete except for its crowning feature. The conception was magnificent: the dome was to span a distance of nearly 42m and rise from a base some 54m above the floor of the nave. It was to be the largest dome ever constructed – but nobody had yet worked out how to build it.

A committee of the masons' guild was set up to ponder the problem, and it was to them that **Filippo Brunelleschi** presented himself. Some seventeen years before, in 1401, Brunelleschi had been defeated by Ghiberti in the competition to design the Baptistry doors, and had spent the intervening time studying classical architecture and developing new theories of engineering. He won the commission on condition that he worked jointly with Ghiberti – a partnership that did not last long. The key to the dome's success was the construction of two shells: a light outer shell about one metre thick, and an inner shell four times thicker. On March 25, 1436 – Annunciation Day, and the Florentine New Year – the completion of the dome was marked by the papal consecration of the cathedral.

The exterior

The Duomo's overblown main **facade** is a nineteenth-century imitation of a Gothic front, its marble cladding quarried from the same sources as the first builders used – white stone from Carrara, red from the Maremma, green from Prato. The south side is the oldest part, but the most attractive adornment is the **Porta della Mandorla**, on the north side. This takes its name from the almond-shaped frame that contains the relief *The Assumption of the Virgin*, sculpted by Nanni di Banco around 1420.

The interior

The Duomo's **interior** is a vast enclosure of bare masonry that makes a stark contrast to the fussy exterior. Initially, the most conspicuous pieces of decoration are two memorials to *condottieri* (mercenary commanders) in the north aisle – Uccello's monument to **Sir John Hawkwood**, painted in 1436, and Castagno's monument to **Niccolò da Tolentino**, created twenty years later. Just beyond, Domenico do Michelino's *Dante Explaining the Divine Comedy* makes the dome only marginally less prominent than the mountain of Purgatory. Judged by mere size, the major work of art in the Duomo is the fresco of *The Last Judgement* inside the dome; painted by Vasari and Zuccari, it merely defaces Brunelleschi's masterpiece. Below the fresco are seven stained-glass roundels designed by Uccello, Ghiberti, Castagno and Donatello; they are best inspected from the gallery immediately below them, which forms part of the route up **inside the dome** – the

entrance is outside, on the north side. The gallery is the queasiest part of the climb, the last part of which winds between the brick walls of the outer and inner shells of the dome; the views from the summit, as you'd expect, are stunning.

In the 1960s remnants of the Duomo's predecessor, **Santa Reparata**, were uncovered beneath the west end of the **nave**. A detailed model helps make sense of the jigsaw of Roman, early Christian and Romanesque remains, areas of mosaic and patches of fourteenth-century frescoes. Also down here is the **tomb of Brunelleschi**, one of the few Florentines honoured with burial inside the Duomo.

The Campanile

Daily 8.15am–7pm • €18 Il Grande Museo del Duomo ticket • ⓦ ilgrandemuseodelduomo.it

Alongside Italy's most impressive cathedral dome is perhaps its most elegant belltower. The **Campanile** was begun in 1334 by **Giotto**, who was no engineer: after his death in 1337 Andrea Pisano and Francesco Talenti took over the teetering, half-built edifice, and immediately doubled the thickness of the walls to stop it collapsing. The first storey is studded with two rows of remarkable bas-reliefs: the lower row, *The Creation of Man* and the *Arts and Industries*, was carved by Pisano himself, the upper by his pupils. The figures of *Prophets* and *Sibyls* in the second-storey niches were created by Donatello and others. (All the sculptures are copies – the originals are in the Museo dell'Opera del Duomo.)

The Baptistry

Mon–Fri 8.15–10.15am & 11.15am–7.30pm, Sat 8.15am–6.30pm, Sun 8.15am–1.30pm • €18 Il Grande Museo del Duomo ticket • ⓦ ilgrandemuseodelduomo.it

Generally thought to date from the sixth or seventh century, the **Baptistry** is the oldest building in Florence, and no building better illustrates the special relationship between Florence and the Roman world. Throughout the Middle Ages the Florentines chose to believe that the Baptistry was originally a Roman temple to Mars, a belief bolstered by the interior's inclusion of Roman granite columns. The pattern of its marble cladding, applied in the eleventh and twelfth centuries, is clearly classical in inspiration, and the Baptistry's most famous embellishments – its gilded bronze doors – mark the emergence of a self-conscious interest in the art of the ancient world.

The doors

After Andrea Pisano's success in 1336 with the **doors** that are now on the south side of the building, the merchants' guild held a competition in 1401 for the job of making a new set. The two finalists were Brunelleschi and **Lorenzo Ghiberti** – and the latter won the day. Ghiberti's **north doors** show a new naturalism and classical sense of harmony, but their innovation is timid in comparison with his sublime **east doors**, which are known as the "Gates of Paradise", supposedly because Michelangelo once remarked that they deserved to be the portals of heaven, though it's more likely that the name came about because the space between a cathedral and its baptistry was called the *paradiso*. Unprecedented in the subtlety of their modelling, these Old Testament scenes are a primer of early Renaissance art, using perspective, gesture and sophisticated grouping of their subjects to convey the human drama of each scene. Ghiberti has included a self-portrait in the frame of the left-hand door – his is the fourth head from the top of the right-hand band. All the panels now set in the door are replicas, with the originals on display in the Museo dell'Opera (the same goes for the north doors); the original competition entries are in the Bargello.

The interior

Inside, both the mosaic floor and the magnificent mosaic ceiling – including a fearsome platoon of demons at the feet of Christ in Judgement – were created in the thirteenth century. To the right of the altar is the **tomb of John XXIII**, the schismatic

9

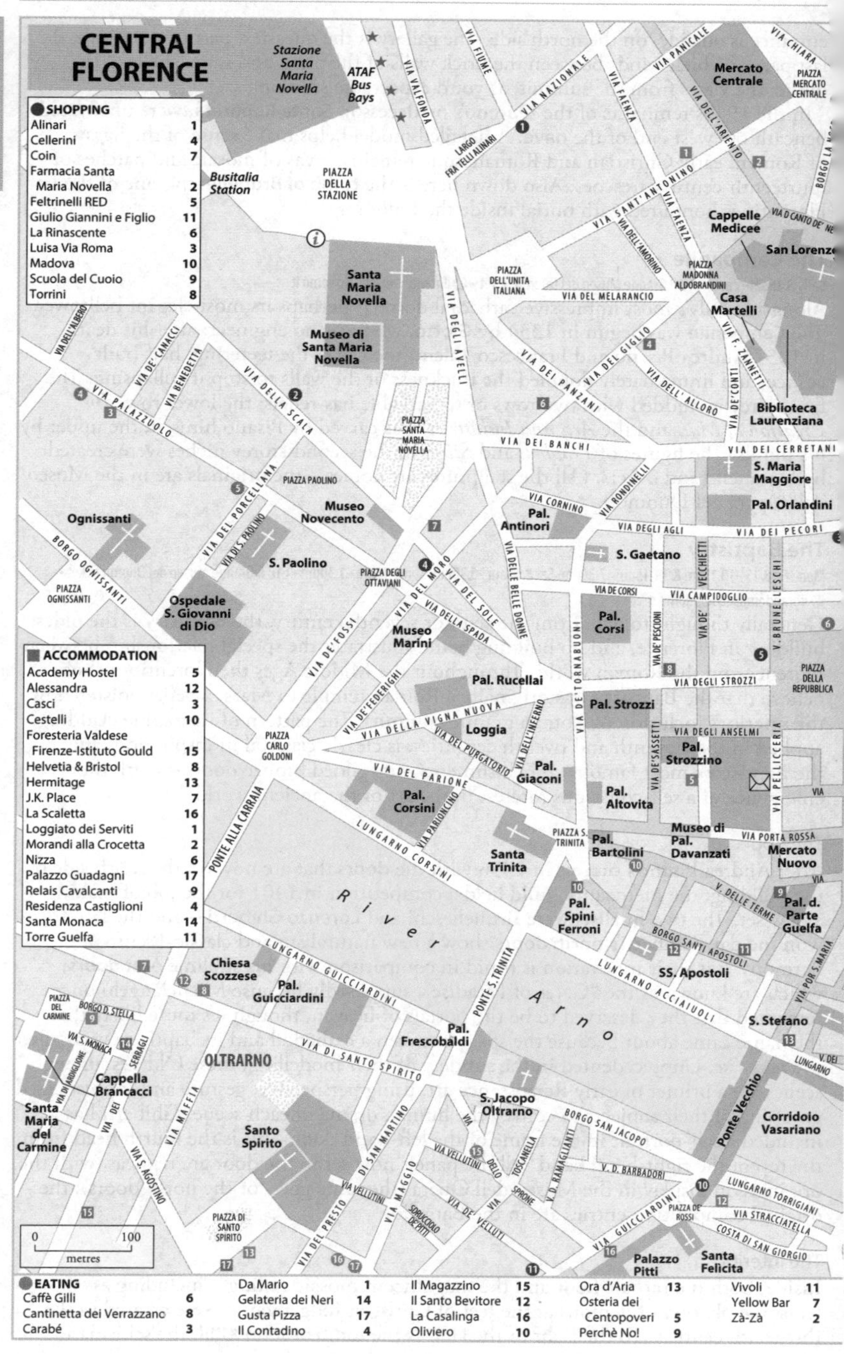
CENTRAL FLORENCE
SHOPPING
Alinari 1
Cellerini 4
Coin 7
Farmacia Santa Maria Novella 2
Feltrinelli RED 5
Giulio Giannini e Figlio 11
La Rinascente 6
Luisa Via Roma 3
Madova 10
Scuola del Cuoio 9
Torrini 8
ACCOMMODATION
Academy Hostel 5
Alessandra 12
Casci 3
Cestelli 10
Foresteria Valdese Firenze-Istituto Gould 15
Helvetia & Bristol 8
Hermitage 13
J.K. Place 7
La Scaletta 16
Loggiato dei Serviti 1
Morandi alla Crocetta 2
Nizza 6
Palazzo Guadagni 17
Relais Cavalcanti 9
Residenza Castiglioni 4
Santa Monaca 14
Torre Guelfa 11
EATING
Caffè Gilli 6
Cantinetta dei Verrazzano 8
Carabé 3
Da Mario 1
Gelateria dei Neri 14
Gusta Pizza 17
Il Contadino 4
Il Magazzino 15
Il Santo Bevitore 12
La Casalinga 16
Oliviero 10
Ora d'Aria 13
Osteria dei Centopoveri 5
Perchè No! 9
Vivoli 11
Yellow Bar 7
Zà-Zà 2
Stazione Santa Maria Novella
ATAF Bus Bays
Busitalia Station
PIAZZA DELLA STAZIONE
Mercato Centrale
PIAZZA MERCATO CENTRALE
Cappelle Medicee
San Lorenzo
Santa Maria Novella
Museo di Santa Maria Novella
PIAZZA DELL'UNITÀ ITALIANA
PIAZZA MADONNA ALDOBRANDINI
Casa Martelli
Biblioteca Laurenziana
PIAZZA SANTA MARIA NOVELLA
S. Maria Maggiore
Pal. Orlandini
Museo Novecento
PIAZZA PAOLINO
Pal. Antinori
S. Gaetano
Ognissanti
S. Paolino
PIAZZA OGNISSANTI
PIAZZA DEGLI OTTAVIANI
Ospedale S. Giovanni di Dio
Museo Marini
Pal. Corsi
PIAZZA DELLA REPUBBLICA
Pal. Rucellai
Pal. Strozzi
Loggia
PIAZZA CARLO GOLDONI
Pal. Strozzino
Pal. Giaconi
Pal. Corsini
Pal. Altovita
Museo di Pal. Davanzati
Mercato Nuovo
PIAZZA S. TRINITA
Santa Trinita
Pal. Bartolini
Pal. Spini Ferroni
Pal. d. Parte Guelfa
River Arno
SS. Apostoli
Chiesa Scozzese
Pal. Guicciardini
Pal. Frescobaldi
S. Stefano
PIAZZA DEL CARMINE
OLTRARNO
Cappella Brancacci
Santa Maria del Carmine
S. Jacopo Oltrarno
Corridoio Vasariano
Ponte Vecchio
Santo Spirito
PIAZZA DI SANTO SPIRITO
PIAZZA DE' ROSSI
Palazzo Pitti
Santa Felìcita
0 100 metres
VIA NAZIONALE
VIA FAENZA
VIA PANICALE
VIA CHIARA
VIA DELL'ARIENTO
VIA VALFONDA
VIA FIUME
LARGO FRA TELLI ALINARI
VIA SANT'ANTONINO
VIA DELL'AMORINO
VIA D CANTO DE' NELLI
VIA DEL MELARANCIO
VIA DEGLI AVELLI
VIA DEL GIGLIO
VIA DEI PANZANI
VIA DELL' ALLORO
VIA F. ZANNETTI
VIA DE' CONTI
VIA DELL'ALBERO
VIA DE' CANACCI
VIA BENEDETTA
VIA PALAZZUOLO
VIA DELLA SCALA
VIA DEI BANCHI
VIA DEI CERRETANI
VIA DEL PORCELLANA
VIA DEL S. PAOLINO
VIA CORNINO
VIA RONDINELLI
VIA DEGLI AGLI
VIA DEI PECORI
BORGO OGNISSANTI
VIA DEL MORO
VIA DEL SOLE
VIA DELLE BELLE DONNE
VIA DE CORSI
VIA CAMPIDOGLIO
VIA DE' VECCHIETTI
V. BRUNELLESCHI
VIA DELLA SPADA
VIA DE' FOSSI
VIA DE' TORNABUONI
VIA DE' PESCIONI
VIA DE' FEDERIGHI
VIA DEGLI STROZZI
VIA DELLA VIGNA NUOVA
VIA DELL'INFERNO
VIA DEL PURGATORIO
VIA DEGLI ANSELMI
VIA DE' SASSETTI
VIA PELLICCERIA
VIA DEL PARIONE
PONTE ALLA CARRAIA
VIA PARIONCINO
LUNGARNO CORSINI
VIA PORTA ROSSA
V. DELLE TERME
BORGO SANTI APOSTOLI
LUNGARNO ACCIAIUOLI
VIA POR S. MARIA
LUNGARNO GUICCIARDINI
PONTE S. TRINITA
BORGO D. STELLA
VIA S. MONACA
VIA DEI SERRAGLI
VIA DI ARDIGLIONE
VIA DI SANTO SPIRITO
VIA MAFFIA
VIA S. AGOSTINO
BORGO SAN JACOPO
VIA DI SAN MARTINO
VIA VELLUTINI
VIA TOSCANELLA
V. D. RAMAGLIANTI
V. D. BARBADORI
LUNGARNO TORRIGIANI
VIA STRACCIATELLA
COSTA DI SAN GIORGIO
VIA GUICCIARDINI
VIA MAGGIO
VIA DEL PRESTO
SDRUCCIOLO DE' PITTI
VIA DE' VELLUTI
VIA DELLO SPRONE
V. DEI LUNGARNO

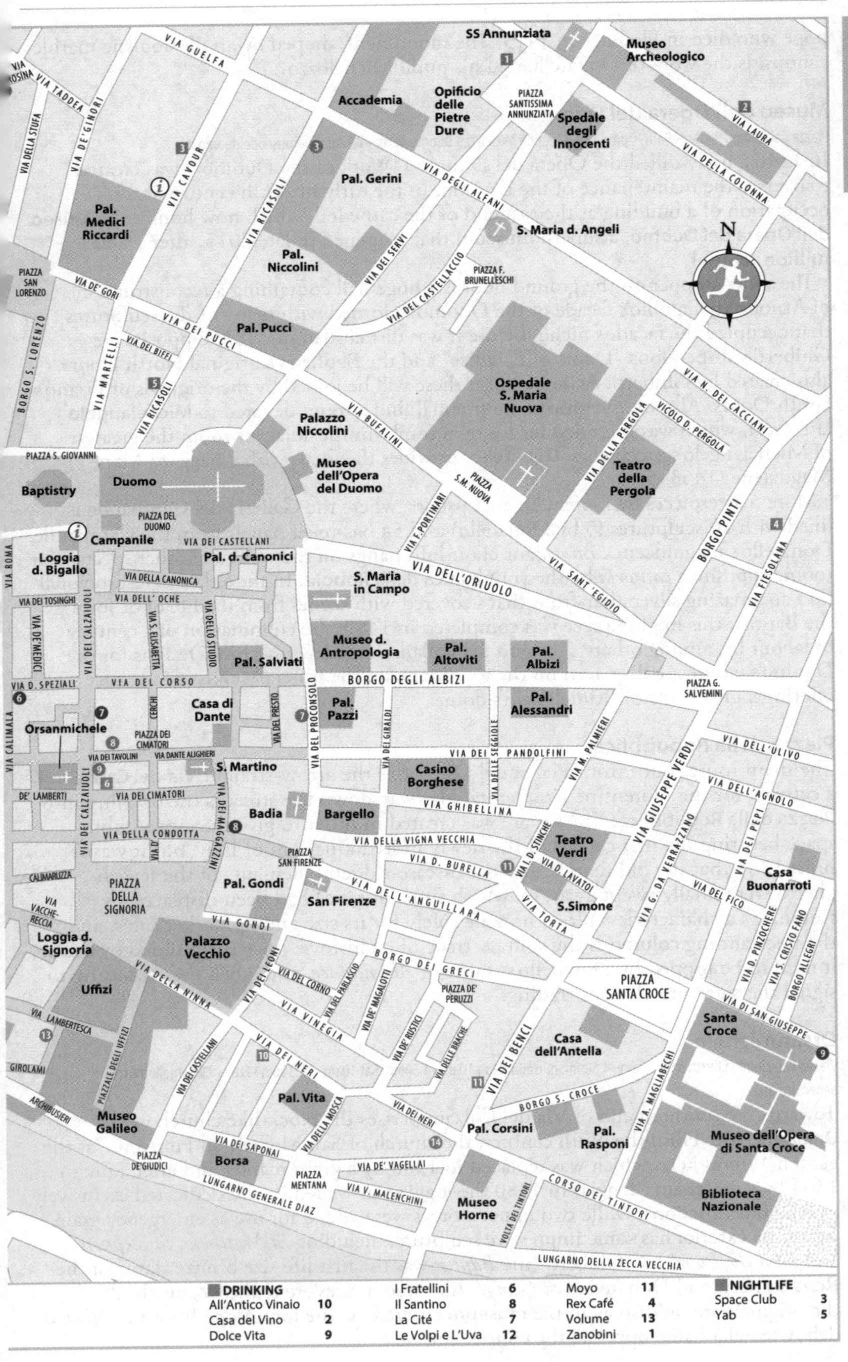
9
SS Annunziata
Museo Archeologico
Accademia
Opificio delle Pietre Dure
PIAZZA SANTISSIMA ANNUNZIATA
Spedale degli Innocenti
Pal. Gerini
Pal. Medici Riccardi
Pal. Niccolini
S. Maria d. Angeli
PIAZZA SAN LORENZO
PIAZZA F. BRUNELLESCHI
Pal. Pucci
Ospedale S. Maria Nuova
Palazzo Niccolini
Museo dell'Opera del Duomo
Teatro della Pergola
PIAZZA S. GIOVANNI
Baptistry
Duomo
PIAZZA DEL DUOMO
Campanile
Loggia d. Bigallo
Pal. d. Canonici
S. Maria in Campo
Museo d. Antropologia
Pal. Altoviti
Pal. Albizi
Pal. Salviati
Casa di Dante
Pal. Pazzi
Pal. Alessandri
Orsanmichele
PIAZZA DEI CIMATORI
S. Martino
Casino Borghese
Badia
Bargello
Teatro Verdi
PIAZZA SAN FIRENZE
Pal. Gondi
San Firenze
S.Simone
Casa Buonarroti
PIAZZA DELLA SIGNORIA
Loggia d. Signoria
Palazzo Vecchio
Uffizi
PIAZZA DE' PERUZZI
PIAZZA SANTA CROCE
Santa Croce
Casa dell'Antella
Pal. Vita
Museo Galileo
Pal. Corsini
Pal. Rasponi
Museo dell'Opera di Santa Croce
PIAZZA DE'GIUDICI
Borsa
PIAZZA MENTANA
Museo Horne
Biblioteca Nazionale
PIAZZA G. SALVEMINI
VIA GUELFA
VIA CAVOUR
VIA RICASOLI
VIA DEGLI ALFANI
VIA DEI SERVI
VIA DEI PUCCI
VIA BUFALINI
VIA DELL'ORIUOLO
VIA SANT'EGIDIO
BORGO PINTI
VIA DELLA PERGOLA
BORGO DEGLI ALBIZI
VIA DEL PROCONSOLO
VIA DEI CALZAIUOLI
VIA DEL CORSO
VIA GHIBELLINA
VIA GIUSEPPE VERDI
VIA DELL'ANGUILLARA
BORGO DEI GRECI
VIA DEI NERI
VIA DEI BENCI
BORGO S. CROCE
CORSO DEI TINTORI
LUNGARNO GENERALE DIAZ
LUNGARNO DELLA ZECCA VECCHIA
DRINKING
All'Antico Vinaio 10
Casa del Vino 2
Dolce Vita 9
I Fratellini 6
Il Santino 8
La Cité 7
Le Volpi e L'Uva 12
Moyo 11
Rex Café 4
Volume 13
Zanobini 1
NIGHTLIFE
Space Club 3
Yab 5

pope who died in Florence in 1419. The monument, draped by an illusionistic marble canopy, is the work of Donatello and his pupil Michelozzo.

Museo dell'Opera del Duomo

Piazza del Duomo 9 • Daily 9am–7pm • €18 Il Grande Museo del Duomo ticket • ⓦ ilgrandemuseodelduomo.it

In 1296 a body called the Opera del Duomo ("Work of the Duomo") was created to oversee the maintenance of the Duomo. In the early fifteenth century it took occupation of a building at the east end of the cathedral, which now houses the **Museo dell'Opera del Duomo**, a superb museum that reopened in late 2015, after a €50 million rebuild.

The show-stopper on the ground floor is a huge hall containing a reconstruction of Arnolfo di Cambio's facade of the Duomo, adorned with many of the sculptures that occupied the facade's niches before it was dismantled in 1587. Opposite are Ghiberti's stupendous "Doors of Paradise" and the Baptistry's original North Doors, also created by Ghiberti. At some point these will be joined by the originals of Pisano's South Doors. Also on the ground floor you'll find a room devoted to **Michelangelo**'s late *Pietà*, which was intended for his own tomb. In the adjacent room the greatest of Michelangelo's precursors, **Donatello**, provides the focus with a haggard Mary Magdalene (1453–5).

More masterpieces by Donatello are upstairs, where the Galleria del Campanile is lined with 16 sculptures (5 by Donatello) and 54 bas-relief panels from the Campanile. Donatello's magnificent *cantoria*, or choir loft, hangs on the wall of another spectacular room, opposite a *cantoria* by the young **Luca della Robbia**. In the Sala del Tesoro you'll find an amazing silver altar-front that's covered with scenes from the life of St John the Baptist; this mighty piece was completed in 1480, the culmination of a century of labour by, among others, Antonio del Pollaiuolo and Verrocchio. Designs for the Duomo's facade are displayed on the top floor, and the itinerary ends on a terrace offering a great view of Brunelleschi's dome.

Piazza della Repubblica

The main route south from Piazza del Duomo is the arrow-straight **Via dei Calzaiuoli**, a catwalk for the Florentine *passeggiata*. Halfway down the street is the opening into **Piazza della Repubblica**. The square was created in order to give the city a public space befitting the first capital of the newly united kingdom of Italy, but it wasn't until 1885 that the old market and the disease-ridden tenements of the Jewish ghetto were finally swept away, by which time Florence had been displaced by Rome. It's a characterless place, notable solely for its size and upmarket cafés, and the freestanding **column** is the solitary trace of its history: once surrounded by stalls, it used to be topped by Donatello's statue of *Abundance*, and a bell that was rung to signal the start and close of trading.

Orsanmichele

Via dei Calzaiuoli • Church daily 10am–4.50pm; museum Mon 10am–4.50pm, Sat 10am–12.30pm • Free • ⓦ bargellomusei.beniculturali.it

Towards the southern end of Via dei Calzaiuoli rises the block-like church of **Orsanmichele**. From the ninth century, the church of San Michele ad Hortum ("at the garden") stood here, which was replaced in 1240 by a grain market and after a fire in 1304 by a merchants' loggia. In 1380 the loggia was walled in and dedicated exclusively to religious functions, while two upper storeys were added for use as emergency grain stores. Its **exterior** has some impressive sculpture, including *St Matthew*, *St Stephen* and *John the Baptist* by Ghiberti (the *Baptist* was the first life-size bronze statue of the Renaissance), and Donatello's *St George*. All these statues are replicas – nearly all of the originals are on display in the **museum** entered via the footbridge from the Palazzo dell'Arte della Lana, opposite the church entrance.

Piazza della Signoria and around

Whereas the Piazza del Duomo provides the focus for the city's religious life, the **Piazza della Signoria** – site of the mighty **Palazzo Vecchio** and forecourt to the **Uffizi** – has always been the centre of its secular existence. The most lavishly decorated rooms of the Palazzo Vecchio are now a museum, but the rest of the building is still the HQ of the city's councillors and bureaucrats, and the piazza in front of it provides the stage for major civic events and political rallies.

The piazza's array of **statuary** starts with Giambologna's equestrian statue of *Cosimo I* and continues with Ammanati's fatuous *Neptune Fountain* and copies of Donatello's *Marzocco* (the city's heraldic lion), his *Judith and Holofernes* and of Michelangelo's *David*. Conceived as a partner piece to *David*, Bandinelli's lumpen **Hercules and Cacus** was designed as a personal emblem of Cosimo I and a symbol of Florentine fortitude; Benvenuto Cellini described the musclebound Hercules as looking like "a sackful of melons". Near Ammanati's fountain is a plaque set into the pavement to mark the site of Savonarola's **Bonfire of the Vanities** and his execution (see page 520). The square's **Loggia della Signoria** was built in the late fourteenth century as a dais for city officials during ceremonies; only in the late eighteenth century did it become a showcase for sculpture, the best of which are Giambologna's *Rape of the Sabine* and Cellini's superb *Perseus*.

Palazzo Vecchio

Piazza della Signoria • **Palazzo and Tracce di Firenze** 1 April–30 Sept Mon–Wed & Fri–Sun 9am–11pm, Thurs 9am–2pm; 1 Oct–31 March Mon–Wed & Fri–Sun 9am–7pm, Thurs 9am–2pm • Palazzo Vecchio €10, Tracce di Firenze free • **Torre di Arnolfo** 1 April–30 Sept Mon–Wed & Fri–Sun 9am–9pm, Thurs 9am–2pm; 1 Oct–31 March Mon–Wed & Fri–Sun 9am–5pm, Thurs 9am–2pm • €10, combined ticket €14 • Ⓦ imuseidifirenze.it

Probably designed by Arnolfo di Cambio, Florence's fortress-like town hall, the **Palazzo Vecchio**, was begun as the Palazzo dei Priori in the last year of the thirteenth century, to provide premises for the highest tier of the city's republican government. Changes in the Florentine constitution over the years entailed alterations to the layout of the palace, the most radical coming in 1540, when Cosimo I moved his retinue here from the Palazzo Medici and grafted a huge extension onto the rear. The Medici remained in residence for only nine years before moving to the Palazzo Pitti; the old (*vecchio*) palace – which they left to their son, Francesco – then acquired its present name.

Tracce di Firenze

The small **Tracce di Firenze** (Traces of Florence) museum, on the ground floor of the *palazzo*, is in essence a collection of maps, prints, photos and topographical paintings that chart the growth of Florence from the fifteenth century to the present. Perhaps the most impressive item is the meticulous nineteenth-century reproduction of a 1472 aerial view of Florence called the *Pianta della Catena* (Chain Map), the original of which was destroyed in Berlin during World War II. It's the oldest accurate representation of Florence's layout. And don't miss the section devoted to the labyrinthine jumble of the Mercato Vecchio, the city's ancient heart, which was demolished to make space for Piazza della Repubblica.

The first floor

Giorgio Vasari, court architect from 1555 until his death in 1574, was responsible for much of the decor in the courtyard, and his limited talents were given full rein in the huge **Salone dei Cinquecento** at the top of the stairs, built at the end of the fifteenth century as a council assembly hall. This room might have become one of Italy's most extraordinary showcases of Renaissance art, when in 1503 Leonardo da Vinci and Michelangelo were commissioned to fresco opposite walls of the chamber. Unfortunately, Leonardo abandoned the project after his experimental fresco technique went wrong, and Michelangelo's work existed only on paper when he was summoned to Rome by Pope Julius II. (The discovery of a cavity behind *The Battle of Marciano*

has raised the possibility that Vasari constructed a false wall over Leonardo's fresco, to preserve his great predecessor's painting. Investigations are proceeding.) A few decades later Vasari stepped in, and covered the room with drearily bombastic murals celebrating Cosimo's military prowess. Michelangelo's *Victory*, facing the entrance door, was sculpted for Julius's tomb but was donated to the Medici by the artist's nephew.

From the Salone del Cinquecento, a roped-off door allows a glimpse of the strangest room in the building, the **Studiolo di Francesco I**. Designed by Vasari towards the end of his career and decorated by no fewer than thirty Mannerist artists (1570–74), this windowless cell was created as a retreat for the introverted son of Cosimo and Eleanor.

The upper floor

Upstairs, you first enter the **Quartiere degli Elementi**, where all five salons are slavishly devoted to a different member of the Medici clan. More interesting are the private apartments of **Eleanor di Toledo**, Cosimo I's wife – especially the tiny and exquisite **chapel**, vividly decorated by Bronzino in the 1540s. Beyond the frescoed Sala dell'Udienza (originally the audience chamber of the Republic) you come to the **Sala dei Gigli**, which takes its name from the lilies (*gigli*) that adorn most of its surfaces. The room has frescoes by Domenico Ghirlandaio, but the highlight is **Donatello**'s original *Judith and Holofernes*. Commissioned by Cosimo il Vecchio, it freezes the moment at which Judith's arm begins the scything stroke that is to cut off Holofernes' head, a dramatic conception that no other sculptor of the period would have attempted.

The two small side-rooms are the Cancelleria, **Machiavelli**'s office for fifteen years and now containing a bust and portrait of the much-maligned political thinker; and the lovely **Sala delle Carte**, decorated with 57 maps painted in 1563 by the Medici court astronomer Fra' Ignazio Danti, depicting what was then the entire known world.

The Torre di Arnolfo

Closed when raining. No access for children under 6.

Outside the Sala dei Gigli, a staircase leads to the **tower** of Palazzo Vecchio; a 223-step climb takes you to the terrace immediately underneath the bellchambers, passing the prison cell known ironically as the Alberghinetto (Little Hotel), where Cosimo il Vecchio and Savonarola were both held for a while. The view from the summit rivals the one you get from the cathedral dome.

The Uffizi

Piazzale degli Uffizi • Tues–Sun 8.15am–6.50pm, but in high summer and at festive periods it sometimes stays open Tues until 10pm (check the website) • 1st March–31st Oct €20, 1st Nov–28th Feb €12, plus €4 booking fee if bought online; booking a time slot in advance strongly recommended (see page 521) • Ⓦ uffizi.it

Attracting well over two million visitors a year, the **Galleria degli Uffizi** is the finest picture gallery in Italy, housed in what were once government offices (*uffizi*) built by Vasari for Cosimo I in 1560. After Vasari's death, work on the building was continued by Buontalenti, who was asked by Francesco I to glaze the upper storey so that it could house his art collection. Each of the succeeding Medici added to the family's trove of art treasures, which was preserved for public inspection by the last member of the family, Anna Maria Lodovica, whose will specified that it should be left to the people of Florence and never be allowed to leave the city. In the nineteenth century a large proportion of the statuary was transferred to the Bargello, while most of the antiquities went to the Museo Archeologico, leaving the Uffizi as essentially a gallery of paintings supplemented with some classical sculptures.

The gallery is in the process of expansion, doubling the number of rooms open to the public in order to show some eight hundred pictures that have been kept in storage. Most of the new galleries have now been finished, as have the improved café and bookshop, but the so-called Nuovo Uffizi is still a work in progress, so the order in which you see things will not exactly correspond to the account that follows.

Pre-Renaissance

You can take a lift up to the galleries, but if you take the staircase instead, you'll pass the entrance to the Uffizi's **prints and drawings** section. The bulk of this vast collection is reserved for scholarly scrutiny but samples are often on public show.

Room 2, the first room of paintings, is dominated by three stunning altarpieces of the *Maestà* (Madonna Enthroned): the *Madonna Rucellai*, *Maestà di Santa Trinità* and *Madonna d'Ognissanti*, by **Duccio**, **Cimabue** and **Giotto** respectively. These great works, which dwarf everything around them, show the softening of the hieratic Byzantine style into a more tactile form of representation.

Painters from fourteenth-century Siena fill Room 3, with several pieces by Ambrogio and Pietro Lorenzetti and **Simone Martini**'s glorious *Annunciation*. In **Room 5**, devoted to the last flowering of Gothic art, **Lorenzo Monaco** is represented by an *Adoration of the Magi* and his greatest masterpiece, *The Coronation of the Virgin*. Equally arresting is another *Adoration of the Magi* by **Gentile da Fabriano** (Room 7), a picture spangled with gold and crammed with incidental detail. Opposite is the *Thebaid*, a beguiling little narrative that depicts monastic life in the Egyptian desert as a sort of holy fairytale; though labelled as being by the young Fra' Angelico, it's also been attributed to the now-obscure Gherardo di Jacopo Starnina.

Early Renaissance

Much of Room 8 is given over to **Fra' Filippo Lippi**, whose *Madonna and Child with Two Angels* is one of the gallery's most popular faces: the model was Lucrezia Buti, a convent novice who became the object of one of his more enduring sexual obsessions. Lucrezia puts in another appearance in Lippi's crowded *Coronation of the Virgin*, where she's the young woman gazing out in the right foreground; Filippo himself, hand on chin, makes eye contact on the left side of the picture. Their liaison produced a son, the aptly named **Filippino** "Little Philip" **Lippi**, whose *Otto Altarpiece* – one of several works by him here – is typical of the more melancholic cast of the younger Lippi's art. In the centre of the room stand **Piero della Francesca**'s paired and double-sided portraits of *Federico da Montefeltro* and *Battista Sforza*, the duke and duchess of Urbino.

The Pollaiuolo brothers and Botticelli

Filippo Lippi's great pupil, Botticelli, steals some of the thunder in Room 9 – *Fortitude*, one of the series of cardinal and theological virtues, is a very early work by him. The rest of the series is by **Piero del Pollaiuolo**, whose brother Antonio (primarily a sculptor) assisted him in the creation of *Sts Vincent, James and Eustace*, their finest collaboration.

It's in the merged rooms 10–14 that the finest of **Botticelli**'s productions are gathered. The identities of the characters in the **Primavera** are clear enough: on the right Zephyrus, god of the west wind, chases the nymph Cloris, who is then transfigured into Flora, the pregnant goddess of spring; Venus stands in the centre, to the side of the three Graces, who are targeted by Cupid; on the left Mercury wards off the clouds of winter. What this all means, however, has occupied scholars for decades, but the consensus seems to be that it shows the triumph of Venus, with the Graces as the physical embodiment of her beauty and Flora the symbol of her fruitfulness.

The **Birth of Venus** is less obscure: it takes as its source the myth that the goddess emerged from the sea after it had been impregnated by the castration of Uranus, an allegory for the creation of beauty through the mingling of the spirit (Uranus) and the physical world.

Botticelli's devotional paintings are equally stunning. *The Adoration of the Magi* is traditionally thought to contain a gallery of Medici portraits: Cosimo il Vecchio as the first king, his sons Giovanni and Piero as the other two kings, Lorenzo the Magnificent on the far left, and his brother Giuliano as the black-haired young man in profile on the right. Only the identification of Cosimo is reasonably certain, along with that of Botticelli himself, on the right in the yellow robe. In later life, influenced by

9

Savonarola's teaching, Botticelli confined himself to religious subjects and moral fables, and his style became increasingly severe. The transformation is clear when comparing the easy grace of the *Madonna of the Magnificat* with the angularity and agitation of the *Calumny of Apelles*.

Not quite every masterpiece in this room is by Botticelli. Set away from the walls is the *Adoration of the Shepherds* by his Flemish contemporary **Hugo van der Goes**. Brought to Florence in 1483 by Tommaso Portinari, the Medici agent in Bruges, it provided the city's artists with their first large-scale demonstration of the realism of Northern European oil painting, and had a great influence on the way the medium was exploited here.

Leonardo to Michelangelo

Works in Room 15 trace the formative years of **Leonardo da Vinci**, whose distinctive touch appears first in the *Baptism of Christ* by his master Verrocchio: the wistful angel in profile is by the 18-year-old apprentice, as is the misty landscape in the background, and Leonardo also worked heavily on the figure of Christ. A similar terrain of soft-focus mountains and water occupies the far distance in Leonardo's slightly later *Annunciation*, in which a diffused light falls on a scene where everything is observed with a scientist's precision. In contrast to the poise of the *Annunciation*, the sketch of *The Adoration of the Magi* – abandoned when Leonardo left Florence for Milan in early 1482 – presents the infant Christ as the eye of a vortex of figures, all drawn into his presence by a force as irresistible as a whirlpool. Most of the rest of the room is given over to Raphael's teacher, **Perugino**.

Beyond the octagonal **Tribuna**, which houses several items from the Medici's collection of **classical sculptures**, comes a sequence of rooms devoted to painters of the early Italian Renaissance. Rooms 20 and 21 are particularly strong, with a pair of gorgeous pictures by **Antonello da Messina**, a perplexing *Sacred Allegory* by **Giovanni Bellini** and a stupendous array of works by **Mantegna**: a swarthy portrait of Carlo de' Medici, the *Madonna delle Cave* – which takes its name from the minuscule quarries (*cave*) in the background – and a triptych which is not in fact a real triptych, but rather a trio of exquisite small paintings shackled together.

When this book went to press the opposite side of the Uffizi from rooms 19–23 was in some disarray, but the new **Michelangelo** room is now finished. The focus of the room is his *Doni Tondo*, the only easel painting he came close to completing. Work by various contemporaries of Michelangelo occupy the rest of the wall space. **Franciabiagio**, **del Sarto** and **Fra' Bartolomeo** all feature strongly, alongside **Albertinelli**'s lustrous *Visitation*.

The Niobe Room and the foreign painters

The majestic **Niobe Room**, which takes its name from the sculptures of *Niobe and her Daughters* (Roman copies of Greek originals, unearthed in a vineyard in Rome in 1583), has two bombastic pictures by Rubens: *Henry IV at the Battle of Ivry* and *The Triumphal Entry of Henry IV into Paris.* Beyond, near the end of this corridor, Room 45 is currently being used as a sort of parking space for pictures that await a new permanent home: **Fra' Angelico**'s gorgeous *Coronation of the Virgin* is here, along with **Paolo Uccello**'s *The Battle of San Romano* and fabulous paintings by Memling.

The lower galleries

Downstairs, you turn left for a new section that's devoted to non-Italian artists from the sixteenth to the eighteenth century. Dutch and Flemish artists occupy most of the wall space, with no fewer than four **Rembrandt** portraits on view; **Goya**, **El Greco** and **Chardin** are just a few of the other great foreigners you'll find here. Most of this floor is taken up with galleries that are given over mainly to Italian art from the sixteenth and seventeenth centuries, with a smattering of later work. Early on you'll pass through

the room that's dedicated to **Andrea del Sarto**, where his sultry *Madonna of the Harpies* takes pride of place. Two of del Sarto's pupils, Rosso Fiorentino and Pontormo, are also given solo rooms, while Pontormo's great protegé, **Bronzino**, gets even more space: his portraits of Cosimo de' Medici, Eleonora di Toledo, Bartolomeo Panciatichi and his wife Lucrezia Panciatichi are all faintly uncanny in their cool precision. Room 66 is packed with pictures by **Raphael**, including his youthful self-portrait, the lovely *Madonna of the Goldfinch* and *Pope Leo X with Cardinals Giulio de' Medici and Luigi de' Rossi* – as shifty a group of ecclesiastics as was ever gathered in one frame.

After Raphael comes Correggio and then **Parmigianino**, whose hyper-elegant and bizarre *Madonna of the Long Neck* is one of the pivotal Mannerist creations. The Venetians are next, with an array of works attributed to **Giorgione**, and **Sebastiano del Piombo**'s *Death of Adonis*, which was reduced to tatters by the Mafia bomb which in 1993 destroyed part of the Uffizi and killed five people. Room 83 is entirely given over to one of the mightiest figures in the story of Venetian art, **Titian**, with no fewer than eleven of his paintings on show. His *Flora* and *A Knight of Malta* are stunning, but most eyes tend to swivel towards the provocative *Urbino Venus*, which was described by Mark Twain as "the foulest, the vilest, the obscenest picture the world possesses".

Room 88 houses a pair of typically idiosyncratic pictures by Lorenzo Lotto and some deeply acute portraits by Moroni, along with **Paolo Veronese**'s *Annunciation* and *Holy Family with St Barbara*. Dramatic images from Salvator Rosa, Luca Giordano and Artemisia Gentileschi make quite an impression in the last rooms, where the presiding genius is **Caravaggio**.

The Museo Nazionale del Bargello

Via del Proconsolo 4 • Daily 8.15am–5pm • €8, €9 during exhibitions • Ⓦ bargellomusei.beneculturali.it

The **Museo Nazionale del Bargello**, which is both an outstanding museum of sculpture and a huge applied art collection, is installed in the daunting Palazzo del Bargello on Via del Proconsolo, halfway between the Duomo and the Palazzo Vecchio. The *palazzo* was built in 1255, and soon became the seat of the Podestà, the chief magistrate. Numerous malefactors were tried, sentenced and executed here; the building acquired its present name in the sixteenth century, after the resident *bargello*, or police chief.

The courtyard and ground floor

From the ticket desk, you enter the beautiful Gothic **courtyard**, which is plastered with the coats of arms of the Podestà and contains, among many other pieces, six allegorical figures by **Ammanati**. At the foot of the courtyard steps is the **Michelangelo Room**, containing his first major sculpture, a tipsy, soft-bellied figure of *Bacchus*, carved at the age of 22 – a year before his great *Pietà* in Rome. Michelangelo's style soon evolved into something less ostentatiously virtuosic, as is shown by the tender *Tondo Pitti*, while the rugged expressivity of his late manner is exemplified by the square-jawed *Bust of Brutus*. Works by Michelangelo's followers and contemporaries are ranged in the immediate vicinity – **Cellini**'s *Bust of Cosimo I* and **Giambologna**'s famous *Mercury* are the best of them.

The upper floors

At the top of the courtyard staircase, the **loggia** has been turned into an aviary for Giambologna's bronze birds, brought here from the Medici villa at Castello. In the adjacent **Salone di Donatello**, vestiges of Donatello's sinuous Gothic manner are evident in the drapery of his marble *David*, placed against the left wall, but there's nothing antiquated in the alert, tense *St George*, carved just eight years later for the tabernacle of the armourers' guild at Orsanmichele and installed here in a replica of its original niche. In front stands Donatello's sexually ambiguous bronze *David*, cast around 1435, as the first freestanding nude figure since classical times. His strange, jubilant figure known as *Amor/Attis* dates from around 1440, while his breathtakingly vivid bust of *Niccolò da Uzzano* shows that he was just as comfortable with portraiture. The less

9

complex humanism of **Luca della Robbia** is embodied in the glazed terracotta Madonnas set round the walls, while Donatello's master, **Ghiberti**, is represented by his relief *The Sacrifice of Isaac*, his successful entry in the competition for the **Baptistry doors**. The treatment of the same theme submitted by **Brunelleschi** is displayed nearby. Most of the rest of this floor is occupied by a collection of **European and Islamic applied art**, of so high a standard that it would constitute an engrossing museum in its own right. Elsewhere on this floor is dazzling carved **ivory** from Byzantium and medieval France.

The sculptural display resumes on the next floor up, where you'll find superb work by the **della Robbia** family, Italy's best assembly of small Renaissance bronzes (with plentiful evidence of Giambologna's virtuosity at table-top scale) and two rooms devoted mainly to Renaissance busts, including magnificent portraits by Verrocchio, Francesco Laurana and Mino da Fiesole.

Museo Galileo

Piazza dei Giudici 1 • Daily 9.30am–6pm • €9 • Ⓦ www.museogalileo.it

Long after Florence had declined from its artistic apogee, the intellectual reputation of the city was maintained by its scientists. Grand Duke Ferdinando II and his brother Leopoldo, both of whom studied with **Galileo**, founded the Accademia del Cimento (Academy of Experiment) in 1657, and the instruments made and acquired by this academy form the core of the excellent **Museo Galileo**. The **first floor** features timepieces and measuring instruments (such as beautiful Arab astrolabes), as well as a massive armillary sphere made for Ferdinando I to demonstrate the veracity of the Ptolemaic model of the universe. Some of Galileo's original instruments are on show here, including the lens with which he discovered the four moons of Jupiter. On the floor above there are all kinds of exquisitely manufactured **scientific and mechanical equipment**, several of which were built to demonstrate the fundamental laws of physics. Dozens of clocks and timepieces are on show too, while the medical section has some alarming surgical instruments and wax anatomical models for teaching obstetrics.

The western city centre

Several streets in central Florence retain their medieval character, especially in the district immediately to the west of Piazza della Signoria. At the edge of this quarter stands the **Mercato Nuovo**, whose souvenir stalls are the busiest in the city. Usually a small group is gathered round the bronze boar known as **Il Porcellino**, trying to gain some good luck by getting a coin to fall from the animal's mouth through the grill below his head.

Palazzo Davanzati

Via Porta Rossa 13 • Mon–Fri 8.15am–1.50pm, Sat & Sun 8.15am–6.50pm closed second & fourth Sun and first, third and fifth Mon of month • €6 • Visitors have unrestricted access to the first floor; visits to the second and third floors are at 10am, 11am & noon, with visits also at 3pm and 4pm on Sat and Sun, and must be prebooked in person or by phone (no extra fee) • Ⓣ 055 238 8610, Ⓦ bargellomusei.beneculturali.it

For an immersion in the world of medieval Florence you should visit the fourteenth-century **Palazzo Davanzati**, nowadays maintained as the **Museo Davanzati**. This huge house is decorated in predominantly medieval style, using furniture from the fourteenth to the nineteenth centuries gathered from various Florentine museums, most notably the Bargello.

The coat of arms of the wealthy Davanzati family, who occupied the house from 1578 until 1838, is still visible on the facade, and you can admire their impressive family tree in the entrance hall. Upstairs are several frescoed rooms – the **Sala dei Pappagalli** (Parrot Room) and the **Camera dei Pavoni** (Peacock Bedroom) are particularly splendid – as well as some interesting reconstructions of day-to-day life in the house, with chests

full of linen in the bedrooms and a clutter of household utensils, tools, looms and spinning wheels in the third-floor kitchen. There are also fine collections of lace work and ceramics on the first floor.

Santa Trìnita

Piazza Santa Trìnita • Mon–Sat 8am–noon & 4–6pm, Sun 8–10.45am & 4–6pm • Free

Via Porta Rossa culminates at Piazza Santa Trìnita, close to the city's most stylish bridge, the **Ponte Santa Trìnita**, which was rebuilt stone by stone after the retreating Nazis had blown up the original in 1944. **Santa Trìnita church** was founded in 1092 by a Florentine nobleman called **Giovanni Gualberto** (scenes from whose life are illustrated in the frescoes in the alcove at the top of the left aisle), but piecemeal additions have lent it a pleasantly hybrid air. The interior is notable above all for **Ghirlandaio**'s frescoes of scenes from the life of St Francis in the **Cappella Sassetti**, which were commissioned by Francesco Sassetti, general manager of the Medici bank. *St Francis Receiving the Rule* sets the action in Piazza della Signoria and features (right foreground) a portrait of Sassetti between his son, Federigo, and Lorenzo il Magnifico. On the steps below them are the humanist Poliziano and three of his pupils, Lorenzo's sons; the blond boy, at the back of the line, is Giovanni, the future Pope Leo X.

Via de' Tornabuoni

In recent years **Via de' Tornabuoni** and nearby Piazza Strozzi have come to be monopolized by high-end designer stores – Versace, Cartier, Armani, Prada, Cavalli, Pucci, Gucci and Ferragamo all have outlets here, to the dismay of those who lament the erosion of Florentine identity by the ever-burgeoning megabrands. (Though the last four in that list are at least Florentine in origin.) Conspicuous wealth is nothing new here, for looming above everything is the vast **Palazzo Strozzi**, the last, the largest and the least subtle of Florentine Renaissance palaces. Filippo Strozzi bought and demolished a dozen townhouses to make space for Giuliano da Sangallo's design (1536). Now administered by the Fondazione Palazzo Strozzi, the building has become a venue for outstanding art exhibitions; it has a nice café too.

Museo Marino Marini and the Cappella Rucellai

Piazza San Pancrazio • **Museo Marino Marini** Sat, Sun & Mon 10am–7pm; permanent collection free, exhibitions €6 • **Cappella Rucellai** Guided tours only Sat, Sun & Mon at 11am, 12pm, 3pm and 4pm; €6 • Ⓦ museomarinomarini.it

The ex-church of San Pancrazio was deconsecrated by Napoleon, then became successively the offices of the state lottery, the magistrates' court, a tobacco factory and an arsenal. It's now the glossy **Museo Marino Marini**, a superbly designed space which holds some two hundred works that were left to the city in Marini's will. Born in Pistoia in 1901, Marini trained at the Accademia and devoted most of his subsequent career to sculpture. His equestrian figures are his best-known works, and variations of the theme make a strong showing here, alongside some potent nudes.

Once part of the church of San Pancrazio and now entered via the Marini museum, the **Cappella Rucellai** was redesigned by Leon Battista Alberti and houses the most delicate of his architectural creations, the **Sacello del Santo Sepolcro**, which was commissioned by Giovanni Rucellai – one of the richest businessmen in the city, and an esteemed scholar too – as his own funerary monument. Giovanni Rucellai's house, **Palazzo Rucellai**, commissioned from Alberti in the 1440s, is around the corner at Via della Vigna Nuova 18.

Ognissanti

Borgo Ognissanti • Mon, Tues & Thurs–Sun 9.30am–noon & 4–7.30pm, Wed 4–7.30pm; refectory Mon, & Sat 9am–1pm • Free • Ⓦ chiesaognissanti.it

In medieval times, a major area of cloth production – the foundation of the Florentine economy – lay in the west of the city, in the parish of **Ognissanti**, five minutes' walk

west of Via de' Tornabuoni. The Baroque facade of the church is not very interesting, but the interior is a different matter. The young face squeezed between the Madonna and the dark-cloaked man in **Ghirlandaio**'s *Madonna della Misericordia* fresco, over the second altar on the right, is said to be that of Amerigo Vespucci – later to set sail on voyages that would give his name to America. Just beyond this, on opposite sides of the nave, are mounted **Botticelli**'s *St Augustine* and Ghirlandaio's *St Jerome*, both painted in 1480. In the same year Ghirlandaio painted the bucolic *Last Supper* that covers one wall of the **refectory**, reached through the cloister entered to the left of the church. And don't miss the dazzling Crucifix that hangs in the left transept: in 2010 it emerged from a seven-year restoration, and in the course of the cleaning it was established that it's almost certainly by **Giotto**.

Santa Maria Novella

Piazza Santa Maria Novella • April–June Mon–Thurs 9am–7pm, Fri 11am–7pm, Sat 9am–5.30pm, Sun 1–5.30pm; July & Aug Mon–Thurs 9am–7pm, Fri 11am–7pm, Sat 9am–6.30pm, Sun noon–6.30pm; Sept Mon–Thurs 9am–7pm, Fri 11am–7pm, Sat 9am–5.30pm, Sun noon–5.30pm; Oct–March Mon–Thurs 9am–5.30pm, Fri 11am–5.30pm, Sat 9am–5.30pm, Sun 1–5.30pm • €7.50 • Ⓦ smn.it

Presiding over the recently refurbished **Piazza Santa Maria Novella**, the marble facade designed by Alberti for the Dominican church of **Santa Maria Novella** is one of the most attractive in the city. The church's interior – designed to enable preachers to address their sermons to as large a congregation as possible – is filled with masterworks, not least **Masaccio**'s extraordinary 1427 fresco of *The Trinity* (left aisle), one of the earliest works in which perspective and classical proportion were rigorously employed. Nearby, Giotto's *Crucifix*, a radically naturalistic and probably very early work (c.1288–90), hangs in what is thought to be its intended position, poised dramatically over the nave.

Filippino Lippi's frescoes for the **Cappella di Filippo Strozzi** (immediately to the right of the chancel) are a fantasy vision of classical ruins in which the narrative (on the life of St Philip the Apostle) often seems to take second place – before starting the project Filippino spent some time in Rome, and this work displays an archeologist's obsession with ancient Roman culture. As a chronicle of fifteenth-century life in Florence, no series of frescoes is more fascinating than **Domenico Ghirlandaio**'s cycle in the Cappella Tornabuoni, behind the high altar; the cycle was commissioned by Giovanni Tornabuoni – which explains why certain ladies of the Tornabuoni family are present at the birth of John the Baptist and of the Virgin. **Brunelleschi**'s *Crucifix*, popularly supposed to have been carved as a response to Donatello's uncouth version at Santa Croce, hangs in the Cappella Gondi, left of the chancel. At the end of the left transept is the raised **Cappella Strozzi**, whose faded frescoes by Nardo di Cione (1350s) include an entire wall of visual commentary on Dante's *Inferno*. The magnificent altarpiece by Nardo's brother Andrea (better known as **Orcagna**) is a piece of propaganda for the Dominicans – Christ is shown bestowing favour simultaneously on St Peter and St Thomas Aquinas, a figure second only to St Dominic in the order's hierarchy.

Museo di Santa Maria Novella

More remarkable paintings are on display in the spacious Romanesque conventual buildings, now the **Museo di Santa Maria Novella**. A door on the left wall of the church takes you into the **Chiostro Verde**, which features frescoes of stories from Genesis by **Paolo Uccello** and his workshop. (A second entrance, shared with the Piazza della Stazione tourist office, takes you directly into the museum.) Leading off from this cloister is the **Cappellone degli Spagnuoli** (Spanish Chapel), which received its new name after Eleanor of Toledo reserved it for the use of her Spanish entourage. Its fresco cycle by Andrea di Firenze was described by Ruskin as "the most noble piece of pictorial philosophy in Italy". The left wall depicts the *Triumph of Divine Wisdom*: Thomas Aquinas is enthroned below the Virgin and Apostles amid winged Virtues and biblical notables. The more spectacular right wall depicts the *Triumph of the Church*, and includes Florence's cathedral, imagined eighty years before its actual completion.

9

Museo Novecento

Piazza Santa Maria Novella 10 • 1st April–30th Sept Thurs 11am–2pm, Fri 11am–11pm, Sat–Wed 11am–8pm; 1 Oct– 31 March Thurs 11am–2pm, Fri–Tues 11am–7pm • €8.50 • Ⓦ museonovecento.it

The colonnaded building that faces Santa Maria Novella – the **Loggia di San Paolo** – has been used as a hospital, a school and a prison, and is now home to Florence's newest civic museum, the **Museo Novecento**, which finally opened its doors in the summer of 2014 after half a century of planning. With around three hundred works on show at any one time, it features some of the heavyweights of Italian **twentieth-century art**, such as Giorgio Morandi, Giorgio de Chirico, Lucio Fontana and Emilio Vedova, and has interesting thematic sections explaining the interactions between music, architecture and the visual arts.

The northern city centre

The busy quarter north of the Duomo and east of the train station is focused on Florence's main food market, the vast **Mercato Centrale** (June–Sept Mon–Fri 7am–2am; Oct–May Mon–Fri 7am–2pm, Sat 7am–5pm). Butchers, *alimentari*, greengrocers and *tavole calde* are gathered on the ground floor, while the upper floor, which reopened in 2014 after a major renovation, has a pizzeria, a birreria and various other places to eat and drink, which keep the building lively long after the market stalls have shut down for the day. Surrounding the building are the stalls of a hectic **street market** (daily 9am–7pm), selling leather bags, belts, clothes and shoes.

San Lorenzo

Piazza San Lorenzo • Mon–Sat 10am–5pm, Sun 1.30–5pm (Nov–Feb closed Sun, slightly longer opening hours in summer) • €6 for Basilica, €8.50 combined ticket with Biblioteca Medicea-Laurenziana (see below) • Ⓦ operamedicealaurenziana.it

Founded in the fourth century, **San Lorenzo** has a claim to be the oldest church in Florence – though the current building dates from the 1420s – and was the city's cathedral for almost three centuries. Although Michelangelo and several other architects laboured to produce a scheme for San Lorenzo's facade, the bare brick of the exterior has never been clad; it's a stark prelude to the powerful simplicity of Brunelleschi's interior, one of the earliest Renaissance church designs. Inside are two amazing **bronze pulpits** by **Donatello**. Covered in densely populated reliefs, chiefly of scenes preceding and following the Crucifixion, these are the artist's last works and were completed by his pupils. Close by, at the foot of the altar steps, a large disc of multicoloured marble marks the grave of Cosimo il Vecchio, the artist's main patron. Further pieces by Donatello adorn the beautiful **Sagrestia Vecchia**, off the left transept.

The Biblioteca Medicea-Laurenziana

Piazza San Lorenzo • Mon–Fri 9.30am–1.30pm • €8.50 combined ticket with San Lorenzo (see above) • Ⓦ operamedicealaurenziana.it

A gateway to the left of the church facade leads to the cloister of San Lorenzo, where one staircase descends to the treasury and the tombs of Cosimo de' Medici and Donatello, and another rises to the **Biblioteca Medicea-Laurenziana**. Wishing to create a suitably grandiose home for the precious manuscripts assembled by Cosimo and Lorenzo de' Medici, Pope Clement VII – Lorenzo's nephew – asked Michelangelo to design a new library in 1524. His Ricetto, or vestibule (1559–71), is a revolutionary showpiece of Mannerist architecture, delighting in paradoxical display: brackets that support nothing, columns that sink into the walls rather than stand out from them, and a flight of steps so large that it almost fills the room. Beyond this eccentric space lies the reading room, which is often used for exhibitions; here, too, almost everything is the work of Michelangelo, even the inlaid desks.

The Cappelle Medicee

Daily 8.15am–5pm, closed first, third & fifth Mon of month, and second & fourth Sun of month • €8 • Ⓦ bargellomusei.beneculturali.it

Some of Michelangelo's most celebrated works are in San Lorenzo's Sagrestia Nuova, part of the **Cappelle Medicee**. The entrance to the chapels is round the back of San Lorenzo, on Piazza Madonna degli Aldobrandini, and leads directly into the low-vaulted **crypt**, last resting place of a clutch of minor Medici. After filing through the crypt, you climb into the **Cappella dei Principi** (Chapel of the Princes), a gloomy, stone-plated octagonal hall built as a mausoleum for Cosimo I and his ancestors. This was the most expensive building project ever financed by the Medici.

A corridor leads to the **Sagrestia Nuova**, begun by Michelangelo in 1520 and intended as a tribute to, and subversion of, Brunelleschi's Sagrestia Vecchia in San Lorenzo. Architectural connoisseurs go into raptures over the complex alcoves and other such sophistications, but you might be more drawn to the fabulous **Medici tombs**, carved by Michelangelo. To the left is the **tomb of Lorenzo**, Duke of Urbino, grandson of Lorenzo il Magnifico. Opposite is the **tomb of Giuliano**, Duke of Nemours, youngest son of Lorenzo il Magnifico. Their effigies were intended to face the equally grand tombs of Lorenzo il Magnifico and his brother Giuliano, two Medici who had genuine claims to fame and honour, but the only part of the project realized by Michelangelo is the serene **Madonna and Child**, the last image of the Madonna he ever sculpted, now flanked by *Cosmas* and *Damian*, patron saints of doctors (*medici*) and thus of the dynasty.

Casa Martelli

Via Zannetti 8 • Thurs 2–7pm, Sat & Sun 9am–2pm; closed second & fourth Sun of month; guided tour every hour, up to 1hr before closing • Free • Ⓦ bargellomusei.beneculturali.it

From the sixteenth century until the death of the last of the Martelli in 1989, **Casa Martelli** – a minute's walk from the Medici chapels – was home to a family that for many years was very closely associated with their near neighbours, the Medici. It was not until 1738 that Casa Martelli took on its present form, when several houses were merged to create this spectacular *palazzo*. The interior was then completely redecorated, and it's the style of this refurbishment that dominates, with room after room of gorgeous trompe l'oeil frescoes, sumptuous furniture, delicate stucco work and shimmering brocades. The family's art collection, stacked almost to the ceiling in the *palazzo*'s picture gallery, includes work by Piero di Cosimo, Salvator Rosa and Luca Giordano.

Palazzo Medici-Riccardi

Via Cavour 1 • Daily except Wed 8.30am–7pm • €7

On the northeastern edge of Piazza San Lorenzo stands the **Palazzo Medici-Riccardi**, built by Michelozzo in the 1440s for Cosimo il Vecchio, and for more than a century the principal seat of the Medici. With its heavily rusticated exterior, this mighty palace was the prototype for such houses as the Palazzo Pitti and Palazzo Strozzi, but was greatly altered in the seventeenth century by its new owners, the Riccardi family, who took over after Cosimo I moved out. Of Michelozzo's original scheme, only the courtyard and upstairs **chapel** remain intact. The chapel's interior is covered by brilliantly colourful and wonderfully detailed **frescoes** of *The Procession of the Magi*, painted around 1460 by Benozzo Gozzoli and featuring several of the Medici household. Only fifteen people are allowed to view these paintings at any one time, so the queues can be long.

After the chapel, you visit the **Riccardi apartments**, including the sumptuous Sala di Carlo VIII and, further on, the Sala di Luca Giordano, a gilded and mirrored gallery notable for Luca Giordano's overblown ceiling fresco, *The Apotheosis of the Medici*, showing Cosimo III with his son, Gian Gastone (d. 1737), the last male Medici. In a nearby room is Fra' Filippo Lippi's *Madonna and Child*.

Off the courtyard, the **Museo dei Marmi** holds the Riccardi's sculpture collection, and a multimedia room explains the history of the chapel frescoes.

9

The Accademia

Via Ricasoli 66 • Tues–Sun 8.15am–6.50pm • €8, or €12.50 when special exhibitions are on; booking advised (see page 521) • galleriaaccademiafirenze.beniculturali.it

Europe's first academy of drawing was founded northeast of San Lorenzo on Via Ricasoli in the mid-sixteenth century by Bronzino, Ammanati and Vasari. In 1784, Grand Duke Pietro Leopoldo opened the adjoining **Galleria dell'Accademia**, which has an impressive collection of paintings, especially of Florentine altarpieces from the fourteenth to the early sixteenth centuries. What pulls the crowds, however, is one of the most famous sculptures in the world: **Michelangelo**'s *David.*

David

Commissioned by the Opera del Duomo in 1501, **David** was conceived to invoke parallels with Florence's freedom from outside domination (despite the superior force of its enemies), and its recent liberation from Savonarola and the Medici. It's an incomparable show of technical bravura, all the more impressive given the difficulties posed by the marble from which it was carved. The 4m block of stone – thin, shallow and riddled with cracks – had been quarried from Carrara forty years earlier. Several artists had already attempted to work with it, notably Agostino di Duccio, Andrea Sansovino and Leonardo da Vinci. Michelangelo succeeded where others had failed, completing the work in 1504 when he was still just 29.

When they gave Michelangelo his commission, the Opera del Duomo had in mind a large statue that would be placed high on the cathedral's facade. Perhaps because the finished *David* was even larger than had been envisaged, it was decided that it should be placed instead at ground level, in the Piazza della Signoria. The statue remained in its outdoor setting, exposed to the elements, until it was sent to the Accademia in 1873, by which time it had lost its gilded hair and the gilded band across its chest. *David* now occupies a specially built alcove, protected by a glass barrier that was built in 1991, after one of its toes was cracked by a hammer-wielding vandal. With its massive head and gangling arms, *David* looks to some people like a monstrous adolescent, but its proportions would not have appeared so graceless in the setting for which it was first conceived, at a rather higher altitude and at a greater distance from the public than the position it occupies here.

The Slaves

Michelangelo once described the process of sculpting as being the liberation of the form from within the stone, a notion that seems to be embodied by the unfinished **Slaves** that line the approach to *David*. His procedure, clearly demonstrated here, was to cut the figure as if it were a deep relief, and then to free the three-dimensional figure; often his assistants would perform the initial operation, working from the master's pencil marks, so it's possible that Michelangelo's own chisel never actually touched these stones. Carved in the 1520s and 1530s, these powerful creations were intended for the tomb of Pope Julius II, but in 1564 the artist's nephew gave them to the Medici, who installed them in the grotto of the Boboli garden.

Museo di San Marco

Piazza San Marco • Mon–Fri 8.15am–1.50pm, Sat & Sun 8.15am–4.50pm; closed second & fourth Mon of month, and first, third & fifth Sun • €4

A whole side of Piazza San Marco is taken up by the Dominican convent and church of San Marco, the first of which is now the **Museo di San Marco**. In the 1430s, the convent was the recipient of Cosimo il Vecchio's most lavish patronage: he financed Michelozzo's enlargement of the buildings, and went on to establish a vast public library here. Ironically, the convent became the centre of resistance to the Medici later in the century – Savonarola was prior of San Marco from 1491. Meanwhile, as Michelozzo was altering and expanding the convent, its walls were being decorated

by one of its friars, **Fra' Angelico**, a painter in whom a medieval simplicity of faith was allied to a Renaissance sophistication of manner. The **Ospizio dei Pellegrini** (Pilgrims' Hospice) contains around twenty paintings by Fra' Angelico, most brought here from other churches in Florence, but the most celebrated work is the glorious **Annunciation** at the summit of the main staircase. All round this upper storey are ranged 44 tiny **dormitory cells**, each frescoed either by Fra' Angelico or his assistants.

Cenacolo di Sant'Apollonia

Via XXVII Aprile 1 • Daily 8.15am–1.50pm • Free

Most of the former Benedictine convent of **Sant'Apollonia,** a few blocks west of San Marco, has been turned into apartments, but one entire wall of the former refectory houses Andrea del Castagno's *Last Supper*, which was painted around 1450 and displays one of the earliest uses of rigorous perspective in Renaissance art. The most commanding figure is the diabolic, black-bearded Judas, who sits on the near side of the table, beneath a panel of hell-fire red marble. Above the illusionistic recess in which the supper takes place are the faded remains of a *Resurrection, Crucifixion and Deposition* by Castagno, who also painted the lunettes of the *Crucifixion* and *Pietà* on the adjacent walls.

Spedale degli Innocenti

Piazza Santissima Annunziata • Daily 10am–7pm • €10 including audio guide • Ⓦ istitutodeglinnocenti.it

To the east of San Marco lies the handsome **Piazza Santissima Annunziata**, whose tone is set by Brunelleschi's **Spedale degli Innocenti**, which opened in 1445 as the first foundlings' hospital in Europe and still incorporates an orphanage – Luca della Robbia's ceramic tondi of swaddled babies advertise the building's function. The convent, centred on two beautiful cloisters, now also contains a miscellany of Florentine Renaissance art including one of Luca della Robbia's most charming Madonnas and an incident-packed *Adoration of the Magi* by Ghirlandaio.

Santissima Annunziata

Piazza Santissima Annunziata • Daily 8am–12.30pm & 4–6.30pm • Free

The church of **Santissima Annunziata** is the mother church of the Servite order, which was founded by seven Florentine aristocrats in 1234. Its dedication took place in the fourteenth century, in recognition of a miraculous image of the Virgin which, left unfinished by the monastic artist, was purportedly completed by an angel. It attracted so many pilgrims that the Medici commissioned **Michelozzo** to rebuild the church in the second half of the fifteenth century in order to accommodate them. In the Chiostro dei Voti, the atrium that Michelozzo built onto the church, are some beautiful frescoes mainly painted in the 1510s, including a *Visitation* by **Pontormo** and a series by **Andrea del Sarto**. Inside the church, the miraculous painting is enshrined in a huge tabernacle to the left; in the second chapel along, there's a striking fresco by Andrea del Castagno, of the *Holy Trinity and St Jerome* (1454). The adjoining Chiostro dei Morti is worth visiting for Andrea del Sarto's *Madonna del Sacco*, painted over the door that connects the cloister to the left transept of the church.

Museo Archeologico

Via della Colonna 36 • Mon, Sat & Sun 8.30am–2pm, Tues–Fri 8.30am–7pm • €4 • Ⓦ polomusealetoscana.beniculturali.it

On the other side of Via della Colonna from Santissima Annunziata, the **Museo Archeologico** houses the finest collection of its kind in northern Italy, but struggles to draw visitors for whom the Renaissance is the beginning and the end of Florence's appeal.

The museum's special strength is its **Etruscan** collection (much of it bequeathed by the Medici), which features two outstanding bronze sculptures – the *Arringatore* (Orator) and the *Chimera*, a triple-headed monster made in the fourth century BC. Much of the **Egyptian collection** is displayed in an uninspiring manner, but a recent renovation

has vastly improved the top storey, where the primary focus is on the **Greek and Roman collections**. The star piece in the huge hoard of Greek vases is the large *François Vase*, a sixth-century-BC *krater* discovered in an Etruscan tomb near Chiusi in 1844. Other attention-grabbing items are the life-size bronze torso known as the *Torso di Livorno*, a large horse's head that was once a feature of the garden of the Palazzo Medici, two beautiful sixth-century-BC Greek *kouroi*, and the bronze statue of a young man known as the *Idilono di Pésaro*, generally thought to be a Roman replica of a Greek figure dating from around 100 BC.

The eastern city centre

The Santa Croce district – the hub of the eastern part of central Florence – was one of the city's more densely populated areas before November 4, 1966, when the Arno burst its banks, with catastrophic consequences for this low-lying zone, which was then packed with tenements and small workshops. Many residents moved out permanently in the following years, but now the more traditional businesses that survived the flood have been joined by an ever-growing number of bars and restaurants. **Piazza Santa Croce**, one of the city's largest squares, has traditionally been used for ceremonies and festivities, and is still used for the annual **Calcio Storico** tournament (see page 553).

Santa Croce

Piazza Santa Croce • Mon–Sat 9.30am–5pm, Sun 2–5pm • €8 • Ⓦ santacroceopera.it

Florence's two most lavish churches after the Duomo were the headquarters of the two preaching orders: the Dominicans occupied Santa Maria Novella, while the Franciscans were based at **Santa Croce**, which also evolved into the mausoleum of Tuscany's most eminent citizens. More than 270 monuments are to be found here, commemorating the likes of Ghiberti, Michelangelo, Alberti, Machiavelli, Galileo and **Dante** – although Dante was actually buried in Ravenna, where he died.

The tombs are not the principal attraction of Santa Croce, however. Far more remarkable are the dazzling chapels at the east end, a compendium of Florentine fourteenth-century art, showing the extent of Giotto's influence and the full diversity of his followers. The two immediately to the right of the chancel are covered with frescoes by **Giotto**: beside the chancel is the **Cappella Bardi**, featuring scenes from the life of St Francis, while next to it is the **Cappella Peruzzi** with a cycle on the lives of St John the Baptist and John the Evangelist. On the south side of the right transept is the **Cappella Baroncelli**, featuring the first night-scene in Western painting, Taddeo Gaddi's *Annunciation to the Shepherds*. On the north side of the left transept, the second **Cappella Bardi** houses a wooden *Crucifix* by **Donatello** – supposedly criticized by Brunelleschi as resembling a "peasant on the Cross".

From the right transept a corridor leads to the **Cappella Medici**, which contains Bronzino's huge *Descent of Christ into Limbo*, Salviati's equally imposing *Deposition* and an altarpiece by Andrea and Giovanni della Robbia. Adjoining the corridor, the beautifully panelled **sacristy** is home to Cimabue's great *Crucifix*, which was half-destroyed in the 1966 flood and has become in effect the emblem of that disaster.

The Cappella dei Pazzi

The door in the south aisle opens onto the Primo Chiostro (First Cloister), at the head of which stands Brunelleschi's **Cappella dei Pazzi**. If one building could be said to typify the spirit of the early Renaissance, this is it: geometrically perfect without seeming pedantic, it's exemplary in the way its decorative detail harmonizes with the design. The polychrome lining of the portico's shallow cupola is by **Luca della Robbia**, as is the tondo of *St Andrew* over the door; inside, Della Robbia also produced the blue-and-white tondi of the *Apostles*.

Museo dell'Opera di Santa Croce

Santa Croce's spacious **Secondo Chiostro** was also designed by Brunelleschi, and is perhaps the most peaceful spot in the centre of Florence. The **Museo dell'Opera di Santa Croce**, between the two cloisters, houses a sizeable miscellany of works of art, the best of which are gathered in the ex-refectory, where Donatello's enormous gilded *St Louis of Toulouse* (1424) occupies a niche like the one it originally filled at Orsanmichele. The detached fresco of the *Last Supper* (1333) on the end wall is considered to be the finest work by Taddeo Gaddi and is the earliest surviving example of the many Last Suppers (*cenacoli*) dotted around the city.

Casa Buonarroti

Via Ghibellina 70 • Daily (except Tues) 10am–5pm (4.30pm 1 Nov–28 Feb) • €6.50 • Ⓦ casabuonarroti.it

The **Casa Buonarroti** occupies a site where **Michelangelo** probably lived intermittently between 1516 and 1525, and contains a smart but low-key museum, mostly consisting of works created in homage to the great man. The two main treasures are to be found upstairs: the *Madonna della Scala* (c.1490–92) is Michelangelo's earliest known work, a delicate relief carved when he was no older than 16; the similarly unfinished *Battle of the Centaurs* was created shortly afterwards, when the boy was living in the Medici household. In an adjacent room you'll find the artist's wooden model (1517) for the facade of San Lorenzo. Close by is the largest of all the sculptural models on display, the torso of a *River God* (1524), a work probably intended for the Medici chapel in San Lorenzo.

South of the river – Oltrarno

Visitors to Florence might perceive the Arno as merely a brief interruption in the urban fabric, but Florentines talk as though a ravine divides their city. North of the river is *Arno di quà* ("over here"), while the south side is *Arno di là* ("over there"), also known as the **Oltrarno**, literally "Beyond the Arno". Traditionally an artisans' quarter, Oltrarno is still home to plenty of small workshops (particularly furniture restorers and leather-workers), and Via Maggio remains the focus of Florence's thriving antiques trade. The ambience is less tourist-centred here than in the zone immediately across the water, which is not to say that Oltrarno doesn't have major sights – **Palazzo Pitti**, **Santa Maria del Carmine**, **San Miniato** and **Santo Spirito** are all essential visits.

The Ponte Vecchio

The direct route from the city centre to the heart of Oltrarno crosses the river on the **Ponte Vecchio**, the only bridge not mined by the retreating Nazis in 1944. Built in 1345 to replace an ancient wooden bridge, it has always been loaded with shops. Up until the sixteenth century, butchers, fishmongers and tanners occupied the bridge, but in 1593 Ferdinando I ejected these malodorous enterprises and installed goldsmiths instead. Today, still replete with jewellery firms, the bridge is crammed with sightseers and big-spending shoppers during the day, and remains busy after the shutters come down.

Santa Felicità

Piazza Santa Felicità • Mon–Sat 9.30am–12.30pm & 3.30–5pm, guided tours Fri, Sat at 3.30pm & 5.30Pm • Free

Just over the Ponte Vecchio, off Via Guicciardini, **Santa Felicità** might well be the oldest church in Florence. It's thought to have been founded in the second century AD close to the Via Cassia, over an early Christian cemetery that's commemorated by the column outside. The interior demands a visit for the amazing paintings by Pontormo in the **Cappella Capponi**. Under the cupola are four tondi of the *Evangelists*, painted with the help of Bronzino (his adoptive son), while on opposite sides of the window on the right wall are the *Virgin* and the angel of Pontormo's delightful *Annunciation*. The centrepiece is the **Deposition** (1525–28), one of the masterworks of Florentine

9

Mannerism, in which there's no sign of the Cross, the thieves, soldiers, or any of the other scene-setting devices usual in paintings of this subject.

Palazzo Pitti

Piazza Pitti • ⓦ imuseidifirenze.it

Although the Medici later took possession of the largest palace in Florence – **Palazzo Pitti** – it still bears the name of the man for whom it was built. Luca Pitti was a prominent rival of Cosimo il Vecchio, and much of the impetus behind the building of his new house came from a desire to trump the Medici. No sooner was the palace completed, however, than the Pitti's fortunes began to decline and by 1549 they were forced to sell. The palace then became the Medici family pile, growing in bulk until the seventeenth century, when it achieved its present gargantuan dimensions.

Galleria Palatina

Tues–Sun 8.15am–6.50pm • €8.50 combined ticket with Galleria d'Arte Moderna, Appartamenti Reali, Museo degli Argenti, Galleria del Costume (see below), or €13 if a special exhibition is on

Today, the *palazzo* and the pavilions of the **Giardino di Boboli** hold eight museums, of which the foremost is the huge art collection of the **Galleria Palatina**. **Andrea del Sarto** is represented by no fewer than seventeen paintings, but even more remarkable is the assembly of work by **Raphael**, including portraits of Angelo and Maddalena Doni, the celebrated *Madonna della Seggiola* and the equally famous *Donna Velata*, for which the model was the painter's mistress, a Roman baker's daughter known to posterity as La Fornarina. An even larger contingent of supreme works by **Titian** includes a number of his most trenchant portraits – among them *Pietro Aretino*, *Cardinal Ippolito de' Medici* and the *Portrait of an Englishman*, a picture that makes the viewer feel as closely scrutinized as was the subject. Elsewhere in the Palatina you'll find masterpieces by Rubens, Fra' Filippo Lippi and Caravaggio, to mention but a few.

Much of the rest of this floor comprises the **Appartamenti Reali** – the Pitti's state rooms, renovated by the dukes of Lorraine in the eighteenth century, and then again by King Vittorio Emanuele when Florence became Italy's capital.

Galleria d'Arte Moderna

Tues–Sat 8.15am–6.50pm • €8.50 combined ticket with Galleria Palatina (see above), or €13 if a special exhibition is on

On the floor above the Galleria Palatina is the **Galleria d'Arte Moderna**, which comprises a chronological survey of primarily Tuscan art from the mid-eighteenth century to 1945. Much space is devoted to the work of the Macchiaioli (the open-air painters who were in some respects the Italian equivalent of the Impressionists), but there's a lot of mediocre stuff here, with ranks of academically proficient portraits, bombastic history paintings and sentimental dross such as Rodolfo Morgari's *Raphael Dying* and Gabriele Castagnola's depiction of Fra' Filippo Lippi on the brink of kissing the lovely young novice, Lucrezia Buti.

Museo degli Argenti and Galleria del Costume

Daily: March 8.15am–5.30pm; April, May, Sept & Oct 8.15am–6.30pm; June–Aug 8.15am–7.30pm; Nov–Feb 8.15am–4.30pm; closed first & last Mon of month • €7 combined ticket for all three museums plus Giardino di Boboli (see opposite) and Giardino Bardini (see page 544); €10 during special exhibitions

Entered from the garden courtyard, the **Museo degli Argenti** is a massive collection of portable (and often hideous) luxury artefacts, including Lorenzo il Magnifico's trove of antique vases, displayed in one of the four splendidly frescoed reception rooms on the ground floor.

Visitors without a specialist interest are unlikely to be riveted by the other Pitti museums. In the Palazzina della Meridiana, the eighteenth-century southern wing of the Pitti, the **Galleria del Costume** provides the opportunity to see the dress that Eleonora di Toledo is wearing in Bronzino's famous portrait of her (in the Palazzo Vecchio).

The Giardino di Boboli

Daily: March 8.15am–5.30pm; April, May, Sept & Oct 8.15am–6.30pm; June–Aug 8.15am–7.30pm; Nov–Feb 8.15am–4.30pm; closed first & last Mon of month • €10 combined ticket with Museo delle Porcellane, which can be entered from the upper part of the Boboli Garden. Reduced entry (€6) 1 Nov–28 Feb.

The delightful formal garden of the Palazzo Pitti, the **Giardino di Boboli** takes its name from the Boboli family, erstwhile owners of much of this area, which was once a quarry. When the Medici acquired the house in 1549 they set to work transforming their back yard into a 111-acre garden. Of all the garden's Mannerist embellishments, the most celebrated is the **Grotta del Buontalenti**, beyond the turtleback figure of Cosimo I's court dwarf. In among the fake stalactites are shepherds and sheep that look like calcified sponges, while embedded in the corners are replicas of Michelangelo's *Slaves*, replacing the originals that were here until 1908. In the deepest recesses of the cave stands Giambologna's *Venus*, leered at by imps.

At the top of the gardens, in the pretty neo-classical Casino del Cavaliere, is a well-presented if esoteric collection of porcelain, the **Museo delle Porcellane**.

La Specola

Via Romana 17 • 1st June–30th Sept Tues–Sun 10am–5.30pm, 1st Oct–31st May Tues–Sun 9.30am–4.30pm; Cere Anatomiche guided tours only Tues–Fri 11.30am & 3pm, Sat & Sun 11.30am & 12.30 & 3pm • €6, plus extra €3 for guided tour • Ⓦ msn.unifi.it

Within a stone's throw of the Pitti, on the third floor of one of the university buildings, you'll find what can reasonably claim to be the strangest museum in the city. Taking its name from the telescope (*specola*) on its roof, **La Specola** is a museum of zoology, with ranks of shells, insects and crustaceans, and a veritable ark of animals stuffed, pickled and desiccated. The exhibits everyone comes to see, however, are the **Cere Anatomiche** (Anatomical Waxworks): wax arms, legs and internal organs cover the walls, arrayed around satin beds on which wax cadavers recline in progressive stages of deconstruction, each muscle fibre and nerve cluster moulded and dyed with scarcely believable precision. They were intended as teaching aids, and most of the six hundred pieces – and nearly all of the amazing full-body models – were made between 1775 and 1791 by one Clemente Susini and his team of assistants.

Santo Spirito

Piazza di Santa Spirito • Mon–Sat 9.30am–12.30pm & 4–5.30pm, Sun 11.30am–12.30pm, 4–5.30pm • Free

With its market stalls, cafés and restaurants, the lively **Piazza di Santo Spirito** is the social hub of Oltrarno. Don't be deterred by the vacant facade of the church of **Santo Spirito** – the interior, one of Brunelleschi's last projects, prompted Bernini to describe it as "the most beautiful church in the world". It's so perfectly proportioned it seems artless, yet the plan is extremely sophisticated – a Latin cross with a continuous chain of 38 chapels round the outside and a line of columns running parallel to the chapels, right round the building. Unfortunately, a Baroque baldachin covers the high altar, but this is the sole disruption of Brunelleschi's arrangement.

A door in the north aisle leads through to Giuliano da Sangallo's stunning vestibule and **sacristy** (1489–93), the latter designed in imitation of Brunelleschi's Pazzi chapel. Hanging above the altar is a delicate wooden crucifix, attributed to **Michelangelo**. It's known that the young Michelangelo was commissioned by the monks of Santo Spirito to make a crucifix for the church in the early 1490s, but many scholars think that this one was made half a century later, by Taddeo Curradi.

The Cappella Brancacci

Piazza del Carmine • Mon & Wed–Sat 9.30am–1pm & 2–5pm, Sun 9.30am–12.30pm • €6 • Ⓦ museicivicifiorentini.comune.fi.it

In 1771 fire wrecked the Carmelite convent and church of **Santa Maria del Carmine** some 300m west of Santo Spirito, but somehow the flames did not damage the frescoes of the church's **Cappella Brancacci**, a cycle of paintings that is one of the essential sights of Florence. The chapel is barricaded off from the rest of the Carmine, and visits are

9

restricted to a maximum of thirty people at a time, for an inadequate fifteen minutes at peak periods.

The decoration of the chapel was begun in 1424 by **Masolino** and **Masaccio**, when the former was aged 41 and the latter just 22. Within a short time the elder artist was taking lessons from the younger, whose grasp of the texture of the real world, of the principles of perspective and of the dramatic potential of the biblical texts they were illustrating far exceeded that of his precursors. In 1428 Masolino was called away to Rome, and was followed by Masaccio a few months later. Neither would return to the chapel. Masaccio died the same year, aged just 27, but, in the words of Vasari, "All the most celebrated sculptors and painters since Masaccio's day have become excellent and illustrious by studying their art in this chapel."

The small scene on the left of the entrance arch is the quintessence of Masaccio's art. Depictions of **The Expulsion of Adam and Eve** had never before captured the desolation of the sinners so graphically – Adam presses his hands to his face in bottomless despair, Eve raises her head and screams. In contrast to the emotional charge of Masaccio's couple, Masolino's dainty *Adam and Eve*, opposite, pose as if to have their portraits painted.

St Peter is chief protagonist of most of the remaining scenes, some of which were left unfinished in 1428 – work did not resume until 1480, when the frescoes were completed by **Filippino Lippi**. One of the scenes finished by Lippi is the *Raising of Theophilus's Son and St Peter Enthroned*, which depicts St Peter bringing the son of the Prefect of Antioch to life and then preaching to the people of the city from a throne. The three figures to the right of the throne are thought to be Masaccio, Alberti and Brunelleschi.

Giardino Bardini

Entrances at Costa di San Giorgio 2 and Via de' Bardi 1r • Daily: March 8.15am–5.30pm; April, May, Sept & Oct 8.15am–6.30pm; June–Aug 8.15am–7.30pm; Nov–Feb 8.15am–4.30pm; closed first & last Mon of month • €10 combined ticket with Museo delle Porcellane and Giardino di Boboli (see page 543) • bardinipeyron.it

The **Giardino Bardini** occupies the slope that was formerly the olive grove of the **Palazzo dei Mozzi**, a colossal house built in the late thirteenth century by the Mozzi family, at that time one of the richest families in Florence. After Stefano Bardini (see page 544) bought the property in 1913 he set about creating a semiformal garden which has now been restored to its original appearance, with a neo-Baroque staircase and terraces dividing the fruit-growing section from the miniature woodland of the "*bosco inglese*". At the summit of the garden, reached by a lovely long pergola of wisteria and hortensia, a colonnaded belvedere gives a splendid view of the city.

Villa Bardini

Costa di San Giorgio 2 • Tues–Sun 10am–7pm • €10 • bardinipeyron.it

At the top of the Giardino Bardini stands the **Villa Bardini**, built in the seventeenth century and extended by Stefano Bardini. Having been thoroughly restored, the villa is used as an exhibition space and also houses a museum dedicated to **Pietro Annigoni** (1910–88), a vehemently anti-Modernist painter who was best known for his portraits of luminaries such as Pope John XXIII and Queen Elizabeth II. Fashionistas may enjoy the villa's collection of **clothes** created by Roberto Capucci (born 1930), dubbed the "Givenchy of Rome" by his admirers.

Museo Stefano Bardini

Piazza de' Mozzi 1 • Mon & Fri–Sun 11am–5pm • €6 • museicivicifiorentini.comune.fi.it

The **Museo Stefano Bardini**, which stands at the end of the handsome Via de' Bardi, houses the collection of **Stefano Bardini** (1836–1922), once the most important art dealer in Italy, whose tireless activity laid the cornerstone of many important European and American museums. Determined that no visitor to his native city should remain unaware of his success, he bought the former monastery of San Gregorio alla Pace, and converted it into a vast house for himself and his collection. Sculpture, paintings,

ceramics, armour, furniture, picture frames, carpets, wooden ceilings, tombstones – Bardini bought it all, and he bequeathed the whole lot to the city.

The Bardini is more like a colossal showroom than a modern museum, with items strewn all about the place, many of them unlabelled. The most interesting items are **upstairs**, where you'll find two reliefs of the *Madonna and Child* that may be by Donatello (in a room that's stacked with similar reliefs), a beautiful terracotta *Virgin Annunciate* from fifteenth-century Siena and some fine drawings by Giambattista Tiepolo and his son Lorenzo.

San Miniato al Monte

Via del Monte alle Croci • Mon–Sat 9.30am–1pm & 3.30–7pm, Sun 3.30–7pm • Free • Ⓦ sanminiatoalmonte.it

The brilliant, multicoloured facade of **San Miniato al Monte** lures hordes of visitors up the hill on which it sits, and it more than fulfils the promise of its appearance from a distance: this is the finest Romanesque church in Tuscany. The church's dedicatee, St Minias, belonged to a Christian community that settled in Florence in the third century; according to legend, after his martyrdom his corpse was seen to carry his severed head over the river and up the hill to this spot, where a shrine was subsequently erected to him. Construction of the present building began in 1013 with the foundation of a Cluniac monastery. The gorgeous marble facade – alluding to the Baptistry in its geometrical patterning – was added towards the end of that century, though the external mosaic *Christ between the Virgin and St Minias* dates from the thirteenth.

The interior

The **interior** is like no other in the city, with the choir raised on a platform above a large crypt. The main structural addition is the Cappella del Cardinale del Portogallo, a paragon of artistic collaboration: the basic design was by Antonio Manetti (a pupil of Brunelleschi), the tomb was carved by Antonio Rossellino, the terracotta decoration of the ceiling is by Luca della Robbia, and the paintings are by Alesso Baldovinetti, except for the altarpiece, which is a copy of a work by the Pollaiuolo brothers (the original is in the Uffizi). Be sure to also visit the sacristy, which is covered in *Scenes from the Life of St Benedict*, painted in the 1380s by Spinello Aretino.

ARRIVAL AND DEPARTURE — FLORENCE

By plane Pisa's Galileo Galilei airport (see page 563) is the main airport for Tuscany. A small number of international air services use Florence's Peretola (aka Amerigo Vespucci) airport (Ⓣ 055 306 1300, Ⓦ aeroporto.firenze.it), 5km northwest of the city centre; the Volainbus service (wataf.net) provides shuttles from here into Florence Santa Maria Novella station every 30min (€6), while by the time this book is published, the new tramline from the airport to Santa Maria Novella should be operational.

By train Nearly all trains arrive at Santa Maria Novella station (Firenze SMN), a few blocks west of the Duomo. A few trains use Campo di Marte, over in the east of the city, from where there are regular buses into the centre. The high speed Freccia Rossa and Freccia Argento lines both pass through Florence, with brilliantly fast – if very expensive – connections with Bologna, Rome, Milan and Venice. If you are trying to save money, and time is not an issue, bear in mind that ticket prices on slower trains are a fraction of those on the Freccias.

Destinations Arezzo (at least hourly; 1hr–1hr30min); Assisi (hourly; 2hr–3hr); Bologna (approx. 3 per hour;35min–1hr 40min); Genoa (approx. hourly, via Pisa; 3hr 15min–4hr 20min); Lucca (approx. 2 per hour; 1hr 15min–1hr 45min); Milan (at least hourly; 1hr 40min–4hr); Naples (approx. two hourly; 2hr 55min–7hr); Perugia (at least hourly; 1hr 30min–2hr 10min); Pisa (approx. 3 hourly; 1hr–1hr 20min); Pisa Aeroporto (changing at Pisa Centrale) (approx. 3 hourly, 1hr10min––1hr25min); Pistoia (1–3 hourly; 40–55min); Prato (1–3 hourly; 20–30min); Rome (at least 2 hourly; 1hr 30min–3hr 40min); Siena (1–2 hourly, often changing at Empoli; 1hr 20min–1hr 45min); Venice (at least 1 hourly; 2hr 5min–4hr.

By bus Services by Busitalia (which include buses to Florence airport) operate from the Busitalia bus station on Via di Santa Caterina da Siena, a few steps west of the train station; other bus companies, CAP, Rama, Lazzi and Copit, operate from the east side of the train station. The main services are listed below; in addition to these, the private bus companies operate services to most Tuscan towns, including Arezzo, Lucca and Pisa. The following timings should be taken as a guideline only and note as well that journey planners don't always come up with the most logical solutions in Florence.

9

FLORENCE ADDRESSES

Florence has a complicated double system of **street numbering**: commercial establishments (such as bars and restaurants) have red numbers (*rosso*), while private buildings have black or blue numbers – and the two systems don't run in tandem. This means, for example, that no. 35r might be next door to no. 89 and a long way from no. 33r.

Destinations Castellina in Chianti (1 daily; 1hr 35min); Certaldo (4 daily; 1hr 40min); Gaiole (2 daily Mon–Fri; 2hr); Greve (around 30 daily; 1hr 5min); Poggibonsi (10 daily; 1hr 20min); Radda in Chianti (1 daily Mon–Sat; 1hr 40min); Siena (20 daily; 1hr 15min–1hr 40min); Volterra (6 daily; 2hr 25min).

By car Only residents are allowed to park in the centre, so you have to leave your car in one of the main car parks, unless you're staying at a hotel with reserved spaces. North of the Arno, the car parks nearest the centre are underneath the train station, just off Piazza della Libertà, and at Piazza Annigoni, near Santa Croce; south of the river the best option is Piazza della Calza, at the southwest tip of the Boboli garden. At the moment it's still possible to park free of charge on Piazzale Michelangelo, but this is unlikely to remain the case forever.

GETTING AROUND

Florence is a small city and walking is the most efficient way of getting around the centre; it's also much more pleasant than it used to be, now that most of the *centro storico*, all the way from the Palazzo Medici-Riccardi to the Palazzo Pitti, has been closed to inessential traffic.

Buses For cross-town journeys you might want to use ATAF buses (ⓦ www.ataf.net). Tickets are valid for unlimited journeys within 90min (€1.50, or 2.50 if bought on board). You can also get a booklet of 10 tickets for €14. Tickets are available from the main ATAF information office at Santa Maria Novella train station (daily 7am–8pm), from shops and stalls displaying the ATAF sign and from automatic machines all over Florence.

The Tramvia The first line of the city's controversial Tramvia tram system was completed in 2010, but it's a commuter line that's of little use to tourists. By the time this book is published, the line from Peretola airport to Santa Maria Novella should be in operation.

INFORMATION

Tourist offices The main tourist office is at Via Cavour 1r, a 5min walk north of the Duomo (Mon–Fri 9am–6pm, Sat 9am–2pm; ⓣ 055 290 832, ⓦ www.firenzeturismo.it); this office provides information not just on the city but on the whole of Florence province. Smaller offices are to be found in the Loggia del Bigallo, on Piazza San Giovanni by the Baptistry (Mon–Sat 9am–7pm, Sun 9am–2pm), and opposite Santa Maria Novella train station, at Piazza della Stazione 5 (Mon–Sat 9am–7pm, Sun 9am–2pm).

Websites, Apps and Magazines A good source of information on events is *Firenze Spettacolo* (ⓦ firenzespettacolo.it; €2), a monthly, partly bilingual online listings magazine and app, with a print version sold at bookshops and larger newsstands. Also useful is bilingual *The Florentine* (ⓦ theflorentine.net) with a print version available at the tourist office and most bookshops. Outstanding among the expat blogs and websites is ⓦ lostinflorence.it, with incisive, bang-up-to-date info on the most enticing places to eat, drink and shop.

ACCOMMODATION

Florence has many hotels but demand is almost limitless, which means that prices are high and the tourist inundation has few slack spots: "**low season**" is defined by most hotels as meaning mid-July to the end of Aug (the weeks during which nearly all Italians head for the beaches or the mountains), and from mid-Nov to mid-March, except for the Christmas and New Year period; between March and Oct, booking ahead is in effect obligatory. In recent years, **boutique hotels** and **B&Bs** have sprung up all over the city, operating under several different labels: places calling themselves a *relais* or a *residenza d'epoca* are generally smart B&Bs, often located in historic *palazzi*. The Via Cavour tourist office has a full accommodation list, or see ⓦ www.firenzeturismo.it.

HOTELS, RESIDENZE AND B&BS

THE CITY CENTRE

★ **Alessandra** Borgo SS. Apostoli 17 ⓣ 055 283 438, ⓦ hotelalessandra.com; map p.524. One of the best and friendliest of the central two-stars, with 27 rooms occupying a sixteenth-century *palazzo* and furnished in a mixture of antique and modern styles. The more expensive en-suite doubles overlook the river; those with shared bathrooms are considerably cheaper. €154

Cestelli Borgo SS. Apostoli 25 ⓣ 055 214 213, ⓦ hotelcestelli.com; map p.524. Spotlessly maintained by its young Florentine-Japanese owners and offering excellent value for money, this eight-roomed one-star

occupies part of a house that once belonged to a minor Medici. The rooms are a good size, and most are en suite. **€100**

★ **Helvetia & Bristol** Via dei Pescioni 2 ⓣ 055 26 651, ⓦ niquesahotels.com; map p.524. In business since 1894, this is a superb five-star hotel. The rooms mix antique furnishings and modern facilities – such as hydromassage baths – to create a style that evokes the belle époque without being suffocatingly nostalgic. The standard rooms are not huge, but have lovely marble bathrooms; the superior rooms and suites are worth the splurge. If you're going to treat yourself, this is a leading contender. **€350**

Hermitage Vicolo Marzio 1/Piazza del Pesce ⓣ 055 287 216, ⓦ hermitagehotel.com; map p.524. Pre-booking is recommended at any time of year to secure one of the 28 rooms in this superbly located three-star hotel, right next to the Ponte Vecchio. The service is friendly, the rooms are cosy, and there are unbeatable views from some rooms, as well as from the flower-filled roof garden. In high season and over busy weekends, there is a minimum 4 night stay. **€220**

Relais Cavalcanti Via Pelliceria 2 ⓣ 055 210 962, ⓦ www.relaiscavalcanti.com; map p.524. Run by Francesca and her sister Anna, the *Relais Cavalcanti* is a homely guesthouse that occupies the fourth floor of a *palazzo* overlooking the Palazzo di Parte Guelfa and Porcellino market. The well-maintained rooms are a good size, and the location excellent. There's a bar on the ground floor, but the glazing more than takes care of any noise. Ingredients for a DIY breakfast are laid out in a small dining room that guests can use at any time of day. Minimum 3 night stay in high season. **€145**

Torre Guelfa Borgo SS. Apostoli 8 ⓣ 055 239 6338, ⓦ hoteltorreguelfa.com; map p.524. There are twenty tastefully furnished rooms crammed into this ancient tower, the tallest private building in the city. Guests can enjoy the marvellous views all over the city from the tower's small roof terrace. Very charismatic and one of the most popular three-stars in Florence – book well ahead. **€120**

THE SANTA MARIA NOVELLA AREA

J.K. Place Piazza S. Maria Novella 7 ⓣ 055 264 5181, ⓦ jkplace.com; map p.524. One of the most appealing – if stratospherically priced – of Florence's designer hotels occupies a fine eighteenth-century building on Piazza Santa Maria Novella. The twenty rooms of this elegant townhouse have been designed by Michele Bönan in hybrid retro-modernist style, and have DVD players and flatscreen TVs. **€1100**

Nizza Via del Giglio 5 ⓣ 055 239 6897, ⓦ hotelnizza.com; map p.524. A smart family-run two-star, with helpful staff and a very central location. All rooms are en suite and are better furnished and decorated than many in this category. **€107**

NORTH OF THE CENTRE

Antica Dimora Firenze Via S. Gallo 72 ⓣ 055 462 7296, ⓦ johanna.it; map p.518. This plush *residenza*, run by the owners of the neighbouring *Antica Dimora Johlea* and *Residenza Johlea*, has six very comfortable double rooms, some with four-poster beds. **€156**

★ **Antica Dimora Johlea** Via S. Gallo 80 ⓣ 055 461 185, ⓦ johanna.it; map p.518. A little pricier and more luxurious than the *Antica Dimora Firenze*, this lovely *residenza* also has a nice roof terrace, giving a roofline view of the Duomo and the hills beyond. **€170**

Casci Via Cavour 13 ⓣ 055 211 686, ⓦ hotelcasci.com; map p.524. It would be hard to find a better two-star in central Florence than this 26-room hotel, which occupies part of a building in which the composer Rossini once lived. Only two (soundproofed) rooms face the busy street; the rest are very quiet, and all are clean and neat. The welcome is warm and the owners very helpful. The big buffet breakfast under the frescoed ceiling of the reception area is a plus. **€170**

Kursaal & Ausonia Via Nazionale 24 ⓣ 055 496 324, ⓦ kursonia.com; map p.518. Welcoming, recently refurbished three-star near the station, with accommodation ranging from spacious "superior" doubles, in faux-antique style, to rather more bland and functional "standard" rooms. **€112**

★ **Loggiato dei Serviti** Piazza Santissima Annunziata 3 ⓣ 055 289 592, ⓦ loggiatodeiservitihotel.it; map p.524. The 38 rooms of this elegant, extremely tasteful three-star hotel have been incorporated into a building designed in the sixteenth century to accommodate Servite priests. All the rooms are decorated with fine fabrics and antiques, and look out onto either the piazza, the peaceful gardens to the rear, or towards the Duomo. The five rooms in the annexe, at Via dei Servi 49, are similarly styled, but don't have the same charm. **€180**

Merlini Via Faenza 56 ⓣ 055 212 848, ⓦ hotelmerlini.it; map p.518. Several budget hotels are crammed into this address, but the family-run *Merlini*, on the third floor (no lift), is the best. Its ten rooms have marble bathrooms – an unexpected bonus in this price bracket – and six give views of the Duomo. **€95**

Morandi alla Crocetta Via Laura 50 ⓣ 055 234 4747, ⓦ hotelmorandi.it; map p.524. An intimate three-star gem, whose small size and friendly welcome ensure a home-from-home atmosphere. Rooms are tastefully decorated with antiques and old prints, and vivid carpets laid on parquet floors. Two rooms have balconies opening onto a modest garden; the best room – with fresco fragments and medieval nooks – was converted from a convent chapel. **€215**

Mr. My Resort Via delle Ruote 14a ⓣ 055 283 955, ⓦ mrflorence.it; map p..518. Run by the same friendly family as *Relais Grand Tour*, this luxury B&B has five bright,

9

quirkily furnished rooms arranged around a tranquil garden, but the real draw is the private, stone-walled spa in the basement, complete with Turkish bath and jacuzzi. €130

★ **Relais Grand Tour & Suites** Via S. Reparata 21 ⓣ 055 283 955, ⓦ florencegrandtour.com; map p.518. The very hospitable owners have done a great job of turning two floors of this old *palazzo* into a superb guesthouse, with two charming rooms on the second floor and three suites on the floor below. Each room is unique: one has a gold-leaf wooden ceiling, and another – formerly a dressing-room – is loaded with mirrors ("suitable for a couple", as the website has it). €180

Residenza Castiglioni Via del Giglio 8 ⓣ 055 239 6013, ⓦ residenzacastiglioni.com; map p.524. This discreet and hugely stylish hideaway has just half a dozen spacious en-suite double rooms (three of them frescoed), on the second floor of a *palazzo* very close to San Lorenzo church. Room 22 is the one to go for, with wall-to-wall frescoes. €212

Residenza Johanna I Via Bonifacio Lupi 14 ⓣ 055 481 896, ⓦ johanna.it; map p.518. The longest-established of the *Johanna/Johlea* family of *residenze*, this genteel place is hidden away in an unmarked apartment building in a quiet, leafy corner of the city, a 5min walk north of San Marco. Rooms are cosy and well kept, and the management are as friendly and helpful as you could hope for. €130

Residenza Johanna II Via Cinque Giornate 12 ⓣ 055 473 377, ⓦ johanna.it; map p.518. The location of this *residenza* – to the north of the Fortezza da Basso – is a little less convenient than that of its siblings (see above and below), but the accommodation is of the same high standard, as is the hospitality. €130

Residenza Johlea Via S. Gallo 76 ⓣ 055 463 3292, ⓦ johanna.it; map p.518. Another venture from the owners of *Residenza Johanna*, offering the same low-cost, high-comfort package. €130

EAST OF THE CENTRE

J & J Via di Mezzo 20 ⓣ 055 263 121, ⓦ jandj.hotelinfirenze.com; map p.518. The bland exterior of this former fifteenth-century convent conceals a romantic nineteen-room four-star hotel. Some rooms are vast, and all of them are furnished brightly, with modern fittings and a few antiques. Common areas are decked with flowers, and retain frescoes and vaulted ceilings from the original building. €289

OLTRARNO

La Scaletta Via Guicciardini 13 ⓣ 055 283 028, ⓦ lascaletta.com; map p.524. Some of the rooms in this spruce sixteen-room two-star give views across to the Boboli garden; those on the Via Guiccardini side are double-glazed against the traffic. Drinks are served on the rooftop terraces, where you look across the Boboli in one direction and the city in the other. €222

★ **Palazzo Guadagni** Piazza di Santo Spirito 9 ⓣ 055 265 8376, ⓦ palazzoguadagni.com; map p.524. A well-presented three-star with huge double rooms overlooking the piazza, some with fantastic frescoed ceilings. The rooftop loggia bar gives spectacular views, though the after-dark liveliness of Piazza di Santo Spirito might trouble light sleepers. €150

HOSTELS

★ **Academy Hostel** Via Ricasoli 9 ⓣ 055 239 8665, ⓦ academyhostel.eu; map p.524. Since opening in 2008, this modern hostel has won awards for its service and excellent facilities: set in a seventeenth-century *palazzo*, it offers airy, high-ceilinged rooms and a common area with huge flatscreen TV, book and DVD library and lots of computer terminals, plus a sunny terrace. All this, and an unbeatable location – just steps from the Duomo. Breakfast and internet included. Dorms €35, doubles (en suite) €90

Archi Rossi Via Faenza 94r ⓣ 055 290 804, ⓦ hostelarchirossi.com; map p.518. A 5min walk from the train station, this privately owned hostel is spotlessly clean and decorated with guests' wall paintings and graffiti. It's popular – the 140 beds fill up quickly – and has a pleasant garden and terrace. There are some basic en-suite doubles (on the third floor; no lift), and a restaurant serving cheap meals. Breakfast and internet included. Dorms from €26, private doubles €80

Foresteria Valdese Firenze–Istituto Gould Via dei Serragli 49 ⓣ 055 212 576, ⓦ firenzeforesteria.it; map p.524. Run by the Waldensian Church, this hostel-evangelical college occupies part of a seventeenth-century *palazzo* between Santo Spirito and the Carmine. It is extremely popular, so book in advance, especially during the academic year. There are singles, doubles, triples and quads, making it idea for a families and groups of friends. Street-front rooms can be noisy (rear rooms cost a little more), but the old courtyard, terracotta floors and stone staircases provide atmosphere throughout. Check-in Mon–Fri 8.45am–1pm & 3–7.30pm, Sat 9am–1.30pm & 2.30–6pm; reception closed Sun. No curfew. Doubles €85

Santa Monaca Via S. Monaca 6 ⓣ 055 268 338, ⓦ ostello.it; map p.524. This privately owned hostel in Oltrarno, close to the Carmine, has 115 beds in rooms sleeping up to 22, both mixed and female-only. Kitchen facilities, washing machines and a useful noticeboard with information on lifts and onward travel. Check-in 6am–2am; bedrooms have to be vacated between 10am and 2pm. Curfew 2am. Discounts in low season and for longer stays. Dorms €21

Villa Camerata Viale Augusto Righi 2–4 ⓣ 055 601 451, ⓦ ostellofirenze.it; buses #17a and #17b from the station; map p.518. Tucked away in a beautiful park northeast of the city, 5km from Santa Maria Novella station, this campsite and HI hostel is one of Europe's most

attractive, set in a sixteenth-century house with frescoed ceilings, fronted by lemon trees. Doors open at 2pm; if you're planning on arriving later, call ahead to make sure there's space. There are 322 dorm beds; breakfast and sheets are included, but there are no kitchen facilities. Films in English are shown every night. Midnight curfew. Dorms **€33**, doubles **€100**

CAMPING

Camping Panoramico Via Peramondo 1, Fiesole ⓣ 055 559 069, ⓦ florencecamping.com; map p.518. Located in Fiesole (see page 556), a short bus ride from central Florence, this 120-pitch three-star site has a bar, restaurant, pool and small supermarket. Mid-March to Nov. Pitches **€8** plus per adult **€13**

EATING

As you'd expect in a major tourist city, Florence has plenty of **restaurants**, but – unsurprisingly – a large number of them are aimed squarely at outsiders, so standards are often patchy. But the situation is nowhere near as bad as some would have it – in fact it's been improving in recent years, with the appearance of several stylish and good-value restaurants. Bear in mind also that simple meals are served in many Florentine **bars** and **cafés**, so if you fancy a quick bite to eat rather than a full-blown restaurant meal, take a look at our listings for cafés and bars.

CAFÉS AND GELATERIE

As elsewhere in Italy, the distinction between Florentine bars and cafés can be tricky to the point of impossibility, as almost every café serves alcohol and almost every bar serves coffee. That said, there are some cafés in which the emphasis is on coffee, cakes and ice cream – these are the places listed below, along with places that are devoted exclusively to ice cream.

CITY CENTRE

Caffè Gilli Piazza della Repubblica 36–39r ⓣ 055 213 896; map p.524. Founded in 1733, *Caffè Gilli* – the most appealing of this square's expensive cafés – moved to its present site in 1910. The lavish belle époque interior is a sight in itself, but most people choose to sit on the big outdoor terrace. Daily 7.30am–midnight.

Cantinetta dei Verrazzano Via dei Tavolini 18–20r ⓣ 055 268 590; map p.524. Owned by Castello dei Verrazzano, a major Chianti vineyard, this wood-panelled place near Orsanmichele is difficult to categorize: part-café, part-bakery, it makes its own excellent focaccia and cakes. A perfect spot for a light lunch or an early evening drink. Mon–Sat 8am–9pm; closes 4.30pm July & Aug.

Gelateria dei Neri Via dei Neri 9–11r; map p.524. Located close to Santa Croce, *Dei Neri* serves what many think is the best ice cream in town, The range of flavours is fantastic – fig and walnut, Mexican chocolate (very spicy), rice – and they also have some non-dairy ice cream. Tues-Sun 10am–midnight.

Perchè No! Via de' Tavolini 19r ⓣ 055 239 8969; map p.524. "Why Not!" is a superb *gelateria* that's been in business since 1939, with seasonal and daily specials: those in the know go for the pistachio and fruit flavours in summer and the *castagna* (chestnut) and *caco* (persimmon) in winter. March–Oct Mon & Wed–Sat 11am–11pm, Tues noon–8pm; Dec–Feb Mon & Wed–Sat noon–7.30pm.

NORTH OF THE CENTRE

Carabé Via Ricasoli 60r ⓣ 055 289 476; map p.524. *Carabé*'s Sicilian ice cream is icier and less smooth than the creations of many other Florentine *gelaterie*, but the flavours are wonderful: try the *Spirito Siciliano*, the most lemony lemon you'll ever taste. Also serves delicious *cannoli* (pastry stuffed with sweet ricotta and candied fruits). Daily: April–Oct 10am–1am; Nov–March 11am–8pm; closed mid-Dec to mid-Jan.

EAST OF THE CENTRE

Caffè Cibrèo Via Andrea del Verrocchio 5r ⓣ 055 234 5853; map p.518. Possibly the prettiest café in Florence, *Caffè Cibrèo* opened in 1989, but the wood-panelled interior gives it the look of a place that's at least two hundred years older. Cakes and desserts are great, and the light meals bear the stamp of the *Cibrèo* restaurant kitchens opposite (see page 550). Tues–Sun 9am–11.30pm.

Vivoli Via Isola delle Stinche 7r ⓣ 055 292 334; map p.524. Operating from deceptively unprepossessing premises in a side street close to Santa Croce, this café has long been one of the best ice-cream makers in Florence. Tues–Sat 7.30am–midnight, Sun 9am–midnight (closes 9pm in winter); closed two weeks in Aug.

PICNIC SUPPLIES

For **picnic supplies** an obvious place to shop is the **Mercato Centrale** by San Lorenzo church, where everything you could possibly need can be bought under one roof: bread, ham, cheese, fruit, wine, ready-made sandwiches. The **Mercato Sant'Ambrogio** over by Santa Croce is smaller but of comparable quality.

9

TOP 5 PLACES FOR OUTDOOR DRINKING

Caffè Gilli see page 549
Dolce Vita see page 552
Fuori Porta see page 552
Le Volpi e L'Uva see page 552
Zoe see page 552

RESTAURANTS

Florence has scores of restaurants, but such is the volume of customers that in high season advance bookings are virtually compulsory – especially on Sun, when many places are closed. And bear in mind that meals – not just snacks – are served in many Florentine bars, so if you're exploring a particular area of the city and fancy a quick bite to eat rather than a full-blown restaurant meal, take a look at the "Cafés and *gelaterie*" and "Drinkings" listings.

THE CITY CENTRE

Oliviero Via delle Terme 51r ⓣ 055 287 643, ⓦ ristorante-oliviero.it; map p.524. *Oliviero* has a welcoming and old-fashioned feel – something like an Italian restaurant of the 1960s – and the menu, though predominantly Tuscan, includes dishes from other regions of Italy. Fresh fish, when available, features strongly – something of a rarity in Florence. Expect to pay upwards of €50 (without wine), which is reasonable for cooking of this calibre. Tues–Sat noon–2.30pm & 7.30–10.30pm; closed Aug.

★ **Ora d'Aria** Via dei Georgofili 11r ⓣ 055 200 1699, ⓦ oradariaristorante.com; map p.524. Marco Stabile, the young boss of the Michelin-starred *Ora d'Aria*, has rapidly established a reputation as one of the city's best restaurateurs, thanks to menus that offer a high-quality mix of the traditional and the innovative. The tasting menus (€75) are very good value for such exceptional cooking; à la carte mains are upward of €30. The bright and cool setting is the very opposite of the faux-rustic style that you often find elsewhere in Florence – the focus here is wholly on the food. Mon 7.30–10pm, Tues–Sat 12.30–2.30pm & 7.30–10pm.

Yellow Bar Via del Proconsolo 39r ⓣ 055 211 766; map p.524. This place looks like a fast-food joint, but the queues of Florentines waiting for a table give you a clue that first impressions are misleading. Inside, the convivial atmosphere in the large dining room is matched by superlative pan-Italian food (including excellent pizzas) in large portions at very reasonable prices. You can often get a table in the mildly less appealing rooms downstairs when the main dining room is busy. Tues–Sun noon–3.30pm & 6.15pm–11.15pm.

WEST OF THE CENTRE

Il Contadino Via Palazzuolo 71r ⓣ 055 238 2673, ⓦ trattoriailcontadino.com; map p.524. This small no-frills trattoria has been popular since it opened for business in the 1970s, and it hasn't changed its style much since then, with its monochrome tiled dining room and refectory-like seating. Service is fast and friendly, and the food is decent and very cheap –with fixed-priced menus from as little as €9. Daily noon–10.30pm.

Osteria dei Centopoveri Via Palazzuolo 31r & 41r ⓣ 055 218 846, ⓦ centopoveri.it; map p.524. This very popular *osteria* offers more fish than is customary with meat-oriented Tuscan menus, and has some excellent set menus (both fish and meat) starting at €28. Established in the 1990s, the operation has expanded in recent years, and pizzas are served at the newer branch, at 41r. Daily noon–3pm & 7–11pm.

NORTH OF THE CENTRE

★ **Da Mario** Via Rosina 2r ⓣ 055 218 550, ⓦ trattoria-mario.com; map p.524. Located close to the Mercato Centrale, *Da Mario* has probably been packed out every lunchtime since the Colsi family started running the place in 1953. For earthy Florentine cooking at very low prices (*ribollita* €4, pork chop €7.50), there's nowhere better. Note that they don't take reservations or credit cards, and are closed in the evenings. Mon–Sat noon–3.30pm; closed Aug.

Da Tito Via S. Gallo 112r ⓣ 055 472 475; map p.518. Full of locals every night and offering excellent food at fair prices, *Da Tito* is well worth the extra few minutes' walk from the centre. Dishes are simple but elegant – beef fillet with rocket pesto, for example – and *secondi* are a reasonable €10–15. But if you don't like your meat the way Florentines like it, go elsewhere – the kitchen refuses to serve anything "well done". Mon–Sat 12.30–3pm & 7–11pm.

Zà-Zà Piazza del Mercato Centrale 26r ⓣ 055 210 756, ⓦ trattoriazaza.it; map p.524. Long-established *Zà-Zà* is one of the best of several trattorias close to the Mercato Centrale. The interior is dark, stone-walled and brick-arched, with a handful of tables – though in summer there's plenty more space on the outside terraces. There's usually a set menu for around €15, with a choice of three or four pastas and mains; otherwise you'll pay around €30/head. Daily 11am–11pm; closed Aug.

EAST OF THE CENTRE

★ **Cibrèo** Via de' Macci 118r ⓣ 055 234 1100, ⓦ cibreo.com; map p.518. Fabio Picchi's restaurant is an obligatory port of call for many foodies, its creative take on Tuscan classics having achieved fame well beyond the city. Some think it's been resting on its laurels for too long, but many still rate it very highly indeed. You'll need to book days in advance for a table in the main part of the restaurant, but next door there's a small, spartan and sometimes overly busy trattoria (*Cibreino*) where the food is virtually the same (though the menu is smaller), no bookings are taken

and the prices are much lower: around €15 for mains, as opposed to €40 in the restaurant. Lunch from 11.50am, dinner from 6.50pm; closed Aug.

Il Pizzaiuolo Via de' Macci 113r ⓣ055 241 171, ⓦilpizzaiuolo.it; map p.518. The Neapolitan pizzas here are the best in the city. Wines and other dishes also have a Neapolitan touch, as does the atmosphere, which is friendly and high-spirited. Booking's a good idea in the evening. Mon–Sat 12.30–3pm & 7pm–midnight; closed Aug.

OLTRARNO

Alla Vecchia Bettola Viale Lodovico Ariosto 32–34r ⓣ055 224 158, ⓦflorence.ala.it/bettola; map p.518. Located on a major traffic intersection a couple of minutes' walk from the Carmine, this place – with its long marble-topped tables – has something of the atmosphere of an old-style drinking den, which is what it once was; nowadays it boasts a good repertoire of Tuscan meat dishes, with pasta from €10 and mains from €14. No credit cards. Tues–Sat noon–2.30pm & 7.30–10.30pm.

Gusta Pizza Via Maggio 46r; map p.524. The wood-fired Neapolitan pizzas served here are the best in Oltrarno – and pizzas are all they do, which is always a good thing. No reservations, and the dining room is not large, so be prepared to queue. Tues–Sun 11.30am–3.30pm & 7–11.30pm.

Il Magazzino Piazza della Passera 2–3 ⓣ055 215 969; map p.524. Occupying a corner of the increasingly lively Piazza Passera, *Il Magazzino* is an earthily authentic osteria-*tripperia*, serving hearty dishes of pasta, tripe and beef at around €10–18. The tourists throng to neighbouring *4 Leoni*, but this place has more of a local following. Daily noon–3pm & 7.30–11pm.

Il Santo Bevitore Via Santo Spirito 64–66r ⓣ055 211 264, ⓦilsantobevitore.com; map p.524. "The Holy Drinker" started out as an *enoteca* with a kitchen but has now shifted the emphasis onto the food and presents itself simply as a restaurant, and a very stylish one at that. The menu is seasonal, small and classy (around €40 for a meal without drinks), and the wine list is enticing. Very busy throughout the year, especially in the evenings. Tues–Sun 12.30–2.30pm & 7.30–11pm, Mon 7.30–11pm; closed three weeks in Aug.

★ **IO – Osteria personale** Borgo San Frediano 167r ⓣ055 933 1341, ⓦio-osteriapersonale.it; map p.518. Matteo Fantini's minimalist restaurant is one of the most innovative to have opened in Florence in recent years. There are no antipasti or pasta courses, and no *bistecca* – what you get instead is an inventive and concise array of seafood and meat dishes (main courses around €20), with the option of selecting your own tasting menus at €40, €49 or €57. Ingredients are seasonal and local, and the wines come from small vineyards. Mon–Sat 7.30–10pm.

La Casalinga Via del Michelozzo 9r ⓣ055 218 624, ⓦtrattorialacasalinga.it; map p.524. Located in a side street off Piazza di Santa Spirito, this long-established family-run trattoria serves up low-cost Tuscan dishes of more than reasonable quality – the pasta isn't the best, but the meat dishes are generally excellent. No frills – paper tablecloths, house wine by the carafe and brisk service – but every night it's filled to bursting, with a mix of regulars and *turisti*. By 8pm there's invariably a queue. Mon–Sat noon–2.30pm & 7–10pm; closed three weeks in Aug.

DRINKING

As you'd expect, Florence has plenty of places where you can sample the produce of Tuscany's fabled vineyards. Nightlife in this city also tends to revolve around its bars, many of which serve food (in some cases full meals), while others – such as *Dolce Vita* and *Negroni* – have an in-house DJ and occasional live music, making them in effect small-scale clubs. After dark, the two liveliest parts of town are Oltrarno (especially Piazza di Santo Spirito) and the Santo Croce area.

CITY CENTRE

All'Antico Vinaio Via dei Neri 65r ⓣ055 238 2723; map p.524. Though recently revamped, this place – located between the Uffizi and Santa Croce – preserves much of the rough-and-ready atmosphere that's made it one of Florence's most popular wine bars for the last hundred years. The panini are famously huge and good. Simple meals are served at the tables in the other branch, over the road at 76r. Tues–Sat 10.30am–11pm, Sun 10.30am–11pm; closed three weeks late July & early Aug.

I Fratellini Via dei Cimatori 38r ⓣ055 239 6096; map p.524. This minuscule stand-up bar – which attracts a melee most lunchtimes – has been in operation since the 1870s; Armando and Michele, the current proprietors, serve 29 varieties of panini, and local wines by the glass. Daily 9am–8pm.

NORTH OF THE CENTRE

★ **Casa del Vino** Via dell'Ariento 16r ⓣ055 215 609; map p.524. Located a few metres south of the Mercato Centrale, the *Casa del Vino* is particularly busy in the middle of the day, when market traders pitch up for a drink, a quick bite and a chat with owner Gianni Migliorini. Mon–Thurs 9.30am–3.30pm, Fri & Sat 10am–10.30pm; closed Aug.

Zanobini Via Sant'Antonino 47r ⓣ055 239 6850; map p.524. Like the nearby *Casa del Vino*, this is an authentic and long-established place, but here the emphasis is much more on the wine: few bars in Florence have a better selection. Mon–Sat 8am–2pm & 3.30–8pm.

EAST OF THE CENTRE

Moyo Via de' Benci 23r ⓣ055 247 9738; map p.524. A young crowd flocks to this bar every evening – the food's

9

pretty good (come for the early-evening *aperitivo* buffet) and the free wi-fi access is a plus, but it's the buzz that really brings them in. Daily 8am–3am, reduced hours in winter.

Rex Café Via Fiesolana 25r 055 248 0331; map p.524. This friendly and extravagantly decorated place has been one of Florence's coolest bars for years. Lots of cosy seating around the central bar, and good cocktails and DJs (from 10.30pm) add to the appeal. The *aperitivi* session is 6–9.30pm. Daily 6pm–3am.

OLTRARNO

Dolce Vita Piazza del Carmine 5 055 284 595, dolcevitafirenze.it; map p.524. This hyper-glossy bar has been going for more than thirty years and has stayed ahead of the game by constantly updating; it reopened in 2015 after a nine-month refit, and is once again the buzziest place in Oltrarno. Install yourself on the terrace or a bar stool and preen with Florence's beautiful young things. There's frequent live music (Latin, rock or jazz) and DJs on other nights, and lavish *aperitivi* from 7.30pm to 10pm. Tues–Sun 7pm–2am.

Fuori Porta Via del Monte alle Croci 10r 055 234 2483; map p.518. If you're climbing up to San Miniato you could take a breather at this superb and justly famous *enoteca-osteria*. There are over four hundred wines by the bottle, and an ever-changing selection by the glass, as well as grappas and malt whiskies. Cheese and cold meats are available, as well as pasta dishes and salads. There's a summertime terrace and large dining area, but it's still wise to book if you're coming here to eat. Daily noon–11.30pm; closed two weeks mid-Aug.

Il Rifrullo Via S. Niccolò 53–57r 055 234 2621, ilrifrullo.com; map p.518. Lying to the east of the Ponte Vecchio–Pitti Palace route, this place attracts fewer tourists than many Oltrarno café-bars. Delicious snacks with the early-evening *aperitivi* (when the music gets turned up), as well as more substantial (and quite pricey) dishes in the restaurant section – the Sun brunch (noon & 3pm) is recommended. There's a pleasant garden terrace, too. Mon–Thurs 7.30am/8am–12.30am, Fri 7.30am–2am, Sat 8.30am–2am, Sun 8am–12.30am; closed two weeks in Aug.

Il Santino Via di Santo Spirito 60r 055 230 2820; map p.524. This small gastronomic *alimentari*-wine bar is an offshoot of the neighbouring *Santo Bevitore* (see page 551), and is proving just as successful. The wines on offer are top-quality (and pricy), as are the snacks. Daily 12.30am–11pm.

La Cité Borgo S. Frediano 20r 055 210 387; map p.524. With its huge windows, mezzanine balcony and shelves of books (to buy or just to browse), this café-bar-bookshop has an arty quasi-Parisian ambience. An area is set aside for live performances (usually music), and food tastings are regular occurrences, too. Daily 8am–11pm.

★ **Le Volpi e L'Uva** Piazza dei Rossi 1r, off Piazza di Santa Felicità 055 239 8132; map p.524. This friendly and highly successful little *enoteca* was founded by a quartet of wine lovers in 1992, and their expertise really shows: at any one time you can choose from at least two dozen different wines by the glass, most of them the produce of small vineyards. A well-assembled selection of tasty cold meats and snacks is on offer, and there are a few tables on the nice little terrace, beside the church of Santa Felicita. Daily 11am–9pm.

Negroni Via dei Renai 17r 055 243 647, negronibar.it; map p.518. Set back from the Arno, on the south side of the Piazza Demidoff, *Negroni* has been a fixture on the Florentine scene for years. It takes its name from the drink created on this spot for Count Camillo Negroni way back at the start of the last century, and cocktails are still a major attraction, along with the early-evening *aperitivo* buffet and the music – there's a DJ most nights. Sun–Wed 1.30am–1am, Thurs–Sat 1.30am–2am; closed two weeks in Aug.

Volume Piazza di Santo Spirito 5r 055 2381 460, volumefirenze.com; map p.524. This is the most unusual of the bar-cafés on Piazza di Santo Spirito – it used to be a workshop used by makers of hat forms, and the walls of the front room are still hung with the tools of the trade. Artworks and craft items are on display in the cosy back room, along with books (*Volume* markets itself as a "Museo Libreria Caffè"), and there's often live music in the evening – otherwise, expect a DJ. Daily 8.30am–1am.

Zoe Via dei Renai 13 055 243 111; map p.518. *Zoe* is perennially popular for summer evening drinks, but also attracts lots of young Florentines right through the day: 8.30am–noon is breakfast time, lunch is noon–3pm, then the cocktail bar kicks into action from 5pm (the Crimson Zoe cocktail is notorious). It also does good snacks and simple meals, there's a DJ in the back room, and it's something of an art venue, too. Mon–Fri 8.30am–2am, Sat & Sun 9am–2am.

NIGHTLIFE AND ENTERTAINMENT

Florence is quite a sedate city, but like every university town it has some decent **clubs** and **live music** venues, and events such as the Maggio Musicale (see below) maintain Florence's standing as the hub of cultural life in Tuscany. The best clubs and music venues are listed below, but for a full picture of the Florence after-dark scene, check the "Bars" listings – many of Florence's **bars** try to keep punters on the premises all night by serving free snacks with the *aperitivi* (usually from about 7–9/10pm) before the music kicks in, either live or (more often) courtesy of the in-house DJ. For information about concerts and shows, check out listings online at firenzespettacolo.it or boxol.it (where you

FLORENCE'S FESTIVALS

Scoppio del Carro The first major festival of the year is Easter Sunday's Scoppio del Carro (Explosion of the Cart), when a cartload of fireworks is hauled by six white oxen from the Porta a Prato to the Duomo; there, during midday Mass, the pile is ignited by a "dove" that whizzes down a wire from the high altar.

Festa del Grillo On the first Sun after Ascension Day (forty days after Easter), the "Festival of the Cricket" is held in the Cascine park. In among the market stalls and the picnickers you'll find people selling tiny mechanical crickets – live crickets were sold until quite recently, a vestige of a ritual that may hark back to the days when farmers had to scour their land for locusts.

Maggio Musicale Fiorentino The highlight of Florence's cultural calendar and one of Europe's leading festivals of opera and classical music, a rich mix of opera and concert; confusingly, it isn't restricted to May (Maggio), but often starts in late April and runs into June. For information and tickets, go to Ⓦ maggiofiorentino.com.

St John's Day and the Calcio Storico The saint's day of John the Baptist, Florence's patron, is June 24 – the occasion for a massive fireworks display on Piazzale Michelangelo, and for the final of the Calcio Storico on Piazza Santa Croce. Played in sixteenth-century costume to commemorate a game played at Santa Croce during the siege of 1530, this uniquely Florentine mayhem is a three-match series between the city's four *quartieri*, with two games in early June preceding the bedlam of June 24. A sort of hybrid of rugby, boxing and wrestling, the game is characterized by incomprehensible rules and an extraordinary degree of violence.

Festa delle Rificolone The "Festival of the Lanterns" takes place on the Virgin's birthday, Sept 7, with a procession of children to Piazza Santissima Annunziata, where a small fair is held. The procession is followed by a parade of floats and street parties.

can also book) or drop in at the **Box Office ticket agency**, which is at Via delle Vecchie Carceri 1, near the Mercato di Sant'Ambrogio (Mon–Fri 9.30am–7pm, Sat 9.30am–2pm; Ⓣ 055 210 804).

CLUBS AND LIVE MUSIC VENUES

Auditorium FLOG Via Michele Mercati 24b Ⓣ 055 477 978, Ⓦ www.auditoriumflog.com; bus #4 or #28 from Santa Maria Novella; map p.518. One of the city's best-known mid-sized venues, and a perennial student favourite for all forms of live music (and DJs), but particularly local indie-type bands. It's usually packed, despite a position way out in the northern suburbs.

Space Club Via Palazzuolo 37 Ⓣ 055 293 082, Ⓦ spaceclubfirenze.com; map p.524. *Space Club* is the archetypal big Continental disco, with a karaoke area downstairs and Florence's biggest dance floor up top. It's fine if all you want to do is dance, though it's a notorious pick-up joint... Daily 10pm–3am.

Tenax Via Pratese 46 Ⓣ 055 632 958, Ⓦ tenax.org; bus #29 or #30 from Santa Maria Novella; map p.518. In business since 1981, this is Florence's biggest club, pulling in the odd jet-setting DJ. With two large floors, it's a major venue for concerts as well. It's located in the northwest of town, near the airport; there's usually a shuttle bus from the train station – otherwise, take a taxi. Admission €20–25. Mid–Sept to Mid–May Thurs–Sat 10pm–3am.

Yab Via Sassetti 5r Ⓣ 055 215 160, Ⓦ yab.it; map p.524. This long-established and very smart basement club (full name: You Are Beautiful) has been popular for years. It doesn't have the most up-to-the-minute playlist in the world, but still offers probably the most relaxed and reliable night's clubbing in central Florence. Oct–May Mon & Wed–Sat 7pm–4am.

FILM

In summer there are often open-air screens at various places – check Ⓦ firenzespettacoli.it for the latest screenings. In July and Aug there's also the Premio Fiesole ai Maestri del Cinema, in which the films of a single director are screened in Fiesole's Roman theatre, 8km northeast of the city (see page 556).

Odeon Original Sound Via de' Sassetti 1 Ⓣ 055 214 068, Ⓦ odeon.intoscana.it. Mainstream films are screened in their original language (with Italian subtitles) at this a/c cinema almost every day. Closed for part of Aug.

CLASSICAL MUSIC, OPERA AND DANCE

The Maggio Musicale (see page 553), Italy's oldest and most prestigious music festival, is the most conspicuous sign of the health of the city's classical music scene, though it should be said that the fare tends towards the conservative. In addition to this and the festival in Fiesole, the Amici della Musica host a season of chamber concerts with top-name international performers from September to April, mostly in the Teatro della Pergola, and the Orchestra da Camera Fiorentina (Florence Chamber Orchestra; Ⓦ orcafi.it) plays concerts from March to Oct, often in Orsanmichele. The Lutheran church on Lungarno Torrigiani regularly holds free chamber music and organ recitals.

CONCERT VENUES

Nuovo Teatro dell'Opera Viale Fratelli Rosselli 1 Ⓣ 055 277 9350, Ⓦ operadifirenze.it; T1 tram from Santa Maria

Novella stops right outside. The city's dramatically hi-tech concert hall has a superb 1800-seat auditorium for operas and other large-scale events, which is complemented by an 1100-seater for recitals and a huge rooftop terrace for open-air performances.

Teatro della Pergola Via della Pergola 18 055 226 4353, teatrodellapergola.com. The beautiful little Pergola was built in 1656 and is Italy's oldest surviving theatre. It plays host to chamber concerts, small-scale operas and some of the best-known Italian theatre companies between October to April.

Teatro Goldoni Via Santa Maria 15 055 210 804, goldoniteatro.it. This exquisite little eighteenth-century theatre, near the Palazzo Pitti, is used for chamber music, opera and dance productions.

Teatro Verdi Via Ghibellina 99–101 055 212 320, teatroverdifirenze.it. This theatre is home to the Orchestra della Toscana, which performs once or twice a month Nov–May; it hosts a variety of concerts during the rest of the year.

SHOPPING

Florence is known as a producer of **luxury items**, notably gold jewellery and top-quality leather goods. The whole Ponte Vecchio is crammed with goldsmiths, but the city's premier shopping thoroughfare is **Via de' Tornabuoni**, where you'll find not only an array of expensive jewellery and shoe shops but also the showrooms of Italy's top fashion designers. For cheap and cheerful stuff there's the plethora of street stalls around the San Lorenzo market (see page 549), while if you want everything under one roof, there's also a handful of **department stores**. Marbled paper is another Florentine speciality, and, as you'd expect in this arty city, Florence is also one of the best places in the country to pick up **books** on Italian art, architecture and culture.

BOOKS AND MAPS

Feltrinelli RED Piazza della Repubblica 27r 055 213 110; map p.524. The Feltrinelli RED format – combining a multi-floor bookshop with a café-restaurant (*Red* stands for "read, eat, dream") – was pioneered in Rome and has now come to Florence, taking over what was formerly the Edison megastore. The stock is more impressive, though, at the city's other Feltrinelli branch, at Via de' Cerretani 30r. Daily 9am–11pm.

DEPARTMENT STORES AND CLOTHING

Coin Via dei Calzaiuoli 56r 055 280 531, coin.it; map p.524. Central, clothes-dominated chain store. Quality is generally high, though styles are conservative except for one or two youth-oriented franchises on the ground floor. Also a good place for linen and other household goods. Mon–Sat 10am–8pm, Sun 10.30am–8pm.

La Rinascente Piazza della Repubblica 1 055 219 113, rinascente.it; map p.524. Like Coin, La Rinascente is part of a countrywide chain, though it's perhaps a touch more upmarket than its nearby rival. It sells clothing, linen, cosmetics, household goods and other staples. Mon–Fri 9am–9pm, Sat 9am–midnight, Sun 10am–8pm.

Luisa Via Roma Via Roma 19–21r 055 217 826, luisaviaroma.com; map p.524. Luisa was founded back in the 1930s and remains Florence's top-end multi-label clothes shop. The interior is one of Florence's more impressive examples of modern architectural design. Daily 10.30am–7.30pm.

PAPER AND STATIONERY

★ **Giulio Giannini e Figlio** Piazza Pitti 36r 055 212 621, giuliogiannini.it; map p.524. Established in 1856, this paper-making and book-binding firm has been honoured with exhibitions dedicated to its work. Once the only place in Florence to make its own marbled papers, it now offers a wide variety of diaries, address books and so forth as well. Mon–Sat 10am–7.30pm, Sun 11am–6.30pm.

Il Torchio Via de' Bardi 17 055 234 2862, legatoriailtorchio.com; map p.518. Now owned by young Sicilian-Canadian Erin Ciulla, Il Torchio produces marbled paper, desk accessories, diaries, albums and other items in paper and leather. Mon–Fri 9.30am–1.30pm & 2.30–7pm, Sat 9.30am–1pm.

PERFUME AND TOILETRIES

★ **Farmacia Santa Maria Novella** Via della Scala 16 055 216 276, smnovella.it; map p.524. Occupying the pharmacy of the Santa Maria Novella monastery, this sixteenth-century shop was founded by Dominican monks as an outlet for their herbal potions, ointments and remedies. Many of these are still in production, together with face creams, shampoos and more esoteric concoctions. Daily 9am–8pm.

PRINTS AND PHOTOS

Alinari Largo Alinari 15 055 23 951, alinari.com; map p.524. Founded in 1852, this is the world's oldest photographic business. They sell books, calendars, posters and cards, and will print any image you choose from their huge catalogue, the largest archive of old photographs in Italy. Mon–Fri 9am–1pm & 2–6pm; closed two weeks in mid-Aug.

Torrini Via della Condotta 20r 055 480 157, torrinifotogiornalismo.it; map p.524. The Torrini archive, founded in 1944 by photojournalist Giulio Torrini, is a great source of unusual postcards and prints of Florence. Mon–Sat 9.30am–7.30pm.

FASHION FACTORY OUTLETS

Armani, Prada, Florence-based Gucci and all the other big Italian names have a massive presence on **Via de Tornabuoni**, but if you want to get hold of top-label clothing without breaking the bank, you'll need to take a trip into Florence's hinterland. Tuscany is the powerhouse of the country's textile industry, and the Arno Valley is the home of many of the factories that manufacture clothes for the top labels. Several **factory outlets** within easy reach of Florence sell each season's leftovers at discounts as high as sixty percent.

Barberino Designer Outlet Via Meucci, Barberino di Mugello ⓣ055 842 161, ⓦmcarthurglen.it/barberino; SITA bus from Via Santa Caterina da Siena or shuttle bus from outside Santa Maria Novella station (2 daily). The biggest range, including Cavalli, D&G, Ferré, Missoni and Prada, plus discounted high-street gear from labels such as Diesel, Benetton and Furla. Daily 10am–9pm.

The Mall Via Europa 8, Leccio Regello ⓣ055 865 7775, ⓦthemall.it; SITA bus from Via Santa Caterina da Siena or shuttle bus from outside Santa Maria Novella station (2 daily). Outlets for Cavalli, Dolce & Gabbana, Pucci, Gucci, Armani, Salvatore Ferragamo and Valentino, among others. Gucci is the dominant presence, with a huge range of bags, shoes and sunglasses. Daily 10am–7pm (June–Aug 8pm).

Space Levanella, Montevarchi ⓣ055 91 901, ⓦprada.com/it; train to Montevarchi, then taxi. On a small industrial estate in the Levanella district (on the SS69), this outlet is stacked with Prada clothes, as well as a good selection from the Miu Miu diffusion label. Mon–Fri & Sun 10.30am–7.30pm, Sat 9.30am–7.30pm.

SHOES AND ACCESSORIES

Cellerini Via del Sole 37r ⓣ055 282 533, ⓦwww.cellerini.it; map p.524. Bags, bags and more bags. Everything is made on the premises under the supervision of the firm's founders, the city's premier exponents of the craft; bags don't come more elegant or durable. Summer Mon–Fri 9am–1pm & 3–7pm, Sat 9am–1pm; winter Mon–Fri 11am–7pm, Sat 10am–1pm.

Madova Via Guicciardini 1r ⓣ055 239 6526, ⓦmadova.com; map p.524. The last word in gloves – every colour, every size, every style, lined with lambswool, silk, cashmere or nothing. Prices range from around €40 to €200. Mon–Fri 10.30am–7pm, Sat 9.30am–7pm.

Scuola del Cuoio Via S. Giuseppe 5r ⓣ055 244 533, ⓦscuoladelcuoio.com; map p.524. This academy for leather-workers at the back of Santa Croce church sells bags, jackets, belts and other accessories at prices that compare very favourably with the shops. You won't find any startlingly original designs, but the quality is very high and the staff knowledgeable and helpful. Summer daily 10am–6pm; winter closed Sun.

DIRECTORY

Banks and exchange Florence's main bank branches are around Piazza della Repubblica.

Consulates The UK consulate for northern Italy is in Milan (see page 244); the US has a consulate in Florence, at Lungarno Amerigo Vespucci 38 (ⓣ055 266 951).

Doctors The Tourist Medical Service is a private service with doctors on call 24hr a day (ⓣ055 475 411, ⓦmedicalservice.firenze.it), or you can visit its clinic at Via Lorenzo il Magnifico 59 (Mon–Fri 11am–noon & 5–6pm, Sat 11am–noon). Note that you'll need insurance cover to recoup the cost of a consultation, which will be at least €50. Florence's central hospital is on Piazza Santa Maria Nuova.

Laundry The Wash & Dry franchise has branches throughout the city, open 8am–10pm daily, including Via dei Servi 105r and Via Ghibellina 143r.

Lost property Lost property handed into the city or railway police ends up at Via Veracini 5 (Mon, Wed & Fri 9am–12.30, Tues & Thurs 9am–12.30 & 2.30–4.30pm; ⓣ055 334 802; bus #17, #29, #30 or #35). There's also a lost property office at Santa Maria Novella station, on platform 16 next to left luggage.

Pharmacies The Farmacia Comunale, on the train station concourse, is open 24hr. All'Insegna del Moro, at Piazza San Giovanni 20r, on the north side of the Baptistry, and Farmacia Molteni, at Via dei Calzaiuoli 7r, alternate their 24hr service every two weeks.

Police To report a theft or other crime, go to the *Carabinieri* at Borgo Ognissanti 48, to the *Questura* at Via Zara 2 (both 24hr), or to the tourist police at Via Pietrapiana 50r (Mon–Fri 8.30am–6.30pm, Sat 8.30am–1pm) – you're more likely to find an English-speaker at the last of these.

Post office The main central post office is near Piazza della Repubblica at Via Pellicceria 3 (Mon–Fri 8.25am–7.10pm, Sat 8.25am–12.35pm).

Around Florence

The greater Florence area has a number of towns and attractions to entice you on a day-trip from the city or even act as a base for exploring the region. City buses run up to the hill-village of **Fiesole**, while inter-town services run south into the hills of **Chianti**, Italy's premier wine region.

Fiesole

A long-established Florentine retreat from the summer heat and crowds, **FIESOLE** spreads over a cluster of hilltops 8km northeast of the city. It predates Florence by several hundred years: the Etruscans held out so long up here that the Romans were forced to set up permanent camp in the valley below – thus creating the beginnings of the settlement that was to become Florence.

The Duomo

Piazza Mino da Fiesole • Daily 8am–noon & 3–6pm; closes 5pm in winter • Free

The central square, **Piazza Mino**, is named after the fifteenth-century sculptor Mino da Fiesole, who has two fine pieces in the **Duomo** that dominates its north side. Nineteenth-century restoration ruined the Duomo's exterior, and the interior is something like a stripped-down version of Florence's San Miniato; the highlight is the Cappella Salutati, to the right of the choir, which contains Mino's panel of the *Madonna and Saints* and tomb of Bishop Salutati. Fiesole's patron saint, St Romulus, is buried underneath the choir in the ancient crypt.

Museo Bandini

Via Dupré 1 • Fri–Sun: April–Sept 10am–7pm; March & Oct 10am–6pm; Nov–Feb 10am–2pm • €5, or one-day ticket for all Fiesole's museums €10 • W fiesole.it

The **Museo Bandini** possesses a collection of glazed terracotta in the style of the della Robbias, the odd piece of Byzantine ivory work and a few thirteenth- and fourteenth-century Tuscan pictures, including pieces by Bernardo Daddi, Lorenzo Monaco and Taddeo Gaddi.

Teatro Romano and the Museo Archeologico

Via Portigiani 1 • April–Sept daily 10am–7pm; March & Oct daily 10am–6pm; Nov–Feb daily (except Tues) 10am–5pm • €7 for Teatro Romano, or €10 for Teatro and museum, or one-day ticket for all Fiesole's museums €12 • W museidifiesole.it

Across the road from the Bandini, the three-thousand-seat **Teatro Romano** was built in the first century BC and excavated towards the end of the nineteenth century. Most of the exhibits in the site's small **Museo Archeologico** were excavated in this area, and encompass pieces from the Bronze Age to Roman occupation; the well-presented Etruscan section is the highlight.

Oratorio di San Jacopo, Sant'Alessandro and San Francesco

Apart from Duomo, Fiesole's other major churches are reached by the narrow Via San Francesco, which rises steeply from Piazza Mino, past the **Oratorio di San Jacopo** (Sat & Sun 10am–5pm), a little chapel containing a fifteenth-century fresco and some ecclesiastical treasures. **Sant'Alessandro** (open for exhibitions only) was founded in the sixth century on the site of Etruscan and Roman temples and has beautiful *marmorino cipollino* (onion marble) columns adorning its basilical interior. The Gothic church of **San Francesco** (daily: 9am–noon & 3–6pm) occupies the site of the acropolis; across one of the tiny cloisters there's a tiny museum of pieces brought back from Egypt and China by missionaries.

San Domenico and the Badia Fiesolana

For a lovely walk, head southwest from Piazza Mino for 1.5km down the narrow, winding Via Vecchia Fiesolana to the hamlet of **San Domenico**. Fra' Angelico was

once prior of the Dominican **monastery** here and the church retains a 1420 *Madonna and Angels* by him (first chapel on the left). Five minutes' walk northwest from San Domenico stands the **Badia Fiesolana** (Mon–Fri 9am–5.30pm, Sat 9am–12.30pm; free), Fiesole's cathedral from the ninth century to the eleventh. Cosimo il Vecchio had the church altered in the 1460s, a project which left the magnificent Romanesque facade embedded in the rough stone frontage while the interior was transformed into a superb Renaissance building.

ARRIVAL AND INFORMATION — FIESOLE

By bus Fiesole is an easy hop from central Florence: bus #7 makes the 30min journey from Via L Pira (off Piazza San Marco) to Piazza Mino da Fiesole every 20min.

Tourist office Via Portigiani 3/5, next to the entrance to the archeological site (Fri, Sat, Sun only 10am–1pm & 2–4pm; ⓣ 055 596 1323, ⓦ fiesoleforyou.it).

Chianti

Ask a sample of middle-class Northern Europeans to define their idea of paradise and the odds are that a hefty percentage will come up with something that sounds a lot like **Chianti**, the territory of vineyards and hill-towns that stretches between Florence and Siena. Life in Chianti seems in perfect balance: the landscape is a softly varied terrain of hills and valleys; the climate for most of the year is sunny; and on top of all this there's the **wine**, the one Italian vintage that's familiar to just about everyone. Visitors from Britain and other similarly ill-favoured climes were long ago alerted to Chianti's charms, and the rate of immigration has been so rapid in recent decades that the region is now wryly dubbed **Chiantishire**. Yet it would be an exaggeration to say that Chianti has completely lost its character: the tone of certain parts has been altered, but concessions to tourism have been more or less successfully absorbed into the rhythm of local life.

If you're relying on **buses** from Florence, the best target is Greve in Chianti; from Siena, you can take a bus to Castellina in Chianti or Radda in Chianti. But the only realistic way to get to know the region is with **your own transport**, following the SS222 (or Chiantigiana), which snakes its way between Florence and Siena through the most beautiful parts of Chianti.

Greve in Chianti

The venue for Chianti's biggest wine fair (the Rassegna del Chianti Classico, usually held in early Sept), **GREVE IN CHIANTI** is a thriving mercantile town where there's wine for sale on every street. The funnel-shaped Piazza Matteotti – venue for the Saturday morning market – is focused on a statue of Giovanni da Verrazzano, the first European to see what became Manhattan; he was born in the nearby Castello di Verrazzano. Greve's only real sight is the **Museo di San Francesco**, at Via San Francesco 14 (April–Oct Tues, Thurs & Fri 4–7pm, Sat & Sun 10–1pm & 4–7pm; Nov–March Sun 10am–1pm & 3–6pm; €5), where the chief exhibit is a painted terracotta *Lamentation*, created in the 1530s.

Castellina in Chianti

Well-heeled **CASTELLINA IN CHIANTI** formerly stood on the front line of the continual wars between Florence and Siena, and its walls and fortress bear testimony to an

AGRITURISMI IN CHIANTI

Hotels in Chianti are rarely inexpensive, but this is prime **agriturismo** territory, with scores of farms offering rooms or apartments (or even self-contained mini-villas), generally for a minimum period of one week, which for an extended stay can provide a good-value alternative to hotel accommodation. We've recommended a small selection in our listings – you'll find hundreds more properties at ⓦ agriturismo.net and ⓦ agriturismo.it.

9

THE CHIANTI AND VALDARNO MUSEUM NETWORK

The Chianti area is littered with small museums like the one in Greve, which have been gathered together as the **Sistema Museale del Chianti e del Valdarno Fiorentino**; the admission ticket to any of these museums includes admission to various others. Details of the scheme can be found at chiantivaldarno.it.

embattled past. Traces of a more distant era can be seen at the **Ipogeo Etrusco di Montecalvario** (daylight hours; free), a complex of subterranean sixth-century-BC Etruscan burial chambers, carved into the summit of a small hill five minutes' walk north of the village. The area's history is illuminated in the **Museo Archeologico del Chianti Senese** (April–Oct daily 10am–6pm; Nov–March Sat & Sun 10am–5pm; €5), which also gives you access to the town's tower. Castellina's one sizeable church is the neo-Romanesque **San Salvatore**, which is notable only for a single fifteenth-century fresco and the mummified remains of the obscure St Fausto. But what really brings in the tourists to Castellina is, of course, wine – as is evident from the power-station bulk of the **wine cooperative** on the main road. The local vintages (and olive oil) can be sampled at several places in town.

Radda in Chianti

The best of Chianti lies east of Castellina and the Chiantigiana, in the less domesticated terrain of the **Monti del Chianti** – the stronghold of the Lega di Chianti, whose power bases were Castellina itself and the two principal settlements of this craggy region, Radda and Gaiole. The nearer of these, the ancient Etruscan-founded town of **RADDA IN CHIANTI**, became the league's capital in 1384, and the imprint of the period is still strong here – though perhaps not quite as strong as the imprint of middle-class tourism, which has almost smothered the town's identity. The minuscule *centro storico* is focused on Piazza Ferrucci, where the frescoed and shield-studded Palazzo Comunale faces a church raised on a high platform.

INFORMATION — CHIANTI

Tourist offices Greve: Piazza Matteotti 10 (March–Oct daily 10.30am–6.30pm; Nov–Feb Mon–Fri 9am–1pm & 3–6.30pm, Sat 10am–5pm, Sun 10am–1pm); Castellina: Via Ferruccio 40 (Mon–Fri 10am-1pm; 0577 741 392.

ACCOMMODATION AND EATING

GREVE IN CHIANTI

Da Verrazzano 28 Piazza Matteotti 055 853 189, albergoverrazzano.it. A plain but characterful three-star hotel which also has a good restaurant, with full meals at around €40; in summer you can eat on the terrace overlooking the piazza. Restaurant Tues–Sun noon–3.30pm & 7–11pm; closed mid-Jan to mid-Feb. **€110**

★ **La Castellana** Via di Montefioralle 2 055 853 134. Located about 500m outside Montefioralle, on the narrow road from neighbouring Greve, this is a perfect Tuscan trattoria: homely, small and utterly genuine, serving delicious food at honest prices – around €25–30 per person. Tues–Sun noon–2.30pm & 7.30–9.30pm

CASTELLINA IN CHIANTI

Albergaccio di Castellina Via Fiorentina 63 0577 741 042, albergacciocast.com. Situated on the outskirts of the village, the rustic *Albergaccio* has a beautiful terrace and a homely stone-walled dining room, and the cooking is of a high standard too, with tasting menus for under €50. Mon–Sat 12.30–2.30pm & 7.30–9.30pm.

★ **Palazzo Squarcialupi** Via Ferruccio 22 0577 741 186, palazzosquarcialupi.com. Pick of Castellina's hotels is the three-star *Palazzo Squarcialupi*, which occupies the upper storeys of a vast fifteenth-century *palazzo*. The rooms are large and well furnished, and there's a sauna in the basement and a pool in the garden, which commands a wonderful view. **€130**

RADDA IN CHIANTI

Palazzo Leopoldo Via Roma 33 0577 735 603, palazzoleopoldo.it. This place was founded as a pilgrims' hostel, then converted into a magnificent townhouse prior to becoming an extremely elegant four-star hotel, with a good restaurant, plus gym, sauna and pool. Restaurant daily except Wed 12.30–2.45pm & 7.30–10pm. **€110**

Relais Vignale Via Pianigiani 9 ⓣ0577 738 012 (hotel), ⓣ0577 738 094 (restaurant), ⓦvignale.it. The elegant 42-room *Relais Vignale* occupies a nicely converted seventeenth-century manor house on the edge of the village; it has a pool in the garden, a wine bar in the cellars and a good if slightly pricey restaurant – but this is a pricey little town. Restaurant April–Nov daily noon–2.30pm & 7–10.30pm. **€200**

Pisa, Lucca and the coast

Thanks to its Leaning Tower, **Pisa** is known by name to just about every visitor to Italy, though it remains an underrated place, seen by most people on a whistle-stop day-trip that takes in nothing of the city except the tower and its immediate environs. Genteel **Lucca** nearby, its walled old town crammed with Romanesque churches, is even less explored.

Tuscany's **coast** is a mixed bag, generally too overdeveloped to be consistently attractive. North of Pisa, the succession of beach resorts enjoys the backdrop of the mighty Alpi Apuane, which harbour the marble quarries of Carrara. South from Pisa, past the untouristed port of Livorno, are a hundred scrubby strips of hotels and campsites. The Tuscan shoreline is at its best in the **Maremma** region, where you'll find the protected **Monti dell'Uccellina** reserve and the wild, wooded peninsula of **Monte Argentario**. Tuscany's main island, **Elba**, also offers a breath of fresh air.

Pisa

For many tourists, **PISA** means just one thing – the **Leaning Tower**, which serves around the world as a shorthand image for Italy. It is indeed a freakishly beautiful building, a sight whose impact no amount of prior knowledge can blunt. Yet it is just a single component of Pisa's breathtaking **Campo dei Miracoli**, or Field of Miracles, where the **Duomo**, **Baptistry** and **Camposanto** complete a dazzling architectural ensemble. These amazing buildings belong to Pisa's Golden Age, from the eleventh to the thirteenth centuries, when the city was one of the maritime powers of the Mediterranean. Decline set in with defeat by the Genoese in 1284, followed by the silting-up of Pisa's harbour, and from 1406 the city was governed by Florence, whose rulers re-established the University of Pisa, one of the great intellectual establishments of the Renaissance – **Galileo** was a teacher here. Subsequent centuries saw Pisa fade into provinciality, though landmarks from its glory days now bring in hundreds of thousands of visitors a year, and the combination of tourism and a large student population give the contemporary city a lively feel.

It has to be said that visiting the Campo in high season is not a calming experience – the tourist maelstrom here can be fierce. Within a short radius of the Campo dei

TICKETS FOR THE CAMPO DEI MIRACOLI MONUMENTS

There are two **ticket offices** for the **Campo dei Miracoli** sights: on the north side of the Leaning Tower, and inside the Museo delle Sinopie. **Tickets** for the Leaning Tower can be bought only from the first of these; tickets for the Campo dei Miracoli's museums and monuments can be bought from either. Single admission to the Baptistry, Museo dell'Opera, Camposanto or Museo delle Sinopie costs €5; admission to any two of these sights is €7, to any three is €8; tickets are valid for the day of issue only. Admission to the **Duomo** is included with each of these tickets, or you can pick up a free voucher for admission to the Duomo on its own.

There's a separate ticket (€18) for the **Leaning Tower**; groups of thirty are allowed in for half an hour, and you should expect a long wait in high season. You can **prebook your visit** online at ⓦopapisa.it, as long as you're making your reservation not more than twenty days and at least one day in advance. Children under the age of 8 are not allowed into the tower.

Miracoli, however, Pisa takes on a quite different character, because very few tourists bother to venture far from the shadow of the Leaning Tower.

The Leaning Tower

Daily: Jan & Dec 10am–5pm; Feb, March & Nov 9am–6pm; April–Sept 9am–8pm; Oct 9am–7pm • Tickets available on site or online (see page 559)

The **Leaning Tower** (Torre Pendente) has always tilted. Begun in 1173, it started to subside when it had reached just three of its eight storeys, but it leaned in the opposite direction to the present one. Odd-shaped stones were inserted to correct this deficiency, whereupon the tower lurched the other way. Over the next 180 years a succession of architects continued to extend the thing upwards, each one endeavouring to compensate for the angle, the end result being that the main part of the tower

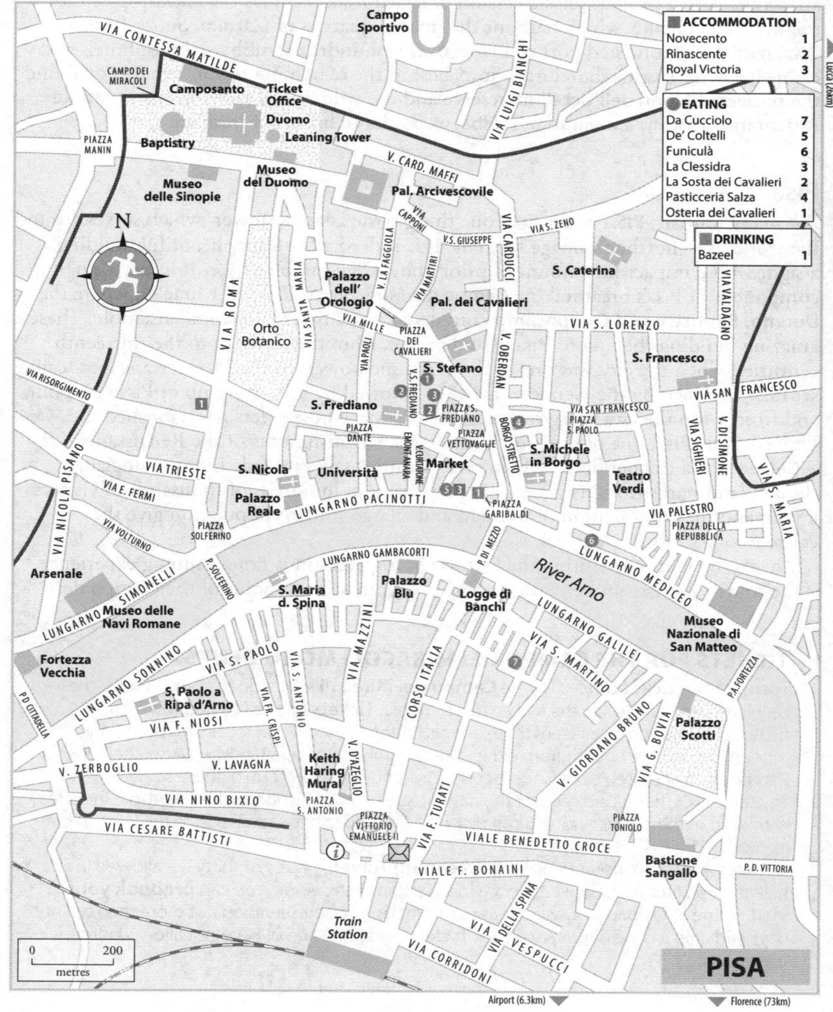

is slightly bent. Around 1350, Tommaso di Andrea da Pontedera completed the magnificent stack of marble and granite arcades by crowning it with a bell chamber, set closer to the perpendicular than the storeys below it, so that it looks like a hat set at a rakish angle.

By 1990 the tower was leaning 4.5m from the upright and nearing its limits. A huge rescue operation was then launched, which involved wrapping steel bands around the lowest section of the tower, placing 900 tonnes of lead ingots at its base to counterbalance the leaning stonework, removing water and silt from beneath the tower's foundations, and finally reinforcing the foundations and walls with steel bars. Eleven years and many millions of euros later, the tower was reopened in November 2001.

The ascent to the bell chamber takes you up a narrow spiral staircase of 294 steps, at a fairly disorientating five-degree angle. It's not for the claustrophobic or those afraid of heights, but you might think the steep admission fee is worth it for the privilege of getting inside one of the world's most famous and uncanny buildings.

The Duomo

Daily: March 10am–6pm; April–Sept 10am–8pm; Oct 10am–7pm; Nov–Feb 10am–6pm; no admittance to tourists before 1pm on Sun • Tickets available on site or online (see page 559)

Pisa's breathtaking **Duomo** was begun in 1064 and completed around a century later. With its four levels of variegated colonnades and its subtle interplay of dark grey marble and white stone, the building is the archetype of Pisan-Romanesque, a model often imitated in buildings across Tuscany, but never surpassed.

Much of the vast interior was redecorated, and some of the chapels remodelled, after a fire in 1595, but a notable survivor is the apse mosaic *Christ in Majesty*, completed by Cimabue in 1302. And don't miss the **pulpit**, which **Giovanni Pisano** began to sculpt in the same year. The last of the great series of pulpits created in Tuscany by Giovanni and his father Nicola (the others are in Siena and Pistoia), it is a work of amazing virtuosity, its whole surface animated by figures almost wholly freed from the stone.

The Baptistry

Daily: March 9am–6pm; April–Sept 8am–8pm; Oct 9am–7pm; Nov–Feb 10am–5pm • Tickets available on site or online (see page 559)

The **Baptistry**, the largest such building in Italy, was begun in 1152 by a certain Diotisalvi ("God Save You"), who left his name on a column to the left of the door; it was continued in the thirteenth century by Nicola and Giovanni Pisano, and completed late in the fourteenth century. Inside you're immediately struck by the plainness of the vast interior (the acoustics are astonishing, as the guard will demonstrate), but take time to admire Nicola Pisano's beautiful **pulpit**, sculpted in 1260, half a century before his son's work in the cathedral.

Camposanto

Daily: March 9am–6pm; April–Sept 8am–8pm; Oct 9am–7pm; Nov–Feb 10am–5pm • Tickets available on site or online (see page 559)

The screen of sepulchral white marble running along the north edge of the Campo dei Miracoli is the perimeter wall of what has been called the most beautiful cemetery in the world – the **Camposanto**. According to legend, the Archbishop Ubaldo Lanfranchi had Pisan knights on the Fourth Crusade of 1203 bring a cargo of soil back to Pisa from the hill of Golgotha, in order that eminent Pisans might be buried in holy earth. The building enclosing this sanctified site was completed almost a century later and takes the form of an enormous Gothic cloister. However, when Ruskin described the Camposanto as one of the most precious buildings in Italy, it was the **frescoes** he was praising. Paintings once covered more than two thousand square metres of cloister wall, but now the brickwork is mostly bare: bombs dropped by Allied planes on July 27, 1944, set the roofing on fire and drenched the frescoes in molten lead. The most important survivor is the remarkable *Triumph of Death* cycle, now displayed in a room attached to the cloister.

9

The museums of the Campo dei Miracoli

Closed for restoration at time of writing; check website for updates (see page 559)

The **Museo dell'Opera del Duomo** is a vast array of statuary from the Duomo and Baptistry, plus ecclesiastical finery, paintings and other miscellaneous pieces. Highlights include the extraordinary bronze doors made for the Duomo by **Bonanno Pisano** (first architect of the Leaning Tower) in 1180, and Giovanni Pisano's affecting *Madonna del Colloquio* (Madonna of the Conversation), so called because of the intensity of the gazes exchanged by the Madonna and Child. On the south side of the Campo, the only gap in the souvenir stalls is for the **Museo delle Sinopie**. After the bomb damage wreaked on the Camposanto, restorers removed its *sinopie* (the sketches over which frescoes are painted) and these great plates of plaster now hang from the walls of this high-tech museum.

Piazza dei Cavalieri to Piazza Garibaldi

If you have time for a wider exploration of the city, head first for **Piazza dei Cavalieri**, the central civic square of medieval Pisa, which opens unexpectedly from the narrow backstreets to the southeast of the Campo. Covered in monochrome sgraffiti and topped with busts of the Medici, the **Palazzo dei Cavalieri** is next to the church of **Santo Stefano**, which still houses banners captured from Turkish ships by the Knights of St Stephen – a grand title for a gang of state-sponsored pirates. From here Via Dini heads east to the arcaded **Borgo Stretto**, Pisa's smartest street; Pisa's market area is west of here, on **Piazza Vettovaglie** and the narrow streets that surround it. The Borgo meets the river at **Piazza Garibaldi**, at the foot of the Ponte di Mezzo.

Museo Nazionale di San Matteo

Piazza S. Matteo 1 • Tues–Sat 8.30am–7pm, Sun 8.30am–1pm • €5, or €8 combined ticket with Palazzo Reale (see below)

East of Piazza Garibaldi, by the river, is the **Museo Nazionale di San Matteo**, where most of the major works of art from Pisa's churches are now gathered. Best of the paintings are polyptychs by Simone Martini and Francesco Traini, a panel of *St Paul* by Masaccio, Gentile da Fabriano's *Madonna of Humility* and a trio of works by Gozzoli. Among the sculptures, two masterpieces stand out – Donatello's reliquary bust of the introspective *St Rossore*, and Andrea and Nino Pisano's *Madonna del Latte*, a touchingly crafted work showing Mary breastfeeding the baby Jesus. The museum also has a stash of fine Middle Eastern ceramics pilfered by Pisan adventurers.

Museo Nazionale di Palazzo Reale

Lungarno Pacinotti 46 • Mon–Sat 9am–2pm • €5, or €8 combined ticket with Museo Nazionale di San Matteo (see above)

The **Museo Nazionale di Palazzo Reale** displays artefacts that once belonged to the Medici, Lorraine and Savoy rulers of the city, who successively occupied the house. Lavish sixteenth-century Flemish tapestries share space with antique weaponry, ivory miniatures, porcelain and a largely undistinguished picture collection; the best-known painting, a version of Bronzino's portrait of Eleanora di Toledo, is displayed alongside a dress that belonged to her.

THE GIOCO DEL PONTE AND GIUGNO PISANO

Pisa's big traditional event is the **Gioco del Ponte**, held on the last Sunday of June, when twelve teams from the north and south banks of the city stage a series of "push-of-war" battles, shoving a seven-tonne carriage over the Ponte di Mezzo. First recorded in 1568, the contest and attendant parades are still held in Renaissance costume. Other celebrations – concerts, regattas, art events – are held throughout June as part of the **Giugno Pisano** (giugnopisano.com). The most spectacular event is the **Luminara di San Ranieri** (June 16), when buildings along both river banks are lit by seventy thousand candles in honour of Pisa's patron saint, and there's a fireworks display at midnight. At 6.30pm the following evening, the various quarters of the city compete in the Palio di San Ranieri, a boat race along the Arno.

PISA AIRPORT

Pisa's **Galileo Galilei airport** (050 849 300, pisa-airport.com) lies about 3km south of the city centre. The **drive** to Florence is straightforward (a slip road takes you directly onto the motorway), but the road into Pisa is so confusing that, without directions from the car-rental desk, you may well end up getting lost.

A new driverless **rail shuttle**, called the **PisaMover**, runs from 6am to midnight every 5–8 min, for 18hr each day (€2.70). You can also take the LAM Rosso city bus (€1.30) from the airport to Pisa Centrale. **Trains to Florence** depart from Pisa Centrale regularly (every 30min; 1hr–1hr 20min; €8). Buses operated by Autostradale (airportbusexpress.it) run almost hourly from the airport to Florence Santa Maria Novella. Journey time is 1hr 10 min and tickets cost €14.

The Arsenale Mediceo

Lungarno Ranieri Simonelli

West along the river from the Palazzo Reale lies the **Arsenale Mediceo**. Built by Cosimo I, it is being converted into the **Museo delle Navi Romane**, which will house the sixteen Roman ships that have been excavated since 1998 from the silt at nearby San Rossore. Almost perfectly preserved in mud for two millennia, the cargo-laden fleet includes what experts believe could be the oldest Roman warship ever found. The museum has been in the works for a decade now, and it's due to open fairly soon; check turismo.pisa.it for the latest situation.

Palazzo Blu

Lungarno Gambacorti 9 • Tues–Fri 10am–7pm, Sat & Sun 10am–8pm • Free, except during special exhibitions • palazzoblu.it

On the south bank of the river, west of the Ponte di Mezzo, the line of *palazzi* is enlivened by the brightly hued **Palazzo Blu**, which holds a permanent collection of regional art from the fourteenth to the twentieth centuries, as well as occasional big-name exhibitions on the ground floor.

Santa Maria della Spina

Lungarno Gambacorti • April–Sept Tues–Fri 10am–1.30pm & 2.30–6pm, Sat & Sun 10am–1.30pm & 2.30–7pm; Oct–March Tues–Sun 10am–2pm • €1.50

West from the Palazzo Blu, just before the Ponte Solferino, is the oratory of **Santa Maria della Spina**. Founded in 1230 but rebuilt in the 1320s by a merchant who had acquired one of the thorns (*spine*) of Christ's crown, this effervescent little church is the finest flourish of Pisan-Gothic. Originally built closer to the water, it was moved here for fear of floods in 1871. The single-naved interior has lost most of its furnishings, but contains a trio of statues by Andrea and Nino Pisano.

ARRIVAL AND INFORMATION — PISA

By air See above.

By train Pisa Centrale train station is about 1km south of the River Arno; the Campo dei Miracoli is about a 30min walk north, or a 5min ride on bus #1, which leaves from outside the station.

Destinations Empoli (approx 2 hourly; 35min; change for Volterra and Siena); Florence (approx 3 hourly; 1hr–1hr 20min); Lucca (approx 2 hourly; 28min).

By bus The main bus terminus is Piazza Sant'Antonio, in front of the train station.

Destinations Florence (from airport: hourly; 1hr 20min); Livorno (hourly; 40min); Lucca (hourly; 50min); Viareggio (hourly; 50min).

Tourist offices Piazza del Duomo 7, by the Leaning Tower (daily 9.30am–5.30pm), comune.pisa.it.

ACCOMMODATION

Novecento Via Roma 37 050 500 323, hotelnovecento.pisa.it; map p.560. This three-star *residenza d'epoca* occupies a handsome old townhouse, but the rooms are immaculately modern in style. The rates are very reasonable (you can pay twice as much for similar accommodation closer to the Campo), the location convenient and quiet, and it has a pleasant garden as well. **€90**

Rinascente Via del Castelletto 28 050 580 460,

9

Ⓦ rinascentehotel.com; map p.560. If you want a cheap and clean room in the city centre, you can't do better than this homely one-star, which occupies an upper floor of a *palazzo* hidden in an alley not far south of Piazza dei Cavalieri – follow the signs from Via San Frediano. Shared or private bathrooms. **€60**

Royal Victoria Lungarno Pacinotti 12 Ⓣ 050 940 111, Ⓦ royalvictoria.it; map p.560. Run by the same family since its foundation in 1837, this old-fashioned and appealingly frayed three-star is the most characterful of central Pisa's hotels – and the best value. The public rooms, with their musty engravings and antique furniture, are redolent of the place's history, but if you're uncharmed by wobbly door handles and patched-up ceilings, it's not the place for you. And there's no double glazing, which might be a problem for light sleepers. **€100**

EATING

Pisa's proximity to the coast means that **seafood** is served in most **restaurants**, with *baccalà alla Pisana* (salt cod in tomato sauce) and *pesce spada* (swordfish) featuring prominently; nearly all menus have two sections, labelled "mare" (for fish) and "terra" (for meat). Avoid the temptation to eat in the vicinity of the Campo dei Miracoli – aimed squarely at the tourist trade, these places are generally of poor quality. Pisa's lively student population means there are plenty of cheap eateries and **bars** around Piazza Dante and Piazza delle Vettovaglie, and between Piazza Garibaldi and Piazza Cairoli.

CAFÉS AND GELATERIE

De' Coltelli Lungarno Pacinotti 23 Ⓣ 345 481 1903; map p.560. The De' Coltelli family are credited with having devised the recipe for ice cream back in the seventeenth century, and the shop that bears their name is one of Italy's top-rank *gelaterie*, with a penchant for adventurous concoctions – anyone for seafood ice cream? Mon–Thurs & Sun 11.30am–10.30pm, Fri & Sat 11.30am–11.30pm.

Pasticceria Salza Borgo Stretto 46 Ⓣ 050 580 144; map p.560. The best-known café-*pasticceria* in Pisa, and rightly so; it has a restaurant section at the back, but the coffee and cakes are the main reason to come. Try the Pisan speciality *torta coi bischeri*, a tart made with dark chocolate, dried fruit and pine nuts. Tues–Sun 8am–8.30pm, till 10pm in summer.

RESTAURANTS

Da Cucciolo Vicolo Rosselmini 9 Ⓣ 050 26 086; map p.560. The family-run *Cucciolo* has been in business for almost half a century, and is one of the city's most reliable trattorias, offering unfussy and delicious traditional meals, from around €12 for a main course. Mon, Thurs, Fri noon–2pm & 7–10.30pm, Tues, Wed noon–2pm, Sat 7–10.30pm.

Funiculà Lungarno Mediceo 43 Ⓣ 050 580 201; map p.560. This place serves the best Neapolitan-style pizzas in Pisa, and though it's central – it's very near the Ponte di Mezzo – its clientele is overwhelmingly local. Daily 8pm–midnight.

La Clessidra Via del Castelletto 26–30 Ⓣ 050 540 160, Ⓦ ristoranteladessidra.net; map p.560. Tucked away in an alley not far from San Frediano, the roomy and atmospheric *Clessidra* offers a small but elegant menu of classic Tuscan dishes, with two tasting menus – one fish, one meat – at around €40 for four courses (minimum two people); à la carte, mains are mostly around €15. Mon–Sat 7.30–10.30pm; closed two weeks in Aug.

La Sosta dei Cavalieri Via San Frediano 3 Ⓣ 050 991 2410, Ⓦ sostadeicavalieri.it; map p.560. This is the smaller, cosier and slightly more refined sibling of the *Osteria dei Cavalieri*, over the road. Mains are around €16–20, and the menu concentrates on classic Pisan meat and fish dishes (using only fresh fish). The two "Sea" and "Land" tasting menus are excellent value at €35. Mon–Sat 12.30–2.30pm & 7.45–10.30pm.

★ **Osteria dei Cavalieri** Via San Frediano 16 Ⓣ 050 580 858, Ⓦ osteriacavalieri.pisa.it; map p.560. The *Osteria dei Cavalieri* has built a solid reputation over the years for its straightforward local food, very reasonable prices (most *secondi* under €15) and hospitable staff; reservations recommended in high season. Mon–Fri 12.30–2pm & 7.45–10.30pm, Sat 7.45–10.30pm; closed most of Aug.

DRINKING

Bazeel Piazza Garibaldi 15 Ⓣ 340 288 1113; map p.560. This café-bar has been one of Pisa's favourite hangouts for some time – the bare-brick interior is spacious, but when the weather's good the punters prefer the outside tables. It serves pizzas and other basic dishes, but this place is not about the food. DJs on Fri and Sat, live music Thurs and Sun. Daily noon–3am.

Lucca

The most graceful of Tuscany's provincial capitals, encircled by an imposing ring of Renaissance walls fronted by gardens and huge bastions, **LUCCA** stands 17km northeast of Pisa. Charming and quiet out of season, Lucca's narrow streets become busier in summer, without ever being as thronged as those of Florence or Siena. The town is a

delightful place in which to wander at random; while workaday and even scruffy in parts, it's consistently lovely, and full of life. Much of the centre is free from traffic, although you will have to keep an eye out for the many cyclists weaving through the crowds (plenty of outlets rent bikes if you wish to join them).

While the focus of Lucca's compact *centro storico* is the vast Piazza Napoleone, its social heart is **Piazza San Michele** just to the north. Once the site of the Roman forum, these days this lively square is fringed with shops and cafés. The "long thread", Via Fillungo, heads northeast, cutting through Lucca's shopping district to reach the extraordinary circular **Piazza Anfiteatro**, while further east, beyond the Fosso ("ditch"), lies San Francesco and Lucca's major art museum, housed in the **Villa Guinigi**. Whatever else you do, be sure to walk – or cycle – at least some of the city **walls**, which are crested by a broad, tree-lined promenade.

Brief history

Set at the heart of one of Italy's richest agricultural regions, Lucca has prospered since Roman times. Its heyday was the eleventh to fourteenth centuries, when the silk trade brought wealth and political power. Lucca first lost its independence to Pisa in 1314, then, under **Castruccio Castracani**, forged an empire in the west of Tuscany. Pisa and Pistoia both fell, and, but for Castracani's untimely death in 1325, Lucca might well have taken Florence. In subsequent centuries it remained largely independent until falling into the hands of Napoleon and then the Bourbons. Composer **Giacomo Puccini** was born here in 1858. Today Lucca is among the wealthiest and most conservative cities in Tuscany, its prosperity gained largely through **silk** and high-quality **olive oil**.

San Michele in Foro

Piazza San Michele • Daily: April–Oct 7.40am–noon & 3–6pm; Nov–March 8.30–10.30am& 3–5pm; closed to tourists during services • Free

Dating mainly from the century following 1070, the church of **San Michele in Foro** boasts one of Tuscany's most exquisite facades. The church is unfinished, as the money ran out before the body of the building could be raised to the level of the facade; the effect is wonderful, the upper loggias and the windows fronting air. Its Pisan-inspired intricacy is a triumph of poetic eccentricity: each of its myriad columns is different – some twisted, others sculpted or candy-striped. The impressive **campanile** is Lucca's tallest. It would be hard to follow this act and the interior barely tries; the best work of art is a beautifully framed painting called *Saints Jerome, Sebastian, Roch and Helena* by Filippino Lippi in the right-hand nave.

Puccini Museum & Bookshop

Corte San Lorenzo 9 • 1 March–30 April & 1Oct–-1 Nov daily 10am–6pm; 1 May–30 Oct daily 10am–7pm; 2 Nov–7 Jan Wed–Mon 10am–1pm & 3–5pm; 8 Jan–28 Feb Wed–Mon 10am–5pm • €7 • Ⓦ puccinimuseum.org

The composer Giacomo Puccini was born on December 22, 1858, about a block from San Michele; his father and grandfather had both been organists at the church. Puccini lived here until 1880, when he moved to Milan to complete his studies. The family home is now the **Puccini Museum**, or **Casa Natale di Giacomo Puccini**, where opera buffs can admire the maestro's original furniture, scores and letters; the splendid gown from a 1926 performance of *Turandot* is the highlight. The museum also organizes a varied programme of Puccini-related **events** (see page 571). Tickets for the museum can be bought a few seconds' walk away to the west at the **Bookshop-Bigliettera** at Piazza Cittadella 3, the small square (with a statue of the composer) off Via di Poggio.

Museo Nazionale di Palazzo Mansi

Via Galli Tassi 43 • Tues–Sat morning entrances scheduled at 9.30am and 11.30am; afternoon entrances scheduled at 2.30pm and 4.30pm • €4, or €6.50 combined ticket with Museo Nazionale di Villa Guinigi (see page 569) • Ⓦ luccamuseinazionali.it

A short way west of the Puccini Museum, the **Museo Nazionale di Palazzo Mansi**, set in a seventeenth-century *palazzo*, is worth seeing for its magnificent Rococo decor:

from a vast, frescoed **music salon**, you pass through three drawing rooms hung with seventeenth-century Flemish **tapestries** to a gilded bridal suite, complete with lavish canopied bed. Rooms 11–14 in the far wing hold an eclectic **Pinacoteca**, the highlights of which are **Pontormo**'s portrait of Alessandro de' Medici, and Sienese Mannerist works by Domenico Beccafumi and Rutilio Manetti.

Duomo di San Martino

Piazza San Martino • Mid-March to Oct Mon–Fri 9.30am–6pm, Sat 9.30am–6.45pm, Sun 9–10am & 11.45am–6pm; Nov to mid-March Mon–Fri 9.30am–5pm, Sat 9.30am–6pm, Sun 11.30am–5pm • €3, or €7 combined ticket with Museo della Cattedrale (see page 568) and San Giovanni e Reparata (see page 568) • museocattedralelucca.it

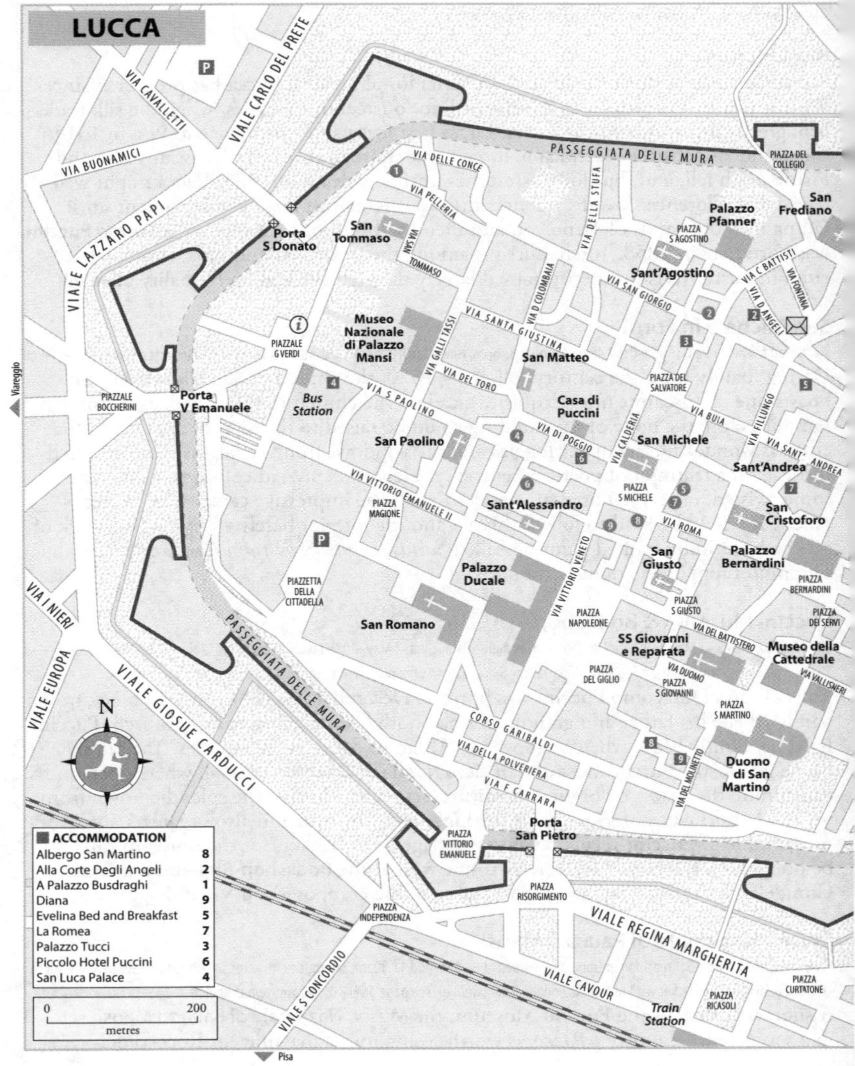

It needs a double take before you realize why the **Duomo** (also known as the Cattedrale di San Martino) looks odd. A severely asymmetric facade fronts the building – its right-hand arch and loggias are squeezed by the belltower, which was already in place from an earlier building. Little however detracts from its overall grandeur, created by the repetition of tiny columns and loggias and by the stunning **atrium**, with its magnificent bas-reliefs. The carvings over the left-hand door – a *Deposition*, *Annunciation*, *Nativity* and *Adoration of the Magi* – are by **Nicola Pisano**. Other panels display a symbolic labyrinth, a *Tree of Life* (with Adam and Eve at the bottom and Christ at the top), a bestiary of grotesques and the months of the year.

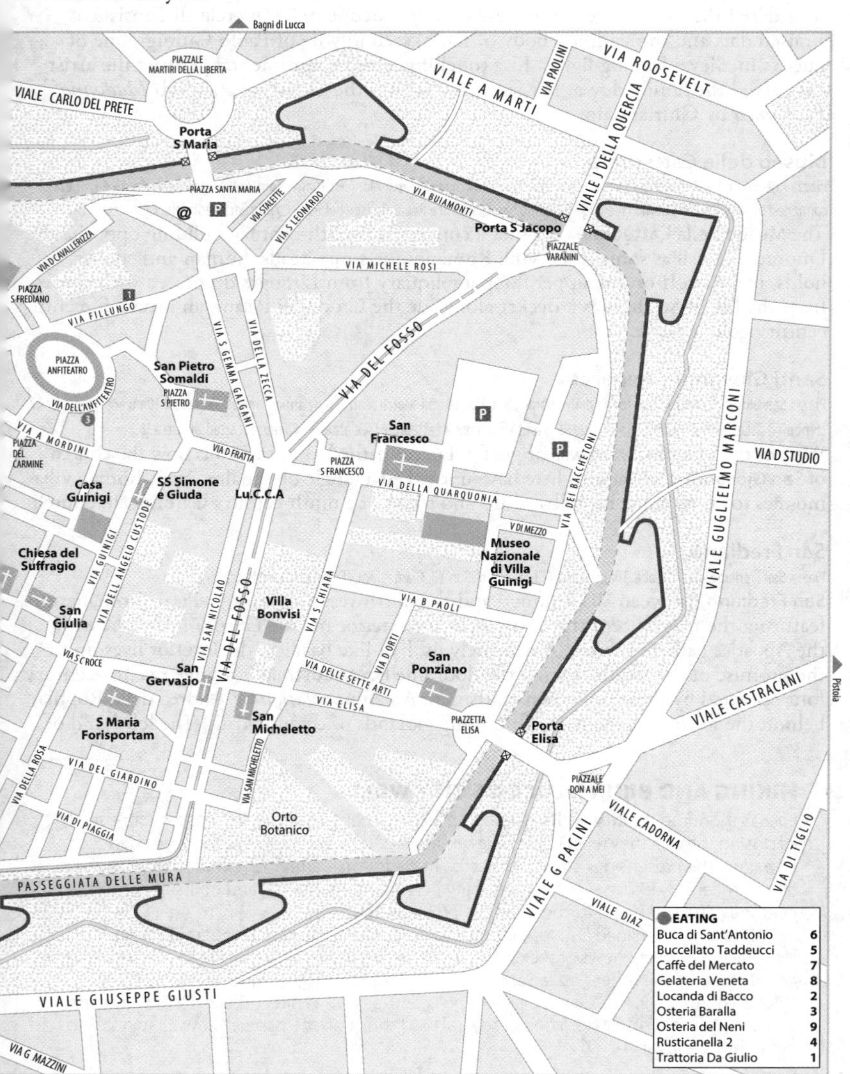

The **interior** is best known for the work of sculptor **Matteo Civitali** (1435–1501). His most celebrated contribution is the *Tempietto*, a gilt-and-marble octagon halfway down the church. Acts of devotion are performed in front of it, directed at the **Volto Santo** (Holy Face) within, a cedar crucifix with bulging eyes and dark brown skin popularly said to be a true effigy of Christ carved by Nicodemus, an eyewitness to the Crucifixion. Legend has it that the *Volto Santo* came to Lucca of its own volition, first journeying by boat from the Holy Land, and then brought by oxen guided by divine will. The effigy attracted pilgrims from all over Europe, including kings – William II of England used to swear by it ("*Per sanctum vultum de Lucca!*").

The **Tomb of Ilaria del Carretto** (1410) in the sacristy off the right (south) nave is considered the masterpiece of Sienese sculptor **Jacopo della Quercia**. It consists of a raised dais and the sculpted body of Ilaria, second wife of Paolo Guinigi, one of Lucca's medieval leading lights. In a touching, almost sentimental gesture, the artist has carved the family dog at her feet. Also within the sacristy is a superb *Madonna Enthroned* by Ghirlandaio.

Museo della Cattedrale

Piazza Antelminelli • Mid-March to Oct daily 10am–6pm; Nov to mid-March Mon–Fri 10am–2pm, Sat & Sun 10am–6pm • €4, or €7 combined ticket with the Duomo (see page 566) and San Giovanni e Reparata (see below) • ⓦ museocattedralelucca.it

The **Museo della Cattedrale** occupies a converted twelfth-century building opposite the Duomo. As well as some unnerving Romanesque stone heads, human and equine, it holds, in Room II on the upper floor, a reliquary from Limoges decorated with stories from the life of St Thomas à Becket alongside the Croce dei Pisani, an ornate fifteenth-century gold crucifix.

Santi Giovanni e Reparata

Piazza San Giovanni • Mid-March to Oct daily 10am–6pm; Nov to mid-March Mon–Fri by appointment, Sat & Sun 10am–6pm • €4, or €7 combined ticket with the Duomo (see page 566) and Museo della Cattedrale (see above) • ⓦ museocattedralelucca.it

West of the Duomo, what was originally Lucca's cathedral until 715 is now the **church of San Giovanni**. Excavations here have unearthed a tangle of remains, from Roman villa mosaics to an eighth-century baptistry and traces of a ninth-century Carolingian church.

San Frediano

Piazza San Frediano • Mon–Sat 8.30am–noon & 3–5.30pm, Sun 10.30am–5pm • Free • ⓦ diocesilucca.it

San Frediano, between Via Fillungo and the northwest city walls, is Pisan-Romanesque, featuring the magnificent thirteenth-century exterior mosaic *Christ in Majesty*, with the Apostles gathered below. A delicately lit, hall-like basilica, the **interior** lives up to the promise of the facade. Facing the door, the **Fonta Lustrale** is a huge twelfth-century font executed by three unknown craftsmen. An *Annunciation* by Andrea della Robbia, behind the font, is festooned with trailing garlands of ceramic fruit. The left-hand of

HIKING AND BIKING LUCCA'S CITY WALLS

Lucca's monumental **city walls** (ⓦ lemuradilucca.it) make a striking first impression: entirely enclosing the city, they're an impressive reminder of Lucca's history as an independent city-state. The present-day structure is actually the fourth – after the Roman, medieval and fifteenth-century efforts – constructed between the mid-sixteenth and mid-seventeenth centuries, and extending further than the previous defences.

The walls are tree-lined and topped by a car-free road – you can walk or cycle the 4.9km loop, taking in lovely views of the city on one side and the walls' grassy flanks and surrounding countryside on the other. Piazza Santa Maria has bike rental outlets including Poli (daily 8.30am–8pm; €3/hr, €15/day; ⓦ biciclettepoli.com), as well as direct access to the ramparts; you can pick up a picnic from one of several food shops off the piazza. Allow 25 minutes to cycle the full circuit.

the two rear chapels houses the apparently incorrupt body of **St Zita** (died 1278), a Lucchese maidservant who achieved sainthood by means of a white lie: she used to give bread from her household to the poor, and when challenged one day by her boss as to the contents of her apron, she replied "only roses and flowers" – into which the bread was transformed. On April 27, a flower market outside the church commemorates her. Lucca's finest frescoes – **Amico Aspertini**'s sixteenth-century scenes of *The Arrival of the Volto Santo*, *The Life of St Augustine* and *The Miracle of St Frediano* – occupy the second chapel of the left aisle. Frediano, an Irish monk, is said to have brought Christianity to Lucca in the sixth century and is depicted here saving the city from flood.

Palazzo Pfanner

Via degli Asili 33 • April–Oct daily 10am–6pm; Nov Mon & Thurs–Sun 11am–4pm • Garden or palace €4.50, garden and palace €6, €0.50 reduction in April, Oct & Nov • ⓦ palazzopfanner.it

A short distance west of San Frediano, **Palazzo Pfanner** houses a collection of period furnishings as well as an exhibition of medical instruments belonging to one Pietro Pfanner, surgeon, philanthropist and mayor of Lucca in the 1920s. More interesting are the rear loggia and exquisite statued gardens with fountain where scenes from Jane Campion's 1996 film *Portrait of a Lady* were filmed. They can also be seen to good effect from the city walls just nearby.

Piazza Anfiteatro

The remarkable **Piazza Anfiteatro**, east of San Frediano, is a ramshackle circuit of medieval buildings that was built on the foundations of a Roman amphitheatre – the original arches and columns can still be discerned – and is now ringed by cafés.

Torre Guinigi

Via Sant'Andrea • Daily: March & Oct 9.30am–5.30pm; April–Sept 9.30am–7.30pm; Nov–Feb 9.30am–4.30pm • €4 • ⓦ lemuradilucca.it

Just south of Piazza Anfiteatro you can't miss the bizarre **Torre Guinigi**, a castellated tower surmounted by a **holm oak** whose roots have grown into the room below. The tower once belonged to Lucca's leading fifteenth-century family, and there are wonderful views from its 44m-high summit, 230 steps up.

Lu.C.C.A.

Via della Fratta 36 • Tues–Sun 10am–7pm; last entry 1hr before closing • €9 • ⓦ luccamuseum.com

Lucca's contemporary arts centre, or **Lu.C.C.A.**, offers slickly presented exhibitions of sculpture, photography, painting and video art. The upper floor is dedicated to temporary exhibitions by established artists; downstairs, amid the remains of the town's medieval walls and some sixteenth-century frescoed columns, are works by emerging talents.

Museo Nazionale di Villa Guinigi

Via della Quarquonia • Tues–Sat 8.30am–7.30pm last admission 7pm, with guided visits at 9.30am, 11.30am, 3.30pm & 5.30pm • €4, or €6.50 combined ticket with Museo Nazionale di Palazzo Mansi (see page 565) • ⓦ luccamuseinazionali.it

Lucca's key collection of painting, sculpture, furniture and applied arts is housed in the Guinigi family's much-restored mansion, the **Museo Nazionale di Villa Guinigi**. Its lower floor holds mainly sculpture and archeological finds, with numerous Romanesque pieces and works by della Quercia and Matteo Civitali. Upstairs are paintings, with several enormous sixteenth-century canvases, and more impressive works by early Lucchese and Sienese masters, as well as fine Renaissance offerings from such as Fra' Bartolomeo.

ARRIVAL AND DEPARTURE — LUCCA

By train Lucca's train station is just south of the city walls, on Piazza Ricasoli.

Destinations Florence (approx 2 per hour; 1hr 15min–1hr 45min); Pisa (approx 2 per hour; 30min); Pistoia (approx hourly; 40min–1hr); Rome (approx hourly; 3hr 15min–5hr); Viareggio (every 30min–1hr; 20–30min).

By bus Buses stop in Piazzale Verdi; see ⓦ www.lucca.cttnord.it for full timetables.

Destinations Florence (12 daily; 1hr 20min); Pisa (every 30min–1hr; 50min); Pisa airport (every 30min–1hr; 1hr); Viareggio (hourly; 45min).

By car Virtually all the centre that isn't pedestrianized is covered by a restricted traffic zone (ZTL), so park at one of the car parks just inside or outside the walls and walk in. There's parking on Piazzale Verdi and Piazza Santa Maria, among other places, but it's only free outside the walls. If you're heading for a hotel, ask the management for directions.

GETTING AROUND AND INFORMATION

By bike Try the bike rental outlets in Piazza Santa Maria (see page 568); bikes are also available to rent at the tourist office in Piazzale Verdi (€3/hr).

By taxi There are ranks on Piazzale Verdi and Piazza Napoleone (T 0583 333 434).

Tourist office Piazzale Verdi (daily: April–Sept 9am–7pm; Oct–March 9am–5pm; T 0583 583 150, W www.luccatourist.it, W www.comune.lucca.it/turismo). The office organizes walking tours of the town (April–Oct daily 2pm; Nov–March Sat & Sun 2pm; €10).

ACCOMMODATION

Albergo San Martino Via della Dogana 9 T 0583 469 181, W albergosanmartino.it; map p.566. Cosy little hotel tucked up an old-town alleyway not far from the Duomo, with spacious, wood-beamed rooms, some of which are painted with bucolic scenes. Exceptionally helpful staff and home-made pastries at breakfast are further draws. **€107**

★ **Alla Corte Degli Angeli** Via degli Angeli 23 T 0583 469 204, W allacortedegliangeli.it; map p.566. Charming, romantic family-run hotel, within the walled town on its northern side. The ten comfortable rooms have delicately frescoed walls and exposed beams; those on the top floor are the nicest. **€163**

A Palazzo Busdraghi Via Fillungo 170 T 0583 950 856, W apalazzobusdraghi.it; map p.566. Ravishing and very central little boutique hotel, overlooking Lucca's main shopping drag; each of its seven antique-furnished rooms has a luxurious bathroom with jacuzzi. Rooms can be on the small side, so it's worth paying extra for a "deluxe". **€150**

Diana Via del Molinetto 11 T 0583 492 202, W albergodiana.com; map p.566. A block west of the Duomo, this unfussy, somewhat austere place has seven double rooms with private bathroom and two singles without. Rooms in the annexe are more spacious (and cost a little more). No breakfast, but there are plenty of cafés nearby. Great value. **€90**

★ **Evelina Bed and Breakfast** Via Streghi 12 T 0583 493 643, W bedandbreakfastevelina.it; map p.566. Tucked away on a tranquil alley off Via Fillungo, this five-room B&B makes a great base. Thoughtful hosts Simona and Giulio provide plenty of local information, and the comfortable, spacious bedrooms (which share three bathrooms) are a relaxing haven after a long day of pounding the pavements. A generous Tuscan breakfast is served on a terrace overlooking the rooftops. **€100**

La Romea Vicolo delle Ventaglie 2 T 0583 464 175, W laromea.com; map p.566. This friendly B&B, in a fourteenth-century *palazzo* just off Via Sant'Andrea, is one of Lucca's most sophisticated options, with just five pretty, intimate rooms. An excellent breakfast is served in the spacious hall. Note that the B&B is up several flights of steps (and there's no lift). **€120**

★ **Palazzo Tucci** Via C. Battisti 13 T 0583 464 279, W palazzotucci.com; map p.566. For an opportunity to stay in a noble *palazzo* in the centre of town, look no further than the six-room *Palazzo Tucci*. From its grand entrance to its vast rooms – all ceiling mouldings, ornate wallpaper and family heirlooms – it has character in spades. It's very central too: everything is within easy walking distance. **€200**

Piccolo Hotel Puccini Via di Poggio 9 T 0583 55 421, W hotelpuccini.com; map p.566. Very friendly, central three-star, just steps from the Puccini Museum and San Michele, with fourteen simple en-suite rooms. The high ceilings, large windows and ceiling fans come into their own in summer (though there's no a/c). **€75**

San Luca Palace Via S. Paolino 103 T 0583 317 446, W sanlucapalace.com; map p.566. Conveniently located just steps from Piazzale Verdi's bus stops, this smart four-star hotel offers large and comfortable if slightly characterless rooms, with swish modern bathrooms. Staff are extremely helpful, and the breakfast is ample. **€200**

EATING

Lucca has a number of high-quality **restaurants**. Keep an eye out for local specialities such as *zuppa di farro*, a thick soup made with spelt (a type of grain); *torta di spinaci*, a sweet spinach tart; and robust pasta dishes such as *pappardelle alla lepre* (with hare). The town's **food shops** are equally good and make great places to stock up for a picnic, or just pick up some foodie souvenirs. Countless **bars** buzz with drinkers come *aperitivo* time (around 7pm), when free snacks are often laid on – just wander the streets and follow the crowds.

CAFÉS AND GELATERIE

Buccellato Taddeucci Piazza S. Michele 34 T 0583 494 933; map p.566. A stunning interior of wood panelling and mosaic tiles matches the great coffee and cakes: try the local speciality *buccellato*, a sweet loaf made with aniseed

and raisins. Daily 8am–8pm.

Caffè del Mercato Piazza S. Michele 17 ⓣ0583 494 127; map p.566. Among the most alluring of the café-bars around the main piazza. A handful of hot dishes – lasagne, risotto and the like – are available, as well as filling sandwiches such as Parma ham with olive pâté (€4). Mon–Thurs 7am–11pm, Fri 7am–1am, Sat 7am–2am, Sun noon–1pm.

Gelateria Veneta Via Vittorio Veneto 74 ⓣ0583 493 727; map p.566. Serving Lucca's finest ice cream since 1927, with four local outlets. The *gelato* here is made with fresh seasonal fruit; try the standout *pinolata* (with pine nuts) and cassata flavours. March–Oct daily 10am–11pm, shorter hours in winter.

RESTAURANTS

Buca di Sant'Antonio Via della Cervia 3 ⓣ0583 55 881, ⓦbucadisantantonio.it; map p.566. Lucca's finest restaurant, in this spot since at least 1782, abounds in old-world charm. Excellent service, top-quality meat or fish menu and delicious house pasta and desserts such as *semifreddo Buccellato*. Reckon on at least €50 a head. Booking essential. Tues–Sat 12.30–3pm & 7.30–11pm, Sun 12.30–3pm.

Locanda di Bacco Via S. Giorgio 36 ⓣ0583 495 692, ⓦwww.locandadibacco.it; map p.566. Set in an elegant wood-panelled space, this local favourite serves quality meals, with the usual meat and fish but also vegetarian options (including a set menu at €20). Pastas start from just €6. The basic tourist menu is good value at €18. Daily noon–midnight.

Osteria Baralla Via dell'Anfiteatro 9 ⓣ0583 440 240, ⓦwww.osteriabaralla.it; map p.566. This much-loved traditional *osteria* serves simple local food in a pair of vaulted dining rooms: come for hearty Tuscan fare such as *peposo* (beef stew in pepper and wine sauce; €15) and braised Chianina beef cooked in spelt beer (€17). Mon–Sat 12.30–2.30pm & 7–10.30pm.

Osteria del Neni Via Pesheria 3 ⓣ0583 492 681, ⓦosteriadelneni.com; map p.566. Tucked away in a side street a minute from Piazza San Michele, this cosy, two-roomed trattoria is traditional in every sense, founded in 1943 and devoted to simple, regional food such as *garmugia* (a Lucchese soup of minced beef, artichokes, fava and other pulses). Service can be slow at busy times, and the handful of tables outside in the shadowy alley are not Lucca's best alfresco dining option, but this is still a great central spot for a leisurely meal for less than €25, a *quartino* (25cl) of wine included. Tues–Sun 12.30–2.30pm & 7.30–10.30pm.

Rusticanella 2 Via S. Paolino 32 ⓣ0583 55 838, ⓦtrattoriarusticanella2.com; map p.566. This wood-panelled restaurant with Italian flags hanging from the rafters and the TV blaring in the bustling back room makes a convivial spot for a cheap meal. Dishes (€8–22) are local and earthy: sausage with beans, or salt cod with chickpeas – and the pizzas (from €7) are good and crispy. The set €10 lunch ("Pranzo di lavoro") is exceptional value. Tues–Sun 11.30am–3pm & 6.45pm–midnight.

Trattoria Da Giulio Via della Conce 45 ⓣ0583 55 948; map p.566. This classic trattoria is always packed in the evenings – the food is not exceptional, but the prices are very reasonable (*primi* from €7, *secondi* €9 and up) and the atmosphere makes it worth it. Mon–Sat noon–2.30pm & 6.30–10.30pm.

DIRECTORY

Hospital San Lucca, Via Guglielmo Lippi Francesconi (ⓣ0583 970111).

Left luggage At the Tourist Center Lucca outside the train station at Piazza Ricasoli 203 (ⓦwww.touristcenterlucca.com). Rates are €3 for up to 3hr or €5/day.

Police Viale Cavour 38 (ⓣ0583 4551).

Post office Via Antonio Vallisneri 2 (Mon–Fri 8.25am–7.10pm, Sat 8.25am–1.10pm).

FESTIVALS AND EVENTS IN LUCCA

The **Settembre Lucchese** festival features plenty of activity throughout September, centred on a **candlelit procession** on the 13th, when the bejewelled Volto Santo (see page 568) is carried through the streets from San Frediano to the Duomo. Consult the tourist office for details of affiliated September events, such as **classical concerts** (including performances of a Puccini opera) at the intimate, four-tiered Teatro Comunale in Piazza del Giglio, as well as **jazz** gigs and **art** exhibitions. Another key musical event is July's **Summer Festival** (ⓦsummer-festival.com) an alternative music beano in which big-name international stars perform (anyone from Nick Cave to Lenny Kravitz), some for free, in Piazza Napoleone.

The **Puccini e la sua Lucca** music festival sees concerts performed daily at 7pm from mid-March to mid-November at the San Giovanni and other churches and small venues (ⓦpuccinielasualucca.com; tickets €25), while the Puccini Museum (see page 565) organizes occasional concerts of the composer's work in atmospheric venues around town, including the botanic gardens.

Every third weekend of the month, an **antiques fair** takes over the central streets and squares, with hundreds of dealers selling everything from secondhand furniture to vintage stamps.

9

North of Pisa

A solid strip of unattractive beach resorts stretches north along the coast from near Pisa to the Ligurian border. This **Riviera della Versilia** ought to be something more special, given the dramatic backdrop of the **Alpi Apuane**, but the beaches share the coastal plain with a railway, autostrada and clogged urban roads, while the sea itself is far from being the cleanest in Italy. The resort of **Viareggio** provides a lively diversion on a coastal journey north to the Cinque Terre. Otherwise, the only real appeal lies inland, exploring the famed marble-quarrying centre of **Carrara**.

Viareggio

Tuscany's largest seaside resort, **VIAREGGIO**, 22km northwest of Pisa, may feature on few independent travellers' itineraries – everyone wants picturesque former fishing villages and converted farmhouses these days – but it does still cling to a certain stately elegance. The problem is that the sheer demand keeps prices high in summer, when many hotels insist on at least half board. Apart from a free stretch south of town, most of the **beach** has been parcelled up into private strips, charging around €20 for a day's use of a sun lounger and parasol.

Life in Viareggio centres on the grand seafront boulevard, **Viale Regina Margherita**; locals and visitors alike promenade each night beneath the palm trees that line this 3km thoroughfare. Interspersed among its imposing old hotels are several fine **Art Nouveau frontages**, as well as a plentiful array of bars and restaurants. On a balmy summer evening, the ensemble has a strip-like neon-lit aesthetic more American in feel than Tuscan. To see Viareggio at its liveliest, come for its famously boisterous **Carnevale** in February, when for four consecutive Sundays it stages an amazing parade of floats, or *carri* – colossal, lavishly designed papier-mâché models of politicians and celebrities (Ⓦviareggio.ilcarnevale.com).

ARRIVAL AND INFORMATION — VIAREGGIO

By train The train station is on Piazza Dante, a 10min walk inland from the seafront. Trains leave for Carrara approximately every 30min (15–25min) and to Lucca and Pisa 2 or 3 times every hour (takes around 20 minutes to either).

By bus Buses stop nearer the centre, on Piazza d'Azeglio and Piazza Mazzini, with services to Lucca (hourly; 45min) and Pisa airport (hourly; 1hr).

By boat In summer, Navigazione Golfo dei Poeti runs boats to Portovenere and the Cinque Terre from Viareggio, calling at Forte dei Marmi, Marina di Massa and Marina di Carrara (mid-June to mid-Sept daily; €40; Ⓣ0187 732 987, Ⓦnavigazionegolfodeipoeti.it).

Tourist office The tourist office faces the sea about 100m north of Piazza Mazzini, at Viale Carducci 10 (Mon–Sat 9am–1pm Tues & Thurs also 3–7pm in July & Aug; Ⓣ0584 962 233, Ⓦturismo.provincia.lucca.it).

ACCOMMODATION AND EATING

Romano Via Giuseppe Mazzini 120 Ⓣ0584 31 382, Ⓦromanoristorante.it. The best local restaurant, specializing in sublime fish and seafood: try the *calamaretti* stuffed with vegetables or the scampi with courgette flowers. A three-course meal will set you back around €70/head, not including wine. Tues–Sun 12.30–2.45pm & 7.30–10.30pm

Tirrenia Via S. Martino 23 Ⓣ0584 49 641, Ⓦtirreniahotel.com. Viareggio's best accommodation option in the heart of town is this gem of a hotel near the seafront. The rooms are spotless and cheerfully furnished, with bright pops of colour and modern art on the walls. The generous breakfast and helpful staff are further bonuses. **€110**

Carrara and around

CARRARA sits just inside the Ligurian border, 28km north of Viareggio, and enjoys a fame that far outstrips its modest size. Ever since the Roman era, the mountains above the town have been a principal source of **marble**; everyone from Michelangelo to Henry Moore has tramped up here in search of the perfect stone. Carrara still ranks among the world's largest producers and exporters of marble, shipping a million tonnes a year of its distinctive white or white-grey stone from the container port in the middle of ugly **Marina di Carrara**. But quiet Carrara itself has a pleasant, rural feel and comes as a relief after the holiday coast.

FERRIES FROM LIVORNO

The major, mostly modern port city of **LIVORNO**, 18km southwest of Pisa, holds little of interest for most casual visitors. However, dozens of **ferries** sail from here to **Corsica**, **Sardinia**, **Sicily** and the **Tuscan islands**. Nearly all ferries to Corsica, Sardinia and Sicily leave from alongside the **Stazione Marittima**, west of the centre behind the Fortezza Vecchia, although some depart from **Varco Galvani**, a long way north of town with no transport connections to the centre. Ferries to Capraia and Gorgona (in the Tuscan archipelago) leave from the central **Porto Mediceo**. For times and prices, check the various companies' websites, or ask at the tourist office on Piazza Municipio (June–Sept Mon–Sat 8am–6pm, Sun 9am–6pm); **reserve** well ahead in summer.

There are **trains** to Livorno from Florence (12 daily; 1hr 20min), La Spezia (13 daily; 55min–1hr 15min), Pisa (every 20min; 15–25min) and Rome (12 daily; 2hr 35min–3hr 45min). Eight daily **buses** run from Piombino (2hr).

There are **trains** to Livorno from Florence (12 daily; 1hr 20min), La Spezia (13 daily; 55min–1hr 15min), Pisa (2–3 hourly; 15–25min) and Rome (12 daily; 2hr 35min–3hr 45min).

FERRY COMPANIES

Corsica Ferries/Sardinia Ferries Stazione Marittima, Calata Carrara (T 199 400 500, W corsica-ferries.co.uk). To Bastia (Corsica) and Golfo Aranci.

Grandi Navi Veloci (Grimaldi) Varco Galvani, Darsena 1 (T 0586 409 804, W grimaldi-lines.com). To Olbia and Palermo.

Moby Lines Stazione Marittima, Calata Carrara (T 199 303 040, W moby.it) To Bastia (Corsica) and Olbia (Sardinia).

From the central **Piazza Matteotti**, pedestrianized Via Roma heads north to the attractive Piazza Accademia, with steps down (west) to the old town and Carrara's Romanesque-Gothic **Duomo** (daily 7am–noon & 3.30–7pm; free), adorned with a lovely Pisan-style marble facade. Gracious **Piazza Alberica**, at the heart of the old town, is the focus for a biennial summer display of contemporary marble sculpture, **Scolpire all'Aperto**, when internationally renowned artists arrive to create new works in public. To get the full low-down on marble, call in at the impressive **Museo del Marmo** on Viale XX Settembre, 2km south of town (Mon–Sat: May–Sept 9.30am–1pm & 3.30–6pm; Oct–April 9am–12.30pm & 2.30–5pm; €4.50).

Colonnata and the marble quarries

There are nine daily buses to Colonnata from Via Minzoni in Carrara; get off when you see the Visita Cave signs

Any short trip into the interior brings you to the startling sight of the **marble quarries**. To get a closer view, head up the twisting road towards **Colonnata**, 8km northeast of Carrara. Once there, you're confronted by a huge, blindingly white marble basin, its floor and sides squared by the enormous saws used to cut the blocks that litter the surroundings. Alternatively, if you have transport, head for the **Frantiscritti mines** (signed from town), where there are a couple of **mine tours**, including Marmo Tours (daily: April, Sept & Oct 11am–5pm; May & June 11am–6pm; July & Aug 10am–6pm; €10), which takes you into the only local mine operating inside the mountains.

ARRIVAL AND DEPARTURE — CARRARA AND AROUND

By train The closest train station is Carrara-Avenza, close to the Marina di Carrara seafront; from the station, regular buses run 4km inland to Carrara's central Piazza Matteotti.

By bus Buses from Florence arrive in Piazza Menconi in Marina di Carrara; more local services stop in Via Don Minzoni.

By boat In summer, Navigazione Golfo dei Poeti runs boats to Portovenere and the Cinque Terre from Marina di Carrara (mid-June to mid-Sept daily; €35; T 0187 732 987, W navigazionegolfodeipoeti.it).

ACCOMMODATION AND EATING

Galleria Ars Apua Via Antica Bergiola 19 T 0585 70 496, W g-arsapua.com. This delightful rural B&B in the hills makes a perfect retreat if you have a car. Marble is everywhere to be seen here: not just in the bathrooms

9

but in the sculptures that decorate the public spaces. The bedrooms have wonderful views of the Alpi Apuane and the nearby quarries. €90

'L Purtunzin d'Ninan Via Lorenzo Bartolini 3 ⓣ 0585 74 741. The pick of the restaurants in Carrara is this cosy little place, with only a handful of tables and bags of charm. It's known for serving up the freshest fish and seafood in town. Expect to pay about €50 à la carte/person or opt for the four-course tasting menu (€40, excluding wine). Wed–Mon noon–11.30pm.

Elba

Nearly 30km long by some 20km wide, **ELBA** is Italy's third-largest island, after Sicily and Sardinia. It has exceptionally clear water, fine white sand beaches, and a lush, wooded interior, superb for walking; almost everyone, including a surge of package tourists in July and August, comes for the beach resorts, so the inland villages remain largely quiet even in high season.

Historically, Elba has been well out of the mainstream. The principal industry until World War II was **mining**, especially of iron ore. The **Romans** wrote of "the island of good wines" – a reputation Elban wines retain to this day – while control in later centuries passed from Pisa to Genoa and on to the Medici, Spain, Turkey and finally France. That cosmopolitan mix has left its mark on both architecture and cultivation. Most people know the island as the place of exile for **Napoleon**, who, after he was banished here in May 1814, revamped education and the legal system, built roads and modernized the economy before escaping back to France in February 1815.

Portoferraio and around

Elba's principal town, **PORTOFERRAIO**, makes an easy and worthwhile day-trip destination from the mainland. If you head straight off to the beaches and resorts, however, you'll hardly see it; the long, unattractive, modern quayside used by the island ferries is well away from the town's atmospheric old quarter, with its stepped alleys and ancient churches.

Wander for a few minutes to the right of the ferry dock, and you'll reach a short flight of steps that leads to the old quarter's "back entrance", the **Porta a Terra**. From here, steep alleys fan out on different levels; zigzag your way up to the first entrance of the **Fortezze**

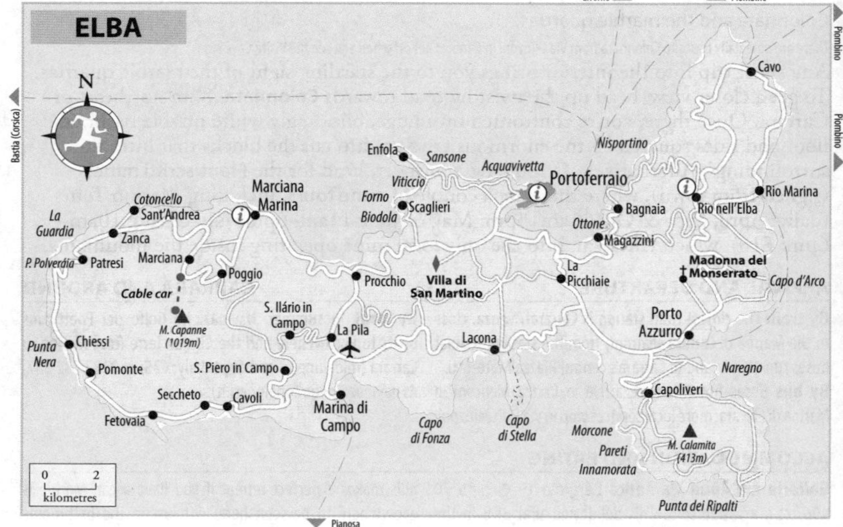

PARCO NAZIONALE DELL'ARCIPELAGO TOSCANO

All seven Tuscan islands, and the seas around them, form the **Parco Nazionale dell'Arcipelago Toscano**, the largest protected marine park in Europe. You can take a ferry from Portoferraio or Porto Azzurro to various smaller islands, and from Marina di Campo in the south you can visit the beautiful island of **Pianosa**, an uninhabited former military base, with great beaches and abundant wildlife. See Ⓦparks.it and Ⓦislepark.it for further information.

Medicee that loom over the town foir fabulous views – at their best at sunset. A ten-minute walk east of here, along Via del Falcone, is the town's main sight: the Villa dei Mulini.

Villa dei Mulini

Piazzale Napoleone • April–Oct Mon–Sat 8.30am–7pm, Sun 8.30am–1.30pm; Nov–March Mon & Wed–Sat 9am–4pm, Sun 9am–1pm • €5, or €8 combined ticket (valid three days) with Villa di San Martino (see below)

At the highest point of the old quarter sits Napoleon's residence-in-exile, the **Villa dei Mulini**. Purpose-built on a well-chosen site with grand views of the bay, the villa is a fair-sized old building, albeit undoubtedly not what the emperor was used to. Inside, you'll find a gallery with Empire-style furniture, a Baroque bedroom with an absurdly over-gilded bed, a library of two thousand books sent over from Fontainebleau, and various items of memorabilia. The peaceful rear garden looks down over the rocky headland. Note that both here and at the Villa di San Martino (see below), only thirty people at a time are allowed inside, so queues build up at busy times.

Villa di San Martino

Via San Martino • April–Oct Tues–Sat 8.30am–7pm, Sun 8.30am–1.30pm; Nov–March Mon–Sat 9am–4pm, Sun 9am–1pm • €5, or €8 combined ticket (valid three days) with Villa dei Mulini (see above) • From Portoferraio's bus station on Viale Elba take bus #1 (hourly)

The arrow-straight avenue leading up to the **Villa di San Martino** is designed to impress, even if the villa itself – bought by Napoleon's sister Elise just before the emperor left the island for good – is a rather chilly affair, with a drab Neoclassical facade enlivened with "N" motifs. The monograms were the idea of Prince Demidoff, husband of Napoleon's niece, and it was he who created the villa's museum, which houses Napoleonic memorabilia. Elsewhere on the site are the handful of Empire-style rooms used by Napoleon as his modest summer retreat; best of them is the **Sala Egizio** (Egyptian Room).

Eastern Elba

Eastern Elba comprises two tongues of land dominated by mountain ridges and a coastline given over entirely to beach tourism. The main road east from Portoferraio heads through the former mining town of **Rio nell'Elba** to **Rio Marina**. Tourism and ferry links have replaced iron ore as the town's principal source of revenue. Some boats stop at picturesque **Cavo**, 9km north of Rio Marina, with a 1km-long sandy beach.

The busy resort of **PORTO AZZURRO** was heavily fortified by Philip III of Spain in 1603; today his fortress is the island's prison. The town's small, pretty, old quarter – closed to traffic – centres on bustling Via d'Alarcon, while broad Piazza Matteotti, lined with pavement cafés, fronts the marina. Plenty of places rent bikes, boats and scooters, while motorboats shuttle across the bay to the sandy beach at Naregno.

Some 3.5km southwest of Porto Azzurro and overlooked by Monte Calamita, **CAPOLIVERI** is the nicest town on Elba's eastern fringe, a prosperous inland centre whose close-knit lanes have made few concessions to tourism. In summer, minibuses run to the nearby beach towns.

Western Elba

The main road west from Portoferraio heads to prim **Marciana Marina**, whose traffic-filled promenade of bars, restaurants and trinket shops does little to lure you into

9

staying. A winding road heads south for 5km into the hills to **Poggio**, a village renowned for its mineral water and medieval centre, with decorated doorways and a patchwork of cheerful gardens.

Marciana

The high, isolated village of **MARCIANA**, up 4km of switchbacks from Poggio, is the oldest settlement and most alluring spot on Elba, perfectly located between great beaches and the mountainous interior. Its steep **old quarter** is a delight of narrow alleys, arches, belvederes and stone stairs festooned with flowers and climbing plants that culminate at the twelfth-century **Fortezza Pisano** (closed to the public, but with great views from its lofty location).

The main draw of Marciana is 500m south of the village – the base station of a **cable car** (*cabinovia*) that climbs 650m to the summit of 1019m **Monte Capanne**, Elba's highest point (daily: mid-April to Sept 10am–1pm & 2.20–6pm; Oct closes 5pm; 15min; €12 one way, €18 return). Note that "cable car" is something of a misnomer: it's a series of small exposed cages, each big enough for two people to stand up in, hooked onto a continually running cable. At the top is a bar at which to soothe jangled nerves and a terrace from which to take in the stupendous panorama; hardy types can take trail #1 from here back down the mountain to Marciana (1hr 30min).

The western coast

The wild **western coast** harbours a handful of small towns, a clutch of stunning **beaches** and little else. The spread-out village of **Sant'Andrea**, 6km west of Marciana, just off the coast road, is the main focus, popular with divers lured by the crystal-clear seas. A little west, the road hugs the coast for a scenic drive that offers breathtaking views at every turn.

ARRIVAL AND DEPARTURE — ELBA

Most ferries to Elba depart from the port of **Piombino**, 75km south of Livorno – not a great place to spend any time, since it was flattened in World War II. If you're arriving by **train**, you'll probably have to change at Campiglia Marittima station, and catch a connecting train to Piombino Marittima. There is one daily **bus** (operated by Tiemme,

ELBA'S BEST BEACHES

No fewer than 156 **beaches** dot Elba's rocky coast, from little-visited shingly coves to broad white sand stretches. The island's best-known beaches can become packed in high season, but if you don't mind negotiating the ranks of baking bodies on sunloungers, they offer all the facilities you could wish for, from snack bars to diving centres. The big five are fine sand **Procchio**; **Fetovaia**, with its crystal-clear water; beautiful **Cavoli**, a sandy arc in a sheltered bay where you can swim well out of season; **Marina di Campo**, a full-blown resort; and **Biodola**, occupying an idyllic sweeping bay near Portoferraio. To avoid the worst of the crowds, however, head to one of the beaches below.

Acquavivetta Not far from Sansone, this shingly beach is backed by high rocks. The gently sloping seashore makes it a good spot for swimming, especially if you have kids in tow.

Cotoncello Reachable from the beach at Sant'Andrea, this small patch of sandy beach has a natural pool of clear, shallow water formed by two tongues of rock.

Forno In the bay of Biodola, sandy Forno is less busy than Biodola beach itself, set in a lovely little bay, surrounded by villas and dense vegetation. There's a restaurant here (though it's the island's most expensive), as well as snack bars.

La Guardia Also known as La Polveraia, this sheltered shingly beach on the island's western coast is always fairly quiet, even in high season. The dark rocks here plunge sheer to the transparent water below.

Sansone A dazzling stretch of shingle, enclosed by sheer white cliffs and lapped by clear water.

Sant'Andrea A lovely, fine sand beach, well set up with sun loungers, parasols and beach bars. A natural rocky barrier keeps the water shallow, and you can rent boats, windsurf and dive here too.

ACTIVITIES ON ELBA

Elba is crisscrossed with **walking** routes for all abilities. Ask at the tourist office for the booklet on local walks (available in English), including a 20km hike round Monte Calamita, where wild orchids thrive, and the 7.6km Monserrato loop from Porto Azzurro, offering splendid views.

For **boat tours** with beach stops, there are several motorboats leaving twice daily from Porto Azzurro for a half-day-trip generally costing around €20. Try Dollaro II Ⓣ 328 689 0227 or Azzurra II, Ⓣ 347 738 4154.

Aquavision runs daily sea cruises around the northern coast and some of the Tuscan islands (€35; Ⓣ 328 709 5470, Ⓦ aquavision.it). Self-drive RIB or motorboat **Boat rental** will cost approx €150 day for a 5m boat, not including fuel; try Bartolini Yachting, which has outlets in Portoferraio, Enfola and Marciana Marina (Ⓣ 348 090 6945, Ⓦ elbarentboat.com).

Part of the biggest marine park in Europe, the waters around Elba offer perfect **diving** conditions. The spots to head for are the islet of La Corbella, off Monte Calamita; the Formiche della Zanca rock formations near Sant'Andrea; the wreck of the *Elviscot* near Pomonte to the southwest; and the Scoglietto north of Portoferraio, with an underwater statue of Christ. Rio Diving at Via Scappini, Rio Marina (Ⓣ 335 570 9947, Ⓦ riodiving.it), offers excursions by boat around little-visited coves where you can snorkel or dive, from €45, while Diving in Elba (Ⓣ 347 371 5788, Ⓦ divinginelba.com) has diving schools in Portoferraio, Procchio and Biodola, with courses at all levels.

Ⓦ tiemmespa.it) from Florence to Piombino's port from June to mid-Sept, currently at 10am (2hr 40min; €13). The ferry terminal at the port – the Stazione Marittima – holds ticket outlets for all ferry companies; it also has ample parking, both paid and free.

ROUTES AND FREQUENCIES

Most ferries head to Portoferraio (1hr), docking at the Calata Italia; island buses leave from Viale Elba just inland of the dock. There are also sailings to Rio Marina (45min) and Cavo (35min). Passenger-only hydrofoils arrive at Cavo (20min) and Portoferraio (35min). Toremar, Moby and Blu Navy ferries run every day of the year, while Corsica Ferries operate a fast ferry (40min) from mid-June to mid-Sept, with the first departure at around 6am and the last around 10.30pm. In summer, there's a huge ferry every 30min or so, but it's still best to book well in advance if you're taking a car; in low season the frequency drops to more like one every 2–3hr. There is excellent information about ferries (in English) at winfoelba.com.

FARES AND BOOKING

Fares Precise fares vary according to the season and the day of the week. The easiest way to be sure of getting the cheapest is to use winfoelba.com's booking system (no booking fee), which lists timings, fares and routes by all companies. In high summer a typical one-way fare to Portoferraio would be around €16–20 passenger, with a car costing €40–60; return fares are double that.

Booking Online via Ⓦ infoelba.com or directly with the ferry companies.

FERRY COMPANY OFFICES

Blu Navy Ⓣ 0565 269710; Ⓦ blunavytraghetti.com.
Corsica Ferries Ⓣ 199 400 500, Ⓦ corsica-ferries.co.uk.
Moby Ⓣ 0565 914 133, Ⓦ mobylines.com.
Toremar Ⓣ 199 117 733, Ⓦ toremar.it.

GETTING AROUND

By boat Boats are much used to reach out-of-the-way beaches, and are well advertised at all ports.

By bus CTT buses serve just about every settlement on the island (Ⓣ 0565 914 783, timetables and link to Elba transport app on Ⓦ infoelba.com; no service after 8pm; single ticket from €1; one day ticket €4).

By minibus The Marebus – a council-run minibus – runs several times a day between town centres and their outlying beaches in the summer season; Marciana is connected with the western beaches and Capoliveri with the eastern beaches, for example.

By bike or scooter All the main agencies are near Portoferraio's ferry dock. The per-day rate for a 50cc scooter €25–40, a mountain bike €15, and an ordinary bike €10.

By car Car rental is not advisable in high season: roads to the beaches and around the resorts get nastily congested. Ouside of July and Aug, however, this can be a great way of exploring the island, particularly the wilder western coast, where the winding roads make for exhilarating driving. Car rental, available through TWN and other agencies (see above), costs around €50–65 for a small car. The car park opposite the bus station on Viale Elba in Portoferraio is free. Cars are banned from Portoferraio's old quarter during the summer.

By taxi In Portoferraio, taxis wait on Calata Italia (Ⓣ 0565 915 112); in Porto Azzurro, Piazza Palestro (Ⓣ 338 860 9896); in Capolivieri at Via Ciro Menotti (Ⓣ 338 268 9417).

9

INFORMATION

Tourist office Calata Italia 44, Portoferraio (Easter–Oct Mon–Sat 9am–6.50pm, Sun 10am–1pm & 3–6pm; rest of the year hours vary; ⓣ 0565 914 671, ⓦ isoleditoscana.it).

Websites Useful online resources include the websites ⓦ elbalink.it, ⓦ visitelba.com and ⓦ infoelba.com.

ACCOMMODATION

Portoferraio has a particularly poor range of **accommodation**, and visitors tend to disperse around the island. Elba has a good selection of **campsites**: see ⓦ campingelba.net for a full list. Most hotels and campsites are open April–Oct only.

AROUND PORTOFERRAIO

Hotel Biodola Biodola beach ⓣ 0565 974 812, ⓦ biodola.it. In an enviable location perched above Biodola beach, this comfortable four-star has breezy, "seaside" decor, with gleaming blue tiles in the bedrooms and a light and airy feel throughout. There's a wealth of activities on offer on site, from swimming pool and tennis courts to a spa, and there's a good restaurant too; many guests stay on a half-board basis. **€394**

Lacona Via del Golfi 71, Lacona ⓣ 0565 964 161, ⓦ camping-lacona.it. The key campsite in Lacona, Elba's camping hot spot on the coast 7km south of Portoferraio. It's set in pinewoods a little away from the flat foreshore crowded with bars and discos, and also has apartments (minimum three night stay, or ten nights in high season). Pitches **€13**, per person **€10**, apartments (per week) **€882**

★ **Le Stanze del Casale** Località S. Giovanni 99 ⓣ 0565 944 340, ⓦ lestanzedelcasale.com. Just a few kilometres from Portoferraio, this beautifully decorated B&B has several well-appointed en-suite rooms combining wood beams and antiques with modern touches. The generous breakfast is served on the shady veranda, which is lit by lanterns in the evenings. **€110**

Relais delle Picchiaie La Picchiaie ⓣ 0565 933 110, ⓦ relaisdellepicchiaie.it. A gorgeous, well-priced hillside retreat, 5km south of town, with plenty of attractions to keep you from the beaches, including a spa, pool and restaurant. The rooms are very comfortable and tastefully decked out. **€135**

EASTERN ELBA

Arrighi Barbarossa ⓣ 0565 95 568, ⓦ campingarrighi.it. This campsite 1km north of town gives straight onto the beach. There are also apartments, caravans and wooden bungalows (three–five people) for rent. Pitches **€13** plus per person **€17.5**, caravans **€90**, apartments **€100** bungalows **€140**

Residence Gavila's Loc. Sassi Turchini 5 ⓣ 0565 958 129, ⓦ gavilas.isoladelba.it. Perched on a hill overlooking Porto Azzurro bay and only 1km from the beach, this rose-pink villa is surrounded by lawns dotted with palm trees. The simply furnished apartments come complete with kitchenette and outdoor terrace, with lovely views. **€98**

Villa Capitorsola Località Colle del Lido di Capoliveri ⓣ 0565 933 546, ⓦ villacapitorsola.it. Just outside Capoliveri, and a short walk from two lovely beaches, this immaculate B&B is in a wonderfully scenic spot with views over the gulf. Cool, simple rooms with tiled floors, a warm welcome and a generous breakfast are further pluses. **€125**

Villa Italia Viale Italia 41 ⓣ 0565 59 119, ⓦ villaitaliahotel.it. This no-frills hotel, just outside the town centre and steps from the beach, offers old-fashioned but spotless rooms of a decent size (a/c costs extra). Staff are friendly and helpful, and there's free parking too. **€190**

WESTERN ELBA

Barsalini Sant'Andrea beach ⓣ 0565 908 920, ⓦ hotelbarsalini.com. At the foot of a lush, forested mountainside and just steps from Sant'Andrea beach, this family-run hotel makes an idyllic escape. The elegant rooms either overlook the sea or the flower-filled garden, and there's a swimming pool and a small spa too. One week minimum stay in high season. **€180**

★ **Ilio** Via Sant'Andrea 5 ⓣ 0565 908 018, ⓦ hotelilio.com. A boutique hotel just above the beach, the ecofriendly *Ilio* has breezy, comfortable rooms with wonderful views; some come with their own little patch of garden, complete with lemon trees. Delicious meals are served in the restaurant (half board available), and breakfast is a five-star feast. **€200**

EATING AND DRINKING

There are plenty of decent **restaurants** scattered across the island. **Market day** in Portoferraio's harbour is Fri; Cavo's is on Wed, Capoliveri's on Thurs and Porto Azzurro's on Sat. There's a big Coop **supermarket** on Via Tesei at Portoferraio's dock (Mon–Sat 8am–8pm, Sun 8am–1pm).

PORTOFERRAIO

Il Castagnacciaio Via del Mercato Vecchio ⓣ 0565 915 845, ⓦ ilcastagnacciaio.com. This authentic place is a Portoferraio institution. There's a host of wood-fired pizzas to choose from, but don't overlook their local specialities, the *torta di ceci* (a kind of focaccia made with chickpea flour) and the *catagnaccio* (similar, but sweet and made with chestnut flour). Mains €6–8. Daily (except Tues) 10.30am–2.30pm & 4.30–10.30pm; Sept–May slightly shorter hours.

★ **Osteria Libertaria** Calata Matteotti 12 ⓣ 0565 914 978. Outdoor tables on the Medici harbourfront, plus

wonderful seafood, including a fabulous gnocchi with swordfish (€10) and tuna fillet with pistachio (€14). Daily noon–2.30pm & 7–10.30pm.

Osteria Pepenero Via dell'Amore 48 ⓣ 0565 916 240. This rustic little place with wood beams and handwritten menus offers *primi* for €10–15, and mains such as fish soup for around €12. Daily 7–11pm; July & Aug daily 7–2am.

★ **Ristorante Pizzeria La Carretta** Località Magazzini 92 ⓣ 0565 933 223. In the little village of Magazzini, not far from Portoferraio, this excellent pizzeria is well worth seeking out. It also serves home-cooked meals, chalked up on the blackboard daily, with an emphasis on fresh fish. Daily 6.30pm–midnight.

EASTERN ELBA

Osteria La Botte Gaia Viale Europa 5/7, Porto Azzurro ⓣ 0565 95 607, ⓦ labottegaia.com. This attractive corner *osteria* is a 5min walk from Porto Azzurro's old centre and offers tasty pastas such as *tonnarelli* with vegetable *caponata* and smoked ricotta (€11), as well as mains like fish soup (€22) served up in a glass bowl. Tues–Sun 7–11pm.

Ristorante Pizzeria Rendez-Vous Lungomare C. Colombo 7, Cavo ⓣ 0565 931 060. This informal local restaurant right on the harbour is perennially popular with locals, who crowd in for a taste of their speciality crêpes, both sweet and savoury; the *covaccini* – pizza stuffed with an array of fillings – are good too. You can get a satisfying meal for well under €20 a head – a bargain. Daily 8am–midnight.

Tamata Via Cesare Battisti 3, Porto Azzurro ⓣ 0565 940 048, ⓦ tamataristorante.it. A wine bar and restaurant with outside tables on an attractive piazza. The creative menu might include octopus served three ways with *pappa al pomodoro* soup, or duck with smoked aubergine, caprino cheese and coffee. Mains €16, tasting menu €60. Daily 12.30–2pm & 6–10pm.

WESTERN ELBA

Da Publius Piazza del Castagneto 11, Poggio ⓣ 0565 99 208, ⓦ ristorantepublius.it. *Da Publius* enjoys fantastic views from its terrace; indoors is rustic but elegant. The steeply priced menu offers refined, beautifully presented dishes such as pink gnocchi with a seafood pesto, or chocolate ravioli with wild boar. Full meals from €50/person and up. April–Nov Tues–Sun noon–2pm & 7.30–10.30pm; mid-June to mid-Sept also open Mon 7.30–10.30pm.

★ **Osteria del Noce** Via della Madonna 14, Marciana ⓣ 0565 901 284, ⓦ osteriadelnoce.it. Book a table on the terrace for the spectacular views and excellent food. Fish is the main draw here, with *primi* such as spaghetti with fish roe and lemon (€10) and the always delicious fish dish of the day chalked up on the blackboard. A full meal will come to around €30 a head, not including wine. Easter–Oct daily noon–2.30pm & 7–11pm.

DIRECTORY

Hospital The hospital is at Località San Rocco, Portoferraio (ⓣ 0565 926 111).

Police Via Manzoni 6, Portoferraio (ⓣ 0565 919 511).

Post office Via Rodolfo Manganaro 7 in Portoferraio (Mon–Fri 8.20am–7.05pm, Sat 8.20am–12.35pm).

The Maremma

The Tuscan shoreline is at its best in the **Maremma** region; the name derives from *Marittima*, referring to the coastal strip and inland hills of the Provincia di Grosseto, Tuscany's southernmost province. The northern heartland of the Etruscans, this became depopulated in the Middle Ages after wars disrupted the drainage schemes and allowed malarial swamps to build up behind the dunes. The area became almost synonymous with disease, and nineteenth-century guides advised strongly against a visit – even so, *butteri* cowboys roamed freely then, as now, taking care of the region's half-feral horses and its celebrated white cattle. Today, the provincial capital of Grosseto remains uninspiring, though there are some patches of fine scenery – notably the **Monti dell'Uccellina**, protected in the **Parco Regionale della Maremma**, and the wooded peninsula of **Monte Argentario**.

Monti dell'Uccellina

Admission to the park €10, payable at the visitor centre or available online; ⓦ parco-maremma.it

Recognized as the last virgin coastal landscape to survive on the Italian peninsula, the hilly **Monti dell'Uccellina**, 12km south of Grosseto, is protected as the **Parco Regionale della Maremma**. This breathtaking piece of countryside combines cliffs, coastal marsh, *macchia*, forest-covered hills, pristine beaches and beautiful stands of umbrella pine. A microcosm of all that's best in the Maremma, it remains devoid of the bars, marinas, hotels and half-finished houses that have destroyed much of the Italian littoral. The

9

best **beach** here (twenty minutes from Pratini, along the Strada degli Olivi) is a beautifully unspoilt, curved bay, backed by lush greenery.

The park authorities have defined half a dozen different **walking itineraries**; some set off from **Alberese** – home to the visitor centre – with the remainder leaving from **Pratini**, 10km into the hills, reached via hourly shuttle bus from the visitor centre. Between mid-June and mid-September, you can only follow the most popular trails on a guided **walk** (no extra charge); these include the circular **Trail A1** (San Rabano; 6km; 5hr), which climbs a ridge from Pratini and passes the eleventh-century ruined abbey of San Rabano. For the rest of the year, you can explore at your own pace. Some trails close altogether in midsummer when the fire risk is high.

ARRIVAL AND GETTING AROUND — MONTI DELL'UCCELLINA

By car There's no public road access – drivers should park in Alberese, near the visitor centre.

By bus Hourly buses run from Grosseto station to the visitor centre. Hourly shuttle buses from the visitor centre run to Pratini, where some of the walking itineraries start (last bus back at 5.30pm, earlier in winter).

INFORMATION AND ACTIVITIES

Tourist information The visitor centre is on Via del Bersagliere 7–9 in Alberese (daily 8.30am–2pm; ⓣ 0564 407 098, ⓦ parco-maremma.it).

Activities and tours The ⓦ parco-maremma.it website has full details of riding, canoeing and mountain-biking opportunities, as well as night tours and birdwatching; most tours cost €10–15.

Monte Argentario

The high, rocky terrain of **Monte Argentario**, 37km south of Grosseto, is as close to wilderness as southern Tuscany gets. The interior is mountainous, reaching 635m at its highest point, while the coast is sectioned dramatically into headlands, bays and shingle beaches. Much of the area is still uninhabited scrub and woodland, badly prone to forest fires but still excellent walking country.

Orbetello

Long ago, Monte Argentario was an island. Over several thousand years, inshore currents built up two narrow sand spits (*tomboli*) between the mountain and the mainland, creating a lagoon between them. The ancient town of **ORBETELLO** occupied a peninsula sticking out into the lagoon; then the Romans built a causeway to link Orbetello to the Argentario, forming a third spit of land and dividing the lagoon in two. Today, Orbetello's strange location is its most exciting feature.

Porto Ercole

On summer weekends the roads over the northern Tombolo della Giannella sandbar and through Orbetello become bottlenecks as tourists pile into resorts such as **PORTO ERCOLE**, which has an attractive old quarter and a fishing-village atmosphere. Though founded by the Romans, its chief historical monuments are two **Spanish fortresses**, facing each other across the harbour. At the entrance to the old town, a plaque on the stone gate commemorates the painter **Caravaggio**, who in 1610 keeled over with sunstroke on a beach nearby and died of a fever; he was buried in the parish church of Sant'Erasmo. From the village, you can easily **walk** across the Tombolo di Feniglia sandbar, barred to traffic and a prime spot for birdwatching over the lagoon.

ARRIVAL AND INFORMATION — MONTE ARGENTARIO

By bus Buses (#2-A) run from Porto Ercole to Orbetello (approx. hourly; 12min; ⓦ tiemmespa.it), from where you can change for Grosseto and destinations further afield.

Tourist office Piazza Roma, Porto Ercole (mid-June to mid-Sept daily 9.30am–12.20pm & 5–8pm; mid-Sept to 1 Nov Fri 3–6pm, Sat 9am–noon & 3–6pm, Sun 9am–noon; irregular hours the rest of the year; ⓣ 0564 811 979; ⓦ comunemonteargentario.gov.it).

SIENA PALIO HORSE RACE

9

ACCOMMODATION AND EATING

Don Pedro Via Panoramica 7, Porto Ercole ⓣ0564 833 914, ⓦhoteldonpedro.it. The best of Porto Ercole's mid-range hotels is the friendly *Don Pedro*, an easy walk down the hill into town. Rooms are basic, but have fantastic views of the harbour. Though small and rocky, the hotel's private beach (a 15min walk away) is a bonus in the height of summer. Rates are reduced by a third in low season. Open Easter–Sept. **€145**

Osteria dei Nobili Santi Via dell'Ospizio 8, Località Le Piane ⓣ0564 833 015. Wonderfully fresh seafood is the order of the day at this slightly kitsch but charming place, a 10min walk out of Porto Ercole's centre. Try the good-value tasting menu (€40 for four courses, including wine). Tues, Wed 7.30–10.30pm, Thurs–Sun 12.15–2pm & 7.30–10.30pm; open daily in Aug; often closed in Nov & Jan.

Siena

Immediately ravishing, and all on a far less daunting scale than Florence, the glorious medieval city of **SIENA** cradles within its ancient walls a majestic Gothic ensemble that can be enjoyed without venturing into a single museum. Far too many visitors breeze through Siena on a day-trip, but it's hard to feel you've even scraped the surface unless you stay at least one night here.

The physical and spiritual heart of the city, and arguably Italy's loveliest square, is the sloping, scallop-shaped piazza **Il Campo**, the setting for the thrilling **Palio** bareback horse race. Siena's **Duomo** and **Palazzo Pubblico** are two of the purest expressions of Italian Gothic architecture; the best of the city's paintings – collected in the **Museo Civico** and **Pinacoteca Nazionale** – are in the same tradition. The finest example of Sienese Gothic is Duccio's *Maestà*, on show in the outstanding **Museo dell'Opera**, while splendid frescoes adorn the walls of **Santa Maria della Scala**.

Brief history

Established as a Roman colony by Augustus, Siena enjoyed its heyday in the twelfth and thirteenth centuries, when it became for a brief period one of the major cities of Europe. Almost as large as Paris, it controlled most of southern Tuscany and its wool industry, dominated the trade routes between France and Rome, and maintained Italy's richest pre-Medici banks. This era climaxed with the defeat of a far superior Florentine army at **Montaperti** in 1260. Although the result was reversed permanently nine years later, Siena embarked on an unrivalled urban development under its mercantile governors, the **Council of Nine**. Between 1287 and 1355, the city underwrote the completion first of its cathedral, and then the Campo and its exuberant Palazzo Pubblico. Prosperity came to an abrupt halt with the **Black Death**, which reached Siena in May 1348; by October, two thirds of the 100,000 inhabitants had died. The city never fully recovered (the population today remains under sixty thousand) and its politics, always factional, descended into chaos. In 1557 Philip II gave up Siena to **Cosimo de' Medici** in lieu of war services, and it became part of Cosimo's Grand Duchy of Tuscany. The lack of subsequent development explains Siena's astonishing state of preservation: little was built and still less demolished.

SIENA ORIENTATION

Everything is easily walkable from Siena's great central square, **Il Campo**, which is built at the intersection of three hills configured like an upside-down Y. Each arm of that Y counts as one of the city's *terzi*, or thirds, and each has its principal thoroughfare, leading from the Campo on elevated ridges: humdrum **Banchi di Sotto** in the Terzo di San Martino on the southeast; bustling, commercial **Via di Città** in the Terzo di Città on the southwest; and elegant **Banchi di Sopra** in the Terzo di Camollia on the north. This central core – almost entirely medieval in plan and appearance, and closed to traffic – can get a little disorienting, but use the Campo as your guide and you can't go far wrong.

THE SIENA PALIO

The **Siena Palio** is Italy's most spectacular festival event: a twice-yearly **bareback horse race** around the Campo, preceded by weeks of preparation, medieval pageantry and chicanery. Only ten of the seventeen *contrade* (neighbourhoods), chosen by lot, take part in any one race; horses, too, are assigned at random. The seven that miss out are automatically entitled to run the next year. The only rule is that riders cannot interfere with each other's reins. Otherwise, anything goes: each *contrada* has a traditional rival, and ensuring that it loses is as important as winning oneself. Jockeys may be bribed to throw the race or whip a rival or a rival's horse; *contrade* have been known to drug horses and even to ambush a jockey on his way to the race.

Held since at least the thirteenth century, the race originally followed a circuit through the town. Since the sixteenth century it has consisted of three laps of the **Campo**, around a track covered with sand and padded with mattresses to minimize injury to riders and horses.

THE RACE

There are two Palios a year, on **July 2 and August 16**, each of which is preceded by all manner of trial races and processions. At around 5pm on the day of the Palio the Palazzo Pubblico's bell rings, and riders and *comparse* – equerries, ensigns, pages and drummers in medieval costume – proceed to the Campo for a display of flag throwing and pageantry. The **race** itself begins at 7.45pm on July 2, or 7pm on August 16, and lasts little more than ninety seconds. At the start all the horses except one are penned between two ropes; the free one charges the group from behind when its rivals least expect it, and the race is on. It's a hectic and violent spectacle; a horse that throws its rider is still eligible to win. The jockeys don't stop at the finishing line but keep going at top speed out of the Campo, pursued by frenzied supporters. A **palio** – or silk banner – is subsequently presented to the winner.

PRACTICALITIES

While seating is available in viciously expensive stands, most spectators crowd for free into the centre of the Campo. For the **best view**, find a position on the inner rail by 2pm (ideally at the start/finish line) then stand your ground; people keep pouring in until just before the race, and the swell of the crowd can be overwhelming. Toilets, shade and refreshments are minimal, and you won't be able to leave the Campo until at least 8.30pm. **Hotel rooms** are very hard to find; if you haven't booked, either visit for the day or stay up all night.

Since World War II, Siena has again become prosperous, thanks partly to **tourism** and partly to the resurgence of the **Monte dei Paschi di Siena**. This bank, founded in Siena in 1472 and currently the city's largest employer, is a major player in Italian finance. It today sponsors much of Siena's cultural life, coexisting, apparently easily, with one of Italy's strongest left-wing councils.

The Campo

The **Campo** is the centre of Siena in every sense: the main streets lead into it, the **Palio** (see above) is held around its perimeter, and every evening visitors and residents alike are drawn to it. Be sure to soak up the atmosphere last thing at night, when the amphitheatre curve of the piazza throws the low hum of café conversation around in an invisible spiral of sound that's drowned out in the daytime. Four hundred years ago, Montaigne described this as the most beautiful square in the world; it's hard to disagree today.

When the Council of Nine were planning the piazza in 1293, this old marketplace, which lay at the convergence of the city quarters but was part of none, was the only possible site. Created in nine segments in honour of the council, the piazza became from the moment it was completed in 1349 the focus of city life, the scene of executions, bullfights, communal boxing matches and, of course, the Palio. St Bernardino preached here, holding before him the monogram of Christ's name in Greek ("IHS"), which the council placed on the facade of the Palazzo Pubblico, alongside the city's she-wolf symbol – a reference to Siena's legendary foundation by Senius, son of Remus.

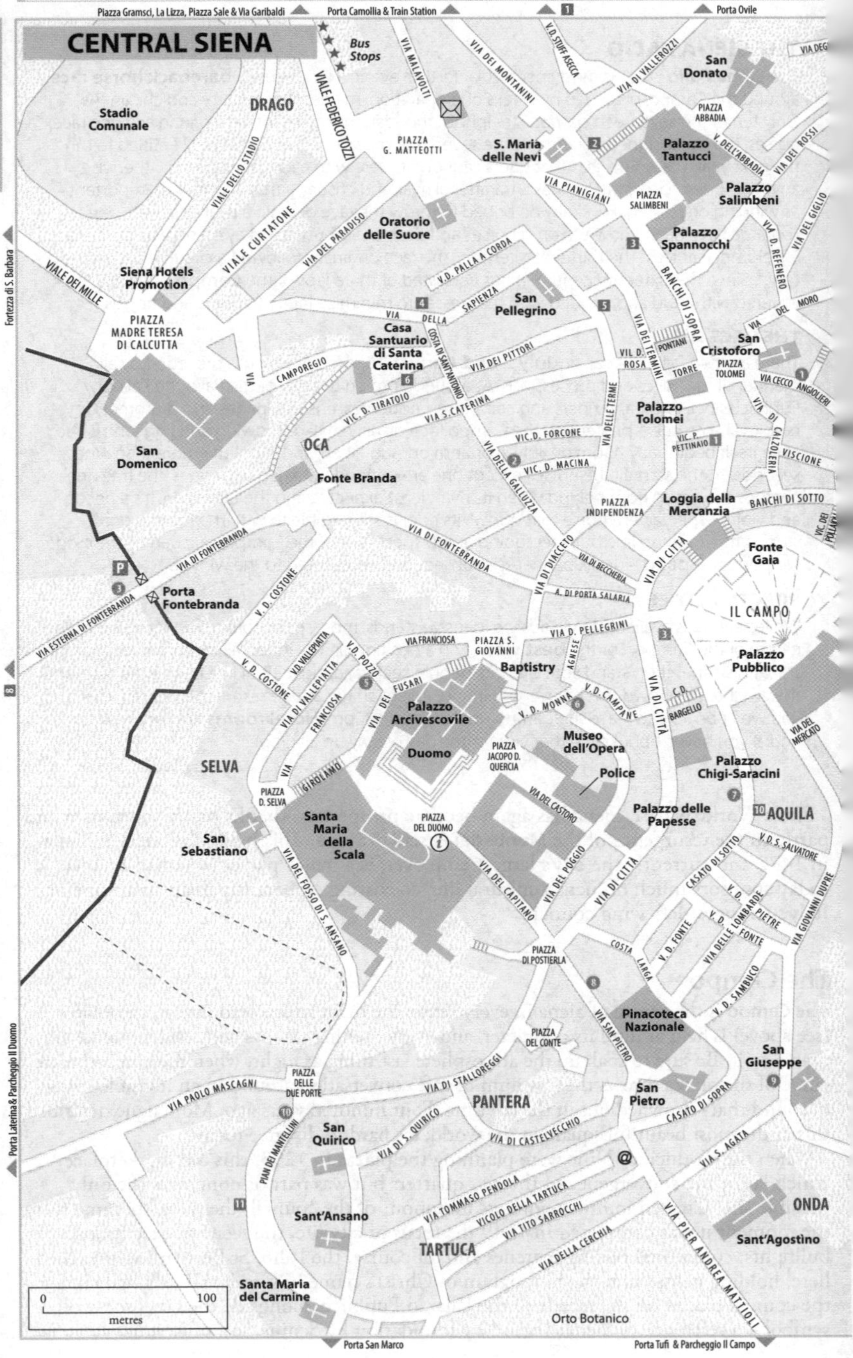

CENTRAL SIENA

Piazza Gramsci, La Lizza, Piazza Sale & Via Garibaldi
Porta Camollia & Train Station
1
Porta Ovile
Fortezza di S. Barbara
8
Porta Laterina & Parcheggio Il Duomo
Porta San Marco
Porta Tufi & Parcheggio Il Campo

Bus Stops
Stadio Comunale
DRAGO
Viale Federico Tozzi
Via Malavolti
Piazza G. Matteotti
Via dei Montanini
V.D. Stuff Asecca
Via di Vallerozzi
San Donato
Piazza Abbadia
Via de Gg
S. Maria delle Nevi
2
Palazzo Tantucci
V. dell'Abbadia
Via dei Rossi
Via Pianigiani
Piazza Salimbeni
Palazzo Salimbeni
Viale dello Stadio
Viale Curtatone
Via del Paradiso
Oratorio delle Suore
Palazzo Spannocchi
3
Via del Giglio
Via D. Refenero
Banchi di Sopra
Viale dei Mille
Siena Hotels Promotion
V.D. Palla a Corda
Sapienza
San Pellegrino
4
5
Via della
Costa di Sant'Antonio
Casa Santuario di Santa Caterina
Via dei Termini
Pontani
Via del Moro
San Cristoforo
Piazza Madre Teresa di Calcutta
Via Camporegio
Via dei Pittori
6
Vil D. Rosa
Torre
Piazza Tolomei
Via Cecco Angiolieri
1
Vic. D. Tiratoio
Via S. Caterina
Via delle Terme
Palazzo Tolomei
Via di Calzoleria
San Domenico
OCA
Vic. D. Forcone
Vic. P. Pettinaio
1
Viscione
Via della Galluzza
2
Vic. D. Macina
Fonte Branda
Piazza Indipendenza
Loggia della Mercanzia
Banchi di Sotto
Vic. dei Pollaioli
Via di Fontebranda
Via di Diacceto
Via di Beccheria
Via di Città
Fonte Gaia
P
3
Porta Fontebranda
Via Esterna di Fontebranda
V. D. Costone
A. di Porta Salaria
IL CAMPO
Via D. Pellegrini
3
Via Franciosa
Piazza S. Giovanni
V.D. Pozzo
V.D. Vallepiatta
Agnese
Baptistry
Palazzo Pubblico
V. D. Costone
5
Via dei Fusari
Via di Vallepiatta
Franciosa
Palazzo Arcivescovile
V. D. Monna
6
V. D. Campane
C.D. Bargello
Via di Città
Via del Mercato
Museo dell'Opera
Duomo
Piazza Jacopo D. Quercia
SELVA
Via Girolamo
Police
Palazzo Chigi-Saracini
Piazza D. Selva
Via del Castoro
7
10
AQUILA
Santa Maria della Scala
Piazza del Duomo
Palazzo delle Papesse
San Sebastiano
V.D. S. Salvatore
Casato di Sotto
Via del Fosso di S. Ansano
Via del Capitano
Via del Poggio
Via di Città
V. D. Pietre
Via Giovanni Dupre
V. D. Fonte
Via delle Lombarde
Costa Larga
V. D. Fonte
Piazza di Postierla
8
Via San Pietro
V. D. Sambuco
Pinacoteca Nazionale
Piazza del Conte
San Giuseppe
9
Via Paolo Mascagni
Piazza delle Due Porte
Via di Stalloreggi
PANTERA
San Pietro
Casato di Sopra
10
Via di S. Quirico
Via di Castelvecchio
San Quirico
Pian dei Mantellini
@
Via S. Agata
11
Via Tommaso Pendola
Vicolo della Tartuca
Sant'Ansano
Via Tito Sarrocchi
ONDA
Via Pier Andrea Mattioli
Sant'Agostino
TARTUCA
Via della Cerchia
Santa Maria del Carmine
0 100 metres
Orto Botanico

9

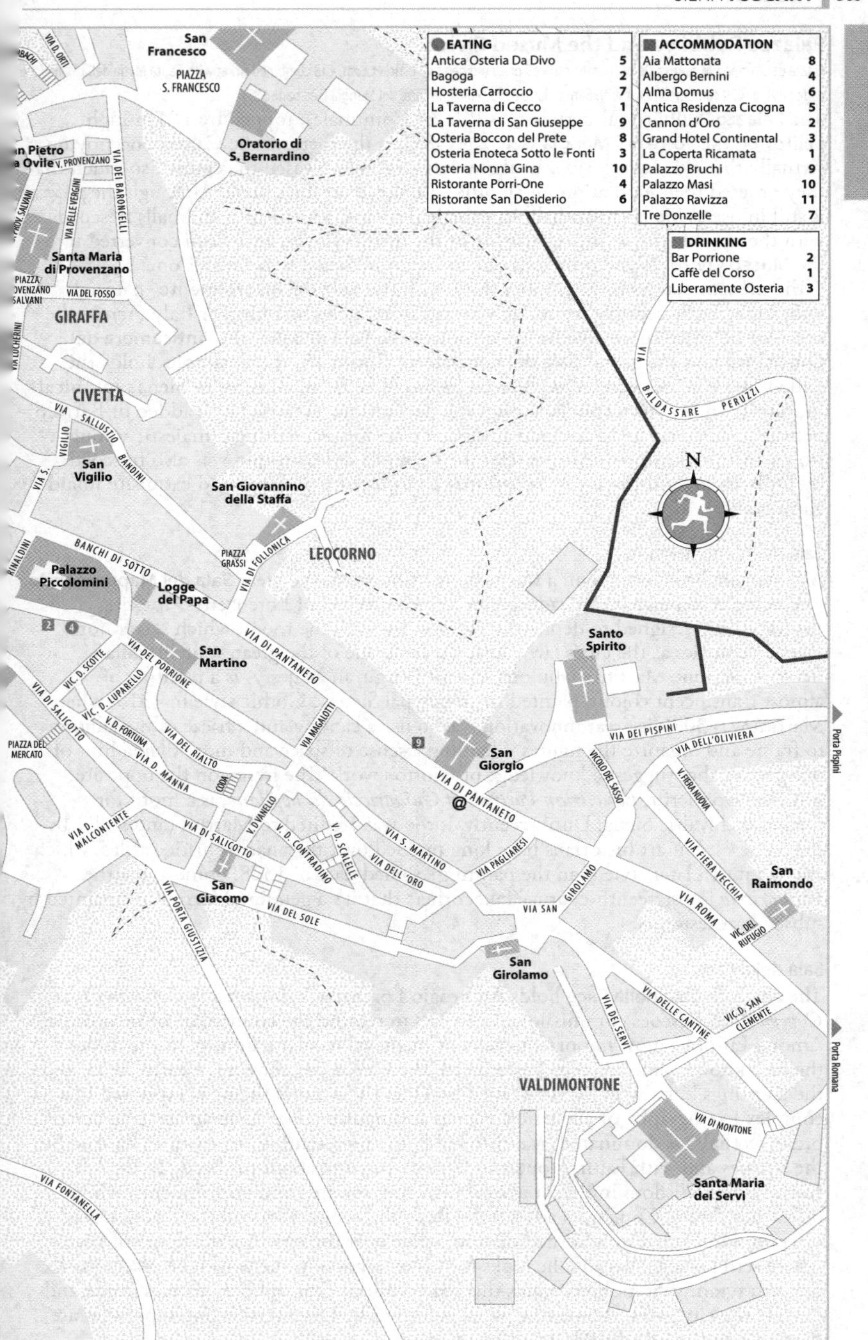
EATING
Antica Osteria Da Divo 5
Bagoga 2
Hosteria Carroccio 7
La Taverna di Cecco 1
La Taverna di San Giuseppe 9
Osteria Boccon del Prete 8
Osteria Enoteca Sotto le Fonti 3
Osteria Nonna Gina 10
Ristorante Porri-One 4
Ristorante San Desiderio 6
ACCOMMODATION
Aia Mattonata 8
Albergo Bernini 4
Alma Domus 6
Antica Residenza Cicogna 5
Cannon d'Oro 2
Grand Hotel Continental 3
La Coperta Ricamata 1
Palazzo Bruchi 9
Palazzo Masi 10
Palazzo Ravizza 11
Tre Donzelle 7
DRINKING
Bar Porrione 2
Caffè del Corso 1
Liberamente Osteria 3
San Francesco
PIAZZA S. FRANCESCO
Oratorio di S. Bernardino
Santa Maria di Provenzano
GIRAFFA
CIVETTA
San Vigilio
San Giovannino della Staffa
LEOCORNO
Palazzo Piccolomini
Logge del Papa
San Martino
Santo Spirito
San Giorgio
San Giacomo
San Girolamo
San Raimondo
VALDIMONTONE
Santa Maria dei Servi
Porta Pispini
Porta Romana
N
VIA DI PANTANETO
BANCHI DI SOTTO
VIA DEL PORRIONE
VIA DI SALICOTTO
VIA ROMA
VIA DEI PISPINI
VIA DELL'OLIVIERA
VIA FIERA VECCHIA
VIA DELLE CANTINE
VIA DEI SERVI
VIA DI MONTONE
VIA BALDASSARE PERUZZI
VIA PORTA GIUSTIZIA
VIA FONTANELLA
VIA DEL SOLE
VIA S. MARTINO
VIA DELL' ORO
VIA PAGLIARESI
VIA SAN GIROLAMO
VIA SALLUSTIO BANDINI
VIA DEL FOSSO
VIA DEI BARONCELLI
VIA DELLE VERGINI
VIA DI FOLLONICA
PIAZZA GRASSI
VIA MAGALOTTI
VIA DEL RIALTO
VIA D. MANNA
VIA D. MALCONTENTE
PIAZZA DEL MERCATO
VICOLO DEL SASSO
V. FIERA NUOVA
VIC. DEL RUFUGIO
VIC. D. SAN CLEMENTE

9 Palazzo Pubblico and the Museo Civico

Piazza del Campo • **Museum** Daily 10am–6pm • €9 or €8 online at Ⓦ b-ticket.com, €13 combined ticket with Santa Maria della Scala (see page 589), or €20 combined ticket with Santa Maria della Scala and Torre del Mangia (see page 587)

The **Palazzo Pubblico** (also known as Palazzo Comunale), topped by a 97m-high belltower, the **Torre del Mangia** (see page 587), is the focus of the Campo, occupying virtually the entire south side. Its three-part windows pleased the council so much that they ordered their emulation on all other buildings on the square. Although the *palazzo* is still in use as Siena's town hall, its principal rooms, a series of grand halls frescoed with themes integral to the secular life of the medieval city, have been converted into the **Museo Civico**. If you only visit one museum in Siena, make it this one.

The museum starts on the upper floor with the **Sala del Risorgimento**, painted with nineteenth-century scenes of Vittorio Emanuele, first king of Italy. Across the corridor lie three successive frescoed rooms: the **Sala di Balia**, the **Anticamera del Concistoro** and the grand **Sala del Concistoro**. Room 13, the **Vestibolo**, holds the gilded *She-Wolf Suckling Romulus and Remus* (1429), an allusion to Siena's mythical founding. In the **Anticappella** alongside, decorations executed by Taddeo di Bartolo between 1407 and 1414 include a huge *St Christopher*. Behind a majestic wrought-iron screen by Jacopo della Quercia, the **Cappella del Consiglio** was also frescoed by Di Bartolo, and holds an exceptional altarpiece by Sodoma and exquisite inlaid choir-stalls.

Sala del Mappamondo

All these are little more than a warm-up for Room 16, the great **Sala del Mappamondo.** The name is somewhat misleading; not a trace survives of Lorenzetti's "rotating contraption", designed to depict the cosmos. Instead, the room, which served for several centuries as the city's law court, contains one of the greatest of all Italian frescoes. Simone Martini's fabulous *Maestà* (Virgin in Majesty) is a painting of almost translucent colour, painted in archetypal Sienese Gothic style in 1315, when Martini was 30. His great innovation was to use a canopy and a frieze of medallions to frame and organize the figures – lending a sense of space and more than a hint of perspective that suggest a knowledge of Giotto's work. The fresco on the opposite wall, the wonderful *Equestrian Portrait of Guidoriccio da Fogliano*, is a motif for medieval chivalric Siena. Until recently, it too was credited to Martini (and still is by the Sienese), but art historians have long puzzled over the anachronistic castles, which are of a much later style than the painting's signed date of 1328. Some argue the *Guidoriccio* is a sixteenth-century fake, others that it's a genuine Martini overpainted by subsequent restorers.

Sala della Pace

The adjacent **Sala della Pace** holds Ambrogio Lorenzetti's *Allegories of Good and Bad Government*, frescoes commissioned in 1338 to remind the councillors of their duties. Among Europe's most important cycles of medieval secular painting, this includes the first-known panorama in Western art. The walled city shown is clearly Siena, and the paintings burst with details of medieval life; their moral theme is expressed in a complex iconography of allegorical virtues and figures. *Good Government* (the better-preserved half) is dominated by a throned figure representing the *comune*, flanked by the Virtues and with Faith, Hope and Charity buzzing about his head. To the left, Justice (with Wisdom in the air above) dispenses rewards and punishments, while below her throne Concordia advises the Republic's councillors on their duties. *Bad Government* is ruled by a horned demon, while over the city flies the figure of Fear, whose scroll reads: "Because he looks for his own good in the world, he places justice beneath tyranny. So nobody walks this road without Fear: robbery thrives inside and outside the city gates." Some fine panel paintings by Lorenzetti's contemporaries are displayed in the **Sala dei Pilastri** to one side.

SIENA TOURIST PASSES

If you're planning to stay a few days, the **OPA SI pass** is worth considering. It includes entry to the Duomo, Museo dell'Opera, baptistry and crypt, and is valid for three consecutive days (€15high season (July/Aug), €13 mid season, €8 Nov–Feb). It's available from the ticket office outside the Museo dell'Opera or by calling ⓣ 0577 286300 or online from various private ticket booking companies (eg ⓦ tiqets.com) for an extra booking fee. **Combined tickets** for the Museo Civico, Santa Maria della Scala and Torre del Mangia are also on offer (€13 for the first two, €20 for all three).

The loggia

Climb the stairs to the rear **loggia** for clear views of quite how abruptly the town ends: buildings rise to the right and left for a few hundred metres along the ridges of the Terzo di San Martino and Terzo di Città, holding a rural valley in their embrace.

Torre del Mangia

Piazza del Campo • Daily: March to mid-Oct 10am–7pm; mid-Oct to Feb 10am–4pm • €10, or €20 combined ticket with Museo Civico (see page 586) & Santa Maria della Scala (see page 589)

Opposite the entrance to the Museo Civico, to the left of the Palazzo Pubblico's internal courtyard, a door leads to the 503 steps of the **Torre del Mangia**, which gives fabulous views across the town and surrounding countryside. The tower takes its name from its first watchman – a slothful glutton (*mangiaguadagni*) commemorated by a statue in the courtyard.

Fonte Gaia

On the uppermost slope of the Campo, the Renaissance makes a fleeting appearance with the **Fonte Gaia** (Gay Fountain), designed and carved by Jacopo della Quercia in the early fifteenth century but now replaced by a poor nineteenth-century reproduction.

Loggia della Mercanzia and Banchi di Sotto

Behind the Fonte Gaia, assorted stairways and alleys between the buildings climb up to where the intersection of Siena's three main streets is marked by the fifteenth-century **Loggia della Mercanzia**. Reluctantly Renaissance, with its Gothic niches for the saints, it was designed as a tribune house for merchants to do their deals.

From the Loggia della Mercanzia, Banchi di Sopra heads north, while Via di Città curves west (see page 590). Follow **Banchi di Sotto** east, and you soon reach the **Logge del Papa** with, alongside it, the **Palazzo Piccolomini**, a committed Renaissance building by Bernardo Rossellino, the architect employed at Pienza by the Sienese Pope Pius II (Aeneas Sylvius Piccolomini).

The Duomo

Piazza del Duomo • 1 March–1 Nov Mon–Sat 10.30am–7pm, Sun 1.30–6pm (March only Sun 1.30–5.30pm); 2 Nov–28 Feb Mon–Sat 10.30am–5.30pm, Sun 1.30–5.30pm • €5, or €8 during the summer uncovering of the marble pavement. The OPA SI pass (see above) gives access to all Duomo sites except the roof. The Porta del Cielo pass (€20) available March–Jan only, includes access to all the Duomo sites, including the roof • ⓦ operaduomo.siena

Siena's **Duomo** is an absolute delight, its exterior an amazing conglomeration of Romanesque and Gothic, delineated by bands of black and white marble. Few buildings can reveal so much of a city's history and aspirations; completed to virtually its present size around 1215, it was subjected to constant plans for expansion. Early in the fourteenth century, attempts were made to double its extent by building a baptistry on the slope below, to serve as a foundation for a rebuilt nave, but work ground to a halt when walls and joints gaped under the pressure. After the Black Death reduced the city's population by two thirds in 1348, funds were suddenly cut off, and the plan

9

abandoned. The part-extension still stands at the north end of the square – a vast structure that would have created the largest church in Italy outside Rome.

The **facade** of the Duomo was designed in 1284 by Giovanni Pisano who, with his workshop, created much of the statuary – philosophers, patriarchs and prophets, now replaced by copies (the originals are in the Museo dell'Opera). In the next century the **Campanile** and a Gothic **rose window** were added. The mosaics in the gables, however, had to wait until the nineteenth century.

The interior

The black-and-white motif of the exterior continues in the sgraffito marble **pavement** that begins outside the church, and takes off into a startling sequence of 56 panels adorning the **interior**. Depicting an eccentric mixture of Biblical themes, secular stories and allegories, the floor panels were completed between 1349 and 1547, with virtually every artist in the city trying his hand on a design. However, you may not see much of the pavement, which these days is only stripped of its protective boarding for a few unpredictable weeks in late summer; check the website for the latest schedule.

The zebra-striped interior is equally arresting above floor level, with its line of popes' heads set above the pillars, the same hollow-cheeked scowls cropping up repeatedly. The greatest individual artistic treasure is Nicola Pisano's **pulpit**, with its elaborate high-relief detail of the *Life of Jesus* and *Last Judgement*. In the north transept is a bronze statue by **Donatello**, the emaciated *St John the Baptist*, companion piece to his equally ragged *Mary Magdalene* in Florence (see page 526), and superb candelabra-carrying angels by Beccafumi flank the Renaissance high altar.

Libreria Piccolomini

Entered off the nave, halfway along on the left, the stunning **Libreria Piccolomini** was commissioned by Francesco Piccolomini (who for ten days was Pius III) as a library for the books of his uncle Aeneas (Pius II). A cycle of crystal-sharp, brilliantly colourful frescoes by **Pinturicchio** celebrates Aeneas's life. It starts to the right of the window, with Aeneas attending the Council of Basel as a secretary, then, in subsequent panels, presenting himself as envoy to James II of Scotland; being crowned poet laureate by Holy Roman Emperor, Frederick II; representing Frederick on a visit to Pope Eugenius IV; and then – as Bishop of Siena – presiding over the meeting of Frederick III and his bride-to-be Eleanora outside Siena's Porta Camollia. The next panels show Aeneas being made a cardinal in 1456; being elected pope two years later; and then launching a call for a crusade against the Turks, who had just seized Constantinople. His best-remembered action was the canonization of St Catherine, shown in the penultimate panel. The final fresco shows his death at Ancona.

The baptistry and crypt

Piazza San Giovanni • 1 March–1 Nov Mon–Sat 10.30am–7pm, Sun 1.30–6pm (March only Sun 1.30–5.30pm); 2 Nov–28 Feb Mon–Sat 10.30am–5.30pm, Sun 1.30–5.30pm • Baptistry €5, crypt €7, or €8 during exhibitions; or OPA SI pass

Behind the Duomo, down some steep steps, is the **baptistry**, beautifully frescoed by Vecchietta and his school in the mid-fifteenth century, and restored in the nineteenth. The main focus is the hexagonal marble **font** (1417–30), with gilded brass panels by Ghiberti, Donatello and Jacopo della Quercia. Donatello's depiction of the *Feast of Herod* is perhaps the finest work: a dramatic scene in which John the Baptist's executioner kneels, carrying the head of the saint on a platter, as Herod recoils in horror.

Accessed through the baptistry, the **crypt** was only discovered in 1999 and is worth a visit for the remains of a marvellous, richly coloured fresco cycle of Old Testament stories (c.1270–80).

Santa Maria della Scala

Piazza del Duomo • 15 March –15 Oct daily 10am–7pm, Thurs 10am–10pm; 16 Oct–14 March Mon, Wed & Fri 10–5pm, Thurs 10am–8pm, Sat & Sun 10am–7pm; 23 Dec–6 Jan daily 10am–7pm • €9, or €13 combined ticket with Museo Civico (see page 586), or €20 combined ticket with Museo Civico and Torre del Mangia (see page 587) • Ⓦ santamariadellascala.com

For nine hundred years until the 1980s, the vast **Santa Maria della Scala** complex, opposite the Duomo, served as Siena's main hospital. Today its wonderful interiors have been converted into a major centre for art and culture, revealing works that remained barely seen for centuries.

Beyond the ticket hall, the first room you enter is a small chapel adorned with fifteenth-century frescoes by Vecchietta. That leads in turn to the larger church of **Santissima Annunziata**, where the same artist's bronze statue of the *Risen Christ* is on the high altar – the figure is so gaunt that the veins show through the skin. Beyond that, the **Cappella del Manto** holds a strikingly beautiful fresco by Beccafumi, *St Anne and St Joachim* (1512). It shows the aged parents of the Virgin who, having failed to conceive in their twenty years of marriage, are told by an angel to meet at Jerusalem's Golden Gate and kiss – a moment that symbolizes the Immaculate Conception of their daughter. The real highlight here, however, is the vast **Sala del Pellegrinaio**. Formerly the main hospital ward, it's entirely frescoed with scenes from the hospital's history, intended to promote charity toward the sick and orphaned. Naturalistic and still vivid, their almost entirely secular content was extraordinary at the time they were painted (after 1440).

Stairs lead down to the **Oratorio di Santa Caterina della Notte**, an oratory that belonged to one of several medieval confraternities which maintained places of worship in the basement of the hospital. It's a dark and strangely spooky place, despite the plethora of decoration – you can easily imagine St Catherine passing nocturnal vigils down here.

Much of the lowest level is given over to the remodelled **Museo Archeologico**. Walkways through the vaults lead past all sorts of Roman and pre-Roman treasures, largely gathered by private Sienese collectors during the nineteenth century.

Museo dell'Opera

Piazza del Duomo • Daily 1 March–1 Nov 10am–7pm; 2 Nov–28 Feb daily 10am–5.30pm; 26 Dec–8 Jan daily 10am–6pm • €7, or included in Opa Sì pass • Ⓦ operaduomo.siena.it

Home to some superlative artworks from the cathedral's history, and also offering amazing views over the city, the impressive **Museo dell'Opera** is tucked into a corner of what was originally intended to be the Duomo's new nave.

As you enter on the ground floor, you're immediately confronted by the **Galleria delle Statue**. Donatello's delicate ochre *Madonna and Child* is at your back as you enter the Galleria, while huge, elongated, twisting figures by Giovanni Pisano loom on all sides. The museum's greatest treasure, Duccio's vast and justly celebrated **Maestà**, dominates a dimly lit air-conditioned gallery upstairs. The Duomo's altarpiece from 1311 until 1505, it's a masterpiece of Sienese art. Its iconic, Byzantine spirituality is accentuated

SIENA'S CONTRADE

Siena takes great pride in its division into neighbourhoods, or **contrade**, ancient self-governing wards that formed a patchwork of tribal identity within the fabric of the city and that still flourish today, helping to foster tight bonds of community and contributing to Siena's surprisingly low crime rate. Each of the seventeen *contrade* has its own church, social club and museum. Each, too, has a heraldic animal **motif**, from caterpillar to unicorn, displayed in a fountain-sculpture in its neighbourhood piazza. Allegiance to one's *contrada* – conferred by birth – remains a strong element of civic life, and identification with the *contrade* is integral to the competition of the Palio. You'll often see groups practising flag-waving and drum-playing around town.

9

by Duccio's flowing composition, his realization of the space in which action takes place, and a new attention to narrative detail in the panels of the predella and the reverse of the altarpiece which are now displayed to its side.

Upstairs again, you can admire the Duomo's original altarpiece, a haunting Byzantine icon known as the **Madonna dagli Occhi Grossi** (of the Big Eyes). A small passageway leads to the open-air **Panorama dal Facciatone**, via steep spiral stairs that climb the walls of the abandoned nave. The sensational view is worth enjoying even if you choose not to venture onto the narrow, exposed, topmost walkway.

Via di Città and around

Via di Città, the main thoroughfare linking the Duomo with the Campo, is lined with shops and plenty of explorable side-alleys, as well as being fronted by some of Siena's finest private *palazzi*. The **Palazzo Chigi-Saracini**, at no. 82, is a Gothic beauty, with its curved facade and rear courtyard.

Pinacoteca Nazionale

Via di S. Pietro 29 • Mon & Sun 9am–1pm, Tues–Sat 8.15am–7.15pm • €4 • Ⓦ pinacotecanazionale.siena.it

Via di Città continues to a small piazza from where Via di San Pietro leads south to the fourteenth-century Palazzo Buonsignori, now the home of the **Pinacoteca Nazionale**. A roll of honour of Sienese Gothic painting, the collection starts on the second floor with the first known Sienese work, an altar frontal from 1215. Romanesque and Byzantine influences dominate the early rooms, with the intricate gilded backgrounds that became so characteristic of Sienese style. Specific artists showcased thereafter include Duccio di Buoninsegna, who together with his school takes up two full rooms, and Simone Martini, whose masterpiece *Blessed Agostino Novello and Four of his Miracles* is in Room 5. On the next floor down you'll find Renaissance works by such as Sodoma, whose panel of the *Deposition* (Room 32) and frescoes from Sant'Agostino (Room 37) show his characteristic drama and delight in costume and landscape.

The gallery's topmost storey is devoted to the **Collezione Spannocchi**. This miscellany of Italian, German and Flemish works includes the only painting in the museum by a female artist – *Bernardo Campi Painting Sofonisba's Portrait* by Sofonisba Anguissola, a neat little joke in which the artist excels in her portrait of Campi, but depicts his portrait of her as a flat stereotype.

Sant'Agostino and around

South of the Pinacoteca Nazionale in the square known as Prato di Sant'Agostino, the church of **Sant'Agostino** – open some years, closed others – holds outstanding paintings by Perugino and Sodoma. A nice walk loops southwest along Via della Cerchia into a student-dominated area around the church of **Santa Maria del Carmine** (which contains a hermaphrodite *St Michael and the Devil* by Beccafumi). Via del Fosso di San Ansano, north of the Carmine square, is a country lane above terraced vineyards that leads to the Selva (Rhinoceros) *contrada*'s square, from where the stepped Vicolo di San Girolamo leads up to the Duomo.

North of the Campo

Exploring beyond the busy central alleys between the Campo and the Duomo reveals much more of the bustling everyday life of Siena. North of the Campo, the **Banchi di Sopra** leads through the commercial heart of town to **Piazza Matteotti**, home of the main post office; north again lies the workaday neighbourhood of the Terzo di Camollia. The city's northwest corner holds the gardens of **La Lizza**, site of Siena's busting town market on Wednesdays (8am–2pm). The gardens lead up to the bastions of the **Fortezza di Santa Barbara**, rebuilt by the Medici and now home to occasional summer concerts.

ST CATHERINE OF SIENA

St Catherine of Siena was born on March 25, 1347, the 24th child of Jacopo Benincasa, a dyer, and Lapa of Duccio de' Piacenti. Her path to beatification began early, with a vision aged 6 of Christ as pope, followed a year later by a vow of perpetual virginity. Her family tried to drill some sense into her by forcing her to work at household chores, but when her father discovered her at prayer one day with a dove fluttering above her head, he realized her holy destiny. Catherine took the Dominican habit aged 16, then began charitable works in post-plague Siena before turning her hand to politics. After preventing Siena and Pisa from joining Florence in rising against Pope Urban V (then absent in Avignon), she travelled herself to Avignon in 1376 to persuade Pope Gregory XI to return to Rome. It was a fulfilment of the ultimate Dominican ideal – a union of the practical and mystical life. Catherine returned to Siena to a life of contemplation, retaining a political role in her attempts to reconcile the 1378 schism between the Popes and Antipopes. She died in Rome in 1380, and was the first woman ever to be **canonized** – by Pius II in 1461. Pius IX made her **co-patron of Rome** in 1866; Pius XII raised her to be **co-patron of Italy** (alongside St Francis) in 1939; and then John Paul II declared her **co-patron of Europe** in 1999.

San Domenico

Piazza San Domenico • Daily: March–Oct 7am–6.30pm; Nov–Feb 9am–6pm • Free • W basilicacateriniana.com

Until the start of the thirteenth century, monasteries were essentially rural, meditative retreats. Then in the space of a few decades, preaching orders of friars were established, which started to found monasteries on the periphery of the major Italian cities. In Siena the two greatest orders, the Dominicans and Franciscans, located themselves respectively to the west and east. Founded in 1125, west of Piazza Matteotti, the vast brick **San Domenico** church remains closely identified with St Catherine of Siena (see box). Inside on the right, a raised chapel holds a contemporary portrait of the saint by her friend Andrea Vanni. Her own chapel, on the south side of the enormous, airy nave, has frescoes by Sodoma of her swooning (to the left of the altar) and in ecstasy (to the right), as well as a reliquary containing her head.

Casa Santuario di Santa Caterina

Costa di Sant'Antonio • Daily 9am–7pm • Free

The **Casa Santuario di Santa Caterina** – St Catherine's family house, where she lived as a Dominican nun – is just south of San Domenico, down the hill. The building has been much adapted, with a Renaissance loggia and a series of oratories – one on the site of her cell.

Fonte Branda

Down the road from the Casa Santuario di Santa Caterina, at the bottom of the hill, through the Oca (Goose) *contrada*, the **Fonte Branda** is the best preserved of Siena's medieval fountains. According to local folklore, it was the haunt of werewolves, who would throw themselves into the water at dawn to return in human form.

Oratorio di San Bernardino

Piazza di S. Francesco 9 • Daily 1 March–31 Oct 1.30–7pm • T 0577 283 048

Born in 1380, the year of St Catherine's death, St Bernardino began his preaching life at the monastic church of **San Francesco**, across the city to the east. Alongside, the **Oratorio di San Bernardino** holds a beautifully wood-panelled upper chapel frescoed by Sodoma and Beccafumi. In the lower chapel are seventeenth-century scenes from the saint's life, which was taken up by incessant travel throughout Italy, preaching against usury and denouncing political strife; his sermons in the Campo frequently went on for the best part of a day. Canonized in 1444, he was made patron saint of advertising in the 1980s – thanks to his dictum on rhetoric, "Make it clear, short and to the point".

ARRIVAL AND DEPARTURE

SIENA

BY TRAIN

Siena's train station is 2km northwest of town. It has a counter selling city bus tickets, as well as tourist information. To get into town, you can either walk, which takes a good 20–25min uphill, and is not recommended, or cross the road and take bus #3 or #9 to Tozzi; #7, #17 or #77 to Garibaldi/Sale; #8 or #10 to Gramsci. All stop at or close to Piazza Matteotti or Piazza Gramsci 100m north. Tickets cost €1.50 (valid for an hour), or €2.50 if bought on board. Day passes are €4.40.

Destinations Buonconvento (10 daily; 22–32min); Chiusi (12 daily; 1hr 35min); Florence (hourly; 1hr 30min direct or 1hr 46min via Empoli); Grosseto (9 daily; 1hr 30min); Pisa (via Empoli; every 30min–1hr; 1hr 45min).

BY BUS

Most intercity buses arrive on or near Viale Federico Tozzi, the road running alongside Piazza Gramsci–Piazza Matteotti, or at nearby La Lizza, but some terminate at the train station or at San Domenico instead. For San Gimignano, you may have to change at Poggibonsi, and for Montepulciano at Buonconvento. Ticket offices beneath Piazza Gramsci (daily 6am–8.30pm) have information on all routes.

Bus companies Siena's buses, as well as those in the local area, are run by Tiemme (T 0577 204 111, W sienamobilita.it), which also runs services to and from Florence; take a "Rapido" rather than "Diretta" service, as these are much quicker.

Destinations Abbadia San Salvatore (3 daily; 1hr 40min–2hr); Arezzo (8 daily; 1hr 30min); Bologna (2 daily; 3hr); Florence (30 daily; 1hr 15min–3hr); Massa Marittima (2 daily; 1hr 55min); Milan (5 daily; 5hr 40min); Montalcino (7 daily; 1hr 15min); Montepulciano (5 daily; 1hr 25min); Perugia (1 daily; 1hr 10min); Pienza (6 daily; 1hr 15min); Pisa airport (1 daily; 1hr 50min); Poggibonsi (hourly; 45min–1hr); Rome (10 daily; 3hr); San Galgano (3 daily; 1hr 5min); San Gimignano (10 daily; 1hr 5min–1hr 15min); Turin (4 weekly; 6hr 45min); Venice (2 daily; 5hr 20min).

BY CAR

Parking There's plentiful free parking outside the walls. The two biggest parking garages (2/hr, €26/day) are misleadingly named: "Parcheggio Il Campo" and "Parcheggio Il Duomo" are a long way south of either the Campo or the Duomo, just inside the Porta Tufi and Porta San Marco respectively (W sienaparcheggi.com). Visitors can drive through the old-town alleys only in order to check in at their hotels.

GETTING AROUND AND INFORMATION

By car, bike and scooter For car, bike and scooter rental, head to Perozzi at Via dei Gazzani 16 (Mon–Fri 8.30am–12.30pm & 3–7pm, Sat 8.30am–12.30pm & 4–6.30pm; T 0577 288 387, W perozzi-siena.com; bikes €15/day, scooters €40/day, cars from €50/day).

On foot See W www.terresiena.it for downloadable walking itineraries (or "urban trekking" as the website calls it).

By taxi Call Radio Taxi (T 0577 49 222), or taxis wait on Piazza Matteotti and Piazza Indipendenza.

Tourist office Santa Maria della Scala, Piazza del Duomo (Daily 9–6pm; T 0577 280 551, W www.terresiena.it).

ACCOMMODATION

Siena is small enough that every hotel within the old walls is within a 15min walk of the main sights. Anyone visiting in summer should **reserve accommodation** as far in advance as possible; hotels are especially booked up at Palio time (early July & mid-Aug), when they charge higher prices. You'll also be glad of air conditioning in the summer heat. A Siena **hotel tax** is charged at €1–5/person/night, depending on the class of the hotel and the time of year, for a maximum of six consecutive nights: the tax is often, but not always, included in the given rate.

Aia Mattonata Strada del Ceraiolo 1, 4km south of the centre T 0577 592 677, W aiamattonata.com; map p.584. Ravishing little hotel in a converted hilltop farmhouse, with six very comfortable rooms and superb views over the city. Swimming pool, jacuzzi and Turkish bath, with massage available and use of mountain bikes. **€245**

Albergo Bernini Via della Sapienza 15 T 0577 289 047, W albergobernini.com; map p.584. Friendly, well-situated one-star hotel near San Domenico, with ten good-value rooms, some of which share bathrooms and lack a/c; the walls are very thin, so earplugs are a good idea. The roof terrace with a fantastic view over Siena is the main draw here. Breakfast costs an extra €3.50. No credit cards. **€70**

★ **Alma Domus** Via Camporegio 37 T 0577 44 177, W hotelalmadomus.it; map p.584. Originally a pilgrim hostel, this fourteenth-century building, reached via a stairway close to San Domenico church, offers great-value and remarkably peaceful accommodation; its en-suite doubles, triples and quads enjoy wonderful views. **€85**

★ **Antica Residenza Cicogna** Via delle Terme 75 T 0577 285 613, W anticaresidenzacicogna.it; map p.584. Charming B&B on the first floor of a medieval *palazzo* not far north of the Campo, with seven a/c, soundproof en-suite rooms, all beautifully decorated. Ask for the Liberty room, a hand-stencilled beauty with four-poster bed and antique furniture. The breakfast is delicious, there's free computer use and wi-fi, and free tea and biscuits add to the home-from-home feel. **€85**

Cannon d'Oro Via Montanini 28 ⓣ0577 44 321, ⓦcannondoro.com; map p.584. Simple, friendly hotel, tucked down an alleyway. Its thirty two-star rooms show signs of age, but they're spacious, high-ceilinged and spotless, and some enjoy fine roofscape views. Breakfast is included but poor. €68

Grand Hotel Continental Via Banchi di Sopra 85 ⓣ0577 56 011, ⓦroyaldemeure.com; map p.584. For years Siena had no luxury five-star hotel – until the hugely expensive restoration of this former palace. The frescoed public spaces are astounding, and the best rooms are also exceptional – vast, entirely frescoed, and with stunning views of the Duomo. Other rooms are superbly appointed, but mostly lack the period details you'll see on the website. Discounts available online or via tour-operator deals. €230

La Coperta Ricamata Via Garibaldi 46 ⓣ0577 43 657 or ⓣ328 808 5491, ⓦlacopertaricamata.it; map p.584. Quiet, clean and friendly B&B, not far north of the centre and within easy walking distance of the bus station, with five large and attractively decorated en-suite rooms. Friendly hostess Luciana is on hand to offer advice. €60

Palazzo Bruchi Via Pantaneto 105 ⓣ0577 287 342, ⓦpalazzobruchi.it; map p.584. Housed in a seventeenth-century *palazzo*, this small B&B, run by a friendly mother-and-daughter team, is a real bargain. Ask for the Camera degli Affreschi, with lovely frescoed ceilings. €100

Palazzo Masi Casato di Sotto 29 ⓣ349 600 9155, ⓦwww.palazzomasi.it; map p.584. In a medieval building, this family-run place is just steps from the Campo. It's worth paying a little more for one of the superior rooms, for extras such as beamed ceilings, tiled floors and antiques. The standard rooms upstairs are more basic and share a bathroom. Breakfast costs an extra €8. €130

★ **Palazzo Ravizza** Pian dei Mantellini 34 ⓣ0577 280 462, ⓦpalazzoravizza.it; map p.584. Elegant, nicely restored hotel in the peaceful southwest corner of the old town, with very pleasant public areas and a lovely garden with stunning views over the surrounding countryside. All rooms have a/c and tasteful furnishings, and many have frescoes; the best are upstairs at the back. Rates include a fine breakfast. Free parking. €140

Tre Donzelle Via Donzelle 5 ⓣ0577 280 358, ⓦtredonzelle.com; map p.584. A very central one-star option close to the Campo, just off Banchi di Sotto. Decent, clean rooms, some with private bathrooms, but book early as the hotel is popular. €68

EATING

Although Siena has no shortage of places where you can eat well, it can feel distinctly provincial after Florence. However, with several new, imaginative *osterie* having raised the general standard of Siena's **restaurants**, you'll have no trouble finding good places in all price ranges – though the Campo is to be avoided unless all you want is an overpriced pizza to go with the view. Putting together a **picnic** in the Campo or elsewhere is easy: you can buy pizza by weight from many central hole-in-the-wall places, or gourmet supplies at the gorgeous old **grocery** De Miccoli, Via di Città 95 (Mon–Sat 9am–8pm), for cheeses and cold meats. More prosaically, there's a La Bottega Simply **supermarket** near the southern end of Via di Città at no.152 (Mon–Sat 7.30am–8pm).

Antica Osteria Da Divo Via Franciosa 29 ⓣ0577 286 054, ⓦosteriadadivo.it; map p.584. Hearty, high-quality Tuscan food, aimed primarily at tourists, a few steps down from the Duomo. There's no pavement seating, but the attractive underground dining rooms incorporate Etruscan vaults, and the upstairs area is pleasant too. First courses at €9 or €12 include a fabulous risotto with courgettes and pecorino; mains €20 or €25. Daily except Tues noon–2.30pm & 7–10.30pm.

Bagoga Via della Galluzza 26 ⓣ0577 282 208, ⓦristorantebagoga.it; map p.584. The full name is the *Grotta di Santa Caterina da Bagoga*, but it's known to all as *Bagoga*, a Sienese dialect word meaning someone from Montalcino, in this case the chef-patron of over forty years, Pierino Fagnoni. It's a fine rustic space with vaulted ceilings and stone walls; the robust Sienese dishes cost from €9 (for a soup of pheasant and lentils), with mains from €12. Tues–Sat 12.30–3pm & 7–10.30pm, Sun 12–3pm; closed last two weeks of Feb and a week in July.

Hosteria Carroccio Via Casato di Sotto 32 ⓣ0577 41 165; map p.584. Popular, good-value little *osteria*, with outdoor tables just a minute's walk from the Campo. Good Sienese dishes such as pasta with salami and broad beans (€8) and rabbit with sausage and olives (€18) are coupled with an extensive wine list. No credit cards. Daily except Wed 12.15–2.45pm & 7.15–9.45pm; closed periods in Feb & Nov.

SWEET TREATS

Siena is famous for its **cakes**, including the trademark **panforte** – a dense and delicious wedge of nuts, fruit and honey – and biscuits such as *cavallucci* (aniseed, nut and spice) and *ricciarelli* (almond). Buy them fresh, by the *etto* (100g), in the bakeries or *pasticcerie* along Banchi di Sopra; the gift-packaged boxes aren't as good.

9

La Taverna di Cecco Via Cecco Angiolieri 19 ☎0577 288 518; map p.584. Attentive service, moderate prices and simple, regional food, with good pasta dishes such as *pappardelle* with rabbit from €10. Daily noon–4pm & 7–11pm.

★ **La Taverna di San Giuseppe** Via Giovanni Duprè 132 ☎0577 42 286, Ⓦwww.tavernasangiuseppe.it; map p.584. Booking ahead is always a good idea at this elegant, brick-vaulted restaurant, which often offers out-of-the ordinary antipasti from around €9 as a prelude to seasonal Tuscan specialities such as impressive *fiorentina* steaks. Have a peek at the Etruscan dwelling downstairs; discovered in 1998, it now helps to keep the wines (including excellent dessert wines) and cheeses cool. Mon–Sat noon–2.30pm & 7–10pm.

Osteria Boccon del Prete Via di S. Pietro 17 ☎0577 280 388, Ⓦosteriaboccondelprete.it; map p.584. A cellar-like little restaurant, with a vaulted ceiling, close to the Pinacoteca. Starters include classic bruschetta and *crostini*, *primi* dishes such as gnocchi with sea bream (from €8), and mains from €10 such as pork fillet with roast potatoes. The food is tasty and well priced, though service can be brusque. Mon–Sat 12.15–3pm & 7.15–10pm.

★ **Osteria Enoteca Sotto le Fonti** Via Esterna di Fontebranda 114 ☎0577 226 446, Ⓦsottolefonti.it; map p.584. This friendly *osteria* with a rustic, homespun feel (and only a handful of tables) offers Tuscan specialities such as *ribollita* (vegetable soup), *pappardelle* with wild boar (€7.50) and an array of meaty mains from €10 – hearty fare that will set you up nicely for the 10min walk uphill back to the centre of the city. It's also an *enoteca*, with over a hundred wines, many offered by the glass. Mon–Sat 12.15–3pm & 7.15–10pm.

Osteria Nonna Gina Piano del Mantellini ☎0577 287 247; map p.584. No-nonsense, ultra-fresh, Italian home cooking in a friendly family atmosphere at the southwest end of town, with some outdoor tables. Most dishes are under €10 (it's renowned for its gnocchi), and the house wine is a real bargain at €6/litre. Tues–Sun 12.30–2.30pm & 7.30–10.30pm.

Ristorante Porri-One Via del Porrione 28 ☎0577 221 442; map p.584. This elegant restaurant with pavement seating in a pedestrian lane just off the Campo is a good option if you've had your fill of traditional Tuscan food: the creative menu includes plenty of culinary curveballs, though they don't come cheap: a full meal without wine will set you back around €50. Daily except Wed noon–3pm & 7–10pm.

Ristorante San Desiderio Piazzetta L. Bonelli 2 ☎0577 286 091, Ⓦristorantesandesiderio.com; map p.584. This cavernous former church, just below the Duomo en route to the Campo, also has a handful of outdoor tables. The menu includes most Tuscan staples such as *pici* pasta, but many dishes change according to the season. *Primi* cost from €9, *secondi* from €14. Daily except Tues noon–2.30pm & 7–10.30pm.

DRINKING

The main action of an evening is the **passeggiata** from Piazza Matteotti along Banchi di Sopra to the Campo – and there's not much in the way of nightlife after that. For most visitors, though, the Campo, the universal gathering place, provides diversion enough, while local students ensure a bit of life in the **bars**, which are scattered all over town. The bar in the garden of the *Palazzo Ravizza* hotel (see page 593) is a tranquil spot on a hot afternoon.

Bar Porrione Via del Porrione 14; map p.584. Just an ordinary bar off the Campo, but it's popular with a studenty crowd at weekends thanks to its late opening hours. Tues–Sun 9am–3am.

Caffè del Corso Banchi di Sopra 25 ☎0577 226 656; map p.584. This diminutive bar serves up a decent *aperitivo* with snacks from 7 to 9pm, and gets lively later on with students thanks to its late hours, loud music and cheap cocktails (€3.50). It has a few tables on the tiny alley outside too. Mon–Sat 8am–2am, Sunday 8am–midnight.

Liberamente Osteria Piazza del Campo 27; map p.584. Of the terrace café-bars ringing the Campo, *Liberamente* is the nicest. With outdoor seating on the corner of the square, it offers a ringside seat for the evening *passeggiata*, and offers drinks (cocktails around €8), as well as breakfast and light meals (sandwiches from €10). Daily 11am–2am (often 3am on Sat & Sun).

SIENA MUSIC FESTIVALS

Siena hosts prestigious classical concerts throughout the year. The **Accademia Musicale Chigiana**, Via di Città 89 (☎0577 22 091, Ⓦwww.chigiana.it), is the driving force, staging the Estate Musicale Chigiana cycle all summer, and the Settimana Musicale Senese in July, often featuring a major opera production. Venues vary from the Teatro dei Rozzi and Sant'Agostino to out-of-town locations such as the atmospheric ruined abbey of Sant'Antimo. Tickets start at €8, bookable through Ⓦwww.chigiana.it from late May onwards, in person at the Accademia Musicale Chigiana (daily 3.30–6pm) or from the venue itself up to two hours before the performance. For jazz fans, **Siena Jazz** (Ⓦsienajazz.it) is a low-key festival in late July and early August, one of several summer events.

DIRECTORY

Hospital Viale Mario Braccci 16, Le Scotte (T 0577 585 111, W www.ao-siena.toscana.it).

Laundry Self-service laundry at Waterland, Via dei Rossi 94 (daily 7am–11pm). Prices include detergent.

Police The *Questura* is at Via del Castoro 6 (T 0577 201 111).

Post office Piazza Matteotti 37 (Mon–Fri 8.20am–7.05pm, Sat 8.20am–12.35pm; T 0577 214 295, W posteitaliane.it).

San Gimignano

SAN GIMIGNANO, 27km northwest of Siena, is perhaps the most visited small village in Italy. Its stunning hilltop skyline of towers, built in aristocratic rivalry by the feuding nobles of the twelfth and thirteenth centuries, evokes the appearance of medieval Tuscany more than any other sight. And the town is all that it's cracked up to be: quietly monumental, beautifully preserved, enticingly rural and with a fine array of religious and secular frescoes. It takes around twenty minutes to walk from one end of town to the other, but it deserves at least a day, both for its frescoes and for its lovely surrounding countryside.

From Easter until October, San Gimignano has very little life of its own, with hordes of day-trippers traipsing up and down its narrow streets and filing in and out of its innumerable olive oil, wine and souvenir shops. If you want to reach beyond its facade of quaintness, try to come out of season; if you can't, then aim to spend the night here – the town takes on a very different pace and atmosphere in the evenings.

Brief history

In the early Middle Ages, San Gimignano was a force to be reckoned with. It was controlled by two great families – the **Ardinghelli** and the **Salvucci** – and its fifteen thousand population (twice the present number) prospered on agricultural holdings and its position on the Lombardy-to-Rome pilgrim route. At its peak, the town's walls enclosed five monasteries, four hospitals, public baths and a brothel. **Feuds**, however, had long wrought havoc: the first Ardinghelli-Salvucci conflict erupted in 1246. Whenever the town itself was united, it picked fights with Volterra, Poggibonsi and other neighbours. These were halted only by the **Black Death**, which devastated first the population and then, as the pilgrim trade collapsed, the economy. Subjection to Florence broke the power of the nobles and so their tower-houses, symbolic in other towns of real control, were not torn down; today, fourteen of an original 72 survive.

Piazza della Cisterna and Piazza del Duomo

From the southern gate, **Porta San Giovanni**, the *palazzo*-lined **Via San Giovanni** leads to the interlocking main squares, the Piazza del Duomo and the Piazza della Cisterna. On the right of the street, about 100m up, is the former church of **San Francesco** – a Romanesque building converted, like many of the *palazzi*, to a wine shop specializing in the local Vernaccia.

You enter the **Piazza della Cisterna** through the **Arco dei Becci**, part of the original fortifications built before the town expanded in the twelfth century. The square itself is flanked by an anarchic cluster of towers and *palazzi*, and is named after the thirteenth-century public **cistern**, still functioning in the centre. Northwest of the square is one of the old Ardinghelli towers; a Salvucci rival rears up behind.

An arch leads from Piazza della Cisterna through to the more austere **Piazza del Duomo**, with further towers and civic *palazzi*.

The Collegiata

Piazza del Duomo • 1 April–31 Oct Mon–Fri 10am–7.30pm, Sat 10am–5.30pm, Sun 12.30–7.30pm; Nov 1–31 March Mon–Sat 10am–5pm, Sun 12.30–5pm • €4, or €6 combined ticket with Museo d'Arte Sacra • T 0577 286 300, W duomosangimignano.it

9

The plain facade of the Duomo, or more properly the **Collegiata**, since San Gimignano no longer has a bishop, could hardly provide a greater contrast with its interior. This is one of the most comprehensively frescoed churches in Tuscany, with cycles of paintings filling every available space, their brilliant colours set off by Pisan-Romanesque arcades of black-and-white-striped marble. Entrance is from the side courtyard, where you'll also find the small **Museo d'Arte Sacra**. While less spectacular, it's still worth a look for its rescued religious art.

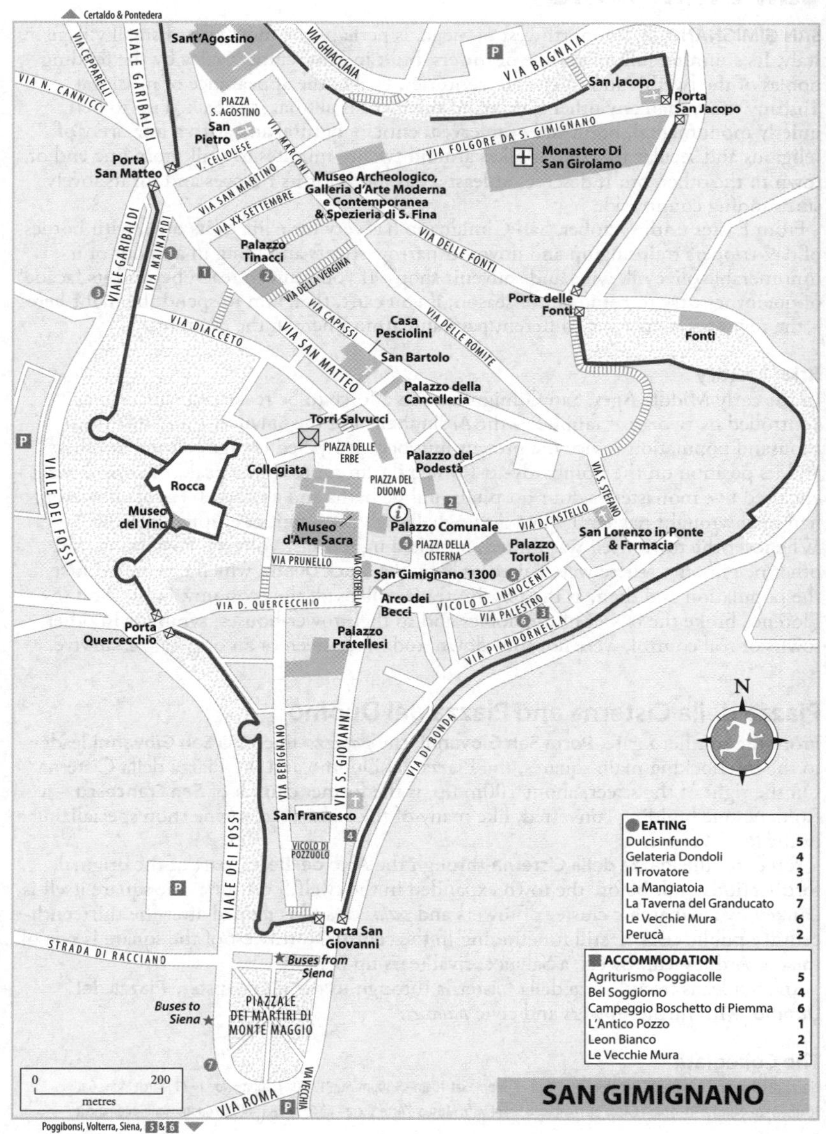

The frescoes

The Collegiata's three principal **fresco cycles** fill the north and south walls, as well as two short side-walls that protrude from the east (exit) wall of the facade. The **Old Testament** scenes on the north wall, completed by Bartolo di Fredi around 1367, are full of medieval detail in the costumes, activities and interiors. They are also quirkily naturalistic: there are few odder frescoes than the depiction of Noah exposing himself in a drunken stupor. The cycle (read from left to right, top to bottom) follows the story of the **Flood** with those of **Abraham and Lot** (their trip to Canaan), **Joseph** (his dream; being let down the well; having his brothers arrested and being recognized by them), **Moses** (changing a stick into a serpent before the Pharaoh; the Red Sea; Mount Sinai) and **Job** (temptation; the devil killing his herds; thanking God; being consoled). Above, note the beautiful fresco depicting the Creation of Eve, in which Eve emerges from the rib of the sleeping Adam.

The **New Testament** scenes opposite (begun 1333), attributed to either Barna da Siena or Lippo Memmi, impress most by the intensity of their emotional expression. In the dramatic *Resurrection of Lazarus*, a dumbstruck crowd witnesses the removal of a coffin-lid to reveal the living Lazarus in the winding bandages of burial. An altogether different vision pervades Taddeo di Bartolo's **Last Judgement** (1410), with paradise to the left and hell to the right. A gruesome depiction of what's always a lurid subject, it features no-holds-barred illustrations of the Seven Deadly Sins.

On the north side of the Collegiata, San Gimignano's most important Renaissance artwork is the superb fresco cycle made by Domenico Ghirlandaio for the small **Cappella di Santa Fina**. The subject, a local saint, born in 1238, was struck by an incurable disease at the age of 10. She gave herself immediately to God, repented her sins (the worst seems to have been accepting an orange from a boy), and insisted on spending the five agonizing years until her death lying on a plank on the floor. The fresco of the right-hand lunette shows Fina experiencing a vision of St Gregory. Opposite it, the *Funeral of St Fina* is an even more accomplished work – Raphael was especially impressed with it – showing the saint on her deathbed with the towers of San Gimignano in the background. Ghirlandaio left a self-portrait: he's the figure behind the bishop who is saying Mass.

Palazzo Comunale

Piazza del Duomo • Daily: 1 April–30 Sept 10am–7.30pm; 1 Oct–31 March 11am–5.30pm • €6 (€7.50 during temporary exhibitions) combined ticket with Museo Archeologico, Spezieria di Santa Fina and Galleria d'Arte Moderna e Contemporanea (see page 598) • Ⓦ sangimignanomusei.it

The **Palazzo Comunale** is a key component of Piazza del Duomo. Its lovely courtyard was built in 1323; a loggia opens on the right, from which judicial and public decrees were occasionally proclaimed (hence the subject matter of its frescoes). Stairs lead up to a picturesque little balcony and the Pinacoteca.

The Pinacoteca

The first room of the **Pinacoteca**, frescoed with hunting scenes, is the **Sala di Dante** – the poet visited as Florence's ambassador to the town in 1299, to plead for Guelph unity. Most of the paintings are Sienese in origin or inspiration, with the highlight being Lippo Memmi's *Maestà* (1317). Off the Sala di Dante are busts of a winsome *Santa Fina* (1496) and *San Gregorio* by Pietro Torrigiano. Highlights upstairs include two outstanding tondi by **Filippino Lippi**. Rooms off to the right hold a painting by **Taddeo di Bartolo**, the *Scenes from the Life of St Gimignano* (1393) – with the saint holding the eponymous town on his lap – and **Lorenzo di Niccolò**'s *Scenes from the Life of St Bartholomew* (1401), which includes a graphic depiction of the saint being flayed alive. The most enjoyable paintings are hidden away in a small room off the stairs. Frescoes of wedding scenes completed in the 1320s by the Sienese painter Memmo di Filipuccio are unique in their subject matter: they show a tournament where the wife

9

rides on her husband's back, followed by the couple taking a shared bath and then climbing into bed – the man managing to retain the same red hat throughout.

Torre Grossa

The entrance ticket also allows access to the **Torre Grossa**, the only one of San Gimignano's towers which you can climb; it's a stiff ascent – the top section involves scrambling up a ladder – but worth it for the great views of the Val d'Elsa, dotted with villages and olive groves.

San Lorenzo in Ponte

From Piazza della Cisterna, Via di Castello continues east past the Romanesque **San Lorenzo in Ponte** (with a dramatic fresco of the *Last Judgement*) to a rural lane that winds down between vineyards to the city walls; just beyond the public wellhouse, or **Fonti**, stretches open countryside.

The Rocca and Wine Museum

Museum April–Oct daily 11.30am–6.30pm • Ⓦ sangimignanomuseovernaccia.com

A signposted lane leads from Piazza del Duomo up to the **Rocca**, the old fortress, with its one surviving tower and wonderful views. It was built, at local expense, by the Florentines "to remove every cause of evil thinking from the inhabitants" after their union with the *comune*. Later, its purpose presumably fulfilled, it was dismantled by Cosimo de' Medici. Nowadays it encloses an orchard-like public garden, with fig and olive trees, and the small **Museo del Vino Vernaccia**, with a small display on the history of local wine production and a bar, the perfect place to sample the local Vernaccia while drinking in the views.

Galleria d'Arte Moderna e Contemporanea, Museo Archeologico and Spezieria di Santa Fina

Via Folgore da San Gimignano • All three museums daily: 1 April–30 Sept 10am–7.30pm; 1 Oct–31 March11am–5.30pm • €6 combined ticket, includes entry to Pinacoteca and Torre Grossa (see page 597) • Ⓦ sangimignanomusei.it

The grand, impressively preserved **Via San Matteo** runs north from Piazza del Duomo. Just before the main **Porta San Matteo** gate, Via XX Settembre heads east towards the former convent of Santa Chiara, which houses both the **Galleria d'Arte Moderna e Contemporanea**, with works by nineteenth- and twentieth-century Tuscan artists, and the dreary **Museo Archeologico**. In the same complex, the fragrant halls of the **Spezieria di Santa Fina** are filled with exhibits from the sixteenth-century spice and herb pharmacy of the Santa Fina hospital.

Sant'Agostino

Piazza Sant'Agostino 10 • Jan–March Mon 4–6pm, Tues–Sun 10am–noon & 3–6pm; April to Oct daily 10am–noon & 3–7pm; Nov & Dec daily 10am–noon & 3–6pm • Free

At the northern end of town is the large church of **Sant'Agostino**. Inside, an outstanding fresco cycle by Benozzo Gozzoli, the *Life of St Augustine* (1465), provides an amazing record of life in Renaissance Florence. As you read from low down on the left, the panels depict the saint – born in what's now Tunisia in 354 – being taken to school and flogged by his teacher, studying grammar at Carthage university, crossing the sea to Italy, teaching in Rome and Milan and being received by Emperor Theodosius. Then comes the turning point, when he hears St Ambrose preach and, while reading St Paul, hears a child's voice extolling him "*Tolle, lege*" (take and read). After this, he was baptized and returned to Africa to found a monastic community.

ARRIVAL AND INFORMATION — SAN GIMIGNANO

9

By train Most visitors see San Gimignano on a day-trip from Siena. Take a train to Poggibonsi (40min) and change there for the 20min bus trip (every 15–30min) up to San Gimignano.

By bus From Siena. Catch one of the direct buses (#130) from Via F. Tozzi (10 daily; 1hr 5min–1hr 20min), or take a bus to Poggibonsi station (hourly; 45min) and change there for the bus to San Gimignano. Buses from Florence to Poggibonsi run at least hourly (50min). The bus stop is just outside the walls, by Porta San Giovanni. Note that despite their proximity, getting a bus between San Gimignano and Volterra is not practical, as it involves an inconvenient change at Colle di Val d'Elsa – a 3hr 45min journey in all.

By car If you're driving, the easiest parking is in the three pay car parks along the road that circles outside the walls; you can only enter the town itself if you have a permit from a hotel.

Tourist office On the south side of Piazza del Duomo (daily: March–Oct 10am–1pm & 3–7pm; Nov–Feb 10am–1pm & 2–6pm; T 0577 940 008, W sangimignano.com). Has information on local wine routes in the surrounding countryside, as well as tastings in cellars and wineries.

ACCOMMODATION

The local hotel tax (€1.50–3/person/night) will be added to your bill, in addition to the room rate.

★ **Agriturismo Poggiacolle** Strada di Montauto 58, a 5min drive south from San Gimignano T 0577 941 537, W poggiacolle.com; map p.596. In an eighteenth-century farmhouse set between an olive grove and a vineyard, this dream of an agriturismo has comfortable, spotless rooms with stunning countryside views, as well as apartments sleeping two to ten people. Lounge by the infinity pool soaking up the views of San Gimignano, tour the farm or have a jaunt through the surrounding countryside – bikes are available free of charge, and there are trekking paths through the estate. **€98**

Bel Soggiorno Via S. Giovanni 91 T 0577 940 375, W hotelbelsoggiorno.it; map p.596. Twenty-one smallish, no-frills rooms in a converted thirteenth-century townhouse on the main street; it's worth paying extra for a room with a view. There's a restaurant with panoramic terrace, too. **€102**

L'Antico Pozzo Via S. Matteo 87 T 0577 942 014, W anticopozzo.com; map p.596. In a tastefully restored *palazzo*, part of which dates back to the Middle Ages, this three-star hotel has comfortable rooms; the "Dante" rooms are superior (and cost €40 more), with hand-painted walls, high ceilings and four-posters. The brick-vaulted bar downstairs makes a cosy spot for a drink, while the sumptuous breakfast is served in what was once the ballroom. **€119**

Leon Bianco Piazza Cisterna 13 T 0577 941 294, W leonbianco.com; map p.596. Tasteful three-star hotel, in a fourteenth-century mansion in the main square. Rooms without views are a little cheaper, but it would be a shame not to make the most of this prime people-watching spot. The roof terrace is a lovely spot for breakfast, drinks and lounging. **€95**

Le Vecchie Mura Via Piandornella 13 T 0577 940 270, W vecchiemura.it; map p.596. Three simply furnished, en-suite doubles above a restaurant (see below), with superb views over vineyards and rolling Tuscan countryside. Friendly owners. **€65**

CAMPING

Campeggio Boschetto di Piemma 2km downhill from Porta San Giovanni at Santa Lucia, off the Volterra road T 0577 940 352, W boschettodipiemma.it; map p.596. The nearest campsite, with camping pitches and chalets as well as a bar, restaurant and pool. Closed Nov to mid-March. Pitches **€11** plus per son **€9**, chalets from **€80**

EATING

San Gimignano has too many visitors and too few locals to ensure high standards in its **restaurants**. However, the tables set out on the car-free squares and lanes, and the good local wines, make for pleasant dining. Good **bars** are similarly thin on the ground, though each of the main piazzas has one or two pleasant places to sit and watch the world go by.

Dulcisinfundo Vicolo degli Innocenti 21 T 0577 941 919, W dulcisinfundo.net; map p.596. A great little restaurant with outdoor tables overlooking the rolling hills. Indoors is elegant, with a smooth jazz soundtrack and a menu of well-executed Tuscan dishes. Mains (from €13) might include roast chicken cooked in Vernaccia wine, rosemary and sage, and grilled beef with rocket and scamorza cheese. March–Nov daily except Wed 12.30–2.30pm & 7–10pm.

★ **Gelateria Dondoli** Piazza della Cisterna 4 T 0577 942 244, W gelateriadipiazza.com; map p.596. This small but extraordinarily popular *gelateria* is renowned for making the best ice cream in Tuscany. Owner Sergio's incomparable pistachio flavour is made from the finest Sicilian nuts, and his trademark *crema di Santa Fina* is perfumed with saffron; but you'd be hard pushed to beat the trio of raspberry and rosemary, champagne with grapefruit, and Vernaccia – a fragrant sorbet made from the crisp local white wine. Fans include Gordon Ramsey. Daily 9am–11am or later.

★ **Il Trovatore** Viale dei Fossi 17 T 0577 942 240,

9

ⓦ trovatoresangimignano.com; map p.596. A cheerful, no-frills place just outside the walls, serving deliciously crispy pizzas cooked in a wood-fired oven (€5.50–10.50). There are some forty types to choose from, including the house special, with salami, Tabasco, mozzarella and olives. They also serve pastas and grilled-meat dishes. Daily (except Wed) 7pm–midnight.

La Mangiatoia Via Mainardi 5 ⓣ 0577 941 528, ⓦ www.capsi.it;see map p.596. Classical music and stained glass compete for attention with some imaginative pasta dishes and wild boar stew at this restaurant, which also has pavement seating, plus a garden that's open for dinner only. Expect to spend about €40/head including wine. Daily except Sun 12.30–2.30pm & 7.30–9.30pm.

La Taverna del Granducato Piazza Martiri di Montemaggio 5 ⓣ 0577 940 824; map p.596. It may not offer the scenic charms of the restaurants inside the walls, but this cavernous place serves up good, old-fashioned pizzas at non-tourist prices (€7; evenings only), as well as a daily menu of two courses for €13. Tues–Sun 12.30–2.30pm & 7–11.30pm (later in summer).

Le Vecchie Mura Via Piandornella 15 ⓣ 0577 940 270, ⓦ vecchiemura.it; map p.596. Housed in an old vaulted stable set into the city walls, this place serves good regional food (*primi* €9–12, *secondi* €13–20), but the real draw is the terrace across the road, offering the best views in town. Daily except Tues 6–10pm.

Perucà Via Capassi 16 ⓣ 0577 943 136, ⓦ peruca.eu; map p.596. *Perucà* has a superb medieval setting in what was once a *cantina* in one of the town's oldest palaces, with a wonderful low, vaulted space. Expect robust Tuscan food, with lots of truffle and mushroom options, and decent prices – pastas around €8 and mains from €10. Daily except Thurs noon–2.30pm, 7–10.30pm.

Volterra

The dramatic location of **VOLTERRA** – built on a high plateau enclosed by volcanic hills midway between Siena and the sea – prompted D.H. Lawrence to write that "it gets all the wind and sees all the world – a sort of inland island", and indeed, you can often find seashells embedded in the paving of streets and squares. Busy but still atmospheric, the town's walled medieval core is made from the yellow-grey stone *panchino*. Tourism has boomed here recently thanks to an unlikely and incongruous source: its fictional role, in Stephenie Meyer's *Twilight* novels, as the home of a 3000-year-old vampire coven known as the Volturi; the tourist office proffers a walking trail of vampire-related sites.

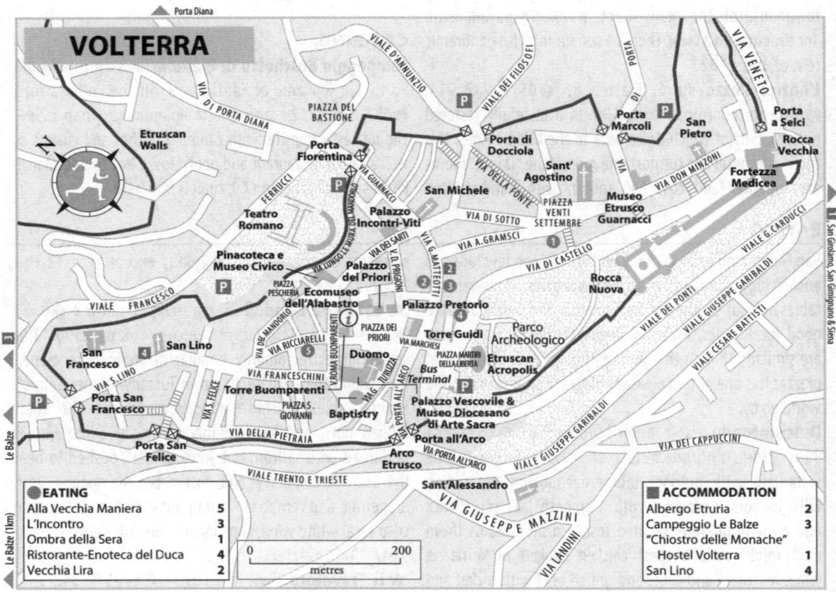

VOLTERRA'S COMBINED TICKET

A **combined ticket** to nine sights in Volterra, including all the sights covered in this guide, valid for 72 hours, is available for €16 from the admissions desk of all participating sights.

Brief history

Volterra is one of the most ancient of all **Etruscan** communities, and still abounds in Etruscan artefacts. Thanks both to its impregnable position and its alabaster mines, the Etruscan settlement of Velathri survived through the Roman era and beyond. In due course, however, its isolation proved to be its downfall. Under **Florentine** control from 1360, Volterra failed to keep pace with changing trade patterns, and the town itself began to subside, its walls and houses slipping away to the west over the **Balze** cliffs, which form a dramatic prospect from the Pisa road. Today, Volterra occupies less than a third of its ancient extent.

Palazzo dei Priori and around

Piazza dei Priori • Sala del Consiglio e della Giunta and tower Mid-March–Oct daily 10.30am–5.30pm; Nov–mid-March Sat & Sun 10am–4.30pm • €16 Volterra combined ticket

Dominating the almost totally medieval square of **Piazza dei Priori**, the **Palazzo dei Priori** is the oldest town hall in Tuscany. Constructed between 1208 and 1257, it may have been the model for Florence's Palazzo Vecchio. Visitors can enjoy great views from its **tower**, while the upstairs **Sala del Consiglio** has served as the town's council chamber without interruption since 1257. Its end wall is frescoed with a huge *Annunciation*, attributed to Jacopo di Cione.

Among the other fine *palazzi* that loom over Piazza dei Priori, the **Palazzo Pretorio** is topped by the **Torre del Porcellino** (Piglet's Tower), named after the weathered carved boar perched on a bracket to the right of the top window.

Museo Diocesano di Arte Sacra

Chiesa di Sant'Agostino, Piazza XX Settembre • Daily: 11am–6pm • €16 Volterra combined ticket

Be sure not to miss the exquisite Museo d'Arte Sacra, housed in the church of Sant'Agostino, whose highlights include a painted terracotta bust of *St Linus* by Andrea della Robbia, and a wonderful stylized, gilded thirteenth-century *Crucifixion*.

The Duomo

Piazza del Duomo • Mon–Sat 8am–12.30pm & 3–6pm, Sun 3–6pm • Free

Via Roma leads into the slightly down-at-heel cathedral square, site of the Pisan-Romanesque Duomo, consecrated in 1120, and baptistry (late thirteenth century). The Duomo's greatest treasure is a sculpture of the *Deposition* (1228) in the south transept, disarmingly repainted in its original bright colours. Behind the baptistry is an old foundling's hospital decorated by della Robbia.

The Duomo

Piazza del Duomo • Mon–Sat 8am–12.30pm & 3–6pm, Sun 3–6pm • Free

Via Roma leads into the slightly down-at-heel cathedral square, site of the Pisan-Romanesque **Duomo**, consecrated in 1120, and **baptistry** (late thirteenth century). The Duomo's greatest treasure is a sculpture of the *Deposition* (1228) in the south transept, disarmingly repainted in its original bright colours. Behind the baptistry is an old foundling's hospital decorated by della Robbia.

Pinacoteca e Museo Civico

Via dei Sarti 1 • Daily: mid-March to Oct 9am–7pm; Nov to mid-March 10am–4.30pm • €16 Volterra combined ticket

9

VOLTERRA'S ALABASTER

The Etruscans and Romans extensively mined Volterra's **alabaster** for sculpting. Until the 1960s, large alabaster factories were scattered throughout the town centre, but – not least because of the quantity of dust they threw up – large-scale production was moved to outlying areas. These days, only about a dozen artisans are permitted to maintain workshops in the town centre, and Volterra's famous **art school** is the only one in Europe to train students to work alabaster.

Most of the plentiful **alabaster shops** in the centre are outlets for factories that produce machined pieces from the tasteful to the tacky.

The beautiful Renaissance Palazzo Minucci-Solaini houses the **Pinacoteca e Museo Civico**, where, unusually, the exhibits are comprehensively captioned in English. Its key works are Florentine: Ghirlandaio's marvellous *Christ in Glory*, set in an imaginary landscape that's very reminiscent of Volterra's own Balze (see page 603); Luca Signorelli's stunning *Annunciation*; and, best of all, Rosso Fiorentino's extraordinary *Deposition*. An altarpiece, painted for the church of San Francesco in 1521, it's a true masterpiece of Mannerism, its figures, without any central focus, creating an agitated tension from sharp lines and blocks of discordant colour.

Ecomuseo dell'Alabastro

Torri Minucci, Piazzetta Minucci • Daily: mid-March to Oct 9am–7pm; Nov to mid-March 10–4.30pm • €16 Volterra combined ticket

The Palazzo Minucci-Solaini contains the Ecomuseo dell'Alabastro, which provides an overview of alabaster-working in the area from Etruscan times to the present day and has a replica sculptor's workshop. The most important pieces are two Etruscan *cinerari* (receptacles for ashes), two capitals that are the only known examples of alabaster work in the Middle Ages and a collection of sculpture from the eighteenth and nineteenth centuries.

Palazzo Incontri-Viti

Via dei Sarti 41 • April–Oct daily 10am–5.30pm, closed 1–2.30pm on Sun; Nov–March by appointment only • €16 Volterra combined ticket • T 0588 84 047, W www.comune.volterra.pi.it

Not far along from the Pinacoteca, the warm sandstone facade of the Palazzo Viti is attributed to Bartolomeo Ammanati. An extensively frescoed Renaissance mansion, the *palazzo* was bought in 1850 by alabaster salesman and traveller Benedetto Giuseppe Viti, who filled his home with beautiful objects in alabaster, everything from 2m-high candelabras to tiles laid in the floor of the ballroom.

Museo Etrusco Guarnacci

Palazzo Desideri Tangassi, Via Don Minzoni 15 • Daily: mid-March to Oct 9am–7pm; Nov to mid-March 10am–4.30pm • €16 Volterra combined ticket

Volterra's Museo Etrusco Guarnacci, 500m east of Piazza dei Priori, ranks among Italy's most important archeological museums, specializing in this region's rich Etruscan history and holding some truly remarkable treasures. The star piece is the so-called Ombra della Sera ("Evening Shadow"), a beautiful bronze statuette of a young boy that was once a votive offering; the elongated nude figure looks uncannily modern, like a proto-Giacometti. Also outstanding is the Urna degli Sposi, a rare and artistically unique clay urn-lid which features a disturbing double portrait of a husband and wife, all piercing eyes and dreadful looks. The bulk of the museum's vast collection consists, however, of around six hundred Etruscan funerary urns. Carved in alabaster, terracotta or local sandstone or limestone, they date from the fourth to first centuries BC, and follow a standard pattern: below a reclining figure of the subject (always leaning on their left side), bas-reliefs depict domestic events, Greek myths or simply a symbolic flower – one for a young person, two for middle-aged, three for elderly.

Parco Archeologico and Teatro Romano

Daily: mid-March to Oct 10.30am–5.30pm; Nov to mid-March 10am–4.30pm • Combined ticket €16

Via Marchesi heads south uphill from the Piazza dei Priori to a lush area of grass, trees and shade known as the **Parco Archeologico**. There's precious little archeology about the place – a few odd lumps of rock, said to be part of a Roman bathhouse – but it's a beautiful area to stroll around. Overlooking the park to the east are the rounded bastions of the Medicean **Fortezza**, a fabulous specimen of Italian military architecture that for the last 150 years has been a prison; while west of the park is an Etruscan **acropolis**. Over on the other side of town, but covered by the same ticket as the Parco Archeologico, are the more impressive remains of the **Teatro Romano** and other Roman-era buildings.

The first turning off Via Marchesi, Via Porta dell'Arco, runs to the **Porta all'Arco**, an Etruscan gateway, third century BC in origin, built in cyclopean blocks of stone. The gate was narrowly saved from destruction in the last war during a ten-day battle between partisans and Nazis.

To the Balze

To reach the eroded **Balze** cliffs, head northwest from the Piazza dei Priori. Beyond the church of **San Francesco**, where fifteenth-century frescoes by Cenni di Francesco depict the *Legend of the True Cross*, you leave town through the Porta San Francesco. From here, follow Borgo Santo Stefano and its continuation, Borgo San Giusto, past the Baroque church and former abbey of **San Giusto**, its striking facade framed by an avenue of cypress trees. At the Balze (almost 2km west of Piazza dei Priori) you gain a real sense of the extent of Etruscan Volterra, whose old walls drop away into the chasms. Gashes in the slopes and the natural erosion of sand and clay are made more dramatic by alabaster mines, ancient and modern. Great tracts of the Etruscan and Roman city lie buried below, and landslips continue – as evidenced by the ruined eleventh-century **Badia** monastery ebbing away over the precipice.

ARRIVAL AND INFORMATION — VOLTERRA

By bus The various, infrequent buses that climb up here arrive on the south side of the walls at Piazza Martiri, a 2min walk from the central square. Note that it takes around 1hr 50min to get here from Florence by bus, and you have to change at Colle Val d'Elsa; and due to the infrequency of buses, travelling between San Gimignano and Volterra (a 3hr 45min round trip) is not advisable.

Destinations Colle Val d'Elsa (for connections to Florence & Siena; at 5.20am, 5.50am, 8am and 1.45pm; 50min).

By car Driving up the spectacular road that twists and turns past endless green hills to reach Volterra from the south is an extraordinary experience. As ever, though, you'll have to park outside the walls, in the free car parks 5, 6 or 8 on the northern side, or the paying underground one to the south.

Tourist office In the centre at Piazza dei Priori 20 (daily: April–Oct 9am–1pm & 2–7pm; Nov–March 10am–1pm, 2–6pm; ☎ 0588 87 257, volterratur.it, comune.volterra.pi.it).

ACCOMMODATION

★ **Albergo Etruria** Via Matteotti 32 ☎ 0588 87 377, albergoetruria.it; map p.600. With a central location, wonderful views from its roof garden, and warm, friendly staff, the *Albergo Etruria* makes a great base. The bathrooms are on the small side and the furnishings a little tired, but it's still the best choice in town. Book ahead to secure the roof garden room. €84

Campeggio Le Balze 1km west of the centre at Via di Mandringa 15 ☎ 0588 87 880, www.campinglebalze.com; map p.600. The well-equipped *Campeggio Le Balze* campsite has shady pitches, a pool and tennis courts. Open late March to mid-Oct. Pitches €9 plus per person €11.50

"Chiostro delle Monache" Hostel Volterra Via del Teatro 4 ☎ 0588 80 050 (March–Oct), ☎ 0588 86 613 (Nov–Feb), www.ostellovolterra.it; map p.600. Youth hostel housed in a converted monastery, 1km (a 15min walk) east of town in the Borgo San Girolamo neighbourhood. Recently refurbished, it has dorms and doubles; all rooms come with private bathroom, and are airy and spacious, with cool tiled floors. Breakfast €6/day for dorms. Half board €16/day. Dorms (mixed) €20, dorms (women-only) €22, doubles €60

San Lino Via S. Lino 26 ☎ 0588 85 250, hotelsanlino.com; map p.600. A converted medieval monastery, just inside the walls at the northwest end of town, a 5min walk from the centre, offering comfortable rooms – some of which come with a terrace overlooking the surrounding countryside – plus a great swimming pool and a pretty courtyard for breakfast. €119

EATING

Alla Vecchia Maniera Via Ricciarelli 38 ⓣ 0588 88 819; map p.600. This unassuming little place doesn't look much from the outside, but locals flock here at lunch for the delicious and inexpensive pizzas with an array of creative toppings. Wed–Mon 11am–3pm & 6.30pm–midnight.

★ **L'Incontro** Via Matteotti 18 ⓣ 0588 80 500; map p.600. A lovely nineteenth-century café, pastry shop and *gelateria*, with a tempting selection of gourmet chocolates and cakes: try the traditional *mandorlato volterrano* (with candied orange, almonds and honey). They also serve light lunches. Daily 6am–midnight; closed Wed in winter.

Ombra della Sera Via Gramsci 70 ⓣ 0588 86 663, ⓦ ristoranteombradellasera.it; map p.600. One of only a few restaurants in Volterra to have outdoor seating, with tables nestling against a tiny chapel – or eat indoors in the wood-beamed dining rooms. Soups and pastas start at €8. The same owners also have a fine pizzeria, *Pizzeria Ombra della Sera*, at Via Guarnacci 16. Tues–Sun noon–3pm & 7–10pm.

Ristorante-Enoteca del Duca Via di Castello 2, cnr Via dei Marchesi ⓣ 0588 81 510, ⓦ enoteca-delduca-ristorante.it; map p.600. On the edge of the old centre, this small restaurant (with an impressive *cantina*) has surprisingly fair prices and decent Tuscan food with a creative twist; the garden is a major plus in summer. Daily 12.30–3pm & 7.30–10.30pm; Oct–June closed Tues; closed late Jan & mid-Nov.

Vecchia Lira Via Matteotti 19 ⓣ 0588 86 180, ⓦ vecchialira.com; map p.600. Particularly good value, this *rosticceria* serves takeaway meals and self-service lunches (soups from €6, pastas from €9), but also offers excellent meals at dinner after 7pm, with most dishes costing €10. Daily except Thurs 11.30am–2.30pm & 7–10.30pm.

Southern Tuscany

The inland hills of **southern Tuscany** display the region at its best, an infinite gradation of trees and vineyards that encompasses the depopulated *crete* before climbing into the hills around Monte Amiata. Southwest of Siena towards the sea, the memorable but little-visited hill-town of **Massa Marittima** presides over a marshy coastal plain. Magnificent monastic architecture survives in the tranquil settings of **San Galgano** and, further east, **Monte Oliveto Maggiore**, which also boasts some marvellous frescoes. The finest of the hill-towns to the south of Siena is **Montepulciano**, with its superb wines and an ensemble of Renaissance architecture that rivals neighbouring **Pienza**.

Further south, the tourist crush is noticeably eased in smaller towns and villages that are often overlooked by visitors gorged on Florentine art and Sienese countryside. Wild **Monte Amiata** offers scenic mountain walks, while the isolated, dramatic medieval town of **Pitigliano** nurtures the amazing story – and scant remains – of what was once Tuscany's strongest Jewish community.

Massa Marittima

The road south from Volterra over the mountains to **MASSA MARITTIMA** is scenically magnificent yet little explored: classic Tuscan countryside which is given an added surreal quality around **Larderello** by the presence of *soffioni* (hot steam geysers), huge silver pipes snaking across the fields and sulphurous smoke rising from chimneys amid the foliage.

The outskirts of Massa have been marred by modern development, but the medieval town itself at the top of the hill, divided between two very distinct levels, remains a splendid ensemble. While visitor numbers are much lower than, say, San Gimignano, Massa is the closest hill-town to several coastal resorts, and on summer evenings it fills up with beach-based day-trippers.

Brief history

Like Volterra, Massa has been a wealthy **mining** town since Etruscan times. In 1225, it passed Europe's first-ever charter for the protection of miners; in the century afterwards, before Siena took over in 1335, its exquisite **Duomo** went up and the population doubled. The trend was reversed in the sixteenth century, and by 1737, after bouts of plague and malaria, it was a virtual ghost town. Massa gained its "Marittima" suffix

in the Middle Ages when it became the leading hill-town of this coastal region, even though the sea is 20km distant across a silty plain. Its recovery began with the draining of coastal marshes in the 1830s. Today, it's a quiet but well-off town, where the effects of mining are less evident than agriculture and low-profile tourism.

Città Vecchia

Piazza Garibaldi, the main square of the **Città Vecchia** – the older, lower part of town – is a perfect example of Tuscan town planning. Its thirteenth-century **Duomo** (daily 8am–noon & 3–7pm; free), set on broad steps at a dramatically oblique angle to the square, is dedicated to the sixth-century St Cerbone, whose claim to fame was to persuade a flock of geese to follow him when summoned to Rome on heresy charges. Behind the altar in its airy interior, the *Arca di San Cerbone* is a marble "ark" carved with bas-reliefs depicting the life of the saint. The Duomo makes a striking backdrop for the Lirica in Piazza **opera festival** in August (tickets at €20, €35 and €50; when they are sold out, standing tickets at €10; ⓦliricainpiazza.it). Performances start at 9.15pm.

Città Nuova

A picturesque lane, Via Moncini, climbs steeply from the northern end of the square up to the quiet Gothic "new" town, known as the **Città Nuova**. Passing through a gateway, you emerge beneath a slender and very spectacular – albeit militarily useless – arch that connects the high town walls to the **Torre del Candeliere** (daily: April–Oct 10.30am–1.30pm & 4–7pm; Nov–March 11am–1pm & 2.30–4.30pm; €3). Set in the centre of **Piazza Matteotti**, and part of the thirteenth-century Fortezza Senese, the tower is open to visitors, who can enjoy a stupendous panorama from the top.

Complesso Museale di San Pietro all'Orto

Corso Diaz • Tues–Sun: April–Oct 10am–1pm & 4–7pm; Nov–March 11am–1pm & 3–5pm • €5 • ⓦmuseidimaremma.it

The chief exhibit in the **Complesso Museale di San Pietro all'Orto** in the Città Nuova is one of the finest altarpieces in Tuscany, a *Maestà* painted in 1335 by **Ambrogio Lorenzetti**. Vivid pink, green and tangerine illuminate the figures of Faith, Hope and Charity below the Madonna, while Cerbone and his devoted geese lurk in the right-hand corner. It also features exhibits from the cathedral and other local churches, including sculptures by Giovanni Pisano removed from the former's facade.

ARRIVAL AND INFORMATION — MASSA MARITTIMA

By bus Buses stop on Via Corridoni near Piazza Garibaldi and run to Piombino (2 daily; 25min) and Siena (2 daily; 1hr 55min).

Tourist office The tourist office is just below Piazza Garibaldi at Via Todini 3/5 (Mon–Sat 10am–4–7pm, Sun also open 10am–1pm April–Sept & 4–7pm June–Sept; ⓣ0566 902 756, ⓦaltamaremmaturismo.it).

ACCOMMODATION AND EATING

Duca del Mare Piazza Dante Alighieri 1 ⓣ0566 902 284, ⓦducadelmare.it. This pleasant, slightly motel-like place a steep downhill walk from the old town has cheery rooms and a nice pool. **€62**

Il Girifalco Via Massetana Nord 25 ⓣ0566 902 177, ⓦilgirifalco.com. Thirty no-frills rooms in a lovely countryside setting, just a 10min walk from the centre. A good choice for the summer months, thanks to its swimming pool surrounded by olive and fruit trees and its flower-filled veranda, where meals are served (half board €22). **€100**

La Tana dei Brilli Vicolo del Ciambellano 4 ⓣ0566 901 274. A lovely little place just off Massa's main street, Via della Libertà, with a couple of outdoor tables. It serves tasty pasta and meat dishes such as *pici* pasta with cacio cheese and pepper (€8) and simple meat dishes from €13. Thurs–Tues noon–3pm & 6.30–10.30pm; closed Nov & Dec–May.

Ostello Sant'Anna Via Gramsci 3 ⓣ0566 901 115, ⓦdigilander.libero.it/leclarisse. A simple, religious-run hostel in the higher part of town, converted from a school. Breakfast costs €1.50. Reception 9am–noon & 5pm–midnight. Dorms **€15**

Vecchio Borgo Via Parenti 12 ⓣ0566 903 950, ⓦmassamarittima.info/vecchioborgo. Excellent-value restaurant with a very charming medieval setting; try the home-made barley soup, juicy game grills or pasta with porcini, made in the local tradition. About €35/person. Tues–Sat 7.30–11pm; closed mid-Feb to mid-March.

9

The crete

The classic Tuscan countryside that stretches south of Siena is known as the **crete**. This tranquil, sparsely populated region of pale clay hillsides, dotted with sheep, cypresses and the odd monumental-looking farmhouse, was a heartland of medieval monasticism in Tuscany. The Vallombrosan order maintained their main house at Torri just south of Siena; the Benedictine order had theirs at Sant'Antimo near Montalcino (see page 613); and the Cistercians founded the convent and abbey of **San Galgano.** Now ruined, this is one of the most alluring sights in Tuscany, complete with its hilltop chapel housing a "sword in the stone". The finest monastery of all lies southeast of Siena, at **Monte Oliveto Maggiore.**

Abbazia di San Galgano

Chiusdino • **Abbey** April, May & Oct daily 9am–6pm; June & Sept daily 9am–7am; July & Aug daily 9am–8pm; Nov–March Mon–Sat 9.30am–5.30pm, Sun 9.30am–6.30pm • €3.50 • **Eremo di Montesiepi** Daily 9am–sunset • Free

The **Abbazia di San Galgano**, surrounded by majestic fields of sunflowers in a peaceful rural setting 26km northeast of Massa Marittima, is perhaps the most evocative Gothic building in all Italy – roofless, with grass for a floor in the nave, nebulous patches of fresco amid the vegetation and panoramas of the sky, clouds and hills through a rose window. The main appeal of the abbey is its general state of ruin, although the basic structure has been stabilized. In summer, it makes a wonderful open-air venue for **opera** performances, staged on various evenings between late June and the end of July.

Brief history

During the twelfth and thirteenth centuries, local **Cistercian** monks were the leading power in Tuscany. The abbots exercised powers of arbitration in city disputes, while the monks in Siena served as the city's accountants. Through them, the ideas of Gothic building were imported to Italy. The order began a hilltop **church** and monastic buildings here in 1218, but their project to build a grand abbey on the fertile land below was doomed to failure. Building work took seventy years up to 1288, but then famine struck in 1329, the Black Death hit in 1348, and mercenaries ran amok in subsequent decades. By 1500, all the monks had moved to the security of Siena. The buildings mouldered until 1786, when the belltower was struck by lightning and collapsed. Three years later, the church was deconsecrated, and the complex was abandoned for good.

Eremo di Montesiepi

Atop the solitary hill near the abbey ruins, the unusual, round, Romanesque **Eremo di Montesiepi** commemorates the spot where Galgano – a local twelfth-century knight – renounced his violent past by thrusting his sword into a stone. Amazingly enough, Galgano's **sword in the stone** has survived, protected under glass as an object of veneration. A side chapel preserves the decaying remains of a man's hands: local legend has it that two wolves – companions of Galgano – tore them from a robber who had broken into the saint's tomb.

ARRIVAL AND DEPARTURE — ABBAZIA DI SAN GALGANO

By car The easiest way to reach the abbey is to drive. From Florence, the quickest route is via Colle Val d'Elsa, but for a more picturesque route take the SP73.

By bus Two daily buses from Siena drop passengers at the abbey (1hr).

ACCOMMODATION AND EATING

Fattoria le Planaie Località Pentolina, Chiusdino ⓣ0577 799 018, ⓦleplanaie.it. This very authentic little agriturismo a few kilometres from the abbey, surrounded by woodland, has comfortable en-suite rooms for if you fancy spending a night or two in this isolated spot. Its restaurant offers huge portions of Tuscan cuisine such as wild boar stew (full meals with wine around €25). **€75**

Abbazia di Monte Oliveto Maggiore

Asciano • Daily: summer 9am–noon & 3–6pm; winter 9.15am–noon & 3.15–5pm • Free • monteolivetomaggiore.it • Train to Buonconvento, then taxi (0577 806 094); one afternoon bus daily runs from Siena's station to the village of Chiusure, 2km east of the abbey

Tuscany's grandest monastery – the **Abbazia di Monte Oliveto Maggiore**, renowned for its absorbing Renaissance **frescoes** – stands 26km southeast of Siena, or roughly 50km east of San Galgano, in a secluded but exceptionally beautiful tract of countryside.

Brief history

When Pius II visited in 1463, it was the overall scene that impressed him: the architecture, in honey-coloured Sienese brick, merging into the woods and gardens that the **Olivetan** or White Benedictine monks had created from the eroded hills of the *crete*. The pope recognized the order within six years, and over the following two centuries this, their principal house, was transformed into one of the most powerful monasteries in the land. Only in 1810, when the monastery was suppressed by Napoleon, did it fall from influence. Today it's maintained by a small group of Olivetan monks, who supplement their state income with a high-tech centre for the restoration of ancient books.

The abbey complex

From the **gatehouse**, an avenue of cypresses leads to the abbey. Signs at the bottom of the slope direct you along a walk to **Blessed Bernardo's grotto** – a chapel built on the site where the founder lived as a hermit.

The abbey is a huge complex, though much of it remains off-limits to visitors. The entrance leads to the **Chiostro Grande**, where the cloister walls are covered by frescoes that depict the *Life of St Benedict*, the founder of Christian monasticism. The fresco cycle, which begins on the east wall, immediately to the left of worshippers emerging from the church itself, was started in 1497 by Luca Signorelli, who painted nine panels in the middle of the series that start with the depiction of a collapsing house. The colourful Antonio Bazzi, known as **Il Sodoma**, painted the remaining 27 scenes between 1505 and 1508. He was by all accounts a lively presence, bringing with him part of his menagerie of pets, which included badgers, depicted at his feet in a self-portrait in the third panel. There's a sensuality in many of the secular figures, especially the young men – as befits the artist's nickname – but also the "evil women" (originally nudes, until the abbot protested).

The **church** was given a Baroque remodelling in the eighteenth century and some superb stained glass in the twentieth. Its main treasure is the choir stalls, inlaid by Giovanni di Verona and others with architectural, landscape and domestic scenes (including a nod to Sodoma's pets with a cat in a window). Stairs lead from the cloister up to the **library**, again with carving by Giovanni; sadly, it has had to be viewed from the door since the theft of sixteen of its twenty codices in 1975.

Montepulciano

Highest of all the major Tuscan hill-towns, at more than 600m, the ravishing, self-contained community of **MONTEPULCIANO** stretches atop a long, narrow ridge 65km southeast of Siena. Its main street, the **Corso**, coils its way between scores of crumbling Renaissance *palazzi* and churches, here clustered around perfect little squares, there towering over tiny alleyways. Wherever stairways or mysterious passages drop down the hillside, you get sudden, stunning glimpses of the quintessential wine-growing countryside rolling off to the horizon; occasionally terraced gardens allow you to contemplate the whole stunning prospect at leisure.

Henry James, who compared Montepulciano to a ship, spent most of his time here drinking – a sound policy, in view of the much-celebrated **Vino Nobile**, production of which dates back well over a thousand years.

Brief history

Montepulciano's rise to eminence began in 1511, when the town finally threw in its lot with Florence rather than Siena. The Florentines thereupon sent **Antonio Sangallo the Elder** to rebuild the town's gates and walls, which he did so impressively that the council took him on to work on the town hall and a series of churches. The local nobles meanwhile hired Sangallo, his nephew Antonio Sangallo the Younger, and later the Modena-born **Vignola**, a founding figure of Baroque, to work on their own *palazzi*. Totally assured in conception and execution, this trio's work makes a fascinating comparison with Rossellino's Pienza (see page 611).

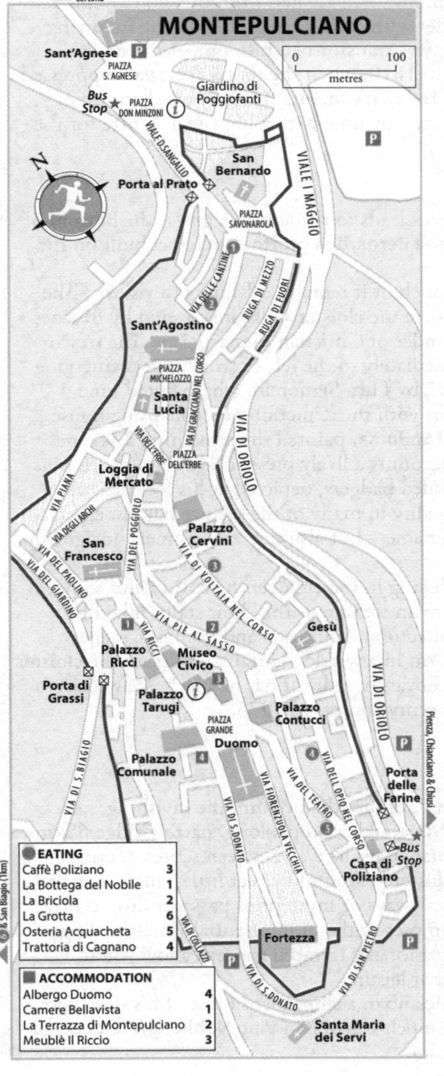

The Corso

The town's bustling main street, the **Corso**, runs from north to south through town. The street begins inside Montepulciano's northern gate, the **Porta al Prato**, Sangallo's first commission. At the first square, Piazza Savonarola, a stone column bears the heraldic lion (*marzocco*) of Florence. The steep climb from this, the lowest point in Montepulciano, up to the highest, the main Piazza Grande, takes around twenty minutes. It's a delightful walk, passing a superb and unusually consistent array of Renaissance architectural treasures.

Sant'Agostino

Via Gracciano del Corso-Piazzale Pasquino da Montepulciano 6 • Daily 8am–noon & 4–7pm • Free

The church of **Sant'Agostino**, just beyond the Porta al Prato, was designed by the earlier Medici protégé, Michelozzo, who also carved the relief above the door. Its interior holds fine Sienese paintings by Lorenzo di Credi and Giovanni di Paolo, and the Crucifix on the high altar is believed to be the work of Donatello.

Santa Lucia and around

The corso forks about 100m further along from Sant'Agostino, where the Renaissance **Loggia di Mercato** overlooks Piazza dell'Erbe. Turning right off the Corso will lead you steeply up to a beautiful little piazza≈fronting the church of **Santa Lucia** (erratic opening hours), where a chapel on the right contains a fabulous *Madonna* by Signorelli.

Museo Civico

Via Ricci 10 • Tues–Sun: 1 April–4 Nov Wed–Mon 10am–7pm, 5 Nov–31 March Sat & Sun 10am–6pm • €6 • Ⓦ museocivicomontepulciano.it

The imposing Via Ricci leads up to the Piazza Grande past the Sienese-Gothic Palazzo Neri-Orselli, home to the **Museo Civico**. Besides an extensive collection of small-town Gothic and Renaissance works, including glazed terracottas by Andrea della Robbia, this hosts substantial temporary exhibitions each year.

Piazza Grande

Piazza Grande, Montepulciano's theatrical flourish of a main square, is built on the highest point of the ridge. Its most distinctive building is the **Palazzo Comunale**, a thirteenth-century Gothic mansion that continues to serve as the town hall. Michelozzo added its **clock tower** (April–Oct Mon–Sat 10am–1pm & 2–6pm; €5) and rustication in imitation of Florence's Palazzo Vecchio; the views across the countryside from here are stunning.

Palazzo Tarugi and Palazzo Contucci

Two of the *palazzi* on Piazza Grande were designed by Sangallo. The highly innovative **Palazzo Tarugi**, alongside the lion and griffin fountain, has a public loggia cut through one corner. The **Palazzo Contucci**, one of the many buildings scattered about Montepulciano that serve as *cantine* for the wine trade, offers free *degustazioni* (tastings) and sale of the **Vino Nobile** (Ⓣ 0578 757 006, Ⓦ contucci.it).

The Duomo

Piazza Grande • Daily 9am–1pm & 3.30–7pm • Free

Sangallo and his contemporaries never got around to building a facade for the plain brick **Duomo** across the square. Its interior is an elegant Renaissance design, scattered with superb sculptures by Michelozzo, while the finest of its paintings is the Sienese **Taddeo di Bartolo**'s iridescent 1401 altarpiece of the *Assumption*, a favourite subject for Sienese artists.

San Biagio

Via di San Biagio • Daily 9am–12.30pm & 3–6/7pm • Free

Sangallo's greatest commission came in 1518, when he was invited to design the pilgrimage church of **San Biagio** just below the town. Set amid lush, pristine lawns, at the end of a long rural avenue, it makes a wonderful fifteen-minute walk down from the centre. This was the second-largest church project of its time after St Peter's in Rome, and exercised Antonio until his death in 1534. The result is one of the most serene Renaissance creations in Italy, constructed from a porous travertine whose soft honey-coloured stone blends perfectly into its niche in the landscape. Its major architectural novelty was the use of freestanding towers to flank the facade (only one was completed). While the interior is somewhat spoiled by Baroque trompe l'oeil decoration, it remains supremely harmonious.

The nearby **Canonica** (rectory), endowed by Sangallo with a graceful portico and double-tiered loggia, is scarcely less perfect.

WINE TASTING IN MONTEPULCIANO

Acclaimed since the medieval era, **Vino Nobile di Montepulciano** today boasts a top-rated DOCG mark, something the townspeople have not been shy in exploiting. Wine shops along the streets of Montepulciano sell gift sets, while local vineyards often offer in-town tastings (usually free, but requiring advance notice). Every restaurant can provide a range of vintages, the very cheapest of which will still set you back at least €20. The tourist office can organize **wine-tasting** rambles for visitors. One of several places to check out is the venerable *Contucci* inside the Palazzo Contucci (see above).

9

FESTIVALS AND EVENTS IN MONTEPULCIANO

From April to September, Palazzo Ricci on Via Ricci hosts a series of **classical music concerts** (☎0578 756 022, Ⓦpalazzoricci.com). Montepulciano comes alive in July during the **Cantiere Internazionale d'Arte** (☎0578 757 007, Ⓦfondazionecantiere.it), which presents exhibitions and concerts around town. The last Sunday in August sees the **Bravìo delle Botti** (☎0578 757 575, Ⓦbraviodellebotti.com), a barrel-race in medieval costume that's the culmination of a week of run-up events. In early September, the five-night, irresistibly named **Live Rock Festival of Beer** (Ⓦliverockfestivalofbeer.it) is celebrated in the tiny village of **Acquaviva**, 10km northeast near Montepulciano's train station.

ARRIVAL AND INFORMATION — MONTEPULCIANO

By train The local train station, on the Siena–Chiusi line, is 10km northeast of town; more frequent services call at the mainline station of Chiusi itself, 22km southeast; connecting buses run from both.

By bus Most buses stop at Porta di Farine and then Porta al Prato, the main "bus station". Note that bus services are very patchy on Sun.

Destinations Buonconvento (7 daily; 1hr); Chiusi (every 30min; 50min); Florence (1–2 daily; 2hr); Pienza (2 daily; 20min); San Quirico (2 daily; 40min); Siena (3–8 daily; 1hr 30min).

By car If you're driving, only enter the town if you have a hotel reservation; failing that, you'll have to park outside the walls – try the free spaces to the east.

Tourist information The main tourist office is outside the walls at the lower end of town, at Piazza Don Minzoni 1 (April–Oct Mon–Sat 9am–1pm & 3–7pm, Sun 9am–1pm; Nov–March Mon–Sat 9.30am–12.30pm & 3–6pm, Sun 9.30am–12.30pm; ☎0578 757 341, Ⓦprolocomontepulciano.it). La Strada del Vino Nobile has an office at Piazza Grande 7 (Mon–Fri 9.30am–1.30pm & 2.30–6pm, Sat 10am–1pm & 2–5pm, Sun 10am–1pm; ☎0578 717 484, Ⓦstradavinonobile.it), offering basic information and details on a wide variety of food and wine-related tours.

ACCOMMODATION

Montepulciano doesn't hold nearly enough **hotels** to meet summer demand, though **private rooms** are also available. Reserve well ahead, and visit the website Ⓦmontepulcianohotels.it. On summer nights, the town's cool hilltop breezes offer a welcome relief from the heat at lower elevations.

Albergo Duomo Via S. Donato 14 ☎0578 757 473, Ⓦalbergoduomomontepulciano.it; map p.608. A short distance from Piazza Grande, the three-star *Duomo* has excellent facilities and smart, clean rooms, plus free private parking and generous breakfasts. **€83**

★ **Camere Bellavista** Via Ricci 25 ☎0578 757 348, Ⓦcamerebellavista.it; map p.608. Ten great-value rooms near the main square, all with en-suite bathrooms, and several with superb countryside views; ask for Room 6 (an extra €25), which comes with a beautiful terrace. Cash only; breakfast is extra. **€70**

La Terrazza di Montepulciano Via Piè al Sasso 16 ☎0578 757 440, Ⓦlaterrazzadimontepulciano.it; map p.608. Peaceful, well-equipped little hotel, in an old house just below the Duomo; breakfast is served on the leafy roof terrace in summer. Owner Roberto is an enthusiastic host. **€97**

Meublè Il Riccio Via Talosa 21 ☎0578 757 713, Ⓦilriccio.net; map p.608. Lovely little B&B in a stunning medieval building just off Piazza Grande, with very comfortable rooms and a mosaic-floored courtyard; it's popular, so book ahead. Next door, *Riccio Suite* is a sister B&B with five elegant, high-ceilinged and light-filled rooms, costing an extra €40–70/night. Breakfast is €8. **€100**

EATING

Caffè Poliziano Via di Voltaia nel Corso 27, Ⓦcaffepoliziano.it; map p.608. This glorious wood-panelled 1868 tearoom, restored to a classic Art Nouveau design, serves tea, coffee and pastries, with free wi-fi, and offers great views from a small terrace at the back. Its adjoining restaurant, *Il Grifon d'Oro*, has a panoramic terrace and serves reasonably-priced Tuscan specialities like *pici* pasta with wild boar *ragù*. Tearoom daily 7am–midnight; restaurant Mon–Sat 7–10.30pm, closed Nov 15–30 & Feb.

La Bottega del Nobile Via di Gracciano nel Corso 95-Via delle Cantine 20 ☎0578 757 016, Ⓦvinonobile.eu; map p.608. *La Bottega* began life as an *enoteca*, and still offers tastings and light meals in fantastic medieval vaulted rooms beneath the Palazzo Avignonesi. It was joined by a restaurant in 2012 serving first-rate Tuscan food such as *ribollita* (€8), *pici* (€9) and rabbit (€13) in an equally appealing period dining room; there are more than sixty Tuscan wines by the glass. Restaurant daily except Thurs 12.30–2.30pm & 7.30–10.30pm; enoteca Mon–Wed & Fri–Sun, Thurs 10am–8pm (later in summer).

La Briciola Via delle Cantine 23 ☎0578 716 903; map p.608. Friendly restaurant with outdoor tables on a quiet

alley just inside the Porta al Prato, with a well-stocked *enoteca* as well as a range of flavourful Tuscan *primi* (€8–12) and *secondi* (€10–18), such as grilled Pienza pecorino with spinach. Daily except Wed 10.30am–2.30pm & 6.30–10.30pm.

La Grotta Via di S. Biagio ⓣ 0578 757 607, ⓦ lagrottamontepulciano.it; map p.608. Opposite San Biagio church, about 1km outside the city walls, this brick-vaulted sixteenth-century restaurant serves refined Tuscan dishes such as rabbit in bacon flavoured with thyme with a courgette flan, and has its own garden. Expect to pay around €50/person (without wine) for a full meal. Daily except Wed 12.30–2.15pm & 7.30–10pm.

★ **Osteria Acquacheta** Via del Teatro 22 ⓣ 0578 717 086, ⓦ acquacheta.eu; map p.608. Small, traditional *osteria*, just down from the Duomo, that's always busy with locals. Lots of cheese and truffle, a changing menu of the day, and home-made pasta dishes from €5.50; you can get a truly memorable meal for under €20. Daily except Tues 12.30–3pm & 7.30–10.30pm.

Trattoria di Cagnano Via dell Opio nel Corso 30 ⓣ 0578 758 757, ⓦ trattoriadicagnano.it; map p.608. Popular and bustling, this place offers a wide range of pizzas, from the simple €5.50 *Margherita* to the €12 *Tartufo*, with mozzarella and fresh truffle, as well as the usual Tuscan *primi* and *secondi*. Outside seating available. Tues–Sun 12.30–2.30pm & 7.30–10pm.

Pienza

The tiny, perfectly preserved village of **PIENZA**, 11km west of Montepulciano, is as complete a Renaissance creation as any in Italy, established as a Utopian "New Town", in an act of considerable vanity, by local boy made good, Enea Silvio Bartolomeo Piccolomini, when he became **Pope Pius II** in 1458. A scion of the leading family of what was formerly Cortignano, he set about transforming his birthplace in 1459, under the architect **Bernardo Rossellino**. The cost was astronomical, but the cathedral, papal and bishop's palaces, and the core of a town (renamed in Pius' honour), were completed in just three years. Pius lived just two more years, and of his successors only his nephew paid Pienza any regard: intended to spread across the hill, the planned city remained village-sized. Today, despite the large number of visitors, it still has an air of emptiness and folly: a natural stage set, where Zeffirelli filmed *Romeo and Juliet*.

Piazza Pio II

Traffic converges on **Piazza Dante**, just outside the main gate, Porta al Murello. From there the **Corso** leads straight to Rossellino's centrepiece, **Piazza Pio II**, which deliberately juxtaposes civic and religious buildings – the Duomo, Palazzo Piccolomini (papal palace), Bishop's Palace and Palazzo Pubblico – to underline the balance between Church and Town. While making the usual medieval nod to Florence in its town hall, the square is otherwise entirely Renaissance in conception.

The Duomo

Piazza Pio II • Daily 7am–1pm & 3–7/8pm • Free

The **Duomo** boasts one of the earliest Renaissance facades in Tuscany; the interior, on Pius' orders, took inspiration from the German hall-churches he had seen on his travels, and remains essentially Gothic. The chapels house an outstanding series of Sienese altarpieces, commissioned from the major painters of the age – Giovanni di Paolo, Matteo di Giovanni, Vecchietta and Sano di Pietro. How long the building itself will remain standing is uncertain, though. Even before completion a crack appeared, and since an earthquake in the nineteenth century the building has required much buttressing – the nave currently dips crazily towards the back of the church.

Palazzo Piccolomini

Piazza Pio II • Tues–Sun: mid-March to mid-Oct 10am–6.30pm; mid-Oct to mid-March 10am–4.30pm, but closed early Jan to mid-Feb & last two weeks of Nov; open Mon on public hols • €7 including guided tours • ⓦ palazzopiccolominipienza.it

The Pope's residence, the **Palazzo Piccolomini** sits alongside the Duomo. Visitors are free to walk into the courtyard and through to the original "hanging garden" behind to the left, where a triple-tiered loggia offers a superb view over the valley. To see the **apartments** above, however, which include Pius II's bedroom, library and other rooms

9

filled with collections of weapons and medals, you have to join one of the frequent half-hour guided tours.

Museo Diocesano

Corso Rossellino 30 • April–mid-Nov daily except Tues 10.30am–1.30pm & 2.30–6pm; mid-Nov to March Sat & Sun 10am–1pm & 2–5pm • €4.50

Mementoes of the pope – notably his English-made embroidered cape – are cherished in the excellent **Museo Diocesano**. The true highlights there, however, are some stunning tapestries and, especially, paintings, including a wonderful anonymous depiction of the life of Christ in 48 tiny panels, one of which shows Jesus meeting a black devil, complete with wings and horns.

ARRIVAL AND INFORMATION — PIENZA

By bus Buses between Montepulciano and Buonconvento stop at both Pienza and San Quirico d'Orcia (see page 612). Buses drop off by Piazza Dante, just outside the walls.

Destinations Buonconvento (8 daily; 35min); Montepulciano (5 daily; 20min); San Quirico d'Orcia (10 daily; 15min); Siena (7 daily; 1hr 15min).

By car Drivers should park outside the city walls in one of the paid car parks.

Tourist office Corso Rossellino 30 (Daily except Tues 9.30am–1pm & 3–6.30pm; ⓣ0578 749 905, ⓦproloco pienza.it or ⓦwww.comune.pienza.siena.it).

ACCOMMODATION AND EATING

La Bandita Podere la Bandita ⓣ333 404 6704, ⓦla-bandita.com. A luxurious, rustic-chic B&B in a scenic location a 15–20min drive from Pienza with serene rooms, an infinity pool and a laidback feel throughout. If you're hankering after total privacy, book the stand-alone Pig-Sty Suite (an extra €200/night), which comes with its own kitchen. The owners have opened a similarly stylish property, the twelve-room *La Bandita Townhouse*, in central Pienza, with rooms from a steep €325 a night. *La Bandita* closed Nov to Easter. **€250**

La Buca di Enea Via della Buca 10 ⓣ0578 748 653. This cosy, hole-in-the-wall *bruschetteria* makes an excellent lunch stop, with delicious toasted Tuscan sandwiches as well as salads and pasta dishes. Pienza is the centre of a region producing sheep's cheese, and this is a great place to sample the local pecorino: a plate of warm pecorino with chestnut honey, pine nuts and walnuts (around €10) hits the spot. Daily 11.30am–10.30pm.

Latte di Luna Just inside the walls at Via S. Carlo 6 ⓣ0578 748 606. This restaurant has a pretty outside seating area screened by flowers, and a menu that offers some tempting Tuscan *primi* (from €8) such as home-made *pici* pasta with wild boar, and mains that might include *maialino arrosto* (roast suckling pig; from €14). Daily except Tues noon–2pm & 7–9pm.

Terrazza di Val d'Orcia Viale Santa Caterina 1–3 19A/B/C ⓣ0578 749 924, ⓦterrazzavaldorcia.com. First choice for lunch, as the views from this restaurant's garden terrace are some of the best in Italy, never mind Tuscany (the interior, though, comes a very poor second). The food doesn't disappoint either, with a fairly priced menu of *pici*, *ribollita* and other Tuscan staples. It's just a minute's walk from the town's western arch. Daily noon–2.30pm & 7.30–10pm; closed Nov.

San Quirico d'Orcia

The rambling old village of **SAN QUIRICO D'ORCIA** stands at a crossroads 8km west of Pienza. Its old town is a quiet and appealing place, whose main attraction is an exceptionally pretty Romanesque **Collegiata** church, its portals sculpted with wild beasts.

ARRIVAL AND INFORMATION — SAN QUIRICO D'ORCIA

By bus Buses stop on Via Cassia, on the eastern side of the village.

Destinations Montepulciano (7 daily; 30min); Pienza (7 daily; 10min); Siena (5 daily; 1hr 10min).

ACCOMMODATION AND EATING

★ **Agriturismo Il Rigo** Località Casabianca 10 ⓣ0577 897 291, ⓦagriturismoilrigo.com. In a wonderfully picturesque position on its own hilltop 5km from San Quirico d'Orcia, this family-run agriturismo has bags of charm, with fifteen rustic, antique-furnished rooms across two buildings (ask for a room in the main house to feel in the thick of things). The home-cooked dinners are a further draw; €23 gets you four courses (wine extra). Doubles **€110**, three-person suites **€170**

Caffè Enoteca Il Pozzo Via Dante Alighieri 24 ⓣ0577

899 085, caffeilpozzo.com. With its beautiful flower-filled garden set around a sixteenth-century well, this place makes an appealing spot for tea, coffee, snacks, a glass of wine or a light meal – tasty home-made pasta costs from €7. There's also wi-fi and occasional live music. Daily (except Tues) 11am–midnight.

Castello Ripa d'Orcia 0577 897 376, castelloripadorcia.com. For drivers, this stunning but inaccessible, isolated castle hotel-restaurant down a gravel road 5km southwest of town makes a wonderfully peaceful place to stay. There are six bedrooms, eight self-catering apartments and a stupendously-sited swimming pool. Minimum stay two nights for rooms, three to five nights for apartments. Closed Nov to mid-March. Doubles €135, apartments (three nights min stay) €110

Montalcino

A classic Tuscan hill-town, **MONTALCINO**, perches 20km west of Pienza. Set within a full circuit of walls and watched over by a fortress, it looks tremendous from below – and from up in the town, the surrounding countryside strewn with vineyards, orchards and olive groves is equally impressive. A quiet place, affluent in an unshowy way from its tourist trade, Montalcino produces a top-notch DOCG **wine**, Brunello di Montalcino, that's reckoned by many to be the finest in Italy. For a spell during the fifteenth century, the town acquired great symbolic importance: this was the last of the Sienese *comuni* to hold out against the Medici, the French and the Spanish, after Siena itself had capitulated. That role is acknowledged at the Siena Palio, where the Montalcino contingent – under its medieval banner proclaiming "The Republic of Siena in Montalcino" – takes pride of place.

Piazza del Popolo

Montalcino's main street, Via Mazzini, leads from **Piazza Cavour** at the north end of town to the **Piazza del Popolo**, an odd little square set beneath the elongated tower of the town hall, based in all but its dimensions on that of Siena. An elegant double-loggia occupies another side with, opposite, a wonderful and rather Germanic nineteenth-century café, the *Fiaschetteria Italiana* (see page 615), which is very much the heart of town life.

TAKING THE WATERS AT BAGNO VIGNONI

The extraordinary ancient site of **Bagno Vignoni** is tucked away 6km southeast of San Quirico. Its central square is entirely taken up by an arcaded Roman *piscina*, or open pool; the springs still bubble up at a steamy 51°C, with a backdrop of the Tuscan hills and Renaissance **loggia** – built by the Medici, who, like St Catherine of Siena, took the sulphur cure here. Bathing in the *piscina* itself is forbidden, but you can still take the waters at the sulphur springs below the village (30°C), or wallow in the mineral-rich waters of one of the nearby spas (advance booking necessary).

Adler Thermae Strada di Bagno Vignoni 1 0577 889 001, adler-thermae.com. Most luxurious of the town's crop of spa hotels, the slick *Adler's* thermal pools bubble at a pleasant 36°C and overlook the rolling hills. The staggering array of treatments ranges from saunas with Tuscan herbs, to steam baths in caves complete with stalactites and stalagmites, to the "Bacchus Ritual", a Vino Nobile-enriched bath and grapeseed peel. Doubles from €234

Albergo le Terme Piazza delle Sorgenti 13 0577 887 150, albergoleterme.it. Facing the *piscina*, Pius II's fifteenth-century summer retreat is now the family-run *Albergo le Terme*. The modern spa in the garden offers treatments such as horse-chestnut peels and lavender steam baths as well as Ayurvedic massages. Day passes for non-residents from €50. Doubles from €300

Hotel Posta Marcucci Via Arca Urcea 43 0577 887 112, hotelpostamarcucci.it. A friendly hotel with indoor and outdoor thermal pools, as well as a sauna and Turkish bath, popular with pensioners. Various treatments are available, most of which tend to be classic rather than cutting-edge. Entrance to the pool for day visitors costs €15; treatments extra. Doubles from €90

9

Musei di Montalcino, Raccolta Archeologica, Medievale, Moderna

Via Ricasoli 31 • Tues–Sun 10am–1pm & 2–5.50pm • €4.50, or €6 combined ticket with the Fortezza di Montalcino (see below)

From Piazza del Popolo, steps (Scale di Via Bandi) near the Fiaschetteria Italiana lead up to the excellent, thoroughly modernized **Musei di Montalcino, Raccolta Archeologica, Medievale, Moderna**. The quality of the art on show is out of all proportion to the size of the town, and takes in a wealth of Sienese painting and early sculpture, including a fabulous twelfth-century *Crucifixion*. Separate basement galleries cover the early archeological history of this site, with a Neolithic burial chamber and some Bronze Age artefacts. The neighbouring church of **Sant'Agostino**, recently incorporated into the complex, is slowly being restored.

Fortezza di Montalcino

Ramparts open daily: April to last Sun in Oct 9am–8pm; Nov–March Tues–Sun 10am–6pm • Courtyard free, ramparts €4, or €6 combined ticket with Musei di Montalcino (see above)

Following Via Ricasoli south from the Musei di Montalcino brings you to the hilltop, fourteenth-century Rocca or **Fortezza di Montalcino**. The open space enclosed within its impressively intact walls makes a great venue for summer concerts. At the foot of one of its towers, a spacious **enoteca** (see page 615) provides access to the **ramparts**. The panorama that unfolds from up here is said to have inspired Leonardo's drawing of a bird's-eye view of the earth; on a clear day you can even see Siena.

ARRIVAL AND INFORMATION — MONTALCINO

By bus Regular buses from Siena stop first at the fortress, then terminate in Piazza Cavour at the north end of town; most pass first through Buonconvento and Torrenieri, from where there are connections to San Quirico, Pienza and Montepulciano.

Destinations Buonconvento (hourly; 20–30min); Siena (7 daily; 1hr 10min).

By car For once, Montalcino's streets are not too narrow to admit cars; there's a car park below the fortress.

Tourist office Just up from the central Piazza del Popolo at Costa del Municipio 1 (Tues–Sun 10am–1pm & 2–6pm; T 0577 849 331, W prolocomontalcino.com). Organizes wine tastings and tours.

ACCOMMODATION

As accommodation is limited, it's wise to book at any time of year. Besides hotels and private Air BnB rooms and apartments, numerous **agriturismi** can be found in the countryside immediately around town.

Castello di Velona Località Castello di Velona, Castelnuovo dell'Abate, about 10km south of Montalcino T 0577 800 101, W castellodivelona.it. Elegant, recently renovated four-star hotel, isolated in lovely open countryside on its own hill and ringed by cypress, close to Castelnuovo dell'Abate. There's a fine dining restaurant and a swanky spa too. Expensive, but rates drop in low season and there are often online deals. **€365**

★ **Il Giglio** Via Soccorso Saloni 5 T 0577 848 167, W gigliohotel.com. Stylish and appealing hotel in a central, sixteenth-century townhouse, where the pleasant a/c rooms come with travertine walls, cast-iron beds and great views; some have frescoed ceilings and terraces, too. **€128**

★ **Palazzina Cesira** Via Soccorso Saloni 2 T 0577 846 055, W montalcinoitaly.com. Set in a medieval building in the centre of town, this place has a home-from-home feel, with comfortable if old-fashioned rooms, some of which (the "mini-suites", worth the extra €16.50) are large and have original frescoes. The breakfast is great too, featuring fluffy omelettes, fresh pastries and home-made jams. Minimum two-night stay. **€125**

Vecchia Oliviera Via Landi 1 T 0577 846 028, W vecchiaoliviera.com. Three-star hotel on the edge of town, where the thirteen fine rooms form part of a well-restored former olive-mill close to Porta Cerbaia and the walls, but do get some traffic noise. There's also a pool, and the patio has excellent views. **€148**

EATING AND DRINKING

Montalcino is filled with good **restaurants**, and also holds a row of fine **enotecas** along Via Matteotti, all of which sell local wines by the glass or bottle and have pavement seating on the town side with sweeping views from the back. There are also plenty of places to pick up a **picnic**: *alimentari* along Via Mazzini sell the usual cheeses and salamis, and *pasticcerie* sell cakes and biscuits made with the local wine.

★ **Castello Banfi La Taverna** Castello di Poggio alle Mura T 0577 877 524, W castellobanfi.com. Set in

28 square kilometres of cultivated land (it's the biggest producer of Brunello di Montalcino), the formidable Banfi wine estate holds a predictably well-stocked *enoteca*, as well as an excellent restaurant whose all-Tuscan menu includes a stellar *pici* with wild boar *ragù*. Reckon on around €40 for a three-course meal, but more if you eat in the more formal *La Sala dei Grappoli* restaurant (outdoor dining in summer). Enoteca daily 10am–7.30pm (closes 6pm Nov–Feb); restaurants Tues–Sat 7.30–10pm.

Enoteca La Fortezza Piazzale Fortezza ⓣ 0577 849 211, ⓦ enotecalafortezza.it. The *enoteca* of the fortress organizes tastings, with 35 different Brunellos to choose from (three glasses €15.50, including cheese and salami, up to €120 for five top wines and three courses in a private cellar), along with light lunches with soups and pastas. Daily: summer 9am–8pm; winter 10am–6pm.

Fiaschetteria Italiana Piazza del Popolo 6 ⓣ 0577 849 043, ⓦ caffefiaschetteriaitaliana.com. In business since 1888, this café has a lovely mosaic-tiled and antique-mirrored interior, as well as outdoor tables perfect for people-watching. It serves simple panini as well as platters of cheeses and cold cuts. Daily 7.30am–midnight; closed Thurs in winter.

Osteria di Porte Al Cassero Via Ricasoli 32 ⓣ 0577 847 196. Indoor and outdoor seating near the fortress, very reasonable prices, and top-notch food, from home-made pastas and soups to a delicious *tiramisù*. A full meal will set you back about €30/head, without wine. Daily except Wed noon–2.30pm & 7–9.30pm.

★ **Taverna Il Grappolo Blu** Via Scale di Moglio 1 ⓣ 0577 847 150, ⓦ grappoloblu.it. Located in a little alley off Via Mazzini, this place has an appealing stone-walled and wood-beamed interior, and excellent pastas, like handmade *pici*, with wild boar *ragù* (€10). Reckon on around €30 a head for two courses, with a glass of wine. Daily noon–3pm & 7–10pm.

Monte Amiata

At 1738m, the extinct volcano of **Monte Amiata** is the highest point in southern Tuscany. Rising in a succession of hills forested in chestnut and fir, it's visible for kilometres around. A circle of towns rings its lower slopes, of which **Abbadia San Salvatore** draws most visitors; in winter these towns are the nearest ski resorts to Rome. Old castles, bucolic countryside and refreshingly cool summer walking make the area a good detour.

Abbadia San Salvatore

The village of **ABBADIA SAN SALVATORE** shelters at its heart a perfect, self-contained medieval quarter. The Benedictine **abbey** around which it developed was founded under the Lombards and rebuilt in 1036. A mere fraction now remains of the original, and most remnants date from the Middle Ages; the highlight is a large and beautiful eighth-century **crypt**, its 35 columns decorated with Lombard motifs. Summer visitors arrive in droves, lured by the landscape, cool breezes and some good, easy walking paths. The best, the 29km-long **Anello della Montagna**, circles the mountain between 900m and 1300m – a long day's walk, or easily manageable in sections round to Arcidosso.

ARRIVAL AND INFORMATION — ABBADIA SAN SALVATORE

By bus If you're visiting Abbadia San Salvatore, avoid the Monte Amiata train station – it's 45km away. Buses serve the village from Siena, Buonconvento, Chiusi and Montepulciano; those from Rome pass first through Arcidosso.

Destinations Arcidosso (10 daily; 45min); Bagno Vignoni (3 daily; 50min); Buonconvento (5 daily; 1hr–1hr 10min); Chiusi (4–5 daily; 1hr 25min); Montalcino (1 daily; 1hr 5min); Montepulciano (2 daily; 1hr); Rome (1 daily; 2hr 50min); San Quirico d'Orcia (5 daily; 1hr); Siena (2–3 daily; 1hr 30min–2hr).

Tourist office Via Roma (ⓣ 0577 775 811). The tourist office is headquarters for the Amiata region, but opening hours are very irregular and limited because of staffing difficulties. Usually open Fri–Sun afternoons in summer.

ACCOMMODATION AND EATING

★ **Castello di Potentino** Seggiano ⓣ 0564 950 014, ⓦ potentino.com. Run by a welcoming English family of wine producers, this hulking, honey-coloured castle is well off the tourist trail, a few kilometres outside the town of Seggiano. It's very much a family home and working farm rather than a hotel, and the family are happy for guests to join in with activities such as harvesting – or simply to relax and enjoy the breathtaking views with a glass of wine. The rooms are splendid: a mix of antiques, well-loved books and family mementoes makes for a cosy, home-from-home atmosphere, and features such as canopy beds and freestanding tubs in some rooms add to the appeal. **€180**

Il Silene Località Pescina, near Seggiano ⓣ 0564 950 805, ⓦ ilsilene.it. A great place for a leisurely meal, this

9

restaurant serves up top-quality cuisine – somewhat unexpectedly considering its unprepossessing location. A typical meal might include poached egg with asparagus and truffle, followed by pigeon-stuffed ravioli and *secondo* of fried rabbit; all beautifully presented (check out their amazing website); a full meal will cost upwards of €50, without wine. Cookery courses are also organized here by the two owner chefs. Tues–Sun 12.30–2pm & 7.30–9.30pm; closed Sun eve in winter.

Pitigliano

Tuscany's deep south, on the Lazio border, is its least visited corner. **PITIGLIANO**, the area's largest town, is best approached along the road from Manciano, 15km west. As you draw close, the town soars above you on a spectacular outcrop of tufa, its quarters linked by the arches of an immense aqueduct. **Etruscan** tombs honeycomb the cliffs, but the town was known for centuries for its flourishing **Jewish** community. Today it has a slightly grim grandeur, owing to its mighty **fortress** and the tall and largely unaltered alleys of the old Jewish ghetto.

The fortress and around

Immediately through the main city gate, **Piazza Garibaldi** is flanked by the **fortress** (1459–62) and aqueduct (1543), with views across houses wedged against the cliffside. Within the fortress, five rooms of the Renaissance **Palazzo Orsini** play host to the **Museo Civico Archeologico della Civiltà Etrusca** (limited opening on several dates per month, listed on the website, Ⓦwww.museidimaremma.it; €3), which holds an interesting collection of Etruscan vases, jewellery and other objects. Part of the cellars beneath the fortress contains the **Museo della Civiltà Giubonnaia** (irregular hours; contact the tourist office), a still evolving collection devoted to folk, domestic and agricultural artefacts from the Maremma.

The fortress backs onto **Piazza della Repubblica**, Pitigliano's elongated main square. From the balcony here you can take in the sweeping views of the surrounding countryside, with Monte Amiata to the north.

The Ghetto

La Piccola Gerusalemme, synagogue and Museo Ebraico daily except Sat: April–Sept 10am–1pm & 2.30–6pm; Oct–March 10am–noon & 3–5pm • €3

Beyond Piazza della Repubblica lies the old town proper, a tight huddle of arches and medieval alleys. This is where you'll find the **old Jewish Ghetto**, centred on Via Zuccarelli, which has been turned into a sort of outdoor museum known as **La Piccola Gerusalemme** (Little Jerusalem). Here, a number of buildings bear witness to the once-thriving community, including a wine cellar, butcher and baker, as well as the eighteenth-century **synagogue**, which part-collapsed in the 1960s, and lay derelict until renovation in 1995; only the grand stone arch and the stairs leading up to the women's gallery survive from the old building, along with plaques commemorating visits made by grand dukes Ferdinand III in 1823 and Leopold II in 1829. The district also has a museum of Jewish culture – the **Museo Ebraico** – and a cemetery. Today virtually no Jewish residents remain in the town.

ARRIVAL AND INFORMATION — PITIGLIANO

By bus Buses from Manciano and Grosseto (3 daily; 1hr 40min–2hr), Orbetello (5 daily; 1hr 25min) and Siena (1 daily; 2hr 55min) drop off on Piazza Petruccioli just outside the city gate.

Tourist office Piazza Garibaldi 51 (Tues–Sat 10am–12.30pm & 3.30–6pm, Sun 10am–12.30pm; limited opening in winter; Ⓣ0564 617 111, Ⓦturismoinmaremma.it). The office has maps of the Vie Cave, ancient Etruscan paths that weave between tombs (mostly free) and cliffside caves all around the town.

ACCOMMODATION AND EATING

Guastini Piazza Petruccioli 16 Ⓣ0564 616 065, Ⓦalbergoguastini.it. The main selling point of this hotel is its excellent location, right in the heart of town. Though somewhat old-fashioned and lacking in mod cons, it has plenty of charm

and stunning views from the rooms. There's also a good restaurant, with outside tables in this attractive square. €66

★Tufo Allegro Vicolo della Costituzione 5 ⓣ0564 616 192, ⓦiltufoallegro.com. A local favourite whose menu is divided into creative, fine dining dishes and more standard, cheaper fare; or opt for one of the five fixed-price menus (€19.50–35), which include hearty dishes such as *buglione di agnello* (a typical lamb stew of the Maremma). Daily (except all day Tues & Wed lunch) 12.30–2.30pm & 7.30–9.30pm.

Eastern Tuscany

The Valdarno (Arno Valley) upstream from Florence is a heavily industrialized tract, with no compelling stop before you reach the provincial capital, **Arezzo**, which is visited by foreigners in their thousands for its Piero della Francesca frescoes, and by Italians in even greater numbers for its antiques trade. South of Arezzo is the ancient hill-town of **Cortona**, whose picturesquely steep streets and sense of hilltop isolation make it an irresistible place for a stopover.

Arezzo

Piero della Francesca's frescoes – which belong in the same company as Masaccio's cycle in Florence and Michelangelo's in Rome – are what makes **AREZZO** a tourist destination, but in Italy the city is equally well known for its jewellers, its goldsmiths and its trade in **antiques**: in the vicinity of the Piazza Grande there are shops filled with museum-quality furniture, and once a month an antiques fair turns the piazza into a vast showroom.

Arezzo has been one of Tuscany's most prosperous towns for a very long time. Occupying a site that controls the major passes of the central Apennines, it was a key settlement of the Etruscan federation, and grew to be an independent republic in the Middle Ages. In 1289, however, its Ghibelline allegiances led to a catastrophic clash with the Guelph Florentines at Campaldino; though Arezzo temporarily recovered under the leadership of the bellicose Bishop Guido Tarlati, it finally came under the control of Florence in 1384. Nowadays, while Florence's economy has become over-reliant on tourist traffic, well-heeled Arezzo goes its own way, though in recent years it has started to market itself more seriously as a place to visit.

There are two distinct parts to Arezzo: the **older quarter**, at the top of the hill, and the businesslike **lower town**, much of which remains hidden from day-trippers, as it spreads behind the train station and the adjacent bus terminal. From the station forecourt, the road straight ahead – Via Guido Monaco – is the traffic axis between the upper and lower town; the parallel, pedestrianized **Corso Italia** is the best route up the hill on foot.

The Basilica di San Francesco

Piazza San Francesco • Half-hourly time-slots April–Oct Mon–Fri 9am–7pm, Sat 9am–6pm, Sun 1–6pm; Nov–March Mon–Fri 9am–6pm, Sat 9am–5.30pm, Sun 1–5.30pm • Reservation obligatory in advance on ⓣ0575 352 727 or ⓦpierodellafrancesca-ticketoffice.it; they can also be reserved at the church's ticket office – in summer you may have to wait 1–2hr for the next available slot, but for most of the year there's rarely any delay • €8, or €12 combined ticket with Casa Vasari (see page 619), Museo Medievale (see page 619) and Museo Archeologico (see page 620)

Built in the 1320s, the plain **Basilica di San Francesco** earned its renown in the early 1450s, when the Bacci family commissioned **Piero della Francesca** to depict **The Legend of the True Cross**, a story in which the wood of the Cross forms the link in the cycle of redemption that begins with humanity's original sin.

Starting with the *Death of Adam* on the right wall, Piero painted the series in narrative sequence, working continuously until about 1457. However, the episodes are not arranged in narrative sequence, as the artist preferred to paint them according to the precepts of symmetry: thus the two battle scenes face each other across the chapel, rather than coming where the story dictates.

The literary source for the cycle, the *Golden Legend* by Jacopo de Voragine, is a very convoluted story, but the outline of the tale is as follows: a sprig from the Tree of

Knowledge is planted in Adam's mouth; Solomon orders a bridge to be built from wood taken from the tree that grew from Adam's grave (below the *Death of Adam*, to the left); the visiting Queen of Sheba kneels, sensing the holiness of the wood, and then later (to the right) tells Solomon of her prophecy that the same wood will be used to crucify a man; Solomon then orders the beam to be buried (back wall, middle right); the Emperor Constantine (back wall, lower right) has a vision of victory under the sign of the Cross; Constantine defeats his rival Maxentius (lower right wall); under torture, Judas the Levite (back wall, middle left) reveals to St Helena, mother of Constantine, the burial place of the crosses from Golgotha, which are then excavated (middle left wall); the True Cross is recognized when it brings about a man's resurrection; and the Persian king Chosroes, who had stolen the Cross, is defeated by Emperor Heraclius (lower left wall), who returns the Cross to Jerusalem (upper left wall).

Pieve di Santa Maria

Corso Italia • Daily 8am–noon & 3–7pm • Free

At the top of the Corso stands one of the finest Romanesque structures in Tuscany, the twelfth-century **Pieve di Santa Maria**. Its arcaded facade, elaborate yet severe, is unusual in presenting its front to a fairly narrow street rather than to the town's main square. Dating from the 1210s, the carvings of the months over the portal are an especially lively group. Known locally as "the tower of the hundred holes", the

campanile was added in the fourteenth century. The oldest section of the chalky grey interior is the raised sanctuary, where the altarpiece is Pietro Lorenzetti's *Madonna and Saints* polyptych, painted in 1320. The unfamiliar saint on the far left, accompanying Matthew, the Baptist and John the Evangelist, is St Donatus, the second bishop of Arezzo, who was martyred in 304. His relics are in the crypt, encased in a beautiful gold and silver bust.

Piazza Grande

The steeply sloping **Piazza Grande** has an unusual assortment of buildings, with the wooden balconied apartments on the east side facing the apse of the Pieve, the Baroque Palazzo dei Tribunali and the Palazzetto della Fraternità dei Laici, which has a Renaissance upper storey and a Gothic lower. The piazza's northern edge is formed by the arcades of the Loggia di Vasari, occupied by restaurants and shops that in some instances still retain their original sixteenth-century stone counters. The **antiques fair** (*fiera antiquaria*) takes over the piazza on the first Sunday of each month and the preceding Saturday.

The Duomo

Piazza del Duomo • Daily 7am–12.30pm & 3–6.30pm • Free

At the highest point of town looms the large and unfussy **Duomo**. Inside, just beyond the organ, is the tomb of Bishop Guido Tarlati, head of the *comune* of Arezzo during its resurgence in the early fourteenth century; the monument, plated with reliefs showing scenes from the militaristic bishop's career, was possibly designed by Giotto. The small fresco nestled against the right side of the tomb is Piero della Francesca's *Magdalene*.

San Domenico

Piazza San Domenico • Daily 8am–1pm & 2pm–7pm • Free

A short distance north of the Duomo, the church of **San Domenico** was constructed mostly in the late thirteenth century but with a Gothic campanile. Inside there are tatters of fifteenth- and sixteenth-century frescoes on the walls, while above the high altar hangs a dolorous *Crucifix* by Cimabue (1260), painted when the artist would have been about twenty years old.

Casa di Giorgio Vasari

Via XX Settembre 55 • Mon & Wed–Sat 8.30am–7pm, Sun 8.30am–1pm • €4, or €12 combined ticket with San Francesco (see page 617), Museo Medievale (see below) and Museo Archeologico (see page 620)

The **Casa di Giorgio Vasari** was designed by the eponymous biographer-architect-artist who was born in Arezzo in 1511, was taught to paint by his distant relative Luca Signorelli, and went on to become general artistic supremo to Cosimo I. The industrious Vasari frescoed much of his house with portraits and mythological characters, a decorative scheme that makes this one of the brashest domestic interiors in Tuscany. Portraits include his wife as the muse of conjugal love (in the Chamber of Apollo) and Michelangelo and Andrea del Sarto (in the Chamber of Fame). Work by other minor artists is strewn all over the place.

Museo d'Arte Medievale e Moderna

Via S. Lorentino 8 • Tues, Wed, Sat 9am–7.30pm, Fri & Sun 3–7.30pm • €4, or €12 combined ticket with San Francesco (see page 617), Casa Vasari (see above) and Museo Archeologico (see below)

The fifteenth-century Palazzo Bruni-Ciocchi houses the **Museo d'Arte Medievale e Moderna**, containing a collection of paintings by local artists and majolica pieces from the thirteenth to the eighteenth centuries, generously spread over three floors. Highlights are the first floor's medieval and Renaissance paintings by the likes of Spinello Aretino, Luca Signorelli and Bartolomeo della Gatta, and the five rooms filled with ceramics from Deruta, Gubbio, Faenza and other major Italian centres of production.

AREZZO'S FESTIVALS

Arezzo's premier folkloric event is the **Giostra del Saracino**, which was first recorded in 1535 and is nowadays held in the Piazza Grande on the first Sunday in September. The day starts off with various costumed parades; at 5pm the action switches to the jousting arena in the piazza, with a procession of some 350 participants leading the way. Each quarter of the city is represented by a pair of knights on horseback, who do battle with a wooden effigy of a Saracen king. In one hand the effigy holds a shield marked with point scores; in the other it has a cat-o'-three-tails which swings round when the shield is hit, necessitating nifty evasive action from the rider. In recent years the event has become so popular that a reduced version of the show is now held on the penultimate Saturday of June; to book tickets, call 0575 377 462 or see giostradelsaracinoarezzo.it.

The musical tradition that began with Guido d'Arezzo (widely regarded as the inventor of modern notation) is kept alive chiefly through the international choral competition that bears his name: the **Concorso Polifonico Guido d'Arezzo**, held in the last week of August. The less ambitious **Pomeriggi Musicali** is a season of free concerts held in various churches, museums and libraries; on average there's one concert a week from mid-January to June.

Museo Archeologico

Via Margaritone • Mon–Sat 8.30am–7.30pm • €6, or €12 combined ticket with San Francesco (see page 617), Casa Vasari and Museo Medievale (see page 619)

All the principal sights are in the upper part of town, with the exception of the **Museo Archeologico**, which occupies part of a monastery built into the wall of the town's Roman amphitheatre. The collection is impressive chiefly for the marvellously coloured coralline vases produced here in the first century BC – the skill of Arezzo's glassblowers achieved a reputation throughout the Roman world.

ARRIVAL AND INFORMATION — AREZZO

By train Sitting on the main line between Florence and Rome, Arezzo is a major hub for train services.

Destinations Assisi (12 daily; 1hr 35min); Florence (hourly; 1hr); Orvieto (7 daily; 1hr 20min); Perugia (every 2hr; 1hr 15min).

By bus Buses into Arezzo all terminate by the train station.

Destinations Città di Castello (at least 12 daily; 1hr 30min); Cortona (hourly; 1hr); Sansepolcro (17 daily, some via Monterchi, most via Anghiari; 1hr); Siena (5 daily Mon–Fri).

Tourist offices Palazzo Comunale, Piazza della Libertà 1 (daily 10am–1pm & 1.30–5.30pm; 0575 401 945, turismo.provincia.arezzo.it).

ACCOMMODATION

Accommodation can be hard to come by, especially when the antiques fair is on (first Sun of each month and preceding Sat). In addition, the town is booked solid at the end of Aug and beginning of Sept, when the Concorso Polifonico Guido d'Arezzo and the Giostra del Saracino follow in quick succession.

Antiche Mura Piaggia di Murello 35 0575 20 410, antichemura.info; map p.618. This cosy six-room B&B has an excellent location, just a short walk from the Duomo, and wood-beamed ceilings and stone walls give it an appealingly rustic feel. The rooms overlooking the internal courtyard are quieter. Breakfast is taken in a nearby bar. **€78**

★ **Graziella Patio** Via Cavour 23 0575 401 962, hotelpatio.it; map p.618. Geared to business travellers, most of central Arezzo's hotels are rather cheerless places, but this small and welcoming four-star, almost next door to San Francesco, is an exception. The rooms are colourful and cosy, and their decor is inspired, apparently, by the work of Bruce Chatwin, hence their names – Utz, Oxiana, Cobra Verde and so on. **€140**

EATING

Antica Osteria L'Agania Via Mazzini 10 0575 29 381, agania.it; map p.618. A very good and informal trattoria with welcoming atmosphere and local dishes (special emphasis on truffles and mushrooms in season) and set menus at €15–25. The *Antica Vineria* next door serves soups, salads, and cheese and meat plates at even lower prices in a bustling dining room. Tues–Sun noon–3pm & 6–10.30pm.

Il Gelato Via de' Cenci 24; map p.618. There are several good *gelaterie* in Arezzo, but none is better than this little place. The *nocciola* (hazelnut), lemon and pistachio are particularly good. Daily except Wed 11am–midnight (8pm in winter); closed Jan & Dec.

Il Saraceno Via Mazzini 6 0575 27 644, ilsaraceno.

com; map p.618. Family-run trattoria, founded in 1946, with a good wine cellar and traditional Aretine specialities (notably duck) at around €35/head for three courses; good wood-oven pizzas too. Noon–2.50pm & 7–9.40pm; closed two weeks in Jan.

★ **Osteria de' Cenci** Via de' Cenci 11 ⓣ0575 24 572; map p.618. Excellent little restaurant, with unpretentious local cooking at fair prices, and an atmosphere that is rather more convivial than that of many restaurants in businesslike Arezzo. The menu is very heavily meat-biased, with main courses averaging around €15. Daily except Tues noon–3pm & 7.30–midnight.

East of Arezzo: the Piero trail

Arezzo is the springboard for one of Italy's most rewarding art itineraries: the **Piero della Francesca trail**, which extends east of the city to **Monterchi** and **Sansepolcro** (the artist's birthplace), and continues through Urbino to Rimini. There's no train link between Arezzo and Sansepolcro, but there is an excellent bus service between the two towns. Most of these buses continue to Città di Castello for train connections to Perugia, and five stop at Monterchi at convenient times to see Piero's Madonna del Parto before continuing.

The Madonna del Parto, Monterchi

Via della Reglia • Daily 9am–1pm & 2–7pm; Nov–March closed Tues • €6.50 combined ticket with Museo delle Bilance (same hours) • ⓦ madonnadelparto.it

MONTERCHI is famous as the home of the **Madonna del Parto** fresco, which is now the focal point of a permanent **exhibition** recounting the technical details of the fresco's restoration, and that of the San Francesco cycle in Arezzo. Images of the pregnant Mary, exemplifying the mystery of the Incarnation, began to appear in Tuscan art some time in the 1330s – Piero's glorious fresco, created around 1467, was one of the last additions to the genre. The picture is still an object of veneration, and the museum is sometimes cleared when local pregnant women come to pray to the Virgin; pregnant tourists are also admitted free.

The ticket also gets you into the village's new **Museo delle Bilance** (Museum of Scales). It's said to be one of the world's most important collections of weighing instruments, a claim that you might be inclined to take on trust.

Museo Civico, Sansepolcro

Via Niccolò Aggiunti 65 • Daily: June 15–Sept 15 10am–1.30pm & 2.30–7pm; Sept 16–June14 10am–1pm & 2.30–6pm • €10 • ⓦ museocivicosansepolcro.it

SANSEPOLCRO, 40km northeast of Arezzo, is where Piero della Francesca was born in the 1410s, and where he spent much of his life. The **Museo Civico** houses a sizeable collection of pictures, including work by Pontormo and Santi di Tito, but the primary focus of attention is inevitably della Francesca's *Resurrection*. Painted for the adjoining town hall in the 1450s and moved here in the sixteenth century, it's one of the most overpowering images of the event ever created, with a muscular Christ stepping onto the edge of the tomb – banner in hand – as if it were the rampart of a conquered city. Elsewhere in the museum, an early della Francesca masterpiece, the *Madonna della Misericordia* polyptych, epitomizes the graceful solemnity of his work.

ACCOMMODATION AND EATING — EAST OF AREZZO

Da Ventura Via Niccolò Aggiunti 30, Sansepolcro ⓣ0575 742 560, ⓦalbergodaventura.it. The family-run *Da Ventura* has for many years been rated as one of town's best places to eat, and it's good value too. It also has inexpensive accommodation upstairs, but the rooms aren't as nice as at *La Locanda del Giglio*. Restaurant open Tues–Sat 12.30–2.30pm & 7–10.30pm, Sun 12.30–2.30pm. €70

★ **La Locanda del Giglio** Via Pacioli 60 Sansepolcro ⓣ0575 742 033, ⓦristorantefiorentino.it. This B&B is the best place to stay in Sansepolcro, with four unfussily modern en-suite rooms, right in the heart of the town. In the same building there's an excellent and well-priced restaurant, the *Fiorentino*, which is also run by the Uccellini family, who have been the proprietors for half a century now. (The adjoining *Fiorentino* hotel is an entirely separate operation.) Restaurant open daily except Wed 12.30–2.30pm & 7–10pm. €85

9

Cortona

Travelling south from Arezzo you enter the **Valdichiana**, reclaimed swampland that is now prosperous farming country. From the valley floor, a 5km-long road winds up through terraces of vines and olives to the ancient hill-town of **CORTONA**, whose heights survey a vast domain: the Valdichiana stretching westwards, with Lago Trasimeno visible over the low hills to the south. The steep streets of Cortona are more or less untouched by modern building: limitations of space have confined almost all later development to the lower suburb of Camucia, which is where the approach road begins.

Even without its monuments and art treasures, this would be a good place to rest up, with decent hotels and excellent restaurants. In recent years, though, Cortona's tourist traffic has increased markedly, in the wake of Frances Mayes' *Under the Tuscan Sun* and *Bella Tuscany*, books that continue to entice coachloads of her readers to the town.

MAEC

Piazza Signorelli • April–Oct daily 10am–7pm; Nov–March Tues–Sun 10am–5pm • €10 • Ⓦ cortonamaec.org

The central **Piazza della Repubblica** adjoins **Piazza Signorelli**, which is named after Luca Signorelli (1441–1523), Cortona's most famous son, and is the site of the Museo dell'Accademia Etrusca e della Città di Cortona – or **MAEC**, for short. On the lowest floor, which charts the development of Cortona from the earliest recorded settlements to Roman times, some spectacular specimens of Etruscan jewellery catch the eye. Upstairs there's a good deal more Etruscan material on show, most notably a bronze lamp from the fourth century BC, which is honoured with a room all to itself. Etruscan and later bronze figurines fill an avenue of cabinets in the middle of the main hall, surrounded by some fairly undistinguished pictures.

The Duomo

Piazza del Duomo • Daily 8am–12.30pm & 3–6.30pm • Free

Piazza Signorelli links with Piazza del Duomo, where the **Duomo** sits hard up against the city walls. The interior is rather chilly, but there's a Pietro da Cortona *Nativity* on the third altar on the left, and a possible Andrea del Sarto (an *Assumption*) to the left of the high altar.

Museo Diocesano

Piazza del Duomo • April–Oct daily 10am–7pm; Nov–March Tues–Sun 10am–5pm • €5

The church that used to face the Duomo now forms part of the **Museo Diocesano**, a tiny but high-quality collection of Renaissance art plus a fine Roman sarcophagus, carved with fighting centaurs. Predictably Luca Signorelli features strongly, though only two works – *Lamentation* (1502) and *The Communion of the Apostles* (1512) – are unequivocally his. Paintings from Sassetta, Bartolomeo della Gatta and Pietro Lorenzetti are also on show, but none measures up to Fra' Angelico, represented by a *Madonna, Child and Saints* and an exquisite *Annunciation*, painted when he was based at Cortona's monastery of San Domenico.

San Francesco

Via Berrettini • Daily 7am–7pm • Free

To get the full taste of Cortona take Via Santucci from Piazza della Repubblica and then clamber along Via Berrettini, at the near end of which stands the crusty and ancient church of **San Francesco.** Designed by St Francis's disciple Brother Elias, this was the first Franciscan church to be built outside Assisi after Francis's death. The church houses a Byzantine ivory reliquary that is said to contain a piece of the True Cross – it's on the high altar, behind which Brother Elias is buried. To the left of the altar are displayed various items that are reputed to have belonged to St Francis, while on the third altar on the left of the nave hangs an *Annunciation* by the man the street is named after, Pietro Berrettini, otherwise known as Pietro da Cortona. (He was born at no. 33, further up the hill).

San Niccolò

Via San Niccolò • 12 April–31 May Sat & Sun 11am–1pm & 2–5pm; 1 June–6 Jan daily 11am–1pm & 2–5/6pm • Donation expected

A work by Signorelli is to be found in the church of **San Niccolò**, a frail little building with a delicate portico and a fine wooden ceiling that's sagging with age. Signorelli's high altarpiece is a standard which he painted on both sides: a characteristically angular *Entombment* on the front and a *Madonna and Saints* on the back – revealed by a neat hydraulic system that swivels the picture away from the wall, as the sacristan will demonstrate.

Santa Margherita

Piazza Santa Margherita • Daily: summer 8am–noon & 3–7pm; winter 9am–noon & 3–6pm • Free

Near the summit of the town stands **Santa Margherita**, resting place of St Margaret of Cortona, the town's patron saint. Her tomb, with marble angels lifting the lid of her sarcophagus, was created in the mid-fourteenth century, and is now mounted on the wall to the left of the chancel, while her remains are on display in a glass coffin directly behind the chancel.

ARRIVAL AND INFORMATION — CORTONA

By train Hourly trains from Florence (1hr 20min) and Arezzo (20min) call at Camucia-Cortona station, from where a shuttle bus (approximately hourly; 10min) runs up to the old town, arriving at either Piazza Garibaldi or Piazza del Mercato; buy tickets at the station bar. Terόntola, 10km south, is the station to get off at if you are approaching from Umbria; it too is served by a shuttle (roughly every hour; 25min).

By bus There are hourly LFI buses between Cortona and Arezzo (50min). Buses terminate at Piazza Garibaldi.

By car The centre is closed to all but essential traffic, so if you're driving you should use one of the free car parks on the periphery.

Tourist office Palazzo Casali, Piazza Signorelli 9 (Mon–Fri 9am–1pm, Tues and Thurs also 3–5pm; T 0575 637 223, W cortonaweb.net).

ACCOMMODATION

Italia Via Ghibellina 5 T 0575 630 254, W hotelitaliacortona.com. An inexpensive three-star, occupying a renovated fifteenth-century house very near Piazza della Repubblica, with 26 rooms and a breakfast terrace that gives terrific views of the Valdichiana and Monte Amiata in the distance. **€119**

★ **San Michele** Via Guelfa 15 T 0575 604 348, W hotelsanmichele.net. The most luxurious central choice, this handsome 43-room four-star has been converted from a rambling medieval townhouse. The rooms are a generous size, and the suites are worth splashing out on – some have private terraces or balconies overlooking the countryside. **€203**

EATING AND DRINKING

Dardano Via Dardano 24 T 0575 601 944, W trattoriadardano.com. The Castelli family are the owners of this excellent, unpretentious, inexpensive and very popular trattoria, and they produce much of the food that's cooked here too. Reservations are advisable, as it's full to bursting most nights. Daily (except Wed) 11.30am–2.30pm & 7–10.30pm.

Fufluns Via Ghibellina 3 T 0575 604 140. If a pizza is all you need, this spacious and bustling place is the first choice. The rest of the menu is more than OK, if not quite as good as you'll find elsewhere in Cortona. Daily except Tues 7.15–10.30pm.

★ **La Bucaccia** Via Ghibellina 17 T 0575 606 039, W labucaccia.it. Husband-and-wife team Romano and Agostina are at the helm of this superlative and refined restaurant, with an atmospheric Etruscan-themed, stone-walled dining room and impressive wine cellar. Main courses are €14–20, and the set menu of Cortona specialities is something of a bargain at under €35. Daily 12–2.30pm & 7–10.30pm.

★ **Osteria del Teatro** Via Maffei 5 T 0575 630 556. Occupying the entire lower floor of a rambling old mansion, this is a good-naturedly busy place, featuring delicious home-made pastas on a meat-heavy menu; portions are generous and prices more than fair – with *ribollita* at €7 and lots of pasta dishes at €8. Daily except Wed 12.30–2.30pm & 7.30–9.30pm.

Umbria

628 Perugia

637 Lago Trasimeno

639 Città di Castello

641 Gubbio

646 Assisi

652 Spello and around

657 Spoleto

663 The Valnerina

665 Terni and around

666 Narni

667 Todi

670 Orvieto

THE PIANO GRANDE

Umbria

10

Often referred to as "the green heart of Italy", Umbria is a beautiful, largely unspoiled landlocked region of rolling hills, woods, streams and valleys. Within its borders are a dozen or so classic hill-towns, each resolutely individual and crammed with artistic and architectural treasures that frequently rival bigger and more famous cities. To the east, pastoral countryside gives way to more rugged scenery, none better than the dramatic twists and turns of the Valnerina and the high mountain landscapes of the Parco Nazionale dei Monti Sibillini.

Historically, Umbria is best known as the birthplace of several saints, **St Benedict** and **St Francis of Assisi** being the most famous, and for a religious tradition that earned the region such names as *Umbra santa*, *Umbra mistica* and *la terra dei santi* ("the land of saints"). The landscape itself has contributed much to this mystical reputation, and even on a fleeting trip it's impossible to miss the strange quality of the Umbrian light, an oddly luminous silver haze that hangs over the hills.

Until the 1990s Umbria was something of an impoverished backwater, but over the past few decades it has become second home to almost as many outsiders as neighbouring Tuscany. This, however, has done nothing to curb the region's renewed sense of identity and youthful enthusiasm, nor to blunt the artistic initiatives that have turned Umbria into one of the most flourishing cultural centres in Italy.

Most visitors head for **Perugia**, **Assisi** – the latter with its extraordinary frescoes by Giotto in the Basilica di San Francesco – or **Orvieto**, whose Duomo is one of the greatest Gothic buildings in the country. For a taste of the region's more understated charms, it's best to concentrate on lesser-known places such as **Todi**, an increasingly chic but still unspoiled hill-town; **Gubbio**, ranked as the most perfect medieval centre in Italy; and **Spoleto**, for many people the outstanding Umbrian town. Although there are few unattractive parts (the factories of Terni and the Tiber Valley being the largest blots), the Umbrian landscape is for the most part enticing: the **Valnerina**, a beautiful valley surrounded by mountains and remote hilltop villages; the **Piano Grande**, a vast, featureless plain best visited in spring, when it's carpeted with wild flowers; and **Lago Trasimeno**, the largest lake in the Italian peninsula, with plenty of opportunities for swimming and watersports.

Brief history

Umbria was named by the Romans after the mysterious **Umbrii**, a tribe cited by Pliny as the oldest in Italy, and one that controlled territory reaching into present-day Tuscany and Le Marche. Although there is scant archeological evidence about them, it seems that their influence was mainly confined to the east of the Tiber; the darker and more sombre towns to the west – such as Perugia and Orvieto – were founded by the **Etruscans**, whose rise forced the Umbrii to retreat into the eastern hills. Roman domination was eventually undermined by the so-called barbarian invasions from northern Europe, in the face of which the Umbrians withdrew into fortified hill-towns, paving the way for a pattern of bloody rivalry between independent city-states that continued through the Middle Ages. Weakened by constant warfare, most towns eventually fell to the papacy, entering a period of economic and cultural stagnation that continued up until the late twentieth century.

GETTING AROUND — UMBRIA

Getting around Umbria by public transport presents no problems. Distances between the main sights are short, and there are excellent rail links both within the region and to Florence and Rome. For travel information, see Ⓦumbriamobilita.it.

BASILICA DI SAN FRANCESCO, ASSISI

Highlights

❶ **Galleria Nazionale dell'Umbria** The region's finest and largest collection of medieval and Renaissance Umbrian paintings. See page 631

❷ **Gubbio** Best-looking of Umbria's medieval hill-towns, and without Assisi's crowds and commercialism. See page 641

❸ **Basilica di San Francesco, Assisi** Burial place of St Francis and one of Italy's great buildings, with frescoes by Giotto and Simone Martini. See page 646

❹ **Valle di Spoleto** A swathe of country with four of the region's most compelling villages: Spello, Bevagna, Trevi and Montefalco. See page 652

❺ **Complesso Museale di San Francesco, Montefalco** One of Umbria's best small galleries, with a major fresco cycle by Benozzo Gozzoli. See page 655

❻ **The Valnerina** A verdant, mountain-edged valley dotted with hill-villages and spectacular views. See page 663

❼ **The Piano Grande** A glorious upland plain, the centrepiece of the Parco Nazionale dei Monti Sibillini. See page 665

❽ **Duomo, Orvieto** On a par with the cathedrals in Milan and Siena, Orvieto's Duomo has a glorious facade and a majestic fresco cycle by Luca Signorelli. See page 670

HIGHLIGHTS ARE MARKED ON THE MAP ON PAGE 628

Perugia

The provincial capital **PERUGIA** is the most obvious place to kick off a tour of Umbria. A bustling university town, known for its chocolate and its jazz festival, it offers at least a day's worth of good sightseeing, and is not a bad place to base yourself if you want to explore the surrounding area: it has big-city amenities, and trains run to all the major highlights, complemented by fast roads and an extensive bus network. The town hinges around a single street, **Corso Vannucci**, named after the city's most celebrated artist, Pietro Vannucci (c.1450–1523), better known as Perugino. Lined with bustling

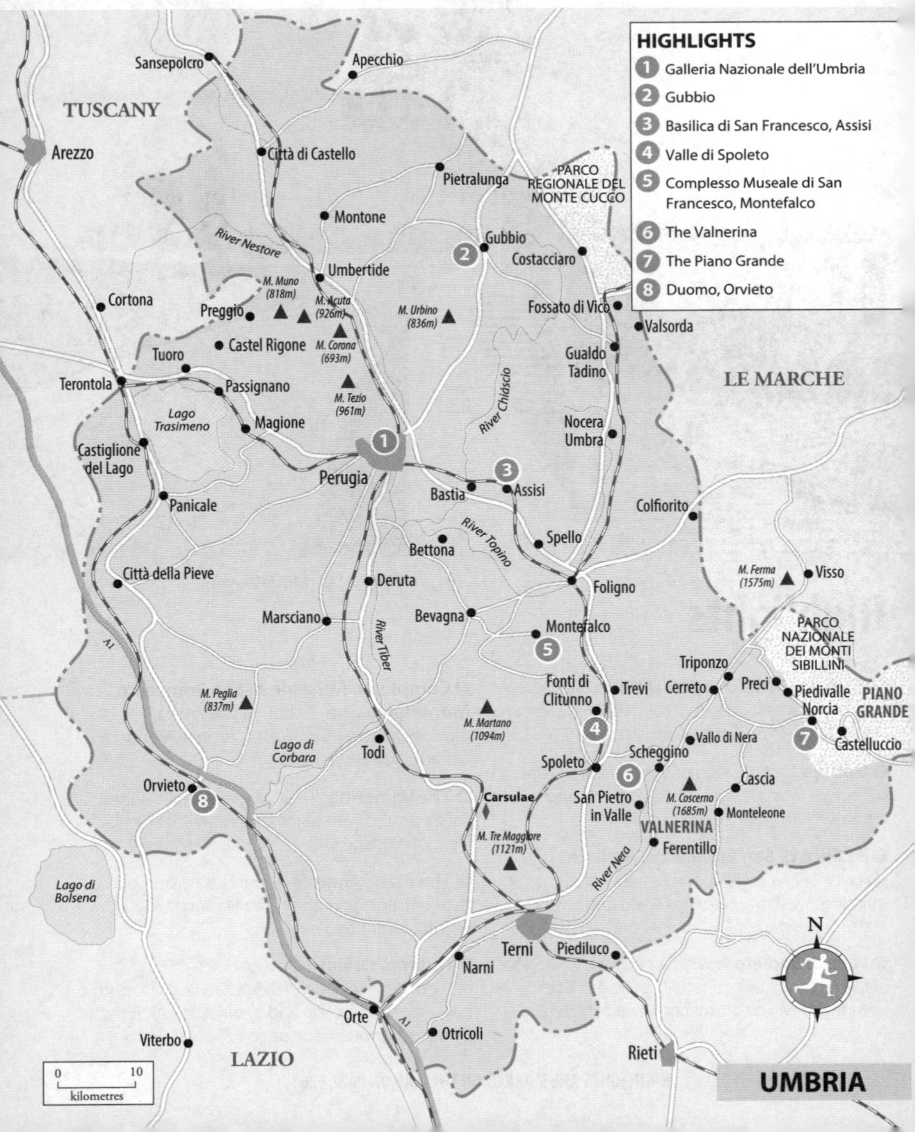

RUSTIC ROASTS AND TRUFFLES – UMBRIAN CUISINE

The traditional cuisine of Umbria relies heavily on rustic staples – pastas and roast meats – and in the past tended to be simple and homely. The region is also the only area outside Piemonte where **truffles** are found in any abundance, and their perfumed shavings, particularly in the east of the region, find their way on to eggs, pasta, fish and meat – but at a price that prohibits overindulgence.

Meat plays a leading role, especially **lamb** and **pork**, which is made into hams, sausage, salami and, most famously, **porchetta** – whole suckling pig stuffed with rosemary or sage, roasted on a spit. **Game** may also crop up on some menus, most often as pigeon, pheasant or guinea fowl. The range of **fish** is restricted by the lack of a coast, but trout can be caught from the Nera River and Clitunno springs, while the lakes of Piediluco and Trasimeno yield eel, pike, tench and grey mullet. **Vegetable** delicacies include much-prized tiny lentils from Castelluccio, beans from Trasimeno and celery and cardoons from around Trevi. Umbrian **olive oil**, though less hyped than Tuscan oils, is of excellent quality. As for desserts, Perugia is renowned for its **chocolate** – it is home to Perugino, Italy's leading chocolate manufacturer – and pastries.

Umbria used to be best known outside Italy for fresh, dry white **wines**. Orvieto, once predominantly a medium-sweet wine, has been revived in a dry style. The wine was beloved of the artists and architects of Orvieto's Duomo: Luca Signorelli requested a thousand litres per year by contract. In recent years the pre-eminence of Orvieto in the domestic market has been successfully challenged by Grechetto, an inexpensive and almost unfailingly decent wine made by countless producers across the region. Umbria's quest for quality is also increasingly reflected in a growing number of small producers, many of whom have followed the lead of Giorgio Lungarotti, one of the pioneers of Umbrian viticulture, and in some outstanding reds, notably the Torgiano Rosso Riserva DOCG and the Sagrantino DOCG of Montefalco. The region has four **wine routes** (*strade del vino*): the Strada del Sagrantino, around Montefalco; the Strada dei Vini del Cantico between Todi, Perugia, Torgiano, Spello and Assisi; the Strada del Vino Colli del Trasimeno; and the Strada dei Vini Etrusco-Romano, in the province of Terni.

pavement cafés, this is one of Italy's greatest people-watching streets, packed from dawn through to the early hours with a parade of tourists, students and trendsetters.

The Duomo

Piazza IV Novembre • Mon–Sat 7.30am–12.30pm & 3.30–7pm, Sun 8am–12.45pm & 4–7pm, except during services • Free

Austere and huge, **Piazza IV Novembre** – once a Roman reservoir and now the old town's main focus – is backed by the unfinished ridged facade of the fifteenth-century **Duomo**. The original intention was to cover it with pink and white scalloped lozenges, but this never happened – there is, however, a trial section around the door, along with the diminutive Cosmati pulpit from which San Bernardino di Siena preached to the Perugini in 1425.

While the cathedral's Baroque interior is big, it's pretty small on works of art, though the curious might like to see what is supposed to be the Virgin's "wedding ring", an unwieldy piece of agate that allegedly changes colour according to the character of the person wearing it. Sadly, there is no chance to test it – it is kept behind a heavy metal grille in the chapel almost immediately to your right as you enter, locked up in fifteen boxes fitted into one another like Russian dolls, each opened with a key held by a different person. In one of the transepts there's an urn holding the ashes of Pope Martin IV, who died in the city after eating too many eels. Urban IV's remains are here too – he was reputedly poisoned with *aquetta*, an imaginative brew made by rubbing white arsenic into pork fat and distilling the unpleasantness that oozes out.

Fontana Maggiore

The centrepiece of Piazza IV Novembre is the **Fontana Maggiore**, designed in the thirteenth century to celebrate the completion of an aqueduct that brought fresh water

to the city from a mountain spring 8km away. It was created by the father-and-son team Nicola and Giovanni Pisano, with sculptures and bas-reliefs depicting episodes from the Old Testament, classical myth, Aesop's fables and the twelve months of the year on the two polygonal basins. By some canny design work they never line up directly, encouraging you to walk round the fountain chasing a point of repose that never comes.

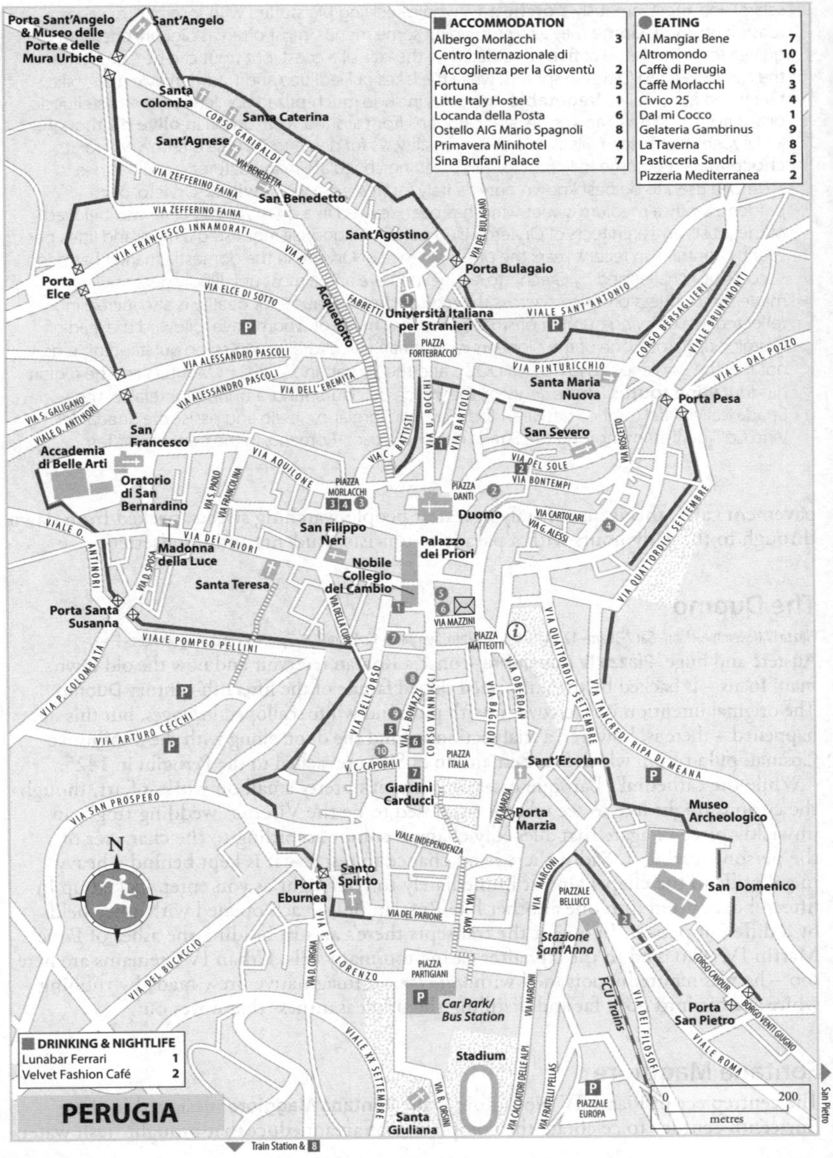

PERUGIA

ACCOMMODATION

Albergo Morlacchi	3
Centro Internazionale di Accoglienza per la Gioventù	2
Fortuna	5
Little Italy Hostel	1
Locanda della Posta	6
Ostello AIG Mario Spagnoli	8
Primavera Minihotel	4
Sina Brufani Palace	7

EATING

Al Mangiar Bene	7
Altromondo	10
Caffè di Perugia	6
Caffè Morlacchi	3
Civico 25	4
Dal mi Cocco	1
Gelateria Gambrinus	9
La Taverna	8
Pasticceria Sandri	5
Pizzeria Mediterranea	2

DRINKING & NIGHTLIFE

Lunabar Ferrari	1
Velvet Fashion Café	2

THE PERUGIA CITTÀ MUSEO CARD

The **Perugia Città Museo Card** (€14 for 48hr; perugiacittamuseo.it) covers twelve major museums and sights in Perugia, including all those mentioned in this chapter; it is valid for five sights and includes admission for one adult and one child under the age of 18. Students are eligible for the U card, also valid for five sights (€10; one month). If you are staying in Perugia for any length of time, and intend to visit lots of museums, the C1 and C2 cards give access to all museums for a year; C1 is for individuals and costs €20, C2 for families and costs €35. Audio and video guides are supplied free of charge at the sights, plus there are discounts at several restaurants in town. Buy the card online, at the tourist office or at participating sights.

Palazzo dei Priori

Just opposite the Duomo on Piazza IV Novembre, and decidedly outdoing it in terms of architectural panache, rises the exquisite Gothic **Palazzo dei Priori**, often – and rightly – described as one of the greatest public palaces in Italy. Sheer bulk aside, it's certainly impressive – with rows of trefoil windows from which convicted criminals were once thrown to their deaths, a majestic Gothic doorway and business-like Guelph crenellations – though the overall effect is rather forbidding; its real beauty derives from the harmony set up by the medieval buildings around it.

Sala dei Notari

Tues–Sat 9.30am–1pm & 3–7pm, Sun 9.30am–1pm; closed at concerts and conventions • Free

The lawyers' meeting hall, the **Sala dei Notari**, at the top of the fan-shaped steps, is noted for its frescoes portraying scenes from the Bible, Aesop's fables and the coats of arms of medieval civic worthies: lots of colour, fancy flags, swirls and no substance – but certainly worth a glance.

Nobile Collegio della Mercanzia

Corso Vannucci 15 • March–Oct Tues–Sat 9am–1pm & 2.30–5.30pm, Sun 9am–1pm; Nov–Feb Tues, Thurs & Fri 8am–2pm, Wed & Sat 8am–4.30pm, Sun 9am–1pm • €1.50 or Perugia Città Museo Card • 075 573 0366

The small **Nobile Collegio della Mercanzia** lies on the Corso side of the palace, hidden behind an innocuous door. The seat of the Merchants' Guild, its walls and vaults are covered entirely with astonishingly intricate fifteenth-century inlaid wood panelling. The decision to have wooden walls instead of the more usual frescoes was not merely aesthetic – wood was far more expensive, and thus provided a subtle way for the Guild to flaunt their wealth and power.

Nobile Collegio di Cambio

Corso Vannucci 25 • Mon–Sat 9am–12.30pm & 2.30–5.30pm, Sun 9am–1pm; Nov–March closed Mon pm • €4.50, or Perugia Città Museo Card • 075 572 8599

A few doors down from Collegio della Mercanzia, the impressive **Nobile Collegio di Cambio** was the town's money exchange in medieval times. The superb frescoes on the walls were executed by Perugino at the height of his powers and are considered the artist's masterpiece; in true Renaissance fashion, they attempt to fuse ancient and Christian culture. Up on the door-side wall there's a famous but unremarkable self-portrait in which the artist looks like he had a bad lunch. Giannicola di Paolo frescoed the small chapel (1519) to the right of the Collegio, the last important Umbrian painter influenced by Perugino.

Galleria Nazionale dell'Umbria

Corso Vannucci 19 • Mon noon–7.30pm, Tues–Sun 8.30am–7.30pm, ticket office closes 6.30pm • €8, or Perugia Città Museo Card • 075 572 1009, gallerianazionaleumbria.it

The **Galleria Nazionale dell'Umbria** is on the upper floor of the palace complex (lift or stairs), with the entrance through its opulently carved doorway. One of central Italy's best and most charming galleries, it takes you on a romp through the history of

Umbrian painting, with masterpieces by Perugino, Pinturicchio and many others, plus one or two stunning Tuscan masterpieces (Duccio, Fra' Angelico, Piero della Francesca) thrown in for good measure. The entrance fee is worth every cent if you're the slightest bit interested in early and mid-Renaissance art.

Pozzo Etrusco

Piazza Danti 18 • April–Oct daily 10am–1.30pm & 2.30–6pm (mid Sept–Oct closed Monday afternoon); Nov–March Tues–Sun 11.30am–1.30pm & 2.30–5pm • €3, €6 combined ticket (valid for a week) with Casa Museo Palazzo Sorbello; or Perugia Città Museo Card

Just east of Piazza Danti behind the Duomo lies the entrance to the **Pozzo Etrusco**, a massive cistern – 36m deep and with a capacity of 424,000 litres – that does more than hint at the dazzling engineering and technical skills of its Etruscan builders. It held water supplies for the entire Etruscan town, and if you look carefully you can see the steps descending to the bottom – used by the Etruscans to fetch water. Visiting is good fun – especially for kids – as you enter the cistern via an underground medieval tunnel, then cross it on a vertiginous bridge.

San Severo

Piazza Raffaello-Porta Sole • April & Aug daily 10am–1.30pm & 2.30–6pm; June & July Tues–Sun 10am-6pm; May, Sept & Oct Tues–Sun 10am–1.30pm & 2.30–6pm; Nov–March Tues–Sun 11am–1.30pm & 2.30–5pm • €4or Perugia Città Museo Card

A few minutes' walk east along Via del Sole from the Pozzo Etrusco brings you to the church of **San Severo** in Piazza Raffaello, known for its painting *Holy Trinity and Saints* by **Raphael**, who spent some five years in Umbria studying with Perugino. According to Vasari, Raphael's mother wept when he was sent away to Perugia from his home in Urbino. She died in 1491, so if Vasari is correct, Raphael must have begun his apprenticeship when he was only 8 years old. *Holy Trinity and Saints* is a fascinating work, painted when he was around 23, its figures displaying the otherworldly pallor shown in paintings by the recently deceased Piero della Francesca, but with some of the same three-dimensional qualities Michelangelo would later demonstrate in the Sistine ceiling. It is the only painting by him still left in the region – Napoleon carted many of the artist's works off to France – except for a painted banner in the art gallery in Città di Castello (see page 639). Perugino, his erstwhile teacher, completed the lower third of the painting, *Six Saints*, in 1521 after Raphael's death.

Via dei Priori and around

The best streets to wander around for a feel of the old city are to the east and west of the Duomo, **Via dei Priori** being the most characteristic. Just behind the Palazzo dei

BLOODLUST IN MEDIEVAL PERUGIA

Medieval Perugia was a hell of a place to be. "The most warlike of the people of Italy", wrote the historian Sismondi, "who always preferred Mars to the Muse." Male citizens played a game (and this was for pleasure) in which two teams, thickly padded in clothes stuffed with deer hair and wearing beaked helmets, stoned each other mercilessly until the majority of the other side were dead or wounded. Children were encouraged to join in for the first two hours to promote "application and aggression".

In 1265 Perugia was also the birthplace of the **Flagellants**, who had half of Europe whipping itself into a frenzy before the movement was declared heretical. In addition to some hearty scourging they took to the streets on moonlit nights, groaning and wailing, dancing in white sheets, singing dirges and clattering human bones together, all as expiation for sin and the wrongs of the world. Then there were the infamous **Baglioni**, the medieval family who misruled the city for several generations, their spellbinding history – full of vendetta, incest and mass slaughter – the stuff of great medieval soap opera.

Priori in **Via della Gabbia** there once hung a large iron cage used to imprison thieves and sometimes even clergy. You can still make out long spikes on some of the lower walls, used as hooks for the heads of executed criminals.

Madonna della Luce

West along Via dei Priori, on the north side beyond the medieval Torre degli Scirri, is the rarely open **Madonna della Luce**, little more than a chapel dominated by an impressive altarpiece by G.B. Caporali, a follower of Perugino. The church takes its name from the story that in 1513 a young barber swore so profusely on losing at cards that a Madonna in a wayside shrine closed her eyes in horror and kept them closed for four days. The miracle prompted celebrations, processions and the building of a new church.

Oratorio di San Bernardino and the ruins of San Francesco

Piazza di San Francesco al Prato • Daily 8.30am–12.30pm & 3.30–5.30pm • Free

Some way beyond the Madonna della Luce, the street bears right towards Agostino di Duccio's colourful **Oratorio di San Bernardino**, whose richly embellished facade (1461) is far and away the best piece of sculpture in the city. To the north is what's left of **San Francesco**, once a colossal church, now ruined by centuries of earthquakes, but with a curiously jumbled and striking facade still just about standing.

The university and Arco di Augusto

From the church of San Francesco, the rather uninspiring Via Alessandro Pascoli passes beneath the much-photographed Acquedotto (a raised walkway from the old centre to the north of the city – well worth taking for the views) and past the ugly university buildings, to the **Università Italiana per Stranieri** (Ⓦunistrapg.it) in the Palazzo Gallenga, at Piazza Fortebraccio 4, one of Italy's most prestigious centres of learning for foreigners.

The big patched-up gateway on one side of the piazza is the **Arco di Augusto**, its lowest section one of the few remaining monuments of Etruscan Perugia. The Romans added the upper remnant when they captured the city in 40 BC.

Sant'Agostino

Corso Garibaldi-Piazza Luppatelli • **Church** Daily 10am–1pm & 5.30–7.30pm; public holidays 8.30am–12.30pm • Free • **Oratorio** Visits Mon–Sat 9am–noon plus Mon & Wed 3.30–5.30pm by advance booking only • Ⓣ 075 572 4815

About a minute's walk north of the university is **Sant'Agostino**, once Romanesque, now botched Baroque and filled with wistful signs explaining what paintings used to hang in the church before they were spirited to France by light-fingered Napoleonic troops. The church, however, is not entirely ruined: there's a beautiful choir (probably based on a drawing by Perugino) and a couple of patches of fresco on the left-hand (north) wall, giving a tantalizing idea of how the place must once have looked. Next door to the north side is the fifteenth-century **Oratorio di Sant'Agostino**, its ludicrously ornate ceiling looking as if it's about to erupt in an explosion of gilt, stucco and chubby plaster cherubs.

Sant'Angelo

Corso Garibaldi • Daily 9am–1pm & 3.30–6.30pm • Free

Fifteen minutes' walk up the street from Sant'Agostino is the fascinating circular fifth-century church of **Sant'Angelo**, situated in a tranquil spot (with a pretty little patch of grass and trees – perfect for picnics and siestas). It was built on the site of a circular Roman temple, itself occupying the site of an ancient Etruscan place of worship; the 24 columns are from the Roman building.

Giardini Carducci

Bustling Corso Vannucci links Piazza IV Novembre to **Piazza Italia** and the small but well-kept **Giardini Carducci**, the best place to appreciate why Henry James called Perugia the "little city of the infinite views". When the usual cloak of haze lifts on crisp winter mornings, half of Umbria is laid out before you, with the mountains of Tuscany in the distance. An **antiques fair** takes place in the gardens and piazza on the last weekend of every month.

Rocca Paolina

The site can be accessed from 6.15am to 1.45am via the escalators from the bus station at Piazza dei Partigiani on the west side of Piazza Italia, at the Porta Marzia and at Via Masi-Viale Indipendenza

During construction work on the escalator (*scala mobile*) linking Piazza Italia and the bus station on Piazza dei Partigiani, the ruins of **Rocca Paolina** – a once-enormous papal fortress destroyed by the Perugians at Unification – and a complex of medieval streets beneath it were unearthed below the Giardini Carducci. Now open to the public, the highlights of this amazing underground labyrinth are the medieval houses along the **Via Baglioni Sotterranea**, and the **Porta Marzia**, a gate that dates back to Etruscan times.

San Domenico

Piazza San Domenico-Piazza Giordano Bruno, Corso Cavour • Daily 7am–noon & 4–7pm • Free

Heading southeast from the Rocca Paolina along Corso Cavour, you come to **San Domenico**, Umbria's biggest church. It has a desolate and unfinished air from the outside, but it's also appealing in a big and rather melancholy sort of way. The original Romanesque interior collapsed in the sixteenth century and the Baroque replacement is vast, cold and bare. Like Sant'Agostino, however, it's full of hints as to how beautiful it must once have been – nowhere more so than in the fourth chapel on the right, where a superb **carved arch** by Agostino di Duccio is spoilt only by a doll-like Madonna. In the east transept, to the right of the altar, is the **tomb of Pope Benedict XI** (1324), who died in Perugia from eating poisoned figs. It's an elegant and well-preserved piece by one of the period's three leading sculptors: Pisano, Lorenzo Maitani or Arnolfo di Cambio, no one knows which. There's also another good choir, together with some impressive **stained-glass** windows – the second biggest in Italy after those in Milan's Duomo.

Museo Archeologico Nazionale dell'Umbria

Piazza Giordano Bruno 10-Convento di San Domenico • Mon 10am–7.30pm, Tues–Sun 8.30am–7.30pm • €5, or Perugia Città Museo Card • ☎ 075 572 7141

Housed in the cloisters of San Domenico is the **Museo Archeologico Nazionale dell'Umbria.** Before being hammered by Augustus, Perugia was a big shot in the twelve-strong Etruscan federation of cities, which is why the city has one of the most extensive Etruscan collections around. The place is definitely worth a visit, even if the Etruscans normally leave you cold, for there's far more here than the usual run of urns and funerary monuments. Particularly compelling are the Carri Etruschi di Castel San Marino, some exquisite sixth-century bronze chariots; a witty collection of eye-opening artefacts devoted to fashion and beauty in the Etruscan era; and the bewildering **Bellucci Collection**, a private hoard of charms and amulets through the ages, ranging from the obvious – lucky horseshoes – to strange and often sinister charms such as snake skins and dried animals.

San Pietro

Borgo XX Giugno 74 • Daily 8am–noon & 3.30–6pm • Free

Beyond the archeological museum and San Domenico, advertised by a rocket-shaped belltower, is the tenth-century basilica of **San Pietro**, the most idiosyncratic of all the town's churches. Tangled up in a group of buildings belonging to the university's agriculture department, the none-too-obvious entrance is through a frescoed doorway in the far left-hand corner of the first courtyard off the road. Few churches can be so sumptuously decorated: every centimetre of available space is covered in gilt, paint or marble, though a guiding sense of taste seems to have prevailed, and in the candlelit gloom it actually feels like the sacred place it's meant to be. All the woodwork is extraordinary; the **choir** has been called the best in Italy, and there is a host of works by Perugino, Fiorenzo di Lorenzo and others.

ARRIVAL AND DEPARTURE — PERUGIA

By plane Arriving by air (Ryanair flies from the UK) you'll land at the Aeroporto "San Francesco d'Assisi" (075 592 1400, airport.umbria.it), 12km east of the centre. ACAP-SULGA shuttles meet incoming flights and run to Piazza Italia (2–4 daily; 15min; €8), with intermediate stops, including Perugia's railway station; these should be booked in advance by phone (075 500 9641). Umbria Mobilità (UM) runs the #E007 service to Assisi (currently 1 daily at 9.54am; €3). A taxi to central Perugia should cost around €30. Florence (see page 545) and Rome's Fiumicino airport (see page 91) are other options; there are four direct SULGA buses to Perugia's bus station daily from Fiumicino (2 on Sun; 3hr 45min; €22 one way).

By train Arriving on the state train network you'll find yourself southwest of the centre at Piazza Vittorio Veneto. Avoid walking into town from here – it's a steep haul on busy roads; the bus takes 15min (anything to Piazza Italia or Piazza Matteotti will do), while the Minimetrò light rail system from the Stazione Fontivegge, 50m to the left of the station exit, has shuttles every 3min and takes 11min. The second stop, "Cupa", drops you just west of the centre near Via dei Priori, while the last stop, "Pincetto", is right in the centre, off Piazza Matteotti.

Destinations Assisi (at least hourly; 20–30min); Florence (6–8 daily; 2hr–2hr 30min); Foligno (13 daily; 40min); Spello (18 daily; 30min); Terontola (16 daily; 40min); Terni (approx hourly; 1hr).

By bus Buses arrive at the terminal at Piazza dei Partigiani, from where you can jump on a *scala mobile* (escalator) as it climbs through weird subterranean medieval streets to Piazza Italia.

Destinations Assisi (3–9 daily; 35–50min); Castiglione del Lago (8–10 daily Mon–Sat; 1hr–1hr 20min); Chiusi (3 daily Mon–Sat; 1hr 35min); Città di Castello (16 daily; 1hr 30min); Florence (1 daily; 2hr–2hr 30min); Foligno (4 daily; 1hr 10min); Gubbio (10 Mon–Sat, 2 Sun; 1hr 10min); Milan (3 weekly; 6hr 50min); Norcia (1 daily; 2hr 50min); Orvieto (2 daily; 2hr 25min); Passignano (6 daily Mon–Sat; 1hr 15min); Rome (5 daily; 2hr 30min); Rome Fiumicino airport (2–4 daily; 3hr 45min); Siena (3–7 daily; 1hr 30min); Sansepolcro (16 daily; 1hr 30min); Spello (4 daily Mon–Sat; 55min); Spoleto (1–2 daily; 1hr 20min); Terni (9 daily; 1hr 40min); Todi (4–8 daily; 1hr 10min).

By car All the town's approaches are up steep hills and the centre is closed to traffic at peak times, so you'll do best to leave your car at the main train station and take a bus. Alternatively head towards one of the big car parks – Piazza dei Partigiani is the largest and most central, or park in the free car park at Pian di Massiano just west of town and take the Minimetrò from there into the centre.

INFORMATION AND GETTING AROUND

City transport is also run by Umbria Mobilità. Tickets are valid on buses and the Minimetrò light rail system. They cost €1.50 for 1hr 10min and are available from the station newsagents and the booth outside the station; you can buy a ticket on the bus for a supplement of €0.50. A 24hr "Turistico" ticket costs €5.40, while a ten-journey ticket is €12.90.

Tourist office Piazza Matteotti 18 (daily 9am–6pm; 075 573 6458, turismo.comune.perugia.it).

PERUGIA'S FESTIVALS

The town's main cultural draw in summer is **Umbria Jazz**, Italy's foremost jazz event. This ten-day extravaganza takes place in early to mid-July and features the top names in the jazz world, performing in atmospheric venues throughout town. Tickets for big names cost around €25 or even less, and there are free events in Piazza IV Novembre and the Giardini Carducci. Book well in advance on umbriajazz.com. In mid-September, the town hosts the **Sagra Musicale Umbra** (perugiamusicaclassica.com), one of Italy's oldest music festivals, with performances of religious orchestral and choir music. In October, **Eurochocolate** (eurochocolate.com) is a large-scale celebration of the world's favourite confectionery – and Perugia's most famous export – with lessons, tasting sessions and exhibitions.

10

ACCOMMODATION

Albergo Morlacchi Via L. Tiberi 2 ⓣ075 572 0319, ⓦhotelmorlacchi.it; map p.630. This central, family-run hotel has comfortable two-star rooms with parquet floors and an eclectic collection of art on the walls. Rooms vary in size, so ask to see a few. **€77**

Centro Internazionale di Accoglienza per la Gioventù Via Bontempi 13 ⓣ075 572 2880, ⓦostello.perugia.it; map p.630. The town's original hostel is perfectly situated in a historic *palazzo* just 2min from the Duomo. It has frescoed common areas and a panoramic terrace that some of the rooms share. There are one hundred beds in four-, six- and eight-bed dorms; the key deposit is €10. Check-in 3.30pm–midnight; closed 11am–3.30pm & mid-Dec to Jan. Dorms **€17**

Fortuna Via Luigi Bonazzi 19 ⓣ075 572 2845, ⓦhotelfortunaperugia.com; map p.630. A central three-star in a historic fourteenth-century *palazzo* with frescoed ceilings in some rooms and a roof garden with good views of the old city. **€77**

Little Italy Hostel Via della Nespola 1 ⓣ075 966 1997, ⓦlittleitalyhostel.it; map p.630. A fine, modern "design" hostel housed in an ancient church, with a bright dorm room for twelve (in three-tier bunks), and a smaller room for eight (with four two-tier bunks) that costs an extra €2. Free, light breakfast. Check-in is 2–6pm, check-out 11am. Dorms **€18**

Locanda della Posta Corso Vannucci 97 ⓣ075 572 8925, ⓦlocandadellaposta.com; map p.630. Perugia's first choice if you want an upmarket treat: it's not as slick as the *Brufani* but is just as central, and the likes of Goethe and Hans Christian Andersen have once stayed in the historic building. **€230**

Ostello AIG Mario Spagnoli Via Cortonese 4, Località Pian di Massiano ⓣ075 501 1366, ⓦhihostels.com; map p.630. Down near the main station, this hostel has 186 beds in 33 four- and six-bed dorms. It has its own restaurant, and breakfast is included. Open 7am–midnight year round. Dorms **€16.10**, doubles **€42.15**

★ **Primavera Minihotel** Via Vincioli 8 ⓣ075 572 1657, ⓦprimaveraminihotel.it; map p.630. In a tranquil alley, this hotel has immaculate en-suite rooms, and the friendly staff are tirelessly helpful. Book well in advance, as it's highly popular. **€100**

Sina Brufani Palace Piazza Italia 12 ⓣ075 573 2541, ⓦbrufanipalace.com; map p.630. Perugia's smartest and most luxurious option, with an equally elegant restaurant, right in the centre of town. An unexpected bonus is the chance to swim over Etruscan ruins in the glass bottomed swimming pool. **€150**

EATING

Perugia's student population ensures that there is a plethora of reasonably priced places to eat out, from the many snack bars around the centre of town to simple trattorias serving traditional Umbrian cuisine. **Local dishes** feature wild mushrooms, truffles and game often succulently combined with home-made egg pasta. The city's liveliest **cafés** are clustered on Corso Vannucci.

CAFÉS, PASTICCERIE AND GELATERIE

Caffè di Perugia Via Mazzini 10 ⓣ075 573 1863, ⓦumbriadeisapori.it; map p.630. A pleasantly smart setting with superb vaulted ceiling from the thirteenth century, as well as lots of outdoor tables. All the café staples, plus a pricey restaurant with *secondi* at around €16, a pizzeria-grill and a wine bar, the last a good early evening retreat. Daily 7.30am–midnight.

Caffè Morlacchi Piazza Morlacchi 6–8 ⓣ075 572 1760; map p.630. This smart but student-oriented café-bar is a pleasant place to hang out during the day, though it's also tempting in the evening when it has occasional live music. Mon–Fri 7.30am–midnight, Sun 10am–midnight. Closed Sat.

Gelateria Gambrinus Via Bonazzi 3 ⓣ075 573 5620, ⓦgelateriagambrinus.it; map p.630. Queues from this ice cream parlour off the Corso often stretch onto the nearby Piazza della Repubblica, especially at the height of the Sun *passeggiata*. A great choice of flavours and very generous scoops. Daily 11am–late.

★ **Pasticceria Sandri** Corso Vannucci 32 ⓣ075 572 4112, ⓦsandridal1860.it; map p.630. Atmospheric, old-world café with a wonderful frescoed ceiling in a perfect position on the main street near the Palazzo dei Priori – a high spot for the sweet-toothed. Sun–Wed 7.30am–9pm, Thurs 7.30am–10pm, Fri 7.30am–11pm, Sat 7.30am–midnight.

RESTAURANTS

★ **Al Mangiar Bene** Via della Luna 21 ⓣ075 573 1047, ⓦalmangiarbene.it; map p.630. Tucked away down a flight of steps off Corso Vannucci, this lovely, brick-vaulted space is a rare find: all organic, with produce sourced from local farms. Sauces for a choice of pastas start from €6 (with pizzas available in the evening only from just €5), while a full and very tasty meal with wine will set you back around €35. Tues–Sat 12.30–2.45pm & 7.30–10.45pm, Mon 7.30–10.30pm. Closed Sun.

Altromondo Via Cesare Caporali 11 ⓣ075 572 6157, ⓦristorante-altromondo-perugia.it; map p.630. Well-priced, traditional Umbrian cooking in a brick-vaulted, airy space. Try *papperdelle* in a juniper-berry spiked wild boar *ragù*, hand-made stuffed *agnolotti*, or the beef tagliata, slices of grilled steak with rocket and tomatoes. *Primi* cost from €9, mains from €12. Mon–Sat noon–3pm & 7–10pm.

Civico 25 Via della Viola 25 ⓣ075 571 6376, ⓦcivico25.com; map p.630. Wine bar with food close to the Università degli Stranieri, great for a glass of wine with a

bruschetta of fava beans, chickpeas or chicken liver pâté, or for a full meal. Dishes on the short menu might include gnocchi with goose *ragù* (or truffle in season), or pasta with fava beans, *guanciale* ham and pecorino. Expect to pay around €35 for a full meal. Mon–Sat 7.30pm–midnight.

Dal mi Cocco Corso Garibaldi 12 ⓣ075 573 2511; map p.630. Simple, decent and amazingly good value, this serves a variety of two-course daily set menus at €13/head plus drinks. Tues–Sun 1–2.15pm & 8.30–10pm.

La Taverna Via delle Streghe 8 ⓣ075 572 4128, ⓦristorantelataverna.com; map p.630. Locals have long patronized this quite formal, rather plain-looking restaurant for its fine, great-value food, but recently tourists have followed suit, meaning that it's now essential to book. There are some outside tables, and the menu offers plenty of Umbrian staples, including truffles and sausages, but also ventures further afield with the odd fish dish and an Italian take on chicken curry. Allow around €30/person for a meal without wine. Daily 7.30–11pm.

Pizzeria Mediterranea Piazza Piccinino 11 ⓣ075 572 4021; map p.630. Simple and tasteful pizzeria with a small wood-fired oven and a couple of brick-vaulted rooms, a few steps beyond the entrance to the Pozzo Etrusco. It has over 25 varieties (from €5 for a Margherita), including the children's crowd-pleaser Nutella pizza. Daily 12.30–2.30pm & 7.30–11pm.

10

DRINKING & NIGHTLIFE

Lunabar Ferrari Via Scura 1 ⓣ075 572 2966; map p.630. Just off Corso Vannucci, this stylish bar attracts an equally stylish crowd. There's moody lighting, a lively *aperitivo* hour (6–9.30pm), DJs and regular theme nights, such as Mojito Night on Fri. There's also an equally contemporary attached restaurant-pizzeria. Daily 8.30am–1.30am.

Velvet Fashion Café Viale Roma 20 ⓣ075 572 1321; map p.630. Perugia's most central club. Smart dining, drinking and occasional live music. Fri-Sun 10.30pm–4.30am.

Lago Trasimeno

The most tempting destination around Perugia – whose surroundings are generally pretty lacklustre – is **LAGO TRASIMENO**, an ideal spot to hole up in for a few days, particularly if you want to get in some swimming, windsurfing or sailing. The lake is about 30km from Perugia and is easy to get to on public transport. It's the biggest inland stretch of water on the Italian peninsula, and, though you wouldn't think so to look at it, never deeper than 7m – hence lovely warm water in summer.

A winning combination of tree-covered hills to the north, Umbria's subtle light and placid lapping water produces some magical moments, but on overcast and squally days the mood can turn melancholy. Not all the reed-lined shore is uniformly pretty, either; steer clear of the northern coast and head for the stretches south of Magione and Castiglione if you're after relative peace and quiet.

ON THE TRAIL OF HANNIBAL

Somewhere along the Lago Trasimeno shore towards the rambling village of Tuoro, probably at Sanguineto ("the Place of Blood") or Ossaia ("the Place of Bones"), is the spot where the Romans suffered their famous clobbering at the hands of the Carthaginian general **Hannibal** in 217 BC. Hannibal was headed for Rome, having just crossed the Alps, when he was met by a Roman force under the Consul Flaminius. Things might have gone better for Flaminius if he'd heeded the omens that piled up on the morning of battle: first he fell off his horse; next the legionary standards had to be dug out of the mud; and finally – and this really should have raised suspicions – the sacred chickens refused their breakfast. (Poultry accompanied all Roman armies and, by some means presumably known to the legionnaire in charge of chickens, communicated the will of the gods to waiting commanders in the field.) Hannibal lured Flaminius into a masterful ambush, with the only escape a muddy retreat into the lake. Sixteen thousand Romans, including the hapless commander, were killed.

A hard-to-find drive and **walkway** have been laid out, starting and finishing just west of Tuoro on the road to Cortona, which take in salient features of the old battlefield; Tuoro's irregularly open Pro Loco office or its website (Piazza Garibaldi 7; ⓣ075 825 220, ⓦprolocotuoroturismosultrasimeno.it) has information on the site, walkway and drive, and occasionally offers guided tours.

ACTIVITIES ON LAGO TRASIMENO

There are plenty of activities on offer from operators based in Castiglione del Lago, including **windsurfing** (contact Club Velico at ⓣ075 953 035, ⓦcvcastiglionese.it), **canoeing**, **waterskiing** and **horseriding** (ask at the tourist office for recommended operators). You can **rent bikes** at Cicli Valentini (Via Firenze 68/B; Mon–Sat 9am–1pm & 4–8pm; ⓣ075 951 663, ⓦciclivalentini.it).

10

Passignano

Strung out along the northern shore, **PASSIGNANO**, a newish town with a medieval heart, is the lake's most accessible point. In summer it can get a bit clogged with traffic, and in the evenings the joint is jumping, with bars, discos and fish restaurants aplenty. The most compelling reason to come, however, is to take the daily boat to Isola Polvese (see below).

Castiglione del Lago

CASTIGLIONE DEL LAGO is the most appealing town on the lake and cuts a fine silhouette from other points around the shore, jutting out into the water on a fortified promontory. A friendly, unpretentious place, Castiglione has enough charm and action to hold anyone's interest for a couple of days, and has plenty of activities available (see page 638). The best of the little **beaches** is at the public lido on the southern side of Castiglione's promontory, with pedaloes for rent. If you want to visit one of the islands on the lake, regular boats make the half-hour trip over to Isola Maggiore.

The islands

The lake's islands include the largely uninhabited **Isola Polvese**, where you can stay at the outstanding *Fattoria* (see page 639), and **Isola Maggiore**, which makes a fun excursion from Castiglione del Lago if you don't mind the summer crowds. There's a pretty walk round the edge of the latter island, and a popular **hotel-restaurant**, *Da Sauro* (see page 639).

ARRIVAL AND DEPARTURE — LAGO TRASIMENO

PASSIGNANO

By train Passignano is served by roughly hourly trains from Perugia (30min) and TerontolaCortona. (10min).

By bus There are six daily buses from Perugia.

CASTIGLIONE DEL LAGO

By train Castiglione del Lago is served by from Terontola-Cortona (6–8min) and Chiusi–Chianciano Terme.

Destinations Arezzo (hourly; 30min); Florence (hourly; 1hr 50min); Rome (9 daily; 2hr 5min).

By bus There are eight or nine buses daily from Perugia.

THE ISLANDS

By boat There are boats (ⓦtrasimeno.ws) to Isola Polvese from Passignano (1 daily; 55 min) and from San Feliciano (10 daily; 10 min; €6 return), on the lake's eastern shore (10 daily; €6 return). Boats to Isola Maggiore run from Castiglione del Lago (6–7 daily; 30min; €8.10 return) and Passignano (2 daily; 45min).

ACCOMMODATION AND EATING

CASTIGLIONE DEL LAGO

Aganoor Via Vittorio Emanuele 91 ⓣ075 953 837, ⓦhotelaganoor.it. Attached to *La Cantina* restaurant, this three-star hotel has comfortable, traditionally styled rooms, as well as a rooftop solarium with lovely views. Ask for one of the four rooms with lake views, but book at least a year in advance for a chance of a room between May and September. **€80**

Badiaccia Via Pratovecchia 91, Località Badiaccia ⓣ075 965 9097, ⓦbadiaccia.com. Most of Castiglione del Lago's campsites are off the main road some way north or south of the town. This is the most highly rated, with excellent and very well maintained facilities, plus a large sandy beach. There are chalets and caravans as well as tent pitches. Pitches **€24**, chalets (four people) **€70**

L'Acquario Via Vittorio Emanuele II 69 ⓣ075 965 2432, ⓦristorantelacquario.it. This is the place to eat game, fish

fresh from the lake and other local dishes, on the old town's single main street. Try lake prawns with almonds and leeks, or duck with figs and raspberry balsamic, and expect to pay around €38 a head for a full meal. Daily 12–2.30pm & 7–10.30pm; closed Wed Sept–June, & periods in Jan & Feb.

La Torre Via Vittorio Emanuele 50 ⓣ075 951 666, ⓦwww.latorretrasimeno.com. A friendly, family-run three-star hotel right on the main street with comfortable, if rather dated, rooms. Doubles €73

ISOLA POLVESE

Fattoria Il Poggio ⓣ075 965 9550, ⓦfattoria isolapolvese.com. Island accommodation with lovely views of the lake, and four- and six-bed dorms (some with private bathroom), doubles and mini-apartments. The restaurant uses produce from the garden, and offers superb value home-cooked food.. It's popular with school groups – so weekdays in April and May are best avoided by those seeking peace and quiet. Check the website for details of weekends devoted to yoga, reiki, canoeing and fishing with the lake's fishermen. Dorm €25, doubles €55, apartments €85

ISOLA MAGGIORE

Da Sauro Via G. Guglielmi 1 ⓣ075 826 168, ⓦdasauro.it. Good, popular rather old-fashioned three-star hotel with plain rooms, which also has a fine restaurant with some good value set meals. €75

10

Città di Castello

CITTÀ DI CASTELLO is a charming and relatively little-visited town 56km north of Perugia in the Upper Tiber Valley, with a sedate and ordered medieval centre that's well worth a few hours. It's also the focus for holidaymakers staying in the many rented villas and farmhouses in the hills to the east and west. In late August and early September the town becomes busier than usual during its renowned **Festival delle Nazioni** (ⓣ075 852 2823, ⓦfestivalnazioni.com), focusing on chamber music and dedicated to a different country each year.

Once an important Roman centre – of which the gridiron of streets is virtually the only legacy – today the town preserves just a handful of fairly mediocre medieval monuments. Its main attractions are its museums and art galleries, along with some quiet, pleasant medieval streets.

Pinacoteca

Via della Cannoniera 22/A • April–Oct daily 10am–1pm & 2.30–6.30pm; Nov–March Tues–Sun 10am–1pm & 3–6pm • €6 • ⓣ0758 554 202

Foremost among the town's museums is the **Pinacoteca** at the southern edge of town, one of the region's best art galleries after Perugia's. The collection makes up in quality what it lacks in quantity, taking in works by **Raphael**, **Signorelli**, **Ghirlandaio** and **Lorenzetti**, plus a wondrous *Maestà* by the anonymous fourteenth-century Maestro di Città di Castello. There are also several sculptures, the most notable by Ghiberti, and a glittering reliquary of Florentine origin, dating from 1420.

Museo del Duomo and Campanile Cilindrico

Piazza Gabriotti 3/A • April–Sept Tues–Sun 10am–1pm & 3–6.30pm; Oct–March Tues–Sun 10am–1pm & 3–5.30pm • €6 combined ticket with Campanile Cilindrico • ⓦmuseoduomocdc.it

The banal, reworked **Duomo** warrants a call for its smart twelve-room museum, the **Museo del Duomo**, entered to the right of the church. It contains a completely unexpected collection of big-name paintings, including major works by Rosso Fiorentino, Giulio Romano and Pinturicchio. Even better is the **Treasure of Canoscio**, a precious hoard of sixth-century silver chalices dug up in 1932.

Nearby in Via del Modello, signposted from the Duomo, the **Campanile Cilindrico** (Tues–Sun 10am–1pm & 3.30–6pm; open daily in Aug; €4, or €7 combined ticket with Museo del Duomo) is a round belltower that's worth the climb for its fine views.

10

Collezione Tessile di Tela Umbra

Via Sant'Antonio 3 • Mon 9am–noon, Tues–Sat 9am–noon & 3.30–6.30pm, Sun 10am–1pm & 3.30–6.30pm • €3.50 • T 075 855 4337, W telaumbra.it.

Just east of Piazza Matteotti, the town's central main square, the fascinating **Collezione Tessile di Tela Umbra** traces the history of textiles in the Upper Tiber Valley, though in many ways the more interesting part of the concern is the original workshop, which continues to employ local women and still – almost uniquely in Italy – uses traditional handworked looms.

Fondazione Palazzo Albizzini

Palazzo Albizzini Via Albizzini 1 • Tues–Sat: April–Sept 9.30am–12.30pm & 2.30–6.30pm, Sun 10.30am–12.30pm & 3–7pm; Oct–March 9.30am–1pm & 2.30–6pm, Sun 10.30am–12.30pm & 3–6pm • **Ex Seccatoi del Tobacco** Via Pierucci • April–Sept same hours; open only to groups the rest of the year • €10 joint ticket • T 075 855 9848, W fonazioneburri.org

Just north of the Collezione Tessile off Piazza Garibaldi is the **Palazzo Albizzini**, home to the **Collezione Burri**, an extensive collection of large sculptural works by local-born artist Alberto Burri, one of the most significant figures of twentieth-century Italian art. Some of Burri's larger works are housed in the distinctive and colossal buildings of the **Ex Seccatoi del Tobacco** (same ticket), a former tobacco factory in the south of the town.

Centro delle Tradizioni Popolari

Località Garavelle • Tues–Sun: April–Oct 9am–12.30pm & 3–6.30pm; Nov–March 9am–12.30pm & 2.30–6pm • €3.70 • Bus from Piazza Garibaldi (5 daily)

A couple of kilometres south of Città di Castello in the hamlet of **Garavelle** is one of Umbria's best folk museums, the **Centro delle Tradizioni Popolari**. It's located in an eighteenth-century farmhouse, preserved with all the accoutrements of daily life – pots, pans, furniture and so forth, plus a range of exhibits covering rural activities such as wine making and weaving.

ARRIVAL AND INFORMATION — CITTÀ DI CASTELLO

By train The train station is east of the *centro storico*, outside the old walls. Città di Castello is on the UM (or FCU) line.
Destinations Perugia (approx. hourly; 1hr 20min); Sansepolcro (approx. hourly; 20min).

By bus Buses arrive at Piazza Garibaldi, inside the walls on the eastern side of town. There are regular connections with Arezzo, Florence, Urbino, Gubbio, Todi and Rome.

By car There is a large, free car park just outside the walls to the west of town.

Tourist office Corso Cavour 5 (Mon–Fri 8.30am–1.30pm & 3–6pm, Sat & Sun 9.30am–12.30pm; T 075 855 4922, W cittadicastelloturismo.it); the office deals with the whole Upper Tiber region. Another useful website is the local council's wcittadicastello.infoaltaumbria.it, in English and Italian, with detailed walking and cycling routes, as well as guides to sights in and around Città di Castello.

ACCOMMODATION

Residenza Antica Canonica Via S. Florido 23 T 075 852 3398, W anticacanonica.it. Restored apartments in a Renaissance *palazzo* right next to the Museo del Duomo, tastefully furnished and with wood beams and frescoes in some rooms. **€70**

Tiferno Piazza Raffaello Sanzio 13 T 075 855 0331, W hoteltiferno.it. Centrally located four-star where the large, traditionally styled rooms have Alberto Burri prints on the walls. There are even some originals in the common areas. **€140**

EATING AND DRINKING

Il Cacciatore Via della Braccina 10 T 075 852 0882. Downstairs in a medieval cellar, this traditionally styled *osteria* has a daily changing menu of simple regional dishes (*secondi* from €8). Wed–Sun 12.30–2.30pm.

L'Accademia Via del Modello 1 T 075 852 3120. Come for a glass of wine and *aperitivo* snacks on the long counter in the front room, or for dinner upstairs. There are local salami and heavenly unpasteurized cheeses, home-made bread with onion, fennel seeds or hazelnuts, and a great choice of handmade pasta – try it stuffed with pork and dressed with *pancetta* and lemon. A full meal without wine will cost around €30. Daily noon–2pm & 8–11pm.

La Lea Via San Florido 38/A ⓣ075 852 1678, ⓦtrattorialea.com. A locals' favourite a short way south of the cathedral, with mains from €9 and a good selection of tasty *primi* from €7. Go for simple dishes like sausages or a *cotoletta* if you're on a budget; otherwise spend a bit more to have the grilled lamb, or, in season, a steak with porcini mushrooms. Tues–Sun 12.30–2.30pm & 7.30–10pm; closed for a period mid-July to mid-Aug.

Gubbio

GUBBIO is the most thoroughly medieval of the Umbrian towns, an immediately likeable place that's hung on to its charm despite an ever-increasing influx of visitors. The streets are picture-book pretty, with houses of rosy-pink stone and seas of orange-tiled roofs; the setting is equally gorgeous with the forest-clad mountains of the Apennines rearing up behind. A broad and largely unspoilt plain stretches out in front of the town, and the whole ensemble – especially on grey, windswept days – maintains Gubbio's tough, mountain-outpost atmosphere.

The town was once a powerful medieval *Comune*, always important as the gateway to Ravenna and the Adriatic and a key point on the Roman Via Flaminia. Buses arrive in the **Piazza dei Quaranta Martiri** at the foot of town, named in memory of forty citizens shot by the Germans in 1944, a reprisal for partisan attacks in the surrounding hills. It's a ten-minute walk uphill from here to the central **Piazza Grande** and Gubbio's main sights.

Palazzo dei Consoli

Centre-stage on the old town's main Piazza Grande is the immense and austere fourteenth-century **Palazzo dei Consoli**, whose crenelated outline and 98m-high campanile immediately grab your attention. Probably designed by Matteo Gattapone, who was also responsible for Spoleto's Ponte delle Torri, the palace took a couple of hundred years to build and required the levelling of vast tracts of the medieval town, mainly to accommodate the huge and windswept Piazza Grande.

Palazzo dei Consoli Museums

Piazza Grande 1 • Daily: April–Oct 10am–1pm & 3–6pm (occasional extended hours June–Aug); Nov–March 10am–1pm & 2.30–5.30pm • €5

Palazzo dei Consoli is home to Gubbio's **museum** collections. The highlight is the **Museo Archeologico,** where the prize exhibit is the famous **Eugubine Tablets**, Umbria's most important archeological find. Discovered in 1444 by an illiterate shepherd, later conned into swapping his priceless treasure-trove for a worthless piece of land, the seven bronze tablets are more or less the only extant record of the ancient Umbrian language, containing for the most part details of sacrifices and other religious rituals. Gubbio was close to the shrine of the so-called Apennine Jove, a major pagan deity visited by pilgrims from all over Italy, so the tablets were probably the work of Roman and Etruscan priests taking advantage of the established order to impose their religious cults in a region where their languages weren't understood. Most importantly, they suggest Romans, Etruscans and Umbrians achieved some sort of coexistence, refuting a long-held belief that succeeding civilizations wiped one another out.

Admission to the museum also gets you into the **Pinacoteca** at the top of the palace, worth a look for works by the Gubbian School – one of central Italy's earliest, and a collection of ponderous fourteenth-century furniture.

Palazzo Pretorio

Piazza Grande 9 • Not usually open to the public

The **Palazzo Pretorio** was built to the same plan as the Palazzo dei Consoli. Deliberately dominating and humbling, it was what medieval civic pride was all about, an attempt to express power and supremacy in bricks and mortar. Behind

a plain, square facade (there's a small hole top-right where criminals were hung in a cage called *la gogna* – from *vergogna* or "shame") is a cavernous baronial hall, the **Salone dell'Arengo**, where council officials and leading citizens met to discuss business; the word "harangue" derives from *arengo*, suggesting proceedings frequently boiled over. The *palazzo* still houses the town's *Comune* and is only rarely open to visitors.

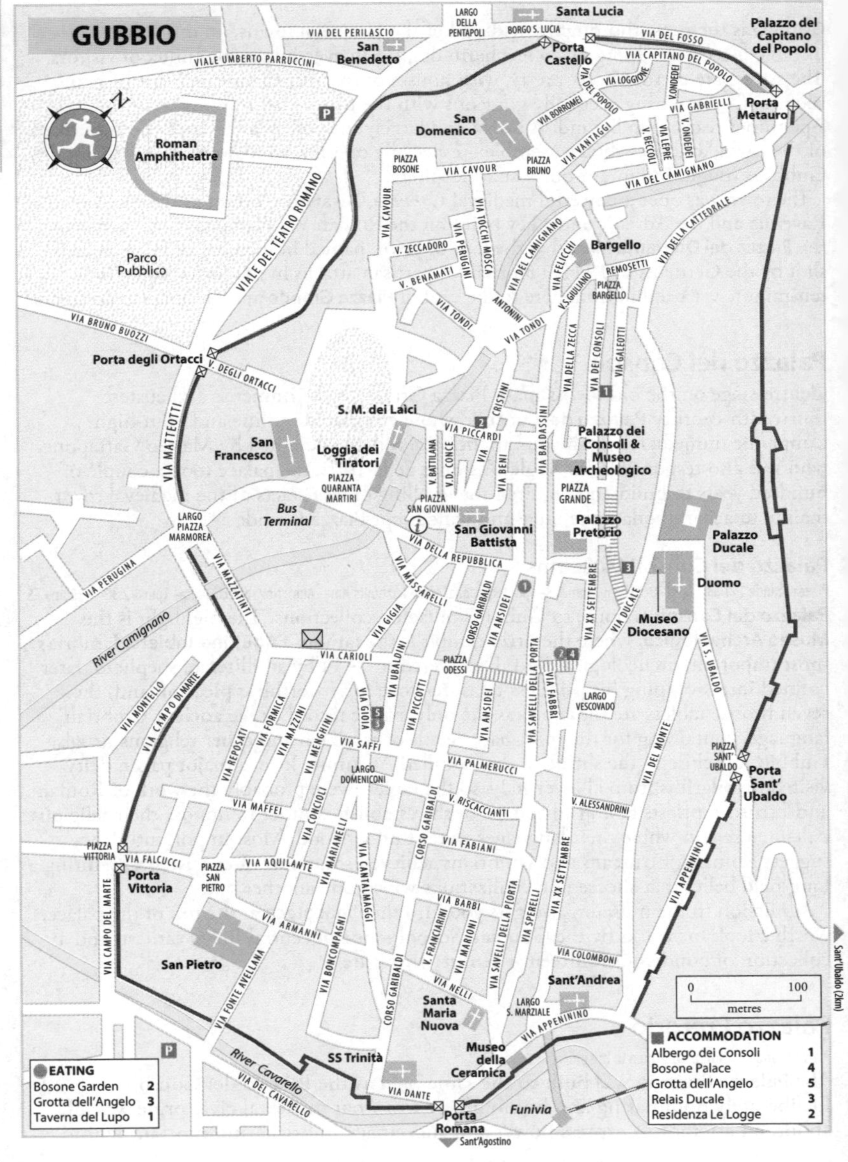

GUBBIO'S DOORS OF DEATH

No one can quite agree on the origins of Gubbio's **Porte della Morte**, the "doors of death". Almost unique to the town (there are a few others in Assisi and southern France), these are narrow, bricked-up doorways wedged into the facades of its medieval townhouses (with the best examples in Via dei Consoli). The party line is that they were used to carry a coffin out of a house, and then, having been tainted with death, were sealed up out of superstitious fear. Nice theory, and very Italian, but judging by the constricted stairways behind the doors, their purpose was probably defensive – the main door could be barricaded, leaving the more easily defended passageway as the only entrance.

The Duomo

Duomo Via Ducale • Daily 9.30am–5pm; closes earlier in winter • Free • **Museo Diocesano** Via Federico da Montefeltro 22 • April–Sept daily 9.30am–5.30pm; Oct–March daily 10am–5pm • €5 • Ⓦ museogubbio.it

To the northeast of the Piazza Grande lurks a not very inspiring thirteenth-century **Duomo**, partly redeemed by the odd fresco, twelfth-century stained glass, and some arches gracefully curved, apparently to emulate the meeting of hands in prayer. There are also a pair of carved **organ lofts** that for once don't look as if they'd be more at home in a fairground. The adjoining **Museo Diocesano**, to the right as you face the facade at the corner of Via Federico da Montefeltro, is well worth a few minutes, mainly for a florid Flemish cope, presented to the cathedral by Pope Marcellus II, who was born in Gubbio.

Museo di Palazzo Ducale (MAD)

Via Federico da Montefeltro • Tues–Sun 8.30am–7.30pm, ticket office closes 30min earlier • €5

The plain-faced Gothic cathedral is overshadowed by the **Palazzo Ducale** opposite, built over an earlier Lombard palace by the Dukes of Montefeltro as a scaled-down copy of their more famous palace in Urbino. The **courtyard** is particularly attractive, but the interior, stripped of most of its original furniture and other trappings, is a trifle dull, despite some fine views from the windows and the harmonious scale of the rooms. The *palazzo* is often used to host temporary exhibitions.

Via dei Consoli

There are dozens of picturesque odds and ends around the streets, which are as wonderfully explorable as any in the region. Along **Via dei Consoli** – the main medieval street (and home to most of the ceramic shops) – it's worth tracking down the **Bargello**, the medieval police station. This also gives you the chance to survey the adjacent **Fontana dei Matti** (the "fountain of the mad"), unremarkable but for the tradition that anyone walking round it three times will end up mad.

Basilica di Sant'Ubaldo

Summer daily 10am–12.30pm & 2.30–5.30pm; winter same hours but closed Tues & Wed mornings • Free

On the Colle Eletto hill above the town stands the **Basilica di Sant'Ubaldo**, which has some great views. There's not much to see in the basilica itself, except the body of the town's patron saint, St Ubaldo, missing three fingers – they were hacked off by his manservant as a religious keepsake. You can't miss the big wooden pillars (*ceri*) featured in Gubbio's annual **Corsa dei Ceri** (see box).

There are several ways up to the basilica, one being via the steep track that strikes off from behind the Duomo. However, it's quicker and far more fun – unless you have no head for heights – to take the cable car (see below). If you are feeling energetic, climb up to the **Rocca**, the remains of the medieval fortress above the basilica, with views right across town to the first-century-BC **Roman theatre** on the outskirts.

10

THE CORSA DEI CERI

Little known outside Italy but second only to Siena's Palio in terms of exuberance and bizarre pageantry, the **Corsa dei Ceri** (ceri.it) takes place on May 15 every year. The rules and rigmarole of the 900-year-old ceremony are mind-boggling, but they boil down to three teams racing from Piazza della Signoria to the basilica, carrying the *ceri* (huge wooden pillars, each representing a different saint) on wooden stretchers. By iron-clad tradition, the *cero* of St Ubaldo always wins, the other teams having to ensure they're in the basilica before the doors are shut by the leaders. The main event starts at 6pm.

The Funivia Colle Eletto

Via San Girolamo • March Mon–Sat 10am–1.15pm & 2.30–5.30pm, Sun till 6pm; April & May Mon–Sat 10am–1.15pm & 2.30–6.30pm, Sun till 7pm; June Mon–Sat 9.30am–1.15pm & 2.30–7pm, Sun 9am–7.30pm; July to mid-Sept daily 9am–8pm; mid-Sept to end Sept Mon–Sat 9.30am–1.15pm & 2.30–7pm, Sun 9am–7.30pm; Oct daily 10am–1.15pm & 2.30–6pm; Nov–Feb daily except Wed 10am–1.15pm & 2.30–5pm • €4 one way, €5 return • funiviagubbio.it

The **cable car** to the basilica, the **Funivia Colle Eletto**, sets off from Porta Romana, over on the eastern side of town; you jump on small, open two-person metal buckets, which then dangle precariously over the woods and crags below as you shudder slowly upwards.

ARRIVAL AND INFORMATION — GUBBIO

By train The nearest train station is at Fossato di Vico, 19km south on the Rome–Foligno–Ancona line; there are connecting shuttle buses to Gubbio (10 daily Mon–Sat, 6 on Sun).

By bus Gubbio is easiest approached by the regular bus from Perugia on the mostly pretty cross-country SS298 road.
Destinations Città di Castello (change at Umbertide; 4 daily Mon–Sat; 1hr 10min); Rome (1 daily; 2hr 40min); Urbino (1 daily; 1hr 30min).

Tourist office Via della Repubblica 15 (April–Nov Mon–Fri 8.30am–1.45pm & 3.30–6.30pm, Sat 9am–1pm & 3–6.30pm, Sun 9.30am–1pm & 3–6pm; Nov–March closes 30min earlier Mon–Sat; mid-Jan to Feb closed Sun pm; 075 922 0693, comune.gubbio.pg.it). If you are in town in summer, ask for details of the (usually Classical-themed) productions at the Roman theatre (www.teatrostabile.umbria.it).

ACCOMMODATION

Albergo dei Consoli Via dei Consoli 59 075 922 0639, consoli.urbaniweb.com; map p.642. A great position just a few steps down the hill from the Palazzo dei Consoli, with comfortable rooms and a decent restaurant. The website offers some excellent-value two night sleep and eat packages. **€100**

Bosone Palace Via XX Settembre 22 075 922 0688, hotelbosone.com; map p.642. A long-established and traditional four-star hotel in a medieval palace with spectacular frescoed ceilings and lots of antiques. There's a nice restaurant, too (see below). **€100**

Grotta dell'Angelo Via Gioia 47 075 927 1747, grottadellangelo.it; map p.642. A reliable little hotel in a peaceful side street; there's also a good and moderately priced restaurant (see below). **€70**

Relais Ducale Via Galeotti 19 075 922 0157, relaisducale.com; map p.642. A classy, intimate four-star just below the cathedral. It's accessed from one of two tiny alleys – Via Ducale or Via Galleotti (signed off the east side of Piazza Grande). **€120**

Residenza Le Logge Via Piccardi 7–9 075 927 7574; map p.642. Pleasant wood-beamed rooms in a lovely medieval building give this *residenza* a homely feel, as does the garden – perfect for a post-sightseeing glass of local wine. **€90**

EATING

Gubbio boasts a good selection of **restaurants**, with some high-quality, if rather expensive, options close to the Palazzo dei Consoli. Cheaper places for **snacks**, sandwiches or pizza *al taglio* are found in the grid of streets to the south, and towards the northern end of Via dei Consoli.

Bosone Garden Via XX Settembre 22 075 922 0688, www.ristorantebosonegarden.com; map p.642. The elegant restaurant of the *Bosone* hotel (see above) is open to non-patrons, and, thanks to its garden, is the nicest place to eat outdoors in the summer. Three tasting menus are available, including truffle and vegetarian options. Full meals without wine cost around €45/person. Thurs–Tues 12–3pm & 7.30–10.30pm.

Grotta dell'Angelo Via Gioia 47 075 927 3438,

ISABET
QVANDO·IHS·F·ESPULIT·DEMES·DE·CIVITATE·ARETII·DIVINA·POTENTIA·ET·PACIFICAVIT·TOTU·POPULU

Ⓦ www.grottadellangelo.it; map p.642. Annexed to the *Grotta dell'Angelo* hotel (see above), this restaurant offers very tasty and reasonably priced dishes such as pasta stuffed with ricotta and wild greens dressed with truffle, served in a wonderful dining room. Reckon on €35/person, without wine, for a three-course meal. Daily except Tues 12.30–2pm & 7.30–10pm.

Taverna del Lupo Via Ansidei 21 ⓣ 075 927 4368; map p.642. A smart and long-established place in a medieval setting, popular for its classic Umbrian dishes and excellent truffle risotto. Three courses will cost around €35. Tues–Sun noon–3pm & 7–10pm; Aug & Sept open daily.

10

Assisi

ASSISI is too well known for its own good, thanks to **St Francis** (see page 650), Italy's premier saint and founder of the Franciscan order, which, with its various splinter groups, forms the world's biggest religious order. Had the man not been born here in 1182 the town wouldn't be thronged with visitors and pilgrims for ten months of the year, but then neither would it have the **Basilica of St Francis**, one of the greatest monuments to thirteenth- and fourteenth-century Italian art. You'll probably feel it's worth putting up with the crowds and increasingly overwhelming commercialism, but you may not want to hang around once you've seen all there is to see – something which can easily be done in a day. That said, Assisi quietens down in the evening, and it does retain considerable medieval hill-town charm.

Basilica di San Francesco

Piazza San Francesco • **Lower Church** Mon–Sat 6am–7pm; Nov–March closes 6pm • Free • **Treasury** April–Oct Mon–Sat 10am–5.30pm • Donation requested • **Upper Church** Mon–Sat 8.30am–7pm; Nov–March closes 6pm; entry may be restricted during services and on Sun morning • Free • Ⓦ sanfrancescoassisi.org

Pilgrims and art lovers alike usually make straight for the **Basilica di San Francesco**, justifiably famed as Umbria's single greatest glory, and one of the most overwhelming collections of art outside a gallery anywhere in the world. Started in 1228, two

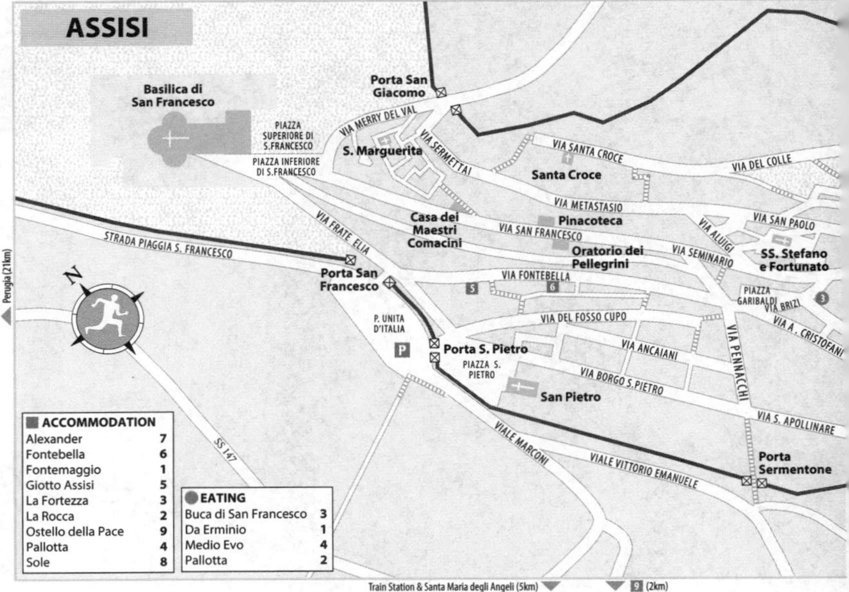

FESTIVALS AND EVENTS IN GUBBIO

Gubbio has a lively calendar of festivals. Apart from the spectacular Corsa dei Ceri (see page 644), the **Summer Festival** sees performances of classical music concerts in atmospheric venues around town (mid-July to mid-Aug; ask at the tourist office for a programme). The **Torneo dei Quartieri** is a few days of medieval fun and games in mid-August, culminating in a costumed parade in Piazza Grande. The medieval theme continues with the **Palio delle Balestre** on the last Sunday in May, with a crossbow contest against neighbouring Sansepolcro.

years after the saint's death, and financed by donations that flooded in from all over Europe, it's not as grandiose as some religious shrines, though it still strikes you as being a long way from the embodiment of Franciscan principles. If you don't mind compromised ideals, the two churches making up the basilica – one built on top of the other – are a treat.

The Lower Church

The sombre **Lower Church** – down the steps to the left – comes earlier, both structurally and artistically. The complicated floor plan and claustrophobic low-lit vaults were intended to create a mood of calm and meditative introspection – an effect added to by brown-robed monks, a ban on photography and a rule of silence. Francis lies under the floor in a **crypt** (entrance midway down the nave) that was only brought to light in 1818 after 52 days of digging. He was hidden after his funeral for safekeeping, and nowadays endures almost continuous Masses in dozens of languages.

Frescoes cover almost every available space and span a century of continuous artistic development. Stilted early works by anonymous painters influenced by the Byzantines sit alongside Roman painters such as Cavallini, who with Cimabue pioneered the move from mosaic to naturalism and the "new" medium of fresco. They were followed by the best of the Sienese School, **Simone Martini** and **Pietro Lorenzetti**, whose paintings are the ones to make a real point of seeing.

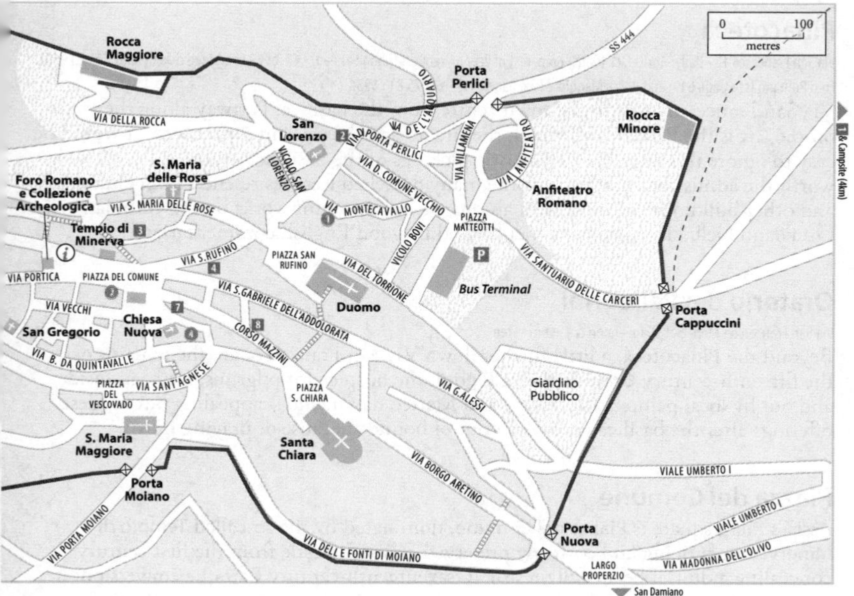

Martini's frescoes are in the **Cappella di San Martino** (1322–26), the first chapel on the left as you enter the nave. He was given free rein in the chapel, and every detail, right down to the floor and stained glass, follows his drawings, adding up to a unified scheme unique in Italy. Lorenzetti's works, dominated by a powerful *Crucifixion*, are in the transept to the left of the main altar. Vaults above the altar itself contain four magnificent frescoes, complicated but colourful allegories of the virtues on which Francis founded his order: Poverty, Chastity and Obedience. Once thought to have been the work of Giotto, they're now attributed to one of the church's army of unknown artists. The big feature in the right transept is Cimabue's over-restored *Madonna, Child and Angels with St Francis*, a painting Ruskin described as "the noblest depiction of the Virgin in Christendom". Look out for the famous portrait of Francis and for the much-reproduced fresco of St Clare on the wall to its left.

If time allows check out the **cloisters**, accessible from the rear right-hand side of the Lower Church, and the Treasury, or **Museo del Tesoro e Collezione F.M. Perkins**, reached via the apse of the Lower Church. The latter, often passed by, contains a rich collection of paintings – including works by Pietro Lorenzetti and Masolino da Panicale.

The Upper Church

The **Upper Church**, built to a light and airy Gothic plan – which was to be followed for countless Franciscan churches – is more straightforward than the Lower Church and a completely different experience. It's less a church than an excuse to show off **Giotto**'s dazzling frescoes on the life of St Francis. *Francis Preaching to the Birds* and *Driving the Devils from Arezzo* are just two of the famous scenes reproduced worldwide on cards and posters. The cycle starts on the right-hand wall up by the main altar and continues clockwise. Giotto was still in his 20s when he accepted the commission, having been recommended for the job by Cimabue, whose own frescoes – almost ruined now by the oxidation of badly chosen pigments and further damaged in the 1997 earthquake – fill large parts of the apse and transepts. In the vaults, several harsh areas of bare plaster stand as graphic monuments to the collapse of that year.

Pinacoteca

Via San Francesco 12 • Daily: April–Oct 10am–6pm, rest of year on request (phone ahead) • €3, or €9 combined ticket (valid 7 days) with Foro Romano (see page 649) and Rocca Maggiore (see page 649) • T 075 815 5234

Via San Francesco leads to the town centre from the basilica. Partway along the street on the left is the Palazzo Vallemani, the site of Assisi's excellent **Pinacoteca**. It would be easy to ignore this after the rich artistic pickings of the basilica, but the gallery is well worth the admission, not least for the many detached frescoes rescued from churches and other buildings around Assisi, among them important works by the Gubbian artist Ottaviano Nelli. The displays are enhanced by good English commentaries.

Oratorio dei Pellegrini

Via San Francesco • Mon–Sat 10am–noon & 4–6pm • Free

Beyond the Pinacoteca, a little further down Via San Francesco, are the remains of the fifteenth-century **Oratorio dei Pellegrini**, the hospice for pilgrims, frescoed inside and out by local painters Mezzastris and Matteo da Gualdo – appealing but modest offerings after the basilica (and often out of bounds because of praying nuns).

Piazza del Comune

Assisi's main square is **Piazza del Comune**, dominated by the so-called **Tempio di Minerva**, an enticing and perfectly preserved classical facade from the first century, concealing a dull, if beautifully restored, seventeenth-century Baroque conversion; it

was the only thing Goethe was bothered about seeing when he came to Assisi – the basilica he avoided, calling it a "Babylonian pile". Francis's birthplace lies just south of the piazza, marked by the **Chiesa Nuova**, a dreary church.

Foro Romano e Collezione Archeologica

Via Portica 2 • Daily: March–May & Oct 10am–6pm; June–Sept 10am–7pm; Nov–Feb 10am–5pm • €5, or €9 combined ticket valid 7 days with Pinacoteca (see page 648) and Rocca Maggiore (see page 649)

The **Foro Romano e Collezione Archeologica**, entered just off Piazza del Comune, is housed in the crypt of the now defunct church of San Niccolò. The classical remains include an excavated street – probably part of the old Roman forum – buried under the Piazza del Comune.

The Duomo

Piazza San Rufino 3 • **Cathedral** Daily: April–Oct 8am–1pm & 3–7pm; Nov–March 8am–1pm & 2–6pm • Free • **Museo Diocesano and crypt**; April–Oct Thurs–Tues 10am–1pm & 3–6pm, Nov–Feb Thurs–Tues 10am–1pm & 2.30–4.30pm • €3.50 • Ⓦ assisimuseodiocesano.com

A short hike from Piazza del Comune up the steep Via di San Rufino brings you to the thirteenth-century **Duomo**, with a typical and very lovely three-tiered Umbrian facade and sumptuously carved central doorway. The only point of interest in a boring interior is the font used to baptize St Francis, St Clare and – by a historical freak – the future Emperor Frederick II, born prematurely in a field outside the town. Off the right (south) nave, there's the small **Museo Diocesano**, with a handful of good paintings, including a 1470 work by Niccolò Alunno, and an atmospheric crypt, the **Cripta di San Rufino**, entered outside down steps to the right of the facade.

Rocca Maggiore

Via della Rocca • Daily 10am–dusk, occasional 9am opening in July & Aug • €5.50, or €9 combined ticket with Pinacoteca (see page 648) and Foro Romano (see above)

The cathedral makes a good point from which to strike off uphill for the **Rocca Maggiore**, one of the bigger and better-preserved castles in the region, rising dramatically from the town walls, with some all-embracing views the reward after a stiff climb.

Basilica di Santa Chiara

Piazza Santa Chiara • Daily 6.30am–noon & 2–7pm; winter closes 6pm • Free • Ⓦ assisisantachiara.it

Below the Duomo, on the pedestrianized Piazza Santa Chiara, stands the **Basilica di Santa Chiara**, burial place of St Francis's devoted early companion, St Clare, who at the age of 17 founded the Order of the Poor Clares, the female wing of the Franciscans. By some peculiar and not terribly dignified quirk she's also the patron saint of television. The church was consecrated in 1265 and is a virtual facsimile of the basilica up the road, down to the simple facade and opulent rose window. The scantily decorated interior has the body of St Clare herself and the Byzantine crucifix famous for having bowed to Francis and commanded him to embark on his sacred mission to repair God's Church (see page 650).

San Damiano

Via San Damiano 85 • Daily 10am–noon & 2–6pm; winter closes 4.30pm • Free • Ⓦ santuariosandamiano.org

You're never long off the St Francis trail in Assisi. **San Damiano**, a peaceful spot of genuine monastic charm, is one of its highlights, and easily reached by taking the Via Borgo Aretino beyond the Santa Chiara basilica and following signs from the Porta Nuova, a steep downhill walk of about fifteen minutes. Original home to the Poor Clares, and one of St Francis's favourite spots (he is thought to have written his much-adored *Canticle to the Sun* here), the church, cloisters and rustic setting preserve a sense of the original Franciscan ideals of humility and simplicity often absent in the rest of the town.

ST FRANCIS

The most extraordinary individual the Italian Church has produced, **St Francis** was a revolutionary figure who took Christianity back to basics. The impact he had on the evolution of the Catholic Church stands without parallel, and everything he accomplished in his short life was achieved by nothing more persuasive than the power of preaching and personal example. Dante placed him alongside another messianic figure, John the Baptist, and his appeal has remained undiminished – Mussolini called him *"il piu santo dei santi"* (the most saintly of the saints).

THE CALL FROM GOD

The events of his life, though doubtless embellished by myth, are well chronicled. He was born in Assisi in 1182, the son of a wealthy merchant and a Provençal woman – which is why he replaced his baptismal name, Giovanni, with Francesco (Little Frenchman). The Occitan literature of Provence, with its troubadour songs and courtly love poems, was later to be the making of Francis as a poet and speaker. One of the earliest writers in the vernacular, Francis laid the foundation of a great **Franciscan literary tradition** – his *Fioretti* and famous *Canticle to the Sun* ("brother sun … sister moon") stand comparison with the best of medieval verse.

In line with the early life of most male saints, his **formative years** were full of drinking and womanizing; he was, says one chronicler, "the first instigator of evil, and behind none in foolishness". Illness and imprisonment in a Perugian jail incubated the first seeds of contemplation. Abstinence and solitary wanderings soon followed. The **call from God**, the culmination of several visions, came in Assisi in 1209, when the crucifix in San Damiano bowed to him and told him to repair God's Church. Francis took the injunction literally, sold his father's stock of cloth and gave the money to Damiano's priest, who refused it.

Francis subsequently renounced his inheritance in the Piazza del Comune: before a large crowd and his outraged father, he stripped naked in a symbolic rejection of wealth and worldly shackles. Adopting the peasant's grey sackcloth (the brown Franciscan habit came later), he began to beg, preach and mix with lepers, a deliberate embodiment of Christ's invocation to the Apostles "to heal the sick, and carry neither purse, nor scrip [money], nor shoes". His **message** was disarmingly simple: throw out the materialistic trappings of daily life and return to a love of God rooted in poverty, chastity and obedience.

THE FRANCISCAN ORDER

In time Francis gathered his own twelve apostles and, after some difficulty, obtained permission from Pope Innocent III to found the **Franciscan Order**, which espoused no dogma and maintained no rule. Francis himself never became a priest. In 1212 he was instrumental in the creation of a second order for women, the **Poor Clares**, and continued the vast travels that took him as far as the Holy Land with the armies of the Crusades. In 1224 Francis received the stigmata on the mountaintop at La Verna. Two years later, he died on the mud floor of his hovel in Assisi, having scorned the offer of grander accommodation at the bishop's palace. His **canonization** followed swiftly, in 1228, in a service conducted by Pope Gregory.

However, a **split** in the Franciscan Order was inevitable. Francis's message and movement had few sympathizers in the wealthy and morally bankrupt papacy of the time, and while his popularity had obliged the Vatican to applaud while he was alive, the papacy quickly moved in after this death to quash the purist elements and encourage more "moderate" tendencies. Gradually it shaped the movement to its own designs, institutionalizing Francis's message in the process. Despite this, Francis's achievement as the first man to fracture the rigid orthodoxy of the hierarchical Church remains beyond question. Moreover, the Franciscans have not lost their ideological edge, and their views on the primacy of poverty are thought by many to be out of favour with the present Vatican administration.

Santa Maria degli Angeli

Via Porzuincola 1 • Daily 6.15am–12.40pm & 2.30–6.30pm • Free • Ⓦ porzuincola.org

From the train station you can see the vast but uninspiring **Santa Maria degli Angeli**, built in the seventeenth century and rebuilt after an earthquake in 1832. Somewhere in its Baroque bowels are the remains of the **Porzuincola**, a tiny chapel that was effectively

the first Franciscan monastery. Francis lived here after founding the order in 1208, attracted by its then remote and wooded surroundings. Today the church is crammed full of largely fourth-rate works of art and is a long way from the Franciscan ideal.

ARRIVAL AND DEPARTURE — ASSISI

By train Bus #C connects the station, which is 5km away to the southwest of the centre, with Piazza Matteotti every 30min.

Destinations Foligno (hourly; 17min); Spello (hourly; 9min); Terontola-Cortona (12 daily; connections to Chiusi, Orvieto, Arezzo, Florence and Rome; 1hr 10min).

By bus Buses connect regularly with surrounding towns – especially Perugia – stopping on Piazza Matteotti, in the east of the town above the Duomo. In addition, there are infrequent buses for Rome and Florence, from Piazza San Pietro.

Destinations Florence (1 daily Mon & Fri; 2hr 30min); Montefalco (from Santa Maria degli Angeli; 1 daily Mon–Sat; 40min); Naples (1 daily; 5hr 15min); Norcia and the Valnerina (from Santa Maria degli Angeli; 1 daily Mon–Sat; 2hr 10min); Rome (2 daily; 3hr 10min); Siena (from Santa Maria degli Angeli; 1–2 daily; 2hr 5min); Spello (2–4 daily Mon–Sat; 25min).

By car If you are driving, note that the centre of town is closed to traffic: your best bet is to park either in Piazza Matteotti at the top (eastern) end of the town, or below the basilica in Piazza dell'Unità d'Italia.

INFORMATION

Tourist office At the western end of Piazza del Comune (April–Oct Mon–Fri 8am–2pm & 3–6pm (closes 6.30pm mid-April to early May, Easter week & July to mid-Oct) Sat 9am–7pm, Sun 9am–6pm; Nov–March Mon–Fri 8am–2pm & 3–6pm, Sat & Sun 9.30am–5pm; ⓣ075 81 38680, ⓦvisit-assisi.it).

ACCOMMODATION

Assisi offers a wide range of accommodation, but the supply is often only just adequate for the number of visitors, so **advance booking** is highly advisable, and essential if you plan to visit over Easter or during the Festa di San Francesco (Oct 3–4) or Calendimaggio (early May). July and Aug are **low season** in Assisi, when hotels will often lower their rates. The **tourist office** has a full list of lodgings, including over thirty rooms for rent and can also supply details of B&Bs, agriturismi and pilgrim hostels. An alternative is to stay at **Spello** (see page 653), which is close enough to make seeing Assisi easy. Wherever you choose to stay, avoid the concentration of rooms and hotels in Santa Maria degli Angeli or the grim village of Bastia, 4km out of Assisi.

★ **Alexander** Piazza Chiesa Nuova 6 ⓣ075 816 190, ⓦhotelalexanderassisi.it; map p.646. This three-star hotel has an excellent position just off Piazza del Comune, but benefits from its location on a quiet piazza. The rooms are wood-beamed and decorated in neutral tones, with spotless en-suite bathrooms. Breakfast is taken in the nearby *Dei Priori* hotel. **€120**

Fontebella Via Fontebella 25 ⓣ075 812 883, ⓦfontebella.com; map p.646. Though a little faded in places, this is still the town's most elegant and intimate choice. Ask for a room on one of the top floors for great panoramas. **€103**

Giotto Assisi Via Fontebella 41 ⓣ075 812 209, ⓦhotelgiottoassisi.it; map p.646. In business since 1899, this four-star has recently been completely renovated. The rooms are very comfortable, if a little bland, and there are fine views from the terrace restaurant. It's the only hotel with parking in the *centro storico*. **€152**

La Fortezza Vicolo della Fortezza 19/B ⓣ075 812 418, ⓦhotelfortezzaassisi.it; map p.646. Friendly little hotel with just seven rooms in a perfect position next to Piazza del Comune, with thoughtful touches such as free water and free tea and coffee in the afternoon; the co-owned restaurant is also excellent. **€65**

La Rocca Via di Porta Perlici 27 ⓣ075 812 284, ⓦhotelarocca.it; map p.646. This one-star situated at the end of the street beyond the Duomo has been managed by the same family since the 1950s. Of the thirty rooms, book one of the five with views; all have private bathroom. Breakfast not included. **€72**

Pallotta Via San Rufino 6 ⓣ075 812 307, ⓦpallottaassisi.it; map p.646. A good location between the Duomo and Piazza del Comune; also has a first-rate co-owned trattoria just off Piazza del Comune (see page 648). **€78**

Sole Corso Mazzini 35 ⓣ075 812 373, ⓦassisihotelsole.com; map p.646. Good-sized medieval-styled rooms just a minute's walk from the Basilica di Santa Chiara. The best rooms have a little balcony or terrace. Breakfast not included (€6 extra). **€72**

HOSTELS AND CAMPING

Fontemaggio 3km east of town on Via S. Rufino Campagna ⓣ075 813 636, ⓦfontemaggio.it; map p.646. Hostel/hotel with a 244-pitch campsite. The fairly rural setting is better than the sites you may see advertised towards Baschi on the other side of Assisi; there's also a decent shop to save you the trek into town for supplies. Breakfast in dorms costs €6. Dorms **€22**, doubles **€54**, pitches **€7** plus per person **€8**

Ostello della Pace Via delle Valecchie 177 ⓣ075 816

10

ASSISI'S FESTIVALS

Assisi's main festivals are the **Festa di San Francesco** (Oct 3–4), commemorating the death of the saint, and **Calendimaggio**, three days of lively games and contests between the two parts of the city – "Parte de Sopra" and "Parte di Sotto" – which takes place in early May.

10

767, ⓦassisihostel.com; map p.646. In a quiet setting a 10min walk downhill from Piazza dell'Unità d'Italia, this hostel (with dorms and two private doubles) occupies an old farmhouse, and has a garden, lots of facilities and welcoming staff. Ask to be dropped at "Villa Guardi" if you're arriving by bus from the station. Dinner costs €10.50. Dorms €13–21, doubles €44–56

EATING

Buca di San Francesco Via Eugenio Brizzi 1 ⓣ075 812 204; map p.646. The *Buca* has been around for ever, and is generally a reliable choice for a decent meal, with typical *primi* (from €10) that might include handmade spaghetti with roast mushroom, beef and herbs, and mains (from €12) such as lamb cooked with wild herbs. Tues–Sun 12–2.30pm & 7–9.30pm.

Da Erminio Via Montecavallo 19 ⓣ075 812 506, ⓦtrattoriadaerminio.it; map p.646. Located above the Duomo in a quiet corner, this restaurant is very good value: eating à la carte, you can expect to pay €30/head. Dishes worth trying include rabbit cooked with ten different herbs, and the Chianina steak spiked with juniper berries. Daily noon–2.30pm & 7–9pm; closed Thurs (except in Aug for lunch), Feb & first half of July.

Medio Evo Via dell'Arco dei Priori 4/B ⓣ075 813 068, ⓦristorantemedioevoassisi.it; map p.646. This place is recommended for its creative cuisine; fixed menus start at €16 (for two courses plus veg at lunch) without wine; otherwise *primi* range from €9 to €14, mains from €12 to €18. The lovely, stone-vaulted space is another plus. March–Oct Tues–Sun 12.30–3pm & 7.30–10.45pm; Nov–Feb Fri–Sun same hours.

★ **Pallotta** Via Volta Piana 2 ⓣ075 812 649; map p.646. An unpretentious and welcoming trattoria with a lovely wood-beamed dining room just south of Piazza del Comune – arrive early for a table at lunchtime, when it's usually packed. *Primi* (€5–10) include *stringozzi alla Pallotta*, handmade pasta (without egg) served with mushroom, chilli flakes and a generous swirl of good, local olive oil. *Secondi* (€6–15) might include suckling pig, lamb chops and braised pigeon. If you are on a budget, go for the daily set tourist menu (€16 with wine) or the more sophisticated €25 tasting menu, or €24 vegetarian menu). Daily except Tues noon–3pm & 7–10pm.

Spello and around

Ranged on broad terraces above the Valle di Spoleto, medieval and pink-stoned **SPELLO** is the best place for a taste of small-town Umbria if you haven't time or means to explore farther, being easy to reach by road and rail from Assisi or Spoleto.

Emperor Augustus gave land in the adjacent valley to faithful legionnaires who had reached the end of their careers, turning the town (Hispellum) into a sort of Roman retirement home in the process, an ambience it still rather retains. The walls and three gateways are the most obvious Roman remnants. Don't bother walking out to the paltry and overgrown remains of the old amphitheatre hidden away beyond the main highway to Assisi: you can see all you need to from the top of the town.

Santa Maria Maggiore

Piazza G. Matteotti 18 • Daily: April–Oct 8.30am–12.30pm & 3–7pm; Nov–March 8.30am–12.30pm & 3–6pm • €2 • ⓦsmariamaggiore.com

By far the most distinguished sight in Spello is **Pinturicchio's fresco cycle** in the thirteenth-century church of **Santa Maria Maggiore**, about a third of the way up the town's winding and steep main street on Piazza Matteotti. The most important Umbrian painter after Perugino, he left other important works in Siena (the Duomo), Rome (the Sistine Chapel, Borgia apartments) and a host of churches scattered over central Italy. The frescoes themselves are fresh and glowing from restoration, with Pinturicchio's famous details and colouring brought out to stunning effect.

Unfortunately they're behind glass, which also means you can't get a closer look at the chapel's praised but faded fifteenth-century **ceramic pavement**.

Pinacoteca Civica

Piazza G. Matteotti 10 • Tues–Sun: April–Sept 10.30am–1pm & 3–6.30pm; Oct–March 10.30am–12.30pm & 3.30–5.30pm • €4 • ⓣ 0742 301 497

Almost immediately to the north of Santa Maria Maggiore stands an excellent little art gallery, the **Pinacoteca Civica**. It contains a handful of masterpieces by local Umbrian painters, notably Niccolò Alunno, as well as some rare pieces of sculpture. One of the works on display is the extremely rare figure of Christ with moveable arms: during Holy Week the arms could be raised for ceremonies involving depictions of the Crucifixion and lowered for those depicting the Deposition and Resurrection.

10

Sant'Andrea

Via Cavour • Daily 10.30am–12.30pm & 3–5pm • Free

Further up the busy, steep main street from Santa Maria Maggiore, on the right, stands **Sant'Andrea**, a striking Gothic church with a dramatic Pinturicchio, Enthroned Madonna with Saints, in the right transept brightening up the gloomy interior. Also look out for the looming crucifix attributed to the School of Giotto.

ARRIVAL AND INFORMATION — SPELLO

By train If you're coming by train from the south, note that you may have to change trains at Foligno for Spello. The station is a 10min walk from the centre of town.

Tourist office Piazza G. Matteotti 3 (April–Oct daily 9.30am–12.30pm & 3.30–5.30pm, but hours are variable; it usually opens and closes a bit later in summer; ⓣ 0742 301 009, ⓦ prospello.it).

ACCOMMODATION

Il Cacciatore Via Giulia 42 ⓣ 0742 651 141, ⓦ ilcacciatorehotel.com. A good-value three-star hotel, with fine views from some rooms and potentially noisier rooms looking out over the street, plus an attached restaurant. €100

La Bastiglia Via dei Molini 17 ⓣ 0742 651 277, ⓦ labastiglia.com. Smart, four-star place, where most of the rooms command a fine view. The standard rooms are on the small side – it's worth paying a bit more for a superior or deluxe room. The two suites come with vast hydromassage baths, and there's a good restaurant too (see page 654). €130

Palazzo Bocci Via Cavour 17 ⓣ 0742 301 021, ⓦ palazzobocci.com. Right in the centre of town, this slightly faded upmarket option has some lovely frescoed ceilings and a tranquil garden – the perfect place for evening *aperitivi* – and is also cosy in winter, with a large fireplace in the communal lounge. Ask for one of the frescoed rooms. €160

EATING AND DRINKING

Bar Giardino Bonci Via Garibaldi 10–12 ⓣ 0742 651 397. There appears nothing special about this small bar until you take your drink or ice cream out to the wonderful panoramic garden terrace at the back. Very reasonably priced light meals are also served. Thurs–Tues summer 7am–midnight; winter 7am–10pm.

Caffè Porta Consolare Piazza Kennedy 7 ⓣ 075 803 9096. At the foot of the old town, this is a great place for a coffee and *cornetto*, plus the usual range of sandwiches, but is known best for its rich and creamy ice cream. Tues–Sun 6am–midnight.

Hostaria de Dadà Via Cavour 47 ⓣ 0742 301 327. A tiny place with a handful of shared tables that's a good choice for cheap, light meals at lunch or dinner. Good for bruschetta, excellent soups and *stringozzi* pasta. Mon–Sat noon–3pm & 7–10pm, Sun noon–3pm.

SPELLO'S CARPETS OF FLOWERS

In early June, Spello is scene of an **Infiorate festival**, when the town's streets are carpeted with flower-petal representations of religious scenes. To find out more, visit ⓦ infioratespello.it.

La Bastiglia Piazza Vallegloria 7-Via Falnitraria 15 ⊕0742 651 277. Attached to the *La Bastiglia* hotel (see page 653), with superb views and a menu focusing on local foods and traditions; there is a good value set tourist menu (€18), *primi* costing from €10–15 and mains from €13–16. Well worth a visit. Daily except Wed 12.30–3pm & 8–10.30pm.

La Cantina Via Cavour 2 ⊕0742 651 775. Spello's most atmospheric restaurant is this fairly smart place, set in a vaulted medieval townhouse a few steps up from Santa Maria Maggiore. First-rate regional cooking, including exceptional truffle dishes; *primi* from €10, mains from around €16. Daily except Tues 12.30–2.30pm & 8–10.30pm.

10

Bevagna

The serene, attractive backwater of **BEVAGNA** is quieter and less visited than Spello, with a windswept central square of stark perfection. Dating from around the thirteenth century, **Piazza S. Silvestri** is flanked by two of Umbria's finest Romanesque churches – both untouched and creaking with age. Look out particularly for the surreal gargoyles over the doorway of the larger church, San Michele. The piazza's fountain, while blending perfectly, was only installed in 1889.

Museo di Bevagna

Corso Matteotti 70 • Daily 10am–1pm & 2.30–5pm, though hours can vary depending on staffing levels• €5

The town's small **Museo di Bevagna** is devoted to the history of the village and is divided into three sections: the archeological collection on the ground floor; maps, letters and other documents on the first floor; and the Pinacoteca on the second floor, with mainly seventeenth-century paintings.

While you're at the museum, inquire about seeing the town's **Roman mosaic** on the north side of Via Porta Guelfa (hours variable; €3), an impressive relic of the town's Roman days that originally formed part of a bath complex. The same ticket admits you to the delightful little nineteenth-century **Teatro Francesco Torti**, just off the main square.

ARRIVAL AND INFORMATION — BEVAGNA

By bus Buses from Montefalco, Foligno, Perugia and Spoleto (all Mon–Sat) arrive in Largo A. Gramsci, just behind the main square.

Destinations Foligno (2–10 daily Mon–Sat; 20min); Montefalco (5 daily Mon–Sat; 35min); Perugia (5 daily Mon–Sat; 1hr); Spoleto (3 daily Mon–Sat; 1hr).

Tourist office Piazza S. Silvestri 1 (Daily 10am–noon & 3–5pm; rest of the year hours vary; ⊕074 236 1667, ⊛prolocobevagna.it).

ACCOMMODATION

Il Chiostro di Bevagna Corso Matteotti 107 ⊕0742 361 987, ⊛ilchiostrodibevagna.com. Simple airy rooms just off Piazza S. Silvestri, in an atmospheric renovated Dominican convent, which retains its original frescoed cloister and airy, pleasant rooms. €80

L'Orto degli Angeli Via dell'Anfiteatro ⊕0742 360 130, ⊛ortoangeli.it. Luxurious accommodation in two porticoed medieval *palazzi*, dripping effortlessly with once-upon-a-time atmosphere, that have been in the same family since 1788. There are gardens, and a fine gourmet restaurant, *Redibis* (see opposite). €130

Ostello Diffuso Torre del Colle ⊕333 320 987, ⊛turriscollis.com. Simple hotel-hostel in a tiny, fortified hamlet in a peaceful spot in the hills 4km northwest of Bevagna. Private doubles and four-bed rooms are available, arranged across three buildings. The hamlet also has a bar and co-owned restaurant, *Serpillo*. Dorms €15, doubles €80

Palazzo Brunamonti Corso Matteotti 79 ⊕0742 361 932, ⊛brunamonti.com. A sumptuous place with a period setting, brocade soft furnishings, beamed ceilings and trompe l'oeil decorations. €90

EATING AND DRINKING

Enoteca di Piazza Onofri Piazza Onofri 1 ⊕0742 361 926. This *enoteca* tucked behind the Palazzo Comunale is a great place to try local food – such as the *pappa al pomodoro* with grilled aubergine and goat cheese, or *taglierini* with a *ragù* of pigeon and truffle. In autumn there should be rabbit with *finferli* (chanterelle mushrooms). Prices are reasonable – €30–35 for a full meal. Mon-Fri 7–10pm, Sat & Sun 12.30–10.30pm; closed two weeks in Aug.

Micheletto Largo Gramsci 1 ⊕ 0742 360 999. Little café-bar with a few tables outside – nice for breakfast, a sandwich lunch or an *aperitivo* with the chance to nibble at a good range of local cheeses and salami. Daily 8am–midnight or later.

Redibis Via dell'Anfiteatro ⓣ 0742 360 130, ⓦ redibis.it. Interesting restaurant, occupying part of a Roman theatre. The cuisine draws equally on family recipes and well-researched local traditions, as well as more inventive fare. Dishes you won't find anywhere else include a soup of spelt and black celery (which is grown only in Trevi), a frittata of cardoons and thyme, and artisanal Gragnano spaghetti served with fresh chilli, garlic and oil. Antipasti cost €9–14, *primi* €14–16, *secondi* €16–24 and desserts €8–10. Daily except Tues 12.30–2.30pm & 8–10.30pm.

Montefalco

MONTEFALCO is a pleasing and intimate medieval village that's home to a superb collection of paintings. Its name, meaning Falcon's Mount, was glorified with the appendage *la ringhiera dell'Umbria* – "the balcony of Umbria" – a tribute to its wonderful views. It was also the birthplace of eight saints, good going even by Italian standards. Nowadays the town is sleepy rather than holy, with only a stupendously ugly water tower and very slight urban sprawl to take the edge off its medieval appeal. The town's lofty location was a godsend to Spoleto's papal governors, left high, dry and terrified by the fourteenth-century defection of the popes to Avignon. They took refuge here, and their cowering presence accounts for some of the rich decoration of Montefalco's **churches**, a richness out of all proportion to the town's size.

The strong, blackberry-flavoured **local wine**, Sagrantino Passito, made from a grape variety found nowhere else in Europe, is well worth a try; it's available in many shops around town. Recommended producers are Adanti and Caprai, also makers of the excellent Rosso di Montefalco. Local events include the **Agosto Montefalchese** (mid-Aug) – two weeks of cultural events and open-air concerts culminating in the Fuga del Bove, a bull race that has taken place here for centuries.

Complesso Museale di San Francesco

Via Ringhiera Umbra 6 • Nov–March Wed–Sun 10.30am–1pm & 2.30–5pm; April, May, Sept daily 10.30am–6pm; June, July, Aug daily 10.30am–7pm • €10 • ⓣ 0742 379 598

The cavernous ex-church of San Francesco, off the central Piazza del Comune, is now the **Complesso Museale di San Francesco**, housing the town's big feature, Benozzo Gozzoli's sumptuous **fresco cycle** on the life of St Francis. With Fra' Angelico, Gozzoli was one of the most prolific and influential Florentine painters to come south and show the backward Umbrians what the Renaissance was all about. Resplendent with colour and detail, the cycle copies many of the ideas and episodes from Giotto's Assisi cycle but, with two hundred years of artistic know-how to draw on, is more sophisticated and more immediately appealing.

Church and convent of Santa Chiara

Via Verdi, 5min walk from San Francesco • Free

Probably the most bizarre sight in town is the mummified body of **St Clare** (St Chiara), which languishes in the otherwise dismal **church of Santa Chiara**. Ring the bell and, if the nuns aren't deep in prayer, they may show you round the adjoining **convent** – a fascinating behind-the-scenes look at monastic life, where you can see the remains of the saint's heart and the scissors used to hack it out. This is a second St Clare, not to be confused with the one in Assisi: the story goes that Christ appeared to Clare, saying the burden of carrying the cross was becoming too heavy; Clare replied she would help by carrying it in her heart, and when she was opened up after her death, a cross-shaped piece of tissue was duly found on her heart. Other strange exhibits include three of her kidney stones and a tree that miraculously grew from a staff planted in the garden here by Christ, during one of his appearances to Clare; the berries are used to make rosaries and are said to have powerful medicinal qualities.

ARRIVAL AND INFORMATION — MONTEFALCO

By bus There are buses from most local towns and villages, including Bevagna (5 daily Mon–Sat) and Perugia (up to 3 daily Mon–Sat). Buses drop off in the large car park below town, from where it's a 5min walk uphill to the centre.

Tourist information The website of the Strada del Sagrantino (ⓦ stradadelsagrantino.it), a body promoting the wines of the region, has a useful map of local *cantine*, perfect if you're planning a tour of the local wineries, and plenty of general background on places to stay, eat and visit. The website ⓦ www.montefalcodoc.it is also worth a look.

ACCOMMODATION AND EATING

L'Alchimista Piazza del Comune 14 ⓣ 0742 378 558, ⓦ montefalcowines.com. A family-run wine bar and restaurant, open early for those who fancy breakfasting, Umbrian-peasant style, on a glass of wine with salami and cheese. At lunchtime and dinner there is more substantial fare on offer – try the *pasta alla carbonara* with local cheese and saffron or with shavings of summer truffle – while puddings are happily accompanied by a glass of local sweet wine, Passito di Sagrantino. Daily 9am/10am–midnight; closed Tues in low season.

10

★ **Palazzo Bontadosi** Piazza del Comune 19 ⓣ 0742 379 357, ⓦ hotelbontadosi.it. Right in the main square, with twelve sumptuously furnished rooms and a swanky spa in the basement. The vast junior suite, with frescoes and a bathtub in the bedroom, plus peerless views of the square, is worth a splurge. €171

Trevi

Road and rail south of Assisi and Spello run down the plain of Spoleto, past the light industrial sites that blight the whole stretch of the valley towards Terni and beyond. Not many people stop before Spoleto itself, giving **TREVI** and its towering position no more than an admiring glance. Its daunting inaccessibility is one of the reasons for its easy-going, old-fashioned charm; the feeling is of a pleasant, ordinary provincial town, unspoilt but beginning to feel the first effects of tourism. All around it are vast expanses of **olive groves**, renowned for producing central Italy's finest oil.

Raccolta d'Arte di San Francesco

Largo Don Bosco 14 • April–July & Sept Tues–Sun 10.30am–1pm & 2.30–6pm; June & July Tues–Sun 10am–12.30pm & 3.30–7pm; Aug daily 10.30am–12.30pm & 3–7.30pm; Oct–March Fri–Sun 10.30am–1pm & 2.30–5pm • €7 • ⓣ 0742 381 628

The key sight in town is the superb **Raccolta d'Arte di San Francesco** in the former Convento di San Francesco, reached by taking Via di San Francesco from the northern end of the main Piazza Mazzini. It houses a well-presented display of coins, ceramics and Roman fragments, several paintings by Umbrian masters and one outstanding work, a *Coronation of the Virgin* (1522) by Lo Spagna. Trevi's medieval governors commissioned this painting as a copy of a more famous work by the Florentine Ghirlandaio, mainly because they couldn't afford the real thing. In the same complex, the **Museo della Civiltà dell'Ulivo** (same hours and ticket) is a smart museum devoted to history of the olive and olive oil production: it's packed with interesting information, in English and Italian.

ARRIVAL AND INFORMATION — TREVI

By train The medieval centre, looming high on its hill, is 4km from the train station, connected by bus service #1 (3–4 daily); check the timetable first on ⓦ umbriamobilita.it before deciding what time to arrive. There are trains approximately every hour from Trevi to Terni, a major junction, with services to Rome and north to Perugia and Città di Castello.

By bus Trevi is not very well connected by bus – bus #430 runs to Foligno (up to 7 daily Mon–Sat).

Tourist office Piazza Mazzini (hours are erratic as the office is volunteer-run; ⓣ 0742 332 222 or ⓣ 0742 332 269, ⓦ treviturismo.it). Has audioguides to the town as well as information on the local olive oil route (ⓦ stradaoliodopumbria.it). Information is also available from the Comune at Piazza Mazzini 21 (Mon–Fri, office hours).

ACCOMMODATION AND EATING

Antica Dimora alla Rocca Piazza della Rocca ⓣ 0742 38 541, ⓦ hotelallarocca.it. Centrally located, this smart four-star hotel occupies part of a historic 1650 building with frescoed ceilings and other period features, all beautifully restored. For atmosphere, ask to be in the main building, rather than the less appealing ten-room annexe. €85

Il Terziere Località Costa 1 ⓣ 0742 78 359, ⓦ ilterziere.com. A very appealingly styled hotel with restaurant whose gorgeous flower-filled garden, outdoor toys for children and swimming pool make it a great choice for families with young children. In addition, most of the rooms on the first floor have their own terrace-balconies. It's about 3km outside town, and although the hotel will pick you up from the station, and organize bike rental, you really do need

your own transport. **€90**

La Vecchia Posta Piazza Mazzini 14 ⓣ0742 381 690. A great little place that makes excellent use of local ingredients – including truffles and the town's rare black celery. The oil hereabouts is excellent as well – shown off to perfection in the very simple *crostini* with local black celery pâté. Truffles turn up in pasta dishes and – most indulgently – encrusting a melting scamorza cheese. A full meal will cost around €25. Daily 12.30–2.30pm & 8–10.30pm.

Fonti del Clitunno and around

Via Flaminia 7, Località Fonti del Clitunno • March & Oct Mon–Fri 9am–1pm & 2–6pm, Sat & Sun 9am–6pm; April daily 9am–7.30pm; May–Aug daily 8.30am–8pm; Sept daily 9am–7pm; Nov–Feb Mon–Fri 10am–1pm & 2–4.30pm, Sat & Sun 10am–4.30pm • €3 • ⓣ0743 521 141, ⓦfontidelclitunno.it • Buses from Foligno (6 daily Mon–Sat; about 25min) and Spoleto (4 daily; about 35min)

The once sacred **Fonti del Clitunno** is an unexpected beauty spot given the pockmarked surroundings. There's a certain amount of commercialized fuss and bother at the entrance, but the springs, streams and willow-shaded lake beyond – painted by Corot and an inspiration to poets from Virgil to Byron – are pure, languid romanticism. The spa waters have attracted people since Roman times – the likes of Caligula and Claudius came here to party – but their major curative effect is allegedly the dubious one of completely extinguishing any appetite for alcohol.

Tempietto del Clitunno

Tues–Sat & first Sun of the month: April–Oct 2.15–7.45pm; Nov–March 12.15–5.45pm • €2 • ⓦtempiettodelclitunno.com

A few hundred metres north of Fonti del Clitunno is the so-called **Tempietto del Clitunno**, looking for all the world like a miniature Greek temple but actually an eighth-century Christian church, cobbled together with a mixture of idiosyncrasy, wishful thinking and old Roman columns. It's only a small, one-off novelty, but still evocative, and with the bonus inside of some faded frescoes said to be the oldest in Umbria.

Spoleto

SPOLETO is among Umbria's most charming large towns, divided into the medieval, hilltop **Upper Town**, home to the Duomo and most of the key museums and galleries, and the predominantly modern **Lower Town**, which nonetheless preserves a handful of Romanesque churches and Roman ruins. Known these days mainly for its big **summer theatre and arts festival** (see page 660), it's also remarkable for its thoroughgoing medievalism, an extremely scenic setting and several of Italy's most ancient Romanesque **churches**. Far more graceful and provincial a city than Perugia, nowadays it plays second fiddle politically to its long-time historical enemy, though for several centuries it was among the most influential of Italian towns.

Two kilometres of well-preserved walls stand as testament to the one-time grandeur of Spoleto's Roman colony, though its real importance dates from the sixth century when the Lombards made it the capital of one of their three Italian dukedoms. The autonomous **Duchy of Spoleto** eventually stretched to Rome, and by 890 its rulers had become powerful enough to lay claim to the imperial throne itself, making Spoleto, for a short time at least, the capital of the entire Holy Roman Empire. Barbarossa flattened the city in a fit of pique in 1155, and in 1499 Pope Alexander VI appointed his daughter, the 19-year-old Lucrezia Borgia, governor. After that it was one long decline until the arrival of the festival almost sixty years ago.

The Lower Town

The **Lower Town** was badly damaged by World War II bombing and its only real interest lies in the remains of a Roman amphitheatre and a couple of first-rate churches. Aficionados of Romanesque architecture – or anyone who fancies staying

in a monastery – might also want to see **San Ponziano** just off Via Cimitero on Via delle Lettere (ring the bell at the adjacent monastery to gain access); it has a simple Romanesque facade, a beautiful tenth-century crypt supported on columns recycled from Roman buildings, and frescoes dating from the fourteenth century.

San Salvatore

Via del Cimitero-Piazza Mario Salmi 1 • Hours vary but generally Mon–Thurs 10am–noon & 4–6pm, Fri–Sun 10am–noon & 3–6pm • Free

The fourth-century paleo-Christian **San Salvatore**, built by Christian monks from the eastern Mediterranean in the fourth century, is one of Umbria's most remarkable buildings. Pretty much untampered with over the centuries, it was conceived at a time when the Western world was still ruled by the Roman emperor, and the only models

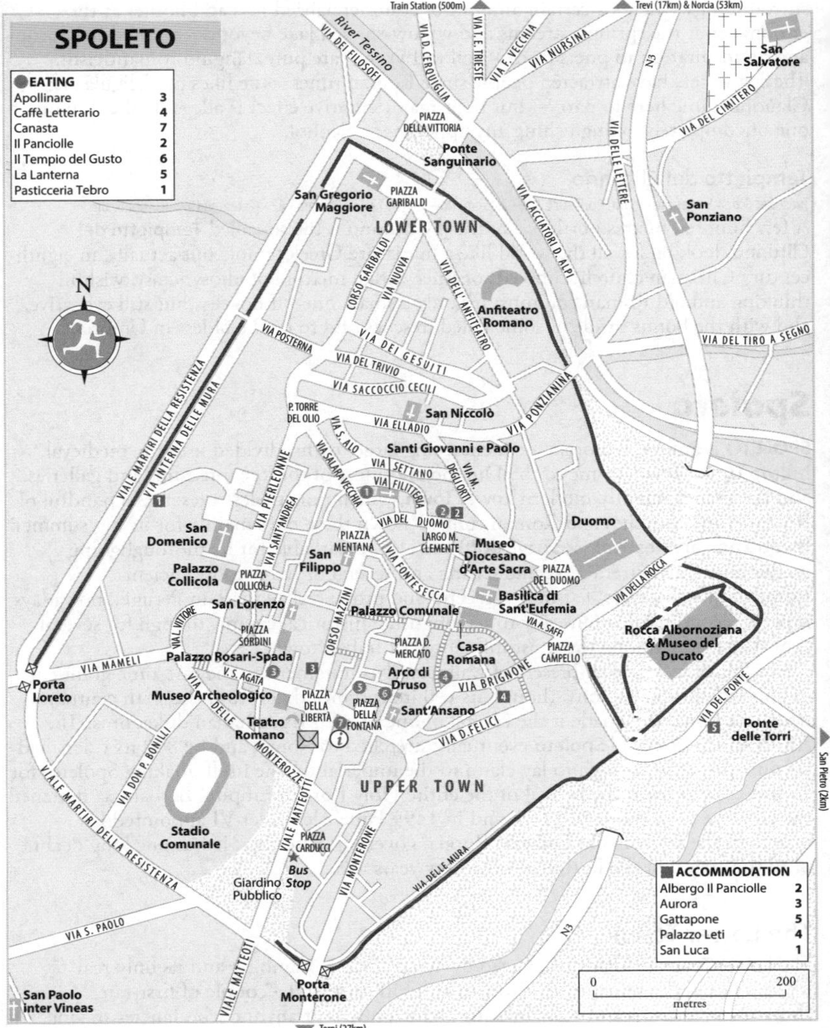

THE SPOLETO CARD

Available from April to September, the **Spoleto Card** (spoletocard.it) provides free entrance to the town's seven museums, as well as free local public transport. The card is valid for seven days and costs €9.50. You can buy it online, from any of the town's museums, or from the bookshop at the Duomo.

for religious buildings were Roman temples. This is pretty much what the monks came up with, the net result leaning more to paganism than Christianity. The walls inside are bare, the floors covered in fallen stone, and the dusty gloom is heavy with an almost eerie antiquity. Crumbling Corinthian columns from different ages are wedged awkwardly alongside one another, and at some point the arches in the nave were filled in to prevent total collapse.

San Gregorio Maggiore

Piazza Garibaldi • Daily 8am–noon & 3.30/4–6pm • Free

In a prominent position on the main Piazza Garibaldi is the church of **San Gregorio Maggiore**, started in 1069. The tower and intriguing portico are made from a patchwork of fragments clearly pinched from earlier Roman remains, but it's the interior that commands most attention. Stripped back to their Romanesque state, the walls are dotted with substantial patches of fresco and interrupted by a series of unusual stone confessionals. The presbytery is raised several metres above the level of the naves to allow for a masterful little crypt, supported by dozens of tiny pillars.

Complesso dell'Anfiteatro Romano

Via dell'Anfiteatro-Vicolo delle Murelle • Not currently open to the public

Tradition has it that somewhere under San Gregorio Maggiore lie the bones of ten thousand Christian martyrs killed by the Romans in Spoleto's **amphitheatre**. Closed for years, and in a sorry state of abandonment, the **Complesso dell'Anfiteatro Romano** now lies within a military barracks on Via dell'Anfiteatro; bear right from the gateway for the best of the amphitheatre's remains. The ever-ingenious Romans apparently constructed special gutters to drain blood from the arena into the nearby Torrente Tessino, which ran crimson as a result.

The Upper Town

There's plenty to explore in the medieval **Upper Town**. Buses drop off at the central Piazza Carducci, and all of the sights are within a fifteen-minute walk of here.

Museo Archeologico

Via Sant'Agata 18/A • Daily 8.30am–7.30pm • €4, or Spoleto Card; free first Sun of the month

A good place to get a sense of Roman Spoleto is the **Museo Archeologico**, evocatively housed in a former monastery on the western edge of the central **Piazza della Libertà**. The museum stylishly documents the Roman presence in the city with artfully presented local finds; included in the ticket is a visit to the exquisite first-century-BC **Teatro Romano** behind the monastery, still used for performances during the Spoleto Festival.

Palazzo Collicola

Piazza Collicola • April–Oct Mon & Wed–Sun 10.30am–1pm & 3.30–7pm; Nov–March Fri–Sun same hours • €4 for permanent collection only, €6 with access to the palace's grandest rooms, €9 with temporary exhibition; Spoleto Card

The **Palazzo Collicola**, northwest of Piazza della Libertà, holds the **Museo Carandente e Appartamento Nobile**, which is devoted primarily to modern Italian artists, though it also contains some works by foreigners who have been connected with the Spoleto Festival over the years, among them Alexander Calder, the man responsible for the

10

THE FESTIVAL DEI DUE MONDI

Hosting Italy's leading international arts festival, the **Festival dei Due Mondi** (Festival of Two Worlds), has been a double-edged blessing for Spoleto – crowds and commercialism being the price it has had to pay for culture. Having already rejected thirty other Italian locations, the influential arts guru Giancarlo Menotti plumped for the town in 1958, attracted by its scenery, small venues and general good vibes. The ensuing jamboree is a great attraction if you're into **music**, **dance** or **theatre**, though the place forgoes a good part of its charm for the duration. While the festival is in progress – for two weeks between June and July – you can expect packed hotels and restaurants, and the chance of higher prices all round. At the same time there's an Edinburgh-influenced **fringe** and plenty of films, jazz, buskers and so on. Organizers, moreover, are increasingly looking to more avant-garde shows to recover the artistic edge of the festival's early days, while Spoleto has spawned an annual sister festival at Charleston in the USA. Check out **information** from the tourist office or the festival's main box office at Piazza della Libertà 10 (T 0743 776 444, W festivaldispoleto.com). For big events, it's worth buying tickets in advance online.

large sculpture by the railway station, and American minimalist Sol LeWit. The top floor hosts some excellent temporary exhibitions.

Piazza del Mercato and around

Nowhere do you get a better sense of Spoleto's market-town roots than in the bustling **Piazza del Mercato**, whose two bars on the west side offer a fine opportunity to take in some streetlife. The *alimentari* on all sides are a cornucopia of goodies, with a definite bias towards truffles and sticky liqueurs.

Straddling the southern entrance to the piazza is the **Arco di Druso** (23 AD), the only one of the town's many Roman arches not embedded in a wall. This is because it was built not as a functional and defendable town gate but as a triumphal, symbolic gateway to the old Forum – to honour the campaign victories of Drusus, son of Tiberius, a heavy-drinking man whose reputation for violence led to the sharpest of gladiator swords being named after him.

The patched-up walls behind the arch are the city's oldest, built in the sixth century BC by the Umbrians. To the right of the arch is what is described as a **Roman temple**, but unless you've a vivid imagination it's difficult to see it as anything other than a ditch. Pop into the adjacent church of **Sant'Ansano** (daily: April–Oct 8.30am–noon & 3.30–5.30pm; Nov–March closes 6.30pm) for a look at more of the temple and the wonderful fresco-covered crypt (down the stairs to the left of the high altar), originally the home of sixth-century monks.

In a tiny side street east of the piazza is the **Casa Romana**, Via di Visiale (daily except Tues 11am–7pm; €3, or Spoleto Card), a dark and atmospheric little corner that contains the impressive remains of a Roman house.

Basilica di Sant'Eufemia

Via Aurelio Saffi Fri–Sun 10am–1pm & 3–6pm; daily in summer • €6, or Spoleto Card • T 0743 231 022

Leaving Piazza del Mercato to the north and turning right on Via A. Saffi brings you to the medieval town's most celebrated **church**, the eleventh-century **Basilica di Sant'Eufemia**. The church is architecturally unique in Umbria for its *matronei*, high-arched galleries above the side-naves that segregated women from the men in the main body of the church. It was built over the site of the eighth-century Lombard ducal palace and appears to have been partly constructed from the remains of this and earlier Roman monuments; one or two of the completely mismatched columns are carved with distinctive Lombard motifs. The general dank solemnity of the place clearly points to an early foundation.

Museo Diocesano

Via Aurelio Saffi 13 • Fri–Sun 10am–1pm & 3-6pm, daily in summer • €6, or Spoleto Card • T 0743 231 022

Sant'Eufemia is best visited in conjunction with the outstanding **Museo Diocesano**, located in the same courtyard as the church. The eight rooms contain several surprisingly good paintings, including a *Madonna* by Fra' Filippo Lippi and an early Domenico Beccafumi, a room of old wooden statues and some wonderfully graphic votive panels offering thanks for salvation from a host of vividly illustrated mishaps.

The Duomo

Piazza del Duomo • Daily: April–Oct 8.30am–12.30pm & 3.30–7pm; Nov–March closes 5.30pm • Free

Close by the Basilica di Sant'Eufemia is the **Duomo**, whose facade of restrained elegance is one of the most memorable in the region. The careful balance of Romanesque and Renaissance elements is framed by a gently sloping piazza and lovely hanging gardens, but the broad background of sky and open countryside is what sets the seal on the whole thing. The church suffered like many in Italy from the desire of rich communities to make their wealth and power conspicuous, a desire usually realized by tearing the guts out of old churches and remodelling them in the latest style. This worked well on the thirteenth-century **facade**, which has an arched portico tacked on in 1491, but less well in the interior where Pope Urban VIII's architect, Luigi Arrigucci, applied great dollops of Baroque midway through the seventeenth century. His "improvements", luckily, are eclipsed by the apse's superlative **frescoes** by the great Florentine artist Fra' Filippo Lippi, dominated by his final masterpiece, a *Coronation of the Virgin* (1469).

You should also make a point of seeing the **Erioli Chapels** at the beginning of the right nave, primarily for a faded *Madonna and Child* (with Lago Trasimeno in the background) by Pinturicchio (1497). At the beginning of the left nave there's a *Crucifix* of 1187, by Alberto Sotio, which is reckoned to be the oldest painting in Umbria, while a colourful chapel further down the left nave contains a framed letter written by St Francis (one of only two to survive). The cathedral also contains the inevitable **icon**, which Federico Barbarossa gave to the town in 1185 to try to make amends for having flattened it thirty years earlier.

Rocca Albornoziana

Piazza Campello • **Rocca** Daily 9.30am–7.30pm, closes earlier in winter; ticket office closes 45min earlier • **Museo Nazionale del Ducato** Tues–Sun 9.30am–7.30pm • €7.50 combined ticket for the Rocca and the Museo Nazionale del Ducato, or Spoleto Card • 0743 224 952

To the east of town, the **Rocca Albornoziana**, everyone's idea of a cartoon castle, with towers, crenellations and sheer walls, was another in the chain of fortresses with which the tireless Cardinal Albornoz hoped to re-establish Church domination in central Italy, a primacy lost during the fourteenth-century papal exile to Avignon. It served until 1982 as a high-security prison – testimony to the skill of its medieval builders – and was home to, among others, Pope John Paul II's would-be assassin and leading members of the Red Brigade. After years of restoration it now houses the sleek **Museo Nazionale del Ducato**, devoted to the Duchy of Spoleto, with paintings including a couple of big canvases by a follower of Perugino, Lo Spagna – one of several local Renaissance artists represented. Both the museum and fortress are well worth seeing, the Rocca in particular for its superb views, the imposing twin courtyards and the sheer scale of the building.

Ponte delle Torri

If you do nothing else in Spoleto you should take the short walk out to the **Ponte delle Torri**, the town's picture-postcard favourite and an astonishing piece of medieval engineering. The bridge is best taken in as part of a circular walk around the base of the Rocca or on the longer trek out to San Pietro (see below). Within a minute of leaving shady gardens in Piazza Campello you suddenly find yourself looking out over superb countryside, with a dramatic panorama across the Tessino gorge and south to the mountains of Castelmonte.

The bridge is genuinely impressive, with a 240m-long span supported by ten 80m-high arches that have been used as a launching pad by jilted lovers for six

THE DISAPPEARING CORPSE OF FRA' FILIPPO LIPPI

Fra' Filippo Lippi died shortly after completing the frescoes in Spoleto's Duomo, the rumour being that he was poisoned for seducing the daughter of a local noble family, his position as a monk having had no bearing on his sexual appetite. The Spoletans, not too perturbed by moral laxity, were delighted at having someone famous to put in their cathedral, being, as Vasari put it, "poorly provided with ornaments, above all with distinguished men", and so refused to send the dead artist back to Lorenzo de' Medici, his Florentine patron. Interred in a **tomb** designed by his son, Filippino Lippi (now in the right transept), the corpse disappeared during restoration two centuries later, the popular theory being that it was spirited away by descendants of the compromised girl – a sort of vendetta beyond the grave.

centuries. Designed by the Gubbian architect Gattapone, who was also responsible for Gubbio's Palazzo dei Consoli, it was initially planned as an aqueduct to bring water from Monteluco, replacing an earlier Roman causeway whose design Gattapone probably borrowed and enlarged upon. In time it also became used as an escape from the Rocca when Spoleto was under siege. The remains of what used to be a covered passageway connecting the two are still visible straggling down the hillside.

San Pietro

From the far side of the Ponte delle Torri, turn right on the road and make for the church of **San Pietro**, whose facade beckons from a not-too-distant hillside. Though the walk is a longish one (2km), it's pleasantly shady with some good glimpses of Spoleto; beware of drivers taking the bends too fast on the country road, where there are no pavements. The church would be undistinguished were it not for the splendid **sculptures** adorning its facade. Taken with Maitani's bas-reliefs in Orvieto, they are the best Romanesque carvings in Umbria, partly Lombard in their inspiration, and drawing variously on the Gospels and medieval legend for their complicated narrative and symbolic purpose. A particularly juicy scene to look out for includes the *Death of a Sinner* (left series, second from the top) where the Archangel Michael abandons the sinner to a couple of demons who bind and torture him before bringing in burning oil to finish the job. Fourth panel from the top (right series) shows a wolf disguised as a friar before a fleeing ram – a dig at dodgy monastic morals.

ARRIVAL AND DEPARTURE — SPOLETO

By train Spoleto is easily reached by train, with regular services on the main Rome–Ancona line, a daily train to Florence and local links with Foligno, Terni, Narni and elsewhere. The train station is just northwest of the Lower Town; shuttle buses (#A, #B, #C) to the centre (Piazza Carducci) depart from outside the station – buy tickets (€1.30, or €2 on board; valid 90min) from the station bar.

Destinations Arezzo (approx. hourly; 2hr 10min–3hr 10min); Florence direct (1 daily; 2hr 50min); Foligno via Trevi (14 daily; connections for Assisi, Spello, Perugia, Terontola-Cortona and Florence; 20min); Fossato di Vico (8 daily; 50min–1hr 15min); Narni (9 daily; 30–40min); Perugia direct (7 daily; 55min–1hr 15min); Rome (14 daily; 1hr 20min–1hr 45min); Terni (17 daily; 25min).

By bus Buses to and from Norcia and the Valnerina pull in at the railway station; other buses arrive at Piazza della Vittoria, just outside the walls to the north of the town.

Destinations Foligno (Mon–Sat 4 daily; 40min); Fonti del Clitunno (8 daily; 20min); Montefalco (1–4 daily Mon–Sat; 50min); Norcia (4–8 daily; 50min); Rome (1 daily; 2hr 20min); Scheggino (4 daily; 1hr 10min); Terni (6 daily; 45min); Trevi (7 daily; 25min).

INFORMATION

Tourist office Piazza della Libertà 7 (April–Oct Mon–Sat 9am–1.30pm & 2–7pm, Sun 9am–1pm & 3–5.30pm; Nov–March Mon–Sat 9am–1.30pm & 2.30–6.15pm, Sun 9.30am–1pm & 3–5pm; ☎0743 218 620 or 621, Ⓦwww.comunespoleto.gov.it/turismoecultura).

ACCOMMODATION

Albergo Il Panciolle Via del Duomo 3 ☎0743 45 677, Ⓦilpanciolle.it; map p.658. Seven decent two-star

rooms (two with a/c) – the best are nos. 3 and 4, with views over the rooftops. It's above the restaurant of the same name (see below), so outdoor eating can make staying here a noisy option in summer. **€85**

Aurora Via dell'Apollinare 3 ⓣ0743 220 315, ⓦhotelauroraspoleto.it; map p.658. A perfectly situated, 23-room hotel in an alley off Piazza della Libertà, which is expensive for what it is in high season, but can be great value in low season. **€110**

★ **Gattapone** Via del Ponte 6 ⓣ0743 223 447, ⓦhotelgattapone.it; map p.658. When this place opened in the 1960s, it rapidly became the hotel of choice for artists and performers at the festival – and its list of past guests is astonishing: Yehudi Menuhin, Leonard Bernstein, Pablo Neruda, Alan Ginsberg, Henry Moore, Audrey Hepburn, Ingrid Bergman. It's a welcoming and beautifully styled family-run hotel with lovely views from most rooms, which are spectacularly situated above the gorge and almost alongside the Ponte delle Torri. Add €30 on to the price during the festival. **€121**

★ **Palazzo Leti** Via degli Eremiti 10 ⓣ0743 224 930, ⓦpalazzoleti.com; map p.658. Set in the palatial residence of the noble Leti family, this gorgeously renovated hotel has elegantly decorated rooms with views of the valley; book one on the top floor for the best panorama. There's also a beautiful formal garden. **€190**

San Luca Via Interna delle Mura 21 ⓣ0743 223 399, ⓦwww.hotelsanluca.com; map p.658. This very tastefully furnished four-star is efficiently run and has the bonus of a large, sunny garden and an internal furnished courtyard. **€130**

10

EATING

★ **Apollinare** Via Sant'Agata 14 ⓣ0743 223 256, ⓦristoranteapollinare.it; map p.658. The blue and gold upholstery is initially off-putting, but the medieval setting is good and the welcome friendly. *Secondi* are around €15, or go for the three-course "Surprise" tasting menu (€25, or €35 for five courses including wine) if you want to try something new. There's a vegetarian menu as well. Don't miss the sublime *caramella* starter – a cheese-and-truffle delight. Daily noon–3pm & 7–10.30pm; closed Tues in winter.

Caffè Letterario Via Brignone ⓣ0743 46 691; map p.658. Literary café in the *palazzo* that houses the town library, offering simple snacks and excellent coffees, along with books and magazines to leaf through. There are regular photo exhibitions and book presentations, and free wi-fi. Tues–Sun 8am–7pm, Mon 2–7pm.

Canasta Piazza della Libertà 14 ⓣ0743 40 205, ⓦcanastaspoleto.it; map p.658. Historic café on the main square, which keeps the townspeople happy with tasty savouries and tempting pastries. Set three-course menus at €18 and €25. A great place to start the day. Daily except Wed, 7am–11pm.

Il Panciolle Via del Duomo 3 ⓣ0743 221 241, ⓦilpanciolle.it; map p.658. Below the hotel of the same name, this is a good choice for a reliable and reasonably priced meal of Umbrian specialities such as *stringozzi* and fire-grilled meats (*secondi* €11–17); it's also known for its selection of cheeses. There's a great outside terrace, and the medieval interior with open fire is cosy in winter. Tues–Sun 12.30–3pm & 7.30pm–midnight.

Il Tempio del Gusto Via Arco del Druso 11 ⓣ0743 47 121, ⓦiltempiodelgusto.com; map p.658. "*The Temple of Taste*" was founded by Eros Patrizi, a former pupil of Vissani, patron of the eponymous restaurant near Baschi, in southern Umbria, that for years has rated as one of Italy's best. Standards – and the often recherché cooking – are similar, and you'll be paying around €50 without wine à la carte, but there are more reasonably charged set menus especially at lunchtime. Daily except Thurs noon–3.30pm & 7–11pm.

La Lanterna Via della Trattoria 6 ⓣ0743 49 815; map p.658. A convivial, central place and the best of the town's mid-price trattorias, on a side street left off the hill between Piazza della Libertà and Piazza Fontana. It serves huge helpings of delicious pasta from €8 and grilled meats and other mains from €9. Daily except Wed 12.30–3pm & 7.30–10.30pm.

Pasticceria Tebro Via Minervia 1 ⓣ0743 45 400, ⓦpasticceriatebro.it; map p.658. Artisan pastries and ice cream in a historic café-*pasticceria*, well worth a visit for breakfast or ice cream, or at *aperitivo* time for a spritz and nibbles. Be sure to try the silky espresso. Daily 7am–9pm.

The Valnerina

The **VALNERINA** is the most beautiful part of Umbria. Strictly translated as the "little valley of the Nera", it effectively refers to the whole eastern part of the region, a self-contained area of high mountains, poor communications, steep wooded valleys, upland villages and vast stretches of barren nothingness. Wolves still roam the summit ridges – with isolated incidences of them savaging sheep making the news every so often – and the area is a genuine "forgotten corner", deserted farms everywhere bearing witness to a century of emigration.

Mountains in the region are 1500m high, creeping up as you move east to about 2500m in the wonderful **Monti Sibillini**, the most outstanding parts of which fall under

the protection of the **Parco Nazionale dei Monti Sibillini**. It's difficult to explore with any sort of plan (unless you stick to the river Nera), and the best approach is to follow your nose, poking into small valleys, tracing high country lanes to remote hamlets. More deliberately, you could make for **Vallo di Nera**, the most archetypal of the **fortified villages** that pop up along the Lower Nera. Medieval **Triponzo** is a natural focus of communications, little more than a quaint staging post and fortified tower (and a better target than modernish Cerreto nearby).

GETTING AROUND

By car The Valnerina is best explored with a car, as public transport is very limited. A road-tunnel links Spoleto to the valley, but for scenery stick to the old and tortuous N395 from Spoleto until you hit the "main" SS209 and the more pastoral run up the Nera Valley towards Norcia.

By bus The easiest way to get to the region without a car is by bus from Spoleto station to Norcia (5–7 daily Mon–Sat; 1hr 15min).

Norcia

The very pleasant mountain retreat of **NORCIA** is the only place of any size or substance in the Valnerina. Noted on the one hand as the birthplace of **St Benedict** – founder of Western monasticism – and on the other as the producer of Italy's top salami, it has an air of charming dereliction, and its low, sturdy houses (built to be earthquake-resistant) are a world away from the pastoral, fairy-tale cities to the west. If transport allows, it could be the base for some good trips into neighbouring territory, particularly the famed Piano Grande (see page 665) and the mountains to the east and north. A major road through the mountains into Le Marche has brought in more visitors – good news for local employment, which is scarce, but a blight on the environment. Hang-gliders and winter-sports enthusiasts have also discovered the area, another mixed blessing. At the time of writing, Norcia is still rebuilding after a severe earthquake in 2016.

It doesn't take long to see the town, but you may want to stay on for the pleasant atmosphere and the surrounding scenery. Most of the action is in the central **Piazza San Benedetto**, site of the Roman forum and presided over by a statue of Benedict. Apart from its facade, you can largely forget about the **Duomo** – destroyed by a series of earthquakes and patched up to look like nothing on earth. The **Castellina** is more captivating: a papal fortress full of gaunt medieval echoes, it contains a fine little **museum** (Oct–April Wed–Sun 10am–1pm & 3–5pm; May–Sept Tues–Sun 10am–1pm & 4–7.30pm; €5)with fascinating old wooden sculptures and several surprisingly accomplished paintings. The ticket also admits you to the **Criptoportico Romano** (same hours), a Roman-era gate and passageway by the present-day Porta Ascolana.

The fortress makes a strange bedfellow for the labyrinthine church of **San Benedetto**, which supposedly was built over the saint's birthplace but was probably raised from the ruins of an earlier Roman temple. Inside there are a few paltry frescoes, nothing more, though the crypt contains the remains of a Roman-era house.

ARRIVAL AND INFORMATION — NORCIA

By bus There are only a few services running to and from Norcia; check umbriamobilita.it for timetables.

Destinations Rome (2 daily Mon–Sat, 1 on Sun; 3hr); Spoleto via Borge Cerretto & Sant'Anatolia di Narco (5 daily Mon–Sat, 3 daily Sun; 1hr); Terni (1 daily; 1hr).

Tourist offices Visitor information is available from the Palazzo Comunale on the main Piazza San Benedetto (Mon–Fri 9.30am–1pm, and possibly some afternoons in summer; 0743 828 173, comune.norcia.pg.it). In summer there's also a branch of the Casa del Parco, with information on the Parco Nazionale dei Monti Sibillini, in the same building (July & Aug daily 9.30am–12.30pm & 3.30–6.30pm; 0743 828 173, www.sibillini.net).

ACCOMMODATION

Norcia has always seen lots of pilgrims, in town for Benedict and trips to Assisi and Loreto in Le Marche for the house of the Virgin (see page 698), but these days its accommodation is under pressure from growing numbers

NORCIA FOR FOODIES

Meat-eaters would be daft not to try the deservedly famous local **pork** products. Anything that can be made from a pig, the Norcians apparently make – and supposedly better than anyone else. For this reason, *alimentari* throughout Italy who pride themselves on their hams and salamis will call themselves a *norcineria*. If finances stretch, you could also indulge in the area's prized black **truffle**. The season runs from January to April (though you may come across the lesser-prized white summer truffles too). Plenty of shops, an attraction in themselves, are on hand to sell you all manner of local specialities, not just truffles, but also hams, the famed lentils of Castelluccio and lots of rare mountain cheeses.

of secular visitors, so it makes sense to **book well in advance**, especially from June to Aug. Prices tend to go up at summer weekends. You should also book ahead during the truffle festival, between the last weekend in Feb and the first weekend in March.

Ostello Il Capisterium Via Manzoni 2 ⓣ 349 300 2091, ⓦ norciaospitalita.it. Fine, recently refurbished hostel popular with pilgrims right in the centre of town in a beautiful ex-monastery with swimming pool. Accommodation in doubles, triples and shared quads. Breakfast included. Dorms €15, doubles €60

★ **Palazzo Seneca** Via Cesare Battisti 12 ⓣ 0743 817 434, ⓦ palazzoseneca.com. This sixteenth-century residence has recently been restored to create an elegant and supremely comfortable hotel. The rooms are tastefully furnished with antiques and four-poster beds, and the marble bathrooms are wonderfully luxurious. There's also a spa and gourmet restaurant, *Vespasia* (see below). €210

EATING AND DRINKING

Trattoria dei Priori Via dei Priori 3 ⓣ 0743 816 282, ⓦ trattoriadeipriori.it. Well-prepared local dishes – such as *fettuccine al cinghiale* (with wild boar) – are served up in a simple, barrel-vaulted space. Fixed-price menus at €31 and €42. Wed–Mon noon–2.30pm & 7.30–10.30pm.

★ **Vespasia** Via Cesare Battisti 12 ⓣ 0743 817 434, ⓦ palazzoseneca.com. Norcia's smartest hotel, *Palazzo Seneca*, has a suitably tasteful (and pricey) Michelin-starred restaurant, serving up refined versions of the local specialities such as *risotto alla crema d'ortica* – risotto with wild nettle. Tasting menus run from €80–150, and the same price range holds for dining à la carte. Daily 12.30–2.30pm & 7.30–9.30pm.

The Piano Grande

The eerie, expansive **Piano Grande**, 20km east of Norcia, is an extraordinary prairie ringed by bare, whaleback mountains and stretching, uninterrupted by tree, hedge or habitation, for kilometres and kilometres. A decade or so ago, it was all but unknown: now, in summer at least, it can be disconcertingly busy. It's much photographed – especially in spring when it's ablaze with wild flowers of every description – and was used by Zeffirelli as a setting for his Franciscan film *Brother Sun, Sister Moon*. The desperately isolated village of **CASTELLUCCIO** hangs above it at around 1400m, and although no longer the sole preserve of shepherds, it remains an unspoilt base and the ideal starting point for any number of straightforward mountain **walks**. To plan routes, get hold of the 1:50,000 Kompass map no. 666 or the more detailed 1:25,000 CAI maps.

Note that there's **no public transport** into the area (save for one bus in and out on a Thurs, market day in Norcia), though you might try your luck at catching lifts in high season.

Terni and around

TERNI was the unlikely birthplace of one of the world's most famous saints, **St Valentine**, bishop of the town until his martyrdom in 273 and now entombed in his personal basilica at San Valentino, a village 2km to the southwest. A less romantic city, however, would be hard to imagine. Terni's important arms and steel industries made it a target for Allied bombing in 1944, and eighty percent of the town was reduced to rubble. Rebuilding replaced what was lost with a grey gridiron; it also put

the arms industry back on its feet – the gun used to assassinate President Kennedy was made here. That said, a swathe of industrial wasteland on the outskirts is undergoing recovery, and an abandoned factory just east of the river at Viale Luigi Campofregoso 98 has been transformed into the **CAOS** complex (ⓦcaos.museum), a centre for contemporary art, which is also home to an archeological museum, a bookshop, theatre and bar.

ARRIVAL AND DEPARTURE — TERNI

By train As might be expected of an industrial town, Terni has great train connections, and sits at the junction between the Ancona–Rome and L'Aquila–Todi–Perugia–Città di Castello–Sansepolcro lines. The station is a 5min walk from the town centre.

Destinations Città di Castello (UM line; up to 6 daily; 2hr 20min–4hr 50min); Foligno (every 30min–1hr; connections to Spello, Assisi, Gualdo Tadino, Fossato di Vico and Perugia; 35–50min); Narni (9 daily; 7min); Orte (11 daily; connections to Rome, Orvieto, Chiusi, Arezzo and Florence; 15–30min); Perugia (UM line up to 7 daily; connections at UM Sant'Anna station in Perugia for Città di Castello and Sansepolcro, shared UM and FS/Trenitalia station at Ponte San Giovanni for connections to Foligno and Terontola; 1hr 30min); Sansepolcro (UM line; 10–16 daily via Perugia Sant'Anna; 2hr 40min–4hr 30min); Todi (UM line; 7 daily; 45min).

By bus Buses stop at the train station, making it easy to move on from Terni without having to enter town, if needed.

Destinations Cascata delle Marmore (at least hourly; 15min); Orvieto (approx. hourly Mon–Sat; 2hr–2hr 20min); Scheggino (8 daily Mon–Sat, 5 Sun; 55min); Todi (3–6 daily Mon–Sat; 1hr 15min–2hr); also long-distance services to Bolsena (connection at Orvieto) and Rome (2 daily; 1hr 25min).

INFORMATION

Tourist office Via Cassian Bon 2–4 – take Viale della Stazione from the station, and it's 400m up, on the right, just beyond Piazza Cornelio Tacito (Mon–Sat 9am–1pm & 3–6pm; ⓣ0744 423 047, ⓦ turismo.comune.terni.it).

Scheggino

By following the SS209 from Terni past the walled, medieval village of **SCHEGGINO** you can pick up the Spoleto road into the Valnerina (see page 663). The village is a pretty spot to stop for lunch, and a better overnight option than Terni and many other places up and down the valley.

ACCOMMODATION AND EATING — SCHEGGINO

★ **Albergo-Trattoria del Ponte** Via del Borgo 11–17 ⓣ0743 61 253, ⓦalbergoristorantedelponte.com. Bright, simple bedrooms, and there is also an excellent restaurant; the trout dishes with truffles, in particular, are superb. Restaurant closed Mon except in Aug. €60, half board/person €50

Narni

NARNI claims to be the geographical centre of Italy, with a hilltop site jutting into the Nera Valley on a majestic spur and crowned by another of Cardinal Albornoz's formidable papal fortresses. Commanding one end of a steep gorge (about ten minutes of fairly spectacular train travel), it was once the gateway into Umbria, the last post before the Tiber Valley and the undefended road to Rome. However, while the town retains a fine medieval character, the views from its heights are marred by steel and chemical works around **Narni Scalo**, the new town in the valley below.

The heart of the **old town** has all the standard fittings: the medieval piazzas, the warren of streets, a modest art gallery, the usual crop of Romanesque churches and a huge *rocca*, open for occasional events. There's a **Roman bridge** on the outskirts, the subject of considerable local hype: when Goethe arrived in Narni in the middle of the night he was peeved not to have seen it, but he was only missing a solitary arch in the middle of the river – just as easily viewed from the train.

Museo della Città di Narni

Via Aurelio Saffi 1 • April–June Tues–Sun 10.30am–1pm & 3.30–6pm; July & Aug Mon 11am–4.30pm, Tues–Sun 10.30am–6.30pm; Sept daily 10am–6pm; Oct–March Fri, Sat, Sun only 10.30am–1pm & 3–5.30pm • €5 • T 0744 717 117

The bulk of the town's paintings and other works of art are housed in the **Museo della Città di Narni** in the Palazzo Eroli. The highlight is a superlative and much-copied *Coronation of the Virgin* by Ghirlandaio, with a collection of good works by minor medieval Umbrian artists.

ARRIVAL, INFORMATION AND TOURS — NARNI

By train It's an easy 30min hop on the train from Terni to Narni, whose station is below the old town in Narni Scalo; there are buses roughly every hour to Piazza Garibaldi in the old town.

By bus Buses from out of town stop at the railway station and at Piazza Garibaldi in the old town; there are frequent services to Terni approx. hourly; 30min).

Tourist office In the town hall at Piazza dei Priori 2 (generally Mon–Fri 9.30am–12.30pm & 4.30–6/7pm, Sat 9.30am–12.30pm, but hours can vary; T 0744 715 362, W turismonarni.it).

Guided tours Some of Narni's most captivating sights lie beneath the streets – parts of Roman cisterns, eighth-century chapels and more, all of which can be seen on 1hr guided tours led by Narni Sotterranea ("Narni Underground"), at Via S. Bernardo 12 (usually 4–6 daily at weekends only, but check the website for the latest programme; €6; T 0744 722 292, W narnisotterranea.it).

ACCOMMODATION AND EATING

Hotel Dei Priori Vicolo del Comune 4 T 0744 726 843, W **loggiadeipriori.it**. Lovely family-run hotel in the heart of Narni, in a medieval building with loggia. Spick-and-span rooms, friendly service and a well-regarded restaurant. **€75**

Todi

TODI is one of the best-known Umbrian hill-towns, its central **Piazza del Popolo** widely held to be among the most perfect medieval piazzas in Italy, and the town itself to be the country's most liveable. At heart a thriving and insular agricultural centre, Todi is also a favoured trendy retreat for foreign expats and Rome's arts and media types. Few places in Umbria can beat it for sheer location – its hilltop position is stunning – and fairy-tale medievalism. Many festivals and events are held in Todi throughout the year, including the increasingly popular **Todi Festival** (late Aug or early Sept; W todifestival.com).

The Duomo

Piazza del Popolo • April–Oct: Mon–Sat 8am–12.30pm & 3–6.30pm, Sun 8.30am–1pm & 3–7pm; Nov–March Mon–Sat 8am–12.30pm & 1.30–5pm, Sun 8.30am–1pm & 3–6pm • Church free, museum €3

The **Duomo** at the far (northern) end of Piazza del Popolo, atop a broad flight of steps, is the town's main feature – a meeting point of the last of the Romanesque and the first of the Gothic forms filtering up from France in the early fourteenth century. The square, three-tiered **facade** is inspired simplicity; just a sumptuous rose window (1520) and ornately carved doorway to embellish the pinky weathered marble – the classic example of a form found all over Umbria. Inevitably the interior is less impressive, though the strikingly carved **choir** (1530) – of incredible delicacy and precision – is the region's best, with panels at floor level near the front depicting the tools used to carve the piece. There's also some delicate nineteenth-century stained glass in the arched nave on the right, and a good altarpiece by Giannicola di Paolo (a follower of Perugino), while a poor sixteenth-century *Last Judgement*, loosely derived from Michelangelo's, defaces the back wall. The crypt and small **museum** contains a rambling collection of ancient Roman – and possibly Etruscan – fragments and religious ephemera.

The palaces

Three **public palaces** square off near the Duomo in deliberately provocative fashion as an expression of medieval civic pride – definitely trying to put one over on the Church. The **Palazzo del Capitano** (1290) and adjacent **Palazzo del Popolo** (begun 1213) are most prominent, thanks mainly to the stone staircase that looks like the setting for a thousand B-movie sword fights.

Museo-Pinacoteca di Todi

Piazza del Popolo 29–30 • Tues–Sun: April–Oct 10am–1.30pm & 3–6pm; Nov–March 10.30am–1pm & 2.30–5pm • €5, or €8.50 combined ticket with Cisterne Romane (see below) and Campanile di San Fortunato (see below) • 075 894 418, coopculture.it

The Palazzo del Capitano houses a superb museum, the **Museo-Pinacoteca di Todi**, which brilliantly weaves an open-plan sequence of rooms into the existing medieval structure. The first section of the museum delves into Todi's history, followed by rooms devoted to archeology, coins and medallions, fabrics, ceramics and a picture gallery. In many cases the rooms are more alluring than their displays – particularly the lovely frescoed salon devoted to ceramics – but numerous individual exhibits merit a closer look, none more so than the museum's star painting: the sumptuous *Coronation of the Virgin* (1507) by Lo Spagna.

Palazzo dei Priori

The **Palazzo dei Priori** (1293–1337) is the southernmost building in Piazza del Popolo, with all the various crenellations, battlements and mullioned windows of the other palaces but with the difference that they've been recently restored. It's been the seat of all the town's various rulers and today is still the town hall; if you can look as if you're on council business you should be able to peep inside.

Cisterne Romane

Via del Monte • Oct–March Fri 2–5pm, Sat, Sun 10am–1pm & 2–5pm; April, May & Sept Mon, Wed, Thurs, Fri 3–6pm, Sat & Sun 10am–6pm; June, July & Aug 10am–6pm • €2, or €8.50 combined ticket with Museo-Pinacoteca di Todi (see above) and Campanile di San Fortunato • 075 894 4148

A side street leads off the west side of Piazza del Popolo to the **Cisterne Romane**, a massive Roman cistern, which offers a graphic illustration of the Romans' prodigious engineering abilities. Though it is possible to visit only a fraction of the site, the tunnels stretch for over 5km.

San Fortunato

Church Tues–Sun: April to mid-Oct 9am–1pm & 3–7pm; mid-Oct to March 10am–1pm & 2.30–5pm • Free • **Campanile** Tues–Sun: April–Oct 10am–1pm & 3–6.30pm; Nov–March 10.30am–1pm & 2.30–5pm; €2, or €8.50 combined ticket with Museo-Pinacoteca di Todi (see above) and Cisterne Romane (see above)

The single most celebrated sight in town after the Piazza del Popolo is the church of **San Fortunato**, set above gardens a very short stroll from the centre. It's an enormous thing given the size of the town – testimony to Todi's medieval wealth and importance. The squat, messy and clearly unfinished facade, an amalgam of Romanesque and Gothic styles, reflects the time it took to build (1292–1462) and at first glance doesn't exactly raise expectations. A florid **Gothic doorway** of arched swirls and carved craziness, however, is the first of several surprises, the second of which is the enormous light, airy interior. It marks the pinnacle of the Umbrian tradition for large vaulted churches, a style based on the smaller and basic "barn churches" common in Tuscany, which were distinguished by a single, low-pitched roof, and naves and aisles of equal height – San Domenico in Perugia is another example (see page 634). It also marks a trend for side-chapels, a habit picked up from Catalonia and southern France in the thirteenth century and made necessary by the rising demand for daily Masses as the Franciscans became a more ministering order.

There's a good **choir**, heavier and with more hints of the Baroque than the one in the Duomo, as well as a few scant patches of Sienese fresco. The fresco by **Masolino di Panicale** in the fourth chapel on the right is a good example of this painter's rare work, though a bit battered. Some lovely **cloisters** to the rear round off a distinctive and worthwhile church. Climb the **campanile** for sweeping views.

The stony track to the west of San Fortunato leads to the rambling **Giardino Pubblico**, an ideal place for a siesta. Full of shady nooks and narrow pathways, it's a cut above the normal town plot. There's also a kids' playground and a very small **Rocca**, both less noteworthy than the views, which are extensive though usually hazy.

Santa Maria della Consolazione

Viale della Consolazione • Daily except Tues: April–Oct 9am–12.30pm & 3–6.30pm; Nov–March 9.30am–12.30pm & 2.30–5pm • Free

A ten-minute walk west of the Tempio di San Fortunato is the **Santa Maria della Consolazione**, completed in 1607. Called the best Renaissance church in Italy by Victorian writers (pretty close to saying the best in the world), it's thought to have been based on an earlier Bramante draft for St Peter's in Rome; the alternating window types in the cupola are a Bramante trademark.

ARRIVAL AND INFORMATION — TODI

By train There are UM trains from Terni and Perugia approximately hourly. Todi's train station, Ponte Rio, is in the middle of nowhere; bus #C runs to the centre roughly hourly. If you want to book a taxi, call ⊕075 894 2375, ⊕075 894 2525 or ⊕347 774 8321.

By bus Buses are less frequent than trains. They stop below the town by the church of Santa Maria della Consolazione, or higher up, just off the main square near San Fortunato.

Destinations Assisi (1 daily; 1hr 40min); Orvieto (1 daily; 2hr 10min); Perugia (4–8 daily; 1hr 15min); Terni (1–3 daily Mon–Sat; 50min).

Tourist office Via del Monte 23 (April–Oct: Mon–Sat 9.30am–1pm & 3.30–6.30pm, Sun 10am–1.30pm; Nov–March Mon–Sat 10am–1pm & 3–6pm, Sun 10am–1pm; ⊕075 895 6529, ⊕visitodi.eu).

ACCOMMODATION

Fonte Cesia Via Lorenzo Leoni 3 ⊕075 894 3737, ⊕fontecesia.it. Converted medieval townhouse at the heart of the historic core. Rooms vary in size and decoration, but all have period details, rich fabrics and up-to-the-minute facilities. **€90**

★ **San Lorenzo Tre** Via S. Lorenzo 3 ⊕075 894 4555, ⊕sanlorenzo3.it. If you don't mind lugging your suitcase up steep flights of steps, this elegantly furnished *residenza* inside a townhouse in the street parallel to Via del Duomo is Todi's most appealing place to stay. Rooms vary in size (and in price); no. 5 is the nicest, beautifully furnished with antiques, and with stunning views of the surrounding countryside. What's more, there's a shady garden and a fabulous roof terrace. **€95**

EATING AND DRINKING

Cavour Corso Cavour 21 ⊕075 894 3730, ⊕ristorante cavour-todi.com. This unpretentious trattoria has stunning views from its outdoor terrace and several cosy rooms indoors. You can eat very well for around €30, or cheaper if you go for one of the generous pizzas (from €5) including asparagus and mushroom, and potato with Gorgonzola. Daily noon–3pm & 7pm–midnight; closed Thurs in winter.

La Mulinella Località Pontenaia 29 ⊕075 894 4779, ⊕ristorantelamulinellatodi.com. Wonderful place on the southern edge of town, where everything is home-made, from the bread (versions with sage, with chilli and with hazelnuts) to the pasta (from €9). Great winter soups (€10) as well. Desserts include a marvellous *zuppa inglese* (trifle). Daily except Wed 12.30–2.30pm & 7.30–10pm.

Pane e Vino Via Ciuffelli 33 ⊕075 894 5448, ⊕www.panevinotodi.com. Just off the main square, this place is perfect for simple lunches and suppers (from €30 for three courses): there's a tremendous choice of antipasti. Try the house special: a sharing platter including smoked duck breast *carpaccio* and cheeses served with honey (€19). *Primi* might include a risotto with pumpkin and saffron, and *taglierini* with tomato and lemon, as well as the usual game, mushroom and truffle dishes. Daily except Wed 12.30–2.30pm & 7.30–10pm.

★ **Umbria** Via San Bonaventura ⊕075 894 2737, ⊕ristoranteumbria.it. The town's best-known restaurant has higher than average prices, but the panorama from the terrace is unbeatable; go for something simple, like a bean soup (€9) or the chargrilled meat (from around €15), and in season, book to be sure of an outside table. Daily except Tues 12.30–2.30pm & 7.30–10pm.

Orvieto

10

Out on a limb from the rest of Umbria, **ORVIETO** is perfectly placed between Rome and Florence to serve as a historical picnic for tour operators. Visitors flood into the town, drawn by the **Duomo**, one of the greatest Gothic buildings in Italy. However, once its facade and Signorelli's frescoes have been admired, the town's not quite as exciting as guides and word of mouth make out. This is partly to do with the gloominess of the dark volcanic rock from which Orvieto is built, and, more poetically, because it harbours something of the characteristic brooding atmosphere of Etruscan towns (it was one of the twelve-strong federation of Etruscan cities). Two thousand years on, it's not difficult to detect a more laidback atmosphere in the cities east of the Tiber – founded by the Umbrians, a sunnier and easier-going people. All the same Orvieto is likeable, the setting superb, the Duomo unmissable and the rest of the town good for a couple of hours' visit. And you could always indulge in its renowned white **wine** if you're stuck with time on your hands. Over New Year there's also the Umbria Jazz Winter festival: five days of marching bands and jazz performances.

It is the first impressions of Orvieto from afar that tend to linger; its position is almost as remarkable and famous as its cathedral. The town, rising 300m sheer from the valley floor, sits on a tabletop plug of volcanic lava, one of four such remnants in the vicinity. It starts to look fairly average again from the dismal town around the train station, but hit the twisting 3km road up to the old centre and you begin to get a sense of its drama and one-off weirdness. Orvieto's old centre is compact and walkable: all of the main sights are within a twenty-minute stroll of the Duomo.

The Duomo

Piazza del Duomo • March & Oct Mon–Sat 9.30am–6pm, Sun 1–5.30pm; April–Sept Mon–Sat 9.30am–7pm; Sun 1–5.30pm; Nov–Feb Mon–Sat 9.30am–1pm & 2.30–5pm, Sun 2.30–4.30pm; Cappella di San Brizio same hours, except Sun: Nov–June closes 5.30pm; July–Oct closes 6.30pm • €4, or €5 combined ticket with Museo dell'Opera del Duomo (see page 672), or Carta Orvieto Unica • Ⓦ opsm.it

Burckhardt described Orvieto's **Duomo** as "the greatest and richest polychrome monument in the world", while Pope Leo XIII called it "the Golden Lily of Italian cathedrals", adding that on the Day of Judgement it would float up to heaven carried by its own beauty. According to a tradition fostered by the Church, it was built to celebrate the so-called **Miracle of Bolsena** of 1263 (see page 673). It was miraculous that the Duomo was built at all. Medieval Orvieto was so violent that at times the population thought about giving up on it altogether. Dante wrote that its family feuds were worse than those between Verona's Montagues and Capulets. The building was also dogged by a committee approach to design – even the plans took thirty years to draw up. Yet though construction dragged on for three centuries and exhausted 33 architects, 152 sculptors, 68 painters and 90 mosaicists, the final product is a surprisingly unified example of the transitional Romanesque-Gothic style. Credit for guiding the work at its most important stage goes to the Sienese architect **Lorenzo Maitani** (c.1270–1330), with the initial plans probably drawn up by Arnolfo di Cambio, architect of Florence's Palazzo Vecchio.

The facade

The **facade** is the star turn, owing its undeniable impact to a decorative richness just the right side of overkill. It's a riot of columns, spires, bas-reliefs, sculptures, dazzling and almost overpowering use of colour, colossally emphasized doorways and hundreds of capricious details just about held together by four enormous fluted columns. Stunning from the dwarfed piazza, particularly at sunset or under floodlights, it's not all superficial gloss. The **four pillars** at the base, one of the highlights of fourteenth-century Italian sculpture, are well worth a close look. The work of Maitani and his pupils, they describe episodes from the Old and New Testaments in staggering detail: lashings of plague,

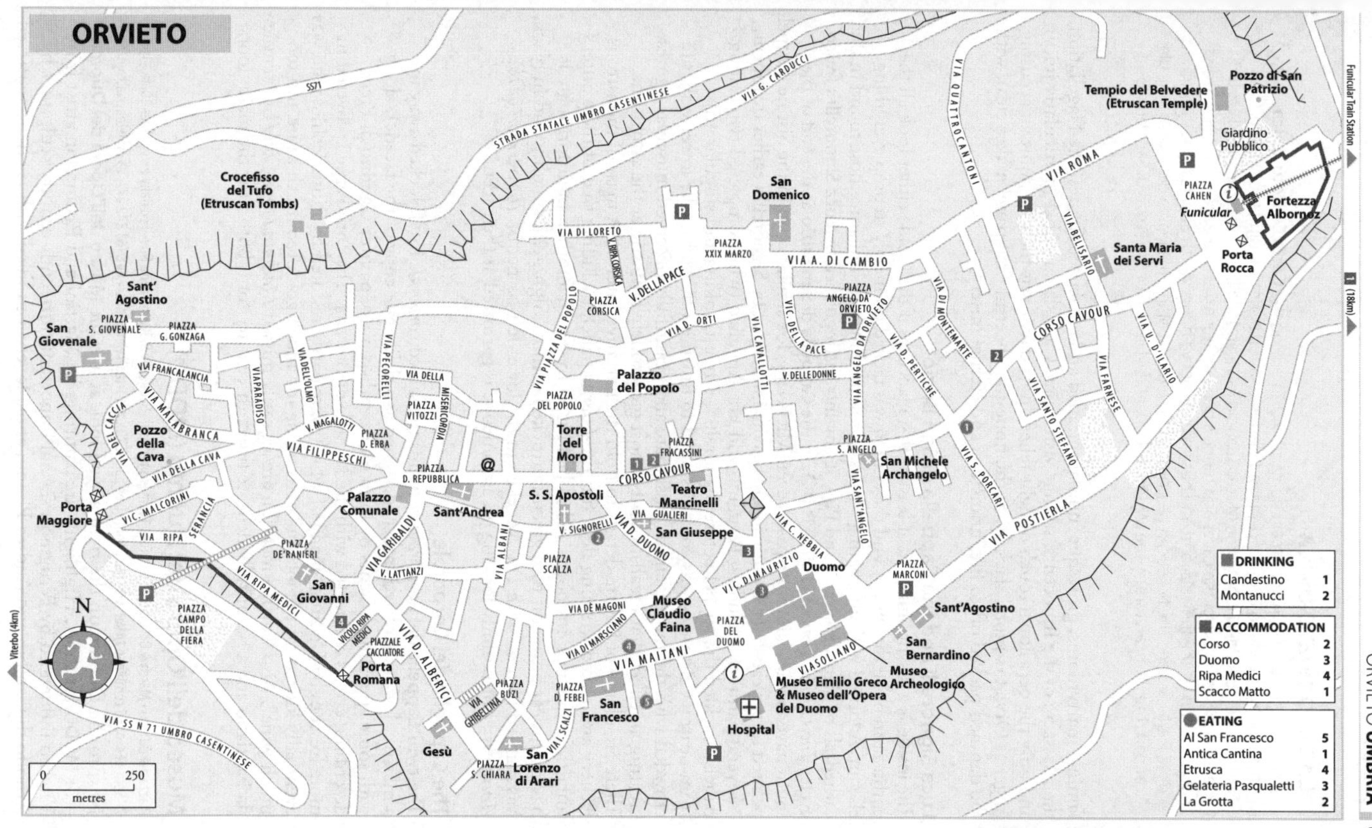
ORVIETO
Funicular Train Station
1 (18km)
Viterbo (4km)
DRINKING
Clandestino 1
Montanucci 2
ACCOMMODATION
Corso 2
Duomo 3
Ripa Medici 4
Scacco Matto 1
EATING
Al San Francesco 5
Antica Cantina 1
Etrusca 4
Gelateria Pasqualetti 3
La Grotta 2
Pozzo di San Patrizio
Tempio del Belvedere (Etruscan Temple)
Giardino Pubblico
Piazza Cahen
Funicular
Fortezza Albornoz
Porta Rocca
Santa Maria dei Servi
San Domenico
Crocefisso del Tufo (Etruscan Tombs)
Sant' Agostino
San Giovenale
Piazza S. Giovenale
Piazza G. Gonzaga
Pozzo della Cava
Porta Maggiore
Palazzo del Popolo
Piazza del Popolo
Torre del Moro
Piazza Fracassini
Piazza Corsica
Piazza XXIX Marzo
Piazza Angelo da' Orvieto
Piazza S. Angelo
San Michele Archangelo
Teatro Mancinelli
S. S. Apostoli
San Giuseppe
Piazza D. Repubblica
Palazzo Comunale
Sant'Andrea
Piazza Vitozzi
Piazza D. Erba
Piazza De'Ranieri
San Giovanni
Piazza Campo della Fiera
Piazzale Cacciatore
Porta Romana
Piazza Scalza
Museo Claudio Faina
Piazza del Duomo
Duomo
Piazza Marconi
Sant'Agostino
San Bernardino
Museo Archeologico
Museo Emilio Greco & Museo dell'Opera del Duomo
Hospital
San Francesco
Piazza D. Febei
Piazza Buzi
Gesù
Piazza S. Chiara
San Lorenzo di Arari
SS71
Strada Statale Umbro Casentinese
Via G. Carducci
Via Quattrocantoni
Via Roma
Via Belisario
Via Farnese
Via U. D'Ilario
Corso Cavour
Via Santo Stefano
Via Postierla
Via S. Porcari
Via di Montemarte
Via D. Pertiche
Via Angelo da Orvieto
Vic. della Pace
V. delle Donne
Via Cavallotti
Via A. di Cambio
Via di Loreto
V. Ripa Corsica
V. della Pace
Via D. Orti
Via Piazza del Popolo
Via Sant'Angelo
Via C. Nebbia
Vic. Dimaurizio
Via D. Duomo
Via Gualieri
V. Signorelli
Via Albani
V. Lattanzi
Via Garibaldi
Via dè Magoni
Via di Marsciano
Via Maitani
Viasoliano
Via D. Alberici
Via Ghibellina
Via I. Scalzi
Via della Misericordia
Via Pecorelli
Via dell'Olmo
Viaparadiso
V. Magalotti
Via Filippeschi
Via Francalancia
Via Malabranca
Via del Caccia
Via della Cava
Vic. Malcorini
Via Ripa Serancia
Via Ripa Medici
Vicolo Ripa Medici
Via SS N 71 Umbro Casentinese
N
0 250 metres

10

CARTA ORVIETO UNICA

If you plan to visit all Orvieto's main sights, it's worth buying the **Carta Orvieto Unica** (inorvieto.it). Costing €20, it provides admission to attractions including the Duomo, the Museo dell'Opera del Duomo, the Museo Claudio Faina and the Etruscan tombs, the Pozzo di San Patrizio and tours of the caves and tunnels beneath the town (see page 674). It also allows you one trip on the funicular and one bus journey, or five hours' worth of parking at the Campo della Fiera car park. The ticket can be bought at the tourist office, the Piazza della Pace funicular car park, the Etruscan tombs, the Museo dell'Opera del Duomo or the Pozzo di San Patrizio.

famine, martyrdoms, grotesque mutilation, mad and emaciated figures, the Flagellation, the Massacre of the Innocents, strange visitations, Cain slaying Abel (particularly juicy), and only the occasional touch of light relief. In its day it was there to point an accusing finger at Orvieto's moral slackers, as the none-too-cheerful final panel makes clear, with the damned packed off to fire, brimstone and eternal misery.

Luca Signorelli and the Cappella di San Brizio

The **inside** is a disappointment at least at first glance, as if the facade either took all the enthusiasm or all the money and the church was tacked on merely to prop everything else up. Adorned with alternating stripes of coloured marble similar to those found in the cathedrals of Siena, Florence and Pisa, it's mainly distinguished by **Luca Signorelli**'s fresco cycle, *The Last Judgement* (1499–1504), in the **Cappella di San Brizio** at the end of the south nave. Some claim it surpasses even Michelangelo's similar cycle in the Sistine Chapel, painted forty years later and obviously heavily influenced by Signorelli's earlier treatment.

Several painters, including Perugino and Fra' Angelico (who completed two ceiling panels), tackled the chapel before Signorelli – a free-thinking and singular artist from nearby Cortona – was commissioned to finish it off. All but the lower walls are crowded with the movement of passionate and beautifully observed muscular figures, creating an effect that's realistic and almost grotesquely fantastic at the same time. There are plenty of bizarre details to hold the narrative interest. A mass of monstrous lechery and naked writhing flesh fills the *Inferno* panel, including that of the painter's unfaithful mistress, immortalized in hell for all to see. In another an unfortunate is having his ear bitten off by a green-buttocked demon. Signorelli, suitably clad in black, has painted himself with Fra' Angelico in the lower left corner of *The Sermon of the Antichrist*, both calmly looking on as someone is garrotted at their feet.

The Cappella del Corporale

The twin **Cappella del Corporale** contains the sacred *corporale* itself, locked away in a massive, jewel-encrusted casket (designed as a deliberate copy of the facade), along with some appealing frescoes by local fourteenth-century painter Ugolino di Prete, describing events connected with the Miracle of Bolsena. The entire apse is covered in more frescoes by Ugolino, many of which were partly restored by Pinturicchio, who was eventually kicked off the job for "consuming too much gold, too much azure and too much wine". Also worth a mention are an easily missed *Madonna and Child* by Gentile da Fabriano and a beautifully delicate fifteenth-century font, both near the main doors.

Museo dell'Opera del Duomo (MODO)

Piazza del Duomo • March & Oct daily except Tues 10am–5pm; April–Sept daily 9.30am–7pm; Nov–Feb daily except Tues 10am–1pm & 2–5pm • €4, or €5 combined ticket with the Duomo (see page 670), or Carta Orvieto Unica • 0763 342 477, orvietoaviva.com/en

Next to the Duomo on the right as you look at it is the **Museo dell'Opera del Duomo** – or **MODO** for short. Highlights are paintings by Martini and Pastura (an artist from Viterbo influenced by Perugino), several important thirteenth-century sculptures by Arnolfo di Cambio and Andrea Pisano, and a lovely font filled with Escher-like carved

fishes. The **Emilio Greco** section of the museum comprises nearly a hundred works donated to the city by the artist who created the Duomo's bronze doors in the 1960s – peek through the door beyond the ground-floor ticket office and you'll see enough of the exhibits to know if you want a closer look.

Museo Claudio Faina and the Etruscan necropolis

Museo Claudio Faina Piazza del Duomo 29 • April–Sept daily 9.30am–6pm; Nov–March Tues–Sun 10am–5pm • €4.50, or Carta Orvieto Unica • ⓣ 0763 341 511, ⓦ museofaina.it • **Etruscan necropolis** Strada della Stazione-SS71 • Daily 8.30am–dusk • €3, or Carta Orvieto Unica • ⓦ orvietoviva.com

The wonderfully restored **Museo Claudio Faina** (incorporating the Museo Civico) has a superbly displayed collection of vases and fragments excavated from sixth-century-BC **tombs**. The tombs themselves are still visible just off the main road that drops towards the station from Piazza Cahen and are worth tracking down for their rows of massive and sombre stone graves.

San Lorenzo di Arari

Piazza Santa Chiara • Daily 9.30am–1pm & 3–6/7pm • Free

As far as the town's **churches** go, they all naturally pale beside the Duomo, though most have something worthwhile to see. The tiny Romanesque **San Lorenzo di Arari** was built in 1291 on the site of a church destroyed by monks from nearby San Francesco because the sound of its bells got on their nerves. Four **frescoes** on the left of the nave depict typically traumatic scenes from the life of St Lawrence. There's also an Etruscan sacrificial slab, which rather oddly serves as the Christian altar (*arari* meaning "altar").

San Giovenale and around

Piazza San Giovenale • Daily 8.30am–noon & 4–6pm • Free

From Piazzale Cacciatore there's a decent **walk** around the city's southern walls (Via Ripa Medici) with views over to a prominent outcrop of rock in the middle distance, part of the old volcanic crater. Ten minutes or so brings you to **San Giovenale**, whose rustic surroundings, on the very western tip of the *rupa*, Orvieto's volcanic plateau, are a far cry from the bustle of the Duomo. It's not much to look at from the outside, but the musty **medieval interior** is the best (and oldest) in the town. The thirteenth-century Gothic transept, with its two pointed arches, rather oddly stands a metre above the rounded Romanesque nave, making for a hybrid and distinctive church, all of it exhaustively decorated with thirteenth- and fifteenth-century **frescoes**. Check out the *Tree of Life* fresco right of the main door and the macabre *Calendar of Funeral Anniversaries* partly covered by the side entrance.

THE MIRACLE OF BOLSENA

The story goes that a Bohemian priest was travelling to Rome to shake off a heretical disbelief in transubstantiation – the idea that the body and blood of Christ are physically present in the Eucharist. While he celebrated Mass in a church near Lago di Bolsena, blood started to drip from the host onto the *corporale*, the cloth underneath the chalice on the altar. The stained linen was whisked off to Pope Urban IV, who like many a pope was in Orvieto to escape the heat and political hassle of Rome. He immediately proclaimed a miracle, and a year later Thomas Aquinas, no less, drew up a papal bull instigating the feast of **Corpus Domini**. The Church at the time, however, was in retreat, and the Umbrian towns were at the height of their civic expansion. It's likely that the building of an awe-inspiring cathedral in one of the region's most powerful *comuni* was less an act to commemorate a miracle than a shrewd piece of political opportunism designed to remind errant citizens of the papacy's power.

10

GOING UNDERGROUND

The fascinating **Orvieto Underground** tours explore the vast labyrinth of **tunnels**, caves and store rooms that riddle the soft volcanic rock on which Orvieto is built: most date back to medieval times, some to the Etruscan era. The ticket office is next to the tourist office at Piazza del Duomo 23. Tours leave daily (except Feb, when they run at weekends only) at 11am, 12.15pm, 4pm and 5.15pm (€6, or **Carta Orvieto Unica**) – more frequently at busy times – and last about an hour. Call T 0347 383 1472 or T 0763 344 891, or see W orvietounderground.it for details and bookings.

Pozzo di San Patrizio and Pozzo della Cava

Pozzo di San Patrizio Viale Sangallo • Daily: March, April, Sept & Oct 9am–6.45pm; May–Aug 9am–7.45pm; Nov–Feb 10am–4.45pm • €5, or €3.50 if you have a ticket to the Pozzo della Cava, or free with Carta Orvieto Unica • **Pozzo della Cava** Via della Cava 28 • Tues–Sun 9am–8pm, closed second half of Jan • €4, or €2 if you have a ticket to the Pozzo di San Patrizio, or free with Carta Orvieto Unica • T 0763 343 768, W pozzodellacava.it

The **Pozzo di San Patrizio**, just off Piazzale Cahen, is the town's novelty act, a huge cylindrical well commissioned in 1527 by Pope Clement VII to guarantee the town's water supply during an expected siege by the Imperial Army (which never came). Water was brought to the surface by donkeys on two broad staircases, cannily designed never to intersect. It's a striking piece of engineering, 13m wide and 62m deep, named after its supposed similarity to the Irish cave where St Patrick died in 493, aged 133.

Another well, the **Pozzo della Cava**, on the western side of town, was discovered in 1984. You can explore the fascinating complex of nine caves, complete with archeological finds, on your own, or take one of the thematic guided tours (see website for details).

ARRIVAL AND DEPARTURE — ORVIETO

By train If you arrive by train, take the restored nineteenth-century funicular (every 10–15min; €1.30; tickets from the funicular ticket office or station newsagent or bar, valid for 90min on city buses; €2 if bought on board a bus) from the station forecourt to Piazza Cahen: it's a pleasant walk from here along Corso Cavour to the centre of town (5–10min), or you can take the regular minibus #A that stops in Piazza Cahen every 10min for the run to Piazza del Duomo; bus #B stops in Piazza della Repubblica before dropping off in Piazza del Duomo. Buses replace the funicular from 8.30pm till midnight. Orvieto has excellent train connections to Rome and into Tuscany, but is less well connected with the rest of Umbria – make connections at Orte for Narni and Spoleto.

Destinations Arezzo (up to 12 daily; 45min–1hr 40min); Chiusi (approx. hourly; 40min; connections to Siena, 1hr 45min–2hr 30min); Florence (at least hourly; 1hr 30min–2hr 45min); Orte (at least hourly; connections to Narni, Terni, Toto and Foligno; 35min); Rome (at least hourly; 1hr 20min); Terontola-Cortona (13 daily; connections to Perugia; 40min–1hr 15min).

By bus Inter-town buses take you directly to Piazza Cahen, Piazza XXIX Marzo or Piazza della Repubblica, depending on the service. However, there are more departures for other Umbrian towns from outside the train station.

Destinations Bolsena (2 daily Mon–Sat; 55min); Narni (4 daily Mon–Sat; 40min); Todi (1 daily Mon–Sat; 2hr 10min).

By car Without a doubt, the best approach is by car through the hills to the southwest from Bolsena (see page 119). You can park at the Campo della Fiera car park, beneath the walls at the southwest corner of town; escalators (7am–9pm) and a lift (7am–midnight) run up to the centre from here.

INFORMATION

Tourist office Piazza del Duomo 24 (Mon–Fri 8.15am–1.50pm & 4–7pm, Sat & Sun 10am–1pm & 3–6pm; T 0763 341 772, W cinorvieto.it or W comune.orvieto.tr.it). A second, summer-only tourist office is on Piazza Cahen, right next to the funicular (April–Sept daily 10am–6pm; T 0763 340 168).

ACCOMMODATION

Most of the town's budget rooms – and nightlife – are in Orvieto Scalo, the unlovely district around the train station, but this is very much a last resort; the hotels below are all in the upper old town.

Corso Corso Cavour 343 ⓣ0763 342 020, ⓦhotelcorso.net; map p.671. A little way from the centre, and therefore relatively quiet, but still within easy walking distance of everything, with cosily decorated rooms. Breakfast is extra. **€84**

Duomo Vicolo di Maurizio 7 ⓣ0763 341 887, ⓦorvietohotelduomo.com; map p.671. This eighteen-room hotel in a restructured medieval building has uninspired but comfortable rooms. It's extremely central and convenient for the Duomo, less than 1min walk away, and there's a garden. The three rooms in the annexe 50m down the road are cheaper. **€120**

★ **Ripa Medici** Vicolo Ripa Medici 14 ⓣ0763 341 343, ⓦripamedici.it; map p.671. This B&B's two bright, airy doubles have been decorated with real attention to detail by friendly owner Sabrina, and there are lovely views and a kitchen for guests' use. **€75**

Scacco Matto 10km away on the SS448 near Lago di Corbora ⓣ0744 950 163, ⓦscaccomatto.net; bus to Baschi/Civitella; map p.671. Orvieto's nearest campsite is on the Lake of Corbara. There's also a hotel with basic rooms and an on-site restaurant (closed Tues). Closed Nov–Feb. Doubles **€65** pitches **€12**

10

EATING

There are plenty of places to eat in Orvieto. For a tourist town, though, many **restaurants** offer very good value and tasty Umbrian food. Restaurants are grouped together at the bottom (eastern end) of Corso Cavour.

RESTAURANTS AND GELATERIE

Al San Francesco Via Bonaventura Cerretti 10 ⓣ0763 343 302, ⓦristorantealsanfrancesco.it; map p.671. A 450-seat canteen affair, with a choice between restaurant and self-service pizzeria; it's deservedly popular for its excellent value and variety, and has shady outdoor tables, too. *Primi* are around €8, *secondi* €9–16 and pizza kicks off at €5. Daily 12.30–3pm, plus usually Fri, Sat & Sun 7.30–10.30pm.

Antica Cantina Corso Cavour 212–Piazza Mondaleschi ⓣ0763 344 746, ⓦanticacantinaorvieto.it; map p.671. Popular with locals and reasonably priced (€20 will buy a good, light meal), this restaurant succeeds in reproducing the old-fashioned trattoria atmosphere and simple, but well-cooked, local seasonal staples. There are soups all year – try the chickpea and chestnut in winter – and the handmade pasta includes *ombrichelli* with sausage and freshly grated truffle, and fresh *fusilli*, made with cheese and black pepper and served with tomato and basil. Tues–Sat 12.30–3pm & 7–10pm, Sun 7–10pm.

Etrusca Via Lorenzo Maitani 10 ⓣ0763 344 016; map p.671. A traditional and relaxed trattoria that takes its cooking seriously, with classic Umbrian dishes (rabbit and pigeon are specialities – both around €12) and an attractive, medieval vaulted dining-room. Check out the ancient wine cellars, carved from the solid rock. Daily 9am–4pm & 7pm–midnight.

Gelateria Pasqualetti Piazza del Duomo 14; map p.671. This ivy-covered *gelateria* in the main piazza is the town's best spot for ice cream. There's a second branch at Corso Cavour 56, open year-round. April–Oct daily 11.30am–midnight.

La Grotta Via Signorelli 5 ⓣ0763 341 348, ⓦtrattorialagrotta.eu; map p.671. Small, reliable trattoria that has been in business for over forty years and is good value for central Orvieto (€25 and up for a meal); the staff are friendly too. Try *tagliatelle* with duck and follow with a hearty wild-boar stew. Daily except Tues noon–3pm & 7–10pm.

DRINKING

The **wine bars** around the Duomo are an expensive way of sampling the well-known Orvietan white.

Clandestino Corso Cavour 40 ⓣ328 972 7472 or ⓣ0763 340 868; map p.671. This bar is a good choice at aperitivo time – with a great range of nibbles to accompany a glass of wine or an Aperol or Campari spritz. They also make good cappuccino, so you might want to consider it for breakfast too. Daily all day till late.

Montanucci Corso Cavour 21–23 ⓣ0763 341 261, ⓦbarmontanucci.it; map p.671. Classic old-fashioned bar on the Corso that makes excellent coffee, and is a good place to sit outside for breakfast. Daily except Wed, all day until late.

Le Marche

678 Urbino and around
686 Pesaro and around
691 Ancona
694 Inland: the Esino Valley
696 The Conero Riviera
698 Loreto
700 Recanati
701 Macerata and around
705 Monti Sibillini National Park
707 Ascoli Piceno

PORTONOVO, CONERO RIVIERA

Le Marche

Wedged between the verdant Apennines and the Adriatic Sea, Le Marche is a varied region, and one you could devote weeks of slow travel to exploring. Sparsely populated inland areas are unspoilt and untouristed, particularly in the southwest, where stone hill-villages make atmospheric bases for hikes into the spectacular Monti Sibillini range. Ancona, the region's capital, is a gritty but engaging port town, while to its south is the jewel of Marche's coast, the dramatic Conero Riviera, where white-pebble beaches are backed by creamy limestone cliffs. In contrast, the rest of the Marche coast is flat and monotonous, a virtually uninterrupted coastal ribbon of sandy beaches hemmed with boxy resorts. Exceptions are Pesaro and Fano, both of which retain rather charming Renaissance cores behind their package-tour seafronts.

Away from the scorching seaside fun, most appealing – and best known – of Le Marche's sights are the small hilltop town of **Urbino**, with its spectacular Renaissance palace, and the dramatic fortress of **San Leo**, just across the border from San Marino. In October 2016 an earthquake measuring 6.6 on the Richter scale, with its epicentre near Norcia, across the border in Umbria, killed more than 300 people (mostly in Amatrice, Lazio). It caused considerable damage in the south of Marche, particularly in medieval university town of Macerata and the hill-villages that dot the foothills of the Monti Sibillini.

Further south, right on the regional border, the engaging town of **Ascoli Piceno** is a worthy stop-off on the way into Abruzzo. **Loreto** just south of Ancona is one of Italy's top pilgrimage sites, the basilica providing shelter for what Catholics claim is Jesus' childhood house, air-freighted to Le Marche, according to local legend, by a posse of angels.

GETTING AROUND — LE MARCHE

Getting around on public transport is relatively easy, though a car is useful in the more remote areas. There are several bus companies. Adriabus (@adriabus.eu) covers Pesaro and Urbino and province; ATMA (@atmaancona.it) covers Ancona and province; CONTRAM (@contram.it) covers Macerata and province; StartSpa (@startspa.it) covers Ascoli Piceno and province; and Trasfer (@trasfer.eu) covers Fermo and province. @orari.trasporti.marche.it is a useful, if rather user-unfriendly, website covering the whole region (in Italian only). There are two main **rail routes**: the Milan–Bari line that hugs the Adriatic coast, and the cross-country Ancona–Rome line. The provincial capitals – Urbino, Pesaro, Macerata, Ancona and Ascoli Piceno – are all well served by public transport, and Ancona is also a major port for **ferries** to Venice, Croatia, Greece and Albania. For hiking in the Sibillini, the little town of Amandola has the best **bus** service; if you don't mind relying on fewer buses, the hill village of Montefortino is a prettier base.

Urbino and around

Walled, austere and mostly built of pale, golden brick, **URBINO** is a jumble of Renaissance and medieval houses, churches and *palazzi* atop a hill, dominated by its stellar attraction, the **Palazzo Ducale**. During the second half of the fifteenth century, it was one of the most prestigious courts in Europe, ruled by the remarkable Federico da Montefeltro, who employed some of the greatest artists and architects of the time to build and decorate his palace. Baldassarre Castiglione, whose sixteenth-century handbook of courtly behaviour, *Il Cortegiane* (The Courtier), is set in the palace,

GROTTE DI FRASASSI

Highlights

❶ **Urbino** "Ideal city" and art capital created by Federico da Montefeltro, the ultimate Renaissance man. See page 678

❷ **Grotte di Frasassi** Get under the region's skin at these impressive, publicly accessible caves bristling with outlandish stalactites and stalagmites. See page 694

❸ **Conero Riviera** A coastline of white cliffs and turquoise seas ideal for walking, cycling and swimming, or just working up a tan. See page 696

❹ **Loreto** Experience religious fervour within the Santa Casa, allegedly Jesus' childhood abode, miraculously carried from Nazareth by angels. See page 698

❺ **Macerata** Catch open-air opera in this attractive old university town surrounded by pretty countryside. See page 701

❻ **Monti Sibillini** Take to the hills in this hiker's mountain paradise. See page 705

❼ **Ascoli Piceno** A relatively undiscovered town of interesting food and architectural gems in southern Le Marche. See page 707

HIGHLIGHTS ARE MARKED ON THE MAP ON PAGE 680

reckoned it to be the most beautiful in all Italy, and it does seem from contemporary accounts that fifteenth-century Urbino was an extraordinarily civilized place, a measured and urbane society in which life was lived without indulgence.

Nowadays Urbino is saved from an existence as an open-air museum by its lively university. In term-time at least, there's a refreshing, energetic feel to the town and plenty of places to eat and drink. Although a new town has grown up in the valley below, it seems to have been almost wilfully designed to be as ugly as possible, so as to better highlight the glories of the walled **upper town**, which, after all, is where you'll want to spend most of your time.

Outside the dour town walls, two places in northern Le Marche – the medieval strongholds of **Sassocorvaro** and **San Leo** – are well worth the effort it takes to reach them.

Palazzo Ducale

Piazza Rinascimento 13 • Mon 8.30am–2pm (last entry 12.30pm), Tues–Sun 8.30am–7.15pm (last entry 6pm) • €8 • Ⓦ palazzoducaleurbino.it

The **Palazzo Ducale**, rising above the town's uniform roofs, is a fitting monument to Federico, the urbane ruler of fifteenth-century Urbino. An elegant combination of the aesthetic and the practical, the facade comprises a triple-decked loggia in the form of a

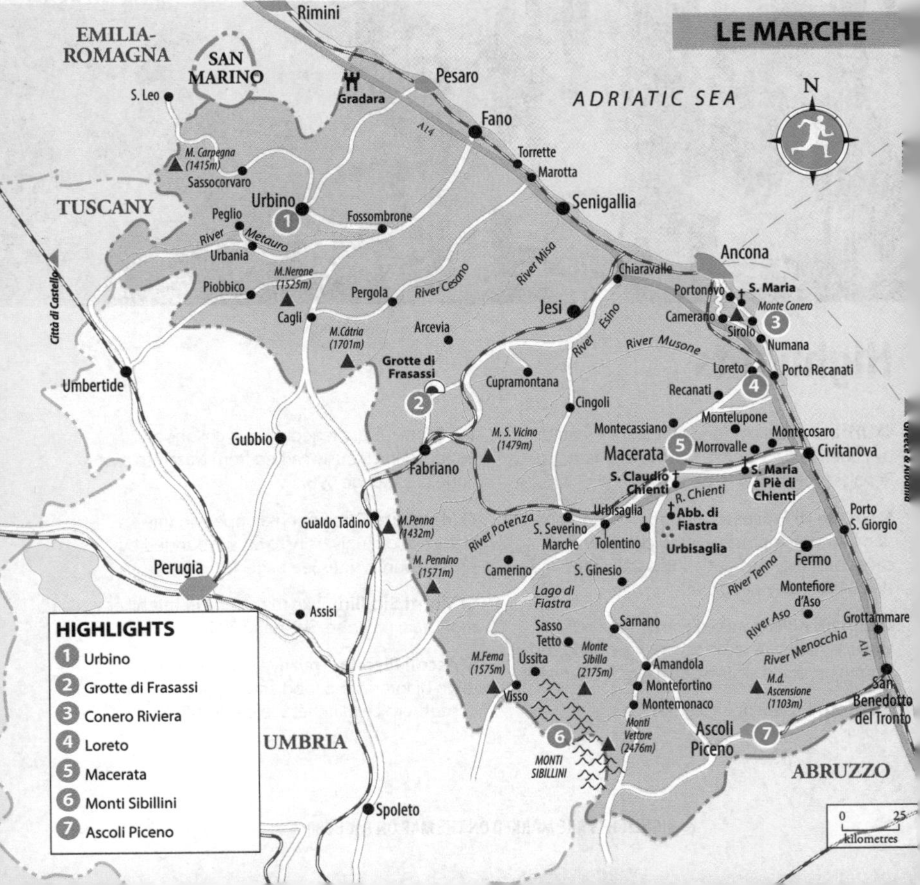

SEAFOOD AND COUNTRY COOKING – THE CUISINE OF LE MARCHE

Le Marche is very much a rural region, its cusine embracing **seafood** from the long coastline and **country cooking** from the interior. Tomatoes and fennel, wild mushrooms, game, nuts and herbs dominate. Rabbit and lamb are popular, as is *pappardelle alla papera*, wide, flat pasta with duck sauce, and, as in many other regions, truffles are considered a delicacy. Unfamiliar items on the antipasti menu include *lonza* (salt-cured pork) and *ciauscolo* (a pork-based spread). Meat grilled *alla brace* (over wood embers) is ubiquitous, and you may even come across *porchetta*, whole roast suckling pig, both in its original large-scale form and in a fast-food version used to fill crisp bread rolls. Don't confuse it with *coniglio in porchetta* though – this is rabbit cooked with fennel. Baked, stuffed dishes such as *vincisgrassi*, a rich layered dish of pasta, minced meat, mushrooms, giblets, brain, bechamel and truffles, are found everywhere. The most popular nibble, served to accompany the evening *aperitivo*, is olive all'asocolana, deep-fried breadcrumbed olives stuffed with meat. A typical seafood dish from Ancona is *zuppa di pesce*, a fish soup flavoured with saffron, though you'll find excellent fish broths – known simply as *brodetto* – all along the coast. Puddings include *cicercchiata*, balls of pasta fried and covered in honey, and *frappe*, fried leaves of filo-like pastry dusted with icing sugar.

Although Marche produces an increasing number of well-regarded **wines**, the region is best known for **Verdicchio**, a crisp greeny-gold white, grown on the hills around Jesi and Matelica, which excellent with fish. March reds include one of Italy's finest, Rosso Conero, a light wine based on the Montepulciano grape and full of fruit; more common is Rosso Piceno, based on the Sangiovese grape.

triumphal arch flanked by twin defensive towers. In contrast, the Palazzo's bare south side, forming one edge of the long central Piazza Rinascimento, looks rather bleak, and it's only inside that you begin to understand its reputation as one of the finest buildings of the Renaissance. The Palazzo houses the **Galleria Nazionale delle Marche**, home to seminal works by Piero della Francesca, along with the equally iconic Ideal City.

The courtyard

Just inside the entrance, the **Cortile d'Onore** is your first real taste of what Urbino is about. The courtyard may not seem immediately striking – the rest of Italy has a host of similar ones – but this is the prototype. Elegant and restrained, it was designed by Dalmatian-born Luciano Laurana, who was selected by Federico after he'd failed to find a suitably bold artist in Florence.

The ground floor

Off the Cortile is the room that housed Federico's **library**, in its day one of the most comprehensive in Europe. He spent fourteen years and over thirty thousand ducats gathering books from across the continent, and employed forty scribes to make illuminated copies on kidskin, which were then covered in crimson and decorated with silver. They disappeared into the vaults of the Vatican after Urbino fell to the papacy in 1631 and now the rooms lie empty.

The first floor

A monumental staircase takes you up to the first floor where the tour starts in the austere, airy rooms of the **Appartamento della Jole**, named for a monumental fireplace featuring exquisite nudes of Hercules and Iole (whose father sensibly refused to allow their marriage, given the fact that Hercules had just murdered his previous wife and children). Dotted with works of art, these rooms are an appetizer for what's to come – look out in particular for the monumental fireplaces and wooden doors inlaid with everything from gyroscopes and mandolins to armour, representing the various facets of Federico's personality.

Passing through two more sets of similarly ornamented suites, you arrive at the elaborately decorated **Appartamento del Duca**. On display here are two of Piero

11

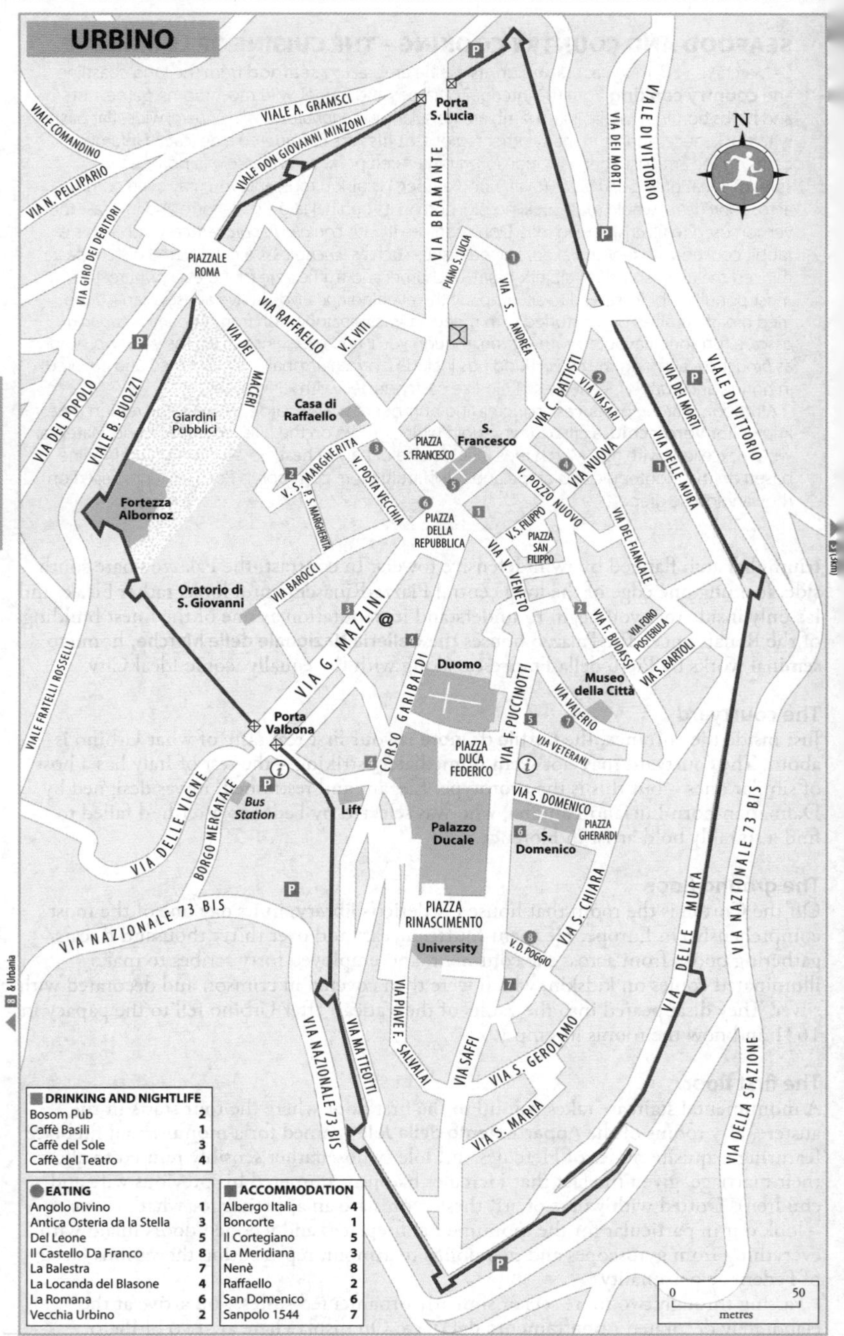
URBINO
Porta S. Lucia
VIALE A. GRAMSCI
VIALE COMANDINO
VIALE DON GIOVANNI MINZONI
VIA N. PELLIPARIO
VIA BRAMANTE
VIA DEI MORTI
VIALE DI VITTORIO
N
VIA GIRO DEI DEBITORI
PIAZZALE ROMA
PIANO S. LUCIA
VIA S. ANDREA
VIA RAFFAELLO
V. T. VITI
VIA DEI MACERI
VIA DEL POPOLO
VIALE B. BUOZZI
Giardini Pubblici
Casa di Raffaello
VIA C. BATTISTI
VIA VASARI
VIA DEI MORTI
VIALE DI VITTORIO
VIA DELLE MURA
PIAZZA S. FRANCESCO
S. Francesco
V. S. MARGHERITA
P. S. MARGHERITA
V. POSTA VECCHIA
VIA NUOVA
V. POZZO NUOVO
Fortezza Albornoz
PIAZZA DELLA REPUBBLICA
V. S. FILIPPO
PIAZZA SAN FILIPPO
VIA DEL FIANCALE
VIA V. VENETO
Oratorio di S. Giovanni
VIA BAROCCI
VIA G. MAZZINI
VIA F. BUDASSI
VIA FORO POSTERULA
VIA S. BARTOLI
Duomo
CORSO GARIBALDI
VIA F. PUCCINOTTI
Museo della Città
VIA VALERIO
VIALE FRATELLI ROSSELLI
Porta Valbona
VIA VETERANI
PIAZZA DUCA FEDERICO
VIA DELLE VIGNE
BORGO MERCATALE
Bus Station
Lift
VIA S. DOMENICO
PIAZZA GHERARDI
Palazzo Ducale
S. Domenico
VIA NAZIONALE 73 BIS
PIAZZA RINASCIMENTO
University
V. D. POGGIO
VIA S. CHIARA
VIA DELLE MURA
VIA PIAVE F. SALVALAI
VIA MATTEOTTI
VIA SAFFI
VIA S. GEROLAMO
VIA NAZIONALE 73 BIS
VIA DELLA STAZIONE
VIA S. MARIA
8 & Urbania
DRINKING AND NIGHTLIFE
Bosom Pub 2
Caffè Basili 1
Caffè del Sole 3
Caffè del Teatro 4
EATING
Angolo Divino 1
Antica Osteria da la Stella 3
Del Leone 5
Il Castello Da Franco 8
La Balestra 7
La Locanda del Blasone 4
La Romana 6
Vecchia Urbino 2
ACCOMMODATION
Albergo Italia 4
Boncorte 1
Il Cortegiano 5
La Meridiana 3
Nenè 8
Raffaello 2
San Domenico 6
Sanpolo 1544 7
0 50
metres

della Francesca's greatest works: the *Madonna of Senigallia*, a haunting depiction of foreboding in which Mary, flanked by two angels, offers up her child; and one of the most famous works of art in the Western world, the perplexing, beguiling *Flagellation*, showing Christ being almost casually beaten in a Renaissance setting of perfect mathematical perspective. Also here is the almost equally famous portrait of Federico by the Spanish artist **Pedro Berruguete**. Painted, as he always was, from the left, in profile (having lost his right eye in battle), Federico is shown as warrior, ruler, scholar and dynast; wearing an ermine-fringed gown over his armour, he sits reading a book, with his pasty and feeble-looking son, Guidobaldo, standing at his feet.

Sometimes on display in the Appartamento del Duca, but occasionally elsewhere in the palace, no painting better embodies the notion of perfection held by Urbino's elite than *The Ideal City*, long attributed to Piero but now thought to be by one of his followers. Probably intended as a design for a stage set, this famous display of perspective skill depicts a perfectly symmetrical, almost space-age cityscape, expressing the desire for a civic order that mirrors that of the heavens.

Proceeding through the Duke's apartment, it's the next few rooms that give the best insight into Federico's personality. A spiral staircase descends to two adjoining chapels, one dedicated to Apollo and the Muses, the other to the Christian God. This dualism typifies a strand of Renaissance thought – known as neo-platonism – in which mythology and Christianity were reconciled by positing a universe in which pagan deities were seen as aspects of the omnipotent Christian deity.

Back on the main floor you come to the most famous and best-preserved of the palace's rooms, Federico's amazing **Studiolo**, a masterpiece of illusory perspective created not with paint but with inlaid wood (intarsia). Shelves laden with geometrical instruments appear to protrude from the walls and books seem about to tumble from cupboards, while doors creak ajar and a suit of armour sways on a wall peg. The upper half of the room is covered with 28 portraits of great men ranging from Homer and Petrarch to Solomon and St Ambrose – another example of Federico's neoplatonic eclecticism.

Beyond the Appartamento del Duca, the cavernous **Throne Room** was a huge roofed space for its time and is bedecked in mammoth Gobelin tapestries depicting the Acts of the Apostles. Some of the most interesting works of art are on show in the

FEDERICO DA MONTEFELTRO

Federico da Montefeltro (1422–82) was a formidable soldier, a shrewd and humane ruler, and a genuine intellectual. As the elder but illegitimate son of the Montefeltro family, he only became ruler of Urbino after his tyrannical half-brother Oddantonio fell victim to an assassin during a popular rebellion. Federico promptly arrived on the scene – fuelling rumours that he'd engineered the uprising himself – and was elected to office after promising to cut taxes, to provide an education and health service, and to allow the people some say in the election of magistrates.

Urbino was a small state with few natural resources a long way from any major trading routes, so selling the military services of his army and himself was Federico's only way of keeping the city solvent. Federico's mercenary activities yielded a huge annual income, a substantial portion of which was used to keep taxes low, thus reducing the likelihood of social discontent during his long absences. When he was at home, he would leave his door open at mealtimes so that any member of his five-hundred-strong court might speak to him between courses, and used to move around his state unarmed (unusual in a time when assassination was common), checking on the welfare of his people.

Between military and political commitments, Federico also found time to indulge his interest in the **arts**. Though he delighted in music, his first love was architecture, which he considered to be the highest form of intellectual and aesthetic activity. A friend of the leading architectural theorist Alberti, he commissioned buildings from Renaissance luminaries such as Francesco di Giorgio Martini and Piero della Francesca.

Appartamento della Duchessa, several by Renaissance Urbino artist Timoteo Viti. This includes a fascinating depiction of a red-robed and rather well fed St Thomas Becket of Canterbury kneeling before Bishop Giovan Pietro Arrivabene and Duke Guidobaldo.

The Duomo

Piazza Pascoli 1 • Museum: daily 7.30am–1pm & 2–7pm • Free

Next door to the Palazzo Ducale, the town's **Duomo** is a pompous Neoclassical replacement for Francesco di Giorgio Martini's Renaissance church, destroyed in an earthquake in 1789. There's a **museum** inside, but the only reason for going in would be to see Barocci's *Last Supper*, with Christ surrounded by the chaos of washers-up, dogs and angels.

Fortezza Albornoz and the Oratorio di San Giovanni

11

A trek up to the gardens dominated by the sixteenth-century fortress, **Fortezza Albornoz** (July & Aug Mon, Thu, Fri Sat & Sun 9.30am–1pm & 3–7pm; April–June, Sept & Oct slightly shorter hours; €2), is rewarded with splendid views of the town and surrounding countryside. The fortress is a summer concert venue but is normally deserted. Close by is the **Oratorio di San Giovanni** (Mon–Sat 10am–12.30pm & 3–5.30pm, Sun 10am–12.30pm; €2.50), behind whose unfortunate modern facade you can see a stunning cycle of early fourteenth-century frescoes, depicting the life of St John the Baptist and the Crucifixion.

Casa Natale di Raffaello

Via Raffaello 57 • March–Oct Mon–Sat 9am–1pm & 3–7pm, Sun 10am–1pm; Nov–Feb Mon–Sat 9am–2pm, Sun 10am–1pm • €3.50

Possibly more interesting as a Renaissance house than anything else, **Casa Natale di Raffaello** the birthplace (in 1483) of Urbino's most famous son, the painter Raphael, proudly displays the "stone" where Raphael and his father Giovanni Santi mixed their pigments. There's one work which may be by Raphael, an early *Madonna and Child*; otherwise the walls are covered with reproductions and minor works by his contemporaries.

ARRIVAL AND INFORMATION — URBINO

By bus Urbino has no train station, and its bus station is at Borgo Mercatale at the foot of the Palazzo Ducale (see details on the lift below). The easiest way to reach the town is by bus from Pesaro train station.

Destinations Fano (at least hourly; 1hr 10min); Pesaro (every 30min; 45min–1hr).

By car Urbino's centre is supposedly car free and even if you are staying in a hotel here you'll still have to leave your car outside the old city walls. Park up at the Borgo Mercatale (€1.20/hr) or one of the other car parks that ring the old centre.

By lift On arrival in Urbino by bus or car, take the lift from Borgo Mercatale (daily 8am–8pm; €0.50) up to the old town, emerging near the Palazzo Ducale. Outside these hours it's a 5min walk along Via Mazzini or a steep climb up ramps and steps next to the lift.

Tourist offices The main tourist office is at Piazza Duca Federico 35, directly opposite the Palazzo Ducale (Mon–Sat 9am–1pm, Tue & Fri also & 2.30–5.30pm, Sat also 2–5pm, Sun 10am–1pm; 0722 2613, turismo.pesarourbino.it). There is also small office at Borgo Mercatale by the entrance to the ramp and lift (daily 7am–9pm).

ACCOMMODATION

CITY CENTRE

Albergo Italia Corso Garibaldi 32 0722 2701, albergo-italia-urbino.it; map p.682. Urbino's oldest hotel has plain, slightly cramped, but attractive rooms. Breakfast is served in the small private garden in summer. €65

★ **Bonconte** Via delle Mura 28 0722 2463, viphotels.it; map p.682. Imaginatively renovated by enthusiastic owners, this is a gem of a place to stay right on top of the town walls. Rooms are all travertine stone, chunky dark wood floors and sumptuous fabrics, oozing

tradition but with all mod cons. However, the icing on the cake is room 306, an exact replica of the Studiolo within the Palazzo Ducale, surely Le Marche's quirkiest hotel room. There's a shady walled garden for breakfast and cosy lounge with real fireplace for the evenings. €210

Il Cortegiano Via Veterani 1 ⊕340 844 1181, ⊛ilcortegiano.it; map p.682. Urbino's best-situated B&B, just across from the Palazzo Ducale above a bar-restaurant, has six large basic rooms, some with shared bathrooms. Free wi-fi and a ten percent discount in the restaurant for guests. €60

Raffaello Via Santa Margherita 40 ⊕0722 4896, ⊛albergoraffaello.com; map p.682. In a typical red-brick, shuttered old-town building, this hotel has fourteen simply furnished rooms with panoramic views over the pantiled roofs of Urbino. Changing art exhibitions in the communal areas. €60

San Domenico Piazza Rinascimento 3 ⊕0722 2626, ⊛viphotels.it; map p.682. Located in a former convent across from the Palazzo Ducale, this hotel has been sumptuously decorated and offers 31 generously proportioned rooms, big beds, polished wood floors and breakfast tables under the porticoes. Despite its location opposite the Palazzo Ducale, there are no palace views. €177

★**Sanpolo 1544** Via Aurelio Saffi 3 ⊕0722 2669, ⊛sanpolo1544.it; map p.682. In a former *palazzo*, this sumptuous B&B is a work of art, packed with antiques and little artistic touches that make staying here a stylishly enjoyable experience. The owners aim to give guests the impression of living in Renaissance Urbino with lots of stone, heavy fabrics and terracotta floors – the effect is impressive. Free wi-fi. €130

OUTSIDE THE CITY

La Meridiana Via Urbinate 43 ⊕0722 320 169, ⊛hotelmeridianaurbino.com; map p.682. About 3km outside Urbino on the road to Pesaro. The interior decoration is bland but it has a swimming pool, restaurant and friendly staff, and is an option of last resort if everything else is full. €98

Nenè Via Strada Rossa 30 ⊕0722 2996, ⊛neneurbino.com; map p.682. This restored stone house, 2km from Urbino, just off the "*strada rossa*" towards Fermignano, is visited as much for its great restaurant – with interesting vegetarian options – as for its simple rooms. The open-air pool is also a big draw card in summer. €60

11

EATING, DRINKING AND NIGHTLIFE

There are plenty of reasonable places to eat in Urbino, with dozens of fast-food and inexpensive self-service places aimed at students. There's also more refined cooking typical of the province in a selection of more formal restaurants. Self-caterers and picnickers have a convenient Conad supermarket at Via Raffaello 37 (Mon–Sat 7.30am–2pm & 4.30–8pm). During termtime, Urbino's late-night **bars** see a brisk trade, and there are reasonable dancing and live music options.

CAFÉS AND RESTAURANTS

Angolo Divino Via Sant'Andrea 14 ⊕0722 327 559; map p.682. Geranium-covered on the outside, and atmospheric within, this *osteria* is located in an dull pink *palazzo* near the Botanical Gardens. It's well known for regional delicacies (including home-made pasta) and there are some good vegetarian choices as well. Antipasti and *primi* around €13, *secondi* from €18. Tues–Sun12.30–3pm & 7pm–midnight.

★**Antica Osteria da la Stella** Via S. Margherita 1 ⊕0722 320 228, ⊛anticaosteriadalastella.com; map p.682. This restaurant offers a constantly changing seasonal menu reflecting chef-owner Giovanna Cecchetti's passion for authentic local produce. Savour dishes such as tagliatelle with local truffles and porcini mushrooms, and pumpkin risotto with goat's cheese and almonds. Some Le Marche restaurants let diners down with unimaginative desserts, but here they're made in house and are just great – try the strawberries with lime yogurt mousse and ginger sauce. *Primi* €10–15, *secondi* €15–25. Tues–Sun 12.30–2.30pm & 7.30–10.30pm.

★**Del Leone** Via C. Battisti 5 ⊕0722 329 894; map p.682. This small, subterranean trattoria under the San Francesco church serves up some of the city's best food. Try the *Gran Piatto del Duca* featuring wild boar stew with organic spelt for €23. Daily 6.30–10.30pm, Sat, Sun & hols also lunchtime 12.30–2pm.

Il Castello Via del Poggio 1 ⊕0722 2492, ⊛ristoranteilcastellourbino.it; map p.682. Relaxed restaurant with *primi* such as home-made *strozzapreti* – "strangled priests" (one can only assume that its twisted shape is supposed to be resonant of a strangled neck) – with vegetables, and *secondi* including rabbit cooked with fennel. Gluten-free, vegetarian and vegan options. Lovely courtyard. A full meal will set you back around €20 including house wine. Mon–Sat noon–3pm, 7–10.30pm.

La Balestra Via Valerio 16 ⊕0722 2942, ⊛labalestraristorante.com; map p.682. Unpretentious back-street restaurant with tables out on decking or in the brick-built dining room bedecked in rural and medieval knick-knacks. Game dishes, truffles and *strozzapreti* are the highlights of the English-language menu. *Primi* €7–9, *secondi* €8–10. Daily 10.30am–3.30pm & 6pm–midnight.

La Locanda del Blasone Via Nuova 3 ⊕0722 2528, ⊛lalocandadelblasone.it; map p.682. Reasonably priced dishes (*primi* around €8 and a good choice of *secondi* for between €8 and €10) with a cluster of chilli-spiked pugliese dishes and several featuring truffles (for slightly

more). There are also generously laden pizzas, some with evocative names like "*bomba*" and "*atomica*" (€3.70–8). Tues–Sun 12.30–3pm & 7.30–11.30pm.

La Romana Via Raffaello 3; map p.682. Urbino's newest *gelateria* is a twenty-first-century affair, all white tiles and spotlights, though the company has been making ice cream since 1947. Only organic milk is used in the 32 flavours, and they also do other snacks and drinks. Try ice cream with a sweet brioche bun, Sicilian style! Daily 11am–midnight.

★ **Vecchia Urbino** Via dei Vasari 3/5 ⓣ 0722 4447, ⓦ vecchiaurbino.it; map p.682. Upmarket but quite inconspicuous place with a wonderful Slow Food influenced menu using lots of carefully sourced and foraged local ingredients including *cappelletti con fegato grasso e tartufo* (hand-made tortelloni-like pasta filled with liver and truffles), pasta with wild greens, and marinated home-made sausage. The puddings are excellent too – don't miss the ice cream made with local saffron – and the wine list is good value. *Primi* €9–16, *secondi* €10.50–32. Daily noon–2pm & 7–11pm.

11

DRINKING AND NIGHTLIFE

Bosom Pub Via Budassi 24 ⓣ 0722 4783; map p.682. Stone-vaulted, garishly lit student pub with a well-stocked bar, including Belgian beers, decent snacks and wi-fi. The main action is Tuesday, Thursday and Saturday nights. Daily 7pm–3.30am.

Caffè Basili Piazza della Repubblica; map p.682. Epicentral (and commonly known as Bar Centrale) and hence madly popular meeting-spot on a busy piazza. Order a *caffè lungo* and watch the trendoids filter by. Daily 6.30am–2am.

Caffè del Sole Via Mazzini 34 ⓣ 0722 2619; map p.682. Up from the bus station on the main drag into town, this café-bar is open from morning till the early hours. Laidback atmosphere, comfy couches and lots of beer and aperitifs. Daily 8am–2am.

Caffè del Teatro Corso Garibaldi; map p.682. The café at the Teatro Sanzio (next to the lift) is a cool drinking hangout, especially at sundown when the views across the Borgo Mercatale and the hills beyond from the terrace come into their own. Daily 8.30am–8.30pm.

Sassocorvaro

La Rocca Ubaldinesca • April–June daily 9.30am–12.30pm & 3–7pm; July & Aug daily 9.30am–7pm; Sept–March Sat, Sun & hols 9.30am–12.30pm & 2.30–6pm. Oct–March Sat & Sun 9am–12.30pm & 2.30–6pm • €5 • Reached by bus from Pesaro (6 daily; 1hr 30min)

Perched above an artificial lake some 30km northwest of Urbino by road, **SASSOCORVARO** is dominated by one of Francesco di Giorgio Martini's most ambitious **fortresses, La Rocca Ubaldinesca**. Built on the orders of Federico da Montefeltro for one of his *condottieri* (mercenary soldiers), Ottaviano degli Ubaldini, it was, like San Leo (see page 511), designed to withstand the onslaught of cannon. As the site lacked San Leo's natural defensive advantages, Francesco was forced to seek a strictly architectural solution, doing away with flat walls (vulnerable to head-on cannonfire) and building instead a grim fortress bulging with rotund prow-like towers. After the functional exterior, the inside comes as something of a surprise, with an elegant Renaissance courtyard and an intimate and frescoed theatre. It's a tribute to the strength of Giorgio Martini's architecture that the fortress was selected as a safe house for 6509 of Italy's greatest works of art during World War II, including Piero della Francesca's *Flagellation* and Giorgione's *La Tempesta*, reproductions of which are on show.

Pesaro and around

The vast majority of tourists come to **PESARO**, an agreeably tranquil backwater, much of which dates from the 1920s and 1930s, for a lazy bake on the long stretch of sandy beach. Though popular with Brits and Germans on cheap packages and blue-collar Italians on annual family holidays, this sometimes overlooked resort has gone slightly more upmarket in recent years. The old town has always had an enjoyably off-the-beaten-track feel, and is a picturesque place to take part in the evening rituals of strolling, window-shopping, *aperitivo*-taking and people-watching. Regular transport connections to Urbino, Sassocorvaro, Gradara and Fano, also make it a feasible and affordable base from which to explore northern Le Marche.

The centre of town is the dignified **Piazza del Popolo**, in which the rituals of the pavement café scene are played out against the sharp lines of Fascist-period buildings and the Renaissance restraint of the Palazzo Ducale. All the main attractions are within a five-minute walk of here.

The beach

Although the town has a clutch of museums, the main attraction is undoubtedly its **beach** of fine sand that shelves gradually into the Adriatic. A tree-lined grid of rather

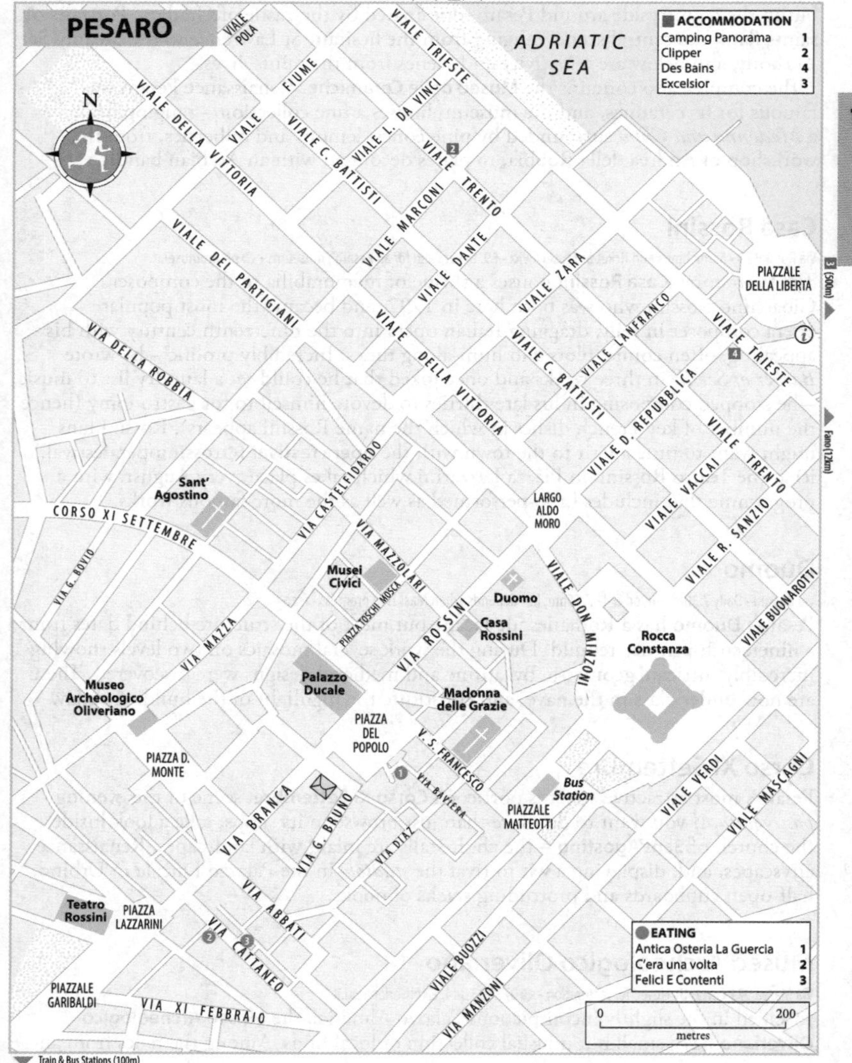

11

bland and boxy looking apartments marks the long sandy beach-front, enlivened here and there by some marvellous Art Nouveau villas, including one on Piazzale della Libertà whose eaves are supported by white stucco lobsters.

Musei Civici

Piazza Toschi Mosca 29 • June–Sept Tues–Sun 10am–1pm & 4.30–7.30pm; Oct–May Tues–Thurs 10am–1pm, Fri–Sun & hols 10am–1pm & 3.30–6.30pm • €9, ticket valid for all Pesaro's museums • Ⓦ pesaromusei.it

The most significant relic of Renaissance Pesaro is Giovanni Bellini's magnificent **Coronation of the Virgin** polyptych, housed in the Pinacoteca of the **Musei Civici**. Painted in the 1470s, the altarpiece situates the coronation not in some starry heaven but in the countryside around Pesaro, dominated by the castle of Gradara. Portraits of saints flank the central scene, ranging from the hesitant St Lawrence to the dreamy St Anthony, and below are a Nativity and scenes from the saints' lives.

11

The complex also contains the **Museo delle Ceramiche**. Renaissance Pesaro was famous for its ceramics, and the museum houses a fine collection – ranging from a *Madonna and Child* surrounded by pine cones, lemons and bilberries, from the workshop of Andrea della Robbia, to plates decorated with an Arabian bandit.

Casa Rossini

Via Rossini 34 • Same hours and ticket as Musei Civici • €9, ticket valid for all Pesaro's museums • Ⓦ pesaromusei.it

The four-storey **Casa Rossini** houses a shrine of memorabilia to the composer Gioachino Rossini who was born here in 1792, and became the most popular opera composer in Italy, dragging Italian opera into the nineteenth century with his appealing, often comic, plots and hum-along tunes. Incredibly prolific – he wrote *Barber of Seville* in three weeks and once joked that he could set a laundry list to music – he stopped composing in his late thirties to devote himself to for gastronomy (hence the number of key French dishes in which the name Rossini appears). Rossini fans might want to time a visit to the town with the **opera festival** (Ⓦ rossinioperafestival.it) at the Teatro Rossini on Piazza Lazzarini which takes place every August, with a programme that includes little-performed as well as the more famous works.

Duomo

Via Rossini • Daily 7.30am–noon & 4–7.15pm, but depends when Mass is in progress • Free

Pesaro's **Duomo** has a Romanesque facade but most of the structure behind dates from a nineteenth-century rebuild. During the work several mosaics on two levels showing incredibly intricate geometric Byzantine and medieval designs were discovered. These are now under glass in the nave, and constitute the highlight of the building today.

Corso XI Settembre

Pesaro's most attractive street is porticoed **Corso XI Settembre**, scene of the evening *passeggiata*. If you want to do more than just browse in its shops, take a look inside the church of **Sant'Agostino** – the choir stalls are inlaid with landscapes, Renaissance cityscapes, and, displaying a wit to rival the *studiolo* in the Palazzo Ducale in Urbino, half-open cupboards and protruding stacks of books.

Museo Archeologico Oliveriano

Via Mazza 97 • Currently closed for restoration • Ⓣ 0721 33 344, Ⓦ oliveriana.pu.it

Installed in the slightly inconspicuous Palazzo Almerici, the **Museo Archeologico Oliveriano** has a small but unusual collection of local finds. Among the relics from an

Iron Age necropolis at nearby Novilara are a child's tomb filled with miniature domestic utensils and a tomb slab carved with pear-shaped figures rowing a square-sailed boat into battle. Even more intriguing is the collection of ex votos – breasts, feet, heads and even a dog – collected not from an early Catholic church but from a Roman sacred grove at San Veneranda (3km from Pesaro), consecrated in the second century BC.

ARRIVAL AND DEPARTURE — PESARO

By train The railway station is 1.5km inland from the sea along arrow-straight Via Montegrappa (which becomes Via Rossini).

Destinations Ancona (approx every 30min; 30–50min); Fano (one or two hourly; 8min); Rimini (at least two or three hourly; 30min).

By bus The bus station is next door to the train station. Local services are run by Adriabus (wadriabus.eu).

Destinations Fano (up to 4 hourly; 18min); Gradara (hourly; 50min); Sassocorvaro (6 daily; 1hr 30min); Urbino (approx every 30min; 1hr).

Tourist office On the seafront on Piazzale della Libertà (Mon–Fri 9am–1pm; ⓣ 0721 69 341, ⓦ turismo.pesarourbino.it).

ACCOMMODATION

Camping Panorama 7km north of Pesaro on the Strada Brisighella ⓣ 0721 20 8145, ⓦ campingpanorama.it; map p.687. This is the closest campsite to town and enjoys a tranquil setting perched on a clifftop above the sea (a path leads down to the beach below). It also has a pool, restaurant, barbeque area and free wi-fi. May–Sept. Pitches €12, per person €10

Clipper Viale Marconi 53 ⓣ 0721 30 915, ⓦ hotelclipper.it; map p.687. Family-run since the 1950s, the *Clipper* lies a block back from the beach. Modernized rooms are crisp and well kept. The buffet breakfasts are served alfresco on the terrace and there's free wi-fi. Closed Oct–April. €104

Des Bains Viale Trieste 221 ⓣ 0721 34 957, ⓦ innitalia.com; map p.687. This friendly, smart and characterful hotel was built in 1905, and though modernized many times since then, still has something of the *belle époque* about it. Some of the rooms are elegantly furnished, others are pretty basic. €80

★ **Excelsior** Lungomare Nazario Sauro 30/34 ⓣ 0721 630 011, ⓦ excelsiorpesaro.it; map p.687. Pesaro's best hotel is this retro-styled new build hugging the beach. Rates for the cool, 21st-century monochrome rooms include free bike rental, use of the pools and some spa facilities, access to the private beach and a humdinger of a continental breakfast. The entire seven-storey building, including the spa, restaurants and lobby, oozes clean-cut chic. €329

EATING AND DRINKING

Antica Osteria La Guercia Via Baviera 33 ⓣ 0721 33 463, ⓦ osterialaguercia.it; map p.687. Located in a tiny courtyard just off Piazza del Popolo, this is one of the town's better choices. Choose between the beautifully beamed and frescoed interior or summer outdoor seating to eat delicious pasta and fish dishes at affordable prices. *Primi* €8–9, mains €8–13. Daily 12.30–3pm & 7.30–11pm.

C'era Una Volta Via Cattaneo 26 ⓣ 0721 30 911; map p.687. Long regarded as the purveyor of the best pizza in town, this place certainly offers plenty of choice with over one hundred different types of imaginatively named pizza on the menu, from simple "Ciclista" (€2.50) to "Billionaire" (€11.50). Other mains €6.50–18. Daily noon–2.30pm & 7pm–12.30am.

Felici e Contenti Via Carlo Cattaneo 37 ⓣ 0721 32 060, ⓦ feliciecontenti.com; map p.687. A long way from the seafront, this sophisticated place with its exposed brick and high ceilings specializes in seafood dishes, though the pizzas are pretty good too. Fish mains such as frittura mista or grilled sole for around €14, pizzas from €4.50 for a margherita. Wed–Sun noon–3pm & midnight, Sun 7–11pm.

Gradara castle

Mon 8.30am–2pm (last entry 1pm), Tues–Sun 8.30am–7pm (last entry 6pm) • €8, ⓣ 0541 964 115, ⓦ castellodigradara.org • Buses from Pesaro bus station

Fifteen kilometres inland from Pesaro, the castle of **GRADARA** is a fairy-tale confection of mellow red brick and swallow-tail turrets, but not the place to go in season if you want to avoid crowds. The castle is said to have been the scene of a thirteenth-century scandal involving Francesca da Rimini, who committed adultery with Paolo da Malatesta, her husband's brother. The lovers were killed for their transgression and later consigned to hell by Dante – he meets their spirits in Canto V of the *Inferno*, where they are caught in a ceaseless whirlwind – though Francesca's unhappy spirit is said to wander the castle when the moon is full.

THE GUARDIAN ANGEL

Not previously regarded as one of his finer works, *The Guardian Angel* by the Emilia-born Renaissance painter, **Guercino**, was quickly elevated to iconic status following a visit to Fano by the British poet, **Robert Browning**, in 1848. The picture, displayed in the Corte Malatestiana, shows a golden-haired child being shown how to pray by a rather chunky-looking angel, and so entranced Browning that he was inspired to write a poem of the same title. Expressing a wistful yearning to take the place of the child, the gushingly sentimental poem became incredibly popular, and Italy was flooded with reproductions of the painting for holidaying Browning fans. The keenest disciples set up a club, membership of which was gained by travelling to Fano and sending the founder a postcard.

Inside the castle is a room decked out as the scene of the crime, with a sumptuously refurbished four-poster bed, fake wall hangings and an open book – Francesca tells Dante in hell that it was while reading the story of Lancelot and Guinevere that she and Paolo first succumbed to their passion. Further reminders of the story are found in two nineteenth-century paintings: one showing the lovers (either dead or in a state of postcoital collapse) watched by the crippled husband; the other, less ambiguous, of the naked couple. Other rooms are furnished as a torture chamber, complete with spiked iron ball, handcuffs and lances, and as the guards' room, a strange mixture of tavern and armoury. After touring the castle, it's well worth taking a walk round the walls for the fine views over the surrounding hills.

Fano

FANO is no longer quite the haven it was when Robert Browning washed up here in 1848, seeking respite from the heat and crowds of Florence. A large swathe of the seafront is dominated by an ugly industrial port, and although its pastel-pebbled beaches remain splendid, they now attract thousands of package tourists every year. Nevertheless, Fano is a pleasant enough place if a little humdrum, and comfortably combines its role as resort with that of small fishing port and minor historical town, the latter very much worth a half-day's wander.

Fano's Roman precursor, named Fanum Fortunae after its Temple of Fortune, lay at the eastern terminus of the Via Flaminia, which traversed the Apennines to Rome. The town is still built around a **Roman crossroads** plan: Via Arco di Augusto and Corso Matteotti follow the routes of the *cardus* and *decumanus*, and their junction is marked with a copy of a Roman milestone stating its distance from the capital (195.4 Roman miles).

The Porta Maggiore and Arco di Augusto

Heading into Fano by bus, you could ask to be dropped off at the old town gate, the crenellated **Porta Maggiore**, to start your sightseeing with the remnants of the medieval defensive walls, on the southwestern side of the town centre. Behind them is a Roman gate, the **Arco di Augusto**, impressive despite having been truncated in the fifteenth century when Federico da Montefeltro blasted away its upper storey. You can see what it used to look like in a relief on the facade of the adjacent church of San Michele, which also houses a tiny – though rarely open – museum.

Corte Malatestiana (Museo Civico Palazzo Malatestiano)

Piazza XX Settembre • Oct–May Tues & Thurs 9am–1pm & 3–6pm, Wed & Fri 9am–1pm, Sat 9am–1pm & 4–7pm, Sun 10.30am–12.30pm & 4–7pm; June–Sept Tues, Thurs, Sat 9am–1pm & 5–8pm, Wed, Fri 9am–1pm, Sun 10.3am–12.30pm & 5–8pm• €4

Overlooking the central Piazza XX Settembre are the reconstructed thirteenth-century Palazzo della Ragione and the fifteenth-century **Corte Malatestiana**, dating from the time Fano was ruled by the Malatesta family. The Corte is at its best nowadays on summer evenings, when its loggias, turrets and trefoil windows provide a backdrop

for concerts. Inside there's a small **archeological museum and art gallery**, where the most sought out exhibit is Guercino's *The Guardian Angel*, which, thanks to Robert Browning's literary intervention, became one of Italy's most famous paintings in the nineteenth century (see page 690).

ARRIVAL AND INFORMATION — FANO

By train The train station is a 10min walk from the seafront, at the end of Via Cavallotti.

Destinations Ancona (every 30min; 30–40min); Pesaro (approx two per hour but some gaps; 8min); Rimini (approx hourly; 40min).

By bus Buses pull in next to the train station. There are regular services to Pesaro (up to 4 hourly; 18min).

Tourist office Piazza XX Settembre (June to mid-Sept daily 10am–noon, 10.30pm–12.30am; rest of the year reduced hours. T 0721 803 534, W turismo.pesarourbino.it).

ACCOMMODATION

Angela Viale Adriatico 13 T 0721 801 239, W hotelangela.it. One of the most reasonably priced three-star hotels, right on the seafront, with 37 modestly equipped rooms, all with TV, and a garden. Half and full-board available. **€85**

Pensione Sassenia Viale Adriatico 86 T 0721 828 229, W hotelsassoniafano.it. This modern guesthouse near the port area has simple, uncluttered bedrooms, a small restaurant, a/c and free wi-fi and bike rental. **€70**

★ **Relais Villa Giulia** Località San Biagio T 0721 823 159, W relaisvillagiulia.com. A good choice if you have your own transport, this country villa sits in extensive grounds with views to the sea, a short walk away. Capably run by its bohemian and cultured aristocratic owners, it has books and magazines everywhere, fires burning in winter and a large swimming pool in summer. The five rooms have frescoed walls, antique furniture and Turkish carpets, and there's an independent apartment to rent in the grounds. **€179**

EATING AND DRINKING

Caffè Centrale Corso Matteotti 102–104 T 0721 801 417, W caffecentralefano.it. With the Roman milestone embedded in its wall, there's no more central caffeine-and-cake halt in all Fano. Sit on the whitewashed outdoor decking or in the classy interior, where you can admire the bakery's miraculous wedding-cake creations. At weekends the place becomes a popular drinking spot. Tues–Sun 6.30am–11.30pm (earlier in low season/on quiet nights), Fri & Sat open until later.

Da Giulio Viale Adriatico 100 T 0721 805 680. Little antique touches, iron-fresh blue-striped table linen, friendly staff and excellent seafood make this a sure-fire choice come mealtimes. *Primi* €7–12, *secondi* €8–18. Daily 12.30–2.30pm & 7.30–10.30pm.

★ **Self Service Al Pesce Azzurro** Viale Adriatico 48 T 0721 803 165, W pesceazzurro.com. Although it enjoys a pretty unprepossessing location at the wrong end of town (at the port), this huge, plasticky, almost industrial place, run by a cooperative of fishermen's wives, offers great-value three-course set meals of the freshest *pesce azzurro* – oily fish such as anchovies, sardines and mackerel – for just €13 a head. Otherwise, pick your dish and take one of the blue and yellow plastic chairs along with the many locals who call the place home at mealtimes. Tues–Sun noon–2pm & 7.30–10pm.

Ancona

War, earthquakes and that transient feel all large port cities possess conspire to make **ANCONA** a less lovable city than others on the Adriatic coast. This busy ferry departure-point attracts an international fleet of fume-belching trucks and tankers from the oil refinery at nearby Falconara that grumble through the port area night and day while lost *arrivés* clog up the station surrounding alleyways. But Ancona has many saving graces embedded in its tangle of commercial buildings and the authorities are making an effort to promote the town as a tourist destination, sprucing up the historic centre and making ambitious improvements to the port area., An increasing number of cruise ships call in here, discharging their crews and guests for a day's wander through the steep streets of the tranquil old quarter and nineteenth-century shopping boulevards below. As you might expect, there are also plenty of extremely well-priced, unpretentious fish trattorias.

For many Ancona is a gateway to the Marche region thanks to Falconara airport, 10km away, used by low-cost flight operators such as Ryanair. There are also decent transport connections to much of Le Marche, though few would plump for the city as a base.

Duomo

Piazza del Duomo • Daily 8am–noon & 3–6pm (until 7pm in summer) • Free • Sporadic bus #11 runs to the Duomo from Piazza Cavour if you don't fancy the climb

A stiff climb from the port area, passing Ancona's well-signposted but essentially disappointing Roman remains along the way, the pink-and-white **Duomo** is mostly built in a restrained Romanesque style, with an outburst of Gothic exuberance in the doorway's cluster of slender columns,. The most memorable feature is the tenth-century marble crypt containing the remains of St Cyriacus, a fourth-century Christian who cared for the slaves forced to work on Rome's Baths of Diocletian where he became known for his power to exorcise demons. When the baths were finished, he and all the slaves were killed. Today, his overdressed skeleton is a macabre sight, the open-mouthed skull eternally taking its last breath. However, it may be the views from here, the ferries lined up in the port and the coast fading into the haze, that remain longest in the memory.

Museo Archeologico Nazionale delle Marche

Via Ferretti 6 • Tues–Sun 8.30am–7.30pm • €4

Ancona's large, three-storey **Museo Archeologico Nazionale delle Marche** in the old quarter is not a bad place to while away an hour or two, its wacky moulded ceilings vaulting over a collection of finds ranging from red- and black-figure Greek *kraters* to a stunning Celtic gold crown found in a Gaulish necropolis near Montefortino. A large section is devoted to the Italic Piceni tribe, who occupied these parts in the seventh century BC.

Museo della Città

Piazza del Plebiscito • Mid-June to mid-Sept Tues–Thurs 5–8pm, Fri 10am–8pm, Sat & Sun 10am–1pm & 5–8pm; mid-Sept to mid-June Tues–Fri 4–7pm, Fri–Sun 10am–7pm • €2; €6 including Pinacoteca

Tucked away at the foot of the flight of steps leading up to Ancona's austere Dominican church, the worthwhile **Museo della Città** displays models, paintings, sculptures and original documents showing key events in Ancona from 2000 BC to 2000 AD. Interestingly, the collections are housed in the former Hospital of St Thomas of Canterbury, dating from the eighteenth century.

Pinacoteca Comunale Francesco Podesti

Via Pizzecolli 17 • Oct–April Tues–Fri 4–7pm, Sat & Sun 10am–7pm; May–Sept Tues–Thurs 5–8pm, Fri 10am–8pm, Sat & Sun 10am–1pm & 5–8pm. €4,60; €6 including Museo della Città.

The undoubted highlight of the **Pinacoteca Comunale Francesco Podesti** is Titian's *Apparition of the Virgin*, a sombre yet impassioned work, with the Virgin appearing to a rotund and fluffy-bearded bishop in a stormy sunset sky. There's also a glorious Holy Conversation by Lotto, and an exquisite yet chilling Madonna and Child by Carlo Crivelli, with a mean-looking Mary pinching the toe of a rather pained Christ.

Santa Maria della Piazza

Piazza Santa Maria • Daily 9am–7pm • Free

A block back from the ferry port, tiny Piazza Maria Santa is dominated by the delightful Romanesque church of **Santa Maria della Piazza**, which dates from the thirteenth century, but was built over the remains of a palaeo-Christian basilica, abandoned in the eleventh century because of the dangers of attacks by Arab pirates. The building's facade is a fantasia of exquisitely carved blind loggias and its portal is decorated with incredibly well preserved floral and animal motifs. When it's open, visitors can admire some early Christian mosaics through glazed sections in the floor.

FERRIES TO VENICE, TRIESTE, CROATIA, ALBANIA AND GREECE

Ferries leave from Ancona's Stazione Marittima, a couple of kilometres north of the train station (bus #1 or #4), close to the centre of town. For the best at-a-glance idea of timetables and routes, visit ⓦ doricaportservices.it (in English and Italian). Each of the main ferry lines has a ticket office (closed 1–3pm) and you can also buy tickets from the agencies all around the port, but booking online gets you the cheapest deals. Always aim to arrive at the Stazione Marittima two hours before departure (3hr if you're taking a camper van).

Ferry companies operating out of Ancona include Superfast (ⓦ superfast.com) and Minoan Lines (ⓦ minoan.it) to Venice (8hr) Igoumenitsa (15hr) and Patras (22hr). Anek (ⓦ anek.gr) to Igoumenitsa (15hr) and Corfu (16hr) in Greece; SNAV (ⓦ snav.it) to Split (Spalato) (9–11hr); Jadrolinija (ⓦ jadrolinija.hr) to Zara (9hr) and Split (Spalato) (8–9hr); and Adria Ferries (ⓦ adriaferries.com) to Trieste (5hr) and Durazzo in Albania (17hr).

San Francesco delle Scale

Piazza San Francesco • Free

Rising sharply from a small square off Via Pizzecolli, the church of **San Francesco delle Scale** is named after the steps leading up to it. Titian's *Apparition* (now in the Pinacoteca Comunale) was painted for this church, but today its rather plain Neoclassical interior still houses works by Lotto, Tibaldi and Lilli.

11

ARRIVAL AND INFORMATION — ANCONA

By plane Ryanair flies direct from the UK to Ancona's Falconara airport. The Aerobus Raffaello (times correspond to flight departures and arrivals 6am–10pm; ⓦ conerobus.it) runs from here to the train station and Piazza Cavour, taking around 30min. Tickets available from the driver. A taxi will cost around €35.

By bus Most buses in Ancona and province are run by ATMA (ⓦ atmaancona.it) and depart from Piazza Cavour, linking up with the train station and the Stazione Marittima, where ferries dock. Services to Sirolo, Numana and Loreto are run by Reni (ⓦ anconarenibus.it) leave from Via Camerini just off the square.

Destinations Jesi (approx every 30min; 45min–1hr); Loreto (7 daily in summer, 5 in winter; 1hr 30min); Macerata (10 daily; 1hr 30min); Numana (approx hourly; 40min); Portonovo (9 daily; 25–30min); Sirolo (approx hourly; 35min).

By train The train station is 1.5km out of town.

Destinations Ascoli Piceno (via San Benedetto; approx hourly; 1hr 30min–2hr); Bologna (at least hourly; 2–3hr); Fano (at least hourly; 30–40min); Jesi (at least hourly; 25min); Loreto (hourly; 15–20min); Pesaro (every 30min; 30–50min); Pescara (at least hourly; 1–2hr); Rome (5 daily; 4hr).

Tourist office Banchina Nazario Sauro (June–Sept daily 9am–6pm; ⓣ 071 2076431, ⓦ turismo.marche.it).

ACCOMMODATION

★ **Ego Hotel** Via Flaminia, 220 ⓣ 071 218 1262, ⓦ egohotelancona.it. A bit out of town on the coast near Ancona Torrette train station, this much-lauded four-star hotel has some of the slickest rooms on the Adriatic coast, all trendy retro browns and beige leather. There's a wellness centre and restaurant on the premises, too. €124

Grand Hotel Passetto Via Thaon de Revel 1 ⓣ 071 31 307, ⓦ hotelpassetto.it. Perched on a hill in a quiet part of town, this luxurious establishment offers excellent service, as well as an outdoor pool, a cocktail bar, health club and great views out over the Adriatic. €177

Milano Via Montebello 1 ⓣ 071 201 147, ⓦ hotelmilanohm.it. This clean, appealing and centrally located hotel is possibly Ancona's best deal. It's understandably very popular, so book ahead. €90

EATING AND DRINKING

Ancona has some great family-run fish places. If you've been in Italy a while and are pining for a curry or just a change from the pizza-pasta routine, a sizeable non-Italian population means there's lots of ethnic food around, most notably from Turkey, Russia and Sri Lanka. Piazza Plebiscito is the place to head for a late-night tipple.

Al Chiosco da Morena Corso Mazzini ⓣ 338 762 8904. Ancona's best street food comes from this tiny stone-built kiosk, a local institution wedged between flashier eateries, that serves some of the city's best local seafood for €6–8 a plate (prices are by weight). Local mussels are the star of the show, washed down with a glass of white wine at the streetside seating area. Tues–Sat 9am–9pm.

Alla Tazza D'Oro Corso Garibaldi 136 ⓣ 071 203 368.

Ancona has ample provision for fans of the bean but this open-all-hours coffee bar is special for its original, quirky interior: dating from 1954, it's all Art Deco ceramics, mirrors, coffee-quaffing Moors and African mosaic scenes. Daily 6am–midnight.

Clarice Via del Traffico 6 ⓣ071 202 926. An old-style, family place in a cobbled alleyway off Corso Garibaldi (on the right as you walk up from the sea). It serves traditional, very reasonably priced food, with local dishes such as *gamberi e pesto* (€9), *trippa alla parmegiana* (€8) and *tagliatelle con vongole* (€9). Mon–Sat 12.15–2.45pm & 7.45–10pm.

★**La Cantineta** Via Gramsci 1/C ⓣ071 201 107, ⓦtrattorialacantineta.it. Almost opposite the theatre, this trattoria may look a little unprepossessing but its speciality, *stoccafisso* (€15.50), traditional salt cod, is well worth sampling, as is the seafood paella and the €20 fixed menu. Mon noon–2.30pm, Tues–Sun noon–2.30pm & 7.30–10pm.

Osteria del Pozzo Via Bonda 2 ⓣ071 207 3996, ⓦosteriadelpozzo.net. This intimate but brightly decorated seafood restaurant, on a narrow lane off the lower end of sloping Piazza del Plebiscito, is the place to tuck into some net-fresh fruits of the Adriatic. There's a four-course tasting menu for €20. Mon–Sat noon–2.30pm & 7.30–10pm.

11

Inland: the Esino Valley

West of Ancona and cutting right across Le Marche, the **Esino Valley** is broad and bland in the east, but narrows to a dramatic limestone gorge, the Gola di Rossa, just before the town of **Fabriano** and the border with Umbria. Famous for two things – paper-making and Gentile da Fabriano, the best of the International Gothic artists – Fabriano is now heavily industrialized and a pretty dismal town – one you're likely to pass straight through on your way to Umbria and Rome. Although Fabriano and **Jesi** are built up, most of the valley is given over to agriculture and is best known for **Verdicchio**, a dry white wine produced in the hilltop villages around Jesi. What most visitors come for, however, are the vast **Grotte di Frasassi** (Frasassi caves).

Jesi

Though its industrial development has led to **JESI** being known as "the little Milan of Le Marche", the historic centre of the town is well preserved. Clinging to a long ridge, it's fringed by medieval walls and retains a scattering of Renaissance and Baroque palaces. Encircling the town are the massive ramparts, restructured in the fourteenth century and built on top of the foundations of Roman walls – an escalator takes you through the ramparts, several metres thick, from the lower town to the upper town (with steps back down again).

Pinacoteca Civica

June–Aug Tues–Sun 10am–7pm; Sept–May Tues–Sat 10am–1pm & 4–7pm, Sun 10am–1pm & 4–7pm • €6

The Palazzo Pianetti houses the **Pinacoteca Civica**, where the highlight of the opulent interior is the magnificent 72m-long stuccoed, gilded and frescoed gallery – a Rococo fantasy of shells, flowers and festoons framing cloud-backed allegorical figures. The collection of paintings is best known for some late works by **Lorenzo Lotto**, including *The Annunciation* and *The Visitation* (both c.1520); his use of colour and the expressive intensity of his portraits are exceptional.

The Grotte di Frasassi

Guided tours only, arrive at booking office 30 min before tour departure time. Closed 24 & 25 Dec & 10–30 Jan. March–Oct daily 10am, 11am, noon, 2.30pm, 4pm & 5pm; Aug daily every 10 min until 6pm; 1–9 Jan & 31 Jan– 28 Feb Mon–Fri 11.30am & 3.30pm, Sat 11.30am, 2.30pm & 4.30pm, Sun (26–31 Dec and 1–6 Jan only a10am, 11am, noon, 2.30pm, 4pm & 5pm; in English June–Sept check website for times • €18 • ⓣ 800 166 250, ⓦ frasassi.com

Some 32km up the Esino valley from Jesi, just after the Gola di Rossa, a road leads up from Genga train station to the Frasassi gorge, carved by the River Sentino, which was

PIAZZA DEL POPOLO, MACERATA

THE GRAPE FESTIVAL OF CUPRAMONTANA

The village of **Cupramontana** in the hills above Jesi is known as the capital of Verdicchio country. The best time to visit is the first Sunday in October, when there's a parade and dancing, and the village streets are lined with stalls of wine and food for the **grape festival** marking the eve of the harvest. A *cantina aperta* ("open cellar") day at the end of May gives you the chance to sample the wines, while the wonderful Istituto Marchigiano Enogastronomia at Via Federico Conti 5 (Tues–Sun10.30am–2pm & 5–8pm; Nov–March 5–9pm; ⓣ0731 213 386, ⓦistitutomarchigianodienogastronomia.it) in Jesi's historic centre (near the top of the escalator) has a fascinating wine museum and holds **tastings** of local wines and produce daily, and organises special food events focussing on anything from wild mussels to single varietal olive oils.

also responsible for creating the 18km of caves beneath it. The largest of the **Grotte di Frasassi**, or Frasassi caves, was discovered only in 1971, and just over a kilometre of its

caverns and tunnels is now open to the public on tours that last seventy minutes – note that the average temperature inside is 14ºC.

Inevitably, the most remarkable stalactite and stalagmite formations have been named: there's a petrified Niagara Falls, a giant's head with a wonderfully Roman profile, a cave whose floor is covered with candles complete with holders, and a set of organ pipes. The vast Cave of the Great Wind, at 240m high, is one of the biggest in Europe – large enough to contain Milan Cathedral – and over the years has been used for a series of experiments, ranging from sensory deprivation (as a possible treatment for drug addicts) to a subterranean version of *Big Brother*.

The Conero Riviera

With its white cliffs, blanched pebble beaches, thick protected forests and easy-going resorts, the **Conero Riviera** to the south of Ancona is the northern Adriatic's most spectacular and enjoyable stretch of coastline. This tranquil holiday paradise is centred around **Monte Conero**, which plunges straight into the sea from an altitude of 572m. The area is easily accessible, with the seaside villages of **Portonovo**, **Sirolo** and **Numana** all linked by bus from Ancona. Sirolo and Numana are now as crowded in July and August as the rest of the Adriatic resorts, the main difference being that their cliff-backed beaches are more picturesque. The most stunning stretch of coast, a series of tiny coves at the base of Monte Conero between Portonovo and Sirolo, is best explored by boat – they leave from both bays. You can go just for the scenery or ask to be dropped off somewhere along the way and be picked up a few hours later.

This stretch of coast is the home of **Rosso Conero wine**, made from the same Montepulciano grape as Chianti, though less well known than its Tuscan counterpart and rarely found outside Italy. There's a chance to sample it at the Rosso Conero **festival** (ⓦfestadelrossoconero.it) at Camerano, 8km inland from Monte Conero, in the first week of September.

Portonovo

A short 11km bus ride from Ancona, **PORTONOVO**, nestling beneath Monte Conero, is a scattered resort made up of a couple of campsites and a clutch of expensive hotels, one of which is sited in the Napoleonic fort that dominates the bay. The main attraction is the unbeatable scenery and the transparent turquoise water, and though the main pebbly pay-beach gets very busy in summer, it's easy enough to escape by walking about 1km to Mezzavalle beach (free) just north of Portonovo bay or clambering over rocks to the few tiny beaches to the south. On the walk south, there's

a beautiful little Romanesque church, **Santa Maria** (Tues–Sun 4.30–6.30pm), perched above the shore at the end of an oleander-lined path. There are lots of **trails** across Monte Conero of varying degrees of difficulty; the tourist office at Sirolo (see below) has hiking maps.

Sirolo

Cliff-top **SIROLO** has an old centre of terraced cottages divided by neat cobbled streets. The main square, **Piazza Veneto**, is on the cliff edge, with good views of the coast and Monte Conero. What used to be a quiet bolthole is now packed out on weekends from June to September, and is exceptionally busy in July and August. In season, buses run roughly every thirty minutes to the two **beaches** below: Sassi Neri, a wide, long, black-pebbled strand, and San Michele, an attractive, narrow, sandy stretch.

Numana

The busiest of the three resorts, **NUMANA** is a small port with a large pebble beach. Up in the old town, a windy headland just beyond the modern church provides some of the coast's most spectacular views and there's an interesting archeology museum nearby. From the port, boats run to the wonderfully secluded beach at **Due Sorelle**, only accessible by water; Traghettatori del Conero (T 071 933 1795, W traghettatoridelconero.it) runs a daily service at 9.30am, with others at 10.30am, 11.30am and 2.30pm according to demand, as well as other boat trips along the coast (full timetable and booking online).

Antiquarium

Via La Fenice 4 • Mon & Tues 1.45–7.15pm, Wed–Sun 8.15am–7.15pm • €2

Away from the beach, Numana's main attraction is the **Antiquarium**, a small but unexpectedly intriguing archeology museum filled mostly with relics of the Piceni tribe, who occupied the area between Senigallia and Pescara from the seventh century BC. Explanations are in English and among the exhibits are burial finds from Sirolo and Numana, Bronze Age helmets and lots of red-and-black pots decorated with scenes from Greek mythology, clearly illustrating the extent to which the Piceni were influenced by the Greeks, who set up a trading post nearby.

ARRIVAL AND INFORMATION — CONERO RIVIERA

By bus Portonovo is linked with Ancona by regular urban buses (mid-June to Aug; every 20min). Buses to Sirolo and Numana (approx hourly; 35–40min) leave from a stop to the left of Ancona's train station (as you leave it) and just off Piazza Cavour.

Tourist offices The main tourist office for the area is in Sirolo at Piazza Vittorio Veneto 6 (Sat & Sun 10am–1pm & 4–7pm; June–Aug longer (erratic) hours; T 071 933 0611. There are also seasonal information offices (July & Aug) on Portonovo's main piazza and in Numana, with the opening hours varying from year to year.

ACCOMMODATION

PORTONOVO

Campeggio La Torre T 071 801 257, W campeggiolatorreportonovo.com. One of two large campsites in Portonovo, the *Torre* is sprinkled across woodland just back from the beach and has a bar-restaurant and games room. June to mid-Sept. Pitches €8.50, per person €9

Fortino Napoleonico T 071 801 450, W hotelfortino.it. Just steps from the lapping turquoise waters of the Adriatic, this luxury four-star establishment began life as a fortress built by Napoleon to stop the English landing to take fresh water from Monte Conero's springs. The hotel retains some military touches here and there among its chi-chi grandeur. €279

SIROLO

Hotel Residence Arturo Via Spiaggia 1 T 071 933 0975, W arturoresidencesirolo.com. Beach lovers should book a room at this superb place right on the white shingle

11

strand of Spiaggia Urbani. The four rooms and two studio apartments have cooking facilities and open out onto small balconies and the sea. There's a restaurant with live music down on the beach, and cars can be left in the public car park above. **€150**

Camping Internazionale ⓣ 071 933 0884, ⓦ campinginternazionale.com. The best campsite on the Conero Riviera is located on a terraced, wooded hillside below Sirolo, with easy access to two beaches. Facilities are kept spotless and there's free internet at reception. Slightly tricky to access with large camper vans and caravans. April–Sept. Pitches **€18**, per person **€12**, bungalows **€110**

Stella Hotel Via Giulietti 9 ⓣ 071 933 0704, ⓦ stellahotel.it. Right in the centre of Sirolo, this freshly refurbished three-star hotel has spacious rooms with balconies and far-reaching sea views. Buses from Ancona stop outside the door. **€173**

11

NUMANA

Scogliera Via del Golfo 21 ⓣ 071 933 0622, ⓦ hotelscogliera.it. A modern, appealing place on a small headland at the northern edge of the bay with a pool, first-rate restaurant and art-covered walls. Some of the 36 rooms have Adriatic views. Half-pension (obligatory) per person **€110**

Sorriso Via Flaminia 109 ⓣ 071 933 0645, ⓦ hotelsorrisonumana.it. Just 50m from the beach, this family-run hotel has 38 decent if unimaginative rooms, half of which enjoy dramatic Adriatic views, and a palm-shaded garden where alfresco breakfast can be taken. Free wi-fi and discounts at some Numana restaurants; 3-night minimum stay in high season. **€140**

Villa Sirena Via del Golfo 24 ⓣ 071 933 0850, ⓦ villasirena.it. Once the only building on the seafront, this exotically red-hued hotel offers 23 freshly modernized rooms, all with balconies and sea views. A snazzy bar-restaurant area, guest terrace, disabled facilities and its very own private beach area make these Numana's top lodgings. Closed Jan–Easter. **€150**

EATING

PORTONOVO

Il Clandestino signposted from car parks ⓣ 071 801 422, ⓦ morenocedroni.it. There's no better place to watch the sun go down than from this baby-blue beach hut bar and restaurant near the tower, serving a fixed menu (€85) of *susci vichinghi* – sushi Viking style: the mind boggles but the reality is pretty amazing, featuring the likes of crab with seaweed pesto. A la carte dishes (€15–25) continue the super-trendy Japanese-Scandi theme with the likes of tataki tuna and salt cod served with fermented cabbage. July & Aug 9am–2am, shorter hours the rest of the year; closed Nov–March.

SIROLO

La Taverna Piazza Veneto 10 ⓣ 071 933 1382. Adriatic views, local wines, home-made fishy pasta dishes (€8–13) and main-course fish (€15–20) make this a madly popular winner on Sirolo's main square. Tues–Sun noon–2.45pm & 7–10.30pm.

Osteria Sara Via Corso Italia 9 ⓣ 071 933 0716. Robust local dishes in a no-nonsense atmosphere; The seafood tagliatelle (€10) and grilled tuna (€16) are highly recommended. Daily 12.30–2.30pm & 7.30–10pm.

NUMANA

La Torre Via La Torre 1 ⓣ 071 933 0747. Boasting bay views from a large new terrace, Numana's top fish restaurant plates up top-notch gourmet fare with a modern twist – there's no pasta, just a series of exquisite fish dishes, most costing around €15. It also runs a relaxed al fresco "Chiosco" in Piazza Nuova open for drinks, sophisticated nibbles and light fish dishes every evening from 7pm. Alternatively you could, literally, push the boat out and treat yourself to a four-hour boat trip with breakfast (€40), lunch (€70), *aperitivo* (€50) and swimming stops (departures at 7am, 10.30am and 6pm). Restuarant daily 12.30–2.30pm & 7.30–10.30pm.

Morelli Via Leopardi. Opposite Numana's modern church and just along from the museum, this is the quintessential Italian café and has been selling coffees and ice creams since 1927. Daily 7am–midnight.

Loreto

The vast majority of people who visit **LORETO** are pilgrims, over four million of whom arrive every year to pay their respects at what they believe is the House of the Virgin Mary where Jesus spent his childhood. The house, which made a miraculous journey from Nazareth to Italy (see page 699), is contained within a huge hilltop basilica visible from miles around. However, away from the religious frenzy, the town, it must be said, has little to offer.

THE MADONNA OF LORETO AND THE JOURNEY OF THE SANTA CASA

Loreto owes its existence to one of the Catholic Church's more surreal legends. The story goes that in 1292, when the Muslims kicked the Crusaders out of Palestine, a posse of angels flew the house of Mary from Nazareth, the **Santa Casa**, to Dalmatia, and then, a few years later, whisked it across the Adriatic to Loreto. In the face of growing scepticism, the Vatican came up with the more plausible story that the Holy House was transported to Loreto on board a Crusader ship. Not surprisingly, though, this new theory doesn't have the same hold on the Catholic imagination, and the **Madonna of Loreto** continues to be viewed as the patron saint of aviators: Lindbergh took an image of her on his landmark Atlantic flight in 1927, and a medallion inscribed with her image also accompanied the crew of Apollo 9. For centuries she was also credited with military victories – presumably she was thought to have power over projectiles.

During the Baroque period the Santa Casa was copied by pious architects across central Europe, most notably in Bohemia and Moravia where tens of replicas were built. The finest of these stands next to Prague Castle.

The House of the Virgin Mary (Santa Casa)

Piazza della Madonna • Daily: April–Sept 6.15am–7.30pm; Oct–March 6.30am–7pm • Free

The primitive stone **House of the Virgin Mary (Santa Casa)** with only three walls, sits within a grand and very far from humble **basilica**, featuring works by such Renaissance luminaries as Bramante, Antonio da Sangallo, Sansovino, Lotto and Luca Signorelli, many of which depict scenes from the life of Mary. Inside the house, pride of place is given to a copy of the famous Black Madonna of Loreto; the medieval original, once crazily attributed to St Luke, was destroyed in a fire in 1921. For the nonbeliever the religious fervour can come as a surprise, with some pilgrims pressing their cheeks against the blackened, crumbling brick walls mumbling tearful prayers, others circling the marble outer shell on their knees. Note that at peak times you may not be able to look around the Holy House as it normally closes from 12.30pm to 2.30pm while a service is conducted for visiting pilgrims.

Over the centuries, Loreto built up a covetable collection of treasures donated by wealthy believers. One of the most costly and idiosyncratic was a golden baby bequeathed by Louis XIII of France, weighing exactly the same as his long-awaited heir, the future Louis XIV. The basilica was ransacked in 1798 by Napoleonic troops, most of the plunder ending up on the shelves of the Louvre in Paris.

Following Napoleon's demise, subsequent popes managed to retrieve many of the valuables, but the majority were stolen again in 1974 in what became known as the "holy theft of the century".

The Antico Tesoro

Palazzo Apostolico, Piazza della Madonna • Mon–Fri 10am–1pm & 3–6pm, Sat & Sun 10am–1pm & 3–7pm • €4

The items left behind in the treasury after the 1974 burglary of the basilica are now kept in the **Antico Tesoro**, well hidden in the west wing of the Palazzo Apostolico (in the far right-hand corner of the square as you look from the basilica). It shouldn't be missed, principally for the eight paintings by Lorenzo Lotto that are held here, nearly all dated between 1549 and 1556, including his final work, *The Presentation in the Temple*. Plagued by neurosis and lack of money, Lotto finally joined the religious community at Loreto, painted some of the canvases on display, and died here in 1556. Looking at *The Presentation*, with its rotund, crumbling priest and frail, almost skeletal nun, it would appear that he never found much inner peace. *Christ and the Adulteress* is an even more powerful work, with Christ surrounded by maniacally intense men and a swooning adulteress.

ARRIVAL AND INFORMATION — LORETO

By train The town is easily accessible by train from Ancona (at least hourly; 15–20min); the station is some way out of town but connected with the centre by an almost hourly bus service.

By bus Buses stop near the tourist office.

Destinations Ancona (5 daily; 1hr 15min); Numana (5 daily; 30min); Sirolo (5 daily; 35min).

Tourist office Via Solari 3 (Tues–Sun 9am–1pm; T 071 970 276, W loretoturismo.info).

ACCOMMODATION

Finding accommodation in Loreto can be difficult, particularly during the main pilgrimage seasons of Dec 8–12 (the anniversary of the legendary flight), Aug 1–20, Sept 5–10, Easter, and from Christmas through to Jan 7. In any case, it's probably best tackled as a day-trip.

Hotel Giardinetto Corso Boccalini 10 T 071 977 135, W hotelgiardinetto.it. Just inside the Porta Romana in a mellow stone building, this pleasingly old-fashioned place has sixty rooms with high ceilings, desks, big beds and cramped bathrooms. Parking is €10 a day but wi-fi is free. **€72**

Pellegrino e Pace Piazza della Madonna T 071 977 106, W pellegrinoepace.com. Sharing the main piazza with the Santa Casa itself, this very reasonably priced and superbly located hotel offers simple rooms in sunny colours, all with tiled floors, wi-fi and a/c. The in-house restaurant does decent pan-Italian favourites. **€69**

11

EATING

Cantina Del Moro Via Vanvitelli 2/4 T 338 964 8533. Pub, *enoteca* and local food haven rolled into one – and there's even a good selection for visiting vegetarians. Daily 12.30–2.15pm & 6.30–10.45pm.

Girarrosto Via Solari T 071 970 173. In the *Centrale* hotel, this family-run place serves reasonably priced antipasti typical of the Conero peninsula, along with a lovely *vincisgrassi* and handmade pasta. Daily noon–10.30pm.

Recanati

Devotees of either tenor Beniamino Gigli, or of eighteenth-century poet Leopardi, will doubtless make a beeline for the small, historic town of **RECANATI**, though most people will find little of excitement here.

Museo Casa Leopardi

Via Leopardi 14 • Mid-March to Oct daily 9am–6pm, Nov to mid-March Tues–Sun 9.30am–1pm & 2–5.30pm • €10 • W giacomoleopardi.it

Still inhabited by his family today, the **Museo Casa Leopardi** was the home of the poet Leopardi. The knowledgeable guides here will show you round his amazing collection of 25,000 books, and can provide a lot of detail on Leopardi's life. Aside from the library, however, the *palazzo* has little else to see.

Museo Beniamino Gigli

Via Cavour • Tues–Sun 11am–1pm & 4–7pm • €3

On the central Piazza Leopardi, the **Museo Beniamino Gigli**, housed in the nineteenth-century Palazzo Comunale, has costumes worn by the great tenor, presents received by him (including a dagger from the poet D'Annunzio), and, best of all, a replica of his dressing room. If you are lucky, the custodian will play some recordings.

Museo Civico Villa Colloredo Mels

Via Gregorio XII • Tues–Sun 10am–1pm & 3–6pm; hours usually extended in summer • €4

It's worth dropping into the patrician house on Via Gregorio XII where the **Museo Civico Villa Colloredo Mels** displays four superb paintings by Lotto, the highlight of the small collection. Among them there's a polyptych, a *Transfiguration* and a dramatic haunting *Annunciation*, better known as *The Madonna of the Cat* for the cat scuttling between the Madonna and angel – thought by some critics to represent the devil.

ARRIVAL AND DEPARTURE **RECANATI**

By bus Buses pull in at Viale del Passero Solitario, near the theatre.

Destinations Ancona (10 daily; 1hr 15min); Numana (10 daily; 30min); Sirolo (10 daily; 35min).

Macerata and around

A hilltop gem built entirely of a soft-coloured brick, the little-known provincial capital of **MACERATA** is one of the region's most attractive and historically well-endowed towns. The comparisons with Urbino are inevitable but what Macerata lacks in Renaissance splendour it more than makes up for with its livelier atmosphere, especially on market day (Wed) when the streets and squares are clogged with stalls and punters. Easy paced and with a large student population, it's an ideal place to wind down in the evenings after exploring the province. For fans of **opera and ballet**, the annual Sferisterio Opera Festival from mid-July to mid-August, held in Italy's best open-air venue outside Verona, is a must (see box).

Piazza della Libertà

Piazza della Libertà is the heart of the old town, an odd square in which contrasting buildings vie for supremacy. The Renaissance **Loggia dei Mercanti** was supplied by Alessandro Farnese, better known as Pope Paul III, the instigator of many architectural improvements to sixteenth-century Rome. It's somewhat overshadowed by the bulky Palazzo del Comune and overlooked by the looming Torre del Comune. Perhaps the square's most striking feature, however, is the mournful brick facade of **San Paolo**, a slowly crumbling, deconsecrated seventeenth-century church now used as an exhibition space.

The Duomo

Piazza Strambi • 7am–7pm • Free

The town's **Duomo** is no architectural showpiece – a workaday chunk of Baroque, which might have looked slightly more appealing had its facade been finished. Inside there's a small statue of Macerata's patron saint (to the left of the altar), Giuliano, to whom the cathedral is dedicated, mounted on a horse. His path to sainthood sounds like something out of the National Enquirer – he arrived home to find two people in his bed and, thinking they were his wife and her lover, promptly killed them. Discovering he'd murdered his parents, he hacked one of his arms off in remorse – the severed limb is now kept in a church strong-room, encased in a sleeve of gold and silver.

Outside the cathedral stands an oriental-looking bronze of Padre Matteo Ricci (1552–1610), a missionary from Macerata who spent the last 27 years of his life in China. *Life* magazine rated him as one of the hundred most influential people of the second millennium.

Palazzo Ricci

Via Domenico Ricci 1 • Visitable on free Italian-language guided tours, but you must call ahead for someone to show you round • ⓣ 0733 261 487, ⓦ palazzoricci.it

OPERA TICKETS

Book **tickets** for the Sferisterio Opera Festival at the Biglietteria dell'Arena Sferisterio, Piazza Mazzini 10 (Mon–Sat 10.30am–12.30pm & 5–7.30pm; ⓣ 0733 230 735, ⓦ sferisterio.it). €10 tickets for the balcony are released daily; bookable tickets range from €25 to €150.

One of Macerata's highlights is the exquisite art collection housed in the magnificent **Palazzo Ricci**, with its frescoed halls and antique furniture. The ever-growing collection of Italian twentieth-century art is exhibited in chronological order, with the three hundred or so works providing a comprehensive overview of the period. Of particular note are works by the socalled Rome School, cofounded by Macerata artist Scipione (Gino Bonichi; 1904–33).

Chiesa San Filippo

Corsa della Repubblica • Daily 7am–8pm • Free

Architecturally Macerata's most interesting place of worship, the **Chiesa San Filippo**, an eighteenth-century brick church with odd, blue onion domes and a small cupola, is the work of Roman architect Giovanni Battista Contini who was also responsible for the town's Palazzo Buonaccorsi. Two notable works of art adorn the interior: *The Crucifixion* by Francesco Mancini and *The Madonna and Saint Gaetano* by Ludovico Trasi.

ARRIVAL AND INFORMATION — MACERATA

By train The train station is a 10min walk south along Viale Don Bosco and connected to central Piazza della Libertà by frequent buses.

Destinations Civitanova (at least hourly; 30min; change here for Ancona); San Severino Marche (approx hourly; 30–40min); Tolentino (approx hourly; 15–25min).

By bus Buses are run by Contram (ⓦ contram.it) and SASP (ⓦ autolineesasp.it). The bus station is just off Giardini Diaz, a short walk west of the town centre.

Destinations Abbazia di Fiastra (up to 12 daily; 10min); Amandola (6 daily; 1hr 15–20min); Ancona (10 daily; 1hr 30min); Loreto (10 daily; 50min); San Severino (5 daily; 35min); Sarnano (12 daily; 55min–1hr 25min); Tolentino (12 daily; 30min); Urbisaglia (12 daily; 10min).

Tourist office The tourist office is at Corso della Repubblica 32 (Mon–Sat 9am–1pm & 3–6pm; July & Aug and during the opera season also Sun 9am–1pm & 3–6pm; ⓣ 0733 234 807.

ACCOMMODATION

Albergo Lauri Via Lauri 6 ⓣ 0733 232 376, ⓦ albergolauri.it. Basic, well-located guesthouse with 28 rooms and six apartments furnished mostly with cheap furniture of the flat-pack variety. A style-free zone but the cheapest deal in town. €60

Arena Vicolo Sferisterio 16 ⓣ 0733 230 931, ⓦ albergoarena.com. Tucked away in a small courtyard behind the opera arena, the friendly *Arena* has an interior dotted with historic prints, antiques and intriguing knick-knacks. Rooms boast minibars, a/c, soundproofing and TVs hooked up to BBC/CNN. €65

Claudiani Via Ulissi 8 ⓣ 0733 261 400, ⓦ hotelclaudiani.it. Macerata's principal four-star option is located just off Corso Matteotti in the historic centre. Its forty rooms are "hotel style" rather than "antique *palazzo*". €70

EATING AND DRINKING

Caffè Venanzetti Via Gramsci 21 ⓣ 0733 236 055. The finest place to get your day's Arabica fix is this stylishly chandeliered, mirrored and marbled café, good for rich cakes and fresh pastries as well as very cheap coffees. Mon–Sat 7am–2am, Sun 8am–2am.

Da Rosa Via Armaroli 17 ⓣ 0733 260 124. A simple trattoria serving beautiful home-made pasta (try the ravioli with ricotta and lemon) and, in season, funghi porcini and truffles. You can eat well for under €25 and house wine comes at €7 per half-litre. Daily noon–2pm & 7.30–11pm.

★ **Da Secondo** Via Pescheria Vecchia ⓣ 0733 260 912, ⓦ ristorantedasecondo.it. It's obvious from the wall snaps of all the illustrious guests to have dined here since 1952 that you've landed in Macerata's most famous restaurant. They do a fabulous *vincisgrassi* along with excellent roast lamb or pigeon with potatoes. Tues–Sun 12.30–3pm & 7.30–11pm.

Il Pozzo Vicolo Costa 5 ⓣ 0733 232 360, ⓦ ilpozzo.com. An old-fashioned pub-birreria dating back to the 1970s where you can listen to live and recorded jazz while sampling Italian beer. Mon–Fri 12.30pm–2.30pm & 7pm–3.30am, Sat & Sun 7pm–3am.

Osteria dei Fiori Via Lauro Rossi 61 ⓣ 0733 260 142, ⓦ osteriadeifiori.it. This sibling-run place specializes in seasonal, local produce, sourcing ingredients from small producers around Macerata. *Vincisgrassi* and rabbit with fennel are the two local dishes you shouldn't miss. Expect to pay €25–30 for a full meal without wine. Mon–Sat noon–3.30pm & 7–10.30pm.

Morrovalle

Rising above the **Chienti Valley**, which runs east from Macerata to the coast, the hill-village of **MORROVALLE** is worth a stop on the way to the sea. The settlement is skirted by a stepped street that disappears through arched gates and hemmed inside the main piazza at the top of the village is the squat Palazzo del Podestà, where Italy's first pawnshop was set up by St Bernard in 1428. The building next to it is the Palazzo Lazzarini, seat of the ruling family who survived their internecine battle for the privilege of ruling Morrovalle. The *palazzo*, though built in the fourteenth century, incorporates an earlier Romanesque-Gothic portal, possibly taken from a local church.

Santa Maria a Piè di Chienti

Daily 8am–8pm • Free • Ⓦ santamariapiedichienti.it

The road and rail track along the Chienti Valley pass the ex-monastery of **Santa Maria a Piè di Chienti** just after the fork for Montecosaro. It was built by Cluniac monks who came to the area in the tenth century, draining the flood-prone river into channels and creating fertile land out of what had been a fever-ridden marsh. Situated close to the coast, the monastery was vulnerable to Saracen invasion, so the monks encircled it with ditches, which could be flooded in the event of a raid. The monastery survived until the early nineteenth century, when it was destroyed by Napoleonic troops, and now all that remains is the church itself.

11

Basilica di San Nicola di Tolentino

Piazza Silveri 2, Tolentino • Daily 9am–noon & 3–6.30pm • Free • Ⓦ sannicoladatolentino.it

Heading southwest of Macerata towards the Sibillini mountain range, you might stop off briefly at the little town of **TOLENTINO** to see the **Basilica di San Nicola**. Its west front is a real feast for the eyes – a curly Baroque facade with a grinning sun instead of a rose window and a fancily twisting Gothic portal topped by an oriental-style arch enclosing a dragon-slaying saint. Inside, the most intriguing feature is the **Cappellone di San Nicola**, a large chapel whose colourful frescoes were painted in 1310–25 under the supervision of Pietro da Rimini and are very much in the style of Giotto.

Castello della Rancia

Tues–Sun 10.30am–6.30pm, slightly shorter hours in winter • €4 • Ⓦ tolentinomusei.it

Some 7km east of Tolentino stands the stately, fourteenth-century **Castello della Rancia**. This vast fort was the main grain store for the Cistercian abbey of Fiastra (see page 704) back in the twelfth century. Transformed into a castle in the fourteenth century, it became the focal point for a number of armed clashes, at one time harbouring the notorious Renaissance mercenary Sir John Hawkwood.

San Severino Marche

Some 12km northwest of Tolentino lies the ancient town of **SAN SEVERINO MARCHE**, a pretty little place whose entre converges on an extraordinary elliptical square, **Piazza del Popolo**, surrounded by porticoes. There's enough to keep history, art and archeology fans busy for half a day here and the town makes for an interesting stop-off on the way to or from Umbria.

Pinacoteca Tacchi Venturi

Via Salimbeni • Tues–Sat 9am–1pm & 3–7pm, Sun 10am–1pm & 3–7pm• €3, €4 with the Museo Civico Archeologico

The town's art gallery, **Pinacoteca Tacchi Venturi**, named after a local historian, is as good a reason as any for a visit, with a memorable assembly of pieces, including works

by Paolo Veneziano and Vittore Crivelli, as well as the Salimbeni brothers, the region's early Renaissance painters who were born and worked in San Severino in the fifteenth century; they are represented by delicate and expressive frescoes detached from local churches, and the wooden polyptych *The Marriage of St Catherine*.

San Lorenzo in Dolìolo

Via Salimbeni • Free

The ancient-looking church of **San Lorenzo in Dolìolo**, at the top of Via Salimbeni, appears slightly odd thanks to a medieval brick tower standing on top of its stone portal. Inside, on the vault of the tenth-century crypt you'll find frescoes by the Salimbeni brothers illustrating the story of St Andrew. The back part of the crypt is thought to be a pagan temple dating back to the time of the refugees from Septempeda.

The Duomo Vecchio

Via Castello al Monte • Free

San Severino's cathedral lurks up in **Castello**, the upper part of town, a long and steep walk, although there are occasional buses from the main square. The **Duomo Vecchio** was founded in the tenth century but has a Romanesque-Gothic facade, simple Gothic cloisters, and a much-rebuilt interior, featuring Salimbeni frescoes in the baptistry.

Museo Civico Archeologico

Via Castello al Monte • Tues–Sat 9am–1pm & 4–7pm, Sun 10am–1pm & 4–7pm • €3, €4 with the Pinacoteca Tacchi Venturi

Finds in the **Museo Civico Archeologico**, located near the cathedral, were excavated from the Roman valley town of Septempeda over the course of the twentieth century. Driven out by barbarian invasions in the sixth century the inhabitants escaped up to what is now the *castello*, thus establishing the town of San Severino.

ARRIVAL AND INFORMATION — SAN SEVERINO MARCHE

By train The train station is 600m east of Piazza del Popolo. Destinations Ancona (10 daily; 1hr 10min); Fabriano (15 daily; 45min); Macerata (10 daily; 40min).

Tourist office The tourist office is at Piazza del Popolo 43 (Tues–Sun 9.30am–12.30pm & 3.30–7pm; ⓣ 0733 638 414, ⓦ prolocossm.sinp.net).

South of Macerata: the road to Sarnano

With the Monti Sibillini on the horizon, snowcapped for most of the year, the route **south from Macerata** towards the spa town of **Sarnano** ranks as one of Le Marche's most beautiful.

Abbazia di Fiastra

June–Sept daily 10am–1pm & 3–7pm; Oct–May Sat, Sun & public hols 10am–1pm & 3–6pm • ⓣ 0733 202 942, ⓦ abbadiafiastra.net

Around 10km to the south of Macerata, on the edge of a dense wood, stands the Romanesque-Gothic complex of the **Abbazia di Fiastra**, a Cistercian abbey with a simple, pantiled brick cloister and monastic quarters adjoining a grandiose, aisled church. Since the 2016 earthquake only the church can be visited, but the trails through its grounds, now a nature reserve, remain a popular Sunday stroll.

Urbs Salvia

Free access

A five-minute bus ride from the Abbazia di Fiastra brings you to the site of **Urbs Salvia** near the modern-day town of Urbisaglia. This was one of Le Marche's most important Roman towns and home to thirty thousand people until it was sacked by Alaric in 409 AD. The Lourdes of its day (Urbs Salvia means "city of health"), its fame continued into the Middle Ages, when Dante invoked it as an example of a city fallen from glory in his *Paradiso*. So far an amphitheatre, theatre, baths and parts of the walls have

been excavated, and frescoes of hunting scenes have been discovered in a *cryptoportico* (underpassage). The theatre was one of the largest in Italy, and could seat 12,600 spectators. Up in modern Urbisaglia, there's also a small **archeological museum** (same hours), visitable on the same ticket, containing finds from the site.

San Ginesio

South of Urbisaglia, the hill-town health resort of **SAN GINESIO** is justifiably known as the balcony of the Sibillini: the panoramic view from the gardens of the Colle Ascarano, just outside the town walls, stretches from the Adriatic and Monte Conero to the Sibillini mountains and the highest of the Apennines, the Gran Sasso in Abruzzo. In the town itself, the central piazza is dominated by one of Le Marche's most unusual churches, the **Collegiata della Annunziata**, whose late-Gothic facade is decorated with filigree-like terracotta moulding. Rising above it are two campaniles, one capped by an onion dome and the other by what looks like a manicured cactus. Gothic frescoes adorn some of the chapels, and the crypt has frescoes by the Salimbeni brothers.

Sarnano

SARNANO, south of San Ginesio, was once a virtually abandoned, pretty down-at-heel village, but in the last three decades or so the authorities have woken up to the potential of its thermal springs – believed since Roman times to have wide-ranging curative properties – and have begun to develop the place into a spa resort and weekend day-trip destination. The medieval core, coiling in concentric circles around a gentle hill, has been subtly restored, and though it's now more of a showpiece than a living village, its narrow interconnecting cobbled streets and picturesque old houses make it an ideal place for an undemanding day's wander.

San Francesco

Just inside the **Porta Brunforte** gate of old Sarnano is the fourteenth-century church of **San Francesco**, decorated with Palestinian plates thought to have been brought to Sarnano by souvenir-collecting Crusaders.

Santa Maria di Piazza

Piazza Alta • Free

The **Piazza Alta** lies at the town's summit and was once the political and religious centre, hemmed with fine medieval *palazzi*, as well as the thirteenth-century church of **Santa Maria di Piazza**. The fifteenth-century frescoes in this austere-looking church include a figure known as the *Madonna with Angels*, for the host of celestial musicians and choristers surrounding her. The wooden statue of Christ on the altar has been saddled with one of popular tradition's strangest myths – if it's about to rain, his beard is supposed to grow. On the second Sunday in August, Santa Maria is the starting point for Sarnano's annual medieval knees-up, or **palio** – though apart from the costumes and processions, it has more in common with a kids' sports day, featuring a tug-of-war, pole climbing and a race in which the competitors have to balance jugs of water on their heads.

Monti Sibillini National Park

With a mountain lake reddened by the blood of the devil, a narrow pass known as the gorge of hell and a cave reputed to have been the lair of an enchantress, the **Monti Sibillini** are not only the most beautiful section of the Apennines, but they teem with ancient legends too. Wolves, chamois and brown bear all live in the national park and

LAGO DI PILATO

According to the legend surrounding the **Lago di Pilato**, Pontius Pilate's body was dispatched from Rome on a cart pulled by two wild oxen which climbed up into the Sibillini and ditched the corpse in the water here. In the Middle Ages it became a favourite haunt for **necromancers** seeking dialogues with the devil – stones inscribed with occult symbols have been found on its shores. Deciding they wanted to be rid of the magicians, one night the local lords put soldiers on guard around its shores. Nothing happened until the morning, when the soldiers discovered that the lake had turned red; assuming it was with the devil's blood, they fled. What in fact turned the water red was a mass of minuscule red *Chircephalus marchesonii*, a species of fish indigenous to Asia; a shoal was stranded here millions of years ago when the sea receded, and its descendants still thrive.

even if you don't come across one of these, you may be lucky enough to see an equally rare golden eagle instead.

The best way to experience the park is by walking, cycling or horseriding, and if you're up for a challenge there's **Il Grande Anello dei Sibillini** (The Great Sibylline Ring), 120km of signposted footpaths that take nine days to walk, or four to five days to cover by mountain bike. Maps and accommodation details, including mountain refuges, are listed on sibillini.net. There are shorter trails too, through meadows filled with wild flowers, for which the most agreeable bases are the medieval hill-villages that crown the Sibillini foothills. Most villages are served by buses, but they're generally few and far between and it's definitely best to have your own transport.

Amandola

The small village of **AMANDOLA** is fairly easy to get to on public transport, making it a good base for seeing the region. The highlight here is the **Museo Antropogeografico** (by appointment only, call 0736 848 598; €5), housed in the ex-convent of the church of San Francesco at Largo Leopardi 4 and chock-full of hands-on exhibits focusing on the wildlife and legends of the park. Otherwise, Amandola is just a great place to kick back after a day's hiking in the Sibillini.

Montefortino

Around 7km by road south of Amandola, the hill-village of **MONTEFORTINO** is a pretty spot, though not that well served by buses and invaded by tourists in season. Primarily a place to wander and admire the Sibillini views, the town also has a small **Pinacoteca** (open on request; call 0736 859 491; free), whose chief attractions are a polyptych by Alemanno – a follower of the Crivelli who clearly took as much delight in painting embroidery as they did – and an arresting twelfth-century portrait of a man with a pipe and candle emerging from the darkness. Appropriately, given the necromantic traditions of this area, there's also an eighteenth-century painting of Circe with her occult apparatus.

Montemonaco and around

A short way south of Montefortino, **MONTEMONACO**, a walled medieval village of cobbled streets and yellow stone houses, is close to some of the Sibillini's most legendary sights. One, the **Grotta della Sibilla** (Sibyl's Cave), whose occupant gave her name to the mountain group, is a two-hour walk west from the village, though periodic rockfalls can block the way. The other, through the **Gola dell'Infernaccio** (Gorge of Hell), a few kilometres southwest of the village, is an easy and spectacular hike in summer – though you should check access locally before leaving as many routes were damaged in the 2016 earthquake and may still not have been repaired. You can take a

bus from Montefortino to the Infernaccio fork, from where it's a three-hour walk to the gorge along a well-defined path. The approach through a narrow valley is atmospheric: silent, except for the distant roar of the River Tenna, with memorial plaques on the cliffs at the entrance to commemorate climbers who've died scaling the walls. The path squeezes its way under jagged rocks, accompanied by the deafening sound of raging water. Once past a second bridge it forks, the lower path leading to the tranquil source of the Tenna while the upper brings you, in about thirty minutes, to the **Hermitage of San Leonardo**, occupied by a solitary monk until not that long ago.

ARRIVAL AND DEPARTURE — MONTI SIBILLINI NATIONAL PARK

By bus The main operator is Trasfer (trasfer.eu/it), with some routes by Madebus (madebus.it). Amandola is the main arrival and departure point for other places within the park.

Destinations Ascoli Piceno (4 daily Mon–Sat; 1hr 10min); Fermo (4 daily; 1hr); Montefortino (daily; 10min); Montemonaco (5 daily; 20–25min); Sarnano (6 daily; 30min).

ACCOMMODATION

Several agriturismi and B&Bs in the area were badly affected by the 2016 earthquake and remained closed at the time of writing. If heading for the area, try searching on Airbnb (airbnb.co.uk).

MONTEMONACO

Agriturismo La Cittadella Località Cittadella 0736 856 361, cittadelladeisibillini.it. Some 2.5km down a dirt road from the northern end of Montemonaco, this rural spot is a peaceful place for an overnight stay, with a decent restaurant to boot. A fitting base for flits into Sibillini backcountry. **€80**

11

Ascoli Piceno

Located between the Monti Sibillini and the Adriatic, **ASCOLI PICENO** is Le Marche's greatest hidden gem and lies well off the tourist trail. This seems odd considering it has plenty of grand architecture and a lovely café-lined central square that's among the most striking in the region. At Mardi Gras it hosts Le Marche's most flamboyant carnival and in August its streets are given over to the Quintana, a medieval **festival** that incorporates a spectacular joust. If that wasn't enough, Ascoli's restaurants and food stalls are the proud purveyors of **olive all'ascolana** (deep-fried breadcrumb-crusted olives stuffed with veal).

Ascoli has a compact centre, surrounded by largely intact walls. Piazza del Popolo is the place to get the feel of the town, while its small number of Roman remains and its churches and museums are scattered throughout the old centre.

Piazza del Popolo and around

Ascoli's historical centre is anchored by the centrepiece **Piazza del Popolo**, a pleasingly petite but beautiful Renaissance square hemmed by grand facades. The western flank is filled by the **Palazzo dei Capitani** which dates from the late twelfth century, when the free *comune* of Ascoli was at its height. That anything of the building has survived is something of a miracle, for in 1535 a certain Giambattista Quieti set it on fire with the intention of incinerating a rebel barricaded inside. The interior was gutted but enough remained of the facade for a swift facelift to suffice. Rectangular windows were slotted into medieval arches, and a grand portal affixed, on top of which sits a statue of Pope Paul III, who reintroduced peace by replacing Quieti with a neutral outsider.

When they weren't slaughtering each other, at least some of Ascoli's rulers found time to collect public money in order to finance city improvements. The sixteenth-century **loggias** that enclose the piazza are one of the results – each of a slightly different width, to correspond to the size of the contribution made by the various merchants and shopkeepers who worked here.

Chiesa di San Francesco

Piazza del Popolo • Free

Abutting Piazza del Popolo is the **Chiesa di San Francesco**, the construction of which was financed by the sale of a Franciscan convent outside the city, after Pope Alexander IV had given the Franciscans permission to move within its walls. The foundations were laid in 1258 but the building wasn't completed until 1549, when the low cupola was added. It's a somewhat restrained church, with little to seize the attention except for the intricate west portal on Via del Trivio, but a good place to take a break from the heat of Ascoli's narrow streets.

Adjoining the south side of the church and overlooking Corso Mazzini is the sixteenth-century **Loggia dei Mercanti**. Formerly the scene of commercial wheeling and dealing, it still features its niches cut into the back wall in which bricks could be checked for size before being purchased. The cloister to the north of the church is now the site of a daily market.

Galleria d'Arte Contemporanea and Museo dell'Arte Ceramica

Corso Mazzini • April 1st–Sept 15th Tues–Sun10am–7pm, 16 Sept–31 Mar Tues–Fri 10am–1pm & 3–6pm, Sat & Sun 11am–6pm • €8 • ascolimusei.it

Following Corso Mazzini from Piazza del Popolo brings you to two of Ascoli's worthwhile museums: the **Galleria d'Arte Contemporanea**, where the beautifully displayed permanent collection includes works by Filippo de Pisis, Lucio Fontana,

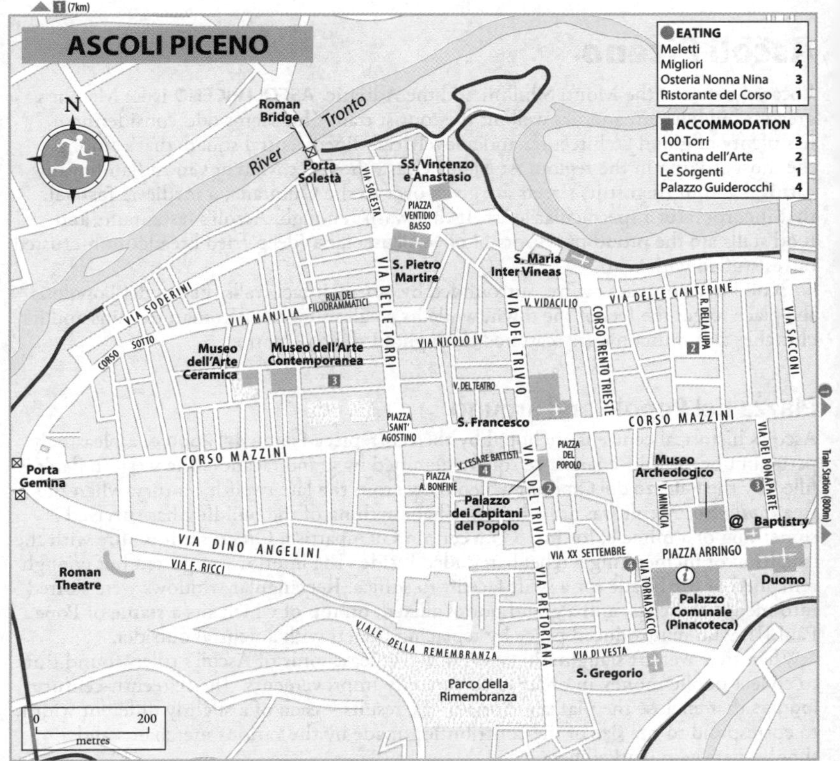

ROMAN ASCOLI

Little of **Roman Ascoli** survives, but beyond the thirteenth-century gate, the **Porta Solestà**, you'll find the Augustan-era **Roman bridge** – one of Italy's largest and most impressively preserved – spanning the River Tronto in a single, 25m-wide arch. Amazingly, it's still used by cars and trucks over two thousand years after it was erected.The only other visitable sites are the sparse remains of a **Roman theatre**, on the southwest edge of town, which stands close to the Roman **Porta Gemina**, or Twin Gate, at the beginning of the road to Rome.

Hans Hart,ng and Gino Severini. It also offers a compelling introduction to the work of local artist Osvaldo Licini, a friend of Modigliani and Picasso, who once saved Picasso from being beaten up by turning on his attackers with the walking stick he had used since being injured in World War I. The **Museo dell'Arte Ceramica** (same hours and ticket) around the corner is of more limited appeal, though the setting, in the ex-convent of San Tommaso, is quite enchanting.

Chiesa dei Santi Vincenzo e Anastasio

Piazza Basso • Sat & Sun only 10am–1pm & 3.30–6.30pm • Free

The **Chiesa dei Santi Vincenzo e Anastasio**, tucked away in the north of the historical centre, is Ascoli's most distinctive church, with an austere fifteenth-century chessboard facade that was once filled in with frescoes. Beneath the mainly eleventh-century body of the building is a primitive crypt erected over a spring that was supposed to have leprosy-curing properties. Although the plunge bath is still there, the spring was diverted elsewhere in the last century.

The Duomo

Piazza Arringo • Daily 7am–noon & 3.30–7.15pm, may close earlier in winter • Free

Ascoli's Baroque **Duomo** is situated on the east side of Piazza Arringo. The interior is one of Italy's more colourful, with panels of North African-style geometric patterns (like fake carpets) painted on the walls, huge shell alcoves, chandeliers suspended on strings of illuminated beads, a blue ceiling studded with gold stars and a cupola decorated with late nineteenth-century frescoes of obscure Ascolani saints. In the Cappella del Sacramento to the right of the altar you'll find a **polyptych** by Carlo Crivelli. The most arresting of the ten panels is the central Pietà, in which the haggard expression of Mary, the torment that distorts Christ's face, and Mary Magdalene's horror as she examines the wound in his hand are given heightened impact by the strict semicircular composition. Held up by some hefty Romanesque pillars, the crypt contains the tomb of St Emidio, to whom the Duomo is dedicated, decorated with some fine mosaic-work.

Museo Archeologico

Piazza Arringo 28 • Tues–Sun 8.30am–7.30pm • €4

If you want to know more about ancient Ascoli, visit the evocative **Museo Archeologico**, across the square from the Duomo. The collection includes Piceni projectiles inscribed with curses against their Roman enemies, jewellery, heavy bronze rings that were placed on the stomachs of dead women, and small test-tube-like containers used to assess the quality of grief by measuring the volume of tears.

Pinacoteca Civica

Piazza Arringo • Tues–Sun 10am–1pm & 3–6pm, Sat & Sun 11am–6pm • €8 • ⓦ ascolimusei.it

As well as housing the tourist office, the Palazzo Comunale next to the Duomo also contains the **Pinacoteca Civica**. The highlights here are works by Crivelli who is thought to have died in Ascoli around 1495. Many consider his finest work to be the polyptych, which can be found next door in the cathedral.

Chiesa di San Gregorio

Piazza San Gregorio • Free

A block behind the Pinacoteca Civile, the fourteenth-century **Chiesa di San Gregorio** was ingeniously built around the remains of a Roman temple. Incorporated into its facade are two lofty Corinthian columns, originally imported by the Romans from Greece, and patches of *opus reticulatum* (diamond brickwork). In the adjoining convent is a tiny revolving door with the inscription *Qui si depositano gli innocenti* ("Here you deposit the innocent"), designed so that parents could remain anonymous when leaving unwanted children to the care of priests and nuns.

ARRIVAL AND INFORMATION — ASCOLI PICENO

By train Ascoli's train station is just east of the town centre, a 10min walk along Viale Indipendenza and Corso Vittorio Emanuele.

Destinations San Benedetto del Tronto (approx hourly; 40min–1hr); Ancona (approx hourly; 1hr 50min).

By bus Buses (mostly run by StartSpa (@startspa.it) stop outside the train station.

Destinations Amandola (4 daily Mon–Sat; 1hr 10min); Montefortino (5 daily Mon–Sat; 1hr 20min); Montemonaco (5 daily Mon–Sat; 1hr 30min); San Benedetto del Tronto (every 30min; 1hr).

Tourist office Well hidden in the entrance to the Palazzo Comunale on Piazza Arringo (Daily 10am–6pm; T 0736 298 334, @comune.ascolipiceno.it).

ACCOMMODATION

★ **100 Torri** Via Mazzoni 6 T 0736 255 123, @centotorri.com; map p.708. If it's chic digs you're after, these nineteen cool, well-appointed rooms within a thirteenth-century building are aimed at affluent tourists and anyone with an appreciation of understated styling. Wi-fi, a ceramic-themed meeting room, a winter-garden breakfast room and extremely courteous service make the experience of staying here even more special. **€114**

Cantina dell'Arte Via Lupa 5/8 T 0736 255 620, @cantinadellarte.it; map p.708. Great-value, cheerful, well-kept hotel in the centre with eleven small rooms and five apartments in an annexe, along with a very reasonably priced, bustling restaurant. **€60**

Le Sorgenti Lago di Castel Trosino T 0736 263 725, @agriturismolesorgenti.org; map p.708. One of several good agriturismi within easy reach of town, this occupies a restored eighteenth-century villa set in rolling countryside 7km north of Ascoli. Rooms are simple and rustic, the food is made from fresh local ingredients (including home-pressed olive oil) and there are plenty of local walks to enjoy. **€60**

★ **Palazzo Guiderocchi** Via Cesare Battisti 3 T 0736 259 710, @palazzoguiderocchi.com; map p.708. This *palazzo* hotel blends aristocratic style with rustic simplicity to create some of the best accommodation in Le Marche. The huge rooms are like medieval bedchambers with canopied beds, convincing replica antiques, full-on fabrics and the highest ceilings you're ever likely to see in a hotel. The hotel also has nine more modern rooms on Piazza del Popolo, five of them with a kitchenette. **€97**

EATING AND DRINKING

★ **Meletti** Piazza del Popolo 20 T 0736 255 559; map p.708. Le Marche's best-located piazza café is *Meletti*, an Ascoli institution. The spacious interior is unadulterated Art Nouveau with huge mirrors, classic marble café tables and lots of Mucha-style detailing. The café makes its own superb anisette liqueur, and serves up delightful sweets and pastries, brought to your table by elegantly uniformed waiters. Mon–Tues 7.30am–9pm, Wed, Thurs & Sun 7.30am–10pm, Fri & Sat 7.30am–midnight.

Migliori Piazza Arringo 2 T 0736 250 042; map p.708. A delightful three-in-one experience comprising a sit-down restaurant that serves local specialities such as *grande fritta* – deep-fried lamb cutlets, vegetables and *olive all'ascolana* for €12 – a well-stocked delicatessen and a small stall out front where you can purchase bags of freshly fried stuffed olives (try the truffle-filled variety) for €4. Tues–Sat noon–11pm.

Osteria Nonna Nina Piazza della Viola 10 T 0736 251 523, @osterianonnanina.com; map p.708. Simple, homely *osteria* in a typical Ascoli vaulted palace plating up dishes such as *fritto misto all'Ascolana* like *nonna* used to make. *Primi* €6.50–10, *secondi* €10–15. Daily noon–4pm & 7pm–midnight.

Ristorante del Corso Corso Mazzini 277 ⓣ 0736 256 760; map p.708. This well-regarded, fish-only restaurant is a modest affair but plates up some of Ascoli's tastiest dishes. The simple *spaghetti alle vongole* and sole (*sogliola*) braised in white wine are the house specialities. For a full three-course meal with wine expect to pay around €35. **Daily 12.30–2.15pm & 8–10pm.**

Abruzzo and Molise

716 Parco Nazionale del Gran Sasso and around

721 Sulmona and around

725 Parco Nazionale d'Abruzzo

727 Teramo and around

730 Pescara and around

733 The coast south of Pescara

735 Inland Molise

SCANNO VILLAGE, L'AQUILA

Abruzzo and Molise

Abruzzo and Molise, united as one region until 1963, together form a kind of transition zone between northern and southern Italy. Both are sparsely populated mountainous regions, which have been outside the mainstream of Italian affairs since the Middle Ages. Bordered by the Apennines, Abruzzo is home to some of Italy's wildest terrain: silent valleys, abandoned hill-villages and vast untamed mountain plains, once roamed by wolves, bears and chamois; sleepy, tiny Molise offers similar attractions, but is even less visited. In recent years Abruzzo has come under international scrutiny after a massive earthquake struck L'Aquila, the regional capital in April 2009, virtually destroying the city, killing over three hundred people and leaving 65,000 homeless. In spite of the widespread destruction, L'Aquila is slowly being pieced back together again, and these two little-visited regions continue to be among the few areas of Italy where there is plenty for visitors to discover.

The Abruzzesi have done much to pull their region out of the poverty trap, developing resorts on the long, sandy Adriatic coastline and exploiting the tourist potential of a large, mountainous national park and some well-stocked historic towns. Since the earthquake, **Sulmona**, to the southeast, makes the most logical base, though **L'Aquila**, at the foot of **Gran Sasso** – the Apennines' highest peak – is still worth a visit, even if it's a slightly unsettling experience.

The rising stars of Abruzzo are the **hill-villages** around L'Aquila, deeply rural places, where time seems to have come to a halt sometime in the fifteenth century, and whose traditions, cuisine and architecture are only now coming to be appreciated. South of Sulmona, in **Scanno** elderly women wear costumes that may have their origins in Asia Minor, and make intricate lace on cylindrical cushions known as *tomboli*. Just down the road, the scruffy hill-village of **Cocullo** celebrates its local saint with an extraordinary annual snake festival (see page 723). The main holiday resort on the Abruzzo coast is **Pescara**, with an impressive stretch of sandy beach that shelves slowly into the Adriatic. It makes a convenient base for excursions inland to **Chieti**, home to an excellent archeological museum. However the best spot for a sun-and-sand break is further south at **Vasto**, with its equally inviting strand and lively old centre.

Gentler, less rugged and somewhat poorer than Abruzzo, **Molise** arguably has more in common with southern than central Italy. The cities, **Isernia** and **Campobasso**, are large and bland, with small historical centres, but Molise has its compensations: a scattering of low-key Roman ruins – most interestingly at **Saepinum**. Wandering among the ruins, and looking out over the green fields to the mountains beyond, you get some inkling of how Italy's first Grand Tourists must have felt. A less-refined but equally interesting attraction takes place in the village of **Ururi**, settled by Albanian refugees in the fifteenth century, where the annual chariot race is as barbaric as anything the Romans dreamed up (see page 735).

Finally, there's the sheer physical aspect of the place. Forty percent of Molise is occupied by **mountains**, and although they are less dramatic than Abruzzo's, they provide almost endless possibilities for hiking. Visitors are also starting to explore the area's ancient sheep-droving routes, known as *tratturi*, which are gaining new life as mountain-bike or horseback-riding trails, served by occasional farmhouse guesthouses and riding stables along the way.

SAEPINUM, SEPINO

Highlights

❶ **Corno Grande** Hike in the wild and craggy Gran Sasso massif, out of which rises Italy's highest peak, the Corno Grande. See page 718

❷ **Driving from Sulmona to Scanno** A spectacular route through the mountains up to the wonderfully unspoilt town of Scanno. See page 724

❸ **Parco Nazionale d'Abruzzo** Get back to nature in this lovely park, which has around one hundred indigenous species of fauna and flora. See page 725

❹ **Museo Archeologico, Chieti** Head here for the best and most comprehensive display of Abruzzese antiquities, including the unique *Capestrano Warrior*. See page 728

❺ **Bull race at Ururi** The ordinary town of Ururi turns into a scene of frenetic activity once a year as horses, bulls and carts career through the streets. See page 735

❻ **Saepinum** This enchanting archeological site in rural Sepino is a throwback to the original Grand Tour, with overgrown Roman ruins dotted with inhabited dwellings. See page 736

HIGHLIGHTS ARE MARKED ON THE MAP ON PAGE 716

GETTING AROUND

ABRUZZO AND MOLISE

Don't expect to rush through Abruzzo and Molise if you're relying on public transport; in both regions, getting around on bus and train demands patience and the careful studying of timetables.

By car The regions are best explored by car and, rarely for Italy, driving here is usually a pleasure: the roads through the national parks are empty and driving through the towns is not as hair-raising an experience as elsewhere.

By bus If you're restricted to public transport, buses are generally better than trains, and services are punctual and cheap. Buses in Abruzzo are run by TUA, buses in Molise by ATM. Check timetables on their respective websites ⓦtuabruzzo.and ⓦatm-molise.it.

By train Train lines run down the coast and into Molise; check timetables on ⓦtrenitalia.com.

Parco Nazionale del Gran Sasso and around

Whether you approach Abruzzo from Le Marche in the north or Rome in the west, your arrival will be signalled by the spectacular bulk of the **Gran Sasso** massif, containing by far the highest of the Apennine peaks as well as a **national park** (ⓦgransassolagapark.it) with its many hiking trails. If you come by autostrada from Le Marche, you'll actually travel underneath the mountains, through a 10km tunnel, passing the entrance to a particle-physics research laboratory bored into the very heart of the mountain range. The massif itself consists of two parallel chains, flanking the **Campo Imperatore** plain that stretches for 27km at over 2000m above sea level.

OLIVE OIL AND WINE – THE CUISINE OF ABRUZZO AND MOLISE

Abruzzo and Molise are mountainous regions where agriculture is difficult and sheep farming dominates. Consequently, **lamb** tends to feature strongly in the local cuisine. You'll come across *abbacchio*, unweaned baby lamb that is usually cut into chunks and roasted or grilled; *arrosticini*, tiny pieces of lamb skewered and flame grilled; and *intingolo di castrato*, lamb cooked as a casserole with tomatoes, wine, herbs, onion and celery.

In Abruzzo, a crucial ingredient is **olive oil**, a product that has gained international acclaim in recent years. Around Sulmona *aglio rosso* (red garlic) is believed by many locals to be a cure for ailments ranging from neuralgia to arthritis; around L'Aquila in particular saffron (*zafferano*) is also found widely in sweet and savoury dishes, grown in fields southeast of the city.

Probably Abruzzo's most famous dish is *maccheroni alla chitarra*, usually referred to on menus as simply *chitarra*, made by pressing a sheet of pasta over a wooden frame of metal strings – hence the name *chitarra*, or guitar – and usually served with a tomato or lamb sauce. Chitarrini are simply extra fine. Cheese tends to be pecorino – either mature and grainy like Parmesan, or still mild, soft and milky.

The **wines** of Molise are rarely found outside the region. The most interesting is the Biferno DOC, which can be red, white or *rosato*. The best-known wine of Abruzzo is Montepulciano d'Abruzzo, a heavy red made from the Montepulciano grape with up to 15 percent Sangiovese. Pecorino, a local varietal and DOC, produces a fresh and mineral white. One of Italy's most important wine events, **Cantine Aperte** (Open Cellars) was born in Abruzzo and takes place the last Sunday in May. Hundreds of producers open their doors to enthusiasts for free tastings and gastronomic events (W movimentoturismovino.it).

12

Fonte Cerreto

FONTE CERRETO is the gateway to the Gran Sasso park. It consists of little more than a few hotels, a restaurant and a campsite clustered around a cable-car station (cable car Mon–Sat 8.30am–5pm, Sun 8am–5pm; every 30min; €10–15 return; T 0862.606143, W ilgransasso.it/la-stazione/la-funivia). Most of these were built in the 1930s as part of Mussolini's scheme to keep Italians fit by encouraging them to take exercise in the mountains. Ironically, he was imprisoned here in 1943, first at the *Villetta* inn (now the *Fior di Gigli*), and then at the *Campo Imperatore*, a decaying Art Deco ski lodge (currently undergoing restoration after earthquake damage) at the top of the cable-car route, in which, eerily, Mussolini's room has been preserved as it was (although the original sheets are now in the cupboard). Il Duce spent twelve days at the hotel on a diet of eggs, rice, boiled onions and grapes, contemplating suicide. Hitler came to his rescue, dispatching an ace pilot to airlift him out in a tiny plane.

ARRIVAL AND INFORMATION — PARCO NAZIONALE DEL GRAN SASSO

By car Fonte Cerreto is just off the A24 motorway. The area is not well connected by public transport, so it's best to drive.

By bus Ama buses from L'Aquila to Funivia call in at Fonte Cerreto (every 2hr; 40min).

Tourist information There's no tourist office, but local hotels are usually a good source of information on walks in the Gran Sasso park, and should be able to supply you with maps of trails and perhaps information on wildlife.

ACCOMMODATION AND EATING

Campo Imperatore

Giampy SS17 bis, Km 18 T 0862 606 225, W hotel giampy.eu. A kilometre from the cable car, this friendly hotel with basic rooms is well placed for hitting both the ski slopes and the local walking trails. There's a decent restaurant too, with a wood-fired pizza oven (evenings only). **€70**

The Campo Imperatore plain

The road continues from Fonte Cerreto across the vast **Campo Imperatore plain**, long the stomping ground of **nomadic shepherds**, who bring their flocks up here for summer grazing after wintering in the south – a practice that has endured since Roman times. The plain is fringed with hill-villages, many of them owing their existence to the medieval wool trade.

GRAN SASSO TRAILS

Snow can continue to fall on the park's highest mountain, **Corno Grande** (2912m), until late May, and remain thick on the ground well into June, so outside July and August, the **ascent** should only be attempted by experienced and fully equipped climbers. At all times you should be prepared for some fairly strenuous scree-climbing and steep descents. If you are fit, but not experienced, it is probably wiser to take a guide: contact Mountain Evolution (T 347 766 1126, W mountainevolution.com). Perhaps the most challenging route is the tough trek from the top of the cable car right across the mountain range, taking in the Corno Grande, and sleeping over at the *Rifugio Franchetti* (T 0861 959 634 or T 333 232 4474, W rifugiofranchetti.it; June–Sept; €30, or €55 for dinner, bed and breakfast). The refuge website has several suggested itineraries (in Italian only), and the staff are also very knowledgeable. If you're going to do any of the Gran Sasso trails, you'll need the CAI *Gran Sasso d'Italia* **map** (on sale in newsagents around the region), and should check out **weather conditions** with your hotel or online at W meteomont.gov.it first.

Castel del Monte

12

Among the hill-villages in the Campo Imperatore is **Castel del Monte**, heavily fortified and crowned with a ruined castle and church, setting for the achingly stylish 2010 film, *The American*, featuring George Clooney as a hitman in midlife crisis. At the beginning of the last century, real life proved even more chilling when village workers discovered a series of caves containing hundreds of clothed skeletons sitting on cane chairs. The skeletons no longer exist, having been burnt as a health precaution, though their discovery perhaps lies behind the town's biggest event of the year, a **festival of witches** that takes place one night in mid-August (see W lanottedellestreghe.org for the exact date), with locals acting out all manner of spooky scenarios.

ACCOMMODATION AND EATING

La Loggia Largo Umberto I, 11 T 338 83 48 150, W ristorantelaloggia.com Despite the frescoed ceiling and chandelier, this is a homely family-run restaurant and pizzeria, serving hearty mountain dishes such as homemade pasta with lentils and spit-roast lamb. They also have three comfy rooms to rent upstairs with a lovely shared living room-kitchen (with open fire in winter). Expect to pay around €25 a head for a full dinner with wine. Rooms per person **€30**

Rocca Calascio and Santo Stefano di Sessanio

The pale-honey castle of **Rocca Calascio** sits crumbling above a village that has recently been restored and repopulated after many years of abandonment, as people realize the potential of its medieval houses as holiday homes. Beyond is **Santo Stefano di Sessanio**, a bustling Medici stronghold in the fifteenth century, then virtually abandoned until the arrival of Daniele Kihlgren in 1999 (see page 719).

L'Aquila

Until April 6, 2009, when an **earthquake** of 5.8 on the Richter scale struck the city (see page 720), **L'AQUILA** was Abruzzo's main cultural attraction. An ancient university town overlooked by the bulk of Gran Sasso, it was founded in 1242 when, according to legend, the Holy Roman Emperor Frederick II drew together the populations from 99 of Abruzzo's villages to form a new city. Each village built its own church, piazza and quarter, and one of the city's most-loved (and surviving) sights is a medieval fountain with 99 spouts. Post-earthquake, some progress has been made in renovating the damaged and destroyed buildings, but areas of the town are still cordoned off and the whole centre is like one permanent building site. You can still wander along the main Corso and into some of the surrounding streets, but the noise, dust and lack of real life doesn't make for a particularly edifying experience.

Castello Cinquecentesco

On the northeast edge of the historic centre, the **Castello Cinquecentesco** was built by the Spanish in the sixteenth century to keep the locals under control.

Santa Maria di Collemaggio

Piazzale Collemaggio • Daily 9.30am–1pm & 4–7pm • Free

East of the centre, outside the city walls, is **Santa Maria di Collemaggio**, recently reopened after extensive rebuilding, its massive rectangular bulk faced with a geometric jigsaw of pink and white stone. The basilica was founded in the thirteenth century by Pietro of Morrone, a hermit unwillingly dragged from his mountain retreat to be made pope by power-hungry cardinals who reckoned he would be easy to manipulate. When he turned out to be too naive even for the uses of the cardinals, he was forced to resign and was posthumously compensated for the ordeal by being canonized.

It was founded in the thirteenth century by Pietro of Morrone, a hermit unwillingly dragged from his mountain retreat to be made pope by power-hungry cardinals who reckoned he would be easy to manipulate. When he turned out to be too naive even for the uses of the cardinals, he was forced to resign and was posthumously compensated for the ordeal by being canonized. Thieves stole his relics in April 1988, intending to hold them to ransom, but they were soon safely retrieved and returned to their grandiose Palladian-style sarcophagus.

Fontana delle 99 Cannelle

Via Madonna del Ponte/Via Borgo Rivera

THE CULTURE OF POVERTY

The son of an Italian mother and Swedish father, **Daniele Kihlgren** was born heir to the vast fortune his mother's family had accrued by producing cement. Like many rich kids, he rebelled, getting himself expelled from school, then dabbling in hard drugs. A motorbike trip around Italy opened his eyes to the immense damage cement – and illegal development – had done to his country, especially in Sicily and the south, but in 1999, biking through Abruzzo, he discovered **Santo Stefano di Sessanio**, a poor hill-village. In other similar villages, those who wanted to make something of their lives had emigrated, often returning to build huge modern houses that had nothing to do with local traditions, materials or landscape. Returnees wanted to demonstrate their wealth by constructing the horrendous Swiss-type chalets or American-style bungalows – mostly built with breezeblocks and cement but no planning permission – that make eyesores of so many small southern villages. Santo Stefano di Sessanio, however, was so insignificant that no one who left bothered to return.

Kihlgren bought a house in Santo Stefano, then promised to make a substantial investment in the village in return for the local authority placing a blanket ban on new building. Kihlgren bought eight more houses in the village, and €4.5 million and eight years later opened **Sextantio**, Via Principe Umberto (T 0835 332 744, W sextantio.it; €225), a hotel whose rooms, restaurant and reception areas are spread among the medieval houses of the village.

Kihlgren was sick of planned cities, big-name architects, high art and culture, preferring anonymous, organic, rural architecture. And though not denying his guests the comfort of under-floor heating (and Philippe Starck bathtubs), he was determined to preserve the spartan realities of rustic life. Walls were stripped back to their ancient plaster and left bare, many preserving blackened patches where a fire once roared. Floors too were left bare, and original oak doors and locks lovingly restored – so that today guests are given iron keys to lug around, the size of a forearm. In the stone-vaulted restaurant, traditional dishes have been revived, and olive oil and pulses produced on the *Sextantio*'s own land are served, along with local cheeses, salamis, home-made liqueurs and locally raised lamb.

Kihlgren has property in nine other villages around the south, but the highest-profile of his recent projects has been the restoration of cave dwellings in Matera, Basilicata (see page 849).

L'AQUILA AND THE QUAKE

At 3.32am on Monday, April 6, 2009, an **earthquake** of 5.8 on the Richter scale rocked central Italy. The shocks were felt as far as Rome and Campania, but the epicentre was **L'Aquila**, the regional capital of Abruzzo, built on the bed of an ancient lake. The geological structure of the terrain amplified the seismic waves.

The city has a history of earthquakes, the worst being in 1703 when five thousand people were killed, and the city virtually flattened. This time, thousands of buildings in the city were badly damaged, and some surrounding villages were pretty much destroyed. However, nearby medieval hill-villages survived almost untouched, and it was clear in the aftermath that much of the damage and many of the deaths were due to shoddy building standards. In all, 308 people died, and over 65,000 were made homeless; 40,000 people were evacuated to tented camps, prompting Prime Minister Berlusconi to make his infamous comment that the earthquake victims should cheer up and consider themselves on a camping weekend.

L'Aquila's famous **Fontana delle 99 Cannelle** is set around three sides of a sunken piazza, each water spout a symbol of one of the villages that formed the city. It was first conceived in 1272 by architect Tancredi da Pentima but has been much altered over the centuries – the last renovation took place in 2008, just a year before the earthquake. Minor damage meant it was out of action until December 2010, but it was one of the first places of interest in the city to be fully restored. L'Aquila's most celebrated sight has sustained the Aquilani through plagues and sieges, and was used for washing clothes until after the war.

12

ARRIVAL AND INFORMATION — L'AQUILA

By train L'Aquila's train station is to the west of the centre, a 5- to 10min walk from the Fontana delle 99 Cannelle.

Destinations Rome via Terni (9 daily; 3hr–4hr 30min); Sulmona (10 daily; 1hr 10min); Terni (9 daily; 2hr).

By bus Long-distance buses arrive at the Collemaggio terminal on Via Giacomo Caldora near Porta Bazzano, a short walk from Santa Maria di Collemaggio.

Destinations Bominaco (5 daily; 1hr–1hr 20min); Pescara (13 daily; 2hr); Rome (hourly; 1hr 50min–2hr 30min); Sulmona (almost hourly, some via Avezzano 1hr 35min–2hr 15min); Teramo (approx hourly; 1hr–1hr 20min).

By car L'Aquila is a difficult place to negotiate by car; the best place to park to visit the centre is Viale Francesco Crispi, a 5min walk from the central Piazza del Duomo.

Tourist office The tourist office (Mon–Sat 9am–1pm & 3–6pm; T0862 410 808, W abruzzoturismo.it) is at Piazza S. Bernardino.

The staff here are enthusiastic and efficient, and have up-to-date information on places to stay and restaurants, as well as accessible sights, so you may like to email them before planning a visit (E iat.aquila@abruzzoturismo.it).

Bominaco

Off the SS17 • 2 buses daily from L'Aquila (1hr)

From L'Aquila, the SS17 follows the ancient route of the local shepherds across the saffron fields south to Sulmona. If you have your own transport, it's worth making a short detour on the way to **BOMINACO**. The village itself is an inauspicious knot of grubby houses in a marvellous setting at the head of a valley, but it's worth a visit to admire two of Abruzzo's most beautiful churches.

Bominaco's churches

To access both churches you have to contact a local guide (tip expected): phone T 086 93 764, or check the information posted on the gate of the San Pellegrino Church.

The endearingly askew and lichen-mottled facade of **San Pellegrino**, founded by Charlemagne, conceals floor-to-ceiling thirteenth-century frescoes in vivid hues reminiscent of a peacock's plume. The frescoes include pictures of the life of Christ, the Virgin and a huge St Christopher, as well as an intriguing calendar with signs of the zodiac. If you put your ear to the hole at the side of the altar, tradition says you'll hear the heartbeat of San Pellegrino buried below.

The church of **Santa Maria Assunta**, just beyond, stands on the foundations of a Roman temple to Venus. Beyond its coolly refined exterior, the creamy-white carvings are so exquisitely precise that it seems the mason has only just put down his chisel; in fact they're eight hundred years old.

Sulmona and around

Flanked by bleak mountains and bristling with legends about its most famous son, Ovid, **SULMONA** is a comfortably affluent provincial settlement that owes its wealth to gold jewellery and sugared almonds. Although it sustained some damage during the 2009 earthquake, most of it was internal, and it remains an atmospheric little place, with a dark tangle of a historical centre lined with imposing palaces and overshadowed by the mountainous bulk of the Majella. Sulmona's sights can be seen in a morning, but the surprisingly undervisited town makes a useful base for exploring the surroundings – from ancient hermitages to towns with snake-infested festivals.

Corso Ovidio, Sulmona's main street, cuts through the centre from the park-side bus terminus, leading up to Piazza XX Settembre. From here, Sulmona's sights are within easy strolling distance.

The Annunziata

Corso Ovidio, T 0864 210216. Palazzo Tues–Sat 9am–1pm & 3.30–6.30pm; church Mon & Wed–Fri 9am–1pm & 3–6pm, Sat & Sun 9am–6pm (until 7pm April–Oct). €3.15

The **Annunziata**, a Gothic-Renaissance *palazzo* adjoining a flamboyant Baroque church rather gloriously dominate Corso Ovidio. Established in 1320 by a religious confraternity to take care of Sulmona's citizens from birth until death, its steps were once crowded with the ill and destitute. These days they are a hangout for Sulmona's teenagers during the evening *passeggiata*, who naturally pay little attention to the external decoration designed to remind onlookers of the cycles of life and death. The most intriguing statue is just inside the entrance: Ovid, metamorphosed from suave erotic poet into an ascetic friar.

Inside the Annunziata are several **museums**, the most interesting of which is the **Museo del Costume Popolare Abruzzese-Molisano e della Transhumanza**, devoted to local costumes and transhumance – the practice of moving sheep to summer pastures – along with examples of work by Sulmona's Renaissance goldsmiths, a trade that continues here to this day, as evidenced by the number of richly supplied jewellers' shops along the Corso. The **Museo Civico** has local sculpture and paintings from the sixteenth to seventeenth centuries; and a third, the **Museo Archeologico** shows the excavations of a Roman villa inhabited from the first century BC to the second century AD, abandoned suddenly along with many other houses in the valley when a landslide or an earthquake

SULMONA'S CONFETTI

As well as gold, the Corso's shops are full of Sulmona's other great product – **confetti** – a confection of sugared almonds or chocolate (a bit like monster M&M's) wired into elaborate flowers and other creations with the aid of coloured cellophane, crepe paper and ribbons. Through ingenious marketing the Sulmonese *confetti* barons have made their intricate sculptures *de rigueur* at christenings, confirmations and weddings throughout Catholic Europe – they are often given to wedding guests as little tokens of appreciation. You can learn about *confetti* manufacture at the town's most famous conveyor of sugary confectionery, the **Fabbrica Confetti Pelino** at Via Stazione Introdacqua 55 (Mon–Sat 9am–12.30pm & 3–7pm; free). Here, the Museo d'Arte Confettiera displays an assortment of antique sweet-making machines and a sixteenth-century laboratory, complete with all manner of mills, toasters and polishing machines.

struck. Among the fragments of fabulously coloured wall-painting are depictions of Pan, Eros, Dionysus and Ariadne, and there are several floor mosaics, all well labelled.

Piazza del Carmine

At the southern end of the Corso is **Piazza del Carmine**, where the hefty Romanesque portal of **San Francesco della Scarpa** was the only part of the church solid enough to withstand the earthquake of 1703. The church gets its name – della Scarpa (of the shoe) – from the fact that Franciscans wore shoes instead of the sandals worn by other monastic orders. Opposite, the impressive Gothic **aqueduct**, built to supply water to the town and power to its wool mills, ends at a small fifteenth-century fountain, the **Fontana del Vecchio**, named for the bust of a chubby-cheeked old man on top.

Piazza Garibaldi

On the other side of the aqueduct, and home to the town's market on Wednesday and Saturday, is **Piazza Garibaldi**, a vast square dominated by the austere, often snow-streaked slopes of **Monte Morrone**, on which the hermit Pietro Morrone lived until he was dragged away to be made Pope Celestine V. There's a former nunnery in the corner – take a look at the courtyard, with its tiny door where unmarried mothers were permitted to abandon their babies. In the church and old refectory, the **Polo Museale di Santa Chiara** (Tues–Sun 9am–1pm & 3.30–6.30pm; €3) holds a collection of religious art, including a fresco cycle with episodes from the lives of Christ and St Francis, wooden sculptures of saints, and a collection of fifteenth-century gold items.

On the last weekend in July, Piazza Garibaldi sees the **Giostra Cavalleresca di Sulmona** (ⓦgiostrasulmona.it), the re-enactment of a Renaissance joust with horses representing the town's seven *borghi* galloping round the square, as well as plenty of costumed pageantry and feasting.

ARRIVAL AND INFORMATION — SULMONA

By car There's covered parking beneath Piazza Garibaldi.

By train The train station is 1.5km outside the centre of town; bus #A runs from the station to the Villa Comunale next to the historic centre. Destinations Avezzano (8 daily; 52min–1hr 20min).

By bus Buses arrive at the Villa Comunale next to the *centro storico*. Destinations Cocullo (3 daily Mon–Fri, 1 daily Sat & Sun; 35 min); Scanno (9–7 daily Mon–Sat; 2 daily Sun 1hr).

Tourist offices The municipal tourist office is Visit Sulmona, Piazza SS Annunziata 3 (daily 9am–12.30pm & 3.30–7pm, closed Sun Sept–May; ⓣ0864 210 216, ⓦvisit-sulmona.it.

ACCOMMODATION

★ B&B Il Marchese Del Grillo Via Corfinio 62 ⓣ327 357 0889, ⓦbebilmarchesedelgrillo.it. Sulmona's best place to stay is this antique-packed town-centre B&B just a short walk west of the Corso. Timber and terracotta floors, hefty ceiling beams, a wonderful courtyard, a breakfast room with real fire and some spectacular mountain views from the roof terrace make this a memorable place to stay. **€90**

Case Bonomini Via Quatrario ⓣ0864 52 308, ⓦbedandbreakfastcasebonomini.com. Comfortable apartments run on a B&B basis with views of the Majella, scattered along Via Quatrario in the historic centre. *Il Rustico* is the pick of the bunch, a rustic, brick-walled apartment on two floors that sleeps up to five. The price includes car access to the city centre. **€75**

Rojan Via degli Agghiacciati 15 ⓣ0864 950 126, ⓦhotelrojan.it. Rooms at this spick-and-span four-star hotel come with wood-beamed ceilings and are soothingly decked out in a palette of neutrals. It's run by the ultra-friendly Casaccia family, whose attention to detail is remarkable: breakfasts are home-made by Rosanna, while Gianluca helps guests plan their itineraries. **€130**

EATING AND DRINKING

Cantina di Biffi Via Barbato 1, off Corso Ovidio ⓣ0864 32 025. A mere 50m off the Corso, this rustic wine cellar-restaurant is dedicated to the Slow Food movement, with an emphasis on local sourcing and traditional dishes. Passionately researched wine list as well. On the menu are handmade pasta dishes such as *rigatoni* with ricotta and

guanciale (a type of bacon; €10), and home-made fruit tarts for dessert. Expect to spend around €35 a head for a full meal with wine. Fri–Wed noon–2.30pm & 6pm–1am.

Clemente Vico Quercia 20 ⓣ 0864 210 679. A bright, family-run place in an old *palazzo* that's been serving home-produced *salumi* and dishes such as *agnello con aglio, rosmarino e pecorino* (pan-seared lamb with garlic, rosemary and pecorino cheese) for over fifty years. For most the antipasti are a meal in themselves, so go easy if you want to last till dessert. *Primi* cost €9, *secondi* €10–16. Mon–Wed, Fri & Sat 12.30–2.30pm & 7.30–10.30pm, Sun 12.30–2.30pm.

★ **Locanda di Gino** Piazza Plebiscito 12 ⓣ 0864 5228, ⓦ lalocandadigino.it. Run by the Allega family since 1962, and open for lunch only, this restaurant serves up some fantastic home-made pasta dishes including courgette-flower *carrati* with local saffron (€10), and traditional mains such as lamb casserole (€11), in a light-filled dining room. The desserts come in for special praise by all who try them. Mon–Sat 12.30–3pm.

Parco Nazionale della Majella

The **Parco Nazionale della Majella**, 10km to the east of Sulmona, is named after the mountain – **Monte Majella** – that dominates the area. Dedicated to the Italic goddess Maja, the mountain was held sacred by the ancient people of Abruzzo, while by the Middle Ages its proliferation of hermitages and abbeys led the poet Petrarch to call it Domus Christi, the "House of Christ". Over a hundred **hermits** made their retreat here; some reused cave dwellings, others built churches into the rock, haunting constructions to this day.

May is a particularly lovely month to visit because of the blossoming **wild flowers**, but its 500km of **walking trails and cycling paths** are a draw all year long. The southern part of the park harbours beautiful beechwood forests, with the possibility of spotting bears, deer and wolves; trails on the eastern side pass through dramatic rocky gorges; while the northern side is full of hermitages and shepherds' huts.

12

Pescocostanzo

Of the park's small towns, **Pescocostanzo** (ⓦ pesconline.it) makes the most enjoyable base, a picture-perfect medieval *borgo* on the slopes of Monte Calvario with a cobbled historic centre, a smattering of places to stay, and access to the ski resort of Vallefura.

ARRIVAL AND INFORMATION — PARCO NAZIONALE DELLA MAJELLA

By bus There are generally two buses a day Mon–Sat to the park's villages from Sulmona, one leaving very early morning, the second at lunchtime. No services on Sundays.

Tourist offices The park has various visitor centres, including one in Pescocostanzo, at Vico delle Carceri 4 (daily 10am–1pm & 4–8pm; ⓣ 333 4291109, ⓦ parcomajella.it), and in Pacentro, at Piazza del Popolo 7 (Mar– May & Oct–Dec: Sat, Sun and public holidays only 10am–1pm & 4–7pm; June–Sept daily 9am–1pm & 4–8pm; ⓣ 0864 41 304).

COCULLO'S SNAKE FESTIVAL

A scrappy hill-village west of Sulmona, **Cocullo** is neglected by outsiders for 364 days of the year. However, every May 1 it's invaded by what seems like half the population of central Italy, come to celebrate the weird **festival of snakes**, an annual event held in memory of St Dominic, the patron saint of the village, who allegedly rid the area of venomous snakes back in the eleventh century.

The festival is an odd mixture of the modern and archaic. After Mass in the main square, a number of snake-charmers in the crowd drape a wooden statue of St Dominic with a writhing bunch of live but harmless snakes, which is then paraded through the streets in a bizarre celebration of the saint's unique powers (he was apparently good at curing snakebites too). It's thought that Cocullo's preoccupation with serpents dates back to before the time of the saint when, in the pre-Christian era, local tribes worshipped their goddess Angitia with offerings of snakes.

Cocullo is connected by train (4 daily; 30min) with Sulmona, though on festival day a special bus service operates. For further information on the festival, ask at Sulmona's tourist office (see above).

ACCOMMODATION AND EATING

★ Al Piccolo Albergo "La Rua" Via Rua Mozza 1/3, Pescocostanzo ⓣ 0864 640 083, ⓦ larua.it. Just steps from the central Piazza Municipio, this friendly, family-run place welcomes guests in from the cold with a roaring fire in the entrance hall. The rooms are generously sized and very comfortable, with stupendous views, and breakfast is a feast of home-made cakes and jams. **€85**

Il Gatto Bianco Viale Appennini 3, Pescocostanzo ⓣ 0864 641 466, ⓦ ilgattobianco.it. Luxuriously appointed rooms with chalet-luxe decor, big bathrooms with a view, and generous breakfasts. There's a spa with sauna, steam room and hot-tub and a smart but relaxed restaurant serves good grilled meat dishes. **€180**

Scanno and around

A popular tourist destination, **SCANNO** is reached by passing through the narrow and rocky **Gole del Sagittario**, a WWF reserve that makes a spectacular drive along galleries of rock and around blind hairpin bends that widen out at the glassy green **Lago di Scanno**. Perched over the lake is a church, the **Madonna del Lago**, with the cliff as its back wall, and nearby there are boats and pedaloes for rent in the summer.

A couple of kilometres beyond, Scanno itself is a well-preserved medieval village encircled by mountains. In 1951, Henri Cartier-Bresson photographed the village, in a series of atmospheric shots focusing on the **traditional dress** worn by Scanno's women. Some elderly women can still be seen wearing the long, dark, pleated skirts and bodices with a patterned apron that suggest a possible origin in Asia Minor; the annual Costume di Scanno festival in April sees the locals taking to the streets in their finery.
12 Scannese **jewellery** also has something of the Orient about it – large, delicately filigreed earrings, and a charm in the form of a star, known as a *presuntosa*, given to fiancées to ward off other men. If you want to see the costume and jewellery at close quarters head for the shops on Strada Roma and Corso Centrale.

The old town

The joy of Scanno is aimless wandering in the **old town**, built into the steep hillside with squares and alleyways lined with solid stone houses that were built by wool barons when business was good. Though shepherding as a way of life is virtually extinct and the population has dwindled, it's still very much a living village. For more background on Scannese jewellery, drop in at Armando di Rienzo, in Via de Angelis, a **jewellery shop** containing a small period workshop preserved as it would have looked between the seventeenth and twentieth centuries.

The chair lift

Mid-June to mid-Sept & mid-Dec to April 9am–6pm • €9 return Via Pescara, ⓣ 0864 576038, ⓦ sciareascanno.it

A **chair lift**, signposted 300m from the centre, takes **skiers** up to a handful of runs on Monte Rotondo. It also operates in the short summer season when it's worth going up just for the view of lake and mountains, especially at sunset.

ARRIVAL AND INFORMATION — SCANNO

By bus Sulmona (7–9 daily Mon–Sat; 2 daily Sun, 1hr); Rome (up to 5 daily, 3hr 35min).

SCANNO'S FESTIVALS

If you're around in August, you might catch Scanno's **summer festival**, with a series of cultural events and fireworks displays held throughout the month: contact the tourist office for details (see page 725). On January 17 the **festival** of local protector of domestic animals, Sant'Antonio Abate is celebrated with the cooking of great cauldrons of sagne (finger-length strips of hand-made pasta) and ricotta outside the door of the church, which is then blessed and doled out with an unholy amount of pushing and shoving.

Tourist office Piazza S. Maria della Valle 12 (summer Mon–Sat 9am–1pm & 4–7pm, Sun 9am–1pm, Aug open longer hours; winter Mon, Wed & Fri 9am–1pm, Tues & Thurs 9am–1pm & 3–6pm; 0864 74 317, abruzzoturismo.it).

ACCOMMODATION AND EATING

Alla Fonte Via Fontana Saracco 3 348 151 3632. Wine bar serving some great, simple food to accompany an interesting selection of wines from all over Italy. There are generous platters of cured hams, salami and cheeses (€10), a couple of daily local pasta dishes (€10) and simple main courses including a wonderful beef carpaccio (€10).

Bio Agriturismo Valle Scannese, Località Valle Scannese 0864 576043, vallescannese.com. Family-run agriturismo set high among the mountains on a glorious biodynamic sheep-farm that makes its own marvellous cheeses, as well as producing meat and wool. Simple, pristine whitewashed rooms, and utterly fabulous home-cooked food. Everything an agriturismo should be. **€70**.

★ **I Lupi** 2km away outside the town of Villalago 0864 740 625, campingilupi.it. A campsite on the shore of the lake; thanks to its picturesque location, it gets packed out in summer. Open all year. Pitches **€14**, bungalows **€45**

La Dimora di D'Annunzio Vico De Angelis 2 0864 747 942, ladimoradidannunzio.it. So named because the poet Gabriele d'Annunzio spent two summer holidays here in the 1880s, Scanno's most central place to stay is located right next to the belltower of the church of Santa Maria della Valle. It offers basic but comfy rooms, free wi-fi and a common room warmed by a real fire in winter. **€75**

Parco Nazionale d'Abruzzo

At four hundred square kilometres, the **PARCO NAZIONALE D'ABRUZZO** is Italy's third-largest national park and holds some of its wildest mountainscapes, providing great walking and a hunter-free haven for wolves, brown bears, chamois, deer, lynx, wild boar and three or four pairs of royal eagles.

12

Pescassèroli

The central village, **PESCASSÈROLI**, is the main hub for visitors, surrounded by campsites, holiday apartments and hotels. The best way to strike out from here is to hike. Take advantage of the comprehensive information service, and get your boots on as quickly as you can: the wild beauty of the Apennine range is only really appreciated as you get further away from the tourist villages. Pescassèroli is also known for its lively **festivals**: the Sagra della Pecora (early Sept) commemorates the work of local nomadic shepherds with a tasting of local products in the town's main square; while the *Festa della Madonna* (July 15 & 16) sees a Black Madonna carried 9km from her sanctuary on Monte Tranquillo to Pescassèroli and back to celebrate the town's miraculous escape from being bombed during World War II after prayers were offered to the Madonna.

Museo Naturalistico

Via Colli dell'Oro, 863 9113221 • Daily July & Aug 10am–6.30pm, Sept–June 10am–5.30pm • €6

In the same building as the park's visitor centre (see below) is the excellent **Museo Naturalistico**, which fills you in on the park's flora and fauna and also acts as a clinic for sick animals such as brown bears and Apennine wolf cubs. There's also a garden where the park's most typical plants and trees are cultivated, home to an array of local wildlife.

Opi

Perched on a hilltop some 6km from Pescassèroli, **OPI** is a charming, unspoilt little town. The centre holds the small **Centro Visita del Camoscio** (Chamois Museum; Daily: July & Aug 9am–7.30pm; Sept–June 9am–12.30pm & 3.30–4.30pm, 3319727262); from a viewpoint near the museum you can observe the chamois in a nearby reserve.

A good time to visit is during the Infiorata **flower festival**, on the festival of Corpus Domini in June, when since the seventeenth century locals have created vast pictures from flower petals all along the main street.

WILDLIFE IN THE PARCO NAZIONALE D'ABRUZZO

The Abruzzo National Park (parcoabruzzo.it) is an area of exceptional biodiversity, with around a hundred indigenous species.

One of the most important animals in the park is the **Marsican brown bear**. Until recently an endangered species, there are now thought to be around thirty to fifty in the park, but they are extremely shy, solitary and lazy, and difficult to spot – you're more likely to find traces of their presence than see an actual bear. The *Centro Visita dell'Orso* (April to mid-June Sat & Sun 9am–1pm & 2.30–6.30pm; mid-June to Sept Tues–Sun 9am–1pm & 2.30–6.30pm; Oct–March Sat & Sun 10.30am–1pm & 2.30–4pm; €3) at Villavallelonga has 3D displays on the evolution of bears in the park, as well as the opportunity to admire some actual bears (from a distance), in the nearby reserve.

Another key park inhabitant is the **Apennine wolf**, of which there are around forty to fifty. As with the bears, the wolves offer no danger to humans, and they are also difficult to spot – the closest you're likely to get to either in the wild are footprints in mud or snow. Look out, too, for chamois, deer and roe deer, wildcats, martens, otters, badgers, polecats and the edible dormouse. Wolves can also be seen at the dedicated *wolf museum* at Civitella Alfadena (daily April–Sept 10am–1.30pm & 3–6.30pm, Oct–Mar daily 10am–1.30, 2–5.30pm; €3); others can be seen close up at the fascinating clinic and natural history museum in Pescassèroli (see page 725).

Among **birds**, the park's species include the golden eagle, the peregrine hawk, the goshawk and the rare white-backed woodpecker. Higher up are snow finch, alpine accentor and rock partridge.

The park's **flora** includes many local orchids, of which the most important variety is Venus's little shoe or Our Lady's slipper, which thrives on the chalky soil in the park. There are also gentians, peonies, violets, irises and columbines, and black pine woods at Villetta Barrea and the Camosciara.

ARRIVAL AND INFORMATION — PARCO NAZIONALE D'ABRUZZO

By train The nearest train station is Avezzano, a stop on the Pescara–Rome rail line. Buses to Pescassèroli leave from outside Avezzano's train station.

By bus Pescassèroli is served by bus from Avezzano (5 daily; 1hr 30min), 30km west of Sulmona. There are also bus services from Castel di Sangro on the border with Molise (6 daily; 1hr 30min), which has connections with Naples. There are five daily buses from Pescassèroli to Opi (10min).

Tourist offices The park's main visitor centre is in Pescassèroli at Via Colli dell'Oro (Daily: April–Sept 10am–6.30pm; Oct–March 10am–5.30pm; 0863 911 3221, parcoabruzzo.it), while the tourist office in town is on Viale Principe di Napoli (summer: Mon–Sat 9am–1pm & 4–7pm, Sun 9am–1pm; winter Mon–Sat 9am–1pm & 3–6pm, Sun 9am–1pm; 0863 910 461).

ACCOMMODATION

In high season, there's little chance of finding a room on arrival; you need to book at least a month in advance and be prepared for compulsory half board in July and Aug. If you're coming here for a week or more, you might consider B&B accommodation in a private house or an apartment rental – the tourist offices can supply you with a list. Campers should manage to find space on one of the campsites, though be warned that night-time temperatures are low even in summer.

Antico Borgo Albergo La Torre Via Castello 3, Civitella Alfedena 0864 890 121, albergolatorre.com. In the medieval centre of Civitella Alfedena near Pescassèroli, this friendly hotel is set in an eighteenth-century palace and has simple, chalet-style rooms and a cosy restaurant. The owner can give advice on local walking routes. **€70**

La Pieja Via Salita la Croce 1, Opi 0863 910 772, lapieja.it. Overlooking picture-perfect Opi, this hotel makes a good base for exploring the park. The food is one of the big draws here; it's worth booking half board (€58/ person) so that you can sample the delicious local dishes cooked up by chef Antonio. **€63**

Paradiso Via Fonte Fracassi 4, Pescassèroli 0863 910 422, albergo-paradiso.it. This delightful hotel, 1.5km from the centre of Pescassèroli, is run by Scottish Geraldine and her Italian husband Marco, with warm rustic decor, good country cooking and a pretty garden. Ask to see Geraldine's pub. Half board (per person) **€65**

★ **Valle del Lupo** Via Collacchi, Pescassèroli 0863 910 534, valledelupo.it. Run by two sisters, this small hotel, around 2km from the centre of Pescassèroli, on its own hilltop surrounded by stunning countryside, is a great place to visit in every season. The ten rooms are basic and sparsely decorated, but spotlessly clean, and there's tasty local food in the restaurant (half board available for €65/ person). **€52**

CAMPING

Le Foci Via Fonte dei Cementi, Opi 0863 912 233, lefoci.it. Just outside Opi, this campsite is well set up with a restaurant, bar and supermarket, and has caravans available to rent. It's open all year round. €5 daily per person plus tent or caravan pitches **€8**, caravan rental per night **€13**.

EATING AND DRINKING

★ La Madonnina SS83, Opi ☎ 0863 916 053. Signora Francesca has been serving up tasty home cooking here for over three decades. On the menu is fresh and hearty mountain fare such as platters of cheeses,pasta with truffle or porcini and sausages with polenta; you can watch your lamb cutlets or veal steaks being grilled on the open fire before you tuck in. A full meal with wine costs around €35. Tues–Sun 12.30–3.30pm & 7–9.30pm.

★ Plistia Via Principe di Napoli 28, Pescassèroli ☎ 0863 910 732. Great for local specialities: you can eat hearty mountain *primi* such as soup with local vegetables and pulses, hand-made pasta or, in spring, gnocchi with asparagus and local saffron, all for around €8; the €36 tasting menu is a good deal. Booking necessary. Tues–Sun 1–3pm & 8–9.30pm; open daily in summer.

Teramo and around

Rising from the Adriatic and rolling towards the eastern slopes of the Gran Sasso, the landscape of **northeast Abruzzo** is gentle, and its inland towns are usually ignored in favour of its long, sandy and highly popular coastline. **TERAMO**, capital of the province of the same name, is a modern town with an elegant centre, and if you're heading for the sea you may well pass through.

The Duomo and around

Piazza Orsini • Daily approximately 7am–noon & 4–8pm • Free

Teramo's main attraction is the **Duomo** at the top of Corso San Giorgio, with its remarkable silver **altarfront** by the fifteenth-century Abruzzese silversmith Nicola da Guardiagrele. It has 35 panels with lively reliefs of religious scenes, starting with the Annunciation and moving through the New Testament, punctuating the narrative with portraits of various saints. The artist was famous enough to feature in a sumptuous polyptych by a Venetian artist, Jacobello del Fiore, in a Baroque chapel to the left. It features a model of Teramo, set against a gilded sky, with Nicola wearing a monk's habit on the left, Jacobello in the red gown on the right.

South of the Duomo, Via Irelli leads to the heart of Roman Teramo, with fragments of the **amphitheatre** and the more substantial walls of the recently renovated **theatre**, where two of the original twenty entrance arches remain.

The Pinacoteca

Viale Bovio 1 • Tues–Thurs 5–8pm, Sat & Sun • €5 with Museo Archeologico

Between Piazza Garibaldi and the Villa Comunale is the town's modest **Pinacoteca.** The collection of local art over the centuries is best represented by the *Madonna Enthroned with Saints* – a polyptych in which the colours are lucid and the forms almost sculpted, the work of local fifteenth-century artist Giacomo da Campli.

HIKING ROUTES

The tourist offices sell maps on which all **hiking routes** in the park are marked, along with an indication of the difficulty involved, the time needed, and the flora and fauna you're likely to see on the way. There are nearly 150 different routes, so making a choice can be difficult. There is also a useful app, downloadable free from ⓦ parcoabruzzo.it. Note that access to certain routes may be forbidden or numbers strictly limited between July and Sept to prevent disturbance to chamois and bears.: for routes where the number of visitors are restricted it's usually sufficient to book the day before. The rest of the year, these routes are open without restriction or fee, though guided walks (€10–15) can still be arranged.

12

Museo Archeologico

Off Via Carducci at Via Delfico 30 • Tues–Sun 10am–1pm, Tues & Thurs also 4–7pm • €5 with Pinacoteca

On a parallel street to the main Corso, the **Museo Archeologico** is strong on Roman finds from excavations in Teramo and includes a reconstruction of the Roman theatre, as well as a first-century mosaic of a lion, among the forum columns and marble busts.

ARRIVAL AND INFORMATION — TERAMO

By train The train station is east of the centre on Via Crispi, linked with Piazza Garibaldi by regular city bus #1.

By bus Buses stop at Piazza Garibaldi.

Destinations Atri (3 daily; 1hr); L'Aquila (12 daily; 1hr 20min); Pescara (via Giulianova; approx hourly; 2hr 20min); Rome (approx hourly, some changing at L'Aquila; 2hr 30min–2hr 55min).

Tourist office Via Oberdan 16, a cross street off the main Corso (Mon–Sat 9am–1pm & 3–6pm; closed Sat afternoon in winter; T 0861 244 222, W abruzzoturismo.it).

ACCOMMODATION, EATING AND DRINKING

Abruzzi Viale Mazzini 18 T 0861 241 043, W hotelabruzziteramo.com. A modern, centrally located hotel with smart, contemporary, if slightly boxy, rooms. There's a restaurant on site, but it's mainly frequented by business travellers, so if you're after a place with atmosphere you're better off hitting the town. €59

★ **Cantina di Porta Romana** Corso Porta Romana 105 T 0861 252 257. An atmospheric wine cellar plastered with photos and retro knick-knacks serving up dishes local to the Teramo area such as deep-fried courgettes (€10), platters of fried fish and *mazzerelle alle Teramana* – parcels of finely chopped offal, wrapped in lettuce leaves and cooked in white wine (€10). The set menu of three courses with wine costs €35. Mon–Sat noon–3.30pm & 7–11pm.

Enoteca Centrale Corso Cerulli 24 T 0861 243 633. On a street leading off from the Duomo, this bustling place has a great wine list – three hundred labels – backed up by excellent local dishes, such as the winter dish *scripelle*, thin crêpes filled with grated cheese and a sprinkle of cinnamon covered in chicken broth. In summer much use is made of seasonal vegetables. All *primi* cost €8–13, *secondi* €8–16. Mon–Sat noon–2.30pm.

12

Atri

The pretty little town of **ATRI**, 24km southeast of Teramo, is well worth a visit for the pleasure of wandering the town and exploring the surrounding countryside, as well as for the fifteenth-century frescoes in its Duomo. Approaching the town from Teramo is like travelling through the backdrop of a Renaissance painting, with gently undulating hills planted with orderly olive groves giving way to a surrealist landscape of sleek clay gullies known as *calanchi*, water-eroded into smooth ripples, wrinkles and folds.

The Duomo

Piazza del Duomo • T 0861 8798140 • Daily June– Sep 10am–noon & 3.30–7pm; March–May& Oct Thurs–Tues 10am–noon & 3–5pm; Nov 15–17th & Feb Fri, Sat & Sun 10am–noon & 3–5pm

Atri's main piazza is dominated by the thirteenth-century **Duomo**. Its facade is understated, pierced by a rose window and perforated by the holes in which scaffolding beams were slotted during construction. The highlight is the cycle of **frescoes** in the apse by Andrea Delitio, known for his sophisticated and realistic portrayal of architecture and landscape. The most emotionally charged scene is the *Slaughter of the Innocents*, in which the horror is intensified by the refined Renaissance architectural setting and the fact that the massacre is coolly observed from a balcony by Herod's party of civic bigwigs.

Museo Capitolare

Via dei Musei • Same hours as Duomo • €5, cloister and cistern only €2 • W museocapitolareatri.it

Inside the Duomo, the **Museo Capitolare** holds a Benedictine cloister dating from the early thirteenth century, with a sixteenth-century well in the centre. Steps lead down to a **cistern** with mosaics from the third century BC, first used as a water supply for the city then as a baths complex. The ten-room **museum** holds various ecclesiastical objects, from reliquaries to paintings.

CORNO GRANDE

Museo Archeologico and Museo Etnografico

Via dei Musei • **Museo Archeologico** Tues–Sun 10.30am–12.30pm & 4.30–7pm • €2 • **Museo Etnografico** Mid-June to mid-Sept Tues–Sun 4.30–7.30pm; mid-Sept to mid-June Tues–Sat 10am–12.30pm • €1.50

Completing Atri's trio of historical museums are the **Museo Archeologico**, displaying local prehistoric and Roman finds, and the **Museo Etnografico**, a huge folk museum which conjures up traditional peasant life with replicas of a bedroom and kitchen, and more than two thousand domestic and rustic objects.

ARRIVAL AND DEPARTURE — ATRI

By bus Buses from Pescara (13 daily; 40min–1hr) stop on Viale Gran Sasso, from where stairs lead up to the centre. Buses from Teramo (3 daily; 1hr) stop on Via Ricciotti, a 5min walk from the centre.

ACCOMMODATION AND EATING

Arco di San Francesco Via San Francesco 8 ⓣ085 87 762, ⓦarcodisanfrancesco.it. Located in the old town, this B&B has four prettily decorated rooms on the second floor of an early twentieth-century *palazzo*, as well as a garden. €60

Hostaria Zedi Piazza R. Tini ⓣ085 87 340. A solid, old-fashioned *osteria* in the historic centre, a few steps from the Museo Etnografico, with a menu of hearty Abruzzese fare such as gnocchi with sausage sauce (€6.50), *chitarra* with meatballs (€6) and grilled meats (€5–11), and a menu of exclusively local wines. Portions are generous. Mon, Tues & Thurs–Sat 12.30–2pm & 7.45–10pm, Sun 12.30–2pm.

Pescara and around

12

Abruzzo's **coastline** stretches for 125km from the border with the Le Marche region down to the seaside resort of Vasto. The main resort on the Abruzzo coast is **Pescara**, also the nearest town to Abruzzo's airport where low-cost flights from the UK touch down. Outside the summer months, it makes a good base for excursions to the atmospheric medieval villages of **Loreto Aprutino** and Atri (see page 728), with the appealing town of **Chieti**, home to a superb archeological museum, being the next stop along the coast.

Pescara

Abruzzo's most commercial city, **PESCARA** is a busy, modern place boasting a 16km stretch of beach. It was heavily bombed in World War II and architecturally there's little of distinction here. Opposite the train station, the main street, **Corso Umberto**, is lined with designer boutiques and packed with the label-conscious Pescaresi, who also hang out in the elegant cafés on **Piazza Rinascita**, known as Pescara's *salone*. The town's main attraction – its **beach** of fine golden sand – is at the end of the Corso, while admirers of eccentric poet **Gabriele D' Annunzio** (see page 293) may want to visit his birthplace, the **Casa Natale di Gabriele D"Annunzio** (Corso Manthonè 116; Daily 8.30am–7.30pm; €2; ⓦcasadannunzio.beniculturali.it).

Museo delle Genti d'Abruzzo

Via delle Caserme 22 • Mon–Fri 9.15am–1.15pm, Sat 9.15am–1.15pm & 4.30–7pm• €6 • ⓦgentidabruzzo.com

In the little that remains of Pescara's historic streets, the town boasts an excellent and child-friendly museum, the **Museo delle Genti d'Abruzzo**, dedicated to the life and popular traditions of the region. Perhaps the most enchanting room is the one devoted to the nomadic shepherds, containing books of their poetry, carved objects and volumes of Ariosto's chivalric romance *Orlando Furioso*.

Museo Civico Basilio Cascella

Viale Marconi 45 • Tues–Sun 9am–1pm, Tues & Thurs also 4–6pm• €2.50

Devotees of Art Nouveau and later twentieth-century art should head for the **Museo Civico Basilio Cascella**. This municipal art museum is home to five hundred lithographic

prints, paintings, ceramics and sculptures, including a stunning set of portraits (mounted on dinner plates) by the prolific Cascella family who lived and worked here.

ARRIVAL AND INFORMATION — PESCARA

By plane Ryanair flights from London Stansted land at Abruzzo airport (abruzzo-airport.it), around 4km southwest of the city; from the airport, city buses #8 and #38 departs for Piazza della Repubblica every 15min (€1.10

By train Pescara has two train stations: Stazione Centrale, at Piazza della Repubblica, close to Corso Umberto and the beach, and Porta Nuova, convenient for the museums and restaurants clustered around Corso Manthonè.

Destinations Ancona (at least hourly; 1–2hr); Chieti (hourly; 15–20min); Rome (6 daily; 4hr); Sulmona (hourly; 1hr–1hr 20min); Termoli (every 30min–1hr; 40min–1hr 25min); Vasto (20 daily; 35min–1hr).

By bus Buses to Rome (quicker than the train) and Naples, as well as regional buses, leave from outside Stazione Centrale, in Piazza della Repubbblica.

Destinations Atri (12 daily; 1hr); Bologna (2 daily; 4hr); Chieti (7 daily; 30min); L'Aquila (8 daily; 1hr 50min–2hr 20min); Naples (4 daily; 4hr); Perugia (1–2 daily; 4hr 15min); Rome (9 daily; 2hr 30min–2hr 50min); Salerno (2 daily; 5hr); Siena (1–2 daily; 5hr 25min); Sulmona (5 daily; 1hr–1h 30min).

Tourist office The tourist office is at Corso V. Emanuele II 301 (Daily 9am–1pm & 4–7pm June–Sept, winter hours vary); 085 4290 0212, abruzzoturismo.it).

ACCOMMODATION

Alba Via M. Forti 14 085 389 145, hotelalba.pescara.it. A fairly upmarket choice for Pescara, a few minutes from the beach – the spacious rooms have a Baroque, old-fashioned touch that takes them beyond the average business hotel, and there are often discounts at weekends. €90

★ **Dimora Novecento** Viale Vittoria Colonna 73 328 088 8691, dimoranovecento.it. This luxurious B&B offers four large and tastefully decorated rooms in the heart of town, each one different: one has a glass-roofed bathroom, another a fireplace and a view of historic *palazzi*. There's also a kitchen for guests' use, and free snacks and drinks to help yourself to during the day. Breakfast is a feast of home-made cakes and pastries. €90

EATING, DRINKING AND ENTERTAINMENT

For meals and nightlife, head for the little that remains of the old town of Pescara near the river. Along Corso Manthonè and Via delle Caserme there are several good bars and restaurants. Frequent live concerts are organized during the summer on the seafront, many of them free. The town's main festival is Pescara Jazz (early July to early Aug; pescarajazz.com), with big-name jazz artists performing in the Teatro Gabriele d'Annunzio.

★ **Flaiano da Alfonso** Corso Manthonè 90–94 085 62 388, ristoranteflaiano.it. This family-run restaurant is a reliable choice, serving tasty dishes such as handmade *orecchiette* pasta with salted ricotta, grilled beef with balsamic vinegar, and pork with cherry tomatoes and wild herbs, all using local, seasonal produce. *Primi* €8–10, *secondi* €14–18. Mon–Fri 7pm–midnight, Sat & Sun noon–3.30pm & 7pm–midnight.

Pésci Corso Manthonè 39 085 453 1183, ristorantepesci.it. An excellent fish restaurant with jazzy, unfussy decor and relaxed and friendly service. Dishes include platters of raw and cooked fishy starters, catch of the day cooked *all'acqua pazza* (in water, with olive oil and tomatoes) and typical Abruzzo *chitarra* spaghetti with lobster. *Primi* €8–18, *secondi* €5–18. Tues–Sat 12.30–3pm & 7.30pm–midnight.

Taverna 58 Corso Manthonè 46 085 690 724, taverna58.it. Handmade pasta with mushrooms and truffles (€10) and some hearty Abruzzo stews (€16), served up in a rurally themed dining room whose windows open out onto the street. The Taste of Abruzzo menu for two (€35) is pretty good value. Mon–Thurs 12.30–2.30pm & 8–10.30pm, Sat 8–10.30pm.

Loreto Aprutino

LORETO APRUTINO is a quiet, medieval hilltop settlement 24km inland from Pescara. The labyrinthine old town is home to a dwindling number of artisans' workshops specializing in handcrafted knives. There are also tiny *cantinas* in the old town selling **olive oil**, for which the area has been awarded a DOP (*denominazione di origine protetta*), the equivalent of the DOC designation for wine. Loreto heaves with people on **market day** (Thurs morning) and in the evenings during the late-running *passeggiata*, when it's a pleasure to simply do nothing and soak up the atmosphere.

12

San Pietro Apostolo

Via del Baio 37 • Daily 9.30am–noon & 4.30–6.30pm • Free

At the top of the old town, on the end of a row of nineteenth-century *palazzi*, stands the church of **San Pietro Apostolo**, with medieval origins and an elegant Renaissance portico. Inside are the relics of the town's patron saint, San Zopito, who is venerated on the first Monday after Pentecost with a procession led by a child riding a white bull.

ARRIVAL AND INFORMATION — LORETO APRUTINO

By bus Regular buses make the trip from Pescara approximately every 30min, dropping you on Via Roma, 150m from the tourist office.

Tourist office Piazza Garibaldi 1 (summer Mon–Fri 10am–noon, Tues & Thurs also 4.30–6.30pm; winter Mon–Fri 10am–noon, Tues & Thurs also 4–6pm; ⓣ 085 829 0213).

ACCOMMODATION AND EATING

★ **B&B Lauretum** Via del Baio 3 ⓣ 085 829 2000, ⓦ bedbreakfastlauretum.com. This B&B is fantastic value for money, with accommodation in a family house near the Castello. The huge, frescoed rooms come with antique furniture and there's a billiards room too. Cash only. **€60**

Ristorante Carmine Contrada Remartello 52 ⓣ 085 820 8553. It might seem strange, but one of the best places to eat fresh fish hereabouts is not along Pescara's coast, but up in Loreto Aprutino. Just west of the *centro storico*, the freshest of fish is expertly prepared. The *coda di rospo con patate e rosmarino*, monkfish with potatoes and rosemary – a typical local dish – is sublime. A full meal will cost from around €45. Tues 7.30–10.30pm, Wed–Sun 12.30–2.30pm & 7.30–10.30pm.

Chieti

12

Inland, 20km southwest of Pescara, is the appealing town of **CHIETI**. Spread over a curving ridge, it offers great views of the Majella and Gran Sasso mountains and – on a clear day – out to sea. It also boasts Abruzzo's finest archeological museum, home to an extraordinary Bronze Age statue. From the chunky and much-reconstructed **cathedral,** the main **Corso Marrucino** cuts through the town centre to Piazza Trento e Trieste. Behind the post office, off Via Spaventa, are the remains of three little **Roman temples.**

Museo Archeologico Nazionale di Abruzzo

Via G. Costanzi • Tues–Sun 8.30am–7pm • €4 • ⓦ archeoabruzzo.beniculturali.it

The **Museo Archeologico Nazionale di Abruzzo**, laid out in the dignified Villa Comunale, displays finds from Abruzzo's major sites: a massive and muscular white marble *Hercules* from his temple at Alba Fucens as well as a miniature bronze statue of him, one of several Roman copies of the Greek original by Lysippus. Most interesting is the *Capestrano Warrior*, a statue of a Bronze Age warrior-prince with strangely feminine hips and thighs, wearing an oversized Mexican-style hat. It dates back to the time (sixth century BC) when a deified, hero-worshipped warrior leader was key to Bronze Age society. Statues like these in characteristic pose with the arms across the torso were set on the top of burial mounds to mark territory throughout the Adriatic and Central Europe and must have made an awesome feature on the landscape. Remains of the occupants of Bronze Age tombs are laid out in the adjacent rooms – the men buried with armour and weapons, the women with jewellery, kitchen utensils, spindles, and in one case even a nail-brush.

La Civitella

Via G. Pianell • Tues–Sun 9am–7.30pm • €4

Further digs in Chieti have uncovered the core of **Teate** – the main town of the Marrucini, an Italic tribe – that became a Roman colony in the first century BC. The site lies on the edge of central Chieti west of the Villa Comunale at **La Civitella archeological park**, where you can see the amphitheatre, thermal baths and a museum with restored temple fragments and remains from Chieti and the nearby river basin.

ARRIVAL AND INFORMATION **CHIETI**

By train Trains stop at Chieti Scalo down in the valley, from where it's 10min on bus #1 up to Chieti proper, 5km away. The #1 stops in the centre along Via Herio and at Largo Cavallerizza near the cathedral.

Destinations Pescara (hourly; 15–20min); Rome (6 daily; 3hr 30min–4hr).

By bus Buses stop in the upper town on Via Asinio Herio, a short walk from Corso Marruccino.

Destinations Pescara (at least hourly; 30min); Rome (9 daily; 2hr 30min).

Tourist office Via B Spaventa 49, just off Corso Marrucino (Mon–Sat 9am–1pm, Tues, Thurs & Fri also 3–6pm; ⓣ 0871 63 640, ⓦ abruzzoturismo.it).

ACCOMMODATION AND EATING

B&B Civico 35 Via Mazzetti 35 ⓣ 0871 452 293. In the town centre, this spotlessly clean, stylish and professionally run B&B is as good as they come for this price. Breakfast is a generous spread and the staff can field almost any question you may have about the town. **€59**

Trattoria Nino Via Principessa di Piemonte 7 ⓣ 0871 63 781. Very good-value meals can be had at this simple trattoria in central Chieti, near Piazza Trento e Trieste, where the service is slow but the family atmosphere and full meals of regional specialities for €25 compensate. Tues–Sun noon–3pm & 7–11pm.

The coast south of Pescara

South of Pescara, the coast becomes less developed, though the long ribbon of sand continues, followed by the train line and punctuated with small resorts. Here, hilltop **Vasto** and the seaside resort **Marina di Vasto** are attractive destinations for a beach holiday, while **Termoli** is a good jumping-off point for trips to the Tremiti islands.

12

Vasto

Some 75km southeast of Pescara and close to the border with Molise, **VASTO** is a fine old city, built on the site of the Roman town Histonium and overlooking the resort of **Marina di Vasto**. There are plenty of campsites, and some reasonable hotels along the broad sandy **beach** – palm-lined and beach-hutted in the centre, wilder and rockier to the north (the ever-shrinking free beach area is central), punctuated by crane-like contraptions of wooden beams and nets, known as *trabocchi*, with a complex system of weights, a landlubberish solution for scooping up fish.

Vasto is all about the beach, though if you're here for a day or so you should definitely take a bus from the train station on the seafront to the **upper town**, whose rooftops and campaniles rise above palms and olive groves. The centre of town is **Piazza Rossetti**, dominated by the massive **Castello Caldoresco**.

Palazzo d'Avalos

Piazza Pudente • Tues–Thurs, Sat & Sun 10am–1pm & 4–7pm, Fri 4–7pm • Museum and garden €5; garden only €1.50

Just off the piazza, next to the small Duomo, stands the Renaissance **Palazzo d'Avalos** and its enchanting Neapolitan garden, a courtyard with orange trees and pillars and gorgeous sea views. The *palazzo* was once the home of the poet and friend of Michelangelo, Vittoria Colonna, who was famous in her time for the bleak sonnets she wrote after her husband's death; nowadays it houses the town **museum**, a somewhat sparse collection of archeological objects and beautiful old costumes, as well as some paintings by the Palizzi brothers.

Portale di San Pietro

Next to the Palazzo d'Avalos, **Piazza del Popolo** opens onto a panoramic promenade that takes you to Vasto's most memorable sight, the **door** of the church of **San Pietro**, all that remains after the rest of the church was destroyed in a landslide in 1956. Surrounded by Romanesque twists and zigzags, the door stands isolated against a backdrop of sky, sea and trees.

ARRIVAL AND INFORMATION — VASTO

By train Trains arrive from Pescara (up to 3 hourly; 40min–1hr) and Termoli (at least hourly; 15min). Get off at Vasto San Salvo, which is on the seafront (not Porto di Vasto). Buses run from Vasto San Salvo to the upper town (#4 or #1 for the Marina and Vasto Centro; roughly every 30min, hourly on Sun, more frequent in summer; 10min).

By bus The bus station is out of town, near the cemetery; bus #4 runs from here to the centre. Buses are run by Di Fonzo here (difonzobus.com).

Destinations Pescara (4 daily Mon–Sat – but 3 of these leave between 6.20am and 7.40am; 1hr 20min); Chieti (11 daily; 1hr–2hr 20min); Rome (5 daily; 3hr 20min).

Tourist office Piazza del Popolo 18 (June–Aug Mon–Sat 9am–1pm & 4–7pm, Sun 9am–1pm; Sept Mon–Sat 9am–1pm & 3–6pm; Oct–May Mon–Fri 9am–1pm, Tues, Thurs & Fri 3–6pm; 0873 367 312, abruzzoturismo.it).

ACCOMMODATION AND EATING

Most of the action is down by the beach in Vasto Marina and further south in San Salvo, with no end of hotels, pizzerias and pubs. Note that the vast majority of hotels insist on half board in July and Aug.

Il Pioppeto SS16 Sud 551 0873 801 466, ilpioppeto.it. There are numerous campsites along the coast, most off the SS16 towards Foggia. *Il Pioppeto* is right on the beach and has pine trees for shade. Mid-May to mid-Sept. Pitches **€14.80**, per person **€7.60**

Locanda dei Baroni Via San Francesco d'Assisi 68–70 0873 370 737, locandadeibaroni.com. Five minutes from the old town in a medieval *palazzo*, this B&B has bright rooms with four-poster beds and antique furniture, plus spotless contemporary bathrooms. The brick-vaulted restaurant serves up well-priced local cuisine. **€93**

Trattoria 21 Largo de Litiis 67 0873 610 988, trattoria21.it. A short walk south of the square in the old town, this long-established family fish trattoria does some great and reasonably priced pasta and seafood dishes, including *spaghetti alle vongole* (€8), and delicious hand-made chitarrina with prawns or scampi, rocket pesto and toasted pistachios (€10). Tues–Sun 12.30pm–2.30pm & 7.30pm–10.30pm.

12

Termoli

Just 6km separate Vasto and Molise's brief stretch of coast, which is less developed than Abruzzo's. Its only real coastal town, **TERMOLI**, a fishing port and low-key resort, makes for a relaxing place to spend a day. The beach is long and sandy and the old town, walled and guarded by a castle, is a pretty *borgo* of pastel-painted houses. It's also a departure point for ferries to the Tremiti islands (see page 813) and in striking distance of the interior towns of **Portocannone** and **Ururi**.

Castello Svevo

The stark **Castello Svevo**, built above the beach in 1247 by Frederick II, lords it over the tiny old town. Outside there's a good viewpoint down to the coast below; beyond, the road follows the old walls around the headland.

The Duomo

Piazza del Duomo • Daily 7.45am–noon & 4.30–7.30pm • Free

The focus of the old town is the **Duomo**, most notable for its Romanesque exterior, decorated all the way round with a series of blind arcades and windows – a feature introduced by Frederick II's Norman-influenced architects. Inside are the relics of St Timothy, Termoli's patron saint, best known for the letters he received from St Paul, who advised him on how to go about converting the Greeks. That he ended up in Termoli is thanks to Termolese Crusaders, who brought his bones back from Constantinople as a souvenir. The Termolese hid them, fearing that if the Turks ever succeeded in penetrating the city they would seize and destroy them. In fact the relics were hidden so well they weren't discovered until 1945, during restoration work to repair bomb damage (the sacristan can show them to you).

ARRIVAL AND INFORMATION — TERMOLI

By train The train station is in the new town, a 5min walk from the Castello and the start of the old town.

Destinations Campobasso (5 daily; 1hr 45min); Foggia (at least hourly; 45min–1hr); Pescara (at least hourly; 45min–

CHARIOT-RACING IN THE ALBANIAN VILLAGES

Buses from Termoli run to the isolated villages of **Portocannone**, 12km south, and **Ururi**, another 15km beyond. Their remoteness is such that, six hundred years after their ancestors emigrated from Albania, the locals still speak an Albanian-Italian dialect incomprehensible to outsiders. The villages receive most visitors during their annual **carressi** – chariot races. Portocannone's takes place the Monday after Pentecost, while Ururi's is at the beginning of May. The *carresse* is a fierce and furious race through the village streets on gladiator-style carts, pulled by bulls and pushed by men on horseback with spiked poles. It's a ruthless business: the horses are fed beer before the race to excite them, and although the riders are supposed to push only the back of the carts, they are not averse to prodding the flanks of the bulls, who have already been given electric shocks to liven them up. The race itself is terrifying, but unforgettable, with bulls, carts and spikes hurtling past the frenzied crowds, nowadays protected by wire fences, though there are almost inevitably injuries. Check Ⓦcomune.ururi.cb.it or Ⓦcomune.portocannone.cb.it for further information.

1hr 20min); Vasto (at least hourly; 15min).

By bus Long-distance buses (run by SATI, Ⓦsatiautobus.com) pull up in Via Martiri della Resistenza, 1km from Termoli's centre. A local bus service connects the bus station with the port and historical centre. Flixbus runs services to Naples airport via Foggia.

Destinations Campobasso (approx hourly; 1hr 10min); Foggia (3 daily; 2hr 5min); Isernia (3 daily; 1hr 45min–2hr 5min); Naples Airport via Naples Metropark (2 daily; 3hr 10min); Pescara (4 daily; 1hr 20min); Portocannone (10 daily; 20min); Rome (3 daily; 4hr 15min); Ururi (2 daily; 40min).

By ferry There are ferries to the Tremiti islands (1–3 ferries and hydrofoils daily in summer, 1 ferry daily in winter; 50min–1hr).

Tourist information The tourist office (July & Aug Mon & Wed 8am–2pm & 3–6pm, Tues, Thurs & Fri 8am–2pm & 4–6pm, Sat 9am–1pm; Sept–June Mon & Wed 8am–2pm & 3–6pm, Tues, Thurs & Fri 8am–2pm; Ⓣ0875 703 913, Ⓦtermoli.net) is on Piazza M. Bega 42, near the train station.

12

ACCOMMODATION AND EATING

Locanda Alfieri Via Duomo 39 Ⓣ0875 708 112, Ⓦlocandalfieri.com. This B&B has comfortable rooms scattered around the *borgo antico*. The rooms come with balconies and lovely sea views, and the more modern ones even boast showers with soothing lighting. **€99**

Residenza Sveva Piazza del Duomo 11 Ⓣ0875 706 803, Ⓦresidenzasveva.com. This self-styled "diffused hotel" offers individual rooms around town, rather than one central structure, but all share the same breezy decor, with gleaming tiled floors and a spacious feel throughout. The simple breakfast is taken on a sunny terrace. Rates include access to the hotel's private beach but in July and Aug there's a minimum stay of seven nights. **€99**

Ristorante Svevia Via Giudicato Vecchio 24 Ⓣ0875 550 284, Ⓦsvevia.it. Termoli has its fair share of pizzerias, but if you're hankering after more refined cuisine, this wonderful fish restaurant, with low lighting and a romantic atmosphere is the place. The menu might include local oysters, *linguine* with clams, and cod with cauliflower and sweet chilli; a five-course tasting menu costs €40. Tues–Sun 12.30–2.30pm & 8–10.30pm.

★ **Trattoria L'Opera** Via Adriatica 32 Ⓣ0875808 001, Ⓦtrattorialopera.com. Traditional Molise cuisine with the odd creative twist, just off the main Corso Nazionale. From antipasto to *dolce*, every dish is prepared and presented with great care by Termoli-born chef Roberto, and the freshness and quality of the ingredients is second to none. Tues–Sun 12.30–2.15pm & 7.30–10pm.

Inland Molise

Much of Molise still seems to be struggling out of its past, its towns and villages victims of either economic neglect or hurried modern development. With few sights as such, the inland areas are little explored, but the unspoiled countryside and glimpses of an authentic, untouristed Italy to be found here are attractions in themselves. Inland from Termoli, while **Campobasso** and **Isernia** win no prizes for their looks, they do possess a certain gritty charm; from the former, you can reach the remarkable ruins at **Saepinum**.

Campobasso

Home of a top-security prison and the National Carabinieri School, **CAMPOBASSO**, Molise's regional capital, is about as appealing as you'd expect – a modern, rather faceless town that was once known for its cutlery industry. It's a good base, though, for the remarkable ruins at **Saepinum**, and if you're around in early June, don't miss the town's spectacular Corpus Christi *Sagra dei Misteri* procession, in which citizens are dressed as saints, angels and devils, inserted into fantastic contraptions and transported, seemingly suspended in mid-air, through the streets. Steep alleys of the old **upper town** lead up to a couple of Romanesque churches – **San Bartolomeo**, which has eerily contorted figures carved around its main door, and **San Giorgio**, whose entrance displays a dragon surrounded by stylized flowers. At the top of the hill are a monastery and sixteenth-century **castle** (Tues–Sun 9.30am–12.30pm & 3.30–6.30pm; free), from which there is a panorama over the environs and the historic centre's *borgo antico* below.

ARRIVAL AND INFORMATION — CAMPOBASSO

By bus Campobasso is generally most easily reached by bus. Destinations Foggia (2 daily Mon–Sat; 1hr 40min); Isernia (hourly; 45min–1hr 20min); Naples (6 daily Mon–Sat, 3 daily Sun; 3hr–4hr); Termoli (every 30min–1hr; 1hr 10min–1hr 45min).

By train The train station is in the centre of town. Destinations Isernia (hourly; 50min–1hr 5min); Naples (4 daily; 2hr 40min–3hr); Rome (10 daily; 3–4hr); Termoli (5 daily; 1hr 45min).

Tourist office Piazza della Vittoria 14 (Mon & Wed 9am–2pm & 3–6pm, Tues, Thurs & Fri 9am–2pm; ☎0874 415 662).

EATING

12

La Grotta Da Concetta Via Larino 7 ☎0874 311 378. Sate yourself on solid home cooking for not much more than €20, with dishes such as meatballs in tomato sauce, and fried aubergines with provola cheese and cherry tomatoes. There's no menu but if you're lucky you'll get to try some of the family's home-produced salami. Mon–Fri 1–2pm & 7.30–10.30pm.

Saepinum

Site Open access • Free • **Museum** Tues–Sun: April–Oct 9.30am–3.30pm & 4–6.30pm; Nov–March 8am–2pm & 2.30–5pm • €2 • Take a bus from Campobasso – some stop right outside the site at Altilia (3 daily Mon–Sat; 35min), others at Sepino (6 daily Mon–Sat; Ⓦ atm-molise.it) from where you can walk the remaining 3km to Saepinum – by car, follow signs to Sepino

SAEPINUM, a ruined **Roman town** to the south of Campobasso, is arguably the most interesting sight in Molise. Surrounded by a lush plain fringed with the foothills of the Matese mountains, it's the best example in Italy of a provincial Roman town.

The main reason Saepinum is so intact is that it was never very important: nothing much happened here, and after the fall of the Roman Empire it carried on as the sleepy backwater it had always been – until the ninth century when it was sacked by Saracens. Over the centuries its inhabitants added only a handful of farms and cottages, incorporating the odd Roman column, and eventually moved south to the more secure hilltop site of present-day Sepino. Some have now moved back and rebuilt the farms and cottages on Saepinum's peripheries, contributing if anything to the site's appeal. Their sheep graze below an ancient mausoleum, chickens scratch around the walls, and the only sound is the tinkling of cowbells.

Depending on whether you arrive by bus or by car, the entrance to Saepinum is through the **Porta Terravecchia** or the **Porta Tammaro**, two of the town's four gates. The site is bisected by the *cardo maximus* (running north–south), still paved with the original stones and crossed by the *decumanus maximus*, once home to the public buildings and trading quarters.

On the left, grass spills through the cracks in the pavement of the **forum**, now used by the few local kids as a football pitch, bordered by the foundations of various municipal buildings: the *comitium* (assembly place), the *curia* (senate house), a temple, baths, and in the centre a fountain with a relief of a griffin. Beyond the forum, on the left of the *decumanus*, the **Casa Impluvio Sannitico** contains a vat to collect rainwater.

Back down the *decumanus* on the other side of the crossroads is the well-preserved **basilica** that served as the main courthouse. Beyond is the most interesting part of the town – the octagonal *macellum* (marketplace), with its small stone stalls and central rain-collecting dish, and a series of houses fronted by workshops, with small living quarters behind.

The *macellum* leads down to the best-preserved gate, the **Porta Boiano**, flanked by cylindrical towers with a relief showing two barbarians and chained prisoners. There is also a small **museum** with artefacts and artwork recovered during excavation.

Isernia

Though unbeguiling in itself, inland **ISERNIA** is a good starting point for exploring the rest of Molise, with good train connections from Rome and Naples. The first settlement dates back to the Samnites, yet very little of old Isernia survives. Earthquakes and wars have wreaked havoc on its historical monuments; much of the centre was destroyed in a bombing raid on September 10, 1943, and a monument to the four thousand who were killed – an anguished nude, ankle-deep in fractured tiles, bricks and gutters – is the centrepiece of the square called, understandably, Piazza X Settembre. In spite of it all, the city has rebuilt its commercial centre so that it's now comparatively busy and bustling. Isernia's most iconic monument is the **Fontana Fraterna** in Piazza Celestino V, a Romanesque fountain built in the thirteenth century by the Rampini family from marble stripped from Roman tombs.

12

La Pineta

Tues–Sun 9am–7pm by reservation only • Free • ⓣ 0865 410 50 • A short ride from Isernia station on the #3 bus

Isernia's main attraction is a prehistoric site called **La Pineta**, an easy 1.5km from the centre. In 1978, road-builders here unearthed traces of a Paleolithic settlement at least 700,000 years old – the most ancient signs of human life yet found in Europe.

Museo Nazionale del Paleolitico di Isernia

Corso Marcelli 48 • Daily 8.30am–7pm • €2 • Bus #2 from the station

Finds from La Pineta form the core of the collection in the former convent of **Santa Maria delle Monache**. Contrary to the misleading publicity, there were no human remains found, just weapons, traps, traces of pigment thought to have been used as body paint, and animal bones, laid out to create a solid platform on the marshy land for the village.

ARRIVAL AND INFORMATION — ISERNIA

By train The train station is on Piazza della Repubblica. Destinations Campobasso (hourly; 1hr); Naples (6 daily; 2hr–3hr); Rome (10 daily; 2hr–3hr 20min).

By bus Local and longer-distance buses, including those to Rome and Naples, depart from outside the train station on Piazza della Repubblica. Destinations Campobasso (at least hourly; 45min–1hr 20min); Naples (9 daily; 1hr 45min); Pescara (3 daily Mon–Sat; 2hr 10min); Rome (8 daily; 2hr 25min); Termoli (13 daily; 1hr 25min–1hr 55min).

Tourist office Via Farinacci 9 (Mon–Sat 8am–2pm; ⓣ 086 53 992, ⓦ iserniaturismo.it).

ACCOMMODATION AND EATING

★ **Antica Dimora 191** Corso Marcelli 191 ⓣ 0865 410 547, ⓦ anticadimora191.com. If you decide to stay overnight, head for this gem of a place, set in a historic *palazzo* in Isernia's old centre. Opulently decorated with paintings, antiques and frescoed ceilings, the rooms have bags of character, and the owners are friendly and helpful. Breakfast is taken in the bar downstairs. **€50**

Nabucco Osteria Verdi Via Marcelli 160 ⓣ 328 632 4215. South of the town centre, this much-lauded *osteria* is as typical as they come with a brief menu of home-style dishes, friendly service and a local clientele who know their food. You could have a *primi*, a *secondo* and a glass of wine for under €20. The interior, with its frescoed vaulting and antiques, really sets the scene for a great regional meal. Tues–Sat 12.30–2.30pm & 7.30–10.30pm. Sun 11am–2.30pm.

Campania

740 Naples

764 The Bay of Naples

776 The islands

787 Inland Campania

791 The Amalfi Coast

GULF OF SALERNO, AMALFI COAST

13

Campania

Immediately below Lazio, Campania marks the real beginning of the Italian South or *mezzogiorno*. It's the part of the South too, perhaps inevitably, that most people see, as it's easily accessible from Rome and home to some of the Italy's most notable features – Roman sites, spectacular stretches of coast, tiny islands. It's always been a sought-after region, first named by the Romans, who tagged it the *campania felix*, or "happy land" (to distinguish it from the rather dull *campagna* further north), and settled down here in villas and palatial estates that stretched right around the Bay of Naples. Later, when Naples became the final stop on northerners' Grand Tours, its bay became no less fabled, the relics of its heady Roman period only adding to the charm for most travellers.

Naples is the obvious focus, an utterly compelling city that dominates the region in every way. Taking one of the fastest trains, you can reach it in a little over an hour from Rome, and there's no excuse for not seeing at least this part of Campania – though of course you need three or four days to begin to absorb the city. The **Bay of Naples**, too, has plenty to occupy you for a good week: there are the ancient sites of **Pompeii** and **Herculaneum** just half an hour away – arguably Italy's best-preserved and most revealing Roman remains; the smouldering volcanic **Campi Flegrei** area to the northwest; the gorgeous islands of **Capri**, **Ischia** and **Procida**; and the cheery and likeable resort town of **Sorrento** at the southern end of the bay.

Inland Campania is, by contrast, a poor and largely unknown region. However, the giant palace and gardens of **Caserta** are worth visiting, as are the ancient treasures of nearby **Capua** and **Santa Maria and Capua Vetere**, as well as – a bit further afield to the east – breezy **Benevento**, an old stop on the Roman route to Brindisi, with a flavour that's quite distinct from the coastal regions.

Beyond the Bay of Naples to the south, a pair of pretty peninsulas bookend the revitalized city of **Salerno** and the impressive Greek temples of **Paestum**: along the first is the **Amalfi Coast**, perhaps Europe's most stunning stretch of coastline, whose enticing and sometimes exclusive resorts – Positano and Amalfi – need little introduction; while Campania's southern border is marked by the quieter, more remote promontory of the **Cilento** region, with plenty of uncrowded beaches.

Naples

The capital of the Italian South, **NAPLES** is a city that comes laden with preconceptions, and most bear some truth. It's huge, filthy, crime-ridden and in some parts appears to be falling apart; it's edgy and atmospheric, with a faint air of menace; and it is definitely like nowhere else in Italy. Yet Naples has bags of charm, making the noise and disorder easily endurable, even enjoyable, for most first-timers. It doesn't yet attract hordes of visitors, and is refreshingly lacking in tourist gloss, yet it's a grand and beautiful place, with monumental squares, world-class museums, down-at-heel churches crammed with Baroque masterpieces and all manner of historic nooks and corners – plus innumerable places to enjoy arguably some of Italy's best food, and without a doubt its best pizza.

NAPLES

Highlights

❶ Centro storico, Naples Still following the street plan of the original Greco-Roman settlement, Naples' ancient centre is unique both above and below ground. See page 743

❷ Museo Archeologico Nazionale, Naples A superb museum with a wealth of Greek and Roman artefacts. See page 754

❸ Herculaneum and Pompeii These sites afford an unparalleled glimpse into ancient Roman daily life and architecture. See pages 767 and 769

❹ Capri The most sought-after destination in the Bay of Naples since Emperor Tiberius' day, this mesmerizingly stunning island is worth braving the crowds to explore. See page 777

❺ Ischia The towering hulk of the Castello Aragonese, perched on a craggy islet linked by a causeway, is just one of this verdant volcanic island's draws. See page 782

❻ Amalfi Coast A staggeringly beautiful stretch of rugged coastline dotted with secluded coves, beaches and a few of the region's most picturesque towns. See page 791

❼ Paestum Check out some of Europe's best-preserved Doric temples and colourful tomb paintings found amid the ruins of this ancient Greek settlement. See page 801

HIGHLIGHTS ARE MARKED ON THE MAP ON PAGE 742

13

Brief history

There was a settlement here, **Parthenope**, as early as the ninth century BC; this was superseded by a Greek colony in 750 BC, which they gave the name Neapolis. It prospered during Greek and later Roman times, and remained independent until the **Normans** took the city in 1139, after which it was passed from one dynasty to the next until Alfonso I of Aragon arrived in 1422, establishing a **Spanish** connection for the city for the next three hundred years.

Following the War of the Spanish Succession, Naples was briefly ceded to the Austrians, before being taken, to general rejoicing, by **Charles of Bourbon** in 1734. Charles was a cultivated and judicious monarch, but his dissolute son Ferdinand presided over a shambolic period in the city's history, abandoning it to the republican French. Their "Parthenopean Republic" here was short-lived, and the British re-installed the Bourbon monarch, carrying out vicious reprisals against the rebels. The instigator of these reprisals was Admiral Nelson – fresh from his victory at the Battle of the Nile. Under continuing Bourbon rule, the city became the second largest in Europe, and a requisite stop on the **Grand Tour**, a position it enjoyed not so much for its proximity to the major classical sites as for the ready availability of sex, giving new meaning (in the days when syphilis was rife) to the phrase "See Naples and die".

THE BIRTHPLACE OF PIZZA – CAMPANIAN CUISINE

The flavour of Naples dominates the whole of Campania. It's the true home of the **pizza**, rapidly baked in searingly hot wood-fired ovens and running with olive oil, as well as fantastic **street food**, served in numerous outlets known as *friggitorie* – sample delicacies such as fried pizzas (*pizzette* or *panzarotti*), heavenly *crocchè* (potato croquettes), *arancini* (rice balls) and *fiorilli* (courgette flowers in batter).

Naples is also the home of pasta and tomato sauce, made with fresh tomatoes and basil, and laced with garlic. Aubergines and courgettes turn up endlessly in pasta sauces, as does the tomato-mozzarella pairing (the regions to the north and east of Naples are the home of mozzarella), the latter particularly good with gnocchi. **Seafood** is excellent all along the coast: clams combine with garlic and oil for superb *spaghetti alle vongole*; mussels are often prepared as *zuppa di cozze* (with hot pepper sauce and croutons); fresh squid and octopus are ubiquitous.

There are loads of great pastries: not to be missed is the *sfogliatella*, a flaky triangular pastry case stuffed with ricotta and candied peel, and the fragrant Easter cake, *pastiera*, made with ricotta and softened wheat grain. Further to the south, the marshy plains of the Cilento produce fabulous strawberries, artichokes and mozzarella cheese – much of the mozzarella that comes from here is made from pure buffalo milk, unmixed with cow's milk.

The volcanic slopes of Vesuvius are among the most ancient **wine-producing** areas in Italy, but despite that the region doesn't have a great reputation for wine. The best choices for a Campanian white are Greco di Tufo, Fiano di Avellino and Falanghina – all fruity yet dry. Ischia also produces good whites, notably Biancolella, while Lacryma Christi, from the slopes of Mount Vesuvius, is available in red and white varieties and is enjoying a resurgence after years of being considered cheap plonk. Among pure reds, there's the unusual but delicious Gragnano, a red sparkling wine that's best served slightly chilled, and Taurasi – like the best wines of the region made from the local Aglianico grape.

More recently, Naples and its surrounding area have received much of the government and EU money that has poured into the Italian South. While a substantial amount of regional power has remained in the hands of organized crime, the **Camorra**, significant gains have been made. **Antonio Bassolino**, mayor of the city from 1993 until 2000 and president of Campania from 2000–10, did much to tackle corruption in the region's entangled bureaucracy, as well as to promote the city's attractions, restoring scores of neglected churches, museums and palaces. Mayor since 2011, former prosecutor **Luigi de Magistris** has kept the forward momentum alive, receiving accolades for his wide-ranging efforts to fight the city's endemic crime and corruption as well as to boost its potential for tourism. While notching a slew of high-profile arrests he has overseen a sweeping revitalization of the city centre, an ambitious expansion of the city's metro and an upsurge of civil society and community activism.

Indeed, tourist arrivals have more than doubled over the past decade, which has also witnessed a burst of creative activity from local filmmakers, songwriters and artists within a thriving contemporary **art scene**. Of course, while there is certainly cause for optimism, there remains plenty of work ahead. Naples and its surrounds continue to struggle with crime, poverty and youth unemployment, while the Camorra still casts a long shadow.

The centro storico

Naples is a large, sprawling city, with a centre that has many different focuses. The area between Piazza Garibaldi and Via Toledo, roughly corresponding to the old Roman Neapolis (much of which is still unexcavated below the ground), makes up the old part of the city – the **centro storico** – with the main streets of **Via dei Tribunali** and **Via San Biagio dei Librai** (the latter also known as "Spaccanapoli") still following the path

13

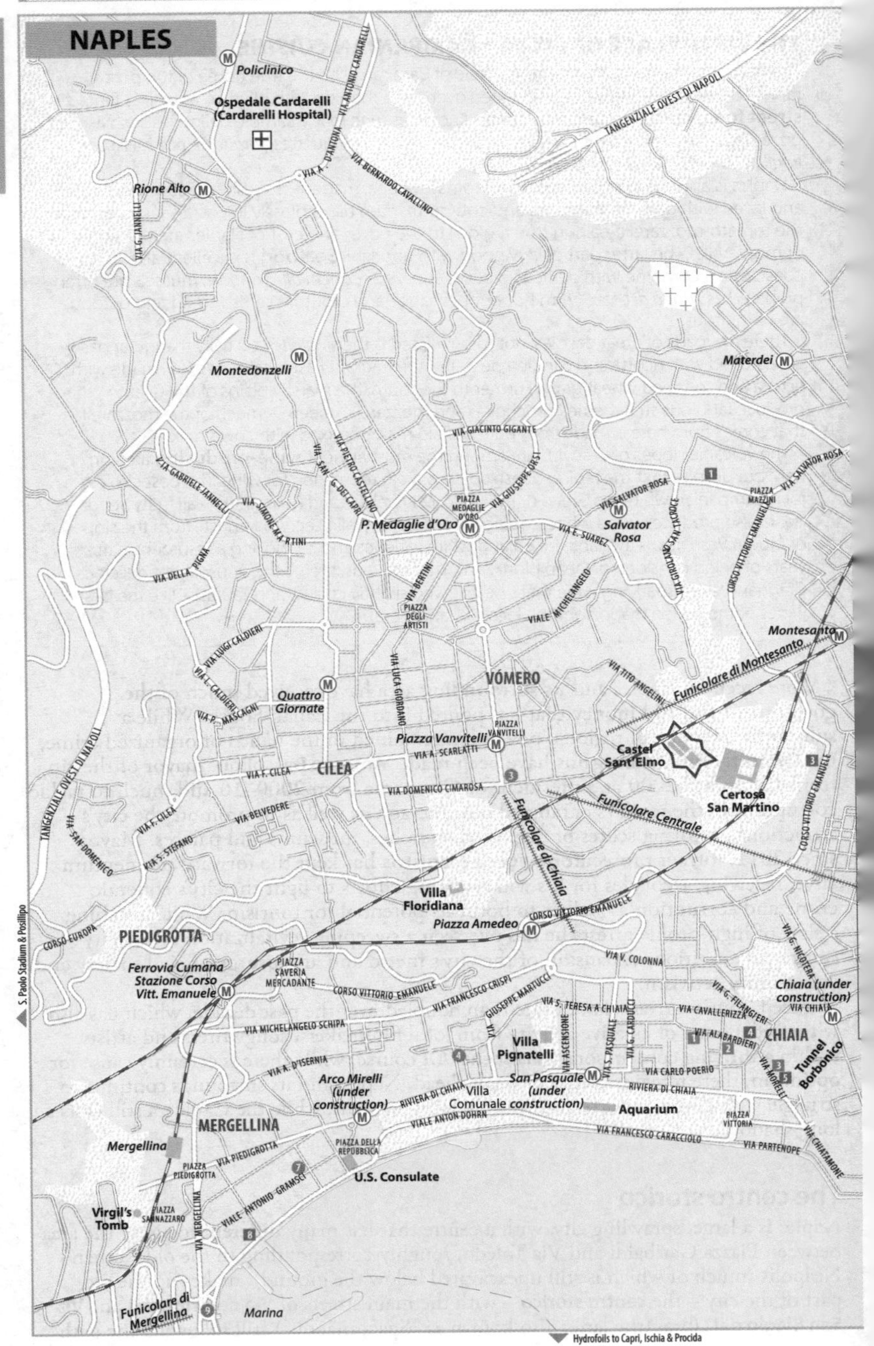
NAPLES
Policlinico
Ospedale Cardarelli
(Cardarelli Hospital)
Rione Alto
Montedonzelli
Materdei
P. Medaglie d'Oro
Salvator Rosa
Montesanto
Quattro Giornate
VÓMERO
Piazza Vanvitelli
CILEA
Castel Sant'Elmo
Certosa San Martino
Funicolare di Montesanto
Funicolare Centrale
Funicolare di Chiaia
Villa Floridiana
Piazza Amedeo
PIEDIGROTTA
Ferrovia Cumana Stazione Corso Vitt. Emanuele
Chiaia (under construction)
CHIAIA
Tunnel Borbonico
Villa Pignatelli
San Pasquale (under construction)
Arco Mirelli (under construction)
Villa Comunale
Aquarium
MERGELLINA
Mergellina
U.S. Consulate
Virgil's Tomb
Funicolare di Mergellina
Marina
S. Paolo Stadium & Posillipo
Hydrofoils to Capri, Ischia & Procida
TANGENZIALE OVEST DI NAPOLI
VIA BERNARDO CAVALLINO
VIA A. D'ANTONA
VIA ANTONIO CARDARELLI
VIA G. JANNELLI
VIA GIACINTO GIGANTE
VIA PIETRO CASTELLINO
VIA S. G. DEI CAPRI
VIA GIUSEPPE ORSI
VIA GABRIELE JANNELLI
VIA SIMONE MARTINI
VIA DELLA PIGNA
VIA SALVATOR ROSA
VIA E. SUAREZ
VIA GIROLAMO SANTACROCE
CORSO VITTORIO EMANUELE
PIAZZA MAZZINI
VIA BERTINI
PIAZZA DEGLI ARTISTI
VIALE MICHELANGELO
VIA LUIGI CALDIERI
VIA L. CALDIERI
VIA P. MASCAGNI
VIA LUCA GIORDANO
VIA TITO ANGELINI
PIAZZA VANVITELLI
VIA A. SCARLATTI
VIA F. CILEA
VIA DOMENICO CIMAROSA
VIA BELVEDERE
VIA S. STEFANO
VIA SAN DOMENICO
CORSO EUROPA
VIA V. COLONNA
PIAZZA SAVERIA MERCADANTE
VIA FRANCESCO CRISPI
VIA GIUSEPPE MARTUCCI
VIA S. TERESA A CHIAIA
VIA MICHELANGELO SCHIPA
VIA ASCENSIONE
VIA S. PASQUALE
VIA G. CARDUCCI
VIA CAVALLERIZZA
VIA G. FILANGIERI
VIA G. NICOTERA
VIA CHIAIA
VIA ALABARDIERI
VIA CARLO POERIO
VIA MORELLI
VIA A. D'ISERNIA
RIVIERA DI CHIAIA
VIALE ANTON DOHRN
VIA FRANCESCO CARACCIOLO
PIAZZA VITTORIA
VIA PARTENOPE
VIA CHIATAMONE
PIAZZA DELLA REPUBBLICA
VIA PIEDIGROTTA
PIAZZA PIEDIGROTTA
VIALE ANTONIO GRAMSCI
PIAZZA SANNAZZARO
VIA MERGELLINA

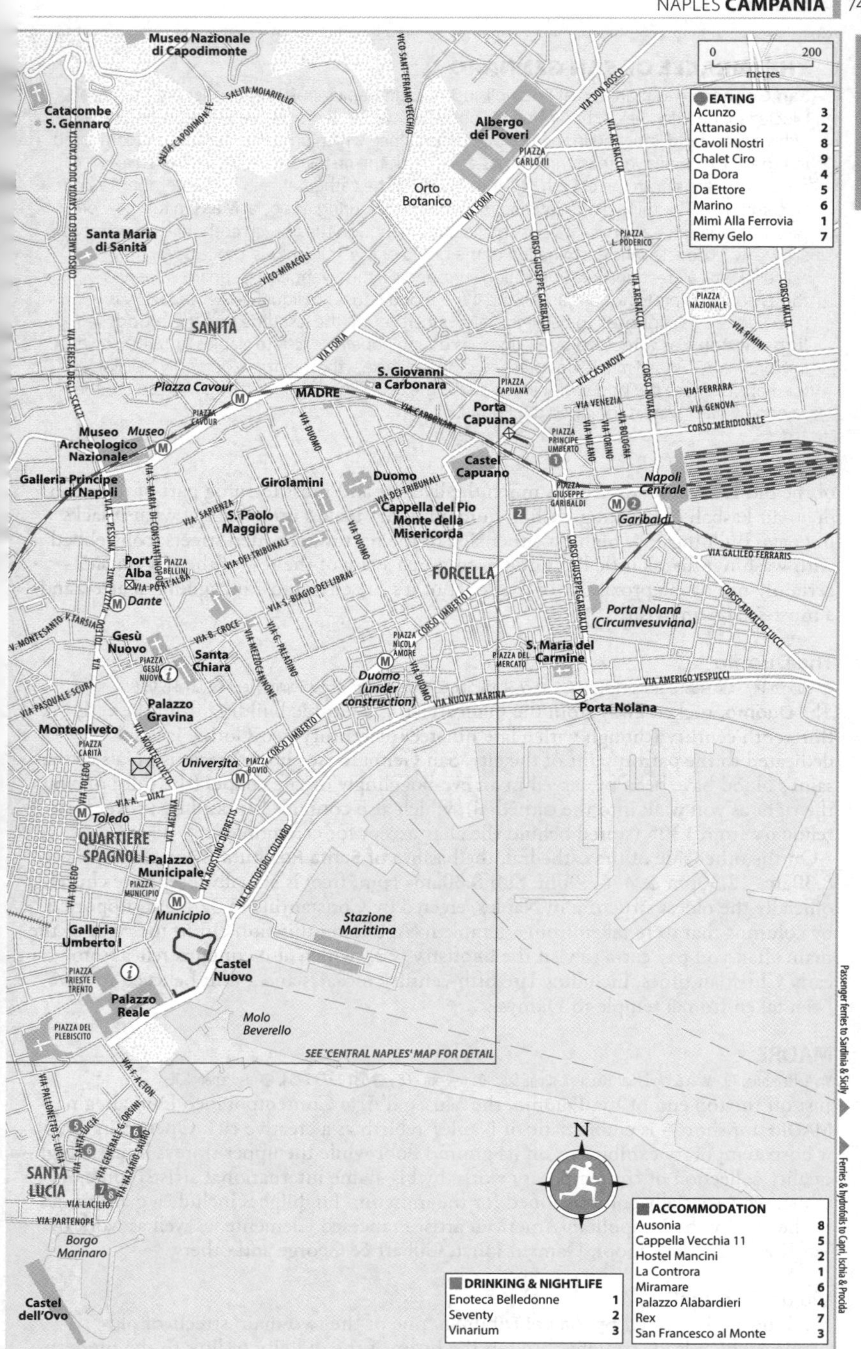

EATING
Acunzo 3
Attanasio 2
Cavoli Nostri 8
Chalet Ciro 9
Da Dora 4
Da Ettore 5
Marino 6
Mimì Alla Ferrovia 1
Remy Gelo 7
DRINKING & NIGHTLIFE
Enoteca Belledonne 1
Seventy 2
Vinarium 3
ACCOMMODATION
Ausonia 8
Cappella Vecchia 11 5
Hostel Mancini 2
La Controra 1
Miramare 6
Palazzo Alabardieri 4
Rex 7
San Francesco al Monte 3
0 200 metres
Museo Nazionale di Capodimonte
Catacombe S. Gennaro
Albergo dei Poveri
Orto Botanico
Santa Maria di Sanità
SANITÀ
S. Giovanni a Carbonara
MADRE
Porta Capuana
Castel Capuano
Piazza Cavour
Museo Archeologico Nazionale
Museo
Galleria Principe di Napoli
Girolamini
Duomo
Cappella del Pio Monte della Misericordia
S. Paolo Maggiore
Port'Alba
Dante
FORCELLA
Napoli Centrale
Garibaldi
Porta Nolana (Circumvesuviana)
Gesù Nuovo
Santa Chiara
S. Maria del Carmine
Duomo (under construction)
Porta Nolana
Palazzo Gravina
Monteoliveto
Università
Toledo
QUARTIERE SPAGNOLI
Palazzo Municipale
Municipio
Stazione Marittima
Galleria Umberto I
Castel Nuovo
Palazzo Reale
Molo Beverello
SEE 'CENTRAL NAPLES' MAP FOR DETAIL
SANTA LUCIA
Borgo Marinaro
Castel dell'Ovo
Passenger ferries to Sardinia & Sicily
Ferries & hydrofoils to Capri, Ischia & Procida
N

13

THE MIRACLE OF SAN GENNARO

San Gennaro was martyred at Pozzuoli, just outside Naples, in 305 AD under the purges of Diocletian. Tradition has it that, when his body was transferred to Naples' Duomo, two phials of his dried blood liquefied in the bishop's hands, since which time the "miracle" has continued to repeat itself no fewer than three times a year – on the first Saturday in May (when a procession leads from the church of Santa Chiara to the cathedral) and on September 19 and December 16. The miraculous liquefaction takes place during a special **Mass** in full view of the congregation – a service it's possible to attend, though the church authorities have yet to allow any close scientific examination of the blood or the "miraculous" process.

There is still a great deal of superstition surrounding this event: San Gennaro is seen as the saviour and protector of Naples, and if the blood refuses to liquefy – which luckily is rare – disaster is supposed to befall the city. Until recently, the last time that the **blood liquefaction** was witnessed by a pope was during Pope Pius' visit to Naples in 1848. However, in March 2015, Pope Francis was present for the miracle – though the blood only half liquified (perhaps because the pope's visit was outside the usual liquefaction dates). "We can see the saint only half loves us", quipped the Pontiff.

of the old Roman roads. This is much the liveliest and most teeming part of town, an open-air kasbah of hawking, yelling humanity that makes up in energy what it lacks in grace. Buildings rise high on either side of the narrow, crowded streets, cobwebbed with washing; there's little light, not even much sense of the rest of the city outside – certainly not of the proximity of the sea. But it's the city's most intriguing quarter, and a must-see on any visit.

The Duomo

Via Duomo 147 • Mon–Sat 8.30am–1.30pm & 2.30–7.30pm, Sun 8.30am–1.30pm & 5–7.30pm • Free • T 081 449 097

The **Duomo**, tucked away from the main street, is a Gothic building from the early thirteenth century (though with a late nineteenth-century neo-Gothic facade) dedicated to the patron saint of the city, San Gennaro (see box). Precious phials of the saint's blood have been preserved in an eye-bogglingly ornate **chapel** (the third one on the right as you walk into the cathedral), which also contains his skull in a silver bust-reliquary from 1305 (stored behind the altar except for ceremonies).

On the other side of the cathedral, the basilica of **Santa Restituta** (Mon–Sat 8.30am–12.30pm & 4–6.30pm, Sun 8.30am–1pm; free) is actually a separate church, officially the oldest structure in Naples, erected by Constantine in 324 and supported by columns that were taken from a temple to Apollo on this site. Off to the right of the main altar, you pay extra to visit the **baptistry** (€2), which also contains relics from very early Christian times, including late fifth-century mosaics and a font believed to have been taken from a temple to Dionysus.

MADRE

Via Settembrini 79 • Mon & Wed–Sat 10am–7.30pm, Sun 10am–8pm • €8 • T 081 1973 7254, W madrenapoli.it

Just off the top end of Via Duomo, the Museo d'Arte Contemporaneo Donnaregina – **MADRE** for short – is emblematic of Naples' rebirth as a creative city. Opened in 2005, it hosts temporary exhibitions on its ground floor while the upper storeys house a high-quality collection of contemporary works by big-name international artists, some of which were specially commissioned for the museum. Highlights include a giant mural of the city by the Neapolitan-American artist Francesco Clemente, as well as work by Jeff Koons, Anish Kapoor, Damien Hirst, Gilbert & George and others.

Via dei Tribunali

Via Duomo is crossed by **Via dei Tribunali**, one of the two main streets of old Naples, which leads straight through the heart of the old city to link to the modern

centre around Via Toledo. It's richer in interest and sights than almost any other street in Naples, and you can spend many happy hours picking your way through its churches, palaces and underground caverns, stopping off for pizza at one of its numerous pizzerias before emerging at Piazza Bellini and strolling up to the archeological museum.

Quadreria e Cappella del Pio Monte della Misericordia

Via dei Tribunali 253 • Mon–Sat 9am–6pm, Sun 9am–2.30pm • €7 • ⓣ 081 446 944, ⓦ piomontedellamisericordia.it

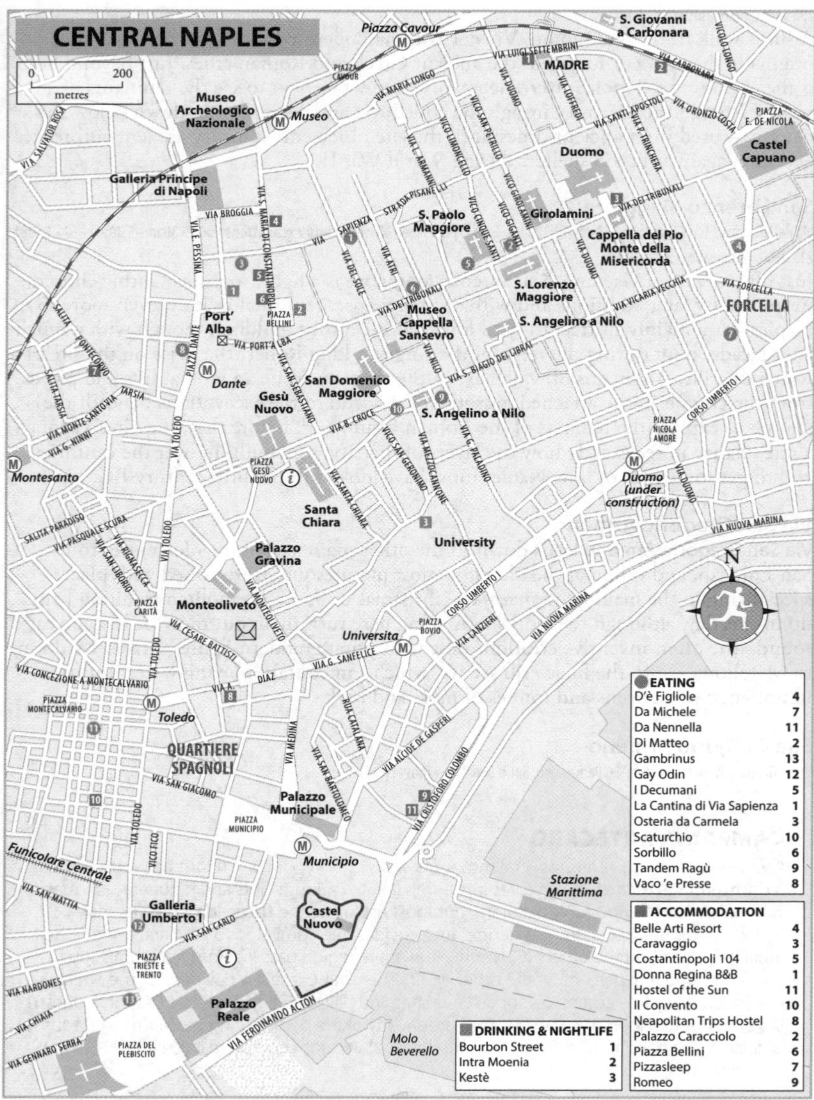

Just around the corner from the Duomo, the **Quadreria e Cappella del Pio Monte della Misericordia** is worth stopping off at before diving into the old city proper. A beautiful octagonal structure, the church is named after and run by a charity, which was founded in the seventeenth-century and still functions today. Inside are paintings by Caravaggio and Luca Giordano, and you can also visit the charity's picture gallery upstairs, which overlooks the church.

Napoli Sotterranea

Piazza S. Gaetano 68 • Daily 2hr tours in English start every other hour 10am–6pm; Thurs also at 9pm by reservation only • €10 • T 081 296 944, W napolisotterranea.org

A short walk from Via Duomo, Via dei Tribunali opens out at **Piazza San Gaetano**, originally the agora or forum of the ancient Greek and Roman cities. Just beyond here is the entrance to **Napoli Sotterranea**, whose tours take you to see the remnants of a nearby Roman theatre and through the aqueducts and cisterns 40m down below the old city – used from ancient times until the late nineteenth-century cholera outbreak, and then again as bomb shelters during World War II.

San Lorenzo Maggiore

Via dei Tribunali 316 • **Church** Daily 8am–12.30pm & 5.30–7pm • Free • **Museum and excavations** Daily 9.30am–5.30pm • €9 • T 081 211 0860, W laneapolissotterrata.it

Just off Piazza San Gaetano, **San Lorenzo Maggiore** is a light, spacious Gothic church, unspoiled by later additions and with a soaring apse – unusual in Italy, even more so in Naples. It's a mainly thirteenth- and fourteenth-century building, though with a much later facade, built during the reign of the Angevin king Robert the Wise on the site of a Roman basilica – remains of which are in the cloisters. You can look at bits and pieces from the church in the attached **museum** or descend to the **excavations** beneath the church to explore the remains of the Roman forum and, before that, the Greek agora – a rare chance to see exactly how the layers of the city were built up over the centuries, and to get some idea of how Naples must have looked in the fifth century BC.

Via San Gregorio Armeno

Via San Gregorio Armeno leads down to the other main axis of the old centre from San Lorenzo, and is one of the old city's most picturesque streets, lined with places specializing in the making of *presepi* or Christmas cribs – a Neapolitan tradition kept up to this day, although the workshops along here turn them out more or less all year round. The often-inventive creations now incorporate modern figures – from Madonna to Maradona – into the huge crib scenes, which can contain moving water features, illuminated pizza ovens and tonnes of moss and bark.

San Gregorio Armeno

Via S. Gregorio Armeno 1 • Mon–Fri 9am–noon, Sat & Sun 9am–1pm • Free

CAMPANIA ARTECARD

If you're considering visiting several museums and sights in Naples, it might be worth buying a **Campania artecard**, which gives free admission to various sights and reductions on many others. There are various combinations, but most useful are the **three-day passes** that include public transport: the city centre one provides free admission to your first three sights and fifty percent off the others (€21); while the entire region pass includes free admission to two sights and fifty percent off the others (€32). There's also a seven-day pass for the entire region, granting free access to your first five sites and half off on others (€34), though it doesn't cover public transport. You can buy the cards at any of the participating museums or at tourist offices and Napoli Stazione Centrale. More details at W campaniartecard.it (T 800 600 601) or at tourist offices.

The church of **San Gregorio Armeno** is a sumptuous Baroque edifice with frescoes above the entrance by the late seventeenth-century Neapolitan artist Luca Giordano, not to mention two stupendously ornate gilded organs, one on each side of the nave. Above the south aisle, you'll notice a series of grilles through which the Benedictine nuns would view the services from the **Chiostro di San Gregorio Armeno** next door, a wonderfully peaceful haven from the noise outside, planted with limes and busy with nuns quietly going about their duties.

Santa Maria delle Anime del Purgatorio ad Arco

Via dei Tribunali 39 • Jan–March Mon–Fri & Sun 10am–2pm, Sat 10am–5pm; April–Dec Mon–Sat 10am–6pm, Sun 10am–2pm • Church free; museum and hypogeum €6 • ⓣ 081 440 438, ⓦ purgatorioadarco.it

Down the street from Piazza San Gaetano, the church of **Santa Maria delle Anime del Purgatorio ad Arco** is the site of a death cult that was outlawed in the 1960s by the Catholic authorities but still lives on in a semi-secret fashion in its downstairs **hypogeum**. Here, dusty chapels hold tiled shrines to the anonymous dead who are revered as intermediaries between the earthly and the divine, and given names that endeared the keepers of their graves to them. Among the intercessors is the virgin-bride Lucia, to whom devotees pray over love-related matters – she's the one with the tiara and bridal veil resting on her skull.

Piazza Bellini

Just past the church of San Pietro a Maiella, **Piazza Bellini** is a pleasant open space marking the end of the old city, and indeed it always has: the ruins of the old Greco-Roman walls can still be seen at the bottom end of the square. It's a leafy, rectangular square lined with terraced cafés, and makes a good spot for a coffee and a break from sightseeing. At night it's a major hub, with the cafés packed and the square full of cool folk hanging out and shooting the breeze.

Spaccanapoli

Running parallel to Via dei Tribunali, **Spaccanapoli** (literally, "Splitting Naples") cuts cleanly through the old city. It's a long street, and changes name several times: at the Via del Duomo end, it's **Via San Biagio dei Librai**, becoming **Via Benedetto Croce** at its western end, where it opens out at the large square of the Gesù Nuovo and the edge of old Naples.

Largo di Corpo di Nilo

The **Largo di Corpo di Nilo** is home to a Roman statue of a reclining old man: sculpted in Nero's time, it's a representation of the Nile and has a habit, it's claimed, of whispering to women as they walk by. The church opposite, on Piazzetta Nilo, **Sant'Angelo a Nilo**, is home to the city's earliest piece of Renaissance art – the funerary monument to Cardinal Rinaldo Brancaccio, made in Pisa in 1426 by Michelozzo and Donatello.

San Domenico Maggiore

Piazza S. Domenico Maggiore 8 • Church Mon–Fri 10am–1pm & 4–6pm, Sat & Sun 9.30am–6.30pm • Free; sacristy €5

Piazza San Domenico Maggiore is marked by the **Guglia di San Domenico**, built in 1737 – one of the whimsical Baroque obelisks originally put up after times of plague or disease or to celebrate the Virgin. The **San Domenico Maggiore church** flanks the north side of the square, a Gothic building from 1289, one of whose chapels holds a miraculous painting of the Crucifixion which is said to have spoken to St Thomas Aquinas during his time at the adjacent monastery. Look also at the Brancaccio chapel, whose clear, bright frescoes by Pietro Cavallini date back to the early fourteenth century, and the sacristry, housing the velvet-clad coffins of Naples' Aragonese rulers, who made this church the centre of their court in Naples.

Cappella Sansevero

Via Francesco de Sanctis 19/21 • Mon & Wed–Sun 9.30am–7pm • €7 • 081 551 8470, museosansevero.it

Off the top end of the Piazza San Domenico, Via de Sanctis leads off right to one of the city's odder monuments, the **Cappella Sansevero**, the tomb-chapel of the Di Sangro family. The centrepiece, sculpted by Giuseppe Sanmartino in the mid-eighteenth century, is a carving of a dead Christ, laid out flat and covered with a veil of stark and remarkable realism, not least because it was carved out of a single piece of marble. Even more accomplished is Antonio Corradini's veiled figure of *Modesty* on the left, and, on the right, its twin *Disillusionment*, by Francesco Queirolo, in the form of a woeful figure struggling with marble netting. Look, too, at the effusive *Deposition*, by Francesco Celebrano, on the high altar, and the memorial above the doorway, which shows one Cecco di Sangro climbing out of his tomb, sword in hand. You might also want to venture downstairs. The man responsible for the chapel, Prince Raimondo, was a well-known eighteenth-century alchemist, and down here are the results of some of his experiments: bodies of an upright man and woman, behind glass, their capillaries and most of their organs preserved by a mysterious liquid developed by the prince – who, incidentally, was excommunicated by the pope for such practices. Even now the black entanglements make for a gruesome sight.

Santa Chiara

Via S. Chiara 49 • **Church** Daily 7.30am–1pm & 4.30–8pm • Free • **Cloister** Mon–Sat 9.30am–5.30pm, Sun 10am–2.30pm • €6 • monasterodisantachiara.eu

Dating from 1328, the church of **Santa Chiara** was completely destroyed by Allied bombs during the last war, then rebuilt in its original bare Gothic austerity. There's not much to see inside, but the medieval tombs of the Angevin monarchs at the far end are fine and include that of Robert the Wise at the altar, showing the king in a monk's habit. And the attached convent has a **cloister** that is truly one of the gems of the city, a shady haven planted with neatly clipped box hedges, and furnished with benches and low walls covered with colourful majolica tiles depicting bucolic scenes of life outside. There's also a giant *presepe* or Christmas crib, and in the far corner a well-put-together museum showing bits from the church before the bombing as well as the excavated remains of a Roman bath complex outside.

Gesù Nuovo

Piazza Gesù Nuovo • Daily 7am–1pm & 4–8pm • Free • gesunuovo.it

Opposite Santa Chiara, the **Gesù Nuovo** church is most notable for its lava-stone facade, originally part of a fifteenth-century palace which stood here, prickled with pyramids that give it an impregnable, prison-like air. The inside is oversized and overdecorated, its most interesting feature being the simple chapel on the far right which is dedicated to San Guiseppe Moscati, a local doctor who died in 1927 and was reputed to perform medical miracles – as you can see from the votive plaques and thanks that plaster the walls.

Piazza Garibaldi and around

Naples' main transport hub is **Piazza Garibaldi**, a giant, bustling square that cuts into the city centre from the modern train station. It's often visitors' first impression of the city, and until recently was an infamously daunting and chaotic sight, made worse by a vast construction zone that took up most of the square. Now that the work is finally done – or at least appears close to it – the square has never looked better. Designed by French architect Dominique Perrault, it now features a striking steel-and-glass canopy covering an underground, open-air shopping centre, beside which lies one of

13

the city's most impressive new metro stations (see page 759). The surrounding area is also a hub for Naples' African community, with a number of African, South Asian and Middle Eastern restaurants and groceries, though don't be surprised to hear Slavic accents as well.

Forcella

On the far side of Piazza Garibaldi is the city's **Forcella** quarter, which spreads down to Corso Umberto I and across as far as Via Duomo. It's an introduction to the old centre of Naples, with an open-air **market**, stamping-ground of contraband seafood sellers and sunglass and headphone hawkers, and a quantity of food stalls that make it one of the city's best places to wander. It's also one of the main city-centre strongholds of the Camorra, and not an especially friendly place at night.

Corso Umberto I

Corso Umberto I spears off the far corner of the square, edging the old part of the city to the port. Known as the "*rettifilo*", it makes its long straight journey southeast from Piazza Garibaldi, passing many of the city's more mainstream shops. Its halfway point is Piazza Nicole Amore – currently disrupted with work on the Duomo metro stop (slated for completion in 2020) – from where Via Duomo heads up the hill to the right, dividing Forcella from the *centro storico* on its left-hand side. At the end of Corso Umberto, **Piazza Bovio** is centered around an eighty-ton statue of Vittorio Emanuelle II.

Via Toledo and the Quartieri Spagnoli

If you asked most people what they thought of as the centre of Naples, they'd say **Via Toledo**, sometimes known as Via Roma: the shop-lined thoroughfare that provides the modern city's spine. Its southern end is anchored by Piazza Trieste e Trento and the city's most monumental buildings: the Palazzo Reale, Galleria Umberto I and the Castel Nuovo. From here, Via Toledo leads north in a dead-straight line, climbing the hill towards the Museo Archeologico Nazionale and separating the city into two very distinct parts.

The streets to the left, scaling the footslopes of the Vomero, are some of the city's most narrow and crowded, a grid of alleys that was laid out to house Spanish troops during the seventeenth century and hence now known as the **Quartieri Spagnoli** – an enticing area, at least for visitors, although it remains a poor part of town, too, and one you might want to avoid wandering too deeply into at night.

Piazza Trieste e Trento and around

Piazza Trieste e Trento is probably as close to central Naples as you can get, though it's more a roundabout than a piazza, whose life you can watch while sipping a pricey drink on the terrace of the sleekly historic *Caffè Gambrinus*, just to the south. North of the square is the **Galleria Umberto I**, an impressive pair of glass-vaulted arcades intersecting at a 57m-high dome, erected in 1887 and modelled after Milan's Galleria Vittorio Emanuele II. It's currently under renovations after decades of neglect, though even with the scaffolding it's a magnificent sight. Across the square, **Piazza del Plebiscito** is a decent attempt to create a grand and symmetrical city-centre space, with matching palaces on either side and a curve of columns resembling Bernini's piazza for St Peter's in Rome. Its focal point, the church of **San Francesco di Paola**, is a copy of Rome's Pantheon – obvious once you're standing under its enormous dome.

The Castel Nuovo

Piazza del Municipio • Mon–Sat 8.30am–7pm • €6 • ☎ 081 795 7722

The brooding hulk of the **Castel Nuovo** – the "Maschio Angioino" – was erected in 1282 by the Angevins and later converted as the royal residence of the Aragon monarchs. The entrance incorporates a triumphal arch from 1454 that commemorates the taking of the city by Alfonso I, the first Aragon ruler, and shows details of his triumph topped by a rousing statue of St Michael. Inside the castle is the **civic museum**, housing within its first floor galleries a smattering of lesser works by Naples' most distinguished artists as well as the castle's original bronze doors from 1468. On the upper floor are some nice nineteenth-century scenes of Naples, but it's the views over the port from the upper terrace that steal the show. Accessed through the courtyard below, it's also worth glimpsing the **Sala dei Baroni**, a huge room with magnificent umbrella-ribbed vaults once covered in frescoes by Giotto, and the **Capella Palatina**, adorned with fourteenth- to sixteenth-century frescoes, Renaissance sculptures and a marble portal.

Teatro di San Carlo

Via S. Carlo 98 • Guided 45min tours daily at 10.30am, 11.30am, 12.30pm, 2.30pm, 3.30pm & 4.30pm • €9 • T 081 797 2468, W teatrosancarlo.it

Just beyond the castle, the **Teatro di San Carlo** is an oddly unimpressive building from the outside. But inside you can see why this theatre was the envy of Europe when it opened in 1737, in time for Charles of Bourbon's birthday, for whom it was built. Destroyed by fire in 1816 and quickly rebuilt, it's one of the largest opera houses in Italy and one of the most distinguished in the world. Tours take in the auditorium itself, backstage areas and the dressing rooms of the principal singers.

The Palazzo Reale

Piazza del Plebiscito • Mon, Tues & Thurs–Sun 9am–8pm • €6 • W palazzorealenapoli.it

The **Palazzo Reale** forms the fourth side of the Piazza del Plebiscito, and manages better than most of the buildings around here to retain some semblance of its former glories, though it's a bland, derivative building for the most part and even a bit of a fake, thrown up hurriedly in 1602 to accommodate Philip III on a visit here and never actually occupied by a monarch long term. Indeed it's more of a monument to monarchies than monarchs, with the various dynasties that ruled Naples by proxy for so long represented in the niches of the facade, from Roger the Norman to Vittorio Emanuele II, taking in among others Alfonso I and a slightly comic Murat on the way.

Upstairs, by way of an impressive white marble double-staircase, the palace's first-floor rooms are decorated with fine Baroque excesses – gilded furniture, trompe l'oeil ceilings, great overbearing tapestries, impressive French Empire pieces and lots and lots of quite creditable seventeenth- and eighteenth-century paintings, including works by Guercino, Carracci and Titian, as well as Flemish old masters. The best bits are the little theatre – the first room on the right – which is refreshingly restrained after the rest of the palace; the vast ballroom; and the terrace, which gives good views over the port and the Castel Nuovo. Look in also on the chapel, on the far side of the central courtyard, which has one of the city's biggest *presepi*, filled with mainly eighteenth-century figures – 210 in all.

Montesanto, La Sanità and Capodimonte

North of Via Toledo spreads the colourful district of **Montesanto**, focusing on the lively intersection of Piazza Pignasecca and the funicular station just beyond. On the right, **Piazza Dante** was designed by Luigi Vanvitelli during the eighteenth century and cuts an elegant semicircle around a graffitied statue of the poet. From here you can cut through the seventeenth-century **Port'Alba** into the old part of the city, or

push straight on up to the **La Sanità** quarter, whose name literally means "health" due to its position outside the walls of the old city. However, the real interest lies in between: at the city's fantastic **archeological museum**, situated at one end of the busy nineteenth-century triangle of **Piazza Cavour.** If you see only one orthodox Naples sight, make it this, though the **Museo Nazionale di Capodimonte**, up on the hill beyond, is a close second.

Museo Archeologico Nazionale

Piazza Museo 19 • Daily (except Tues) 9am–7.30pm • €12 • ⓣ 848 800 288, ⓦ museoarcheologiconapoli.it

Naples' **Museo Archeologico Nazionale** is home to the Farnese collection of antiquities from Lazio and Campania, the best of the finds from the nearby Roman sites of Pompeii and Herculaneum. It seems to be under almost constant reorganization, and some of the displays are tired and old-fashioned, but it's certainly one of the highlights of the city.

Ground floor

The **ground floor** of the museum has sculpture from the **Farnese collection**, displayed at its best in the mighty Great Hall, which holds imperial-era figures like the *Farnese Bull* and *Farnese Hercules* from the Baths of Caracalla in Rome – the former the largest piece of classical sculpture ever found. Don't miss *Ephesian Artemis*, an alabaster and bronze statue with rows of bulbous objects peeling off her chest – variously interpreted as breasts, eggs, bulls' scrota, dates or pollen sacs – and bees, mini-beasts and sphinxes adorning her lower half.

Campanian mosaics

The mezzanine floor holds the museum's collection of **Campanian mosaics** – remarkably preserved works that give a superb insight into ordinary Roman customs, beliefs and humour. Most were lifted from the villas of Pompeii, including a 5m-wide depiction of Alexander the Great battling Darius (no. 10020), an urbane meeting of the Platonic Academy (no. 124545), and a marvellously captured scene from a comedy – *The Consultation of the Fattucchiera* (no. 9987), with a soothsayer giving a dour and doomy prediction. At the far end of the hall, the fascinating **Gabinetto Segreto** (Secret Room) displays erotic material taken from the brothels, bathhouses and taverns of Pompeii and Herculaneum – languidly sensual wall paintings, preposterously phallic lamps and the like.

Campanian wall paintings

Upstairs is the cavernous **Gran Salone della Meridiana**, with its mesmerizing frescoed ceiling and fine assortment of Roman figures. It also displays a collection of colourful and inventive **Campanian wall paintings**, brought from Pompeii and Herculaneum, as well as works from the Sacrarium – part of Pompeii's Egyptian temple of Isis, the most celebrated mystery cult of antiquity. Look out, too, for a paternal *Achilles and Chirone* (no. 9109); the *Sacrifice of Iphiginia* (no. 9112), one of the best preserved of all the murals; and a group of four small pictures, the best of which is a depiction of a woman gathering flowers entitled *Allegoria della Primavera* – a fluid, impressionistic piece of work capturing both the gentleness of Spring and the graceful beauty of the woman.

Other Campanian finds

Beyond the murals are the actual **finds from the Campanian cities** – everyday items like glass, silver, ceramics, charred pieces of rope, even foodstuffs (petrified cakes, figs, fruit and nuts), together with a model layout of Pompeii in cork. On the other side of the first floor, there are finds from the **Villa dei Papiri** in Herculaneum – sculptures in

bronze mainly. The *Hermes at Rest* in the centre of the second room is perhaps the most arresting item, boyishly rapt and naked except for wings on his feet, while all around are other adept statues – a languid *Resting Satyr*, the convincingly woozy *Drunken Silenus* and a pair of youthful *Runners*.

The Egyptian Section

Hidden below the museum – down to the right from the ground floor's main staircase – is a trove of ancient **Egyptian artefacts**, re-opened in 2016 after six years of closure. There are more than two thousand items on display, spanning from the Old Kingdom to the Ptolemaic-Roman age. The most substantial portions were gathered by late eighteenth-century antiquarian Cardinal Stefano Borgia and early nineteenth-century and collector Giuseppe Picchianti, who spent six years exploring the Nile down to the Nubian desert. Perhaps most intriguing are its four human **mummies** and a mummified crocodile.

Santa Maria della Sanità and the Catacombe di San Gaudioso

Piazza Sanità 14 • Mon–Sun 10am–1pm; guided tours every hour • €9, including Catacombe di San Gennaro • T 081 744 3714, W catacombedinapoli.it

The church of **Santa Maria della Sanità**, on the piazza of the same name, is a Dominican church from the early seventeenth century whose design was based loosely on Bramante's for St Peter's in Rome. There are paintings by Giordano and other Neapolitan artists inside, although perhaps of more interest are the **Catacombe di San Gaudioso**, an intriguing, early Christian burial ground that's home to the fifth-century tomb of St Gaudioso, a bishop known as the "African", as he was from North Africa, and the final resting places of the Dominicans themselves, who were decapitated and buried sitting down.

Catacombe di San Gennaro

Via Tondo di Capodimonte 11 • Mon–Sat 10am–5pm, Sun 10am–2pm, guided tours every hour • €9, including Catacombe di San Gaudioso • T 081 744 3714, W catacombedinapoli.it • Bus #R4 from Via Toledo, or #178 from the Archeological Museum

Lifts link Sanità with Corso Amedeo up above, the main road up to Capodimonte, and you can walk up from here in ten minutes or so to another burial place, the **Catacombe di San Gennaro**, next door to the huge Madre del Buon Consiglio church, halfway up the hill to Capodimonte. This is a very different sort of catacomb, bigger and more open than San Gaudioso, and best known for being the final resting place of San Gennaro, whose body was brought here in the fifth century. There are some early Christian frescoes and mosaics, newly restored and amazingly bright.

Museo Nazionale di Capodimonte

Via Miano 2 • Daily (except Wed) 8.30am–7.30pm • €12; €16 combined with return shuttle; audioguides €5 • T 081 749 9111, W museocapodimonte.beniculturali.it • Bus #R4 from Via Toledo, #178 from the Archeological Museum, or Museo Capodimonte shuttle bus from Piazza Trieste e Trento & the Archeological Museum (one-way/return €5/8)

At the top of the hill, the **Palazzo Reale di Capodimonte** was the royal residence of the Bourbon King Charles III. Built in 1738, it now houses the picture gallery of the Naples museum, the superb **Museo Nazionale di Capodimonte**, arguably one of the best collections of art in the country, with many important works by Campanian and other, mainly Italian artists, as well as curious objets d'art and fine pieces of Capodimonte porcelain.

First floor

The three-storey museum is organized roughly chronologically, but also by its various collections, which were built up by the Borgia, Farnese and Bourbon rulers of the city. It begins on the **first floor** with the Farnese collection, and a grouping of

13

portraits of the Farnese pope, Paul III, by Titian, alongside the same artist's portrayal of Charles V and Philip II, which face his portrait of Alessandro Farnese and Andre del Sarto's glowering depiction of Leo X. Beyond are more works by Renaissance masters: Bellini's impressively coloured and composed *Transfiguration*; Lotto's odd *Madonna with St Peter*; Giulio Romano's dark and powerful *Madonna of the Cat*; Sebastiano del Piombo's haughty *Clement VII*; Marcello Venusti's small-scale 1549 copy of Michelangelo's *Last Judgement* – probably the only chance you'll get to see the painting this close up; and Titian's lascivious *Danaë*. There are also two rooms mainly devoted to the Carracci brothers, full of magnificent pieces like Annibale's *Mystical Marriage of St Catherine*.

If you have time to spare, take a walk around the **royal apartments** on this floor. They're kept much as they would have been in the eighteenth century, and high spots include the airy, mirrored ballroom, lined with portraits of various Bourbon monarchs and other European despots, and an entire room decked out entirely with dripping, colourful porcelain, sprouting three-dimensional Chinese scenes, monkeys, fruit and flowers.

Second floor

On the **second floor** are some outstanding Italian paintings from the fourteenth and fifteenth centuries, of which the most famous is *St Ludovic of Toulouse* by Simone Martini, a fascinating Gothic painting glowing with gold leaf. Elsewhere there are paintings that used to hang in Naples' churches: Niccolò Colantonio's *St Jerome in his Study* was painted for the altar of San Lorenzo Maggiore, and the same artist's *Deposition* used to hang in San Domenico Maggiore. Further on, Vasari's dramatic, almost snapshot-like *Presentation in the Temple* was done for the city's Monteoliveto church, and a series of smaller works by the same painter for the sacristry of San Giovanni Carbonara; while Titian's *Annuncation*, further on, was for the church of San Domenico Maggiore. The long series of rooms ends in fine style with one of Caravaggio's best-known works, his dark and brutal *Flagellation*, beyond which is the museum's collection of seventeenth- and eighteenth-century Neapolitan paintings, including a generally wonderful grouping of all the shining lights of the Neapolitan Baroque – Caracciolo, Ribera, the prolific Luca Giordano and later work by Francesco de Mura and Solimena. Finally, upstairs is a smattering of **twentieth-century works**, of which the most notable is a painting of an erupting *Vesuvius* by Andy Warhol.

Chiaia, Santa Lucia and Mergellina

Lined with the city's fanciest shops, **Via Chiaia** leads west from Piazza Trieste e Trento to the elegant circle of **Piazza dei Martiri** – named after the nineteenth-century revolutionary martyrs commemorated by the column in its centre. This part of town is the wealthy **Chiaia** neighbourhood, its buildings well preserved and displaying a sense of order and classical elegance. From Piazza dei Martiri, you can stroll down to the waterfront and **Villa Comunale**, Naples' most central city park, richly adorned with classical sculpture and the best place to appreciate the city's maritime side with views stretching right around the bay to the distinctive silhouette of Vesuvius in the east.

Galleria Borbonico

Vico del Grottone 4 • Standard tours Fri–Sun tours at 10am, noon, 3.30pm & 5.30pm (1hr) • ⓣ 081 764 5808, ⓦ galleriaborbonica.com

Accessed through an alley off Via Serra, a short stroll from Piazza del Plebescito, the **Galleria Borbonico** is really three sights in one: a tunnel built by the nervous king Ferdinand II in the 1850s as a means of escape from the Palazzo Reale; a series of cisterns used as the main water supply for this part of the city until the 1880s; and a series of bomb shelters from World War II which were fashioned out of the tunnel

and a number of disused cisterns. Among many things to see are a host of abandoned cars mainly from the 1940s and 1950s; the cisterns themselves, including the steps hollowed out of the rock that the "*pozzari*" or water attendants would use to get in and out; and the bomb shelters, full of moving graffiti written by the folk who once sheltered here.

There's a second entrance to the site inside the Parcheggo Morelli on Via Morelli, near Piazza Vittoria – you can arrive at either entrance for the tunnel **tours**. There's no need to reserve for the standard tour, but book ahead for the more adventurous options (see website for up-to-date schedules), which include rafting beneath the city through an abandoned metro tunnel and zip-lining above the old cisterns.

Castel dell'Ovo

Via Partenope • June–Sept Mon–Sat 9am–7.30pm, Sun 9am–2pm; Oct–May Mon–Sat 9am–6.30pm, Sun 9am–2pm • Free • ⓦ comune.napoli.it/casteldellovo

Down on the waterfront in the swanky **Santa Lucia** district, the grey mass of the **Castel dell'Ovo** or "egg-castle" takes its name from the legend that it was built over an egg placed here by Virgil in Roman times: it is believed that if the egg breaks, Naples will fall. Actually it was built by the Hohenstaufen king Frederick II and extended by the Angevins. There's not much to see or do inside; it's just a series of terraces and views, really. But the **views** are the best in town: a 360-degree panorama over the entire bay and back over Naples itself. When you're done you can go for drinks or dinner at one of the quayside restaurants in the **Borgo Marinaro** below.

Villa Comunale and around

The **Villa Comunale** park stretches around the bay for a good 1.5km and is a nice way to walk to Mergellina, particularly in the early evening when the city lights enhance the views. About halfway along the park on the inland side is the **Villa Pignatelli** (daily except Tues 8.30am–5pm; €5; ⓣ 081 761 2356, ⓦ polomusealenapoli.beniculturali.it), a museum that was once the home of a prominent Naples family and a meeting place for the city's elite in the nineteenth century. It's tastefully furnished and by Naples standards low-key, its handful of rooms holding books, porcelain, the odd painting and a set of photos signed by various aristocrats and royal personages. The northern side of the complex houses a collection of old carriages while there's a photography exhibit on the first floor, which also plays regular host to local cultural events.

Mergellina

At the far end of the Villa Comunale lie the harbour and main square – **Piazza Sannazzaro** – of the **Mergellina** district, a good place to eat at night and a terminus for hydrofoils to the bay's islands. The little church of **Santa Maria in Piedigrotta** (daily 9am–noon & 5–7pm; free), next door to the train station, is home to the Madonna that gets carried through the streets every September in one of the city's most popular festivals. Just behind the church is the **Parco Virgiliano a Piedigrotta** (mid-April to mid-Oct Mon & Wed–Sun 9am–7pm; mid-Oct to mid-April 10am–2.50pm; free), the starting point of a 700m-long Roman tunnel that was cut through the hillside.

Vomero

Vomero – the district topping the hill immediately above the old city – is one of Naples' more modern additions, a light, airy and relatively peaceful quarter connected with the teeming morass below by funicular railway. It's mostly residential, and you're unlikely to stray beyond the streets that fan out from each of the three funicular stations, centring on the grand symmetry of **Piazza Vanvitelli**. Come up on the Montesanto funicular and you're well placed for a visit to two of the buildings that dominate Naples, way above the old city.

13

Castel Sant'Elmo

Via Tito Angelini 22 • **Castle** Daily 8.30am–7.30pm • €5 • **Museum** Daily (except Tues) 9.30am–5pm • Entry included in castle ticket • ⓣ 081 229 4401, ⓦ polomusealecampania.beniculturali.it

Five minutes' walk from the funicular station, the **Castel Sant'Elmo** occupies Naples' highest point and is an impressive fortification, a fourteenth-century structure once used for incarcerating political prisoners and now lording it grandly over the streets below. Not surprisingly it has the very best views of Naples, and you can enjoy them from the top terrace of the castle before visiting the **Napoli Novecento** museum in the centre – a collection of painting and sculpture by Neapolitan artists from the early twentieth century to the 1980s.

Certosa San Martino

Largo S. Martino 5 • Daily (except Wed) 8.30am–7.30pm • €6 • ⓣ 081 229 4502, ⓦ polomusealecampania.beniculturali.it

Beyond Castel Sant'Elmo, the fourteenth-century **Certosa San Martino** has the next-best views over the bay and is home to the **Museo Nazionale di San Martino**. The views from its cunningly constructed terraced gardens are well worth the entrance fee alone but you also get to see the monastery's church, with a colourful pavement and an *Adoration of the Shepherds* by Reni above the altar, as well as works by some of the greats of Neaopolitan painters in most of the chapels and in the rooms off the high altar. In the museum proper, there are more paintings by Neapolitan masters – Ribera, Stanzione, Vaccaro – as well as sculpture by Pietro Bernini; the frescoed library and prior's apartments; and an unparalleled collection of *presepi* or Christmas cribs. The Baroque cloisters are lovely, too, though a little gone to seed, but they're surrounded by historical and maritime sections displaying models of ships, and documents, coins and costumes recording the era of the Kingdom of Naples.

Villa Floridiana

Via Cimarosa 77 • **Park & Gardens** Daily: April–Oct 8.30am–7pm; Nov–March 8.30am–5.15pm • Free • **Museum** Daily (except Tues) 8.30am–5pm • €4 • ⓣ 081 578 8418, ⓦ polomusealecampania.beniculturali.it

One of Vomero's most popular sights is the Neoclassical **Villa Floridiana**, close to the Chiaia funicular, whose lush grounds make a good place for a picnic. The **Museo Duca di Martina** is of fairly specialist interest, however, with a porcelain collection varying from the beautifully simple to the outrageously kitsch – teapots, ceramic asparagus sticks and the like. There are examples of Capodimonte and Meissen, and eighteenth-century English, French, German and Viennese work – as well as a few pieces of Qing Dynasty Chinese porcelain and Murano glass, and exquisite non-ceramic items like inlaid ivory boxes and panels.

ARRIVAL AND DEPARTURE NAPLES

By plane Naples' Capodichino airport (ⓣ 081 789 6259, ⓦ aeroportodinapoli.it) is about 7km north of the city centre. The official airport bus, Alibus, run by ANM (ⓣ 081 763 1111, ⓦ anm.it), connects with both Piazza Garibaldi (20min) and Piazza Municipio (30min), with departures every 20min from 6am–11.40pm (€5 from *tabacchi* or on board). Taxis take about as long as buses to reach the centre, and cost €18 between the airport and Garibaldi. There are also direct buses linking Sorrento (at least 8 daily; 1hr 20min; €10), operated by Curreri Viaggi (ⓦ curreriviaggi.it), and Salerno (1hr; €4–5.50), operated by Buonotourist (9 daily Mon–Sat; ⓦ buonobus.it) and Sita Sud (2–3 daily; ⓦ sitasudtrasporti.it).

By train The most-used station is Napoli Centrale, which welcomes roughly four hundred trains/day. It's on the edge of the city centre at one end of Piazza Garibaldi, which is the main hub for city and suburban transport services; there's a left luggage office at the station (daily 7am–8pm). Some trains also pull into Stazione Mergellina, on the opposite side of the city centre, which is connected with Piazza Garibaldi by the old metro (line 2).

Destinations Agropoli (18 daily; 1hr 20min); Benevento (4 direct daily; 8 daily via Caserta; 1hr 20min–2hr 20min); Caserta (every 15min; 35–45min); Foggia (8 daily; via Caserta 2hr 20min–3hr); Formia (roughly every 30min; 50min–1hr 15min); Rome (every 10–30min; 1hr 10min–2hr 30min); Salerno (every 20–30min; 40min–1hr 30min).

By bus City and suburban buses also stop on Piazza

Garibaldi. ATC (ⓦ atcbus.it), CTP (ⓦ ctp.na.it) and Angelino Bus (ⓦ angelinobus.it) all run buses to Caserta, and SITA (ⓣ 081 552 2176, ⓦ sitabus.it) connects with Pompeii, the Amalfi Coast and Salerno.

Destinations Amalfi (4 daily; 2hr); Bari (8 daily; 3hr); Benevento (12 daily; 1hr 40min); Caserta (every 20min; 40–50min); Pompeii (every 30min; 45min); Salerno (every 15–30min; 1hr 15min).

By ferry and hydrofoil Ferries – to the islands and other places in the Bay of Naples, including Sorrento, and along the Amalfi Coast – run from the Molo Beverello main ferry terminal, next to Piazza Municipio. In summer, departures are frequent enough for the main destinations that you can just show up at the port. Slow ferries generally depart from the adjacent Calata Porta di Massa, 200m to the north, while there are also a few hydrofoils departing from Mergellina. For updated schedules from each company, visit ⓦ inaples.it. Caremar (ⓣ 081 1896 6690, ⓦ caremar.it) and SNAV (ⓣ 081 428 5555, ⓦ snav.it) run ferries and hydrofoils to the islands, while Alilauro (ⓣ 081 497 2222, ⓦ alilauro.it) runs ferries to Ischia (departing from Mergellina) and Sorrento. SNAV and Tirrenia (ⓣ +49 6111 4020, ⓦ tirrenia.it) run to Sardinia and Sicily, while the Aeolian islands are linked by two weekly slow ferries run by Siremar (ⓣ 081 251 4721, ⓦ siremar.it) and fast ferries run by SNAV (June–early Sept only) – the latter departing from Mergellina.

Destinations Aeolian islands (June–early Sept 1–2 daily; ferry 13hr; hydrofoil 4hr 30min); Cagliari (2 weekly; 13hr 30min); Capri (every 30min in high season; 1hr–1hr 30min); Ischia (every 15–30min in high season; 40min–1hr); Palermo (2–3 daily in high season; 10–13hr); Procida (19 daily in high season; 35min–1hr); Sorrento (5 daily; 40min).

INFORMATION AND TOURS

Tourist offices There are two offices in the centre of the city: on Piazza del Gesù Nuovo (Mon–Sat 9am–5pm, Sun 9am–1pm; ⓣ 081 551 2701), and at Via S. Carlo 9, on the south side of Galleria Umberto I across from Teatro San Carlo (Mon–Sat 9am–5pm, Sun 9am–1pm; ⓣ 081 402 394). At each of them you can pick up a free city map, a decent free transport map and an English-language copy of the monthly *Qui Napoli* what's-on guide.

Tours CitySightseeing Napoli (ⓣ 055 901 938, ⓦ city-sightseeing.it/en/naples) operates a hop-on-hop-off service covering several routes around town (April–Oct; €23; tickets valid 24hr); tours leave from just in front of the Castel Nuovo.

GETTING AROUND

ON FOOT

The best way to get around central Naples is to walk. Driving can be a nightmare, and to negotiate the narrow streets, hectic squares and racetrack boulevards on a moped or scooter takes years of training. In any case, not to walk would mean you'd miss a lot – Naples is the kind of place best appreciated at street level.

BY PUBLIC TRANSPORT

Naples' transport system, most of which is run by ANM, is conveniently integrated. If you have a smartphone, download the Gira Napoli app for real-time updates on metro lines, buses and funiculars. For out-of-town trips – around the bay in either direction – or to get from one side of the centre to another, the Circumvesuviana and Cumana train lines are very useful, operated by EAV (ⓣ 081 1980 5000, ⓦ eavsrl.it).

Metro lines and city buses Though crowded and slow, buses will get you pretty much everywhere, but are most useful in areas where the *metropolitana* has yet to reach. The latter is generally the most useful way of getting around Naples (departures roughly every 9min 6am–11pm. Two urban lines are handy for visitors, each snaking across the city centre from Piazza Garibaldi. The older Line 2, run by Trenitalia, has three stops between Garibaldi and Mergellina before continuing on to Pozzuoli Solfatara. The newer Line 1, operated by ANM, has useful stops at Municipio (for the harbour), Toledo, Museo (beside the Museo Archeologico), Dante and Vanvitelli (for Vomero). When completed, this line will trace a full circle around the city, taking in the airport – the next station in the pipeline is the Duomo station,

NAPLES TRANSPORT TICKETS

TIC tickets (issued by UnicoCampania; ⓦ unicocampania.it) are valid on all city buses, metro lines and funiculars as well as the Circumvesuviana and Cumana lines (within Naples), and can be bought in advance from *tabacchi*, newsstands or metro stations. **Fares** cost a flat €1.60 for all journeys (valid 90min), or you can buy an all-day ticket (€4.50) or a weekly ticket (€16). Alternatively, the three-day or one-week Artecard (see page 748) includes select transport throughout the city and region, including the airport bus, island buses and beyond.

13

as evidenced by the construction chaos on Piazza Nicola Amore.

Funiculars Three funiculars scale the hill of the Vomero every 10min (daily 7am–10pm): the Funicolare di Chiaia (from Piazza Amedeo), the Funicolare Centrale (from the Augusteo station, just off the bottom end of Via Toledo) and the Funicolare di Montesanto (from the station on Piazza Montesanto). A fourth, the Funicolare di Mergellina, runs up the hill above Mergellina from Via Mergellina (same hours).

The Circumvesuviana This train service runs from Porta Nolana station, on Corso Garibaldi, just off Piazza Garibaldi, and from Napoli Centrale, right around Vesuvius and the southern part of the Bay of Naples (roughly every 30min), with stops in Ercolano (15min), Pompeii (35min), and at its southern end in Sorrento (1hr 10min).

The Ferrovia Cumana and Circumflegrea these two train lines both depart roughly every 15min from Piazza Montesanto: Cumana heads west along the coast to Bagnoli (15min) and Pozzuoli (25min), ending at Torregaveta (40min), while the Circumflegrea follows a more inland route from Montesanto to the same terminus.

BY TAXI

If you need to take a taxi make sure the driver switches on the meter when you start, or request a flat fare at the beginning of the journey (there are published rates to key locations that taxi drivers have to adhere to if requested); otherwise fares start at €3.50 for the initial journey, €6.50 after 10pm or on weekends. The minimum fare is €4.50. Note that certain journeys command a flat fare, for example between the airport and the train station (€18), Municipio (for ferry connections; €21) and Chiaia and Vomero (€23). There are taxi ranks at the train station, on Piazza Dante, Piazza del Gesù, Piazza Trieste e Trento, at Mergellina station and other places. Reliable numbers are ⓣ081 5522 5252, ⓣ081 570 7070, ⓣ081 0101, ⓣ081 2222 and ⓣ081 556 4444.

BY CAR

Unless you are picking up a rental car, driving in Naples should be avoided, particularly in the city centre, which is always congested and anarchic, even by Italian standards. Car rental companies include Avis (ⓣ081 780 5790); Europcar (ⓣ081 780 5643); Hertz (ⓣ081 231 1200); Maggiore (ⓣ081 780 3011); Sixt (ⓣ02 9475 7979).

ACCOMMODATION

Accommodation prices in Naples may come as a refreshing change after the north of Italy, but they're still not cheap, and you need to choose carefully from among the budget options around Piazza Garibaldi. A better bet is the lively and more atmospheric *centro storico*, with its good supply of boutique hotels and small B&Bs.

HOTELS AND B&BS

CENTRO STORICO AND PIAZZA GARIBALDI

Belle Arti Resort Via S. Maria di Costantinopoli 27 ⓣ081 557 1062, ⓦbelleartiresort.com; map p.747. Contemporary design meets historic elegance at this boutique B&B near Piazza Bellini. Rooms are individually decorated with modern artworks and some have original seventeenth-century ceiling frescoes. **€75**

Caravaggio Piazza Riario Sforza 157 ⓣ081 211 0066, ⓦcaravaggiohotel.it; map p.747. Right in the thick of things on the edge of Forcella, just around the corner from the Duomo, but quiet enough, on its own small square – which some of the nicer rooms in this elegant old *palazzo* overlook. **€110**

★ **Costantinopoli 104** Via S. Maria di Costantinopoli 104 ⓣ081 557 1035, ⓦcostantinopoli104.it; map p.747. A contemporary boutique hotel with its own garden and small swimming pool in a secluded location at the back of a Piazza Bellini *palazzo*. Some of the rooms open onto the garden, others on the upstairs terrace. Very peaceful, but also very convenient. **€230**

Donna Regina B&B Via L. Settembrini 80 ⓣ081 446 799, ⓦdiscovernaples.net; map p.747. Inside the former Donnaregina convent, each room of this welcoming B&B is spacious and uniquely decorated. There's art all over the walls and a lovely terrace off a communal kitchen where Neapolitan dinners are served on request. **€95**

Il Convento Via Speranzella 137/A ⓣ081 403 997, ⓦhotelilconvento.com; map p.747. Situated in the Quartieri Spagnoli, just a couple of blocks from Via Toledo, this three-star has decent, cosy rooms with tiny balconies and a couple of suites with their own roof terraces (€170). **€105**

Palazzo Caracciolo Via Carbonara 112 ⓣ081 016 0111, ⓦaccorhotels.com.com; map p.747. Only 2min from Piazza Garibaldi and handy for the *centro storico*, this place is a bit of a haven from the noisy streets outside; it's a conversion of a venerable old palace with lovely, peaceful courtyards and very comfortable rooms in contemporary style. **€120**

★ **Piazza Bellini** Via S. Maria di Costantinopoli 101 ⓣ081 451 732, ⓦhotelpiazzabellini.com; map p.747. Stylish yet unpretentious and friendly contemporary hotel housed in a light-flooded high-ceilinged Renaissance *palazzo*, a short walk from both the archeological museum and Spaccanapoli. There's a big courtyard, and 48 spacious rooms with unfussy custom-designed furniture – the best have huge terraces looking over the city to Vesuvius. **€130**

Pizzasleep Piazzetta Sant'Alfonso e Sant'Antonio a Tarsia 11/G ⓣ081 549 6766, ⓦpizzasleepbeb.it; map p.747. Set in a peaceful neighbourhood a short walk to the west of Piazza Dante, this welcoming, family-run B&B

UNDERGROUND ART

Even if you aren't taking a ride, it's worth descending to some of the metro stations along Line 1, comprising the *Stazioni dell'Arte* (Art Stations), which hold permanent modern art installations. The Toledo station is the most striking, its wavy blue walls reflecting the natural light that finds its way down a deep, smooth crater in the ceiling – Robert Wilson's Crater de Luz. At Dante, just one stop to the north, are floor-to-ceiling mosaics by Nicola De Maria, while the next station, **Museo**, houses classical statues from the nearby Archeological Museum. Some stops cleverly incorporate chance archeological finds inevitably made during the metro's construction, such as the Aragonese walls at Toledo and the ancient Roman port at **Municipio**. At the ultra-futuristic **Garibaldi** station, designed by Dominique Perrault, you'll find a pair of installations by Michelangelo Pistoletto, while the tech-themed **Università** station is adorned with the vivid art of Karim Rashid.

somehow manages to tastefully incorporate a pizza theme, using refurbished bits and bobs from local pizzerias. Each of the three well-appointed rooms is bright and airy with a pleasant balcony overlooking Vesuvius and the harbour. **€70**

Romeo Via Cristoforo Colombo 45 ☎081 6041 580, ⓦromeohotel.it; map p.747. A standout building on this grungy stretch of the waterfront opposite the cruise-ship terminal, the *Romeo* is the ultimate Naples boutique hotel, complete with weird-looking furniture and a range of very well appointed rooms, the best with views over the bay (€480). Even better views from the ninth storey pool, bar and Michelin-starred restaurant. **€420**

SANTA LUCIA, CHIAIA AND MERGELLINA

Ausonia Via Caracciolo 11 ☎081 682 278, ⓦhotel ausonianapoli.it; map p.744. A two-star hotel decorated to give the impression you're on a yacht, neatly placed in Mergellina, next to the stop for hydrofoils to Ischia and the Pontine islands. **€85**

Cappella Vecchia 11 Vicolo S. Maria a Cappella Vecchia 11 ☎081 240 5117, ⓦcappellavecchia11.it; map p.744. Just off Piazza dei Martiri, this small B&B has six simple but brightly furnished en-suite rooms, some with balconies. A warm welcome, too, from the young, friendly owners. **€110**

Miramare Via N. Sauro 24 ☎081 764 7589, ⓦhotel miramare.com; map p.744. A great location on the waterfront a little way down from the Palazzo Reale, this Art Nouveau gem is a good alternative to the giant, less personal palaces nearby, with a more homely feel and warmer welcome as well as a good breakfast buffet served on the rooftop. Deluxe rooms with front seaviews cost €280. **€220**

★ **Palazzo Alabardieri** Via Alabardieri 38 ☎081 415 278, ⓦpalazzoalabardieri.it; map p.744. In the heart of Chiaia, this hotel is geared towards business travellers and discerning tourists looking for luxury and courteous service. The well-appointed rooms are decorated with parquet floors, marble and rich fabrics. **€190**

★ **Rex** Via Palepoli 12 ☎081 764 9389, ⓦhotel-rex.it; map p.744. In a striking Art Nouveau-style building designed by the renowned Italian architect Coppedè, this family-run hotel in Santa Lucia has some of the friendliest staff around. It has simple but clean rooms and a large sitting room in the reception area, frequented by the owner's family and friends. **€110**

★ **San Francesco al Monte** Corso Vittorio Emanuele 328 ☎081 423 9111, ⓦsanfrancescoalmonte.it; map p.744. Occupying a commanding position on the slopes leading up to Vomero, not far from the funicular, this converted sixteenth-century monastery is an exceptional hotel – each of the 45 rooms is beautifully decorated with panoramic views of the city. There's a pool, bar, tranquil gardens and three restaurants in the grounds. **€250**

HOSTELS

Hostel Mancini Via Mancini 33 ☎081 200 800, ⓦhostelmancininaples.com; map p 744. A few minutes' walk from the train station and the Forcella district's famous pizzerias, this good value hostel offers tidy, all-a/c dorms and private rooms, helpful staff, a small communal kitchen and a balcony overlooking the rough streets. Dorms **€25**, doubles **€70**

★ **Hostel of the Sun** Via Melisurgo 15 ☎081 420 6393, ⓦhostelnapoli.com; map p.747. Just off the main waterfront, this is perhaps the best hostel in the city, with a range of a/c dorms and nicely furnished doubles, a cosy common area and bar, free communal dinners on Tues and Thurs, and plenty of its own well-priced tours on offer. It's also well placed for going out, and there's no curfew. Breakfast included. Dorms **€24**, doubles **€65**

La Controra Piazzetta Trinità della Cesarea 231 ☎081 549 4014, ⓦlacontrora.com; map p.744. A 5min walk downhill from the Salvator Rosa metro stop and a 15min walk uphill from Montesanto station, this welcoming hostel centres around a peaceful garden, hidden away from the noise of the busy street. Rooms and dorms are all a/c and clean, and there's a communal kitchen and bar that's great for meeting fellow travellers – perhaps less so for those trying to sleep. Dorms **€20**, doubles **€65**

Neapolitan Trips Hostel Via dei Fiorentini 10 ☎081

13

551 8977, neapolitantrips.com; map p.747. Well-situated between the port and Via Toledo, this cavernous new hostel has fifteen large, a/c dorms, a bar, and cosy common areas inside and out on a big, sofa-decked terrace. Breakfast costs an extra €3.50, while guests have free access to the kitchen and its basic food supplies. They also run a spotless B&B and hotel on the upper floors. Dorms €20, doubles €57

EATING

Neapolitan cuisine consists of simple dishes cooked with fresh, healthy ingredients (see page 743). As Naples is not primarily a tourist-geared city, most restaurants are family-run places used by locals and as such generally serve good food at very reasonable prices. There's no better place in Italy to eat pizza, at a solid core of almost obsessively unchanging places that still serve only the (very few) traditional varieties, and you're never far from a food stall for delectable snacks on the move at one of the city's many *friggitorie*.

CAFÉS, SNACKS AND GELATERIE

Attanasio Vico Ferrovia 1-4, off Via Milano sfogliatelleattanasio.it; map p.744. Around the corner from the bus station at Piazza Garibaldi, this well-known bakery specializes in delectable *sfogliatelle* (ricotta-stuffed pastries). Tues–Sun 6.30am–7.30pm.

Chalet Ciro Via Caracciolo 1–2 chaletciro.it; map p.744. This Mergellina institution is known for its *babà* and other pastries as well as delicious ice cream. Its marathon opening hours make it a dependable early morning or after-dinner pit stop for sweets. Mon, Tues & Thurs–Sun 7am–2.30am.

Gambrinus Via Chiaia 1–2 grancaffegambrinus.com; map p.747. The oldest and best-known Neapolitan café, founded in 1861, *Gambrinus* was once a gathering place for the city's artists and intellectuals. It's not cheap, but the aura of chandeliered gentility – and outside seating on Piazza Trieste e Trento – make it worth a visit. Daily 7am–1am.

Gay Odin Via Benedetto Croce 61 gay-odin.it; map p.747. One of nine locations around town, the century-old Spaccanapoli branch of this long-established chocolatier also sells decadent ice cream. Daily 10am–8.30pm.

★ **Remy Gelo** Via F. Galiani 9; map p.744. Two minutes off Via Caracciolo, near the hydrofoil terminal in Mergellina, this little shop has served up superb ice creams and *granite* since 1919. Mon–Fri 10am–10pm, Sat & Sun 10am–midnight.

Scaturchio Piazza S. Domenico; map p.747. Another elegant old Naples standard, this café has been serving coffee and pastries in the heart of Spaccanapoli for decades. Daily 7am–10pm.

Vaco 'e Presse Piazza Dante 84 081 549 9424; map p.747. True to its name ("I'm in a hurry"), this *friggitoria* on Via Toledo sells cheap, delicious Neapolitan street food like *zeppole* (fried doughballs) and *arancini* (rice balls) to a hungry university crowd. Mon–Fri 7am–9pm, Sat 7am–11.30pm.

RESTAURANTS AND PIZZERIAS

CENTRO STORICO AND PIAZZA GARIBALDI

D'è Figliole Via Giudecca Vecchia 39 081 286 721; map p.747. Hole-in-the-wall pizzeria right in the heart of Forcella, with a tiny menu of fried pizzas (€5–6) – a Neapolitan speciality – that hasn't changed much since 1860. Mon–Fri 10.30am–2.30pm & 4.30–10.30pm, Sat 10.30am–2.30pm & 4.30–midnight.

★ **Da Michele** Via Cesare Sersale 1–3 081 553 9204, damichele.net; map p.747. Considered one of Italy's best, *Da Michele* is certainly the most traditional pizzeria in Naples. Tucked away off Corso Umberto I in the Forcella district, it offers just two varieties (allegedly the only two worth eating) – Marinara and Margherita – for €4 or €5. Arrive early to beat the crowds – they sometimes run out of dough. Mon–Sat 11am–10.30pm.

★ **Da Nennella** Vico Lungo Teatro Nuovo 103–105 081 414 338; map p.747. This humble trattoria is a local favourite deep in the old Spanish Quarter, and a riot of Neapolitan charm, where the playful comedian waiters and occasional stand-up performances by the owner can ignite the entire dining room with laughter. Though perhaps not the main attraction, the food is good and the daily menu a bargain (€12 including wine). Mon–Sat noon–4pm & 7pm–midnight.

Di Matteo Via dei Tribunali 94 081 455 262, pizzeriadimatteo.com; map p.747. One of the best and most famous pizzerias in the city, a bit low on atmosphere, but the enormous, mouth-watering pizzas (from €4) more than make up for it – when Bill Clinton was in town, this is where he came to sample proper Neapolitan pizza. Mon–Sat 9am–midnight, Sun 9am–4pm.

★ **I Decumani** Via dei Tribunali 58–61 081 557 1309, pizzeriadecumani.it; map p.747. One of several excellent pizzerias along this stretch and commonly recognized as among Naples' best. The *fritti misti* are a must, as are the huge, delicious pizzas, which average €4–5, although prices start at €3 for a Marinara. Tues–Sun noon–4pm & 7pm–midnight.

★ **La Cantina di Via Sapienza** Via Sapienza 40–41 081 459 078; map p.747. Proprietor Gaetano's no-nonsense food and service draws a busy lunch crowd to feast on hearty home-cooked classics like *polpette* (meatballs; €6) and a staggering array of seasonal vegetable side dishes. Two courses cost €10–12. Mon–Sat noon–3pm.

Mimì alla Ferrovia Via A. d'Aragona 21 081 57 6883; map p.744. A real old-fashioned bustling restaurant and

something of a haven in the none-too-desirable streets off Piazza Garibaldi. The walls are adorned with pictures of celebrity diners – from Maradona to Fellini – and there's good traditional Neapolitan food at reasonable prices; pasta from €6, and mains from €10. Mon–Sat noon–3pm & 7–11pm.

Osteria da Carmela Via Conte di Ruovo 11/12 ⓣ081 549 9738, ⓦosteriadacarmela.it; map p.747. Next door to the Teatro Bellini, this is just one room, serving variations on traditional Neapolitan cuisine – great fish, excellent antipasti and tasty pasta and meat, too (seafood risotto €12), in an intimate and friendly setting. Mon–Sat 11.45am–3.30pm & 7–11.45pm; also open Sun May & Dec; closed most of Aug.

Sorbillo Via dei Tribunali 32 ⓣ081 446 643, ⓦsorbillo.it; map p.747. In business since 1935, this place has a cult following and is a scrum most nights – you may have to give your name and wait for a table. The pizzas (from €3.80) are great and made from the highest-quality ingredients. Mon–Sat noon–3.30pm & 7pm–11.30pm.

★ **Tandem Ragù** Via G. Paladino 51 ⓣ081 1900 2468, ⓦtandem.napoli.it; map p.747. Run by a young and hip team, this new restaurant just off Spaccanapoli prides itself on an old Neapolitan specialty: slow-cooked, flavoursome ragù – served in pastas (from €6) and bowls with bread for dipping (€5). Alternatively, pick up a delicious meatball sandwich (€4) at their nearby takeaway branch around the block at Via Mezzocannone 75 (and open until 3am on weekends). Daily 12.30–3.30pm & 7–11.30pm.

CHIAIA, SANTA LUCIA, MERGELLINA AND VOMERO

Acunzo Via D. Cimarosa 60–62 ⓣ081 578 5362, ⓦacunzo1964.it; map p.744. Family-run since 1936, this low-key trattoria and wood-oven pizzeria is set just off Piazza Vanvitelli near to the Centrale and Chiaia, with good pastas (from €8) and perhaps Vomero's best pizzas (margherita €5.50). There are dozens to choose from. Daily 1–3.30pm & 7–11.30pm.

Cavoli Nostri Via Palepoli 32 ⓣ081 1948 5739 ⓦcavolinostriveg.com; map p.744. Sleek, modern all-veg restaurant in the heart of Santa Lucia, with friendly service and a fresh, creative menu including pasta with seaweed and pistachio (€9); quinoa burgers €9). Save room for the soy-milk tiramisu (€5), which is surprisingly convincing. Mon–Sat noon–3.30pm & 7–11.45pm, Sun noon–4.30pm & 7–11.45pm.

★ **Da Dora** Via Palasciano 30 ⓣ081 680 519, ⓦristorantedora.it; map p.744. Not cheap, but perhaps the best place in the city to eat seafood and fish. One room, more or less, tiled and decorated in nautical fashion, and presided over by the implacable Dora in her pink pinny, who serves up wonderful seafood *linguine* (€24) and mixed fried fish. Three-course menus for €40. Mon 8pm–midnight, Tues–Sat 12.30pm–4pm & 8pm–midnight, Sun 12.30–4pm; closed Aug.

Da Ettore Via S. Lucia 56 ⓣ081 764 0498; map p.744. In the heart of Santa Lucia, this casual and lively neighbourhood restaurant is famous for its *pagnotielli* (*calzone* stuffed with mozzarella, ham and mushrooms; €8–9), and there is a wide selection of pizza (from €7) plus traditional pasta dishes, too. Mon–Sat noon–3pm & 7pm–midnight.

Marino Via S. Lucia 118 ⓣ081 764 0280; map p.744. A warm and welcoming family-style place in Santa Lucia with good pizzas (margherita €5) and reliable Neapolitan dishes like *scialatielli* (long, home-made pasta) with aubergine, tomato and mozzarella (€8). Tues–Sun noon–3.30pm & 7.30–11.30pm.

DRINKING

Enoteca Belledonne Vico Belledonne a Chiaia 18 ⓣ081 403 162, ⓦenotecabelledonne.it; map p.744. Right in the heart of the Chiaia bar scene, this unpretentious *enoteca* serves an exhaustive collection of Italian wines and delicious selections of cheeses and *salumi* – and without the full-on noise of its nearby rivals. Mon 4.30pm–2am, Tues–Sat 10am–1.30pm & 4.30pm–2am, Sun 7pm–2am.

Intra Moenia Piazza Bellini 70; map p.747. One of several trendy haunts on Piazza Bellini, where tables spread across the square, this is a lovely place to sit and read under the wisteria on a sunny day, or for an early evening *aperitivo*. Daily 10am–2am.

Seventy Via Bisignano 19 ⓣ081 1956 6482; map p.744. There's a decent early-evening buffet at this cosy, wood-panelled lounge bar, decked with vintage, flea-market couches and playing thumping garage to a cool or just plain hungry clientele. Mon–Sat 6.30pm–2.30am.

Vinarium Vicolo S. Maria a Cappella Vecchia 7 ⓣ081 764 4114, ⓦvinariumnapoli.it; map p.744. Busy wine bar just off Piazza dei Martiri that has a good selection of wines and serves food from an ever-changing menu. Mon–Fri noon–3.30pm & 7pm–1.30am, Sat & Sun 7pm–1.30am.

Kestè Via Largo S. Giovanni Maggiore Pignatelli 27 ⓣ081 781 0034, ⓦkeste.it; map p.747. Laid-back bar and café that spills onto a square just west of the university. Go early for the *aperitivo* buffet and stay for the band or DJ set. Mon–Thurs & Sun 6pm–1.30am, Fri & Sat 6pm–3am; closed Aug.

NIGHTLIFE AND ENTERTAINMENT

Neapolitan **nightlife** is largely concentrated in two neighbourhoods – the *centro storico* and the Chiaia district,

13

FOOTBALL IN NAPLES

Football is something of a religion in Naples, and support for the local side, **Napoli**, reached its pinnacle in the 1987 season when they won the *scudetto* with Diego Maradona as their star player. Since then the team dropped down two divisions after going bankrupt, but have since been rescued by movie mogul Aurelio De Laurentiis and are thriving in the top flight. The club plays at the **Stadio di San Paolo** in Fuorigrotta; take the Ferrovia Cumana from Montesanto to Mostra and the stadium is right in front of you. You can also take Line 2 of the metro – the stadium is a five-minute walk from the Napoli Campi Flegri stop. Match tickets are available from the windows on the ground floor, and cost from around €40 for seats in the end stands or "Curve" and up to around €100 for the side or "Tribuna" stands.

with the latter in particular a buzzing concentration of bars and clubs well into the small hours – though many clubs close down for the summer from June to Sept, when they move out around the bay to Posillipo, Bacoli, Fusaro or Pozzuoli. For **listings** of Naples nightlife, pick up *Zero* (ⓦ zero.eu), a free monthly publication available in bars.

Bourbon Street Via Bellini 52/53 ⓣ 338 825 3756, ⓦ bourbonstreetjazzclub.com; map p.747. A premier venue for Italian and international jazz acts, bringing a slice of New Orleans to the heart of Naples' *centro storico*. Sept–May Tues–Sun 8pm–4am.

DIRECTORY

Consulates US, Piazza della Repubblica 2 (ⓣ 081 583 8111).

Hospital To call an ambulance, dial ⓣ 118. The most central hospitals with A&E departments are Ascalesi, Via Egiziaca Forcella 31 (ⓣ 081 254 2111); Cardarelli, Via Cardarelli 9 (ⓣ 081 747 1111); and Santa Maria di Loreto Nuovo, Via Vespucci 15 (ⓣ 081 254 2111).

Pharmacies The pharmacy at Napoli Centrale is open 24hr and there's a list of those open at night in the newspaper *Il Mattino*.

Police ⓣ 112 or ⓣ 113; you can speak to an operator in English. The main police station (Questura) is at Via Medina 5 (ⓣ 081 794 1111); you can also report crimes at the small police station in the Stazione Centrale. To report the theft of a car, call ⓣ 081 794 1435.

Post office The main post office is in the enormous building on Piazza Matteotti, just off Via Toledo (Mon–Fri 8.20am–7.05pm, Sat 8.20am–12.35pm).

The Bay of Naples

Naples spreads right around its **bay** in an almost unbroken ribbon of docks, housing and development whose appeal is hard to discern, and only really becomes apparent the further away from the city you get. It's one of the most geologically unstable regions in the world, a fact that becomes obvious west of the city, where volcanic craters, hot springs and fumaroles make up the area known as the **Campi Flegrei**, the Phlegrean Fields of classical times, a mysterious place in turn mythologized by Homer and Virgil as the entrance to Hades. These days most of the mystery is gone – like most of the bay, the presence of Naples dominates in the form of new, mostly illegal, construction – and much of the volcanic activity is extinct, or at least dormant. But parts of the area still retain some of the doomy associations that first drew the ancients here, and there are some substantial remains of their presence at **Pozzuoli**, **Baia** and **Cumae**. In the opposite direction, the coast east from Naples is even more built up, the Circumvesuviana train edging out through derelict industrial buildings and dense housing that squeezes ever closer to the track. Most people come here for the ancient sights of **Herculaneum** and **Pompeii**, or to scale **Vesuvius** – or they skip the lot for the resort town of **Sorrento**. All are easy day-trips, and Sorrento, though overdeveloped, is worth a little more time and makes a good springboard for the Amalfi Coast.

Pozzuoli

As you head west, the first town that can really be considered free of Naples' sprawl is **POZZUOLI**, which sits on a stout promontory jutting out from the slender crescent of volcanic hills behind. Aside from being the hometown of screen goddess Sophia Loren, it's not a particularly glamorous place, though scattered around and underneath the town are some striking and worthwhile remnants of its heyday as the main port of the Roman Empire (up until Emperor Trajan expanded the port of Ostia). Most visitors, however, only stay long enough to catch a ferry to the islands of Procida and Ischia.

Rione Terra

Largo Sedile di Porta • Tours Sat & Sun (40min) 11am, noon, 2.20pm & 4.20pm • €5 • ⓣ 081 853 0626, ⓦ associazionenemea.it • Entrance is above tourist office, off Via Marconi

Buried within the hill on the south side of the port, the **Rione Terra** is a vast and ongoing excavation site, offering an accessible look at the old Roman town – complete with streets, taverns, apartments, cisterns, brothels and public terraces overlooking the sea. The tour ends up just outside the entrance to the baroque **Cathedral of San Procolo** (Sat 10am–noon & 5.30–7.30pm, Sun 10am–1pm & 5.30–7.30pm; free), which incorporates the massive Corinthian columns of a much earlier Temple of Augustus as well as the foundations of the *Capitoleum*, an even earlier Roman temple dedicated to the triad of Jupiter, Juno and Minerva.

Temple of Serapide

Beyond the Cumana station, between Via Roma and Via Sacchini, just east of the port, the so-called **Temple of Serapide** sits enclosed within a small park, often flooded in winter, but otherwise accessible. Its name derives from the unearthing here of a statue of the Pluto-esque Egyptian god, *Serapis Enthroned* (now in the Naples archeological museum), but in fact the structure has since proved to be not a temple but a richly embellished produce market from the first to the third centuries AD, one of the largest known to have been excavated.

Anfiteatro Flavio

Via Terracciano 75 • Mon & Wed–Sun 9am–1hr before sunset • €4 combined ticket with Cumae, Parco Archeologico and Museo Archeologico in Baia (valid 48hr)

A five-minute walk above the town centre, Pozzuoli's best-known sight is the **Antifeatro Flavio**, which was at one time the third largest Roman amphitheatre in Italy, holding some twenty thousand spectators. It was here that the patron saint of Naples, San Gennaro, is said to have been thrown to the lions. As the story goes, he survived the ordeal before being promptly taken to **Solfatara** (see below) and decapitated. The amphitheatre is still reasonably intact, though visitors are not allowed on the seating area: the subterranean chambers for gladiators and wild beasts are especially complete, and lying around everywhere is an abundance of beautifully carved architectural fragments.

Solfatara

ⓦ vulcanosolfatara.it/en

Just north of town (a ten-minute walk uphill from the *metropolitana* station), the **Solfatara** offers the most dramatic evidence of the volcanic nature of the Pozzuoli area, the exposed crater of a semi-extinct volcano that hasn't erupted for a couple of thousand years; in fact, it was a major tourist attraction in Roman times, too. Not surprisingly, it's a weird place: sulphur fumes rise from the rocks, fumaroles and mud pools, and the grey-yellow ground is hot to the touch (and sounds hollow underfoot), emitting eerily silent – and pungent – jets of steam. In the 1800s some of the fumaroles were covered with brick, creating an almost unbearably warm, sauna-like environment into which you can bend if you can stand it, while others are

13

just left open. At the time of writing, the site was closed indefinitely for renovations, though you can still glimpse the steaming crater by following the narrow road up to the left of the entrance.

ARRIVAL AND INFORMATION — POZZUOLI

By train You can get to Pozzuoli from Naples on the *metropolitana* (Line 2), or on the Ferrovia Cumana line from Montesanto station; both take about 20min. Pozzuoli's Cumana station is in the centre of town, not far from the Temple of Serapide, while its *metropolitana*/FS station is situated above the main town, off Via Solfatara, a 10min walk from the port – so is better if you're just going to see the Solfatara.

By bus Bus #M1B runs direct to Pozzuoli from Piazzale Tecchio in Naples' Fuorigrotta district, stopping right outside the Solfatara before descending to the town centre.

Tourist office A little east of the port at Piazza Matteotti 1 (June–Oct daily Mon–Fri 9am–7pm, Nov–May Mon–Sat 9am–3pm; ☎ 081 526 6639, ⓦ infocampiflegrei.it).

ACCOMMODATION AND EATING

Bobo Via Cristoforo Colombo 20 ☎ 081 526 2034, ⓦ ristorantebobo.com. Moderate- to high-priced harbourside restaurant which does great fish and has an excellent wine list. Try the pasta with sea urchins or mussels and zucchini (€18). Mon & Wed–Fri 8–11.45pm, Sat & Sun noon–4pm & 7–11.45pm.

Darsena Via Magazzini 35/37 ☎ 081 303 1281, ⓦ hoteldarsenapozzuoli.it. Just a short walk from the ferry terminal with clean, simply furnished rooms, some with views over the harbour. Discounted parking about 1km away (€10 including free transfer). €70

Baia

The next town along from Pozzuoli is **BAIA**, a small port with a set of imperial-era Roman ruins piling up on the hill above. This was one of the bay's most favoured spots in Roman times, a trendy resort at which all the most fashionable of the city's patricians had villas: the Emperor Hadrian died here in 138 AD and Nero was rumoured to have murdered his mother in Baia.

Parco Archeologico delle Terme di Baia

Via Sella di Baia 22 • Tues–Sun 9am–1hr before sunset • €4 combined ticket with Cumae, Museo Archeologico and Anfiteatro Flavio di Pozzuoli • ☎ 081 868 7592

Baia's extensive and evocative **Parco Archeologico delle Terme di Baia** lies at the top of a flight of steps off the main street. It consists of a collection of buildings from various eras – from the first century BC to the third century AD – and is quiet even in season, with plenty of shade and seats to rest on. Structured across several levels, it has a central villa with the remains of baths on either side. The villa has a series of rooms arched around a central fountain and what would have been a large courtyard below, around which you can see traces of frescoes and, beyond, a well-preserved stretch of mosaic floor. Beyond here is a small baths complex but the real treat lies on the other side, through an arched corridor – a wonderfully intact, domed frigidarium from the first century BC, water-filled and hauntingly atmospheric in the filtered sunlight.

Museo Archeologico

Via Castello 39 • Tues–Sun 9am–2.30pm • €4 combined ticket with Parco Archeologico, Cumae and Anfiteatro Flavio di Pozzuoli • ☎ 081 081 523 3797

Many of the finds from Baia and around are in the **Museo Archeologico**, housed in part of the town's mammoth fifteenth-century Aragon castle, a fifteen-minute walk up the main road towards Bacoli. Among the displays here is a *sacellum* – a shrine dedicated to the imperial cult – from the forum of ancient Misenum on Capo Miseno, rebuilt here on the ground floor, and a *nymphaeum* or monumental fountain, partially reconstructed on the top floor.

Cumae

Further up the coast from Baia, the town of **Cumae** was the first Greek colony on the Italian mainland, a source of settlers for other colonies (Naples was originally settled by Greeks from Cumae) and a centre of Hellenistic civilization. Later it was home to the so-called Cumaean Sibyl, from whom Tarquinius purchased the Sibylline Books that laid down the laws for the Republic. The **site**, a short walk from the bus stop at Via Monte di Cuma 3 (daily 9am–1hr before sunset; €4 combined ticket with Parco Archeologico, Museo Archeologico and Anfiteatro Flavio; ⓣ081 804 0430), is spread over a large area and not at all comprehensively excavated. But the only part you're likely to want to see forms a tight nucleus close to the entrance.

Grotto of the Sibyl

The best-known feature is the **Grotto of the Sibyl**, a long, dark corridor that was home to the most famous of the ancient oracles. The cave is rectangular in shape, with light admitted from a series of openings in the western wall; the Sibyl used to dispense her wisdom from the three large chambers at the far end of the 12m passageway, the most famous occasion being when Aeneas came here to consult her – an event recorded by the lines of Virgil posted up either side of the entrance.

The acropolis and temple to Jupiter

Steps lead up from the Sibyl's cave to the main part of the site, where the Via Sacra winds past a belvedere on the left and the scanty remains of a temple of Apollo at the centre of Cumae's old **acropolis** on the right. Keep going and you'll find the remains of a **temple to Jupiter** at the summit of the hill, with tremendous views south across the shellfish-filled **Lago Fusaro** and the bottom corner of the coast; and, if you clamber down from the far side of the temple, north up the curving coast to the Gulf of Gaeta.

Herculaneum

Daily: April–Oct 8.30am–7.30pm; Nov–March 8.30am–5pm • €11, combined ticket for four sites including Pompeii valid 3 days, €22 • ⓣ 081 777 7008, ⓦ ercolano.beniculturali.it

East of Naples the first real point of any interest is the town of **Ercolano**, the modern offshoot of the ancient site of **Herculaneum**, which was destroyed by the eruption of Vesuvius on August 24, 79 AD, and is situated at the seaward end of Via IV Novembre, straight ahead when exiting the Circumvesuviana station. In its heyday, Herculaneum was a residential town, much smaller than Pompeii, and as such it makes a more manageable site, more easily taken in on a single visit.

Cardo III

Because Herculaneum wasn't a commercial town, there was no central open space or forum, just streets of villas and shops, cut as usual by two very straight main thoroughfares that cross in the centre. Start your tour just inside the site entrance at the bottom end of **Cardo III**, where you'll see the **House of the Argus** (Casa d'Argo) on the left, a very grand building, judging by its once-impressive courtyard. However, this is dwarfed by the so-called **Hotel** (Casa del Albergo) across the street, which covers a huge area – you can get a true impression of its size from the rectangle of stumpy columns that made up its atrium. At the street's far end, the **College of the Augustales** (Sede degli Augustali), once a centre dedicated to the imperial cult, has well-preserved wall paintings depicting Hercules.

DISCOVERING HERCULANEUM

The **site of Herculaneum** was discovered in 1709, when a well-digger accidentally struck the stage of the buried theatre. Excavations were undertaken throughout the eighteenth and nineteenth centuries, during which period much of the marble and bronze from the site was carted off to Naples to decorate the city's palaces, and it wasn't until 1927 that digging and preservation began in earnest. Archeologists held for a long time that unlike in Pompeii, on the other side of the volcano, most of the inhabitants of Herculaneum managed to escape. However, discoveries of entangled skeletons found at what was the shoreline of the town suggest otherwise, and it's now believed that most of the population was buried by huge avalanches of volcanic mud, which later hardened into the tufa-type rock that preserved much of the town so well. In early 2000 the remains of another 48 people were found; they were carrying coins, which suggests they were attempting to flee the disaster.

Cardo IV

Cardo III joins the Decumanus Inferiore, just beyond which is the large **Thermae** or bath complex on the corner of **Cardo IV** – the domed frigidarium of its men's section decorated with a floor mosaic of dolphins, its caldarium containing a plunge bath and a scallop-shell apse. Still intact are the benches where people sat and the wooden, partitioned shelves for clothing. On the far side of the baths, the **House of Neptune and Amphitrite** (Casa di Nettuno ed Anfitrite) holds sparklingly preserved and richly ornamental wall mosaics. From here you can stroll back down to the seaward end of Cardo IV, where the **House of the Wooden Partition** still has its original partition doors (now under glass).

Cardo V

Turning right at the top of Cardo IV takes you around to **Cardo V** and most of the rest of the town's **shops** – including a baker's, complete with ovens and grinding mills, a weaver's, with loom and bones, and a dyer's, with a huge pot for dyes. Behind the ones on the left you can see the **Palestra**, where public games were held, opposite which there's a well-preserved **Taverna** with counters and, further down Cardo V on the right, another tavern, the **Taverna del Priapo**, with a priapic painting behind its counter.

Further down Cardo V, the **House of the Deer** (Casa dei Cervi) was another luxury villa, its two storeys built around a central courtyard and containing corridors decorated with richly coloured still lifes. From here, the end of Cardo V, the path descends under a covered passageway down to the so-called **Suburban Baths** on the left: one of the most impressive – and intact – structures in Herculaneum, complete with extremely well-preserved stuccowork and a pretty much intact set of baths; it also has a complete original Roman door, the only one in Herculaneum that wasn't charred by fire.

Mount Vesuvius

Since its first eruption in 79 AD, when it buried the towns and inhabitants of Pompeii and Herculaneum, **Mount Vesuvius** (1281m) has dominated the lives of those who live on the Bay of Naples, its brooding bulk forming a stately backdrop to the ever-growing settlements that group around its lower slopes. It's still an active volcano, and the only one on mainland Europe. There have been more than a hundred eruptions over the years, but only two others of real significance – one in December 1631 that engulfed many nearby towns and killed three thousand people; and the last, in March 1944, which caused widespread devastation in the towns around, though no one was actually killed. The people who live here still fear the reawakening of the volcano, and with

good cause – scientists calculate it should erupt every thirty years or so. It's carefully monitored, of course, and there is apparently no reason to expect any movement for some time. But the subsidence in towns like Ercolano below is a continuing reminder of the instability of the area, one of southern Italy's most densely populated: about 600,000 people live in the red zone – where the impact of another eruption could be quick and devastating.

The ascent

Daily: Jan & Feb, Nov & Dec 9am–3pm; March & Oct 9am–4pm; April & May, June & Sept 9am–6pm; July & Aug 9am–6pm • €10 • ⓦ parconazionaledelvesuvio.it

It's a twenty- to thirty-minute **ascent** from the car park to the crater – a stony and mildly strenuous stroll across reddened, barren gravel and rock along a marked-out path that is roped off to minimize the chance of stumbling down the sheer drop to the right. At the top is a deep, wide, jagged ashtray of red rock swirled over by midges and emitting the odd plume of smoke, though since the last eruption effectively sealed up the main crevice, this is much less evident than it once was. There's also a small kiosk selling drinks and trinkets, and the path continues halfway around the crater so you can get a view from the other side – a further fifteen minutes or so on foot.

ARRIVAL AND DEPARTURE — MOUNT VESUVIUS

From Ercolano Turn left out of the train station for buses run by Vesuvio Express (ⓣ 081 739 3666, ⓦ vesuvioexpress.it), which head to the car park by the crater every 40min from 9.45am–4pm (€10 return); the last bus back to Ercolano departs at 5.30pm.

From Pompeii EAV buses leave roughly every other hour from Piazza Anfiteatro between 8am and 3.30pm (€6.50 return); the journey takes just over an hour and the last bus back is at 5.40pm.

From Two daily EAV buses depart from Naples' Molo Beverello (9.10am & 10.10am), and from Piazza Garibaldi 10min later, taking about 1hr 10min to reach the top and returning at 12.30pm and 2pm (€7.20 return). There is a fixed fare of €100 for taxis from Naples city centre to Veuvius, including a 2hr wait at the summit.

Pompeii

The other Roman town to be destroyed by Vesuvius – **Pompeii** – was a much larger affair than Herculaneum and one of Campania's most important commercial centres – a moneyed resort for wealthy patricians and a trading town that exported wine and fish. In effect the eruption froze the town's way of life as it stood at the time. Indeed, the excavations, which have continued more or less without interruption from 1748 to the present day, have probably yielded more information about the ordinary life of Roman citizens during the imperial era than anywhere else: their social conventions, class structure, domestic arrangements and (very high) standard of living. Some of the buildings are even covered with ancient graffiti, either referring to contemporary

MOUNTAIN VIEWS WITHOUT THE EFFORT

For a spectacular view over the whole of the Bay of Naples, take the **funivia** or cable car up to the summit of the 1131m-high **Monte Faito**. Between April and early Nov it leaves every 20–30 minutes from just west of the train station in Castellammare di Stabia, a few stops south on the Circumvesuviana from Pompeii (one-way/return €5.50/€8). It's only an eight-minute journey but definitely not for those of a delicate disposition, giving increasingly stupendous views of the bay and of the deepening gulf between you and the beech-covered hillside below. At the top are a few bars selling drinks and sandwiches, and if you can't face the trip down, it's comforting to know that several roads meet here and there's a Circumvesuviana bus stop nearby (linking to the Vico Equense station) – though it's debatable which is the more hair-raising ride.

AUGUST 24, 79 AD: THE DAY POMPEII DIED

Vesuvius had been spouting smoke and ash for several days before the **eruption** on August 24. Fortunately most of Pompeii had already been evacuated when disaster struck: out of a total population of twenty thousand it's thought that only two thousand actually perished, asphyxiated by the toxic fumes of the volcanic debris, their homes buried in several metres of volcanic ash and pumice. Pliny, the Roman naturalist, was one of the casualties – he died at nearby Stabiae (now Castellammare di Stabia) of a heart attack. But his nephew, **Pliny the Younger**, described the full horror of the scene in two vivid letters to the historian Tacitus, who was compiling a history of the disaster, writing that the sky turned dark like "a room when it is shut up, and the lamp put out".

political events or simply to the romantic entanglements of the inhabitants; and the full horror of their way of death is apparent in plaster casts made from the shapes their bodies left in the volcanic ash – with faces tortured with agony, or shielding themselves from the dust and ashes.

The site

Daily: April–Oct 8.30am–7.30pm, last entry 6pm; Nov–March 8.30am–5pm, last entry 3.30pm • €15, combined ticket for four sites including Herculaneum, valid three days €22 • ⓣ 081 857 5347, ⓦ pompeiisites.org

The **site** covers a wide area, and seeing it properly takes half a day at the very least. Unlike Herculaneum there's little shade, and the distances involved are quite large: breaks along the way: flat, comfortable shoes are a must. Since there is so much to see here, it is worth studying the **site map**, which you'll find at every entrance – pins on the map indicate which areas are currently closed, as the site is in continuous restoration. Many of the most interesting structures are kept locked and only opened when a large group forms or a tip is handed over to one of the custodians. To be sure of seeing as much as possible you could consider taking a tour, although one of the pleasures of Pompeii is to escape the hordes and absorb the strangely still quality of the town, which, despite the large number of visitors, it is quite possible to do.

The western sector: from the Forum to the House of the Vettii

Entering the site from the Pompeii-Villa dei Misteri side, through the Porta Marina, the **Forum** is the first real feature of significance, a long, slim, open space surrounded by the ruins of what would have been some of the town's most important official buildings – a basilica, temples to Apollo and Jupiter and a market hall. Walking north from here, up the so-called Via di Mercurio, takes you towards some of the town's more luxurious houses. On the left, the **House of the Tragic Poet** (Casa del Poetica Tragico) is named for its mosaics of a theatrical production and a poet inside, though the "Cave Canem" (Beware of the Dog) mosaic by the main entrance is more eye-catching. Close by, the residents of the **House of the Faun** (Casa del Fauno) – one of Pompeii's most luxurious residences – must have been a friendlier lot, its "Ave" (Welcome) mosaic outside beckoning you in to view the atrium and the copy of a tiny, bronze, dancing faun (the original is in Naples) that gives the villa its name.

On the street behind, the **House of the Vettii** (Casa dei Vettii) is one of the most delightful houses in Pompeii and one of the best maintained, a merchant villa ranged around a lovely central peristyle that gives the best possible impression of the domestic environment of the city's upper middle classes. The first room on the right off the peristyle holds some of the best of Pompeii's murals: the one on the left shows the young Hercules struggling with serpents. There are more paintings beyond here, through the villa's kitchen in a small room that's normally kept locked – erotic works showing various techniques of lovemaking together with an

absurdly potent-looking statue of Priapus from which women were supposed to drink to be fertile.

The eastern sector: the Grand Theatre to the Amphitheatre

Cross over to the other side of the site for the so-called **new excavations**, which began in 1911 and uncovered some of the town's most important quarters. The **Grand Theatre**, for one, is very well preserved and is still used for performances, overlooking the small, grassy, column-fringed square of the **Samnite Palestra** – a refectory and meeting place for spectators from the theatre. Walk around to the far left side of the Grand Theatre, down the steps and up again, and you're in front of the **Little Theatre** – a smaller, more intimate venue also still used for summer performances and with a better-kept corridor behind the stage space. Walk up from here to rejoin the Via dell' Abbondanza, where there's lots of interest – the Lararium has a niche with a delicate relief showing scenes from the Trojan War; the **Fullonica Stephani** is a well-preserved laundry, with a large tiered tub for washing; the **House of the Venus in the Shell** is named after the excellently preserved painting on its back wall; while next door, the **House of Octavius Quartio** is a gracious villa fronted by great bronze doors, with paintings of Narcissus gazing rapt at his reflection in the villa's lovely garden, which has been replanted with vines and shrubs.

Just beyond here is the town's **Amphitheatre** – one of Italy's most intact and accessible, and also its oldest, dating from 80 BC; it once had room for a crowd of some twelve thousand – well over half the town's population. Next door, the **Palestra** is a vast parade ground that was used by Pompeii's youth for sport and exercise – still with its square of swimming pool in the centre. It must have been in use when the eruption struck Pompeii, since its southeast corner was found littered with the skeletons of young men trying to flee the disaster.

Villa dei Misteri

One last place you shouldn't miss at Pompeii is the **Villa dei Misteri** (Villa of the Mysteries). Recently restored, this is probably the best preserved of all Pompeii's palatial houses, an originally third-century-BC structure with a warren of rooms and courtyards that derives its name from a series of paintings in one of its larger chambers: depictions of the initiation rites of a young woman into the Dionysiac Mysteries, an outlawed cult of the early imperial era. Not much is known about the cult itself, but the paintings are marvellously clear, remarkable for the surety of their execution and the brightness of their tones and colours.

ARRIVAL AND INFORMATION — POMPEII

By train The Circumvesuviana is the easiest way to reach Pompeii, linking Pompeii Scavi-Villa dei Misteri – just outside the western, Porta Marina entrance to the site – with Naples (35min) and Sorrento (30min). There are two other train stations to the west of the site, just above and below the new city, with services to Naples (40min).

Tourist office Via Sacra 1, just off the modern town's main square (June–Oct Mon–Sat 8.30am–8pm; Nov–May Mon–Sat 8.30am–3.30pm; ⓣ 081 850 7255).

ACCOMMODATION

Agora Hostel Via Duca d'Aosta 15 ⓣ 081 058 2826, ⓦ agorapompei.com. The best hostel in town, situated in the centre of modern Pompeii, with wonderfully friendly owners, well-kept, all a/c dorms and doubles and a pleasant, shady common area out back. Dorms **€22**, doubles **€50**

Fortuna Village Via Plinio 115, south of the main entrance ⓣ 081 850 8439, ⓦ fortunavillagepompei.it. This campground is within easy reach of old Pompeii, with a decent restaurant, laundry facilities and a/c doubles (€80). Open all year. Pitches **€11**, plus per adult **€14**

13

Sorrento

Topping the rocky cliffs close to the end of its peninsula, 25km south of Pompeii, the last town of significance on the southern side of the bay, **SORRENTO** is solely and unashamedly a resort, its inspired location and mild climate drawing foreigners from all over Europe for close on two hundred years. Ibsen wrote part of *Peer Gynt* in Sorrento, Wagner and Nietzsche had a well-publicized row here, and Maxim Gorky lived for over a decade in the town. Nowadays it's strictly package-tour territory, but not too much the worse for it, with little of the brashness of its Spanish and Greek equivalents but all their vigour, a bright, lively place that retains its southern Italian roots. There are only a few sites of interest in Sorrento, though it makes a pleasant base for exploring the rugged peninsula (even parts of the Amalfi Coast) and the islands of the bay.

Piazza Tasso and around

It's nice to wander through the streets that feed into the central square, **Piazza Tasso**, built astride the gorge that runs through the centre of town and named after the wayward sixteenth-century Italian poet whose statue stands in the far corner. Running west of here is the backbone to Sorrento's small grid of old-town streets, **Corso Italia**, pedestrianized for the lively evening *passeggiata* and lined with restaurants, *gelaterie* and shops selling souvenirs and *limoncello*.

Villa Comunale and San Francesco

It's worth strolling down from the Piazza Tasso to linger in the shady gardens of the **Villa Comunale**, whose terrace has lovely views out to sea. Off to the right, you can also peek into the small thirteenth-century cloister of the church of **San Francesco** just outside, planted with vines and bright bougainvillea – a peaceful escape from the bustle of the rest of Sorrento.

The Cattedrale

Corso Italia 1 • Daily 8am–12.30pm & 4.30–8pm • Free

Skirting the northern edge of the old town, Sorrento's busiest artery is **Corso Italia**, which is pedestrianized after 7.30pm on summer evenings for the lively *passeggiata* (only on Sat from mid-Oct to May). A little way down on the left, Sorrento's **Cattedrale** has been much rebuilt, and the real challenge of its gaudy interior is how to tell the fake marble from the real. The bishop's throne, on the main aisle, is certainly authentic, dating from the late sixteenth century, as are the inlaid wood scenes on the main doors and choir stalls, which add a genuine Sorrentine touch. Take a look also at the large *presepe* just inside the main doors, and the chapel in the left aisle, which is dedicated to San Giuseppe Moscati – a Neapolitan doctor who died in 1927 and is venerated in Naples' Gesù church (see page 750).

Museo Bottega della Tarsialignea

Via San Nicola 28 • Daily: April–Oct 10am–6.30pm; Nov–March 10am–5pm • €8 • Ⓣ 081 877 1942, Ⓦ museomuta.it

The **Museo Bottega della Tarsialignea**, housed in an ancient mansion in the artisanal quarter of the old town, is a shrine to Sorrento's craft speciality of inlaid woodwork – cheap and pretty awful examples of which you see all over town. Don't let the tourist tat put you off: the ground floor here has some clever and stylish examples of contemporary *intarsio* work (it's for sale, but not at all cheap), while upstairs displays the work of Sorrento's late nineteenth-century *intarsio* greats.

Museo Correale di Terranova

Via Correale 50 • April–Oct Mon–Sat 9.30am–6.30pm & Sun 9.30am–1.30pm; Nov–March Tues–Sun 9.30am–1.30pm • €8 • Ⓣ 081 878 1846, Ⓦ museocorreale.it

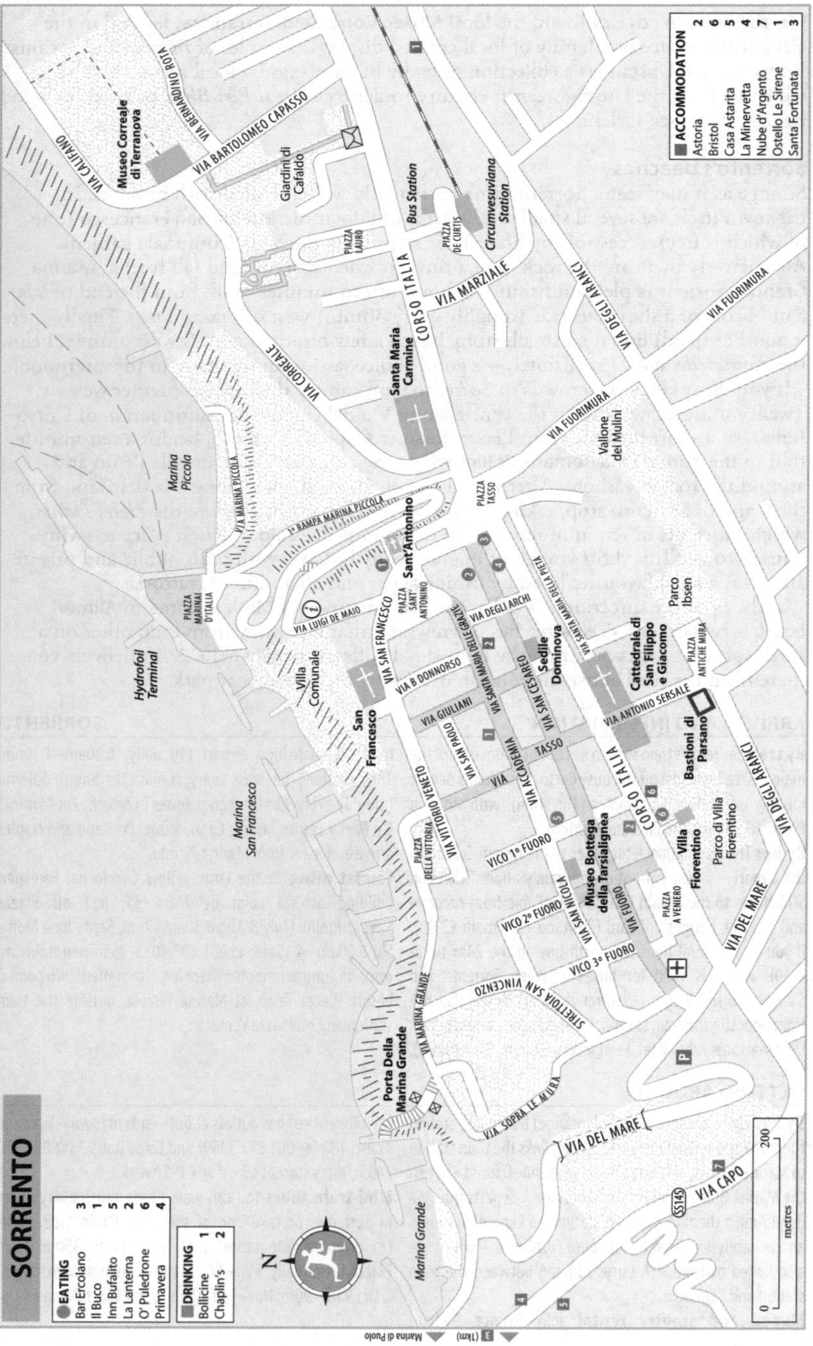

SORRENTO
EATING
Bar Ercolano 3
Il Buco 1
Inn Bufalito 5
La Lanterna 2
O' Puledrone 6
Primavera 4
DRINKING
Bollicine 1
Chaplin's 2
ACCOMMODATION
Astoria 2
Bristol 6
Casa Astarita 5
La Minervetta 4
Nube d'Argento 7
Ostello Le Sirene 1
Santa Fortunata 3
N
Marina Grande
Porta Della Marina Grande
Marina San Francesco
Villa Comunale
Hydrofoil Terminal
Marina Piccola
Museo Correale di Terranova
Giardini di Cafaldo
Bus Station
Circumvesuviana Station
Santa Maria Carmine
Vallone dei Mulini
Sant'Antonino
San Francesco
Sedile Dominova
Cattedrale di San Filippo e Giacomo
Parco Ibsen
Bastioni di Parsano
Museo Bottega della Tarsialignea
Villa Fiorentino
Parco di Villa Fiorentino
VIA CALIFANO
VIA BERNARDINO ROTA
VIA BARTOLOMEO CAPASSO
VIA CORREALE
CORSO ITALIA
VIA MARZIALE
VIA DEGLI ARANCI
VIA FUORIMURA
PIAZZA LAURO
PIAZZA DE CURTIS
PIAZZA TASSO
VIA MARINA PICCOLA
1° RAMPA MARINA PICCOLA
PIAZZA MARINAI D'ITALIA
VIA LUIGI DE MAIO
VIA SAN FRANCESCO
PIAZZA SANT' ANTONINO
VIA DEGLI ARCHI
VIA SANTA MARIA DELLE GRAZIE
VIA SANTA MARIA DELLA PIETÀ
VIA B DONNORSO
VIA SAN CESAREO
PIAZZA ANTICHE MURA
VIA ANTONIO SERSALE
VIA GIULIANI
VIA SAN PAOLO
VIA TASSO
VIA ACCADEMIA
VIA VITTORIO VENETO
PIAZZA DELLA VITTORIA
VICO 1° FUORO
VICO 2° FUORO
VICO 3° FUORO
VIA SAN NICOLA
VIA FUORO
PIAZZA A VENIERO
VIA DEL MARE
STRETTOIA SAN VINCENZO
VIA MARINA GRANDE
VIA SOPRA LE MURA
SS145
VIA CAPO
0
200
metres
Capri & Positano
Marina di Puolo

13

On the western edge of town, the local **Museo Correale di Terranova**, housed in the airy former palace of a family of local counts, displays examples of *intarsio* and various Roman finds. Upstairs is a collection of badly lit paintings by local artists, best of which by far is the late eighteenth-century roulette game, *Il Biri Bisso*, painted on wood by one Francesco Celebrano.

Sorrento's beaches

Strange as it may seem, Sorrento isn't particularly well provided with **beaches.** In the town itself are several small sandy strips of lido at the **Marina San Francesco** (one of which is free), accessible by lift (€1) or steps from the Villa Comunale gardens. Alternatively there are the rocks and a tiny, crowded strip of sand (all free) at **Marina Grande**, Sorrento's pleasant fishing harbour, fifteen minutes' walk from the end of Via San Nicola or a short bus ride (roughly every 30min) west of Piazza Tasso. Finally there is another (paid) lido on a small, stony **beach** a few hundred metres west of town below the *Tonnarella* and *Désirée* hotels – a good choice, as it is quite shady in the afternoon.

If you don't fancy the crowds in Sorrento, you can try the beaches further west. Twenty minutes' walk from the centre along Via del Capo (the continuation of Corso Italia), or a short bus ride from Piazza Tasso to Capo di Sorrento, begins a ten-minute trail to the **Ruderi Villa Romana Pollio**, where the ruins of a Roman villa lie on and around the rocky seashore. Alternatively, stroll 100m further along Via del Capo from the Capo di Sorrento stop, taking a path off to the right just before the *Hotel Dania*, which shortcuts in ten minutes or so to the **Marina di Puolo**, the best place to swim outside town. This short stretch of mainly sandy beach – with both public and private areas – is a local favourite lined by fishing boats and a handful of trattorias.

In the opposite direction, the adjacent-but-one town of **Meta** is home to **Alimuri** beach – two decent-sized stretches of grey sand that face away from each other on a small spit that sticks out from the high-sided cliffs of the bay here. A lift delivers you there from the road above, or you can drive down to a small car park.

ARRIVAL AND INFORMATION — SORRENTO

By train Sorrento's train station lies about 300m east of the main Piazza Tasso just off the busy Corso Italia. Trains depart roughly every 30min to Naples (1hr 5min), with stops in Pompeii (30min) and Ercolano (50min).

By bus The bus station – for buses to the Amalfi Coast and the airport – is just in front of the train station. Tickets on SITA buses to the Amalfi Coast are available from *tabacchi* and can't be bought onboard (Positano €2; Amalfi €2.90); if you plan several hops it's worth buying the 24hr ticket (€10), which is valid for buses between Sorrento and Salerno. Curreri Viaggi (ⓦ curreriviaggi.it) buses also run from opposite the train station, linking Naples' airport.

Destinations Amalfi (at least every 30min; 1hr 30min); Naples Capodichino airport (10 daily; 6.30am–4.30pm; 1hr); Positano (at least every 30min; 1hr 5min); Salerno (roughly every 30min; change buses in Amalfi; 2hr 45min).

By Ferry Ferries linking Capri, Ischia, Positano and Naples arrive and leave from Marina Piccola.

Tourist office In the large yellow Circolo dei Forestieri building at Via Luigi de Maio 35, just off Piazza Sant'Antonino (July & Aug 8.30am–7pm, Sept–June Mon–Sat 8.30am–4.15pm; ⓣ 081 807 4033, ⓦ sorrentotourism.com). In summer months there are also staffed "info points" beside Piazza Tasso, at Marina Piccola, outside the train station and on Piazza Veniero.

GETTING AROUND

By bus There are several useful (orange) bus routes around the town and surrounding area. Line B links the train station to Marine Piccola, via Piazza Tasso, while line D runs between the Marina Grande and Piazza Tasso. Line A departs from Via degli Aranci (behind the train station) to Capo di Sorrento, and is handy for *Désirée* and *Santa Fortunata* – which are also linked by blue SITA buses running between the train station and Sant'agata.

Moped and scooter rental Jolly Service & Rent (ⓦ jollyrent.eu) has outlets at both ends of town – Via degli Aranci 180 (ⓣ 081 877 3450) and Corso Italia 3 (ⓣ 081 878 2403); rates start at €35/day, €195/week.

Mini-train tours You can walk pretty much everywhere in Sorrento, or take one of the 30min mini-train tours (ⓦ sorrentotraintour.com) that leave every 35min from Piazza Tasso (daily: May–Sept 9am–midnight; March, April & Oct 9am–9pm; Nov–Feb 10am–6pm; €6, children €4).

ACCOMMODATION

★ **Astoria** Via S. Maria delle Grazie 24 ⓣ081 807 4030, ⓦhotelastoriasorrento.com; map p.773. Right in the heart of old Sorrento, this place is quite special, with reasonably sized doubles that are well equipped and nicely furnished with beautiful tiles; the best of them overlook a peaceful garden. The price includes an excellent buffet breakfast, and there's discounted parking nearby for guests (€20 per night). **€180**

Bristol Via Capo 22 ⓣ081 878 4522, ⓦbristolsorrento.com; map p.773. About a ten-minute walk west of the centre, this hotel is pressed high against the cliffs above Marina Grande, with breathtaking views over the bay from its rooftop pool and bar. The upper rooms are best for escaping the noise from the adjacent road, some of them featuring their own private jacuzzi (€400). **€300**

Casa Astarita Corso Italia 67 ⓣ081 877 4906, ⓦcasastarita.com; map p.773. Six brightly-coloured rooms overlooking the street, all with bathroom, flatscreen TV, fridge and a good breakfast around a communal table each morning. Cosy, welcoming and in a central position, it's one of Sorrento's best options at this price. **€140**

La Minervetta Via Capo 25 ⓣ081 877 4455, ⓦlaminervetta.com; map p.773. Perched on the cliff overlooking Marina Grande, *La Minervetta* is Sorrento's top boutique hotel, with a lovely lounge terrace overlooking the sea. Below that is a plunge pool and jacuzzi, with steps leading down to Marina Grande's beaches and restaurants. The rooms are gorgeous – prices start at around €400 for one of their superior rooms. **€350**

Ostello Le Sirene Via degli Aranci 160 ⓣ081 877 1371, ⓦhostellesirene.net; map p.773. A 5min walk west of the train station, this recently renovated hostel has clean and bright double, triple and quadruple rooms and dormitories, with breakfast served in the cosy downstairs café and bar (open 24hr). Dorms **€23**, doubles **€80**

CAMPING

Nube d'Argento Via del Capo 21 ⓣ081 878 1344, ⓦnubedargento.com; map p.773. Scenic site with a nice pool, restaurant and bar just to the west of town, about 200m from the end of Corso Italia. March–Nov. Bungalows **€90**, pitches **€9**, plus **€13** per adult

Santa Fortunata Via del Capo 41 ⓣ081 807 3579, ⓦwww.santafortunata.com; map p.773. Just over 1km out of Sorrento on the way to Massa Lubrense (linked to town by orange bus A and blue SITA buses), this camping site has a tiny private beach and superb sea views, as well as somewhat cramped bungalows (€49), some of them with private bathrooms (€63). There is also a big pool, restaurant and bar. April–Oct. Pitches **€11**, plus **€14** per adult

EATING

CAFÉS AND GELATERIE

Bar Ercolano Piazza Tasso 28 ⓣ081 807 2951; map p.773. The smaller and friendlier of the two main bars on Piazza Tasso – with not such good views of the parading crowds, but a lot shadier when it's hot. A good place to start the day with a pastry. Daily 6.30am–midnight.

Primavera Corso Italia 142 ⓣ081 807 3252, ⓦprimaverasorrento.it; map p.773. There's a great choice of flavours at this veteran *gelateria*, just off Piazza Tasso. Check out the photos of the famous and infamous who have stopped by for a quick *cono*. Daily 10am–1am.

RESTAURANTS

O' Puledrone Via Marina Grande 150 ⓣ081 012 4134, ⓦopuledrone.com; map p.773. With a menu as short as those in the upper town are long, this friendly trattoria is right on the waterfront in Marina Grande, run by a consortium of fishermen. Good value for excellent seafood (grilled fish €10). No credit cards. Daily April–Oct noon–3pm & 6.30–10pm.

Il Buco Rampa Marina Piccola 11, Piazza San Antonino ⓣ081 878 2354, ⓦilbucoristorante.it; map p.773. Housed in the wine cellar of a former monastery, this is Sorrento at its gastronomic best, with a real variety of antipasti and *primi* that focus on local ingredients and a *secondi* menu that is mainly about fish. You can order à la carte and pay around €25 for *primi* and around €30 for *secondi*, or choose from menus that range from €80 for five courses to €120 for eight. Daily except Wed 12.30–2.30pm & 7.30–11pm.

★ **Inn Bufalito** Vico Fuoro I 21 ⓣ081 365 6975, ⓦinnbufalito.it; map p.773. Warm, friendly mozzarella bar and restaurant that's passionate about buffalo dishes – cheese, steaks, sausages and "slow" local and seasonal produce. Great pasta dishes and inventive mains, big baskets of country breads, cheese platters, delicious *antipasti misti*, and buffalo steaks (€18). They also run a produce shop on Piazza Tasso. Daily noon–midnight; closed Jan & Feb.

La Lanterna Via S. Cesareo 23 ⓣ081 878 1355, ⓦlalanternasorrento.it; map p.773. Down a dead end just off Piazza Tasso and built over the ruins of a Roman bathhouse (partly visible beneath a plate of glass), this has long been one of the better restaurants in the centre of town, with moderate prices, excellent service, tables outside and consistently good food – great fish (catch of the day €22), and much else besides, including pizzas (from €6). March–Oct daily except Wed noon–3pm & 7pm–midnight.

13

DRINKING

Bollicine Via Accademia 9/11 ⓣ081 878 4616; map p.773. Run by friendly and knowledgeable wine connoisseur Luigi, this small, wood-panelled wine bar in the heart of the old town has a wide range of good Campanian wines, draught beer, a cosy atmosphere, good sandwiches (€4.50) and happy hour on selected wines (7–9pm). Daily noon–3pm & 6pm–1am May–early Oct, 6pm–1pm mid Oct–April.

Chaplin's Corso Italia 18 ⓣ081 807 2551; map p.773. Run by three delightful cousins, Sorrento's original Irish pub offers a warm Italian welcome, with a well-stocked bar and a mixed, international crowd. The walls are decked with an array of TVs airing live sport. Daily 11am–2am.

The islands

Guarding each prong of the Bay of Naples, the **islands** of Capri, Ischia and Procida between them make up the best-known group of Italian islands. Each is a very different creature, though. **Capri** is a place of legend, home to the mythical Sirens and a much-eulogized playground of the super-rich in the years since – though now settled down to a lucrative existence as a target for day-trippers from the mainland. Visit by all means, but bear in mind that you have to hunt hard these days to detect the origins of much of the purple prose. **Ischia** is a target for package tours and weekenders from Naples, but its size means that it doesn't feel as crowded as Capri, and plentiful hot springs, sandy beaches and a green volcanic interior make the island well worth a few days' visit. Pretty **Procida**, the smallest of the islands and the best place for peaceful lazing, remains relatively untouched.

GETTING THERE — THE ISLANDS

Ferries, hydrofoils and catamarans There are regular services to all the islands throughout the year, though they run more frequently and from more ports between April and Oct. The principal point of departure is Naples' main port, the Molo Beverello at the bottom of Piazza Municipio; car ferries leave from Calata Porta di Massa, about 200m further east. Hydrofoils and catamarans also run from Naples Mergellina (for Ischia), Pozzuoli (for Procida and Ischia), Castellammare (Capri), Salerno (Capri and Ischia) and Sorrento (Capri). There are also services between Capri and Ischia, and Ischia and Procida, although, curiously, the islands are not as well connected as you might expect. Note that you can't take a car to Capri, nor, in summer months, to Ischia or Procida; there's a useful car park in Naples' Calata di Massa port (daily 6am–10pm; €25 for 24hr; ⓣ081 551 4988, ⓦtirreniparking.it).

Tickets All the operators below offer online booking but, in general, there's no need to book tickets in advance; just make sure you arrive at the docks 15min before departure. It's usually better to buy a single rather than a return ticket – it's no more expensive and you retain more flexibility on the time you come back, and the service you use. Having said that, on summer Sun (especially on Capri and Procida, and especially by hydrofoil), it's a good idea to buy your return ticket as soon as you arrive, to avoid the risk of finding the last service fully booked.

Timings Ferry timings are published daily in newspaper *Il Mattino*, as well as being available from local tourist offices. Online, you can visit the island-specific websites, those belonging to the ferry lines themselves, or all of them lumped together at ⓦnaplesbayferry.com. Day-trips are feasible to all the islands; usually the last connection delivers you back to the mainland in time for dinner.

FERRY AND HYDROFOIL LINES

Alilauro ⓣ081 497 2222, ⓦalilauro.it. Naples–Ischia (Porto and Forío), Sorrento; Capri–Ischia (Porto); Castellammare–Capri; Sorrento–Capri and Ischia (Porto); Salerno–Capri and Ischia (Porto); Positano and Amalfi–Capri and Ischia (Porto).

Caremar ⓣ081 551 3882, ⓦcaremar.it. Naples–Capri, Ischia (Porto and Casamicciola) and Procida; Pozzuoli–Ischia (Porto and Casamicciola); Procida–Ischia (Porto and Casamicciola); Sorrento–Capri.

Gescab ⓣ081 704 1911, ⓦgescab.it. Naples, Sorrento, Ischia (Porto), Castellamare, Positano, Amalfi, Salerno and Castellammare–Capri.

Med Mar ⓣ081 333 4411, ⓦmedmargroup.it. Naples and Pozzuoli–Ischia (Porto and Casamicciola); Ischia, Naples and Pozzuoli–Procida.

NLG ⓣ081 552 0763, ⓦnavlib.it. Naples, Sorrento, Positano, Amalfi, Salerno and Castellammare–Capri.

SNAV ⓣ081 428 5555, ⓦsnav.it. Naples–Capri, Ischia (Casamicciola) and Procida; Castellammare–Capri; Sorrento–Capri.

Capri

Sheering out of the sea just off the far end of the Sorrentine peninsula, the island of **Capri** has long been the most sought-after part of the Bay of Naples. During Roman times Augustus retreated to the island's gorgeous cliffbound scenery to escape the cares of office; later Tiberius moved the imperial capital here, indulging himself in legendarily debauched antics until his death in 37 AD. After the Romans left, Capri was rather neglected until the early nineteenth century, when the discovery of the Blue Grotto and the island's remarkable natural landscape coincided nicely with the rise of tourism. The English especially have always flocked here: D.H. Lawrence and George Bernard Shaw were among its more illustrious visitors; Graham Greene and Gracie Fields had houses here; and even Lenin visited for a time after the failure of the 1905 uprising.

Capri tends to get a mixed press these days, the consensus being that while it might have been an attractive place once, it's been pretty much ruined by the crowds and the prices. And Capri *is* crowded, to the degree that in July and August, and on all summer weekends, you might want to give it a miss, though the island does still have a unique charm, and it would be hard to find a place with more inspiring views.

Marina Grande

Marina Grande is almost certainly where you will arrive on Capri, a busy harbour that receives day-trippers on ferries and other vessels before dispatching them onward by bus, funicular or taxi. Beyond the port area and the bus terminal is a sand and shingle beach of mixed quality. It's often crowded but is possibly the easiest place to swim on the island. There are lots of free spots too, though you can pay for the usual facilities if you prefer.

Capri Town and around

CAPRI is the main town of the island, nestled between two mountains. Its houses are connected by winding, hilly alleyways that give onto the dinky main square of **Piazza Umberto I**, or "La Piazzetta", crowded with café tables and lit by twinkling fairy lights in the evenings. Don't neglect the maze of charming streets behind La Piazzetta, or the covered walkways up the steps to the right as you enter the square – these lead to

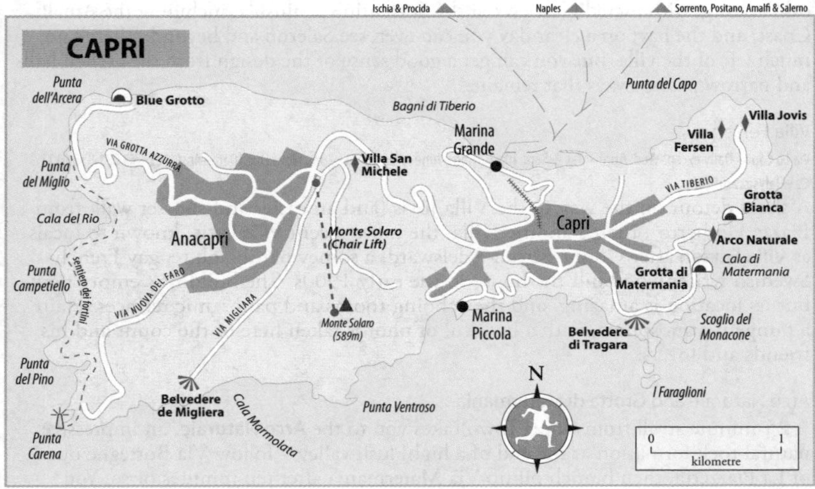

13

the domed seventeenth-century parish church of **Santo Stefano** (daily 9am–1pm & 4–7pm; free), worth a look for its marble floor, originally from the ancient Roman Villa Jovis and the ruins of other Tiberian villas.

Certosa di San Giacomo

Via Certosa 11 • Tues–Sun 9am–2.30pm • €6 • ⓣ 081 837 6218

On the far side of town is the **Certosa di San Giacomo**, a restored monastery with a small collection of 31 metaphysical paintings and five sculptures by Karl Wilhelm Diefenbach, a German Symbolist artist who lived on the island until his death in 1913.

Giardini di Augusto

Daily 9am–7.30pm • Easter to mid-Nov €1; mid-Nov to Easter free

Beyond the monastery, on the other side of the island, the **Giardini di Augusto** give tremendous views of the coast below and the towering, jagged cliffs above. From the gardens, you can look down on a spectacular zigzag pathway, **Via Krupp**, commissioned by German industrialist Friedrich Alfred Krupp in 1900 to link the area around the Certosa di San Giacomo, near his suite at the *Hotel Quisisana*, to Marina Piccola, where he moored his yacht. It's often closed these days, due to the danger of falling rocks.

Belvedere del Cannone

Up above the Certosa, and a further pleasant walk fifteen minutes through Capri Town, the **Belvedere del Cannone** has marvellous views, especially over the **Faraglioni** rocks to the east and Marina Piccola to the west.

Villa Jovis

Via Tiberio • April, May & Oct: Mon & Wed–Sun 10am–5pm; June–Sept daily 10am–7pm; Nov & Dec: Mon & Wed–Sun 10am–4pm • €6, free first Sun of the month • From the Piazzetta take Via Le Botteghe, followed by Via Fuorlovado and Via Croce, then head up to the end of Via Tiberio

It's a steep forty-minute hike uphill to the ruins of the **Villa Jovis**, on the eastern edge of the island. It was here that Tiberius retired in 27 AD, reportedly to lead a life of vice and debauchery and to take revenge on his enemies, many of whom he apparently had thrown off the cliff face. You can see why he chose the site: it's among Capri's most exhilarating, with incredible views of the Sorrentine peninsula, including the Amalfi Coast, and the bay; on a clear day you can even see Salerno and beyond. There's not much left of the villa, but you can get a good sense of the design from the arched halls and narrow passageways that remain.

Villa Fersen

Via Lo Capo • Daily except Wed: April–May & Sept 10am–6pm, June–Aug 10am–7pm, Nov–Dec 10am–4pm • €2 • ⓣ 081 838 6111, ⓦ villalysiscapri.com

A short detour on the way to the Villa Jovis (and an easier and shorter walk from Piazza Umberto), there's another villa, the more recent **Villa Lysis**, known to locals as **Villa Fersen** after Count Fersen-Adelsward, a somewhat dissolute, gay French-Swedish writer who built the house in the early 1900s. The building's empty now, but its location is amazing, and the echoing rooms and panoramic terraces retain a pungent atmosphere, with a handful of photos taken here of the count and his friends and lovers.

Arco Naturale and Grotta di Matermania

A 25-minute stroll from Capri Town takes you to the **Arco Naturale**, an impressive natural rock formation at the end of a high, lush valley – follow Via Botteghe out of La Piazzetta, then branch off up Via Matermania after ten minutes or so. You

can get quite close to the arch owing to the specially constructed viewing platforms. Just before the path descends towards the arch, steps lead down to the **Grotta di Matermania**, ten minutes away down quite a few steps – a dusty cutaway out of the rock that was converted to house a shrine to the goddess Cybele by the Romans. Steps lead on down from the cave, sheer through the trees, before flattening into a fine path that you can follow to the **Belvedere di Tragara**, affording some of the island's best views along the way, and, eventually, back to Capri Town – reachable in about half an hour from the belvedere.

Marina Piccola

Buses from Capri town run to Marina Piccola, or you can walk, following Via Mulo from Via Roma, or taking Via Krupp if it is open (see page 778); either walk takes about 20min

A small huddle of houses and restaurants around patches of pebble beach, **Marina Piccola** is reasonably uncrowded out of season, though in July or August you might as well forget it. This is the one place on the island where you can rent **kayaks** (about €16/hr) and do a circuit of the island – about a five-hour trip, including stops and swims.

Anacapri and around

The island's other main settlement, **ANACAPRI**, is more sprawling than Capri itself and less obviously picturesque, though quieter and greener. Its main square, **Piazza della Vittoria**, is flanked by souvenir shops, bland fashion boutiques and restaurants decked with tourist menus – Capri without the chic.

San Michele

Piazza San Nicola • Daily: April–Sept 9am–7pm; Oct–March 10am–3pm • €2

A short walk from Piazza della Vittoria down Via G. Orlandi, the church of **San Michele** is one of Anacapri's two principal sights. Its tiled floor is painted with an eighteenth-century depiction of the Fall that you view from an upstairs balcony – a lush work after a drawing by the Neapolitan painter **Solimena**, in rich blues and yellows, showing cats, unicorns and other creatures.

Villa San Michele

Via Axel Munthe 34 • Daily: March 9am–4.30pm; April & Oct 9am–5pm; May–Sept 9am–6pm; Nov–Feb 9am–3.30pm • €8 • Ⓣ 081 837 1401, Ⓦ villasanmichele.eu

It's a short walk from Piazza della Vittoria, past a long gauntlet of souvenir stalls, to Axel Munthe's **Villa San Michele**, a light, airy house with lush and fragrant gardens that is one of the highlights of the island. A nineteenth-century Swedish writer and physician to the elite, Munthe lived here for a number of years, and the place is filled with his furniture and knick-knacks, as well as Roman artefacts and columns plundered from a ruined villa on the site. There's also an attractive, small natural history exhibition in the gardens, which fills you in on local flora and fauna.

Monte Solaro

Piazza Vittoria • Daily: March–Oct 9.30am–5.30pm; Nov–Feb 10.30am–3pm • €8 one-way, €11 return • Ⓦ capriseggiovia.it • The chair lift takes 12min; hiking up takes 1hr 30min, or it's around 1hr downhill

A chair lift runs from Piazza della Vittoria up to **Monte Solaro**, the island's highest point (596m). There's not much at the top – a ruined castle and a café – but the ride and the location are very tranquil and the 360-degree views are marvellous – perhaps the bay's very best.

13

The Blue Grotto

Daily 9am–1hr before sunset, but closed in bad weather • Rowing boat into the grotto plus admission €14 • Some round-island excursions include the Grotto (see page 780), or you can take a boat from Marina Grande (€14 round-trip; 10min each way), or a bus from Anacapri's Piazza della Vittoria (every 15–20min; 15min); alternatively, it's a good 45min hike from Anacapri, starting off down Via Lo Pozzo

The **Blue Grotto**, or Grotta Azzurra, is probably the island's best-known feature – though also its most touristy, with the boatmen here whisking visitors onto boats and in and out of the grotto in about five minutes flat. It's best to plan a visit in the **morning**, as it's more likely to be closed after 1pm due to high tide.

People enter the grotto in twos, and you have to duck below its low opening. Once you're inside, the grotto is quietly impressive, the blue of its innards caused by sunlight entering the cave through the water.

ARRIVAL AND INFORMATION — CAPRI

By boat All hydrofoils and ferries arrive at Marine Grande. If you've booked a hotel, you can arrange for a porter to meet you at the port. Otherwise, it's a steep walk up three hundred or so steps to Capri Town (20–45min depending on your stamina), or you can take the funicular (daily 6.30am–8.30pm; departures every 15min; €2 one-way; wait in line at the kiosk to get tickets) or a bus.

Tourist offices There are offices in Marina Grande (April–Oct Mon–Sat 9am–1pm & 3–6pm, Sun 9.30am–1.30pm; Nov–March Mon–Sat 9am–3pm; ☎081 837 0634, capritourism.com); in Capri Town in the Piazzetta (April–Oct Mon–Sat 9.30am–1.30pm & 4–6.45pm, Sun 9.30am–1.30pm; Oct–April closed Sun; ☎081 837 0686); and Anacapri, at Via G. Orlandi 59 (Mon–Sat 9am–3pm; ☎081 837 1524).

GETTING AROUND

By bus Capri's main bus station is on Via Roma, near the Piazzetta. The bus service runs every 15min, connecting all the island's main centres – Marina Grande, Capri Town, Marina Piccola and Anacapri. Tickets are available from ticket booths, newsstands and *tabacchi* (€2 to anywhere on the island), as well as upon boarding (in which case they cost €2.50).

By boat Capri Boat, located to the right of Marina Grande as you arrive, next to the ferry ticket booths (☎081 837 5188), rents boats for a minimum of 2hr (mid-April to mid-Oct 9.30am–6.30pm; €90/boat for a maximum of five people). There are also operators at Marina Grande offering boat excursions around the island, taking in the Blue Grotto, for €17, not including entry to the grotto; trips last 2hr, or 1hr if the Blue Grotto is closed.

By scooter You can rent scooters in Marina Grande for around €50 a day from Oasi, at Via Cristoforo Colombo 47 (☎081 837 7138 or ☎334 353 2975), and Capri Scooter (☎081 362 0083 capriscooter.com), at various locations including just up from the port at Via Marina Grande 280 and at Piazza Barile 26, Anacapri.

By taxi Non-residents' cars are not allowed to disembark on Capri, and you can't rent a car, so the island's stylish – and very expensive – convertible taxis are the only private option. There are ranks on the right as you walk out of the port at Marina Grande (☎081 837 0543) and in Anacapri (☎081 837 1175).

ACCOMMODATION

CAPRI TOWN AND AROUND

★ **'A Pazziella** Via Fuorlovado 36 ☎081 837 0044, royalgroup.it. Cool and breezy even on the hottest day, this place has a palpable serenity, yet it's located conveniently in the middle of town. The rooms are elegant and comfortable, many with private balconies and sea views, and there are lovely gardens and free use of the next-door *Sirene* hotel's pool (May–Sept). Closed mid-Oct to April. **€320**

JK Place Capri Via Marina Grande 225 ☎081 838 4001, jkcapri.com. Lording it over Marina Grande from its own clifftop perch, this is easily Capri's most lavish option, with chic, breezy decor in all of its rooms and suites, each perfumed with freshly cut blooms. There's a wraparound terrace with dazzling views, a beautiful pool and a top-notch restaurant, and it's all set a safe distance from the hustle and bustle of the port below. It's the perfect place to unwind – so long as someone else is paying. Closed mid-Oct to mid-April. **€1200**

★ **La Tosca** Via Dalmazio Birago 5 ☎081 837 0989, latoscahotel.com. Genuine bargains on Capri are few and far between, but this place is a real find. A short walk from the Giardini di Augusto on a quiet lane, this whitewashed house has eleven en-suite doubles, some with sea views, kept in spick-and-span condition. Service is ultra-friendly and breakfast on the tiny terrace overlooking Faraglioni is a treat. Closed Nov–late March. **€165**

Weber Ambassador Via Marina Piccola ☎081 837

0141, ⓦhotelweber.com. This quiet, comfortable choice offers great views from its multi-levelled terraces. The decor is cosy and elegant, with warm terracotta accents, and steps lead directly down to the Marina Piccola beach. The frequent shuttle to Capri town (every 5min until 3am) is a bonus. Closed Nov–March. **€280**

ANACAPRI AND AROUND

★ **Da Gelsomina** Via Migliara 72 ⓣ081 837 1499, ⓦdagelsomina.com. In a peaceful location, just a short walk from the belvedere at the end of Via Migliara, this lovely hotel enjoys a pool, a restaurant and easy access to some of the island's best hiking trails. Rooms are simple and fresh, plus each has its own terrace. Fills up fast in summer months so book ahead, and call ahead upon arrival for the complimentary shuttle service – otherwise, it's a 20min walk from the centre of Anacapri. **€200**

La Bussola Via Traversa la Vigna 14 ⓣ081 838 2010, ⓦbussolahermes.com. This boutiquey hotel is a true oasis of peace, a 10min walk from the centre of Anacapri. Cool, stylish rooms, all with balconies – the upper-floor ones are best – and a friendly, welcoming vibe. Closed Oct–March. **€165**

Villa Eva Via La Fabbrica 8 ⓣ081 837 1549, ⓦvillaeva.com. For a long time now, *Villa Eva* has been the cult budget option of the island, and the legend only gets better. It has a wide choice of individually styled rooms, most of them spacious and light, in the main building, as well as others scattered around the gardens, and a grand-piano shaped pool. No dinner, but there are snacks available by the pool, where breakfast is served too. Take the Grotta Azzurra bus and ask to be let off at *Villa Eva*. Closed Nov–March. **€150**

EATING

CAPRI TOWN AND AROUND

★ **Buonocore Gelateria** Via Vittorio Emanuele 35 ⓣ081 837 7826. A fantastic family-run *gelateria* serving up the creamiest ice cream in town, made with fresh fruit – figs, prickly pears, mandarins – from their own garden. Specialities include the rich *fantasia di Capri* (vanilla with Nutella and almonds) and cones are made to order from a generations-old family recipe. Mid-March to mid-Nov daily except Tues 8am–10pm; closes 2am in high season.

Capri Pasta Via Parroco Roberto Canale 12 ⓣ081 837 0147, ⓦcapripasta.com. A family-run, hole-in-the-wall takeaway serving delicious, crispy pizza, as well as a handful of hot dishes – the likes of spinach pie, meatballs or *melanzane alla parmigiana* – for a few euros. Everything's home-made, delicious and very cheap. Mon–Sat 9am–8pm, Sun 11am–2pm; closed Jan & Feb.

Da Giorgio Via Roma 34 ⓣ081 837 0898, ⓦdagiorgiocapri.com. This popular local hangout has a great, very central yet picturesque location on Capri Town's main street, with lovely views through its picture windows. Service is brash but efficient and the prices moderate by Capri standards (pasta dishes around €15) – try the *linguine* with prawns (€23). There are also rooms available (from €195) with half-board options. Daily noon–3.30pm & 7pm–midnight; closed Tues April, May & Oct; closed Nov–March.

★ **Da Tonino** Via Dentecala ⓣ081 837 6718. Tucked away in the hills above Capri Town near the Arco Naturale (it's about a 15min walk from the Piazzetta), *Da Tonino* is worth the trek. Campanian cuisine with a gourmet twist – such as risotto in a beer reduction, or courgette-flower tempura (€12) – is on the menu, and the wine list is exceptional. Ask for a tour of the cellar, which holds over fifteen thousand bottles from all over Italy. Tues–Sun noon–3pm & 7–11pm.

ANACAPRI

Café Casa Oliv Viale Axel Munthe 34 ⓣ081 837 1401. This treetop terrace oasis nestled amid maritime pines is a fine place for a drink. You have to pay the *Villa San Michele* entry fee (see page 779), but you can savour the good life and sea views while sipping a coffee or cocktail (€6–8), and also enjoy a simple but lovely lunch (sandwiches €8) in this tranquil setting. April–Nov 9.30am–6pm.

★ **Il Solitario** Via G. Orlandi 96 ⓣ081 837 1382, ⓦtrattoriailsolitario.it. Take the little walkway back from the street and discover an arboured garden patio decorated with appealingly kitsch statues and coloured fairy lights. A family-run restaurant where the food is excellent – they do a very generous *spaghetti alle vongole* (€18) with home-made pasta, and great pizzas too; the prices are moderate, and the service very friendly. Mon, Tues & Thurs–Sun noon–3.30pm & 7pm–midnight; closed two months in winter.

Lido del Faro Località Punta Carena ⓣ081 837 1798, ⓦlidofaro.com/it/ristorante. Set above the dramatic rocky cove below Anacapri's lighthouse, this is a great place for lunch; ladders lead down into the cove for sea swimming, but there is a pool as well (no children after 3pm). Meals are expensive – you could easily spend €60 on three courses, without wine, but the food (tender octopus salad, crisp fried *baccalà*) is really good, and the setting is gorgeous. Daily mid April–Oct noon–sunset.

L'Olivo Via Capodimonte 2/b ⓣ081 978 0560, ⓦcapripalace.com. The only restaurant on Capri to be awarded two Michelin stars, this plush place in the *Capri Palace Hotel* is renowned for its creative nouvelle

13

Mediterranean cuisine (seven-course tasting menu €130; a la carte dishes around €40). Natural textiles in neutral tones, Murano glassware and handmade dishes complete a very luxurious picture. **April–Oct daily 7.30–10.30pm.**

Ischia

Largest of the islands in the Bay of Naples, **Ischia** (pronounced Iss-kee-a) rises out of the sea in a series of pointy green hummocks, with the cone of a dormant volcano in the centre. German, Scandinavian and British tourists flock here in large numbers during peak season, attracted by its charming beach resorts and thermal springs. Although its reputation has always been poorer than Capri's – it is perhaps not so dramatically beautiful – you can at least be sure of being alone in exploring parts of the mountainous interior, and **La Mortella**, the exotic garden cultivated by the British composer William Walton and his wife Susana, is an unmissable attraction. Indeed, if you're after some beach lounging, good walking and lively nightlife within striking distance of Naples and the rest of the bay, it might be just the place.

Ischia Porto and Ponte

The main town of Ischia is **ISCHIA PORTO**, where the ferries dock, an appealing stretch of hotels, ritzy boutiques and beach shops planted with lemon trees and Indian figs fronted by golden sands: **Spiaggia San Pietro** is to the right of the port, accessible by following Via Buonocore off Via Roma, while the **Spiaggia degli Inglesi**, on the other side, is reachable by way of a narrow path that leads over the headland from the end of Via Iasolino. Apart from sunbathing the main thing to do is to window-shop and stroll along the main Corso Vittoria Colonna, either branching off to a further beach, the **Spiaggia dei Pescatori**, or following it all the way down to the other part of Ischia's main town, **ISCHIA PONTE** (also reachable by bus #7), a quieter and less commercialized centre. Ischia Ponte is home to the island's **Museo del Mare** (daily: April–June, Sept & Oct 10.30am–12.30pm & 3–7pm; July & Aug 10.30am–12.30pm & 6.30–10pm; Nov–Jan & March 10.30am–12.30pm; €2.50; Ⓦ museodelmareischia.it), which traces the community's seafaring roots with ancient, barnacle-encrusted pottery retrieved from the sea and samples of marine fauna.

Castello Aragonese

Ischia Ponte • Daily 9am–8pm; Oct–April until 4pm• €10 • Ⓦ castelloaragonese.it

Accessible from Ischia Ponte via a short causeway, the stunningly distinctive pyramid of the **Castello Aragonese** was one of the backdrops in the film *The Talented Mr Ripley*. The citadel itself is rather tumbledown now and some of it is closed to the public, but below is a complex of buildings, almost a separate village really, around which you can stroll by way of olive-shaded paths and lush terraces. There's the weird open shell of a cathedral destroyed by the British in 1806, a prison that held political prisoners during the Unification struggle and a small torture museum atop the stairs leading out, its disturbing artefacts bearing witness to the depths of medieval cruelty – and admittedly, ingenuity. By far the castle's best-known feature, however, lies within the dark rooms of its old convent, which are ringed with a set of commode-like seats that once served as an open-air cemetery for the dead sisters – placed here to putrefy in front of the living members of the community. The rest of the convent has been converted into a rather nice hotel (see page 785), while there are a couple of pleasant café-restaurants nearby, offering plenty of shady spots to enjoy the stunning views.

Casamicciola Terme

The island is at its most developed along its northern and western shores. Heading west from Ischia Porto, the first village you reach, **CASAMICCIOLA TERME**, is a spa centre with many hotels and a crowded central beach – though you can find a quieter one on the far side of the village. Ibsen spent a summer here, and the waters are said to be full of iodine (apparently beneficial for the skin and the nervous system).

Lacco Ameno

LACCO AMENO is a bright little town, with a beach and spa waters that are said to be the most radioactive in Italy. It's known for the 10m-tall offshore tufa rock, affectionately nicknamed **Il Fungo**, and the **Museo Archeologico di Pithecusae**, housed in the eighteenth-century Villa Arbusto just above the centre (Tues–Sun: June–Sept 9am–5pm; €5; ⓣ 081 333 0288, ⓦ pithecusae.it). The museum's most celebrated piece is the Coppa di Nestore (Nestor's Cup), engraved with a light-hearted challenge to the cup mentioned in Homer's *Iliad*.

La Mortella

Via Francesco Calise 39 • End March–Oct Tues, Thurs, Sat & Sun 9am–7pm • €12; concerts including garden visit €20 • ⓣ 081 986 220, ⓦ lamortella.org • Bus #CS from Ischia Porto, Casamicciola and Lacco Ameno, or #CD from Forío – ask the bus driver to drop you off; taxis from Forío or Casamicciola cost about €10; free parking at upper entrance, in Via Zaro

The stunning garden of **La Mortella** is one of Ischia's highlights, created by the English composer William Walton and his Argentinian wife Susana, who lived here until her death in 2010. The Waltons moved to Ischia, then sparsely populated and little known to tourists, in 1949. With the garden designer Russell Page, they created La Mortella from an unpromising volcanic stone quarry.

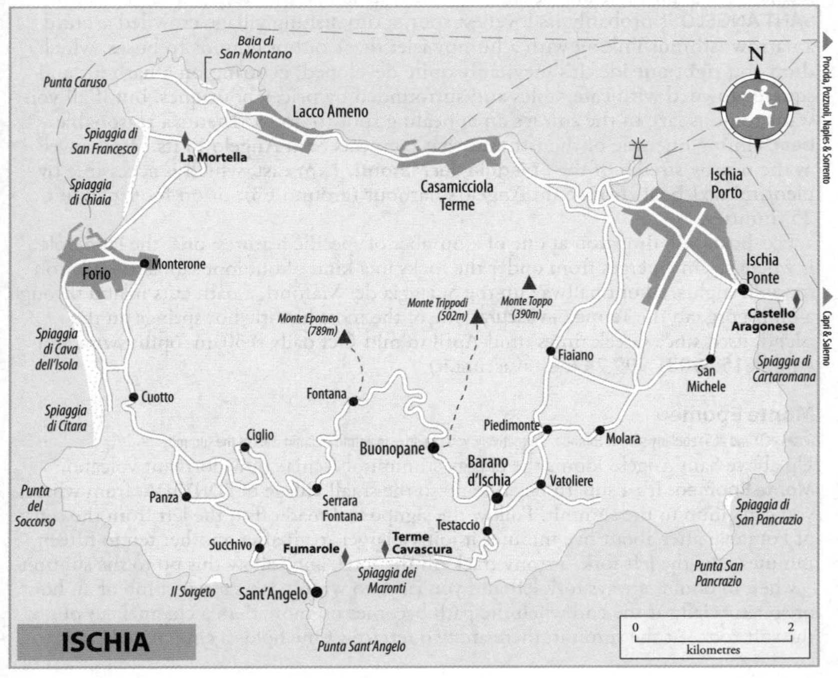

Paths wind up through the abundant site, which is home to some three hundred rare and exotic plants. Near the entrance is a glasshouse sheltering the world's largest water lily, while above the glasshouse is a charming terraced **tearoom**, where the strains of Walton's music can be heard. Paths loop through luxuriant foliage to the memorial to Susana Walton and, beyond, the pyramid-shaped rock that holds Walton's ashes, a cascade guarded by a sculpted crocodile and a pretty **Thai pavilion** surrounded by heavy-headed purple agapanthus. At the garden's summit, a belvedere provides superb views across the island.

Forío

The growing resort of **FORÍO** sprawls around its bay, and is quite pretty behind a seafront of bars and pizzerias, focusing around the busy main street of Corso Umberto. Out on the point on the far side of the old centre (turn right at the end of Corso Umberto), the simple **Chiesa Soccorso** is a bold, whitewashed landmark from which to survey the town. There are good **beaches** either side of Forío: the **Spiaggia di Chiaia**, a short walk to the north, followed immediately by the **Spiaggia di San Francesco** (both buses #1, #2 or #CS); to the south **Cava dell'Isola**, popular with a young crowd; and the **Spiaggia di Citara**, a somewhat longer walk to the south along Via G. Mazzella (both bus #2).

Further south of Forío, at the bottom of a steep path that begins about a twenty-minute walk to the south of Panza (buses #1 or #CS; ask to be let out at Il Ritrovo), is one of the island's most attractive natural springs, **Il Sorgeto**. It's a popular spot around midnight, when the whole bay glimmers in the moonlight – canny locals take a bottle of wine and make a night of it.

Sant'Angelo and around

Ischia is most pleasant on the southern side, its landscape steeper and greener. **SANT'ANGELO** is probably its loveliest spot, a tiny fishing village crowded around a narrow isthmus linking with a humpy islet that's out of bounds to buses, which drop you right outside. It's inevitably quite developed, centring on a harbour and square crowded with café tables and surrounded by pricey boutiques, but if all you want to do is laze in the sun it's an appealing spot to do so. There's a reasonable **beach** lining one side of the isthmus that connects Sant'Angelo to its islet, as well as the nearby stretch of the **Spiaggia dei Maronti**, 1km east, which is accessible by plentiful taxi-boats from Sant'Angelo's harbour (around €3), or on foot in about 25 minutes.

Taxi-boats will drop you at one of a number of specific features: one, the **Fumarole**, is where steam emerges from under the rocks in a kind of outdoor sauna, popular on moonlit nights. About halfway up the Spiaggia dei Maronti, a path cuts inland through a mini-gorge to the **Terme Cavascura**, one of the most historic hot springs on the island, used since Greek times (mid-April to mid-Oct daily 8.30am–6pm; swim and sauna €15; ⓣ081 999 242, ⓦcavascura.it).

Monte Epomeo

Buses #CD and #CS regularly stop at Fontana; alternatively, you can drive to within a 20min walk of the summit

Up above Sant'Angelo looms the craggy summit of Ischia's now dormant volcano, **Monte Epomeo**. It's a superb bus ride up to the small village of **FONTANA**, from where you can climb to the summit. Follow the signposted road off to the left from the centre of Fontana: after about five minutes it joins a larger road; after another ten to fifteen minutes take the left fork, a stony track off the road, and follow this up to the summit – when in doubt, always fork left and you can't go wrong. It's a steep climb of an hour or so, especially at the end when the path becomes no more than a channel cut out of the soft rock. At the summit, there are two terraces. One holds a **church** dedicated to

San Nicola di Bari, built in 1459; on the other terrace, there's a scenic **café** (Feb–Nov daily 9am–6pm).

ARRIVAL AND INFORMATION — ISCHIA

By boat Ferries and hydrofoils from various points around the bay (see page 776) arrive at three points: the main port, Ischia Porto (from Naples, Capri, Procida and Pozzuoli, and seasonally from Sorrento and the Amalfi Coast); Casamicciola Terme (from Naples, Procida and Pozzuoli); and on the western end of the island at Forío (from Naples).

Tourist offices Ischia Porto, right by the quayside ferry ticket offices in the old Terme Comunali building at Via Sogliuzzo 72 (March–Oct daily 9am–2pm & 3–8pm; ⓣ 081 507 4231, ⓦ infoischiaprocida.it); Panza, between Forío and Sant'Angelo (daily 9am–1pm & 7–10pm; ⓣ 081 908 436, ⓦ prolocopanzaischia.it).

GETTING AROUND

You can rely on the efficient bus system to get to all of the major towns and some of the other popular spots, such as the Spiaggia dei Maronti and the various departure points for hikes. Outsiders are prohibited from bringing cars from Easter to the end of the summer.

By bus The main buses, #CS (anticlockwise) and #CD (clockwise), circle the island at 30min intervals; a round trip takes around 1hr 30min. Twenty lesser lines give access to various byways and smaller settlements; the tourist office has timetables. Tickets cost €1.50 (or €2 on board) for a single journey; €1.80 for 1hr 40min; day-tickets are available for €4.50, weekly tickets for €14.50.

By car or scooter Autonoleggio Ischia, at Via Iasolino 27, Ischia Porto (ⓣ 081 992 444, ⓦ autonoleggioischia.it) rents cars for around €40/day and scooters for around €30/day.

ACCOMMODATION

ISCHIA PORTO AND ISCHIA PONTE

★ **Il Monastero** Castello Aragonese, Ponte ⓣ 081 992 433, ⓦ albergoilmonastero.it. Located on the upper floors of the Castello Aragonese, this is the place to stay in Ischia Ponte, with twenty-odd guestrooms in former nuns' cells, which are suitably spare but cool and stylishly furnished. There's a five percent discount if you pay cash and half board is available for €35/person. Closed Nov to mid-April. **€145**

La Marticana Via Quercia 48–50, Porto ⓣ 081 333 4431, ⓦ lamarticana.it. An easy walk from Ischia Porto, this B&B has thirteen comfortable, airy rooms set in a tranquil garden filled with lemon, orange and fig trees. It's worth paying an extra €20 for a room with a terrace or balcony. Hosts Giancarlo and Anna are very welcoming, and discounts for the island's best spas are available too. **€120**

Locanda sul Mare Via Jasolino 80, Porto ⓣ 081 981 470, ⓦ locandasulmare.it. Right on the waterfront just beyond the ferry terminal port (ask for a room with a view to enjoy the comings and goings of the boats), this tiny, idiosyncratically decorated and very pleasant hotel is a great bargain, with simple but spacious rooms and a decent restaurant. **€125**

Macrí Via Iasolino 78/a, Porto ⓣ 081 992 603, ⓦ albergomacri.it. Down a narrow street just steps from the arrival docks of Ischia Porto, this family-run, nicely furnished place has its own bar, terrace, garden and parking, and is handy for a night out in lively Porto. **€110**

FORÍO

★ **Paradise Beach Backpackers Hostel** Via Provinciale Panza 387, Cuotto Forío ⓦ paradisebeachhostel.com. Just a 5min walk from Forío and 10min from Citara beach, this scenically sited hostel is hemmed in by vineyards and has lovely sea views from the simple, spotless rooms. The owner is passionate about the hostel, planting herbs for guests to use in the communal kitchen and organizing events such as barbecues in the sunny garden (complete with fumaroles), beach parties and trips to nearby Il Sorgeto. There's a bar and a good-sized pool too. Dorms **€25**, doubles **€100**

SANT'ANGELO

Casa Giuseppina Via Gaetano D'Iorio 11 ⓣ 081 907 771, ⓦ casagiuseppina.it. Up in Succhivo, a 10min walk from the centre in the direction of Forío (the bus passes right by), this family-run, pleasantly rustic garden villa has a swimming pool and hot tub, and organizes mountain-bike excursions through the surrounding countryside. A/c costs an extra €7/day. No credit cards. Half-board available for an extra €36. Closed Nov–April. **€104**

Camping Mirage Spiaggia dei Maronti ⓣ 081 990 551, ⓦ campingmirage.com. A pleasant, eucalyptus-shaded campsite set right on Maronti Beach about a 20min walk east of Sant'Angelo. There's a bar and restaurant at the hotel and several more along the beach, though there's little else besides – best to stock up on supplies before you arrive. Take bus #5 from Ischia Porto. Pitches **€7** plus **€13** per person

★ **Villa Mario** Via Succhivo 46, Panza ⓣ 081 907 775, ⓦ villamario.it. A calm, restful retreat with wonderful views of Sant'Angelo, this little hotel is expertly run by Tiberio and his family. There's a thermal pool and a flower-filled terrace, and the restaurant is excellent – dishes

13

are prepared with ingredients from the family's garden. Located in Succhivo, just outside Sant'Angelo, the hotel has direct access to the lovely Cava Grado beach. Closed Dec–Feb. €102

EATING AND DRINKING

ISCHIA PORTO AND ISCHIA PONTE

Ischia Salumi Via Luigi Mazzella 100, Ponte ⊕081 906 011, ⓦischiasalumi.com . Run by the family of one of the island's longest-running butchers, this friendly little *salumeria* in the centre of Ischia Ponte offers excellent cold cuts, including cured, smoked rabbit, an Ischian specialty, as well as a range of fresh Campanian classics like pickled artichokes, grilled aubergines and buffalo mozzarella, combining for delicious – and generously portioned – *panini* (€5). April to mid-Oct daily 9am–9pm.

Calise Caffè Concerto Piazza degli Eroi 69, Porto ⊕081 991 270, ⓦbarcalise.com. An island institution with many locations, this branch is set in the midst of a veritable jungle oasis and is an all-purpose venue, serving everything from excellent ice cream to scrumptious cakes and sandwiches, *tavola calda* dishes and pizzas. After hours, it becomes a lounge bar and music venue. April–Oct daily 7.30am–3am; Nov–March closed Tues.

Da Coco' Piazzale Aragonese, Ponte ⊕081 981 823. In an enviable position just below the Castello Aragonese, this bar-restaurant boasts lovely sea views and great seafood from (*spaghetti alle vongole* €14), with home-made ice cream for afters. April–Sept daily 12.30–2.30pm & 7.30–11pm; Oct–March closed Wed.

L'Altra Mezzanotte Via Porto 71, Porto ⊕081 981 711, ⓦristorantelaltramezzanotte.it. The best of the harbourfront's string of upscale restaurants, with friendly service to match the excellent menu – mussel soup for €12, seafood pastas from €15, and grilled fish from €18. Very busy later in the evening, so call ahead. Mid-March to Oct daily 11am–midnight.

CASAMICCIOLA TERME

★ **Il Focolare** Via Cretajo al Crocefisso 3, Barano d'Ischia ⊕081 902 944, ⓦtrattoriailfocolare.it. This is the Casamicciola area's most celebrated restaurant, with a warm welcome and great views of the port from its hilltop perch. Refreshingly, the menu focuses on ingredients other than seafood, with lots of produce from the hills, like their speciality *coniglio all'ischitana* (rabbit stew). Expect to pay about €45/person for a full meal. From Casamicciola's port it's a 5min taxi ride or a 15min bus ride (bus #16; get off at Cretaio). June–Oct Mon–Wed 7.30pm–midnight, Thurs–Sun noon–3pm & 7pm–midnight; Nov–May Mon, Tues & Thurs 7.30pm–midnight, Fri–Sun noon–3pm & 7pm–midnight.

FORÍO

La Casareccia Via Baiola ⊕081 987 756. Set above Forío, on the foothills of Epomeo, this restaurant is worth the trip (call ahead and someone will give you a lift from town and back). Mamma Tina turns out dish after dish of superbly inventive yet deeply authentic Ischian cookery – home-made pizza (margherita €5), creamy tagliolini al limone (€8) and grilled rabbit marinated in wine and herbs (one portion €12; whole rabbit €35). Daily noon–3.30pm & 7pm–midnight.

★ **Umberto a Mare** Via Soccorso 4 ⊕081 997 171, ⓦumbertoamare.it. Established in 1936, this restaurant sits atop a promontory just beside the Chiesa del Soccorso, and the light changes over the water are dazzling. The elegantly presented fish menu changes daily and is accompanied by a large wine selection. It's not cheap – reckon on about €65 a head for a meal with wine – but the food is excellent, and although the terrace has only ten tables, both dining rooms overlook the sea. Rooms are available, and moorings for small boats too, if you arrive by sea. Easter–Oct daily noon–3pm & 7.30–10.30pm.

SANT'ANGELO

Da Pasquale Via Sant'Angelo 79 ⊕081 904 208, ⓦdapasquale.it. Restaurants in Sant'Angelo don't come cheap, but you could do worse than stoke up on the fine pizzas (margherita €6.50) and simple pastas (parmigiana di melanzane €9) they serve at this unpretentious pizzeria in the old centre of the village. April–Nov daily 12.30–3pm & 7pm–midnight.

Procida

A serrated hunk of volcanic rock that's the smallest (population ten thousand) and nearest island to Naples, **Procida** stills manages to fend off the kind of tourist numbers that have flooded into Capri and Ischia. It lacks the spectacle, or variety, of both islands, though it compensates with extra room and extra peace. For the most part, Procida's appeal lies in its opportunities to swim and eat in relative peace.

Marina Grande

The island's main town, **MARINA GRANDE**, where you arrive by ferry, is a slightly run-down but picturesque conglomeration of tall pastel-painted houses rising from the waterfront to a network of steep streets winding up to the fortified tip of the island – the so-called **Terra Murata**. Part of this was once given over to a rather forbidding prison, now abandoned, but it's worth walking up anyway to see the abbey church of **San Michele** (Mon 10am–12.45pm, Tues–Sat 10am–12.45pm & 3–5pm; €2 donation expected), whose ceilings and domes are decorated with paintings by Nicola Russo, pupil of Baroque master Luca Giordano, several depicting St Michael as he beats back the Saracens from Procida's shore. The views, too, from the nearby belvedere are among the region's best.

Corricella

The island's most atmospheric spot, **CORRICELLA** featured as a lost-in-time island town in the Oscar-winning film *Il Postino*. A picturesque little harbour overlooked by pastel-painted houses, it's known as the "Borgo dei Pescatori" as it's still used by local fisherman; you can watch them mending their nets as you tuck into the day's catch at one of the restaurant tables that line the waterfront.

The beaches

There are **beaches** in Marina Grande, on the far side of the jetty, and, in the opposite direction, beyond the fishing harbour, though there are better options elsewhere. **Spiaggia Chiaia**, just beyond the fishing harbour of nearby Corricella and reached by 186 steps, is a reasonable bathing beach but can get crowded; from Marina Grande, buses #L1, #L2 and #C1 stop nearby at Piazza dell'Olmo. If you want to swim you're better off heading to **Spiaggia del Pozzo Vecchio** (bus #C1; 10min), which spreads beneath a bowl of cliffs just beyond the island's cemetery. Further south and at least as popular is the island's longest beach, **Spiaggia di Ciraccio**, a two-minute walk to the west of the pretty, yacht-crammed marina of **Chiaiolella** (bus #L1 or #L2; 15min).

ARRIVAL AND INFORMATION — PROCIDA

By boat Ferries and hydrofoils from Naples and Ischia (see page 776) arrive at the port of Marina Grande; buses #L1 and #L2 coincide with all arrivals and run to Chiaiolella roughly every 20min (€1.20 single; tickets sold in *tabacchi* and newsstands, *Bar Capriccio* in Marina Grande and on board).

Tourist office There is currently no office on the island dedicated to tourist information, but you can find plenty online – including ferry and bus timetables – at procida.net and visitprocida.com.

ACCOMMODATION AND EATING

Crescenzo Via Marina Chiaiolella 33 081 896 7255, hotelcrescenzo.it. This pink brick hotel, fronted by its whitewashed, on-site restaurant and pizzeria, marks the centre of Chiaiolella. Rooms are simple but bright and well-kept, some of them with views over the harbour. A friendly, family-run place with plenty of repeat guests. **€120**

La Casa sul Mare Via Salita Castello 13, Terra Murata 081 896 8799, lacasasulmare.it. One of the island's top choices, consisting of ten bright, elegant guest rooms with private balcony and incredible views over Corricella, set within a seventeenth-century villa with gardens and terraces. There's a free shuttle to the beaches, too. **€170**

★ **La Conchiglia** Via Pizzaco 10, Spiaggia Chiaia 081 896 7602, laconchigliaristorante.com. Above Chiaia beach (there's a handy boat shuttle from Marina di Corricella), this restaurant is an ideal lunch spot, where locals come to tuck into tasty pasta dishes like *cappelletti* filled with provolone cheese and aubergine (€14), or delicious grilled fish. Book ahead. April–Oct daily 12.30–3.15pm & 8.30–10pm.

★ **La Locanda del Postino** Via Marina di Corricella 45, Corricella 081 810 1887, facebook.com/lalocandadelpostino. Set in the fishermen's cove of Corricella, with outside tables under big umbrellas. A plate of pasta costs €7–15, and the delicious fish soup (prebooking necessary) is about €25 for two. The interior remembers the eponymous film, with pictures of its beloved star, the late Neapolitan actor Massimo Troisi. Daily: Sept–June 9.30am–10pm; July & Aug 8am–2/3am.

13

LAND OF FIRES

Illicit waste disposal has long been an important mainstay of the Camorra – netting the group around 600 million euros per year – and the area just north and northeast of Naples has borne most of the brunt of it. Since the early nineties, millions of tons of toxic waste have been dumped here, and the common practice of waste burning has earned it the nickname **"Land of Fires"**.

In more recent years, however, the area has received a good deal of scholarly attention and become one of the most closely-monitored parts of Italy. Considering that other parts of the country have been similarly impacted by heavy dumping, some scholars have rightly pointed out that the contamination of Campania's environment has perhaps been outstripped by that of its reputation.

Inland Campania

As most people head to the coast, few visitors reach **inland Campania**. Indeed the suburbs that sprawl to the north of Naples are rather grim and uninviting (see page 788). Beyond these, however, lies a surprising array of attractions to make the trip worthwhile. Certainly the best-known of the region's attractions is found in Caserta, under an hour north of Naples: a breathtakingly vast, eighteenth-century Palazzo Reale known simply as **La Reggia**. The adjoining towns of **Capua** and **Santa Maria Capua Vetere** to the west boast some significant ancient sites, as does the spruced-up historic centre of **Benevento**, a breezy provincial capital less than two hours to the east.

Caserta and around

A short train or bus ride direct from Naples, **CASERTA**, incongruously surrounded by a sprawl of industrial complexes and warehouses that seems to stretch all the way back to Naples, is known as the "Versailles of Naples" for its vast eighteenth-century **Reggia di Caserta**. Most visitors come solely for the palace, though to its east spreads Caserta's pleasant old town, offering a good selection of cafés, restaurants and bars. Further afield lies the older and much smaller medieval town of **Casertavecchia**, founded in the ninth century by Lombards on the hilltops to the northeast of town (a twenty-minute bus ride from the train station). The views over Caserta from up here are perhaps only rivaled by those from the grand terrace of the **Real Fabbrica della Seta** (Wed–Mon 9.30am–6pm; €6; no public transport); a giant silk factory complex in the hills just northwest of the palace, built by Ferdinand IV in the late eighteenth century as a bold experiment in utopian socialism.

La Reggia di Caserta

Viale Giulio Douhet • Daily (except Tues) 8.30am–7.30pm, park closes between 2.30pm & 6pm, depending on time of year • €12 for apartments, park and English Garden; €9 apartments only; €8 park and English Garden only • ⓣ 0823 277 111, ⓦ reggiadicaserta.beniculturali.it

Begun in 1752 for the Bourbon King Charles III to plans drawn up by Vanvitelli, and completed a little over twenty years later, **La Reggia di Caserta** is an awesomely large complex, built around four courtyards, with a facade 245m long. However, it's a dull structure that generally substitutes size for inspiration.

Only the majestic central staircases up to the **royal apartments** hit exactly the right note. The apartments themselves are a grand parade of heavily painted and stuccoed rooms, sparsely furnished in French Empire style, with great, overbearing classical statues and smug portraits of the Bourbon dynasty – look out for the one of the podgy Francis I with his brat-like children.

The Parco Reale and English Garden

Regular shuttle buses (€2.50) run up and down the park and to the English Garden, dropping off at regular intervals along the way; bike rental €4/hr, e-bike rental €6/hr

Behind the palace, the **Parco Reale** is on no less huge a scale, stretching out behind along a central axis punctured by myth-inspired fountains. Stretching about three kilometres, it's certainly longer than it looks from the palace (it's a good thirty-minute walk), culminating in the main cascade at the top. Completed in 1779, the falls are the backdrop for a set of statues that depict Diana turning Actaeon into a stag. On your left as you face back to the palace from here is the **English Garden**, with pathways that curve through groves and meadows adorned with a smattering of would-be ancient ruins.

Santa Maria Capua Vetere

About 6km west of Caserta • Bus #1 and #22 link with Caserta's train station (every 40min; 15min)

Bang on the old Via Appia, ancient Capua boasts numerous wonders of the age, including the ruins of Italy's second largest Roman **amphitheatre** (Tues–Sun 9am–1hr before sunset) – from which Spartacus supposedly began his famous revolt in 73 AD – and a fascinating **mithraeum** (same hours): a mysterious temple of cult worship. Combined tickets (€2.50) include entrance to the amphitheatre, the mithraeum (Tues–Sun 9am–6pm) and the **Museo Archeologico dell'Antica Capua**, which houses a smattering of Bronze Age, Etruscan, Greek and Roman finds uncovered in the area.

Capua

About 10km west of Caserta • Bus #1 and #22 link with Caserta's train station (every 40min; 30min)

Nestled in a lazy bend of the Volturno River about four kilometres west of Santa Maria Capua Vetere, the **walled medieval town** of Capua is more picturesque than its Roman counterpart. Originally called Casilinum, it became Capua in the ninth century AD, when the Capuans resettled here after Saracen invaders razed their city. The town centres on **Piazza dei Giudici**, bordered to the south by the sixteenth-century Palazzo Municipale, adorned with seven heads of Roman deities removed from the Capuan amphitheatre. The best reason to visit, however, lies a few blocks north of here – a superb **museum** with one of Campania's very best historical collections.

Museo Provinciale Campano di Capua

Tues & Thurs 9am–1.30pm & 3–6pm, Wed, Fri & Sat 9am–1.30pm, Sun 9am–1pm • €6 • ⓣ 0823 961 042, ⓦ museocampano.it

Three thousand years are on display in this captivating museum, including much of the remaining wealth of ancient Capua. Worth the visit alone is the collection of sixth- to first-century **mothers**, discovered in a nearby temple dedicated to Mater Matuta, an early Italic deity (later equated with Aurora, the Roman goddess of dawn). There are about two hundred votive statues of mothers, almost all of them bearing swaddled children in their earthen laps. The old goddess herself sits at the back, holding not a child but a dove and a pomegranate, symbols of peace and fertility. The museum also has an impressive store of terracotta figurines and vases, funeral stele and medieval and Renaissance works of art.

Sant'Agata de' Goti

About 10km west of Caserta • Buses run to and from Naples' Piazza Garibaldi (3 daily; 1hr); there's only one daily bus connecting Benevento, departing in the afternoon (1hr)

About halfway between Caserta and Benevento lies inland Campania's prettiest hill-town, **Sant'Agata de' Goti**. The old town is built on a raised table of tufa, divided from the newer part of town by a deep, verdant gorge, while the bridge leading across is the vantage point for its most photographed **view**. It's worth popping

into its old churches or simply wandering for an hour or two, though there are at least several accommodation options in case you'd like to stay the night – the town's narrow cobblestone streets and handful of piazzas are at their most charming after dark.

ACCOMMODATION AND EATING

Agriturismo Mustilli Piazza Trento 4 ☎ 0823 718 142, Ⓦ hotelvillatraiano.it. Six comfortable rooms furnished with family antiques set with an old palazzo in the heart of the old town. There's also a beautiful garden courtyard and a restaurant where the friendly hosts serve full meals including home-made wine (€35). **€85**

Benevento

Appealing **BENEVENTO** was another important Roman settlement, a key point on the Via Appia between Rome and Brindisi and, as such, a thriving trading town. Founded in 278 BC, it was at the time the farthest point from Rome to be colonized, and even now it has a remote air about it, circled by forested hills. The old centre was bombed to smithereens in the last war, but it's been beautifully restored.

Museo del Sannio

Corso Garibaldi 6 • Tues–Sun 9am–1pm & 4–7.30pm • €4; €2 cloister only • ☎ 0824 47 360, Ⓦ museodelsannio.it

The excellent **Museo del Sannio**, in the cloister behind the eighth-century church of Santa Sofia, holds an impressive selection of Hellenistic and Roman finds from the local area, including exquisite bas-reliefs, terracotta votive figurines and Greek vases. The twelfth-century cloister itself is worth a look, ringed with Moorish arches divided by Romanesque capitals carved with energetic scenes of animals, humans and strange beasts, hunting, riding and attacking.

ARCOS

Corso Garibaldi 1 • Tues–Fri 10am–6pm, Sat & Sun 10am–1pm & 3–6pm • €2 • ☎ 0824 312 465

Set beneath the town prefecture opposite the Museo del Sannio, **ARCOS**, a small contemporary art museum, is best known for its unique collection of ancient Egyptian-style artefacts gathered from a nearby temple dedicated to Isis. Alongside the objects themselves – various sphinxes, falcons, bulls, an effigy of Emperor Domitian as a Pharaoh, two headless statues of priests of Isis and the granite head of the goddess herself – are detailed descriptions of the peculiar pagan cult that once swept much of the Mediterranean world, a final pagan flourish before the rise of Christianity.

Arch of Trajan

Further along Corso Garibaldi, off to the right, the **Arch of Trajan** is the major remnant of the Roman era, a marvellously preserved triumphal arch boasting much more distinct images than Rome's arches, and you can get close enough to study its friezes. Built to guard the entrance to Benevento from the Appian Way, it's actually as heavy-handed a piece of self-acclaim as there ever was, showing the Emperor Trajan in various scenes of triumph, power and generosity.

The Duomo

Piazza Orsini • Daily 7.15am–noon & 4.30–7pm (opens 4pm on days when museum is open); museum Tues–Sat 9am–noon & 4–7pm • Duomo free; museum €3 • ☎ 0824 323 315, Ⓦ diocesidibenevento.it

The city's star-crossed **Duomo** is an almost total reconstruction of a thirteenth-century Romanesque original, but a few cobbled-together fragments of the original Lombard structure now form the hotchpotch facade along with a celebrated set of twelfth-century Byzantine bronze doors that have been recently restored. Take a look, too, at the bell tower, with its line-up of Roman busts scavenged from local funerary

sites, and the eighth-century crypt, which has thirteenth-century frescoes and hosts a small **museum**.

Teatro Romano

Piazza Ponzio Telesino • Daily 9am–sunset • €2 • ⓦ comune.benevento.it

Benevento has a shabby but picturesque medieval quarter, the **Triggio**, off to the left of Corso Garibaldi beyond the cathedral, where there's a substantial but indifferently maintained **Teatro Romano**, inaugurated in 126 AD. Built during the reign of Hadrian, it seated twenty thousand people in its heyday, and it's still an atmospheric sight, with views over the rolling green countryside of the province.

ARRIVAL AND INFORMATION — BENEVENTO

By train There are trains from Naples about every hour (1hr 45min); most change at Caserta. The station is a 30min walk from the centre, but there are frequent buses in.

By bus Six daily buses make the 90min trip from Naples, dropping off in a car park below Benevento's centre.

Tourist office Via Nicola Sala 31 (Mon–Fri 9am–1.30pm & 3–4pm; ⓣ 0824 319 911).

ACCOMMODATION AND EATING

Villa Traiano Viale dei Rettori 9 ⓣ 0824 326 241, ⓦ hotelvillatraiano.it. Housed in a lovely belle époque building just a short distance the famous arch, with finely furnished guestrooms, a tranquil terrace garden and a bar. Free underground parking available. **€150**

La Casa sul Mare Via Giuseppe Manciotti 48–50 ⓣ 0824 21 568, ⓦ facebook.com/pg/ristorantetraiano1985. Dining inside this friendly restaurant and pizzeria feels more like eating at home; meanwhile, its tables in the piazza overlook the famous Arch of Trajan. Excellent pastas and pizzas (margherita €5). Mon & Wed–Sun 9am–4pm & 6.45pm–11.45pm.

The Amalfi Coast

Occupying the southern side of Sorrento's peninsula, the **Amalfi Coast** (Costiera Amalfitana) lays claim to being Europe's most beautiful stretch of coast, its corniche road winding around the towering cliffs that slip almost sheer into the sea. By car or bus it's an incredible ride (though it can get mighty congested in summer), with some of the most spectacular stretches between Salerno and Amalfi. If you're staying in Sorrento especially, it shouldn't be missed on any account; in any case the towns along here hold the beaches that Sorrento lacks. The coast as a whole has become rather developed, and these days it's one of Italy's ritzier bits of shoreline, villas atop its precarious slopes fetching a bomb in both cash and kudos. While it's home to some stunning hotels, budget travellers should be aware that you certainly get what you pay for here.

Positano

There's not much to **POSITANO**, only a couple of decent beaches, an interesting Duomo, and a great many boutiques; the town has long specialized in clothes made from linen, georgette and cotton, as well as handmade shoes and sandals. But its location, heaped up in a pyramid high above the water, has inspired a thousand postcards and helped to make it a moneyed resort that runs a close second to Capri in the celebrity stakes. Since John Steinbeck wrote up the place in glowing terms back in 1953, the town has enjoyed a fame quite out of proportion to its size. Franco Zeffirelli is just one of many famous names who have villas nearby, and the people who come here to lie on the beach consider themselves a cut above your average sun-worshipper.

13

The beaches

Positano is, of course, expensive, but its beaches are nice enough and don't get too crowded. The main beach, the **Spiaggia Grande** right in front of the village, is reasonable, although you'll be sunbathing among the fishing boats unless you want to pay over the odds for the pleasanter bit on the far left. There's also another, larger stretch of beach, **Spiaggia del Fornillo**, around the headland to the west, accessible in five minutes by a pretty path that winds around from above the hydrofoil jetty – although its main section is also a pay area. Nonetheless the bar-terrace of the *Pupetto* hotel (see page 792), which runs along much of its length, is a cheaper place to eat and drink than anywhere in Positano proper.

ARRIVAL AND INFORMATION — POSITANO

By bus Buses stop at various points along the main coastal road, Via Marconi, which skirts the top of the old town of Positano. There's a stop on the Amalfi side of town, from where it's a steep walk or a short bus ride down to Piazza dei Mulini, the little square at the bottom of Via Cristoforo Colombo – a 5min walk from the seafront; or you could get off on the other side of the centre, by the *Bar Internazionale*, from where Viale Pasitea winds down to the Fornillo part of town. You must purchase tickets for SITA buses from *tabacchi* (you can't buy them on board); one-way trips cost €2 to both Sorrento and Amalfi; 24hr tickets cost €10, valid for buses between Sorrento and Salerno. Alternatively, open-top City Sightseeing buses (T 081 877 4707, W city-sightseeing.it) run hourly from late March–Oct between Sorrento, Positano and Amalfi; you can buy tickets (€10) on board.

By boat Ferries and hydrofoils from Capri, Naples and Amalfi pull in at the jetty just to the right of the main beach, where there are also plenty of ticket booths.

By car Arriving by car, you'll shell out a lot on garage space as parking is very limited; reckon on at least €20 a day.

Tourist office Just back from the beach by the church steps at Via del Saracino 4 (May–Sept daily 8.30am–7.30pm; Oct–April Mon–Sat 9am–7pm, Sun 9am–2pm; T 089 875 067, W aziendaturismopositano.it).

ACCOMMODATION

Hostel Brikette Via G. Marconi 358 T 089 875 857, W hostel-positano.com. A couple of minutes' walk up from the *Bar Internazionale* on the main coastal road, this is easily Positano's cheapest option. It's clean and welcoming, with a cozy bar and a pretty terrace offering stunning Mediterranean views, though it's quite a climb down to the beach. Dorm rooms are clean but spartan, and private rooms are available too. Hearty breakfast options available (€5–7). Dorms **€40**, rooms **€150**

★ **Maria Luisa** Via Fornillo 42 T 089 875 023, W pensionemarialuisa.com. Perched high above Fornillo beach, *Maria Luisa* offers good value, with clean, simple a/c rooms equipped with mini-fridges. It's the five-star views from the shared terrace that make it really special, and perhaps worth paying a bit more for one of the private terraces (€173). Breakfast available for an additional €8. Closed Nov–March. **€123**

★ **Palazzo Murat** Via dei Mulini 23 T 089 875 177, W palazzomurat.it. Right in the heart of things – you can almost touch the tin-glazed Duomo from its gorgeous pool – and just 2min from the beach. It has thirty good-sized and well-equipped rooms – though most of them are not in the old *palazzo* itself but in the newer extension. **€400**

Pupetto Via Fornillo 37 T 089 875 087, W hotelpupetto.it. Right on Fornillo beach and with access for guests, this bright spot offers a huge terrace and pastel rooms, some overlooking a garden and others with sea views (from €200). Full-range restaurant, from wood-fired pizza to catch of the day. Parking available for €15/day. **€180**

Buca di Bacco Via Rampa Teglia 4 T 089 875 699, W buccadibacco.it. This charming old-timer sits right on Spiaggia Grande, with bright tiled floors throughout and spacious, traditionally-styled rooms with marble bathrooms. The pricier ones come with private terraces that boast some of the best views in town. **€350**

EATING AND DRINKING

Bruno Via C. Colombo 157 T 089 875 392, W brunopositano.it. Some way from the more touristy places near the beach, both in distance and in price, this street-side restaurant has lovely views over the town and the beach. Friendly staff and good food, with main courses heavily weighted towards fish and seafood (pasta with lobster €25). April–Oct daily 12.30–11pm.

Chez Black Spiaggia Grande T 089 875 036, W chezblack.it. With an unbeatable central setting, right across from Positano's beach, this long-established seafood restaurant is perhaps a bit over-branded these days, but the food is unfalteringly good. Lots of great seafood options – try the *paccheri* with cuttlefish and octopus (€22). Good

PATH OF THE GODS

Offering unparalleled views over the rugged Amalfi Coast, the well-marked **Path of the Gods** (Il Sentiero degli Dei) undulates along ridges beside terraced slopes and sheer karst walls. The 6km trail starts from the main square in mountaintop Bomerano (634m) – reachable by bus from Amalfi – and ends in Nocelle (440m), with a side trail branching off to Praiano from roughly the halfway point. From Nocelle, a pretty little town with great views over Positano, you can catch a bus down to the main road – unless you still have the energy to tackle the 1700-step descent to Positano. The trail takes roughly three hours and can be uncomfortably hot in summer – start early and pack plenty of water. Pick up a map at the tourist office in Positano or Praiano.

pizza, too (from €10). First two weeks of Jan & March–Oct daily noon–6pm & 6.30–11.30pm.

★ **Da Vincenzo** Via Pasitea 172–178 ⓣ 089 875 128, ⓦ davincenzo.it. Welcoming, family-run place in the centre of town with warm service, a lively local atmosphere and tasty homemade pasta dishes (*tagliolini al limone* with shrimp €25; *maccheroncelli alla Genovese* €17). April–Oct Mon & Wed–Sun 12.15–2.45 & 6.15–10.45pm, Tues 6.30–11pm.

★ **Lo Guarracino** Via Positanesi d'America 12 ⓣ 089 875 794, ⓦ loguarracinopositano.it. Set above the footpath to Fornillo beach, *Lo Guarracino* makes a welcoming escape from the bustle of town, with wonderful views from a bright, flower-fringed terrace overlooking the sea. It has a delicious, varied and well-priced menu – try the *Scialatielli Lo Guarracino* (€21) – pasta with clams, mussels, shrimps and squids in a cherry tomato sauce. There are also excellent pizzas from €9. April–Oct daily noon–3.30pm & 7–11pm.

Praiano and around

Around 6km east of Positano, **PRAIANO** consists of two tiny centres: Vettica Maggiore, which is Praiano proper, scattered along the main road from Positano high above the sea; and Marina di Praia, squeezed into a cleft in the rock down at shore level, a couple of kilometres further along towards Amalfi. Praiano is much smaller and quieter than Positano, and although there's not much to either bit of the village, it does make a more peaceful and authentic place to stay than its more renowned neighbour. There are a few decent places to swim, the closest being immediately below town at the **Spiaggia Gavitella** – reachable from the main road along the path from the *San Gennaro* restaurant – and there's a small patch of shingly beach at **Marina di Praia**, surrounded by a couple of restaurants and places offering rooms. There's also a marked trail from here that connects to the Path of the Gods (see above).

The Grotta dello Smeraldo

Conca dei Marini • Daily: April–Oct 9.30am–4pm; Nov–March 9.30am–3pm • €5 • Taxi-boat from either Praiano or Amalfi €10 return

About 4km out of Praiano, the **Grotta dello Smeraldo** is one of the most highly touted local natural features around here, a flooded cavern in which the sunlight turns the water a vivid shade of green. It's not unimpressive, but is basically one huge chamber and it doesn't take long for the boatman to whisk you around the main features, best of which is the intense colour of the water, and the stalagmites and stalactites that puncture, and drip from, every surface.

ARRIVAL AND INFORMATION **PRAIANO**

By bus Local buses link Positano with Praiano (April to mid-June, Oct & late Dec to early Jan 9 daily; mid-June to Sept roughly every 30min; Nov & Dec 4 daily; 25min), with stops in both Vettica Maggiore and Marina di Praia, as do SITA buses (year-round), which also run to Sorrento (1hr 15min) and Amalfi (25min).

Tourist office Across from San Gennaro at Via Capriglione 116/B (Mon–Sat 9am–1pm & 4.30–8.30pm; ⓣ 089 874 4557, ⓦ praiano.org).

ACCOMMODATION AND EATING

Casa Angelina Via Capriglione 147 ⓣ089 813 1333, ⓦcasangelina.com. Stylish boutique hotel perched on the cliffs at the Positano end of town, with spectacular views up the coast from the beautiful pool deck and rooftop restaurant. It has a lobby full of contemporary art and a selection of beautiful rooms decorated with stark, modern white minimalism – the pricier rooms include large balconies or terraces with sunbeds. **€780**

★ **Costa Diva** Via Roma 12 ⓣ089 813 076, ⓦlocandacostadiva.it. Up above Marina di Praia, this hotel spills down a leafy series of terraces from the road; almost all the rooms have lovely tilework, balconies and sea views, which you can enjoy – in a few select rooms – from the comfort of your own hot tub (€200). Even if you're not staying here you can enjoy views from the pergola-draped terrace of its superb restaurant (mains for around €14). Closed Nov–early March. **€160**

Trattoria San Gennaro Via Capriglione 75 ⓣ089 874 293, ⓦfacebook.com/rossellamilano90p. Right next to the church, this is as central as you get in Vettica Maggiore, and serves huge portions of *antipasti di mare* and *primi* like *linguine alla carbonara* for €12. There are also decent pizzas from €7 and a terrace with a great view over the church square and sea. Fri–Wed 12.40–4pm & 6–10.30pm.

Amalfi and Atrani

Cradled in a wide cleft in the cliffs, **AMALFI**, a mere 10km or so east of Praiano, is the largest town and perhaps the highlight of the coast. It has been an established seaside resort since Edwardian times, when the British upper classes found the town a pleasant spot to spend their winters. Actually, Amalfi's credentials go back much further: it was an independent republic during Byzantine times and one of the great naval powers, with a population of some seventy thousand; Webster's *Duchess of Malfi* was set here, and the city's traders established outposts all over the Mediterranean, setting up the Order of the Knights of St John of Jerusalem. Amalfi was finally vanquished by the Normans in 1131, and the town was devastated by an earthquake in 1343, but there is still the odd remnant of Amalfi's past glories around today, and the town has a crumbly attractiveness to its whitewashed courtyards and alleys that makes it fun to wander through. Plus there is a decent, mostly sandy beach to the left of the busy seafront, as well as in the attractive next-door resort of Atrani.

The Duomo

Piazza Duomo • Daily: March–June & Oct 9am–6.45pm; July–Sept 9am–7.45pm; Nov–Feb 10am–1pm & 2.30–4.30pm • €3

The **Duomo**, at the top of a steep flight of steps, utterly dominates the town's main piazza, its tiered, almost gaudy facade topped by a glazed tiled cupola that's typical of the area. The bronze doors of the church came from Constantinople and date from 1066. Inside it's a mixture of Saracen and Romanesque styles, though now heavily restored, and the cloister – the so-called **Chiostro del Paradiso** – is the most appealing part of the building, oddly Arab in feel with its whitewashed arches and palms. The adjacent **museum**, housed in an ancient, bare basilica, dates back to the sixth century and has various medieval and episcopal treasures, most intriguingly an eighteenth-century sedan chair from Macau, used by the bishop of Amalfi, a thirteenth-century mitre sewn with myriad seed pearls and a lovely fourteenth-century bone-and-ebony inlaid box, made by the renowned Embriarchi studio in Venice. Steps lead down from the museum to the heavily decorated **crypt**, where the remains of the apostle St Andrew lie under the altar, brought here (minus head) from Constantinople by the Knights of Malta in 1204.

The Arsenale

Largo Cesareo • Tues–Sun 10am–1pm & 4–7pm • €4 • ⓣ334 917 7814

Facing the waterfront square, the town's ancient, vaulted **Arsenale** is a reminder of the former military might of Amalfi, used to build the maritime republic's fleet. Now it hosts temporary exhibitions and a small museum containing bits and pieces

including the costumes worn by the great and the good of the town for the Regatta of the Maritime Republics, and the city banner, showing the emblems of Amalfi – the diagonal red strip and Maltese cross you see everywhere.

Museo della Carta

Via delle Cartiere 23 • March–Oct daily 10am–6.30pm; Nov–Feb Tues, Wed & Fri–Sun 10am–3.30pm • €4 • ⓣ 089 830 4561, ⓦ museodellacarta.it

At the top of Via Genova, a fifteen-minute walk from the main square, the **Museo della Carta** is housed in a paper mill that dates from 1350 and claims to be the oldest in Europe. The valley beyond the museum is still known as the **Valle dei Mulini** (Valley of Mills), because it was once the heart of Amalfi's paper industry, with around fifteen functioning mills. This is the only one to survive, and it makes all the high-spec paper you see on sale around town. Tours take in the tools of the trade and the original paper-making process and equipment, including that in use when the mill shut down in 1969.

Atrani

Just a short walk around the headland from Amalfi – or an even shorter walk through the pedestrian tunnel from Piazza Municipio – **ATRANI** is to all extents and purposes an extension of Amalfi. Indeed, it was another part of the maritime republic, with a similarly styled church also sporting a set of bronze doors from Constantinople, manufactured in 1086; it's here that the Regatta of the Maritime Republics (see page 36) begins every four years (next due to be held in Amalfi in 2020). It's a quiet place, with a pretty, almost entirely enclosed little square, Piazza Umberto, giving onto a smallish sandy beach – a little more developed than it once was, but still gloriously peaceful compared to Amalfi.

ARRIVAL AND INFORMATION — AMALFI AND ATRANI

By bus Regular SITA buses stop at Piazza Flavio Gioia on the seafront in Amalfi and directly above Piazza Umberto I in Atrani. From late March to October open-top City Sightseeing buses run hourly to Positano (25min) and Sorrento (1hr 25min) for €10 one-way and to Ravello (30min) for €5 one-way; it's worth joining the queue early.

By boat Ferries and hydrofoils from Salerno, Positano, Capri, Ischia and Sorrento arrive and leave at the landing stages in Amalfi's harbour, right by the main bus terminal, as do the smaller boats to the Grotta dello Smeraldo and other points along the coast.

Tourist office In a courtyard on the seafront next door to the post office, the tourist office (Mon–Sat: April–Oct 9am–1pm & 3–7pm, Nov–March 8am–1pm ⓣ 089 871 107, ⓦ amalfitouristoffice.it) can provide a map of the town and answer basic questions.

ACCOMMODATION

A'Scalinatella Piazza Umberto 1, Atrani ⓣ 089 871 492, ⓦ hostelscalinatella.com. As good a reason as any for coming to Atrani is this friendly hotel, one of the cheapest places to stay on the coast, a friendly, family-run establishment that offers excellent-value hostel beds and private en-suite rooms in various buildings around town. Dorms **€40**, doubles **€100**

Aurora Piazzale dei Protontini 7 ⓣ 089 871 209, ⓦ aurora-hotel.it. Right in the corner of the harbour and a 5min walk from the centre of Amalfi, this newly refurbished hotel has bright rooms with large balconies as well as a spacious lounge and terrace. Access to the hotel's private beach €15/day. Closed Nov to mid-April. **€230**

Marina Riviera Via Pantaleone Comite 19 ⓣ 089 871 104, ⓦ marinariviera.it. Directly overlooking the beach and the town from the east side of town, this family-run hotel has 34 bright, spacious and well-equipped rooms. The views from its rooftop pool and bar – where a generous breakfast is served, weather permitting – are some of the best in town, as are those from the terrace of its adjacent *Eolo* restaurant.

★ **Palazzo Ferraioli** Via Campo 16, Atrani ⓣ 089 872 652, ⓦ palazzoferraioli.it. Up through the whitewashed passages off Atrani's main square, the coolly contemporary rooms of this ingeniously converted *palazzo* are each decorated uniquely, with a stylish, modern theme, some with great views over the town and bay. Perhaps the best view is from the fancy rooftop terrace bar. Closed Nov–March. **€200**

13

Residenza del Duca Via Mastalo del Duca 3 ⓣ089 873 6365, ⓦresidencedelduca.it. Tiny *pensione* tucked away at the top of a building among the alleys and tiny courtyards off to the left of Amalfi's main street. All rooms are uniquely decorated with period furniture, partial sea views, bathrooms with jacuzzi-style showers and flatscreen TVs and a/c. **€150**

EATING AND DRINKING

A'Paranza Via Dragone 2, Atrani ⓣ089 871 840, ⓦristoranteparanza.com. On the road that leads inland from the main square, this friendly seafood trattoria serves fabulous home-made pasta and a speciality of *zuppa di pesce* (€65 for two). Mon & Wed–Sun 12.30–3pm & 7–11pm; open until 2am in summer months.

Il Mulino Via della Cartiere 36, Amalfi ⓣ089 872 223. At the top of the main street and worth the 10min walk from the Duomo, this down-to-earth, family-run restaurant with an outside terrace does great home-made seafood pasta from €8–14 and good pizzas too (from €6). March–Oct Tues–Sun 11.30–4pm & 6.30–midnight.

La Caravella Via Matteo Camera 12, Amalfi ⓣ089 871 029, ⓦristorantelacaravella.it. One of the town's posher options, this Michelin-starred stalwart serves great, individual takes on traditional dishes, made with local ingredients. A cut above the rest in price as well as tone, with four-course tasting menus starting at €50. Mon & Wed–Sun noon–2.30pm & 7–11pm.

Pizzeria Donna Stella Salita Rascica 2, Amalfi ⓣ338 358 8483. About a 5min walk up the main street from the coast, with a good range of inventive pizzas served on a trellised patio with a roof of overhanging lemon trees. Most pizzas between €8–14. Come early or book ahead. Mon & Wed–Sun noon–3pm & 6.30–10.30pm.

★**Taverna Buonvicino** Largo S. Maria Maggiore 13, Amalfi ⓣ089 873 6385, ⓦtavernabuonvicino.com. A couple of minutes' walk left of the Duomo steps, this restaurant and wine bar makes the most of its atmospheric little square – perhaps Amalfi's prettiest – offering a well-priced seasonal menu, with local favourites such as lamb with wild Mediterranean herbs (€18) and squid stuffed with potatoes (€14). Book ahead. March–Oct & mid- to late Dec daily 11.45am–2.30pm & 6.30–10.30pm.

Trattoria da Gemma Via Fra Gerardo Sasso 11, Amalfi ⓣ089 871 345, ⓦtrattoriadagemma.com. The oldest restaurant in town, it's still one of the best and most charming – and pricey – places to eat, with a lovely terrace overlooking the main street. Its small, carefully considered menu is strong on fish and seafood – pasta and *primi* start at €16 and mains at €23. The fish soup is especially tasty (€80 for two). Daily noon–3pm & 7–11pm.

Ravello

The best views of the coast can be had inland, high above Amalfi in **RAVELLO**: a renowned spot "closer to the sky than the seashore", wrote André Gide – with some justification. Ravello was also an independent republic for a while, and for a time an outpost of the Amalfi city-state. Now it's not much more than a large village, but its unrivalled location, spread across the top of one of the coast's mountains, makes it more than worth the thirty-minute bus ride through the steeply cultivated terraces up from Amalfi. Wagner set part of Parsifal, one of his last operas, here; D.H. Lawrence wrote some of *Lady Chatterley's Lover* here; John Huston filmed his languid movie *Beat the Devil* in town; and more recently the writer and political polemicist Gore Vidal lived here for many years.

THE RAVELLO FESTIVAL

Ravello's annual **arts festival** (ⓦravellofestival.com) dominates the summer months, with performances all over town from the end of June to early September. The festival's prime venue, the **Oscar Niemeyer Auditorium**, is something of an attraction itself – a sleek, modern, white wave below the crown of the hill to the east of the centre. Concentrating on classical music, dance, film and the visual arts, the festival makes the most of the town's spectacular settings and attracts an impressive array of international performers. From March to October, the Ravello Concert Society (ⓦravelloarts.org) also hosts several concerts a week in the Anunziata Church.

The Duomo

Piazza Duomo • **Church** Daily 9am–noon & 5.30–7pm • Free • **Museum** Daily 9am–7pm • €3 • ⓣ 089 858 311

Everything in Ravello revolves around the main **Piazza Duomo**, where the **Duomo**, a bright eleventh-century church, renovated in 1786, is dedicated to St Pantaleone, a fourth-century saint whose blood – kept in a chapel on the left-hand side – is supposed to liquefy (like Naples' San Gennaro and others) once a year on July 27. It's a richly decorated church, with a pair of twelfth-century bronze doors, cast with 54 scenes of the Passion; inside, there are two monumental thirteenth-century *ambones* (pulpits), both wonderfully adorned with intricate and glittering mosaics. The more elaborate one to the right of the altar, dated 1272, sports dragons and birds on spiral columns supported by six roaring lions, while the one on the left illustrates the story of Jonah and the whale. Downstairs in the crypt, the **museum** holds the superb bust of Sigilgaita Rufolo and the silver reliquary of St Barbara, alongside a collection of highly decorative, fluid mosaic and marble reliefs from the same era.

Villa Rufolo

Piazza Duomo • Daily: April–Oct 9am–9pm; Nov–March 9am–5pm • €7 • ⓣ 089 857 621, ⓦ villarufolo.it

The Rufolos figure on the other side of the square from the Duomo, where various remains of their **Villa Rufolo** lie scattered among rich gardens overlooking the precipitous coastline. The rambling villa offers some of Ravello's most iconic views and hosts many of the Ravello Festival's top events. If the crowds (best avoided by coming early in the morning) put you off, turn left by the entrance and walk up the steps over the tunnel for the best (free) view over the shore, from where it's a pleasant stroll through the back end of Ravello to the main square.

Villa Cimbrone

Via S. Chiara 26 • Daily 9am–sunset • €7 • ⓣ 089 857 459

It's just a ten-minute walk from the centre of Ravello to perhaps its most celebrated sight, the **Villa Cimbrone**, whose formal gardens spread across the furthest tip of Ravello's ridge. Most of the villa itself is now a luxury hotel but you can peep into the flower-hung cloister and crypt as you go in. The gardens are dotted with statues and little temples and lead down to what must be the most gorgeous spot in Ravello – a belvedere that looks over Atrani below and the sea beyond.

ARRIVAL AND INFORMATION — RAVELLO

By bus SITA buses run to Ravello from Piazza Flavio Gioia in Amalfi (every 30min; 25min) and drop off the other side of the tunnel from Piazza del Duomo, outside the *Garden* hotel at the top of Via della Repubblica. From late March to Oct City Sightseeing buses also link Amalfi (hourly; 30min) for €5 one-way.

By car There's a useful car park that often has space just below the main square (€3 for first 3hr, then €1/hr). Taxis stop just through the tunnel outside the *Garden* hotel, and cost around €40 one way from Amalfi.

Tourist office Piazza Fontana Moresca 10, just beside *Parsifal* hotel (Mon–Sat 9.30am–7pm; ⓣ 089 857 096, ⓦ ravellotime.it).

ACCOMMODATION

Auditorium Rooms Via Crocelle 23 ⓣ 339 418 2233, ⓦ auditoriumrooms.it. A Just a 2min stroll east of town, this tiny, two-room B&B is perfectly placed for a summer concert at the auditorium. Both of the a/c, majolica-floored rooms are spotless and attractively furnished, with private terraces that offer stunning views over the vineyards and olive groves tumbling down the coast. €160

Garden Via Boccaccio 4 ⓣ 089 857 226, ⓦ gardenravello.com. The other side of the tunnel from central Ravello, this small family-run hotel and restaurant occupies a prime spot looking up the coast, and makes the most of it with a large airy lobby, a small pool and ten rooms that all have sea views. The rooms aren't huge, but they have small terraces and are well kept and well equipped – and the views, of course, are great. €220

Parsifal Viale Gioacchino d'Anna 5 ⓣ 089 857 144,

13

hotelparsifal.it. Housed in a former convent (originally built in 1288), this family-run hotel offers traditional-style rooms, wonderful terraces decked with flowers and one of the town's top restaurants to boot; eat on a bijou terrace under the stars in summer with breathtaking views over Minori and Maiori. **€175**

★ **Villa Amore** Via dei Fusco 5 089 857 135, villaamore.it. Down a short path off the main route between the centre of Ravello and the Villa Cimbrone, the rooms here are simply furnished but comfortable while the views from the communal terrace are among the best in town – quite something by Ravello standards. The drawback is that you have to carry your luggage from the nearest parking 10min walk away back on the main piazza – or pay €6/piece for the hotel to do it for you. Closed Nov to mid-April. **€130**

EATING AND DRINKING

Confalone Via San Giovanni del Toro 16 089 857 244, hotelpalumbo.it. Housed in the seventh-century salon of the *Palumbo Hotel*, this upmarket restaurant has high stucco ceilings adorned with frescoes, gold-framed mirrors and an incredible view over the bay from a lovely terrace. It serves mostly fish and seafood, with antipasti like swordfish *carpaccio* with strawberry tartar (€16) and *primi* such as lemon risotto with cuttlefish (€18). You can also choose the catch of the day, cooked any way you like and served with vegetable ratatouille (€32). March–Oct daily noon–3pm & 7.30–11pm; Nov–Feb closed Mon.

Da Salvatore Via della Repubblica 2 089 857 227. In business for over fifty years, *Da Salvatore* has fantastic views from the restaurant and outside terrace, and an intriguing, daily-changing menu – tuna *carbonara*, gnocchi with cod and rabbit doughnuts, to name some of the more bizarre items. The food is excellent and not all weird – it serves *spaghetti alle vongole* and steak too – with *primi* from €13 and mains around €18. There's a cheaper pizzeria downstairs, which does starters and pizzas (from €4) only in the evenings. Tues–Sun 12.30–3pm & 7.15–11pm.

Il Flauto di Pan Via Santa Chiara 26 089 857 459, hotelvillacimbrone.com. This elegant restaurant takes advantage of its breathtaking setting at the edge of *Villa Cimbrone*'s celebrated gardens, with wonderful views from its terrace. The food is excellent as well, generously portioned and prepared with homegrown produce, though it's certainly on the pricey side – *primi* from €30, *secondi* for around €40 and a seafood tasting menu for €130. Daily 7.30–10.30pm.

Salerno

Capital of Campania's southernmost province, the lively port of **SALERNO** is much less chaotic than Naples and is well off most travellers' itineraries, giving it a pleasant, relaxed air. During medieval times the town's medical school was the most eminent in Europe; more recently, it was the site of the Allied landing of September 9, 1943 – a landing that reduced much of the centre to rubble. Today it reflects a hodgepodge of architectural eras, from the ramshackle old medieval core on the west end of town – filled with intriguingly dark corners and alleys – to the cutting-edge modern port just to the south. Stretching east from the old quarter to the train station is the pedestrianized main shopping drag of **Corso V. Emanuele**, parallel to the lively seafront promenade, each of which makes a pleasant place for a stroll. There's a good supply of shops, nightlife and relatively cheap accommodation, rendering it a reasonable base for exploring the Amalfi Coast and the ancient site of Paestum to the south.

Pinacoteca Provinciale di Salerno

Via dei Mercanti 63 • Tues–Sun 9am–7.45pm • Free

Snaking through the heart of Salerno's old quarter, its main street is the narrow **Via dei Mercanti**, which has been spruced up over recent years and is home to the seventeenth-century Palazzo Pinto. Inside the *palazzo* is the **Pinacoteca Provinciale di Salerno**, with half a dozen rooms displaying one or two nice fifteenth-century altarpieces and a couple of works by Carlo Rosa and other Neapolitan Baroque artists.

The Duomo

Via del Duomo • Mon–Sat 10am–6.30pm, Sun 1–6.30pm • Free • cattedraledisalerno.it

Off to the right of Via dei Mercanti, up Via del Duomo, the **Duomo** is Salerno's highlight, an enormous church built in 1076 by Robert Guiscard and dedicated to

St Matthew. Entrance is through a cool and shady courtyard, built with columns plundered from Paestum, and centring on a gently gurgling fountain set in an equally ancient bowl. In the heavily restored interior, the two elegant mosaic pulpits are the highlight, the one on the left dating from 1173, the other, with its matching paschal candlesticks, a century later. Immediately behind there's more sumptuous mosaic-work in the screens of the choir, as well as the quietly expressive fifteenth-century tomb of Margaret of Anjou, wife of Charles III of Durazzo, in the left aisle. Be sure not to skip the stunning polychrome marble **crypt**, set down some steps off the right aisle – it is believed to hold the body of St Matthew himself, brought here in the tenth century.

Museo Diocesano

Largo Plebiscito 12 • Mon, Tues & Thurs–Sun 9am–1pm & 3–7pm • €2 • ⓦ museodiocesanodisalerno.it

Next door to the cathedral, the main attraction at the **Museo Diocesano** is a set of 69 ivory panels depicting Biblical scenes from a large eleventh-century altar-front – said to be the largest work of its kind in the world. They're amazing, minutely crafted pieces, showing everything from Creation and the Expulsion from Paradise to the Last Supper – a sort of Biblical comic strip in ivory.

Museo Archeologico Provinciale

Via S. Benedetto 26 • Tues–Sun 9am–7.30pm • €4 • ⓦ museoarcheologicosalerno.it

Five minutes' walk from the cathedral, the **Museo Archeologico Provinciale** occupies two floors of a restored Romanesque palace. It's full of local finds, and has an array of terracotta heads and votive figurines, jewellery, lamps and household objects, from Etruscan as well as Roman times, but its most alluring piece is a sensual *Head of Apollo* upstairs, a Roman bronze fished from the Gulf of Salerno in the 1930s.

Giardini della Minerva

Via Ferrante Sanseverino 1 • Tues–Sun: Jan & Nov–Dec 9.30am–4.30pm; Feb 9.30am–1pm; March 9.30am–5pm; April & Sept 9.30am–7pm; May 9.30am–7.30pm; June–Aug 9.30am–8pm; Oct 9.30–6pm • €3 • ⓦ giardinodellaminerva.it

After the cathedral, Salerno's most interesting attraction is the **Giardini della Minerva** on Via Ferrante Sanseverino, a medicinal garden laid out according to medieval medical principles and traversed by channels of tinkling water. It's a gloriously fragrant place, its shady terraces wonderfully soothing in summer, and there's even a café serving herbal tea to ensure you leave healthier than when you arrived.

ARRIVAL AND DEPARTURE — SALERNO

By train Salerno's train station lies at the southeastern end of the town centre on Piazza Vittorio Veneto, about a 10min walk from the old town.

Destinations Naples (every 15–20min; 40min–1hr 20min); Paestum/Agropoli (15 daily; 30–40min).

By bus Buses to Amalfi depart from the square directly in front of the train station, and arrive from Amalfi at the Piazza della Concordia, a few hundred metres south of the station by the waterside. Buses departing for and arriving from Naples use the bus station on Via Vinciprova, about 500m east of the train station.

Destinations Agropoli (hourly; 1hr 20min); Amalfi (every 30min–1hr; 1hr 10min); Naples (every 15–30min; 1hr 15min); Padula (1 daily; 2hr 30min); Paestum (15 daily; 50min–1hr 20min).

By boat There are two points of arrival and departure for ferries and hydrofoils from Salerno to the Amalfi Coast, Bay of Naples and elsewhere arrive in the harbour: Piazza della Concordia, a few minutes' walk south of the train station, has the most frequent services, while the futuristic Molo Manfredi is about a 10min walk south of Salerno's medieval quarter. For departure times, check ⓦ livesalerno.com/ferry-connections.

Destinations Amalfi (April to mid-Oct 15 daily hydrofoils; 35min); Positano (10 daily hydrofoils; 1hr 10min).

13

INFORMATION

Tourist office Corso Vittorio Emanuele 193, inside the Galleria Capitol (Mon, Wed & Fri 10am–2pm & 3.30–7.30pm; Tues & Thurs 10am–1pm & 4.30–7.30pm, Sat 9am–1pm; ⓣ 089 662 951).

ACCOMMODATION

Ave Gratia Plena Via dei Canali ⓣ 089 234 776, ⓦ ostellodisalerno.it. Housed in a former church and cloister complex, Salerno's best-value hostel is right in the centre of town – a clean and welcoming place with a mixture of worn but well-kept dorms and private rooms set around a lovely central courtyard. Dorms €16, doubles €60

Bruman Piazza Piazza Vittorio Veneto 30 ⓣ 089 842 4100, ⓦ hotelbrumansalerno.it. Sleek, modern B&B just to the left of the train station as you exit: as well as being handy for transport connections (both by rail and sea), it's the most comfortable of the hotels around the station, with welcoming staff and clean, spacious rooms that are surprisingly well-insulated against the noise from the street. €110

Salerno Antico Via Masuccio Salernitano 8 ⓣ 089 253 156. Friendly B&B situated on the edge of the old town in a former monastery that was also the owner's childhood home. The three rooms are bright and airy with good a/c, and two of them have views over a charming street. Plentiful breakfast served in the family dining room. €120

EATING AND DRINKING

Botteghelle 65 Via Botteghelle 65 ⓣ 089 232 992, ⓦ botteghelle65.blogspot.com. Great value little *enoteca* with a rustic dining room out back, where owner Pino Adinolfi, a cheesemaster and sommelier, serves up tasty meat and cheese platters as well as rice and pasta salads, for around €5 a plate. Mon–Sat 9am–3pm & 8–11pm.

Caffè dei Mercanti Via dei Mercanti 114 ⓣ 089 232 731. Small and cosy bar in the city's historic centre – it's good for a quick coffee or a few drinks, as well as bar snacks or a light lunch. Daily 8am–10pm.

Hostaria Il Brigante Via Fratelli Linguiti 4 ⓣ 089 226 592. A great, old-fashioned *osteria* near the Duomo with communal tables and a handwritten menu featuring pasta and fish – try the *sangiovannara* (pasta with mozzarella, aubergine, peppers and basil; €5). A full meal with wine starts at around €20. Tues–Sun 1.30–2.30pm & 8–11pm.

CILENTO: THE ANTI-AMALFI

Just beyond Paestum to the south, the plain collides with the mountainous promontory of Cilento, where the Alburni range – sometimes called the "Dolomites of Campania" – runs down into the sea. The area is now Italy's second-largest national park, with an untamed beauty and low-key charm far removed from the gloss of the Amalfi Coast's resorts. Popular with holidaying Italians in high summer, it offers swathes of pristine sandy beach and a handful of pretty coastal towns at which to base yourself. Its largest and liveliest town, Agropoli, is the gateway to the region, situated at the Cilento's northern end, while a bit further south is Castellabate with its picturesque fortified hilltop. Other charming spots around the coast are Acciaroli, Pisciotta and Palinuro – the latter's dramatic cliffs, caves and natural arches have provided the backdrop for many a film over the years, from Jason and the Argonauts to Wonderwoman.

Beyond its beaches, Cilento is also home to a couple of UNESCO-protected sites. About halfway along the coast is **Velia** (Mon & Wed–Sun 9am to 1hr before sunset; €3), the ruins of the ancient Greek colony of Elea, founded around 540 BC. Set further inland just off the Salerno-ReggioCalabria motorway is the **Certosa di Padula** (Mon & Wed–Sun 9am–7pm; €4), a sprawling monastic complex founding in 1306 which boasts the world's largest cloister.

ARRIVAL AND GETTING AROUND

The region's refreshing isolation also means that getting there and around isn't always straightforward. While Cilento's towns are all well-linked with Salerno and Naples by bus routes (excepting those further south of Acciaroli), most routes are cut completely outside the summer high season. The train line connects Paestum with Agropoli, though if you hope to explore the area in any depth it's just about essential to have your own set of wheels. A few metres from Agropoli's train station, Agropoli Rent (Via Gasperi 75; ⓣ 0974 826 301, ⓦ agropolirent.it) offers good deals on car, motorbike and scooter rental.

Paestum

Daily 8.30am–7.30pm; special openings June–Aug: Thurs until 10.30pm, Fri until 11pm • €9.50 combined ticket for ancient site and museum; €7 site only (only when museum is closed) • ⓦ paestum.it

About 45km south of Salerno, the ancient site of **Paestum** spreads across a large area at the bottom end of the **Piana del Sele** – a wide, flat plain grazed by the buffalo that produce a good quantity of southern Italy's mozzarella cheese. Paestum, or Poseidonia as it was known, was founded by Greeks from Sybaris in the sixth century BC, and later, in 273 BC, colonized by the Romans, who Latinized the name. But by the ninth century a combination of malaria and Saracen raids had decimated the population and left the buildings deserted and gradually overtaken by thick forest – the site wasn't rediscovered until the eighteenth century during the building of a road through here. It's a desolate, open place even now ("inexpressibly grand", Shelley called it), mostly unrecognizable ruins but with three golden-stoned **temples** that are among the best-preserved Doric temples in Europe. Of these, the Temple of Neptune, dating from about 450 BC, is the most complete, with only its roof and parts of the inner walls missing. The Basilica of Hera, built a century or so earlier, retains its double rows of columns, while the Temple of Ceres at the northern end of the site was used as a Christian church for a time. In between, the forum is little more than an open space, and the buildings around are mere foundations.

The museum

Via Magna Grecia 919 • Same hours as the park, except for first & third Mon of each month: closes 1.40pm • €9.50 combined ticket for ancient site and museum; €4 museum only (only when site is closed) • ⓦ museopaestum.beniculturali.it

The splendid **museum**, across the road, displays Greek and Roman finds from the site and around. At the back on the right are some stunning sixth-century bronze vases (*hydriae*), decorated with rams, lions and sphinxes; to the left is more bronze – gleaming helmets, breastplates and greaves. Make a point of seeing the rare Greek tomb paintings, the best of which are from the Tomb of the Diver, graceful and expressively naturalistic pieces of work, including a diver in mid-plunge, said to represent the passage from life to death, and male lovers banqueting. Nearby, attractive fourth-century terracotta plates depict all sorts of comestibles – sweets, fruit and cheese, and a set of weathered archaic-period Greek metopes from another temple at the mouth of the Sele River, a few kilometres north, shows scenes of fighting and hunting. The first floor hosts Neolithic, Bronze and early Stone Age daggers and pots plus other prehistoric bits and bobs, while the second floor is devoted to Roman finds: the highlights here include a statue of an abstracted-looking Pan with his pipes, a third-century relief showing a baby in pointed hat and amulets, and a sarcophagus cover of a tenderly embracing couple.

ARRIVAL AND INFORMATION — PAESTUM

By bus Buses to and from Salerno (15 daily; 50min–1hr 20min) and Agropoli (15 daily; 15min) stop beside the train station.

By train It's quicker to take the train from Salerno (15 daily; 30–40min). It's a 10min walk from the train station to the site.

Puglia

806 The Tavoliere

809 The Gargano promontory

813 The Tremiti islands

814 Trani

815 Bari

819 Le Murge

821 Down the coast from Bari

822 The FSE line: Grotte di Castellana to Martina Franca

825 Taranto and around

828 Brindisi

832 Ostuni

833 Salento

LECCE

Puglia

14

Stretching 400km from north to south, Puglia's long, narrow peninsula forms the heel of Italy. For centuries it was a strategic province, colonized, invaded and conquered by just about every major power of the day – from the ancient Greeks through to the Spanish. These days clean seas and reliable sunshine are the draws for holiday-makers both Italian and foreign, and acres of campsite-and-bungalow-type tourist villages stud the shoreline, though there are still quiet spots to be found. Low-cost flights to Bari and Brindisi have opened up the area to British tourists, many of whom have been buying and doing up *trulli* – ancient storehouses (see page 823) – and *masserie* (farm estates) as holiday accommodation. There's a brisk air of investment in many resorts, from the new top-of-the-range spa hotels in converted *masserie* to agriturismo places where you can holiday among olive groves and orchards. B&Bs continue to spring up everywhere, often in the historic centres of towns, some simple, some splendid, all of them better value for money than most hotels.

Puglia has plenty of architectural interest, as each ruling dynasty left its own distinctive mark on the landscape – the Romans their agricultural schemes and feudal lords their fortified medieval towns. Perhaps most distinctive are the kasbah-like quarters of many towns and cities, a vestige of the Saracen conquest of the ninth century – the one at Bari is the biggest and most atmospheric. The Normans endowed Puglia with splendidly ornate cathedrals, while the **Baroque** exuberance of towns like Lecce and **Martina Franca** are testament to the Spanish legacy. But if there's one symbol of Puglia that stands out, it's the imposing castles built by the Swabian Frederick II all over the province – foremost of which are the **Castel del Monte** (immortalized on the Italian 5 cent coin) and the remnants of the palace at **Lucera**.

Puglia's cities also merit some exploration. **Taranto** and its surroundings have fought a losing battle with the local steel industry, but **Lecce** is worth a visit for its crazed confection of Baroque churches and laidback café life. Though **Bari** is not a traditional tourist destination, reinvestment in its maze-like old city is drawing visitors in-the-know for its ambience and excellent restaurants; while **Brindisi**, best known for its ferry connections with Greece, lies just 15km away from the dunes of the **Torre Guaceto** nature reserve.

Puglia is geographically diverse, though it has to be said that the **Tavoliere** (tableland) of the north with mile upon mile of wheatfields, is hardly the most exciting of landscapes. More alluring is the hilly, forested **Gargano promontory** jutting out to the east, fringed by gently shelving, sandy beaches, seaside hotels and campsite villages that make good places for a family holiday – though you'll need to catch a ferry to the **Tremiti islands** for the clearest sea. The best escape is to the southernmost tip, the **Salentine peninsula** where the terrain is rocky and dry, more Greek than Italian, and there are some beautiful coves and sea caves to swim in.

GETTING AROUND — PUGLIA

Getting around Puglia by public transport is fairly easy, at least as far as the main towns and cities go. FS **trains** connect nearly all the major places, while small, private lines head into more remote areas – in the Gargano and on the edges of Le Murge. Most other places can be reached by **bus**, although isolated village services can be infrequent or inconveniently early – a problem that can only really be solved by having your own **transport**. In July and Aug buses connect coastal towns.

OTRANTO

Highlights

❶ **Vieste** For sun and sea, head to this resort on the dramatic Gargano promontory, which also serves as a gateway to the remote Tremiti islands. See pages 810 and 805

❷ **Castel del Monte** Puglia's greatest Swabian castle is a testament to thirteenth-century engineering. See page 820

❸ **Martina Franca** This lively town with its Moorish feel makes a good base for exploring the surrounding area's *trulli* – Puglia's traditional conical whitewashed buildings. See page 824

❹ **Ostuni** One of the most stunning hilltop towns in southern Italy, with a sun-bleached old quarter and a sandy coastline 7km away. See page 832

❺ **Lecce** Dubbed the "Florence of the South", Lecce is an exuberant city of Baroque architecture and opulent churches. See page 833

❻ **Otranto** Pressed against clear Adriatic waters at Italy's easternmost point, Otranto's whitewashed medieval core makes a great base for getting around Salento's windswept coast. See page 837

HIGHLIGHTS ARE MARKED ON THE MAP ON PAGE 806

The Tavoliere

The province of Foggia, known also as the **Tavoliere** (tableland), occupies a broad **plain** stretching from the foothills of the Apennines in the west and the Gargano massif in the east. **FOGGIA**, the capital and transport hub of the province, is not somewhere to linger – for more of an idea of what the Tavoliere is like, head for the walled town of **Lucera** or the little village of **Troia**.

Lucera

LUCERA (pronounced Loosh-airer) makes a wonderful introduction to Puglia. A charming small town dominated by a mighty Angevin-Svevian fortress with a bright, bustling centre and a lively *passeggiata* on summer evenings, it was once the capital of the Tavoliere – a thriving Saracen hub. Frederick II, having forced the Arabs out of Sicily, resettled twenty thousand of them here, on the site of an abandoned Roman town, allowing them complete freedom in religious worship – an almost unheard-of act of liberalism for the early thirteenth century.

The Duomo

Piazza del Duomo • Daily 7am–noon & 4–7pm • Free

Lucera's timber-roofed **Duomo** was built in the early fourteenth century after Frederick II's death, when the Angevins arrived and a conflict with the Saracens began. The Angevins won and built the cathedral on the site of a mosque; by the end of their rule, few of the town's original Arab-influenced buildings were left. However, the Arabic layout of Lucera survived and there's a powerful atmosphere here – best appreciated by wandering the narrow streets of the old town, peering into the courtyards and alleyways.

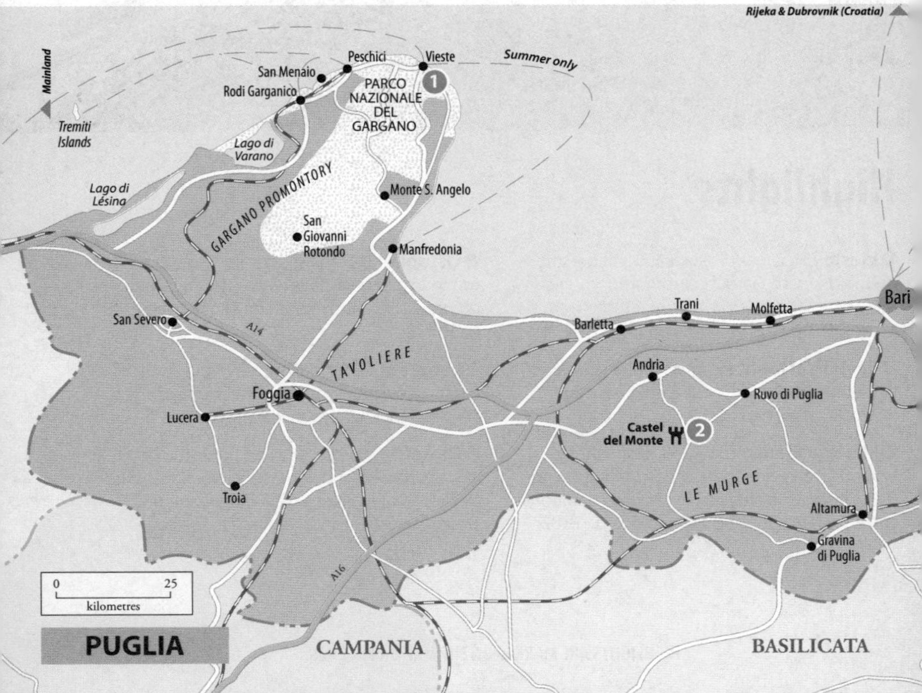

Museo Civico

Via De Nicastri 74 • Tues–Sat 9.30am–1pm & 3.30–7.30pm, Sun 9am–1pm • €3 • ☎ 0881 522 762

Housed in Palazzo de Nicastri behind the cathedral, the **Museo Civico** has an appealing collection ranging from Roman portrait busts, mosaics and a pair of muscly miniature gladiators tensed for battle, to moulds used by the town's medieval artisans to create terracotta Madonnas.

Fortezza Angioino Svevo

Piazza Padre Angelo Cuomo • Tues–Sun 9am–1pm, Tues and Thurs also & 3.30–7.30pm • €3 • From Piazza del Duomo, follow Via Bovio and Via Federico II to Piazza Matteotti and look for the signs; it's a 15min walk west of the centre

The main sights are outside the old centre, most notably the vast **fortress** built by Frederick and designed to house a lavish court that included a collection of exotic wild beasts. The castle commands spectacular views over the Tavoliere, stretching across to the Apennines to the west and the mountains of Gargano to the east. Contained within the kilometre-long walls are the remains of Frederick's great palace, evocative fragments of mosaic-work and fallen columns now surrounded by wild flowers.

The Roman amphitheatre

Viale Augusteo • Same hours as Fortezza • €3

At the **Roman amphitheatre**, a fifteen-minute walk east of the old centre, audiences of eighteen thousand once watched gladiatorial battles; there are guides on hand to show you round, but often in Italian only.

ARRIVAL AND INFORMATION — LUCERA

By train and bus Ferrovia del Gargano (ⓦ ferroviadelgargano.com) buses and trains run every 30min from Foggia East. Buses are slightly more convenient as they stop at both the train station (20min walk south of the centre)

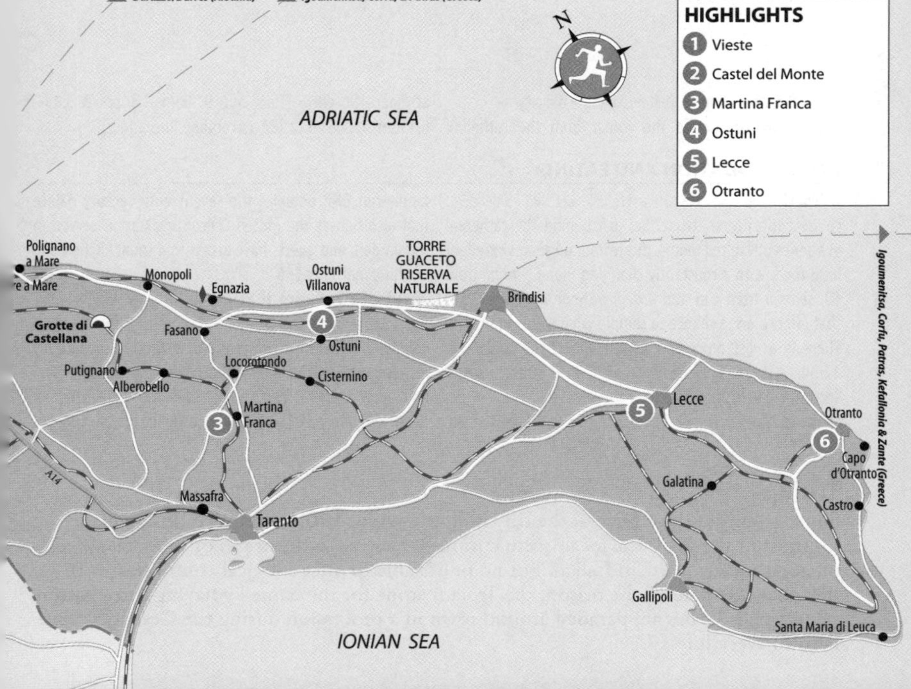

14

PUGLIA – ITALY'S BREADBASKET

Puglia is known as the breadbasket of Italy. It's the source of 80 percent of Europe's pasta and much of Italy's fish; it produces more wine than Germany and more olive oil than all the other regions of Italy combined. It's famous for olives (from Cerignola), almonds (from Ruvo di Puglia), dark juicy tomatoes (often sun-dried), *cime di rapa* (turnip tops), fava beans, figs (fresh and dried), *cotognata* (a moulded jam made from quince) and for its melons, grapes and green cauliflower. The influence of Puglia's former rulers is still evident in the region's food. Like the **Greeks**, Pugliesi eat lamb and goat spit-roast over herb-scented fires and deep-fried doughnut-like cakes steeped in honey; and like the **Spanish** they drink almond milk, *latte di mandorla*.

The most distinctive local **pasta** is *orecchiette*, ear-shaped pasta that you will still see women making in their doorways in the old part of Bari. Look out, too, for *panzarotti alla barese*, deep-fried pockets of dough stuffed with tomato or prosciutto and ricotta. Otherwise, there is a marked preference for short, stubby varieties of pasta, which you'll find served with peppers, cauliflower and *cime di rapa*. Not surprisingly, fish and shellfish dominate coastal menus. There are some good fish soups (*zuppe di pesce*) whose ingredients and style vary from place to place – the Brindisi version, for example, is dominated by eel. Vegetarians are well catered for with a range of meat-free antipasti, and combining pasta and vegetables is a typically Pugliese trait.

A local meat dish is *gnummerieddi*: resembling haggis, it's made by stuffing a lamb gut with minced offal, herbs and garlic – best grilled over an open fire. There is little beef or pork eaten in Puglia, and poultry is uncommon, aside from small game birds in season; as a result, horsemeat is popular, especially in the Salento area. To confound your prejudices, go for *pezzetti di cavallo*, bits of horsemeat stewed in a rich tomato sauce.

Cheeses are a strong point, including ricotta, cacioricotta, canestrato (sheep's-milk cheese formed in baskets) and burrata (cream encased in mozzarella, a speciality of Andria). Pair these with the local durum-wheat breads, the most famous of which, *pane di Altamura*, carries the DOP seal of quality.

Puglia also produces some of Italy's best-value wines, particularly its formidable reds – Primitivo di Manduria (aka red Zinfandel), Salice Salentino, and Negroamaro. Locorotondo is a straightforward, fresh white from Salento, a region known also for its *rosati* (rosé) called Salento Rosato and dessert wine called Aleatico.

and in Piazza del Popolo, just outside the old city.

Tourist office Around the corner from the cathedral at Piazza Nocelli 6 (Tues–Sun 9.30am–1.30pm & 3.15–6.45pm; T 0881 522 762, W comune.lucera.fg.it).

ACCOMMODATION AND EATING

Il Cortiletto Via De' Nicastri 26 T 0881 542 554, W ristoranteilcortiletto.it. Set just behind the cathedral in a series of vaulted rooms, this restaurant serves excellent local food, with a constantly changing menu – *primi* from €8, *secondi* from €15 and a *degustazione* menu (€27.50) that offers a great chance to sample whatever is in season. There is a vast array of Pugliese wines, too. Mon–Sat 12.30–2.15pm & 8–9.30pm, Sun 8–9.30pm; closed second week of July.

Mimosa Via De' Nicastri 6 T 338 457 0070. This small, family-run B&B occupies the seventeenth-century palace that also houses the Museo Civico; breakfast is served in the garden, and guests have access to a small kitchen and washing machine. €65

Residenza Federico II Piazza del Popolo T 0881 201 421, W residenzadifedericosecondo.it. Fifteen well-equipped rooms near the centre of town, in a beautifully restored medieval building with its own hydromassage pool and sauna, as well as a pizzeria. If it's full, try its cheaper sister hotel, *Villa Imperiale* (€80), just opposite the piazza. €66

Troia

Some 18km south of Lucera, the tiny hilltop town of **TROIA** is a quiet, dusty village for most of the year. The locals seem curiously blasé as to the origin of their village's name; it means "slut" in Italian, but no one is able to offer a logical connection with the village. Whatever the reason, the Troiani atone for the name by having three patron saints, whose relics are paraded around town in a procession during the Gesta dei Santi Patroni every July 17.

The Duomo

Via Regina Margherita 77 • Daily 9am–12.30 & 4–8pm • Free

Troia's only sight is the fine **Duomo**, an intriguing eleventh-century blend of Byzantine and Apulian-Romanesque styles, with a generous hint of Saracen. Its great bronze doors are covered with reliefs of animals and biblical figures, while above, surrounded by a frenzy of carved lions frozen in stone, is an extraordinary rose window. Distinctly Saracen, the window resembles a finely worked piece of oriental ivory, composed of eleven stone panels, each one delicately carved. There's more exact detail inside, too, including a curiously decorated pulpit and some ornate capitals.

ARRIVAL AND DEPARTURE — TROIA

There are 4 daily **buses** from Lucera (about 30min) and at least one per hour from Foggia (about 30min).

The Gargano promontory

The **Gargano promontory** rises like an island from the flat plains of the Tavoliere. It has a remarkably diverse landscape: beaches and lagoons to the north, a rocky, indented eastern coast and a mountainous, green heartland of oak and beech trees – more reminiscent of a Germanic forest than a corner of southern Italy. For centuries the promontory was extremely isolated, visited only by pilgrims making their way along the valley to **Monte Sant'Angelo** and its shrine. Tourism has taken off in a big way, especially around the seaside resort of **Vieste**, but in 1991 the whole peninsula became a national park, helping to protect it from overbearing development and ensuring that much of the interior remains supremely unspoiled and quiet.

It may seem as though the promontory is one long strip of private beach, but bear in mind that by Italian law everyone has access to the actual seashore, as well as zones between the reserved areas. Check with your hotel – often the price of a sunbed and umbrella at the nearest beach is included in the cost of an overnight stay.

ARRIVAL AND DEPARTURE — THE GARGANO PROMONTORY

By bus and train Approaches to the promontory are pretty straightforward. FS trains run from Foggia to Manfredonia on the southeast side of Gargano, from where it's only 16km by bus to Monte Sant'Angelo. To get to the north of the peninsula, Ferrovie del Gargano (T 0881 587 211, W ferroviedelgargano.com) runs trains from Foggia to San Severo, where you change for onward travel to Peschici–Calanelle: here a bus connects to Peschici (5km). Note that most FG stations are quite a distance from the towns and villages they serve, so always go for the connecting bus if there is one.

GETTING AROUND

By bus and train Getting around the interior can be a little more tortuous. Buses are run by two companies: SITA SUD (T 0881 5790111, W sitasudtrasporti.it) which serves the inland towns and operates the inland route to Vieste; and Ferrovie del Gargano (see above), which runs the trains and connecting buses in northern Gargano.

Monte Sant'Angelo

Perched almost 800m up in the hills, **MONTE SANT'ANGELO** is the highest – and coldest – settlement in the Gargano. Pilgrims have trudged up the switchback paths and roads for centuries to visit the spot where the archangel Michael is said to have made four separate appearances, mostly at the end of the fifth century – making the sanctuary here one of the earliest Christian shrines in Europe and one of the most important in Italy. Today, the pilgrims come by bus, and the village is a bit of a tourist trap. But the annual major **festivals** on May 8 and September 28, 29 and 30 attract locals from far and wide, some of whom turn up in traditional dress.

Santuario di San Michele Arcangelo

Via Reale Basilica • July–Sept Mon–Sat 7.30.am–7.30pm, Sun 7am–8pm; April–June & Oct Mon–Sat 7.30am–12.30pm & 2.30–7pm, Sun 7am–1pm & 2.30-8pm; Nov–March Mon–Sat 7.30am–12.30pm & 2.30–5pm, Sun 7am–1pm & 2.30–5pm • Free • ⓣ 0884 561 150, ⓦ santuariosanmichele.it

From the central Piazza Duca d'Aosta the road runs uphill to the edge of the old town and the Via Reale Basilica, where you'll find the famous **Santuario di San Michele Arcangelo**. From the small courtyard on the right a flight of stone steps leads down to the crypts that form the entrance to the church, built on the site of the cave in which the archangel first appeared (in 490).

14

Tomba di Rotari and the Castello

Opposite the sanctuary, a set of steps leads down to the nearby ruins of the **Complesso di San Pietro**, behind which is the so-called **Tomba di Rotari** (daily 10am–1pm & 3.15–7pm; €1) – an imposing domed tower that contained a baptistry; the large baptismal font is just on the right as you enter the tower. Little remains of the church itself, wrecked by an earthquake, but the rose window – a Catherine wheel of entwined mermaids – survives.

Back on Via Reale Basilica, it's an easy clamber up to the ruined Norman **Castello** (daily: July & Aug 8am–1pm & 2.30–7pm; Sept–June 9am–1pm & 2.30–6pm; €2; ⓣ 0884 562 062), whose views over the town and valley make a nice finale to a visit – especially at sunset.

ACCOMMODATION AND EATING **MONTE SANT'ANGELO**

If you intend to stay overnight, don't count on finding anywhere to sleep at the last minute during the main festival times. For snacks, ignore the touristy places in the lower town and head instead for the bakery outside the castle.

Casa del Pellegrino Via Carlo d'Angio ⓣ 0884 562 363, ⓦ santuariosanmichele.it. A three-star hotel right next to the sanctuary, run by a religious institution but open to everybody. The rooms are modern and well looked after, and there's a set lunch and dinner menu for €15. Only downside is the midnight curfew. **€65**

Hotel Sant'Angelo 1km out of town on the road to Pulsano ⓣ 0884 562 146, ⓦ hotelsantangelo.com. Comfortable hotel with a swimming pool, and its own restaurant and pizzeria, and a panoramic view from most of the rooms' balconies. A good choice for families. **€69**

Medioevo Via Castello 21 ⓣ 0884 565 356, ⓦ ristorantemedioevo.it. One of the best restaurants in town, serving excellent seasonal local dishes such as *pancotto con cavoli, patate e fave* (bread soup baked with cabbage, potatoes and fava beans; €8), *fave e cicora* (broad bean and wild chicory soup; €8), and delicious home-made desserts (€3–5). Daily 12–2.30pm & 8–11.30pm; Oct–July closed Mon.

Taverna Li Jalantuùmene Piazza di Galganis ⓣ 0884 565 484, ⓦ li-jalantuumene.it. Set in a pretty piazza with an ever-changing menu to reflect seasonal produce, this restaurant features both traditional and innovative recipes, with the *mucca podolica*, a rare-breed Pugliese cow, featuring prominently. You can eat à la carte, or choose one of the fixed menus – a vegetarian menu at €24 or a tasting menu at €48, both excluding wine. There are also two competitively priced suites, furnished with antiques. Daily Noon–2.45pm & 7–10.30pm, closed Mon lunch. **€100**

Vieste and around

The best base on the Gargano peninsula is **VIESTE**, jutting out into the Adriatic on two promontories. Fifty years ago there wasn't even a proper road here, but today Vieste, with its excellent beaches, is the holiday capital of Gargano, and the streets and sands are packed in August. Despite the crowds, it is a lively and inviting town, with an interesting historic core and, in summer at least, a fairly lively nightlife.

The **old town** sits on the easternmost of the two promontories, at the tip of which stands the **Chiesa di San Francesco**, once a thriving monastery, and a *trabucco* – used by fishermen to catch mullet. Probably Phoenician in origin, these cantilevered arrangements of wooden beams, winches and ropes are found on the rocky Gargano coast and further north around Vasto in Abruzzo (see page 733).

From the church, climb up Via Mafrolla, walking through the old town to Piazza Seggio. Straight ahead, Via Duomo is the site of the so-called **Chianca Amara**, the

THE PILGRIM ROUTE: SAN GIOVANNI ROTONDO

The ancient **pilgrim route** weaved its way along the Stignano Valley between San Severo in the west and Monte Sant'Angelo, and until comparatively recently was the only road that linked the villages of the Gargano interior. With your own transport, it's still a good route for exploring a couple of the region's most important religious centres. If you want to follow any part of the pilgrim route by bus, you'll have to plan your itinerary carefully and be prepared to travel in leisurely fashion.

Nestling under Monte Calvo, the highest peak hereabouts, **San Giovanni Rotondo** is a modern centre for pilgrimage on a massive scale: it's the burial place of Padre Pio, a local priest who died in 1968 and was canonized in 2002. Pio received the stigmata and won an immense following – especially among Italian Catholics – for his piety and legendary ability to heal the sick. Proof of his divinity was announced in 2008 when his body was exhumed and pronounced to be in good condition and without signs of the stigmata, forty years after his burial. Two years later, his jewel-encrusted, silver coffin was moved to his own golden crypt.

Padre Pio is hugely popular in Italy, and you'll see his image – bearing an uncanny resemblance to the late John Peel – stuck on the walls of bars, shops and petrol stations throughout the south. A whole industry has grown up around him in San Giovanni Rotondo, fuelled by the seven million and more pilgrims who pass through every year, making it the most visited pilgrimage site in the world after Lourdes. In 2004, renowned architect Renzo Piano completed a striking new church, the shape of which resembles a large snail – its "shell" forming the roof and enveloping the pilgrims below. The town takes its name from the Rotonda di San Giovanni, a building of indeterminate origin on the edge of the old town – like the Tomba di Rotari (see page 810), it's thought to have been a baptistry, built on the site of an earlier pagan temple.

"bitter stone", where five thousand local people were beheaded when the Turks sacked the town in 1554. Further down, past the stone, the **Cattedrale**, eleventh century in origin but tampered with in the nineteenth, provides a cool retreat from the fierce glare of the sun in the whitewashed streets.

ARRIVAL AND INFORMATION — VIESTE

By bus All buses arrive at Piazzale Also Muro, to the west of the town centre. Vieste is a stop on the Pugliair service (May–Sept, Ⓦ aeroportidipuglia.it,) linking the Gargano peninsula with the airports of Bari, Brindisi and Foggia.

Destinations Bari (4 daily; 3hr); Foggia (5 daily; 2hr 45min); Rome (daily at 3.30pm; 7hr 15min).

By ferry In summer 1 April–30 Sept there is at least one departure daily from Vieste to the Tremiti islands, returning in the late afternoon. (Ⓦ navitremiti.com). Tickets from their call centre (Ⓣ 0884 962732) or the Gargano Viaggi office at Piazza Roma 7 (Ⓣ 0884 708 501, Ⓦ garganoviaggi.it).

Tourist office Piazza Kennedy, on the seafront at the end of the main drag, Viale XXIV Maggio/Corso Lorenzo Fazzini (June to mid-Sept daily 8am–2pm & 4–8pm; mid-Sept to May Mon–Sat 8am–2pm, Tues & Thurs also 3–7pm; Ⓣ 0884 708 806, Ⓦ viaggiareinpuglia.it).

ACCOMMODATION

Giada Lungomare Europa 18 Ⓣ 0884 706 593. Easily among the cheapest options in Vieste, this welcoming family-run apartments place is a few steps from the beach and a 10min walk from the old town, with simple but clean rooms, decent free wi-fi and free parking. Closed mid Sept–mid June. Apartments rented by the week. **€450**

Punta San Francesco Via S. Francesco 2 Ⓣ 0884 701 422, Ⓦ hotelpuntasanfrancesco.it. Though showing its age, this hotel enjoys a quiet position in the old town with lovely views over the promontory from the rooftop terrace. All rooms are en suite. Closed Nov–March. **€83**

Rocca sul Mare Via Mafrolla 32 Ⓣ 0884 702 719, Ⓦ roccasulmare.it. Housed in a charming eighteenth-century building with a great old town location overlooking the sea, this friendly family-run hotel has simple rooms and a wonderful terrace with views across to the lighthouse. Piano and violin performances are held on summer nights in the restaurant, and the helpful staff can arrange activities – they will even show you how to make pasta. Big discounts outside Aug. **€104**

Seggio Via Veste 7 Ⓣ 0884 708 123, Ⓦ hotelseggio.it. An upmarket option in the old town with vertiginous views down to its swimming pool, and its own private sandy beach and lagoon. Closed Nov–March. **€130**

14

DAY-TRIPS FROM VIESTE

Beaches The most obvious day-trip is to the beaches. Head for the small one between the promontories; north to San Lorenzo, with fine, soft, gently shelving sand; or just south of town, to sandy Pizzomunno. They all go in for the grill-pan variety of sunbathing with rows and rows of sunbeds. Slightly less crowded, if you're lucky, is the marvellous Scialmarino beach, 4.5km up the coast towards Peschici. Nicest of all is the small Baia di San Felice, squeezed between two headlands and backed by pine trees, just before you get to the Testa del Gargano, several kilometres south of town.

Boat trips If you want to swim away from the crowds, consider an organized boat trip to the grotto-ridden coastline around the headland of Testa del Gargano. Boats leave for the three-hour grotto excursion from next to San Francesco church at around 9am and 3.30pm; tickets cost €15. Alternatively, you can rent your own boat for the day from Noleggio Gommoni, at the port (T 347 133 9215, W marinavieste.it), from €120/day (four–six people).

The interior Inland, the Gargano promontory can make a cool break from its busy coast, although there's not much public transport, apart from the odd bus from Vieste. The tourist office in Monte Sant'Angelo, however, can help organize mountain bike rental, jeep safaris and pony trekking, and Noleggio Gommoni rents scooters for €10/ hour and €50/ day.

EATING AND DRINKING

There are plenty of fish restaurants to choose from in and around the old town. If you're on a budget, try the pair of cheerful pizzerias in Piazza Vittorio Emanuele II. The terrace bar at *Seggio* (see page 811) is a perfect place for a pre-dinner drink.

★ **Al Dragone** Via Duomo 8 T 0884 701 212, W aldragone.it. Located in a once-inhabited cave, *Al Dragone* is good for fish dishes, such as the antipasto of marinated grey mullet (€9), and twists on local dishes you won't find anywhere else, such as *orecchiette* with turnip greens, salted anchovies scattered with *bottarga* and shards of thin crispy bread spiked with capers, parsley, basil, garlic and chilli (€9). Tasting menus cost €35 including drinks, and there are some unusual desserts too, such as *mostazzuoli* – made with almonds, wine must (the syrup made by boiling down what is left of the grapes after making wine) and egg white. Daily 12–2.30pm & 7–11pm; closed Nov–end of March, plus Tues in April, May & Oct.

Osteria degli Archi Via Ripe 2 T 0884 705 199, W osteriadegliarchivieste.it. Occupying a restored stone building in the sea wall at the Punta di San Francesco end of the old town, this restaurant specializes in locally caught, grilled seafood. *Primi* (€7–11) include a fine dish of *troccoli* (local pasta) with stuffed cuttlefish (€10), and the fish soup (€22) is good. March–Nov daily 1–3pm & 7–11pm; Oct–April closed Mon.

Peschici and northern Gargano

Atop its rocky vantage point overlooking a beautiful sandy bay, **PESCHICI** is a little smaller than Vieste and one of the most attractive village resorts in the Gargano. Though originally built in 970 AD as a buffer against Saracen incursions, its labyrinth of tiny streets and houses sporting domed roofs has a distinctly Arab flavour. Beach-lazing is the focus, although the town also makes a good base for exploring some of the caves and defensive medieval towers of the nearby coastline. The easiest trips are to the grotto at **San Nicola**, 3km east of town (some buses), or 5km west to the **Torre di Monte Pucci** for fine coastal views (and where there's a *trabucco* restaurant for refreshments in summer).

ARRIVAL AND INFORMATION — PESCHICI

By train The FG train line ends at Calanelle, 6km west of Peschici, but there's an almost hourly bus connection to the town (15min).

By bus All buses drop you along Via Montesanto in the newer, beach-resort part of Peschici, from where it's a short walk down to the main street – Corso Garibaldi – and the sea. Destinations Rome and Florence (FlixBus, W flixbus.com daily at 11am; 11hr 30min); Vieste (9 daily; 45min).

ACCOMMODATION

Camping Baia San Nicola Località S. Nicola T 0884 964 231, W baiasannicola.it. Along the coast at Punta San Nicola, 2km east of Peschici, this campsite features sandy beaches and shady pine groves. Mid-May–mid-Oct. Pitches

€8.50, per person €8

★ **Locanda Al Castello** Via Castello 29 ⊕ 0884 964 038, ⓦ peschicialcastello.it. Perched at the far edge of the old town, down a narrow lane of whitewashed houses, *Locanda Al Castello* has very friendly staff and simple but well-kept rooms with some of Peschici's best views. There's also a restaurant offering five or six daily specials, and a neighbouring pizzeria with a pretty terrace. Closed Jan–March. €144

EATING AND DRINKING

Fra Stefano Via Forno 8 ⊕ 0884 964 141. An informal place in the heart of the old town, serving moderately priced, delicious raw and cooked seafood antipasti, *cavatelli* (home-made pasta with seafood; €10), *ruoto* (baby goat or lamb roasted with onions and potatoes; €16) and good tasting menus from €25–30 (drinks excluded). Daily 12.30–2.30pm & 8–10.30pm; closed mid-Jan to Feb.

Grotta delle Rondini Via al Porto 64 ⊕ 0884 964 007. Built in a natural cave overlooking the port outside the old town, this restaurant specializes in fish and the antipasti are especially good. Reasonably priced local dishes include sautéed clams (€10), and if you choose carefully you can have a full meal for €25 including wine. March–Oct daily 12.30–2.30pm & 8–10.30pm (usually stays open later in high summer).

West along the coast

A string of white sandy beaches stretches from San Menaio to **RODI GARGANICO** – originally a Greek settlement ("Rodi" is derived from Rhodes) and now a highly popular summer resort. It's busy and expensive in August, but a couple of months either side it can be delightful. **SAN MENAIO** is much quieter than Rodi – more compact and with fewer villas – and even in high season it's easy to get away from it all by walking a few hundred metres south along the strand.

From Rodi Garganico, both road and rail skirt the large **Lago di Varano**, a once-malarial swamp that swallowed the ancient Athenian town of Uria in the fourth century BC. The preserve of eel fishermen, it's the least-visited region on the Gargano promontory, and consequently attracts a great variety of birdlife, particularly curlew and warbler. Further west, the thin **Lago di Lesina** is a highly saline, shallow lagoon, cut off from the sea by a 27km stretch of sand dunes. It's still mercifully free from development – unlike the northern spit of Varano, which has a growing number of campsites and hotels.

The Tremiti islands

A tiny cluster of rugged islands 40km off the Gargano coast, the **Tremiti islands** – Isole Tremiti – are almost entirely given over to tourism in the summer, when the tiny population is swamped by visitors. Despite this, they remain relatively unspoilt and the sea crystal clear. The main Tremiti group consists of three islands: **San Nicola**, **San Domino** – the biggest – and **Capraia**, of which only the first two are inhabited.

Brief history

The islands were traditionally a place of exile and punishment. Augustus banished his granddaughter Julia to the islands, while Charlemagne packed his father-in-law off here (minus eyes and limbs) in the eighth century. Monks from Montecassino, on the mainland, first set about building a formidable fortress-abbey on one of the islands in the eleventh century, which managed to withstand frequent assault by the Turks. Later, during the eighteenth century, the islands returned to their old role as a place of confinement for political prisoners, though the Bourbons, concerned at the decline in the local population, shipped in two hundred single women from Naples to encourage a recovery.

San Nicola

Most **ferries** arrive at **SAN NICOLA**, where you can wander around the monastic fortress and the tiny church of **Santa Maria a Mare**, built by the monks in the eleventh century

14

on the site of an earlier ninth-century hermitage. San Nicola is barren and rocky with no beaches, although there is nude bathing on its east side and good swimming off the whole island.

San Domino

14

Ignore the offers of pricey boat-trips to the other islands and instead jump on the regular ferry that takes about a minute to cross to **SAN DOMINO**. It's a greener island than its neighbour, its pines offering welcome shade from the heat. Although there's a sandy **beach** – Cala delle Arene – right where the ferry lands on the northeast side of the island, it's packed in the summer. Your best bet is to follow the signs for the *Villaggio TCI* and make for the west of the island and the quieter coves, such as Cala dello Spido. If you're **walking**, head for the Punta di Diamante; maps are pinned up in some of the bars or can be bought from souvenir shops.

ARRIVAL AND DEPARTURE — THE TREMITI ISLANDS

By helicopter Year round, there is at least one helicopter trip daily to San Domino heliport from Foggia airport, operated by Alidaunia (T 0881 024 024, W alidaunia.it; €57.20 one way).

By ferry There is at least one daily ferry service (mid-June to mid-Sept) to the Tremiti islands from Vieste (see page 810). Ferries and fast ferries for foot passengers run throughout the year from Termoli (W tirrenia.it, see page 812). There are also summer services from the Abruzzo ports of Vasto (see page 733) and Ortona. In summer, you'll find plenty of tour boats in Vieste, Peschici and Rodi Garganico touting day-trips to the islands.

Destinations Ortona (end June–early Sept 1 daily; 2hr); Termoli (June–Sept 2–3 daily; 50min–1hr 25min; Oct–May 1–2 daily; 1hr 25min); Vasto (early April–early Sept 1 daily; 1hr); Vieste (June–Sept 1 daily; 1hr).

ACCOMMODATION

Accommodation on the islands is limited to San Domino and is largely full board in high season: count on paying at least €60 a night/person. Finding a place on spec in low season won't be a problem, but in high season you should book in advance. Bear in mind that mosquitoes can be a serious problem in summer and that, as provisions have to be ferried across from the mainland, eating out can be costly – shop on the mainland before you leave.

La Vela Via Amerigo Vespucci 17, San Domino T 338 882 1583, W hotel-lavela.it. One of the best of the island's small hotels, set among the pine trees just a few minutes' walk from the town and port. Rooms are simply appointed but spotless, and there's a great sundeck overlooking a pretty beach. Rates are half board only. Per person **€80**

Trani

The initial part of the coastal route south from Manfredonia is unremarkable, with flat lands given up to saline extraction. The first town of note down the coast is **TRANI**, a beautiful stone-built port and fishing village with an unusually cosmopolitan air. One of the most important medieval Italian ports, it was a prosperous trading centre with a large mercantile and Jewish community, and rivalled Bari as a commercial port. A wander through the streets around the harbour gives an impression of the medieval city, not least in the names that echo the town's mercantile and Jewish origins – Via Sinagoga, Via Doge Vecchia (the port had strong – not always amicable – links with Venice) and Via Cambio (Street of the Moneychangers).

The Duomo

Piazza del Duomo • Daily: Nov–March 8.30am–12.30pm & 3.30–6pm; April–Oct 9am–12.30pm & 3.30–7.pm • Free but donation appreciated • **Belltower** €5

Centrepiece of the town is the cream-coloured, eleventh-century **Duomo**, right on the sea at the edge of the old town. Dedicated to San Nicola Pellegrino, it consists of no fewer than three churches, stacked on top of each other like an inverted wedding

cake – the facade austere but lightened by a pretty rose window. The interior has been restored to its original Norman state, the stark nave displaying a timbered ceiling, with the original doorway standing in the back corner. You also can climb the **belltower** for great views over the town.

ARRIVAL AND DEPARTURE — TRANI

By train Trani is on the main train line between Bari (40min) and Foggia (50min) and well served by services from both cities.

By bus Buses arrive and depart from Piazza XX Settembre, outside the train station, a 10–15min walk from the port. There are regular services to Bari and Foggia.

ACCOMMODATION AND EATING

Corteinfiore Via Ognissanti 18 ⓣ0883 508 402. Inspired contemporary fish dishes that change according to the day's catch, in a tree-filled patio (heated in winter). A selection of five antipasti (€10) makes for a stunning lunch – there might be sea bass with a salsa of orange and courgette, swordfish rolled around ricotta, or grilled octopus on couscous, for example – while a full meal should cost around €35/head. **Tues–Sat 1pm–2.15pm & 8–10.15pm, Sun lunch only.**

Bari

The commercial and administrative capital of Puglia, a university town and southern Italy's second city, **BARI** is an economically vibrant place, with few pretensions to being a major tourist attraction. People come here primarily for work or to leave for Greece, Croatia and Albania on its many ferries, though the regenerated old city is well worth exploring – in recent years it's made considerable strides to shake off its image as a den of thieves rife with bag-snatchers (though it's best to keep your wits about you in the narrow old alleyways).

Brief history

Bari was already a thriving centre when the Romans arrived. Later, the city was the seat of the Byzantine governor of southern Italy, while, under the Normans, it rivalled Venice both as a maritime centre and, following the seizure of the remains of St Nicholas, as a place of pilgrimage. Since those heady days, Bari has declined considerably. Its fortunes revived briefly in 1813 when the king of Naples foisted a planned expansion on the city – giving the centre its contemporary gridded street pattern, wide avenues and piazzas. And Mussolini instituted a university and left a legacy of strident Fascist architecture. However, the city was heavily bombed during the last war, and today its compact and dynamic centre is a symbol of the south's zeal for commercial growth. Fortunately, heavy investment in redeveloping the old centre has given Bari a new lease of life.

The old town

Even if you're only in Bari to catch a ferry, try to make time to explore the **old town**, an entrancing jumble of streets that's possibly the most perplexing place to walk around in southern Italy. Situated at the far end of Corso Cavour, its labyrinth of seemingly endless passages weaving through courtyards and under arches was originally designed to spare the inhabitants from the wind and to throw invaders into a state of confusion. This it still does admirably, and even with the best of maps you're going to get lost. Life is lived very much outdoors, and on summer evenings it's full of people sitting outside their kitchen doors.

Basilica di San Nicola

Largo Abate Elia • Mon–Sat 7am–8.30pm, Sun 7am–10pm • Free

The **Basilica di San Nicola**, in the heart of the old town, was, as an inscription at the side of the main door testifies, consecrated in 1197 to house the relics of the saint

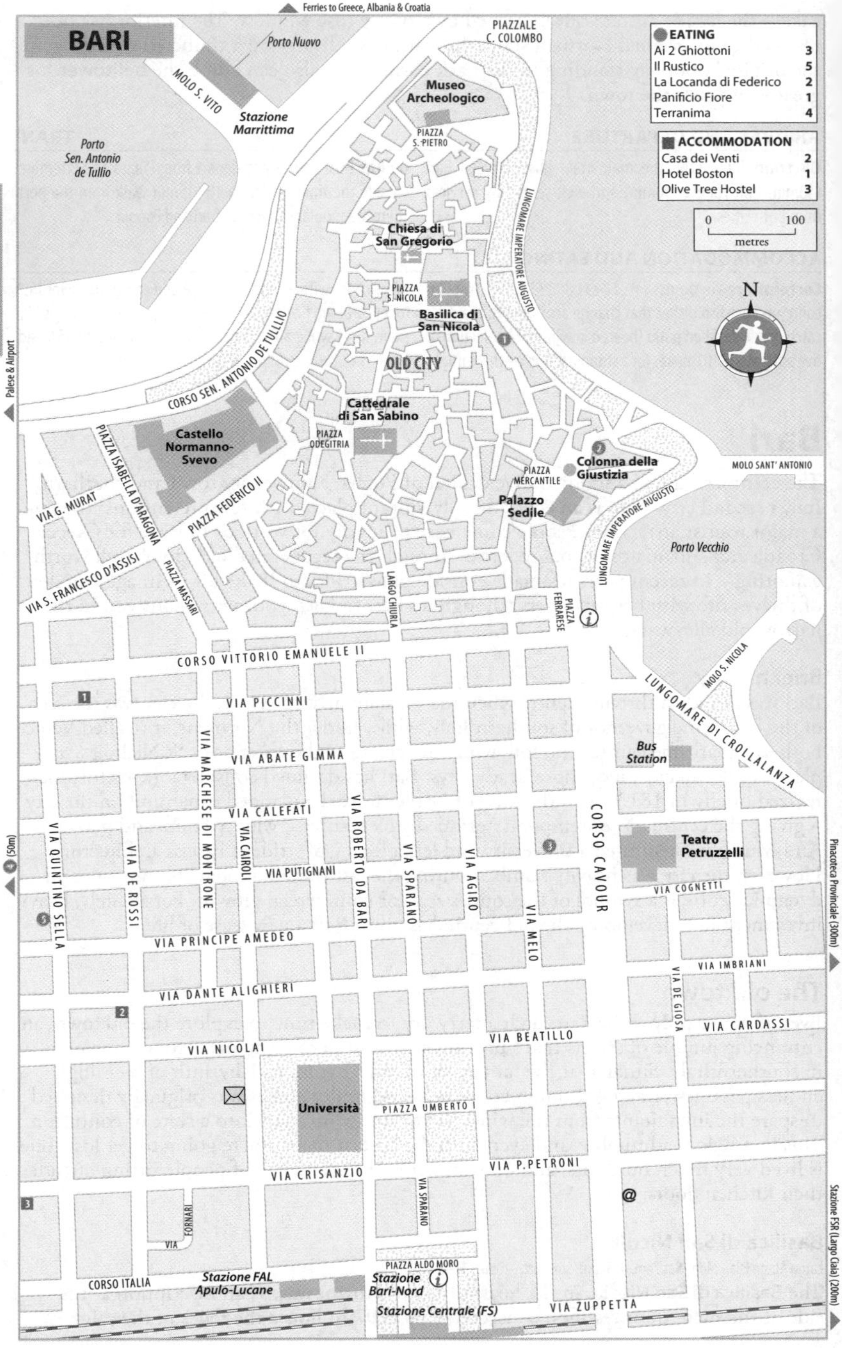

BARI

EATING

Ai 2 Ghiottoni	3
Il Rustico	5
La Locanda di Federico	2
Panificio Fiore	1
Terranima	4

ACCOMMODATION

Casa dei Venti	2
Hotel Boston	1
Olive Tree Hostel	3

0 100 metres

N

Ferries to Greece, Albania & Croatia

Porto Nuovo

Molo S. Vito

Stazione Marrittima

Porto Sen. Antonio de Tullio

Piazzale C. Colombo

Museo Archeologico

Piazza S. Pietro

Lungomare Imperatore Augusto

Chiesa di San Gregorio

Piazza S. Nicola

Basilica di San Nicola

Old City

Corso Sen. Antonio de Tullio

Palese & Airport

Cattedrale di San Sabino

Piazza Odegitria

Castello Normanno-Svevo

Piazza Isabella d'Aragona

Piazza Federico II

Via G. Murat

Via S. Francesco d'Assisi

Piazza Massari

Largo Chiurla

Piazza Mercantile

Colonna della Giustizia

Palazzo Sedile

Molo Sant' Antonio

Lungomare Imperatore Augusto

Porto Vecchio

Piazza Ferrarese

Corso Vittorio Emanuele II

Molo S. Nicola

Lungomare di Crollalanza

Via Piccinni

Via Abate Gimma

Bus Station

Via Marchese di Montrone

Via Calefati

Via Roberto da Bari

Corso Cavour

Via Quintino Sella

Via de Rossi

Via Cairoli

Via Sparano

Via Agiro

Teatro Petruzzelli

4 (50m)

Via Putignani

Via Cognetti

Via Melo

Pinacoteca Provinciale (300m)

Via Principe Amedeo

Via Imbriani

Via Dante Alighieri

Via de Giosa

Via Cardassi

Via Beatillo

Via Nicolai

Università

Piazza Umberto I

Via P. Petroni

Via Crisanzio

Via Sparano

Via Fornari

Stazione FSR (Largo Ciaia) (200m)

Piazza Aldo Moro

Corso Italia

Stazione FAL Apulo-Lucane

Stazione Bari-Nord

Stazione Centrale (FS)

Via Zuppetta

plundered a century earlier from southern Turkey. The real beauty of the church lies in its stonework, with the twelfth-century altar canopy one of the finest in Italy. The motifs around the capitals are the work of stonemasons from Como, while the lovely twelfth-century carved doorway and simple, striking mosaic floor behind the altar are heavily influenced by the Saracens. Best of all is the twelfth-century episcopal throne behind the altar, a superb piece of work supported by small figures wheezing beneath its weight. Down in the crypt are the remains of the saint – patron of Bari and many surrounding towns, plus orphans, pawnbrokers, thieves, sailors and Russians.

Cattedrale di San Sabino

Piazza dell'Odegitria • Daily 8am–1pm & 4–8pm, 8am–8pm in summer • Free

It's not far from the basilica to Bari's other important church, the **Cattedrale di San Sabino**, off Piazza dell'Odegitria, dedicated to the original patron saint of Bari, before he was usurped by Nicholas, and built at the end of the twelfth century. Come just for the contrast: uncluttered by arches, it retains its original medieval atmosphere and – unlike the basilica – a timbered roof. The cathedral houses an eighth-century icon known as the *Madonna Odegitria*, brought here for safety from Constantinople by Byzantine monks. It's said to be the most authentic likeness of the Madonna in existence, having been taken from an original sketch by Luke the Apostle, and is paraded around the city at religious festivals.

Castello Normanno-Svevo

Piazza Federico II di Svevia • Daily (except Tues) 8.30am–6.30pm • €6 • T 080 521 3704

Due west of the Piazza dell'Odegitria, the **Castello Normanno-Svevo** sits on the site of an earlier Roman fort. Built by Frederick II, much of it is closed to the public, but it has a vaulted hall that provides a cool escape from the afternoon sun. You can also see a gathering of some of the best of past Pugliese artistry in a display of plaster-cast reproductions from churches and buildings throughout the region – particularly from the cathedrals at Altamura and Bari, and an animated frieze of griffins devouring serpents from the church of San Leonardo at Siponto.

The new town

There's not a lot to the "**new town**" of Bari: straight streets are lined with shops and offices, relieved occasionally by the odd bit of greenery. Bordered with trees, **Corso Cavour**, Bari's main commercial street, leads down to the waterfront.

The **Pinacoteca Provinciale** on Via Spalato (Tues–Sat 9am–7pm, Sun 9am–1pm; €3) contains mostly southern Italian art ranging from the twelfth to nineteenth centuries, but there are also works by Tintoretto and Paolo Veronese that were moved here from the cathedral, and a small collection of paintings by the twentieth-century Bolognese painter, Giorgio Morandi. If your timing is right, it's also worth visiting the town's most prestigious performance venue, the extravagant **Teatro Petruzzelli** (guided tours €5, dates and times listed on website W www.fondazionepetruzzelli.com), whose design was influenced by Naples' San Carlo and the Paris Opera.

ARRIVAL AND DEPARTURE — BARI

BY PLANE

Bari airport (T 080 580 0200, W aeroportidipuglia.it) is 25km northwest of the city centre and served by low-cost airlines from the UK. Autobus Tempesta (T 080 521 9172, W autoservizitempesta.it) runs shuttle buses from the airport to Bari Centrale (at least hourly 5am–midnight; 30min; €4), and there's a slightly faster train connection to the same station (15min; €5). Pugliairbus (W pugliairbus.aeroportidipuglia.it) connects Bari airport with those of Brindisi and Foggia, and with Lecce, Taranto, Matera and the Gargano promontory.

BY TRAIN

Bari has excellent rail connections and three train stations.

14

Stazione Centrale This station in Piazza Aldo Moro is on the southern edge of the modern centre and serves regular FS trains and those of the private Ferrovia del Sud-Est line (080 546 2111, fseonline.it), which run down to Taranto via Alberobello, Locorotondo and Martina Franca (see page 824).

Stazione Bari-Nord Just to the west, also on Piazza Aldo Moro, the separate Stazione Bari-Nord is for trains run by the private FerroTramViaria company (080 529 9342, ferrovienordbarese.it), connecting Bari with the airport, Andria, Barletta, Bitonto and Ruvo di Puglia.

Stazione FAL Apulo-Lucane Adjacent to Stazione Bari-Nord, on Corso Italia, is the Stazione FAL Apulo-Lucane; trains and buses from here are run by Ferrovia Appulo-Lucane (080 572 5211, fal-srl.it) and go to Altamura, Gravina, and Matera and Potenza in Basilicata.

Destinations Alberobello (FSE, every 30min–1hr; 1hr 30min); Altamura (FAL, at least one hourly; 1hr15min); Andria (Ferrovia del Nord Barese, hourly; 1hr); Barletta (at least two hourly; 55min); Brindisi (2–3 hourly; 1hr 20min); Fasano (2–3 hourly; 40min); Grotte Castellana (FSE, every 30min–1hr; 1hr); Lecce (2–3 hourly; 1hr 30min–2hr); Locorotondo (2–3 hourly; 1hr 40min); Martina Franca (1–2 hourly; 1hr 50min); Matera (FAL, 14 daily; 1hr 30min); Ostuni (approx. 2 hourly daily; 1hr); Polignano a Mare (2–3 hourly ; 30min); Putignano (2–3 hourly daily; 1hr); Rome (5 daily; 4hr 40min); Ruvo di Puglia (Ferrovia del Nord Barese, 13 daily; 1hr); Taranto (at least 1 hourly; 1hr 20min); Trani (2–3 hourly ; 40min).

BY BUS

From the coastal towns north of Bari you'll arrive at Piazza Eroi del Mare; SITA SUD buses from inland and southern towns, Miccolis buses from Rome and FAL buses from Basilicata pull up in Largo Sorrentino (behind the train station). FSE buses from Brindisi pull in at Largo Ciaia (Mon–Sat), and on Largo Sorrentino (Sun), when they substitute for the train service. Bus services to Naples (3hr) are quicker than the train.

BY FERRY

Ferries all use the Stazione Marittima, next to the old city, which is connected with the main FS train station by bus #20.

INFORMATION

Tourist office The main tourist office is at Piazza del Ferrarese 29 (daily 10am–1pm & 4–7pm; 080 990 9341, infopointbari.com.

Bike tours Puglia in Movimento (327 824 0564, pugliainmovimento.com) hires bikes (€20 per day pedal bike, €35 per day electric bike) and runs bike tours to a different city each day, among them Alberobello, Ostuni, Polignano a Mare (€50/person). Meet in front of the main tourist office.

ACCOMMODATION

Most accommodation is in the modern part of Bari although some small B&Bs are opening up in the old city (see infopointbari.com for a comprehensive list). The most affordable hotels are found around the train station, though the area takes a turn for the worse after dark.

Casa dei Venti Via Dante 182 345 740 6687, casadeiventi.com; map p.816. Stylish new B&B in the modern town, about a 10min walk from the train station. Five spacious rooms and a suite, with classic furniture and contemporary decor, all with a/c, fridges and TV. Large breakfasts, including scrambled eggs and other savouries on request, are served in a splendid room wallpapered with Nina Campbell butterflies. **€104**

Hotel Boston Via Piccinni 155 080 521 6633, bostonbari.it; map p.816. A stone's throw from the old city, this business travellers' hotel has comfortable, if characterless, rooms and is in a safe area convenient for an evening *passeggiata*. **€89**

★ **Olive Tree Hostel** Via Scipione Crisanzio 90 0331 196 3949, hostelabari.com; map p.816. Sparkling hostel situated about 5min walk from the central train station, with dormitories and private rooms, and welcoming, helpful staff. There's wi-fi, lockers, a/c (at night), a laundry service, a communal kitchen and a nice shared patio. Dorms **€22**, doubles **€50**

EATING

There are lots of colourful choices of places to eat in and around the old town of Bari. Most offer traditional Pugliese dishes and seafood, along with the Bari speciality of *orecchiette*, ear-shaped pasta, usually served with broccoli or *cime di rapa* (turnip greens). In the evenings, stalls sell *panzarotti* and *sgagliozze* (fried polenta cubes) around Piazza Mercantile and Piazza del Ferrarese.

Ai 2 Ghiottoni Via Putignani 11 080 523 2240, ai2ghiottoni.it; map p.816. One of the town's best restaurants, serving good shellfish and a refined version of Pugliese cuisine in attractive surroundings just outside the old town. There are mixed fish plates from €17: expect to pay €45 for a full meal. Daily 12–2.30pm & 7pm–midnight; closed Aug.

Il Rustico Via Quintino Sella 95 080 521 6727; map p.816. Friendly and hugely popular local trattoria and pizzeria, where heaps of appetizers arrive at your table in waves, followed by the pizza of your choice. Excellent value meal deals, too. Mon–Sat 7pm–2am.

La Locanda di Federico Piazza Mercantile 63–64 080 522 7705, lalocandadifederico.com; map p.816. Lively *osteria* in the old town, attracting a young crowd with mixed appetizer plates, such as mozzarella, fava beans and chicory flan, and house specials like seafood

14

FERRIES FROM BARI

International ferry services run from Bari to Greece, Albania and Croatia; for information and timetables call ⓣ080 578 8511 or visit ⓦaplevante.org, which also has an updated list of the day's arrivals and departures. Travel agents often have special offers on **tickets**, so it is worth comparing the prices they can offer with those you find on the websites. As a general rule, you will save twenty percent if you buy a return ticket. Once you've got your ticket, you must report to the relevant desk at the Stazione Marittima at least two hours before departure. Prices given below are for travel in high season.

ALBANIA

Ventouris (ⓣ0805 217 609, ⓦventourisferries.com) and Adria (ⓣ0805 211 069, ⓦagemar.it) run car ferries to Durazzo/Durres in **Albania** daily all year round; the journey takes eight or nine hours overnight (from €50 one way for a reclining seat, €90 for a car).

CROATIA

Jadrolinija (ⓦjadrolinija.hr) operates services (March–Nov) to Dubrovnik in **Croatia**, and Bar in Montenegro. Tickets on both routes start at €48 for reclining seat, €58 for a car one way, though you will pay slightly more in high season.

GREECE

Ferry services to **Greece** are operated by Ventouris (see above), Anek Superfast (ⓦanek.gr), and Agoudimos (ⓦagoudimoslines.it). All three companies offer online booking. Ventouris runs services almost daily to Corfu and Igoumenitsa; one-way prices start at €58/person on deck, €50 extra for a car, plus port fees. The service to Igoumenitsa takes about twelve hours and to Corfu about ten hours. Anek Superfast runs afternoon and occasional overnight trips to Corfu (9hr), Igoumenitsa (10hr 30min) and Patras (16hr 30min) year-round. Prices start at €58 for deck passage to Corfu in low season, rising to €71 in July and August, while vehicles cost from €60 in low season to €96 in July and August.

calamarata (ring shaped pasta; €12) and *orecchiette* with rocket pesto (€8). Daily 12.45–3pm & 7.45pm–midnight.

Panificio Fiore Strada Palazzo di Città 38; map p.816. Locals queue for their delicious focaccia *barese*, simply garnished with tomatoes, olives, salt and olive oil (€1.50). Mon–Wed, Fri & Sat 8am–2pm & 5–8pm, Sun and Thurs 8am–2pm.

Terranima Via Putignani 213–215 ⓣ080 521 9725; map p.816. Informal café-restaurant serving a daily changing menu of regional specialities, with mixed antipasti for €8, *primi* such as *orecchiette* with aubergine and Martina Franca sausage (€9.50), and *secondi* like fava bean purée and baby squid (€12). There's often live Pugliese music in the evening. Mon–Sat 10am–11.30pm, Sun 10am–5pm; closed first week of Aug.

DIRECTORY

Police Via Paolo Aquilino 3 (ⓣ080 549 1331).

Post office The main office is near the university in Piazza Umberto I 33/A (Mon–Fri 8.20am–6.20pm, Sat 8.30am–12.30pm).

Taxis Taxi Bari (ⓣ080 554 3333, ⓦtaxibari.it; 24hr).

Le Murge

Rising gently from the Adriatic coast, **Le Murge** – a low limestone plateau – dominates the landscape to the south and west of Bari. The towns in the region are not natural holiday destinations: the area is sparsely populated and the small settlements that exist are rural backwaters with a slow pace of life. But they do make an interesting day out or a good stopover if you're heading for the region of Basilicata.

GETTING AROUND — LE MURGE

By train Andria and Ruvo di Puglia are on the Nord Barese train line from Bari, and Altamura and Gravina on the FAL line. Trains run at least hourly, sometimes half-hourly. For the more out-of-the-way places, it's much easier with a car.

Andria and the Low Murge

Easily reached from Barletta or Bari, the main town of the Low Murge is **ANDRIA**, a large agricultural centre at its best during the Monday morning market. There's little here to entice you to stay, unless you are heading to Castel del Monte on public transport.

Castel del Monte

14

Via Castel del Monte, Contrada Castel del Monte • Daily: 1 April–30 Sept 10.15am–7.45pm; 1 Oct–31 March 9am–6.30pm; ticket office closes 30min earlier • €10 • T 0883 569 997, W casteldelmonte.beniculturali.it • From 1 April–1 Nov a shuttle bus (W autolineeandriesi.it) runs from the train station in Andria every half hour; 9am–7.45pm; €1)

Despite its lack of obvious appeal today, Andria was a favourite haunt of Frederick II, who was responsible for the major local attraction, the **Castel del Monte**, 17km south – the most extraordinary of all Puglia's castles and one of the finest surviving examples of Swabian architecture.

Begun by Frederick in the 1240s, the castle is a high, isolated fortress built around an octagonal courtyard in two storeys of eight rooms. A mystery surrounds its intended purpose. Although there was once an iron gate that could be lowered over the main entrance, there are no other visible signs of fortification, and the castle may have served merely as a hunting lodge. Nonetheless, the mathematical precision involved in its construction, and the preoccupation with the number eight, have intrigued writers for centuries. It's argued the castle is in fact an enormous astrological calendar, or that Frederick may have had the octagonal Omar mosque in Jerusalem in mind when he designed it; yet, despite his recorded fascination with the sciences, no one really knows the truth. There is only one record of its use. The defeat of Manfred, Frederick's illegitimate son, at the battle of Benevento in 1266 signalled the end of Swabian power in Puglia; and Manfred's sons and heirs were imprisoned in the castle for more than thirty years – a lonely place to be incarcerated.

Ruvo di Puglia

Southeast of Andria, the old centre of **RUVO DI PUGLIA** is an attractive stop, with a quiet, timeless atmosphere. In autumn, the pavements of the old town are strewn with almonds, spread out to dry in the sun. Ruvo's thirteenth-century **Duomo**, tucked into the tightly packed streets of the town's old quarter, is well worth a look. Its beautiful portal is guarded by animated griffins balancing on fragile columns, with a staggering amount of decoration on the outer walls, a fine rose window and arches that taper off into human and animal heads.

ACCOMMODATION AND EATING — THE LOW MURGE

Antichi Sapori Piazza Sant'Isidoro 9, Montegrosso T 0883 569 529. On the main road from Andria to Montegrosso, this restaurant serves fine local produce, with dishes prepared by internationally renowned chef Pietro Zito: try *troccoli*, a local pasta, with aubergine, tomato, wild fennel and seasoned ricotta (€8). Mon–Fri 12.30–2.30pm & 8–10pm, Sat 12.30–2.30pm.

Lama di Luna Località Montegrosso T 0883 569 505, W lamadiluna.com. This luxurious and engaging agriturismo, 10km southwest of Andria on the road to Canosa di Puglia, may well tempt you to stay for a while. Serene, minimalist, but very comfortable rooms occupy an eighteenth-century house on an estate producing organic olive oil and fruit. Sheets are unbleached cotton, soaps are natural olive oil, and you breakfast on jams of organic fruit and wood-baked bread. There is also a good-sized swimming pool, set among a vast olive grove where some of the trees are more than a thousand years old, and free use of mountain bikes. €200

Altamura and the High Murge

Around 45km south of Bari (and reachable by FAL train), **ALTAMURA** is the largest town in the High Murge: originally a fifth-century-BC Peucetian settlement, you can still see some parts of the old town. Given its many historical layers, it's perhaps

appropriate that Altamura is home to one of southern Italy's best **archeological museums** (Mon–Fri 8am–7.45pm, Sat & Sun 8am–1.45pm; free; ⊕080 314 6409,) at Via Santeramo 88. The collection here traces the history of the people of the Murge from prehistory to late medieval times, with plenty of exciting finds from all over the peninsula.

Altamura's most striking feature is its **Duomo**, a mixture of styles varying from Apulian-Romanesque to Gothic and Baroque. Take a look, too, at the tiny church of **San Niccolò dei Greci** on Corso Federico di Svevia; built by the Greek colonists in the thirteenth century, it housed their Orthodox religious ceremonies for more than four hundred years.

Down the coast from Bari

The coast **south of Bari** is a craggy stretch, with rock-hewn villages towering above tiny sandy coves, offering easy escapes from the city. In summer, and on hot weekends, expect beaches to be crowded.

Torre a Mare and Polignano a Mare

About 10km down the coast from Bari, **TORRE A MARE** is situated on a rocky ledge high above two large caves. Being so close to the city, the village can become quite crowded, but things are quieter at the small, low-key port of **POLIGNANO A MARE**, a further twenty minutes or so. Its whitewashed medieval centre, sprinkled with bars, souvenir and *focacciarie* shops, is perched on the edge of the limestone cliffs, where people head on a Sunday to watch the waves crashing against the rocks or to sunbathe on the clifftops.

ARRIVAL AND DEPARTURE — TORRE A MARE AND POLIGNANO A MARE

By train and bus Both villages are on the FS train line south of Bari, though services to Torre are slightly more frequent. The journey takes around 12min to Torre, 20min to Polignano.

ACCOMMODATION AND EATING

Casa Dorsi Via Porto 58, Polignano ⊕080 425 1168, ⊕casadorsi.com. A beautifully renovated bed and breakfast in the heart of the old town, with rooms equipped with a/c, LCD TVs, wi-fi, kitchens and patios overlooking the sea. Staff rent out boats and offer cooking courses, and there is parking available about 300m away (€10/night). Minimum stay 2 nights in high season. **€100**

Covo dei Saraceni Via Conversano 1, Polignano ⊕080 424 1177, ⊕covodeisaraceni.com. An appealing hotel which sits right above the rocks with comfortable rooms – some with large balconies and private terraces (from €185) – and a continental breakfast buffet in its restaurant with panoramic views. Excellent deals online as long as you book a couple of months in advance. **€209**

Da Tuccino Via S. Caterina 69/F, Polignano ⊕080 424 1560, ⊕tuccino.it. One of the region's most renowned seafood restaurants, *Da Tuccino* is popular with aged celebrities, though unless you are a keen follower of 1970s and 1980s Italian pop music you probably won't have heard of any of them. What they come to eat is the magnificent, fresh raw fish, which you can select from a tank. The menu varies according to the catch of the day and booking is essential. Expect to pay around €100 a head for a full meal. Tues–Sat 12.30–3.30pm & 8–11pm, Sun lunch only.

Egnazia

Contrada Losciale near Fasano • Daily 8.30am to 1hr before sunset • €6 including museum • ⊕egnaziaonline.it

Some 10km south of the commercial port of Monopoli is the site of the ancient city of **Egnazia**. Here, an on-site **museum** houses an array of artefacts, including a stunning mosaic of the three Graces, an exquisite white-marble head of the Egyptian fertility god, Attis, and examples of the distinctive earthenware for which the ancient town was

BURRATA – A LUXURY MADE FROM LEFTOVERS

In some of the fancy restaurants around Egnazia, you'll see **burrata** on the menu, a local delicacy in which still-hot mozzarella is formed into a pouch, which is then filled with scraps of leftover mozzarella and fresh cream before closing. It seems to have been invented on a farm in Andria in the early twentieth century, as a way of using up the spare scraps of mozzarella at the end of the day's cheese making. It's at its best when eaten within 24 hours, which has led to its becoming a prestige food, with upmarket delis throughout Italy vying to have the cheese flown in fresh from Puglia.

prized. Right next to the seafront excavations, the water is tempting and clear, so bring swimming stuff and a picnic.

Brief history

Egnazia (also known as Gnathia) was an important Messapian centre during the fifth century BC, fortified with more than 2km of walls, large parts of which still stand in the northern corner of the ruined town – up to 7m high. It was later colonized by the Greeks and then the Romans (in 244 BC), who built a forum, amphitheatre, colonnaded public hall and temples: one was dedicated to Syria, a popular early Roman goddess, who, according to Lucian, was worshipped by men dressed as women. Horace is known to have dropped by here to see the city's famous altar, which ignited wood without a flame.

With the collapse of the Roman Empire, the city fell to subsequent barbarian invasions, and was almost completely destroyed by the Gothic king Totila in 545 AD. A community struggled on here, seeking refuge in the Messapian tombs, until the tenth century when the settlement was finally abandoned.

ARRIVAL AND DEPARTURE — EGNAZIA

By train The nearest train station to Egnazia is at Fasano, 4km or so inland: there's currently no bus service from here to the site.

ACCOMMODATION AND EATING

La Silvana Viale dei Pini 87, Selva di Fasano ⓣ 080 433 1161, ⓦ sierrasilvana.com. An unpretentious family-run hotel with large, simply decorated rooms, balconies and plenty of terrace space. The restaurant serves good, genuine local food. Half-board per person **€120**

Masseria Torre Maizza, Contrada Coccaro, between Fasano and Savelletri ⓣ 080 482 7838, ⓦ masseriatorremaizza.com. Stylish resort hotel with spacious rooms in outbuildings once used to house passing pilgrims. There's an Aveda spa, a chic heated pool, a Moroccan-influenced roof terrace and a restaurant that serves sophisticated Pugliese food. Facilities also include a golf course within the grounds, cooking classes, a beach club 4km away, and the chance to sail on the hotel's 14m yacht. **€430**

Pescheria Due Mari Piazza Amati, Savelletri ⓣ 080 482 9161, ⓦ pescheria2mari.it. Don't miss the chance to sample spanking-fresh fish in a stylish glass cube on the seafront in the little resort of Savelletri, where the local fishmonger serves raw seafood and deftly cut slivers of fish, accompanied by a glass of chilled white or sparkling wine. . Daily 111m–4pm & 4.30–10.30pm; closed Sun in winter.

The FSE line: Grotte di Castellana to Martina Franca

Meandering lazily down towards the **Valle d'Itria**, the Ferrovia Sud-Est (FSE) train passes through some of the prettiest of Puglia's landscapes. Olives gradually lose ground to vineyards and cherry and peach orchards, neatly partitioned by dry-stone walls. The barren limestone terrain of Le Murge swallows rivers whole producing a landscape cut by deep ravines and pitted with caverns and grottoes.

Grotte di Castellana

Piazzale Anelli, Castellana Grotte • Daily hourly tours: April–July & Sept 9am–5pm; Aug 9am–8pm; Oct 10am–4pm; March 10am–noon; Nov–Feb by reservation only • €17.50 for a 3km/2hr tour, €11.50 for 1km/50min tour excluding Grotta Bianca • T 0804 998 211, W grottedicastellana.it • From Castellana-Grotte station, it's about 500m to the grotto

About 40km out of Bari are the **Grotte di Castellana**, a spectacular set of underground caves. A lift takes you down to the largest of the caverns, La Grave, 60m below ground. From here, there's more than 1km of strangely formed caves to explore, ending in the most impressive, the Grotta Bianca – a shimmering sea of white stalagmites and stalactites.

Alberobello

Beyond Putignano, traditional *trulli* (see page 823) dominate the landscape, with around 1500 of them packing the narrow streets of **ALBEROBELLO**: most are south of Largo Martellotta in the Rione Monti zone, the rest to the north in Rione Aia Piccola. You can pick up a town map from the tourist office. Inevitably, a rampant tourist industry has grown up around the cute, conical stone huts, and the proprietors of *trulli* given over to displays of woolly shawls, liqueurs and other souvenirs practically drag in passers-by and don't let them go until they've bought something.

ARRIVAL AND INFORMATION — ALBEROBELLO

By train The FSE line connects Bari (approx. hourly; 1hr 30min) and Martina Franca (approx. hourly; 15min); trains do not run on Sun.

Tourist office Just off Largo Martellotta at Via Montenero 1, (daily 9am–1pm & 3–7pm; Nov–March Fri–Sun only; T 080 432 6030, W prolocoalberobello.it).

ACCOMMODATION AND EATING

Guesthouse Tipico Trulli Suite Via Monte S. Marco 28 T 349 565 0106. Complete your *trulli* experience by staying in one of the three rooms in this beautifully restored set of *trulli* – it's a bit like sleeping in a giant stone igloo. Breakfast is served on a panoramic patio. **€170**

L'Aratro Via Monte San Michele 25–29 T 080 432 2789. Inside a *trullo*, this is a stellar option, rigorously sourcing all its ingredients locally, and serving a dizzying number of vegetable and cheese antipasti and local specialities including that Pugliese staple, *purè di fave e cicoria* (puréed broad bean and wild chicory; €10) and *orecchiete con cime di rapa* (pasta with turnip tops and salty anchovies; €10). Three-course meals from €18. Daily noon–3pm & 7.30–10.30pm.

Locorotondo and Cisternino

Just a few kilometres south of Alberobello, **LOCOROTONDO**, which owes its name to its circular layout, has good views over the whole area, speckled with red- and grey-roofed *trulli* in a sea of vines and olive and almond trees. It's a great place to wander for an hour or so.

TRULLI

Curious-looking **trulli** are dotted throughout the Murge area of Puglia. Cylindrical, whitewashed buildings with grey conical roofs tapering out to a point or sphere, they are often adorned with painted symbols. Unique to Puglia, their ancient origins are obscure, but are probably connected to feudal lords who made people working their land build their houses without mortar so they could easily be pulled down if tax inspectors came round. The thick walls insulate equally against the cold in winter and the summer heat, while local limestone is used to make the two-layered roofs watertight. Most *trulli* have just one room but when more space was needed, a hole was simply knocked in the wall and an identical structure built next door. Although originally they were both dwellings and storehouses, these days they're being snapped up as holiday homes, and some are rented out as self-catering or B&B accommodation. An organization called Trullidea (T 080 432 3860, W trullidea.it), based in Alberobello, rents basic *trulli* in town and in the countryside for short- and long-term stays (from around €100/night) and can also arrange wine-tasting tours, cycling excursions and cooking courses.

14

THE FESTIVAL DELLA VALLE D'ITRIA

Southern Italy's top performing-arts festival, the annual **Festival della Valle d'Itria** (080 480 5100, festivaldellavalleditria.it), takes place in Martina Franca from mid July to early August. On a par with the Maggio Musicale in Florence (see page 553), the festival is mainly operatic, with performances – often of rarely performed works – in the appropriately grand Palazzo Ducale, as well as classical concerts and film screenings. It's a congenial and unpretentious event, though tickets aren't cheap – full-price tickets at main event operas are around €50; they're available online and from the festival office in the Palazzo Ducale.

Beyond, on the road between Locorotondo and Ostuni, **CISTERNINO** rejoices in the nickname "La Vera" ("the Real Thing") and is a marvellous antidote to touristy Alberobello: it's a pleasure to wander around the tiny, whitewashed alleyways of its old town. A series of **open-air concerts** is held in the main square, Piazza Vittorio Emanuele, between late June and September: among them is *Pietre che Cantano* ("The Stones that Sing"; pietrechecantano.com) in August.

Martina Franca

Trulli are still plentiful by the time you reach **MARTINA FRANCA**, a surprising town with a jubilant Baroque sensibility and a lively *passeggiata* at weekends. It is reputed to have been founded by settlers from Taranto fed up with constant Saracen attacks during the tenth century, but it was the Angevin prince of Taranto who bolstered the community in the early fourteenth century by granting it certain tax privileges. The town derives its name from this – *franca* meaning duty or stamp. Today its medieval core is adorned with some of the most subtle and least overbearing examples of architecture from the Baroque period you'll find.

Through the **Porta di Santo Stefano**, which marks the entrance to the old town, Piazza Roma is dominated by the hulking **Palazzo Ducale** which dates from 1688, and is now the town hall. A handful of rooms are open to the public most mornings (Mon–Fri) – most of them smothered in classical eighteenth-century Arcadian murals. Just across the square, the narrow Via Vittorio Emanuele leads right into the old town and Piazza Plebiscito, fronted by the undulating Baroque facade of the **Chiesa di San Martino** (daily 9am–11pm), an eighteenth-century church built on the site of an earlier Romanesque structure, of which only the campanile survives. From adjacent Piazza Immacolata you can either bear left down Via Cavour, with its Baroque *palazzi* and balconied streets, or wander further into the old town; the roads running around the edge of the surviving fourteenth-century town walls offer an excellent panorama of the Valle d'Itria, with its neatly ordered fields dotted with *trulli*.

ARRIVAL AND INFORMATION — MARTINA FRANCA

By train From the FSE train station it's a 15min walk to the town centre – go left out of the station and up Viale della Libertà to Corso Italia, which leads to the old town centre.

Tourist office Piazza XX Settembre 3 (June–Sept Mon–Fri 8.30am–2.30pm & 5–8pm, Sat & Sun 10.30am–-12.30pm & 5–8pm; Oct–May Mon–Sat 9am–1pm, Tues & Thurs also 4–7pm; 080 480 5702).

ACCOMMODATION AND EATING

Macelleria Lisi Via Verdi 57 080 480 1547. It is a summer tradition in the Murge for butchers to light a stove in the back of their shops, set a few tables outside, and serve a limited selection of hot dishes – along with some of the excellent local cured meats. *Lisi* keeps the tradition alive – expect to find the likes of grilled lamb kebabs, beef *tagliata* (a steak grilled rare, and cut into thin slices) and home-made sausages. Daily 8–11pm; Sept–June closed Tues.

Villagio In Via Arco Grassi 8 080 480 5911, villaggioincasesparse.it. The most atmospheric accommodation in Martina Franca is in these traditional apartments scattered around in various historic houses the old town, which are run like a B&B. Studios include breakfast. €75

Taranto and around

Straddling two harbours and set beside the deep blue waters of the Ionian, **TARANTO** is an unpretentious city with a thriving fish market, fabulous restaurants and a top-notch archeological museum. It also makes a good base to visit the nearby caves and grottoes of **Massafra**.

The city divides neatly into three distinct parts: the northern spur is the industrial area, home of the steel works and train station. Cross the Ponte di Porta Napoli and you're on the central island containing the old town. The southern spur holds the modern city centre (Borgo Nuovo), the administrative and commercial hub of Taranto, linked to the old town by a swing bridge.

Brief history

Known as **Taras** to the ancient Greeks, the port became the first city of Magna Graecia (the area of southern Italy colonized by the Greeks) and was renowned for its oysters, mussels and dyes – the imperial purple was the product of decayed Tarentine molluscs. Resplendent with temples, its acropolis harboured a vast bronze of Poseidon that was one of the wonders of the ancient world. Sadly, little remains of ancient Taras or even of later Roman Tarentum, although their monuments and relics are on display in the city's magnificent museum. After being destroyed by the Romans, Taranto was for years little more than a small fishing port, its strategic position on the sea only being recognized in Napoleonic times. It was home to the Italian fleet after Unification, and consequently heavily bombed during World War II; attempts to rejuvenate the town have left its medieval heart girdled by heavy industry, including the vast and ailing Ilva steel plant that throws its flames and lights into the skies above.

The old town

In Greek times the island holding the **old town** wasn't an island at all but part of the southern peninsula, connected by an isthmus to the southern spur. The Greeks raised temples and the acropolis here, while further south lay the residential districts. There's one extant fragment of ancient Taranto – the Doric **columns**, re-erected in a corner of **Piazza Castello**, which once adorned a temple of Poseidon. The rest of the tiny island is a mass of poky streets and alleyways tunnelling between massive *palazzi*, buttressed by scaffolding seemingly to prevent the whole place from falling down. Now owned by the navy, the Aragonese **Castello**, at the southern end (daily 9.30am–3am with sporadic breaks throughout the day; free; Ⓦcastelloaragonesetaranto.it), surveys the comings and goings of warships and fishing boats. The narrow canal they slide through, between the city's two inland "seas", was built in the late nineteenth century, on the site of the castle's old moat. "Seas" is a bit of a misnomer: the Mare Piccolo is really a large lagoon, home to Taranto's famous oysters and the Italian navy; and the Mare Grande is actually a vast bay, protected by sea walls and the offshore fortified island of San Pietro.

The Duomo and the fish market

Piazza Duomo • Daily 8am–noon & 4–8pm • Ⓦcattedraletaranto.it

At the heart of the old town lies the eleventh-century **Duomo**, which once did duty as a mosque – dedicated to Taranto's patron saint, Cataldo (Cathal), a seventh-century Irish monk who on returning from a pilgrimage to the Holy Land was so shocked by the licentiousness of the town's inhabitants that he decided to stay and clean the place up. His remains lie under the altar of a small chapel. As for the rest of the church, restoration has stripped away most of the Baroque alterations, and fragments of a Byzantine mosaic floor have been revealed. A few blocks away, check out the city's **fish market**, on Via Cariati, a lively affair where the best of the local catch is displayed at the crack of dawn.

The Borgo Nuovo

It's a short walk across the swing bridge to Taranto's modern centre or **Borgo Nuovo** – its wide streets laid out on a grid pattern that forms the focus of the city's *passeggiata*, around piazzas Vittoria and Archita. Nearby, the **Villa Peripato** was *the* place for the Tarentini to take their early evening stroll at the beginning of the last century, but today the city's gardeners seem to be fighting a losing battle with the ponds and undergrowth.

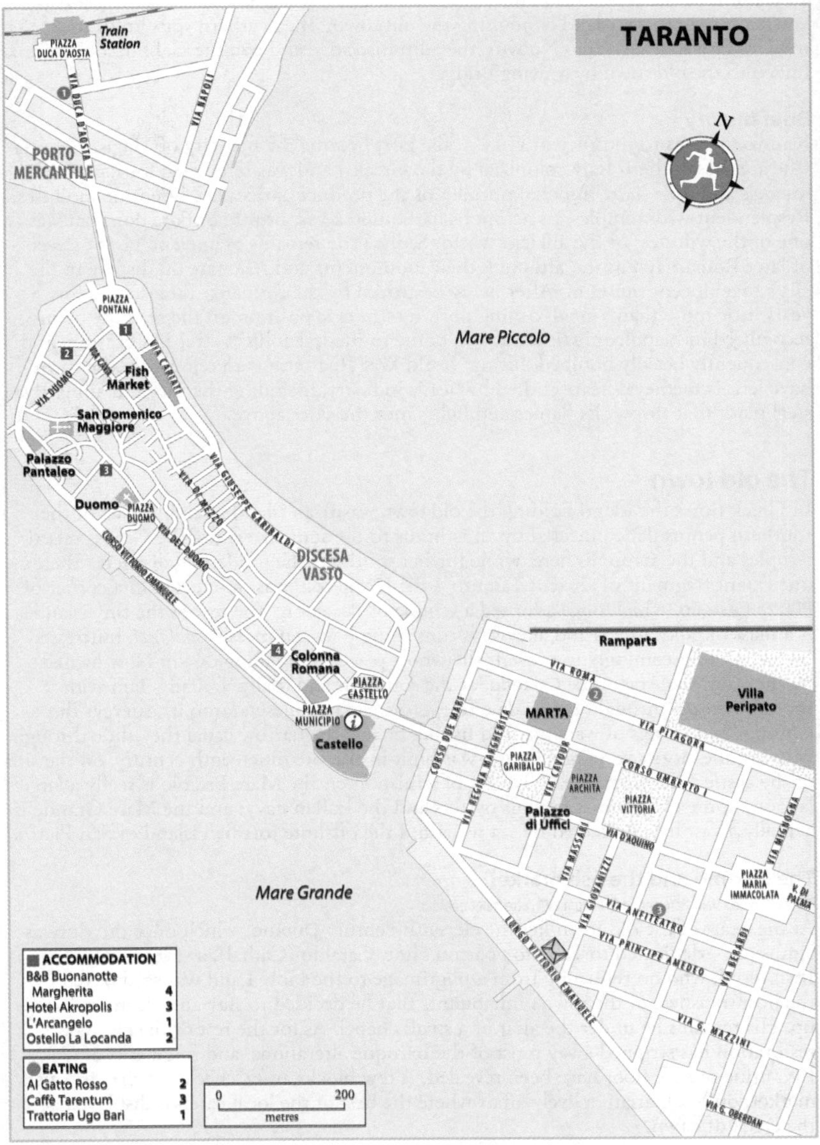

TARANTO

ACCOMMODATION

B&B Buonanotte Margherita	4
Hotel Akropolis	3
L'Arcangelo	1
Ostello La Locanda	2

EATING

Al Gatto Rosso	2
Caffè Tarentum	3
Trattoria Ugo Bari	1

0 200 metres

Museo Nazionale Archeologico di Taranto (MARTA)

Piazza Cavour • Daily 8.30am–7.30pm • €8 • Ⓦ museotaranto.beniculturali.it

The only real attraction in the modern part of town – and it's a gem – is the recently renovated **Museo Nazionale Archeologico di Taranto (MARTA)**, which offers a fascinating insight into the splendour of ancient Taras. The work of the goldsmiths of Taras is a particular highlight, all delicately patterned and finely worked in gold filigree. Several finds from Greek tombs are also worth a look, including a tiny terracotta model of Aphrodite emerging from the sea (dated end of fourth/early third century BC).

ARRIVAL AND INFORMATION — TARANTO

By train The train station is on Piazza Duca d'Aosta, with the old town a 400m walk across the bridge. Most buses from the station run to Corso Umberto I, useful for the archeological museum.

Destinations Bari (1–2 hourly; 1hr 15min); Brindisi (12 daily; 1hr); Lecce (1 direct train daily; 1hr 15min; plus Mon–Sat 10 daily via Brindisi; 1hr 40min–2hr 20min); Martina France (Mon–Sat 9 daily; 40min).

By bus Buses for most destinations (including Gallipoli and Martina Franca) arrive at and depart from Porto Mercantile, except FS connections with Metaponto and Potenza, which arrive at Piazza Duca d'Aosta, just outside the train station. Timetables for city buses can be found at Ⓦ amat.taranto.it.

Tourist office Piazza Castello (April–Sept daily 9am–-7pm; Oct–March Mon–Sat 9am–3pm, Sun 9am–1pm; Ⓣ 334 284 4098, Ⓦ viaggiareinpuglia.it).

ACCOMMODATION

B&B Buonanotte Margherita Piazzetta S. Francesco Ⓣ 349 295 8959, Ⓦ buonanottemargherita.it; map p.826. One of the very few B&Bs in the old town, this recently renovated little place has two spick-and-span rooms with balconies plus a living room with tea-making facilities and a small fridge: breakfast can be taken at a nearby bar. **€60**

Hotel Akropolis Vico I Seminario 3 Ⓣ 099 470 4110, Ⓦ hotelakropolis.it; map p.826. A modern-style hotel with fourteen rooms in an old building: it's aimed more at business travellers than tourists, though it has a picturesque wine bar in an ancient corn-store underground, and good views of the old town from its rooftop restaurant. **€94**

L'Arcangelo Via Garibaldi 3 Ⓣ 099 471 5940, Ⓦ hotelarcangelotaranto.it; map p.826. Just steps from the bridge over to the train station, this business hotel – renovated a couple years ago – is easily among the most comfortable options in the crumbling old town, facing onto Piazza Fontana. The rooms are spotless, some with balconies and sea views (€90), and all with wi-fi. **€74**

Ostello La Locanda Vico Civitanova Ⓣ 099 476 0033, Ⓦ ostellolalocanda.it; map p.826. About 100m from Piazza Fontana, near the entrance to the old city, this bare-bones hostel has beds in single and triple rooms and dorms. There's internet access, a sun terrace and a laundry for guest use. Guests get discounts at the restaurant downstairs. Dorms **€22**, singles **€30**

EATING

Al Gatto Rosso Via Cavour 2 Ⓣ 099 452 9875; map p.826. Refined, long-established fish restaurant near the archeological museum that delivers friendly service, excellent antipasti and inventive pasta dishes – try *gnocchetti* with prawns, basil and crispy aubergine (€12), and for a main course, go for deep-fried catch of the day (*frittura mista di paranza*; €13). Tues–Sat 12.30–3pm & 7.30pm–midnight. Sun 7.30pm–midnight.

Caffè Tarentum Via Anfiteatro 97 Ⓣ 099 453 3956; map p.826. Come here for excellent coffee, lovely *cornetti*, wicked *krapfen* (pastries filled with home-made jam) and typical almond-based sweets like *mustazzueli* as well as savoury snacks. Tue–Sun 6am–10pm.

Trattoria Ugo Bari Via Duca D'Aosta 27 Ⓣ 099 460 8736; map p.826. Don't leave Taranto without eating at this trattoria, known universally as "Da Ugo al Orologio", which has served fish at rock-bottom prices for more than seventy years. Wine costs €2 a litre, antipasti and *primi* cost €3, and *secondi* such as pasta with calamari and olives cost €5. You'll sit at long shared tables beside families, fishermen and bank clerks, and the fish is straight from the sea and freshly cooked. Mon–Fri noon–2.30pm & 8–10.30pm, Sat noon–2.30pm.

Around Taranto: Massafra

At first glance, **MASSAFRA**, some 15km from Taranto, appears to be the kind of unprepossessing, shabby dust-blown town you drive through as quickly as possible. However, it's split in two by a ravine, the Gravina di San Marco, that is lined with grottoes dating mainly from the ninth to the fourteenth centuries. Many contain cave-churches, hewn out of the rock by Greek monks and decorated with lavish frescoes.

The **Santuario della Madonna della Scala** is built onto an earlier cave-church; a Baroque staircase runs down to the eighteenth-century church, which features a beautiful fresco of a Madonna and Child, dating from the twelfth to the thirteenth centuries; more steps lead down to an eighth-century crypt.

The nearby **Cripta della Buona Nuova** houses a thirteenth-century fresco of the Madonna and a striking painting of Christ Pantocrator. About 200m away, at the bottom of the ravine, is a mass of interconnected caves known as the **Farmacia del Mago Greguro**, now in a pretty pitiful state but once used by the medieval monks as a herbalist's workshop.

ARRIVAL AND DEPARTURE — MASSAFRA

There are regular **trains** (Mon–Sat 12 daily, Sun 6 daily; 15min) and FSE **buses** (Mon–Sat 12–19 daily; 15min) from Taranto's Porto Mercantile to Massafra, though the town's sites are only visitable by **guided tours** arranged with Massafra's tourist office at Piazza Garibaldi (Mon–Fri 10am–12.30 & 3.30–5.30pm; ☎ 099 880 4695, ⓦ massafraturismo.it).

Brindisi

Across the peninsula, 60km east of Taranto on the opposite coast, lies **BRINDISI**, once a bridging point for crusading knights and still a town that makes its living from people passing through. The natural harbour here, the safest on the Adriatic coast, made Brindisi an ideal choice for early settlers. In Roman times, the port became the main crossing point between the eastern and western empires, and later, under the Normans, there came a steady stream of pilgrims heading east towards the Holy Land. The route is still open, and now Brindisi – primarily – is where you come if you're **heading for Greece** from Italy. On arrival, you may well think that the entire town is full of shipping agents: this, when all is said and done, is its main business. But even if you're leaving the same night you'll almost certainly end up with time on your hands. You could just while away time in a bar or restaurant in the old town – it is pretty compact and, although it isn't brimming with ancient monuments, has a pleasant, almost oriental flavour about it, and a few hidden gems tucked down its narrow streets.

Scalinata Virgiliana

The top of **Scalinata Virgiliana** (Virgil's Steps) marks the end of the ancient Via Appia, which ran all the way from the Porta Capena in Rome. Two columns stood here for years – useful navigation points for ships coming into harbour. The single column that remains has been restored, as has the area around it; the other column was carried off to Lecce.

The Duomo and Museo Archeologico Provinciale

Via Colonne, with its seventeenth- and eighteenth-century *palazzi*, runs up to the **Duomo** (daily 8am–9pm; free) – a remarkable building, if only for the fact that it's survived seven earthquakes since its construction in the eleventh century. Just outside is the **Museo Archeologico Provinciale** (Tues–Sat 9.30am–1.30pm, Tues also 3.30–6.30pm; free), which displays ornaments and statues from the necropolises that lined the Via Appia in Roman times. There are also several rooms with bronzes recovered in nearby underwater explorations, as well as finds from the excavations at Egnazia (see page 821).

San Giovanni al Sepolcro

Piazza San Giovanni al Sepolcro • Fri–Wed 8am–13 & 5–9pm; closes much earlier in winter • Free

Follow Via Tarentini from the Duomo and bear left for the tiny, round church of **San Giovanni al Sepolcro**, an eleventh-century baptistry. It's a little dark and decrepit inside, but you can just make out some of the original thirteenth-century frescoes. And there are more frescoes, this time a century older, in the **Chiesa di Santa Lucia**, just off Piazza del Popolo.

Chiesa di Santa Maria del Casale

Via Ruggero de Simone • Daily 8am–8pm • Free • Take airport bus or #4 or #5 from the train station, and ask the driver when to get off

Brindisi's most important medieval monument, the **Chiesa di Santa Maria del Casale** is a 3km bus ride from town. Built by Philip of Anjou at the end of the thirteenth century, it's an odd mixture of styles: the facade is adorned with an Arabic mass of geometric patterns, worked in two shades of sandstone, and the portal has an almost Art Deco touch to it. The stark interior is rescued from gloom by some fourteenth-century

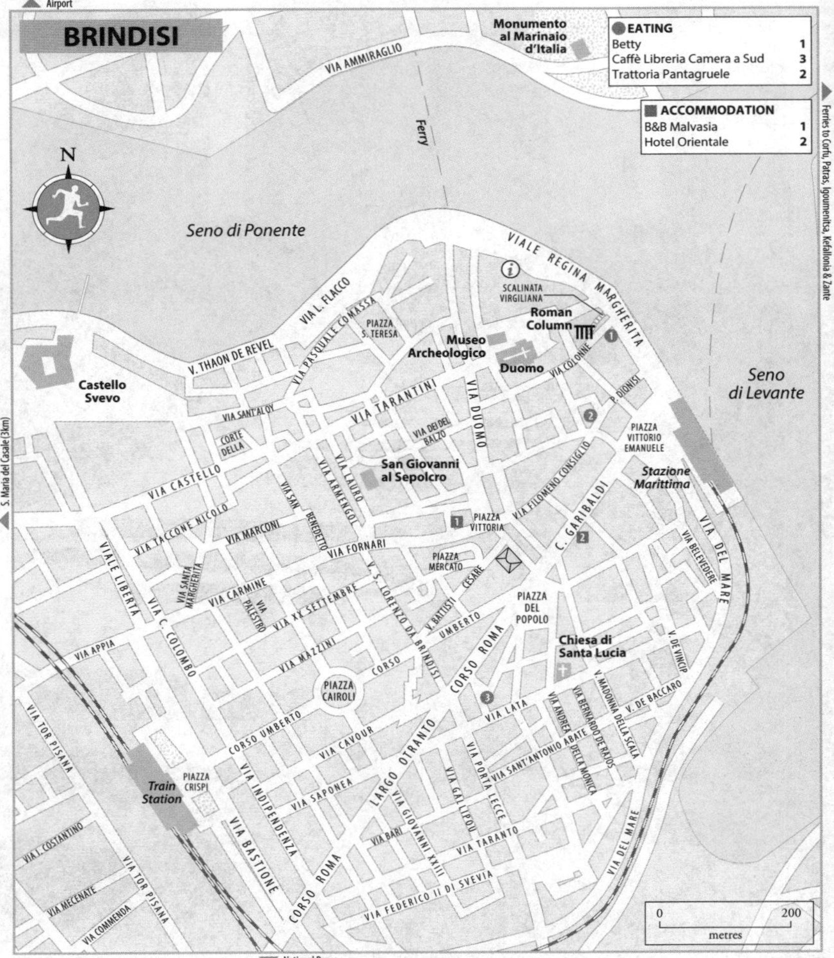

frescoes depicting frightening allegorical scenes relating to the Last Judgement, a vision of hell designed to scare the living daylights out of the less devout.

ARRIVAL AND DEPARTURE — BRINDISI

By plane Brindisi's airport (T 080 580 0200, W aeroportidipuglia.it), served by Ryanair from Stansted, is 7km from the city centre. A shuttle bus runs to the Stazione Centrale every 30min (8.15am–8.45pm; €1), taking 10min to town and continuing to Costa Morena (20min). There are also buses from the airport direct to Lecce (€8), Bari (€10) and Taranto (€7); the service is run by COTRAP (W pugliairbus.aeroportidipuglia.it). If you want to rent a car, all major operators have booths at the airport.

By train The train station is on Piazza Crispi, at the foot of Corso Umberto, a 10- to 15min walk from the port.

Destinations Lecce (2–3 hourly; 30min); Ostuni (1–2 hourly daily; 25min); Taranto (13 daily; 1hr).

By bus Services to Rome, Florence and Pisa (Marozzi buses) and Naples (Miccolis buses) arrive at, and depart from, Viale P. Togliatti, a continuation of Viale A. Moro in the new part of town.

Destinations Florence (1 daily; 13hr); Naples (3 daily; 5hr 30min); Pisa (1 daily; 14hr); Rome (4 daily; 7hr).

By ferry Arriving by ferry from Greece leaves you at Costa Morena, a couple of kilometres southeast of town; a shuttle bus run by the port authority links this with the town centre, dropping off and picking up at the intersection of Corso Garibaldi and Lungomare Regina Margherita, in front of the maritime station, before continuing to the airport.

INFORMATION AND GETTING AROUND

By bus Central Brindisi is small enough to walk around, but for transport around town, lots of buses run down Corso Umberto and Corso Garibaldi.

By taxi If you need a taxi call T 0831 597 901 or T 0831 597 503.

Tourist office There's a very helpful office at Lungomare Regina Margherita 44 (Mon 10am–6pm, Tues–Sun 8am–8pm; T 0831 523 072, W viaggiareinpuglia.it), and one in the airport arrivals hall (daily 8am–8pm; T 0831 412 975).

ACCOMMODATION

B&B Malvasia Vico Scalese, behind Piazza della Vittoria T 349 380 0689, W malvasiabrindisi.com; map p.830. Two comfy rooms above a cultural association with a bar, where you can listen to blues and browse the bookshelves.

FERRIES TO ALBANIA AND GREECE

A staggering array of **agents** sell **ferry tickets** to Albania and Greece, and you should take care to avoid getting ripped off. Ignore the touts clustered around the train station in high season, who specialize in selling imaginary places on non-existent boats, and always buy your ticket direct from the company's office or an approved agent. Discovery, Via Provinciale per Lecce 27 (T 0831 573 800, W discoveryto.it), is a reliable **general agent** which also sells onward ferry tickets to the Cyclades and Crete. You can also buy tickets at Costa Morena.

ROUTES

A variety of **routes** operate most of the year, although less frequently outside peak season – roughly defined as between mid-July and mid-August. **Services** – including some high-speed catamarans – sail to Vlore in Albania and Corfu, Igoumenitsa, Patras, Cephallonia and Zante in Greece. Visit W aferry.it for **timetables** and **prices**. As a rule, nearly all the reliable companies sail in the evening.

PRICES AND BOARDING

Prices vary considerably according to season but there's not much difference between the companies: for a one-way, high-season fare to Corfu/Igoumenitsa, expect to pay around €50/person on deck or €72 for a reclining seat (cabins are available for a higher charge), from €54 extra for a car; in low season prices almost halve. High-speed links are more expensive. When you buy your ticket, check whether it includes **embarkation tax** – €10/person or car.

Leaving Italy, you should arrive at least one hour – preferably two hours in high season – before your ship's departure. Free shuttle buses link the Stazione Marittima with Costa Morena (about 20min), but only when cruise ships arrive, so check the bus schedule beforehand. Make sure that any stopover you are making on the way to Patras is clearly marked on your ticket. **Stock up on food and drink** in Brindisi's supermarkets to avoid the inevitable mark-ups on board.

It's good for families or a group of friends (you can even bring a pet). €75

Hotel Orientale Corso Garibaldi 40 ⓣ0831 568 451, ⓦhotelorientale.it; map p.830. Right in the thick of things on Brindisi's main drag, this newly renovated high-rise hotel has clean, comfortable rooms, a small fitness centre and parking. €99

EATING

Betty Viale Regina Margherita 6 ⓣ0831 563 465; map p.830. Great café close to the port with tasty pastries and ice cream. A good choice for an evening *aperitivo*, as it has a tempting spread of nibbles. Open till the early hours too, so it's the perfect place to sit and wait till your ferry leaves. Daily 7am–midnight.

Caffè Libreria Camera a Sud Largo Otranto 1 ⓣ0831 529 733; map p.830. This bookshop café makes a nice place to while away a few hours. It's a good place for a lazy breakfast or civilized *aperitivo* – and look out for the regular gastronomic evenings. Daily 7.30am until late; closed 5pm Sat & all Sun in summer.

Trattoria Pantagruele Via Salita di Ripalta 1 ⓣ0831 560 605; map p.830. Well-regarded restaurant serving excellent Pugliese dishes and local seafood: they do a great version of puréed fava beans with tender wild chicory (€7) and the spaghetti with pistachio, anchovies and breadcrumbs or the *orecchiette* with a *ragù* made of octopus (€10) is delicious. Look out for local specialities such as the purple prawns from Gallipoli. Mon–Sat 12.30–2.45pm & 7.30–10.45pm,

Around Brindisi: Torre Guaceto

Just 15km northwest of Brindisi is a beautiful nature reserve and protected marine area known as **Torre Guaceto** (visitor centre ⓣ0831 989 885, ⓦriservaditorreguaceto.it). You'll need a car to get here outside summer, when there are buses from town, but it's a lovely spot for biking through maquis and olive groves, scuba diving over small reefs of coral and sea grass or chilling out on the sandy beach.

Ostuni

OSTUNI, 40km northwest of Brindisi (35min by train), is known as the "white city" and is one of southern Italy's most stunning small towns. Situated on three hills at the southernmost edge of Le Murge, it was an important Greco-Roman city in the first century AD. The old centre spreads across the highest of the hills, a gleaming white splash of sun-bleached streets and cobbled alleyways dominating the plains below. Seven kilometres away, the popular sandy coastline has Blue Flag beaches.

The maze of well-preserved winding streets provides a fascinating amble, and there are some exceptional views – particularly from Largo Castello over the woods to the north. Bits of cavorting Baroque twist out of unexpected places, including an ornamented eighteenth-century obelisk, 21m high, dedicated to St Oronzo, which stands in **Piazza della Libertà** (or Piazza Sant'Oronzo) on the southern edge of the old town. This is the focal point on summer Saturday nights for hordes of people who drive in from the countryside, meet their friends and pack out the bars and cafés. From here, follow Via Cattedrale uphill, past a series of monumental palaces and churches that trim the ascent. One of these, the **Chiesa di San Vito**, houses an **ethnography museum**, newly reopened after a long restoration (July–Dec daily 10am–1pm & 4–7pm; Jan–June Mon–Fri 10am–1pm, Sat, Sun 10am–1pm & 4–7pm, Tues–Fri 10am–1pm, Sat & Sun 10am–1pm & 5–8pm; €6) – its highlight is "Delia", the skeleton of a young pregnant woman found in a crouched position, her bones decorated before burial. At the top of the hill, the fifteenth-century **Duomo** nestles into a charming piazza dominated by the Palazzo Vescovile and the Palazzo del Seminario.

ARRIVAL AND INFORMATION — OSTUNI

By train Trains from Brindisi and Bari arrive at the station a couple kilometres out of town, though there's a connecting bus service (departing roughly every 30min) to Piazza della Libertà at the foot of the old town.

By bus Buses stop outside the centre, on Viale dello Sport: from here, you can take a local bus into town or it's a 20min walk.

Tourist Corso Mazzini 8 just off Piazza della Libertá (July & Aug daily 8am–2pm & 4.30–10.30pm; Sept–June daily 8am–2pm & 3.30–8pm; 0831.301.268). Shares an office with InfoPoint, a very helpful information service that can give advice on accommodation, eating and excursions (daily 10am–1pm & 3–8pm, 0831 1798833, www.borgostuni.it).

ACCOMMODATION

Bienbi Via G. Pinto 11 393 930 4223, bienbi.it. A boutique B&B with four serene rooms, fittingly furnished in white, and a roof terrace with views over the old town to the coast. Home-cooked meals featuring local produce can be arranged on request, served in a lovely sitting room. **€130**

I 7 Archi Via Bixio Continelli 102 347 616 0297, i7archi.com. Beautifully designed and well-equipped little rooms in a whitewashed stone building along Via Bixio, also known as the road of seven arches. Some of the rooms have great terraces with views over the rooftops, and breakfast (€5 extra) is brought to your room on a tray. **€81**

Il Frantoio SS16 km 874 0831 330 276, masseriailfrantoio.it. A traditional white farmhouse in 72 hectares of olive grove, a 5min drive from Ostuni, with sixteen rooms furnished with family furniture and heirlooms. The estate produces organic olive oil, fruits and vegetables, and they make delicious meals. Rates include access to selected lidos on nearby beaches. **€230**

EATING AND DRINKING

Osteria del Tempo Perso Via G. Tanzarella Vitale 47 0831 304 819, osteriadeltempoperso.com. Set in a charming cave in the heart of the old city, with antipasti including tuna tartare (€15) and *primi* such as *orecchiette* with clams, mussels, chickpeas and fennel (€12). Tues–Sun 12.30–3pm & 7.30–11pm.

★ **Osteria Piazzetta Cattedrale** Largo Arcidiacono 0831 335 026, piazzettacattedrale.it. Elegant restaurant opposite the cathedral, which uses locally sourced ingredients to great creative effect – try the stunning *cestino di crepe con crema di cavolfiori, pancetta crocante e vincotto di Primitivo*, a crêpe basket filled with cauliflower purée and crisp bacon and drizzled with sweet wine must – on a constantly evolving seasonal menu. *Degustazione* menus cost €30/head excluding wine, or you can lunch on a selection of six antipasti for €15/head. Daily 12.30–2pm & 7.30–11pm; closed Tues in June.

Porta Nova Via G. Petrarolo 38 0831 338 983, ristoranteportanova.com. Set in a fifteenth-century stone city gate overlooking olive groves and the sea, this is a fine place for fish and shellfish, with a following for its raw fish (the raw fish tasting menu costs €35), as well as marvellous dishes such as black *trofie* served with turnip tops, baby squid, anchovy and toasted breadcrumbs (€15). Daily 12.30–3.30pm & 7–11pm.

Salento

Some 40km south from Brindisi, Baroque **Lecce** makes a good starting-point for excursions around **Salento**, the name given to the very tip of Italy's heel extending from just south of Ostuni to **Santa Maria di Leuca**. Here the landscape begins to take on a distinctive Greek flavour, a mildly undulating region planted with carob, prickly pear and tobacco. The Adriatic coast is pitted with cliffs topped with ruined watchtowers, and rugged coves and caves trail right the way down to the **southern cape**. The hinterland, by comparison, is more barren, although again there's a Greek feel to it, with tiny, sun-blasted villages growing out of the dry, stony, red earth and flat-roofed houses painted in bright pastel colours.

Lecce

Dubbed the "Florence of the South", **LECCE** is a place to linger, with a wealth of fine architecture scattered about an appealing old town, as well as a few diverting Roman remains. The exuberant building styles here are the legacy of religious orders (Jesuits, the Teatini and Franciscans) who came to the region at the end of the sixteenth century, bringing an influx of wealth which paid for the opulent churches and *palazzi* that still pervade today's city. The flowery style of "Leccese Baroque" owed as much to the materials to hand as to the skills of the architects: the soft local sandstone could be intricately carved and then became hard with age.

Piazza Sant'Oronzo

Start at **Piazza Sant'Oronzo**, the hub of the old town, named after the first-century bishop of Lecce who went to the lions under Nero. His bronze statue lurches unsteadily from the top of the **Colonna di Sant'Oronzo** that once stood at the end of the Via Appia in Brindisi. It reappeared here in 1666 to honour Oronzo, who was credited with having spared the town from plague ten years earlier. The south side of the piazza is taken up by the **Anfiteatro Romano**, which probably dates from the time of Hadrian. In its heyday it seated twenty thousand spectators; today it's used for the Christmas nativity scene.

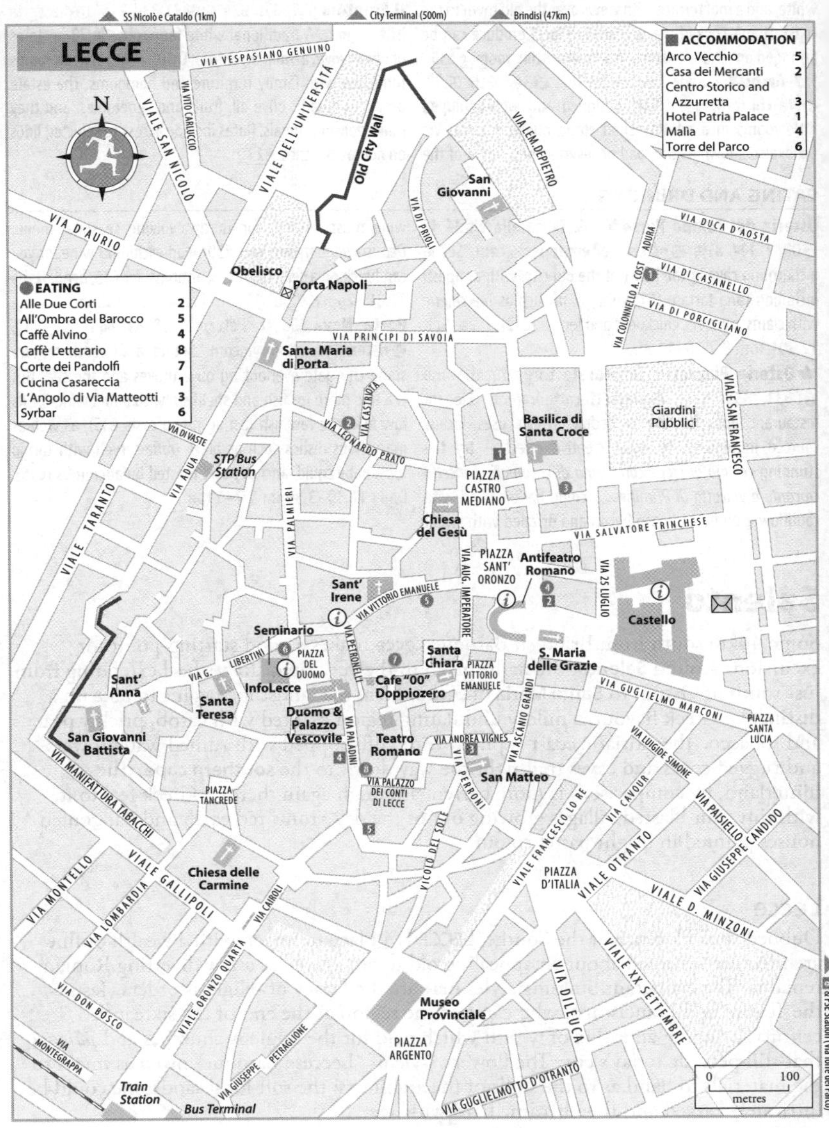

Sadly, most of its decorative bas-reliefs of fighting gladiators and wild beasts have been removed for safekeeping, and nowadays it looks rather depleted. Just behind the piazza is another relic of Roman Lecce, the well-preserved **Teatro Romano**, the only one of its kind to be found in Puglia, with rows of seats and orchestra floor still remarkably intact.

Basilica di Santa Croce

Piazzetta Gabriele Riccardi • Daily 9am–noon & 5–8pm • Free

The finest and most ornate of Lecce's Baroque churches is the **Basilica di Santa Croce**, just to the north, whose florid facade was the work of the local architects Zimbalo and Penna and took around 150 years to complete; its upper half is a riot of decorative garlands and flowers around a central rose window.

Piazza del Duomo

Head west from Piazza Sant'Oronzo along the bustling Via Vittorio Emanuele to **Piazza del Duomo**. Facing onto the square, the **Seminario** holds an impressively ornate well, with carved stone resembling delicately wrought iron. The balconied **Palazzo Vescovile** adjoins the **Duomo** itself (daily 9am–noon & 4–6.30pm; free), twelfth century in origin but rebuilt entirely in the mid-seventeenth by Zimbalo. He tacked on two complex facades and an enormous five-storey campanile that towers 70m above the square.

San Giovanni Battista

Via Giuseppe Libertini • Daily 9am–1pm & 4–8pm; 3.30–7.30pm in winter • Free

There is further work by Zimbalo in the **Church of San Giovanni Battista** (or del Rosario), by the Porta Rudiae in the southwest corner of town. The ornate facade and twisting columns front some extremely odd altars, while dumpy cherubim dive for cover amid scenes resembling an exploding fruit bowl.

Museo Provinciale

Viale Gallipoli • Daily 9am–1.30pm & 2.30–7.30pm, Sun 9.30am–1.30pm • Free • ⓣ 0832 307 415

The imaginative displays in Salento's recently revamped **Museo Provinciale** bring the city's history – and prehistory – to life. There are also frequent exhibitions, and an annual programme of evening openings with concerts, guided tours and other cultural events – see the Provincia di Lecce website (ⓦprovincia.le.it) for details.

SS Nicolò e Cataldo

Viale San Nicola • Sat afternoons & Mon mornings • Free

If the Baroque trappings of the town are beginning to pall, you might want to check out the fine Romanesque church of **SS Nicolò e Cataldo**, a ten-minute walk north along Viale San Nicola from Porta Napoli. Built by the Normans in 1190, its cool interior reveals a generous hint of Saracen in the arches and the octagonal rounded dome. Little remains of the frescoes that once covered its walls, though an image of St Nicolò can be found on the south side, together with a delicately carved portal.

Along the coast: Roca Vecchia

From Lecce follow the Littoranea Otranto coast road through pinewoods where several paths lead to long stretches of dunes and little rocky coves. Continue south to **Roca Vecchia**, where a 1960s-style resort has grown up behind the **Grotte Basiliane**, a fascinating honeycomb of man-made caves carved into the soft sandstone dating back to the seventh century. There's a gorgeous natural sea pool here known as the **Grotta della Poesia**, a favourite spot for locals to launch themselves off the cliffs.

ARRIVAL AND DEPARTURE — LECCE

By bus Regional buses arrive at the City Terminal (north of Porta Napoli), and the train station. Between June 25 and Sept 5, Salento in Treno e Bus (ⓣ0833 541 025, ⓦsalentointrenoebus.it) services depart from Viale Gallipoli,

near the FS station, to Otranto, Santa Maria di Leuca (via Gallipoli) and the seaside resort of Porto Cesareo and Roca. There are transfers from Brindisi airport (see page 831).
Destinations Gallipoli (10 daily; 1–2hr); Otranto (11 daily; 1hr); Porto Cesareo (8 daily; 1hr); Roca (9 daily; 50min); San Cataldo (8 daily; 30min); Santa Maria di Leuca (10 daily; 1hr 45min).

By train FSE (fseonline.it) and FS trains use the same station, 1km south of the centre at the end of Via Oronzo Quarta. FSE services (Mon–Sat) link Gallipoli, Alberobello, Otranto, Ostuni, Galatina and Martina Franca, while regular daily FS trains link Bari, Brindisi and Rome.

14

INFORMATION

Tourist offices There are three helpful tourist offices (ilecce.it) around the city centre, the main one being at Corso Vittorio Emanuele 24 (daily: June–Sept 9.30am–-1.30pm & 3.30–7.30pm; Oct–May 10am–1pm & 4–6pm; 0832 682 985). The other two (both daily: June–Sept 9.30am–1.30pm & 3.30–7.30pm; Oct–May 9.30am–1.30pm & 3.30pm–7.30pm) are at Piazza Sant'Oronzo (0832 242 099) and in the castle, at Viale 25 July (0832 246 517).

InfoLecce Piazza del Duomo 2 (Mon–Fri 9.30am–1.30pm & 3.30–7.30pm, Sat & Sun 10am–7pm; 0832 521 877). A well-run private information office offering several guided tours of the city and Salento, bikes to rent (€3/hr or €12/day) and a well-researched website (infolecce.it).

ACCOMMODATION

Arco Vecchio Via Quinto Fabio Balbo 5 0832 243 620 or 333 941 4114, arcovecchio.com; map p.834. Spruce, restored *palazzo* just off the very pleasant Via Paladini, with nine neat, contemporary, minimalist rooms, with flatscreen TVs, satellite and wi-fi. There's also a suite with a fully equipped kitchen and its own terrace, ideal for families. **€101**

Casa dei Mercanti Piazza Sant'Oronzo 44 0832 277 299, casadeimercanti.it; map p.834. Nine elegantly renovated apartments, smart and international in style, with glossy parquet floors and modern furniture, overlooking Piazza Sant'Oronzo. All apartments have flatscreen TVs and full kitchens, and there's a daily cleaning service. **€102**

Centro Storico and Azzurretta Via Vignes 2/B 0832 242 727, centrostoricolecce.it (Centro Storico); 0832 242 211, bblecce.it (Azzurretta); map p.834. These two appealing B&Bs share the same sixteenth-century building with vaulted ceilings, balconies, a reading room and a pair of big sun terraces looking out over the city's monuments. Rooms in the *Centro Storico* are a bit more upmarket, with tea-making facilities and a jacuzzi, while the owner of *Azzurretta* organizes occasional concerts in summer and tastings of wine and local produce. Both places offer a simple breakfast at the *Cin Cin* bar on Piazza Sant'Oronzo. *Azzurretta* **€80**, *Centro Storico* **€100**

Hotel Patria Palace Piazza Riccardi 0832 245 111, patriapalacelecce.com; map p.834. A smart, conventional hotel in an eighteenth-century palace near Santa Croce, aimed at business travellers and tourists wanting five-star service and facilities such as minibars, Sky and a fitness room. Rooms are all blue and gold, and give little sense of the historic building, the main concession to design being a Liberty-style lily motif. The five best rooms have private terraces; seventeen rooms look onto Santa Croce, and guests have access to the roof terrace. Substantial discounts on website. **€124**

★ **Malìa** Via Paladini 33 329 571 663, maliabb.com; map p.834. Fabulous TV-free boutique B&B designed by owner-architect Laura Aguglia – the huge, elegant sitting room has a star-vaulted ceiling, parquet floor, a vast calico sofa and an ample choice of art and design books and magazines to leaf through. There are only three rooms, but each is gorgeous, different, and imaginatively lit, especially the romantic double with a four-poster bed designed by Laura. Breakfast is served at the nearby trendy *"00" Doppiozero Café*. **€110**

Torre del Parco Viale Torre del Parco 1 0832 347 694, torredelparco.com; map p.834. Set in a medieval fortress about 10min walk from the old centre, with nine rooms converted from a seventh-century convent. There's a generous breakfast served on a big and beautiful terrace, well-kept gardens and an attached tower that was once the prince's palace, still surrounded by a deep moat. Sometimes reserved for events, so book ahead. **€118**

EATING

CAFÉS

All'Ombra del Barocco Corte dei Cicala 9 0832 245 524, liberrima.it; map p.834. Cool – if expensive – wine bar, café and restaurant linked to the Liberrima bookshop next door. Salads, antipasti and an abundant and elegantly presented *aperitivo* with nibbles including fresh ricotta, tiny *pizze* and *crostini* with artichokes and roast almonds. Eat inside to an accompaniment of jazz (during the winter), or outside on the *piazzetta*. Daily 7am–midnight.

Caffè Alvino Piazza Sant'Oronzo 30 0832 246 748, caffealvino.it; map p.834. *Caffè Alvino* serves some of the city's most astonishingly jewel-like sweet confections and savoury snacks. Sample their vast array of *paste di mandorla* (almond-paste cookies). Wed–Mon 7am–midnight.

Caffè Letterario Via G. Paladini 46 ⓣ832 242 351, ⓦcaffeletterario.org; map p.834. An arty little bookshop-café perfect for an *aperitivo* (from €5) or after-dinner drinks, with cosy outdoor seating along Via Paladini, a DJ on Thurs and Sun, and occasional live music or theatre; check the website for a full programme of events. Tues–Sat 7am–late, Sun 5pm–late.

Syrbar Via Giuseppe Libertini 67/A, Piazza del Duomo; map p.834. A laidback café-restaurant, with tables on the main pedestrian drag and windows looking onto Piazza del Duomo. A fine place for breakfast, lunch or a light dinner, with a daily vegetable soup and a large choice of panini (from €5) and *crostini* (€8–10) served with inspired combinations of local cheeses, hams, salamis and fish. In winter, you can warm up with a hot grog of Cognac infused with cinnamon and orange peel. Daily 8.30am–midnight; Nov–March closed Wed.

RESTAURANTS

Alle Due Corti Corte dei Giugni 1 ⓣ0832 242 223, ⓦalleduecorti.com; map p.834. Simple, traditional Salentino dishes and mouthwatering antipasti draw locals and tourists alike. Try the *taieddha* (oven-baked potatoes, rice, tomatoes, onions and mussels; €10) in summer, or *cocule de marangiana allu sucu* year round (€8). Mon–Sat 12.30–2.10pm & 7.45–10.30pm.

★**Corte dei Pandolfi** Piazzetta Orsini ⓣ0832 332 309, ⓦcortedeipandolfi.com; map p.834. Intimate place in a charming piazza off Via Paladini, gaining a reputation for creative twists on traditional cuisine, using fresh ingredients, shown off to perfection in several raw fish dishes. Other meals worth trying are the mixed seasonal vegetables (€11) and handmade spaghetti with fresh anchovies, capers and tomato (€12). Daily 1–3pm, 8pm–midnight. Shorter hours in winter.

Cucina Casareccia Via Col. A. Costadura 19 ⓣ0832 245 178; map p.834. Be sure to call ahead for one of the dozen tables at this Leccese favourite, known for its home-style cooking and atmosphere – locals also call it *Le Zie* (the aunts). The pasta is made on site and the accompanying sauces change according to the season – try the excellent stuffed squid (€11), the rib-warming winter dish *ciceri e tria* (pasta with chickpeas; €8) or *pezzetti di cavallo* (horse stew; €10), a Leccese speciality. Tues–Sat 12.30–2.30pm & 7.45–10.30pm, Sun 12.30–2.30pm.

L'Angolo di Via Matteotti Via Matteotti 25 ⓣ346 836 1999; map p.834. Cheap and friendly little place around the corner from Santa Croce, usually busy with locals who come for the good selection of *puccia* (*puccia con pezzetti di cavallo* €6). Daily 11am–3pm & 6.30–11.30pm; Oct–Feb closed Mon.

Otranto

OTRANTO, a kasbah-like town nestling around a harbour, is only an hour by train from Lecce, set in an arid, rocky and windblown landscape, with translucent seas to swim in. The port overflows with tourists in August, when Otranto's nightlife is at its peak and the town is most entertaining, but the picturesque location and slow pace will reward visitors year-round, even if the number of gaudy souvenir shops detracts a little from the charm of its winding whitewashed lanes. A variety of musical and theatrical events are held in Otranto throughout the summer, usually centred around the castle, among them the annual commemoration of the "800 Martyrs" on August 13–15.

Brief history

Otranto's **history** is decidedly grim. One of the last Byzantine towns to fall to the Normans in 1070, it remained a thriving port for Crusaders, pilgrims and traders. But in 1480 a Turkish fleet laid siege to the town, which held out for fifteen days before capitulating. It's said that as a punishment the archbishop, on capture, suffered the indignity of being sawn in half, a popular Turkish spectacle at that time. Nearly twelve thousand people lost their lives and the eight hundred survivors, refusing to convert, were taken up a nearby hill and beheaded. Otranto never really recovered, though the town does feature one glorious survivor of the Turkish attack inside its cathedral: an extraordinary **mosaic floor**.

Cattedrale di Santa Maria Annunziata

Piazza Basilica • Daily 7.30am–noon & 3–7pm, closes 5pm 31 Oct–30 March • Free

The town's Romanesque **Cattedrale di Santa Maria Annunziata** is worth a visit, its marble-columned nave adorned by an incredible multi-coloured mosaic. The theme

is the "Tree of Life". Historical and animal figures are shown as a mix of myth and reality – Alexander the Great, King Arthur, the Queen of Sheba, crabs, serpents and mermaids. The work of a twelfth-century monk, its rough simplicity is empowered by a delightful child-like innocence. The rose window was added in the fifteenth century.

The Castello

Via Nicola d'Otranto • Mon–Sat: June 10am–10pm; July & Aug 8am–midnight; Sept–May 10am–8pm • €10

Not far from the cathedral, the town's Aragonese **Castello** juts out into the bay, defending the harbour. Large parts of it have recently undergone renovation, and its hulking walls incorporate fragments of Roman and medieval inscriptions, while Charles V's coat of arms looms from its portal. Just beyond is a small museum with various historical displays and – in summer – art exhibits.

Chiesa di San Francesco di Paola

Out on the southern edge of town is the cypress-tree-covered hill where the survivors of the Turkish siege were beheaded. At the top of the hill, the sixteenth-century **Chiesa di San Francesco di Paola** holds the names of the victims, together with a vivid description of the terrible events of July 1480.

Basilica di San Pietro e Paolo

Via San Pietro • Daily 9am–noon & 3–7pm, closes 5pm 31 Oct–31 March • Free

On the Bastione dei Pelasgi, the newly restored **Basilica di San Pietro e Paolo** is one of the most important Byzantine monuments in the Salento. This tiny chapel has frescoes, some with Greek inscriptions dating from the tenth to the thirteenth centuries, including a *Last Supper*.

ARRIVAL AND INFORMATION — OTRANTO

By train Otranto marks the end of the rail line from Maglie, with connections to Lecce (10 daily via Maglie and Zollino; 1hr 10min) and Gallipoli (7 daily via Maglie and Zollino). The station is a 15min walk north of Otranto centre.

By bus The Salento in Treno e Bus service (June 25–Sept 5) links Otranto to Lecce (9 daily via Maglie; 1hr 40min; 9 daily via the coast road; 1hr 40min) and Gallipoli (3 daily; 1hr 30min), while year-round FSE buses run to Lecce (3 daily; 1hr 30min).

Tourist office Piazza Castello (Mon–Sat 9am–1pm & 4–6pm; ⓣ 0836 801 436, ⓦ viaggiareinpuglia.it).

ACCOMMODATION

B&B Palazzo de Mori Bastione dei Pelasgi ⓣ 0836 801 088, ⓦ palazzodemori.it. Set in the heart of the historical centre overlooking the harbour, with ten pleasant whitewashed rooms, white beds, white linen and white mosquito nets. There is also a lovely roof terrace for breakfast or drinks, and free parking nearby. **€153**

Bellavista Via Vittorio Emanuele 18 ⓣ 0836 801 058, ⓦ hotelbellavistaotranto.it. Conventional rooms in a light, modern hotel right in the centre of things just steps from the beach and 100m from entrance to the old town. The nicest rooms have balconies with sea views (from €110). **€105**

EATING

Boomerang Via Vittorio Emanuele II 13/14 ⓣ 0836 802 619. Self-service restaurant with a/c and outdoor seating by the park next to the beach; serves delicious, low-priced, simple meals, as well as fresh antipasti and pasta. Daily noon–3pm & 7.30–10.30pm; closed in winter.

Da Sergio Corso Garibaldi 9 ⓣ 0836 801 408. Unlike many Otranto restaurants, *Da Sergio* focuses on honest, reasonably priced local cuisine (seafood risotto €10, grilled prawns €13). March–mid-Nov & mid-Dec–mid-Jan daily 12.30–2.30pm & 8–10.30pm; closed Wed in low season.

The southern cape

From Otranto, all the way down to the cape at Santa Maria di Leuca, the coastline is steep and rugged. The unmissable journey along the winding road takes you past one spectacular view of sheer cliffs and blue sea after another.

Capo d'Otranto

CAPO D'OTRANTO, 5km south of Otranto, is the easternmost point on the Italian peninsula, topped by a lighthouse and the rather desolate ruins of a seventh-century abbey. This is the first place in Italy to see the sun rise, and is a popular spot to welcome in the New Year. On clear mornings there's a commanding view across the straits – the mountains of Albania are visible about 80km away – and on seriously clear days they say you can even see Corfu, 100km away. If you want to stop and swim, there are a couple of inlets at Porto Badiso and La Fraula, though the first place of any size is **Santa Cesarea Terme**, a spa town boasting some extraordinarily opulent Moorish-style villas and the reek of sulphur. Old-fashioned **Castro**, perched high above the sea, is a cluster of white- and pastel-washed houses around an Aragonese castle. **Marittima**, despite its name, lies a little inland, and is dominated by a splendid Baroque palace, while the coast road leads down to Puglia's southernmost point, Santa Maria di Leuca.

ARRIVAL AND DEPARTURE — THE SOUTHERN CAPE

By train From Lecce, trains run to the end of the FSE rail line at Gagliano del Capo (Mon–Sat 2–3 hourly ; 1hr 40min, just 5km from the cape.

By bus The Salento in Treno e Bus service (see page 838) runs from Otranto to Santa Cesarea Terme (3 daily; 30min) and Santa Maria di Leuca (3 daily; 1hr 50min), and from Lecce to the cape via Gallipoli, or inland via Maglie.

ACCOMMODATION

Camping Porto Miggiano 16km from Otranto, just south of Santa Cesarea Terme ☎ 0836 944 303, 🌐 campingportomiggiano.it. A simple but beautiful campsite set among olive trees with steps leading down to a gorgeous beach surrounded by cliffs. Small bungalows are also available, and there's a restaurant on site. Open March–Oct. 2 Adults plus tent pitch **€27**, bungalows **€101**

Hotel degli Ulivi Via Litoranea per S. Cesarea Terme, Castro Marina ☎ 0836 943 037, 🌐 hoteldegliulivi.it. Located in Castro's seaside satellite, this has pleasant rooms with big balconies, a pool and a restaurant with a view over the sea. Half board (obligatory in mid-Aug) €60/ person. **€65**

Il Giardino Via Sant'Antonio 207, Castro ☎ 340 603 5400, 🌐 ilgiardinonelsalento.it. A lovely B&B with spotless rooms, a family-friendly atmosphere, cooking facilities for guests and a large garden where a breakfast of home-made pastries, buns and fresh fruit is served. **€50**

Galatina

GALATINA, 30km south of Lecce, is an intriguing Salentine town on the edge of an area known as Grecia Salentina, a key Greek colony in medieval times that has retained Greek customs and language up until the present. It's an important centre of the Italian tobacco industry today, with much of the weed grown in the fields around. It's also famed for being the centre of the *tarantella* (see page 840) and for its excellent local **wine.** In the old part of town, the church of **Santa Caterina di Alessandria** (daily 8.30am–12.30pm & 4.30–6.45pm; free) is well worth a look for the stunning fourteenth-century frescoes that cover its interior.

ARRIVAL AND INFORMATION — GALATINA

By train Galatina is about 30min down the FSE rail line from Lecce. Trains run approximately hourly.

Tourist office At Via V. Emanuele II 35, the tourist office (Mon–Fri 9am–12.30pm & 3–7pm; ☎ 0836 569 984, 🌐 comune.galatina.le.it) has the lowdown on events surrounding the town's *festa*.

ACCOMMODATION AND EATING

Anima & Cuore Corso Garibaldi 7 ☎ 0836 564 301, 🌐 animaecuore. Just steps from the church of San Paolo on Piazza San Pietro, this rambling restaurant takes up the first floor of a beautiful old building with vaulted ceilings, a mosaic floor and a spacious outdoor patio. The traditional Salentino menu includes *orecchiette* with aubergine, ricotta and olives (€10) and seafood brought daily from Gallipoli (if you are lucky there may be pasta with sea urchins €18). Daily noon–2.30pm & 7.30pm–midnight; Nov–April closed Thurs.

Il Covo della Taranta Corso Garibaldi 13 ☎ 0836 210 265. This lively pub/pizzeria/trattoria in an eighteenth-

century building serves pizzas from €4 and *puccia* from €5, with world music jam sessions at weekends. Daily 7pm–midnight, closes earlier in winter.

Palazzo Baldi Corte Baldi ⓣ0836 568 345, ⓦhotel palazzobaldi.it. Plush, elegant hotel with its own little courtyard for a quiet *aperitivo*. Rooms are romantic, with exposed stone walls and antique furniture giving them a medieval feel, and some – rather more practically – have cooking facilities. Good deals online. **€80**

14

Gallipoli

First impressions of **GALLIPOLI** (not the World War I battlefield in Turkey) are fairly uninspiring. The new town sprouted on the mainland once the population outgrew its original island site in the eighteenth century, and all that remains of the once-beautiful Greek city (the Kale' polis) is the rather weather-beaten **Fontana Ellenica**, a fountain from the third century BC (restored in the sixteenth century), which sits in the new town near the bridge. Immediately over the bridge is the imposing Aragonese castle, beyond which things become more interesting: the old town itself is a maze of meandering and twisting whitewashed streets, with tiny tomatoes hanging on the walls to dry providing a sudden blaze of colour alongside the fishing nets. The work of Zimbalo, the Baroque-style **Cattedrale di Sant'Agata** and its adjoining piazza mark the centre of the island. It's also worth visiting the early morning **fish market**, between the castle and the bridge, or stepping into one of the old town's 35 underground **olive presses** (*frantoi*; daily: April–June 10am–1pm & 3.30–6.30pm; July–March 10am–10pm; €1.50 each). The consistently warm, damp atmosphere (and plenty of slave-like labour in horrid working conditions) made the presses ideal for producing the *oro verde* (green gold), one of the city's largest industries until the advent of electricity.

ARRIVAL AND INFORMATION — GALLIPOLI

By train and bus From Lecce, regular FSE trains (Mon–Sat 12 daily; 1hr) and buses (Mon–Sat 7 daily, Sun 2 daily; 1hr) run to Gallipoli.

THE DANCE OF THE SPIDER

The small town of Galatina has long been a pilgrimage centre for *tarantate* – women (mostly) who have been "possessed" by the mythical spider of Puglia. **Tarantism** dates back centuries in this region, with the earliest known accounts of it appearing in manuscripts from the fifteenth century. Victims believed that they had been bitten by the Italian tarantula, or the European black widow spider. After descending into a funk of symptoms that included vomiting and sweating, fear and delirium, depression and paranoia, the only cure was the rite of the tarantula, which involved trance-dancing to the local *tarantella*, or *pizzica*, for days on end. The *pizzica* musicians – typically a violinist, guitarist, accordion and tambourine player – would perform fast and feverishly, engaging the victim in a call-and-response ritual until eventually they were released from their misery.

The cult has continued to fascinate Salentines and others into this century, with the myth and music being both preserved and reinvented. St Paul, patron saint of the *tarantate*, is revered and celebrated to this day in Galatina and surrounding villages. On the night of June 28 around 10.30pm there is a **procession** from Piazza San Pietro to the chapel of St Paul, followed by performances by drummers and musicians from across the region, lasting until dawn of June 29 – the feast day of saints Peter and Paul. Around 4.30 or 5am, the musicians, dancers, *tarantate* and tourists gather at St Paul's chapel to pay their respects before the crowds arrive for the official early morning Mass. Today, *pizzica* music is enjoying a boom in the Salento and elsewhere. It's worth timing your visit to coincide with the all-night music festival **The Night of the Tarantula** (*La Notte della Taranta*; ⓦlanottedellataranta.it), held in late August at Melpignano, between Galatina and Otranto.

ACCOMMODATION AND EATING

Il Bastione Riviera N. Sauro 28 ⓣ0833 263 836, ⓦilbastionegallipoli.it. Great place to sample the catch of the day – raw, grilled, fried, baked or cooked in salt – on a panoramic seafront terrace. Prices start at €12 for *primi* and around €40 for a full meal excluding wine. Tues–Sun 11am–2.30pm & 7pm–midnight.

Basilicata and Calabria

844 Melfi

848 Venosa

849 Matera and around

853 Basilicata's Ionian coast

856 Parco Nazionale Pollino

856 Maratea

857 Calabria's Tyrrhenian coast

860 Reggio Calabria and around

863 Cosenza and around

864 The Sila

866 Calabria's Ionian coast

MATERA, BASILICATA

Basilicata and Calabria

More than any other regions, Basilicata and Calabria represent the quintessence of the *mezzogiorno*, the historically underdeveloped southern tracts of the Italian peninsula. After Unification in 1861, the area was largely neglected and sank into abject poverty that was worsened by emigration. Conditions here were immortalized in Carlo Levi's *Christ Stopped at Eboli* – a vivid account of his internment in Basilicata during the Fascist era in which he describes a land characterized by apathy, where malaria is endemic and the peasants' way of life is deeply rooted in superstition. His account forced politicians to address the problem of the poor south. Things have improved, although tourism is yet to bring the riches found in neighbouring Puglia and Campania.

In Basilicata, the greatest draw is **Matera** (one of the places Levi was interned) whose distinctive Sassi – cave-like dwellings in the heart of the town – give it a uniquely dramatic setting. In the northern part of the region, **Melfi** and **Venosa** are bastions of medieval charm with important relics from the Byzantine and Norman eras. Of the region's two coasts, the mountainous **Tyrrhenian** is most engaging, with spots like **Maratea** offering crystal-clear water, a bustling marina and opportunities to discover remote sea grottoes. The flatter **Ionian** coast is less charming, though worth a visit for its ancient sites in **Metaponto** and **Policoro** – ruins of the once mighty states that comprised Magna Graecia.

While conditions in Basilicata have improved, **Calabria** remains arguably more marginalized than it was before Unification. Since the war, a massive channelling of funds to finance huge irrigation and land-reclamation schemes, industrial development and a modern system of communications has brought built-up sprawl to previously isolated towns such as **Crotone** – often hand in hand with the forces of organized crime. The **'Ndrangheta** Mafia – reckoned to be far more powerful and dangerous than the Neapolitan Camorra – continues to maintain a stranglehold across parts of the region.

Although unchecked development financed by the 'Ndrangheta has marred parts of the coastline, resorts such as **Scilla**, **Tropea** and **Capo Vaticano** are still charming, and have become favourite hideaway resorts for discerning Italian and foreign visitors. The interior of the region is dominated by the mountain grandeur of the **Pollino**, **Sila** and **Aspromonte** ranges, offering excellent hiking and rustic local cuisine.

GETTING AROUND AND INFORMATION — BASILICATA AND CALABRIA

By car Although good transport services exist in Basilicata, a car is useful in hilly and coastal areas. The roads are narrow and winding, so allow more time than you think. In Calabria too, your own transport will be necessary for reaching remoter spots in the mountainous interior.

By public transport In Calabria, train services connect the coastal towns, supplemented by regular buses. Most trains are run by the national operator, FS (W trenitalia.com), though much of Basilicata is served by FAL (Ferrovia Appulo Lucane; W ferrovieappulolucane.it). Different bus companies operate in different parts of the region; the main one is SITASUD (T 0835 385 007, W sitasudtrasporti.it); others are detailed in the text.

Websites The website W basilicataturistica.it is a mine of information for the Basilicata region.

Melfi

Way up in the northernmost reaches of Basilicata, in the foothills of the imposing **Monte Vulture** (1326m), the town of **MELFI** was long a centre of strategic importance,

CRIPTA DEL PECCATO ORIGINALE, MATERA

Highlights

1. **Matera** Sliced by a ravine containing thousands of Sassi – cave dwellings gouged out of rock – Matera's unique city-landscape fusion never ceases to astonish. See page 849

2. **Cripta del Peccato Originale, Contrada Petrapenta** The best example of Basilicata's distinctive rock-hewn churches, with vibrant eighth-century frescoes inside. See page 853

3. **Tropea promontory** This region has it all: white sandy beaches, turquoise water, hills tumbling down to the coast and – in Tropea town and Pizzo – two of Calabria's most engaging resorts. See page 858

4. **Bronzi di Riace** Two extraordinary, 2m-high, bronze statues of Greek athletes fished out of the sea and displayed in Reggio Calabria. See page 861

5. **Purple Codex, Rossano** History buffs shouldn't miss this illustrated manuscript from the sixth century with fascinating early depictions of the life of Christ. See page 867

6. **Museo Archeologico Nazionale, Crotone** The best of the collections featuring finds from Magna Graecia is small but well presented, displaying fascinating remnants of the Greek settlements on the Ionian coast. See page 868

HIGHLIGHTS ARE MARKED ON THE MAP ON PAGE 846

BASILICATA & CALABRIA
HIGHLIGHTS
1 Matera
2 Cripta del Peccato Originale, Contrada Petrapenta
3 Tropea promontory
4 Bronzi di Riace
5 Purple Codex, Rossano
6 Museo Archeologico Nazionale, Crotone
0 25 kilometres
N
PUGLIA
BASILICATA
CAMPANIA
CALABRIA
TYRRHENIAN SEA
IONIAN SEA
SICILY
Aeolian Islands
Foggia
Bari
Naples
Melfi
Venosa
Monte Vulture
Altamura
Matera
Contrada Petrapenta
Montescaglioso
Potenza
Ferrandina
Taranto
Metaponto
Lido di Metaponto
R. Agri
Policoro
R. Sinni
Lago Moliterno
PARCO NAZIONALE POLLINO
Pollino
R. Noce
Maratea
Laino Borgo
Laino Castello
Papasidero
R. Lao
Sybaris
Diamante
Belvedere
R. Crati
Rossano
Rossano Scalo
Sila Greca
Luzzi
Camigliatello
Paola
Cosenza
Rende
San Lucido
Lorica
Sila Grande
R. Neto
Santa Severina
PARCO NAZIONALE DELLA SILA
Sila Piccola
Crotone
Capo Colonna
R. Savuto
Nocera Tirinese
Isola Capo Rizzuto
Le Castella
Catanzaro
Sant'Eufemia-Lamezia
Lamezia Airport
Catanzaro Lido
La Roccelletta
Squillace
Soverato
Pizzo
Tropea
Capo Vaticano
Nicótera
Serre
R. Mésima
Rosarno
Gerace
Scilla
Villa San Giovanni
Santo Stefano
Santuario della Madonna di Polsi
Locri Epizefiri
Messina
Reggio Calabria
Aspromonte
Reggio Calabria Airport
A3
SS407
SS106
SS18
SS107

PORK, PRESERVES AND PEPPERS – THE CUISINE OF BASILICATA AND CALABRIA

The cuisine of **Basilicata**, also known as **cucina lucana** (Lucanian cuisine), derives from a poor tradition that depended heavily on preserving food, especially pork and fruit, which are dried, and vegetables, which are preserved in oil. **Arab influence** still pervades in the form of aubergines and desserts incorporating figs, almonds and honey. Basilicata is an important producer of durum wheat, used to make fresh pasta, rustic breads prepared in wood-fired ovens, and *friselle*, stale bread softened with water, oil and tomatoes. **Strong cheeses**, like matured or smoked ricotta and aged caciocavallo are favoured. A rare breed of cow, the *mucca podolica*, grazes around Matera, and the milk and meat they produce are full of flavour.

The trademark of **Calabrian** cuisine is *peperoncino*, spicy chilli pepper, used liberally in many dishes, and thought to ward off illness and misfortune. Try the spicy *sorpressata* salami, **'Nduia**, a hot *peperoncino* and pork fat spread. As in all southern cuisine, cheeses such as caciocavallo, mature provola and pecorino are ubiquitous. The *cipolla rossa* from Tropea is a sweet red onion used in rustic pies, meat dishes and in sweet preserves called **composte**. For dessert, try *mostazzolo*, an almond cookie sweetened with honey or wine must, or anything containing *bergamotto*, a citrus fruit that grows along the south coast. Dried figs are popular stuffed, dipped in chocolate, or arranged in braids or wheels.

Cirò is the success story of Calabrian **winemaking**. Made from the ancient **gaglioppo** grape, it has been given some modern touches and is now respected outside its home territory. Calabria also turns out sweet whites such as Greco di Bianco. The **aglianico** grape makes a star appearance in Basilicata: Aglianico del Vulture is the region's only DOCG; it's been dubbed "the Barolo of the south" for its complexity, late ripening and long maturation. Other wines worth trying are the sweet Malvasia and Moscato.

15

taken by the Normans in 1041 and their first capital in the south of Italy. Repeatedly damaged by earthquakes, the town preserves an attractive historic centre with a formidable Norman castle that now holds a good museum.

Museo Archeologico

Via Castello • Mon 2–8pm, Tues–Sun 9am–8pm • €2.50 • ⓣ 0972 238 726

Melfi's hilltop castle now contains an **archeological museum** with prehistoric finds and objects from the Greek, Roman and Byzantine eras. The museum's most celebrated item is an exquisitely carved Roman sarcophagus from the second century, showing the image of the dead girl for whom it was made, reclining on cushions, with five statuettes of gods and heroes on the sides. Look out for the paws carved on the left-hand side of the top of the sarcophagus – all that's left of the girl's pet puppy.

The Duomo

Piazza del Duomo • Daily: summer 8am–1pm & 4–8pm; winter 8am–12.30pm & 3.30–7.30pm • Free, campanile €2

In the centre of town off Via Vittorio Emanuele II, the **Duomo** was originally twelfth-century but was almost entirely rebuilt in 1700. After the 1930 earthquake, a Byzantine-style thirteenth-century *Madonna and Child* fresco was brought to light, which you can see to the left of the altar; to the left of this is another Madonna, in her role as protector of the city. Opposite the fresco, a door provides access to the cathedral's **campanile**, which has miraculously survived the various cataclysms; the two black stone griffins near the top symbolized the Norman hegemony in the region and are visible everywhere in Melfi, having been adopted as the town's emblem.

ARRIVAL AND DEPARTURE — MELFI

Trains Melfi is on the FS line between Potenza and Foggia, but trains have currently been replaced by buses. The station lies a little way west of the centre, connected by local buses. For connections to Matera, change at Potenza.

Destinations Bus replacements almost hourly Foggia (8 daily; 55min–1hr 10min); Potenza (1hr 15min–1hr 45min).

Buses SITASUD is the main bus company serving this area (T 0971 506 811). There are stops at the station and on Valle Verde.

Destinations Venosa (Mon–Fri 5 daily; 45min).

ACCOMMODATION AND EATING

Delle Rose Via Vittorio Emanuele 29 T 0972 21 682. A friendly, family-run restaurant with garden seating a little way down from the cathedral, where you can try such local dishes as *baccalà alla trainera* – salt cod with dried pepperoni. First courses cost €11, mains are €11–15, and pizzas are served in the evening. Daily (except Thurs) noon–3pm & 7pm–11.30pm.

Il Tetto Piazza IV Novembre T 0972 236 837, W hosteliltetto.com. Behind the Duomo, this former seminary retains its plain character, offering clean and spacious en-suite rooms (including family rooms) and a restaurant. €50

Venosa

15

If Melfi preserves the appearance of a dark medieval town, **VENOSA**, 25km east, has an attractive airiness: a harmonious place surrounded by green rolling hills and neatly divided parcels of farmland. Known in antiquity as Venusia, it was in its time the largest colony in the Roman world, and is most famous today as the birthplace of the poet Quintus Horatius Flaccus – Orazio in Italian, and known to English speakers as **Horace** (65–8 BC). His supposed house lies off Via Vittorio Emanuele in the *centro storico*, where one large room shows a reconstruction of his living quarters, with a bed and kitchen utensils; free visits can be arranged through Associazione La Quadriga, around the corner at Via Frusci 7 (T 0972 36 542 or 339 480 7431).

Parco Archeologico

Località San Rocco • Wed–Mon 9am–8pm, Tues 2–8pm • Free • T 329 260 7541

Venosa's **Parco Archeologico**, located just outside the old centre at the bottom of the Corso, consists of ruins from the Roman era including housing, shops and mosaics. Much of the stone here was recycled to build the next-door abbey.

Abbazia della Trinità

Località San Rocco • Call T 0972 34211 for access • Free but donation appreciated

Adjacent to the archeological park, the sprawling **Abbazia della Trinità** is a rich treasury of remains from different historical periods. An eleventh-century Benedictine abbey was superimposed upon a sixth-century construction – of which substantial traces remain – and this was in turn extended to create a much larger building begun in 1135 but never completed (the perimeter walls and some decorations survive). The eleventh-century church includes a mosaic floor, numerous murals and the tombs of various Norman bigwigs including the great Robert Guiscard.

Castello Aragonese

Piazza Umberto I • Mon & Wed–Sun 9am–8pm, Tues 2–8pm • Free • T 0972 36 095

The old town's main piazza at the top of Via Vittorio Emanuele is dominated by the **Castello Aragonese**, a moated castle dating from 1470 with stout towers at each corner. Finds from Venosa's archeological park and abbey can be seen in the museum within, and there's a sixteenth-century loggia.

ACCOMMODATION AND EATING VENOSA

★ **Al Baliaggio** Via Vittorio Emanuele 136 T 0972 35 081. Sharing a courtyard with the *Orazio* hotel, this semiformal restaurant specializes in delicious grilled meat (€10–13) and fish (€13–18) dishes, and has excellent

desserts. Tues–Sun noon–2.30pm & 8-10.30pm.

★ **Orazio** Via Vittorio Emanuele 142 ⊕ 0972 31 135, ⓦ hotelorazio.it. Elegant small hotel in the heart of the old town, once a *palazzo* belonging to the Knights of Malta and still preserving old frescoes and vaulted ceilings. It has just been renovated and some rooms have balconies with great valley views. €65

Matera and around

The town of **MATERA**, situated on the edge of a ravine at the eastern end of Basilicata, dates from the Middle Ages when Byzantine and Benedictine monks built rock-hewn churches and monasteries into what are now called the **Sassi** – literally "stones" – an intricate series of terraced caves. Later, farmers, seeking safety from invasions, also settled in the Sassi, fashioning their homes, stables and shops out of the rock, creating one of Italy's oddest townscapes and its most significant troglodyte settlement. During the Spanish Bourbon era, wealthy Sassi-dwellers were able to move out of the cave dwellings to the plain above, while the masses were left in squalor below. The area was graphically described in Carlo Levi's 1945 memoir *Christ Stopped at Eboli*, in which the Sassi were compared to Dante's *Inferno*, with their impoverished, malaria-ridden inhabitants. During the 1950s twenty thousand people were forcibly removed from the Sassi and rehoused in modern districts in the new town.

Today, it's hard to picture the conditions that previously existed here; EU funds and private investment have poured in, and the area has been cleaned up and repopulated with homes, B&Bs, hotels, restaurants and workshops. In 1993, the city and its grotto-filled outskirts were declared a UNESCO World Heritage Site, in 2003 Mel Gibson filmed his controversial *The Passion of the Christ* here, and Matera has been declared a European Capital of Culture for 2019.

15

The Sassi

Divided into two sections – Sasso Caveoso and Sasso Barisano – the **Sassi** district can be entered from a number of different points around the centre of town, some signposted, some not. Via Buozzi weaves through the Caveoso zone and Via Fiorentini through the Barisano zone – both make useful reference points, although most of the points of interest, such as the *chiese rupestri*, or **cave churches** (most open daily 10am–7pm or 10am–2pm; €3 each), lie in the warren of steps and lanes above.

To get the most out of the area, pick up an *itinerario turistico* and a map from the various tourist kiosks, or take a tour (see page 852). Note that there's little shade, so take some water with you, and wear comfortable shoes for the numerous cobbled steps.

Santa Maria de Idris and the Convicinio di Sant'Antonio

Santa Maria de Idris Daily 10:30am–1:30pm (April–Nov: also 2:30–7pm) • €3 • **Convicinio di Sant'Antonio** Daily 10am–2pm • €5

The most spectacularly sited of Matera's *chiese rupestri*, **Santa Maria de Idris**, is perched on the conical Monte Errone that rises in the midst of the Sassi. Inside are frescoes dating from the fourteenth century. Behind and below it, the **Convicinio di Sant'Antonio** holds the most interesting interior. This former monastery complex of four interlinking thirteenth-century churches was turned into wine cellars in 1700 – look for the spouts for wine emerging from what appears to be an altar – and later into houses. Of particular interest are tombs in the floor converted into water tanks that demonstrate considerable ingenuity: the porous stone had to be waterproofed, and rainwater channelled into the tanks.

The Duomo

Daily 7.30am–noon & 4–7pm, 3–6pm in winter • Free

Built on a rocky spur rising above the Sassi, Matera's thirteenth-century **Duomo** retains a strong Apulian-Romanesque flavour. Between the figures of saints Peter and Paul on

the cathedral's facade is a sculpture of the patron of Matera, the Madonna della Bruna. Every July 2, a painting of the saint is carried through the streets on a papier-mâché float which, at the end of the day-long festivities, is stormed by onlookers and torn apart, in the belief that the pieces offer protection and blessings.

MUSMA

Via San Giacomo • Tues–Sun: April–Sept 10am–2pm & 4–8pm; Oct–5 Nov & 15-31 March 10am–6pm; 7 Nov–14 March 10am-2pm • €5 • T 366 935 7768, W musma.it

Housed within the seventeenth-century Palazzo Pomarici, **MUSMA** is a museum of contemporary sculpture appropriately and strikingly set in rooms gouged out of the

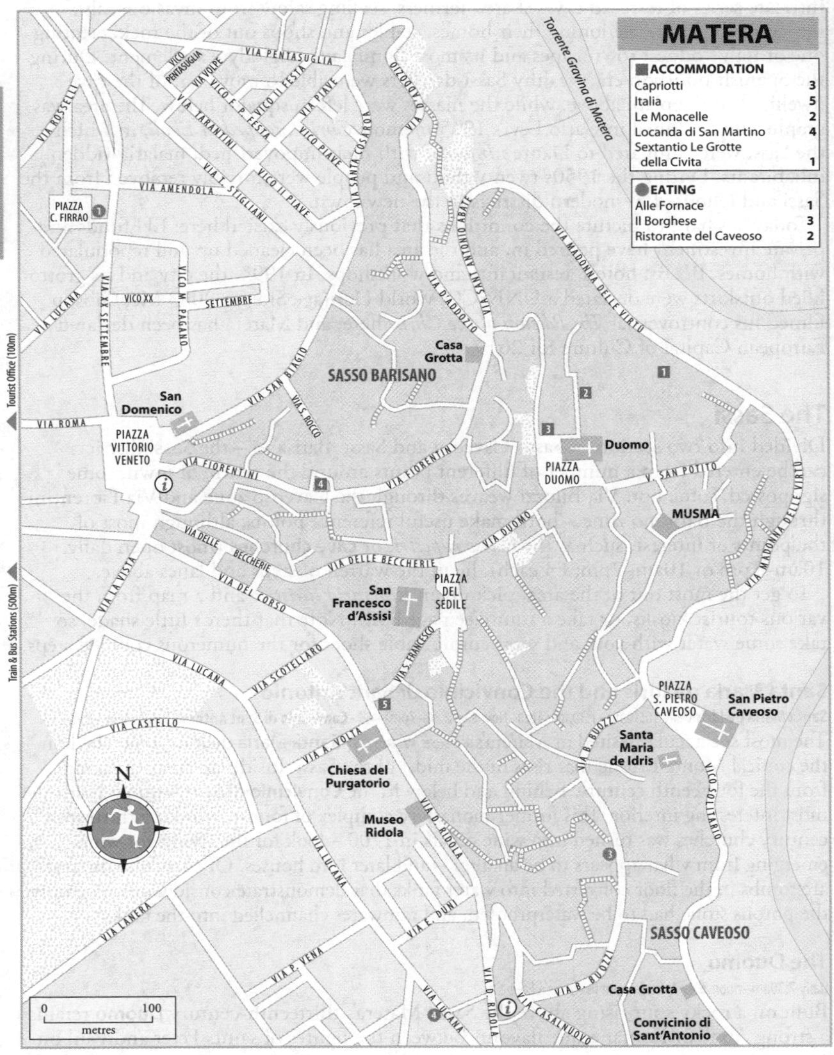

rock. Its permanent collection includes works by Lorenzetti, Pomodoro and Magnoni and there are regular temporary exhibitions.

Casa Grotta

Vicinato di Vico Solitario, 11 • Open 9am–6pm Mon–Sat & 9:30–6:40pm Sun • W www.casagrotta.it • €3

For a glimpse of what life was like for the Sassi-dwellers, head to this traditional sasso dwelling reconstructed with the help of the family who lived here until the 1950s. There is an iron bed, under which chickens were kept, and a single dish, from which the whole family ate. The huge chests, in which bread was kept to keep it from mice, became beds at night, with straw mattresses placed on top.

Ticket also includes entry to a former neviera, or snow cellar, close by which screens a fascinating documentary about Matera; and a Rupestrian Church dated back to the ninth century.

Parco della Murgia

T 0835 336 166, W parcomurgia.it

If you want to explore the **caves** and more *chiese rupestri* in the **Parco della Murgia** on the far side of the ravine, you can do so via several entrances from SS7 northwest of Matera. The park is best seen with a guide – Ferula Viaggi (see page 852) organizes excursions – who can lead you to some of the hundreds of hypogeums and rock-hewn churches in its eight thousand hectares.

15

The new town: Matera Piano

Most visitors to Matera head straight for the atmospheric Sassi, and understandably so, but **Matera Piano** – the "new" town above begun in the seventeenth century – is worthy of exploration, too, with a host of churches and a lively feel.

The centre of Matera Piano is **Piazza Vittorio Veneto**, a large and stately square, which in the evening is given over to a long procession of shuffling promenaders. The Materani take their evening stroll seriously, and the din of the crowds rising up out of this square can be like the noise from a stadium. Matera's modern quarters stretch out to the north and west of here, but most of the things worth seeing are along Via Ridola and its extension Via del Corso, winding off from the bottom end of the piazza.

San Francesco d'Assisi

Piazza San Francesco • Daily: summer 8.30am–12.30pm & 5.30–8pm; winter 7.30am–noon & 4–6pm • Free

Off Via del Corso, the seventeenth-century church of **San Francesco d'Assisi** has an ornate Baroque style that was superimposed on two older churches, traces of which, including some eleventh-century frescoes, can be visited through a passage in the fourth chapel on the left. Set above the altar in the main church are eight panels of a polyptych by Lorenzo Bastiani, a fifteenth-century follower of Bartolomeo Vivarini. From San Francesco, you can head to the bar-strewn Piazza del Sedile just above the Sassi, or on to Via Ridola to admire the **Chiesa del Purgatorio** (daily 8.30am–12.30pm & 4–7pm (closes earlier in winter), its elliptical facade gruesomely decorated with skulls and with a tall, domed interior.

Museo Ridola

Via Ridola 24 • Mon 9am–2pm, Tues–Sun 9am–8pm • €2.50 • T 0835 310 058

Matera's archeological collection, the **Museo Ridola** is home to some choice fourth-century-BC Greek amphoras and ceramics from the nearby sites of Timmari and Montescaglioso. It also displays Bronze Age remains, a reconstructed farmstead from that era, and some atmospheric black-and-white photos – one portraying Eustachio Chita (1862–96), said to be the last of Basilicata's brigands.

15

ARRIVAL AND DEPARTURE — MATERA

By train Matera's central train station is on Piazza Matteotti and is served by the FAL line, linked to Altamura (Mon–Sat every 1–2hr; 30min) and Bari in Puglia (Mon–Sat 12 daily; 1hr 20min); for Potenza change at Altamura on the FAL line, or take a bus to Ferrandina to pick up the FS line Metaponto–Potenza.

By bus SITASUD buses stop on Piazza Matteotti, connecting Matera to Montescaglioso, Metaponto and Policoro. The ticket office is below the piazza off Via Don Minzoni. Marino (T 080 311 2335, W marinobus.it), operating services to and from Naples, stop on the northwest edge of town near the Matera Nord station, Villa Longo, connected to the centre by local buses (every 20–30min).

Destinations Metaponto (Mon–Sat 5-6 daily; 50min); Montescaglioso (Mon–Sat almost hourly, Sun 3 daily; 35min); Naples (9 daily; 3hr 45min–4hr 20min); Policoro (Mon–Sat 5-6 daily; 1hr 30min); Potenza (Mon–Sat 5-6 daily; 1hr 40min).

INFORMATION, TOURS AND ACTIVITIES

Tourist information Matera's only official tourist office is the Pro Loco at Via Lucana 184C (Mon–Fri 8.30am–1pm; T 0835 335508, W prolocomatera2019.it). There are numerous other independent "info points" scattered around the centre, all primarily interested in promoting their own services but useful for tips and maps.

Tours For access to parts of the Sassi you might miss on your own, it's worth joining a tour with English-speaking guides: the pro loco (see above) and the website aptbasilicata.it have a list of operators, or try the excellent Ferula Viaggi, on Via Cappelluti 34 in the new town (T 0835 336 572, W ferulaviaggi.it), which charges around €90 for a tour (up to six people) lasting 3hr (price remains the same – i.e. charged per tour not per person) plus the entrance charges (€2 or €3 to the various *chiese rupestri visited)*.

Bike rental Ferula Viaggi (see above) rents out bikes for €15/day, and arranges self-guided cycle tours.

ACCOMMODATION

A lot of new B&Bs and some classy hotels have recently opened in the Sassi, which is unarguably the most atmospheric place to stay – although the numerous steps and lack of nearby parking may put off some. Booking a few days ahead is recommended in busy periods.

Capriotti Piazza del Duomo 75 T 329 619 3757, W capriotti-bed-breakfast.it; map p.850. Three tastefully decorated, light-flooded rooms, each with its own private entrance and outdoor space (and one with a terrace), in the vaulted rooms of a restored sixteenth-century *sasso* close to the Duomo. No credit cards. Closed Nov–Feb. €80

Italia Via Ridola 5 T 0835 333 561, W albergoitalia.com; map p.850. Matera Piano's most convenient hotel, where Mel Gibson and his cast stayed, and the best option if you don't fancy sleeping in a cave. Transfers to and from Bari and Ferrandina can be arranged. €129

★ **Le Monacelle** Via Riscatto 9/10 T 0835 344 097, W lemonacelle.com; map p.850. Built into a former convent and conservatory, this small hotel near the Duomo has spacious rooms, a large panoramic terrace and a garden. €98

★ **Locanda di San Martino** Via Fiorentini 71, Sasso Barisano T 0835 256 600, W locandadisanmartino.it; map p.850. A lovely hotel in the Sassi incorporating a former carpenter's workshop and a deconsecrated chapel. The rooms – mostly in grottoes – are beautifully furnished, and there's a luxurious pool and sauna in the basement. €163

★ **Sextantio Le Grotte della Civita** Via Civita 28, Sasso Barisano T 0835 332 744, W sextantio.it; map p.850. This ultra-stylish hotel in the Sassi incorporates a range of rooms fashioned out of the grottoes, with Philippe Starck baths, rainfall showers and furnishings reclaimed from abandoned rural buildings. Breakfast and aperitifs are served in a former cave-church or on the terrace overlooking the gorge. €700

EATING

Alle Fornace Piazza Cesare Firrao T 0835 335 037; map p.850. This sober-looking spot in the new town is one of the few places in Matera to specialize in seafood, traditionally prepared but with creative twists, such as *baccalà con polenta* (cod with polenta). Meals from around €25. Tues–Sat 12.30–2.30pm & 7.30–10pm, Sun 12.30–2.30pm.

Il Borghese Via Lucana 202 T 0835 314 223; map p.850. Popular with locals, this restaurant with a garden has great antipasti and typical *lucana* dishes such as *cavatelli con peperoni cruschi* (pasta with sun-dried peppers) and *agnello grigliato* (grilled lamb). Pasta dishes are around €10, mains €10–18. Summer daily noon–3pm & 7.30pm–11pm; closed Wed lunch; winter closed Wed.

★ **Ristorante del Caveoso** Via Buozzi 21 T 0835 312 374; map p.850. Enjoy the Sassi experience at this atmospheric spot over a meal of *tagliolini con cicerchie e funghi* (pasta with legumes and mushrooms) and *salsiccia con cime di rapa* (sausage with turnip tops). A full meal without drinks should cost €25-30. Thurs–Tues 12.30–3pm & 7.30–11pm.

Cripta del Peccato Originale

Tours: Oct–March Tues–Sun at 9.30am, 11am, 12.30pm & 3.30pm; April–Sept also 5pm & 6.30pm • €8 • T 320 535 0910, W criptadelpeccatooriginale.it

Some 14km south of Matera in **CONTRADA PETRAPENTA**, the **Cripta del Peccato Originale** (Crypt of the Original Sin) is lauded as the "Sistine Chapel of cave churches". Inside, late eighth-century frescoes depict surprisingly dynamic Old Testament scenes, saints and angels on a white background embellished with tendrils of red flowers. Note that you need to **book by phone** in order to visit; tours last around an hour.

San Michele Arcangelo, Montescaglioso

Piazza del Popolo • April–Oct Mon 10am–1pm, Tues–Sun 10am–1pm & 3–7pm; Nov–March Tues–Sun 10am–1pm & 3–5pm • Tours €4 • Book at T 334 836 0098 • Buses from Matera Mon–Sat hourly, Sun 3 daily; 35min

Twenty kilometres southeast of Matera, the hilltop village of **MONTESCAGLIOSO** was once a Greek settlement and is now the site of the magnificent eleventh-century Benedictine abbey of **San Michele Arcangelo**, where the hourly tours take in sixteenth- and seventeenth-century frescoes. You could easily spend a few hours here exploring the town's winding backstreets, and there are great views over the Bradano Valley.

ACCOMMODATION AND EATING — MONTESCAGLIOSO

Caveosus Via Chiesa Maggiore 1 T 0835 208 836. Simple backstreet trattoria that serves up a delicious home-cooked lunch for around €15. Meat is the speciality – in particular, horsemeat steaks. Tues–Sun 12.30–2.30pm & 7.30–10.30pm.

L'Orto di Lucania Contrada Dogana T 333 980 0730, W ortodilucania.it. This agriturismo on the SP175 3km west of Montescaglioso has a renowned restaurant that focuses on local and seasonal food (booking essential). Should you want to stay, you'll find well-kitted-out rooms and apartments in lovely grounds with fruit trees and a pool. €77

Basilicata's Ionian coast

A leisurely thirty-minute drive from Matera, **Basilicata's Ionian coast** from **Metaponto** to **Policoro** consists of a mountainous interior backing onto a seaboard punctuated only by holiday resorts, a plethora of campsites – overflowing in the summer months – and some notable historical sites. Of these, the most significant are connected with the periods of Greek occupation, the most recent of which was that of the Byzantines who administered the area on and off for five hundred years.

Metaponto

The most extensively excavated of Baslicata's Greek sites, **METAPONTO** was settled in the eighth century BC and owed its subsequent prosperity to the fertility of the surrounding land – perfect for cereal production (symbolized by the ear of corn stamped on its coinage). In about 510 BC, Pythagoras, banished from Kroton, established a school here that contributed to an enduring philosophical tradition. Metapontum's downfall came as a result of a series of catastrophes: absorbed by Rome, embroiled in the Punic Wars, sacked by the slave-rebel Spartacus, and later desolated by a combination of malaria and Saracen raids.

Metaponto today is a straggling, amorphous place, lacking much charm but with sandy beaches at **Metaponto Lido** that attract holiday-makers in summer. There's a train station at **Metaponto Scalo**, and **Metaponto Borgo**, some 800m from Scalo and 3km northwest of Lido, has an important archeological museum, otherwise the place mostly consists of the huge archeological park and modern villas, apartments and hotels.

15

Museo Archeologico Nazionale

Via Aristea 21 • Mon 2–8pm, Tues–Sun 9am–8pm • €2.50 • ☎ 0835 745 327

A ten-minute walk north of the train station, the **Museo Archeologico Nazionale** has mainly fifth- and fourth-century-BC exhibits, consisting of statuary, ceramics and jewellery dug up from the archeological park. There's a small but fascinating section on the new insights revealed by the study of fingerprints on shards found in the artisans' quarter.

Parco Archeologico and Tavole Palatine

Daily 9am–1hr before sunset (best to phone ahead to confirm opening times) • Free • ☎ 0835 745 327 • From Metaponto Borgo station to the Parco Archeologico, it's a 20min walk, or take a taxi to accompany you to all the sites (€35) and drop you back at the station (☎ 338 865 9918).

From Metaponto Borgo, follow Via di Apollo 500m east to the entrance of the **Parco Archeologico**, which has the remains of a theatre and a Temple of Apollo Licius. The latter is a sixth-century-BC construction that once possessed 32 columns, but you need some imagination to picture its original appearance.

In a better state of preservation, the **Tavole Palatine**, or Temple of Hera, is around 5km northwest where the main SS106 crosses the River Bradano. With fifteen of its columns remaining, the fifth-century-BC temple is the most evocative remnant of this once mighty state.

ARRIVAL AND INFORMATION — METAPONTO

By train Trains have been replaced by FS buses which depart from Metaponto Borgo station. SITASUD buses stop at the station and at Piazza Giovanni XXIII.

Destinations Policoro (Mon–Sat 7 daily, Sun 1 daily; 20min); Sibari (Mon–Sat 8 daily, Sun 1 daily; 53min–1hr 30min); Taranto (Mon–Sat 17 daily, Sun 1 daily; 30min–1hr 10min). Matera (Mon–Sat 5 daily; 50min).

Tourist office The very helpful volunteer-run Pro Loco on Piazza Giovanni XXIII (☎ 0835 748 903 or ☎ 328 421 3933) keeps flexible hours but is usually open Mon–Sat 9 mornings only.

ACCOMMODATION

Camping Internazionale Viale delle Nereidi Grecia ☎ 0835 741 916, @villageinternazionale.com. This campsite is small but clean, right opposite the beach, and has bungalows (€80) as well as pitches for tents and camper vans. There's a bar and pizzeria. Pitches €8, per person €9

Kennedy Via Ionio 1 ☎ 0835 741 960. About 1km from the station and 200m from the sea, off the Lido road, this modern holiday hotel is excellent value. It has some apartments as well as rooms, and may be half board only in Aug. €72

Policoro

Twenty kilometres south of Metaponto, the area between the Sinni and Agri rivers was in its time one of the richest areas on this coast and site of the Greek colonies of **Siris** and **Herakleia**. The latter was where Pyrrhus, king of Epirus, first introduced elephants to the Romans, and, although winning the first of two battles in 280 BC, suffered such high losses that he is said to have declared another such victory would cost him the war – so bequeathing to posterity the term "Pyrrhic victory". The ruins of Herakleia are in modern-day **POLICORO**, just behind the museum (see below) and although in a poor state, they're worth a wander.

Museo Nazionale della Siritide

Via Colombo 8 • Mon & Wed–Sun 9am–8pm, Tues 2am–8pm • €2.50 • ☎ 0835 972 154 • It's a 15min walk from the centre of Policoro, or a 5min walk from the nearest local bus stop

Artefacts unearthed from the area can be seen at the **Museo Nazionale della Siritide**, which has a good collection of clay figurines and images of Demeter. There are also specimens of fine jewellery from the seventh and eighth centuries BC recovered from tombs, some made from amber and ivory. You'll need some knowledge of Italian to read the descriptions, though.

EATING **POLICORO**

★ **Pitty** Piazza della Pace ⓣ 0835 981 203. For quality seafood, try this terrific restaurant in Policoro's centre, near the bus terminal. Standout dishes incude *spaghetti con le vongole* (with clams). A full meal will cost €30–40. Oct–May daily noon–4pm & 7–midnight pm; closed Mon in winter.

Parco Nazionale Pollino

Straddling Basilicata and Calabria, the **Parco Nazionale Pollino** is one of Italy's largest national parks, covering an area of nearly two thousand square kilometres. It is named for the **Massiccio del Pollino**, a massif in the southern Apennines that reaches a height of 2248m, offering spectacular views over pine forests, plains, limestone slopes and beyond to both the Tyrrhenian and Ionian seas. That, and its other major peaks such as the **Serra Dolcedorme** (2267m), are best explored on organized hiking excursions (see page 856) aimed at seeking out the park's rare flora and fauna, which include the cuirassed pine (the park's symbol), the roe deer and the golden eagle.

15

The park's lower slopes are home to nearly sixty villages, best seen by car, as public transport connections are irregular. Near the park's eastern boundary are several settlements – Acquaformosa, Civita, San Basile, San Costantino Albanese and San Paolo Albanese among them – founded between 1470 and 1540 by **Albanian refugees** fleeing persecution by the Turks. Here language, costume and religious customs have a decidedly eastern flavour.

From the western side, one logical gateway is **LAINO BORGO**, just off the A3 autostrada, known for its **Santuario delle Cappelle**, fifteen chapels frescoed with scenes from the life of Christ. From here, it is a short drive to **Laino Castello**, an eerie medieval hamlet abandoned after an earthquake in the 1980s that provides commanding views over the Lao River Valley.

The park's limestone terrain is particularly susceptible to erosion, which gives rise to its many grottoes, including the **Grotta del Romito** in **PAPASIDERO**. Many guided excursions depart to the Pollino massif from Papasidero, though the town itself is worth a stroll for its elaborately carved portals that precede churches and *palazzi nobili*.

Maratea

The brief stretch of Basilicata's **Tyrrhenian coast** is the most visually ravishing part of the entire region, its tall, sheer cliffs rising dramatically above rocky coves and some first-rate **beaches**. Though these get overcrowded in summer, the encircling mountains mean that there has been minimal development by the holiday industry. The obvious stop here is **MARATEA**, a dispersed settlement stretching for some 20km along the

ACTIVITIES IN THE PARCO NAZIONALE POLLINO

From **horseriding** to **hiking**, there are plenty of activities on offer in the park. Try the following operators:

CAI (Club Alpino Italiano) Via C. Pepe 74, Castrovillari (ⓣ 334 100 5054, ⓦ caicastrovillari.it). The Italian Alpine Club can arrange hikes and nature trails with English-speaking guides – or just join in their regular programme of walks.

Ente Parco Complesso Monumentale Santa Maria della Consolazione, Rotonda (ⓣ 0973 669 311, ⓦ parcopollino.it). The official national park office has information on activities and hiking maps – excellent, but in Italian only.

Ferula Viaggi Via Cappelluti 34, Matera (ⓣ 0835 336 572, ⓦ ferulaviaggi.it). Multiday hiking or biking excursions with guides and lodging.

Viaggiare nel Pollino (ⓣ 347 2631462, ⓦ viaggiarenelpollino.com. Themed tours, hiking, biking and rafting excursions. The website has lots of information on the park.

beautiful rocky coastline, including the hamlets of Castrocucco, Marina, Porto, Fiumicello, Cersuta and Acquafredda. Most of the action – and accommodation – is in or around the little seaside area of **Fiumicello**, 5km north of **Maratea Paese** (the inland centre), though the chic elite who have colonized much of the area prefer to be seen in the bars and restaurants of **Marina di Maratea**, directly south of Maratea Paese – if nothing else, a pleasant place to stroll around and gawp at the yachts.

The whole area is well endowed with sandy **beaches**, including those at Fiumicello and Acquafredda; most are well signposted, but don't hesitate to explore the less obvious ones. The coast is also home to fifty or so **grottoes**, most accessible only by boat; enquire at the tourist office (see below) for boat rental agencies.

If you fancy some exercise, try climbing up to **Monte San Biagio** (624m), the highest point above Maratea. The peak is dominated by the **Redentore**, an enormous marble Christ symbolically positioned with its back to the sea, looking towards the mountains of the interior. Opposite the statue, and looking as if it were about to be crushed under the giant's feet, is an eighteenth-century church, the **Santuario di San Biagio**, dedicated to the town's patron saint. On the second Sunday of May, a statue of the saint is carried up the hill in a large procession.

15

ARRIVAL AND INFORMATION — MARATEA

By train Most trains between Salerno and Paola stop at the main Maratea station (Maratea Scalo), below Maratea Paese, from where it's a 5min minibus or taxi ride (or a 20min walk) to Fiumicello. There are also stations at Acquafredda and Marina di Maratea – a nice way of exploring the coast.

By bus or minibus SITASUD (sitasudtrasporti.it) runs buses along the coast and to other towns in Basilicata year-round, and also operates a minibus service between late June and Aug that connects Marina di Maratea, Fiumicello, Maratea Scalo and Maratea Paese (hourly; tickets on board €0.75).

Tourist office Municipio, Piazza Vitolo 1, Maratea Paese (July & Aug daily 9am–1pm & 5–10pm; Sept–June Mon–Fri 8am–2pm; 0973 030 366, aptbasilicata.it).

ACCOMMODATION

Hotel Martino Via Citrosello 16, Marina di Maratea 0973 879 126. One of Maratea's cheapest hotels, this provides great value for its position overlooking the coast and its spacious rooms – those with a sea view cost extra. There's a shuttle service to a private beach. Closed early Nov to March. **€83**

La Casa del Gelso Via Timpone 47, Acquafredda 0973 878 108 or 340 838 2898, lacasadelgelso.it. This peaceful spot near two beaches has three fresh, airy rooms and a terrace (where generous breakfasts are served) with stunning sea views. No credit cards. Closed Nov. **€70**

★ **La Locanda delle Donne Monache** Via C. Mazzei 4, Maratea Paese 0973 876 139, locandamonache.com. Maratea's most distinctive hotel is sited in an elegantly renovated eighteenth-century convent in the old town, with stunning views, a pool and a private beach – just the place for a romantic splurge. Closed mid-Oct to April. **€200**

EATING

El Sol Via Santa Venere 151, Fiumicello 0973 873 192. This casual place signposted off the main road generally pulls in a local crowd for its pizzas and seafood dishes, such as mussels and swordfish. You'll pay around €6 for a pizza, €14 for grilled fish. Daily noon–2.30pm & 6.30–11.30pm.

Il Sacello La Locanda delle Donne Monache (see above). This hotel's chic garden restaurant prepares modern interpretations of the region's cuisine, both land- and sea-based – try the *tagliolini del golfo* (fresh pasta with mixed seafood and cherry tomatoes). It's pricey though: expect to pay around €100 for two including wine. May to mid-Oct daily 7–10pm.

Calabria's Tyrrhenian coast

The northern stretch of the **Tyrrhenian coast** in **Calabria** is peppered with holiday complexes that crowd the flat littoral. There are some attractive places to break the journey, notably the towns of **Diamante**, **Belvedere** and **San Lucido**.

South of the Savuto River the **Piana di Sant'Eufemia** plain is the narrowest part of the Calabrian peninsula, much of it reclaimed only in the last hundred years from malarial swamp: the mosquitoes remain but they no longer carry the disease. Heading south,

past the high tableland of the Tropea promontory, the Autostrada del Sole winds round and through the mountains with glimpses of Sicily to the south.

GETTING AROUND **CALABRIA'S TYRRHENIAN COAST**

The towns dotted along Calabria's long Tyrrhenian coast are connected by the SS18, the Naples–Reggio train line (though the frequent trains don't always stop at smaller places) and by local independent bus companies. From the Savuto River down to Reggio, the SS18, autostrada and main rail line all run parallel along the coast, apart from the stretch of the Tropea promontory. Just north of here, **Lamezia** has Calabria's main **airport** (T 0968 414 111, W lameziaairport.it), mainly used for domestic and seasonal flights, while nearby **Sant'Eufemia-Lamezia** is the **rail and road junction** for Catanzaro and the Ionian coast.

Pizzo

If you are following the railway or the SS18 southward, the picturesque little town of **PIZZO**, overlooking the sea, merits a stop.

15

Castello Murat

Piazza del Castello • April to mid-July, Sept & Oct daily 9am–7pm; mid- to end-July Mon–Fri 9am–7pm, Sat & Sun 9am–midnight; Aug daily 9am–midnight; Nov–March Mon–Fri 9am–7pm, Sat & Sun 9am–1pm & 3–7pm • €3 or €4.50 with Chiesetta di Piedigrotta • T 0963 532 523

Off the main Piazza della Repubblica, the small, well-preserved **Castello Murat** was built in 1486 by Ferdinand I of Aragon, and is now named after **Joachim Murat**, Napoleon's brother-in-law and one of his ablest generals. Murat met his end here after attempting to rouse the people against the Bourbons to reclaim the throne of Naples given to him by Napoleon; the people of Pizzo ignored him, and he was arrested and court-martialled. In the castle you can see the room in which Murat was imprisoned, with some of his personal effects and copies of the last letters he wrote, and the terrace where he was shot in October 1815.

Chiesetta di Piedigrotta

Daily: April–June, Sept & Oct 9am–1pm & 3–6pm; July & Aug 9am–1pm & 3–7.pm; Nov–March 11am–1pm & 3–5pm • €3, or €4.50 with Castello Murat T 392 058 0111

A couple of kilometres north of the town centre, signposted opposite the *Bar Aquarium* on the main road into town, the **Chiesetta di Piedigrotta** is a curious rock-hewn church next to a sandy beach. Created in the seventeenth century by Neapolitan sailors rescued from a shipwreck, the church was later enlarged and its interior festooned with eccentric statuary depicting episodes from the Bible. Most of this was the work of a local father-and-son team, and it was augmented by another scion of the family in 1969, who restored the works and contributed a scene of his own, a double portrait of Pope John XXIII and President Kennedy.

ARRIVAL AND INFORMATION **PIZZO**

By train Pizzo has two stations: Pizzo, by the sea at the bottom of the town, for the local coastal line to Tropea and Lamezia Terme, and Vibo Valentia-Pizzo, about 5km southwest, connected to the main network for fast trains to Naples and Reggio Calabria.

Destinations from Pizzo Lamezia Terme (hourly; 20min, with bus connections from Lamezia to airport); Tropea (4–7 daily; 30min).

Destinations from Vibo Valentia-Pizzo Cosenza (6–10 daily; 1hr 20min); Reggio Calabria (approx. hourly; 1hr 15min).

By bus Various private companies serve Pizzo, with frequent links to Tropea and the coastal resorts.

Tourist office Pro Loco, Piazza della Repubblica (usually Tues–Sun 10am–12.30pm & 3.30–7pm; T 0963 531 310, W prolocopizzo.it).

ACCOMMODATION

Casa Armonia Via Armonia 9 T 339 374 3731, W casaarmonia.com. Central B&B very close to the castle, with a friendly owner, three clean, modern rooms with private bathrooms, and a terrace overlooking the sea. No credit cards. Closed Jan. €77

Pepe Nero Via G. Marconi, 3, T 390963531076. Friendly

modern place in the historic centre, for spanking fresh fish, and some deftly cooked seafood pasta dishes. Try perfectly deep-fried seppioline (baby squid) and home-made tagliolini with tuna roe and bottarga (€15) or paccheri with lobster (min 2 people, €18) or play modest with a seafood risotto or mezzo maniche pasta with clams and potatoes (both €12). Summer daily lunch & dinner; winter Thurs–Sun lunch & dinner.

Tropea

Southwest of Pizzo, **TROPEA** is the prettiest town on the southern Tyrrhenian coast, built right on the edge of steep cliffs, towering high over its beach. It is also (after Maratea in Basilicata) the most fashionable, with a certain seaside charm, though this can wear pretty thin with the summer tourist influx.

There are numerous **beaches** below the town, all within walking distance, and the old centre has plenty of character – see particularly the lovely Norman **cathedral** at the bottom of Via Roma, whose interior harbours a couple of unexploded American bombs from the last war, a Renaissance ciborium and a statue of the Madonna and Child from the same period.

15

The views from the upper town over the sea and the church of **Santa Maria dell'Isola** on its rock are superb, and on a clear evening you can see the cone of Stromboli shimmering on the horizon.

ARRIVAL AND INFORMATION — TROPEA

By train Local trains from Lamezia, Reggio Calabria and Pizzo arrive at Tropea's station located on the outskirts of the *centro storico*, 1km from the beach.

Destinations Lamezia Terme (hourly; 50min); Pizzo (12 daily; 30min); Reggio Calabria (15 daily; 1hr 50min–2hr 45min).

By bus In summer, regular bus services link Tropea with the local coastal resorts, but transport is more infrequent out of season.

By taxi With the often inadequate public transport services, local taxis are often the only means to get around; call T 347 557 2100 or T 340 625 8642. A ride from Tropea to Capo Vaticano will cost around €20.

Tourist information Pro Loco, Piazza Ercole (April–Sept daily 9am–1pm & 2–8pm, reduced hours in winter; T 0963 61 475, W prolocotropea.eu).

ACCOMMODATION

Camping Marina del Convento Via Marina del Convento T 0963 62 501 (summer), T 329 919 1865 (winter), W marinadelconvento.it. One of two campsites right on the beach at the base of the cliff below Tropea's centre, both with very similar facilities, though *Marina del Convento* also has small, simple bungalows and apartments from €400 a week in high season, more in Aug. Late May–Oct. Pitches €10, per person €10

La Porta del Mare Via Libertà 52 T 0963 666 481, W hotellaportadelmare.it. An old, remodelled *palazzo* provides modern comforts near the centre, with a large terrace overlooking the sea where breakfast is served in summer (otherwise it's in your room). Rooms are small and simple; four have balconies. Closed Nov–Feb. €110

Terrazzo sul Mare Via Libertà 52 T 0963 61 020. Few Tropea hotels have sea views from the bedrooms, but most rooms in this modern three-star near the centre boast not just sea views but balconies, and the terrace where buffet breakfasts are taken enjoys a similarly sweeping vista. There's a private beach, too. Closed Nov–March. €120

Villa Antica Via Ruffo 37 T 0963 607 176, W villaanticatropea.it. Right in the centre of Tropea, this villa from 1906 has quiet grounds and antique pieces. Rooms are all different, accessed from a courtyard or the garden, and some have murals. €122

★ **Villa Vittoria** Via della Vittoria 7 T 0963 666 194, W villavittoria.com This bright, modern B&B in a beautifully restored Liberty villa near the centre (behind the post office) provides spacious rooms with a/c, TV and private bathrooms. Breakfast is served in the garden in summer. €180

EATING AND DRINKING

Genius Loci Largo Vaccari 51 T 0963 666 883. Boasting one of Tropea's most romantic views from its terrace, this friendly place serves local dishes expertly prepared – try the *orecchiette* with clams or the *pesce spada alla calabrese* (swordfish with olives, capers and lemon). *Primi* are €10–12, *secondi* €12–20. April–Oct daily noon–2.30pm & 7–10.45pm; Nov–March Fri–Sun eves only.

La Munizione Largo Duomo 12 T 346 382 7594. Chic cocktail bar behind the cathedral, with a roof terrace offering sweeping views. It serves around 130 wines, and cocktails from €8. June to mid-Sept daily 6pm–5am.

Le Volpi e L'Uva Via Pelliccia 2/4, signed off Corso

Vittorio Emanuele II ☎ 0963 61 900. Secluded, simple *enoteca* and trattoria with red-check tablecloths, run by two brothers (the chef also teaches cookery courses). Seafood dishes are around the €10 mark, and there are some sixty different Southern Italian wines to choose from. Daily noon–2.30pm & 6.30pm–midnight.

Osteria del Pescatore Via del Monte 7 ☎ 0963 603 018. Excellent, good-value fish is served up in the evenings in this vaulted cellar near the cathedral; a big plate of *filea alla tropeana* local pasta is €9. Easter–Nov daily 7.30–11pm.

Vecchio Forno Via Caivano, off Corso Vittorio Emanuele II ☎ 347 311 2416. The most historic place to eat in town, serving crisp, freshly baked pizza for €3.50–7 at outdoor tables. Try one with Tropea's famous *cipolle rosse* (red onions). Easter–Oct daily 7pm–late.

Capo Vaticano

Further around the promontory beyond Tropea, **Capo Vaticano** holds some of the area's most popular beaches, including **Grotticelle** and **Tonicello**, both spacious enough to allow you to get away from the bustle.

15

Scilla

As you head south along the coast, the proximity of Sicily becomes the dominant feature. This stretch of the autostrada can claim to be one of the most panoramic in Italy, burrowing high up through mountains with the Strait of Messina glittering below. Travelling by train or following the old coastal road, you pass through **SCILLA**, with a fine sandy **beach** and lots of action in the summer. Known as Scylla in classical times, this was the legendary location of a six-headed cave monster, one of two hazards to mariners mentioned in the **Odyssey**, the other being the whirlpool Charybdis, corresponding to the modern Cariddi located 6km away on the other side of the strait. Crowning a hefty rock, a **castle** separates the main beach from the fishing village of Chianalea to the north.

Castello Ruffo

Piazza del Castello • Daily 9.30am–1.40pm & 3–7.15pm • €2 • ☎ 0965 704 207

Standing sentinel over Scilla, the **Castello Ruffo** has existed in one form or another for at least eight centuries, while the rock on which it stands has revealed fortifications dating back to the fifth century BC. Today, the castle offers the best views in town, and holds exhibitions on the fauna and flora of the Strait and fishing – specifically the rituals of swordfishing.

ARRIVAL AND DEPARTURE — SCILLA

By train Scilla's station is close to the beach and hotels on Via Nazionale.

Destinations Cosenza (Mon–Sat 10 daily, Sun 2 daily; 2hr 10min–2hr 47min); Reggio Calabria (13 daily Mon–Sat, Sun 8 daily ; 25min).

By bus Various companies operate in Scilla, with bus stops on Via Nazionale.

Destinations Reggio Calabria (every 30min–1hr; 20–35min).

ACCOMMODATION AND EATING

Bleu de Toi Via Grotte 40 ☎ 0965 790 585. Scilla's best fish restaurants are in Chianalea, and this is the top choice, where you can sample grilled swordfish, tuna and grilled prawns. Pasta dishes are around €10, mains about €15. July & Aug daily 1–3pm & 8–11.30pm; Sept–Dec & March–June closed Tues. Closed Jan & Feb.

Le Sirene Via Nazionale 57 ☎ 0965 754 019, ⓦ hotellesirenescilla.com. Try this small, airy hotel if you want to stay centrally in Scilla, right opposite the station and with a wide panoramic terrace overlooking the beach. Four of the rooms are sea-facing. €87

Reggio Calabria and around

REGGIO CALABRIA was one of the first ancient Greek settlements on the Italian mainland; in recent years, it's become synonymous with urban decline and the influence of the

local mafia, or **'Ndrangheta**, though foreign visitors are unlikely to come into contact with the city's seamier side. The most attractive areas are the long, mainly pedestrianized **Corso Garibaldi** – the venue for Calabria's liveliest *passeggiata* – and the **lungomare**, the seafront esplanade that affords wonderful views of the Sicilian coastline and, occasionally, Mount Etna. At the southern end of the Corso, you can see remains of sixth-century-BC **city walls** and a **Roman bathing complex**. Just off the Corso lies Reggio's **Duomo**, an airy building heavily restored after the 1908 earthquake.

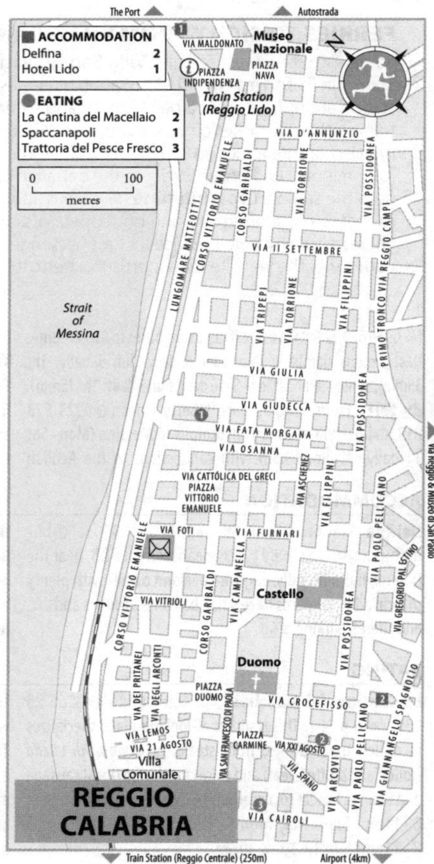

Museo Nazionale di Reggio di Calabria

Piazza De Nava, at the northern end of Corso Garibaldi • Daily April–Oct 9am–8pm, Nov–March closed Mon • €8 • ⓣ 0965 812 255, ⓦ archeocalabria.beniculturali.it

Reggio's main draw, the **Museo Nazionale** is home to Calabria's most important collection of archeological finds from the Hellenic period. Over five floors, the museum displays examples from all the major Greek sites in the region, including the famous *pinakes* or carved tablets from the sanctuary of Persephone at Locri. The biggest crowd-puller, however, is the **Bronzi di Riace**: two bronze statues dragged out of the Ionian Sea in 1972 near the village of Riace. These shapely examples of the highest period of Greek art (fifth century BC) are especially prized because there are so few finds from this period in such a good state of repair. Other rooms in the museum display items relating to daily life in Magna Graecia and to the indigenous cultures prior to the Greek settlement: there's also a panoramic roof terrace with a restaurant.

Piccolo Museo di San Paolo

Via Reggio Campi 4 (Sorgonà crossroads) • By appointment only, call ⓣ 388 106 6926 • Free but donation appreciated

After the Museo Nazionale, Reggio's other must-see attraction is the **Piccolo Museo di San Paolo**, an impressive private collection of religious art including some 160 Russian icons and a *St Michael* attributed to Antonello da Messina.

ARRIVAL AND INFORMATION — REGGIO CALABRIA

By train If you're arriving by train, get off at Reggio Lido for the port or museum.

Destinations Cosenza (4–7 daily; 2hr 35min); Naples (8–9 daily; 3hr 50min–5hr 30min); Scilla (Mon–Sat 13 daily, Sun 8 daily; 30min).

By bus Buses end up at Reggio Centrale station, 1km or so down the long Corso Garibaldi. Almost all buses stop at the museum too, so you can make use of ATAM city buses for getting from one end of town; tickets cost €1.50 from kiosks and *tabacchi*, valid for 75min, day tickets are €4.50. ATAM

FERRIES TO SICILY FROM VILLA SAN GIOVANNI

Some 9km southwest of Scilla, **Villa San Giovanni** is the main embarkation point for **Sicily**. State-run FS **ferries** (T 340 984 8540, W bluferries.it) leave from directly behind the train station about nine times a day Mon–Fri and six times daily Sat & Sun and arrive at Messina's train station; the ticket office is in front of Villa's train station. There are more services on the private Caronte ferries (T 800 627 414, W carontetourist.it), which leave approximately every forty minutes and pull in closer to the entrance of the autostrada; the ticket office is across from the station. **Crossing time** for each is about forty minutes. For a car with two people, expect to pay around €40, and both operators charge around €2.50 for foot passengers. There's also a hydrofoil service for foot passengers between Reggio Calabria and Messina (see page 907). The website W trasportisullostretto.it has information on all crossings.

15

(T 0965 620 121, W atam-rc.it) also runs buses to Aspromonte.
Destinations Gambarie (Mon–Sat 6 daily, Sun 3 daily; 1hr 35min); Santo Stefano (Mon–Sat 6 daily, Sun 3 daily; 1hr 15min).
By ferry From Reggio's port, Liberty Lines (T 0923 873 813, W libertylines.it) runs hydrofoils to Messina (Mon–Sat 11 daily; 35min; €3.50) with connections to the Aeolian islands.
Taxi Call T 347 676 6562 or T 0965 27 450.
Tourist information There is an information desk at Reggio's airport (Mon–Sat 8am–8pm; T 0965 630 301), and in town there's a kiosk near Reggio Lido train station that keeps erratic hours.

ACCOMMODATION

Delfina Via Crocefisso 58 T 334 161 3905, W bb-delfina.com; map p.861. This clean, central B&B, near the Duomo, has a friendly, English-speaking owner with plenty of local advice. Rooms have small balconies, fridges and a/c, and there's parking. **€68**

Hotel Lido Via F. Cananzi 6 T 0965 25 001, W hotellidoreggiocalabria.it; map p.861. It's not exactly bursting with character, but this three-star hotel near the museum and Lido station has reasonable rates, cheerful rooms with modern facilities and a garage. **€75**

EATING

La Cantina del Macellaio Via Arcovito 26 T 0965 23 932; map p.861. This traditional-looking place specializes in grilled meat dishes, from steaks to *involtini di vitello* (rolled and stuffed veal) and *salsiccia e fagioli* (local sausage and beans). Expect to pay around €25. June–Aug Mon–Sat 8–11pm; Sept–May Mon & Wed–Sat 12.30–2.30pm & 8–11pm, Sun 12.30–2.30pm.

Spaccanapoli Via Fata Morgana 3 T 0965 312 276; map p.861. Just off Corso Garibaldi, this easy-going place serves up great-value Neapolitan-style pizzas for €4.50–9. The antipasti and desserts are also worth sampling. Gets very busy at weekends. Daily 12.30-3pm & 7.30pm–1am.

Trattoria del Pesce Fresco Via Cairoli 7 T 0965 890 420; map p.861. This is the town's top choice for excellent fresh seafood, including grilled prawns, squid and whatever else has been freshly caught. They also do a memorable spicy spaghetti with swordfish, capers and olives, and all for €30–35 for a full meal including drinks. Mon–Sat 1–2.30pm & 8–10.30pm; June–Sept also Sun noon–3pm.

Aspromonte

On the tip of Italy's boot, the great massif of **Aspromonte** is the last spur of the Apennines, where you can pass from the brilliant, almost tropical vegetation of the coast to dense forests of beech and pine that rise to nearly 2000m. Although it has been a national park since 1989, the thickly forested mountain is not an established tourist destination – mostly due to its reputation as the stronghold of the **'Ndrangheta**, the Calabrian Mafia. On top of this, the area remains virtually unsigned, and the oppressive tree cover rarely breaks to provide views. If you're in a car, note the *Strada Interotta* ("Road interrupted") signs at the entrances, and only attempt the rocky dirt tracks across the range in an off-road vehicle.

Santo Stefano

Access to the Aspromonte range is easiest from the Tyrrhenian side, with several buses a day leaving Reggio's Piazza Garibaldi for Gambarie and winding their way up the

highly scenic SS184 from Gallico, through profusely terraced groves of vine and citrus. The road passes through the village of **SANTO STEFANO**, famous as the birthplace and final resting place of the last of the great brigands who roamed these parts, **Giuseppe Musolino** (1875–1956). A sort of local Robin Hood, Musolino was a legend in his own lifetime, the last thirty years of which he spent in jail and, finally, a lunatic asylum – the penalty for having led the *carabinieri* on a long and humiliating dance up and down the slopes of Aspromonte during his profitable career. Just above the village, in the cemetery, you can see Musolino's grave, now renovated but until recently daubed with the signatures of people come to pay their respects.

Cosenza and around

In Calabria's interior, **COSENZA** is a burgeoning city with a small and atmospheric historic centre surrounded by rings of featureless modern construction. Tradition has it that **Alaric the Goth**, the barbarian who prised open the gates of Rome in 410 AD, is buried under the Busento River. Struck down for his sins by malaria while journeying south, he was interred here along with his booty, and the course of the river diverted to cover the traces, lending Cosenza a place in history and giving rise to countless, fruitless projects to discover the tomb's whereabouts.

In the new town, you might take a stroll around the pedestrianized main axis, Corso Mazzini, and Piazza Bilotti to see half a dozen open-air sculptures by the likes of Dalí, De Chirico and Pietro Consagra, part of a bequest that makes up the **Museo all'Aperto Bilotti**, or **MAB**. At the top of the old town, the mainly thirteenth-century **Castello Svevo** (Tues–Sun 9.30am–1pm & 4–8pm; €4; T 0984 813 806) affords excellent views over the city and occasionally holds exhibitions and concerts.

Duomo

Piazza del Duomo • Daily 8.30am–noon & 4–7pm • Free

Cosenza's chief sight is the stately **Duomo** in the historic town centre off the main Corso Telesio. Consecrated on the occasion of Frederick II's visit to the city in 1222, it contains the lovely tomb of Isabella of Aragon, who died in Cosenza in 1271 while returning with her husband Philip III – seen kneeling beside her – from an abortive Crusade in Tunisia, as well as a copy of a thirteenth-century Byzantine icon, the *Madonna del Pilerio*, which was once carried around the country during times of plague.

ARRIVAL AND INFORMATION — COSENZA

By train Arriving by train, you have to take a bus (every 20min) from the train station a little way outside town – buy tickets from the bar inside the station. For onward journeys, change at Paola for faster and more frequent services.

Destinations Diamante (5–7 daily; 1hr); Naples (3–4 daily; 4hr 15min); Paola (every 30min–1hr; 25min); Reggio Calabria (2–6 daily; 2hr 40min).

By bus The bus station is below Piazza Fera, from where it's a 20min walk along the length of Corso Mazzini to the hotels and the *centro storico*. Buses are run by a number of companies. The best one-stop source of bus times is the website W silaonline.it

Destinations Camigliatello (Mon–Sat every 30min–1hr; 45min); Lorica (Mon–Sat 2 daily; 1hr 25min); Luzzi (Mon–

THE SANTUARIO DELLA MADONNA DI POLSI

A boisterous **fair** takes place every year in Aspromonte on the first two days of September at the **Santuario della Madonna di Polsi**, a 10km hike from the park entrance. It's an unashamedly pagan event that involves the sale and slaughter of large numbers of goats – the fair is also known to provide a convenient cover for the meeting of 'Ndrangheta cells from all over the world.

Sat 10–15 daily; 50min); Rende (Mon–Sat 10 daily; 30min).
Tourist office There's an office by the Busento River on Piazza T. Campanella (daily 10am–1pm & 4–7pm; ⓣ328 175 4422, ⓦcosenzaturismo.it), and a kiosk off the main Corso Mazzini at Piazza XI Settembre (daily 10am–1pm & 5–8pm).

ACCOMMODATION

Old Garden Re Alarico Vicolo Fiorentino 10 ⓣ0984 181 1102 or ⓣ328 114 9430, ⓦoldgardenrealarico.com. In an alley above the River Crati, this B&B and hostel occupies an eighteenth-century *palazzo* with antique furnishings, accommodation in double rooms or dormitories and the use of a large kitchen and internet. There's a garden for summer barbecues. Dorms **€21**, doubles **€38**

Via dell'Astrologo Via R. Benincasa 16 ⓣ338 920 5394, ⓦviadellastrologo.com. Elegant B&B in a tastefully restored *palazzo* in the heart of the old town, with two spacious en-suite rooms and wi-fi. No credit cards. **€85**

EATING AND DRINKING

Calabria Bella Piazza del Duomo ⓣ349 585 9445. Old-town trattoria next to the Duomo, which serves traditional, mainly meaty local dishes. A generous mixed plate of antipasti can be had for about €8; mains are around €12. Daily 12.30–2.30pm & 7.30pm–11.30pm.

Gran Caffè Renzelli Corso Umberto ⓣ0984 26 814. The best aperitif in the *centro storico* is found at this old-fashioned coffee house above the Duomo, with marble-top tables and local pastries. Mon–Sat 7.30am–9pm; Oct–March daily 7.30am–9pm.

15

Around Cosenza

From Cosenza, you can make excursions into the **Sila highlands** (see page 864), or visit some of the villages dotted around the surrounding hills. In summer, the streets are lively until late, and at night the views over the bowl of the valley are magnificent. In summer, too, the village **festas** normally take place, with each *comune* vying to outdo the others in terms of spectacle and expense.

Northwest of Cosenza, the well-preserved hilltop village of **RENDE** is easily reached, and worth a stroll for its good views and an absorbing pair of museums, both on Via de Bártolo: the **Museo Civico**, in the Palazzo Zagarese (Tues–Sat 9am–1pm & 3–7pm Sun by appointment; free; ⓣ0984 813 806), devoted to local folk art, costumes, cuisine, music, the Albanian community and emigration, and **Maon** in Palazzo Vitari (Tues–Sat 10am–1.30pm & 4.30–8pm; free; ⓣ0984 444 113), showing nineteenth- and twentieth-century works of art.

Further north, above the village of **Luzzi**, stands the **Abbazia di Sambucina**. A Cistercian abbey founded in the twelfth century and long the centre of this order of monks throughout the south, it has a beautiful, lightly pointed portal (rebuilt in the fifteenth century) and the original presbytery.

EATING — AROUND COSENZA

Hostaria de Mendoza Piazza degli Eroi 3, Rende ⓣ0984 444 022. Rustic-looking place that offers a range of authentically Calabrese meat dishes, many of them with fresh mushrooms and truffles. First courses are €8–9, mains €15–20. Daily (except Tues) 1–2.30pm & 8–10.30pm.

The Sila

Covering the widest part of the Calabrian peninsula, the **Sila** massif, east of Cosenza, is more of an extensive plateau than a mountain range, though the peaks on its western flank reach heights of nearly 2000m. Protected by the Parco Nazionale della Sila (ⓦparcosila.it), it's divided into three main groups: the Sila Greca, Sila Grande and Sila Piccola, of which the Sila Grande is of most interest to tourists.

At one time the Sila was one huge forest and was exploited from earliest times to provide fuel and material for the construction of fleets, fortresses and even for church-building in Rome, resulting in a deforestation that helped bring about the malarial

THE STRADA DELLE VETTE

Camigliatello is a useful starting point for a tough hike that takes in the area's highest peaks, following the **Strada delle Vette** ("road of the peaks") for 13km through pine- and beechwoods before forking off and up to the three **peaks** of Monte Scuro, Monte Curcio and, highest of all, Monte Botte Donato (1928m). The trail, which is often snowbound between December and May, continues down to **Lago Arvo** and the resort of **Lorica**, from where it's a shorter distance than following the Strada delle Vette to Botte Donato. Or you can save the sweat and take the chair lift from Località Cavaliere, just outside town.

conditions that for centuries blighted much of Calabria. The cutting of trees is now strictly controlled, and **ancient pines** (the so-called **Giganti della Sila**), which can live for several hundred years, are among the region's chief attractions. There's plenty here, too, for the outdoors enthusiast: in summer the area provides relief from the heat of the towns, and in winter there's downhill and cross-country skiing.

The Sila Grande

Densely forested, and the highest, most extensive part of the Sila range, the **Sila Grande** is home to Calabria's main **ski slopes** as well as the region's three principal **lakes** – all artificial (for hydroelectric purposes) and much loved by fishing enthusiasts, who come out in force at weekends. The **campsites** here enjoy good lakeside locations, while the hotels are mainly in the towns and villages, and many close out of season.

Camigliatello

The functional town of **CAMIGLIATELLO** is the best known of the resorts, though it lacks any intrinsic charm. Centred on Via Roma, the town has three ski slopes, and another in the satellite town of Contrada Moccone, 3km west, plus plenty of hotels, restaurants and souvenir shops. **Ski** passes are available from around €20 for a half-day, €25 for a day, and there are facilities for renting equipment and tuition (group lessons) from various ski clubs, including the Scuola Sci Camigliatello, Località Tasso, Spezzano della Sila, ⊕333.25 66 588 ⓦscuolascicamigliatello.it. The Sila terrain also makes ideal **riding** country; most stables are open in summer only.

ARRIVAL AND INFORMATION — CAMIGLIATELLO

By bus Camigliatello has good bus connections with Cosenza (Mon–Sat every 30min–1hr; 45min).

Tourist office The volunteer-run Pro Loco at the top of Via Roma (roughly 10am–12.30pm & 4–6.30pm, reduced hours in winter; ⊕0984 578 159) has maps of the area and suggestions for walking routes in the park.

ACCOMMODATION AND EATING

Da Fulvio Contrada Moccone ⊕0984 578 790. This great-value trattoria-grocery shop and deli is known for simple, good-value local cooking, using wild mushrooms and wild boar. You'll pay €20–25 for a full lunch. Tues–Sun noon–2.30pm.

Lo Sciatore Via Roma 126 ⊕0984 578 105, ⓦhotellosciatore.it. Outdated but centrally located hotel with clean, comfortable and spacious rooms and a good pizzeria-*ristorante*. The staff are friendly and buffet breakfasts abundant. **€52**

★ **San Lorenzo Si Alberga** Campo San Lorenzo 14 ⊕0984 570 809, ⓦsanlorenzosialberga.it. Some 4km northeast of Camigliatello on the SS177 towards Lago Cecita, this modern hotel makes the best of its great views. Rooms are minimally furnished, breakfasts are abundant and there's a top-notch restaurant *La Tavernetta*, renowned for its gourmet versions of regional specialities using local ingredients. Tasting menus cost €50 or €60, but you can eat a la carte as well. Tues–Sun 12.30–3pm & 7.3010pm; closed two weeks in March & Nov. **€85**

Lorica

Like Camigliatello, **LORICA**, 26km southeast, is dedicated to tourism in the height of the winter and summer seasons, but its lakeside location makes it a more relaxed spot,

with lots of places for picnicking under the pines and observing the antics of the black squirrels that inhabit them.

ACCOMMODATION **LORICA**

Park 108 Via Nazionale 86 ⓣ0984 537 077, ⓦhotelpark108.it. Comfortable four-star hotel, which has a garden with lake views, a sauna and a fitness centre. Look out for special deals. €95

Calabria's Ionian coast

15

Calabria's Ionian coast is a mainly flat sandy strip, sometimes monotonous but less developed than the Tyrrhenian side of the peninsula, and generally with cleaner seawater. At the border with Basilicata, mountainous slopes soon give way to the wide **Piana di Sibari**, the most extensive of the Calabrian coastal plains, bounded by Pollino to the north, the Sila Greca to the west and the Sila Grande in the south. The rivers flowing off these mountains, which for centuries kept the land well watered and rich, also helped to transform it into a stagnant, malarial mire, and although land reclamation has restored the area's fertility, without visiting the museum and excavations at **Sybaris** you could pass through the area with no inkling of the civilization that once flourished on these shores. Southeast of here, the old Byzantine centre of **Rossano** and **Crotone**, another ancient Greek city, provide further interest as you travel along the coastline.

The southern part of Calabria's Ionian seaboard is less developed than the rest of the region and less scenic, with a string of mostly unappealing seaside towns and villages. There are sandy **beaches**, though – either wild and unpopulated, or glitzy and brochure-style, as at **Soverato.** At **Locri**, you'll find the region's best collection of Greek ruins and, overlooking the coast a short way inland, the craggy medieval strongholds of **Squillace** and **Gerace.**

GETTING AROUND **CALABRIA'S IONIAN COAST**

The **SS106** runs along the whole Ionian coast, passing through every coastal town: consequently it's often very slow. Just one or two **trains** a day run along the coastal line between Taranto and Reggio Calabria, but there are frequent **bus** services connecting the coastal and inland towns run by various independent companies.

Sybaris

July–Sept daily 9am to 1hr before sunset; Oct–June closed Mon • Free

Long one of the great archeological mysteries tantalizing generations of scholars, the site of ancient **SYBARIS** (Sibari) was only definitely identified in the late 1960s, when aerial and X-ray photography confirmed that the site previously known to be that of Roman Thurium was also that of Sybaris. There are in fact three separate levels of construction that have been unearthed here, one Greek and two Roman, one on top of the other. Together these make up one of the world's largest archeological sites, covering a thousand hectares (compared with Pompeii's fifty), though only ten hectares have so far been dug up.

The **excavations** lie signposted off the SS106, on the right-hand side. Most of them belong to the Roman period, but something of the earlier site might still be turned up – the silt and sand of the river bed have yet to be explored properly, work having stopped owing to shortage of funds. Of the Roman city, the remains are impressively displayed and maintained, including baths, a patrician's house with mosaics, and a *decumanus* – main street – claimed to be the widest in existence.

There's plenty more to be seen, from here and other local sites, at the **Museo della Sibaritide** (Tues–Sun 9am–7.30pm; €2; ⓣ0981 79 392), about 2km before the excavations on the banks of the River Crati, where a series of rooms holds an assortment of coins, statuettes, amphorae and mosaic floors.

A LIFE OF LUXURY

The inhabitants of Sybaris – said to number 100,000 – were so fond of luxury and their excesses so legendary that we derive the modern word **sybaritic** from their reputation. The city's laws and institutions were apparently made to ensure the greatest comfort and wellbeing of its citizens, including the banning from the city of all noisy traders, such as metalworkers, and the planting of trees along every street for shade. Cooks were so highly prized that they were apparently bought and sold in the marketplace for great sums and were allowed to patent their recipes, while inventions ascribed to the Sybarites include pasta and the chamberpot. This was all too much for the Crotonians, who under their general Milo destroyed the city in 510 BC, diverting the waters of the river over the site to complete the job.

Rossano Calabro

Thirty kilometres down the coast from Sibari, **ROSSANO** was the foremost Byzantine centre in the south, and the focus of a veritable renaissance of literature, theology and art between the eighth and eleventh centuries, a period to which the town's greatest treasures belong. These days, its coastal offshoot of **Rossano Scalo** (site of the train station) has far outstripped its inland parent in terms of size and bustle, and most of the holiday-makers who frequent its beaches never get round to visiting the hilltop town, 7km up an awkward winding road – something that has helped to preserve the old centre from excessive development.

Duomo

Piazza del Duomo • Daily 8am–noon & 5–8pm • Free

Rossano's majolica-tiled **Duomo** is an Angevin construction largely rebuilt after an 1836 earthquake, but it does have a much-venerated ninth-century **Byzantine fresco** encased in an elaborate marble setting in the nave. Its Greek epithet, *Madonna Achiropita*, meaning "not painted by hand", refers to its divine authorship.

Museo Diocesano e del Codex

Via Arcivescovado • July–mid-Sept daily 9.30am–1pm & 4.30–8pm; mid-Sept to June Tues–Sat 9.30am–12.30pm & 3–6pm, Sun 10am–noon & 4–6pm • €5 • ☎ 340 475 9406

Behind the cathedral, the **Museo Diocesano** contains the famed **codex purpureus Rossanensis**, or Purple Codex, a unique sixth-century manuscript on reddish-purple parchment illustrating the life of Christ. The book, which was brought from Palestine by monks fleeing the Muslim invasions, is open at one page, but you can leaf through a copy and see, among other things, how the Last Supper was originally depicted, with Christ and his disciples not seated but reclining on cushions round the table, and all eating from the same plate.

San Marco

Corso Garibaldi • Daily 9am to 1hr before sunset • Free

In contrast to the cathedral's grandiosity, the diminutive church of **San Marco**, above a gorge on the edge of town, retains a primitive spirituality. The five cupolas of the tenth- or eleventh-century construction and the cool white interior impart an almost Middle Eastern flavour.

INFORMATION — ROSSANO CALABRO

Tourist office Pro Loco, Palazzo Bernardino, Piazza Plebiscito, *centro storico* (Mon–Fri 8am–2pm; ☎ 349 252 1291, Ⓦ prolocorossano.it).

ACCOMMODATION

Casa Mazzei Via T. Mandatoriccio 31 ☎ 347 581 0142, Ⓦ bbcasamazzei.it. A short walk from both the Duomo and San Marco in the old town, this B&B is in an antique *palazzo* filled with thoughtfully chosen furniture and ancestral portraits. No credit cards. **€60**

★ **La Terrazza** Via Salita Ospedale 11 ☎ 0983 525 428

or ☎338 774 6255, ⓦlaterrazzabeb.com. At the top of a flight of steps in the old town, this B&B has two rooms with large bathrooms, a/c and free wi-fi. There are great views from the terrace after which it's named. €71

EATING

★ **La Bizantina** Corso Garibaldi 246 ☎0983 525 340. Right next to San Marco, this trattoria with tables outside has a rustic, almost medieval-looking interior. There are abundant and delicious antipasti (try the *peperoni e patate* – roast red peppers and potatoes) and pizzas. A full meal should cost around €25 a head. Sept–June Tues–Sun 8pm–midnight; July & Aug open daily.

La Villa Via San Bartolomeo ☎0983 522 214. Just off Piazza SS. Anargiri in the old town, you can enjoy alfresco eating on a panoramic veranda in summer here. It serves typical Calabrese food, with fresh pasta and lots of local sausage, mushrooms and tomatoes (mains €7–12), though most come for the pizzas (€3.50–6). No credit cards. Sept–July Thurs–Tues 7pm–midnight; Aug daily 12.30–2.30pm & 7pm–midnight.

Crotone

15

South of Rossano lies an empty stretch of beach, with, inland, the vineyards of Cirò, the source of Calabria's best-known **wine**. Crossing the River Neto into the fertile **Marchesato** region, you'll find the approach to **CROTONE** (the ancient Greek city of Kroton) blighted by a smoky industrial zone – not the most alluring entry into a city, but a rare thing in Calabria, and a reminder of the false hopes once vested in the industrialization of the region. In spite of this, Crotone today has a pleasant, unspoiled old centre and a great museum, and makes a good base for the **beaches** that spread to the south and for the Greek ruins at **Capo Colonna**.

Brief history

In its day ancient **Kroton** was among the most important colonial settlements of Magna Graecia. The mathematician and metaphysician **Pythagoras** lived here in 530 BC, the city's army overwhelmed and destroyed its powerful neighbour Sybaris in 510 BC, and Kroton's school of medicine was famous throughout the classical world – closely linked with the prowess of the city's athletes, who regularly scooped all the honours at the Olympic Games in Greece. Increasingly destabilized by internal conflicts, however, the city was eventually conquered by the Romans in 194 BC.

Kroton continued to be an important trading centre until the eighth century AD, and a resurgence of sorts occurred in the thirteenth century when it was made the main town of the Marchesato region, a vast feudal domain held by the powerful Ruffo family of Catanzaro. But its prosperity was always hindered by the scourge of malaria, provoking the author George Gissing – himself a victim of malaria during his visit in 1897 – to condemn Crotone as "a squalid little town".

Museo Archeologico Nazionale

Via Risorgimento • Sept–June Tues–Sun 9am–7.30pm • €2 • ☎0962 23 082

The town's **Museo Archeologico Nazionale** holds the best collection of finds from Magna Graecia on the Ionian coast. Most noteworthy is the so-called **Treasure of Hera Lacinia**, a beautifully restored group of bronze statuettes – including a sphinx, a gorgon, a horse, a winged siren and a rare Nuraghic boat from Sardinia dating from the seventh to the fifth centuries BC. The most dazzling item is a gold diadem, expertly worked with garlands of leaves and sprigs of myrtle.

INFORMATION — CROTONE

Tourist office Via Molo Sanità, near the port (Mon–Fri 8.30am–7.30pm, reduced hours in winter; ☎329 815 4963, ⓦprolococrotone.it).

ACCOMMODATION

Aprile Dolce Dormire Via Cavour 26 ☎392 906 1366, ⓦairbnb.com. Near the museum in the old town, this

B&B has three colourful rooms decorated by local artists on musical themes – punk, reggae, soul. Breakfast is self-serve. No credit cards. **€75**

Concordia Via Messinetti 12 ⓣ0962 23 910. Round the corner from Piazza della Vittoria in the old town, this old-fashioned hotel has a dingy entrance but the rooms are clean and functional. The writers George Gissing and Norman Douglas both stayed here, as did the archeologist François Lenormant. **€72**

EATING AND DRINKING

★ **Da Ercole** Viale Gramsci 122 ⓣ0962 901 425, ⓦristorantedaercole.eu. Classic seafront restaurant run by Ercole Villirillo, where you can sample such dishes as *linguine a pitagora* (which features *prine*, a kind of sea anemone) or *ricciola con carciofi selvatici* (amberjack fish with wild artichokes). A meal will probably weigh in at around €50. Mon–Sat 12.30–2.30pm 12.30–2.20pm & 8.30–11pm.

La Pignata Vico Orfeo 8, off Viale Regina Margherita ⓣ0962 22 984. Small fish restaurant on the edge of the old town with friendly service. The *antipasto di mare* is spectacular and abundant. Expect to pay around €30–35 including drinks. Noon–2.30pm & 8–10pm.

15

Santa Severina

Thirty-five kilometres inland of Crotone, off the road to San Giovanni in Fiore, **SANTA SEVERINA** lies on the eastern fringes of the Sila Piccola. A Byzantine fortified town built on a hilltop, it's a pretty place with great views, but is chiefly worth a detour for the Norman castle that dominates it.

The castle

Piazza Campo • Easter to mid-Sept daily 9.30am–12.30pm & 3–6.30pm (3.30–7.30pm in summer); mid-Sept to Easter Tues–Sun 9.30am–12.30pm & 3–6pm • €3.10 • ⓣ0962 51 069

Rebuilt by Robert Guiscard on the ruins of a Byzantine stronghold and remodelled by the Swabians and Angevins, the renovated **castle** holds a first-rate **museum**, taking in all parts of the construction from the foundations to the first-floor rooms, holding weaponry, costumes and temporary exhibitions. From the stout battlemented walls long views extend over the hilly surroundings towards the mountains of the Sila.

The Duomo and baptistry

Piazza Campo • Daily 8am–noon & 5–8pm • Free

From the castle, cross the piazza – whose flagstones are studded with symbols of the zodiac – to the spacious **Duomo**. Adjacent to it, the eighth-century Byzantine **baptistry** preserves traces of frescoes of the saints, Greek inscriptions on the capitals and its original font. If it's closed, ask in the cathedral for access.

Museo Diocesano

Piazza Campo • Daily 9am–1pm & 3–6pm • €2.50 • ⓣ339 405 1632

Next to the Duomo, the **Museo Diocesano** repays a visit for a painfully graphic Christ on the Cross from the fifteenth century, an early printed edition of the Bible, and – its greatest treasure – the *Spilla Angioina*, a brooch from about 1300, studded with gold, pearls and rubies.

ACCOMMODATION AND EATING — SANTA SEVERINA

★ **Le Puzelle** Località Puzelle, SS107bis ⓣ0962 51 004, ⓦlepuzelle.it. Less than 1km south of town, this smart agriturismo offers calm, spacious rooms with a/c, a small pool, fantastic views and amiable, professional service. The restaurant – open to all – is the best in the area, offering full meals (without drinks) for €22/person. Open daily for lunch and dinner. **€63**

Locanda del Re Via Orsi 6 ⓣ0962 51 662. On the steps below the castle, this trattoria focuses on food rooted in the medieval traditions of the area, so expect handmade pasta, lots of wild mushroom, boar, ricotta and pecorino on the fixed-price menus (€13–27). Pizzas are also available. Daily noon–3pm & 7.30–11pm.

Capo Colonna

On Calabria's extreme eastern point, 11km south of Crotone, the famed column at **CAPO COLONNA** is a solitary remnant of a vast structure that served as the temple for all the Greeks in Calabria. Dedicated to Hera Lacinia, the temple originally possessed 48 of these Doric columns and was the repository of immense wealth before being repeatedly sacked as Magna Graecia and Hellenism itself declined.

There are some excellent **bathing spots** not far south of here. The **Isola Capo Rizzuto** is a spit of land, not an island, with a choice of sandy or rocky inlets to swim from. During the winter the resort is dead, but it can get quite congested in the height of summer and difficult to find a place to stay.

Le Castella

West of Capo Rizzuto, **LE CASTELLA** gets very busy in summer, but it would be hard to spoil the beautifully sited Aragonese **fortress** (April–June daily 9.30am–1pm & 3–7.30pm; July & Aug daily 9am–12.30am; early Sept daily 9.30am–11.30pm; late Sept daily 9.30am–8.30pm; Oct Tues–Sun 9.30am–1pm & 3–7.30pm; Nov–March Tues–Sun 10am–noon & 3–5pm; €3.10; ⓣ0962 795 160) on an islet just off the main town. There's not much to see inside, but you could wander round the outside of the castle and swim off the rocks, though you'll probably be more tempted by the arc of beach to the south.

La Roccelletta and the ruins of Scolacium

South of Catanzaro Lido, the ruined basilica of Santa Maria della Roccella, or **La Roccelletta**, stands amid an olive grove 100m down the road signposted towards San Floro and Borgia, branching off the SS106. The partly restored redbrick shell is all that remains of what was once the second-largest church in Calabria (after Gerace). Of uncertain date, though probably Norman in origin and founded by Basilian monks, it still has a mighty impact. In summer the site is used for open-air contemporary art exhibitions and for concerts.

The church lies adjacent to a large **Zona Archeologica** (daily 8am–1hr before sunset; free) holding the ruins of the Roman town of Scolacium, built over the Greek town of Skylletion. The best-preserved item here is a **teatro**, once able to hold some 3500 spectators, and thought to have been abandoned following a fire some time after 350 AD. A **museum** (same hours) displays finds from the site.

Squillace

Some 5km south of La Roccelletta, at Lido di Squillace, turn right off SS106 for the old town of **SQUILLACE**, 8km up in the hills. Now a rather isolated mountain village, this was once an important centre, probably most renowned for its associations with the scholar **Cassiodorus** (480–570), who used his position as secretary to the Ostrogoth, Theodoric, to preserve much of Italy's classical heritage against the onset of the Dark Ages and the book-burning propensities of the Christians. Retiring to spend the last thirty years of his life in seclusion in a monastery located in the vicinity – all trace of it has long since disappeared – Cassiodorus composed histories and collections of documents that have been of invaluable use to historians.

On its high crag, Squillace affords lofty views over the Golfo di Squillace and beyond Catanzaro as far as the Sila Píccola mountain range, best enjoyed from its **castle** (May–Sept daily 8.30am–12.30pm & 4–8.30pm; Oct–April reduced hours; €3; ⓣ0961 912 040) – a candidate for one of Calabria's most romantic collections of ruins.

Locri Epizefiri

On the SS106, 5km south of Locri • Oct–June Tues–Sun 9am–8pm; July–Sept also Mon 9am–8pm • €4 • ⓣ 0964 390 023, ⓦ locriantica.it

Founded in the seventh century BC, the city of **Locri Epizefiri** was responsible for the first written code of law throughout the Hellenic world. Its moment of glory came in the second half of the sixth century when, supposedly assisted by Castor and Pollux, ten thousand Locrians defeated 130,000 Crotonians on the banks of the River Sagra, 25km north. The walls of the city, traces of which can still be seen, measured some 8km in circumference, and the excavations within are now interspersed over a wide area among farms and orchards. A car is useful to reach some of the more far-flung features, though the most interesting can be visited on foot, including a fifth-century-BC Ionic **temple**, a Roman **necropolis** and a well-preserved Greco-Roman **theatre**. Stop at the **museum** to consult a plan of the site, and examine the most recent finds, including a good collection of **pinakes**, or votive ceramics – though most of the best items are displayed at the Museo Nazionale in Reggio (see page 861).

15

Gerace

After the Saracens devastated Locri in the seventh century AD, the survivors fled inland to found **GERACE**, on an impregnable site that was later occupied and strengthened by the Normans. At the end of a steep and tortuous road 10km up from modern Locri, its ruined **castle** stands at one end of the town on a sheer cliff; it's usually accessible, though officially out of bounds due to the precarious state of the paths and walls.

The Duomo

Daily 9.30am–1pm & 3–7.30pm • ⓣ 0964 356 323

Gerace's **Duomo** was founded in 1045 by Robert Guiscard, enlarged by Frederick II in 1222 and is still the biggest church in Calabria. Its simple and well-preserved interior has twenty columns of granite and marble, each different and with various capitals: the one on the right nearest the altar in *verde antico* marble that changes tone according to the weather.

Sicily

877 Palermo and around

891 The Tyrrhenian coast

895 The Aeolian islands

906 The Ionian coast

926 The southern coast and the interior

935 Trapani and the west

TEATRO GRECO, TAORMINA

Sicily

The largest island in the Mediterranean, and with a strategically vital position, Sicily has a history and outlook derived from its erstwhile foreign rulers – from the Greeks who first settled the east coast in the eighth century BC, through a dazzling array of Phoenicians, Carthaginians, Romans, Arabs, Normans, French and Spanish, to the Bourbons seen off by Garibaldi in 1860.

Substantial **relics** of these ages remain, with temples, theatres and churches scattered about the whole island. But there are other, more immediate hints of Sicily's unique past. Sicilian dialect, for example, is still widely spoken in cities and countryside, varying from place to place; and the food is noticeably different from elsewhere in Italy, spicier and with more emphasis on fish and vegetables; even the flora echoes the change of temperament – oranges, lemons (introduced by the Arabs), prickly pears and palms are ubiquitous.

Most Sicilians consider themselves, and their island, a separate entity, and a visit here still induces a real sense of **arrival**. The standard approach for those heading south from the mainland is to cross the Strait of Messina, from Villa San Giovanni or Reggio di Calabria: this way, the train-ferry pilots a course between Scylla and Charybdis, the twin hazards of rock and whirlpool that were a legendary threat to sailors. Coming in by plane, too, there are spectacular approaches to the coastal airports at Palermo, Trapani and Catania.

Once you're on land, deciding **where to go** is largely a matter of time. Inevitably, most points of interest are on the coast: the interior of the island is mountainous, sparsely populated and relatively inaccessible, though in parts extremely beautiful. The capital, **Palermo**, is a filthy, bustling, noisy city with an unrivalled display of Norman art and architecture and Baroque churches, combined with a warren of medieval streets and markets. To the east, there's no better place in Sicily for a traditional family sea, sun and sand holiday than **Cefalù**, with a magnificent golden sandy beach and a mellow medieval core overlooked by a beetling castle-topped crag. An hour or so further east is the workaday port of Milazzo, departure point for the **Aeolian islands**, an archipelago of seven islands. Here you can climb two active volcanoes, laze on lava beaches, snorkel over bubbling underwater fumaroles and wallow in warm, reeking, sulphurous mud baths.

The islands are also linked by hydrofoil with the major port of **Messina**, separated from mainlaind Italy by the Strait of Messina. If you are travelling to Sicily overland from Italy, Messina will unavoidably be your point of arrival. Devastated by an earthquake and tidal wave in 1908, it is a modern city of little charm and unlikely to hold your interest for long. The most obvious target from here is the almost too charming hill-town of **Taormina**, spectacularly located on a rocky bluff between the Ionian Sea and the soaring peak of Mount Etna. For a gutsier taste of Sicily, head to **Catania**, the island's second city, intellectual and cultured, with a compact Baroque core of black lava and white limestone, and two exuberant markets. From Taormina or Catania, a skirt around the foothills, and even better, up to the craters of **Mount Etna**, is a must.

In the south of the island is **Siracusa**, once the most important city of the Greek world, and beyond it, the Val di Noto, with an alluring group of Baroque towns centring on **Ragusa**. The south coast's greatest draw is the cluster of Greek temples at **Agrigento**, while the nearby **Piazza Armerina** boats some impressive Roman mosaics. To the west, most of Sicily's fishing industry – and much of the continuing Mafia activity (see page 880) – focuses on the area around **Trapani**, itself a salty old port with connections to the rough, sunblasted islands of the Egadi archipelago and Pantelleria.

CRATER AT MOUNT ETNA

Highlights

❶ **The Aeolian Islands** An archipelago of seven islands with active volcanoes, lava beaches, fractured coastlines and whitewashed villages. See page 895

❷ **Mount Etna** It's an eerie climb up the blackened lunar landscape of this smoking volcano that dominates eastern Sicily. See page 910

❸ **Siracusa** Classical dramas are staged every summer in the city's spectacular ancient Greek theatre, while Ortigia, surrounded by sea, has year-round appeal. See page 916

❹ **Val di Noto** This valley, stretching from Noto to Ragusa, is full of splendid Baroque towns, built after an earthquake, and now enjoying a renaissance, spurred on by UNESCO. See pages 926 and 930

❺ **Coastal nature reserves** Nature reserves such as Vendicari and Zingaro provide respite from the overdevelopment of much of the island's coast. See pages 927 and 939

❻ **Valley of the Temples, Agrigento** A spectacular sight, especially at night when the towering Doric columns are artfully floodlit. See page 932

❼ **Villa Romana del Casale** The extravagant country residence of an unknown Roman, holding the most lavish late Roman mosaics in Italy. See page 935

HIGHLIGHTS ARE MARKED ON THE MAP ON PAGE 876

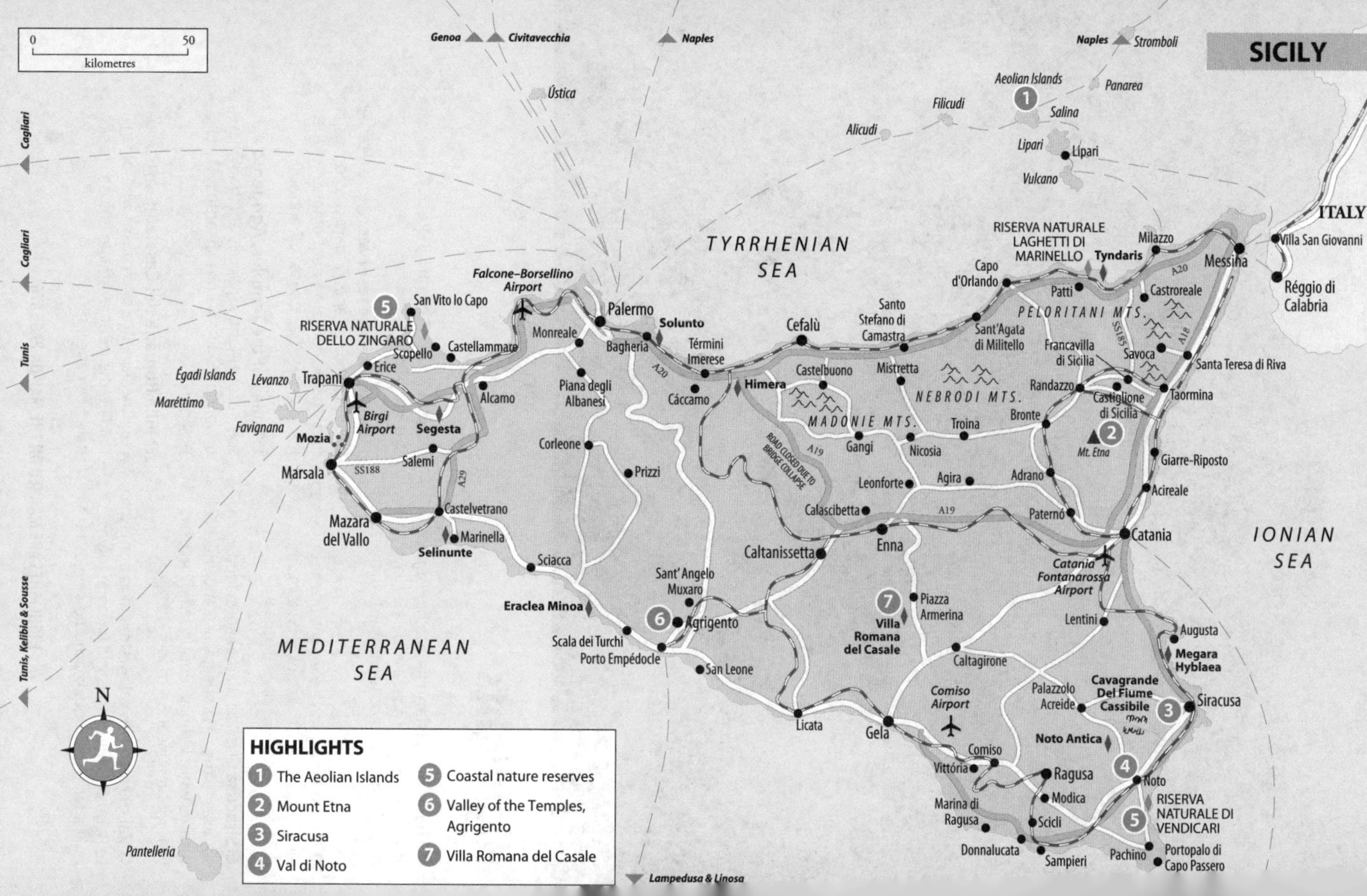

SICILY
0
50
kilometres
Genoa
Civitavecchia
Naples
Naples
Stromboli
Ústica
Aeolian Islands
Panarea
Filicudi
Salina
Alicudi
Lipari
Lipari
Vulcano
ITALY
Villa San Giovanni
Réggio di Calabria
Cagliari
Cagliari
Tunis
Tunis, Kelibia & Sousse
TYRRHENIAN SEA
IONIAN SEA
MEDITERRANEAN SEA
RISERVA NATURALE LAGHETTI DI MARINELLO
Tyndaris
Milazzo
Messina
Capo d'Orlando
Patti
Castroreale
Falcone–Borsellino Airport
San Vito lo Capo
RISERVA NATURALE DELLO ZINGARO
Palermo
Solunto
Santo Stefano di Camastra
Cefalù
PELORITANI MTS.
Sant'Agata di Militello
Francavilla di Sicilia
Savoca
Santa Teresa di Riva
Scopello
Castellammare
Monreale
Bagheria
Términi Imerese
Erice
Égadi Islands
Lévanzo
Trapani
Castelbuono
Mistretta
Randazzo
Castiglione di Sicilia
Taormina
Maréttimo
Alcamo
Piana degli Albanesi
Cáccamo
Himera
NEBRODI MTS.
Favignana
Birgi Airport
Segesta
MADONIE MTS.
Troina
Bronte
Mt. Etna
Mozia
Corleone
Gangi
Nicosia
Salemi
Giarre-Riposto
Marsala
SS188
Prizzi
ROAD CLOSED DUE TO BRIDGE COLLAPSE
A19
Leonforte
Agira
Adrano
A29
Acireale
Mazara del Vallo
Castelvetrano
Calascibetta
A19
Paternò
Marinella
Catania
Selinunte
Sciacca
Caltanissetta
Enna
Catania Fontanarossa Airport
Sant' Angelo Muxaro
Eraclea Minoa
Piazza Armerina
Agrigento
Villa Romana del Casale
Lentini
Augusta
Scala dei Turchi
Porto Empédocle
Megara Hyblaea
San Leone
Caltagirone
Cavagrande Del Fiume Cassibile
Palazzolo Acreide
Comiso Airport
Siracusa
Licata
Gela
Noto Antica
Comiso
Vittória
Ragusa
Noto
Modica
RISERVA NATURALE DI VENDICARI
Marina di Ragusa
Scicli
Donnalucata
Sampieri
Pachino
Portopalo di Capo Passero
Pantelleria
Lampedusa & Linosa
N
A20
A20
A18
SS185
HIGHLIGHTS
1 The Aeolian Islands
2 Mount Etna
3 Siracusa
4 Val di Noto
5 Coastal nature reserves
6 Valley of the Temples, Agrigento
7 Villa Romana del Casale

SICILIAN CUISINE – SWEETS, STREET FOOD AND SARDINES

Sicily's food has been influenced by the island's endless list of invaders, including Greeks, Arabs, Normans and Spanish, even the English, each of them leaving behind them traces of their gastronomy. Dishes such as orange salads, unctuous sweet-sour aubergine and, of course, couscous evoke North Africa, while Sicily's most distinctive pasta dish, *spaghetti con le sarde* – with sardines, pine nuts, wild fennel and raisins – is thought to date back to the first foray into Sicily, at Mazara, by an Arab force in 827. The story goes that the army cooks were ordered to forage around for food, and found sardines at the port, wild fennel growing in the fields and raisins drying in the vineyards. Religious festivals too, are often associated with foods: for example at San Giuseppe, on March 19, altars are made of bread, and at Easter you will find *pasticcerie* full of sacrifical lambs made of marzipan, and Gardens of Adonis (trays of sprouting lentils, chickpeas and other pulses) placed before church altars to symbolize the rebirth of Christ. The last has its roots in fertility rites that predate even the arrival of the Greeks to the island.

Sicily is famous for its **sweets** too, like rich cassata, sponge cake filled with sweet ricotta cream and covered with pistachio marzipan, and cannoli – crunchy tubes of deep-fried pastry stuffed with sweet ricotta. **Street food** is ubiquitous in cities such as Palermo, dating back to the eighteenth century when wood was rationed, and few people were able to cook at home: deep-fried rice balls, potato croquettes and chickpea-flour fritters compete with dinky-sized pizzas. Naturally, **fish** such as anchovies, sardines, tuna and swordfish are abundant – indeed, it was in Sicily that the technique of canning tuna was invented. **Cheeses** are pecorino, provolone, caciocavallo and, of course, the sheep's-milk ricotta which goes into so many of the sweet dishes.

Traditionally wine-making in Sicily was associated mainly with sweet wines such as Malvasia and the fortified Marsala – in the nineteenth century many a fortune was made providing Malvasia to the Napoleonic army – but the island has also made a name for itself as a producer of quality everyday wines found in supermarkets throughout Italy, such as Corvo, Regaleali, Nicosia, Settesoli and Tria. There are superb wines too – notably Andrea Franchetti's prize-winning Passopisciaro, from the north slopes of Etna – as well as wines across a wide price range from producers such as Tasca d'Almerita, Baglio Hopps, Planeta, Morgante and Murgo.

GETTING AROUND — SICILY

By train Getting around Sicily by train can be a protracted business. Services along the northern and eastern coasts (Messina–Palermo and Messina–Siracusa) are extensions of – or connect with – trains from Rome and Naples, and delays of over an hour are frequent.

By bus Buses are quicker than trains, though you should expect little (if any) service anywhere on a Sun. Local operators include AST (T 091 620 8111, W aziendasicilianatrasporti.it); Cuffaro (T 091 616 1510, W cuffaro.info); Inter-bus (T 091 616 7919, W interbus.it); Giuntabus (Milazzo to Catania airport) (T 090 673 782, W giuntabus.com); Giuntabus Trasporti (Milazzo to Messina) (T 090 675 749, W giuntabus trasporti.com); SAIS (T 091 616 6028, W saisautolinee.it); SAIStrasporti (T 091 617 1141, W saistrasporti.it); Salemi (T 091 617 5411, W autoservizisalemi.it); Segesta (T 092 398 1120, W segesta.it).

Palermo and around

PALERMO is fast, brash, filthy and – at times – insane. Exotic Arabic cupolas float above exuberant Baroque facades, high-fashion shops compete with raffish street markets, and walls of graffitied municipal cement abut the crumbling shells of collapsing *palazzi* sprouting clusters of prickly pear. Add to this a constant soundtrack of sputtering, swirling traffic, and some of the most anarchic driving in Europe, and you'll quickly see that this is not a city for the faint-hearted. With Sicily's greatest concentration of sights, and the biggest historic centre in Italy bar Rome, Palermo is a complex, multilayered city that can easily feel overwhelming if you try to do or see too much. The best thing to do here is just to wander as the fancy takes you, sifting through the city's jumbled layers of crumbling architecture, along deserted back alleys, then suddenly emerging in

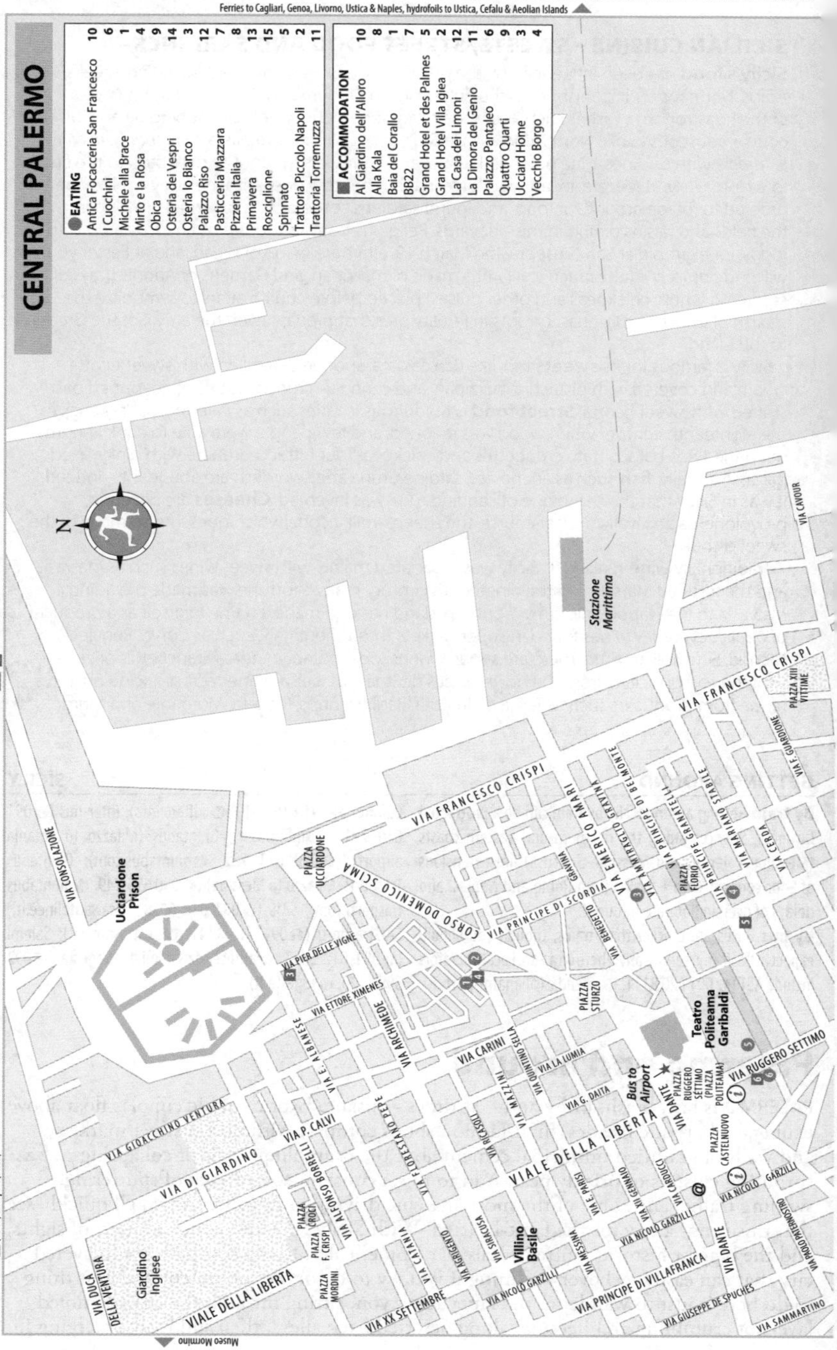

16

CENTRAL PALERMO

EATING

Antica Focacceria San Francesco	10
I Cuochini	6
Michele alla Brace	1
Mirto e la Rosa	4
Obica	9
Osteria dei Vespri	14
Osteria lo Bianco	3
Palazzo Riso	12
Pasticceria Mazzara	7
Pizzeria Italia	8
Primavera	13
Rosciglione	15
Spinnato	5
Trattoria Piccolo Napoli	2
Trattoria Torremuzza	11

ACCOMMODATION

Al Giardino dell'Alloro	10
Alla Kala	8
Baia del Corallo	1
BB22	7
Grand Hotel et des Palmes	5
Grand Hotel Villa Igiea	2
La Casa dei Limoni	12
La Dimora del Genio	11
Palazzo Pantaleo	6
Quattro Quarti	9
Ucciard Home	3
Vecchio Borgo	4

Ferries to Cagliari, Genoa, Livorno, Ustica & Naples, hydrofoils to Ustica, Cefalù & Aeolian Islands

2

1 (12km) & Airport (31km)

Museo Mormino

N

Stazione Marittima

Ucciardone Prison

Piazza Ucciardone

Giardino Inglese

Villino Basile

Teatro Politeama Garibaldi

Bus to Airport

Piazza Ruggero Settimo (Piazza Politeama)

Piazza Castelnuovo

Piazza Sturzo

Piazza Florio

Piazza XIII Vittime

Piazza Croci

Piazza F. Crispi

Piazza Mordini

Via Consolazione

Via Francesco Crispi

Via Cavour

Corso Domenico Scina

Via Principe di Scordia

Via Emerico Amari

Via Gravina

Via Ammiraglio Gravina

Via Principe di Belmonte

Via Principe Granatelli

Via Mariano Stabile

Via Cerda

Via F. Guardione

Via Benedetto

Via Pier delle Vigne

Via Ettore Ximenes

Via E. Albanese

Via Archimede

Via Carini

Via Quintino Sella

Via La Lumia

Via Mazzini

Via G. Daita

Via Ruggero Settimo

Via Dante

Viale della Libertà

Via Ricasoli

Via Gioacchino Ventura

Via di Giardino

Via P. Calvi

Via Alfonso Borrelli

Via Florestano Pepe

Via Duca della Verdura

Via Catania

Via Agrigento

Via Siracusa

Via Messina

Via E. Parisi

Via XII Gennaio

Via Carducci

Via Nicolò Garzilli

Via Paolo Paternostro

Via XX Settembre

Via Principe di Villafranca

Via Giuseppe de Spuches

Via Sammartino

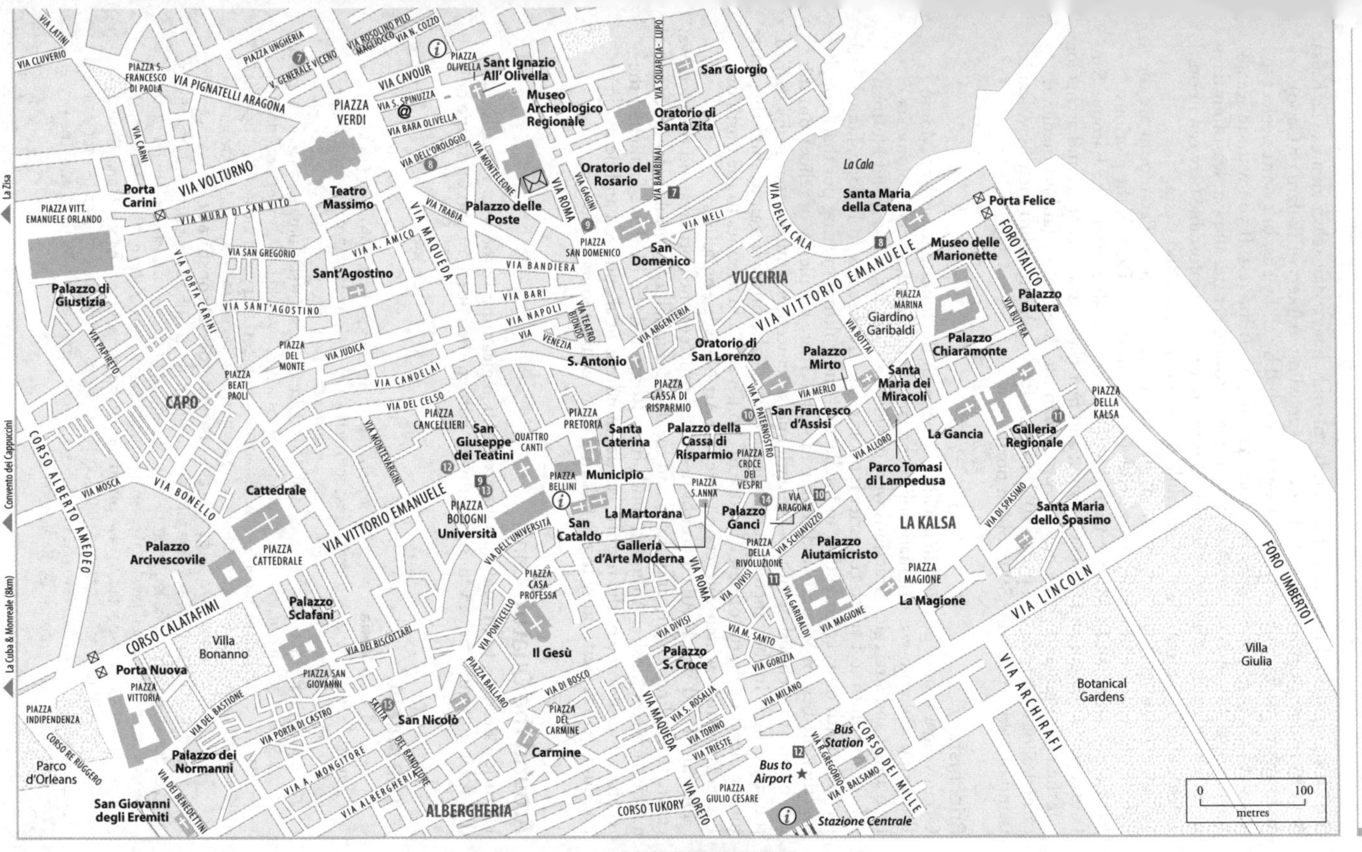
La Zisa
Convento dei Cappuccini
La Cuba & Monreale (8km)
VIA LATINI
VIA CLUVERIO
PIAZZA S. FRANCESCO DI PAOLA
VIA PIGNATELLI ARAGONA
PIAZZA UNGHERIA
V. GENERALE VICENO
VIA ROSOLINO PILO MAGLIOCCO
VIA N. COZZO
VIA CAVOUR
PIAZZA OLIVELLA
Sant Ignazio All' Olivella
Museo Archeologico Regionale
VIA SQUARCIA - LUPO
San Giorgio
Oratorio di Santa Zita
PIAZZA VERDI
VIA S. SPINUZZA
VIA BARA OLIVELLA
VIA DELL'OROLOGIO
VIA CARNI
VIA VOLTURNO
Porta Carini
Teatro Massimo
VIA MONTELEONE
Palazzo delle Poste
VIA ROMA
VIA GAGINI
Oratorio del Rosario
VIA BAMBINAI
La Cala
VIA DELLA CALA
Santa Maria della Catena
Porta Felice
FORO ITALICO
PIAZZA VITT. EMANUELE ORLANDO
VIA MURA DI SAN VITO
VIA TRABIA
VIA MAQUEDA
VIA A. AMICO
PIAZZA SAN DOMENICO
San Domenico
VIA MELI
Museo delle Marionette
VIA SAN GREGORIO
VIA BANDIERA
Sant'Agostino
VUCCIRIA
VIA VITTORIO EMANUELE
Palazzo Butera
VIA BUTERA
Palazzo di Giustizia
VIA PORTA CARINI
VIA SANT'AGOSTINO
VIA BARI
VIA NAPOLI
VIA TEATRO BIONDO
VIA ARGENTERIA
PIAZZA MARINA
Giardino Garibaldi
VIA BOTTAI
Palazzo Chiaramonte
VIA PAPIRETO
PIAZZA DEL MONTE
VIA JUDICA
VIA VENEZIA
Oratorio di San Lorenzo
Palazzo Mirto
Santa Maria dei Miracoli
S. Antonio
PIAZZA BEATI PAOLI
VIA CANDELAI
PIAZZA CASSA DI RISPARMIO
VIA MERLO
VIA A. PATERNOSTRO
PIAZZA DELLA KALSA
CAPO
VIA DEL CELSO
PIAZZA PRETORIA
San Francesco d'Assisi
La Gancia
Galleria Regionale
PIAZZA CANCELLIERI
VIA MONTEVARGINI
San Giuseppe dei Teatini
QUATTRO CANTI
Santa Caterina
Palazzo della Cassa di Risparmio
PIAZZA CROCE DEI VESPRI
VIA ALLORO
Parco Tomasi di Lampedusa
CORSO ALBERTO AMEDEO
VIA MOSCA
VIA BONELLO
Cattedrale
PIAZZA BELLINI
Municipio
PIAZZA S. ANNA
VIA ARAGONA
VIA DI SPASIMO
Santa Maria dello Spasimo
PIAZZA BOLOGNI
Università
La Martorana
Palazzo Ganci
LA KALSA
Palazzo Arcivescovile
PIAZZA CATTEDRALE
VIA DELL'UNIVERSITÀ
San Cataldo
Galleria d'Arte Moderna
VIA SCHIAVUZZO
PIAZZA DELLA RIVOLUZIONE
Palazzo Aiutamicristo
FORO UMBERTO I
PIAZZA CASA PROFESSA
VIA DIVISI
PIAZZA MAGIONE
La Magione
VIA GARIBALDI
VIA MAGIONE
VIA LINCOLN
CORSO CALATAFIMI
Palazzo Sclafani
Villa Bonanno
VIA PONTICELLO
VIA DEI BISCOTTARI
Il Gesù
VIA M. SANTO
Palazzo S. Croce
VIA GORIZIA
Villa Giulia
Porta Nuova
PIAZZA VITTORIA
PIAZZA SAN GIOVANNI
PIAZZA BALLARO
VIA DI BOSCO
VIA MILANO
VIA ARCHIRAFI
Botanical Gardens
PIAZZA INDIPENDENZA
VIA DEL BASTIONE
SALITA
San Nicolò
PIAZZA DEL CARMINE
VIA S. ROSALIA
VIA TORINO
CORSO RE RUGGERO
VIA PORTA DI CASTRO
Carmine
VIA TRIESTE
Bus Station
CORSO DEI MILLE
Parco d'Orleans
Palazzo dei Normanni
VIA A. MONGITORE
DEL BANDITORE
Bus to Airport
VIA R. GREGORIO
VIA P. BALSAMO
VIA DEI BENEDETTINI
VIA ALBERGHERIA
PIAZZA GIULIO CESARE
0
100
metres
San Giovanni degli Eremiti
ALBERGHERIA
CORSO TUKORY
VIA ORETO
Stazione Centrale

the midst of an ebullient street market. If you only have a day, select an area (La Kalsa, with its two museums, for example, or the sprawling markets of Ballarò or Capo), and explore: have a couple of target sights in mind by all means, but don't neglect to wander up any particular alley or street that takes your interest. If you want to see all the major sights and explore the labyrinthine historical centre, allow at least four days in cool weather. In summer, Palermo is far too hot to be comfortable between noon and around 5pm, so avoid it or schedule in a leisurely lunch and siesta.

The essential sights are pretty central and easy to cover on foot. Paramount are the hybrid Cattedrale and nearby Palazzo dei Normanni (Royal Palace); the glorious Norman churches of La Martorana and San Giovanni degli Eremiti; the Baroque San Giuseppe dei Teatini and Santa Caterina; and first-class museums of art and archeology.

If the urban grit and grime become overwhelming, head to the famous medieval cathedral of Monreale (see page 890), or take a ferry or hydrofoil to the tiny volcanic island of Ustica (see page 890), 60km northwest.

Brief history

Occupying a superb position in a wide bay beneath the limestone bulk of Monte Pellegrino, Palermo was originally a Phoenician, then a Carthaginian colony. Its mercantile and strategic attractions were obvious, and under Saracen and Norman rule in the ninth to twelfth centuries it became the greatest city in Europe, famed both for the wealth of its court and as an intellectual and cultural melting pot that brought together the best of Western and Arabic thought. There are plenty of relics from this era, but it's the rebuilding of the sixteenth and seventeenth centuries that really shaped the city centre. In the nineteenth century, wealthy Palermitani began to shun the centre for the elegant suburbs of new "European" boulevards and avenues to the north of Piazza Politeama, which still retain some fine Art Nouveau buildings.

During World War II Allied bombs destroyed much of the port area and the medieval centre (including seventy churches), and for decades much of central Palermo remained a ramshackle bombsite. Although funds from Rome and the EU have facilitated the regeneration of some of the historic centre, hundreds of abandoned and decaying buildings remain testimony to the fact that there is still a long way to go.

Around the Quattro Canti

Historic Palermo sits around the **Quattro Canti**, a gleaming Baroque crossroads that divides it into quadrants. On the southwest corner, the church of **San Giuseppe dei**

THE MAFIA

Whatever else the **Mafia** is, it isn't an organization that impinges upon the lives of tourists. For most Sicilians, mafia with a small *m* is so much a way of life and habit of mind that they don't even think about it. If a Sicilian lends a neighbour a bag of sugar, for example, both will immediately be aware of a favour owed, and the debtor uncomfortable until the favour has been returned, and balance restored. As for allegiance to friends, it would be very rare indeed for a Sicilian, asked to recommend a hotel or restaurant, to suggest that you go to one that does not belong to a friend, relative, or someone who forms part of his personal network of favours.

The Mafia, with a capital M, began life as an **early medieval conspiracy**, created to protect the family from oppressive intrusions of the state. Existing to this day, Sicily continues to endure this system of allegiance, preferment and patronage of massive self-perpetuating proportions, from which few local people profit. In many parts of the region, owners of shops and businesses are expected to give **pizzo** (protection money) to the local Mafia. Though efforts to resist the Mafia continue, with local businesses in Palermo and Siracusa, for example, banding together to refuse to pay pizzo, it is not uncommon for the Mafia to have the power to close down the enterprises of refuseniks.

Teatini (mid-July to mid-Sept Mon–Sat 7.30–11am & 6.15–8pm, Sun 8.30am–1.15pm & 6–8pm; mid-Sept to mid-July Mon–Sat 7.30am–noon & 5.30–8pm, Sun 8.30am–1.15pm & 6–8pm), begun in 1612, is the most harmonious of the city's Baroque churches, its grey columns cutting through the opulence of stucco, fresco and coloured marble. Outside, across Via Maqueda, is **Piazza Pretoria**, floodlit at night to highlight the nude figures of its great central fountain, a racy Florentine design, bought secondhand by the city's dignitaries in 1573. The piazza also holds the restored **Municipio**, while towering above both square and fountain is the massive flank of **Santa Caterina** (April–Oct Mon–Sat 9.30am–1.30pm & 3–7pm, Sun 9.30am–1.30pm; Nov Mon–Sat 9.30am–1pm & 3–5.30pm, Sun 9.30am–1pm; Dec–March daily 9.30am–1pm), Sicilian Baroque at its most exuberant, every centimetre of the enormous interior iced with white stucco and pastel frescoes.

San Cataldo

Piazza Bellini 3 • March–Oct Mon–Sat 9am–1pm & 3.30–6.30pm, Sun 9am–1pm; Nov–Feb daily 9am–1pm, Dec 22–Jan 6 daily 9am–5pm • €2.50

Around the corner from Santa Caterina, Piazza Bellini is the site of two contrasting churches. Here, the little Saracenic red domes belong to **San Cataldo**, a perfectly proportioned twelfth-century Byzantine chapel flooded with light. Never decorated, it retains a good mosaic floor.

La Martorana

Piazza Bellini 3 • Mon–Sat 9.30am–1pm & 3.30–5.30pm (6.30pm in summer), Sun 9–10.30am • €2 • T 091 616 1692

San Cataldo's understatement is more than offset by the splendid intricacy of the adjacent **La Martorana** – one of the finest survivors of the medieval city. With a Norman foundation, the church received a Baroque makeover in 1588. Happily, the alterations don't detract from the power of the interior, entered through the slim twelfth-century campanile, which retains its ribbed arches and slender columns. A series of spectacular, twelfth-century Greek **mosaics** is laid on and around the columns supporting the main cupola. Two original mosaic panels have been set in frames on the walls just inside the entrance to the church: a kneeling George of Antioch (the church's founder) dedicating La Martorana to the Virgin, and King Roger being crowned by Christ.

16

The Albergheria

The **Albergheria** district just to the northwest of the train station hasn't changed substantially for several hundred years. A maze of tiny streets and tall leaning buildings, it's an engaging place to wander, with much of the central area taken up by the exuberant chaos of the **Ballarò street market** (Mon–Sat 7am–2pm). On Piazza Casa Professa, the Baroque church of **Il Gesù**, or Casa Professa (Daily 6.30am–1.30pm) was the first Jesuit foundation in Sicily, its interior an iconic example of Palermo Baroque. In nearby **Piazza del Carmine**, with its heaving vegetable stalls, unmarked drinking dens and gutsy snack-stalls, you should look upwards to glimpse the glinting majolica-tiled dome of the **Chiesa del Carmine**, supported by muscle-bound stucco telamons.

San Giovanni degli Eremiti

Via dei Benedettini • Tues–Sun 9am–6.30pm • €6 • T 091 651 5019

At the westernmost edge of the Albergheria, the deconsecrated church of **San Giovanni degli Eremiti** (St John of the Hermits) is the most obviously Arabic of the city's Norman relics, with five ochre domes topping a small church that was built in 1132 upon the remains of a mosque. It was founded by Roger II, who favoured the monks of San Giovanni by granting them 21 barrels of tuna a year. A path leads up through citrus trees to the church, behind which lie delicate late thirteenth-century cloisters – perfect twin columns with slightly pointed arches surrounding a garden.

Palazzo dei Normanni

Piazza Indipendenza • Mon–Sat 8.15am–5.40pm, Sun 8.15am–1pm; last entry 45min before closing; the palace is currently undergoing restoration and is also the seat of the Sicilian government, so opening hours can be irregular; check the website for updates • €12; €10 Tues–Thurs when the Royal Apartments are closed during Sicilian parliament sessions • 091 626 2833, federicosecondo.org

Originally built by the Saracens, the **Palazzo dei Normanni** was enlarged considerably by the Normans (hence its name), under whom it housed the most magnificent of medieval European courts – a noted centre of poetic and artistic achievement. Most of the interior is now taken up by the Sicilian Regional Parliament, which explains the security guards and frequent closures of all or part of the complex – be prepared to queue.

Sala di Ruggero and the Cappella Palatina

The showpiece of the Royal Apartments is the **Sala di Ruggero**, one of the earliest parts of the palace and richly covered with a twelfth-century mosaic of hunting scenes. The highlight of the palace, however, is the beautiful **Cappella Palatina**, the private royal chapel of Roger II, built between 1132 and 1143, and the undisputed artistic gem of central Palermo, its cupola, three apses and nave entirely covered in mosaics of outstanding quality. The oldest are those in the cupola and apses, probably completed in 1150 by Byzantine artists; those in the nave are made by local craftsmen, finished twenty-odd years later and depicting Old and New Testament scenes. The colours are vivid and, as usual in Byzantine art, the powerful image of Christ as Pantocrator (creator of everything) dominates. Aside from the mosaics, the chapel has a delightful and recently restored Arabic ceiling with richly carved wooden stalactites, a patterned marble floor and an impressive marble Norman candlestick (by the pulpit), 4m high and contorted by manic carvings.

Cattedrale

Via Vittorio Emanuele • Mon–Sat 9am–5.30pm, Sun 9am-1pm; treasury Nov–Feb Mon–Sat 9.30am–1.30pm; March–Oct Mon–Sat 9.30am–5.30pm • Free; treasury and crypt €3, roof €5• 091 334373

Spanning Corso Vittorio Emanuele, the early sixteenth-century **Porta Nuova** commemorates Charles V's Tunisian crusade with grim, moustachioed, turbaned prisoners adorning the western entrance. This gate marked the extent of the late medieval city, and the long road beyond heads to Monreale.

The Corso runs back towards the centre, past the huge bulk of the Norman **Cattedrale.** The triple-apsed eastern end and graceful matching towers date from 1185, and despite the Catalan-Gothic facade and arches, there's enough Norman carving and detail to rescue the exterior from mere curiosity value. The same is not true, however, of the sterile Neoclassical interior. The only items of interest are the fine fifteenth-century portal and wooden doors and **royal tombs**, containing the remains of Sicilian monarchs – including Frederick II and his wife, Constance of Aragon.

There's also a **treasury** to the right of the choir, the highlights of which are a jewel-and-pearl-encrusted skullcap and three simple, precious rings, all enterprisingly removed from the tomb of Constance in the eighteenth century. In recent years it has become possible to climb to the roof, for an incredible rooftop vista of the city.

The Capo

From the cathedral you can bear left, around the apses, and up into the **Capo** quarter, whose tight web of impoverished streets is home to yet another market. Just around the corner from Piazza del Monte is the fine church of **Sant'Agostino** (Mon–Sat 7am–noon & 4–6pm, Sun 7am–noon; free), built in the thirteenth century. Above its main door (on Via Raimondo) there's a latticework rose window, and inside, a tranquil sixteenth-century cloister. The stalls of the daily **clothes market** along **Via Sant'Agostino** run all the way down to Via Maqueda and beyond, the streets off to the left gradually

becoming wider and more nondescript as they broach the area around the monumental Neoclassic **Teatro Massimo**, supposedly the largest theatre in Italy. To appreciate the interior fully, take a **tour** (Tues–Sun 9.30am–6pm, except during rehearsals; €8; T091 605 3267, Ⓦteatromassimo.it), or attend one of the classical concerts or operas held here between October and June.

The theatre marks the dividing line between old and new Palermo. Via Maqueda becomes the far smarter **Via Ruggero Settimo**, which cuts up through the gridded shopping streets to the huge double square made up of **Piazza Castelnuovo** and **Piazza Ruggero Settimo** (commonly referred to as Piazza Politeama). Dominating the whole lot is Palermo's other massive theatre, the **Politeama Garibaldi**, topped by a flamboyant statue group of sword-brandishing figures on leaping horses.

The Vucciria and around

Tucked into the wedge of streets between Via Roma and Corso Vittorio Emanuele, the morning **Vucciria market**, once the most famous market in Palermo, is now a shadow of its former self, though it still has several basic bars and fish trattorias. Beyond the market, the thumb-shaped inlet of **La Cala** was once Palermo's main port, stretching as far inland as Via Roma: during the sixteenth century silting caused the water to recede to its current position, and La Cala now does duty as a yachting marina.

The northern limit of the market is marked by the distinctive church of **San Domenico** (Tues–Sat: 9am–noon, also open Mon in May and Oct; free), with a fine eighteenth-century facade and tombs inside containing a host of famous Sicilians. Behind the church, the **Oratorio del Rosario** (Mon–Sat 9am–1pm; free but tipping is usual) contains exuberant decor by the seventeeth-century maestro of stucco, Giacomo Serpotta (see below), and a masterful Van Dyck altarpiece, painted in 1628 before the artist fled Palermo for Genoa to escape the plague.

16

Museo Archeologico Regionale

Piazza Olivella 24 • Partially closed for restoration; ground floor only open Tues–Sat 9am–6pm, Sun 9am–1pm • €6 • Ⓣ091 611 6806 • Tickets also available online at Ⓦcoopculture.it

Although the **Museo Archeologico Regionale** has been closed for restoration for years, small sections open sporadically, while occasional **temporary exhibitions** offer a chance to see some of its magnificent collection of artefacts, which spans the island's Phoenician, Greek and Roman heritage. Highlights include the immense Punic tombs bearing the sculptured forms of their occupants; spectacular finds from the Greek temples of Selinunte, including sculpted panels of Perseus beheading Medusa; and beautifully preserved Roman mosaics from Marsala.

Oratorio di Santa Zita

Via Squarcialupo • Mon–Fri 9am–1pm; ring the bell if closed, or ask in the church in front • €5 • Ⓣ091 332779

The **Oratorio di Santa Zita** (also known as Santa Cita or San Mamiliano) holds one of Giacomo Serpotta's finest stucco extravaganzas – the *Battle of Lepanto*. Born in Palermo in 1656, Serpotta specialized in decorating oratories with moulded plasterwork in ornamental frames, creating three-dimensional extravaganzas featuring life-sized figures surrounded by plaster draperies, swags of fruit, bouquets of flowers and other Baroque exotica.

La Kalsa

The regenerated **La Kalsa** district, in old Palermo's southeastern quarter, is the city's most appealing area for nightlife (see page 888), in particular the streets between Piazza Garibaldi and Piazza Magione, which are packed with bars and pubs. It's here too, that you'll find some of Palermo's most remarkable buildings and churches, as

well as the city's only central park, **Villa Giulia**, which is home to an extensive **botanical garden** (daily 9am–1hr before sunset; €5; ⓦortobotanico.unipa.it).

La Magione and Santa Maria dello Spasimo

Built in 1151, the simple, sparse Norman church of **La Magione** (Piazza Magione 44; Mon–Sat 8.30am–noon & 3–6.30pm, Sun 9am–1.30pm; Donation requested; ⓣ091 617 0596), has beautiful cloisters and a chapel, a rare plaster preparation of a crucifixion fresco and a lovely small Arab-Norman column carved with a Koranic inscription. The church backs onto the desolate square of **La Kalsa** (its name is from the Arabic *khalisa*, meaning "pure"), at the centre of the eponymous area. La Kalsa was subjected to saturation bombing during World War II, because of its proximity to the port, with the area now occupied by the square taking the brunt of it.

Across the square is the atmospheric complex of **Santa Maria dello Spasimo** (Piazza Kalsa; Daily 8–11am & 4.30–6pm, closed Thurs morning; ⓣ091 6171658), a former church, now roofless except for its late Gothic apse, once used as a leper house and warehouse. It holds night-time jazz concerts in the courtyard.

Galleria Regionale di Palazzo Abatellis

Via Alloro 4 • Tues–Fri 9am–6pm, Sat, Sun 9am–1.30pm • €8, €10 with Palazzo Mirto • ⓣ091 623 0011, ⓦregione.sicilia.it/beniculturali/palazzoabatellis

Housed in the fifteenth-century Palazzo Abatellis, Sicily's Galleria Regionale is a stunning medieval art collection. Inside, there's sculpture downstairs, and paintings upstairs, the one exception being a magnificent fifteenth-century fresco, the *Triumph of Death*, which covers an entire wall of the former chapel. The other masterpiece on the ground floor is a calm, perfectly studied, white marble bust of *Eleanora of Aragon* by the fifteenth-century artist Francesco Laurana. Upstairs, there are thirteenth- and fourteenth-century Sicilian works, Byzantine in style, and a fine collection of works by Antonello da Messina (1430–79), including three small portraits of Sts *Gregory*, *Jerome* and *Augustine* and a ground-breaking*Annunciation* in which the angel is off-canvas.

16

Galleria d'Arte Moderna

Via Sant'Anna 21 • Tues–Sun 9.30am–6.30pm; ticket office closes at 5.30pm • €7 • ⓣ091 843 1605, ⓦgampalermo.it

The Convento di Sant'Anna, on Piazza Sant'Anna, has been stunningly restored to house the **Galleria d'Arte Moderna**, a collection of nineteenth- and twentieth-century Sicilian art. The works here are displayed thematically (portraits, nudes, mythology, seascapes, landscapes, etc) to great effect. Its café, spilling into the courtyard in summer, is a lovely place for lunch or an aperitif.

Palazzo Mirto

Via Merlo 2 • Tues–Sat 9am–6pm, Sun 10am–1pm • €6, €10 with with Galleria Regionale

NIGHTMARE IN PALERMO: THE CATACOMBS

Home to some eight thousand mummified bodies, the gruesome **Catacombe dei Cappuccini** (daily 9am–1pm & 3–6pm; Nov–March closed Sun afternoon; €3; ⓣ091 652 4156, ⓦcatacombepalermo.it) is a popular attraction for horror-movie fans. The bodies were preserved by various chemical and drying processes – including the use of vinegar and arsenic baths – then dressed in a suit of clothes and placed in niches along rough-cut subterranean corridors. In different caverns reserved for men, women, clergy, lawyers and surgeons, some of the bodies are decomposed beyond recognition, others complete with skin, hair and eyes. Those that aren't arranged along the walls lie in stacked glass coffins, and it's an unnerving experience to walk among them. The *Catacombe* lie on the outskirts of Palermo, in Piazza dei Cappuccini: take bus #327 from Piazza Indipendenza southwest along Via dei Cappuccini as far as Via Pindemonte.

The late-eighteenth-century **Palazzo Mirto** is one of Palermo's few buildings to retain its original furnishings. The exquisite ceilings, intimate Chinese Room, imposing baldacchino, vibrant tapestries and overblown Baroque fountain give an insight into palazzo life, though the family's more modest living quarters have also been preserved, while visits also take in the servants' kitchen and the carriages in the stables.

ARRIVAL AND DEPARTURE — PALERMO

BY PLANE

Palermo's Falcone Borsellino airport (☎800 541 880, ⓦgesap.it) is at Punta Raisi, 31km west of the city. Buses (Prestia & Comandè; ☎091 580 457, ⓦprestiaecomande.it) run into the city (5am, then every 30min 6.30am–12.30am; 45min), and stop outside Politeama theatre, Stazione Marittima, and at Stazione Centrale; tickets €6.30 online or on board, €11 return. From Stazione Centrale, departures are at 4am, and then every 30min from 5am until 10.30pm. Trains (€5.80) run from the airport to Stazione Centrale from 7.27am until 9.42pm, leaving at 27 and 42 past the hour in between. From Stazione Centrale they leave at 5.45am, 6.05 am and then every 30 minutes until 8.20pm.

BY TRAIN

All trains arrive at the Stazione Centrale at the southern end of Via Roma. Bus #101 runs from the station along Via Roma to Via della Libertà. It has its own priority lane, so is somewhat faster than most of the city's other services. In general bus connections within Sicily are faster, more frequent and reliable than the trains, but the following destinations have good services.

Destinations Agrigento (12 daily; 2hr 15min); Cefalù (hourly; 45min–1hr); Messina (13 daily; 3hr–4hr); Milazzo (14 daily; 2hr 30min–3hr).

BY BUS

Bus station The majority of country- and island-wide buses operate from the recently opened Piazza Cairoli bus station alongside the train station.

Destinations Agrigento (5 daily; 2hr 30min); Castelbuono (5 daily Mon–Sat, 1 daily Sun; 1hr 40min–2hr 30min); Castellammare del Golfo (6 daily Mon–Sat, 1–3 daily Sun; 50min); Catania (hourly; 2hr 40min); Cefalù (5 daily; 1hr); Corleone (hourly Mon–Sat; 1hr 30min); Enna (5–7 daily; 1hr 35min–1hr 50min); Marsala (hourly; 2hr 30min); Messina (5 daily Mon–Sat; 2hr 40min); Piana degli Albanesi (6 daily Mon–Sat; 1hr); Piazza Armerina (hourly; 2hr 15min); Siracusa (3 daily; 3hr 15min); Trapani (Segesta; every 30min–1hr; 2hr).

BY FERRY OR HYDROFOIL

All ferry and hydrofoil services dock at the Stazione Marittima, just off Via Francesco Crispi. A free *navetta* bus meets arrivals and will take you to the port entrance, from where it's a 10min walk up Via E. Amari to Piazza Castelnuovo. Bus #139 connects the port with Stazione Centrale, though it is rather infrequent, so it is better to walk up Via E. Amari to Piazza Politeama from where buses #101 or #102, and the *linea rossa*, run regularly to the train station. The services detailed here refer to the period from June to Sept; expect frequencies to be greatly reduced or suspended outside these months. Hydrofoils are run by Liberty Lines (ⓦlibertylines.it).

Ferry destinations Cagliari (1 or less weekly; 12hr; ⓦtirrenia.it); Civitavecchia (1–3 weekly; 14hr; ⓦgnv.it); Genoa (1 daily; 21hr); Naples (1–2 daily; 10hr; ⓦgnv.it and ⓦtirrenia.it); Tunis (1 weekly; 10hr; ⓦgnv.it); Ustica (1 daily; 2hr 20min; ⓦcarontetourist.it).

Hydrofoil destinations Aeolian islands (all 1 daily June–Sept only) – Alicudi (2hr), Filicudi (2hr 30min), Rinella (3hr 15min), Santa Marina Salina (3hr 30min), Lipari (4hr), Vulcano (4hr 25min), Panarea (4hr 40min), Stromboli (5hr 15min); Ustica (2 daily; 90min).

16

GETTING AROUND

BY BUS

City buses (AMAT; ☎091 350 111, infoline ☎848 800 817 or from a mobile ☎199 240 800, ⓦwww.amat.pa.it) cover every corner of Palermo as well as Monreale and Mondello. There's a flat fare of €1.40 valid for 90min, or you can buy an all-day ticket for €3.50. Buy them from AMAT booths outside Stazione Centrale, at the southern end of Viale della Libertà, in *tabacchi* and anywhere else you see the AMAT sign, or from the driver for a supplement of €0.40. Validate tickets in the machine at the back of the bus as you board – spot checks are carried out by plainclothes inspectors. The main city bus rank is outside Stazione Centrale and buses run until midnight (11.30pm on Sun).

BY TRAM

Palermo has a new tram system, also run by Amat, but it is of little use to most tourists, with routes designed to connect to the suburbs.

BY CAR

Driving in the city is best avoided. Overtaking on both sides is the norm, and indicating virtually unheard of. Black-

market parking attendants will guide you to a space and charge you a small amount (around €1/hr), while meters are installed in some parts of the centre.

Car rental Avis, right by the port at Via Francesco Crispi 115 (t 091 586 940); Hertz, Via Messina 7/E (t 091 323 439); Sicily By Car, Via Mariano Stabile 6/A (t 091 581 045). All of these also have desks at the airport.

BY TAXI

There are taxi ranks at the airport, train and bus stations, and all the main squares. Palermo's two taxi companies – Auto Radio Taxi (t 091 513 311, w autoradiotaxi.it) and Radio Taxi Trinacria (t 255 455 or t 091 6878, w radiotaxitrinacria.it) – both charge the same rates. Anywhere within the city centre there is a fixed rate of €7. A taxi to the airport will cost between €35 and €40.

BY BIKE OR SCOOTER

If you're adept on two wheels, biking is not a bad option: as long as you realize the rules of the road – he who hesitates is lost, and go for the gap – weaving your way in and out of the traffic can be an exhilarating way to save time and legwork. For the more adventurous, scooter rental is also available.

Bike rental There are good bike rental outfits all over the centre. Social Bike (Discesa dei Giudici, 21, t 328 284 3734, daily 9.30am–6.30pm) has reliable folding bikes, tandems, electric bikes and city bikes rentable by the hour, half-day, day or week. Prices from €3 per hour, €15 per day for a folding or city bike.

INFORMATION

Tourist offices Palermo's city-centre tourist office is at Via Principe di Belmonte 92 (Mon–Fri 8.30am–7.30pm, Sat 8.30am–6pm; t 091 585 172). Information kiosks run by the council (all Sat–Wed 9am–1pm & 3–7pm, Thurs & Fri 9am–1pm & 3–6pm, though hours and sites may be reduced because of budget restraints) are scattered around the city centre, in places like Piazza Politeama, Piazza Bellini and at the Stazione Centrale.

Listings information For a more detailed look at arts and entertainment, there are several websites including w palermoweb.com, w palermoviva.it, w balarm.it and w palermotoday.it, while w visitpalermo.it is a useful source of information in English, covering everything from guided tours and wine tastings to where to stay and where to eat.

16

ACCOMMODATION

Most of Palermo's traditional budget hotels lie on and around the southern ends of Via Maqueda and Via Roma, close to Stazione Centrale, but you'll get far more for your money in the city's B&Bs, many of which are charming and extremely well run. Prices tend to stay the same year-round (except out on the nearby coast, where usual summer rates apply), but advance reservations are recommended, particularly around the time of Palermo's annual festival, July 11–15. The two nearest campsites, as well as Palermo's youth hostel, are all at the beachside town of Sferracavallo, 16km northwest of the city or a good half an hour on the bus – convenient for the beach or airport but not really for city sightseeing.

CITY CENTRE

Al Giardino dell'Alloro Vicolo S. Carlo 8 t 338 224 3541, w giardinodellalloro.it; map p.878. Lovely B&B in the heart of La Kalsa with books for guests to borrow, a courtyard where breakfast is served and a living room used as an exhibition space for contemporary Sicilian artists. The five rooms feature original works of art, and have kettles and mugs. There is a small kitchen for guests' use. €80

Alla Kala Via Vittorio Emanuele 71 t 091 743 4763, w allakala.it; map p.878. This excellent, centrally located, spick-and-span B&B has five stylish designer rooms and a suite with magnificent views of the sailing marina. It's popular, so book in advance. €94

★ **BB22** Palazzo Pantelleria, Largo Cavalieri di Malta 22 t 091 611 1610 or t 335 790 8733, w bb22.it; map p.878. Milanese designer-chic (resinated cement floors, perspex chairs, walls painted in matt stone hues) blended with a feeling of being at home (free wi-fi, coffee and water) in a historic *palazzo* a few steps from the Vucciria market. Breakfast is served on a small roof terrace. The owners also organize food and wine tours, plus boat trips to the beach at Mondello. €140

Grand Hotel et des Palmes Via Roma 398 t 091 602 811, w grandhotel-et-des-palmes.com; map p.878. Although it may no longer have its former cachet, when guests included Wagner, the Des Palmes remains an extremely comfortable four-star chain hotel conveniently located on the main Via Roma. What's more, online discounts can result in room rates that compete with those of many B&Bs. €140

La Casa dei Limoni Piazza Giulio Césare 9 t 334 834 3888 or t 338 967 8907, w lacasadeilimoni.it; map p.878. A friendly B&B right opposite the train station that's great value for money, and a good choice if you're catching an early train. €50

La Dimora del Genio Via Garibaldi 58 t 347 658 7664, w ladimoradelgenio.it; 5min walk from Stazione Centrale; map p.878. Three cosy rooms in a seventeenth-century *palazzetto*, furnished with a tasteful blend of antiques, modern furniture and original paintings. The friendly owner offers cooking courses for guests, as well as a splendid Sun dinner for €30 a head. €90

★ **Palazzo Pantaleo** Via Ruggero Settimo 74/H t091

325 471 or ☎335 700 6091, @palazzopantaleo.it; map p.878. Set on a quiet square close to Piazza Politeama, this outstanding B&B has seven huge, light, airy rooms in an eighteenth-century *palazzo*. It's perfect for business travellers – instant internet access in all rooms, adaptors for charging mobile phones in all sockets, and a small kitchen to make drinks or snacks. €103

Quattro Quarti Palazzo Arone di Valentino, Via Vittorio Emanuele 376 ☎347 854 7209, @quattroquarti.it; map p.878. A superior B&B with four smart, elegant rooms in part of a huge *palazzo* owned by the Arone di Valentino family. Guests are very well looked after, making this a great choice if you're a little nervous about finding your feet in Palermo. €98

Ucciard Home Via Enrico Albanese 34–36 ☎091 348 426, @hotelucciardhome.hotelsinsicily.it; map p.878. Trendy designer hotel opposite the prison, with sixteen comfortable, stylish rooms and lovely, luxurious bathrooms. Staff are excellent, breakfasts good and website deals can be fantastic. €108

Vecchio Borgo Via Quintino Sella 1–7 ☎091 611 8330, @ghshotels.it/vecchioborgo; map p.878. A smart and appealing hotel, whose comfortable rooms have bold printed fabrics and all amenities (including internet points). Excellent breakfast, including home-made cakes. Garage €10 a night, outdoor car park free, but spaces are limited. Website deals can make it cheaper than many B&Bs. €90

OUT OF THE CENTRE

Baia del Corallo Via Plauto 27, Sferracavallo ☎091 679 7807, @www.ostellopalermo.it; bus #101 from the train station to Piazza de Gaspari, and then bus #628 to Punta Matese; map p.878. Palermo's youth hostel is by the sea 12km northwest of the city – not the most convenient choice for sightseeing, but handy for the airport and a good cheap option for a first or last night. It was closed for restoration at the time we went to print, but worth calling to see if it has opened by the time you are reading this.

★ **Grand Hotel Villa Igiea** Via Belmonte 43 ☎091 631 2111, @villa-igiea.com; bus #731 or #721 from Piazza Santa Croce, halfway along Via della Libertà; map p.878. This classic Art Nouveau building was designed by Ernesto Basile in 1900, and stands outside the city centre above the Acquasanta marina. It has a swimming pool overlooking the port, shady gardens, a tennis court and sweeping terraces – best enjoyed at *aperitivo* time. Boat trips and food tours available. €230

16

EATING

CAFÉS AND STREET FOOD

I Cuochini Via Ruggero Settimo 68 ☎091 581 158; map p.878. Diminutive, spick-and-span *frigittoria* – all gleaming white tiles and zinc – founded in 1826, and concealed within an arched gateway (the only sign is a small ceramic plaque). *Panzerotti* (deep-fried pastries, stuffed with tomato, mozzarella and anchovy, or aubergine, courgette and cheese), *arancini* (with *ragù*, or cheese and ham), *pasticcino* (a sweet pastry with minced meat), *timballini di pasta* (deep-fried pasta), *besciamelle fritte* (breadcrumbed and deep-fried *béchamel*) and the like – most at less than €1 a portion. Mon–Sat 8.30am–2.30pm.

Michele alla Brace Piazza Borgo Vecchio; map p.878. At the tiny market of Piazza Borgo Vecchio, you can't miss this huge grill with a couple of plastic tables and a steaming cauldron of vegetables. Buy your fish from one of the nearby stalls and bring it to Michele, who will grill it, and provide you with veg, drinks and a table. Thurs–Tues approx. noon–2pm.

Obica Fourth floor Rinascente, Via Roma/Piazza S. Domenico ☎091 601 7861, @obica.com; map p.878. The Palermo branch of an exclusive chain of bars specializing in *mozzarella di bufala*, which appears in exquisitely presented salads and other light dishes, though there are vegan options too. A great lunchtime escape from the heat and chaos of Palermo, and a good place for an aperitif (daily 6.30–9pm), the drinks accompanied by a selection of mouthwatering mozzarella tasters. Daily 10am–11pm.

Palazzo Riso Via Vittorio Emanuele 365 ☎091 320 532, @palazzoriso.it; map p.878. Cool, white, minimalist bar belonging to Palermo's contemporary art museum. Hazelnut- and chocolate-flavoured coffees, tisanes, *cornetti* with forest fruits, light lunches and *aperitivi*. Eat in the bar, or outside in the shady courtyard. Free wi-fi and use of computers. Daily 9am–approx. 1am.

Pasticceria Mazzara Via Magliocco 15 (off Via Ruggero Settimo ☎091 321 443; map p.878. Long-established bar-*pasticceria* serving light brunches and lunches plus delicious pastries and ice creams: try the rare roast beef with rocket and shaved Parmesan. Tues–Sun 6am–8.30pm.

Rosciglione Via Gian Luca Barbieri 5 ☎091 651 2959; map p.878. Watch *cannoli* being made as you eat them at this bakery, on the edge of the Ballarò market. Mon–Fri 8am–1pm & 12–5pm, Sat 8am–1pm.

Spinnato Via Principe di Belmonte 107–115 ☎091 749 5104, @spinnato.it; map p.878. With tables outside on a pedestrianized street, this is the perfect place for breakfast, delicious cakes and ice creams, or an *aperitivo* served with an aesthetic cascade of roast almonds, shelled pistachios and crisps. Daily 7.30am–8.30pm or later.

RESTAURANTS

Antica Focacceria San Francesco Via A. Paternostro 58 ☎091 320 264, @afsf.it; map p.878. This old-

fashioned place has been in the same family for five generations. Downstairs they serve traditional Palermitano street food, such as focaccia with offal and cheese, or pizza with onion, tomato, caciocavallo and breadcrumbs: upstairs you can eat full meals (try the *pasta con le sarde*). There are also several fixed-price menus: *pannelle, crocchè*, an *arancina* or slice of pizza, *cannolo* and a drink for €7.50; or the same, with pasta instead of the *arancina* or pizza for €9. In summer you can eat outside. Wed–Mon 11am–11pm.

★ **Mirto e la Rosa** Via Principe di Granitello 30 ⓣ 091 324 353; map p.878. This began life as a vegetarian restaurant, and although carefully sourced local fish and meat have now joined the menu, the emphasis on vegetables remains. Signature dishes include *caponata* with pistachio-spiked couscous, and home-made *tagliolini* with tomato sauce, grilled aubergine and cheese from the Nebrodi mountains. Choose from various menu deals (€10 for a *primo, secondo* and salad; €13 for antipasto, *primo* and dessert, or *primo* and *secondo*). Mon–Sat noon–3pm & 7–11pm.

★ **Osteria dei Vespri** Piazza Croce dei Vespri ⓣ 091 617 1631, ⓦ osteriadeivespri.it; map p.878. Possibly Palermo's best restaurant is run with passion by brothers Andrea and Alberto Rizzo, who cook complex meals using Sicilian ingredients. Dishes might include rabbit terrine with pistachios, black *tagliolini* served with red mullet, ginger, red onion and fava beans, or quail stuffed with prunes. There are fantastic-value lunch menus at €35 including a glass of wine, plus *degustazione* menus at €80/person, excluding wine. Mon–Sat 12.30–2.30pm & 7.30–10.30pm.

16

★ **Osteria lo Bianco** Via E. Amari 104 ⓣ 091 251 4906; map p.878. Decorated with Juventus souvenirs and religious bric-a-brac, this is one of the cheapest places to eat in town. Traditional Palermitano food, such as *pasta con sarde*, meatballs in tomato sauce, *ricciola* in a spicy tomato sauce, or a stew of beef, peas and carrots.Antipasto are €4, *primi* €5, meat *secondi* €7 and fish *secondi* €8. Daily 12.30–3.30pm & 7.30–10.30pm.

Pizzeria Italia Via Orologio 54 ⓣ 091 589 885; map p.878. Attracting large queues, this is the best place in town for light, oven-blistered pizzas (€5–12). Try the "Palermitana" with tomato, anchovies, onion, artichokes, caciocavallo cheese and breadcrumbs. Tues–Sun 8–10.30pm.

Primavera Piazza Bologni 4 ⓣ 091 329 408; map p.878. With outdoor seating in a lovely little piazza, this popular trattoria serves home-style cooking such as *pasta con le sarde* and *bucatini con broccoli* (both €10), as well as bottles of good, inexpensive local wine. Tues–Sun 12.30–2.30pm & 8–10.30pm.

Trattoria Piccolo Napoli Piazzetta Mulino di Vento 4 ⓣ 091 320 431; map p.878. Lively trattoria off the Vecchio Borgo market, founded in 1951 and run by three generations of the same family. They have two boats at Terrasini, and the fish is brought in daily. Try raw prawns, pasta with *neonati* (newborn fish) when it's in season (€14), or what may be the best *caponata* you will ever taste (€5). Mon–Sat 12.30–2.30pm & 7.30–11pm.

★ **Trattoria Torremuzza** Via Torremuzza 17 ⓣ 091 252 5532; map p.878. Eat at streetside tables in summer at this bustling, no-frills trattoria where fish is grilled on an outside brazier. There is a huge set menu for €20 including wine. Antipasti (mussel soup, seafood salad, etc) and *primi* (pasta with mussels and clams, or swordfish and aubergine) are all €5, except for a couple of special dishes such as spaghetti with sea urchin (€10). Meat *secondi* are also €5, while fish dishes (mixed fried or grilled fish or grilled prawns) cost from €7 to €10. Wine is a dangerous €3 a litre. Daily noon–midnight.

DRINKING

After dark and over much of the city, Palermo's frenetic lifestyle stops, pedestrians flit quickly through the shadows, and the main roads are given over to speeding traffic and screaming police sirens. The only place for a civilized, fume-free *aperitivo al fresco* is the pedestrianized **Via Principe di Belmonte**, off the upper part of Via Roma, which has a glitzy selection of bars and *pasticcerie*. For a livelier scene, head to the clutch of bars in the streets behind the **Museo Archeologico** – Via Spinuzza, Via Bara all'Olivella and Piazza Olivella – while things are grungier in the student-filled bars along and around **Via Candelai**, not far from the Quattro Canti, off Via Maqueda. There's also a burgeoning bar scene down in La Kalsa, on and off Via Alloro.

DIRECTORY

Hospital Pronto Soccorso at Ospedale Policlinico, Via del Vespro 129 (ⓣ 091 655 1111). For an ambulance call ⓣ 118.

Left luggage Stazione Marittima (daily 7am–8pm; ⓣ 091 611 3257).

Pharmacist All-night service opposite the train station at Via Roma 1, Via Roma 207, and near the port at Via Mariano Stabile 177.

Police Central city station, the Questura, at Piazza della Vittoria ⓣ 112.

Post office Main post office is the Palazzo delle Poste on Via Roma (Mon–Sat 8am–6.30pm).

BAROQUE TOWN OF RAGUSA IBLA

17 57

Monreale

Best know for its impressive Norman cathedral, the small hill-town of **MONREALE** (Royal Mountain), 8km southwest of Palermo, has a dense latticework of medieval streets. From its **belvedere**, you get commanding views down the Conca d'Oro Valley to Palmermo in the distance, while the main **Via Roma** pulses with life at *passeggiata* time.

Duomo

Piazza Guglielmo II • Nov–March Mon–Sat 8.30am–12.30pm & 2.30–4.30pm, Sun 8am–9.30am & 2.30–4.30pm • April–Oct Mon–Sat 8.30am–12.45pm & 2–4.45pm, Sun 8am–9.15am & 2.30–4.45pm • €4 duomo only, €10 for entire complex, max. visiting time within main Duomo is 30 min, max. 350 people at a time, if you are not deemed to be decently dressed, you will be given a second hand shirt to wear; • Cloisters Daily 9am–6.30pm, Sun 9am–1.30pm • €6 or €10 including Duomo; also bookable online via coopculture.it

Monreale's severe, square-towered **Duomo** holds the most impressive and extensive area of Christian medieval mosaic-work in the world. What immediately draws your attention is the half-figure of Christ in the central apse, the head and shoulders alone almost 20m high. Beneath sit an enthroned Madonna and Child, attendant angels and, below, ranks of saints, each individually and subtly coloured and identified by name. The remarkable series of nave mosaics starts with the Creation (to the right of the altar) and runs around the whole church. Most scenes are instantly recognizable: Adam and Eve, Abraham on the point of sacrificing his son, a jaunty Noah's Ark; even the Creation, shown in a set of glorious, simplistic panels portraying God filling his world with animals, water, light and people.

The cloisters

16

It's also worth visiting the **cloisters**, part of the original Benedictine monastery established here in 1174. The formal garden is surrounded by an elegant arcaded quadrangle, each column capital a riot of detail and imagination: armed hunters doing battle with winged beasts, flowers, birds, snakes and foliage. Entrance to the cloisters is from Piazza Guglielmo, in the corner by the right-hand tower of the cathedral.

ARRIVAL AND DEPARTURE — MONREALE

By bus Bus #389 runs frequently from Palermo's Piazza dell'Indipendenza, outside the Palazzo dei Normanni (20min), reached by bus #109 from Stazione Centrale.

By taxi A taxi from Palermo costs around €120 return, including 3 hours visiting time.

By car Parking is restricted in Monreale's old town and visitors are advised to use one of the signposted car parks (€1 an hour; free overnight after 8pm).

ACCOMMODATION AND EATING

Locanda Re Ruggero Via Arcivescovado 348 524 1341, locandareruggero.it. Four stylish contemporary rooms with deep purple or blue walls setting off white furniture, plus a neat apartment (sleeping four) with kitchen. All rooms have a/c and wi-fi. Close to the Duomo, just off Via Cappuccini. Rooms **€60**, apartment **€80**

Peppino Via B. Civiletti 12 091 640 7770. Popular local pizzeria tucked away down a side street off Via Roma, beyond San Giuseppe church. It has a shady summer terrace, decent antipasti and crisp pizzas (€6–12) – the pizzas with buffalo mozzarella are well worth the extra. Mon & Wed–Sun noon–2pm & 7.30–10pm.

Ustica

A volcanic, turtle-shaped island 60km northwest of Palermo, **USTICA** is somewhere you could spend an entire holiday, though it is close enough to Palermo for a day-trip. Ustica's fertile uplands are perfect for a day's ambling, and there's a path running round the entire rocky coastline, with just a brief stretch where you have to follow the road. The main reason people come here, however, is to dive in its clear waters, bursting with fish, sponges, weed and coral. Less adventurous types can take a boat trip through Ustica's rugged grottoes and lava outcrops. The small, rather dishevelled port of **Ustica town**, where the boats dock, has a few bars, a bank, several restaurants and a handful of places to stay. All these sit around a sloping double piazza, just five minutes' walk uphill from the harbour.

DIVING ON USTICA

The waters around Ustica are protected by a natural marine reserve, divided into several zones with restrictions on where you can swim, dive and fish. It's well set up for divers, and facilities include a decompression chamber, though medical facilities are limited to the pharmacy and the *guardia medica*. The excellent **Profondo Blu** (T 091 844 9609 or T 349 672 6529, W ustica-diving.it) is the island's most organized and experienced dive operator, arranging guided dives and packages – a single dive costs €45, a night dive €50, a ten-dive package €380, and a six-day Open Water PADI course €430. It also offers accommodation in a very pleasant and friendly resort of self-catering apartments outside town (May–Oct; €490–660/week in an apartment for 2 people), with meals available too (breakfast €5, lunch, €15, dinner €35).

ARRIVAL AND DEPARTURE — USTICA

By boat Siremar operates one ferry daily from Palermo to Ustica (2hr 30min), while both Liberty Lines runs 2–5 hydrofoils daily between Easter and Oct (fewer in winter; 1hr 15min). Travel doesn't come cheap; expect to pay around €40 return by ferry, almost €60 by hydrofoil.

ACCOMMODATION

Da Umberto Piazza della Vittoria T 091 844 9542, W usticatour.it. As well as running the *Da Umberto* restaurant, Gigi Tranchina rents out rooms in over twenty apartments and houses around Ustica, some with great sea views, others in more rustic locations. Prices depend on size and quality of the accommodation. From **€65**

Giulia Via S. Francesco 16 T 091 844 9007, W giuliahotel.com. Open year-round, with ten two-star rooms right off the main piazza (single rooms also available), above a lovely restaurant. Weekend packages include certain meals and excursions: see website for details. No credit cards. **€80**

Stella Marina Residence Via Cristoforo Colombo 35 T 091 844 8121, W stellamarinaustica.it. Seventeen smart, self-catering mini-apartments in a small complex above the port. There's a nice big terrace and a small spa. Rentals are €500–1000/week for a two-person apartment, including breakfast, but they're also available on a two-nightly basis May–July, Sept & Oct. **€150**

EATING

Da Umberto Piazza della Vittoria T 091 844 9542. Tables on the terrace and a menu chiefly consisting of spaghetti dishes (from around €8), plus seafood main courses that depend on the day's catch (€12–18). Daily 12.30–2.30pm & 8–10.30pm; closed winter.

Giulia Via S. Francesco 13 T 091 844 9007. This simple trattoria is the best bet on the island for genuine home cooking. Try *pennette al usticese* (with herbs, chilli, garlic, pine nuts, raisins, anchovies, capers and olives), *polpettine* (fish balls) with local capers and olives, or *totano* (a big squid) stuffed with shrimp, tomatoes, cheese and breadcrumbs. Fish couscous is available for a minimum of two people. Expect to spend around €35–40/person. No credit cards. Daily 12.30–2.30pm & 8–10.30pm; closed winter.

The Tyrrhenian coast

From Palermo, the whole of the rugged **Tyrrhenian coast** is hugged by rail, road and autostrada, and for the most part, pretty built up. The first attraction is **Cefalù**, a beach resort and cathedral town. Beyond Cefalù, there are several resorts tucked along the narrow strip of land between the Nebrodi mountains and the sea, most of them not worth going out of your way for. Most people tend to head straight for the port of **Milazzo** – Sicily's second-largest port – the main departure point for ferries and hydrofoils to the seven fascinating islands of the **Aeolian archipelago**.

Cefalù

Despite being one of Sicily's busiest international beach resorts, **CEFALÙ** has a parallel life as a small-scale fishing port, tucked onto every available centimetre of a shelf of land beneath a fearsome crag, **La Rocca**. Roger II founded a mighty cathedral here in 1131 and his church dominates the skyline, the great twin towers of the facade rearing

up above the flat roofs of the medieval quarter. Naturally, the fine long sandy **beach** beyond the harbour is the major attraction, but Cefalù is a pleasant town, with a tangibly Arabic central grid of streets.

Duomo

Daily Mon–Sat 10am–6pm, Sun 10am–1pm & 3–6pm • Free; cloister €3 • cattedraledicefalu.com

Central to Cefalù's historic existence is its majestic **Duomo**, set back in a pretty square under the cliffs. Apocryphally, it was built in gratitude by Roger II, who found refuge at the town's safe beach in a violent storm, though it's more likely that the cathedral owed its foundation to his power struggle with Pope Innocent II. Dating from 1148 (forty years older than those at Monreale), it is also covered with mosaics, once again thoroughly Byzantine in concept: Christ Pantocrator, right hand outstretched in benediction, dominates the central apse, looking, it has to be said, rather more military than spiritual; in the vaults above him are the eight-winged heads of cherubim and seraphim; below is the Madonna flanked by archangels, then the twelve Apostles, ranked in two rows of six.

Overlooked by the sheer limestone cliff of La Rocca, and ringing with bird-song, the cloisters retain a tranquil magic. Only two sides remain, of slender, intriguingly mismatched pairs of columns with eroded capitals – look carefully and you can make out the once extraordinary detail of lizards, monsters and salamanders.

Museo Mandralisca

16

Via Mandralisca 13 • Daily: Jan–July & Sept–Dec 9am–7pm; Aug 9am–11pm • €6 • 0921 421 547, fondazionemandralisca.it

The splendid little **Museo Mandralisca** has its origins in the private collection of nineteenth-century aristocrat and benefactor, Barone Enrico Pirajno di Mandralisca. On the first floor, the star exhibit is a wry and inscrutable *Portrait of an Unknown Man* by the fifteenth-century Sicilian master **Antonello da Messina**. Look out, too, for the quirky Greek *krater* (fourth century BC) showing a robed tuna-fish salesman, knife in hand, disputing the price of his fish.

La Rocca and the Tempio di Diana

Tempio di Diana Daily: April–Oct 9am–6.45pm; Nov–March closes at least 1hr before sunset • Free

Towering above Cefalù, the mountain of **La Rocca** is home to the **Tempio di Diana**, a mesolithic structure, which was adapted by the Greeks in the fifth century BC by the addition of classical doorways. The temple is accessed by a steep twenty-minute climb up the footpath at the side of the Banco di Sicilia on Piazza Garibaldi. From the temple a path continues around the crag, through pinewoods, dipping in and out of a stretch of medieval wall to the sketchy fortifications at the top. The round walk to the top takes a little over an hour – take water with you, as it's a strenuous climb.

ARRIVAL AND INFORMATION — CEFALÙ

By train and bus All trains between Palermo and Messina pull in to the station to the south of the town centre, a 10min walk from the main drag, Corso Ruggero. Buses also arrive and leave from here.

Tourist office Piazza Duomo (Mon–Sat 9am–7pm; 0921 421 508). The website cefalu.it is also useful for accommodation, restaurants and local services.

ACCOMMODATION

Most of the resort hotels are out of the town centre, by the beaches and bays to either side of Cefalù. There are, however, lots of central B&Bs, though vacancies are few in Aug (when prices everywhere double). Self-catering apartments are widely available, though again summer is very busy and there's often a minimum stay of three or even seven nights: try casevacanzecefalu.it or ask at the tourist office.

HOTELS AND B&BS

Al Pescatore Località Caldura 0921 421 572, **hotelalpescatore.it**. Around the headland, near the port, this family-run hotel is pretty good value for most

of the year, with simply furnished rooms with tile floors offering sea or mountain views. There's no restaurant, though, and it's a fair walk into town. **€150**

★ **Dolce Vita** Via C.O. Bordonaro 8 ⓣ 0921 923 151, ⓦ dolcevitabb.it. The top choice for B&B – right in the heart of the old town but with the sea on one side. Two rooms face the street, three the sea, and all are en suite and spacious (sleeping up to four), with high ceilings and restored tile floors. Best of all is the glorious terrace, with uninterrupted sea views, while the cheery owner can arrange boat trips, airport transfers, etc. Breakfast is taken in a bar in the cathedral piazza. **€100**

Le Calette Via Vincenzo Cavallaro 12, Contrada Caldura ⓣ 0921 424 144, ⓦ lecalette.it. On the eastern side of the headland, overlooking the hydrofoil port, this four-star villa-style hotel is beautifully sited above a little cove, and has its own pool, restaurant and gardens. All rooms face the sea and those on the second floor have large balconies. Good deals online outside the main season. **€252**

★ **Palazzo** Villelmi Corso Ruggero 149 ⓣ 0921 923 057 or ⓣ 339 852.0161, ⓦ hotelscombined.it/Hotel/Villelmi_BB.htm. Stylish, elegant B&B in a beautifully restored old *palazzo* on the main street, very near the Duomo. High painted ceilings give a hint of its former grandeur, and a rooftop breakfast terrace looks right onto the cathedral. **€100**

EATING AND DRINKING

There are dozens of restaurants in Cefalù, though many trade on their sea view and are overpriced. Menus are broadly similar – fish and seafood, of course, is the highlight – and the best deals are often in the form of set menus aimed at tourists for €20–30 a head. The cafés in Piazza del Duomo are a nice place to start the day, with breakfast in front of the cathedral. For sunset drinks and views, there's a line of restaurants, bars and *gelaterie* along the prom by the beach, while the local *passeggiata* runs all the way up the main Corso to Piazza Garibaldi and its streetside bars and ice-cream shops.

CAFÉS AND RESTAURANTS

Al Gabbiano Lungomare G. Giardina ⓣ 0921 421 495. Best of the seafront promenade restaurants, this place has a good *antipasto al buffet*, spicy *zuppa di cozze* and pizzas (€6–10), as well as fish and seafood mains (mostly €10–12). June–Sept daily noon–midnight; Oct–May Thurs–Tues noon–2pm & 7.30–10pm.

Caffè di Noto Via Bagno Cicerone 3 ⓣ 0921 422 654. This *gelateria*, on the edge of the *centro storico* and the beginning of the Lungomare, has fabulous ice creams in flavours including mango, raspberry, prickly pear and chocolate with chilli. Easter–Oct daily 10am–late.

Le Chat Noir Via XXV Novembre 17 ⓣ 0921 420 697. An atmospheric setting in the whitewashed, plant-filled courtyard of a sixteenth-century building a short walk from the Duomo. The menu features memorable executions of Sicilian dishes such as aubergine *parmigiana* with salty ricotta, swordfish *involtini* and an orange salad spiked with chilli. Count on spending €35 for a meal including wine if you eat fish, €25 if you opt for meat. Thurs–Tues noon–2pm & 7.30–10pm.

★ **Tivitti** Via Lungomare G Giardina 7 ⓣ 0921 922 642. Contemporary twist on a traditional wine bar with wines by the bottle or glass (from €5 a glass including antipasti nibbles), as well as excellent pizzas (€5–12), many of them using local produce and ingredients such as Madonie white truffles to great effect. There are also hamburgers using Sicilian beef served with tasty combinations of sundried tomatoes, local cheeses and olives. For a beach picnic, buy a bottle and cold cuts to take away. There are tables inside and out, overlooking the beach. Daily from 10am–late.

16

Milazzo

If it weren't for the chimneys of the oil refinery on its periphery **MILAZZO** it wouldn't be a bad-looking place. A long plane- and palm-tree-lined promenade looks across the sea, while a rambling castle caps the town's ancient acropolis. Most people, though, are put off by the unsightly oil refinery, and only stop long enough to take the first ferry or hydrofoil to the Aeolian islands (see page 895), for which Milazzo is the major embarkation point. If you are self-catering on the islands, you can stock up with food at the morning **market** behind the post office on Via G Medici.

The Castello

Via del Castello • Tues–Sun: July 9.30am–1.30pm & 4.30pm–10pm; Aug 9.30am–1.30pm & 4.30pm– midnight; Sept–June times vary, so check at tourist office • €6 • ⓣ 090 922 1291

If there's time to kill, you might like to poke around the streets of the **Borgo**, the old town on the top of the hill, where the magnificently preserved Spanish

Castello sits inside a much larger and older walled city, complete with its own cathedral. Built by Frederick II in the thirteenth century, over Arab foundations on the site of the ancient Greek acropolis, it's one of Sicily's best castles, with views stretching to the Aeolian islands and beyond. The steps that run down the far side of the castle walls lead to the Spiaggia di Ponente, a long **beach** of grey gravel with crystal-clear waters.

Capo Milazzo and the Piscina di Venere

Bus #6 from the stop to the left as you leave the hydrofoil station

A thin promontory 6km out of town, **Capo Milazzo** is the focus of most of the town's summertime activity. There are plenty of good little beaches here, but the loveliest spot to swim and snorkel is at the tip of the cape, where the road ends and a path leads down to a natural sea-pool known as the **Piscina di Venere**, or pool of Venus. From here, a path runs along the west coast to a longer, sand and shingle beach, which is rarely busy, even in summer.

ARRIVAL AND INFORMATION — MILAZZO

By bus Buses to Messina stop at the port-side car park by the hydrofoil station, with timings pretty much arranged to tie in with hydrofoil arrivals and departures.

Destinations Catania airport (April–Oct 2–4 daily; 1hr 50min; giuntabus.com); Messina (fast service hourly Mon–Sat, 3 daily Sun; 50min; giuntabustrasporti.it).

16

By train The train station is 3km south of the centre. Local buses should run from here into town every 30min during the day, dropping you on the quayside or further up in Piazza della Repubblica, but they are unreliable so don't count on it. And don't rely on finding a taxi outside the station either.

Destinations Cefalù (9–12 daily; 1hr 20min–2hr 30min); Messina (12–18 daily; 20–30min); Palermo (9–11 daily; 2hr 10min–3hr 30min).

Tourist information Milazzo's tourist office is at Piazza Duilio 20 (Mon–Fri 8.30am–1.30pm & 3.30–6pm, Sat 8.30am–1.30pm; 090 922 2865), just back from the harbour.

ACCOMMODATION

★ Cassisi Via Cassisi 5 090 922 9099, cassisihotel.com. Elegant, minimalist, family-run hotel, with a touch of contemporary oriental style. The buffet breakfast is abundant, with local cheese and salamis, typical pastries and biscuits, and lots of fresh fruit. Five minutes' walk from the port, and close to the main shopping area. **€92**

★ Petit Hotel Via dei Mille 37 090 928 6784, petithotel.it. Eco-hotel in a nineteenth-century building on the seafront overlooking the hydrofoil dock. Staff go out of their way to be helpful, and breakfasts include local salamis and cheeses, organic yogurt, eggs and jams, and home-made cakes. **€90**

Locanda del Bagatto Via M. Regis 11 090 922 4212, locandadelbagatto.com. Sexy, chic, modern rooms above Milazzo's best restaurant – just the place to cheer yourself up if your hydrofoil to the Aeolians has been cancelled. Comfy beds, chromatic showers, mini bars and vaguely erotic photos on the walls. **€100**

Giardino di Sicilia Via Santa Maria Maggiore 29 090 922 2191. Five simple rooms with en-suite facilities, belonging to one of Milazzo's most appealing restaurants. The location is perfect for those who want to discover the hidden delights of the town, right at the foot of the Borgo, a few steps from the seafront, and a short walk to the first beach of Capo Milazzo. **€60**

EATING AND DRINKING

Al Bagatto Via M. Regis 11 090 922 4212. Amiable wine bar with restaurant where you can sample local salami and cheeses, as well as more substantial dishes – try the fabulous *tagliata* of beef (€16). Thurs–Tues 12.30–2.30pm & 8–10.30pm.

Giardino di Sicilia Via Santa Maria Maggiore 29 090 922 2191, giardinodisicilia.net. Family-run restaurant and pizzeria, with a garden courtyard in summer. It serves tasty pizzas (from €4.50) with crisp, featherlight bases made from dough fermented for 48 hours. The emphasis is on quality ingredients – even a simple *pepata di cozze* (€9) is an unforgettable experience. Daily 7.30–10.30pm.

Il Spizzico Via dei Mille s/n. This waterfront takeaway does the best *arancini* hereabouts, including versions filled with spinach and mozzarella or aubergine. Daily 7.30–8.30pm.

The Aeolian islands

Volcanic in origin, the **Aeolian islands** are named after Aeolus, the Greek god who kept the winds he controlled shut tight in one of the islands' many caves. According to Homer, Odysseus put into the Aeolians and was given a bag of wind to help him home, but his sailors opened it too soon and the ship was blown straight back to port. More verifiably, the islands were coveted for their mineral wealth, the mining of obsidian (hard, glass-like lava) providing the basis for early prosperity, because it was the sharpest material available until people learned the art of smelting metals. Later their strategic importance attracted the Greeks, who settled on Lipari in 580 BC, but they later became a haven for pirates and a place of exile, a state of affairs that continued right into the twentieth century with the Fascists exiling their political opponents to Lipari.

The twentieth century saw mass emigration, mostly to Australia, and even now islands such as Panarea and Alicudi have just a hundred or so year-round inhabitants. It's only recently that the islanders stopped scratching a subsistence living and started welcoming tourists, and these days during the summer months the population of the islands can leap from 10,000 to 200,000. Every island is **expensive**, with prices in shops as well as restaurants reflecting the fact that most food is imported. But get out to the minor isles or come in blustery winter for a taste of what life was like on the islands twenty – or a hundred – years ago: unsophisticated, rough and beautiful.

ARRIVAL AND DEPARTURE

THE AEOLIAN ISLANDS

16

Sailings from Milazzo operate daily and are frequent enough to make it unnecessary to book ahead (for which there is a surcharge) except in high season (unless you're taking a car), although bear in mind that there is a reduced service between Oct and May – and that even moderately rough weather can disrupt the schedules. Hydrofoils are more frequent and twice as quick, but almost twice the price of the ferries. The islands can be reached hydrofoil from Palermo (in summer) and Messina (year round), and (weather permitting) from Naples year round by ferry and in summer by hydrofoil.

Ferry and hydrofoil operators Hydrofoils are all run by Liberty Lines, except for the Naples route which is run by SNAV (ⓦ snav.it). **Ferries** from Milazzo are (currently at least) run by Siremar (ⓦ carontetourist.it) and NGI (ⓦ ngi-spa.it).

Tickets Tickets are sold online and from the port terminal building before departure; up-to-date schedules are also available online. In July and August, and at the beginning and end of public holidays you might need to buy tickets in advance (for which there is a surcharge); otherwise, services are rarely full.

Fares One-way high-season fares from Milazzo are around €16 by hydrofoil or €10 by ferry to Lipari; €18/€12 to Salina; €21/14 to Stromboli; and €28/16 to Alicudi. Hydrofoils from Messina to Lipari cost around €23, while from Palermo you'll pay around €26 to Alicudi, €38 to Lipari and €54 to Stromboli. All islands charge a €6 tourist tax on top of the ticket price, which is paid at the time of booking. Transporting a car on the car-ferry starts at around €30 one-way (Milazzo to Lipari), while on all services children under 4 go free and under-12s go half-price. Note that in recent summers there have been severe restrictions on tourists bringing their own cars to the islands, so don't count on it! If you have more than one large suitcase you may be charged an extra €2 on the hydrofoils.

GETTING AROUND

Getting around in summer is easy, as ferries (*traghetti*) and hydrofoils (*aliscafi*) link all the islands. In winter, services are reduced and in rough weather cancelled altogether, particularly on the routes out to Stromboli, Alicudi and Filicudi. Cars, bikes and scooters can be rented on all islands except Alicudi and Panarea (on Alicudi you walk, on Panarea there are golf carts): the islands are very popular with cyclists, though you need to enjoy hills.

ESSENTIALS

In high season (Easter & July–Aug), accommodation is scarce and many places insist on half board, so you'd be wise to book in advance. From Oct to March prices can drop by up to fifty percent. There are campsites on Vulcano, Salina and Lipari – but camping rough is illegal. There are ATMs on all the islands except Alicudi. Power cuts are commonplace, caused by storms in winter, and in Aug by over-demand, so a torch is a good idea, especially in winter. Don't be surprised if hotels ask you to be sparing with the water, as it is imported by tanker.

16

DRIVING IN THE AEOLIANS

In a measure designed to cut down on the density of tourist traffic on the islands, **cars** are banned from Stromboli, Panarea and Alicudi. In July and August, cars belonging to non-residents can disembark from ferries to Lipari, Vulcano and Filicudi only if drivers can prove they are staying on the island for at least a week, whether in a hotel or in private accommodation. Ferry companies will ask for proof of a hotel booking before issuing tickets to those wanting to take their own car.

However, it's easy enough to manage without your own transport. Lipari and Salina have a good **bus** network, while you can **rent bicycles**, **mopeds** and **scooters** on all the main islands, or simply walk around the smaller ones.

If you need to leave a car in Milazzo, you can do so at one of several **garages**, the most convenient of which are listed below; expect to pay around €15 per day (worth negotiating for longer periods). Some offer a shuttle service to the port.

GARAGES

Central Garage Via Cumbo Borgia 60 ⊕ 090 928 2472. By the Duomo Nuovo, 5min from the port.

Garage delle Isole Via San Paolino 66 ⊕ 090 928 8585. About 10min walk from the port, just off the SP68B.

HYDROFOILS FROM MILAZZO

Mid-June–mid-Sept to: Alicudi (2 daily; 2hr 35hr–3hr 15min); Filicudi (2 daily; 2hr 20min–2hr 35min); Ginostra (4 daily; 1hr 20min–2hr 30min); Lipari (16 daily; 1hr); Panarea (8 daily; 1hr 15min–2hr); Rinella (7 daily; 1hr 35min–1hr 40min); Santa Marina (13 daily; 1hr 25min); Stromboli (8 daily; 1hr 5min–2hr 50min); Vulcano (15 daily; 40min).

Mid-Sept–mid-June to: Alicudi (1 daily; 2hr 35min); Filicudi (1 daily; 2hr); Ginostra (2 daily; 1hr 20min–2hr 30min); Lipari (12 daily; 1hr); Panarea (4 daily; 1hr 40min–2hr 5min); Rinella (8 daily; 1hr 40min–2hr 20min); Santa Marina (12 daily; 1hr 20min–2hr); Stromboli (4 daily; 1hr 5min–2hr 45min); Vulcano (12 daily; 45min).

FERRIES FROM MILAZZO

June–Sept to: Alicudi (7 weekly; 6hr); Filicudi (7 weekly; 5hr); Ginostra (4 weekly; 5hr 20min); Lipari (5–8 daily; 2hr–2hr 30min); Panarea (4 weekly; 4hr 20min); Rinella (8 weekly; 3hr 30min); Santa Marina (4–5 daily; 3hr–3hr 30min); Stromboli (6 weekly; 5hr 50min–6hr 40min); Vulcano (5–8 daily; 1hr 30min–2hr).

Oct–May to: Alicudi (6 weekly; 6hr–6hr 30min); Filicudi (6 weekly; 5hr 10min); Ginostra (3 weekly; 5hr 45min); Lipari (3–5 daily; 2hr–2hr 30min); Panarea (4 weekly; 4hr 10min–5hr); Rinella (6 weekly; 3hr 45min); Santa Marina (2–4 daily; 3hr–3hr 30min); Stromboli (5 weekly; 5hr 45min–7hr); Vulcano (3–5 daily; 1hr 30min–2hr).

HYDROFOILS FROM MESSINA

Mid-June to mid-Sept to: Lipari (5 daily; 1 hr 10min–3hr 35min); Panarea (3 daily; 2hr 5min–2hr 40min); Rinella (2 daily; 2hr 20min–3hr); Santa Marina Salina (4 daily; 2hr 10min–3hr); Stromboli (3 daily; 1hr 25min–2hr 25min); Vulcano (4 daily; 1hr 25min–2hr 35min).

Mid-Sept to mid-June to: Lipari (1 daily; 1hr 45min); Rinella (1 daily; 2hr 40min); Santa Marina Salina (1 daily; 2hr 20min); Vulcano (1 daily; 1hr 25min).

HYDROFOILS FROM PALERMO

June to mid-Sept 1 daily to: Alicudi (2hr); Filicudi (2hr 30min); Lipari (4hr); Panarea (4hr 40 min); Rinella (3hr 15min); Santa Marina Salina (3hr 30min); Stromboli (5hr 15min); Vulcano (4hr 25min).

Vulcano

Closest to the Sicilian mainland, **VULCANO** is the first port of call for ferries and hydrofoils, and you know when you are approaching it from the rotten-egg reek of sulphur. The novelty value of its smouldering volcano, and the chance to wallow in warm mud baths and swim above bubbling mid-sea fumaroles, make it a popular destination. Consequently Vulcano has been carelessly developed, its little town ugly, and the promontory of Vulcanello studded with bland mass-market hotels. High prices and mass

tourism make Vulcano best seen on a day-trip and as the cost of food on the island is exorbitant, and the restaurants are unexceptional, you're better off bringing a picnic.

The crater

The path up to the **crater** (access €4 in summer, unmanned in winter) begins about 1km out of town on the road to Gelso, marked by a sign warning of the dangers of inhaling volcanic gases. The ascent should take less than an hour. Wear hiking boots, as the ashy track is slippery, and follow the crater in an anticlockwise direction, so you are going downhill rather than up through the clouds of sulphurous emissions on the northern rim. Alternatively, there is an easier hike to **Vulcanello**, the volcanic pimple just to the north of the port, spewed out of the sea in 183 BC: start at the port and head past the Fanghi di Vulcano.

Fanghi di Vulcano and spa treatments

The **Fanghi di Vulcano**, or mud baths (small entrance fee in season), and offshore fumaroles lie a couple of minutes' walk from the port – if you bathe, be prepared to stink of sulphur for a couple of days. There's a black sand beach, five minutes' walk beyond. Alternatively, at Via Lentia 1, the *Oasi della Salute* is a naouveau riche spa with three thermal hydromassage pools and a beauty centre (May–Sept; ❶ 090 985 2093).

Lipari

LIPARI is the biggest and most heavily populated of the islands. Development has not been carefully controlled, and although parts of the island are beautiful and unspoilt, getting there inevitably means passing through villages cluttered with brassy holiday houses. The main port and capital, **Lipari Town** is a busy little place bunched between two harbours.

16

Lipari Town

The upper town within the fortress walls, the **Castello**, has been continuously occupied since Neolithic times. Alongside the well-marked **excavations**, there's a tangle of churches flanking the main cobbled street, and several buildings that make up the separate sections of the **Museo Archeologico Eoliano** (Mon–Sat 9am–7.30pm, Sun 9am–1.30pm; €6; ❶ 090 988 0174) – a lavish collection of Neolithic pottery, late Bronze Age artefacts and decorated Greek and Roman vases and statues. Highlights are the towering pyramids of amphorae rescued from ancient shipwrecks, a stunning array of miniature Greek theatrical masks found in tombs, and unique polychrome painted pottery by an artist known as the Lipari Painter, the colours tinted with volcanic clays.

Quattrocchi and San Calogero

As you head out of town to the west coast, **Quattrocchi** ("Four Eyes") provides much-photographed views over spiky *faraglioni* rocks to Vulcano. Beyond, just after the village of Pianoconte, a side road slinks down to the ancient thermal baths at **San Calogero** hidden behind a long-disused spa hotel: there's usually an unofficial guide to show you around and allow you a dip, if you dare, in the scummy 57°C Roman pool.

Monte Pilato

Above Campobianco, where pumice workings have left huge white scars on the hillside, a path leads up the slopes of **Monte Pilato** (476m), thrown up in the eruption from which all the island's pumice originally came. The volcano last erupted around 700 AD, leading to the virtual abandonment of Lipari town and creating the obsidian flows of Rocche Rosse and Forgia Vecchia, both of which can be climbed. Although it is overgrown with vegetation, you can still make out the outline of the crater at the top, and find black veins of obsidian.

Porticello

From the main road above the stony beach at **Porticello**, a road (and a quicker, more direct path) winds down to a small bay, which sunbathers share with the forlorn Heath Robinson-style pumice-work machinery that connects the white hillside with the pier. The deep blue waters here with their bed of white pumice sand are great for snorkelling, but be aware that there's no shade and the pebble beach can reach scalding temperatures. A couple of summer vans sell cool drinks and snacks.

ARRIVAL AND INFORMATION — LIPARI

By ferry or hydrofoil Hydrofoils and ferries dock at the Marina Lunga, while excursion boats use the smaller Marina Corta, formed by a church-topped pier and dwarfed by the castle that crowns the hill above. To get to Marina Corta walk straight along the main *corso* and turn right near the end at Via Maurolico.

Tourist office Corso Vittorio Emanuele 202 (Mon–Fri 8.30am–1.30pm & 4–7.30pm; July & Aug also Sat 8.30am–1.30pm; ⓣ 090 988 0095, ⓦ comunelipari.gov.it).

GETTING AROUND

By bus From Lipari Town, the rest of the island is easy to reach on a network of buses, which leave regularly from a stop by Marina Lunga, opposite the Esso service station. Buses run in two directions around the island, clockwise to Quattropani, and anticlockwise to Canneto, Porticello and Acquacalda. There are enough departures (up to 10 daily in summer) to be able to get around the whole island easily in a day. Ticket prices vary from €1.30 to €2.40 depending on your destination, and return tickets always work out cheaper.

ACCOMMODATION

16

In July and Aug it's a good idea to listen to the offers of rooms as you step off the boat. Expect to pay around €40/person in Aug, €20–30 at other times of the year, for something with a shower, kitchen, and balcony or terrace. The nearest campsite is in Canneto, a 10min bus ride from the port.

LIPARI TOWN

Carasco Porto delle Genti ⓣ 090 981 1605, ⓦ carasco.it. Best choice in town if you have children, as this big 1960s hotel, fused to a cliff on the edge of town, has a vast pool. All the rooms have terraces, and virtually all have sea views. Facilities include a decent restaurant and a poolside bar. **€150**

★ **Diana Brown** Vico Himera 3 ⓣ 090 981 2584, ⓦ dianabrown.it. Spotless place on a quiet alley off the main *corso*, run by a charming South African lady who has lived on the island for thirty years, and gives good advice on anything you need to know. Rooms come with fridges and kettles; breakfast is served in a sunny roof garden; and there is a well-stocked book exchange. **€100**

Enza Marturano Via Maurolico 35 ⓣ 368 322 4997, ⓦ enzamarturano.it. Four a/c rooms, with fridges, kitchens and private terraces close to the Marina Corta. It is worth checking the website for off-season deals. No credit cards. **€90**

Hotel Tritone Via Mendolita ⓣ 090 981 1595, ⓦ bernardigroup.it. Comfortable hotel in a quiet part of town, but just a 5min walk from the centre, built around a swimming pool with thermally heated spring water. There is also a well-equipped spa centre, with a wide range of massage therapies and beauty treatments. It is owned by the same people as the excellent *Il Filippino* restaurant (see page 899). **€150**

Villa Meligunis Via Marte 7 ⓣ 090 981 2426, ⓦ villameligunis.it. If you fancy staying in the lap of luxury, push the boat out at this gorgeous converted *palazzo* with excellent views of the citadel and sea from its rooftop restaurant, and a pool alongside; it offers great off-season discounts. **€140**

CANNETO

Baia Unci Via Marina Garibaldi ⓣ 090 981 1909, ⓦ campingbaiaunci.it. At the busy resort of Canneto, 3km from the port, this campsite has bungalows and tents to rent (€10–19) as well as pitches. There are communal cooking facilities (including fridges) and a restaurant. The bus from Lipari stops outside. Mid-March to mid-Oct. Camping per person including tent pitch and water **€15**, two-person bungalow **€90**

EATING AND DRINKING

LIPARI TOWN

★ **Al Kasbah** Vico Selinunte 16 ⓣ 090 981 1075. Stylish but unpretentious restaurant, with a beautiful garden, where the Anglo-Aeolian owner Sasha will advise on the best ways to sample the spanking-fresh fish. Antipasti (€7–10) and *primi* (€9–12) make creative use of local ingredients – try the handmade ravioli stuffed with fish. They also make their own bread – and the island's best pizza (€6–12), using

stoneground flour. April–Oct Thurs–Tues 8–10.30pm.

★ **Il Filippino** Piazza Municipio ⓣ090 981 1002, ⓦfilippino.it. This stupendous fish restaurant – Lipari's best, in business since 1910 – is in the upper town and has a shaded outdoor terrace where you can eat classy Aeolian specialities like borlotti bean, sardine and fennel soup (€13.50), *risotto nero* (€13.50), grouper-stuffed *ravioloni* and local fish in a tomato sauce (€14). Choose carefully and you might get away with €50 a head, though you could easily spend €70 – and more if you give any serious thought to the massive wine list. Jan to mid-Nov daily 12.30–2.30pm & 8–10.30pm; Oct to mid-Nov & Jan closed Mon.

Subba Corso Vittorio Emanuele 92 ⓣ090 981 1352. The island's best and most traditional café, since 1930, has a nice shaded terrace at the rear in the square. Try Lulus, clouds of *crema*-filled choux pastry, or the pistachio- and almond-studded *eoliana* ice cream. Daily 7.30am–8.30pm.

Trattoria d'Oro Via Umberto I 32 ⓣ090 981 1304. A cut above the town's cheaper trattorias, this shady, rustic place is a cool haven on a hot day, and it's very welcoming to families. *Pasta con le sarde* and stuffed squid are typical dishes, with pasta from €8.50 and fish mains from €10. Daily 12.30–2.30pm & 8–10.30pm.

Salina

North of Lipari, **SALINA**'s two extinct volcanic cones rise out of a fertile land that produces capers and white Malvasia. It's excellent **walking** country, with marvellous vantage points over the other islands. Tourism came to Salina far later than Lipari and Vulcano, with the happy result that development and building have been strictly controlled. Although you can bring a car in low season, there is a reliable bus service between all the main villages.

Santa Marina di Salina

16

The principal island port is **SANTA MARINA DI SALINA** on the east coast – a relaxed village ranged along Via Risorgimento, a single, pedestrianized main street where chic boutiques and down-to-earth food shops occupy the ground floors of substantial nineteenth-century houses built by those who made their fortune selling sweet wine (*malvasia*) to the British. Most lost their fortunes in 1890 when phylloxera arrived, destroying ninety percent of the vines, and prompting a mass exodus to Australia. At the end of Via Risorgimento, cut down to the Lungomare – where steps lead down to Punta Barone, a little beach with swimming in front of the perplexing remains of an ancient Roman fish farm. As you head back to the port along the Lungomare, there are more swimming spots in waters protected by the sea defences, and another beach in front of the main piazza, close enough to the port to let you have a last swim as you wait for your ferry or hydrofoil.

Lingua

LINGUA, sitting by a pretty lagoon 3km south, makes a pleasant alternative base to Santa Marina. It has two small **museums** in exquisitely restored Aeolian houses

LIPARI BOAT TRIPS

Tour operators all over town offer year-round **boat trips**, both around Lipari and to all the other islands. The boats mostly run from Marina Corta, but agencies are prominent at the main port too. Universally recommended is Da Massimo, Via Maurolico 2 (ⓣ338 369, ⓦdamassimo.it), with clean, well-maintained boats with freshwater showers and sun shades; English is spoken. They also run a boat trip to Stromboli with the excellent Magmatrek (see page 904), including a night ascent of the volcano (from €80).

Prices for boat trips are roughly the same everywhere, from €15 for a Lipari and Vulcano tour; Lipari and Salina €30; Alicudi and Filicudi for €40; and €45 to Panarea and Stromboli. If you want to rent a gommone (rubber boat) and putter around yourself, expect to pay €80 a day in low season, and up to €200 in August for a 50m boat with shower, canopy and space for six people. Most operators also run **beach shuttles** in summer to Lipari's beaches that are otherwise tricky to reach, like Praia Vinci.

overlooking the lagoon with its skewwhiff lighthouse: a small **ethnographic museum** (May–Oct Tues–Sun 9am–1pm & 3–6pm; free) displays examples of rustic art and island culture – mainly kitchen utensils and mill equipment, much of it fashioned from lavic rock, while the **archeological museum** (May–Oct Tues–Sun 9am–1pm & 3–6pm; free) has finds from Bronze Age and Roman Salina. Head through the alleyway at the side of the ethnographic museum and you'll be bang in the centre of Lingua's seafront piazza, hub of Salina summer life, with several little flights of steps leading down to a pebble beach.

Capo Faro and Malfa

Salina's only road climbs from the harbour at Santa Marina and traces the coast north, turning west at **Capo Faro**, with its vineyards and a lighthouse. A couple of kilometres beyond here, the road winds in to **MALFA**, Salina's largest village, set back from the sea. Though quite busy with traffic in the centre, it has an appealing little fishing port tucked away at the foot of cliffs, reached by either a devilishly twisting road or paved stepped footpaths. Its stony beach, backed by dramatic cliffs, is officially closed because of the danger of falling rocks. If this is still the case, do as the locals do and swim instead from the harbour. If you're around in late afternoon, don't miss watching the sunset from the cliff-top bar of the *Santa Isabel* hotel (Easter–Oct).

Pollara

Just out of Malfa, a minor road (served by several buses a day) snakes off west to secluded **POLLARA**, raised on a cliff above the sea and occupying a crescent-shaped crater from which Salina's last eruption took place some 13,000 years ago. Scenes from the 1994 film *Il Postino* were shot in a house here which you can occasionally rent: call Pippo Cafarella (**T** 339 425 3684). Pollara's beach, which also featured in *Il Postino*, diminishes every year, and it has now been closed because of the danger of falling rocks. Swim instead from the ancient fishing-boat ramps reached by a cobbled stepped footpath from below the *Postino* house. *Bar L'Oasis* has lilos, kayaks, sun umbrellas and masks to rent, and will bring sandwiches and drinks down from the bar.

Rinella

Most ferries and hydrofoils call at the little port of **RINELLA**, on the island's south coast. It's a drowsy place with something of a Greek island feel, its higgledy-piggledly fishermen's houses clustered above a black sand beach. A couple of good bars make it a tempting destination for an aperitif watching the sunset over Filicudi. Buses meet most boat arrivals on the quayside (and call here several times a day). Spilling along a ridge above the town, the little village of **Leni** has an appealingly sleepy feel and fantastic views over to Lipari and Vulcano.

ACTIVITIES ON SALINA

Walking trails cut right across Salina. Most accessible are the several tracks from the main port, Santa Marina and Lingua up to the peak of **Monte Fossa delle Felci** (962m). Look out for trailheads signed from the road between Santa Marina and Lingua, and also from the Circonvalazione that cuts behind Santa Marina. Paths are not very well used, and tend to get overgrown, so cover your legs if you don't want to get scratched by prickly scrub. The easiest ascent, however, is from the sanctuary of **Madonna del Terzito** in the lush village of Valdichiesa, in the saddle between the two mountains. A broad, easy-to-follow jeep track leads off from directly behind the sanctuary; it's about 10km to the top, and should take a couple of hours.

ACCOMMODATION

SALINA

SANTA MARINA DI SALINA

I Cinque Balconi Via Risorgimento 38 ⓣ 090 094 3517, ⓦ icinquebalconi.it. Simple rooms in an eighteenth-century townhouse on Santa Marina's pedestrianized main street, with striking floors of subtle, carefully preserved original tiles. Behind the hotel, there's an enchanting secluded garden, shaded by citrus and fig trees. It has eight rooms, several with sea views, plus a romantic suite overlooking the garden, with its own terrace. **€160**

★ **Mamma Santina** Via Sanità ⓣ 090 984 3054, ⓦ mammasantina.it. The affable Mario presides over a relaxed boutique-style hotel, set on wide terraces around a swimming pool high above the town with views over to Stromboli and Panarea. The sixteen rooms are in bright seaside colours, with Mediterranean ceramic tile floors and big bathrooms, and there are hammocks on the covered terraces. Call to be picked up from the port, or find the hotel signposted to the left off Via Risorgimento (after no. 66). Excellent deals negotiable in low season. Closed mid-Dec to mid-March. **€230**

Mercanti di Mare Piazza Santa Marina 7 ⓣ 090 984 3536, ⓦ hotelmercantidimare.it. Harbourfront three-star hotel with nine, white, airy rooms and an attractive terrace that overlooks the water. **€180**

LINGUA

A Cannata Via Umberto I ⓣ 090 984 3161 or ⓣ 339 575 4240, ⓦ acannata.it. Simple rooms above a restaurant a few metres back from the sea near the church, plus apartments of various sizes just across the road and around the village (€500/week). Good deals in low season. There's a decent restaurant, too. **€170**

Il Delfino Via Marina Garibaldi ⓣ 090 984 3024, ⓦ ildelfinosalina.it. Smart new rooms with marvellous terraces and views, set back from Lingua's *lungomare*; older rooms that open directly onto it are a good bet if you have children. Good deals in low season. The restaurant is lovely, with tables on the *lungomare*. **€160**

La Salina Borgo di Mare Via Manzoni ⓣ 090 984 3441, ⓦ lasalinahotel.com. This impressive four-star hotel is set in the restored buildings of the old salt-works, by Lingua's lagoon. The rooms are lovely, individually furnished, most with sea views and private terraces, while traditional tile- and stonework enhances public areas. There's no restaurant, but you can eat at nearby *Il Gambero* on a half-board basis. **€160**

CAPO FARO AND MALFA

Capo Faro Halfway between Santa Marina Salina and Malfa on the main road ⓣ 090 984 4330, ⓦ capofaro.it. At the five-star Tasca d'Almerita Malvasia wine estate a series of stunning, contemporary rooms occupy seven Aeolian-style houses that look down across the vineyards, and the converted buildings of the (still-operating) lighthouse. Facilities are top-notch, from a magnificent pool to classy bar and restaurant, and you can tour the vineyards on request. No children under 12. **€380**

★ **Signum** Via Scalo 15, Malfa ⓣ 090 984 4222, ⓦ hotelsignum.it. Island hotels don't come much better than this, deftly balancing style and luxury with friendly and relaxed service. Thirty comfortable rooms blend antique furniture with contemporary style and have either terraces or balconies, sea or garden views. There are sea views too, from the splendid infinity pool – indeed swimming here at night and catching sight of Stromboli erupting takes some beating. The exquisite spa, tapping into a hot volcanic spring, and offering treatments such as an anti-cellulite caper-rub, is not to be missed. There's also what is probably the island's best restaurant (reservations recommended for non-guests), serving Aeolian specialities. **€380**

16

EATING AND DRINKING

SANTA MARINA DI SALINA

★ **Mamma Santina** Via Sanità ⓣ 090 984 3054. This lovely hotel restaurant serves genuine island dishes, such as *linguine* with flakes of fish, wine, chilli, garlic and parsley and pasta with a pesto of fourteen herbs. They also do a delicious pasta with melted cheese and courgettes (two people or more). *Secondi* are mostly fish. Pasta dishes from €10, fish from €16.. Be sure to try the hot chocolate pudding and the pistacchio *semifreddo*. Mid-March–mid-Dec daily 12.30–2.30pm & 8–10.30pm.

Nni Lausta Via Risorgimento 188 ⓣ 090 984 3486. Cool bar-restaurant whose New York-trained owner-chef gives an adventurous twist to local dishes – like raw tuna dressed with wild fennel and capers, or crispy fish cakes made from the day's catch. That said, quality and service can be a bit erratic, and a full meal will cost at least €40 without wine, though you can just have a drink at the bar (until 2am); €6 at *aperitivo* will buy you a glass of decent Salina wine, with crostini and home-made dips, pestos and salsas, best sipped and nibbled at low tables outside watching life pass by. April–Oct daily 12.30–2.30pm & 8–10.30pm.

Porto Bello Via Bianchi 1 ⓣ 090 984 3125. Right above the harbour, with a terrace looking out to Lipari, this is a reliable and longstanding restaurant owned by a local writer. It serves excellent local antipasti – don't miss the chef's own *pasta al fuoco* with chopped cherry tomatoes, chilli and grated ricotta or the raw prawns with yogurt salsa. Main courses depend on the catch of the day. A four-course meal costs around €50

or so without wine. A good choice for a splash-out meal. Easter–Oct daily 12.30–2.30pm & 8–10.30pm.

LINGUA

★Da Alfredo Piazza Marina Garibaldi ⓣ090 984 3075. Right on the seafront piazza, this little café is known for its fresh fruit granitas (€3.50) – the summer yachties and boat-trippers queue up for a taste, while Dolce and Gabbana have on occasion brought Naomi Campbell along to try one. The other speciality is *pane cunzato* (from €10), a huge round of grilled bread piled with various combinations of home-cured tuna, capers, tomatoes, baked ricotta and olives. One between two will satisfy most. Easter–early Nov daily 7.30am–late.

Franco Manca Via Marina Garibaldi ⓣ090 984 3070 Giuseppe Mascoli, founder of the burgeoning UK pizza chain, spends his holidays in Salina, hence the Lingua outpost! The trademark scorched pizzas, topped with high-quality ingredients – along with sensationally speedy service – have made it a true winner. June–September, noon–late.

16

MALFA

★Signum Via Scalo 15 ⓣ090 984 4222, ⓦhotelsignum.it. Young, enthusiastic and attentive staff plus great cooking make dinner at the *Signum* special. Signature dishes include a *sformata* of raw prawns with pistachios, light and succulent fish *polpette*, and home-made ravioli stuffed with ricotta, orange and lemon zest, sprinkled with finely chopped lemon leaves. Hotel guests have priority until 4pm, after which bookings are taken from non-residents. Easter–late Oct daily 12.30–2.30pm & 8–10.30pm.

POLLARA

Al Cappero ⓣ090 984 3968. Simple, family-run place, with something of a Greek taverna feel – make sure you arrive in time to watch the sun set over the islands of Filicudi and Alicudi. *Frittelle di zucchine* (deep-fried courgette fritters) come free, after which there will be two or three pasta dishes (€8–10) of the day, invariably including one dressed with a pesto of their own capers. Fish (€10–14) comes grilled or fried, but the signature dish is a tasty *coniglio in agrodolce (€12)*, rabbit stewed in a Sicilian sweet–sour sauce. Easter–Nov daily 8–10.30pm.

RINELLA

Il Glicine Via Rotabile. Run with verve and passion by three siblings, this friendly bar does a great *tavola calda* of home-cooked food (and yummy cakes for afterwards). A great hangout at any time of day, but especially in the evening, when you can sit on the terrace and watch the sun set. Daily–late.

Panarea

Only 3km by 1.5km, **PANAREA** is the smallest, loveliest, most stylish and ridiculously expensive of the Aeolians, and in summer its harbours, hotels and villas overflow with an international crowd of designers, models, pop stars, film stars, royalty and their lackeys. In low season, however, the island is an utter delight, accommodation prices are relatively sane, and the three-hour walk up the peak of Pizzo Corvo and hugging the fractured coastline is one of the most stunning anywhere in Italy.

Cars are banned, and the only transport is by Vespa or electric golf cart. Panarea's couple of hundred year-round inhabitants live in three linked hamlets on the eastern side of the island, Ditella, San Pietro and Drauto, with the boats docking at **San Pietro**. Thirty minutes' walk south of San Pietro, clearly signposted, Zimmari is the island's one sandy **beach**. From here, a steep path leads up to **Punta Milazzese**, where you can see the foundations of 23 Bronze Age huts, with the glorious cove of Cala Junco below. Just before the Bronze Age village is the beginning of the well-marked track up Pizzo Corvo, circling the entire island and ending up at **Calcara** to the north of town, where there are steaming fumaroles on the beach.

DIVING IN THE AEOLIANS

There's plenty of fun to be had snorkelling in Aeolian waters. At **Panarea** you can snorkel over the submerged foundations of a Roman port, or head to the Salinan village of **Pollara**, where a giant offshore crater offers easy diving with lots to see. There are some great scuba dives as well – including the chance to explore the wreck of a Roman ship off **Filicudi**; a rope guides you down to the archeological area – a true underwater museum.

The islands' most professional diving outfit is Amphibia, with bases at the ports of Panarea and Salina (ⓣ335 613 8529, ⓦamphibia.it).

ACCOMMODATION — PANAREA

Albergo Girasole Via Drauto ⓣ090 983 018 or ⓣ328 861 8595, ⓦhotelgirasole-panarea.it. Family-run hotel at Drauto, out on the way to the sandy beach at Zimmari. Great place to stay in low season, but even this part of the island is busy in Aug. **€240**

Lisca Bianca Via Lani ⓣ090 983 004, ⓦliscabianca.it. This typical Aeolian building – covered wide terraces, blue shutters, white walls – has gorgeous views, with stylish rooms overlooking either the sea or the bougainvillea-clad gardens and port. You can see Stromboli from the breakfast terrace, and the bar is one of the best on the island. The *Casa Nonna* annexe has a few cheaper rooms in the village on Via Iditella, and if you can avoid Aug, prices aren't too bad at all (check website for promotions). Closed Nov–March. **€240**

Pippo and Maria Soldini Via Iditella ⓣ090 983 061 or ⓣ334 703 5010. Up the hill behind the port in Iditella beyond the Carabinieri barracks, these spotlessly clean rooms are among the least expensive places to stay on Panarea. They have their own terraces and are set in a garden and, out of season, owners Pippo and Maria will cook for you. **€120**

Quartara Via S. Pietro ⓣ090 983 027, ⓦquartarahotel.com. Very classy four-star boutique hotel run by a cheerful family: its thirteen fashionable rooms have elegant wood furniture and stone floors, with a terrace jacuzzi out the back overlooking the port. There's also a well-regarded restaurant. Closed Nov–March. **€300**

Raya Via S. Pietro ⓣ090 983 013, ⓦhotelraya.it. The hotel that put Panarea on the party map. Opened in the 1960s, it remains the hippest, sexiest and most expensive hotel in Sicily, even though owner Myriam Beltrami's refusal to install TVs and telephones means that it has only two stars. The place is built entirely of natural materials and food is organic, though the hotel's claim to be a simple retreat for nature lovers seems a little disingenuous when the place is crawling with party animals. Bar, club and restaurant are down above the harbour, rooms (whitewashed walls, teak furniture, hand-batiked textiles, citronella candles) are built into the hillside above the village, with great views to the sea over groves of olives, hibiscus and bougainvillea. **€540**

EATING AND DRINKING

16

Da Adelina Via Comunale Mare 28 ⓣ090 983 246, ⓦadelina-panarea.com. Intimate candlelit restaurant, with a romantic roof terrace overlooking Panarea's port. Relaxing and unpretentious, with a simple menu of seasonal dishes, such as *moscardini*, tiny octopus cooked with tomato, capers, wild fennel and chilli (€15), appearing alongside year-round dishes like *pennette adelina*, dressed with anchovies, aubergine, capers, olives, mint and basil (€10). For the main course opt for the mixed fish of the day, either fried or grilled (priced by weight, but expect to pay from €20 up for a whole fish). If you are staying in a villa, they also have a great chef at home catering service. March–Oct daily 12.30–2.30pm & 8–10.30pm.

Da Francesco Via S. Pietro ⓣ090 983 023, ⓦdafrancescopanarea.com. Overlooking the harbour, and pretty good value for meals of pasta (around €10–14), including the signature dish *"disgraziata"* with peppers, chilli, capers, olives, aubergine, tomatoes and baked ricotta, and fish (from €15). It also has rooms to rent in summer (€90–120), and a smart clothes boutique. March–Nov daily 12.30–2.30pm & 8–10.30pm.

Da Paolino Via Iditella 75 ⓣ090 983 008. Walking north towards Ditella, after 10min or so you'll reach this family-run restaurant whose terrace has fine views of Stromboli. You can spend quite a bit here, but an unpretentious meal of pasta and salad and a glass of wine will cost you €25–30 – try the handmade *mille baci* pasta with greens (€10.50) – and the fish is whatever the family have caught that day. April–Oct daily 12.30–2.30pm & 8–10.30pm.

Stromboli

Despite the regularity of the volcanic explosions, people have always lived on **STROMBOLI**. It is in a constant state of activity, throwing up fountains of fire and glowing rock every twenty minutes or so. A full eruption happens on average every ten years. A flow of lava is often visible from afar, slowly sliding down the northwest side of the volcano into the sea. In January 2003 there was a colossal landslide, triggering a 10m-high tsunami that inundated the coasts of Sicily and Calabria.

Most of the many hotels and rooms to let on the island are on the eastern side, in the adjacent parishes of San Vincenzo, San Bartolo and Piscità, often grouped together as **Stromboli Town** and something of a chic resort since Rossellini and Ingrid Bergman immortalized the place in the 1949 film *Stromboli*. From the quayside, the lower coastal road runs around to the beach of **Ficogrande** and, further on, **Piscità**, where there's a series of tiny lava coves with ashy sand. It's around 25 minutes on foot from the port to here. The other road from the dock

cuts up to the **Piazza di San Vincenzo**, which offers glorious views of the offshore islet of Strombolicchio.

On the other side of the island, accessible by hydrofoil, the hamlet of **Ginostra** is a laidback place of steeply terraced, white Aeolian houses, where the only way of getting about is on foot or donkey. **Hydrofoils** run back to Stromboli Town twice a day in summer (once daily in winter), but these are susceptible to cancellation because of rough waters.

GETTING AROUND AND TOURS — STROMBOLI

Taxis and lapas The only transport on the island is three-wheeler pick-up (known as a *lapa*), motorbike or electric car. The only official taxis are the electric golf carts, though unofficial *lapas* may offer their services. Despite this, as the electric cars take 10hr to charge for every 2hr driving, demand often outstrips supply. Of the official taxis, Sabbia Nera (090 986 399), based near the port, are reliable and friendly.

Boat trips The best boat trips are the tours around the island, calling at Ginostra and Strombolicchio (around 2hr 30min; €35), and trips out at night to see the Sciara del Fuoco (around 1hr 20min; €35). Try Pippo (338 985 7883), who has a stand in front of the *Beach Bar*, or Paola and Giovanni (338 431 2803), who work from opposite the *Sirenetta Park* hotel in Ficogrande.

ACCOMMODATION

In summer, the quayside is thick with three-wheelers and touts offering rooms; prices start at around €40/person. If you have a booking and are arriving in summer, ask your hotel to arrange a pick-up if you are far from the port or have baggage.

Casa del Mulino Piscità 338 540 8931, michele.wegner@gmail.com. Friendly, laidback, scruffy-bohemian place with four simple rooms (including two adjacent triples with their own terrace and kitchen) in an old windmill perched right on the lava-cliff edge above a black sandy cove. **€100**

Casa del Sole Via Soldato Cincotta, Piscità 090 986 300. A cheapie in an old building metres from the sea. Simple four- to six-bed apartments are available all year (both with en-suite bathrooms and without), and the accommodation is pretty flexible, whether you want a single or multi-bed room. Kitchen facilities are available, and there's a sun terrace. Great deals in low season. No credit cards. **€90**

La Sirenetta Park Via Marina 33, Ficogrande 090 986 025, lasirenettahotel.it. Four-star hotel set opposite the black sands of Ficogrande. It's got a decent-sized outdoor pool, a summer nightclub and access to watersports facilities. The room rates drop considerably outside summer and at the beginning or end of the season you can stay for around €120. **€240**

Petrusa Ginostra 090 981 2305. Ginostra's only official accommodation (though you may find rooms if you ask around) has three large rooms with their own terraces, sharing a bathroom. No credit cards. Closed Oct–April. **€120**

Vilaggio Stromboli Via Regina Elena 090 986 018, villaggiostromboli.it. With simple rooms jutting up against the breaking waves, this pleasant, quiet place is one of the nicest seaside stays; it also has a good terrace restaurant where you can gaze out over the water. **€200**

EATING AND DRINKING

La Lampara Via Vittorio Emanuele 090 986 009. Dine on the large raised terrace beneath a pergola of climbing vines among huge pots of basil and rosemary. Dishes include pizza (from €6), pasta and grilled meat and fish. April–Oct daily 12.30–2.30pm & 8–10.30pm.

Zurro Via Marina s/n 090 986 283. Not exactly

CLIMBING STROMBOLI

Guides for the **ascent of the volcano** cost around €30/person from all companies, though if eruptions are thought to be dangerous, the mountain is closed; try Magmatrek on Via Vittorio Emanuele (090 986 5768, magmatrek.it), where the staff are well informed and in constant radio contact with the volcanologists at the control centre. The climb up takes three hours, and you are expected to go at a fair whack; at first, it is no different from climbing any mountain, then suddenly all vegetation stops, giving way to black ash strewn with small jagged boulders spewed out by the volcano. At the top, all you can see at first are clouds of white steam – then suddenly there will be a resounding clash, the clouds glow red, and spouts of fire shoot into the air, the glowing boulders drawing tracks of red light across the night sky. You should not attempt the climb alone. Be equipped for a tough-ish hike, and for a night climb bring warm clothes and a torch.

romantic, with its startlingly bright lights, but you eat well at *Zurro*, named after its bearded, piratical-looking chef, a one-time fisherman. Choose from razor-thin slices of raw aubergine, flecked with chilli flakes served with balsamic-dressed rocket and parmesan; *spaghetti alla strombolana*, with cherry tomatoes, anchovies, mint, chilli and garlic (€15); or *pietre di mare* – black ravioli stuffed with *ricciola* and dressed with capers, cherry tomatoes and basil (€15). The chocolate cake is a must. **April–Oct daily 12.30–2.30pm & 8pm–late.**

Filicudi

FILICUDI, the larger of the two most westerly islands, is a fascinating place, the contours of its sheer slopes traced with steep stone terraces and crisscrossed by stone mule tracks. It is an island best explored on foot, which is just as well, as there is no public transport. The tarmac road that connects the several small settlements gives a false impression of the island, making villages seem far apart when they are, in fact, just a few minutes' walk away: most of the tracks are pretty steep, though, occasionally following, but mostly cutting between, the ancient terraces carved into the slopes of maquis and prickly pear.

The main settlement, **Filicudi Porto**, has a couple of shops, bars, hotels and a pharmacy. Inland, accessible by road or mule track, are three whitewashed villages, **Valdichiesa**, **Rocche Ciauli** and **Pecorini**. And down on the west coast, about 3km by road from the port, is the lovely little seaside village of **Pecorini Mare**.

GETTING AROUND — FILICUDI

There is no public transport. If you are not up to walking, use the red minivan-taxi that meets most boat arrivals (€14/person to Pecorini Mare). If it's not there, or if you want to book in advance, call D&G Servizio Navetta (347 757 5916). Although distances by road can seem considerable, the island is crisscrossed with a series of mule tracks, which – as long as you don't mind a steepish climb – can get you from one village to another far more quickly than you might imagine.

16

ACCOMMODATION AND EATING

★ **La Canna** Via Rosa 43, Rocche Ciauli 090 988 9956, lacannahotel.it. The best choice near the port, though it's a stiff climb up the steps to Rocche Ciauli; call ahead and they'll pick you up from the dock. Ten lovely bright rooms with tiled bathrooms open onto a spacious terrace with a magnificent view over the bay below. There's a small pool (summer only), and the food is excellent – home-made pasta, fresh fish, local caper salads and plenty of home-produced wine and fruit. **€120**

★ **La Sirena** Pecorini Mare 090 988 9997, pensionelasirena.it. An oasis you won't want to leave, this cosy inn sits right on the Pecorini Mare seafront, with the fishing boats drawn up alongside. A varied selection of rooms is available, some with antique furniture and little waterfront balconies, others in self-contained houses not far away. Out on the shaded terrace is the island's most relaxed restaurant (lunch and dinner, non-guests welcome). It gets very busy in Aug, but at most times of year all you can hear is the sound of lapping water as you tuck into the likes of spaghetti with almond sauce and fresh grilled tuna. Half-board-only July & Aug (€110–120/person). Closed Oct–May. **€180**

Alicudi

End-of-the-line Europe doesn't come much more remote than **ALICUDI**, a stark cone rising from the sea two and a half hours from Milazzo by hydrofoil. Electricity arrived only in the 1990s, and the sole way of getting about is on foot, although there are six donkeys to carry heavy loads. There are just eighty year-round inhabitants, while superstitions and sightings of ghosts abound – as does the conviction that some Alicudari are blessed with the power to control the weather and divert cyclones. Up the sheer slope behind the tiny port, terraced smallholdings and whitewashed flat-roofed houses linked by lava-paved paths cling on for dear life, among bursts of bougainvillea.

Hiking on Alicudi

Most of the **hiking** here is up stepped tracks that seem to have been designed with giants in mind, so be prepared for a good deal of calf-work. If you don't fancy hauling

yourself to the top of the island (675m; 2hr), you'll still get plenty of exercise climbing up to the church of San Bartolomeo. Otherwise, follow the path north out of the port behind the church of the Carmine, from where it's an easy walk to the narrow stony beach of Bazzina, with a couple of smallholdings behind it.

ACCOMMODATION AND EATING — ALICUDI

Silvio Taranto Via Regina Elena ⓣ090 988 9922. Although there is a modern hotel in the port, the most interesting option is to call Silvio, a local who speaks English and can put you in touch with people who have rooms to rent. For twenty years he and his wife have been cooking dinner at their house above the port for whoever needs a place to eat. There's no menu and no choice, and everyone eats the same, sitting at long tables on the family's terrace, drinking locally produced red wine. Expect to pay around €25–30 per person for dinner depending on the menu on offer that day. €55

The Ionian coast

Sicily's eastern **Ionian coast** draws the largest number of visitors, attracted by **Taormina**, most chic of the island's resorts and famed for its remarkable Greco-Roman theatre; **Mount Etna**, Europe's highest volcano; and the island's second city, **Catania**. Further south, out of the lee of Etna, **Siracusa** was formerly the most important and beautiful city in the Hellenistic world, its enchanting *centro storico* surrounded by water.

16

Messina

MESSINA may well be your first sight of Sicily, and – from the ferry – it's a fine one, the glittering town spread up the hillside beyond the sickle-shaped harbour. Sadly, the image is shattered almost as soon as you step into the city, bombed and shaken to a shadow of its former self by plague, cholera and earthquakes. The great earthquake of 1908 killed 84,000 people, levelled the city and made the shore sink by half a metre overnight. Allied bombing raids in 1943 didn't help, undoing much of the post-earthquake restoration.

Today, the remodelled city guards against future natural disasters, with wide streets and low, reinforced concrete buildings. Few people hang around for long, but if you do need to stay overnight, Messina has a couple of worthwhile sights – the impressivly reconstructed Norman **Duomo** and the **Museo Regionale**, home to some of Sicily's best fifteenth- to seventeenth-century art. It's also a good place to be on the feast of the Assumption, or **Ferragosto** (Aug 15), when a towering carriage, the Vara – an elaborate column supporting dozens of papier-mâché *putti* and angels, topped by the figure of Christ – is hauled through the city centre, followed by a firework display on the seafront.

The Duomo

Piazza del Duomo • **Duomo:** Daily 9am–12.30pm & 4–7pm; **Treasury:** Aug daily 9.30am–1pm & 4–7.30pm; Sept–July usually Mon–Sat 9.30am–1pm • €4, or €6 including campanile

Messina's most important monument, the **Duomo**, epitomizes the city's phoenix-like ability to re-create itself from the ashes of its last disaster. It's the reconstruction of a twelfth-century cathedral erected by Roger II, one of a series of great Norman churches that included the sumptuous cathedrals of Palermo and Cefalù. Devastated by the earthquake in 1908, it was rebuilt in the years following World War I, only to fall victim to a firebomb in 1943 that reduced it once more to rubble. What you see today is mostly a faithful copy, which took years to complete, with few elements remaining of the original fabric.

The Romanesque facade is its best aspect, the lower part mostly authentic and dominated by a richly decorated, late-Gothic **central portal**, extravagantly pointed, with

good detail, and flanked by two smaller contemporary doors. Almost everything in the undeniably grand **interior** is a reproduction, from the marble floor to the sturdy columns lining the nave, topped by cement capitals faithfully copied from originals, some of which can still be seen in the Museo Regionale. Of the **mosaicwork** in the three grand apses, only the mosaic on the left – of the Virgin Mary with St Lucy – is original.

The **tesoro** holds precious reliquaries, the bejewelled *Manta d'Oro* – a holy adornment for sacred images, of a kind more commonly used in Orthodox rites – and a collection of skilfully crafted silverware.

Museo Regionale

Via della Libertà 465 • Tues–Sat 9am–7pm (last entry 6.30pm), Sun 9am–1pm (last entry 12.30pm) • €8 • T 090 361292, W www.regione.sicilia.it • It's a 45min walk along Via della Libertà, or take tram #28 to the terminus, Annunziata; the museum is on the left, immediately after the Regina Margherita hospital

Messina's **Museo Regionale** is a repository for some of the city's greatest works of art, many of them carefully rescued from earthquake rubble, and includes what is perhaps Sicily's finest collection of fifteenth- to seventeenth-century art.

The highlight of the collection is the *St Gregory* polyptych, in room 4, by Sicily's greatest native artist, **Antonello da Messina** – a masterful synthesis of Flemish and Italian Renaissance styles that's a good example of the various influences that reached Messina in the fifteenth century. A sixteenth-century statue of *Scilla*, who terrorized sailors from the Calabrian coast (as described in Homer's *Odyssey*), is on display in **room 6** – a suitably alarming spectacle, she originally formed part of the Neptune fountain down on the city's waterfront. There are also two works (room 10) by **Caravaggio**, *Raising of Lazarus* and *Adoration of the Shepherds*, commissioned by the city in 1609, when Caravaggio arrived in Messina, on the run from the Knights of Malta.

ARRIVAL AND INFORMATION — MESSINA

By train Messina is connected by direct train with Milazzo, Catania, Taormina, Siracusa, Cefalù and Palermo. It is also the last station in Sicily for trains heading to Italy across the Strait – the trains shunt onto ferries, which carry them over to Villa San Giovanni. All trains pass through the Stazione Centrale, adjacent to the Stazione Marittima by the harbour, where train-ferries from Calabria dock.

By bus Buses stop outside the train station. If you are going to the Aeolian islands it is easier to take the bus than the train to Milazzo, as it stops right at Milazzo's port.

Destinations Catania (approx hourly; 1hr 35min); Catania airport (approx hourly; 1hr 50min); Milazzo (approx hourly; 50min); Palermo (6 daily; 2hr 40min); Taormina (9 daily; 1hr–1hr 50min).

By hydrofoil To get to the hydrofoil dock (for the Aeolian islands and Reggio di Calabria) from Messina Centrale walk straight along platform 1, which brings you to the Stazione Marittima. The hydrofoil dock is straight across the road. Allow 10min on foot if you have luggage. On no account take a taxi from outside the station – they will attempt to fleece you. There is one hydrofoil daily to Reggio di Calabria and the Aeolian islands throughout the year, and four–five daily in summer (mid-June to mid-Sept).

By car ferry Car ferries (to and from Villa San Giovanni and Reggio di Calabria) dock and depart several times an hour from quays about 1km north of the hydrofoil dock on Via della Libertà, and are well signposted.

Tourist information Inside the Palazzo Civile, Via dei Mille 270 (Mon–Fri 9.30am–1.30pm, Wed (when staffing permits) also 3.30–4.30pm; T 090 293 5292).

GETTING AROUND

By tram You can walk easily from the station or harbour to the centre of town, but to venture anywhere further, take the city's single tram line (#28), running between Annunziata in the north (for the Museo Regionale) to Gazzi in the south, with departures from Piazza della Repubblica, Piazza Cairoli and Piazza Municipio every 10min (every 30min on Sun). Tickets (€1.20 for a single journey; €1.25 valid 90min; €1.70 valid two journeys a day, or €2.60 all day) are available at *tabacchi*.

By bus A fun, easy way to see the city is on the hop-on-hop-off open-top red double decker bus run by City Sightseeing Messina, which stops at Piazza Duomo, Via Garibaldi, the Museo Regionale and Cristo Re. Tickets cost €15 online or from the office at Via Cesare Battisti 7 (daily 9am–6pm). In summer they also run a shuttle service (€5 daily ticket) out to the lidos that line the Strait to the west of the city.

By taxi Ranks at Piazza Cairoli (T 090 293 4880), Piazza della Repubblica, outside Stazione Centrale (T 090 673 703), and at the Caronte terminal; 24hr radio taxi (T 090 6505).

ACCOMMODATION

Messina Guest House Via Reitano Spadafora 1 T 090 958 6266, W guesthousemessina.it. Smart, stylish B&B occupying the first floor of an apartment on busy Corso Europa. Rooms are soundproofed, with dark wood fittings and furniture. The bathrooms are spacious and some rooms have terraces. **€90**

Sole Luna Via Solferino 9 T 328 678 7901, W bbsoleluna.it. Perfect central location, on a small street between Viale San Martino and Via Garibaldi, a hop and a skip from the hydrofoil port and Piazza Cairoli. The three rooms are cheerfully decorated and spotlessly clean. **€65**

Town House Messina Via Giordano Bruno 66 T 090 293 6097, W townhousemessina.it. Bijou B&B just off Piazza Cairoli, with minimalist rooms decorated in subtle shades of mink, white and grey. Fabulous bathrooms and contemporary art on the walls. **€90**

EATING AND DRINKING

Al Gattopardo Via Santa Cecilia 184 T 090 673 076. With tables outside on a tree-lined avenue, *Al Gattopardo* is a Messinese institution. The pizzas are some of the best in town (try the Messinese with escarole, mozzarella, anchovies and black pepper; €8) but there are other tempting choices too – including a fine *zuppe di cozze* (mussel soup) for €9. Tues–Sun noon–2pm & 8–10.30pm (later in summer).

Fratelli La Bufala Corso Vittorio Emanuele 1 T 090 662 513, W fratellilabufala.eu. A branch of the superior Neapolitan pizza chain committed to using no hydrogenated fats or genetically modified ingredients: it is handy for the hydrofoil dock and serves great pizza (with buffalo mozzarella, of course) along with buffalo-meat *secondi* and Campanian wines. Two could eat a pizza and have a glass of wine for less than €20. Daily 12.30–2.30pm & 8–10.30pm.

Irrera Piazza Cairoli 12 T 090 673 823, W irrera.it. Founded in 1910, this historic *pasticceria* makes excellent Sicilian biscuits, cakes, pastries, *cornetti* and *cannoli*, while slick service during lunch (good sandwiches) and the *aperitivo* hour make this a popular spot throughout the day. Daily 7.30am–late.

Taormina

TAORMINA, perched high on Monte Tauro, with Mount Etna as backdrop, looks down on two grand, sweeping bays and is Sicily's best-known resort. D.H. Lawrence was so enraptured that he lived here from 1920–23, in a house at the top of the valley cleft, behind the remains of the Greek theatre. Although international tourism has taken its toll, Taormina is still a very charming town, peppered with small, intimate piazzas. The single traffic-free main street is an unbroken line of fifteenth- to nineteenth-century *palazzi* decked out with flower-filled balconies, and there is an agreeably crumbly castle. The downside is that between June and August it's virtually impossible to find anywhere to stay, and the narrow alleys are shoulder-to-shoulder with tourists. April, May or September are slightly better, but to avoid the crowds completely come between October and March, when it's often still warm enough to swim in the sea.

As well as the **Greek theatre**, there are several vestiges of Roman Taormina around town, including a small **Odeon** (used for musical recitations) next to the tourist office. Really, though, Taormina's attractions are all to do with strolling and window-shopping along the Corso. Centre of town is **Piazza IX Aprile**, with its restored twelfth-century **Torre dell'Orologio** and fabulous views of Etna and the bay from the terraces of its pricey cafés.

The Teatro Greco

Daily 9am–1hr before sunset • €10 • W teatrogrecotaormina.com

The views from the **Teatro Greco** are arguably more stunning than the ruins themselves, encompassing southern Calabria, the Sicilian coastline down to Siracusa and the smouldering heights of Etna. The theatre was founded by the Greeks in the third century BC but the visible remains are almost entirely Roman, dating from the end of the first century AD, when Taormina thrived under imperial Roman rule. The theatre was converted to stage gladiatorial combat and a deep trench was dug in the orchestra to accommodate animals and fighters. Between July and August the theatre hosts an international **arts festival** including opera, film, drama and rock and classical music: check Wteatrogrecotaormina.com for the programme, tickets and information.

Taormina's beaches

The huge resort of **Giardini-Naxos**, just to the south of Taormina, is a favourite with international package companies, and best avoided: **Mazzarò**, the closest beach to town is lovelier by far. With a much-photographed offshore islet, several fish trattorias and a **cable car** that runs every fifteen minutes from Via Pirandello (the road that encircles old Taormina), it's an ideal place to relax after sightseeing or shopping.

ARRIVAL AND DEPARTURE — TAORMINA

By train Taormina is a stop on the main Messina–Catania–Siracusa line. Trains pull up at the handsome Taormina-Giardini station on the water's edge, below town. It's a very steep 30min walk up to Taormina (turn right out of the station and then, after 200m, left through a gap in the buildings, marked "Centro") and the road is extremely busy. Much better to take one of the Interbus buses (every 30min–1hr) that pick up outside the train station.

By bus Buses arrive at the terminal on Via Luigi Pirandello in the centre of town.

Destinations Catania (16 daily; 1hr 40min); Catania airport (6 daily Mon–Sat; 1hr 25min).

By car If you're arriving by car, make for the Porta Catania multistorey car park, below Piazza S. Antonio.

Tourist office Palazzo Corvaja, off Piazza Vittorio Emanuele (Mon–Fri 8.30am–2.15pm & 3.30–6.45pm; Easter–Oct also Sat 9am–1pm & 4–6.30pm; June–Sept also Sun 9am–1pm; T 0942 23 243, W comune.taormina.me.it).

16

ACCOMMODATION

Pensione Svizzera Via Pirandello 26 T 0942 23 790, W hotelpensionesvizzera.com. Just up from the bus terminal and cable-car station, this comfortable hotel has excellent views from its spacious rooms (sea-view rooms cost extra), 24hr bar service, free wi-fi throughout and a shuttle to a private beach. Excellent value for money. **€160**

San Domenico Palace Piazza S. Domenico 5 T 0942 613 111, W san-domenico-palace.com. The last word in luxury. One of the most celebrated hotels in Italy, housed in a fifteenth-century convent, with gorgeous formal gardens, unsurpassable views, a Michelin-starred restaurant and stratospheric prices. Staff are refreshingly relaxed and gracious. The luxury suites cost €3000/night, but check the website as there are deals on rooms for a fraction of that. **€350**

Taormina's Odyssey Via Paterno di Biscaria 13, near Porta Catania T 0942 24 533, W taorminaodyssey.it. Homely and comfortable, with four double rooms and two dorms. There is a kitchen for guest use, rooms have a/c and TV, and there's even a terrace. It is understandably popular, so book well ahead. Dorms **€20**, doubles **€40**

★ **Villa Angela** Via Leonardo da Vinci T 0942 27 038, W hotelvillaangela.com. Ever wondered what rock stars do in their spare time? Jim Kerr of Simple Minds plumped for opening a boutique four-star hotel, high on the Castelmola road above town. It's a swish, contemporary take on a traditional villa, with terrific views from soaring picture windows, an open-air pool and a terrace restaurant. The staff are especially friendly. It's a steep walk from Taormina itself, but the hotel lays on an efficient shuttle to town and beach, and there's a bus stop directly outside. **€195**

Villa Carlotta Via Pirandello 81 T 0942 626 058, W hotelvillacarlottataormina.com. Splendidly sited above the sea among abundant subtropical vegetation, this hotel could has a roof garden with spectacular views (very romantic and candlelit at night), and a terraced garden with a small pool set among citrus and olive trees, bougainvillea and mint. There's a comfortable, homely sitting room with books, games and sofas, and all the stylish rooms but one have bathtubs. **€250**

Villa Floresta Via Damiano Rosso 1 T 0942 620 184, W villafloresta.it. Pleasant, family-run B&B in a nineteenth-century *palazzo* tucked into a courtyard with a crumbling fifteenth-century staircase behind Piazza del Duomo. Most rooms have balconies, with views of the sea or the Duomo. **€90**

★ **Villa Greta** Via Leonardo da Vinci 41 T 0942 28 286, W villagreta.it. Family-run place 15min walk out of town on the road up to Castelmola, with superb balcony views. The dining room serves good home cooking, and in winter, there's tea with complimentary home-made cakes and biscuits. **€108**

Villa Schuler Piazzetta Bastione T 0942 23 481, W villaschuler.com. This lovely old hotel has been in the same family of German émigrés for a century, and retains the feel of an elegant family-run *pensione* (they take no tour groups). There are great views from its rooms and terrace, and a beautiful garden behind. Worth checking the website for special offers. **€160**

EATING, DRINKING AND NIGHTLIFE

Eating in Taormina can be expensive. For snacks or picnic ingredients, head to the indoor market off Via Cappuccini (Mon–Sat mornings only). Nightlife in Taormina is focused on the gay bars around gorgeous Piazza Paladini, just off the Corso, moving down to various beach clubs in the summer – whose names tend to change from season to season.

Al Grappola d'Uva Via Bagnoli Croce 6–8 T 0942 625 874. Friendly, unpretentious wine bar – a good place to

sample Etna wines with olives and local cheeses (from €5 a glass including nibbles). They can also organize tours of Etna's vineyards. Daily 9am–8pm.

Re di Bastoni Corso Umberto I ⊕0942 23 037. For unpretentious after-dinner boozing head for the boho *Re di Bastoni*, quite alternative for Taormina and attracting a lively crowd. Around noon–late; closed Mon in winter.

Trattoria da Nino Via Luigi Pirandello 37 ⊕0942 21 265. Welcoming place that, despite its touristy appearance, is popular with locals for its fresh food: the mixed vegetable (€13) or mixed fish (€18) antipasti are particularly good – and enough for a light lunch for two. There are plenty of *primi* for €10, though plenty others that cost considerably more, while *secondi* run from €14 for meat and €16 for fish. Daily 12.30–2.30pm & 8–10.30pm.

Vecchia Taormina Vico Ebrei 3 ⊕0942 625 589. Popular pizzeria in an alley across from the Duomo serving light, blistered pizzas (from €6.50) from its wood-fired oven. Daily 12.30pm–late.

Wunderbar Café Piazza IX Aprile ⊕0942 625 302. Once the haunt of Garbo and Fassbinder, this is the place to splash out on an Aperol Spritz at aperitif time or an after-dinner drink. Daily 7.30am–midnight or later.

Mount Etna

16

The bleak lava wilderness around the summit of **Mount Etna** is one of the most memorable landscapes Italy has to offer. The volcano's height is constantly shifting, depending on whether eruptions are constructive or destructive, and over the last century it has ranged from 3263m to the present estimate of 3340m. Whatever its exact height, Etna is a substantial mountain, one of the world's biggest active volcanoes, and on a clear day it can be seen from well over half of Sicily. Some of its eruptions have been disastrous: in 1169, 1329 and 1381 the lava reached the sea and in 1669 Catania was wrecked and its castle surrounded by molten rock. The volcano has been in an almost continual **state of eruption** since 1998, meaning that, at times, access is strictly limited. Note that the **ski season** on Etna lasts from around November to March, though obviously this can vary from year to year.

ARRIVAL AND DEPARTURE — MOUNT ETNA

By car There are several approaches to the volcano. If you have a car, you can enjoy some of the best scenery on the north side of the volcano by taking the circular road that leads up from Linguaglossa to Piano Provenzana, a good place to bring the kids in winter to learn to ski or toboggan.

By bus On public transport, you'll be limited to exploring Etna from the southern side, though this does at least give you easy access by cable car to the summit. There are frequent buses to the village of Nicolosi from Catania; one (8am from outside Catania train station) continues to the *Hotel/Rifugio Sapienza* at the end of the negotiable road up the south side of Etna. Arriving on the early-morning bus, you should have enough time to make it to the top and get back for the return bus to Catania – it leaves for Catania again at around 4.30pm.

By cable car The Funivia dell'Etna cable car (daily, weather and volcano permitting: summer 9am–5.30pm; winter 9am–3.30pm; €30 return; ⓦfuniviaetna.com) runs from the *Hotel Rifugio Sapienza* (see below) to an altitude of 2500m at Monte Montagnola.

On foot You can walk all the way up from the *Hotel Rifugio Sapienza* but it will take around four hours, and is a dull trudge up slopes of lava. So you are better off taking the cable car to Monte Montagnola and walking from there. Once at the top paths are clearly marked, though not signposted, giving various views of the three central craters and Valle di Bove, though as ever, how far you are permitted to go depends on volcanic activity.

By 4WD minbus These leave from the top of the cable-car station, with routes as ever depending on the volcanic activity (April–Oct daily 9am–5pm, weather permitting; ⊕095 914 141). The total journey (including cable car, minibus and guide) takes around two and a half hours and costs €64/person. When the wind is up, or conditions are otherwise difficult, the entire journey is undertaken from *Hotel Rifugio Sapienza* by minibus.

ACCOMMODATION AND EATING

Hotel/Rifugio Sapienza Piazzale Rifugio Sapienza, Nicolosi Nord, Etna Sud ⊕095 915 321, ⓦrifugiosapienza.com. Simple, but comfortable (with central heating in winter) this *rifugio* right by the cable-car station is more like a little Alpine hotel than a refuge. It doesn't have the "away from it all" feel of *Ragabo* or *Citelli*, but is the only refuge accessible on public transport. There are 25 rooms, all with TV and private bathroom, and a restaurant too – half board deals available on request. €80

Rifugio Citelli Clearly signposted and marked on all maps ⊕095 930 000, ⓦrifugiocitelli.net. A tiny, spartan *rifugio* dating back to the 1930s, from which the views on a

clear day stretch to the Aspromonte mountains of Calabria. When it is open, there is basic accommodation – and occasional mountain-sausage dinners – plus an annual programme of excursions ranging from trekking to snow-shoeing. Half board €55/person. **€70**

Rifugio Ragabo Strada Mareneve, Pineta Bosco Ragabo, Linguaglossa ⓣ 095 647 841, ⓦ ragabo.it. Cosy and warm, this Alpine-style *rifugio*, 1450m above sea level, is the perfect place to get away from it all. It has little pine bedrooms and a restaurant where you can keep the cold at bay with hearty mountain fare. There are excursions and treks available, and they can help you organize skiing. Half-board is €55/person. **€70**

The Alcantara Valley

The dramatic riverscapes of the **Alcantara Valley** lie between the northern slopes of Etna and the foothills of the Peloritani mountains. Around 2400 BC, the volcano of Monte Moia, at the head of the valley, erupted, smothering the river and filling the valley with lava. Over four millennia, the river has carved its way through the deposits of slick grey basalt, scooping it into all manner of strange, sculptural rock formations. As you head along the SS185 from the coast just south of Taormina, the most theatrical (and touristy) part of the gorge is at **Motta Camastra**. There's a **visitor centre** (daily 9am–sunset) with a restaurant and souvenir shops. Here you pay €10 (€13 in August) to descend in a lift to the bottom and follow a geological and botanical itinerary, extending for 1.5km above the river. River-trekking and body rafting expeditions (€30 and €40 respectively) can be booked at the ticket office. A couple of hundred metres beyond the visitor centre, there is free public access to the gorge, down a flight of steps.

Francavilla di Sicilia

If you want to escape the crowds, continue from Motta Camastra another 4km to the largely modern town of **Francavilla di Sicilia**. Here, following brown signs to *Le Gurne*, you twist up to the ancient, and largely abandoned, centre of town, from where a well-marked path winds down to the river, through groves of citrus and nut trees overlooked by a toothy old castle. Here you'll find a series of waterfalls and natural round ponds where you can swim.

Castiglione di Sicilia

The nicest place to stay in the Alcantara Valley is **Castiglione di Sicilia**. On a hilltop above the valley, the town's lovely weather-eroded houses with pantiled roofs cluster below the remains of a castle founded in the fifth century BC by Greek exiles from nearby Naxos. There are plenty of old churches, including a perfectly restored Byzantine chapel in the valley below, known as "La Cuba" for its perfect symmetry. Behind "La Cuba" a path leads to the river, where there are more little waterfalls and pools.

ACCOMMODATION AND EATING — **CASTIGLIONE DI SICILIA**

Hotel Federico II Via Maggiore Baracca 2 ⓣ 0942 980 368, ⓦ hotelfedericosecondo.com. A chic yet reasonably priced little hotel just off the main piazza, with an excellent restaurant, *Sine Tempore* (open to non-residents) serving local

HIKING ON ETNA

There are some fantastic **trails** on Etna, but bear in mind that the topography here changes rapidly, maps can be out of date, and conditions challenging even for experienced trekkers. Trekking with an authorized guide is a good idea, especially on the upper slopes and craters, and has the advantage that you will find out far more about the volcano than you would walking alone: Etna Walks (ⓣ 339 256 3014; English spoken) is highly recommended. However you go, take warm clothes, a hat, good shoes or boots and – especially if you wear contact lenses – glasses to keep the flying grit out of your eyes. Weather conditions higher up are often different to those at the *rifugio*, so you might want to take advantage of the padded jackets (€3) that are available to rent from the minibus guides. Food on the mountain is poor and overpriced, so bring a picnic.

produce in simple, tasty dishes. The mixed antipasto (€10) is a great way of trying lots of local goodies, while to follow there is *tagliatelle Federico Secondo* (with porcini mushrooms, courgettes and pancetta; €9) or handmade ravioli dressed with pistachios from Bronte (€10). Restaurant sometimes closes on Wed if there are no guests in the hotel. **€100**

Catania

Bang in the middle of the Ionian coast, **CATANIA** is Sicily's second-largest city, a major transport hub, a thriving commercial centre, and a lively, energetic place with a more international outlook than Palermo. Defined by Etna – even the city's main street is named after the volcano – and the ubiquitous black-grey volcanic stone in pavements and buildings, Catania has more openness and space than in Palermo, but far less to see, as the ancient and medieval city was engulfed by lava in 1669, and then devastated

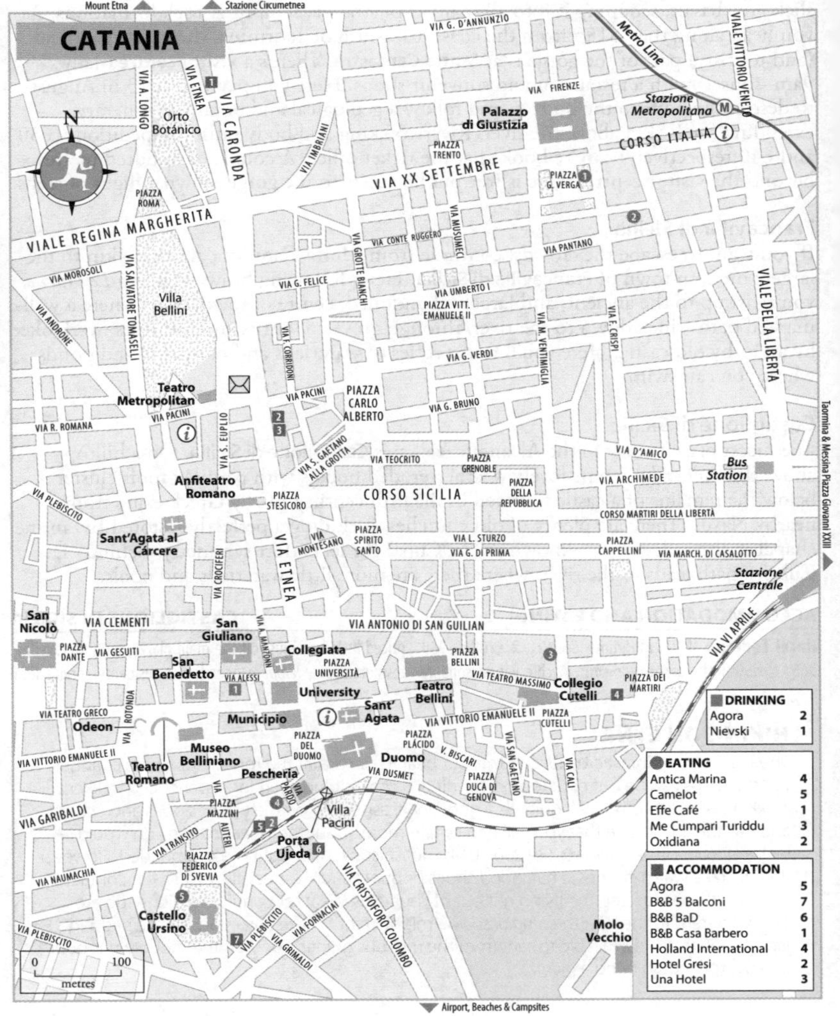

by an earthquake in 1693. Spearheaded by architect Giovanni Vaccarini, Catania was rebuilt swiftly and on a grand scale, making full use of the lava that had been the old city's nemesis.

Piazza del Duomo

Catania's main square, **Piazza del Duomo**, is a handy orientation point and a stop for most city buses: **Via Etnea** heads north, lined with the city's most fashionable shops and cafés; the fish market and port lie behind to the south; the train station to the east; and the best of the Baroque quarter to the west. It's also one of Sicily's most attractive city squares, rebuilt completely in the first half of the eighteenth century by Vaccarini. Most striking of the buildings is the **Municipio** on the northern side, best seen from the central reserve of the piazza beside the **elephant fountain**, the city's symbol, an eighteenth-century lava elephant supporting an Egyptian obelisk on its back.

The Duomo

Piazza del Duomo • Mon–Sat 9am–noon & 4–6pm, Sun 7.30am–12.30pm & 4–7pm • Free

The **Duomo,** on the piazza's eastern flank, retains marvellous volcanic-rock medieval apses (seen through the gate at Via Vittorio Emanuele 159), though the rest was remodelled by Vaccarini, who incorporated granite columns from Catania's Roman amphitheatre onto the facade. The interior has a series of richly adorned chapels, notably the Cappella di Sant'Agata to the right of the choir, which holds the relics of the saint paraded through the city on her feast day.

Museo Diocesano and the Terme Achilliane

16

Piazza Duomo • Mon–Fri 9am–2pm, Tues & Thurs 9am–2pm & 3–6pm, Sat 9am–1pm • Museum €7, Terme Achilliane €5, joint ticket €10 • ⓣ 095 281 636, ⓦ museodiocesanocatania.com

To the right of the Duomo, the **Museo Diocesano** is home to the cathedral's collection of religious art and silverware. Beautifully presented as the museum is, most people will find more appeal in the remains of the **Terme Achilliane**, Catania's Imperial Roman baths, which form part of the museum. They're perhaps not quite as alluring as they were in the days of eighteenth-century French traveller Jean Houel, who, discovering a hall covered with stuccoes of Cupids, vines, grapes and animals, concluded that it must have been a Temple to Bacchus. It was actually a Roman baths complex which originally stretched right across the piazza as far as the Pescheria.

Pescheria

Mon–Sat 7am–2pm

Catania's best-known food and fish market, the **Pescheria**, is reached from the back of Piazza del Duomo by nipping down the steps behind a gushing marble fountain. This takes you right into the main part of the fish market, where vendors shout across slabs and buckets full of twitching fish, eels, crabs and shellfish. Brandishing wicked-looking knives, they slice off swordfish steaks to order, while others shuck oysters, mussels and sea urchins for browsing customers. The side alleys off the fish market are dense with stalls selling fruit, vegetables, dried goods and herbs, as well as cheese counters and bloody butchers' tables.

The Museo Civico

Piazza Federico di Svevia • Mon–Sat 9am–7pm (last entry 6.30pm), Sun 9am–1.30pm (last entry 1pm) • €6 • ⓣ 095 345 830

Castello Ursino, once the proud fortress of Frederick II, stands at the heart of an atmospheric, if dilapidated, neighbourhood beyond the market. Originally the castle stood on a rocky cliff, over the beach, but following the 1669 eruption, which reclaimed this entire area from the sea, all that remains is the blackened keep. It now houses the **Museo Civico**, part of whose ground floor hosts temporary exhibitions, while its permanent display includes retrieved mosaic fragments, stone inscriptions, elegant

painted Greek amphorae and terracotta statuettes. Upstairs the Pinacoteca (art gallery) shows mainly religious art from the seventeenth century.

Via Crociferi and the Museo Belliniano

Just above Piazza del Duomo, **Via Crociferi** is lined with some of the most arresting religious and secular Baroque buildings in the city, best seen on a slow amble, peering in the eighteenth-century courtyards and churches. At the bottom of the street, the house where composer Vincenzo Bellini was born in 1801 now houses the **Museo Belliniano**, a collection including photographs, original scores, his death mask and other memorabilia(Pizza S. Francesco 3; Mon–Sat 9am–7pm, Sun 9am–1pm; €5; T 095 715 0535).

The Ancient Theatre

West from here, the **Teatro Greco Romano e Odeon** (or Ancient Theatre) was built of lava in the second century AD on the site of an earlier Greek theatre, and much of the seating and the underground passageways are preserved (Via V. Emanuele 266; Mon–Sat 9am–7pm (last entry 6.30pm), Sun 9am–1.30pm (last entry 1pm; €6; T 095 715 0508).

ARRIVAL AND DEPARTURE — CATANIA

16

By plane Catania airport, Fontanarossa (T 095 340 505, W aeroporto.catania.it), is 5km south of the centre. The Alibus #457 (5am–midnight; every 20min; €4 runs from right outside to the central Piazza Stesicoro (on Via Etnea) and to Stazione Centrale in around 20min. A taxi from the rank outside the airport costs around €15 for the same. If you're heading straight to the Aeolian islands, there are direct buses (April, May & Sept 2 daily; June, July & Aug 4 daily) from the airport to the port of Milazzo. Times vary from year to year, so check first (T 090 673 782, W giuntabus.com).

By train The Stazione Centrale (T 892 021), where all mainline trains arrive, is in Piazza Giovanni XXIII, northeast of the centre. To get into the centre, take one of the AMT (T 095 751 9111, W amt.ct.it) city buses from the ranks outside the station: #1/4 (not Sun), #4/7, #432 and #448 run along Via VI Aprile and Via Vittorio Emanuele to Piazza del Duomo.

Destinations Enna (Mon–Sat 7 daily; 1hr 20min); Messina (approx. hourly; 1hr 30min); Palermo (3 daily; 3hr 45min); Siracusa (approx hourly; 1hr 30min); Taormina (at least hourly; 40min).

By bus The bus station is on Via Archimede, a grotty 5min walk from the train station, up Viale della Libertà, and the ticket offices are inconveniently located on the other side of the street, so buy them before going in. Virtually all long-distance services stop at the airport as well – a far easier place to change buses. Local operators include AST (T 095 723 0535; *Rifugio Sapienza*, Nicolosi, Modica, Piazza Armerina and Siracusa); Interbus/Etna Trasporti (T 095 532 716; Enna, Noto, Piazza Armerina, Ragusa, Siracusa and Taormina); and SAIS (T 095 536 201; Agrigento, Enna, Messina and Palermo).

Destinations Agrigento (approx. hourly; 2hr 50min); Enna (almost hourly; 1hr 30min–2hr 25min); Messina (approx. hourly; 1hr 35min); Nicolosi (hourly; 40min); Noto (5–7 daily; 2hr 25min–2hr 15min); Palermo (approx. hourly; 2hr 40min); Piazza Armerina (3–6 daily; 1hr 50min); Ragusa (12 daily; 2hr); Rifugio Sapienza (1 daily; 2hr); Rome (2–3 daily; 11hr); Siracusa (approx. hourly; 1hr 20min); Taormina (16 daily; 1hr 40min).

GETTING AROUND

By bus Catania is served by a network of AMT city buses (W amt.ct.it), whose main ranks are outside the Stazione Centrale. Other central pick-up points are Piazza del Duomo, Piazza Stesicoro and Piazza Borsellino (below Piazza del Duomo), where there's a stop for the airport. Tickets (€1) are valid for any number of journeys within 90min and are

THE CATANIA PASS

The **Catania Pass** offers unlimited travel on public transport and free access to museums run by the city council (Museo Civico, Museo Belliniano, Museo Diocesiano, Terme Achilliane). The pass is available from any participating museum, AMT booth or InfoPoint. There are single and family (two adults and two children under 13) cards available in one-, three- and five-day versions (single €12.50/€16.50/€20; family €23/€30.50/€38).

CATANIA CITY TOURS

To see a lot of Catania in a short time and without too much walking, join one of the **bus tours** operated by Katane Live (095 354 704, katanelive.it), which offers a hop-on, hop-off service (daily 9am–7pm; €5, plus €2 for audioguide; tickets sold on board) around the centre, taking in Via Etnea, Piazza del Duomo and Villa Bellini, with additional stops at the train station, Piazza Stesicoro and Piazza Verga, among other places. There is also a nice hop-on, hop-off Sea Tour, which will take you to Acitrezza, Acicastello and other beaches (€15; leaving at 11am, 2pm, 4pm and 6pm).

available from *tabacchi*, the newsagents inside Stazione Centrale or the booth outside the station. The same outlets also sell a *biglietto giornaliero* (€2.50), valid for one day's unlimited travel on all local AMT bus routes.

By metro The city has a metro system which operates every 15min (7am–8.30pm) on a limited route running from the main Stazione Centrale (beyond Platform 11) south to Catania Porto and north and northwest to Catania Borgo, the terminal for the Stazione Circumetnea on Via Caronda. Bus tickets are valid on metros as well and must be punched at machines before boarding the train.

By taxi There are ranks at Stazione Centrale, Piazza del Duomo and Via Etnea (Piazza Stesicoro); call 095 330 966 or 095 338 282 for 24hr service.

By car Driving and parking in Catania is a stressful experience: ask at your hotel where to park. If you want to rent a car, note that all the major agencies have branches at the airport.

INFORMATION

Tourist offices There are useful InfoPoints run by the city council at Via Vittorio Emanuele 172, near the Duomo, and at the airport (both open Mon–Sat 8.15am–7pm; 800 841 042, comune.catania.it/turismo).

16

ACCOMMODATION

Agora Piazza Currò 095 723 3010, agorahostel.com; map p.912. Catania's youth hostel has dorm bunks and a couple of double rooms, plus internet access and laundry facilities. It shares a building with the lively *Agora* pub (see page 916). Dorms **€22**, doubles **€60**

B&B 5 Balconi Via del Plebiscito 133 338 727 2701, 5balconi.it; map p.912. Stylish B&B run by a friendly young Italo-English couple in an old-fashioned, neighbourly quarter behind Castello Ursino. The three rooms are furnished with elegant flea-market finds. As the name implies, it has five balconies. Breakfast includes traditional Catanese pastries. **€60**

B&B BaD Via C. Colombo 24 095 346 903, badcatania.it; map p.912. Four rooms and an apartment in a self-styled designer B&B owned by a couple of graphic designers, conveniently located behind the Pescheria and Piazza del Duomo. **€70**, apartment **€100**

★ **B&B Casa Barbero** Via Caronda 209 095 820 6301, casabarbero.it; map p.912. Deft use of contemporary colours and design in a beautifully restored Liberty-era *palazzo* with six quiet rooms set around a courtyard. Breakfast is served either in the courtyard, or in the elaborately stuccoed and frescoed dining room, at tables elegantly laid with Japanese-style ceramics and modern pewter. Bikes for guest use (free but €100 deposit). **€85**

Holland International Via Vittorio Emanuele 8 095 533 605, hollandintrooms.it; map p.912. Old-fashioned *pensione*, convenient for the station, and with competitive prices for rooms on the first floor of an old *palazzo* with vaulted frescoed ceilings. The a/c rooms come with and without bathroom and all have satellite TV and tea- and coffee-making facilities. There is free wi-fi, and the friendly Dutch owner speaks good English. **€50**

Hotel Gresi Via Pacini 28 095 322 709, gresihotel.com; map p.912. Newly refurbished traditional hotel, with a pleasantly old-fashioned atmosphere, where the spacious rooms have frescoed ceilings. Good location between Via Etnea and the bustling Piazza Carlo Alberto market. **€70**

Una Hotel Via Etnea 218 095 250 5111, unahotels.it; map p.912. Chic designer hotel belonging to a national chain, whose decor reflects the dominant black and cream tones of the city's Baroque architecture: floors of Etna lava and Comiso limestone; beds laid with cream cotton and black velvet; and Baroque-style chairs sprayed gold and upholstered in black velvet. Facilities include a roof terrace and restaurant-bar with spectacular views of Etna, plus a gym with steam bath. **€230**

EATING

They take food seriously in Catania, as the city centre's bustling markets testify. For the best snacks, try the markets in Piazza Carlo Alberto and the stall-heavy streets through the Porta Uzeda, to the south of the Duomo. Another popular area for food is lively Piazza Federico di Svevia outside the Castello Ursino. Don't miss the chance to sample

the Catanese speciality *selz* – fruit (and nuts such as almond and pistacchio) syrups with soda water – served at kiosks throughout the city, most famously on Piazza Vittorio Emanuele (corner of Corso Umberto and Via Oberdan).

Antica Marina Via Pardo 29 ☎ 095 348 197; map p.912. Trattoria buzzing with old fashioned atmosphere bang in the heart of the fish market where you can eat reasonably priced, fresh fish on tables laid with paper cloths. Go for one of the set menus – a mixed antipasto plus two kinds of pasta or an antipasto plus mixed fried fish for €30 including a lemon sorbet and coffee. Mon–Sat 12.30–2.30pm & 8–10.30pm.

Camelot Piazza Federico di Svevia 75 ☎ 095 723 2103; map p.912. Lively place understandably popular with students where you can feast for a song on Sicilian antipasti (€5) and barbecued sausages and meat (from €3.50) and drink local wine from plastic cups. Tues–Sun 8–10.30pm.

Effe Café Piazza Giovanni Verga 21 ☎ 095 532 334; map p.912. Chic little café that wouldn't look out of place in New York or London, serving juiced fruit and veg, coffees, drinks, snacks and light meals. It is set across from the main courts, so it's popular with lawyers. Daily 7am–9pm (later in summer).

Me Cumpari Turiddu Via Ventimiglia 15 ☎ 095 532 585; map p.912. One for the foodies. Rigorously sourced ingredients in simple, intelligent dishes. Try the *sformato* of spiny artichokes (a local delicacy), deep-fried ricotta with Salina capers, olives and an orange sauce, or the home-made pasta with a sauce of Nebrodi black pork. Mon–Sat 7.30am–10.30pm.

Oxidiana Via Conte Ruggero 4/A ☎ 095 532 585, ⓦ oxidiana.it; map p.912. Scores of different sushi and California rolls, along with *tataki*, *tempuras*, stir-fries and a marvellous sesame-crusted tuna (try it in May or June, at the height of the tuna season, if you can). There are vegetarian options, and lots of gluten-free dishes too. Fab cocktails as well, plus more than sixty different rums to try. A great place, and they deliver too (orders taken daily 6.30–8.30pm). Daily 6.30am–11pm.

DRINKING AND NIGHTLIFE

16

Catania's city council operates *café-concerto* periods during the summer, when the streets and squares of the old town, between Piazza Università and Piazza Bellini, are closed to traffic between 9pm and 2am. The bars here all spill tables out onto the squares and alleys, and live bands keep things swinging until late. Catania's student population ensures a fair choice of youthful bars and pubs – some with live music – that stay open late.

Agora Piazza Currò ☎ 095 723 3010; map p.912. One of Catania's most popular and atmospheric pubs, that attracts a mix of locals and travellers from the youth hostel above (see page 915). Here you can eat and drink till the early hours outside, or in an underground grotto with a river running through it. They make nice *bruschette* too, to soak up the booze. Daily noon–late.

Nievski Via Alessi 15 ☎ 095 313 792; map p.912. Occupying several floors of a labyrinthine, ramshackle building, this bar-restaurant hosts cultural events, book readings, art exhibitions and live music as well as being a popular meeting place for Catania's alternative set. Tues–Sat noon–late, Sun 6pm–late.

DIRECTORY

Hospital Ospedale Garibaldi, Piazza Maria di Gesù 7, Pronto Soccorso (☎ 095 759 4368).

Pharmacies Croce Rossa, Via Etnea 274 (☎ 095 317 053); Cutelli, Via Vittorio Emanuele II 54 (☎ 095 531 400); Europa, Corso Italia 111 (☎ 095 383 536). All open daily 8.30am–1pm & 5–8pm; late openings are indicated by a rota posted on the shop windows.

Police Emergencies ☎ 112; Carabinieri, Piazza Giovanni Verga 8, or Vigili Urbani, Via Veniero 7 (☎ 095 531 333). The Questura (police station) is in Piazza S. Nicolella 8 (☎ 095 736 7111).

Post office Main post office at Via Etnea 215, close to the Villa Bellini (Mon–Sat 8.15am–6.30pm).

Siracusa

Under ancient Greek rule, **SIRACUSA** was the most important city in the Western world. Today it is one of Sicily's main draws, thanks to its extensive archeological park, a Greek theatre where plays are still performed and a charming historic centre occupying an offshore island where Greek, Roman, medieval and Baroque buildings of mellow golden limestone tangle along a labyrinth of cobbled streets. In between the two is modern Siracusa, a busy and functional city of undistinguished apartment-lined boulevards.

Brief history

It's hardly surprising that Siracusa attracted **Greek** colonists from Corinth, who settled the site in 733 BC. An easily defendable offshore island with fertile plains across on

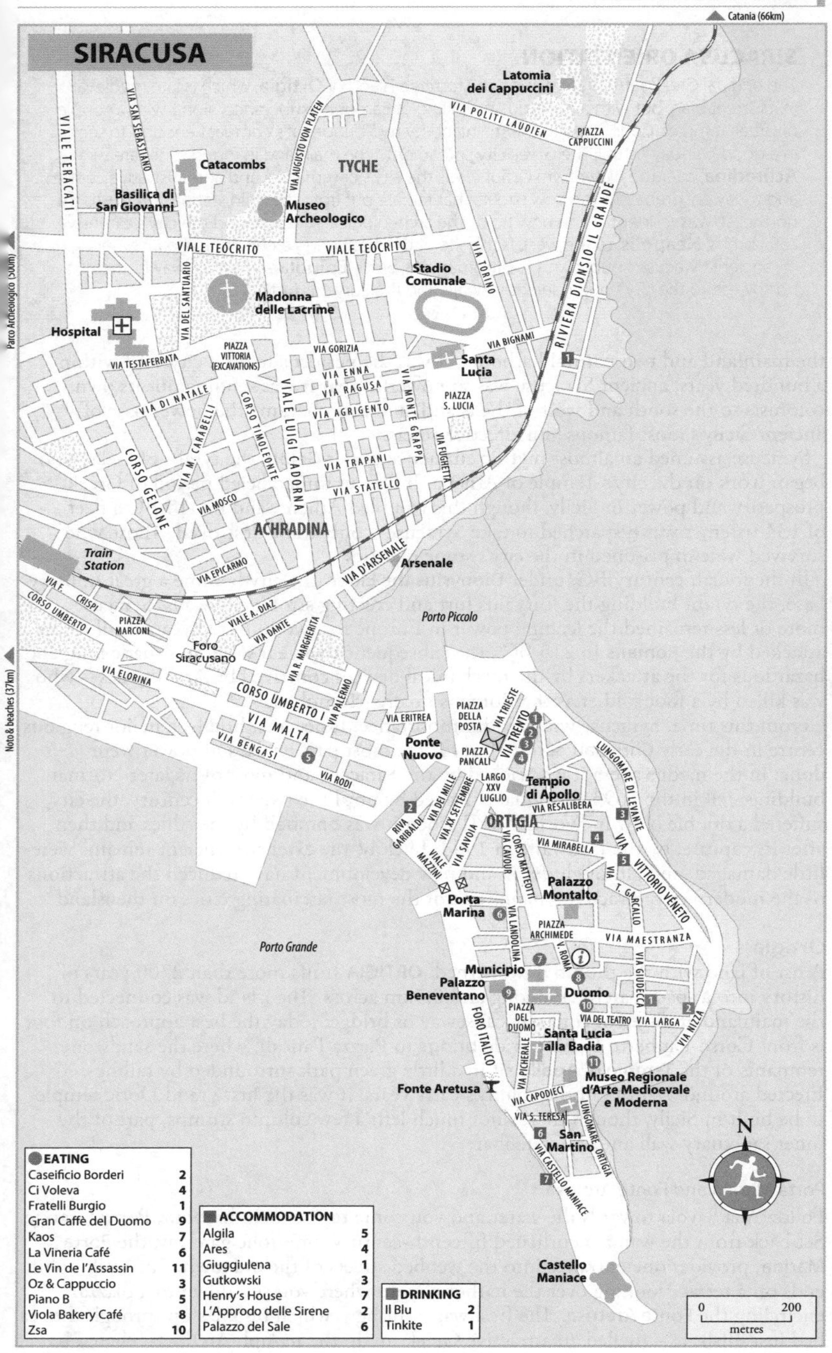
SIRACUSA
Catania (66km)
Latomia dei Cappuccini
Catacombs
Basilica di San Giovanni
Museo Archeologico
TYCHE
Stadio Comunale
Madonna delle Lacrime
Hospital
Santa Lucia
ACHRADINA
Train Station
Arsenale
Porto Piccolo
Foro Siracusano
Ponte Nuovo
Tempio di Apollo
ORTIGIA
Palazzo Montalto
Porta Marina
Porto Grande
Municipio
Palazzo Beneventano
Duomo
Santa Lucia alla Badia
Fonte Aretusa
Museo Regionale d'Arte Medioevale e Moderna
San Martino
Castello Maniace
Parco Archeologico (500m)
Noto & beaches (37km)
EATING
Caseificio Borderi 2
Ci Voleva 4
Fratelli Burgio 1
Gran Caffè del Duomo 9
Kaos 7
La Vineria Café 6
Le Vin de l'Assassin 11
Oz & Cappuccio 3
Piano B 5
Viola Bakery Café 8
Zsa 10
ACCOMMODATION
Algila 5
Ares 4
Giuggiulena 1
Gutkowski 3
Henry's House 7
L'Approdo delle Sirene 2
Palazzo del Sale 6
DRINKING
Il Blu 2
Tinkite 1
0 200 metres
N

16

SIRACUSA ORIENTATION

The original Greek settlement was on the fortified island of **Ortigia**, which is late medieval in its street plan, but with a generous sprinkling of Baroque exuberance, along with a couple of Greek temples. Connected to the mainland by two bridges, it's compact enough to see in a good half-day's stroll. The Greek city spread onto the mainland in four distinct areas: **Achradina**, over the water from Ortigia, was the city's commercial and administrative centre and today encompasses the new streets that radiate out from the train station; **Tyche**, to the northeast, was residential and now holds the archeological museum and the city's extensive catacombs; **Neapolis**, to the west, is the site of the fascinating archeological park based on ancient Syracuse's public and social amenities; while **Epipolae** stretches way to the northwest, to the city's outer defensive walls and the Euryalus fort.

the mainland and two natural harbours, it was the perfect site for a city, and within a hundred years, ancient Syracuse was so powerful that it was sending out its own colonists to the south and west of the island, and soon became the power base of ancient Sicily's most famous and effective rulers.

Syracuse assumed an almost mythic eminence under **Gelon**, the tyrant of Gela, who began work on the city's Temple of Athena. It was an unparalleled period of Greek prosperity and power in Sicily, though this troubled Athens, and in 415 BC a fleet of 134 triremes was dispatched to take Syracuse – only to be destroyed. Those who survived were imprisoned in the city's stone quarries.

In the fourth century BC, under **Dionysius the Elder**, the city became a great military base, the tyrant building the Euryalus fort and erecting strong city walls. Syracuse more or less remained the leading power in Europe for two hundred years until it was attacked by the **Romans** in 215 BC. The subsequent **two-year siege** was made long and hazardous for the attackers by the mechanical devices contrived by Archimedes – who was killed by a foot soldier as the Romans finally triumphed.

From this time, Syracuse withered in importance. It became, briefly, a major religious centre in the early **Christian period**, but for the most part its days of power were done: in the medieval era it was sacked by the Saracens and most of its later Norman buildings fell in the 1693 earthquake. Passed by until the twentieth century, the city suffered a double blow in World War II when it was **bombed** by the Allies and then, after its capture, by the Luftwaffe in 1943. Luckily, the extensive ancient remains were little damaged, and although decay and new development have reduced the attractions of the modern city, Siracusa remains one of the most fascinating cities on the island.

Ortigia

A fist of land with the thumb downturned, **ORTIGIA** stuffs more than 2700 years of history into a space barely 1km long and 0.5km across. The island was connected to the mainland at different times by causeway or bridge: today the best approach on foot is from Corso Umberto I over a wide **bridge** to Piazza Pancali, where the sandstone remnants of the **Tempio di Apollo** sit in a little green park surrounded by railings. Erected around 570 BC in the colony's early years, it was the first grand Doric temple to be built in Sicily, though there's not much left: a few column stumps, part of the inner sanctuary wall and the stereobate.

Porta Marina and Fonte Aretusa

Follow Via Savoia towards the water and you come to the main harbour, Porto Grande. Set back from the water, a curlicued fifteenth-century limestone gateway, the **Porta Marina**, provides one entrance into the webbed streets of the **old town**. The walk uphill ends on a terrace looking over the harbour, from where you slip down to a piazza encircling the **Fonte Aretusa.** The freshwater spring – which bubbles up through the sea bed just offshore – fuelled an attractive Greek myth: the nymph Arethusa, chased by

the river god Alpheus, was changed into a spring by the goddess Artemis and, jumping into the sea off the Peloponnese, reappeared as a fountain in Siracusa. The landscaped, papyrus-covered fountain – complete with fish and ducks – is undeniably pretty, and a favourite place to lean and watch the sun set over the Porto Grande. Admiral Nelson took on water supplies here before the Battle of the Nile.

The old town's roads lead on, down the "thumb" of Ortigia, as far as the **Castello Maniace** on the island's southern tip. Built by Frederick II in 1239, the solid, square keep is now a barracks and usually off-limits, although occasionally concerts are held here, publicized by notices around town.

Museo Regionale d'Arte Medioevale e Moderna

Via Capodieci 14–16 • Tues–Sat 9am–7pm, Sun 9am–1pm • €8, or combined ticket (see page 920) • ☎ 0931 69 511

Back on the main chunk of Ortigia, the **Museo Regionale d'Arte Medioevale e Moderna** on Via Capodieci is housed in the austere thirteenth-century **Palazzo Bellomo**. Inside is a marvellous collection of gilded Byzantine and Gothic altarpieces, though the highlight is an exquisite, fifteenth-century *Annunciation* by Antonello da Messina, brought back to life by a deft restoration, and occupying a room on its own on the upper floor. Antonello created the painting in Siracusa – the outline of the Cava Grande mountain, which you can see rising behind the Porto Grande, is clearly visible in the background.

Piazza del Duomo

Ortigia's most impressive architecture is Baroque, best displayed in the splendid **Piazza del Duomo**, Sicily's greatest square. A theatrical, elongated space, it is flanked by magnificent buildings, including the seventeenth-century **Municipio** with the remains of an early Ionic temple in its basement. This was abandoned in the fifth century BC, when work began on the **Temple of Athena**, possibly the most extravagant temple of its time, with doors of ivory and gold, walls painted with war scenes and portraits of tyrants, and its roof crowned with a statue of Athena bearing a golden shield designed to catch the sun and serve as a beacon for sailors.

The ivory, paintings and gold have long gone, yet much of the rest survives, preserved within the **Duomo** (daily 8am–noon & 4–8pm; €3), which incorporated the temple in its structure. Twelve of the temple's fluted columns and their architrave are embedded in the Duomo's battlemented Norman wall, while inside, the nave was formed by hacking eight arches in the *cella* walls. Along the north aisle, columns distorted by the 1693 earthquake show how close the entire structure came to toppling then. Indeed, the Norman facade was completely destroyed, and replaced with the rhythmic Baroque that dominates the piazza today.

At the far end of the square, behind the barley-sugar Baroque facade of **Santa Lucia alla Badia** (Tues–Sun 11am–4pm; free) is one of Caravaggio's most ground-breaking

SWIMMING IN SIRACUSA

Every summer, towards the end of June, the local council erects wooden swimming platforms on the so-called Solarium rocks on the eastern coast of Ortigia, and at two points along the cycle path that runs along the coast from the Latomie dei Cappuccini. Access is free, and the platforms remain until the end of September – sometimes later.In Ortigia there is also a tiny beach at Cala Rossa; entrance by steps right below the Royal Maniace hotel. There are also smart lidos (€25 a day for sunbed and umbrella) in Ortigia, one on the east coast (entry opposite the end of Via Maestranze), the other just below Fontana Arethusa. If you prefer a long, sandy beach, head to Arenella (a 40 minute ride on bus #23). For a wild rocky coast with several secluded swimming spots, catch the same bus and ask the driver to let you off at the 'Villa Arlecchino'. From here, a side road leads down to a sheltered cove with two tiny sandy beaches. It is also the starting point for the cliff path that traces its way across the Plemmirio peninsula to the Murro del Porco lighthouse – the walk should take about 1 and a half hours.

THE SIRACUSA COMBINED TICKET

If you're planning to see Siracusa's major sights, it's worth buying a **combined ticket**, which is valid for two days. A combined ticket for the Museo Archeologico Paolo Orsi and Parco Archeologico di Neapolis is €13.50.

masterpieces, the bleak *Burial of St Lucy*, an astonishingly pared down, almost monochromatic work in which all the action is limited to the bottom third of the canvas (see page 921).

Achradina: Corso Umberto I and the Foro Siracusano

Directly across the bridge from Ortigia's Piazza Pancali is the area known in ancient times as **Achradina**, the commercial centre of old Syracuse. Nineteenth-century **Corso Umberto I** leads up to **Foro Siracusano**, site of the Greek city's marketplace and forum, a few mysterious remains of which are scattered about the garden and playground in its centre. From here, you could either head up the main shopping street, Corso Gelone, towards the archeological park and museum, or cross over to Via Rubino, behind the station, where buses will take you out to the beaches of Arenella and Fontane Bianche.

Tyche: the modern town

16

The district of **Tyche**, north of the train station, is of little interest in itself, but it is home to the impressive **Museo Archeologico** and a series of **catacombs**. It's about thirty minutes' walk from Ortigia, or take one of the council's Siracusa d'Amare electric minibuses that run round the city (see page 924).

Museo Archeologico Paolo Orsi

Via Teocrito 66 • Tues–Sat 9am–7pm, Sun 9am–1pm; last entry 1hr before closing • €8, or combined ticket (see page 920) • T 0931 464 022 • Minibus #2

The well-organized **Museo Archeologico Paolo Orsi** starts with geological and prehistoric finds, then moves through rooms devoted to the colonies of Naxos, Lentini, Zancle and Megara Hyblaea, and to the main body of the collection: an immensely detailed catalogue of life in ancient Syracuse. The most famous exhibit is a headless **Venus** arising from the sea, the clear white marble almost palpably dripping. Look out, too, for the section dealing with the temples of Syracuse; fragments from each (like the seven lion-gargoyles from the Tempio di Atena) are displayed alongside model and video reconstructions.

Catacombe di San Giovanni

Piazza San Giovanni • Daily 9.30am–12.30pm & 2.30–5pm • Tour of catacombs €8 • T 0931 64 694 • Minibus #2

Tyche is riddled with **catacombs**, since the Romans forbade burial within the walls of a city. All are now inaccessible apart from those beneath the **Basilica di San Giovanni**, built over the burial site of Roman martyr St Marcian. The presence of the saint made this a hugely popular burial place, and there are thousands of niches hollowed into the walls to contain the remains of Roman Syracuse's Christians.

Santuario della Madonna delle Lacrime

Daily 7am–12.30pm & 4–7pm • Free • Minibus #2

Opposite the archeological museum, across Viale Teocrito, the monolithic **Santuario della Madonna delle Lacrime** is the newest and least harmonious addition to the city's skyline. Completed in 1994 to house a statue of the Madonna that allegedly wept for five days in 1953, it was designed to resemble a giant teardrop.

Parco Archeologico di Neapolis

Viale Paradiso • Daily 9am–1hr before sunset • €10, or combined ticket (see page 920) • T 0931 66 206 • Minibus #2

To the west of Tyche, the **Parco Archeologico Di Neapolis** is an extensive area that's worth at least half a day, so bring water and a picnic (though you'll need to eat fairly discreetly). The **Ara di Ierone II**, an enormous third-century-BC altar on a solid white plinth, is the first thing you see, across the way from which is the entrance to the theatre and quarries. The **Teatro Greco** is prettily sited, cut out of the rock and looking down into trees below. It's much bigger than the one at Taormina, capable of holding

CARAVAGGIO'S SICILIAN ADVENTURES

In October 1608, the most famous artist of his time, **Michelangelo Merisi da Caravaggio**, arrived in Siracusa. He came to the city not to fulfil a prestigious commission, but as a fugitive from justice. He was a wanted man with a charge of murder on his head and had just escaped from a high-security prison in Malta.

So how did a prestigious artist end up as a felon on the run? A wild, turbulant soul, mired in Roman lowlife, Caravaggio killed a notorious pimp, Ranuccio Tomassoni, in a duel in 1606. **Sentenced to death** for homicide, he left Rome, escaping first to Naples and then to Malta, where he hoped the patronage of Alof de Wignacourt, Grand Master of the Knights of Malta, might help him secure a pardon. De Wignacourt was thrilled to have the most famous artist in Italy on the island, and immediately commissioned him to paint his portrait. Caravaggio portrayed him in full armour (with a beguiling young page at his side) as a powerful, menacing figure full of his own importance. De Wignacourt was apparently delighted with the work, for he secured Caravaggio a pardon from the Pope and in July 1608 made him a knight.

But a few weeks later Caravaggio was in trouble again. After seriously injuring a high-ranking knight in a brawl he was thrown on August 18 into a cell reserved for those who had committed serious crimes, carved into the rock below Valletta's Fort Sant'Angelo, and sealed by a small trapdoor. The castle itself was fused to a 60m precipice above the sea. Escape seemed impossible.

16

Miraculously, however, Caravaggio did manage to escape. On October 6, 1608, he was officially declared missing. Wignacourt alerted Knights of Malta throughout Europe to the artist's disappearance, and ordered galleys belonging to the Order to keep the coast of Sicily under close surveillance. Caravaggio was a wanted man once again. He disembarked secretly somewhere along the Sicilian coast and made his way to Siracusa, distracted, restless, penniless and fearing for his life, seeking refuge at the house of his former student, model – and lover – **Mario Minniti**. Fully armed, reported his biographer Susinno, "he looked more like a swordsman than an artist" and slept in his clothes with a dagger by his side, accompanied by an aggressive black dog.

Minniti set about finding Caravaggio a commission. He struck lucky. The church of **Santa Lucia al Sepolcro**, outside the city walls on the site of the tomb where Santa Lucia had been buried, had recently been restored, and was in need of a new painting for its main altar (see page 919). The deadline was the saint's feast day, December 13, less than two months away. Caravaggio set to work.

Bathed in shaft of sunlight, dwarfed by stark, scorched bare plaster walls, the **painting** depicts two mighty gravediggers bracing themselves to lower the coccoon-like corpse of the saint into her tomb, watched by a bishop and mourners. According to the writer Jeremy Dummett, the brutish, bearded gravedigger to the left is a portrait of Alof de Wignacourt. It has been suggested that Caravaggio identified himself with St Lucy, at the mercy of the gravedigger consigning her to burial.

By December 6, 1608, Caravaggio was in Messina. But the strait was full of Maltese galleys. Uneasy – although not before he had completed a couple more canvasses – Caravaggio left. By the following autumn he was in Naples, where he was offered shelter in the palace of his former patrons. One night he left the safety of the palace for a notorious brothel and tavern. On leaving, he was set upon by four men. Three of them held him down, while the fourth cut him across the face, in a deliberate, **cold-blooded attack**. According to historian and Caravaggio expert Professor Vincenzo Pacelli, the only likely candidates are the Knights of Malta, with the secret approval of the Vatican, who were seeking revenge for the artist's attack on a knight in 1608. Seriously injured, Caravaggio seems to have headed for Rome in a small boat with his three canvasses for his patron Scipione Borghese. He never got there, and neither his body – nor the paintings – were ever retrieved.

THEATRE IN SIRACUSA

Classical Greek drama is performed each year (May & June, usually Tues–Sun from around 6.45pm) at the Teatro Greco in the Parco Archeologico. Although performances are in Italian, plot outlines are provided in English so, you can still enjoy a fabulous – often haunting – spectacle. Tickets are available from the box office of the **Istituto Nazionale del Dramma Antico** (INDA), Palazzo Greco, Corso Matteotti 29 (T 800 542 644 or T 0931 487 200, W indafondazione.org) or online, and cost €30–65, with cheaper last-minute tickets available for some performances. Further details can be found on the INDA website or from Siracusa's tourist office.

For a more quirky theatre experience, you might like to try and catch one of the traditional **puppet shows** run by the Vaccaro-Mauceri family, Siracusa's puppeteers. They take place at the thriving Piccolo Teatro dei Pupi, Via della Giudecca 17 (T 0931 465 540, W pupari.com) at least twice weekly from March to October; twice daily in August; and daily from late December to early January: tickets cost €8.50. Behind-the-scenes tours and special shows also take place throughout the year: check up-to-date schedules on the website.

around fifteen thousand people. Around the top of the middle gangway is a set of carved names which marked the various seat blocks occupied by the royal family. Greek dramas are still performed here in May and June.

Walk back through the theatre and another path leads down into a leafy **quarry**, the **Latomia del Paradiso**, best known for an unusually shaped cavern that the tyrant Dionysius is supposed to have used as a prison. This, the **Orecchio di Dionisio** (or "Ear of Dionysius"), is a high, S-shaped cave 65m long: Caravaggio, a visitor in 1586, coined the name after the shape of the entrance, but the acoustic properties are such that it's thought that Dionysius may have used it to eavesdrop on his prisoners from above. Look out, too, for the elliptical **Anfiteatro Romano**, dating from the third century AD. It's a substantial relic with the tunnels for animals and gladiators clearly visible and, again, some of the seats are inscribed with the owners' names.

Castello Eurialo

Frazione Belvedere • Daily 9am until 1hr before sunset • €4 • T 0931 711 773 • Bus #25 makes the 15min ride from Ortigia, past the archeological park, to the village of Belvedere; the site is just before the village, on the right – to come back, take bus #26

For terrific views over the city head a few kilometres west of Siracusa to the military and defensive works begun under Dionysius the Elder to defend the port from land attack. They basically consisted of a **great wall**, which defended the ridge of Epipolae (the city's western limit), and the massive **Castello Eurialo** – the most important surviving Greek fortification in the Mediterranean. There are three defensive trenches, the innermost leading off into a system of tunnels and passages. Climb up to the castle proper for hearty **views** down to the oil refineries and tankers of the coast north of the city, and over Siracusa itself.

Bars and **pizzerias** share the view, and make this a great place for an evening out.

ARRIVAL AND INFORMATION — SIRACUSA

By train The train station is on the mainland, a 20min walk from both Ortigia and the archeological park.

Destinations Catania (10 daily; 1hr 30min); Messina (9 daily; 3hr); Noto (9 daily; 30min); Ragusa (4 daily; 2hr 10min); Taormina (10 daily; 2hr).

By bus All regional buses – run by AST and Interbus – stop across the road from the train station, on Via Rubino.

Destinations Catania (via Catania airport; hourly; 1hr 20min); Noto (12 daily; 55min); Palermo (3 daily; 3hr 15min); Ragusa (5 daily; 2hr 15min–3hr); Rome (4 daily; 11hr).

By car Siracusa's drivers are as undisciplined as any in Sicily, but nevertheless drivers will find the city a breeze after Palermo and Catania. Parking on the street in Ortigia is for residents only, so leave your car at the Talete car park on the east coast of the island (a signposted left turn as you drive across the Via Malta bridge or park it at the mainland carpark Molo Sant'Antonio, a couple of minutes' walk from the Via Malta bridge. Ortigia is completely closed to traffic

(except for residents) from 8pm Mon–Fri, from 4pm Sat and from 11am Sun – and on certain other occasions – a traffic signal at the foot of Corso Matteotti indicates whether access is permitted or not.

Tourist office There is an InfoPoint inside the provincial offices at Via Roma 30 (daily 9am–8pm; T 0931 462 946, E infoturistico@provsr.it).

GETTING AROUND

By bus Siracusa has the worst bus service in Sicily. Apart from the buses to the beaches, routes will be cancelled without warning, and so if you have to be anywhere at a certain time, either walk or get a taxi. There is nowhere in Ortigia to buy tickets. The closest ticket outlet is the newsagent inside the train station. Sometimes tickets can be bought onboard, sometimes drivers just shrug and let you travel for free.

Conventional city buses are run by AST and depart from from Via Rubino. All buses run on circular routes. Tickets cost €1.20 for 2hr.

By electric minibus In theory the electric minibuses, run by the city council and called Siracusa d'Amare (W siracusadamare.it), which do a well-marked circuit of Ortigia, then link the island with strategic points on the mainland, such as the Museo Archeologico, the Parco Archeologico di Neapolis, the Teatro Greco, the Riviera Dionisio il Grande and the car park at Molo Sant'Antonio. Sadly these are also suspended without warning at times. Every bus stop has the stopping points along the route marked clearly, so it is easy to use. Tickets (€0.50) can be bought on board and are valid for 90min.

ACCOMMODATION

16

Siracusa has a good choice of accommodation available, but in high summer and during the theatre season (May–June) it's wise to book in advance.

Algila Via Vittorio Veneto 93 T 0931 465 186, W algila.it; map p.917. On the eastern seafront of Ortigia, with all the comforts of a four-star hotel, plus friendly, helpful staff. The design has a Maghreb feel, with Tunisian tiles in the bathrooms, kilims on the floors, watercolours of sun-scorched palms and North African piazzas, and a tiny decorative courtyard with fountain. Prices depend on availability rather than season. **€205**

Ares Via Mirabella 49 T 0931 461 145, W aresbedandbreakfast.it; map p.917. Comfortable B&B on a quiet street, near the sea, on the less touristy east side of Ortigia. Rooms are smart and spotless, there's a lovely roof terrace, and owner Enzo is a great source of information on Ortigia. Breakfast is by voucher at the fabulous Bar del Duomo opposite the cathedral, just a few minutes' walk away. **€80**

★ **Giuggiulena** Via Pitagora da Reggio 35 T 0931 468 142, W giuggiulena.it; map p.917. Belonging to the same owners as Palazzo del Sale, Giuggiulena is a chic, but friendly and relaxed B&B in a cliff-top villa, along the eastern seafront of Siracusa, and ideal for families. The main living/eating area has floor-to-ceiling windows, and is flooded with light, with a glass cube suspended above the ocean, and a bookcase stuffed with a tempting selection of English paperbacks. All six rooms have balconies overlooking the sea, and you can swim off rocks or forage in rock pools (the hotel has a supply of chairs, mats and beach shoes), yet Ortigia is just a 15min walk away. Breakfasts are abundant and delicious, and eaten on a balcony overhanging the sea. **€90**

★ **Gutkowski** Lungomare Vittorini 26 T 0931 465 861, W guthotel.it; map p.917. Chic simplicity and intelligent design make this hotel overlooking the sea on the eastern edge of Ortigia a good restful choice in the *centro storico*. It's worth booking in advance to secure one of the rooms with private terrace. Great breakfasts, with freshly squeezed orange juice and, in summer, home-made almond granita. There is also a little wine bar, and private dinners can be arranged for four or more guests. **€110**

Henry's House Via del Castello Maniace 68 T 0931 21 361, W hotelhenryshouse.com; map p.917. A wonderful bijou hotel overlooking the serene waters of the Porto Grande, *Henry's House* sports a gorgeous terrace awash with flowers and voluptuous Baroque interiors furnished with antiques – imagine *The Leopard* remade by the Downton Abbey team. Perfect for a romantic escape or honeymoon. Breakfasts and aperitivi on the terrace are unforgettable. **€165**

★ **L'Approdo delle Sirene** Riva Garibaldi 15 T 0931 24 857, W approdo delle sirene.com; map p.917. Owned and run by a charming mother-and-son team, this tastefully renovated waterfront *palazzo* overlooks the channel between Ortigia and the mainland. Great home-made breakfasts with abundant fresh fruit are served on a terrace overlooking the sea. Facilities include mini-laptops in rooms and free wi-fi, and you can borrow bikes, free of charge. **€130**

★ **Palazzo del Sale** Via S. Teresa 25 T 0931 69 558, W palazzodelsale.it; map p.917. Stylish, relaxed B&B in a nineteenth-century salt-merchant's home and warehouse on a quiet street behind Piazza del Duomo. The six spacious rooms have wooden floors, architect-designed beds, and intriguing touches such as mirrors framed with driftwood Mon–Fri & Sun, and lamps with palm-bark shades. Breakfasts are superb, and service is unfussy and friendly. Free wi-fi – though the hefty stone walls mean that the signal can be weak in some rooms – and a PC for guests' use. **€130**

EATING

Ortigia holds the city's best array of cafés and restaurants. Prices are on the high side for Sicily, though there are few nicer places to sit outside in a medieval street or courtyard and while the evening away. Ortigia also has excellent bars – from Italian-style pubs to cocktail joints. Most of the late-night action is concentrated on the streets and alleys near the Fonte Aretusa, particularly around Piazzetta San Rocco and along Lungomare Alfeo.

CAFES AND SNACK BARS

Caseificio Borderi Via De Benedictis 6 ☎329 985 2500; map p.917. An Ortigia institution, this theatrical family of cheesemakers produce their own ricotta, tricotta (baked ricotta with a pleasant custardy texture and sweet-savoury caramel crust) and mozzarella daily, as well as provole (smoked – with almond shells – and unsmoked) and pecorino spiked with pistachio. They also stock some excellent artisan cheeses from the Ragusa area, and three Sicilian DOP cheeses. Nothing is wasted – cheese whey is fed to the Borderis' pigs, who are eventually made into salami and sausages. Try also the gigantic, custom-made sandwiches (€3.50–5) – watching Andrea make them is part of the shop's theatre – and enjoy the generous cheese tasting samples. Mon–Sat 7am–3pm.

Fratelli Burgio Piazza Cesare Battisti 4 ☎0931 60 069; map p.917. A mecca for foodies, this deli in the heart of the market is the place to come for artisan, DOP and Slow Food Presidio cheeses and cured meats from all over Italy. Look out for speck matured in myrtleberry grappa, a Sicilian *suino nero prosciutto crudo* from the Nebrodi mountains, handmade salami from Trentino's Val di Non or a blue buffalo-milk cheese from Piemonte. At lunchtime they serve a range of cheeses, cold meats and condiments on wooden platters – best savoured with a glass of chilled white wine (€15/person). There is not much seating, so you may need to stand. Mon–Sat 7am–3.30pm, evenings in summer.

Gran Caffè del Duomo Piazza del Duomo 18 ☎0931 21 584; map p.917. Right in front of the cathedral, this is the place to sit and watch life pass by over a lazy breakfast or aperitif – staff are friendly and attentive and prices are so reasonable that even street-sweepers and dustmen stop by for a coffee on their morning rounds. Try the *cornetti* filled to order with fresh ricotta. Daily 8am–late; Sept–June closed Mon.

Viola Bakery Café Via Roma 43 ☎331 861 8415; map p.917. A contemporary urban look, free, reliable wi-fi and friendly staff have made the Via Roma branch of *Viola* popular with locals and travellers alike. The food is good too – nice light *cornetti*, and at lunchtime there are salads, focaccia and *scacce* (a kind of bread pie stuffed with combinations of vegetables, cheeses and ham) all priced at €5 and under. Daily 7.30am–9pm.

RESTAURANTS

Ci Voleva Via Trento 14, ☎339 120 5261; map p.917. Just some tables out on the pavement in a side street off the market, but this little place does the best *spaghetti alla siracusana* (spaghetti with anchovies, capers, tomato, currants and crispy breadcrumbs) you may ever taste (€10). They also do a fab plate of roast tiger prawns (€12). Great service too. Mon–Sat daily 9am–midnight, Sun 9am–4pm.

Kaos Piazza Minerva 7 ☎338 612 9831; map p.917. The pizza (from €6) here is astonishingly light, with a crisp crunch and not a hint of sogginess – even when piled with a rich tangle of juicy Mediterranean vegetables. With tables outside, on a pedestrianized piazza looking on to the ancient Greek columns embedded in the Duomo wall, this really is very hard to beat. Daily 7.30–10.30pm.

La Vineria Café Via Cavour 9 ☎0931 185 6049; map p.917. A stylish but relaxed fusion of café, wine bar and restaurant, using carefully sourced ingredients in unusual ways. Look for ravioli with Puglian burrata, prawn *carpaccio* with ginger or Sicilian pork marinaded in Hyblaean honey and peppercorns. *Primi* start at €10, and you can expect to pay around €40/head for dinner, but there are less expensive options at lunch, including a superior kids' menu. Daily noon–2pm & 6.30–10.30pm.

16

Le Vin de l'Assassin Via Roma 115 ☎333 288 4189; map p.917. Relaxed, romantic and contemporary, this small French bistro welcomes couples, groups of friends and families with children. Its menu is chalked on blackboards, though the standard of the cooking can vary – try the French onion soup (€8.50), or honey-roast duck breast (€14.50), and save room for dessert. Tues–Sat 7.30pm–midnight, Sun noon–3pm & 7.30pm–midnight.

Oz & Cappuccio Via Giaracà 8 ☎39 0931 196 0301, facebook.com/ozecappuccio; map p.917. Joint venture between a musician from Berlin and the son of the market's biggest fishmongers. There's no booking, and no frills, just spanking fresh fish served in biodegradable cardboard boxes at little tables. Wine made by Oz on his vineyard outside Siracusa goes down a treat too. Try the super-crispy mixed fried fish (squid, anchovies and prawns), or the tuna burger. Expect to queue, but pass the time while you are waiting with a glass of Oz's rose. March–May 12–3.30pm; June–Sept 12–3.30pm & 7–11pm; Oct 12–3.30pm.

Piano B Via Cairoli 18 (off Via Malta, across the bridge from Ortigia) ☎0931 66 851; map p.917. Fantastic light pizza made of slow-risen dough (from €6), fine quality burgers cooked over charcoal (€11) and traditional Roman dishes (a homage to the owner's mother) such as *carciofi alla giudia* (deep-fried artichokes), *fiori di zucca fritti* (deep-fried zucchini flowers) and *baccalà in pastella* (battered salt cod). Tues–Sun 7.30pm–late.

Zsa Via Roma 73 ☎0931 22 204; map p.917. Good pizza – the dough is made with a light touch, and comes blistered from the wood oven, and the ingredients on top are good quality and abundant. Pizzas start at €4.50. Feast on a *vegetariana*, laden with grilled vegetables laced with radicchio, or a *stufata*, scattered with chilli and fennel-seed-scented sausages and potatoes. There's takeaway too – just show up and order. Tues–Sat 12.30–2.30pm & 8–10.30pm.

DRINKING

Il Blu Via Nizza 50 ☎0931 445 052; map p.917. Charismatic and unpretentious, *Il Blu* is a great restaurant-bar serving fresh fruit gremolatas (€3.50; try white peach, or black fig with chilli), superior sandwiches and light lunches in the shade of their terrace. Come *aperitivo* time, there are prosecco cocktails made with fresh fruit (€5; try pineapple, strawberry, peach or black mulberry) and top-notch daiquiris and mojitos. Easter–Nov daily 6–11pm or later; May–late Sept 12.30–2.30pm & 6–11pm or later.

Tinkite Via della Giudecca 61–63 ☎348 597 5369; map p.917. This Giudecca institution attracts a laidback international crowd.They also have a huge choice of speciality teas (served with little biscuits) along with hot chocolate and coffee. Heaters outside (and blankets) in winter. June–Sept 9.30am–1.30pm & 7–11pm (or later if busy); Oct–May 8.30am–1pm & 5–10pm (or later if busy); closed Wed morning.

The southern coast and the interior

Sicily's **southern coast** and hinterland mark a welcome break from the blacker volcanic lands to the north. A calamitous **earthquake in 1693** utterly destroyed the original towns and villages of Sicily's southeastern bulge, which were rebuilt as new planned towns in an opulent Baroque style. All were harmonious creations, and eight of them are now protected by UNESCO as World Heritage Sites. Funding has poured into the area, and in recent years there has been an explosion of new hotels and B&Bs. **Noto**, recently restored to perfection, is the most eagerly promoted by the tourist board, while **Ragusa Ibla**, a Baroque town built on a medieval plan, has become a destination for the stylish international set, with a couple of Michelin-starred restaurants. Also worth a visit is the bustling little town of **Modica**, famous for the production of chocolate. The coast, too, has some jewels: 10km south of Noto is the magical **Riserva Naturale di Vendicari**. Further west still, is **Agrigento**, sitting on a rise overlooking the sea above its famed series of Greek temples.

Slow cross-country trains and limited-exit autostradas do little to encourage stopping in the island's **interior**. The obvious target is **Piazza Armerina** and the fabulous Roman mosaics.

Noto and around

NOTO, half an hour by train or bus from Siracusa, is easily the most harmonious town of those rebuilt after the earthquake, and during the mid-nineteenth century, it replaced Siracusa as provincial capital. Planned and laid out by Giovanni Battista Landolina and adorned by Gagliardi, there's not a town to touch Noto for uniform excellence in design and execution. Each year more monuments are restored, regaining their original apricot- and honey-hued limestone facades, and each year more tour groups visit.

The pedestrianized main Corso is lined with some of Sicily's most captivating buildings, from the flat-fronted church of **San Francesco**, on the right, along as far as Piazza XVI Maggio and the graceful, curving church of **San Domenico**. And **Piazza Municipio** is one of Sicily's finest piazzas, with its perfectly proportioned, tree-planted expanses. The **Duomo**, a striking example of Baroque at its most muscular, has reopened following the collapse of its dome in 1996. Its refreshingly unadorned interior is a striking example of how well the best of Baroque architects knew how to articulate space. Opposite, the **Municipio**, Palazzo Ducezio, is flanked by its own green spaces, the arcaded building presenting a lovely, simple facade of columns and long stone balconies. Head up the steep Via Corrado Nicolaci, an eighteenth-century street that contains the extraordinary **Palazzo Villadorata** at no. 18, its six balconies supported by a panoply of griffins, galloping horses and fat-cheeked cherubs.

Noto Antica

16km northwest of Noto • Open access • Free • It's signposted from the western end of the Corso in Noto (there's no bus) – take the turn-off to the convent of Santa Maria delle Scale, and Noto Antica is 5km beyond the convent; be warned, the remote car park here is a favourite target for thieves – do not leave anything visible in your car

Before being abandoned after the 1693 earthquake, **Noto Antica**, or ancient Netum, had been inhabited for some 3500 years. Fused to a jagged ridge teetering on the brink of a rugged ravine, it was first inhabited in the Bronze Age. According to legend, Daedalus stopped here on his flight over the Ionian Sea, and Hercules rested here after killing the Minotaur. It was also the last bastion of Arab Sicily before the Norman conquest of the island. You park outside the dramatic surviving **castle gate** (occupied from the eleventh to the seventeenth century), where some of the original circular tower has been rebuilt. Early Christian catacombs honeycomb the rock beneath the tumbling walls that line the valley cliff, above a lovely shady area with stone barbecues and picnic tables.

An unsurfaced lane – the one-time high street – pushes through the castle gate past the evocative remains of an **abandoned city** – square-cut stone blocks, fragments of carved arches, bramble-covered courtyards, a castle keep and crumbling walls. The keep was once used as a prison – peer through the (usually locked) metal grille-gate to see the carved graffiti of seventeenth-century prisoners. Behind the castle, a path runs along the edge of the gorge – the second stile along the path leads into the valley below, with the remains of tanneries and watermills and lovely pools for river swimming.

Cava Grande del Fiume Cassibile

16

10km northeast of Noto • Open access • Free • Head up the SS287, past the turn-off for Noto Antica (no public transport)

A spectacular winding route northwest of the ramshackle agricultural town of Avola climbs up to the magnificent gorge and nature reserve of the **Cava Grande del Fiume Cassibile.** There's parking by a sensational viewpoint over the Grand Canyon-esque Cassibile River gorge, with sheer rock walls visible across the divide, birds of prey circling and the river glistening far below. The very steep path that leads down to the valley bottom is closed at times of high fire risk, and an information booth posts warnings of the dangers of the descent – you certainly need to be properly shod, fit enough to climb back out, and to carry plenty of water. The round trip takes a good three hours, plus any time you spend splashing in the natural swimming pools or following the footpath alongside the river, which runs for most of the gorge's 11km length. At the parking area at the top, you can get a drink or a meal from a rustic tavern, the *Trattoria Cava Grande*.

Villa Romana del Tellaro

Contrada Vaddeddi • Daily 9am–7pm • €6 • ⓣ 0931 573 883, ⓦ villaromanadeltellaro.com • There are no buses: it's clearly signposted off the SS115, just before the Vendicari entrance

In 1971 the remains of an Imperial-era Roman country villa dating from the fourth century AD, were discovered on land above the River Tellaro, 3km south of Noto town. Though on a smaller scale than the Villa Romana del Casale (see page 935), **Villa Romana del Tellaro** has some fantastic mosaics, including scenes from *The Odyssey* and a wonderful hunting scene in which people and wild animals are shown wading through water. There is a magnificent tiger, too – suggesting that these mosaics, like those at Casale, were the work of North African craftsmen.

Riserva Naturale di Vendicari

10km south of Noto • Daily: summer 7am–8pm; winter 7am–6.30pm • Free entry; parking €3, camper vans €12 • There's no public transport; it's off the main SS115 coast road and is well signed from Noto and the autostrada

A line of small-town resorts stretches south from Siracusa to Vittoria, with several sweeps of pristine sands in between – most notably at the **Riserva Naturale di Vendicari,**

a lovely coastal nature reserve. Paths lead to unspoilt beaches of white-gold sand and salt lakes that, between October and March, attract flamingoes, herons, cranes, black storks and pelicans. In the middle of the last century turtles disappeared from the area, perhaps thanks to the local appetite for turtle soup, but thanks to careful management, they have now been encouraged back to Vendicari: at times, the local beaches are closed to allow them to breed in peace.

ARRIVAL AND INFORMATION

By train Although it is fun to take the single-coach train from Siracusa, the train station is a good 10–15min walk out of Noto town centre down Via Principe di Piemonte, and has no facilities – not even a bench: it's often unmanned, so don't show up early. If you have luggage, you may need a taxi (T 338 945 8206 or T 0931 838 713).

Destinations Siracusa (8 daily; 30min); Ragusa (4 daily; 1hr 30min).

By bus Buses stop at the Giardino Pubblico at the eastern end of the historic centre, close to the Porta Reale.

Destinations Modica (4 daily; 1hr 45min); Ragusa (2 daily; 2hr 15min); Siracusa (11 daily Mon–Sat, 4 daily Sun; 55min).

By car Traffic through town is all one-way and it's easy enough to drive in (follow "centro" signs) or out (destinations are all well signposted).

Tourist information There's a well-informed tourist office in Piazza XVI Maggio, just off the main Corso Vittorio Emanuele, behind the Hercules fountain (April–Oct Mon–Sat & most Sun 9am–1pm & 2.30–7.30pm; Nov–March daily 8.30am–1pm & 2.30–7pm; T 0931 573 779, W comune.noto.sr.it).

ACCOMMODATION

16

NOTO

Il Castello Via Fratelli Bandiera 2 W ostellodinoto.it. Youth hostel in a converted *palazzo* in the upper part of town with wonderful views, small dormitories and double, triple and family rooms (with private facilities). It's accessible from the centre in a few minutes up signposted steps from Via Cavour, behind the Duomo. You might want to pay extra for a room with a view over the town. Dorms **€22**, doubles **€80.**

La Fontanella Via Rosolino Pilo 3 T 0931 894 735, W albergolafontanella.it. Thirteen rooms in a sympathetically restored nineteenth-century *palazzo* on a busy road on the northern edge of Noto Alta. It's a three-star place, and the only hotel within walking distance of the centre (10min). Often cheaper than the B&Bs, though lacking some of their charm. Parking is easy around here. **€75**

Macrina Vico Grillo, corner of Via Fabrizi T 0931 837 202, W b-bmacrina.com. Family-run B&B in a neighbourly street, with three spacious and airy rooms, each with its own terrace. There's also a huge walled garden with a couple of swings plus use of a barbecue, making this a good choice if you have kids. The small breakfast terrace is useful if you want to rustle up a snack or *aperitivo*. **€80**

★ Montandon Via A. Sofia 50 T 0931 836 389 or T 339 524 4607, W b-bmontandon.com. A real gem, this B&B in a grand *palazzo* in the higher town has three huge rooms, each with its own terrace. Guests have access to an enchanting garden (with swings), which makes a welcome summer retreat from heat and crowds. The owner is a marvellous host, and serves outstanding breakfasts, including eggs, local ricotta, salami, ham, pastries, fruit and home-made jams. **€80**

Villa Canisello Via Cesare Pavese 1 T 0931 835 793, W villacanisello.it. An old farmhouse on the western outskirts of town in a quiet residential suburb; rooms open onto a patio or terrace, and there's parking. Signs direct you from the western end of the Corso – it seems like a bit of a slog, but it's actually only a 10min walk to the centre. Closed Nov–Easter. **€85**

NORTH OF NOTO

Masseria degli Ulivi 12km north of Noto, SS287 T 0931 813 019, W masseriadegliulivi.com. This estate deep in the countryside has been beautifully restored using traditional materials, and there's a good restaurant, plus an outdoor pool under the olive trees. Closed Dec–March. **€160**

NOTO ANTICA

★ Borgo Alveria Contrada Noto Antica T 0931 810 003, W borgoalveria.com. Stylish agriturismo set enticingly close to the evocative ruins of Noto Antica – perfect for anyone wanting to get completely away from it all. Lava-stone floors, exposed sandstone walls and high dark-wood ceilings act as a foil to contemporary designer furniture and fittings – the suite comes with a Japanese bath and waterfall shower. There is a good restaurant and pool surrounded by olive groves. **€160**

RISERVA NATURALE DI VENDICARI

Agriturismo Calamosche Oasi di Vendicari T 347 858 7319, W agriturismocalamosche.it. This little agriturismo is just inside the reserve at the Cala Mosche entrance: look out for a hand-painted sign off the main road. They have

seven simple rooms and produce their own vegetables, almonds, lemons and oil, which are served along with local hams and cheeses, fish and game in the reasonably priced open-air trattoria set in the shade of carob trees (around €16 for an antipasto and pasta, with a glass of wine). Closed Nov–March. **€60**

EATING AND DRINKING

Caffè Sicilia Corso Vittorio Emanuele 125. The *Caffè Sicilia Corso* is the more radical of Noto's two prize-winning *gelaterie*, with flavours such as lemon and saffron, and even basil. Tues–Sun 7.30am–8pm or later.

★**Carmine** Via Ducezio 1 ⓣ0931 838 705. Locals recommend this trattoria for a good low-cost meal and it's certainly pretty remarkable value, with rustic antipasto and pasta dishes at €7, grilled fish from around €11 and a mixed grill at €13. The house wine is challenging to say the least and the interconnected rooms get very busy, but it defines perfectly the phrase "cheap and cheerful". July & Aug daily noon–3pm & 7–11pm; Sept–May Tues–Sun noon–3pm & 7–11pm.

Costanzo Via Silvio Spaventa 7–11. *Pasticceria* and *gelateria*, known for producing what may be the best ice cream in Italy in flavours such as mandarin, ricotta, jasmine and rose, as well as sweets and pastries, including dreamy *cassata*. The almond milk is joyous. Thurs–Tues 7.30am–8pm or later.

Trattoria Baglieri Il Crocifisso Via Principe Umberto 46 ⓣ0931 571 151. Nationally recognized super-chic trattoria using seasonal local ingredients in ways that make the taste buds zing: spaghetti with white prawns and Siracusan lemon, rabbit with orange blossom honey, wild greens, celery, carrot and peppers, tuna in a pistachio and sesame crust. There is a €45 tasting menu; otherwise expect to pay between €50 and €60 a head without wine. Thurs 7.30–10.15pm, Fri–Tues 12.30–2.30pm & 7.30–10.15pm.

Modica

A dynamic little town, with solid left-wing allegiances, **MODICA** was the provincial capital until Mussolini shifted base to the more conservative Ragusa. Linked by both train and bus with Siracusa and Ragusa, this Baroque town is well worth a visit, with some great places to stay and eat, and to taste the local speciality, **chocolate**. Modican chocolate is powerful, gritty stuff, made as the Mayans did, a technique introduced to Sicily by the Spanish, without cocoa butter, and without heat, so that the sugar doesn't melt and the texture remains crunchy. Traditional flavours are vanilla and cinnamon; innovations include sea salt and chilli.

Arriving by car you have to negotiate your way through the confusing and badly signposted streets of the modern town, known as Sordo, before winding down to the old town, cascading down the sides of a narrow gorge. A powerful medieval base of the Chiaramonte, Baroque Modica is watched over by the magnificent eighteenth-century facade of **San Giorgio**, at the head of a vast flight of steps. It's thought that Gagliardi was responsible for this: the elliptical facade is topped by a belfry, the church approached by a symmetrical double staircase which switchbacks up across the upper roads of the town.

16

ARRIVAL AND DEPARTURE — MODICA

By train Modica is on the Siracusa–Ragusa train line, with the station a good 10min walk from the town centre – walk up to the ornamental fountain at Piazza Rizone and bear left for the Corso.

Destinations Ragusa (4 daily; 20min); Scicli (5 daily; 10min); Siracusa (5 daily; 1hr 35min–1hr 54min).

By bus Regional buses drop you right in Modica's centre on Corso Umberto I.

Destinations Catania Airport (1 daily; 2hr 30min); Ragusa (4 daily; 30min); Scicli (3 daily; 40min).

By car Drivers can park on the street, but in most central areas you need to buy a parking voucher (from *tabacchi*) to put in your window (charges apply Mon–Sat 9am–1pm & 4–8pm; €0.80/hour, €2.50/half day).

Tourist information The tourist office is at Corso Umberto I 141 (Mon–Sat 8am–1.30pm & 3–7pm; ⓣ346 655 8227).

ACCOMMODATION

Casa Talia Via Exaudinos 1 ⓣ0932 752 075, ⓦcasatalia.it. Occupying a cluster of restored houses in what was once the Jewish ghetto of Modica, *Casa Talia* is far removed from the bustle of the city centre, yet just a 5min walk down steps and alleyways to the main Corso. A garden planted with fruit trees adds to the feeling of getting away from it all. Rooms, designed by their architect owners, who live on site, are stylish and practical. Breakfasts are excellent (freshly squeezed juices, home-made cakes, jams and breads), served in a whitewashed room occupying what were once

caves used as a cistern and stables. **€150**

I Tetti di Siciliando Via Cannata 24 ⓣ0932 942 843, ⓦsiciliando.it. Simple, friendly and unpretentious hotel popular with budget travellers in the tangle of historic streets above Corso Umberto. Rooms are pretty basic, but it's reasonably priced and sociable and the helpful owners have rental bikes (€15/day) and can organize bike tours of the surrounding area. Look for the sign opposite the Agip petrol station towards the top of the Corso (where you'll have to park), and follow the steps up around the passageway for the signposted "bed, bike and breakfast". **€55**

L'Orangerie Vico de Naro 5 ⓣ0932 754 703, ⓦlorangerie.it. Tranquil, refined B&B with three huge suites, with kitchens (€126) and four spacious rooms in a *palazzo* with frescoed ceilings and private flower-filled terraces. **€90**

Palazzo Failla Via Blandini 5 ⓣ0932 941 059, ⓦpalazzofailla.it. A handsome upper-town palace, by the Santa Teresa church, reborn as a comfortable four-star hotel: with just seven rooms, it retains the intimate feel of a gracious aristocratic *palazzo*. Rooms are elegant and traditional, with tiled floors, high frescoed ceilings and antique beds. There are also three contemporary minimalist rooms in an annexe. The website has some great last-minute deals. **€140**

Palazzo Il Cavaliere Corso Umberto I 259 ⓣ0932 947 219, ⓦpalazzoilcavaliere.it. A down-to-earth aristocratic family run their eighteenth-century palace as a B&B. The building is splendid and authentic, with original Caltagirone tiled floors, frescoed ceilings and antique furniture. There are eight rooms, three of which open on to a courtyard. **€99**

EATING AND DRINKING

16

La Locanda del Colonnello Vico Biscari 6 ⓣ0932 752 423. Done-up like a traditional *locanda*, with chequered tiled walls and a local limestone floor below cantilevered white vaults, with evocative photos of old Modica on its walls. Antipasti (€9–11), *primi* (€13–15) and *secondi* (€16–20) make great use of local produce, including pork, cured hams, vegetables, legumes, ricotta and seafood. Wed & Fri–Mon noon–2pm & 7.30–10.30pm, Tues & Thurs 7.30–10.30pm.

Osteria dei Sapori Perduti Corso Umberto 1 228–230 ⓣ0932 944 247. Marvellous value, right on the Corso, where you can eat reasonably priced traditional rustic dishes, inside or out, with an emphasis on beans and pulses. The abundant mixed antipasto is a good way to start, and enough for two people, followed by *lolli con le fave* (handmade pasta with fava bean purée) or pasta with broth and meatballs. *Primi* and *secondi* are all priced between €5 and €9. The menu is in Sicilian, but translations are available, and you can eat well for €10–15. Wed–Mon noon–3pm & 7.30–11pm.

Taverna Nicastro Via S. Antonino 30 ⓣ0932 945 884. For traditional meat (and especially pork) dishes, this delightfully old-fashioned and very reasonably priced trattoria has tables outside on a flight of steps in the upper part of the old town. Specialities include sausages and salamis made on the premises, and ravioli stuffed with ricotta and dressed in a sauce of tomato, pancetta, sausage and pork (classic Modican fare). There are also some good hearty legume dishes. Secondi include rabbit with potato, olives, tomato and pork, and lamb stewed with tomato, capers, cherry tomatos and onion. You could eat a four-course meal (including a cannolo or a lemon, cinnamon or almond jelly) for under €20, while house wine is €3/litre. It's signposted from outside San Giorgio, but it's quite a walk, and you may have to ask the way before you find it. Tues–Sat 6.30–11pm, Sun noon–3pm.

Ragusa

RAGUSA is a town with two identities, literally split in two by the earthquake: the old town of **Ragusa Ibla**, on a jut of land above its valley, was flattened, and within a few years a new town, **Ragusa Superiore**, was built on a grand, planned grid, on a higher ridge to the west. Meanwhile, Ibla was rebuilt – in Baroque style – along its old medieval street plan.

In the second half of the last century people began to move out of Ibla for the modern comforts of life in the apartment buildings rapidly sprouting up in Ragusa Superiore. All commercial and social activity shifted here, and until the end of the last century Ibla was all but abandoned. Since then, thanks to generous European and government funding, Ibla has been painstakingly restored, and scores of B&Bs and stylish second homes now occupy its lovely limestone Baroque houses and palaces. However, with a population of just two thousand (out of a total of 70,000), and little in the way of ordinary shops or bars, Ibla is very much a museum town, virtually pedestrianized and dedicated only to tourism. Ragusa Superiore, on the other hand, is busy and mostly modern, but with a good slice of Baroque on the edge of the cleft between the two cities.

Ragusa Superiore

Ragusa Superiore is essentially a gridded Baroque town, slipping off to right and left on either side of the steeply sloping **Corso Italia**. To the right, down the Corso on a wide terrace above Piazza San Giovanni, stands the **Duomo**, conceived on a grand, symmetrical scale. Finished in 1774, its tapered columns and fine doorways are a fairly sombre background to the vigorous small-town atmosphere around.

Museo Archeologico

Via Natalelli • Mon–Sat 9am–6.30pm • Free • ⓣ 0932 622 963

Regusa's **Museo Archeologico** displays local archeological finds spanning the centuries from Neolithic (incised bowls and scythes) to Greek (some fantastic black figure vases), offering a fascinating insight into the rich, multilayered history of the province.

Santa Maria della Scala

Corso Mazzini

The restored fifteenth-century church of **Santa Maria della Scala** features the remains of an unusual exterior pulpit. From the church terrace, you get a mighty view of the weatherbeaten roofs of Ragusa Ibla straddling an outcrop of rock, rising to the prominent dome of San Giorgio (see below). From here, steps descend beneath the winding road to another church, the **Chiesa del Purgatorio**, from where alleyways climb back into the heart of Ragusa Ibla.

Ragusa Ibla

16

It's **Ragusa Ibla**, the original **lower town**, where most people head, its weather-beaten roofs straddling an outcrop of rock. The whole town – often deathly quiet – is ripe for aimless wandering. Rosario Gagliardi gets a credit for the elegant rounded facade of the church of **San Giuseppe** in Piazza Pola, a few steps below the Duomo (see below), while Corso XXV Aprile continues down past abandoned *palazzi* to the **Giardino Iblei** (daily 8am–1 hour before sunset), gardens occupying the very edge of the spur on which the town is built.

Duomo di San Giorgio

Piazza del Duomo • Mon & Wed–Sun 10am–12.30pm & 4–6.30pm, Tues 4–6.30pm, may stay open a little later in summer • Free

The main attraction, situated in the gleaming central core of the town, is Ibla's Duomo, **San Giorgio**, a masterpiece of Sicilian Baroque, built by Gagliardi and finished in 1784. The glorious three-tiered facade, sets of triple columns climbing up the wedding-cake exterior to a balconied belfry, is an imaginative work, though typically not much enhanced by venturing inside. As with Gagliardi's other important church in Modica (see page 929), all the beauty is in the immediacy of the powerful exterior.

ARRIVAL AND INFORMATION — RAGUSA

By train The train station is in Ragusa Superiore: from here, a left turn takes you along the main road and over the exposed Ponte Nuovo, one of three bridges spanning a huge gully in the ridge.

Destinations Modica (8 daily; 20min); Noto (5 daily; 1hr 30min).

By bus The bus terminus is also in Ragusa Superiore at Via Zama. From here buses #11 and #33, among others, will take you to Ibla, running around every 30min and stopping at Largo Kamerina and the Giardini Iblei.

Destinations Catania Airport (1 daily; 3hr); Modica (4 daily; 25min).

Tourist office There is an information point (erratic hours) in the Giardini Iblei.

ACCOMMODATION

Eremo della Giubiliana 7.5km out of Ragusa, along the road to Marina di Ragusa ⓣ 0932 669 119, ⓦ eremodellagiubiliana.com. An upmarket agriturismo (with its own 700m private airstrip, no less) housed in the restored buildings of a feudal estate dating back to the twelfth century. The grounds are gorgeous, and you can dine on their own organically grown food. **€200**

Locanda Don Serafino Via XI Febbraio 15, Ragusa Ibla ⓣ 0932 220 065, ⓦ locandadonserafino.it. A small, exclusive hotel, beautifully set within the hefty stone walls of

a nineteenth-century mansion. Two of the rooms, occupying the former stables, are carved straight into the bare rock, and one of them (room 8) has a bathroom inside a cave. **€150**

L'Orto sul Tetto Via Ten. Distefano 56, Ragusa Ibla ⓣ0932 247 785 or ⓣ338 478 0484, ⓦlortosultetto.it. A warm, friendly place a short walk from the Duomo with three serene bedrooms, run by a mother and son. Breakfasts, served on a roof terrace full of plants, include pastries fresh from the bakery. **€90**

Villa del Lauro Via Ecce Homo, Ragusa Superiore ⓣ0932 655 177, ⓦvilladellauro.it. Minimalist style within the exposed limestone walls of an eighteenth-century *palazzo* in the historic part of Ragusa Superiore. Excellent choice in summer, when you can while away afternoons in the serene, stylish garden with swimming pool. **€130**

EATING AND DRINKING

Ibla has two internationally renowned rival restaurants, each of them well worth splashing out on. However, if you are on a budget, a good alternative is a picnic; wander down narrow, curving Corso 25 Aprile, lined with fancy shops selling local produce.

I Banchi Via Orfanotrofio 39 ⓣ0932 655 000, ⓦibanchiragusa.it. Styled as a "basilica of taste" by its creator, Ciccio Sultano of *Duomo* (see below). At the root of it all is their fantastic home-made bread and pasta, along with meticulously sourced deli produce – all on sale. Then there's café-style service for traditional (but exceptional) street food and pastries; and a more sophisticated set lunch for €30. There are also special events, worth looking out for on the I Banchi Facebook page.

Pasticceria di Pasquale Corso Vittorio Veneto 104, Ragusa Superiore ⓣ0932 624 635, ⓦpasticceriadipasquale.com. Ragusa's best ice cream, plus utterly divine pastries and cakes, can be found in the nineteenth-century part of the upper town, just downhill from the Duomo of San Giovanni. Daily 7am–9pm.

Ristorante Duomo Via Capitano Bocchieri 31, Ragusa Ibla ⓣ0932 651 265. Meticulously sourced Sicilian ingredients reworked to stunning effect – black truffle ice cream, a savoury *cannolo* with a dab of caviar, for example – in what is arguably Sicily's greatest restaurant. Put yourself in the hands of chef Ciccio Sultano, and opt for one of the tasting menus (€135 and €150). Daily 12.30–2.30pm & 8–10.30pm; closed all day Sun & Mon lunch in summer, Sun eve & all day Mon in winter.

Ristorante Locanda Don Serafino Via Orfanotrofio 39, Ragusa Ibla ⓣ0932 248 778. In a vaulted medieval wine cellar, lit by candles, this is a place to feast on simple, well-executed dishes like handmade black spaghetti with squid ink, squid and ricotta, or an Angus steak with roasted vegetables and a red pepper ketchup. There are tasting menus at €120, €130 and €150 without wine, but there is a three-course lunch menu for €55. Wed–Mon 12.30–2.30pm & 8–10.30pm.

Trattoria la Bettola Largo Kamarina, Ragusa Ibla ⓣ0932 653 377. A rarity in Ibla: a simple, inexpensive family-run trattoria with red-and-white tablecloths that has been around for thirty years. Antipasti (from €5) include deep-fried and breadcrumbed morsels of local cheeses, aubergine *polpette* and a lemon-scented *tortino* of courgettes. *Primi* (all around €9) include *tagliatelle* with cream and saffron, *secondi* (€8–10) feature *maiale ubriaco*, pork braised in wine and wild herbs, in winter, and pork chops with citrus in summer. There is horsemeat too, if you feel like going totally local. Tues–Sun 7.30–11pm, Sun also lunch 12.30–2.30pm.

Agrigento

Modern **AGRIGENTO**, sited on a ridge high above the coast, is rarely visited for the town itself. The interest instead focuses on the substantial **remains** of Pindar's "most beautiful city of mortals", a couple of kilometres below. Here, strung out along a ridge facing the sea, is a series of **Doric temples** – the most captivating of Sicilian Greek remains and a grouping unique outside Greece.

In 581 BC colonists from nearby Gela and from Rhodes founded the city of **Akragas** between the rivers of Hypsas and Akragas. They surrounded it with a mighty wall, formed in part by a higher ridge on which the acropolis stood (today occupied by the modern town). The southern limit of the ancient city was a second, lower ridge and it was here, in the "**Valle dei Templi**", that the city architects erected their sacred buildings during the fifth century BC.

Valle dei Templi (Valley of the Temples)

Via dei Templi • Daily 8.30am–7pm; July–Sept, the temples of Juno, Concord and Hercules also open Mon–Fri 7.30–10pm, Sat & Sun 7.30pm–midnight • €10, €13.50 with Museo Archeologico • ⓦvalleyofthetemples.com or for online tickets ⓦcoopculture.it • Buses #1, #2 and #3 run to the main entrance from outside Agrigento train station (tickets from the bar inside station) – open entry on summer nights is at the Temple of Juno entrance, accessible from the main entrance by shared taxi (€2/person); a taxi from Agrigento costs €15

A road winds down from the modern city to the **Valle dei Templi**, which is divided into two zones. The more spectacular remains are in the eastern zone – to avoid crowds come in the early morning or (in summer) for the night openings. The western zone may be less architecturally impressive, but gives more of a sense of discovery – and holds the lovely gardens of Kolymbetra.

The eastern zone

The **eastern zone** is unenclosed and is at its crowd-free best in early morning or late evening. A path climbs up to the oldest of Akragas's temples, the **Tempio di Ercole** (Hercules). Probably begun in the last decades of the sixth century BC, nine of the original 38 columns have been re-erected, everything else is scattered around like the pieces of a jigsaw puzzle. Retrace your steps back to the path that leads to the glorious **Tempio della Concordia**, dated to around 430 BC: perfectly preserved and beautifully sited, with fine views to the city and the sea, the tawny stone lends the structure warmth and strength. That it's still so complete is explained by its conversion in the sixth century AD to a Christian church. Restored to its (more or less) original layout in the eighteenth century, it has kept its lines and slightly tapering columns, although it's fenced off to keep the crowds at bay. The path continues, following the line of the ancient city walls, to the **Tempio di Giunone** (Juno or Hera), an engaging half-ruin standing at the very edge of the ridge. The patches of red visible here and there on the masonry denote fire damage, probably from the sack of Akragas by the Carthaginians in 406 BC.

The western zone

The **western zone**, back along the path and beyond the car park, is less impressive, a vast tangle of stone and fallen masonry from a variety of temples. Most notable is the mammoth construction that was the **Tempio di Giove**, or Temple of Olympian Zeus. The largest Doric temple ever known, it was never completed, left in ruins by the Carthaginians and further damaged by earthquakes. Still, the stereobate remains, while on the ground, face to the sky, lies an 8m-high telamone: a supporting column sculpted as a male figure, arms raised and bent to bear the temple's weight. Other scattered remains litter the area, including the so-called **Tempio dei Dioscuri** (Castor and Pollux), rebuilt in 1832 and actually made up of unrelated pieces from the confused rubble on the ground. When you've had your fill of the ruins, make for the **Giardino Kolymbetra**, an enchanting sunken garden of shady citrus, almond and olive groves, with a stream running through it, set between cave-pocked tufa cliffs that once formed part of the city's irrigation system.

Museo Nazionale Archeologico di Agrigento

Mon–Sat 9am–7.30pm, Sun 9am–1.30pm • €8 or €13.50 with Valley of the Temples

Via dei Templi leads back to the town from the car park via the excellent **Museo Nazionale Archeologico di Agrigento**. The extraordinarily rich collection is devoted to finds from the city and the surrounding area; the best displays are the cases of vases (sixth to third century BC) and a reassembled telamone stacked against one wall. Nip over the road on the way out for the **Hellenistic-Roman quarter** (daily 9am until 1hr before sunset; free), which contains lines of houses, inhabited intermittently until the fifth century AD, many with mosaic designs still discernible.

ARRIVAL AND INFORMATION — AGRIGENTO

By train Trains arrive at Agrigento Centrale station at the edge of the old town; don't get out at Agrigento Bassa which is 3km north of town. There are excellent services (for Sicily) to Palermo (12 daily; 2hr min), but for other destinations the bus is usually faster.

By bus Regional buses use the terminal in Piazza Rosselli, near the post office. City buses to the temples and the beach at San Leone can be picked up here or at the train station. Buy city bus tickets (€1.20 valid 90 min, €3.40 valid all day) from kiosks or tabacchi. Tickets bought on board cost €1.70 valid for 90 min.

Destinations Catania and Catania airport (hourly; 2hr

50min); Palermo (5 daily; 2hr 30min); Trapani (3 daily; 3hr 20min–4hr).

Tourist office Via Atene 272 (Mon–Fri 9.30am–1.30pm plus Tues & Thurs 3.30–7.30pm; ⓣ 0922 596 168).

ACCOMMODATION

Arco Ubriaco Via Sferri 12 ⓣ 335 745 6532, ⓦ arcoubriaco.com. Three rooms in a welcoming family house on the edge of Rabato, named for the tilting medieval arch leading off the living room. There's wi-fi, and all rooms have a bathroom, a/c and a fridge. The motherly owner is adept at making guests feel part of the family. **€80**

Mille e Una Notte Via Garibaldi 46 ⓣ 320 483 5856, ⓦ milleeunanottebeb.it. Sensitively run B&B with spick-and-span rooms including two sleeping four and five and a small apartment. **€70**

★ **Peppe e Romina Melisenda Giambertoni** Via Passeggiata Archeologica 29 ⓣ 3487 622 790, ⓔ casinagiambertoni@gmail.com. There is no better place to stay in Agrigento than these three simple apartments on the ground floor of a nineteenth-century villa set just between an olive grove and the Roman-Hellenistic area of the archeological zone, a short walk from the museum. They may not be luxurious, but you have everything you need, and the opportunity to sit outside your apartment at night, looking at the temples, is priceless. **€75**

EATING AND DRINKING

There are two distinct areas for cafés and bars. The town-centre *passeggiata* focuses on Via Atenea, and once the shops reopen in the late afternoon the whole street is packed. To watch the action, choose a seat at one of the little bars in Piazzale Aldo Moro, at the beginning of Via Atenea, a nice place to sit in the early evening, despite the occasional burst of organ music from a local crooner. For sunsets and views, stroll along the leafy Viale della Vittoria, where four or five cafés cater to a local family crowd.

Antica Panelleria Musicò Viale della Vittoria s/n. No phone. This little van parked at the beginning of Viale della Vittoria is an Agrigento institution, selling *pane e panelle* (chickpea flour fritters in soft bread rolls) since 1954. Daily 8.30am–1pm & 5–8.30pm.

Caffeteria Nobel Viale della Vittoria 11. A relaxing spot for breakfast that serves amazing pastries, ice creams or a beer under the shady trees of the avenue. Daily 6am–late.

Capotavola Viale della Vittoria 15–17 ⓣ 0922 21 484. Perfect for families – it even has a play area screened from the main restaurant by a glass window, so you can keep an eye on the kids while you eat in peace. There are pizzas (€5–8), including the crowd-pleasing *ricottina*, with mozzarella, ricotta, ham and Parmesan. On the restaurant menu you'll find risotto with crustaceans; lemon-scented spaghetti with seafood and toasted breadcrumbs; and fish dishes such as red prawns from Mazara, further up the coast. From Tues to Fri you can have as much pasta as you can eat (though you have to finish one plate before ordering another) for €15 a head including a drink. Otherwise a full meal will cost around €35. Daily noon–2pm & 7.30–10.30pm.

Le Cuspidi Piazza Cavour 19. Come to this *gelateria* for the best ice creams in town – some say even in Sicily. Try the fresh ricotta, pistachio or almond, or one of the mouthwatering fruit flavours. Daily 9am–late.

★ **Posata di Federico Secondo** Piazza Cavour 19 ⓣ 0922 28 289. Lovely, elegant restaurant, just off the elegant, tree-lined Viale della Vittoria. The food is superb, strictly seasonal, with the menu divided according to the main ingredient (artichoke, veal etc). The signature dish is an amazing beef fillet served with Gorgonzola and honey. Expect to pay €35–40 for a full meal, but you could have a light lunch for less than €15. Mon–Sat noon–4pm & 7–11pm.

Terracotta Via Francesco Crispi 34 ⓣ 0922 29 742 or ⓣ 329 091 4850. Lovely relaxed setting in the garden of playwright Luigi Pirandello's former summer villa, with an unpretentious menu and wine list inspired by the Slow Food ethos. The menu is seasonal, using Sicilian produce – try *linguine* lightly dressed with mussels, cherry tomatoes and courgette plant fronds. Around €45 a head. Tues–Sun noon–3.30pm & 7–11pm (later in July & Aug).

Piazza Armerina

A thirty-minute drive to the south of Enna, **PIAZZA ARMERINA** lies amid densely planted hills; it's a quiet, unassuming place, mainly seventeenth and eighteenth century in appearance, with a skyline pierced by towers and houses huddled together under the joint protection of castle and cathedral. All in all, it's a thoroughly pleasant place to idle around, though the real local draw is the imperial **Villa Romana del Casale** that stands in rugged countryside at Casale, 5km southwest of Piazza Armerina. It was hidden under mud for seven hundred years, until excavations in the 1950s revealed a lavish villa, probably a hunting lodge and summer home, decorated with polychromatic mosaic floors that are unique in the Roman world for their quality and extent.

Villa Romana del Casale

Strada Provinciale 15 • Daily 9am–6pm • €10 • ⊕ 0935 680 036, ⊛ villaromanadelcasale.it • Buses leave Piazza Senatore Marescalchi in Piazza Armerina for the Villa Romana, with a stop at Piazza Generale Cascino (hourly May–Sept 9am–noon & 3–6pm; 30min): the return service is on the half-hour, starting at 9.30am; a taxi from Piazza Generale Cascino in Piazza Armerina costs €15 one way

The **Villa Romana del Casale** dates from the early fourth century BC and was used right up until the twelfth century when a mudslide left it largely covered until the 1950s. The **mosaics** themselves are identifiable as fourth-century Roman-African school, which explains many of the more exotic scenes and animals portrayed; they also point to the villa having had an important owner, possibly Maximianus Herculeus, one of four co-emperors with Diocletian, who divided the Roman world up between them.

The **main entrance** leads into a wide courtyard with fountains, where the **thermae** (baths) group around an octagonal frigidarium and a central mosaic showing a lively marine scene. A walkway leads out of the baths and into the villa proper, to the massive central court or **peristyle**, whose surrounding corridors are decorated with animal-head mosaics. From here, a balcony looks down on one of the villa's most interesting pictures, a boisterous circus scene showing a chariot race. Small rooms beyond, on either side of the peristyle, reveal only fragmentary geometric patterns, although one contains probably the villa's most famous image, a two-tiered scene of ten realistically muscular **Roman girls in "bikinis"**, taking part in various gymnastic and athletic activities.

Beyond the peristyle, a long, covered corridor contains the most extraordinary of the mosaics: the **great hunting scene**, which sets armed and shield-bearing hunters against a panoply of wild animals. Along the entire 60m length of the mosaic are tigers, ostriches, elephants, even a rhino, being trapped, bundled up and down gangplanks and into cages, destined for the Games back in Rome. The square-hatted figure overseeing the operation is probably Maximianus himself: his personal area of responsibility in the imperial Tetrarchy was North Africa, where much of the scene is set.

Other rooms beyond are nearly all on a grand scale. The **triclinium**, a dining room with three apses, features the labours of Hercules, and a path leads around the back to the **private apartments**, based around a large basilica. The best mosaics here are a children's circus, where tiny chariots are drawn by colourful birds, and a children's hunt, the kids chased and pecked by the hares and peacocks they're supposed to snare.

16

ARRIVAL AND DEPARTURE — PIAZZA ARMERINA

By bus Buses drop you in Piazza Senatore Marescalchi, a large square on the main road in the lower, modern town, 15min walk from the old centre.

Destinations Enna (4–6 daily; 30min); Palermo (5 daily Mon–Sat; 2hr 15min).

ACCOMMODATION AND EATING

Amici Miei Largo Capodarso 5 ⊕ 0935 683 541. Despite the distance from the sea, the fish is excellent here, from baked bream to sautéed mussels (dishes €7–16.50). There are also pizzas in the evening, which you can eat on a charming terrace. Fri–Wed noon–3pm & 7pm–midnight, Tues 7pm–midnight only.

Suite d'Autore Piazza Duomo ⊕ 0935 688 553, ⊛ suitedautore.it. Top choice in town is the fabulously quirky "art-hotel" opposite the cathedral, whose fun-filled rooms mix contemporary design, stylish artefacts, retro objects, original art and photography. Highlight is a circular bed! €100

Trattoria del Goloso Via Garao 4, just off Piazza Garibaldi ⊕ 0935 685 693. An excellent choice for good-value seasonal regional dishes such as handmade pasta with cherry tomatoes, aubergine and basil served with a dollop of fresh ricotta (€6.50). Noon–3pm & 7–10pm; closed Wed in winter.

Trapani and the west

The **west** of Sicily is a land apart. Skirting around the coast from **Trapani** – the provincial capital – the cubic whitewashed houses, palm trees, active fishing harbours and sunburned lowlands seem more akin to Africa than Europe, and historically, the

west of the island has always looked south. The earliest of all Sicilian sites, the mountain haunt of **Erice** was dominated by Punic influence. The Carthaginians themselves entrenched themselves in **Marsala**, at Sicily's westernmost point, for several hundred years, while in medieval times the Saracen invaders took their first steps onto the island at **Mazara del Vallo**, a town still strongly Arabic at heart. The Greeks never secured the same foothold in Sicily's west as elsewhere, although the remains at **Segesta** count among the island's best. Also worth seeing are the three islands of the **Egadi** archipelago, and the stunning stretch of coastline protected by the **Riserva Naturale dello Zingaro**.

Trapani and around

Out on a limb, and with more than a little North African atmosphere about it, **TRAPANI** is an attractive old port town, rediscovering its charms after years of neglect. Halfway point between Europe and Tunis, it was a rich trading centre throughout the early Middle Ages, then flourished again in the nineteenth and early twentieth centuries as a stronghold of the tuna-canning industry. After that, it went into decline, and became a salty old port with a crumbling, sun-scorched historic centre high on atmosphere, but with few creature comforts. Then, it was selected to host the 2004 Americas Cup and received a massive injection of cash – buildings were restored, streets in the historic centre pedestrianized – giving the town and its people a new confidence. These days Trapani is a thoroughly pleasant and authentic place to hang out for a couple of days. Its **Easter celebrations** are justly famous, involving dramatic processions around town, particularly poignant on Good Friday.

The centro storico

The nicest way to approach the **centro storico** is along pedestrianized **Via Garibaldi**, which begins opposite the northwest corner of the Villa Margherita gardens across from the train station. Lined with palaces, churches and little pavement cafés, it leads to Via Torrearsa, a pedestrianized shopping street, which neatly splits the old town in two. West of here Trapani's layout becomes more regularly planned, while the main drag and shopping street, the elegant, pedestrianized **Corso Vittorio Emanuele**, changes its name to Via Carolina and then Via Torre di Ligny as it runs towards the **Torre di Ligny** – utmost point of the scimitar of land that holds the old town.

Back on Via Torrearsa, Corso Italia leads back towards the station via a trio of little piazzas, enlivened by their surrounding churches: the sixteenth-century **Chiesa di Santa Maria di Gesù** (Via San Pietro) is defiantly Renaissance in execution, while the fourteenth-century church of **Sant'Agostino** retains a Gothic portal and delicate rose window.

Chiesa del Purgatorio

Via Francesco d'Assisi • In theory open daily 9am–noon • Free

South of the Corso, Via Francesco d'Assisi holds the exuberantly sculpted **Chiesa del Purgatorio**, at the junction with Via Domenico Giglio, where the **Misteri**, a group of life-sized eighteenth-century wooden figures representing scenes from the Passion, are displayed when they're not being wheeled around town during Easter commemorations.

ARRIVAL AND DEPARTURE — TRAPANI

By plane Trapani's airport, 15km south of the centre at Birgi, has flights from Italian cities and Pantelleria (1–3 daily; 40min), as well as several Ryanair services from mainland Italy, Prague, Frankfurt and Karlsruhe. AST also has a regular (hourly) service to Trapani port and station, although the future of the very useful and currently suspended Terravision service to Palermo is uncertain.

By train Trains stop at the Stazione Centrale just around the corner from the bus station.

Destinations Marsala (12 daily; 30min); Mazara del Vallo (12 daily; 40min–1hr); Palermo (8 daily; 3hr–3hr 49min); Segesta Tempio (4 daily; 20min).

By bus Most buses (including those to and from Erice) pull up at the terminal in Piazza Malta. If you're heading straight off

to the Egadi islands, note that the fast buses from the airport, Palermo, Palermo airport and Agrigento stop at the ferry and hydrofoil terminals, as well as the bus station. Bus companies include S. Lumia (T 0922 20 414, W autolineelumia.it) from Piazza Malta and Trapani airport to Agrigento; Segesta (T 091 342 525, W segesta.it) from Piazza Garibaldi to Palermo and Palermo airport; Salemi (T 0923 981 120, W autoservizisalemi.it) from Trapani airport to Marsala and Palermo; Tarantola (T 0924 31 020) from Piazza Malta to Segesta; and Terravision (T 0923 981 120, W terravision.eu) from the port, bus station and airport to Palermo.

Destinations Agrigento (3 daily; 3hr 10min–3hr 40min); Castellammare (4 daily Mon–Sat; 1hr 20min); Erice (8 daily; 45min); Palermo (every 30min–1hr Mon–Sat, approx hourly Sun; 2hr); Palermo airport (4 daily; 1hr); Segesta (6 daily; 1hr 10min).

By boat Ferries for the Egadi Islands, Pantelleria, Cagliari and Tunis dock at the Molo di Sanità, while Libertylines hydrofoils for the Egadi islands, Naples and Ustica dock to the east of the Molo, on Via A. Stati. The frequencies given below are year-round. Services usually increase between June 10 and September 10.

Ferry and hydrofoil companies Siremar ferries (T 0923 031911, W carontetourist.it) sails to the Egadi Islands and Pantelleria; and Liberty Lines (T 347.8734219, W libertylines.it) to the Egadi Islands, and (usually summer only) Pantelleria, Ustica and Naples.

Ferry destinations Favignana (1–2 daily; 1hr–1hr 25min); Lévanzo (1–2 daily; 50min–1hr 40min); Marettimo (1 daily; 2hr 35min–2hr 50min); Pantelleria (6 weekly; 5hr 45min).

Hydrofoil destinations Favignana (roughly hourly; 15–40min); Lévanzo (11 daily; 20–40min); Marettimo (4 daily; 1hr); Naples (1 on Sat June–Sept; 7hr); Pantelleria (1 daily except Tues June–Sept); Ustica (1 on Sat usually June–Sept; 2hr 30min).

INFORMATION

Tourist office The tourist office is at Via S. Francesco D'Assisi, 29 (Mon–Sat 9am–1pm & 4–7pm, Sun 9am–1pm; reduced hours out of season; T 0923 545511).

Website Good online source of information on Trapani and surroundings are W turismo.trapani.it, and, for those interested in exploring the region's vineyards and wines, W stradadelvinoericedoc.com.

16

ACCOMMODATION

Ai Lumi Corso Vittorio Emanuele 71 T 0923 540 922, W ailumi.it. Five small but pristine rooms entered through a flower-filled courtyard. They also own the trattoria of the same name at street level. **€120**

Lido Valderice Località Lido Valderice T 0923 573 477 or T 349 854 2190, W campinglidovalderice.it; around 5 buses daily (except Sun in winter) from Trapani bus station (direction San Vito via Sciare) to the turn-off, from where it's a 10min walk. Appealing campsite near the beach at Lido Valderice, a 25min bus ride away, with bungalows and caravans to rent as well as tent pitches. Pitches **€7.40**, per person **€6.90**

Maccotta Via degli Argentieri 4 T 0923 28 418, W albergomaccotta.it. Smart and friendly place with spacious, modern rooms with comfortable beds but small bathrooms; a/c and wi-fi available. **€50**

Nuovo Russo Via Tintori 4 T 0923 22 163. Trapani's oldest hotel is in a great position on the main Corso, just a few minutes walk from the port. It has recently restored 36 rooms, with shutters to cut out most of the street noise, and the corridors are sprinkled with a random assortment of family heirlooms. **€120**

Residence La Gancia Piazza Mercato del Pesce T 0923 438 060, W lagancia.com. Smart, if slightly sterile, contemporary rooms and mini apartments (with and without cooking facilities), a great roof terrace (where breakfast is served) and a superb position on the northern seafront right above the town beach at the head of Via Torrearsa. **€125**

Tonnara di Bonagia Piazza Tonnara di Bonagia T 0923 431 111, W tonnaradibonagia.it. Excellent choice for families, this hotel occupies the buildings of an old tuna fishery (complete with beached tuna boats and Saracen watchtower) and has accommodation in apartments with a kitchen, as well as conventional rooms. There is a huge pool, a tennis court, laidback activities for kids, local produce for sale and little paths leading straight out of the grounds to the shore, where you can swim off rocks or a wooden jetty. **€200**

EATING AND DRINKING

Ai Lumi Corso Vittorio Emanuele 71–77 T 0923 872 418. Romantic setting in the brick-vaulted rooms of a Baroque palace with a pretty terrace for summer. Good home-made pasta – try it with shrimp, asparagus tips and sea urchin. €35/head. Wed–Mon noon–2.30pm & 8–10.30pm (later in summer).

I Grilli Corso Vittorio Emanuele 69 T 0923 20 663. Carefully sourced meats cooked on a charcoal grill, along with French and Italian cheeses, salami and cured hams, plus over 150 wines. Its terrace is on the main Corso. Daily 5.30–11pm, open all day from noon till late in summer.

La Bettolaccia Via Gen. Enrico Fardella 25 T 0923 25932. Popular with locals, this informal but sophisticated *osteria* is known for its excellent pasta dishes (wonderful spaghetti with red prawns, cherry tomatoes and almonds, and *busiate alla trapanese* or with smoked cheese and

sundried tomatoes are both lovely) which will have anyone who likes cooking making notes. Expect to pay €30–40 per head, including good local wine. Delicious desserts include *parfait al pistacchio*. Book, or arrive early. Mon–Fri 12.45–3pm & 8–11pm, Sat & Sun 8–11pm.

Pizzeria Calvino Via N. Nasi 77 ⓣ 0923 21 464. A Trapani institution, this bustling bakery has been making pizza since 1946. Try the local speciality, *rianata* with tomato, pecorino and oregano, or a hearty plate of sausages and potatoes roasted with onions in the pizza oven. Wed–Mon 7pm–midnight.

Erice

The nearest and most exhilarating ride from Trapani is to **ERICE**, fifteen minutes away by **cable car** (*funivia*). It's a mountain town with creeping hillside alleys, stone buildings, silent charm and powerful associations. Founded by Elymnians, who claimed descent from the Trojans, the original city was known to the ancient world as Eryx, and a magnificent temple, dedicated to Venus Erycina, Mediterranean goddess of fertility, once topped the mountain. Though the city was considered impregnable, Carthaginian, Roman, Arab and Norman invaders all forced entry. But all respected the sanctity of Erice: the Romans rebuilt the temple and set two hundred soldiers to serve as guardians of the shrine, while the Arabs renamed the town Gebel-Hamed, or "Mohammed's mountain".

Scout around the town at random: the most convoluted of routes is only going to take you a couple of hours and every street and piazza is a delight. You enter through the Norman **Porta Trapani**, just inside which is the **Duomo**, or Chiesa Matrice, and its battlemented fourteenth-century campanile, the **Torre di Re Federico**, which did service as a lookout tower for Frederick III of Aragon.

Castello di Venere

April–Oct daily 10am–1hr before sunset; Nov–March Sat & Sun 10am–4pm • €4

At the far end of town, the ivy-clad **Castello di Venere** is a Norman castle built on the site of the famed ancient temple, chunks of which are incorporated in the walls. When it's fine, the **views** from the terraces of Erice are phenomenal – over Trapani and the slumbering whales of the Egadi islands.

ARRIVAL AND INFORMATION — ERICE

By bus To get to Erice from Trapani, take bus #21 or #23 (direction Ospedale S. Antonio Abbate) and get off at the stop before the hospital, from where it's a short walk to the *funivia* station (ⓦ funiviaerice.it, the cable car operates Mon 1–8.30pm, Tues–Fri 8.10am–8.30pm, Sat 9am–9pm, Sun 10am–8pm, or later in summer; the service may be cancelled if it's very windy). The trip costs €5.50 one way, €9 return, and you arrive at the Porta Trapani in Erice.

ACCOMMODATION

Il Carmine Piazza del Carmine 23 ⓣ 0923 869 089 or ⓣ 0923 194 1532, ⓦ ilcarmine.com. Spacious, bright rooms in a former Carmelite convent in the heart of town, with separate private bathrooms. €90

San Domenico Via Tommaso Guerrasi 26 ⓣ 0923 860 128, ⓦ hotel-sandomenico.it. Engaging family-run hotel in a medieval house in the heart of Erice – with the owners' children's toys in evidence in the sitting room along with some robust rustic antiques. Two sets of connecting rooms, and a triple. Breakfast is in a tiny courtyard. €120

Ulisse Camere Via S. Lucia 2 ⓣ 0923 860 155 or ⓣ 389 985 6089, ⓦ sitodiulisse.it. Nicely furnished rooms dispersed over two buildings, with private bathrooms. The best are grouped around a tranquil central courtyard. They also have a restaurant in Via Chiaramonte serving local dishes. €65

EATING AND DRINKING

Caffè Maria Via Vittorio Emanuele 4. Don't leave town without a visit to the café or its sister *pasticceria* a few doors down, for marzipan goodies and exquisite *cannoli*. The café's founder, Maria Grammatico, learned her trade as a girl in a convent, and has co-written a recipe book with writer Mary Taylor Simeti. Daily 7.30am–8.30pm; closed Tues in winter.

La Pentolaccia Via Guarnotti 17 ⓣ 0923 869 099. Atmospherically housed in an old monastery, this moderately priced place serves excellent home-made pasta and couscous. Try the ravioli stuffed with cernia (grouper) in a sauce of cherry tomato, swordfish, mint and prawns (€12.50). Daily noon–10.30pm.

Monte San Giuliano Vicolo S. Rocco 7 ⓣ 0923 869

595. Really excellent food in a restaurant entered through a medieval stone archway. Wed–Sun 12.30–2.30pm & 7.30–10.30pm, Tues open eve only; closed three weeks in Nov & Jan.

The Temple of Segesta

Daily 9am to 1hr before sunset • €6

One of the most evocative Doric temples anywhere, the **temple** of **Segesta** lies 35km southeast of Trapani. Although unfinished, this Greek construction of 424 BC is virtually the only relic of an ancient city whose roots – like those of Erice – go back to the twelfth century BC. Unlike Erice, though, ancient Segesta was eventually Hellenized and spent most of the later period disputing its borders with Selinus to the south. The temple dates from a time of prosperous alliance with Athens, the building abandoned when a new dispute broke out with Selinus in 416 BC.

The **temple** itself crowns a low hill, beyond a café and car park. From a distance you could be forgiven for thinking that it's complete: the 36 regular white stone columns, entablature and pediment are all intact, and all it lacks is a roof. However, get closer and you see just how unfinished the building is: stone studs, always removed on completion, still line the stylobate, the tall columns are unfluted and the cella walls are missing. Below the car park, a road winds up through slopes of wild fennel to the small **theatre** on a higher hill beyond. There's a **minibus** service every thirty minutes – handy if you don't fancy the twenty-minute climb. The view from the top is justly lauded, across green slopes and the plain to the sea, the deep blue of the bay a lovely contrast to the theatre's white stone.

ARRIVAL AND DEPARTURE — THE TEMPLE OF SEGESTA

16

By bus To get to Segesta, catch one of the direct Tarantola buses from Piazza Malta in Trapani (6 daily; 1hr 10min). There are also buses from Castellamare del Golfo (1 daily in summer; 30min) and Palermo (4 daily; 1hr 30min).

Northeast of Trapani

The main reason for heading out **northeast of Trapani** is to get away from it all in the beguiling surroundings of what is probably Sicily's most beautiful coastal nature reserve, **Zingaro**, which is approached via the pretty village of **Scopello**.

Scopello

The road to Scopello forks just before arriving at the village, with one strand running the few hundred metres down to the **Tonnara do Scopello**, set in its own tiny cove, an old tuna fishery where the writer Gavin Maxwell lived and worked in the 1950s, basing his *Ten Pains of Death* on his experiences here. It's almost too picturesque to be true – not least the row of abandoned buildings on the quayside and the ruined old watchtowers tottering on jagged pinnacles of rock above the sea. The actual village of **SCOPELLO** perches on a ridge a couple of hundred metres above the coastline, comprising little more than a paved square and a fountain, off which run a couple of alleys. A stone's throw away is the lovely bay of **Cala Bianca**, where there's good swimming.

Riserva Naturale dello Zingaro

Just 2km from Scopello is the southern entrance to the **Riserva Naturale dello Zingaro**, Sicily's first nature reserve, comprising a completely unspoiled 7km stretch of **coastline** backed by steep mountains. At the entrance, there's an **information hut**, where you can pick up a plan showing the **trails** through the reserve. It's less than twenty minutes to the first beach, Punta della Capreria, and 3km to the successive coves of Disa, Berretta and Marinella, which should be a little more secluded.

ARRIVAL AND DEPARTURE — SCOPELLO AND ZINGARO

By bus To get to Scopello you have to go via the seaside resort of Castellammare. Buses run from Trapani to

Castellammare (4 daily Mon–Sat; 1hr 20min), then from Castellammare's Piazza della Repubblica to Scopello (mid-June to mid-Sept 4 daily; mid-Sept to mid-June Mon–Sat 4 daily; 30min). From Scopello it's an easy 2km walk to the reserve's nearest entrance, though there is a bus in summer.

ACCOMMODATION AND EATING

La Tavernetta Via A. Diaz 3 0924 541 129, albergo latavernetta.it. Run by friendly, accommodating owners, this hotel has twelve very pleasant, refurbished rooms, all with balconies, sea views and pretty stencilled furniture. Its restaurant, in a huge garden of olives, prickly pear and citrus trees, specializes in local dishes like couscous (€11.50) and *spaghetti con le sarde* (€10); half board €75/person. €85

La Tranchina Via A. Diaz 7 0924 541 099, pensione tranchina.com. Simple rooms with a friendly English-speaking owner. You'll eat well here too – fresh fish, and interesting pasta dishes such as pasta with peppers and home-cured *bottarga* (tuna-fish egg roe); half board €75/person. €85

The Egadi islands

Of the various islands, islets and rock stacks that fan out from the west coast of Sicily, the three **Egadi islands** (Isole Egadi) are best for a quick jaunt – connected by ferry and hydrofoil with Trapani. The islands have been saved from depopulation by tourism, so in season at least you're not going to be alone, certainly on the main island, **Favignana**, where in August every scrap of flat rock and sand is filled. But a tour of the islands is worthwhile, not least for the caves that perforate the splintered coastlines. Out of season things are noticeably quieter, and in May or June you may witness the bloody **Mattanza**, an age-old slaughter in this noted centre of tuna fishing, though its future is uncertain.

16

ARRIVAL AND DEPARTURE — THE EGADI ISLANDS

By Ferry Ferries to the islands depart from Trapani's Molo di Sanità.

By Hydrofoil Hydrofoils leave from further east along Via Ammiraglio Staiti (see page 937).

Favignana

FAVIGNANA, island and port town, is first stop for the boats from Trapani, and makes a good base since it has virtually all the accommodation and the Egadis' only campsites. Just 25 minutes by hydrofoil from the mainland, the island attracts a lot of day-trippers, keen to get onto its few rocky beaches. But get out of the main port and it's easy enough to escape the crowds, even easier with a bike (which can be rented from dozens of outlets in the centre of town). **Caves** all over the island bear prehistoric traces and many are accessible if you're determined enough. Otherwise, the two wings of the island invite separate **walks**; best is the circuit around the eastern part, past the bizarre ancient quarries at Cala Rossa, over the cliffs to Cala Azzurra and then following the coast past the ugly tourist village at Punta Fanfalo to Lido Burrone, one of the island's best beaches, only 1km from the port. Other beaches worth checking out are **Cala Rossa** and **Cala Azzurra**, on the eastern end of the island.

ACCOMMODATION — FAVIGNANA

Aegusa Via Garibaldi 11 0923 922 430, aegusa hotel.it. Favignana's longest-established hotel is a central but quiet choice in town, with 28 cheerful rooms and a well-regarded restaurant. €140

Cave Bianche Cala Azzurra 0923 925 451, cave bianchehotel.it. Built inside one of the island's tufa quarries, this original hotel has chic, minimalist rooms, plus the added draw of a swimming pool and restaurant. You can find excellent deals through the website. €300

Hotel delle Cave Contrada Torretta, Str Vic. della Madonna (but known locally as Zona Cavallo) 0923 925 423, hoteldellecave.it. Designer hotel with just fourteen rooms built on the lip of an abandoned quarry, with two mini-hydromassage pools and gardens inside the quarry itself. You can find excellent deals through the website. €230

EATING

Il Giardino delle Aloe Contrada Grotta Perciata 348 412 3040. Fish fresh from the island's fleet served in a garden

of aloe near the dramatic bay of Cala Rossa. The menu depends on the catch – handmade twisted pasta with mussels, for example, or a slice of the famous Favignana tuna. There is a free minibus from town, but during the day it is a nice cycle ride. They also have some lovely apartments. €30/head without wine. Noon–2.30pm, plus dinner on request.

La Bettola Via Nicotera 47 ⓣ0923 921 988. With a terrace for eating alfresco, this popular spot serves up a memorable *couscous di pesce* (€19). As an antipasto, the *fritelle di gámberi* (prawn fritters) are also good. Prices are reasonable, with starters at €8–10, mains €10–16. Daily noon–2pm & 8–10pm or later.

Levanzo

LEVANZO, to the north of Favignana, looks immediately inviting, its white houses against a turquoise sea reminiscent of the Greek islands. The steep coast is full of inlets and riddled with caves: the **Grotta del Genovese** was discovered in 1949 and contains some remarkable Paleolithic incised drawings, six thousand years old, as well as later Neolithic pictures. Tours to the cave (€23.50/person) leave twice daily in summer by boat, less frequently in winter by jeep, and must be booked in advance, by phone or at Via Calvario 11, above the quay (ⓣ339 741 8800, ⓦgrottadelgenovese.it). The island's **interior** has some great **walks** along old cart tracks, and there's a paved (and virtually traffic-free) cornice road leading to a lovely white pebble **beach** by the jagged rocks of the Faraglioni.

ACCOMMODATION AND EATING — LEVANZO

Lisola Residence Contrada Case ⓣ0923 194 1530 or ⓣ320 180 9090, ⓦlisola.eu. Seven apartments (sleeping two–four) in simple tufa cottages originally built by a nineteenth-century tuna-canning magnate for his workers, 400m outside the port. There's a large pool, canvas sun umbrellas and loungers, and free transport to the port whenever you need it. Minimum stay three nights or a week in summer. Closed Nov–March. **€95**

Paradiso Via Lungomare 6 ⓣ0923 26 235. Lovely sea views and simple fish, seafood and pasta at the tiny island's only restaurant. Try *tuna polpette*, spaghetti with pesto *trapanese* (with basil, tomatoes and almonds) or the catch of the day. Around €30/head without wine. Easter–Oct daily noon–2pm & 8–10pm or later.

16

Marettimo

MARETTIMO, furthest out of the Egadi islands, is the place to come for solitude. Very much off the beaten track, it's visisted by only a few tourists. White houses are scattered across the rocky island, and there's a bar in the main piazza, along with two restaurants. The spectacular fragmented coastline is pitted with rocky coves sheltering hideaway **beaches**, and there are numerous gentle **walks**, which will take you all over the island.

ACCOMMODATION AND EATING — MARETTIMO

Caffe Tramontana Via Scalo Vecchio. Marettimo's main hangout. Breakfast on almond, mulberry or watermelon granita, or come for an evening *aperitivo* accompanied by a plate of raw fish as you watch the sun set over the fishing harbour and castle. Daily from 8am.

Il Veliero Corso Umberto ⓣ0923 923 274. Cane-covered terrace right on the water, serving traditional pasta dishes, and fish caught by the owner. Arrive early for a good table and call in advance to reserve lobster. €30–35/head without wine, if you resist the lobster. Easter–Oct daily noon–2pm & 8–10pm, longer hours in high season.

Marettimo Residence ⓣ0923 923 202, ⓦmarettimoresidence.it. An appealing little cluster of resort cottages available for weekly rental above a stony beach south of the main port, or ask at the café in the main square. Per week from **€890** in high season, from **€360** in low season.

Rosa dei Venti Punta S. Simone ⓣ0923 923 249, ⓦisoladimarettimo.it. Six rooms with bathrooms, as well as apartments with cooking facilities, run by friendly owners who can also arrange boat trips. **€65**

Sardinia

949 Cagliari

954 Nora and around

955 Sant'Antioco

958 Oristano

960 Tharros

960 Bosa

961 Nuoro

963 Monte Ortobene

964 The interior and the east coast

967 Olbia

969 The Costa Smeralda and around

970 The Maddalena islands

972 Santa Teresa Gallura and around

973 Castelsardo

973 Sassari

976 Stintino and around

976 Alghero

SA SARTIGLIA FESTIVAL, ORISTANO

17

Sardinia

Closer to the North African coast at Tunisia than the Italian mainland and with a fierce sense of independence, Sardinia (Sardegna) can feel distinctly un-Italian. D.H. Lawrence found it exotically different when he passed through here in 1921 – "lost", as he put it, "between Europe and Africa and belonging to nowhere". The island may seem less remote nowadays – and it's certainly more accessible, with frequent flights serving Cagliari, Olbia and Alghero – but large tracts remain remarkably untouched by tourism, particularly the interior. The island's main draw, however, is its dazzling coastline, with some of the cleanest beaches in Italy, which can be packed in peak season (particularly August), when ferries bring in a steady stream of sun-worshippers from what the islanders call *il continente*, or mainland Italy. The weather is generally warm enough for a swim as early as May, however, and October is bright and sunny – reason enough to avoid the summer crowds.

Although more famed for its beaches than its cultural riches, the island does hold some surprises, not least the remains of the various civilizations that passed through here. Its central Mediterranean position ensured that it was never left alone for long, and from the Carthaginians onwards the island was ravaged by a succession of invaders, each of them leaving some imprint behind: Roman and Carthaginian ruins, Genoan fortresses and a string of elegant Pisan churches, not to mention some impressive Spanish Baroque architecture. Perhaps most striking of all, however, are the remnants of Sardinia's most significant native culture, known as the **Nuraghic** civilization after the seven-thousand-odd *nuraghi* (ancient stone towers) that litter the landscape.

On the whole, Sardinia's smaller centres are the most attractive, but the lively capital, **Cagliari** – for many the arrival point – shouldn't be written off. With plenty of accommodation and restaurants, it makes an excellent base for exploring the southern third of the island. The other main ferry port is **Olbia** in the north, little more than a transit town but conveniently close to the pristine beaches of the jagged northern coast. The **Costa Smeralda**, a few kilometres distant, is Sardinia's best-known resort area and lives up to its reputation for glitzy opulence.

Both Olbia and Cagliari have airports, as does the vibrant resort of **Alghero** in the northwest of the island, which retains its distinctive Catalan flavour and a friendly, unspoiled air despite its year-round tourist industry. Sardinia's biggest interior town, **Nuoro**, makes a useful stopover for visiting some of the remoter mountain areas. Of these, the **Gennargentu** range, covering the heart of the island, holds the highest peaks and provides rich evidence of the island's traditional culture, in particular the numerous village **festivals**.

Brief history

Of all the phases in Sardinia's chequered history, the prehistoric **Nuraghic era** is perhaps the most intriguing. Although little is known about the society, plenty of traces survive, most conspicuous of which are the mysterious, stone-built constructions known as *nuraghi*, mainly built between 1500 and 500 BC both for defensive purposes and as dwellings, and unique to Sardinia. The Nuraghic culture peaked between the tenth and eighth centuries BC, trading with the **Phoenicians**, among others, from the eastern Mediterranean. But from the sixth century BC, the more warlike **Carthaginians** settled

CAGLIARI OLD TOWN

Highlights

❶ **Cagliari's old town** Cagliari's Castello quarter is the most atmospheric part of town, a dense warren of alleys girded by thick walls. See page 949

❷ **Nora** Although much of this Carthaginian and Roman archeological site is submerged under the sea, what remains – including mosaics, a theatre and baths – gives a good indication of the town's former importance. See page 954

❸ **Su Nuraxi** Sardinia's mysterious prehistoric *nuraghi* are strewn throughout the island, and this is one of the most impressive. See page 958

❹ **Sa Sartiglia, Oristano** One of the island's most spectacular festivals, involving brilliant feats of equestrian prowess, fabulous costumes and lashings of medieval pageantry. See page 960

❺ **Tiscali** A vast mountain cave housing the remains of a prehistoric village. See page 965

❻ **Beaches** Sardinia has secluded beaches along every coast; among the finest are those at La Pelosa, near Stintino, and around Chia, south of Cagliari. See page 976

HIGHLIGHTS ARE MARKED ON THE MAP ON PAGE 946

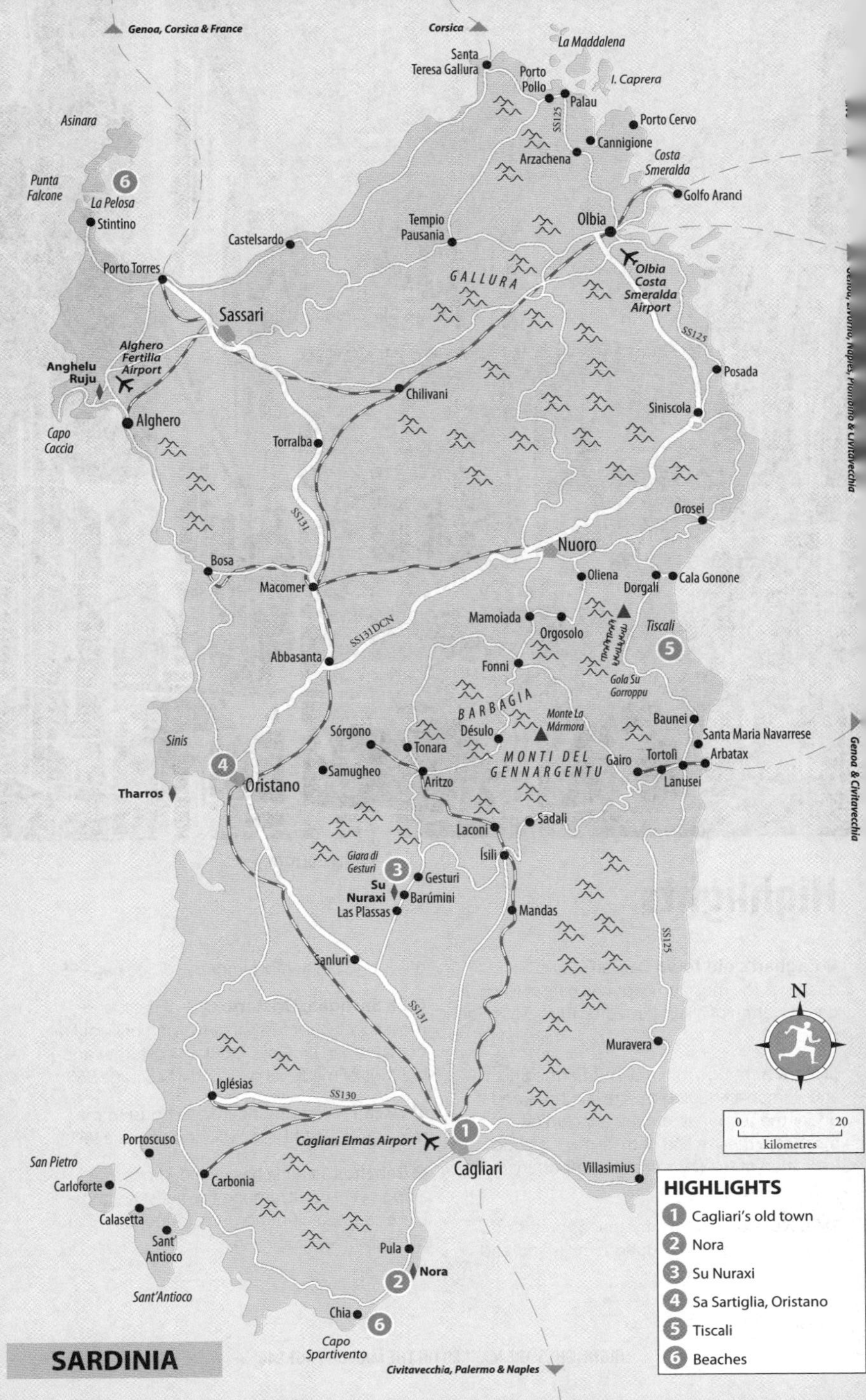

SARDINIA
Genoa, Corsica & France
Corsica
La Maddalena
Santa Teresa Gallura
Porto Pollo
Palau
I. Caprera
SS125
Porto Cervo
Cannigione
Arzachena
Costa Smeralda
Golfo Aranci
Asinara
Punta Falcone
La Pelosa
Stintino
Castelsardo
Tempio Pausania
Olbia
Porto Torres
GALLURA
Olbia Costa Smeralda Airport
Sassari
Alghero Fertilia Airport
Anghelu Ruju
Alghero
Capo Caccia
Chilivani
Posada
Siniscola
Torralba
SS131
Orosei
Nuoro
Bosa
Macomer
Oliena
Dorgali
Cala Gonone
Mamoiada
Orgosolo
Tiscali
SS131DCN
Abbasanta
Fonni
Gola Su Gorroppu
BARBAGIA
Monte La Mármora
Baunei
Santa Maria Navarrese
Sinis
Sórgono
Tonara
Désulo
MONTI DEL GENNARGENTU
Gairo
Tortolì
Arbatax
Lanusei
Genoa & Civitavecchia
Oristano
Samugheo
Aritzo
Tharros
Laconi
Sadali
Ísili
Giara di Gesturi
Gesturi
Su Nuraxi
Barúmini
Las Plassas
Mandas
SS125
Sanluri
SS131
N
Muravera
Iglésias
SS130
0
20
kilometres
Portoscuso
Cagliari Elmas Airport
Cagliari
San Pietro
Carloforte
Carbonia
Villasimius
Calasetta
Sant' Antioco
Pula
Nora
Sant'Antioco
Chia
Capo Spartivento
Civitavecchia, Palermo & Naples
HIGHLIGHTS
1 Cagliari's old town
2 Nora
3 Su Nuraxi
4 Sa Sartiglia, Oristano
5 Tiscali
6 Beaches

SEAFOOD AND SUCKLING PIG – SARDINIAN CUISINE

Sardinian cooking revolves around the freshest of ingredients simply prepared: seafood – especially **lobster** – is grilled over open fires scented with myrtle and juniper, as is meltingly tender **suckling pig**. A few wild boar escape the fire long enough to be made into prosciutto *di cinghiale*, a ham with a strong flavour of game. Being surrounded by sparkling seas, Sardinians also make rich, Spanish-inspired **fish stews** and produce *bottarga*, a version of caviar made with mullet eggs. **Pasta** is substantial here, taking the form of *culurgiones* (massive ravioli filled with cheese and egg) or *malloreddus* (saffron-flavoured, gnocchi-like shapes), while cheeses tend to be made from ewe's milk and are either fresh and herby or pungent and salty – like the famous *pecorino sardo*. The island is also famous for the quality and variety of its bread, ranging from parchment-thin *pane carasau* to chunky rustic loaves intended to sustain shepherds on the hills. As in Sicily, there is an abundance of light and airy **pastries**, frequently flavoured with lemon, almonds or orange-flower water.

Vernaccia is the most famous Sardinian **wine**: a hefty drink reminiscent of sherry and treated in a similar way – the bone-dry version as an aperitif and the sweet variant as a dessert wine. The standout red is the Cannonau di Sardegna, a heady number much favoured by locals. Among the whites, look out for dry Torbato or the full-flavoured Trebbiano Sardo, both perfect accompaniments to local fish and seafood.

on the island, with their capital less than 200km away near present-day Tunis, and their occupation continued gradually until it was challenged by the emergence of **Rome.** Caught in the middle, the Sards fought on both sides until their decisive defeat by the Romans in 177–176 BC. A core of survivors fled into the impenetrable central and eastern mountains, where they retained their independence in an area called Barbaria by the Romans, known today as the **Barbagia.**

The most impressive remains left by the Romans can be seen in **Cagliari**, at nearby **Nora**, and at **Tharros**, west of Oristano – all Carthaginian sites later enlarged by Roman settlers – and strong Latin traces still survive in the Sard dialect today. After the Roman withdrawal around the fifth century, the destructive effects of malaria and corsair raids from North Africa prompted the abandonment of the island's coasts in favour of more secure inland settlements. The numerous coastal watchtowers still surviving testify to the constant threat of piracy and invasion.

In the eleventh century ecclesiastical rights over Sardinia were granted to the rising city-state of **Pisa**, with its influence mainly concentrated in the south, based in **Cagliari**, and Pisan churches can be found throughout Sardinia. By the end of the thirteenth century, however, Pisa's rival **Genoa** had established itself in the north of the island, with power bases in Sassari and on the coast. The situation was further complicated in 1297, when Pope Boniface VIII gave James II of Aragon exclusive rights over both Sardinia and Corsica in exchange for surrendering his claims to Sicily. Local resistance to the Aragonese was led by **Arborea**, the area around present-day Oristano, and championed in particular by **Eleanor of Arborea**, whose forces succeeded in stemming the Spanish advance. Following her death in 1404, however, Sardinian opposition crumbled, beginning three centuries of **Spanish occupation**. Traces of Spain's long dominion survive in Sardinia's dialects and in the sprinkling of Gothic and Baroque churches and palaces, with **Alghero**, in particular, still retaining a strong Catalan dialect.

In the wake of the War of the Spanish Succession (1701–20), Victor Amadeus, Duke of Savoy, took possession of the island, which became the new **Kingdom of Sardinia. Garibaldi** embarked on both his major expeditions from his farm on one of Sardinia's outlying islands, **Caprera**, and the Kingdom of Sardinia ended with the **Unification of Italy** in 1861. Since then, Sardinia's integration into the modern nation-state has not always been easy. Outbreaks of **banditry**, for example, associated with the Gennargentu mountains in particular, were ruthlessly suppressed, but there was little money available to address the root causes of the problem, nor much interest in doing so. The island

17

FERRIES TO SARDINIA

From	To	Line	No. per week	Duration
Bonifacio	S. Teresa Gallura	Blu Navy & Moby	14–49	1hr
Civitavecchia	Arbatax	Tirrenia	2	10hr
Civitavecchia	Cagliari	Tirrenia	7	13–15hr
Civitavecchia	Olbia	Tirrenia, Grimaldi & Moby	7–23	5–8hr
Civitavecchia	Porto Torres	Grimaldi	2–5	7hr 15min
Genoa	Arbatax	Tirrenia	2 (mid-July to early Sept)	16hr 30min
Genoa	Olbia	Tirrenia & Moby	5–8	10–12hr 15min
Genoa	Porto Torres	Tirrenia	7	12hr
Livorno	Golfo Aranci	Corsica	7–14	6hr 30min –10hr
Livorno	Olbia	Grimaldi	14	8hr
Livorno	Olbia	Moby	14 (Feb–Oct)	8–9hr
Marseille	Porto Torres	Corsica Linea & La Meridionale	Sporadic	17hr
Naples	Cagliari	Tirrenia	2	14hr 30min
Palermo	Cagliari	Tirrenia	1–2	12hr
Piombino	Olbia	Moby	4	8hr 30min
Propriano	Porto Torres	Corsica Linea & La Meridionale	2 (May–Oct)	4hr

benefited from the **land reforms** of Mussolini, however, which included the harnessing and damming of rivers, the draining of land, and the introduction of agricultural colonies from the mainland.

After **World War II**, Sardinia was granted semi-autonomous status, and the island was saturated with enough DDT to rid it of malaria forever. Such improvements, together with the increasing revenues from tourism, have helped marginalize local opposition towards the central government, at the same time creating a bolthole for wealthy mainlanders which soon grew to become a mass-market destination.

ARRIVAL AND DEPARTURE — SARDINIA

By plane From the UK, flights operated by Ryanair, Tui and easyJet to Alghero, Olbia and Cagliari are hard to beat for price. From the Italian mainland there are frequent daily flights to the island's airports from Rome, Milan and Bologna, with less frequent connections from smaller centres. Most routes are served by Alitalia, Air Italy, easyJet and Ryanair; prices start at around €40 for a one-way Milan–Alghero ticket.

By ferry Regular, year-round ferries sail to Sardinia from mainland Italy, Sicily, Corsica and France (see box). Reserve well in advance for summer crossings, especially if you have a car or bike; Aug sailings can be fully booked by May. Prices in high season start from about €40/person, depending on the route. The cheapest tickets (*"Ponte"*) involve sleeping on deck; pricier tickets include a reclining armchair; a berth adds another €45 or so. The charge for a medium car is around €130 in high season. Look out for discounts on return tickets bought in advance within certain periods, and for special deals for a car plus two or three passengers.

GETTING AROUND

By car Much the most convenient way of getting around the island is by car; there are rental offices in all the major towns including Cagliari (see page 953).

By bus The island-wide bus service is run by ARST (T 800 865 042, W arst.sardegna.it), supplemented by smaller independent operators covering specific long-distance routes, for example Turmo (T 0789 21 487, W gruppoturmotravel.com) between Cagliari and Olbia.

By train Trains connect the major towns of Cagliari, Oristano, Sassari and Olbia, operated by Trenitalia (T 892 021, W trenitalia.com). Smaller narrow-gauge lines linking Nuoro and Alghero with the main network are run by ARST (see above). From mid-June to mid-Sept, the Trenino Verde trains (W treninoverde.com) take slow but scenic routes to various destinations around the island, including Bosa, Tempio Pausania and Láconi.

Cagliari

Viewing **CAGLIARI**, Sardinia's capital, from the sea at the start of his Sardinian sojourn in 1921, D.H. Lawrence compared it to Jerusalem: "strange and rather wonderful, not a bit like Italy", and the city still makes a striking impression today. Crowned by its historic nucleus squeezed within a protective ring of Pisan fortifications, its setting is enhanced by the calm lagoons (*stagni*) on either side of the city, a habitat for cranes, cormorants and flamingos. In the centre, the evening promenades along Via Manno are the smartest you'll see in Sardinia, dropping down to the noisier Piazza Yenne and Largo Carlo Felice, around which most of the shops, restaurants, banks and hotels are located. At the bottom of the town, the arcades of portside Via Roma shelter more shops and bars.

Cagliari's main attractions are the **archeological museum** with its captivating collection of Nuraghic statuettes, the city walls with their two **Pisan towers** looking down over the port, and the **cathedral** – all within easy distance of each other. There is also a sprinkling of Roman remains, including an impressive **amphitheatre**.

Bastione di Saint Remy

Almost all the sights you'll want to see in Cagliari are within the old **Castello** quarter, on the hill overlooking the port. Traditionally, this was the seat of the administration, aristocracy and highest ecclesiastical offices. The most evocative entry is from the monumental, late nineteenth-century **Bastione di Saint Remy** rising up from Piazza Costituzione. At the top of the grandiose flight of steps inside, you can enjoy Cagliari's best views over the port and the lagoons beyond – sunset is a good time to be here, and there are some chic bars for whiling away an evening.

The Cattedrale

Piazza Palazzo • Mon–Sat 8am–8pm, Sun 8am–1pm & 4.30–8.30pm • Free • T 070 663 837, W duomodicagliari.it

From the Bastione, you can wander off in any direction to explore the intricate maze of Cagliari's citadel, for the most part little altered since the Middle Ages. Its greatest monument, the **Cattedrale**, has undergone numerous changes since its original construction, however, with its tidy Romanesque facade added in the twentieth century in the old Pisan style.

Inside, a pair of massive stone **pulpits** flank the main doors: they were crafted as a single piece in around 1160 to grace Pisa's cathedral, but were later presented to Cagliari along with the same sculptor's set of lions, which now adorn the outside of the building. Other features of the cathedral include the ornate seventeenth-century **tomb** of Martin II of Aragon (in the left transept), the **aula capitolare** (off the right transept), containing some good religious art and, under the altar, a **crypt** densely adorned with carvings of Sardinian saints by Sicilian artists.

Museo del Duomo

Via del Fossario 5 • Sat & Sun 10am–1pm & 4.30–7.30pm; July & Aug Tues–Fri 4.30–7.30pm • €4 • T 328 268 7731, W museoduomodicagliari.it

Behind the cathedral, the **Museo del Duomo** is primarily worth seeing for two items: the fifteenth-century *Tríttico di Clemente VII*, a painting of unknown authorship, but possibly a copy of a lost painting by Rogier van der Weyden, and the powerful *Retablo della Crocefissione*, a six-panelled polyptych attributed to Michele Cavaro (1517–84).

Palazzo di Città

Piazza Palazzo • Tues–Sun 10am–9pm; mid-Sept to mid-June closes 6pm • €4 • T 070 677 6482, W museicivicicagliari.it

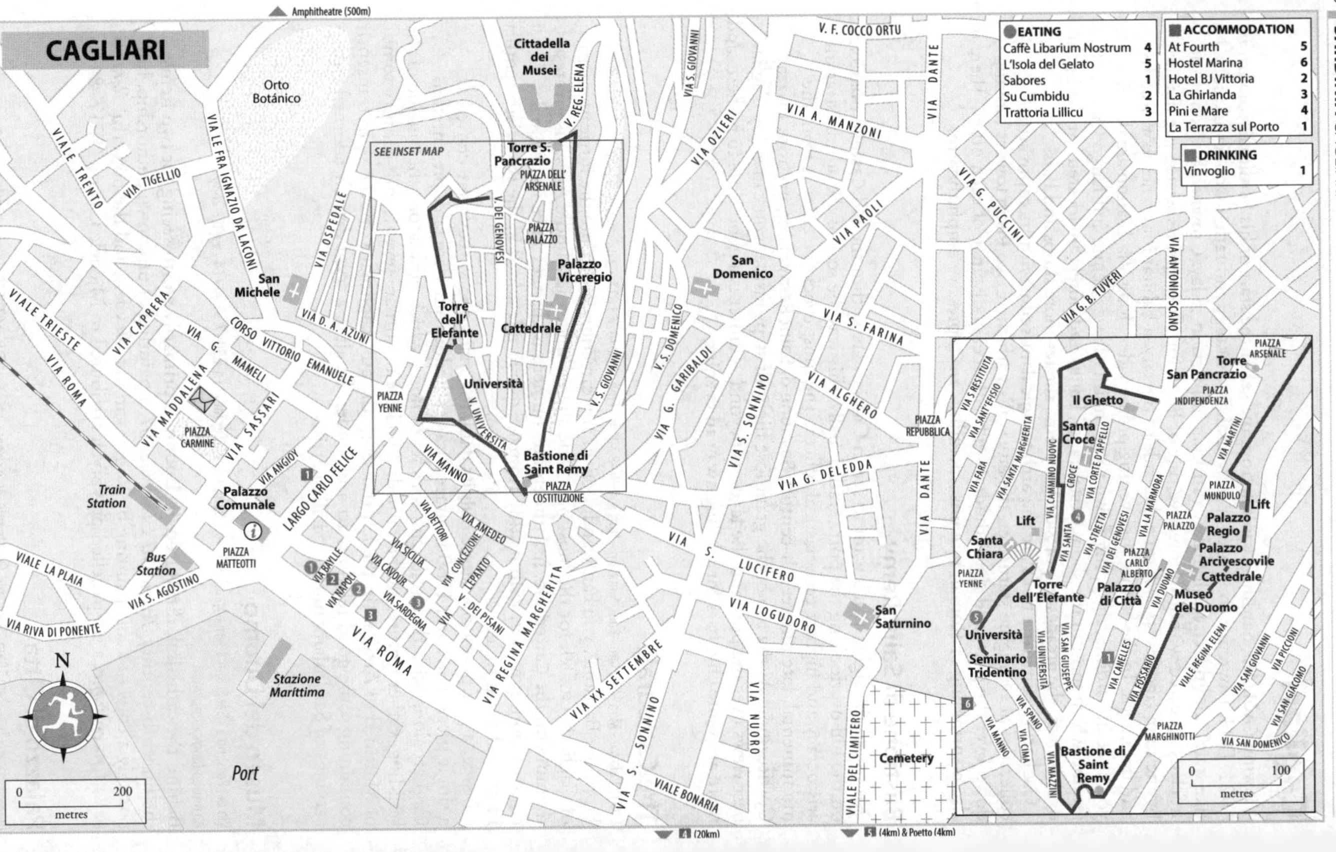
CAGLIARI
EATING
Caffè Librarium Nostrum 4
L'Isola del Gelato 5
Sabores 1
Su Cumbidu 2
Trattoria Lillicu 3
ACCOMMODATION
At Fourth 5
Hostel Marina 6
Hotel BJ Vittoria 2
La Ghirlanda 3
Pini e Mare 4
La Terrazza sul Porto 1
DRINKING
Vinvoglio 1
Amphitheatre (500m)
Airport (6km) & SS131
4 (20km)
5 (4km) & Poetto (4km)
Orto Botánico
Cittadella dei Musei
San Michele
See Inset Map
Torre S. Pancrazio
Piazza dell' Arsenale
Piazza Palazzo
V. dei Genovesi
Palazzo Viceregio
Torre dell' Elefante
Cattedrale
Università
Piazza Yenne
V. Università
Bastione di Saint Remy
Piazza Costituzione
San Domenico
San Saturnino
Cemetery
Train Station
Palazzo Comunale
Bus Station
Piazza Matteotti
Piazza Carmine
Stazione Marittima
Port
Piazza Repubblica
V. F. Cocco Ortu
Via Dante
Via A. Manzoni
Via Ozieri
V. Reg. Elena
Via S. Giovanni
Via G. Puccini
Via Paoli
Via G. B. Tuveri
Via Antonio Scano
Via S. Farina
Via Alghero
Via S. Sonnino
Via G. Garibaldi
V. S. Domenico
V. S. Giovanni
Via G. Deledda
Via S. Lucifero
Via Logudoro
Via XX Settembre
Via Nuoro
Viale del Cimitero
Viale Bonaria
Via Regina Margherita
Via Roma
Largo Carlo Felice
Via Manno
Via Dettori
Via Amedeo
Via Sicilia
Via Concezione
Lepanto
Via Cavour
Via Sardegna
V. dei Pisani
Via Baylle
Via Napoli
Via Angioy
Via Sassari
Via Maddalena
Via G. Mameli
Corso Vittorio Emanuele
Via D. A. Azuni
Via Ospedale
Viale Trento
Via Tigellio
Via le Fra Ignazio da Laconi
Viale Trieste
Via Caprera
Viale la Plaia
Via S. Agostino
Via Riva di Ponente
0 200 metres
Piazza Arsenale
Torre San Pancrazio
Piazza Indipendenza
Il Ghetto
Santa Croce
Via Corte d'Appello
Via Martini
Piazza Mundulo
Lift
Palazzo Regio
Piazza Palazzo
Palazzo Arcivescovile
Cattedrale
Lift
Santa Chiara
Piazza Yenne
Torre dell'Elefante
Palazzo di Città
Piazza Carlo Alberto
Museo del Duomo
Università
Seminario Tridentino
Bastione di Saint Remy
Piazza Marghinotti
Via S. Restituta
Via Sant'Efisio
Via Fara
Via Santa Margherita
Via Cammino Nuovo
Croce
Via Santa
Via Stretta
Via dei Genovesi
Via la Marmora
Via Duomo
Via Università
Via San Giuseppe
Via Canelles
Via Fossario
Viale Regina Elena
Via San Giovanni
Via Piccioni
Via San Giacomo
Via San Domenico
Via Spano
Via Manno
Via Cima
Via Mazzini
0 100 metres

Next to the cathedral, Cagliari's old town hall, the **Palazzo di Città**, has been restored to house an excellent gallery of local and regional art and crafts. You'll see lacework, embroidered fabrics, ceramics and paintings on the first floor, sacred art on the top floor, and temporary exhibitions in the basement, which also reveals traces of the building's original fourteenth-century construction.

Torre di San Pancrazio and Torre dell'Elefante

Piazza dell'Indipendenza (S. Pancrazio) and Via S. Croce (Elefante) • May–Sept 10am–7pm; Oct–April Tues–Sun 10am–5pm; no under-7s • €3 each • T 366 256 2826

At the far end of Piazza Palazzo a road leads into the smaller Piazza dell'Indipendenza, location of the **Torre di San Pancrazio**, one of the main bulwarks of the city's defences erected by Pisa after it had wrested the city from the Genoans in 1305 (though these did not prevent the Aragonese from walking in just fifteen years later). It's worth ascending the tower for the magnificent views seawards over the old town and port.

From here it's a short walk southwest to the city's second watchtower, the **Torre dell'Elefante**, named after a small carving of an elephant on one side. Like the other tower, it has a half-finished look, with the side facing the old town completely open.

The Cittadella dei Musei

Through the arch at the top of Piazza dell' Indipendenza, Piazza dell'Arsenale leads to **Cittadella dei Musei** museum complex, on the site of the former royal arsenal.

Museo Archeologico

Cittadella dei Musei • Tues–Sun 9am–8pm, last entry 7.15pm • €7, €9 with Pinacoteca (see below) • T 070 655 911, W museoarcheocagliari.beniculturali.it

Cagliari's most important collection is its **Museo Archeologico**, a must for anyone interested in Sardinia's past. The island's most significant Phoenician, Carthaginian and Roman finds are gathered here, including busts and statues of muses and gods, jewellery and coins, and funerary items from the sites of Nora and Tharros. But the museum's greatest pieces are from Sardinia's prehistoric **Nuraghic** culture, including the formidable stone sculptures known as the **Giganti di Mont'e Prama**, thought to represent archers, warriors and boxers, and a series of bronze statuettes, ranging from about 10 to 30cm in height, spindly and highly stylized but packed with invention and quirky humour.

Pinacoteca

Cittadella dei Musei • 9am–8pm, last entry 7.15pm • €4, €9 with Museo Archeologico • T 070 662 496, W pinacoteca.cagliari.beniculturali.it

The excellent **Pinacoteca** contains mostly Catalan and Italian religious art from the fifteenth and sixteenth centuries. Look out in particular for the trio of panel paintings next to each other on the top level: the *Retablo di San Bernardino* by Joan Figuera and Rafael Thomas, *Annunciation* by Joan Mates and *Visitation* by Joan Barcelo.

Museo d'Arte Siamese

Cittadella dei Musei • Tues–Sun: June–Aug 10am–8pm; Sept–May 10am–6pm • €2 • T 070 651 888, W museicivicicagliari.it

The **Museo d'Arte Siamese** offers the opportunity to make a long cultural leap, with its fascinating array of items from Southeast Asia originally collected by a Cagliari engineer who spent twenty years in the region. Exhibits include Siamese paintings of Hindu and Buddhist legends, Chinese bowls and boxes, Japanese statuettes and a fearsome array of weaponry.

Museo delle Cere Anatomiche

Cittadella dei Musei • Tues–Sun 9am–1pm & 4–7pm • €1.50 • T 070 675 7624, W pacs.unica.it/cere

17

The smallest and most offbeat of the Cittadella's museums is the **Museo delle Cere Anatomiche**, which displays 23 gruesome wax models of anatomical sections crafted by the Florentine Clemente Susini in the nineteenth century.

The Anfiteatro Romano

Via Sant'Ignazio da Láconi • Daily: May–Sept 10am–7pm; Oct–April 9am–5pm; months may alter depending on demand • €3 • ⊤ 366 256 2826, ⓦ beniculturalicagliari.it

Cut out of solid rock in the second century AD, the city's **Anfiteatro Romano** could at one time hold Cagliari's entire population of about ten thousand. Much of the site was cannibalized to build churches in the Middle Ages, but you can still see the trenches for the animals, the underground passages and several rows of seating.

The Orto Botanico

Via Sant'Ignazio • Tues–Sun: April–Oct 9am–6pm; Nov–March 9am–4pm • €4 • ⊤ 070 675 3522, ⓦ www.ccb-sardegna.it/hbk/hbk.htm

Below Cagliari's amphitheatre, you can find shady relief on a sizzling afternoon in the **Orto Botanico**, one of Italy's most famous botanical gardens, with around two thousand species of Mediterranean and tropical plants. Also here are a spring, a rock pool swarming with turtles and Carthaginian and Roman remains, including four cisterns.

San Saturnino

Piazza San Cosimo • Mon & Thurs–Sat 9am–1pm • Free • ⊤ 070 662496

East of the centre, the main sight in Cagliari's traffic-thronged new town is the fifth-century remains of **San Saturnino**, one of Sardinia's oldest churches and one of the most important surviving examples of early Christian architecture in the Mediterranean. Set in its own piazza off busy Via Dante, looking Middle Eastern with its palm trees and cupola, the basilica was erected on the spot where the Christian martyr Saturninus met his fate during the reign of Diocletian. The sturdy walls suffered severe bombardment during World War II and the interior is bare, but various relics from the past lie scattered about, including fragments of Roman sarcophagi, slabs of stone carved with Latin inscriptions, cannonballs and the excavated remains of a paleo-Christian necropolis.

ARRIVAL AND INFORMATION — CAGLIARI

By plane Cagliari's airport (ⓦ sogaer.it) has banks and an information desk (daily 9am–9pm; ⊤ 070 2112 1281) and is linked to town by train (every 10–20min; 5–10min); a taxi costs €15–20.

By ferry Cagliari's Stazione Marittima is a short walk from Via Roma and the train and bus stations. Tirrenia's ticket office is at Via Riva di Ponente (⊤ 070 666 065 or ⊤ 199 303 040, ⓦ tirrenia.it).

Destinations Civitavecchia (1 daily; 11hr–15hr 30min); Naples (2 weekly; 14hr 30min); Palermo (1–2 weekly; 12hr).

By train Cagliari's main station is centrally located on Piazza Matteotti, used by Trenitalia trains. Gottardo station for trains to Mandas, operated by ARST, is in Monserrato, north of the centre, reachable by tram from Piazza della Repubblica (bus #8 or #M from Piazza Matteotti).

Destinations Macomer (6–9 daily; 1hr 45min–2hr 15min); Olbia (4–6 daily, some with change; 3hr 30min–4hr); Oristano (10 daily; 1hr 10min); Sassari (5–7 daily, some with change; 3hr–3hr 45min).

By bus The bus station is next to the train station on Piazza

THE BEACHES AT POETTO

It's just a fifteen-minute bus ride (#PF, #PQ and Poetto Express) from Cagliari's Piazza Matteotti to the marina at the western end of **Poetto**, where a fine sandy **beach** extends for some 6km, dotted with bars and public showers. Some sections are lidos charging a standard daily rate for entry (€5–10), with sunbeds and parasols available for rent, along with pedalos and windsurfing equipment.

Matteotti. ARST operates almost all services, apart from those run by Turmo for Oristano, Nuoro, Olbia and Santa Teresa Gallura.
Destinations Barumini (Mon–Sat 2 daily; 1hr 20min–1hr 50min); Nuoro (3 daily; 2hr 40min); Olbia (1 daily; 4hr 45min); Oristano (Mon–Sat 3 daily, Sun 1 daily; 2hr); Sant'Antioco (1–2 daily; 2hr 15min).

Tourist office The main office is in the Palazzo Cívico on Piazza Matteotti (April–Oct daily 9am–8pm; Nov–March Mon–Sat 10am–1pm & 2–5pm, Sun 10am–1pm; ⊕070 677 7397 or ⊕338 649 8498, ⊕cagliariturismo.it). In summer, an information kiosk sometimes opens outside the Stazione Marittima when cruise ships dock at the port.

GETTING AROUND

By bus or tram Piazza Matteotti is the terminus for most local buses, operated by CTM (⊕800 078 870, ⊕ctmcagliari.it). Tickets are sold at a booth in the piazza (€1.30 for 1hr 30min, €2 for 2hr or €3.30 for a day's travel); useful routes include #7 running up to the museums and cathedral from Piazza Yenne, and #8 and #8A for the Roman amphitheatre and Orto Botanico.

Car rental Hertz, Piazza Matteotti 8 ⊕070 651 078 and airport ⊕070 240 037, ⊕hertz.it; Ruvioli, airport ⊕070 240 323, ⊕ruvioli.it; Sixt, airport ⊕0294 757 979, ⊕sixt.it.

Taxis Rank at Piazza Matteotti; Radiotaxi 4 Mori (⊕070 400 101) operates 24hr.

ACCOMMODATION

At Fourth Via Ísola Strómboli 3, Poetto ⊕388 320 9394, ⊕atfourthbb.com; map p.950. A brief hop from the beach at Poetto and easily reached by buses from the centre, this B&B has two rooms with private but separate bathrooms and a/c, and a back garden planted with citrus trees where breakfast is taken (including home-made cakes and jams). Bikes are available. Closed Dec & Jan. **€90**

★ **Hostel Marina** Scalette San Sepolcro ⊕070 670 818, ⊕hostelmarinacagliari.it; map p.950. Modern hostel in the heart of the Marina quarter, with dorms sleeping from three to six, family rooms and doubles. Non-members must pay for temporary membership (€3). All prices include breakfast. Dorms **€24**, doubles **€60**

Hotel BJ Vittoria Via Roma 75 ⊕070 667 970, ⊕hotelbjvittoria.it; map p.950. Right across from the port, on the second floor (there's a lift), this *pensione* has spotless a/c rooms, mostly en suite, with solid wood furnishings and antique tiled floors. Larger rooms facing the front have great views and cost extra, but can be noisy. The host family is friendly, and there's a ten-percent discount on presentation of this book. **€92**

★ **La Ghirlanda** Via Baylle 7 ⊕070 204 0610 or ⊕339 889 2648, ⊕laghirlandacagliari.it; map p.950. Smart and central B&B in a late nineteenth-century building with painted ceilings and welcoming hosts. The five large rooms are equipped with TV, a/c, fridges and bathrooms; breakfast is at a bar on Via Roma. **€85**

★ **La Terrazza sul Porto** Largo Carlo Felice 36 ⊕070 658 997 or ⊕339 876 0155, ⊕laterrazzasulporto.com; map p.950. Three brightly coloured rooms with TVs and CD players in this easy-going B&B, with shared or private bathrooms, self-service breakfasts, a washing machine and a panoramic roof terrace with great views. No credit cards. **€65**

CAMPING

Pini e Mare Capitana ⊕070 803 103, ⊕piniemare.com; map p.950. The nearest campsite to Cágliari is close to some choice beaches, around 20km east of the capital (about 40min on any Villasimius-bound bus). Bungalows are available for €80. Closed Oct–Easter. Pitches **€28**

EATING

RESTAURANTS

★ **Sabores** Via Baylle 6 ⊕070 653 216, ⊕saborescagliari.com; map p.950. This tiny place is choc-full of cheeses, salamis, wines and other delicacies, which can be bought to take away or eaten on the spot. It's a perfect snack stop – and good for an *aperitivo* too. Mon–Wed 10am–10pm, Thurs–Sat 10am–11pm, Sun 5–11pm.

Su Cumbidu Via Napoli 11 ⊕070 670 712; map p.950. This wood-beamed restaurant serves heaving plates of antipasti, pasta and meaty Sardinian specialities. Set-price menus €15–25. Daily noon–midnight.

★ **Trattoria Lillicu** Via Sardegna 78 ⊕070 652 970; map p.950. This Cagliari institution with marble tables serves sensational antipasti, pastas and a limited choice of mainly fishy Sard specialities (€15–22). Daily 1–3pm & 8.30–11pm.

CAFÉS AND GELATERIE

Caffè Libarium Nostrum Via Santa Croce 33 ⊕346 522 0212; map p.950. With tables and divans outside on the old city walls, affording marvellous views, this is an excellent nook for a drink and a snack. June–Oct daily 7.30am–2am; Nov–May closed Mon.

★ **L'Isola del Gelato** Piazza Yenne 35 ⊕070 659 824; map p.950. This *gelateria* offers a staggering variety of ice cream flavours – including vegan and gluten-free varieties – as well as yoghurt with fresh fruit, making it a great breakfast stop too. Daily 6am–midnight; closed Jan.

17

DRINKING

Vinvoglio Via Lamarmora 45–47 ☎ 328 359 2877. Squeezed into a tiny space in Castello, this "wine jazz bar" has a cool, late-night ambience and live jazz most weekends. There's a great selection of wines and beers, and you can eat here too (booking recommended). Mon–Sat 7pm–3am.

DIRECTORY

Festivals Sant'Efísio: May 1–4, including a procession to the saint's church at Nora.

Hospital San Giovanni di Dio, Via Ospedale 54 (☎ 070 6091).

Laundry Lavanderia San Giacomo, Via Piccioni 4 (daily 9am–9pm; €5/11kg, dryer €2/16min).

Left luggage Bus station (daily 7am–7.30pm; €2/bag/hr).

Pharmacy Farmacia Scanu, Largo Carlo Felice 46 (Mon–Fri 8.30am–1.30pm & 4.30–8pm, Sat 9am–1pm; at other times, consult the list of open pharmacies by the door).

Post office Piazza del Carmine (Mon–Fri 8.20am–7.05pm, Sat 8.20am–12.35pm).

Nora and around

Daily: mid-Feb to March 10am–6pm; April–Sept 10am–8pm; Oct 10am–6.30pm; Nov to mid-Feb 10am–5.30pm; last entry 1hr before closing • €7.50 • ☎ 070 920 9138, Ⓦ nora.sardegna.it

Thirty-five kilometres south of Cagliari, 3km outside the small town of **PULA**, the ancient remains of **Nora** constitute one of Sardinia's most important archeological sites. Founded by the Phoenicians and settled later by Carthaginians and Romans, Nora was abandoned around the third century AD, possibly as a result of a natural disaster. Now partly submerged under the sea, the remains on land include houses, Carthaginian warehouses, a temple, baths with some well-preserved mosaics, and a theatre which hosts summer performances. The rest is rubble, though its waterside position gives it plenty of atmosphere. The archeological **museum** at Corso Vittorio Emanuele 69 in Pula (currently closed) gives background and displays some of the finds.

Beside the site is a lovely sandy bay lapped by crystal-clear water, but packed with day-trippers in season. Behind the beach stands the rather ordinary looking eleventh-century church of **Sant'Efísio**, site of the martyrdom of Cagliari's patron saint and the destination of an annual procession from Cagliari on May 1.

Ten kilometres further south, around **Chia**, lie some of Sardinia's finest beaches – acres of untrammelled sand (but with little or no shade).

ARRIVAL AND DEPARTURE — NORA AND AROUND

By bus ARST buses connect Pula with Cagliari roughly every hour, less frequently on Sun (50min). From Pula, a local minibus runs to Nora and the campsites at Santa Margherita di Pula (5–9 daily; mid-Sept to mid-May Mon–Sat only).

ACCOMMODATION AND EATING

Cala d'Ostia Santa Margherita di Pula ☎ 070 921 470, Ⓦ campingcaladostia.com. The coast 3km south of Pula holds two similar campsites sheltered by pinewoods and right by the sea; this one has access to a slightly wilder beach, while *Flumendosa* (☎ 070 461 5332, Ⓦ campingflumendosa.com) lies slightly closer to town. Both have caravans to rent (€55–70) and are connected to Pula by local buses. April to late Oct. Pitches €35

Glemerald Hostel Via Sant'Efisio, Pula ☎ 371 333 9821, Ⓦ glemeraldhostel.it. Independent hostel near the centre of Pula with modern rooms, shared or private facilities and a pizzeria (summer only). No credit cards. Dorms €20; doubles €60

Su Furriadroxu Via XXIV Maggio 11, Pula ☎ 070 924 6148. With an arcaded courtyard, this place specializes in dishes from the Campidano area. Try the ravioli stuffed with ricotta and saffron, cooked in butter and orange, or a mixed meat grill. Pastas and soups are under €10, mains €12–15. Thurs–Tues 8–10.15pm.

Su Gunventeddu Località Su Gunventeddu ☎ 070 920 9092, Ⓦ sugunventeddu.com. Just 100m from the beach and surrounded by greenery, this rather dated *pensione* has spacious and quiet rooms and a decent restaurant. It's 1km from Nora; local buses stop outside. Closed Dec & Jan. €93

Villa Madau Via Nora 84, Pula ☎ 070 924 9033, Ⓦ villamadau.it. Chic hotel in the centre of Pula with colourful modern decor, a courtyard and a relaxed, indoor/outdoor café-restaurant. €110

Sant'Antioco

Joined to the mainland by a road causeway and bridge, **Sant'Antioco** is the larger of Sardinia's southwest islands, measuring about 15km by 10km at its longest and widest. The main town – also called **SANT'ANTIOCO** – has a sheltered harbour that made this an important base for the Phoenicians, Carthaginians and Romans, allowing them control over the whole of Sardinia's southwest coast. The second town, **CALASETTA**, on the island's northern tip, lies close to some good beaches and is the port for the island of **San Pietro**.

The catacombs

Piazza Parrochia • Tours Mon–Sat 9.30am–12.30pm, 3.30–5.30pm, Sun 3.30–5.30pm & 7–8pm (also open 7–8pm in summer; reduced hours in winter) • €5 • T 0781 83 044

In the upper part of town, the twelfth-century **Basilica of Sant'Antioco** was built over Christian **catacombs**, which were in turn enlarged from an existing Carthaginian burial place. You can join a guided tour round these dingy corridors, with authentic skeletons and reproductions of ceramic objects unearthed during excavation.

The archeological zone and around

A combination ticket that includes all the sites below costs €13, and is available from any of the sites • T 0781 82 105, W archeotur.it

Dating from the eighth century BC, the earliest traces of Sulki – as Sant'Antioco was then known – are visible in the extensive **archeological zone**, occupying a hillside at the top of the town. Signposted up a side road outside the basilica, it's less than a 1km walk from the sea.

Museo Archeologico

Daily 9am–7pm • €6

At the bottom of the archeological zone, the **Museo Archeologico** displays finds from the Phoenician, Carthaginian and Roman cities. Among the stelae, amphoras, plates, ceramics and jewellery, the highlights include sculptures of human figures and bulls' heads, and a mosaic showing panthers drinking from a plant pot (second to third century AD).

Punic tophet

Daily 9am–7pm • €4

The extensive **Punic tophet**, or burial site, was dedicated to the Carthaginian goddess Tanit and once covered the entire hill where the old city now stands. The numerous urns scattered about here are mostly modern reproductions – the originals contained the ashes of children who died from natural causes.

Museo Etnografico

Via Necrópoli • Daily: April–Sept 9am–8pm; early Oct 9am–1pm & 3.30–8pm; mid-Oct to March 9.30am–1pm & 3–6pm • €2.50

Just outside the archeological zone, the small but engrossing **Museo Etnografico** consists of one capacious room crammed to the rafters with examples of rural culture – tools, agricultural implements, crafts, bread- and pasta-making equipment – all enthusiastically explained (in Italian) by a guide.

Villaggio Ipogeo and Forte Su Pisu

Via Necrópoli • Daily: April–Sept 9am–8pm; early Oct 9am–1pm & 3.30–8pm; mid-Oct to March 9.30am–1pm & 3–6pm • €2.50 each

The **Villaggio Ipogeo**, or Punic necropolis, is worth a glance for its restored *hypogea* (underground chambers) that once held Carthaginian tombs and were later converted into plain dwellings by local townsfolk. The nearby **Forte Su Pisu**, built in 1812, was

17

stormed by corsairs three years later, resulting in the massacre of the entire garrison. There's not much to see here, but it's been tidily restored and is a panoramic spot.

ARRIVAL AND INFORMATION — SANT'ANTIOCO

By bus ARST buses stop in Piazza della Repubblica and in Calasetta. For Cagliari, it's best to catch a bus to Carbonia or Iglesias and take a bus or train from there.
Destinations Cagliari (Mon–Sat 1 daily; 2hr); Carbonia (8–12 daily; 30–40min); Iglesias (4–5 daily; 1hr 20min).

Pro Loco Piazza della Repubblica (erratic hours; ⓣ0781 840 592, ⓦprolocosantantioco.it).

Bike and scooter rental Euromoto, Via Nazionale 57 (ⓣ0781 840 907, ⓦeuromoto.info), rents out bikes (from €12/day) and scooters (from €30/day).

ACCOMMODATION

Hotel del Corso Corso Vittorio Emanuele 32 ⓣ0781 800 265, ⓦhoteldelcorso.it. On the town's main promenading route, this old-fashioned three-star hotel above a bar has fairly standard but spacious rooms. Some street noise. €92

La Jacaranda Via Risorgimento 22 ⓣ0781 82 008, ⓦlajacaranda.it. In a quiet lane a short walk from Piazza Garibaldi and the port, this B&B has helpful hosts, six spacious rooms and a garden where breakfast and dinners are served in summer. €80

Tonnara Cala Sapone ⓣ0781 809 058, ⓦcampingtonnara.it. Clean and well-run campsite on the western side of the island, with a pool and direct access to the sheltered Cala Sapone beach. There's a restaurant and shop, plus caravans and bungalows to rent. Late April to Nov. Pitches €41

EATING AND DRINKING

La Sulcitana Lungomare Colombo 66 ⓣ329 196 7803. Run by a fishermen's cooperative, this no-frills trattoria serves simple but delicious seafood dishes using whatever the boats have brought in. All dishes are €6–10. Mon 8–11pm, Tues–Sun 12.30–2.30pm & 8–11pm.

Magazzino dello Spirito Via Regina Margherita 162 ⓣ0781 921840. Laid-back place with rustic-style decor and a few tables outside, offering boards of cold meats and cheeses, seafood dishes and grills. Mains are around €15. Daily 7–11.30pm.

★ **Rubiu** Via Bologna 22 ⓣ346 723 4605, ⓦrubiubirra.it. An industrial-style place specializing in *birre artigianali* (artisan beers) brewed here or elsewhere in Italy, and served with cold meats and seafood, salads, *focaccia* (€8–14) and the island's best pizzas (mostly €6–10). Daily 7pm–1am.

San Pietro

A 5km ferry ride from Calasetta – and also accessible from the small industrial port of Portovesme, on the mainland – the island of **San Pietro** has a history and culture distinct from that of Sant'Antioco. The largely Ligurian local dialect is due to the island's settlement two and a half centuries ago by a colony of Genoans after they were evicted from the island of Tabarca, near Tunisia. The only town, **CARLOFORTE**, is both prettier and more compact than Sant'Antioco, with pastel seafront *palazzi* overlooking a palm-fringed port, and narrow balconied alleys beyond. It's lively in summer, particularly during May and June's **La Mattanza** festival, celebrating the local speciality found in all restaurants, tuna. The island's secluded coves and beauty spots are within easy reach.

ARRIVAL AND INFORMATION — SAN PIETRO

By ferry Delcomar (ⓣ0781 857 123, ⓦdelcomar.it) runs a ferry service from Calasetta roughly every 90min (30min; €25–30 for two people and a car) and hourly from Portovesme on the mainland (40min; €20–25). In summer, drivers should join the queue in good time – especially for the return crossing.

Tourist office Piazza Carlo Emanuele III, opposite the port (Mon–Sat 10.30am–12.30pm & 6–8pm, Sun 10.30am–12.30pm; ⓣ0781 854 009, ⓦcarloforteturismo.it).

ACCOMMODATION AND EATING

★ **Al Tonno di Corsa** Via Marconi 47 ⓣ0781 855 106. This excellent seafood restaurant with sea views is dedicated to the local *cucina tabarkina*, and tuna dishes in particular. Mains cost around €20, and there's a tasting menu for €35. Tues–Sun 12.30–2.30pm & 8–10.30pm; Aug also open Mon.

17

Hieracon Corso Cavour 62 ⓣ0781 854 028, ⓦhotelhieracon.com. At the quiet end of the seafront, this hotel has a stylish, old-world ambience, with period furnishings and an internal garden. Some rooms have harbour views. **€100**

★ **Il Ghiro** Piazza della Repubblica 7 ⓣ338 205 0553, ⓦcarlofortebedandbreakfast.it. Ecofriendly B&B overlooking the town's liveliest square, with two wood-beamed rooms, arty decor and organic breakfasts. No credit cards. **€85**

Pizzeria Lo Scugnizzo Via Garibaldi 8 ⓣ0781 186 3102. With old photos on the walls and tables outside, this little place has the best pizzas and *calzoni* on the island, and rock-bottom prices. Daily 5–11.30pm; closed Wed in winter.

Oristano

The province of Oristano roughly corresponds to the much older entity of **Arborea**, the medieval *giudicato* which championed the Sardinian cause in the struggle against the Spaniards. Then as now, **ORISTANO** was the region's main town, and today it retains more than a hint of medieval atmosphere, with a relaxed and elegant old centre. It makes an attractive base for visiting the nearby Sinis peninsula, home to the impressive Punic and Roman ruins of **Tharros** and a string of wild beaches.

Antiquarium Arborense

Piazzetta Corrias • Mon–Fri 9am–8pm, Sat & Sun 9am–2pm & 3–8pm • €5 • ⓣ0783 791 262, ⓦantiquariumarborense.it

One of Sardinia's finest collections, Oristano's **Antiquarium Arborense** is housed in a sixteenth-century merchant's house in a secluded square in the centre of town. As well as rotating exhibitions of its extensive collection of Nuraghic, Phoenician, Roman and Greek artefacts, there are scaled-down reconstructions of Roman Tharros and thirteenth-century Oristano, and an absorbing collection of medieval and Renaissance art.

The Duomo

Piazza del Duomo • Daily 8.30am–7pm (closes 6pm in winter) • Free • ⓣ0783 78 684

Oristano's **Duomo** stands in a spacious square up a short walk from Piazza Eleonora. Construction started in the thirteenth century, but most of the present building is a Baroque reworking, retaining only parts of the apses from the original building. With

VISITING SU NURAXI

If you only see one of Sardinia's *nuraghi* (ancient tower constructions) you should make it the biggest and most famous: **Su Nuraxi**, between Cagliari and Oristano. The majestic UNESCO-protected complex (daily 9am–dusk; €12) is a compelling sight, surrounded by the brown hills of the interior, and a good taste of the primitive grandeur of the island's only indigenous civilization.

Su Nuraxi's dialect name means simply "the nuragh", and not only is it the largest Nuraghic complex on the island, but it's also thought to be the oldest, dating probably from around 1500 BC. Comprising a bulky fortress surrounded by the remains of a village, Su Nuraxi was a palace complex at the very least – possibly even a capital city. The central tower once reached 21m (now shrunk to less than 15m), and its outer defences and inner chambers are connected by passageways and stairs. The whole complex is thought to have been covered with earth by Sards and Carthaginians at the time of the Roman conquest, which may account for its excellent state of preservation: if it weren't for a torrential rainstorm that washed away the slopes in 1949, the site may never have been revealed at all.

The site lies five minutes' drive west of **Barumini**, 50km north of Cagliari: the village is served by two daily ARST buses (excluding Sun) from Cagliari (1hr 30min). **Accommodation** possibilities include *Sa Lolla* (ⓣ070 936 8419; €75), a small hotel on Via Cavour with a basic **restaurant** with outdoor seating.

ELEONORA DI ARBOREA

Oristano's finest hour is recalled in the marble statue of **Eleonora d'Arborea** that presides over the piazza named after her in the old centre. Eleonora was the *giudice* of the Arborea region from 1384 to 1404 and is the best loved of Sardinia's medieval rulers, having been the only one who enjoyed any success against the Aragonese invaders. She died from plague in 1404, though her most enduring legacy survived her by several centuries: the formulation of a **Code of Laws**, which was eventually extended throughout the island. Eleonora's statue, carved in 1881, shows her bearing the scroll on which the laws were written, while inset panels depict her various victories.

its fifteenth-century belltower topped by a multicoloured-tiled cupola and the next-door seminary dating from 1712, it forms a harmonious ensemble.

ARRIVAL AND DEPARTURE — ORISTANO

By train Oristano's train station is at the eastern end of town, a 20min walk from the centre, also linked by local buses (Mon–Sat about every 25min) – buy tickets from the machine or the bar outside the station.

Destinations Cagliari (11–16 daily; 1hr 5min); Macomer (11–16 daily; 55min–1hr 20min); Olbia (5–6 daily, some with change; 2hr 25min–3hr); Sassari (5–7 daily, some with change; 2hr–2hr 30min).

By bus The bus station is on Via Cagliari, near the Duomo.

Destinations Bosa (Mon–Sat 5 daily; 2hr); Cagliari (Mon–Sat 2 daily; 2hr 10min); Sassari (Mon–Sat 2 daily; 2hr 5min).

INFORMATION

Tourist offices The tourist office, Piazza Eleonora 19 (April–Sept daily 10am–2pm & 3–7pm; Oct–March Mon–Thurs 10am–1pm & 3–6pm, Fri 10am–1pm, Sat 10am–1.30pm & 4–8pm, Sun 10am–1.30pm; ⓣ 0783 368 3210, ⓦ gooristano.com), covers the whole province; the Pro Loco, Via Ciutadella de Menorca 14 (erratic hours; usually Mon–Fri 9am–1pm; ⓣ 0783 70 621), has some information on the city.

ACCOMMODATION

Hostel Rodia Viale della Repubblica ⓣ 0783 251 881, ⓦ hostelrodia.it. Around a 15min walk from the old centre, this modern complex has hostel and hotel rooms, though there's little to distinguish them except the latter have minibars, TVs and private bathrooms. Breakfast costs €2–5, meals are €18 and bikes are available to rent (book ahead). Shared rooms **€30**, doubles **€90**

Hotel Regina d'Arborea Piazza Eleonora d'Arborea 4 ⓣ 0783 302 101, ⓦ hotelreginadarborea.com. Right on Oristano's central (pedestrianized) square, this hotel of just seven rooms is a glorious evocation of nineteenth-century splendour, with frescoed ceilings, period furnishings and antiques. Breakfasts are equally sumptuous. **€130**

L'Arco Vico Ammirato 12 ⓣ 0783 72 849, ⓦ arcobedandbreakfast.it. Centrally located off Piazza Martiri, this spotless, wood-beamed and relaxed B&B has two good-size rooms with a/c and a shared bathroom. There's a small terrace, too. No credit cards. **€60**

Spinnaker Marina di Torre Grande ⓣ 0783 22 074, ⓦ spinnakervacanze.com. The nearest campsite lies 6km away at Oristano's seaside resort, accessible on frequent buses from the bus and train stations. It's well equipped, with a private beach, pool, and huts and bungalows (from €40). Mid-May to Oct. Pitches **€28**

EATING AND DRINKING

Cocco & Dessi Via Tirso 31 ⓣ 0783 252 648, ⓦ coccoedessi.it. Retro-style restaurant serving quality meat and seafood dishes and pizzas (mains €11–15). You might finish your meal with a glass of Oristano's celebrated Vernaccia dessert wine. Daily 12.30–2.30pm & 7.30–11.30pm.

La Torre Piazza Roma ⓣ 0783 301 494. For down-to-earth pizza and pasta at low prices head for *La Torre*; the speciality is *pizza ai funghi porcini*. Most pizzas are around €7, mains €10–18. Tues–Sun noon–3pm & 7–11pm; Aug also open Mon.

Lolamundo Piazzetta Corrias ⓣ 0783 301 284. For daytime snacks or an evening drink, this contemporary café in a quiet piazza next to the Antiquarium has a cool vibe and tables outside in summer. Mon–Thurs 7.30am–1am, Fri & Sat 7.30am–3am; closes 11pm in winter.

Trattoria Gino Via Tirso 13 ⓣ 0783 71 428. A reliable little place featuring traditional Sardinian dishes such as *ravioli sardi* (made with butter and sage) and *sebadas* (warm, cheese-filled pastries topped with honey). Pastas are €8–10, mains €10–15. Mon–Sat 12.30–3pm & 8–11pm.

17

SA SARTIGLIA

The rituals of Oristano's flamboyant **Sa Sartiglia** festival (ⓦ sartiglia.info) perhaps originated with knights on the Second Crusade, who in the eleventh century may well have imported the trappings of Saracen tournaments to Sardinia. In the period of the Spanish domination, similarly lavish feasts were held for the ruling knights. In time, these celebrations took on a more theatrical aspect and merged with the annual Carnival – Sa Sartiglia is now a three-day festival ending on **Shrove Tuesday**. With all the participants masked and costumed, the whole affair exudes a drama unrivalled by Sardinia's other festivals. The climax of proceedings, in Piazza Eleonora, is the joust after which the festival is named, when mounted contestants attempt to lance a ring, or *sartiglia*, suspended in the air, charging towards it at full gallop.

Tharros

Località San Giovanni di Sinis • April, May & Oct daily 9am–6pm; June, July & Sept daily 9am–7pm; Aug daily 9am–8pm; Nov–March Tues–Sun 9am–5pm • €5 • ⓣ 0783 370 019, ⓦ tharros.sardegna.it • July & Aug 5 buses daily from Oristano (35min)

About 20km west of Oristano, the Punic and Roman ruins at **Tharros** are spread across an isthmus that forms the northern tip of the mouth of the Golfo di Oristano. Now overlooked by a sturdy Spanish watchtower, the site was settled by Phoenicians as early as 800 BC, and consists mostly of Punic and Roman houses arranged on a grid of streets, of which the broad-slabbed Decumanus Maximus is the most impressive. The two solitary Corinthian columns marking the site of a first-century-BC Roman temple are in fact a modern reconstruction. A Spanish watchtower (€2) allows a bird's eye view of the site. Like Nora (see page 954), there is much more submerged underwater, the result of subsidence.

Next to the car park for the site stands the fifth-century church of **San Giovanni di Sinis**, which vies with Cagliari's San Saturnino (see page 952) for the title of oldest Christian church in Sardinia.

Bosa

Some 60km north of Oristano, **BOSA** presents an appealing picture of pastel houses huddled around a hilltop castle on the banks of the Temo River. Exploring the mazey lanes of its medieval centre is the chief pleasure here, and it makes a pleasant, if sleepy place to hole up for a few days.

Running parallel to the river, Bosa's long main street, Corso Vittorio Emanuele, cuts through **Sa Piana**, the lower town, site of the **cathedral** at the Corso's eastern end, by the old bridge. From Sa Piana, the cobbled lanes of **Sa Costa**, or upper town, straggle up the hill towards the **castle**. For a swim, head to **Bosa Marina**, 2km west, where a crescent of sandy beach is backed by restaurants and bars.

Castello Malaspina

Via Castello • Mid- to late-March & early-Nov Mon–Fri 10am–1pm, Sat & Sun 10am–4pm; April–June daily 10am–7pm; July & Aug daily 10am–7.30pm; Sept daily 10am–6pm; mid-Nov to mid-March Sat & Sun 10am–1pm • €4 • ⓣ 340 395 5048, ⓦ castellodibosa.it

Erected by the Malaspina family in 1122, the **Castello Malaspina** offers stunning views over the town, river and sea. Inside, the church of **Nostra Signora di Regnos Altos** contains some rare Catalan frescoes dating from around 1300. Take any alley leading up from the Corso to get here, a steep twenty-minute climb, otherwise take the road skirting the back of town that winds round to the castle gate.

Museo delle Conce

Via delle Conce • July to mid-Sept daily 9.30am–12.30pm, 4–6pm; mid-Sept to June Tues–Sun 9.30am–12.30pm & 3.30–5.30pm • €3.50 • 0785 376 220

Leather tanning was central to Bosa's economy until World War II, and one of the former riverside tanneries now houses the **Museo delle Conce.** The ground floor displays the original *vasche*, or basins, where the leather was soaked and washed. Upstairs, you can view more equipment and old photos.

Bosa Marina

Before Bosa's inhabitants shifted to a more defensible position inland, the town's original site was at what is now **BOSA MARINA**, at the mouth of the Temo, where there's now a small choice of hotels and bars behind a broad swathe of clean, sandy **beach.** You can also swim from numerous sandy coves on the beautiful rocky coast further north, accessible from the spectacular Alghero road. Protected from development, this highly panoramic stretch is one of the last habitats in Sardinia of the griffon vulture.

ARRIVAL AND DEPARTURE — BOSA

By bus Buses stop at Piazza Zanetti, a short walk from Bosa's centre. Tickets are sold at *Gold Bar*, Via Azuni.

Destinations Alghero (2–5 daily; 1hr); Macomer, for Nuoro (Mon–Sat 11 daily, Sun 4–8 daily; 40min–1hr 5min); Oristano (Mon–Sat 5–6 daily; 2hr).

By train Bosa Marina is a terminal for the narrow-track Trenino Verde tourist train to the village of Sindia, 15km inland (mid-June to early Sept Sat at 3.30pm; 2hr 50min; 0785 743 044, treninoverde.com). The return journey is by bus (included in the ticket; €18).

ACCOMMODATION

★ **Corte Fiorita** Lungo Temo De Gásperi 45 0785 377 058, albergo-diffuso.it. With rooms distributed among three buildings, this hotel has its main base overlooking the river. Rooms have rafters, tiled floors, exposed stonework and opulent trimmings. **€99**

Sa Balza Corso Vittorio Emanuele II 45 0785 374 391, sabalza.it. On Bosa's main street, the four rooms here are located around a quiet courtyard. They don't have views but are clean and spacious, each with a/c, a fridge and a modern bathroom. There's no breakfast. **€65**

★ **Sa Pischedda** Via Roma 8 0785 373 065, hotelsapischedda.com. Just across the river from the centre, this fine old *palazzo* has a grand staircase leading up to attractive, a/c rooms, some with balcony (and some quite small). There's a classy restaurant and pizzeria, too. **€112**

S'Ammentu Via del Cármine 55 346 500 4719, samentu.com. Old-town B&B on four floors (there's a lift), with lots of character. The six en-suite rooms are small but comfortable, with a/c and TVs. Abundant breakfasts are served in a separate building nearby. **€80**

EATING AND DRINKING

Borgo Sant'Ignazio Via Sant'Ignazio 33 0785 374 129. Rustic restaurant in an alley above the Corso serving local specialities such as *brasato di cinghiale* (wild boar cooked in white wine): main courses €12–16. March to early Nov daily 12.30–3pm & 7.30–11pm; early Dec to Feb closed Mon.

★ **La Taverna** Piazza Cármine 331 850 4785. This secluded bar makes a quiet retreat for a pause over a beer and/or an ample and delicious panino, inside or on the terrace. Daily 7am–11pm, closes midnight in summer; mid-Oct to mid-June closed Thurs.

★ **Locanda di Corte** Via del Pozzo 7 340 247 4823, ristorantebosa.it. No-frills trattoria in the heart of Sa Costa with tables in the piazza (in summer) and a great atmosphere. The menu offers such items as *fregola* (semolina pasta) with clams, mussels and tomatoes. Main courses are around €12. Daily 12.30–2.30m & 7.30–10.30pm; closed Mon Sept–June.

Sa Nassa Via Lungotemo De Gasperi 81 347 781 4166. Traditional, low-vaulted trattoria located right next to the old bridge, offering delicious antipasti, fresh fish dishes and friendly service. Pasta courses cost around €10–12, mains €8–14. Tues–Sun 12.30–3pm & 7.30–11pm.

Nuoro

"There is nothing to see in Nuoro: which to tell the truth, is always a relief. Sights are an irritating bore," wrote D.H. Lawrence of the town he visited in

1921, though he was impressed by its appearance – "as if at the end of the world, mountains rising sombre behind". **NUORO**'s superb backdrop – beneath the soaring peak of Monte Ortobene and opposite the sheer and stark heights of Monte Corrasi – is still a major part of its appeal. Some absorbing museums and a vibrant old centre bisected by the pedestrianized **Corso Garibaldi** are added reasons to spend time here.

Evident everywhere are reminders of Nuoro's distinguished literary and artistic heritage, notably in connection with the locally born **Sebastiano Satta** (1867–1914), Sardinia's best-known poet; **Grazia Deledda** (1871–1936), who won the Nobel Prize for Literature in 1926 in recognition of a writing career that chronicled the day-to-day trials and passions of local life; and the modernist sculptor **Francesco Ciusa** (1883–1949). The town is also home to one of Sardinia's most spectacular festivals, the annual **Festa del Redentore** (last ten days of Aug), where enthusiastic dancing and singing in dialect culminate in a costumed procession to Monte Ortobene (see page 963).

MAN (Museo d'Arte Provincia di Nuoro)

Via Satta 27 • Tues–Sun: late June to Oct 10am–8pm; Nov to late June 10am–1pm & 3–7pm • €5, €6 with Museo Tribu, free 1st Sun of month • T 0784 252 110, W museoman.it

Housed in a modern building off Corso Garibaldi, **MAN (Museo d'Arte Provincia di Nuoro)** displays mainly twentieth-century art from the whole island, with a preponderance of Nuorese artists. The works are refreshingly diverse, though mainly focusing on rural and village life, and there are also regular exhibitions of contemporary Italian art.

Museo Tribu (Museo Ciusa)

Piazza Santa Maria della Neve • Tues–Sun: May–Sept 11am–8pm; Oct–April 10am–1pm & 3–7pm • €3, or €6 with MAN • T 0784 253 052, W tribunuoro.it

Next to Nuoro's Duomo at the top of the Corso, the **Museo Tribu** is mainly devoted to the work of Nuoro's most celebrated artist, Francesco Ciusa, whose early twentieth-century sculptures invest lowly peasant figures with heroic stature. His most famous work, *La Madre dell'Ucciso* ("The Mother of the Murdered Man"), is a moving study of grief. The rest of the gallery holds temporary exhibitions of pieces by other local figures in the fields of graphic art, ceramics, embroidery and jewellery.

Museo Etnografico Sardo

Via Mereu 56 • Tues–Sun: mid-March to Sept 9am–1pm & 3–8pm; Oct to mid-March 10am–1pm & 3–7pm • €5, €7 with Casa di Grazia Deledda • T 0784 257 035, W isresardegna.it

Nuoro's impressive **Museo Etnográfico Sardo** holds Sardinia's most comprehensive range of local costumes, jewellery, masks, carpets and other handicrafts, as well as an array of traditional musical instruments from around the island, including *launeddas* (Sardinian pipes).

Casa di Grazia Deledda and Museo Archeologico

Casa di Grazia Deledda Via Deledda 42 • Tues–Sun: mid-March to Sept 10am–1pm & 3–8pm; Oct to mid-March 10am–1pm & 3–7pm • €3, €7 with Museo Etnografico • T 0784 258 088 • **Museo Archeologico** Piazza Asproni • Wed–Sat 9am–6.30pm (Oct–May closed 1–4pm) • €4, free 1st Sun of month • T 0784 31 688

Anyone interested in literature and how local people lived a century ago should drop into the **Casa di Grazia Deledda**, the restored home of Nuoro's famous author,

displaying various photos and mementoes. From here, it's a brief walk to the **Museo Archeologico**, which takes in everything from rocks and skulls to carved vases, Neolithic jewellery and Nuraghic art.

ARRIVAL AND INFORMATION — NUORO

By train ARST runs trains along a narrow-gauge line from Macomer (on the main train line) to Nuoro (Mon–Sat 6–7 daily; 1hr 15min). The station is on Via Lamarmora, a city bus ride or 15min walk from the old centre.

By bus The bus station is on Via Sardegna, a 10min walk south of the train station. Frequent city buses for the centre stop outside.

Destinations Aritzo (1–2 daily; 1hr 55min–2hr 20min); Cagliari (4 daily; 2hr 40min–4hr 50min); Cala Gonone (Mon–Sat 6–7 daily, Sun 3–4 daily; 1hr 10min); Fonni (Mon–Sat 1–2 hourly, Sun 3 daily; 40min–1hr 30min); Macomer (4 daily; 1hr–1hr 35min); Olbia & Olbia airport (3–12 daily; 1hr 45min–3hr 50min); Orgosolo (Mon–Sat 9–10 daily, Sun 3 daily; 35min); Oristano (1 daily; 1hr 40min); Sassari (4–5 daily; 1hr 45min–2hr 20min); Tonara (1–2 daily; 1hr 30min–1hr 55min).

Tourist office Piazza Italia 19, on the edge of the old quarter (Mon & Fri 9am–2pm, Tues–Thurs 9am–2pm & 3–6pm; T 0784 238 878).

ACCOMMODATION

Nughe 'e' Oro Via Matteotti 14 T 340 805 2769, W nugheoro.it. On the sixth floor of a modern block near the Duomo, this B&B has bright rooms with or without private facilities, and there's a panoramic terrace. No credit cards. €55

Silvia e Paolo Corso Garibaldi 58 T 0784 31 280 or T 328 921 2199, W silviaepaolo.it. In the heart of the old centre, this B&B has three modern, spotless rooms with shared or en-suite bathrooms, plus a spacious roof terrace overlooking the Corso. €55

EATING AND DRINKING

Caffè Tettamanzi Corso Garibaldi 71. Nuoro's oldest bar (from 1875) has the usual tables outside, but the mirrored interior is unique, with a painted ceiling and cherubs flitting about. The coffee's good too. Daily 6am–2am.

Il Rifugio Via Mereu 28 T 0784 232 355. Nuoro's best choice for regional specialities, such as *filindeu nel brodo di pecora* (stringy pasta in a mutton broth), as well as delicious pizzas. Most main courses cost €13–18. Service is brisk but friendly, and the place is usually packed. Thurs–Tues 12.45–3pm & 7.45–11.30pm.

La Locanda Via Brofferio 31 T 0784 31 032. There are no airs or graces in this traditional *osteria* in a large, plain room, which offers Sard dishes at rock-bottom prices. You won't spend more than €25 including drinks, and the fixed-price lunchtime menu is a popular draw. Mon–Sat 12.30–2.45pm & 8.30–10.30pm.

Su Nugoresu Piazza San Giovanni 9 T 0784 258 017. This trattoria on a cobbled piazza off the Corso has tables outside in summer, and such dishes as *bavette alle vongole* (pasta with clams and a creamy pistachio sauce). There are pizzas, too. Summer daily 1–3pm & 7.45–11pm; winter Tues–Sat 7.45–11pm.

Monte Ortobene

Signposted west of town, a lane climbs through the forested slopes of **Monte Ortobene** to its summit (955m), 8km away, presided over by a bronze **statue** of the Redeemer. From here there are majestic views over the gorge separating Nuoro from the Supramonte massif, while the woods are perfect for walks, picnics or a dip in the open-air pool at Farcana (summer only). During Nuoro's **Festa del Redentore** (see page 962) a procession from town weaves up the mountain.

ARRIVAL AND DEPARTURE — MONTE ORTOBENE

By bus Between mid-June and mid-Sept bus #8 runs once or twice hourly from Nuoro's Via Manzoni and the Duomo up to the summit of Monte Ortobene (not Sun). In winter the service operates just twice daily.

ACCOMMODATION

★ **Casa Solotti** T 0784 33 954, W casasolotti.it. Monte Ortobene has an excellent, friendly B&B, offering wonderful mountain views from its clean and spacious rooms, and great breakfasts. It's just after the Farcana turn-off, near the bus stop – ring ahead for directions or a pick-up from Nuoro. No credit cards. €70

17

The interior and the east coast

Though little travelled by tourists, Sardinia's **interior** is in many ways the most interesting part of the island, dominated by thick forests and rugged peaks. The local inhabitants have retained a fierce sense of independence and loyalty to their traditions, and this is especially true in the ring of the once almost impenetrable **Monti del Gennargentu**, centred on the island's highest peak, La Mármora (1834m). The range forms the core of the **Barbagia** region, called Barbaria by the Romans who, like their successors, were never able to subdue it, foiled by the guerrilla warfare for which its hidden recesses proved ideal. More recently, the isolation and economic difficulties of the Barbagia's villages led to widescale emigration and, among those who stayed behind, a wave of sheep-rustling, internecine feuding and the kidnapping of wealthy industrialists or their families that continued until the last decades of the twentieth century. Today, the Barbagia's main appeal is to **outdoors enthusiasts**, particularly mountain hikers: Oliena's tourist office (see below) has routes and lists of guides.

Sardinia's long **eastern seaboard** is highly developed around the resorts of Siniscola and Posada, but further south it preserves its desolate beauty, virtually untouched apart from a couple of isolated spots around **Cala Gonone**, and, further down, around the port of **Arbatax**, in Ogliastra province.

Oliena and around

Though famed as the haunt of bandits until relatively recently, **OLIENA**, 12km southeast of Nuoro, prefers its reputation as the producer of one of the island's best **wines**, Nepente – a variety of the prized Cannonau – a dry, almost black concoction that turns lighter and stronger over time. The best place to sample it is the **Cantina Oliena** winery, at Via Nuoro 112 (T 0784 287 509, W cantinasocialeoliena.it).

Oliena lies on the steep slopes of **Monte Corrasi**, a dramatically rugged limestone elevation which forms part of the Supramonte massif and rises to 1363m. There are numerous organized **excursions** you can make around its various caves and crags, the most famous of which is to the remote Valle Lanaittu and the Nuraghic village of Tiscali (see box).

ARRIVAL AND INFORMATION — OLIENA

By bus Buses depart once or twice hourly from Nuoro (4–6 on Sun), taking 20min.

Tourist office Corso Deledda 32 (Mon–Sat 9am–1pm & 4–7pm; Oct–Easter closed Sat; T 0784 286 078).

ACCOMMODATION AND EATING

B&B Barbagia Corso M. Luther King 4 T 0784 288 024, W cikappa.it. Friendly place on the main drag, with four colour-themed en-suite rooms. The lively restaurant below offers traditional rural dishes incorporating wild mushrooms and boar, as well as excellent pizzas. Fixed-price menus are €20–30. Daily 12.30–3pm & 7.30pm–midnight. **€70**

★ **Santa Maria** Corso Deledda 76 T 328 117 8551, W bbsantamaria.it. Modern, central B&B with spacious rooms including a traditionally styled suite with its own balcony. All rooms have private bathrooms and a/c, and there's a large, panoramic roof terrace. No credit cards. **€70**

★ **S'Enis** Località Maccione T 0784 288 363, W coopenis.it. Up a steep hill 3km south of Oliena, this hotel, campsite and restaurant complex is perfectly situated for mountain walks. The clean rooms, basic pitches and terrace restaurant all have lofty views over the valley. Pizzas are available alongside such dishes as rabbit stew and roast suckling pig (mains around €15). Daily 12.30–3pm & 8–10.30pm; no pizzas Oct–March. Rooms **€60**, pitches **€20**

Orgosolo

Some 18km south of Oliena, connected by frequent buses from Nuoro, **ORGOSOLO** is stuck with its label of erstwhile bandit capital of the island. The village's most infamous son, Graziano Mesina – the so-called "Scarlet Rose" – won local hearts in the 1960s by robbing from the rich to give to the poor. Roaming at will through the mountains,

even granting interviews to reporters and television journalists, he was eventually captured and is currently serving a life sentence.

Today, the only traces of Orgosolo's violent past are in its vivid, graffiti-style **murals**, some covering whole buildings. Portraying village culture and history, many of the paintings are peopled with gun-toting locals and illustrate the oppression of the landless by the landowners.

The Gennargentu massif

The central region of the Barbagia holds the **Gennargentu** chain of mountains – the name means "silver gate", referring to the snow that covers them every winter. Here, you'll find the island's only skiing facilities on **Monte Bruncu Spina**, Sardinia's second-highest peak (1829m). In spring and summer, you can explore this and other areas on **mountain treks**, best undertaken with a guide: the tourist office in Nuoro (see page 963) can supply a list.

Buried within chestnut forests, the isolated villages of the region make useful bases for both skiers and trekkers; for example **FONNI**, 36km south of Nuoro and at 1000m the island's highest village. Try to combine your visit with one of Fonni's costumed **festivals**, principally the Madonna dei Mártiri, on the Monday following the first Sunday in June, and on San Giovanni's day on June 24. Other centres for excursions and to get a flavour of the mountain culture include **TONARA**, a quiet, traditional village some 30km southwest of Fonni, famed for its chestnuts and *torrone* (a sticky, sweet nougat confection), and **ARITZO**, 15km further south.

ACCOMMODATION — THE GENNARGENTU MASSIF

La Baita Via Ceredi 36, Aritzo ☎338 248 4172, labaita.org. Surrounded by greenery at the southern end of Aritzo, this stylishly renovated villa with a very cordial owner offers B&B in three comfortable rooms sharing a bathroom. You can breakfast on home-made cakes and jams in the garden. No credit cards. **€60**

Sa Orte Via Roma 14, Fonni ☎0784 58 020, hotelsaorte.it. This smartly restored hotel in the centre of the village has impersonal but well-equipped rooms with modern bathrooms. The pizzeria/*ristorante* is open to non-residents too. **€80**

Tia Zicca Via Galusè 2, Tonara ☎346 012 3114, tiazicca.com. In the older part of the village, this simple B&B has two en-suite rooms, a garden and a panoramic terrace where breakfast can be served. Closed Nov & Jan. No credit cards. **€55**

HIKES FROM OLIENA, DORGALI AND CALA GONONE

South of Oliena and Dorgali, the Supramonte massif provides lots of opportunities for mountain **hikes**. The most popular excursion is to the Nuraghic village of **Tiscali** (daily: May–Oct 9am–7pm; Nov–April 9am–5pm; €5), spectacularly sited within a vast mountaintop cavern: allow 4–6 hours for the return walk from Su Gologone on the Oliena side, slightly less from the Flumineddu River on the Dorgali side (an easier ascent). The trickier route from Su Gologone is best accomplished with a guide – contacts for guides are available from the tourist offices at Oliena (see page 964) and Dorgali (Via Lamarmora 108; Mon–Fri 10am–1pm & 4–8pm; ☎0784 96 243, enjoydorgali.it). The **Gola di Gorropu gorge**, through which the Flumineddu river flows, constitutes one of Sardinia's most dramatic mountain landscapes and is one of southern Europe's deepest canyons. You'll get stunning views of the Flumineddu valley from the SS125, running high above it, but you should hook up with a guide to experience it more directly. Even for shorter hikes, you'll need hardy footwear with a secure grip and ankle support, and preferably some head protection against bumps and falls: the boulders can be extremely slippery, especially when wet.

Along the coast, you can make half- or full-day hikes from **Cala Gonone** to the beaches at Cala Luna and Cala Sisine. From Cala Sisine, the route wanders inland up the Sisine canyon, as far as the solitary church of San Pietro, from where a track leads to the village of Baunei. Again, guides are advised for all but the most straightforward coastal routes.

BOAT TOURS FROM CALA GONONE

Tickets for a range of **boat trips** from Cala Gonone to the beaches and deep grottoes that pit the shore are sold at the port. Most famous of the grottoes is the **Grotta del Bue Marino**, formerly home to a colony of Mediterranean monk seals, or "sea ox". It's among Sardinia's most spectacular caves, a luminescent gallery filled with remarkable natural sculptures, resembling organ pipes, wedding cakes and even human heads – one of them is known as Dante, after a fondly imagined resemblance to the poet. Trips here cost €22 including entry to the grotto. Other sea excursions provide access to various beaches along the coast, the most popular of which are **Cala Luna** and **Cala Sisine** – for more solitude, opt for tours with remoter swimming and snorkelling stops.

Cala Gonone

On the east coast, the small resort of **CALA GONONE** was until recently accessible only by boat – now it's reached via a tunnel through the 900m-high rock wall off the SS125, from which the road zigzags steeply down to the bay. The rapid development of the settlement has not spoilt the sense of isolation, and it is worth a stay if only to take advantage of the numerous boat tours to the secluded beaches and grottoes along the coast.

ARRIVAL AND INFORMATION — CALA GONONE

By bus ARST buses and Deplano services to and from Olbia airport stop on Viale Bue Marino.
Destinations Dorgali (4–14 daily; 20min); Nuoro (2–7 daily; 1hr 10min); Olbia airport (June–Sept 4 daily; 2hr 15min).

Tourist office Viale Bue Marino (daily: April–Oct 9am–1pm & 3–7pm; ☎ 0784 93 696, ⓦ enjoydorgali.it).

ACCOMMODATION AND EATING

Cala Luna Lungomare Palmasera ☎ 0784 93 133, ⓦ calalunahotel.com. Bougainvillea-covered hotel with direct access to the beach, modern art on the walls and a great roof terrace where the restaurant is located. It's worth spending extra on a sea-facing room with balcony. Closed Nov to mid-April. **€144**

Camping Cala Gonone Via Collodi ☎ 0784 93 476, ⓦ calagononecamping.com. Shady but often crowded campsite a brief walk from the bus stop and tourist office, and 300m up from the seafront. Bungalows can be rented (€75), and a pool and tennis court are available in summer. Closed early Nov to late March. Pitches **€30**

Il Pescatore Via Acquadolce 7 ☎ 0784 93 174, ⓦ ristoranteilpescatorecalagonone.com. Gourmet seafood parlour right on the sea, pricey but worth it for the lobster pasta, linguini with clams, and grilled fish platters. The €35 tourist menu is good value, otherwise reckon on €45–60 for a full meal. April–Oct noon–3pm & 7.30–11pm.

La Favorita Lungomare Palmasera 30 ☎ 0784 93 169, ⓦ lafavoritahotel.com. Facing the beach, this two-star hotel offers great value, with functional, spacious rooms and an excellent restaurant. Closed Nov to late April. **€80**

Roadhouse Blues Lungomare Palmasera ☎ 0784 93 187. Overlooking the sea, this bar-restaurant has a rock'n'roll theme, with "Led Zeppelin" and "Hendrix" among the pizzas listed (around €10). The menu extends from burgers to red snapper Sardinian style, and cocktails and beers are served until late. March to mid-Nov daily 11.30am–11.30pm.

Su Recreu Piazza Andrea Doria ☎ 0784 93 135. Up from the port, this café-bar serves the town's best ice cream as well as smoothies and cocktails, and sandwiches, salads and grills are available till late; basic tourist menus cost €16. There's live salsa music on summer evenings from 9.30pm. Mid-March to early Nov daily 11am–late.

Arbatax and around

South of Cala Gonone and the majestic Gorropu gorge, the SS125 descends steeply to **TORTOLI**, the fairly nondescript provincial capital of Ogliastra. The ferry port of **ARBATAX** lies around 5km west, with a small beach that's famous for its red rocks, but there are much better **beaches** outside town – 6km north at **Santa Maria Navarrese**, 2km south at **Porto Frailis** and 5km south at **Lido Orrì**.

ARRIVAL AND DEPARTURE — ARBATAX AND AROUND

By train Arbatax station, by the port, is a terminus of the narrow-gauge Trenino Verde railway (mid-June to early Sept Thurs–Sun 1 daily at 8am; ⓦ treninoverde.com), a tourist service which follows a scenic inland

route to Lanusei (2hr) and Gairo (3hr 15min). The STS agency located within Arbatax station (393 930 3736, sardiniantouristservices.com) offers Trenino Verde packages including a forest walk and lunch for €45, and the helpful staff also provide information on the area.

By bus Buses to Santa Maria Navarrese, Cagliari and Nuoro leave from Tortoli. An hourly local bus service links Arbatax, Tortoli and Porto Frailis, also stopping at Lido Orri between mid-June and mid-Sept.

By ferry Ferry tickets are available from the Tirrenia office near the port, on your right as you head towards the station (0782 667 067).

Destinations Civitavecchia (2 weekly; 10hr 30min); Genoa (late July to early Sept 2 weekly; 17hr 30min).

ACCOMMODATION AND EATING

Entula Via Sindaco Lorrai 2, Porto Frailis 329 348 1855, entula.com. Comfortable B&B 5min from the beach and good restaurants: the spacious rooms have a/c and there's a garden where breakfast is served. Closed early Dec to early Jan. €55

Il Faro Porto Frailis 0782 667 499. There are a few restaurants in Arbatax, but you're better off heading to this place overlooking the beach, which has a good choice of grilled fish and a lively atmosphere. Mains are €12–15. April–Oct Tues–Sun 12.30–2.30pm & 7.15–10pm, also Mon in Aug; Nov–March Tues–Fri & Sun 12.30–2.15pm, Sat 12.30–2.30pm & 7.15–10pm.

Ostello Bellavista Via Pedra Longa, Santa Maria Navarrese 0782 614 039, ostelloinogliastra.com. Independent hotel-hostel in a great position above Santa Maria. Each of the plain white doubles has a private bathroom and a sea view. Closed Nov to late March. €74

Telis Porto Frailis 0782 667 140, campingtelis.com. Close to the beach, this campsite has good facilities (including two pools), bungalows to rent (€90/night sleeping two) and mobile homes (€105/night). Pitches €38

Olbia

The largest town in northeastern Sardinia, **OLBIA** is in some ways the least Sardinian of the island's major centres, predominantly modern and usually busy with tourists, many of them bound for one of the Mediterranean's most famous stretches of coast, the **Costa Smeralda** (see page 969). But there's more to Olbia than its port and airport – it has one of Sardinia's most significant Romanesque churches, a good museum and a lively selection of bars and restaurants.

Museo Archeologico

Molo Brin • Wed–Sun 10am–1pm & 5–8pm • Free • 0789 28 290

Olbia's **Museo Archeologico** is a fortress-like construction on a miniature island by the port. The displays range from Proto-Sard prehistory through to the Carthaginian, Greek and Roman eras, and include the remains of fifth-century shipwrecks and a magnificent terracotta head of Hercules wearing a lion's mane – a Roman copy of a Greek original.

San Simplicio

Via S. Símplicio • Mon–Fri 9.30am–5.30pm, Sat 9.30am–1pm • €4 • 342 512 9458

Part of the great Pisan reconstruction programme of the eleventh and twelfth centuries, the basilica of **San Simplicio** has three aisles separated by pillars and columns recycled from Roman constructions – even the table on the right as you enter has been adapted from an ancient urn that once held cremated ashes. The church is the venue for Olbia's biggest **festa**, six days of processions, costumed dancing and fireworks around May 15, commemorating San Simplicio's martyrdom in the fourth century. Across the square you can also visit the newly-revealed remains of a subterranean **Roman necropolis** (Mon & Thurs 10am–1pm, Wed, Fri & Sat 5–8pm, €5, aspo.it).

ARRIVAL AND DEPARTURE — OLBIA

By plane Olbia's airport (olbiairport.it) is connected by buses #2 and #10 to Via Mameli or Piazza Regina Margherita (every 10–30min until 11.40pm; 10min; tickets €1 from the tourist information desk in the terminal, €1.50 on board). Taxis cost €15–20. There are bus services (June–Sept 4 daily) from the airport to the resorts of Porto Cervo (1hr

20min), Cannigione (1hr 50min) and Cala Gonone (2hr 15min), plus year-round buses to Santa Teresa Gallura (1–6 daily; 1hr 25min) and Nuoro (3–11 daily; 1hr 45min–2hr 30min); other destinations can be reached from Olbia city.

By ferry Ferries (see page 948) dock at the Stazione Marittima, Isola Bianca, 2km from the centre, connected by city bus #9 every 30min (€1 from the information office, or €1.50 on board), or you can take one of the infrequent trains to Olbia's main station. The Stazione Marittima holds the ticket offices for Tirrenia, Grimaldi and Moby Lines. Corsica Ferries to Livorno leave from Golfo Aranci, 15km up the coast. Book early for all departures.

Destinations Civitavecchia (1–2 daily; 8hr); Genoa (1 daily; 12hr 15min); Livorno (1–2 daily; 8hr 30min); Piombino (4–7 weekly; 8hr 30min).

By train Trains run several times daily from the station just off Corso Umberto.

Destinations Cagliari (5–6 daily, some with change; 3hr 35min–4hr 30min); Golfo Aranci (3–6 daily; 25min); Oristano (5–6 daily, some with change; 2hr 40min–3hr 15min); Sassari (7–8 daily, some with change; 2hr).

By bus The stop for ARST buses is on Via Vittorio Veneto, past the level crossing at the bottom of Corso Umberto. Tickets are sold at *Bar della Caccia*, by the stop on Via Vittorio Veneto (corner of Via Fiume d'Italia). Turmo buses to Nuoro, Arzachena, Palau and Santa Teresa and summer-only Sun Lines buses to Porto Cervo leave from Piazza Crispi (off the seafront) and from the Stazione Marittima. Caramelli Tours (0789 709 083, caramellitours.it) operates a year-round service leaving from the Stazione Marittima and Via San Simplicio to Porto Cervo (1–3 daily).

Destinations Arzachena (7–16 daily; 50min); Cagliari (Mon–Sat 1 daily; 4hr 20min); Golfo Aranci (mid-June to mid-Sept 4–7 daily; 25min); Nuoro (5–8 daily; 1hr 45min –2hr 40min); Palau (8–13 daily; 50min–1hr 10min); Porto Cervo (June–Sept 7–8 daily; Oct–May Mon–Sat 2 daily; 35min–1hr 50min); Santa Teresa Gallura (7–8 daily; 1hr 20min–2hr).

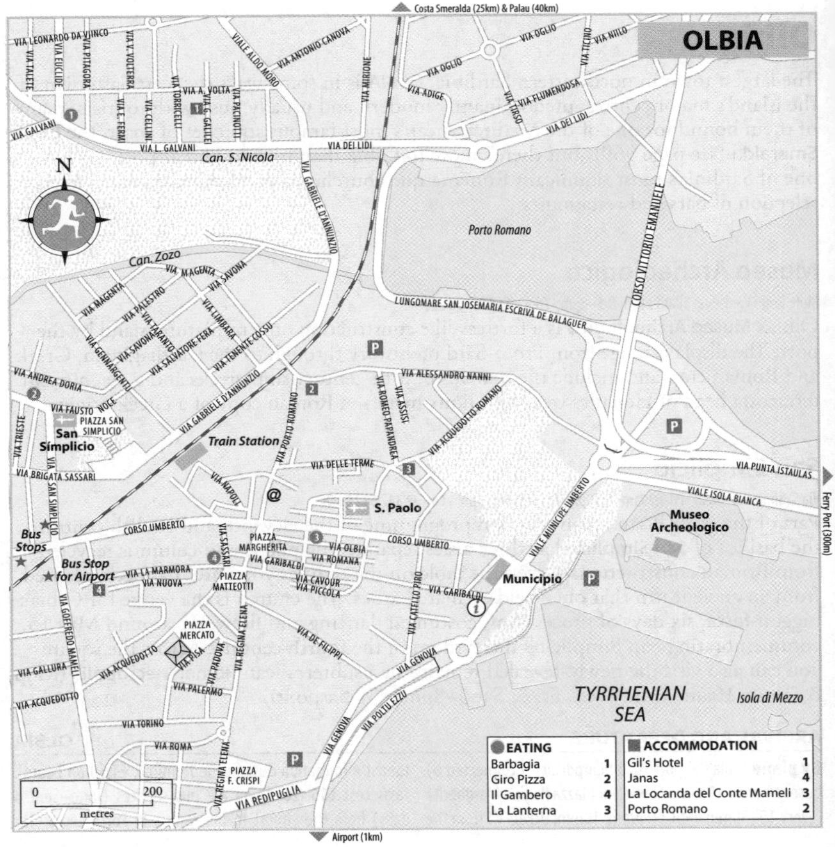

INFORMATION

Tourist office Tourist information for the city is dispensed at the Municipio at the bottom of Corso Umberto (April–Sept Mon–Sat 9am–8pm, Sun 9am–1pm & 4–8pm; Oct–March Mon–Fri 9am–1pm & 2–6pm; ⊕0789 52 206, ⓦolbiaturismo.it).There's also an information desk at the airport (daily 8am–11.30pm; ⊕0789 563 444).

Left luggage Stazione Marittima (daily: summer 6am–10pm; winter 6.30–9.30am, 12.30–3.30pm & 4–10pm).

ACCOMMODATION

Gil's Hotel Via Galilei 16 ⊕0789 58 869, ⓦgilshotel.com; map p.968. Functional but pleasant modern hotel with eight spacious rooms, located slightly off the beaten track by Olbia's main public gardens. Breakfast is in the nearby restaurant, where you check in. **€80**

Janas Via Lamarmora 61 ⊕349 872 8140, ⓦjanasaffittacamere.com; map p.968. This B&B in a renovated old house has three spacious ground-floor rooms, all with private bathrooms, and one giving onto the shady garden where self-service breakfasts can be taken. No credit cards. **€90**

La Locanda del Conte Mameli Via delle Terme 8 ⊕0789 23 008, ⓦlalocandadelcontemameli.com; map p.968. In a quiet back-street in the centre, this period-furnished hotel has exposed-stone walls and rooms (some quite small) with modern, marbled bathrooms. Guests have access to spa facilities. **€130**

★ **Porto Romano** Via Nanni 2 ⊕349 192 7996, ⓦbedandbreakfastportoromano.it; map p.968. Friendly B&B in a central but secluded position, offering doubles with private or en-suite bathrooms (and one with cooking facilities). Breakfast is served on the terrace in summer. No credit cards. **€75**

EATING

Barbagia Via Galvani 94 ⊕0789 51 640, ⓦristorantebarbagia.com; map p.968. With a large, beamed dining area and tables outdoors, this traditional place offers a tasty array of antipasti, mainly meat-based dishes and pizzas. Service is friendly, and there are tourist menus at €15–25. July–Sept daily 12.30–3pm & 7–11pm; Oct–June closed Wed.

★ **Giro Pizza** Via Fausto Noce 34 ⊕347 134 4026; map p.968. Olbia's best pizzas are served at this buzzing place by San Simplicio church, with a wood-fired oven – it's music-themed, with posters of 1960s icons and a grooving soundtrack. Most pizzas are €8–12, and meat and seafood dishes are also available (around €12). May–Oct Mon–Sat noon–2pm & 7–11.30pm, Sun 7–11.30pm; open daily in summer.

Il Gambero Via Lamarmora 6 ⊕0789 23 874; map p.968. Brass pots, ceramics and hangings adorn the walls of this centrally located restaurant, where you'll find delicious antipasti and seafood including *affumicati di mare* (smoked tuna and swordfish). Count on €60–70 for a full meal for two. Tues–Sun 12.30–2.15pm & 7.30–10.30pm; June–Aug also Mon 7.30–10.30pm.

La Lanterna Via Olbia 13 ⊕0789 23 082; map p.968. Tucked away in an alley off the Corso, this cellar restaurant offers superb pizzas (mostly €10) alongside an impressive menu that includes grilled mussels, *fregola sarda* (semolina pasta) and outstanding antipasti. July–Sept daily 6pm–midnight; Sept–June closed Wed.

The Costa Smeralda and around

Long a magnet for Italy's glitziest celebrities, the five-star development of the **Costa Smeralda** in the 1960s helped to transform the economy of the entire island. A coastline this beautiful inevitably comes at a price, however: budget accommodation is virtually nonexistent, while the high-end hotels are mostly devoid of much character. **Arzachena** and **Cannigione** are cheaper bases from which to explore the area.

The Costa Smeralda begins about 12km north of Olbia and is defined as the 10km strip between the gulfs of Cugnana and Arzachena. Although strict rules were imposed to prevent overzealous development – you won't see any multistorey hotels, advertising hoardings or fast-food chains – the area has little in common with the rest of Sardinia, and the luxurious holiday villages have a bland, almost suburban feel. This hasn't kept the mega-rich away – Silvio Berlusconi owns six properties here.

Porto Cervo and around

The "local"-style rustic-red architecture of **PORTO CERVO**, the main centre of the Costa Smeralda, embodies the dream of an idyllic Mediterranean village without any of the

17

irritations of real life. Graffiti- and litter-free, Porto Cervo exults in its exclusivity, with a glittering yachting marina as its centrepiece.

You'll need your own transport to reach the sandy **beaches** dotted down the coast south of Porto Cervo. None is clearly marked; just follow any dirt track down to the sea – the rougher the track, the more likely it is to lead to an attractive, promising and not too busy stretch of sand. Both **Cappriccioli** and **Liscia Ruia**, 6km south of Porto Cervo, are good bets.

ARRIVAL AND DEPARTURE — PORTO CERVO

By bus Caramelli Tours (see page 968) operates services connecting Porto Cervo and other points on the Costa Smeralda with Olbia, Arzachena and Santa Teresa Gallura, Sun Lines operates buses between Porto Cervo and Olbia in summer, and ARST runs a year-round link to Arzachena. Destinations Arzachena (Mon–Sat 4–9 daily, Sun mid-June to mid-Sept 1 daily; 30–40min); Olbia (Mon–Sat 2–7 daily, Sun mid-June to mid-Sept 5 daily; 1hr 10min).

ACCOMMODATION

Cugnana Porto Rotondo Località Cugnana ⊕0789 33 184, ⓦcampingcugnana.it. Just south of the Costa Smeralda, 12km north of Olbia, this campsite has a pool, bungalows (€90/night) and a shuttle service to nearby beaches. ARST and, in summer, Sun Lines buses stop right outside. May–Sept. Pitches **€24**

Arzachena and around

Inland **ARZACHENA** is the nearest "normal" town to the Costa Smeralda, not particularly inspiring in itself but well equipped with banks, shops and restaurants. It's a transport hub for local bus services, and close to **CANNIGIONE**, a small yachting resort on the **Golfo di Arzachena**. This deep, narrow bay shares many of the Costa Smeralda's natural features, but without the air of exclusivity.

ARRIVAL AND INFORMATION — ARZACHENA AND AROUND

By bus ARST services run to most places along the coast, and there are daily Turmo connections to Olbia, Palau and Santa Teresa. In summer, Linea Blu and Linea Smeralda buses link Arzachena with beaches around Cannigione and along the Costa Smeralda (⊕349 388 5580), while Sun Lines buses connect Olbia and Porto Cervo with Cannigione. Destinations Cannigione (Mon–Sat 4–9 daily; 10min); Olbia (1–2 hourly; 30–50min); Palau (1–2 hourly; 20min); Porto Cervo (Mon–Sat 1–5; 40min); Santa Teresa Gallura (5–11 daily; 55min–1hr 10min).

Tourist offices There are information offices at Piazza Risorgimento, Arzachena (Mon & Wed 8.30am–2pm & 3–6pm, Tues, Thurs & Fri 8.30am–2pm; ⊕0789 844 055); Malchittu, between Arzachena and Cannigione (daily 9am–7pm; ⊕0789 83 306) and Via Orecchioni, Cannigione (Mon–Sat 9am–2pm & 3–7pm, Sun 9am–noon; ⊕0789 88 229).

ACCOMMODATION AND EATING

Centro Vacanze Isuledda La Conia ⊕0789 86 003, ⓦcampingisuledda.com. A couple of kilometres north of Cannigione, this campsite is right on the shore and has rooms and bungalows to rent (from €105). It gets a bit overwhelmed in August, and there's not much shade. Local buses stop outside in summer. Late March–early Nov. Pitches **€48**

Hotel del Porto Via Nazionale 94, Cannigione ⊕0789 88 011, ⓦhoteldelporto.com. On the seafront, this hotel has balconied rooms overlooking the marina and a café and restaurant. Daily 12.30–2.30pm & 7.30–9.30pm. **€146**

★ **La Tavola Blu** Via Vasco da Gama 12, Cannigione ⊕347 121 5328. Below the church, this *rosticceria* has a brisk, authentic feel, offering delicious portions of fresh seafood and other hot snacks for €3–6 each (pastas from €12). April to mid-Oct daily 9am–2.30pm & 5–11pm.

Santa Lucia Via Cagliari 11, Arzachena ⊕0789 83 012 or ⊕338 269 3640, ⓦbbslucia.it. This B&B in a quiet backstreet has a peaceful walled garden, spacious rooms and freshly baked cakes for breakfast. No credit cards. **€80**

The Maddalena islands

The profusion of minor **islands** off Sardinia's northeastern coast, more than sixty in all, form part of **La Maddalena national park**, which can be explored on various boat tours

from the mainland or from the archipelago's only port, **La Maddalena**, reachable on ferries from **Palau** (10km up the coast from Cannigione).

The island invites aimless wandering and offers a variety of sandy and rocky beaches in mostly undeveloped coves. The **beaches** on the northern and western coasts are most attractive, particularly those around the tiny port of Madonetta, 5km west of La Maddalena, and at Cala Lunga, 5km north of town. Attached to the main island by a causeway is neighbouring **Caprera**, the island on which Garibaldi spent his last years.

La Maddalena

The attractive, upbeat town of **LA MADDALENA** gets very busy in July and August but you'll find little open here in winter. Most of the action takes place in the warren of narrow lanes between Piazza Umberto I and Cala Gavetta (the marina for small boats), a five-minute walk from the ferry port heading left. Prices are notably higher than on the Sardinian mainland.

ARRIVAL AND DEPARTURE — LA MADDALENA

By ferry Various operators run ferries from Palau to La Maddalena (every 15–30min in peak season, every 30min–1hr in winter; 15min). Tickets are sold at Palau's Stazione Marittima and cost around €12 return per person, €40 return for two people in a medium-sized car.

INFORMATION AND GETTING AROUND

By bus Local buses run to various parts of the island and to Caprera from Piazza Umberto I near the port (once or twice hourly in summer, less frequently in winter). Tickets are €1 from vendors or €1.50 on board.

By bike or moped Bikes and mopeds can be rented from any of the outlets on the seafront towards Cala Gavetta for around €20/day for a bike, or €30–50/day for a scooter (prices drop outside peak season).

Tourist office Via Venti Settembre (June–Sept daily 9am–10pm; Oct–May Mon & Wed 9am–1.30pm & 3.30–5.30pm, Tues, Thurs & Fri 9am–1.30pm; ⓣ0789 736 321, ⓦcomune.lamaddalena.ot.it).

ACCOMMODATION AND EATING

Il Gabbiano Via Giulio Césare 20 ⓣ0789 722 507, ⓦhotel-ilgabbiano.it. A 10min walk west of the centre beyond Cala Gavetta, this refurbished 1960s hotel enjoys a fantastic location right on the sea. Rooms are pretty standard (some without a/c), though some have balconies. **€100**

Il Ghiottone Via Oberdan 5 ⓣ320 181 3107. This central trattoria has a small menu, but the choices are usually excellent, including *trofie casarecce mari e monti* (home-made pasta with meat and seafood) and *tagliatelle con cozze e menta* (with mussels and mint). Full meals cost around €40/head, drinks included. Booking essential. April–Oct daily 7pm–midnight.

★**La Petite Maison** Via Livenza ⓣ0789 738 432 or ⓣ340 646 3722, ⓦlapetitmaison.net. Quirky and welcoming B&B 5min from the centre, dotted with antiques and artworks (some by the owner). Breakfast is served in the shady courtyard garden. No credit cards. Closed Dec–Feb. **€85**

Maddalena Località Moneta ⓣ0789 728 051, ⓦcampingmaddalena.it. The best equipped of the island's campsites lies close to town and Caprera, and has chalets and bungalows to rent (from €70). June–Sept. Pitches **€28**

Sergent Pepper's Via G. Bruno 6 ⓣ331 509 0091, ⓦsergentpeppers.it. Off Piazza Garibaldi with a few outdoor tables, this is ideal for a fast and tasty pizza (€4–14) with a jug of beer. There's a good choice; the pizzas are thin-crust and fairly large. You can't book, so you may have to wait for a table in summer. May–Sept daily noon–11pm; Oct–April Wed–Mon 7.15pm–midnight.

Caprera

Undeveloped and largely uninhabited – apart from Garibaldi's house in the centre and a couple of secluded, self-contained tourist complexes – **Caprera** mainly consists of protected wooded parkland surrounded by an inhospitable rocky shore. Perhaps attracted by its austerity, **Giuseppe Garibaldi** (1807–82) came to live on the island in 1855, after a twenty-year exile from Italy. It was from here that he embarked on his spectacular conquest of Sicily and Naples in 1861, accompanied by his thousand Red Shirts, and it was here that he returned after his campaigns to resume a simple farming

17

life. Having bought the northern part of the island for £360, he spent much of his time writing his memoirs and some bad novels. In 1864 a group of English admirers provided the money for Garibaldi to buy the rest of Caprera from local landowners.

Compendio Garibaldino

July & Aug Tues–Sun 9am–8pm; Sept–June Mon–Sat 9am–8pm (but open 1st Sun of month and closed following Mon; last entry at 7.15pm) • €7, €11 with Memoriale Garibaldi • ⓣ 0789 727 162, ⓦ compendiogaribaldino.it • Buses from Colonna Garibaldi, Via Amendola (every 30min–1hr, less frequent in winter; €1)

Garibaldi's old house, the elegant South American-style Casa Bianca, has been preserved pretty much as he left it, though it now houses the **Compendio Garibaldino** museum. Visitors are escorted past the bed where he slept, a smaller one where he died, various scrolls, manifestos and pronouncements, as well as an array of personal memorabilia. A stopped clock and a wall calendar indicate the precise time and date of his death. The tour ends with Garibaldi's **tomb** in the garden, its rough granite contrasting with the more pompous tombs of his last wife and five of his children. Garibaldi had requested cremation, but following the wishes of his son Menotti, his corpse was embalmed. In 1932, fifty years after his death, his tomb was opened to reveal the body perfectly intact.

Memoriale Giuseppe Garibaldi

Daily 10.15am–7.15pm, last entry at 6.15pm; closed Weds • €6, €11 with Compendio Garibaldino • ⓣ 0789 727 162, ⓦ compendiogaribaldino.it

Housed in a hilltop fort about 4km north of the Compendio, the **Memoriale Giuseppe Garibaldi** provides a detailed account of Garibaldi's life and his various campaigns, using multimedia presentations, documents, newspaper cuttings and photos. There are also stunning views of the Maddalena archipelago and Corsica. You'll need your own transport to get here, or else walk.

Santa Teresa Gallura and around

The road northwest from Arzachena passes a succession of lovely bays, some dramatic rocky coastline and a handful of campsites. Six kilometres west of Palau, the slender isthmus of **Porto Pollo** is Sardinia's busiest watersports centre, with ideal conditions for **windsurfing** and **kitesurfing**. There are numerous surf schools and rental outfits, while the sheltered, dune-backed beaches will equally appeal to non-surfers.

Some 15km further west, **SANTA TERESA GALLURA** is Sardinia's northernmost port. The town gets extremely lively in summer, with a buzzing nightlife, but the main draw is the **beaches**, many enjoying superb views over to Corsica, just 11km away. There's one stretch of sand right at the edge of town, but some of the finest beaches on the whole island are a short bus-ride away, with **Punta Falcone** and **La Marmorata** to the east, and **Capo Testa**, with its wind-sculpted granite rock formations, 3km west of Santa Teresa.

ARRIVAL AND INFORMATION — SANTA TERESA GALLURA

By bus

Destinations Arzachena (8–13 daily; 1hr); Olbia (7–12 daily; 1hr 20min–1hr 50min); Palau (7–12 daily; 30–40min); Sassari (2–5 daily; 2hr 30min).

By ferry From the port on the eastern side of town, Moby Lines and Blu Navy sail to Bonifacio in Corsica (2–7 daily; 50min; around €25 one way, plus €30–40/car).

Tourist office Piazza Vittorio Emanuele (mid-July to mid-Sept daily 9am–1pm & 4.30–8pm; mid-Sept to mid-July Mon, Thurs & Fri 10am–1pm, Tues & Wed 4–5.30pm; seasonal variations; ⓣ 0789 754 127, ⓦ comunesantateresagallura.it).

GETTING AROUND

By bus Between mid-June and mid-Sept, frequent local buses link Santa Teresa with the beaches of Marmorata and Capo Testa; tickets on board, €5/day.

By bike, scooter or car Tibula Rent, at Via Maria Teresa 41 (ⓣ 0789 189 5239, ⓦ tibularent.it), has bikes (from €15/day), scooters (from €30/day) and cars (from €65/day) to rent.

ACCOMMODATION

Comfort Scano Inn Via Lazio 4 ⊕0789 754 447, ⊕albergoscano.it. Small and functional, family-run *pensione* off the Capo Testa road, with standard rooms with a/c and a decent restaurant. In summer, the same family runs a nearby hotel with slightly smarter and pricier rooms. €72

★**La Chicca di Francesca** Via Basilicata 4 ⊕347 335 0779, ⊕lachiccadifrancesca.com. Set in lush gardens a 5min walk from the centre, this B&B has three rooms with wood furnishings, balconies, private bathrooms and a/c. No credit cards. Closed mid-Nov to mid-March. €80

La Liccia SP90 ⊕0789 755 190, ⊕campinglaliccia.com. The nearest campsite to Santa Teresa lies 6km south, signposted off the Castelsardo road and a 10min walk from a good beach. Pitches are large, terraced and shady, and there are caravans and bungalows (from €42). Mid-May to Sept. Pitches €24

★**Moderno** Via Umberto 39 ⊕0789 754 233, ⊕modernohotel.eu. This friendly, centrally located hotel has airy rooms in pale blues and greens with Sardinian motifs, spacious bathrooms and a/c. Family rooms are also available. Closed Oct to late April. €90

EATING AND DRINKING

Balajana Piazza Villa Marina ⊕0789 754 332. This pizzeria doles out super-size pizzas (mostly €12–16) – if one is too much, you can order one to share with two different toppings. Daily: March and April noon–2.30pm & 6–11pm; May–Oct noon–11pm.

Gallura Grill Via Carlo Felice 51 ⊕347 571 4281, ⊕galluragrill.it. Grilled meats are the speciality here, from Sardinian sausages and steaks to *porchetto sardo* (spit-roast pork; €25), but seafood feasts such as *grigliata di mare* are available too. Set-price menus are €15 and €20. Easter–Sept daily noon–3pm & 7–11pm; April & Oct closed Wed.

Castelsardo

On Sardinia's north coast, 70km southwest from Santa Teresa Gallura, **CASTELSARDO** lies picturesquely draped over a promontory overlooking the **Golfo dell'Asinara**. The town was the Sardinian power base of the Doria family of Genoa for nearly 250 years, and the historic centre preserves a pungent medieval flavour, crowned by a **castle** that now holds a museum of basketwork. This local speciality, combined with the town's photogenic setting, has helped to transform Castelsardo into a fully-fledged holiday resort, with numerous hotels, restaurants and handicrafts shops.

Museo dell'Intreccio Mediterraneo

Castello di Castelsardo, Via Marconi • Easter–April & Oct 9am–7pm; May, June & Sept 9am–9pm; July 9am–midnight; Aug 9am–1am; Nov–Easter 10.30am–4.30pm • €3 • ⊕347 111 8547, ⊕mimcastelsardo.it

Artfully incorporated into the small chambers of Castelsardo's castle, the **Museo dell'Intreccio Mediterraneo** showcases the local mastery in the craft of basketweaving. There's much to admire in this assortment of bowls, bottles, lobster traps and even boats, often skilfully patterned. Some of the most prized items are woven from the leaves of the local dwarf-palm, others use rushes and asphodel. Elsewhere in the castle you'll come across replicas of medieval **weaponry** and sweeping coastal views.

ARRIVAL AND DEPARTURE — CASTELSARDO

Castelsardo has **bus** connections with Sassari (4–13 daily; 1hr) and Santa Teresa Gallura (2–5 daily; 1hr 30min).

Sassari

Sardinia's second city, **SASSARI** combines an insular, traditional feel, as embodied in its well-preserved old quarter, with a forward-looking, confident air that is most evident in its modern centre. Here, leading off from the grandiose Piazza Italia, the café-lined Via Roma holds the city's principal sight, the **Museo Sanna**, displaying some of the island's most important archeological finds.

17

Brief history

While Cagliari was Pisa's base of operations in Sardinia during the Middle Ages, Sassari was the Genoan capital, ruled by the Doria family, whose power reached throughout the Mediterranean. Under the Aragonese it became an important centre of Spanish hegemony, and the Spanish stamp is still strong, not least in its churches. In the sixteenth century the Jesuits founded Sardinia's first **university** here, which continues to excel in the spheres of law, medicine and politics.

The old quarter

Sassari's **old quarter**, a network of alleys and piazzas bisected by the main Corso Vittorio Emanuele, is an absorbing area for a stroll. At its heart is the **Duomo** (Mon–Sat 8.45am–noon & 4.30–7pm, Sun 9–11.30am & 5–7pm), whose florid facade is Sardinia's most imposing example of Baroque architecture, added to a simpler Aragonese-Gothic base from the fifteenth and sixteenth centuries.

Behind the Duomo, the eighteenth-century **Palazzo Ducale** houses the town hall and a small city museum (Tues–Fri 10am–1pm & 3–6pm, Sat 10am–1pm; €4), and **Mus'a** on Via Santa Caterina displays the best of the city's art (Tues–Sat 9am–6pm; €4, 1st Sun of month free). On the other side of the Corso, **Piazza Tola** retains its medieval feel and is the venue of a morning market and lively bar-life in the evening.

Museo Sanna

Via Roma 64 • Tues–Sat 9am–8pm, 1st Sun of month 9am–8pm • €3, free 1st Sun of month • ☎ 079 272 203

Organized chronologically from prehistoric through Nuraghic to Phoenician, Carthaginian and Roman items, the **Museo Sanna** offers a fascinating review of Sardinia's distant past. Alongside the coins, jewellery and amphorae from the classical period, the most impressive displays are connected with the Nuraghic period, notably a collection of **bronze statuettes**, including warriors with boldly stylized ox-head helmets, boats with equally extravagant prows, and a shepherd holding either a dog or goat on the end of a lead.

LA CAVALCATA

One of Sardinia's showiest festivals – **La Cavalcata** – takes place in Sassari on the penultimate Sunday of May, the highlight of a month of cultural activities. Originally staged for the benefit of visiting Spanish kings or other dignitaries, it attracts hundreds of richly costumed participants from villages throughout the province and beyond. The festival is divided into three stages: the morning features a horseback parade and a display of the embroidered and decorated costumes unique to each village, after which there is a show of stirring horsemanship at the local Ippodromo racecourse. The day ends with traditional songs and dances back in Piazza Italia.

Fonte Rosello

Corso Trinità • Tues & Sun 10am–1pm, Wed–Sat 10am–1pm & 3–6pm • Free

On the edge of the old quarter outside Porta Rosello, the **Fonte Rosello** appears somewhat stranded at the bottom of a flight of grassy steps. Built in 1606 in late Renaissance style by Genoan stonemasons, the fountain is elaborately carved with dolphins and four statues representing the seasons. The city's old **washhouse** stands adjacent.

ARRIVAL AND INFORMATION — SASSARI

By train Coming to Sassari by train, you'll usually have to change at Ozieri-Chilivani, though journeys from Alghero are direct. The station is at the bottom of the old town's Corso Vittorio Emanuele.

Destinations Alghero (9–14 daily; 40min); Cagliari (5–7 daily; 3hr–3hr 35min); Macomer (5–8 daily; 1hr 10min–1hr 40min); Olbia (6–8 daily; 1hr 45min); Oristano (5–7 daily; 2hr 20min).

By bus The bus stands for all long-distance buses as well as the ARST link with Alghero airport (aeroportodialghero.it) are on Via Padre Zirano – turn right out of the train station.

Destinations Alghero (4–10 daily; 45min–1hr); Alghero (Fertilia) airport (9 daily; 30min); Bosa (Mon–Sat 1–4 daily; 1hr 10min–2hr 10min); Cagliari (late June to late Oct 2 daily; 3hr 10min); Castelsardo (4–12 daily; 1hr–1hr 30min); Nuoro (4–6 daily; 1hr 45min–2hr 30min); Oristano (Mon–Sat 1–3 daily, Sun late June to late Oct 2 daily; 2hr); Santa Teresa Gallura (2–5 daily; 2hr 40min); Stintino (2–6 daily; 1hr 15min).

Tourist office Via Sebastiano Satta 13 (Tues–Fri 9am–-1.30pm & 3–6pm, Sat 10am–1.30pm; 079 200 8072, turismosassari.it).

ACCOMMODATION

Altair Piazza Matteotti 11 079 200 060 or 338 569 9122, bbaltair.com; map p.974. Sixth-floor B&B in a modern apartment with lofty views of the city. The three rooms with private or shared bathrooms are spacious and have a/c. Parking is available. No credit cards. **€60**

Hotel Vittorio Emanuele Corso Vittorio Emanuele 100 079 235 538, hotelvittorioemanuele.ss.it; map p.974. This smartly renovated old-town *palazzo* has comfortable if rather bland rooms but no car park. **€70**

★ **La Serra sui Tetti** Via al Cármine 18 334 121 7623, laserrasuitetti.it; map p.974. This slightly bohemian B&B in the old centre has loads of character, but its greatest assets are its airy top-floor lounge and its roof terrace. No credit cards. **€60**

Tanina Viale Trento 14 346 181 2404, taninabandb.com; map p.974. First-floor B&B furnished with antiques, 5min walk from Piazza Italia in the new town. The three en-suite rooms are spacious, quiet and bright, and there's a kitchen and terrace for guests' use. No credit cards. **€50**

EATING

Fainè Sassu Via Usai 17 079 236 402; map p.974. The menu here is confined to a Ligurian and *sassarese* speciality: *fainè*, a sort of pancake made of chickpea flour, either plain or cooked with onions, sausage or anchovies. It's ideal for a snack, costing €5–8. Sept–May Mon–Sat 7–11.30pm.

★ **Il Vecchio Mulino** Via Frigaglia 5 079 492 0324; map p.974. A former olive mill makes an unusual venue for this excellent restaurant, where the menu focuses on traditional meat dishes (all around €13). Mon 8–11pm, Tues–Sat 1–3pm & 8–11pm.

PizzaImetro Via Usai 10 079 492 0837; map p.974. Sizzling pizzas are served by the metre to eat in or take away – just point out how much you want. Half a metre will cost €6.50–15. Tues–Sun 7pm–midnight.

Taberna Santona Piazza Tola 22 347 546 6752; map p.974. Basic trattoria with tables outside on the piazza. Delicious rural dishes such as vegetable soup and lamb stew are available in two sizes (€5 and €8). No credit cards. Mon–Sat 7.30–11pm.

TRIPS TO ASINARA

Previously a prison island, the elongated offshore isle of **Asinara** is now a national park and nature reserve. Boat trips leave Stintino daily between Easter and October at around 9/10am, returning at 5/6pm. A simple return ticket to the island is €20; a package that might include bike rental or other transport on the island, swimming stops, lunch and a guide costs €45–60. Book tickets at least one day before from the kiosks by the port or an agency in town such as La Nassa, Via Sassari 39 (T 0789 520 060, W escursioniasinara.it).

Stintino and around

The coast north of Sassari is lined with beaches, the most alluring of them lying around the port and resort of **STINTINO**, on Sardinia's northwestern tip. Until recently nothing more than a remote jumble of fishermen's cottages jammed between two narrow harbours, Stintino remains a small, laidback village for most of the year, but is transformed into a busy holiday centre in the tourist season. With no beaches to speak of in the resort itself, most of the sunning and swimming takes place to either side – 4km south at the beach of **Le Saline** or the same distance north at La Pelosa (see page 976) – though most of the area's bars, restaurants and reasonably priced accommodation lie in Stintino.

ARRIVAL AND INFORMATION — STINTINO AND AROUND

By bus Stintino and La Pelosa are linked to Sassari by ARST buses (2–6 daily; 1hr 15min).

Tourist information See W webstintino.com).

ACCOMMODATION AND EATING

Al Martin Pescatore Via Tonnara 30 T 079 523 330 or 335 872 5872, W almartinpescatore.it. Central B&B with the same owners as La Nassa agency, offering fairly basic but clean and spacious en-suite rooms. Breakfast is taken at a nearby restaurant. **€80**

Il Porto Vecchio Via Tonnara 69 T 339 435 3582, W bbstintino.com. This simple B&B has six mostly spacious rooms (some facing the port) with Sardinian decoration. Breakfasts are served at the bar below. **€75**

Lina Via Lepanto 30 T 079 523 505. The best thing about this trattoria (next to a hotel of the same name) is its location, with a terrace overlooking the fishing boats moored in Portu Minori. The food is good but pricey; lunchtime menus cost €15 and €18. Daily noon–5pm & 7–11pm; closed Tues or Wed in winter.

★ **Silvestrino** Via Sassari 14 T 079 523 007, W silvestrino.it. On the town's main street, this hotel has a touch of luxury in its rooms, some of which have their own terrace and terrific views. The restaurant (open to all) is one of Stintino's best, renowned for its seafood – try the clam soup. First courses and mains cost €10–15. March to mid-Oct daily 12.30–2.30pm & 7.30–10.30pm; March–May and early to mid-Oct closed Tues. **€100**

La Pelosa

Some 4km up the road from Stintino a clutter of tourist villages backs the otherwise idyllic promontory of **La Pelosa**, location of one of Sardinia's most tropical-looking **beaches**. With its fine sand, turquoise water and views out to the isles of Piana and Asinara, it can get horribly crowded in the peak tourist season, but nothing can spoil its setting. The beach can be reached by hourly bus from Stintino (June–Sept 8am–midnight; €1).

Alghero

ALGHERO, 40km southwest of Sassari, is one of Sardinia's most charming towns, and one of its busiest resorts. The predominant flavour here is Catalan, owing to a wholesale Hispanicization that followed the overthrow of the Doria family by Pedro IV of Aragon in 1354, a process so thorough that the town became known as "Barcelonetta". The traces are still strong in the old town today, with its flamboyant churches and narrow

cobbled lanes named in both Italian and Catalan, all sheltered within a stout girdle of walls that now hold bars and restaurants – a fine venue for watching the sunset.

The Cattedrale

Piazza del Duomo • **Cattedrale** Daily 7am–7.30pm • Free • **Campanile** May–early Sept Mon–Fri 11am–1.30pm & 5.30–8pm; late Sept 5–7.30pm; may close in bad weather • €4 • 079 973 3041

In the heart of the old quarter, Alghero's predominantly sixteenth-century **Cattedrale** sports an incongruously Neoclassical facade. In the lofty nave, alternating pillars and

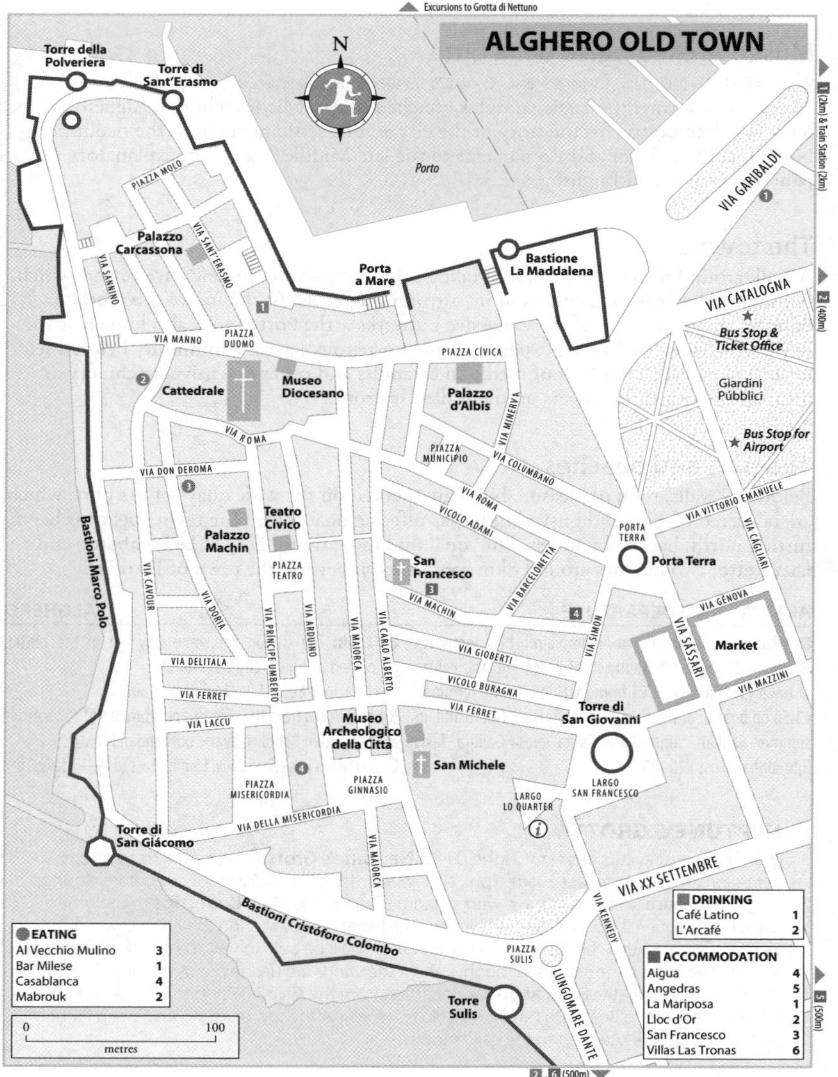

17

columns rise to an impressive octagonal dome. To get the full picture, take a look at the Gothic entrance at the back of the building on Via Umberto. Climb the **campanile** for superb city views.

Palazzo d'Albis and the Palazzo Carcassona

Two of the best examples of the Catalan-Gothic style that characterizes some of Alghero's finest architecture are the **Palazzo d'Albis** on Piazza Civica and the elegantly austere Jewish palace **Palazzo Carcassona** in Via Sant'Erasmo (now a restaurant), both from the sixteenth century.

Museo Archeologico della Città

Via Carlo Alberto 72 • Daily 11am–1.30pm & 5–8pm • €5 • Ⓣ 070 973 4045, Ⓦ fondazionemeta.eu

Housed in a former monastic complex attached to San Michele church, Alghero's **Museo Archeologico** tells the story of the city and its settlements from the neolithic, Nuraghic, Phoenician and Roman eras to the late Middle Ages, with explanatory panels in Italian and English.

The towers

A walk around the old town should take in the circuit of seven defensive **towers** which dominate Alghero's old centre and its surrounding walls. At the top of the **Giardini Pubblici** stands the first of these massive bulwarks – the **Porta Terra**, also known as the Jewish Tower, erected at the expense of the prosperous Jewish community before their expulsion in 1492. Replicas of medieval catapults and other defensive machinery are displayed between the towers on the walled seafront.

The port and beaches

Below the walls, rows of pleasure boats are moored off the wide quays of the **port**, which are bordered by bars and busy with kiosks offering boat tours. The town's **beaches** begin further north, backed by hotels, but you'll find more tranquillity at **Le Bombarde** and **Lazzaretto**, two beaches around 8km west of town beyond the town of Fertilia.

ARRIVAL AND DEPARTURE — ALGHERO

By plane Visitors arriving at Alghero airport (Ⓦ aeroporto dialghero.it) can catch hourly local buses into the centre of town (30min; tickets €1 from machines in the terminal, €1.50 on board), or direct services to Sassari, Nuoro and, in summer, Cagliari, Stintino and Santa Teresa Gallura. Taxis into Alghero cost €20–25.

By train The station lies some way out of the centre, connected by hourly city bus #Al.F.A.

Destinations Sassari (9–14 daily; 35min).

By bus Buses from the airport and from out of town arrive at the Giardini Pubblici, by the port and old centre.

Destinations Bosa (2–5 daily; 55min); Sassari (4–10 daily; 1hr).

NEPTUNE'S GROTTO

One of the best excursions from Alghero is to **Neptune's Grotto** (daily: April to mid-Sept 9am–8pm; mid-Sept to Oct 10am–7pm; Nov–March 10am–4pm; last tour 1hr before closing; €13), a dramatically lit marine cave with stalagmites and stalactites. **Boat trips** to the grotto leave from Alghero's port between March and October (€16 excluding the entry charge). Before buying tickets, check with the operator that you'll be able to visit the grotto on that day, as you can't enter if the sea is too rough – and if the winds are up, be prepared for a choppy ride (30min). Alternatively, **local buses** departing from the Giardini Pubblici (1–3 daily; €4.50 return), the Alghero Beach Bus and Il Trottolo leave you at the top of a long and steep flight of steps that corkscrews down to the cave mouth.

INFORMATION AND GETTING AROUND

Tourist office Largo Lo Quarter (a courtyard off Largo San Francesco, near Piazza Sulis (Mon–Sat 8am–8pm, Sun 10am–1pm & 5–8pm; 079 979 054, algheroturismo.eu).

By bus The hourly Alghero Beach Bus connects the centre of town with all the beaches north and west of town as far as Capo Caccia (mid-June to mid-Sept 9.20am–7.20pm; €3 for one trip, €5 for a day ticket, €15 for 4 days). Il Trottolo, a hop-on, hop-off tourist bus (April–Oct; €18 valid for 24hr, €25 for 48hr, €12/€18 for children aged 6–14, €56/€70 family ticket; 329 875 5555, trottolo.it), also stops at all the sights and beaches along the coast including Capo Caccia.

By bike Raggi di Sardegna, Via Maiorca 119 (334 305 2480, algherorentabike.com; €8–18/day).

ACCOMMODATION

Aigua Via Machin 22 340 077 7688, aigua.it; map p.977. Six mini-apartments buildings, with exposed stonework, wooden floors and ceilings, and basic kitchen facilities for self-service breakfasts are available here. **€85**

Angedras Via Frank 2 079 973 5034, angedras.it; map p.977. In a quiet spot a 15min walk south of the centre, this modern three-star hotel has bright, spacious rooms (some with small balconies) and attentive, friendly staff. A bus shuttles guests to Maria Pia beach in summer. Low-season rates are a steal. **€145**

La Mariposa Via Lido 22 079 950 480, lamariposa.it; map p.977. Some 2km north of Alghero, this busy campsite has shady pitches and private rooms and bungalows (from €32), plus a shop, restaurant and private beach. Closed early Oct to late April. Pitches **€30**

★ **Lloc d'Or** Via Logudoro 26 334 289 7130, llocdor.com; map p.977. Friendly B&B a short walk from the old town, with two large, airy rooms and a self-contained apartment. Breakfasts on the patio include fresh fruit and yoghurt. No credit cards. Closed Nov–March. **€75**

San Francesco Via Machin 2 079 980 330, sanfrancescohotel.com; map p.977. The only hotel in the old town lies just behind the San Francesco church, with clean, simply furnished and quiet en-suite rooms, and breakfast in the cloister. Closed Nov & Dec. **€100**

Villa Las Tronas Lungomare Valencia 1 079 981 818, hotelvillalastronas.it; map p.977. Grandly sited on a promontory a 10min walk south of the centre, this castellated five-star hotel from 1884 is full of character, still retaining a baronial air with its old-fashioned furnishings. There's also an excellent restaurant, a spa and a saltwater pool. **€420**

EATING

★ **Al Vecchio Mulino** Via Don Deroma 3 079 977 254; map p.977. In the heart of the old town, this locals' favourite serves up tasty sea- and land-based dishes (mostly €12–16) and pizzas in low-vaulted rooms: it also has a good selection of white wines. Daily 6.30–11.30pm; mid-Sept to mid-June closed Tues; closed mid-Nov to mid-Dec.

Bar Milese Via Garibaldi 11 079 952 419, barmilese.it; map p.977. Locals flock here for the *focacce* – enormous chunks of filled crusty rolls. There's a full bar service and seating outside. Order first at the till, then present your receipt at the counter. July & Aug daily 7am–1am; Sept–June closed Tues.

Casablanca Via Principe Umberto 72 079 601 5123; map p.977. With vaulted rooms, this is a great venue for a straight-forward pizza (also available at lunchtime) or pasta dish in a convivial atmosphere; mains are €10–15. Daily noon–2.30 & 7–11.30pm; Oct–May closed Wed.

★ **Mabrouk** Via Santa Barbara 4 079 970 000; map p.977. There's no written menu in this lively trattoria: everyone gets the same €40 fixed-price seafood dinner (including drinks) – and it's superb. Mid-March to Oct Tues–Sun 8–11pm; July & Aug daily 8–11pm.

DRINKING

Café Latino Piazza del Duomo 6 079 976 541; map p.977. A great place for an evening aperitif, with parasols on the walls overlooking the port. Snacks and ice creams are also served. June–Sept daily 9am–2am; Oct–May closed Tues.

★ **L'Arcafé** Lungomare Dante 6 328 174 4091; map p.977. Seafront hangout with regular DJs and live music throughout the year. There's a long list of cocktails, beers and other drinks, along with excellent panini, salads and other nibbles. Gets very lively in summer. June–Sept daily 6pm–2am.

MARBLE IMITATION IN SCROVEGNI CHAPEL, PADUA

Contexts

981 History

998 Italian art

1007 Italian architecture

1014 An A–Z of Italian film

1019 Books

1024 Italian

1030 Glossary of artistic and architectural terms

History

A smattering of remains exist from the Neanderthals who occupied the Italian peninsula half a million years ago, but the main period of colonization began after the last Ice Age, with evidence of Paleolithic and Neolithic settlements dating from around 20,000 BC and 4000 BC respectively. More sophisticated tribes developed towards the end of the prehistoric period, between 2400 and 1800 BC; those who left the most visible traces were the Ligurians (who inhabited a much greater area than modern Liguria), the Siculi of southern Italy and Latium, and the Sards, who farmed and raised livestock on Sardinia. More advanced still were migrant groups from the eastern Mediterranean, who introduced the techniques of working copper. Later, various Bronze Age societies (1600–1000 BC) built a network of farms and villages in the Apennines, and on the Sicilian and southern coasts, the latter population trading with Mycenaeans in Greece.

Other tribes brought Indo-European languages into Italy. The Veneti, Latins and Umbrii moved down the peninsula from the north, while the Piceni and the Messapians in Puglia crossed the Adriatic from what is now Croatia. The artificial line between prehistory and history is drawn around the eighth century BC with the arrival of the **Phoenicians** and their trade links between Carthage and southern Italy. This soon encouraged the arrival of the **Carthaginians** in Sicily, Sardinia and the Latium coast – just when **Greeks** and **Etruscans** were gaining influence.

Etruscans and Greeks

Greek settlers colonized parts of the Tuscan coast and the Bay of Naples in the eighth century BC, moving on to **Naxos** on Sicily's Ionian coast, and founding the city of Syracuse in the year 736 BC. The colonies they established in Sicily and southern Italy came to be known as **Magna Graecia**. Along with Etruscan cities to the north they were the earliest Italian civilizations to leave substantial buildings and written records.

The Greek settlements were hugely successful, introducing the vine and the olive to Italy, and establishing a high-yielding agricultural system. Cities like **Syracuse** and **Tarentum** were wealthier and more sophisticated than those on mainland Greece, dominating trade in the central Mediterranean, despite competition from Carthage. Ruins such as the temples of **Agrigento** and **Selinunte**, the fortified walls around Gela, and the theatres at Syracuse and Taormina on Sicily attest to a great prosperity, and Magna Graecia became an enriching influence on the culture of the Greek homeland – Archimedes, Aeschylus and Empedocles were all from Sicily. Yet these colonies suffered from the same factionalism as the Greek states, and the cities of Tarentum, Metapontum, Sybaris and Croton were united only when faced with the threat of

2000 BC	**Eighth century BC**	**736 BC**	**44 BC**
Bronze Age societies established across the peninsula.	Etruscans establish sophisticated civilizations in various centres, notably around the Arno and Tiber rivers.	The city of Syracuse is founded by Greek settlers.	Julius Caesar is assassinated.

outside invasion. From 400 BC, after Sybaris was razed to the ground, the other colonies went into irreversible economic decline, to become satellite states of Rome.

The **Etruscans** were the other major civilization of the period, mostly living in the area between the **Tiber** and **Arno** rivers. Their language, known mostly from funerary texts, is one of the last relics of an ancient language common to the Mediterranean. Some say they arrived in Italy around the ninth century BC from western Anatolia, others that they came from the north, and a third hypothesis places their origins in Etruria. Whatever the case, they set up a cluster of **twelve city-states** in northern Italy, traded with Greek colonies to the south and were the most powerful people in northern Italy by the sixth century BC, edging out the indigenous population of Ligurians, Latins and Sabines. Tomb frescoes in Umbria and Lazio depict a refined and luxurious culture with highly developed systems of divination, based on the reading of animal entrails and the flight of birds. Herodotus wrote that the Etruscans recorded their ancestry along the female line, and tomb excavations in the nineteenth century revealed that women were buried in special sarcophagi carved with their names. Well-preserved chamber tombs with wall paintings exist at **Cerveteri** and **Tarquinia**, the two major sites in Italy. The Etruscans were technically advanced, creating new agricultural land through irrigation and building their cities on ramparted hilltops – a pattern of settlement that has left a permanent mark on central Italy. Their kingdom contracted, however, after invasions by the **Cumans**, **Syracusans** and **Gauls**, and was eventually forced into alliance with the embryonic Roman state. Almost none of their towns have survived the archeological record – the only exception being modern-day Marzabotto or Misa, a fine example of Etruscan urban planning.

Roman Italy

The growth of **Rome**, a border town between the Etruscans and the Latins, gained impetus around 600 BC from a coalition of Latin and Sabine communities. The **Tarquins**, an Etruscan dynasty, oversaw the early expansion, but in 509 BC the Romans ejected the Etruscan royal family and became a **republic**, with power shared jointly between two consuls, both elected for one year. Further changes came half a century later, after a protracted class struggle that resulted in the **Law of the Twelve Tables**, which made patricians and plebeians equal. Thus stabilized, the Romans set out to systematically conquer the northern peninsula and, after the fall of Veii in 396 BC, succeeded in capturing **Sutri** and **Nepi**, towns which Livy considered the "barriers and gateways of Etruria". Various wars and truces with other cities brought about agreements to pay harsh tributes.

The **Gauls** captured Rome in 390, refusing to leave until they had received a vast payment, but this proved a temporary reversal. The Romans took **Campania** and the fertile land of Puglia after defeating the **Samnites** in battles over a period of 35 years. They then set their sights on the wealthy Greek colonies to the south, including Tarentum, whose inhabitants turned to the Greek king, **Pyrrhus of Epirus**, for military support. He initially repelled the Roman invaders, but lost his advantage and was defeated at **Beneventum** in 275 BC. The Romans had by then established their rule in most of southern Italy, and now became a threat to Carthage. In 264 they had the chance of obtaining **Sicily**, when the Mamertines, a

79 AD	**First to second century AD**	**313 AD**
Vesuvius erupts, covering Pompeii and Herculaneum.	Peace and prosperity under Roman rule sees agriculture and cities flourish across much of Europe.	Christianity is declared the state religion by Constantine in the Edict of Milan.

mercenary army in control of Messina, appealed to them for help against the Carthaginians. The Romans obliged – sparking off the **First Punic War** – and took most of the island, together with Sardinia and Corsica. With their victory in 222 BC over the Gauls in the Po Valley, all Italy was now under Roman control.

They also turned a subsequent military threat to their advantage, in what came to be known as the **Second Punic War**. The Carthaginians had watched the spread of Roman power across the Mediterranean with some alarm, and at the end of the third century BC they allowed **Hannibal** to make an Alpine crossing into Italy with his army of infantry, horsemen and elephants. Hannibal crushed the Roman legions at Lago Trasimeno and Cannae (216 BC), and then halted at Capua. With remarkable cool, considering Hannibal's proximity, **Scipio** set sail on a retaliatory mission to the Carthaginian territory of **Spain**, taking Cartagena, and continuing his journey into **Africa**. It was another fifty years before Carthage was taken, closely followed by all of Spain, but the Romans were busy in the meantime adding **Macedonian Greece** to their territory.

These conquests gave Roman citizens a tax-free existence subsidized by captured treasure, but society was sharply divided between those enjoying the benefits and those who were not. The former belonged mostly to the **senatorial party**, who ignored demands for reform by their opposition, the popular party. The radical reforms sponsored by the tribune **Gaius Gracchus** came too close to democracy for the senatorial party, whose declaration of martial law was followed by the assassination of Gracchus. The majority of people realized that the only hope of gaining influence was through the army, but **General Gaius Marius**, when put into power, was ineffective against the senatorial clique, who systematically picked off the new regime.

The first century BC saw civil strife on an unprecedented scale. Although Marius was still in power, another general, **Sulla**, was in the ascendancy, leading military campaigns against northern invaders and rebellious subjects in the south. Sulla subsequently took power and established his dictatorship in Rome, throwing out a populist government which had formed while he was away on a campaign in the east. Murder and exile were common, and cities which had sided with Marius during their struggle for power were punished with massacres and destruction. Thousands of Sulla's war veterans were given confiscated land, but much of it was laid to waste. In 73 BC a gladiator named **Spartacus** led seventy thousand dispossessed farmers and escaped slaves in a revolt, which lasted two years before they were defeated by the legions.

Julius Caesar and Augustus

Rome became calmer only after Sulla's death, when **Pompey**, another general, and **Licinus Crassus**, a rich builder, became masters of Rome. Pompey's interest lay in lucrative wars elsewhere, so his absence from the capital gave **Julius Caesar** the chance to make a name for himself as an orator and raiser of finance. When Pompey returned in 60 BC, he made himself, Crassus and Caesar rulers of the **first Triumvirate**.

Caesar bought himself the post of consul in 59 BC, then spent the next eight years on campaigns against the **Gauls**. His military success needled Pompey, and he eventually turned against his colleague, giving Caesar the chance to hit back. In 49 BC he crossed the river **Rubicon**, committing the offence of entering Roman territory with an army without first informing the Senate, but when he reached the city there was no

410 AD

The decline of the Roman Empire leads to the Sack of Rome.

754 AD

Pepin the Short removes the Lombards from Rome and lays the foundation for the Papal States.

800 AD

Charlemagne is crowned Holy Roman Emperor. By his death the empire stretches from below Rome to the Italian Lakes.

resistance – everyone had fled, and Caesar became absolute ruler of Rome. He spent the next four years on civil reforms, writing his history of the Gallic wars, and chasing Pompey and his followers through Spain, Greece and Egypt. A group of enemies within the Senate, including his adopted son **Brutus**, conspired to murder him in 44 BC, a few months after he had been appointed ruler for life. **Octavian**, Caesar's nephew and heir, Lepidus and Marcus Antonius (**Mark Antony**) formed the **second Triumvirate** the following year. Again, the arrangement was fraught with tensions, the battle for power this time being between Antony and Octavian. While Antony was with **Cleopatra**, Octavian spent his time developing his military strength and the final, decisive battle took place at **Actium** in 31 BC, where Antony committed suicide.

As sole ruler of the new regime, Octavian, renaming himself **Augustus Caesar**, embarked on a series of reforms and public works, giving himself complete powers despite his unassuming official title of "First Citizen".

The emperors

Tiberius (14–37 AD), the successor to Augustus, ruled wisely, but thereafter began a period of decadence. During the psychopathic reign of **Caligula** (37–41) the civil service kept the empire running; **Claudius** (41–54) conquered southern Britain, and was succeeded by his stepson **Nero** (54–68), who violently persecuted the **Christians.** Nero committed suicide when threatened by a coup, leading to a rapid succession of four emperors in the year 68. The period of prosperity during the rule of the **Flavian** emperors (Vespasian and his sons Titus and Domitian) was a forerunner for the **Century of the Antonines**, a period named after the successful reigns of Nerva, Trajan, Hadrian, Antonius and **Marcus Aurelius**. These generals consolidated the empire's infrastructure, and created an encouraging environment for artistic achievement. A prime example is the formidable bronze equestrian statue of Marcus Aurelius in Rome – a work not equalled in sophistication until the Renaissance.

A troubled period followed under the rule of Marcus Aurelius's son **Commodus** (180–193) and his successors, none of whom were wholly in control of the legions. Artistic, intellectual and religious life stagnated, and the balance of economic development tilted in favour of the north, while the agricultural south grew ever more impoverished.

Barbarians and Byzantines

In the middle of the third century, incursions by **Goths** in Greece, the Balkans and Asia, and the **Franks** and **Alamanni** in Gaul, foreshadowed the collapse of the empire. **Aurelian** (270–275) re-established some order after terrible civil wars, to be followed by **Diocletian** (284–305), whose persecution of Christians produced many of the Church's present-day saints. **Plagues** had decimated the population, but problems of a huge but static economy were compounded by the doubling in size of the army at this time to about half a million men. To ease administration, Diocletian **divided the empire** into two halves, east and west, basing himself as ruler of the western empire in Mediolanum (Milan). This measure brought about a relative recovery, coinciding with the rise of **Christianity**, which was declared the state religion during the reign of **Constantine** (306–337). **Constantinople**, capital of the eastern empire, became a thriving trading and manufacturing city, while Rome itself went into decline as the enlargement of the

1176	1200–1550	1346
Battle of Legnano. An affiliation of northern cities defeats Barbarossa, making way for a string of independent city-states.	Powerful city-states keep relative peace, which enables the flourishing of the arts known as the Renaissance.	The Black Death decimates the population of Europe; Florence's population is cut by half.

senatorial estates and the impoverishment of the lower classes gave rise to something comparable to a primitive feudal system.

Barbarians (meaning outsiders, or foreigners) had been crossing the border into the empire since 376 AD, when the **Ostrogoths** were driven from their kingdom in southern Russia by the **Huns**, a tribe of ferocious horsemen. The Huns went on to attack the **Visigoths**, seventy thousand of whom crossed the border and settled inside the empire. When the Roman aristocracy saw that the empire was no longer a shield against barbarian raids, they were less inclined to pay for its support, seeing that a more comfortable future lay in being on good terms with the barbarian successor states.

By the fifth century, many legions were made up of troops from conquered territories, and several posts of high command were held by outsiders. With little will or loyalty behind it, the **empire floundered**, and on New Year's Eve of 406, Vandals, Alans and Sueves crossed the frozen Rhine into Gaul, chased by the Huns from their kingdoms in what are now Hungary and Austria. By 408, the imperial government in Ravenna could no longer hold off **Alaric** (commander of Illyricum – now Croatia) who went on to **sack Rome** in 410, causing a crisis of morale in the West. "When the whole world perished in one city," wrote Saint Jerome, "then I was dumb with silence."

The bitter **end of the Roman Empire** in the west came after **Valentinian III**'s assassination in 455. His eight successors over the next twenty years were finally ignored by the Germanic troops in the army, who elected their general **Odoacer** as king. The remaining Roman aristocracy hated him, and the eastern emperor, **Zeno**, who in theory now ruled the whole empire, refused to recognize him. In 487, Zeno rid himself of the Ostrogoth leader **Theodoric** by persuading him to march on Odoacer in Italy. By 493, Theodoric had succeeded, becoming ruler of the western territories.

A lull followed. The Senate in Rome and the civil service continued to function, and the remains of the empire were still administered under Roman law. Ostrogothic rule of the west continued after Theodoric's death, but in the 530s the eastern emperor, **Justinian**, began to plan the reunification of the Roman Empire "up to the two oceans". In 536 his general **Belisarius** landed in Sicily and moved north through Rome to Ravenna; complete reconquest of the Italian peninsula was achieved in 552, after which the Byzantines retained a presence in the south and in Sardinia for five hundred years.

During this time the **Christian Church** developed as a more or less independent authority, since the emperor was at a safe distance in Constantinople. Continual invasions had led to an uncertain political scene in which the **bishops of Rome** emerged with the strongest voice – justification of their primacy having already been given by Pope Leo I (440–461), who spoke of his right to "rule all who are ruled in the first instance by Christ". A confused period of rule followed, as armies from northern Europe tried to take more territory from the old empire.

Lombards and Franks

During the chaotic sixth century, the **Lombards**, a Germanic tribe, were driven southwest into Italy, and by the eighth century, when the **Franks** arrived from Gaul, they were extending their power throughout the peninsula. The Franks were orthodox Christians, and therefore acceptable to Gallo-Roman nobility, integrating quickly and taking over much of the provincial administration. They were ruled by the

1498	1380	1508	1559
Leonardo da Vinci paints *The Last Supper* in Milan.	Venice defeats Genoa in the War of Chioggia and is established as Italy's supreme maritime trading nation.	Pope Julius II commissions Michelangelo to paint the ceiling frescoes of the Sistine Chapel in Rome.	Sicily, Sardinia, Naples, the Duchy of Milan and parts of Tuscany come under Spanish rule.

Merovingian royal family, but the mayors of the palace – the Carolingians – began to take power in real terms. Led by **Pepin the Short**, they saw an advantage in supporting the papacy, giving Rome large endowments and forcibly converting pagans in areas they conquered. When Pepin wanted to oust the Merovingians, and become King of the Franks, he appealed to the pope in Rome for his blessing, who was happy to agree, anointing the new Frankish king with holy oil.

This alliance was useful to both parties. In 755 the pope called on the Frankish army to confront the Lombards. The Franks forced them to hand over treasure and 22 cities and castles, which then became the northern part of the **Papal States**. Pepin died in 768, with the Church indebted to him. According to custom, he divided the kingdom between his two sons, one of whom died within three years. The other was Charles the Great, or **Charlemagne**.

An intelligent and innovative leader, Charlemagne was proclaimed King of the Franks and of the Lombards, and patrician of the Romans, after a decisive war against the Lombards in 774. On Christmas Day of the year 800, Pope Leo III expressed his gratitude for Charlemagne's political support by crowning him **Emperor of the Holy Roman Empire**, an investiture that forged an enduring link between the fortunes of Italy and those of northern Europe. By the time Charlemagne died, all of Italy from south of Rome to Lombardy, including Sardinia, was part of the huge **Carolingian Empire**. The parts that didn't come under his domain were Sicily and the southern coast, which were gradually being reconquered by Arabs from Tunisia; and Puglia and Calabria, colonized by Byzantines and Greeks.

The task of holding these gains was beyond Charlemagne's successors, and by the beginning of the tenth century the family was extinct and the rival Italian states had become prizes for which the western (French) and eastern (German) Frankish kingdoms competed. Power switched in 936 to **Otto**, king of the eastern Franks. Political disunity in Italy invited him to intervene, and in 962 he was crowned emperor; Otto's son and grandson (Ottos II and III) set the seal on the renewal of the Holy Roman Empire.

Popes and emperors

On the death of **Otto III** in 1002, Italy was again without a recognized ruler. In the north, noblemen jockeyed for power, and the papacy was manipulated by rival Roman families. The most decisive events were in the south, where Sicily, Calabria and Puglia were captured by the **Normans**, who proved effective administrators and synthesized their own culture with the existing half-Arabic, half-Italian south. In **Palermo** in the eleventh century they created the most dynamic culture of the Mediterranean world.

Meanwhile, in Rome, a series of reforming popes began to strengthen the Church. **Gregory VII**, elected in 1073, was the most radical, demanding the right to depose emperors if he so wished. **Emperor Henry IV** was equally determined for this not to happen. The inevitable quarrel broke out, over a key appointment to the archbishopric of Milan. Henry denounced Gregory as "now not pope, but false monk"; the pope responded by excommunicating him, thereby freeing his subjects from their allegiance. By 1077 Henry was aware of his tactical error and tried to make amends by visiting the pope at **Canossa**, where the emperor, barefoot and penitent, was kept waiting outside

1633	**1693**	**1740–96**
Galileo is sentenced to house arrest for the rest of his life for maintaining that the Earth moves around the sun.	A powerful earthquake and subsequent tsunami destroys much of Sicily and kills around sixty thousand.	Austrian rule over northern Italy, Naples and Sardinia introduces wide-ranging administrative, judicial and educational reforms.

for three days. The formal reconciliation did nothing to heal the rift, and Henry's son, **Henry V**, continued the feud, eventually coming to a compromise in which the emperor kept control of bishops' land ownership, while giving up rights over their investiture.

After this symbolic victory, the papacy developed into the most comprehensive and advanced centralized government in Europe in the realms of law and finance, but it wasn't long before unity again came under attack. This time, the threat came from **Emperor Frederick I** (Barbarossa), who besieged many northern Italian cities from his base in Germany from 1154. **Pope Alexander III** responded with ambiguous pronouncements about the imperial crown being a "benefice" which the pope conferred, implying that the emperor was the pope's vassal. The issue of papal or imperial supremacy was to polarize the country for the next two hundred years, almost every part of Italy being torn by struggles between **Guelphs** (supporting the pope) and **Ghibellines** (supporting the emperor).

Henry VI's son, **Frederick II**, assumed the imperial throne at the age of 3 and a half, inheriting the Norman **Kingdom of Sicily**. Later linked by marriage to the great **Hohenstaufen** dynasty in Germany, he inevitably turned his attentions to northern Italy. However, his power base was small, and opposition from the Italian commune and the papacy snowballed into civil war. His sudden death in 1250 marked a major downturn in imperial fortunes.

The emergence of city-states

Charles of Anjou, brother of King Louis IX of France, defeated Frederick II's heirs in southern Italy, and received **Naples and Sicily** as a reward from the pope. His oppressive government finally provoked an uprising on Easter Monday 1282, a revolt that came to be known as the **Sicilian Vespers**, as some two thousand occupying soldiers were murdered in Palermo at the sound of the bell for vespers. For the next twenty years the French were at war with **Peter of Aragon**, who took Sicily and then tried for the southern mainland.

If imperial power was on the defensive, the papacy was in even worse shape. Knowing that the pontiff had little military backing or financial strength left, **Philip of France** sent his men to the pope's summer residence in 1303, subjecting the old man to a degrading attack. Boniface died within a few weeks; his French successor, Clement V, promptly moved the papacy to **Avignon** in southern France.

The declining political power of the major rulers was countered by the growing autonomy of the cities. By 1300, a broad belt of some three hundred virtually **independent city-states** stretched from central Italy to the northernmost edge of the peninsula. In the middle of the century the population of Europe was savagely depleted by the **Black Death** – brought into Europe by a Genoese ship returning from the Black Sea – but the city-states survived, developing a concept of citizenship quite different from the feudal lord-and-vassal relationship. By the end of the fourteenth century the richer and more influential states had swallowed up the smaller *comune*, leaving four as clear political frontrunners. These were **Genoa** (controlling the Ligurian coast), **Florence** (ruling Tuscany), **Milan**, whose sphere of influence included Lombardy and much of central Italy, and **Venice**. Smaller principalities, such as Mantua and Ferrara, supported armies of mercenaries, ensuring their security by building impregnable fortress-palaces.

1796	**1805**	**1815**	**1849**
Napoleon invades northern Italy.	Napoleon is crowned King of Italy in Milan's Duomo.	Settlement of Vienna. With Napoleon's decline the Austrians rule again, but unrest is rife.	Revolutions throughout Italy are crushed.

Perpetual vendettas between the propertied classes often induced the citizens to accept the overall rule of one **signore** in preference to the bloodshed of warring clans. A despotic form of government evolved, sanctioned by official titles from the emperor or pope, and by the fifteenth century most city-states were under princely rather than republican rule. In the south of the fragmented peninsula was the **Kingdom of Naples**; the **States of the Church** stretched up from Rome through modern-day Le Marche, Umbria and the Romagna; **Siena**, **Florence**, **Modena**, **Mantua** and **Ferrara** were independent states, as were the **Duchy of Milan**, and the maritime republics of **Venice** and **Genoa**, with a few odd pockets of independence like Lucca, for example, and Rimini.

The commercial and secular city-states of late medieval times were the seedbed for the **Renaissance**, when urban entrepreneurs (such as the Medici) and autocratic rulers (such as Federico da Montefeltro) enhanced their status through the financing of architectural projects, paintings and sculpture. It was also at this time that the Tuscan dialect – the language of Dante, Petrarch and Boccaccio – became established as Italy's literary language; it later became the nation's official spoken language.

By the mid-fifteenth century the five most powerful states – Naples, the papacy, Milan and the republics of Venice and Florence – reached a tacit agreement to maintain the new balance of power. Yet though there was a balance of power at home, the history of each of the independent Italian states became inextricably bound up with the power politics of other European countries.

French and Spanish intervention

The inevitable finally happened when an Italian state invited a larger power in to defeat one of its rivals. In 1494, at the request of the Duke of Milan, **Charles VIII** of France marched south to renew the Angevin claim to the Kingdom of Naples. After the accomplishment of his mission, Charles stayed for three months in Naples before heading back to France; the kingdom was then acquired by **Ferdinand II of Aragon**, subsequently ruler of all Spain.

The person who really established the Spanish in Italy was the Habsburg **Charles V** (1500–58), who within three years of inheriting both the Austrian and Spanish thrones bribed his way to being elected Holy Roman Emperor. In 1527 the imperial troops sacked **Rome**, a calamity widely interpreted at the time as God's punishment of the disorganized and dissolute Italians. The French remained troublesome opposition, but they were defeated at Pavia in 1526 and Naples in 1529. With the treaty of Cateau-Cambrésis in 1559, Spain held Sicily, Naples, Sardinia, the Duchy of Milan and some Tuscan fortresses, and they were to exert a stranglehold on Italian political life for the next 150 years. The remaining smaller states became satellites of either Spanish or French rule; only the papacy and Venice remained independent.

Social and economic troubles were as severe as the political upheavals. While the papacy combated the spread of the **Reformation** in northern Europe, the major manufacturing and trading centres were coming to terms with the opening up of the Atlantic and Indian Ocean trade routes – discoveries which meant that northern Italy would increasingly be bypassed. Mid-sixteenth-century **economic recession** prompted wealthy Venetian and Florentine merchants to invest in land rather than business,

1861

Italy is declared a unified nation under King Vittorio Emanuele II; Venice and Rome are added ten years later.

1908

An earthquake destroys Messina in Sicily.

1915

Italy enters World War I on the side of Britain, France and Russia.

1922

Mussolini becomes prime minister and within three years has declared himself Il Duce, dictator of Italy.

while in the south high taxes and repressive feudal regimes produced an upsurge of banditry and even the raising of peasant militias – resistance that was ultimately suppressed brutally by the Spanish.

The seventeenth century was a low point in Italian political life, with little room for manoeuvre between the papacy and colonial powers. The Spanish eventually lost control of Italy at the start of the eighteenth century when, as a result of the War of the Spanish Succession, Lombardy, Mantua, Naples and Sardinia all came under Austrian control. The machinations of the major powers led to **frequent realignments** in the first half of the century. Piemonte, ruled by the Duke of Savoy, Victor Amadeus II, was forced in 1720 to surrender Sicily to the Austrians in return for Sardinia. In 1734 Naples and Sicily passed to the Spanish Bourbons, and three years later the House of Lorraine acquired Tuscany on the extinction of the Medici.

Relatively enlightened Bourbon rule in the south did little to arrest the economic polarization of society, but the northern states advanced under the intelligent if autocratic rule of Austria's **Maria Theresa** (1740–80) and her son **Joseph II** (1780–90), who prepared the way for early industrialization. Lightning changes came in April 1796, when the French armies of **Napoleon** invaded northern Italy. Within a few years the French had been driven out again, but by 1810 Napoleon was in command of the whole peninsula, and his puppet regimes remained in charge until Waterloo. Napoleonic rule had profound effects, reducing the power of the papacy, reforming feudal land rights and introducing representative government to Italy. Elected assemblies were provided on the French model, giving the emerging middle class a chance for political discussion and action.

Unification

The fall of Napoleon led to the Vienna Settlement of 1815, by which the Austrians effectively restored the old ruling class. **Metternich**, the Austrian Chancellor, did all he could to foster any local loyalties that might weaken the appeal of unity, yet the years between 1820 and 1849 became years of revolution. Uprisings began in Sicily, Naples and Piemonte, when **King Ferdinand** introduced measures that restricted personal freedom and destroyed many farmers' livelihoods. A makeshift army quickly gained popular support in Sicily, and forced some concessions, before Ferdinand invited the Austrians in to help him crush the revolution. In the north, the oppressive laws enacted by **Vittorio Emanuele I** in the Kingdom of Piemonte sparked off student protests and army mutinies in Turin. Vittorio Emanuele abdicated in favour of his brother, Carlo Felice, and his son, **Carlo Alberto**; the latter initially gave some support to the radicals, but Carlo Felice then called in the Austrians, and thousands of revolutionaries were forced into exile. Carlo Alberto became King of Sardinia in 1831. A secretive, excessively devout and devious character, he did a major volte-face when he assumed the throne by forming an alliance with the Austrians.

In 1831 further uprisings occurred in Parma, Modena, the Papal States, Sicily and Naples. Their lack of coordination, and the readiness with which Austrian and papal troops intervened, ensured that revolution was short-lived. But even if these actions were unsustained, their influence grew.

1929	**1930s**	**1940**
The Lateran Pact recognizes the Vatican as an autonomous Church state within the Kingdom of Italy.	Italy invades Ethiopia and sends aircraft and weapons to aid Franco's Nationalist side in the Spanish Civil War.	Italy declares war on France and Britain, announces a Tripartite Pact with Japan and Germany and invades France, Albania and Greece.

One person profoundly influenced by these insurgencies was **Giuseppe Mazzini**. Arrested as Secretary of the Genoese branch of the Carbonari (a secret radical society) in 1827 and jailed for three months in 1830, he formulated his political ideology and set up "**Young Italy**" on his release. Among the many to whom the ideals of "Young Italy" appealed was **Giuseppe Garibaldi**, soon to play a central role in the **Risorgimento,** as the movement to reform and unite the country was known.

Crop failures in 1846 and 1847 produced widespread **famine and cholera outbreaks.** In Sicily an army of peasants marched on the capital, burning debt collection records, destroying property and freeing prisoners. Middle- and upper-class moderates were worried, and formed a government to control the uprising, but Sicilian **separatist** aims were realized in 1848. Fighting spread to Naples, where **Ferdinand II** made some temporary concessions, but nonetheless he retook Sicily the following year. At the same time as the southern revolution, serious disturbances took place in Tuscany, Piemonte and the Papal States. Rulers fled their duchies, and Carlo Alberto altered course again, prompted by Metternich's fall from power in Vienna: he granted his subjects a constitution and declared war on Austria. In Rome, the pope fled from rioting and Mazzini became a member of the city's republican triumvirate in 1849, with Garibaldi organizing the defences.

None of the uprisings lasted long. Twenty thousand revolutionaries were expelled from Rome, Carlo Alberto abdicated in favour of his son Vittorio Emanuele II after military defeats at the hands of the Austrians, and the dukes returned to Tuscany, Modena and Parma. One thing that survived was Piemonte's constitution, which throughout the 1850s attracted political refugees to the cosmopolitan state.

Cavour and Garibaldi

Nine years of radical change began when **Count Camillo Cavour** became prime minister of Piemonte in 1852. The involvement of Piemontese troops in the Crimean War brought Cavour into contact with Napoleon III at the Congress of Paris, at which the hostilities were ended, and in July 1858 the two men had secret talks on the "Italian question". Napoleon III had decided to support Italy in its fight against the Austrians – the only realistic way of achieving Unification – as long as resistance was non-revolutionary. Having bargained over the division of territory, they waited for a chance to provoke Austria into war. This came in 1859, when Cavour wrote an emotive anti-Austrian speech for Vittorio Emanuele at the opening of parliament. His battle cry for an end to the **grido di dolore** (cry of pain) was taken up all over Italy. The Austrians ordered demobilization by the Piemontese, who did the reverse.

The war was disastrous from the start, and thousands died at Magenta and Solferino. In July 1859, Napoleon III made a truce with the Austrians without consulting Cavour, who resigned in fury. Provisional governments remained in power in Tuscany, Modena and the Romagna. Cavour returned to government in 1860, and soon France, Piemonte and the papacy agreed to a series of plebiscites, a move that ensured that by mid-March of 1860, **Tuscany** and the new state of **Emilia** (duchies of Modena and Parma plus the Romagna) had voted for **union with Piemonte.** A secret treaty between Vittorio Emanuele and Napoleon III ceded Savoy and Nice to France, subject to plebiscites. The result was as planned, no doubt due in part to the presence of the French Army during voting.

1943

US and UK troops land in Sicily. Italy declares an armistice with the Allied forces.

Mussolini is rescued from Italian captivity by German forces and establishes a puppet government on Lake Garda.

1944

Rome is liberated but bloody hand-to-hand fighting continues throughout the rest of northern Italy. Around 50,000 Allied soldiers and 45,000 Italian partisans die.

Garibaldi promptly set off for Nice with the aim of blowing up the ballot boxes, only to be diverted when he reached Genoa, where he heard of an **uprising in Sicily**. Commandeering two old paddle steamers and obtaining just enough rifles for his thousand Red Shirts, he headed south. More support came when they landed in Sicily, and Garibaldi's army outflanked the twelve thousand Neapolitan troops to take the island. After that, they crossed to the mainland, easily occupied Naples, then struck out for Rome. Cavour, anxious that he might lose the initiative, hastily dispatched a Piemontese army to **annex the Papal States**, except for the Patrimony around Rome. Worried by the possibility that the anti-Church revolutionaries who made up the Red Shirt army might stir up trouble, Cavour and Vittorio Emanuele travelled south to Rome, accompanied by their army, and arranged plebiscites in Sicily, Naples, Umbria and the Papal Marches that offered little alternative but to vote for annexation by Piemonte. After their triumphal parade through Naples, they thanked Garibaldi for his trouble, took command of all territories and held elections to a new parliament. In February 1861, the members formally announced the **Kingdom of Italy**.

Cavour died the same year, before the country was completely unified, since Rome and Venice were still outside the kingdom. Garibaldi marched unsuccessfully on Rome in 1862, and again five years later, by which time Venice had been subsumed. It wasn't until Napoleon III was defeated by Prussia in 1870 that the French troops were ousted from Rome. Thus by 1871 **Unification** was complete.

The world wars

After the Risorgimento, some things still hadn't changed. The ruling class were slow to move towards a broader-based political system, while living standards actually worsened in some areas, particularly in Sicily. When Sicilian peasant farmers organized into **fasci** – forerunners of trade unions – the prime minister sent in thirty thousand soldiers, closed down newspapers and interned suspected troublemakers without trial. In the 1890s capitalist methods and modern machinery in the Po Valley created a new social structure, with rich **agrari** at the top of the pile, a mass of farm labourers at the bottom, and an intervening layer of estate managers.

In the 1880s Italy's **colonial expansion** began, initially concentrated in bloody – and ultimately disastrous – campaigns in Abyssinia and Eritrea in 1886. In 1912 Italy wrested the Dodecanese islands and Libya from Turkey, a development deplored by many, including **Benito Mussolini**, who during this war was the radical secretary of the PSI (Partito Socialista Italiano) in Forlì.

World War I and the rise of Mussolini

Italy entered **World War I** in 1915 with the chief aims of settling old scores with Austria and furthering its colonial ambitions through French and British support. A badly equipped, poorly commanded army took three years to force Austria into defeat, finally achieved in the last month of the war at Vittorio Veneto. Some territory was gained – Trieste, Gorizia, and what became Trentino-Alto Adige – but at the cost of over half a million dead, many more wounded, and a mountainous war debt.

1945

Mussolini is captured on Lake Como trying to escape to Switzerland with his mistress, executed and strung up from a petrol station in Milan the following day.

German armies in Italy sign their surrender. Roberto Rossellini films *Rome, Open City* in war-torn Rome and kick-starts Italian Neorealism.

1946

Italians vote for a republic and an end to the monarchy.

The middle classes, disillusioned with the war's outcome and alarmed by inflation and social unrest, turned to Mussolini, now a figurehead of the Right. In 1921, recently elected to parliament, Mussolini formed the Partito Nazionale Fascista, whose **squadre** terrorized their opponents by direct personal attacks and the destruction of newspaper offices, printing shops, and socialist and trade union premises. By 1922 the party was in a position to carry out an insurrectionary "**March on Rome**". Plans for the march were leaked to prime minister Facta, who needed the king's signature on a martial law decree if the army were to meet the march. Fears of civil war led to the king's refusal. Facta resigned, Mussolini made it clear that he would not join any government he did not lead, and on October 29 was awarded **the premiership**. Only then did the march take place.

Zealous **squadristi** now urged Mussolini towards **dictatorship**, which he announced early in 1925. Political opposition and trade unions were outlawed, the free press disintegrated under censorship and Fascist takeovers, elected local governments were replaced by appointed officials, powers of arrest and detention were increased, and special courts were established for political crimes. In 1929, Mussolini ended a sixty-year feud between Church and State by reorganizing the **Vatican** as an autonomous Church state within the Kingdom of Italy. (As late as 1904, anyone involved in the new regime, even as a voter, had been automatically excommunicated.) By 1939, the motto "Everything within the State; nothing outside the State; nothing against the State" had become fact, with the government controlling the larger part of Italy's steel, iron and shipbuilding industries, as well as every aspect of political life.

World War II

Mussolini's involvement in the **Spanish Civil War** in 1936 brought about the formation of the "**Axis**" with Nazi Germany. Italy entered **World War II** totally unprepared and with outdated equipment, but in 1941 invaded Yugoslavia to gain control of the Adriatic coast. Before long, though, Mussolini was on the defensive. Tens of thousands of Italian troops were killed on the Russian Front in the winter of 1942, and in July 1943 the Allied forces gained a first foothold in Europe, when Patton's American Seventh Army and the British Eighth Army under Montgomery landed in Sicily. A month later they controlled the island.

In the face of these and other reversals Mussolini was overthrown by his own Grand Council, who bundled him away to the isolated mountain resort of Gran Sasso, and replaced him with the perplexed **Marshal Badoglio**. The Allies wanted Italy's surrender, for which they secretly offered amnesty to the king, Vittorio Emanuele III, who had coexisted with the Fascist regime for 21 years. On September 8 a radio broadcast announced that an **armistice** had been signed, and on the following day the Allies crossed onto the mainland. As the Anglo-American army moved up through the peninsula, German divisions moved south to meet them, springing Mussolini from jail to set up the **republic of Salò** on Lago di Garda. It was a total failure, and increasing numbers of men and women from Communist, Socialist or Catholic parties swelled the opposing partisan forces to 450,000. In April 1945 Mussolini fled for his life, but was caught by partisans before reaching Switzerland. He and his lover, Claretta Petacci, were shot and strung upside down from a filling-station roof in Milan's Piazzale Loreto.

1958

Italy is a founder member of the European Economic Community (EEC) which is renamed the European Community (EC) in 1992 and becomes part of the European Union (EU) in 2009.

1969

Bomb in Milan's Piazza Fontana kills sixteen people and marks the beginning of ten years during which a toxic mix of the Italian secret service, far-right and far-left terrorist groups attempt to destabilize the country.

The postwar years

A popular mandate declared Italy a republic in 1946, and Alcide de Gasperi's **Democrazia Cristiana (DC)** party formed a government. During the 1950s Italy became a front-rank industrial nation, massive firms such as Fiat and Olivetti helping to double the GDP and triple industrial production. American financial aid – the Marshall Plan – was an important factor in this expansion, as was the availability of a large and compliant workforce, a substantial proportion of which was drawn from the villages of the south.

The DC at first operated in alliance with other right-wing parties, but in 1963, in a move precipitated by the increased politicization of the blue-collar workers, they were obliged to share power for the first time with the **Partito Socialista Italiano (PSI)**. The DC politician who was largely responsible for sounding out the socialists was **Aldo Moro**, the dominant figure of Italian politics in the 1960s. Moro was prime minister from 1963 to 1968, a period in which the economy was disturbed by inflation and the removal of vast sums of money by wealthy citizens alarmed by the arrival in power of the PSI. The decade ended with the "**autunno caldo**" ("hot autumn") of 1969, when strikes, occupations and demonstrations paralyzed the country.

The 1970s and 1980s

In the 1970s the situation continued to worsen. More extreme forms of unrest broke out, instigated in the first instance by the far right, who were almost certainly behind a bomb which killed sixteen people in Piazza Fontana, Milan, in 1969, and the Piazza della Loggia bombing in Brescia five years later. **Neo-fascist terrorism** continued throughout the next decade, reaching its hideous climax in 1980, when 85 people were killed and 200 wounded in a bomb blast at Bologna train station. At the same time, a plethora of left-wing terrorist groups sprang up, many of them led by disaffected intellectuals at the northern universities. The most active of these were the **Brigate Rosse** (Red Brigades). They reached the peak of their notoriety in 1978, when a Red Brigade group kidnapped and killed Aldo Moro himself. A major police offensive in the early 1980s nullified most of the Brigate Rosse, but a number of hardline splinter groups from the various terrorist organizations are still in existence.

Inconsistencies and secrecy beset those trying to discover who was really responsible for the terrorist activity of the 1970s. One Red Brigade member who served eighteen years in jail for his part in the assassination of Aldo Moro recently asserted that it was spies working for the **Italian secret services** who masterminded the operation. A report prepared by the PDS (Italy's party of the democratic left) in 2000 stirred up further controversy: it alleged that in the 1970s and 1980s the Establishment pursued a "**strategy of tension**" and that indiscriminate bombing of the public and the threat of a right-wing coup were devices to stabilize centre-right political control of the country. The perpetrators of bombing campaigns were rarely caught, said the report, because "those massacres, those bombs, those military actions had been organized or promoted or supported by men inside Italian state institutions and, as has been discovered more recently, by men linked to the structures of United States intelligence". "Other bombing campaigns were attributed to the left to prevent the Communist Party from achieving power by democratic means," said Valter Bielli, PDS MP, and one of the

1978

Aldo Moro, leader of the Christian Democrats and ex-prime minister, is kidnapped and murdered by Red Brigade terrorists after 55 days of imprisonment.

1980

Bomb in Bologna train station kills 85 people.

1992

Anti-Mafia judges Giovanni Falcone and Paolo Borsellino murdered.

report's authors. The report drew furious rebuttals from centre-right groups and the US embassy in Rome.

By whatever means, the DC government certainly clung to power. It was partly sustained by the so-called "historic compromise" negotiated in 1976 with **Enrico Berlinguer**, leader of the **Partito Comunista Italiano (PCI)**. By this arrangement the PCI – polling 34 percent of the national vote, just three points less than the DC – agreed to abstain from voting in parliament in order to maintain a government of national unity. The pact was rescinded in 1979, and after Berlinguer's death in 1984 the PCI's share of the vote dropped to around 27 percent. The combination of this withdrawal of popular support and the collapse of the Communist bloc led to a realignment of the PCI under the leadership of **Achille Occhetto**, who turned the party into a democratic socialist grouping along the lines of left-leaning parties in Germany or Sweden – a transformation encapsulated by the party's new name – the **Partito Democratico della Sinistra** ("Democratic Party of the Left").

In its efforts to exclude the left wing from power, the DC had been obliged to accede to demands from minor parties such as the **Radical Party**, which gained eighteen seats in the 1987 election, one of them going to the porn star Ilona Staller, better known as **La Cicciolina**. Furthermore, the DC's reputation was severely damaged in the early 1980s by a series of scandals, notably the furore surrounding the activities of the P2 Masonic Lodge, when links were discovered between corrupt bankers, senior DC members and fanatical right-wing groups. As its popularity fell, the DC was forced to offer the premiership to politicians from other parties. In 1981 Giovanni Spadolini of the Republicans became the first non-DC prime minister since the war, and in 1983 **Bettino Craxi** was installed as the first premier from the PSI, a position he held for four years.

Even through the upheavals of the 1970s the national income of Italy continued to grow, and there developed a national obsession with **Il Sorpasso**, a term signifying the country's overtaking of France and Britain in the economic league table. Experts disagreed as to whether Il Sorpasso actually happened (most thought it hadn't), and calculations were complicated by the huge scale of tax evasion and other illicit financial dealings in Italy. All strata of society were involved in the withholding of money from central government, but the ruling power in this **economia sommersa** (submerged economy) was, and to a certain extent still is, the **Mafia**, whose contacts penetrate to the highest levels in Rome. The most traumatic proof of the Mafia's infiltration of the political hierarchy came in May 1992, with the murders of anti-Mafia judges **Giovanni Falcone** and **Paolo Borsellino**, whose killers could only have penetrated the judges' security with the help of inside information.

Mani Pulite

The murders of the immensely respected Falcone and Borsellino marked a faultline in the political history of modern Italy, and the late 1980s and early 1990s saw the rise of a number of new political parties, as people became disillusioned with the old DC-led consensus. One was the right-wing Lega Nord (Northern League), whose autocratic leader, Umberto Bossi, capitalized on concerns that the hard-working, law-abiding North was supporting the corrupt South, while the Fascist MSI, renamed the Alleanza

1994

Silvio Berlusconi's centre-right Forza Italia party wins the general election with the National Alliance and the Lega Nord. It falls after eight months when the Lega withdraws support for the coalition.

2001–06

A second government headed by Silvio Berlusconi becomes the longest post-war government.

2002

The euro replaces the lira as Italy's currency.

Nazionale (AN), or National Alliance, and now a wide coalition of right-wingers led by the persuasive Gianfranco Fini, has gained ground in recent years.

In 1992 the new government of Giuliano Amato – a politician untainted by any hint of corruption – instigated the biggest roundup of Mafia members in nearly a decade, leading to the arrest of Salvatore "Toto" Riina, the Mafia *capo di tutti capi* (boss of bosses) and the man widely believed to have been behind the Falcone and Borsellino killings. The arrest of Riina followed the testimony of numerous supergrasses, who also implicated key members of the Establishment in Mafia activities, including the former prime minister Giulio Andreotti, who was brought to trial.

Bettino Craxi once called Andreotti a fox, adding "sooner or later all foxes end up as fur coats", but it was Craxi himself who was one of the first to fall from grace. Craxi was at the centre of the powerful Socialist establishment that ran the key city of Milan, when in February 1992 a minor party official was arrested on corruption charges. This represented just the tip of a long-established culture of kickbacks and bribes that went right to the top of the Italian political establishment, not just in Milan but across the entire country, and was nicknamed Tangentopoli ("Bribesville"). By the end of that year thousands were under arrest and what came to be known as the **Mani Pulite** or "Clean Hands" investigation, led by the crusading Milan judge, Antonio di Pietro, was under way. In January 1999, Craxi was convicted with twenty others of corruption and sentenced to five years in prison, dying a year later in exile in Tunisia.

Italy today: Berlusconi and after

The established Italian parties, most notably the Christian Democrats and the Socialists, were almost wiped out in the municipal elections of 1993, and the national elections of 1994 saw yet another political force emerge to fill the vacuum: the centre-right **Forza Italia** ("Come on Italy"), led by the media mogul **Silvio Berlusconi**, who swept to power in a populist alliance with Bossi's Lega Nord and the post-fascist National Alliance. The fact that Berlusconi was not a politician was perhaps his greatest asset, and most Italians, albeit briefly, saw this as the end of the old, corrupt regime, and the birth of a truly modern Italian state.

Although he went on to win three more elections in the following eight years and was head of Italy's **longest-lasting postwar government**, Berlusconi proved no more successful at ruling the country than his predecessors. On a personal front not only did he resist all attempts to reduce the scope of his media business and its blatant conflict of interest with his premiership, but also his time in the public eye was accompanied by a constantly evolving charge sheet covering money laundering, corruption, sex scandals, gerrymandering and forcing through backdated legislation to get himself out of sticky court cases. (You can find a summary of his legal travails at en.wikipedia.org/wiki/Trials_and_allegations_involving_Silvio_Berlusconi. It's quite a list.)

But perhaps more worrying was his effect on the state of the nation: the media-mogul-turned-politician's promises of freedom and prosperity were shown to be empty, as economic decline, social stagnation and stifling bureaucracy continued to afflict the country. Faced with global financial crises, and Italy on the verge of bankruptcy, Berlusconi was finally forced to quit in November 2011, and an emergency

2006

Italy wins the football World Cup for the fourth time (previously in 1934, 1938 and 1982).

2008

Roberto Saviano's book and subsequent film *Gomorrah* document the influence of the Camorra on every aspect of Neapolitan life.

In the general election, as leader of the People of Freedom political party, Berlusconi is returned for his fourth term as prime minister.

FROM CRUISE SHIP TO PREMIERSHIP: SILVIO BERLUSCONI

Italy has had more than sixty different governments since World War II, which perhaps indicates that this is a country that does not trust its politicans, and might explain how it came to choose the cruise-ship crooner and self-made media tycoon **Silvio Berlusconi** as prime minister for four terms. The gaffes, scandals and sleaze that characterized his time in power did nothing for Italy's wider reputation, and his shameless womanizing almost brought him down in 2009 when a series of prostitutes went public about their relationships with him. However, he held on as premier, even while the papers ran stories about a 17-year-old "entertainer" who was released from arrest after his intervention, and printed details of his wild "bunga bunga" parties.

Berlusconi also got into trouble when representing Italy abroad, famously accusing a German MEP of acting like a Nazi camp guard. At home his battle with the Italian judiciary (a quasi-communist "cancerous growth" in his view) combined with attempts (mostly successful) to change the law to protect him from prosecution for corruption, arguably occupied more of his political time than any other issues. But, unlike most politicians, he didn't seem to care what people thought, which kept him popular with much of the Italian electorate. As for the fact that as head of a media business and prime minister he virtually controlled all mainstream television, he simply said: "If I, taking care of everyone's interests, also take care of my own, you can't talk about a conflict of interest."

Since finally being ejected from office in 2011, Berlusconi has been found guilty of tax fraud and convicted of paying for sex with an underage prostitute – though the latter conviction was overturned on an appeal. A new anti-corruption law barred him from serving in any legislative office for six years (until 2019), but he has remained leader of Forza Italia throughout his ban. With Berlusconi it never ends.

government of technocrats was put together under the economist **Mario Monti**, who remained in power until the election of February 2013.

Political deadlock followed this election, which made comedian Beppe Grillo's anti-Establishment **Five Star Movement** the largest party in the Chamber of Deputies. But with Grillo refusing to play any part in governing the country, **Enrico Letta** was invited by President Giorgio Napolitano to form a coalition government. This lasted until February 2014, when the Democratic Party withdrew its support for Letta in favour of the telegenic **Matteo Renzi**, the 39-year-old mayor of Florence.

As likely to denounce trade union privileges as to deplore the sins of big business, Renzi practised a soft-left pragmatism that drew comparison with Tony Blair and Bill Clinton. After losing a referendum in late 2016 on constitutional reform Renzi was forced to resign. In the **general election** of March 2018 half of Italian voters opted for two populist parties offering radical change – the **Five Star Movement**, led by **Luigi di Maio**, and the Northern League, rebranded as simply "**Lega**", led by **Matteo Salvini**. An awkward union of left and right wing populism, FSM and the Lega shared a scorn for Italy's elites, a rejection of the EU's austerity policies, and a fierce xenophobia. FSM proposed a basic "citizenship income" of €780 a month for all Italians, while the Lega offered a flat tax of 15–20 percent, and a lower retirement age. Both railed at North African immigrants. Though FSM and the Lega cobbled together a coalition in the summer of 2018 with a policy "contract" and a caretaker prime minister, Giuseppe Conte, Italy's situation remains as uncertain as ever. The coalition's spendthrift policies

2009

An earthquake strikes L'Aquila in Abruzzo killing over three hundred people.

2011

In the dock again, after years of trials for fiscal impropriety, Silvio Berlusconi resigns as Italy teeters on the edge of bankruptcy. Mario Monti is invited to steer Italy through the financial crisis.

and friendliness towards Russia seemed certain to bring them into conflict with EU rules and institutions. Salvini rapidly proved the more dynamic partner, and the formerly separatist Lega saw its support rise throughout Italy, bringing tensions to the coalition. And Italy's underlying problems may be the rock on which this government, like all its predecessors, founders. Though still the Eurozone's third largest economy, Italy's is one of its worst-performing, crippled by chronically low growth and one of the world's highest levels of public debt. Two million Italians, mostly the educated and skilled, have left in the past decade. Unemployment is over eleven percent. Immigration from North Africa continues to rise. The conditions are ripe for further populist strongmen like Salvini – and the solutions seem as far away as ever.

2014

Matteo Renzi becomes Italy's youngest prime minister.

2018

A hung parliament results in an uneasy coalition between two anti-establishment parties: Lega and Five Star Movement.

Italian art

Pick up any history of Western art and you'll find the biggest chapter by far will be on Italy. The country's contribution to the pantheon of creativity through the past three thousand years is immense, whether it's the legacy of the Romans and the early Christian era or the enormous and unprecedented achievements of the Renaissance in Florence and Rome. It's the reason many people visit Italy in the first place, and this short history is designed to give you the most basic of backgrounds to enhance your trip.

The Etruscans

A sensible way to begin any account of Italian art is with the **Etruscans**, who lived in central Italy – in Etruria – from around 900 BC until their incorporation into the Roman world in 88 BC. The Romans borrowed heavily from their civilization, and thus in many ways the influence of the Etruscans is still felt today: our alphabet, for example, is based on the Etruscan system; and bishops' crooks and the "fasces" symbol, of a bundle of rods with an axe – found, among other places, behind the speaker's rostrum in the US House of Representatives – are just two other Etruscan symbols that endure. The Etruscans were also master craftsmen, working in terracotta, gold and bronze, and accomplished carvers in stone, and it is these skills – together with their obvious sensuality and the ease with which they enjoyed life – that make their civilization so beguiling. A lot of Etruscan objects have survived from tombs, particularly those found in the sites of Tarquinia and Cerveteri – terracotta sculptures such as the sculpture of the married couple or *Apollo* and *Hercules* in the Villa Giulia museum in Rome, or bronzes like the *Orator* and the *Chimera* in the archeological museum in Florence.

The Romans

The militaristic **Romans**, who wrested control of the region from the Etruscans, are not usually known as great artists. There were great builders, certainly, and the wall paintings and mosaics of Pompeii and Herculaneum demonstrate that there were gifted artists around. But the fact is that a great deal of Roman art and sculpture is in fact copied from ancient Greek originals – most famously the *Laocoön* and *Apollo Belvedere* in the Vatican or any number of sculptures in the Palazzo Nuovo of the Capitoline Museums in Rome. There's no doubting the skill of Roman sculptors who re-created these works, though, and the Romans as a whole were prolific creators of sculptural art. Above all they were good portraitists, and there are lots of likenesses of both ordinary people and most of the great emperors still with us today, including a huge hoard in the Vatican Museums, as well as fantastic sarcophagi portraying battle scenes in relief – a medium which was also used to adorn triumphal arches and other architectural features.

Early Christian and Byzantine art

The **early Christians** borrowed the tendency to decorate sarcophagi with relief sculptures from the Romans, though by now these depicted fundamental Christian themes like the shepherd and the lamb, Christ enthroned or the alpha and omega symbols. Early Christian paintings were done in the catacombs and other burial places, mainly depictions of saints but again often borrowing colour and other styles

from the Romans. However, mosaics were the more commonly used medium as the decoration in churches, especially during the reign of the Emperor Justinian, whose period in power during the middle of the sixth century marks the high point of early **Byzantine** art. These usually depicted a group of saints lined up with the church's donor, centring on a figure of Christ enthroned in glory, for example in the basilica of Santa Maria Maggiore in Rome, whose mosaics are a fifth-century comic strip of the Old Testament, or, a little later, in the new Christian Roman capital of Ravenna, where the sixth-century basilicas of San Vitale and Sant'Apollinaire Nuovo hold stupendous cycles of mosaics.

The Middle Ages

The medium of mosaic stayed in use for hundreds of years, and indeed was the principal method used to decorate the basilica of San Marco in Venice (see page 353) in the thirteenth century. However, mosaic was an inevitably monumental and static medium, and before long frescoes became preferred in churches, albeit following the rather stiff and formal styles of the mosaicists, along with panel paintings depicting Christ or the Madonna and a group of saints.

Nicola Pisano (1220–85) was the first great sculptor of the Middle Ages in what we now call Italy, a native of Pisa and famous for his work on the pulpit in Pisa's baptistry, whose sculptural complexity bears comparison with the best pre-Christian sarcophagi. He passed on his talent to his son, **Giovanni Pisano** (1250–1315), who continued to work in the same Gothic tradition but with more fluidity and skill, creating pulpits in both Pistoia and Pisa cathedrals as well as a series of statues for the facade of Siena's cathedral and another pulpit inside. One of Nicola Pisano's assistants on this, **Arnolfo di Cambio** (1240–1310) was also very active at this time. He produced the famous statue of *St Peter* in St Peter's in Rome, whose foot is worn smooth by worshippers, and developed the design for funerary tombs which was followed for the next couple of centuries, but he's perhaps best known as the architect responsible for the construction of the cathedral in Florence in the late 1200s.

At about the same time, **Pietro Cavallini** (1250–1330) introduced a new level of realism into the mosaics he designed and the frescoes he painted, moving away somewhat from the stiff Byzantine figures people were used to – as evidenced by the frescoes in the basilica of St Francis in Assisi, in the church of Santa Cecilia in Rome, and some fragmentary frescoes in Naples. **Cimabue**, too (1240–1302), was a pioneer of his time, namechecked by Dante in his *Purgatorio* as being eclipsed in talent only by his pupil, **Giotto di Bondone** (1267–1337) – no disgrace as Giotto, as he is now known, was certainly the greatest artist of this time, widely regarded as the link between Gothic art and everything else that followed. This is due to the fact that he was the first to truly break away from the heavily stylized forms of the Byzantine and Gothic era and give his figures proper, human form. His frescoes in the Scrovegni Chapel in Padua are justifiably famous, and have a humane power that makes them one of the great unmissable sights of Italy, although most other works by him are lost or disputed – apart from his frescoes in the basilica of St Francis in Assisi, an altarpiece in the Uffizi, a crucifix in Rimini and one or two other small-scale works.

Despite the influence of Giotto, the dominant school of painting at the time was in fact in Siena, headed up by **Duccio di Buoninsegna** (1255–1318) and **Simone Martini** (1284–1344), both of whom followed a more traditional path, engaging with the more formal Byzantine style to some extent but making it into a more refined and elegant style of their own. Duccio's masterpiece is probably his *Maestà*, currently in the museum of Siena's cathedral, which was so admired on its completion that it was carried around the town in a procession. Simone Martini was a pupil of Duccio and painted the same subject in the town hall of Siena; he is also known for his frescoes in the church of St Francis in Assisi and his *Annunciation* in the Uffizi.

The Renaissance

The fifteenth century in Italy really belongs to what we now call the **Renaissance**, a remarkable time, centred on Florence and Tuscany in particular. In architecture this involved an attempt to get back to classical ideas coupled with ingenious new building methods and techniques, while in the visual arts there was a move away from a more iconic style of painting towards an approach that placed man centre stage in as realistic a fashion as possible, with perspective, elements of portraiture and landscape. At the same time artists in general began to gain a new respect, moving gradually away from being considered as mere artisans to take their place as members of the professional classes.

If the Renaissance begins anywhere it's with **Lorenzo Ghiberti** (1378–1455), whose victory in a competition sponsored by the Florentine authorities to design the doors of the city's baptistry arguably kick-started the movement, and occupied the artist for the best part of the next fifty years, with a design that exhibited more drama, naturalism and perspective than had been previously seen, and spawning a legacy of Florentine sculptors who would blaze a trail through the rest of the fifteenth century. The runner-up in the competition, **Filippo Brunelleschi** (1377–1446), went on to specialize in architecture, and added a dome to the city's cathedral that would prove to be one of the engineering wonders of the century (see page 522), while Ghiberti's pupil **Donatello** (1386–1466) became arguably the greatest sculptor of his age, with an appreciation of nature and an ability to render it in marble that upstaged everyone who had gone before. His skill is manifest in numerous examples around the country, but most notably in his early sculptures of the *Evangelists* in Orsanmichele in Florence, now split between the church and the Bargello, where his iconic figure of *David* also resides. In 1425 Donatello began to work with another sculptor, **Michelozzo** (1396–1472), producing the tomb of Cardinal Brancacci in Naples, among other things; Michelozzo also worked on Ghiberti's bronze doors. Another sculptor who entered the baptistry doors competition was **Jacopo della Quercia** (1374–1438), a Sienese artist who was influenced by the work of Nicola Pisano and Arnolfo di Cambio. He is responsible for the Fonte Gaia in Siena's main square, and work in the churches of San Frediano and San Petronio, in Lucca and Bologna respectively.

The invention of perspective is sometimes credited to **Paolo Uccello** (1397–1475), whose most famous work, in the National Gallery in London, shows the foreshortened body of the "soldier who died for perspective" in his *Battle Scene* there. But Uccello was more interested in perspective for its own sake (hence a painting like this) rather than using it to create more realistic pictures, and it was **Masaccio** (1401–28) who in fact developed it properly – most potently in his fresco of the *Trinity* in the church of Santa Maria Novella, whose extraordinary depth and realism were revolutionary at the time. His contemporary **Masolino da Panicale** (1383–1447) was another veteran of Ghiberti's doors, but he painted in a more traditional style that harkened back to his Gothic predecessors.

Masaccio's only pupil, **Fra Filippo Lippi** (1406–69), was a clear follower of his master, but he was influenced by the Flemish masters too, as we can see in his dramatic and naturalistic frescoes in Prato's cathedral. At the same time, **Fra Angelico** (1395–1455) painted more monumental and in some ways more staid creations, though with a greater emphasis on colour – as you can see if you visit the home of his greatest works, painted in the monastery at which he was a Dominican monk – San Marco in Florence. Meanwhile, in Verona, Fra Angelico's contemporary **Antonio Pisanello** (1395–1455) was decorating some of the principal churches of his home town in a well-developed Gothic style, along with a series of frescoes in the Palazzo Ducale in Mantua.

One of the painters closest in style to Masaccio was **Domenico Ghirlandaio** (1449–94), whose frescoes adorn the church of Santa Maria Novella among other churches in Florence. However, perhaps the greatest of the next generation of Renaissance artists

was **Luca Signorelli** (1445–1523), who in fact painted Fra Angelico's portrait (as well as his own) into his amazing *Last Judgement*, in a chapel in Orvieto cathedral – a work which is said to have influenced Michelangelo's later work on the same subject in the Sistine Chapel.

To the south of Florence, in Arezzo, another contemporary of Mantegna, **Piero della Francesca** (1410–92), was experimenting with perspective in the same way, but his work today looks less archaic, almost modern, in its outlook compared to others of the time, with calm, understated colours and cool sense of form – best seen in his series of paintings depicting the *Legend of the True Cross* in Arezzo's church of San Francesco.

Piero della Francesca was a big influence on the Umbrian painter, **Melozzo da Forlì** (1438–94), who worked in Rome in the last two decades of the fifteenth century, decorating a number of churches, including Santi Apostoli and San Marco – the latter including a famous picture showing his patron Pope Sixtus IV that's now in the Vatican Pinacoteca. Among fellow Umbrians, **Pietro Perugino** (1446–1524) was known for his harmoniously composed paintings – less full of drama than some of his contemporaries, but theatrically staged nonetheless, as serene, beautifully coloured tableaux that almost epitomize the symmetrical beauty of much of Renaissance art. His assistant, **Pinturricchio** (1454–1513), also produced beautifully composed works of great form and colour, but made no attempt at any sort of profound vision; some of his best-known and most accessible work is in the church of Santa Maria del Popolo in Rome.

Andrea Mantegna (1431–1506), who worked in the north of Italy, in Padua and then Mantua, was one of the most inventive practitioners of the new Renaissance techniques, peopling his paintings with living, breathing human beings and setting them against backdrops that had realism and perspective – much more so, say, than his contemporary **Benozzo Gozzoli** (1421–97), whose frescoes in the chapel in Florence's Palazzo Medici-Ricciardi are more decorative than naturalistic. Some of Mantegna's best work is in the Palazzo Ducale in Mantua, where he painted a series of marvellous family frescoes for the Gonzagas.

Towards the end of the fifteenth century, **Sandro Botticelli** (1445–1510), too, developed a style of his own, apprenticed at a young age to Fra Filippo Lippi but increasingly creating pictures which married naturalism with elegance. He also worked as much for wealthy merchants as the Church, painting canvases rather than frescoes, and as such his work is smaller-scale and less concerned with monumental religious themes than others, and overall more decorative, using ancient Greek and Roman stories as his subject matter instead.

Botticelli's best-known contemporary was **Leonardo da Vinci** (1452–1519), a Florentine who died in France and is now known as the ultimate "Renaissance Man", as comfortable designing weaponry or writing a learned thesis as with drawing or painting. Precious little work has survived from Leonardo, partly because he was so busy with other projects, and partly because he insisted on deciding when something was completed himself, and so works were often left unfinished or never delivered. *The Last Supper* in Milan's Santa Maria delle Grazie is probably his most famous piece of work in Italy, and is incredibly naturalistic for its time, not only realistically depicting the characters in the story, but also actually telling the story.

The sixteenth century

At the end of the fifteenth century the emphasis shifted from Florence to Rome and to Venice. The **High Renaissance** is generally used to describe a period of time during the first half of the sixteenth century when all the ideas of the Renaissance were in tune, and there was a group of artists – led by Michelangelo and Raphael in Rome, and Titian in Venice – who were at the height of their powers, interpreting the humanist principles of the time with an almost divine virtuosity and skill, until the mid-century backlash started with the more empty showiness of **Mannerism**.

At the turn of the sixteenth century Ghirlandaio's studio took on a young and hungry Florentine painter called **Michelangelo Buonarotti** (1475–1564), who from the outset was something special, studying anatomy so as to get the draughtsmanship of his figures exactly right, as can be seen in his early – and renowned – figure of *David* in the Uffizi. Michelangelo preferred sculpture to painting, but his fame quickly spread, and he was still a relatively young man when he was called to Rome to decorate the Sistine Chapel for Pope Julius II in 1506 – a feat which took four years, and to this day is perhaps the most heroic and accomplished single piece of work that any painter has achieved. He was an artist who never let up, and it's possible to follow the development of his style around Italy, taking in early works like the figure of *Bacchus* in Florence's Bargello and his pietà in St Peter's in Rome right up to the Sistine Chapel's dark *Last Judgement*, which he painted more than thirty years after the ceiling. It's perhaps testament to Michelangelo's originality and uncompromising approach that both Sistine Chapel works caused an equal level of outcry at the time.

His contemporary **Raphael** (1483–1520), a native of Perugia, represents with Michelangelo the high point of the Renaissance, the point at which the era's ideas and inventions with regards to form, light, naturalism and composition all converged. Unlike Michelangelo, Raphael was an out-and-out painter, and naturally he was called to work for the pope as well, his best work probably being the suite of rooms he decorated for the same Pope Julius II in the Vatican Palace. It seems almost incredible that these two great artists were for a period working in the same building at the same time, creating arguably the two greatest pieces of Renaissance painting ever within a few metres of each other. Yet that is what happened, although Raphael enjoyed a much shorter life than Michelangelo, and works by him are scarce by comparison. However, his later work in the nearby Villa Farnesina in Rome is also among his best, and there are paintings by him in a number of different Italian galleries.

Venice was a booming city at this time, and it first embraced the Renaissance in the elderly figure of **Giovanni Bellini** (1430–1516). He had been influenced by Andrea Mantegna, who had married his sister, and became known for introducing naturalistic details into his religious paintings. He also headed up a large workshop, one that was responsible for turning out the next generation of Venetian painters, including Sebastiano del Piombo, Giorgione and Titian. **Giorgione** (1476–1510) died young and there's hardly any work by him in existence now, but what there is marks him out as one of the greatest Venetian painters, in particular a mysterious painting that has been named *The Tempest* due to the fact that no one really knows what it depicts or what it is about. It was a revolutionary painting for its time, principally in the way it incorporates nature into the composition, almost as a character in its own right. The second great Venetian painter of this time was **Titian** (1487–1576), a talent so revered that it was said that even the Holy Roman Emperor Charles V had stopped to pick up one of his brushes – a story which perhaps says as much about the evolving status of artists during the Renaissance as it does about Titian. Titian was a colourist, and brilliant, too, at composition, and he rewrote the rules of both in his great painting of *The Assumption* in the Frari church in Venice. He was also a great portraitist, as can be seen in his depiction of the Farnese pope Paul III, which hangs in the Capodimonte Museum in Naples, as well as many other great portraits he painted during his long careeer. **Sebastian del Piombo** (1485–1547) is thought to have finished some of Giorgione's paintings after he died, and he also worked with Raphael on the Villa Farnesina, but he became closest of all to Michelangelo, whose influence can be seen in his later works, for example the two that hang in the Trinità dei Monti church in Rome.

Of the Venetians that followed this group, **Lorenzo Lotto** (1480–1556) followed in the footsteps of Giorgione, as did his friend **Palma il Vecchio** (1480–1528), although it's **Tintoretto** who stands out. His distinctive, dramatic style prefigured the Baroque with its theatrical lighting and dashing, almost unfinished style – all a far cry from the cool delivery of Titian, but typical of the time in his determination to break free of the

dominant Renaissance approach and forge a style of his own. He was a prolific artist and his work can be found everywhere, all over Italy, but the four paintings he did for the Scuola di San Marco in Venice are among his best, as are those in the Scuola di San Rocco, also in Venice.

The third great sixteenth-century Venetian painter was arguably **Paolo Veronese**, who was also a great stylist, painting big narrative works that decorated the Palladian Villa Barbaro in Maser and the church of San Giovanni e Paolo in Venice. Meanwhile in Parma, **Correggio** (1489–1534) was busily decorating the churches and the cathedral in a soft flowing style in which he perfected his *sotto in su* technique, in which figures are depicted on domes and ceiling as if floating in the sky – an effect which was to be taken up with a vengeance in the decades to come.

Mannerism

Veronese and Correggio worked towards the end of the sixteenth century, and in some way their styles anticipate what has become known as **Mannerism**, a somewhat derogatory term derived from the Italian word *maniera* or "style". This alluded to the fact that the artists who followed on from the Renaissance greats had to find a way of distinguishing themselves, which they did by using increasingly flashy techniques of perspective and draughtsmanship – all style and no substance, if you like. Mannerist paintings tended to go for cheap and immediate effects – in colour, subject matter and delivery – and as such they prefigure the equally dramatic Baroque era that was to follow. Perhaps the ultimate Mannerist painter is **Giulio Romano** (1499–1546), whose frescoes in Mantua's Palazzo del Te are still quite shocking today. But other painters fall into this post-Renaissance category, for example **Francesco Parmigianino** (1503–40), who worked alongside Correggio in Parma and is probably best known for a painting that has become known as the *Madonna with the Long Neck*, in the Uffizi in Florence, a very elegant work that typifies the Mannerist approach to the human form.

Other so-called Mannerist painters include **Giorgio Vasari** (1511–74), whose work is common in Italy – he was quite prolific – although he is probably best known for his biographies of the various Renaissance artists, from which we know a great deal about these men and their time. **Agnolo Bronzino** (1503–72) was another gifted Mannerist painter who worked mainly in Florence and concentrated on portraiture. His contemporary, **Benvenuto Cellini** (1500–71) was an artist turned writer who made beautiful pieces in bronze and gold that still survive today but who is more renowned for his racy autobiography which describes his life in Rome during the sixteenth century. Giovanni da Bologna or **Giambologna** (1529–1608), as he's better known, was a Florentine sculptor who also worked in bronze and marble, and whose aim to produce a piece that could be viewed from all angles was Mannerist to its core, and can be seen at its best in Florence's Bargello.

The Baroque

The end of the sixteenth century saw upheaval in Europe, with the Reformation gaining pace in Northern Europe and the Catholic Church forced to retrench in its southern heartlands, giving way to another new style that got stuck with a derogatory name: the **Baroque**, a term which literally meant grotesque, and was coined to describe the grand and theatrical style in painting and architecture that swept Europe at the beginning of the seventeenth century.

The first artist of the Baroque age was perhaps **Annibale Carracci** (1560–1609), of Bologna, whose work in the Palazzo Farnese, depicting a series of mythological scenes, prefigures the style with its overtones of fantasy, illusion and mild titillation. **Guido Reni** (1575–1642), also from Bologna, focused more on religious themes, but with a sentimentality that made his pictures popular everywhere and his work much

in demand. Less sentimental but equally dramatic, the works of **Michelangelo Merisi da Caravaggio** (d.1610) have stood the test of time better, as has his reputation, perhaps because his story fits the archetype of artist-as-outlaw that's very much in tune with modern tastes. Nonetheless his pictures were strikingly original at the time, using models from the streets for religious figures and making street life, clothes and the nitty-gritty of the human form, warts and all, a fit subject for religious art – as can be seen in his paintings in the church of Santa Maria del Popolo and other churches in Rome, where he worked for much of his life. Caravaggio was a great dramatist, composing his pictures in a theatrical manner that was increasingly typical of the times. He was also a superb technician, particularly with regard to light, and perhaps the greatest exponent of a technique known as chiaroscuro – basically the interplay of light and dark on the canvas. This style was taken up with relish by the artists of the Baroque era, and done to death by some of them, not least a group of painters from Naples – **Luca Giordano** (1632–1705), **Massimo Stanzione** (1585–1656) and **Battistello Caracciolo** (d.1637) – who raised the city's status in the art world at a time when it was becoming one of the most populous and important cities in Europe. Giordano in particular was a massively prolific painter, and you can't move for his work in Naples, though perhaps the best place to see it is the Cappella del Pio Monte della Misericordia, where one of his finest paintings hangs alongside a great work by Caravaggio, both done for the same church. Hot on the heels of these artists in Naples was **Francesco Solimena** (1657–1747), a Neapolitan late-Baroque painter who was hugely successful, and whose work is also ubiquitous, but at its best in the city's Gesù Nuovo.

A pupil of Carracci, **Domenichino** (1581–1641) also worked on the Farnese Palace, and decorated the church of Sant'Andrea delle Valle in Rome along with another student of Carracci, **Giovanni Lanfranco** (1582–1647), though the two fell out shortly after this, after which Domenichino went to Naples and relative obscurity. Lanfranco meanwhile went on to bigger and better things, becoming an expert in *sotto in su* technique and as such landing commissions for all kinds of domes and ceilings, both in Rome and in Naples. Another follower of Carracci, and also from Bologna, Giovanni Francesco Barbieri, known as **Guercino** or "the squinter" because he was cross-eyed (1591–1666), fell out with Reni, who accused him of stealing all his ideas, but who still managed to produce a fair body of work, most famous of which is his *St Petronilla* altarpiece which he painted for St Peter's but which now hangs in Rome's Capitoline Museums.

Working alongside Lanfranco in Rome, **Pietro da Cortona** (1596–1669) was another great illusionist, whose ceiling in the Palazzo Barberini in Rome is perhaps the ultimate in Baroque *sotto in su* trickery – a mass of writhing figures, clouds and drapery that are at once in the room with you and at the same time escaping into the sky beyond. The Barberini pope, Urban VIII, was the greatest pope of the Baroque age, not least because he was the patron of **Gianlorenzo Bernini** (1598–1680), who was without question the greatest Baroque artist of all, producing a lifetime's work of sculpture and architecture that more than any other defines what Baroque really means. The best of his small-scale statues – in Rome's Galleria Borghese – are virtuosic pieces of dynamic sculpture, intensely theatrical, that invite you to study them from all angles, while Bernini's work for Rome's church of Santa Maria in Vitorria, depicting the *Ecstasy of St Theresa*, is the very essence of Baroque drama.

All those who came into contact with Bernini were influenced by him, and **Giovanni Baciccia** (1639–1709) was no exception, taking on the illusionistic challenge of the age and decorating the Gesù church in Rome with a vigour and invention that rivalled even Cortona's Palazzo Barberini work. **Andrea Pozzo** (1642–1709), too, took the style's illusionism to an extreme, decorating another Jesuit Rome church, Sant'Ignazio, with one of the biggest fakes of the era – painting in a trompe l'oeil dome which from one point in the nave looks exactly like the real thing.

The eighteenth century

The late Baroque style became what is known as the **Rococo** in the early eighteenth century – basically an ornate style of interior decoration that is a toned-down and more domestic version of the Baroque. In comparison to what had gone before, the period, and indeed the eighteenth century in general, was not a great era for Italian art, partly because interior decoration was indeed what artists increasingly came to specialize in, working for the aristocracy and the wealthy merchant classes rather than their traditional patron, the Church. Landscape painting became popular, as seen in the Venetian scenes of **Francesco Guardi** (1712–93) and **Antonio Canaletto** (1697–1768), the latter of whom churned out views of Venice that were extremely popular, though he never reproduced the same quality when painting other cities. Guardi, too, painted only Venice, though with a more impressionistic style that may be more suited to modern tastes. Perhaps the greatest Italian Rococo artist, however, was **Giambattista Tiepolo** (1696–1770), whose flamboyant frescoes were sought after in palaces and castles all over Italy, although they were essentially fantasy works, used as decoration rather than for any deeper meaning – an approach that was ably continued by his son **Giandomenico Tiepolo** (1727–1804).

Later eighteenth-century Italian art took many forms – the architectural fantasies and complex etchings of **Giambattista Piranesi** (1720–78), for example, or the Venetian genre scenes of **Pietro Longhi** (1702–85). But ultimately the style that caught on was the one that prevailed over the rest of Europe, **Neoclassicism** – a movement inspired by the art and architecture of the ancient world, which at the time was being excavated in sites around Rome and in Pompeii and Herculaneum, and which for most people meant a return to truly civilized artistic ideals. **Antonio Canova** (1757–1822) was the best-known and most prolific Italian Neoclassical artist; he produced a huge body of work, although he is perhaps most famous for his renderings of Napoleon at the beginning of the nineteenth century, and in particular of Napoleon's famously sluttish sister, Pauline, in the Galleria Borghese.

The nineteenth century to the modern day

The nineteenth century, too, was not an especially auspicious time for Italian art, and the international focus was by now firmly in France and elsewhere. After Canova, the mantle of Neoclassical sculpture had been taken up by **Pietro Canonica** (1869–1959), a Rome-based sculptor who specialized in civic and public sculpture as well as busts of the rich and famous, and **Vincenzo Gemito** (1859–1929), known for his genre studies of Naples lowlife. Another Neapolitan artist, **Domenico Morelli** (1823–1901), also specialized in historical and religious themes, passing on his penchant for drama to his student **Antonio Mancini** (1852–1930). Mancini quickly developed a style of his own which had more in common with the realist movement that by this time was sweeping through France and other parts of Europe. Shortly after, around the middle of the nineteenth century, a group of painters based in Tuscany, the **Macchiaioli** movement, also tried to get away from a more traditional approach, prefiguring to some extent the French Impressionists, though they were much less influential. They saw their brief as loosening the chains of figurative painting while also depicting real-life themes, and one of their best-known figures, **Giovannia Fattori** (1825–1908), while initially concentrating on historical scenes and portraits, eventually became a painter of landscapes in a style that was influenced by the French Barbizon school.

Giovanni Fattori taught the young **Amedeo Modigliani** (1884–1920), a painter from Livorno who lived fast and died young after he decided to ditch the relatively wholesome landscapes of the Macchiaioli to concentrate on idiosyncratic depictions of the lowlife of Paris, where he died at the age of 35. The big homegrown Italian movement of the twentieth century, however, was the **Futurists**, a quasi-fascist group of abstract painters led by the poet Filippo Marinetti, who believed in the purity

of the modern world and all that went with it, including war, weaponry and in particular World War I, which unfortunately claimed their most talented painter **Umberto Boccioni** (1882–1916) as a victim. Other Futurists included **Giacomo Balla** (1871–1958) and **Carlo Carra** (1881–1966), and you can see much of their work in Rome's Galleria Nazionale d'Arte Moderna, along with selected works by perhaps the greatest and most influential Italian artist of the twentieth century, **Giorgio de Chirico** (1888–1978), who with Carra set up the **Metafisicamovement** after World War I – a reaction against Cubism and abstraction and a precursor of Dadaism and the Surrealist movement and work of Magritte. De Chirico is known for his strange dreamlike landscapes – figurative and yet unreal – which display an almost dysfunctional vision of the modern world.

Italian architecture

The architecture of Italy perhaps doesn't dominate the Western world in the same way the country's art does, but the fact remains that tracing the history of Italy's buildings is akin to tracing that of Europe in general. The Renaissance and Baroque periods are the most distinctive, but buildings and architecture from all eras make up the fabric of the Italian landscape – more, perhaps, than any other European country.

The Greeks and the Etruscans

The first great Italian builders were the **Greeks**, who, during the Hellenistic age – between the third and first century BC – left an indelible mark on the Italian regions they occupied. Greek architecture followed a very rigid system, one that has been subsequently followed on and off by just about every architectural era at some point, so it's hard to overstate their importance, which was based on the three classical orders: the Doric, the oldest and lowest; Ionic, the middle order; and Corinthian, the highest and most florid. You can find examples of each in the various **temples** the Greeks left in the south – at Paestum, just south of Naples, and at Agrigento and Siracusa in Sicily, the latter of which has been incorporated into the city's cathedral. The Greeks built small **theatres** too, two examples of which remain in Sicily, in Taormina and Siracusa.

At the same time as the Greeks were leaving their mark on the south, the **Etruscans** occupied parts of central Italy, though they didn't leave much in the way of architecture apart from a series of necropolises, at Cerveteri and Tarquinia in Lazio, and a third-century-BC gateway in Volterra in Tuscany, part of a set of walls that once encircled this ancient Etruscan city.

The Romans

The **Romans** were great and ingenious builders, and they moved architectural forms on from the Greeks, still using columns and pediments but often making these more decorative than supportive. That they could do this was down to the invention of concrete, which allowed the Romans more flexibility in what they built, and their use of the arch, the innate strength of which allowed them to build more solid yet more diverse structures. As with everything else, the Romans were less interested in aesthetics than the Greeks, and favoured function above form at all times; they also liked to build on a large scale, preferring big, grandiose, imperial structures that showed off the power of their system and empire. The Pantheon and Colosseum in Rome are just two examples of this love of size for its own sake, but really any Roman site demonstrates it.

The Roman love of order is also evident in the planned nature of their **towns**, which had their random, poor quarters but whose commercial heart, around the main forum, had a uniform style across the empire. You can see this in Rome itself, and in the ruins at nearby Ostia Antica; while settlements like Pompeii and Herculaneum demonstrate how rigid the Roman street grid could be, with three horizontal main streets – the *decumanus inferior*, *major* and *superior* – crossed at right angles by other main streets or *cardos*. The forums were surrounded by shops and businesses, law courts usually in the form of a basilica – a long building with aisles either side and at least one temple, usually a rectangular colonnaded building topped with a triangular pediment with steps leading up to the main entrance.

The Romans also built for their leisure time, constructing theatres and more usually **amphitheatres** for the staging of gladiatorial games and other spectacles. The

Colosseum in Rome is the best-known and largest example of this kind of building, but there are other impressive amphitheatres dotted all over Italy – in Pompeii and Pozzuoli near Naples, and in Verona, to name just the most intact examples.

Roman militarism led to the building of some structures that had no more purpose than to celebrate a famous victory or conquest of a new territory, the **triumphal arch** – a form which, interestingly, stayed with us right up to the nineteenth century (for example in Paris and New York). Usually they would be decorated with frieze sculptures illustrating the heroic battles. There are three intact triumphal arches in and around the Forum in Rome, and others in Benevento near Naples, in Aosta, and in Rimini and Ancona on the Adriatic coast. Another way of celebrating imperial triumphs was to decorate a **column** with sculpted friezes, but far fewer of these survive – only two in fact, in Rome, dedicated by and to the emperors Trajan and Marcus Aurelius.

Finally there are the **mausoleums** that were raised by emperors to hold the remains of themselves and their families – planned as large and fitting tributes to their imperial dynasties. As you might expect the best of these are in Rome, and most impressive is probably the mausoleum of Hadrian, which has been adapted as the Castel Sant'Angelo and is as much a medieval and Renaissance monument as a Roman one.

The early Christian and Byzantine era

The first **Christian** structures in Italy were probably the **catacombs**. A series of artificial underground tunnels and caverns, they're not strictly architecture as such, but some of the features – altars, arches and so on, used in underground places of worship – were later adopted when Christianity became the dominant religion and Christian buildings were erected above ground, too.

The first Christian buildings adopted the Roman **basilica** as their model, for example in Santa Sabina or Santa Maria Maggiore in Rome, with one main and two side aisles, and were often built on the site of a saint's martyrdom or final resting place, for example St Peter's on the Vatican Hill. Often they incorporated ancient columns from previous Roman buildings, and were quite bare. Later, the capital of the Church moved to Ravenna and early Christian architecture moved to a **Byzantine** style, with round churches, mosaics rather than paintings, and often a dome – a style which caught on quickly, and, as you can tell from looking at the skyline of Rome today, never really went away.

The Middle Ages

The first style of the **Middle Ages**, predominant during the tenth and eleventh centuries, was the **Romanesque**, identifiable by its round arches and a return to the basic basilical plan, often with transepts added – not only to add extra space but also so that the footprint of the church made the shape of a cross. There was also a tendency to build campaniles or belltowers separate from the church, and sometimes a separate baptistry too – as can be seen in Pisa, where the Duomo, Baptistry and famous leaning belltower form a perfect Romanesque ensemble. There are other superb examples of the Romanesque style in Parma and Modena, and in the south at Monreale in Sicily, whose Norman cathedral still bears a large Byzantine strain in its impressive mosaics – a bit like another Romanesque-Byzantine hybrid, the basilica of San Marco in Venice. Another fine Romanesque Italian church, and one which formed something of a blueprint for many that followed, is the church of Sant'Ambrogio in Milan.

By the twelfth century, the **Gothic** style began to dominate across Europe, characterized by its use of pointed arches, vaulting, and an emphasis on verticality, space and light. However, it never took hold in Italy to the extent it did in France or England, and as a result there are relatively few Gothic buildings here, and those that

DOMESTIC ARCHITECTURE

Italian architecture isn't just about palaces and churches: **domestic architecture** is also a source of interest and the layout of small towns and farming settlements have had as much impact on Italy's landscape as the country's better-known monuments and buildings.

HILL-TOWNS

Throughout the Middle Ages, the countryside was unsafe, unhealthy and, in many places, uncultivated, but its topography, with an abundance of hills and mountains rising steeply from fertile plains, provided natural sites for **fortified settlements** which could both remove the population from malarial swamps and bandits, and preserve the limited fertile land for cultivation.

In the period of their greatest expansion – between the twelfth and fourteenth centuries – **hill-towns** sprang up all over the peninsula. Many were superimposed on early Etruscan cities – Chiusi and Cortona – or were cave dwellings, such as Matera, in Basilicata. Most hill-towns were built within high and sometimes battlemented walls, the sheer drop afforded by these sites (often extended by the use of towers) enabling inhabitants to make good use of gravity by dropping a crushing blow onto the heads of enemies attempting to scale the walls. It was also a good way of dispatching the dead, as well as a simple form of rubbish disposal. Houses were densely packed together and constructed with materials found on or near their site, which adds to the impression that they arise naturally from their geological foundations. Most day-to-day activities were carried out in the streets, traces of which are still visible in the surviving evidence of public fountains and washhouses, wells and communal ovens. Although many hill-towns were genuinely self-contained communities, they were often under the political and economic control of the cities, particularly in north and central Italy. Each city-state set up **satellite towns** of its own, to protect trade routes or to operate as garrisons for soldiers, weaponry and food in case of war. For example, Siena established the fortified hill-town of Monteriggioni in the early thirteenth century along an important route from Rome into France, which also passed through **San Gimignano**. At roughly the same time, Florence founded similar frontier outposts, including San Giovanni Valdarno, Scarperia and Firenzuola.

VILLAS AND FARMHOUSES

If you're travelling through Tuscany, Umbria or Le Marche, you're likely to see another classic Italian structure – the **country villa** or *Casa della Mezzadria*, which became widespread during the Renaissance. Usually square in plan, it was built using a combination of brick, stone and terracotta under a tent-like roof with a dove tower (*la torre colombaia*) at its apex – doves and pigeons were adept at killing snakes and consuming weeds and also provided valuable meat for the table. The house derives its name from the system of sharecropping or *mezzadria* (based on the word *mezza* – "half"), under which the peasant farmer yielded up half his produce to the landowner. Used only occasionally by the landlord, these houses were the primary residence of the estate manager (*il fattore*), who oversaw the landlord's interests.

In contrast, the architecture of the **farming complex** (*la cascina*) was stark, with high rectangular porticoes supported by square columns. The estate accommodated four architecturally distinct elements: the owner-manager's house, which was more elaborate in design and often taller than the other buildings; housing for workers, tenement-like in character, with external balconies running along the upper floors used to dry and store crops; cow barns; and stables for horses with hay lofts above. Today, many farmhouses have been converted into tourist accommodation or agriturismi. In southern Italy the **masseria** is a more common type of farming settlement – massive, complex structures that dominate vast tracts of countryside. Consisting of a dense cluster of separate buildings, *masserie* were sometimes enclosed by a high-perimeter wall with defence towers built into it. At its largest a *masseria* virtually operated as a self-contained village incorporating church, school, medical clinic and shop, in addition to accommodating the full range of agricultural requirements for stabling, housing (of day-labourers called *braccianti*) and storage. In their purest, least altered form, village *masserie* are still visible in parts of Sicily. **Trulli**, found along the coast of Puglia and inland, form one of the most remote, curious and ancient types of farm settlement in Italy. Of uncertain origin, they consist of clusters of single circular rooms, each covered by a conical roof (see page 823).

exist have often been dulled by the heavier lines of the Renaissance style that succeeded it. The style was adopted most successfully in Venice, where a particular form of florid Gothic architecture took root and is in evidence throughout the city – in the Palazzo Ducale most prominently, but also in some of the buildings on the Grand Canal; the Ca' Foscari and Palazzo Giustinian, for example. Otherwise there are isolated examples of the Gothic style throughout the country: Cistercian abbeys like that of Fossanova in Lazio; some of the French-looking churches of the Angevin monarchs of Naples, in particular the monastic complex of Santa Chiara; and the cathedral in Siena, which exhibits a peculiarly Italian form of the Gothic style – very ornate on the outside, much like the nearby cathedral of Orvieto in Umbria. Perhaps the most impressive Gothic building in Italy, at least from a purists' point of view, is the cathedral of Milan, a vast building which took five hundred years to build but exhibits all the classic features of the style, with a facade and roof that is a forest of pinnacles.

The Renaissance

Spreading through Italy from the fifteenth century onwards, the **Renaissance** was perhaps the high point of Italian architecture, as it was in the arts and most other disciplines, and its influence on building methods and styles remains to this day. Essentially, the Renaissance ushered in the period of the professional architect rather than a collection of masons, whose vision of a building was paramount; it also led to a spread of architectural ideas and techniques to domestic as well as religious and royal buildings.

Florence was at the heart of the Renaissance and the architect who led its revival was **Filippo Brunelleschi** (1377–1446), who became famous for designing an elegant dome to top the city's Gothic cathedral – a dome which was not only a magnificent engineering feat at the time but is still the most enduring symbol of the city today. Brunelleschi was familiar with and keen to emulate the building methods and feats of ancient Rome and Greece but was also successful in creating his own style, which incorporated the methods of the past but in an increasingly modern way. As such, he more than anyone is responsible for the fact that so many modern buildings still incorporate the columns and capitals, pediments and frames of ancient Greece and Rome.

Another Florentine, **Michelozzo di Bartolomeo** (1396–1471), succeeded Brunelleschi as chief architect of the cathedral, and built the seminal Medici-Ricciardi palace – a prototype for the classic Renaissance palace, with its rustic basement and more refined first floor. He worked on a number of other Florentine buildings at the time including the "tribune" of the Annunziata church, which he designed as an ancient Roman temple – a design which was finished off by **Leone Battista Alberti** (1404–72). Alberti was like Leonardo da Vinci in that he was the complete Renaissance man, skilled in all disciplines but perhaps excelling at architecture, although unlike his contemporaries he had nothing to do with the actual building of any of his designs. His focus was on the aesthetic of a building rather than what made it stand up, and as such he could let his imagination run riot, which he did in buildings like the Palazzo Rucellai in Florence, the Tempio Malatestiano in Rimini and the church of Sant'Andrea in Mantua.

The building of the Palazzo Rucellai was overseen by **Bernardo Rossellino** (1409–64), another architect who had a big influence both in Florence and beyond. He also completed the work on Brunelleschi's cathedral dome and is perhaps best known for the design and creation of the Renaissance "new town" of Pienza for Pope Pius II.

The High Renaissance

Arguably the greatest architect of the **High Renaissance** was **Donato Bramante** (1443–1514), who learned a lot from his Florentine predecessors but spun it into a style of his

own, in the ingenious rebuildings of the churches of San Satiro and Santa Marie delle Grazie in Milan, and most famously in his little Tempietto in Rome, which faithfully turned back to the classical orders of the past but with a small-scale sensibility that was very much of its time. Bramante's best years were in Rome, and he was commissioned to develop the buildings of the Vatican Palace as well as rebuilding St Peter's itself. The Greek-cross plan he came up with for the latter never saw the light of day, but the building was started while he was alive and as such he must take credit for at least part of it.

The St Peter's project spanned more than a century, and Bramante's place was taken by **Michelangelo** (1475–1564), who added the dome but died before he could achieve very much. In Rome, the other great artist of the High Renaissance, **Raphael** (1483–1520), undertook architectural commissions too, designing the Chigi chapel in the church of Santa Maria del Popolo and encouraging his pupil **Giulio Romano** (1499–1546) to take on vast projects such as the Palazzo del Te in Mantua. Raphael decorated another building for the Chigi family in Rome, the Villa Farnesina, which was built to the designs of **Baldassare Peruzzi** (1481–1536), an important architect who designed much in his native Siena, and who worked on the Villa Farnese in Caprarola in Lazio with **Antonio Sangallo the Younger** (1483–1546) – the most talented member of a family of architects. Sangallo was very much the successor of Bramante and Raphael in Rome, and was responsible – again along with a very aged Michelangelo – for perhaps the city's finest Renaissance palace, the supremely elegant and dignified Palazzo Farnese, in 1514.

Meanwhile **Jacopo Sansovino** (1486–1570) was the principal architect at the time in Venice, and was responsible for many of the large public buildings around Piazza San Marco, most notably the Library and Loggetta, as well as several churches, all of which display an inventiveness that plays well with the fripperies of the existing Venetian-Gothic buildings there. Not far from Venice, in Vicenza, **Andrea Palladio** (1508–80) achieved an influence that stretched far and wide, with his refined take on Renaissance principles, building a number of palaces and villas between 1540 and 1580 that became the apotheosis of the refined country house – a symmetrical central block, with a columned portico and a central dome. Palladio rigorously followed classical rules and while this means his buildings sometimes appear dull, it is also perhaps the reason why his principles are still alive today.

In Rome, **Giacomo Vignola** (1507–73) took over as the latest architect to oversee the progress of St Peter's and at the same time built the influential church of the Gesù in the city, to a striking new design that dispensed with aisles and focused everything on the enormous cupola and the high altar. The church, or at least its facade, was finished by **Giacomo della Porta** (1533–1602), who unwittingly came up with a design that more or less every Roman church would follow for a century or more – one which used all the columns and pediments of the classical orders, but mixed them up in a new and freer way than before, with scrollwork and other features that heralded the new, flashier age of the Baroque.

The Baroque era

As in painting and sculpture, the **Baroque era** was one of massive change, with the Church defiant in the face of the Reformation sweeping across the rest of Europe, and looking for new ways to keep the faithful on message. The theatrical and dramatic nature of the painting and sculpture at the time seeped into architecture, too, and nowhere more so than in Rome, where the Baroque became the dominant architectural style – and the one that most defines the city today (much as Florence is above all defined by the Renaissance).

The chief architect of this time was **Carlo Maderno** (1556–1629), and it was he who took over and at long last finished St Peter's, some would say by ruining its original

design and converting it to a Latin cross, which undermined the original dome-focused plan. It's the St Peter's of Maderno that you see today, and the church is in many ways a Baroque church inside and out – much like the piazza outside, whose columned arms are the brainchild of the greatest sculptor and architect of the Baroque age, **Gianlorenzo Bernini** (1598–1680). Bernini was a prodigy of the most amazing kind, the son of a sculptor and extremely successful – as a sculptor – while still very young. He was enormously talented and incredibly prolific, which means that he more than anyone else may have shaped the Rome you see today. Patronized as he was by the pope at the time, Urban VIII, Bernini created the features that define the interior of St Peter's, not least the vast and flashy baldachino under the dome, and although he only gravitated towards architecture later in life he is responsible for a variety of buildings and architectural features around the rest of the city. He restored Piazza Navona and added the massive Fountain of the Four Rivers as its centrepiece; he built the small oval church of Sant'Andrea delle Quirinale; and he worked on the enormous Palazzo Barberini, the seat of his benefactor Urban VIII, as well as the Montecitorio and Chigi palaces.

It's said that the figure in Bernini's Fountain of the Four Rivers in Rome is shielding its eyes from the horrors of the nearby church of Sant'Agnese in Agone, because it was built by **Francesco Borromini** (1599–1667), his greatest rival, and the only one who came close to Bernini in talent at the time. As well as being more of an architect, Borromini was a very different sort of man to Bernini: more troubled, and much less of a man about town, but he, too, left his mark on Rome, becoming known as an architect who could come up with ingenious solutions to thorny architectural problems, often shoehorning grand buildings into sites for which they were ill suited – for example the churches of San Carlo alle Quattro Fontane and Sant'Ivo alla Sapienza, both of which are clever and unique designs. He also worked with Bernini on the Palazzo Barberini, adding a lovely circular staircase as a counterpart to Bernini's more traditional rectangular one.

The other great Baroque architect active in Rome was **Pietro da Cortona** (1596–1669), who contributed to the Palazzo Barberini (see page 73), but who also designed the clever and very theatrical church of Santa Maria della Pace and its small piazza. Outside of Rome, the big centres for the Baroque were in southern Italy – in **Naples**, where architects like **Cosimo Fanzago** (1591–1678) and **Fernando Sanfelice** (1675–1748) were active, and in **Lecce**, whose central core is a Baroque extravaganza, with an array of exuberant buildings fashioned from the soft local sandstone.

Neoclassicism

Like much of the rest of Europe, Italy entered a relatively bland era after the Baroque – deliberately so, for the spirit of the **Neoclassical** movement that followed was essentially a revolt against the excesses of the Baroque style, and at heart a return to the solid principles of classicism. **Luigi Vanvitelli** (1700–73) was probably the foremost eighteenth-century Italian architect. The son of a Dutch landscape painter living in Naples, he worked with **Nicola Salvi** (1697–1751) on the Rococo fantasy, Rome's Trevi Fountain, and later, after a handful of small commissions in Rome, designed and built the enormous Royal Palace at Caserta in 1752, a massive Versailles-like blend of both perfect symmetry and ludicrous grandiloquence, as well as remodelling the more restrained Palazzo Reale in nearby Naples. His successor as most prominent Italian architect was **Giuseppe Valadier** (1762–1839), a purer exponent of Neoclassical principles, who taught architecture at Rome's Accademia San Luca and laid out many key parts of the city centre, including the great open space of the Piazza del Popolo, the Pincio and the streets leading off it.

The nineteenth century saw the construction of a series of **shopping arcades** in the big Italian cities – the Galleria Umberto in Naples, what is now the Galleria Sordi

in Rome and perhaps most successfully the Galleria Vittorio Emanuele II in Milan, built in 1865 by **Giuseppe Mengoni** (1829–77), who unfortunately died when he fell from the roof a few days before it opened. Around this time, the era of the Unification of Italy, Rome was remodelled as a capital fit for the new country, and it saw a huge amount of construction. Much of it was a mixture of the functional nineteenth-century apartment buildings that you find in most European capitals and the odd piece of faux-grandeur like the semicircular Piazza della Repubblica at the top of Via Nazionale, or, most strikingly, the hideous Vittoriano monument overlooking Piazza Venezia, the work of one **Giuseppe Sacconi** (1854–1905) in 1895 – though even this monstrosity has become accepted over the years.

The modern era

The early **twentieth century** saw several international styles touch Italy in some way, for example Art Nouveau, but none really caught on and there wasn't a new indigenous architectural movement until the **Futurists**. Chief architect of the Futurists was **Antonio Sant'Elia** (1888–1916), who never really built anything but had far-reaching ideas about the modern city that at the time were more science fiction than anything else. **Giuseppe Terragni** (1904–43) was his true heir, an arch-rationalist who built the Casa del Fascio in Como in 1936, and was the designer of an unrealized project in Rome based on Dante's *Divine Comedy* as a tribute to the Italian poet. Terragni worked under Mussolini but died young, after which Mussolini's preferred architect became **Marcello Piacentini** (1881–1960), who was responsible for some of the most celebrated of Il Duce's architecture – the Stadio dei Marmi, the housing complex of Garbatella and EUR, all in Rome, as well as the chilling open space of Brescia's Piazza della Vittoria. Piacentini worked on EUR's Palazzo dello Sport with **Pier Luigi Nervi** (1891–1979), a celebrated Italian architect who specialized in buildings based around prefabricated and reinforced concrete and who later became known for enormous works such as aircraft hangars, the trade-fair halls in Turin, and the Olympic Stadium and the Papal Audience Chamber in Rome. Nervi worked with another Italian architect, **Gio Ponti** (1891–1979), on the prestigious and at the time – 1950 – audacious Pirelli Tower in Milan, until recently still the tallest building in Italy. Ponti was a great Italian designer as well as architect and set up the bilingual design magazine *Domus*, which is still in circulation today.

Perhaps the best-known Italian architect of the current era is **Renzo Piano** (b.1937), though more for his work outside Italy than in his home country. Famous initially for his Paris Beaubourg collaboration with Richard Rogers, he has since worked on numerous prestige projects around the world – Hong Kong's airport, the redesign of Potsdamer Platz in Berlin, London's Shard and many big museum projects and extensions. But he returned to his roots at the start of the new century, designing the hugely successful Auditorium Parco della Musica in Rome and the Padre Pio pilgrimage church at San Giovanni Rotondo.

An A–Z of Italian film

From the earliest days of cinema, the Italians have always been passionate movie-lovers and movie makers. But Italy's films really came to the forefront of world cinema in the postwar period; this was partly due to the location shift from studio-based films to the country's towns and landscape. Their style and technique were groundbreaking, and the use of real sites added a dimension, a mood, which made Italian cinema linger in the memory.

8 1/2 (1963). Fellini's most autobiographical film, about a "blocked" film director recalling his past life, loves and successes. It's also perhaps his most revered movie, though you could at a pinch call it self-indulgent. The title refers to the number of films Fellini had directed up to that point.

Amarcord (1973). One of several Fellini films that uses the director's home town of Rimini as a location, this time under Fascism. Also very autobiographical, it's a tale of youth and a satire of the Church and Mussolini all rolled into one.

Aprile (1998). Nanni Moretti appears to be continually questioning the worth of everything, including his own work, and in fact went too far for some critics in this movie, which focuses on his inability to decide how to finish his films – or even whether to finish them. Although poorly received, it's still a very funny film.

Bicycle Thieves (1948). A young boy is the witness to his father's humiliation in De Sica's classic movie, set in the poorer quarters of Rome, when he sees him steal a bicycle out of desperation (to get his job back) and immediately get caught. The child's illusions are dashed, and the blame is laid on society for not providing the basic human requirements, although in retrospect its message seems politically ambiguous – the masses are seen as hostile, and the only hope seems to lie in the family unit, which the hero falls thankfully back on at the end.

The Brownnose (1991). Daniele Luchetti's film satirizes the favoured Italian way of outwitting the system and getting things done – and the oiling of the wheels of bureaucracy by means of gifts and bribery involves the antihero in all manner of scrapes.

Cabiria (1914). The Italians were once famous for their silent costume epics, often set in the period of the Roman Empire, anticipating the Fascist nostalgia for ancient Rome by at least a decade. This film by Giovanni Pastrone, set in ancient Carthage, was the most sophisticated and innovative of the genre, with spectacular sets and lighting effects that were imitated by the American director D.W. Griffith.

Casanova (1976). Fellini's take on the notorious womanizer is an oddly (and deliberately) artificial-looking film. It wasn't actually shot in Venice, and the water in the lagoon is, in fact, a shaken plastic sheet – an odd backlash against the real landscapes of the Neorealists.

Christ Stopped at Eboli (1979). A surprisingly unincisive critique of "the problem of the south", set in a poverty-stricken mountain village in Basilicata.

Cinema Paradiso (1988). Giuseppe Tornatore's Oscar-winning movie was shot in the director's native village near Palermo, and tells its story through a series of flashbacks. The central figure, a successful film director named Salvatore, returns to the village for the funeral of the projectionist of the magical Cinema Paradiso of his childhood, only to find that it is about to be razed to make way for a car park.

The City of Women (1980). This dream-like, late Fellini film explores the great Italian director's own sexual fantasies, using Marcello Mastroianni to act them out.

Come Te Nessuno Mai (1999). This coming-of-age story by Gabriele Muccino is an interesting take on the US high-school comedy genre; his very Italian students are highly politicized youngsters, planning strikes and taking part in a 24-hour sit-in, both of which provide a backdrop for the inevitable angst and first love.

The Conformist (1970). One of Bertolucci's early films, adapted from the novel by Alberto Moravia, with a spiritually empty hero searching for father substitutes in Fascist Rome in a dream-like jumble of flashbacks. *The Conformist* was Bertolucci's first step on the path to world recognition.

Dear Diary (1993). Director, actor and screenwriter Nanni Moretti achieved great acclaim with this film in three parts, covering such diverse subjects as twentieth-century archi-tecture, children and telephones, Pasolini's unsolved murder, the myth of rural idyll, and Moretti's own fight against cancer. Much of the film is spent following Moretti on his scooter through Rome, or travelling by ferry from one island to another.

Death in Venice (1971). Style constantly threatened to overtake content in Visconti's work, and this film version of Thomas Mann's novella about a washed-up writer obsessed by a young boy is perhaps the best example, dripping with emotion and visual set pieces. Mann's writer is a composer in Visconti's film, enabling the director to lay on the strings of Mahler with a trowel.

Decameron (1971). Pasolini's film of the Italian literary classic was a record hit at the box office because of its explicit sex scenes, although the director's intention had been

political rather than salacious, with Boccaccio's fourteenth-century tales transposed from their original middle-class Florentine setting to the dispossessed of Naples.

The Earth Trembles (1948). This version of the nineteenth-century Sicilian author Giovanni Verga's novel *The House by the Medlar Tree* is about a family of fishermen destroyed by circumstance, and was shot on location on the stark Sicilian coast, using an entire village as cast, speaking in their native Sicilian (with an Italian voice-over and subtitles). There's a pervading atmosphere of stoic fatalism and a truly sophisticated visual style incorporating stunning tableaux.

The Eclipse (1962). Antonioni used the impersonal Stock Exchange building in Rome as the background to this slow-moving tale of doomed love. Short on plot, but with a memorable visual subtlety.

The Garden of the Finzi-Continis (1970). Vittorio De Sica's film about a Jewish family living in prewar Ferrara captures perfectly the elegiac, dreamy quality of Giorgio Bassani's great novel.

Germany, Year Zero (1947). The final, desolate film of Rossellini's "War Trilogy", set in the ruins of postwar Berlin, and telling the story of a child whom circumstances push to suicide.

Gold of Naples (1955). A film about Naples basically, directed by Vittorio De Sica, following six different Neapolitan characters whose lives are ultimately interconnected. It stars two of the most successful Neapolitan actors of all time – Sophia Loren and Totò.

Gomorrah (2008). Based on Roberto Saviano's bestselling book about the Neapolitan Camorra, this is a tough film, portraying a Naples you're unlikely to see on any visit – it's shot in the housing projects north of the city and uses locals as actors.

Good Morning Babylon (1987). Perhaps the Taviani brothers' best film, tracking the life journeys of two brothers who make their fortune in Hollywood during the silent-movie era but end up fighting on opposite sides in World War I. A big, epic film, beautifully made.

The Gospel According to Matthew (1964). Pasolini's film is a radical inter-pretation of a familiar story – the life of Christ as detailed in the gospel of St Matthew. As you might expect in a Pasolini film, Christ is a radical, intent on changing the world, and not necessarily by peaceful means either.

Hands Over the City (1963). This docudrama by Francesco Rosi and starring Rod Steiger is a brutal critique of the mob-dominated construction industry in Naples. Perhaps the most shocking thing about it is that it could still be made today.

Ignorant Fairies (2001). Themes of love, loss and deception wrapped up in a soundtrack of Middle Eastern and Latin music. Commenting on the current changes in Italian film, the director Ozpetek says, "The public is more demanding now. At the same time, people have become more willing to experiment. Before they would have looked to foreign films for that type of cinema."

Il Divo (2008). Paolo Sorrentino's biopic of the power-addicted and most influential figure of postwar Italian politics, Giulio Andreotti, which pulled no punches and perhaps should be judged by the reaction of its subject, who walked out halfway through.

Il Postino (1994). Michael Radford's film is a humorous tale set in 1930s Italy, which follows the artistic and political awakening of the central character, played by Italian comic Massimo Troisi (who sadly died soon after the film's completion).

I Vitelloni (1953). All through his long career Fellini used films as a kind of personal notebook in which to hark back to his youth. This is set in an unrecognizable Rimini, his birthplace, before the days of mass tourism.

Journey to Italy (1953). A well-to-do couple visit Italy – specifically Naples – and inherit an estate, running into problems in their relationship. A powerful film, much of which was scripted on location or improvised, it's full of brooding atmosphere and is perhaps Rossellini's best work.

Kaos (1984). An adapation of Pirandello stories shot in scenic Sicily, both loving of the Italian landscape and redolent of a time past.

La Dolce Vita (1960). Marcello Mastroianni is the now-iconic *paparazzo* in Fellini's stylish 1960s classic about celebrity, style – and ultimately emptiness.

La Grande Bellezza (2013). Paolo Sorrentino's masterpiece – a luscious *Dolce Vita* for the Berlusconi era – is the most widely lauded Italian film of the last decade. The central character, a world-weary writer hitting a late-life crisis, finds some solace in memory and the beauties of Rome, which has never looked more seductive than here.

La Luna (1979). Jill Clayburgh stars in this tale of the tortured son of a tortured opera singer, directed by Bertolucci at the beginning of his career. It's hard to care about the characters, but it's undeniably beautifully put together.

La Notte (1961). The bleak townscape of industrial Milan is the backdrop for this Francesco Rosi film. Not a lot happens, but it's deftly done, with slow, lingering scenes and dialogue.

La Sconosciuta (2006). Tornatore's film involves an East European prostitute forced to abandon her children as she tries to earn a living in an Italian town.

The Last Kiss (2001). Muccino's romantic comedy, dealing with panic at parenthood and the chasing of vanishing youth, won a flurry of awards and universal approval.

La Strada (1954). One of Fellini's early films, and following a recogniz-ably realistic storyline (unlike his later movies). Also, his characters are motivated by human values rather than social ones – searching for love instead of solidarity.

L'Avventura (1960). The volcanic landscape of Sicily is the sensuous backdrop for this typically bleak yet perceptive

Antonioni tale of middle-class relationships and ultimately amoral choices.

Le Quattro Volte (2010). Set in the depths of rural Calabria, Michelangelo Frammartino's quasi-documentary is a meditation on life, death and rebirth, beginning with the final decline of an elderly goatherd, before moving through episodes that focus on the animal, vegetable and mineral worlds. Slow-moving and almost devoid of dialogue, this is austerely beautiful and deeply moving.

Life is Beautiful (1997). Roberto Benigni's film stars himself and his wife, Nicoletta Braschi, as parents striving to protect the innocence of their child amid the horrors of the Holocaust. For many, the combination of sentimental comedy and genocide was unbearably poignant; others found it unbearably crass.

Light of My Eyes (2001). Set in Rome, this is a haunting exploration of the alienation that many feel in their lives and their romantic relationships. The story is particularly strong thanks to the character of Maria, the female lead, free of the usual stereo-types and beautifully acted and directed by Giuseppe Piccioni.

Luna Rossa (2001). Neapolitan director Antonio Capuano's mesmeriz-ing portrayal of a Camorra family from the inside, borrowing from Greek tragedy for its structure and with a soundtrack by indie-rockers Almamegretta. Visually rich, brooding, confusing and violent, the film is artistically assured in a way that few others have been in recent years.

Many Wars Ago (1970). Rosi's film about the inhumanity of war depicts a mutiny among Italian troops on the Austrian front during World War I.

Mario's War (2005). Capuano's gritty film looks at a well-to-do Neapolitan family who foster a disturbed boy.

Marrakech Express (1989). Not the Crosby, Stills & Nash song, but a Salvatores' road movie telling the story of a group of seven young Italians setting off for Morocco in search of their friend.

Mediterraneo (1991). This Gabriele Salvatores film shows eight reluctant Italian sailors stranded on a Greek island in 1941, and recounts their gradual integration into local life. It won an Oscar for Best Foreign Language Film the year of its release.

Mery per Sempre (1989). Marco Risi films deal with specific social problems, and this follows the lives of half a dozen youngsters in prison. Its sequel, *Ragazzi Fuori* (1990), shows them fresh out of jail.

Mid-August Lunch (2008). The directorial debut of *Gomorrah* scriptwriter Gianni di Gregorio, and it couldn't be more different: a gentle comedy about a hapless middle-aged man who cares for his mother in a Trastevere flat and ends up making lunch for a group of elderly ladies. For once, a movie that celebrates being old.

Miracle in Milan (1951). Vittorio De Sica's fantastic fable, about a young man who is given a white dove which possesses the power to grant the wishes of everyone living in his slummy suburb. Surreal special effects are used to create a startling impact, for example in a shot of the hero and heroine flying high above the pinnacles of Milan cathedral on a broomstick.

Novecento (1976). Bertolucci's historical masterpiece spans the first half of the twentieth century and is deliberately epic in scale, following the fates of two brothers as they make their way through World War I, the rise of Fascism and beyond. It's six hours long (though split into two parts), but the story is well told with a compelling narrative.

Obsession (1943). Luchino Visconti's adaptation of the American novel *The Postman Always Rings Twice* – a lowlife story of adultery and murder transposed to northern Italy – was something new in Italian cinema: it had an honesty and intensity, a lack of glamour, that pointed the way to the Neorealist films of the immediate postwar period.

Open Doors (1990). Gianni Amelio's political drama is set in Fascist Palermo just before World War II, but its subject matter – a liberal judge being obstructed in his investigations of all-pervasive corruption – was particularly apposite at the time.

Padre Padrone (1977). The Taviani brothers' mini-epic set in Sardinia details the showdown between an overbearing father and his rebellious son.

Paisà (1946). The second film of Rossellini's "War Trilogy" traces the Allied Occupation north from Sicily to the Po Valley, in six self-contained episodes.

Pinocchio (2002). Adapted from the Italian writer Carlo Collodi's 1880 fable, this Roberto Benigni film grossed US$7m in its first weekend, a new record at the Italian box office. Benigni doubles as star and director, playing opposite his wife, Braschi, who is the blue-haired fairy.

Puerto Escondido (1992). A slightly far-fetched plot, in which an ordinary man is shot by bank robbers and ends up living in a commune in Mexico. But, as in all Salvatores' movies, the story is well told and ultimately meaningful.

Red Desert (1964). The alienating oil refineries and power plants at Ravenna make a perfect setting for this movie in what is the cinematic equivalent of an existential novel.

Roma (1972). Religion is a major theme in Fellini's work, and he's at his best when satirizing the Roman Catholic Church, as in the grotesque clerical fashion parade in this, one of his best-known movies.

Rome, Open City (1945). As the tanks were rolling out of Rome in 1945, Roberto Rossellini cobbled together the bare minimum of finances, crew and equipment and started shooting this movie, using real locations, documentary footage and low-grade film, and coming up with a grainy, idiosyncratic style that influenced not only his Italian contemporaries, but also the American film noir of the late 1940s.

Sailing Home (2001). Vincenzo Marra's movie was made on a shoestring budget: it uses fishermen rather than

REALISM AND NEOREALISM IN ITALIAN CINEMA

The Fascist regime was surprisingly slow to recognize the potential of the cinema, but in 1937 Mussolini inaugurated **Cinecittà**, the film studio complex just outside Rome that is still the nerve centre of the Italian movie industry, to produce a stream of propagandist films.

The late 1930s and early 1940s saw an element of documentary-style **realism** creep into film-making: contemporary social themes were addressed; nonprofessional actors were sometimes used; and directors – even those with the official stamp of approval – made the occasional realistic documentary, with none of the bombast or gloss of the typical Fascist film. It was on films such as these that future Neorealist directors such as Luchino Visconti, Roberto Rossellini and Vittorio De Sica worked their apprenticeships, learning techniques that they would draw on a few years later when they were allowed to unleash their creative imaginations.

In 1945, Rossellini's groundbreaking *Rome, Open City* ushered in a new wave of **Neorealism**. This movement had no manifesto, but its main exponents – again, Rossellini, De Sica and Visconti – intended their films to present the everyday stuff of life and not romantic dreams. They developed specific aims (even if they didn't always stick to them), to show real people rather than conventional heroes, real time, real light and real places – using nonactors and shooting on location, not in studios.

professional actors, is spoken in Neapolitan dialect (at home it was released with Italian subtitles) and was shot in semidocumentary style.

Salvatore Giuliano (1962). Francesco Rosi's film traces the story of a bandit from Sicily's mountains who became a hero on the island after his violent death in the 1950s. One of the best films about Sicily and the Mafia you'll ever see, and perhaps the only one that never mentions the M-word.

Senso (1954). This adaptation of a nineteenth-century novel opens to the strains of Verdi in the Venice opera house, La Fenice, one night in 1866, and is Visconti's view of the politically controversial Unification, portrayed through the lives of a few aristocrats. It was the first major Italian film to be made in colour.

Shoeshine (1946). An anatomy of a friendship between two Roman boys, destroyed first by black-marketeers, then by the police. Like many Neorealist films, children are seen as the innocent victims of adult corruption.

The Son's Room (2001). Winner of the Palme d'Or at Cannes, Nanni Moretti's exploration of a family's bereavement is a much darker work than his more famous *Dear Diary*.

The Spider's Strategem (1970). Filmed in the strange, star-shaped Renaissance town of Sabbioneta near Mantua, this was the first of many feature films sponsored by RAI, the Italian state TV network, and is about a destructive father-son relationship with flashbacks to the Fascist era.

Splendor (1989). The owner of the cinema in a small provincial town is forced to sell up to a property developer in Ettore Scola's nostalgic film.

Stolen Children (1992). One of Gianni Amelio's best-known films outside Italy deals with corrupt society as seen through the eyes of a child.

Theorem (1968). Pasolini's film intercuts shots of a spiritually empty middle-class Milanese family, into which a mysterious young stranger insinuates himself, with desolate scenes of a volcanic wasteland.

Three Brothers (1981). Three different political attitudes, as the brothers of the title, reunited for their mother's funeral back home in Puglia, argue, reminisce and dream.

Toto Che Visse Due Volte (1998). Daniele Cipri and Franco Maresco's film, set in Sicily, ruffled a few feathers with its violation of religious and sexual taboos, but this iconoclastic work didn't trouble the Establishment. When the film censors banned its release, the deputy prime minister – a film buff – stepped in and disbanded their board.

Totò Looks for a Home (1949). The Neapolitan comic actor Totò had a colossal career spanning several decades. Here, he and his family search for somewhere to live in the postwar ruins of Rome, in a comic variation on a Neorealist theme.

The Tree of Wooden Clogs (1978). Ermanno Olmi's film has a cast from Bergamo speaking dialect with Italian subtitles, and was a worldwide hit.

Vento di Terra (2004). Vincenzo Marra's follow up to *Sailing Home* was shot in Naples, and depicts life in the city as hard and unrewarding.

The Way We Laughed (1998). One of Amelio's most successful recent films, this is the story of two brothers leaving rural Sicily for Turin in the late 1950s – a nostalgic film that suggests the present-day malaises Italy is experienc-ing have their roots in the late 1950s and early 1960s.

We Have a Pope (2011). Nanni Moretti is seen by some as Rome's Woody Allen, chronicling the lives and neuroses of the city's inhabitants with a series of gentle, well-acted and sophisticated human comedies. This film follows a man elected against his will as the new pope, and how he deals with the panic that ensues.

The White Sheikh (1952). The heroine of this film falls in love with the Valentino-type actor playing the romantic lead for "photo romance" comics (being shot on the coast outside Rome), and has her illusions dashed when reality intervenes and he makes a bungling attempt to seduce her.

Yesterday, Today, Tomorrow (1965). This Vittorio De Sica comedy tells the stories of three Italian women: a cigarette seller in Naples, a prostitute in Rome and the wife of an industria-list in Milan. Marcello Mastroianni is superb, as is Sophia Loren, who also gets her kit off (well, almost).

Books

TRAVEL CLASSICS

Henry James *Italian Hours*. Urbane travel pieces from the young James; perceptive about particular monuments and works of art, superb on the different atmospheres of Italy.

D.H. Lawrence *D.H. Lawrence and Italy*. Lawrence's three Italian travelogues collected into one volume. *Sea and Sardinia* and *Twilight in Italy* combine the author's seemingly natural ill temper when travelling with a genuine sense of regret for a way of life almost visibly passing away. *Etruscan Places*, published posthumously, consists of his more philosophical musings on Etruscan art and civilization.

Norman Lewis *Naples '44*. Lewis was among the first Allied troops to move into Naples following the Italian surrender in World War II, and this is his diary of his experiences there – it is without question the finest thing you can read on World War II in Italy. Lewis's more recent *In Sicily* is a broad contemporary portrait of the island he has married into and returns to frequently.

Mary McCarthy *The Stones of Florence/Venice Observed*. Published now in a single volume, this mixture of high-class reporting on the contemporary cities and anecdotal detail on their histories is one of the few accounts of these two cities that doesn't read as if it's been written in a library.

Jan Morris *Venice* (titled *The World of Venice* in US). Some people think this is the most acute modern book written about any Italian city, while others find it unbearably fey. At least give it a look. The author has more recently published what she claims is her final book, *Trieste and the Meaning of Nowhere*, an aptly elegiac salute to this curious frontier city.

CONTEMPORARY TRAVEL AND IMPRESSIONS

Matthew Fort *Eating Up Italy*. Food writer Fort's voyage around Italy on a Vespa, discovering the mainland by eating its food from region to region, and painting an eloquent picture of the contemporary country. See also his more recent *Sweet Honey, Bitter Lemons*, which focuses on Sicily.

Annie Hawes *Extra Virgin*. Belonging to the Mayes/Mayle school of expats abroad, but superior to most of the genre, this relates how two sisters overcome various adversities and much local incomprehension to find their idyll on a Ligurian mountain. It's funny and smart, interspersed with plenty of culinary culture and peasant lore.

Frances Mayes *Under the Tuscan Sun*; *Bella Tuscany*. The trials and triumphs of American author and her boyfriend as they renovate a farmhouse near Cortona, interspersed with recipes.

Peter Moore *Vroom with a View*. Moore is an entertaining and honest travel companion on this Bryson-like tour of Italy on a battered scooter, sharing all the highs and lows along the way. A fun and light-hearted holiday read.

★ **Tim Parks** *Italian Neighbours*; *An Italian Education*; *A Season with Verona*. Novelist Tim Parks has lived in Italy since 1981. The first two of these deftly told tales of family life examine what it means to be Italian, and how national identity is absorbed. *A Season with Verona* relates his passion for his local football team, but draws in much more besides.

HISTORY

Jérôme Carcopino *Daily Life in Ancient Rome*. Detailed but never dull, this is a seminal work of Roman social history, with background on everything from education and religion to domestic daily rituals.

Edward Gibbon *The History of the Decline and Fall of the Roman Empire*. Awe-inspiring in its erudition, Gibbon's masterpiece is one of the greatest histories ever written, and one of the finest compositions of English prose. Penguin publishes an abridged version for those without the time to tackle the entire work.

David Gilmour *The Pursuit of Italy*. This one-volume paperback is easily the most digestible history of Italy you can buy. It's full of interesting contemporary insights, and what it lacks in detail it more than makes up for in readability.

★ **Paul Ginsborg** *A History of Contemporary Italy*. A scholarly but readable account of postwar Italian history, illustrating the complexity of contending economic, social and political currents. Bringing the story up to date, Ginsborg's *Italy and Its Discontents* unravels the knotty background to Berlusconi's rise to power.

Robert Hughes *Rome*. The Australian art historian's stab at writing a definitive, chronological guide to the city's art and architecture, and not a bad effort – a big book, but beautifully written and very engaging, with lots of cultural and historical background, anecdote and opinion.

Valerio Lintner *A Traveller's History of Italy*. A brief history of the country, from the Etruscans right up to the present day. Well written and sensibly concise, it's just the thing for the dilettante historian of the country.

★ **Mark Thompson** *The White War*. Italy's role in World War I is just a sideshow in many non-Italian histories of the conflict, and is often misrepresented within the country. Thompson's book is a magisterial account of the catastrophes and triumphs of the Italian campaign, and a brilliant expli-cation of the part the war has played in forming the nation's self-image.

ITALIAN CRIME FICTION

Andrea Camilleri *The Shape of Water*; *The Terracotta Dog*; *The Snack Thief*; and others. Camilleri is perhaps the best known and most translated of the current wave of Italian crime writers, and his Inspector Montalbano series, set in Sicily, has achieved worldwide popularity. Rightly so – the plots, characterization (Montelbano is a classic maverick cop with a complicated personal life), and contemporary Sicilian background make for an absorbing and entertaining read.

Michael Dibdin *Cabal*; *Ratking*; and others. Not all of the late Michael Dibdin's novels are set in Rome, but the author was as interested in Italy as in his characters, with the result that his Aurelio Zen novels tell us plenty about the way Italian society operates – and they're well-plotted whodunnits to boot, with Zen as a classically eccentric, loner detective.

Michele Giuttari *A Florentine Death*; *A Death in Tuscany*; *The Death of a Mafia Don*. Giuttari is the former police chief of Florence, and he uses all his knowledge and experience to put together these tightly plotted police procedurals, with lots of local colour.

Donna Leon *Death at La Fenice*; *A Venetian Reckoning*; *Fatal Remedies*; and others. Venice-based crime thrillers featuring Guido Brunetti, the honest police *commissario* in a world of high-level intrigue and corruption.

Iain Pears *The Raphael Affair*; *The Bernini Bust*; *The Titian Committee*; *Death and Restoration*; and others. Recently reissued, and rightly so, Pears' successful series of thrillers with an art historical theme are all set in Rome and make great holiday reading. There are plenty of local settings and descriptions, not to mention fast-paced art-world intrigue, with robbery, forgery and general skulduggery.

CRIME AND SOCIETY

★ **Tobias Jones** *The Dark Heart of Italy*. Written during a three-year period in Parma, this is an interconnected sequence of essays dealing with various aspects of modern Italian society. Bewildered and fascinated at every turn, Jones reveals a culture in which evasiveness and ethical malleability are as significant as the much-celebrated virtues of vivacity, charm and sophistication.

Norman Lewis *The Honoured Society*. Lewis's classic account of the Mafia, originally written in the 1960s, is still the most enjoyable introduction to the subject available.

Douglas Preston with Mario Spezi *The Monster of Florence*. Between 1974 and 1985 the area around Florence was terrorized by Italy's most notorious serial killer. The crimes were truly monstrous, but Preston describes them without undue prurience, in a gripping book which develops into a hard-hitting indictment of the still unfinished investigation. Essentially a modern Italian tale of incompetent officials, deranged conspiracy theorists and unbelievable witnesses.

★ **Peter Robb** *Midnight in Sicily*. The Australian Robb spent fifteen years in the Italian South and this book focuses on the structure of the Mafia, the trials of the bosses in the 1980s and the high-profile assassinations that ensued. It's a thorough, fast-paced study, providing deep insights into the dynamics of Sicilian society.

★ **Robert Saviano** *Gomorrah*. Saviano's exposé of the Neapolitan Camorra is the first to have dished the dirt on the most violent grouping of Italy's various organized criminal gangs, and he is currently in hiding because of it. At heart it's a passionate protest against a problem which only seems to get worse, and has been made into a well-received movie.

Alexander Stille *Excellent Cadavers*. Stille traces the rise, successes, failures and eventual assassinations of anti-Mafia magistrates Giovanni Falcone and Paolo Borsellino, as well as blowing the cover of Andreotti and Craxi.

ART, ARCHITECTURE AND ARCHEOLOGY

★ **Frederick Hartt** *History of Italian Renaissance Art: Painting, Sculpture and Architecture*. If one book on this vast subject can be said to be indispensable, this is it – due to both the comprehensiveness of its coverage and the range of its illustrations.

Anthony Hughes *Michelangelo*. An ideal single-volume introduction to arguably the greatest artist of the Renaissance, which sets Michelangelo within his historical and political context.

Ross King *Brunelleschi's Dome*. An intriguing account of the archi-tectural innovations and intense rivalries behind the construction of Florence's Duomo. It also paints an engaging picture of life in the medieval city.

Peter Murray *The Architecture of the Italian Renaissance*. Begins with Romanesque buildings and finishes with Palladio – valuable both as a gazetteer of the main monuments and as a synopsis of the underlying concepts.

Catherine Puglisi *Caravaggio*. An intelligent and engaging study of one of the most innovative artists of the Renaissance, enhanced with sumptuous colour plates throughout.

Nigel Spivey *Etruscan Art*. An in-depth look at the art of the elusive Etruscans, whose history and lives are told through

their tomb art. Sumptuously illustrated throughout, this is an intriguing story of a long-lost race.

Giorgio Vasari *Lives of the Artists*. The sixteenth-century artist's classic work on his predecessors and contemporaries, with essays on Giotto, Brunelleschi, Mantegna, Leonardo, Michelangelo, Raphael and more. The first real work of art history and still among the most penetrating books you can read on Italian Renaissance art.

FOOD AND DRINK

★ **Accademia Italiana della Cucina** *La Cucina*. Perhaps the widest selection of authentic Italian recipes you can find in one volume, and certainly the best available introduction to the regional variations in Italian cuisine. A lovely lesson in the simplicity and diversity of Italian food, though perhaps not quite as practical as Marcella Hazan's book.

Elizabeth David *Italian Food*. The writer who introduced Italian cuisine – and ingredients – to Britain. Ahead of its time when it was published in the 1950s, and imbued with all the enthusiasm and diversity of Italian cookery. An inspirational book.

★ **Marcella Hazan** *The Classic Italian Cookbook*. A step-by-step guide that never compromises the spirit or authenticity of the recipes. Hazan draws her recipes from all over the peninsula, emphasizing the intrinsi-cally regional nature of Italian food. The best Italian cookbook for the novice in the kitchen.

Fred Plotkin *Italy for the Gourmet Traveller*. Comprehensive, region-by-region guide to the best of Italian cuisine, with a foodie's guide to major towns and cities, a gazetteer of restaurants and specialist food and wine shops, and descriptions of local dishes, with recipes.

Claudia Roden *The Food of Italy*. A culinary classic, this regional guide takes in local recipes from the people for whom they are second nature. Authentic and accessible.

Michèle Shah *Wines of Italy*. An excellent pocket guide to the regional wines and winemaking techniques of Italy, with up-to-date information on the best current producers and labels.

ANCIENT AND ITALIAN CLASSICS

Dante Alighieri *The Divine Comedy*. No work in any other language bears comparison with Dante's poetic exegesis of the moral scheme of God's Creation; in late medieval Italy it was venerated both as a book of almost scriptural authority and as the ultimate refinement of the vernacular Tuscan language.

Giovanni Boccaccio *The Decameron*. Set in the plague-racked Florence of 1348, this assembly of one hundred short stories is a fascinating social record as well as a constantly diverting comic sequence.

Benvenuto Cellini *Autobiography*. The shamelessly egocentric record of the travails and triumphs of the sculptor and goldsmith's career – one of the freshest literary productions of its time.

Livy *The Early History of Rome*. Lively chronicle of the city's evolution from the days of Romulus and Remus.

Alessandro Manzoni *The Betrothed*. No poolside thriller, but a skilful melding of the romance of two young lovers and a sweeping historical drama, all suffused with an almost religious sense of human destiny. First published in 1823, but reissued in 1840 after Manzoni had improved the novel's diction through study of the Tuscan dialect – a landmark in the transition towards linguistic nationalism.

Suetonius *The Twelve Caesars*. The inside story of Caligula, Nero, Domitian and others, elegantly written and very enjoyable, by the private secretary to Hadrian, who made the most of his unique access to the annals of recent imperial history.

Virgil *The Aeneid*. The central work of Latin literature, depicting the adventures of Aeneas after the fall of Troy, and thus celebrating Rome's heroic lineage.

MODERN ITALIAN LITERATURE

Niccolò Ammaniti *I'm Not Scared; Steal You Away; The Crossroads; Me & You; Let the Games Begin*. One of the bright young lights of contemporary Italian literature, the Roman Ammaniti is a bit of a star in his own country, and becoming increasingly popular overseas, with five of his shortish novels available in translation. His style is haunting, usually in the first person, and full of suspense, as it deals with the secret, distasteful and frequently horrifying side of life, often through the eyes of children.

Giorgio Bassani *The Garden of the Finzi-Continis*. Gentle, elegiac novel, set in the Jewish community of Ferrara during the Fascist period, on the eve of the mass deportations to Germany. Infused with a sense of regret for a Europe that died with the war.

Italo Calvino *If on a Winter's Night a Traveller*. Calvino's fiction became increasingly concerned with the nature of fiction itself, and this witty novel marks the culmination of the process. Other titles include *The Castle of Crossed Destinies*, *Invisible Cities*, *Difficult Loves* and *Mr Palomar*.

Gabriele d'Annunzio *Notturno*. In English translation, d'Annunzio can come across as a mere windbag, but Stephen Sartarelli's translation of *Notturno* is different. It's an extraordinary memoir-cum-prose poem, written in extraordinary circumstances – d'Annunzio composed it on small scraps of paper, while immobilized and almost blinded after crash-landing a plane. Newcomers to d'Annunzio might start with Lucy Hughes-Hallett's brilliant biography, *The Pike*, which doesn't gloss over his absurdity

ANCIENT ROME IN FICTION

Robert Graves *I Claudius*; *Claudius the God*. Having translated Suetonius' *Twelve Caesars*, Graves used the madness and corruption of the Imperial Age to create a gripping, if not necessarily historically accurate, tale.

Robert Harris *Imperium*; *Lustrum*. No one brings to life the Roman Republic quite as vividly as Harris, viewing the power struggles and intrigues of the main protagonists through the eyes of Cicero's faithful secretary, the freed slave Tiro.

Conn Iggulden *The Gates of Rome*; *The Death of Kings*; *The Field of Swords*; *The Gods of War*. Iggulden's engaging four-book series, *Emperor*, is a historical romp documenting the rise and fall of Julius Caesar, from the rites of passage of the young man during the turmoil of the last decades of the Republic to his eventual murder in Pompey's theatre.

Allan Massie *Augustus*; *Tiberius*; *Caesar*; *Caligula*. Massie's series of novels aspires to re-create the Roman Empire at its height through the imagined memoirs of its key figures, and does so with great success, in a series of novels that offers a well-researched but palatable way into the minutiae of the era.

Thornton Wilder *The Ides of March*. A suppositional reconstruction of the last year of the life of Julius Caesar through his letters, writings and reports.

and ghastliness, while making sense of his allure.

Umberto Eco *The Name of the Rose*. An allusive, tightly plotted, monastic detective story. Check out also his equally hyped, though rather more impenetrable, *Foucault's Pendulum* and *Baudolino*, another medieval fable, this time interspersed with reflections on the postmodern age.

Elena Ferrante *My Brilliant Friend*. This is the first of Ferrante's four "Neapolitan novels", an immense feminist personal-political saga that has been a huge success at home and abroad. "The best modern portrait of a female friendship" one publisher remarked, and many have agreed. "Elena Ferrante" is a nom de plume, and there's a lot of speculation in Italy as to her true identity.

Carlo Emilio Gadda *That Awful Mess on Via Merulana*. Superficially a detective story, this celebrated modernist novel is so dense a weave of physical reality and literary diversions that the reader is led away from a solution rather than towards it; it enjoys the sort of status in Italian fiction that *Ulysses* has in English.

Natalia Ginzburg *The Things We Used to Say*. The constraints of family life are a dominant theme in Ginzburg's writing, and her own upbringing is the source material for this characteristically rigorous yet lyrical work.

Giuseppe di Lampedusa *The Leopard*. Perhaps the most famous Sicilian novel, recounting the dramatic nineteenth-century transition from Bourbon to Piemontese rule from an aristocrat's point of view. A good character study and rich with incidental detail.

Carlo Levi *Christ Stopped at Eboli*. First published in 1945, this memoir, describing Levi's exile to a remote region of Basilicata by the Fascists, was the first to awaken modern Italy to the plight of its southern regions.

★ **Primo Levi** *If This is a Man/The Truce*; *The Periodic Table*. Levi's experiences in Auschwitz are the main subject of *If This is a Man*, while *The Truce* records his journey back to Turin after his liberation. Levi's training as a chemist forms the background of *The Periodic Table*, a mixture of autobiographical reflection and practical observation. All show an unwavering exactitude of recollection and judgement.

Margaret Mazzantini *Don't Move*. Intense psychological novel of midlife crisis, sex and obsession in Rome that was a massive bestseller in Italy and made into a movie directed by the author's husband. The city and its outskirts form a bleak, rain-soaked backdrop.

Elsa Morante *History*. Capturing daily Roman life during the last war, this is probably the most vivid fictional picture of the conflict as seen from the city.

★ **Alberto Moravia** *The Conformist*. A psychological novel about a man sucked into the abyss of Fascism by his desperation to conform; *The Woman of Rome* is an earlier work, a teeming and sensual novel, centred on the activities of a Roman prostitute.

Pier Paolo Pasolini *A Violent Life*. This supernaturalistic evocation of life in the slum areas of Rome caused a scandal when it was published in 1959, but is now considered one of the classics of Italian postwar fiction.

Cesare Pavese *Moon and the Bonfire*; *Devil in the Hills*. Exploring the difficulties of achieving an acceptance of one's past, *Moon and the Bonfire* was written shortly before Pavese's suicide at the age of 42; *Devil in the Hills* is an early collection of tales of adolescence in and around Turin.

★ **Leonardo Sciascia** *Sicilian Uncles*; *The Wine Dark Sea*; *The Day of the Owl*. Writing again and again about his native Sicily, Sciascia has made of that island "a metaphor of the modern world". Economically written, Sciascia's short stories are packed with incisive insights and infused with the author's humane and sympathetic views of its people. *The Moro Affair* is an illuminating account of the kidnapping of the ex-prime minister Aldo Moro by the Brigate Rosse in 1978.

Ignazio Silone *Fontamara; Bread and Wine; The Seed Beneath the Snow*. From his exile in Switzerland, Silone wrote about his native Abruzzo, and these three novels have now been published in one volume by Steerforth Press, titled *The Abruzzo Trilogy*. *Fontamara* tells the tale of a small village driven to revolt against its landlords and the Fascist thugs sent to enforce their rule, while *Bread and Wine* is a more introspective work, examining Silone's political commitment and religious beliefs.

Italo Svevo *Zeno's Conscience*. Complete critical indifference to his early efforts so discouraged Svevo that he gave up writing altogether, until encouraged by James Joyce, who taught him English in Trieste. The resultant novel is a unique creation, a comic portrait of a character at once wistful, helpless and irrepressible.

Giovanni Verga *Cavalleria Rusticana; Sparrow; The House by the Medlar Tree*. Verga, born in the nineteenth century in Catania, spent several years in various European salons before coming home to write his best work. Much of it is a reaction against the pseudo-sophistication of society circles, stressing the simple lives of ordinary people, accompanied by a heavy smattering of emotion, wounded honour and feuds to the death.

Elio Vittorini *Conversations in Sicily*. A Sicilian emigrant returns from the north of Italy after fifteen years to see his mother on her birthday. The conversations of the title are with the people he meets on the way, and reveal a poverty- and disease-ridden Sicily.

William Weaver (ed) *Open City: Seven Writers in Postwar Rome*. A nicely produced anthology of pieces by the cream of Italy's twentieth-century novelists – Bassani, Silone, Ginzburg, Moravia, among others – selected and with an introduction by one of the most eminent Italian translators of recent years.

LITERATURE SET IN ITALY

Jonathan Buckley *Nostalgia*. A novel by a *Rough Guide* author. Selecting it as a Book of the Year in 2013, the *Sunday Times* wrote: "From a multitude of angles – history, geography, present and past residents, flora, fauna, festivals – a small Tuscan town is brought to teeming, vivid life. With a central storyline about an English expat painter, it's as exhilarating as an Italian holiday."

E.M. Forster *A Room with a View*. Set in and around Florence, this is the ultimate novel about how the nature of the Italian light, temperament and soul can make the English upper classes lose their heads.

James Hamilton-Paterson *Cooking with Fernet-Branca*. An excellent comic novel which is packed full of laughs at everyone's expense – sad middle-aged writers, foodies, and most of all the middle-class English expat community in Tuscany.

Nathaniel Hawthorne *The Marble Faun*. A nineteenth-century take on the lives of Anglo-American expats in the Eternal City: sculptors, passionate lovers – the usual mad mix and excessive goings-on that you'll still find today.

Ernest Hemingway *A Farewell to Arms*. Hemingway's first novel is partly based on his experiences as a teenage ambulance-driver on Italy's northeast front during World War I – a terse account of the futility of this particular corner of the conflict.

Patricia Highsmith *The Talented Mr Ripley*. The novel follows the fortunes of the eponymous hero through Italy as he exchanges his own identity for that of the man he has murdered. Good locations in the film of the book, starring Matt Damon and directed by Anthony Minghella.

Thomas Mann *Death in Venice*. Irascible and ultra-traditional old novelist visits Venice to recover after a breakdown and becomes obsessed with a beautiful young boy, awakening an internal debate about the nature of beauty and art to which the city is a fitting and resonant backdrop.

Ian McEwan *The Comfort of Strangers*. An ordinary young English couple fall foul of a sexually ambiguous predator in a Venice which is never named, but evoked by means of arch little devices such as quotes from Ruskin.

Stendhal *The Charterhouse of Parma*. A panoramic nineteenth-century French novel that dramatizes the struggles and intrigues of the Italian Papal States before Unification. A wonderful read, and a good insight into the era to boot.

Irving Stone *The Agony and the Ecstasy*. Stone's dramatized life of Michelangelo, popular "faction" that is entertaining even if it doesn't exactly get to the root of the artist's work and times.

Barry Unsworth *After Hannibal; Stone Virgin*. *After Hannibal* is a black comedy of expat life, set in Umbria, where the author lives. The earlier *Stone Virgin*, set in Venice, is about a conservation expert who falls under the spell of a statue of the Madonna he is working on.

Salley Vickers *Miss Garnet's Angel*. The unique atmosphere of Venice is captured in this tale of a desiccated spinster awakened by the city to the finer things in life. The author's sound knowledge of the place and its art triumphs over a potentially hackneyed tale.

Italian

The ability to speak English confers prestige in Italy, and there's often no shortage of people willing to show off their knowledge. But using at least some Italian, however tentatively, can mark you out from the masses in a country used to hordes of tourists. The words and phrases below should help you master the basics, and the *Rough Guide Italian Phrasebook* – which packs a huge amount of vocabulary into a handy dictionary format – is a useful backup. There are lots of good pocket dictionaries – the Collins range represents the best all-round choice.

Pronunciation

Italian is one of the easiest European languages to learn, especially if you already have a smattering of French or Spanish. **Pronunciation** is straightforward: Italian words are generally stressed on the penultimate syllable unless an accent (´ or `) denotes otherwise, and words are usually enunciated with exaggerated, open-mouthed clarity.

The only difficulties you're likely to encounter are the few consonants that are different from English:

c before e or i is pronounced as in **ch**urch, while **ch** before the same vowels is hard, as in **c**at.

sci or **sce** are pronounced as in **sh**eet and **sh**elter respectively.

g is soft before e or i, as in **g**eranium; hard before h, as in **g**arlic.

gn has the ni sound of o**ni**on.

gl in Italian is softened to something like li in English, as in stal**li**on.

h is not aspirated, as in **h**onour.

When speaking to strangers, the third person is the polite form (ie *lei* instead of *tu* for "you"). It's also worth remembering that Italians don't use "please" and "thank you" half as much as English speakers: it's all implied in the tone, though if in doubt, err on the polite side.

WORDS AND PHRASES

BASICS

good morning buongiorno
good afternoon/evening buonasera
goodnight buonanotte
hello/goodbye ciao (informal; to strangers use phrases above)
goodbye arrivederci
yes si
no no
please per favore
thank you (very much) (molte/mille) grazie
you're welcome prego
all right/that's ok va bene
how are you? come stai/sta? (informal/formal)
I'm fine bene
do you speak English? parla Inglese?
I don't understand non ho capito
I don't know non lo so
excuse me mi scusi
excuse me (in a crowd) permesso
I'm sorry mi dispiace
I'm here on holiday Sono qui in vacanza
I'm English/Irish/Welsh/Scottish/American/Australian/Canadian/a New Zealander Sono Inglese/Irlandese/Gallese/Scozzese/Americano/a (m/f)/Australiano/a (m/f)/Canadese/Neozelandese
What's your name? Come ti chiami/si chiama? (informal/formal)
wait a minute! aspetta!
let's go! andiamo!
here/there qui/là
good/bad buono/cattivo
big/small grande/píccolo
cheap/expensive economico/caro

early/late presto/tardi
hot/cold caldo/freddo
near/far vicino/lontano
quickly/slowly velocemente/lentamente

QUESTIONS

where? dove?
where is/are…? dov'è/dove sono…?
when? quando?
what? cosa?
what is it? cos'è?
how much/many? quanto/quanti?
why? perché?
is it/is there…? c'è…?
What time does it open/close? A che ora apre/chiude?
What's it called in Italian? Come si chiama in Italiano?

Travel and directions

Where is…? Dov'è…?
How do I get to…? Per arrivare a…?
the centre il centro
the (main) square la piazza (principale)
the station la stazione
the bus station l'autostazione
the port il porto
Turn left/right Giri a sinistra/destra
Go straight on Vai sempre diritto
How far is it to…? Quant'è lontano a…?
What time does the…arrive/leave? A che ora arriva/ parte…?
bus l'autobus
coach il pullman
ferry il traghetto
hydrofoil l'aliscafo
plane l'aereo
train il treno
Do I have to change? Devo cambiare?
Which platform does it leave from? Da quale binario parte?
How long does it take? Quanto ci vuole?
Can you tell me when to get off? Mi può dire dove scendere?
I'd like a ticket to… Vorrei un biglietto per…
one-way solo andata
return andata e ritorno

SIGNS

entrance/exit entrata/uscita
arrivals/departures arrivi/partenze
free entrance ingresso líbero
gentlemen/ladies signori/signore
wc gabinetto/bagno
vacant/engaged libero/occupato
no smoking vietato fumare
open/closed aperto/chiuso
closed for restoration chiuso per restauro
closed for holidays chiuso per ferie
pull/push tirare/spingere
cash desk cassa
out of order guasto
ring the bell suonare il campanello

ACCOMMODATION

I'd like to book a room Vorrei prenotare una cámera
I have a booking Ho una prenotazione
Is there a hotel nearby? C'è un albergo qui vicino?
Do you have…? Ha…?
a single/double/triple una cámera singola/doppia/ tripla
a bed un letto
for one/two/three night/s per una/due/tre notti
for one/two week/s per una/due settimana/e
with a double bed con un letto matrimoniale
with twin beds con due letti
with a shower/bath con doccia/bagno
with a balcony con balcone
hot/cold water acqua calda/fredda
How much is it? Quanto costa?
Is breakfast included? È compresa la prima colazione?
Do you have anything cheaper? Ha qualcosa che costa di meno?
Can I see the room? Posso vedere la cámera?
I'll take it Lo/La prendo (m/f)
hotel albergo
hostel ostello
campsite campeggio
lift ascensore
key chiave
full/half board pensione completa/ mezza pensione

RESTAURANTS

I'd like to reserve a table (for two) Vorrei riservare una távola (per due)
Can we sit outside? Possiamo sederci fuori?
Can I order? Posso ordinare?

I'm a vegetarian Sono vegetariano/a (m/f)
Does it contain meat? C'è carne dentro?
It's good È buono
The bill, please Il conto, per favore
Is service included? Il servizio è incluso?
(set) menu menù (fisso)
waiter/waitress cameriere/a
knife coltello
fork forchetta
spoon cucchiaio
plate piatto
bicchiere glass

SHOPPING AND SERVICES

I'd like to buy… Vorrei comprare…
How much does it cost/do they cost? Quanto costa/ cóstano?
It's too expensive È troppo caro
with/without con/senza
more/less più/meno
enough, no more basta
I'll take it Lo/la prendo (m/f)
Do you take credit cards? Accettate carte di credito?
bank banca
money exchange cambio
post office posta
tourist office ufficio turistico
shop negozio
supermarket supermercato
market mercato
ATM Bancomat

DAYS, TIMES AND MONTHS

What time is it? Che ore sono?
It's nine o'clock Sono le nove
today oggi
tomorrow domani
day after tomorrow dopodomani
yesterday ieri
now adesso
later più tardi
in the morning di mattina
in the afternoon nel pomeriggio
in the evening di sera
Monday lunedì
Tuesday martedì
Wednesday mercoledì
Thursday giovedì
Friday venerdì
Saturday sabato
Sunday domenica
January gennaio
February febbraio
March marzo
April aprile
May maggio
June giugno
July luglio
August agosto
September settembre
October ottobre
November novembre
December dicembre

NUMBERS

1 uno
2 due
3 tre
4 quattro
5 cinque
6 sei
7 sette
8 otto
9 nove
10 dieci
11 undici
12 dodici
13 tredici
14 quattordici
15 quindici
16 sedici
17 diciassette
18 diciotto
19 diciannove
20 venti
21 ventuno
22 ventidue
30 trenta
40 quaranta
50 cinquanta
60 sessanta
70 settanta
80 ottanta
90 novanta
100 cento
101 centuno
110 centodieci
200 duecento
500 cinquecento
1000 mille
5000 cinquemila

Italian menu reader

BASICS AND SNACKS

aceto vinegar
aglio garlic
biscotti biscuits
burro butter
caramelle sweets
cioccolato chocolate
formaggio cheese
frittata omelette
marmellata jam
olio oil
olive olives
pane bread
pepe pepper
riso rice
sale salt
uova eggs
yogurt yoghurt
zucchero sugar
zuppa soup

THE FIRST COURSE (IL PRIMO)

brodo clear broth
minestrina clear broth with small pasta shapes
minestrone thick vegetable soup
pasta al forno baked pasta, usually with minced meat, tomato and cheese
pasta e fagioli soup with pasta and beans
pastina in brodo pasta in clear broth
stracciatella broth with egg

PASTA

bucatini thick, hollow spaghetti- type pasta common in Rome and Lazio
cannelloni thick pasta tubes usually filled with veal
capellini thin noodles of pasta, thicker than *capelli d'angeli*
conchiglie seashell-shaped pasta shapes, good for capturing thick sauces
farfalle literally "butterflies", or bow ties
fettuccine flat, ribbon-like egg noodles
fusilli tight spirals of pasta
gnocchi potato and pasta dumplings, often served "*alla sorrentina*", or with tomato and basil sauce
lasagne big squares of egg noodles, most commonly baked in the oven with white sauce and beef *ragù*
linguini thin, flat noodles, often served with seafood
macaroni small tubes of pasta
maltagliati flat triangles of pasta, often used in soup
orecchiette small ear-shaped pieces of pasta
paccheri large tubes of pasta
panzarotti filled pasta shapes from Puglia
pappardelle thick, flat egg noodles
penne the most common tubes of pasta
pici thick Tuscan spaghetti
ravioli literally "little turnips" – flat, square parcels of filled pasta
rigatoni large, curved and ridged tubes of pasta – larger than *penne* but smaller than *paccheri*
spaghetti the most common pasta shape of all – long, thin, non-egg noodles
tagliatelle flat ribbon egg noodles, slightly thinner than *fettuccine*
tonnarelli another name for *bucatini*
tortellini/tortolloni triangles of filled pasta folded into rounded shapes
tortiglioni narrow *rigatoni*

PASTA SAUCE (SALSA)

amatriciana cubed bacon and tomato
arrabbiata ("angry") spicy tomato with chillies
bolognese meat
burro butter
carbonara cream, ham and beaten egg
funghi mushroom
panna cream
parmigiano Parmesan cheese
peperoncino olive oil, garlic and fresh chillies
pesto ground basil, garlic and pine nuts
pomodoro tomato
puttanesca "whorish", with tomato, anchovy, olive oil and oregano
ragù meat
vongole clams

THE SECOND COURSE (IL SECONDO)

MEAT (CARNE)

agnello lamb
bistecca steak
carpaccio slices of raw beef
cervello brain, usually calves'
cinghiale wild boar
coniglio rabbit
costolette cutlet, chop
fegato liver
maiale pork
manzo beef
ossobuco shin of veal
pancetta bacon
pollo chicken
polpette meatballs
rognoni kidneys

salsiccia sausage
saltimbocca veal with ham
spezzatino stew
trippa tripe
vitello veal

FISH (PESCE) AND SHELLFISH (CROSTACEI)
acciughe anchovies
anguilla eel
aragosta lobster
baccalà dried salted cod
calamari squid
cefalo grey mullet
cozze mussels
dentice sea bream
gamberetti shrimps
gamberi prawns
granchio crab
merluzzo cod
ostriche oysters
pesce spada swordfish
polpo octopus
rospo monkfish
sampiero John Dory
sarde sardines
sogliola sole
tonno tuna
trota trout
vongole clams

VEGETABLES (CONTORNI) AND SALAD (INSALATA)

asparagi asparagus
carciofi artichokes
carciofini artichoke hearts
cavolfiori cauliflower
cavolo cabbage
cipolla onion
erbe aromatiche herbs
fagioli beans
fagiolini green beans
finocchio fennel
funghi mushrooms
insalata verde/mista green salad/mixed salad
lenticchie lentils
melanzane aubergine
patate potatoes
peperoni peppers
piselli peas
pomodori tomatoes
radicchio red salad leaves
spinaci spinach

COOKING TERMS

al dente firm, not overcooked
al ferri grilled without oil
al forno baked
al sangue rare
alla brace barbecued
alla griglia grilled
alla milanese fried in egg and breadcrumbs
alla pizzaiola cooked with tomato sauce
allo spiedo on the spit
arrosto roast
ben cotto well done
bollito/lesso boiled
cotto cooked
crudo raw
fritto fried
in umido stewed
ripieno stuffed
stracotto braised, stewed

CHEESE (FORMAGGIO)

dolcelatte creamy blue cheese
fontina northern Italian cheese, often used in cooking
Gorgonzola soft, strong, blue-veined cheese
mozzarella soft white cheese, traditionally made from buffalo's milk
pecorino strong, hard sheep's cheese
provola/provolone smooth, round mild cheese, made from buffalo or sheep's milk; sometimes smoked
ricotta soft, white sheep's cheese

DESSERTS (DOLCI), FRUIT (FRUTTA) AND NUTS (NOCI)

amaretti macaroons
ananas pineapple
anguria watermelon
arachidi peanuts
arance oranges
banane bananas
cacchi persimmons
ciliegie cherries
coccomero watermelon
crostata pastry tart with jam or chocolate topping
fichi figs
fichi d'india prickly pears
frágole strawberries
gelato ice cream

limone lemon
macedonia fruit salad
mandorle almonds
mele apples
melone melon
pere pears
pesche peaches
pinoli pine nuts
pistacchio pistachio nut
sorbetto sorbet
torta cake, tart
uva grapes
zabaglione dessert made with eggs, sugar and Marsala wine
zuppa inglese trifle

DRINKS

acqua minerale (con gas/senza gas) mineral water (fizzy/still)
aranciata orangeade
birra beer
bottiglia bottle
caffè coffee
cioccolato caldo hot chocolate
ghiaccio ice
granita iced drink with coffee or fruit
latte milk
limonata lemonade
spremuta fresh fruit juice
spumante sparkling wine
succo concentrated fruit juice with sugar
tè tea
tonica tonic water
vino wine
rosso red
bianco white
rosato rosé
secco dry
dolce sweet
litro litre
mezzo half
quarto quarter
caraffa carafe
salute! cheers!

Glossary of artistic and architectural terms

agora square or marketplace in an ancient Greek city
ambo a kind of simple pulpit, popular in Italian medieval churches
apse semicircular recess at the altar (usually eastern) end of a church
architrave the lowest part of the entablature
atrium inner courtyard
baldacchino a canopy on columns, usually placed over the altar in a church
basilica originally a Roman administrative building, adapted for early churches; distinguished by lack of transepts
belvedere a terrace or lookout point
caldarium the steam room of a Roman bath
campanile belltower, sometimes detached, usually of a church
capital top of a column
Catalan-Gothic hybrid form of architecture, mixing elements of fifteenth-century Spanish and Northern European styles
cella sanctuary of a temple
chancel part of a church containing the altar
chiaroscuro the balance of light and shade in a painting, and the skill of the artist in depicting the contrast between the two
ciborium another word for baldacchino, see above
cornice the top section of a classical facade
cortile galleried courtyard or cloisters
cosmati work decorative mosaic-work on marble, usually highly coloured, found in early Christian Italian churches, especially in Rome; derives from the name Cosma, a common name among families of marble workers at the time
cryptoporticus underground passageway
cyclopean walls fortifications built of huge, rough stone blocks, common in the pre-Roman settlements of Lazio
Decumanus Maximus the main street of a Roman town – the second cross street was known as the Decumanus Inferiore
entablature the section above the capital on a classical building, below the cornice
ex voto artefact designed in thanksgiving to a saint
fresco wall-painting technique in which the artist applies paint to wet plaster for a more permanent finish
loggia roofed gallery or balcony
metope a panel on the frieze of a Greek temple
Mithraism pre-Christian cult associated with the Persian god of light, who slew a bull and fertilized the world with its blood
nave central space in a church, usually flanked by aisles
Pantocrator usually refers to an image of Christ, portrayed with outstretched arms
piano nobile main floor of a *palazzo*, usually the first
polyptych painting on several joined wooden panels
portico covered entrance to a building, or porch
presepio/presepe Christmas crib
putti cherubs
reliquary receptacle for a saint's relics, usually bones; often highly decorated
sgraffito decorative technique whereby one layer of plaster is scratched to form a pattern
stereobate visible base of any building, usually a Greek temple
stucco plaster made from water, lime, sand and powdered marble, used for decorative work
thermae baths, usually elaborate buildings in Roman villas
triptych painting on three joined wooden panels
trompe l'oeil work of art that deceives the viewer by means of tricks with perspective

Small print and index

1032 Small print

1032 About the author

1034 Index

1045 Map symbols

A ROUGH GUIDE TO ROUGH GUIDES

Published in 1982, the first Rough Guide – to Greece – was a student scheme that became a publishing phenomenon. Mark Ellingham, a recent graduate in English from Bristol University, had been travelling in Greece the previous summer and couldn't find the right guidebook. With a small group of friends he wrote his own guide, combining a contemporary, journalistic style with a thoroughly practical approach to travellers' needs.

The immediate success of the book spawned a series that rapidly covered dozens of destinations. And, in addition to impecunious backpackers, Rough Guides soon acquired a much broader readership that relished the guides' wit and inquisitiveness as much as their enthusiastic, critical approach and value-for-money ethos. These days, Rough Guides include recommendations from budget to luxury and cover more than 120 destinations around the globe, from Amsterdam to Zanzibar, all regularly updated by our team of roaming writers.

Browse all our latest guides, read inspirational features and book your trip at **roughguides.com**.

Rough Guide credits

Editors: Aimee White, Siobhan Warwicker
Cartography: Katie Bennett
Managing editor: Rachel Lawrence
Picture editor: Michelle Bhatia
Cover photo research: Tom Smyth
Senior DTP coordinator: Dan May
Head of DTP and Pre-Press: Rebeka Davies

Publishing information

Thirteenth edition 2019

Distribution
UK, Ireland and Europe
Apa Publications (UK) Ltd; sales@roughguides.com
United States and Canada
Ingram Publisher Services; ips@ingramcontent.com
Australia and New Zealand
Woodslane; info@woodslane.com.au
Southeast Asia
Apa Publications (SN) Pte; sales@roughguides.com
Worldwide
Apa Publications (UK) Ltd; sales@roughguides.com
Special Sales, Content Licensing and CoPublishing
Rough Guides can be purchased in bulk quantities at discounted prices. We can create special editions, personalised jackets and corporate imprints tailored to your needs. sales@roughguides.com.

roughguides.com
Printed in China by CTPS

A catalogue record for this book is available from the British Library

Help us update

We've gone to a lot of effort to ensure that this edition of **The Rough Guide to Italy** is accurate and up-to-date. However, things change – places get "discovered", opening hours are notoriously fickle, restaurants and rooms raise prices or lower standards. If you feel we've got it wrong or left something out, we'd like to know, and if you can remember the address, the price, the hours, the phone number, so much the better.

Please send your comments with the subject line **"Rough Guide Italy Update"** to mail@uk.roughguides.com. We'll credit all contributions and send a copy of the next edition (or any other Rough Guide if you prefer) for the very best emails.

Acknowledgements

Robert Andrews Many thanks are due to the staff of Sardinia's local tourist offices, and at Rough Guides to Aimee White for her excellent edit.
Kiki Deere would like to thank Erika Carpaneto from Turismo Torino for her wonderful support, advice and assistance; Claudia Macrì in Valle d'Aosta for her patience and expert advice on the region; Paola Dalla Valentina from InfoMilano for double checking pesky travel info; the friendly tourist information team from all around Lake Como; on Lake Maggiore, thank you to Silvia Lorenzini from the Distretto Turistico dei Laghi and Giorgia Meretti from the Isole Borromee; many thanks to Francesca Blench for her useful advice on all things Lake Orta and Lake Maggiore; on Lake Garda, many thanks to Daniele Tonelli, Francesca Campagnari and Gianluca Ginepro; a big thank you also to Anna Ferlinghetti on Lake Iseo; finally, in Friuli Venezia Giulia, a huge thank you to Tatjana Familio and Giulia Cantone.
Natasha Foges Thanks to research assistants Will, Joe and Laurie for joining me on the road.

Photo credits

(Key: T-top; M-middle; B-bottom; L-left; R-right)

Alamy 17BR, 214/215, 363, 449, 844/845, 942/943
Francesco Iacobelli/ AWL Images 5
Getty Images 1, 15B, 645
iStock 2, 4, 11T, 11B, 12, 13TR, 13B, 14B, 14T, 14M, 15T, 16T, 16B, 18B, 18T, 19T, 19M, 19B, 22, 44/45, 130/131, 133, 143, 170/171, 173, 195, 217, 247, 279, 304/305, 307, 346/347, 439, 464/465, 467, 512/513, 533, 581, 626/627, 676/677, 695, 712/713, 729, 738/739, 741, 751, 802/803, 805, 829, 889, 945
Ken Scicluna / AWL Images 477
Natascha Sturny / Rough Guides 13M
Shutterstock 9, 17T, 17BL, 20, 47, 67, 111, 325, 349, 411, 436/437, 515, 624/625, 679, 715, 842/843, 855, 872/873, 875, 923, 957, 980
Uffizi Galleries 13TL

Cover: Duomo Santa Maria del Fiore, Florence **Pietro Canali/4Corners Images**

ABOUT THE AUTHORS

Robert Andrews has previously lived in Calabria and Sardinia and still visits those regions regularly. He has worked on various Rough Guides for Italy and the UK, and orgnanizes culture and activity holidays in both places. He is currently based in Bristol.

Ros Belford co-authored the first edition of this guide, and has since written and broadcast extensively about Italy and the Mediterranean. She has two daughters and spends as much time as she can on the Aeolian Island of Salina.

Jonathan Buckley has written and contributed to several Rough Guides on Italy and music. He has also published ten novels, and was shortlisted for the 2015 BBC National Short Story award. He lives in Brighton.

Kiki Deere is a travel writer raised bilingually in London and Turin who writes regularly about all things Italy for a number of travel publications including Rough Guides and UK broadsheets. She is an expert on the Italian Lakes region, and regularly writes about hotels, restaurants and attractions in the area.

Natasha Foges packed her bags and moved to Rome on a whim, and stayed four years. Now based in London, she misses the food, the sun and the scooter rides, but escapes back to Italy as often as she can to revisit old haunts and overindulge on ice cream. Natasha is also author of *Pocket Rough Guide Rome*.

Anthon Jackson is a roaming writer and photographer based in Aarhus, Denmark. He has contributed to numerous Rough Guides over the years – from Italy to India and Indonesia – and spent years along the Mediterranean coast, returning as often as he can find the excuse.

Index

A

Abbazia di Fiastra 704
Abbazia di Monte Oliveto Maggiore 607
Abbazia di San Galgano 606
Abbazia San Nilo 120
Abruzzo and Molise 714
Abruzzo National Park 725, 726
accommodation 29
accommodation prices 30
AC Milan 245
activities 37
Aeolian islands 895
Agrigento 932
agriturismi in Chianti 557
agriturismo 31
Agropoli 800
air travel 23
alabaster 602
Alagna 159
Alba 153
Albanian villages 735
Albenga 193
Alberobello 823
Alcantara Valley 911
Alghero 976
Alicudi 905
Alpe di Siusi 333
Altamura 820
Alta Via dei Monti Liguri 198
Alto Lario 271
Amalfi 793
Amalfi Coast 791
Amandola 706
Anacapri 779
Ancona 691
Andalo 318
Andria 820
Anzio 125
Aosta 161
apartments 30
Aquileia 452
Arbatax 966
architecture 1007
Arcipelago Toscano National Park 575
Arcos 790
Arezzo 617
Arezzo festivals 620
Ariccia 121
art 998
Arzachena 970
Ascoli Piceno 707
Asinara 976
Asolo 431
Aspromonte 862
Assisi 646
Assisi festivals 652
Asti 155
Atrani 793
Atri 728
Augustus 983

B

Bagno Vignoni 613
Baia 766
banking hours 42
Barbarians 984
Barcola 451
Bardolino 301
Bari 815
Barolo 154
Baroque architecture 1011
Baroque art 1003
bars 33
Basilicata 844
basketball 37
Bassano del Grappa 429
Bassano war memorials 430
Bassa Valle 160
Bay of Naples 764
bears 726
bed and breakfasts 30
beer 34
Bellagio 272
Bellini, Giovanni 1002
Belluno 434
Benevento 789
Bergamo 276
Berlusconi, Silvio 222, 995, 996
Bernini, Gianlorenzo 1004, 1012
Bevagna 654
Biella 158
birds 726
Blue Grotto, Capri 779
Bologna 466
Bologna festivals and events 481
Bologna's porticoes 474
Bolsena miracle 673
Bolzano 327
Bominaco 720
books 1019
Borromean islands 258
Borromini, Francesco 1012
Bosa 960
Botticelli, Sandro 1001
Bracciano 114
Bramante, Donato 1010
breakdowns 28
breakfast 32
Brenta Massif 319
Brenta, the 402
Brenzone 299
Brescia 285
Bressanone 335
Brigate Rosse 993
Brindisi 828
Brisighella 494
Brixen Card 336
Browning, Robert 690
Brunico 337
burrata 822
buses 26
buses to Italy 24
Bussana Vecchia 198
Byzantine art 998
Byzantines 984

C

cable cars, Bolzano 332
Cagliari 949
Calabria 857
Cala Gonone 965, 966
Calcio 106
Caldaro 333
Camigliatello 865
Camogli 199
Campania 740
Campania artecard 748
camper van rental 28
camping 31
Campobasso 736
Campo Imperatore plain 717
Canazei 324
Canevaworld 289
Cannobio 260
canoeing 38, 159
Canova, Antonio 1005
canyoning 38, 298
Capo Colonna 870
Capo d'Otranto 839
Capo Faro 900
Capoliveri 575
Capo Vaticano 860
Caprarola 117
Caprera 971
Capri 776

Capriz Feinkäserei 337
Capua 789
Caravaggio 921, 1004
Carrara 572
car rental 28
Carso, the 448
car travel 27
Casamicciola Terme 782
Cascata di Nardis 318
Casella by train 191
Caserta 787
Cash Passports 42
Cassino 123
Castel del Monte 718
Castel Firmiano/Sigmundskron 332
Castelfranco 429
Castel Gandolfo 120
Castell'Arquato 491
Castelli Romani 119
Castello d'Appiano 332
Castello della Rancia 703
Castello di Fénis 161
Castello di Issogne 161
Castello di Miramare 451
Castello di Racconigi 152
Castello di Sarre 164
Castello Eurialo 922
Castello Juval 343
Castelluccio 665
Castel Roncolo 331
Castelsardo 973
Castel Tirolo 342
Castiglione del Lago 638
Castiglione di Sicilia 911
catacombs 1008
Catania 912
Catinaccio 323
Cava Grande del Fiume Cassibile 927
Cavalese 321
Cavallini, Pietro 999
Cavour, Count Camillo 990
Cefalù 891
cellphones 43
Certosa di Pavia 244
Cerveteri 112
chariot-racing 735
Charlemagne 986
Charles of Anjou 987
Charles of Bourbon 742
cheese 222, 337, 469, 808, 877
Chianti 557
Chianti and Valdarno museum network 558
Chieti 732
children, travelling with 43
chocolate 147
Churburg 343
churches 42
Ciampino airport 92
Cilento 800
cinema 1014
Cinque Terre 206, 207
Circeo National Park 126
Circumflegrea train 760
Circumvesuviana train 760
Cisternino 823
Cittadella 429
Città di Castello 639
city-states 987
Cividale del Friuli 461
Cividale del Friuli festivals 463
Civitavecchia 113
climate 10, 39
climbing 37, 160, 298, 311, 904
Cocullo 723
Cocullo snake festival 723
coffee 33, 446
Colle del Gran San Bernardo 164
Colonnata 573
Comacchio 499
Como 265
Como, Lake 265
Compaccio 333
Conegliano 432
Conero Riviera 696
convent accommodation 30
Corniglia 206
Corniglio 491
Correggio 1003
Corricella 786
Corsa dei Ceri 644
Cortina d'Ampezzo 338
Cortona 622
Corvara 326
Cosenza 863
Costa Smeralda 969
costs 39
Courmayeur 168
credit cards 38
Cremona 246
crete, the 606
crime and personal safety 39
Cripta del Peccato Originale 853
Crotone 868
cultural tours 25
Cumae 766
Cupramontana grape festival 696
currency 42
cycling 29, 37, 302, 496. *See also* mountain biking
  Lombardy and the Lakes 302
  Riviera dei Fiori 193
  Tuscany 568

D

da Cortona, Pietro 1004, 1012
da Montefeltro, Federico 683
d'Annunzio, Gabriele 293
da Vinci, Leonardo 225, 1001
  The Last Supper 233, 235
debit cards 38
dentists 40
di Arborea, Eleonora 959
disabilities, travellers with 43
diving 37, 577, 891, 902
Dolomites 306
Dolomiti di Brenta 316
Dolomiti Superski 311
Domaso 271
Domodossola 160
Donatello 1000
Dorgali 965
drinks 31, 33
driving 27
Duino 452

E

Early Christian art 998
earthquakes 473, 718, 720
Egadi islands 940
Egnazia 821
Elba 574
Elba's best beaches 576
electricity 40
emergencies 40
Emilia-Romagna 466
emperors 984, 986
enoteche 33
entry requirements 40
Erice 938
Esino Valley 694
essentials 39
Etna 910
Etruria 112
Etruscan art 998
Etruscans 981
Eurail 24
European Health Insurance Card (EHIC) 40

F

fact file 8
Faenza 493
Fano 690
fashion factory outlets 555
Favignana 940
Ferdinand II of Aragon 988
Ferrara 494
Ferrara festivals and events 498
Ferrari 484
ferries 29
  Bay of Naples 776
  from La Spezia 210

Liguria coastal routes 200
Lombardy lakes 256
to Albania 693, 819, 831
to Corsica 573
to Croatia 693, 819
to Elba 576
to Greece 693, 819, 831
to Sardinia 113, 573, 948
to Sicily 113, 573, 862
to the Aeolian Islands 895
to the Tuscan islands 573
to Trieste 693
to Venice 693
Ferrovia Cumana train 760
festival calendar 35
Festival dei Due Mondi, Spoleto 660
Festival della Valle d'Itria 824
festivals 35
Fiera di Primiero 320
Fiesole 556
Filicudi 905
film 1014
Finale Ligure 192
Fiumicino airport 91
flights 23
domestic 29
from Australia, New Zealand and South Africa 23
from the UK and Ireland 23
from the US and Canada 23
Florence 518
Accademia 538
accommodation 546
addresses 546
airport 545
apps 546
arrival and departure 545
bars 551
Biblioteca Medicea-Laurenziana 536
buses 546
bus station 545
cafés 549
camping 549
Cappella Brancacci 543
Cappella Rucellai 534
Cappelle Medicee 536
Casa Buonarroti 541
Casa Martelli 537
Cenacolo di Sant'Apollonia 539
central 524
classical music, opera and dance 553
clubs 553
concert venues 553
directory 555
drinking 551
Duomo 522
eating 549
entertainment 552
festivals 553
film 553
gelaterie 549
Giardino Bardini 544
Giardino di Boboli 543
history 517
hostels 548
hotels 546
live music venues 553
magazines 546
Museo Archeologico 539
Museo dell'Opera del Duomo 526
Museo di San Marco 538
Museo Galileo 532
Museo Marino Marini 534
Museo Nazionale del Bargello 531
Museo Novecento 536
Museo Stefano Bardini 544
museums tickets and information 521
nightlife 552
Ognissanti 534
Oltrarno 541
Orsanmichele 526
outdoor drinking 550
Palazzo Davanzati 532
Palazzo Medici-Riccardi 537
Palazzo Pitti 542
Palazzo Vecchio 527
parking 546
Piazza del Duomo 521
Piazza della Repubblica 526
Piazza della Signoria 527
picnic supplies 549
Ponte Vecchio 541
restaurants 549, 550
San Lorenzo 536
San Miniato al Monte 545
Santa Croce 540
Santa Felicità 541
Santa Maria Novella 535
Santa Trìnita 534
Santissima Annunziata 539
Santo Spirito 543
shopping 554
Specola 543
Spedale degli Innocenti 539
Torre di Arnolfo 528
tourist offices 546
Tracce di Firenze 527
train station 545
Tramvia 546
transport 546
Uffizi, the 528
Via de' Tornabuoni 534
websites 546
Fonte Cerreto 717
Fonti del Clitunno 657
food and drink 31. *See also* wine
Abruzzo and Molise cuisine 717
aperitivo 239
Basilicata and Calabria cuisine 847
birthplace of pizza 743
Campanian cuisine 743
confetti 721
Emilia-Romagna cuisine 469
Friuli Venezia Giulia cuisine 441
gourmet trail 486
Le Marche cuisine 681
Ligurian cuisine 177
Lombardy and the Lakes cuisine 222
Norcia specialities 665
Piemonte and Valle d'Aosta cuisine 135
Rome's cuisine 49
Sardinian cuisine 947
Sicilian cuisine 877
Trentino-Alto Adige cuisine 310
Tuscan cuisine 517
Umbrian cuisine 629
Veneto cuisine 351
football 10, 37, 106, 764
Forío 783
Forte di Bard 160
Forte di Fenestrelle 150
Francavilla di Sicilia 911
Franciacorta 284
Franciacorta wineries 284
Franks 985
Frascati 120
Friuli Venezia Giulia 438
Futurists 1005

G

Galatina 839
Galileo Galilei airport 545, 563
Gallipoli 840
Garda, Isola del 291
Garda, Lake 288, 298
Gardaland 289
Gardone Riviera 292
Gargano promontory 809
Gargnano 294
Garibaldi, Giuseppe 990, 971, 991
Gennargentu massif 965
Genoa 172
Gerace 871
Gioco del Ponte, Pisa 562
Giotto 999
glaciers 318
Glorenza 343
glossary 1030
Golfo dei Poeti 209
Golfo dei Poeti islands 212
Gonzaga,The 251
Gorizia 455

gourmet trail 486
Gradara castle 689
Grado 454
Gran Paradiso National Park 165
Gran Sasso 716
Gran Sasso National Park 716
Gran Sasso trails 718
grappa 431
Gravedona ed Uniti 271
Greeks, ancient 981
Greenway, The 270
Greve in Chianti wine fair 557
Grotta dello Smeraldo 793
Grottaferrata 120
Grotta Gigante 448
Grotte di Castellana 822
Grotte di Frasassi 694
Gruppo di Sella 323
Guardian Angel, The 690
Gubbio 641
Gubbio's doors of death 643
Guercino 690

H

haggling 38
Hannibal 637
health 40
Herculaneum 767, 768
hiking 37
- Abruzzo and Molise 714, 716, 718, 727
- Basilicata and Calabria 844, 856, 865
- Campania 793
- Emilia Romagna 491
- Fruli-Venezia Giulia 450
- Gran Paradiso National Park 165, 166
- Le Marche 697, 706
- Liguria 191, 198, 203, 207
- Lombardy and the Lakes 219, 270, 271, 298
- maps 42, 311
- Parco Nazionale del Circeo 126
- Piemonte 159
- Po Valley 153
- Sardinia 964, 965
- Sicily 897, 904, 905, 911
- Trentino-Alto Adige 306, 310, 316, 318, 319, 322, 323, 326, 333, 336, 339
- Tuscany 568, 577

hill-towns 1009
history 981
holidays, public 42
horseriding 38
hostels 30
hotels 29
hydrofoils 29

I

ice cream 9
Imer 320
Imperia 196
insurance 41
Inter Milan 245
international dialing codes 43
internet 41
Interrail 24
Ionian coast 853, 866
Ischia 781
Ischia Ponte 782
Ischia Porto 782
Iseo, Lake 283
Isernia 737
Isola Bella 258
Isola del Garda 291
Isola del Tinetto 212
Isola del Tino 212
Isola Madre 259
Isola Palmaria 212
Isola San Giulio 263
Isola Superiore 259
Italian Lakes 219
Ivrea 157

J

Jesi 694
Joyce, James 445
Julius Caesar 983

K

Kihlgren, Daniele 719

L

La Cavalcata festival 975
Lacco Ameno 782
Ladins, the 324
Lago Carezza 323
Lago di Bolsena 118
Lago di Bracciano 115
Lago di Braies 338
Lago di Lesina 813
Lago di Pilato 706
Lago di Toblino 314
Lago di Tovel 319
Lago di Varano 813
Lago di Vico 117
Lago Maggiore Express 258
Lago Trasimeno 637
Laguna di Grado 454
Lake Como 265
Lake Garda 288, 298
Lake Iseo 283
Lake Maggiore 256
Lake Orta 263
La Maddalena 971
La Mortella 783
Land of Fires 788
Langhe Roero hills 153
language 1024
- timetable reading 27

La Pelosa 976
L'Aquila 718
La Roccelletta 870
La Spezia 209
La Thuile 167
laundries 41
Laveno 262
Lazio 112
Lazio public transport 112
Leaning Tower, Pisa 560
Le Castella 870
Lecce 833
Lemon houses 294
Le Murge 819
Lerici 212
Levanto 205
Levanzo 941
LGBTQ 41, 105, 242
Liguria 172
Limone sul Garda 295
Linate airport 235
Lingua 899
Lipari 897, 899
Lippi, Fra' Filippo 662
liqueurs 34
Locorotondo 823
Locri Epizefiri 871
Lombards 985
Lombardy and the Lakes 216
Loreto 698
Loreto Aprutino 731
Lorica 865
Lotto, Lorenzo 1002
Lucca 559, 564
Lucca festivals and events 571
Lucera 806
Luino 261

M

Macerata 701
Maddalena islands 970
Madonna di Campiglio 318
Madonna of Loreto 699
Mafia 880
Maggiore, Lake 256

mail 41
Majella National Park 723
Malfa 900
Malpensa airport 235
Manarola 206
Mani Pulite 994
Mannerism 1001, 1003
Mantua 249
maps 41
Abruzzo & Molise 716
Alghero Old Town 977
Aosta 162
Arezzo 618
Ascoli Piceno 708
Assisi 646
Bari 816
Basilicata & Calabria 846
Bergamo 277
Bologna 470
Bolzano 328
Brescia 286
Brindisi 830
Cagliari 950
Campania 742
Canal Grande 371
Cannaregio 376
Capri 777
Catania 912
Centro Storico 55
Como 266
Elba 574
Emilia-Romagna 468
Ferrara 495
Florence 518
Friuli-Venezia Giulia 440
Genoa 176
Genoa Old Town 179
Gubbio 642
hiking 42, 311
Ischia 783
Italy 6
Itineraries 21
Lecce 834
Le Marche 680
Liguria 174
Lombardy & the Lakes 218
Lucca 566
Mantua 250
Matera 850
Milan 220
Milan meto 236
Modena 483
Montepulciano 608
Naples 744
Olbia 968
Orvieto 671
Padua 404
Parma 488
Perugia 630
Pesaro 687
Piemonte & Valle d'Aosta 134
Pisa 560
Puglia 806
Ravenna 500
Regio Calabria 861
Rimini 507
Rome 50
Rome & Lazio 48
Rome metro 93
San Gimignano 596
Sardinia 946
Sassari 974
Sicily 876
Siracusa 917
Sorrento 773
Spoleto 658
Taranto 826
Trentino-Alto Adige 308
Trento 312
Trieste 442
Turin 136
Tuscany 516
Udine 458
Umbria 628
Urbino 682
Venice 352
Venice & the Veneto 350
Verona 419
Vicenza 413
Volterra 600
Maratea 856
marble quarries 573
Marche, Le 678
Marciana 576
Marciana Marina 575
Marco Polo airport 387
Maremma, the 579
Marettimo 941
Marina Grande 786
markets 38
Marmolada 326
Martina Franca 822, 824
MART, Rovereto 316
Massafra 827
Massa Marittima 604
Matera 849
media 34
Medici dynasty 520
medieval art 999
Melfi 844
Menaggio 270
menus 32
Merano 340
Messina 906
Messner Mountain Museum 337
Messner, Reinhold 337
Metaponto 853
Mezzano 320
Mezzegra 269
Michelangelo 1002, 1011
Milan 216
accommodation 237
AC Milan 245
airports 235
apartments 238
aperitivo 239
Archeological Area 225
arrival and departure 235
bars 241
bed-and-breakfasts 238
Biblioteca Pinacoteca Ambrosiana 225
bike-sharing services 237
boat trips 232, 237
buses 236
bus station 236
cafés 239
camping 238
canals 232
Cappella Portinari 232
car rental 237
Castello Sforzesco 227
central 223
clubs 241
cycling 237
directory 244
drinking 241
driving 236, 237
Duomo 224
eating 239
fashion and design 222, 242
football 245
Galleria Vittorio Emanuele II 226
Gallerie d'Italia 226
gelaterie 239
Giardini Pubblici 231
history 219
hostels 238
Inter Milan 245
La Scala 226, 242
Last Supper, The 233, 234, 235
LGBTQ & Milan 242
live music venues 241
metro 236
Moscova 228
Museo Archeologico 234
Museo Bagatti Valsecchi 230
Museo del Duomo 224
Museo del Novecento 225
Museo Poldi Pezzoli 230
Navigli 232
Naviglio Grande 233
Naviglio Pavese 233
nightlife 241
opera 242
Parco Sempione 228
parking 237
Piazza Castello 227
Piazza dei Mercanti 225
Piazza del Duomo 222

Pinacoteca di Brera 229
Porta Genova 233
Quadrilatero d'Oro 230
restaurants 239
San Lorenzo Maggiore 231
Santa Maria delle Grazie 233
Sant'Ambrogio 234
Sant'Eustorgio 231
shopping 242
soccer 245
Stadio San Siro stadium 245
Studio Museo Achille Castiglioni 228
taxis 237
Ticinese district 231
tourist office 237
tours 237
train stations 235
trams 236
transport 236
Triennale 228
Via Brera 228
Villa Necchi Campiglio 231
Milazzo 893
mobile phones 43
Modena 482
modern art 1005
Modica 929
Modigliani, Amedeo 1005
Molise 714
Molveno 318
monastery accommodation 30
money 42
Monreale 890
Montalcino 613
Mont Blanc 167
Monte Amiata 615
Monte Argentario 580
Monte Capanne 576
Montecassino, Abbazia di 123
Monte Epomeo 784
Monte Faito 769
Montefalco 655
Montefortino 706
Monte Isola 284
Monte Malpasso 491
Montemonaco 706
Monte Ortobene 963
Montepulciano 607
Montepulciano festivals and events 610
Montepulciano wine tasting 609
Monterchi 621
Monterosso 206
Monte Sant'Angelo 809
Monti dell'Uccellina 579
Monti Sibillini 663
Monti Sibillini National Park 664, 705
Morrovalle 703
motorbikes 29
motor racing 37
motorways 28
mountain biking 37, 193
mountain refuges 31
Mount Etna 910
Mount Vesuvius 768
Muggia 451
Museumobil card 330
Mussolini, Benito 991

N

Naples 740
accommodation 760
airport 758
arrival and departure 758
bars 763
B&Bs 760
buses in 759
buses to 758
cafés 762
Campania artecard 748
Capodichino airport 758
Capodimonte 753
Cappella Sansevero 750
Castel dell'Ovo 757
Castel Nuovo 752
Castel Sant'Elmo 758
Catacombe di San Gaudioso 755
Catacombe di San Gennaro 755
central 747
centro storico 743
Certosa San Martino 758
Chiaia 756
Circumflegrea train 760
Circumvesuviana train 760
Corso Umberto I 752
directory 764
drinking 763
driving 760
Duomo 746
eating 762
entertainment 763
ferries 759
Ferrovia Cumana train 760
football 764
Forcella 752
funiculars 760
Galleria Borbonico 756
gelaterie 762
Gesù Nuovo 750
history 742
hostels 761
hotels 760
hydrofoils 759
Largo di Corpo di Nilo 749
La Sanità 753
MADRE 746
Mergellina 756, 757
metro 759
metro station art 761
Montesanto 753
Museo Archeologico Nazionale 754
Museo Nazionale di Capodimonte 755
Napoli Sotterranea 748
nightlife 763
Palazzo Reale 753
Piazza Bellini 749
Piazza Garibaldi 750
Piazza Trieste e Trento 752
pizzerias 762
Quadreria e Cappella del Pio Monte della Misericordia 747
Quartieri Spagnoli 752
restaurants 762
Roman remains 748
San Domenico Maggiore 749
San Gregorio Armeno 748
San Lorenzo Maggiore 748
Santa Chiara 750
Santa Lucia 756
Santa Maria della Sanità 755
Santa Maria delle Anime del Purgatorio ad Arco 749
Santa Restituta 746
Spaccanapoli 749
taxis 760
Teatro di San Carlo 753
tourist offices 759
train stations 758
transport 759
transport tickets 759
Via dei Tribunali 746
Via San Gregorio Armeno 748
Via Toledo 752
Villa Comunale 757
Villa Floridiana 758
Vomero 757
walking 759
Naples Capodichino airport 758
Napoleon 351, 574, 989
Narni 666
national parks
Abruzzo 725, 726
Circeo 126
dell'Arcipelago Toscano 575
Gran Paradiso 165
Gran Sasso 716
Majella 723
Monti Sibillini 664
Pollino 856
Sila 864
Stelvio 342
Neapolis 920
Nemi 121
Neoclassical architecture 1012
Neptune's Grotto 978
newspapers 34

Night of the Tarantula 840
Noli 191
Nora 954
Norcia 664
Northern Lazio 112
Noto 926
Noto Antica 927
Numana 697
Nuoro 961

O

Olbia 967
Oliena 964, 965
opening hours 42
Opi 725
Orbetello 580
orchids 726
Orgosolo 964
Orient Express 24
Oristano 958
Orta, Lake 263
Orta San Giulio 263
Ortigia 918
Orvieto 670
Ostia Antica 108
Ostuni 832
Otranto 837
Ötzi Cult 329
outdoor pursuits 37

P

package and special interest holidays 25
Padua 403
Paestum 800
Palazzo Barberini 122
Palazzo Farnese 117
Palermo 877
 Palermo, central 878
Palestrina 122
Palladio, Andrea 415, 1011
Panarea 902
paragliding 298
Parco dei Mostri, Bomarzo 118
Parco Faunistico di Spormaggiore 319
Parco Naturale Fanes-Sannes-Braies 338
Parco Naturale Paneveggio 321
Parco Nazionale d'Abruzzo 725, 726
Parco Nazionale dei Monti Sibillini 664
Parco Nazionale del Circeo 126
Parco Nazionale del Gran Sasso 716
Parco Nazionale della Majella 723
Parco Nazionale dell'Arcipelago Toscano 575
Parco Nazionale della Sila 864
Parco Nazionale dello Stelvio 342
Parco Nazionale Gran Paradiso 165
Parco Nazionale Pollino 856
parking 28
Parma 487
Parma ham 469
parmesan 469
Passignano 638
Passo dello Stelvio 343
Passo di Sella 324
Passo Pordoi 324
pasta 808
Path of the gods 793
pedestrian crossings 28
Perugia 628
Perugia festivals 635
Pesaro 686
Pescallo 272
Pescara 730
Pescassèroli 725
Peschici 812
Peschiera del Garda 302
Pescocostanzo 723
petrol stations 27
pharmacists 40
phones 43
 international dialling codes 43
Piano Grande 665
Piano, Renzo 1013
Piazza Armerina 934
Piemonte 157
Pienza 611
Piero trail 621
Pinzolo 317
Pisa 559
Pisa airport 563
Pisano, Nicola 999
Pitigliano 616
pizza 32
Pizzo 858
Po Delta 498
Po Delta boat trips 499
Poetto beaches 952
Poggio 576
police 39
Policoro 854
Polignano a Mare 821
politics 216, 993
Pollara 900
Pollenzo 155
Pollino National Park 856
Pompeii 769, 770
Pont d'Aël 164
Ponte Verde 318
Pontine islands 128
Pontine Marshes 124
Ponza 128
popes 986
Porto Azzurro 575
Portocannone 735
Porto Cervo 969
Porto Ercole 580
Portoferraio 574
Portofino 201, 203
Portonovo 696
Portovenere 211
Positano 791
post offices 41
Pozzuoli 764
Praiano 792
Predazzo 321
Procida 786
Puglia 804, 808
Punta San Vigilio 301

R

radio 35
rafting 38, 159
Ragusa 930
rail passes 24, 26
rail travel 24, 191
 in Italy 26
 ticket validation 26
 to Italy 24
rainfall 40
Ramo di Lecco 275
Rapallo 203
Raphael 1002, 1011
Ravello 796
Ravenna 499
Ravenna festivals 505
Recanati 700
Red Brigade 993
refuges 31, 311
Reggio Calabria 860
Reggio Emilia 485
Renaissance architecture 1010
Renaissance art 1000
restaurants 32
Rimini 506
Rinella 900
Riomaggiore 207
Riserva Naturale dello Zingaro 939
Riva del Garda 296
Riviera del Limone 294
Riviera di Levante 199
Riviera di Ponente 190
Rocca Calascio 718
Rocca di Angera 262
rock carvings 300

Rococo art 1005
Rodi Garganico 813
Roman art 998
Roman Italy 982
Rome 46
accommodation 94
airports 91
Ancient Rome 65
Ara Pacis 71
Arch of Constantine 66
Arch of Septimius Severus 66
Arch of Titus 68
arrival and departure 91
Aventine Hill 80
bars 97, 103
Basilica of Maxentius 68
Baths of Caracalla 81
bed-and-breakfasts 94
bike rentals 94
bookshops 107
buses 92, 95
bus stations 92
camping 98
Campo de' Fiori 59
Capitoline Hill 63
Capitoline Museums 63
Carcer Tullianum 64
Case Romane 79
Castel Sant'Angelo 91
Catacombe di San Sebastiano 83
Catacombs of San Callisto 83
Celian Hill 79
central 53
Centrale Montemartini 82
centro storico 54
Circus Maximus 69
classical music 106
clubs 105
Colosseum 65
Convento dei Cappuccini 74
cuisine 49
Curia 66
cycling 94
directory 107
Domus Aurea 75
drinking 103
driving 92
eating 98
Elephant Statue 54
emergency numbers 107
entertainment 106
Esquiline 75
film 106
flea market 84
Fontana dei Quattro Fiumi 58
football 106
Galleria Borghese 85
Galleria Colonna 72
Galleria Doria Pamphilj 70
Galleria Nazionale d'Arte Antica, Palazzo Barberini 73
Galleria Nazionale d'Arte Moderna 86
Galleria Nazionale di Arte Antica – Palazzo Corsini 84
Galleria Spada 60
Gesù 61
Ghetto 59
history 49
hostels 98
hotels 94
House of the Vestal Virgins 68
ice cream 99
Imperial Forums 69
Isola Tiberina 61
Janiculum Hill 83, 85
Keats-Shelley House 70
Largo di Torre Argentina 60
LGBTQ bars and clubs 105
live music venues 105
magazines 94
Mamertine Prison 64
MAXXI 87
metro 92
Monti 75, 76
Museo di Roma 59
Museo di Scultura Antica Giovanni Barracco 60
Museo Ebraico 61
Museo Nazionale di Palazzo Venezia 62
Museo Nazionale Etrusco di Villa Giulia 86
Museo Storico della Liberazione 80
newspapers 94
nightbuses 95
nightlife 105
Omnia Card 56
opera 106
Palatine Hill 68
Palazzo Altemps 57
Palazzo Barberini 73
Palazzo Corsini 84
Palazzo delle Esposizioni 77
Palazzo del Quirinale 75
Palazzo di Montecitorio 56
Palazzo Farnese 60
Palazzo Massimo 78
Palazzo Valentini 63
Pantheon 54
passes 56
Piazza Barberini 73
Piazza Bocca della Verità 64
Piazza Colonna 70
Piazza della Repubblica 77
Piazza del Popolo 71
Piazza di Spagna 70
Piazza Navona 58
Piazza Pasquino 59
Piazza San Pietro 87
Piazza Venezia 62
Pincio Gardens 85
Porta Portese flea market 84
Protestant Cemetery 81
pyramid of Caius Cestius 82
Quirinale 73
Raphael Rooms 90
restaurants 98
Roman Forum 66
Roma Pass 56
Rooms of St Ignatius 61
San Carlino alle Quattro Fontane 74
San Clemente 79
Sancta Sanctorum 80
San Giovanni 79
San Giovanni in Laterano 79
San Gregorio Magno 79
San Lorenzo fuori le Mura 78
San Luigi dei Francesi 58
San Marco 62
San Paolo fuori le Mura 82
San Pietro in Carcere 64
San Pietro in Vincoli 76
Santa Cecilia in Trastevere 84
Sant'Agnese in Agone 58
Sant'Agostino 57
Santa Maria degli Angeli 77
Santa Maria della Concezione 74
Santa Maria della Vittoria 75
Santa Maria del Popolo 71
Santa Maria in Aracoeli 63
Santa Maria in Cosmedin 64
Santa Maria in Trastevere 83
Santa Maria Maggiore 76
Santa Maria sopra Minerva 56
Sant'Andrea al Quirinale 74
Santa Prassede 77
Santa Sabina 80
Santi Giovanni e Paolo 79
Sant'Ignazio 56
Sant'Ivo alla Sapienza 59
Scala Santa 80
scooter rentals 94
Scuderie del Quirinale 75
shopping 107
Sistine Chapel 90
Spanish Steps 71
Stadio di Domiziano 58
St Peter's 87
Synagogue 61
taxis 94
Temple of Castor and Pollux 68
Terme di Diocleziano 77
Termini 75
Termini station 78, 92
Testaccio 81
Time Elevator 72
tourist buses 95
tourist information kiosks 94

tourist information line 94
tourist office 94
tourist passes 56
tours 65
train stations 92
Trajan's Markets 69
trams 95
transport 92
transport tickets 94
transport, useful routes 95
Trastevere 83
travel cards 94
Trevi Fountain 72
Tridente 69
Trinità dei Monti 71
Vatican City 87
Vatican Museums 88, 89
Via Appia Antica 82
Via dei Coronari 57
Via del Corso 69
Via del Governo Vecchio 59
Via Giulia 60
Via Portico d'Ottavia 61
Via Sacra 66
Via Veneto 74
Villa Borghese 85
Villa Farnesina 84
Vittoriano 62
websites 94
Romeo and Juliet 421
Rossano Calabro 867
Rossano Scalo 867
Rovereto 315
rules of the road 27
Rupingrande 448
Ruvo di Puglia 820

S

Sacra di San Michele 150
Sacro Monte di San Francesco 263
Sacro Monte di Varallo 159
Saepinum 736
safety, personal 39
sailing 37
Salento 833
Salerno 798
Salina 899, 900
Salò 291
Saltria 333
Saluzzo 151
San Daniele del Friuli 461
San Domino 814
San Felice Circeo 125
San Fruttuoso 200
San Gennaro 746
San Gimignano 595
San Ginesio 705
San Giovanni Rotondo 811
San Leo 511
San Marino 510
San Martino di Castrozza 320
San Menaio 813
San Nicola 813
San Pietro 956
San Quirico d'Orcia 612
San Remo 196
Sansepolcro 621
San Severino Marche 703
Santa Caterina del Sasso 262
Santa Margherita Ligure 202
Santa Maria a Piè di Chienti 703
Santa Maria Capua Vetere 788
Santa Marina di Salina 899
Sant'Andrea 576
Sant'Angelo 784
Sant'Antioco 955
Santa Severina 869
Santa Teresa Gallura 972
Santo Stefano 862
Santo Stefano di Sessanio 718, 719
Santuario della Madonna di Polsi 863
Santuario di Oropa 158
Santuario di San Luca 482
Santuario di Vicoforte 153
Santuario Madonna della Corona 300
Sardinia 944
Sarnano 705
Sa Sartiglia festival 960
Sassari 973
Sassocorvaro 686
Savona 190
Scanno 724
Scheggino 666
Schloss Taufers 337
Scilla 860
Scopello 939
scuba diving 37
Segesta 939
self-catering 30
Sentiero Rilke 452
Sermoneta 124
Sestri Levante 204
Sferisterio Opera Festival 701
shopping 38
Sicily 874
Siena 582
Seina, Central 584
Siena Palio 583
Sila Grande 865
Sila National Park 864
Sila, the 864
Siracusa 916, 919, 922
Sirmione 289
Sirolo 697
skiing 37, 159, 167, 168
Dolomites 311, 338
ski resorts, Piemonte 151
Skyway Monte Bianco 168
smoking 32
snorkelling 902
snowboarding 37
soccer 10, 37, 106, 764
soft drinks 34
Solfatara 765
Sorrento 771
Southern Lazio 119
Southern Lombardy 244
souvenirs, foodie 480
Spello 652
Sperlonga 127
spirits 34
Spoleto 657
sports 37
Squillace 870
St Benedict 626
St Catherine of Siena 591
Stelvio National Park 342
St Francis of Assisi 646, 650, 626
Stintino 976
St Mark 351
Strada delle Vette 865
Strada del Vino 332
Strada Vicentina 450
Stradivari, Antonio 246
Stresa 256
Stromboli 903, 904
student accommodation 30
studying in Italy 38
St Valentine 665
Subiaco 122
Sulmona 721
Su Nuraxi 958
Sybaris 866
Sybarites 867

T

Taormina 908
tarantism 840
Taranto 825
Tarquinia 113
Tarquinia Lido 114
Tavoliere 806
tax 38
tea 33
Tellaro 212
temperatures 40
Temple of Segesta 939
Teramo 727
Termeno 333
Termoli 734
Terni 665
Terracina 126

terrorism 993
Tesero 321
Tharros 960
theme parks 289
Tiepolo, Giambattista 1005
time zone 43
Tintoretto 1002
tipping 32
Titian 1002
Tivoli 109
Todi 667
Toirano caves 194
Tolentino 703
Torbole sul Garda 297
Törggelen season 333
Torino 132
Torre a Mare 821
Torrechiara 491
Torre Guaceto 832
Torri del Benaco 299
Toscolano Maderno 293
tourist information 43
tour operators 25
trains 24. *See also* rail travel
Trani 814
transport 25
Trapani 935
travel agents 25
travellers' cheques 42
Tre Cime di Lavaredo 339
Tremiti islands 813
Tremosine 295
Trentino-Alto Adige 306
Trento 311
Trevi 656
Treviso 427
Treviso Airport 388
Trieste 438
Trieste festivals and events 447
Triestine Riviera 450
Troia 808
Tropea 859
trulli 823
Turin 132
Turin festivals 148
Turin Shroud 141
Tuscany 514
TV 35
Tyche 920
Tyrol, Italianization of 327
Tyrrhenian coast 857

U

Udine 457
Udine festivals and events 461
Umbria 626
Urbino 678
Urbs Salvia 704
Ururi 735
Ustica 890

V

Val di Cogne 165
Val di Rhêmes 167
Val di Solda 344
Val di Trafoi 344
Val d'Ultimo 342
Valeggio sul Mincio 302
Val Gardena 333
Val Genova 317
Valle d'Aosta 160
Valle dei Templi 932
Val Martello 343
Valnerina 663
Valnontey 165
Val Pusteria 336
Val Rosandra 450
Valsavarenche 166
Valsesia 159
Val Venosta 343
Varenna 274
Vasto 733
VAT 38
Vatican City 87
vegetarians and vegans 33
Veneto, the 401
Venice 348
Accademia 364
accommodation 390
arrival and departure 387
Arsenale 381
bars 397
Basilica di San Marco 353
B&Bs 393
Biennale 400
Bridge of Sighs 357
Burano 384
buses 387
bus station 388
Ca' d'Oro 376
cafés 394
Campanile 360
camping 393
Campo San Bartolomeo 362
Campo San Fantin 362
Campo San Luca 362
Campo Santa Margherita 367
Canal Grande 372
Cannaregio 374
Ca' Pésaro 370
Ca' Rezzonico 368
Carnevale 400
car parks 388
Castello 378
central 358
cinemas 400
Colleoni monument 379
directory 400
Dorsoduro 364
drinking 397
eating 393
entertainment 399
Festa della Salute 401
Festa del Redentore 401
festivals and events 401
Film Festival 401
flooding 356
Frari 371
Galleria Internazionale d'Arte Moderna 370
gelaterie 394
Gesuati 366
Gesuiti 378
Ghetto 375
Giudecca, La 386
gondolas 390
Guggenheim Collection 366
history 350
hostels 392
hotels 390
La Fenice 362
La Sensa 400
Libreria Sansoviniana 360
Lido 387
listings magazines 390
locande 390
Madonna dell'Orto 375
Marco Polo airport 387
Miracoli 378
motoscafi 388
Murano 383
Museo Archeologico 360
Museo Correr 360
Museo del Merletto 384
Museo del Vetro 384
Museo Dipinti Sacri Bizantini 381
Museo di Storia Naturale 370
Museo Ebraico 375
Museo Fortuny 362
Museo Orientale 370
Museo Storico Navale 382
opera and classical music 399
outdoor drinking 397
outdoor eating 395
Palazzo Ducale 356
Palazzo Grassi 364
Palazzo Grimani 380
Palazzo Labia 374
passes 354
pasticcerie 394
Piazzetta 361
picnicking 394
Pietà 381
Pinacoteca Querini-Stampalia 380
Procuratie 360

Punta della Dogana 366
Regata Storica 401
restaurants 393, 395
Rialto Bridge 369
Rialto district 369
Rialto market 369
San Cassiano 369
San Francesco della Vigna 380
San Geremia e Lucia 374
San Giacomo di Rialto 369
San Giorgio dei Greci 381
San Giorgio Maggiore 386
San Giovanni Crisostomo 377
San Lazzaro degli Armeni 387
San Marco 353
San Michele 383
San Michele in Isola 383
San Moisè 362
San Pantalon 368
San Pietro di Castello 382
San Polo 368, 370
San Rocco 374
San Salvador 361
San Sebastiano 366, 367
Santa Croce 368
Sant'Alvise 375
Santa Maria del Carmelo 367
Santa Maria del Giglio 364
Santa Maria della Salute 366
Santa Maria Formosa 380
Santi Giovanni e Paolo 378
Santo Stefano 364
San Trovaso 367
San Zaccaria 381
Scalzi 374
Scuola di San Giorgio degli Schiavoni 381
Scuola Grande dei Carmini 367
Scuola Grande di San Marco 379
Scuola Grande di San Rocco 372
scuole of Venice 368
self-catering 393
sestieri 353
shopping 399
taxis 388, 389
Teatro Malibran 399
Torcello 385
Torre dell'Orologio 360
tourist office 390
tourist passes 354
tours 357
traghetti 388
train station 388
transport 388
travel cards 387
Treviso Airport 388
vaporetti 388
Vogalonga 400
water-buses 388, 389
water-taxis 389
Zattere 366
Venice Simplon-Orient-Express 24
Venosa 848
Verbania 259
Verdi country 492
Verdi, Giuseppe 492
Vernazza 206
Verona 418
Verona carnival 426
Verona opera festival 420
Vesuvius 768
Via Emilia 492
Viareggio 572
Vicenza 412
vie ferrate 317
Viel del Pan 326
Vieste 810, 812
Villa Adriana, Tivoli 110
Villa del Balbianello 269
Villa d'Este, Tivoli 109
Villa Fóscari 402
Villa Gregoriana, Tivoli 109
Villa Lante, Bagnaia 118
Villa Melzi 273
Villa Pisani 402
Villa Romana del Casale 935
Villa Romana del Tellaro 927
villas 31
Villa Serbelloni 272
Vinitaly 425
violins 246, 248
Vipiteno 338
Viterbo 115
Vittorio Emanuele I 989
Vittorio Veneto 433
Volterra 600
Vulcano 896

W

walking. *See also* hiking
Elba 577
Monti dell'Uccellina 580
water 34
watersports 298, 638
wi-fi 41
wildlife 165
windsurfing 37
wine 34
Abruzzo and Molise 717
Basilicata and Calabria 847, 868
Campania 743
Emilia Romagna 469
Friuli Venezia Giulia 441
Le Marche 681, 696
Lombardy 219, 284, 301
Piemonte and Valle d'Aosta 135
Puglia 808, 823
Sardinia 947, 964
Sicily 877
Trentino-Alto Adige 306, 310, 313, 331, 332, 333
Tuscany 517, 557, 574, 607, 609, 613
Umbria 629, 655, 656, 670
Veneto 351, 425, 432
wine festivals 313, 425, 461, 505, 557, 696
wine bars 33
wine road, Bolzano 332
wolves 726
working in Italy 38
World War I 991
World War II 124, 992

Z

Zingaro, Riserva Naturale dello 939

Map symbols

The symbols below are used on maps throughout the book

- International boundary
- Provincial boundary
- Chapter boundary
- Motorway
- Road
- Pedestrianized road
- Steps
- Path
- Railway
- Cable car
- Funicular
- Ferry route
- Traghetto
- Tram line
- Wall

- Airport
- Transport stop
- Metro station
- Ferry/boat stop
- Internet access
- Information office
- Telephone office
- Parking
- Hospital
- Post office
- Place of interest
- National Park
- Ruin
- Refuge

- Statue
- Monastery
- Abbey
- Synagogue
- Church
- Castle
- Archeological site
- Swimming
- Gate
- Fountains
- Cave
- Viewpoint
- Lighthouse
- Arc

- Mountain peak
- Mountain range
- Church (town map)
- Building
- Park
- Stadium
- Beach
- Glacier
- Christian cemetery
- Jewish cemetery

Listings key

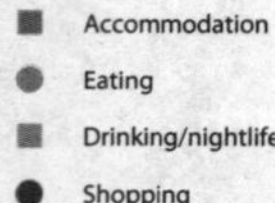

BENEFITS OF PLANNING AND BOOKING AT ROUGHGUIDES.COM/TRIPS

PLAN YOUR ADVENTURE WITH LOCAL EXPERTS

Rough Guides' English-speaking local experts are hand-picked, based on their experience in the travel industry and their impeccable standards of customer service.

SAVE TIME AND GET ACCESS TO LOCAL KNOWLEDGE

When a local expert plans your trip, you save time and money when you book, even during high season. You won't be charged for using a credit card either.

MAKE TRAVEL A BREEZE: BOOK WITH PIECE OF MIND

Enjoy stress-free travel when you use Rough Guides' secure online booking platform. All bookings come witha money-back guarantee.

WHAT DO OTHER TRAVELLERS THINK ABOUT ROUGH GUIDES TRIPS?

Trip to Spain

This Spain tour company did a fantastic job to make our dream trip perfect. We gave them our travel budget, told them where we would like to go, and they did all of the planning. Our drivers and tour guides were always on time and very knowledgable. The hotel accommodations were better than we would have found on our own. Only one time did we end up in a location that we had not intended to be in. We called the 24 hour phone number, and they immediately fixed the situation.

Don A, USA ★★★★★

Trip to Morocco

Our trip was fantastic! Transportation, accommodations, guides - all were well chosen! The hotels were well situated, well appointed and had helpful, friendly staff. All of the guides we had were very knowledgeable, patient, and flexible with our varied interests in the different sites. We particularly enjoyed the side trip to Tangier! Well done! The itinerary you arranged for us allowed maximum coverage of the country with time in each city for seeing the important places.

Sharon, USA ★★★★★

PLAN AND BOOK YOUR TRIP AT ROUGHGUIDES.COM/TRIPS

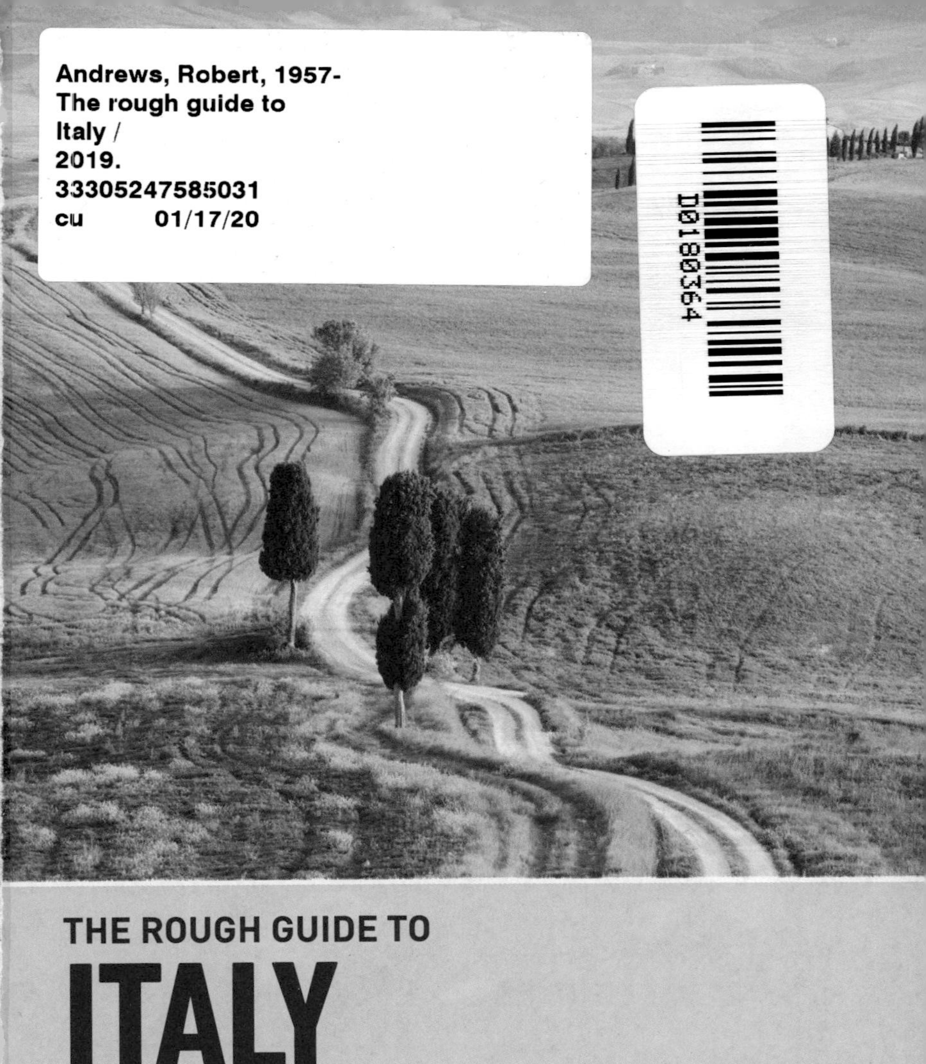

THE ROUGH GUIDE TO ITALY

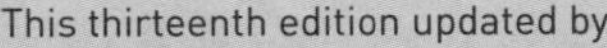

This thirteenth edition updated by

Robert Andrews, Ros Belford, Jonathan Buckley, Kiki Deere, Natasha Foges and Anthon Jackson